Official 2006
National Football League
Record
& Fact Book

NATIONAL FOOTBALL LEAGUE
280 Park Avenue, New York, N.Y. 10017 (212) 450-2000. NFL Internet Address: http://www.NFL.com

Compiled by the NFL Communications Department and Seymour Siwoff, Elias Sports Bureau.
Statistics by Elias Sports Bureau.

Edited by Randall Liu, NFL Communications Department, and Matt Marini. Layout by William Tham. Proofread by Jon Zimmer. Cover design by NFL Creative.
Produced by NFL Communications Department.

Cover photograph of Ben Roethlisberger of the Super Bowl XL champion Pittsburgh Steelers by Jonathan Ferrey/GETTY IMAGES SPORTS.

Time Inc.
HOME ENTERTAINMENT

Time Inc. Home Entertainment
1271 Avenue of the Americas, New York, N.Y. 10020
Manufactured in the United States of America.
First printing, July 2006.
10 9 8 7 6 5 4 3 2 1

A National Football League Book
Time Inc. Home Entertainment

TABLE OF CONTENTS

All times local. Dates and times subject to change.
Nationally televised games indicated by network in parentheses.

| | **Sunday, August 6** | Hall of Fame Game at Canton, Ohio | |
| | | Oakland _____ vs. Philadelphia _____ | (NBC) 8:00 |

PRESEASON/WEEK 1

	Thursday, August 10	Indianapolis _____ at St. Louis _____	(FOX) 7:00
		Cleveland _____ at Philadelphia _____	7:30
	Friday, August 11	New England _____ at Atlanta _____	(CBS) 8:00
		Denver _____ at Detroit _____	7:30
		New York Jets _____ at Tampa Bay _____	7:30
		New York Giants _____ at Baltimore _____	8:00
		Chicago _____ at San Francisco _____	7:00
	Saturday, August 12	Pittsburgh _____ at Arizona _____	1:00
		Buffalo _____ at Carolina _____	7:30
		Jacksonville _____ at Miami _____	7:30
		Kansas City _____ at Houston _____	7:00
		New Orleans _____ at Tennessee _____	7:00
		Dallas _____ at Seattle _____	7:00
		Green Bay _____ at San Diego _____	7:00
	Sunday, August 13	Washington _____ at Cincinnati _____	(NBC) 8:00
	Monday, August 14	Oakland _____ at Minnesota _____	(ESPN) 7:00

PRESEASON/WEEK 2

	Thursday, August 17	Kansas City _____ at New York Giants _____	(FOX) 8:00
		Philadelphia _____ at Baltimore _____	8:00
	Friday, August 18	San Diego _____ at Chicago _____	(CBS) 7:00
		Cincinnati _____ at Buffalo _____	7:00
		Detroit _____ at Cleveland _____	7:30
	Saturday, August 19	Arizona _____ at New England _____	(NFLN) 8:00
		Carolina _____ at Jacksonville _____	7:30
		Miami _____ at Tampa Bay _____	7:30
		Atlanta _____ at Green Bay _____	7:00
		Houston _____ at St. Louis _____	7:00
		Minnesota _____ at Pittsburgh _____	8:00
		New York Jets _____ at Washington _____	8:00
		Tennessee _____ at Denver _____	7:00
	Sunday, August 20	Seattle _____ at Indianapolis _____	(NBC) 8:00
		San Francisco _____ at Oakland _____	5:00
	Monday, August 21	Dallas _____ at New Orleans _____	(ESPN) 7:00
		(at Shreveport, Louisiana)	

PRESEASON/WEEK 3

	Thursday, August 24	Miami _____ at Carolina _____	(FOX) 8:00
	Friday, August 25	Pittsburgh _____ at Philadelphia _____	(ESPN) 8:00
		Arizona _____ at Chicago _____	7:00
		Baltimore _____ at Minnesota _____	7:00
		New York Giants _____ at New York Jets _____	8:00
		Detroit _____ at Oakland _____	7:00
	Saturday, August 26	Tampa Bay _____ at Jacksonville _____	(CBS) 8:00
		Cleveland _____ at Buffalo _____	6:00
		Indianapolis _____ at New Orleans _____	6:00
		(at Jackson, Mississippi)	
		Atlanta _____ at Tennessee _____	7:00
		San Francisco _____ at Dallas _____	7:00
		Washington _____ at New England _____	8:00
		St. Louis _____ at Kansas City _____	7:30
		Seattle _____ at San Diego _____	8:00
	Sunday, August 27	Houston _____ at Denver _____	(NFLN) 6:00
	Monday, August 28	Green Bay _____ at Cincinnati _____	(ESPN) 8:00

PRESEASON/WEEK 4

	New England _____ at New York Giants _____	(TBD)
	Philadelphia _____ at New York Jets _____	(TBD)
Thursday, August 31	Buffalo _____ at Detroit _____	7:30
	Carolina_____ at Pittsburgh _____	7:30
	Jacksonville _____ at Atlanta _____	7:30
	St. Louis _____ at Miami _____	7:30
	Baltimore _____ at Washington _____	8:00
	Chicago _____ at Cleveland _____	8:00
	Minnesota _____ at Dallas _____	7:00
	Tampa Bay _____ at Houston _____	7:00
	New Orleans _____ at Kansas City _____	7:30
	Denver _____ at Arizona _____	7:00
	Oakland _____ at Seattle _____	7:00
Friday, September 1	Tennessee _____ at Green Bay _____	3:00
	Cincinnati _____ at Indianapolis _____	7:00
	San Diego _____ at San Francisco _____	7:00

KICKOFF WEEKEND

Thursday, September 7	Miami_____ at Pittsburgh _____	(NBC) 8:30
Sunday, September 10	Atlanta_____ at Carolina _____	1:00
FOX-TV National Weekend	New Orleans_____ at Cleveland _____	1:00
	Seattle_____ at Detroit _____	1:00
	Philadelphia_____ at Houston _____	12:00
	Cincinnati_____ at Kansas City _____	12:00
	Buffalo_____ at New England _____	1:00
	Denver_____ at St. Louis _____	12:00
	Baltimore_____ at Tampa Bay _____	1:00
	N.Y. Jets_____ at Tennessee _____	12:00
	San Francisco_____ at Arizona _____	1:15
	Chicago_____ at Green Bay _____	3:15
	Dallas_____ at Jacksonville _____	4:15
	Indianapolis_____ at N.Y. Giants _____	(NBC) 8:15
Monday, September 11	Minnesota_____ at Washington _____	(ESPN) 7:00
	San Diego_____ at Oakland _____	(ESPN) 7:15

SECOND WEEKEND

Sunday, September 17	Tampa Bay_____ at Atlanta _____	1:00
CBS-TV National Weekend	Oakland_____ at Baltimore _____	1:00
	Detroit_____ at Chicago _____	12:00
	Cleveland_____ at Cincinnati _____	1:00
	New Orleans_____ at Green Bay _____	12:00
	Houston_____ at Indianapolis _____	1:00
	Buffalo_____ at Miami _____	1:00
	Carolina_____ at Minnesota _____	12:00
	N.Y. Giants_____ at Philadelphia _____	1:00
	St. Louis _____ at San Francisco _____	1:05
	Arizona_____ at Seattle _____	1:05
	Kansas City_____ at Denver _____	2:15
	New England_____ at N.Y. Jets _____	4:15
	Tennessee_____ at San Diego _____	1:15
	Washington_____ at Dallas _____	(NBC) 7:15
Monday, September 18	Pittsburgh_____ at Jacksonville _____	(ESPN) 8:30

THIRD WEEKEND
Open Dates:
Dallas, Kansas City, Oakland, San Diego

Sunday, September 24	N.Y. Jets_____ at Buffalo _____	1:00
FOX-TV National Weekend	Green Bay_____ at Detroit _____	1:00
	Washington_____ at Houston _____	12:00
	Jacksonville_____ at Indianapolis _____	1:00
	Tennessee_____ at Miami _____	1:00
	Chicago_____ at Minnesota _____	12:00
	Cincinnati_____ at Pittsburgh _____	1:00
	Carolina_____ at Tampa Bay _____	1:00
	Baltimore_____ at Cleveland _____	4:05
	St. Louis_____ at Arizona _____	1:15
	Philadelphia_____ at San Francisco _____	1:15
	N.Y. Giants_____ at Seattle _____	1:15
	Denver_____ at New England _____	(NBC) 8:15
Monday, September 25	Atlanta_____ at New Orleans _____	(ESPN) 7:30

FOURTH WEEKEND
Open Dates:
Denver, N.Y. Giants, Pittsburgh, Tampa Bay

Sunday, October 1
CBS-TV National Weekend

Arizona_____ at Atlanta _____	1:00
San Diego_____ at Baltimore _____	1:00
Minnesota_____ at Buffalo _____	1:00
New Orleans_____ at Carolina _____	1:00
Miami_____ at Houston _____	12:00
San Francisco_____ at Kansas City _____	12:00
Indianapolis_____ at N.Y. Jets _____	1:00
Dallas_____ at Tennessee _____	12:00
Detroit_____ at St. Louis _____	3:05
New England_____ at Cincinnati _____	4:15
Cleveland_____ at Oakland _____	1:15
Jacksonville_____ at Washington _____	4:15
Seattle_____ at Chicago _____	(NBC) 7:15
Monday, October 2 Green Bay_____ at Philadelphia _____	(ESPN) 8:30

FIFTH WEEKEND
Open Dates:
Atlanta, Cincinnati, Houston, Seattle

Sunday, October 8
FOX-TV National Weekend

Cleveland_____ at Carolina _____	1:00
Buffalo_____ at Chicago _____	12:00
St. Louis_____ at Green Bay _____	12:00
Tennessee_____ at Indianapolis _____	1:00
Detroit_____ at Minnesota _____	12:00
Miami_____ at New England _____	1:00
Tampa Bay_____ at New Orleans _____	12:00
Washington_____ at N.Y. Giants _____	1:00
Kansas City_____ at Arizona _____	1:05
N.Y. Jets_____ at Jacksonville _____	4:05
Oakland_____ at San Francisco _____	1:05
Dallas_____ at Philadelphia _____	4:15
Pittsburgh_____ at San Diego _____	(NBC) 5:15
Monday, October 9 Baltimore_____ at Denver _____	(ESPN) 6:30

SIXTH WEEKEND
Open Dates:
Cleveland, Green Bay, Indianapolis,
Jacksonville, Minnesota, New England

Sunday, October 15
CBS-TV National Weekend

N.Y. Giants_____ at Atlanta _____	1:00
Carolina_____ at Baltimore _____	1:00
Houston_____ at Dallas _____	12:00
Buffalo_____ at Detroit _____	1:00
Philadelphia_____ at New Orleans _____	12:00
Seattle_____ at St. Louis _____	12:00
Cincinnati_____ at Tampa Bay _____	1:00
Tennessee_____ at Washington _____	1:00
Miami_____ at N.Y. Jets _____	4:15
Kansas City_____ at Pittsburgh _____	4:15
San Diego_____ at San Francisco _____	1:15
Oakland_____ at Denver _____	(NBC) 6:15
Monday, October 16 Chicago_____ at Arizona _____	(ESPN) 5:30

SEVENTH WEEKEND
Open Dates:
Baltimore, Chicago, New Orleans,
St. Louis, San Francisco, Tennessee

Sunday, October 22
FOX-TV National Weekend

Pittsburgh_____ at Atlanta _____	1:00
New England_____ at Buffalo _____	1:00
Carolina_____ at Cincinnati _____	1:00
Jacksonville_____ at Houston _____	12:00
San Diego_____ at Kansas City _____	12:00
Green Bay_____ at Miami _____	1:00
Detroit_____ at N.Y. Jets _____	1:00
Philadelphia_____ at Tampa Bay _____	1:00
Denver_____ at Cleveland _____	4:05
Washington_____ at Indianapolis _____	4:15
Arizona_____ at Oakland _____	1:15
Minnesota_____ at Seattle _____	1:15
Monday, October 23 N.Y. Giants_____ at Dallas _____	(ESPN) 7:30

EIGHTH WEEKEND
Open Dates:
Buffalo, Detroit, Miami, Washington

Sunday, October 29	San Francisco_____ at Chicago _____	12:00
CBS-TV National Weekend	Atlanta_____ at Cincinnati _____	1:00
	Arizona_____ at Green Bay _____	12:00
	Seattle_____ at Kansas City _____	12:00
	Baltimore_____ at New Orleans _____	12:00
	Tampa Bay_____ at N.Y. Giants _____	1:00
	Jacksonville_____ at Philadelphia _____	1:00
	Houston_____ at Tennessee _____	12:00
	St. Louis_____ at San Diego _____	1:05
	N.Y. Jets_____ at Cleveland _____	4:15
	Indianapolis_____ at Denver _____	2:15
	Pittsburgh_____ at Oakland _____	1:15
	Dallas_____ at Carolina _____	(NBC) 8:15
Monday, October 30	New England_____ at Minnesota _____	(ESPN) 7:30

NINTH WEEKEND
Open Dates:
Arizona, Carolina, N.Y. Jets, Philadelphia

Sunday, November 5	Cincinnati_____ at Baltimore _____	1:00
CBS-TV National Weekend	Green Bay_____ at Buffalo _____	1:00
	Miami_____ at Chicago _____	12:00
	Atlanta_____ at Detroit _____	1:00
	Tennessee_____ at Jacksonville _____	1:00
	Houston_____ at N.Y. Giants _____	1:00
	Kansas City_____ at St. Louis _____	12:00
	New Orleans_____ at Tampa Bay _____	1:00
	Dallas_____ at Washington _____	1:00
	Minnesota_____ at San Francisco _____	1:05
	Denver_____ at Pittsburgh _____	4:15
	Cleveland_____ at San Diego _____	1:15
	Indianapolis_____ at New England _____	(NBC) 8:15
Monday, November 6	Oakland_____ at Seattle _____	(ESPN) 5:30

TENTH WEEKEND

Sunday, November 12	Cleveland_____ at Atlanta _____	1:00
FOX-TV National Weekend	San Diego_____ at Cincinnati _____	1:00
	San Francisco_____ at Detroit _____	1:00
	Buffalo_____ at Indianapolis _____	1:00
	Houston_____ at Jacksonville _____	1:00
	Kansas City_____ at Miami _____	1:00
	Green Bay_____ at Minnesota _____	12:00
	N.Y. Jets_____ at New England _____	1:00
	Chicago_____ at N.Y. Giants _____	1:00
	Washington_____ at Philadelphia _____	1:00
	New Orleans_____ at Pittsburgh _____	1:00
	Baltimore_____ at Tennessee _____	12:00
	Denver_____ at Oakland _____	1:05
	Dallas_____ at Arizona _____	2:15
	St. Louis_____ at Seattle _____	1:15
	NBC Game TBD*	(NBC) 8:15 ET
Monday, November 13	Tampa Bay_____ at Carolina _____	(ESPN) 8:30

ELEVENTH WEEKEND

Sunday, November 19	Atlanta_____ at Baltimore _____	1:00
CBS-TV National Weekend	St. Louis_____ at Carolina _____	1:00
	Pittsburgh_____ at Cleveland _____	1:00
	Indianapolis_____ at Dallas _____	12:00
	New England_____ at Green Bay _____	12:00
	Buffalo_____ at Houston _____	12:00
	Oakland_____ at Kansas City _____	12:00
	Minnesota_____ at Miami _____	1:00
	Cincinnati_____ at New Orleans _____	12:00
	Chicago_____ at N.Y. Jets _____	1:00
	Tennessee_____ at Philadelphia _____	1:00
	Washington_____ at Tampa Bay _____	1:00
	Detroit_____ at Arizona _____	2:05
	Seattle_____ at San Francisco _____	1:05
	San Diego_____ at Denver _____	2:15
	NBC Game TBD*	(NBC) 8:15 ET
Monday, November 20	N.Y. Giants_____ at Jacksonville _____	(ESPN) 8:30

TWELFTH WEEKEND

NFL THANKSGIVING CLASSICS 2006

Thursday, November 23	Miami_____ at Detroit _____	(CBS) 12:30
FOX-TV National Weekend	Tampa Bay_____ at Dallas _____	(FOX) 3:15
	Denver_____ at Kansas City _____	(NFLN) 7:00
Sunday, November 26	New Orleans_____ at Atlanta _____	1:00
	Pittsburgh_____ at Baltimore _____	1:00
	Jacksonville_____ at Buffalo _____	1:00
	Cincinnati_____ at Cleveland _____	1:00
	Philadelphia_____ at Indianapolis _____	1:00
	Arizona_____ at Minnesota _____	12:00
	Chicago_____ at New England _____	1:00
	Houston_____ at N.Y. Jets _____	1:00
	San Francisco_____ at St. Louis _____	12:00
	N.Y. Giants_____ at Tennessee _____	12:00
	Carolina_____ at Washington _____	1:00
	Oakland_____ at San Diego _____	1:05
	NBC Game TBD*	(NBC) 8:15 ET
Monday, November 27	Green Bay_____ at Seattle _____	(ESPN) 5:30

THIRTEENTH WEEKEND

Thursday, November 30	Baltimore_____ at Cincinnati _____	(NFLN) 8:00
Sunday, December 3	San Diego_____ at Buffalo _____	1:00
FOX-TV National Weekend	Minnesota_____ at Chicago _____	12:00
	Kansas City_____ at Cleveland _____	1:00
	N.Y. Jets_____ at Green Bay _____	12:00
	Jacksonville_____ at Miami _____	1:00
	Detroit_____ at New England _____	1:00
	San Francisco_____ at New Orleans _____	12:00
	Dallas_____ at N.Y. Giants _____	1:00
	Tampa Bay_____ at Pittsburgh _____	1:00
	Arizona_____ at St. Louis _____	12:00
	Indianapolis_____ at Tennessee _____	12:00
	Atlanta_____ at Washington _____	1:00
	Houston_____ at Oakland _____	1:05
	Seattle_____ at Denver _____	2:15
	NBC Game TBD*	(NBC) 8:15 ET
Monday, December 4	Carolina_____ at Philadelphia _____	(ESPN) 8:30

FOURTEENTH WEEKEND

Thursday, December 7	Cleveland_____ at Pittsburgh _____	(NFLN) 8:00
Sunday, December 10	N.Y. Giants_____ at Carolina _____	1:00
CBS-TV National Weekend	Oakland_____ at Cincinnati _____	1:00
	New Orleans_____ at Dallas _____	12:00
	Minnesota_____ at Detroit _____	1:00
	Tennessee_____ at Houston _____	12:00
	Indianapolis_____ at Jacksonville _____	1:00
	Baltimore_____ at Kansas City _____	12:00
	New England_____ at Miami _____	1:00
	Buffalo_____ at N.Y. Jets _____	1:00
	Atlanta_____ at Tampa Bay _____	1:00
	Philadelphia_____ at Washington _____	1:00
	Seattle_____ at Arizona _____	2:05
	Green Bay_____ at San Francisco _____	1:05
	Denver_____ at San Diego _____	1:15
	NBC Game TBD*	(NBC) 8:15 ET
Monday, December 11	Chicago_____ at St. Louis _____	(ESPN) 7:30

FIFTEENTH WEEKEND

Thursday, December 14	San Francisco_____ at Seattle _____	(NFLN) 5:00
Saturday, December 16	Dallas_____ at Atlanta _____	(NFLN) 8:00
Sunday, December 17	Cleveland_____ at Baltimore _____	1:00
FOX-TV National Weekend	Miami_____ at Buffalo _____	1:00
	Pittsburgh_____ at Carolina _____	1:00
	Tampa Bay_____ at Chicago _____	12:00
	Detroit_____ at Green Bay _____	12:00
	N.Y. Jets_____ at Minnesota _____	12:00
	Houston_____ at New England _____	1:00
	Washington_____ at New Orleans _____	12:00
	Philadelphia_____ at N.Y. Giants _____	1:00
	Jacksonville_____ at Tennessee _____	12:00
	Denver_____ at Arizona _____	2:05
	Kansas City_____ at San Diego _____	1:05
	St. Louis_____ at Oakland _____	1:15
	NBC Game TBD*	(NBC) 8:15 ET
Monday, December 18	Cincinnati_____ at Indianapolis _____	(ESPN) 8:30

SIXTEENTH WEEKEND

Thursday, December 21	Minnesota_____ at Green Bay _____	(NFLN) 7:00
Saturday, December 23	Kansas City_____ at Oakland _____	(NFLN) 5:00
Sunday, December 24	Carolina_____ at Atlanta _____	1:00
CBS-TV National Weekend	Tennessee_____ at Buffalo _____	1:00
	Tampa Bay_____ at Cleveland _____	1:00
	Chicago_____ at Detroit _____	1:00
	Indianapolis_____ at Houston _____	12:00
	New England_____ at Jacksonville _____	1:00
	New Orleans_____ at N.Y. Giants _____	1:00
	Baltimore_____ at Pittsburgh _____	1:00
	Washington_____ at St. Louis _____	12:00
	Arizona_____ at San Francisco _____	1:05
	Cincinnati_____ at Denver _____	2:15
	San Diego_____ at Seattle _____	1:15
Monday, December 25	Philadelphia_____ at Dallas _____	(NBC) 4:00
	N.Y. Jets_____ at Miami _____	(ESPN) 8:30

SEVENTEENTH WEEKEND

Saturday, December 30	N.Y. Giants_____ at Washington _____	(NFLN) 8:00
Sunday, December 31	Buffalo_____ at Baltimore _____	1:00
CBS-TV National Weekend &	Green Bay_____ at Chicago _____	12:00
FOX-TV National Weekend	Pittsburgh_____ at Cincinnati _____	1:00
	Detroit_____ at Dallas _____	12:00
	Cleveland_____ at Houston _____	12:00
	Miami_____ at Indianapolis _____	1:00
	Jacksonville_____ at Kansas City _____	12:00
	St. Louis_____ at Minnesota _____	12:00
	Carolina_____ at New Orleans _____	12:00
	Oakland_____ at N.Y. Jets _____	1:00
	Atlanta_____ at Philadelphia _____	1:00
	Seattle_____ at Tampa Bay _____	1:00
	New England_____ at Tennessee _____	12:00
	San Francisco_____ at Denver _____	2:15
	Arizona_____ at San Diego _____	1:15
	NBC Game TBD*	(NBC) 8:15 ET

The 2006 season signals the advent of primetime "flexible scheduling" in the NFL. That process will take place on Sunday nights on NBC in seven of the season's final eight weeks, from Weeks 10-15 and in Week 17.
The Sunday night game in those weeks is listed as "TBD." One game from that Sunday afternoon will be moved to Sunday night at 8:15 PM ET. The move will be announced 12 days before the game. For Week 17, the move may be announced six days before the game. Flexible scheduling will ensure quality matchups on Sunday night in those weeks and give surprise teams a chance to play their way onto primetime.

PLAYOFFS

Wild Card Playoff Games
Site Priorities
Two Wild Card teams (division non-champions with best two records) from each conference and the division champions with the third and fourth-best record in each conference will enter the first round of the playoffs. The division champion with the third-best record will play host to the Wild Card team with the second-best record. The division champion with the fourth-best record will play host to the Wild Card team with the best record. There are no restrictions on intra-division games.

Saturday, January 6, 2007 American Football Conference

_____ at _____ (NBC)

National Football Conference

_____ at _____ (NBC)

Sunday, January 7, 2007 American Football Conference

_____ at _____ (CBS)

National Football Conference

_____ at _____ (FOX)

Divisional Playoff Games
Site Priorities
In each conference, the two division champions with the highest won-lost-tied percentage during the regular season will play host to the Wild Card winners. The division champion with the best record in each conference is assured of playing the lowest seeded Wild Card survivor. There are no restrictions on intra-division games.

Saturday, January 13, 2007 American Football Conference

_____ at _____ (CBS)

National Football Conference

_____ at _____ (FOX)

Sunday, January 14, 2007 American Football Conference

_____ at _____ (CBS)

National Football Conference

_____ at _____ (FOX)

Championship Games
Site Priorities for
Championship Games
The home teams will be the surviving playoff winners with the best won-lost-tied percentage during the regular season. A Wild Card team cannot play host unless two Wild Card teams are in the game, in which case the Wild Card team that was seeded highest in the first round of the playoffs will be the home team.

Sunday, January 21, 2007 American Football Conference

_____ at _____ (CBS)

National Football Conference

_____ at _____ (FOX)

Super Bowl XLI

Sunday, February 4, 2007 Super Bowl XLI at Dolphin Stadium, South Florida

_____ vs. _____ (CBS)

AFC-NFC Pro Bowl

Saturday, February 10, 2007 AFC-NFC Pro Bowl at Aloha Stadium, Honolulu, Hawaii

AFC_____ vs. NFC_____ (CBS)

2006 NATIONALLY TELEVISED GAMES AT A GLANCE

All times ET.

Thursday, Sept. 7	Miami at Pittsburgh (NBC)	8:30 P.M.
Sunday, Sept. 10	Dallas at Jacksonville (FOX)	4:15 P.M.
	Indianapolis at N.Y. Giants (NBC)	8:15 P.M.
Monday, Sept. 11	Minnesota at Washington (ESPN)	7:00 P.M.
	San Diego at Oakland (ESPN)	10:15 P.M.
Sunday, Sept. 17	Kansas City at Denver (CBS)	4:15 P.M.
	Washington at Dallas (NBC)	8:15 P.M.
Monday, Sept. 18	Pittsburgh at Jacksonville (ESPN)	8:30 P.M.
Sunday, Sept. 24	N.Y. Giants at Seattle (FOX)	4:15 P.M.
	Denver at New England (NBC)	8:15 P.M.
Monday, Sept. 25	Atlanta at New Orleans (ESPN)	8:30 P.M.
Sunday, Oct. 1	New England at Cincinnati (CBS)	4:15 P.M.
	Seattle at Chicago (NBC)	8:15 P.M.
Monday, Oct. 2	Green Bay at Philadelphia (ESPN)	8:30 P.M.
Sunday, Oct. 8	Dallas at Philadelphia (FOX)	4:15 P.M.
	Pittsburgh at San Diego (NBC)	8:15 P.M.
Monday, Oct. 9	Baltimore at Denver (ESPN)	8:30 P.M.
Sunday, Oct. 15	Kansas City at Pittsburgh (CBS)	4:15 P.M.
	Oakland at Denver (NBC)	8:15 P.M.
Monday, Oct. 16	Chicago at Arizona (ESPN)	8:30 P.M.
Sunday, Oct. 22	Washington at Indianapolis (FOX)	4:15 P.M.
Monday, Oct. 23	N.Y. Giants at Dallas (ESPN)	8:30 P.M.
Sunday, Oct. 29	Indianapolis at Denver (CBS)	4:15 P.M.
	Dallas at Carolina (NBC)	8:15 P.M.
Monday, Oct. 30	New England at Minnesota (ESPN)	8:30 P.M.
Sunday, Nov. 5	Denver at Pittsburgh (CBS)	4:15 P.M.
	Indianapolis at New England (NBC)	8:15 P.M.
Monday, Nov. 6	Oakland at Seattle (ESPN)	8:30 P.M.
Sunday, Nov. 12	To be determined (FOX)	4:15 P.M.
	To be determined (NBC)*	8:15 P.M.
Monday, Nov. 13	Tampa Bay at Carolina (ESPN)	8:30 P.M.
Sunday, Nov. 19	To be determined (CBS)	4:15 P.M.
	To be determined (NBC)*	8:15 P.M.
Monday, Nov. 20	N.Y. Giants at Jacksonville (ESPN)	8:30 P.M.
Thursday, Nov. 23	Miami at Detroit (CBS)	12:30 P.M.
	Tampa Bay at Dallas (FOX)	4:15 P.M.
	Denver at Kansas City (NFL Network)	8:00 P.M.
Sunday, Nov. 26	To be determined (FOX)	4:15 P.M.
	To be determined (NBC)*	8:15 P.M.
Monday, Nov. 27	Green Bay at Seattle (ESPN)	8:30 P.M.
Thursday, Nov. 30	Baltimore at Cincinnati (NFL Network)	8:00 P.M.
Sunday, Dec. 3	To be determined (FOX)	4:15 P.M.
	To be determined (NBC)*	8:15 P.M.
Monday, Dec. 4	Carolina at Philadelphia (ESPN)	8:30 P.M.
Thursday, Dec. 7	Cleveland at Pittsburgh (NFL Network)	8:00 P.M.
Sunday, Dec. 10	To be determined (CBS)	4:15 P.M.
	To be determined (NBC)*	8:15 P.M.
Monday, Dec. 11	Chicago at St. Louis (ESPN)	8:30 P.M.
Thursday, Dec. 14	San Francisco at Seattle (NFL Network)	8:00 P.M.
Saturday, Dec. 16	Dallas at Atlanta (NFL Network)	8:00 P.M.
Sunday, Dec. 17	To be determined (FOX)	4:15 P.M.
	To be determined (NBC)*	8:15 P.M.
Monday, Dec. 18	Cincinnati at Indianapolis (ESPN)	8:30 P.M.
Thursday, Dec. 21	Minnesota at Green Bay (NFL Network)	8:00 P.M.
Saturday, Dec. 23	Kansas City at Oakland (NFL Network)	8:00 P.M.
Sunday, Dec. 24	Cincinnati at Denver (CBS)	4:15 P.M.
Monday, Dec. 25	Philadelphia at Dallas (NBC)	5:00 P.M.
	N.Y. Jets at Miami (ESPN)	8:30 P.M.
Saturday, Dec. 30	N.Y. Giants at Washington (NFL Network)	8:00 P.M.
Sunday, Dec. 31	To be determined (CBS)	4:15 P.M.
	To be determined (FOX)	4:15 P.M.
	To be determined (NBC)*	8:15 P.M.

POSTSEASON GAMES

Saturday, January 6	AFC and NFC Wild Card Playoffs (NBC)
Sunday, January 7	AFC and NFC Wild Card Playoffs (CBS and FOX)
Saturday, January 13	AFC and NFC Divisional Playoffs (CBS and FOX)
Sunday, January 14	AFC and NFC Divisional Playoffs (CBS and FOX)
Sunday, January 21	AFC and NFC Championship Games (CBS and FOX)
Sunday, February 4	Super Bowl XLI at Dolphin Stadium, South Florida (CBS)
Saturday, February 10	AFC-NFC Pro Bowl in Honolulu, Hawaii (CBS)

* The 2006 season signals the advent of primetime "flexible scheduling" in the NFL. That process will take place on Sunday nights on NBC in seven of the season's final eight weeks, from Weeks 10-15 and in Week 17.
The Sunday night game in those weeks is listed as "TBD." One game from that Sunday afternoon will be moved to Sunday night at 8:15 PM ET. The move will be announced 12 days before the game. For Week 17, the move may be announced six days before the game. Flexible scheduling will ensure quality matchups on Sunday night in those weeks and give surprise teams a chance to play their way onto primetime.

2006

July 5	Claiming period of 24 hours begins in waiver system.
Mid-July	Preseason training camps open. Clubs not permitted to open official preseason camp earlier than July 5. Veteran players cannot be required to report earlier than 15 days prior to club's first preseason game.
July 22#	Signing period ends at 4 P.M., New York time, for Unrestricted Free Agents to whom a June 1 tender was made by Old Club, and for Transition Players. After this date and through 4 P.M., New York time, on November 15, Old Club has exclusive negotiating rights to these players.
	#or the first scheduled day of the first NFL training camp, whichever is later.
August 5-6	Hall of Fame Weekend.
August 6	Pro Football Hall of Fame Game, Canton, Ohio: Oakland vs. Philadelphia
August 8	If a Drafted Rookie has not signed with his club by this date, he may not be traded to any other club in 2006.
August 8	Deadline for players under contract to report to earn a season of free-agency credit.
August 10-14	First Preseason Weekend.
August 12-16	Deadline for club to provide written notice to certain unsigned players and the NFLPA of its intent to place them on the Exempt List if they fail to report no later than one day prior to the club's second preseason game. Any player who fails to report prior to the deadline will be ineligible to play or receive compensation for at least three games (preseason or regular season) from the time that he reports.
August 29	Roster cut-down to maximum of 75 players on Active List by 4 P.M., New York time.
August 30	All tryouts on this date and for the remainder of the season must be reported to the League office.
September 2	Roster cut-down to maximum of 53 players on Active/Inactive List by 4 P.M., New York time. Clubs may dress minimum of 42 and maximum of 45 players and Third Quarterback for each regular-season and postseason game.
September 2	Simultaneously with the cut-down to 53, clubs that have players in the categories of Active/Physically Unable to Perform or Active/Non-Football Injury or Illness must take one of the following options: place player on Reserve/Physically Unable to Perform or Reserve/Non-Football Injury or Illness, whichever is applicable; ask waivers; terminate; trade; or continue to count him on Active List.
September 3	After 12 noon, New York time, clubs may establish a Practice Squad of eight players by signing free agents who do not have an accrued season of free-agency credit or who were on the 45-player Active List for less than nine regular-season games during their only Accrued Season(s). A player cannot

	participate on the Practice Squad for more than two seasons.
September 5	All clubs are required to file a personnel (injury) report with their conference Director of Information by 1 P.M., New York time, on this Tuesday and thereafter on each Wednesday before a regular-season game. Such report is to be updated by 1 P.M., New York time, each Thursday. An update must also be reported if there is any change in a player's condition after Thursday.
September 6	Beginning at 4 P.M., New York time, Team Salary includes all players receiving compensation under their 2006 contracts. Top 51 rule is no longer in effect.
September 7-11	Regular Season opens.
September 7-11	Beginning on these dates vested veterans terminated from the Active List or Inactive List (and from Reserve/Injured if the player is placed on Reserve/Injured after the beginning of the regular season) are entitled to receive, after the end of the regular-season schedule, Termination Pay pursuant to the terms of the 1993 CBA.
September 26	Priority on multiple waiver claims is now based on the current season's standing.
October 17	Beginning the day after the conclusion of the sixth regular-season weekend and continuing through the day after the conclusion of the ninth regular-season weekend, clubs are permitted to begin practicing players on Reserve/Physically Unable to Perform and Reserve/Non-Football Injury or Illness for a period not to exceed 21 days. Players may be activated during the 21-day practice period or until 4 P.M., New York time, on the day after the conclusion of the 21-day period.
October 17	All trading ends at 4 P.M., New York time.
October 18	Players with at least four previous pension-credited seasons are subject to the waiver system for the remainder of the regular season and postseason.
November 6	Deadline at 4 P.M., New York time, for an increase in a player's 2006 Salary to be counted as Salary for the current year. Any notice of an increase in a player's 2006 Salary received by the NFLMC after this deadline will be treated as a Signing Bonus.
November 14	Signing period ends at 4 P.M., New York time, for Franchise Players who are eligible to receive Offer Sheets.
November 14	Deadline for clubs to sign by 4 P.M., New York time, their unsigned Franchise and Transition Players, including Franchise Players who were eligible to receive Offer Sheets until this date. If still unsigned after this date, such players are prohibited from playing in NFL in 2006.
November 14	Deadline for clubs to sign by 4 P.M., New York time, their Unrestricted Free Agents to whom June 1 tender was made. If still unsigned after this date, such players are prohibited from playing in NFL in 2006.

November 14	Deadline for clubs to sign by 4 P.M., New York time, their Restricted Free Agents to whom June 1 tender was made. If such players remain unsigned, they are prohibited from playing in NFL in 2006.
November 14	Deadline for clubs to sign Drafted players by 4 P.M., New York time. If such players remain unsigned, they are prohibited from playing in NFL in 2006.
December 1	Deadline for reinstatement of players in Reserve List categories of Retired, Did Not Report, and Exclusive Rights, and of players who were placed on Reserve/Left Squad in a previous season.
December 29	Deadline for waiver requests in 2006, except for "special waiver requests," which have a 10-day claiming period, with termination or assignment delayed until after the Super Bowl.

2007

January 1	Clubs may begin signing free-agent players for the 2007 season.
January 6-7	Wild Card Playoff Games.
January 13-14	Divisional Playoff Games.
January 21	AFC and NFC Championship Games.
February 4	Super Bowl XLI, Dolphin Stadium, South Florida.
February 10	AFC-NFC Pro Bowl, Honolulu, Hawaii.

2008

| February 3 | Super Bowl XLII, Cardinals Stadium, Arizona. |

2009

| February 1* | Super Bowl XLIII, Raymond James Stadium, Tampa, Florida. |

2010

| February 7* | Super Bowl XLIV, Dolphin Stadium, South Florida. |

*Tentative date

The NFL is online to provide fans and media quick and easy access to all the latest professional football information.

NFL.COM—(http://NFL.com or AOL Keyword: NFL.com)

NFL.com, the league's year-round home page on the Internet, enters its tenth season in cyberspace. The site provides NFL information during the regular season, postseason, and offseason, including:

NEWS/STATS: Up-to-the-minute news from around the league, plus game previews, injury reports, and player and team stats.

TEAM AREAS: Customized areas for all 32 clubs, featuring updated rosters, depth carts, and all the latest news from the teams.

GAMEDAY COVERAGE: Live game coverage with play-by-play, scores, and statistics, including graphical drive charts and comprehensive scoreboard that does not require reloading to get the latest information.

VIDEO HIGHLIGHTS: The site showcases NFL Films video highlights of the previous week's games as well as upcoming matchups. Video also supports feature stories and team highlight clips from every game last season.

SUPERBOWL.COM—(http://SuperBowl.com)

Look for SuperBowl.com in late December for complete coverage of the playoffs and Super Bowl XLI. The multimedia site follows all postseason action and features audio and video clips of past Super Bowls.

During the week leading up to Super Bowl XLI, the site will go 'live' from South Florida, providing coverage of events, press conferences, and chats with Super Bowl players and coaches.

On Super Bowl Sunday, SuperBowl.com will showcase a live Internet cybercast, complete with online commentators calling the action. The site also features digital photos from the game, live public address audio and press-box announcements, and live audio from foreign broadcasts.

NFLEUROPE.COM—(http://NFLEurope.com)

The official site of NFL Europe League provides in-depth information on the six teams and their players, and weekly video highlights of game action. In addition, the site includes weekly player diaries from NFL allocated players, as well as a complete league stats package.

NFLYOUTHFOOTBALL.COM—(http://nflyouthfootball.com)

NFLyouthfootball.com is the NFL's official youth football website. Boys and girls ages 6-18 can be a part of something big by getting involved nationwide with one of the NFL's Youth Football programs. Coaches, parents, and youth organizations can learn how to host their own local NFL Punt, Pass, and Kick event and can learn how to get children involved with an NFL FLAG league in their local community. Our website is also a resource for coaches and parents to help them promote a positive experience for all youth participants. The NFL's youth football programs follow our Seven Guiding Principles, which are posted on our website, and were developed from feedback from kids, parents, and coaches.

PLAYFOOTBALL.COM—(http://playfootball.com)

PlayFootball.com is the NFL's official Website for kids. It offers boys and girls an interactive sports destination where kids and their families can get actively involved with the NFL. Youths also can find profiles on NFL players and people behind the scenes of the NFL, vote on weekly MVPs and Plays of the Week, play challenging games, and learn about football strategy and skill.

NFLHS.COM—(http://NFLHS.com)

The League's Website dedicated to high school football. NFLHS.com covers high school football on a nation-wide basis and also looks into the high school careers of current and former NFL players and coaches. NFLHS.com goes behind the scenes at major NFL events, such as the Super Bowl and the Draft, and provides coverage from a high school perspective. The site is packed with tips and drills, health and safety information, academic tips and news on the NFL's and its teams' efforts in the community. Whatever you are looking for regarding high school football, we've got it!

JOINTHETEAM.COM—(http://JoinTheTeam.com)

JointheTeam.com is the official Website dedicated to the off-the-field community work of the NFL and the member clubs. The site provides news and information regarding how the NFL gives back and serves as a useful tool for individuals who are looking for a way to make a difference in their communities. As part of the NFL's Join The Team platform, the site encourages people to unite with NFL teams, players and partners to give back to communities across America. Join The Team is a "call to action" —a way for everyone to come together and make a difference through community involvement.

PROFOOTBALLHOF.COM—(http://profootballhof.com)

Profootballhof.com is the official site of the Pro Football Hall of Fame in Canton, Ohio. In addition to a complete visitor's guide to the Hall, the site features bios, stories and Q & A's with Hall of Fame inductees, a detailed archive of football history, and information on appearances by members of the Hall.

OFFICIAL NFL TEAM SITES

In addition to a dedicated area on NFL.com, all 32 teams have their own Websites, which have separate URLs, and are linked from NFL.com.

Arizona Cardinals (www.azcardinals.com)
Atlanta Falcons (www.atlantafalcons.com)
Baltimore Ravens (www.baltimoreravens.com)
Buffalo Bills (www.buffalobills.com)
Carolina Panthers (www.panthers.com)
Chicago Bears (www.chicagobears.com)
Cincinnati Bengals (www.bengals.com)
Cleveland Browns (www.clevelandbrowns.com)
Dallas Cowboys (www.dallascowboys.com)
Denver Broncos (www.denverbroncos.com)
Detroit Lions (www.detroitlions.com)
Green Bay Packers (www.packers.com)
Houston Texans (www.houstontexans.com)
Indianapolis Colts (www.colts.com)
Jacksonville Jaguars (www.jaguars.com)
Kansas City Chiefs (www.kcchiefs.com)
Miami Dolphins (www.miamidolphins.com)
Minnesota Vikings (www.vikings.com)
New England Patriots (www.patriots.com)
New Orleans Saints (www.neworleanssaints.com)
New York Giants (www.giants.com)
New York Jets (www.newyorkjets.com)
Oakland Raiders (www.raiders.com)
Philadelphia Eagles (www.philadelphiaeagles.com)
Pittsburgh Steelers (www.steelers.com)
St. Louis Rams (www.stlouisrams.com)
San Diego Chargers (www.chargers.com)
San Francisco 49ers (www.sf49ers.com)
Seattle Seahawks (www.seahawks.com)
Tampa Bay Buccaneers (www.buccaneers.com)
Tennessee Titans (www.titansonline.com)
Washington Redskins (www.redskins.com)

NFL Network provides fans with a network to call their own. Seven days a week, 24 hours a day, 365 days a year, fans turn to NFL Network to receive information and insight straight from team headquarters, league offices and wherever else the NFL is making news.

NFL Network gives fans unprecedented year-round access to all NFL events, including the preseason, regular season, playoffs, Super Bowl, Pro Bowl, Scouting Combine, league meetings, the playing schedule, NFL Draft, mini-camps and training camps. And for the 2006 season, NFL Network has a new package of eight live games and will replay 75 key games. NFL Network also expands its college football programming to include a weekly Saturday highlights show, multiple midweek spotlights, live telecast of the Insight Bowl in December, and complete coverage of the Senior Bowl game and the accompanying week of events for the top pro prospects.

NFL Network is available on cable and satellite television through your local service provider. If your provider doesn't currently offer NFL Network, please call (866) NFL-NETWORK to make them aware of your interest in receiving it.

KEY PROGRAMMING

EXCLUSIVE LIVE PRIMETIME GAMES
NFL Network's new late season "Run to the Playoffs" eight-game Thursday-Saturday night package kicks off in high definition on Thanksgiving night with award-winning broadcasters Bryant Gumbel and Cris Collinsworth calling the game. Each game, at 8:00 PM ET, will be preceded by a special NFL Total Access pregame show, and followed by a live post-game show.

NFL TOTAL ACCESS
NFL Network's signature show is THE football show of record. NFL Total Access is uniquely structured to see the game through the participants' eyes, airing at 7:00 PM ET/PT every Monday through Saturday and hosted by Rich Eisen.

Covering all 32 teams, NFL Total Access features interviews with players, coaches and other key league personnel. Using the most advanced technology, NFL Total Access has the ability to go live to any NFL team headquarters at any time.

NFL GAMEDAY
After each Sunday's final game, the new 90-minute NFL GameDay delivers comprehensive coverage of the day's action. Hosted by Rich Eisen, GameDay kicks off at 11:30 PM ET and features highlights, post-game press conferences, on-field interviews, analysis and more in wrapping up each NFL Sunday. GameDay runs in a continuous loop until 1:00 PM ET each Monday.

NFL REPLAY
For the first time, NFL games will be re-aired with the original television announcers and cameras. This offering features the four most-exciting games each week in a 90-minute format (eliminating halftime and other non-critical elements) at 5:30 PM ET and 8:30 PM ET each Tuesday and Wednesday. Enhancements to each broadcast include additional camera angles, sideline sound and post-game interviews.

AT THE MIC
NFL Network brings you inside the interview rooms of the NFL and top college teams each weekday at 3:00 PM ET with At the Mic. Former NFL head coach Jim Mora, Sr. serves as analyst for At the Mic which focuses on the NFL on Mondays, Wednesdays and Fridays, and college football on Tuesdays and Thursdays.

POINT AFTER
After Sunday's early games conclude, NFL Network's Point After takes viewers around the league for post-game press conferences and game highlights. Point After airs at 4:00 PM ET on Sundays and will air through the Sunday evening game.

NFL SCOREBOARD
NFL Network provides the best place on television to get up-to-the-minute scores, statistics and news each game day during the season. A three-hour program airing at 1:00 PM ET on Sundays, NFL Scoreboard features continuously scrolling real-time game statistics with audio from Sirius NFL Radio's Around the League program.

AMERICA'S GAME
On Friday November 17, NFL Network kicks off a 40-part series featuring first-person accounts, behind-the-scenes access and Hollywood narrators profiling the winning team of each of the NFL's 40 Super Bowls. Each 60-minute episode of America's Game will air on a Friday night at 9:00 PM ET with the greatest 20 Super Bowl champions, as chosen by a blue-ribbon panel, revealed in reverse order with the final episode airing just before Super Bowl XLI.

COLLEGE SCOREBOARD
Kicking off at 4:00 PM ET each Saturday, College Scoreboard is NFL Network's first college football highlights show. A four-hour program, College Scoreboard recaps all the early action while looking ahead at the upcoming contests.

NFL NETWORK GAME OF THE WEEK
Every Friday at 9:00 PM ET on NFL Network Game of the Week, a 60-minute condensed version of a current or classic NFL game takes fans inside the game in a way they do not see on a weekend broadcast. Using unique NFL Films camera angles, microphones on the field and in the locker room, GOTW tells the story of the game from the inside out. This show is available in High Definition.

PRESEASON GAMES
NFL Network is the only place on television where fans can view the majority of NFL preseason games. NFL Network televises every game that does not appear on the four NFL broadcast partners (CBS, FOX, NBC, and ESPN) during the preseason, more than 50 games each summer.

Log on to www.NFL.com/NFLnetwork for more information on NFL Network.

SCHEDULING FORMULA

The NFL expanded to 32 teams in 2002 with the addition of the Houston Texans. In addition, the NFL realigned for the first time since 1970—into eight divisions of four teams each—and the scheduling formula that was introduced guarantees for the first time that all teams play each other on a regular, rotating basis. Although the number of teams has increased to 32, the number of playoff teams remains the same at 12.

Under the NFL scheduling formula, every team within a division plays 16 games as follows:

- Home and away against its three division opponents (6 games).
- The four teams from another division within its conference on a rotating three-year cycle (4 games).
- The four teams from a division in the other conference on a rotating four-year cycle (4 games).
- Two intraconference games based on the prior year's standings (2 games). These games will match a first-place team against the first-place teams in the two same-conference divisions the team is not scheduled to play that season. The second-place, third-place, and fourth-place teams in a conference will be matched in the same way each year.

"The scheduling formula is one of the most positive aspects of realignment," says NFL Commissioner Paul Tagliabue. "The formula guarantees that NFL fans will see every team play each other on a regular, rotating basis. The formula will eliminate the many aberrations of the past in which teams either did not play for long periods of time or did not play in another team's stadium for many years."

The schedule format takes each team through a cycle of games—home and away—against every other team in the league. From 2002-2009, every team will play every other team at least twice—once home and once away. After the 2009 season, a decision will be made on whether to continue with the same rotation or modify it.

In determining how to begin the divisional rotation in 2002, the displacement of teams from their old divisions in the new alignment was taken into account. Preference was given to scheduling games with former division rivals and other regional opponents for clubs realigned from otherwise intact divisions.

FUTURE SCHEDULING ROTATION

		2006	2007	2008	2009
AFC EAST	Intraconference	AFCS	AFCN	AFCW	AFCS
	Interconference	NFCN	NFCE	NFCW	NFCS
AFC NORTH	Intraconference	AFCW	AFCE	AFCS	AFCW
	Interconference	NFCS	NFCW	NFCE	NFCN
AFC SOUTH	Intraconference	AFCE	AFCW	AFCN	AFCE
	Interconference	NFCE	NFCS	NFCN	NFCW
AFC WEST	Intraconference	AFCN	AFCS	AFCE	AFCN
	Interconference	NFCW	NFCN	NFCS	NFCE
NFC EAST	Intraconference	NFCS	NFCN	NFCW	NFCS
	Interconference	AFCS	AFCE	AFCN	AFCW
NFC NORTH	Intraconference	NFCW	NFCE	NFCS	NFCW
	Interconference	AFCE	AFCW	AFCS	AFCN
NFC SOUTH	Intraconference	NFCE	NFCW	NFCN	NFCE
	Interconference	AFCN	AFCS	AFCW	AFCE
NFC WEST	Intraconference	NFCN	NFCS	NFCE	NFCN
	Interconference	AFCW	AFCN	AFCE	AFCS

AFC EAST NON-DIVISIONAL OPPONENTS 2006-2009

BUFFALO BILLS

	2006 Home	Away	2007 Home	Away
Intraconference by Division	JAX	HOU	BALT	CLE
	TENN	IND	CIN	PITT
Interconference by Division	GB	CHI	DALL	PHIL
	MINN	DET	NYG	WASH
Intraconference by Position	AFCW	AFCN	AFCW	AFCS

	2008 Home	Away	2009 Home	Away
Intraconference by Division	OAK	DEN	HOU	JAX
	SD	KC	IND	TENN
Interconference by Division	SF	ARIZ	NO	ATL
	SEA	STL	TB	CAR
Intraconference by Position	AFCN	AFCS	AFCN	AFCW

MIAMI DOLPHINS

	2006 Home	Away	2007 Home	Away
Intraconference by Division	JAX	HOU	BALT	CLE
	TENN	IND	CIN	PITT
Interconference by Division	GB	CHI	DALL	PHIL
	MINN	DET	NYG	WASH
Intraconference by Position	AFCW	AFCN	AFCW	AFCS

	2008 Home	Away	2009 Home	Away
Intraconference by Division	OAK	DEN	HOU	JAX
	SD	KC	IND	TENN
Interconference by Division	SF	ARIZ	NO	ATL
	SEA	STL	TB	CAR
Intraconference by Position	AFCN	AFCS	AFCN	AFCW

NEW ENGLAND PATRIOTS

	2006 Home	Away	2007 Home	Away
Intraconference by Division	HOU	JAX	CLE	BALT
	IND	TENN	PITT	CIN
Interconference by Division	CHI	GB	PHIL	DALL
	DET	MINN	WASH	NYG
Intraconference by Position	AFCW	AFCN	AFCW	AFCS

	2008 Home	Away	2009 Home	Away
Intraconference by Division	DEN	OAK	JAX	HOU
	KC	SD	TENN	IND
Interconference by Division	ARIZ	SF	ATL	NO
	STL	SEA	CAR	TB
Intraconference by Position	AFCN	AFCS	AFCN	AFCW

NEW YORK JETS

	2006 Home	Away	2007 Home	Away
Intraconference by Division	HOU	JAX	CLE	BALT
	IND	TENN	PITT	CIN
Interconference by Division	CHI	GB	PHIL	DALL
	DET	MINN	WASH	NYG
Intraconference by Position	AFCW	AFCN	AFCW	AFCS

	2008 Home	Away	2009 Home	Away
Intraconference by Division	DEN	OAK	JAX	HOU
	KC	SD	TENN	IND
Interconference by Division	ARIZ	SF	ATL	NO
	STL	SEA	CAR	TB
Intraconference by Position	AFCN	AFCS	AFCN	AFCW

AFC NORTH NON-DIVISIONAL OPPONENTS 2006-2009

BALTIMORE RAVENS

	2006			2007	
	Home	Away		Home	Away
Intraconference by Division	OAK	DEN		NE	BUFF
	SD	KC		NYJ	MIA
Interconference by Division	ATL	NO		ARIZ	SF
	CAR	TB		STL	SEA
Intraconference by Position	AFCE	AFCS		AFCS	AFCW

	2008			2009	
	Home	Away		Home	Away
Intraconference by Division	JAX	HOU		DEN	OAK
	TENN	IND		KC	SD
Interconference by Division	PHIL	DALL		CHI	GB
	WASH	NYG		DET	MINN
Intraconference by Position	AFCW	AFCE		AFCS	AFCE

CINCINNATI BENGALS

	2006			2007	
	Home	Away		Home	Away
Intraconference by Division	OAK	DEN		NE	BUFF
	SD	KC		NYJ	MIA
Interconference by Division	ATL	NO		ARIZ	SF
	CAR	TB		STL	SEA
Intraconference by Position	AFCE	AFCS		AFCS	AFCW

	2008			2009	
	Home	Away		Home	Away
Intraconference by Division	JAX	HOU		DEN	OAK
	TENN	IND		KC	SD
Interconference by Division	PHIL	DALL		CHI	GB
	WASH	NYG		DET	MINN
Intraconference by Position	AFCW	AFCE		AFCS	AFCE

CLEVELAND BROWNS

	2006			2007	
	Home	Away		Home	Away
Intraconference by Division	DEN	OAK		BUFF	NE
	KC	SD		MIA	NYJ
Interconference by Division	NO	ATL		SF	ARIZ
	TB	CAR		SEA	STL
Intraconference by Position	AFCE	AFCS		AFCS	AFCW

	2008			2009	
	Home	Away		Home	Away
Intraconference by Division	HOU	JAX		OAK	DEN
	IND	TENN		SD	KC
Interconference by Division	DALL	PHIL		GB	CHI
	NYG	WASH		MINN	DET
Intraconference by Position	AFCW	AFCE		AFCS	AFCE

PITTSBURGH STEELERS

	2006			2007	
	Home	Away		Home	Away
Intraconference by Division	DEN	OAK		BUFF	NE
	KC	SD		MIA	NYJ
Interconference by Division	NO	ATL		SF	ARIZ
	TB	CAR		SEA	STL
Intraconference by Position	AFCE	AFCS		AFCS	AFCW

	2008			2009	
	Home	Away		Home	Away
Intraconference by Division	HOU	JAX		OAK	DEN
	IND	TENN		SD	KC
Interconference by Division	DALL	PHIL		GB	CHI
	NYG	WASH		MINN	DET
Intraconference by Position	AFCW	AFCE		AFCS	AFCE

AFC SOUTH NON-DIVISIONAL OPPONENTS 2006-2009

HOUSTON TEXANS

	2006		2007	
	Home	Away	Home	Away
Intraconference by Division	BUFF	NE	DEN	OAK
	MIA	NYJ	KC	SD
Interconference by Division	PHIL	DALL	NO	ATL
	WASH	NYG	TB	CAR
Intraconference by Position	AFCN	AFCW	AFCE	AFCN

	2008		2009	
	Home	Away	Home	Away
Intraconference by Division	BALT	CLE	NE	BUFF
	CIN	PITT	NYJ	MIA
Interconference by Division	CHI	GB	SF	ARIZ
	DET	MINN	SEA	STL
Intraconference by Position	AFCE	AFCW	AFCW	AFCN

INDIANAPOLIS COLTS

	2006		2007	
	Home	Away	Home	Away
Intraconference by Division	BUFF	NE	DEN	OAK
	MIA	NYJ	KC	SD
Interconference by Division	PHIL	DALL	NO	ATL
	WASH	NYG	TB	CAR
Intraconference by Position	AFCN	AFCW	AFCE	AFCN

	2008		2009	
	Home	Away	Home	Away
Intraconference by Division	BALT	CLE	NE	BUFF
	CIN	PITT	NYJ	MIA
Interconference by Division	CHI	GB	SF	ARIZ
	DET	MINN	SEA	STL
Intraconference by Position	AFCE	AFCW	AFCW	AFCN

JACKSONVILLE JAGUARS

	2006		2007	
	Home	Away	Home	Away
Intraconference by Division	NE	BUFF	OAK	DEN
	NYJ	MIA	SD	KC
Interconference by Division	DALL	PHIL	ATL	NO
	NYG	WASH	CAR	TB
Intraconference by Position	AFCN	AFCW	AFCE	AFCN

	2008		2009	
	Home	Away	Home	Away
Intraconference by Division	CLE	BALT	BUFF	NE
	PITT	CIN	MIA	NYJ
Interconference by Division	GB	CHI	ARIZ	SF
	MINN	DET	STL	SEA
Intraconference by Position	AFCE	AFCW	AFCW	AFCN

TENNESSEE TITANS

	2006		2007	
	Home	Away	Home	Away
Intraconference by Division	NE	BUFF	OAK	DEN
	NYJ	MIA	SD	KC
Interconference by Division	DALL	PHIL	ATL	NO
	NYG	WASH	CAR	TB
Intraconference by Position	AFCN	AFCW	AFCE	AFCN

	2008		2009	
	Home	Away	Home	Away
Intraconference by Division	CLE	BALT	BUFF	NE
	PITT	CIN	MIA	NYJ
Interconference by Division	GB	CHI	ARIZ	SF
	MINN	DET	STL	SEA
Intraconference by Position	AFCE	AFCW	AFCW	AFCN

AFC WEST NON-DIVISIONAL OPPONENTS 2006-2009

DENVER BRONCOS

	2006			2007	
	Home	Away		Home	Away
Intraconference by Division	BALT	CLE		JAX	HOU
	CIN	PITT		TENN	IND
Interconference by Division	SF	ARIZ		GB	CHI
	SEA	STL		MINN	DET
Intraconference by Position	AFCS	AFCE		AFCN	AFCE

	2008			2009	
	Home	Away		Home	Away
Intraconference by Division	BUFF	NE		CLE	BALT
	MIA	NYJ		PITT	CIN
Interconference by Division	NO	ATL		DALL	PHIL
	TB	CAR		NYG	WASH
Intraconference by Position	AFCS	AFCN		AFCE	AFCS

KANSAS CITY CHIEFS

	2006			2007	
	Home	Away		Home	Away
Intraconference by Division	BALT	CLE		JAX	HOU
	CIN	PITT		TENN	IND
Interconference by Division	SF	ARIZ		GB	CHI
	SEA	STL		MINN	DET
Intraconference by Position	AFCS	AFCE		AFCN	AFCE

	2008			2009	
	Home	Away		Home	Away
Intraconference by Division	BUFF	NE		CLE	BALT
	MIA	NYJ		PITT	CIN
Interconference by Division	NO	ATL		DALL	PHIL
	TB	CAR		NYG	WASH
Intraconference by Position	AFCS	AFCN		AFCE	AFCS

OAKLAND RAIDERS

	2006			2007	
	Home	Away		Home	Away
Intraconference by Division	CLE	BALT		HOU	JAX
	PITT	CIN		IND	TENN
Interconference by Division	ARIZ	SF		CHI	GB
	STL	SEA		DET	MINN
Intraconference by Position	AFCS	AFCE		AFCN	AFCE

	2008			2009	
	Home	Away		Home	Away
Intraconference by Division	NE	BUFF		BALT	CLE
	NYJ	MIA		CIN	PITT
Interconference by Division	ATL	NO		PHIL	DALL
	CAR	TB		WASH	NYG
Intraconference by Position	AFCS	AFCN		AFCE	AFCS

SAN DIEGO CHARGERS

	2006			2007	
	Home	Away		Home	Away
Intraconference by Division	CLE	BALT		HOU	JAX
	PITT	CIN		IND	TENN
Interconference by Division	ARIZ	SF		CHI	GB
	STL	SEA		DET	MINN
Intraconference by Position	AFCS	AFCE		AFCN	AFCE

	2008			2009	
	Home	Away		Home	Away
Intraconference by Division	NE	BUFF		BALT	CLE
	NYJ	MIA		CIN	PITT
Interconference by Division	ATL	NO		PHIL	DALL
	CAR	TB		WASH	NYG
Intraconference by Position	AFCS	AFCN		AFCE	AFCS

NFC EAST NON-DIVISIONAL OPPONENTS 2006-2009

DALLAS COWBOYS

	2006			2007	
	Home	Away		Home	Away
Intraconference by Division	NO	ATL		GB	CHI
	TB	CAR		MINN	DET
Interconference by Division	HOU	JAX		NE	BUFF
	IND	TENN		NYJ	MIA
Intraconference by Position	NFCN	NFCW		NFCW	NFCS

	2008			2009	
	Home	Away		Home	Away
Intraconference by Division	SF	ARIZ		ATL	NO
	SEA	STL		CAR	TB
Interconference by Division	BALT	CLE		OAK	DEN
	CIN	PITT		SD	KC
Intraconference by Position	NFCS	NFCN		NFCW	NFCN

NEW YORK GIANTS

	2006			2007	
	Home	Away		Home	Away
Intraconference by Division	NO	ATL		GB	CHI
	TB	CAR		MINN	DET
Interconference by Division	HOU	JAX		NE	BUFF
	IND	TENN		NYJ	MIA
Intraconference by Position	NFCN	NFCW		NFCW	NFCS

	2008			2009	
	Home	Away		Home	Away
Intraconference by Division	SF	ARIZ		ATL	NO
	SEA	STL		CAR	TB
Interconference by Division	BALT	CLE		OAK	DEN
	CIN	PITT		SD	KC
Intraconference by Position	NFCS	NFCN		NFCW	NFCN

PHILADELPHIA EAGLES

	2006			2007	
	Home	Away		Home	Away
Intraconference by Division	ATL	NO		CHI	GB
	CAR	TB		DET	MINN
Interconference by Division	JAX	HOU		BUFF	NE
	TENN	IND		MIA	NYJ
Intraconference by Position	NFCN	NFCW		NFCW	NFCS

	2008			2009	
	Home	Away		Home	Away
Intraconference by Division	ARIZ	SF		NO	ATL
	STL	SEA		TB	CAR
Interconference by Division	CLE	BALT		DEN	OAK
	PITT	CIN		KC	SD
Intraconference by Position	NFCS	NFCN		NFCW	NFCN

WASHINGTON REDSKINS

	2006			2007	
	Home	Away		Home	Away
Intraconference by Division	ATL	NO		CHI	GB
	CAR	TB		DET	MINN
Interconference by Division	JAX	HOU		BUFF	NE
	TENN	IND		MIA	NYJ
Intraconference by Position	NFCN	NFCW		NFCW	NFCS

	2008			2009	
	Home	Away		Home	Away
Intraconference by Division	ARIZ	SF		NO	ATL
	STL	SEA		TB	CAR
Interconference by Division	CLE	BALT		DEN	OAK
	PITT	CIN		KC	SD
Intraconference by Position	NFCS	NFCN		NFCW	NFCN

NFC NORTH NON-DIVISIONAL OPPONENTS 2006-2009

CHICAGO BEARS

	2006		2007	
	Home	Away	Home	Away
Intraconference by Division	SF	ARIZ	DALL	PHIL
	SEA	STL	NYG	WASH
Interconference by Division	BUFF	NE	DEN	OAK
	MIA	NYJ	KC	SD
Intraconference by Position	NFCS	NFCE	NFCS	NFCW

	2008		2009	
	Home	Away	Home	Away
Intraconference by Division	NO	ATL	ARIZ	SF
	TB	CAR	STL	SEA
Interconference by Division	JAX	HOU	CLE	BALT
	TENN	IND	PITT	CIN
Intraconference by Position	NFCE	NFCW	NFCE	NFCS

DETROIT LIONS

	2006		2007	
	Home	Away	Home	Away
Intraconference by Division	SF	ARIZ	DALL	PHIL
	SEA	STL	NYG	WASH
Interconference by Division	BUFF	NE	DEN	OAK
	MIA	NYJ	KC	SD
Intraconference by Position	NFCS	NFCE	NFCS	NFCW

	2008		2009	
	Home	Away	Home	Away
Intraconference by Division	NO	ATL	ARIZ	SF
	TB	CAR	STL	SEA
Interconference by Division	JAX	HOU	CLE	BALT
	TENN	IND	PITT	CIN
Intraconference by Position	NFCE	NFCW	NFCE	NFCS

GREEN BAY PACKERS

	2006		2007	
	Home	Away	Home	Away
Intraconference by Division	ARIZ	SF	PHIL	DALL
	STL	SEA	WASH	NYG
Interconference by Division	NE	BUFF	OAK	DEN
	NYJ	MIA	SD	KC
Intraconference by Position	NFCS	NFCE	NFCS	NFCW

	2008		2009	
	Home	Away	Home	Away
Intraconference by Division	ATL	NO	SF	ARIZ
	CAR	TB	SEA	STL
Interconference by Division	HOU	JAX	BALT	CLE
	IND	TENN	CIN	PITT
Intraconference by Position	NFCE	NFCW	NFCE	NFCS

MINNESOTA VIKINGS

	2006		2007	
	Home	Away	Home	Away
Intraconference by Division	ARIZ	SF	PHIL	DALL
	STL	SEA	WASH	NYG
Interconference by Division	NE	BUFF	OAK	DEN
	NYJ	MIA	SD	KC
Intraconference by Position	NFCS	NFCE	NFCS	NFCW

	2008		2009	
	Home	Away	Home	Away
Intraconference by Division	ATL	NO	SF	ARIZ
	CAR	TB	SEA	STL
Interconference by Division	HOU	JAX	BALT	CLE
	IND	TENN	CIN	PITT
Intraconference by Position	NFCE	NFCW	NFCE	NFCS

NFC SOUTH NON-DIVISIONAL OPPONENTS 2006-2009

ATLANTA FALCONS

	2006		2007	
	Home	Away	Home	Away
Intraconference by Division	DALL	PHIL	SF	ARIZ
	NYG	WASH	SEA	STL
Interconference by Division	CLE	BALT	HOU	JAX
	PITT	CIN	IND	TENN
Intraconference by Position	NFCW	NFCN	NFCE	NFCN

	2008		2009	
	Home	Away	Home	Away
Intraconference by Division	CHI	GB	PHIL	DALL
	DET	MINN	WASH	NYG
Interconference by Division	DEN	OAK	BUFF	NE
	KC	SD	MIA	NYJ
Intraconference by Position	NFCW	NFCE	NFCN	NFCW

CAROLINA PANTHERS

	2006		2007	
	Home	Away	Home	Away
Intraconference by Division	DALL	PHIL	SF	ARIZ
	NYG	WASH	SEA	STL
Interconference by Division	CLE	BALT	HOU	JAX
	PITT	CIN	IND	TENN
Intraconference by Position	NFCW	NFCN	NFCE	NFCN

	2008		2009	
	Home	Away	Home	Away
Intraconference by Division	CHI	GB	PHIL	DALL
	DET	MINN	WASH	NYG
Interconference by Division	DEN	OAK	BUFF	NE
	KC	SD	MIA	NYJ
Intraconference by Position	NFCW	NFCE	NFCN	NFCW

NEW ORLEANS SAINTS

	2006		2007	
	Home	Away	Home	Away
Intraconference by Division	PHIL	DALL	ARIZ	SF
	WASH	NYG	STL	SEA
Interconference by Division	BALT	CLE	JAX	HOU
	CIN	PITT	TENN	IND
Intraconference by Position	NFCW	NFCN	NFCE	NFCN

	2008		2009	
	Home	Away	Home	Away
Intraconference by Division	GB	CHI	DALL	PHIL
	MINN	DET	NYG	WASH
Interconference by Division	OAK	DEN	NE	BUFF
	SD	KC	NYJ	MIA
Intraconference by Position	NFCW	NFCE	NFCN	NFCW

TAMPA BAY BUCCANEERS

	2006		2007	
	Home	Away	Home	Away
Intraconference by Division	PHIL	DALL	ARIZ	SF
	WASH	NYG	STL	SEA
Interconference by Division	BALT	CLE	JAX	HOU
	CIN	PITT	TENN	IND
Intraconference by Position	NFCW	NFCN	NFCE	NFCN

	2008		2009	
	Home	Away	Home	Away
Intraconference by Division	GB	CHI	DALL	PHIL
	MINN	DET	NYG	WASH
Interconference by Division	OAK	DEN	NE	BUFF
	SD	KC	NYJ	MIA
Intraconference by Position	NFCW	NFCE	NFCN	NFCW

NFC WEST NON-DIVISIONAL OPPONENTS 2006-2009

ARIZONA CARDINALS

	2006 Home	Away	2007 Home	Away
Intraconference by Division	CHI	GB	ATL	NO
	DET	MINN	CAR	TB
Interconference by Division	DEN	OAK	CLE	BALT
	KC	SD	PITT	CIN
Intraconference by Position	NFCE	NFCS	NFCN	NFCE

	2008 Home	Away	2009 Home	Away
Intraconference by Division	DALL	PHIL	GB	CHI
	NYG	WASH	MINN	DET
Interconference by Division	BUFF	NE	HOU	JAX
	MIA	NYJ	IND	TENN
Intraconference by Position	NFCN	NFCS	NFCS	NFCE

ST. LOUIS RAMS

	2006 Home	Away	2007 Home	Away
Intraconference by Division	CHI	GB	ATL	NO
	DET	MINN	CAR	TB
Interconference by Division	DEN	OAK	CLE	BALT
	KC	SD	PITT	CIN
Intraconference by Position	NFCE	NFCS	NFCN	NFCE

	2008 Home	Away	2009 Home	Away
Intraconference by Division	DALL	PHIL	GB	CHI
	NYG	WASH	MINN	DET
Interconference by Division	BUFF	NE	HOU	JAX
	MIA	NYJ	IND	TENN
Intraconference by Position	NFCN	NFCS	NFCS	NFCE

SAN FRANCISCO 49ERS

	2006 Home	Away	2007 Home	Away
Intraconference by Division	GB	CHI	NO	ATL
	MINN	DET	TB	CAR
Interconference by Division	OAK	DEN	BALT	CLE
	SD	KC	CIN	PITT
Intraconference by Position	NFCE	NFCS	NFCN	NFCE

	2008 Home	Away	2009 Home	Away
Intraconference by Division	PHIL	DALL	CHI	GB
	WASH	NYG	DET	MINN
Interconference by Division	NE	BUFF	JAX	HOU
	NYJ	MIA	TENN	IND
Intraconference by Position	NFCN	NFCS	NFCS	NFCE

SEATTLE SEAHAWKS

	2006 Home	Away	2007 Home	Away
Intraconference by Division	GB	CHI	NO	ATL
	MINN	DET	TB	CAR
Interconference by Division	OAK	DEN	BALT	CLE
	SD	KC	CIN	PITT
Intraconference by Position	NFCE	NFCS	NFCN	NFCE

	2008 Home	Away	2009 Home	Away
Intraconference by Division	PHIL	DALL	CHI	GB
	WASH	NYG	DET	MINN
Interconference by Division	NE	BUFF	JAX	HOU
	NYJ	MIA	TENN	IND
Intraconference by Position	NFCN	NFCS	NFCS	NFCE

TOP ACTIVE PASSERS
1,000 or more attempts

		Yrs.	Att.	Comp.	Pct. Comp.	Yards	TD	Pct. TD	Had Int.	Pct. Int.	Ratings Pts.
1.	Kurt Warner, Ari.	8	2,340	1,537	65.7	19,214	119	5.1	78	3.3	94.1
2.	Peyton Manning, Ind.	8	4,333	2,769	63.9	33,189	244	5.6	130	3.0	93.5
3.	Chad Pennington, NYJ	6	1,174	767	65.3	8,621	55	4.7	30	2.6	92.1
4.	Daunte Culpepper, Mia.	7	2,607	1,678	64.4	20,162	135	5.2	86	3.3	91.5
5.	Marc Bulger, St.L.	4	1,518	987	65.0	11,932	71	4.7	51	3.4	90.6
6.	Tom Brady, N.E.	6	2,548	1,577	61.9	18,035	123	4.8	66	2.6	88.5
7.	Trent Green, K.C.	8	3,329	2,022	60.7	25,621	150	4.5	92	2.8	88.3
8.	Matt Hasselbeck, Sea.	7	2,205	1,342	60.9	15,925	96	4.4	57	2.6	86.6
9.	Brett Favre, G.B.	15	7,610	4,678	61.5	53,615	396	5.2	255	3.4	86.0
10.	Jeff Garcia, Phi.	7	2,785	1,695	60.9	19,076	126	4.5	71	2.5	85.8
11.	Drew Brees, N.O.	5	1,809	1,125	62.2	12,348	80	4.4	53	2.9	84.9
12.	Brian Griese, Chi.	8	2,318	1,463	63.1	16,344	103	4.4	78	3.4	84.8
13.	Jake Delhomme, Car.	5	1,503	888	59.1	11,160	75	5.0	52	3.5	84.5
14.	Brad Johnson, Min.	12	3,798	2,350	61.9	25,798	155	4.1	102	2.7	84.4
15.	Donovan McNabb, Phi.	7	2,943	1,718	58.4	19,433	134	4.6	66	2.2	84.1
16.	Mark Brunell, Was.	12	4,334	2,576	59.4	30,037	174	4.0	102	2.4	84.1
17.	Steve McNair, Ten.	11	3,871	2,305	59.5	27,141	156	4.0	103	2.7	83.3
18.	Byron Leftwich, Jax.	3	1,161	681	58.7	7,883	44	3.8	31	2.7	80.8
19.	Aaron Brooks, Oak.	6	2,771	1,563	56.4	19,156	120	4.3	84	3.0	79.7
20.	Jeff Blake, *	13	3,241	1,827	56.4	21,711	134	4.1	99	3.1	78.0
21.	Drew Bledsoe, Dal.	13	6,548	3,749	57.3	43,447	244	3.7	198	3.0	77.3
22.	Jay Fiedler, *	8	1,717	1,008	58.7	11,844	69	4.0	66	3.8	77.1
23.	Charlie Batch, Pit.	8	1,370	770	56.2	9,309	50	3.6	41	3.0	76.9
24.	Michael Vick, Atl.	5	1,342	726	54.1	9,031	51	3.8	39	2.9	75.8
25.	Gus Frerotte, St.L.	12	2,635	1,426	54.1	18,093	95	3.6	79	3.0	75.3

TOP ACTIVE SCORERS
(number in parantheses represents 2-point conversions scored)

		Yrs.	TD	FG	PAT	TP
1.	John Carney, N.O.	18	0	390	464	1,634
2.	Matt Stover, Bal.	15	0	380	454	1,594
3.	Jason Elam, Den.	13	0	341	534	1,557
4.	Jason Hanson, Det.	14	0	327	439	1,420
5.	John Kasay, Car.	15	0	310	375	1,305
6.	Jeff Wilkins, St.L.	12	0	251	435	1,188
7.	Adam Vinatieri, Ind.	10	0	263	367(1)	1,158
8.	Ryan Longwell, Min.	9	0	226	376	1,054
9.	Todd Peterson, *	12	0	235	338	1,043
10.	Mike Vanderjagt, Dal.	8	0	217	344	995
11.	Olindo Mare, Mia.	9	0	219	291	948
12.	John Hall, Was.	9	0	194	271	853
13.	Marshall Faulk, St.L.	12	136	0	0(7)	830
14.	David Akers, Phi.	8	0	155	224	689
15.	Kris Brown, Hou.	7	0	158	201	675
16.	Marvin Harrison, Ind.	10	110	0	0(5)	670
17.	Joe Nedney, S.F.	10	0	153	210	669
18.	Sebastian Janikowski, Oak.	6	0	138	227	641
19.	Terrell Owens, Dal.	10	103	0	0(2)	622
20.	Curtis Martin, NYJ	11	100	0	0(3)	606
21.	Shaun Alexander, Sea.	6	100	0	0(3)	600
	Randy Moss, Oak.	8	99	0	0(3)	600
23.	Martin Gramatica, N.E.	6	0	137	181	592
24.	Jay Feely, NYG	5	0	133	185	584
25.	Phil Dawson, Cle.	7	1	135	170	581

TOP ACTIVE RUSHERS

		Yrs.	Att.	Yards	TD
1.	Curtis Martin, NYJ	11	3,518	14,101	90
2.	Marshall Faulk, St.L.	12	2,836	12,279	100
3.	Corey Dillon, N.E.	9	2,419	10,429	69
4.	Edgerrin James, Ari.	7	2,188	9,226	64
5.	Tiki Barber, NYG	9	1,890	8,787	50
6.	Fred Taylor, Jax.	8	1,831	8,367	51
7.	Warrick Dunn, Atl.	9	1,970	8,321	39
8.	Priest Holmes, K.C.	9	1,734	8,035	86
9.	Stephen Davis, *	10	1,905	7,875	65
10.	Shaun Alexander, Sea.	6	1,717	7,817	89
11.	Ahman Green, G.B.	8	1,605	7,432	49
12.	LaDainian Tomlinson, S.D.	5	1,702	7,361	72
13.	Antowain Smith, Hou.	8	1,784	6,881	54
14.	Jamal Lewis, Bal.	5	1,508	6,669	36
15.	Clinton Portis, Was.	4	1,258	5,930	45
16.	Duce Staley, Pit.	9	1,430	5,785	24
17.	Mike Alstott, T.B.	10	1,299	4,917	55
18.	Michael Pittman, T.B.	8	1,198	4,776	20
19.	Deuce McAllister, N.O.	5	1,054	4,529	34
20.	Travis Henry, Ten.	5	1,051	4,184	27
21.	Thomas Jones, Chi.	6	1,053	4,174	28
22.	Rudi Johnson, Cin.	5	930	3,936	33
23.	Mike Anderson, Bal.	5	865	3,822	36
24.	Kevan Barlow, S.F.	5	891	3,614	24
25.	Steve McNair, Ten.	11	614	3,439	36

Free agent; subject to developments.

TOP ACTIVE PASS RECEIVERS

	Yrs.	No.	Yards	TD
1. Marvin Harrison, Ind.	10	927	12,331	110
2. Keenan McCardell, S.D.	14	825	10,680	62
3. Isaac Bruce, St.L.	12	813	12,278	77
4. Rod Smith, Den.	11	797	10,877	65
5. Marshall Faulk, St.L.	12	767	6,875	36
6. Keyshawn Johnson, Car.	10	744	9,756	60
7. Terrell Owens, Dal.	10	716	10,535	101
8. Eric Moulds, Hou.	9	675	9,096	48
9. Ricky Proehl, *	16	666	8,848	54
10. Tony Gonzalez, K.C.	9	648	7,810	56
11. Muhsin Muhammad, Chi.	10	642	8,501	48
12. Randy Moss, Oak.	8	634	10,147	98
13. Johnnie Morton, *	12	624	8,719	43
14. Torry Holt, St.L.	7	619	9,487	54
15. Hines Ward, Pit.	8	574	7,030	52
16. Joey Galloway, T.B.	11	550	8,501	64
17. Joe Horn, N.O.	10	539	7,822	53
Derrick Mason, Bal.	9	539	7,187	40
19. Amani Toomer, NYG	10	529	7,797	44
20. Tiki Barber, NYG	9	528	4,718	12
21. Terry Glenn, Dal.	10	523	7,776	38
22. Troy Brown, N.E.	13	514	5,982	27
23. Curtis Martin, NYJ	11	484	3,329	10
24. Eddie Kennison, K.C.	10	482	7,384	37
25. Bobby Engram, Sea.	10	480	5,764	28

TOP ACTIVE INTERCEPTORS

	Yrs.	No.	Yards	TD
1. Terrell Buckley, *	14	50	793	6
2. Troy Vincent, Buf.	14	47	711	3
3. Ty Law, *	11	46	778	7
4. Darren Sharper, Min.	9	45	953	7
5. Aaron Glenn, Dal.	12	39	525	5
6. Sammy Knight, K.C.	9	37	606	4
7. Tory James, Cin.	9	35	333	0
8. Patrick Surtain, K.C.	8	33	355	2
9. Rodney Harrison, N.E.	12	31	357	2
Sam Madison, NYG	9	31	487	2
Dewayne Washington, *	12	31	569	5
12. Dre' Bly, Det.	7	30	497	5
Dexter McCleon, *	9	30	160	0
Tony Parrish, S.F.	8	30	670	2
15. Champ Bailey, Den.	7	29	263	3
Deltha O'Neal, Cin.	6	29	354	3
17. Brent Alexander, *	12	28	253	0
Ronde Barber, T.B.	9	28	449	3
Brian Dawkins, Phi.	10	28	451	2
20. John Lynch, Den.	13	26	204	0
Shawn Springs, Was.	9	26	354	2
Greg Wesley, K.C.	6	26	503	0
Willie Williams, *	13	26	302	4
24. Marcus Coleman, Dal.	10	25	476	2
Duane Starks, Oak.	8	25	245	2

TOP ACTIVE PUNT RETURNERS

40 or more punt returns

	Yrs.	No.	Yards	Avg.	TD
1. Rod Smith, Den.	11	52	645	12.4	1
2. Santana Moss, Was.	5	95	1,092	11.5	2
3. B.J. Sams, Bal.	2	88	976	11.1	2
4. Michael Lewis, N.O.	5	126	1,371	10.9	1
5. Allen Rossum, Atl.	8	207	2,229	10.8	3
6. Az-Zahir Hakim, *	8	165	1,773	10.7	3
7. Phillip Buchanon, Hou.	4	84	891	10.6	3
8. Dennis Northcutt, Cle.	6	174	1,837	10.6	3
9. Troy Brown, N.E.	13	244	2,554	10.5	3
10. Bobby Engram, Sea.	10	101	1,053	10.4	2
11. Hank Poteat, N.E.	5	76	788	10.4	1
12. Dante Hall, K.C.	6	161	1,642	10.2	4
13. Eddie Kennison, K.C.	10	142	1,430	10.1	3
14. Deltha O'Neal, Cin.	6	135	1,358	10.1	2
15. Reggie Swinton, *	5	132	1,311	9.9	2
16. Wes Welker, Mia.	2	86	854	9.9	0
17. Lamont Brightful, *	4	69	681	9.9	1
18. Joey Galloway, T.B.	11	136	1,332	9.8	5
19. Steve Smith, Car.	5	160	1,559	9.7	4
20. Amani Toomer, NYG	10	109	1,060	9.7	3
21. Tim Dwight, NYJ	8	162	1,573	9.7	3
22. Tiki Barber, NYG	9	122	1,181	9.7	1
23. Eddie Drummond, Det.	4	80	762	9.5	4
24. R.W. McQuarters, NYG	8	168	1,596	9.5	3
25. Nate Clements, Buf.	5	65	617	9.5	2

TOP ACTIVE KICKOFF RETURNERS

40 or more kickoff returns

	Yrs.	No.	Yards	Avg.	TD
1. Jerome Mathis, Hou.	1	54	1,542	28.6	2
2. Terrence McGee, Buf.	3	106	2,921	27.6	4
3. Willie Ponder, NYG	3	71	1,872	26.4	2
4. Justin Miller, NYJ	1	60	1,577	26.3	1
5. Pacman Jones, Ten.	1	43	1,127	26.2	0
6. Koren Robinson, Min.	5	47	1,221	26.0	1
7. Bethel Johnson, N.E.	3	102	2,557	25.1	2
8. Reuben Droughns, Cle.	5	51	1,272	24.9	0
9. Steve Smith, Car.	5	96	2,372	24.7	2
10. Tyson Thompson, Dal.	1	57	1,399	24.5	0
11. Tab Perry, Cin.	1	64	1,562	24.4	0
12. Eddie Drummond, Det.	4	151	3,677	24.4	2
13. Ladell Betts, Was.	4	78	1,898	24.3	1
14. Josh Cribbs, Cle.	1	45	1,094	24.3	1
15. Terry Fair, *	6	111	2,698	24.3	2
16. Kevin Kasper, Sea.	5	77	1,869	24.3	0
17. Darren Sproles, S.D.	1	63	1,528	24.3	0
18. Deuce McAllister, N.O.	5	45	1,091	24.2	0
19. Jerry Azumah, *	7	119	2,885	24.2	2
20. Dante Hall, K.C.	6	307	7,437	24.2	6
21. Michael Lewis, N.O.	5	206	4,989	24.2	3
22. Najeh Davenport, G.B.	4	46	1,110	24.1	0
23. Duce Staley, Pit.	9	48	1,158	24.1	0
24. Jonathan Carter, T.B.	5	44	1,060	24.1	1
25. Chris Carr, Oak.	1	73	1,752	24.0	0

TOP ACTIVE PUNTERS
50 or more punts

		Yrs.	No.	Avg.	LG
1.	Shane Lechler, Oak.	6	442	45.9	73
2.	Chris Kluwe, Min.	1	71	44.1	62
3.	Todd Sauerbrun, Den.	11	832	44.0	73
4.	Ben Graham, NYJ	1	74	43.7	59
5.	Tom Rouen, Sea.	13	810	43.4	76
6.	Brian Moorman, Buf.	5	379	43.4	84
7.	Mike Scifres, S.D.	3	140	43.4	71
8.	Tom Tupa, *	17	873	43.4	73
9.	Hunter Smith, Ind.	7	425	43.4	69
10.	Chris Hanson, Jax.	6	356	43.3	74
11.	Sean Landeta, *	21	1,401	43.3	74
12.	Mitch Berger, N.O.	11	710	43.2	75
13.	Josh Miller, N.E.	10	704	43.1	75
14.	Craig Hentrich, Ten.	12	896	42.9	78
15.	Scott Player, Ari.	8	648	42.9	67
16.	Chris Gardocki, Pit.	15	1,112	42.8	72
17.	Leo Araguz, Bal.	7	322	42.6	64
18.	Kyle Larson, Cin.	2	143	42.6	75
19.	Mat McBriar, Dal.	2	156	42.4	68
20.	Matt Turk, StL.	10	790	42.4	77
21.	Michael Koenen, Atl.	1	78	42.3	67
22.	Donnie Jones, Mia.	2	114	42.2	63
23.	Josh Bidwell, T.B.	6	480	42.2	68
24.	Bryan Barker, *	16	1,132	42.1	83
25.	Brad Maynard, Chi.	9	837	42.0	75

TOP ACTIVE QUARTERBACK SACKERS

		Yrs.	No.
1.	Michael Strahan, NYG	13	129.5
2.	Simeon Rice, T.B.	10	119.0
3.	Jason Taylor, Mia.	9	92.5
4.	Kevin Carter, Mia.	11	92.0
5.	Warren Sapp, Oak.	11	84.5
6.	Chad Brown, *	13	78.0
7.	Willie McGinest, Cle.	12	78.0
8.	Bryant Young, S.F.	12	77.5
9.	La'Roi Glover, St.L.	10	71.5
10.	Peter Boulware, *	9	70.0
11.	Lance Johnstone, Oak.	10	70.0
12.	Marco Coleman, *	14	65.5
13.	Trevor Pryce, Bal.	9	64.0
14.	Jevon Kearse, Phi.	7	62.5
15.	Leonard Little, St.L.	8	61.0
16.	Kabeer Gbaja-Biamila, G.B.	6	58.5
17.	Dan Wilkinson, Det.	12	54.5
18.	John Abraham, Atl.	6	53.5
19.	Phillip Daniels, Was.	10	53.5
20.	Patrick Kerney, Atl.	7	53.5
21.	Joey Porter, Pit.	7	53.0
22.	Greg Ellis, Dal.	8	52.0
23.	Junior Seau, *	16	52.0
24.	Dwight Freeney, Ind.	4	51.0
25.	Rod Coleman, Atl.	7	50.5

COACHES RECORDS

ACTIVE COACHES' CAREER RECORDS (Order Based on Career Victories)
Start of 2006 Season

Coach	Team(s)	Yrs.	Regular Season Won	Lost	Tied	Pct.	Postseason Won	Lost	Pct.	Career Won	Lost	Tied	Pct.
Marty Schottenheimer	Cleveland Browns, Kansas City Chiefs, Washington Redskins, San Diego Chargers	20	186	124	1	.600	5	12	.294	191	136	1	.584
Bill Parcells	New York Giants, New England Patriots, New York Jets, Dallas Cowboys	18	163	123	1	.570	11	7	.611	174	130	1	.572
Joe Gibbs	Washington Redskins	14	140	76	0	.648	17	6	.739	157	82	0	.657
Bill Cowher	Pittsburgh Steelers	14	141	82	1	.632	12	9	.571	153	91	1	.627
Mike Holmgren	Green Bay Packers, Seattle Seahawks	14	138	86	0	.616	11	9	.550	149	95	0	.611
Mike Shanahan	Los Angeles Raiders, Denver Broncos	13	122	74	0	.622	8	5	.615	130	79	0	.622
Dennis Green	Minnesota Vikings, Arizona Cardinals	12	108	83	0	.565	4	8	.333	112	91	0	.552
Bill Belichick	Cleveland Browns, New England Patriots	11	99	77	0	.563	11	2	.846	110	79	0	.582
Tony Dungy	Tampa Bay Buccaneers, Indianapolis Colts	10	102	58	0	.638	5	5	.385	107	66	0	.618
Jeff Fisher	Tennessee Titans	11	97	85	0	.533	5	4	.556	102	89	0	.534
Tom Coughlin	Jacksonville Jaguars, New York Giants	10	85	75	0	.531	4	5	.444	89	80	0	.527
Jon Gruden	Oakland Raiders, Tampa Bay Buccaneers	8	73	55	0	.570	5	3	.625	78	58	0	.574
Andy Reid	Philadelphia Eagles	7	70	42	0	.625	7	5	.583	77	47	0	.621
Brian Billick	Baltimore Ravens	7	62	50	0	.554	5	2	.714	67	52	0	.563
Art Shell	Los Angeles/Oakland Raiders	6	54	38	0	.587	2	3	.400	56	41	0	.577
John Fox	Carolina Panthers	4	36	28	0	.563	5	2	.714	41	30	0	.577
Herm Edwards	New York Jets, Kansas City Chiefs	5	39	41	0	.488	2	3	.400	41	44	0	.482
Dick Jauron	Chicago Bears, Detroit Lions, Buffalo Bills	6	36	49	0	.424	0	1	.000	36	50	0	.419
Marvin Lewis	Cincinnati Bengals	3	27	21	0	.563	0	1	.000	27	22	0	.551
Jack Del Rio	Jacksonville Jaguars	3	26	22	0	.542	0	1	.000	26	23	0	.531
Jim Mora	Atlanta Falcons	2	19	13	0	.594	1	1	.500	20	14	0	.588
Lovie Smith	Chicago Bears	2	16	16	0	.500	0	1	.000	16	17	0	.485
Nick Saban	Miami Dolphins	1	9	7	0	.563	0	0	—	9	7	0	.563
Romeo Crennel	Cleveland Browns	1	6	10	0	.375	0	0	—	6	10	0	.375
Mike Nolan	San Francisco 49ers	1	4	12	0	.250	0	0	—	4	12	0	.250
Brad Childress	Minnesota Vikings	0	0	0	0	—	0	0	—	0	0	0	—
Gary Kubiak	Houston Texans	0	0	0	0	—	0	0	—	0	0	0	—
Scott Linehan	St. Louis Rams	0	0	0	0	—	0	0	—	0	0	0	—
Eric Mangini	New York Jets	0	0	0	0	—	0	0	—	0	0	0	—
Rod Marinelli	Detroit Lions	0	0	0	0	—	0	0	—	0	0	0	—
Mike McCarthy	Green Bay Packers	0	0	0	0	—	0	0	—	0	0	0	—
Sean Payton	New Orleans Saints	0	0	0	0	—	0	0	—	0	0	0	—

COACHES WITH 100 CAREER VICTORIES (Order Based on Career Victories)
Start of 2006 Season

Coach	Team(s)	Yrs.	Regular Season				Postseason			Career			
			Won	Lost	Tied	Pct.	Won	Lost	Pct.	Won	Lost	Tied	Pct.
Don Shula	Baltimore Colts, Miami Dolphins	33	328	156	6	.677	19	17	.528	347	173	6	.666
George Halas	Chicago Bears	40	318	148	31	.682	6	3	.667	324	151	31	.682
Tom Landry	Dallas Cowboys	29	250	162	6	.607	20	16	.556	270	178	6	.603
Earl (Curly) Lambeau	Green Bay Packers, Chicago Cardinals, Washington Redskins	33	226	132	22	.631	3	2	.600	229	134	22	.631
Chuck Noll	Pittsburgh Steelers	23	193	148	1	.566	16	8	.667	209	156	1	.572
Dan Reeves	Denver Broncos, New York Giants, Atlanta Falcons	23	190	165	2	.535	11	9	.550	201	174	2	.536
Chuck Knox	Los Angeles Rams, Buffalo Bills, Seattle Seahawks	22	186	147	1	.558	7	11	.389	193	158	1	.550
Marty Schottenheimer	Cleveland Browns, Kansas City Chiefs, Washington Redskins, San Diego Chargers	20	186	124	1	.600	5	12	.294	191	136	1	.584
Bill Parcells	New York Giants, New England Patriots, New York Jets, Dallas Cowboys	18	163	123	1	.570	11	7	.611	174	130	1	.572
Paul Brown	Cleveland Browns, Cincinnati Bengals	21	166	100	6	.624	4	8	.333	170	108	6	.612
Bud Grant	Minnesota Vikings	18	158	96	5	.621	10	12	.455	168	108	5	.608
Joe Gibbs	Washington Redskins	14	140	76	0	.648	17	6	.739	157	82	0	.657
Marv Levy	Kansas City Chiefs, Buffalo Bills	17	143	112	0	.561	11	8	.579	154	120	0	.562
Bill Cowher	Pittsburgh Steelers	14	141	82	1	.632	12	9	.571	153	91	1	.627
Steve Owen	New York Giants	23	151	100	17	.602	2	8	.200	153	108	17	.586
Mike Holmgren	Green Bay Packers, Seattle Seahawks	14	138	86	0	.616	11	9	.550	149	95	0	.611
Hank Stram	Kansas City Chiefs, New Orleans Saints	17	131	97	10	.574	5	3	.625	136	100	10	.576
Weeb Ewbank	Baltimore Colts, New York Jets	20	130	129	7	.502	4	1	.800	134	130	7	.508
Mike Shanahan	Los Angeles Raiders, Denver Broncos	13	122	74	0	.622	8	5	.615	130	79	0	.622
Mike Ditka	Chicago Bears, New Orleans Saints	14	121	95	0	.560	6	6	.500	127	101	0	.557
Dick Vermeil	Philadelphia Eagles, St. Louis Rams, Kansas City Chiefs	15	120	109	0	.524	6	5	.545	126	114	0	.525
Jim Mora	New Orleans Saints, Indianapolis Colts	15	125	106	0	.541	0	6	.000	125	112	0	.527
George Seifert	San Francisco 49ers, Carolina Panthers	11	114	62	0	.648	10	5	.667	124	67	0	.649
Sid Gillman	Los Angeles Rams, Los Angeles-San Diego Chargers, Houston Oilers	18	122	99	7	.552	1	5	.167	123	104	7	.542
George Allen	Los Angeles Rams, Washington Redskins	12	116	47	5	.712	2	7	.222	118	54	5	.686
Don Coryell	St. Louis Cardinals, San Diego Chargers	14	111	83	1	.572	3	6	.333	114	89	1	.561
John Madden	Oakland Raiders	10	103	32	7	.759	9	7	.563	112	39	7	.739
Dennis Green	Minnesota Vikings, Arizona Cardinals	12	108	83	0	.565	4	8	.333	112	91	0	.552
Bill Belichick	Cleveland Browns, New England Patriots	11	99	77	0	.563	11	2	.846	110	79	0	.582
Tony Dungy	Tampa Bay Buccaneers, Indianapolis Colts	10	102	58	0	.638	5	8	.385	107	66	0	.618
Ray (Buddy) Parker	Chicago Cardinals, Detroit Lions, Pittsburgh Steelers	15	104	75	9	.581	3	1	.750	107	76	9	.585
Vince Lombardi	Green Bay Packers, Washington Redskins	10	96	34	6	.739	9	1	.900	105	35	6	.750
Tom Flores	Oakland-Los Angeles Raiders, Seattle Seahawks	12	97	87	0	.527	8	3	.727	105	90	0	.538
Bill Walsh	San Francisco 49ers	10	92	59	1	.609	10	4	.714	102	63	1	.617
Jeff Fisher	Tennessee Titans	11	97	85	0	.533	5	4	.556	102	89	0	.534

Active coaches in bold.

The **Green Bay Packers** need 10 victories to become the second team (Chicago Bears, 671) with 650 total victories. Green Bay's all-time record is 640-506-36.

The **New York Giants** need 12 regular-season victories to become the third team (Chicago Bears, 657 and Green Bay Packers, 616) with 600 regular-season victories. New York's all-time regular-season record is 588-492-33.

The **Pittsburgh Steelers** need 10 regular-season victories to reach 500 regular-season victories. Pittsburgh's all-time regular-season record is 490-470-20.

The **St. Louis Rams** need 10 regular-season victories to reach 500 regular-season victories. St. Louis' all-time regular-season record is 490-433-20.

The **Oakland Raiders** need six regular-season victories to reach 400 regular-season victories. Oakland's all-time regular-season record is 394-287-11.

The **Dallas Cowboys** need eight regular-season victories to reach 400 regular-season victories. Dallas' all-time regular-season record is 392-292-6.

The **Indianapolis Colts** need 10 regular-season victories to reach 400 regular-season victories. Indianapolis' all-time regular-season record is 390-377-7.

Marty Schottenheimer, San Diego, needs three victories to pass Chuck Knox (193) to move into seventh place all-time in career victories and needs nine victories to become the seventh coach with 200 career victories. In 20 seasons, Schottenheimer has 191 career victories.

Schottenheimer has 13 winning seasons in his 20-year career and needs one more to pass Chuck Noll for sole possession of third place all-time.

Bill Belichick, New England, needs one regular-season victory to reach 100 regular-season victories. In 11 seasons, Belichick has 99 regular-season victories.

Jeff Fisher, Tennessee, needs three regular-season victories to reach 100 regular-season victories. In 11 seasons, Fisher has 97 regular-season victories.

Brett Favre, Green Bay, needs 25 touchdown passes to pass Dan Marino (420) for the most touchdown passes in NFL history and needs four touchdown passes to join Marino as the only players in NFL history with 400 touchdown passes. In his 15-year career, Favre has 396 touchdown passes.

Favre needs 290 pass completions to pass Dan Marino (4,967) and move into first place all-time. In 15 seasons, Favre has 4,678 pass completions.

Favre needs 1,385 passing yards to join Dan Marino (61,361) as the only players in NFL history with 55,000 passing yards. In 15 seasons, Favre has passed for 53,615 yards.

Favre has passed for 3,000 yards in a season 14 times in his 15-year career and can extend his NFL-record streak with another 3,000-yard season. Favre also holds the record for the most consecutive seasons with 3,000 passing yards with 14 (active).

Favre has led the league in touchdown passes four times in his 15-year career and can pass Johnny Unitas, Len Dawson and Steve Young (4) for the most seasons leading the league in touchdown passes.

Favre needs 20 touchdown passes to extend his NFL-best streak to 13 consecutive seasons with 20 touchdown passes. Favre has thrown for 20 touchdowns in 12 consecutive seasons, the longest streak in NFL history.

In his 15-year career, Favre has passed for four touchdowns in a game 19 times. Favre needs three more four-touchdown games to pass Dan Marino (21) for the most games with four touchdown passes in NFL history.

Favre needs 10 wins to pass Dan Marino (147) and John Elway (148) for the most wins by a quarterback. In 15 seasons, Favre has won 139 games.

Drew Bledsoe, Dallas, needs 251 pass completions to become the fourth player (Dan Marino, Brett Favre and John Elway) in NFL history with 4,000 pass completions. In 13 seasons, Bledsoe has completed 3,749 passes.

Bledsoe has passed for 400 yards in a game six times in his 13-year NFL career. Bledsoe needs one 400-yard passing game to tie Joe Montana and Warren Moon (7) for the second-most games with 400 yards passing in NFL history (see Manning note).

Peyton Manning, Indianapolis, needs 4,000 passing yards to pass Dan Marino (6) for the most career 4,000-yard passing seasons in NFL history. In his eight-year career, Manning has six 4,000-yard passing seasons.

Manning needs 25 touchdown passes to become the first player in NFL history to throw 25 touchdown passes in nine consecutive seasons. Manning is the only player to have eight consecutive seasons with 25 touchdown passes.

Manning has passed for 3,000 yards in each of the past eight seasons and can tie Dan Marino (9) for the second-longest streak of consecutive 3,000-yard seasons. Manning is the only player in NFL history to start a career with eight consecutive 3,000-yard seasons.

Manning has passed for 400 yards in a game six times in his eight-year NFL career. Manning needs one 400-yard passing game to tie Joe Montana and Warren Moon (7) for the second-most games with 400 yards passing in NFL history (see Bledsoe note).

Manning has thrown 94 touchdown passes to wide receiver Marvin Harrison, the most touchdowns by a quarterback-receiver tandem in NFL history. They need six touchdowns to become the first duo to combine for 100 touchdowns.

Manning and Harrison have combined for 783 completions and 10,542 yards. The duo owns the NFL record for the most completions and yards by a tandem and needs 17 completions and 458 yards to become the first quarterback-receiver combination in NFL history with 800 completions and 11,000 yards.

Daunte Culpepper, Miami, needs 3,000 passing yards and 400 rushing yards this season to become the first quarterback in NFL history with five seasons with 3,000 passing yards and 400 rushing yards. Culpepper is the only player to accomplish the feat in four seasons.

Curtis Martin, New York Jets, needs 1,000 rushing yards to join Emmitt Smith as the only players in NFL history with 11 seasons with 1,000 rushing yards. In his 11-year career, Martin has rushed for 1,000 yards 10 times.

Martin has rushed for 14,101 yards in 11 seasons. Martin needs 1,169 rushing yards to pass Barry Sanders (15,269) to move into fourth place all-time and needs 899 yards to become the fourth player (Emmitt Smith, Walter Payton and Sanders) in NFL history with 15,000 rushing yards.

Martin needs 10 rushing touchdowns to become the seventh player in NFL history to rush for 100 touchdowns (see Alexander note). In 11 seasons, Martin has rushed for 90 touchdowns.

Shaun Alexander, Seattle, needs 11 rushing touchdowns to become the seventh player in NFL history to rush for 100 touchdowns (see Martin note). In six seasons, Alexander has rushed for 89 touchdowns.

Marshall Faulk, St. Louis, needs 10 touchdowns to pass Marcus Allen (145) to move into third place all-time. In 12 seasons, Faulk has scored 136 touchdowns.

Faulk has rushed for 100 touchdowns in his 12-year career and needs 11 rushing touchdowns to pass John Riggins (104), Jim Brown (106) and Walter Payton (110) to move into third place all-time.

Faulk has led the league in scoring two times in his 12-year NFL career and can tie Earl "Dutch" Clark, Pat Harder and Paul Hornung (3) for third place all-time for the most seasons leading the league in scoring.

In his 12-year career, Faulk has rushed for 200 yards in a game three times. Faulk needs one 200-yard rushing game to tie Tiki Barber, Jim Brown, Earl Campbell, Barry Sanders and LaDainian Tomlinson (4) for second place all-time (see Dillon note).

Faulk needs 846 total yards from scrimmage to become the fourth player in NFL history with 20,000 scrimmage yards. In 12 seasons, Faulk has gained 19,154 total yards from scrimmage.

Faulk has gained 2,000 scrimmage yards four times in his career, tied for the most in NFL history. With one more 2,000-scrimmage yard season, Faulk will pass Eric Dickerson and Walter Payton (4) for the most all-time (see James note).

Faulk needs 810 combined yards to become the fifth player in NFL history with 20,000 combined yards. In 12 seasons, Faulk has gained 19,190 combined yards.

Faulk has gained 2,000 combined yards four times in his career, tied for the most in NFL history. Faulk needs one more season with 2,000 combined yards to pass Eric Dickerson, Dante Hall, Brian Mitchell and Walter Payton (4) for the most all-time (see Hall note).

LaDainian Tomlinson, San Diego, needs 10 rushing touchdowns to extend his NFL-record streak of consecutive seasons to begin a career with 10 rushing touchdowns to six.

Tomlinson needs 1,200 rushing yards to join Eric Dickerson (1983-89) as the only players in NFL history to begin a career with six 1,200-yard rushing seasons.

Tomlinson has rushed for 200 yards in a game four times in his five-year career. Tomlinson needs one 200-yard rushing game to pass Tiki Barber, Jim Brown, Earl Campbell and Barry Sanders (4) to move into sole possession of second place all-time and needs two to tie O.J. Simpson (6) for the NFL record (see Barber note).

Edgerrin James, Arizona, has gained 2,000 scrimmage yards three times in his seven-year career. With one more 2,000-scrimmage yard season, James will tie Eric Dickerson, Marshall Faulk and Walter Payton (4) for the most all-time (see Faulk note).

James has gained 2,000 combined yards three times in his career. James needs one more season with 2,000 combined yards to tie Eric Dickerson, Marshall Faulk, Dante Hall, Brian Mitchell and Walter Payton (4) for the most all-time (see Faulk, Hall and Barber notes).

Tiki Barber, New York Giants, has gained 2,000 combined yards three times in his career. Barber needs one more season with 2,000 combined yards to tie Eric Dickerson, Marshall Faulk, Dante Hall, Brian Mitchell and Walter Payton (4) for the most all-time (see Faulk, Hall and James notes).

Barber has rushed for 200 yards in a game four times in his nine-year career. Barber needs one 200-yard rushing game to pass Jim Brown, Earl Campbell, Barry Sanders and LaDainian Tomlinson (4) to move into sole possession of second place all-time and needs two to tie O.J. Simpson (6) for the NFL record (see Tomlinson note).

Corey Dillon, New England, has rushed for 200 yards in a game three times in his nine-year career. Dillon needs one 200-yard rushing game to tie Tiki Barber, Jim Brown, Earl Campbell, Barry Sanders and LaDainian Tomlinson (4) for second place all-time (see Faulk note).

Marvin Harrison, Indianapolis, needs 100 receptions to pass Jerry Rice (4) to become the first player in NFL history with five 100-catch seasons. In 10 seasons, Harrison has four seasons with 100 receptions.

Harrison has 927 career receptions in his first 10 seasons and needs 16 receptions to pass Jerry Rice (942) for the most receptions in a player's first 11 seasons.

Harrison needs 73 receptions to become the fourth player (Jerry Rice, Cris Carter and Tim Brown) in NFL history with 1,000 receptions and needs 25 receptions to pass Art Monk (940) and Andre Reed (951) to move into fourth place all-time.

Harrison has three 1,500-receiving yard seasons in his 10-year career and needs 1,500 receiving yards to tie Jerry Rice (4) for the most 1,500-receiving yard seasons.

Harrison has 110 career touchdowns and needs 17 to pass Lenny Moore (113), John Riggins (116), Walter Payton (125) and Jim Brown (126) to move into sixth place all-time.

Terrell Owens, Dallas, needs 14 touchdowns to pass Tim

Brown (105), Don Hutson (105), Barry Sanders (109), Marvin Harrison (110), Lenny Moore (113) and John Riggins (116) to move into eighth place all-time (see M. Harrison note). In 10 seasons, Owens has 103 career touchdowns.

Rod Smith, Denver, needs 1,000 receiving yards to pass Cris Carter and Steve Largent (8) to move into a second place tie with Tim Brown and Jimmy Smith in 1,000-yard receiving seasons. In 12 seasons, Smith has eight 1,000-yard seasons.

Smith has recorded 100 receptions in a season two times in his 12-year NFL career. Smith can join Marvin Harrison and Jerry Rice (4) as the only players in NFL history with three seasons with 100 receptions (see Boldin, Holt and Moss notes).

Randy Moss, Oakland, needs two receiving touchdowns to become the seventh player with 100 receiving touchdowns. In his eight-year career, Moss has 98 receiving touchdowns.

Moss has recorded 100 receptions in a season two times in his eight-year NFL career. Moss can join Marvin Harrison and Jerry Rice (4) as the only players in NFL history with three seasons with 100 receptions (see Boldin, Holt and Smith notes).

Torry Holt, St. Louis, has recorded 100 receptions in a season two times in his seven-year NFL career. Holt can join Marvin Harrison and Jerry Rice (4) as the only players in NFL history with three seasons with 100 receptions (see Boldin, Moss and Smith notes).

Anquan Boldin, Arizona, has recorded 100 receptions in a season two times in his three-year NFL career. Boldin can join Marvin Harrison and Jerry Rice (4) as the only players in NFL history with three seasons with 100 receptions (see Holt, Moss and Smith notes).

Tony Gonzalez, Kansas City, needs seven touchdowns to pass Jerry Smith (60) and Shannon Sharpe (62) to become the all-time leader in touchdowns by a tight end in NFL history. In nine seasons, Gonzalez has 56 touchdown receptions.

Dante Hall, Kansas City, has six kickoff-return touchdowns in his six-year career, tied for the most all-time. Hall needs one kickoff-return touchdown to pass Mel Gray, Ollie Matson, Gale Sayers and Travis Williams (6) for sole possession of first place in NFL history.

Hall needs 2,000 combined yards to become the first player in NFL history to gain 2,000 combined yards in five consecutive seasons. Hall and Marshall Faulk (1998-2001) are the only players to gain 2,000 combined yards in four consecutive seasons.

Hall has gained 2,000 combined yards four times in his career, tied for the most in NFL history. Hall needs one more season with 2,000 combined yards to pass Eric Dickerson, Marshall Faulk, Brian Mitchell and Walter Payton (4) for the most all-time (see Faulk note).

Michael Strahan, New York Giants, needs 8.5 sacks to pass Leslie O'Neal (132.5), Lawrence Taylor (132.5), Richard Dent (137.5) and John Randle (137.5) to move into fifth place all-time. In 13 seasons, Strahan has 129.5 sacks.

Rodney Harrison, New England, needs 2.5 sacks to become the first player in NFL history with 30 interceptions and 30.0 sacks. In his 12-year career, Harrison has 31 interceptions and 27.5 sacks.

Jason Elam, Denver, has scored 100 points in each of his first 13 seasons, the longest streak all-time. Elam needs 100 points to tie Morten Andersen and Gary Anderson (14) for the most seasons with 100 points in NFL history.

Adam Vinatieri, Indianapolis, has scored 100 points in each of his first 10 seasons and needs 100 points to become the second player (Jason Elam, 13) in NFL history with 100 points in each of his first 11 seasons.

Jeff Wilkins, St. Louis, has successfully kicked 311 consecutive points after touchdowns, the second-longest streak in NFL history. Wilkins needs to convert 61 in a row to pass Jason Elam (371) for the longest streak all-time.

71st Annual NFL Draft, April 29-30, 2006
+Denotes Compensatory Selection
#Denotes Underclassman Selection

ARIZONA CARDINALS

1. Matt Leinart—10, QB, Southern California
2. Taitusi Lutui—41, G, Southern California
3.# Leonard Pope—72, TE, Georgia
4. Gabe Watson—107, DT, Michigan
5. Brandon Johnson—142, LB, Louisville
6. Jonathan Lewis—177, DT, Virginia Tech
7. Todd Watkins—218, WR, Brigham Young

ATLANTA FALCONS

2. Jimmy Williams—37, DB, Virginia Tech,
   from San Francisco through Denver and Green Bay
3. Jerious Norwood—79, RB, Mississippi State
5. Quinn Ojinnaka—139, T, Syracuse, from Green Bay
6. Adam Jennings—184, WR, Fresno State
7. D.J. Shockley—223, QB, Georgia

BALTIMORE RAVENS

1.# Haloti Ngata—12, DT, Oregon, from Cleveland
2. Chris Chester—56, C, Oklahoma, from New York Giants
3. David Pittman—87, DB, Northwestern (La.) State,
   from New York Giants
4. Demetrius Williams—111, WR, Oregon
 + P.J. Daniels—132, RB, Georgia Tech
5. Dawan Landry—146, DB, Georgia Tech
 + Quinn Sypniewski—166, TE, Colorado
6.+ Sam Koch—203, P, Nebraska
 # + Derrick Martin—208, DB, Wyoming
7. Ryan LaCasse—219, LB, Syracuse

BUFFALO BILLS

1.# Donte' Whitner—8, DB, Ohio State
 # John McCargo—26, DT, North Carolina State,
   from Chicago
3.# Ashton Youboty—70, DB, Ohio State, from Tennessee
4.# Ko Simpson—105, DB, South Carolina
5. Kyle Williams—134, DT, Louisiana State, from Houston
   Brad Butler—143, T, Virginia
6. Keith Ellison—178, LB, Oregon State
7. Terrance Pennington—216, T, New Mexico
 + Aaron Merz—248, G ,California

CAROLINA PANTHERS

1. DeAngelo Williams—27, RB, Memphis
2.# Richard Marshall—58, DB, Fresno State
3. James Anderson—88, LB, Virginia Tech, from Chicago
   Rashad Butler—89, T, Miami
4. Nate Salley—121, DB, Ohio State
5. Jeff King—155, TE, Virginia Tech
7. Will Montgomery—234, G, Virginia Tech
 # Stanley McClover—237, DE, Auburn, from Denver

CHICAGO BEARS

2.# Danieal Manning—42, DB, Abilene Christian, from Buffalo
 # Devin Hester—57, DB, Miami
3. Dusty Dvoracek—73, DT, Oklahoma, from Buffalo
4. Jamar Williams—120, LB, Arizona State
5. Mark Anderson—159, DE, Alabama
6. J.D. Runnels—195, RB, Oklahoma
   Tyler Reed—200, G, Penn State, from Seattle

CINCINNATI BENGALS

1.# Johnathan Joseph—24, DB, South Carolina
2. Andrew Whitworth—55, T, Louisiana State
3. Frostee Rucker—91, DE, Southern California
4. Domata Peko—123, DT, Michigan State
5. A.J. Nicholson—157, LB, Florida State
6. Reggie McNeal—193, WR, Texas A&M
7. Ethan Kilmer—209, DB, Penn State, from Houston
   Bennie Brazell—231, WR, Louisiana State

CLEVELAND BROWNS

1. Kamerion Wimbley—13, DE, Florida State,
   from Baltimore
2. D'Qwell Jackson—34, LB, Maryland, from New Orleans
3. Travis Wilson—78, WR, Oklahoma
4. Leon Williams—110, LB, Miami
   Isaac Sowells—112, G, Indiana, from Atlanta
5. Jerome Harrison—145, RB, Washington State
   DeMario Minter—152, DB, Georgia, from New England
6. Lawrence Vickers—180, RB, Colorado
   Babatunde Oshinowo—181, DT, Stanford, from Baltimore
7. Justin Hamilton—222, DB, Virginia Tech

DALLAS COWBOYS

1. Bobby Carpenter—18, LB, Ohio State
2.# Anthony Fasano—53, TE, Notre Dame,
   from Washington through New York Jets
3. Jason Hatcher—92, DE, Grambling State,
   from Jacksonville
4. Skyler Green—125, KR, Louisiana State,
   from Jacksonville
5. Pat Watkins—138, DB, Florida State, from New York Jets
6. Montavious Stanley—182, DT, Louisville,
   from Philadelphia
7. Pat McQuistan—211, T, Weber State,
   from New York Jets
   E.J. Whitley—224, C,Texas Tech

DENVER BRONCOS

1. Jay Cutler—11, QB, Vanderbilt, from St. Louis
2. Tony Scheffler—61, TE, Western Michigan
4. Brandon Marshall—119, WR, Central Florida,
   from Washington
   Elvis Dumervil—126, DE, Louisville
 + Domenik Hixon—130, WR, Akron
5. Chris Kuper—161, T, North Dakota
6. Greg Eslinger—198, C, Minnesota

DETROIT LIONS

1.# Ernie Sims—9, LB, Florida State
2. Daniel Bullocks—40, DB, Nebraska
3.# Brian Calhoun—74, RB, Wisconsin
5. Jonathan Scott—141, T, Texas
6. Dee McCann—179, DB, West Virginia
7.# Fred Matua—217, G, Southern California
 + Anthony Cannon—247, LB, Tulane

GREEN BAY PACKERS
1. A.J. Hawk—5, LB, Ohio State
2. Daryn Colledge—47, T, Boise State, from Atlanta
   Greg Jennings—52, WR, Western Michigan,
     from New England
3. Abdul Hodge—67, LB, Iowa
   Jason Spitz—75, G, Louisville,
     from Baltimore through New England
4.# Cory Rodgers—104, WR, TCU
   Will Blackmon—115, DB, Boston College,
     from Minnesota through Philadelphia
5. Ingle Martin—148, QB, Furman, from Atlanta
+ Tony Moll—165, T, Nevada
6. Johnny Jolly—183, DT, Texas A&M, from St. Louis
   Tyrone Culver—185, DB, Fresno State,
     from Minnesota through Philadelphia
7.+ Dave Tollefson—253, DE, Northwest Missouri State

HOUSTON TEXANS
1.# Mario Williams—1, DE, North Carolina State
2. DeMeco Ryans—33, LB, Alabama
3. Charles Spencer—65, T, Pittsburgh
   Eric Winston—66, T, Miami, from New Orleans
4. Owen Daniels—98, TE, Wisconsin
6. Wali Lundy—170, RB, Virginia
7.+ David Anderson—251, WR, Colorado State

INDIANAPOLIS COLTS
1. Joseph Addai—30, RB, Louisiana State
2. Tim Jennings—62, DB, Georgia
3. Freddie Keiaho—94, LB, San Diego State
5. Michael Toudouze—162, T, TCU
6. Charlie Johnson—199, T, Oklahoma State
+ Antoine Bethea—207, DB, Howard
7. T.J. Rushing—238, DB, Stanford 238,
   reacquired from Tennessee

JACKSONVILLE JAGUARS
1. Marcedes Lewis—28, TE, UCLA
2.# Maurice Jones-Drew—60, RB, UCLA
3. Clint Ingram—80, LB, Oklahoma, from Dallas
5. Brent Hawkins—160, LB, Illinois State
7. James Wyche—213, DE, Syracuse, from San Francisco
 # Dee Webb—236, DB, Florida,
   reacquired from San Francisco

KANSAS CITY CHIEFS
1. Tamba Hall—20, DE, Penn State
2.# Bernard Pollard—54, DB, Purdue
3. Brodie Croyle—85, QB, Alabama
5. Marcus Maxey—154, DB, Miami
6. Tre' Stallings—186, G ,Mississippi, from Dallas
   Jeff Webb—190, WR, San Diego State
7. Jarrad Page—228, DB, UCLA

MIAMI DOLPHINS
1. Jason Allen—16, DB, Tennessee
3. Derek Hagan—82, WR, Arizona State
4. Joe Toledo—114, T, Washington
5. Choice Exercised in 2005 Supplemental Draft,
   for Manuel Wright, DT, Southern California
7. Fred Evans—212, NT, Texas State-San Marcos,
     from Green Bay
   Rodrique Wright—226, NT, Texas
   Devin Aromashodu—233, WR, Auburn, from Chicago

MINNESOTA VIKINGS
1. Chad Greenway—17, LB, Iowa
2. Cedric Griffin—48, DB, Texas
   Ryan Cook—51, C, New Mexico, from Miami
   Tarvaris Jackson—64, QB, Alabama State,
     from Pittsburgh
4.# Ray Edwards—127, DE, Purdue,
     from Indianapolis through Philadelphia
5. Greg Blue—149, DB, Georgia

NEW ENGLAND PATRIOTS
1.# Laurence Maroney—21, RB, Minnesota
2.# Chad Jackson—36, WR, Florida, from Green Bay
3. David Thomas—86, TE, Texas
4. Garrett Mills—106, RB, Tulsa, from Detroit
   Stephen Gostkowski—118, K, Memphis
5. Ryan O'Callaghan—136, T, California, from Oakland
6. Jeremy Mincey—191, LB, Florida
+ Dan Stevenson—205, G, Notre Dame
+ Le Kevin Smith—206, DT, Nebraska
7. Willie Andrews—229, DB, Baylor

NEW ORLEANS SAINTS
1.# Reggie Bush—2, RB, Southern California
2. Roman Harper—43, DB, Alabama, from Cleveland
4. Jahri Evans—108, T, Bloomsburg, from Philadelphia
5. Rob Ninkovich—135, DE, Purdue
6. Mike Hass—171, WR, Oregon State
   Josh Lay—174, DB, Pittsburgh, from Green Bay
7. Zach Strief—210, T, Northwestern
+ Marques Colston—252, WR, Hofstra

NEW YORK GIANTS
1. Mathias Kiwanuka—32, DE, Boston College,
     from Pittsburgh
2. Sinorice Moss—44, WR, Miami, from Baltimore
3. Gerris Wilkinson—96, LB, Georgia Tech,
     from Pittsburgh
4. Barry Cofield—124, DT, Northwestern
   Guy Whimper—129, T, East Carolina, from Pittsburgh
5. Charlie Peprah—158, DB, Alabama
7. Gerrick McPhearson—232, DB, Maryland

NEW YORK JETS
1. D'Brickashaw Ferguson—4, T, Virginia
   Nick Mangold—29, C, Ohio State, from Denver
2. Kellen Clemens—49, QB, Oregon, from Dallas
3. Anthony Schlegel—76, LB, Ohio State,
     from Philadelphia
+ Eric Smith—97, DB, Michigan State
4. Brad Smith—103, WR, Missouri
   Leon Washington—117, RB, Florida State,
     from Kansas City
5. Jason Pociask—150, TE, Wisconsin, from Dallas
6. Drew Coleman—189, DB, TCU
     from Washington through New York Jets and Dallas
7. Titus Adams—220, DE, Nebraska, from Philadelphia

OAKLAND RAIDERS
1. Michael Huff—7, DB, Texas
2. Thomas Howard—38, LB, Texas-El Paso
3. Paul McQuistan—69, G, Weber State
4.# Darnell Bing—101, LB, Southern California
6. Kevin Boothe—176, G, Cornell
7. Chris Morris—214, C, Michigan State
+ Kevin McMahan—255, WR, Maine

PHILADELPHIA EAGLES
1. Brodrick Bunkley—14, DT, Florida State
2.# Winston Justice—39, T, Southern California,
    from Tennessee
3. Chris Gocong—71, LB, Cal Poly-San Luis Obispo,
    from New York Jets
4. Max Jean-Gilles—99, G, Georgia, from New Orleans
    Jason Avant—109, WR, Michigan,
    from St. Louis through Green Bay
5. Jeremy Bloom—147, WR, Colorado
  + Omar Gaither—168, LB, Tennessee
6.+ LaJuan Ramsey—204, DT, Southern California

PITTSBURGH STEELERS
1.# Santonio Holmes—25, WR, Ohio State,
    from New York Giants
3. Anthony Smith—83, DB, Syracuse, from Minnesota
    Willie Reid—95, WR, Florida State,
    from Seattle through Minnesota
4.+ Willie Colon—131, G, Hofstra
  + Orien Harris—133, DE, Miami
5.+ Omar Jacobs—164, QB, Bowling Green
  + Charles Davis—167, TE, Purdue
6. Marvin Philip—201, C, California
7. Cedric Humes—240, RB, Virginia Tech

ST. LOUIS RAMS
1. Tye Hill—15, DB, Clemson, from Atlanta through Denver
2. Joe Klopfenstein—46, TE, Colorado
3. Claude Wroten—68, DT, Louisiana State,
    from San Francisco through Denver
    Jon Alston—77, LB, Stanford
    Dominique Byrd—93, TE, Southern California,
    from Denver through Atlanta and Green Bay
4. Victor Adeyanju—113, DE, Indiana, from San Diego
5. Marques Hagans—144, WR, Virginia
7. Tim McGarigle—221, LB, Northwestern
  + Mark Setterstrom—242, G, Minnesota
  + Tony Palmer—243, G, Missouri

SAN DIEGO CHARGERS
1.# Antonio Cromartie—19, DB, Florida State
2. Marcus McNeill—50, T, Auburn
3. Charlie Whitehurst—81, QB, Clemson
5. Tim Dobbins—151, LB, Iowa State
6. Jeromey Clary—187, T, Kansas State
    Kurt Smith—188, K, Virginia, from Miami
7. Chase Page—225, DT, North Carolina
    Jimmy Martin—227, T, Virginia Tech, from Minnesota

SAN FRANCISCO 49ERS
1.# Vernon Davis—6, TE, Maryland
    Manny Lawson—22, DE, North Carolina State,
    from Washington through Denver
3. Brandon Williams—84, WR Wisconsin, from Washington
4. Michael Robinson—100, RB, Penn State
5. Parys Haralson—140, LB, Tennessee
6. Delanie Walker—175, WR, Central Missouri
    Marcus Hudson—192, DB, North Carolina State,
    from Tampa Bay
    Melvin Oliver—197, DE, Louisiana State,
    from Jacksonville
7.+ Vickiel Vaughn—254, DB, Arkansas

SEATTLE SEAHAWKS
1. Kelly Jennings—31, DB, Miami
2. Darryl Tapp—63, DE, Virginia Tech
4. Rob Sims—128, G, Ohio State
5. David Kirtman—163, RB, Southern California
7. Ryan Plackemeier—239, P, Wake Forest
  + Ben Obomanu—249, WR, Auburn

TAMPA BAY BUCCANEERS
1. Davin Joseph—23, G, Oklahoma
2. Jeremy Trueblood—59, T, Boston College
3. Maurice Stovall—90, WR, Notre Dame
4. Alan Zemaitis—122, DB, Penn State
5. Julian Jenkins—156, DE, Stanford
6. Bruce Gradkowski—194, QB, Toledo,
    from New York Giants
  + T.J. Williams—202, TE, North Carolina State
7. Justin Phinisee—235, DB, Oregon
  + Charles Bennett—241, DE, Clemson
  + Tim Massaquoi—244, TE, Michigan

TENNESSEE TITANS
1.# Vince Young—3, QB, Texas
2.# LenDale White—45, RB, Southern California,
    from Philadelphia
4. Calvin Lowry—102, DB, Penn State
  # Stephen Tulloch—116, LB, North Carolina State,
    from Dallas through Philadelphia
5. Terna Nande—137, LB, Miami (Ohio)
  + Jesse Mahelona—169, DT, Tennessee
6. Jonathan Orr—172, WR, Wisconsin
7. Cortland Finnegan—215, DB, Samford
  + Spencer Toone—245, LB, Utah
  + Quinton Ganther—246, RB, Utah

WASHINGTON REDSKINS
2. Rocky McIntosh—35, LB, Miami, from New York Jets
5. Anthony Montgomery—153, DT, Minnesota
6. Reed Doughty—173, DB, Northern Colorado,
    from New York Jets
    Kedric Golston—196, DT, Georgia, from Carolina
7. Kili Lefotu—230, G, Arizona
  + Kevin Simon—250, LB, Tennessee

NUMBER OF PLAYERS DRAFTED— 2006

BY POSITION:
Defensive Backs	49
Linebackers	34
Wide Receivers	30
Tackles	25
Defensive Ends	21
Defensive Tackles	19
Running Backs	19
Guards	18
Tight Ends	15
Quarterbacks	11
Centers	7
Kickers	2
Nose Tackle	2
Punters	2
Kick Returner	1

BY COLLEGE:
Southern California	11
Miami	9
Ohio State	9
Virginia Tech	9
Florida State	8
Georgia	7
Louisiana State	7
North Carolina State	6
Oklahoma	6
Penn State	6
Texas	6
Alabama	5
Tennessee	5
Virginia	5
Wisconsin	5
Auburn	4
Colorado	4
Louisville	4
Minnesota	4
Nebraska	4
Oregon	4
Purdue	4
Stanford	4
Syracuse	4
Boston College	3
California	3
Clemson	3
Florida	3
Fresno State	3
Georgia Tech	3
Maryland	3
Michigan	3
Michigan State	3
Northwestern	3
Notre Dame	3
TCU	3
UCLA	3
Arizona State	2
Hofstra	2
Indiana	2
Iowa	2
Memphis	2
Missouri	2
New Mexico	2
Oregon State	2
Pittsburgh	2
San Diego State	2
South Carolina	2
Texas A&M	2
Utah	2
Weber State	2
Western Michigan	2
Abilene Christian	1
Akron	1
Alabama State	1
Arizona	1
Arkansas	1
Baylor	1
Bloomsburg (Pa.)	1
Boise State	1
Bowling Green	1
Brigham Young	1
Cal Poly-San Luis Obispo	1
Central Florida	1
Central Missouri	1
Colorado State	1
Cornell	1
East Carolina	1
Furman	1
Grambling State	1
Howard	1
Illinois State	1
Iowa State	1
Kansas State	1
Maine	1
Miami (Ohio)	1
Mississippi	1
Mississippi State	1
Nevada	1
North Carolina	1
North Dakota	1
Northern Colorado	1
Northwest Missouri State	1
Northwestern (La.) State	1
Oklahoma State	1
Samford	1
Texas-El Paso	1
Texas State-San Marcos	1
Texas Tech	1
Toledo	1
Tulane	1
Tulsa	1
Vanderbilt	1
Wake Forest	1
Washington	1
Washington State	1
West Virginia	1
Wyoming	1

BY CONFERENCE:
Atlantic Coast	51
Big Ten	41
Southeastern	37
Pacific 10	32
Big 12	29
Mountain West	12
Big East	11
Conference USA	7
Mid-American	6
Western Athletic	5
Atlantic 10	3
Independent	3
Big Sky	2
Great West Football	2
Mid-America Intercollegiate Athletic	2
Southland	2
Southwestern Athletic	2
Gateway Football	1
Ivy League	1
Lone Star	1
Mid-Eastern Athletic	1
North Central Intercollegiate Athletic	1
Ohio Valley	1
Pennsylvania State Athletic	1
Southern	1

UNDERCLASSMEN IN THE DRAFT

Year	Entered	Drafted	In Top 10
1989	25	12	3
1990	38	18	5
1991	33	22	2
1992	48	25	5
1993	46	24	5
1994	43	26	6
1995	42	22	2
1996	46	21	4
1997	44	27	7
1998	41	20	3
1999	42	27	5
2000	31	20	4
2001	54	31	5
2002	43	26	5
2003	54	32	5
2004	44	35	5
2005	57	38	4
2006	62	34	6

WAIVERS

The waiver system is a procedure by which player contracts or NFL rights to players are made available by a club to other clubs in the League. During the procedure, the 31 other clubs either file claims to obtain the players or waive the opportunity to do so—thus the term "waiver." Claiming clubs are assigned players on a priority based on the inverse of won-and-lost standing. The claiming period is three business days from the beginning of the League Year through the last business day before July 4, and 24 hours after July 4 through the conclusion of the regular season. If a player passes through waivers unclaimed, he becomes a free agent. All waivers are no recall and no withdrawal. Under the Collective Bargaining Agreement, from the beginning of the waiver system each year through the trading deadline (October 17, 2006), any veteran who has acquired four years of pension credit is not subject to the waiver system if the club desires to release him. After the trading deadline, such players are subject to the waiver system.

ACTIVE/INACTIVE LIST

The Active/Inactive List is the principal status for players participating for a club. It consists of all players under contract who are eligible for preseason, regular-season, and postseason games. Teams are permitted to open training camp with no more than 80 players under contract and thereafter must meet two mandatory roster reductions prior to the season opener. Teams will be permitted an Active List of 45 players and an Inactive List of eight players for each regular-season and postseason game. Provided that a club has two quarterbacks on its 45-player Active List, a third quarterback from its Inactive List is permitted to dress for the game, but if he enters the game during the first three quarters, the other two quarterbacks are thereafter prohibited from playing. Teams also are permitted to establish Practice Squads of up to eight players who are eligible to participate in practice, but these players remain free agents and are eligible to sign with any other team in the league.

August 29.....................Roster reduction to 75 players
September 2.................Roster reduction to 53 players
September 3.................Teams establish a Practice Squad of up to eight players

In addition to the squad limits described above, the overall roster limit of 80 players remains in effect throughout the regular season and postseason. The overall limit is applicable to players on a team's Active, Inactive, and certain Exempt Lists, players on the Practice Squad, and players on the Reserve List as Injured, Physically Unable to Perform, Non-Football Illness/Injury, and Suspended by Club.

RESERVE LIST

The Reserve List is a status for players who, for reasons of injury, retirement, military service, or other circumstances, are not immediately available for participation with a club. Players on Reserve/Injured are not eligible to practice or return to the Active/Inactive List in the same season that they are placed on Reserve. Players in the category of Reserve/Retired, Reserve/Did Not Report, Reserve/Exclusive Rights, and players who were placed in the category of Reserve/Left Squad in a previous season may not be reinstated during the period from 30 days before the end of the regular season through the postseason.

TRADES

Unrestricted trading between the AFC and NFC is allowed in 2006 through October 17, after which trading will end until 2007.

ANNUAL ACTIVE PLAYER LIMITS

NFL

Year(s)	Limit
1991-2006	45**
1985-90	45
1983-84	49
1982	45†-49
1978-81	45
1975-77	43
1974	47
1964-73	40
1963	37
1961-62	36
1960	38
1959	36
1957-58	35
1951-56	33
1949-50	32
1948	35
1947	35*-34
1945-46	33
1943-44	28
1940-42	33
1938-39	30
1936-37	25
1935	24
1930-34	20
1926-29	18
1925	16

** 45 plus a third quarterback
† 45 for first two games
* 35 for first three games

AFL

Year(s)	Limit
1966-69	40
1965	38
1964	34
1962-63	33
1960-61	35

NFL FREE AGENCY MOVEMENT

The following chart details veteran free agents who signed with new teams:

	Unrestricted	Restricted	Transition	Franchise	TOTALS
1993	108	8	4	1	121
1994	121	7	4	0	132
1995	171	6	2	0	179
1996	100	4	2	0	106
1997	86	2	2	0	90
1998	112	4	1	2	119
1999	115	2	1	0	118
2000	107	4	0	0	111
2001	93	4	0	0	97
2002	130	1	0	0	131
2003	111	5	1	0	117
2004	124	1	1	0	126
2005	104	3	0	0	107

The following procedures will be used to break standings ties for postseason playoffs and to determine regular-season schedules.

Note: Tie games count as one-half win and one-half loss for both clubs.

TO BREAK A TIE WITHIN A DIVISION

If, at the end of the regular season, two or more clubs in the same division finish with the best won-lost-tied percentage, the following steps will be taken until a champion is determined:

TWO CLUBS

1. Head-to-head (best won-lost-tied percentage in games between the clubs.)
2. Best won-lost-tied percentage in games played within the division.
3. Best won-lost-tied percentage in common games.
4. Best won-lost-tied percentage in games played within the conference.
5. Strength of victory.
6. Strength of schedule.
7. Best combined ranking among conference teams in points scored and points allowed.
8. Best combined ranking among all teams in points scored and points allowed.
9. Best net points in common games.
10. Best net points in all games.
11. Best net touchdowns in all games.
12. Coin toss.

THREE OR MORE CLUBS

(Note: If two clubs remain tied after a third club is eliminated during any step, tie-breaker reverts to Step 1 of the two-club format.)

1. Head-to-head (best won-lost-tied percentage in games among the clubs.)
2. Best won-lost-tied percentage in games played within the division.
3. Best won-lost-tied percentage in common games.
4. Best won-lost-tied percentage in games played within the conference.
5. Strength of victory.
6. Strength of schedule.
7. Best combined ranking among conference teams in points scored and points allowed.
8. Best combined ranking among all teams in points scored and points allowed.
9. Best net points in common games.
10. Best net points in all games.
11. Best net touchdowns in all games.
12. Coin toss.

TO BREAK A TIE FOR THE WILD-CARD TEAM

If it is necessary to break ties to determine the two Wild Card clubs from each conference, the following steps will be taken:

A. If all the tied clubs are from the same division, apply division tie-breaker.

B. If the tied clubs are from different divisions, apply the following steps:

TWO CLUBS

1. Head-to-head, if applicable.
2. Best won-lost-tied percentage in the games played within the conference.
3. Best won-lost-tied percentage in common games, minimum of four.
4. Strength of victory.
5. Strength of schedule.
6. Best combined ranking among conference teams in points scored and points allowed.
7. Best combined ranking among all teams in points scored and points allowed.
8. Best net points in conference games.
9. Best net points in all games.
10. Best net touchdowns in all games.
11. Coin toss.

THREE OR MORE CLUBS

1. Apply division tie-breaker to eliminate all but highest ranked club in each division prior to proceeding to Step 2. The original seeding within a division upon application of the division tie-breaker remains the same for all subsequent applications of the procedure that are necessary to identify the Wild Card participants.
2. Head-to-head sweep (apply only if one club has defeated each of the others or one club has lost to each of the others).
3. Best won-lost-tied percentage in games played within the conference.
4. Best won-lost-tied percentage in common games, minimum of four.
5. Strength of victory.
6. Strength of schedule.
7. Best combined ranking among conference teams in points scored and points allowed.
8. Best combined ranking among all teams in points scored and points allowed.
9. Best net points in conference games.
10. Best net points in all games.
11. Best net touchdowns in all games.
12. Coin toss.

When the first Wild Card team has been identified, the procedure is repeated to name the second Wild Card (i.e., eliminate all but the highest ranked club in each division prior to proceeding to Step 2.) In situations where three teams from the same division are involved in the procedure, the original seeding of the teams remains the same for subsequent applications of the tie-breaker if the top-ranked team in that division qualifies for a Wild Card berth.

OTHER TIE-BREAKING PROCEDURES

1. Only one club advances to the playoffs in any tie-breaking step. Remaining tied clubs revert to the first step of the applicable division or Wild Card tie-breakers. As an example, if two clubs remain tied in any tie-breaker step after all other clubs have been eliminated, the procedure reverts to Step 1 of the two-club format to determine the winner. When one club wins the tie-breaker, all other clubs revert to Step 1 of the applicable two-club or three-club format.
2. In comparing records against common opponents among tied teams, the best won-lost-tied percentage is the deciding factor since teams may have played an unequal number of games.
3. To determine home-field priority among division-titlists, apply Wild Card tie-breakers.
4. To determine home-field priority for Wild Card qualifiers, apply division tie-breakers (if teams are from the same division) or Wild Card tie-breakers (if teams are from different divisions).

TIE-BREAKING PROCEDURE FOR SELECTION MEETING

If two or more clubs are tied in the selection order, the strength-of-schedule tie-breaker is applied, subject to the following exceptions for playoff clubs:

1. The Super Bowl winner is last and the Super Bowl loser next-to-last.
2. Any non-Super Bowl playoff club involved in a tie shall be assigned priority within its segment below that of non-playoff clubs and in the order that the playoff club exited from the playoffs. Thus, within a tied segment a playoff club that loses in the Wild Card game will have priority over a playoff club that loses in the Divisional playoff game, which in turn will have priority over a club that loses in the Conference Championship game. If two tied clubs exited the playoffs in the same round, the tie is broken by strength of schedule.

If any ties cannot be broken by strength of schedule, the divisional or conference tie-breakers, whichever are applicable, are applied. Any ties that still exist are broken by a coin flip.

For the 2004-08 seasons, the NFL will continue to employ a system of Referee Replay Review to aid officiating.

Prior to the two-minute warning of each half, a Coaches' Challenge System will be in effect. After the two-minute warning, and throughout any overtime period, a Referee Review will be initiated by a Replay Assistant from a Replay Booth.

The following procedures will be used:

REVIEWS BY REFEREE: All Replay Reviews will be conducted by the Referee on a field-level monitor after consultation with the other covering official(s), prior to review. A decision will be reversed only when the Referee has *indisputable visual evidence* available to him that warrants the change.

COACHES' CHALLENGE: In each game, a team will be permitted two challenges that will initiate Referee Replay reviews. Each challenge will require the use of a team time out. If a challenge is upheld, the time out will be restored to the challenging team. If both challenges are upheld, a third challenge will be awarded to the challenging team. No challenges will be recognized from a team that has exhausted its time outs.

REPLAY ASSISTANT'S REQUEST FOR REVIEW: After the two-minute warning of each half, and throughout any overtime period, any review will be initiated by a Replay Assistant. There is no limit to the number of reviews that may be initiated by the Replay Assistant. His ability to initiate a review will be unrelated to the number of time outs that either team has remaining, and no time out will be charged for any review initiated by the Replay Assistant.

TIME LIMIT: Each review will be a maximum of 60 seconds in length, timed from when the Referee begins his review of the replay at the field-level monitor.

REVIEWABLE PLAYS: The Replay System will cover the following play situations only:

A) PLAYS GOVERNED BY SIDELINE, GOAL LINE, END ZONE, AND END LINE:
1. Scoring plays, including a runner breaking the plane of the goal line.
2. Pass complete/incomplete/intercepted at sideline, goal line, end zone, and end line.
3. Runner/receiver in or out of bounds.
4. Recovery of loose ball in or out of bounds.

B) PASSING PLAYS:
1. Pass ruled complete/incomplete/intercepted in the field of play.
2. Touching of a forward pass by an ineligible receiver.
3. Touching of a forward pass by a defensive player.
4. Quarterback (Passer) forward pass or fumble.
5. Illegal forward pass beyond line of scrimmage.
6. Illegal forward pass after change of possession.
7. Forward or backward pass thrown from behind line of scrimmage.

C) OTHER DETECTABLE INFRACTIONS:
1. Runner ruled not down by defensive contact.
2. Forward progress with respect to first down.
3. Touching of a kick.
4. Number of players on the field.
5. Recovery of loose ball in the field of play.

INSTANT REPLAY HISTORY
From 1986-1991, a limited system of Instant Replay was used on a year-by-year basis. Replay also was experimented with during the 1996 and 1998 preseasons. For the 1999 season, the NFL introduced a system of Referee Replay Review to aid officiating. That system was extended on a one-year basis for the 2000 season and and then approved for the next three years through 2003. In March 2004, the system was extended for five seasons through 2008.

Following are the results of the different systems:

REGULAR SEASON, 1986-1991

Year	Games	Plays Closely Reviewed	Reversals
1986	224	374	38
1987	210	490	57
1988	224	537	53
1989	224	492	65
1990	224	504	73
1991	224	570	90
TOTAL	1,330	2,967	376

PRESEASON, 1996, 1998

Year	Games	Challenges	Reversals
1996	10	13	3
1998	10	10	3
TOTAL	20	23	6

REGULAR SEASON, 1999-2005

Year	Games	Total Replay Reviews	Challenges	Reversals
1999	248	195	133	57
2000	248	247	179	84
2001	248	258	191	89
2002	256	294	208	94
2003	256	255	184	66
2004	256	283	233	88
2005	256	295	223	92
TOTAL	1,768	1,827	1,351	570

The AFC

American Football Conference
North Division
Team Colors: Black, Purple, and Metallic
Gold
1 Winning Drive
Owings Mills, Maryland 21117
Telephone: (410) 701-4000

2006 SCHEDULE
PRESEASON
Aug. 11 **New York Giants** 8:00
Aug. 17 **Philadelphia** 8:00
Aug. 25 at Minnesota 7:00
Aug. 31 at Washington 8:00

REGULAR SEASON
Sept. 10 at Tampa Bay 1:00
Sept. 17 **Oakland** 1:00
Sept. 24 at Cleveland 4:05
Oct. 1 **San Diego**.........................1:00
Oct. 9 at Denver (Mon.) 6:30
Oct. 15 **Carolina**............................1:00
Oct. 22 Open Date
Oct. 29 at New Orleans................12:00
Nov. 5 **Cincinnati** 1:00
Nov. 12 at Tennessee 12:00
Nov. 19 **Atlanta**...............................1:00
Nov. 26 **Pittsburgh**.........................1:00
Nov. 30 at Cincinnati (Thu.).............8:00
Dec. 10 at Kansas City 12:00
Dec. 17 **Cleveland** 1:00
Dec. 24 at Pittsburgh......................1:00
Dec. 31 **Buffalo**...............................1:00

Stadium: M&T Bank Stadium
(opened in 1998)
•**Capacity:** 70,107
1101 Russell Street
Baltimore, Maryland 21230
Playing Surface: Sportexe Momentum
Training Camp: McDaniel College
2 College Hill
Westminster, Maryland
21157

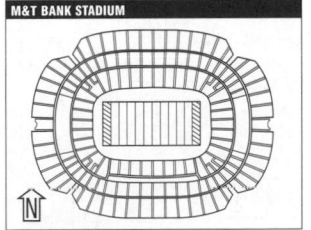

M&T BANK STADIUM

CLUB OFFICIALS
Owner: Steve Bisciotti
President: Dick Cass
Executive Vice President/General
Manager: Ozzie Newsome
Senior Vice President/Public and
Community Relations: Kevin Byrne
Senior Vice President/Business Ventures:
Dennis Mannion
Vice President of Football Administration:
Pat Moriarty
Chief Financial Officer: Jeff Goering
Vice President of Medical Services:
Bill Tessendorf
Senior Director of Operations: Bob Eller
Senior Director of Publications:
Francine Lubera
Director of Pro Personnel: George Kokinis
Director of College Scouting:
Eric DeCosta
Director of Player Development:
O.J. Brigance
Director of Media Relations:
Chad Steele
Assistant Director of Pro Personnel:
Vince Newsome
Scouts: Chad Alexander, Joe Douglas,
Joe Hortiz, Daniel Jeremiah,
Lionel Vital, Jeremiah Washburn,
Andrew Weidel
Equipment Manager: Ed Carroll
Video Director: Jon Dubé
Senior Director, Media Sales and
Business Development: Mark Burdett
Senior Director, Information Technology:
Bill Jankowski
Senior Director, Ticket Sales and
Operations: Baker Koppelman
Senior Director, Stadium Operations:
Roy Sommerhof
Senior Director of Broadcasting:
Larry Rosen
Director of Premium Services/Suites:
Theresa Abato
Director, Community Relations:
Kenny Abrams
Director, Corporate Partnerships:
Ed Burchell
Director, Marketing: Lisa Dixon
Director, Corporate Sales: Kevin Rochlitz
Director, Security: Darren Sanders
Director, Corporate Sales Administration:
Erin Stewart

COACHING HISTORY
(83-83-1)
Records include postseason games
1996-98   Ted Marchibroda 16-31-1
1999-2005 Brian Billick 67-52-0

ATTENDANCE
Home 554,222   Away 519,018
Total 1,073,240
Single-game home record,
70,604 (12/19/05)
Single-season home record, 554,222
(2005)

2006 DRAFT CHOICES
Round	Name	Pos.	College
1	Haloti Ngata	DT	Oregon
2	Chris Chester	C	Oklahoma
3	David Pittman	DB	Northwestern (La.) St.
4	Demetrius Williams	WR	Oregon
	P.J. Daniels	RB	Georgia Tech
5	Dawan Landry	DB	Georgia Tech
	Quinn Sypniewski	TE	Colorado
6	Sam Koch	P	Nebraska
	Derrick Martin	DB	Wyoming
7	Ryan LaCasse	LB	Syracuse

2005 TEAM RECORD

PRESEASON (2-2)

Date	Result		Opponent
8/13	L	3-16	at Atlanta
8/20	L	14-20	Philadelphia
8/26	W	21-6	at New Orleans
9/1	W	26-20	Washington

REGULAR SEASON (6-10)

Date	Result		Opponent	Att.
9/11	L	7-24	Indianapolis	70,501
9/18	L	10-25	at Tennessee	69,149
10/2	W	13-3	New York Jets	70,479
10/9	L	17-35	at Detroit	61,201
10/16	W	16-3	Cleveland	70,196
10/23	L	6-10	at Chicago	62,102
10/31	L	19-20	at Pittsburgh	64,178
11/6	L	9-21	Cincinnati	70,540
11/13	L	3-30	at Jacksonville	66,107
11/20	W	16-13	Pittsburgh (OT)	70,601
11/27	L	29-42	at Cincinnati	65,680
12/4	W	16-15	Houston	69,909
12/11	L	10-12	at Denver	75,651
12/19	W	48-3	Green Bay	70,604
12/25	W	30-23	Minnesota	70,246
1/1	L	16-20	at Cleveland	69,871

(OT) Overtime

SCORE BY PERIODS

Ravens	50	77	44	91	3 —	265
Opponents	54	75	90	80	0 –	299

2005 TEAM STATISTICS

	Ravens	Opp.
Total First Downs	286	277
Rushing	97	79
Passing	163	161
Penalty	26	37
3rd Down: Made/Att	95/243	79/219
3rd Down Pct.	39.1	36.1
4th Down: Made/Att	11/19	4/12
4th Down Pct.	57.9	33.3
Possession Avg.	30:22	29:38
Total Net Yards	4,693	4,549
Avg. Per Game	293.3	284.3
Total Plays	1,056	998
Avg. Per Play	4.4	4.6
Net Yards Rushing	1,605	1,591
Avg. Per Game	100.3	99.4
Total Rushes	452	431
Net Yards Passing	3,088	2,958
Avg. Per Game	193.0	184.9
Sacked/Yards Lost	42/293	42/270
Gross Yards	3,381	3,228
Att./Completions	562/335	525/296
Completion Pct.	59.6	56.4
Had Intercepted	21	11
Punts/Average	86/42.8	89/40.5
Net Punting Avg.	86/35.6	89/33.0
Penalties/Yards	139/1067	110/844
Fumbles/Ball Lost	28/15	28/15
Touchdowns	25	30
Rushing	5	8
Passing	17	18
Returns	3	4

2005 INDIVIDUAL STATISTICS

PASSING	Att.	Comp.	Yds.	Pct.	TD	Int.	Tkld.	Rate
Boller	293	171	1,799	58.4	11	12	23/146	71.8
Wright	266	164	1,582	61.7	6	9	19/147	71.7
Hymes	2	0	0	0.0	0	0	0/0	39.6
Clayton	1	0	0	0.0	0	0	0/0	39.6
Ravens	562	335	3,381	59.6	17	21	42/293	71.3
Opponents	525	296	3,228	56.4	18	11	42/270	77.4

SCORING	TD R	TD P	TD Rt	PAT	FG	Saf	PTS
Stover	0	0	0	23/23	30/34	0	113
Heap	0	7	0	0/0	0/0	0	42
J. Lewis	3	1	0	0/0	0/0	0	24
Clayton	1	2	0	0/0	0/0	0	18
Mason	0	3	0	0/0	0/0	0	18
A. Thomas	0	0	3	0/0	0/0	0	18
Hymes	0	2	0	0/0	0/0	0	12
Boller	1	0	0	0/0	0/0	0	6
Taylor	0	1	0	0/0	0/0	0	6
Wilcox	0	1	0	0/0	0/0	0	6
J. Green	0	0	0	0/0	0/0	0	2
Elling	0	0	0	10-12	0/1	0	0
Ravens	5	17	3	23/23	30/35	0	265
Opponents	8	18	4	28/29	29/31	1	299

2-Pt. Conversions: J. Green.
Ravens 1-2, Opponents 1-1.

RUSHING	Att.	Yds.	Avg.	LG	TD
J. Lewis	269	906	3.4	25	3
Taylor	117	487	4.2	52	0
Wright	18	68	3.8	22	0
Boller	23	66	2.9	9	1
Clayton	8	33	4.1	11t	1
Stewart	4	24	6.0	13	0
White	6	17	2.8	5	0
J. Green	5	4	0.8	4	0
Sanders	1	0	0.0	0	0
Zastudil	1	0	0.0	0	0
Ravens	452	1,605	3.6	52	5
Opponents	431	1,591	3.7	77t	8

RECEIVING	No.	Yds.	Avg.	LG	TD
Mason	86	1,073	12.5	39t	3
Heap	75	855	11.4	48	7
Clayton	44	471	10.7	47t	2
Taylor	41	292	7.1	20	1
J. Lewis	32	191	6.0	15t	1
Wilcox	20	154	7.7	17t	1
Hymes	11	132	12.0	21	2
J. Green	7	32	4.6	8	0
Dinkins	6	55	9.2	15	0
Moore	3	59	19.7	24	0
Mughelli	3	13	4.3	6	0
Mu. Smith	3	5	1.7	4	0
P. Johnson	2	31	15.5	19	0
Ricard	2	18	9.0	11	0
Ravens	335	3,381	10.1	48	17
Opponents	296	3,228	10.9	56	18

INTERCEPTIONS	No.	Yds.	Avg.	LG	TD
Sanders	2	57	28.5	33	0
A. Thomas	2	48	24.0	28	1
Suggs	2	38	19.0	38	0
Reed	1	23	23.0	23	0
Ch. Williams	1	14	14.0	14	0
Rolle	1	11	11.0	11	0
R. Lewis	1	0	0.0	0	0
McAlister	1	0	0.0	0	0
Ravens	11	191	17.4	48	1
Opponents	21	256	12.2	37	3

PUNTING	No.	Yds.	Avg.	In 20	LG
Zastudil	84	3,653	43.5	11	60
Elling	1	32	32.0	1	32
Ravens	86	3,685	42.8	12	60
Opponents	89	3,605	40.5	30	61

PUNT RETURNS	No.	FC	Yds.	Avg.	LG	TD
Sams	33	10	401	12.2	51	0
Clayton	6	2	30	5.0	10	0
Sanders	0	1	0	—	—	0
Ravens	39	13	431	11.1	51	0
Opponents	55	12	481	8.7	62t	1

KICKOFF RETURNS	No.	Yds	Avg	LG	TD
Sams	44	998	22.7	87	0
Taylor	12	253	21.1	45	0
White	2	18	9.0	9	0
Dinkins	1	10	10.0	10	0
J. Green	1	10	10.0	10	0
Ravens	60	1,289	21.5	87	0
Opponents	62	1,352	21.8	59	0

FIELD GOALS	1-19	20-29	30-39	40-49	50+
Stover	1/1	8/8	10/11	11/14	0/0
Elling	0/0	0/0	0/0	0/0	0/1
Ravens	1/1	8/8	10/11	11/14	0/1
Opponents	0/0	12/12	9/9	8/10	0/0

SACKS	No.
A. Thomas	9.0
Suggs	8.0
Polley	4.0
Scott	4.0
Boulware	2.5
Gregg	2.5
R. Green	2.0
Weaver	2.0
TEAM	2.0
J. Johnson	1.5
Ch. Williams	1.5
Franklin	1.0
Kemoeatu	1.0
R. Lewis	1.0
Ravens	42.0
Opponents	42.0

RECORD HOLDERS
INDIVIDUAL RECORDS—CAREER

Category	Name	Performance
Rushing (Yds.)	Jamal Lewis, 2000-05	6,669
Passing (Yds.)	Vinny Testaverde, 1996-97	7,148
Passing (TDs)	Vinny Testaverde, 1996-97	51
Receiving (No.)	Todd Heap, 2001-05	243
Receiving (Yds.)	Todd Heap, 2001-05	2,893
Interceptions	Ed Reed, 2002-05	22
Punting (Avg.)	Greg Montgomery, 1996-97	43.2
Punt Return (Avg.)	Jermaine Lewis, 1996-2001	11.8
Kickoff Return (Avg.)	Corey Harris, 1998-2001	24.0
Field Goals	Matt Stover, 1996-2005	272
Touchdowns (Tot.)	Jamal Lewis, 2000-05	38
Points	Matt Stover, 1996-2005	1,114

INDIVIDUAL RECORDS—SINGLE SEASON

Category	Name	Performance
Rushing (Yds.)	Jamal Lewis, 2003	2,066
Passing (Yds.)	Vinny Testaverde, 1996	4,177
Passing (TDs)	Vinny Testaverde, 1996	33
Receiving (No.)	Derrick Mason, 2005	86
Receiving (Yds.)	Michael Jackson, 1996	1,201
Interceptions	Ed Reed, 2004	9
Punting (Avg.)	Kyle Richardson, 1998	43.9
Punt Return (Avg.)	Jermaine Lewis, 2000	16.1
Kickoff Return (Avg.)	Corey Harris, 1998	27.6
Field Goals	Matt Stover, 2000	35
Touchdowns (Tot.)	Michael Jackson, 1996	14
	Jamal Lewis, 2003	14
Points	Matt Stover, 2000	135

INDIVIDUAL RECORDS—SINGLE GAME

Category	Name	Performance
Rushing (Yds.)	Jamal Lewis, 9-14-03	*295
Passing (Yds.)	Vinny Testaverde, 10-27-96	429
Passing (TDs)	Tony Banks, 9-10-00	5
Receiving (No.)	Priest Holmes, 10-11-98	13
Receiving (Yds.)	Qadry Ismail, 12-12-99	268
Interceptions	Many times	2
	Last time by Deion Sanders, 10-24-04	
Field Goals	Matt Stover, 9-21-97, 12-26-99, 10-28-00	5
Touchdowns (Tot.)	Marcus Robinson, 11-23-03	4
Points	Marcus Robinson, 11-23-03	24

*NFL Record

2006 VETERAN ROSTER

No.	Name	Pos.	Ht.	Wt.	Birthdate	NFL Exp.	College	Hometown	How Acq.	'05 Games/ Starts
38	Anderson, Mike	RB	6-0	230	9/21/73	7	Utah	Fairfield, S.C.	FA-'06	15/15*
2	Araguz, Leo	P	5-11	190	1/19/70	7	Stephen F. Austin	Harlingen, Texas	FA-'06	4/0*
94	Bannan, Justin	DT	6-3	305	4/18/79	5	Colorado	Orangeale, Calif.	UFA(Buff)-'06	16/7*
7	Boller, Kyle	QB	6-3	220	6/17/81	4	California	Newhall, Calif.	D1b-'03	9/9
60	Brown, Jason	G/T	6-3	320	5/5/83	2	North Carolina	Henderson, N.C.	D4-'05	6/1
14	Bryant, Romby	WR	6-1	181	12/21/79	2	Tulsa	Oklahoma City, Okla.	FA-'05	3/0*
89	Clayton, Mark	WR	5-10	195	7/2/82	2	Oklahoma	Arlington, Texas	D1-'05	14/10
53	Cody, Dan	LB/DE	6-5	255	12/1/81	2	Oklahoma	Ada, Okla.	D2a-'05	0*
81	Darling, Devard	WR	6-1	215	4/16/82	3	Washington State	Houston, Texas	D3-'04	10/0
93	Edwards, Dwan	DT	6-3	315	5/16/81	3	Oregon State	Columbus, Mont.	D2-'04	12/1
8	Elling, Aaron	K	6-2	201	5/31/78	4	Wyoming	Lander, Wyo.	FA-'05	9/0
62	Flynn, Mike	C	6-3	305	6/15/74	9	Maine	Springfield, Mass.	FA-'97	16/16
91	Franklin, Aubrayo	DT	6-1	320	8/27/80	4	Tennessee	Johnson City, Tenn.	D5a-'03	15/1
33	Green, Justin	FB	5-11	251	4/30/82	2	Montana	San Diego, Calif.	D5-'05	12/4
54	Green, Roderick	LB	6-2	250	4/26/82	3	Central Missouri State	Brenham, Texas	D5-'04	16/0
97	Gregg, Kelly	DT	6-0	310	11/1/76	7	Oklahoma	Edmond, Okla.	FA-'00	16/16
86	Heap, Todd	TE	6-5	252	3/16/80	6	Arizona State	Mesa, Ariz.	D1-'01	16/16
35	Ivy, Corey	CB	5-9	188	3/29/77	6	Oklahoma	Moore, Okla.	UFA(StL)-'06	16/5*
95	Johnson, Jarret	DE	6-3	285	8/14/81	4	Alabama	Chiefland, Fla.	D4a-'03	16/12
50	Johnson, Tim	LB	5-11	235	2/7/78	4	Youngstown State	Fairfield, Ala.	FA-'06	16/0*
70	Katula, Matt	LS	6-6	272	8/22/82	2	Wisconsin	Brookfield, Wis.	FA-'05	16/0
31	Lewis, Jamal	RB	5-11	245	8/29/79	7	Tennessee	Atlanta, Ga.	D1a-'00	15/15
52	Lewis, Ray	LB	6-1	245	5/15/75	11	Miami	Lakeland, Fla.	D1b-'96	6/6
85	Mason, Derrick	WR	5-10	192	1/17/74	10	Michigan State	Detroit, Mich.	FA-'05	16/16
21	McAlister, Chris	CB	6-1	206	6/14/77	8	Arizona	Pasadena, Calif.	D1-'99	14/14
84	Moore, Clarence	WR	6-6	211	9/24/82	3	Northern Arizona	Buena Park, Calif.	D6-'04	4/1
34	Mughelli, Ovie	FB	6-1	255	6/10/80	4	Wake Forest	Charleston, S.C.	D4b-'03	13/6
64	Mulitalo, Edwin	G	6-3	345	9/1/74	8	Arizona	Daly City, Calif.	D4b-'99	16/15
42	Norton, Zach	CB	5-11	183	11/19/81	2	Cincinnati	Lloyd, Fla.	FA-'04	3/0
75	Ogden, Jonathan	T	6-9	345	7/31/74	11	UCLA	Washington, D.C.	D1a-'96	16/16
79	Pashos, Tony	T	6-6	337	8/3/80	4	Illinois	Lock Port, Ill.	D5b-'03	16/7
90	Pryce, Trevor	DE	6-5	286	8/3/75	10	Clemson	Winter Park, Fla.	FA-'06	16/16*
20	Reed, Ed	S	5-11	200	9/11/78	5	Miami	St. Rose, La.	D1-'02	10/10
39	Ricard, Alan	FB	5-11	237	1/17/77	6	Northeast Louisiana	Amite, La.	FA-'00	2/2
69	Rimpf, Brian	G	6-5	319	2/11/81	3	East Carolina	Raleigh, N.C.	D7b-'04	15/7
22	Rolle, Samari	CB	6-0	175	8/10/76	9	Florida State	Miami, Fla.	FA-'05	16/16
12	St. Pierre, Brian	QB	6-3	230	11/28/79	4	Boston College	Danvers, Mass.	FA-'05	0*
36	Sams, B.J.	RB	5-10	185	10/29/80	3	McNeese State	Mandeville, La.	FA-'04	14/0
57	Scott, Bart	LB	6-2	235	8/18/80	5	Southern Illinois	Detroit, Mich.	FA-'02	16/10
51	Smith, Mike	LB	6-1	235	9/2/81	2	Texas Tech	Lubbock, Texas	D7-'05	6/0
32	Smith, Musa	RB	6-0	232	5/31/82	4	Georgia	West Perry, Pa.	D3-'03	1/0
56	Stills, Gary	LB/DE	6-2	250	7/11/74	8	West Virginia	Valley Forge, Pa.	FA-'06	16/0*
3	Stover, Matt	K	5-11	178	1/27/68	17	Louisiana Tech	Dallas, Texas	PB(NYG)-'91	16/0
55	Suggs, Terrell	LB	6-3	260	10/11/82	4	Arizona State	Chandler, Ariz.	D1a-'03	16/16
63	Szalay, Thatcher	C	6-4	303	1/18/79	3	Montana	Whitefish, Mont.	FA-'05	4/0
78	Terry, Adam	T	6-8	330	9/1/82	2	Syracuse	Queensbury, N.Y.	D2b-'05	7/0
96	Thomas, Adalius	LB	6-2	270	8/18/77	7	Southern Mississippi	Equality, Ala.	D6a-'00	16/16
68	Vincent, Keydrick	G	6-5	325	4/13/78	6	Mississippi	Bartow, Fla.	UFA(Pitt)-'05	9/9
46	Ward, B.J.	S	6-3	208	11/4/81	2	Florida State	Dallas, Texas	FA-'05	15/0
83	Wilcox, Daniel	TE	6-1	245	3/23/77	4	Appalachian State	Atlanta, Ga.	FA-'04	13/3

* Anderson played 15 games with Denver in '05; Araguz played 4 games with Seattle; Bannan played 16 games with Buffalo; Bryant played 3 games with Atlanta; Cody missed '05 season because of injury; Ivy played 16 games with St. Louis; T. Johnson played 16 games with Oakland; Pryce played 16 games with Denver; St. Pierre inactive for 4 games; Stills played 16 games with Kansas City.

Players lost through free agency (7): S Will Demps (NYG; 11 games in '05), DT Maake Kemoeatu (Car; 16), RB Chester Taylor (Minn; 15), DE Anthony Weaver (Hou; 10), DB Chad Williams (SF; 16), QB Anthony Wright (Cin; 9), P Dave Zastudil (Cle; 16).

Also played with Ravens in '05—T Orlando Brown (9 games), LB Peter Boulware (15), CB Dale Carter (15), TE Darnell Dinkins (16), LB Dennis Haley (4), WR Randy Hymes (16), WR Patrick Johnson (6), TE Terry Jones (1), LB Jim Nelson (2), LB Tommy Polley (16), CB Deion Sanders (16), QB Kordell Stewart (1), RB Jamel White (5).

2006 FIRST-YEAR ROSTER

Name	Pos.	Ht.	Wt.	Birthdate	College	Hometown	How Acq.
Abiamiri, Rob (1)	TE	6-2	240	12/21/82	Maryland	Baltimore, Md.	FA-'05
Blizzard, Bobby (1)	TE	6-4	272	3/22/80	North Carolina	Hampton, Va.	FA-'05
Bratton, Brian (1)	WR	5-10	186	7/31/82	Furman	Evans, Ga.	FA-'05
Butler, Robb (1)	DB	6-0	207	9/14/81	Robert Morris	Pittsburgh, Pa.	FA-'05
Chester, Chris	G/C	6-3	305	1/12/83	Oklahoma	Tustin, Calif.	D2
Cottrell, Jim	LB/DE	6-2	257	1/13/83	New Mexico State	Castle Rock, Colo.	FA
Daniels, P.J.	RB	5-10	214	12/21/82	Georgia Tech	Houston, Texas	D4b
Dean, B.J.	FB	5-11	246	12/2/82	Florida State	Tuscaloosa, Ala.	FA
Droege, Rob (1)	G/T	6-6	302	12/15/81	Missouri	St. Louis, Mo.	FA-'05
Haley, Dennis (1)	LB	6-1	247	2/18/82	Virginia	Salem, Va.	FA-'05
James, Shannon	S	5-9	193	12/28/83	Massachusetts	Stratford, Conn.	FA
Koch, Sam	P	6-1	230	8/13/82	Nebraska	Seward, Neb.	D6a
Kracalik, Michael (1)	T	6-8	337	9/9/82	San Diego State	San Diego, Calif.	FA-'05
LaCasse, Ryan	LB/DE	6-2	257	2/6/83	Syracuse	Stoughton, Mass.	D7
Landry, Dawan	S	6-0	220	12/30/82	Georgia Tech	Boutte, La.	D5a
Leaders, Nick	DT	6-1	290	3/31/84	Iowa State	Omaha, Neb.	FA
Martin, Derrick	CB	5-10	202	5/16/85	Wyoming	Denver, Colo.	D6b
Meadow, Robin	T	6-5	324	8/4/83	Washington	Concord, Calif.	FA
Moses, Tres	WR	5-9	196	10/18/82	Rutgers	Delray Beach, Fla.	FA
Ngata, Haloti	DT	6-4	340	1/21/84	Oregon	Salt Lake City, Utah	D1
Oglesby, Evan (1)	CB	5-10	185	12/18/81	North Alabama	Tocca, Ga.	FA-'05
Olson, Drew	QB	6-2	222	6/6/83	UCLA	Piedmont, Calif.	FA
Paris, Steve	S	6-0	201	1/7/83	Iowa State	Dallas, Texas	FA
Pittman, David	CB	5-11	182	10/14/83	Northwestern State (La.)	Gramercy, La.	D3
Prude, Ronnie	CB	5-11	178	6/4/82	Louisiana State	Shreveport, La.	FA
Roper, Kyle	G	6-3	291	2/19/83	Arkansas	Powder Springs, Ga.	FA
Ross, Cory	RB	5-6	201	9/22/82	Nebraska	Denver, Colo.	FA
Schrage, Landon	LS	6-5	225	6/1/82	Iowa State	Parkersburg, Iowa	FA
Skillern, Rufus	WR	6-0	184	5/12/82	San Jose State	Oakland, Calif.	FA
Sypniewski, Quinn	TE	6-6	270	4/14/82	Colorado	Johnston, Iowa	D5b
Thomas, Benard (1)	DE	6-4	273	4/10/81	Nebraska	Mountain View, Calif.	FA-'05
Thompson, Duvol (1)	CB	5-9	183	1/28/82	Pennsylvania	Cleveland, Ohio	FA-'05
Williams, Demetrius	WR	6-2	197	3/28/83	Oregon	Concord, Calif.	D4a
Winborne, Jamaine (1)	CB/S	5-10	202	12/26/80	Virginia	Chesapeake, Va.	FA-'05
Woodfin, Zac (1)	LB	6-1	235	3/19/83	Alabama-Birmingham	Montgomery, Ala.	FA-'05

The term NFL Rookie is defined as a player who is in his first season of professional football and has not been on the roster of another professional football team for any regular-season or postseason games. A Rookie is designated by an "R" on NFL rosters. Players who have been active in another professional football league or players who have NFL experience, including either preseason training camp or being on an Active List or Inactive List, or on Reserve/Injured or Reserve/Physically Unable to Perform for fewer than six regular-season games, are termed NFL First-Year Players. An NFL First-Year Player is designated by a "1" on NFL rosters. Thereafter, a player is credited with an additional year of experience for each season in which he accumulates six games on the Active List or Inactive List, or on Reserve/Injured or Reserve/Physically Unable to Perform.

Log on to www.baltimoreravens.com for an up-to-date roster.

COACHING STAFF
Head Coach,
Brian Billick

Pro Career: Entering his eighth season, Brian Billick is tied for fourth in longevity with one team in the NFL. Billick and the Eagles' Andy Reid trail only the Steelers' Bill Cowher (15), Titans' Jeff Fisher (12), and Broncos' Mike Shanahan (12). Billick led the Ravens to the Super Bowl XXXV title in 2000, his second season with the club. Baltimore defeated the New York Giants, 34-7, on January 28, 2001. That season, Billick's Ravens allowed the fewest points in NFL history (165) in a 16-game season and also became the first team since 1978 to allow fewer than 1,000 rushing yards (970) in a regular season. His teams made the playoffs in 2000 (Super Bowl XXXV champions), 2001 (lost in Divisional playoff to the AFC champion Steelers) and 2003 (lost to Titans in Wild Card playoff). Prior to becoming the Ravens' head coach, Billick spent five years as Minnesota's offensive coordinator, where in 1998, the Vikings' offense scored an NFL single-season record 556 points. Billick was named the second head coach in Ravens history on January 19, 1999. Career record: 67-52.

Background: Billick was an honorable mention All-America tight end in 1976 at Brigham Young. Played linebacker at Air Force as a freshman before transferring to BYU. Drafted by the 49ers in the eleventh round of the 1977 draft, was released, and had a brief stint with the Dallas Cowboys, but did not play. Coached collegiately at Redlands (1977), Brigham Young (1978), San Diego State (1981-85), Utah State (1986-88), and Stanford (1989-1991). From 1979-1980 Billick was the San Francisco 49ers' assistant director of public relations.

Personal: Born February 28, 1954 in Fairborn, Ohio. He and his wife, Kim, have two daughters—Aubree and Keegan. Billick has co-authored two books: *Competitive Leadership: Twelve Principles for Success* (with Dr. James A. Peterson) and *Finding the Winning Edge* with Pro Football Hall of Fame coach Bill Walsh.

ASSISTANT COACHES

Clarence Brooks, defensive line; born May 20, 1951, New York, N.Y. Guard Massachusetts 1970-73. No pro playing experience. College coach: Massachusetts 1976-1980, Syracuse 1981-89, Arizona 1990-92. Pro coach: Chicago Bears 1993-98, Cleveland Browns 1999, Miami Dolphins 2000-04, joined Ravens in 2005.

Mark Carrier, secondary; born April 28, 1968, Lake Charles, La. Cornerback Southern California 1987-89. Pro cornerback Chicago Bears, 1990-96, Detroit Lions 1997-99, Washington Redskins 2000. College coach: Arizona State 2004-05. Pro coach: Joined Ravens in 2006.

Jim Fassel, offensive coordinator; born August 31, 1949, Anaheim, Calif. Quarterback Fullerton College 1967-68, Southern California 1969-1972. No pro game experience. College coach: Fullerton College 1973, Utah 1976, 1985-89, Weber State 1977-78, Stanford 1979-1983. Pro coach: Hawaii Hawaiians (World League) 1974, New Orleans Breakers (USFL) 1984, New York Giants 1991-92, Denver Broncos 1993-94, Oakland Raiders 1995, Arizona Cardinals 1996, New York Giants 1997-2003 (head coach), joined Ravens in 2004.

John Fassel, special teams assistant; born January 10, 1974, Anaheim, Calif. Wide receiver/quarterback Pacific 1994-95, Weber State 1996-98. No pro playing experience. College coach: Bucknell 1999, 2001, Idaho State 2000, New Mexico Highlands 2002-03. Pro coach: Amsterdam Admirals (NFLE) 2000, joined Ravens in 2005.

Jedd Fisch, asst. wide receivers/quarterbacks; born May 5, 1976, Livingston, N.J. Attended Florida. No college or pro playing experience. College coach: Florida 1999-2000. Pro coach: Houston Texans 2001-2003, joined Ravens in 2004.

Jeff FitzGerald, linebackers; born April 18, 1960, Burbank, Calif. Linebacker Oregon State 1980. No pro playing experience. College coach: Cincinnati 1985-86, Alabama 1987-89, San Diego State 1994-97. Pro coach: Tampa Bay Buccaneers 1990-93, Washington Redskins 1998-99, Arizona Cardinals 2000-2003, joined Ravens in 2004.

Chris Foerster, offensive line/asst. head coach; born October 12, 1961, Milwaukee, Wis. Center Colorado State 1979-1982. No pro playing experience. College coach: Colorado State 1983-87, Stanford 1988-1991, Minnesota 1992. Pro coach: Minnesota Vikings 1993-95, Tampa Bay Buccaneers 1996-2001, Indianapolis Colts 2002-03, Miami Dolphins 2004, joined Ravens in 2005.

Jeff Friday, strength and conditioning; born October 11, 1966, Milwaukee, Wis. Attended Wisconsin-Milwaukee. No college or pro playing experience. College coach: Illinois State 1991-92, Northwestern 1992-95. Pro coach: Minnesota Vikings 1996-98, joined Ravens in 1999.

Frank Gansz, Jr., special teams coordinator; born August 8, 1962, Greenville, S.C. Defensive back The Citadel 1981-84. No pro playing experience. College coach: Kansas 1987, Pittsburgh 1988-89, Army 1990-91, Houston 1993-97. Pro coach: New York/New Jersey Knights (WLAF) 1992, Oakland Raiders 1998-99, Kansas City Chiefs 2001-2005, joined Ravens in 2006.

Wade Harman, tight ends/asst. offensive line; born October 1, 1963, Corydon, Iowa. Linebacker Drake 1985, Utah State 1986. No pro playing experience. College

coach: Utah State 1987-1991, Pacific 1992-95, Morningside 1996. Pro coach: Minnesota Vikings 1997-98, joined Ravens in 1999.

Mike Johnson, wide receivers; born May 2, 1967, Los Angeles. Quarterback Arizona State 1985-86, Akron 1988-89. Pro quarterback Arizona Cardinals 1990, San Antonio Riders (World League) 1991-92, British Columbia Lions (CFL) 1992-93, Shreveport Pirates (CFL) 1994-95. College coach: Oregon State 1997-99. Pro coach: San Diego Chargers 2000-01, Atlanta Falcons 2002-2005, joined Ravens in 2006.

Tony Nathan, running backs; born December 14, 1956, Birmingham, Ala. Running back Alabama 1975-78. Pro running back Miami Dolphins 1979-1987. College coach: Florida International 2003-05. Pro coach: Miami Dolphins 1988-1995, Tampa Bay Buccaneers 1996-2001, joined Ravens in 2006.

Rick Neuheisel, quarterbacks; born February 7, 1961, Madison, Wis. Quarterback UCLA 1979-1983. Pro quarterback San Antonio Gunslingers (USFL) 1984-85, San Diego Chargers 1987, Tampa Bay Buccaneers 1987. College coach: UCLA 1988-1994, Colorado 1995-98 (head coach), Washington 1999-2002 (head coach). Pro coach: Joined Ravens in 2005.

Mike Pettine, outside linebackers; born September 25, 1966, Doylestown, Pa. Safety Virginia 1984-87. No pro playing experience. College coach: Pittsburgh 1993-94. Pro coach: Joined Ravens in 2002.

Paul Ricci, asst. strength and conditioning; born November 15, 1969, Elmer, N.J. Offensive lineman Penn State 1988-89. Pro coach: Seattle Seahawks 1993, Philadelphia Eagles 1995-96, Arizona Cardinals 1996-97, joined Ravens in 2002.

Greg Roman, asst. offensive line; born August 19, 1972, Atlantic City, N.J. Defensive line/linebacker John Carroll 1990-94. No pro playing experience. Pro coach: Carolina Panthers 1995-2001, Houston Texans 2002-2005, joined Ravens in 2006.

Rex Ryan, defensive coordinator; born December 13, 1962, Ardmore, Okla. Defensive end Southwest Oklahoma State 1983-86. No pro playing experience. College coach: Eastern Kentucky 1987-88, New Mexico Highlands 1989, Morehead State 1990-93, Cincinnati 1996-97, Oklahoma 1998. Pro coach: Arizona Cardinals 1994-95, joined Ravens in 1999.

Dennis Thurman, secondary; born April 13, 1956, Santa Monica, Calif. Safety Southern California 1974-77. Pro defensive back Dallas Cowboys 1978-1985, St. Louis Cardinals 1986. College coach: Southern California 1993-2000. Pro coach: Phoenix Cardinals 1988-89, joined Ravens in 2002.

American Football Conference
East Division
Team Colors: Dark Navy, Red, Royal, and Nickel
One Bills Drive
Orchard Park, New York 14127-2296
Telephone: (716) 648-1800

2006 SCHEDULE
PRESEASON
Aug. 12 at Carolina.........................7:30
Aug. 18 **Cincinnati** 7:00
Aug. 26 **Cleveland** 6:00
Aug. 31 at Detroit............................7:00

REGULAR SEASON
Sept. 10 at New England 1:00
Sept. 17 at Miami........................ 1:00
Sept. 24 **N.Y. Jets**..........................1:00
Oct. 1   **Minnesota** 1:00
Oct. 8   at Chicago.......................12:00
Oct. 15 at Detroit 1:00
Oct. 22 **New England** 1:00
Oct. 29 Open Date
Nov. 5   **Green Bay**........................1:00
Nov. 12 at Indianapolis 1:00
Nov. 19 at Houston 12:00
Nov. 26 **Jacksonville**......................1:00
Dec. 3   **San Diego**........................1:00
Dec. 10 at N.Y. Jets 1:00
Dec. 17 **Miami**............................ 1:00
Dec. 24 **Tennessee** 1:00
Dec. 31 at Baltimore.......................1:00

Stadium: Ralph Wilson Stadium
(opened in 1973)
 • **Capacity:** 73,967
One Bills Drive
Orchard Park, New York
14127-2296
Playing Surface: AstroPlay
Training Camp: St. John Fisher College
Rochester, New York
14618

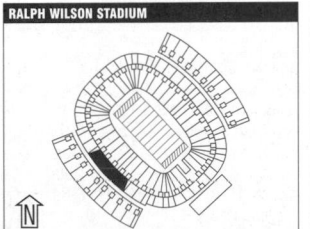

RALPH WILSON STADIUM

CLUB OFFICIALS
Owner and President:
Ralph C. Wilson, Jr.
General Manager/Football Operations:
Marv Levy
Assistant General Manager: Tom Modrak
Vice President/Assistant Director of
College and Pro Scouting:
Linda Bogdan
Treasurer: Jeffrey C. Littmann
Executive Vice President of Business
Operations: Russ Brandon
Vice President of Communications:
Scott Berchtold
Vice President of Stadium Operations:
Joe Frandina
Vice President of Business Development:
Pete Guelli
Vice President of Marketing and
Broadcasting: Marc Honan
Vice President of Public Affairs:
Bill Munson
Vice President of Football Administration:
Jim Overdorf
Vice President of Strategic Planning:
Mary Owen
Vice President of Business Operations
and Ticketing: Dave Wheat
Director of Pro Personnel: John Guy
Consultant: Christy Wilson Hofmann
Executive Director of Community
Relations: Gretchen Geitter
Executive Director of Information
Technology: Dan Evans
Director of Football Administration:
Don Purdy
Director of Merchandise: Tim Kehoe
Director of Player Programs:
Paul Lancaster
Director of Security: Chris Clark
Controller: Frank Wojnicki
Strength and Conditioning Assistant:
Ambar Paranjape
Equipment Manager: Dave Hojnowski
Assistant Equipment Managers:
Randy Ribbeck, Jeff Mazurek
Head Athletic Trainer: Bud Carpenter
Athletic Trainers: Chris Fischetti,
Shone Gipson, Greg McMillen
Video Director: Henry Kunttu
Assistant Video Director: Greg Estes
Video Assistant: Kevin Shearer
Scouts: Brad Forsyth, Joe Haering,
Shawn Heilen, Doug Majeski,
Marc Ross, Tom Roth,
(emeritus) Bob Ryan,
(emeritus) David G. Smith,
(emeritus) David W. Smith,
Terry Wooden

COACHING HISTORY
(341-372-8)
Records include postseason games
1960-61   Buster Ramsey 11-16-1
1962-65   Lou Saban 38-18-3
1966-68   Joe Collier*................13-17-1
1968   Harvey Johnson 1-10-1
1969-1970 John Rauch...................7-20-1
1971   Harvey Johnson 1-13-0
1972-76   Lou Saban** 32-29-1
1976-77   Jim Ringo.......................3-20-0
1978-1982 Chuck Knox 38-38-0
1983-85   Kay Stephenson*** 10-26-0
1985-86   Hank Bullough****....4-17-0
1986-1997 Marv Levy..................123-78-0
1998-2000 Wade Phillips 29-21-0
2001-03   Gregg Williams.........17-31-0
2004-05   Mike Mularkey.............14-18-0
    *Released after two games in 1968
  **Resigned after five games in 1976
 ***Released after four games in 1985
****Released after nine games in 1986

ATTENDANCE
Home 562,559   Away 508,013
Total 1,070,572
Single-game home record,
80,368 (10/4/92)
Single-season home record,
635,889 (1991)

2006 DRAFT CHOICES
Round	Name	Pos.	College
1	Donte' Whitner	DB	Ohio State
	John McCargo	DT	North Carolina St.
3	Ashton Youboty	DB	Ohio State
4	Ko Simpson	DB	South Carolina
5	Kyle Williams	DT	Louisiana State
	Brad Butler	T	Virginia
6	Keith Ellison	LB	Oregon State
7	Terrance Pennington	T	New Mexico
	Aaron Merz	G	California

BUFFALO BILLS

2005 TEAM RECORD
PRESEASON (3-1)

Date	Result		Opponent
8/13	W	17-10	at Indianapolis
8/20	W	27-7	Green Bay
8/26	L	12-16	at Chicago
9/2	L	7-21	Detroit

REGULAR SEASON (5-11)

Date	Result		Opponent	Att.
9/11	W	22-7	Houston	71,781
9/18	L	3-19	at Tampa Bay	64,777
9/25	L	16-24	Atlanta	72,032
10/2	L	7-19	at New Orleans	58,688
10/9	W	20-14	Miami	72,160
10/16	W	27-17	New York Jets	72,045
10/23	L	17-38	at Oakland	42,779
10/30	L	16-21	at New England	68,756
11/13	W	14-3	Kansas City	72,093
11/20	L	10-48	at San Diego	65,602
11/27	L	9-13	Carolina	71,440
12/4	L	23-24	at Miami	72,051
12/11	L	7-35	New England	71,810
12/17	L	17-28	Denver	71,887
12/24	W	37-27	at Cincinnati	65,485
1/1	L	26-30	at New York Jets	76,822

SCORE BY PERIODS

Bills	80	86	46	59	0	—	271
Opponents	34	135	75	123	0	—	367

2005 TEAM STATISTICS

	Bills	Opp.
Total First Downs	259	343
Rushing	96	146
Passing	129	169
Penalty	34	28
3rd Down: Made/Att	74/201	93/200
3rd Down Pct.	36.8	46.5
4th Down: Made/Att	6/16	7/12
4th Down Pct.	37.5	58.3
Possession Avg.	29:04	30:56
Total Net Yards	4,122	5,496
Avg. Per Game	257.6	343.5
Total Plays	930	1030
Avg. Per Play	4.4	5.3
Net Yards Rushing	1,607	2,205
Avg. Per Game	100.4	137.8
Total Rushes	428	489
Net Yards Passing	2,515	3,291
Avg. Per Game	157.2	205.7
Sacked/Yards Lost	43/337	38/269
Gross Yards	2,852	3,560
Att./Completions	459/269	503/314
Completion Pct.	58.6	62.4
Had Intercepted	16	17
Punts/Average	71/45.7	62/40.2
Net Punting Avg.	71/39.1	62/34.4
Penalties/Yards	120/897	124/904
Fumbles/Ball Lost	26/10	24/13
Touchdowns	26	44
Rushing	6	22
Passing	18	19
Returns	2	3

2005 INDIVIDUAL STATISTICS

PASSING

PASSING	Att.	Comp.	Yds.	Pct.	TD	Int.	Tkld.	Rate
Holcomb	230	155	1,509	67.4	10	8	17/140	85.6
Losman	228	113	1,340	49.6	8	8	26/197	64.9
Parrish	1	1	3	100.0	0	0	0/0	79.2
Bills	459	269	2,852	58.6	18	16	43/337	75.4
Opponents	503	314	3,560	62.4	19	17	38/269	82.1

SCORING

SCORING	TD R	TD P	TD Rt	PAT	FG	Saf	PTS
Lindell	0	0	0	26/26	29/35	0	113
Evans	0	7	0	0/0	0/0	0	42
McGahee	5	0	0	0/0	0/0	0	30
Moulds	0	4	0	0/0	0/0	0	24
McGee	0	0	2	0/0	0/0	0	12
Reed	0	2	0	0/0	0/0	0	12
Burns	0	1	0	0/0	0/0	0	6
Holcomb	1	0	0	0/0	0/0	0	6
Parrish	0	1	0	0/0	0/0	0	6
Peters	0	1	0	0/0	0/0	0	6
Shelton	0	1	0	0/0	0/0	0	6
J. Smith	0	1	0	0/0	0/0	0	6
Fletcher	0	0	0	0/0	0/0	1	2
Bills	6	18	2	26/26	29/35	1	271
Opponents	22	19	3	44/44	19/25	1	367

2-Pt. Conversions: None.
Bills 0-0, Opponents 0-0.

RUSHING

RUSHING	Att.	Yds.	Avg.	LG	TD
McGahee	325	1,247	3.8	27	5
S. Williams	45	161	3.6	28	0
Losman	31	154	5.0	30	0
Evans	4	38	9.5	39	0
Holcomb	18	11	0.6	8	1
J. Smith	1	1	1.0	1	0
Shelton	1	0	0.0	0	0
Parrish	2	-2	-1.0	4	0
Reed	1	-3	-3.0	-3	0
Bills	428	1,607	3.8	39	6
Opponents	489	2,205	4.5	59	22

RECEIVING

RECEIVING	No.	Yds.	Avg.	LG	TD
Moulds	81	816	10.1	55t	4
Evans	48	743	15.5	65	7
Reed	32	449	14.0	51t	2
McGahee	28	178	6.4	19	0
Campbell	19	139	7.3	27	0
S. Williams	17	118	6.9	23	0
Parrish	15	148	9.9	28	1
Shelton	13	98	7.5	21	1
J. Smith	5	56	11.2	19	1
Aiken	4	57	14.3	22	0
Euhus	3	17	5.7	9	0
Peters	2	5	2.5	4	1
Burns	1	19	19.0	19t	1
Neufeld	1	9	9.0	9	0
Bills	269	2,852	10.6	65	18
Opponents	314	3,560	11.3	57	19

INTERCEPTIONS

INTERCEPTIONS	No.	Yds.	Avg.	LG	TD
McGee	4	97	24.3	46t	1
Vincent	4	78	19.5	42	0
Crowell	2	3	1.5	2	0
Clements	2	0	0	0	0
Fletcher	1	20	20.0	20	0
R. Baker	1	18	18.0	18	0
Kelsay	1	17	17.0	17	0
Milloy	1	0	0.0	0	0
Schobel	1	0	0.0	0	0
Bills	17	233	13.7	46t	1
Opponents	16	209	13.1	42	2

PUNTING

PUNTING	No.	Yds.	Avg.	In 20	LG
Moorman	71	3,242	45.7	22	68
Bills	71	3,242	45.7	22	68
Opponents	62	2,492	40.2	22	61

PUNT RETURNS

PUNT RETURNS	No.	FC	Yds.	Avg.	LG	TD
Parrish	14	9	186	13.3	43	0
Clements	8	3	52	6.5	13	0
J. Smith	6	5	41	6.8	17	0
Bills	28	17	279	10.0	43	0
Opponents	42	10	285	6.8	29	0

KICKOFF RETURNS

KICKOFF RETURNS	No.	Yds.	Avg.	LG	TD
McGee	46	1,391	30.2	99t	1
Parrish	10	261	26.1	45	0
J. Smith	5	124	24.8	44	0
Reed	4	69	17.3	24	0
Burns	3	46	15.3	19	0
Neufeld	3	39	13.0	23	0
Shelton	2	26	13.0	16	0
Leonhard	1	36	36.0	36	0
Euhus	1	0	0.0	0	0
Bills	75	1,992	26.6	99t	1
Opponents	64	1,308	20.4	95t	1

FIELD GOALS

FIELD GOALS	1-19	20-29	30-39	40-49	50+
Lindell	0/0	8/9	11/13	7/10	3/3
Bills	0/0	8/9	11/13	7/10	3/3
Opponents	0/0	10/10	5/6	4/9	0/0

SACKS

SACKS	No.
Schobel	12.0
Denney	4.0
Fletcher	4.0
Adams	3.0
Crowell	3.0
Posey	3.0
Kelsay	2.5
Bannan	1.5
T. Anderson	1.0
R. Baker	1.0
Greer	1.0
Milloy	1.0
Spikes	1.0
Bills	38.0
Opponents	43.0

RECORD HOLDERS
INDIVIDUAL RECORDS—CAREER

Category	Name	Performance
Rushing (Yds.)	Thurman Thomas, 1988-1999	11,938
Passing (Yds.)	Jim Kelly, 1986-1996	35,467
Passing (TDs)	Jim Kelly, 1986-1996	237
Receiving (No.)	Andre Reed, 1985-1999	941
Receiving (Yds.)	Andre Reed, 1985-1999	13,095
Interceptions	George (Butch) Byrd, 1964-1970	40
Punting (Avg.)	Brian Moorman, 2001-05	43.4
Punt Return (Avg.)	Clifford Hicks, 1990-92	12.2
Kickoff Return (Avg.)	O.J. Simpson, 1969-1977	30.0
Field Goals	Steve Christie, 1992-2000	234
Touchdowns (Tot.)	Andre Reed, 1985-1999	87
	Thurman Thomas, 1988-1999	87
Points	Steve Christie, 1992-2000	1,011

INDIVIDUAL RECORDS—SINGLE SEASON

Category	Name	Performance
Rushing (Yds.)	O.J. Simpson, 1973	2,003
Passing (Yds.)	Drew Bledsoe, 2002	4,359
Passing (TDs)	Jim Kelly, 1991	33
Receiving (No.)	Eric Moulds, 2002	100
Receiving (Yds.)	Eric Moulds, 1998	1,368
Interceptions	Billy Atkins, 1961	10
	Tom Janik, 1967	10
Punting (Avg.)	Brian Moorman, 2005	45.7
Punt Return (Avg.)	Keith Moody, 1977	13.1
Kickoff Return (Avg.)	Terrence McGee, 2005	30.24
Field Goals	Steve Christie, 1998	33
Touchdowns (Tot.)	O.J. Simpson, 1975	23
Points	Steve Christie, 1998	140

INDIVIDUAL RECORDS—SINGLE GAME

Category	Name	Performance
Rushing (Yds.)	O.J. Simpson, 11-25-76	273
Passing (Yds.)	Drew Bledsoe, 9-15-02	463
Passing (TDs)	Jim Kelly, 9-8-91	6
Receiving (No.)	Andre Reed, 11-20-94	15
Receiving (Yds.)	Jerry Butler, 9-23-79	255
Interceptions	Many times	3
	Last time by Nate Clements, 10-20-02	
Field Goals	Steve Christie, 10-20-96	6
Touchdowns (Tot.)	Cookie Gilchrist, 12-8-63	5
Points	Cookie Gilchrist, 12-8-63	30

2006 VETERAN ROSTER

No.	Name	Pos.	Ht.	Wt.	Birthdate	NFL Exp.	College	Hometown	How Acq.	'05 Games/ Starts
89	Aiken, Sam	WR	6-2	204	12/14/80	4	North Carolina	Kenansville, N.C.	D4b-'03	16/2
66	Anderson, Bennie	G/T	6-5	345	2/17/77	6	Tennessee State	St. Louis, Mo.	FA-'05	16/15
77	Anderson, Tim	DT	6-3	304	11/22/80	3	Ohio State	Clyde, Ohio	D3-'04	16/12
26	Baker, Rashad	S	5-10	198	2/22/82	3	Tennessee	Camden, N.J.	FA-'04	14/0
41	Bowen, Matt	S	6-1	203	11/12/76	7	Iowa	Glen Ellyn, Ill.	FA-'06	13/1*
35	Burns, Joe	FB/RB	5-9	215	9/15/79	4	Georgia Tech	Thomasville, Ga.	FA-'02	16/0
22	Clements, Nate	CB	6-0	209	12/12/79	6	Ohio State	Shaker Heights, Ohio	D1-'01	16/16
55	Crowell, Angelo	LB	6-1	235	8/16/81	4	Virginia	Winston-Salem, N.C.	D3-'03	15/13
18	Davis, Andre'	WR	6-1	195	6/12/79	5	Virginia Tech	Niskayuna, N.Y.	UFA(NE)-'06	9/4*
92	Denney, Ryan	DE	6-7	275	6/15/77	5	Brigham Young	Thornton, Colo.	D2b-'02	16/0
87	Euhus, Tim	TE	6-5	249	10/2/80	3	Oregon State	Eugene, Ore.	D4-'04	11/3
83	Evans, Lee	WR	5-10	197	3/11/81	3	Wisconsin	Bedford, Ohio	D1a-'04	16/15
85	Everett, Kevin	TE	6-4	241	6/5/82	2	Miami	Kilgore, Texas	D3-'05	0*
50	Ezekiel, Liam	LB	6-0	249	10/30/82	2	Northeastern	Arlington, Mass.	FA-'05	2/0
59	Fletcher, London	LB	5-10	245	5/19/75	9	John Carroll	Cleveland, Ohio	FA-'02	16/16
67	Fowler, Melvin	G/T	6-3	295	3/31/79	5	Maryland	Wheatly Heights, N.Y.	UFA(Minn)-'06	11/9*
69	Gandy, Mike	G/T	6-4	310	1/3/79	6	Notre Dame	Dallas, Texas	FA-'04	16/16
25	Gates, Lionel	RB	6-0	233	3/13/82	2	Louisville	Jacksonville, Fla.	D7-'05	0*
73	Geisinger, Justin	G/T	6-3	322	5/24/82	2	Vanderbilt	Pittsburgh, Pa.	D6-'05	0*
74	Gibson, Aaron	G/T	6-6	375	9/27/77	7	Wisconsin	Indianpolis, Ind.	FA-'06	0*
33	Greer, Jabari	CB	5-11	169	2/11/82	3	Tennessee	Jackson, Tenn.	FA-'04	16/2
53	Haggan, Mario	LB	6-3	248	3/3/80	4	Mississippi State	Clarksdale, Miss.	D7-'03	16/0
10	Holcomb, Kelly	QB	6-2	212	7/9/73	10	Middle Tennessee State	Fayetville, Tenn.	UFA(Cle)-'05	10/8
99	Jefferson, Jason	DT	6-1	310	12/20/81	2	Wisconsin	Chicago, Ill.	FA-'05	5/0
76	Jerman, Greg	G/T	6-5	310	1/24/79	5	Baylor	El Paso, Texas	FA-'05	10/3
90	Kelsay, Chris	DE	6-4	275	10/31/79	4	Nebraska	Auburn, Neb.	D2-'03	16/16
29	King, Eric	CB	5-10	185	5/10/82	2	Wake Forest	Woodstock, Md.	D5-'05	16/1
42	Leonhard, Jim	S	5-8	190	10/27/82	2	Wisconsin	Tony, Wis.	FA-'05	10/0
9	Lindell, Rian	K	6-3	235	1/20/77	7	Washington State	Vancouver, Wash.	FA-'03	16/0
7	Losman, JP	QB	6-2	217	3/12/81	3	Tulane	Venice, Calif.	D1b-'04	9/8
79	McFarland, Dylan	T	6-5	290	7/11/80	2	Montana	Kalispell, Mont.	D7a-'04	1/0
21	McGahee, Willis	RB	6-0	228	10/21/81	3	Miami	Miami, Fla.	D1-'03	16/15
24	McGee, Terrence	CB	5-9	195	10/14/80	4	Northwestern State (La.)	Athens, Texas	D4a-'03	15/14
8	Moorman, Brian	P	6-0	175	2/5/76	6	Pittsburg State	Sedgwick, Kan.	FA-'01	16/0
16	Nall, Craig	QB	6-3	230	4/21/79	5	Northwestern State	Alexandria, La.	UFA(GB)-'06	0*
88	Neufeld, Ryan	TE	6-4	250	11/22/75	6	UCLA	Morgan Hill, CA	FA-'03	13/0
11	Parrish, Roscoe	WR	5-9	168	7/16/82	2	Miami	Miami, Fla.	D2-'05	10/1
71	Peters, Jason	G/T	6-4	328	1/22/82	3	Arkansas	Queen City, Texas	FA-'04	16/10
96	Posey, Jeff	LB	6-4	241	8/14/75	9	Southern Mississippi	Bassfield, Miss.	FA-'03	16/15
75	Preston, Duke	G/T	6-5	311	6/12/82	2	Illinois	San Diego, CA	D4-'05	15/1
81	Price, Peerless	WR	5-11	190	10/27/76	8	Tennessee	Dayton, Ohio	FA-'06	7/0*
82	Reed, Josh	WR	5-10	208	5/1/80	5	Louisiana State	Rayne, La.	D2a-'02	16/6
70	Reyes, Tutan	G/T	6-3	310	10/28/77	7	Mississippi	Queens, N.Y.	UFA(Car)-'06	16/16*
84	Royal, Robert	TE	6-4	260	5/15/78	4	Louisiana State	New Orleans, La.	UFA(Wash)-'06	15/14*
93	Sape, Lauvale	DT	6-1	296	8/29/80	3	Utah	Leilehua, Hawaii	D6-'03	9/0
54	Schneck, Mike	LS	6-1	237	8/4/77	8	Wisconsin	Whitefish Bay, Wis.	FA-'05	16/0
94	Schobel, Aaron	DE	6-4	262	9/1/77	6	Texas Christian	Columbus, Texas	D2a-'01	16/16
31	Shelton, Daimon	FB	6-0	262	9/15/72	9	Sacramento State	Duarte, Calif.	FA-'04	16/11
19	Smith, Jonathan	WR	5-10	194	11/28/81	3	Georgia Tech	Argyle, Ga.	D7b-'04	7/1
51	Spikes, Takeo	LB	6-2	242	12/17/76	9	Auburn	Sandersville, Ga.	FA-'03	3/3
57	Stamer, Josh	LB	6-2	238	10/11/77	4	South Dakota	Sutherland, Iowa	FA-'03	16/0
28	Thomas, Anthony	RB	6-2	225	11/7/77	6	Michigan	Pineville, La.	UFA(NO)-'06	9/2*
37	Thomas, Kiwaukee	DB	5-11	192	6/19/77	7	Georgia Southern	Perry, Ga.	UFA(Mia)-'06	10/0*
98	Tripplett, Larry	DT	6-2	295	1/18/79	5	Washington	Los Angeles, Calif.	UFA(Ind)-'06	16/4*
58	Villarrial, Chris	G/T	6-3	318	6/9/73	11	Indiana (Pa.)	Hershey, Pa.	FA-'04	15/15
23	Vincent, Troy	S	6-1	200	6/8/71	15	Wisconsin	Trenton, N.J.	FA-'04	16/16
20	Williams, Shaud	RB	5-7	193	10/02/80	3	Alabama	Andrews, Texas	FA-'04	16/0
15	Wilson, George	WR	6-0	210	3/14/81	2	Arkansas	Paducah, KY	FA-'04	3/0
27	Wire, Coy	S	6-0	205	11/7/78	5	Stanford	Camp Hill, Pa.	D3-'02	13/0
2	Woodbury, Tory	QB	6-2	208	7/12/78	3	Winston Salem	Winston-Salem, N.C.	FA-'06	0*
63	Word, Mark	DE	6-5	295	11/23/75	3	Jacksonville State	Miami, Fla.	FA-'06	0*

* Bowen played 13 games with Washington in '05; Davis played 9 games with New England; Everett missed '05 season because of injury; Fowler played 11 games with Minnesota; Gates did not play in 2 games; Geisinger did not play in 2 games; Gibson last active with Chicago in '04; Nall inactive for 16 games with Green Bay; Price played 7 games with Dallas; Reyes played 16 games with Carolina; Royal played 15 games with Washington; A. Thomas played 9 games with New Orleans; K. Thomas played 10 games with Miami; Tripplett played 16 games with Indianapolis; Woodbury last active with N.Y. Jets in '02; Word last active with Cleveland in '03.

Players lost through free agency (3): DT Justin Bannan (Balt; 16 games in '05), DT Ron Edwards (KC; 4), C Trey Teague (NYJ; 16).

Traded—WR Eric Moulds (Hou; 15 games in '05).

Also played with Bills in '05—DT Sam Adams (14 games), TE Mark Campbell (14), S Lawyer Milloy (16), T Mike Williams (9).

2006 FIRST-YEAR ROSTER

Name	Pos.	Ht.	Wt.	Birthdate	College	Hometown	How Acq.
Bassey, Eric	CB	6-1	200	1/23/83	Oklahoma	Garland, Texas	FA
Bethea, James (1)	CB/S	6-0	180	9/24/82	California	Reseda, Calif.	FA
Brown, LaWaylon (1)	DT	6-5	305	6/12/80	Oklahoma State	Whitehouse, Texas	FA-'05
Butler, Brad	G/T	6-7	309	9/18/83	Virginia	Lynchburg, Va.	D5b
Carothers, Greg (1)	S/LB	6-2	228	7/13/81	Washington	Great Falls, Mont.	FA
Cieslak, Brad (1)	TE	6-3	262	7/1/82	Northern Illinois	Long Grove, Ill.	FA-'05
Denney, Chris	WR	6-3	219	1/25/83	Nebraska-Omaha	Norfolk, Neb.	FA
DiGiorgio, John	LB	6-2	225	6/29/82	Saginaw Valley State	Shelby Twp.,	FA
Ellison, Keith	LB	6-0	228	2/6/84	Oregon State	Redondo Beach, Calif.	D6
Goldsberry, Jon (1)	FB	6-1	246	12/4/81	Purdue	Santa Claus, Ind.	FA-'05
Hall, Jason	DE/DT	6-3	260	10/31/83	Tennessee	Marietta, Ga.	FA
Hunter, Wendell (1)	LB	6-0	228	4/19/82	California	Carson, Calif.	FA-'05
Jackson, Fred (1)	RB	6-1	210	2/20/81	Coe College	Fort Worth, Texas	FA
Lee, Rob (1)	CB	6-0	193	2/11/81	Northern Illinois	Port Washington, Wis.	FA-'05
McCargo, John	DT	6-2	295	8/19/83	North Carolina State	Drake's Branch, Va.	D1b
Merz, Aaron	G/T	6-4	340	8/27/83	California	Wasco, Calif.	D7b
Ming, Derrick	FB	5-11	245	7/16/82	Missouri	Webster Groves, Mo.	FA
Morgan, Matt (1)	G/T	6-6	304	12/3/80	Pittsburgh	Pittsburgh, Pa.	FA
Nance, Martin	WR	6-3	212	5/26/83	Miami (Ohio)	Maryland Heights, Mich.	FA
Neill, Ryan	DE/DT	6-3	265	12/12/82	Rutgers	Wayne Hills, N.J.	FA
Ochs, Craig (1)	QB	6-2	210	8/20/81	Montana	Boulder, Colo.	FA
Pennington, Terrance	G/T	6-7	325	9/25/83	New Mexico	Compton, Calif.	D7a
Powell, Eric (1)	DE/DT	6-3	268	11/16/79	Florida State	Orlando, Fla.	FA-'05
Rice, Matthew	DE/DT	6-4	256	2/12/82	Penn State	Baltimore, Md.	FA
Setta, Nicholas (1)	K	6-0	194	5/6/81	Notre Dame	Lockport, Ill.	FA
Simpson, Ko	S	6-1	201	11/9/83	South Carolina	Rock Hill, S.C.	D4
Thomas, Jason (1)	G/T	6-4	325	6/10/77	Hampton	Savannah, Ga.	FA
Tupa'i, Faafetai (1)	DT	6-3	330	5/24/81	Washingon State	Monterey, Calif.	FA
Whitner, Donte	S	5-10	204	7/24/85	Ohio State	Cleveland, Ohio	D1a
Williams, Kyle	DT	6-1	295	6/10/83	Louisiana State	Ruston, La.	D5a
Youboty, Ashton	CB	5-11	189	7/7/84	Ohio State	Klein, Texas	D3

The term NFL Rookie is defined as a player who is in his first season of professional football and has not been on the roster of another professional football team for any regular-season or postseason games. A Rookie is designated by an "R" on NFL rosters. Players who have been active in another professional football league or players who have NFL experience, including either preseason training camp or being on an Active List or Inactive List, or on Reserve/Injured or Reserve/Physically Unable to Perform for fewer than six regular-season games, are termed NFL First-Year Players. An NFL First-Year Player is designated by a "1" on NFL rosters. Thereafter, a player is credited with an additional year of experience for each season in which he accumulates six games on the Active List or Inactive List, or on Reserve/Injured or Reserve/Physically Unable to Perform.

Log on to www.buffalobills.com for an up-to-date roster.

COACHING STAFF
Head Coach,
Dick Jauron

Pro Career: Became the fourteenth coach in franchise history on January 23, 2006. Jauron enters his third stint as an NFL head coach after serving as the head coach of the Chicago Bears (1999-2003) and as interim head coach of the Detroit Lions for the final five games of 2005. The highlight of his Bears' tenure career came in 2001 when Chicago finished 13-3 and claim its first division championship since 1990. Under Jauron's leadership, the 2001 Bears were 8-0 in games decided by seven points or less, and engineered five second half, come-from-behind victories. The Bears defense ranked first in the NFL in points allowed and second in rushing yards allowed. For his efforts, Jauron was selected as the *Associated Press* NFL Coach of the Year. He was just the third coach in team history to win 13 games in a season. The 2001 season marked the greatest single-season turnaround in team history improving from 5-11 in 2000 to 13-3. In his five seasons in Chicago, Jauron accumulated a 35-46 (.432) record. He became the first Bears coach to defeat the Green Bay Packers in Lambeau Field on his first two trips. Jauron began his coaching career with the Buffalo Bills (1985, defensive backs), Green Bay Packers (1986-1994, defensive backs), and Jacksonville Jaguars (1995-98, defensive coordinator). As Jacksonville's inaugural defensive coordinator, he was instrumental in the early success of the franchise which included three playoff berths in the franchise's first four seasons and a run to the 1996 AFC Championship game. He served as the Lions' defensive coordinator from 2004-05. Career record: 36-50.

Background: A three-sport (football, basketball, and baseball) standout at Swampscott (Mass.) High School. Named one of the top 10 prep athletes of the 20th Century in the state of Massachusetts by the *Boston Globe*. Played running back at Yale (1970-72) where, for 27 years, he held the school's career rushing mark with 2,947 yards. Drafted by the Detroit Lions in the fourth round of the 1973 draft. Played defensive back for Detroit (1973-77) and was named to the Pro Bowl following the 1974 season after leading the NFC in punt return average (16.8). He finished his career with the Cincinnati Bengals (1978-1980).

Personal: Born October 7, 1950, Peoria, Ill. Dick and his wife Gail have two daughters—Kacy and Amy.

ASSISTANT COACHES

John Allaire, strength and conditioning; born December 3, 1970, Woonsocket, R.I. Attended Springfield College. No college or pro playing experience. College coach: Boston College 1992, Clemson 1993-95, Tulsa 1996-2001. Pro coach: Joined Bills in 2002.

Bobby April, asst. head coach/special teams; born April 15, 1963, New Orleans. Linebacker/defensive end Nicholls State 1972-75. No pro playing experience. College coach: Southern Mississippi 1978, Tulane 1979, Arizona 1980-86, Southern California 1987-1990. Pro coach: Atlanta Falcons 1991-93, Pittsburgh Steelers 1994-95, New Orleans Saints 1996-99, St. Louis Rams 2001-02, joined Bills in 2004.

George Catavolos, defensive backs; born May 8, 1945, Chicago. Defensive back Purdue 1964-67. No pro playing experience. College coach: Purdue 1967-68, 1971-76, Middle Tennessee State 1969, Louisville 1970, Kentucky 1977-81, Tennessee 1982-83. Pro coach: Indianapolis Colts 1984-1994, 1998-2001, Carolina Panthers 1995-97, Washington Redskins 2002-03, Detroit Lions 2004-05, joined Bills in 2006.

Charlie Coiner, tight ends; born April 24, 1960, Wayensboro, Va. Attended Catawba College, Appalachian State. No college or pro playing experience. College coach: Appalachian State 1983-86, Minnesota 1987, Louisville 1995-97, Tennessee-Chattanooga 1998, Louisiana State 1999, Texas Southern 2000. Pro coach: Chicago Bears 2001-05, joined Bills in 2006.

DeMontie Cross, defensive/special teams assistant; born February 26, 1974, St. Louis, Mo. Free safety Missouri 1994-96. No pro playing experience. College coach: Missouri 1998-99, Sam Houston State 2000, Iowa State 2001-05. Pro coach: Joined Bills in 2006.

Steve Fairchild, offensive coordinator; born June 21, 1958, Decatur, Ill. Quarterback San Diego Mesa C.C. 1978-79, Colorado State 1980-81. No pro playing experience. College coach: San Diego Mesa C.C. 1982-83, Ferris State 1984-85, San Diego State 1991-92, Colorado State 1997-2000. Pro coach: Buffalo Bills 2001-02, St. Louis Rams 2003-05, rejoined Bills in 2006.

Perry Fewell, defensive coordinator; born September 7, 1962, Gastonia, N.C. Defensive back Lenoir-Rhyne 1981-84. No pro playing experience. College coach: North Carolina 1985-86, Army 1987, 1992-94, Kent State 1988-91, Vanderbilt 1995-97. Pro coach: Jacksonville Jaguars 1998-2002, St. Louis Rams 2003-04, Chicago Bears 2005, joined Bills in 2006.

Sean Hayes, asst. strength and conditioning; born October 25, 1975, Peabody, Mass. No college or pro playing experience. College coach: Springfield College 1997-98, Tulsa 1999-2000, Harvard 2001-03, Clemson 2004-05. Pro coach: Joined Bills in 2006.

Bill Kollar, defensive line; born November 27, 1952, Warren, Ohio. Defensive end Montana State 1971-74. Pro defensive end Cincinnati Bengals 1974-76, Tampa Bay Buccanneers 1977-1981. College coach: Illinois: 1985-87, Purdue 1988-89. Pro coach: Tampa Bay Buccaneers 1984, Atlanta Falcons 1990-2000, St. Louis Rams 2001-2005, joined Bills in 2006.

Chuck Lester, asst. to the head coach/defensive assistant; born May 18, 1955, Chicago. Linebacker Oklahoma 1974. No pro playing experience. College coach: Iowa State 1980-81, Oklahoma 1982-84. Pro coach: Kansas City Chiefs 1984-86 (scout), joined Bills in 1987.

Jim McNally, offensive line; born December 13, 1943, Buffalo. Guard Buffalo 1961-65. No pro playing experience. College coach: Buffalo 1966-1970, Marshall 1971-74, Boston College 1975-77, Wake Forest 1978-79. Pro coach: Cincinnati Bengals 1980-94, Carolina Panthers 1995-98, New York Giants 1999-2003, joined Bills in 2004.

Turk Schonert, quarterbacks; born January 15, 1957, Torrance, Calif. Quarterback Stanford 1975-79. Pro quarterback Cincinnati Bengals 1980-85, 1987-89, Atlanta Falcons 1986. Pro coach: Tampa Bay Buccaneers 1992-95, Buffalo Bills 1998-2000, Carolina Panthers 2001, New York Giants 2003, New Orleans Saints 2005, rejoined Bills in 2006.

Matt Sheldon, linebackers; born February 26, 1969, Berwyn, Ill. Cornerback Minnesota 1987-1991. No pro playing experience. College coach: Wisconsin 1997-99. Pro coach: St. Louis Rams 2001-05, joined Bills in 2006.

Eric Studesville, running backs; born May 29, 1967, Madison, Wis. Defensive back Wisconsin-Whitewater 1985-88. No pro playing experience. College coach: Wingate 1994, Kent State 1995-96. Pro coach: Chicago Bears 1997-2000, New York Giants 2001-03, joined Bills in 2004.

Tyke Tolbert, wide receivers; born September 15, 1967, Conroe, Texas. Wide receiver Louisiana State 1988-1990. No pro playing experience. College coach: Louisiana-Monroe 1994-97, Auburn 1998, Louisiana-Lafayette 1999-2001, Florida 2002. Pro coach: Arizona Cardinals 2003, joined Bills in 2004.

Alex Van Pelt, offensive quality control; born May 1, 1970, Pittsburgh. Quarterback Pittsburgh 1990-94. College coach: Buffalo 2005. Pro coach: Frankfurt Galaxy (NFLE) 2005, joined Bills in 2006.

Larry Zierlein, asst. offensive line; born July 12, 1945, Lenora Kan. Attended Fort Hays State College. No college or pro playing experience. College coach: Fort Hays (Kan.) State College 1970-71, Houston 1978-1986, Tulane 1988-1990, 1995-96, Louisiana State 1993-94, Cincinnati 1997-2000. Pro coach: Washington Commandos (Arena League) 1987, New York/New Jersey Knights (WLAF) 1991-92, Cleveland Browns 2001-2004, joined Bills in 2006.

**American Football Conference
North Division
Team Colors:** Black, Orange, and White
**One Paul Brown Stadium
Cincinnati, Ohio 45202-3492
Telephone:** (513) 621-3550
Ticket Office (513) 621-TDTD (8383)

**2006 SCHEDULE
PRESEASON**
Aug. 13 **Washington** 8:00
Aug. 18 at Buffalo 7:00
Aug. 28 **Green Bay**.........................8:00
Sept. 1 at Indianapolis 7:00

REGULAR SEASON
Sept. 10 at Kansas City 12:00
Sept. 17 **Cleveland** 1:00
Sept. 24 at Pittsburgh.......................1:00
Oct. 1 **New England** 4:15
Oct. 8 Open Date
Oct. 15 at Tampa Bay 1:00
Oct. 22 **Carolina**.............................1:00
Oct. 29 **Atlanta** 1:00
Nov. 5 at Baltimore........................1:00
Nov. 12 **San Diego**.........................1:00
Nov. 19 at New Orleans.................12:00
Nov. 26 at Cleveland 1:00
Nov. 30 **Baltimore** (Thu.) 8:00
Dec. 10 **Oakland** 1:00
Dec. 18 at Indianapolis (Mon.).........8:30
Dec. 24 at Denver 2:15
Dec. 31 **Pittsburgh**...........................1:00

Stadium: Paul Brown Stadium
        (opened in 2000)
        •**Capacity:** 65,378
        One Paul Brown Stadium
        Cincinnati, Ohio 45202-3492
Playing Surface: Synthetic
Training Camp: Georgetown College
            Georgetown, Kentucky
            40324

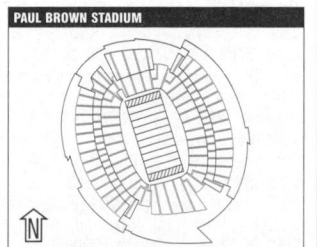

PAUL BROWN STADIUM

CLUB OFFICIALS
President: Mike Brown
Senior Vice President: Pete Brown
Executive Vice President: Katie Blackburn
Vice President: Paul Brown
Vice President: John Sawyer
Business Development: Troy Blackburn
Business Manager: Bill Connelly
Chief Financial Officer: Bill Scanlon
Director of Development—Paul Brown
    Stadium: Bob Bedinghaus
Managing Director of Paul Brown
    Stadium: Eric Brown
Directors of Technology: Michael Kayes,
    Jo Ann Ralstin
Bengals.com Editor: Geoff Hobson
Director of Sales and Public Affairs:
    Jeff Berding
Director of Corporate Sales and
    Marketing: Vince Cicero
Ticket Manager: Tim Kelly
Director of Ticket Sales: Kevin Lane
Director of Player Relations: Eric Ball
Director of Football Operations:
    Jim Lippincott
Director of Player Personnel: Duke Tobin
Public Relations Director: Jack Brennan
Athletic Trainer: Paul Sparling
Equipment Manager: Rob Recker
Video Director: Travis Brammer

COACHING HISTORY
(258-334-1)
Records include postseason games
1968-1975 Paul Brown.................55-59-1
1976-78   Bill Johnson* 18-15-0
1978-79   Homer Rice.................8-19-0
1980-83   Forrest Gregg 34-27-0
1984-1991 Sam Wyche................64-68-0
1992-96   Dave Shula**.............19-52-0
1996-2000 Bruce Coslet*** 21-39-0
2000-02   Dick LeBeau.............12-33-0
2003-05   Marvin Lewis...............27-22-0
   * Resigned after five games in 1978
  ** Released after seven games in 1996
*** Resigned after three games in 2000

ATTENDANCE
Home 514,751   Away 531,915
Total 1,046,666
Single-game home record,
    65,362 (12/28/03)
Single-season home record, 514,751
    (2005)

2006 DRAFT CHOICES
Round	Name	Pos.	College
1	Johnathan Joseph	DB	South Carolina
2	Andrew Whitworth	T	Louisiana State
3	Frostee Rucker	DE	So. California
4	Domata Peko	DT	Michigan State
5	A.J. Nicholson	LB	Florida State
6	Reggie McNeal	WR	Texas A&M
7	Ethan Kilmer	DB	Penn State
	Bennie Brazell	WR	Louisiana State

2005 TEAM RECORD

PRESEASON (2-2)

Date	Result	Opponent
8/12	L 13-23	New England
8/19	W 24-17	at Washington
8/26	L 17-27	at Philadelphia
9/2	W 38-0	Indianapolis

REGULAR SEASON (11-5)

Date	Result	Opponent	Att.
9/11	W 27-13	at Cleveland	73,013
9/18	W 37-8	Minnesota	65,763
9/25	W 24-7	at Chicago	62,045
10/2	W 16-10	Houston	65,714
10/09	L 20-23	at Jacksonville	66,137
10/16	W 31-23	at Tennessee	69,149
10/23	L 13-27	Pittsburgh	66,104
10/30	W 21-14	Green Bay	65,940
11/6	W 21-9	at Baltimore	70,540
11/20	L 37-45	Indianapolis	65,995
11/27	W 42-29	Baltimore	65,680
12/04	W 38-31	at Pittsburgh	63,044
12/11	W 23-20	Cleveland	65,788
12/18	W 41-17	at Detroit	61,749
12/24	L 27-37	Buffalo	65,485
1/1	L 3-37	at Kansas City	77,211

POSTSEASON (0-1)

1/8	L 17-31	Pittsburgh	65,870

SCORE BY PERIODS

Team	84	147	98	92	0	—	421
Opponents	60	102	89	99	0	—	350

2005 TEAM STATISTICS

	Bengals	Opp.
Total First Downs	342	321
Rushing	109	109
Passing	203	185
Penalty	30	27
3rd Down: Made/Att	84/196	81/190
3rd Down Pct.	42.9	42.6
4th Down: Made/Att	3/10	6/14
4th Down Pct.	30.0	42.9
Possession Avg.	30:52	29:09
Total Net Yards	5,730	5,419
Avg. Per Game	358.1	338.7
Total Plays	1,018	976
Avg. Per Play	5.6	5.6
Net Yards Rushing	1,910	1,850
Avg. Per Game	119.4	115.6
Total Rushes	459	429
Net Yards Passing	3,820	3,569
Avg. Per Game	238.8	223.1
Sacked/Yards Lost	21/115	28/180
Gross Yards	3,935	3,749
Att./Completions	538/362	519/324
Completion Pct.	67.3	62.4
Had Intercepted	14	31
Punts/Average	61/42.5	50/42.1
Net Punting Avg.	61/35.6	50/37.4
Penalties/Yards	110/920	110/985
Fumbles/Ball Lost	18/6	31/13
Touchdowns	48	39
Rushing	15	16
Passing	32	21
Returns	1	2

2005 INDIVIDUAL STATISTICS

PASSING	Att.	Comp.	Yds.	Pct.	TD	Int.	Tkld.	Rate
Palmer	509	345	3,836	67.8	32	12	19/105	101.1
Kitna	29	17	99	58.6	0	2	2/10	36.4
Bengals	538	362	3,935	67.3	32	14	21/115	97.6
Opponents	519	324	3,749	62.4	21	31	28/180	72.8

SCORING	TD R	TD P	TD Rt	PAT	FG	Saf	PTS
Graham	0	0	0	47/47	28/32	0	131
R. Johnson	12	0	0	0/0	0/0	0	72
C. Johnson	0	9	0	0/0	0/0	0	54
Houshmandzadeh	1	7	0	0/0	0/0	0	48
Henry	0	6	0	0/0	0/0	0	36
J. Johnson	0	3	0	0/0	0/0	0	18
C. Perry	0	2	0	0/0	0/0	0	12
T. Perry	1	1	0	0/0	0/0	0	12
Schobel	0	1	0	0/0	0/0	0	8
Kelly	0	1	0	0/0	0/0	0	6
Palmer	1	0	0	0/0	0/0	0	6
Thurman	0	0	1	0/0	0/0	0	6
Walter	0	1	0	0/0	0/0	0	6
Washington	0	1	0	0/0	0/0	0	6
Bengals	15	32	1	47/47	28/32	0	421
Opponents	16	21	2	37/37	25/28	0	350

2-Pt. Conversions: Schobel.
Bengals 1-1, Opponents 2-2.

RUSHING	No.	Yds	Avg	LG	TD
R. Johnson	337	1,458	4.3	33	12
C. Perry	61	279	4.6	30	0
Houshmandzadeh	8	62	7.8	17	1
Palmer	34	41	1.2	14	1
C. Johnson	5	33	6.6	11	0
J. Johnson	8	14	1.8	5	0
Kitna	2	14	7.0	11	0
T. Perry	3	9	3.0	7	1
Luchey	1	0	0.0	0	0
Bengals	459	1,910	4.2	33	15
Opponents	429	1,850	4.3	49t	16

RECEIVING	No.	Yds	Avg	LG	TD
C. Johnson	97	1,432	14.8	70t	9
Houshmandzadeh	78	956	12.3	43t	7
C. Perry	51	328	6.4	28	2
Henry	31	422	13.6	47	6
R. Johnson	23	90	3.9	15	0
Walter	19	211	11.1	33	1
Schobel	18	193	10.7	28	1
Kelly	15	90	6.0	16	1
J. Johnson	12	65	5.4	27t	3
Washington	10	101	10.1	18t	1
Stewart	4	26	6.5	10	0
T. Perry	4	21	5.3	13	1
Bengals	362	3,935	10.9	70t	32
Opponents	324	3,749	11.6	68t	21

INTERCEPTIONS	No.	Yds	Avg	LG	TD
O'Neal	10	103	10.3	37	0
Thurman	5	59	11.8	30t	1
James	5	5	1.0	5	0
Ratliff	3	52	17.3	35	0
Kaesviharn	3	9	3.0	6	0
Simmons	2	15	7.5	16	0
Ohalete	1	15	15.0	15	0
M. Williams	1	2	2.0	2	0
Thornton	1	0	0.0	0	0
Bengals	31	260	8.4	37	1
Opponents	14	247	17.6	55	1

PUNTING	No.	Yds.	Avg.	In 20	LG
Larson	60	2,591	43.2	13	75
Bengals	61	2,591	42.5	13	75
Opponents	50	2,106	42.1	18	56

PUNT RETURNS	Ret	FC	Yds	Avg	LG	TD
Ratliff	28	14	157	5.6	13	0
Bengals	28	14	157	5.6	13	0
Opponents	32	7	260	8.1	27	0

KICKOFF RETURNS	No.	Yds	Avg	LG	TD
T. Perry	64	1,562	24.4	94	0
Schobel	2	4	2.0	4	0
O'Neal	1	14	14.0	14	0
Bengals	67	1,580	23.6	94	0
Opponents	85	1,787	21.0	99t	1

FIELD GOALS	1-19	20-29	30-39	40-49	50+
Graham	0/0	11/11	10/11	7/9	0/1
Bengals	0/0	11/11	10/11	7/9	0/1
Opponents	1/1	12/12	7/8	3/4	2/3

SACKS	No.
J. Smith	6.0
Pollack	4.5
Simmons	4.0
Geathers	3.0
Clemons	2.0
Thornton	2.0
TEAM	2.0
Thurman	1.5
Kaesviharn	1.0
Mitchell	1.0
Powell	1.0
Bengals	28.0
Opponents	21.0

RECORD HOLDERS
INDIVIDUAL RECORDS—CAREER

Category	Name	Performance
Rushing (Yds.)	Corey Dillon, 1997-2003	8,061
Passing (Yds.)	Ken Anderson, 1971-1986	32,838
Passing (TDs)	Ken Anderson, 1971-1986	197
Receiving (No.)	Carl Pickens, 1992-99	530
Receiving (Yds.)	Isaac Curtis, 1973-1984	7,101
Interceptions	Ken Riley, 1969-1983	65
Punting (Avg.)	Dave Lewis, 1970-73	43.8
Punt Return (Avg.)	Mike Martin, 1983-89	9.9
Kickoff Return (Avg.)	Lemar Parrish, 1970-77	24.7
Field Goals	Jim Breech, 1980-1992	225
Touchdowns (Tot.)	Pete Johnson, 1977-1983	70
Points	Jim Breech, 1980-1992	1,151

INDIVIDUAL RECORDS—SINGLE SEASON

Category	Name	Performance
Rushing (Yds.)	Rudi Johnson, 2005	1,458
Passing (Yds.)	Boomer Esiason, 1986	3,959
Passing (TDs)	Carson Palmer, 2005	32
Receiving (No.)	Carl Pickens, 1996	100
Receiving (Yds.)	Chad Johnson, 2005	1,432
Interceptions	Deltha O'Neal, 2005	10
Punting (Avg.)	Dave Lewis, 1970	46.2
Punt Return (Avg.)	Lemar Parrish, 1974	18.8
Kickoff Return (Avg.)	Tremain Mack, 1999	27.1
Field Goals	Doug Pelfrey, 1995	29
Touchdowns (Tot.)	Carl Pickens, 1995	17
Points	Shayne Graham, 2005	131

INDIVIDUAL RECORDS—SINGLE GAME

Category	Name	Performance
Rushing (Yds.)	Corey Dillon, 10-22-00	278
Passing (Yds.)	Boomer Esiason, 10-7-90	490
Passing (TDs)	Boomer Esiason, 12-21-86	5
	Boomer Esiason, 10-29-89	5
Receiving (No.)	Carl Pickens, 10-11-98	13
Receiving (Yds.)	Eddie Brown, 11-6-88	216
Interceptions	Many times	3
	Last time by Deltha O'Neal, 9-18-05	
Field Goals	Doug Pelfrey, 11-6-94	6
Touchdowns (Tot.)	Larry Kinnebrew, 10-28-84	4
	Corey Dillon, 12-4-97	4
Points	Larry Kinnebrew, 10-28-84	24
	Corey Dillon, 12-4-97	24

2006 VETERAN ROSTER

No.	Name	Pos.	Ht.	Wt.	Birthdate	NFL Exp.	College	Hometown	How Acq.	'05 Games/ Starts
95	Adams, Sam	DT	6-4	335	6/13/73	13	Texas A&M	Houston, Texas	UFA(Buff)-'06	14/9*
71	Anderson, Willie	T	6-5	340	7/11/75	11	Auburn	Whistler, Ala.	D1-'96	16/16
79	Andrews, Stacy	T	6-7	350	6/2/81	3	Mississippi	Camden, Ark.	D4c-'04	14/0
96	Askew, Matthias	DT	6-5	302	7/1-/82	3	Michigan State	Fort Lauderdale, Fla.	D4a-'04	1/0
21	Bauman, Rashad	CB	5-8	184	5/7/79	5	Oregon	Phoenix, Ariz.	W(Wash)-'04	11/1
41	Body, Patrick	CB	6-2	192	1/17/82	2	Toledo	Pittsburgh, Pa.	FA-'05	6/0
74	Braham, Rich	C	6-4	305	11/6/70	13	West Virginia	Morgantown, W. Va.	W(Ariz)-'94	15/15
27	Brooks, Greg	CB	5-11	177	12/16/80	3	Southern Mississippi	New Orleans, La.	D6-'04	11/0
13	Broussard, Jamall	WR	5-9	175	8/19/81	2	San Jose State	Kingwood, Texas	FA-'05	0*
26	Bua, Tony	S	5-11	218	2/11/80	2	Arkansas	River Ridge, La.	FA-'05	0*
83	Chatman, Antonio	WR	5-9	185	2/12/79	4	Cincinnati	Los Angeles, Calif.	FA-'06	16/3*
68	Fanene, Jonathan	DE	6-4	291	3/19/82	2	Utah	Pago Pago, American Samoa	D7-'05	3/1
91	Geathers, Robert	DE	6-3	280	8/11/83	3	Georgia	Georgetown, S.C.	D4b-'04	16/16
53	Ghiaciuc, Eric	C	6-4	302	5/28/81	2	Central Michigan	Oxford, Mich.	D4-'05	5/1
17	Graham, Shayne	K	6-0	197	12/9/77	6	Virginia Tech	Dublin, Va.	W(Car)-'03	16/0
15	Henry, Chris	WR	6-4	200	5/17/83	2	West Virginia	Belle Chasse, La.	D3-'05	14/5
84	Houshmandzadeh, T.J.	WR	6-1	197	9/26/77	6	Oregon State	Barstow, Calif.	D7-'01	14/12
28	Jackson, Dexter	S	6-0	210	7/28/77	8	Florida State	Quincy, Fla.	UFA(TB)-'06	11/10*
20	James, Tory	CB	6-2	192	5/18/73	11	Louisiana State	New Orleans, La.	FA-'03	16/16
85	Johnson, Chad	WR	6-1	192	1/9/78	6	Oregon State	Miami, Fla.	D2-'01	16/16
11	Johnson, Doug	QB	6-2	220	10/27/77	6	Florida	Gainesville, Fla.	FA-'06	0*
31	Johnson, Jeremi	FB	5-11	265	9/4/80	4	Western Kentucky	Louisville, Ky.	D4b-'03	16/11
59	Johnson, Landon	LB	6-2	227	3/13/81	3	Purdue	Lubbock, Texas	D3b-'04	16/10
32	Johnson, Rudi	HB	5-10	225	10/1/79	6	Auburn	Ettrick, Va.	D4-'01	16/14
76	Jones, Levi	T	6-5	300	8/24/79	5	Arizona State	Eloy, Ariz.	D1-'02	15/15
34	Kaesviharn, Kevin	S	6-1	196	8/29/76	6	Augustana (S.D.)	Lakewood, Calif.	FA-'01	16/16
82	Kelly, Reggie	TE	6-4	255	2/22/77	8	Mississippi State	Aberdeen, Miss.	UFA(Atl)-'03	15/14
70	Kieft, Adam	T	6-7	337	8/21/82	2	Central Michigan	Rockford, Mich.	D5-'05	0*
75	Kooistra, Scott	G	6-6	320	10/14/80	4	North Carolina State	Cary, N.C.	D7a-'03	15/1
6	Krenzel, Craig	QB	6-4	228	7/1/81	3	Ohio State	Sterling Heights, Mich.	W(Chi)-'05	0*
19	Larson, Kyle	P	6-1	204	9/2/80	3	Nebraska	Funk, Neb.	FA-'04	16/0
30#	Luchey, Nick	FB	6-2	273	3/30/77	8	Miami	Farmington Hills, Mich.	FA-'05	3/0
58	Miller, Caleb	LB	6-3	228	9/3/80	3	Arkansas	Sulphur Springs, Texas	D3a-'04	7/0
42	Mitchell, Anthony	S	6-1	215	12/13/74	7	Tuskegee	Atlanta, Ga.	FA-'04	16/0
50	Moore, Larry	G/C	6-3	300	6/1/75	9	Brigham Young	San Diego, Calif.	FA-'04	4/0
57	Navies, Hannibal	LB	6-3	245	7/19/77	8	Colorado	Berkeley, Calif.	FA-'05	15/1
26#	Ohalete, Ifeanyi	S	6-2	221	5/22/79	6	Southern California	Los Alamitos, Calif.	FA-'05	15/12
24	O'Neal, Deltha	CB	5-11	194	1/30/77	7	California	Milpitas, Calif.	T(Den)-'04	15/14
9	Palmer, Carson	QB	6-5	230	12/27/79	4	Southern California	Mission Viejo, Calif.	D1-'03	16/16
23	Perry, Chris	HB	6-0	224	12/27/81	3	Michigan	Advance, N.C.	D1-'04	14/2
88	Perry, Tab	WR	6-3	215	1/20/82	2	UCLA	Milpitas, Calif.	D6-'05	16/0
99	Pollack, David	LB	6-2	255	6/19/82	2	Georgia	Snellville, Ga.	D1-'05	14/5
72#	Powell, Carl	DE	6-2	278	1/4/74	8	Louisville	Detroit, Mich.	UFA(Wash)-'03	11/1
25	Ratliff, Keiwan	CB	5-11	185	4/19/81	3	Florida	Columbus, Ohio	D2a-'04	16/3
98	Robinson, Bryan	DT	6-4	304	6/22/74	10	Fresno State	Toledo, Ohio	UFA(Mia)-'05	10/9
48	St. Louis, Brad	LS/TE	6-3	243	8/19/76	7	Southwest Missouri State	Belton, Mo.	D7-'00	16/0
18	Sam, P.K.	WR	6-3	210	2/26/83	2	Florida State	Buford, Ga.	FA-'06	0*
47	Sanders, Darnell	TE	6-5	260	3/16/79	4	Ohio State	Warrensville Heights, Ohio	FA-'06	0*
56	Simmons, Brian	LB	6-3	244	6/21/75	9	North Carolina	New Bern, N.C.	D1b-'98	16/16
90	Smith, Justin	DE	6-4	275	9/30/79	6	Missouri	Holts Summit, Mo.	D1-'01	16/16
66	Smith, Shaun	DT	6-2	320	8/19/81	3	South Carolina	Brooklyn, N.Y.	W(NO)-'04	13/5
65	Steinbach, Eric	G/T	6-6	295	4/4/80	4	Iowa	Lockport, Ill.	D2-'03	16/16
86	Stewart, Tony	TE	6-5	260	8/9/79	6	Penn State	Allentown, Pa.	W(Phil)-'02	14/3
97	Thornton, John	DT	6-3	297	10/2/76	8	West Virginia	Philadelphia, Pa.	UFA(Tenn)-'03	16/16
51	Thurman, Odell	LB	6-0	235	7/9/83	2	Georgia	Monticello, Ga.	D2-'05	16/15
67	Vieira, Steven	G	6-6	311	1/22/82	2	UCLA	Carlsbad, Calif.	FA-'05	0*
87	Washington, Kelley	WR	6-3	216	8/21/79	4	Tennessee	Stephens City, Va.	D3-'03	7/0
33	Watson, Kenny	HB	5-11	220	3/13/78	5	Penn State	Harrisburg, Pa.	FA-'03	1/0
55	Wilkins, Marcus	LB	6-2	231	1/2/80	5	Texas	Austin, Texas	W(Ariz)-'04	15/0
63	Williams, Bobbie	G	6-4	340	9/25/76	7	Arkansas	Jefferson, Texas	UFA(Phil)-'04	16/16
40	Williams, Madieu	S	6-1	195	10/18/81	3	Maryland	Lanham, Md.	D2b-'04	4/3
2	Wright, Anthony	QB	6-1	211	2/14/76	8	South Carolina	Vanceboro, N.C.	UFA(Balt)-'06	9/7*

*   Adams played 14 games with Buffalo in '05; Broussard last active with Carolina in '04; Bua last active with Miami in '04; Chatman played 16 games with Green Bay; Jackson played 11 games with Tampa Bay; D.Johnson inactive for 2 games with Cleveland; Kieft missed '05 season because of injury; Krenzel inactive for 16 games; Sam last active with New England in '04; Sanders last active with Atlanta in '04; Vieira on the Reserve/Physically Unable to Perform list for 8 games; Wright played 9 games with Baltimore.

\#   Unrestricted free agent; subject to developments.

  Players lost through free agency (4): QB Jon Kitna (Det; 3 games in '05), TE Matt Schobel (Phil; 16), WR Kevin Walter (Hou; 16), LB Nate Webster (Den; 1).

  Also played with Bengals in '05—DE Duane Clemons (10 games), S Kim Herring (16), LB Caleb Moore (7), S Reggie Myles (10), CB Terrell Roberts (4), LB Larry Stevens (7), C Ben Wilkerson (16).

2006 FIRST-YEAR ROSTER

Name	Pos.	Ht.	Wt.	Birthdate	College	Hometown	How Acq.
Baugher, Danny	P	5-10	194	1/24/84	Arizona	Phoenix, Ariz.	FA
Bennett, A.J.	WR	5-9	190	1/17/84	Eastern Michigan	Delray Beach, Fla.	FA
Boone, Jesse	C	6-5	297	1/28/82	Utah	Fillmore, Utah	FA
Brazell, Bennie	WR	6-0	176	6/2/82	Louisiana State	Houston, Texas	D7b
Busing, John	S	6-3	231	9/1/83	Miami (Ohio)	Alpharetta, Ga.	FA
Dorsey, DeDe	HB	5-10	194	8/1/84	Lindenwood	Broken Arrow, Okla.	FA
Estandia, Greg	TE	6-8	264	11/18/82	Nevada-Las Vegas	Moorpark, Calif.	FA
Gayer, Wyatt	LB	6-0	259	4/22/84	Anderson	Leopold, Ind.	FA
Ghent, Ronnie (1)	TE	6-2	253	1/5/80	Louisville	Lakeland, Fla.	FA-'04
Hamby, Ryan	TE	6-3	246	10/30/81	Ohio State	Cincinnati, Ohio	FA
Henderson, Eric	DE	6-2	270	1/8/83	Georgia Tech	New Orleans, La.	FA
Jeanty, Rashad	LB	6-2	235	4/17/83	Central Florida	Miami, Fla.	FA
Jones, David	TE	6-3	259	9/15/83	Louisiana State	Silver Springs, Md.	FA
Jones, Herana-Daze (1)	S	5-11	205	4/15/82	Indiana	Louisville, Ky.	FA-'05
Joseph, Johnathan	CB	5-11	193	4/16/84	South Carolina	Rock Hill, S.C.	D1
Kilmer, Ethan	S	6-0	204	1/31/83	Penn State	Wyalusing, Pa.	D7a
Lewis, Marcus	DT	6-2	296	10/3/80	Urbana	Lithonia, Ga.	FA
Livings, Nate	G	6-4	309	3/16/82	Louisiana State	Lake Charles, La.	FA
Lougheed, Pete (1)	T	6-5	300	11/5/79	Purdue	Fort Wayne, Ind.	FA-'04
Manderino, Chris	FB	6-0	231	12/22/82	California	Newport Beach, Calif.	FA
McNeal, Reggie	WR	6-2	198	9/20/83	Texas A&M	Lufkin, Texas	D6
Meyer, Erik	QB	6-1	210	12/28/82	Eastern Washington	La Mirada, Calif.	FA
Nicholson, A.J.	LB	6-1	245	6/25/83	Florida State	Winston-Salem, N.C.	D5
Olomua, Bristol	TE	6-5	268	5/20/81	Texas Tech	Laie, Hawaii	FA
Peko, Domata	DT	6-3	307	11/27/84	Michigan State	Pago Pago, American Samoa	D4
Rucker, Frostee	DE	6-3	267	9/14/83	Southern California	Tustin, Calif.	D3
Tahi, Naufahu	FB	6-0	254	10/30/81	Brigham Young	West Valley City, Utah	FA
Takavitz, Kyle (1)	G	6-3	310	11/1/81	Cincinnati	Powell, Ohio	FA-'05
Warfield, Mike	WR	6-1	190	10/30/82	Duquesne	Washington, D.C.	FA
Whitehead, Terrence	HB	5-10	209	5/31/83	Oregon	Los Angeles, Calif.	FA
Whitworth, Andrew	T	6-7	334	12/12/81	Louisiana State	West Monroe, La.	D2
Wilkerson, Ben (1)	C	6-4	305	11/22/82	Louisiana State	Hemphill, Texas	FA-'05
Wilson, Quincy (1)	HB	5-9	225	4/26/81	West Virginia	Weirton, W. Va.	W(Atl)-'04

The term NFL Rookie is defined as a player who is in his first season of professional football and has not been on the roster of another professional football team for any regular-season or postseason games. A Rookie is designated by an "R" on NFL rosters. Players who have been active in another professional football league or players who have NFL experience, including either preseason training camp or being on an Active List or Inactive List, or on Reserve/Injured or Reserve/Physically Unable to Perform for fewer than six regular-season games, are termed NFL First-Year Players. An NFL First-Year Player is designated by a "1" on NFL rosters. Thereafter, a player is credited with an additional year of experience for each season in which he accumulates six games on the Active List or Inactive List, or on Reserve/Injured or Reserve/Physically Unable to Perform.

Log on to www.bengals.com for an up-to-date roster.

CINCINNATI BENGALS

COACHING STAFF
Head Coach, Marvin Lewis

Pro Career: After establishing himself as a record-setting NFL defensive coordinator, Lewis was named the ninth head coach in Bengals history on January 14, 2003. He is now in his fourth season, coming off a 2005 campaign in which he guided the team to the AFC North title. The Bengals gained the No. 3 seed in the AFC playoffs with an 11-5 record before losing to Pittsburgh, the eventual Super Bowl winner, in the Wild Card round. Lewis is the only Bengals head coach not to experience a losing season. Taking over after the 2002 club had posted a franchise-worst 2-14 record, he led a pair of 8-8 finishes before breaking through to claim the division title last year. In club history, Lewis' .551 winning percentage (27-22) trails only Forrest Gregg's .561 percentage (32-25 from 1980-83). The 2005 Bengals posted a club-record and NFL-best turnover differential of plus-24, and set a club record for the fewest sacks allowed (21). In 2003, the Bengals were the NFL's most improved team (six-game increase), and Lewis finished second in *Associated Press* voting for NFL Coach of the Year while also being named Rookie Coach of the Year by *Football Digest*. Prior to his arrival, Lewis was the Washington Redskins' defensive coordinator (2002), serving as assistant head coach in addition to his coordinator's role. He spent six seasons (1996-2001) as defensive coordinator with the Baltimore Ravens, a tenure that included a Super Bowl victory following the 2000 season. In the 2000 regular season, Lewis' Baltimore defense set the NFL record for fewest points allowed in a 16-game campaign (165). Lewis' 2000 defensive unit has been widely considered as one of the best NFL defenses of all time. The 970 rushing yards allowed were the fewest in NFL history for a 16-game season. The Ravens' four shutouts were the most in the NFL since 1976. Prior to joining Baltimore, he spent four seasons (1992-95) with Pittsburgh as linebackers coach. Career record: 27-22.

Background: Earned All-Big Sky Conference honors as a linebacker at Idaho State for three years (1978-1980), and saw action at quarterback and free safety. Received his bachelor's degree in physical education from Idaho State in 1981, and earned his Master's degree in athletic administration from the school in 1982. Inducted into Idaho State's Hall of Fame in 2001. Began his coaching career at Idaho State (1981-84). The team finished 12-1 during his first season and won the NCAA Division I-AA championship. Was also the linebackers coach at Long Beach State (1985-86), New Mexico (1987-89), and Pittsburgh (1990-91).

Personal: Born September 23, 1958, McDonald, Pa. Lewis and his wife, Peggy, have two children—Whitney and Marcus.

ASSISTANT COACHES

Paul Alexander, asst. head coach/offensive line; born February 12, 1960, Rochester, N.Y. Tackle Cortland State 1979-1981. No pro playing experience. College coach: Penn State 1982-84, Michigan 1985-86, Central Michigan 1987-1991. Pro coach: New York Jets 1992-93, joined Bengals in 1994.

Jim Anderson, running backs; born March 27, 1948, Harrisburg, Pa. Linebacker/defensive end California Western 1967-69. No pro playing experience. College coach: California Western 1970-71, Scottsdale (Ariz.) C.C. 1973, Nevada-Las Vegas 1974-75, Southern Methodist 1976-1980, Stanford 1981-83. Pro coach: Joined Bengals in 1984.

Bob Bratkowski, offensive coordinator; born December 2, 1955, San Angelo, Texas. Wide receiver Washington State 1975-77. No pro playing experience. College coach: Missouri 1978-1980, Weber State 1981-85, Wyoming 1986, Washington State 1987-88, Miami 1989-1991. Pro coach: Seattle Seahawks 1992-98, Pittsburgh Steelers 1999-2000, joined Bengals in 2001.

Chuck Bresnahan, defensive coordinator; born September 8, 1960, Springfield, Mass. Linebacker Navy 1979-1982. No pro playing experience. College coach: Navy 1983, 1986, Georgia Tech 1987-1991, Maine 1992-93. Pro coach: Cleveland Browns 1994-95, Indianapolis Colts 1996-97, Oakland Raiders 1998-2003, joined Bengals in 2004.

Louie Cioffi, asst. defensive backs; born September 21, 1973, Greenlawn, N.Y. Attended SUNY-Stony Brook. No college or pro playing experience. College coach: C.W. Post 1995-96. Pro coach: New York Jets 1993-94, joined Bengals in 1997.

Kevin Coyle, defensive backs; born January 14, 1956, Staten Island, N.Y. Defensive back Massachusetts 1975-77. No pro playing experience. College coach: Cincinnati 1978-79, Arkansas 1980, U.S. Merchant Marine Academy 1981, Holy Cross 1982-1990, Syracuse 1991-93, Maryland 1994-96, Fresno State 1997-2000. Pro coach: Joined Bengals in 2001.

Paul Guenther, staff assistant; born Nov. 22, 1971, Richboro, Pa. Linebacker Ursinus College 1990-93. No pro playing experience. College coach: Western Maryland 1994-95, Ursinus College 1996, 1997-2001 (head coach 1997-2001), Jacksonville 1997. Pro coach: Washington Redskins 2002-03, joined Bengals in 2005.

Jay Hayes, defensive line; born March 3, 1960, South Fayette, Pa. Defensive end Idaho 1978-1981. Pro defensive end/linebacker Michigan Panthers (USFL) 1984, Memphis Showboats (USFL) 1985. College coach: Notre Dame 1988-1991, California 1992-94, Wisconsin 1995-98. Pro coach: Pittsburgh Steelers 1999-2001, Minnesota Vikings 2002, joined

Bengals in 2003.

Jonathan Hayes, tight ends; born Aug. 11, 1962, South Fayette, Pa. Linebacker/tight end Iowa 1981-84. Pro tight end Kansas City Chiefs 1985-1993, Pittsburgh Steelers 1994-96. College coach: Oklahoma 1999-2002. Pro coach: Joined Bengals in 2003.

Ricky Hunley, linebackers; born November 11, 1961, Petersburg, Va. Linebacker Arizona 1980-83. Pro linebacker Denver Broncos 1984-87, Los Angeles Raiders 1989-1990. College coach: Southern California 1992-93, Missouri 1994-2000, Florida 2001. Pro coach: Washington Redskins 2002, joined Bengals in 2003.

Hue Jackson, wide receivers; born October 22, 1965, Los Angeles. Quarterback Pacific 1985-86. No pro playing experience. College coach: Pacific 1987-89, Cal State-Fullerton 1990, Arizona State 1992-95, California 1996, Southern California 1997-2000. Pro coach: London Monarchs (WFL) 1991, Washington Redskins 2001-03, joined Bengals in 2004.

Chip Morton, strength and conditioning; born November 27, 1962, Hamden, Conn. Attended North Carolina. No college or pro playing experience. College coach: Ohio State 1985-86, Penn State 1987-1991. Pro coach: San Diego Chargers 1992-94, Carolina Panthers 1995-98, Baltimore Ravens 1999-2001, Washington Redskins 2002, joined Bengals in 2003.

Ray Oliver, asst. strength and conditioning; born June 6, 1961, Cincinnati. Defensive back Ohio State 1980-81. College coach: Pittsburgh 1985-88, Kentucky 1989-1991, South Carolina 1993-95, Memphis 2001-03. Pro coach: Tampa Bay Buccaneers 1992, New Jersey Nets (NBA) 1996-97, joined Bengals in 2004.

Darrin Simmons, special teams; born April 9, 1973, Elkhart, Kan. Punter Kansas 1993-95. No pro playing experience. College coach: Kansas 1996, Minnesota 1997. Pro coach: Baltimore Ravens 1998, Carolina Panthers 1999-2002, joined Bengals in 2003.

Bob Surace, offensive assistant; born April 25, 1968, Harrisburg, Pa. Center Princeton 1987-89. No pro playing experience. College coach: Springfield College 1990-91, Maine Maritime Academy 1992-93, Rensselaer Polytechnic Institute 1995, Western Connecticut State 1996-2001 (head coach 2000-01). Pro coach: Shreveport Pirates (CFL) 1994, joined Bengals in 2002.

Ken Zampese, quarterbacks; born July 19, 1967, Santa Maria, Calif. Wide receiver San Diego 1985-88. No pro playing experience. College coach: San Diego 1989, Southern California 1990-91, Northern Arizona 1992-95, Miami (Ohio) 1996-97. Pro coach: Philadelphia Eagles 1998, Green Bay Packers 1999, St. Louis Rams 2000-02, joined Bengals in 2003.

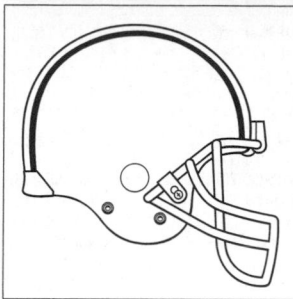

**American Football Conference
North Division
Team Colors:** Brown, Orange, and White
**76 Lou Groza Blvd.
Berea, Ohio 44017
Telephone: (440) 891-5000**

2006 SCHEDULE
PRESEASON
Aug. 10 at Philadelphia 7:30
Aug. 18 **Detroit** 7:30
Aug. 26 at Buffalo 6:00
Aug. 31 **Chicago** 8:00

REGULAR SEASON
Sept. 10 **New Orleans** 1:00
Sept. 17 at Cincinnati 1:00
Sept. 24 **Baltimore**...........................4:05
Oct. 1 at Oakland 1:15
Oct. 8 at Carolina...........................1:00
Oct. 15 Open Date
Oct. 22 **Denver**................................4:05
Oct. 29 **N.Y. Jets** 4:15
Nov. 5 at San Diego 1:15
Nov. 12 at Atlanta 1:00
Nov. 19 **Pittsburgh**...........................1:00
Nov. 26 **Cincinnati** 1:00
Dec. 3 **Kansas City** 1:00
Dec. 7 at Pittsburgh (Thu.) 8:00
Dec. 17 at Baltimore.......................1:00
Dec. 24 **Tampa Bay**.........................1:00
Dec. 31 at Houston 12:00

Stadium: Cleveland Browns Stadium
(opened in 1999)
• **Capacity:** 73,300
100 Alfred Lerner Way
Cleveland, Ohio 44114
Playing Surface: Grass
Headquarters/Training Camp:
76 Lou Groza Boulevard
Berea, Ohio 44017

CLEVELAND BROWNS STADIUM

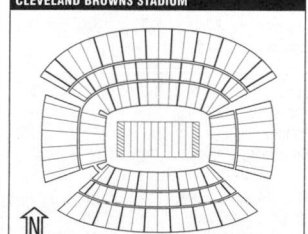

CLUB OFFICIALS
Owner: Randy Lerner
Senior Vice President and General
   Manager: Phil Savage
Head Coach: Romeo Crennel
Executive Vice President and Chief
   Financial Officer: Doug Jacobs
Executive Vice President and Chief
   Operating Officer: Lew Merletti
Vice President, Communications:
   Bill Bonsiewicz
Vice President, Administration:
   Diane Downing
Vice President, Finance and
   Administration: Mike Keenan
Vice President, Security, Logistics and
   Information Technology: Carl Meyer
Vice President, Corporate Sales and
   Partnership Marketing: Joey Porcelli
Vice President, Event and Stadium
   Operations: Don Renzulli
Vice President, Broadcasting and
   Production: George Veras
Director, Business Development:
   Lorne Novick
Director, Corporate Sales and Partnership
   Marketing: Brett Reynolds
Director, Direct Marketing and Customer
   Service: John Schulze
Director, Media Information:
   Ken Mather
Head Athletic Trainer: Marty Lauzon
Equipment Manager: Brad Melland
Video Director: Pat Dolan
Head Groundskeeper: Chris Powell

COACHING HISTORY
(421-362-10)
Records include postseason games
1950-1962 Paul Brown 115-49-5
1963-1970 Blanton Collier 79-38-2
1971-74 Nick Skorich 30-26-2
1975-77 Forrest Gregg* 18-23-0
1977 Dick Modzelewski 0-1-0
1978-1984 Sam Rutigliano** 47-52-0
1984-88 Marty Schottenheimer ..46-31-0
1989-1990 Bud Carson*** 12-14-1
1990 Jim Shofner......................1-6-0
1991-95 Bill Belichick 37-45-0
1999-2000 Chris Palmer 5-27-0
2001-04 Butch Davis****.........24-36-0
2004 Terry Robiskie 1-4-0
2005 Romeo Crennel 6-10-0
*Resigned after 13 games in 1977
**Released after eight games in 1984
***Released after nine games in 1990
****Resigned after 11 games in 2004

ATTENDANCE
Home 564,911   Away 493,192
Total 1,058,103
Single-game home record,
   85,073 (9/21/70)
Single-season home record, 620,496
   (1980)

2006 DRAFT CHOICES
Round	Name	Pos.	College
1	Kamerion Wimbley	DE	Florida State
2	D'Qwell Jackson	LB	Maryland
3	Travis Wilson	WR	Oklahoma
4	Leon Williams	LB	Miami
	Isaac Sowells	G	Indiana
5	Jerome Harrison	RB	Washington St.
	DeMario Minter	CB	Georgia
6	Lawrence Vickers	FB	Colorado
	Babatunde Oshinowo	DT	Stanford
7	Justin Hamilton	DB	Virginia Tech

CLEVELAND BROWNS

2005 TEAM RECORD
PRESEASON (3-1)

Date	Result	Opponent
8/13	W 17-14	N.Y. Giants
8/20	W 21-13	at Detroit
8/26	L 20-23	Carolina
9/1	W 16-6	at Chicago

REGULAR SEASON (6-10)

Date	Result	Opponent	Att.
9/11	L 13-27	Cincinnati	73,013
9/18	W 26-24	at Green Bay	70,400
9/25	L 6-13	at Indianapolis	57,127
10/9	W 20-10	Chicago	73,079
10/16	L 3-16	at Baltimore	70,196
10/23	L 10-13	Detroit	72,923
10/30	L 16-19	at Houston	70,064
11/6	W 20-14	Tennessee	72,594
11/13	L 21-34	at Pittsburgh	63,491
11/20	W 22-0	Miami	72,773
11/27	L 12-24	at Minnesota	63,814
12/4	L 14-20	Jacksonville	70,941
12/11	L 20-23	at Cincinnati	65,788
12/18	W 9-7	at Oakland	41,862
12/24	L 0-41	Pittsburgh	73,136
1/1	W 20-16	Baltimore	69,871

SCORE BY PERIODS

Browns	56	65	52	59	0	—	232
Opponents	58	102	81	60	0	—	301

2005 TEAM STATISTICS

	Browns	Opp.
Total First Downs	241	292
Rushing	76	116
Passing	149	161
Penalty	16	15
3rd Down: Made/Att	67/203	87/215
3rd Down Pct.	33.0	40.5
4th Down: Made/Att	7/18	8/18
4th Down Pct.	38.9	44.4
Possession Avg.	28:00	32:00
Total Net Yards	4,550	5,069
Avg. Per Game	284.4	316.8
Total Plays	938	1021
Avg. Per Play	4.9	5.0
Net Yards Rushing	1,503	2,202
Avg. Per Game	93.9	137.6
Total Rushes	395	527
Net Yards Passing	3,047	2,867
Avg. Per Game	190.4	179.2
Sacked/Yards Lost	46/276	23/142
Gross Yards	3,323	3,009
Att./Completions	497/297	471/279
Completion Pct.	59.8	59.2
Had Intercepted	17	15
Punts/Average	80/40.4	72/42.5
Net Punting Avg.	80/33.8	72/35.1
Penalties/Yards	99/770	97/716
Fumbles/Ball Lost	27/13	21/8
Touchdowns	22	31
Rushing	4	11
Passing	15	19
Returns	3	1

2005 INDIVIDUAL STATISTICS

PASSING	Att.	Comp.	Yds.	Pct.	TD	Int.	Tkld.	Rate
Dilfer	333	199	2,321	59.8	11	12	23/139	76.9
Frye	164	98	1,002	59.8	4	5	22/135	72.8
Jackson	0	0	0	—	0	0	1/2	—
Browns	497	297	3,323	59.8	15	17	46/276	75.5
Opponents	471	279	3,009	59.2	19	15	23/142	78.2

SCORING	TD R	TD P	TD Rt	PAT	FG	Saf	PTS
P. Dawson	0	0	0	19/21	27/29	0	100
Bryant	0	4	0	0/0	0/0	0	24
Edwards	0	3	0	0/0	0/0	0	18
Heiden	0	3	0	0/0	0/0	0	18
Northcutt	0	2	1	0/0	0/0	0	18
Droughns	2	0	0	0/0	0/0	0	12
Bodden	0	0	1	0/0	0/0	0	6
Cribbs	0	0	1	0/0	0/0	0	6
Frye	1	0	0	0/0	0/0	0	6
Jackson	0	1	0	0/0	0/0	0	6
Shea	0	1	0	0/0	0/0	0	6
Smith	0	1	0	0/0	0/0	0	6
Wright	1	0	0	0/0	0/0	0	6
Browns	4	15	3	19/21	27/29	0	232
Opponents	11	19	1	31/31	28/35	0	301

2-Pt. Conversions: Team 0-1, Opponents 0-0.

RUSHING	No.	Yds	Avg	LG	TD
Droughns	309	1,232	4.0	75t	2
Green	20	78	3.9	17	0
Frye	18	60	3.3	16	1
Dilfer	20	46	2.3	12	0
Northcutt	2	33	16.5	31	0
Wright	11	27	2.5	6t	1
Suggs	8	15	1.9	7	0
Smith	6	9	1.5	4	0
Bryant	1	3	3.0	3	0
Browns	395	1,503	3.8	75t	4
Opponents	527	2,202	4.2	80t	11

RECEIVING	No.	Yds	Avg	LG	TD
Bryant	69	1,009	14.6	54	4
Heiden	43	401	9.3	62t	3
Northcutt	42	441	10.5	58t	2
Droughns	39	369	9.5	51	0
Edwards	32	512	16.0	80t	3
Jackson	24	287	12.0	68t	1
Shea	18	153	8.5	27	1
Smith	12	58	4.8	9	1
Suggs	6	26	4.3	8	0
Green	5	30	6.0	14	0
Wright	3	15	5.0	15	0
Irons	2	16	8.0	14	0
Cribbs	1	7	7.0	7	0
Faine	1	-1	-1.0	-1	0
Browns	297	3,323	11.2	80t	15
Opponents	279	3,009	10.8	51t	19

INTERCEPTIONS	No.	Yds	Avg	LG	TD
Russell	3	50	16.7	37	0
Bodden	3	6	2.0	6	0
Crocker	2	35	17.5	24	0
McCutcheon	2	14	7.0	14	0
Baxter	2	10	5.0	10	0
Davis	1	14	14.0	14	0
Pool	1	1	1.0	1	0
Stewart	1	0	0.0	0	0
Browns	15	130	8.7	37	0
Opponents	17	215	12.6	72	0

PUNTING	No.	Yds.	Avg.	In 20	LG
Richardson	78	3,181	40.8	22	61
P. Dawson	2	53	26.5	2	31
Browns	80	3,234	40.4	24	61
Opponents	72	3,058	42.5	19	60

PUNT RETURNS	Ret	FC	Yds	Avg	LG	TD
Northcutt	35	13	368	10.5	62t	1
Cribbs	1	0	5	5.0	5	0
Jones	1	0	0	0.0	0	0
Browns	37	13	373	10.1	62t	1
Opponents	36	9	347	9.6	51	0

KICKOFF RETURNS	No.	Yds	Avg	LG	TD
Cribbs	45	1,094	24.3	90t	1
Droughns	5	119	23.8	35	0
Green	5	79	15.8	22	0
Perkins	3	82	27.3	35	0
McIntyre	3	47	15.7	17	0
Shea	3	29	9.7	13	0
Smith	2	24	12.0	13	0
Wright	1	17	17.0	17	0
Jackson	1	15	15.0	15	0
Browns	68	1,506	22.1	90t	1
Opponents	56	1,182	21.1	63	0

FIELD GOALS	1-19	20-29	30-39	40-49	50+
P. Dawson	2/2	11/11	9/11	5/5	0/0
Browns	2/2	11/11	9/11	5/5	0/0
Opponents	0/0	10/10	11/12	6/10	1/3

SACKS	No.
McKinley	5.0
Thompson	5.0
Roye	3.0
Crocker	2.0
Davis	2.0
Eason	2.0
Lang	2.0
Kelley	1.0
Pool	1.0
Browns	23.0
Opponents	46.0

RECORD HOLDERS
INDIVIDUAL RECORDS—CAREER

Category	Name	Performance
Rushing (Yds.)	Jim Brown, 1957-1965	12,312
Passing (Yds.)	Brian Sipe, 1974-1983	23,713
Passing (TDs)	Brian Sipe, 1974-1983	154
Receiving (No.)	Ozzie Newsome, 1978-1990	662
Receiving (Yds.)	Ozzie Newsome, 1978-1990	7,980
Interceptions	Thom Darden, 1972-74, 1976-1981	45
Punting (Avg.)	Horace Gillom, 1950-56	43.8
Punt Return (Avg.)	Greg Pruitt, 1973-1981	11.8
Kickoff Return (Avg.)	Greg Pruitt, 1973-1981	26.3
Field Goals	Lou Groza, 1950-59, 1961-67	234
Touchdowns (Tot.)	Jim Brown, 1957-1965	126
Points	Lou Groza, 1950-59, 1961-67	1,349

INDIVIDUAL RECORDS—SINGLE SEASON

Category	Name	Performance
Rushing (Yds.)	Jim Brown, 1963	1,863
Passing (Yds.)	Brian Sipe, 1980	4,132
Passing (TDs)	Brian Sipe, 1980	30
Receiving (No.)	Ozzie Newsome, 1983	89
	Ozzie Newsome, 1984	89
Receiving (Yds.)	Webster Slaughter, 1989	1,236
Interceptions	Thom Darden, 1978	10
	Anthony Henry, 2001	10
Punting (Avg.)	Gary Collins, 1965	46.7
Punt Return (Avg.)	Leroy Kelly, 1965	15.6
Kickoff Return (Avg.)	Billy Lefear, 1975	31.7
Field Goals	Matt Stover, 1995	29
Touchdowns (Tot.)	Jim Brown, 1965	21
Points	Jim Brown, 1965	126

INDIVIDUAL RECORDS—SINGLE GAME

Category	Name	Performance
Rushing (Yds.)	Jim Brown, 11-24-57	237
	Jim Brown, 11-19-61	237
Passing (Yds.)	Brian Sipe, 10-25-81	444
Passing (TDs)	Frank Ryan, 12-12-64	5
	Bill Nelsen, 11-2-69	5
	Brian Sipe, 10-7-79	5
	Kelly Holcomb, 11-28-04	5
Receiving (No.)	Ozzie Newsome, 10-14-84	14
Receiving (Yds.)	Ozzie Newsome, 10-14-84	191
Interceptions	Many times	3
	Last time by Anthony Henry, 11-18-01	
Field Goals	Don Cockroft, 10-19-75	5
	Matt Stover, 10-29-95	5
	Phil Dawson, 1-2-05	5
Touchdowns (Tot.)	Dub Jones, 11-25-51	*6
Points	Dub Jones, 11-25-51	36

*NFL Record

2006 VETERAN ROSTER

No.	Name	Pos.	Ht.	Wt.	Birthdate	NFL Exp.	College	Hometown	How Acq.	'05 Games/ Starts
3	Anderson, Derek	QB	6-6	245	6/15/83	2	Oregon State	Portland, Ore.	W(Balt)-'05	0*
63	Andruzzi, Joe	T/G	6-3	315	8/23/75	10	Southern Connecticut State	Staten Island, N.Y.	UFA(NE)-'05	13/13
24	Baxter, Gary	CB/S	6-2	210	11/24/78	6	Baylor	Tyler, Texas	UFA(Balt)-'05	5/5
00	Bentley, LeCharles	G/C	6-2	313	11/7/79	5	Ohio State	Cleveland, Ohio	UFA(NO)-'06	14/14*
28	Bodden, Leigh	CB/S	6-1	190	9/24/81	4	Duquesne	Upper Marlborough, Md.	FA-'03	13/11
65	Chambers, Kirk	T/G	6-7	314	3/19/79	3	Stanford	Provo, Utah	D6-'04	15/0
2	Chandler, Jeff	K	6-2	215	6/18/79	3	Florida	Jacksonville, Fla.	FA-'06	0*
60	Coleman, Cosey	T/G	6-4	310	10/27/78	7	Tennessee	New Orleans, La.	UFA(TB)-'05	14/14
16	Cribbs, Joshua	WR	6-1	192	6/9/83	2	Kent State	Washington, D.C.	FA-'05	14/0
54	Davis, Andra	LB	6-1	250	12/23/78	5	Florida	Live Oak, Fla.	D5-'02	16/16
4	Dawson, Phil	K	5-11	200	1/23/75	8	Texas	Dallas, Texas	FA-'99	16/0
87	Dinkins, Darnell	TE	6-2	255	1/20/77	5	Pittsburgh	Pittsburgh, Pa.	UFA(Balt)-'06	16/4*
5	Dorsey, Ken	QB	6-4	218	4/22/81	4	Miami	Orinda, Calif.	T(SF)-'06	3/3*
70	Dorsey, Nat	T/G	6-7	322	9/9/83	3	Georgia Tech	New Orleans, La.	T(Minn)-'05	9/0
34	Droughns, Reuben	RB	5-11	215	8/21/78	7	Oregon	Chicago, Ill.	T(Den)-'05	16/16
71	Dunn, Jonathan	T/G	6-7	328	12/12/81	2	Virginia Tech	Norfolk, Va.	D7-'05	0*
98	Eason, Nick	DE/DT	6-3	310	5/29/80	4	Clemson	Lyons, Ga.	FA-'04	16/0
17	Edwards, Braylon	WR	6-3	211	2/21/83	2	Michigan	Detroit, Mich.	D1-'05	10/7
75	Fraser, Simon	DE/DT	6-6	288	3/27/83	2	Ohio State	Upper Arlington, Ohio	FA-'05	16/0
9	Frye, Charlie	QB	6-4	217	8/28/81	2	Akron	Willard, Ohio	D3-'05	7/5
31	Green, William	RB	6-0	214	12/17/79	5	Boston College	Atlantic City, N.J.	D1-'02	8/0
62	Hallen, Bob	T/G	6-3	295	3/9/75	9	Kent State	Mentor, Ohio	UFA(SD)-'06	9/3*
82	Heiden, Steve	TE	6-5	267	9/21/76	8	South Dakota State	Rushford, Minn.	T(SD)-'02	15/13
20	Hunter, Pete	CB/S	6-2	208	5/25/80	4	Virginia Union	Atlantic City, N.J.	FA-'05	4/0
88	Jackson, Frisman	WR	6-3	217	6/12/79	5	Western Illinois	Chicago, Ill.	FA-'04	12/0
26	Jones, Sean	CB/S	6-1	212	3/2/82	3	Georgia	Atlanta, Ga.	D2-'04	16/0
84	Jurevicius, Joe	WR	6-5	230	12/23/74	9	Penn State	Mentor, Ohio	UFA(Sea)-'06	16/11*
78	Kelley, Ethan	DE/DT	6-2	310	2/12/80	2	Baylor	Sugarland, Texas	W(NE)-'05	11/2
56	Kurpeikis, Justin	LB	6-3	248	7/17/77	3	Penn State	Pittsburgh, Pa.	FA-'05	0*
37	Mayer, Shawn	LB	6-0	202	3/4/79	2	Penn State	Hillsborough, N.J.	FA-'06	0*
33	McCutcheon, Daylon	CB/S	5-10	190	12/9/76	8	Southern California	La Puente, Calif.	D3a-'99	16/16
55	McGinest, Willie	LB	6-5	270	12/11/71	13	Southern California	Long Beach, Calif.	FA-'06	16/16*
36	McIntyre, Corey	FB	6-0	246	1/25/79	2	West Virginia	Indiantown, Fla.	FA-'04	15/1
97	McKinley, Alvin	DE/DT	6-3	294	6/9/78	7	Mississippi State	Jackson, Miss.	FA-'01	16/16
90	McMillan, David	LB	6-3	262	9/20/81	2	Kansas	Killeen, Texas	D5-'05	4/0
86	Northcutt, Dennis	WR	5-11	171	12/27/77	7	Arizona	Los Angeles, Calif.	D2-'00	16/7
85	Owens, John	TE	6-3	255	1/10/80	4	Notre Dame	Washington, D.C.	FA-'05	0*
30	Perkins, Antonio	CB/S	5-11	188	1/9/82	2	Oklahoma	Lawton, Okla.	D4-'05	1/0
64	Pontbriand, Ryan	LS	6-2	248	10/1/79	4	Rice	Houston, Texas	D5a-'03	11/0
21	Pool, Brodney	CB/S	6-2	208	5/24/84	2	Oklahoma	Houtson, Texas	D2-'05	13/0
11	Rideau, Brandon	WR	6-3	200	10/18/82	2	Kansas	Beaumont, Texas	FA-'05	0*
99	Roye, Orpheus	DE/DT	6-4	305	1/21/73	11	Florida State	Carrol City, Fla.	UFA(Pitt)-'00	16/16
27	Russell, Brian	CB/S	6-2	207	2/5/78	5	San Diego State	West Covina, Calif.	RFA(Minn)-'05	16/16
77	Shaffer, Kevin	T/G	6-5	290	3/2/80	5	Tulsa	Salisbury, Md.	UFA(Atl)-'06	16/16*
42	Smith, Terrelle	FB	6-0	242	3/12/78	7	Arizona State	West Covina, Calif.	UFA(NO)-'04	16/15
59	Speegle, Nick	LB	6-6	250	11/29/81	2	New Mexico	Albuquerque, N.M.	D6a-'05	14/0
52	Stewart, Matt	LB	6-3	236	8/31/79	6	Vanderbilt	Columbus, Ohio	UFA(Atl)-'05	14/12
44	Suggs, Lee	RB	6-0	206	8/11/80	4	Virginia Tech	Roanoke, Va.	D4-'03	8/0
51	Thompson, Chaun	LB	6-2	242	5/22/80	4	West Texas A&M	Mt. Pleasant, Texas	D2-'03	16/15
72	Tucker, Ryan	T/G	6-6	314	6/12/75	10	Texas Christian	Midland, Texas	UFA(StL)-'02	16/16
53	Unck, Mason	LB	6-3	238	3/30/80	3	Arizona State	Ogden, Utah	FA-'04	16/0
92	Washington, Ted	DT	6-5	365	4/13/68	16	Louisville	Tampa, Fla.	FA-'06	16/16*
80	Winslow, Kellen	TE	6-4	254	7/21/83	3	Miami	San Diego, Calif.	D1-'04	0*
29	Wright, Jason	RB	5-10	210	7/12/82	2	Northwestern	Diamond Bar, Calif.	FA-'05	3/0
68	Yovanovits, Dave	G/T	6-3	294	3/6/81	4	Temple	Stanhope, N.J.	W(NYJ)-'05	2/1
15	Zastudil, Dave	P	6-3	215	10/26/78	5	Ohio	Bay Village, Ohio	UFA(Balt)-'06	16/0*

* Anderson inactive for 14 games; Bentley played 14 games with New Orleans in '05; Chandler last active with Washington in '04; Dinkins played 16 games with Baltimore, K. Dorsey played 3 games with San Francisco; Dunn missed '05 season because of injury; Hallen played 9 games with San Diego; Jurevicius played 16 games with Seattle; Kurpeikis last active with New England in '04; Mayer last active with New England in '04; McGinest played 16 games with New England; Owens last active with Chicago in '04; Rideau inactive for 10 games; Shaffer played 16 games with Atlanta; Washington 16 games with Oakland; Winslow missed '05 season because of injury; Zastudil played 16 games with Baltimore.

t- Browns traded for K. Dorsey (SF).

Traded—C Jeff Faine (NO; 14 games in '05), QB Trent Dilfer (SF; 11).

Players lost through free agency (5): WR Antonio Bryant (SF; 16 games in '05), C Mike Pucillo (Wash; 10), TE Aaron Shea (SD; 12), T L.J. Shelton (Mia; 16), LB Ben Taylor (GB; 16).

Also played with Browns in '05—NT Jason Fisk (14 games), DE/DT Kenard Lang (16), CB/S Michael Lehan (10), LB Jody Littlejohn (5), CB Ray Mickens (16), TE Billy Miller (3), P Kyle Richardson (16), LB Orlando Ruff (16).

2006 FIRST-YEAR ROSTER

Name	Pos.	Ht.	Wt.	Birthdate	College	Hometown	How Acq.
Almond, Dustin	QB	6-2	214	2/5/83	Southern Mississippi	Orange Park, Fla.	FA
Ashley, Jermial	DT/DE	6-5	260	1/28/83	Kansas	Keller, Texas	FA
Barclay, Chris	RB	5-10	180	10/15/83	Wake Forest	Louisville, Ky.	FA
Basler, Kyle	P	6-3	238	12/27/82	Washington State	Olympia, Wash.	FA
Brewster, Carlton	WR	5-11	214	2/12/83	Ferris State	Grand Rapids, Mich.	FA
Brielmaier, Ben	T/G	6-4	310	10/24/83	Princeton	Mankato, Minn.	FA
Butler, Lance	T/G	6-7	298	4/13/83	Florida	Princeton, N.J.	FA
Campbell, Darrell (1)	DT/DE	6-4	290	7/6/81	Notre Dame	South Holland, Ill.	FA
Campbell, Lang (1)	QB	6-1	199	9/25/81	William & Mary	Winchester, Va.	FA
Farris, Blake	CB/S	6-0	202	9/28/81	North Alabama	Jasper, Ala.	FA
Hackney, Darrell	QB	6-0	240	8/7/83	Alabama-Birmingham	Atlanta, Ga.	FA
Hall, Charles	CB/S	5-11	182	4/10/82	Southeastern Louisiana	Gulfport, Miss.	FA
Hamilton, Justin	CB/S	6-3	217	9/17/82	Virginia Tech	Norton, Va.	D7
Harrison, Jerome	RB	5-9	199	2/26/83	Washington State	Kalamazoo, Mich.	D5a
Herrion, Atlas (1)	T/G	6-4	313	12/3/80	Alabama	Daphne, Ala.	FA-'05
Hoffman, Andrew (1)	DT/DE	6-4	296	2/15/82	Virginia	Fairfax, Va.	D6b- 05
Hughley, Willie	CB/S	5-11	170	11/24/82	Florida Atlantic	Haines City, Fla.	FA
Hurley, Ricardo	LB	6-1	242	9/15/83	South Carolina	Greenwood, S.C.	FA
Irons, Paul (1)	TE	6-2	242	12/23/83	Florida State	New Orleans, La.	FA-'05
Jackson, D'Qwell	LB	6-0	228	9/26/83	Maryland	Largo, Fla.	D2
Kern, Kenny	LB	6-0	235	2/1/84	Delaware State	Clarksdale, Miss.	FA
Little, Brent	WR	6-0	185	4/3/83	Southern Illinois	Poplar Bluff, Mo.	FA
McMahon, Pete (1)	T/G	6-8	330	10/15/81	Iowa	Dubuque, Iowa	FA-'05
Minter, DeMario	CB/S	5-11	190	2/20/84	Georgia	Stone Mountain, Ga.	D5b
Modkins, Jeremy	CB/S	6-1	198	5/18/82	Texas Christian	Marlin, Texas	FA
Mosley, Kendrick (1)	WR	6-2	197	7/21/81	Western Michigan	Pahokee, Fla.	FA-'05
Oshinowo, Babatunde	DT	6-1	302	1/14/83	Stanford	Naperville, Ill.	D6b
Pace, Andrew	CB/S	6-0	198	10/7/83	Vanderbilt	Birmingham, Ala.	FA
Parker, J'Vonne (1)	DT/DE	6-4	310	6/7/82	Rutgers	Newark, N.J.	FA-'05
Perry, Jereme	CB/S	6-0	190	12/15/81	Eastern Michigan	Saginaw, Mich.	FA
Sanders, Steve	WR	6-3	201	12/23/82	Bowling Green	Cleveland, Ohio	FA
Smith,Clifton (1)	LB	6-3	267	7/21/80	Syracuse	Freeport, N.Y.	FA-'05
Smith, Rob	T/G	6-4	306	3/8/84	Tennessee	Fort Thomas, Ky.	FA
Sowells, Isaac	T/G	6-3	324	5/4/82	Indiana	Louisville, Ky.	D4b
Stith, Walter	T/G	6-9	320	1/2/83	North Carolina A&T	Atlanta, Ga.	FA
Thornton, James (1)	CB/S	5-11	185	9/9/79	Morris Brown	La Grange, Ga.	FA-'05
Vickers, Lawrence	FB	6-0	233	5/8/83	Colorado	Beaumont, Texas	D6a
Williams, Leon	LB	6-2	238	7/30/83	Miami	Brooklyn, N.Y.	D4a
Wilson, Travis	WR	6-1	213	2/11/84	Oklahoma	Carrollton, Texas	D3
Wimbley, Kamerion	LB	6-3	245	10/13/83	Florida State	Wichita, Kan.	D1

The term NFL Rookie is defined as a player who is in his first season of professional football and has not been on the roster of another professional football team for any regular-season or postseason games. A Rookie is designated by an "R" on NFL rosters. Players who have been active in another professional football league or players who have NFL experience, including either preseason training camp or being on an Active List or Inactive List, or on Reserve/Injured or Reserve/Physically Unable to Perform for fewer than six regular-season games, are termed NFL First-Year Players. An NFL First-Year Player is designated by a "1" on NFL rosters. Thereafter, a player is credited with an additional year of experience for each season in which he accumulates six games on the Active List or Inactive List, or on Reserve/Injured or Reserve/Physically Unable to Perform.

Log on to www.clevelandbrowns.com for an up-to-date roster.

COACHING STAFF

Head Coach,
Romeo Crennel

Pro Career: Romeo Crennel was named head coach of the Cleveland Browns on Feb. 8, 2005, the eleventh full-time head coach in franchise history. Crennel returned to Cleveland in 2005 after serving as the Browns defensive coordinator in 2000 and along with Phil Savage helped rebuild the football operations. Crennel led the Browns to a respectable 6-10 record in his first year as a head coach. His resumé includes 36 years of coaching experience, including 25 years in the NFL. In 2005, Crennel brought a 3-4 defensive scheme to Cleveland and witnessed his squad rank fourth in the NFL in pass defense. Prior to joining the Browns, Crennel was widely recognized as one of the top assistant coaches in the NFL. He crafted the defense for the New England Patriots and helped the Patriots win three Super Bowl's (2001, 2003-04). The 2004 Patriots finished the season with a 24-21 victory over Philadelphia in Super Bowl XXXIX. In 2003, he was recognized by the Pro Football Writers of America as the NFL's Assistant Coach of the Year. The New England defense was among the best units in NFL history, propelling the Patriots to a 15-game winning streak that culminated with a 32-29 victory over Carolina in Super Bowl XXXVIII. New England allowed a league-low and franchise-record 14.9 points per game, while also leading the league with 29 interceptions and added three shutouts. In 2001, the Patriots defeated the Rams 20-17 in Super Bowl XXXVI. Crennel and Bill Belichick worked together for 18 seasons, during which time they earned five Super Bowl titles, six conference titles and eight division titles. Crennell had previously coached in the NFL with Cleveland (2000), the New York Jets (1997-99), New England (1993-96), the New York Giants (1981-1992), where he was the defensive line coach for the Giants' Super Bowl XXV title. Career record: 6-10.

Background: Crennel was a four-year starter (1966-69) as a defensive lineman at Western Kentucky. He earned team MVP honors as a senior. Earned his bachelor's degree in physical education from Western Kentucky, and then earned his master's degree while serving as a graduate assistant. Crennel coached collegiately at Western Kentucky (1970-74), Texas Tech (1975-77), Mississippi (1978-79), Georgia Tech (1980).

Personal: Born June 18, 1947 in Lynchburg, Va. He and his wife, Rosemary, have three daughters, Lisa Tulley, Tiffany Crennel and Kristin Cullinane.

ASSISTANT COACHES

Dave Atkins, running backs; born May 18, 1949, Victoria, Texas. Running back Texas El-Paso 1970-72. Pro running back San Francisco 49ers 1973, Honolulu Hawaiians (WFL) 1974, San Diego Chargers 1975. College coach: Texas El-Paso 1979-1980, San Diego State 1981-85. Pro coach: Philadelphia Eagles 1986-1992, New England Patriots 1993, Arizona Cardinals 1994-95, New Orleans Saints 1996, 2000-04, Minnesota Vikings 1997-99, joined Browns in 2005.

Maurice Carthon, offensive coordinator; born April 24, 1961, Chicago. Running back Arkansas State 1979-1982. Pro running back New Jersey Generals (USFL) 1983-85, N.Y. Giants 1985-1991, Indianapolis Colts 1992. Pro coach: New England Patriots 1994-96, N.Y. Jets 1997-2000, Detroit Lions 2001-02, Dallas Cowboys 2003-04, joined Browns in 2005.

Ben Coates, tight ends; born Aug. 16, 1969, Greenwood, S.C. Tight end Livingstone College 1987-1990. Pro tight end New England Patriots 1991-99, Baltimore Ravens 2000. College coach: Livingstone College 2001-04. Pro coach: Joined Browns in 2005.

Carl Crennel II, offensive quality control; born Sept. 7, 1974, Montreal, Quebec, Canada. Attended Robert Morris. No college or pro playing experience. College coach: Robert Morris 1998-2000, Duquesne 2002, West Virginia Tech 2003-04. Pro coach: Erie Invaders (IFL) 2000, Jacksonville Tomcats (AFL2) 2001, joined Browns in 2005.

Jeff Davidson, asst. head coach/offensive line; born Oct. 3, 1967 in Akron, Ohio. Offensive lineman Ohio State 1986-89. Pro offensive lineman Denver Broncos 1990-92, New Orleans Saints 1994. Pro coach: New Orleans Saints 1995-96, New England Patriots 1997-2004, joined Browns in 2005.

Todd Grantham, defensive coordinator; born Sept. 13, 1966, Pulaski, Va. Offensive lineman Virginia Tech 1984-88. No pro playing experience. College coach: Virginia Tech 1990-95, Michigan State 1996-98. Pro coach: Indianapolis Colts 1999-2001, Houston Texans 2002-04, joined Browns in 2005.

Mike Haluchak, linebackers; born Nov. 28, 1949, Concord, Calif. Linebacker Southern California 1967-1970. No pro playing experience. College coach: Southern California 1976-77, Cal State-Fullerton 1978, Pacific 1979-1980, California 1981, North Carolina State 1982. Pro coach: Oakland Invaders (USFL) 1983-85, San Diego Chargers 1986-1991, Cincinnati Bengals 1992-93, Washington Redskins 1994-96, New York Giants 1997-99, St. Louis Rams 2000-02, Jacksonville Jaguars 2003-04, joined Browns in 2005.

John Lott, strength and conditioning; born May 9, 1964, Denton, Texas. Offensive lineman North Texas 1983-86. Pro offensive lineman Pittsburgh Steelers 1987. College coach: North Texas 1990, Houston 1991-96. Pro coach: New York Jets 1997-2004, joined Browns in 2005.

Randy Melvin, defensive line; born April 3, 1959, Aurora, Ill. Defensive line Eastern Illinois 1978-1981. No pro playing experience. College coach: Eastern Illinois 1988-1994, Wyoming 1995-96, Purdue 1997-99, Rutgers 2002-04, Illinois 2005. Pro coach: New England 2000-01, joined Browns in 2005.

Terry Robiskie, wide receivers; born Nov. 12, 1954, New Orleans. Running back Louisiana State 1973-76. Pro running back Oakland Raiders 1977-79, Miami Dolphins 1980-81. Pro coach: Los Angeles Raiders 1982-1993, Washington Redskins 1994-2000 (interim head coach 2000), joined Browns in 2001 (interim head coach 2004).

Jerry Rosburg, special teams coordinator; born Nov. 24, 1955, Fairmont, Minn. Linebacker North Dakota State 1974-77. No pro playing experience. College coach: Northern Michigan 1981-86, Western Michigan 1987-1991, Cincinnati 1992-95, Minnesota 1996, Boston College 1997-98, Notre Dame 1999-2000. Pro coach: Joined Browns in 2001.

Rip Scherer, quarterbacks; born Aug. 3, 1952. Quarterback William & Mary 1970-74. No pro playing experience. College coach: Penn State 1974-75, North Carolina State 1976, Hawaii 1977-78, Virginia 1979, Georgia Tech 1980-86, Alabama 1987, Arizona 1988-1990, James Madison 1991-94, Memphis 1995-2000, Kansas 2001, Southern Mississippi 2003-04. Pro coach: Joined Browns in 2005.

Bob Trott, defensive assistant; born March 19, 1954, Concord, N.C. College safety North Carolina 1973-75. No pro playing experience. College coach: North Carolina 1976-77, Air Force 1978-1983, Arkansas 1984-89, Clemson 1990, Duke 1996-2001, Baylor 2002, Louisiana-Monroe 2003-04. Pro coach: New York Giants 1991-92, New England Patriots 1993-95, joined Browns in 2005.

Mel Tucker, secondary; born Jan. 4, 1972, Cleveland. College defensive back Wisconsin 1992-95. No pro playing experience. College coach: Michigan State 1997, Miami (Ohio) 1998-99, Louisiana State 2000, Ohio State 2001-04. Pro coach: Joined Browns in 2005.

Jeff Uhlenhake, asst. offensive line; born Jan. 28, 1966, Newark, Ohio. College offensive lineman Ohio State 1985-88. Pro offensive lineman Miami Dolphins 1989-1993, New Orleans Saints 1994-96, Washington Redskins 1996-99. College coach: Ohio State 2003, Cincinnati 2004. Pro coach: Joined Browns in 2005.

Cory Undlin, defensive quality control; born June 29, 1971, St. Cloud, Minn. Safety California Lutheran 1990-94. No pro playing experience. College coach: California Lutheran 1998-2002, Fresno State 2002-03. Pro coach: New England 2004, joined Browns in 2005.

**American Football Conference
West Division
Team Colors:** Orange, Broncos Navy
Blue, and White
**13655 Broncos Parkway
Englewood, Colorado 80112
Telephone:** (303) 649-9000

2006 SCHEDULE
PRESEASON
Aug. 11 at Detroit...........................7:30
Aug. 19 Tennessee 7:00
Aug. 27 **Houston**...........................6:00
Aug. 31 at Arizona.........................7:00

REGULAR SEASON
Sept. 10 at St. Louis 12:00
Sept. 17 **Kansas City** 2:15
Sept. 24 at New England................8:15
Oct. 1   Open Date
Oct. 9   **Baltimore** (Mon.) 6:30
Oct. 15 **Oakland**...........................6:15
Oct. 22 at Cleveland 4:05
Oct. 29 **Indianapolis** 2:15
Nov. 5   at Pittsburgh 4:15
Nov. 12 at Oakland.........................1:05
Nov. 19 **San Diego** 2:15
Nov. 23 at Kansas City (Thu.) 7:00
Dec. 3   **Seattle**.............................2:15
Dec. 10 at San Diego 1:15
Dec. 17 at Arizona.........................2:05
Dec. 24 **Cincinnati** 2:15
Dec. 31 **San Francisco** 2:15

Stadium: INVESCO Field at Mile High
         (opened in 2001)
         • **Capacity:** 76,125
         1701 Bryant Street
         Denver, Colorado 80204
Playing Surface: Grass (PAT)
Training Camp: 13655 Broncos Parkway
         Englewood, Colorado
         80112

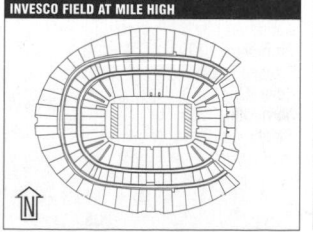
INVESCO FIELD AT MILE HIGH

CLUB OFFICIALS
President-Chief Executive Officer:
  Pat Bowlen
Executive Vice President of Football
  Operations/ Head Coach:
  Mike Shanahan
Executive Vice President of Business
  Operations: Joe Ellis
FOOTBALL STAFF
General Manager: Ted Sundquist
Assistant General Manager: Rick Smith
Director of Player Personnel:
  Jim Goodman
Coordinator of Football Administration:
  Mike Bluem
Trainer: Steve Antonopulos
Equipment Manager: Chris Valenti
Video Director: Kent Erickson
BUSINESS STAFF
General Counsel/Senior Vice President of
  Administration: Rich Slivka
Vice President of Public Relations:
  Jim Saccomano
Vice President of Marketing: Greg Carney
Vice President of Finance: Jim Barlow
Vice President of Community
  Development: Cindy Galloway-Kellogg
STADIUM MANAGEMENT COMPANY
Vice President and General Manager:
  Mac Freeman

COACHING HISTORY
(379-335-10)
Records include postseason games
1960-61	Frank Filchock	7-20-1
1962-61	Jack Faulkner*	9-22-1
1964-66	Mac Speedie**	6-19-1
1966	Ray Malavasi	4-8-0
1967-1971	Lou Saban***	20-42-3
1971	Jerry Smith	2-3-0
1972-76	John Ralston	34-33-3
1977-1980	Robert (Red) Miller	42-25-0
1981-1992	Dan Reeves	117-79-1
1993-94	Wade Phillips	16-17-0
1995-2005	Mike Shanahan	122-67-0

  *Released after four games in 1964
  **Resigned after two games in 1966
  ***Resigned after nine games in 1971

ATTENDANCE
Home 595,671   Away 551,594
Total 1,147,265
Single-game home record,
  76,643 (11/11/00)
Single-season home record, 595,671
  (2005)

2006 DRAFT CHOICES
Round	Name	Pos.	College
1	Jay Cutler	QB	Vanderbilt
2	Tony Scheffler	TE	Western Michigan
4	Brandon Marshall	WR	Central Florida
	Elvis Dumervil	DE	Louisville
	Domenik Hixon	WR	Akron
5	Chris Kuper	G	North Dakota
6	Greg Eslinger	C	Minnesota

DENVER BRONCOS

2005 TEAM RECORD

PRESEASON (4-0)

Date	Result	Opponent
8/13	W 20-14	at Houston
8/20	W 26-21	San Francisco
8/27	W 37-24	Indianapolis
9/2	W 30-21	at Arizona

REGULAR SEASON (13-3)

Date	Result	Opponent	Att.
9/11	L 10-34	at Miami	72,324
9/18	W 20-17	San Diego	75,310
9/26	W 30-10	Kansas City	76,381
10/2	W 20-7	at Jacksonville	66,045
10/9	W 21-19	Washington	75,880
10/16	W 28-20	New England	76,571
10/23	L 23-24	at N.Y. Giants	78,516
10/30	W 49-21	Philadelphia	76,530
11/13	W 31-17	at Oakland	62,779
11/20	W 27-0	New York Jets	76,255
11/24	W 24-21	at Dallas (OT)	63,273
12/4	L 27-31	at Kansas City	78,261
12/11	W 12-10	Baltimore	75,651
12/17	W 28-17	at Buffalo	71,887
12/24	W 22-3	Oakland	76,212
12/31	W 23-7	at San Diego	65,513

(OT) Overtime

POSTSEASON (1-1)

Date	Result	Opponent	
1/14	W 27-13	New England	76,238
1/22	L 17-34	Pittsburgh	76,775

SCORE BY PERIODS

Broncos	81	143	83	85	3	—	395
Opponents	44	61	37	116	0	—	258

2005 TEAM STATISTICS

	Broncos	Opp.
Total First Downs	330	295
Rushing	145	82
Passing	162	183
Penalty	23	30
3rd Down: Made/Att	76/210	76/207
3rd Down Pct.	36.2	36.7
4th Down: Made/Att	14/19	10/19
4th Down Pct.	73.7	52.6
Possession Avg.	32:37	27:23
Total Net Yards	5,766	5,006
Avg. Per Game	360.4	312.9
Total Plays	1,030	985
Avg. Per Play	5.6	5.1
Net Yards Rushing	2,539	1,363
Avg. Per Game	158.7	85.2
Total Rushes	542	344
Net Yards Passing	3,227	3,643
Avg. Per Game	201.7	227.7
Sacked/Yards Lost	23/146	28/190
Gross Yards	3,373	3,833
Att./Completions	465/279	613/344
Completion Pct.	60.0	56.1
Had Intercepted	7	20
Punts/Average	73/43.2	81/44.9
Net Punting Avg.	73/38.0	81/38.2
Penalties/Yards	97/756	139/989
Fumbles/Ball Lost	19/9	29/16
Touchdowns	46	31
Rushing	25	10
Passing	18	20
Returns	3	1

2005 INDIVIDUAL STATISTICS

PASSING

PASSING	Att.	Comp.	Yds.	Pct.	TD	Int.	Tkld.	Rate
Plummer	456	277	3,366	60.7	18	7	22/135	90.2
Van Pelt	8	2	7	25.0	0	0	0/0	39.6
Smith	1	0	0	0.0	0	0	1/11	39.6
Broncos	465	279	3,373	60.0	18	7	23/146	88.9
Opponents	613	344	3,833	56.1	20	20	28/190	72.2

SCORING

SCORING	TD R	TD P	TD Rt	PAT	FG	Saf	PTS
Elam	0	0	0	43/44	24/32	0	115
Mi. Anderson	12	1	0	0/0	0/0	0	78
Bell	8	0	0	0/0	0/0	0	48
Johnson	1	5	0	0/0	0/0	0	36
Smith	0	6	0	0/0	0/0	0	36
Bailey	0	0	2	0/0	0/0	0	12
Carswell	0	2	0	0/0	0/0	0	12
Plummer	2	0	0	0/0	0/0	0	12
S. Alexander	0	1	0	0/0	0/0	0	6
Dayne	1	0	0	0/0	0/0	0	6
Devoe	0	1	0	0/0	0/0	0	6
Duke	0	1	0	0/0	0/0	0	6
Lelie	0	1	0	0/0	0/0	0	6
Van Pelt	1	0	0	0/0	0/0	0	6
Da. Williams	0	0	1	0/0	0/0	0	6
Putzier	0	0	0	0/0	0/0	0	2
Veal	0	0	0	0/0	0/0	0	2
Broncos	25	18	3	43/44	24/32	1	395
Opponents	10	20	1	30/30	14/18	0	258

2-Pt. Conversions: Putzier.
Team 1-2, Opponents 0-1.

RUSHING

RUSHING	No.	Yds	Avg	LG	TD
Mi. Anderson	239	1,014	4.2	44t	12
Bell	173	921	5.3	68	8
Dayne	53	270	5.1	55	1
Plummer	46	151	3.3	22	2
Lelie	5	84	16.8	39	0
Van Pelt	11	48	4.4	11	1
Sapp	5	21	4.2	10	0
Adams	5	14	2.8	13	0
Johnson	4	9	2.3	4	1
Smith	1	7	7.0	7	0
Broncos	542	2,539	4.7	68	25
Opponents	344	1,363	4.0	61	10

RECEIVING

RECEIVING	No.	Yds	Avg	LG	TD
Smith	85	1,105	13.0	72	6
Lelie	42	770	18.3	56	1
Putzier	37	481	13.0	32	0
Adams	21	203	9.7	21	0
S. Alexander	21	170	8.1	15	1
Mi. Anderson	18	212	11.8	66t	1
Bell	18	104	5.8	14	0
Johnson	17	160	9.4	33	5
Devoe	9	87	9.7	44t	1
Dayne	3	17	5.7	7	0
Duke	2	22	11.0	21	1
Watts	2	22	11.0	12	0
Sapp	2	17	8.5	12	0
Carswell	2	3	1.5	2t	2
Broncos	279	3,373	12.1	72	18
Opponents	344	3,833	11.1	91t	20

INTERCEPTIONS

INTERCEPTIONS	No.	Yds	Avg	LG	TD
Bailey	8	139	17.4	65t	2
Ferguson	5	59	11.8	30	0
Da. Williams	2	108	54.0	80t	1
Foxworth	2	23	11.5	23	0
Lynch	2	2	1.0	1	0
Cox	1	48	48.0	48	0
Broncos	20	379	19.0	80t	3
Opponents	7	43	6.1	25	0

PUNTING

PUNTING	No.	Yds.	Avg.	In 20	LG
Sauerbrun	72	3,157	43.8	24	66
Broncos	73	3,157	43.2	24	66
Opponents	81	3,633	44.9	25	64

PUNT RETURNS

PUNT RETURNS	Ret	FC	Yds	Avg	LG	TD
Da. Williams	17	12	148	8.7	52	0
Adams	16	5	133	8.3	32	0
Broncos	33	17	281	8.5	52	0
Opponents	36	15	266	7.4	20	0

KICKOFF RETURNS

KICKOFF RETURNS	No.	Yds	Avg	LG	TD
Da. Williams	18	431	23.9	36	0
R. Alexander	12	261	21.8	31	0
Adams	10	218	21.8	32	0
Sapp	2	28	14.0	20	0
Mi. Anderson	1	18	18.0	18	0
Johnson	1	8	8.0	8	0
Veal	1	6	6.0	6	0
Engelberger	1	5	5.0	5	0
Carswell	1	0	0.0	0	0
Broncos	47	975	20.7	36	0
Opponents	67	1,696	25.3	87	0

FIELD GOALS

FIELD GOALS	1-19	20-29	30-39	40-49	50+
Elam	0/0	9/10	5/5	9/13	1/4
Broncos	0/0	9/10	5/5	9/13	1/4
Opponents	0/0	3/3	6/8	4/5	1/2

SACKS

SACKS	No.
Ekuban	4.0
Lynch	4.0
Pryce	4.0
Gold	3.0
Warren	3.0
Wilson	3.0
Brown	2.0
Coleman	1.0
M. Myers	1.0
Veal	1.0
Da. Williams	1.0
TEAM	1.0
Broncos	28.0
Opponents	23.0

RECORD HOLDERS
INDIVIDUAL RECORDS—CAREER

Category	Name	Performance
Rushing (Yds.)	Terrell Davis, 1995-2001	7,607
Passing (Yds.)	John Elway, 1983-1998	51,475
Passing (TDs)	John Elway, 1983-1998	300
Receiving (No.)	Rod Smith, 1995-2005	797
Receiving (Yds.)	Rod Smith, 1995-2005	10,877
Interceptions	Steve Foley, 1976-1986	44
Punting (Avg.)	Jim Fraser, 1962-64	45.2
Punt Return (Avg.)	Darrien Gordon, 1997-98	12.5
Kickoff Return (Avg.)	Abner Haynes, 1965-66	26.3
Field Goals	Jason Elam, 1993-2005	341
Touchdowns (Tot.)	Rod Smith, 1995-2005	66
Points	Jason Elam, 1993-2005	1,557

INDIVIDUAL RECORDS—SINGLE SEASON

Category	Name	Performance
Rushing (Yds.)	Terrell Davis, 1998	2,008
Passing (Yds.)	Jake Plummer, 2004	4,089
Passing (TDs)	John Elway, 1997	27
	Jake Plummer, 2004	27
Receiving (No.)	Rod Smith, 2001	113
Receiving (Yds.)	Rod Smith, 2000	1,602
Interceptions	Goose Gonsoulin, 1960	11
Punting (Avg.)	Tom Rouen, 1998	46.9
Punt Return (Avg.)	Floyd Little, 1967	16.9
Kickoff Return (Avg.)	Bill Thompson, 1969	28.5
Field Goals	Jason Elam, 1995, 2001	31
Touchdowns (Tot.)	Terrell Davis, 1998	23
Points	Terrell Davis, 1998	138

INDIVIDUAL RECORDS—SINGLE GAME

Category	Name	Performance
Rushing (Yds.)	Mike Anderson, 12-3-00	251
Passing (Yds.)	Jake Plummer, 10-31-04	499
Passing (TDs)	Frank Tripucka, 10-28-62	5
	John Elway, 11-18-84	5
	Gus Frerotte, 11-19-00	5
Receiving (No.)	Rod Smith, 9-23-01	14
Receiving (Yds.)	Shannon Sharpe, 10-20-02	214
Interceptions	Goose Gonsoulin, 9-18-60	*4
	Willie Brown, 11-15-64	*4
	Deltha O'Neal, 10-7-01	*4
Field Goals	Gene Mingo, 10-6-63	5
	Rich Karlis, 11-20-83	5
	Jason Elam, 9-3-95, 10-13-02	5
Touchdowns (Tot.)	Clinton Portis, 12-7-03	5
Points	Clinton Portis, 12-7-03	30

*NFL Record

2006 VETERAN ROSTER

No.	Name	Pos.	Ht.	Wt.	Birthdate	NFL Exp.	College	Hometown	How Acq.	'05 Games/ Starts
21	Abdullah, Hamza	S	6-2	213	8/20/83	2	Washington State	Pomona, Calif.	W(TB)-'05	1/0
81	Adams, Charlie	WR	6-2	190	10/23/79	4	Hofstra	Mechanicsburg, Pa.	FA-'04	16/2
69	Alexander, P.J.	G	6-4	297	12/23/78	4	Syracuse	Tallahassee, Fla.	FA-'03	0*
45	Alexander, Roc	CB	5-10	190	9/23/81	3	Washington	Colorado Springs, Colo.	FA-'04	10/0
82	Alexander, Stephen	TE	6-4	250	11/7/75	9	Oklahoma	Chickasha, Okla.	UFA(Det)-'05	16/15
24	Bailey, Champ	CB	6-0	192	6/22/78	8	Georgia	Folkston, Ga.	T(Wash)-'04	14/14
26	Bell, Tatum	RB	5-11	213	3/2/81	3	Oklahoma State	Dallas, Texas	D2a-'04	15/1
68	Bibla, Martin	G	6-3	306	10/4/79	4	Miami	Mountaintop, Penn.	FA-'06	0*
42	Brandon, Sam	S	6-2	200	7/5/79	5	Nevada-Las Vegas	Riverside, Calif.	D4-'02	14/0
98	Brown, Courtney	DE	6-4	285	2/14/78	7	Penn State	Alvin, S.C.	FA-'05	14/13
29	Browner, Brandon	CB	6-4	221	8/2/84	2	Oregon State	Sylmar, Calif.	FA-'05	0*
51	Burns, Keith	LB	6-2	235	5/16/72	13	Oklahoma State	Alexandria, Va.	UFA(TB)-'05	15/1
65	Carlisle, Cooper	G/T	6-5	295	8/11/77	7	Florida	McComb, Miss.	D4b-'00	16/16
77	Carswell, Dwayne	G	6-3	290	1/18/72	13	Liberty	Jacksonville, Fla.	FA-'94	7/0
54	Chukwurah, Patrick	LB	6-1	250	3/1/79	6	Wyoming	Irving, Texas	FA-'04	14/0
70	Collins, Javiar	T	6-6	307	4/13/78	5	Northwestern	Mendota Heights, Minn.	FA-'06	0*
40	Cox, Curome	S	6-1	199	2/28/81	2	Maryland	Washington, D.C.	FA-'04	13/1
33	Dayne, Ron	RB	5-10	245	3/14/78	7	Wisconsin	Berlin, N.J.	UFA(NYG)-'05	10/0
14	Devoe, Todd	WR	6-2	198	4/5/80	2	Central Missouri State	Fort Lauderdale, Fla.	FA-'05	14/0
84	Duke, Wesley	TE	6-5	225	6/21/81	2	Mercer	Norcross, Ga.	FA-'05	3/0
91	Ekuban, Ebenezer	DE	6-4	275	5/29/76	8	North Carolina	Bowie, Md.	T(Cle)-'05	16/4
1	Elam, Jason	K	5-11	200	3/8/70	14	Hawaii	Ft. Walton Beach, Fla.	D3b-'93	16/0
60	Engelberger, John	DE	6-4	268	10/18/76	7	Virginia Tech	Springfield, Va.	T(SF)-'05	14/0
3	Ernster, Paul	P/K	6-0	217	1/26/82	2	Northern Arizona	Glendale, Ariz.	D7-'05	1/0
25	Ferguson, Nick	S	5-11	201	11/27/74	7	Georgia Tech	Miami, Fla.	FA-'03	16/16
72	Foster, George	T	6-5	338	6/9/80	4	Georgia	Macon, Ga.	D1-'03	16/16
22	Foxworth, Domonique	CB	5-11	180	3/27/83	2	Maryland	Catonsville, Md.	D3b-'05	16/7
52	Gold, Ian	LB	6-0	223	8/23/78	7	Michigan	Belleville, Mich.	FA-'05	16/16
94	Gordon, Amon	DL	6-2	305	10/13/81	3	Stanford	San Diego, Calif.	W(Cle)-'06	0*
74	Green, Cornell	T	6-6	315	8/25/76	7	Central Florida	St. Petersburg, Fla.	UFA(TB)-'04	14/0
53	Green, Louis	LB	6-3	228	9/23/79	3	Alcorn State	Vicksburg, Miss.	FA-'03	14/0
50	Hamilton, Ben	G/C	6-4	283	8/18/77	6	Minnesota	Minneapolis, Minn.	D4a-'01	16/16
89	Jackson, Nate	TE	6-3	235	6/4/79	4	Menlo	San Jose, Calif.	T(SF)-'03	2/0
39	Johnson, Kyle	FB	6-0	242	12/15/78	4	Syracuse	Woodbridge, N.J.	FA-'03	16/14
87	Kircus, David	WR	6-2	190	2/19/80	3	Grand Valley State	Imlay City, Mich.	FA-'06	0*
76	Lang, Kenard	DE	6-3	257	1/31/75	10	Miami	Orlando, Fla.	FA-'06	16/5*
83	Leach, Mike	TE/LS	6-2	245	10/18/76	7	William & Mary	Jefferson Township, N.J.	FA-'02	16/0
85	Lelie, Ashley	WR	6-3	200	2/16/80	5	Hawaii	Honolulu, Hawaii	D1-'02	16/13
78	Lepsis, Matt	T	6-4	290	1/13/74	10	Colorado	Conroe, Texas	FA-'97	16/16
47	Lynch, John	S	6-2	220	9/25/71	14	Stanford	Del Mar, Calif.	FA-'04	16/16
31	Miree, Brandon	RB	5-11	237	4/14/81	2	Pittsburgh	Cincinnati, Ohio	D7b-'04	0*
75	Mustard, Chad	T	6-6	288	10/8/77	3	North Dakota	Columbus, Neb.	FA-'06	0/0
62	Myers, Chris	C/G	6-4	300	9/15/81	2	Miami	Miami, Fla.	D6-'05	9/0
96	Myers, Michael	DT	6-2	300	1/20/76	9	Alabama	Vicksburg, Miss.	T(Cle)-'05	16/15
66	Nalen, Tom	C	6-3	286	5/13/71	13	Boston College	Foxboro, Mass.	D7c-'94	16/16
5	Parsons, Preston	QB	6-4	229	2/19/79	3	Northern Arizona	Portland, Ore.	FA-'06	0*
41	Paymah, Karl	CB	6-0	200	11/29/82	2	Washington State	Culver City, Calif.	D3a-'05	13/0
16	Plummer, Jake	QB	6-2	212	12/19/74	10	Arizona State	Boise, Idaho	UFA(Ariz)-'03	16/16
37	Sapp, Cecil	RB	5-11	229	12/23/78	4	Colorado State	Miami, Fla.	FA-'03	16/0
10	Sauerbrun, Todd	P	5-10	215	1/4/73	12	West Virginia	East Setauket, N.Y.	T(Car)-'05	16/0
28	Shoate, Jeff	CB	5-10	189	3/23/81	3	San Diego State	San Diego, Calif.	D5-'04	0/0
80	Smith, Rod	WR	6-0	200	5/15/70	12	Missouri Southern	Texarkana, Ark.	FA-'94	16/16
13	Terrell, David	WR	6-3	212	3/13/79	6	Michigan	Richmond, Va.	FA-'05	1/0
86	Trusty, Landon	TE	6-7	260	10/9/81	3	Central Arkansas	Hot Springs, Ark.	FA-'06	0*
11	Van Pelt, Bradlee	QB	6-2	220	7/3/80	2	Colorado State	Santa Barbara, Calif.	D7c-'04	3/0/1
95	Vaughn, Khaleed	DE	6-4	270	5/20/81	2	Clemson	North Atlanta, Ga.	FA-'06	0*
97	Veal, Demetrin	DT	6-2	288	8/11/81	4	Tennessee	Paramount, Calif.	FA-'04	15/0
19	t- Walker, Javon	WR	6-3	215	10/14/78	5	Florida State	Lafayette, La.	T(GB)-'06	1/1*
61	Warren, Gerard	DT	6-4	325	7/25/78	6	Florida	Raiford, Fla.	T(Cle)-'05	16/16
17	Watts, Darius	WR	6-2	190	12/19/81	3	Marshall	Atlanta, Ga.	D2b-'04	6/0
58	Webster, Nate	LB	6-0	240	11/29/77	7	Miami	Miami, Fla.	UFA(Cin)-'06	1/0*
59	Wells, Ray	LB	6-1	234	8/20/80	3	Arizona	Spring Valley, Calif.	FA-'06	0*
59	Whitley, Taylor	G	6-4	315	2/21/80	4	Texas A&M	Sudan, Texas	FA-'05	2/0
55	Williams, D.J.	LB	6-1	242	7/20/82	3	Miami	Concord, Calif.	D1-'04	16/14
27	Williams, Darrent	CB	5-8	188	9/27/82	2	Oklahoma State	Fort Worth, Texas	D2-'05	12/9
56	Wilson, Al	LB	6-0	240	6/21/77	8	Tennessee	Jackson, Tenn.	D1-'99	15/15

* P.J. Alexander missed '05 season because of injury; Bibla last active with Atlanta in '04; Browner missed '05 season because of injury; Collins last active with Dallas in '03; Gordon missed '05 season with Cleveland because of injury; Kircus last active with Detroit in '04; Lang played 16 games with Cleveland in '05; Miree missed '04 season with Denver because of injury; Mustard last active with Cleveland in '04; Parsons last active with Arizona in '03; Shoate missed '05 season because of injury; Trusty inactive for 4 games with San Diego; K. Vaughn last active with Atlanta in '04; Walker played 1 game with Green Bay; Webster played 1 game with Cincinnati; Wells last active with San Francisco in '04.

t- Broncos traded for Walker (GB).

Players lost through free agency (1). DT Monsanto Pope (NYJ; 2 games in '05).

Also played with Broncos in '05—S Marques Anderson (6 games), RB Mike Anderson (15), DE Marco Coleman (7), DE Trevor Pryce (16), TE Jeb Putzier (16), CB Lenny Walls (7).

2006 FIRST-YEAR ROSTER

Name	Pos.	Ht.	Wt.	Birthdate	College	Hometown	How Acq.
Bell, Mike	RB	6-0	215	4/23/83	Arizona	Tolleson, Ariz.	FA
Buhl, Josh (1)	LB	6-0	210	5/4/81	Kansas State	Mesquite, Texas	FA-'05
Burton, Antwon	DT	6-2	315	7/11/83	Temple	Cheektowaga, N.Y.	FA
Clark, Brian	WR	6-2	211	12/26/83	North Carolina State	Tampa, Fla.	FA
Cobbs, Cedric (1)	RB	6-0	225	1/9/81	Arkansas	Little Rock, Ark.	FA-'05
Cutler, Jay	QB	6-3	226	4/29/83	Vanderbilt	Lincoln City, Ind.	D1
Dumervil, Elvis	DE	5-11	258	1/19/84	Louisville	Miami, Fla.	D4b
Eslinger, Greg	C	6-3	285	4/23/83	Minnesota	Bismarck, N.D.	D6
Everett, Tyler	S	5-11	202	11/4/83	Ohio State	Canton, Ohio	FA
Fredrickson, Tyler (1)	P/K	6-3	220	2/26/81	California	Goleta, Calif.	FA
Gause, George (1)	DE	6-5	275	6/20/82	South Carolina	Conway, S.C.	FA-'05
Hixon, Domenik	WR	6-2	192	10/8/84	Akron	Columbus, Ohio	D4c
Hunt, Rob (1)	G/C	6-3	298	3/3/81	North Dakota State	Cavalier, N.D.	FA-'05
Jackson, Corey (1)	DE	6-6	265	11/6/78	Nevada	Kershaw, S.C.	FA-'05
Kuper, Chris	G	6-4	305	12/19/82	North Dakota	Anchorage, Alaska	D5
Majondo-Mwamba, Patrice (1)	DT/DE	6-4	293	7/29/79	Texas Tech	Republic of Congo	FA-'05
Marshall, Brandon	WR	6-4	230	3/23/84	Central Florida	Lake Howell, Fla.	D4a
Pears, Erik (1)	T	6-8	305	6/25/82	Colorado State	Denver, Colo.	FA-'05
Powers-Neal, Rashon	FB	6-3	238	4/3/83	Notre Dame	St. Paul, Minn.	FA
Rogers, Antwaun (1)	CB	6-2	172	8/29/82	Purdue	Middletown, Ohio	FA-'05
Scheffler, Tony	TE	6-5	254	2/15/83	Western Michigan	Morenci, Mich.	D2
Vaughn, Cameron	LB	6-4	237	2/27/84	Louisiana State	Marrero, La.	FA

The term NFL Rookie is defined as a player who is in his first season of professional football and has not been on the roster of another professional football team for any regular-season or postseason games. A Rookie is designated by an "R" on NFL rosters. Players who have been active in another professional football league or players who have NFL experience, including either preseason training camp or being on an Active List or Inactive List, or on Reserve/Injured or Reserve/Physically Unable to Perform for fewer than six regular-season games, are termed NFL First-Year Players. An NFL First-Year Player is designated by a "1" on NFL rosters. Thereafter, a player is credited with an additional year of experience for each season in which he accumulates six games on the Active List or Inactive List, or on Reserve/Injured or Reserve/Physically Unable to Perform.

Log on to www.denverbroncos.com for an up-to-date roster.

COACHING STAFF

Head Coach,
Mike Shanahan
Pro Career: Became the eleventh head coach in Broncos history on January 31, 1995. Mike Shanahan led the Broncos to back-to-back Super Bowl championships in 1997 and 1998, becoming just the fifth head coach to accomplish that feat, and is the only coach to win seven consecutive postseason games in a two-year period. No NFL head coach has won more games than Mike Shanhan's 130 victories since the start of the 1995 season. During his NFL career, Shanahan has been a part of teams that have played in nine conference championship games and six Super Bowls. In 27 seasons as a pro and college coach, Shanahan's teams have participated in postseason or bowl games 22 times. Under Shanahan's guidance, Denver has set and NFL record by posting the most victories in both a two-year (33, 1997-98) and three-year (46, 1996-98) period. In the last twelve years (nine with Denver and three as offensive coordinator with the San Francisco 49ers), Shanahan's offenses have finished number one in the NFL four times, second twice, and third twice. Shanahan was an assistant with Denver (1984-87, 1989-1991) and San Francisco (1992-94). Returned to Denver as quarterbacks coach on October 16, 1989, after posting 8-12 record as the Los Angeles Raiders' head coach. Career record: 130-79.
Background: Shanahan coached at Oklahoma (1975-76), Northern Arizona (1977), Eastern Illinois (1978), Minnesota (1979), and Florida (1980-83).
Personal: Born in Oak Park, Illinois, on August 24, 1952. He was a wishbone quarterback-defensive back at Eastern Illinois. Mike and his wife, Peggy, have two children—Kyle and Krystal.

ASSISTANT COACHES

Jeremy Bates, offensive assistant, born August 27, 1976, Manhattan, Kan. Quarterback Tennessee 1995, Rice 1996-99. No pro playing experience. Pro coach: Tampa Bay Buccaneers 2002-04, New York Jets 2005, joined Broncos in 2006.
Ronnie Bradford, special teams; born October 1, 1970, Minot, N.D. Defensive back Colorado 1989-1992. Pro defensive back Denver Broncos 1993-95, Arizona Cardinals 1996, Atlanta Falcons 1997-2001, Minnesota Vikings 2002. Pro coach: Joined Broncos in 2003.
Tim Brewster, tight ends; born October 13, 1960, Phillipsburg, N.J. Tight End Illinois 1980-1983. No pro playing experience. College coach: Purdue 1986, North Carolina 1989-1997, Texas 1998-2001. Pro coach: San Diego Chargers 2002-04, joined Broncos in 2005.
Jacob Burney, defensive line/ends; born January 24, 1959, Chattanooga, Tenn. Defensive tackle Tennessee-Chattanooga

1977-1980. No pro playing experience. College coach: New Mexico 1983-86, Tulsa 1987, Mississippi State 1988, Wisconsin 1989, UCLA 1990-92, Tennessee 1993. Pro coach: Cleveland Browns/Baltimore Ravens 1994-98, Carolina Panthers 1999-2001, joined Broncos in 2002.
Larry Coyer, defensive coordinator; born April 19, 1943, Huntington, W. Va. Linebacker Marshall 1962-64. No pro playing experience. College coach: Marshall 1965-67, Iowa 1974-77, Oklahoma State 1978, Iowa State 1979-1983, 1995-96, UCLA 1987-89, Houston 1990, Ohio State 1991-92, East Carolina 1993, Pittsburgh 1997-99. Pro coach: Michigan Panthers (USFL) 1984-85, Memphis Showboats (USFL) 1986, New York Jets 1994, joined Broncos in 2000.
Rick Dennison, offensive coordinator; born June 22, 1958, in Kalispell, Mont. Tight end Colorado State 1976-79. Pro linebacker Denver Broncos 1982-1990. Pro coach: Joined Broncos in 1995.
Kirk Doll, linebackers; born September 24, 1951, Wichita, Kan. Defensive end-tackle East Carolina 1971-72. No pro playing experience. College coach: Wichita State 1975-76, Iowa State 1979, Tulsa 1980-84, Arizona State 1985-87, Texas A&M 1988-1994, Notre Dame 1994-2001, Louisiana State 2002-03. Pro coach: Joined Broncos in 2004.
Mike Heimerdinger, asst. head coach, born October 13, 1952, DeKalb, Ill. Wide receiver Eastern Illinois 1970-1974. No pro playing experience. College coach: Florida 1980, Air Force 1981, North Texas State 1982, Florida 1983-87, Cal State-Fullerton 1988, Rice 1989-1993, Duke 1994. Pro coach: Denver Broncos 1995-99, Tennessee Titans 2000-04, New York Jets 2005, re-joined Broncos in 2006.
Thomas McGaughey, special teams assistant; born May 8, 1973, Chicago. Safety Houston 1991-95. Pro safety Philadelphia Eagles 1996, Barcelona Dragons (NFLE) 1997. College coach: Houston 1997, 2003-04. Pro coach: Scottisch Claymores (NFLE) 2002, Kansas City Chiefs 2002, joined Broncos in 2005.
Pat McPherson, quarterbacks; born April 15, 1969, Santa Clara, Calif. Linebacker Santa Clara 1991-92. No pro playing experience. Pro coach: Joined Broncos in 1998.
Andre Patterson, defensive line/tackles; born June 12, 1960, Camdon, Ark. Offensive lineman Contra Costa (Calif.) J.C. 1978-1980, Montana 1981. No pro playing experience. College coach: Montana 1982, Weber State 1988, Cornell 1990-91, Washington State 1992-93, Cal Poly-San Luis Obispo 1994-96. Pro coach: New England Patriots 1997, Minnesota Vikings 1998-99, Dallas Cowboys 2000-02, Cleveland Browns 2003-04, joined Broncos in 2005.

Jim Ryan, defensive assistant; born May 18, 1957, Bellmawr, N.J.. Linebacker William & Mary 1974-1978. Linebacker Denver Broncos 1979-1988. Pro coach: Joined Broncos in 2005.
Greg Saporta, asst. strength and conditioning; born February 2, 1957, New York, N.Y. Wide receiver Buffalo State 1977-79. No pro playing experience. College coach: Florida 1981-88, 1993-94, North Carolina 1989-1992. Pro coach: Joined Broncos in 1995.
Cedric Smith, asst. strength and conditioning; born May 27, 1968, Enterprise, Ala. Running back Florida 1986-89. Pro fullback Minnesota Vikings 1990, New Orleans Saints 1991, Washington Redskins 1994-95, Arizona Cardinals 1996-98. Pro coach: Joined Broncos in 2001.
Bob Slowik, defensive backs; born May 16, 1954, Pittsburgh. Defensive back Delaware 1973-76. No pro playing experience. College coach: Delaware 1977-78, Florida 1979-1982, Drake 1983, Rutgers 1984-89, East Carolina 1990-91. Pro coach: Dallas Cowboys 1992, Chicago Bears 1993-98, Cleveland Browns 1999, Green Bay Packers 2000-04, joined Broncos in 2005.
Ryan Slowik, defensive assistant; born Dec. 27, 1980, Chicago. Safety Wisconsin-Oshkosh 2002-03. No pro playing experience. College coach: Wisconsin-Oshkosh 2004. Pro coach: Joined Broncos in 2005.
Jimmy Spencer, asst. defensive backs; born March 29, 1969, Manning, S.C. Cornerback Florida 1988-1990. Pro cornerback Washington Redskins 1991, New Orleans Saints 1992-95, Cincinnati Bengals 1996-97, San Diego Chargers 1998-99, Denver Broncos 2000-current. Pro coach: Joined Broncos in 2003.
Bobby Turner, running backs; born May 6, 1949, East Chicago, Ind. Defensive back Indiana State 1968-1971. No pro playing experience. College coach: Indiana State 1975-1982, Fresno State 1983-88, Ohio State 1989-1990, Purdue 1991-94. Pro coach: Joined Broncos in 1995.
Rich Tuten, strength and conditioning; born December 30, 1953, Columbia, S.C. Nose guard Clemson 1976-78. No pro playing experience. College coach: Florida 1979-1988, 1993-94, North Carolina 1989-1992. Pro coach: Joined Broncos in 1995.
Steve Watson, wide receivers; born May 28, 1957, Baltimore. Wide receiver Temple 1975-78. Pro wide receiver Denver 1979-1987. Pro coach: Joined Broncos in 2001.

**American Football Conference
South Division**
Team Colors: Deep Steel Blue, Battle
Red, and Liberty White
Two Reliant Park
Houston, Texas 77054
Telephone: (832) 667-2000

2006 SCHEDULE
PRESEASON
Aug. 12 **Kansas City** 7:00
Aug. 19 at St. Louis...........................7:00
Aug. 27 at Denver.............................6:00
Aug. 31 **Tampa Bay**.........................7:00

REGULAR SEASON
Sept. 10 **Philadelphia** 12:00
Sept. 17 at Indianapolis 1:00
Sept. 24 **Washington** 12:00
Oct. 1 **Miami** 12:00
Oct. 8 Open Date
Oct. 15 at Dallas........................... 12:00
Oct. 22 **Jacksonville**....................12:00
Oct. 29 at Tennessee 12:00
Nov. 5   at N.Y. Giants.....................1:00
Nov. 12 at Jacksonville....................1:00
Nov. 19 **Buffalo**...........................12:00
Nov. 26 at N.Y. Jets 1:00
Dec. 3   at Oakland 1:05
Dec. 10 **Tennessee** 12:00
Dec. 17 at New England 1:00
Dec. 24 **Indianapolis**....................12:00
Dec. 31 **Cleveland** 12:00

Stadium: Reliant Stadium
(opened in 2002)
• **Capacity:** 71,054
Houston, Texas 77054
Playing Surface: Grass
Training Camp: Reliant Park Practice
Facility

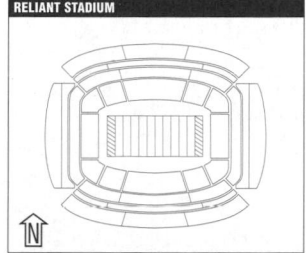

RELIANT STADIUM

CLUB OFFICIALS
Chairman and CEO: Robert C. McNair
Vice Chairman: Philip Burguieres
Senior Vice President and General
Manager/Football Operations:
TBD
President, Business Operations:
Jamey Rootes
Senior Vice President, Treasurer and
Chief Financial Officer:
Scott Schwinger
Senior Vice President, General Counsel
and Chief Administrative Officer:
Suzie Thomas
Vice President, Ticket Operations:
John Schriever
Vice President, Communications:
Tony Wyllie
Vice President, Sales and Marketing:
John Vidalin
Vice President, Marketing:
Kim Babiak Phillips
Vice President, Operations: Barry Asimos
Controller: Marilan Logan
Vice President, Football Administration:
Dan Ferens
Director of Pro Scouting: Chuck Banker
Associate Directors of Pro Scouting:
Bobby Grier, Miller McCalmon
Pro Scout: Rob Kisiel
Coordinator of College Scouting:
Mike Maccagnan
National Scout: George Saimes
College Scouts: Larry Bryan,
Eugene Armstrong, Pete Russell,
Dave Sears, Rob Lohman,
Tom Throckmorton
Pro and College Scouting Administrator:
Brian Hudspeth
Director of Corporate Development:
Ted Major, Greg Grissom
Director of Security: Ryan Reichert
Director of Community Relations:
Regina Woolfolk
Director of Internet Services &
Publications: Carter Toole
Director of Media Relations:
Kevin Cooper
Director of Player Programs:
Marcus Heard
Director of Information Technology:
Nick Ignatiev
Executive Director, Houston Texans
Foundation: Joanie Haley
Director of Finance: Greg Watson
Assistant Treasurer: Jan Southern
Human Resources Manager:
Glenda Morrison
Corporate Counsel: Greg Kondritz
Risk Manager: Jan Kelly
Head Athletic Trainer: Kevin Bastin
Coordinator of Rehabilitation: Tom Colt
Assistant Athletic Trainer: Jon Ishop
Director of Equipment Services:
Jay Brunetti
Assistant Equipment Managers:
Matt Grupp, Christian Snell
Director of Video Operations:
Ken Sparacino
Assistant Director of Video Operations:
Joe Malota
Video Operations Assistant: Robert Wells

COACHING HISTORY
(18-46-0)
2002-05   Dom Capers.................18-46-0

ATTENDANCE
Home 547,677   Away 511,891
Total 1,059,568
Single-game home record,
70,758 (12/21/03)
Single-season home record,
555,421 (2004)

2006 DRAFT CHOICES
Round	Name	Pos.	College
1	Mario Williams	DE	North Carolina St.
2	DeMeco Ryans	LB	Alabama
3	Charles Spencer	T	Pittsburgh
	Eric Winston	T	Miami
4	Owen Daniels	TE	Wisconsin
6	Wali Lundy	RB	Virginia
7	David Anderson	WR	Colorado State

2005 TEAM RECORD
PRESEASON (1-3)

Date	Result	Opponent
8/13	L 14-20	Denver
8/20	W 19-17	Oakland
8/27	L 9-21	at Dallas
9/1	L 14-38	at Tampa Bay

REGULAR SEASON (2-14)

Date	Result	Opponent	Att.
9/11	L 7-22	at Buffalo	71,781
9/18	L 7-27	Pittsburgh	70,742
10/2	L 10-16	at Cincinnati	65,714
10/9	L 20-34	Tennessee	70,430
10/16	L 10-42	at Seattle	66,196
10/23	L 20-38	Indianapolis	70,621
10/30	W 19-16	Cleveland	70,064
11/6	L 14-21	at Jacksonville	64,613
11/13	L 17-31	at Indianapolis	57,209
11/20	L 17-45	Kansas City	70,481
11/27	L 27-33	St. Louis (OT)	70,010
12/4	L 15-16	at Baltimore	69,909
12/11	L 10-13	at Tennessee	69,149
12/18	W 30-19	Arizona	70,024
12/24	L 20-38	Jacksonville	70,025
1/1	L 17-20	at S.F. (OT)	67,970

(OT) Overtime

SCORE BY PERIODS

Texans	40	111	64	45	0 —	260
Opponents	84	115	83	140	9 —	431

2005 TEAM STATISTICS

	Texans	Opp.
Total First Downs	243	348
Rushing	89	123
Passing	142	188
Penalty	12	37
3rd Down: Made/Att	75/219	75/196
3rd Down Pct.	34.2	38.3
4th Down: Made/Att	8/17	13/20
4th Down Pct.	47.1	65.0
Possession Avg.	28:10	31:50
Total Net Yards	4,053	5,824
Avg. Per Game	253.3	364.0
Total Plays	954	1,012
Avg. Per Play	4.2	5.8
Net Yards Rushing	1,816	2,303
Avg. Per Game	113.5	143.9
Total Rushes	437	506
Net Yards Passing	2,237	3,521
Avg. Per Game	139.8	220.1
Sacked/Yards Lost	68/424	37/206
Gross Yards	2,661	3,727
Att./Completions	449/270	469/304
Completion Pct.	60.1	64.8
Had Intercepted	13	7
Punts/Average	77/38.8	63/40.1
Net Punting Avg.	77/35.7	63/34.4
Penalties/Yards	106/854	105/846
Fumbles/Ball Lost	30/11	24/9
Touchdowns	26	50
Rushing	9	21
Passing	15	24
Returns	2	5

2005 INDIVIDUAL STATISTICS

PASSING	Att.	Comp.	Yds.	Pct.	TD	Int.	Tkld.	Rate
Carr	423	256	2,488	60.5	14	11	68/424	77.2
Banks	25	14	173	56.0	1	2	0/0	57.6
D. Davis	1	0	0	0.0	0	0	0/0	39.6
Texans	449	270	2,661	60.1	15	13	68/424	76.0
Opponents	469	304	3,727	64.8	24	7	37/206	100.0

SCORING	TD R	TD P	TD Rt	PAT	FG	Saf	PTS
K. Brown	0	0	0	24/24	26/34	0	102
D. Davis	2	4	0	0/0	0/0	0	36
Bradford	0	5	0	0/0	0/0	0	32
Wells	4	0	0	0/0	0/0	0	24
Mathis	0	1	2	0/0	0/0	0	18
Gaffney	0	2	0	0/0	0/0	0	12
A. Johnson	0	2	0	0/0	0/0	0	12
Morency	2	0	0	0/0	0/0	0	12
Carr	1	0	0	0/0	0/0	0	6
Norris	0	1	0	0/0	0/0	0	6
Texans	9	15	2	24/24	26/34	0	260
Opponents	21	24	5	47/47	28/32	0	431

2-Pt. Conversions: Bradford.
Texans 1-2, Opponents 0-2.

RUSHING	No.	Yds	Avg	LG	TD
D. Davis	230	976	4.2	44	2
Wells	90	325	3.6	14t	4
Carr	56	308	5.5	20	1
Morency	46	184	4.0	25t	2
Gaffney	4	13	3.3	10	0
A. Johnson	6	10	1.7	5	0
K. Brown	1	4	4.0	4	0
Stanley	1	0	0.0	0	0
Banks	2	-2	-1.0	-1	0
Bradford	1	-2	-2.0	-2	0
Texans	437	1,816	4.2	44	9
Opponents	506	2,303	4.6	49	21

RECEIVING	No.	Yds	Avg	LG	TD
A. Johnson	63	688	10.9	53t	2
Gaffney	55	492	8.9	29	2
D. Davis	39	337	8.6	33	4
Bradford	34	436	12.8	50t	5
Rivers	24	168	7.0	20	0
Wells	22	179	8.1	20	0
Morency	10	87	8.7	16	0
Armstrong	9	115	12.8	28	0
Mathis	5	65	13.0	34t	1
Morgan	4	42	10.5	14	0
Murphy	2	26	13.0	14	0
Bruener	2	22	11.0	19	0
Norris	1	4	4.0	4t	1
Texans	270	2,661	9.9	53t	15
Opponents	304	3,727	12.3	56t	24

INTERCEPTIONS	No.	Yds	Avg	LG	TD
Earl	2	2	1.0	2	0
Sanders	1	29	29.0	29	0
Coleman	1	6	6.0	6	0
C. Brown	1	5	5.0	5	0
T. Evans	1	3	3.0	3	0
Robinson	1	1	1.0	1	0
Texans	7	46	6.6	29	0
Opponents	13	225	17.3	57t	3

PUNTING	No.	Yds.	Avg.	In 20	LG
Stanley	77	2,990	38.8	29	61
Texans	77	2,990	38.8	29	61
Opponents	63	2,528	40.1	17	59

PUNT RETURNS	Ret	FC	Yds	Avg	LG	TD
Buchanon	12	6	101	8.4	37	0
Mathis	12	0	68	5.7	19	0
D. Davis	3	1	24	8.0	21	0
Morgan	3	0	30	10.0	23	0
Texans	30	7	223	7.4	37	0
Opponents	33	27	219	6.6	52t	1

KICKOFF RETURNS	No.	Yds	Avg	LG	TD
Mathis	54	1,542	28.6	99t	2
Morency	20	437	21.9	31	0
Wells	5	106	21.2	40	0
Hollings	2	46	23.0	28	0
D. Davis	1	29	29.0	29	0
Bruener	1	11	11.0	11	0
Norris	1	2	2.0	2	0
Texans	84	2,173	25.9	99t	2
Opponents	55	1,194	21.7	71	0

FIELD GOALS	1-19	20-29	30-39	40-49	50+
K. Brown	0/0	9/9	12/17	4/6	1/2
Texans	0/0	9/9	12/17	4/6	1/2
Opponents	0/0	9/9	11/11	7/10	1/2

SACKS	No.
Orr	7.0
Peek	6.0
Babin	4.0
Payne	4.0
Polk	3.5
Greenwood	2.0
Smith	1.5
C. Anderson	1.0
DeLoach	1.0
T. Johnson	1.0
Malone	1.0
McKenzie	1.0
Robinson	1.0
Simmons	1.0
G. Walker	1.0
Wong	1.0
Texans	37.0
Opponents	68.0

RECORD HOLDERS
INDIVIDUAL RECORDS—CAREER

Category	Name	Performance
Rushing (Yds.)	Domanick Davis, 2003-05	3,195
Passing (Yds.)	David Carr, 2002-05	10,624
Passing (TDs)	David Carr, 2002-05	48
Receiving (No.)	Andre Johnson, 2003-05	208
Receiving (Yds.)	Andre Johnson, 2003-05	2,806
Interceptions	Marcus Coleman, 2002-05	11
	Aaron Glenn, 2002-04	11
Punting (Avg.)	Chad Stanley, 2002-05	40.9
Punt Return (Avg.)	Avion Black, 2002	13.4
Kickoff Return (Avg.)	Jerome Mathis, 2005	28.6
Field Goals	Kris Brown, 2002-05	78
Touchdowns (Tot.)	Domanick Davis, 2003-05	28
Points	Kris Brown, 2002-05	339

INDIVIDUAL RECORDS—SINGLE SEASON

Category	Name	Performance
Rushing (Yds.)	Domanick Davis, 2004	1,188
Passing (Yds.)	David Carr, 2004	3,531
Passing (TDs)	David Carr, 2004	16
Receiving (No.)	Andre Johnson, 2004	79
Receiving (Yds.)	Andre Johnson, 2004	1,142
Interceptions	Marcus Coleman, 2003	7
Punting (Avg.)	Chad Stanley, 2003	41.5
Punt Return (Avg.)	Avion Black, 2002	13.4
Kickoff Return (Avg.)	Jerome Mathis, 2005	28.6
Field Goals	Kris Brown, 2005	26
Touchdowns (Tot.)	Domanick Davis, 2004	14
Points	Kris Brown, 2005	102

INDIVIDUAL RECORDS—SINGLE GAME

Category	Name	Performance
Rushing (Yds.)	Domanick Davis, 12-26-04	158
Passing (Yds.)	David Carr, 10-10-04	372
Passing (TDs)	David Carr, 10-10-04	3
	David Carr, 11-27-05	3
Receiving (No.)	Andre Johnson, 10-10-04	12
	Andre Johnson, 11-27-05	12
Receiving (Yds.)	Andre Johnson, 10-10-04	170
Interceptions	Aaron Glenn, 12-8-02	2
	Marcus Coleman, 9-7-03	2
	Kenny Wright, 9-28-03	2
	Dunta Robinson, 10-3-04	2
Field Goals	Kris Brown, 9-7-03	5
Touchdowns (Tot.)	Many times	2
	Last time by Jonathan Wells, 12-18-05	
Points	Kris Brown, 9-7-03	15
	Kris Brown, 12-4-05	15

2006 VETERAN ROSTER

No.	Name	Pos.	Ht.	Wt.	Birthdate	NFL Exp.	College	Hometown	How Acq.	'05 Games/ Starts
50	Anderson, Charlie	LB	6-4	246	12/8/81	3	Mississippi	Jackson, Miss.	D6c-'04	16/0
88	Armstrong, Derick	WR	6-2	206	4/2/79	4	Arkansas-Monticello	Dallas, Texas	FA-'03	13/3
93	Babin, Jason	LB	6-2	252	5/24/80	3	Western Michigan	Kalamazoo. Mich.	D1b-'04	12/3
68	Bedell, Brad	T	6-4	318	2/12/77	5	Colorado	Arcadia, Calif.	FA-'06	0*
24	Brown, C.C.	S	6-0	199	1/27/83	2	Louisiana-Lafayette	Greenwood, Miss.	D6-'05	13/13
3	Brown, Kris	K	5-11	205	12/23/76	8	Nebraska	Southlake, Texas	RFA(Pitt)-'02	16/0
87	Bruener, Mark	TE	6-4	258	9/16/72	12	Washington	Olympia, Wash.	UFA(Pitt)-'04	16/15
31	Buchanon, Phillip	CB	5-10	187	9/19/80	5	Miami	Ft. Meyers, Fla.	T(Oak)-'05	10/6
8	Carr, David	QB	6-3	215	7/21/79	5	Fresno State	Bakersfield, Calif.	D1-'02	16/16
43	Cook, Jameel	FB	5-10	237	2/8/79	6	Illinois	Miami, Fla.	UFA(TB)-'06	16/0*
57	Cowart, Sam	LB	6-2	245	2/26/75	9	Florida State	Jacksonville, Fla.	UFA(Minn)-'06	15/14*
39	Curtis, Kevin	S	6-2	210	7/28/80	2	Texas Tech	Lubbock, Texas	FA-'06	0*
37	Davis, Domanick	RB	5-9	223	10/1/80	4	Louisiana State	Breaux Bridge, La.	D4-'03	11/11
86	Doering, Chris	WR	6-4	201	5/19/73	11	Florida	Gainesville, Fla.	FA-'06	0*
26	Earl, Glenn	S	6-1	216	6/10/81	3	Notre Dame	Naperville, Ill.	D4-'04	10/7
54	Evans, Troy	LB	6-1	238	12/3/77	5	Cincinnati	Cincinnati, Ohio	FA-'02	16/0
38	Faggins, Demarcus	CB	5-10	178	6/13/79	5	Kansas State	Irving, Texas	D6a-'02	13/10
10	Filipovic, Filip	P	6-2	221	11/5/77	2	South Dakota	Youngstown, Ohio	FA-'06	0*
58	Flanagan, Mike	C	6-5	301	11/10/73	11	UCLA	Sacramento, Calif.	UFA(GB)-'06	14/14*
36	Floyd, Anthony	S	5-10	202	2/1/81	2	Louisville	Youngstown, Ohio	FA-'06	0*
56	Greenwood, Morlon	LB	6-0	236	7/17/78	6	Syracuse	Freeport, N.Y.	UFA(Mia)-'05	16/16
63	Hodgdon, Drew	C	6-3	292	11/15/81	2	Arizona State	Palo Alto, Calif.	D5-'05	4/3
80	Johnson, Andre	WR	6-3	219	7/11/81	4	Miami	Miami, Fla.	D1-'03	13/13
75	Johnson, Travis	DT	6-3	314	4/26/82	2	Florida State	Sherman Oaks, Calif.	D1-'05	15/3
83	Joppru, Bennie	TE	6-4	234	1/5/80	4	Michigan	Minnetonka, Minn.	D2-'03	0*
94	Kalu, N.D.	DE	6-3	265	8/3/75	10	Rice	San Antonio, Texas	UFA(Phil)-'06	15/8*
20	Lord, Jammal	S	6-2	225	1/10/82	2	Nebraska	Bayonne, N.J.	D6b-'04	0*
62	Loverne, David	G	6-3	299	5/22/76	8	San Jose State	Concord, Calif.	FA-'06	0*
13	Mathis, Jerome	WR	5-11	192	7/26/83	2	Hampton	Petersburg, Va.	D4-'05	12/0
28	McKenzie, Chris	CB	5-8	178	3/17/82	2	Arizona State	Queens, N.Y.	FA-'05	3/0
76	McKinney, Steve	G	6-4	300	10/15/75	9	Texas A&M	Friendswood, Texas	UFA(Ind)-'02	16/16
34	Morency, Vernand	RB	5-9	213	2/4/80	2	Oklahoma State	Miami, Fla.	D3-'05	13/1
11	Morgan, Donovan	WR	6-2	190	7/29/82	2	Louisiana-Lafayette	New Orleans, La.	FA-'05	3/0
84 t-	Moulds, Eric	WR	6-2	210	7/17/73	11	Mississippi State	Lucedale, Miss.	T(Buff)-'06	15/15*
79	Murphy, Matt	T	6-5	277	2/23/80	4	Maryland	New Haven, Mich.	FA-'03	9/2
53	Orr, Shantee	LB	6-0	235	5/28/81	4	Michigan	Detroit, Mich.	FA-'03	16/12
91	Payne, Seth	DT	6-4	302	2/12/75	10	Cornell	Victor, N.Y.	ED(Jax)-'02	16/14
98+	Peek, Antwan	LB	6-3	237	10/29/79	4	Cincinnati	Cincinnati, Ohio	D3-'03	16/16
55	Pettway, Kenneth	LB	6-3	239	11/13/82	2	Grambling State	Gilmer, Texas	D7-'05	0*
95	Pierce, Terry	LB	6-1	252	7/21/81	3	Kansas State	Fort Worth, Texas	FA-'06	0*
48	Pittman, Bryan	LS	6-3	278	1/20/77	4	Washington	Auburn, Wash.	FA-'03	16/0
69	Pitts, Chester	G	6-4	323	6/26/79	5	San Diego State	Inglewood, Calif.	D2-'02	16/16
51	Polk, DaShon	LB	6-2	238	3/13/77	7	Arizona	Pacoima, Calif.	UFA(Buff)-'04	16/11
89	Putzier, Jeb	TE	6-4	256	1/20/79	5	Boise State	Eagle, Idaho	FA-'06	16/4*
15	Ragone, Dave	QB	6-3	226	10/3/79	4	Louisville	Middleberg, Ohio	D3c-'03	0*
96	Rainer, Wali	LB	6-2	240	4/19/77	8	Virginia	Charlotte, N.C.	UFA(Det)-'06	16/5*
23	Robinson, Dunta	CB	5-10	172	4/11/82	3	South Carolina	Athens, Ga.	D1a-'04	16/16
18	Rosenfels, Sage	QB	6-4	224	3/6/78	6	Iowa State	Maquoketa, Iowa	UFA(Mia)-'06	4/1*
74	Salaam, Ephraim	T	6-7	300	6/19/76	9	San Diego State	Sacramento, Calif.	UFA(Jax)-'06	5/2*
21	Sanders, Lewis	CB	6-1	208	6/22/78	7	Maryland	Staten Island, N.Y.	UFA(Cle)-'05	12/4
19	Schifino, Jake	WR	6-1	201	11/15/79	4	Akron	Penn Hills, Pa.	FA-'06	0*
30	Simmons, Jason	S	5-9	202	3/30/76	9	Arizona State	Lawndale, Calif.	UFA(Pitt)-'02	14/1
32	Smith, Antowain	RB	6-2	232	3/14/72	10	Houston	Millbrook, Ala.	UFA(NO)-'06	16/7*
99	Smith, Robaire	DT	6-4	315	11/15/77	7	Michigan State	Flint, Mich.	UFA(Tenn)-'04	16/16
7	Stanley, Chad	P	6-3	210	1/29/76	7	Stephen F. Austin	Ore City, Texas	FA-'02	16/0
82	Steele, Ben	TE	6-5	260	5/27/78	3	Mesa College	Denver, Colo.	FA-'06	2/0*
42	Stone, Michael	S	6-0	201	2/13/78	5	Memphis	Southfield, Mich.	UFA(NE)-'06	13/3*
71	Wade, Todd	T	6-8	314	10/30/76	7	Mississippi	Jackson, Miss.	UFA(Mia)-'04	9/9
22	Walker, Ramon	S	6-0	210	11/8/79	5	Pittsburgh	Akron, Ohio	D5b-'02	16/0
85	Walter, Kevin	WR	6-3	219	8/4/81	4	Eastern Michigan	Vernon Hills, Ill.	RFA(Cin)-'06	16/2*
78	Wand, Seth	T	6-7	337	8/6/79	4	Northwestern Missouri State	Springfield, Mo.	D3b-'03	13/0
70	Weary, Fred	G	6-4	313	9/30/77	5	Tennessee	Montgomery, Ala.	D3a-'02	4/4
92	Weaver, Anthony	DE/DT	6-3	282	7/28/80	5	Notre Dame	Saratoga, N.Y.	UFA(Balt)-'06	10/8*
32#	Wells, Jonathan	RB	6-1	252	7/21/79	5	Ohio State	River Ridge, La.	D4-'02	15/6
72	Wiegert, Zach	T	6-5	296	8/16/72	12	Nebraska	Fremont, Neb.	UFA(Jax)-'03	12/12
52	Wong, Kailee	LB	6-2	245	5/23/76	8	Stanford	Eugene, Ore.	UFA(Minn)-'02	5/5

* Bedell last active with Green Bay in '04; Cook played 16 games for Tampa Bay in '05; Cowart played 15 games for Minnesota; Curtis last active with San Francisco in '02; Doering last active with Pittsburgh in '04; Filipovic last active with Dallas in '02; Flanagan played 14 games for Green Bay; Floyd last active with Indianapolis in '04; Joppru spent '05 season on reserve/physically unable to perform list; Kalu played 15 games for Philadelphia; Lord inactive for 1 game; Loverne missed '05 season with Detroit because of injury; Moulds played 15 games with Buffalo; Pettway inactive for 4 games; Pierce last active with Denver in '04; Putzier played 16 games for Denver; Ragone inactive for 16 games with Detroit; Rosenfels played 4 games with Miami; Salaam played 5 games with Jacksonville; Schifino last active with Tennessee in '04; A. Smith played 16 games with New Orleans; Steele played 2 games with Green Bay; Stone played 13 games with New England; Walter played 16 games with Cincinnati; Weaver played 10 games with Baltimore.

+ Restricted free agent; subject to developments.

Unrestricted free agent; subject to developments.

t- Texans traded for Moulds (Buff).

Players lost through free agency (6): CB Jason Bell (NYG; 16 games in '05), WR Corey Bradford (Det; 16), G Milford Brown (Ariz; 13), WR Jabar Gaffney (Phil; 16), TE Marcellus Rivers (Oak; 16), G Tyson Walter (Wash; 0).

Also played with Texans in '05—RB Jason Anderson (1 game), QB Tony Banks (1), LB Frank Chamberlin (9), S Marcus Coleman (15), DE Jerry DeLoach (11), RB Tony Hollings (2), DT Junior Ioane (12), FB Moran Norris (16), T Victor Riley (10), DE Gary Walker (11), C Todd Washington (15).

2006 FIRST-YEAR ROSTER

Name	Pos.	Ht.	Wt.	Birthdate	College	Hometown	How Acq.
Alexander, Phillip	DE	6-4	265	6/1/83	Duke	Bronx, N.Y.	FA
Anderson, David	WR	5-10	193	7/28/83	Colorado State	Thousand Oaks, Calif.	D7
Baker, Matt	QB	6-3	210	5/11/83	North Carolina	Rochester Hills, Mich.	FA
Brisiel, Mike	G	6-5	282	3/14/83	Colorado State	Fayetteville, Ark.	FA
Brock, Fred	LB	6-4	233	10/10/83	Texas Southern	San Antonio, Texas	FA
Chaisson, Kelvin	G	6-4	290	10/3/82	Oklahoma	Beaumont, Texas	FA
Charleston, Jeff	DE	6-4	260	1/19/83	Idaho State	Monmouth, Ore.	FA
Chick, John	DE	6-4	257	11/20/82	Utah State	Gillette, Wyo.	FA
Daniels, Owen	TE	6-3	247	11/9/82	Wisconsin	Naperville, Ill.	D4
Davis, Jason (1)	DE	6-3	320	5/12/80	West Virginia	Ft. Lauderdale, Fla.	FA
Estelle, Mark (1)	CB	5-10	180	7/29/81	Utah State	Carson, Calif.	FA
Halterman, Aaron (1)	TE	6-5	255	3/31/82	Indiana	Greenwood, Ind.	FA
Harris, Elliott (1)	DE	6-3	285	10/29/81	Arkansas	Marianna, Ark.	FA
Hill, Quadtrine	FB	6-2	228	11/18/82	Miami	Sunrise, Fla.	FA
Lundy, Wali	RB	5-10	214	9/8/83	Virginia	Delran, N.J.	D6
Malone, Alfred (1)	DT	6-5	311	2/21/82	Troy	Frisco City, Ala.	FA-'05
Porter, Quinton	QB	6-5	233	12/28/82	Boston College	Portland, Maine	FA
Rhodes, Damien	RB	6-0	217	4/26/84	Syracuse	Manlius, N.Y.	FA
Ross, Richie	WR	6-4	205	8/28/82	Nebraska-Kearney	Lincoln, Neb.	FA
Ryans, DeMeco	LB	6-1	229	7/28/84	Alabama	Bessemer, Ala.	D2
Scandrett, Devarick	DE	6-4	276	1/23/84	Middle Tennessee State	Forsythe, Ga.	FA
Spencer, Charles	T	6-4	352	3/17/82	Pittsburgh	Poughkeepsie, N.Y.	D3a
Starling, Kendrick (1)	WR	6-0	193	12/27/79	San Jose State	Marshall, Texas	FA
Taylor, Chris	RB	6-0	220	11/7/83	Indiana	Memphis, Tenn.	FA
Torrey, Andre (1)	LB	6-4	245	1/28/82	Arizona	Alameda, Calif.	FA
Walker, John	CB	6-1	200	4/25/83	Southern California	North Hills, Calif.	FA
Weaver, Jarrell (1)	S	6-2	207	12/28/80	Miami	Miami, Fla.	FA
Weaver, Scott	FB	6-4	260	4/7/83	Portland State	Eugene, Ore.	FA
Williams, Mario	DE	6-6	291	1/31/85	North Carolina State	Richlands, N.C.	D1
Williams, Tramon	CB	5-11	181	3/16/83	Louisiana Tech	Houma, La.	FA
Winston, Eric	T	6-5	310	11/17/83	Miami	Midland, Texas	D3b

The term NFL Rookie is defined as a player who is in his first season of professional football and has not been on the roster of another professional football team for any regular-season or postseason games. A Rookie is designated by an "R" on NFL rosters. Players who have been active in another professional football league or players who have NFL experience, including either preseason training camp or being on an Active List or Inactive List, or on Reserve/Injured or Reserve/Physically Unable to Perform for fewer than six regular-season games, are termed NFL First-Year Players. An NFL First-Year Player is designated by a "1" on NFL rosters. Thereafter, a player is credited with an additional year of experience for each season in which he accumulates six games on the Active List or Inactive List, or on Reserve/Injured or Reserve/Physically Unable to Perform.

Log on to www.houstontexans.com for an up-to-date roster.

COACHING STAFF

Head Coach,
Gary Kubiak

Pro Career: Gary Kubiak was introduced as the second head coach in Houston Texans history on January 26, 2006. Kubiak returns to Houston to start his head coaching career after spending 20 of the past 23 years in the Denver area, first as a player and then later as an assistant coach. For the last 11 years, Kubiak served as Denver's offensive coordinator, helping guide the Broncos to back-to-back World Championships in Super Bowls XXXII and XXXIII and three AFC West Division titles. Kubiak tutored Hall of Fame quarterback John Elway from 1995-98 and oversaw the most dominant rushing attack in the NFL. In 1998, running back Terrell Davis was named NFL Most Valuable Player after becoming the fourth player in league history to rush for over 2,000 yards. In Kubiak's 11 years in Denver, the Broncos had 28 Pro Bowl players on the offensive side of the ball. Kubiak began his coaching career in 1992 at his alma mater, Texas A&M, as running backs coach. There he guided Greg Hill to second-team All-America honors in 1993. Kubiak started his NFL coaching career with the San Francisco 49ers as the quarterbacks coach. In his lone season in San Francisco, he guided Hall of Fame quarterback Steve Young to league MVP honors. Under Kubiak's tutelage, Young posted an NFL-record 112.8 quarterback rating and was named MVP of Super Bowl XXIX after tossing a Super Bowl-record six touchdown passes. Kubiak is a veteran of six Super Bowls—three as a player and three as a coach—and has coached three World Championship teams. Career record: 0-0.

Background: Kubiak starred at quarterback for Texas A&M from 1979-1982, earning all-Southwest Conference honors as a senior. He played for the Broncos from 1983-1991 as the backup to Elway. Kubiak played in 119 games during his career and tossed 14 touchdowns in that span. During his time as a player in the Mile High City, he was a part of three teams that reached the Super Bowl.

Personal: Born August 15, 1961 in Houston. He and his wife, Rhonda, have three sons—Klint, Klay and Klein.

ASSISTANT COACHES

Martin Bayless, asst. defensive backs; born October 11, 1962, Dayton, Ohio. Defensive back Bowling Green 1981-83. Pro defensive back St. Louis Cardinals 1984, Buffalo Bills 1984-86, San Diego Chargers 1987-1991, Kansas City Chiefs 1992-93, 1995-96, Washington Redskins 1994. College coach: North Carolina 2001. Pro coach: Amsterdam Admirals (NFLEL) 2002-03, Carolina Panthers 2003, Oakland Raiders 2004-05, joined Texans in 2006.

John Benton, offensive line; born December 13, 1963, Los Angeles. Offensive lineman Colorado State 1986-1990. No pro playing experience. College coach: California University (Pa.) 1990-94, Colorado State 1996-2003. Pro coach: St. Louis Rams 2004-05, joined Texans in 2006.

Troy Calhoun, offensive coordinator/quarterbacks; born September 26, 1966, McMinnville, Ore. Quarterback Air Force 1986-89. No pro playing experience. College coach: Air Force 1989, 1993-94, Ohio University 1994-2000, Wake Forest 2001-02. Pro coach: Denver Broncos 2003-05, joined Texans in 2006.

Chick Harris, running backs; born September 21, 1945, Durham, N.C. Running back Northern Arizona 1966-69. No pro playing experience. College coach: Colorado State 1970-71, Long Beach State 1972-73, Washington 1975-1980. Pro coach: Detroit Wheels (WFL) 1974, Buffalo Bills 1981-82, Seattle Seahawks 1983-1991, Los Angeles Rams 1992-94, Carolina Panthers 1995-2001, joined Texans in 2002.

Jon Hoke, defensive backs; born January 24, 1957, Kettering, Ohio. Defensive back Ball State 1976-1979. Pro defensive back Chicago Bears 1980. College coach: Bowling Green 1983-86, San Diego State 1987-88, Kent State 1989-1993, Missouri 1994-98, Florida 1999-2001. Pro coach: Joined Texans in 2002.

Johnny Holland, linebackers; born March 11, 1965, Belleville, Texas. Linebacker Texas A&M 1983-86. Pro linebacker Green Bay Packers 1987-1993. Pro coach: Green Bay Packers 1995-99, Seattle Seahawks 2000-02, Detroit Lions 2003-05, joined Texans in 2006.

Bob Karmelowicz, defensive line; born July 22, 1949, New Britain, Conn. Nose tackle Bridgeport 1968-1971. No pro playing experience. College coach: Arizona State 1975-79, Massachusetts 1980, Texas-El Paso 1981, Nevada-Las Vegas 1982, Illinois 1983-86, Washington State 1987-88, Miami 1989-1991. Pro coach: Cincinnati Bengals 1992-93, Washington Redskins 1994-96, Kansas City Chiefs 1997-2005, joined Texans in 2006.

Joe Marciano, special teams coordinator; born February 10, 1954, Dunmore, Pa. Quarterback Temple 1972-75. No pro playing experience. College coach: East Stroudsburg State 1977, Rhode Island 1978-79, Villanova 1980, Penn State 1981, Temple 1982. Pro coach: Philadelphia/Baltimore Stars (USFL) 1983-85, New Orleans Saints 1986-1995, Tampa Bay Buccaneers 1996-2001, joined Texans in 2002.

Mike McDaniel, offensive quality control; born March 6, 1983, Greeley, Colo. Wide receiver Yale 2001-04. No pro playing experience. Pro coach: Joined Texans in 2006.

Brian Pariani, tight ends; born July 2, 1965, San Francisco. No college or pro playing experience. College coach: UCLA 1989, Syracuse 2005. Pro coach: San Francisco 49ers 1991-94, Denver Broncos 1994-2004, joined Texans in 2006.

Robert Saleh, defensive quality control; born January 31, 1979, Dearborn, Mich. Tight end Northern Michigan 1997-2000. No pro playing experience. College coach: Michigan State 2002-03, Central Michigan 2004. Pro coach: Joined Texans in 2005.

Kyle Shanahan, wide receivers; born December 14, 1979, Minneapolis. Wide receiver Duke 1998-99, Texas 2000-02. No pro playing experience. College coach: UCLA 2003. Pro coach: Tampa Bay Buccaneers 2004-05, joined Texans in 2006.

Mike Sherman, asst. head coach/offense; born December 19, 1954, Norwood, Mass. Guard/tackle/linebacker Central Connecticut State 1974, 1976-77. No pro playing experience. College coach: Pittsburgh 1981-82, Tulane 1983-84, Holy Cross 1985-88, Texas A&M 1989-1993, 1995-96, UCLA 1994. Pro coach: Green Bay 1995-96, 2000-05 (head coach 2000-05), joined Texans in 2006.

Tracy Simien, asst. defensive line; born May 21, 1967, Sweeny, Texas. Center/nose tackle/defensive end Texas Christian 1985-89. Pro linebacker Montreal Machine (WLAF) 1991, Kansas City Chiefs 1991-97, San Diego Chargers 1999. Pro coach: Cologne Centurions (NFLEL) 2005, joined Texans in 2006.

Richard Smith, defensive coordinator; born October 17, 1955, Los Angeles. Offensive lineman Rio Hondo (Calif.) J.C. 1975-76, Fresno State 1977-78. No pro playing experience. College coach: Rio Hondo (Calif.) J.C. 1979-1980, Cal State-Fullerton 1981-83, California 1984-86, Arizona 1987. Pro coach: Houston Oilers 1988-1992, Denver Broncos 1993-96, San Francisco 49ers 1997-2002, Detroit Lions 2003-04, Miami Dolphins 2005, joined Texans in 2006.

**American Football Conference
South Division
Team Colors:** Royal Blue and White
**P.O. Box 535000
Indianapolis, Indiana 46253
Telephone:** (317) 297-2658

2006 SCHEDULE
PRESEASON
Aug. 10 at St. Louis.........................7:00
Aug. 20 **Seattle**............................. 8:00
Aug. 27 at New Orleans (Jackson, MS)..6:00
Sept. 1 **Cincinnati** 7:00

REGULAR SEASON
Sep. 10 at N.Y. Giants.....................8:15
Sep. 17 **Houston** 1:00
Sep. 24 **Jacksonville**......................1:00
Oct. 1   at N.Y. Jets........................1:00
Oct. 8   **Tennessee** 1:00
Oct. 15 Open Date
Oct. 22 **Washington** 4:15
Oct. 29 at Denver 2:15
Nov. 5   at New England 8:15
Nov. 12 **Buffalo**.............................1:00
Nov. 19 at Dallas.......................... 12:00
Nov. 26 **Philadelphia** 1:00
Dec. 3   at Tennessee 12:00
Dec. 10 at Jacksonville....................1:00
Dec. 18 **Cincinnati** (Mon.)...............8:30
Dec. 24 at Houston 12:00
Dec. 31 **Miami**............................. 1:00

Stadium: RCA Dome (opened in 1983)
• **Capacity:** 55,531
100 South Capitol Avenue
Indianapolis, Indiana 46225
Playing Surface: FieldTurf
Training Camp: Rose-Hulman Institute
5500 Wabash Avenue
Terre Haute, IN 47803

RCA DOME

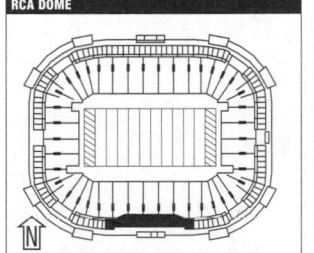

CLUB OFFICIALS
Owner and CEO: James Irsay
President: Bill Polian
Head Coach: Tony Dungy
Senior Executive Vice President:
Pete Ward
Executive Vice President: Bob Terpening
Senior Vice President of Sales and
Marketing: Tom Zupancic
Vice President of Football Operations:
Chris Polian
Assistant General Manager/Scouting:
Dom Anile
Vice President-Finance: Kurt Humphrey
Vice President-Ticket Operations/Guest
Relations: Larry Hall
Vice President-Public Relations:
Craig Kelley
Vice President of Sponsorship Sales:
Jay Souers
Vice President of Premium Seating and
Ticket Sales: Greg Hylton
Director of Pro Player Personnel:
Clyde Powers
Director of College Scouting: Mike Butler
Director of Player Development:
Steve Champlin
Executive Director of Administration:
Bill Brooks
Director of Community Relations/
Marketing: Nicole Duncan
Equipment Manager: Jon Scott
Video Director: Marty Heckscher
Head Trainer: Hunter Smith
Assistant Director of Public Relations:
Vernon Cheek
Assistant Equipment Managers:
Mike Mays, Sean Sullivan,
Brian Seabrooks
Assistant Trainers: Dave Hammer,
Dave Walston, Bryant Baugh
Assistant Video Director: John Starliper
Purchasing Administrator: Dave Filar

COACHING HISTORY
Baltimore 1953-1983
(403-393-7)
Records include postseason games

Year	Coach	Record
1953	Keith Molesworth	3-9-0
1954-1962	Weeb Ewbank	61-52-1
1963-69	Don Shula	73-26-4
1970-72	Don McCafferty*	26-11-1
1972	John Sandusky	4-5-0
1973-74	Howard Schnellenberger**	4-13-0
1974	Joe Thomas	2-9-0
1975-79	Ted Marchibroda	41-36-0
1980-81	Mike McCormack	9-23-0
1982-84	Frank Kush***	11-28-1
1984	Hal Hunter	0-1-0
1985-86	Rod Dowhower****	5-24-0
1986 1991	Ron Meyor#	36-36-0
1991	Rick Venturi	1-10-0
1992-95	Ted Marchibroda	32-35-0
1996-97	Lindy Infante	12-21-0
1998-2001	Jim Mora	32-34-0
2002-05	Tony Dungy	51-20-0

*Released after five games in 1972
**Released after three games in 1974
***Resigned after 15 games in 1984
****Released after 13 games in 1986
#Released after five games in 1991

ATTENDANCE
Home 442,644   Away 535,548
Total 978,192
Single-game home record,
61,139 (10/20/97)
Single-season home record, 481,305
(1984)

2006 DRAFT CHOICES
Round	Name	Pos.	College
1	Joseph Addai	RB	Louisiana State
2	Tim Jennings	DB	Georgia
3	Freddie Keiaho	LB	San Diego St.
5	Michael Toudouze	T	Texas Christian
6	Charlie Johnson	T	Oklahoma State
	Antoine Bethea	DB	Howard
7	T.J. Rushing	DB	Stanford

INDIANAPOLIS COLTS

2005 TEAM RECORD

PRESEASON (0-5)

Date	Result	Opponent
8/6	L 21-27	at Atlanta
8/13	L 10-17	Buffalo
8/20	L 17-24	Chicago
8/27	L 24-37	at Denver
9/2	L 0-38	at Cincinnati

REGULAR SEASON (14-2)

Date	Result	Opponent	Att.
9/11	W 24-7	at Baltimore	70,501
9/18	W 10-3	Jacksonville	56,460
9/25	W 13-6	Cleveland	57,127
10/2	W 31-10	at Tennessee	69,149
10/9	W 28-3	at San Francisco	68,084
10/17	W 45-28	St. Louis	57,307
10/23	W 38-20	at Houston	70,621
11/7	W 40-21	at New England	68,756
11/13	W 31-17	Houston	57,209
11/20	W 45-37	at Cincinnati	65,995
11/28	W 26-7	Pittsburgh	57,442
12/4	W 35-3	Tennessee	57,228
12/11	W 26-18	at Jacksonville	67,164
12/18	L 17-26	San Diego	57,389
12/24	L 13-28	at Seattle	67,855
1/1	W 17-13	Arizona	57,211

POSTSEASON (0-1)

1/15	L 18-21	Pittsburgh	57,449

SCORE BY PERIODS

Colts	90	122	119	108	0	—	439
Opponents	61	63	47	76	0	—	247

2005 TEAM STATISTICS

	Colts	Opp.
Total First Downs	363	269
Rushing	116	91
Passing	217	163
Penalty	30	15
3rd Down: Made/Att	91/187	76/207
3rd Down Pct.	48.7	36.7
4th Down: Made/Att	8/13	14/24
4th Down Pct.	61.5	58.3
Possession Avg.	30:22	29:38
Total Net Yards	5,799	4,913
Avg. Per Game	362.4	307.1
Total Plays	1,000	953
Avg. Per Play	5.8	5.2
Net Yards Rushing	1703	1762
Avg. Per Game	106.4	110.1
Total Rushes	465	398
Net Yards Passing	4,096	3,151
Avg. Per Game	256.0	196.9
Sacked/Yards Lost	20/95	46/318
Gross Yards	4,191	3,469
Att./Completions	515/347	509/343
Completion Pct.	67.4	67.4
Had Intercepted	11	18
Punts/Average	52/44.3	67/41.7
Net Punting Avg.	52/37.1	67/36.9
Penalties/Yards	94/690	119/857
Fumbles/Ball Lost	14/8	32/13
Touchdowns	53	27
Rushing	18	9
Passing	31	17
Returns	4	1

2005 INDIVIDUAL STATISTICS

PASSING	Att.	Comp.	Yds.	Pct.	TD	Int.	Tkld.	Rate
Manning	453	305	3,747	67.3	28	10	17/81	104.1
Sorgi	61	42	444	68.9	3	1	3/14	99.4
Smith	1	0	0	0.0	0	0	0/0	39.6
Colts	515	347	4,191	67.4	31	11	20/95	103.3
Opponents	509	343	3,469	67.4	17	18	46/318	83.0

SCORING	TD R	TD P	TD Rt	PAT	FG	Saf	PTS
Vanderjagt	0	0	0	52/52	23/25	0	121
James	13	1	0	0/0	0/0	0	84
Harrison	0	12	0	0/0	0/0	0	72
Wayne	0	5	0	0/0	0/0	0	30
Clark	0	4	0	0/0	0/0	0	24
Rhodes	4	0	0	0/0	0/0	0	24
Fletcher	0	3	0	0/0	0/0	0	18
Walters	0	3	0	0/0	0/0	0	18
June	0	0	2	0/0	0/0	0	12
Utecht	0	2	0	0/0	0/0	0	12
Carthon	1	0	0	0/0	0/0	0	6
Reagor	0	0	1	0/0	0/0	0	6
Stokley	0	1	0	0/0	0/0	0	6
Tripplett	0	0	1	0/0	0/0	0	6
Rayner	0	0	0	0/0	0/1	0	0
Colts	18	31	4	52/52	23/26	0	439
Opponents	9	17	1	24/24	19/27	0	247

2-Pt. Conversions: None.
Colts 0-1, Opponents 2-3.

RUSHING	No.	Yds	Avg	LG	TD
James	360	1,506	4.2	33	13
Rhodes	40	118	3.0	24	4
Manning	33	45	1.4	12	0
Carthon	13	18	1.4	7	1
Mungro	7	15	2.1	7	0
Sorgi	12	1	0.1	6	0
Colts	465	1,703	3.7	33	18
Opponents	398	1,762	4.4	83t	9

RECEIVING	No.	Yds	Avg	LG	TD
Wayne	83	1,055	12.7	66t	5
Harrison	82	1,146	14.0	80t	12
James	44	337	7.7	20	1
Stokley	41	543	13.2	45	1
Clark	37	488	13.2	56	4
Fletcher	18	202	11.2	23	3
Walters	14	152	10.9	39	3
Rhodes	12	88	7.3	15	0
Moorehead	7	75	10.7	24	0
Utecht	3	59	19.7	26t	2
Mungro	3	28	9.3	17	0
Hartsock	2	8	4.0	7	0
Carthon	1	10	10.0	10	0
Colts	347	4,191	12.1	80t	31
Opponents	343	3,469	10.1	68t	17

INTERCEPTIONS	No.	Yds	Avg	LG	TD
June	5	115	23.0	36	2
Brackett	3	50	16.7	31	0
Harper	3	41	13.7	21	0
David	2	13	6.5	13	0
Doss	2	8	4.0	8	0
Gardner	1	16	16.0	16	0
Jackson	1	16	16.0	16	0
Sanders	1	0	0.0	0	0
Colts	18	259	14.4	36	2
Opponents	11	136	12.4	36	0

PUNTING	No.	Yds.	Avg.	In 20	LG
Smith	52	2,301	44.3	23	58
Colts	52	2,301	44.3	23	58
Opponents	67	2,791	41.7	17	62

PUNT RETURNS	Ret	FC	Yds	Avg	LG	TD
Walters	21	25	172	8.2	29	0
David	1	0	0	0.0	0	0
Harrison	1	0	10	10.0	10	0
Jackson	1	0	0	0.0	0	0
Colts	24	25	182	7.6	29	0
Opponents	25	15	272	10.9	29	0

KICKOFF RETURNS	No.	Yds	Avg	LG	TD
Rhodes	41	855	20.9	39	0
Carthon	5	92	18.4	25	0
Mungro	2	39	19.5	22	0
Walters	1	13	13.0	13	0
Jefferson	1	11	11.0	11	0
Utecht	1	7	7.0	7	0
Colts	51	1017	19.9	39	0
Opponents	89	1978	22.2	89t	1

FIELD GOALS	1-19	20-29	30-39	40-49	50+
Vanderjagt	1/1	9/9	6/7	7/8	0/0
Rayner	0/0	0/0	0/0	0/0	0/1
Colts	1/1	9/9	6/7	7/8	0/1
Opponents	0/0	8/8	3/5	8/12	0/2

SACKS	No.
Mathis	11.5
Freeney	11.0
Brock	6.5
Reagor	5.5
Tripplett	4.0
Thomas	3.0
Thornton	2.0
Brackett	1.0
Gardner	1.0
Labinjo	0.5
Colts	46.0
Opponents	20.0

RECORD HOLDERS
INDIVIDUAL RECORDS—CAREER

Category	Name	Performance
Rushing (Yds.)	Edgerrin James, 1999-2005	9,226
Passing (Yds.)	Johnny Unitas, 1956-1972	39,768
Passing (TDs)	Johnny Unitas, 1956-1972	287
Receiving (No.)	Marvin Harrison, 1996-2005	927
Receiving (Yds.)	Marvin Harrison, 1996-2005	12,331
Interceptions	Bob Boyd, 1960-68	57
Punting (Avg.)	Chris Gardocki, 1995-98	44.8
Punt Return (Avg.)	Ron Gardin, 1970-71	13.5
Kickoff Return (Avg.)	Jim Duncan, 1969-1971	32.6
Field Goals	Mike Vanderjagt, 1998-2005	217
Touchdowns (Tot.)	Lenny Moore, 1956-1967	113
Points	Mike Vanderjagt, 1998-2005	995

INDIVIDUAL RECORDS—SINGLE SEASON

Category	Name	Performance
Rushing (Yds.)	Edgerrin James, 2000	1,709
Passing (Yds.)	Peyton Manning, 2004	4,557
Passing (TDs)	Peyton Manning, 2004	*49
Receiving (No.)	Marvin Harrison, 2002	*143
Receiving (Yds.)	Marvin Harrison, 2002	1,722
Interceptions	Tom Keane, 1953	11
Punting (Avg.)	Rohn Stark, 1985	45.9
Punt Return (Avg.)	Clarence Verdin, 1989	12.9
Kickoff Return (Avg.)	Jim Duncan, 1970	35.4
Field Goals	Mike Vanderjagt, 2003	37
Touchdowns (Tot.)	Lenny Moore, 1964	20
Points	Mike Vanderjagt, 2003	157

INDIVIDUAL RECORDS—SINGLE GAME

Category	Name	Performance
Rushing (Yds.)	Edgerrin James, 10-15-00	219
Passing (Yds.)	Peyton Manning, 10-31-04	472
Passing (TDs)	Peyton Manning, 9-28-03, 11-25-04	6
Receiving (No.)	Marvin Harrison, 12-26-99, 11-17-02	14
Receiving (Yds.)	Raymond Berry, 11-10-57	224
Interceptions	Many times	3
	Last time by Mike Prior, 12-20-92	
Field Goals	Many times	5
	Last time by Mike Vanderjagt, 12-7-03	
Touchdowns (Tot.)	Many times	4
	Last time by Eric Dickerson, 10-31-88	
Points	Many times	24
	Last time by Eric Dickerson, 10-31-88	

*NFL Record

2006 VETERAN ROSTER

No.	Name	Pos.	Ht.	Wt.	Birthdate	NFL Exp.	College	Hometown	How Acq.	'05 Games/ Starts
58	Brackett, Gary	LB	5-11	235	5/23/80	4	Rutgers	Glassboro, N.J.	FA-'03	16/16
79	Brock, Raheem	DE	6-4	274	6/10/78	5	Temple	Philadelphia, Pa.	FA-'02	16/16
	Burns, Vincent	DT	6-2	260	6/21/81	2	Kentucky	Valdosta, Ga.	D3-'05	0*
	Campbell, Cody	G	6-4	305	9/29/81	2	Texas Tech	Lubbock, Texas	FA-'05	0*
31	Chapman, Kory	RB	6-1	202	7/13/80	2	Jacksonville State	Batesville, Miss.	FA-'05	3/0
44	Clark, Dallas	TE/FB	6-3	252	6/12/79	4	Iowa	Livermore, Iowa	D1-'03	15/14
42	David, Jason	CB/S	5-8	172	6/12/82	3	Washington State	Covina, Calif.	D4c-'04	16/16
71	Diem, Ryan	T	6-6	331	7/1/79	6	Northern Illinois	Carol Stream, Ill.	D4-'01	14/14
20	Doss, Mike	S	5-10	207	3/24/81	4	Ohio State	Canton, Ohio	D2-'03	15/14
81	Fletcher, Bryan	TE	6-5	230	3/23/79	2	UCLA	St. Louis, Mo.	FA-'05	16/12
93	Freeney, Dwight	DE	6-1	268	2/19/80	5	Syracuse	Hartford, Conn.	D1-'02	16/13
76	Freitas, Makoa	T	6-4	307	11/23/79	4	Arizona	Honolulu, Hawaii	D6c-'03	0*
57	Gandy, Dylan	G	6-3	302	3/8/82	2	Texas Tech	Harlingen, Texas	D4a-'05	16/2
51	Gardner, Gilbert	LB	6-1	228	5/9/82	3	Purdue	Angleton, Texas	D3b-'04	11/3
43	Giordano, Matt	CB/S	5-11	192	10/16/82	2	California	Fresno, Calif.	D4b-'05	15/0
78	Glenn, Tarik	T	6-5	332	5/25/76	10	California	Oakland, Calif.	D1-'97	16/6
96	Goddard, Johnathan	LB	6-0	242	5/11/81	2	Marshall	Jacksonville, Fla.	FA-'05	1/0
25	Harper, Nick	CB/S	5-10	182	9/10/74	6	Ft. Valley State	Baldwin, Ga.	FA-'01	15/15
88	Harrison, Marvin	WR	6-0	175	8/25/72	11	Syracuse	Philadelphia, Pa.	D1-'96	16/6
80	Hartsock, Ben	TE	6-4	262	7/5/80	3	Ohio State	Chillicothe, Ohio	D3a-'04	7/0
26	Hayden, Kelvin	CB/S	6-0	195	7/23/83	2	Illinois	Chicago, Ill.	D2-'05	16/0
27	Hutchins, Von	CB/S	5-9	181	2/14/81	3	Mississippi	Natchez, Miss.	D6a-'04	3/0
28	Jackson, Marlin	CB/S	6-0	196	6/30/83	2	Michigan	Sharon, Pa.	D1-'05	15/1
59	June, Cato	LB	6-0	227	11/18/79	4	Michigan	Washington, D.C.	D6a-'03	13/13
65	Lilja, Ryan	G	6-2	285	10/15/81	3	Kansas State	Shawnee, Kan.	W(KC)-'04	16/16
18	Manning, Peyton	QB	6-5	230	3/24/76	9	Tennessee	New Orleans, La.	D1-'98	16/16
98	Mathis, Robert	DE	6-2	235	2/26/81	4	Alabama A&M	Atlanta, Ga.	D5a-'03	13/0
85	Moorehead, Aaron	WR	6-3	200	11/5/80	4	Illinois	Deerfield, Ill.	FA-'03	2/0
94	Morris, Rob	LB	6-2	243	1/18/75	7	Brigham Young	Nampa, Idaho	D1-'00	14/0
23	Mungro, James	RB	5-9	214	2/13/78	5	Syracuse	E. Stroudsburg, Pa.	W(Det)-'02	12/0
53	O'Neil, Keith	LB	6-0	240	8/26/80	4	Northern Arizona	Amherst, N.Y.	W(Dall)-'05	11/0
55	Pope, Kendyll	LB	6-1	220	5/9/81	3	Florida State	Fort White, Fla.	D4a-'04	0*
90	Reagor, Montae	DT	6-3	285	6/29/77	8	Texas Tech	Waxahachie, Texas	UFA(Den)-'03	13/12
95	Reid, Darrell	DT	6-2	288	6/20/82	2	Minnesota	Freehold, N.J.	FA-'05	8/1
36	Reid, Dexter	CB/S	5-11	203	3/18/81	3	North Carolina	Norfolk, Va.	FA-'05	16/0
33	Rhodes, Dominic	RB	5-9	203	1/17/79	6	Midwestern State (Texas)	Abilene, Texas	FA-'01	13/1
21	Sanders, Bob	CB/S	5-8	206	2/24/81	3	Iowa	Erie, Pa.	D2b-'04	14/14
38	Sapp, Gerome	CB/S	6-1	216	2/8/81	4	Notre Dame	Houston, Texas	FA-'04	16/2
63	Saturday, Jeff	C	6-2	295	6/8/75	8	North Carolina	Tucker, Ga.	FA-'99	16/16
73	Scott, Jake	G	6-5	280	4/16/81	3	Idaho	Lewiston, Idaho	D5a-'04	16/16
97	Simon, Corey	DT	6-2	293	3/2/77	7	Florida State	Pompano Beach, Fla.	UFA(Phil)-'05	13/13
17	Smith, Hunter	P	6-2	209	8/9/77	8	Notre Dame	Sherman, Texas	D7a-'99	16/0
48	Snow, Justin	TE	6-3	240	12/21/76	7	Baylor	Abilene, Texas	FA-'00	16/0
12	Sorgi, Jim	QB	6-5	196	12/3/80	3	Wisconsin	Fraser, Mich.	D6b-'04	9/0
83	Stokley, Brandon	WR	5-11	197	6/23/76	8	Southwestern Louisiana	Dallas, Texas	UFA(Balt)-'03	15/4
91	Thomas, Josh	DE	6-5	271	6/26/81	3	Syracuse	Orchard Park, N.Y.	FA-'04	12/2
69	Ulrich, Matt	G/T	6-2	309	12/30/81	2	Northwestern	Streamwood, Ill.	FA-'05	5/0
86	Utecht, Ben	TE	6-6	251	6/30/81	3	Minnesota	Hastings, Minn.	FA-'04	1/0
4	Vinatieri, Adam	K	6-0	202	12/28/72	11	South Dakota State	Rapid City, S.D.	UFA(NE)-'06	16/0*
87	Wayne, Reggie	WR	6-0	198	11/17/78	6	Miami	New Orleans, La.	D1b-'01	16/16
99	Welsh, Jonathan	DE	6-4	228	6/9/82	2	Wisconsin	Houston, Texas	D5a-'05	6/0
52	Whiteside, Keyon	LB	6-0	229	1/31/80	3	Tennessee	Forest City, N.C.	FA-'03	0*

* Burns missed '05 season because of injury; Campbell missed '05 season because of injury; Freitas missed '05 season because of injury; Hagler missed '05 season because of injury; Pope last active with Indianapolis in '04; Vinatieri played 16 games with New England in '05; Whiteside missed '05 season because of injury.

Players lost through free agency (5): RB Edgerrin James (Ariz; 15 games in '05), LB David Thornton (Tenn; 16), DT Larry Tripplett (Buff; 15), K Mike Vanderjagt (Dall; 16), WR Troy Walters (Ariz;16).

Also played with Colts in '05—RB Ran Carthon (6 games), K Jose Cortez (2), T Joaquin Gonzalez (5), CB/S Joseph Jefferson (4), LB Mike Labinjo (2), K Dave Rayner (14), CB/S Donald Strickland (1), T Kurt Vollers (2), DT Josh Williams (4).

2006 FIRST-YEAR ROSTER

Name	Pos.	Ht.	Wt.	Birthdate	College	Hometown	How Acq.
Addai, Joseph	RB	5-11	214	5/3/83	Louisiana State	Houston, Texas	D1
Andrus, Shane (1)	K	5-10	190	10/2/80	Murray State	Murray, Ky.	FA
Bethea, Antoine	CB/S	5-11	203	7/7/84	Howard	Newport News, Va.	D6b
Betts, Josh	QB	6-1	225	8/25/82	Miami (Ohio)	Vandalia, Ohio	FA
Bimper, Albert	C	6-1	303	7/26/83	Colorado State	Arlington, Texas	FA
Brown, Justin (1)	DE	6-2	260	4/16/82	East Central Oklahoma	Fletcher, Okla.	FA
Crosby, Roscoe (1)	WR	6-2	210	2/6/83	Clemson	Buffalo, S.C.	FA
Culton, Montiese (1)	WR	6-2	180	1/18/82	Tulsa	Dallas, Texas	FA
Davis, Ashlan	KR	5-8	179	2/15/83	Tulsa	Mesquite, Texas	FA
Davis, Tanard	CB/S	6-0	186	1/27/83	Miami	Miami, Fla.	FA
Federkeil, Daniel	T	6-7	275	11/9/83	Calgary	Medicine Hat, Alberta, Canada	FA
Goodwin, Jamie	WR	5-10	173	7/2/82	Northern Iowa	Duquesne, Pa.	FA
Hagler, Tyjuan (1)	LB	6-0	236	12/3/81	Cincinnati	Kankakee, Ill.	D5c-'05
Hannah, Nick (1)	LB	6-1	220	10/3/81	Eastern Oregon	East Wenetchee, Wash.	FA
Hare, Brian	WR	6-3	190	8/18/83	Purdue	Arlington Heights. Ill.	FA
Hawkins, Joey (1)	TE	6-9	252	12/16/81	Texas Tech	Gilmer, Texas	FA
Hill, Eric (1)	CB/S	6-0	190	5/22/80	Colorado State	Denver, Colo.	FA
Hoyte, Brandon	LB	5-11	235	9/26/83	Notre Dame	Parlin, N.J.	FA
Jennings, Tim	CB/S	5-8	185	12/24/83	Georgia	Orangeburg, S.C.	D2
Johnson, Charlie	T	6-4	305	5/2/84	Oklahoma State	Sherman, Texas	D6a
Johnson, Mike (1)	C	6-3	296	3/26/82	Kansas State	Boulder, Colo.	FA
Johnson, Tom	DT	6-2	277	8/30/84	Southern Mississippi	Moss Point, Miss.	FA
Keiaho, Freddie	LB	5-11	232	12/18/82	San Diego State	Ventura, Calif.	D3
Killion, Kyle	LB	6-0	225	2/1/84	Indiana	Kingwood, Texas	FA
Koral, David	QB	6-3	216	11/27/82	UCLA	Santa Monica, Calif.	FA
Lacy, Bo (1)	G/T	6-4	300	11/22/80	Arkansas	New Port, Ark.	FA
Laskowski, Chris (1)	CB/S	5-9	210	9/12/81	Florida Atlantic	Melbourne, Fla.	FA
Marsh, Antwan	CB/S	6-2	216	7/7/83	Pikeville College	Polkton, N.C.	FA
Myrick, Chip	G	6-4	290	6/1/82	Clemson	Atlanta, Ga.	FA
Nyenhuis, Gabe (1)	DE	6-3	269	6/26/81	Colorado	St. Charles, Ill.	FA
Pearson, Vashon (1)	RB	5-10	205	1/23/83	Mississippi	Ripley, Miss.	FA
Roberts, Corey	TE	6-5	235	10/23/82	Sam Houston State	Carthage, Texas	FA
Robinson, Dale	LB	6-0	230	9/7/83	Arizona State	Jamaica, N.Y.	FA
Rushing, T.J.	CB/S	5-10	180	6/8/83	Stanford	Pauls Valley, Okla.	D7
Sheldon, Dan (1)	WR	5-11	173	5/23/82	Northern Illinois	Burlington, Ill.	FA
Snyder, Cole	LB	5-11	230	2/23/82	Idaho	Kamiah, Idaho	FA
Standeford, John (1)	WR	6-4	206	4/15/82	Purdue	Monrovia, Ind.	FA
Tanner, Russ	C	6-4	297	10/27/82	Georgia	Wrightsville, Ga.	FA
Toudouze, Michael	T	6-7	310	4/27/83	Texas Christian	San Antonio, Texas	D5
Walker, Gerran	WR	5-10	185	10/2/83	Lehigh	Atlanta, Ga.	FA

The term NFL Rookie is defined as a player who is in his first season of professional football and has not been on the roster of another professional football team for any regular-season or postseason games. A Rookie is designated by an "R" on NFL rosters. Players who have been active in another professional football league or players who have NFL experience, including either preseason training camp or being on an Active List or Inactive List, or on Reserve/Injured or Reserve/Physically Unable to Perform for fewer than six regular-season games, are termed NFL First-Year Players. An NFL First-Year Player is designated by a "1" on NFL rosters. Thereafter, a player is credited with an additional year of experience for each season in which he accumulates six games on the Active List or Inactive List, or on Reserve/Injured or Reserve/Physically Unable to Perform.

Log on to www.colts.com for an up-to-date roster.

COACHING STAFF
Head Coach,
Tony Dungy

Pro Career: Tony Dungy was named head coach of the club on January 22, 2002. This season marks Dungy's fifth with the Colts and eleventh as an NFL head coach. Dungy became the 35th coach in NFL history to earn 100 career victories (including playoffs) with a 38-20 win at Houston on October 23, 2005. Dungy is only the sixth coach to win 100-plus regular-season games in the first 10 years as a head coach (113, George Seifert; 105, Don Shula; 103, John Madden; 102, Dungy; 101, Joe Gibbs; 101, Mike Ditka). He is the NFL's winningest head coach from 1999-2005 with a mark of 78-34 (30-18 with Tampa Bay, 48-16 with Colts), and his .638 winning percentage ranks second among active head coaches. He has directed the Colts to 10-6, 12-4, 12-4 and 14-2 records, becoming the only coach in club history to produce 10-plus victories and playoff berths in the first four seasons with the team. In 2005, Dungy led the Colts to a franchise-record 14 wins and a third consecutive divisional title, the fifth for the club in its 22-year Indianapolis era. Dungy has seven career double-digit victory seasons and stands as the only NFL head coach to defeat all 32 NFL teams. Dungy held a 54-42 record as head coach with Tampa Bay from 1996-2001, qualifying for the playoffs four times in six seasons. At 25, Dungy was the NFL's youngest assistant coach with Pittsburgh in 1981. In 1982, he was promoted from defensive assistant to defensive backs coach, before becoming the league's youngest defensive coordinator in 1984 at age 28. He served as defensive backs coach at Kansas City (1989-1991) and as defensive coordinator at Minnesota (1992-95). Dungy signed with Pittsburgh as a free agent in 1977 and played safety for two seasons. He had 9 interceptions in 30 games for Pittsburgh and played in the club's Super Bowl XIII victory over Dallas. He was traded to San Francisco in 1979. Career record: 107-66.

Background: Starred as a quarterback at University of Minnesota from 1973-76. Finished career as school's all-time leader in attempts, completions, passing yards and touchdown passes. Two-time team most valuable player, played in Hula Bowl, East-West Shrine Game and Japan Bowl.

Personal: Born October 6, 1955, in Jackson, Mich. Tony and his wife, Lauren, are the parents of five children, daughters Tiara and Jade, and sons, Eric and Jordan, and the late James Dungy.

ASSISTANT COACHES

Jim Caldwell, asst. head coach/quarterbacks; born January 16, 1955, Beloit, Wis. Defensive back Iowa 1973-76. No pro playing experience. College coach: Iowa 1977, Southern Illinois 1978-1980, Northwestern 1981, Colorado 1982-84, Louisville 1985, Penn State 1986-1992, Wake Forest 1993-2000 (head coach). Pro coach: Tampa Bay Buccaneers 2001, joined Colts in 2002.

Clyde Christensen, wide receivers; born January 28, 1956, Covina, Calif. Quarterback Fresno (Calif.) J.C. 1975, North Carolina 1976-78. No pro playing experience. College coach: Mississippi 1979, East Tennessee State 1980-82, Temple 1983-85, East Carolina 1986-88, Holy Cross 1989-1990, South Carolina 1991, Maryland 1992-93, Clemson 1994-95. Pro coach: Tampa Bay Buccaneers 1996-2001, joined Colts in 2002.

Leslie Frazier, special assistant to the head coach/defensive backs; born April 3, 1959, Columbus, Miss. Defensive back Alcorn State 1977-1980. Pro defensive back Chicago Bears 1981-86. College coach: Trinity (Ill.) College 1988-1996 (head coach), Illinois 1997-98. Pro coach: Philadelphia Eagles 1999-2002, Cincinnati Bengals 2003-04, joined Colts in 2005.

Richard Howell, asst. strength and conditioning; born February 19, 1972, Bladenboro, N.C. Quarterback Davidson 1990-93. No pro playing experience. College coach: Davidson 1994-98, North Carolina 1998-99. Pro coach: Barcelona Dragons (NFLE) 1999, joined Colts in 2000.

Gene Huey, running backs; born July 20, 1947, Uniontown, Pa. Defensive back-wide receiver Wyoming 1965-68. Pro running back San Diego Chargers 1969. College coach: Wyoming 1970-73, New Mexico 1974-76, Nebraska 1977-1986, Arizona State 1987, Ohio State 1988-1991. Pro coach: Joined Colts in 1992.

Ron Meeks, defensive coordinator; born August 27, 1954, Jacksonville. Defensive back Arkansas State 1972-76. Pro defensive back Hamilton Tiger-Cats (CFL) 1977-79, Ottawa Rough Riders (CFL) 1979, Toronto Argonauts (CFL) 1980-81. College coach: Arkansas State 1984-85, Miami 1986-87, New Mexico State 1988, Fresno State 1989-1990. Pro coach: Dallas Cowboys 1991, Cincinnati Bengals 1992-96, Atlanta Falcons 1997-99, Washington Redskins 2000, St. Louis Rams 2001, joined Colts in 2002.

Pete Metzelaars, offensive quality control; born May 24, 1960, Three Rivers, Mich. Tight end Wabash College 1978-1981. Pro tight end Seattle Seahawks 1982-84, Buffalo Bills 1985-1994, Carolina Panthers 1995, Detroit Lions 1996-97. College coach: Wingate 2003. Pro coach: Barcelona Dragons (NFLE) 2003, joined Colts in 2004.

Tom Moore, offensive coordinator; born November 7, 1938, Owatanna, Minn. Quarterback Iowa 1957-1960. No pro playing experience. College coach: Iowa 1961-62, Dayton 1965-68, Wake Forest 1969, Georgia Tech 1970-71, Minnesota 1972-73, 1975-76. Pro coach: New York Stars (WFL) 1974, Pittsburgh Steelers 1977-1989, Minnesota Vikings 1990-93, Detroit Lions 1994-96, New Orleans Saints 1997, joined Colts in 1998.

Howard Mudd, offensive line; born February 10, 1942, Midland, Mich. Guard Hillsdale (Mich.) College 1960-63. Pro offensive lineman San Francisco 49ers 1964-69, Chicago Bears 1969-1971. College coach: California 1972-73. Pro coach: San Diego Chargers 1974-76, San Francisco 49ers 1977, Seattle Seahawks 1978-1982, 1993-97, Cleveland Browns 1983-88, Kansas City Chiefs 1989-1992, joined Colts in 1998.

Mike Murphy, linebackers; born September 25, 1944, New York, N.Y. Guard-linebacker Huron (S.D.) 1963-66. No pro playing experience. College coach: Vermont 1970-73, Idaho State 1974-76, Western Illinois 1977-78. Pro coach: Saskatchewan Rough Riders (CFL) 1979-1983, Chicago Blitz (USFL) 1984, Detroit Lions 1985-89, Arizona Cardinals 1990-93, Seattle Seahawks 1995-97, joined Colts in 1998.

Russ Purnell, special teams; born June 12, 1948, Chicago. Center Orange Coast (Calif.) J.C. 1966-67, Whittier College 1968-69. No pro playing experience. College coach: Whittier College 1970-71, Southern California 1982-85. Pro coach: Seattle Seahawks 1986-1994, Tennessee Oilers/Titans 1995-98, Baltimore Ravens 1999-2001, joined Colts in 2002.

Diron Reynolds, defensive quality control; born February 23, 1971, Aiken, S.C. Linebacker Wake Forest 1989-1993. No pro playing experience. College coach: Wake Forest 1997-2000; Indiana 2001. Pro coach: Joined Colts in 2002.

John Teerlinck, defensive line; born April 9, 1951, Rochester, N.Y. Defensive lineman Western Illinois 1970-73. Pro defensive tackle San Diego Chargers 1974-77. College coach: Iowa Lakes J.C. 1977, Eastern Illinois 1978-79, Illinois 1980-82. Pro coach: Chicago Blitz (USFL) 1983-84, Arizona Wranglers/Outlaws (USFL) 1985-86, Cleveland Browns 1989-1990, Los Angeles Rams 1991, Minnesota Vikings 1992-94, Detroit Lions 1995-96, Denver Broncos 1997-2001, joined Colts in 2002.

Ricky Thomas, tight ends; born March 29, 1965, London, England. Safety Alabama 1983-86. College coach: Kentucky 1996, Gardner-Webb 1997. Pro coach: Tampa Bay Buccaneers 1997-2001, joined Colts in 2002.

Jon Torine, strength and conditioning; born November 16, 1973, Livingston, N.J. Linebacker Springfield (Mass.) College 1991. No pro playing experience. Pro coach: Buffalo Bills 1995-97, joined Colts in 1998.

Alan Williams, defensive backs; born November 4, 1969, Norfolk, Va. Running back William & Mary 1988-1991. No pro playing experience. College coach: William & Mary 1996-2000. Pro coach: Tampa Bay Buccaneers 2001, joined Colts in 2002.

American Football Conference
South Division
Team Colors: Teal, Black, and Gold
Alltel Stadium
One Alltel Stadium Place
Jacksonville, Florida 32202
Telephone: (904) 633-6000

2006 SCHEDULE
PRESEASON
Aug. 12 at Miami 7:30
Aug. 19 **Carolina** 7:30
Aug. 26 **Tampa Bay** 8:00
Aug. 31 at Atlanta 7:30

REGULAR SEASON
Sept. 10 **Dallas** 4:15
Sept. 18 **Pittsburgh** (Mon.) 8:30
Sept. 24 at Indianapolis 1:00
Oct. 1   at Washington 4:15
Oct. 8   **N.Y. Jets** 4:05
Oct. 15   Open Date
Oct. 22   at Houston 12:00
Oct. 29   at Philadelphia 1:00
Nov. 5   **Tennessee** 1:00
Nov. 12   **Houston** 1:00
Nov. 20   **N.Y. Giants** (Mon.) 8:30
Nov. 26   at Buffalo 1:00
Dec. 3   at Miami 1:00
Dec. 10   **Indianapolis** 1:00
Dec. 17   at Tennessee 12:00
Dec. 24   **New England** 1:00
Dec. 31   at Kansas City 12:00

Stadium: Alltel Stadium
          (opened in 1995)
          •**Capacity:** 67,164
          One Alltel Stadium Place
          Jacksonville, Florida 32202
Playing Surface: Grass
Training Camp: Alltel Stadium
              One Alltel Stadium Place
              Jacksonville, Florida 32202

ALLTEL STADIUM

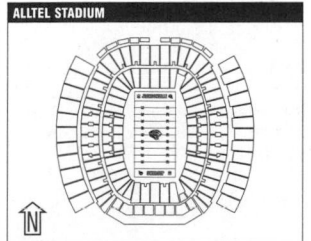

CLUB OFFICIALS
Chairman and Chief Executive Officer:
    Wayne Weaver
Senior Vice President/Football
    Operations: Paul Vance
Senior Vice President/Chief Financial
    Officer: Bill Prescott
Senior Vice President/Business
    Development: Tim Connolly
Vice President/Player Personnel:
    James Harris
Vice President/Communications and
    Media: Dan Edwards
Executive Director of Ticket Sales and
    Marketing: Scott Loft
Executive Director of Corporate
    Sponsorship: Macky Weaver
Executive Director of Football Operations:
    Skip Richardson
Executive Director of Information
    Technology: Bruce Swindell
Director of Pro Personnel: Charles Bailey
Director of College Scouting: Gene Smith
Director of Ticket Operations: Tim Bishko
Director of Marketing: Jennifer Perkins
Director of Broadcasting: Chris Sinclair
Associate General Counsel: Sashi Brown
Head Athletic Trainer: Michael Ryan
Video Director: Mike Perkins
Equipment Manager: Drew Hampton
Assistant Director of Pro Personnel:
    Louis Clark
Executive Scouts: Terry McDonough,
    Tim Mingey
Regional Scouts: Andy Dengler,
    Chris Driggers, Art Perkins
BLESTO Representative: Kadar Hamilton
Scouts: Marty Miller, Larry Wright
Scouting Assistant: Chris Prescott
Coordinator, Communications:
    Hunter Robinson
Coordinator, Communications:
    Ryan Robinson
Executive Assistant to VP,
    Communications and Media:
    Alisa Abbott
Chair & Chief Executive Officer, Jaguars
    Foundation: Delores Barr Weaver
Executive Director: Peter Racine

COACHING HISTORY
(98-87-0)
Records include postseason games
1995-2002 Tom Coughlin 72-64-0
2003-05   Jack Del Rio 26-23-0

ATTENDANCE
Home 477,809   Away 500,657
Total 978,466
Single-game home record,
    74,143 (12/28/98)
Single-season home record, 561,472
    (1998)

2006 DRAFT CHOICES
Round	Name	Pos.	College
1	Marcedes Lewis	TE	UCLA
2	Maurice Jones-Drew	RB	UCLA
3	Clint Ingram	LB	Oklahoma
5	Brent Hawkins	LB	Illinois State
7	James Wyche	DE	Syracuse
	Dee Webb	DB	Florida

2005 TEAM RECORD
PRESEASON (2-2)

Date	Result	Opponent
8/13	W 27-17	Miami
8/20	W 20-17	at Tampa Bay
8/25	L 7-23	Atlanta
9/1	L 20-27	at Dallas

REGULAR SEASON (12-4)

Date	Result	Opponent	Att.
9/11	W 26-14	Seattle	65,204
9/18	L 3-10	at Indianapolis	56,460
9/25	W 26-20	at N.Y. Jets (OT)	77,422
10/2	L 7-20	Denver	66,045
10/9	W 23-20	Cincinnati	66,137
10/16	W 23-17	at Pittsburgh (OT)	63,891
10/30	L 21-24	at St. Louis	65,251
11/6	W 21-14	Houston	64,613
11/13	W 30-3	Baltimore	66,107
11/20	W 31-28	at Tennessee	69,149
11/27	W 24-17	at Arizona	39,198
12/4	W 20-14	at Cleveland	70,941
12/11	L 18-26	Indianapolis	67,164
12/18	W 10-9	San Francisco	64,764
12/24	W 38-20	at Houston	70,025
1/1	W 40-13	Tennessee	65,485

(OT) Overtime

POSTSEASON (0-1)

Date	Result	Opponent	
1/7	L 3-28	at New England	68,756

SCORE BY PERIODS

Jaguars	67	70	113	99	12	—	361
Opponents	30	117	36	86	0	—	269

2005 TEAM STATISTICS

	Jaguars	Opp.
Total First Downs	301	273
Rushing	97	79
Passing	170	158
Penalty	34	36
3rd Down: Made/Att	93/225	67/205
3rd Down Pct.	41.3	32.7
4th Down: Made/Att	4/10	4/14
4th Down Pct.	40.0	28.6
Possession Avg.	31:33	28:27
Total Net Yards	5,149	4,655
Avg. Per Game	321.8	290.9
Total Plays	1,021	963
Avg. Per Play	5.0	4.8
Net Yards Rushing	1,959	1,709
Avg. Per Game	122.4	106.8
Total Rushes	502	434
Net Yards Passing	3,190	2,946
Avg. Per Game	199.4	184.1
Sacked/Yards Lost	32/162	47/277
Gross Yards	3,352	3,223
Att./Completions	487/283	482/285
Completion Pct.	58.1	59.1
Had Intercepted	6	19
Punts/Average	83/42.4	88/42.8
Net Punting Avg.	83/36.9	88/36.7
Penalties/Yards	121/1006	130/1055
Fumbles/Ball Lost	27/11	21/9
Touchdowns	42	30
Rushing	18	4
Passing	21	22
Returns	3	4

2005 INDIVIDUAL STATISTICS

PASSING

	Att.	Comp.	Yds.	Pct.	TD	Int.	Tkld.	Rate
Leftwich	302	175	2,123	57.9	15	5	23/110	89.3
Garrard	168	98	1,117	58.3	4	1	8/45	83.9
Gray	14	8	100	57.1	2	0	1/7	119.0
M. Jones	3	2	12	66.7	0	0	0/0	74.3
Jaguars	487	283	3,352	58.1	21	6	32/162	88.4
Opponents	482	285	3,223	59.1	22	19	47/277	78.0

SCORING

	TD R	TD P	TD Rt	PAT	FG	Saf	PTS
Scobee	0	0	0	38/39	23/30	0	107
Wilford	0	7	0	0/0	0/0	0	42
J. Smith	0	6	0	0/0	0/0	0	36
M. Jones	0	5	0	0/0	0/0	0	30
G. Jones	4	0	0	0/0	0/0	0	24
Toefield	4	0	0	0/0	0/0	0	24
Garrard	3	0	0	0/0	0/0	0	20
Taylor	3	0	0	0/0	0/0	0	18
Leftwich	2	0	0	0/0	0/0	0	12
Wimbush	1	0	1	0/0	0/0	0	12
Wrighster	0	2	0	0/0	0/0	0	12
Brady	0	1	0	0/0	0/0	0	6
Mathis	0	0	1	0/0	0/0	0	6
Pearman	1	0	0	0/0	0/0	0	6
Peterson	0	0	1	0/0	0/0	0	6
Jaguars	18	21	3	38/39	23/30	0	361
Opponents	4	22	4	29/30	20/27	0	269

2-Pt. Conversions: Garrard.
Jaguars 1-1, Opponents 0-0.

RUSHING

	No.	Yds	Avg	LG	TD
Taylor	194	787	4.1	71t	3
G. Jones	151	575	3.8	27	4
Garrard	31	172	5.5	28	3
Pearman	39	149	3.8	45	1
Toefield	36	142	3.9	32t	4
Leftwich	31	67	2.2	9	2
M. Jones	12	51	4.3	25	0
Wimbush	3	12	4.0	7	1
R. Williams	2	3	1.5	10	0
Gray	3	1	0.3	3	0
Jaguars	502	1,959	3.9	71t	18
Opponents	434	1,709	3.9	51	4

RECEIVING

	No.	Yds	Avg	LG	TD
J. Smith	70	1,023	14.6	45t	6
Wilford	41	681	16.6	39	7
M. Jones	36	432	12.0	42	5
R. Williams	35	445	12.7	41	0
Pearman	32	240	7.5	19	0
Brady	18	157	8.7	33	1
Wrighster	13	120	9.2	27	2
Taylor	13	83	6.4	13	0
G. Jones	10	65	6.5	10	0
Wimbush	5	26	5.2	6	0
B. Jones	3	49	16.3	41	0
Toefield	3	17	5.7	11	0
Hankton	3	15	5.0	8	0
Manuwai	1	-1	-1.0	-1	0
Jaguars	283	3,352	11.8	45t	21
Opponents	285	3,223	11.3	83t	22

INTERCEPTIONS

	No.	Yds	Avg	LG	TD
Mathis	5	79	15.8	41t	1
Cousin	4	18	4.5	14	0
Peterson	3	54	18.0	26t	1
Grant	3	29	9.7	29	0
Wright	2	4	2.0	4	0
Cooper	1	0	0.0	0	0
D. Smith	1	0	0.0	0	0
Jaguars	19	184	9.7	41t	2
Opponents	6	90	15.0	37	0

PUNTING

	No.	Yds.	Avg.	In 20	LG
Hanson	82	3,517	42.9	33	74
Jaguars	83	3,517	42.4	33	74
Opponents	88	3,763	42.8	22	75

PUNT RETURNS

	Ret	FC	Yds	Avg	LG	TD
Pearman	49	15	410	8.4	24	0
Owens	3	0	6	2.0	6	0
Mathis	1	0	-1	-1.0	-1	0
Jaguars	53	15	415	7.8	24	0
Opponents	29	15	236	8.1	72t	1

KICKOFF RETURNS

	No.	Yds	Avg	LG	TD
Wimbush	39	955	24.5	91t	1
Pearman	8	187	23.4	34	0
Alexis	1	31	31.0	31	0
Brady	1	24	24.0	24	0
G. Jones	1	0	0.0	0	0
Jaguars	50	1,197	23.9	91t	1
Opponents	56	1,327	23.7	85	0

FIELD GOALS

	1-19	20-29	30-39	40-49	50+
Scobee	0/0	9/9	7/8	5/10	2/3
Jaguars	0/0	9/9	7/8	5/10	2/3
Opponents	0/0	2/2	8/10	9/14	1/1

SACKS

	No.
Hayward	8.5
Spicer	7.5
Meier	6.0
Peterson	6.0
McCray	5.5
D. Smith	4.0
Henderson	3.0
Ayodele	2.5
Grant	1.5
Maddox	1.0
Stroud	1.0
Cousin	0.5
Jaguars	47.0
Opponents	32.0

RECORD HOLDERS
INDIVIDUAL RECORDS—CAREER

Category	Name	Performance
Rushing (Yds.)	Fred Taylor, 1998-2005	8,367
Passing (Yds.)	Mark Brunell, 1995-2003	25,698
Passing (TDs)	Mark Brunell, 1995-2003	144
Receiving (No.)	Jimmy Smith, 1995-2005	862
Receiving (Yds.)	Jimmy Smith, 1995-2005	12,287
Interceptions	Aaron Beasley, 1996-2001	15
Punting (Avg.)	Bryan Barker, 1995-2000	43.5
Punt Return (Avg.)	Chris Hudson, 1995-98	10.9
Kickoff Return (Avg.)	Derrick Wimbush, 2005	24.5
Field Goals	Mike Hollis, 1995-2001	175
Touchdowns (Tot.)	Jimmy Smith, 1995-2005	69
Points	Mike Hollis, 1995-2001	764

INDIVIDUAL RECORDS—SINGLE SEASON

Category	Name	Performance
Rushing (Yds.)	Fred Taylor, 2003	1,572
Passing (Yds.)	Mark Brunell, 1996	4,367
Passing (TDs)	Mark Brunell, 1998	20
Receiving (No.)	Jimmy Smith, 1999	116
Receiving (Yds.)	Jimmy Smith, 1999	1,636
Interceptions	Aaron Beasley, 1999	6
	Marlon McCree, 2002	6
Punting (Avg.)	Bryan Barker, 1998	45.0
Punt Return (Avg.)	Reggie Barlow, 1998	12.9
Kickoff Return (Avg.)	Reggie Barlow, 1998	24.9
Field Goals	Mike Hollis, 1997, 1999	31
Touchdowns (Tot.)	Fred Taylor, 1998	17
Points	Mike Hollis, 1997	134

INDIVIDUAL RECORDS—SINGLE GAME

Category	Name	Performance
Rushing (Yds.)	Fred Taylor, 11-19-00	234
Passing (Yds.)	Mark Brunell, 9-22-96	432
Passing (TDs)	Mark Brunell, 11-29-98	4
Receiving (No.)	Keenan McCardell, 10-20-96	16
Receiving (Yds.)	Jimmy Smith, 9-10-00	291
Interceptions	Many times	2
	Last time by Terry Cousin, 11-13-05	
Field Goals	Mike Hollis, 12-1-96, 11-30-97, 9-10-00	5
Touchdowns (Tot.)	James Stewart, 10-12-97	5
Points	James Stewart, 10-12-97	30

2006 VETERAN ROSTER

No.	Name	Pos.	Ht.	Wt.	Birthdate	NFL Exp.	College	Hometown	How Acq.	'05 Games/ Starts
69	Barnes, Khalif	T	6-5	315	4/21/82	2	Washington	Spring Valley, Calif.	D2-'05	13/12
80	Brady, Kyle	TE	6-6	278	1/14/72	12	Penn State	New Cumberland, Pa.	UFA(NYJ)-'99	16/15
61	Connolly, Dan	G	6-4	318	9/2/82	2	SE Missouri State	St. Louis, Mo.	FA-'05	4/0
58	Cordova, Jorge	LB/DE	6-1	241	9/25/81	3	Nevada	Murrieta, Calif.	D3-'04	0*
21	Cousin, Terry	CB	5-9	185	4/11/75	10	South Carolina	Miami, Fla.	FA-'05	16/5
20	Darius, Donovin	S	6-1	225	8/12/75	9	Syracuse	Camden, N.J.	D1b-'98	2/2
68	Fletcher, Derrick	OL	6-6	350	9/9/75	5	Baylor	Houston, Texas	FA-'04	13/1
9	Garrard, David	QB	6-1	244	2/14/78	5	East Carolina	Durham, N.C.	D4a-'02	7/5
50	Gilbert, Tony	LB	6-0	239	10/16/79	4	Georgia	Macon, Ga.	W(Ariz)-'03	16/0
37	Grant, Deon	S	6-2	210	3/14/79	7	Tennessee	Augusta, Ga.	UFA(Car)-'04	16/16
5	Gray, Quinn	QB	6-3	240	5/21/79	3	Florida A&M	Fort Lauderdale, Fla.	FA-'03	1/0
55	Greisen, Nick	LB	6-1	245	8/10/79	5	Wisconsin	Sturgeon Bay, Wisc.	UFA(NYG)-'06	16/12*
85	Hankton, Cortez	WR	6-0	200	1/20/81	4	Texas Southern	New Orleans, La.	FA-'03	5/0
2	Hanson, Chris	P	6-2	223	10/25/76	6	Marshall	Senioa, Ga.	FA-'01	16/0
97	Hayward, Reggie	DE	6-5	280	3/14/79	6	Iowa State	Dolton, Ill.	UFA(Den)-'05	15/15
98	Henderson, John	DT	6-7	328	1/9/79	5	Tennessee	Nashville, Tenn.	D1-'02	16/15
86	Jones, Brian	TE	6-3	252	8/23/81	3	Arkansas-Pine Bluff	Bastrop, La.	FA-'04	13/1
33	Jones, Greg	FB/RB	6-1	250	5/9/81	3	Florida State	Beaufort, S.C.	D2b-'04	14/13
18	Jones, Matt	WR	6-6	229	4/22/83	2	Arkansas	Fort Smith, Ark.	D1-'05	16/1
7	Leftwich, Byron	QB	6-5	240	1/14/80	4	Marshall	Washington D.C.	D1-'03	11/11
91	Maddox, Anthony	DT	6-1	305	11/22/78	2	Delta State	Funston, Ga.	D4a-'04	5/0
67	Manuwai, Vince	G	6-2	312	7/12/80	4	Hawaii	Honolulu, Hawaii	D3-'03	16/16
27	Mathis, Rashean	CB	6-1	195	8/27/80	4	Bethune-Cookman	Jacksonville, Fla.	D2-'03	16/16
93	McCray, Bobby	DE	6-6	261	8/8/81	3	Florida	Miami, Fla.	D7-'04	16/1
73	McDougle, Stockar	T	6-6	348	1/11/77	7	Oklahoma	Deerfield Beach, Fla.	UFA(Mia)-'06	7/2*
63	Meester, Brad	C	6-3	300	3/23/77	7	Northern Iowa	Parkersburg, Iowa	D2-'00	12/12
92	Meier, Rob	DT	6-5	293	8/29/77	7	Washington State	W. Vancouver, B.C.	D7b-'00	16/2
65	Naeole, Chris	G	6-3	330	12/25/74	10	Colorado	Kaaava, Hawaii	UFA(NO)-'02	15/15
62	Norman, Dennis	C	6-5	312	1/26/80	5	Princeton	Marlton, N.J.	FA-'04	16/4
78	Patterson, Elton	DE	6-2	271	6/3/81	3	Central Florida	Orlando, Fla.	FA-'06	0*
34	Pearman, Alvin	RB/KR	5-10	206	8/10/82	2	Virginia	Charlotte, N.C.	D4-'05	16/0
54	Peterson, Mike	LB	6-1	235	6/17/76	8	Florida	Gainesville, Fla.	UFA(Ind)-'03	16/16
26	Richardson, David	CB	6-0	202	9/9/81	3	Cal Poly-San Luis Obispo	Los Angeles, Calif.	FA-'04	7/0
38	Roberson, Chris	CB	5-11	185	6/3/83	2	Eastern Michigan	Farmington Hills, Mich.	D7-'05	6/0
66	Romberg, Brett	C	6-2	298	10/10/79	3	Miami	Windsor, Ontario, Canada	FA-'03	0*
10	Scobee, Josh	K	6-1	190	6/23/82	3	Louisiana Tech	Longview, Texas	D5a-'04	16/0
43	Sensabaugh, Gerald	S	6-0	210	6/13/83	2	North Carolina	Kingsport, Tenn.	D5-'05	16/2
52	Smith, Daryl	LB	6-2	242	3/14/82	3	Georgia Tech	Albany, Ga.	D2a-'04	16/16
41	Sorensen, Nick	S	6-3	210	7/31/78	6	Virginia Tech	Vienna, Va.	FA-'03	10/0
95	Spicer, Paul	DE	6-4	295	8/18/75	7	Saginaw Valley State	Indianapolis, Ind.	FA-'00	15/14
31	Starks, Scott	CB	5-9	174	6/27/83	2	Wisconsin	St. Louis, Mo.	D3-'05	16/0
99	Stroud, Marcus	DT	6-6	312	6/25/78	6	Georgia	Barney, Ga.	D1-'01	16/16
28	Taylor, Fred	RB	6-1	234	1/27/76	9	Florida	Belle Glade, Fla.	D1a-'98	11/11
53	Thomas, Pat	LB	6-2	243	1/26/83	2	North Carolina State	Miami, Fla.	D6b-'05	9/0
22	Toefield, LaBrandon	RB	5-11	232	9/24/80	4	Louisiana State	Independence, La.	D4b-'03	9/2
75	Wiley, Marcellus	DE	6-4	275	11/30/74	10	Columbia	Santa Monica, Calif.	FA-'05	11/1
19	Wilford, Ernest	WR	6-4	218	1/14/79	3	Virginia Tech	Richmond, Va.	D4b-'04	16/8
29	Williams, Brian	CB	5-11	198	7/2/79	5	North Carolina State	High Point, N.C.	UFA(Minn)-'06	14/9*
74	Williams, Maurice	T	6-5	310	1/26/79	6	Michigan	Detroit, Mich.	D2-'01	16/16
77	Williams, Mike	T	6-6	370	1/11/80	5	Texas	The Colony, Texas	FA-'06	9/5*
11	Williams, Reggie	WR	6-4	214	5/17/83	3	Washington	Tacoma, Wash.	D1-'04	16/7
94	Williams, Tony	DT	6-2	296	7/9/75	9	Memphis	Memphis, Tenn.	UFA(Cin)-'05	0*
36	Wimbush, Derrick	RB/KR	6-1	220	8/26/80	2	Fort Valley State	Mauk, Ga.	FA-'05	14/1
87	Wrighster, George	TE	6-3	254	4/1/81	4	Oregon	Van Nuys, Calif.	D4a-'03	16/6
83	Yoder, Todd	TE	6-4	255	3/18/78	7	Vanderbilt	New Palestine, Ind.	UFA(TB)-'04	0*
88	Zelenka, Joe	LS/TE	6-3	265	3/9/76	8	Wake Forest	Cleveland, Ohio	FA-'01	16/0

* Cordova missed '05 season with injury; Greisen played 16 games with N.Y. Giants in '05; McDougle played 7 games with Miami; Patterson last active with Jacksonville in '04; Romberg inactive for 4 games; B. Williams played 14 games with Minnesota; M. Williams played 9 games with Buffalo; T. Williams last active with Cincinnati in '05; Yoder missed '05 season with injury

Retired—Jimmy Smith, 13-year wide receiver, 16 games in '05.

Players lost through free agency (6): LB Akin Ayodele (Dall; 16 games in '05), S Deke Cooper (Mia; 16), T Mike Pearson (Mia; 4), T Ephraim Salaam (Hou; 5), LB Jamie Winborn (TB; 5), CB Kenny Wright (Wash; 16).

Also played with Jaguars in '05—RB Rich Alexis (2 games), DT Martin Chase (1), DE Jim Davis (1), LB Greg Favors (1), WR Chad Owens (1), LB Tracy White (15).

2006 FIRST-YEAR ROSTER

Name	Pos.	Ht.	Wt.	Birthdate	College	Hometown	How Acq.
Alexis, Rich (1)	RB	6-0	213	3/6/81	Washington	Coral Springs, Fla.	FA
Collier, Richard	T	6-7	358	10/23/81	Valdosta State	Shreveport, La.	FA
Curry, Walter (1)	DT/DE	6-4	275	6/18/81	Albany State	Daytona Beach, Fla.	FA-'05
Davis, Jim (1)	DE	6-3	275	10/4/81	Virginia Tech	Highland Springs, Va.	FA-'05
Economos, Andrew (1)	LS	6-1	250	6/24/82	Georgia Tech	Atlanta, Ga.	FA-'05
Fudge, Jamaal	S	5-9	196	5/17/83	Clemson	Jacksonville, Fla.	FA
George, Trestin	CB	5-9	179	8/24/83	San Jose State	Berkeley, Calif.	FA
Gibbons, Ryan	T	6-6	318	3/13/83	Northeastern	Marshfield, Mass.	FA
Hand, Omari (1)	DE	6-4	265	7/3/80	Tennessee	Tallahassee, Fla.	FA
Hawkins, Brent	LB	6-2	240	9/1/83	Illinois State	Godfrey, Ill.	D5
Hill, Kahlil (1)	WR	6-2	200	3/18/79	Iowa	Iowa City, Iowa	FA-'05
Huggins, Felton	WR	6-2	181	2/15/83	Southeastern Louisiana	Zachary, La.	FA
Ingram, Clint	LB	6-2	245	3/21/83	Oklahoma	Hallsville, Texas	D3
Iwuh, Brian	LB	6-0	224	3/8/84	Colorado	Houston, Texas	FA
Jones-Drew, Maurice	RB/KR	5-7	207	3/23/85	UCLA	Antioch, Calif.	D2
Joseph, Carlos (1)	T	6-6	342	7/14/80	Miami	Miami, Fla.	FA
Lewis, Marcedes	TE	6-6	262	5/19/84	UCLA	Lakewood, Calif.	D1
McCullough, Edorian	CB	5-9	194	1/6/82	Texas	Dallas, Texas	FA
McDaniel, Tony	DT	6-7	295	1/20/85	Tennessee	Columbia, S.C.	FA
Owens, Chad (1)	WR/KR	5-7	183	4/3/82	Hawaii	Honolulu, Hawaii	D6a-'05
Owens, Montell	RB	5-10	219	5/4/84	Maine	Wilmington, Del.	FA
Pinegar, Paul	QB	6-5	230	3/10/82	Fresno State	Woodland, Calif.	FA
Sharon, Charles	WR	6-0	184	4/4/83	Bowling Green	Palatka, Fla.	FA
Stamps, Fred (1)	WR	6-1	180	12/10/80	Lousiana-Lafayette	New Orleans, La.	FA-'05
Twito, Brandon	TE	6-5	256	8/21/81	Pittsburg State	Sanger, Texas	FA
Webb, Dee	CB	5-11	186	12/8/84	Florida	Jacksonville, Fla.	D7b
Wyche, James	DE	6-5	262	4/19/82	Syracuse	Roosevelt, N.Y.	D7a

The term NFL Rookie is defined as a player who is in his first season of professional football and has not been on the roster of another professional football team for any regular-season or postseason games. A Rookie is designated by an "R" on NFL rosters. Players who have been active in another professional football league or players who have NFL experience, including either preseason training camp or being on an Active List or Inactive List, or on Reserve/Injured or Reserve/Physically Unable to Perform for fewer than six regular-season games, are termed NFL First-Year Players. An NFL First-Year Player is designated by a "1" on NFL rosters. Thereafter, a player is credited with an additional year of experience for each season in which he accumulates six games on the Active List or Inactive List, or on Reserve/Injured or Reserve/Physically Unable to Perform.

Log on to www.jaguars.com for an up-to-date roster.

COACHING STAFF
Head Coach,
Jack Del Rio

Pro Career: Jack Del Rio was named head coach of the Jaguars on January 17, 2003, becoming the second head coach in franchise history. At 43, Del Rio is the sixth-youngest head coach in the NFL. In 2005, Jacksonville finished with a 12-4 record and Del Rio guided the franchise to its first postseason appearance since 1999. In 2004, the Jaguars registered a 9-7 record for the franchise's first winning season since 1999. In 2003, six of the Jaguars' eleven losses were by seven points or less. Del Rio was the defensive coordinator for the Carolina Panthers in 2002, and the team's defense ranked second in the league after finishing thirty-first in 2001. From 1999-2001, he was the linebackers coach for the Baltimore Ravens, helping the team win Super Bowl XXXV. Del Rio previously coached in New Orleans (1997-98). He previously spent 11 years as an NFL linebacker. In 1985, he was a third-round choice of the New Orleans Saints and was named to the NFL's All-Rookie team. Del Rio also played for the Kansas City Chiefs (1987-88), Dallas Cowboys (1989-1991), and Minnesota Vikings (1992-95). He played in the Pro Bowl following the 1994 season. Career record: 26-23.

Background: Four-year starter at linebacker from 1981-84 at Southern California, where he earned consensus All-America honors as a senior and was runner-up for the Lombardi Award. He was co-MVP of the 1985 Rose Bowl. Drafted by baseball's Toronto Blue Jays in 1981, Del Rio batted .340 while playing catcher on USC's baseball team. He has a political science degree from Kansas.

Personal: Born April 4, 1963 in Castro Valley, Calif. Jack and his wife, Linda, live in Jacksonville, and have three daughters, Lauren, Hope, and Aubrey, and a son, Luke.

ASSISTANT COACHES

Ken Anderson, quarterbacks; born February 15, 1949, Batavia, Ill. Quarterback Augustana (Ill.) 1967-1970. Pro quarterback Cincinnati Bengals 1971-1986. Pro coach: Cincinnati Bengals 1992-2002, joined Jaguars in 2003.

Mark Asanovich, strength and conditioning; born May 20, 1959, Duluth, Minn. Attended St. Cloud State. No college or pro playing experience. College coach: Ohio State 1984-85, The Citadel 1986. Pro coach: Minnesota Vikings 1995, Tampa Bay Buccaneers 1996-2001, Baltimore Ravens 2002, joined Jaguars in 2003.

Dave Campo, asst. head coach/secondary; born July 18, 1947, Groton, Conn. Defensive back Central Connecticut State 1967-1970. No pro playing experience. College coach: Central Connecticut State 1971-72, Albany 1973, Bridgeport 1974, Pittsburgh 1975, Washington State 1976, Boise State 1977-79, Oregon State 1980, Weber State 1981-82, Iowa State 1983, Syracuse 1984-86, Miami 1987-88. Pro coach: Dallas Cowboys 1989-2002 (head coach 2000-2002), Cleveland Browns 2003-2004, joined Jaguars in 2005.

Mark Duffner, linebackers; born July 19, 1953, Annadale, Va. Defensive lineman William & Mary 1972-74. No pro playing experience. College coach: Ohio State 1975-76, Cincinnati 1977-1980, Holy Cross 1981-1991 (head coach 1986-1991), Maryland 1992-1996 (head coach). Pro coach: Cincinnati Bengals 1997-2002, Green Bay Packers 2003-2005, joined Jaguars in 2006.

Les Ebert, asst. strength and conditioning; born October 1, 1972, Brainerd, Minn. Attended Minnesota-Duluth. No college or pro playing experience. Pro coach: Tampa Bay Buccaneers 1999-2002, joined Jaguars in 2003.

Ray Hamilton, defensive line; born January 20, 1951, Omaha, Neb. Nose tackle Oklahoma 1969-1972. Pro defensive lineman New England Patriots 1973-1981. College coach: Tennessee 1992. Pro coach: New England Patriots 1985-89, Tampa Bay Buccaneers 1991, Los Angeles Raiders 1993-94, New York Jets 1994-96, 2000, New England Patriots 1997-99, Cleveland Browns 2001-02, joined Jaguars in 2003.

Andy Heck, offensive line; born January 1, 1967, Fargo, N.D. Tackle Notre Dame 1985-88. Pro tackle Seattle 1989-1993, Chicago 1994-98, Washington 1999-2000. College coach: Virginia 2001-03. Pro coach: Joined Jaguars in 2003.

Mark Michaels, asst. special teams; born August 15, 1963, Kingston, Pa. Defensive lineman Connecticut 1983-86. No pro playing experience. College coach: New Haven 1987-1990, Brown 1993-97, Massachusetts 1998. Pro coach: Helsinki Roosters (Finnish Maple League) 1991, Utah Pioneers (Professional Spring Football League) 1992, Cleveland Browns 1999-2000, Seattle Seahawks 2001-2004, joined Jaguars in 2005.

Ted Monachino, asst. defensive line; born October 15, 1966, Council Bluffs, Iowa. Defensive lineman Missouri 1984-1990. No pro playing experience. College coach: Texas Christian 1998, Southwest Missouri State 1999, Boise State 2000, Arizona State 2001-2005. Pro coach: Joined Jaguars in 2006.

Kennedy Pola, running backs; born November 22, 1963, Pago, Pago, American Samoa. Fullback Southern California 1982-85. No pro playing experience. College coach: UCLA 1992-93, San Diego State 1994-96, Colorado 1997-98, San Diego State 1999, Southern California 2000-2005. Pro coach: Cleveland Browns 2004, joined Jaguars in 2005.

Alvin Reynolds, defensive backs; born June 24, 1959, Pineville, La. Safety Indiana State 1978-1981. No pro playing experience. College coach: Indiana State 1982-1992. Pro coach: Denver Broncos 1993-95, Baltimore Ravens 1996-98, Carolina Panthers 1999-2002, joined Jaguars in 2003.

Alfredo Roberts, tight ends; born March 17, 1965, Fort Lauderdale, Fla. Tight end Miami 1983-87. Pro tight end Kansas City Chiefs 1988-1990, Dallas Cowboys 1991-93. College coach: Florida Atlantic 1999-2002. Pro coach: Joined Jaguars in 2003.

Pete Rodriguez, special teams coordinator, born July 25, 1940, Chicago. Guard-linebacker Denver 1959-1960, Western State (Colo.) 1961-63. College coach: Arizona 1968-69, Western Illinois 1970-73, 1979-1982 (head coach 1979-1982), Florida State 1974-75, Iowa State 1976-78, Northern Iowa 1986. Pro coach: Michigan Panthers (USFL) 1983-84, Denver Gold (USFL) 1985, Jacksonville Bulls (USFL) 1986, Ottawa Rough Riders (CFL) 1987, Los Angeles Raiders 1988-89, Phoenix Cardinals 1990-93, Washington Redskins 1994-97, Seattle Seahawks 1998-2003, joined Jaguars in 2004.

Carl Smith, offensive coordinator; born April 28, 1948, Wasco, Calif. Quarterback Bakersfield College 1966-67, defensive back Cal-Poly San Luis Obispo 1969-70. No pro playing experience. College coach: Colorado 1972-73, Southwestern Louisiana 1974-78, Lamar 1979-1981, North Carolina State 1982, Southern California 2004. Pro coach: Philadelphia/Baltimore Stars (USFL) 1983-85, New Orleans Saints 1986-1996, New England Patriots 1997-2000, Cleveland Browns 2001-2003, joined Jaguars in 2005.

Mike Smith, defensive coordinator; born November 30, 1959, Chicago. Linebacker East Tennessee 1977-1981. Pro linebacker Winnipeg Blue Bombers (CFL) 1982. College coach: San Diego State 1982-85, Morehead State (Ky.) 1986, Tennessee Tech 1987-1998. Pro coach: Baltimore Ravens 1999-2002, joined Jaguars in 2003.

Mike Tice, asst. head coach/offense; born February 2, 1959, Bayshore, N.Y. Quarterback Maryland 1977-1980. Pro tight end Seattle Seahawks 1981-1988, 1990-91, Washington Redskins 1989, Minnesota Vikings 1992-1993, 1995. Pro coach: Minnesota Vikings 1996-2005 (head coach 2001-2005), joined Jaguars in 2006.

Steve Walters, wide receivers; born June 16, 1948, Jonesboro, Ark. Quarterback-defensive back Arkansas 1967-1970. No pro playing experience. College coach: Tampa 1973, Northeastern Louisiana 1974-75, Morehead State 1976, Tulsa 1977-78, Memphis State 1979, Southern Methodist 1980-81, Alabama 1985. Pro coach: New England Patriots 1982-84, 1997-98, New Orleans Saints 1986-1996, Tennessee Titans 1999-2004, joined Jaguars in 2005.

American Football Conference
West Division
Team Colors: Red, Gold, and White
One Arrowhead Drive
Kansas City, Missouri 64129
Telephone: (816) 920-9300

2006 SCHEDULE
PRESEASON
Aug. 12 at Houston 7:00
Aug. 17 at New York Giants 8:00
Aug. 26 **St. Louis** 7:30
Aug. 31 **New Orleans**......................7:30

REGULAR SEASON
Sept. 10 **Cincinnati** 12:00
Sept. 17 at Denver 2:15
Sept. 24 Open Date
Oct. 1 **San Francisco** 12:00
Oct. 8 at Arizona...........................1:05
Oct. 15 at Pittsburgh.......................4:15
Oct. 22 **San Diego**.......................12:00
Oct. 29 **Seattle**............................12:00
Nov. 5 at St. Louis.......................12:00
Nov. 12 at Miami........................... 1:00
Nov. 19 **Oakland** 12:00
Nov. 23 **Denver** (Thu.) 7:00
Dec. 3 at Cleveland 1:00
Dec. 10 **Baltimore**........................12:00
Dec. 17 at San Diego 1:05
Dec. 23 at Oakland (Sat.) 5:00
Dec. 31 **Jacksonville**....................12:00

Stadium: Arrowhead Stadium
(opened in 1972)
  •Capacity: 79,451
  One Arrowhead Drive
  Kansas City, Missouri 64129
Playing Surface: Grass
Training Camp: University of
  Wisconsin-River Falls
  River Falls, Wisconsin
  54022

ARROWHEAD STADIUM

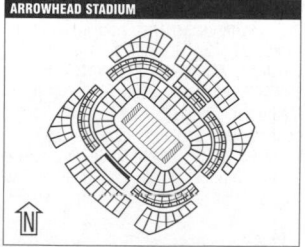

CLUB OFFICIALS
Founder: Lamar Hunt
Chairman of the Board: Clark Hunt
Vice Chairman of the Board:
  Jack Steadman
President: Carl Peterson
Executive Vice President/Chief Operating
  Officer: Denny Thum
Vice President of Player Personnel:
  Bill Kuharich
Vice President of Football Operations:
  Lynn Stiles
Senior Vice President of Administration:
  Bill Newman
Secretary: Jim Seigfreid
Director of Finance/Treasurer: Dale Young
Vice President of Sales and Marketing:
  Tammy Fruits
Director of College Scouting: Chuck Cook
Director of Public Relations: Bob Moore
Associate Director of Public Relations:
  Pete Moris
Director of Stadium Operations:
  Steve Schneider
Director of Development: Ken Blume
Director of Corporate Sponsorship:
  Anita Bailey
Director of Sales: Gary Spani
Director of Player Development:
  Lamonte Winston
Director of Community Relations:
  Brenda Sniezek
Director of Ticket Operations:
  Doug Hopkins
Equipment Manager: Mike Davidson
Asst. Equipment Managers: Allen Wright,
  Chris Shropshire
Head Athletic Trainer: David Price
Assistant Athletic Trainers: David Glover,
  Dan Lorenz, Jimmy Ntelekos
Director of Video Operations: Pat Brazil
Assistant Director of Video Operations:
  Andrew Hearne
Video Assistant: Ken Radino

COACHING HISTORY
Dallas Texans 1960-62
(374-326-12)
Records include postseason games
1960-1974	Hank Stram	129-79-10
1975-77	Paul Wiggin*	11-24-0
1977	Tom Bettis	1-6-0
1978-1982	Marv Levy	31-42-0
1983-86	John Mackovic	30-35-0
1987-88	Frank Gansz	8-22-1
1989-1998	Marty Schottenheimer	...104-65-1
1999-2000	Gunther Cunningham	16-16-0
2001-05	Dick Vermeil	44-37-0

*Released after seven games in 1977

ATTENDANCE
Home 625,081   Away 552,499
Total 1,177,580
Single-game home record,
  82,893* (10/2/00)
Single-season home record,
  629,569 (1999)
*Arrowhead Stadium attendance: 78,502;
Kauffman Stadium attendance: 4,391

2006 DRAFT CHOICES
Round	Name	Pos.	College
1	Tamba Hali	DE	Penn State
2	Bernard Pollard	DB	Purdue
3	Brodie Croyle	QB	Alabama
5	Marcus Maxey	DB	Miami
6	Tre' Stallings	G	Mississippi
	Jeff Webb	WR	San Diego St.
7	Jarrad Page	DB	UCLA

2005 TEAM RECORD

PRESEASON (0-4)

Date	Result	Opponent
8/12	L 16-27	at Minnesota
8/20	L 17-24	Arizona
8/27	L 17-23	Seattle
9/2	L 23-27	at St. Louis

REGULAR SEASON (10-6)

Date	Result	Opponent	Att.
9/11	W 27-7	New York Jets	78,014
9/18	W 23-17	at Oakland	62,273
9/26	L 10-30	at Denver	76,381
10/2	L 31-37	Philadelphia	78,742
10/16	W 28-21	Washington	78,083
10/21	W 30-20	at Miami	68,350
10/30	L 20-28	at San Diego	65,750
11/6	W 27-23	Oakland	79,033
11/13	L 3-14	at Buffalo	72,093
11/20	W 45-17	at Houston	70,481
11/27	W 26-16	New England	78,025
12/4	W 31-27	Denver	78,261
12/11	L 28-31	at Dallas	63,432
12/17	L 17-27	at N.Y. Giants	78,625
12/24	W 20-7	San Diego	75,956
1/1	W 37-3	Cincinnati	77,211

SCORE BY PERIODS

Chiefs	85	136	79	103	0	—	403
Opponents	51	110	76	88	0	—	325

2005 TEAM STATISTICS

	Chiefs	Opp.
Total First Downs	347	292
Rushing	138	84
Passing	182	189
Penalty	27	19
3rd Down: Made/Att	91/213	78/206
3rd Down Pct.	42.7	37.9
4th Down: Made/Att	10/16	7/19
4th Down Pct.	62.5	36.8
Possession Avg.	32:09	27:51
Total Net Yards	6,192	5,249
Avg. Per Game	387.0	328.1
Total Plays	1,059	971
Avg. Per Play	5.8	5.4
Net Yards Rushing	2,382	1,570
Avg. Per Game	148.9	98.1
Total Rushes	520	383
Net Yards Passing	3,810	3,679
Avg. Per Game	238.1	229.9
Sacked/Yards Lost	32/204	29/183
Gross Yards	4,014	3,862
Att./Completions	507/317	559/325
Completion Pct.	62.5	58.1
Had Intercepted	10	16
Punts/Average	65/39.4	69/45.7
Net Punting Avg.	65/35.2	69/40.0
Penalties/Yards	115/890	90/805
Fumbles/Ball Lost	23/13	33/15
Touchdowns	46	38
Rushing	26	11
Passing	17	25
Returns	3	2

2005 INDIVIDUAL STATISTICS

PASSING	Att.	Comp.	Yds.	Pct.	TD	Int.	Tkld.	Rate
Green	507	317	4,014	62.5	17	10	32/204	90.1
Chiefs	507	317	4,014	62.5	17	10	32/204	90.1
Opponents	559	325	3,862	58.1	25	16	29/183	82.3

SCORING	TD R	TD P	TD Rt	PAT	FG	Saf	PTS
L. Johnson	20	1	0	0/0	0/0	0	126
Tynes	0	0	0	44/45	27/33	0	125
Holmes	6	1	0	0/0	0/0	0	42
Kennison	0	5	0	0/0	0/0	0	30
D. Hall	0	3	1	0/0	0/0	0	24
Parker	3	0	0	0/0	0/0	0	18
Gonzalez	0	2	0	0/0	0/0	0	12
Brown	0	1	0	0/0	0/0	0	6
Knight	0	0	1	0/0	0/0	0	6
Richardson	0	1	0	0/0	0/0	0	6
Warfield	0	0	1	0/0	0/0	0	6
Boerigter	0	0	0	0/0	0/0	2	2
Chiefs	26	17	3	44/45	27/33	0	403
Opponents	11	25	2	33/33	20/26	0	325

2-Pt. Conversions: Boerigter.
Chiefs 1-1, Opponents 2-5.

RUSHING	No.	Yds	Avg	LG	TD
L. Johnson	336	1,750	5.2	49t	20
Holmes	119	451	3.8	35t	6
Green	35	82	2.3	13	0
Kennison	7	43	6.1	23	0
Brown	7	21	3.0	7	0
Richardson	6	20	3.3	8	0
D. Hall	7	11	1.6	7	0
Wilson	1	6	6.0	6	0
Collins	2	-2	-1.0	-1	0
Chiefs	520	2,382	4.6	49t	26
Opponents	383	1,570	4.1	65t	11

RECEIVING	No.	Yds	Avg	LG	TD
Gonzalez	78	905	11.6	39	2
Kennison	68	1,102	16.2	55	5
Parker	36	533	14.8	49	3
D. Hall	34	436	12.8	52t	3
L. Johnson	33	343	10.4	36	1
Holmes	21	197	9.4	60t	1
Horn	18	187	10.4	50	0
Richardson	9	68	7.6	22	1
Boerigter	8	119	14.9	38	0
Dunn	5	53	10.6	24	0
Wilson	3	33	11.0	16	0
Brown	3	23	7.7	9	1
Cruz	1	15	15.0	15	0
Chiefs	317	4,014	12.7	60t	17
Opponents	325	3,862	11.9	78t	25

INTERCEPTIONS	No.	Yds	Avg	LG	TD
Wesley	6	106	17.7	51	0
Surtain	4	57	14.3	53	0
Knight	2	12	6.0	12	0
McCleon	2	0	0.0	0	0
Warfield	1	57	57.0	57t	1
K. Mitchell	1	0	0.0	0	0
Chiefs	16	232	14.5	57t	1
Opponents	10	196	19.6	40t	1

PUNTING	No.	Yds.	Avg.	In 20	LG
Colquitt	65	2,564	39.4	27	62
Chiefs	65	2,564	39.4	27	62
Opponents	69	3,155	45.7	19	61

PUNT RETURNS	Ret	FC	Yds	Avg	LG	TD
D. Hall	42	6	276	6.6	52	0
Kennison	1	1	17	17.0	17	0
Chiefs	43	7	293	6.8	52	0
Opponents	23	21	179	7.8	47	0

KICKOFF RETURNS	No.	Yds	Avg	LG	TD
D. Hall	65	1,560	24.0	96t	1
Horn	3	31	10.3	11	0
Chiefs	68	1,591	23.4	96t	1
Opponents	83	2,053	24.7	99t	1

FIELD GOALS	1-19	20-29	30-39	40-49	50+
Tynes	1/1	8/8	12/13	4/8	2/3
Chiefs	1/1	8/8	12/13	4/8	2/3
Opponents	0/0	7/9	6/7	6/8	1/2

SACKS	No.
Allen	11.0
Hicks	4.0
Sapp	2.5
Browning	2.0
D. Johnson	2.0
Knight	2.0
K. Mitchell	2.0
Bell	1.5
Dalton	1.0
C. Hall	1.0
Chiefs	29.0
Opponents	32.0

RECORD HOLDERS
INDIVIDUAL RECORDS—CAREER

Category	Name	Performance
Rushing (Yds.)	Priest Holmes, 2001-05	5,933
Passing (Yds.)	Len Dawson, 1962-1975	28,507
Passing (TDs)	Len Dawson, 1962-1975	237
Receiving (No.)	Tony Gonzalez, 1997-2005	648
Receiving (Yds.)	Tony Gonzalez, 1997-2005	7,810
Interceptions	Emmitt Thomas, 1966-1978	58
Punting (Avg.)	Jerrel Wilson, 1963-1977	43.4
Punt Return (Avg.)	Noland Smith, 1967-69	11.1
Kickoff Return (Avg.)	Noland Smith, 1967-69	26.8
Field Goals	Nick Lowery, 1980-1993	329
Touchdowns (Tot.)	Priest Holmes, 2001-05	83
Points	Nick Lowery, 1980-1993	1,466

INDIVIDUAL RECORDS—SINGLE SEASON

Category	Name	Performance
Rushing (Yds.)	Larry Johnson, 2005	1,750
Passing (Yds.)	Trent Green, 2004	4,591
Passing (TDs)	Len Dawson, 1964	30
Receiving (No.)	Tony Gonzalez, 2004	102
Receiving (Yds.)	Derrick Alexander, 2000	1,391
Interceptions	Emmitt Thomas, 1974	12
Punting (Avg.)	Jerrel Wilson, 1965	45.4
Punt Return (Avg.)	Dante Hall, 2003	16.3
Kickoff Return (Avg.)	Dave Grayson, 1962	29.7
Field Goals	Nick Lowery, 1990	34
Touchdowns (Tot.)	Priest Holmes, 2003	27
Points	Priest Holmes, 2003	162

INDIVIDUAL RECORDS—SINGLE GAME

Category	Name	Performance
Rushing (Yds.)	Larry Johnson, 11-20-05	211
Passing (Yds.)	Elvis Grbac, 11-5-00	504
Passing (TDs)	Len Dawson, 11-1-64	6
Receiving (No.)	Tony Gonzalez, 1-2-05	14
Receiving (Yds.)	Stephone Paige, 12-22-85	309
Interceptions	Bobby Ply, 12-16-62	*4
	Bobby Hunt, 10-4-64	*4
	Deron Cherry, 9-29-85	*4
Field Goals	Many times	5
	Last time by Nick Lowery, 9-20-93	
Touchdowns (Tot.)	Abner Haynes, 11-26-61	5
Points	Abner Haynes, 11-26-61	30

*NFL Record

2006 VETERAN ROSTER

No.	Name	Pos.	Ht.	Wt.	Birthdate	NFL Exp.	College	Hometown	How Acq.	'05 Games/ Starts
	Allen, Ian	T	6-5	310	7/22/78	5	Purdue	Atlanta, Ga.	UFA(Ariz)-'06	2/0*
69	Allen, Jared	DE	6-6	265	4/3/82	3	Idaho State	Los Gatos, Calif.	D4b-'04	16/15
24	Bartee, William	S	6-1	200	6/25/77	7	Oklahoma	Daytona Beach, Fla.	D2-'00	16/0
26	Battle, Julian	CB	6-2	205	7/11/81	4	Tennessee	West Palm Beach, Fla.	D3-'03	0*
99	Bell, Kendrell	LB	6-1	245	7/2/80	6	Georgia	Augusta, Ga.	UFA(Pitt)-'05	16/14
65	Black, Jordan	T	6-5	304	1/28/80	4	Notre Dame	Mesquite, Texas	D5-'03	16/10
67	Bober, Chris	C/T	6-5	310	12/24/76	7	Nebraska-Omaha	Omaha, Neb.	UFA(NYG)-'04	16/2
22	Brown, Dee	RB	5-10	210	5/12/78	4	Syracuse	Altamonte Springs, Fla.	FA-'05	8/0
93	Browning, John	DT	6-5	297	9/30/73	11	West Virginia	Miami, Fla.	D3-'96	16/12
2	Colquitt, Dustin	P	6-1	191	5/6/82	2	Tennessee	Knoxville, Tenn.	D3-'05	16/0
42	Cruz, Ronnie	RB	6-0	237	6/11/81	2	Northern State	Lakeport, Calif.	FA-'05	14/0
75	Dalton, Lional	DT	6-1	315	2/21/75	9	Eastern Michigan	Detroit, Mich.	FA-'04	16/14
89	Dunn, Jason	TE	6-6	274	11/15/73	10	Eastern Kentucky	Harrodsburg, Ky.	FA-'00	16/1
95	Edwards, Ron	DT	6-3	293	7/12/79	6	Texas A&M	Houston, Texas	UFA(Buff)-'06	4/4*
97	Fox, Keyaron	LB	6-3	235	1/24/82	3	Georgia Tech	Atlanta, Ga.	D3-'04	2/0
71	Freeman, Eddie	DE	6-5	310	1/4/78	3	Alabama-Birmingham	Mobile, Ala.	FA-'06	0*
83	Gammon, Kendall	TE	6-4	255	10/23/68	15	Pittsburg State	Rose Hill, Kan.	UFA(NO)-'00	10/0
46	Garrett, Kevin	CB	5-9	194	7/29/80	3	Southern Methodist	Brazoria, Texas	FA-'06	0*
88	Gonzalez, Tony	TE	6-5	251	2/27/76	10	California	Huntington Beach, Calif.	D1-'97	16/16
10	Green, Trent	QB	6-3	217	7/9/70	13	Indiana	St. Louis, Mo.	T(StL)-'01	16/16
53	Griffin, Kris	LB	6-3	232	5/27/81	2	Indiana (Pa.)	Rochester, Pa.	FA-'05	8/0
34	Griffin, Quentin	RB	5-7	195	1/12/81	3	Oklahoma	Houston, Texas	FA-'06	0*
51	Grigsby, Boomer	LB	5-11	249	11/15/81	2	Illinois State	Canton, Ill.	D5a-'05	16/0
92	Hall, Carlos	DE	6-4	259	1/16/79	5	Arkansas	Marianna, Ark.	T(Tenn)-'05	14/2
82	Hall, Dante	WR	5-8	187	9/20/78	7	Texas A&M	Houston, Texas	D5a-'00	16/2
98	Hicks, Eric	DE	6-6	280	6/17/76	9	Maryland	Erie, Pa.	FA-'98	16/14
9	Hill, Darrell	WR	6-2	187	6/19/79	4	Northern Illinois	Chicago, Ill.	FA-'06	0*
47	Hodge, Alphonso	CB	5-10	203	5/30/82	2	Miami (Ohio)	Lakewood, Ohio	D5b-'05	0*
31	Holmes, Priest	RB	5-9	213	10/7/73	10	Texas	San Antonio, Texas	UFA(Balt)-'01	7/7
11	Huard, Damon	QB	6-3	212	7/9/73	10	Washington	Puyallup, Wash.	FA-'04	0*
66	Ingram, Johnathan	C	6-2	300	9/20/80	2	San Diego State	La Quinta, Calif.	FA-'06	4/0
39	Johnson, Chris	CB	6-0	198	9/25/79	4	Louisville	Longview, Texas	FA-'06	14/1*
56	Johnson, Derrick	LB	6-3	242	11/22/82	2	Texas	Waco, Texas	D1-'05	16/16
27	Johnson, Larry	RB	6-1	230	11/19/79	4	Penn State	State College, Pa.	D1-'03	16/9
87	Kennison, Eddie	WR	6-1	201	1/20/73	11	Louisiana State	Lake Charles, La.	FA-'01	16/16
29	Knight, Sammy	S	6-1	215	9/10/75	10	Southern California	Riverside, Calif.	UFA(Mia)-'05	16/16
72	Mitchell, Clint	DE	6-7	257	9/21/80	2	Florida	Clearwater, Fla.	FA-'06	0*
50	Mitchell, Kawika	LB	6-1	253	10/10/79	4	South Florida	Lake Howell, Fla.	D2-'03	16/16
18	Parker, Samie	WR	5-11	190	3/25/81	3	Oregon	Long Beach, Calif.	D4a-'04	12/9
72	Parquet, Jeremy	T	6-6	321	4/11/82	2	Southern Mississippi	Norco, La.	D7b-'05	0*
77	Roaf, Willie	T	6-5	320	4/18/70	14	Louisiana Tech	Pine Bluff, Ark.	T(NO)-'02	10/10
79	Sampson, Kevin	T	6-4	312	6/19/81	3	Syracuse	Westwood, N.J.	D7-'04	4/1
20	Sapp, Benny	CB	5-9	190	1/20/81	3	Northern Iowa	Ft. Lauderdale, Fla.	FA-'04	16/3
91	Scanlon, Rich	LB	6-2	249	12/23/80	3	Syracuse	Oradell, N.J.	FA-'04	16/0
68	Shields, Will	G	6-3	320	9/15/71	14	Nebraska	Lawton, Okla.	D3-'93	16/16
94	Siavii, Junior	DT	6-5	336	11/14/78	3	Oregon	Pago Pago, American Samoa	D2a-'04	14/0
90	Sims, Ryan	DT	6-4	315	5/4/80	5	North Carolina	Spartanburg, S.C.	D1-'02	6/5
23	Surtain, Patrick	CB	5-11	195	6/19/76	9	Southern Mississippi	New Orleans, La.	T(Mia)-'05	15/15
71	Svitek, Will	T	6-6	300	1/8/82	2	Stanford	Newbury, Calif.	D6a-'05	1/0
1	Tynes, Lawrence	K	6-1	202	5/3/78	3	Troy State	Milton, Fla.	FA-'04	16/0
43	Walls, Lenny	CB	6-4	192	9/26/79	5	Boston College	San Francisco, Calif.	FA-'06	7/3*
54	Waters, Brian	G	6-3	318	2/18/77	3	North Texas	Waxahachie, Texas	FA-'00	16/16
76	Welbourn, John	G/T	6-5	310	3/30/76	8	California	Rolling Hills, Calif.	T(Phil)-'04	12/9
25	Wesley, Greg	S	6-2	206	3/19/78	7	Arkansas-Pine Bluff	England, Ark.	D3-'00	16/16
62	Wiegmann, Casey	C	6-2	285	7/20/73	11	Iowa	Parkersburg, Iowa	UFA(Chi)-'01	16/16
96	Wilkerson, Jimmy	DE	6-2	280	1/4/81	4	Oklahoma	Omaha, Texas	D6-'03	16/2
84	Wilson, Kris	TE	6-2	251	8/22/81	3	Pittsburgh	Lancaster, Pa.	D2b-'04	14/1

* Allen played 2 games with Arizona in '05; Battle missed '05 season because of injury; Edwards played 4 games with Buffalo; Freeman last active with Jacksonville in '04; Garrett last active with St. Louis in '04; Q. Griffin inactive for 1 game with Denver; Hill last active with Tennessee in '04; Hodge inactive for 6 games; Huard did not play in 1 game; C. Johnson played 14 games with St. Louis; C. Mitchell last active with Denver in '03; Parquet did not play in 2 games; Walls played 7 games with Denver.

Players lost through free agency (3): WR Marc Boerigter (GB; 10), QB Todd Collins (Wash; 1), FB Tony Richardson (Minn; 16).

Also played with Chiefs in '05—LB Shawn Barber (3 games), WR Chris Horn (14), DE Khari Long (1), CB Dexter McCleon (11), TE Ed Perry (6), LB Gary Stills (16), CB Eric Warfield (11), CB Dewayne Washington (16), S Jerome Woods (7).

2006 FIRST-YEAR ROSTER

Name	Pos.	Ht.	Wt.	Birthdate	College	Hometown	How Acq.
Barnett, Thomas (1)	T	6-4	314	10/21/78	Kansas State	Oklahoma City, Okla.	FA
Bragg, Michael (1)	CB	6-1	183	12/31/81	Texas A&M-Kingsville	Lakewood, Calif.	FA
Brown, Kyle	WR	6-0	200	12/31/83	Michigan State	West Bloomfield, Mich.	FA
Connot, Scott (1)	S	6-3	216	6/24/81	South Dakota State	Spencer, Neb.	FA
Croyle, Brodie	QB	6-2	206	2/6/83	Alabama	Rainbow City, Ala.	D3
Curry, Nathaniel (1)	WR	5-10	196	3/11/82	Georgia Tech	Miami, Fla.	FA
Dixon, Arrion (1)	DT	6-4	308	10/21/81	Arkansas	Wynne, Ark.	FA
Docherty, Robert	TE	6-5	274	7/26/83	Wisconsin-Oshkosh	Oshkosh, Wis.	FA
Franklin, Steve	G	6-2	302	6/9/83	Syracuse	Dover, Del.	FA
Golliday, Aaron (1)	TE	6-3	282	12/3/79	Nebraska	York, Neb.	FA
Guerrero, Alex	DT	6-1	303	2/16/84	Boise State	Brea, Calif.	FA
Guillory, Brandon	LB	6-4	253	6/28/83	Louisiana-Monroe	New Orleans, La.	FA
Hali, Tamba	DE	6-3	275	11/3/83	Penn State	Teaneck, N.J.	D1
Hannon, Chris	WR	6-3	205	2/18/84	Tennessee	Sarasota, Fla.	FA
Helms, Gabriel (1)	CB	5-10	221	3/25/80	Northwest Missouri State	St. Louis, Mo.	FA
Howard, De Arrius	RB	5-11	229	6/7/83	Arkansas	Memphis, Ark.	FA
Jamison, Jermaine	WR	6-2	201	4/9/83	Fresno State	Los Angeles, Calif.	FA
Johnson, Adam (1)	TE	6-5	235	11/11/79	Buffalo	Rancho Cucamonga, Calif.	FA
Kershaw, William	LB	6-3	240	12/15/83	Maryland	Raeford, N.C.	FA
Kilian, James (1)	QB	6-3	218	10/24/80	Tulsa	Medford, Okla.	FA
Maxey, Marcus	CB	6-0	192	2/2/83	Miami	Navasota, Texas	D5
McIntyre, Jeris (1)	WR	6-0	203	7/4/81	Auburn	Tampa, Fla.	D6-'04
Melendez, Dan	WR	6-2	173	2/16/84	Maryland	Lancaster, Pa.	FA
Metcalf, Terrance	WR	6-3	207	5/20/80	South Carolina State	Seattle, Wash.	FA
Niswanger, Rudy	C	6-5	301	11/9/82	Louisiana State	Monroe, La.	FA
Page, Jarrad	S	6-0	225	10/19/84	UCLA	San Leandro, Calif.	D7
Perkins, Justin (1)	CB	5-10	186	7/9/82	Connecticut	Sunrise, Fla.	FA
Pollard, Bernard	S	6-1	224	12/23/84	Purdue	Ft. Wayne, Ind.	D2
Printers, Casey (1)	QB	6-2	222	5/16/81	Florida A&M	DeSoto, Texas	FA
Reid, Nick	LB	6-3	234	11/18/83	Kansas	Derby, Kan.	FA
Ross, Derrick	RB	5-10	226	12/29/83	Tarleton State	Huntsville, Texas	FA
Slaughter, Jake	FB	6-1	242	9/4/82	Auburn	New Orleans, La.	FA
Smith, McKenzi (1)	RB	5-8	196	10/19/81	Washington State	Pasadena, Calif.	FA
Stallings, Tre	G	6-3	315	1/8/83	Mississippi	Magnolia, Miss.	D6a
Thorpe, Craphonso (1)	WR	6-0	187	6/27/83	Florida State	Tallahassee, Fla.	D4-'05
Ville, Zach (1)	DE	6-1	291	4/24/82	Missouri	Miami, Fla.	FA
Webb, Jeff	WR	6-2	211	1/31/82	San Diego State	La Quinta, Calif.	D6b
Williams, Steve	DT	6-2	306	9/1/82	Northwest Missouri State	Bolingbrook, Ill.	FA
Wilson, Travis (1)	FB	6-3	256	5/31/81	Kansas State	Howell, Mich.	FA

The term NFL Rookie is defined as a player who is in his first season of professional football and has not been on the roster of another professional football team for any regular-season or postseason games. A Rookie is designated by an "R" on NFL rosters. Players who have been active in another professional football league or players who have NFL experience, including either preseason training camp or being on an Active List or Inactive List, or on Reserve/Injured or Reserve/Physically Unable to Perform for fewer than six regular-season games, are termed NFL First-Year Players. An NFL First-Year Player is designated by a "1" on NFL rosters. Thereafter, a player is credited with an additional year of experience for each season in which he accumulates six games on the Active List or Inactive List, or on Reserve/Injured or Reserve/Physically Unable to Perform.

Log on to www.kcchiefs.com for an up-to-date roster.

COACHING STAFF
Head Coach,
Herm Edwards

Pro Career: Herm Edwards was named the tenth head coach in Chiefs franchise history on January 9, 2006. He enters his sixth year as an NFL head coach and his twenty-seventh season in the league as either a player, a scout, or coach. He began his pro coaching career as a participant in the NFL's Minority Coaching Fellowship program with Kansas City in 1989 and is the first graduate of the program to go on to become the head coach of the franchise for which he served his fellowship. He rejoins the Chiefs after spending six seasons with Kansas City as a scout (1990-91), defensive backs coach (1992-94) and pro personnel scout (1995). During his tenure as Kansas City's defensive backs coach, Edwards oversaw a Chiefs secondary that helped the club force a league-high 115 turnovers from 1992-94. Edwards joined Tony Dungy's staff in Tampa Bay as assistant head coach/defensive backs coach, spending five seasons (1996-2000) in that capacity. Edwards then enjoyed a five-year stint as the head coach of the N.Y. Jets (2001-05). He led the Jets to 41 wins, equalling the third-highest victory total in that franchise's history. He was on the sideline for a Jets-best five postseason games. Edwards originally entered the NFL as a rookie free agent with Philadelphia in 1977 and went on to start 135 consecutive regular season contests at cornerback, producing a franchise-record 38 combined interceptions in regular and postseason action. He also played in Super Bowl XV. He concluded his career with the L.A. Rams and Atlanta in 1986. Career record: 41-44.

Background: Edwards played cornerback collegiately for California (1972, 1974), Monterey Peninsula (Calif.) J.C. (1975) and San Diego State (1976). He played 10 NFL seasons with Philadelphia (1977-85), the L.A. Rams (1986) and Atlanta Falcons (1986). Collegiately, he was the defensive backs coach at San Jose State (1987-89).

Personal: Born April 27, 1954 in Fort Monmouth, N.J. He and his wife Lia have a son, Marcus and a daughter, Gabrielle.

ASSISTANT COACHES

Don Blackmon, linebackers; born March 14, 1958, Pompano Beach, Fla. Linebacker Tulsa 1977-1980. Pro linebacker New England Patriots 1981-87. Pro coach: New England Patriots 1988-1990, Cleveland Browns 1991, N.Y. Giants 1993-96, Atlanta Falcons 1997-2001, Buffalo Bills 2003-05, joined Chiefs in 2006.

Gunther Cunningham, defensive coordinator; born June 19, 1946, Munich, Germany. Linebacker/placekicker Oregon 1966-68. No pro playing experience. College coach: Oregon 1969-1971, Arkansas 1972, Stanford 1973-76, California 1977-1980. Pro coach: Hamilton Tiger-Cats (CFL) 1981, Baltimore/Indianapolis Colts 1982-84, San Diego Chargers 1985-1990, L.A. Raiders 1991-94, Kansas City Chiefs 1995-2000 (head coach 1999-2000), Tennessee Titans 2001-03, rejoined Chiefs in 2004.

Dick Curl, asst. to the head coach/offense; born May 4, 1940, Chester, Pa. Quarterback Richmond 1960-62. No pro playing experience. College coach: Trenton State 1973-74 (head coach 1974), Rutgers 1975-1980, 1983-89, Virginia 1981-82, Boston College 1990. Pro coach: Barcelona Dragons (NFLEL) 1991-97, Frankfurt Galaxy (NFLEL) 1998-2000 (head coach), N.Y. Jets 2003-05, joined Chiefs in 2006.

Jon Embree, tight ends; born October 15, 1965, Los Angeles. Tight end Colorado 1983-86. Pro tight end L.A. Rams 1987-88. College coach: Colorado 1991, 1993-2002, UCLA 2003-05. Pro coach: Joined Chiefs in 2006.

David Gibbs, defensive backs; born January 10, 1968, Mount Airy, N.C. Defensive back Colorado 1987-1990. No pro playing experience. College coach: Oklahoma 1991-92, Colorado 1993-94, Kansas 1995-96, Minnesota 1997-2000, Auburn 2005. Pro coach: Denver Broncos 2001-04, joined Chiefs in 2006.

Jeff Hurd, strength and conditioning; born April 24, 1958, Pomona, Calif. Attended Fort Hays State. No college or pro playing experience. College coach: Fort Hays State 1984, Delta State 1985-86, Clemson 1986-87, Western Michigan 1987-1992, Tulsa 1994. Pro coach: Jacksonville Jaguars 1995-97, joined Chiefs in 1998.

Charlie Joiner, receivers; born October 14, 1947, Many, La. Wide receiver Grambling State 1965-68. Pro defensive back-wide receiver Houston Oilers 1969-1972, Cincinnati Bengals 1972-75, San Diego Chargers 1976-1986. Inducted into Pro Football Hall of Fame 1996. Pro coach: San Diego Chargers 1987-1991, Buffalo Bills 1992-2000, joined Chiefs in 2001.

Kaz Kazadi, strength and conditioning assistant; born December 20, 1973, Zaire, Africa. Linebacker Tulsa 1993-96. Pro linebacker St. Louis Rams 1997, Montreal Alouettes (CFL) 1999, Barcelona Dragons (NFLE) 2001. College coach: Missouri 2004. Pro coach: Joined Chiefs in 2005.

Mike Ketchum, offensive assistant/quality control; born July 2, 1977, Ft. Benning, Ga. Offensive/defensive lineman University of the South 1995-98. College coach: Cumberland 1999-2000, Vanderbilt 2001-02, Iowa 2003-05. Pro coach: Joined Chiefs in 2006.

Tim Krumrie, defensive line; born May 20, 1960, Menomonie, Wis. Defensive tackle Wisconsin 1979-1982, Pro defensive tackle Cincinnati Bengals 1983-1994, Pro coach: Cincinnati Bengals 1995-2002, Buffalo Bills 2003-05, joined Chiefs in 2006.

Billy Long, asst. strength and conditioning; born June 23, 1959, Phenix City, Ala. Guard Alabama State 1977-1980. College coach: Alabama State 1981-86, Arkansas-Pine Bluff 1987-1991, Southern 1992-2000. Pro coach: Joined Chiefs in 2001.

John Matsko, offensive line; born February 2, 1951, Cleveland. Fullback Kent State 1970-73. No pro playing experience. College coach: Kent State 1973, Miami (Ohio) 1974-75, 1977, North Carolina 1978-1984, Navy 1985, Arizona 1986, Southern California 1987-1991. Pro coach: Phoenix Cardinals 1992-93, New Orleans Saints 1994-96, N.Y. Giants 1997-98, St. Louis Rams 1999-2005, joined Chiefs in 2006.

Mike Priefer, special teams; born August 21, 1966, Cleveland. Attended U.S. Naval Academy. No college or pro playing experience. College coach: Navy 1994-96, Youngstown State 1997-98, Virginia Military Institute 1999, Northern Illinois 2000-01. Pro coach: Jacksonville Jaguars 2002, N.Y. Giants 2003-05, joined Chiefs in 2006.

James Saxon, running backs; born March 23, 1966, Beaufort, S.C. Running back American River (Calif.) J.C. 1984-85, San Jose State 1986-87. Pro running back Kansas City Chiefs 1988-1991, Miami Dolphins 1992-94, Philadelphia Eagles 1995. College coach: Rutgers 1997-98, Menlo College 1999. Pro coach: Buffalo Bills 2000, joined Chiefs in 2001.

Terry Shea, quarterbacks; born June 12, 1946, San Mateo, Calif. Quarterback Oregon 1965-67. No pro playing experience. College coach: Oregon 1968-69; Mt. Hood (Ore) J.C. 1970-75, Utah State 1976-1983, San Jose State 1984-86, 1990-91 (head coach 1990-91), California 1987-89, Stanford 1992-94, Rutgers 1996-2000 (head coach). Pro coach: British Columbia Lions (CFL) 1995, Kansas City Chiefs 2001-03, Chicago Bears 2004, re-joined Chiefs in 2005.

Mike Solari, offensive coordinator; born January 16, 1955, Daly City, Calif. Offensive lineman San Diego State 1975-76. No pro playing experience. College coach: Mira Vista (Calif.) J.C. 1978, U.S. International 1979, Boise State 1980, Cincinnati 1981-82, Kansas 1983-85, Pittsburgh 1986, Alabama 1990-91. Pro coach: Dallas Cowboys 1987-88, Phoenix Cardinals 1989, San Francisco 49ers 1992-96, joined Chiefs in 1997.

Nate Wainwright, manager of football administration; born July 28, 1975, Wilton, Iowa. Attended Iowa. No college or pro playing experience. Pro coach: N.Y. Jets 2001-05, joined Chiefs in 2006.

Darvin Wallis, defensive assistant/quality control; born February 14, 1949, Ft. Branch, Ind. Defensive end Arizona 1970-71. No pro playing experience. College coach: Adams State 1976-77, Tulane 1978-79, Mississippi 1980-81. Pro coach: Cleveland Browns 1982-88, joined Chiefs in 1989.

**American Football Conference
East Division**
Team Colors: Aqua, Coral, Blue, and
White
**7500 S.W. 30th Street
Davie, Florida 33314**
Telephone: (954) 452-7000

2006 SCHEDULE
PRESEASON
Aug. 12 **Jacksonville**......................7:30
Aug. 19 at Tampa Bay 7:30
Aug. 24 at Carolina.........................8:00
Aug. 31 **St. Louis** 7:30

REGULAR SEASON
Sept. 7 at Pittsburgh (Thu.) 8:30
Sept. 17 **Buffalo**...............................1:00
Sept. 24 **Tennessee** 1:00
Oct. 1 at Houston 12:00
Oct. 8 at New England 1:00
Oct. 15 at N.Y. Jets 4:15
Oct. 22 **Green Bay**.........................1:00
Oct. 29 Open Date
Nov. 5 at Chicago.......................12:00
Nov. 12 **Kansas City** 1:00
Nov. 19 **Minnesota** 1:00
Nov. 23 at Detroit (Thu.)................12:30
Dec. 3 **Jacksonville**.......................1:00
Dec. 10 **New England** 1:00
Dec. 17 at Buffalo 1:00
Dec. 25 **N.Y. Jets** (Mon.).................8:30
Dec. 31 at Indianapolis 1:00

Stadium: Dolphin Stadium
(opened in 1987)
• **Capacity:** 75,192
2269 Dan Marino Blvd.
Miami Gardens, Florida 33056
Playing Surface: Grass (PAT)
Training Camp: Nova Southeastern Univ.
7500 S.W. 30th Street
Davie, Florida 33314

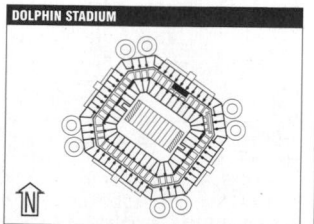

DOLPHIN STADIUM

CLUB OFFICIALS
Owner/Chairman of the Board:
H. Wayne Huizenga
Chief Executive Officer, Dolphins
Enterprises: Joe Bailey
Head Coach: Nick Saban
President & Chief Operating Officer:
Bryan Wiedmeier
Senior Vice President-Finance &
Administration: Jill R. Strafaci
Senior Vice President-Operations:
Bill Galante
Senior Vice President-Media Relations:
Harvey Greene
Senior Vice President-Sales & Marketing:
Jim Ross
General Manager: Randy Mueller
Coordinator of Football Operations/
Assistant to the Head Coach:
Scott O'Brien
Special Assistant to the Head Coach/
Director of Player Development:
John Gamble
Director of Pro Personnel: George Paton
Director of College Scouting:
Ron Labadie
Assistant Director of Player Personnel:
Mike Baugh
Staff Counsel: Matt Thomas
Senior Director of Ticket Operations:
Andy Major
Senior Director of Internet & Publications:
Scott Stone
Director of Alumni Relations: Jamie Allen
Director of Media Relations: Neal Gulkis
Director of Information Technology:
Tery Howard
Director of Cheerleaders & Event
Entertainment: Dorie Grogan
Director of Programming & Production:
Jeff Griffith
Director of Records & Archives:
Kristin Hingston
Head Athletic Trainer: Kevin O'Neill
Equipment Manager: Tony Egues
Video Director: Dave Hack
Team Security Investigator:
Stuart Weinstein

COACHING HISTORY
(382-261-4)
Records include postseason games
1966-69   George Wilson.............15-39-2
1970-1995 Don Shula 274-147-2
1996-99   Jimmy Johnson...........38-31-0
2000-04   Dave Wannstedt* 43-33-0
2004   Jim Bates.........................3-4-0
2005   Nick Saban.....................9-7-0
*Resigned after nine games in 2004

ATTENDANCE
Home 575,256   Away 529,767
Total 1,105,023
Single-game home record,
75,283 (10/27/96)
Single-season home record, 592,161
(1999)

2006 DRAFT CHOICES
Round	Name	Pos.	College
1	Jason Allen	CB	Tennessee
3	Derek Hagan	WR	Arizona State
4	Joe Toledo	T	Washington
7	Fred Evans	NT	Texas St.-San Marcos
	Rodrique Wright	NT	Texas
	Devin Aromashodu	WR	Auburn

2005 TEAM RECORD

PRESEASON (1-4)

Date	Result	Opponent
8/8	L 24-27	Chicago
8/13	L 17-27	at Jacksonville
8/20	L 3-17	at Pittsburgh
8/27	W 17-14	Tampa Bay
9/1	L 17-20	Atlanta

REGULAR SEASON (9-7)

Date	Result	Opponent	Att.
9/11	W 34-10	Denver	72,324
9/18	L 7-17	at New York Jets	77,918
9/25	W 27-24	Carolina	72,288
10/9	L 14-20	at Buffalo	72,160
10/16	L 13-27	at Tampa Bay	65,168
10/21	L 20-30	Kansas City	68,350
10/30	W 21-6	at New Orleans	61,643
11/6	L 10-17	Atlanta	72,187
11/13	L 16-23	New England	73,405
11/20	L 0-22	at Cleveland	72,773
11/27	W 33-21	at Oakland	49,097
12/4	W 24-23	Buffalo	72,051
12/11	W 23-21	at San Diego	65,026
12/18	W 24-20	New York Jets	72,650
12/24	W 24-10	Tennessee	72,001
1/1	W 28-26	at New England	68,756

SCORE BY PERIODS

Dolphins	44	78	57	139	0 —	318
Opponents	94	67	71	85	0 —	317

2005 TEAM STATISTICS

	Dolphins	Opp.
Total First Downs	274	319
Rushing	93	94
Passing	159	183
Penalty	22	42
3rd Down: Made/Att	79/225	95/236
3rd Down Pct.	35.1	40.3
4th Down: Made/Att	6/15	8/19
4th Down Pct.	40.0	42.1
Possession Avg.	27:25	32:35
Total Net Yards	5,198	5,078
Avg. Per Game	324.9	317.4
Total Plays	1,026	1,078
Avg. Per Play	5.1	4.7
Net Yards Rushing	1,898	1,771
Avg. Per Game	118.6	110.7
Total Rushes	444	480
Net Yards Passing	3,300	3,307
Avg. Per Game	206.3	206.7
Sacked/Yards Lost	26/158	49/375
Gross Yards	3,458	3,682
Att./Completions	556/291	549/323
Completion Pct.	52.3	58.8
Had Intercepted	16	14
Punts/Average	89/43.1	92/43.0
Net Punting Avg.	89/39.0	92/37.0
Penalties/Yards	132/1,055	105/827
Fumbles/Ball Lost	31/14	35/17
Touchdowns	34	35
Rushing	11	11
Passing	22	23
Returns	1	1

2005 INDIVIDUAL STATISTICS

PASSING	Att.	Comp.	Yds.	Pct.	TD	Int.	Tkld.	Rate
Frerotte	494	257	2,996	52.0	18	13	26/158	71.9
Rosenfels	61	34	462	55.7	4	3	0/0	81.5
Booker	1	0	0	0.0	0	0	0/0	39.6
Dolphins	556	291	3,458	52.3	22	16	26/158	72.8
Opponents	549	323	3,682	58.8	23	14	49/375	82.4

SCORING	TD R	TD P	TD Rt	PAT	FG	Saf	PTS
Mare	0	0	0	33/33	25/30	0	108
Chambers	0	11	0	0/0	0/0	0	66
Williams	6	0	0	0/0	0/0	0	36
Brown	4	1	0	0/0	0/0	0	30
McMichael	0	5	0	0/0	0/0	0	30
Booker	0	3	0	0/0	0/0	0	18
Taylor	0	0	1	0/0	0/0	1	8
Gilmore	0	1	0	0/0	0/0	0	6
Heller	0	1	0	0/0	0/0	0	6
Morris	1	0	0	0/0	0/0	0	6
Carter	0	0	0	0/0	0/0	1	2
Howard	0	0	0	0/0	0/0	1	2
Dolphins	11	22	1	33/33	25/30	3	318
Opponents	11	23	1	31/32	24/24	1	317

2-Pt. Conversions: None.
Dolphins 0-1, Opponents 1-3.

RUSHING	No.	Yds	Avg	LG	TD
Brown	207	907	4.4	65t	4
Williams	168	743	4.4	35	6
Chambers	12	92	7.7	61	0
Frerotte	27	61	2.3	14	0
Morris	16	58	3.6	9t	1
Minor	5	17	3.4	9	0
Rosenfels	6	15	2.5	12	0
Welker	1	5	5.0	5	0
Evans	1	0	0.0	0	0
D. Jones	1	0	0.0	0	0
Dolphins	444	1,898	4.3	65t	11
Opponents	480	1,771	3.7	75t	11

RECEIVING	No.	Yds	Avg	LG	TD
Chambers	82	1,118	13.6	77t	11
McMichael	60	582	9.7	30t	5
Booker	39	686	17.6	60t	3
Brown	32	232	7.3	38	1
Welker	29	434	15.0	47	0
Williams	17	93	5.5	19	0
Diamond	8	54	6.8	18	0
Morris	8	54	6.8	18	0
Gilmore	5	105	21.0	44t	1
Boston	4	80	20.0	54	0
Evans	4	17	4.3	5	0
Holmes	1	2	2.0	2	0
Heller	1	1	1.0	1t	1
Minor	1	0	0.0	0	0
Dolphins	291	3,458	11.9	77t	22
Opponents	323	3,682	11.4	60t	23

INTERCEPTIONS	No.	Yds	Avg	LG	TD
Schulters	4	78	19.5	37	0
Tillman	3	38	12.7	22	0
Madison	2	11	5.5	11	0
Howard	1	5	5.0	5	0
Daniels	1	4	4.0	4	0
Bell	1	0	0.0	0	0
Spragan	1	0	0.0	0	0
Z. Thomas	1	0	0.0	0	0
Dolphins	14	136	9.7	37	0
Opponents	16	127	7.9	33	0

PUNTING	No.	Yds.	Avg.	In 20	LG
D. Jones	88	3,827	43.5	31	63
Mare	1	8	8.0	0	8
Dolphins	89	3,835	43.1	31	63
Opponents	92	3,957	43.0	31	63

PUNT RETURNS	Ret	FC	Yds	Avg	LG	TD
Welker	43	23	390	9.1	47	0
Dolphins	43	23	390	9.1	47	0
Opponents	46	14	227	4.9	37	0

KICKOFF RETURNS	No.	Yds	Avg	LG	TD
Welker	61	1,379	22.6	46	0
Gilmore	3	84	28.0	29	0
Minor	2	22	11.0	19	0
Heller	1	11	11.0	11	0
Bowens	1	5	5.0	5	0
Dolphins	68	1,501	22.1	46	0
Opponents	56	1,425	25.4	65	0

FIELD GOALS	1-19	20-29	30-39	40-49	50+
Mare	0/0	9/10	9/12	6/6	1/2
Dolphins	0/0	9/10	9/12	6/6	1/2
Opponents	0/0	7/7	7/7	7/7	3/3

SACKS	No.
Taylor	12.0
Bowens	6.0
Carter	6.0
Holliday	5.0
Bell	3.0
Howard	2.0
T. Jones	2.0
Schulters	2.0
Z. Thomas	2.0
Traylor	2.0
Zgonina	2.0
Roth	1.0
Seau	1.0
Spragan	1.0
Wright	1.0
TEAM	1.0
Dolphins	49.0
Opponents	26.0

RECORD HOLDERS
INDIVIDUAL RECORDS—CAREER

Category	Name	Performance
Rushing (Yds.)	Larry Csonka, 1968-1974, 1979	6,737
Passing (Yds.)	Dan Marino, 1983-1999	*61,361
Passing (TDs)	Dan Marino, 1983-1999	*420
Receiving (No.)	Mark Clayton, 1983-1992	550
Receiving (Yds.)	Mark Duper, 1982-1992	8,869
Interceptions	Jake Scott, 1970-75	35
Punting (Avg.)	John Kidd, 1994-97	44.2
Punt Return (Avg.)	Jeff Ogden, 2000-01	13.7
Kickoff Return (Avg.)	Mercury Morris, 1969-1975	26.5
Field Goals	Olindo Mare, 1997-2005	219
Touchdowns (Tot.)	Mark Clayton, 1983-1992	82
Points	Olindo Mare, 1997-2005	948

INDIVIDUAL RECORDS—SINGLE SEASON

Category	Name	Performance
Rushing (Yds.)	Ricky Williams, 2002	1,853
Passing (Yds.)	Dan Marino, 1984	*5,084
Passing (TDs)	Dan Marino, 1984	48
Receiving (No.)	O.J. McDuffie, 1998	90
Receiving (Yds.)	Mark Clayton, 1984	1,389
Interceptions	Dick Westmoreland, 1967	10
Punting (Avg.)	John Kidd, 1996	46.3
Punt Return (Avg.)	Jeff Ogden, 2000	17.0
Kickoff Return (Avg.)	Duriel Harris, 1976	32.9
Field Goals	Olindo Mare, 1999	39
Touchdowns (Tot.)	Mark Clayton, 1984	18
Points	Olindo Mare, 1999	144

INDIVIDUAL RECORDS—SINGLE GAME

Category	Name	Performance
Rushing (Yds.)	Ricky Williams, 12-1-02	228
Passing (Yds.)	Dan Marino, 10-23-88	521
Passing (TDs)	Bob Griese, 11-24-77	6
	Dan Marino, 9-21-86	6
Receiving (No.)	Chris Chambers, 12-4-05	15
Receiving (Yds.)	Chris Chambers, 12-4-05	238
Interceptions	Dick Anderson, 12-3-73	*4
Field Goals	Olindo Mare, 10-17-99	6
Touchdowns (Tot.)	Paul Warfield, 12-15-73	4
	Mark Ingram, 11-27-94	4
Points	Paul Warfield, 12-15-73	24
	Mark Ingram, 11-27-94	24

*NFL Record

2006 VETERAN ROSTER

No.	Name	Pos.	Ht.	Wt.	Birthdate	NFL Exp.	College	Hometown	How Acq.	'05 Games/ Starts
79	Alabi, Anthony	T	6-5	315	2/16/81	2	Texas Christian	San Antonio, Texas	D5-'05	0*
25	Allen, Will	CB	5-10	196	8/5/78	6	Syracuse	Syracuse, N.Y.	UFA(NYG)-'06	16/16*
36	Barnes, Darian	FB	6-2	240	2/29/80	5	Hampton	Toms River, N.J.	FA-'05	9/6
40	Beasley, Fred	FB	6-0	245	9/18/74	9	Auburn	Montgomery, Ala.	UFA(SF)-'06	9/7*
37	Bell, Yeremiah	S	6-0	200	3/3/78	3	Eastern Kentucky	Winchester, Ky.	D6-'03	16/0
65	Berger, Joe	G	6-5	305	5/25/82	2	Michigan Tech	Newaygo, Mich.	FA-'05	3/0
86	Booker, Marty	WR	6-0	210	7/31/76	8	Louisiana-Monroe	Jonesboro, La.	T(Chi)-'04	15/12
#	Boston, David	WR	6-2	228	8/19/78	8	Ohio State	Humble, Texas	FA-'05	5/0
96	Bowens, David	DE	6-3	265	7/3/77	7	Western Illinois	Detroit, Mich.	FA-'01	16/0
69	Brooks, C.J.	G	6-5	310	8/21/82	2	Maryland	Morrow, Ga.	FA-'05	0*
23	Brown, Ronnie	RB	6-0	232	12/12/81	2	Auburn	Cartersville, Ga.	D1-'05	15/14
80	Campbell, Kelly	WR	5-10	175	7/23/80	4	Georgia Tech	Atlanta, Ga.	FA-'06	0*
72	Carey, Vernon	T	6-5	335	7/31/81	3	Miami	Miami, Fla.	D1-'04	16/14
93	Carter, Kevin	DE	6-6	305	9/21/73	12	Florida	Tallahassee, Fla.	FA-'05	16/16
84	Chambers, Chris	WR	5-11	210	8/12/78	6	Wisconsin	Cleveland, Ohio	D2-'01	16/16
35	Cooper, Deke	S	6-2	210	10/18/77	5	Notre Dame	Evansville, Ind.	UFA(Jax)-'06	16/12*
52	Crowder, Channing	LB	6-2	245	12/2/83	2	Florida	Atlanta, Ga.	D3-'05	16/13
8 t-	Culpepper, Daunte	QB	6-4	265	1/28/77	8	Central Florida	Ocala, Fla.	T(Minn)-'06	7/7*
21	Daniels, Travis	CB	6-1	192	9/8/82	2	Louisiana State	Hollywood, Fla.	D4-'05	16/14
97	Denney, John	LS	6-5	270	12/13/78	2	Brigham Young	Thornton, Colo.	FA-'05	16/0
#	Glenn, Jason	LB	6-0	231	8/20/79	6	Texas A&M	Humble, Texas	FA-'05	16/0
29	Goodman, Andre	CB	5-10	185	8/11/78	5	South Carolina	Greenville, S.C.	UFA(Det)-'06	15/8*
95	Green, Howard	DT	6-2	320	1/12/79	3	Louisiana State	Donaldsonville, La.	FA-'06	0*
66	Hadnot, Rex	G	6-2	325	1/28/82	3	Houston	Lufkin, Texas	D6-'04	16/16
3 t-	Harrington, Joey	QB	6-4	220	10/21/78	5	Oregon	Portland, Ore.	T(Det)-'06	12/11*
24	Hill, Renaldo	CB	5-11	190	11/12/78	6	Michigan State	Detroit, Mich.	UFA(Oak)-'06	16/13*
50	Hodge, Sedrick	LB	6-4	246	9/13/78	6	North Carolina	Atlanta, Ga.	UFA(NO)-'06	13/12*
91	Holliday, Vonnie	DT	6-5	288	12/11/75	9	North Carolina	Camden, S.C.	FA-'05	16/16
89	Holmes, Alex	TE	6-2	270	8/22/81	2	Southern California	N. Hollywood, Calif.	FA-'05	8/0
20	Jackson, Eddie	CB	6-0	200	12/19/80	3	Arkansas	Richardson, Texas	W(Car)-'05	15/1
78	James, Jeno	G	6-4	320	1/12/77	7	Auburn	Montgomery, Ala.	UFA(Car)-'04	16/16
47	Johnson, Teyo	TE	6-6	245	11/29/81	3	Stanford	San Diego, Calif.	FA-'06	6/3*
5	Jones, Donnie	P	6-3	222	7/5/80	3	Louisiana State	Baton Rouge, La.	FA-'05	16/0
53	Labinjo, Mike	LB	6-1	255	7/8/80	2	Michigan State	Toronto, Ontario, Canada	W(Ind)-'05	7/1*
42	LeJeune, Norman	S	6-0	210	5/10/80	2	Louisiana State	Brusly, La.	FA-'05	5/0
17	Lemon, Cleo	QB	6-2	215	8/16/79	3	Arkansas State	Greenwood, Miss.	T(SD)-'05	0*
10	Mare, Olindo	K	5-11	190	6/6/73	10	Syracuse	Cooper City, Fla.	FA-'97	16/0
77	McIntosh, Damion	T	6-4	320	3/25/77	7	Kansas State	Pembroke Pines, Fla.	UFA(SD)-'04	16/16
68	McKinney, Seth	C	6-3	310	6/12/79	5	Texas A&M	Austin, Texas	D3-'02	13/13
81	McMichael, Randy	TE	6-3	255	6/28/79	5	Georgia	Fort Valley, Ga.	D4-'02	16/16
28	Minor, Travis	RB	5-10	203	6/30/79	6	Florida State	Baton Rouge, La.	D3a-'01	16/0
58	Moore, Eddie	LB	6-1	235	7/5/80	4	Tennessee	South Pittsburg, Tenn.	D2-'03	5/0
31	Morris, Sammy	RB	6-0	218	3/23/77	7	Texas Tech	San Antonio, Texas	UFA(Buff)-'04	16/2
71	Pearson, Mike	T	6-7	302	8/22/80	5	Florida	Seffner, Fla.	UFA(Jax)-'06	4/2*
87	Peelle, Justin	TE	6-4	255	3/15/79	5	Oregon	Dublin, Calif.	UFA(SD)-'06	16/4*
27	Poole, Will	CB	5-10	192	7/24/81	3	Southern California	Queens, N.Y.	D4-'04	0*
56	Pope, Derrick	LB	6-0	232	5/4/82	3	Alabama	Galveston, Texas	D7b-'04	12/2
#	Rogers, Nick	LB	6-2	250	5/31/79	5	Georgia Tech	East Point, Ga.	FA-'05	3/0
98	Roth, Matt	DE	6-4	272	10/14/82	2	Iowa	Villa Park, Ill.	D2-'05	16/0
88	Russell, Cliff	WR	5-11	190	2/8/79	5	Utah	Fayetteville, N.C.	FA-'05	2/0
#	Schulters, Lance	S	6-2	202	5/27/75	9	Hofstra	Brooklyn, N.Y.	FA-'05	16/16
38	Shabazz, Siddeeq	S	5-11	200	2/5/81	3	New Mexico State	Gadsden, N.M.	FA-'06	2/0*
76	Shaw, Josh	DT	6-3	305	9/17/79	3	Michigan State	Ft. Lauderdale, Fla.	FA-'06	0*
70	Shelton, L.J.	T	6-6	345	3/21/76	8	Eastern Michigan	Rochester, Mich.	UFA(Cle)-'06	16/16*
74	Smith, Wade	C	6-4	318	4/26/81	4	Memphis	Dallas, Texas	D3a-'03	0*
59	Spragan, Donnie	LB	6-3	242	7/12/76	6	Stanford	Union City, Calif.	UFA(Den)-'05	16/9
99	Taylor, Jason	DE	6-6	255	9/1/74	10	Akron	Woodland Hills, Pa.	D3a-'97	16/16
54	Thomas, Zach	LB	5-11	228	9/1/73	11	Texas Tech	Pampa, Texas	D5c-'96	14/14
26	Tillman, Travares	S	6-1	205	10/8/77	6	Georgia Tech	Lyons, Ga.	UFA(Car)-'05	16/10
#	Towns, Lester	LB	6-1	245	8/27/77	6	Washington	Pasadena, Calif.	FA-'05	6/1
94	Traylor, Keith	DT	6-2	337	9/3/69	16	Central State (Okla.)	Malvern, Ark.	FA-'05	13/13
92	Vickerson, Kevin	DT	6-5	305	1/8/83	2	Michigan State	Detroit, Mich.	D7-'05	0/0
83	Welker, Wes	WR	5-9	185	5/1/81	3	Texas Tech	Oklahoma City, Okla.	FA-'04	16/1
15	Willis, Jason	WR	6-1	196	7/26/80	2	Oregon	Los Angeles, Calif.	FA-'05	0*
75	Wright, Manuel	DT	6-6	329	4/13/84	2	Southern California	Compton, Calif.	D5(Supp.)-'05	3/0
90	Zgonina, Jeff	DT	6-2	290	5/24/70	14	Purdue	Mundelein, Ill.	UFA(StL)-'03	16/3

* Alabi inactive for 16 games; Allen played 16 games with N.Y. Giants in '05; Beasley played 9 games with San Francisco; Brooks inactive for 5 games; Campbell missed '05 season with Minnesota because of injury; Cooper played 16 games with Jacksonville; Culpepper played 7 games with Minnesota; Goodman played 15 games with Detroit; Green last active with New Orleans in '04; Harrington played 12 games with Detroit; Hill played 16 games with Oakland; Hodge played 13 games with New Orleans; Johnson played 6 games with Arizona; Labinjo played 5 games with Philadelphia and 2 games with Indianapolis; Lemon inactive for 6 games with San Diego and 11 games with Miami; Pearson played 4 games with Jacksonville; Peelle played 16 games with San Diego; Poole last active with Miami in '04; Shabazz played 2 games with New Orleans; Shaw inactive for 5 games; Shelton played 16 games with Cleveland; Smith missed '05 season because of injury; Willis last active with Seattle in '04.

\# Unrestricted free agent; subject to developments.

t- Dolphins traded for Culpepper (Minn), Harrington (Det).

Players lost through free agency (4): WR Bryan Gilmore, (SF; 15 games in '05), T Stockar McDougle (Jax; 9), QB Sage Rosenfels (Hou; 4), CB Kiwaukee Thomas (Buff; 10).

Also played with Dolphins in '05—TE Lorenzo Diamond (16 games), G Alonzo Ephraim (13), FB Heath Evans (6), QB Gus Frerotte (16), TE Will Heller (7), CB Reggie Howard (1), S Tebucky Jones (6), CB Sam Madison (15), LB Junior Seau (7), RB Ricky Williams (12).

2006 FIRST-YEAR ROSTER

Name	Pos.	Ht.	Wt.	Birthdate	College	Hometown	How Acq.
Allen, Jason	CB	6-1	213	7/5/83	Tennessee	Muscle Shoals, Ala.	D1
Aromashodu, Devin	WR	6-2	200	5/23/84	Auburn	Miami Springs, Fla.	D7c
Berlin, Brock (1)	QB	6-1	215	7/4/81	Miami	Shreveport, La.	FA
Bray, Trent	LB	6-0	227	9/28/82	Oregon State	Pullman, Wash.	FA
Davis, Chris (1)	WR	6-2	200	10/9/81	Southern	Greensburg, La.	FA-'05
Evans, Fred	DT	6-4	305	11/6/83	Texas State	Morgan Park, Ill.	D7a
Fifita, Steve	DT	6-0	327	5/16/82	Utah	Fountain Valley, Calif.	FA
Gibson, Fred (1)	WR	6-4	202	10/26/81	Georgia	Waycross, Ga.	FA-'05
Hagan, Derek	WR	6-2	203	9/21/84	Arizona State	Palmdale, Calif.	D3
Harris, Kay-Jay (1)	RB	6-0	235	3/27/79	West Virginia	Tampa, Fla.	FA-'05
Holland, Justin	QB	6-2	219	4/16/83	Colorado State	Lakewood, Colo.	FA
Hunt, Jack (1)	S	6-0	195	11/30/81	Louisiana State	Ruston, La.	FA-'05
Ishola, Ben	DE	6-3	248	6/8/80	Indiana	Berlin, Germany	FA
Kimble, Eric	WR	5-11	195	6/8/83	Eastern Washington	Tacoma, Wash.	FA
Kimrin, Ola (1)	K	6-3	230	2/29/72	Texas-El Paso	Malmo, Sweden	FA-'05
McGrew, Sam	LB	6-2	244	7/28/84	Florida State	Crawfordville, Fla.	FA
McNeil, Chris	C	6-3	307	2/18/83	Mississippi State	Petal, Miss.	FA
Mitchell, Shirdonya (1)	CB	5-11	183	5/16/82	Missouri	Arlington, Texas	FA-'05
Olmsted, Thomas	P	6-4	214	12/28/83	Troy	Lake City, Fla.	FA
Pape, Tony (1)	T	6-6	310	9/29/81	Michigan	Clarendon Hills, Ill.	D7a-'04
Rader, Jason (1)	TE	6-4	274	4/12/81	Marshall	St. Albana, W. Va.	FA-'05
Riggs, Gerald Jr.	RB	5-11	229	9/28/83	Tennessee	Chattanooga, Tenn.	FA
Sinclair, Matt (1)	LB	6-1	245	7/24/82	Illinois	St. Louis, Mo.	FA
Thomas, Art (1)	CB	6-3	214	9/24/79	Virginia	Mechanicsburg, Pa.	FA
Thompson, Orrin (1)	T	6-6	310	11/11/82	Duke	Camden, N.J.	FA-'05
Toledo, Joe	T	6-5	330	10/20/82	Washington	Carlsbad, Calif.	D4
Vick, Marcus (1)	QB/WR	6-0	216	3/20/84	Virginia Tech	Newport News, Va.	FA
Wright, Rodrique	DT	6-5	305	7/31/84	Texas	Houston, Texas	D7b

The term NFL Rookie is defined as a player who is in his first season of professional football and has not been on the roster of another professional football team for any regular-season or postseason games. A Rookie is designated by an "R" on NFL rosters. Players who have been active in another professional football league or players who have NFL experience, including either preseason training camp or being on an Active List or Inactive List, or on Reserve/Injured or Reserve/Physically Unable to Perform for fewer than six regular-season games, are termed NFL First-Year Players. An NFL First-Year Player is designated by a "1" on NFL rosters. Thereafter, a player is credited with an additional year of experience for each season in which he accumulates six games on the Active List or Inactive List, or on Reserve/Physically Unable to Perform.

Log on to www.miamidolphins.com for an up-to-date roster.

COACHING STAFF
Head Coach,
Nick Saban
Pro Career: Signed a five-year contract on December 27, 2004 to become the sixth coach in Dolphins history. Led the Dolphins to a record of 9-7 in 2005, as the team won its final six games in Saban's initial season at the helm. Joined the Dolphins following a 10-year stint as a collegiate head coach, including the previous five at Louisiana State where he led the Tigers to a composite record of 48-16 and a national championship following the 2003 season. Prior to his tenure at LSU, Saban guided Michigan State to a five-year record of 35-24-1 (1995-99). Began his NFL career as defensive backs coach with the Houston Oilers from 1988-89. After one year (1990) as head coach at Toledo, was named defensive coordinator with the Cleveland Browns in 1991, and spent four years (1991-94) on Bill Belichick's staff. Career record: 9-7.
Background: Saban served as an assistant at the collegiate level at Kent State (1973-76), Syracuse (1977), West Virgina (1978-79), Ohio State (1980-81), Navy (1982) and Michigan State (1983-87). Saban lettered three seasons (1970-72) as a defensive back at Kent State, where he also played shortstop on the school's baseball team.
Personal: Born October 31, 1951 in Fairmont, West Virginia. He and his wife, Terry, have a son, Nicholas, and a daughter, Kristen.

ASSISTANT COACHES
Keith Armstrong, special teams; born December 15, 1963, Trenton, N.J. Running back/defensive back Temple 1983-86. No pro playing experience: College coach: Temple 1987, Miami 1988, Akron 1989, Oklahoma State 1990-92, Notre Dame 1993. Pro coach: Atlanta Falcons 1994-96, Chicago Bears 1997-2000, joined Dolphins in 2001.
Charlie Baggett, asst. head coach/wide receivers; born January 21, 1953, Fayetteville, N.C. Quarterback Michigan State 1972-75. No pro playing experience. College coach: Bowling Green 1977-1980, Minnesota 1981-82, Michigan State 1983-1992, 1995-98. Pro coach: Houston Oilers 1993-94, Green Bay Packers 1999, Minnesota Vikings 2000-04, joined Dolphins in 2005.
Dom Capers, special assistant to the head coach; born August 5, 1950, Cambridge, Ohio. Defensive back Mount Union College 1968-1971. No pro playing experience. College coach: Kent State 1972-74, Hawaii 1975-76, San Jose State 1977, California 1978-79, Tennessee 1980-81, Ohio State 1982-83. Pro coach: Philadelphia/Baltimore Stars (USFL) 1984-85, New Orleans Saints 1986-1991, Pittsburgh Steelers 1992-94, Carolina Panthers 1995-98 (head coach),

Jacksonville Jaguars 1999-2000, Houston Texans 2001-05 (head coach), joined Dolphins in 2005.
James Coley, offensive quality control; born April 14, 1973, Miami. Attended Florida State. No college or pro playing experience. College coach: Louisiana State 2003-04. Pro coach: Joined Dolphins in 2005.
Bo Davis, asst. strength and conditioning/assist with the defensive line; born May 17, 1970, Magee, Miss. Defensive lineman Louisiana State 1990-92. No pro playing experience. College coach: Louisiana State 1995-97, 2002-05. Pro coach: Joined Dolphins in 2006.
Tim Davis, asst. offensive line; born June 17, 1958. Tackle Utah 1978-1980. No pro playing experience. College coach: Wisconsin 1983-86, Arizona 1987, Walla Walla (Wash.) C.C. 1988, Idaho State 1989, Utah 1990-96, Wisconsin 1997-2001, Southern California 2002-04. Pro coach: Joined Dolphins in 2005.
Derek Dooley, tight ends; born June 10, 1968, Athens, Ga. Wide receiver Virginia 1987-1990. No pro playing experience. College coach: Georgia 1996, Southern Methodist 1997-99, Louisiana State 2000-04. Pro coach: Joined Dolphins in 2005.
George Edwards, linebackers; born January 16, 1967, Siler City, N.C. Linebacker Duke 1985-89. No pro playing experience. College coach: Florida 1990-91, Appalachian State 1992-95, Duke 1996, Georgia 1997. Pro coach: Dallas Cowboys 1998-2001, Washington Redskins 2002-03, Cleveland Browns 2004, joined Dolphins in 2005.
Jason Garrett, quarterbacks; born March 28, 1966, Abington, Pa. Quarterback Princeton 1987-88. Pro quarterback Ottawa Rough Riders (CFL) 1991, Dallas Cowboys 1993-99, New York Giants 2000-03, Tampa Bay Buccaneers 2004, Miami Dolphins 2004. Pro coach: Joined Dolphins in 2005.
Bert Hill, strength & conditioning; born January 25, 1958, Montgomery, Ala. Linebacker Marion (Ala.) Military Institute 1976-77, Wichita State 1978. No pro playing experience. College coach: Nicholls State 1981, Auburn 1982, Texas A&M 1983-87, 1989, Ohio State 1988. Pro coach: Detroit Lions 1990-2000, joined Dolphins in 2005.
Hudson Houck, offensive line; born January 7, 1943, Los Angeles. Center Southern California 1962-64. No pro playing experience. College coach: Southern California 1970-72, 1976-82, Stanford 1973-75. Pro coach: Los Angeles Rams 1983-91, Seattle Seahawks 1992, Dallas Cowboys 1993-2001, San Diego Chargers 2002-04, joined Dolphins in 2005.
Travis Jones, asst. defensive line; born June 6, 1972, Milledgville, Ga. Linebacker Georgia 1991-94. Pro line-

backer Baltimore Stallions (CFL) 1995. College coach: Georgia 1997, Appalachian State 1998-2000, Kansas 2001-02, Louisiana State 2003-04. Pro coach: Joined Dolphins in 2005.
Mike Mularkey, offensive coordinator; born November 19, 1961, Ft. Lauderdale, Fla. Tight end Florida 1979-1982. Pro tight end Minnesota Vikings 1983-88, Pittsburgh Steelers 1989-1991. College coach: Concordia 1993. Pro coach: Tampa Bay Buccaneers 1994-95, Pittsburgh Steelers 1996-2003, Buffalo Bills, 2004-05 (head coach), joined Dolphins in 2006.
Mel Phillips, secondary; born January 6, 1942, Shelby, N.C. Defensive back/running back North Carolina A&T 1964-65. Pro defensive back San Francisco 49ers 1966-1977. Pro coach: Detroit Lions 1980-84, joined Dolphins in 1985.
Glenn Pires, defensive quality control; born September 13, 1958, New Bedford, Mass. Offensive lineman Springfield College 1976-79. No pro playing experience. College coach: Dartmouth 1985-88, Syracuse 1989-1994, Michigan State 1995. Pro coach: Arizona Cardinals 1996-2000, Detroit Lions 2001-02, joined Dolphins in 2003.
Dan Quinn, defensive line; born September 11, 1970, Orange, N.J. Defensive lineman Salisbury State 1990-93. No pro playing experience. College coach: William & Mary 1994, Virginia Military Institute 1995, Hofstra 1997-2000. Pro coach: San Francisco 49ers 2001-04, joined Dolphins in 2005.
Kirby Smart, safeties; born December 28, 1975, Bainbridge, Ga. Defensive back Georgia 1995-98. No pro playing experience. College coach: Valdosta State 2000-01, Florida State 2002-03, Louisiana State 2004, Georgia 2005. Pro coach: Joined Dolphins in 2006.
Patrick Suddes, defensive assistant; born May 1, 1982, Alabama. Attended Alabama. No college or pro playing experience. Pro coach: Joined Dolphins in 2005.
Bobby Williams, running backs; born November 21, 1958, St. Louis, Mo. Running back/defensive back Purdue 1978-1981. No pro playing experience. College coach: Purdue 1982, Ball State 1983-84, Eastern Michigan 1985-89, Michigan State 1990-2002 (head coach, 2000-02), Louisiana State 2004. Pro coach: Detroit Lions 2003, joined Dolphins in 2005.

American Football Conference
East Division
Team Colors: Blue, Red, Silver, and White
Gillette Stadium
One Patriot Place
Foxborough, Massachusetts 02035
Telephone: (508) 543-8200

2006 SCHEDULE
PRESEASON
Aug. 12   at Atlanta............................8:00
Aug. 18   **Arizona** 8:00
Aug. 26   **Washington** 8:00
TBD   at New York Giants.............TBD

REGULAR SEASON
Sept. 10   **Buffalo**................................1:00
Sept. 17   at N.Y. Jets 4:15
Sept. 24   **Denver**............................. 8:15
Oct. 1   at Cincinnati 4:15
Oct. 8   **Miami**............................. 1:00
Oct. 15   Open Date
Oct. 22   at Buffalo 1:00
Oct. 30   at Minnesota (Mon.) 7:30
Nov. 5   **Indianapolis**......................8:15
Nov. 12   **N.Y. Jets** 1:00
Nov. 19   at Green Bay 12:00
Nov. 26   **Chicago** 1:00
Dec. 3   **Detroit** 1:00
Dec. 10   at Miami............................ 1:00
Dec. 17   **Houston** 1:00
Dec. 24   at Jacksonville....................1:00
Dec. 31   at Tennessee 12:00

Stadium: Gillette Stadium
   (opened in 2002)
   •Capacity: 68,756
   One Patriot Place
   Foxborough, Massachusetts 02035
Playing Surface: Grass
Training Camp: Gillette Stadium
                       Foxborough,
                       Massachusetts 02035

GILLETTE STADIUM

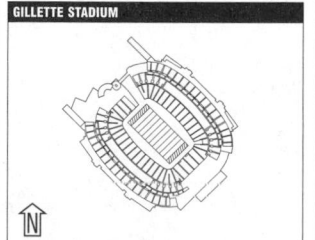

CLUB OFFICIALS
Chairman and CEO: Robert K. Kraft
Vice Chairman and President:
   Jonathan A. Kraft
Chief Operating Officer: Ray Sullivan
Vice President, Player Personnel:
   Scott Pioli
Vice President, Community Affairs and
   Corporate Philanthropy: Rena Clark
Vice President, Finance: Jim Hausmann
Vice President, Marketing Operations:
   Jennifer Ferron
Chief Administrative Counsel: Jack Mula
Vice President, Human Resources:
   Robin Boudreau
Executive Director of Media Relations:
   Stacey James
Executive Director of Sales: Murray Kohl
Executive Director of Corporate
   Development: David Pearlstein
Publisher/Editor-in-Chief and Director of
   Interactive Media: Fred Kirsch
Director of Football/Head Coach
   Administration: Berj Najarian
Equipment Manager: Don Brocher
Video Director: Jimmy Dee
Head Athletic Trainer: Jim Whalen
Director of Pro Personnel: Nick Caserio
Director of College Scouting:
   Thomas Dimitroff
Director of Premium Seating:
   Melissa Aghjayian
Director of Strategic Initiatives:
   Brian Bilello
Director of Supply Chain Management:
   Ken Flanders
Director of Business Development:
   Jessica Gelman
Director of Entertainment and Broadcast
   Production: Gary Grodecki
Director of Ticketing: Maryruth Hughey
Director of Sales: Jon Levy
Director of Sales: Joe Mariani
Director of Research: Richard Miller
Director of Corporate Relationships:
   Bill Nelsen
Director of Human Resources:
   Joanne Nichols
Director of Cheerleaders: Tracy Sormanti
Director of Football Development and
   Promotions for Community Affairs:
   Andre Tippett
Director of Customer and Sponsor
   Services: Gail Titus
Director of Finance: Jim Wilson
Kraft Group, Vice President of
   Information Technology: Pat Curley
Gillette Stadium, Vice President of
   Security and Front of House
   Operations: Mark Briggs
Gillette Stadium, Vice President of
   Business Development and External
   Affairs: Dan Murphy
Gillette Stadium, Vice President of
   Operations: Jim Nolan

COACHING HISTORY
Boston 1960-1970
(355-356-9)
Records include postseason games
1960-61   Lou Saban*....................7-12-0
1961-68   Mike Holovak 53-47-9
1969-1970   Clive Rush**....................5-16-0
1970-72   John Mazur***..............9-21-0
1972   Phil Bengtson...................1-4-0
1973-78   Chuck Fairbanks****....46-41-0
1978   Hank Bullough-Ron Erhardt# ...0-1-0
1979-1981   Ron Erhardt 21-27-0
1981-84   Ron Meyer## 18-16-0
1984-89   Raymond Berry 51-41-0
1990   Rod Rust.........................1-15-0
1991-92   Dick MacPherson 8-24-0
1993-96   Bill Parcells 34-34-0
1997-99   Pete Carroll 28-23-0
2000-05   Bill Belichick.................73-34-0
Records include postseason games
   *Released after five games in 1961
   **Released after seven games in 1970
   ***Resigned after nine games in 1972
****Suspended for final regular-season game in 1978
   #Co-coaches
   ##Released after eight games in 1984

ATTENDANCE
Home 567,714   Away 579,133
Total 1,146,847
Single-game home record,
   70,262 (12/12/04)
Single-season home record,
   567,714 (2005)

2006 DRAFT CHOICES

Round	Name	Pos.	College
1	Laurence Maroney	RB	Minnesota
2	Chad Jackson	WR	Florida
3	Dave Thomas	TE	Texas
4	Garrett Mills	TE	Tulsa
	Stephen Gostkowski	K	Memphis
5	Ryan O'Callaghan	T	California
6	Jeremy Mincey	LB	Florida
	Dan Stevenson	G	Notre Dame
	Le Kevin Smith	DT	Nebraska
7	Willie Andrews	DB	Baylor

2005 TEAM RECORD
PRESEASON (2-2)

Date	Result	Opponent
8/12	W 23-13	at Cincinnati
8/18	L 27-37	New Orleans
8/26	W 27-3	at Green Bay
9/1	L 3-27	N.Y. Giants

REGULAR SEASON (10-6)

Date	Result	Opponent	Att.
9/8	W 30-20	Oakland	68,756
9/18	L 17-27	at Carolina	73,528
9/25	W 23-20	at Pittsburgh	64,868
10/2	L 17-41	San Diego	68,756
10/9	W 31-28	at Atlanta	71,079
10/16	L 20-28	at Denver	76,571
10/30	W 21-16	Buffalo	68,756
11/7	L 21-40	Indianapolis	68,756
11/13	W 23-16	at Miami	73,405
11/20	W 24-17	New Orleans	68,756
11/27	L 16-26	at Kansas City	78,025
12/4	W 16-3	New York Jets	68,756
12/11	W 35-7	at Buffalo	71,810
12/17	W 28-0	Tampa Bay	68,756
12/26	W 31-21	at New York Jets	77,569
1/1	L 26-28	Miami	68,756

POSTSEASON (1-1)

Date	Result	Opponent	
1/7	W 28-3	at Jacksonville	68,756
1/14	L 13-27	at Denver	76,238

SCORE BY PERIODS

Patriots	90	74	97	118	0	—	379
Opponents	55	117	56	110	0	—	338

2005 TEAM STATISTICS

	Patriots	Opp.
Total First Downs	334	306
Rushing	101	94
Passing	204	179
Penalty	29	33
3rd Down: Made/Att	93/221	92/219
3rd Down Pct.	42.1	42.0
4th Down: Made/Att	13/17	3/9
4th Down Pct.	76.5	33.3
Possession Avg.	30:19	29:41
Total Net Yards	5,632	5,283
Avg. Per Game	352.0	330.2
Total Plays	1,031	997
Avg. Per Play	5.5	5.3
Net Yards Rushing	1,512	1,580
Avg. Per Game	94.5	98.8
Total Rushes	439	437
Net Yards Passing	4,120	3,703
Avg. Per Game	257.5	231.4
Sacked/Yards Lost	28/202	33/223
Gross Yards	4,322	3,926
Att./Completions	564/352	527/296
Completion Pct.	62.4	56.2
Had Intercepted	15	10
Punts/Average	77/44.6	81/43.7
Net Punting Avg.	77/38.3	81/37.8
Penalties/Yards	110/921	132/1068
Fumbles/Ball Lost	19/9	13/8
Touchdowns	46	38
Rushing	16	11
Passing	28	25
Returns	2	2

2005 INDIVIDUAL STATISTICS

PASSING	Att.	Comp.	Yds.	Pct.	TD	Int.	Tkld.	Rate
Brady	530	334	4,110	63.0	26	14	26/188	92.3
Cassel	24	13	183	54.2	2	1	1/1	89.4
Flutie	10	5	29	50.0	0	0	1/13	56.3
Patriots	564	352	4,322	62.4	28	15	28/202	91.5
Opponents	527	296	3,926	56.2	25	10	33/223	87.8

SCORING	TD R	TD P	TD Rt	PAT	FG	Saf	PTS
Vinatieri	0	0	0	40/41	20/25	0	100
Dillon	12	1	0	0/0	0/0	0	78
Branch	0	5	0	0/0	0/0	0	30
Vrabel	0	3	1	0/0	0/0	0	24
Watson	0	4	0	0/0	0/0	0	24
Dwight	0	3	0	0/0	0/0	0	18
Graham	0	3	0	0/0	0/0	0	18
Pass	3	0	0	0/0	0/0	0	18
T. Brown	0	2	0	0/0	0/0	0	12
Fauria	0	2	0	0/0	0/0	0	12
Givens	0	2	0	0/0	0/0	0	12
Ashworth	0	1	0	0/0	0/0	0	6
Brady	1	0	0	0/0	0/0	0	6
A. Davis	0	1	0	0/0	0/0	0	6
Johnson	0	1	0	0/0	0/0	0	6
Sanders	0	0	1	0/0	0/0	0	6
Evans	0	0	0	0/0	0/0	1	2
Flutie	0	0	0	1/1	0/0	0	1
Patriots	16	28	2	41/42	20/25	0	379
Opponents	11	25	2	34/34	24/30	1	338

2-Pt. Conversions: Evans.
Patriots 1-4, Opponents 1-4.

RUSHING	No.	Yds	Avg	LG	TD
Dillon	209	733	3.5	29	12
Pass	54	245	4.5	31	3
Evans	51	192	3.8	21	0
Faulk	51	145	2.8	13	0
Brady	27	89	3.3	15	1
Cloud	23	59	2.6	15	0
Zereoue	7	14	2.0	12	0
Givens	2	13	6.5	9	0
Cassel	6	12	2.0	9	0
Dwight	4	11	2.8	12	0
Flutie	5	-1	-0.2	2	0
Patriots	439	1,512	3.4	31	16
Opponents	437	1,580	3.6	68	11

RECEIVING	No.	Yds	Avg	LG	TD
Branch	78	998	12.8	51	5
Givens	59	738	12.5	40	2
T. Brown	39	466	11.9	71	2
Watson	29	441	15.2	35	4
Faulk	29	260	9.0	23	0
Pass	22	227	10.3	39	0
Dillon	22	181	8.2	25	1
Dwight	19	332	17.5	59	3
Graham	16	235	14.7	45t	3
Evans	10	88	8.8	19	0
A. Davis	9	190	21.1	60t	1
Fauria	8	57	7.1	18	2
Johnson	4	67	16.8	55t	1
Childress	3	32	10.7	21	0
Vrabel	3	4	1.3	2t	3
Zereoue	1	5	5.0	5	0
Ashworth	1	1	1.0	1t	1
Patriots	352	4,322	12.3	71	28
Opponents	296	3,926	13.3	85t	25

INTERCEPTIONS	No.	Yds	Avg	LG	TD
Samuel	3	15	5.0	15	0
Hobbs	3	8	2.7	8	0
Vrabel	2	23	11.5	24t	1
Sanders	1	39	39.0	39t	1
Wilson	1	0	0.0	0	0
Patriots	10	85	8.5	39t	2
Opponents	15	188	12.5	74t	2

PUNTING	No.	Yds.	Avg.	In 20	LG
Miller	76	3,431	45.1	22	59
Patriots	77	3,431	44.6	22	59
Opponents	81	3,537	43.7	27	68

PUNT RETURNS	Ret	FC	Yds	Avg	LG	TD
Dwight	32	13	273	8.5	29	0
T. Brown	7	5	30	4.3	7	0
Johnson	1	0	11	11.0	11	0
Patriots	40	18	314	7.9	29	0
Opponents	42	14	405	9.6	76	0

KICKOFF RETURNS	No.	Yds	Avg	LG	TD
Johnson	31	694	22.4	54	0
Hobbs	15	361	24.1	37	0
Dwight	10	250	25.0	38	0
Faulk	4	81	20.3	26	0
A. Davis	3	108	36.0	65	0
Pass	2	31	15.5	21	0
Cloud	1	15	15.0	15	0
Banta-Cain	1	14	14.0	14	0
Watson	1	1	1.0	1	0
Izzo	1	0	0.0	0	0
Stone	1	0	0.0	0	0
Patriots	70	1,555	22.2	65	0
Opponents	68	1,487	21.9	46	0

FIELD GOALS	1-19	20-29	30-39	40-49	50+
Vinatieri	0/0	7/7	9/10	4/6	0/2
Patriots	0/0	7/7	9/10	4/6	0/2
Opponents	0/0	6/6	9/12	6/8	3/4

SACKS	No.
Colvin	7.0
McGinest	6.0
Vrabel	4.5
Seymour	4.0
Green	2.5
Bruschi	2.0
Warren	1.5
Beisel	1.0
Chatham	1.0
Hawkins	1.0
Poteat	1.0
Banta-Cain	0.5
Klecko	0.5
Wilfork	0.5
Patriots	33.0
Opponents	28.0

RECORD HOLDERS
INDIVIDUAL RECORDS—CAREER

Category	Name	Performance
Rushing (Yds.)	Sam Cunningham, 1973-79, 1981-82	5,453
Passing (Yds.)	Drew Bledsoe, 1993-2001	29,657
Passing (TDs)	Steve Grogan, 1975-1990	182
Receiving (No.)	Stanley Morgan, 1977-1989	534
Receiving (Yds.)	Stanley Morgan, 1977-1989	10,352
Interceptions	Raymond Clayborn, 1977-1989	36
	Ty Law, 1995-2004	36
Punting (Avg.)	Tom Tupa, 1996-98	44.7
Punt Return (Avg.)	Mack Herron, 1973-75	12.0
Kickoff Return (Avg.)	Allen Carter, 1975-76	27.2
Field Goals	Adam Vinatieri, 1996-2005	263
Touchdowns (Tot.)	Stanley Morgan, 1977-1989	68
Points	Adam Vinatieri, 1996-2005	1,158

INDIVIDUAL RECORDS—SINGLE SEASON

Category	Name	Performance
Rushing (Yds.)	Corey Dillon, 2004	1,635
Passing (Yds.)	Drew Bledsoe, 1994	4,555
Passing (TDs)	Vito (Babe) Parilli, 1964	31
Receiving (No.)	Troy Brown, 2001	101
Receiving (Yds.)	Stanley Morgan, 1986	1,491
Interceptions	Ron Hall, 1964	11
Punting (Avg.)	Tom Tupa, 1997	45.8
Punt Return (Avg.)	Mack Herron, 1974	14.8
Kickoff Return (Avg.)	Raymond Clayborn, 1977	31.0
Field Goals	Tony Franklin, 1986	32
Touchdowns (Tot.)	Curtis Martin, 1996	17
Points	Gino Cappelletti, 1964	155

INDIVIDUAL RECORDS—SINGLE GAME

Category	Name	Performance
Rushing (Yds.)	Tony Collins, 9-18-83	212
Passing (Yds.)	Drew Bledsoe, 11-13-94	426
Passing (TDs)	Vito (Babe) Parilli, 11-15-64	5
	Vito (Babe) Parilli, 10-15-67	5
	Steve Grogan, 9-9-79	5
Receiving (No.)	Troy Brown, 9-22-02	16
Receiving (Yds.)	Terry Glenn, 10-3-99	214
Interceptions	Many times	3
	Last time by Roland James, 10-23-83	
Field Goals	Gino Cappelletti, 10-4-64	6
Touchdowns (Tot.)	Many times	3
	Last time by Antowain Smith, 11-3-02	
Points	Gino Cappelletti, 12-18-65	28

2006 VETERAN ROSTER

No.	Name	Pos.	Ht.	Wt.	Birthdate	NFL Exp.	College	Hometown	How Acq.	'05 Games/ Starts
49	Alexander, Eric	LB	6-2	240	2/8/82	2	Louisiana State	Port Arthur, Texas	FA-'04	1/0
95	Banta-Cain, Tully	LB	6-2	250	8/28/80	4	California	Sunnyvale, Calif.	D7b-'03	13/0
52	Beisel, Monty	LB	6-3	238	8/20/78	6	Kansas State	Douglass, Kan.	UFA(KC)-'05	15/6
12	Brady, Tom	QB	6-4	225	8/3/77	7	Michigan	San Mateo, Calif.	D6b-'00	16/16
83	Branch, Deion	WR	5-9	193	7/18/79	5	Louisville	Albany, Ga.	D2-'02	16/15
80	Brown, Troy	WR	5-10	196	7/2/71	14	Marshall	Blackville, S.C.	D8-'93	13/3
54	Bruschi, Tedy	LB	6-1	247	6/9/73	11	Arizona	Roseville, Calif.	D3-'96	9/9
87	Caldwell, Reche	WR	6-0	215	3/28/79	5	Florida	Tampa, Fla.	UFA(SD)-'06	16/2*
16	Cassel, Matt	QB	6-4	222	5/17/82	2	Southern California	Northridge, Calif.	D7a-'05	2/0
47	Claridge, Ryan	LB	6-2	254	4/12/81	2	Nevada-Las Vegas	Almont, Mich.	D5-'05	0*
59	Colvin, Rosevelt	LB	6-3	250	9/5/77	8	Purdue	Indianapolis, Ind.	UFA(Chi)-'03	16/11
51	Davis, Don	LB	6-1	235	12/17/72	11	Kansas	Olathe, Kan.	UFA(StL)-'03	16/0
28	Dillon, Corey	RB	6-1	225	10/24/74	10	Washington	Seattle, Wash.	T(Cin)-'04	12/10
44	Evans, Heath	FB	6-0	250	12/30/78	6	Auburn	West Palm Beach, Fla.	FA-'05	12/3*
33	Faulk, Kevin	RB	5-8	202	6/5/76	8	Louisiana State	Carencro, La.	D2-'99	8/2
21	Gay, Randall	CB	5-11	186	5/5/82	3	Louisiana State	Brusly, La.	FA-'04	5/2
76	Gorin, Brandon	T	6-6	308	7/17/78	5	Purdue	Muncie, Ind.	FA-'03	11/8
82	Graham, Daniel	TE	6-3	257	11/16/78	5	Colorado	Denver, Colo.	D1-'02	11/9
7	Gramatica, Martin	K	5-8	170	11/27/75	8	Kansas State	LaBelle, Fla.	FA-'06	0*
97	Green, Jarvis	DT/DE	6-3	290	1/12/79	5	Louisiana State	Donaldsonville, La.	D4b-'02	15/5
37	Harrison, Rodney	S	6-1	220	12/15/72	13	Western Illinois	Chicago, Ill.	FA-'03	3/3
25	Hawkins, Artrell	CB/S	5-10	190	11/24/76	9	Cincinnati	Johnstown, Pa.	FA-'05	5/4
91	Hill, Marquise	DE	6-6	300	8/7/82	3	Louisiana State	New Orleans, La.	D2-'04	8/0
27	Hobbs, Ellis	CB	5-9	188	5/16/83	2	Iowa State	DeSoto, Texas	D3a-'05	16/8
71	Hochstein, Russ	C	6-4	305	10/7/77	6	Nebraska	Hartington, Neb.	FA-'02	16/7
53	Izzo, Larry	LB	5-10	228	9/26/74	11	Rice	Houston, Texas	UFA(Mia)-'01	16/0
81	Johnson, Bethel	WR	5-11	200	2/11/79	4	Texas A&M	Corsicana, Texas	D2b-'03	11/1
34	Jones, Tebucky	S	6-2	218	10/6/74	9	Syracuse	New Britain, Conn.	FA-'06	6/6*
77	Kaczur, Nick	T	6-4	319	7/28/79	2	Toledo	Brantford, Ontario	D3b-'05	14/11
90	Klecko, Dan	DT/DE	5-11	275	1/12/81	4	Temple	Colts Neck, N.J.	D4a-'03	10/0
67	Koppen, Dan	C	6-2	296	9/12/79	4	Boston College	Whitehall, Pa.	D5-'03	9/9
72	Light, Matt	T	6-4	305	6/23/78	6	Purdue	Greenville, Ohio	D2-'01	3/3
70	Mankins, Logan	G/T	6-4	307	3/10/82	2	Fresno State	Catheys Valley, Calif.	D1-'05	16/16
15	McGrew, Michael	WR	6-2	201	5/17/82	2	Virginia	Birmingham, Ala.	FA-'05	0*
8	Miller, Josh	P	6-4	225	7/14/70	11	Arizona	Rockaway, N.Y.	FA-'04	16/0
24	Mitchell, Mel	S	6-1	222	2/10/79	5	Western Kentucky	Rockledge, Fla.	UFA(NO)-'06	13/0*
64	Mruczkowski, Gene	G/C	6-2	305	6/6/80	4	Purdue	Cleveland, Ohio	FA-'03	7/0
61	Neal, Stephen	G	6-4	305	10/9/76	5	Cal State-Bakersfield	San Diego, Calif.	FA-'01	16/16
35	Pass, Patrick	FB	5-10	217	12/31/77	7	Georgia	Tucker, Ga.	D7b-'00	12/4
66	Paxton, Lonie	LS	6-2	260	3/13/78	7	Sacramento State	Corona, Calif.	FA-'00	16/0
32	Poteat, Hank	CB	5-10	192	8/30/77	5	Pittsburgh	Harrisburg, Pa.	FA-'04	10/1
	Roehl, Jeff	T	6-4	300	5/18/80	2	Northwestern	Evergreen Park, Ill.	FA-'06	0*
22	Samuel, Asante	CB	5-10	185	1/6/81	3	Central Florida	Ft. Lauderdale, Fla.	D4b-'03	15/15
36	Sanders, James	S	5-10	207	11/11/83	2	Fresno State	Porterville, Calif.	D4-'05	10/2
30	Scott, Chad	CB	6-1	202	9/6/74	10	Maryland	Capitol Heights, Md.	FA-'05	3/0
29	Scott, Guss	S	5-10	205	5/21/82	3	Florida	Jacksonville, Fla.	D3-'04	5/2
93	Seymour, Richard	DT	6-6	310	10/6/79	6	Georgia	Gadsden, S.C.	D1-'01	12/12
	Smith, Zuriel	WR	5-11	174	1/15/80	2	Hampton	Mechanicsville, Va.	FA-'06	0*
14	Stone, John	WR	5-11	180	7/7/79	2	Wake Forest	Somers Point, N.J.	FA-'06	0*
69	Tucker, Ross	C/G	6-4	316	3/2/79	5	Princeton	Wyomissing, Pa.	FA-'05	1/0
50	Vrabel, Mike	LB	6-4	261	8/14/75	10	Ohio State	Akron, Ohio	UFA(Pitt)-'01	16/16
23	Warfield, Eric	CB	6-0	200	3/3/76	9	Nebraska	Vicksburg, Miss.	FA-'06	11/10*
94	Warren, Ty	DT/DE	6-5	300	2/6/81	4	Texas A&M	Bryan, Texas	D1-'03	16/16
84	Watson, Benjamin	TE	6-3	253	12/18/80	3	Georgia	Rock Hill, S.C.	D1b-'04	15/9
75	Wilfork, Vince	DT/DE	6-2	325	11/4/81	3	Miami	Boynton Beach, Fla.	D1a-'04	16/16
26	Wilson, Eugene	S	5-10	195	8/17/80	4	Illinois	Merrillville, Ind.	D2a-'03	16/16
99	Wright, Mike	DE/DT	6-4	295	3/1/82	2	Cincinnati	Cincinnati, Ohio	FA-'05	13/0
74	Yates, Billy	G	6-2	305	4/15/80	3	Texas A&M	Fort Worth, Texas	FA-'04	4/0

* Caldwell played 16 games with San Diego in '05; Claridge missed '05 season because of injury; Evans played 6 games with Miami and 6 games with New England; Gramatica last active with Indianapolis in '04; Jones played 6 games with Miami; McGrew missed '05 season because of injury; Mitchell played 13 games with New Orleans; Roehl last active with N.Y. Giants in '03; Z. Smith last active with Dallas in '03; Stone last active with Oakland in '04; Warfield played 11 games with Kansas City.

Retired—Doug Flutie, 12-year quarterback, 5 games in '05.

Players lost through free agency (8): T Tom Ashworth (Sea; 14 games in '05), LB Matt Chatham (NYJ; 15), WR Andre' Davis (Buff; 9), WR Tim Dwight (NYJ; 16), TE Christian Fauria (Wash; 16), WR David Givens (Tenn; 13), S Michael Stone (Hou: 13), K Adam Vinatieri (Ind; 16).

Also played with Patriots in '05—LB Chad Brown (15 games), RB Mike Cloud (6), S Arturo Freeman (2), LB Wesly Mallard (3), LB Willie McGinest (16), CB Duane Starks (7), RB Amos Zereoue (3).

2006 FIRST-YEAR ROSTER

Name	Pos.	Ht.	Wt.	Birthdate	College	Hometown	How Acq.
Andrews, Willie	DB	5-10	193	11/2/83	Baylor	Longview, Texas	D7
Ayodele, Remi	NT	6-2	300	4/22/83	Oklahoma	Grand Prairie, Texas	FA
Barthelmes, Brian	C	6-6	288	1/28/83	Virginia	Parkman, Ohio	FA
Bramlet, Corey	QB	6-4	219	1/17/83	Wyoming	Wheatland, Wyo.	FA
Britt, Wesley (1)	T	6-8	314	11/21/81	Alabama	Cullman, Ala.	FA-'05
Brown, Vernell	CB	5-8	165	12/10/82	Florida	Gainesville, Fla.	FA
Charles, Earl (1)	RB	6-1	215	9/11/82	Marshall	Brooklyn, N.Y.	FA
Childress, Bam (1)	WR	5-10	185	3/31/82	Ohio State	Warrensville Heights, Ohio	FA-'05
Condo, Jon (1)	LS	6-3	250	8/26/81	Maryland	Philipsburg, Pa.	FA
Davis, Erik	WR	6-2	192	2/21/84	Vanderbilt	Nashville, Tenn.	FA
Drame, Kader	DE	6-5	290	3/22/83	Syracuse	New Haven, Conn.	FA
Gostkowski, Stephen	K	6-1	212	1/28/84	Memphis	Madison, Miss.	D4b
Hand, Randy	T	6-6	305	1/10/84	Florida	Fort Myers, Fla.	FA
Herring, Jarvis	S	5-11	205	1/19/83	Florida	Live Oak, Fla.	FA
Jackson, Chad	WR	6-1	202	3/6/85	Florida	Hoover, Ala.	D2
Jackson, Keon	S	5-11	206	5/12/83	Toledo	East Chicago, Ind.	FA
Maroney, Laurence	RB	5-11	211	2/5/85	Minnesota	St. Louis, Mo.	D1
Mays, Corey	LB	6-1	234	11/27/83	Notre Dame	Chicago, Ill.	FA
Mills, Garrett	FB	6-1	232	10/12/83	Tulsa	Jenks, Okla.	D4a
Mincey, Jeremy	LB	6-3	263	12/14/83	Florida	Statesboro, Ga.	D6a
Mortensen, Todd (1)	QB	6-4	225	7/12/79	San Diego	Tempe, Ariz.	FA
Musinski, Rich (1)	WR	5-11	199	10/12/80	William & Mary	Wilkes-Barre, Pa.	FA
O'Callaghan, Ryan	T	6-7	344	7/19/83	California	Redding, Calif.	D5
Roach, Freddie	LB	6-2	248	6/3/83	Alabama	Killen, Ala.	FA
Shelton, Matt	WR	6-0	172	4/1/82	Notre Dame	Collierville, Tenn.	FA
Smith, Le Kevin	NT/DE	6-1	307	7/21/82	Nebraska	Macon, Ga.	D6c
Smith, Sam	S	6-0	200	9/7/82	Delaware State	St. Petersburg, Fla.	FA
Spann, Antwain (1)	CB	6-0	185	2/22/83	Louisiana-Lafayette	El Camino, Calif.	FA-'05
Steitz, Nick (1)	G	6-3	315	9/18/82	Oregon	Los Banos, Calif.	FA
Stevenson, Dan	G	6-5	300	10/4/82	Notre Dame	Barrington, Ill.	D6b
Thomas, David	TE	6-3	246	7/5/83	Texas	Wolfforth, Texas	D3
Thomas, Santonio (1)	NT/DE	6-4	308	7/2/81	Miami	Belle Glade, Fla.	FA-'05
Ventrone, Raymond (1)	S	5-10	200	10/21/82	Villanova	Pittsburgh, Pa.	FA-'05
Williams, Gemara	CB	5-8	180	4/30/83	Buffalo	Oak Park, Mich.	FA
Woods, Pierre	LB	6-5	249	1/6/82	Michigan	Cleveland, Ohio	FA

The term NFL Rookie is defined as a player who is in his first season of professional football and has not been on the roster of another professional football team for any regular-season or postseason games. A Rookie is designated by an "R" on NFL rosters. Players who have been active in another professional football league or players who have NFL experience, including either preseason training camp or being on an Active List or Inactive List, or on Reserve/Injured or Reserve/Physically Unable to Perform for fewer than six regular-season games, are termed NFL First-Year Players. An NFL First-Year Player is designated by a "1" on NFL rosters. Thereafter, a player is credited with an additional year of experience for each season in which he accumulates six games on the Active List or Inactive List, or on Reserve/Injured or Reserve/Physically Unable to Perform.

Log on to www.patriots.com for an up-to-date roster.

COACHING STAFF

Head Coach,
Bill Belichick

Pro Career: Bill Belichick is in his thirty-second season as an NFL coach and is the only head coach in league history to win three Super Bowl championships in a four-year span. Coach Belichick's Patriots teams own all of the major winning streaks in NFL history: consecutive overall wins (21 from 2003-04), consecutive regular season wins (18 from 2003-04), and consecutive playoff wins (10 from 2001-05). Hired as the fourteenth head coach in Patriots' history by Chairman and CEO Robert Kraft on January 27, 2000, Belichick is in his seventh season as New England's head coach. In 2001, just his second season at the helm, Belichick guided the Patriots to their first league title with a dramatic victory in Super Bowl XXXVI. In the seasons since then, he has directed New England to sustained on-field success through an instilled philosophy of maintaining short-term focus to deliver long-term goals. Belichick directed the Patriots to victories in Super Bowls XXXVI (2001), XXXVIII (2003), and XXXIX (2004), and enters the 2006 season as the only NFL head coach to record nine or more victories in each of the last five years. Additionally, his teams have won the AFC East title and advanced in the playoffs in three straight seasons and four of the last five years. The Patriots' three straight years of playoff advancement mark the longest current streak in the NFL and their string of three straight division crowns is a team record and is tied for the longest current streak in the league. Belichick's accomplishments have placed him among the NFL's elite coaches. Only one coach (Pittsburgh's Chuck Noll, 4) has won more Super Bowls than Belichick, and his three Super Bowl titles tie Washington's Joe Gibbs and San Francisco's Bill Walsh for second place on the NFL's all-time list. Including regular season and playoff games, Belichick enters 2006 as the winningest head coach in the NFL over the last five seasons and is also the Patriots' all-time leader in victories (73) and winning percentage (.682). Since 2001, Belichick has directed the Patriots to a 68-23 (.747) record, including a 10-1 postseason mark. Belichick owns a career playoff record of 11-2, a mark that ranks second in NFL history behind only the legendary Vince Lombardi (9-1). From 2003-04, Belichick directed the Patriots through the most prosperous two-year period for any team in NFL history, netting back-to-back Super Bowl victories and consecutive 17-2 campaigns. The team's 34 victories in 2003-04 mark the highest two-year win total in the NFL's 86-year history. Belichick's recent accomplishments are the latest triumphs in a career during which he has helped produce five Super Bowl titles, six conference championships and 11 division titles since entering the NFL in 1975. Now in his thirty-second season, he has more years of NFL experience than any of the other 31 head coaches. He won his first two Super Bowls as the defensive coordinator for the New York Giants in 1986 and 1990. George Seifert is the only other man to have won multiple Super Bowls both as a head coach and as an assistant coach. Belichick launched his career in 1975 as a special assistant with the Baltimore Colts, then became an assistant special teams coach with Detroit (1976-77) and Denver (1978). In 1979, he joined the New York Giants to begin a 12-season stint. Belichick was named head coach of the Cleveland Browns in 1991, becoming the youngest head coach in the NFL at age 37. By 1994, Belichick returned the Browns to the playoffs, finishing 11-5 and advancing to the second round, while allowing a league-low 204 total points. In 1996, Belichick joined New England and was a key contributor to the team's rebound from a 6-10 season in 1995 to an 11-5 season and the team's first division title in 10 years en route to the Patriots' appearance in Super Bowl XXXI. Belichick then spent three seasons with the Jets from 1997 to 1999, helping New York improve from a 1-15 season in 1996 to reach the AFC Championship Game in 1998. Career record: 110-79.

Background: Belichick was a center/tight end at Wesleyan 1971-74.

Personal: Born April 16, 1952, Nashville.

ASSISTANT COACHES

Joel Collier, secondary; born December 25, 1963, Buffalo. Linebacker Northern Colorado 1984-87. No pro playing experience. College coach: Syracuse 1988-89. Pro coach: Tampa Bay Buccaneers 1990, New England Patriots 1991-93, Miami Dolphins 1994-2004, rejoined Patriots in 2005.

Brian Daboll, wide receivers; born Welland, Ontario. Safety Rochester 1994-96. No pro playing experience. College coach: William & Mary 1997, Michigan State 1998-99. Pro coach: Joined Patriots in 2000.

Ivan Fears, running backs; born November 15, 1954, Portsmouth, Va. Running back William & Mary 1973-75. No pro playing experience. College coach: William & Mary 1977-79, Syracuse 1980-1990. Pro coach: New England Patriots 1991-92, Chicago Bears 1993-98, rejoined Patriots in 1999.

Pepper Johnson, defensive line; born July 29, 1964, Detroit. Linebacker Ohio State 1982-85. Pro linebacker New York Giants 1986-1992, Cleveland Browns 1993-95, Detroit Lions 1996, New York Jets 1997-98. Pro coach: Joined Patriots in 2001.

Pete Mangurian, tight ends; born June 17, 1955, Los Angeles. Defensive lineman Louisiana State 1975-78. No pro playing experience. College coach: Southern Methodist 1979-1980, New Mexico State 1981, Stanford 1982-83, Louisiana State 1984-87, Cornell 1998-2000 (head coach). Pro coach: Denver Broncos 1988-1992, New York Giants 1993-96, Atlanta Falcons 1997, 2001-03, joined Patriots in 2005.

Josh McDaniels, offensive coordinator/quarterbacks; born April 22, 1976, Canton, Ohio. Wide receiver John Carroll 1995-98. No pro playing experience. College coach: Michigan State 1999-2000. Pro coach: Joined Patriots in 2001.

Harold Nash, asst. strength and conditioning; born May 5, 1970, New Orleans. Defensive back Louisiana-Lafayette 1988-1993. Pro defensive back Shreveport Pirates (CFL) 1994-95, Montreal Alouettes (CFL) 1996-99, Winnipeg Blue Bombers (CFL) 1999-2003, Edmonton Eskimos (CFL) 2004. Pro coach: Joined Patriots in 2005.

Matt Patricia, linebackers; born Sept. 13, 1974. Center-guard Rensselaer 1992-96. No pro playing experience. College coach: Rensselaer 1996, Amherst 1999-2000, Syracuse 2001-03. Pro coach: Joined Patriots in 2004.

Dean Pees, defensive coordinator; born September 4, 1949, Dunkirk, Ohio. Attended Bowling Green. No college or pro playing experience. College coach: Findlay 1979-1982, Miami (Ohio) 1983-86, Navy 1987-89, Toledo 1990-93, Notre Dame 1994, Michigan State 1995-97, Kent State 1998-2003. Pro coach: Joined Patriots in 2004.

Dante Scarnecchia, asst. head coach/offensive line; born February 15, 1948, Los Angeles. Center/guard California Western 1968-1970. No pro playing experience. College coach: California Western 1970-72, Iowa State 1973-74, Southern Methodist 1975-76, 1980-81, Pacific 1977-78, Northern Arizona 1979. Pro coach: New England Patriots 1982-88, Indianapolis Colts 1989-1990, rejoined Patriots in 1991.

Brad Seely, special teams; born September 6, 1956, Vinton, Iowa. Tackle-guard South Dakota State 1974-77. No pro playing experience. College coach: Colorado State 1980, Southern Methodist 1981, North Carolina State 1982, Pacific 1983, Oklahoma State 1984-88. Pro coach: Indianapolis Colts 1989-1993, New York Jets 1994, Carolina Panthers 1995-98, joined Patriots in 1999.

Mike Woicik, strength and conditioning; born September 26, 1956, Baltimore. Attended Boston College. No college or pro playing experience. College coach: Springfield College 1978-79, Syracuse 1980-89. Pro coach: Dallas Cowboys 1990-96, New Orleans Saints 1997-99, joined Patriots in 2000.

**American Football Conference
East Division**
Team Colors: Green and White
1000 Fulton Avenue
Hempstead, New York 11550
Telephone: (516) 560-8100

2006 SCHEDULE
PRESEASON
Aug. 11 at Tampa Bay 7:30
Aug. 19 at Washington 8:00
Aug. 25 **New York Giants** 8:00
TBD   **Philadelphia** ....TBD

REGULAR SEASON
Sept. 10 at Tennessee 12:00
Sept. 17 **New England** 4:15
Sept. 24 at Buffalo 1:00
Oct. 1   **Indianapolis** 1:00
Oct. 8   at Jacksonville 4:05
Oct. 15   **Miami**.............................. 4:15
Oct. 22   **Detroit** 1:00
Oct. 29   at Cleveland 4:15
Nov. 5   Open Date
Nov. 12   at New England 1:00
Nov. 19   **Chicago** 1:00
Nov. 26   **Houston** 1:00
Dec. 3   at Green Bay 12:00
Dec. 10   **Buffalo**..............................1:00
Dec. 17   at Minnesota 1:00
Dec. 25   at Miami (Mon.) 8:30
Dec. 31   **Oakland** 1:00

Stadium: Meadowlands
(opened in 1976)
• **Capacity:** 80,062
East Rutherford, New Jersey
07073
Playing Surface: FieldTurf
Training Camp: 1000 Fulton Avenue
Hempstead, New York
11550

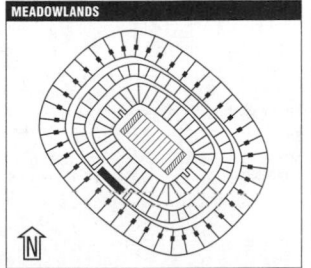

MEADOWLANDS

CLUB OFFICIALS
Chairman and CEO:
Robert Wood Johnson IV
President: Jay Cross
General Manager: Mike Tannenbaum
Senior V.P. for Public Affairs:
Matt Higgins
Senior V.P. for New Meadowlands
Stadium Project: Bill Senn
Senior V.P. for Finance: Thad Sheely
Senior V.P. for Sales: Lee Stacey
Director, Pro Personnel: JoJo Wooden
Assistant Director, Pro Personnel:
Brendan Prophett
Senior Director, Football Administration:
David Socie
Manager, Football Administration:
Ari Nissim
Pro Personnel Assistant: Tom Frawley
Pro Personnel Assistant: Carrine Marrino
Senior Director, College Scouting:
Jesse Kaye
National Scout: Joey Clinkscales
Coordinator, College Scouting:
John Griffin
Personnel Scouts: Jeff Bauer,
Matt Bazirgan, Joe Bommarito,
Ron Brockington, Jim Cochran,
Michael Davis, Sid Hall, Gary Smith
Scouting Consultant: Dick Haley
Personnel Consultant: Terry Bradway
Assistant, College Scouting:
Kirwan Watson
College Scouting Assistant: Kerri Stork
Head Athletic Trainer: John Mellody
Assistant Athletic Trainer: TBA
Assistant Athletic Trainer: TBA
Assistant Equipment Manager:
Gus Granneman
V.P., Media Relations: Ron Colangelo
Director, Media Relations: Douglas Miller
Senior Director, Information Technology:
Tom Murphy
Senior Director, Operations:
Clay Hampton
Senior Director, Security: Steve Yarnell
Director, Internet & Publications: TBA
Director, Video: Steve Scarnecchia
Director, Player Development:
Jerome Henderson
Director, Ticket Operations:
John Buschhorn
Manager, Community Relations:
Jesse Linder

COACHING HISTORY
New York Titans 1960-62
(316-386-8)
Records include postseason games
1960-61   Sammy Baugh............14-14-0
1962   Clyde (Bulldog) Turner 5-9-0
1963-1973 Weeb Ewbank..............73-78-6
1974-75   Charley Winner* 9-14-0
1975   Ken Shipp.......................1-4-0
1976   Lou Holtz**.................3-10-0
1976   Mike Holovak..................0-1-0
1977-1982 Walt Michaels 41-49-1
1983-89   Joe Walton 54-59-1
1990-93   Bruce Coslet...............26-39-0
1994   Pete Carroll....................6-10-0
1995-96   Rich Kotite....................4-28-0
1997-99   Bill Parcells.................30-20-0
2000   Al Groh..........................9-7-0
2001-05   Herman Edwards.........41-44-0
*Released after nine games in 1975
**Resigned after 13 games in 1976

ATTENDANCE
Home 619,842   Away 577,382
Total 1,197,224
Single-game home record,
78,920 (11/10/02)
Single-season home record,
628,773 (2002)

2006 DRAFT CHOICES

Round	Name	Pos.	College
1	D'Brickashaw Ferguson	T	Virginia
	Nick Mangold	C	Ohio State
2	Kellen Clemens	QB	Oregon
3	Anthony Schlegel	LB	Ohio State
	Eric Smith	DB	Michigan State
4	Brad Smith	WR	Missouri
	Leon Washington	RB	Florida State
5	Jason Pociask	TE	Wisconsin
6	Drew Coleman	DB	Texas Christian
7	Titus Adams	DF	Nebraska

2005 TEAM RECORD
PRESEASON (3-1)

Date	Result		Opponent
8/12	W	10-3	Detroit
8/19	W	28-21	Minnesota
8/26	L	14-15	at N.Y. Giants
9/1	W	37-14	at Philadelphia

REGULAR SEASON (4-12)

Date	Result		Opponent	Att.
9/11	L	7-27	at Kansas City	78,014
9/18	W	17-7	Miami	77,918
9/25	L	20-26	Jacksonville (OT)	77,422
10/2	L	3-13	at Baltimore	70,479
10/9	W	14-12	Tampa Bay	77,852
10/16	L	17-27	at Buffalo	72,045
10/24	L	14-27	at Atlanta	70,995
11/6	L	26-31	San Diego	77,662
11/13	L	3-30	at Carolina	73,529
11/20	L	0-27	at Denver	76,255
11/27	L	19-21	New Orleans	77,152
12/4	L	3-16	at New England	68,756
12/11	W	26-10	Oakland	77,561
12/18	L	20-24	at Miami	72,650
12/26	L	21-31	New England	77,569
1/1	W	30-26	Buffalo	76,822

(OT) Overtime

SCORE BY PERIODS

Jets	23	83	50	84	0	—	240
Opponents	85	109	58	97	6	—	355

2005 TEAM STATISTICS

	Jets	Opp.
Total First Downs	251	321
Rushing	74	136
Passing	146	151
Penalty	31	34
3rd Down: Made/Att	72/204	88/212
3rd Down Pct.	35.3	41.5
4th Down: Made/Att	8/19	14/17
4th Down Pct.	42.1	82.4
Possession Avg.	26:37	33:23
Total Net Yards	3,970	4,940
Avg. Per Game	248.1	308.8
Total Plays	907	1,047
Avg. Per Play	4.4	4.7
Net Yards Rushing	1,328	2,185
Avg. Per Game	83.0	136.6
Total Rushes	384	554
Net Yards Passing	2,642	2,755
Avg. Per Game	165.1	172.2
Sacked/Yards Lost	53/347	30/193
Gross Yards	2,989	2,948
Att./Completions	470/268	463/284
Completion Pct.	57.0	61.3
Had Intercepted	15	21
Punts/Average	75/43.3	62/45.0
Net Punting Avg.	75/37.7	62/39.5
Penalties/Yards	98/801	115/981
Fumbles/Ball Lost	36/19	24/7
Touchdowns	25	38
Rushing	10	19
Passing	11	17
Returns	4	2

2005 INDIVIDUAL STATISTICS

PASSING

PASSING	Att.	Comp.	Yds.	Pct.	TD	Int.	Tkld.	Rate
Bollinger	266	150	1,558	56.4	7	6	32/193	72.9
Testaverde	106	60	777	56.6	1	6	12/102	59.4
Pennington	83	49	530	59.0	2	3	9/52	70.9
Fiedler	13	8	107	61.5	1	0	0/0	113.3
Kingsbury	2	1	17	50.0	0	0	0/0	79.2
Jets	470	268	2,989	57.0	11	15	53/347	70.6
Opponents	463	284	2,948	61.3	17	21	30/193	73.1

SCORING

SCORING	TD R	TD P	TD Rt	PAT	FG	Saf	PTS
Nugent	0	0	0	24/24	22/28	0	90
Coles	0	5	0	0/0	0/0	0	30
Martin	5	0	0	0/0	0/0	0	30
Sowell	1	2	0	0/0	0/0	0	18
Houston	2	0	0	0/0	0/0	0	12
McCareins	0	2	0	0/0	0/0	0	12
Testaverde	2	0	0	0/0	0/0	0	12
Baker	0	1	0	0/0	0/0	0	6
Brown	0	0	1	0/0	0/0	0	6
Jolley	0	1	0	0/0	0/0	0	6
Law	0	0	1	0/0	0/0	0	6
Miller	0	0	1	0/0	0/0	0	6
Reed	0	0	1	0/0	0/0	0	6
Jets	10	11	4	24/24	22/28	0	240
Opponents	19	17	2	37/37	30/35	0	355

2-Pt. Conversions: None.
Jets 0-1, Opponents 0-0.

RUSHING

RUSHING	No.	Yds	Avg	LG	TD
Martin	220	735	3.3	49	5
Houston	81	302	3.7	17	2
Bollinger	35	135	3.9	15	0
Askew	13	59	4.5	14	0
Blaylock	17	53	3.1	11	0
Pennington	6	27	4.5	14	0
McCareins	1	8	8.0	8	0
Cotchery	1	4	4.0	4	0
Testaverde	7	4	0.6	2	2
Sowell	1	1	1.0	1t	1
Fiedler	1	0	0.0	0	0
Graham	1	0	0.0	0	0
Jets	384	1,328	3.5	49	10
Opponents	554	2,185	3.9	65	19

RECEIVING

RECEIVING	No.	Yds	Avg	LG	TD
Coles	73	845	11.6	43	5
McCareins	43	713	16.6	45	2
Jolley	29	324	11.2	60t	1
Sowell	28	155	5.5	28	2
Martin	24	118	4.9	14	0
Cotchery	19	251	13.2	45	0
Baker	18	269	14.9	47	1
Chrebet	15	153	10.2	20	0
Houston	8	66	8.3	16	0
Dreessen	5	41	8.2	17	0
Blaylock	3	17	5.7	10	0
Ridgeway	2	26	13.0	17	0
Askew	1	11	11.0	11	0
Jets	268	2,989	11.2	60t	11
Opponents	284	2,948	10.4	50t	17

INTERCEPTIONS

INTERCEPTIONS	No.	Yds	Avg	LG	TD
Law	10	195	19.5	74t	1
Barrett	5	28	5.6	13	0
Brown	2	51	25.5	33t	1
Coleman	2	4	2.0	4	0
Vilma	1	1	1.0	1	0
Rhodes	1	0	0.0	0	0
Jets	21	279	13.3	74t	2
Opponents	15	147	9.8	53	1

PUNTING

PUNTING	No.	Yds.	Avg.	In 20	LG
Graham	74	3,233	43.7	18	59
Nugent	1	18	18.0	1	18
Jets	75	3,251	43.3	19	59
Opponents	62	2,787	45.0	17	60

PUNT RETURNS

PUNT RETURNS	Ret	FC	Yds	Avg	LG	TD
Cotchery	23	7	182	7.9	18	0
Miller	6	1	9	1.5	12	0
McCareins	5	4	28	5.6	12	0
Jets	34	12	219	6.4	18	0
Opponents	36	15	305	8.5	23	0

KICKOFF RETURNS

KICKOFF RETURNS	No.	Yds	Avg	LG	TD
Miller	60	1,577	26.3	95t	1
Cotchery	4	105	26.3	30	0
Houston	2	18	9.0	18	0
Baker	2	11	5.5	11	0
Blaylock	1	17	17.0	17	0
Barrett	1	0	0.0	0	0
Lawton	1	0	0.0	0	0
Jets	71	1,728	24.3	95t	1
Opponents	60	1,250	20.8	50	0

FIELD GOALS

FIELD GOALS	1-19	20-29	30-39	40-49	50+
Nugent	0/0	8/9	7/7	7/10	0/2
Jets	0/0	8/9	7/7	7/10	0/2
Opponents	1/1	10/12	9/10	8/9	2/3

SACKS

SACKS	No.
Abraham	10.5
Robertson	3.5
Thomas	3.5
Legree	3.0
Ellis	2.5
Reed	2.0
Brown	1.0
Hobson	1.0
Rhodes	1.0
Washington	1.0
Vilma	0.5
Jets	30.0
Opponents	53.0

RECORD HOLDERS
INDIVIDUAL RECORDS—CAREER

Category	Name	Performance
Rushing (Yds.)	Curtis Martin, 1998-2005	10,302
Passing (Yds.)	Joe Namath, 1965-1976	27,057
Passing (TDs)	Joe Namath, 1965-1976	170
Receiving (No.)	Don Maynard, 1960-1972	627
Receiving (Yds.)	Don Maynard, 1960-1972	11,732
Interceptions	Bill Baird, 1963-69	34
Punting (Avg.)	Ben Graham, 2005	43.7
Punt Return (Avg.)	Dick Christy, 1961-63	16.2
Kickoff Return (Avg.)	Chad Morton, 2001-02	25.0
Field Goals	Pat Leahy, 1974-1991	304
Touchdowns (Tot.)	Don Maynard, 1960-1972	88
Points	Pat Leahy, 1974-1991	1,470

INDIVIDUAL RECORDS—SINGLE SEASON

Category	Name	Performance
Rushing (Yds.)	Curtis Martin, 2004	1,697
Passing (Yds.)	Joe Namath, 1967	4,007
Passing (TDs)	Vinny Testaverde, 1998	29
Receiving (No.)	Al Toon, 1988	93
Receiving (Yds.)	Don Maynard, 1967	1,434
Interceptions	Dainard Paulson, 1964	12
Punting (Avg.)	Curley Johnson, 1965	45.3
Punt Return (Avg.)	Dick Christy, 1961	21.3
Kickoff Return (Avg.)	Bobby Humphery, 1984	30.7
Field Goals	Jim Turner, 1968	34
Touchdowns (Tot.)	Art Powell, 1960	14
	Don Maynard, 1965	14
	Emerson Boozer, 1972	14
	Curtis Martin, 2004	14
Points	Jim Turner, 1968	145

INDIVIDUAL RECORDS—SINGLE GAME

Category	Name	Performance
Rushing (Yds.)	Curtis Martin, 12-3-00	203
Passing (Yds.)	Joe Namath, 9-24-72	496
Passing (TDs)	Joe Namath, 9-24-72	6
Receiving (No.)	Clark Gaines, 9-21-80	17
Receiving (Yds.)	Don Maynard, 11-17-68	228
Interceptions	Many times	3
	Last time by Ty Law, 1-1-06	
Field Goals	Jim Turner, 11-3-68	6
	Bobby Howfield, 12-3-72	6
Touchdowns (Tot.)	Wesley Walker, 9-21-86	4
Points	Wesley Walker, 9-21-86	24

2006 VETERAN ROSTER

No.	Name	Pos.	Ht.	Wt.	Birthdate	NFL Exp.	College	Hometown	How Acq.	'05 Games/ Starts
35	Askew, B.J.	FB	6-3	233	8/19/80	4	Michigan	Cincinnati, Ohio	D3-'03	10/1
86	Baker, Chris	TE	6-3	258	11/18/79	5	Michigan State	Queens, N.Y.	D3-'02	8/8
96	Ball, Dave	DE	6-5	277	1/4/81	3	UCLA	Fairfield, Calif.	FA-'05	3/0
36	Barrett, David	CB	5-10	195	12/22/77	7	Arkansas	Osceola, Ark.	UFA(Ariz)-'04	13/8
50	Barton, Eric	LB	6-2	245	9/29/77	8	Maryland	Alexandria, Va.	UFA(Oak)-'04	4/3
23	Blaylock, Derrick	RB	5-9	205	8/23/79	5	Stephen F. Austin	Atlanta, Texas	UFA(KC)-'05	7/1
5	Bollinger, Brooks	QB	6-1	205	11/15/79	4	Wisconsin	Grand Forks, N.D.	D6-'03	11/9
58	Chatham, Matt	LB	6-4	250	6/28/77	7	South Dakota	Sioux City, Iowa	UFA(NE)-'06	15/0*
68	Clement, Anthony	T	6-8	320	4/10/76	9	Southwestern Louisiana	Lafayette, La.	UFA(SF)-'06	14/6*
26	Coleman, Erik	S	5-10	200	5/6/82	3	Washington State	Spokane, Wash.	D5-'04	16/16
87	Coles, Laveranues	WR	5-11	193	12/29/77	7	Florida State	Jacksonville, Fla.	T(Wash)-'05	16/16
89	Cotchery, Jerricho	WR	6-0	207	6/16/82	3	North Carolina State	Birmingham, Ala.	D4a-'04	16/1
85	Dearth, James	TE/LS	6-4	270	1/22/76	6	Tarleton State	Scurry, Texas	FA-'01	16/0
83	Dreessen, Joel	TE/LS	6-4	260	7/26/82	2	Colorado State	Fort Morgan, Colo.	D6b-'05	14/0
17	Dwight, Tim	WR	5-8	180	7/13/75	9	Iowa	Iowa City, Iowa	UFA(NE)-'06	16/1*
24	Dyson, Andre	CB	5-10	183	5/25/79	6	Utah	Clearfield, Utah	FA-'06	10/5*
92	Ellis, Shaun	DE	6-5	285	6/24/77	7	Tennessee	Anderson, S.C.	D1a-'00	13/13
7	Graham, Ben	P	6-5	230	11/27/3	2	Deakin (Australia)	Geelong/Victoria, Australia	FA-'05	15/7
54	Hobson, Victor	LB	6-0	252	2/3/80	4	Michigan	Mt. Laurel, N.J.	D2-'03	16/16
34	Houston, Cedric	RB	6-0	220	6/28/82	2	Tennessee	Clarendon, Ark.	D6a-'05	12/4
32	Johnson, Darrien	DB	5-11	215	5/3/80	2	Iowa	Chicago, Ill.	FA-'05	8/0
97	Johnson, Trevor	DE/LB	6-4	260	2/26/81	3	Nebraska	Lincoln, Neb.	D7b-'04	9/0
88	Jolley, Doug	TE	6-4	250	1/2/79	5	Brigham Young	Sandy, Utah	T(Oak)-'05	16/7
79	Jones, Adrian	T	6-4	296	6/10/81	3	Kansas	Dallas, Texas	D4b-'04	16/16
55	Kassell, Brad	LB	6-3	242	1/7/80	5	North Texas	Llano, Texas	UFA(Tenn)-'06	16/14*
64	Katnik, Norm	C	6-4	298	7/2/81	2	Southern California	Santa Ana, Calif.	FA-'05	1/0
66	Kendall, Pete	G/C	6-5	280	7/9/73	11	Boston College	Weymouth, Mass.	UFA(Ariz)-'04	16/16
3	Kingsbury, Kliff	QB	6-4	220	8/9/79	2	Texas Tech	San Antonio, Texas	FA-'05	1/0
44	Lawton, Luke	FB	5-11	237	8/26/80	2	McNeese State	Lafayette, La.	FA-'05	4/0
28	Martin, Curtis	RB	5-11	210	5/1/73	12	Pittsburgh	Pittsburgh, Pa.	RFA(NE)-'98	6/6
81	McCareins, Justin	WR	6-2	215	12/11/78	6	Northern Illinois	Naperville, Ill.	T(Tenn)-'04	16/16
95	McChesney, Matt	DT	6-4	292	11/6/81	2	Colorado	Santa Cruz, Calif.	FA-'05	3/0
57	McClover, Darrell	LB	6-2	226	8/25/81	2	Miami	Ft. Lauderdale, Fla.	D7a-'04	0*
22	Miller, Justin	CB	5-10	202	2/14/84	2	Clemson	Owensboro, KY	D2b-'05	16/8
65	Moore, Brandon	G	6-3	295	6/3/80	4	Illinois	Gary, IN	FA-'03	16/16
76	Morley, Steve	T/G	6-7	330	8/18/81	2	St. Mary's (Canada)	Halifax, Nova Scotia, Canada	T(GB)-'05	7/0
45	Myers, Ryan	LB	6-2	245	2/27/80	2	Akron	Wellington, Ohio	FA-'05	15/0
71	Neinhuis, Doug	G	6-6	307	2/16/82	2	Oregon State	Irvine, Calif.	FA-'05	7/0
1	Nugent, Mike	K	5-9	182	3/2/82	2	Ohio State	Centerville, Ohio	D2a-'05	16/0
10	Pennington, Chad	QB	6-3	225	6/26/76	7	Marshall	Knoxville, Tenn.	D1c-'00	3/3
75	Pope, Monsanto	DT	6-3	300	1/27/78	4	Virginia	Norfolk, Va.	UFA(Den)-'06	2/0*
91	Pouha, Sione	DT	6-3	325	2/3/79	2	Utah	Salt Lake City, Utah	D3-'05	14/0
11 t-	Ramsey, Patrick	QB	6-2	225	2/14/79	5	Tulane	Ruston, La.	T(Wash)-'06	4/1*
25	Rhodes, Kerry	S	6-3	210	8/2/82	2	Louisville	Bessemer, Ala.	D4-'05	16/16
84	Ridgeway, Dante	WR	6-1	200	4/18/84	2	Ball State	Decatur, Ill.	W(Cin)-'05	7/0
63	Robertson, Dewayne	DT	6-1	317	10/16/81	4	Kentucky	Memphis, Tenn.	D1-'03	13/12
21	Strait, Derrick	CB	5-11	189	8/27/80	3	Oklahoma	Austin, Texas	D3-'04	16/2
70	Teague, Trey	C	6-5	300	12/27/78	9	Tennessee	Jackson, Tenn.	UFA(Buff)-'06	16/16*
99	Thomas, Bryan	DE	6-4	266	6/7/79	5	Alabama-Birmingham	Birmingham, Ala.	D1-'02	16/4
51	Vilma, Jonathan	LB	6-1	230	4/16/82	3	Miami	South Miami, Fla.	D1-'04	16/16
67	von Oelhoffen, Kimo	DT	6-4	299	1/30/71	13	Boise State	Kaunakakai, Hawaii	UFA(Pitt)-'06	16/15*
42	Washington, Rashad	S	6-1	217	3/15/80	3	Kansas State	Wichita, Kan.	D7d-'04	16/0

* Chatham played 15 games with New England in '05; Clement played 14 games with San Francisco; Dwight played 16 games with New England; Dyson played 10 games with Seattle; Kassell played 16 games with Tennessee; McClover missed '05 season because of injury; Pope played 2 games with Denver in '05; Ramsey played 4 games with Washington; Teague played 16 games with Buffalo; von Oelhoffen played 16 games with Pittsburgh.

t- Jets traded for Ramsey (Wash).

Traded—DE John Abraham (16 games in '05) to Atlanta.

Retired—Vinny Testaverde, 19-year quarterback, 6 games in '05; Wayne Chrebet, 11-year wide receiver, 8 games.

Players lost through free agency (1): G Jonathan Goodwin (NO; 16 games in '05).

Also played with Jets in '05—LB Mark Brown (15 games), S Oliver Celestin (12), T Jason Fabini (9), QB Jay Fiedler (2), LB Barry Gardner (16), T Scott Gragg (15), LB T.J. Hollowell (2), CB Ty Law (16), DE/DT Lance Legree (16), CB/S Jeremy LeSueur (3), C Kevin Mawae (6), DT James Reed (16), FB Jerald Sowell (16), WR Harry Williams (1), LB Kenyatta Wright (15).

2006 FIRST-YEAR ROSTER

Name	Pos.	Ht.	Wt.	Birthdate	College	Hometown	How Acq.
Adams, Darrell	DE/DT	6-5	282	9/16/83	Villanova	Bayshore, N.Y.	FA
Adams, Titus	DT	6-4	305	1/28/83	Nebraska	Omaha, Neb.	D7
Alailefaleula, Tui	DL/OL	6-4	350	11/5/82	Washington	Anchorage, Alaska	FA
Bailey, Craig	DE/LB	6-4	265	11/6/83	Nevada	Harbor City, Calif.	FA
Blanton, Ed	T	6-9	330	10/23/82	UCLA	Winfield, Ill.	FA
Brown Jr., Michael	LB	6-4	250	9/21/84	Howard	Baltimore, Md.	FA
Butler, Terry (1)	RB	6-1	200	8/2/82	Villanova	Syracuse, N.Y.	FA-'05
Cavka, Marko (1)	T	6-7	294	4/4/84	Sacramento State	Cypress, Calif.	D6-'04
Clemens, Kellen	QB	6-2	223	6/6/83	Oregon	Burns, Ore.	D2
Coleman, Drew	CB	5-9	175	4/22/83	Texas Christian	Henderson, Texas	D6
Costanzo, Blake	LB	6-1	235	4/14/84	Lafayette	Franklin Lakes, N.J.	FA
Dada, Omowale	CB	5-11	194	5/31/83	Washington State	Orland Park, Ill.	FA
Davis, Mondoe (1)	LB	6-1	225	3/19/82	Delaware	Newport News, Va.	FA-'05
Enzor, Jamar (1)	LB	6-1	237	12/28/06	Cincinnati	Tallahassee, Fla.	FA-'05
Ferguson, D'Brickashaw	T	6-6	312	12/10/83	Virginia	Freeport, N.Y.	D1a
Fitzpatrick, D.J.	P/K	6-1	208	11/18/82	Notre Dame	Granger, Ind.	FA
King, Michael (1)	G	6-3	298	6/15/82	Northwestern State	Natchitoches, La.	FA-'05
Kowalewski, Joe	TE	6-4	250	11/15/82	Syracuse	Warners, N.Y.	FA
Maddox, Andre (1)	S	6-1	200	10/8/82	North Carolina State	Miami, Fla.	D5-'05
Mangold, Nick	C	6-4	300	1/13/84	Ohio State	Kettering, Ohio	D1b
Missant, Charles (1)	C	6-3	295	4/23/81	Western Michigan	Grosse Pointe, Mich.	FA-'05
Mobley, Deqawn	WR	6-2	210	7/17/84	Texas A&M	Bronx, N.Y.	FA
Moore, DonTrell	RB	5-10	208	9/25/82	New Mexico	Roswell, N.M.	FA
Pociask, Jason	TE	6-2	259	2/9/83	Wisconsin	Plainfield, Ind.	D5
Schlegel, Anthony	LB	6-1	251	3/1/81	Ohio State	Dallas, Texas	D3a
Schmidt, Brennan	DT	6-3	290	3/17/83	Virginia	Washington, D.C.	FA
Smith, Brad	WR	6-2	210	12/12/83	Missouri	Liberty, Ohio	D4a
Smith, Eric	S	6-1	209	3/17/83	Michigan State	Groveport, Ohio	D3b
Snell, Isaac (1)	T	6-6	288	11/4/81	North Dakota State	Piperstone, Minn.	FA-'05
Thompson, Jamie	S	6-0	192	5/25/83	Oklahoma State	Sparr, Fla.	FA
Thompson, Will	LB	6-3	255	12/26/81	Georgia	Columbus, Ga.	A
Tutt, Stacy	RB	6-2	235	8/8/82	Richmond	Fredricksburg, Va.	FA
Washington, Leon	RB	5-8	202	8/29/82	Florida State	Jacksonville, Fla.	D4b
Witherspoon, Jovan (1)	WR	6-3	210	8/13/81	Central Michigan	Fort Wayne, Ind.	FA-'05
Wright, Wallace	WR	6-0	191	2/1/84	North Carolina	Sayetteville, N.C.	FA

The term NFL Rookie is defined as a player who is in his first season of professional football and has not been on the roster of another professional football team for any regular-season or postseason games. A Rookie is designated by an "R" on NFL rosters. Players who have been active in another professional football league or players who have NFL experience, including either preseason training camp or being on an Active List or Inactive List, or on Reserve/Injured or Reserve/Physically Unable to Perform for fewer than six regular-season games, are termed NFL First-Year Players. An NFL First-Year Player is designated by a "1" on NFL rosters. Thereafter, a player is credited with an additional year of experience for each season in which he accumulates six games on the Active List or Inactive List, or on Reserve/Injured or Reserve/Physically Unable to Perform.

Log on to www.newyorkjets.com for an up-to-date roster.

COACHING STAFF
Head Coach,
Eric Mangini
Pro Career: Eric Mangini was named the fourteenth full-time head coach of the New York Jets on January 17, 2006. He rejoins the Jets following six seasons with the New England Patriots (2000-05), the first five of which he served as the defensive backs coach before earning a promotion to the defensive coordinator's position. Mangini, a coaching veteran of 14 seasons, is entering his twelfth season in the NFL and his first as a head coach. He has been a part of five division titles, three conference titles, and three Super Bowl championships in his career. In his first five seasons with the Patriots, he tutored a secondary that earned five Pro Bowl selections and evolved into one of the NFL's most successful defensive backfields despite suffering numerous injuries. Prior to joining the Patriots, Mangini served as an assistant on Bill Parcells' coaching staff with the Jets (1997-1999), where he worked primarily as the defensive assistant/quality control coach. During that time, he worked closely with Bill Belichick, who was the Jets' assistant head coach/secondary coach. Mangini was also responsible for advance opponent film breakdowns and analysis. In 1999, the Jets' defense ranked third in the AFC with 24 interceptions, the team's highest total since 1969 (29). In 1998, the Jets' defense surrendered just 16.6 points per game, helping the Jets to a 12-4 overall record and their first division title, while advancing to the AFC Championship game. In 1996, he served as a quality control/offensive assistant on Ted Marchibroda's coaching staff with the Baltimore Ravens. Mangini's first NFL coaching opportunity came in 1995 as an assistant on Belichick's Cleveland Browns staff. While completing his Wesleyan degree in Melbourne, Australia, Mangini served as the head coach and defensive coordinator for the Kew Colts, a semi-professional football team, and led them to back-to-back titles. Career record: 0-0.
Background: Mangini set a school record with 36.5 sacks as a nose tackle in college for Wesleyan (Conn.) from 1989-1990, 92-93. He was voted a first-team all-star by NESCAC and ECAC New England Division III.
Personal: Born January 19, 1971, Hartford, Conn. Mangini and his wife, Julie, have two sons, Jake and Luke.

ASSISTANT COACHES
Richie Anderson, tight ends/asst. wide receivers; born September 13, 1971, Sandy Spring, Md. Running back Penn State 1989-1992. Pro running back New York Jets 1993-2002, Dallas Cowboys 2003-04. Pro coach: Joined Jets in 2006.
Brett Bech, asst. strength and conditioning; born August 20, 1971, Slidell, La.
Wide receiver Louisiana State 1991-94. Pro wide receiver New Orleans Saints 1996-99. Pro coach: Joined Jets in 2006.
Corwin Brown, defensive backs; born April 25, 1970, Chicago. Safety Michigan 1989-1992. Pro safety New England Patriots 1993-96, New York Jets 1997-98, Detroit Lions 1999-2000. College coach: Virginia 2001-03. Pro coach: Joined Jets in 2004.
Bryan Cox, asst. defensive line; born February 17, 1968, East St. Louis, Ill. Linebacker Western Illinois 1987-1990. Pro linebacker Miami Dolphins 1991-95, Chicago Bears 1996-97, New York Jets 1998-2000, New England Patriots 2001, New Orleans Saints 2002. Pro coach: Joined Jets in 2006.
Mike Devlin, tight ends/asst. offensive line; born November 16, 1969, Blacksburg, Va. Offensive line Iowa 1989-1992. Pro offensive lineman Buffalo Bills 1993-95, Arizona Cardinals 1996-99. College coach: Toledo 2004-05. Pro coach: Arizona Cardinals 2000-03, joined Jets in 2006.
Andy Dickerson, coaching assistant; born January 29, 1982, Wilmington, Del. Offensive lineman Tufts 1999-2002. No pro playing experience. College coach: Tufts 2003. Pro coach: Joined Jets in 2006.
Sam Gash, asst. running backs/special teams; born March 7, 1969, Hendersonville, N.C. Fullback Penn State 1987-1991. Pro fullback New England Patriots 1992-97, Buffalo Bills 1998-99, 2003, Baltimore Ravens 2000-02. Pro coach: Joined Jets in 2005.
Jim Herrmann, linebackers; born December 8, 1960, Hollywood, Calif. Linebacker Michigan 1979-1982. No pro playing experience. College coach: Michigan 1983, 1986-2005. Pro coach: Joined Jets in 2006.
Rick Lyle, asst. strength and conditioning; born February 26, 1971, Monroe, La. Defensive lineman Missouri 1989-1993. Pro defensive lineman Cleveland Browns 1994-95, Baltimore Ravens 1996, New York Jets 1997-2001, New England Patriots 2002-03. Pro coach: Joined Jets in 2006.
Denny Marcin, defensive line; born April 24, 1942, Cleveland. Defensive/offensive lineman Miami (Ohio) 1961-64. No pro playing experience. College coach: Miami (Ohio) 1974-77, North Carolina 1978-1987, Illinois 1988-1996. Pro coach: New York Giants 1997-2003, joined Jets in 2004.
Jay Mandolesi, defensive quality control; born August 23, 1982, Springfield, Mass. Attended Springfield College. No college or pro playing experience. Pro coach: Joined Jets in 2005.
Noel Mazzone, wide receivers; born March 21, 1957, Mt. Vernon, Wash. Quarterback New Mexico 1975-79. No pro playing experience. College coach: New Mexico 1980-81, Colorado State 1982-86, Texas Christian 1987-1991, Minnesota 1992-94, Mississippi 1994-
98, Auburn 1999-2001, Oregon State 2002, North Carolina State 2003-05. Pro coach: Joined Jets in 2006.
Jason Michael, offensive quality control; born October 15, 1978, Portsmouth, Ohio. Quarterback Western Kentucky 1999-2002. No pro playing experience. College coach: Tennessee 2003-04. Pro coach: Oakland Raiders 2005, joined Jets in 2006.
Markus Paul, head strength and conditioning; born April 1, 1966, Orlando, Fla. Safety Syracuse 1984-88. Pro safety Chicago Bears 1989-1993, Tampa Bay Buccaneers 1993. Pro coach: New Orleans Saints 1998-99, New England Patriots 2000-04, joined Jets in 2005.
Jimmy Raye, running backs; born March 26, 1946, Fayetteville, N.C. Quarterback Michigan State 1964-68. Pro defensive back Philadelphia Eagles 1969. College coach: Michigan State 1971-75, Wyoming 1976. Pro coach: San Francisco 49ers 1977, Detroit Lions 1978-79, Atlanta Falcons 1980-82, 1987-89, Los Angeles Rams 1983-84, 1991, Tampa Bay Buccaneers 1985-86, New England Patriots 1990, Kansas City Chiefs 1992-2000, Washington Redskins 2001, New York Jets 2002-03, Oakland Raiders 2004-2005, re-joined Jets in 2006.
Brian Schottenheimer, offensive coordinator; born October 16, 1973, Denver. Quarterback Kansas 1992, Florida 1993-96. No pro playing experience. College coach: Syracuse 1999, Southern California 2000. Pro coach: St. Louis Rams 1997, Kansas City Chiefs 1998, Washington Redskins 2001, San Diego Chargers 2002-05, joined Jets in 2006.
Bob Sutton, defensive coordinator; born January 28, 1951, Ypsilanti, Mich. Attended Eastern Michigan. No college or pro playing experience. College coach: Michigan 1972-73, Syracuse 1974, Western Michigan 1975-76, 1980-81, Illinois 1977-79, North Carolina State 1982, Army 1983-1999 (head coach 1991-99). Pro coach: Joined Jets in 2000.
Mike Westhoff, special teams coordinator; born January 10, 1948, Pittsburgh. Center/linebacker Wichita State 1967-69. No pro playing experience. College coach: Indiana 1974-75, Dayton 1976, Indiana State 1977, Northwestern 1978-1980, Texas Christian 1981. Pro coach: Baltimore/Indianapolis Colts 1982-84, Arizona Outlaws (USFL) 1985, Miami Dolphins 1986-2000, joined Jets in 2001.
Tony Wise, offensive line; born December 28, 1951, Albany, N.Y. Offensive lineman Ithaca College 1969-1972. No pro playing experience. College coach: Albany State 1973, Bridgeport 1974, Central Connecticut State 1975, Washington State 1976, Pittsburgh 1977-78, Oklahoma State 1979-83, Syracuse 1984, Miami 1985-88. Pro coach: Dallas Cowboys 1989-1992, Chicago Bears 1993-98, Carolina Panthers 1999-2000, Miami Dolphins 2001-04, joined Jets in 2006.

**American Football Conference
West Division**
Team Colors: Silver and Black
**1220 Harbor Bay Parkway
Alameda, California 94502
Telephone:** (510) 864-5000

2006 SCHEDULE
PRESEASON
Aug. 6   vs. Philadelphia at Canton, OH 8:00
Aug. 14   at Minnesota 7:00
Aug. 20   **San Francisco** 5:00
Aug. 25   **Detroit** 7:00
Aug. 31   at Seattle. 7:00

REGULAR SEASON
Sept. 11 **San Diego** (Mon.) 7:15
Sept. 17 at Baltimore 1:00
Sept. 24 Open Date
Oct. 1   **Cleveland** 1:15
Oct. 8   at San Francisco 1:05
Oct. 15   at Denver 6:15
Oct. 22   **Arizona** 1:15
Oct. 29   **Pittsburgh** 1:15
Nov. 6   at Seattle (Mon.) 5:30
Nov. 12   **Denver** 1:05
Nov. 19   at Kansas City 12:00
Nov. 26   at San Diego 1:05
Dec. 3   **Houston** 1:05
Dec. 10   at Cincinnati 1:00
Dec. 17   **St. Louis** 1:15
Dec. 23   **Kansas City** (Sat.) 5:00
Dec. 31   at N.Y. Jets 1:00

Stadium: McAfee Coliseum
         (opened in 1966)
         •**Capacity:** 63,132
         7000 Coliseum Way
         Oakland, CA 94621-1917
Playing Surface: Grass
Training Camp: Napa Valley Marriott
         Napa, California 94558

MCAFEE COLISEUM

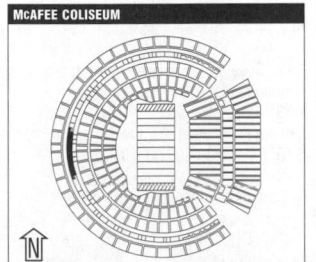

CLUB OFFICIALS
Owner: Al Davis
Chief Executive: Amy Trask
Personnel Executive: Michael Lombardi
Legal: Jeff Birren, Dan Ventrelle
Finance: Marc Badain, Tom Blanda,
   Derek Person, Ed Villanueva
Special Projects: Jim Otto
Senior Executive: John Herrera
Public Relations: Mike Taylor
Ticket Operations: Rob Sullivan,
   Peter Eiges
Multi-Cultural Initiatives: Patty Herrera,
   Elena Valenzuela
Internet: Jerry Knaak
Suites: Rachel Venrick, Andrea Stamps,
   Jay Campbell
Marketing: Craig Purcell,
   Morris Bradshaw, Dawn French,
   Kevin Kimball, Michael Campbell,
   Jesse Diaz
Community Relations: Scott Fink
Youth Initiatives: Rosie Bone
Raiderettes: Karen Kovac
Trainers: H. Rod Martin, Mark Mayer,
   Scott Touchet
Equipment: Bob Romanski,
   Richard Romanski, Danny Molina
Video Operations: Dave Nash, Jim Otten,
   John Otten
Broadcasting: Chris Gargano,
   Vittorio DeBartolo
Computer Operations: Moses Cathey,
   Matt Pasco

COACHING HISTORY
Oakland 1960-1981
Los Angeles 1982-1994
(419-305-11)
Records include postseason games
1960-61   Eddie Erdelatz* 6-10-0
1961-62   Marty Feldman** 2-15-0
1962   Red Conkright 1-8-0
1963-65   Al Davis 23-16-3
1966-68   John Rauch 35-10-1
1969-1978 John Madden 112-39-7
1979-1987 Tom Flores 91-56-0
1988-89   Mike Shanahan*** 8-12-0
1989-1994 Art Shell 56-41-0
1995-96   Mike White 15-17-0
1997   Joe Bugel 4-12-0
1998-2001 Jon Gruden 40-28-0
2002-03   Bill Callahan 17-18-0
2004-05   Norv Turner 9-23-0
   *Released after two games in 1961
   **Released after five games in 1962
   ***Released after four games in 1989

ATTENDANCE
Home 401,373   Away 591,020
Total 992,393
Single-game home record,
   62,660 (11/3/02)
Single-season home record,
   471,151 (2002)

2006 DRAFT CHOICES
Round	Name	Pos.	College
1	Michael Huff	DB	Texas
2	Thomas Howard	LB	Texas-El Paso
3	Paul McQuistan	G	Weber State
4	Darnell Bing	LB	So. California
6	Kevin Boothe	G	Cornell
7	Chris Morris	C	Michigan State
	Kevin McMahan	WR	Maine

2005 TEAM RECORD
PRESEASON (1-3)

Date	Result	Opponent
8/13	L 13-21	at San Francisco
8/20	L 17-19	at Houston
8/26	L 16-17	Arizona
9/1	W 13-6	New Orleans

REGULAR SEASON (4-12)

Date	Result	Opponent	Att.
9/8	L 20-30	at New England	68,756
9/18	L 17-23	Kansas City	62,273
9/25	L 20-23	at Philadelphia	67,735
10/2	W 19-13	Dallas	62,400
10/16	L 14-27	San Diego	52,666
10/23	W 38-17	Buffalo	42,779
10/30	W 34-25	at Tennessee	69,149
11/6	L 23-27	at Kansas City	79,033
11/13	L 17-31	Denver	62,779
11/20	W 16-13	at Washington	90,129
11/27	L 21-33	Miami	49,097
12/4	L 10-34	at San Diego	66,436
12/11	L 10-26	at New York Jets	77,561
12/18	L 7-9	Cleveland	41,862
12/24	L 3-22	at Denver	76,212
12/31	L 21-30	New York Giants	44,594

SCORE BY PERIODS

Raiders	64	81	48	97	0	—	290
Opponents	75	132	84	92	0	—	383

2005 TEAM STATISTICS

	Raiders	Opp.
Total First Downs	294	299
Rushing	80	100
Passing	189	165
Penalty	25	34
3rd Down: Made/Att	85/214	92/226
3rd Down Pct.	39.7	40.7
4th Down: Made/Att	7/14	3/9
4th Down Pct.	50.0	33.3
Possession Avg.	28:07	31:53
Total Net Yards	4,951	5,292
Avg. Per Game	309.4	330.8
Total Plays	997	1,029
Avg. Per Play	5.0	5.1
Net Yards Rushing	1369	2049
Avg. Per Game	85.6	128.1
Total Rushes	361	507
Net Yards Passing	3,582	3,243
Avg. Per Game	223.9	202.7
Sacked/Yards Lost	45/301	36/238
Gross Yards	3,883	3,481
Att./Completions	591/316	486/296
Completion Pct.	53.5	60.9
Had Intercepted	14	5
Punts/Average	82/45.7	76/41.5
Net Punting Avg.	82/37.9	76/37.8
Penalties/Yards	147/1132	101/825
Fumbles/Ball Lost	26/9	22/14
Touchdowns	33	40
Rushing	11	18
Passing	21	18
Returns	1	4

2005 INDIVIDUAL STATISTICS

PASSING

PASSING	Att.	Comp.	Yds.	Pct.	TD	Int.	Tkld.	Rate
Collins	565	302	3,759	53.5	20	12	39/261	77.3
Tuiasosopo	26	14	124	53.8	1	2	6/40	47.6
Raiders	591	316	3,883	53.5	21	14	45/301	76.0
Opponents	486	296	3,481	60.9	18	5	36/238	90.7

SCORING

SCORING	TD R	TD P	TD Rt	PAT	FG	Saf	PTS
Janikowski	0	0	0	30/30	20/30	0	90
Jordan	9	2	0	0/0	0/0	0	68
Moss	0	8	0	0/0	0/0	0	48
Porter	0	5	0	0/0	0/0	0	30
Anderson	0	3	0	0/0	0/0	0	18
Gabriel	0	3	0	0/0	0/0	0	18
Collins	1	0	0	0/0	0/0	0	6
Cooper	0	0	1	0/0	0/0	0	6
Crockett	1	0	0	0/0	0/0	0	6
Raiders	11	21	1	30/30	20/30	0	290
Opponents	18	18	4	34/37	35/38	1	383

2-Pt. Conversions: Jordan.

Raiders 1-3, Opponents 1-3.

RUSHING

RUSHING	No.	Yds	Avg	LG	TD
Jordan	272	1,025	3.8	26	9
Crockett	60	208	3.5	24	1
Whitted	2	51	25.5	27	0
Collins	17	39	2.3	18t	1
Fargas	5	28	5.6	15	0
Tuiasosopo	2	19	9.5	10	0
Gabriel	1	5	5.0	5	0
Lechler	1	2	2.0	2	0
Porter	1	-8	-8.0	-8	0
Raiders	361	1,369	3.8	27	11
Opponents	507	2,049	4.0	95t	18

RECEIVING

RECEIVING	No.	Yds	Avg	LG	TD
Porter	76	942	12.4	49t	5
Jordan	70	563	8.0	28	2
Moss	60	1,005	16.8	79	8
Gabriel	37	554	15.0	38	3
Anderson	24	303	12.6	36	3
Whitted	14	183	13.1	26	0
R. Williams	13	164	12.6	34	0
Crockett	13	111	8.5	23	0
Foschi	6	37	6.2	11	0
Curry	2	12	6.0	8	0
Fargas	1	9	9.0	9	0
Raiders	316	3,883	12.3	79	21
Opponents	296	3,481	11.8	78t	18

INTERCEPTIONS

INTERCEPTIONS	No.	Yds	Avg	LG	TD
Schweigert	2	35	17.5	33	0
Sapp	1	3	3.0	3	0
Hill	1	0	0.0	0	0
Woodson	1	0	0.0	0	0
Raiders	5	38	7.6	33	0
Opponents	14	336	24.0	80t	4

PUNTING

PUNTING	No.	Yds.	Avg.	In 20	LG
Lechler	82	3,744	45.7	26	64
Raiders	82	3,744	45.7	26	64
Opponents	76	3,156	41.5	32	71

PUNT RETURNS

PUNT RETURNS	Ret	FC	Yds	Avg	LG	TD
Carr	34	7	186	5.5	34	0
Woodson	3	0	20	6.7	15	0
Raiders	37	7	206	5.6	34	0
Opponents	39	16	460	11.8	58	0

KICKOFF RETURNS

KICKOFF RETURNS	No.	Yds	Avg	LG	TD
Carr	73	1,752	24.0	62	0
Gabriel	4	64	16.0	21	0
Flemister	2	16	8.0	8	0
Hulsey	1	0	0.0	0	0
Raiders	80	1,832	22.9	62	0
Opponents	56	1,369	24.4	60	0

FIELD GOALS

FIELD GOALS	1-19	20-29	30-39	40-49	50+
Janikowski	1/1	7/8	5/6	7/12	0/3
Raiders	1/1	7/8	5/6	7/12	0/3
Opponents	0/0	14/14	14/15	7/8	0/1

SACKS

SACKS	No.
Burgess	16.0
Sapp	5.0
Kelly	4.5
Hamilton	2.0
Jasper	2.0
Brayton	1.0
Clark	1.0
Gibson	1.0
Grant	1.0
Routt	1.0
Sands	1.0
Cooper	0.5
Raiders	36.0
Opponents	45.0

RECORD HOLDERS
INDIVIDUAL RECORDS—CAREER

Category	Name	Performance
Rushing (Yds.)	Marcus Allen, 1982-1992	8,545
Passing (Yds.)	Ken Stabler, 1970-79	19,078
Passing (TDs)	Ken Stabler, 1970-79	150
Receiving (No.)	Tim Brown, 1988-2003	1,070
Receiving (Yds.)	Tim Brown, 1988-2003	14,734
Interceptions	Willie Brown, 1967-1978	39
	Lester Hayes, 1977-1986	39
Punting (Avg.)	Shane Lechler, 2000-05	*45.9
Punt Return (Avg.)	Claude Gibson, 1963-65	12.6
Kickoff Return (Avg.)	Jack Larscheid, 1960-61	28.4
Field Goals	Chris Bahr, 1980-88	162
Touchdowns (Tot.)	Tim Brown, 1988-2003	104
Points	George Blanda, 1967-1975	863

INDIVIDUAL RECORDS—SINGLE SEASON

Category	Name	Performance
Rushing (Yds.)	Marcus Allen, 1985	1,759
Passing (Yds.)	Rich Gannon, 2002	4,689
Passing (TDs)	Daryle Lamonica, 1969	34
Receiving (No.)	Tim Brown 1997	104
Receiving (Yds.)	Tim Brown, 1997	1,408
Interceptions	Lester Hayes, 1980	13
Punting (Avg.)	Shane Lechler, 2003	46.9
Punt Return (Avg.)	Claude Gibson, 1964	14.4
Kickoff Return (Avg.)	Harold Hart, 1975	30.5
Field Goals	Jeff Jaeger, 1993	35
Touchdowns (Tot.)	Marcus Allen, 1984	18
Points	Jeff Jaeger, 1993	132

INDIVIDUAL RECORDS—SINGLE GAME

Category	Name	Performance
Rushing (Yds.)	Napoleon Kaufman, 10-19-97	227
Passing (Yds.)	Cotton Davidson, 10-25-64	427
Passing (TDs)	Tom Flores, 12-22-63	6
	Daryle Lamonica, 10-19-69	6
Receiving (No.)	Tim Brown, 12-21-97	14
Receiving (Yds.)	Art Powell, 12-22-63	247
Interceptions	Many times	3
	Last time by Rod Woodson, 9-20-02	
Field Goals	Jeff Jaeger, 12-11-94	5
	Sebastian Janikowski, 10-29-00	5
Touchdowns (Tot.)	Art Powell, 12-22-63	4
	Marcus Allen, 9-24-84	4
	Harvey Williams, 11-16-97	4
Points	Art Powell, 12-22-63	24
	Marcus Allen, 9-24-84	24
	Harvey Williams, 11-16-97	24

*NFL Record

2006 VETERAN ROSTER

No.	Name	Pos.	Ht.	Wt.	Birthdate	NFL Exp.	College	Hometown	How Acq.	'05 Games/ Starts
83	Anderson, Courtney	TE	6-6	270	11/19/80	3	San Jose State	Richmond, Calif.	D7-'04	14/13
21	Asomugha, Nnamdi	CB	6-2	210	7/6/81	4	California	Los Angeles, Calif.	D1-'03	16/16
70	Badger, Brad	G	6-4	320	1/11/75	10	Stanford	Corvallis, Ore.	UFA(Minn)-'02	16/8
91	Brayton, Tyler	DE	6-6	280	11/20/79	4	Colorado	Pasco, Wash.	D1-'03	16/3
2	Brooks, Aaron	QB	6-4	220	3/24/76	8	Virginia	Newport News, Va.	FA-'06	13/13*
56	Burgess, Derrick	DE	6-2	260	8/12/78	6	Mississippi	Greenbelt, Md.	UFA(Phil)-'05	16/12
23	Carr, Chris	CB	5-10	180	4/30/83	2	Boise State	Reno, Nev.	FA-'05	16/0
55	Clark, Danny	LB	6-2	245	5/9/77	7	Illinois	Blue Island, Ill.	UFA(Jax)-'04	16/15
40	Cooper, Jarrod	S	6-1	215	3/31/78	6	Kansas State	Pearland, Texas	FA-'04	16/10
32	Crockett, Zack	RB	6-2	240	12/2/72	12	Florida State	Pompano Beach, Fla.	UFA(Jax)-'99	16/10
89	Curry, Ronald	WR	6-2	210	5/28/79	5	North Carolina	Hampton, Va.	D7-'02	2/0
50	Ekejiuba, Isaiah	LB	6-4	240	10/5/81	2	Virginia	Somerset, N.J.	FA-'05	10/0
25	Fargas, Justin	RB	6-1	220	1/25/80	4	Southern California	Sherman Oaks, Calif.	D3-'03	14/0
49	Foschi, John Paul	RB	6-4	270	5/19/82	2	Georgia Tech	Atlanta, Ga.	FA-'05	10/5
82	Francis, Carlos	WR	5-10	190	1/3/81	3	Texas Tech	Fort Worth, Texas	D4-'04	0*
85	Gabriel, Doug	WR	6-2	215	8/27/80	4	Central Florida	Orlando, Fla.	D5-'03	16/2
76	Gallery, Robert	T	6-7	325	7/26/80	3	Iowa	Masonville, Iowa	D1-'04	16/16
69	Garmon, Kelvin	G	6-2	350	10/26/76	7	Baylor	Fort Worth, Texas	FA-'06	0*
36	Gibson, Derrick	S	6-2	215	3/22/79	6	Florida State	Miami, Fla.	D1-'01	6/6
64	Grove, Jake	C	6-4	300	1/22/80	3	Virginia Tech	Forest, Va.	D2-'04	10/8
98	Hamilton, Bobby	DE	6-5	285	7/1/71	12	Southern Mississippi	Columbus, Miss.	UFA(NE)-'04	14/13
77	Hawthorne, Anttaj	DT	6-3	310	11/15/81	2	Wisconsin	New Haven, Conn.	D6a-'05	2/0
71	Hulsey, Corey	G	6-4	325	7/26/77	5	Clemson	Gainesville, Ga.	FA-'04	11/0
96	Irons, Grant	LB	6-6	285	7/7/79	5	Notre Dame	The Woodlands, Texas	FA-'03	15/1
11	Janikowski, Sebastian	K	6-2	250	3/2/78	7	Florida State	Daytona Beach, Fla.	D1-'00	16/0
51	Johnstone, Lance	DE	6-5	250	6/11/73	11	Temple	Philadelphia, Pa.	UFA(Minn)-'06	15/1*
34	Jordan, LaMont	RB	5-10	230	11/11/78	6	Maryland	Suitland, Md.	UFA(NYJ)-'05	14/14
93	Kelly, Tommy	DT	6-6	300	12/27/80	3	Mississippi State	Jackson, Miss.	FA-'04	16/12
9	Lechler, Shane	P	6-2	225	8/7/76	7	Texas A&M	Sealy, Texas	D5-'00	16/0
42	Lee, ReShard	RB	5-10	220	10/12/80	3	Middle Tennessee State	Brunswick, Ga.	FA-'06	7/1*
92	McNeal, Bryant	DE	6-4	250	7/13/79	3	Clemson	Swansea, S.C.	FA-'06	0*
97	Moore, Rashad	DT	6-3	325	3/16/79	3	Tennessee	Huntsville, Ala.	FA-'06	0*
19	Morant, Johnnie	WR	6-4	220	12/7/81	3	Syracuse	Parsippany, N.J.	D5-'04	1/0
52	Morrison, Kirk	LB	6-2	240	2/19/82	2	San Diego State	Oakland, Calif.	D3b-'05	16/15
18	Moss, Randy	WR	6-4	215	2/13/77	9	Marshall	Rand, W. Va.	T(Minn)-'05	16/15
38	Poole, Tyrone	CB	5-8	190	2/3/72	12	Fort Valley State	LaGrange, Ga.	FA-'06	1/1*
84	Porter, Jerry	WR	6-2	220	7/14/78	7	West Virginia	Washington, D.C.	D2-'00	16/14
57	Riddle, Ryan	LB	6-2	250	7/5/81	2	California	Culver City, Calif.	D6b-'05	12/0
88	Rivers, Marcellus	TE	6-4	250	10/26/78	6	Oklahoma State	Oklahoma City, Okla.	UFA(Hou)-'06	16/5*
26	Routt, Stanford	CB	6-1	195	7/26/83	2	Houston	Austin, Texas	D2-'05	14/2
90	Sands, Terdell	DT	6-7	335	10/31/79	4	Tennesse-Chattanooga	Chattanooga, Tenn.	WA-'03	9/0
99	Sapp, Warren	DT	6-2	300	12/19/72	12	Miami	Apopka, Fla.	UFA(TB)-'04	10/10
30	Schweigert, Stuart	S	6-1	210	6/21/81	3	Purdue	Saginaw, Mich.	D3-'04	16/13
65	Sims, Barry	T	6-5	300	12/1/74	8	Utah	Park City, Utah	FA-'99	16/16
78	Slaughter, Chad	T	6-8	340	6/4/78	6	Alcorn State	Dallas, Texas	FA-'02	11/0
39	Smart, Rod	RB	5-11	205	1/9/77	6	Western Kentucky	Lakeland, Fla.	UFA(Car)-'06	12/0*
68	Spikes, Cameron	G	6-4	320	11/6/76	7	Texas A&M	Bryan, Texas	FA-'06	0*
22	Starks, Duane	CB	5-10	175	5/23/74	9	Miami	Miami, Fla.	FA-'06	7/6*
58	Thomas, Robert	LB	6-0	235	7/17/80	5	UCLA	El Centro, Calif.	FA-'06	10/9*
62	Treu, Adam	C	6-5	300	6/24/74	10	Nebraska	Lincoln, Neb.	D3-'97	16/10
8	Tuiasosopo, Marques	QB	6-1	220	3/22/79	6	Washington	Woodinville, Wash.	D2-'01	1/1
66	Walker, Langston	T	6-8	345	9/3/79	5	California	Oakland, Calif.	D2-'02	6/6
16	Walter, Andrew	QB	6-6	230	5/11/82	2	Arizona State	Grand Junction, Colo.	D3a-'05	0*
27	Washington, Fabian	CB	5-11	185	6/9/83	2	Nebraska	Bradenton, Fla.	D1-'05	16/11
87	Whitted, Alvis	WR	6-0	185	9/4/74	9	North Carolina State	Hillsborough, N.C.	FA-'02	15/0
86	Williams, Randal	TE	6-3	235	5/21/78	6	New Hampshire	Bronx, N.Y.	FA-'05	16/4
54	Williams, Sam	LB	6-5	260	7/28/80	4	Fresno State	Clayton, Calif.	D3-'03	0*
20	Williams, Walter	RB	6-1	215	9/8/77	4	Grambling State	Baton Rouge, La.	FA-'06	2/0*

* Brooks played 13 games with New Orleans in '05; Francis inactive for 16 games; Garmon last active with Cleveland in '04; Johnstone played 15 games with Minnesota; Lee played 7 games with Green Bay; McNeal inactive for 2 games with Tampa Bay in '04; Moore last active with Seattle in '04; Poole played 1 game with New England; Rivers played 16 games with Houston; Smart played 12 games with Carolina; Spikes last active with Arizona in '04; Starks played 7 games with New England; Thomas played 10 games with Green Bay; Walter inactive for 16 games; S. Williams missed '05 season because of injury; W. Williams played 2 games with Green Bay.

Players lost through free agency (3): CB Renaldo Hill (Mia; 16 games in '05), DT Ed Jasper (Phil; 11), CB Charles Woodson (GB; 6).

Also played with Raiders in '05—S Calvin Branch (6 games), QB Kerry Collins (15), RB Omar Easy (16), TE Zeron Flemister (12), LB DeLawrence Grant (9), LB Tim Johnson (16), T Brad Lekkerkerker (1), G Ron Stone (16), S Reggie Tongue (4), CB Denard Walker (9), DT Ted Washington (16).

2006 FIRST-YEAR ROSTER

Name	Pos.	Ht.	Wt.	Birthdate	College	Hometown	How Acq.
Adkisson, James (1)	TE	6-5	230	1/11/80	South Carolina	St. Louis, Mo.	FA-'04
Bing, Darnell	LB	6-2	230	9/10/84	Southern California	Long Beach, Calif.	D4
Boothe, Kevin	G	6-4	315	7/5/83	Cornell	Plantation, Fla.	D6
Boyd, Jayson	WR	6-4	200	9/29/83	Texas-El Paso	Riverside, Calif.	FA
Brown, Ricky	LB	6-2	230	12/27/83	Boston College	Cincinnati, Ohio	FA
Buchanon, Will	WR	6-1	180	4/5/83	Southern California	Oceanside, Calif.	FA
Cooper, Roger (1)	LB	6-2	250	6/4/81	Montana State	Port Orchard, Wash.	FA
Davis, Dennis	CB	5-10	190	11/24/82	Georgia Tech	Sicklerville, N.J.	FA
Duncan, Tim (1)	K	6-1	215	6/12/79	Oklahoma	Clinton, Okla.	FA
Eugene, Hiram (1)	CB/S	6-2	200	11/24/80	Louisiana Tech	Jeanerette, La.	FA
Gatewood, Rick	WR	5-11	190	8/3/83	Montana State	El Cerrito, Calif.	FA
Green, DeJuan	RB	5-11	205	5/13/80	South Florida	Jacksonville, Fla.	FA-'04
Green, Jeff (1)	DE	6-2	245	11/3/80	Florida A&M	Cairo, Ga.	FA
Green, Roderick (1)	G/T	6-5	290	6/23/82	Arkansas Pine Bluff	El Dorado, Ark.	FA
Hall, Joe (1)	RB	6-2	300	11/3/79	Kansas State	Lakewood, Calif.	FA
Howard, Thomas	LB	6-3	240	7/14/83	Texas-El Paso	Lubbock, Texas	D2
Huff, Michael	CB/S	6-1	205	3/6/83	Texas	Irving, Texas	D1
Huntley, Kevin (1)	DT	6-7	270	4/8/82	Kansas State	Washington, D.C.	FA
Kimball, David (1)	K	6-1	205	1/13/82	Penn State	State College, Pa.	FA
Lekkerkerker, Brad (1)	T	6-7	330	5/8/78	California-Davis	Chino, Calif.	FA-'04
Lemon, J.R.	RB	6-1	225	6/6/83	Stanford	Fayetteville, Ga.	FA
Levey, Jabari	T	6-6	315	7/16/84	South Carolina	Moncks Corner, S.C.	FA
Madsen, John	WR	6-5	220	5/9/83	Utah	West Valley City, Utah	FA
McMahan, Kevin	WR	6-2	200	3/2/83	Maine	Rochester, N.Y.	D7b
McQuistan, Paul	T	6-6	315	4/30/83	Weber State	Lebanon, Ore.	D3
Miller, Derek	TE	6-8	268	6/10/83	Maryland	Carlisle, Pa.	FA
Morgan, Shawn (1)	LB	6-3	250	11/6/78	Fayetteville State	Havelock, N.C.	FA
Morris, Chris	G/T	6-4	305	2/22/83	Michigan State	Lambertville, Mich.	D7a
Nanton, Javon	DE	6-5	265	1/25/83	Miami	Miami Springs, Fla.	FA
Nnabuife, Alvin	DB	6-1	205	4/3/83	Southern Methodist	Missouri City, Texas	FA
Obeng, William (1)	T	6-7	325	4/14/83	San Jose State	Chicago, Ill.	FA
Pakulak, Glenn (1)	P	6-3	220	4/9/80	Kentucky	Lapeer, Mich.	FA
Quarshie, Michael (1)	DT	6-2	295	11/13/79	Columbia	Helsinki, Finland	FA-'05
Robertson, Reggie (1)	QB	6-2	200	1/28/82	California	Tucson, Ariz.	FA
Rose, Shaun (1)	G/T	6-6	325	7/17/80	East Carolina	Wilson, N.C.	FA
Smith, Kent	QB	6-5	215	9/5/83	Central Michigan	Toledo, Ohio	FA
Toler, Burl	WR	6-2	185	4/7/83	California	Oakland, Calif.	FA
Tuiasosopo, Zach (1)	FB	6-2	245	12/19/81	Washington	Woodinville, Wash.	FA-'05
Washington, Raymond	CB	6-0	210	6/2/83	Fresno State	Long Beach, Calif.	FA
Wusu, Timi	LB	6-3	210	6/10/83	Stanford	Palo Alto, Calif.	FA

The term NFL Rookie is defined as a player who is in his first season of professional football and has not been on the roster of another professional football team for any regular-season or postseason games. A Rookie is designated by an "R" on NFL rosters. Players who have been active in another professional football league or players who have NFL experience, including either preseason training camp or being on an Active List or Inactive List, or on Reserve/Injured or Reserve/Physically Unable to Perform for fewer than six regular-season games, are termed NFL First-Year Players. An NFL First-Year Player is designated by a "1" on NFL rosters. Thereafter, a player is credited with an additional year of experience for each season in which he accumulates six games on the Active List or Inactive List, or on Reserve/Injured or Reserve/Physically Unable to Perform.

Log on to www.raiders.com for an up-to-date roster.

COACHING STAFF
Head Coach,
Art Shell

Pro Career: Named the fifteenth head coach in Raiders history. He is the first person to hold the post two times for the Raiders, previously holding the position from the fifth game of the 1989 season through 1994. Shell's .577 career winning percentage is the highest of any coach hired this offseason, and his 56 career victories are more than any other new coach. He guided the Raiders to the playoffs three times, advancing to the AFC Championship Game in his first full season (1990). Shell coached the offensive line for Kansas City (1995-96) and Atlanta (1997-2000). Prior to being named Raiders head coach, Shell worked five years as the Senior Vice President for Football Operations and Development in the National Football League office. He has also served on the USA Football Board of Directors. He was Raiders' offensive line coach for seven years (1983-89), including 1983 world championship season. He first joined the coaching staff after 15 seasons (1968-1982) as one of the greatest offensive tackles in pro football history. He came to the Raiders in 1968 as a third-round pick out of Maryland State (now Maryland-Eastern Shore) and went on to play in 207 games, including the first 156 in a row—and 24 playoff games—for the Raiders. Was starting left tackle in Super Bowl XI and XV victories for Silver and Black, and was selected to Pro Bowl eight times. Inducted into Pro Football Hall of Fame on August 5, 1989. Also named to state of South Carolina Sports Hall of Fame. Career record: 56-41.

Background: All-America as junior and senior and three-year All-Conference on both offense and defense at Maryland State 1965-67. Also lettered in basketball.

Personal: Born November 26, 1946, Charleston, S.C. Art and his wife Janice have two sons, Arthur III and Christopher.

ASSISTANT COACHES

Fred Biletnikoff, wide receivers; born February 23, 1943, Erie, Pa. Receiver Florida State 1962-64. Pro wide receiver Oakland Raiders 1965-1978, Montreal Alouettes (CFL) 1980. Inducted into Pro Football Hall of Fame in 1988. College coach: Palomar (Calif.) J.C. 1983, Diablo Valley (Calif.) J.C. 1984, 1986. Pro coach: Oakland Invaders (USFL) 1985, Calgary Stampeders (CFL) 1987-88, joined Raiders in 1989.

Willie Brown, squad development, defensive backs; born December 2, 1940, Yazoo City, Miss. Defensive back Grambling State 1959-1962. Pro defensive back Denver Broncos 1963-66, Oakland Raiders 1967-1978. Inducted into Pro Football Hall of Fame in 1984. College coach: Long Beach State 1990-91 (head coach 1991). Pro coach: Oakland/Los Angeles Raiders 1979-

1988, rejoined Raiders in 1995.

Ted Daisher, special teams; born February 2, 1955, Taylor, Mich. Wide receiver/defensive back Western Michigan 1975-77. No pro playing experience. College coach: Illinois 1980-84, Eastern Michigan 1985-88, Cincinnati 1989-1992, Army 1995-97, Indiana 1998-2000, East Carolina 2001-2002. Pro coach: Philadelphia Eagles 2004-05, joined Raiders in 2006.

Irv Eatman, offensive line; born January 1, 1961, Birmingham Ala. Defensive end/offensive tackle UCLA 1979-1982. Pro offensive tackle Philadelphia/Baltimore Stars (USFL) 1983-85, Kansas City Chiefs 1986-1990, New York Jets 1991-92, Los Angeles Rams 1993. Atlanta Falcons 1994, Houston Oilers 1995-96. Pro coach: Green Bay Packers 1999, Pittsburgh Steelers 2000, Kansas City Chiefs 2001-05, joined Raiders in 2006.

Jeff Fish, strength & conditioning; born June 6, 1966, Ithaca, N.Y. Wide receiver Western Carolina 1986-88. No pro playing experience. College coach: Clemson 1991-92, Kent State 1993-94, Tulsa 1995-96, Missouri 2001-02. Pro coach: Tampa Bay Buccaneers 1997, Kansas City Chiefs 1998-2000, joined Raiders in 2004.

Robert Ford, quality control, offense; born June 21, 1951, Belton, Texas. Wide receiver Houston 1970-72. No pro playing experience. College coach: Western Illinois 1974-76, New Mexico 1977-79, Oregon State 1980-81, Mississippi State 1982-83, Kansas 1986, Texas Tech 1987-88, Texas A&M 1989-1990. Pro coach: Houston Gamblers (USFL) 1985, Dallas Cowboys 1991-97, Miami Dolphins 1998-2003, Arizona Cardinals 2004, joined Raiders in 2006.

Don Martindale, linebackers; born May 19, 1963, Dayton, Ohio. Linebacker Defiance College 1984-86. No pro playing experience. College coach: Defiance College 1987, Notre Dame 1994-95, Cincinnati 1996-98, Western Illinois 1999, Western Kentucky 2000-02. Pro coach: Joined Raiders in 2004.

George Martinez, quality control, defense; born August 5, 1951, Fort Bragg, N.C. Quarterback Northwestern Oklahoma State 1969-1972. No pro playing experience. College coach: East Central (Okla.) 1981-87, Panhandle State 1988. New Mexico Highlands 1989-1991 (head coach). Pro coach: Arizona Cardinals 1993-94, joined Raiders in 2006.

Jim McElwain, quarterbacks; born in 1962, Missoula, Mont. Quarterback Eastern Washington 1980-83. No pro playing experience. College coach: Eastern Washington 1985-1994, Montana State 1995-99, Louisville 2000-02. Pro coach: Joined Raiders in 2006.

Keith Millard, defensive line; born March 18, 1962, Pleasanton, Calif. Defensive lineman Washington State 1980-84. Pro defensive lineman Minnesota Vikings 1985-1991, Seattle Seahawks 1992, Green Bay

Packers 1992, Philadelphia Eagles 1993. College coach: Fort Lewis 1996, Menlo College 1997-2000. Pro coach: San Francisco Demons (XFL) 2001, Denver Broncos 2002-04, joined Raiders in 2005.

Chuck Pagano, defensive backs; born October 2, 1960, Boulder, Colo. Safety Wyoming 1980-83. No pro playing experience. College coach: Southern California 1984-85, Miami 1986, Boise State 1987-88, East Carolina 1989, Nevada-Las Vegas 1990-91, East Carolina 1992-94, Miami 1995-2000. Pro coach: Cleveland Browns 2001-04, joined Raiders in 2005.

Skip Peete, running backs; born January 30, 1963, Mesa, Ariz. Wide receiver Arizona 1981-82, Kansas 1984-85. Pro wide receiver New York Jets 1987. College coach: Pittsburgh 1988-1992, Michigan State 1993-94, Rutgers 1995, UCLA 1996-97. Pro coach: Joined Raiders in 1998.

Rob Ryan, defensive coordinator; born December 13, 1962, Ardmore, Okla. Linebacker Oklahoma State 1984, Southwestern Oklahoma State 1985-86. No pro playing experience. College coach: Western Kentucky 1987, Ohio State 1988, Tennessee State 1989-1993, Hutchinson (Kan.) C.C. 1996, Oklahoma State 1997-99. Pro coach: Arizona Cardinals 1994-95, New England Patriots 2000-03, joined Raiders in 2004.

John Shoop, tight ends; born August 1, 1969, Pittsburgh. Quarterback University of South 1987-1990. No pro playing experience. College coach: Dartmouth 1991, Vanderbilt 1992-94. Pro coach: Carolina Panthers 1995-98, Chicago Bears 1999-2003, Tampa Bay Buccaneers 2004, joined Raiders in 2005.

Darryl Sims, asst. defensive line; born July 23, 1961, Winston-Salem, N.C. Defensive lineman Wisconsin 1981-84. Pro defensive lineman Pittsburgh Steelers 1985-86, Cleveland Browns 1987-1991. College coach: Wisconsin-Oshkosh 1999. Pro coach: Amsterdam Admirals (NFLEL) 2000-05, joined Raiders in 2006

Jackie Slater, offensive line; born May 27, 1954, Jackson, Miss. Offensive lineman, Jackson State 1972-75. Pro offensive tackle, Los Angeles/St. Louis Rams, 1976-1996. Inducted into Pro Football Hall of Fame in 2001. Pro coach: Joined Raiders in 2006.

Tom Walsh, offensive coordinator; born April 16, 1949, Vallejo, Calif. Attended UC Santa Barbara. No college or pro playing experience. College coach: San Diego 1972-76, U.S. International 1979 (head coach), Murray State 1980, Cincinnati 1981. Pro coach: Raiders 1990-94, rejoined Raiders in 2006.

Lorenzo Ward, asst. defensive backs, asst. special teams; born April 26, 1967, Greensboro Ala. Defensive back Alabama 1986-1990. No pro playing experience. College coach: Alabama 1991-93, UT-Chattanooga 1994-98, Virginia Tech 1999-2005. Pro coach: Joined Raiders in 2006.

**American Football Conference
North Division
Team Colors:** Black and Gold
3400 South Water Street
Pittsburgh, Pennsylvania 15203
Telephone: (412) 432-7800

2006 SCHEDULE
PRESEASON
Aug. 12 at Arizona............................1:00
Aug. 19 **Minnesota**..........................8:00
Aug. 25 at Philadelphia....................8:00
Aug. 31 **Carolina**.............................8:00

REGULAR SEASON
Sept. 7 **Miami** (Thu.)......................8:30
Sept. 18 at Jacksonville (Mon.)........8:30
Sept. 24 **Cincinnati**..........................1:00
Oct. 1 Open Date
Oct. 8 at San Diego......................5:15
Oct. 15 **Kansas City**......................4:15
Oct. 22 at Atlanta............................1:00
Oct. 29 at Oakland..........................1:15
Nov. 5 **Denver**.............................4:15
Nov. 12 **New Orleans**....................1:00
Nov. 19 at Cleveland.......................1:00
Nov. 26 at Baltimore........................1:00
Dec. 3 **Tampa Bay**......................1:00
Dec. 7 **Cleveland** (Thu.)..............8:00
Dec. 17 at Carolina..........................1:00
Dec. 24 **Baltimore**.........................1:00
Dec. 31 at Cincinnati........................1:00

Stadium: Heinz Field (opened in 2001)
•**Capacity:** 64,350
100 Art Rooney Avenue
Pittsburgh, Pennsylvania 15212
Playing Surface: DD GrassMaster
Training Camp: St. Vincent College
Latrobe, Pennsylvania
15650

HEINZ FIELD

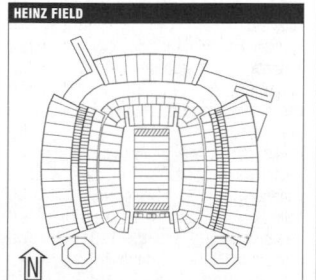

CLUB OFFICIALS
Chairman: Daniel M. Rooney
President: Arthur J. Rooney II
Vice President: John R. McGinley
Vice President: Arthur J. Rooney Jr.
Administration Advisor: Charles H. Noll
Director of Business: Mark Hart
Business Operations: Omar Khan
Director of Football Operations:
Kevin Colbert
College Scouting Coordinator:
Ron Hughes
Pro Scouting Coordinator: Doug Whaley
Head Athletic Trainer: John Norwig
Director of Marketing: Tony Quatrini
Communications Coordinator:
Dave Lockett
Public Relations/Media Manager:
Burt Lauten
Director of Stadium Management:
Jim Sacco
Video Coordinator: Bob McCartney
Human Relations/Office Coordinator:
Geraldine Glenn
Ticket Manager: Ben Lentz

COACHING HISTORY
**Pittsburgh Pirates 1933-1940
(523-502-21)**
Records include postseason games
1933	Forrest (Jap) Douds	3-6-2
1934	Luby DiMelio	2-10-0
1935-36	Joe Bach	10-14-0
1937-39	Johnny (Blood) McNally*	6-19-0
1939-1940	Walt Kiesling	3-13-3
1941	Bert Bell**	0-2-0
	Aldo (Buff) Donelli***	0-5-0
1941-44	Walt Kiesling****	13-20-2
1945	Jim Leonard	2-8-0
1946-47	Jock Sutherland	13-10-1
1948-1951	Johnny Michelosen	20-26-2
1952-53	Joe Bach	11-13-0
1954-56	Walt Kiesling	14-22-0
1957-1964	Raymond (Buddy) Parker	51-47-6
1965	Mike Nixon	2-12-0
1966-68	Bill Austin	11-28-3
1969-1991	Chuck Noll	209-156-1
1992-2005	Bill Cowher	153-91-1

*Released after three games in 1939
**Resigned after two games in 1941
***Released after five games in 1941
****Co-coach with Earle (Greasy) Neale in
Philadelphia-Pittsburgh merger in 1943 and
with Phil Handler in Chicago Cardinals-
Pittsburgh merger in 1944

ATTENDANCE
Home 509,841   Away 532,483
Total 1,042,324
Single-game home record,
64,046 (12/26/04)
Single-season home record,
509,841 (2005)

2006 DRAFT CHOICES
Round	Name	Pos.	College
1	Santonio Holmes	WR	Ohio State
3	Anthony Smith	DB	Syracuse
	Willie Reid	WR	Florida State
4	Willie Colon	G	Hofstra
	Orien Harris	DE	Miami
5	Omar Jacobs	QB	Bowling Green
	Charles Davis	TE	Purdue
6	Marvin Philip	C	California
7	Cedric Humes	RB	Virginia Tech

2005 TEAM RECORD
PRESEASON (3-1)
Date	Result	Opponent
8/15	W 38-31	Philadelphia
8/20	W 17-3	Miami
8/26	L 10-17	at Washington
9/1	W 21-17	at Carolina

REGULAR SEASON (11-5)
Date	Result	Opponent	Att.
9/11	W 34-7	Tennessee	62,931
9/18	W 27-7	at Houston	70,742
9/25	L 20-23	New England	64,868
10/10	W 24-22	at San Diego	68,537
10/16	L 17-23	Jacksonville (OT)	63,891
10/23	W 27-13	at Cincinnati	66,104
10/31	W 20-19	Baltimore	64,178
11/6	W 20-10	at Green Bay	70,607
11/13	W 34-21	Cleveland	63,491
11/20	L 13-16	at Baltimore (OT)	70,601
11/28	L 7-26	at Indianapolis	57,442
12/4	L 31-38	Cincinnati	63,044
12/11	W 21-9	Chicago	61,237
12/18	W 18-3	at Minnesota	64,136
12/24	W 41-0	at Cleveland	73,136
1/1	W 35-21	Detroit	63,794

(OT) Overtime

POSTSEASON (4-0)
Date	Result	Opponent	
1/8	W 31-17	at Cincinnati	65,870
1/15	W 21-18	at Indianapolis	57,449
1/22	W 34-17	at Denver	76,775
2/5	W 21-10	vs. Seattle at Detroit	68,206

SCORE BY PERIODS
Steelers	99	121	103	66	0 —	389
Opponents	78	49	54	68	9 —	258

2005 TEAM STATISTICS
	Steelers	Opp.
Total First Downs	297	275
Rushing	120	75
Passing	144	179
Penalty	33	21
3rd Down: Made/Att	68/192	92/232
3rd Down Pct.	35.4	39.7
4th Down: Made/Att	5/12	6/17
4th Down Pct.	41.7	35.3
Possession Avg.	31:16	28:44
Total Net Yards	5,149	4,544
Avg. Per Game	321.8	284.0
Total Plays	960	998
Avg. Per Play	5.4	4.6
Net Yards Rushing	2,223	1,376
Avg. Per Game	138.9	86.0
Total Rushes	549	402
Net Yards Passing	2,926	3,168
Avg. Per Game	182.9	198.0
Sacked/Yards Lost	32/178	47/312
Gross Yards	3,104	3,480
Att./Completions	379/228	549/315
Completion Pct.	60.2	57.4
Had Intercepted	14	15
Punts/Average	69/41.7	80/43.3
Net Punting Avg.	69/34.5	80/34.7
Penalties/Yards	99/876	120/1031
Fumbles/Ball Lost	22/9	30/15
Touchdowns	45	27
Rushing	21	10
Passing	21	15
Returns	3	2

2005 INDIVIDUAL STATISTICS
PASSING
	Att.	Comp.	Yds.	Pct.	TD	Int.	Tkld.	Rate
Roethlisberger	268	168	2,385	62.7	17	9	23/129	98.6
Maddox	71	34	406	47.9	2	4	8/43	51.7
Batch	36	23	246	63.9	1	1	1/6	81.5
Randle El	3	3	67	100.0	1	0	0/0	158.3
Gardocki	1	0	0	0.0	0	0	0/0	39.6
Steelers	379	228	3,104	60.2	21	14	32/178	89.4
Opponents	549	315	3,480	57.4	15	15	47/312	74.0

SCORING
	TD R	TD P	TD Rt	PAT	FG	Saf	PTS
Reed	0	0	0	45/45	24/29	0	117
Ward	0	11	0	0/0	0/0	0	66
Bettis	9	0	0	0/0	0/0	0	54
Miller	0	6	0	0/0	0/0	0	36
Parker	4	1	0	0/0	0/0	0	30
Haynes	3	0	0	0/0	0/0	0	18
Randle El	0	1	2	0/0	0/0	0	18
Roethlisberger	3	0	0	0/0	0/0	0	18
Morgan	0	2	0	0/0	0/0	0	12
Batch	1	0	0	0/0	0/0	0	6
Polamalu	0	0	1	0/0	0/0	0	6
Staley	1	0	0	0/0	0/0	0	6
Foote	0	0	0	0/0	0/0	1	2
Steelers	21	21	3	45/45	24/29	1	389
Opponents	10	15	2	24/25	24/30	0	258

2-Pt. Conversions: None.
Steelers 0-0, Opponents 0-1.

RUSHING
	No.	Yds	Avg	LG	TD
Parker	255	1,202	4.7	80t	4
Bettis	110	368	3.3	39	9
Haynes	74	274	3.7	20	3
Staley	38	148	3.9	17	1
Randle El	12	73	6.1	43	0
Roethlisberger	31	69	2.2	13	3
Batch	11	30	2.7	15	1
Maddox	8	26	3.3	16	0
Kreider	3	21	7.0	12	0
Ward	3	10	3.3	7	0
Herron	3	2	0.7	1	0
Wilson	1	0	0.0	0	0
Steelers	549	2,223	4.0	80t	21
Opponents	402	1,376	3.4	36	10

RECEIVING
	No.	Yds	Avg	LG	TD
Ward	69	975	14.1	85t	11
Miller	39	459	11.8	50	6
Randle El	35	558	15.9	63t	1
Wilson	26	451	17.3	46	0
Parker	18	218	12.1	48	1
Haynes	11	113	10.3	18	0
Morgan	9	150	16.7	31t	2
Kreider	7	43	6.1	9	0
Staley	6	34	5.7	9	0
Bettis	4	40	10.0	16	0
Tuman	3	57	19.0	27	0
Kranchick	1	6	6.0	6	0
Steelers	228	3,104	13.6	85t	21
Opponents	315	3,480	11.0	80t	15

INTERCEPTIONS
	No.	Yds	Avg	LG	TD
Hope	3	60	20.0	55	0
Polamalu	2	42	21.0	36	0
Townsend	2	26	13.0	26	0
Porter	2	9	4.5	9	0
J. Harrison	1	25	25.0	25	0
Colclough	1	14	14.0	14	0
Carter	1	3	3.0	3	0
McFadden	1	0	0.0	0	0
A. Smith	1	0	0.0	0	0
Taylor	1	0	0.0	0	0
Steelers	15	179	11.9	55	0
Opponents	14	194	13.9	41t	1

PUNTING
	No.	Yds	Avg	In 20	Lg
Gardocki	67	2,803	41.8	22	65
Roethlisberger	2	72	36.0	1	39
Steelers	69	2,875	41.7	23	65
Opponents	80	3,463	43.3	19	58

PUNT RETURNS
	Ret	FC	Yds	Avg	LG	TD
Randle El	44	12	448	10.2	81t	2
Iwuoma	1	0	3	3.0	3	0
Taylor	1	0	19	19.0	19	0
J. Harrison	0	1	0	—	—	0
Steelers	46	13	470	10.2	81t	2
Opponents	37	12	336	9.1	36	0

KICKOFF RETURNS
	No.	Yds	Avg	LG	TD
Morgan	23	583	25.3	74	0
Colclough	22	473	21.5	63	0
Taylor	3	59	19.7	24	0
Wilson	3	53	17.7	29	0
Keisel	2	23	11.5	12	0
Randle El	1	16	16.0	16	0
Kreider	1	3	3.0	3	0
J. Harrison	1	-2	-2.0	-2	0
Steelers	56	1,208	21.6	74	0
Opponents	77	1,685	21.9	94	0

FIELD GOALS
	1-19	20-29	30-39	40-49	50+
Reed	0/0	9/9	9/9	6/9	0/2
Steelers	0/0	9/9	9/9	6/9	0/2
Opponents	0/0	8/8	5/8	11/13	0/1

SACKS
	No.
Porter	10.5
Haggans	9.0
von Oelhoffen	3.5
Foote	3.0
J. Harrison	3.0
Keisel	3.0
Polamalu	3.0
Townsend	3.0
J. Farrior	2.0
A. Smith	2.0
Carter	1.0
Colclough	1.0
Frazier	1.0
Kirschke	1.0
McFadden	1.0
Steelers	47.0
Opponents	32.0

RECORD HOLDERS
INDIVIDUAL RECORDS—CAREER

Category	Name	Performance
Rushing (Yds.)	Franco Harris, 1972-1983	11,950
Passing (Yds.)	Terry Bradshaw, 1970-1983	27,989
Passing (TDs)	Terry Bradshaw, 1970-1983	212
Receiving (No.)	Hines Ward, 1998-2005	574
Receiving (Yds.)	John Stallworth, 1974-1987	8,723
Interceptions	Mel Blount, 1970-1983	57
Punting (Avg.)	Bobby Joe Green, 1960-61	45.7
Punt Return (Avg.)	Bobby Gage, 1949-1950	14.9
Kickoff Return (Avg.)	Lynn Chandnois, 1950-56	29.6
Field Goals	Gary Anderson, 1982-1994	309
Touchdowns (Tot.)	Franco Harris, 1972-1983	100
Points	Gary Anderson, 1982-1994	1,343

INDIVIDUAL RECORDS—SINGLE SEASON

Category	Name	Performance
Rushing (Yds.)	Barry Foster, 1992	1,690
Passing (Yds.)	Terry Bradshaw, 1979	3,724
Passing (TDs)	Terry Bradshaw, 1978	28
Receiving (No.)	Hines Ward, 2002	112
Receiving (Yds.)	Yancey Thigpen, 1997	1,398
Interceptions	Mel Blount, 1975	11
Punting (Avg.)	Bobby Joe Green, 1961	47.0
Punt Return (Avg.)	Bobby Gage, 1949	16.0
Kickoff Return (Avg.)	Lynn Chandnois, 1952	35.2
Field Goals	Norm Johnson, 1995	34
Touchdowns (Tot.)	Louis Lipps, 1985	15
Points	Norm Johnson, 1995	141

INDIVIDUAL RECORDS—SINGLE GAME

Category	Name	Performance
Rushing (Yds.)	John Fuqua, 12-20-70	218
Passing (Yds.)	Tommy Maddox, 11-10-02	473
Passing (TDs)	Terry Bradshaw, 11-15-81	5
	Mark Malone, 9-8-85	5
Receiving (No.)	Courtney Hawkins, 11-1-98	14
Receiving (Yds.)	Plaxico Burress, 11-10-02	253
Interceptions	Jack Butler, 12-13-53	*4
Field Goals	Gary Anderson, 10-23-88	6
	Jeff Reed, 12-1-02	6
Touchdowns (Tot.)	Ray Mathews, 10-17-54	4
	Roy Jefferson, 11-3-68	4
Points	Ray Mathews, 10-17-54	24
	Roy Jefferson, 11-3-68	24

*NFL Record

2006 VETERAN ROSTER

No.	Name	Pos.	Ht.	Wt.	Birthdate	NFL Exp.	College	Hometown	How Acq.	'05 Games/ Starts
93	Bailey, Rodney	DE	6-3	305	10/7/79	6	Ohio State	Cleveland, Ohio	UFA(Sea)-'06	8/0*
82	Baker, Eugene	WR	6-1	167	3/18/76	4	Kent State	Monroeville, Pa.	FA-'06	0*
16	Batch, Charlie	QB	6-2	216	12/5/74	9	Eastern Michigan	Homestead, Pa.	FA-'02	4/2
72	Brooks, Barrett	T	6-5	325	5/5/72	12	Kansas State	Florissant, Mo.	FA-'03	16/0
23	Carter, Tyrone	S	5-8	195	3/31/76	7	Minnesota	Pompano Beach, Fla.	FA-'04	16/0
25	Clark, Ryan	S	5-11	205	10/12/79	5	Louisiana State	Merraro, La.	UFA(Wash)-'06	13/13*
21	Colclough, Ricardo	CB	5-11	195	4/18/82	3	Tusculum	Sumter, S.C.	D2-'04	14/0
79	Essex, Trai	T	6-4	324	12/5/82	2	Northwestern	Fort Wayne, Ind.	D3-'05	6/4
66	Faneca, Alan	G	6-5	307	12/7/76	8	Louisiana State	New Orleans, La.	D1-'98	16/16
51	Farrior, James	LB	6-2	243	1/6/75	10	Virginia	Ettrick, Va.	UFA(NYJ)-'02	14/14
	Farrior, Matt	LB	6-1	230	8/6/81	2	Florida	Petersburg, Va.	FA-'06	0*
50	Foote, Larry	LB	6-1	239	6/12/80	5	Michigan	Detroit, Mich.	D4-'02	16/16
94	Frazier, Andre	LB	6-5	234	6/29/82	2	Cincinnati	Cincinnati, Ohio	FA-'05	11/0
17	Gardocki, Chris	P	6-1	192	2/7/70	16	Clemson	Stone Mountain, Ga.	UFA-'04	16/0
53	Haggans, Clark	LB	6-4	243	1/10/77	7	Colorado State	Torrance, Calif.	D5a-'00	13/13
98	Hampton, Casey	DT	6-1	325	9/3/77	6	Texas	Galveston, Texas	D1-'01	16/15
92	Harrison, James	LB	6-0	242	5/4/78	3	Kent State	Akron, Ohio	FA-'04	16/3
64	Hartings, Jeff	C	6-3	299	9/7/72	11	Penn State	St. Henry, Ohio	UFA(Det)-'01	16/16
34	Haynes, Verron	RB	5-10	222	2/17/79	5	Georgia	Bronx, N.Y.	D5-'02	14/0
76	Hoke, Chris	DT	6-2	305	4/6/76	6	Brigham Young	Long Beach, Calif.	FA-'02	15/0
29	Iwuoma, Chidi	CB	5-9	184	2/19/78	6	California	Pasadena, Calif.	FA-02	15/0
99	Keisel, Brett	DE	6-5	285	9/19/78	5	Brigham Young	Greybull, Wyo.	D7b-'02	16/0
90	Kirschke, Travis	DE	6-3	298	9/6/74	10	UCLA	Highland Ranch, Colo.	UFA(SF)-'04	16/0
35	Kreider, Dan	FB	5-11	255	3/11/77	6	New Hampshire	Mount Joy, Pa.	FA-'00	16/7
57	Kriewaldt, Clint	LB	6-1	248	3/16/76	8	Wisconsin-Stevens Point	Shiocton, Wis.	UFA(Det)-'03	16/2
31	Logan, Mike	S	6-1	211	9/15/74	10	West Virginia	Pittsburgh, Pa.	UFA(Jax)-'01	12/1
89	Mays, Lee	WR	6-2	193	11/18/78	4	Texas-El Paso	Houston, Texas	FA-'05	0*
20	McFadden, Bryant	CB	6-0	190	11/21/81	2	Florida State	Hollywood, Fla.	D2-'05	12/1
83	Miller, Heath	TE	6-5	256	10/22/82	2	Virginia	Swords Creek, Va.	D1-'05	16/15
81	Morey, Sean	WR	5-11	200	2/26/76	5	Brown	Marshfield, Mass.	FA-'04	15/0
11	Morgan, Quincy	WR	6-1	215	9/23/77	6	Kansas State	Dallas, Texas	UFA(Dall)-'05	16/0
56	Okobi, Chukky	C	6-1	305	10/18/78	6	Purdue	Pittsburgh, Pa.	D5-'01	16/0
39	Parker, Willie	RB	5-10	209	11/11/80	3	North Carolina	Clinton, N.C.	FA-'04	15/15
43	Polamalu, Troy	S	5-10	212	4/19/81	4	Southern California	Roseburg, Ore.	D1-'03	16/16
55	Porter, Joey	LB	6-3	250	3/22/77	8	Colorado State	Bakersfield, Calif.	D3a-'99	16/16
3	Reed, Jeff	K	5-11	225	4/9/79	5	North Carolina	Charlotte, N.C.	FA-'02	16/0
7	Roethlisberger, Ben	QB	6-5	241	3/2/82	3	Miami (Ohio)	Findlay, Ohio	D1-'04	12/12
5	Rutherford, Rod	QB	6-2	223	12/12/80	2	Pittsburgh	Pittsburgh, Pa.	FA-'05	0*
95	Seigler, Richard	LB	6-2	238	10/19/80	2	Oregon State	Las Vegas, Nev.	FA-'05	0*
73	Simmons, Kendall	G	6-3	319	3/11/79	5	Auburn	Ripley, Miss.	D1-'02	16/16
91	Smith, Aaron	DE	6-5	298	4/9/76	8	Northern Colorado	Colo. Springs, Colo.	D4-'99	16/16
77	Smith, Marvel	T	6-5	321	8/6/78	7	Arizona State	Oakland, Calif.	D2-'00	12/12
22	Staley, Duce	RB	5-11	242	2/27/75	10	South Carolina	Columbia, S.C.	UFA(Phil)-'04	5/1
78	Starks, Max	T	6-8	337	1/10/82	3	Florida	Orlando, Fla.	D3-'04	16/16
24	Taylor, Ike	CB	6-1	191	5/5/80	4	Louisiana-Lafayette	Gretna, La.	D4-'03	16/15
26	Townsend, Deshea	CB	5-10	190	9/8/75	9	Alabama	Batesville, Miss.	D4a-'98	16/15
84	Tuman, Jerame	TE	6-4	253	3/24/76	8	Michigan	Liberal, Kan.	D5-'99	16/9
54	Wallace, Rian	LB	6-3	243	5/24/82	2	Temple	Pottstown, Pa.	D5-'05	4/0
86	Ward, Hines	WR	6-0	205	3/8/76	9	Georgia	Forest Park, Ga.	D3b-'98	15/15
60	Warren, Greg	LS	6-3	252	10/18/81	2	North Carolina	Goldsboro, N.C.	FA-'05	16/0
85	Washington, Nate	WR	6-1	185	8/28/83	2	Tiffin	Toledo, Ohio	FA-'05	1/0
80	Wilson, Cedrick	WR	5-10	183	12/17/78	6	Tennessee	Memphis, Tenn.	UFA(SF)-'05	16/1
18	Young, Walter	WR	6-4	220	12/7/79	2	Illinois	Park Forest, Ill.	FA-'04	0*

* Bailey played 8 games with Seattle in '05; Baker did not play in 1 game with Carolina; Clark played 13 games with Washington; M. Farrior missed '05 season because of injury; Mays last active with Pittsburgh in '05; Rutherford last active with Carolina in '04; Seigler last active with San Francisco in '04; Young last active with Carolina in '03.

Players lost through free agency (3): S Chris Hope (Tenn; 16 games in '05), WR Antwaan Randle El (Wash; 16), DE Kimo von Oelhoffen (NYJ; 16).

Also played with Steelers in '05—HB Jerome Bettis (16 games), RB Noah Herron (2), TE Matt Kranchick (4), QB Tommy Maddox (4), S Russell Stuvaints (4), CB Willie Williams (4).

2006 FIRST-YEAR ROSTER

Name	Pos.	Ht.	Wt.	Birthdate	College	Hometown	How Acq.
Andrews, Kyle (1)	LS	5-11	254	9/10/81	Ohio State	Middletown, Ohio	FA
Baker, Zach	S	6-2	212	7/27/83	East Carolina	Tucson, Ariz.	FA
Barr, Mike (1)	P	6-2	230	12/8/78	Rutgers	Lynchburg, Va.	FA
Booker, Ulish (1)	T	6-6	319	8/14/79	Michigan State	West Haven, Conn.	FA-'05
Boyd, Shane (1)	QB	6-1	232	9/17/82	Kentucky	Lexington, Ky.	FA
Brown, Tim (1)	C	6-5	313	5/12/80	West Virginia	Harrisburg, Pa.	FA-'05
Brubaker, Mark	K	6-0	189	2/11/84	East Stroudsburg	Stouchsburg, Pa.	FA
Colon, Willie	T	6-3	315	4/9/83	Hofstra	Bronx, N.Y.	D4a
Davis, Charles	TE	6-6	260	3/13/83	Purdue	Fraser, Mich.	D5b
Dekker, Jonathan	TE	6-5	250	5/15/83	Princeton	Greenfield, Wis.	FA
Easlick, Doug (1)	FB	5-11	243	12/4/80	Virginia Tech	Marlton, N.J.	FA
Hagemann, Nick	T	6-7	295	9/9/82	South Dakota	New Vienna, Iowa	FA
Harris, Orien	DE	6-3	302	6/3/83	Miami	Newark, Del.	D4b
Harrison, Arnold (1)	LB	6-3	236	9/20/82	Georgia	Augusta, Ga.	FA-'05
Herzing, Adam (1)	WR	6-3	190	9/23/80	Cal-Poly	San Jose, Calif.	FA
Holmes, Santonio	WR	5-11	189	3/3/84	Ohio State	Belle Glade, Fla.	D1
Humes, Cedric	HB	6-1	233	8/7/83	Virginia Tech	Virginia Beach, Va.	D7
Jacobs, Omar	QB	6-4	224	3/3/84	Bowling Green	Delray Beach, Fla.	D5a
Jemison, Mike (1)	RB	5-11	216	6/3/83	Indiana (Pa.)	Greencastle, Pa.	FA
Joe, Branden (1)	FB	6-0	242	10/12/81	Ohio State	Westerville, Ohio	FA
Kemoeatu, Chris (1)	G	6-3	344	1/4/83	Utah	Kahuka, Hawaii	D6-'05
Kudla, Mike	LB	6-3	265	3/8/84	Ohio State	Medina, Ohio	FA
Kuhn, John (1)	RB	6-0	255	11/9/82	Shippensburg	York, Pa.	FA-'05
Landrom, Jamar	S	6-3	215	2/16/84	Tennessee State	Pontiac, Mich.	FA
Lorello, Mike	S	5-11	208	10/15/84	West Virginia	Powell, Ohio	FA
Love, Grayling	G	6-3	296	9/30/83	Arizona State	Lansing, Mich.	FA
Madison, Anthony	CB	5-9	180	10/8/81	Alabama	Thomasville, Ala.	FA
Newton, Brandon (1)	C	6-2	296	4/1/81	Hofstra	Lauderdale Lakes, Fla.	FA
Nua, Shaun (1)	DE	6-5	280	5/2/81	Brigham Young	Pago Pago, American Samoa	D7a-'05
Paxson, Scott	DT	6-4	292	2/3/83	Penn State	Philadelphia, Pa.	FA
Philip, Marvin	C	6-1	307	2/3/82	California	Redwood City, Calif.	D6
Postell, Malcolm (1)	LB	6-1	231	8/3/82	Pittsburgh	Keyport, N.J.	FA
Reid, Willie	WR	5-10	186	9/19/82	Florida State	Kathleen, Ga.	D3b
Smith, Anthony	S	5-11	192	9/20/83	Syracuse	Hubbard, Ohio	D3a
Smolko, Isaac	TE	6-5	257	2/28/83	Penn State	Youngstown, Ohio	FA
Stanley, Ronald (1)	LB	6-0	244	3/6/83	Michigan State	Saginaw, Mich.	FA-'05
Torrey, Brandon (1)	T	6-6	277	5/18/83	Howard	Durham, N.C.	FA
Vickers, Lee	DE	6-6	270	3/13/81	North Alabama	Athens, Ala.	FA
West, Isaac (1)	WR	6-0	187	4/5/82	Furman	Hampton, Va.	FA

The term NFL Rookie is defined as a player who is in his first season of professional football and has not been on the roster of another professional football team for any regular-season or postseason games. A Rookie is designated by an "R" on NFL rosters. Players who have been active in another professional football league or players who have NFL experience, including either preseason training camp or being on an Active List or Inactive List, or on Reserve/Injured or Reserve/Physically Unable to Perform for fewer than six regular-season games, are termed NFL First-Year Players. An NFL First-Year Player is designated by a "1" on NFL rosters. Thereafter, a player is credited with an additional year of experience for each season in which he accumulates six games on the Active List or Inactive List, or on Reserve/Injured or Reserve/Physically Unable to Perform.

Log on to www.steelers.com for an up-to-date roster.

PITTSBURGH STEELERS

COACHING STAFF
Head Coach,
Bill Cowher
Pro Career: Became the fifteenth head coach in Steelers history when he replaced Chuck Noll on January 21, 1992. Last season, Cowher guided the Steelers to their first Super Bowl victory in 26 years by capturing the team's fifth Lombardi Trophy after defeating the Seattle Seahawks, 21-10, in Super Bowl XL. In 1995, at age 38, he became the youngest coach to lead his team to a Super Bowl. Cowher is only the second coach in NFL history to lead his team to the playoffs in each of his first six seasons as head coach, joining Pro Football Hall of Fame member Paul Brown. During Cowher's 21-year coaching career, teams he has been associated with have made the postseason 16 times. Began his NFL career as a free-agent linebacker with the Philadelphia Eagles in 1979, and then signed with the Cleveland Browns the following year. Cowher played three seasons (1980-82) in Cleveland before being traded back to the Eagles, where he played two more years (1983-84). Cowher began his coaching career in 1985 at age 28 under Marty Schottenheimer with the Browns. He was the Browns' special teams coach in 1985-86 and secondary coach in 1987-88 before following Schottenheimer to the Kansas City Chiefs in 1989 as defensive coordinator. Career record: 153-91-1.
Background: Excelled in football, basketball, and track for Carlynton High in Crafton, Pa. Was a three-year starter at linebacker for North Carolina State, serving as captain and earning team MVP honors as a senior. Graduated in 1979 with education degree.
Personal: Born in Pittsburgh, on May 8, 1957. His wife Kaye, also a North Carolina State graduate, played professional basketball for the New York Stars of the Women's Professional Basketball League with twin sister Faye. Bill and Kaye live in Pittsburgh and have three daughters—Meagan Lyn, Lauren Marie, and Lindsay Morgan.

ASSISTANT COACHES
Bruce Arians, wide receivers; born October 3, 1952, Paterson, N.J. Quarterback Virginia Tech 1970-74. No pro playing experience. College coach: Virginia Tech 1975-77, Mississippi State 1978-1980, Alabama 1981-82, Temple 1983-88 (head coach), Mississippi State 1993-95, Alabama 1997. Pro coach: Kansas City Chiefs 1989-1992, New Orleans Saints 1996, Indianapolis Colts 1998-2000, Cleveland Browns 2001-03, joined Steelers in 2004.
Keith Butler, linebackers; born May 16, 1956, Anniston, Ala. Linebacker Memphis 1974-77. Pro linebacker Seattle Seahawks 1978-1987. College coach: Memphis 1990-97, Arkansas State 1998. Pro coach: Cleveland Browns 1999-2002, joined Steelers in 2003.
James Daniel, tight ends; born January 17, 1953, Wetumpka, Ala. Guard Alabama State 1970-73. No pro playing experience. College coach: Auburn 1981-1992. Pro coach: New York Giants 1993-96, Atlanta Falcons 1997-2003, joined Steelers in 2004.
Russ Grimm, asst. head coach/offensive line; born May 2, 1959, Scottdale, Pa. Center Pittsburgh 1977-1980. Pro guard Washington Redskins 1981-1991. Pro coach: Washington Redskins 1992-2000, joined Steelers in 2001.
Dick Hoak, running backs; born December 8, 1939, Jeannette, Pa. Halfback-quarterback Penn State 1958-1960. Pro running back Pittsburgh Steelers 1961-1970. Pro coach: Joined Steelers in 1972.
Ray Horton, asst. defensive backs; born April 12, 1960, Tacoma, Wash. Defensive back Washington 1979-1982. Pro defensive back Cincinnati Bengals 1983-88, Dallas Cowboys 1989-1992. Pro coach: Washington Redskins 1994-96, Cincinnati Bengals 1997-2001, Detroit Lions 2002-03, joined Steelers in 2004.
Dick LeBeau, defensive coordinator; born September 9, 1937, London, Ohio. Defensive back Ohio State 1955-58. Pro cornerback Detroit Lions 1959-1972. Pro coach: Philadelphia Eagles 1973-75, Green Bay Packers 1976-79, Cincinnati Bengals 1980-1991, 1997-2002 (head coach 2000-02), Pittsburgh Steelers 1992-96, Buffalo Bills 2003, re-joined Steelers in 2004.
John Mitchell, defensive line; born October 14, 1951, Mobile, Ala. Defensive end Eastern Arizona J.C. 1969-1970, Alabama 1971-72. No pro playing experience. College coach: Alabama 1973-76, Arkansas 1977-1982, Temple 1986, Louisiana State 1987-1990. Pro coach: Birmingham Stallions (USFL) 1983-85, Cleveland Browns 1991-93, joined Steelers in 1994.
Darren Perry, defensive backs; born December 29, 1968, Chesapeake, Va. Safety Penn State 1987-1991. Pro safety Pittsburgh Steelers 1992-98, New Orleans Saints 2000. Pro coach: Cincinnati Bengals 2002, joined Steelers in 2003.
Kevin Spencer, special teams; born November 2, 1953, Queens, N.Y. Outside linebacker Springfield College 1971. No pro playing experience. College coach: SUNY-Cortland 1975-76, Cornell 1979-1980, Ithaca 1981-86, Wesleyan 1987-1991. Pro coach: Cleveland Browns 1991-94, Oakland Raiders 1995-97, Indianapolis Colts 1998-2001, joined Steelers in 2002.
Mark Whipple, quarterbacks; born April 1, 1957, Tarrytown, N.Y. Quarterback Brown 1976-78. No pro playing experience. College coach: St. Lawrence 1980, Union College 1981-82, Brown 1983, New Hampshire 1986-87, New Haven 1988-1993 (head coach), Brown 1994-97 (head coach), Massachusetts 1998-2003 (head coach). Pro coach: Arizona Wranglers 1984 (USFL), joined Steelers in 2004.
Ken Whisenhunt, offensive coordinator; born February 28, 1962, Atlanta. Tight end-quarterback Georgia Tech 1980-84. Pro tight end Atlanta Falcons 1985-88, Washington Redskins 1989-1990, New York Jets 1991-93. College coach: Vanderbilt 1995-96. Pro coach: Baltimore Ravens 1997-98, Cleveland Browns 1999, New York Jets 2000, joined Steelers in 2001.

American Football Conference
West Division
Team Colors: Navy Blue, White, and Gold
P.O. Box 609609
San Diego, California 92160-9609
Telephone: (858) 874-4500

2006 SCHEDULE
PRESEASON
Aug. 12	**Green Bay**	7:00
Aug. 21	at Chicago	7:00
Aug. 26	at Minnesota	7:00
Sept. 1	**San Francisco**	7:00

REGULAR SEASON
Sept. 11	at Oakland (Mon.)	7:15
Sept. 17	**Tennessee**	1:15
Sept. 24	Open Date	
Oct. 1	at Baltimore	1:00
Oct. 8	**Pittsburgh**	5:15
Oct. 15	at San Francisco	1:15
Oct. 22	at Kansas City	12:00
Oct. 29	**St. Louis**	1:05
Nov. 5	**Cleveland**	1:15
Nov. 12	at Cincinnati	1:00
Nov. 19	at Denver	2:15
Nov. 26	**Oakland**	1:05
Dec. 3	at Buffalo	1:00
Dec. 10	**Denver**	1:15
Dec. 17	**Kansas City**	1:05
Dec. 24	at Seattle	1:15
Dec. 31	**Arizona**	1:15

Stadium: Qualcomm Stadium
(opened in 1967)
• **Capacity:** 70,000
9449 Friars Road
San Diego, California 92108
Playing Surface: Grass
Training Camp: Chargers Park
4020 Murphy Canyon Rd.
San Diego, CA 92123

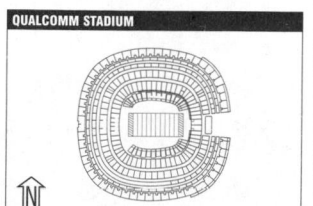
QUALCOMM STADIUM

CLUB OFFICIALS
Owner: Alex G. Spanos
President/CEO: Dean A. Spanos
Executive Vice President:
Michael A. Spanos
Executive Vice President-General
Manager: A.J. Smith
Executive Vice President-Chief Operating
Officer: Jim Steeg
Executive Vice President:
Jeremiah T. Murphy
Executive Vice President of Football
Operations: Ed McGuire
Executive Vice President-Chief Financial
Officer: Jeanne M. Bonk
Vice President-Chief Marketing Officer:
Ken Derrett
Assistant General Manager-Director of
Player Personnel: Buddy Nix
Director of College Scouting:
Jimmy Raye
Assistant Director of College Scouting:
John Spanos
Director of Pro Scouting:
Dennis Abraham
Head Athletic Trainer: James Collins
Director of Video Operations:
Brian Duddy
Equipment Manager: Bob Wick
Director of Player Development:
Arthur Hightower
Senior Director of Marketing
Partnerships: Dennis O'Leary
Senior Director of Ticket Sales and
Service: Todd Poulsen
Director of Marketing Programs and
Business Development: A.G. Spanos
Director of Business Operations:
John Hinek
Director of Public Relations: Bill Johnston
Director of Public Affairs &
Corporate/Community Relations:
Kimberley Layton
Director of Security: Dick Lewis
Director of Stadium/Game Operations &
Events: Sean O'Connor
Controller: Marsha Wells
Director of Ticket Operations:
Michael L. Dougherty

COACHING HISTORY
Los Angeles 1960
(336-364-11)
Records include postseason games
1960-69	Sid Gillman*	83-51-6
1969-1970	Charlie Waller	9-7-3
1971	Sid Gillman**	4-6-0
1971-73	Harland Svare***	7-17-2
1973	Ron Waller	1-5-0
1974-78	Tommy Prothro****	21-39-0
1978-1986	Don Coryell#	72-60-0
1986-88	Al Saunders	17-22-0
1989-1991	Dan Henning	16-32-0
1992-96	Bobby Ross	50-36-0
1997-98	Kevin Gilbride	6-16-0
1998	June Jones	3-7-0
1999-2001	Mike Riley	14-34-0
2002-05	Marty Schottenheimer	33-32-0

*Retired after nine games in 1969
**Resigned after 10 games in 1971
***Resigned after eight games in 1973
****Resigned after four games in 1978
#Resigned after six games in 1986
##Released after six games in 1998

ATTENDANCE
Home 547,937	Away 560,903

Total 1,108,840
Single-game home record,
69,288 (11/7/99)
Single-season home record,
547,937 (2005)

2006 DRAFT CHOICES
Round	Name	Pos.	College
1	Antonio Cromartie	DB	Florida State
2	Marcus McNeill	T	Auburn
3	Charlie Whitehurst	QB	Clemson
5	Tom Dobbins	LB	Iowa State
6	Jeromey Clary	T	Kansas State
	Kurt Smith	K	Virginia
7	Chase Page	DT	North Carolina
	Jimmy Martin	T	Virginia Tech

2005 TEAM RECORD
PRESEASON (2-2)

Date	Result	Opponent
8/11	L 7-10	at Green Bay
8/21	W 36-21	St. Louis
8/26	L 16-19	at Minnesota
9/1	W 28-24	San Francisco

REGULAR SEASON (9-7)

Date	Result	Opponent	Att.
9/11	L 24-28	Dallas	67,679
9/18	L 17-20	at Denver	75,310
9/25	W 45-23	N.Y. Giants	65,373
10/2	W 41-17	at New England	68,756
10/10	L 22-23	Pittsburgh	68,537
10/16	W 27-14	at Oakland	52,666
10/23	L 17-20	at Philadelphia	67,747
10/30	W 28-20	Kansas City	65,750
11/6	W 31-26	at N.Y. Jets	77,662
11/20	W 48-10	Buffalo	65,602
11/27	W 23-17	at Washington (OT)	84,930
12/4	W 34-10	Oakland	66,436
12/11	L 21-23	Miami	65,026
12/18	W 26-17	at Indianapolis	57,389
12/24	L 7-20	at Kansas City	75,956
12/31	L 7-23	Denver	65,513

(OT) Overtime

SCORE BY PERIODS

Chargers	93	139	74	106	6	—	418
Opponents	36	126	77	73	0	—	312

2005 TEAM STATISTICS

	Chargers	Opp.
Total First Downs	337	306
Rushing	116	90
Passing	191	189
Penalty	30	27
3rd Down: Made/Att	88/208	79/212
3rd Down Pct.	42.3	37.3
4th Down: Made/Att	11/17	10/20
4th Down Pct.	64.7	50.0
Possession Avg.	31:34	28:26
Total Net Yards	5,567	4,948
Avg. Per Game	347.9	309.3
Total Plays	1,022	999
Avg. Per Play	5.4	5.0
Net Yards Rushing	2,072	1,349
Avg. Per Game	129.5	84.3
Total Rushes	465	386
Net Yards Passing	3,495	3,599
Avg. Per Game	218.4	224.9
Sacked/Yards Lost	31/243	46/289
Gross Yards	3,738	3,888
Att./Completions	526/338	567/338
Completion Pct.	64.3	59.6
Had Intercepted	16	10
Punts/Average	71/43.7	78/42.0
Net Punting Avg.	71/38.0	78/37.6
Penalties/Yards	110/890	110/831
Fumbles/Ball Lost	22/12	23/10
Touchdowns	51	36
Rushing	22	14
Passing	27	20
Returns	2	2

2005 INDIVIDUAL STATISTICS

PASSING	Att.	Comp.	Yds.	Pct.	TD	Int.	Tkld.	Rate
Brees	500	323	3,576	64.6	24	15	27/223	89.2
Rivers	22	12	115	54.5	0	1	3/16	50.4
Tomlinson	4	3	47	75.0	3	0	0/0	153.1
McCardell	0	0	0		0	0	1/4	
Chargers	526	338	3,738	64.3	27	16	31/243	89.7
Opponents	567	338	3,888	59.6	20	10	46/289	84.7

SCORING	TD R	TD P	TD Rt	PAT	FG	Saf	PTS
Tomlinson	18	2	0	0/0	0/0	0	120
Kaeding	0	0	0	49/49	21/24	0	112
Gates	0	10	0	0/0	0/0	0	60
McCardell	0	9	0	0/0	0/0	0	54
Parker	0	3	0	0/0	0/0	0	18
Turner	3	0	0	0/0	0/0	0	18
Hart	0	0	2	0/0	0/0	0	12
Brees	1	0	0	0/0	0/0	0	6
Caldwell	0	1	0	0/0	0/0	0	6
Neal	0	1	0	0/0	0/0	0	6
Peelle	0	1	0	0/0	0/0	0	6
Chargers	22	27	2	49/49	21/24	0	418
Opponents	14	20	2	34/35	20/29	1	312

2-Pt. Conversions: None.
Chargers 0-1, Opponents 0-1.

RUSHING	No.	Yds	Avg	LG	TD
Tomlinson	339	1,462	4.3	62	18
Turner	57	335	5.9	83t	3
Neal	29	98	3.4	9	0
Parker	4	55	13.8	30	0
Sproles	8	50	6.3	21	0
Brees	21	49	2.3	9	1
Caldwell	2	10	5.0	7	0
McCardell	2	6	3.0	3	0
Osgood	1	4	4.0	4	0
Pinnock	1	4	4.0	4	0
Rivers	1	-1	-1.0	-1	0
Chargers	465	2,072	4.5	83t	22
Opponents	386	1,349	3.5	46	14

RECEIVING	No.	Yds	Avg	LG	TD
Gates	89	1,101	12.4	38	10
McCardell	70	917	13.1	54	9
Parker	57	725	12.7	49	3
Tomlinson	51	370	7.3	41	2
Caldwell	28	352	12.6	43	1
Neal	24	145	6.0	21	1
Peelle	11	38	3.5	11	1
Jackson	3	59	19.7	21	0
Sproles	3	10	3.3	6	0
Osgood	2	21	10.5	15	0
Chargers	338	3,738	11.1	54	27
Opponents	338	3,888	11.5	56	20

INTERCEPTIONS	No.	Yds	Avg	LG	TD
Jue	3	28	9.3	20	0
Edwards	2	15	7.5	14	0
Hart	1	110	110.0	70t	2
Fletcher	1	19	19.0	19	0
Jammer	1	14	14.0	14	0
Wilhelm	1	10	10.0	10	0
Florence	1	9	9.0	9	0
Chargers	10	205	20.5	70t	2
Opponents	16	230	14.4	51	1

PUNTING	No.	Yds.	Avg.	In 20	LG
Scifres	71	3,104	43.7	25	71
Chargers	71	3,104	43.7	25	71
Opponents	78	3,274	42.0	19	65

PUNT RETURNS	Ret	FC	Yds	Avg	LG	TD
Parker	18	9	106	5.9	15	0
Sproles	18	5	108	6.0	23	0
McCardell	3	3	31	10.3	14	0
Chargers	39	17	245	6.3	23	0
Opponents	26	19	244	9.4	52	0

KICKOFF RETURNS	No.	Yds	Avg	LG	TD
Sproles	63	1528	24.3	58	0
Caldwell	3	99	33.0	60	0
Pinnock	1	24	24.0	24	0
Parker	1	16	16.0	16	0
Turner	1	0	0.0	0	0
Chargers	69	1,667	24.2	60	0
Opponents	83	1,856	22.4	54	0

FIELD GOALS	1-19	20-29	30-39	40-49	50+
Kaeding	1/1	3/3	9/9	8/11	0/0
Chargers	1/1	3/3	9/9	8/11	0/0
Opponents	0/0	8/9	6/7	5/5	1/8

SACKS	No.
Merriman	10.0
Phillips	7.0
Foley	4.5
Scott	4.5
Castillo	3.5
Edwards	3.0
Olshansky	3.0
Leber	2.0
Cooper	1.5
Cesaire	1.0
Davis	1.0
Fletcher	1.0
Godfrey	1.0
Harris	1.0
Kiel	1.0
Wilhelm	1.0
Chargers	46.0
Opponents	31.0

RECORD HOLDERS
INDIVIDUAL RECORDS—CAREER

Category	Name	Performance
Rushing (Yds.)	LaDainian Tomlinson, 2001-05	7,361
Passing (Yds.)	Dan Fouts, 1973-1987	43,040
Passing (TDs)	Dan Fouts, 1973-1987	254
Receiving (No.)	Charlie Joiner, 1976-1986	586
Receiving (Yds.)	Lance Alworth, 1962-1970	9,585
Interceptions	Gill Byrd, 1983-1992	42
Punting (Avg.)	Darren Bennett, 1995-2003	43.8
Punt Return (Avg.)	Darrien Gordon, 1993-96	13.6
Kickoff Return (Avg.)	Leslie (Speedy) Duncan, 1964-1970	25.3
Field Goals	John Carney, 1990-2000	261
Touchdowns (Tot.)	Lance Alworth, 1962-1970	83
Points	John Carney, 1990-2000	1,076

INDIVIDUAL RECORDS—SINGLE SEASON

Category	Name	Performance
Rushing (Yds.)	LaDainian Tomlinson, 2002	1,683
Passing (Yds.)	Dan Fouts, 1981	4,802
Passing (TDs)	Dan Fouts, 1981	33
Receiving (No.)	LaDainian Tomlinson, 2003	100
Receiving (Yds.)	Lance Alworth, 1965	1,602
Interceptions	Charlie McNeil, 1961	9
Punting (Avg.)	Darren Bennett, 2000	46.2
Punt Return (Avg.)	Leslie (Speedy) Duncan, 1965	15.5
Kickoff Return (Avg.)	Keith Lincoln, 1962	28.4
Field Goals	John Carney, 1994	34
Touchdowns (Tot.)	LaDainian Tomlinson, 2005	20
Points	John Carney, 1994	135

INDIVIDUAL RECORDS—SINGLE GAME

Category	Name	Performance
Rushing (Yds.)	LaDainian Tomlinson, 12-28-03	243
Passing (Yds.)	Dan Fouts, 10-19-80, 12-11-82	444
Passing (TDs)	Dan Fouts, 11-22-81	6
Receiving (No.)	Kellen Winslow, 10-7-84	15
Receiving (Yds.)	Wes Chandler, 12-20-82	260
Interceptions	Many times	3
	Last time by Dwayne Harper, 11-27-95	
Field Goals	John Carney, 9-5-93, 9-18-93	6
	Greg Davis, 10-5-97	6
Touchdowns (Tot.)	Kellen Winslow, 11-22-81	5
Points	Kellen Winslow, 11-22-81	30

2006 VETERAN ROSTER

No.	Name	Pos.	Ht.	Wt.	Birthdate	NFL Exp.	College	Hometown	How Acq.	'05 Games/ Starts
97	Bingham, Ryon	DT	6-3	303	6/6/81	2	Nebraska	Sandy, Utah	D7a-'04	1/0
50	Binn, David	LS	6-3	223	2/6/72	13	California	San Mateo, Calif.	FA-'94	16/0
93	Castillo, Luis	DE	6-3	303	8/4/83	2	Northwestern	Garfield, N.J.	D1b-'05	16/15
74	Cesaire, Jacques	DE	6-2	295	8/30/80	4	Southern Connecticut State	Gardner, Mass.	FA-'03	16/5
54	Cooper, Stephen	LB	6-1	235	6/19/79	4	Maine	Wareham, Mass.	FA-'03	16/2
32	Croom, Larry	RB	5-10	210	10/29/81	2	Nevada-Las Vegas	Long Beach, Calif.	FA-'06	0*
68	Dielman, Kris	G	6-4	310	2/3/81	4	Indiana	Troy, Ohio	FA-'03	16/14
59	Edwards, Donnie	LB	6-2	227	4/6/73	11	UCLA	Chula Vista, Calif.	UFA(KC)-'02	16/16
7	Feeley, A.J.	QB	6-3	220	5/16/77	6	Oregon	Ontario, Ore.	T(Mia)-'05	0*
29	Florence, Drayton	CB	6-0	195	12/19/80	4	Tuskegee	Ocala, Fla.	D2a-'03	13/12
53	Foley, Steve	LB	6-4	265	9/11/75	9	Louisiana-Monroe	Little Rock, Ark.	UFA(Hou)-'04	13/13
85	Gates, Antonio	TE	6-4	260	6/18/80	4	Kent State	Detroit, Mich.	FA-'03	15/15
94	Gbaja-Biamila, Akbar	LB	6-5	260	5/6/79	3	San Diego State	Los Angeles, Calif.	FA-'06	0*
58	Godfrey, Randall	LB	6-2	245	4/6/73	11	Georgia	Valdosta, Ga.	UFA(Sea)-'04	14/14
79	Goff, Mike	G	6-5	311	1/6/76	9	Iowa	Peru, Ill.	UFA(Cin)-'04	16/16
61	Hardwick, Nick	C	6-4	295	9/2/81	3	Purdue	Indianapolis, Ind.	D3b-'04	13/13
92	Harris, Marques	LB	6-1	231	9/20/81	2	Southern Utah State	Grand Junction, Colo.	FA-'05	11/0
42	Hart, Clinton	S	6-0	205	7/20/77	4	Central Florida C.C.	Bushnell, Fla.	W(Phil)-'04	16/5
83	Jackson, Vincent	WR	6-5	241	1/14/83	2	Northern Colorado	Colorado Springs, Colo.	D2-'05	8/0
23	Jammer, Quentin	CB	6-0	204	6/19/79	5	Texas	Angleton, Texas	D1-'02	16/16
75	Jordan, Leander	T	6-4	320	9/15/77	7	Indiana (Pa.)	Pittsburgh, Pa.	UFA(Jax)-'04	13/9
27	Jue, Bhawoh	FS	6-0	200	5/24/79	6	Penn State	Chantilly, Va.	UFA(GB)-'05	14/14
10	Kaeding, Nate	K	6-0	187	3/26/82	3	Iowa	Coralville, Iowa	D3a-'04	16/0
48	Kiel, Terrence	SS	5-11	207	11/24/80	4	Texas A&M	Lufkin, Texas	D2b-'03	12/12
89	Krause, Ryan	TE	6-3	256	6/16/81	3	Nebraska-Omaha	Omaha, Neb.	D6-'04	3/0
71	Lekkerkerker, Cory	T	6-7	323	7/25/81	2	California-Davis	Chino, Calif.	FA-'05	0*
24	Lott, Andre	S	5-10	197	5/31/79	4	Tennessee	Memphis, Tenn.	FA-'06	0*
49 t-	Manumaleuna, Brandon	TE	6-2	288	1/4/80	6	Arizona	Torrance, Calif.	T(StL)-'06	14/14*
87	McCardell, Keenan	WR	6-1	191	1/6/70	15	Nevada-Las Vegas	Houston, Texas	T(TB)-'04	16/16
20	McCree, Marlon	S	5-11	202	3/17/77	6	Kentucky	Daytona Beach, Fla.	UFA(Car)-'06	16/15*
56	Merriman, Shawne	LB	6-4	272	5/25/84	2	Maryland	Upper Marlboro, Md.	D1a-'05	15/10
31	Milligan, Hanik	S	6-3	200	11/3/79	4	Houston	Coconut Creek, Fla.	D6-'03	16/0
63	Mruczkowski, Scott	C	6-5	318	4/5/82	2	Bowling Green	Garfield Heights, Ohio	D7-'05	6/0
41	Neal, Lorenzo	FB	5-11	255	12/27/70	14	Fresno State	Hanford, Calif.	UFA(Cin)-'03	16/15
72	Oben, Roman	T	6-4	305	10/9/72	11	Louisville	Washington D.C.	T(TB)-'04	8/8
70	Olivea, Shane	T	6-4	312	10/7/81	3	Ohio State	Long Beach, N.Y.	D7B-'04	15/15
99	Olshansky, Igor	DE	6-6	309	5/3/82	3	Oregon	San Francisco, Calif.	D2-'04	14/12
81	Osgood, Kassim	WR	6-5	220	5/20/80	4	San Diego State	Salinas, Calif.	FA-'03	12/3
88	Parker, Eric	WR	6-0	180	4/14/79	5	Tennessee	Shorewood, Ill.	FA-'02	15/9
95	Phillips, Shaun	LB	6-3	262	5/13/81	3	Purdue	Willingboro, N.J.	D4-'04	15/3
34	Pinnock, Andrew	FB	5-10	250	3/12/80	4	South Carolina	Bloomfield, Conn.	D7-'03	12/0
28	Pippens, Jerrell	S	6-3	200	6/30/80	2	Nebraska	Philadelphia, Pa.	FA-'05	2/0
52	Polk, Carlos	LB	6-2	262	2/22/77	6	Nebraska	Rockford, Ill.	D4-'01	0*
17	Rivers, Philip	QB	6-5	228	12/8/81	3	North Carolina State	Athens, Ala.	T(NYG)-'04	2/0
98	Robinson, Derreck	DE	6-4	289	3/3/82	2	Iowa	Minneapolis, Minn.	FA-'05	2/0
5	Scifres, Mike	P	6-2	236	10/8/80	4	Western Illinois	Destrehan, La.	D5-'03	16/0
84	Shea, Aaron	TE	6-4	250	12/5/76	7	Michigan	Ottawa, Ill.	UFA(Cle)-'06	12/4*
60	Sims, Wes	G	6-4	317	4/8/81	2	Oklahoma	Weatherford, Okla.	D6-'05	1/0
43	Sproles, Darren	RB/KR	5-6	181	6/20/83	2	Kansas State	Olathe, Kan.	D4-'05	15/0
21	Tomlinson, LaDainian	RB	5-10	221	6/23/79	6	Texas Christian	Waco, Texas	D1-'01	16/16
33	Turner, Michael	RB	5-10	237	2/13/82	3	Northern Illinois	Chicago, Ill.	D5b-'04	16/0
22	Walls, Raymond	CB	5-10	189	7/24/79	6	Southern Mississippi	Kentwood, La.	UFA(Ariz)-'06	7/0*
57	Wilhelm, Matt	LB	6-4	245	2/2/81	4	Ohio State	Elyria, Ohio	D3-'03	16/0
76	Williams, Jamal	DT	6-3	348	4/28/76	9	Oklahoma State	Washington, D.C.	D2(Supp)-'98	16/16
86 t-	Woods, Rashaun	WR	6-2	202	10/17/80	3	Oklahoma State	Oklahoma City, Okla.	T(SF)-'06	0*

* Croom last active with Arizona in '04; Feely inactive for 5 games with Miami and 10 games with San Diego; Gbaja-Biamila last active with Oakland in '04; Lekkerkerker did not play in 1 game; Lott last active with Washington in '04; Manumaleuna played 14 games with St. Louis in '05; McCree played 16 games for Carolina; Polk missed '05 season because of injury; Shea played 12 games with Cleveland; Walls played 7 games with Arizona; Woods inactive for 3 games with San Francisco.

t- Chargers traded for Manumaleuna (StL), Woods (SF).

Traded—CB Sammy Davis (16 games in '05) to San Francisco.

Players lost through free agency (7): QB Drew Brees (NO; 16 games in '05); WR Reche Caldwell (NE; 16); CB Jamar Fletcher (Det; 14); C/G Bob Hallen (Cle; 9); LB Ben Leber (Minn; 9); TE Justin Peelle (Mia; 16); DE DeQuincy Scott (Minn; 16).

Also played with Chargers in '05—DE Dave Ball (2 games), G Toniu Fonoti (2).

2006 FIRST-YEAR ROSTER

Name	Pos.	Ht.	Wt.	Birthdate	College	Hometown	How Acq.
Archer, Phil (1)	LB	6-2	245	4/22/81	Western Illinois	St. Paul, Minn.	FA
Camarillo, Greg (1)	WR	6-1	190	4/18/82	Stanford	Menlo Park, Calif.	FA-'05
Clary, Jeromey	T	6-6	306	11/5/83	Kansas State	Mansfield, Texas	D6a
Coffey, Sean	WR	6-4	216	7/12/83	Missouri	East Cleveland, Ohio	FA
Cromartie, Antonio	CB	6-2	203	4/15/84	Florida State	Tallahassee, Fla.	D1
Curry, Markus (1)	CB	5-11	181	4/7/81	Michigan	Detroit, Mich.	FA-'05
Dobbins, Tim	LB	6-1	246	10/10/82	Iowa State	Nashville, Tenn.	D5
Elliott, Brett	QB	6-3	210	6/11/82	Linfield	Lake Oswego, Ore.	FA
Evans, Jonathan (1)	RB	6-1	245	10/10/81	Baylor	Duncanville, Texas	FA
Farmer, Derek (1)	RB	5-11	205	10/24/82	Stephen F. Austin	Tyler, Texas	FA
Floyd, Malcom (1)	WR	6-5	225	9/8/81	Wyoming	Sacramento, Calif.	FA-'04
Gordon, Cletis	CB	6-1	197	7/17/82	Jackson State	Amite, La.	FA
Gregory, Steve	CB	5-11	185	1/8/83	Syracuse	Staten Island, N.Y.	FA
Griffeth, Kelly	TE	6-5	298	4/11/82	Fort Hays State	Jewell, Kan.	FA
Gross, Tyronne	RB	5-9	213	5/14/83	Eastern Oregon	Stockton, Calif.	FA
Henry, Keron (1)	WR	6-2	218	8/20/82	Connecticut	Brooklyn, N.Y.	FA
Johnson, Ben (1)	T	6-6	329	4/7/80	Wisconsin	Brussels, Wis.	FA-'05
Martin, Jimmy	C/G	6-5	306	10/19/82	Virginia Tech	Chantilly, Va.	D7b
Massey, Patrick	DE	6-8	290	8/23/82	Michigan	Cleveland, Ohio	FA
McKinney, Brandon	DT	6-2	324	8/24/83	Michigan State	Dayton, Ohio	FA
McNeill, Marcus	T	6-7	336	11/16/83	Auburn	Decatur, Ga.	D2
Meeuwsen, Mitch	CB	6-3	210	4/20/82	Oregon State	Forest Grove, Ore.	FA
Mihlhauser, Nick	C	6-3	291	7/6/84	Washington State	Arroyo Grande, Calif.	FA
Mims, Anthony	CB	6-0	194	7/27/83	West Virginia	Los Angeles, Calif.	FA
Murphy, Jason	G	6-2	304	8/7/82	Virginia Tech	Baltimore, Md.	FA
Ortiz, Robert	WR	6-1	188	5/30/83	San Diego State	San Diego, Calif.	FA
Page, Chase	T	6-5	296	5/20/83	North Carolina	Summerville, S.C.	D7a
Perkins, Ray (1)	RB	5-10	205	11/6/82	Southeastern Louisiana	Ft. Lauderdale, Fla.	FA-'05
Pollard, Jonathan (1)	LB	6-1	255	11/19/81	Oregon State	Las Vegas, Nev.	FA
Simmons, Mark	WR	5-10	187	1/16/84	Kansas	DeSoto, Texas	FA
Smith, Alvin	DT	6-2	307	6/16/82	Oregon State	Atlanta, Ga.	FA
Smith, Kurt	K	6-0	182	1/9/83	Virginia	Chattanooga, Tenn.	D6b
Sumlin, Bryson	RB	5-11	201	12/3/82	Fresno State	Bakersfield, Calif.	FA
Whitehurst, Charlie	QB	6-4	227	8/6/82	Clemson	Alpharetta, Ga.	D3
Willis, Shawn	FB	6-1	267	1/28/83	Oklahoma State	Flatonia, Texas	FA

The term NFL Rookie is defined as a player who is in his first season of professional football and has not been on the roster of another professional football team for any regular-season or postseason games. A Rookie is designated by an "R" on NFL rosters. Players who have been active in another professional football league or players who have NFL experience, including either preseason training camp or being on an Active List or Inactive List, or on Reserve/Injured or Reserve/Physically Unable to Perform for fewer than six regular-season games, are termed NFL First-Year Players. An NFL First-Year Player is designated by a "1" on NFL rosters. Thereafter, a player is credited with an additional year of experience for each season in which he accumulates six games on the Active List or Inactive List, or on Reserve/Injured or Reserve/Physically Unable to Perform.

Log on to www.chargers.com for an up-to-date roster.

COACHING STAFF
Head Coach,
Marty Schottenheimer
Pro Career: Marty Schottenheimer is entering his fifth season as the head coach of the San Diego Chargers. He was named the NFL Coach of the Year by the *Associated Press* in 2004 after leading the Chargers to a 12-4 record and their first AFC West title since 1994. In 19 full seasons as a head coach in the NFL, Schottenheimer has led his teams to 14 winning seasons. He is tied for seventh on the NFL's all-time list with 186 regular-season wins. Schottenheimer is 33-32, including playoffs, in four seasons as head coach of the Chargers. He spent 2001 as the Washington Redskins head coach and director of football operations. In his 10 years as head coach of the Kansas City Chiefs (1989-1998), he had a record of 104-65-1 and advanced to the playoffs seven times. The Cleveland Browns went to the playoffs all four full seasons (1985-88) he was the head coach. In 1986, Schottenheimer was the consensus AFC coach of the year. He coached with the Portland Storm (WFL) in 1974, New York Giants (1975-77), and Detroit Lions (1978-79), and Cleveland Browns (1980-84). In 1984, he took over as the Browns' head coach midway through the season. Played linebacker for Buffalo (1965-68) and Boston Patriots (1969-1970). Career record: 191-136-1.
Background: Schottenheimer was an All-America linebacker at Pittsburgh (1962-64). After leaving the Chiefs in 1998, he joined ESPN as a pro football analyst.
Personal: Born September 23, 1943 in Canonsburg, Pa. Marty and his wife Patricia have one daughter, Kristen, one son, Brian, who is the offensive coordinator for the New York Jets, and four grandchildern, Brandon, Catherine, Sutton, and Savannah.

ASSISTANT COACHES
Cam Cameron, offensive coordinator; born February 6, 1961, Chapel Hill, N.C. Quarterback Indiana 1980-83. No pro playing experience. College coach: Michigan 1984-1993, Indiana 1997-2001 (head coach). Pro coach: Washington Redskins 1994-96, joined Chargers in 2002.
Rob Chudzinski, tight ends; born May 12, 1968, Toledo, Ohio. Tight end Miami 1986-1990. No pro playing experience. College coach: Miami 1994-2003. Pro Coach: Cleveland Browns 2004, joined Chargers in 2005.
Steve Crosby, special teams; born July 3, 1950, Great Bend, Kan. Running back Fort Hayes State 1970-73. Pro running back New York Giants 1974-76. College coach: Vanderbilt 1998-2001. Pro coach: Miami Dolphins 1979-1982, Atlanta Falcons 1983-84, 1986-89, Cleveland Browns 1985, 1991-95, New England Patriots

1990, joined Chargers in 2002.
John (Jack) Henry, offensive line; born March 14, 1946, Houston, Pa. Linebacker Penn State 1964-65, guard Indiana (Pa.) 1967-68. No pro playing experience. College coach: West Virginia 1970, 1978-79, Edinboro 1973, Louisville 1974, Millersville 1975-76, Southern Illinois 1977, Appalachian State 1980, Wake Forest 1981-85, Indiana (Pa.) 1986-89, Pittsburgh 1993-95. Pro coach: Pittsburgh Steelers 1990-91, San Diego Chargers 1996, Detroit Lions 1997-99, New Orleans Saints 2000-05, re-joined Chargers in 2006.
Hal Hunter, asst. offensive line; born July 8, 1959, Canonsburg, Pa. Linebacker Northwestern 1978. College coach: William & Mary 1982, Pittsburgh 1983-84, Columbia 1985, Indiana (Pa.) 1986, Akron 1987-1990, Vanderbilt 1991-94, Louisiana State 1995-99, Indiana 2000-01, North Carolina 2002-05. Pro coach: Joined Chargers in 2006.
James Lofton, wide receivers; born July 5, 1956, Fort Ord, Calif. Wide receiver Stanford 1975-77. Pro wide receiver Green Bay Packers 1978-1986, Los Angeles Raiders 1987-88, Buffalo Bills 1989-1992, Los Angeles Rams 1993, Philadelphia Eagles 1993. Pro coach: Joined Chargers in 2002.
Greg Manusky, linebackers; born August 12, 1966, Wilkes-Barre, Pa. Linebacker Colgate 1983-87. Pro linebacker Washington Redskins 1988-1990, Minnesota Vikings 1991-93, Kansas City Chiefs 1994-99. Pro coach: Washington Redskins 2001, joined Chargers in 2002.
Wayne Nunnely, defensive line; born March 29, 1952, Los Angeles. Fullback Nevada-Las Vegas 1972-75. No pro playing experience. College coach: Nevada-Las Vegas 1976, 1982-89 (head coach 1986-89), Cal Poly-Pomona 1977-78, Cal State-Fullerton 1979, Pacific 1980-81, Southern California 1991-92, UCLA 1993-94. Pro coach: New Orleans Saints 1995-96, joined Chargers in 1997.
John Pagano, asst. linebackers/quality control; born March 30, 1967, Boulder, Colo. Linebacker Mesa State College 1985-88. No pro playing experience. College coach: Mesa State College 1989, Nevada-Las Vegas 1990-91, Louisiana Tech 1994, Mississippi 1995. Pro coach: New Orleans Saints 1996-97, Indianapolis Colts 1998-2001, joined Chargers in 2002.
Wade Phillips, defensive coordinator; born June 21, 1947, Orange, Texas. Linebacker Houston 1966-68. No pro playing experience. College coach: Houston 1969, Oklahoma State 1973-74, Kansas 1975. Pro coach: Houston 1976-1980, New Orleans 1981-85 (head coach of last four games in 1985), Philadelphia 1986-88, Denver 1989-1994 (head coach 1993-94), Buffalo 1995-2000 (head coach 1998-2000), Atlanta 2002-03

(head coach last three games of 2003), joined Chargers in 2004.
John Ramsdell, quarterbacks; born August 16, 1954, Lafayette, Ind. Running back Springfield (Mass.) College 1972-75. No pro playing experience. College coach: San Francisco State 1976-77, Long Beach State 1978, Pacific 1979-1982, Oregon 1983-1994. Pro coach: St. Louis Rams 1995-2005, joined Chargers in 2006.
Dave Redding, strength and conditioning; born June 14, 1952, North Platte, Neb. Defensive end Nebraska 1972-75. No pro playing experience. College coach: Nebraska 1976, Washington State 1977, Missouri 1978-1981. Pro coach: Cleveland Browns 1982-88, Kansas City Chiefs 1989-1997, Washington Redskins 2001, joined Chargers in 2002.
Matt Schiotz, asst. strength and conditioning; born June 8, 1971, Menomonie, Wis. Attended Wisconsin-La Crosse. No college or pro playing experience. College coach: Kansas 1995-96, Southern California 1998-2000. Pro coach: Kansas City Chiefs 1997, Washington Redskins 2001, joined Chargers in 2002.
Clarence Shelmon, running backs; born September 17, 1952, Bossier City, La. Running back Houston 1971-75. No pro playing experience. College coach: Army 1978-1980, Indiana 1981-83, Arizona 1984-86, Southern California 1987-1990. Pro coach: Los Angeles Rams 1991, Seattle Seahawks 1992-97, Dallas Cowboys 1998-2001, joined Chargers in 2002.
Brian Stewart, secondary; born December 4, 1964, San Diego. Cornerback Northern Arizona 1983, 1986-87, Santa Monica City College 1984-85. No pro playing experience. College coach: Cal Poly-San Luis Obispo 1993-94, Northern Arizona 1995, Missouri 1996, 1999-2000, San Jose State 1997-98, Syracuse 2001. Pro coach: Houston 2002-03, joined Chargers in 2004.
John Wuehrmann, coaching administrator; born January 21, 1956, Chicago. Attended Wyoming. No college or pro playing experience. Pro coach: Joined Chargers in 2003.

American Football Conference
South Division
Team Colors: Navy, Titans Blue, Red, Silver
460 Great Circle Road
Nashville, Tennessee 37228
Telephone: (615) 565-4000

2006 SCHEDULE
PRESEASON
Aug. 12 **New Orleans** 7:00
Aug. 19 at Denver.............................7:00
Aug. 26 at San Francisco.................7:00
Sept. 1 **Green Bay** 3:00

REGULAR SEASON
Sept. 10 **N.Y. Jets** 12:00
Sept. 26 Atlanta................................7:00
Sept. 24 at Miami..............................1:00
Oct. 1 **Dallas** 12:00
Oct. 8 at Indianapolis 1:00
Oct. 15 at Washington 1:00
Oct. 22 Open Date
Oct. 29 **Houston** 12:00
Nov. 5 at Jacksonville...................1:00
Nov. 12 **Baltimore**........................12:00
Nov. 19 at Philadelphia...................1:00
Nov. 26 **N.Y. Giants** 12:00
Dec. 3 **Indianapolis**....................12:00
Dec. 10 at Houston 12:00
Dec. 17 **Jacksonville**....................12:00
Dec. 24 at Buffalo 1:00
Dec. 31 **New England** 12:00

Stadium: LP Field
(opened in 1999)
•**Capacity:** 68,809
One Titans Way
Nashville, Tennessee 37213
Playing Surface: Natural Grass
Training Camp: Baptist Sports Park
460 Great Circle Road
Nashville, Tennessee
37228

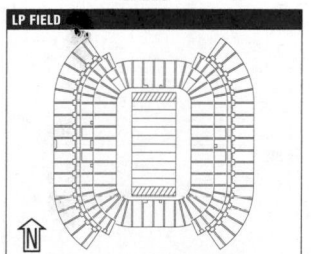

CLUB OFFICIALS
Owner/Chairman of the Board/CEO/
President: K.S. (Bud) Adams, Jr.
Executive V.P./General Manager and
Director Of Football Operations:
Floyd Reese
Executive V.P. of Administration/Facilities:
Don MacLachlan
Executive V.P./General Counsel:
Steve Underwood
Asst. General Counsel: Elza Bullock
Vice President/Finance:
Robert McBurnett
Vice President/Community Affairs:
Bob Hyde
Director of Player Personnel:
Rich Snead
Director of College Scouting:
Mike Ackerley
Director of Sales and Operations:
Stuart Spears
Asst. Director of Sales and Operations:
Brent Akers
Director of Broadcasting: Mike Keith
Director of Marketing: Ralph Ockenfels
Controller: Jenneen Kaufman
Director of Information Systems:
Russ Hudson
Director of Internet
Operations/Publications: Gary Glenn
Director of Media Relations:
Robbie Bohren
Asst. Director of Media Relations:
Dwight Spradlin
Director of Security: Steve Berk
Director of Ticket Operations:
Marty Collins
Director of Pro Personnel: Al Smith
Director of Player Development:
Marcus Robertson
Director of Cheerleading: Stacie Kinder
Director of Suite and Club Services:
Bill Wainwright
Head Athletic Trainer: Brad Brown
Assistant Athletic Trainers:
Don Moseley, Geoff Kaplan
Equipment Manager: Paul Noska
Video Director: Anthony Pastrana
General Manager of Coliseum:
Walter Overton

COACHING HISTORY
Houston 1960-1996
(346-371-6)
Records include postseason games
1960-61 Lou Rymkus* 12-7-1
1961 Wally Lemm 10-0-0
1962-63 Frank (Pop) Ivy 17-12-0
1964 Sammy Baugh................4-10-0
1965 Hugh Taylor.................4-10-0
1966-1970 Wally Lemm 28-40-4
1971 Ed Hughes.......................4-9-1
1972-73 Bill Peterson** 1-18-0
1973-74 Sid Gillman....................8-15-0
1975-1980 O.A. (Bum) Phillips 59-38-0
1981-83 Ed Biles*** 8-23-0
1983 Chuck Studley 2-8-0
1984-85 Hugh Campbell**** 8-22-0
1985-89 Jerry Glanville..............35-35-0
1990-94 Jack Pardee#.............44-35-0
1994-2005 Jeff Fisher..................102-89-0
* Released after five games in 1961
** Released after five games in 1973
*** Resigned after six games in 1983
**** Released after 14 games in 1985
# Released after 10 games in 1994

ATTENDANCE
Home 533,721   Away 493,009
Total 1,026,730
Single-game home record,
68,809, many times (last: 12/28/03)
Single-season home record,
537,496 (2001)

2006 DRAFT CHOICES
Round	Name	Pos.	College
1	Vince Young	QB	Texas
2	LenDale White	RB	So. California
4	Calvin Lowry	DB	Penn State
	Stephen Tulloch	LB	North Carolina St.
5	Terna Nande	LB	Miami (Ohio)
	Jesse Mahelona	DT	Tennessee
6	Jonathan Orr	WR	Wisconsin
7	Cortland Ferguson	DB	Samford
	Spencer Toone	LB	Utah
	Quinton Ganther	RB	Utah

2005 TEAM RECORD
PRESEASON (1-3)

Date	Result	Opponent
8/12	L 17-20	Tampa Bay
8/19	W 24-21	at Atlanta
8/26	L 13-16	at San Francisco
9/1	L 17-21	Green Bay

REGULAR SEASON (4-12)

Date	Result	Opponent	Att.
9/11	L 7-34	at Pittsburgh	62,931
9/18	W 25-10	Baltimore	69,149
9/25	L 27-31	at St. Louis	65,835
10/2	L 10-31	Indianapolis	69,149
10/9	W 34-20	at Houston	70,430
10/16	L 23-31	Cincinnati	69,149
10/23	L 10-20	at Arizona	39,482
10/30	L 25-34	Oakland	69,149
11/6	L 14-20	at Cleveland	72,594
11/20	L 28-31	Jacksonville	69,149
11/27	W 33-22	San Francisco	69,149
12/4	L 3-35	at Indianapolis	57,228
12/11	W 13-10	Houston	69,149
12/18	L 24-28	Seattle	69,149
12/24	L 10-24	at Miami	72,001
1/1	L 13-40	at Jacksonville	65,485

SCORE BY PERIODS

Titans	50	88	83	78	0 —	299
Opponents	79	132	108	102	0 —	421

2005 TEAM STATISTICS

	Titans	Opp.
Total First Downs	279	294
Rushing	72	89
Passing	191	180
Penalty	16	25
3rd Down: Made/Att	75/218	71/200
3rd Down Pct.	34.4	35.5
4th Down: Made/Att	9/31	7/11
4th Down Pct.	29.0	63.6
Possession Avg.	31:13	28:47
Total Net Yards	5,122	5,110
Avg. Per Game	320.1	319.4
Total Plays	1,022	960
Avg. Per Play	5.0	5.3
Net Yards Rushing	1,525	1,894
Avg. Per Game	95.3	118.4
Total Rushes	397	449
Net Yards Passing	3,597	3,216
Avg. Per Game	224.8	201.0
Sacked/Yards Lost	31/200	41/246
Gross Yards	3,797	3,462
Att./Completions	594/358	470/296
Completion Pct.	60.3	63.0
Had Intercepted	14	9
Punts/Average	78/43.2	85/44.1
Net Punting Avg.	78/37.8	85/37.5
Penalties/Yards	125/1002	95/718
Fumbles/Ball Lost	27/12	20/11
Touchdowns	33	51
Rushing	8	12
Passing	20	33
Returns	5	6

2005 INDIVIDUAL STATISTICS

PASSING

PASSING	Att.	Comp.	Yds.	Pct.	TD	Int.	Tkld.	Rate
McNair	476	292	3,161	61.3	16	11	20/134	82.4
Volek	88	50	474	56.8	4	2	9/45	77.6
Mauck	27	15	136	55.6	0	1	1/8	53.9
Hentrich	2	1	26	50.0	0	0	0/0	95.8
Bennett	1	0	0	0.0	0	0	0/0	39.6
P. Jones	0	0	0	—	0	0	1/13	—
Titans	594	358	3,797	60.3	20	14	31/200	80.3
Opponents	470	296	3,462	63.0	33	9	41/246	100.7

SCORING

SCORING	TD R	TD P	TD Rt	PAT	FG	Saf	PTS
Bironas	0	0	0	30/32	23/29	0	99
Brown	5	2	0	0/0	0/0	0	42
Bennett	0	4	0	0/0	0/0	0	24
Troupe	0	4	0	0/0	0/0	0	24
B. Jones	0	2	0	0/0	0/0	0	12
Kinney	0	2	0	0/0	0/0	0	12
Odom	0	0	2	0/0	0/0	0	12
Payton	2	0	0	0/0	0/0	0	12
Scaife	0	2	0	0/0	0/0	0	12
R. Williams	0	2	0	0/0	0/0	0	12
Fleming	0	1	0	0/0	0/0	0	6
Hill	0	0	1	0/0	0/0	0	6
P. Jones	0	0	1	0/0	0/0	0	6
Kassell	0	0	1	0/0	0/0	0	6
McNair	1	0	0	0/0	0/0	0	6
Roby	0	1	0	0/0	0/0	0	6
Reynolds	0	0	0	0/0	0/0	1	2
Titans	8	20	5	30/32	23/29	1	299
Opponents	12	33	6	48/49	21/27	0	421

2-Pt. Conversions: Titans 0-1, Opponents 2-2.

RUSHING

RUSHING	No.	Yds	Avg	LG	TD
Brown	224	851	3.8	38t	5
Henry	88	335	3.8	29	0
McNair	32	139	4.3	19	1
Payton	33	105	3.2	15	2
Mauck	7	39	5.6	12	0
Nash	6	32	5.3	8	0
Roby	2	16	8.0	11	0
Bennett	1	3	3.0	3	0
Volek	1	3	3.0	3	0
B. Jones	1	1	1.0	1	0
Wade	1	1	1.0	1	0
Hentrich	1	0	0.0	0	0
Titans	397	1,525	3.8	38t	8
Opponents	449	1,894	4.2	52	12

RECEIVING

RECEIVING	No.	Yds	Avg	LG	TD
Bennett	58	738	12.7	55t	4
Kinney	55	543	9.9	27	2
Troupe	55	530	9.6	35	4
Scaife	37	273	7.4	19	2
Brown	25	327	13.1	57	2
B. Jones	23	299	13.0	38t	2
Calico	22	191	8.7	18	0
R. Williams	21	299	14.2	50t	2
Roby	21	289	13.8	32	1
Henry	13	117	9.0	42	0
Fleming	10	69	6.9	18	1
Payton	6	30	5.0	9	0
Wade	4	40	10.0	15	0
Nash	3	14	4.7	7	0
Guenther	2	13	6.5	8	0
Nickey	1	26	26.0	26	0
Small	1	6	6.0	6	0
Roos	1	-7	-7.0	-7	0
Titans	358	3,797	10.6	57	20
Opponents	296	3,462	11.7	63t	33

INTERCEPTIONS

INTERCEPTIONS	No.	Yds	Avg	LG	TD
Hill	3	88	29.3	52t	1
Bulluck	2	16	8.0	16	0
Kassell	1	21	21.0	21t	1
Woolfolk	1	3	3.0	3	0
Ta. Williams	1	1	1.0	1	0
Thompson	1	0	0.0	0	0
Titans	9	129	14.3	52t	2
Opponents	14	293	20.9	85t	4

PUNTING

PUNTING	No.	Yds.	Avg.	In 20	LG
Hentrich	78	3,371	43.2	21	59
Titans	78	3,371	43.2	21	59
Opponents	85	3,746	44.1	16	74

PUNT RETURNS

PUNT RETURNS	Ret	FC	Yds	Avg	LG	TD
P. Jones	29	8	272	9.4	52t	1
Thurman	9	5	31	3.4	11	0
B. Jones	5	0	75	15.0	32	0
Thompson	1	0	31	31.0	31	0
Ta. Williams	1	0	9	9.0	9	0
Titans	45	13	418	9.3	52t	1
Opponents	32	20	144	4.5	15	0

KICKOFF RETURNS

KICKOFF RETURNS	No.	Yds	Avg	LG	TD
P. Jones	43	1127	26.2	85	0
Roby	22	495	22.5	59	0
Thurman	2	42	21.0	25	0
Payton	2	24	12.0	24	0
Fleming	1	9	9.0	9	0
Titans	70	1,697	24.2	85	0
Opponents	57	1,290	22.6	50	0

FIELD GOALS

FIELD GOALS	1-19	20-29	30-39	40-49	50+
Bironas	0/0	10/10	6/7	5/7	2/5
Titans	0/0	10/10	6/7	5/7	2/5
Opponents	1/1	6/6	9/14	5/5	0/1

SACKS

SACKS	No.
Vanden Bosch	12.5
LaBoy	6.5
Bulluck	5.0
Long	3.5
Haynesworth	3.0
Starks	3.0
Sirmon	2.5
Odom	2.0
Schobel	1.0
Thompson	1.0
Clauss	0.5
Waddell	0.5
Titans	41.0
Opponents	31.0

RECORD HOLDERS
INDIVIDUAL RECORDS—CAREER

Category	Name	Performance
Rushing (Yds.)	Eddie George, 1996-2003	10,009
Passing (Yds.)	Warren Moon, 1984-1993	33,685
Passing (TDs)	Warren Moon, 1984-1993	196
Receiving (No.)	Ernest Givins, 1986-1994	542
Receiving (Yds.)	Ernest Givins, 1986-1994	7,935
Interceptions	Jim Norton, 1960-68	45
Punting (Avg.)	Greg Montgomery, 1988-1993	43.6
Punt Return (Avg.)	Billy Johnson, 1974-1980	13.2
Kickoff Return (Avg.)	Bobby Jancik, 1962-67	26.5
Field Goals	Al Del Greco, 1991-2000	246
Touchdowns (Tot.)	Eddie George, 1996-2003	74
Points	Al Del Greco, 1991-2000	1,060

INDIVIDUAL RECORDS—SINGLE SEASON

Category	Name	Performance
Rushing (Yds.)	Earl Campbell, 1980	1,934
Passing (Yds.)	Warren Moon, 1991	4,690
Passing (TDs)	George Blanda, 1961	36
Receiving (No.)	Charley Hennigan, 1964	101
Receiving (Yds.)	Charley Hennigan, 1961	1,746
Interceptions	Fred Glick, 1963	12
	Mike Reinfeldt, 1979	12
Punting (Avg.)	Craig Hentrich, 1998	47.2
Punt Return (Avg.)	Billy Johnson, 1977	15.4
Kickoff Return (Avg.)	Ken Hall, 1960	31.3
Field Goals	Al Del Greco, 1998	36
Touchdowns (Tot.)	Earl Campbell, 1979	19
Points	Al Del Greco, 1998	136

INDIVIDUAL RECORDS—SINGLE GAME

Category	Name	Performance
Rushing (Yds.)	Billy Cannon, 12-10-61	216
	Eddie George, 8-31-97	216
Passing (Yds.)	Warren Moon, 12-16-90	527
Passing (TDs)	George Blanda, 11-19-61	*7
Receiving (No.)	Charley Hennigan, 10-13-61	13
	Haywood Jeffires, 10-13-91	13
	Drew Bennett, 12-19-04	13
Receiving (Yds.)	Charley Hennigan, 10-13-61	272
Interceptions	Many times	3
	Last time by Samari Rolle, 12-26-99	
Field Goals	Roy Gerela, 9-28-69	5
	Al Del Greco, 12-3-00	5
Touchdowns (Tot.)	Billy Cannon, 12-10-61	5
Points	Billy Cannon, 12-10-61	30

*NFL Record

2006 VETERAN ROSTER

No.	Name	Pos.	Ht.	Wt.	Birthdate	NFL Exp.	College	Hometown	How Acq.	'05 Games/ Starts
54	Amano, Eugene	C	6-3	310	3/1/82	3	Southeast Missouri State	San Diego, Calif.	D7-'04	16/0
58	Amato, Ken	LB/LS	6-2	245	5/18/77	4	Montana State	Miami, Fla.	FA-'03	7/0
60	Bell, Jacob	G/T	6-4	295	3/2/81	3	Miami (Ohio)	Cleveland, Ohio	D5-'04	9/1
83	Bennett, Drew	WR	6-5	206	8/26/78	6	UCLA	Orinda, Calif.	FA-'01	13/10
2	Bironas, Rob	K	6-0	205	1/29/78	2	Georgia Southern	Louisville, Ky.	FA-'05	16/0
29	Brown, Chris	RB	6-3	220	4/17/81	4	Colorado	Naperville, Ill.	D3-'03	15/14
53	Bulluck, Keith	LB	6-3	235	4/4/77	7	Syracuse	New City, N.Y.	D1-'00	16/16
87	Calico, Tyrone	WR	6-4	220	11/9/80	4	Middle Tenn. State	Memphis, Tenn.	D2-'03	12/6
96	Clauss, Jared	DT	6-4	290	4/7/81	3	Iowa	W. Des Moines, Iowa	D7-'04	15/1
44	Fleming, Troy	FB	6-0	245	10/1/80	3	Tennessee	Franklin, Tenn.	D6-'04	13/2
22	Fuller, Vincent	S	6-1	190	8/3/82	2	Virginia Tech	Baltimore, Md.	D4a-'05	2/0
30	Gardner, Rich	CB	5-10	194	2/1/81	3	Penn State	Chicago, Ill.	D3-'04	13/0
89	Givens, David	WR	6-0	215	8/16/80	5	Notre Dame	Humble, Texas	UFA(NE)-'06	13/10*
85	Guenther, Gregg	TE	6-8	255	1/29/82	2	Southern California	Van Nuys, Calif.	FA-'05	5/0
92	Haynesworth, Albert	DT	6-6	320	6/17/81	5	Tennessee	Hartsville, S.C.	D1-'02	14/14
20	Henry, Travis	RB	5-9	215	10/29/78	6	Tennessee	Frostproof, Fla.	T(Buff)-'05	10/1
15	Hentrich, Craig	P/K	6-3	213	5/18/71	13	Notre Dame	Alton, Ill.	UFA(GB)-'98	16/0
21	Hill, Reynaldo	CB	5-11	185	8/28/82	2	Florida	Ft. Lauderdale, Fla.	D7-'05	15/10
24	Hope, Chris	S	5-11	206	9/20/80	5	Florida State	Rock Hill, S.C.	UFA(Pitt)-'06	16/16*
81	Jones, Brandon	WR	6-1	212	10/6/82	2	Oklahoma	Texarkana, Texas	D3b-'05	10/8
32	Jones, Pacman	CB	5-10	185	9/30/83	2	West Virginia	Atlanta, Ga.	D1-'05	15/13
88	Kinney, Erron	TE	6-6	275	7/28/77	7	Florida	Ashland, Va.	D3a-'00	14/14
91	LaBoy, Travis	DE	6-3	260	8/10/81	3	Hawaii	San Rafael, Calif.	D2-'04	15/7
99	Long, Rien	DT	6-6	300	8/7/81	4	Washington State	Anacortes, Wash.	D4-'03	16/1
70	Loper, Daniel	T	6-6	320	1/15/82	2	Texas Tech	Houston, Texas	D5b-'05	0*
8	Mauck, Matt	QB	6-2	220	2/12/79	2	Louisiana State	Evansville, Ind.	FA-'05	2/1
68	Mawae, Kevin	C	6-4	289	1/23/71	13	Louisiana State	Savannah, Ga.	FA-'06	6/6*
9	McNair, Steve	QB	6-2	230	2/14/73	12	Alcorn State	Mt. Olive, Miss.	D1-'95	14/14
42	Nash, Damien	RB	5-10	220	4/14/82	2	Missouri	St. Louis, Mo.	D5a-'05	3/0
23	Nickey, Donnie	S	6-3	210	4/25/80	4	Ohio State	Plain City, Ohio	D5-'03	16/0
98	Odom, Antwan	DE	6-4	274	9/24/81	3	Alabama	Bayou La Batre, Ala.	D2-'04	16/9
75	Olson, Benji	G	6-4	320	6/5/75	9	Washington	Port Orchard, Wash.	D5-'98	16/16
33	Payton, Jarrett	RB	6-0	220	12/26/80	2	Miami	Arlington, Ill.	FA-'05	13/0
69	Piller, Zach	G	6-5	315	5/2/76	8	Florida	Tallahassee, Fla.	D3-'99	16/16
51	Reynolds, Robert	LB	6-3	247	5/20/81	3	Ohio State	Bowling Green, Ky.	D5-'04	15/1
82	Roby, Courtney	WR	6-0	189	1/10/83	2	Indiana	Indianapolis, Ind.	D3a-'05	13/6
71	Roos, Michael	T	6-7	315	10/5/82	2	Eastern Washington	Vancouver, Wash.	D2-'05	16/16
40	Sandy, Justin	S	6-0	207	2/22/82	2	Northern Iowa	Sioux City, Iowa	FA-'04	2/1
80	Scaife, Bo	TE	6-3	249	1/6/81	2	Texas	Denver, Colo.	D6-'05	16/5
95	Schobel, Bo	DE	6-5	264	3/24/81	3	Texas Christian	Columbus, Texas	D4-'04	8/0
59	Sirmon, Peter	LB	6-2	237	2/18/77	7	Oregon	Walla Walla, Wash.	D4b-'00	14/13
56	Spencer, Cody	LB	6-2	245	6/1/81	3	North Texas	Port Lavaca, Texas	FA-'04	16/0
90	Starks, Randy	DT	6-3	312	12/14/83	2	Maryland	Waldorf, Md.	D3-'04	16/16
76	Stewart, David	T	6-7	318	8/28/82	2	Mississippi State	Moulton, Ala.	D4b-'05	0*
16	Thomas, Sloan	WR	6-1	203	12/22/81	2	Texas	Houston, Texas	FA-'05	1/0
28	Thompson, Lamont	S	6-1	220	7/30/78	5	Washington State	Richmond, Calif.	FA-'03	16/16
50	Thornton, David	LB	6-2	225	11/1/78	5	North Carolina	Goldsboro, N.C.	UFA(Ind)-'06	16/16*
84	Troupe, Ben	TE	6-4	270	9/1/82	3	Florida	Augusta, Ga.	D2-'04	15/11
93	Vanden Bosch, Kyle	DE	6-4	278	11/17/78	6	Nebraska	Larchwood, Iowa	UFA(Ariz)-'05	16/16
7	Volek, Billy	QB	6-2	214	4/28/76	7	Fresno State	Fresno, Calif.	FA-'00	6/1
36	Waddell, Michael	CB	5-10	180	1/9/81	3	North Carolina	Ellerbe, N.C.	D4-'04	16/1
19	Wade, Bobby	WR	5-10	186	2/25/81	4	Arizona	Phoenix, Ariz.	W(Chi)-'05	14/1*
86	Williams, Roydell	WR	6-0	187	3/14/81	2	Tulane	New Orleans, La.	D4c-'05	10/2
26	Woolfolk, Andre	CB	6-2	197	1/26/80	4	Oklahoma	Denver, Colo.	D1-'03	13/7

* Givens played 13 games with New England in '05; Hope played 16 games with Pittsburgh; Loper did not play in 1 game; Mawae played 6 games with N.Y. Jets; Stewart inactive for 16 games; Thornton played 16 games with Indianapolis; Wade played 12 games with Chicago and 2 games with Tennessee.

Players lost through free agency (4): LB Rocky Boiman (Dall; 15 games in '05); C Justin Hartwig (Car; 16); LB Brad Kassell (NYJ; 16); S Tank Williams (Minn; 16).

Also played with Titans in '05—CB Tony Beckham (15 games), LS Jon Dorenbos (9), T Brad Hopkins (15), WR Andrae Thurman (5), T Todd Williams (1).

2006 FIRST-YEAR ROSTER

Name	Pos.	Ht.	Wt.	Birthdate	College	Hometown	How Acq.
Allred, Colin	LB	6-1	238	4/15/83	Baylor	Dallas, Texas	FA
Appel, Jaxson	S	5-10	198	4/21/82	Texas A&M	Friendswood, Texas	FA
Bryan, Copeland	DE	6-3	253	7/14/83	Arizona	San Jose, Calif.	FA
Conover, Sean	DE	6-5	262	7/31/84	Bucknell	Whitman, Mass.	FA
Dickens, Wayne	DT	6-1	296	8/20/83	Auburn	Lakeland, Fla.	FA
Douglas, Cody	G	6-4	312	11/25/83	Tennessee	LaMarque, Texas	FA
Erickson, Mike (1)	G/T	6-4	304	5/8/82	Nebraska	Omaha, Neb.	FA
Finnegan, Cortland	CB	5-10	188	2/2/84	Samford	Milton, Fla.	D7a
Ganther, Quinton	RB	5-9	214	7/15/84	Utah	Richmond, Calif.	D7c
Hall, Tramain	WR	5-10	190	12/14/81	North Carolina State	Deerfield Beach, Fla.	FA
Harris, Antoine (1)	CB	5-10	190	4/8/82	Louisville	Columbus, Ohio	FA
Herring, Chris	DT	6-0	311	12/20/82	Southern Arkansas	Batesville, Miss.	FA
Hill, Mario	WR	5-11	196	1/23/82	Mississippi	Meridian, Miss.	FA
Hodges, Cody	QB	6-0	207	11/20/82	Texas Tech	Hereford, Texas	FA
Holt, Cedric	CB	5-10	187	12/30/83	North Carolina	Wadesboro, N.C.	FA
Littlejohn, Jeff	DT	6-1	314	2/14/83	Middle Tennessee	Gaffney, S.C.	FA
Lowry, Calvin	S	5-11	200	2/13/83	Penn State	Fayetteville, N.C.	D4a
Mahelona, Jesse	DT	6-0	311	4/7/83	Tennessee	Kailua-Kona, Hawaii	D5b
Mattos, Grant (1)	WR	6-2	220	3/12/81	Southern California	Mountain View, Calif.	FA
McLemore, Daniel	CB	5-7	161	11/1/82	Oklahoma State	Duncanville, Texas	FA
Nande, Terna	LB	6-0	230	6/17/83	Miami (Ohio)	Grand Rapids, Mich.	D5a
Newberry, Jared (1)	LB	6-1	238	11/11/81	Stanford	Minneapolis, Minn.	FA
Olds, Rod	C	6-1	305	10/30/82	Jacksonville State	Panama City, Fla.	FA
Orr, Jonathan	WR	6-1	193	3/20/83	Wisconsin	Detroit, Mich.	D6
Osemwegie, Moses	LB	6-0	230	10/13/82	Vanderbilt	Nashville, Tenn.	FA
Petrowski, Jamie	TE	6-4	250	7/12/82	Indiana State	Terre Haute, Ind.	FA
Randall, Marcus (1)	LB	6-2	219	3/14/82	Louisiana State	Baton Rouge, La.	FA
Raymond, Keon	CB	5-9	190	11/27/82	Middle Tennessee	St. Louis, Mo.	FA
Reid, Lamont	RB	6-1	221	11/28/83	Western Carolina	Maiden, N.C.	FA
Rhoades, Brad	T	6-5	285	10/14/82	Montana	Bellingham, Wash.	FA
Roberts, Adam	DE	6-2	249	8/28/82	Cincinnati	Brooklyn, N.Y.	FA
Rodriguez, Joel (1)	C	6-3	289	6/27/82	Miami	Miami, Fla.	FA
Singletary, Wendell	T	6-6	300	6/24/83	Western Carolina	Whiteville, N.C.	FA
Small, O.J. (1)	WR	6-1	223	8/18/82	Florida	Jacksonville, Fla.	FA
Thompson, Tim	DE	6-3	250	8/4/81	Valdosta State	Sparta, Ga.	FA
Toone, Spencer	LB	6-2	240	8/25/80	Utah	Blackfoot, Idaho	D7b
Tulloch, Stephen	LB	5-11	235	1/1/85	North Carolina State	Miami, Fla.	D4b
Warford, Derrick	G	6-3	315	4/1/82	Alabama State	Macon, Ga.	FA
White, LenDale	RB	6-1	235	12/20/84	Southern California	Denver, Colo.	D2
White, Marcus (1)	DT	6-5	303	11/13/81	Murray State	Theodore, Ala.	FA
Young, Vince	QB	6-4	233	5/18/83	Texas	Houston, Texas	D1

The term NFL Rookie is defined as a player who is in his first season of professional football and has not been on the roster of another professional football team for any regular-season or postseason games. A Rookie is designated by an "R" on NFL rosters. Players who have been active in another professional football league or players who have NFL experience, including either preseason training camp or being on an Active List or Inactive List, or on Reserve/Injured or Reserve/Physically Unable to Perform for fewer than six regular-season games, are termed NFL First-Year Players. An NFL First-Year Player is designated by a "1" on NFL rosters. Thereafter, a player is credited with an additional year of experience for each season in which he accumulates six games on the Active List or Inactive List, or on Reserve/Injured or Reserve/Physically Unable to Perform.

Log on to www.titansonline.com for an up-to-date roster.

COACHING STAFF
Head Coach,
Jeff Fisher

Pro Career: Officially became the franchise's fifteenth head coach on January 5, 1995, after closing his first campaign with the Oilers as head coach/defensive coordinator. He replaced Jack Pardee on November 14, 1994, coaching the remaining six games as head coach. Fisher holds the franchise mark for wins with 102 over his 11-year coaching career and ranks fifth among NFL head coaches (Dungy, Reid, Cowher, and Shanahan) with 65 victories since 1999. Last year, he became the 34th coach in NFL history to reach the 100-win plateau. In 2004, he became the fourth youngest coach (46) since 1960 to reach 90 regular-season victories (John Madden, Don Shula, and Bill Cowher). Over the last seven seasons, Fisher has led the Titans to four playoff appearances, two AFC Championship Games, two division titles and a berth in Super Bowl XXXIV. In 2000, Fisher became only the fifth coach in NFL history to lead his team to consecutive 13-win seasons, joining Mike Holmgren, George Seifert, Marv Levy, and Mike Ditka. Fisher originally joined the Oilers in 1994 as the defensive coordinator, after serving as defensive backs coach for the San Francisco 49ers (1992-93). Prior to heading up the 49ers secondary, Fisher served as the defensive coordinator for the Los Angeles Rams (1991). He began his coaching career with the Philadelphia Eagles in 1986, where he handled defensive backs until becoming the NFL's youngest defensive coordinator in 1988. Drafted by Chicago in seventh round in 1981, he spent five seasons as a cornerback and kick returner for the Bears (1981-85). Assisted defensive coordinator Buddy Ryan in Bears' 1985 Super Bowl championship season after being placed on injured reserve with ankle injury. Career record: 102-89.

Background: Played at Southern California (1977-1980) for John Robinson in a star-studded defensive backfield that included Ronnie Lott, Dennis Smith, and Joey Browner. Member of the USC team that won the national championship in 1978. Also served as the Trojans' backup placekicker and was a Pac-10 All-Academic selection in 1980.

Personal: Born February 25, 1958, in Culver City, Calif. Jeff and his wife, Juli, have three children, sons Brandon and Trenton, and daughter Tara.

ASSISTANT COACHES

Matt Burke, defensive assistant/quality control, born March 25, 1976, Hudson, Mass. Safety Dartmouth 1994-97. No pro playing experience. College coach: Boston College 2000-02, Harvard 2003. Pro coach: Joined Titans in 2006.

Chuck Cecil, asst. coach/safeties and nickel backs; born November 8, 1964, Red Bluff, Calif. Defensive back Arizona 1983-87. Pro safety Green Bay Packers 1988-1992, Phoenix Cardinals 1993, Houston Oilers 1995. Pro coach: Joined Titans in 2001.

Norm Chow, offensive coordinator; born May 3, 1946, Honolulu, Hawaii. Guard Utah 1965-67. No pro playing experience. College coach: Brigham Young 1973-1999, North Carolina State 2000, Southern California 2001-04. Pro coach: Joined Titans in 2005.

Marty Galbraith, asst. special teams; born February 3, 1950, Joplin, Mo. Defensive back Missouri Southern 1971-73. No pro playing experience. College coach: Purdue 1977, Wake Forest 1978-1982, Louisiana State 1987-88, Wake Forest 1989-1990, Pittsburgh 1991, Georgia Tech 1992-93, Marshall 1998-99, North Carolina State 2000-02, Duke 2004. Pro coach: Tampa Bay Bandits (USFL) 1983-84, Kansas City Chiefs 1985, Arizona Outlaws (USFL) 1986, Arizona Cardinals 2003, joined Titans in 2005.

Craig Johnson, quarterbacks; born March 3, 1960, Rome, N.Y. Quarterback Wyoming 1978-1982. No pro playing experience. College coach: Wyoming 1983, Arkansas 1984, Army 1985, Rutgers 1986-88, Virginia Military Institute 1989-1991, Northwestern 1992-96, Maryland 1997-99. Pro coach: Joined Titans in 2000.

Alan Lowry, special teams; born November 21, 1950, Miami, Okla. Defensive back-quarterback Texas 1970-72. No pro playing experience. College coach: Virginia Tech 1974, Wyoming 1975, Texas 1977-1981. Pro coach: Dallas Cowboys 1982-1990, Tampa Bay Buccaneers 1991, San Francisco 49ers 1992-95, joined Titans/Oilers in 1996.

Dave McGinnis, linebackers; born August 7, 1951, Independence, Kan. Defensive back Texas Christian 1970-72. No pro playing experience. College coach: Texas Christian 1973-74, 1982, Missouri 1975-77, Indiana State 1978, 1980-81, Kansas State 1983-85. Pro coach: Chicago Bears 1986-1995, Arizona Cardinals 1996-2003 (head coach 2000-2003), joined Titans in 2004.

Mike Munchak, offensive line; born March 5, 1960, Scranton, Pa. Guard-tackle Penn State 1979-1981. Pro guard Houston Oilers 1982-1993. Inducted into Pro Football Hall of Fame 2001. Pro coach: Joined Titans/Oilers in 1994.

Jim Schwartz, defensive coordinator; born June 2, 1966, Baltimore. Linebacker Georgetown 1984-88. No pro playing experience. College coach: Maryland 1989, Minnesota 1990, North Carolina Central 1991, Colgate 1992. Pro coach: Cleveland Browns/Baltimore Ravens 1995-98, joined Titans in 1999.

Ray Sherman, wide receivers; born November 27, 1951, Berkeley, Calif. Wide receiver Laney (Calif.) J.C. 1969-1970, Fresno State 1971-72. No pro playing experience. College coach: San Jose State 1974, California 1975, 1981, Michigan State 1976-77, Wake Forest 1978-1980, Purdue 1982-85, Georgia 1986-87. Pro coach: Houston Oilers 1988-89, Atlanta Falcons 1990, San Francisco 49ers 1991-93, New York Jets 1994, Minnesota Vikings 1995-97, 1999, Pittsburgh Steelers 1998, Green Bay Packers 2000-04, re-joined Titans in 2005.

Sherman Smith, asst. head coach/offense; born November 1, 1954, Youngstown, Ohio. Quarterback Miami (Ohio) 1972-75. Pro running back Seattle Seahawks 1976-1982, San Diego Chargers 1983-84. College coach: Miami (Ohio) 1990-91, Illinois 1992-94. Pro coach: Joined Titans/Oilers in 1995.

Jim Washburn, defensive line; born December 2, 1949, Shelby, N.C. Offensive lineman Gardner-Webb 1969-1973. No pro playing experience. College coach: Southern Methodist 1976, Lees McRae (N.C.) J.C. 1977-78, Livingston 1979, New Mexico 1980-82, South Carolina 1983-88, Purdue 1989, Arkansas 1994-97, Houston 1998. Pro coach: London Monarchs (WLAF) 1991, Charlotte Rage (AFL) 1993, joined Titans in 1999.

Steve Watterson, strength and rehabilitation; born November 27, 1956, Newport, R.I. Attended Rhode Island. No college or pro playing experience. Pro coach: Philadelphia Eagles 1984-85, joined Titans/Oilers in 1986.

Everett Withers, defensive backs; born June 15, 1963, Charlotte. Defensive back Appalachian State 1981-85. No pro playing experience. College coach: Austin Peay 1988-1990, Tulane 1991, Southern Mississippi 1992-93, Louisville 1995-97, Texas 1998-2000. Pro coach: New Orleans Saints 1994, joined Titans in 2001.

John Zernhelt, tight ends, born January 4, 1954, Pottsville, Pa. Offensive lineman Maryland 1974-77. No pro playing experience. College coach: Ferrum 1977-1980, Marshall 1981, East Carolina 1982-86, Maryland 1987-1991, Rice 1992-93, Duck 1994-95, South Carolina 1996-98, James Madison 1999-2002, The Citadel 2003-04. Pro coach: New York Jets 2005, joined Titans in 2006.

The NFC

National Football Conference
West Division
Team Colors: Cardinal Red, Black, and
White
P.O. Box 888
Phoenix, Arizona 85001-0888
Telephone: (602) 379-0101

2006 SCHEDULE
PRESEASON
Aug. 12	**Pittsburgh**	1:00
Aug. 20	at New England	8:00
Aug. 25	at Chicago	7:00
Aug. 31	**Denver**	7:00

REGULAR SEASON
Sept. 10	**San Francisco**	1:15
Sept. 17	at Seattle	1:05
Sept. 24	**St. Louis**	1:15
Oct. 1	at Atlanta	1:00
Oct. 8	**Kansas City**	1:05
Oct. 16	**Chicago** (Mon.)	5:30
Oct. 22	at Oakland	1:15
Oct. 29	at Green Bay	12:00
Nov. 5	Open Date	
Nov. 12	**Dallas**	2:15
Nov. 19	**Detroit**	2:05
Nov. 26	at Minnesota	12:00
Dec. 3	at St. Louis	12:00
Dec. 10	**Seattle**	2:05
Dec. 17	**Denver**	2:05
Dec. 24	at San Francisco	1:05
Dec. 31	at San Diego	1:15

Stadium: Cardinals Stadium
(opens 2006)
•**Capacity:** 63,400
Maryland Avenue
Glendale, Arizona 85305
Playing Surface: Grass
Training Camp: Northern Arizona University
Flagstaff, Arizona 86011

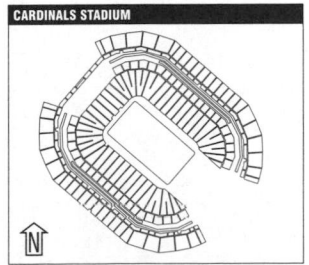

CARDINALS STADIUM

CLUB OFFICIALS
President: William V. Bidwill
Vice President/General Counsel:
Michael Bidwill
Vice President: William V. Bidwill, Jr.
Vice President-Football Operations:
Rod Graves
Vice President-Sales and Marketing:
Ron Minegar
Senior Vice President-Finance:
Jim Jacobs
Senior Director of Football Operations:
John Idzik
Treasurer and Chief Financial Officer:
Charley Schlegel
Video Director: Benny Greenberg
Director of Media Relations: Mark Dalton
Senior Director of Marketing and
Promotions: Lisa Manning
Senior Director of Business
Development: Steve Ryan
Director of Players Programs:
Anthony Edwards
Director of Community Relations:
Luis Zendejas
Director of Cardinals Charities:
Pat Tankersley
Information Services Director: Mark Feller
Director of Broadcasting/Executive
Producer: Tom Hanny
Director of Ticketing: Steve Bomar
Director of Ticket Sales: Jamie Brandt
Director of Cheerleading: Heather Shrake
Head Trainer: John Omohundro
Assistant Trainers:
Jim Shearer, Jeff Herndon,
Freddie Carbajal
Equipment Manager: Mark Ahlemeier
Assistant Equipment Manager:
Steve Christensen

COACHING HISTORY
Chicago 1920-1959, St. Louis 1960-1987
(453-653-39)
Records include postseason games

1920-22	John (Paddy) Driscoll	17-8-4
1923-24	Arnold Horween	13-8-1
1925-26	Norman Barry	16-8-2
1927	Guy Chamberlin	3-7-1
1928	Fred Gillies	1-5-0
1929	Dewey Scanlon	6-6-1
1930	Ernie Nevers	5-6-2
1931	LeRoy Andrews*	0-1-0
1931	Ernie Nevers	5-3-0
1932	Jack Chevigny	2-6-2
1933-34	Paul Schissler	6-15-1
1935-38	Milan Creighton	16-26-4
1939	Ernie Nevers	1-10-0
1940-42	Jimmy Conzelman	8-22-3
1943-45	Phil Handler**	1-29-0
1946-48	Jimmy Conzelman	27-10-0
1949	Phil Handler-Buddy Parker***	2-4-0
1949	Raymond (Buddy) Parker	4-1-1
1950-51	Earl (Curly) Lambeau****	7-15-0
1951	Phil Handler-Cecil Isbell#	1-1-0
1952	Joe Kuharich	4-8-0
1953-54	Joe Stydahar	3-20-1
1955-57	Ray Richards	14-21-1
1958-1961	Frank (Pop) Ivy##	15-31-2
1961	Chuck Drulis-Ray Prochaska-Ray Willsey###	2-0-0
1962-65	Wally Lemm	27-26-3
1966-1970	Charley Winner	35-30-5
1971-72	Bob Hollway	8-18-2
1973-77	Don Coryell	42-29-1
1978-79	Bud Wilkinson####	9-20-0
1979	Larry Wilson	2-1-0
1980-85	Jim Hanifan	39-50-1
1986-89	Gene Stallings@	23-34-1
1989	Hank Kuhlmann	0-5-0
1990-93	Joe Bugel	20-44-0
1994-95	Buddy Ryan	12-20-0
1996-2000	Vince Tobin@@	29-44-0
2000-03	Dave McGinnis	17-40-0
2004-05	Dennis Green	11-21-0

* Resigned after one game in 1931
** Co-coach with Walt Kiesling in Chicago
Cardinals-Pittsburgh merger in 1944
*** Co-coaches for first six games in 1949
**** Resigned after 10 games in 1951
# Co-coaches
Resigned after 12 games in 1961
Co-coaches
Released after 13 games in 1979
@ Released after 11 games in 1989
@@ Released after seven games in 2000

ATTENDANCE
Home 389,131	Away 511,285
Total 900,416	

Single-game home record, 73,025*
(9/19/93)
Single-season home record, 497,330
(1994)
*Team holds NFL attendance record of 103,467 for
home game at Azteca Stadium, Mexico City, Mexico

2006 DRAFT CHOICES
Round	Name	Pos.	College
1	Matt Leinart	QB	So. California
2	Taitusi Lutui	G	So. California
3	Leonard Pope	TE	Georgia
4	Gabriel Watson	DT	Michigan
5	Brandon Johnson	LB	Louisville
6	Jon Lewis	DT	Virginia Tech
7	Todd Watkins	WR	Brigham Young

2005 TEAM RECORD
PRESEASON (3-1)

Date	Result	Opponent
8/13	W 13-11	Dallas
8/20	W 24-17	at Kansas City
8/26	W 17-16	at Oakland
9/2	L 21-30	Denver

REGULAR SEASON (5-11)

Date	Result	Opponent	Att.
9/11	L 19-42	at N.Y. Giants	78,387
9/18	L 12-17	St. Louis	45,160
9/25	L 12-37	at Seattle	64,843
10/2	W 31-14	San Francisco	103,467
10/9	L 20-24	Carolina	38,809
10/23	W 20-10	Tennessee	39,482
10/30	L 13-34	at Dallas	62,068
11/6	L 19-33	Seattle	43,542
11/13	L 21-29	at Detroit	61,091
11/20	W 38-28	at St. Louis	65,750
11/27	L 17-24	Jacksonville	39,198
12/4	W 17-10	at San Francisco	60,439
12/11	L 13-17	Washington	46,654
12/18	L 19-30	at Houston	70,024
12/24	W 27-21	Philadelphia	44,723
1/1	L 13-17	at Indianapolis	57,211

SCORE BY PERIODS

Cardinals	27	111	74	99	0	—	311
Opponents	87	105	103	92	0	—	387

2005 TEAM STATISTICS

	Cardinals	Opp.
Total First Downs	304	272
Rushing	58	83
Passing	224	158
Penalty	22	31
3rd Down: Made/Att	91/239	67/196
3rd Down Pct.	38.1	34.2
4th Down: Made/Att	5/16	4/11
4th Down Pct.	31.3	36.4
Possession Avg.	31:20	28:40
Total Net Yards	5575	4729
Avg. Per Game	348.4	295.6
Total Plays	1075	936
Avg. Per Play	5.2	5.1
Net Yards Rushing	1138	1632
Avg. Per Game	71.1	102.0
Total Rushes	360	411
Net Yards Passing	4437	3097
Avg. Per Game	277.3	193.6
Sacked/Yards Lost	45/286	37/217
Gross Yards	4723	3314
Att./Completions	670/419	488/301
Completion Pct.	62.5	61.7
Had Intercepted	21	15
Punts/Average	74/43.3	85/44.1
Net Punting Avg.	74/37.0	85/37.8
Penalties/Yards	145/1184	103/819
Fumbles/Ball Lost	26/16	24/11
Touchdowns	26	46
Rushing	2	22
Passing	21	17
Returns	3	7

2005 INDIVIDUAL STATISTICS

PASSING

PASSING	Att.	Comp.	Yds.	Pct.	TD	Int.	Tkld.	Rate
Warner	375	242	2,713	64.5	11	9	23/158	85.8
McCown	270	163	1,836	60.4	9	11	18/101	74.9
Navarre	24	14	174	58.3	1	1	4/27	77.4
Boldin	1	0	0	0.0	0	0	0/0	39.6
Cardinals	670	419	4,723	62.5	21	21	45/286	81.0
Opponents	488	301	3,314	61.7	17	15	37/217	80.6

SCORING

SCORING	TD R	TD P	TD Rt	PAT	FG	Saf	PTS
Rackers	0	0	0	20/20	40/42	0	140
Fitzgerald	0	10	0	0/0	0/0	0	60
Boldin	0	7	0	0/0	0/0	0	44
Arrington	2	0	0	0/0	0/0	0	12
Dansby	0	0	2	0/0	0/0	0	12
Novak	0	0	0	0/0	3/3	0	9
Bergen	0	1	0	0/0	0/0	0	6
Edwards	0	1	0	0/0	0/0	0	6
B. Johnson	0	1	0	0/0	0/0	0	6
Macklin	0	0	1	0/0	0/0	0	6
McCoy	0	1	0	0/0	0/0	0	6
Ayanbadejo	0	0	0	0/0	0/0	0	4
Cardinals	2	21	3	20/20	43/45	0	311
Opponents	22	17	7	44/45	21/24	1	387

2-Pt. Conversions: Ayanbadejo 2, Boldin.
Cardinals 3-6, Opponents 1-1.

RUSHING

RUSHING	Att.	Yds.	Avg.	LG	TD
Shipp	157	451	2.9	19	0
Arrington	112	370	3.3	32	2
McCown	29	139	4.8	12	0
Ayanbadejo	22	46	2.1	11	0
Boldin	12	45	3.8	11	0
Fitzgerald	8	41	5.1	15	0
Warner	13	28	2.2	13	0
Jackson	4	11	2.8	3	0
Anderson	2	7	3.5	6	0
B. Johnson	1	0	0.0	0	0
Cardinals	360	1,138	3.2	32	2
Opponents	411	1,632	4.0	88t	22

RECEIVING

RECEIVING	No.	Yds	Avg	LG	TD
Fitzgerald	103	1,409	13.7	47	10
Boldin	102	1,402	13.7	54t	7
B. Johnson	40	432	10.8	41	1
Shipp	35	255	7.3	28	0
Ayanbadejo	34	231	6.8	18	0
Bergen	28	270	9.6	32	1
Arrington	25	139	5.6	15	0
McCoy	18	191	10.6	24	1
Edwards	12	133	11.1	63	1
Lee	11	152	13.8	49	0
Newhouse	4	45	11.3	17	0
T. Johnson	3	29	9.7	13	0
Jackson	2	31	15.5	19	0
Baxter	1	4	4.4	4	0
Warner	1	0	0.0	0	0
Cardinals	419	4,723	11.3	63	21
Opponents	301	3,314	11.0	65t	17

INTERCEPTIONS

INTERCEPTIONS	No.	Yds	Avg	LG	TD
Dansby	3	31	10.3	18t	2
Macklin	2	79	39.5	60t	1
Tate	2	47	23.5	25	0
Darling	2	22	11.0	15	0
Wilson	1	36	36.0	36	0
Rolle	1	29	29.0	29	0
Dockett	1	14	14.0	14	0
Green	1	13	13.0	13	0
Griffith	1	11	11.0	11	0
Huff	1	3	3.0	3	0
Cardinals	15	285	19.0	60t	3
Opponents	21	334	15.9	71	1

PUNTING

PUNTING	No.	Yds.	Avg.	In 20	LG
Player	73	3,206	43.9	18	60
Cardinals	74	3,206	43.3	18	60
Opponents	85	3,752	44.1	26	58

PUNT RETURNS

PUNT RETURNS	Ret	FC	Yds	Avg	LG	TD
Swinton	42	14	334	8.0	32	0
Moses	7	0	40	5.7	12	0
B. Johnson	1	2	9	9.0	9	0
Cardinals	50	16	383	7.7	32	0
Opponents	39	14	328	8.4	52t	1

KICKOFF RETURNS

KICKOFF RETURNS	No.	Yds	Avg	LG	TD
Swinton	63	1,456	23.1	90	0
Moses	7	177	25.3	35	0
B. Johnson	2	45	22.5	24	0
Ayanbadejo	1	16	16.0	16	0
Jackson	1	14	14.0	14	0
Anderson	1	7	7.0	7	0
Green	1	4	4.0	4	0
Cardinals	76	1,719	22.6	90	0
Opponents	60	1,700	28.3	95t	3

FIELD GOALS

FIELD GOALS	1-19	20-29	30-39	40-49	50+
Rackers	0/0	11/11	10/10	13/14	6/7
Novak	1/1	0/0	2/2	0/0	0/0
Cardinals	1/1	11/11	12/12	13/14	6/7
Opponents	0/0	10/10	3/4	7/7	1/3

SACKS

SACKS	No.
Wilson	8.0
Okeafor	7.5
Berry	6.0
Dansby	4.0
Kolodziej	3.0
Smith	3.0
Blackstock	1.0
Darling	1.0
Huff	1.0
Moore	1.0
Pace	1.0
Dockett	0.5
Cardinals	37.0
Opponents	45.0

RECORD HOLDERS
INDIVIDUAL RECORDS—CAREER

Category	Name	Performance
Rushing (Yds.)	Ottis Anderson, 1979-1986	7,999
Passing (Yds.)	Jim Hart, 1966-1983	34,639
Passing (TDs)	Jim Hart, 1966-1983	209
Receiving (No.)	Larry Centers, 1990-98	535
Receiving (Yds.)	Roy Green, 1979-1990	8,497
Interceptions	Larry Wilson, 1960-1972	52
Punting (Avg.)	Jerry Norton, 1959-1961	44.9
Punt Return (Avg.)	Charley Trippi, 1947-1955	13.7
Kickoff Return (Avg.)	Ollie Matson, 1952, 1954-58	28.5
Field Goals	Jim Bakken, 1962-1978	282
Touchdowns (Tot.)	Roy Green, 1979-1990	70
Points	Jim Bakken, 1962-1978	1,380

INDIVIDUAL RECORDS—SINGLE SEASON

Category	Name	Performance
Rushing (Yds.)	Ottis Anderson, 1979	1,605
Passing (Yds.)	Neil Lomax, 1984	4,614
Passing (TDs)	Charley Johnson, 1963	28
	Neil Lomax, 1984	28
Receiving (No.)	Larry Fitzgerald, 2005	103
Receiving (Yds.)	David Boston, 2001	1,598
Interceptions	Bob Nussbaumer, 1949	12
Punting (Avg.)	Jerry Norton, 1960	45.6
Punt Return (Avg.)	John (Red) Cochran, 1949	20.9
Kickoff Return (Avg.)	Ollie Matson, 1958	35.5
Field Goals	Neil Rackers, 2005	*40
Touchdowns (Tot.)	John David Crow, 1962	17
Points	Neil Rackers, 2005	140

INDIVIDUAL RECORDS—SINGLE GAME

Category	Name	Performance
Rushing (Yds.)	LeShon Johnson, 9-22-96	214
Passing (Yds.)	Boomer Esiason, 11-10-96 (OT)	522
Passing (TDs)	Jim Hardy, 10-2-50	6
	Charley Johnson, 9-26-65, 11-2-69	6
Receiving (No.)	Sonny Randle, 11-4-62	16
Receiving (Yds.)	Sonny Randle, 11-4-62	256
Interceptions	Bob Nussbaumer, 11-13-49	*4
	Jerry Norton, 11-20-60	*4
	Kwamie Lassiter, 12-27-98	*4
Field Goals	Jim Bakken, 9-24-67	*7
Touchdowns (Tot.)	Ernie Nevers, 11-28-29	*6
Points	Ernie Nevers, 11-28-29	*40

*NFL Record

2006 VETERAN ROSTER

No.	Name	Pos.	Ht.	Wt.	Birthdate	NFL Exp.	College	Hometown	How Acq.	'05 Games/ Starts
22	Anderson, Damien	RB	5-11	211	7/17/79	5	Northwestern	Wilmington, Ill.	FA-'05	5/0
28	Arrington, J.J.	RB	5-9	214	1/23/83	2	California	Nashville, N.C.	D2-'05	5/0
30	Ayanbadejo, Obafemi	FB	6-2	233	3/5/75	8	San Diego State	Santa Cruz, Calif.	UFA(Mia)-'04	16/2
89	Bergen, Adam	TE	6-4	263	9/3/83	2	Lehigh	Seaford, N.Y.	FA-'05	16/9
92	Berry, Bertrand	DE	6-3	277	8/15/75	9	Notre Dame	Houston, Texas	UFA(Den)-'04	8/8
55	Blackstock, Darryl	LB	6-3	240	5/30/83	2	Virginia	Newport News, Va.	D3b-'05	14/1
81	Boldin, Anquan	WR	6-1	220	10/3/80	4	Florida State	Pahokee, Fla.	D2-'03	14/14
41	Brewer, Jack	S	6-0	192	1/8/79	5	Minnesota	Grapevine, Texas	UFA(Phil)-'06	6/0*
73	Bridges, Jeremy	G	6-4	323	4/19/80	4	Southern Mississippi	McComb, Miss.	FA-'05	7/3
85	Bronson, John	TE	6-3	260	7/8/82	2	Penn State	Kent, Wash.	FA-'05	1/0
61	Brown, Elton	G	6-4	339	5/22/82	2	Virginia	Hampton, Va.	D4-'05	9/9
	Brown, Mark	LB	6-0	238	5/19/80	3	Auburn	Germantown, Tenn.	FA-'05	15/11*
67	Brown, Milford	G	6-4	325	8/15/80	5	Florida State	Montgomery, Ala.	UFA(Hou)-'06	13/12*
93	Bulman, Tim	DT	6-3	290	10/31/82	2	Boston College	Milton, Mass.	FA-'05	8/1
69	Cantu, Rolando	G	6-5	361	2/25/81	2	ITESM Monterey	Monterey, Mexico	NFL-ID	1/0
38	Carter, Dyshod	CB	5-10	194	6/18/78	4	Kansas State	Denver, Colo.	FA-'05	3/0
70	Clancy, Kendrick	DT	6-1	305	8/17/78	7	Mississippi	Tuscaloosa, Ala.	UFA(NYG)-'06	16/15*
58	Dansby, Karlos	LB	6-4	243	11/3/81	3	Auburn	Birmingham, Ala.	D2-'04	15/15
51	Darling, James	LB	6-1	247	12/29/74	10	Washington State	Kettle Falls, Wash.	UFA(NYJ)-'03	14/14
6	Davey, Rohan	QB	6-2	245	4/14/78	5	Louisiana State	Miami, Fla.	FA-'05	0*
75	Davis, Leonard	T	6-6	366	9/5/78	6	Texas	Wortham, Texas	D1-'01	15/15
90	Dockett, Darnell	DT	6-4	293	5/27/81	3	Florida State	Burtonsville, MD	D3-'04	16/16
83	Edwards, Eric	TE	6-5	257	8/4/80	3	Louisiana State	Monroe, La.	FA-'04	16/9
68	Ellington, Dante	T	6-6	330	2/29/80	2	Alabama	Leighton, Ala.	FA-'05	2/0
11	Fitzgerald, Larry	WR	6-3	221	8/31/83	2	Pittsburgh	Minneapolis, Minn.	D1-'04	16/16
47	Francisco, Aaron	S	6-2	212	7/5/83	2	Brigham Young	Laie, Hawaii	FA-'05	11/0
25	Green, Eric	CB	5-11	188	3/16/82	2	Virginia Tech	Pahokee, Fla.	D3a-'05	12/5
34	Griffith, Robert	S	6-0	200	11/30/70	13	San Diego State	San Diego, Calif.	UFA(Cle)-'05	16/16
54	Hayes, Gerald	LB	6-1	247	10/10/80	4	Pittsburgh	Paterson, N.J.	D3-'03	0*
48	Hodel, Nathan	LS	6-2	248	11/12/77	5	Illinois	Fairview Heights, Ill.	FA-'01	16/0
42	Hodgins, James	FB	6-1	264	4/30/77	8	San Jose State	San Jose, Calif.	UFA(StL)-'03	1/0
15	Holiday, Caryle	WR	6-1	207	10/4/81	2	Notre Dame	San Antonio, Texas	FA-'05	1/0
57	Huff, Orlando	LB	6-3	250	8/14/78	6	Fresno State	Upland, Calif.	UFA(Sea)-'05	16/12
32	James, Edgerrin	RB	6-0	214	8/1/78	8	Miami	Immokalee, Fla.	UFA(Ind)-'06	15/15*
80	Johnson, Bryant	WR	6-3	214	3/7/81	4	Penn State	Baltimore, Md.	D1a-'03	14/4
53	Keys, Isaac	LB	6-3	247	6/6/78	4	Morehouse	St. Louis, Mo.	FA-'05	6/0
95	King, Kenny	DT	6-4	291	4/23/81	4	Alabama	Daphine, Ala.	D5-'03	0*
60	Leckey, Nick	C/G	6-3	298	3/12/82	3	Kansas State	Grapevine, Texas	D6-'04	14/9
65	Lynch, Shawn	C	6-4	294	7/25/79	2	Duke	West Palm Beach, Fla.	FA-'05	2/1
27	Macklin, David	CB	5-10	200	7/14/78	7	Penn State	Newport News, Va.	UFA(Ind)-'04	16/15
19	McCoy, LeRon	WR	6-1	205	1/24/82	2	Indiana (Pa.)	Harrisburg, Pa.	D7-'05	10/4
52	Mitchell, Lance	LB	6-2	250	10/9/81	2	Oklahoma	Los Banos, Calif.	D5-'05	12/0
91	Moore, Langston	DT	6-1	303	7/17/81	4	South Carolina	Charleston, S.C.	W(Cin)-'05	8/1
16	Navarre, John	QB	6-6	251	9/9/80	3	Michigan	Cudahy, Wis.	D7-'04	1/0
3	Novak, Nick	K	6-0	190	8/21/81	2	Maryland	Charlottesville, Va.	FA-'05	5/0
56	Okeafor, Chike	DE	6-5	265	3/27/76	8	Purdue	Grand Rapids, Mich.	UFA(Sea)-'05	16/16
97	Pace, Calvin	DE	6-4	270	10/28/80	4	Wake Forest	Douglasville, Ga.	D1b-'03	5/1
96	Palepoi, Anton	DE	6-3	283	1/19/78	5	Nevada-Las Vegas	Salt Lake City, Utah	FA-'05	3/0
10	Player, Scott	P	6-1	211	12/17/69	9	Florida State	St. Augustine, Fla.	FA-'98	16/0
1	Rackers, Neil	K	6-1	207	8/16/76	7	Illinois	St. Louis, Mo.	FA-'03	15/0
20	Reid, Lamont	CB	5-11	187	5/4/82	2	North Carolina State	Concord, N.C.	FA-'05	10/1
66	Reuber, Alan	T	6-6	314	1/26/81	2	Texas A&M	Plano, Texas	FA-'05	0*
21	Rolle, Antrel	CB	6-0	206	12/16/82	2	Miami	Homestead, Fla.	D1-'05	5/4
79	Ross, Oliver	T	6-4	324	9/27/74	8	Iowa State	Los Angeles, Calif.	UFA(Pitt)-'05	12/12
35	Shazor, Ernest	S	6-4	231	7/4/83	2	Michigan	Detroit, Mich.	FA-'05	2/0
31	Shipp, Marcel	RB	5-11	225	8/8/78	6	Massachusetts	Paterson, N.J.	FA-'01	15/11
94	Smith, Antonio	DE	6-4	272	10/21/81	2	Oklahoma State	Oklahoma City, Okla.	D5-'04	12/8
71	Stepanovich, Alex	C	6-4	304	9/25/81	3	Ohio State	Berea, Ohio	D4-'04	9/9
26	Tate, Robert	CB	5-11	192	10/19/73	8	Cincinnati	Harrisburg, Pa.	FA-'05	13/5
78	Wakefield, Fred	G/T	6-7	312	9/17/78	6	Illinois	Tuscola, Ill.	FA-'01	15/9
86	Walters, Troy	WR	5-7	172	12/15/76	7	Stanford	College Station, Texas	UFA(Ind)-'06	16/1*
13	Warner, Kurt	QB	6-2	219	6/22/71	9	Northern Iowa	Burlington, Iowa	UFA(NYG)-'05	10/10
74	Wells, Reggie	G	6-4	320	11/3/80	4	Clarion (Pa.)	Library, Pa.	D6a-'03	9/9
24	Wilson, Adrian	S	6-3	230	10/12/79	6	North Carolina State	High Point, N.C.	D3-'01	16/16

* Brewer played 6 games with Philadelphia in '05; Ma. Brown played 15 games with N.Y. Jets; Mi. Brown played 13 games with Houston; Clancy played 16 games with N.Y. Giants; Davey inactive for 4 games; Hayes missed '05 season because of injury; James played 15 games for Indianapolis; King missed '05 season because of injury; Reuber last active with Arizona in '04; Walters played 16 games for Indianapolis.

Players lost through free agency (5): T Ian Allen (KC; 2 games in '05), DT Russell Davis (Sea; 3), CB Quentin Harris (NYG; 16), QB Josh McCown (Det; 9), CB Raymond Walls (SD; 7).

Also played with Cardinals in '05—FB Jarrod Baxter (8 games), DE Antonio Cochran (3), G Adam Haayer (12), RB James Jackson (8), LB Eric Johnson (3), TE Teyo Johnson (6), DT Ross Kolodziej (16), WR Charles Lee (6), S Adrian Mayes (3), FB Harold Morrow (14), KR J.J. Moses (2), WR Reggie Newhouse (3), KR Reggie Swinton (15), LB Lester Towns (2), DE R-Kal Truluck (7).

2006 FIRST-YEAR ROSTER

Name	Pos.	Ht.	Wt.	Birthdate	College	Hometown	How Acq.
Bilbo, Damarius	WR	6-2	222	12/3/82	Georgia Tech	Moss Point, Miss.	FA
Brown, Mark	LB	6-0	238	5/19/80	Auburn	Lawrenceville, Ga.	FA
Capshaw, Fred (1)	P	5-11	195	12/27/79	Miami	Rock Springs, Wyo.	FA
Harrell, Chris	S	6-2	209	1/29/83	Penn State	Cleveland, Ohio	FA
Hall, Ben (1)	TE	6-5	265	7/27/82	Clemson	Welford, S.C.	FA-'05
Hunter, Darrell	CB	5-11	211	11/29/83	Miami (Ohio)	Middletown, Ohio	FA
Johnson, Brandon	LB	6-5	223	5/5/83	Louisville	Birmingham, Ala.	D5
King, Tyler (1)	DE	6-5	266	9/5/80	Connecticut	Attleboro, Mass.	FA-'05
Lee, Greg	WR	6-1	202	10/19/84	Pittsburgh	Tampa, Fla.	FA
Leinart, Matt	QB	6-4	224	5/11/83	Southern California	Santa Ana, Calif.	D1
Lewis, Jonathan	DT	6-0	304	7/12/84	Virginia Tech	Richmond, Va.	D6
Lutui, Deuce	G	6-4	334	5/5/83	Southern California	Ha'api, Tonga	D2
McCareins, Jay	CB	6-0	190	3/13/83	Princeton	Naperville, Ill.	FA
Otis, Jeff	QB	6-1	206	1/30/83	Columbia	St. Louis, Mo.	FA
Pinson, Lawrence	LB	6-1	240	12/9/83	Oklahoma State	Jenks, Okla.	FA
Pope, Leonard	TE	6-7	256	9/9/83	Georgia	Americus, Ga.	D3
Robinson, Roger (1)	RB	5-9	199	4/22/82	Northern Arizona	Apple Valley, Calif.	FA-'05
Schable, A.J.	DE	6-4	285	5/18/84	South Dakota	Ida Grove, Iowa	FA
Schmitt, Kyle (1)	C	6-4	295	8/12/81	Maryland	Derry, Pa.	FA
Shor, Alex	TE	6-8	255	1/29/83	Syracuse	Panama City, Fla.	FA
Spurlock, Michael	WR	5-11	200	1/31/83	Mississippi	Indianola, Miss.	FA
Stokes, Andy (1)	TE	6-4	257	6/2/81	William Penn	Moapa Valley, Nev.	FA-'05
Watkins, Todd	WR	6-2	191	6/22/83	Brigham Young	San Diego, Calif.	D7
Watson, Gabe	DT	6-4	341	9/24/83	Michigan	Southfield, Mich.	D4
Wyatt, Justin	CB	5-9	186	1/27/84	Southern California	Compton, Calif.	FA

The term NFL Rookie is defined as a player who is in his first season of professional football and has not been on the roster of another professional football team for any regular-season or postseason games. A Rookie is designated by an "R" on NFL rosters. Players who have been active in another professional football league or players who have NFL experience, including either preseason training camp or being on an Active List or Inactive List, or on Reserve/Injured or Reserve/Physically Unable to Perform for fewer than six regular-season games, are termed NFL First-Year Players. An NFL First-Year Player is designated by a "1" on NFL rosters. Thereafter, a player is credited with an additional year of experience for each season in which he accumulates six games on the Active List or Inactive List, or on Reserve/Injured or Reserve/Physically Unable to Perform.

Log on to www.azcardinals.com for an up-to-date roster.

COACHING STAFF
Head Coach,
Dennis Green

Pro Career: Named the thirty-third head coach of the Arizona Cardinals on January 7, 2004. Posted 101-70 (.591) composite record in 10 seasons (1992-2001) as head coach of the Minnesota Vikings. Led club to eight postseason berths (four NFC Central Division titles) and two NFC championship games. Green is one of four NFL coaches to achieve a 15-victory season (15-1 in 1998), joining Bill Walsh (San Francisco, 1984), Mike Ditka (Chicago, 1985) and Bill Cowher (Pittsburgh, 2004), and is one of just eight coaches in NFL history to lead his team to the playoffs in each of his first three seasons (1992-94) as an NFL head coach. Green's eight postseason appearances with the Vikings were accomplished with seven different quarterbacks—Sean Salisbury (1992), Jim McMahon (1993), Warren Moon (1994), Brad Johnson (1996), Randall Cunningham (1997-98), Jeff George (1999), and Daunte Culpepper (2000). The Vikings were the only NFL team to qualify for the playoffs each season from 1996-2000 and posted the NFL's best winning percentage (.639, 92-52) from 1992-2000. Green's first professional coaching opportunity came as special teams coach for San Francisco in 1979. Career record: 112-91.

Background: Green was an all-Pennsylvania running back at John Harris High School in Harrisburg, Pa. before attending Iowa where he started for one season as a flanker (1968) followed by two at running back (1969-70 where he was honorable mention all-Big Ten both years) for the Hawkeyes. Green played defensive back briefly for the British Columbia Lions of the Canadian Football League in 1971. Green was a college assistant coach at Iowa (1972, 1974-76), Dayton (1973), and Stanford (1977-78, 1980). During his six seasons (1981-85) as head coach at Northwestern, he was named Big Ten Conference coach-of-the-year in 1982. As head coach at Stanford from 1989-1991, Green led the Cardinal to the 1991 Aloha Bowl.

Personal: Born February 17, 1949 in Harrisburg, Pa., Green earned his degree in recreation from Iowa. He and his wife, Marie, have a daughter, Vanessa, and son, Zachary. Green also has a daughter, Patti, and a son, Jeremy.

ASSISTANT COACHES

Larry Brooks, defensive line; born June 10, 1950, Prince George, Va. Defensive lineman Virginia State 1968-1971. Pro defensive tackle Los Angeles Rams 1972-1982. College coach: Virginia State 1992-93. Pro coach: Los Angeles Rams 1983-1990, Green Bay Packers 1994-98, Seattle Seahawks 1999-2002, Chicago Bears 2003, Detroit Lions 2004-05, joined Cardinals in 2006.

Frank Bush, asst. head coach-linebackers; born January 10, 1963, Athens, Ga. Linebacker North Carolina State 1981-84. Pro linebacker Houston Oilers 1985-86. Pro coach: Houston Oilers 1987-1991 (scout), 1992-94, Denver Broncos 1995-2003, joined Cardinals in 2004.

Rick Courtright, defensive quality control; born Jan. 4, 1961, Miami. Linebacker Wheaton College 1980-83. No pro playing experience. College coach: Washington 1991-92, Minnesota-Morris 1993, Ohio 1994, Idaho State 1995, Idaho 1996-99, Murray State 2000, Western Illinois 2001-03. Pro coach: Joined Cardinals in 2004.

Carl Hargrave, tight ends; born November 8, 1954, Frankfurt, Germany. Defensive back Upper Iowa 1972-75. No pro playing experience. College coach: Upper Iowa 1977-1980, Northwestern 1981-85, Pittsburgh 1986, Houston 1987-1991, Iowa 1992-93, Lindenwood 2002-03. Pro coach: Minnesota Vikings 1994-2001, joined Cardinals in 2004.

Bill Khayat, offensive quality control; born March 26, 1973, York, Pa. Tight end Duke 1992-95. Pro tight end Kansas City Chiefs 1996, Carolina Panthers 1997, Barcelona Dragons (NFLE) 1998. College coach: Tennessee State 2000-03. Pro coach: Joined Cardinals in 2004.

Mike Kruczek, quarterbacks; born March 15, 1953, Washington, D.C. Quarterback Boston College 1973-75. Pro quarterback Pittsburgh Steelers 1976-79, Washington Redskins 1980. College coach: Florida State 1982-83 Central Florida 1985-2003 (head coach 1998-2003). Pro coach: Jacksonville Bulls (USFL) 1984, joined Cardinals in 2004.

Daryl Lawrence, asst. strength and conditioning; born October 20, 1965, Chicago Heights, Ill. Attended Illinois State. No college or pro playing experience. College coach: Illinois State 1995-96, Army 1998-99. Pro coach: Minnesota Vikings 1997, 2000-03, joined Cardinals in 2004.

Steve Loney, offensive line; born April 26, 1952, Marshalltown, Iowa. Offensive line Iowa State 1970-73. No pro playing experience. College coach: Missouri Western College 1975-76, Morehead State 1979-1983, The Citadel 1984-86, Colorado State 1989-1992, Connecticut 1994, Iowa State 1995-97, 2000-01, Minnesota 1998-99. Pro coach: Phoenix Cardinals 1993, Minnesota Vikings 2002-05, re-joined Cardinals in 2006.

Clancy Pendergast, defensive coordinator; born November 29, 1967, Phoenix. Attended Arizona. No college or pro playing experience. College coach: Mississippi State 1991, Southern California 1992, Oklahoma 1993-94, Alabama-Birmingham 1995. Pro coach: Houston Oilers 1995, Dallas Cowboys 1996-2002, Cleveland Browns 2003, joined Cardinals in 2004.

Keith Rowen, offensive coordinator; born September 2, 1952, New York, N.Y. Tackle Stanford 1972-74. No pro playing experience. College coach: Stanford 1975-76, Long Beach State 1977-78, Arizona 1979-1982. Pro coach: Boston/New Orleans Breakers (USFL) 1983-84, Cleveland Browns 1984, Indianapolis Colts 1985-88, New England Patriots 1989, Atlanta Falcons 1990-93, Minnesota Vikings 1994-96, Oakland Raiders 1997-98, Kansas City Chiefs 1999-2004, joined Cardinals in 2005.

Richard Solomon, defensive backs; born December 8, 1949, New Orleans. Running back-defensive back Iowa 1970-72. No pro playing experience. College coach: Dubuque 1973-75, Southern Illinois 1976, Iowa 1977-78, Syracuse 1979, Illinois 1980-86, Western Illinois 2003. Pro coach: New York Giants 1987-1991 (scout), Minnesota Vikings 1992-2001, joined Cardinals in 2004.

Keith Vulgamott, asst. strength and conditioning; born January 15, 1981, Jewell Iowa. Defensive end Iowa State 1999, linebacker Simpson College 2001-02. No pro playing experience. College coach: Texas Tech 2005. Pro coach: Joined Cardinals in 2006.

Steve Wetzel, strength and conditioning; born May 11, 1963, Washington, D.C. Attended Slippery Rock. No college or pro playing experience. College coach: Maryland 1985-89, George Mason 1990. Pro coach: Washington Redskins 1990-91, Minnesota Vikings 1991-2003, joined Cardinals in 2004.

Kirby Wilson, running backs; born August 24, 1961, Los Angeles, Calif. Running back-wide receiver Pasadena (Calif.) C.C. 1979-1980, Illinois 1981-82. Pro cornerback Winnipeg Blue Bombers (CFL) 1983, Toronto Argonauts (CFL) 1984. College coach: Pasadena (Calif.) C.C. 1989-1990, Southern Illinois 1991-92, Wyoming 1993-94, Iowa State 1995-96, Southern California 2001. Pro coach: New England Patriots 1997-99, Washington Redskins 2000, Tampa Bay Buccaneers 2002-03, joined Cardinals in 2004.

Mike Wilson, wide receivers; born December 19, 1958, Los Angeles, Calif. Wide receiver Washington State 1978-1980. Pro wide receiver San Francisco 49ers 1981-1990. College coach: Stanford 1992-94, Southern California 1997-2000. Pro coach: Oakland Raiders 1995-96, joined Cardinals in 2004.

Gary Zauner, special teams coordinator; born November 2, 1950, Milwaukee, Wis. Punter Wisconsin-La Crosse 1968-1972. No pro playing experience. College coach: Brigham Young 1979-1980, San Diego State 1981-86, New Mexico 1987-88, Long Beach State 1990-91. Pro coach: Minnesota Vikings 1994-2001, Baltimore Ravens 2002-05, joined Cardinals in 2006.

National Football Conference
South Division
Team Colors: Red, Black, Silver, and White
4400 Falcon Parkway
Flowery Branch, Georgia 30542
Telephone: (770) 965-3115

2006 SCHEDULE
PRESEASON
Aug. 13 **New England** 8:00
Aug. 19 at Green Bay 7:00
Aug. 26 at Tennessee 7:00
Sept. 1 **Jacksonville**.......................7:30

REGULAR SEASON
Sept. 10 at Carolina...........................1:00
Sept. 17 **Tampa Bay**.........................1:00
Sept. 25 at New Orleans (Mon.) 7:30
Oct. 1 **Arizona**..............................1:00
Oct. 8 Open Date
Oct. 15 **N.Y. Giants**........................1:00
Oct. 22 **Pittsburgh**...........................1:00
Oct. 29 at Cincinnati 1:00
Nov. 5 at Detroit 1:00
Nov. 12 **Cleveland** 1:00
Nov. 19 at Baltimore........................1:00
Nov. 26 **New Orleans**.......................1:00
Dec. 3 at Washington 1:00
Dec. 10 at Tampa Bay 1:00
Dec. 16 **Dallas** (Sat.) 8:00
Dec. 24 **Carolina**.............................1:00
Dec. 31 at Philadelphia 1:00

Stadium: Georgia Dome
(opened in 1992)
•**Capacity:** 71,228
One Georgia Dome Drive
Atlanta, Georgia 30313
Playing Surface: FieldTurf
Training Camp: Atlanta Falcons
4400 Falcon Parkway
Flowery Branch, GA 30542

GEORGIA DOME

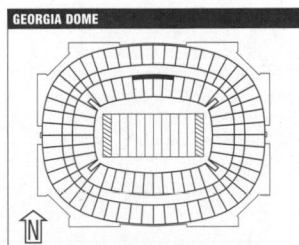

CLUB OFFICIALS
Owner & CEO: Arthur M. Blank
President-General Manager: Rich McKay
Executive Vice President-Head Coach:
Jim Mora
Executive Vice President-Chief
Administrative Officer: Ray Anderson
Executive Vice President-Marketing:
Dick Sullivan
Vice President-Human Resources:
Tim Bolton
Vice President & CFO: Greg Beadles
Manager-Payroll and Employee Benefits:
Wallace Norman
Vice President of Football
Communications: Reggie Roberts
Vice President of Information Technology
& Store Development: Danny Branch
Vice President of Marketing: Jim Smith
Vice President of Sales: Dave Cohen
Senior Director of Media Relations:
Frank Kleha
Senior Director of Player Development:
Kevin Winston
Senior Personnel Executive:
Billy Devaney
Executive Director of the Atlanta Falcons
Youth Foundation: Scott Doll
Director of Logistics and Facilities:
Spencer Treadwell
Controller: Rob Geoffroy
Director of Ticket Operations:
Jack Ragsdale
Director of Football Operations: Nick Polk
Director of Football Administration:
Brian Xanders
Director of Pro Personnel: Les Snead
Director of College Scouting: Phil Emery
Coordinator-Program Development/
Player Outreach: Chris Demos
Area Scouts: Matt Berry, Boyd Dowler,
Bob Harrison, Taylor Morton,
Mark Olson, Alex Page,
Bruce Plummer
Pro Scouts: Ray Farmer
Head Athletic Trainer: Ron Medlin
Assistant Athletic Trainers: Harold King,
Thomas Reed
Video Director: Mike Crews
Video Assistant: Rocky Sabbatini
Equipment Manager: Brian Boigner
Senior Equipment Director/Gameday
Coordinator: Horace Daniel
Director of Event Marketing and Client
Services: Roddy White
Manager of New Media: Dan Levak
Football Communications Manager:
Ted Crews
Football Communications Coordinator:
Ryan Moore

COACHING HISTORY
(251-365-6)
Records include postseason games

Years	Coach	Record
1966-68	Norb Hecker*	4-26-1
1968-1974	Norm Van Brocklin**	37-49-3
1974-76	Marion Campbell***	6-19-0
1976	Pat Peppler	3-6-0
1977-1982	Leeman Bennett	47-44-0
1983-86	Dan Henning	22-41-1
1987-89	Marion Campbell****	11-32-0
1989	Jim Hanifan	0-4-0
1990-93	Jerry Glanville	28-38-0
1994-96	June Jones	19-30-0
1997-2003	Dan Reeves#	52-61-1
2003	Wade Phillips	2-1-0
2004-05	Jim Mora	20-14-0

*Released after three games in 1968
**Released after eight games in 1974
***Released after five games in 1976
****Retired after 12 games in 1989
#Released after 13 games in 2003

ATTENDANCE
Home 550,511   Away 529,501
Total 1,080,012
Single-game home record,
71,079 (10/9/05)
Single-season home record,
553,979 (1992)

2006 DRAFT CHOICES
Round	Name	Pos.	College
2	Jimmy Williams	DB	Virginia Tech
3	Jerious Norwood	RB	Mississippi St.
5	Quinn Ojinnaka	T	Syracuse
6	Adam Jennings	WR	Fresno State
7	D.J. Shockley	QB	Georgia

2005 TEAM RECORD
PRESEASON (4-1)

Date	Result	Opponent
8/6	W 27-21	vs. Indianapolis at Tokyo
8/13	W 16-3	Baltimore
8/19	L 21-24	Tennessee
8/25	W 23-7	at Jacksonville
9/1	W 20-17	at Miami

REGULAR SEASON (8-8)

Date	Result	Opponent	Att.
9/12	W 14-10	Philadelphia	70,806
9/18	L 18-21	at Seattle	66,030
9/25	W 24-16	at Buffalo	72,032
10/2	W 30-10	Minnesota	69,552
10/9	L 28-31	New England	71,079
10/16	W 34-31	at New Orleans	65,562
10/24	W 27-14	New York Jets	70,995
11/6	W 17-10	at Miami	72,187
11/13	L 25-33	Green Bay	71,001
11/20	L 27-30	Tampa Bay	70,794
11/24	W 27-7	at Detroit	62,390
12/4	L 6-24	at Carolina	73,661
12/12	W 36-17	New Orleans	70,083
12/18	L 3-16	at Chicago	62,170
12/24	L 24-27	at Tampa Bay (OT)	65,482
1/1	L 11-44	Carolina	70,796

(OT) Overtime

SCORE BY PERIODS

Falcons	78	132	49	92	0	—	351
Opponents	79	111	57	91	3	—	341

2005 TEAM STATISTICS

	Falcons	Opp.
Total First Downs	313	319
Rushing	139	122
Passing	149	167
Penalty	25	30
3rd Down: Made/Att	94/219	58/192
3rd Down Pct.	42.9	30.2
4th Down: Made/Att	5/14	10/16
4th Down Pct.	35.7	62.5
Possession Avg.	29:58	30:02
Total Net Yards	5,225	52,00
Avg. Per Game	326.6	325.0
Total Plays	1,021	1,001
Avg. Per Play	5.1	5.2
Net Yards Rushing	2,546	2,063
Avg. Per Game	159.1	128.9
Total Rushes	531	438
Net Yards Passing	2,679	3,137
Avg. Per Game	167.4	196.1
Sacked/Yards Lost	39/228	37/257
Gross Yards	2,907	3,394
Att./Completions	451/247	526/320
Completion Pct.	54.8	60.8
Had Intercepted	13	16
Punts/Average	78/42.3	79/43.1
Net Punting Avg.	78/36.9	79/39.0
Penalties/Yards	114/1043	114/981
Fumbles/Ball Lost	26/16	22/13
Touchdowns	39	38
Rushing	17	18
Passing	19	18
Returns	3	2

2005 INDIVIDUAL STATISTICS

PASSING	Att.	Comp.	Yds.	Pct.	TD	Int.	Tkld.	Rate
Vick	387	214	2,412	55.3	15	13	33/201	73.1
Schaub	64	33	495	51.6	4	0	6/27	98.1
Falcons	451	247	2,907	54.8	19	13	39/228	76.6
Opponents	526	320	3,394	60.8	18	16	37/257	78.4

SCORING	TD R	TD P	TD Rt	PAT	FG	Saf	PTS
Peterson	0	0	0	35/35	23/25	0	104
Duckett	8	0	0	0/0	0/0	0	48
Vick	6	0	0	0/0	0/0	0	36
Crumpler	0	5	0	0/0	0/0	0	32
Dunn	3	1	0	0/0	0/0	0	24
Finneran	0	2	0	0/0	0/0	0	18
Griffith	0	3	0	0/0	0/0	0	18
Jenkins	0	3	0	0/0	0/0	0	18
R. White	0	3	0	0/0	0/0	0	18
Blakley	0	1	0	0/0	0/0	0	6
Davis	0	0	1	0/0	0/0	0	6
Hall	0	0	1	0/0	0/0	0	6
D. White	0	1	0	0/0	0/0	0	6
D. Williams	0	0	1	0/0	0/0	0	6
Koenen	0	0	0	0/0	1/2	0	3
Lake	0	0	0	0/0	0/0	1	2
Falcons	17	19	3	35/35	24/27	1	351
Opponents	18	18	2	38/38	25/30	0	341

2-Pt. Conversions: Finneran 3, Crumpler.
Falcons 4-4, Opponents 0-0.

RUSHING	Att.	Yds.	Avg.	LG	TD
Dunn	280	1,416	5.1	65	3
Vick	102	597	5.9	32	6
Duckett	121	380	3.1	25	8
Schaub	9	76	8.4	23	0
Griffith	15	65	4.3	19	0
R. White	4	12	3.0	16	0
Falcons	531	2,546	4.8	65	17
Opponents	438	2,063	4.7	70t	18

RECEIVING	No.	Yds.	Avg.	LG	TD
Crumpler	65	877	13.5	48	5
Finneran	50	611	12.2	53	2
Jenkins	36	508	14.1	58	3
R. White	29	446	15.4	54t	3
Dunn	29	220	7.6	24	1
Griffith	21	111	5.3	17	3
Duckett	6	63	10.5	19	0
Blakley	4	30	7.5	10	1
McCrary	3	12	4.4	11	0
D. White	2	25	12.5	14t	1
Pathon	1	18	18.0	18	0
Vick	1	-14	-14.0	-14	0
Falcons	247	2,907	11.8	58	19
Opponents	320	3,394	10.6	55t	18

INTERCEPTIONS	No.	Yds	Avg	LG	TD
Hall	6	177	29.5	65	0
Brooking	4	50	12.5	22	0
D. Williams	2	6	3.0	6	0
Carpenter	2	1	0.5	1	0
Webster	1	19	19.0	19	0
Scott	1	15	15.0	15	0
Falcons	16	268	16.8	65	0
Opponents	13	163	12.5	51	0

PUNTING	No.	Yds.	Avg.	In 20	LG
Koenen	78	3,300	42.3	23	67
Falcons	78	3,300	42.3	23	67
Opponents	79	3,401	43.1	30	65

PUNT RETURNS	No.	FC	Yds.	Avg.	LG	TD
Rossum	17	12	145	8.5	29	0
Hall	8	2	82	10.3	27	0
Jenkins	3	0	19	6.3	15	0
Finneran	2	8	7	3.5	5	0
Cobb	1	0	8	8.0	8	0
Torrence	0	1	0	—	—	0
Falcons	31	23	261	8.4	29	0
Opponents	35	14	238	6.8	28	0

KICKOFF RETURNS	No.	Yds.	Avg.	LG	TD
Rossum	31	702	22.6	47	0
Cobb	16	359	22.4	39	0
Griffith	8	149	18.6	23	0
Bryant	8	137	17.1	23	0
Pathon	3	54	18.0	21	0
Hall	2	45	22.5	23	0
Duckett	2	36	18.0	18	0
Falcons	70	1,482	21.2	47	0
Opponents	59	1,138	19.3	45	0

FIELD GOALS	1-19	20-29	30-39	40-49	50+
Peterson	0/0	9/10	11/11	3/4	0/0
Koenen	0/0	0/0	0/0	0/0	1/2
Falcons	0/0	9/10	11/11	3/4	1/2
Opponents	2/2	5/6	6/6	9/13	3/3

SACKS	No.
Coleman	10.5
Kerney	6.5
Brooking	3.5
Lake	3.5
Smith	3.0
D. Williams	3.0
Lavalais	2.5
Shropshire	2.0
Davis	1.0
Scott	1.0
Babineaux	0.5
Falcons	37.0
Opponents	39.0

RECORD HOLDERS
INDIVIDUAL RECORDS—CAREER

Category	Name	Performance
Rushing (Yds.)	Gerald Riggs, 1982-88	6,631
Passing (Yds.)	Steve Bartkowski, 1975-1985	23,468
Passing (TDs)	Steve Bartkowski, 1975-1985	154
Receiving (No.)	Terance Mathis, 1994-2001	573
Receiving (Yds.)	Terance Mathis, 1994-2001	7,349
Interceptions	Rolland Lawrence, 1973-1980	39
Punting (Avg.)	Rick Donnelly, 1985-89	42.6
Punt Return (Avg.)	Darrien Gordon, 2001	14.1
Kickoff Return (Avg.)	Darrick Vaughn, 2000-01	25.7
Field Goals	Morten Andersen, 1995-2000	139
Touchdowns (Tot.)	Terance Mathis, 1994-2001	57
Points	Morten Andersen, 1995-2000	620

INDIVIDUAL RECORDS—SINGLE SEASON

Category	Name	Performance
Rushing (Yds.)	Jamal Anderson, 1998	1,846
Passing (Yds.)	Jeff George, 1995	4,143
Passing (TDs)	Steve Bartkowski, 1980	31
Receiving (No.)	Terance Mathis, 1994	111
Receiving (Yds.)	Alfred Jenkins, 1981	1,358
Interceptions	Scott Case, 1988	10
Punting (Avg.)	Billy Lothridge, 1968	44.3
Punt Return (Avg.)	Darrien Gordon, 2001	14.1
Kickoff Return (Avg.)	Darrick Vaughn, 2000	27.7
Field Goals	Jay Feely, 2002	32
Touchdowns (Tot.)	Jamal Anderson, 1998	16
Points	Jay Feely, 2002	138

INDIVIDUAL RECORDS—SINGLE GAME

Category	Name	Performance
Rushing (Yds.)	Gerald Riggs, 9-2-84	202
Passing (Yds.)	Steve Bartkowski, 11-15-81	416
Passing (TDs)	Wade Wilson, 12-13-92	5
Receiving (No.)	William Andrews, 11-15-81	15
Receiving (Yds.)	Terance Mathis, 12-13-98	198
Interceptions	Many times	2
	Last time by Ashley Ambrose, 11-18-01	
Field Goals	Norm Johnson, 11-13-94	6
Touchdowns (Tot.)	T.J. Duckett, 12-12-04	4
Points	T.J. Duckett, 12-12-04	24

2006 VETERAN ROSTER

No.	Name	Pos.	Ht.	Wt.	Birthdate	NFL Exp.	College	Hometown	How Acq.	'05 Games/ Starts
55 t-	Abraham, John	DE	6-4	258	5/6/78	7	South Carolina	Timmonsville, S.C.	T(NYJ)-'06	16/15*
95	Babineaux, Jonathan	DT	6-2	286	10/12/81	2	Iowa	Port Arthur, Texas	D2-'05	16/6
52	Beck, Jordan	LB	6-2	233	4/18/83	2	Cal Poly	Santa Cruz, Calif.	D3-'05	0*
80	Beverly, Eric	TE	6-3	300	3/28/74	10	Miami (Ohio)	Cleveland, Ohio	UFA(Det)-'04	16/2
85	Blakley, Dwayne	TE	6-4	257	8/10/79	3	Missouri	St. Joseph, Mo.	W(Tenn)-'04	16/1
59	Boley, Michael	LB	6-3	236	8/24/82	2	Southern Mississippi	Athens, Ala.	D5-'05	16/11
56	Brooking, Keith	LB	6-2	245	10/30/75	9	Georgia Tech	Senoia, Ga.	D1-'98	16/16
29	Cash, Chris	CB	5-10	185	7/13/80	5	Southern California	Stockton, Calif.	FA-'05	3/0
67	Clabo, Tyson	G	6-6	314	10/17/81	3	Wake Forest	Knoxville, Tenn.	FA-'06	0*
69	Claxton, Ben	G	6-2	301	7/30/80	2	Mississippi	Dublin, Ga.	W(Pitt)-'05	2/0
34	Cobb, DeAndra	RB	5-10	196	5/18/81	2	Michigan State	Las Vegas, Nev.	D6-'05	3/0
75	Coleman, Rod	DT	6-2	285	8/16/76	8	East Carolina	Vicksburg, Miss.	UFA(Oak)-'04	16/16
25	Crocker, Chris	S	5-11	192	3/9/80	4	Marshall	Chesapeake, Va.	FA-'06	16/16*
83	Crumpler, Alge	TE	6-2	262	12/23/77	6	North Carolina	Wilmington, N.C.	D2-'01	16/16
92	Davis, Chauncey	DE	6-2	277	1/27/81	2	Florida State	Bartow, Fla.	D4-'05	16/5
79	Draper, Shawn	T	6-3	275	7/5/79	2	Alabama	Huntsville, Ala.	FA-'06	0*
45	Duckett, T.J.	RB	6-0	254	2/17/81	5	Michigan State	Kalamazoo, Mich.	D1-'02	14/0
28	Dunn, Warrick	RB	5-9	180	1/5/75	10	Florida State	Baton Rouge, La.	UFA(TB)-'02	16/16
86	Finneran, Brian	WR	6-5	217	1/31/76	8	Villanova	Mission Viejo, Calif.	FA '00	16/7
65	Forney, Kynan	G	6-3	307	9/8/78	6	Hawaii	Nacogdoches, Texas	D7b-'01	16/16
72 t-	Gandy, Wayne	T	6-5	308	2/10/71	13	Auburn	Haines City, Fla.	T(NO)-'06	16/16*
33	Griffith, Justin	FB	5-11	232	4/13/81	4	Mississippi State	Magee, Miss.	D4-'03	16/15
21	Hall, DeAngelo	CB	5-10	197	11/19/83	3	Virginia Tech	Chesapeake, Va.	D1a-'04	15/15
50	Hartwell, Edgerton	LB	6-1	250	5/27/78	6	Western Illinois	Las Vegas, Nev.	UFA(Balt)-'05	5/5
12	Jenkins, Michael	WR	6-4	217	6/18/82	3	Ohio State	Tampa, Fla.	D1b-'04	14/12
11	Johnson, Kerry	WR	6-3	200	3/6/82	2	Mississippi	Oxford, Miss.	FA-'05	0*
73	Jones, Garrick	T	6-5	306	12/2/78	3	Arkansas State	Little Rock, Ark.	FA-'06	0*
97	Kerney, Patrick	DE	6-5	273	12/30/76	8	Virginia	Newtown, Pa.	D1-'99	16/16
66	King, Austin	C	6-5	303	4/11/81	4	Northwestern	Cincinnati, Ohio	FA-'04	16/1
9	Koenen, Michael	P	5-11	195	7/13/82	2	Western Washington	Ferndale, Wash.	FA-'05	16/0
96	Lake, Antwan	DE	6-4	308	7/10/79	4	West Virginia	Cambridge, Md.	FA-'03	13/2
93	Lavalais, Chad	DT	6-1	293	4/15/79	3	Louisiana State	Marksville, La.	D5-'04	14/14
53	Leake, John	LB	6-0	228	8/28/81	2	Clemson	Plano, Texas	FA-'06	11/0*
61	Lehr, Matt	G	6-2	304	4/25/79	6	Virginia Tech	Jacksonville, Fla.	UFA(StL)-'05	15/15
26	Lowe, Omare	S	6-1	195	4/20/78	5	Washington	Seattle, Wash.	W(Sea)-'05	16/1
77	Mallard, Josh	DE	6-2	259	3/21/79	2	Georgia	Savannah, Ga.	FA-'06	0*
11	Marler, Seth	K	6-1	200	3/27/81	3	Tulane	Atlanta, Ga.	FA-'06	0*
23	Mathis, Kevin	CB	5-9	185	4/29/74	10	Texas A&M-Commerce	Gainesville, Texas	FA-'02	0*
62	McClure, Todd	C	6-1	286	2/16/77	8	Louisiana State	Baton Rouge, La.	D7-'99	16/16
44	McCrary, Fred	FB	6-0	247	9/19/72	10	Mississippi State	Naples, Fla.	FA-'04	15/0
36	Milloy, Lawyer	S	6-0	210	11/14/73	11	Washington	St. Louis, Mo.	FA-'06	16/16*
39	Newton, Cam	S	6-1	203	5/19/82	2	Furman	Darlington, S.C.	FA-'05	6/0
70	Omiyale, Frank	T	6-4	310	11/23/82	2	Tennessee Tech	Nashville, Tenn.	D5b-'05	0*
82	Pathon, Jerome	WR	6-0	195	12/16/75	9	Washington	Cape Town, South Africa	FA-'06	8/0
48	Rackley, Derek	TE	6-4	250	7/18/77	7	Minnesota	Apple Valley, Minn.	FA '00	16/0
98	Reese, Ike	LB	6-2	222	10/16/73	9	Michigan State	Jacksonville, N.C.	UFA(Phil)-'05	16/0
20	Rossum, Allen	CB	5-8	178	10/22/75	9	Notre Dame	Dallas, Texas	UFA(GB)-'02	10/0
94	Savage, Josh	DE	6-4	276	9/28/80	2	Utah	Hillcrest, Utah	FA-'05	1/0
8	Schaub, Matt	QB	6-5	237	6/25/81	3	Virginia	Westchester, Pa.	D3-'04	16/1
71	Shropshire, Darrell	DT	6-2	301	3/18/83	2	South Carolina	Kershaw, S.C.	D7-'05	10/0
22	Torrence, Leigh	CB	6-0	183	1/4/82	2	Stanford	Raleigh, N.C.	FA-'05	10/0
7	Vick, Michael	QB	6-0	215	6/26/80	6	Virginia Tech	Newport News, Va.	D1-'01	15/15
27	Webster, Jason	CB	5-9	187	9/8/77	7	Texas A&M	Houston, Texas	UFA(SF)-'04	15/13
74	Weiner, Todd	T	6-4	297	9/16/75	9	Kansas State	Coral Springs, Fla.	UFA(Sea)-'02	16/15
84	White, Roddy	WR	6-0	208	11/2/81	2	Alabama-Birmingham	James Island, S.C.	D1-'05	16/8
51	Williams, Demorrio	LB	6-0	232	7/6/80	3	Nebraska	Beckville, Texas	D4-'04	16/16

* Abraham played 16 games with N.Y. Jets in '05; Beck missed '05 season because of injury; Clabo inactive 2 games with Denver in '04; Crocker played 16 games with Cleveland; Gandy played 16 games with New Orleans; Johnson missed '05 season because of injury; Jones last active with Houston in '04; Leake played 8 games with Atlanta and 3 games with Green Bay; Mallard last active with Indianapolis in '02; Marler last active with Jacksonville in '03; Mathis missed '05 season because of injury; Milloy played 16 games with Buffalo; Omiyale inactive 16 games with Atlanta.

t- Falcons traded for Abraham (NYJ); Gandy (NO).

Players lost through free agency (3): S Kevin McCadam (Car; 16 games in '05), T Kevin Shaffer (Cle; 16), T Barry Stokes (Det; 16).

Also played with Falcons in '05—WR Romby Bryant (3 games), S Keion Carpenter (15), LB Antoine Cash (3), S Antuan Edwards (4), DE Junior Glymph (3), S/CB Ronnie Heard (16), CB Christian Morton (4), K Todd Peterson (16), DE Constantin Ritzmann (1), S/CB Bryan Scott (16), DE Brady Smith (5), LB Artie Ulmer (9), WR Dez White (6).

2006 FIRST-YEAR ROSTER

Name	Pos.	Ht.	Wt.	Birthdate	College	Hometown	How Acq.
Alinen, Klaus (1)	TE	6-6	275	2/22/81	None	Pori, Finland	FA
Ballard, Derrick (1)	LB	6-2	206	12/8/81	Memphis	Madison, Ga.	FA
Bergeron, Troy	WR	6-2	190	12/3/83	Middle Tennessee State	Columbus, Ga.	FA
Bonner, Cedric (1)	WR	6-1	170	12/14/78	Texas A&M-Commerce	Dallas, Texas	FA-'05
Bowers, Ryan	S	6-1	210	8/8/80	Presbyterian	Evans, Ga.	FA
Bozeman, Michael	DT	6-2	290	12/9/82	Mississippi	Hawkinsville, Ga.	FA
Carrington, Paul	DE	6-7	250	11/11/82	Central Florida	Guyton, Ga.	FA
Cecil, Toby (1)	C	6-4	290	12/26/80	Texas Tech	Lubbock, Texas	FA
Derr, Zac (1)	K	5-9	180	3/8/79	Akron	Pittsburgh, Pa.	FA
Dudley, Kevin (1)	FB	6-0	238	1/2/82	Michigan	Brookville, Ind.	FA
Fells, Daniel	TE	6-4	252	9/23/83	California-Davis	Anaheim, Calif.	FA
Ferentz, Brian	C	6-3	282	3/28/83	Iowa	Iowa City, Iowa	FA
Ferri, Diamond (1)	RB	5-10	223	8/6/81	Syracuse	Everett, Mass.	FA
Jackson, Jonathan (1)	DE	6-3	250	10/17/82	Oklahoma	Houston, Texas	FA
Jackson, Tommy	DT	6-1	311	12/13/83	Auburn	Opelika, Ala.	FA
Jennings, Adam	WR	5-9	181	11/17/82	Fresno State	Granite Bay, Calif.	D6
Jones, Garrick (1)	T	6-5	306	12/2/78	Arkansas State	Little Rock, Ark.	FA
Magner, Cole (1)	WR	6-2	196	11/11/82	Bowling Green	Ojai, Calif.	FA
McGee, Chris	G	6-4	285	9/2/82	Tulane	Beaumont, Texas	FA
Miller, Brook	DT	6-4	295	8/11/81	San Diego State	Bakersfield, Calif.	FA
Norwood, Jerious	RB	5-11	204	7/29/83	Mississippi State	Brandon, Mich.	D3
Ojinnaka, Quinn	T	6-5	292	4/23/84	Syracuse	Seabrook, Md.	D5
Pannozzo, John	FB	5-11	235	12/5/84	Indiana	Brooklyn, N.Y.	FA
Patterson, Martin (1)	LB	6-1	243	2/18/83	Texas Christian	Dallas, Texas	FA
Randall, Bryan (1)	QB	6-0	222	8/16/83	Virginia Tech	Williamsburg, Va.	FA
Randall, Jason (1)	TE	6-5	280	12/26/82	Michigan State	Muskegon Heights, Mich.	FA
Redd, Robert (1)	CB	5-10	200	11/1/80	Bowling Green	Dayton, Ohio	FA
Reis, Chris	S	6-1	215	9/19/83	Georgia Tech	Roswell, Ga.	FA
Rossner, Ryan (1)	K	6-3	230	3/30/82	Stephen F. Austin	Marrero, La.	FA
Shockley, D.J.	QB	6-0	214	3/25/83	Georgia	College Park, Ga.	D7
Tarquinio, Gavin	LS	6-3	250	10/24/83	Georgia Tech	Marietta, Ga.	FA
Threat, Greg	S	6-0	196	8/8/81	Miami	Tallahassee, Fla.	FA
Treaudo, Ahmad (1)	CB	5-10	181	4/15/82	Southern	New Orleans, LA	FA-'05
Turnbull, Nick	S	6-2	216	7/28/81	Florida International	Miramar, Fla.	FA
Williams, Jimmy	CB	6-2	216	3/8/84	Virginia Tech	Hampton, Va.	D2
Williams, Travis	LB	6-1	213	1/20/83	Auburn	Columbia, S.C.	FA
Yelk, Tony	K	6-1	205	9/29/81	Iowa State	Arlington, Wis.	FA
Youngblood, Kevin (1)	WR	6-5	215	11/22/80	Clemson	Jacksonville, Fla.	FA

The term NFL Rookie is defined as a player who is in his first season of professional football and has not been on the roster of another professional football team for any regular-season or postseason games. A Rookie is designated by an "R" on NFL rosters. Players who have been active in another professional football league or players who have NFL experience, including either preseason training camp or being on an Active List or Inactive List, or on Reserve/Injured or Reserve/Physically Unable to Perform for fewer than six regular-season games, are termed NFL First-Year Players. An NFL First-Year Player is designated by a "1" on NFL rosters. Thereafter, a player is credited with an additional year of experience for each season in which he accumulates six games on the Active List or Inactive List, or on Reserve/Injured or Reserve/Physically Unable to Perform.

Log on to www.atlantafalcons.com for an up-to-date roster.

COACHING STAFF

Executive Vice President/Head Coach, Jim Mora

Pro Career: Third-year head coach Jim Mora was hired by the Falcons on January 9, 2004. In 2004, set franchise record for the most wins by a first year head coach and became eleventh rookie head coach in NFL history to capture a division title. Directed team to second NFC championship game in franchise history in his first year. Led the NFL in rushing offense for the past two seasons and the defense led NFL in quarterback sacks (48) in 2004. In 2003, in his fifth season as defensive coordinator of the San Francisco 49ers, Mora's unit finished fourth in the NFC in total defense and tied for fourth in the NFL with 42 quarterback sacks. In 2001, the defense ranked sixth in the NFL in scoring defense, allowing only 16.3 points per game. The team also registered three shutouts, the most in 49ers history. Mora served as the 49ers' secondary coach (1997-98). He was named as the Saints' secondary coach in 1992. During his five years in New Orleans (1992-96), the team twice led the NFL in fewest passing yards allowed (1992-93). Mora spent seven seasons in the Chargers' organization as a member of the pro personnel department (1985), defensive assistant in the secondary (1986-88), and defensive backs coach (1989-1991). Career record: 20-14.

Background: Mora played defensive back for Washington (1980-83), appearing in two Rose Bowls. He served as an assistant for one season (1984) on Don James' staff, helping the squad earn a berth in the Orange Bowl.

Personal: Born November 19, 1961 in Los Angeles. Mora attended Interlake High in Bellevue, Wash. He is the son of former NFL head coach Jim Mora. He and his wife, Shannon, have four children: Cole, Lillia, Ryder, and Trey.

ASSISTANT COACHES

Sal Alosi, strength and conditioning; born May 11, 1977, Massapequa, N.Y. Linebacker Hofstra 1996-2000. No pro playing experience. College coach: Hofstra 2001. Pro coach: New York Jets 2002-05, joined Falcons in 2006.

Clancy Barone, tight ends; born July 26, 1963, San Andreas, Calif. Offensive lineman Cal State-Sacramento 1981-82, Nevada 1985-86. No pro playing experience. College coach: American River (Calif.) J.C. 1987-1989, Cal State-Sacramento 1990-92, Texas A&M 1993, Eastern Illinois 1994-96, Wyoming 1997-1999, Houston 2000-02, Texas State 2003. Pro coach: Joined Falcons in 2004.

Chris Beake, linebackers; born September 10, 1972, Kansas City, Mo. Quarterback Air Force 1990-92. No pro playing experience. College coach: Air Force 1994-95. Pro coach: San Francisco 49ers 1999-2003, joined Falcons in 2004.

Tom Cable, offensive line; born November 26, 1964, Merced, Calif. Offensive lineman Idaho 1982-86. Pro offensive lineman Indianapolis Colts 1987. College coach: Idaho 1987-88, San Diego State 1989, Cal State-Fullerton 1990, UNLV 1991, California 1992-97, Colorado 1998-99, Idaho 2000-03, UCLA 2004-05. Pro coach: Joined Falcons in 2006.

Chris Dalman, offensive assistant; born March 15, 1970, Salinas, Calif. Guard/center Stanford 1989-1992. Pro center San Francisco 49ers 1993-2000. Pro coach: Joined Falcons in 2005.

Joe DeCamillis, special teams coordinator; born June 29, 1965, Arvada, Colo. Attended Wyoming. No college or pro playing experience. College coach: Wyoming 1988. Pro coach: Denver Broncos 1989, Miami Dolphins 1990, New York Giants 1993-96, joined Falcons in 1997.

Ed Donatell, defensive coordinator; born February 4, 1957, Akron, Ohio. Defensive back Glenville (W. Va.) State 1975-78. College coach: Kent State 1979-1980, Washington 1981-82, Pacific 1983-85, Idaho 1986-88, Cal State-Fullerton 1989. Pro coach: New York Jets 1990-94, Denver Broncos 1995-99, Green Bay Packers 2000-03, joined Falcons in 2004.

Alex Gibbs, consultant/offensive line; born February 22, 1941 Morganton, N.C. Running back/defensive back Davidson College 1959-1963. No pro playing experience. College coach: Duke 1969-1970, Kentucky 1971-72, West Virginia 1973-74, Ohio State 1975-78, Auburn 1979-1981, Georgia 1982-83. Pro coach: Denver Broncos 1984-87, Oakland Raiders 1988-89, San Diego Chargers 1990-91, Indianapolis Colts 1992, Kansas City Chiefs 1993-94, Denver Broncos 1995-2003, joined Falcons in 2004.

Steve Hoffman, kickers; born September 8, 1958, Camden, N.J. Quarterback/running back/wide receiver Dickinson College 1977-1980. Pro punter Washington Federals (USFL) 1983. College coach: Miami 1985-87. Pro coach: Dallas Cowboys 1989-2004, joined Falcons in 2006.

Bill Johnson, defensive line; born June 23, 1955, Monroe, La. Defensive lineman Northwestern (La.) State 1976-79. No pro playing experience. College coach: Northwestern (La.) State 1980-81, McNeese State 1985-86, Miami 1987, Louisiana Tech 1988-89, Arkansas 1990-91, 2000, Texas A&M 1992-99. Pro coach: Joined Falcons in 2001.

Billy 'Whiteshoes' Johnson, asst. strength and conditioning; born January 21, 1952, Boothwyn, Pa. Wide receiver Widener 1971-74. Pro wide receiver Houston Oilers 1974-1980, Atlanta Falcons 1982-87, Washington Redskins 1988. Pro coach: Joined Falcons in 2006.

Greg Knapp, offensive coordinator; born March 5, 1963, Long Beach, Calif.

Quarterback Cal State-Sacramento 1982-85. No pro playing experience. College coach: Cal State-Sacramento 1986-1994. Pro coach: San Francisco 49ers 1995-2003, joined Falcons in 2004.

Joe Lombardi, defensive assistant; born June 6, 1981, Seattle. Tight end Air Force 1992-94. No pro playing experience. College coach: Dayton 1996-98, Virginia Military Institute 1999, Bucknell 2000, Mercyhurst 2002-05. Pro coach: Joined Falcons in 2006.

Brett Maxie, defensive backs; born January 13, 1962, Dallas. Safety Texas Southern 1982-85. Pro safety New Orleans Saints 1985-1993, Atlanta Falcons 1994, Carolina Panthers 1995-96, San Francisco 49ers 1997. Pro coach: Carolina Panthers 1998, San Francisco 49ers 1999-2003, joined Falcons in 2004.

Bill Musgrave, quarterbacks; born November 11, 1967, Grand Junction, Colo. Quarterback Oregon 1987-1990. Pro quarterback San Francisco 49ers 1991-94, Denver Broncos 1995-96. College coach: Virgnia 2001-02. Pro coach: Oakland Raiders 1997, Philadelphia Eagles 1998, Carolina Panthers 1999-2000, Jacksonville Jaguars 2003-04, Washington Redskins 2005, joined Falcons in 2006.

Robert Prince, asst. quarterbacks; born May 8, 1965, Okinawa, Japan. Wide receiver Humboldt State 1985-86. No pro playing experience. College coach: Humboldt State 1989-1990, Montana State 1991, Cal State-Sacramento 1992-93, Fort Lewis College 1994-95, Recruit Seagulls (X League Japan) 1996-97, Portland State 1998-2000, Boise State 2001-03. Pro coach: Joined Falcons in 2004.

George Stewart, wide receivers; born December 29, 1958, Little Rock, Ark. Guard Arkansas 1977-1980. No pro playing experience. College coach: Minnesota 1984-85, Notre Dame 1986-88. Pro coach: Pittsburgh Steelers 1989-1991, Tampa Bay Buccaneers 1992-95, San Francisco 49ers 1996-2002, joined Falcons in 2003.

Emmitt Thomas, senior defensive assistant/secondary; born June 3, 1943, Angleton, Texas. Quarterback/receiver Bishop (Texas) College 1963-65. Pro defensive back Kansas City Chiefs 1966-1978. College coach: Central Missouri State 1979-1980. Pro coach: St. Louis Cardinals 1981-85, Washington Redskins 1986-1994, Philadelphia Eagles 1995-98, Green Bay Packers 1999, Minnesota Vikings 2000-01, joined Falcons in 2002.

Ollie Wilson, running backs; born March 3, 1951, Worcester, Mass. Wide receiver Springfield 1971-73. No pro playing experience. College coach: Springfield 1975, Northeastern 1976-1982, California 1983-1990. Pro coach: Atlanta Falcons 1991-96, San Diego Chargers 1997-2001, rejoined Falcons in 2002.

**National Football Conference
South Division
Team Colors:** Black, Panther Blue, and
Silver
**800 South Mint Street
Charlotte, North Carolina 28202-1502
Telephone:** (704) 358-7000

2006 SCHEDULE
PRESEASON
Aug. 12 **Buffalo** 7:30
Aug. 19 at Jacksonville...................7:30
Aug. 24 **Miami** 8:00
Aug. 31 at Pittsburgh.......................7:30

REGULAR SEASON
Sept. 10 **Atlanta**.............................1:00
Sept. 17 at Minnesota 12:00
Sept. 24 at Tampa Bay 1:00
Oct. 1 **New Orleans**.....................1:00
Oct. 8 **Cleveland** 1:00
Oct. 15 at Baltimore.......................1:00
Oct. 22 at Cincinnati 1:00
Oct. 29 **Dallas** 8:15
Nov. 5 Open Date
Nov. 13 **Tampa Bay** (Mon.) 8:30
Nov. 19 **St. Louis** 1:00
Nov. 26 at Washington 1:00
Dec. 4 at Philadelphia (Mon.).......8:30
Dec. 10 **N.Y. Giants**.........................1:00
Dec. 17 **Pittsburgh**.........................1:00
Dec. 24 at Atlanta............................1:00
Dec. 31 at New Orleans................12:00

Stadium: Bank of America Stadium
(opened in 1996)
• **Capacity:** 73,298
Charlotte, North Carolina
28202-1502
Playing Surface: Grass
Training Camp: Wofford College
Spartanburg,
South Carolina 29303

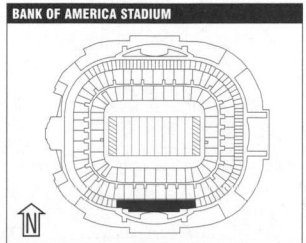

BANK OF AMERICA STADIUM

CLUB OFFICIALS
Owner/Founder: Jerry Richardson
President, Panthers Football LLC:
Mark Richardson
President Panthers Stadium LLC:
Jon Richardson
General Manager: Marty Hurney
General Counsel: Richard Thigpen
Chief Financial Officer: Dave Olsen
Controller: Mike Dudan
Director of Pro Scouting: Mark Koncz
Pro Scouts: Trent Kirchner, Tag Ribary,
Brandon Taylor
Director of College Scouting: Tony Softli
College Scouts: Brian Adams,
Bucky Brooks, Ryan Cowden,
Khary Darlington, Jeff Morrow,
Joe Schoen, Mike Szabo,
Gerald Williams
Director of Communications:
Charlie Dayton
Communications Assistant:
Bruce Speight
Public Relations Assistant: Deedee Mills
Media Relations Assistant:
Steven Drummond
Director of Ticket Operations:
Phil Youtsey
Director of Player Relations: Donnie Shell
Director of Community Relations and
Cheerleader/Mascot Programs:
Riley Fields
Cheerleader/Mascot Program Manager:
Tina Becker
Director of Sales and Sponsor Services:
Kyle Caddell
Director of Broadcast Administration:
Henry Thomas
Executive Producer-Television:
Greg Brannon
Executive Producer-Radio: David Langton
Director of Information Systems:
Troy Bigelow
Salary Cap Analyst/Negotiatior:
Rob Rogers
Video Director: Mark Hobbs
Assistant Video Director: Jeff Mueller
Head Trainer: Ryan Vermillion
Assistant Trainers: Mark Shermansky,
Reggie Scott
Equipment Manager: Jackie Miles
Assistant Equipment Manager: Don Toner
Director of Security: Gene Brown
Stadium Operations Manager: Scott Paul
Director of Entertainment and
Panthervision: Kyle Ritchie
Facilities Manager: Matthew Getz
Head Groundskeeper: Tom Vaughan
Human Resources/Office Manager:
Tracy Rivers

COACHING HISTORY
(88-97-0)
Records include postseason games
1995-98   Dom Capers 31-35-0
1999-2001 George Seifert 16-32-0
2002-05   John Fox.....................41-30-0

ATTENDANCE
Home 578,033   Away 464,135
Total 1,042,168
Single-game home record,
76,136 (12/10/95)
Single-season home record, 578,033
(2005)

2006 DRAFT CHOICES
Round	Name	Pos.	College
1	DeAngelo Williams	RB	Memphis
2	Richard Marshall	DB	Fresno State
3	James Anderson	LB	Virginia Tech
	Rashad Butler	T	Miami
4	Nate Salley	DB	Ohio State
5	Jeff King	TE	Virginia Tech
7	Will Montgomery	G	Virginia Tech
	Stanley McClover	DE	Auburn

2005 TEAM RECORD

PRESEASON (2-2)

8/13	W	28-10	Washington
8/20	L	21-27	at N.Y. Giants
8/26	W	23-20	at Cleveland
9/1	L	17-21	Pittsburgh

REGULAR SEASON (11-5)

Date	Result		Opponent	Att.
9/11	L	20-23	New Orleans	72,920
9/18	W	27-17	New England	73,528
9/25	L	24-27	at Miami	72,288
10/3	W	32-29	Green Bay	73,657
10/9	W	24-20	at Arizona	38,809
10/16	W	21-20	at Detroit	61,083
10/30	W	38-13	Minnesota	73,502
11/6	W	34-14	at Tampa Bay	65,014
11/13	W	30-3	New York Jets	73,529
11/20	L	3-13	at Chicago	62,156
11/27	W	13-9	at Buffalo	71,440
12/4	W	24-6	Atlanta	73,661
12/11	L	10-20	Tampa Bay	73,467
12/18	W	27-10	at New Orleans	32,551
12/24	L	20-24	Dallas	73,436
1/1	W	44-11	at Atlanta	70,796

POSTSEASON (2-1)

1/8	W	23-0	at N.Y. Giants	79,378
1/15	W	29-21	at Chicago	62,209
1/22	L	14-34	at Seattle	67,837

SCORE BY PERIODS

Panthers	96	117	53	125	0	—	391
Opponents	72	73	42	72	0	—	259

2005 TEAM STATISTICS

	Panthers	Opp.
Total First Downs	278	262
Rushing	82	72
Passing	157	160
Penalty	39	30
3rd Down: Made/Att	92/218	90/221
3rd Down Pct.	42.2	40.7
4th Down: Made/Att	2/6	5/16
4th Down Pct.	33.3	31.3
Possession Avg.	30:48	29:12
Total Net Yards	4,950	4,522
Avg. Per Game	309.4	282.6
Total Plays	964	981
Avg. Per Play	5.1	4.6
Net Yards Rushing	1,679	1,465
Avg. Per Game	104.9	91.6
Total Rushes	487	408
Net Yards Passing	3,271	3,057
Avg. Per Game	204.4	191.1
Sacked/Yards Lost	28/214	45/294
Gross Yards	3,485	3,351
Att./Completions	449/269	528/305
Completion Pct.	59.9	57.8
Had Intercepted	16	23
Punts/Average	73/43.2	79/45.1
Net Punting Avg.	73/38.6	79/37.4
Penalties/Yards	91/732	128/1045
Fumbles/Ball Lost	23/10	25/19
Touchdowns	45	27
Rushing	17	9
Passing	25	15
Returns	3	3

2005 INDIVIDUAL STATISTICS

PASSING	Att.	Comp.	Yds.	Pct.	TD	Int.	Tkld.	Rate
Delhomme	435	262	3,421	60.2	24	16	28/214	88.1
Weinke	13	7	64	53.8	1	0	0/0	93.1
Foster	1	0	0	0.0	0	0	0/0	39.6
Panthers	449	269	3,485	59.9	25	16	28/214	88.1
Opponents	528	305	3,351	57.8	15	23	45/294	68.0

SCORING	TD R	TD P	TD Rt	PAT	FG	Saf	PTS
Kasay	0	0	0	43/44	26/34	0	121
S. Smith	1	12	0	0/0	0/0	0	78
S. Davis	12	0	0	0/0	0/0	0	72
Proehl	0	4	0	0/0	0/0	0	24
Foster	2	1	0	0/0	0/0	0	18
Colbert	0	2	0	0/0	0/0	0	12
Gaines	0	2	0	0/0	0/0	0	12
Mangum	0	2	0	0/0	0/0	0	12
Carter	0	1	0	0/0	0/0	0	6
Delhomme	1	0	0	0/0	0/0	0	6
Gamble	0	0	1	0/0	0/0	0	6
Gardner	0	1	0	0/0	0/0	0	6
Manning	0	0	1	0/0	0/0	0	6
Robertson	1	0	0	0/0	0/0	0	6
Witherspoon	0	0	1	0/0	0/0	0	6
Panthers	17	25	3	43/44	26/34	0	391
Opponents	9	15	3	22/22	23/27	0	259

2-Pt. Conversions: Team 0-1, Opponents 3-5.

RUSHING	Att.	Yds.	Avg.	LG	TD
Foster	205	879	4.3	70t	2
S. Davis	180	549	3.1	39	12
Goings	37	133	3.6	17	0
Robertson	14	41	2.9	11	1
Delhomme	24	31	1.3	12	1
S. Smith	4	25	6.3	20t	1
Hoover	10	22	2.2	4	0
Colbert	1	6	6.0	6	0
Smart	3	6	2.0	6	0
Weinke	8	-5	-0.6	1	0
Proehl	1	-8	-8.0	-8	0
Panthers	487	1,679	3.4	70t	17
Opponents	408	1,465	3.6	58	9

RECEIVING	No.	Yds.	Avg.	LG	TD
S. Smith	103	1,563	15.2	80t	12
Foster	34	372	10.9	47	1
Proehl	25	441	17.6	69	4
Colbert	25	282	11.3	42	2
Mangum	23	202	8.8	24	2
Goings	14	151	10.8	30	0
Hoover	14	87	6.2	12	0
Gaines	12	155	12.9	38	2
Gardner	9	84	9.3	15	1
Carter	5	103	20.6	40	1
S. Davis	5	45	9.0	21	0
Panthers	269	3,485	13.0	80t	25
Opponents	305	3,351	11.0	86	15

INTERCEPTIONS	No.	Yds.	Avg.	LG	TD
Gamble	7	157	22.4	61t	1
Lucas	6	70	11.7	32	0
McCree	3	73	24.3	46	0
Wallace	2	38	19.0	38	0
Witherspoon	2	35	17.5	35t	1
Manning	2	20	10.0	10	0
Minter	1	47	47.0	47	0
Panthers	23	440	19.1	61t	2
Opponents	16	335	20.9	64t	3

PUNTING	No.	Yds.	Avg.	In 20	LG
Baker	72	3,118	43.3	23	59
Kasay	1	36	36.0	0	36
Panthers	73	3,154	43.2	23	59
Opponents	79	3,562	45.1	18	69

PUNT RETURNS	No.	FC	Yds.	Avg.	LG	TD
S. Smith	27	6	286	10.6	44	0
Gamble	14	5	158	11.3	76	0
Panthers	41	11	444	10.8	76	0
Opponents	36	20	235	6.5	31	0

KICKOFF RETURNS	No.	Yds.	Avg.	LG	TD
Smart	29	615	21.2	60	0
Robertson	16	343	21.4	42	0
S. Smith	3	61	20.3	33	0
Gaines	2	24	12.0	13	0
Goings	1	21	21.0	21	0
Hoover	1	10	10.0	10	0
Mangum	1	9	9.0	9	0
Panthers	53	1,083	20.4	60	0
Opponents	80	1,702	21.3	47	0

FIELD GOALS	1-19	20-29	30-39	40-49	50+
Kasay	1/1	8/8	8/8	6/9	3/8
Panthers	1/1	8/8	8/8	6/9	3/8
Opponents	0/0	6/6	9/11	7/9	1/1

SACKS	No.
Peppers	10.5
Rucker	7.5
Moorehead	5.0
Wallace	5.0
Carstens	4.0
Morgan	3.0
Witherspoon	2.5
Draft	2.0
T. Davis	1.5
Minter	1.5
Buckner	1.0
TEAM	1.0
Short	0.5
Panthers	45.0
Opponents	28.0

RECORD HOLDERS
INDIVIDUAL RECORDS—CAREER

Category	Name	Performance
Rushing (Yds.)	Tshimanga Biakabutuka, 1996-2001	2,530
Passing (Yds.)	Steve Beuerlein, 1996-2000	12,690
Passing (TDs)	Steve Beuerlein, 1996-2000	86
Receiving (No.)	Muhsin Muhammad, 1996-2004	578
Receiving (Yds.)	Muhsin Muhammad, 1996-2004	7,751
Interceptions	Eric Davis, 1996-2000	25
Punting (Avg.)	Todd Sauerbrun, 2001-04	45.5
Punt Return (Avg.)	Winslow Oliver, 1996-98	10.7
Kickoff Return (Avg.)	Michael Bates, 1996-2000	25.7
Field Goals	John Kasay, 1995-2005	228
Touchdowns (Tot.)	Wesley Walls, 1996-2002	44
	Muhsin Muhammad, 1996-2004	44
Points	John Kasay, 1995-2005	964

INDIVIDUAL RECORDS—SINGLE SEASON

Category	Name	Performance
Rushing (Yds.)	Stephen Davis, 2003	1,444
Passing (Yds.)	Steve Beuerlein, 1999	4,436
Passing (TDs)	Steve Beuerlein, 1999	36
Receiving (No.)	Steve Smith, 2005	103
Receiving (Yds.)	Steve Smith, 2005	1,563
Interceptions	Doug Evans, 2001	8
Punting (Avg.)	Todd Sauerbrun, 2001	47.5
Punt Return (Avg.)	Winslow Oliver, 1996	11.5
Kickoff Return (Avg.)	Michael Bates, 1996	30.2
Field Goals	John Kasay, 1996	37
Touchdowns (Tot.)	Muhsin Muhammad, 2004	16
Points	John Kasay, 1996	145

INDIVIDUAL RECORDS—SINGLE GAME

Category	Name	Performance
Rushing (Yds.)	Stephen Davis, 10-26-03	178
Passing (Yds.)	Steve Beuerlein, 12-12-99	373
Passing (TDs)	Steve Beuerlein, 1-2-00	5
Receiving (No.)	Steve Smith, 11-20-05	14
Receiving (Yds.)	Steve Smith, 10-30-05	201
Interceptions	Deon Grant, 9-22-02	3
Field Goals	John Kasay, 12-5-04	6
Touchdowns (Tot.)	Many times	3
	Last time by Steve Smith, 9-25-05	
Points	Fred Lane, 11-2-97	18
	Tshimanga Biakabutuka, 10-3-99	18
	Muhsin Muhammad, 12-18-99, 11-14-04	18
	Steve Smith, 12-8-02, 9-25-05	18
	Nick Goings, 11-21-04	18
	Stephen Davis, 9-18-05	18

2006 VETERAN ROSTER

No.	Name	Pos.	Ht.	Wt.	Birthdate	NFL Exp.	College	Hometown	How Acq.	'05 Games/ Starts
50	Adams, Keith	LB	5-11	223	11/22/79	6	Clemson	Atlanta, Ga.	UFA(Phil)-'06	16/16*
7	Baker, Jason	P	6-2	205	5/17/78	6	Iowa	Fort Wayne, Ind.	T(Den)-'05	16/0
	Beasley, Chad	T	6-5	302	11/13/78	4	Virginia Tech	Gate City, Va.	FA-'06	0*
28	Branch, Colin	S	5-11	205	3/2/80	4	Stanford	Carlsbad, Calif.	D4-'03	0*
	Brown, Tony	DT	6-1	280	9/29/80	2	Memphis	Chattanooga, Tenn.	FA-'06	0*
67	Carstens, Jordan	DT	6-5	300	1/22/81	3	Iowa State	Bagley, Iowa	FA-'04	16/15
18	Carter, Drew	WR	6-3	200	9/5/81	3	Ohio State	Solon, Ohio	D5-'04	3/0
54	Ciurciu, Vinny	LB	6-0	235	5/2/80	4	Boston College	Paramus, N.J.	FA -'03	15/1
83	Colbert, Keary	WR	6-1	200	5/21/82	3	Southern California	Oxnard, Calif.	D2-'04	16/16
49	Cramer, Casey	FB	6-2	250	1/5/82	3	Dartmouth	Middleton, Wis.	FA-'05	1/0
58	Davis, Thomas	S	6-0	231	3/22/83	2	Georgia	Shellman, Ga.	D1-'05	16/1
17	Delhomme, Jake	QB	6-2	215	1/10/75	8	Louisiana-Lafayette	Lafayette, La.	UFA(NO)-'03	16/16
53	Diggs, Na'il	LB	6-4	240	7/8/78	7	Ohio State	Los Angeles, Calif.	FA-'06	9/6*
52	Draft, Chris	LB	5-11	232	2/26/76	8	Stanford	Placentia, Calif.	FA-'05	16/3
98	Ellison, Atiyyah	DT	6-3	303	9/29/81	2	Missouri	St. Louis, Mo.	FA-'05	0*
78	Fordham, Todd	T	6-5	319	10/9/73	10	Florida State	Atlanta, Ga.	T(Pitt)-'04	16/0
26	Foster, DeShaun	RB	6-0	222	1/10/80	5	UCLA	Tustin, Calif.	D2-'02	15/5
84	Gaines, Michael	TE	6-3	280	3/30/80	3	Central Florida	Tallahassee, Fla.	D7-'04	11/6
20	Gamble, Chris	CB	6-1	200	3/11/83	3	Ohio State	Sunrise, Fla.	D1-'04	15/15
37	Goings, Nick	RB	6-0	225	1/26/78	6	Pittsburgh	Dublin, Ohio	FA-'01	16/1
	Grigsby, Otis	DE	6-3	260	11/19/80	2	Kentucky	Converse, Texas	FA-'06	0*
69	Gross, Jordan	T	6-4	300	7/20/80	4	Utah	Fruitland, Idaho	D1-'03	16/16
63	Hangartner, Geoff	C	6-5	301	4/22/82	2	Texas A&M	New Braunfels, Texas	D5b-'05	6/0
88	Hankton, Karl	WR	6-2	202	7/24/70	8	Trinity College (Ill.)	New Orleans, La.	FA-'00	16/0
75	Hartwig, Justin	C	6-4	312	11/21/78	5	Kansas	West Des Moines, IA	UFA(Tenn)-'06	16/16*
92	Haye, Jovan	DE	6-2	290	6/21/82	2	Vanderbilt	Fort Lauderdale, Fla.	D6a-'05	2/0
45	Hoover, Brad	FB	6-0	245	11/11/76	7	Western Carolina	Thomasville, N.C.	FA-'00	15/15
23	Howard, Reggie	CB	6-0	185	5/17/77	7	Memphis	Memphis, Tenn.	FA-'06	15/7*
48	Jenkins, Corey	LB	6-1	228	8/25/76	3	South Carolina	Columbia, S.C.	FA-'06	0*
77	Jenkins, Kris	DT	6-4	335	8/3/79	6	Maryland	Ypsilanti, Mich.	D2-'01	1/1
19	Johnson, Keyshawn	WR	6-4	211	7/22/72	11	Southern California	Los Angeles, Calif.	FA-'06	16/14*
61	Kadela, Dave	T	6-6	304	5/6/78	5	Virginia Tech	Dearborn, Mich.	FA-'04	0*
4	Kasay, John	K	5-10	198	10/27/69	16	Georgia	Athens, Ga.	UFA(Sea)-'95	16/0
99	Kemoeatu, Maake	DT	6-5	350	1/10/79	5	Utah	Kahuku, Hawaii	UFA(Pitt)-'06	16/16*
6	Knorr, Micah	P	6-2	199	1/9/75	6	Utah State	Orange, Calif.	FA-'06	0*
56	Kyle, Jason	LB	6-3	242	5/12/72	12	Arizona State	Tempe, Ariz.	UFA(SF)-'01	16/0
3	LeFors, Stefan	QB	6-0	201	6/7/81	2	Louisville	Baton Rouge, La.	D4-'05	0*
97	Leverette, Otis	DE	6-7	278	5/31/78	4	Alabama-Birmingham	Americus, Ga.	FA-'06	0*
91	Lewis, Damione	DT	6-2	301	3/1/78	6	Miami	Sulphur Springs, Texas	UFA(StL)-'06	16/7*
21	Lucas, Ken	CB	6-0	205	1/23/79	6	Mississippi	Cleveland, Miss.	UFA(Sea)-'05	15/15
86	Mangum, Kris	TE	6-4	252	8/15/73	9	Mississippi	Magee, Miss.	D7-'97	14/9
71	Mathis, Evan	G	6-5	304	11/1/81	2	Alabama	Homewood, Ala.	D3a-'05	9/0
25	McCadam, Kevin	S	6-1	219	3/6/79	5	Virginia Tech	Lakeside, Calif.	UFA(Atl)-'06	16/0*
30	Minter, Mike	S	5-10	195	1/15/74	10	Nebraska	Lawton, Okla.	D2-'97	16/16
60	#Mitchell, Jeff	C	6-4	300	1/29/74	10	Florida	Dallas, Texas	UFA(Balt)-'01	16/16
94	Moorehead, Kindal	DT	6-2	285	10/14/78	4	Alabama	Memphis, Tenn.	D5-'03	15/0
55	Morgan, Dan	LB	6-2	245	12/19/78	6	Miami	Coral Springs, Fla.	D1-'01	13/13
	Peck, Jared	T	6-5	290	5/6/79	2	North Dakota State	Bloomington, Minn.	FA-'06	0*
90	Peppers, Julius	DE	6-7	283	1/18/80	5	North Carolina	Bailey, N.C.	D1-'02	16/16
64	Peters, Scott	G	6-3	300	11/23/78	3	Arizona State	Pleasanton, Calif.	FA-'05	0*
81	#Proehl, Ricky	WR	6-0	190	3/7/68	17	Wake Forest	Hillsborough, N.J.	UFA(StL)-'03	16/0
22	Robertson, Jamal	RB	5-10	210	1/10/77	5	Ohio Northern	Washington, D.C.	FA-'04	7/0
93	Rucker, Micheal	DE	6-5	275	2/28/75	8	Nebraska	St. Joseph, Mo.	D2b-'99	15/14
82	Seidman, Mike	TE	6-4	261	2/11/81	4	UCLA	Westlake Village, Calif.	D3a-'03	12/1
59	Seward, Adam	LB	6-2	248	6/15/82	2	Nevada-Las Vegas	Las Vegas, Nev.	D5a-'05	4/0
32	Shelton, Eric	RB	6-1	246	6/23/83	2	Louisville	Lexington, Ky.	D2-'05	0*
89	Smith, Steve	WR	5-9	185	5/12/79	6	Utah	Lynwood, Calif.	D3-'01	16/16
57	Tufts, Sean	LB	6-4	245	3/26/82	3	Colorado	Aurora, Colo.	FA-'05	12/0
68	Wahle, Mike	G	6-6	304	3/29/77	9	Navy	Lake Arrowhead, Calif.	UFA(GB)-'05	16/16
96	Wallace, Al	DE	6-5	275	3/25/74	7	Maryland	West Palm Beach, Fla.	T(Mia)-'02	16/2
16	Weinke, Chris	QB	6-4	232	7/31/72	6	Florida State	St. Paul, Minn.	D4-'01	3/0
70	Wharton, Travelle	T	6-4	312	5/19/81	3	South Carolina	Simpsonville, S.C.	D3-'04	16/16
36	Williams, Shaun	S	6-2	218	10/10/76	9	UCLA	Encino, Calif.	UFA(NYG)-'06	8/0*

* Adams played 16 games with Philadelphia in '05; Beasley missed '04 season with Cleveland because of injury; Branch missed
'05 season because of injury; Brown last active with San Francisco in '04; Diggs played 9 games with Green Bay; Ellison inactive for
10 games; Grigsby last active with Miami in '03; Hartwig played 16 games with Tennessee; Howard played 15 games with Miami;
Jenkins last active with Miami in '04; Johnson played 16 games with Dallas; Kadela inactive for 16 games; Kemoeatu played 16 games
with Baltimore; Knorr last active with Denver in '04; LeFors inactive for 16 games; Leverette last active with San Francisco in '04; Lewis
played 16 games with St. Louis; McCadam played 16 games with Atlanta; Peck last active with Atlanta in '04; Peters last active with
San Francisco in '04; Shelton missed '05 season because of injury; Williams played 8 games with N.Y. Giants.

\# Unrestricted free agent, subject to developments.

Players lost through free agency (7): S Idrees Bashir (Det; 11 games in '05), CB Ricky Manning Jr. (Chi; 16),
S Marlon McCree (SD; 16), DE Kemp Rasmussen (Sea; 15), G/T Tutan Reyes (Buff; 16), CB Dante Wesley (Chl; 16);
LB Will Witherspoon (StL; 15).

Also played with Carolina in '05—DT Brentson Buckner (16 games), RB Stephen Davis (13), WR Rod Gardner (11),
LB Brandon Short (16), RB Rod Smart (12).

2006 FIRST-YEAR ROSTER

Name	Pos.	Ht.	Wt.	Birthdate	College	Hometown	How Acq.
Alexander, Lorenzo (1)	DT	6-1	301	5/31/83	California	Berkeley, Calif.	FA-'05
Anderson, James	LB	6-2	232	9/26/83	Virginia Tech	Chesapeake, Va.	D3a
Basanez, Brett	QB	6-2	210	5/11/83	Northwestern	Arlington Heights, Ill.	FA
Bergeron, David (1)	LB	6-3	245	12/4/81	Stanford	Lake Oswego, Ore.	FA-'05
Biddle, Taye	WR	6-1	175	2/27/83	Mississippi	Decatur, Ala.	FA
Bouknight, Jovon	WR	6-1	191	7/15/83	Wyoming	Denver, Colo.	FA
Bush, Jarrett	CB	6-1	192	5/21/84	Utah State	Vacaville, Calif.	FA
Butler, Rashad	T	6-4	293	2/10/83	Miami	Palm Beach Gardens, Fla.	D3b
Cassel, Marcus	CB	6-0	189	1/6/83	UCLA	Carson, Calif.	FA
Cherry, Matt (1)	WR	6-1	203	12/14/81	Akron	Wilmette, Ill.	FA-'05
Evwaraye, Seppo	G	6-5	320	6/1/82	Nebraska	Laurel, Neb.	FA
Fitzhugh, Shannon (1)	CB	5-11	202	9/19/81	Western Illinois	Schaumburg, Ill.	FA-'05
Hardy, Jermaine (1)	S	5-10	213	3/20/82	Virginia	Roanoke, Va.	FA-'05
Hawkins, Phil (1)	G	6-4	325	2/26/82	Houston	Chicago, Ill.	FA-'05
Haynes, Alex (1)	RB	5-10	223	2/13/82	Central Florida	Orlando, Fla.	FA-'05
Hill, Efrem (1)	WR	6-0	179	7/23/83	Samford	Atlanta, Ga.	FA-'05
Jackson, Lynzell	WR	6-2	193	1/31/82	Weber State	Tempe, Ariz.	FA
King, Jeff	TE	6-3	253	2/19/83	Virginia Tech	Pulaski, Va.	D5
Long, Devan	DE	6-4	258	8/31/83	Oregon	Anacortes, Wash.	FA
Marshall, Richard	CB	5-11	189	12/12/84	Fresno State	Los Angeles, Calif.	D2
McClover, Stanley	DE	6-2	263	12/16/84	Auburn	Fort Lauderdale, Fla.	D7b
McCullum, Justin	WR	6-4	220	10/5/82	Stanford	Mercer Island, Wash.	FA
Montgomery, Will	C	6-3	312	2/13/83	Virginia Tech	Clifton, Va.	D7a
Mulcahy, Sean (1)	TE	6-5	297	2/14/82	Connecticut	Westport, Conn.	FA-'05
O'Connor, Adam	G	6-8	270	1/27/83	William & Mary	Greensboro, N.C.	FA
Parker, Billy (1)	CB	6-0	195	5/17/81	William & Mary	Mechanicsville, Va.	FA-'05
Salley, Nate	S	6-1	216	2/5/84	Ohio State	Fort Lauderdale, Fla.	D4
Samp, Chris (1)	WR	6-3	217	7/12/80	Winona State	Green Bay, Wis.	FA-'05
Smith, Daniel	WR	6-1	210	5/5/83	Idaho	Houston, Texas	FA
Stenavich, Adam	T	6-5	317	3/11/83	Michigan	Marshfield, Wis.	FA
Toeaina, Albert	T	6-6	355	6/26/84	Tennessee	Antioch, Calif.	FA
Wilds, Garnell (1)	CB	5-11	189	6/8/81	Virginia Tech	Tampa, Fla.	FA-'05
Williams, DeAngelo	RB	5-9	217	4/25/83	Memphis	Wynne, Ark.	D1

The term NFL Rookie is defined as a player who is in his first season of professional football and has not been on the roster of another professional football team for any
regular-season or postseason games. A Rookie is designated by an "R" on NFL rosters. Players who have been active in another professional football league or players
who have NFL experience, including either preseason training camp or being on an Active List or Inactive List, or on Reserve/Injured or Reserve/Physically Unable to
Perform for fewer than six regular-season games, are termed NFL First-Year Players. An NFL First-Year Player is designated by a "1" on NFL rosters. Thereafter, a player
is credited with an additional year of experience for each season in which he accumulates six games on the Active List or Inactive List, or on Reserve/Injured or
Reserve/Physically Unable to Perform.

Log on to www.panthers.com for an up-to-date roster.

COACHING STAFF
Head Coach,
John Fox

Pro Career: Became third coach in Carolina Panthers history on January 25, 2002. In 2005, directed team to second NFC championship appearance in three seasons. Became the fifth head coach in NFL history to record four career postseason road wins. Equaled an NFL record with four consecutive postseason road wins. In 2004, directed Carolina team that overcame a 1-7 record to end the regular season with mark of 7-9. Of the 28 NFL teams that began season with 1-7 record since 1990, Panthers became only third team to finish season with seven victories. In 2003, guided Panthers to Super Bowl XXXVIII two years after inheriting team that won one game in 2001. Joined Vince Lombardi and Bill Parcells as the only coaches in NFL history to inherit a one-win team and guide it to the playoffs in their second season. In 2002, engineered a six-game turn-around that ranks second for rookie head coaches since 1978. In 2002, the Panthers became the only team since 1970 to improve from thirty-first to second in total defense in one season. Prior to joining Carolina he served as the defensive coordinator for the N.Y. Giants (1997-2001). In 2000, Fox helped the Giants reach Super Bowl XXXV, including posting the first shutout in a conference title game since 1986. Before joining the Giants, Fox was a consultant for the Rams (1996), defensive coordinator for the Raiders (1994-95), defensive backs coach for the Chargers (1992-93) and Steelers (1989-1991), and secondary coach for the USFL's Los Angeles Express (1985). Career record: 41-30.

Background: Defensive back at San Diego State (1976-77). Coached at San Diego State (1978), U.S. International (1979), Boise State (1980), Long Beach State (1981), Utah (1982), Kansas (1983), Iowa State (1984), and Pittsburgh (1986-88). Received bachelor's degree in physical education and earned a teaching credential from San Diego State.

Personal: Born February 8, 1955, in Virginia Beach, Va. He and his wife, Robin, have four children—Mathew, Mark, Cody, and Halle.

ASSISTANT COACHES

Geep Chryst, quality control/offense; born June 25, 1962, Madison, Wis. Linebacker Princeton 1981-84. Pro linebacker Orlando Thunder (WFL) 1992. College coach: Wisconsin-Platteville 1987, Wisconsin 1988, Wyoming 1989-1990. Pro coach: Orlando Thunder (WL) 1991, Chicago Bears 1991-95, Arizona Cardinals 1996-98, 2001-03, San Diego Chargers 1999-2000, joined Panthers in 2006.

Danny Crossman, special teams; born January 17, 1967, El Paso, Texas. Defensive back Kansas 1985, Pittsburgh 1987-89. Pro defensive back Washington

Redskins 1990, Detroit Lions 1991-92. College coach: U.S. Coast Guard Academy 1993, Western Kentucky 1994-96, Central Florida 1997-98, Georgia Tech 1999-2001, Michigan State 2002. Pro coach: Joined Panthers in 2003.

Ken Flajole, linebackers; born October 4, 1954, Seattle. Linebacker Wenatchee Valley (Wash.) C.C. 1973-74, Pacific Lutheran 1975-76. No pro playing experience. College coach: Pacific Lutheran 1977-78, Washington 1979, Montana 1980-85, Texas-El Paso 1986-88, Missouri 1989-1993, Richmond 1994, Hawaii 1995, Nevada 1996-97. Pro coach: Green Bay Packers 1998, Seattle Seahawks 1999-2002, joined Panthers in 2003.

Mike Gillhamer, secondary/safeties; born February 20, 1956, Oakland. Defensive back Carroll College 1972, Wenatchee (Wash.) J.C. 1973, Humboldt State 1974-75. No pro playing experience. College coach: College of the Sequoias 1979-1983, Weber State 1984, Utah 1985-89, San Jose State 1990-93, Nevada 1994-95, Oregon 2001-02, Louisville 2003. Pro coach: New York Giants 1997-2000, joined Panthers in 2004.

Dan Henning, offensive coordinator; born June 21, 1942, Bronx, N.Y. Quarterback William & Mary 1962-64. Pro quarterback San Diego Chargers 1964, 1966-67. College coach: Florida State 1968-1970, 1974, Virginia Tech 1971, 1973, Boston College 1994-96 (head coach). Pro coach: Houston Oilers 1972, New York Jets 1976-78, 1998-2000, Miami Dolphins 1979-1980, Washington Redskins 1981-1982, 1987-88, Atlanta Falcons 1983-86 (head coach), San Diego Chargers 1989-1991 (head coach), Detroit Lions 1992-93, Buffalo Bills 1997, joined Panthers in 2002.

Tony Levine, special teams assistant/asst. strength and conditioning; born October 28, 1972, St. Paul, Minn. Wide receiver Minnesota 1991-95. Pro wide receiver Minnesota (AFL) 1996. College coach: Southwest Texas State 1997-99, Aubun 2000-01, Louisiana Tech 2002, Louisville 2003-05. Pro coach: Joined Panthers in 2006.

David Magazu, tight ends; born June 10, 1957, Taunton Mass. Defensive tackle Springfield College 1976-79. No pro playing experience. College coach: Ithaca 1980, Western Michigan 1981, Eastern Michigan 1982, Michigan 1983, Northern Illinois 1984, Ball State 1985-86, Navy 1987-89, Indiana State 1990-91, Colorado State 1992-94, Kentucky 1995-96, Memphis 1997-98, Boston College 1999-2002. Pro coach: Joined Panthers in 2003.

Mike Maser, offensive line; born March 2, 1947, Clayton N.Y. Guard Buffalo 1967-1970. No pro playing experience. College coach: Marshall 1973, Bluefield State College 1974-78, Maine 1979-1980, Boston College 1981-1993. Pro coach: Jacksonville Jaguars 1995-2002, joined Panthers in 2003.

Mike McCoy, quarterbacks; born April 1, 1972, San Francisco. Quarterback Long Beach State 1990-91, Utah 1992-94. Pro quarterback Amsterdam Admirals (NFLE) 1997, Calgary Stampeders (CFL) 1999. Pro coach: Joined Panthers in 1999.

Sam Mills III, quality control/defense; born May 20, 1978, Long Branch, N.J. Cornerback Montclair State 1997-98. Pro coach: Joined Panthers in 2006.

Rod Perry, secondary/cornerbacks; born September 11, 1953, Fresno, Calif. Defensive back Colorado 1972-74. Pro cornerback Los Angeles Rams 1975-1982, Cleveland Browns 1983-84. College coach: Columbia 1985, Fresno C.C. 1986, Fresno State 1987-88. Pro coach: Seattle Seahawks 1989-1991, Los Angeles Rams 1992-94, Houston Oilers 1995-96, San Diego Chargers 1997-2001, joined Panthers in 2002.

Jerry Simmons, strength and conditioning; born June 15, 1954, Elkhart, Kan. Linebacker Fort Hays State 1976-77. No pro playing experience. College coach: Fort Hays State 1978, Clemson 1980, Rice 1981-82, Southern California 1983-87. Pro coach: New England Patriots 1988-1990, Cleveland Browns/Baltimore Ravens 1991-98, joined Panthers in 1999.

Jim Skipper, asst. head coach/running backs; born January 23, 1949, Breaux Bridge, La. Defensive back Whittier College 1971-72. No pro playing experience. College coach: Cal Poly-Pomona 1974-76, San Jose State 1977-78, Pacific 1979, Oregon 1980-82. Pro coach: Philadelphia/Baltimore Stars (USFL) 1983-85, New Orleans Saints 1986-1995, Arizona Cardinals 1996, New York Giants 1997-2000, San Francisco Demons (XFL) 2001 (head coach), joined Panthers in 2002.

Sal Sunseri, defensive line; born August 1, 1959, Pittsburgh. Linebacker Pittsburgh 1979-1981. College coach: Pittsburgh 1985-1992, Iowa Wesleyan 1993, Louisville 1995-97, Alabama A&M 1998-99, Louisiana State 2000, Michigan State 2001. Pro coach: Joined Panthers in 2002.

Mike Trgovac, defensive coordinator; born February 27, 1959, Youngstown, Ohio. Defensive lineman Michigan 1977-1980. No pro playing experience. College coach: Michigan 1984-85, Ball State 1986-88, Navy 1989, Colorado State 1990-91, Notre Dame 1992-94. Pro coach: Philadelphia Eagles 1995-98, Green Bay Packers 1999, Washington Redskins 2000-01, joined Panthers in 2002.

Richard Williamson, wide receivers; born April 13, 1941, Ft. Deposit, Ala. Receiver Alabama 1961-62. No pro playing experience. College coach: Alabama 1963-67, 1970-71, Arkansas 1968-69, 1972-74, Memphis State 1975-1980 (head coach). Pro coach: Kansas City Chiefs 1983-86, Tampa Bay Buccaneers 1987-1991 (interim head coach 1990, head coach 1991), Cincinnati Bengals 1992-94, joined Panthers in 1995.

**National Football Conference
North Division**
Team Colors: Navy Blue, Orange, and
White
Halas Hall at Conway Park
1000 Football Drive
Lake Forest, Illinois 60045
Telephone: (847) 295-6600

2006 SCHEDULE
PRESEASON
Aug. 11 at San Francisco.................7:00
Aug. 18 **San Diego**...........................7:00
Aug. 25 **Arizona**...............................7:00
Aug. 31 at Cleveland.......................8:00

REGULAR SEASON
Sept. 10 at Green Bay......................3:15
Sept. 17 **Detroit**.............................12:00
Sept. 24 at Minnesota....................12:00
Oct. 1 **Seattle**..............................7:15
Oct. 8 **Buffalo**.............................12:00
Oct. 16 at Arizona (Mon.)...............5:30
Oct. 22 Open Date
Oct. 29 **San Francisco**.................12:00
Nov. 5 **Miami**............................. 12:00
Nov. 12 at N.Y. Giants......................1:00
Nov. 19 at N.Y. Jets.........................1:00
Nov. 26 at New England...................1:00
Dec. 3 **Minnesota**.......................12:00
Dec. 11 at St. Louis (Mon.)..............7:30
Dec. 17 **Tampa Bay**.......................12:00
Dec. 24 at Detroit.............................1:00
Dec. 31 **Green Bay**........................12:00

Stadium: Soldier Field
(opened in 1924)
•**Capacity:** 61,500
1410 S. Museum Campus Dr.
Chicago, Illinois 60605
Playing Surface: Natural Grass
Training Camp: Olivet-Nazarene Univ.
Bourbonnais, Illinois
60901

SOLDIER FIELD

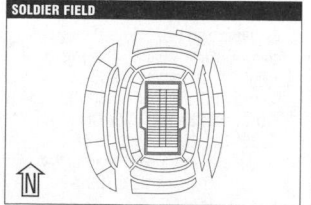

CLUB OFFICIALS
Chairman of the Board:
Michael B. McCaskey
Secretary: Virginia H. McCaskey
President and CEO: Ted Phillips
General Manager: Jerry Angelo
Vice President: Tim McCaskey
Senior Director of Special Projects:
Pat McCaskey
Senior Director of Ticket Operations:
George McCaskey
Senior Director of Business Development
& Alumni Relations: Brian McCaskey
Senior Director of Administration:
John Bostrom
Senior Director of Finance & Treasurer:
Karen Murphy
Senior Director of Corporate Sales &
Marketing: TBA
Senior Director of Corporate
Communications: Scott Hagel
Director of Pro Personnel: Bobby DePaul
Director of College Scouting:
Greg Gabriel
Director of Player Contracts and Legal
Affairs: Cliff Stein
Assistant Director of Pro Personnel:
Morocco Brown
Director of Player Development:
Bobbie Howard
Director of Community Relations:
Caroline Guip
Director of Broadcasting: Greg Miller
Media Services Manager: Jim Christman
Media Information Manager:
Roger Hacker
Media Relations Assistant: Brian Hardin
Video Director: Dean Pope
Assistant Video Directors:
Dave Hendrickson, Dan Tuohy
Head Athletic Trainer: Tim Bream
Assistant Trainers: Scott DeGraff,
Chris Hanks
Director of Rehabilitation: Bobby Slater
Head Equipment Manager: Tony Medlin
Assistant Equipment Managers:
Carl Piekarski, Brad Camp
Scouts: Chris Ballard, Marty Barrett,
Rex Hogan, Ted Monago,
Mark Sadowski, Jeff Shiver

COACHING HISTORY
Decatur Staleys 1920,
Chicago Staleys 1921
(671-495-42)
Records include postseason games
1920-29   George Halas.............84-31-19
1930-32   Ralph Jones................24-10-7
1933-1942 George Halas*............88-24-4
1942-45   Hunk Anderson-
Luke Johnsos**..........24-12-2
1946-1955 George Halas..............76-43-2
1956-57   John (Paddy) Driscoll......14-10-1
1958-1967 George Halas..............76-53-6
1968-1971 Jim Dooley..................20-36-0
1972-74   Abe Gibron..................11-30-1
1975-77   Jack Pardee.................20-23-0
1978-1981 Neill Armstrong.............30-35-0
1982-1992 Mike Ditka.................112-68-0
1993-98   Dave Wannstedt..........41-57-0
1999-2003 Dick Jauron.................35-46-0
2004-05   Lovie Smith.................16-17-0
*Retired after five games to enter U.S. Navy
**Co-coaches

ATTENDANCE
Home 486,503   Away 511,687
Total 998,190
Single-game home record,
66,900 (9/5/93)
Single-season home record, 527,769
(1999)

2006 DRAFT CHOICES
Round	Name	Pos.	College
2	Danieal Manning	DB	Abilene Christian
	Devin Hester	WR	Miami
3	Dusty Dvoracek	DT	Oklahoma
4	Jamar Williams	LB	Arizona State
5	Mark Anderson	DE	Alabama
6	J.D. Runnels	RB	Oklahoma
	Tyler Reed	G	Penn State

2005 TEAM RECORD

PRESEASON (3-2)

Date	Result	Opponent
8/8	W 27-24	vs. Miami in Canton, OH
8/12	L 13-17	at St. Louis
8/20	W 24-17	at Indianapolis
8/26	W 16-12	Buffalo
9/1	L 6-16	Cleveland

REGULAR SEASON (11-5)

Date	Result	Opponent	Att.
9/11	L 7-9	at Washington	90,138
9/18	W 38-6	Detroit	62,019
9/25	L 7-24	Cincinnati	62,045
10/9	L 10-20	at Cleveland	73,079
10/16	W 28-3	Minnesota	62,143
10/23	W 10-6	Baltimore	62,102
10/30	W 19-13	at Detroit (OT)	61,814
11/6	W 20-17	at New Orleans	32,637
11/13	W 17-9	San Francisco	62,153
11/20	W 13-3	Carolina	62,156
11/27	W 13-10	at Tampa Bay	65,506
12/4	W 19-7	Green Bay	62,177
12/11	L 9-21	at Pittsburgh	61,237
12/18	W 16-3	Atlanta	62,170
12/25	W 24-17	at Green Bay	69,757
1/1	L 10-34	at Minnesota	64,023

(OT) Overtime

POSTSEASON (0-1)

1/15	L 21-29	Carolina	62,209

SCORE BY PERIODS

Bears	54	82	54	64	6	—	260
Opponents	35	69	34	64	0	—	202

2005 TEAM STATISTICS

	Bears	Opp.
Total First Downs	233	259
Rushing	99	83
Passing	111	153
Penalty	23	23
3rd Down: Made/Att	62/215	76/238
3rd Down Pct.	28.8	31.9
4th Down: Made/Att	7/16	6/20
4th Down Pct.	43.8	30.0
Possession Avg.	28:41	31:19
Total Net Yards	4,101	4,509
Avg. Per Game	256.3	281.8
Total Plays	937	1,034
Avg. Per Play	4.4	4.4
Net Yards Rushing	2,099	1,637
Avg. Per Game	131.2	102.3
Total Rushes	488	443
Net Yards Passing	2,002	2,872
Avg. Per Game	125.1	179.5
Sacked/Yards Lost	31/199	41/275
Gross Yards	2,201	3,147
Att./Completions	418/219	550/313
Completion Pct.	52.4	56.9
Had Intercepted	15	24
Punts/Average	98/40.5	97/41.1
Net Punting Avg.	98/35.0	97/35.1
Penalties/Yards	105/850	118/1016
Fumbles/Ball Lost	32/13	26/10
Touchdowns	28	20
Rushing	11	9
Passing	11	10
Returns	6	1

2005 INDIVIDUAL STATISTICS

PASSING

PASSING	Att.	Comp.	Yds.	Pct.	TD	Int.	Tkld.	Rate
Orton	368	190	1,869	51.6	9	13	30/190	59.7
Grossman	39	20	259	51.3	1	2	1/9	59.7
Blake	9	8	55	88.9	1	0	0/0	129.2
Maynard	2	1	18	50.0	0	0	0/0	81.3
Bears	418	219	2,201	52.4	11	15	31/199	61.5
Opponents	550	313	3,147	56.9	10	24	41/275	61.2

SCORING

SCORING	TD R	TD P	TD Rt	PAT	FG	Saf	PTS
Gould	0	0	0	19/20	21/27	0	82
Jones	9	0	0	0/0	0/0	0	54
Muhammad	0	4	0	0/0	0/0	0	24
Clark	0	2	0	0/0	0/0	0	12
M. Edwards	0	2	0	0/0	0/0	0	12
Gage	0	2	0	0/0	0/0	0	12
Peterson	2	0	0	0/0	0/0	0	12
Vasher	0	0	2	0/0	0/0	0	12
Brien	0	0	0	7/7	1/4	0	10
Briggs	0	0	1	0/0	0/0	0	6
M. Brown	0	0	1	0/0	0/0	0	6
Gilmore	0	1	0	0/0	0/0	0	6
Tillman	0	0	1	0/0	0/0	0	6
Wade	0	0	1	0/0	0/0	0	6
Bears	11	11	6	26/27	22/31	0	260
Opponents	9	10	1	19/20	21/29	0	202

2-Pt. Conversions: Team 0-0, Opponents 0-0.

RUSHING

RUSHING	Att.	Yds.	Avg.	LG	TD
Jones	314	1,335	4.3	42	9
Peterson	76	391	5.1	36	2
Benson	67	272	4.1	36	0
Orton	24	44	1.8	15	0
Berrian	2	31	15.5	37	0
McKie	3	22	7.3	13	0
B. Johnson	1	5	5.0	5	0
Blake	1	-1	-1.0	-1	0
Bears	488	2,099	4.3	42	11
Opponents	443	1,637	3.7	61t	9

RECEIVING

RECEIVING	No.	Yds.	Avg.	LG	TD
Muhammad	64	750	11.7	33	4
Gage	31	346	11.2	25	2
Jones	26	143	5.5	41	0
Clark	24	229	9.5	31	2
Bradley	18	230	12.8	54	0
Berrian	13	246	18.9	54	0
Wade	10	80	8.0	17	0
M. Edwards	10	66	6.6	13	2
Peterson	7	48	6.9	18	0
B. Johnson	5	15	3.0	7	0
McKie	4	15	3.8	11	0
Reid	3	20	6.7	10	0
Berlin	2	9	4.5	9	0
Benson	1	3	3.0	3	0
Gilmore	1	1	1.0	1t	1
Bears	219	2,201	10.1	54	11
Opponents	313	3147	10.1	56	10

INTERCEPTIONS

INTERCEPTIONS	No.	Yds.	Avg.	LG	TD
Vasher	8	145	18.1	46	1
Tillman	5	172	34.4	95	1
M. Brown	3	116	38.7	72	1
C. Harris	3	44	14.7	44	0
Briggs	2	30	15.0	20	1
M. Green	1	14	14.0	14	0
Scott	1	3	3.0	3	0
Hillenmeyer	1	0	0.0	0	0
Bears	24	524	21.8	95	4
Opponents	15	66	4.4	25	0

PUNTING

PUNTING	No.	Yds.	Avg.	In 20	LG
Maynard	96	3,937	41.0	24	63
Gould	1	28	28.0	0	28
Bears	98	3,965	40.5	24	63
Opponents	97	3,982	41.1	27	59

PUNT RETURNS

PUNT RETURNS	No.	FC	Yds.	Avg.	LG	TD
Wade	33	9	317	9.6	73t	1
Berrian	8	3	69	8.6	24	0
Davis	5	1	31	6.2	21	0
Bears	46	13	417	9.1	73t	1
Opponents	39	13	312	8.0	85t	1

KICKOFF RETURN

KICKOFF RETURN	No.	Yds.	Avg.	LG	TD
Azumah	32	705	22.0	40	0
Davis	11	251	22.8	34	0
Bradley	4	70	17.5	23	0
McKie	3	29	9.7	17	0
Peterson	2	32	16.0	19	0
Gilmore	1	5	5.0	5	0
Idonije	1	0	0.0	0	0
Vasher	1	0	0.0	0	0
Bears	55	1092	19.9	40	0
Opponents	63	1255	19.9	45	0

FIELD GOALS

FIELD GOALS	1-19	20-29	30-39	40-49	50+
Gould	0/0	9/9	9/10	3/8	0/0
Brien	0/0	0/0	0/2	1/2	0/0
Bears	0/0	9/9	9/12	4/10	0/0
Opponents	2/2	7/8	7/10	4/6	1/3

SACKS

SACKS	No.
Ogunleye	10.0
A. Brown	6.0
Urlacher	6.0
Ta. Johnson	5.0
T. Harris	3.0
Briggs	2.0
Boone	1.5
Haynes	1.5
Azumah	1.0
M. Brown	1.0
C. Harris	1.0
Hillenmeyer	1.0
Idonije	1.0
Tillman	1.0
Bears	41.0
Opponents	31.0

RECORD HOLDERS
INDIVIDUAL RECORDS—CAREER

Category	Name	Performance
Rushing (Yds.)	Walter Payton, 1975-1987	16,726
Passing (Yds.)	Sid Luckman, 1939-1950	14,686
Passing (TDs)	Sid Luckman, 1939-1950	137
Receiving (No.)	Walter Payton, 1975-1987	492
Receiving (Yds.)	Johnny Morris, 1958-1967	5,059
Interceptions	Gary Fencik, 1976-1987	38
Punting (Avg.)	George Gulyanics, 1947-1952	44.5
Punt Return (Avg.)	George McAfee, 1940-41, 1945-1950	*12.8
Kickoff Return (Avg.)	Gale Sayers, 1965-1971	*30.6
Field Goals	Kevin Butler, 1985-1995	243
Touchdowns (Tot.)	Walter Payton, 1975-1987	125
Points	Kevin Butler, 1985-1995	1,116

INDIVIDUAL RECORDS—SINGLE SEASON

Category	Name	Performance
Rushing (Yds.)	Walter Payton, 1977	1,852
Passing (Yds.)	Erik Kramer, 1995	3,838
Passing (TDs)	Erik Kramer, 1995	29
Receiving (No.)	Marty Booker, 2001	100
Receiving (Yds.)	Marcus Robinson, 1999	1,400
Interceptions	Mark Carrier, 1990	10
Punting (Avg.)	Bobby Joe Green, 1963	46.5
Punt Return (Avg.)	Harry Clark, 1943	15.8
Kickoff Return (Avg.)	Gale Sayers, 1967	37.7
Field Goals	Kevin Butler, 1985	31
Touchdowns (Tot.)	Gale Sayers, 1965	22
Points	Kevin Butler, 1985	144

INDIVIDUAL RECORDS—SINGLE GAME

Category	Name	Performance
Rushing (Yds.)	Walter Payton, 11-20-77	275
Passing (Yds.)	Johnny Lujack, 12-11-49	468
Passing (TDs)	Sid Luckman, 11-14-43	*7
Receiving (No.)	Jim Keane, 10-23-49	14
Receiving (Yds.)	Harlon Hill, 10-31-54	214
Interceptions	Many times	3
	Last time by Mark Carrier, 12-9-90	
Field Goals	Roger LeClerc, 12-3-61	5
	Mac Percival, 10-20-68	5
Touchdowns (Tot.)	Gale Sayers, 12-12-65	*6
Points	Gale Sayers, 12-12-65	36

*NFL Record

CHICAGO BEARS

2006 VETERAN ROSTER

No.	Name	Pos.	Ht.	Wt.	Birthdate	NFL Exp.	College	Hometown	How Acq.	'05 Games/ Starts
94	Ayanbadejo, Brendon	LB	6-1	228	9/6/76	4	UCLA	Santa Cruz, Calif.	T(Mia)-'05	16/0
32	Benson, Cedric	RB	5-10	222	12/28/82	2	Texas	Midland, Texas	D1-'05	9/1
80	Berrian, Bernard	WR	6-1	185	12/27/80	3	Fresno State	Winton, Calif.	D3-'04	11/2
70	Boone, Alfonso	DT	6-4	318	1/11/76	6	Mt. San Antonio (CA) J.C.	Saginaw, Mich.	FA-'00	16/1
16	Bradley, Mark	WR	6-2	201	1/29/82	2	Oklahoma	Pine Bluff, Ark.	D2-'05	7/4
55	Briggs, Lance	LB	6-1	238	11/12/80	4	Arizona	Sacramento, Calif.	D3-'03	16/16
96	Brown, Alex	DE	6-3	262	6/4/79	5	Florida	White Springs, Fla.	D4-'02	16/16
30	Brown, Mike	S	5-10	212	2/13/78	7	Nebraska	Scottsdale, Ariz.	D2-'00	12/12
74	Brown, Ruben	G	6-3	300	2/13/72	12	Pittsburgh	Lynchburg, Va.	FA-'04	12/12
58	Cain, Jeremy	LB	6-1	235	4/24/80	3	Massachusetts	Ft. Lauderdale, Fla.	FA-'04	3/0
88	Clark, Desmond	TE	6-3	254	4/20/77	8	Wake Forest	Lakeland, Fla.	UFA(Mia)-'03	16/16
81	Davis, Rashied	WR	5-9	180	7/24/79	2	San Jose State	Granada Hills, Calif.	FA-'05	12/0
79	Edwards, Steve	T	6-5	330	2/20/79	4	Central Florida	Chicago, Ill.	FA-'03	6/0
62	Friedman, Lennie	G	6-3	295	8/13/76	7	Duke	West Milford, N.J.	FA-'05	11/0*
87	Gage, Justin	WR	6-4	210	1/25/81	4	Missouri	Jefferson City, Mo.	D5b-'03	15/11
90	Garay, Antonio	DT	6-3	310	11/30/79	3	Boston College	Rahway, N.J.	FA-'05	0*
63	Garza, Roberto	G/C	6-2	296	3/26/79	6	Texas A&M-Kingsville	Rio Hondo, Texas	UFA(Atl)-'05	16/7
85	Gilmore, John	TE	6-4	262	9/21/79	5	Penn State	West Lawn, Pa.	FA-'02	16/0
9	Gould, Robbie	K	6-0	181	12/30/81	2	Penn State	Lock Haven, Pa.	FA-'05	13/0
67	Green, Jamaal	DE	6-2	272	6/5/80	2	Miami	Camden, N.J.	FA-'05	0*
14	Griese, Brian	QB	6-3	214	3/18/75	9	Michigan	Miami, Fla.	FA-'06	6/6*
8	Grossman, Rex	QB	6-1	218	8/23/80	4	Florida	Bloomington, Ind.	D1b-'03	2/1
46	Harris, Chris	S	6-1	206	8/6/82	2	Louisiana-Monroe	Little Rock, Ark.	D6-'05	14/13
91	Harris, Tommie	DT	6-3	300	4/29/83	3	Oklahoma	Killeen, Texas	D1-'04	16/16
97	Haynes, Michael	DE	6-4	274	9/13/80	4	Penn State	Columbus, N.J.	D1a-'03	11/0
92	Hillenmeyer, Hunter	LB	6-4	238	10/28/80	4	Vanderbilt	Nashville, Tenn.	FA-'03	13/12
25	Hollings, Tony	RB	5-11	219	12/1/81	4	Georgia Tech	Jeffersonville, Ga.	FA-'05	2/0*
49	Hollowell, T.J.	LB	6-0	235	4/8/81	2	Nebraska	Copperas Cove, Tex.	FA-'05	2/0*
26	Holly, Daven	CB	5-10	192	8/8/82	2	Cincinnati	Clairton, Pa.	W(SF)-'05	3/0
71	Idonije, Israel	DT	6-7	290	11/17/80	3	Manitoba	Brandon, Manitoba, Canada	FA-'03	11/1
53	Joe, Leon	LB	6-1	235	10/26/81	3	Maryland	Fort Washington, Md.	W(Ariz)-'05	14/1
47	Johnson, Bryan	FB	6-1	242	1/18/78	6	Boise State	Pocatello, Id.	T(Wash)-'04	7/6
99	Johnson, Tank	DT	6-3	300	12/7/81	3	Washington	Tempe, Ariz.	D2-'04	16/4
35	Johnson, Todd	S	6-1	200	12/18/78	3	Florida	Sarasota, Fla.	D4a-'03	14/2
20	Jones, Thomas	RB	5-10	220	8/19/78	7	Virginia	Big Stone Gap, Va.	FA-'04	15/15
57	Kreutz, Olin	C	6-2	292	6/9/77	9	Washington	Honolulu, Hawaii	D3-'98	16/16
65	Mannelly, Patrick	T/LS	6-5	265	4/18/75	9	Duke	Atlanta, Ga.	D6b-'98	16/0
24	Manning, Jr., Ricky	CB	5-9	185	11/18/80	4	UCLA	Fresno, Calif.	FA-'06	16/16*
31	Marshall, Alfonso	CB	6-0	188	1/17/81	2	Miami	Clewiston, Fla.	D7-'04	0*
4	Maynard, Brad	P	6-1	186	2/9/74	10	Ball State	Sheridan, Ind.	UFA(NYG)-'01	16/0
36	McGowan, Brandon	S	5-11	200	9/16/83	2	Maine	Jersey City, N.J.	D4-'05	8/3
37	McKie, Jason	FB	5-11	240	5/22/80	5	Temple	Gulf Breeze, Fla.	W(Dall)-'03	8/2
60	Metcalf, Terrence	G/T	6-3	318	1/28/78	5	Mississippi	Clarksdale, Miss.	D3-'02	13/13
69	Miller, Fred	T	6-7	320	2/6/73	11	Baylor	Aldine, Texas	FA-'05	15/15
72	Mitchell, Qasim	T	6-6	355	12/3/79	5	North Carolina A&T	Jacksonville, N.C.	FA-'03	4/0
87	Muhammad, Muhsin	WR	6-2	217	5/5/73	11	Michigan State	Lansing, Mich.	FA-'05	15/15
59	Odom, Joe	LB	6-1	235	12/14/79	4	Purdue	Bethalto, Ill.	D6a-'03	2/0
93	Ogunleye, Adewale	DE	6-4	260	8/9/77	6	Indiana	Staten Island, N.Y.	T(Mia)-'04	15/15
18	Orton, Kyle	QB	6-4	226	11/14/82	2	Purdue	Runnels, Iowa	D4-'05	15/15
29	Peterson, Adrian	RB	5-10	210	7/1/79	5	Georgia Southern	Alachua, Fla.	D6a-'02	16/0
48	Reid, Gabe	TE	6-4	260	5/28/77	4	Brigham Young	American Samoa	FA-'03	16/3
78	St. Clair, John	T	6-5	318	7/15/77	7	Virginia	Roanoke, Va.	FA-'05	13/2
95	Scott, Ian	DT	6-3	305	11/8/81	4	Florida	Gainesville, Fla.	D4b-'03	14/13
48	Smith, Justin	LB	6-0	218	6/5/79	2	Indiana	Indianapolis, Ind.	FA-'05	0*
76	Tait, John	T	6-6	315	1/26/75	8	Brigham Young	Tempe, Ariz.	RFA(KC)-'04	15/15
27	Thompson, Chris	CB	6-0	187	5/19/82	3	Nicholls State	New Orleans, La.	W(Jax)-'05	12/1
33	Tillman, Charles	CB	6-1	196	2/23/81	4	Louisiana-Lafayette	Copperas Cove, Texas	D2-'03	15/15
54	Urlacher, Brian	LB	6-4	258	5/25/78	7	New Mexico	Lovington, N.M.	D1-'00	16/16
31	Vasher, Nathan	CB	5-10	180	11/17/81	3	Texas	Texarkana, Texas	D4-'04	16/15
21	Wesley, Dante	CB	6-1	211	4/5/79	5	Arkansas-Pine Bluff	Pine Bluff, Ark.	UFA(Car)-'06	16/0*
44	Worrell, Cameron	S	5-11	199	12/14/79	3	Fresno State	Chowchilla, Calif.	FA-'03	0*

* Friedman played 10 games with Washington and 1game with Chicago in '05; Garay spent '04 season with Cleveland on physically unable to perform list; Green last active with Philadelphia in '04; Griese played 6 games with Tampa Bay; Hollings played 2 games with Houston; Hollowell played 2 games with N.Y. Jets; Manning played 16 games with Carolina; Marshall spent '05 season on physically unable to perform list; Smith missed '05 season with Carolina because of injury; Wesley played 16 games with Carolina; Worrell missed '05 season because of injury.

Players lost through free agency (0): None.

Also played with Bears in '05—CB Jerry Azumah (15 games), WR Eddie Berlin (5), QB Jeff Blake (2), K Doug Brien (3), T Marc Colombo (1), FB Marc Edwards (8), WR Carl Ford (10), S Michael Green (16), WR Bobby Wade (12).

2006 FIRST-YEAR ROSTER

Name	Pos.	Ht.	Wt.	Birthdate	College	Hometown	How Acq.
Anderson, Mark	DE	6-4	258	5/26/83	Alabama	Tulsa, Okla.	D5
Amos, Willie (1)	CB	6-0	186	7/28/82	Nebraska	Sweetwater, Texas	FA-'05
Belton, Keith (1)	FB	6-0	232	6/1/81	Syracuse	West Charlotte, N.C.	W(Det)-'04
Bragg, Craig (1)	WR	6-1	195	3/15/82	UCLA	San Jose, Calif.	W(GB)-'05
Bunce, Nate	G	6-6	321	8/4/82	Miami (Ohio)	Hamilton, Ohio	FA
Byrum, Dion	CB	5-10	192	2/18/83	Ohio	Matthews, N.C.	FA
Currie, Airese (1)	WR	5-10	186	11/16/82	Clemson	Columbia, S.C.	D5-'05
Day, Tim	TE	6-3	265	9/3/83	Oregon	Las Vegas, Nev.	FA
Dean, Josh (1)	LB	6-0	213	11/7/82	San Diego State	Oakland, Calif.	FA-'05
Dvoracek, Dusty	DT	6-3	305	3/3/81	Oklahoma	Lake Dallas, Texas	D3
Elimimian, Abraham (1)	CB	5-10	190	3/2/82	Hawaii	Los Angeles, Calif.	W(SD)-'05
Harmon, Jason (1)	S	5-11	209	4/3/82	Michigan State	Ironton, Ohio	FA-'05
Harrell, Reggie (1)	WR	6-3	210	1/28/81	Texas Christian	Arlington, Texas	FA-'05
Hester, Devin	CB	5-11	189	11/4/82	Miami	Riviera Beach, Fla.	D2b
Huston, Josh	K	6-1	195	2/28/82	Ohio State	Findlay, Ohio	FA
Larsen, Stephen (1)	LB	6-1	235	4/13/82	San Diego State	Chandler, Ariz.	FA-'05
Leffew, Travis	G	6-4	301	1/27/82	Louisville	Danville, Ky.	FA
LeVoir, Mark	T	6-7	315	7/29/82	Notre Dame	Eden Prairie, Minn.	FA
Long, Khari (1)	DE	6-4	257	5/23/82	Baylor	Wichita Falls, Texas	W(KC)-'05
Manning, Danieal	S	5-11	201	8/9/82	Abilene Christian	Corsicana, Texas	D2a
McMeans, Tyler	G	6-4	329	4/4/80	Miami	Shippenville, Pa.	FA
Oakley, Anthony (1)	G/T	6-4	295	8/16/81	Western Kentucky	Houston, Texas	W(Cle)-'05
Philmore, Mark	WR	5-10	185	8/8/84	Northwestern	Reynoldsburg, Ohio	FA
Pope, P.J.	RB	5-9	212	2/26/84	Bowling Green	Fairfield, Ohio	FA
Reed, Tyler	G/T	6-4	307	10/6/82	Penn State	Jefferson Borough, Pa.	D6b
Runnels, J.D.	FB	5-11	237	6/19/84	Oklahoma	Midwest City, Okla.	D6a
Slay, Dwayne	S	6-3	215	6/21/84	Texas Tech	Brunswick, Ga.	FA
Stelly, Joel	P	5-10	200	1/13/84	Louisiana-Monroe	Cecilia, La.	FA
Symons, B.J. (1)	QB	6-1	210	11/19/80	Texas Tech	Houston, Texas	W(Hou)-'05
Wallace, Cooper	TE	6-3	265	4/26/82	Auburn	Nashville, Tenn.	FA
Williams, Jamar	LB	6-0	250	6/14/84	Arizona State	Houston, Texas	D4
Wilson, Rod (1)	LB	6-2	217	11/12/81	South Carolina	Cross, S.C.	D7-'05

The term NFL Rookie is defined as a player who is in his first season of professional football and has not been on the roster of another professional football team for any regular-season or postseason games. A Rookie is designated by an "R" on NFL rosters. Players who have been active in another professional football league or players who have NFL experience, including either preseason training camp or being on an Active List or Inactive List, or on Reserve/Injured or Reserve/Physically Unable to Perform for fewer than six regular-season games, are termed NFL First-Year Players. An NFL First-Year Player is designated by a "1" on NFL rosters. Thereafter, a player is credited with an additional year of experience for each season in which he accumulates six games on the Active List or Inactive List, or on Reserve/Injured or Reserve/Physically Unable to Perform.

Log on to www.chicagobears.com for an up-to-date roster.

COACHING STAFF

Head Coach,
Lovie Smith

Pro Career: Named the thirteenth head coach in Chicago Bears history on January 15, 2004. Smith was named the *Associated Press* NFL Coach of the Year for 2005. His 11 victories in 2005 are the most by a second-year coach in club annals, and he became the franchise's first second-year coach to win a division title, earning the NFC's second seed. Fueled by an eight-game win streak, Smith led a worst-to-first revival in the NFC North division as the Bears six-win improvement from the previous season was tied for the biggest in the NFL in 2005. Chicago posted a 5-11 record in 2004 in Smith's first season as head coach as he presided over the NFL's youngest team. During Smith's first two seasons at the helm, Chicago ranked second in the NFL having allowed 16.7 points per game while leading the league during that time by allowing the lowest opponent passer rating, opponent third-down and fourth-down conversion percentage, and opponent red zone touchdown percentage in the league. From 2004-05, the Bears had a league-high 10 touchdowns via defensive return—including a franchise-record 6 in 2004. Allowing the fewest points in the NFL in 2005, Chicago ranked second in overall defense. Smith came to Chicago from St. Louis (2001-03), where he served as defensive coordinator. In 2001 he helped the Rams return to the Super Bowl after missing the playoffs the previous season. Smith previously coached the linebackers for the Tampa Bay Buccaneers (1996-2000). Career record: 16-17.

Background: Played at Tulsa (1976-79), where he was a linebacker before moving to strong safety and earning two-time All-America and three-time All-Missouri Conference defensive back honors. Began his coaching career at his hometown high school (Big Sandy, Texas) in 1980 before moving to Cascia Hall Prep in Tulsa the following year. Two years later Smith began coaching collegiately at Tulsa (1983-86), Wisconsin (1987), Arizona State (1988-1991), Kentucky (1992), Tennessee (1993-94), and Ohio State (1995).

Personal: Born May 8, 1958, Gladewater, Texas. Lovie and his wife MaryAnne have three sons—Mikal, Matthew and Miles and twin grandsons—Malachi and Noah.

ASSISTANT COACHES

Jim Arthur, strength and conditioning assistant; born July 12, 1978. Attended Springfield (Mass.) College. No college or pro playing experience. College coach: Springfield (Mass.) College 2000, Louisiana Tech 2001, Boston College 2002. Pro coach: Joined Bears in 2005.

Bob Babich, asst. head coach/linebackers; born February 20, 1961, Aliquippa, Pa. Linebacker Mesa (Colo.) C.C. 1979-

1980, Tulsa 1981-82. No pro playing experience. College coach: Tulsa 1984-87, 1990, Wisconsin 1988-89, Bowling Green 1991, East Carolina 1992-93, Pittsburgh 1994-96, North Dakota State 1997-2002 (head coach). Pro coach: St. Louis Rams 2003, joined Bears in 2004.

Mike Bajakian, offensive quality control; born August 4, 1974, River Vale, N.J. Quarterback Williams College 1993-96. No pro playing experience. College coach: Rutgers 1998-99, Sacred Heart 2000, Michigan 2000-01, Central Michigan 2002-03. Pro coach: Joined Bears in 2004.

Rob Boras, tight ends; born September 30, 1970, Glen Ellyn, Ill. Center DePauw 1988-1991. No pro playing experience. College coach: DePauw 1992-93, Texas 1994-97, Benedictine 1998 (head coach), Nevada-Las Vegas 1999-2003. Pro coach: Joined Bears in 2004.

Gill Byrd, asst. defensive backs; born February 20, 1961, San Francisco. Cornerback San Jose State 1979-1982. Pro cornerback San Diego Chargers 1983-1992. Pro coach: St. Louis Rams 2003-05, joined Bears in 2006.

Darryl Drake, wide receivers; born December 11, 1956, Louisville, Ky. Wide receiver Western Kentucky 1975-78. Pro wide receiver Washington Redskins 1979, Ottawa Rough Riders (CFL) 1981, Cincinnati Bengals 1983. College coach: Western Kentucky 1983-1991, Georgia 1992-96, Baylor 1997, Texas 1998-2003. Pro coach: Joined Bears in 2004.

Harold Goodwin, asst. offensive line; born November 14, 1973, Columbia, S.C. Offensive lineman Michigan 1992-94. No pro playing experience. College coach: Eastern Michigan 1998-99, Central Michigan 2000-03. Pro coach: Joined Bears in 2004.

Harry Hiestand, offensive line; born November 19, 1958, Malvern, Pa. Offensive lineman Springfield College 1978-79, East Stroudsburg 1980. No pro playing experience. College coach: East Stroudsburg 1981-85, Pennsylvania 1986, Southern California 1987, Toledo 1988, Cincinnati 1989-1993, Missouri 1994-96, Illinois 1997-2004. Pro coach: Joined Bears in 2005.

Don Johnson, defensive line; born November 3, Newark, N.J. Defensive lineman Jersey City State 1973-76. Pro defensive lineman New Jersey Generals (USFL) 1977. College coach: Jersey City State 1984-85, Riverside (Calif.) C.C. 1987-1990, 1993-94, Cal State-Fullerton 1991-92, Nevada-Reno 1995-99, UCLA 2000-04. Pro coach: Joined Bears in 2005.

Rusty Jones, strength and conditioning coordinator; born August 14, 1953. Attended Springfield (Mass.) College. No college or pro playing experience. College coach: Springfield (Mass.) College 1979-82. Pro coach: Buffalo Bills 1985-2004, joined Bears in 2005.

Lloyd Lee, defensive assistant; born

August 10, 1976, Minneapolis. Safety Dartmouth 1994-97. Pro safety San Diego Chargers 1998-99. Pro coach: Tampa Bay Buccaneers (scout) 2001-03, joined Bears in 2004.

Kevin O'Dea, asst. special teams; born June 9, 1960, Williamsport, Pa. Wide receiver/defensive back Lock Haven 1983-85. No pro playing experience. College coach: Lock Haven 1986, Cornell 1987, Virginia 1988-1990, Penn State 1991-93. Pro coach: San Diego Chargers 1994-95, Tampa Bay Buccaneers 1996-2001, Detroit Lions 2002-03, Arizona Cardinals 2004-05, joined Bears in 2006.

Ron Rivera, defensive coordinator; born January 7, 1962, Fort Ord, Calif. Linebacker California 1980-83. Pro linebacker Chicago Bears 1984-1992. Pro coach: Chicago Bears 1997-98, Philadelphia Eagles 1999-2003, re-joined Bears in 2004.

Tim Spencer, running backs; born December 10, 1960, Martin Ferry, Ohio. Running back Ohio State 1979-1982. Pro running back Chicago Blitz (USFL) 1983, Arizona Wranglers (USFL) 1984, Memphis Showboats (USFL) 1985, San Diego Chargers 1985-1990. College coach: Ohio State 1994-2003. Pro coach: Joined Bears in 2004.

Dave Toub, special teams coordinator; born June 1, 1962, Ossining, N.Y. Offensive lineman Springfield College 1980-81, Texas-El Paso 1983-84. No pro playing experience. College coach: Texas El-Paso 1987-89, Missouri 1989-2000. Pro coach: Philadelphia Eagles 2001-03, joined Bears in 2004.

Ron Turner, offensive coordinator; born December 5, 1953, Martinez, Calif. Wide receiver Diablo Valley (Calif.) C.C. 1973-74, Pacific 1975-76. No pro playing experience. College coach: Pacific 1977, Arizona 1978-1980, Northwestern 1981-82, Pittsburgh 1983-84, Southern California 1985-87, Texas A&M 1988, Stanford 1989-1991, San Jose State 1992 (head coach), Illinois 1997-2004 (head coach). Pro coach: Chicago Bears 1993-96, re-joined Bears in 2005.

Steven Wilks, defensive backs; born August 8, 1969, Charlotte. Defensive back Appalachian State 1987-1991. Pro defensive back/wide receiver Charlotte Rage (AFL) 1993. College coach: Johnson C. Smith 1995-96, Savannah State 1997-99, Illinois State 2000, Appalachian State 2001, East Tennessee State 2002, Bowling Green State 2003, Notre Dame 2004, Washington 2005. Pro coach: Joined Bears in 2006.

Wade Wilson, quarterbacks; born February 1, 1959, Commerce, Texas. Quarterback East Texas State 1977-1980. Pro quarterback Minnesota Vikings 1981-1991, Atlanta Falcons 1992, New Orleans Saints 1993-94, Dallas Cowboys 1995-97, Oakland Raiders 1998-99. Pro coach: Dallas Cowboys 2000-02, joined Bears in 2004.

**National Football Conference
East Division**
Team Colors: Royal Blue, Metallic Silver
Blue, and White
**Cowboys Center
One Cowboys Parkway
Irving, Texas 75063
Telephone: (972) 556-9900**

2006 SCHEDULE
PRESEASON
Aug. 12 at Seattle.............................7:00
Aug. 21 at New Orleans (Shreveport, LA) 7:00
Aug. 26 **San Francisco**....................7:00
Aug. 31 **Minnesota** 7:00

REGULAR SEASON
Sept. 10 at Jacksonville....................4:15
Sept. 17 **Washington** 7:15
Sept. 24 Open Date
Oct. 1   at Tennessee 12:00
Oct. 8   at Philadelphia....................4:15
Oct. 15   **Houston** 12:00
Oct. 23   **N.Y. Giants** (Mon.) 7:30
Oct. 29   at Carolina.........................8:15
Nov. 5   at Washington 1:00
Nov. 12   at Arizona...........................2:15
Nov. 19   **Indianapolis**.....................12:00
Nov. 23   **Tampa Bay** (Thu.) 3:15
Dec. 3   at N.Y. Giants.....................1:00
Dec. 10   **New Orleans**....................12:00
Dec. 16   at Atlanta (Sat.) 8:00
Dec. 25   **Philadelphia** (Mon.)...........4:00
Dec. 31   **Detroit** 12:00

Stadium: Texas Stadium (opened in 1971)
•**Capacity:** 65,529
2401 E. Airport Freeway
Irving, Texas 75062
Playing Surface: Sportfield Realgrass
Training Camp: Marriott Residence Inn
Oxnard, California 93030

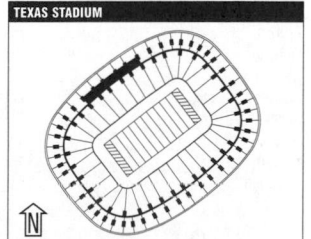

TEXAS STADIUM

CLUB OFFICIALS
Owner/President/General Manager:
Jerry Jones
Chief Operating Officer/Executive Vice
President/Director of Player Personnel:
Stephen Jones
Vice President/Director of Charities and
Special Events: Charlotte Anderson
Chief Sales and Marketing Officer/Vice
President: Jerry Jones Jr.
CFO: George Mitchell
Vice President of College and Pro
Scouting: Jeff Ireland
General Counsel: Alec Scheiner
Director of Public Relations:
Rich Dalrymple
Director of Corporate Communications:
Brett Daniels
Director of Community Relations:
Emily Robbins
Assistant Director of College Scouting:
Tom Ciskowski
Assistant Director of Pro Scouting:
Brian Gaine
Director of Operations: Bruce Mays
Director of Player Development:
Steve Carichoff
Chief Human Resources and Diversity
Officer: Vincent Thompson
Director of Information Technology:
Peter Walsh
Director of Broadcasting: Scott Purcel
Internet Director: Derek Eagleton
Director of Ticket Operations:
Carol Padgett
Director of Sales, Promotions and
Advertising: Joel Finglass
Head Athletic Trainer: Jim Maurer
Equipment Manager: Mike McCord
Video Director: Robert Blackwell
Cheerleader Director: Kelli Finglass

COACHING HISTORY
(424-314-6)
Records include postseason games
1960-1988 Tom Landry 270-178-6
1989-1993 Jimmy Johnson 51-37-0
1994-97   Barry Switzer 45-26-0
1998-99   Chan Gailey 18-16-0
2000-02   Dave Campo 15-33-0
2003-05   Bill Parcells 25-24-0

ATTENDANCE
Home 497,364   Away 567,508
Total 1,064,872
Single-game home record,
65,180 (11/12/95)
Single-season home record,
518,167 (1995)

2006 DRAFT CHOICES
Round	Name	Pos.	College
1	Bobby Carpenter	LB	Ohio State
2	Anthony Fasano	TE	Notre Dame
3	Jason Hatcher	DE	Grambling St.
4	Skyler Green	KR	Louisiana St.
5	Pat Watkins	DB	Florida State
6	Montavious Stanley	DT	Louisville
7	Pat McQuistan	T	Weber State
	E.J. Whitley	C	Texas Tech

2005 TEAM RECORD
PRESEASON (3-1)

Date	Result	Opponent
8/13	L 11-13	at Arizona
8/22	W 18-10	at Seattle
8/27	W 21-9	Houston
9/1	W 27-20	Jacksonville

REGULAR SEASON (9-7)

Date	Result	Opponent	Att.
9/11	W 28-24	at San Diego	67,679
9/19	L 13-14	Washington	65,207
9/25	W 34-31	at San Francisco	68,247
10/2	L 13-19	at Oakland	62,400
10/9	W 33-10	Philadelphia	63,199
10/16	W 16-13	N.Y. Giants (OT)	62,278
10/23	L 10-13	at Seattle	67,046
10/30	W 34-13	Arizona	62,068
11/14	W 21-20	at Philadelphia	67,739
11/20	W 20-7	Detroit	62,670
11/24	L 21-24	Denver (OT)	63,273
12/4	L 10-17	at N.Y. Giants	78,645
12/11	W 31-28	Kansas City	63,432
12/18	L 7-35	at Washington	90,588
12/24	W 24-20	at Carolina	73,436
1/1	L 10-20	St. Louis	63,131

(OT) Overtime

SCORE BY PERIODS

	1	2	3	4	OT		Total
Cowboys	69	99	54	100	3	—	325
Opponents	68	112	61	64	3	—	308

2005 TEAM STATISTICS

	Cowboys	Opp.
Total First Downs	318	256
Rushing	97	87
Passing	177	150
Penalty	44	19
3rd Down: Made/Att	94/232	73/211
3rd Down Pct.	40.5	34.6
4th Down: Made/Att	7/13	7/11
4th Down Pct.	53.8	63.6
Possession Avg.	32:24	27:36
Total Net Yards	5,202	4,814
Avg. Per Game	325.1	300.9
Total Plays	1,071	946
Avg. Per Play	4.9	5.1
Net Yards Rushing	1,861	1,731
Avg. Per Game	116.3	108.2
Total Rushes	521	414
Net Yards Passing	3,341	3,083
Avg. Per Game	208.8	192.7
Sacked/Yards Lost	50/298	37/236
Gross Yards	3,639	3,319
Att./Completions	500/300	495/271
Completion Pct.	60.0	54.7
Had Intercepted	17	15
Punts/Average	82/42.4	95/41.0
Net Punting Avg.	82/36.9	95/37.1
Penalties/Yards	99/739	142/1015
Fumbles/Ball Lost	36/14	21/11
Touchdowns	38	35
Rushing	13	13
Passing	23	18
Returns	2	4

2005 INDIVIDUAL STATISTICS

PASSING

PASSING	Att.	Comp.	Yds.	Pct.	TD	Int.	Tkld.	Rate
Bledsoe	499	300	3,639	60.1	23	17	49/295	83.7
K. Johnson	1	0	0	0.0	0	0	0/0	39.6
Barber	0	0	0	—	0	0	1/3	—
Cowboys	500	300	3,639	60.0	23	17	50/298	83.6
Opponents	495	271	3,319	54.7	18	15	37/236	75.1

SCORING

	TD R	TD P	TD Rt	PAT	FG	Saf	PTS
Cortez	0	0	0	13/14	12/16	0	49
T. Glenn	1	7	0	0/0	0/0	0	48
K. Johnson	0	6	0	0/0	0/0	0	38
Witten	0	6	0	0/0	0/0	0	36
Barber	5	0	0	0/0	0/0	0	30
J. Jones	5	0	0	0/0	0/0	0	30
Cundiff	0	0	0	14/14	5/8	0	29
Suisham	0	0	0	8/8	3/4	0	17
Bledsoe	2	0	0	0/0	0/0	0	12
Crayton	0	2	0	0/0	0/0	0	12
Campbell	0	1	0	0/0	0/0	0	6
Henry	0	0	1	0/0	0/0	0	6
Polite	0	1	0	0/0	0/0	0	6
Williams	0	0	1	0/0	0/0	0	6
Cowboys	13	23	2	35/36	20/28	0	325
Opponents	13	18	4	35/35	21/27	0	308

2-Pt. Conversions: K. Johnson.
Team 1-2, Opponents 0-0

RUSHING

RUSHING	No.	Yds	Avg	LG	TD
J. Jones	257	993	3.9	51	5
Barber	138	538	3.9	28t	5
Thompson	46	182	4.0	16	0
Thomas	36	80	2.2	12	0
Bledsoe	34	50	1.5	9	2
P. Price	1	9	9.0	9	0
Polite	2	8	4.0	6	0
Newman	1	4	4.0	4	0
K. Johnson	1	3	3.0	3	0
Crayton	1	0	0.0	0	0
Romo	2	-2	-1.0	-1	0
T. Glenn	2	-4	-2.0	6t	1
Cowboys	521	1,861	3.6	51	13
Opponents	414	1,731	4.2	55	13

RECEIVING

RECEIVING	No.	Yds	Avg	LG	TD
K. Johnson	71	839	11.8	34	6
Witten	66	757	11.5	34	6
T. Glenn	62	1,136	18.3	71t	7
J. Jones	35	218	6.2	26	0
Crayton	22	341	15.5	63t	2
Barber	18	115	6.4	21	0
Polite	9	72	8.0	15	1
P. Price	6	96	16.0	58	0
Campbell	3	24	8.0	18	1
Thompson	3	16	5.3	8	0
Pierce	2	15	7.5	10	0
Thomas	2	5	2.5	5	0
Copper	1	5	5.0	5	0
Cowboys	300	3,639	12.1	71t	23
Opponents	271	3,319	12.2	89t	18

INTERCEPTIONS

INTERCEPTIONS	No.	Yds	Avg	LG	TD
A. Glenn	4	10	2.5	10	0
Henry	3	102	34.0	58t	1
Williams	3	52	17.3	46t	1
Newman	3	16	5.3	12	0
Nguyen	1	7	7.0	7	0
Singleton	1	0	0.0	0	0
Cowboys	15	187	12.5	58t	2
Opponents	17	326	19.2	65t	2

PUNTING

PUNTING	No.	Yds.	Avg.	In 20	LG
McBriar	81	3439	42.5	28	63
Cundiff	1	35	35.0	0	35
Cowboys	82	3,474	42.4	28	63
Opponents	95	3,892	41.0	26	59

PUNT RETURNS

PUNT RETURNS	Ret	FC	Yds	Avg	LG	TD
Crayton	23	9	166	7.2	25	0
P. Price	12	6	63	5.3	11	0
Newman	10	6	55	5.5	26	0
Cowboys	45	21	284	6.3	26	0
Opponents	33	18	250	7.6	32	0

KICKOFF RETURNS

KICKOFF RETURNS	No.	Yds	Avg	LG	TD
Thompson	57	1,399	24.5	49	0
Barber	3	58	19.3	21	0
Copper	2	32	16.0	21	0
A. Glenn	1	20	20.0	20	0
Campbell	1	14	14.0	14	0
Cowboys	64	1,523	23.8	49	0
Opponents	66	1,432	21.7	49	0

FIELD GOALS

FIELD GOALS	1-19	20-29	30-39	40-49	50+
Cortez	0/0	5/6	4/4	3/6	0/0
Cundiff	1/1	1/1	2/5	0/0	1/1
Suisham	0/0	3/3	0/0	0/1	0/0
Cowboys	1/1	9/10	6/9	3/7	1/1
Opponents	0/0	8/9	2/3	7/8	4/7

SACKS

SACKS	No.
Ellis	8.0
Ware	8.0
Glover	3.0
Canty	2.5
James	2.5
Williams	2.5
Fujita	2.0
Shanle	1.5
Spears	1.5
Burnett	1.0
Ferguson	1.0
Newman	1.0
Nguyen	1.0
Ratliff	1.0
Coleman	0.5
Cowboys	37.0
Opponents	50.0

RECORD HOLDERS
INDIVIDUAL RECORDS—CAREER

Category	Name	Performance
Rushing (Yds.)	Emmitt Smith, 1990-2002	*17,162
Passing (Yds.)	Troy Aikman, 1989-2000	32,942
Passing (TDs)	Troy Aikman, 1989-2000	165
Receiving (No.)	Michael Irvin, 1988-1999	750
Receiving (Yds.)	Michael Irvin, 1988-1999	11,904
Interceptions	Mel Renfro, 1964-1977	52
Punting (Avg.)	Toby Gowin, 1997-99, 2003	41.7
Punt Return (Avg.)	Deion Sanders, 1995-99	13.3
Kickoff Return (Avg.)	Mel Renfro, 1964-1977	26.4
Field Goals	Rafael Septien, 1978-1986	162
Touchdowns (Tot.)	Emmitt Smith, 1990-2002	164
Points	Emmitt Smith, 1990-2002	986

INDIVIDUAL RECORDS—SINGLE SEASON

Category	Name	Performance
Rushing (Yds.)	Emmitt Smith, 1995	1,773
Passing (Yds.)	Danny White, 1983	3,980
Passing (TDs)	Danny White, 1983	29
Receiving (No.)	Michael Irvin, 1995	111
Receiving (Yds.)	Michael Irvin, 1995	1,603
Interceptions	Everson Walls, 1981	11
Punting (Avg.)	Sam Baker, 1962	45.4
Punt Return (Avg.)	Bob Hayes, 1968	20.8
Kickoff Return (Avg.)	Mel Renfro, 1965	30.0
Field Goals	Richie Cunningham, 1997	34
Touchdowns (Tot.)	Emmitt Smith, 1995	25
Points	Emmitt Smith, 1995	150

INDIVIDUAL RECORDS—SINGLE GAME

Category	Name	Performance
Rushing (Yds.)	Emmitt Smith, 10-31-93	237
Passing (Yds.)	Don Meredith, 11-10-63	460
Passing (TDs)	Many times	5
	Last time by Troy Aikman, 9-12-99	
Receiving (No.)	Lance Rentzel, 11-19-67	13
Receiving (Yds.)	Bob Hayes, 11-13-66	246
Interceptions	Many times	3
	Last time by Terance Newman, 12-14-03	
Field Goals	Chris Boniol, 11-18-96	*7
	Billy Cundiff, 9-15-03	*7
Touchdowns (Tot.)	Many times	4
	Last time by Emmitt Smith, 9-4-95	
Points	Many times	24
	Last time by Emmitt Smith, 9-4-95	

*NFL Record

2006 VETERAN ROSTER

No.	Name	Pos.	Ht.	Wt.	Birthdate	NFL Exp.	College	Hometown	How Acq.	'05 Games/ Starts
76	Adams, Flozell	T	6-7	335	5/18/75	9	Michigan State	Bellwood, Ill.	D2-'98	6/6
50	Ayodele, Akin	LB	6-2	246	9/17/79	5	Purdue	Irving, Texas	UFA(Jax)-'06	16/11*
24	Barber, Marion	RB	6-0	218	6/10/83	2	Minnesota	Wayzata, Minn.	D4a-'05	13/2
11	Bledsoe, Drew	QB	6-5	238	2/14/72	14	Washington State	Ellensburg, Wash.	FA-'05	16/16
59	Boiman, Rocky	LB	6-4	236	1/24/80	5	Notre Dame	Cincinnati, Ohio	UFA(Tenn)-'06	15/2*
57	Burnett, Kevin	LB	6-3	240	12/24/82	2	Tennessee	Carson, Calif.	D2-'05	13/0
99	Canty, Chris	DE	6-7	295	11/10/82	2	Virginia	Charlotte, N.C.	D4b-'05	16/2
93	Coleman, Kenyon	DE	6-5	295	4/10/79	5	UCLA	Alta Loma, Calif.	T(Oak)-'03	12/5
32	Coleman, Marcus	S	6-2	210	5/24/74	11	Texas Tech	Dallas, Texas	FA-'06	15/11*
75	Colombo, Marc	T	6-8	325	10/8/78	5	Boston College	Bridgewater, Mass.	FA-'05	4/0
18	Copper, Terrance	WR	6-0	210	3/12/82	3	East Carolina	Washington, N.C.	FA-'04	16/0
84	Crayton, Patrick	WR	6-0	205	4/7/79	3	Northwestern Oklahoma State	DeSoto, Texas	D7b-'04	11/0
29	Davis, Keith	S	5-11	207	12/30/78	4	Sam Houston	Italy, Texas	FA-'04	16/15
98	Ellis, Greg	DE	6-6	280	8/14/75	9	North Carolina	Wendell, N.C.	D1-'98	16/13
69	Fabini, Jason	T	6-7	304	8/25/74	9	Cincinnati	Fort Wayne, Ind.	FA-'06	9/9*
95	Ferguson, Jason	DT	6-3	310	11/28/74	10	Georgia	Nettleton, Miss.	FA-'05	16/5
55	Fowler, Ryan	LB	6-3	250	5/20/82	3	Duke	Redington Shores, Fla.	FA-'04	14/3
26	Glenn, Aaron	CB	5-9	185	7/16/72	13	Texas A&M	Humble, Texas	FA-'05	16/7
83	Glenn, Terry	WR	5-11	195	7/23/74	11	Ohio State	Columbus, Ohio	T(GB)-'03	16/16
78	Glymph, Junior	LB	6-6	270	9/2/80	3	Carson-Newman	Newberry, S.C.	FA-'06	3/0*
65	Gurode, Andre	G/C	6-4	314	3/6/78	5	Colorado	Houston, Texas	D2a-'02	16/2
48	Hannam, Ryan	TE	6-2	248	2/24/80	5	Northern Iowa	St. Ansgar, Iowa	UFA(Sea)-'06	16/5*
42	Henry, Anthony	CB	6-1	207	11/3/76	6	South Florida	Fort Myers, Fla.	UFA(Cle)-'05	12/10
7	Henson, Drew	QB	6-4	233	2/13/80	3	Michigan	Brighton, Mich.	T(Hou)-'04	0*
56	James, Bradie	LB	6-2	250	1/17/81	4	Louisiana State	Monroe, La.	D4-'03	16/16
52	Johnson, Al	C	6-5	305	1/27/79	3	Wisconsin	Brussels, Wis.	D2-'03	16/16
92	Johnson, Thomas	DT	6-2	300	6/24/81	2	Middle Tennessee State	Memphis, Tenn.	FA-'05	2/0
21	Jones, Julius	RB	5-10	211	8/14/81	3	Notre Dame	Big Stone Gap, Va.	D2a-'04	13/12
33	Jones, Nathan	CB	5-10	192	6/15/82	3	Rutgers	Scotch Plains, N.J.	D7a-'04	16/0
63	Kosier, Kyle	T/G	6-5	305	11/27/78	5	Arizona State	Peoria, Ariz.	UFA(Det)-'06	16/11*
91	Ladouceur, Louis-Philippe	LS	6-4	257	3/13/81	2	California	Pointe-Claire, Quebec	FA-'05	13/0
1	McBriar, Mat	P	6-1	220	7/8/79	3	Hawaii	East Brighton, Australia	FA-'04	16/0
86	Merritt, Ahmad	WR	5-10	195	2/5/77	4	Wisconsin	Chicago, Ill.	FA-'06	0*
41	Newman, Terence	CB	5-11	195	9/4/78	4	Kansas State	Salina, Kan.	D1-'03	16/16
81	Owens, Terrell	WR	6-3	226	12/7/73	11	Tennessee-Chattanooga	Alexander City, Ala.	FA-'06	7/7*
72	Peterman, Stephen	G	6-4	323	1/11/82	2	Louisiana State	Waveland, Miss.	D3-'04	3/0
79	Petitti, Rob	T	6-6	325	5/21/82	2	Pittsburgh	Rumson, N.J.	D6b-'05	16/16
88	Pierce, Brett	TE	6-5	265	1/7/81	3	Stanford	Vancouver, Wash.	FA-'04	10/1
20	Pile, Willie	S	6-2	206	5/25/80	3	Virginia Tech	Alexandria, Va.	FA-'05	16/1
39	Polite, Lousaka	FB	6-0	246	9/14/81	2	Pittsburg	Woodland Hills, Pa.	FA-'04	14/3
71	Proctor, Cory	G	6-4	295	10/18/82	2	Montana	Gig Harbor, Wash.	FA-'05	1/0
66	Ratliff, Jay	DE	6-4	293	8/29/81	2	Auburn	Valdosta. Ga.	D7-'05	4/1
35	Reeves, Jacques	CB	5-11	192	10/8/82	3	Purdue	Lancaster, Texas	D7c-'04	16/0
62	Rivera, Marco	G	6-4	307	4/26/72	11	Penn State	Elmont, N.Y.	UFA(GB)-'05	14/14
9	Romo, Tony	QB	6-2	219	4/21/80	4	Eastern Illinois	Burlington, Wis.	FA-'03	16/0
80	Ryan, Sean	TE	6-5	257	3/27/80	3	Boston College	Buffalo, N.Y.	D5-'04	3/1
58	Shanle, Scott	LB	6-2	245	11/23/79	4	Nebraska	St. Edward, Neb.	W(StL)-'05	15/7
51	Singleton, Al	LB	6-2	250	8/7/75	10	Temple	Irvington, N.J.	UFA(TB)-'03	8/7
96	Spears, Marcus	DE	6-4	294	3/8/83	2	Louisiana State	Baton Rouge, La.	D1b-'05	16/10
4	Suisham, Shaun	K	6-0	199	12/29/81	2	Bowling Green	Wallaceburg, Ontario	FA-'05	3/0
28	Thompson, Tyson	RB	6-1	220	5/21/81	2	San Jose State	Irving, Texas	FA-'05	15/0
53	Thornton, Kalen	LB	6-3	245	5/12/82	2	Texas	Dallas, Texas	FA-'04	0*
87	Tolver, J.R.	WR	6-1	200	1/13/80	2	San Diego State	San Diego, Calif.	FA-'06	0*
13	Vanderjagt, Mike	K	6-5	211	3/24/70	9	West Virginia	Oakville, Ontario	UFA(Ind)-'06	16/0*
94	Ware, DeMarcus	LB	6-4	255	7/31/82	2	Troy State	Auburn, Ala.	D1a-'05	16/16
31	Williams, Roy	S	6-0	226	8/14/80	5	Oklahoma	Union City, Calif.	D1-'02	16/16
82	Witten, Jason	TE	6-5	261	5/6/82	4	Tennessee	Elizabethton, Tenn.	D3-'03	16/16

* Ayodele played 16 games with Jacksonville in '05; Boiman played 15 games with Tennessee; Coleman played 15 games with Houston; Fabini played 9 games with N.Y. Jets; Glymph played 3 games with Atlanta; Hannam played 16 games with Seattle; Henson inactive for 16 games; Kosier played 16 games with Detroit; Merritt last active with Chicago in '03; Owens played 7 games with Philadelphia; Thornton missed '05 season because of injury; Tolver last active with Miami in '03; Vanderjagt played 16 games with Indianapolis.

Retired—Dat Nguyen, seven-year linebacker, 8 games with Dallas in '05.

Players lost through free agency (3): TE Dan Campbell (Det; 16 games in '05), LB Scott Fujita (NO; 16), T Torrin Tucker (TB; 16).

Also played with Cowboys in '05—G Larry Allen (16 games), LB Mike Barrow (2), T Ethan Brooks (1), LB Quinton Caver (8), LS Jon Condo (3), K Jose Cortez (7), K Billy Cundiff (6), DT La'Roi Glover (16), WR Keyshawn Johnson (16), G Ben Noll (4), LB Eric Ogbogu (6), WR Peerless Price (7), S Lynn Scott (6), RB Anthony Thomas (5).

2006 FIRST-YEAR ROSTER

Name	Pos.	Ht.	Wt.	Birthdate	College	Hometown	How Acq.
Austin, Miles	WR	6-3	219	6/30/84	Monmouth College	Garfield, N.J.	FA
Beriault, Justin (1)	S	6-3	208	8/23/81	Ball State	Indianapolis, Ind.	D6a-'05
Bowen, Stephen	DE	6-5	271	3/28/84	Hofstra	Wheatley Heights, N.Y.	FA
Brooks, Darrell	S	6-1	192	3/11/83	Arizona	Moreno Valley, Calif.	FA
Butler, Quincy	CB	6-1	191	11/25/81	Texas Christian	San Antonio, Texas	FA
Carpenter, Bobby	LB	6-2	255	8/1/83	Ohio State	Lancaster, Ohio	D1
Crowder, Tom (1)	WR	6-1	212	1/21/81	Arkansas	Camden, Ark.	FA
Curtis, Tony (1)	TE	6-5	265	2/11/83	Portland State	Seaside, Calif.	FA
Elam, Abram	S	6-0	205	10/15/81	Kent State	Riviera Beach, Fla.	FA
Fasano, Anthony	TE	6-4	250	4/20/84	Notre Dame	Verona, N.J.	D2
Gill, Erik	TE	6-5	275	3/24/82	Pittsburgh	Belle Vernon, Pa.	FA
Green, Skyler	WR	5-9	197	9/12/84	Louisiana State	Harvey, La.	D4
Hatcher, Jason	DE	6-6	285	7/13/82	Grambling State	Alexandria, La.	D3
Horne, JJ	LB	6-2	240	7/25/83	Pittsburgh	Franklin, Pa.	FA
Hoyte, Oliver	LB	6-3	247	10/5/84	North Carolina State	Tampa, Fla.	FA
Hurd, Sam	WR	6-2	187	4/24/85	Northern Illinois	San Antonio, Texas	FA
Jamison, Vontrell (1)	DE	6-6	277	7/26/82	Clemson	Holly Hill, S.C.	FA-'05
Kincade, Keylon (1)	RB	5-11	204	8/20/82	Southern Methodist	Troup, Tex.	FA
McQuistan, Pat	T	6-6	314	4/30/83	Weber State	Lebanon, Ore.	D7
Mroz, Jeff	QB	6-5	230	7/11/83	Yale	Greensburg, Pa.	FA
Parham, Kai	LB	6-3	253	3/15/84	Virginia	Virginia Beach, Va.	FA
Parker, Byron (1)	CB	5-11	197	3/7/81	Tulane	Madisonville, Ky.	FA
Rector, Jamaica (1)	WR	5-10	186	8/10/81	Northwest Missouri State	Celeste, Texas	FA
Roland, Dennis	T	6-9	309	3/10/83	Georgia	Bolivar, Mo.	FA
Saldi, John	LB	6-5	233	6/14/82	Texas Tech	Southlake, Texas	FA
Snell, Shannon (1)	G	6-2	310	4/27/82	Florida	Tampa, Fla.	FA
Stanley, Montavious	DT	6-2	313	9/10/81	Louisville	Albany, Ga.	D6
Tarullo, Matthew (1)	G/C	6-5	314	8/13/82	Syracuse	Albany, N.Y.	FA
Watkins, Patrick	S	6-5	211	12/18/82	Florida State	Tallahassee, Fla.	D5
Whitley, E.J.	G/C	6-6	293	2/16/82	Texas Tech	Texas City, Texas	D7
Williams, Lenny (1)	CB	5-10	190	12/16/81	Southern	Lake Charles, La.	FA
Young, Danny (1)	TE/LS	6-5	265	1/13/82	North Carolina State	San Diego, Calif.	FA

The term NFL Rookie is defined as a player who is in his first season of professional football and has not been on the roster of another professional football team for any regular-season or postseason games. A Rookie is designated by an "R" on NFL rosters. Players who have been active in another professional football league or players who have NFL experience, including either preseason training camp or being on an Active List or Inactive List, or on Reserve/Injured or Reserve/Physically Unable to Perform for fewer than six regular-season games, are termed NFL First-Year Players. An NFL First-Year Player is designated by a "1" on NFL rosters. Thereafter, a player is credited with an additional year of experience for each season in which he accumulates six games on the Active List or Inactive List, or on Reserve/Injured or Reserve/Physically Unable to Perform.

Log on to www.dallascowboys.com for an up-to-date roster.

COACHING STAFF
Head Coach,
Bill Parcells

Pro Career: Named head coach on January 2, 2003, Parcells has accumulated a 174-130-1 record, including two Super Bowl victories (XXI and XXV with the Giants) and another Super Bowl appearance (XXXI with New England) in 18 seasons as an NFL head coach. His 174 career victories make him the second winningest active coach in the NFL, trailing only Marty Schottenheimer (191). Parcells has guided his teams to 12 winning seasons, nine playoff berths, and posted an 11-7 postseason record. Parcells-led teams have finished in either first or second place in their division ten times. With the Cowboys' postseason appearance in 2003, Parcells became the first coach in NFL history to lead four different teams to the playoffs. He is one of only five coaches (Don Shula, Dan Reeves, Dick Vermeil, and Mike Holmgren) in NFL history to have led two separate teams to the Super Bowl. Parcells, Denver's Mike Shanahan, Washington's Joe Gibbs, and New England's Bill Belichick are the only active coaches to have claimed two-or-more Super Bowl titles, and he is one of just eight active coaches to have ever won a Super Bowl title. In his first season at the helm in Dallas, Parcells took a team that had posted three consecutive 5-11 seasons and posted a 10-6 mark in the regular season, as well as an NFC Wild Card playoff berth. In 2004, the Cowboys posted a 6-10 record in his second season, and then rebounded in 2005 with a 9-7 record. Under his direction, the N.Y. Jets (1997-99)—who won a combined four games the two seasons prior to his arrival—improved to 9-7 his first season and 12-4 with a trip to the AFC Championship Game his second season. This success marked the first time in NFL history that a team had won one game and within two years was playing for a conference championship. He took over the New England Patriots (1993-96) following a 2-14 season by the Patriots. Within two years, Parcells coached the team to a 10-6 mark and its first playoff game in eight years. In his fourth year, the Patriots went 11-5 and advanced to Super Bowl XXXI against Green Bay. Parcells began his NFL head coaching career with the N.Y. Giants (1983-1990), who had posted one winning season in its previous 10 years. After an initial campaign of 3-12-1, he improved the club's victory total to 9, 10, 14, 10, 12, and 13 between 1984 and 1990. In the process, the Giants were able to win two Super Bowl titles—Super Bowl XXI over Denver and Super Bowl XXV over Buffalo. During his time at the Giants helm, the club won two Super Bowls, three division titles, and had only one losing season. For his accomplishment, Parcells was honored with NFL Coach of the Year honors in both 1986 and 1989. Career record: 174-130-1.

Background: Played linebacker at Wichita State 1961-63. Served as college coach at: Hastings (Neb.) 1964, Wichita State 1965, Army 1966-69, Florida State 1970-72, Vanderbilt 1973-74, Texas Tech 1975-77, and was head coach at Air Force in 1978.

Personal: Born August 22, 1941, in Englewood, N.J. Parcells resides in Irving, Texas. He has three daughters—Suzy, Jill, and Dallas.

ASSISTANT COACHES

Todd Bowles, secondary; born November 18, 1963, Elizabeth, N.J. Defensive back Temple 1982-85. Pro defensive back Washington Redskins 1986-1990, 1992-93, San Francisco 49ers 1991. College coach: Morehouse College 1997, Grambling State 1998-99. Pro coach: New York Jets 2000, Cleveland Browns 2001-04, joined Cowboys in 2005.

Vincent Brown, inside linebackers; born January 9, 1965, Atlanta. Linebacker Mississippi Valley State 1984-87. Pro linebacker New England Patriots 1988-1995. Pro coach: Joined Cowboys in 2006.

Bruce DeHaven, special teams; born September 6, 1948, Trousdale, Kan. Attended Southwestern (Kan.) College. No pro playing experience. College coach: Kansas 1979-1981, New Mexico State 1982. Pro coach: New Jersey Generals (USFL) 1983, Pittsburgh Maulers (USFL) 1984, Orlando Renegades (USFL) 1985, Buffalo Bills 1987-1999, San Francisco 49ers 2000-02, joined Cowboys in 2003.

Todd Haley, wide receivers/passing game; born February 28, 1967, Atlanta. Attended Florida and Miami. No college or pro playing experience. Pro coach: New York Jets 1996-2000, Chicago Bears 2001-2003, joined Cowboys in 2004.

Joe Juraszek, strength and conditioning; born June 8, 1958, Chicago. Linebacker/defensive end New Mexico 1976-1980. No pro playing experience. College coach: Oklahoma 1981-86, 1993-96, Texas Tech 1987-1992. Pro coach: Joined Cowboys in 1997.

Freddie Kitchens, tight ends; born November 29, 1974, Gadsden, Ala. Quarterback Alabama 1994-97. No pro playing experience. College coach: Glenville State College 1999, Louisiana State 2000, North Texas 2001-03, Mississippi State 2004-05. Pro coach: Joined Cowboys in 2006.

David Lee, offensive quality control; born July 2, 1953, Cape Girardeau, Mo. Quarterback Vanderbilt 1971-74. No pro playing experience. College coach: Tennessee-Martin 1975-76, Vanderbilt 1977, Mississippi 1978-1982, New Mexico 1983, Arkansas 1984-88, 2001-02, Texas-El Paso 1989-1993 (head coach), Rice 1994-2000. Pro coach: Joined Cowboys in 2003.

Anthony Lynn, running backs; born December 21, 1968, McKinney, Texas. Fullback Texas Tech 1987-1990. Pro fullback Denver Broncos 1993, 1997-1999, San Francisco 49ers 1995-96. Pro coach: Denver Broncos 2000-02, Jacksonville Jaguars 2003-2004, joined Cowboys in 2005.

Mike MacIntyre, safeties; born March 14, 1965, Miami. Safety Vanderbilt 1985-86, Georgia Tech 1987-88. No pro playing experience. College coach: Georgia 1990-91, Davidson 1992, Tennessee-Martin 1993-96, Temple 1997-98, Mississippi 1999-2002. Pro coach: Joined Cowboys in 2003.

Chris Palmer, quarterbacks; born: September 23, 1949, Brewster, N.Y. Quarterback Southern Connecticut State 1968-1971. No pro playing experience. College coach: Connecticut 1972-74, Lehigh 1975, Colgate 1976-1982, New Haven 1986-87 (head coach), Boston 1988-89 (head coach). Pro coach: Montreal Concordes (CFL) 1983, New Jersey Generals (USFL) 1984-85, Houston Oilers 1990-92, New England Patriots 1993-96, Jacksonville Jaguars 1997-98, Cleveland Browns 1999-2000 (head coach), Houston Texans 2001-05, joined Cowboys in 2006.

Paul Pasqualoni, linebackers; born August 16, 1949, New Haven, Conn. Linebacker Penn State 1968-1971. No pro playing experience. College coach: Southern Connecticut State 1976-1981, Western Connecticut 1982-86 (head coach), Syracuse 1987-2004 (head coach 1991-2004). Pro coach: Joined Cowboys in 2005.

Kacy Rodgers, defensive line; born June 24, 1969, Humboldt, Tenn. Linebacker/defensive end Tennessee 1988-1991. Pro linebacker Shreveport Pirates (CFL) 1994. College coach: Tennessee-Martin 1994-97, Louisiana-Monroe 1998, Middle Tennessee State 1999-2001, Arkansas 2002. Pro coach: Joined Cowboys in 2003.

Tony Sparano, asst. head coach/offensive line/running game; born October 7, 1961, West Haven, Conn. Center New Haven 1978-1981. No pro playing experience. College coach: New Haven 1984-87, 1994-98 (head coach 1994-98), Boston University 1988-1993. Pro coach: Cleveland Browns 1999-2000, Washington Redskins 2001, Jacksonville Jaguars 2002, joined Cowboys in 2003.

Mike Zimmer, defensive coordinator; born June 5, 1956, Peoria, Ill. Quarterback/linebacker Illinois State 1974-76. No pro playing experience. College coach: Missouri 1979-1980, Weber State 1981-88, Washington State 1989-1993. Pro coach: Joined Cowboys in 1994.

National Football Conference
North Division
Team Colors: Honolulu Blue and Silver
Detroit Lions Practice &
Training Facility
222 Republic Drive
Allen Park, Michigan 48101
Telephone: (313) 216-4000

2006 SCHEDULE
PRESEASON
Aug. 11	**Denver**	7:30
Aug. 20	at Cleveland	7:30
Aug. 25	at Oakland	7:00
Aug. 31	**Buffalo**	7:30

REGULAR SEASON
Sept. 10	**Seattle**	1:00
Sept. 17	at Chicago	12:00
Sept. 24	**Green Bay**	1:00
Oct. 1	at St. Louis	3:05
Oct. 8	at Minnesota	12:00
Oct. 15	**Buffalo**	1:00
Oct. 22	at N.Y. Jets	1:00
Oct. 29	Open Date	
Nov. 5	**Atlanta**	1:00
Nov. 12	**San Francisco**	1:00
Nov. 19	at Arizona	2:05
Nov. 23	**Miami** (Thu.)	12:30
Dec. 3	at New England	1:00
Dec. 10	**Minnesota**	1:00
Dec. 17	at Green Bay	12:00
Dec. 24	**Chicago**	1:00
Dec. 31	at Dallas	12:00

Stadium: Ford Field (opened in 2002)
    •**Capacity:** 64,500
    2000 Brush Street
    Detroit, Michigan 48226
Playing Surface: FieldTurf
Training Camp: 222 Republic Drive
      Allen Park, Michigan
      48101

FORD FIELD

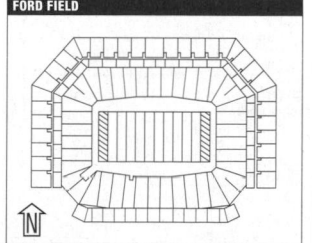

CLUB OFFICIALS
Chairman and Owner: William Clay Ford
Vice Chairman: William Clay Ford, Jr.
President and CEO: Matt Millen
Executive Vice President/COO:
  Tom Lewand
Senior Vice President & Assistant GM:
  Martin Mayhew
Senior Vice President: Bill Keenist
Senior Vice President/CFO: Tom Lesnau
Secretary: David Hempstead
Director of Pro Personnel: Sheldon White
Director of College Scouting:
  Scott McEwen
Scouts: Bob Beers, Chad Henry,
  Silas McKinnie, Bob Merrit,
  Dennis Murphy, Lance Newmark,
  Dave Uyrus, Dennis Gentry
Senior Director of Community Affairs:
  Tim Pendell
Director of Media Relations:
  Matt Barnhart
Director of Broadcasting: Bryan Bender
Director of Ticket Operations:
  Mark Graham
Head Athletic Trainer: Al Bellamy
Equipment Manager: Tim O'Neill
Video Director: Robert Yanagi

COACHING HISTORY
Portsmouth Spartans 1930-33
(485-541-32)
Records include postseason games
1930	Hal (Tubby) Griffen	5-6-3
1931-36	George (Potsy) Clark	49-20-6
1937-38	Earl (Dutch) Clark	14-8-0
1939	Elmer (Gus) Henderson	6-5-0
1940	George (Potsy) Clark	5-5-1
1941-42	Bill Edwards*	4-9-1
1942	John Karcis	0-8-0
1943-47	Charles (Gus) Dorais	20-31-2
1948-1950	Alvin (Bo) McMillin	12-24-0
1951-56	Raymond (Buddy) Parker	50-24-2
1957-1964	George Wilson	55-45-6
1965-66	Harry Gilmer	10-16-2
1967-1972	Joe Schmidt	43-35-7
1973	Don McCafferty	6-7-1
1974-76	Rick Forzano**	15-17-0
1976-77	Tommy Hudspeth	11-13-0
1978-1984	Monte Clark	43-63-1
1985-88	Darryl Rogers***	18-40-0
1988-1996	Wayne Fontes	67-71-0
1997-2000	Bobby Ross****	27-32-0
2000	Gary Moeller	4-3-0
2001-02	Marty Mornhinweg	5-27-0
2003-05	Steve Mariucci#	15-28-0
2005	Dick Jauron	1-4-0

    *Released after three games in 1942
   **Resigned after four games in 1976
  ***Released after 11 games in 1988
 ****Resigned after nine games in 2000
    # Released after 11 games in 2005

ATTENDANCE
Home 492,607   Away 515,149
Total 1,007,756
Single-game home record,
  80,444 (12/20/81)
Single-season home record, 644,904
  (1980)

2006 DRAFT CHOICES
Round	Name	Pos.	College
1	Ernis Sims	LB	Florida State
2	Daniel Bullocks	S	Nebraska
3	Brian Calhoun	RB	Wisconsin
5	Jonathan Scott	T	Texas
6	Alton McCann	CB	West Virginia
7	Fred Matua	G	So. California
	Anthony Cannon	LB	Tulane

2005 TEAM RECORD
PRESEASON (1-3)

Date	Result		Opponent
8/12	L	3-10	at N.Y. Jets
8/20	L	13-21	Cleveland
8/29	L	13-37	St. Louis
9/2	W	21-7	at Buffalo

REGULAR SEASON (5-11)

Date	Result		Opponent	Att.
9/11	W	17-3	Green Bay	61,877
9/18	L	6-38	at Chicago	62,019
10/2	L	13-17	at Tampa Bay	64,994
10/9	W	35-17	Baltimore	61,201
10/16	L	20-21	Carolina	61,083
10/23	W	13-10	at Cleveland	72,923
10/30	L	13-19	Chicago (OT)	61,814
11/6	L	14-27	at Minnesota	63,813
11/13	W	29-21	Arizona	61,091
11/20	L	7-20	at Dallas	62,670
11/24	L	7-27	Atlanta	62,390
12/4	L	16-21	Minnesota	61,375
12/11	L	13-16	at Green Bay (OT)	70,019
12/18	L	17-41	Cincinnati	61,749
12/24	W	13-12	at New Orleans	63,747
1/1	L	21-35	at Pittsburgh	63,794

(OT) Overtime

SCORE BY PERIODS

Lions	69	72	43	70	0	—	254
Opponents	84	136	66	50	9	—	345

2005 TEAM STATISTICS

	Lions	Opp.
Total First Downs	258	308
Rushing	69	109
Passing	151	166
Penalty	38	33
3rd Down: Made/Att	87/224	82/208
3rd Down Pct.	38.8	39.4
4th Down: Made/Att	7/17	6/11
4th Down Pct.	41.2	54.5
Possession Avg.	29:13	30:47
Total Net Yards	4,319	5,158
Avg. Per Game	269.9	322.4
Total Plays	955	1,006
Avg. Per Play	4.5	5.1
Net Yards Rushing	1,471	2,040
Avg. Per Game	91.9	127.5
Total Rushes	404	488
Net Yards Passing	2,848	3,118
Avg. Per Game	178.0	194.9
Sacked/Yards Lost	31/173	31/187
Gross Yards	3,021	3,305
Att./Completions	520/297	487/295
Completion Pct.	57.1	60.6
Had Intercepted	18	19
Punts/Average	84/43.5	72/40.3
Net Punting Avg.	84/36.9	72/34.5
Penalties/Yards	115/838	130/953
Fumbles/Ball Lost	21/12	24/12
Touchdowns	28	39
Rushing	10	15
Passing	15	19
Returns	3	5

2005 INDIVIDUAL STATISTICS

PASSING

	Att.	Comp.	Yds.	Pct.	TD	Int.	Tkld.	Rate
Harrington	330	188	2,021	57.0	12	12	24/136	72.0
Garcia	173	102	937	59.0	3	6	6/34	65.1
Orlovsky	17	7	63	41.2	0	0	1/3	51.8
Lions	520	297	3,021	57.1	15	18	31/173	69.1
Opponents	487	295	3,305	60.6	19	19	31/187	77.6

SCORING

	TD R	TD P	TD Rt	PAT	FG	Saf	PTS
Hanson	0	0	0	27/27	19/24	0	84
R. Williams	0	8	0	0/0	0/0	0	48
Jones	5	0	0	0/0	0/0	0	30
Pinner	3	0	0	0/0	0/0	0	18
Pollard	0	3	0	0/0	0/0	0	18
Bailey	0	0	1	0/0	0/0	0	6
Bryson	1	0	0	0/0	0/0	0	6
Fitzsimmons	0	1	0	0/0	0/0	0	6
Garcia	1	0	0	0/0	0/0	0	6
Kennedy	0	0	1	0/0	0/0	0	6
C. Rogers	0	1	0	0/0	0/0	0	6
S. Rogers	0	0	1	0/0	0/0	0	6
Schlesinger	0	1	0	0/0	0/0	0	6
M. Williams	0	1	0	0/0	0/0	0	6
Wilkinson	0	0	0	0/0	0/0	1	2
Hamilton	0	0	0	0/1	0/0	0	0
Lions	10	15	3	27/28	19/24	1	254
Opponents	15	19	5	37/37	24/30	0	345

2-Pt. Conversions: Team 0-0, Opponents 1-1.

RUSHING

	No.	Yds	Avg	LG	TD
Jones	186	664	3.6	40	5
Pinner	106	349	3.3	19	3
Bryson	64	306	4.8	77t	1
Harrington	24	80	3.3	15	0
Garcia	17	51	3.0	14	1
P. Smith	4	16	4.0	6	0
Vines	1	7	7.0	7	0
Schlesinger	1	1	1.0	1	0
Drummond	1	-3	-3.0	-3	0
Lions	404	1,471	3.6	77t	10
Opponents	488	2,040	4.2	64t	15

RECEIVING

	No.	Yds	Avg	LG	TD
Pollard	46	516	11.2	86	3
R. Williams	45	687	15.3	51t	8
Vines	40	417	10.4	40	0
Bryson	37	284	7.7	63	0
M. Williams	29	350	12.1	49	1
Pinner	21	181	8.6	24	0
Jones	20	109	5.5	28	0
K. Johnson	17	133	7.8	25	0
C. Rogers	14	197	14.1	35t	1
Fitzsimmons	10	45	4.5	11	1
Schlesinger	8	31	3.9	8	1
P. Smith	6	49	8.2	11	0
T. Edwards	2	15	7.5	8	0
Martinez	1	11	11.0	11	0
Harrington	1	-4	-4.0	-4	0
Lions	297	3,021	10.2	86	15
Opponents	295	3,305	11.2	80t	19

INTERCEPTIONS

	No.	Yds	Avg	LG	TD
Bly	6	54	9.0	28	0
Goodman	3	17	5.7	21	0
Kennedy	2	64	32.0	64t	1
Holt	2	51	25.5	51	0
McQuarters	2	25	12.5	19	0
Bailey	1	34	34.0	34t	1
Bra. Walker	1	22	22.0	22	0
Lehman	1	21	21.0	17	0
Wayne	1	20	20.0	20	0
Lions	19	308	16.2	64t	2
Opponents	18	271	15.1	41t	2

PUNTING

	No.	Yds.	Avg.	In 20	LG
Harris	84	3,656	43.5	34	60
Lions	84	3,656	43.5	34	60
Opponents	72	2,899	40.3	20	61

PUNT RETURNS

	Ret	FC	Yds	Avg	LG	TD
Drummond	26	11	157	6.0	38	0
McQuarters	10	2	117	11.7	49	0
Lions	36	13	274	7.6	49	0
Opponents	50	17	520	10.4	81t	2

KICKOFF RETURNS

	No.	Yds	Avg	LG	TD
Drummond	49	1,077	22.0	48	0
McQuarters	16	381	23.8	73	0
Bryson	4	55	13.8	25	0
Martinez	2	42	21.0	24	0
K. Johnson	1	14	14.0	14	0
DeVries	1	7	7.0	7	0
Lions	73	1,576	21.6	73	0
Opponents	55	1,239	22.5	90t	1

FIELD GOALS

	1-19	20-29	30-39	40-49	50+
Hanson	1/1	9/9	3/3	4/7	2/4
Lions	1/1	9/9	3/3	4/7	2/4
Opponents	1/1	8/8	7/9	5/7	3/5

SACKS

K. Edwards	7.0
S. Rogers	5.5
Hall	5.0
DeVries	3.0
Wilkinson	3.0
TEAM	2.0
Cody	1.5
Bailey	1.0
Redding	1.0
K. Smith	1.0
Woods	1.0
Lions	31.0
Opponents	31.0

RECORD HOLDERS
INDIVIDUAL RECORDS—CAREER

Category	Name	Performance
Rushing (Yds.)	Barry Sanders, 1989-1998	15,269
Passing (Yds.)	Bobby Layne, 1950-58	15,710
Passing (TDs)	Bobby Layne, 1950-58	118
Receiving (No.)	Herman Moore, 1991-2001	670
Receiving (Yds.)	Herman Moore, 1991-2001	9,174
Interceptions	Dick LeBeau, 1959-1972	62
Punting (Avg.)	Yale Lary, 1952-53, 1956-1964	44.3
Punt Return (Avg.)	Jack Christiansen, 1951-58	12.8
Kickoff Return (Avg.)	Pat Studstlll, 1961-67	25.7
Field Goals	Jason Hanson, 1992-2005	327
Touchdowns (Tot.)	Barry Sanders, 1989-1998	109
Points	Jason Hanson, 1992-2005	1,420

INDIVIDUAL RECORDS—SINGLE SEASON

Category	Name	Performance
Rushing (Yds.)	Barry Sanders, 1997	2,053
Passing (Yds.)	Scott Mitchell, 1995	4,338
Passing (TDs)	Scott Mitchell, 1995	32
Receiving (No.)	Herman Moore, 1995	123
Receiving (Yds.)	Herman Moore, 1995	1,686
Interceptions	Don Doll, 1950	12
	Jack Christiansen, 1953	12
Punting (Avg.)	Yale Lary, 1963	48.9
Punt Return (Avg.)	Pat Studstill, 1962	15.8
Kickoff Return (Avg.)	Mel Gray, 1994	28.4
Field Goals	Jason Hanson, 1993	34
Touchdowns (Tot.)	Barry Sanders, 1991	17
Points	Jason Hanson, 1995	132

INDIVIDUAL RECORDS—SINGLE GAME

Category	Name	Performance
Rushing (Yds.)	Barry Sanders, 11-13-94	237
Passing (Yds.)	Charlie Batch, 11-18-01	436
Passing (TDs)	Gary Danielson, 12-9-78	5
Receiving (No.)	Herman Moore, 12-4-95	14
Receiving (Yds.)	Cloyce Box, 12-3-50	302
Interceptions	Don Doll, 10-23-49	*4
Field Goals	Garo Yepremian, 11-13-66	6
	Jason Hanson, 10-17-99	6
Touchdowns (Tot.)	Dutch Clark, 10-22-34	4
	Cloyce Box, 12-3-50	4
	Barry Sanders, 11-24-91	4
Points	Dutch Clark, 10-22-34	24
	Cloyce Box, 12-3-50	24
	Barry Sanders, 11-24-91	24

*NFL Record

2006 VETERAN ROSTER

No.	Name	Pos.	Ht.	Wt.	Birthdate	NFL Exp.	College	Hometown	How Acq.	'05 Games/ Starts
76	Backus, Jeff	T	6-5	305	9/21/77	6	Michigan	Norcross, Ga.	D1-'01	16/16
97	Bailey, Boss	LB	6-3	235	10/14/79	4	Georgia	Folkston, Ga.	D2-'03	11/11
28	Bashir, Idrees	S	6-2	198	12/7/78	6	Memphis	Decatur, Ga.	UFA(Car)-'06	11/0*
94	Bell, Marcus	DT	6-2	325	6/1/79	6	Memphis	Memphis, Tenn.	UFA(Ariz)-'04	15/0
32	Bly, Dré	CB	5-10	188	5/22/77	8	North Carolina	Chesapeake, Va.	UFA(StL)-'03	12/11
17	Bradford, Corey	WR	6-1	201	12/8/75	9	Jackson State	Clinton, La.	UFA(Hou)-'06	16/6*
25	Bryant, Fernando	CB	5-11	175	3/26/77	8	Alabama	Murfeesboro, Tenn.	UFA(Jax)-'04	2/2
24	Bryson, Shawn	RB	6-1	230	11/30/76	8	Tennessee	Franklin, N.C.	UFA(Buff)-'03	16/2
79	Butler, Kelly	T	6-7	330	7/24/82	3	Purdue	Grand Rapids, Mich.	D6-'04	16/16
89	Campbell, Dan	TE	6-5	265	4/13/76	7	Texas A&M	Glen Rose, Texas	UFA(Dall)-'06	16/12*
75	Cody, Shaun	DT	6-4	310	1/22/83	2	Southern California	Hacienda Heights, Calif.	D2-'05	16/2
55	Curry, Donté	LB	6-1	240	7/22/78	6	Morris Brown	College Park, Ga.	W(Wash)-'02	13/2
52	Davis, James	LB	6-1	240	4/26/79	4	West Virginia	Stuart, Fla.	D5b-'03	16/14
64	DeMulling, Rick	G	6-4	310	7/21/77	6	Idaho	Cheney, Wash.	UFA(Ind)-'05	13/5
95	DeVries, Jared	DE	6-4	275	6/11/76	8	Iowa	Aplington, Iowa	D3-'99	16/0
18	Drummond, Eddie	WR	5-9	190	4/12/80	5	Penn State	Pittsburgh, Pa.	FA-'02	12/0
98	Edwards, Kalimba	DE	6-6	265	12/26/79	5	South Carolina	Atlanta, Ga.	D2-'02	16/2
82	FitzSimmons, Casey	TE	6-4	258	10/10/80	4	Carroll College (Mont.)	Helena, Mont.	FA-'03	14/2
41	Fletcher, Jamar	CB	5-10	186	8/28/79	6	Wisconsin	St. Louis, Mo.	UFA(SD)-'06	14/0*
36	Fox, Vernon	S	5-10	200	10/9/79	5	Fresno State	Las Vegas, Nev.	FA-'04	14/0
87	Furrey, Mike	WR	6-0	205	5/12/77	4	Northern Iowa	Grove City, Ohio	FA-'06	16/11*
93	Gregory, Damian	DE	6-2	305	1/21/77	4	Illinois State	Lansing, Mich.	FA-'06	0*
63	Gutierrez, Brock	G/C	6-3	304	9/25/73	10	Central Michigan	Charlotte, Mich.	UFA(SF)-'05	16/0
96	Hall, James	DE	6-2	280	2/4/77	7	Michigan	New Orleans, La.	FA-'00	14/14
4	Hanson, Jason	K	6-0	190	6/17/70	15	Washington State	Spokane, Wash.	D2b-'92	15/0
33	Harris, Arlen	RB	5-10	212	4/22/80	4	Virginia	Downington, Pa.	FA-'06	16/0*
2	Harris, Nick	P	6-2	218	7/23/78	6	California	Avondale, Ariz.	W(Cin)-'03	16/0
42	Holt, Terrence	S	6-2	208	3/5/80	4	North Carolina State	Raleigh, N.C.	D5a-'03	10/10
69	Hopson, Tyrone	G/C	6-2	300	5/28/76	5	Eastern Kentucky	Owensboro, Ky.	FA-'06	0*
91	Jackson, Tyoka	DT	6-2	280	11/22/71	12	Penn State	Forrestville, Md.	UFA(StL)-'06	16/2*
34	Jones, Kevin	RB	6-0	228	8/21/82	3	Virginia Tech	Chester, Pa.	D1b-'04	13/13
26	Kennedy, Kenoy	S	6-1	218	11/15/77	7	Arkansas	Terrell, Texas	UFA(Den)-'05	16/16
10	King, Shaun	QB	6-1	228	5/29/77	7	Tulane	St. Petersberg, Fla.	FA-'06	0*
8	Kitna, Jon	QB	6-2	225	9/21/72	11	Central Washington	Tacoma, Wash.	UFA(Cin)-'06	3/0*
54	Lehman, Teddy	LB	6-1	242	11/18/81	3	Oklahoma	Fort Gibson, Okla.	D2-'04	5/0
53	Lenon, Paris	LB	6-2	240	11/26/77	6	Richmond	Lynchburg, Va.	UFA(GB)-'06	16/12*
59	Lewis, Alex	LB	6-0	235	6/11/81	3	Wisconsin	Delran, N.J.	D5-'04	1/1
12	McCown, Josh	QB	6-4	213	7/4/79	5	Sam Houston State	Jacksonville, Texas	UFA(Ariz)-'06	9/6*
38	McGraw, Jon	S	6-3	206	4/2/79	5	Kansas State	Manhattan, Kan.	T(NYJ)-'05	8/2
48	Muhlbach, Don	LS	6-4	260	8/17/81	3	Texas A&M	Newark, Ohio	FA-'04	13/0
6	Orlovsky, Dan	QB	6-5	230	8/18/83	2	Connecticut	Shelton, Conn.	D5-'05	2/0
67	Pinkney, Cleveland	DT	6-1	300	9/14/77	3	South Carolina	Sumpter, S.C.	FA-'06	0*
21	Pinner, Artose	RB	5-10	232	1/5/78	4	Kentucky	Hopkinsville, Ky.	D4-'03	16/2
81	Pollard, Marcus	TE	6-3	250	2/8/72	12	Bradley	Valley, Ala.	FA-'05	16/16
51	Raiola, Dominic	C	6-1	295	12/30/78	6	Nebraska	Honolulu, Hawaii	D2a-'01	16/16
78	Redding, Cory	DE	6-4	295	11/15/80	4	Texas	Austin, Texas	D3-'03	16/16
80	Rogers, Charles	WR	6-4	218	5/23/81	4	Michigan State	Saginaw, Mich.	D1-'03	9/3
92	Rogers, Shaun	DT	6-4	340	3/12/79	6	Texas	LaPorte, Texas	D2b-'01	14/14
71	Rogers, Victor	T	6-6	330	11/10/78	4	Colorado	Federal Way, Wash.	FA-'05	0*
30	Schlesinger, Cory	FB	6-0	247	6/23/72	12	Nebraska	Duncan, Neb.	D6b-'95	11/8
23	Smith, Keith	CB	5-11	191	3/20/80	3	McNeese State	Leesville, La.	D3-'04	15/2
68	Stokes, Barry	G	6-4	310	12/20/73	7	Eastern Michigan	Davison, Mich.	UFA(Atl)-'06	16/1*
90	Swancutt, Bill	DE	6-4	265	9/4/82	2	Oregon State	Salem, Ore.	D6a-'05	8/0
74	Tucker, Rex	T	6-5	315	12/20/76	8	Texas A&M	Midland, Texas	UFA(StL)-'06	8/3*
77	Van Buren, Courtney	T	6-6	350	2/22/80	4	Arkansas-Pine Bluff	St. Louis, Mo.	FA-'06	0*
83	Vines, Scottie	WR	6-2	220	4/17/79	3	Wyoming	Alexander City, Ala.	FA-'05	13/11
72	Wilkinson, Dan	DT	6-4	340	3/13/73	13	Ohio State	Dayton, Ohio	UFA(Wash)-'03	16/16
88	Williams, Mike	WR	6-5	234	1/4/84	2	Southern California	Tampa, Fla.	D1-'05	14/4
11	Williams, Roy	WR	6-3	220	12/20/81	3	Texas	Odessa, Texas	D1a-'04	13/12
31	Wilson, Stanley	CB	5-11	189	11/5/82	2	Stanford	Carson, Calif.	D3-'05	9/0
57	Woods, LeVar	LB	6-2	244	3/15/78	6	Iowa	Inwood, Iowa	FA-'05	6/3
65	Woody, Damien	G	6-3	335	11/3/77	8	Boston College	Beaverdam, Va.	UFA(NE)-'04	16/16

* Bashir played 11 games with Carolina in '05; Bradford played 16 games with Houston; Campbell played 16 games with Dallas; Fletcher played 14 games with San Diego; Furrey played 16 games with St. Louis; Gregory last active with Tampa Bay in '04; A. Harris played 16 games for St. Louis; Hopson inactive for 4 games; Jackson played 16 games for St. Louis; King last active with Arizona in '04; Kitna played 3 games with Cincinnati; Lenon played 16 games with Green Bay; McCown played 9 games with Arizona; Pinkney last active with Carolina in '04; V. Rogers did not play in 1 game; Stokes played 16 games with Atlanta; Tucker played 8 games with St. Louis; Van Buren missed '05 season with San Diego because of injury.

Traded—QB Joey Harrington (12 games in '05) to Miami.

Players lost through free agency (6): QB Jeff Garcia (Phil; 6 games in '05); CB André Goodman (Mia; 15); T Kyle Kosier (Dall; 16); CB R.W. McQuarters (NYG; 16); LB Wali Rainer (Hou; 16), RB Paul Smith (StL; 12).

Also played with Lions in '05—WR Troy Edwards (3 games), LB Matt Grootegoed (3), K Remy Hamilton (1), LB Earl Holmes (11), WR Kevin Johnson (6), LB Alex Lewis (1), C Joe Maese (3), S Bracy Walker (16), LB Nate Wayne (5).

2006 FIRST-YEAR ROSTER

Name	Pos.	Ht.	Wt.	Birthdate	College	Hometown	How Acq.
Anderson, Adam (1)	P	6-0	190	6/26/81	Western Michigan	Grand Rapids, Mich.	FA
Battle, Andrew (1)	LB	6-4	235	7/21/81	Indiana (Pa.)	Allentown, Pa.	FA
Benoit, Sarth (1)	LB	6-2	250	2/6/79	Southern Connecticut State	Nyack, N.Y.	FA-'05
Bernstein, Matt	FB	6-0	260	12/26/82	Wisconsin	Scarsdale, N.Y.	FA
Bodiford, Shaun	WR	5-11	187	5/4/82	Portland State	Federal Way, Wash.	FA
Bullocks, Daniel	S	6-0	212	2/28/83	Nebraska	Chattanooga, Tenn.	D2
Calhoun, Brian	RB	5-10	194	5/8/84	Wisconsin	Oak Creek, Wisc.	D3
Cannon, Anthony	LB	6-0	224	12/31/84	Tulane	Stone Mountain, Ga.	D7b
Carberry, Kevin (1)	DT	6-4	269	5/19/83	Ohio	Oak Lawn, Ill.	FA-'05
Davis, Frank	G	6-3	329	8/22/81	South Florida	Panama City, Panama	FA
Demps, Marcus	S	6-0	198	8/19/83	San Diego State	Palmdale, Calif.	FA
Dickerson, Kori (1)	TE	6-4	240	12/6/78	Southern California	Los Angeles, Calif.	FA
Downer, Cole	TE	6-3	262	2/2/83	Clemson	Chantilly, Vir.	FA
Ellis, Devale	WR	5-10	174	4/2/84	Hofstra	Brooklyn, N.Y.	FA
Fischer, Brett (1)	WR	5-11	192	6/12/81	Missouri-Rolla	St. Louis, Mo.	FA
Hamilton, Paris (1)	WR	6-1	195	7/26/81	Minnesota	Katy, Texas	FA-'05
Hicks, LaMarcus	CB/S	6-0	189	4/15/83	Iowa State	Clarksdale, Miss.	FA
Jasmin, Marcus (1)	DT	6-5	325	11/15/82	Texas A&M	New Orleans, La.	FA
Kaleita, Tom (1)	T	6-6	320	5/29/83	Eastern Michigan	Kingsley, Mich.	FA
Malone, Antonio	CB/S	6-0	200	1/24/84	Toledo	Portsmouth, Ohio	FA
Martinez, Glenn (1)	WR	6-1	183	11/30/81	Saginaw Valley State	Tampa, Fla.	FA-'05
Matthews, Will (1)	FB	6-3	250	4/30/81	Texas	Austin, Texas	FA-'05
Matua, Fred	G	6-2	306	1/14/84	Southern California	Wilmington Calif.	D7a
McCann, Dee	CB	5-10	200	4/24/83	West Virginia	Greene County, Miss.	D6
McGhghy, Matt (1)	G	6-3	296	1/26/82	Northern Illinois	Keokuk, Iowa	FA
McHugh, Sean (1)	TE	6-5	265	5/27/82	Penn State	Springfield, Mass.	FA-'05
Newton, Levi (1)	G	6-4	310	6/30/83	South Florida	Jacksonville, Fla.	FA-'05
Pearson, Dave (1)	C	6-3	287	3/29/81	Michigan	Brighton, Mich.	FA-'05
Prater, Matt	K	5-9	166	8/10/84	Central Florida	Estero, Fla.	FA
Scott, Jonathan	T	6-6	315	1/10/83	Texas	Dallas, Texas	D5
Shaw, Bryant (1)	DE	6-3	287	7/17/78	Mississippi	Ocean Springs, Miss.	FA
Sims, Ernie	LB	6-0	221	12/23/84	Florida State	Tallahassee, Fla.	D1
Smith, Harrison	CB/S	6-2	199	2/28/83	California	Oakland, Calif.	FA
Stickdorn, Clint (1)	T	6-5	307	4/30/82	Cincinnati	Toledo, Ohio	FA-'05

The term NFL Rookie is defined as a player who is in his first season of professional football and has not been on the roster of another professional football team for any regular-season or postseason games. A Rookie is designated by an "R" on NFL rosters. Players who have been active in another professional football league or players who have NFL experience, including either preseason training camp or being on an Active List or Inactive List, or on Reserve/Injured or Reserve/Physically Unable to Perform for fewer than six regular-season games, are termed NFL First-Year Players. An NFL First-Year Player is designated by a "1" on NFL rosters. Thereafter, a player is credited with an additional year of experience for each season in which he accumulates six games on the Active List or Inactive List, or on Reserve/Injured or Reserve/Physically Unable to Perform.

Log on to www.detroitlions.com for an up-to-date roster.

COACHING STAFF

Head Coach,
Rod Marinelli

Pro Career: Named Lions' twenty-fourth head coach January 19, 2006. Marinelli joined the Lions after spending 10 seasons with Tampa Bay (1996-2005) as defensive line coach and holding the additional duties of assistant head coach for the last four seasons. In Marinelli's 10-year tenure, the Buccaneers recorded 416 sacks, with 328.5 coming courtesy of his defensive line. The 328.5 sacks registered by Marinelli's line ranked first in the NFL among all defensive lines during that span. Additionally, the Buccaneers' defensive front four garnered top 5 rankings in sacks during six of the 10 seasons under Marinelli. Among individual leaders, a Tampa Bay defensive lineman ranked in the league's top 15 in sacks on eight occasions and in the top 10 six times. The defensive line also played a major role in setting an NFL record for consecutive games with a sack (69) from 1999-2003. Career record: 0-0.

Background: Marinelli's college playing career was split due to a one-year tour of duty in Vietnam. In 1968, he played offensive and defensive tackle at Utah. After his service in the military, he attended California Lutheran from 1970-72, earning NAIA All-America honors as an offensive tackle his senior season. He began his coaching career at his high school alma mater, Rosemead (San Gabriel Valley, Calif.) from 1973-75. Collegiately, Marinelli coached defensive line at Utah State (1976), California (1983-91), Arizona State (1992-94), and Southern California (1995).

Personal: Born July 13, 1949, in Rosemead, Calif., He and his wife, Barbara, have two daughters, Chris and Gina. Chris is married to Joe Barry, linebackers coach for the Tampa Bay Buccaneers. Marinelli also has two granddaughters and two grandsons.

ASSISTANT COACHES

Jason Arapoff, strength and conditioning; born July, 8 1965, Weymouth, Mass. Defensive back Springfield College 1985-88. No college or pro playing experience. Pro coach: Washington Redskins 1992-2000, joined Lions in 2001.

Mike Barry, asst. offensive line; born October 18, 1946, Brooklyn, N.Y. Center Nebraska 1964-66, Southern Illinois 1966-69. No pro playing experience. College coach: Southern Illinois 1977-1980, Arizona 1980-83, Iowa State 1986, Colorado 1987-1992, Southern California 1993-97, Tennessee 1998-2002, North Carolina State 2003-05. Pro coach: San Antonio Gunslingers (USFL) 1984, New Orleans/Portland Breakers (USFL) 1984-85, joined Lions in 2006.

Larry Beightol, offensive line; born November 21, 1942 in Pittsburgh, Pa.

Guard/linebacker Catawba College 1960-63. No pro playing experience. College coach: Williams & Mary 1968-71, North Carolina State 1972-75, Auburn 1976, Arkansas 1977-78, 1980-82, Louisiana Tech 1979 (head coach), Missouri 1983-84. Pro coach: Atlanta Falcons 1985-86, Tampa Bay Buccaneers 1987-88, San Diego Chargers 1989, New York Jets 1990-94, Houston Oilers 1995, Miami Dolphins 1996-98, Green Bay Packers 1999-2005, joined Lions in 2006.

Malcolm Blacken, asst. strength and conditioning; born October 12, 1965, Richmond, Va. Running back Virginia Tech 1984-88. No pro playing experience. College coach: South Carolina 1990-91, George Mason 1992-94, Virginia 1995. Pro coach: Washington Redskins 1996-2000, joined Lions in 2001.

Kippy Brown, wide receivers; born March 6, 1955, Sweetwater, Tenn. Quarterback Memphis State 1974-77. No pro playing experience. College coach: Memphis State 1978-1980, Louisville 1982, Tennessee 1983-89, 1993-94. Pro coach: New York Jets 1990-92, Tampa Bay Buccaneers 1995, Miami Dolphins 1996-99, Green Bay Packers 2000, Memphis Maniax (XFL head coach) 2001, Houston Texans 2002-05, joined Lions in 2006.

Pat Carter, tight ends; born August 1, 1966, Sarasota, Fla. Tight end Florida State 1984-87. Pro tight end Detroit Lions 1988, Los Angeles Rams 1989-1994, Houston Oilers 1995-96, Arizona Cardinals 1997. Pro coach: St. Louis Rams 2005, joined Lions in 2006.

Don Clemons, defensive quality control; born February 15, 1954, Newark, N.J. Defensive end Muhlenberg (Pa.) 1973-76. No pro playing experience. College coach: Kutztown State 1977-78, New Mexico 1979, Arizona State 1980-84. Pro coach: Joined Lions in 1985.

Joe Cullen, defensive line; born December 15, 1967, Quincy, Mass. Nose Guard Massachusetts 1986-89. No pro playing experience. College coach: Massachusetts 1990-91, Richmond 1992-98, 2000, Louisiana State 1999, Memphis 2001, Indiana 2002-04, Illinois 2005. Pro coach: Joined Lions in 2006.

Adam Gase, offensive quality control; born March 29, 1978, Ypsilanti, Mich. Attended Michigan State. No college or pro playing experience. College coach: Louisiana State 2000-02. Pro coach: Joined Lions in 2003.

Donnie Henderson, defensive coordinator; born May 17, 1957, Baltimore. Defensive back Utah State 1978-79. No pro playing experience. College coach: Utah State 1983-88, Idaho 1989-1990, California 1992-97, Houston 1998. Pro coach: Baltimore Ravens 1999-2003, N.Y. Jets 2004-05, joined Lions in 2006.

Shawn Jefferson, offensive assistant; born February 22, 1969, Jacksonville. Wide receiver Central Florida 1988-1990.

Pro wide receiver San Diego Chargers 1991-95, New England Patriots 1996-99, Atlanta Falcons 2000-02, Detroit Lions 2003. Pro coach: Joined Lions in 2005.

Stan Kwan, special teams assistant/offensive assistant; born November 2, 1967, Phoenix. Attended South Mountain (Ariz.) C.C. No college or pro playing experience. Pro coach: San Diego Chargers 1991-96, Detroit Lions 1997-2000, Arizona Cardinals 2001-2003, re-joined Lions in 2004.

Clayton Lopez, defensive backs; born May 26, 1971, Los Angeles. Safety Nevada 1991-94. No pro playing experience. College coach: Nevada 1995-98. Pro coach: Seattle Seahawks 1999-2003, Oakland Raiders 2004-2005, joined Lions in 2006.

Mike Martz, offensive coordinator; born May 13, 1951, Sioux Falls, S.D. Tight end Fresno State 1972. No pro playing experience. College coach: San Diego Mesa C.C. 1974, 1976-77, San Jose State 1975, Santa Ana College 1978, Fresno State 1979, Pacific 1980-81, Minnesota 1982, Arizona State 1983-91. Pro coach: St. Louis Rams 1992-96, 1999-2005 (head coach 2000-05), Washington Redskins 1997-98, joined Lions in 2006.

Wilbert Montgomery, running backs; born September 16, 1954, Greenville, Miss. Running back Abilene Christian 1973-76. Pro running back Philadelphia Eagles 1977-1984, Detroit Lions 1985. Pro coach: St. Louis Rams 1997-2005, joined Lions in 2006.

Chuck Priefer, special teams; born July 26, 1944, Cleveland. Attended John Carroll. No college or pro playing experience. College coach: Miami (Ohio) 1977, North Carolina 1978-1983, Kent State 1986, Georgia Tech 1987-1991. Pro coach: Green Bay Packers 1984-85, San Diego Chargers 1992-96, joined Lions in 1997.

Fred Reed, defensive assistant; born July 31, 1967, Meridian, Miss. Safety Mesa State (Colo.) College 1991-92. No pro playing experience. College coach: South Dakota 1994, Nebraska-Omaha 1995, 2000-04, Minnesota, Morris 1996, Michigan Tech 1997-99, Ohio 2005. Pro coach: Joined Lions in 2006.

Phil Snow, linebackers; born December 22, 1955, Woodland, Calif. Quarterback Sacramento City College 1974-75, Cal State Hayward 1977-78. No pro playing experience. College coach: Laney (Calif.) College 1979-1981, Boise State 1982-86, California 1987-1991, Arizona State 1992-2000, UCLA 2001-2002, Washington 2003-2004. Pro coach: Joined Lions in 2005.

National Football Conference
North Division
Team Colors: Dark Green, Gold, and White
Lambeau Field Atrium
1265 Lombardi Avenue
Green Bay, Wisconsin 54304
Telephone: (920) 569-7500

2006 SCHEDULE
PRESEASON
Aug. 12	at San Diego	7:00
Aug. 19	**Atlanta**	7:00
Aug. 28	at Cincinnati	8:00
Aug. 31	**Tennessee**	3:00

REGULAR SEASON
Sept. 10	**Chicago**	3:15
Sept. 17	**New Orleans**	12:00
Sept. 24	at Detroit	1:00
Oct. 2	at Philadelphia (Mon.)	8:30
Oct. 8	**St. Louis**	12:00
Oct. 15	Open Date	
Oct. 22	at Miami	1:00
Oct. 29	**Arizona**	12:00
Nov. 5	at Buffalo	1:00
Nov. 12	at Minnesota	12:00
Nov. 19	**New England**	12:00
Nov. 27	at Seattle (Mon.)	5:30
Dec. 3	**N.Y. Jets**	12:00
Dec. 10	at San Francisco	1:05
Dec. 17	**Detroit**	12:00
Dec. 21	**Minnesota** (Thu.)	7:00
Dec. 31	at Chicago	12:00

Stadium: Lambeau Field (opened in 1957)
   • **Capacity:** 72,922
   1265 Lombardi Avenue
   Green Bay, Wisconsin 54304
Playing Surface: Grass
Training Camp: St. Norbert College
   De Pere, Wisconsin 54115

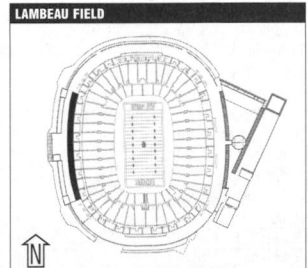
LAMBEAU FIELD

CLUB OFFICIALS
Chairman of the Board and
  Chief Executive Officer: Bob Harlan
President and Chief Operating Officer:
  John Jones
Vice President: John Fabry
Secretary: Peter Platten
Treasurer: Larry Weyers
Executive Vice President/General
  Manager/Director of Football
  Operations: Ted Thompson
Vice President of Player Finance/General
  Counsel: Andrew Brandt
Dir. of College Scouting: John Dorsey
Dir. of Pro Personnel: Reggie McKenzie
Personnel Analyst to General Manager:
  John Schneider
Director of Player Development:
  George Koonce
Director of Public Relations: Jeff Blumb
Assistant Director of Public Relations:
  Zak Gilbert
Public Relations Coordinators:
  Sarah Quick, Adam Woullard
Corporate Communications Specialist:
  Aaron Popkey
Ticket Director: Mark Wagner
Director of Marketing and Corporate
  Sales: Craig Benzel
Director of Premium Guest Services:
  Jennifer Ark
Director of Atrium Business
  Development: Steve Klegon
Director of Retail Operations:
  Kate Hogan
Team Historian: Lee Remmel
Director of Administrative Affairs:
  Mark Schiefelbein
Director of Finance:
  Vicki Vannieuwenhoven
Director of Information Technology:
  Wayne Wichlacz
Director of Facility Operations:
  Ted Eisenreich
Director of Corporate Security:
  Jerry Parins
Assistant Director of Security:
  Doug Collins
Corporate Counsel: Jason Wied
Manager of Community Relations:
  Cathy Dworak
Assistant Director of College Scouting:
  Shaun Herock
College Scouts: Lee Gissendaner,
  Brian Gutekunst, Alonzo Highsmith,
  Lenny McGill, Sam Seale,
  Jon-Eric Sullivan
Scouting Coordinator: Danny Mock
Pro Personnel Assistants: Tim Terry,
  Eliot Wolf
Director of Research and Development:
  Mike Eayrs
Football Administration Coordinator:
  Matt Klein
Video Director: Bob Eckberg
Head Trainer: Pepper Burruss
Equipment Manager: Gordon (Red) Batty

COACHING HISTORY
(640-506-36)
Records include postseason games
1921-1949	Earl (Curly) Lambeau	.212-106-21
1950-53	Gene Ronzani*	14-31-1
1953	Hugh Devore-	
	Ray (Scooter) McLean**	..0-2-0
1954-57	Lisle Blackbourn	17-31-0
1958	Ray (Scooter) McLean	1-10-1
1959-1967	Vince Lombardi	98-30-4
1968-1970	Phil Bengtson	20-21-1
1971-74	Dan Devine	25-28-4
1975-1983	Bart Starr	53-77-3
1984-87	Forrest Gregg	25-37-1
1988-1991	Lindy Infante	24-40-0
1992-98	Mike Holmgren	84-42-0
1999	Ray Rhodes	8-8-0
2000-05	Mike Sherman	59-43-0

  *Resigned after 10 games in 1953
**Co-coaches

ATTENDANCE
Home 562,399   Away 527,294
Total 1,089,693
Single-game home record,
  70,688 (9/19/04)
Single-season home record,
  564,344 (2004)

2006 DRAFT CHOICES
Round	Name	Pos.	College
1	A.J. Hawk	LB	Ohio State
2	Daryn Colledge	T	Boise State
	Greg Jennings	WR	Western Michigan
3	Abdul Hodge	LB	Iowa
	Jason Spitz	G	Louisville
4	Cory Rodgers	WR	Texas Christian
	Will Blackmon	DB	Boston College
5	Ingle Martin	QB	Furman
	Tony Moll	T	Nevada
6	Johnny Jolly	DT	Texas A&M
	Tyrone Culver	DB	Fresno State
7	Dave Tollefson	DE	Northwest Missouri St.

2005 TEAM RECORD
PRESEASON (2-2)

Date	Result		Opponent
8/11	W	10-7	San Diego
8/20	L	7-27	at Buffalo
8/26	L	3-27	New England
9/1	W	21-17	at Tennessee

REGULAR SEASON (4-12)

Date	Result		Opponent	Att.
9/11	L	3-17	at Detroit	61,877
9/18	L	24-26	Cleveland	70,400
9/25	L	16-17	Tampa Bay	70,518
10/3	L	29-32	at Carolina	73,657
10/9	W	52-3	New Orleans	70,580
10/23	L	20-23	at Minnesota	64,278
10/30	L	14-21	at Cincinnati	65,940
11/6	L	10-20	Pittsburgh	70,607
11/13	W	33-25	at Atlanta	71,001
11/21	L	17-20	Minnesota	70,610
11/27	L	14-19	at Philadelphia	67,665
12/4	L	7-19	at Chicago	62,177
12/11	W	16-13	Detroit (OT)	70,019
12/19	L	3-48	at Baltimore	70,604
12/25	L	17-24	Chicago	69,757
1/1	W	23-17	Seattle	69,928

(OT) Overtime

SCORE BY PERIODS

Packers	77	100	36	82	3	—	298
Opponents	88	100	59	97	0	—	344

2005 TEAM STATISTICS

	Packers	Opp.
Total First Downs	318	280
Rushing	76	107
Passing	206	143
Penalty	36	30
3rd Down: Made/Att	91/221	74/206
3rd Down Pct.	41.2	35.9
4th Down: Made/Att	9/19	3/8
4th Down Pct.	47.4	37.5
Possession Avg.	30:48	29:12
Total Net Yards	5,118	4,690
Avg. Per Game	319.9	293.1
Total Plays	1,051	969
Avg. Per Play	4.9	4.8
Net Yards Rushing	1,352	2,010
Avg. Per Game	84.5	125.6
Total Rushes	398	504
Net Yards Passing	3,766	2,680
Avg. Per Game	235.4	167.5
Sacked/Yards Lost	27/198	35/196
Gross Yards	3,964	2,876
Att./Completions	626/383	430/252
Completion Pct.	61.2	58.6
Had Intercepted	30	10
Punts/Average	70/38.9	85/42.3
Net Punting Avg.	70/33.5	85/36.9
Penalties/Yards	119/918	98/975
Fumbles/Ball Lost	31/15	33/11
Touchdowns	34	37
Rushing	11	10
Passing	20	22
Returns	3	5

2005 INDIVIDUAL STATISTICS

PASSING

	Att.	Comp.	Yds.	Pct.	TD	Int.	Tkld.	Rate
Favre	607	372	3,881	61.3	20	29	24/170	70.9
Rodgers	16	9	65	56.3	0	1	3/28	39.8
Fisher	1	1	14	100.0	0	0	0/0	118.8
Sander	1	1	4	100.0	0	0	0/0	83.3
Gado	1	0	0	0.0	0	0	0/0	39.6
Packers	626	383	3,964	61.2	20	30	27/198	70.1
Opponents	430	252	2,876	58.6	22	10	35/196	86.2

SCORING

	TD R	TD P	TD Rt	PAT	FG	Saf	PTS
Longwell	0	0	0	30/31	20/27	0	90
Gado	6	1	0	0/0	0/0	0	42
Chatman	0	4	1	0/0	0/0	0	30
Driver	0	5	0	0/0	0/0	0	30
Ferguson	0	3	0	0/0	0/0	0	20
Martin	0	3	0	0/0	0/0	0	20
Davenport	2	0	0	0/0	0/0	0	12
Fisher	1	1	0	0/0	0/0	0	12
Herron	2	0	0	0/0	0/0	0	12
D. Lee	0	2	0	0/0	0/0	0	12
Barnett	0	0	1	0/0	0/0	0	6
Franks	0	1	0	0/0	0/0	0	6
Harris	0	0	1	0/0	0/0	0	6
Packers	11	20	3	30/31	20/27	0	298
Opponents	10	22	5	33/35	29/34	0	344

2-Pt. Conversions: Ferguson, Martin.
Team 2-3, Opponents 1-2.

RUSHING

	No.	Yds	Avg	LG	TD
Gado	143	582	4.1	64t	6
Green	77	255	3.3	13	0
Fisher	60	173	2.9	17	1
Herron	45	121	2.7	17	2
Davenport	30	105	3.5	24	2
Favre	18	62	3.4	20	0
Chatman	8	34	4.3	11	0
R. Lee	11	16	1.5	4	0
Driver	2	13	6.5	9	0
Rodgers	2	7	3.5	8	0
Henderson	1	-5	-5.0	-5	0
Sander	1	-11	-11.0	-11	0
Packers	398	1,352	3.4	64t	11
Opponents	504	2,010	4.0	43	10

RECEIVING

	No.	Yds	Avg	LG	TD
Driver	86	1,221	14.2	59	5
Chatman	49	549	11.2	25	4
Fisher	48	347	7.2	15	1
D. Lee	33	294	8.9	27	2
Henderson	30	264	8.8	32	0
Ferguson	27	366	13.6	51	3
Martin	27	224	8.3	21t	3
Franks	25	207	8.3	24	1
Green	19	147	7.7	20	0
Gado	10	77	7.7	30	1
Thurman	7	92	13.1	33	0
Murphy	5	36	7.2	12	0
Leach	5	19	3.8	9	0
Gardner	4	67	16.8	33	0
Walker	4	27	6.8	9	0
Davenport	2	3	1.5	2	0
Wa. Williams	1	19	19.0	19	0
R. Lee	1	5	5.0	5	0
Packers	383	3,964	10.3	59	20
Opponents	252	2,876	11.4	80t	22

INTERCEPTIONS

	No.	Yds	Avg	LG	TD
Harris	3	30	10.0	22t	1
Carroll	2	38	19.0	38	0
Roman	2	18	9.0	12	0
Barnett	1	95	95.0	95t	1
R. Thomas	1	24	24.0	24	0
Collins	1	0	0.0	0	0
Packers	10	205	20.5	95t	2
Opponents	30	370	12.3	95	3

PUNTING

	No.	Yds.	Avg.	In 20	LG
Sander	64	2,508	39.2	11	53
Flinn	6	218	36.3	0	42
Packers	70	2,726	38.9	11	53
Opponents	85	3,597	42.3	29	63

PUNT RETURNS

	Ret	FC	Yds	Avg	LG	TD
Chatman	45	18	381	8.5	85t	1
Packers	45	18	381	8.5	85t	1
Opponents	49	12	339	6.9	49	0

KICKOFF RETURNS

	No.	Yds	Avg	LG	TD
Carroll	19	390	20.5	57	0
R. Lee	15	319	21.3	35	0
Davenport	10	189	18.9	27	0
Thurman	8	136	17.0	23	0
Chatman	5	91	18.2	33	0
Murphy	5	91	18.2	29	0
Jones	4	80	20.0	25	0
Leach	3	39	13.0	20	0
Ferguson	2	44	22.0	22	0
Henderson	2	20	10.0	10	0
Co. Williams	1	14	14.0	14	0
Peterson	1	5	5.0	5	0
Packers	75	1,418	18.9	57	0
Opponents	65	1,404	21.6	73	0

FIELD GOALS

	1-19	20-29	30-39	40-49	50+
Longwell	0/0	7/7	6/10	3/5	4/5
Packers	0/0	7/7	6/10	3/5	4/5
Opponents	1/1	11/11	10/10	6/10	1/2

SACKS

	No.
Gbaja-Biamila	8.0
Kampman	6.5
Harris	3.0
Jenkins	3.0
Peterson	3.0
Cole	2.0
Poppinga	2.0
Co. Williams	2.0
Lenon	1.5
Barnett	1.0
Jackson	1.0
Montgomery	1.0
TEAM	1.0
Packers	35.0
Opponents	27.0

RECORD HOLDERS
INDIVIDUAL RECORDS—CAREER

Category	Name	Performance
Rushing (Yds.)	Jim Taylor, 1958-1966	8,207
Passing (Yds.)	Brett Favre, 1992-2005	53,615
Passing (TDs)	Brett Favre, 1992-2005	396
Receiving (No.)	Sterling Sharpe, 1988-1994	595
Receiving (Yds.)	James Lofton, 1978-1986	9,656
Interceptions	Bobby Dillon, 1952-59	52
Punting (Avg.)	Craig Hentrich, 1994-97	42.8
Punt Return (Avg.)	Desmond Howard, 1996, 1999	13.8
Kickoff Return (Avg.)	Travis Williams, 1967-1970	26.7
Field Goals	Ryan Longwell, 1997-2005	226
Touchdowns (Tot.)	Don Hutson, 1935-1945	105
Points	Ryan Longwell, 1997-2005	1,054

INDIVIDUAL RECORDS—SINGLE SEASON

Category	Name	Performance
Rushing (Yds.)	Ahman Green, 2003	1,883
Passing (Yds.)	Lynn Dickey, 1983	4,458
Passing (TDs)	Brett Favre, 1996	39
Receiving (No.)	Sterling Sharpe, 1993	112
Receiving (Yds.)	Robert Brooks, 1995	1,497
Interceptions	Irv Comp, 1943	10
Punting (Avg.)	Craig Hentrich, 1997	45.0
Punt Return (Avg.)	Billy Grimes, 1950	19.1
Kickoff Return (Avg.)	Travis Williams, 1967	*41.1
Field Goals	Chester Marcol, 1972	33
	Ryan Longwell, 2000	33
Touchdowns (Tot.)	Ahman Green, 2003	20
Points	Paul Hornung, 1960	*176

INDIVIDUAL RECORDS—SINGLE GAME

Category	Name	Performance
Rushing (Yds.)	Ahman Green, 12-28-03	218
Passing (Yds.)	Lynn Dickey, 10-12-80	418
Passing (TDs)	Many times	5
	Last time by Brett Favre, 9-27-98	
Receiving (No.)	Don Hutson, 11-22-42	14
Receiving (Yds.)	Billy Howton, 10-21-56	257
Interceptions	Bobby Dillon, 11-26-53	*4
	Willie Buchanon, 9-24-78	^4
Field Goals	Chris Jacke, 11-11-90, 10-14-96	5
	Ryan Longwell, 9-24-00	5
Touchdowns (Tot.)	Paul Hornung, 12-12-65	5
Points	Paul Hornung, 10-8-61	33

*NFL Record

2006 VETERAN ROSTER

No.	Name	Pos.	Ht.	Wt.	Birthdate	NFL Exp.	College	Hometown	How Acq.	'05 Games/ Starts
97	Allen, Kenderick	DT	6-5	328	9/14/78	4	Louisiana State	Bogalusa, La.	FA-'06	14/0*
56	Barnett, Nick	LB	6-2	232	5/27/81	4	Oregon State	Fontana, Calif.	D1-'03	16/16
71	Barry, Kevin	T	6-4	332	7/20/79	5	Arizona	Racine, Wis.	FA-'02	16/1
83	Boerigter, Marc	WR	6-3	220	5/4/78	5	Hastings	Hastings, Neb.	UFA(KC)-'06	10/0*
52	Campbell, Kurt	LB	6-1	227	7/30/82	2	Albany	Kingston, Jamaica	D7a-'05	0*
28	Carroll, Ahmad	CB	5-10	190	8/4/83	3	Arkansas	Atlanta, Ga.	D1-'04	16/16
76	Clifton, Chad	T	6-5	330	6/26/76	7	Tennessee	Martin, Tenn.	D2-'00	16/16
90	Cole, Colin	DT	6-2	325	6/24/80	3	Iowa	Ft. Lauderdale, Fla.	FA-'04	16/4
36	Collins, Nick	S	5-11	200	8/16/83	2	Bethune-Cookman	Cross City, Fla.	D2a-'05	16/16
62	Coston, Junius	G	6-3	317	11/5/83	2	North Carolina A&T	Raleigh, N.C.	D5a-'05	2/0
2	Cundiff, Billy	K	6-1	201	3/30/80	5	Drake	Harlan, Iowa	FA-'06	6/0*
44	Davenport, Najeh	RB	6-1	247	2/8/79	5	Miami	Miami, Fla.	D4-'02	5/1
60	Davis, Rob	LS	6-3	284	12/10/68	11	Shippensburg	Greenbelt, Md.	FA-'97	16/0
34	Dendy, Patrick	CB	6-0	190	3/10/82	2	Rice	Austin, Texas	FA-'05	4/0
80	Driver, Donald	WR	6-0	190	2/2/75	8	Alcorn State	Houston, Texas	D7b-'99	16/16
4	Favre, Brett	QB	6-2	222	10/10/69	16	Southern Mississippi	Kiln, Miss.	T(Atl)-'92	16/16
89	Ferguson, Robert	WR	6-1	219	12/17/79	6	Texas A&M	Houston, Texas	D2-'01	11/7
88	Franks, Bubba	TE	6-6	265	1/6/78	7	Miami	Big Spring, Texas	D1-'00	10/8
43#	Franz, Todd	S	6-0	205	4/12/76	5	Tulsa	Weatherford, Okla.	FA-'05	5/0
35	Gado, Samkon	RB	5-10	226	11/13/82	2	Liberty	Columbia, S.C.	FA-'05	8/5
82	Gardner, Rod	WR	6-2	215	10/26/77	6	Clemson	Jacksonville, Fla.	W(Car)-'05	2/1
94	Gbaja-Biamila, Kabeer	DE	6-4	250	9/24/77	7	San Diego State	Los Angeles, Calif.	D5-'00	16/16
30	Green, Ahman	RB	6-0	218	2/16/77	9	Nebraska	Omaha, Neb.	T(Sea)-'00	5/5
31	Harris, Al	CB	6-1	185	12/7/74	9	Texas A&M-Kingsville	Pompano Beach, Fla.	T(Phil)-'03	16/16
37	Hawkins, Mike	CB	6-1	180	7/15/83	2	Oklahoma	Carrollton, Texas	D5b-'05	11/1
33	Henderson, William	FB	6-1	252	2/19/71	12	North Carolina	Chester, Va.	D3b-'95	16/8
23	Herron, Noah	RB	5-11	224	4/3/82	2	Northwestern	Mattawan, Mich.	FA-'05	5/0
26	Horton, Jason	CB	6-0	190	2/16/80	3	North Carolina A&T	Ahoskie, N.C.	FA-'04	9/0
75#	Jackson, Grady	DT	6-2	345	1/21/73	10	Knoxville	Greensboro, Ala.	W(NO)-'03	16/16
77	Jenkins, Cullen	DT/DE	6-3	290	1/20/81	3	Central Michigan	Belleville, Mich.	FA-'04	16/12
74	Kampman, Aaron	DE	6-4	278	11/30/79	5	Iowa	Parkersburg, Iowa	D5a-'02	16/16
70	Klemm, Adrian	T/G	6-4	318	5/21/77	7	Hawaii	Santa Monica, Calif.	UFA(NE)-'05	16/8
48	Leach, Vonta	FB	6-0	250	11/6/81	3	East Carolina	Rowland, N.C.	FA-'04	16/5
86	Lee, Donald	TE	6-4	248	8/31/80	4	Mississippi State	Maben, Miss.	FA-'05	15/5
61	Lucier, Wayne	C	6-4	315	12/5/79	3	Colorado	Salem, N.H.	FA-'06	0*
54	Manning, Roy	LB	6-2	245	12/4/81	2	Michigan	Saginaw, Mich.	FA-'05	15/2
22	Manuel, Marquand	S	6-0	209	7/11/79	5	Florida	Miami, Fla.	UFA(Sea)-'06	16/11*
87	Martin, David	TE	6-4	265	3/13/79	6	Tennessee	Norfolk, Va.	D6-'01	12/8
96	Montgomery, Michael	DE	6-5	275	8/18/83	2	Texas A&M	Center, Texas	D6a-'05	12/0
98	Peterson, Kenny	DE/DT	6-3	285	11/21/78	4	Ohio State	Canton, Ohio	D3-'03	16/0
79	Pickett, Ryan	DT	6-2	322	10/8/79	6	Ohio State	Zephyrhills, Fla.	UFA(StL)-'06	16/16*
51	Poppinga, Brady	LB	6-3	245	9/21/79	2	Brigham Young	Evanston, Wyo.	D4b-'05	12/1
16	Rayner, Dave	K	6-2	210	10/26/82	2	Michigan State	Oxford, Mich.	W(Ind)-'06	14/0*
12	Rodgers, Aaron	QB	6-2	223	12/2/83	2	California	Chico, Calif.	D1-'05	3/0
20	Roman, Mark	S	5-11	201	3/26/77	7	Louisiana State	New Iberia, La.	UFA(Cin)-'04	16/16
11	Sander, B.J.	P	6-4	218	7/29/80	3	Ohio State	Cincinnati, Ohio	D3c-'04	14/0
65	Tauscher, Mark	T	6-4	315	6/17/77	7	Wisconsin	Auburndale, Wis.	D7a-'00	16/16
58	Taylor, Ben	LB	6-2	238	8/31/78	5	Virginia Tech	Bellaire, Ohio	UFA(Cle)-'06	16/16*
38	Thornburg, Jeremy	S	6-0	196	5/7/82	2	Northern Arizona	Cathedral City, Calif.	W(SF)-'05	4/0
25	Underwood, Marviel	S	5-10	197	2/17/82	2	San Diego State	San Leandro, Calif.	D4a-'05	16/0
95	Washington, Donnell	DT	6-6	328	2/6/81	3	Clemson	Beaufort, S.C.	D3b-'04	0*
63	Wells, Scott	C	6-2	304	1/7/81	3	Tennessee	Brentwood, Tenn.	FA-'04	16/10
68	White, Chris	CB	6-2	285	2/28/83	2	Southern Mississippi	Winona, Miss.	FA-'05	1/0
59	White, Tracy	LB	6-0	236	4/14/81	4	Howard	St. Stephen, S.C.	FA-'06	15/0*
78	Whitticker, William	G	6-5	338	8/2/82	2	Michigan State	Marion, Ind.	D7b-'05	15/14
42	Williams, Chaz	RB	5-9	210	7/9/82	2	Georgia Southern	Apopka, Fla.	FA-'05	0*
99	Williams, Corey	DT	6-4	313	8/17/80	3	Arkansas State	Camden, Ark.	D6-'04	12/0
41	Wishom, Jerron	CB	6-0	197	3/1/82	2	Louisiana Tech	Lutcher, La.	FA-'05	5/0
21	Woodson, Charles	CB	6-1	208	10/7/76	9	Michigan	Fremont, Ohio	UFA(Oak)-'06	6/6*

* Allen played 14 games with N.Y. Giants in '05; Boerigter played 10 games with Kansas City; Campbell missed '05 season because of injury; Cundiff played 6 games with Dallas; Lucier last active with N.Y. Giants in '04; Manuel played 16 games with Seattle; Pickett played 16 games with St. Louis; Rayner played 14 games with Indianapolis; Taylor played 16 games with Cleveland; Washington did not play in 1 game; T. White played 15 games with Jacksonville; C. Williams missed '05 season because of injury; Woodson played 6 games with Oakland.

Traded—WR Javon Walker (1 game in '05) to Denver.

Players lost through free agency (6): RB Tony Fisher (StL; 14 games in '05), C Mike Flanagan (Hou; 14), LB Paris Lenon (Det; 16), K Ryan Longwell (Minn; 16), QB Craig Nall (Buff; 0), G/C Grey Ruegamer (NYG; 13).

Also played with Packers in '05—WR/KR Antonio Chatman (Cin; 16 games), LB Na'il Diggs (9), P Ryan Flinn (2), WR/KR Jamal Jones (2), LB John Leake (3), RB ReShard Lee (7), S Earl Little (4), WR Chad Lucas (1), WR Terrence Murphy (3), TE Ben Steele (2), CB Joey Thomas (6), LB Robert Thomas (10), WR Andrae Thurman (10), WR Taco Wallace (1), RB Walter Williams (2).

2006 FIRST-YEAR ROSTER

Name	Pos.	Ht.	Wt.	Birthdate	College	Hometown	How Acq.
Alcorn, Zac	TE	6-4	260	8/24/80	Black Hills State	Chadron, Neb.	FA
Arth, Tom (1)	QB	6-3	227	5/11/81	John Carroll	Cleveland, Ohio	FA
Beach, Arliss	RB	5-10	219	3/28/84	Kentucky	Ashland, Ky.	FA
Bigby, Atari (1)	S	5-11	211	9/19/81	Central Florida	Miami, Fla.	FA-'05
Blackmon, Will	CB	6-0	198	10/27/84	Boston College	Warwick, R.I.	D4b
Boger, Tra	S	5-11	210	6/25/83	Tulane	Decatur, Ga.	FA
Bookman, Leo	WR	6-2	212	1/3/82	Kansas	Dickinson, Texas	FA
Bourke, Josh	T	6-7	314	10/16/82	Grand Valley State	Orchard Lake, Mich.	FA
Brown, Ben	FB	6-1	246	10/26/80	Tabor	Los Banos, Calif.	FA
Butler, Vince (1)	WR	6-0	195	5/9/81	Northwestern Oklahoma State	Tampa, Fla.	FA
Colledge, Daryn	T/G	6-4	299	2/11/82	Boise State	North Pole, Alaska	D2a
Cooper, A.J.	FB	6-2	240	4/14/84	North Dakota State	Phoenix, Ariz.	FA
Cross, Garrett (1)	TE	6-4	245	11/30/82	California	Chico, Calif.	FA-'05
Culver, Tyrone	S	6-1	200	7/6/83	Fresno State	Palmdale, Calif.	D6b
Fontenot, Therrian (1)	CB	5-11	187	6/20/82	Fresno State	Lawndale, Calif.	FA-'05
Francies, Chris	WR	6-1	193	7/26/82	Texas-El Paso	Houston, Texas	FA
Gafford, Thomas	LS	6-2	252	1/29/83	Houston	Friendswood, Texas	FA
Goodwell, Tim	LB	6-0	243	1/30/84	Memphis	Tucker, Ga.	FA
Hawk, A.J.	LB	6-1	246	1/6/84	Ohio State	Centerville, Ohio	D1
Hodge, Abdul	LB	6-0	236	9/9/82	Iowa	Lauderdale Lakes, Fla.	D3a
Humphrey, Tory (1)	TE	6-2	257	1/20/83	Central Michigan	Saginaw, Mich.	FA-'05
Hunter, Jason	DE	6-4	243	8/28/83	Appalachian State	Fayetteville, N.C.	FA
Jennings, Greg	WR	5-11	197	9/21/83	Western Michigan	Kalamazoo, Mich.	D2b
Jolly, Johnny	DT	6-3	317	2/21/83	Texas A&M	Houston, Texas	D6a
Lucas, Chad (1)	WR	6-1	201	11/7/81	Alabama State	Tuskegee, Ala.	FA
Martin, Ingle	QB	6-2	220	8/15/82	Furman	Nashville, Tenn.	D5a
Martin, Ruvell (1)	WR	6-4	217	8/10/82	Saginaw Valley State	Muskegon, Mich.	FA
McGill, Tim (1)	DT	6-2	316	6/24/79	Illinois	Chicago, Ill.	FA
Moll, Tony	T/G	6-5	308	8/23/83	Nevada	Sonoma, Calif.	D5b
Murphy, Montez	DE	6-6	256	1/6/82	Baylor	East St. Louis, Ill.	FA
Nichols, Jerome (1)	DT	6-3	285	5/27/80	Wake Forest	Washington, D.C.	FA
Rodgers, Cory	WR/KR	6-0	186	2/22/83	Texas Christian	Houston, Texas	D4a
Russell, Calvin	WR	6-0	190	6/14/83	Tuskegee	Fairburn, Ga.	FA
Ryan, Jon (1)	P	6-0	202	11/26/81	Regina (Canada)	Regina, Saskatchewan, Canada	FA
Santiago, Byron	LB	6-1	242	8/2/82	Louisiana Tech	St. Bernard, La.	FA
Schimmelmann, Kevin	LB	6-3	228	12/31/82	Stanford	Marietta, Ga.	FA
Spitz, Jason	G/C	6-4	313	12/9/82	Louisville	Jacksonville, Fla.	D3b
Tollefson, Dave	DE	6-4	255	5/19/81	Northwest Missouri State	Concord, Calif.	D7
Traynor, Pete (1)	G	6-3	311	1/16/80	Iowa	Milton, Wis.	FA
Wrobel, Brian (1)	QB	6-2	197	4/4/82	Winona State	De Soto, Wis.	FA

The term NFL Rookie is defined as a player who is in his first season of professional football and has not been on the roster of another professional football team for any regular-season or postseason games. A Rookie is designated by an "R" on NFL rosters. Players who have been active in another professional football league or players who have NFL experience, including either preseason training camp or being on an Active List or Inactive List, or on Reserve/Injured or Reserve/Physically Unable to Perform for fewer than six regular-season games, are termed NFL First-Year Players. An NFL First-Year Player is designated by a "1" on NFL rosters. Thereafter, a player is credited with an additional year of experience for each season in which he accumulates six games on the Active List or Inactive List, or on Reserve/Injured or Reserve/Physically Unable to Perform.

Log on to www.packers.com for an up-to-date roster.

COACHING STAFF
Head Coach,
Mike McCarthy

Pro Career: Named the fourteenth head coach in Packers history January 12, 2006. Returned to Green Bay after serving as the team's quarterbacks coach in 1999. Subsequently was a highly successful offensive coordinator for the New Orleans Saints (2000-04). With McCarthy calling plays, the Saints racked up 10 offensive team records and 25 individual marks. He was named NFC Assistant Coach of the Year by *USA Today* in 2000, and New Orleans led the league with 432 points and 49 touchdowns in 2002. The list of quarterbacks he has coached includes Joe Montana, Elvis Grbac, Rich Gannon, Brett Favre, Matt Hasselbeck, Aaron Brooks, Jake Delhomme and Marc Bulger—a collection that combines for 25 career Pro Bowl selections and eight Super Bowl starts. Favre threw for 4,091 yards, the third-highest total of his career, in 1999 as Green Bay ranked seventh in the league in passing and ninth overall. Career record: 0-0.

Background: Graduated with a degree in business administration from Baker University following a two-year playing career (1985-86). Was an all-conference tight end, helping the school to a NAIA Division II runner-up finish as a senior captain. Coached collegiately at Fort Hays State (1987-88) and Pittsburgh (1989-1992), before moving to the the NFL with the Kansas City Chiefs (1993-98), Green Bay Packers (1999), New Orleans Saints (2000-04) and San Francisco 49ers (2005).

Personal: Born November 10, 1963, in Pittsburgh. Has a daughter, Alexandra.

ASSISTANT COACHES

Edgar Bennett, running backs; born February 15, 1969, Jacksonville. Running back Florida State 1987, 1989-1991. Pro running back Green Bay Packers 1992-96, Chicago Bears 1998-99. Pro coach: Joined Packers in 2001.

James Campen, asst. offensive line; born June 11, 1964, Sacramento, Calif. Center Sacramento City (Calif.) J.C. 1982-83, Tulane 1984-85. Pro center New Orleans Saints 1987-88, Green Bay Packers 1989-1993. Pro coach: Joined Packers in 2004.

Tom Clements, quarterbacks; born June 18, 1953, McKees Rocks, Pa. Quarterback Notre Dame 1972-74. Pro quarterback Ottawa Rough Riders (CFL) 1975-78, Hamilton Tiger-Cats (CFL) 1979, 1981-82, Kansas City Chiefs 1980, Winnipeg Blue Bombers (CFL) 1983-87. College coach: Notre Dame 1992-95. Pro coach: New Orleans Saints 1997-99, Kansas City Chiefs 2000, Pittsburgh Steelers 2001-03, Buffalo Bills 2004-05, joined Packers in 2006.

Rock Gullickson, strength & conditioning; born April 11, 1955, Moorhead, Minn.

Guard Moorhead (Minn.) State 1973-76. No pro playing experience. College coach: Moorhead State 1978, Mayville (N.D.) State 1979-1980, South Dakota State 1981, Montana State 1982-89, Rutgers 1990-92, Texas 1993-97, Louisville 1988-1999. Pro coach: New Orleans Saints 2000-05, joined Packers in 2006.

Carl Hairston, defensive ends; born December 15, 1952, Martinsville, Va. Defensive end Maryland-Eastern Shore 1972-75. Pro defensive end Philadelphia Eagles 1976-1983, Cleveland Browns 1984-89, Phoenix Cardinals 1990. Pro coach: Kansas City Chiefs 1995-96, 2001-05, St. Louis Rams 1997-2000, joined Packers in 2006.

Jeff Jagodzinski, offensive coordinator; born October 12, 1963, Milwaukee, Wis. Fullback Wisconsin-Whitewater 1981-84. No pro playing experience. College coach: Wisconsin-Whitewater 1985, Northern Illinois 1986, Louisiana State 1987-88, East Carolina 1989-1996, Boston College 1997-98. Pro coach: Green Bay Packers 1999-2003, Atlanta Falcons 2004-05, rejoined Packers in 2006.

Ty Knott, offensive quality control; born December 9, 1965, Los Angeles. Defensive back Oregon Tech 1988-89. No pro playing experience. College coach: Whittier College 1994-95, Indiana University (Pa.) 1997-99, Mt. San Antonio (Calif.) J.C. 2000, Greenville 2001. Pro coach: Jacksonville Jaguars 2002, New Orleans Saints 2003-05, joined Packers in 2006.

Eric Lewis, defensive quality control; born January 2, 1976, East Lansing, Mich. Defensive back San Diego State 1995-98. No pro playing experience. College coach: Michigan State 2001, Bucknell 2002, Ball State 2003-05. Pro coach: Joined Packers in 2006.

Ben McAdoo, tight ends; born July 7, 1977, Homer City, Pa. Attended Indiana University (Pa.). No college or pro playing experience. College coach: Michigan State 2001-02, Fairfield 2002, Pittsburgh 2003, Akron 2003, Stanford 2005. Pro coach: New Orleans Saints 2004, San Francisco 49ers 2005, joined Packers in 2006.

Winston Moss, linebackers; born December 24, 1965, Miami. Linebacker Miami 1983-86. Pro linebacker Tampa Bay Buccaneers 1987-1990, Los Angeles Raiders 1991-94, Seattle Seahawks 1995-97. Pro coach: Seattle Seahawks 1998, New Orleans Saints 2000-05, joined Packers in 2006.

Robert Nunn, defensive tackles; born June 10, 1965, Apache, Okla. Linebacker Oklahoma State 1983-84, 1986-87. No pro playing experience. College coach: Northeastern Oklahoma 1988, Tennessee 1989-1990, Georgia Military College 1991-99 (head coach 1992-99). Pro coach: Miami Dolphins 2000-02, 2004, Washington Redskins 2003, joined Packers in 2005.

Joe Philbin, offensive line; born July 2,

1961, Springfield, Mass. Tight end Washington & Jefferson 1980. No pro playing experience. College coach: Tulane 1984-85, Worcester Tech 1986-87, U.S. Merchant Marine Academy 1988-89, Allegheny 1990-93, Ohio University 1994, Northeastern 1995-96, Harvard 1997-98, Iowa 1999-2002. Pro coach: Joined Packers in 2003.

Jimmy Robinson, wide receivers; born January 3, 1953, Atlanta. Wide receiver Georgia Tech 1972-74. Pro wide receiver New York Giants 1976-79, San Francisco 49ers 1980, Denver Broncos 1981. College coach: Georgia Tech 1987-89. Pro coach: Memphis Showboats (USFL) 1984-85, Atlanta Falcons 1990-93, Indianapolis Colts 1994-97, New York Giants 1998-2003, New Orleans Saints 2004-05, joined Packers in 2006.

Bob Sanders, defensive coordinator; born December 5, 1953, Jacksonville, N.C. Linebacker Davidson College 1973-75. No pro playing experience. College coach: Georgia Tech 1978, East Carolina 1980-82, Richmond 1983-84, Duke 1985-89, Florida 1990-2000. Pro coach: Miami Dolphins 2001-04, joined Packers in 2005.

Kurt Schottenheimer, secondary; born October 1, 1949, McDonald, Pa. Quarterback Coffeyville (Kan.) J.C. 1967-68, defensive back Miami (Fla.) 1969-70. No pro playing experience. College coach: William Patterson 1974, Michigan State 1978-1982, Tulane 1983, Louisiana State 1984-85, Notre Dame 1986. Pro coach: Cleveland Browns 1987-88, Kansas City Chiefs 1989-2000, Washington Redskins 2001, Detroit Lions 2002-03, Green Bay Packers 2004, St. Louis Rams 2005, rejoined Packers in 2006.

Shawn Slocum, asst. special teams; born February 21, 1965, Bryan, Texas. Linebacker Texas A&M 1983-84. No pro playing experience. College coach: Texas A&M 1989, 1991-97, 2000-02, Pittsburgh 1990, Southern California 1998-99, Mississippi 2005. Pro coach: Joined Packers in 2006.

Mike Stock, special teams coordinator; born September 29, 1939, Barberton, Ohio. Fullback Northwestern 1961. Pro running back Saskatchewan Roughriders (CFL) 1961. College coach: Northwestern 1961, Buffalo 1966-67, Navy 1968, Notre Dame 1969-1974, 1983-86, Wisconsin 1975-77, Eastern Michigan 1978-1982 (head coach), Ohio State 1992-94. Pro coach: New Jersey Generals (USFL) 1983, Cincinnati Bengals 1987-1991, Kansas City Chiefs 1995-2000, Washington Redskins 2001-03, St. Louis Rams 2004, joined Packers in 2006.

Lionel Washington, defensive nickel package/cornerbacks; born October 21, 1960, New Orleans. Defensive back Tulane 1979-1982. Pro defensive back St. Louis Cardinals 1983-86, Los Angeles/Oakland Raiders 1987-1994, 1997, Denver Broncos 1995-96. Pro coach: Joined Packers in 1999.

National Football Conference
North Division
Team Colors: Purple, Gold, and White
9520 Viking Drive
Eden Prairie, Minnesota 55344
Telephone: (952) 828-6500

2006 SCHEDULE
PRESEASON
Aug. 14 **Oakland** 7:00
Aug. 19 at Pittsburgh......................8:00
Aug. 25 **Baltimore**.........................7:00
Aug. 31 at Dallas............................7:00

REGULAR SEASON
Sept. 11 at Washington (Mon.).........7:00
Sept. 17 **Carolina**..........................12:00
Sept. 24 **Chicago** 12:00
Oct. 1   at Buffalo 1:00
Oct. 8   **Detroit** 12:00
Oct. 15   Open Date
Oct. 22   at Seattle............................1:15
Oct. 30   **New England** (Mon.).......7:30
Nov. 5   at San Francisco................1:05
Nov. 12   **Green Bay**......................12:00
Nov. 19   at Miami............................ 1:00
Nov. 26   **Arizona** 12:00
Dec. 3   at Chicago........................12:00
Dec. 10   at Detroit 1:00
Dec. 17   **N.Y. Jets** 12:00
Dec. 21   at Green Bay (Thu.) 7:00
Dec. 31   **St. Louis** 12:00

Stadium: Hubert H. Humphrey Metrodome
 (opened in 1982)
 •**Capacity:** 64,121
 500 11th Avenue South
 Minneapolis, Minnesota 55415
Playing Surface: FieldTurf
Training Camp: Minnesota State-Mankato
 Mankato, Minnesota
 56001

HUBERT H. HUMPHREY METRODOME

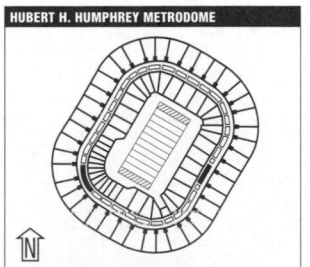

CLUB OFFICIALS
Owner/Chairman: Zygi Wilf
Owner/President: Mark Wilf
Owner/Vice Chairman: Leonard Wilf
Ownership Partners: Reggie Fowler,
 Alan Landis, David Mandelbaum
Vice President of Public Affairs/Stadium
 Development: Lester Bagley
Vice President of Football Operations:
 Rob Brzezinski
Vice President of Sales and Marketing:
 Steve LaCroix
Vice President of Finance: Steve Poppen
Vice President of Operations and Legal
 Counsel: Kevin Warren
Director of College Scouting:
 Scott Studwell
Senior Consultant/Pro Personnel:
 Paul Wiggin
Director of Football Administration:
 Dave Blando
Director of Public Relations: Bob Hagan
Director of Community Relations:
 Brad Madson
Director of Operations: TBD
Director of Ticket Sales: Phil Huebner
Director of Video: Bob Marcus
Director of Player Development/Legal:
 Les Pico
Head Athletic Trainer: Eric Sugarman
Senior Consultant/Medical Services:
 Fred Zamberletti
Equipment Manager: Dennis Ryan

COACHING HISTORY
(389-322-9)
Records include postseason games
1961-66   Norm Van Brocklin 29-51-4
1967-1983 Bud Grant 161-99-5
1984   Les Steckel 3-13-0
1985   Bud Grant 7-9-0
1986-1991 Jerry Burns................55-46-0
1992-2001 Dennis Green* 101-70-0
2001-05   Mike Tice..................33-34-0
*Resigned after 15 games in 2001

ATTENDANCE
Home 497,984   Away 545,057
Total 1,043,041
Single-game home record,
 64,482 (11/2/03)
Single-season home record,
 510,741 (1998)

2006 DRAFT CHOICES
Round	Name	Pos.	College
1	Chad Greenway	LB	Iowa
2	Cedric Griffin	DB	Texas
	Ryan Cook	C	New Mexico
	Tarvaris Jackson	QB	Alabama State
4	Ray Edwards	DE	Purdue
5	Greg Blue	DB	Georgia

2005 TEAM RECORD
PRESEASON (3-1)

Date	Result	Opponent
8/12	W 27-16	Kansas City
8/19	L 21-28	at N.Y. Jets
8/26	W 19-16	San Diego
9/2	W 23-21	at Seattle

REGULAR SEASON (9-7)

Date	Result	Opponent	Att.
9/11	L 13-24	Tampa Bay	63,939
9/18	L 8-37	at Cincinnati	65,763
9/25	W 33-16	New Orleans	63,952
10/2	L 10-30	at Atlanta	69,552
10/16	L 3-28	at Chicago	62,143
10/23	W 23-20	Green Bay	64,278
10/30	L 13-38	at Carolina	73,502
11/6	W 27-14	Detroit	63,813
11/13	W 24-21	at N.Y. Giants	78,637
11/21	W 20-17	at Green Bay	70,610
11/27	W 24-12	Cleveland	63,814
12/4	W 21-16	at Detroit	61,375
12/11	W 27-13	St. Louis	64,005
12/18	L 3-18	Pittsburgh	64,136
12/25	L 23-30	at Baltimore	70,246
1/1	W 34-10	Chicago	64,023

SCORE BY PERIODS

Vikings	54	89	82	81	0	—	306
Opponents	51	136	60	97	0	—	344

2005 TEAM STATISTICS

	Vikings	Opp.
Total First Downs	285	304
Rushing	83	96
Passing	169	177
Penalty	33	31
3rd Down: Made/Att	64/196	95/221
3rd Down Pct.	32.7	43.0
4th Down: Made/Att	4/9	5/13
4th Down Pct.	44.4	38.5
Possession Avg.	28:46	31:14
Total Net Yards	4,613	5,173
Avg. Per Game	288.3	323.3
Total Plays	945	1,029
Avg. Per Play	4.9	5.0
Net Yards Rushing	1,467	1,841
Avg. Per Game	91.7	115.1
Total Rushes	381	462
Net Yards Passing	3,146	3,332
Avg. Per Game	196.6	208.3
Sacked/Yards Lost	54/303	34/207
Gross Yards	3,449	3,539
Att./Completions	510/323	533/319
Completion Pct.	63.3	59.8
Had Intercepted	16	24
Punts/Average	81/43.3	72/41.8
Net Punting Avg.	81/35.7	72/36.8
Penalties/Yards	128/1013	137/990
Fumbles/Ball Lost	25/14	22/11
Touchdowns	33	37
Rushing	10	14
Passing	18	23
Returns	5	0

2005 INDIVIDUAL STATISTICS

PASSING	Att.	Comp.	Yds.	Pct.	TD	Int.	Tkld.	Rate
B. Johnson	294	184	1,885	62.6	12	4	23/134	88.9
Culpepper	216	139	1,564	64.4	6	12	31/169	72.0
Vikings	510	323	3,449	63.3	18	16	54/303	81.7
Opponents	533	319	3,539	59.8	23	24	34/207	75.2

SCORING	TD R	TD P	TD Rt	PAT	FG	Saf	PTS
Edinger	0	0	0	31/31	25/34	0	106
M. Robinson	0	5	0	0/0	0/0	0	32
M. Bennett	3	2	0	0/0	0/0	0	30
Fason	4	0	0	0/0	0/0	0	24
Moore	1	2	1	0/0	0/0	0	24
T. Taylor	0	4	0	0/0	0/0	0	24
K. Robinson	1	1	1	0/0	0/0	0	18
Sharper	0	0	2	0/0	0/0	0	12
Williamson	0	2	0	0/0	0/0	0	12
Burleson	0	1	0	0/0	0/0	0	6
Culpepper	1	0	0	0/0	0/0	0	6
Do. Edwards	0	0	1	0/0	0/0	0	6
Wiggins	0	1	0	0/0	0/0	0	6
Vikings	10	18	5	31/31	25/34	0	306
Opponents	14	23	0	34/34	28/33	1	344

2-Pt. Conversions: M. Robinson.
Vikings 1-2, Opponents 1-3.

RUSHING	No.	Yds	Avg	LG	TD
Moore	155	662	4.3	33	1
M. Bennett	126	473	3.8	61t	3
Culpepper	24	147	6.1	18	1
Fason	32	62	1.9	15	4
B. Johnson	18	53	2.9	16	0
Williamson	3	28	9.3	11	0
K. Robinson	4	27	6.8	13t	1
M. Williams	13	20	1.5	9	0
T. Taylor	2	3	1.5	5	0
Hill	2	-2	-1.0	-1	0
Burleson	2	-6	-3.0	-2	0
Vikings	381	1,467	3.9	61t	10
Opponents	462	1,841	4.0	71t	14

RECEIVING	No.	Yds	Avg	LG	TD
Wiggins	69	568	8.2	24	1
T. Taylor	50	604	12.1	31	4
Moore	37	339	9.2	29	2
M. Robinson	31	515	16.6	68	5
Burleson	30	328	10.9	20	1
M. Bennett	27	124	4.6	20	2
Williamson	24	372	15.5	56	2
K. Robinson	22	347	15.8	80t	1
Kleinsasser	22	171	7.8	15	0
M. Williams	8	52	6.5	25	0
Owens	2	18	9.0	12	0
Angulo	1	11	11.0	11	0
Vikings	323	3,449	10.7	80t	18
Opponents	319	3,539	11.1	70t	23

INTERCEPTIONS	No.	Yds	Avg	LG	TD
Sharper	9	276	30.7	92t	2
B. Williams	4	59	14.8	31	0
Winfield	4	5	1.3	4	0
Chavous	2	0	0.0	0	0
Smoot	2	0	0.0	0	0
Do. Edwards	1	51	51.0	51t	1
Newman	1	1	1.0	1	0
Offord	1	0	0.0	0	0
Vikings	24	392	16.3	92t	3
Opponents	16	220	13.8	55	0

PUNTING	No.	Yds.	Avg.	In 20	LG
Kluwe	71	3,130	44.1	17	62
D. Bennett	8	300	37.5	1	53
Edinger	2	75	37.5	1	40
Vikings	81	3,505	43.3	19	62
Opponents	72	3,013	41.8	25	60

PUNT RETURNS	Ret	FC	Yds	Avg	LG	TD
Moore	21	9	245	11.7	71t	1
Howry	12	5	78	6.5	19	0
Burleson	5	0	21	4.2	10	0
K. Robinson	2	0	0	0.0	0	0
T. Taylor	1	0	0	0.0	0	0
Vikings	41	14	344	8.4	71t	1
Opponents	45	17	495	11.0	72	0

KICKOFF RETURNS	No.	Yds	Avg	LG	TD
K. Robinson	47	1,221	26.0	86t	1
Williamson	12	192	16.0	28	0
Moore	4	72	18.0	27	0
Owens	3	25	8.3	16	0
Fason	2	4	2.0	4	0
M. Williams	1	16	16.0	16	0
Henderson	1	13	13.0	13	0
Herrera	1	6	6.0	6	0
Vikings	71	1,549	21.8	86t	1
Opponents	67	1,416	21.1	48	0

FIELD GOALS	1-19	20-29	30-39	40-49	50+
Edinger	0/0	11/11	3/8	8/10	3/5
Vikings	0/0	11/11	3/8	8/10	3/5
Opponents	1/1	9/10	9/9	7/8	2/5

SACKS	No.
Johnstone	7.5
James	4.0
Scott	4.0
K. Williams	4.0
Mosley	3.0
Newman	3.0
Cowart	2.0
P. Williams	1.5
Harris	1.0
Henderson	1.0
R. Smith	1.0
Udeze	1.0
B. Williams	1.0
Vikings	34.0
Opponents	54.0

RECORD HOLDERS
INDIVIDUAL RECORDS—CAREER

Category	Name	Performance
Rushing (Yds.)	Robert Smith, 1993-2000	6,818
Passing (Yds.)	Fran Tarkenton, 1961-66, 1972-78	33,098
Passing (TDs)	Fran Tarkenton, 1961-66, 1972-78	239
Receiving (No.)	Cris Carter, 1990-2001	1,004
Receiving (Yds.)	Cris Carter, 1990-2001	12,383
Interceptions	Paul Krause, 1968-1979	53
Punting (Avg.)	Harry Newsome, 1990-93	43.8
Punt Return (Avg.)	David Palmer, 1994-2000	9.4
Kickoff Return (Avg.)	Charlie West, 1968-1973	25.5
Field Goals	Fred Cox, 1963-1977	282
Touchdowns (Tot.)	Cris Carter, 1990-2001	110
Points	Fred Cox, 1963-1977	1,365

INDIVIDUAL RECORDS—SINGLE SEASON

Category	Name	Performance
Rushing (Yds.)	Robert Smith, 2000	1,521
Passing (Yds.)	Daunte Culpepper, 2004	4,717
Passing (TDs)	Daunte Culpepper, 2004	39
Receiving (No.)	Cris Carter, 1994, 1995	122
Receiving (Yds.)	Randy Moss, 2003	1,632
Interceptions	Paul Krause, 1975	10
Punting (Avg.)	Bobby Walden, 1964	46.4
Punt Return (Avg.)	David Palmer, 1995	13.2
Kickoff Return (Avg.)	John Gilliam, 1972	26.3
Field Goals	Gary Anderson, 1998	35
Touchdowns (Tot.)	Chuck Foreman, 1975	22
Points	Gary Anderson, 1998	164

INDIVIDUAL RECORDS—SINGLE GAME

Category	Name	Performance
Rushing (Yds.)	Chuck Foreman, 10-24-76	200
Passing (Yds.)	Tommy Kramer, 11-2-86	490
Passing (TDs)	Joe Kapp, 9-28-69	*7
Receiving (No.)	Rickey Young, 12-16-79	15
Receiving (Yds.)	Sammy White, 11-7-76	210
Interceptions	Many Times	3
	Last time by Darren Sharper, 11-13-05	
Field Goals	Rich Karlis, 11-5-89	*7
Touchdowns (Tot.)	Chuck Foreman, 12-20-75	4
	Ahmad Rashad, 9-2-79	4
Points	Chuck Foreman, 12-20-75	24
	Ahmad Rashad, 9-2-79	24

*NFL Record

2006 VETERAN ROSTER

No.	Name	Pos.	Ht.	Wt.	Birthdate	NFL Exp.	College	Hometown	How Acq.	'05 Games/ Starts
86	Angulo, Richard	TE	6-8	270	11/13/80	4	Western New Mexico	Albuquerque, N.M.	W(StL)-'03	2/0
78	Birk, Matt	C	6-4	309	7/23/76	9	Harvard	St. Paul, Minn.	D6-'98	0*
50	Davis, Rod	LB	6-2	239	4/2/81	3	Southern Mississippi	Gulfport, Miss.	D5-'04	16/1
83	Dugan, Jeff	TE	6-4	258	4/8/81	3	Maryland	Pittsburgh, Pa.	D7-'04	1/0
22	Echemandu, Adimchinobe	RB	5-10	226	11/21/80	3	California	Hawthorne, Calif.	FA-'05	2/0
36	Edwards, Dovonte	CB	6-0	182	10/17/82	2	North Carolina State	Chapel Hill, N.C.	FA-'05	12/0
59	Farwell, Heath	LB	6-0	235	12/31/81	2	San Diego State	Corona, Calif.	FA-'05	7/0
35	Fason, Ciatrick	RB	6-0	207	10/29/82	2	Florida	Jacksonville, Fla.	D4-'05	13/0
37	Fox, Dustin	CB	5-11	190	10/8/82	2	Ohio State	Canton, Ohio	D3-'05	0*
28	Gallishaw, Laroni	S	6-0	190	4/4/81	2	Murray State	Lakeland, Fla.	FA-'05	5/0
73	Goldberg, Adam	G	6-7	310	8/12/80	3	Wyoming	Edina, Minn.	FA-'03	16/12
44	Goodspeed, Joey	FB	6-1	247	2/22/78	4	Notre Dame	Oswego, Ill.	FA-'06	0*
58	Harris, Napoleon	LB	6-2	255	2/25/79	5	Northwestern	Harvey, Ill.	T(Oak)-'05	15/3
56	Henderson, E.J.	LB	6-1	245	8/3/80	4	Maryland	Aberdeen, Md.	D2-'03	15/14
64	Herrera, Anthony	G	6-2	315	6/14/80	3	Tennessee	Naples, Fla.	FA-'04	10/6
79 t-	Hicks, Artis	G	6-4	335	11/28/78	5	Memphis	Jackson, Tenn.	T(Phil)-'06	14/14*
31	Hunter, Will	S	5-10	190	3/24/79	2	Syracuse	Chester, Pa.	FA-'04	13/0
76	Hutchinson, Steve	G	6-5	313	11/1/77	6	Michigan	Ft. Lauderdale, Fla.	RFA(Sea)-'06	16/16*
99	James, Erasmus	DE	6-4	266	11/4/82	2	Wisconsin	Hollywood, Fla.	D1b-'05	15/9
14	Johnson, Brad	QB	6-5	226	9/13/68	15	Florida State	Black Mountain, N.C.	FA-'05	15/9
72	Johnson, Marcus	T	6-6	321	12/1/81	2	Mississippi	Coffeeville, Miss.	D2-'05	14/8
97	Johnson, Spencer	DT	6-3	286	12/12/81	3	Auburn	Silas, Ala.	FA-'04	10/2
40	Kleinsasser, Jim	TE	6-3	272	1/31/77	8	North Dakota	Carrington, N.D.	D2-'99	16/16
5	Kluwe, Chris	P	6-4	215	12/24/81	2	UCLA	Los Alamitos, Calif.	W(Sea)-'05	15/0
51	Leber, Ben	LB	6-3	244	12/7/78	5	Kansas State	Vermillion, S.D.	UFA(SD)-'06	9/6*
67	Liwienski, Chris	G	6-5	325	8/2/75	8	Indiana	Sterling Heights, Mich.	FA-'99	15/9
46	Loeffler, Cullen	LS	6-5	241	1/27/81	2	Texas	Ingram, Texas	FA-'04	16/0
8	Longwell, Ryan	K	6-0	200	8/16/74	10	California	Bend, Ore.	UFA(GB)-'06	16/0*
74	McKinnie, Bryant	T	6-8	335	9/23/79	5	Miami	Woodbury, N.J.	D1-'02	16/16
4	McMahon, Mike	QB	6-2	215	2/8/79	6	Rutgers	Wexford, Pa.	FA-'06	9/7*
30	Moore, Mewelde	RB	5-11	209	7/24/82	3	Tulane	Baton Rouge, La.	D4b-'04	16/8
96	Mosley, C.J.	DT	6-2	314	8/6/83	2	Missouri	Waynesville, Mo.	D6-'05	12/2
7	O'Sullivan, J.T.	QB	6-2	227	8/25/79	5	California-Davis	Carmichael, Calif.	FA-'05	0*
24	Offord, Willie	S	6-1	216	12/22/78	5	South Carolina	Palatka, Fla.	D3-'02	3/1
45	Owens, Richard	FB	6-4	273	11/4/80	3	Louisville	Middleburg, Fla.	FA-'04	16/2
17	Redmond, Jimmy	WR	6-0	190	8/18/77	3	McNeese State	Blue Springs, Mo.	FA-'06	0*
49	Richardson, Tony	FB	6-1	238	12/17/71	12	Auburn	Daleville, Ala.	UFA(KC)-'06	16/16*
81	Robinson, Koren	WR	6-1	205	3/19/80	6	North Carolina State	South Point, N.C.	FA-'05	14/5
87	Robinson, Marcus	WR	6-3	215	2/27/75	10	South Carolina	Fort Valley, Ga.	UFA(Balt)-'04	15/9
75	Rosenthal, Mike	T	6-7	318	6/10/77	8	Notre Dame	Mishawaka, Ind.	UFA(NYG)-'03	16/12
98	Scott, Darrion	DE	6-3	289	10/25/81	3	Ohio State	Charleston, W. Va.	D3-'04	16/15
92	Scott, DeQuincy	DE	6-1	260	3/5/78	5	Southern Mississippi	LaPlace, La.	UFA(SD)-'06	16/0*
42	Sharper, Darren	S	6-2	210	11/3/75	10	William & Mary	Richmond, Va.	FA-'05	14/14
21	Smoot, Fred	CB	5-11	178	4/17/79	6	Mississippi State	Jackson, Miss.	UFA(Wash)-'05	11/8
29	Taylor, Chester	RB	5-11	213	9/22/79	5	Toledo	River Rouge, Mich.	UFA(Balt)-'06	15/1*
89	Taylor, Travis	WR	6-1	210	3/30/79	7	Florida	Jacksonville, Fla.	UFA(Balt)-'05	16/13
54	Thomas, Dontarrious	LB	6-2	241	9/2/80	3	Auburn	Perry, Ga.	D2-'04	14/2
95	Udeze, Kenechi	DE	6-3	281	3/5/83	3	Southern California	Los Angeles, Calif.	D1-'04	3/2
65	Whittle, Jason	G	6-4	305	3/7/75	9	Southwest Missouri State	Camdenton, Mo.	FA-'06	14/0*
85	Wiggins, Jermaine	TE	6-2	260	1/18/75	7	Georgia	East Boston, Mass.	UFA(Car)-'04	16/8
93	Williams, Kevin	DT	6-5	311	8/16/80	4	Oklahoma State	Fordyce, Ark.	D1-'03	14/14
94	Williams, Pat	DT	6-3	317	10/24/72	10	Texas A&M	Monroe, La.	UFA(Buff)-'05	16/16
25	Williams, Tank	S	6-2	223	6/30/80	5	Stanford	Bay St. Louis, Miss.	UFA(Tenn)-'06	16/16*
82	Williamson, Troy	WR	6-1	203	4/30/83	2	South Carolina	Aiken, S.C.	D1a-'05	14/3
63	Wilson, Mark	T	6-6	318	11/11/80	2	California	McArthur, Calif.	FA-'05	0*
26	Winfield, Antoine	CB	5-9	180	6/24/77	8	Ohio State	Akron, Ohio	UFA(Buff)-'04	16/16

* Birk missed '05 season because of injury; Fox missed '05 season because of injury; Goodspeed last active with St. Louis in '04; Hicks played 14 games with Philadelphia in '05; Hutchinson played 16 games with Seattle; Leber played 9 games with San Diego; Longwell played 16 games with Green Bay; McMahon played 9 games with Philadelphia; O'Sullivan inactive for 8 games; Redmond last active with Jacksonville in '03; Richardson played 16 games with Kansas City; De. Scott played 16 games with San Diego; Taylor played 15 games with Baltimore; Whittle played 14 games with N.Y. Giants; T. Williams played 16 games with Tennessee; Wilson last active with Washington in '04.

t- Vikings traded for Hicks (Phil).

Traded—QB Daunte Culpepper (7 games in '05) to Miami.

Players lost through free agency (9): RB Michael Bennett (NO; 16 games in '05), WR Nate Burleson (Sea; 12), S Corey Chavous (StL; 16), LB Sam Cowart (Hou; 15), G Toniu Fonoti (TB; 1), C Melvin Fowler (Buff; 11), DE Lance Johnstone (Oak; 15), LB Raonall Smith (StL; 16), CB Brian Williams (Jax; 14),

Also played with Vikings in '05—P Darren Bennett (1 game), CB Ralph Brown (16), K Paul Edinger (16), QB Shaun Hill (1), WR Keenan Howry (4), CB Ken Irvin (7), LB Keith Newman (13), RB Moe Williams (6), C Cory Withrow (16).

2006 FIRST-YEAR ROSTER

Name	Pos.	Ht.	Wt.	Birthdate	College	Hometown	How Acq.
Baskett, Hank	WR	6-4	220	9/4/82	New Mexico	Clovis, N.M.	FA
Blue, Greg	S	6-2	216	3/12/82	Georgia	Atlanta, Ga.	D5
Bubin, Sean (1)	T	6-6	305	1/26/81	Illinois	Rantoul, Ill.	FA
Carter, Jason	WR	6-0	205	9/15/82	Texas A&M	Caldwell, Texas	FA
Cobbs, R.J.	CB	5-11	190	7/26/82	Massachusetts	Parsippany Hills, N.J.	FA
Cook, Ryan	C/G	6-6	328	5/8/83	New Mexico	Albuquerque, N.M.	D2b
Dozier, Ukee (1)	CB	6-1	190	3/10/82	Minnesota	Bradenton, Fla.	FA
Edwards, Ray	DE	6-5	268	1/1/85	Purdue	Indianapolis, Ind.	D4
Foliaki, Lee	LB	6-2	242	2/20/82	Texas A&M	Euless, Texas	FA
Gordon, Charles	CB	5-11	180	7/18/74	Kansas	Santa Monica, Calif.	FA
Greenway, Chad	LB	6-2	242	1/12/83	Iowa	Mount Vernon, S.D.	D1
Griffin, Cedric	CB	6-0	203	11/11/82	Texas	San Antonio, Texas	D2a
Henderson, Taurean	RB	5-10	210	1/20/83	Texas Tech	Gatesville, Texas	FA
Hoag, Ryan (1)	WR	6-2	200	11/23/79	Gustavus Adolphus	Minneapolis, Minn.	FA
Hopoi, Manase	DT	6-4	290	9/23/83	Washington	Sacramento, Calif.	FA
Hosack, Aaron (1)	WR	6-5	210	11/28/81	Minnesota	Chino, Calif.	FA
Jackson, Steven	FB	6-2	260	5/11/84	Clemson	Columbia, S.C.	FA
Jackson, Tarvaris	QB	6-2	232	4/21/83	Alabama State	Montgomery, Ala.	D2c
Jones, Chris (1)	WR	6-3	203	7/17/82	Jackson State	Mason, Miss.	FA
Kight, Kelvin (1)	WR	6-0	213	7/2/82	Florida	Lithonia, Ga.	FA
Mathis, Wendell	RB	5-9	185	9/28/83	Fresno State	Merced, Calif.	FA
McKenzie, Kyle	LB	6-1	235	2/5/83	Minnesota	Detroit, Mich.	FA
Mitchell, Jayme	DE	6-6	285	3/15/84	Mississippi	Jackson, Miss.	FA
Nealy, Barrick	WR	6-5	230	8/7/83	Texas State	Dallas, Texas	FA
Palermo, Jason	C/G	6-3	307	10/16/82	Wisconsin	Madison, Wis.	FA
Penn, Donald	T	6-5	305	4/27/83	Utah State	Playa del Rey, Calif.	FA
Smith, Kyle	WR	6-0	170	10/15/84	Youngstown State	Buffalo, N.Y.	FA
Stinson, Albert	RB	6-5	330	6/24/83	Jackson State	Tuscaloosa, Ala.	FA
Taylor, Eric (1)	DE	6-2	305	12/14/81	Memphis	Winchester, Tenn.	FA
Torp, John	P	6-2	205	0/19/82	Colorado	Louisville, Colo.	FA
Ward, Marvin (1)	CB	5-11	208	8/7/82	Northwestern	Landover, Md.	FA
Whitaker, Ronyell (1)	CB	5-9	196	3/19/79	Virginia Tech	Norfolk, Va.	FA

The term NFL Rookie is defined as a player who is in his first season of professional football and has not been on the roster of another professional football team for any regular-season or postseason games. A Rookie is designated by an "R" on NFL rosters. Players who have been active in another professional football league or players who have NFL experience, including either preseason training camp or being on an Active List or Inactive List, or on Reserve/Injured or Reserve/Physically Unable to Perform for fewer than six regular-season games, are termed NFL First-Year Players. An NFL First-Year Player is designated by a "1" on NFL rosters. Thereafter, a player is credited with an additional year of experience for each season in which he accumulates six games on the Active List or Inactive List, or on Reserve/Injured or Reserve/Physically Unable to Perform.

Log on to www.vikings.com for an up-to-date roster.

COACHING STAFF
Head Coach,
Brad Childress

Pro Career: Named the seventh head coach in Vikings' history on January 6, 2006. Childress enters his twenty-ninth season of coaching, including his ninth in the NFL. He joins the Vikings following seven years with the Philadelphia Eagles, including the past four seasons as offensive coordinator. During his tenure in Philadelphia, the Eagles reached Super Bowl XXXIX, played in four straight NFC Championship games, won four straight NFC East titles, and amassed a 70-42 (.625) record in the regular season. During Childress' time as offensive coordinator (2002-05), the Eagles' 43 victories were the most in the NFC over that span. The Eagles' offense since 2000 featured seven players who earned 14 berths in the Pro Bowl. Childress got his first taste of NFL coaching in 1985 when he served as the quarterbacks coach for the Indianapolis Colts. Career record: 0-0.

Background: Coached at Illinois (1978-84), Northern Arizona (1986-89), Utah (1990), and Wisconsin (1991-98). The coaching staff at Northern Arizona included future NFL head coaches Bill Callahan, Marty Mornhinweg, and Andy Reid. Childress briefly played quarterback and wide receiver at Illinois before transferring to Eastern Illinois, where he graduated with a bachelor's degree in psychology.

Personal: Born June 27, 1956 in Aurora, Ill. He and his wife Dru-Ann have four children: Cara, Kyle, Andrew, and Christopher.

ASSISTANT COACHES

Juney Barnett, asst. strength and conditioning; born January 11, 1979, Philadelphia. Defensive back Bloomsburg 1997-2000. College coach: Bloomsburg 2001, Army 2005. Pro coach: Rhein Fire (NFLE) 2004-05, joined Vikings in 2006.

Darrell Bevell, offensive coordinator; born January 6, 1970, Yuma, Ariz. Quarterback Northern Arizona 1989, Wisconsin 1992-95. No pro playing experience. College coach: Westmar 1996, Iowa State 1997, Connecticut 1998-99. Pro coach: Green Bay Packers 2000-05, joined Vikings in 2006.

Eric Bieniemy, running backs; born August 15, 1969, New Orleans. Running back Colorado 1987-1990. Pro running back San Diego Chargers 1991-94, Cincinnati Bengals 1995-98, Philadelphia Eagles 1999. College coach: Colorado 2001-02, UCLA 2003-05. Pro coach: Joined Vikings in 2006.

Brendan Daly, defensive quality control; born September 10, 1975, Chicago. Tight end Drake 1993-96. No pro playing experience. College coach: Drake 1998, Villanova 1999, 2005, Maryland 2000, Oklahoma State 2001-03, Illinois State 2004. Pro coach: Joined Vikings in 2006.

Karl Dunbar, defensive line; born May 18, 1967, Plaisance, La. Defensive lineman Louisiana State 1986-89. Pro defensive lineman Pittsburgh Steelers 1990, New Orleans Saints 1992-93, Arizona Cardinals 1994-95. College coach: Nicholls State 1998-99, Louisiana State 2001-01, 2005, Oklahoma State 2002-03. Pro coach: Chicago Bears 2004, joined Vikings in 2006.

Paul Ferraro, special teams coordinator; born April 30, 1959, Ridgewood, N.J. Defensive back Springfield College 1980-82. No pro playing experience. College coach: Massachusetts 1982, Syracuse 1983, Villanova 1984-86, Dartmouth 1987, Catholic 1988, Maine 1989, Ohio 1990, Bowling Green 1991-98, Georgia Tech 1999-2000, Rutgers 2001-04. Pro coach: Carolina Panthers 2005, joined Vikings in 2006.

Jim Hueber, asst. offensive line; born August 14, 1948, Philadelphia. Center South Dakota 1966-67. No pro playing experience. College coach: Cincinnati 1974, Dodge City (Kan.) C.C. 1975-78, Wichita State 1979-1980, Temple 1981-82, Memphis State 1983, Minnesota 1984-1991, Wisconsin 1992-2005. Pro coach: Joined Vikings in 2006.

Jeff Imamura, defensive assistant; born May 22, 1974, Lubbock, Texas. Attended Texas Christian. No college or pro playing experience. College coach: Texas Christian 1997-99, Northern Arizona 2000-02, Saginaw Valley State 2003. Pro coach: Joined Vikings in 2006.

Jimmie Johnson, tight ends; born October 6, 1966, Augusta, Ga. Tight end Howard 1985-88. Pro tight end Washington Redskins 1989-1991, Detroit Lions 1992-93, Kansas City Chiefs 1994, Philadelphia Eagles 1995-98. College coach: South Carolina State 2001, Shaw 2002-03, Texas Southern 2004-05. Pro coach: Joined Vikings in 2006.

Tom Kanavy, strength and conditioning; born April 8, 1970, Archibald, Pa. Attended Penn State. No college or pro playing experience. College coach: Miami 1993, Penn State 1993-95. Pro coach: Philadelphia Eagles 1995-2005, joined Vikings in 2006.

Clay Matchett, offensive assistant; born June 11, 1980, Houston. Safety Louisiana College 2000-04. Pro coach: Joined Vikings in 2006.

Pat Morris, offensive line; born April 7, 1954, Cleveland. Offensive lineman Southern California 1972-75. College coach: Southern California 1976-77, 1983-86, Northern Arizona 1978, Minnesota 1979-1982, Michigan State 1987-1994, Stanford 1995-96. Pro coach: San Francisco 49ers 1997-2003, Detroit Lions 2004-05, joined Vikings in 2006.

Brian Murphy, asst. special teams; born July 17, 1969, Elmwood Park, Ill. Defensive lineman Lehigh 1988-1991. No pro playing experience. College coach: Benedictine 1992, Wisconsin 1994-96, 2002-05, Baylor 1997, San Diego 1998, Lehigh 1999. Pro coach: Joined Vikings in 2006.

Chad O'Shea, offensive quality control; born December 18, 1972, Houston. Quarterback Marshall 1991-93, Houston 1994-95. No pro playing experience. College coach: Houston 1996-99, Southern Mississippi 2000-02. Pro coach: Kansas City Chiefs 2004-05, joined Vikings in 2006.

Fred Pagac, linebackers; born April 26, 1952, Richeyville, Pa. Tight end Ohio State 1971-73. Pro tight end Chicago Bears 1974, Tampa Bay Buccaneers 1976. College coach: Ohio State 1978-2000. Pro coach: Oakland Raiders 2001-03, Kansas City Chiefs 2004-05, joined Vikings in 2006.

Kevin Rogers, quarterbacks; born September 7, 1951, Brooklyn, N.Y. Linebacker Massanutten Academy 1969-1970, William & Mary 1971-73. College coach: Ohio State 1977-78, William & Mary 1980-82, Navy 1983-1990, Syracuse 1991-98, Notre Dame 1999-2001, Virginia Tech 2002-05. Pro coach: Joined Vikings in 2006.

Kevin Stefanski, asst. to the head coach; born May 8, 1982, Philadelphia. Safety Pennsylvania 2000-04. College coach: Pennsylvania 2005. Pro coach: Joined Vikings in 2006.

Martin Streight, asst. strength and conditioning; born June 20, 1969, Trenton, N.J. Attended Indiana (Penn.). No college or pro playing experience. College coach: Penn State 1994, Princeton 1995-96. Pro coach: Philadelphia Eagles 1995-96, Arizona Cardinals 1997-2003, Scottish Claymores (NFLE) 2003, Berlin Thunder (NFLE) 2004-05, joined Vikings in 2006.

Mike Tomlin, defensive coordinator; born March 15, 1972, Hampton, Va. Wide receiver William & Mary 1991-94. College coach: Virginia Military Institute 1995, Memphis 1996, Tennessee-Martin 1997, Arkansas State 1997-98, Cincinnati 1999-2000. Pro coach: Tampa Bay Buccaneers 2001-05, joined Vikings in 2006.

Joe Woods, defensive backs; born June 25, 1970, Natrona Heights, Pa. Safety Illinois State 1988-1991. College coach: Muskingum 1992, Eastern Michigan 1993-94, Northwestern (La.) State 1994, Grand Valley State 1994-96, Kent State 1997, Hofstra 1998-2000, Western Michigan 2001-03. Pro coach: Tampa Bay Buccaneers 2004-05, joined Vikings in 2006.

Darrell Wyatt, wide receivers; born June 18, 1966, Killeen, Texas. Wide receiver Trinity Valley (Texas) C.C. 1985-86, Kansas State 1987-88. College coach: Trinity Valley (Texas) C.C. 1990-91, Sam Houston State 1992-94, Wyoming 1995, Baylor 1996, Kansas 1997-2000, Oklahoma State 2001, Oklahoma 2002-05. Pro coach: Joined Vikings in 2006.

National Football Conference
South Division
Team Colors: Old Gold, Black, and White
5800 Airline Drive
Metairie, Louisiana 70003
Telephone: (504) 733-0255

2006 SCHEDULE
PRESEASON
Aug. 12 at Tennessee 7:00
Aug. 21 **Dallas (Shreveport, LA)**.....7:00
Aug. 26 **Indianapolis (Jackson, MS)**.6:00
Aug. 31 at Kansas City 7:30

REGULAR SEASON
Sept. 10 at Cleveland 1:00
Sept. 17 at Green Bay 12:00
Sept. 25 **Atlanta** (Mon.) 7:30
Oct. 1   at Carolina..........................1:00
Oct. 8   **Tampa Bay**......................12:00
Oct. 15   **Philadelphia** 12:00
Oct. 22   Open Date
Oct. 29   **Baltimore**........................12:00
Nov. 5   at Tampa Bay 1:00
Nov. 12   at Pittsburgh.......................1:00
Nov. 19   **Cincinnati** 12:00
Nov. 26   at Atlanta............................1:00
Dec. 3   **San Francisco** 12:00
Dec. 10   at Dallas........................... 12:00
Dec. 17   **Washington** 12:00
Dec. 24   at N.Y. Giants.....................1:00
Dec. 31   **Carolina**...........................12:00

Stadium: Louisiana Superdome
(opened in 1975)
• **Capacity:** 65,000
1500 Poydras Street
New Orleans, Louisiana 70112
Playing Surface: Sportexe Momentum
Training Camp: TBD

LOUISIANA SUPERDOME

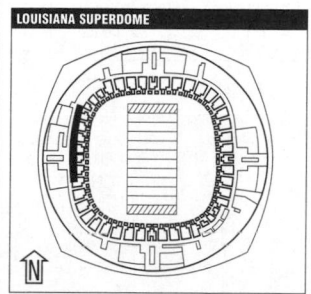

CLUB OFFICIALS
Owner: Tom Benson
Owner/Executive Vice-President of
  Administration: Rita Benson LeBlanc
Executive Vice President/General
  Manager: Mickey Loomis
Senior Vice President/Chief Financial
  Officer: Dennis Lauscha
Vice President of Marketing and
  Business Development: Ben Hales
Vice President/General Counsel:
  Vicky Neumeyer
Vice President of Ticket and Suite Sales:
  Mike Stanfield
Director of Player Personnel:
  Rick Mueller
Senior Football Administrator: Russ Ball
Director of Operations: James Nagaoka
Director of College Scouting:
  Rick Reiprish
College Scouting Coordinator:
  Rick Thompson
Pro Scouts: Ryan Pace, Bill Quinter,
  Terry Fontenot
Area Scouts: Hal Athon, David Hinson,
  James Jefferson, Jim Monos,
  Dwaune Jones, Barrett Wiley
Combine Scout: Ryan Powell
Scouting Assistant: Josh Lucas
Equipment Manager: Dan Simmons
Assistant Equipment Manager:
  Glennon (Silky) Powell
Equipment Assistants: Eddie Falgout,
  John Baumgartner, Corey Gaudet
Head Athletic Trainer: Scottie B. Patton
Assistant Athletic Trainers: Duane
  Brooks, Kevin Mangum, Reggie Stone
Video Director: Dave Desposito
Director of Player Development:
  Ricky Porter
Coaching Assistants: Joe Alley,
  Josh Constant, Carter Sheridan
Director of Media & Public Relations:
  Greg Bensel
Assistant Director of Media & Public
  Relations: Ricky Zeller
Media & Public Relations Manager:
  Justin Macione
Media & Public Relations Assistant:
  Nicholas Karl
Director of Security: Geoff Santini
Director of Photography:
  Michael C. Hebert
Director of Community Affairs: TBA
Director of New Media: Chris Pika
Information Technology/Network
  Manager: Jeff Huffman
Facilities Manager: Terry Ashburn

COACHING HISTORY
(238-357-5)
Records include postseason games
1967-70 Tom Fears*...................13-34-2
1970-72 J.D. Roberts 7-25-3
1973-75 John North**................11-23-0
1975   Ernie Hefferle 1-7-0
1976-77 Hank Stram.......................7-21-0
1978-80 Dick Nolan***...............15-29-0
1980   Dick Stanfel 1-3-0
1981-85 O.A. (Bum) Phillips**** 27-42-0
1985   Wade Phillips 1-3-0
1986-96 Jim Mora# 93-78-0
1996   Rick Venturi 1-7-0
1997-99 Mike Ditka.....................15-33-0
2000-05 Jim Haslett....................46-52-0
     *Released after seven games in 1970
     **Released after six games in 1975
     ***Released after 12 games in 1980
     ****Released after 12 games in 1985
     #Resigned after eight games in 1996

ATTENDANCE
Home 399,485   Away 547,231
Total 946,716
Single-game home record,
  70,940 (9/2/79)
Single-season home record,
  548,728 (1992)

2006 DRAFT CHOICES
Round	Name	Pos.	College
1	Reggie Bush	RB	So. California
2	Roman Harper	DB	Alabama
4	Jahri Evans	T	Bloomsburg
5	Rob Ninkovich	DE	Purdue
6	Mike Hass	WR	Oregon State
	Josh Lay	DB	Pittsburgh
7	Zach Strief	T	Northwestern
	Marques Colston	WR	Hofstra

2005 TEAM RECORD

PRESEASON (1-3)

Date	Result	Opponent
8/12	L 15-34	Seattle
8/18	W 37-27	at New England
8/26	L 6-21	Baltimore
9/1	L 6-13	at Oakland

REGULAR SEASON (3-13)

Date	Result	Opponent	Att.
9/11	W 23-20	at Carolina	72,920
9/19	L 10-27	New York Giants	68,031
9/25	L 16-33	at Minnesota	63,952
10/2	W 19-7	Buffalo	58,688
10/9	L 3-52	at Green Bay	70,580
10/16	L 31-34	Atlanta	65,562
10/23	L 17-28	at St. Louis	64,586
10/30	L 6-21	Miami	61,643
11/6	L 17-20	Chicago	32,637
11/20	L 17-24	at New England	68,756
11/27	W 21-19	at New York Jets	77,152
12/4	L 3-10	Tampa Bay	34,411
12/12	L 17-36	at Atlanta	70,083
12/18	L 10-27	Carolina	32,551
12/24	L 12-13	Detroit	63,747
1/1	L 13-27	at Tampa Bay	65,379

SCORE BY PERIODS

Saints	47	97	22	69	0	—	235
Opponents	103	126	59	110	0	—	398

2005 TEAM STATISTICS

	Saints	Opp.
Total First Downs	312	281
Rushing	89	103
Passing	182	145
Penalty	41	33
3rd Down: Made/Att	82/211	89/220
3rd Down Pct.	38.9	40.5
4th Down: Made/Att	2/12	3/4
4th Down Pct.	16.7	75.0
Possession Avg.	30:32	29:28
Total Net Yards	5,031	4,994
Avg. Per Game	314.4	312.1
Total Plays	1,017	946
Avg. Per Play	4.9	5.3
Net Yards Rushing	1,688	2,145
Avg. Per Game	105.5	134.1
Total Rushes	423	503
Net Yards Passing	3,343	2,849
Avg. Per Game	208.9	178.1
Sacked/Yards Lost	41/261	25/165
Gross Yards	3,604	3,014
Att./Completions	553/308	418/241
Completion Pct.	55.7	57.7
Had Intercepted	24	10
Punts/Average	71/43.2	76/45.6
Net Punting Avg.	71/38.7	76/39.0
Penalties/Yards	135/1130	127/985
Fumbles/Ball Lost	23/19	19/9
Touchdowns	23	43
Rushing	8	16
Passing	15	20
Returns	0	7

2005 INDIVIDUAL STATISTICS

PASSING

	Att.	Comp.	Yds.	Pct.	TD	Int.	Tkld.	Rate
Brooks	431	240	2,882	55.7	13	17	33/202	70.0
Bouman	122	68	722	55.7	2	7	8/59	54.7
Saints	553	308	3,604	55.7	15	24	41/261	66.6
Opponents	418	241	3,014	57.7	20	10	25/165	86.2

SCORING

	TD R	TD P	TD Rt	PAT	FG	Saf	PTS
Carney	0	0	0	22/22	25/32	0	97
Stallworth	0	7	0	0/0	0/0	0	42
Henderson	0	3	0	0/0	0/0	0	18
McAllister	3	0	0	0/0	0/0	0	18
A. Smith	3	0	0	0/0	0/0	0	18
Brooks	2	0	0	0/0	0/0	0	12
Hakim	0	2	0	0/0	0/0	0	12
Conwell	0	1	0	0/0	0/0	0	6
Hilton	0	1	0	0/0	0/0	0	6
Horn	0	1	0	0/0	0/0	0	6
Saints	8	15	0	22/22	25/32	0	235
Opponents	16	20	7	43/43	31/39	2	398

2-Pt. Conversions: None.

Team 0-1, Opponents 0-0.

RUSHING

	No.	Yds	Avg	LG	TD
A. Smith	166	659	4.0	42	3
Stecker	95	363	3.8	32	0
McAllister	93	335	3.6	26	3
Brooks	45	281	6.2	22	2
Bouman	8	15	1.9	6	0
A. Thomas	7	12	1.7	4	0
Karney	6	12	2.0	3	0
Henderson	1	9	9.0	9	0
Stallworth	2	2	1.0	3	0
Saints	423	1,688	4.0	42	8
Opponents	503	2,145	4.3	64	16

RECEIVING

	No.	Yds	Avg	LG	TD
Stallworth	70	945	13.5	43	7
Horn	49	654	13.3	30	1
Hilton	35	396	11.3	29	1
Stecker	35	281	8.0	41	0
Hakim	34	489	14.4	42	2
Henderson	22	343	15.6	66	3
McAllister	17	117	6.9	22	0
Conwell	13	165	12.7	31	1
A. Smith	12	46	3.8	8	0
Karney	10	61	6.1	10	0
Hall	6	36	6.0	8	0
Poole	3	63	21.0	42	0
A. Thomas	2	8	4.0	6	0
Saints	308	3,604	11.7	66	15
Opponents	241	3,014	12.5	68	20

INTERCEPTIONS

	No.	Yds	Avg	LG	TD
Craft	3	63	21.0	39	0
D. Smith	2	53	26.5	28	0
F. Thomas	2	4	2.0	4	0
Bullocks	1	51	51.0	51	0
McKenzie	1	11	11.0	11	0
Slaughter	1	0	0.0	0	0
Saints	10	182	18.2	51	0
Opponents	24	456	19.0	95t	3

PUNTING

	No.	Yds.	Avg.	In 20	LG
Berger	71	3,066	43.2	28	69
Saints	71	3,066	43.2	28	69
Opponents	76	3,462	45.6	23	59

PUNT RETURNS

	Ret	FC	Yds	Avg	LG	TD
Hakim	34	4	260	7.6	42	0
Stallworth	7	1	52	7.4	27	0
Lewis	4	0	8	2.0	5	0
F. Thomas	1	0	0	0.0	0	0
Saints	46	5	320	7.0	42	0
Opponents	33	26	260	7.9	23	0

KICKOFF RETURNS

	No.	Yds	Avg	LG	TD
Stecker	31	672	21.7	46	0
McAfee	22	485	22.0	34	0
Hakim	9	171	19.0	29	0
Lewis	8	137	17.1	20	0
Whitehead	2	12	6.0	12	0
Hall	2	9	4.5	5	0
A. Smith	1	30	30.0	30	0
Saints	75	1,516	20.2	46	0
Opponents	61	1,404	23.0	82	0

FIELD GOALS

	1-19	20-29	30-39	40-49	50+
Carney	1/1	12/13	4/6	8/12	0/0
Saints	1/1	12/13	4/6	8/12	0/0
Opponents	0/0	10/10	13/15	8/12	0/2

SACKS

	No.
W. Smith	8.5
Bryant	4.0
Howard	3.5
F. Thomas	3.0
Grant	2.5
Craft	1.0
D. Smith	1.0
Watson	1.0
Whitehead	0.5
Saints	25.0
Opponents	41.0

RECORD HOLDERS
INDIVIDUAL RECORDS—CAREER

Category	Name	Performance
Rushing (Yds.)	Deuce McAllister, 2001-2005	4,529
Passing (Yds.)	Archie Manning, 1971-1982	21,734
Passing (TDs)	Aaron Brooks, 2000-05	120
Receiving (No.)	Eric Martin, 1985-1993	532
Receiving (Yds.)	Eric Martin, 1985-1993	7,854
Interceptions	Dave Waymer, 1980-89	37
Punting (Avg.)	Mark Royals, 1997-98	45.7
Punt Return (Avg.)	Mel Gray, 1986-88	13.4
Kickoff Return (Avg.)	Walter Roberts, 1967	26.3
Field Goals	Morten Andersen, 1982-1994	302
Touchdowns (Tot.)	Dalton Hilliard, 1986-1993	53
Points	Morten Andersen, 1982-1994	1,318

INDIVIDUAL RECORDS—SINGLE SEASON

Category	Name	Performance
Rushing (Yds.)	George Rogers, 1981	1,674
Passing (Yds.)	Jim Everett, 1995	3,970
Passing (TDs)	Aaron Brooks, 2002	27
Receiving (No.)	Joe Horn, 2000, 2004	94
Receiving (Yds.)	Joe Horn, 2004	1,399
Interceptions	Dave Whitsell, 1967	10
Punting (Avg.)	Mark Royals, 1997	45.9
Punt Return (Avg.)	Mel Gray, 1987	14.7
Kickoff Return (Avg.)	Don Shy, 1969	27.9
	Mel Gray, 1986	27.9
Field Goals	Morten Andersen, 1985	31
	John Carney, 2002	31
Touchdowns (Tot.)	Dalton Hilliard, 1989	18
Points	John Carney, 2002	130

INDIVIDUAL RECORDS—SINGLE GAME

Category	Name	Performance
Rushing (Yds.)	George Rogers, 9-4-83	206
Passing (Yds.)	Aaron Brooks, 12-3-00	441
Passing (TDs)	Billy Kilmer, 11-2-69	6
Receiving (No.)	Tony Galbreath, 9-10-78	14
Receiving (Yds.)	Wes Chandler, 9-2-79	205
Interceptions	Tommy Myers, 9-3-78	3
	Dave Waymer, 10-6-85	3
	Reggie Sutton, 10-18-87	3
	Gene Atkins, 12-22-91	3
	Sammy Knight, 9-9-01	3
Field Goals	Many times	5
	Last time by John Carney, 9-26-04	
Touchdowns (Tot.)	Joe Horn, 12-14-03	4
Points	Joe Horn, 12-14-03	24

2006 VETERAN ROSTER

No.	Name	Pos.	Ht.	Wt.	Birthdate	NFL Exp.	College	Hometown	How Acq.	'05 Games/ Starts
50	Allen, James	LB	6-2	240	11/11/79	5	Oregon State	Portland, Ore.	D3-'02	3/0
60	Archibald, Ben	T	6-3	320	8/26/78	2	Brigham Young	Tacoma, Wash.	FA-'05	5/0
20	Bellamy, Jay	S	5-11	200	7/8/72	13	Rutgers	Aberdeen, N.J.	UFA(Sea)-'01	3/3
28	Bennett, Michael	RB	5-9	209	8/13/78	6	Wisconsin	Milwaukee, Wis.	UFA(Minn)-'06	16/6*
17	Berger, Mitch	P	6-4	228	6/24/72	12	Colorado	Kamloops, B.C.	UFA(StL)-'03	16/0
57	Bockwoldt, Colby	LB	6-1	237	4/14/81	3	Brigham Young	Sunset, Utah	D7-'04	16/16
4	Bouman, Todd	QB	6-2	226	8/1/72	9	St. Cloud State	Ruthton, Minn.	T(Minn)-'03	16/3
9	Brees, Drew	QB	6-0	209	1/15/79	6	Purdue	Austin, Texas	UFA(SD)-'06	16/16*
70	Brown, Jammal	T	6-6	313	3/30/81	2	Oklahoma	Lawton, Okla.	D1-'05	13/13
92	Bryant, Tony	DE	6-6	282	9/3/76	7	Florida State	Marathon, Fla.	FA-'03	16/1
29	Bullocks, Josh	S	6-1	207	2/28/83	2	Nebraska	Chattanooga, Tenn.	D2-'05	16/13
80	Campbell, Mark	TE	6-6	260	12/6/75	9	Michigan	Clawson, Mich.	FA-'06	14/10*
3	Carney, John	K	5-11	185	4/20/64	17	Notre Dame	West Palm Beach, Fla.	FA-'01	16/0
85	Conwell, Ernie	TE	6-2	255	8/17/72	11	Washington	Kent, Wash.	UFA(StL)-'03	8/8
21	Craft, Jason	CB	5-10	187	2/13/76	8	Colorado State	Denver, Colo.	T(Jax)-'04	16/4
59 t-	Faine, Jeff	C	6-3	291	4/6/81	4	Notre Dame	Sanford,Fla.	T(Cle)-'06	14/14*
56	Fincher, Alfred	LB	6-1	238	8/15/83	2	Connecticut	Norwood, Mass.	D3-'05	11/0
52	Fujita, Scott	LB	6-5	250	4/28/79	5	California	Oxnard, Calif.	UFA(Dall)-'06	16/8*
37	Gleason, Steve	S	5-11	212	3/19/77	6	Washington State	Gonzaga, Calif.	FA-'01	13/1
76	Goodwin, Jonathan	G/C	6-3	318	12/2/78	5	Michigan	Richland, S.C.	UFA(NYJ)-'06	16/10*
94	Grant, Charles	DE	6-3	290	9/3/78	5	Georgia	Colquitt, Ga.	D1b-'02	16/14
19	Henderson, Devery	WR	5-11	200	3/26/82	3	Louisiana State	Opelousas, La.	D2a-'04	14/3
86	Hilton, Zachary	TE	6-8	268	7/2/80	4	North Carolina	Silver Spring, Md.	FA-'03	15/6
61	Holland, Montrae	G	6-2	322	5/21/80	4	Florida State	Ore City, Texas	D4-'03	15/10
81	Horn, Chris	WR	5-11	195	7/13/77	3	Rocky Mountain College	Notus, Idaho	FA-'06	14/3*
87	Horn, Joe	WR	6-1	213	1/16/72	11	Itawamba (Miss.) J.C.	Fayetteville, N.C.	UFA(KC)-'00	13/13
47	Houser, Kevin	LS	6-2	252	8/23/77	7	Ohio State	Westlake, Ohio	D7-'00	16/0
44	Karney, Mike	FB	5-11	258	7/6/81	3	Arizona State	Kent, Wash.	D5b-'04	16/14
82	Lawrie, Nate	TE	6-7	256	10/7/81	2	Yale	Indianapolis, Ind.	W(TB)-'05	5/0*
69	Ledford, Dwayne	G	6-4	300	11/2/76	3	East Carolina	Morgantown, N.C.	FA-'06	0*
77	Leisle, Rodney	DT	6-3	315	2/5/81	3	UCLA	Bakersfield, Calif.	D5a-'04	1/0
84	Lewis, Michael	WR	5-8	173	11/14/71	6	None	New Orleans, La.	FA-'01	2/0
15	Lyman, Chase	WR	6-4	210	9/4/82	2	California	Los Altos Hills, Calif.	D4-'05	0*
10	Martin, Jamie	QB	6-2	205	2/8/70	12	Weber State	Arroyo Grande, Calif.	UFA(StL)-'06	8/5*
75	Mayberry, Jermane	G	6-4	325	8/29/73	11	Texas A&M-Kingsville	Floresville, Texas	UFA(Phil)-'05	11/8
25	McAfee, Fred	RB	5-10	197	6/20/68	15	Mississippi College	Philadelphia, Miss.	FA-'04	16/0
26	McAllister, Deuce	RB	6-1	232	12/27/78	6	Mississippi	Lena, Miss	D1-'01	5/5
34	McKenzie, Mike	CB	6-0	194	4/26/76	8	Memphis	Miami, Fla.	T(GB)-'04	15/15
5	McPherson, Adrian	QB	6-3	218	5/8/83	2	Florida State	Bradenton, Fla.	D5-'05	0*
51	Melton, Terrence	LB	6-1	235	1/1/77	3	Rice	Houston, Texas	FA-'04	15/2
67	Nesbit, Jamar	T	6-4	328	12/17/76	8	South Carolina	Summerville, S.C.	UFA(Jax)-'04	16/4
88	Poole, Nate	WR	6-2	204	2/1/77	5	Marshall	Danville, Va.	FA-'05	7/0
38 t-	Scott, Bryan	S	6-1	219	4/13/81	4	Penn State	Doylestown, Pa.	T(Atl)-'06	16/13*
63	Setterstrom, Chad	T	6-3	310	6/13/80	2	Northern Iowa	Northfield, Minn.	FA-'05	0*
58	Simmons, Anthony	LB	6-0	240	6/6/76	8	Clemson	Spartanburg, S.C.	FA-'06	0*
24	Smith, Dwight	S	5-10	201	8/13/78	6	Akron	Detroit, Mich.	UFA(TB)-'05	15/15
91	Smith, Will	DE	6-3	282	7/4/81	3	Ohio State	Utica, N.Y.	D1-'04	16/9
83	Stallworth, Donté	WR	6-0	196	11/10/80	5	Tennessee	Sacramento, Calif.	D1a-'02	16/13
27	Stecker, Aaron	RB	5-10	213	11/13/75	7	Western Illinois	Green Bay, Wis.	UFA(TB)-'04	15/5
78	Stinchcomb, Jon	T	6-5	315	8/27/79	4	Georgia	Lilburn, Ga.	D2-'03	0*
23	Stoutmire, Omar	S	5-11	205	7/9/74	10	Fresno State	Long Beach, Calif.	UFA(Wash)-'06	10/0*
97	Sullivan, Johnathan	DT	6-3	315	1/21/81	4	Georgia	Griffin, Ga.	D1-'03	15/0
22	Thomas, Fred	CB	5-9	185	9/11/73	11	Tennessee-Martin	Bruce, Miss.	UFA(Sea)-'00	16/11
99 t-	Thomas, Hollis	DT	6-0	306	1/10/74	11	Northern Illinois	St. Louis, Mo.	T(Phil)-'06	16/12*
31	Thomas, Joey	CB	6-1	190	9/29/80	3	Montana State	Burien, Wash.	W(GB)-'05	11/1*
79	Verdon, Jimmy	DE	6-3	280	11/14/81	2	Arizona State	Pomona, Calif.	D7-'05	4/0
55	Watson, Courtney	LB	6-1	246	9/18/80	3	Notre Dame	Sarasota, Fla.	D2b-'04	9/6
98	Whitehead, Willie	DT	6-3	300	1/26/73	8	Auburn	Tuskegee, Ala.	FA-'99	16/15
95	Woodard, Cedric	DT	6-2	310	9/5/77	7	Texas	Sweeny, Texas	FA-'05	0*
66	Young, Brian	DT	6-2	298	7/8/77	7	Texas-El Paso	El Paso, Texas	UFA(StL)-'04	16/16

* Bennett played 16 games with Minnesota in '05; Brees played 16 games with San Diego; Campbell played 14 games with Buffalo; Faine played 14 games with Cleveland; Fujita played 16 games with Dallas; Goodwin played 16 games with N.Y. Jets; C. Horn played 14 games with Kansas City; Lawrie played 5 games with Tampa Bay; Ledford last active with San Francisco in '04; Lyman missed '05 season because of injury; Martin played 8 games with St. Louis; McPherson inactive for 16 games; Scott played 16 games with Atlanta; Setterstrom inactive for 1 game; Simmons last active with Seattle in '04; Stinchcomb missed '05 season because of injury; Stoutmire played 10 games with Washington; H. Thomas played 16 games with Philadelphia; J. Thomas played 6 games with Green Bay and 5 games with New Orleans; Woodard inactive for 5 games.

t- Saints traded for Faine (Cle), Scott (Atl), and H. Thomas (Phil).

Traded—T Wayne Gandy (16 games in '05) to Atlanta.

Players lost through free agency (8): C LeCharles Bentley (Cle; 14 games in '05), CB Fakhir Brown (StL; 12), LB Sedrick Hodge (Mia; 13), DE Darren Howard (Phil; 12), S Mel Mitchell (NE; 13), LB T.J. Slaughter (SF; 10), RB Antowain Smith (Hou; 16), RB Anthony Thomas (Buff; 4).

Also played with Saints in '05—CB Fred Booker (12 games), QB Aaron Brooks (13), WR Az-Zahir Hakim (12), TE Lamont Hall (16), G Kendyl Jacox (15), LB Ron McKinnon (16), TE Shad Meier (1), S Sideeq Shabazz (2).

2006 FIRST-YEAR ROSTER

Name	Pos.	Ht.	Wt.	Birthdate	College	Hometown	How Acq.
Bienemann, Troy	TE	6-4	258	2/19/83	Washington State	Mountain View, Calif.	FA
Boykin, McKinley	DT	6-1	289	3/24/83	Mississippi	Bessemer, Ala.	FA
Branch, Jamaal	RB	5-11	230	1/30/81	Colgate	New Hampton, N.H.	FA
Bush, Reggie	RB	6-0	203	3/2/85	Southern California	Spring Valley, Calif.	D1
Colston, Marques	WR	6-4	231	6/5/83	Hofstra	Harrisburg, Pa.	D7b
Davis, Tommy	DE	6-2	257	10/18/82	North Carolina	Dudley, N.C.	FA
Eugene, Bruce	QB	6-0	268	6/20/82	Grambling State	New Orleans, La.	FA
Evans, Jahri	G	6-4	318	8/22/83	Bloomsburg	Philadelphia, Pa.	D4
Harper, Roman	S	6-1	200	12/11/82	Alabama	Prattville, Ala.	D2
Hass, Mike	WR	6-1	209	1/2/83	Oregon State	Tualatin, Ore.	D6a
Hoffmann, Augie (1)	G	6-2	315	2/23/81	Boston College	Park Ridge, N.J.	FA
Hudson, Ray	RB	5-9	191	12/31/80	Alabama	Bonifay, Fla.	FA
Hughes, Connor	K	5-10	172	10/4/83	Virginia	Williamsburg, Pa.	FA
Iwuchukwu, Bobby	LB	6-2	246	8/1/83	Purdue	Arlington, Texas	FA
Jones, Jamal (1)	WR	5-11	205	4/24/81	North Carolina A&T	Washington, D.C.	FA
Joseph, Keith (1)	RB	6-2	223	12/9/81	Texas A&M	Houston, Texas	FA
Kuale, E.J.	LB	6-2	232	6/22/83	Louisiana State	Daytona Beach, Fla.	FA
Lay, Josh	CB	6-1	197	9/8/82	Pittsburgh	Aliquippa, Pa.	D6b
Mason, Grant	CB	6-0	192	8/18/83	Michigan	Pontiac, Mich.	FA
Matha, Pascal	C	6-4	315	2/4/81	Eastern Illinois	Voorburg, Netherlands	FA
Moore, Chris	LB	6-1	235	8/12/82	East Carolina	Havelock, N.C.	FA
Moore, Lance (1)	WR	5-9	177	8/31/83	Toledo	Westerville, Ohio	FA
Ninkovich, Rob	DE	6-2	252	2/1/84	Purdue	New Lenox, Ill.	D5
Phillips, Anwar	CB	6-0	187	10/25/82	Penn State	Germantown, Md.	FA
Rabe, Russel (1)	LB	6-2	228	6/21/82	Minnesota-Duluth	Lake Holcombe, Wis.	FA
Schurman, Nate (1)	FB	6-2	247	11/8/81	Southwest Missouri State	St. Joseph, Mo.	FA
Strief, Zach	T	6-7	349	9/22/83	Northwestern	Milford, Ohio	D7a
Thomas, Levon (1)	WR	6-1	201	7/7/83	Georgia Tech	College Park, Ga.	FA
Villarreal, Brandon	DT	6-1	289	6/1/83	Purdue	Allen, Texas	FA
Weatherford, Steve	P	6-3	215	12/17/82	Illinois	Terre Haute, Ind.	FA
Williams, Ray	CB	6-1	205	11/11/83	Purdue	Scotch Plains, N.J.	FA

The term NFL Rookie is defined as a player who is in his first season of professional football and has not been on the roster of another professional football team for any regular-season or postseason games. A Rookie is designated by an "R" on NFL rosters. Players who have been active in another professional football league or players who have NFL experience, including either preseason training camp or being on an Active List or Inactive List, or on Reserve/Injured or Reserve/Physically Unable to Perform for fewer than six regular-season games, are termed NFL First-Year Players. An NFL First-Year Player is designated by a "1" on NFL rosters. Thereafter, a player is credited with an additional year of experience for each season in which he accumulates six games on the Active List or Inactive List, or on Reserve/Injured or Reserve/Physically Unable to Perform.

Log on to www.neworleanssaints.com for an up-to-date roster.

COACHING STAFF

Head Coach,
Sean Payton

Pro Career: Named the fourteenth head coach in Saints history on Jan. 18, 2006. Arrives in New Orleans following a three-year stint with Dallas Cowboys, serving as the assistant head coach/passing game coordinator in 2005 after spending his first two seasons as assistant head coach/quarterbacks. Considered one of the NFL's brightest offensive minds, he has led a resurgence in his unit's productivity at each career stop. Additional experience includes four years with the New York Giants (1999-2002), the last three seasons as offensive coordinator. Also previously worked for the Philadelphia Eagles (1997-98) as quarterbacks coach. Career record: 0-0.

Background: Earned a degree in communications at Eastern Illinois, where he departed with a school-record 10,665 passing yards, the third-highest total in NCAA Division I-AA history. A three-time All-American, Payton had brief playing stops with Chicago of the Arena Football League, the Ottawa Rough Riders of the Canadian Football League and the Chicago Bears in 1987. Inducted into the Eastern Illinois Hall of Fame in 2000, Payton entered the NFL after two coaching stints at San Diego State (1988-89, 1992-93) around a stop at Indiana State (1990-91). He also was quarterbacks coach/co-offensive coordinator at Miami (Ohio) from 1994-95.

Personal: Born Dec. 29, 1963 in San Mateo, Calif. and raised in Naperville, Ill, Payton and his wife, Beth, have a daughter, Meghan, and a son, Connor Thomas.

ASSISTANT COACHES

Dennis Allen, asst. defensive line; born Sept. 22, 1972, Atlanta. Safety Texas A&M 1992-95. No pro playing experience. College coach: Texas A&M 1996-99, Tulsa 2000-01. Pro coach: Atlanta Falcons 2002-05, joined Saints in 2006.

Adam Bailey, asst. strength and conditioning; born March 30, 1976, Tyler, Texas. Attended Louisville. No college or pro playing experience. College coach: Texas 1996-1997, Louisville 1998-1999, Auburn 2000-2001, Missouri 2002-2003. Pro coach: New Orleans VooDoo (AFL) 2004-2005, joined Saints in 2005.

John Bonamego, special teams coordinator; born Aug. 14, 1963, Waynesboro, Pa. Wide receiver/quarterback Central Michigan 1985-86. No pro playing experience. College coach: Maine 1988-1991, Lehigh, 1992, Army 1993-98. Pro coach: Jacksonville Jaguars 1999-2002, Green Bay Packers 2003-05, joined Saints 2006.

Pete Carmichael Jr., quarterbacks; born October 6, 1971, Farmingham, Mass. Attended Boston College. No college or pro playing experience. College coach: New Hampshire 1994, Louisiana Tech 1995-99. Pro coach: Cleveland Browns 2000, Washington Redskins 2001, San Diego Chargers 2002-05, joined Saints in 2006.

Dan Dalrymple, head strength and conditioning; born Aug. 26, 1965, Cleveland. Offensive lineman Miami (Ohio) 1983-86. No pro playing experience. College coach: Miami (Ohio) 1983-86. Pro coach: Joined Saints in 2006.

Gary Gibbs, defensive coordinator; born Aug. 13, 1952, Beaumont, Texas. Linebacker Oklahoma, 1972-75. No pro playing experience. College coach: Oklahoma 1975-1994 (head coach 1989-1994), Georgia 2000, Louisiana State 2001. Pro coach: Dallas Cowboys 2002-04, joined Saints in 2006.

Tom Hayes, defensive backs; born March 26, 1949, Keokuk, Iowa. Defensive back Iowa 1967-1971. No pro playing experience. College coach: Coe College 1973, Iowa 1977-78, Cal State-Fullerton 1979, UCLA 1980-88, Texas A&M 1989, Oklahoma 1990-94, Kansas 2001, Stanford 2005. Pro coach: Washington Redskins 1995-2000, joined Saints in 2006.

George Henshaw, senior assistant/running backs; born Jan. 22, 1948, Richmond, Va. Defensive tackle West Virginia 1967-69. No pro playing experience. College coach: West Virginia 1970-75, Florida State 1976-1982, Alabama 1983-86, Tulsa 1987 (head coach). Pro coach: Denver Broncos 1988-1992, New York Giants 1993-96, Tennessee Oilers 1997-98, Tennessee Titans 1999-2005, joined Saints in 2006.

Marion Hobby, defensive line; born November 7, 1966, Birmingham, Ala. Defensive end Tennessee 1985-89. Pro defensive end New England Patriots 1990-92. College coach: Tennessee-Martin 1995, Southwestern Louisiana 1996-97, Tennessee 1998, Mississippi 1999-2004, Clemson 2005. Pro coach: Joined Saints in 2006.

Curtis Johnson, wide receivers; born November 5, 1961, New Orleans. Wide receiver Idaho 1979-1983. No pro playing experience. College coach: Idaho 1987-88, San Diego State 1989-93, Southern Methodist 1994, California 1995, Miami 1996-2005. Pro coach: Joined Saints in 2006.

Terry Malone, tight ends; born February 26, 1960, Buffalo. Tight end Holy Cross 1978-1982. No pro playing experience. College coach: Arizona 1983-84, Holy Cross 1985, Bowling Green 1986-1995, Boston College 1996, Michigan 1997-2005. Pro coach: Joined Saints in 2006.

Doug Marrone, offensive coordinator/offensive line, born July 25, 1964, Bronx, N.Y. Offensive lineman Syracuse 1983-85. Pro offensive lineman Miami Dolphins 1987, New Orleans Saints 1989, London Monarchs (NFLE) 1992. College coach: Cortland College 1992, U.S. Coast Guard Academy 1993, Northeastern 1994, Georgia Tech 1995-99, Georgia 2000, Tennessee 2001. Pro coach: New York Jets 2002-05, joined Saints in 2006.

Greg McMahon, asst. special teams, born Jan. 2, 1960, Rantoul, Ill. Defensive back Eastern Illinois 1978-81. College coach: Eastern Illinois 1982, Minnesota 1983-84, North Alabama 1985-87, Southern Illinois 1988, Valdosta State 1989, Nevada Las-Vegas 1990-91, Illinois 1992-2004, East Carolina 2005. Pro coach: Joined Saints in 2006.

John Morton, offensive assistant/passing game; born Sept. 24, 1969, Rochester Hills, Mich. Wide receiver Western Michigan 1991-92. Pro wide receiver Toronto Argonauts (CFL) 1995-96, Frankfurt Galaxy (World League) 1997. College coach: San Diego 2005. Pro coach: Oakland Raiders 2002-04, joined Saints in 2006.

Tony Oden, defensive assistant/secondary; born June 30, 1973, Cleveland. Linebacker Baldwin-Wallace College 1991-1995. No pro playing experience. College coach: Millersville (Penn.) 1996, Boston College 1997, Army 1998-99, East Carolina 2000-02, Eastern Michigan 2003. Pro coach: Houston Texans 2004-05, joined Saints in 2006.

Joe Vitt, asst. head coach/linebackers, born August 23, 1954, Syracuse, N.Y. Linebacker Towson State 1974-78. No pro playing experience. Pro coach: Baltimore Colts 1979-1981, Seattle Seahawks 1982-1991, Los Angeles Rams 1992-94, Philadelphia Eagles 1995-98, Green Bay Packers 1999, Kansas City Chiefs 2000-03, St. Louis Rams 2004-05 (head coach, final 11 games of 2005), joined Saints in 2006.

National Football Conference
East Division
Team Colors: Blue, Red, and White
Giants Stadium
East Rutherford, New Jersey 07073
Telephone: (201) 935-8111

2006 SCHEDULE
PRESEASON

Aug. 11	at Baltimore	8:00
Aug. 17	**Kansas City**	8:00
Aug. 25	at New York Jets	8:00
TBD	**New England**	TBD

REGULAR SEASON

Sep. 10	**Indianapolis**	8:15
Sep. 17	at Philadelphia	1:00
Sep. 24	at Seattle	1:15
Oct. 1	Open Date	
Oct. 8	**Washington**	1:00
Oct. 15	at Atlanta	1:00
Oct. 23	at Dallas (Mon.)	7:30
Oct. 29	**Tampa Bay**	1:00
Nov. 5	**Houston**	1:00
Nov. 12	**Chicago**	1:00
Nov. 20	at Jacksonville (Mon.)	8:30
Nov. 26	at Tennessee	12:00
Dec. 3	**Dallas**	1:00
Dec. 10	at Carolina	1:00
Dec. 17	**Philadelphia**	1:00
Dec. 24	**New Orleans**	1:00
Dec. 30	at Washington (Sat.)	8:00

Stadium: Giants Stadium (opened in 1976)
 • **Capacity:** 80,242
  East Rutherford, New Jersey
  07073
Playing Surface: FieldTurf
Training Camp: University at Albany
   1400 Washington Avenue
   Albany, New York 12222

GIANTS STADIUM

CLUB OFFICIALS
President/CEO: John Mara
Chairman/EVP: Steve Tisch
Executive Vice President and Chief
  Operating Officer/General Counsel:
  John K. Mara, Esq.
Treasurer: Jonathan Tisch
Senior Vice President-General Manager:
  Ernie Accorsi
Vice President-Player Evalutions:
  Chris Mara
Vice President-Chief Financial Officer:
  Christine Procops
Vice President-Marketing: Rusty Hawley
Vice President-Medical Services:
  Ronnie Barnes
Vice-President-Communications:
  Pat Hanlon
Assistant General Manager:
  Kevin Abrams
Director of Player Personnel: Jerry Reese
Director of Pro Player Personnel:
  David Gettleman
Assistant Director of Pro Player
  Personnel: Ken Sternfeld
Director of College Scouting: Jerry Shay
Director of Research and Development:
  Raymond J. Walsh, Jr.
Director of Player Development:
  Charles Way
Director of Marketing Partnerships:
  Glenn Todd
Pro Personnel Assistants: Tom Polifroni,
  Matthew Shauger
Director of Promotions: Frank Mara
Ticket Manager: John Gorman
Director of Administration: Jim Phelan
Controller: Steven Hamrahi
Director of Community Relations:
  Allison Stangeby
Director of Creative Services:
  Doug Murphy
Director of Public Relations:
  Peter John-Baptiste
Assistant Director of Communications:
  Avis Roper
Head Athletic Trainer: Ronnie Barnes
Assistant Athletic Trainers:
  John Johnson, Steve Kennelly,
  Byron Hansen
Equipment Manager: Ed Wagner, Jr.
Assistant Equipment Managers:
  Joseph Skiba, Ed Skiba, Tim Slaman
Video Director: Dave Maltese
Assistant Video Directors:
  Carmen Pizzano, Ed Triggs
Assistant Director of Community
  Relations: Ethan Medley
Broadcast Production Manager:
  Stephen Venditti
Director of Information Technology:
  Jon Berger
Director of Marketing Services & Youth
  Programs: Beth Roche

COACHING HISTORY
(604-514-33)
Records include postseason games

1925	Bob Folwell	8-4-0
1926	Joe Alexander	8-4-1
1927-28	Earl Potteiger	15-8-3
1929-1930	LeRoy Andrews*	24-5-1
1930	Benny Friedman-Steve Owen	2-0-0
1931-1953	Steve Owen	153-108-17
1954-1960	Jim Lee Howell	55-29-4
1961-68	Allie Sherman	57-51-4
1969-1973	Alex Webster	29-40-1
1974-76	Bill Arnsparger**	7-28-0
1976-78	John McVay	14-23-0
1979-1982	Ray Perkins	24-35-0
1983-1990	Bill Parcells	85-52-1
1991-92	Ray Handley	14-18-0
1993-96	Dan Reeves	32-34-0
1997-2003	Jim Fassel	60-56-1
2004-05	Tom Coughlin	17-16-0

*Released after 15 games in 1930
**Released after seven games in 1976

ATTENDANCE
Home 628,527 Away 524,145
Total 1,152,672
Single-game home record,
  78,907 (9/15/03)
Single-season home record,
  629,874 (2004)

2006 DRAFT CHOICES

Round	Name	Pos.	College
1	Mathias Kiwanuka	DE	Boston College
2	Sinorice Moss	WR	Miami
3	Gerris Wilkinson	LB	Georgia Tech
4	Barry Cofield	DT	Northwestern
	Guy Whimper	T	East Carolina
5	Charlie Peprah	DB	Alabama
7	Gerrick McPhearson	DB	Maryland

2005 TEAM RECORD
PRESEASON (3-1)

Date	Result	Opponent
8/13	L 14-17	at Cleveland
8/20	W 27-21	Carolina
8/26	W 15-14	N.Y. Jets
9/1	W 27-3	at New England

REGULAR SEASON (11-5)

Date	Result	Opponent	Att.
9/11	W 42-19	Arizona	78,387
9/19	W 27-10	at New Orleans	68,031
9/25	L 23-45	at San Diego	65,373
10/2	W 44-24	St. Louis	78,453
10/16	L 13-16	at Dallas (OT)	62,278
10/23	W 24-23	Denver	78,516
10/30	W 36-0	Washington	78,630
11/6	W 24-6	at San Francisco	63,820
11/13	L 21-24	Minnesota	78,637
11/20	W 27-17	Philadelphia	78,626
11/27	L 21-24	at Seattle (OT)	67,102
12/4	W 17-10	Dallas	78,645
12/11	W 26-23	at Philadelphia (OT)	67,443
12/17	W 27-17	Kansas City	78,625
12/24	L 20-35	at Washington	90,477
12/31	W 30-21	at Oakland	44,594

(OT) Overtime

POSTSEASON (0-1)

Date	Result	Opponent	
1/8	L 0-23	Carolina	79,378

SCORE BY PERIODS

Giants	84	136	84	115	3	—	422
Opponents	55	95	95	63	6	—	314

2005 TEAM STATISTICS

	Giants	Opp.
Total First Downs	312	302
Rushing	106	83
Passing	172	189
Penalty	34	30
3rd Down: Made/Att	90/227	94/236
3rd Down Pct.	39.6	39.8
4th Down: Made/Att	6/13	6/12
4th Down Pct.	46.2	50.0
Possession Avg.	30:26	29:34
Total Net Yards	5,787	5,240
Avg. Per Game	361.7	327.5
Total Plays	1,055	1,049
Avg. Per Play	5.5	5.0
Net Yards Rushing	2,209	1,656
Avg. Per Game	138.1	103.5
Total Rushes	469	428
Net Yards Passing	3,578	3,584
Avg. Per Game	223.6	224.0
Sacked/Yards Lost	28/184	41/268
Gross Yards	3,762	3,852
Att./Completions	558/294	580/329
Completion Pct.	52.7	56.7
Had Intercepted	17	17
Punts/Average	73/42.1	88/41.5
Net Punting Avg.	73/37.0	88/35.7
Penalties/Yards	143/1115	136/1180
Fumbles/Ball Lost	17/8	29/20
Touchdowns	45	36
Rushing	17	12
Passing	24	20
Returns	4	4

2005 INDIVIDUAL STATISTICS

PASSING

	Att.	Comp.	Yds.	Pct.	TD	Int.	Tkld.	Rate
Manning	557	294	3,762	52.8	24	17	28/184	75.9
Barber	1	0	0	0.0	0	0	0/0	39.6
Giants	558	294	3,762	52.7	24	17	28/184	75.7
Opponents	580	329	3,852	56.7	20	17	41/268	76.3

SCORING

	TD R	TD P	TD Rt	PAT	FG	Saf	PTS
Feely	0	0	0	43/43	35/42	0	148
Barber	9	2	0	0/0	0/0	0	68
Shockey	0	7	0	0/0	0/0	0	44
Burress	0	7	0	0/0	0/0	0	42
Jacobs	7	0	0	0/0	0/0	0	42
Toomer	0	7	0	0/0	0/0	0	42
Blackburn	0	0	1	0/0	0/0	0	6
Manning	1	0	0	0/0	0/0	0	6
Morton	0	0	1	0/0	0/0	0	6
Pierce	0	0	1	0/0	0/0	0	6
Ponder	0	0	1	0/0	0/0	0	6
Tyree	0	1	0	0/0	0/0	0	6
Giants	17	24	4	43/43	35/42	0	422
Opponents	12	20	4	35/35	21/30	0	314

2-Pt. Conversions: Barber, Shockey.
Giants 2-2, Opponents 0-1.

RUSHING

	No.	Yds	Avg	LG	TD
Barber	357	1,860	5.2	95t	9
Ward	35	123	3.5	12	0
Jacobs	38	99	2.6	21	7
Manning	29	80	2.8	14	1
Carter	6	46	7.7	22	0
Ponder	1	4	4.0	4	0
Cloud	1	0	0.0	0	0
Hasselbeck	2	-3	-1.5	-1	0
Giants	469	2,209	4.7	95t	17
Opponents	428	1,656	3.9	62	12

RECEIVING

	No.	Yds	Avg	LG	TD
Burress	76	1,214	16.0	78t	7
Shockey	65	891	13.7	59	7
Toomer	60	684	11.4	37	7
Barber	54	530	9.8	48	2
Finn	13	98	7.5	15	0
Carter	10	186	18.6	44	0
Shiancoe	8	91	11.4	17	0
Tyree	5	52	10.4	18	1
Ward	2	13	6.5	8	0
Berton	1	3	13.0	3	0
Giants	294	3,762	12.8	78t	24
Opponents	329	3,852	11.7	72t	20

INTERCEPTIONS

	No.	Yds	Avg	LG	TD
Alexander	4	45	11.3	24	0
Pierce	2	41	20.5	24	0
Wilson	2	36	18.0	19	0
Williams	2	34	17.0	34	0
Butler	2	16	8.0	16	0
F. Walker	1	71	71.0	71	0
Torbor	1	37	37.0	37	0
Blackburn	1	31	31.0	31t	1
Deloatch	1	20	20.0	20	0
Emmons	1	6	6.0	6	0
W. Allen	0	17	—	17	0
Giants	17	354	20.8	71	1
Opponents	17	302	17.8	92t	2

PUNTING

	No.	Yds.	Avg.	In 20	LG
Feagles	73	3,070	42.1	26	56
Giants	73	3,070	42.1	26	56
Opponents	88	3,651	41.5	30	61

PUNT RETURNS

	Ret	FC	Yds	Avg	LG	TD
Morton	47	16	453	9.6	58	1
Blackburn	1	0	0	0.0	0	0
Butler	1	0	0	0.0	0	0
Giants	49	16	453	9.2	58	1
Opponents	36	15	309	8.6	71t	1

KICKOFF RETURNS

	No.	Yds	Avg	LG	TD
Ponder	35	905	25.9	95t	1
Morton	24	559	23.3	41	0
Jacobs	2	58	29.0	33	0
Shiancoe	1	5	5.0	5	0
K. Allen	1	2	2.0	2	0
Giants	63	1,529	24.3	95t	1
Opponents	85	1,867	22.0	86t	1

FIELD GOALS

	1-19	20-29	30-39	40-49	50+
Feely	0/0	11/13	13/14	8/10	3/5
Giants	0/0	11/13	13/14	8/10	3/5
Opponents	1/1	6/7	4/6	8/14	2/2

SACKS

	No.
Umenyiora	14.5
Strahan	11.5
Wilson	3.0
Pierce	2.5
K. Allen	2.0
Clancy	2.0
Joseph	2.0
Robbins	1.5
Greisen	1.0
Tuck	1.0
Giants	41.0
Opponents	28.0

RECORD HOLDERS
INDIVIDUAL RECORDS—CAREER

Category	Name	Performance
Rushing (Yds.)	Tiki Barber, 1997-2005	8,787
Passing (Yds.)	Phil Simms, 1979-1993	33,462
Passing (TDs)	Phil Simms, 1979-1993	199
Receiving (No.)	Amani Toomer, 1996-2005	530
Receiving (Yds.)	Amani Toomer, 1996-2005	7,797
Interceptions	Emlen Tunnell, 1948-1958	74
Punting (Avg.)	Don Chandler, 1956-1964	43.8
Punt Return (Avg.)	Ward Cuff, 1941-45	12.1
Kickoff Return (Avg.)	Rocky Thompson, 1971-73	27.2
Field Goals	Pete Gogolak, 1966-1974	126
Touchdowns (Tot.)	Frank Gifford, 1952-1964	78
Points	Pete Gogolak, 1966-1974	646

INDIVIDUAL RECORDS—SINGLE SEASON

Category	Name	Performance
Rushing (Yds.)	Tiki Barber, 2005	1,860
Passing (Yds.)	Kerry Collins, 2002	4,073
Passing (TDs)	Y.A. Tittle, 1963	36
Receiving (No.)	Amani Toomer, 2002	82
Receiving (Yds.)	Amani Toomer, 2002	1,343
Interceptions	Otto Schnellbacher, 1951	11
	Jim Patton, 1958	11
Punting (Avg.)	Don Chandler, 1959	46.6
Punt Return (Avg.)	Merle Hapes, 1942	15.5
Kickoff Return (Avg.)	John Salscheider, 1949	31.6
Field Goals	Ali Haji-Sheikh, 1983	35
	Jay Feely, 2005	35
Touchdowns (Tot.)	Joe Morris, 1985	21
Points	Jay Feely, 2005	148

INDIVIDUAL RECORDS—SINGLE GAME

Category	Name	Performance
Rushing (Yds.)	Tiki Barber, 12-17-05	220
Passing (Yds.)	Phil Simms, 10-13-85	513
Passing (TDs)	Y.A. Tittle, 10-28-62	*7
Receiving (No.)	Tiki Barber, 1-2-00	13
Receiving (Yds.)	Del Shofner, 10-28-62	269
Interceptions	Many times	3
	Last time by Terry Kinard, 9-20-87	
Field Goals	Joe Danelo, 10-18-81	6
Touchdowns (Tot.)	Ron Johnson, 10-2-72	4
	Earnest Gray, 9-7-80	4
	Rodney Hampton, 9-24-95	4
Points	Ron Johnson, 10-2-72	24
	Earnest Gray, 9-7-80	24
	Rodney Hampton, 9-24-95	24

*NFL Record

2006 VETERAN ROSTER

No.	Name	Pos.	Ht.	Wt.	Birthdate	NFL Exp.	College	Hometown	How Acq.	'05 Games/ Starts
55	Arrington, LaVar	LB	6-3	255	6/20/78	7	Penn State	Pittsburgh, Pa.	FA-'06	13/8*
95	Awasom, Adrian	DE	6-5	275	10/25/83	2	North Texas	Fort Bend, Texas	FA-'05	5/0
21	Barber, Tiki	RB	5-10	200	4/7/75	10	Virginia	Roanoke, Va.	D2-'97	16/16
33	Bell, Jason	CB	6-0	186	4/1/78	6	UCLA	Long Beach, Calif.	UFA(Hou)-'06	16/0*
57	Blackburn, Chase	LB	6-3	247	6/10/83	2	Akron	Marysville, Ohio	FA-'05	15/2
17	Burress, Plaxico	WR	6-5	226	8/12/77	7	Michigan State	Virginia Beach, Va.	UFA(Pitt)-'05	16/15
37	Butler, James	S	6-3	210	9/7/82	2	Georgia Tech	Climax, Ga.	FA-'05	16/1
84	Carter, Tim	WR	6-0	200	9/21/79	5	Auburn	Lakewood, Fla.	D2-'02	15/1
39	Deloatch, Curtis	CB	6-2	217	10/4/81	3	North Carolina A&T	Murfreesboro, N.C.	FA-'04	16/13
47	Demps, Will	S	6-0	205	11/7/79	5	San Diego State	Palmdale, Calif.	UFA(Balt)-'06	11/11*
66	Diehl, David	G	6-5	315	9/15/80	4	Illinois	Oak Lawn, Ill.	D5-'03	16/16
	Dorsch, Travis	P/K	6-6	221	9/4/79	2	Purdue	Bozeman, Mont.	FA-'06	0*
99	Duckett, Damane	DT	6-6	300	1/21/81	3	East Carolina	Lexington, N.C.	FA-'04	8/0
51	Emmons, Carlos	LB	6-5	250	9/3/73	11	Arkansas State	Greenwood, Miss.	UFA(Phil)-'04	9/8
18	Feagles, Jeff	P	6-1	215	3/7/66	19	Miami	Phoenix, Ariz.	UFA(Sea)-'03	16/0
2	Feely, Jay	K	5-10	206	5/23/76	5	Michigan	Odessa, Fla.	UFA(Atl)-'05	16/0
20	Finn, Jim	FB	6-0	245	12/9/76	7	Pennsylvania	Fair Lawn, N.J.	UFA(Ind)-'03	16/13
26	Harris, Quentin	S	6-1	213	1/26/77	5	Syracuse	Wilkes-Barre, Pa.	UFA(Ariz)-'06	16/0*
8	Hasselbeck, Tim	QB	6-1	211	4/6/78	5	Boston College	Westwood, Mass.	W(Wash)-'05	2/0
27	Jacobs, Brandon	RB	6-4	256	7/6/82	2	Southern Illinois	Napoleanville, La.	D4-'05	16/0
94	Joseph, William	DT	6-5	315	9/3/79	4	Miami	Miami, Fla.	D1-'03	10/10
61	Kelly, Lewis	G/T	6-4	306	4/21/77	5	South Carolina State	Lithonia, Ga.	FA-'05	1/0
83	Kranchick, Matt	TE	6-7	260	12/13/79	3	Penn State	Carlisle, Pa.	FA-'05	2/0
90	Kuehl, Ryan	LS	6-5	280	1/18/72	10	Virginia	Potomac, Md.	UFA(Cle)-'03	16/0
19	Lorenzen, Jared	QB	6-4	275	2/14/81	2	Kentucky	Ft. Thomas, Ky.	FA-'04	0*
19	Luke, Triandos	WR	5-10	195	12/24/81	2	Alabama	Phenix City, Ala.	FA-'06	0*
22	Madison, Sam	CB	5-11	180	4/23/74	10	Louisville	Tallahassee, Fla.	FA-'06	16/15*
10	Manning, Eli	QB	6-4	218	1/3/81	3	Mississippi	New Orleans, La.	T (SD)-'04	16/16
43	Mayes, Adrian	S	6-1	215	11/17/80	2	Louisiana State	Houston, Texas	FA-'06	3/0
67	McKenzie, Kareem	T	6-6	327	5/24/79	6	Penn State	Willingboro, N.J.	UFA(NYJ)-'05	14/14
25	McQuarters, R.W.	CB	5-10	195	12/21/76	9	Oklahoma State	Tulsa, OK	UFA(Det)-'06	16/11*
93	Moore, Eric	DE	6-4	268	2/28/81	2	Florida State	Pahokee, Fla.	D6-'05	8/0
29	Morton, Chad	RB	5-8	203	4/4/77	7	Southern California	Torrance, Calif.	FA-'05	16/0
60	O'Hara, Shaun	C/G	6-3	306	6/23/77	7	Rutgers	Hillsborough, N.J.	UFA(Cle)-'04	16/16
24	Peterson, Will	CB	6-0	200	6/15/79	6	Western Illinois	Uniontown, Pa.	D3-'01	2/2
77	Petitgout, Luke	T	6-6	310	6/16/76	8	Notre Dame	Georgetown, Del.	D1-'99	15/15
58	Pierce, Antonio	LB	6-1	240	10/26/78	6	Arizona	Ontario, Calif.	UFA(Wash)-'05	13/13
87	Ponder, Willie	WR	6-0	205	2/14/80	4	Southeast Missouri State	Tulsa, Okla.	D6a-'03	11/0
98	Robbins, Fred	DT	6-4	325	3/25/77	7	Wake Forest	Pensacola, Fla.	UFA(Minn)-'04	16/6
65	Ruegamer, Grey	G	6-4	305	6/11/76	8	Arizona State	Las Vegas, Nev.	UFA(GB)-'06	14/10*
69	Seubert, Rich	G	6-3	305	3/30/79	6	Western Illinois	Rozellville, Wis.	FA-'01	4/1
82	Shiancoe, Visanthe	TE	6-4	250	6/18/80	4	Morgan State	Laurel, Md.	D3-'03	16/5
80	Shockey, Jeremy	TE	6-5	253	8/18/80	5	Miami	Ada, Okla.	D1-'02	15/15
54	Short, Brandon	LB	6-3	253	7/11/77	7	Penn State	McKeesport, Pa.	FA-'06	16/15*
76	Snee, Chris	G	6-3	314	1/8/82	3	Boston College	Montrose, Pa.	D2-'04	16/16
92	Strahan, Michael	DE	6-5	275	11/21/71	14	Texas Southern	Westbury, Texas	D2-'93	16/16
86	Taylor, Jamaar	WR	6-0	197	2/25/81	3	Texas A&M	Mission, Texas	D6-'04	5/0
81	Toomer, Amani	WR	6-3	208	9/8/74	11	Michigan	Berkeley, Calif.	D2-'96	16/15
53	Torbor, Reggie	LB	6-2	254	1/25/81	3	Auburn	Baton Rouge, La.	D4-'04	14/8
91	Tuck, Justin	DE	6-5	268	3/29/83	2	Notre Dame	Kellyton, Ala.	D3-'05	14/1
85	Tyree, David	WR	6-0	205	1/3/80	4	Syracuse	Montclair, N.J.	D6c-'03	13/0
72	Umenyiora, Osi	DE	6-3	280	11/16/81	4	Troy State	Auburn, Ala.	D2-'03	16/16
41	Walker, Frank	CB	5-10	198	8/6/81	4	Tuskegee	Tuskegee, Ala.	D6b-'03	7/0
34	Ward, Derrick	RB	5-11	233	8/30/80	3	Ottawa	Moreno Valley, Calif.	FA-'04	14/0
23	Webster, Corey	CB	6-0	204	3/2/82	2	Louisiana State	Vacherie, La.	D2-'05	15/2
71	Whitfield, Bob	T	6-5	310	10/18/71	15	Stanford	Carson, Calif.	UFA(Jax)-'05	16/1
28	Wilson, Gibril	S	6-0	197	11/12/81	3	Tennessee	San Jose, Calif.	D5-'04	16/16

* Arrington played 13 games with Washington in '05; Bell played 16 games with Houston; Demps played 11 games with Baltimore; Dorsch last active with Cincinnati in '02; Harris played 16 games with Arizona; Lorenzen inactive for 16 games; Luke last active with Denver in '04; Madison played 16 games with Miami; McQuarters played 16 games with Detroit; G Grey Ruegamer played 13 games with Green Bay; Short played 16 games with Carolina.

Players lost through free agency (4): CB Will Allen (Mia; 16 games in '05), DT Kendrick Clancy (Ariz; 16), LB Nick Greisen (Jax; 16), S Shaun Williams (Car; 8).

Also played with Giants in '05—S Brent Alexander (16 games), DT Kenderick Allen (14), TE Sean Berton (14), CB Terrell Buckley (4), RB Mike Cloud (1), LB Barrett Green (1), LB Alonzo Jackson (8), LB Kevin Lewis (1), Roman Phifer (2), G Jason Whittle (14).

2006 FIRST-YEAR ROSTER

Name	Pos.	Ht.	Wt.	Birthdate	College	Hometown	How Acq.
Anderson, Sir Henry	DT	6-4	308	10/16/82	Oregon State	Oakland, Calif.	FA
Carroll, Thomas	DE	6-4	239	1/26/83	Miami	Lakewood, N.J.	FA
Cofield, Barry	DT	6-4	306	3/19/84	Northwestern	Cleveland Heights, Ohio	D4a
Coley, Kevis	LB	6-1	231	6/23/82	Southern Mississippi	Palatka, Fla.	FA
Coley, Trevis	S	6-1	227	6/23/82	Southern Mississippi	Palatka, Fla.	FA
Dockery, Kevin	CB	5-8	188	1/8/84	Mississippi State	Hernando, Miss.	FA
Evans, Willie	DE	6-1	269	3/5/84	Mississippi State	Waynesboro, Miss.	FA
Fletcher, Wade (1)	TE	6-5	243	4/30/82	Columbia	Denver, Colo.	FA-'05
Goddard, Na'Shan	G/T	6-5	315	4/23/83	South Carolina	Dayton, Ohio	FA
Green, Marcus	DT	6-1	285	9/27/83	Ohio State	Louisville, Ky.	FA
Hanoian, Greg (1)	FB	6-2	255	12/9/81	Syracuse	Providence, R.I.	FA
Jackson, Tony (1)	FB	6-2	266	7/5/82	Iowa	Ypsilanti, Mich.	FA
Jennings, Michael (1)	WR	5-11	175	9/7/79	Florida State	Jacksonville, Fla.	FA-'04
Johnson, Darcy	TE	6-5	252	2/11/83	Central Florida	Palatka, Fla.	FA
Kiwanuka, Mathias	DE	6-5	261	3/8/83	Boston College	Indianapolis, Ind.	D1
Lentz, Matthew	G	6-6	320	11/19/82	Michigan	Ortonville, Mich.	FA
Lewis, Jai	G/T	6-5	292	2/13/83	George Mason	Aberdeen, Md.	FA
Londot, Todd	G/T	6-5	301	4/4/83	Miami (Ohio)	Utica, Ohio	FA
McNeil, Nick (1)	LB	6-2	245	8/19/81	Western Carolina	Leland, N.C.	FA
McPhearson, Gerrick	CB	5-10	197	12/29/83	Maryland	Columbia, Md.	D7
Mix, Anthony	WR	6-4	235	1/20/83	Auburn	Bay Minette, Ala.	FA
Moss, Sinorice	WR	5-8	185	12/28/83	Miami	Miami, Fla.	D2
Peprah, Charles	S	5-11	202	2/24/83	Alabama	Plano, Texas	D5
Seawright, Jonas (1)	DT	6-6	312	4/12/82	North Carolina	Orangeburg, S.C.	FA-'05
Sims, James	RB	6-0	211	2/14/83	Washington	Las Vegas, Nev.	FA
Tella, Tony	G	6-4	306	12/5/82	Miami	Houston, Texas	FA
Underwood, E.J.	CB	6-1	185	8/4/83	Pikeville	Cincinatti, Ohio	FA
Void, Jerod	RB	6-0	220	1/29/83	Purdue	Clinton, Md.	FA
Whimper, Guy	T	6-5	302	5/21/83	East Carolina	Havelock, N.C.	D4b
Wilkinson, Gerris	LB	6-3	231	4/5/83	Georgia Tech	Oakland, Calif.	D3
Williams, Harry (1)	WR	6-2	184	8/10/82	Tuskegee	Birmingham, Ala.	FA

The term NFL Rookie is defined as a player who is in his first season of professional football and has not been on the roster of another professional football team for any regular-season or postseason games. A Rookie is designated by an "R" on NFL rosters. Players who have been active in another professional football league or players who have NFL experience, including either preseason training camp or being on an Active List or Inactive List, or on Reserve/Injured or Reserve/Physically Unable to Perform for fewer than six regular-season games, are termed NFL First-Year Players. An NFL First-Year Player is designated by a "1" on NFL rosters. Thereafter, a player is credited with an additional year of experience for each season in which he accumulates six games on the Active List or Inactive List, or on Reserve/Injured or Reserve/Physically Unable to Perform.

Log on to www.giants.com for an up-to-date roster.

COACHING STAFF
Head Coach,
Tom Coughlin
Pro Career: Was named the sixteenth head coach in Giants history on January 6, 2004. Coached the Giants to an 11-5 record, the NFC East title and the playoffs in 2005, his second season with the team. Coughlin previously spent eight years (1995-2002) with the Jacksonville Jaguars. Under Coughlin, the Jaguars had the most victories of any NFL expansion team in its first seven seasons. They were also the only expansion team in NFL history to advance to the playoffs four times in their first five seasons. Coughlin's team went 9-7 in 1996 and an NFL-best 14-2 in 1999, both times reaching the AFC Championship Game. Coughlin previously coached the Philadelphia Eagles (1984-85), Green Bay Packers (1986-87), and Giants (1988-1990). He was a member of the Giants' Super Bowl XXV champion coaching staff. Career record: 89-80.
Background: Served as head coach at Boston College (1991-93), where he posted a 21-13-1 record, and coached at Syracuse (1969, 1974-1980), Rochester Institute of Technology 1970-73 (head coach), and Boston College (1981-83). Played wingback for Syracuse (1965-67), with Larry Csonka and Floyd Little. Received Syracuse 1967 Orange Key Award as outstanding scholar athlete, and graduated with bachelor's and master's degree.
Personal: Born August 31, 1947, Waterloo, N.Y. Tom and his wife, Judy, have two daughters, Keli and Katie, two sons, Brian and Tim, a daughter-in-law, Andrea (Tim's wife), and two grandchildren, Emma Rose and Dylan.

ASSISTANT COACHES
Andy Barnett, asst. strength and conditioning; born January 12, 1960, Des Moines, Iowa. Attended Wyoming, Calgary. No college or pro playing experience. College coach: Wyoming 1988-1991, Calgary 1993-95, Olympic Training Center, Calgary 1995-2000, International Performance Institute 2000-2003. Pro coach: Joined Giants in 2004.
Andre Curtis, defensive assistant; born December 8, 1976, Richmond, Va. Linebacker Virginia Military Institute 1996-1999. No pro playing experience. College coach: Virginia Military Institute 2002-03, Georgia Southern 2004-05. Pro coach: Joined Giants in 2006.
John DeFilippo, offensive quality control; born April 12, 1978, Youngstown, Ohio. Quarterback James Madison 1996-99. No pro playing experience. College coach: Fordham 2000, Notre Dame 2001-02, Columbia 2003-04. Pro coach: Joined Giants in 2005.
Dave DeGuglielmo, asst. offensive line; born July 15, 1968, Cambridge, Mass. Attended Boston University. No college or pro playing experience. College coach: Boston College 1991-92, Boston

University 1993-96, Connecticut 1997-98, South Carolina 1999-2003. Pro coach: Joined Giants in 2004.
Pat Flaherty, offensive line; born April 27, 1956, Hanover, Pa. Center East Stroudsburg 1974-77. No pro playing experience. College coach: East Stroudsburg 1980-81, Penn State 1982-83, Rutgers 1984-1991, East Carolina 1992, Wake Forest 1993-98, Iowa 1999. Pro coach: Washington Redskins 2000, Chicago Bears 2001-03, joined Giants in 2004.
Kevin Gilbride, quarterbacks; born August 27, 1951, New Haven, Conn. Quarterback/tight end Southern Connecticut State 1971-73. No pro playing experience. College coach: Idaho State 1974-75, Tufts 1976-77, American International 1978-79. Southern Connecticut State 1980-84, East Carolina 1987-88. Pro coach: Ottawa Rough Riders (CFL) 1985-86, Houston Oilers 1989-1994, Jacksonville Jaguars 1995-96, San Diego Chargers 1997-98 (head coach), Pittsburgh Steelers 1999-2000, Buffalo Bills 2002-2003, joined Giants in 2004.
Peter Giunta, secondary/corners; born August 11, 1956, Salem, Mass. Running back/defensive back Northeastern 1974-77. No pro playing experience. College coach: Penn State 1981-83, Brown 1984-87, Lehigh 1988-1990. Pro coach: Philadelphia Eagles 1991-94, N.Y. Jets 1995-96, St. Louis Rams 1997-2000, Kansas City Chiefs 2001-2005, joined Giants in 2006.
John Hufnagel, offensive coordinator; born September 13, 1951, Pittsburgh. Quarterback Penn State 1969-1972. Pro quarterback Denver Broncos 1973-75, Calgary Stampeders (CFL) 1976-79, Saskatchewan Roughriders (CFL) 1980-83, 1987, Winnipeg Blue Bombers (CFL) 1984-86. Pro coach: Saskatchewan Roughriders (CFL) 1988, Calgary Stampeders (CFL) 1990-96, New Jersey Red Dogs (AFL) 1997-98, Cleveland Browns 1999-2000, Indianapolis Colts 2001, Jacksonville Jaguars 2002, New England Patriots 2003, joined Giants in 2004.
Jerald Ingram, running backs; born December 24, 1960, Dayton, Ohio. Fullback Michigan 1979-1983. College coach: Michigan 1984, Ball State 1985-1990, Boston College, 1991-93. Pro coach: Jacksonville Jaguars 1994-2002, joined Giants in 2004.
Tim Lewis, defensive coordinator; born December 18, 1961, Quakertown, Pa. Defensive back Pittsburgh 1979-1982. Pro cornerback Green Bay Packers 1983-86. College coach: Texas A&M 1987-88, Southern Methodist 1989-1992, Pittsburgh 1993-94. Pro coach: Pittsburgh Steelers 1995-2003, joined Giants in 2004.
David Merritt Sr., secondary/safeties; born September 8, 1971, Raleigh, N.C. Linebacker North Carolina State 1989-1992. Pro linebacker Miami Dolphins 1993, Arizona Cardinals 1993-96, Rhein

Fire (NFLE) 1997. College coach: Chattanooga 1997, Virginia Military Institute 1998-2000. Pro coach: New York Jets 2001-2003, joined Giants in 2004.
Jerry Palmieri, strength and conditioning; born October 30, 1958, Englewood, N.J. Attended Montclair State. No college or pro playing experience. College coach: North Carolina 1982-83, Oklahoma State 1984-86, Kansas State 1987-1992, Boston College 1993-94. Pro coach: Jacksonville Jaguars 1995-2002, New Orleans Saints 2003, joined Giants in 2004.
Michael Pope, tight ends; born March 15, 1942, Monroe, N.C. Quarterback Lenoir-Rhyne 1962-64. No pro playing experience. College coach: Florida State 1970-74, Texas Tech 1975-77, Mississippi 1978-1982. Pro coach: New York Giants 1983-1991, Cincinnati Bengals 1992-93, New England Patriots 1994-96, Washington Redskins 1997-99, re-joined Giants in 2000.
Tom Quinn, asst. special teams; born January 27, 1968, Pasadena, Calif. Linebacker Arizona 1986-1990. No pro playing experience. College coach; Davidson College 1991, James Madison 1992-94, Boston 1995, Holy Cross 1996-98, San Jose State 1999-01, Stanford 2002-05. Pro coach: Joined Giants in 2006.
Bill Sheridan, linebackers; born January 27, 1959, Detroit. Linebacker Grand Valley State 1979-1982. No pro playing experience. College coach: Michigan 1985-86, Maine 1987-88, Cincinnati 1989-1991, Army 1992-97, Michigan State 1998-2000, Notre Dame 2001, Michigan 2002-04. Pro coach. Joined Giants in 2005.
Mike Sullivan, wide receivers; born January 28, 1967, Santa Maria, Calif. Defensive back Army 1987-88. No pro playing experience. College coach: Mt. San Jacinto (Calif.) J.C. 1993, Humboldt State 1993-94, Army 1995-96, 1999-2000, Youngstown State 1997-98, Ohio 2001. Pro coach: Jacksonville Jaguars 2002-03, joined Giants 2004.
Mike Sweatman, special teams coordinator; born October 23, 1946, Kansas City, Mo. Linebacker Kansas 1964-67. Linebacker Quantico Marines 1969. College coach: Okinawa Devil Dogs 1970, Quantico Marines 1971-72, Kansas 1973-74, 1979-1982, Coffeyville (Kan.) C.C. 1975-76, Tulsa 1977-78, Tennessee 1983. Pro coach: Minnesota Vikings 1984, New York Giants 1985-1992, New England Patriots 1993-96, New York Jets 1997-2000, Chicago Bears 2001-2003, re-joined Giants in 2004.
Mike Waufle, defensive line; born June 27, 1954, Hornell, N.Y. U.S. Marines 1972-75. Defensive lineman Bakersfield (Calif.) J.C. 1975-76, Utah State 1977-78. No pro playing experience. College coach: Alfred 1979, Utah State 1980-84, Fresno State 1985-88, UCLA 1989, Oregon State 1990-91, California 1992-97. Pro coach: Oakland Raiders 1998-2003, joined Giants in 2004.

**National Football Conference
East Division**
Team Colors: Midnight Green, Silver, Black, and White
**NovaCare Complex
One NovaCare Way
Philadelphia, Pennsylvania 19145**
Telephone: (215) 463-2500

2006 SCHEDULE
PRESEASON
Aug. 6   vs. Oakland in Canton, OH..8:00
Aug. 10 **Cleveland** 7:30
Aug. 17 at Baltimore........................8:00
Aug. 25 **Pittsburgh**.........................8:00
TBD   at New York Jets ....TBD

REGULAR SEASON
Sept. 10 at Houston 12:00
Sept. 17 **N.Y. Giants**........................1:00
Sept. 24 at San Francisco.................1:15
Oct. 2   **Green Bay** (Mon.) 8:30
Oct. 8   **Dallas** 4:15
Oct. 15 at New Orleans................12:00
Oct. 22 at Tampa Bay 1:00
Oct. 29 **Jacksonville**......................1:00
Nov. 5   Open Date
Nov. 12 **Washington** 1:00
Nov. 19 **Tennessee** 1:00
Nov. 26 at Indianapolis 1:00
Dec. 4   **Carolina** (Mon.) 8:30
Dec. 10 at Washington 1:00
Dec. 17 at N.Y. Giants.....................1:00
Dec. 25 at Dallas (Mon.) 4:00
Dec. 31 **Atlanta**..............................1:00

Stadium: Lincoln Financial Field
        (opened in 2003)
        •**Capacity:** 68,400
        One Lincoln Financial Field Way
        Philadelphia, Pennsylvania 19148
Playing Surface: Natural Grass
Training Camp: Lehigh University
                Bethlehem, PA 18015

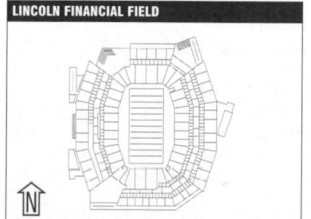

LINCOLN FINANCIAL FIELD

CLUB OFFICIALS
Chairman/Chief Executive Officer:
    Jeffrey Lurie
President: Joe Banner
Head Coach/Executive Vice President of
    Football Operations: Andy Reid
General Manager: Tom Heckert
Vice President of Player Personnel:
    Jason Licht
Senior Vice President of Business
    Operations: Mark Donovan
Senior Vice President/Chief Financial
    Officer: Don Smolenski
Vice President of Football Administration:
    Howie Roseman
Vice President of Sales and Service:
    Bill Manning
Vice President of Stadium Operations and
    Facility Management: Scott Jenkins
Executive Director of Eagles Youth
    Partnership: Sarah Martinez-Helfman
Director of Pro Personnel: Scott Cohen
Director of Football Media Relations:
    Derek Boyko
Assistant Director of Football Media
    Services: Rich Burg, Bob Lange
Senior Director of Marketing:
    Tim McDermott
Manager of Community Relations:
    Julie Dubin
Director of Human Resources:
    Eric Newman
Director of Stadium Operations:
    Dave Duernberger
Director, Broadcasting: Rob Alberino
Director of Events: Leonard Bonacci
Director of Ticket Operations:
    Laini Delawter
Director of Ticket Client Relations:
    Leo Carlin
Director of Merchandise:
    Steve Strawbridge
Travel Manager: Tracey Detweiler
Director of Team Security:
    Anthony (Butch) Buchanico
Director of Facility and Stadium Security:
    Victor Cooper
Head Athletic Trainer: Rick Burkholder
Asst. Athletic Trainers: Steve Condon,
    Chris Peduzzi
Video Director: Mike Dougherty
Head Equipment Manager: John Hatfield

COACHING HISTORY
(477-526-25)
Records include postseason games

Year	Coach	Record
1933-35	Lud Wray	9-21-1
1936-1940	Bert Bell	10-44-2
1941-1950	Earle (Greasy) Neale*	66-44-5
1951	Alvin (Bo) McMillin**	2-0-0
1951	Wayne Millner	2-8-0
1952-55	Jim Trimble	25-20-3
1956-57	Hugh Devore	7-16-1
1958-1960	Lawrence (Buck) Shaw	20-16-1
1961-63	Nick Skorich	15-24-3
1964-68	Joe Kuharich	28-41-1
1969-1971	Jerry Williams***	7-22-2
1971-72	Ed Khayat	8-15-2
1973-76	Mike McCormack	16-25-1
1976-1982	Dick Vermeil	57-51-0
1983-85	Marion Campbell****	17-29-1
1985	Fred Bruney	1-0-0
1986-1990	Buddy Ryan	43-38-1
1991-94	Rich Kotite	37-29-0
1995-98	Ray Rhodes	30-36-1
1999-2005	Andy Reid	77-47-0

*Co-coach with Walt Kiesling in Philadelphia-
        Pittsburgh merger in 1943
**Retired after two games in 1951
***Released after three games in 1971
****Released after 15 games in 1985

ATTENDANCE
Home 531,195   Away 559,316
Total 1,090,511
Single-game home record,
    72,111 (11/1/81)
Single-season home record,
    557,325 (1980)

2006 DRAFT CHOICES

Round	Name	Pos.	College
1	Brodrick Bunkley	DT	Florida State
2	Winston Justice	T	So. California
3	Chris Gocong	LB	Cal Poly
4	Max Jean-Gilles	G	Georgia
	Jason Avant	WR	Michigan
5	Jeremy Bloom	WR	Colorado
	Omar Gaither	LB	Tennessee
6	LaJuan Ramsey	DT	So. California

2005 TEAM RECORD

PRESEASON (2-2)

Date	Result	Opponent
8/15	L 31-38	at Pittsburgh
8/20	W 20-14	at Baltimore
8/26	W 27-17	Cincinnati
9/1	L 14-37	N.Y. Jets

REGULAR SEASON (6-10)

Date	Result	Opponent	Att.
9/12	L 10-14	at Atlanta	70,806
9/18	W 42-3	San Francisco	67,727
9/25	W 23-20	Oakland	67,735
10/2	W 37-31	at Kansas City	78,742
10/9	L 10-33	at Dallas	63,199
10/23	W 20-17	San Diego	67,747
10/30	L 21-49	at Denver	76,530
11/6	L 10-17	at Washington	90,298
11/14	L 20-21	Dallas	67,739
11/20	L 17-27	at N.Y. Giants	78,626
11/27	W 19-14	Green Bay	67,665
12/5	L 0-42	Seattle	67,637
12/11	L 23-26	N.Y. Giants (OT)	67,443
12/18	W 17-16	at St. Louis	65,382
12/24	L 21-27	at Arizona	44,723
1/1	L 20-31	Washington	67,700

(OT) Overtime

SCORE BY PERIODS

Eagles	62	88	81	79	0 —	310
Opponents	113	119	50	103	3 —	388

2005 TEAM STATISTICS

	Eagles	Opp.
Total First Downs	282	290
Rushing	73	91
Passing	182	171
Penalty	27	28
3rd Down: Made/Att	72/220	80/233
3rd Down Pct.	32.7	34.3
4th Down: Made/Att	3/12	7/11
4th Down Pct.	25.0	63.6
Possession Avg.	28:22	31:38
Total Net Yards	5,109	5,206
Avg. Per Game	319.3	325.4
Total Plays	1,027	1,038
Avg. Per Play	5.0	5.0
Net Yards Rushing	1432	1883
Avg. Per Game	89.5	117.7
Total Rushes	365	506
Net Yards Passing	3,677	3,323
Avg. Per Game	229.8	207.7
Sacked/Yards Lost	42/226	29/184
Gross Yards	3,903	3,507
Att./Completions	620/337	503/297
Completion Pct.	54.4	59.0
Had Intercepted	20	17
Punts/Average	100/40.7	104/41.9
Net Punting Avg.	100/37.0	104/35.7
Penalties/Yards	134/1130	112/910
Fumbles/Ball Lost	34/14	25/10
Touchdowns	35	46
Rushing	11	15
Passing	21	24
Returns	3	7

2005 INDIVIDUAL STATISTICS

PASSING	Att.	Comp.	Yds.	Pct.	TD	Int.	Tkld.	Rate
McNabb	357	211	2,507	59.1	16	9	19/112	85.0
McMahon	207	94	1,158	45.4	5	8	19/96	55.2
Detmer	56	32	238	57.1	0	3	3/15	45.1
Westbrook	0	0	0	—	0	0	1/3	—
Eagles	620	337	3,903	54.4	21	20	42/226	71.5
Opponents	503	297	3,507	59.0	24	17	29/184	82.2

	TD	TD	TD					
SCORING	R	P	Rt	PAT	FG	Saf	PTS	
Akers	0	0	0	23/23	16/22	0	71	
Westbrook	3	4	0	0/0	0/0	0	44	
Owens	0	6	0	0/0	0/0	0	36	
R. Brown	0	4	0	0/0	0/0	0	24	
France	0	0	0	5/5	6/7	0	23	
McMahon	3	0	0	0/0	0/0	0	18	
Moats	3	0	0	0/0	0/0	0	18	
Smith	0	3	0	0/0	0/0	0	18	
Bartrum	0	2	0	0/0	0/0	0	12	
S. Brown	0	0	2	0/0	0/0	0	12	
Gordon	1	0	0	0/0	0/0	0	6	
G. Lewis	0	1	0	0/0	0/0	0	6	
McMullen	0	1	0	0/0	0/0	0	6	
McNabb	1	0	0	0/0	0/0	0	6	
Ware	0	0	1	0/0	0/0	0	6	
Cortez	0	0	0	3/3	0/0	0	3	
Simoneau	0	0	0	1/2	0/0	0	1	
Eagles	11	21	3	32/33	22/29	0	310	
Opponents	15	24	7	46/46	22/27	0	388	

2-Pt. Conversions: Westbrook.
Eagles 1-2, Opponents 0-0.

RUSHING	No.	Yds	Avg	LG	TD
Westbrook	156	617	4.0	31	3
Moats	55	278	5.1	59t	3
Gordon	54	182	3.4	11	1
McMahon	34	118	3.5	19	3
Mahe	20	87	4.4	13	0
Perry	16	74	4.6	11	0
McNabb	25	55	2.2	11	1
G. Lewis	2	13	6.5	8	0
R. Brown	1	5	5.0	5	0
Owens	1	2	2.0	2	0
Detmer	1	1	1.0	1	0
Eagles	365	1,432	3.9	59t	11
Opponents	506	1,883	3.7	67t	15

RECEIVING	No.	Yds	Avg	LG	TD
Smith	61	682	11.2	48	3
Westbrook	61	616	10.1	62	4
G. Lewis	48	561	11.7	34	1
Owens	47	763	16.2	91t	6
R. Brown	43	571	13.3	56t	4
McMullen	18	268	14.9	38	1
Parry	13	89	6.8	13	0
Mahe	12	68	5.7	12	0
Gordon	11	79	7.2	18	0
Spach	7	42	6.0	8	0
McCants	5	87	17.4	22	0
C. Lewis	5	64	12.8	17	0
Moats	4	7	1.8	9	0
Bartrum	2	6	3.0	3t	2
Eagles	337	3,903	11.6	91t	21
Opponents	297	3,507	11.8	61t	24

INTERCEPTIONS	No.	Yds	Avg	LG	TD
S. Brown	4	67	16.8	40t	1
Sheppard	3	72	24.0	34	0
Dawkins	3	24	8.0	24	0
Hood	3	17	5.7	17	0
M. Lewis	2	13	6.5	13	0
Trotter	1	2	2.0	2	0
D. Jones	1	0	0.0	0	0
Eagles	17	195	11.5	40t	1
Opponents	20	339	17.0	72t	4

PUNTING	No.	Yds.	Avg.	In 20	LG
Johnson	39	1,615	41.4	11	59
Landeta	34	1,483	43.6	7	56
Hodges	19	699	36.8	6	51
Murphy	7	275	39.3	1	44
Eagles	100	4,072	40.7	25	59
Opponents	104	4,361	41.9	27	62

PUNT RETURNS	Ret	FC	Yds	Avg	LG	TD
Wynn	22	10	110	5.0	27	0
Mahe	21	9	269	12.8	44	0
Westbrook	8	2	60	7.5	23	0
Sheppard	2	3	9	4.5	8	0
Eagles	53	24	448	8.5	44	0
Opponents	57	18	310	5.4	25	0

KICKOFF RETURNS	No.	Yds	Avg	LG	TD
Hood	38	900	23.7	53	0
Wynn	16	284	17.8	27	0
Perry	10	273	27.3	49	0
Gordon	3	64	21.3	25	0
Moats	2	26	13.0	15	0
Mahe	1	19	19.0	19	0
Patterson	1	12	12.0	12	0
Eagles	71	1,578	22.2	53	0
Opponents	67	1,416	21.1	96t	1

FIELD GOALS	1-19	20-29	30-39	40-49	50+
Akers	0/0	3/3	7/8	5/9	1/2
France	0/0	3/3	1/1	2/3	0/0
Eagles	0/0	6/6	8/9	7/12	1/2
Opponents	0/0	12/12	8/9	1/4	1/2

SACKS	No.
Kearse	7.5
Cole	5.0
Dawkins	3.5
Patterson	3.5
Walker	2.5
Kalu	2.0
S. Brown	1.0
M. Lewis	1.0
Rayburn	1.0
Sheppard	1.0
Trotter	1.0
Eagles	29.0
Opponents	42.0

RECORD HOLDERS
INDIVIDUAL RECORDS—CAREER

Category	Name	Performance
Rushing (Yds.)	Wilbert Montgomery, 1977-1984	6,538
Passing (Yds.)	Ron Jaworski, 1977-1986	26,963
Passing (TDs)	Ron Jaworski, 1977-1986	175
Receiving (No.)	Harold Carmichael, 1971-1983	589
Receiving (Yds.)	Harold Carmichael, 1971-1983	8,978
Interceptions	Bill Bradley, 1969-1976	34
	Eric Allen, 1988-1994	34
Punting (Avg.)	Joe Muha, 1946-1950	42.9
Punt Return (Avg.)	Ernie Steele, 1942-48	16.8
Kickoff Return (Avg.)	Steve Van Buren, 1944-1951	26.7
Field Goals	David Akers, 1999-2005	155
Touchdowns (Tot.)	Harold Carmichael, 1971-1983	79
Points	Bobby Walston, 1951-1962	881

INDIVIDUAL RECORDS—SINGLE SEASON

Category	Name	Performance
Rushing (Yds.)	Wilbert Montgomery, 1979	1,512
Passing (Yds.)	Donovan McNabb, 2004	3,875
Passing (TDs)	Sonny Jurgensen, 1961	32
Receiving (No.)	Irving Fryar, 1996	88
Receiving (Yds.)	Mike Quick, 1983	1,409
Interceptions	Bill Bradley, 1971	11
Punting (Avg.)	Joe Muha, 1948	47.2
Punt Return (Avg.)	Steve Van Buren, 1944	15.3
Kickoff Return (Avg.)	Al Nelson, 1972	29.1
Field Goals	Paul McFadden, 1984	30
	David Akers, 2002	30
Touchdowns (Tot.)	Steve Van Buren, 1945	18
Points	David Akers, 2002	133

INDIVIDUAL RECORDS—SINGLE GAME

Category	Name	Performance
Rushing (Yds.)	Steve Van Buren, 11-27-49	205
Passing (Yds.)	Donovan McNabb, 12-5-04	464
Passing (TDs)	Adrian Burk, 10-17-54	*7
Receiving (No.)	Don Looney, 12-1-40	14
Receiving (Yds.)	Tommy McDonald, 12-10-60	237
Interceptions	Russ Craft, 9-24-50	*4
Field Goals	Tom Dempsey, 11-12-72	6
Touchdowns (Tot.)	Many times	4
	Last time by Irving Fryar, 10-20-96	
Points	Bobby Walston, 10-17-54	25

*NFL Record

2006 VETERAN ROSTER

No.	Name	Pos.	Ht.	Wt.	Birthdate	NFL Exp.	College	Hometown	How Acq.	'05 Games/ Starts
2	Akers, David	K	5-10	200	12/9/74	8	Louisville	Lexington, Ky.	FA-'99	12/0
73	Andrews, Shawn	T/G	6-4	340	12/25/82	3	Arkansas	Camden, Ark.	D1-'04	16/16
76	Armstrong, Calvin	T	6-7	325	3/31/82	2	Washington State	Centralia, Wash.	D6-'05	0*
56	Barber, Shawn	LB	6-2	240	1/14/75	9	Richmond	Richmond, Va.	FA-'06	3/0*
88	Bartrum, Mike	TE/LS	6-4	245	6/23/70	13	Marshall	Pomeroy, Ohio	FA-'00	16/0
86	Brown, Reggie	WR	6-1	197	1/13/81	2	Georgia	Carrollton, Ga.	D2a-'05	16/11
24	Brown, Sheldon	CB	5-10	200	3/19/79	5	South Carolina	Ft. Lawn, S.C.	D2b-'02	16/16
28	Buckhalter, Correll	RB	6-0	222	10/6/78	6	Nebraska	Collins, Miss.	D4-'01	0*
61	Clarke, Adrien	G	6-5	330	3/26/81	3	Ohio State	Shaker Heights, Ohio	D7a-'04	14/4
58	Cole, Trent	LB/DE	6-3	270	10/5/82	2	Cincinnati	Xenia, Ohio	D5a-'05	15/7
37	Considine, Sean	S	6-0	212	10/28/81	2	Iowa	Byron, Ill.	D4a-'05	6/0
66	Darilek, Trey	G/C	6-5	310	4/23/81	3	Texas-El Paso	San Antonio, Texas	D4b-'04	15/0
20	Dawkins, Brian	S	6-0	210	10/13/73	11	Clemson	Jacksonville, Fla.	D2b-'96	16/16
10	Detmer, Koy	QB	6-1	195	7/5/73	10	Colorado	San Antonio, Texas	D7a-'97	16/0
50	#Ena, Justin	LB	6-3	247	11/20/77	5	Brigham Young	Shelton, Wash.	FA-'05	6/0
19	Ford, Carl	WR	6-0	182	10/8/80	3	Toledo	Monroe, Mich.	W(Chi)-'05	10/0*
63	Fraley, Hank	C/G	6-2	300	9/21/77	7	Robert Morris	Gaithersburg, Md.	W(Pitt)-'00	8/8
84	Gaffney, Jabar	WR	6-1	205	12/1/80	5	Florida	Jacksonville, Fla.	UFA(Hou)-'06	16/13*
7	Garcia, Jeff	QB	6-1	200	2/24/70	8	San Jose State	Gilroy, Calif.	UFA(Det)-'06	6/5*
25	#Gordon, Lamar	RB	6-1	223	1/7/80	5	North Dakota State	Milwaukee, Wis.	W(Mia)-'05	14/4
96	Grasmanis, Paul	DT	6-3	298	8/2/74	11	Notre Dame	Jenison, Mich.	UFA(Den)-'00	2/0
79	Herremans, Todd	T	6-6	321	10/13/82	2	Saginaw Valley State	Ravenna, Mich.	D4b-'05	4/4
29	Hood, Roderick	CB	5-11	196	10/3/81	4	Auburn	Columbus, Ga.	FA-'03	16/6
90	Howard, Darren	DE	6-3	275	11/19/76	7	Kansas State	St. Petersburg, Fla.	UFA(NO)-'06	12/9*
67	Jackson, Jamaal	C/G	6-4	330	5/8/80	3	Delaware State	Miami, Fla.	FA-'03	8/8
94	Jasper, Ed	DT	6-2	295	1/18/73	10	Texas A&M	Troup, Texas	UFA(Oak)-'06	15/1*
16	Jenkins, Justin	WR	6-0	207	12/10/80	2	Mississippi State	Pearl, Miss.	FA-'04	0*
8	Johnson, Dirk	P	6-0	205	6/1/75	4	Northern Colorado	Montrose, Colo.	FA-'03	7/0
55	Jones, Dhani	LB	6-1	240	2/22/78	7	Michigan	Potomac, Md.	UFA(NYG)-'04	16/16
93	Kearse, Jevon	DE	6-4	265	9/3/76	8	Florida	Ft. Myers, Fla.	UFA(Tenn)-'04	15/15
7	#Landeta, Sean	P	6-0	215	1/6/62	21	Towson State	Towson, Md.	FA-'05	5/0
89	#Lewis, Chad	TE	6-6	252	10/5/71	9	Brigham Young	Orem, Utah	FA-'05	8/0
83	Lewis, Greg	WR	6-0	180	2/12/80	4	Illinois	Matteson, Ill.	FA-'03	16/16
32	Lewis, Michael	S	6-1	222	4/29/80	5	Colorado	Richmond, Texas	D2a-'02	16/16
34	Mahe, Reno	RB	5-10	212	6/3/80	4	Brigham Young	Salt Lake City, Utah	FA-'03	15/0
65	Marshall, Keyonta	DT	6-1	325	8/13/81	2	Grand Valley State	Saginaw, Mich.	D7a-'05	1/0
85	McCants, Darnerien	WR	6-3	215	8/1/78	5	Delaware State	Gambrills, Md.	FA-'05	12/0
51	McCoy, Matt	LB	5-11	230	10/14/82	2	San Diego State	Tustin, Calif.	D2b-'05	4/0
95	McDougle, Jerome	DE	6-2	264	12/15/78	4	Miami	Pompano Beach, Fla.	D1-'03	0*
80	McMullen, Billy	WR	6-4	215	3/8/80	4	Virginia	Richmond, Va.	D3-'03	16/0
5	McNabb, Donovan	QB	6-2	240	11/25/76	8	Syracuse	Chicago, Ill.	D1-'99	9/9
27	Mikell, Quintin	S	5-10	206	9/16/80	4	Boise State	Eugene, Ore.	FA-'03	16/0
23	Moats, Ryan	RB	5-8	210	12/17/82	2	Louisiana Tech	Dallas, Texas	D3-'05	7/1
49	Parry, Josh	FB	6-2	250	4/5/78	3	San Jose State	Sonora, Calif.	FA-'04	16/11
98	Patterson, Mike	DT	6-0	292	9/1/83	2	Southern California	Los Alamitos, Calif.	D1-'05	16/7
35	Perry, Bruce	RB	5-10	200	3/22/81	2	Maryland	Philadelphia, Pa.	D7b-'04	2/1
87	Pinkston, Todd	WR	6-3	180	4/23/77	7	Southern Mississippi	Forest, Miss.	D2a-'00	0*
91	Rayburn, Sam	DT	6-3	303	10/20/80	4	Tulsa	Chickasha, Okla.	FA-'03	16/2
30	Reed, J.R.	S	5-11	202	2/11/82	3	South Florida	Tampa, Fla.	D4a-'04	0*
50	Richmond, Greg	LB	6-1	235	7/15/81	2	Oklahoma State	Oklahoma City, Okla.	FA-'04	0*
59	Roper, Dedrick	LB	6-2	245	7/31/81	2	Northwood	Milpitas, Calif.	FA-'05	6/0
69	Runyan, Jon	T	6-7	330	11/27/73	11	Michigan	Flint, Mich.	UFA(Tenn)-'00	16/16
89	Schobel, Matt	TE	6-5	255	11/4/78	5	Texas Christian	Columbus, Texas	UFA(Cin)-'06	16/1*
26	Sheppard, Lito	CB	5-10	194	4/8/81	5	Florida	Jacksonville, Fla.	D1-'02	10/10
52	Short, Jason	LB	6-4	254	7/15/78	3	Eastern Michigan	Painesville, Ohio	FA-'03	6/0
53	Simoneau, Mark	LB	6-0	245	1/16/77	7	Kansas State	Smith Center, Kan.	T(Atl)-'03	16/0
82	Smith, L.J.	TE	6-3	258	5/13/80	4	Rutgers	Highland Park, N.J.	D2-'03	16/16
41	Spach, Stephen	TE	6-4	250	7/18/82	2	Fresno State	Clovis, Calif.	FA-'05	13/1
33	Strickland, Donald	CB	5-10	187	11/24/80	4	Colorado	San Francisco, Calif.	FA-'05	4/0*
38	Tapeh, Thomas	FB	6-1	243	3/28/80	3	Minnesota	St. Paul, Minn.	D5-'04	0*
75	Thomas, Juqua	DE	6-2	250	5/15/78	6	Oklahoma State	Houston, Texas	FA-'05	16/1
72	Thomas, William	T	6-7	335	11/20/74	9	Florida State	Deland, Fla.	D1-'98	10/10
54	Trotter, Jeremiah	LB	6-1	262	1/20/77	8	Stephen F. Austin	Hooks, Texas	FA-'04	15/15
97	Walker, Darwin	DT	6-3	294	6/15/77	7	Tennessee	Walterboro, S.C.	W(Ariz)-'00	13/12
21	Ware, Matt	CB	6-2	210	12/2/82	3	UCLA	Los Angeles, Calif.	D3-'04	16/0

No.	Name	Pos.	Ht.	Wt.	Birthdate	NFL Exp.	College	Hometown	How Acq.	'05 Games/ Starts
36	Westbrook, Brian	RB	5-8	203	9/2/79	5	Villanova	Ft. Washington, Md.	D3-'02	12/12
31	Wynn, Dexter	CB	5-9	177	2/25/81	3	Colorado State	Colorado Springs, Colo.	D6b-'04	10/0
71	Young, Scott	G	6-4	312	7/15/81	2	Brigham Young	Salt Lake City, Utah	D5b-'05	0*

* Armstrong did not play in 3 games; Barber played 3 games with Kansas City in '05; Buckhalter missed '05 season because of injury; Ford played 10 games with Chicago; Gaffney played 16 games with Houston; Garcia played 6 games with Detroit; Howard played 6 games with New Orleans; Jasper played 15 games with Oakland; Jenkins missed '05 season because of injury; McDougle missed '05 season because of injury; Pinkston missed '05 season because of injury; Reed missed '05 season because of injury; Richmond missed '05 season because of injury; Schobel played 16 games with Cincinnati; Strickland played 1 game with Indianapolis in '05, Tapeh missed '05 season because of injury; Young inactive for 6 games.

\# Unrestricted free agent; subject to developments.

Traded—G/T Artis Hicks (14 games in '05) to Minnesota; DT Hollis Thomas (16) to New Orleans.

Players lost through free agency (3): LB Keith Adams (Car; 16 games in '05), S Jack Brewer (Ariz; 6), DE N.D. Kalu (Hou; 15).

Also played with Eagles in '05—K Jose Cortez (4 games), K Todd France (3), P Reggie Hodges (3), DE Alonzo Jackson (1), LB Mike Labinjo (5), QB Mike McMahon (9), LB Zeke Moreno (4), P Nick Murphy (1), WR Terrell Owens (7).

2006 FIRST-YEAR ROSTER

Name	Pos.	Ht.	Wt.	Birthdate	College	Hometown	How Acq.
Avant, Jason	WR	6-0	212	4/20/83	Michigan	Chicago, Ill.	D4b
Bloom, Jeremy	WR	5-9	180	4/2/82	Colorado	Loveland, Colo.	D5a
Bunkley, Brodrick	DT	6-2	306	11/23/83	Florida State	Tampa, Fla.	D1
Canonico, Eddie (1)	CB	6-1	180	9/17/78	Sacramento State	Las Vegas, Nev.	FA-'05
Caudill, Jeremy (1)	DT	6-2	318	11/22/81	Kentucky	Prestonburg, Ky.	FA
Chang, Timmy (1)	QB	6-1	207	10/9/81	Hawaii	Honolulu, Hawaii	FA
Cochrane, E.J.	K	5-11	196	10/31/80	Montana State	Philadelphia, Pa.	FA
Cole, Nick	C	6-0	350	7/28/84	New Mexico State	Lawton, Okla.	FA
Crafts, Jonas (1)	TE	6-3	250	12/29/81	Texas-El Paso	San Antonio, Texas	FA-'05
Daniels, Torrance	LB	6-3	248	12/27/81	Harding	Clarendon, Ark.	FA
Davis, Jason	FB	5-10	240	11/2/83	Illinois	St. Louis, Mo.	FA
Gaither, Omar	LB	6-1	234	3/18/84	Tennessee	Charlotte, N.C.	D5b
Gasperson, Michael (1)	WR	6-4	220	6/10/82	San Diego	Monterey, Calif.	FA-'05
Gocong, Chris	LB	6-2	263	11/16/83	Cal Poly	Carpinteria, Calif.	D3
Hodges, Reggie (1)	P	6-0	226	4/18/84	Ball State	Champaign, Ill.	FA-'05
Jean-Gilles, Max	G	6-3	358	11/19/83	Georgia	Miami, Fla.	D4a
Justice, Winston	T	6-6	320	9/14/84	Southern California	Long Beach, Calif.	D2
Loo, Darrell (1)	DE	6-4	273	6/28/82	Florida	Kirkwood, Mo.	FA-'05
McCoy, Pat	T	6-5	328	12/14/80	West Texas	Fairfield, Calif.	FA
Outlaw, J.J.	WR	5-9	187	2/8/84	Villanova	Columbia, Md.	FA
Peoples, Corey (1)	S	6-2	212	7/23/81	South Carolina	Bishopville, S.C.	FA-'05
Pinderhughes, Brandon (1)	S	5-11	195	8/21/82	Nebraska-Omaha	St. Paul, Minn.	FA
Ramsey, LaJuan	DT	6-3	291	3/19/84	Southern California	Compton, Calif.	D6
Rowan, Levonne	CB	5-11	198	11/2/82	Wisconsin	Erie, Pa.	FA
Sampy, Bill	WR	5-11	192	5/10/83	Louisiana-Lafayette	Carencro, La	FA
Skinner, Dejuan	T	6-5	349	11/30/79	West Texas	Starkville, Miss.	FA
Thorn, Andy (1)	TE	6-5	250	2/4/82	Northern Iowa	Warren, Mich.	FA-'05
Ware, Scott	S	6-1	218	5/5/85	Southern California	Santa Rosa, Calif.	FA

The term NFL Rookie is defined as a player who is in his first season of professional football and has not been on the roster of another professional football team for any regular-season or postseason games. A Rookie is designated by an "R" on NFL rosters. Players who have been active in another professional football league or players who have NFL experience, including either preseason training camp or being on an Active List or Inactive List, or on Reserve/Injured or Reserve/Physically Unable to Perform for fewer than six regular-season games, are termed NFL First-Year Players. An NFL First-Year Player is designated by a "1" on NFL rosters. Thereafter, a player is credited with an additional year of experience for each season in which he accumulates six games on the Active List or Inactive List, or on Reserve/Injured or Reserve/Physically Unable to Perform.

Log on to www.philadelphiaeagles.com for an up-to-date roster.

COACHING STAFF

Head Coach/Executive Vice President of Football Operations, Andy Reid

Pro Career: Reid has earned NFL coach of the year honors twice, compiled the highest win total (77) and winning percentage (.621) in team history, captured four consecutive division titles and four trips to the NFC Championship game (2001-04) for the first time in franchise history, and registered the most playoff wins (7) in club history. In his 14-year NFL coaching career, Reid's teams have made the playoffs 11 times (16-10 record in those games). He has coached in the Super Bowl three times, in the NFC Championship game seven times, and in the Pro Bowl four times. Reid became the twentieth head coach in franchise history on January 11, 1999, and was promoted to head coach/executive vice president of football operations in 2001. He was named NFL coach of the year in 2000 and 2002. He joined the Eagles after a seven-year stint as an assistant coach with Green Bay (1992-98) under Mike Holmgren. With Green Bay, Reid helped the Packers earn a Super Bowl XXXI victory over the New England Patriots. Career record: 77-47.

Background: Coached at Brigham Young (1982), San Francisco State (1983-85), Northern Arizona (1986), Texas-El Paso (1987-88), and Missouri (1989-1991). Reid first met Holmgren, who was a member of BYU's coaching staff, when Reid was an offensive tackle and guard on three Cougar Holiday Bowl teams. Reid graduated with a bachelor's degree in physical education. He also received a master's degree in professional leadership in physical education and athletics.

Personal: Born in Los Angeles on March 19, 1958, Reid and his wife Tammy have five children—Garrett, Britt, Crosby, Drew Ann, and Spencer.

ASSISTANT COACHES

Juan Castillo, offensive line; born October 8, 1959, Port Isabel, Texas. Linebacker Texas A&I (now Texas A&M-Kingsville) 1978-1980. Pro linebacker San Antonio Gunslingers (USFL) 1984-85. College coach: Texas A&I/Texas A&M-Kingsville 1982-85, 1990-94. Pro coach: Joined Eagles in 1995.

David Culley, wide receivers; born September 17, 1955, Sparta, Tenn. Quarterback Vanderbilt 1973-77. No pro playing experience. College coach: Austin Peay 1978, Vanderbilt 1979-1981, Middle Tennessee State 1982, Tennessee-Chattanooga 1983, Western Kentucky 1984, Southwestern Louisiana 1985-88, Texas-El Paso 1989-1990, Texas A&M 1991-93. Pro coach: Tampa Bay Buccaneers 1994-95, Pittsburgh Steelers 1996-1998, joined Eagles in 1999.

John Harbaugh, special teams; born September 23, 1962, Perrysburg, Ohio. Defensive back Miami (Ohio) 1980-83. No pro playing experience. College coach: Western Michigan 1984-86, Pittsburgh 1987, Morehead State 1988, Cincinnati 1989-1996, Indiana 1997. Pro coach: Joined Eagles in 1998.

Pete Jenkins, defensive line; born August 27, 1941, Macon, Ga. Linebacker/nose tackle Western Carolina 1963-64. No pro playing experience. College coach: Troy State 1968-1970, South Carolina 1971-74, Southern Mississippi 1975-77, Oklahoma State 1978, Florida 1979, Louisiana State 1980-1990, 2000-02, Mississippi State 1991-94, Auburn 1995-1999. Pro coach: Joined Eagles in 2006.

Jim Johnson, defensive coordinator; born May 26, 1941, Maywood, Ill. Quarterback Missouri 1959-1962. Pro tight end Buffalo Bills 1963-64. College coach: Missouri Southern 1967-68 (head coach), Drake 1969-1972, Indiana 1973-76, Notre Dame 1977-1980. Pro coach: Oklahoma Outlaws (USFL) 1984, Jacksonville Bulls (USFL) 1985, Phoenix Cardinals 1986-1993, Indianapolis Colts 1994-97, Seattle Seahawks 1998, joined Eagles in 1999.

Sean McDermott, secondary/safeties; born March 21, 1974, Omaha, Neb. Safety William & Mary 1994-97. No pro playing experience. College coach: William & Mary 1998. Pro coach: Joined Eagles in 1998.

Tom Melvin, tight ends; born October 1, 1961, Redwood City, Calif. Offensive lineman San Francisco State 1982-83. No pro playing experience. College coach: San Francisco State 1984-85, Northern Arizona 1986-87, California-Santa Barbara 1988-1990, Occidental College 1991-98. Pro coach: Joined Eagles in 1999.

Marty Mornhinweg, asst. head coach/offensive coordinator; born March 29, 1962, Edmond, Okla.. Quarterback Montana 1981-84. Pro quarterback Denver Dynamite (AFL) 1987. College coach: Montana 1985, Texas-El Paso 1986-87, Northern Arizona 1988, 1994, Southeast Missouri State 1989-1990, Missouri 1991-93. Pro coach: Green Bay Packers 1995-96, San Francisco 49ers 1997-2000, Detroit Lions 2001-02 (head coach), joined Eagles in 2003.

Mike Reed, defensive assistant/quality control; born August 16, 1972, Wilmington, Del. Defensive back Boston College 1991-94. Pro defensive back Carolina Panthers 1995-96, Frankfurt Galaxy (NFL Europe) 1998-99. College coach: Richmond 2000-02. Pro coach: Joined Eagles in 2003.

Ryan Segrest, special teams quality control; born May 20, 1973, Waycross, Ga. Tackle Alabama 1991-93. No pro playing experience. College coach: Alabama 1994-97, Auburn 1997-98, Southeast Missouri State 1999-2001, Samford 2002-05. Pro coach: Joined Eagles in 2006.

Bill Shuey, offensive assistant/quality control; born October 5, 1974, Bethlehem, Pa. Attended Slippery Rock. No college or pro playing experience. Pro coach: Joined Eagles in 2003.

Pat Shurmur, quarterbacks; born April 14, 1965, Dearborn Heights, Mich. Center Michigan State 1983-87. No pro playing experience. College coach: Michigan State 1988-1997, Stanford 1998. Pro coach: Joined Eagles in 1999.

Steve Spagnuolo, linebackers; born December 21, 1959, Witinsville, Mass. Wide receiver Springfield College 1979-1981. No pro playing experience. College coach: Massachusetts 1982-83, Lafayette 1984-86, Connecticut 1987-1991, Maine 1993, Rutgers 1994-95, Bowling Green 1996-97. Pro coach: Barcelona Dragons (World League) 1992, Frankfurt Galaxy (NFLE) 1998, joined Eagles in 1999.

Trent Walters, secondary; born November 20. 1943, Knoxville, Tenn. Defensive back Indiana 1963-65. Pro defensive back Edmonton Eskimos (CFL) 1966-67. College coach: Indiana 1968-1971, Louisiana 1972, 1986-1990, Indiana 1973-1980, Washington 1981-83, Pittsburgh 1985, Texas A&M 1991-93, Notre Dame 2002-03. Pro coach: Cincinnati Bengals 1984, Minnesota Vikings 1994-2001, joined Eagles in 2004.

Ted Williams, running backs; born November 17, 1943, Lyons, Texas. Attended Cal Poly-Pomona. No college or pro playing experience. College coach: UCLA 1980-89, Washington State 1991-93, Arizona 1994. Pro coach: Joined Eagles in 1995.

Mike Wolf, strength and conditioning; born May 15, 1966, Allentown, Pa. Center Penn State 1983-87. No pro playing experience. College coach: Vanderbilt 1988-89, Lehigh 1990, Penn State 1991. Pro coach: Minnesota Vikings 1992-94, joined Eagles in 1995.

National Football Conference
West Division
Team Colors: New Century Gold,
　　　　Millennium Blue, and White
One Rams Way
St. Louis, Missouri 63045
Telephone: (314) 982-7267

2006 SCHEDULE
PRESEASON
Aug. 10	Indianapolis	7:00
Aug. 19	Houston	7:00
Aug. 26	at Kansas City	7:30
Aug. 31	at Miami	7:30

REGULAR SEASON
Sept. 10	**Denver**	12:00
Sept. 17	at San Francisco	1:05
Sept. 24	at Arizona	1:15
Oct. 1	**Detroit**	3:05
Oct. 8	at Green Bay	12:00
Oct. 15	**Seattle**	12:00
Oct. 22	Open Date	
Oct. 29	at San Diego	1:05
Nov. 5	**Kansas City**	12:00
Nov. 12	at Seattle	1:15
Nov. 19	at Carolina	1:00
Nov. 26	**San Francisco**	12:00
Dec. 3	**Arizona**	12:00
Dec. 11	**Chicago** (Mon.)	7:30
Dec. 17	at Oakland	1:15
Dec. 24	**Washington**	12:00
Dec. 31	at Minnesota	12:00

Stadium: Edward Jones Dome
　　　　(opened in 1995)
　　　　• **Capacity:** 66,000
　　　　701 Convention Plaza
　　　　St. Louis, Missouri 63101
Playing Surface: FieldTurf
Training Camp: Rams Park
　　　　Training Facility
　　　　St. Louis, Missouri 63045

EDWARD JONES DOME

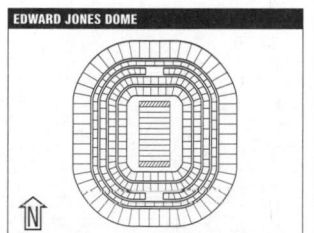

CLUB OFFICIALS
Owner/Chariman: Georgia Frontiere
Owner/Vice Chairman: Stan Kronke
President: John Shaw
President, Football Operations:
　　Jay Zygmunt
Executive Vice President and General
　　Counsel: Bob Wallace
Treasurer: Jeff Brewer
Vice President, Finance: Adrian Bracy
General Manager: Charlie Armey
Vice President, Sales and Marketing:
　　Phil Thomas
Vice President, Business Administration
Vice President, Ticket Operations:
　　Michael T. Naughton
Vice President, Operations: John Oswald
Vice President, Public Relations:
　　Rick Smith
Director, Football Administration:
　　Samir Suleiman
Head Trainer: Jim Anderson
Assistant Trainers: Dake Walden,
　　Ron DuBuque, James Lomax
Equipment Manager: Todd Hewitt
Scouts: Dave Boller, Dick Daniels,
　　Luke Driscoll, Mel Foels,
　　John Mancini, Tom Marino,
　　Dave Razzano

COACHING HISTORY
Cleveland 1937-1945,
Los Angeles 1946-1994
(509-457-20)
Records include postseason games
1937-38	Hugo Bezdek*	1-13-0
1938	Art Lewis	4-4-0
1939-1942	Earl (Dutch) Clark	16-26-2
1944	Aldo (Buff) Donelli	4-6-0
1945-46	Adam Walsh	16-5-1
1947	Bob Snyder	6-6-0
1948-49	Clark Shaughnessy	14-8-3
1950-52	Joe Stydahar**	19-9-0
1952-54	Hamp Pool	23-11-2
1955-59	Sid Gillman	28-32-1
1960-62	Bob Waterfield***	9-24-1
1962-65	Harland Svare	14-31-3
1966-1970	George Allen	49-19-4
1971-72	Tommy Prothro	14-12-2
1973-77	Chuck Knox	57-20-1
1978-1982	Ray Malavasi	43-36-0
1983-1991	John Robinson	79-74-0
1992-94	Chuck Knox	15-33-0
1995-96	Rich Brooks	13-19-0
1997-99	Dick Vermeil	25-26-0
2000-05	Mike Martz****	56-36-0
2005	Joe Vitt	4-7-0

　* Released after three games in 1938
　** Resigned after one game in 1952
　*** Resigned after eight games in 1962
　**** Took medical leave after five games in 2005

ATTENDANCE
Home 510,718　　　　Away 498,587
Total 1,009,305
Single-game home record,
　　66,273 (12/10/00)
Single-season home record,
　　520,926 (1999)

2006 DRAFT CHOICES
Round	Name	Pos.	College
1	Tye Hill	DB	Clemson
2	Joe Klopfenstein	TE	Colorado
3	Claude Wroten	DT	Louisiana State
	Jon Alston	LB	Stanford
	Dominique Byrd	TE	So. California
4	Victor Adeyanju	DE	Indiana
5	Marques Hagans	WR	Virginia
7	Tim McGarigle	LB	Northwestern
	Mark Setterstrom	G	Minnesota
	Tony Palmer	G	Missouri

ST. LOUIS RAMS

2005 TEAM RECORD
PRESEASON (3-1)

Date	Result	Opponent
8/12	W 17-13	Chicago
8/21	L 21-36	at San Diego
8/29	W 37-13	at Detroit
9/2	W 27-23	Kansas City

REGULAR SEASON (6-10)

Date	Result	Opponent	Att.
9/11	L 25-28	at San Francisco	67,918
9/18	W 17-12	at Arizona	45,160
9/25	W 31-27	Tennessee	65,835
10/2	L 24-44	at N.Y. Giants	78,453
10/9	L 31-37	Seattle	65,707
10/17	L 28-45	at Indianapolis	57,307
10/23	W 28-17	New Orleans	64,586
10/30	W 24-21	Jacksonville	65,251
11/13	L 16-31	at Seattle	67,192
11/20	L 28-38	Arizona	65,750
11/27	W 33-27	at Houston (OT)	70,010
12/4	L 9-24	Washington	65,701
12/11	L 13-27	at Minnesota	64,005
12/18	L 16-17	Philadelphia	65,382
12/24	L 20-24	San Francisco	65,473
1/1	W 20-10	at Dallas	63,131

(OT) Overtime

SCORE BY PERIODS

Rams	67	123	54	113	6	—	363
Opponents	110	124	92	103	0	—	429

2005 TEAM STATISTICS

	Rams	Opp.
Total First Downs	314	321
Rushing	82	116
Passing	209	178
Penalty	23	27
3rd Down: Made/Att	77/211	80/199
3rd Down Pct.	36.5	40.2
4th Down: Made/Att	14/21	2/9
4th Down Pct.	66.7	22.2
Possession Avg.	30:14	29:46
Total Net Yards	5,571	5,602
Avg. Per Game	348.2	350.1
Total Plays	1,025	1,007
Avg. Per Play	5.4	5.6
Net Yards Rushing	1,535	2,178
Avg. Per Game	95.9	136.1
Total Rushes	380	459
Net Yards Passing	4,036	3,424
Avg. Per Game	252.3	214.0
Sacked/Yards Lost	46/315	41/195
Gross Yards	4,351	3,619
Att./Completions	599/392	507/314
Completion Pct.	65.4	61.9
Had Intercepted	24	13
Punts/Average	73/41.2	68/40.0
Net Punting Avg.	73/33.9	68/36.0
Penalties/Yards	131/941	117/1066
Fumbles/Ball Lost	24/13	27/14
Touchdowns	40	50
Rushing	13	22
Passing	23	26
Returns	4	2

2005 INDIVIDUAL STATISTICS

PASSING	Att.	Comp.	Yds.	Pct.	TD	Int.	Tkld.	Rate
Bulger	287	192	2,297	66.9	14	9	26/188	94.4
Martin	177	124	1,277	70.1	5	7	11/78	83.5
Fitzpatrick	135	76	777	56.3	4	8	9/49	58.2
Rams	599	392	4,351	65.4	23	24	46/315	83.0
Opponents	507	314	3,619	61.9	26	13	41/195	89.8

SCORING	TD R	TD P	TD Rt	PAT	FG	Saf	PTS
Wilkins	0	0	0	36/36	27/31	0	117
S. Jackson	8	2	0	0/0	0/0	0	60
Holt	0	9	0	0/0	0/0	0	54
Curtis	1	6	0	0/0	0/0	0	42
Bruce	0	3	0	0/0	0/0	0	18
Fitzpatrick	2	0	0	0/0	0/0	0	12
M. Faulk	0	1	0	0/0	0/0	0	8
Harris	1	0	0	0/0	0/0	0	8
Archuleta	0	0	1	0/0	0/0	0	6
Cason	1	0	0	0/0	0/0	0	6
Chillar	0	0	1	0/0	0/0	0	6
Cleeland	0	1	0	0/0	0/0	0	6
Furrey	0	0	1	0/0	0/0	0	6
Johnson	0	0	1	0/0	0/0	0	6
Manumaleuna	0	1	0	0/0	0/0	0	6
Rams	13	23	4	36/36	27/31	1	363
Opponents	22	26	2	49/49	26/33	0	429

2-Pt. Conversions: M. Faulk, Harris.
Rams 2-3, Opponents 1-1.

RUSHING	No.	Yds	Avg	LG	TD
S. Jackson	254	1,046	4.1	51	8
M. Faulk	65	292	4.5	20	0
Cason	10	65	6.5	14	1
Fitzpatrick	14	64	4.6	14t	2
Bulger	9	29	3.2	9	0
Harris	13	21	1.6	10	1
McDonald	1	7	7.0	7	0
Martin	9	6	0.7	9	0
Curtis	1	5	5.0	5t	1
Holt	1	2	2.0	2	0
Manumaleuna	1	2	2.0	2	0
Hedgecock	1	0	0.0	0	0
Wilkins	1	-4	-4.0	-4	0
Rams	380	1,535	4.0	51	13
Opponents	459	2,178	4.7	73t	22

RECEIVING	No.	Yds	Avg	LG	TD
Holt	102	1,331	13.0	44	9
Curtis	60	801	13.4	83t	6
McDonald	46	523	11.4	31	0
M. Faulk	44	291	6.6	18	1
S. Jackson	43	320	7.4	27	2
Bruce	36	525	14.6	46t	3
Looker	23	237	10.3	23	0
Manumaleuna	13	129	9.9	33	1
Hedgecock	9	69	7.7	15	0
Cleeland	5	17	3.4	9t	1
Harris	4	34	8.5	17	0
R. Williams	3	21	7.0	12	0
Robinson	1	28	28.0	28	0
Thompson	1	13	13.0	13	0
Cason	1	11	11.0	11	0
Bulger	1	1	1.0	1	0
Rams	392	4,351	11.1	83t	23
Opponents	314	3,619	11.5	52	26

INTERCEPTIONS	No.	Yds	Avg	LG	TD
Furrey	4	143	35.8	67t	1
Tinoisamoa	2	35	17.5	20	0
Groce	2	0	0.0	0	0
Archuleta	1	85	85.0	85t	1
Atogwe	1	42	42.0	42	0
Hawthorne	1	24	24.0	24	0
Ivy	1	19	19.0	19	0
Coakley	1	16	16.0	16	0
Rams	13	364	28.0	85t	2
Opponents	24	268	11.2	37	0

PUNTING	No.	Yds.	Avg.	In 20	LG
Barker	50	2,137	42.7	13	63
Hodges	22	836	38.0	3	55
Wilkins	1	35	35.0	0	35
Rams	73	3,008	41.2	16	63
Opponents	68	2,722	40.0	18	55

PUNT RETURNS	Ret	FC	Yds	Avg	LG	TD
Looker	8	2	69	8.6	17	0
McDonald	8	6	33	4.1	14	0
Allen	7	6	38	5.4	12	0
Furrey	4	2	28	7.0	13	0
Fair	3	6	7	2.3	8	0
Atogwe	0	1	0	—	—	0
Rams	30	23	175	5.8	17	0
Opponents	39	14	410	10.5	75t	1

KICKOFF RETURNS	No.	Yds	Avg	LG	TD
Johnson	38	857	22.6	99t	1
Allen	23	472	20.5	32	0
Fair	10	182	18.2	35	0
Cason	2	48	24.0	29	0
Harris	1	21	21.0	21	0
Rams	74	1,580	21.4	99t	1
Opponents	70	1,781	25.4	90	0

FIELD GOALS	1-19	20-29	30-39	40-49	50+
Wilkins	0/0	6/7	8/8	9/11	4/5
Rams	0/0	6/7	8/8	9/11	4/5
Opponents	0/0	7/7	13/13	4/11	2/2

SACKS	No.
Little	9.5
Hargrove	6.5
Archuleta	3.5
Green	3.0
Kennedy	3.0
TEAM	3.0
T. Jackson	2.5
Coakley	2.0
Ivy	2.0
Pickett	2.0
Tinoisamoa	1.5
Atogwe	1.0
Lewis	1.0
Claiborne	0.5
Rams	41.0
Opponents	46.0

RECORD HOLDERS
INDIVIDUAL RECORDS—CAREER

Category	Name	Performance
Rushing (Yds.)	Eric Dickerson, 1983-87	7,245
Passing (Yds.)	Jim Everett, 1986-1993	23,758
Passing (TDs)	Roman Gabriel, 1962-1972	154
Receiving (No.)	Isaac Bruce, 1994-2005	813
Receiving (Yds.)	Isaac Bruce, 1994-2005	12,278
Interceptions	Ed Meador, 1959-1970	46
Punting (Avg.)	Danny Villanueva, 1960-64	44.3
Punt Return (Avg.)	Az-Zahir Hakim, 1998-2001	11.4
Kickoff Return (Avg.)	Ron Brown, 1984-89, 1991	26.3
Field Goals	Jeff Wilkins, 1997-2005	209
Touchdowns (Tot.)	Marshall Faulk, 1999-2005	85
Points	Jeff Wilkins, 1997-2005	995

INDIVIDUAL RECORDS—SINGLE SEASON

Category	Name	Performance
Rushing (Yds.)	Eric Dickerson, 1984	*2,105
Passing (Yds.)	Kurt Warner, 2001	4,830
Passing (TDs)	Kurt Warner, 1999	41
Receiving (No.)	Isaac Bruce, 1995	119
Receiving (Yds.)	Isaac Bruce, 1995	1,781
Interceptions	Dick (Night Train) Lane, 1952	*14
Punting (Avg.)	Danny Villanueva, 1962	45.5
Punt Return (Avg.)	Woodley Lewis, 1952	18.5
Kickoff Return (Avg.)	Verda (Vitamin T) Smith, 1950	33.7
Field Goals	Jeff Wilkins, 2003	39
Touchdowns (Tot.)	Marshall Faulk, 2000	26
Points	Jeff Wilkins, 2003	163

INDIVIDUAL RECORDS—SINGLE GAME

Category	Name	Performance
Rushing (Yds.)	Willie Ellison, 12-5-71	247
Passing (Yds.)	Norm Van Brocklin, 9-28-51	*554
Passing (TDs)	Many times	5
	Last time by Kurt Warner, 10-10-99	
Receiving (No.)	Tom Fears, 12-3-50	18
Receiving (Yds.)	Willie Anderson, 11-26-89	*336
Interceptions	Many times	3
	Last time by Keith Lyle, 12-15-96	
Field Goals	Bob Waterfield, 12-9-51	5
	Jeff Wilkins, 10-1-00	5
Touchdowns (Tot.)	Many times	4
	Last time by Marshall Faulk, 10-20-02	
Points	Many times	24
	Last time by Marshall Faulk, 10-20-02	

*NFL Record

2006 VETERAN ROSTER

No.	Name	Pos.	Ht.	Wt.	Birthdate	NFL Exp.	College	Hometown	How Acq.	'05 Games/ Starts
20	Anderson, Dwight	CB	5-10	172	7/5/81	3	South Dakota	Bloomfield, Conn.	FA-'05	3/0
21	Atogwe, Oshiomogho	S	5-11	203	6/23/81	2	Stanford	Windsor, Ontario, Canada	D3a-'05	12/0
70	Barron, Alex	T	6-7	320	9/28/82	2	Florida State	Orangeburg, S.C.	D1-'05	12/11
32	Bartell, Ron	CB	6-1	208	2/22/82	2	Howard	Detroit, Mich.	D2-'05	10/7
55	Brooks, Jamal	LB	6-2	238	11/9/76	5	Hampton	Grenada Hills, Calif.	FA-'06	0*
34	Brown, Fakhir	CB	5-11	192	9/21/77	7	Grambling State	Mansfield, La.	UFA(NO)-'06	12/4*
80	Bruce, Isaac	WR	6-0	188	11/10/72	13	Memphis State	Fort Lauderdale, Fla.	D2a-'94	11/10
10	Bulger, Marc	QB	6-3	215	4/5/77	6	West Virginia	Pittsburgh, Pa.	FA-'01	8/8
23	Butler, Jerametrius	CB	5-10	181	11/28/78	6	Kansas State	Dallas, Texas	D5-'01	0*
90	Calahan, Jeremy	DT	6-2	298	7/7/83	2	Rice	Pflugerville, Texas	FA-'05	1/0
27	Carpenter, Dwaine	S	6-1	203	11/4/76	4	North Carolina A&T	Wadeville, N.C.	FA-'05	3/0*
42	Carter, Jerome	S	5-11	219	10/25/82	2	Florida State	Lake City, Fla.	D4a-'05	14/2
25	Chavous, Corey	S	6-1	205	1/5/76	9	Vanderbilt	Aiken, S.C.	UFA(Minn)-'06	16/16*
54	Chillar, Brandon	LB	6-3	253	10/21/82	3	UCLA	Carlsbad, Calif.	D4-'04	16/7
52	Coakley, Dexter	LB	5-10	236	10/20/72	10	Appalachian State	Mt. Pleasant, S.C.	FA-'05	12/9
48	Collins, James	TE	6-4	267	8/18/82	2	Notre Dame	Warrenville, Ill.	D5-'05	3/0
83	Curtis, Kevin	WR	5-11	186	7/17/78	4	Utah State	South Jordan, Utah	D3-'03	16/9
96	Dukes, Clifford	DE	6-3	270	6/26/81	2	Michigan State	Lexington Park, Md.	FA-'05	0*
28	Faulk, Marshall	RB	5-10	211	2/26/73	13	San Diego State	New Orleans, La.	T(Ind)-'99	16/1
57	Faulk, Trev	LB	6-3	254	8/6/81	5	Louisiana State	Lafayette, La.	FA-'03	16/5
30	Fisher, Tony	RB	6-1	222	10/12/79	5	Notre Dame	Euclid, Ohio	UFA(GB)-'06	14/4*
22	Fisher, Travis	CB	5-10	189	9/12/79	5	Central Florida	Tallahassee, Fla.	D2-'02	8/8
12	Fitzpatrick, Ryan	QB	6-2	221	11/24/82	2	Harvard	Gilbert, Ariz.	D7a-'05	4/3
11	Frerotte, Gus	QB	6-3	233	7/31/71	13	Tulsa	Ford City, Pa.	FA-'06	16/15*
97	Glover, La'Roi	DT	6-2	290	7/4/74	11	San Diego State	San Diego, Calif.	FA-'06	16/13*
53	Goolsby, Mike	LB	6-3	244	9/10/82	2	Notre Dame	Joliet, Ill.	FA-'05	2/0
93	Green, Brandon	DE	6-3	264	9/5/80	4	Rice	Vanderbilt, Texas	FA-'05	16/1
24	Groce, DeJuan	CB	5-10	192	2/17/80	4	Nebraska	Garfield Heights, Ohio	D4b-'03	15/15
95	Hargrove, Anthony	DE	6-3	269	7/20/83	3	Georgia Tech	Punta Gorda, Fla.	D3-'03	16/15
44	Hedgecock, Madison	TE	6-3	266	8/27/81	2	North Carolina	Wallburg, N.C.	D7b-'05	16/7
81	Holt, Torry	WR	6-0	190	6/5/76	8	North Carolina State	Greensboro, N.C.	D1-'99	14/14
98	Howard, Brian	DT	6-4	278	9/9/81	3	Idaho	Kent, Wash.	FA-'04	5/0
68	Incognito, Richie	G	6-3	305	7/5/83	2	Nebraska	Glendale, Ariz.	D3b-'05	0*
39	Jackson, Steven	RB	6-2	231	7/22/83	3	Oregon State	Las Vegas, Nev.	D1-'04	15/15
73	Kennedy, Jimmy	DT	6-4	320	11/15/79	4	Penn State	Yonkers, N.Y.	D1-'03	15/9
91	Little, Leonard	DE	6-3	261	10/19/74	9	Tennessee	Asheville, N.C.	D3-'98	14/14
89	Looker, Dane	WR	6-0	194	5/5/76	6	Washington	Puyallup, Wash.	FA-'02	16/0
45	Massey, Chris	RB/LS	6-0	245	8/21/79	5	Marshall	Chesapeake, W. Va.	D7-'02	16/0
67	McCollum, Andy	C	6-4	300	6/2/70	13	Toledo	Richfield, Ohio	UFA(NO)-'99	16/16
84	McDonald, Shaun	WR	5-10	183	6/13/81	4	Arizona State	Phoenix, Ariz.	D4a-'03	16/2
64	Noll, Ben	G/T	6-4	317	11/14/81	3	Pennsylvania	St. Louis, Mo.	W(Dall)-'05	4/0*
76	Pace, Orlando	T	6-7	325	11/4/75	10	Ohio State	Sandusky, Ohio	D1-'97	16/16
88	Pyatt, Brad	WR	5-11	195	4/16/80	4	Northern Colorado	Arvada, Colo.	FA-'06	0*
60	Saipaia, Blaine	G/T	6-3	310	8/25/78	3	Colorado State	Oxnard, Calif.	FA-'04	9/3
31	Smith, Paul	FB	5-11	235	1/31/78	7	Texas-El Paso	El Paso, Texas	UFA(Det)-'06	12/5*
56	Smith, Raonall	LB	6-2	241	10/22/78	5	Washington State	Gig Harbor, Wash.	UFA(Minn)-'06	16/6*
9	Smoker, Jeff	QB	6-3	223	6/13/81	3	Michigan State	Manheim, Pa.	D6-'04	0*
79	Steussie, Todd	T	6-6	320	12/1/70	13	California	Agoura, Calif.	UFA(TB)-'06	15/0*
75	Terrell, Claude	G	6-2	343	4/20/82	2	New Mexico	LaMarque, Texas	D4b-'05	14/10
17	Thompson, Dominique	WR	5-11	197	12/28/82	2	William & Mary	Durham, N.C.	FA-'05	2/0
62	Timmerman, Adam	G	6-4	310	8/14/71	12	South Dakota State	Cherokee, Iowa	UFA(GB)-'99	16/16
50	Tinoisamoa, Pisa	LB	6-1	235	7/15/81	4	Hawaii	Vista, Calif.	D2-'03	16/15
1	Turk, Matt	P	6-5	243	6/16/70	12	Wisconsin-Whitewater	Greenville, Wis.	FA-'06	0*
63	Turner, Larry	G/C	6-2	290	3/8/82	3	Eastern Kentucky	Huber Heights, Ohio	FA-'05	6/0
58	Wahlroos, Drew	LB	6-3	235	6/7/80	3	Colorado	Poway, Calif.	FA-'04	15/0
87	Walker, Aaron	TE	6-6	252	3/14/80	4	Florida	Titusville, Fla.	FA-'05	0
14	Wilkins, Jeff	K	6-2	205	4/19/72	13	Youngstown State	Austintown, Ohio	RFA(SF)-'97	16/0
51	Witherspoon, Will	LB	6-1	231	8/19/80	5	Georgia	Panama City, Fla.	UFA(Car)-'06	15/15*

* Brooks last active with Cleveland in '03; Brown played 12 games with New Orleans in '05; Butler missed '05 season because of injury; Carpenter played 2 games with San Francisco and 1 game with St. Louis; Chavous played 16 games with Minnesota; Dukes inactive for 3 games; To. Fisher played 14 games with Green Bay; Frerotte played 16 games with Miami; Glover played 16 games with Dallas; Incognito missed '05 season because of injury; Noll played 4 games with Dallas; Pyatt missed '05 season with Indianapolis because of injury; P. Smith played 12 games with Detroit; R. Smith played 16 games with Minnesota; Smoker did not play in 1 game; Steussie played 15 games with Tampa Bay; Turk missed '05 season with Miami because of injury; Witherspoon played 15 games with Carolina.

Players lost through free agency (11): S Adam Archuleta (Wash; 14 games in '05), S Mike Furrey (Det; 16), RB Arlen Harris (Det; 16), CB Corey Ivy (Balt; 16), DE/DT Tyoka Jackson (Det; 16), CB Chris Johnson (KC; 14), DT Damione Lewis (Car; 16), QB Jamie Martin (NO; 8), T Matt Morgan (Buff; 1), DT Ryan Pickett (GB; 16), G/T Rex Tucker (Det; 8).

Also played with Rams in '05—RB David Allen (4 games), P Bryan Barker (11), RB Aveion Cason (2), LB Chris Claiborne (14), TE Cameron Cleeland (9), CB Terry Fair (5), S Michael Hawthorne (5), LB Jeremy Loyd (4), TE Brandon Manumaleuna (16), G Tom Nutten (8), TE Roland Williams (4).

2006 FIRST-YEAR ROSTER

Name	Pos.	Ht.	Wt.	Birthdate	College	Hometown	How Acq.
Adeyanju, Victor	DE	6-4	268	2/11/83	Indiana	Chicago, Ill.	D4
Alston, Jon	LB	6-0	218	6/4/83	Stanford	Shreveport, La.	D3b
Bagwell, Antoine	RB	5-11	186	9/13/84	California (Pa.)	Lansing, Mich.	FA
Byrd, Dominique	TE	6-2	260	2/7/84	Southern California	Golden Valley, Minn.	D3c
Carter, Jeremy (1)	WR	5-11	194	11/20/79	Western Carolina	Raleigh, N.C.	FA-'05
Cummings, Josh	K	5-10	175	2/20/83	Pittsburgh	Newhall, Calif.	FA
Eiland, Deandre	S	6-0	209	6/4/82	South Carolina	Tupelo, Miss.	FA
Groom, Andy	P	6-0	196	9/10/79	Ohio State	Columbus, Ohio	FA
Hagans, Marques	WR	5-10	209	12/29/82	Virginia	Hampton, Va.	D5
Hill, Tye	CB	5-10	185	6/3/82	Clemson	St. George, S.C.	D1
Hilliard, Jason	T	6-6	328	6/29/81	Louisville	Jeffersonville, Ind.	FA
Klopfenstein, Joe	TE	6-5	251	11/9/83	Colorado	Aurora, Colo.	D2
McGarigle, Tim	LB	6-0	240	10/25/83	Northwestern	Chicago, Ill.	D7a
Middleton, Brandon (1)	WR	5-10	190	1/2/81	Houston	Houston, Texas	FA-'05
Palmer, Tony	G	6-2	330	2/23/83	Missouri	Midwest City, Okla.	D7c
Raiola, Donovan	C	6-2	300	12/13/82	Wisconsin	Honolulu, Hawaii	FA
Russell, Fred	RB	5-10	195	9/14/80	Iowa	Romulus, Mich.	FA
Sandidge, Tim	DT	6-1	310	6/12/83	Virginia Tech	Madison Heights, Va.	FA
Setterstrom, Mark	G	6-4	314	3/3/84	Minnesota	Northfield, Minn.	D7b
Solomon, Clinton	WR	6-3	214	10/21/83	Iowa	Fort Worth, Texas	FA
Strojny, Drew (1)	T	6-7	327	6/30/81	Duke	Westwood, Mass.	FA-'05
Stubblefield, Taylor	WR	5-11	172	1/21/82	Purdue	Yakima, Wash.	FA
Trafford, Rod	TE	6-3	250	11/28/78	South Carolina	Morristown, N.J.	FA
Washington, John David	RB	5-9	190	7/28/84	Morehouse	Toluca Lake, Calif.	FA
Williams, Jonathan	TE	6-3	246	4/23/83	New Hampshire	Rochester, N.Y.	FA
Wroten, Claude	DT	6-2	292	9/16/83	Louisiana State	Bastrop, La.	D3a

The term NFL Rookie is defined as a player who is in his first season of professional football and has not been on the roster of another professional football team for any regular-season or postseason games. A Rookie is designated by an "R" on NFL rosters. Players who have been active in another professional football league or players who have NFL experience, including either preseason training camp or being on an Active List or Inactive List, or on Reserve/Injured or Reserve/Physically Unable to Perform for fewer than six regular-season games, are termed NFL First-Year Players. An NFL First-Year Player is designated by a "1" on NFL rosters. Thereafter, a player is credited with an additional year of experience for each season in which he accumulates six games on the Active List or Inactive List, or on Reserve/Injured or Reserve/Physically Unable to Perform.

Log on to www.stlouisrams.com for an up-to-date roster.

COACHING STAFF

Head Coach,
Scott Linehan

Pro Career: Named twenty-second head coach in franchise history by Owner/Chairman Georgia Frontiere on January 19, 2006. Joins the Rams after one season as offensive coordinator of the Miami Dolphins (2005). In one season, Dolphins went from 29th in total offense to 14th last season as Gus Frerotte had the best season of his career, passing for 2,996 yards and 18 touchdowns. Prior to that, Linehan spent three seasons (2002-04) as offensive coordinator for the Minnesota Vikings. Minnesota ranked second, first, and fourth, respectively in total offense during that time. In 2004, Daunte Culpepper posted the fourth-highest single season passer rating in NFL history (110.9), and the fifth-highest single season passing yards total in league history (4,717). A college quarterback, Linehan was a free agent signee with the Dallas Cowboys before a shoulder injury ended his active career. Career record: 0-0.

Background: Linehan was an assistant coach on the collegiate level at Idaho (1989-90, 1992-93), Nevada-Las Veags (1991), Washington (1994-1998) and Louisville (1999-2001). Played quarterback at Idaho under Dennis Erickson (1982-86). The Vandals won the Big Sky Championship (1985) and made three consecutive playoff appearances (1984-86).

Personal: Born September 17, 1963 in Sunnyside, Wash. He and his wife, Kristen, have three sons: Matthew, Michael, and Marcus.

ASSISTANT COACHES

Brian Baker, defensive line; born June 20, 1962, Baltimore. Linebacker Maryland 1980-83. No pro playing experience. College coach: Maryland 1984-85, Army 1986, Georgia Tech 1987-1995. Pro coach: San Diego Chargers 1996, Detroit Lions 1997-2000, Minnesota Vikings 2001-05, joined Rams in 2006.

Joe Baker, defensive quality control; born June 29, 1969, Glen Ridge, N.J. Wide receiver Princeton 1987-1990. No pro playing experience. College coach: East Stroudsburg 1991, Samford 1993, Wisconsin 1999. Pro coach: Birmingham Fire (WLAF) 1992, Jacksonville Jaguars 1994-98, New Orleans Saints 2000-04, Green Bay Packers 2005, joined Rams in 2006.

Paul Boudreau, offensive line; born December 30, 1949, Arlington, Mass. Offensive lineman Boston College 1971-73. No pro playing experience. College coach: Boston College 1974-75, Maine 1976-78, Dartmouth 1979-1981, Navy 1982. Pro coach: Edmonton Eskimos (CFL) 1983-86, New Orleans Saints 1987-1993, Detroit Lions 1994-96, New England Patriots 1997-98, Miami Dolphins 1999-2000, Carolina Panthers 2001-02, Jacksonville Jaguars 2003-05, joined Rams in 2006.

Jim Chaney, asst. offensive line; born January 12, 1962, Warrensburg, Mo. Guard Central Missouri State 1981-85. No pro playing experience. College coach: Cal State-Fullerton 1985-1992, Wyoming 1993-1996, Purdue 1997-2005. Pro coach: Joined Rams in 2006.

Todd Downing, coaching/special teams assistant; born July 22, 1980, Eden Prairie, Minn. Attended Minnesota. No college or pro playing experience. Pro coach: Minnesota Vikings 2003-05, joined Rams in 2006.

Henry Ellard, wide receivers; born July 21, 1961, Fresno, Calif. Wide receiver Fresno State 1979-1982. Pro wide receiver/punt returner Los Angeles Rams 1983-1993, Washington Redskins 1994-97, New England Patriots 1998, Washington Redskins 1998. College coach: Fresno State 2000. Pro coach: Joined Rams in 2001.

Judd Garrett, tight ends; born June 25, 1967, Abington, Pa. Running back Princeton 1987-89. Pro running back London Monarchs (WLAF) 1991-92, Dallas Cowboys 1993, Las Vegas Posse (CFL) 1994, San Antonio Texans (CFL) 1995. College coach: Princeton 1990. Pro coach: New Orleans Saints 1997-99, Miami Dolphins 2000-05, joined Rams in 2006.

Randy Hanson, offensive quality control; born January 17, 1968, Sacramento, Calif. Quarterback Pacific 1990-92. No pro playing experience. College coach: Eastern Washington 1993-95, 1998-99, Washington 1996-97, Portland State 2000-02. Pro coach: Minnesota Vikings 2003-05, joined Rams in 2006.

Jim Haslett, defensive coordinator; born December 9, 1955, Pittsburgh. Defensive end Indiana (Pa.) 1975-1978. Pro linebacker Buffalo Bills 1979-1986, N.Y. Jets 1987. College coach: Buffalo 1988-1990, Pittsburgh 1997-99. Pro coach: Sacramento Surge (NFLE) 1991-92, Los Angeles Raiders 1993-94, New Orleans Saints 1995-96, 2000-05 (head coach 2000-05), joined Rams in 2006.

Jeff Horton, special assistant/offense; born July 13, 1957, Tulsa, Okla. Attended Nevada. No college or pro playing experience. College coach: Minnesota 1984, Nevada 1985-89, 1992-93, Nevada-Las Vegas 1990-91, 1994-98 (head coach 1994-98), Wisconsin 1999-2005, Iowa State 2006. Pro coach: Joined Rams in 2006.

Dana LeDuc, strength and conditioning; born March 22, 1953, Tacoma, Wash. Attended Texas. No college or pro playing experience. College coach: Texas 1977-1992, Miami 1993-94. Pro coach: Seattle Seahawks 1995-98, joined Rams in 1999.

Bob Ligashesky, special teams; born June 2, 1962, Pittsburgh. Linebacker Indiana (Pa.) 1983-84. No pro playing experience. College coach: Wake Forest 1985, Arizona State 1986-89, Kent State 1990, Bowling Green 1991-99, Pittsburgh 2000-03. Pro coach: Jacksonville Jaguars 2004, joined Rams in 2005.

Ron Milus, asst. secondary; born November 25, 1963, Tacoma, Wash. Cornerback-punt returner Washington 1982-1985. No pro playing experience. College coach: Washington 1991-98, Texas A&M 1999. Pro coach: Denver Broncos 2000-02, Arizona Cardinals 2003, New York Giants 2004-05, joined Rams in 2006.

Wayne Moses, running backs, born January 11, 1955, New Gulf, Texas. Washington 1975-78. No pro playing experience. College coach: Cal State-Fullerton 1978, Chaffey (Calif) J.C. 1980, Bowling Green 1981-83, Rutgers 1984-1985, San Diego State 1986-88, New Mexico 1989, UCLA 1990-95, 2001, California 1996, Washington 1997-2000, Stanford 2002-03, 2005. Pro coach: Joined Rams in 2006.

Doug Nussmeier, quarterbacks, born December 11, 1970, Portland, Ore. Quarterback Idaho 1990-93. Pro quarterback New Orleans Saints 1994-97, Indianapolis Colts 1998, British Columbia Lions (CFL) 2000. College coach: Michigan State 2003-05. Pro coach: British Columbia Lions (CFL) 2001, Ottawa Renegades (CFL) 2002, joined Rams in 2006.

Greg Olson, offensive coordinator; born March 1, 1963, Richland, Wash. Quarterback Central Washington 1983-86. No pro playing experience. College coach: Washington State 1987-89, Central Washington 1990-93, Idaho 1994-96, Purdue 1997-2000, 2002. Pro coach: San Francisco 49ers 2001, Chicago Bears 2003, Lions 2004-05, joined Rams in 2006.

Willy Robinson, secondary; born February 10, 1956, Ft. Carson, Colo. Defensive back Fresno State 1976-77. College coach: Fresno State 1978, 1980-1993, San Jose State 1979, Miami 1994, Oregon State 1999. Pro coach: Seattle Seahawks 1995-98, Pittsburgh Steelers 2000-03, San Francisco 49ers 2004, New Orleans Saints 2005, joined Rams in 2006.

Brad Roll, asst. strength & conditioning; born July 4, 1958, Houston. Center Blinn (Tex.) J.C. 1976-77, Stephen F. Austin 1978-79. No pro playing experience. College coach: Stephen F. Austin 1980, Southwestern Louisiana 1981-86, Kansas 1987-88, Miami 1989-1992. Pro coach: Tampa Bay Buccaneers 1993-95, Miami Dolphins 1996-2003, Buffalo Bills 2004-05, joined Rams in 2006.

Rick Venturi, asst. head coach/linebackers; born February 23, 1946, Taylorville, Ill. Quarterback/defensive back Northwestern 1965-67. No pro playing experience. College coach: Northwestern 1968-1972, 1978-1980 (head coach 1978-1980), Purdue 1973-76, Illinois 1977. Pro coach: Hamilton Tiger-Cats (CFL) 1981, Indianapolis Colts 1982-1993 (interim head coach for final 11 games of 1991), Cleveland Browns 1994-95, Saints 1996-2005 (interim head coach for final eight games of 1996), joined Rams in 2006.

**National Football Conference
West Division
Team Colors:** Metalllic Gold,
Cardinal Red, and Beige
**4949 Centennial Boulevard
Santa Clara, California 95054
Telephone:** (408) 562-4949

2006 SCHEDULE
PRESEASON
Aug. 11	**Chicago**	7:00
Aug. 20	at Oakland	5:00
Aug. 26	at Dallas	7:00
Sept. 1	**San Diego**	7:00

REGULAR SEASON
Sept. 10	at Arizona	1:15
Sept. 17	**St. Louis**	1:05
Sept. 24	**Philadelphia**	1:15
Oct. 1	at Kansas City	12:00
Oct. 8	**Oakland**	1:05
Oct. 15	**San Diego**	1:15
Oct. 22	Open Date	
Oct. 29	at Chicago	12:00
Nov. 5	**Minnesota**	1:05
Nov. 12	at Detroit	1:00
Nov. 19	**Seattle**	1:05
Nov. 26	at St. Louis	12:00
Dec. 3	at New Orleans	12:00
Dec. 10	**Green Bay**	1:05
Dec. 14	at Seattle (Thu.)	5:00
Dec. 24	**Arizona**	1:05
Dec. 31	at Denver	2:15

Stadium: Monster Park (opened in 1958)
• **Capacity:** 69,732
San Francisco, California
94124
Playing Surface: Natural Grass
Training Camp: Marie P. DeBartolo
Sports Center
4949 Centennial Boulevard
Santa Clara, CA 95054

MONSTER PARK

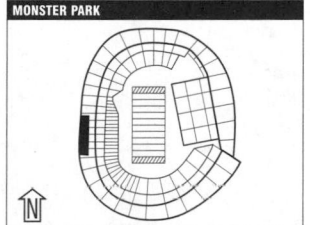

CLUB OFFICIALS
OWNERSHIP
Owner: The DeBartolo Corporation
Owner: Denise DeBartolo York
Owner: Dr. John York
Limited Partner: Franklin Mieuli
Limited Partner: Rick and Carla Morabito
MANAGEMENT
Executive Vice President of Football
Operations: Lal Heneghan
Vice President of Player Personnel:
Scot McCloughan
Vice President/Operations: Murlan Fowell
Vice President of Business
Affairs/General Counsel: Ed Goines
Vice President Communications:
Lisa Lang
Vice President/CFO: Larry MacNeil
Vice President/Sales And Marketing:
David Peart
Director of Football Operations:
Paraag Marathe
Director of Football Administration:
Terry Tumey
Ticket Manager: Lynn Carrozzi
Director of Security: Fred Formosa
Director of Information Technology:
Alexander Ignacio
Director of Stadium Operations:
Jim Mercurio
Director of Public Relations: Aaron Salkin
Equipment Manager: Steve Urbaniak
Video Operations Director: Keith Yanagi

COACHING HISTORY
(463-376-13)
Records include postseason games
1950-54	Lawrence (Buck) Shaw	33-25-2
1955	Norman (Red) Strader	4-8-0
1956-58	Frankie Albert	19-17-1
1959-1963	Howard (Red) Hickey*	27-27-1
1963-67	Jack Christiansen	26-38-3
1968-1975	Dick Nolan	56-56-5
1976	Monte Clark	8-6-0
1977	Ken Meyer	5-9-0
1978	Pete McCulley**	1-8-0
1978	Fred O'Connor	1-6-0
1979-1988	Bill Walsh	102-63-1
1989-1996	George Seifert	108-35-0
1997-2002	Steve Mariucci	60-43-0
2003-04	Dennis Erickson	9-23-0
2005	Mike Nolan	4-12-0

*Resigned after three games in 1963
**Released after nine games in 1978

ATTENDANCE
Home 512,060	Away 573,265

Total 1,085,325
Single-game home record,
69,014 (11/13/94)
Single-season home record,
544,228 (1999)

2006 DRAFT CHOICES
Round	Name	Pos.	College
1	Vernon Davis	TE	Maryland
	Manny Lawson	DE	North Carolina St.
3	Brandon Williams	WR	Wisconsin
4	Michael Robinson	RB	Penn State
5	Parys Haralson	DE	Tennessee
6	Delanie Walker	WR	Central Missouri St.
	Marcus Hudson	DB	North Carolina St.
	Melvin Oliver	DE	Louisiana State
7	Vickiel Vaughn	DB	Arkansas

2005 TEAM RECORD

PRESEASON (2-2)

Date	Result	Opponent
8/13	W 21-13	Oakland
8/20	L 21-26	at Denver
8/26	W 16-13	Tennessee
9/1	L 24-28	at San Diego

REGULAR SEASON (4-12)

Date	Result	Opponent	Att.
9/11	W 28-25	St. Louis	67,918
9/18	L 3-42	at Philadelphia	67,727
9/25	L 31-34	Dallas	68,247
10/2	L 14-31	at Arizona	103,467
10/09	L 3-28	Indianapolis	68,084
10/23	L 17-52	at Washington	90,224
10/30	W 15-10	Tampa Bay	63,358
11/6	L 6-24	N.Y. Giants	63,820
11/13	L 9-17	at Chicago	62,153
11/20	L 25-27	Seattle	63,590
11/27	L 22-33	at Tennessee	69,149
12/4	L 10-17	Arizona	60,439
12/11	L 3-41	at Seattle	66,690
12/18	L 9-10	at Jacksonville	64,764
12/24	W 24-20	at St. Louis	65,473
1/1	W 20-17	Houston (OT)	67,970

(OT) Overtime

SCORE BY PERIODS

49ers	44	94	51	47	3 —	239
Opponents	70	150	91	117	0 —	428

2005 TEAM STATISTICS

	49ers	Opp.
Total First Downs	191	335
Rushing	70	115
Passing	96	205
Penalty	25	15
3rd Down: Made/Att	49/204	87/226
3rd Down Pct.	24.0	38.5
4th Down: Made/Att	5/8	11/19
4th Down Pct.	62.5	57.9
Possession Avg.	27:18	32:42
Total Net Yards	3,587	6,259
Avg. Per Game	224.2	391.2
Total Plays	865	1,090
Avg. Per Play	4.1	5.7
Net Yards Rushing	1,689	1,832
Avg. Per Game	105.6	114.5
Total Rushes	428	486
Net Yards Passing	1,898	4,427
Avg. Per Game	118.6	276.7
Sacked/Yards Lost	48/292	28/193
Gross Yards	2,190	4,620
Att./Completions	389/204	576/374
Completion Pct.	52.4	64.9
Had Intercepted	21	16
Punts/Average	108/41.2	71/40.1
Net Punting Avg.	108/36.3	71/33.7
Penalties/Yards	106/780	120/961
Fumbles/Ball Lost	31/14	18/10
Touchdowns	23	49
Rushing	9	19
Passing	8	28
Returns	6	2

2005 INDIVIDUAL STATISTICS

PASSING	Att.	Comp.	Yds.	Pct.	TD	Int.	Tkld.	Rate
A. Smith	165	84	875	50.9	1	11	29/185	40.8
Rattay	97	56	667	57.7	5	6	10/63	70.3
Dorsey	90	48	481	53.3	2	2	6/28	66.9
Pickett	35	14	140	40.0	0	2	3/16	28.3
Battle	2	2	27	100.0	0	0	0/0	118.8
49ers	389	204	2,190	52.4	8	21	48/292	53.6
Opponents	576	374	4,620	64.9	28	16	28/193	94.2

SCORING	TD R	TD P	TD Rt	PAT	FG	Saf	PTS
Nedney	0	0	0	19/19	26/28	0	97
Lloyd	0	5	0	0/0	0/0	0	30
Barlow	3	0	0	0/0	0/0	0	18
Battle	0	3	0	0/0	0/0	0	18
Gore	3	0	0	0/0	0/0	0	18
Hicks	3	0	0	0/0	0/0	0	18
M. Adams	0	0	1	0/0	0/0	0	6
Amey	0	0	1	0/0	0/0	0	6
D. Johnson	0	0	1	0/0	0/0	0	6
Parrish	0	0	1	0/0	0/0	0	6
D. Smith	0	0	1	0/0	0/0	0	6
Spencer	0	0	1	0/0	0/0	0	6
Cortez	0	0	0	2/2	0/1	0	2
Jackson	0	0	0	0/0	0/0	0	2
49ers	9	8	6	21/21	26/29	0	239
Opponents	19	28	2	43/44	29/36	0	428

2-Pt. Conversions: Jackson.
49ers 1-2, Opponents 2-5.

RUSHING	No.	Yds	Avg	LG	TD
Gore	127	608	4.8	72t	3
Barlow	176	581	3.3	29	3
Hicks	59	308	5.2	73t	3
A. Smith	30	103	3.4	19	0
Pickett	13	42	3.2	12	0
Rattay	7	18	2.6	13	0
Battle	8	11	1.4	9	0
Dorsey	4	11	2.8	6	0
Jackson	2	11	5.5	11	0
Hetherington	1	3	3.0	3	0
Marshall	1	-7	-7.0	-7	0
49ers	428	1,689	3.9	73t	9
Opponents	486	1,832	3.8	40	19

RECEIVING	No.	Yds	Avg	LG	TD
Lloyd	48	733	15.3	89t	5
Battle	32	363	11.3	39	3
Barlow	31	241	7.8	24	0
Morton	21	288	13.7	30	0
Gore	15	131	8.7	47	0
Hicks	12	47	3.9	11	0
Jackson	10	67	6.7	12	0
Jones	9	76	8.4	21	0
McAddley	7	125	17.9	38	0
Bajema	5	54	10.8	24	0
Hetherington	5	26	5.2	11	0
Bush	3	21	7.0	10	0
T. Smith	3	7	2.3	6	0
Beasley	2	12	6.0	6	0
Marshall	1	-1	-1.0	-1	0
49ers	204	2,190	10.7	89t	8
Opponents	374	4,620	12.4	78t	28

INTERCEPTIONS	No.	Yds	Avg	LG	TD
Spencer	4	85	21.3	61t	1
M. Adams	4	36	9.0	40t	1
Parrish	2	34	17.0	34t	1
Thornton	2	0	0.0	0	0
Emanuel	1	38	38.0	35	0
D. Smith	1	13	13.0	13	0
Moore	1	12	12.0	12	0
Lewis	1	2	2.0	2	0
49ers	16	220	13.8	61t	3
Opponents	21	265	12.6	34	1

PUNTING	No.	Yds.	Avg.	In 20	LG
Lee	107	4,447	41.6	15	58
49ers	108	4,447	41.2	15	58
Opponents	71	2,846	40.1	22	56

PUNT RETURNS	Ret	FC	Yds	Avg	LG	TD
Marshall	17	10	87	5.1	13	0
Amey	11	2	125	11.4	75t	1
49ers	28	12	212	7.6	75t	1
Opponents	62	20	471	7.6	25	0

KICKOFF RETURNS	No.	Yds	Avg	LG	TD
Hicks	34	689	20.3	40	0
Marshall	26	488	18.8	29	0
Amey	14	241	17.2	25	0
McAddley	7	122	17.4	22	0
49ers	81	1,540	19.0	40	0
Opponents	48	960	20.0	35	0

FIELD GOALS	1-19	20-29	30-39	40-49	50+
Nedney	0/0	4/4	10/11	10/10	2/3
Cortez	0/0	0/0	0/1	0/0	0/0
49ers	0/0	4/4	10/12	10/10	2/3
Opponents	1/1	8/8	7/9	9/10	4/8

SACKS	No.
Young	8.0
Moore	5.0
Carter	4.5
Peterson	3.0
A. Adams	2.5
M. Adams	1.0
Douglas	1.0
D. Johnson	1.0
TEAM	1.0
Emanuel	0.5
Hall	0.5
49ers	28.0
Opponents	48.0

RECORD HOLDERS

INDIVIDUAL RECORDS—CAREER

Category	Name	Performance
Rushing (Yds.)	Joe Perry, 1950-1960, 1963	7,344
Passing (Yds.)	Joe Montana, 1979-1992	35,124
Passing (TDs)	Joe Montana, 1979-1992	244
Receiving (No.)	Jerry Rice, 1985-2000	1,281
Receiving (Yds.)	Jerry Rice, 1985-2000	19,247
Interceptions	Ronnie Lott, 1981-1990	51
Punting (Avg.)	Tommy Davis, 1959-1969	44.7
Punt Return (Avg.)	Dana McLemore, 1982-87	10.8
Kickoff Return (Avg.)	Abe Woodson, 1958-1964	29.4
Field Goals	Ray Wersching, 1977-1987	190
Touchdowns (Tot.)	Jerry Rice, 1985-2000	187
Points	Jerry Rice, 1985-2000	1,130

INDIVIDUAL RECORDS—SINGLE SEASON

Category	Name	Performance
Rushing (Yds.)	Garrison Hearst, 1998	1,570
Passing (Yds.)	Jeff Garcia, 2000	4,278
Passing (TDs)	Steve Young, 1998	36
Receiving (No.)	Jerry Rice, 1995	122
Receiving (Yds.)	Jerry Rice, 1995	*1,848
Interceptions	Dave Baker, 1960	10
	Ronnie Lott, 1986	10
Punting (Avg.)	Tommy Davis, 1965	45.8
Punt Return (Avg.)	Dana McLemore, 1982	22.3
Kickoff Return (Avg.)	Joe Arenas, 1953	34.4
Field Goals	Jeff Wilkins, 1996	30
Touchdowns (Tot.)	Jerry Rice, 1987	23
Points	Jerry Rice, 1987	138

INDIVIDUAL RECORDS—SINGLE GAME

Category	Name	Performance
Rushing (Yds.)	Charlie Garner, 9-24-00	201
Passing (Yds.)	Joe Montana, 10-14-90	476
Passing (TDs)	Joe Montana, 10-14-90	6
Receiving (No.)	Terrell Owens, 12-17-00	*20
Receiving (Yds.)	Jerry Rice, 12-18-95	289
Interceptions	Dave Baker, 12-4-60	*4
Field Goals	Ray Wersching, 10-16-83	6
	Jeff Wilkins, 9-29-96	6
Touchdowns (Tot.)	Jerry Rice, 10-14-90	5
Points	Jerry Rice, 10-14-90	30

*NFL Record

2006 VETERAN ROSTER

No.	Name	Pos.	Ht.	Wt.	Birthdate	NFL Exp.	College	Hometown	How Acq.	'05 Games/ Starts
91	Adams, Anthony	DT	6-0	297	6/18/80	4	Penn State	Detroit, Mich.	D2-'03	16/16
20	Adams, Mike	S	5-11	192	3/24/81	3	Delaware	Paterson, N.J.	FA-'04	14/10
71	Allen, Larry	G	6-3	325	11/27/71	13	Sonoma State	Compton, Calif.	FA-'06	16/16
18	Amey, Otis	WR	5-10	192	12/4/81	2	Sacramento State	Union City, Calif.	FA-'05	11/0
64	Baas, David	G	6-4	312	9/28/81	2	Michigan	Sarasota, Fla.	D2-'05	13/5
47	Bajema, Billy	TE	6-4	255	10/31/82	2	Oklahoma State	Oklahoma City, Okla.	D7d-'05	15/7
32	Barlow, Kevan	RB	6-1	234	1/7/79	6	Pittsburgh	Pittsburgh, Pa.	D3-'01	12/12
83	Battle, Arnaz	WR	6-1	206	2/22/80	4	Notre Dame	Shreveport, La.	D6-'03	10/8
81	Bryant, Antonio	WR	6-2	188	3/9/81	5	Pittsburgh	Miami, Fla.	UFA(Cle)-'06	16/15
31	t- Davis, Sammy	CB	6-1	195	4/8/80	4	Texas A&M	Humble, Texas	T(SD)-'06	16/4
	t- Dilfer, Trent	QB	6-4	234	3/13/72	13	Fresno State	Aptos, Calif.	T(Cle)-'06	11/11
94	Douglas, Marques	DE	6-2	286	3/15/77	6	Howard	Greensboro, N.C.	UFA(Balt)-'05	16/15
38	Emanuel, Ben	S	6-2	213	6/18/82	2	UCLA	Friendswood, Texas	FA-'05	11/8
78	Estes, Patrick	T	6-7	283	2/4/83	2	Virginia	Richmond, Va.	D7c-'05	7/0
95	Fields, Ronald	DT	6-2	310	9/13/81	2	Mississippi State	Bogalusa, La.	D5a-'05	4/0
10	Fleck, P.J.	WR	5-10	191	11/29/80	2	Northern Illinois	Sugar Grove, Ill.	FA-'04	0*
84	Gilmore, Bryan	WR	6-1	193	7/21/78	6	Midwestern State	Lufkin, Texas	UFA(Mia)-'06	15/1
21	Gore, Frank	RB	5-9	215	5/14/83	2	Miami	Coral Gables, Fla.	D2-'05	14/1
88	Hamilton, Derrick	WR	6-4	207	11/30/81	3	Clemson	Dillon, S.C.	D3-'04	0*
77	Harris, Kwame	T	6-7	306	3/15/82	4	Stanford	Newark, Del.	D1-'03	16/16
27	Harris, Walt	CB	5-11	190	8/10/74	11	Mississippi State	LaGrange, Ga.	FA-'06	13/11
66	Heitmann, Eric	G/C	6-3	307	2/24/80	5	Stanford	Katy, Texas	D7a-'02	16/16
41	Hetherington, Chris	FB	6-3	253	11/27/72	11	Yale	North Branford, Conn.	UFA(Oak)-'05	16/6
43	Hicks, Maurice	RB	5-11	196	7/22/78	3	North Carolina A&T	Emporia, Va.	FA-'04	14/4
22	Jackson, Terry	FB	6-0	221	1/10/76	8	Florida	Gainesville, Fla.	D5-'99	16/0
86	Jennings, Brian	TE/LS	6-5	233	10/14/76	7	Arizona State	Mesa, Ariz.	D7b-'00	16/0
75	Jennings, Jonas	T	6-3	323	11/21/77	6	Georgia	College Park, Ga.	FA-'05	3/3
23	Johnson, Derrick	CB	5-10	186	2/9/82	3	Washington	Riverside, Calif.	D6-'05	14/5
82	Johnson, Eric	TE	6-3	252	9/15/79	6	Yale	Needham, Mass.	D7b-'01	0*
49	Jones, Terry	TE	6-3	260	12/3/79	5	Alabama	Tuscaloosa, Ala.	FA-'05	7/5
4	Lee, Andy	P	6-0	183	8/11/82	3	Pittsburgh	Westminster, N.C.	D6a-'04	16/0
28	Lewis, Keith	S	6-0	210	10/20/81	3	Oregon	Sacramento, Calif.	D6b-'04	16/4
89	Marshall, Rasheed	WR	6-1	183	7/11/81	2	West Virginia	Pittsburgh, Pa.	D5b-'05	12/0
57	Maxwell, Jim	LB	6-4	242	8/8/81	3	Gardner-Webb	Johnsonville, S.C.	FA-'05	11/2
19	Maxwell, Marcus	WR	6-4	205	7/8/83	2	Oregon	Berkeley, Calif.	D7b-'05	4/0
15	McAddley, Jason	WR	6-2	200	7/28/79	5	Alabama	Oak Ridge, Tenn.	FA-'05	12/2
56	Moore, Brandon	LB	6-1	246	1/16/79	5	Oklahoma	Baldwin, N.Y.	FA-'02	16/10
6	Nedney, Joe	K	6-5	235	3/22/73	10	San Jose State	San Jose, Calif.	FA-'05	15/0
62	Newberry, Jeremy	C	6-5	313	3/23/76	9	California	Antioch, Calif.	D2-'98	10/10
7	Palmer, Jesse	QB	6-2	219	10/5/78	6	Florida	Toronto, Ontario, Canada	FA-'06	0*
33	Parrish, Tony	S	6-0	209	11/23/75	9	Washington	Huntington Beach, Calif.	FA-'02	9/9
3	Pickett, Cody	QB	6-3	217	6/30/80	3	Washington	Caldwell, Idaho	D7a-'04	5/2
35	Richard, Kris	CB	5-11	190	10/28/05	5	Southern California	Carson, Calif.	FA-'05	1/0
24	Rumph, Mike	CB	6-2	206	11/8/79	5	Miami	Boynton Beach, Fla.	D1-'02	3/3
52	Slaughter, T.J.	LB	6-1	233	2/20/77	7	Southern Mississippi	Birmingham, Ala.	UFA(NO)-'06	9/1*
65	Smiley, Justin	G	6-3	300	11/11/81	3	Alabama	Ellabel, Ga.	D2a-'04	16/16
11	Smith, Alex	QB	6-4	210	5/7/84	2	Utah	San Diego, Calif.	D1-'05	9/7
58	Smith, Corey	LB	6-2	261	10/2/79	4	North Carolina State	Richmond, Va.	FA-'04	14/0
50	Smith, Derek	LB	6-2	237	1/18/75	10	Arizona State	American Fork, Utah	UFA(Wash)-'01	16/16
48	Smith, Trent	TE	6-5	238	9/15/79	3	Oklahoma	Norman, Okla.	FA-'05	5/2
68	Snyder, Adam	T/G	6-6	312	1/30/82	2	Oregon	Fullerton, Calif.	D3b-'05	16/8
60	Sobieski, Ben	G	6-5	307	5/3/79	2	Iowa	Mahtomedi, Minn.	FA-'05	0*
90	Sopoaga, Isaac	DT	6-2	332	9/4/81	2	Hawaii	Pago Pago, American Samoa	D4a-'04	16/1
36	Spencer, Shawntae	CB	6-1	179	2/22/82	3	Pittsburgh	Rankin, Pa.	D2b-'04	15/14
26	Thornton, Bruce	CB	5-10	195	1/31/80	3	Georgia	Atlanta, Ga.	FA-'05	12/11
30	Tucker, B.J.	CB	5-10	188	10/12/80	2	Wisconsin	Sierra Leone, W. Africa	FA-'05	6/0
53	Ulbrich, Jeff	LB	6-0	240	2/17/77	7	Hawaii	San Jose, Calif.	D3b-'00	5/5
25	Williams, Chad	S	5-9	207	1/22/79	5	Southern Mississippi	Birmingham, Ala.	UFA(Balt)-'06	16/3*
59	Williams, Renauld	LB	6-0	238	2/23/81	3	Hofstra	Stonybrook, N.Y.	FA-'05	2/0
69	Wragge, Tony	G	6-4	320	8/14/79	2	New Mexico State	Creighton, Neb.	FA-'05	0*
97	Young, Bryant	DE	6-3	297	1/27/72	13	Notre Dame	Chicago Heights, Ill.	D1-'94	13/13

* Fleck missed '05 season because of injury; Hamilton last active with San Francisco in '04; E. Johnson inactive for 2 games; Palmer did not play in 3 games; Slaughter played 9 games with New Orleans in '05; Sobieski last active with Buffalo in '03; C. Williams played 16 games with Baltimore; Wragge did not play in 5 games.

t- 49ers traded for Davis (SD), Dilfer (Cle).

Traded—QB Ken Dorsey (3 games in '05) to Cleveland, WR Brandon Lloyd (16) to Washington, WR Rashaun Woods (0) to San Diego.

Players lost through free agency (3): FB Fred Beasley (Mia; 9 games in '05); LB Andre Carter (Wash; 16); LB Julian Peterson (Sea; 14).

Also played with 49ers in '05—TE Steve Bush (16 games), K Jose Cortez (1), DE Travis Hall (16), CB Willie Middlebrooks (5), CB Ahmed Plummer (3), LB Saleem Rasheed (9), QB Tim Rattay (4), CB/S Jeremy Thornburg (2), LB Jamie Winborn (3), LB Jamie Winborn (3),

2006 FIRST-YEAR ROSTER

Name	Pos.	Ht.	Wt.	Birthdate	College	Hometown	How Acq.
Baker, Chris	WR	6-5	200	3/16/83	Rutgers	Jersey City, N.J.	FA
Brewer, C.J.	WR	6-2	205	5/12/82	Wyoming	Denver, Colo.	FA
Dahl, Harvey (1)	T	6-5	302	6/24/81	Nevada	Fallon, Nev.	FA-'05
Davis, Vernon	TE	6-3	253	1/31/84	Maryland	Washington, D.C.	D1
Haralson, Parys	DE/LB	6-1	250	1/24/84	Tennessee	Flora, Miss.	D5
Harris, Bobby	T	6-4	310	6/15/83	Mississippi	Decatur, Ga.	FA
Hudson, Marcus	S	6-2	200	11/15/82	North Carolina State	Miami, Fla.	D6b
Ibekwe, Onye	TE	6-8	254	1/19/84	Long Beach State	Los Angeles, Calif.	FA
Jacas, Andrew (1)	K	5-11	185	7/27/82	Fort Valley State	Kingston, Jamaica	FA
Keasey, Zak (1)	FB	6-0	236	3/19/82	Princeton	Lake Orion, Mich.	FA-'05
Lawson, Manny	LB	6-5	240	7/3/84	North Carolina State	Goldsboro, N.C.	D1b
Malone, Tom	P	6-0	205	3/29/84	Southern California	Lake Elsinore, Calif.	FA
Oliver, Melvin	DE	6-3	279	7/25/83	Louisiana State	Opelika, Ala.	D6c
Parker, Arnold (1)	S	6-2	201	7/1/81	Utah	Las Vegas, Nev.	FA
Payne, Bobby	DT	6-4	286	12/18/83	Middle Tennessee State	Morrilton, Ark.	FA
Robinson, Michael	RB	6-1	218	2/6/83	Penn State	Richmond, Va.	D4
Scharff, Scott (1)	DE	6-3	272	2/7/82	Stanford	Wisconsin Rapids, Wis.	FA-'05
Spinner, Bryson (1)	QB	6-3	235	11/7/80	Richmond	Lorton, Va.	FA
Vaughn, Vickiel	S	6-1	204	10/24/83	Arkansas	Plano, Texas	D7
Walker, Delanie	RB	6-1	237	8/12/84	Central Missouri State	Pomona, Calif.	D6a
Washington, Tavares	T	6-3	320	4/20/83	Florida	Greenville, Miss.	FA
Wilder, Sam (1)	T	6-5	297	1/10/82	Colorado	Dallas, Texas	FA-'05
Williams, Brandon	WR	5-11	175	2/24/84	Wisconsin	St. Louis, Mo.	D3

The term NFL Rookie is defined as a player who is in his first season of professional football and has not been on the roster of another professional football team for any regular-season or postseason games. A Rookie is designated by an "R" on NFL rosters. Players who have been active in another professional football league or players who have NFL experience, including either preseason training camp or being on an Active List or Inactive List, or on Reserve/Injured or Reserve/Physically Unable to Perform for fewer than six regular-season games, are termed NFL First-Year Players. An NFL First-Year Player is designated by a "1" on NFL rosters. Thereafter, a player is credited with an additional year of experience for each season in which he accumulates six games on the Active List or Inactive List, or on Reserve/Injured or Reserve/Physically Unable to Perform.

Log on to www.sf49ers.com for an up-to-date roster.

COACHING STAFF

Head Coach,
Mike Nolan

Pro Career: Named the fifteenth head coach in 49ers history on January 19, 2005 Mike Nolan enters his second season as head coach of the San Francisco 49ers. Nolan is in his nineteenth year in the league and twenty-fifth year in coaching. Nolan joins San Francisco after an impressive stint as defensive coordinator of the Baltimore Ravens, a position he has held with three other teams: New York Jets (2000), Washington Redskins (1997-99), and New York Giants (1993-96). In Baltimore, Nolan's defense was among the NFL's best, finishing third overall. Baltimore ranked first in the AFC with 17 fumble recoveries and led the NFL in sacks (47) and tied for first in the AFC and second in the NFL with 41 takeaways. Nolan joined the Ravens after a one-year stay as the New York Jets defensive coordinator in 2000. Under Nolan's tutelage, the Jets defense rebounded to tenth overall (tied with Philadelphia) in the league—an improvement of 11 spots from the previous year. From 1997-99 Nolan was the defensive coordinator of the Washington Redskins. In 1997, the Redskins allowed the eighth-fewest points in NFL and finished third overall in pass defense. He also spent four seasons as defensive coordinator under then-head coach Dan Reeves for the New York Giants (1993-96). In his first season, the Giants' defense allowed the fewest points in the NFL (205). Nolan also worked on Reeves' staff from 1987-1992 with the Denver Broncos as linebackers coach and as special teams coach/defensive assistant. Career record: 4-12.

Background: Nolan participated in the Broncos' 1981 training camp as a defensive back under Dan Reeves. He joined the Broncos after earning three letters as free safety for the Oregon Ducks (1978-1980). Nolan graduated from Woodside (Calif.) high school. He is the son of former NFL head coach Dick Nolan (San Francisco and New Orleans).

Personal: Born March 7, 1959, Baltimore. He and wife Kathy, have four children: sons, Michael and Christopher, and daughters, Laura and Jennifer.

ASSISTANT COACHES

Duane Carlisle, asst. strength and conditioning; born Nov. 13, 1965, Haverhill, Mass. Attended Maryland. No college or pro playing experience. Pro coach: Speed development consultant for Philadelphia Eagles 2000-04, joined 49ers in 2005.

Billy Davis, defensive coordinator; born November 5, 1965, Youngstown, Ohio. Quarterback Cincinnati 1984-88. College coach: Michigan State 1990-91. Pro coach: Pittsburgh Steelers 1992-94, Carolina Panthers 1995-98, Cleveland Browns 1999, Green Bay Packers 2000, Atlanta Falcons 2001-03, New York Giants

2004, joined 49ers in 2005.

Gary Emanuel, defensive line; born October 30, 1958, Philadelphia. Offensive lineman West Chester (Pa.) C.C. 1976-78, Plymouth State 1979-1980. College coach: Plymouth State 1981-84, West Chester C.C. 1985, Massachusetts 1986-87, Dartmouth 1988-90, Syracuse 1991-93, Washington State 1994-96, Purdue 1997-2004. Pro coach: Joined 49ers in 2005.

Pep Hamilton, offensive assistant/quarterbacks: born September 19, 1974, Charlotte, N.C. Quarterback Howard 1993-96. College coach: Howard 1997-2002. Pro coach: N.Y. Jets 2003-05, joined 49ers in 2006.

Bishop Harris, running backs; born November 23, 1941, Phenix City, Ala. Running back/defensive back North Carolina College 1960-63. College coach: Duke 1972-75, North Carolina State 1977-79, Louisiana State 1980-83, Notre Dame 1984-85, Minnesota 1986-1990, North Carolina Central 1991-92 (head coach). Pro coach: Denver Broncos 1993-94, Oakland Raiders 1995-97, Buffalo Bills 1998-99, New York Jets 2001-04, joined 49ers in 2005.

Pete Hoener, tight ends; born June 14, 1954, Peoria, Ill. Tight end/defensive end Bradley 1969-1970. College coach: Missouri 1975-76, Illinois State 1977, Indiana State 1978-1984, Illinois 1986-88, Purdue 1989-1990, Texas Christian 1991-97, Iowa State 1998-99, Texas A&M 2000. Pro coach: St. Louis Cardinals 1985-86, Arizona Cardinals 2003, Chicago Bears 2004, joined 49ers in 2005.

Jim Hostler, quarterbacks; born November 11, 1966, Pittsburgh. Defensive back Indiana (Pa.) 1986-89. College coach: Indiana (Pa.) 1990-92, 1994-99, Juanita (Pa.) 1993. Pro coach: Kansas City Chiefs 2000, New Orleans Saints 2001-02, New York Jets 2003-04, joined 49ers in 2005.

Vance Joseph, secondary assistant; born September 20, 1972, Marrero, La. Defensive back Colorado 1990-94. Pro defensive back New York Jets 1995, Indianapolis Colts 1996. College coach: Colorado 1999-2001, 2002-03, Wyoming 2002, Bowling Green State 2004. Pro coach: Joined 49ers in 2005.

Johnnie Lynn, secondary; born December 19, 1956, Los Angeles. Defensive back UCLA 1975-78. Pro defensive back New York Jets 1979-1986. College coach: Arizona 1988-1993. Pro coach: Tampa Bay Buccaneers 1994-95, San Francisco 49ers 1996, New York Giants 1997-2003, Baltimore Ravens 2004-05, joined 49ers in 2006.

Larry Mac Duff, special teams coordinator; born June 22, 1948, Clinton, Iowa. Defensive end Fullerton (Calif.) J.C. 1966-67, Oklahoma 1968-69. No pro playing experience. College coach: Stanford 1980-83, Hawaii 1984-86, Arizona 1987-

96, 2001-02. Pro coach: New York Giants 1997-2000, joined 49ers in 2003.

Johnny Parker, strength & conditioning; born February 1, 1947, Greenville, S.C. Attended Mississippi. No college or pro playing experience. College coach: South Carolina, 1974-76, Indiana 1977-79, Louisiana State 1980, Mississippi 1981-83. Pro coach: New York Giants 1984-92, New England Patriots 1993-99, Tampa Bay Buccaneers 2002, joined 49ers in 2005.

Jeff Rodgers, special teams assistant; born January 12, 1978, St. Paul, Minn. Linebacker North Texas 1997-2000. No pro playing experience. College coach: Arizona 2001-02. Pro coach: Joined 49ers in 2003.

Mike Singletary, asst. head coach/linebackers; born October 9, 1958, Houston. Linebacker Baylor 1977-1980. Pro linebacker Chicago Bears 1981-1992. Inducted into Pro Football Hall of Fame 1998. Pro coach: Baltimore Ravens 2003-04, joined 49ers in 2005.

Jerry Sullivan, wide receivers; born July 13, 1944, Miami, Fla. Quarterback Florida State 1963-64. No pro playing experience. College coach: Kansas State 1971-72, Texas Tech 1973-75, South Carolina 1976-1982, Indiana 1983, Louisiana State 1984-1990, Ohio State 1991. Pro coach: San Diego Chargers 1992-96, Detroit Lions 1997-2000, Arizona Cardinals 2001-03, Miami Dolphins 2004, joined 49ers in 2005.

Jason Tarver, defensive quality control/defensive assistant; born August 28, 1974, Stanford, Calif. Defensive back West Valley College 1994-95. No pro playing experience. College coach: West Valley College 1996-97, UCLA 1998-2000. Pro coach: Joined 49ers in 2001.

Norv Turner, offensive coordinator; born May 17, 1952, LeJeune, N.C. Quarterback Oregon 1972-74. College coach: Oregon 1975, Southern California 1976-1984. Pro coach: Los Angeles Rams 1985-1990, Dallas Cowboys 1991-93, Washington Redskins 1994-2000 (head coach), San Diego Chargers 2001, Miami Dolphins 2002, Oakland Raiders 2003-04 (head coach), joined 49ers in 2006.

George Warhop, offensive line; born September 19, 1961, Riverside, Ca. Guard/center Mt. San Jacinto (Calif.) J.C. 1979-1980, Cincinnati 1981-82. College coach: Cincinnati 1983, Kansas 1984-86, Vanderbilt 1987-89, New Mexico 1990, Southern Methodist 1993, Boston College 1994-95. Pro coach: London Monarchs (WL) 1991-92, St. Louis Rams 1996-97, Arizona Cardinals 1998-2002, Dallas Cowboys 2003-04, joined 49ers in 2005.

**National Football Conference
West Division**
Team Colors: Seahawks Blue, Seahawks
Navy, Seahawks Bright Green
**11220 N.E. 53ᴿᴰ Street
Kirkland, Washington, 98033
Telephone:** (425) 827-9777

2006 SCHEDULE
PRESEASON
Aug. 12 **Dallas** 7:00
Aug. 20 at Indianapolis 8:00
Aug. 26 at San Diego.......................8:00
Aug. 31 **Oakland** 7:00

REGULAR SEASON
Sept. 10 at Detroit 1:00
Sept. 17 **Arizona** 1:05
Sept. 24 **N.Y. Giants** 1:15
Oct. 1   at Chicago.........................7:15
Oct. 8   Open Date
Oct. 15 at St. Louis......................12:00
Oct. 22 **Minnesota** 1:15
Oct. 29 at Kansas City 12:00
Nov. 6   **Oakland** (Mon.)..................5:30
Nov. 12 **St. Louis** 1:15
Nov. 19 at San Francisco................1:05
Nov. 27 **Green Bay** (Mon.) 5:30
Dec. 3   at Denver 2:15
Dec. 10 at Arizona..........................2:05
Dec. 14 **San Francisco** (Thu.) 5:00
Dec. 24 **San Diego**.......................1:15
Dec. 31 at Tampa Bay 1:00

Stadium: Qwest Field
(opened in 2002)
• **Capacity:** 67,000
Playing Surface: FieldTurf
Training Camp: Eastern Washington Univ.
Cheney, Washington 99004

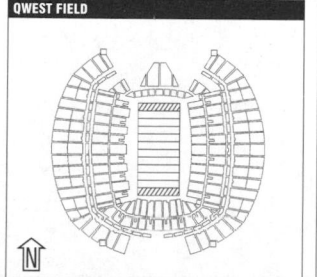

CLUB OFFICIALS
Chairman: Paul Allen
CEO: Tod Leiweke
President of Football Operations:
Tim Ruskell
Executive VP of Football Operations/
Head Coach: Mike Holmgren
VP/Player Personnel: Ruston Webster
VP/Community Outreach: Mike Flood
VP/Corporate Partnership/Legal Affairs:
Lance Lopes
VP/Corporate Sales: Scott Patrick
VP/Administration: Gary Wright
Director of Marketing, Suite Sales and
Service: Ron Jenkins
Director of Pro Personnel: Will Lewis
Director of Communications and
Broadcasting: Dave Pearson
Asst. Director of Communications:
Lane Gammel
Director of Community Outreach:
Sandy Gregory
Director of Ticket Sales/Operations:
Chuck Arnold
Gameday Presentation: Rick Crawford
Video Director Football: Thom Fermstad
Head Athletic Trainer: Sam Ramsden
Equipment Manager: Erik Kennedy
Team Travel: Jeremy Young

COACHING HISTORY
(232-249-0)
Records include postseason games
1976-1982 Jack Patera*................35-59-0
1982   Mike McCormack 4-3-0
1983-1991 Chuck Knox 83-67-0
1992-94   Tom Flores...................14-34-0
1995-98   Dennis Erickson...........31-33-0
1999-2005 Mike Holmgren 65-53-0
*Released after two games in 1982

ATTENDANCE
Home 519,967   Away 518,271
Total 1,038,238
Single-game home record,
68,681 (12/16/00)
Single-season home record,
522,656 (1999)

2006 DRAFT CHOICES
Round	Name	Pos.	College
1	Kelly Jennings	DB	Miami
2	Darryl Tapp	DE	Virginia Tech
4	Rob Sims	G	Ohio State
5	David Kirtman	FB	So. California
7	Ryan Plackemeier	P	Wake Forest
	Ben Obomanu	WR	Auburn

2005 TEAM RECORD
PRESEASON (2-2)

Date	Result	Opponent
8/12	W 34-15	at New Orleans
8/22	L 10-18	Dallas
8/27	W 23-17	at Kansas City
9/2	L 21-23	Minnesota

REGULAR SEASON (13-3)

Date	Result	Opponent	Att.
9/11	L 14-26	at Jacksonville	65,204
9/18	W 21-18	Atlanta	66,030
9/25	W 37-12	Arizona	64,843
10/2	L 17-20	at Washington (OT)	90,215
10/9	W 37-31	at St. Louis	65,707
10/16	W 42-10	Houston	66,196
10/23	W 13-10	Dallas	67,046
11/6	W 33-19	at Arizona	43,542
11/13	W 31-16	St. Louis	67,192
11/20	W 27-25	at San Francisco	63,590
11/27	W 24-21	N.Y. Giants (OT)	67,102
12/5	W 42-0	at Philadelphia	67,637
12/11	W 41-3	San Francisco	66,690
12/18	W 28-24	at Tennessee	69,149
12/24	W 28-13	Indianapolis	67,855
1/1	L 17-23	at Green Bay	69,928

(OT) Overtime

POSTSEASON (2-1)

Date	Result	Opponent	
1/14	W 20-10	Washington	67,551
1/22	W 34-14	Carolina	67,837
2/5	L 10-21	vs. Pittsburgh at Detroit	68,206

SCORE BY PERIODS

Seahawks	93	148	121	87	3	—	452
Opponents	44	80	83	61	3	—	271

2005 TEAM STATISTICS

	Seahawks	Opp.
Total First Downs	361	295
Rushing	142	78
Passing	192	194
Penalty	27	23
3rd Down: Made/Att	76/192	89/234
3rd Down Pct.	39.6	38.0
4th Down: Made/Att	7/8	12/19
4th Down Pct.	87.5	63.2
Possession Avg.	29:17	30:43
Total Net Yards	5,915	5,069
Avg. Per Game	369.7	316.8
Total Plays	1,020	1,041
Avg. Per Play	5.8	4.9
Net Yards Rushing	2,457	1,510
Avg. Per Game	153.6	94.4
Total Rushes	519	420
Net Yards Passing	3,458	3,559
Avg. Per Game	216.1	222.4
Sacked/Yards Lost	27/174	50/302
Gross Yards	3,632	3,861
Att./Completions	474/307	571/331
Completion Pct.	64.8	58.0
Had Intercepted	10	16
Punts/Average	80/41.0	77/40.1
Net Punting Avg.	80/34.7	77/36.0
Penalties/Yards	94/846	123/909
Fumbles/Ball Lost	18/7	25/11
Touchdowns	57	24
Rushing	29	5
Passing	25	18
Returns	3	1

2005 INDIVIDUAL STATISTICS

PASSING	Att.	Comp.	Yds.	Pct.	TD	Int.	Tkld.	Rate
Hasselbeck	449	294	3,459	65.5	24	9	24/154	98.2
Wallace	25	13	173	52.0	1	1	3/20	70.9
Seahawks	474	307	3,632	64.8	25	10	27/174	96.8
Opponents	571	331	3,861	58.0	18	16	50/302	77.4

SCORING	TD R	TD P	TD Rt	PAT	FG	Saf	PTS
Alexander	27	1	0	0/0	0/0	0	168
J. Brown	0	0	0	56/57	18/25	0	110
Jurevicius	0	10	0	0/0	0/0	0	60
Stevens	0	5	0	0/0	0/0	0	30
Engram	0	3	0	0/0	0/0	0	18
Jackson	0	3	0	0/0	0/0	0	18
Dyson	0	0	2	0/0	0/0	0	12
Hackett	0	2	0	0/0	0/0	0	12
Hannam	0	1	0	0/0	0/0	0	6
Hasselbeck	1	0	0	0/0	0/0	0	6
Morris	1	0	0	0/0	0/0	0	6
Tatupu	0	0	1	0/0	0/0	0	6
Seahawks	29	25	3	56/57	18/25	0	452
Opponents	5	18	1	21/21	34/42	0	271

2-Pt. Conversions: None.
Seahawks 0-0, Opponents 2-3.

RUSHING	No.	Yds	Avg	LG	TD
Alexander	370	1,880	5.1	88t	27
Morris	71	288	4.1	49	1
Hasselbeck	36	124	3.4	23	1
Weaver	17	80	4.7	24	0
Strong	17	78	4.6	16	0
Jackson	1	7	7.0	7	0
Warrick	1	5	5.0	5	0
Wallace	6	-5	-0.8	0	0
Seahawks	519	2,457	4.7	88t	29
Opponents	420	1,510	3.6	50	5

RECEIVING	No.	Yds	Avg	LG	TD
Engram	67	778	11.6	56	3
Jurevicius	55	694	12.6	52	10
Stevens	45	554	12.3	35t	5
Jackson	38	482	12.7	48	3
Hackett	28	400	14.3	47	2
Strong	22	166	7.5	27	0
Alexander	15	78	5.2	9	1
Hannam	13	89	6.8	20	1
Warrick	11	180	16.4	42	0
Urban	7	151	21.6	46	0
Morris	5	48	9.6	20	0
Weaver	1	12	12.0	12	0
Seahawks	307	3,632	11.8	56	25
Opponents	331	3,861	11.7	63	18

INTERCEPTIONS	No.	Yds	Avg	LG	TD
Boulware	4	107	26.8	40	0
Babineaux	3	56	18.7	25	0
Tatupu	3	55	18.3	38t	1
Herndon	2	12	6.0	10	0
Williams	2	6	3.0	6	0
Dyson	1	72	72.0	72t	1
Trufant	1	7	7.0	7	0
Seahawks	16	315	19.7	72t	2
Opponents	10	93	9.3	33	0

PUNTING	No.	Yds.	Avg.	In 20	LG
Rouen	61	2,539	41.6	20	62
Araguz	18	723	40.2	4	53
J. Brown	1	20	20.0	1	20
Seahawks	80	3,282	41.0	25	62
Opponents	77	3,091	40.1	23	67

PUNT RETURNS	Ret	FC	Yds	Avg	LG	TD
Williams	24	22	139	5.8	24	0
Warrick	6	0	29	4.8	10	0
Engram	1	1	9	9.0	9	0
Seahawks	31	23	177	5.7	24	0
Opponents	41	16	343	8.4	44	0

KICKOFF RETURNS	No.	Yds	Avg	LG	TD
Scobey	59	1,326	22.5	53	0
Morris	1	21	21.0	21	0
Tafoya	1	0	0.0	0	0
Seahawks	61	1,347	22.1	53	0
Opponents	82	1,802	22.0	99t	1

FIELD GOALS	1-19	20-29	30-39	40-49	50+
J. Brown	0/0	5/5	4/5	4/7	5/8
Seahawks	0/0	5/5	4/5	4/7	5/8
Opponents	0/0	8/9	16/18	7/10	3/5

SACKS	No.
Fisher	9.0
Bernard	8.5
Hill	7.5
Tubbs	5.5
Tatupu	4.0
Wistrom	4.0
TEAM	3.0
Darby	2.5
Boulware	2.0
Terrill	2.0
Tafoya	1.0
Trufant	1.0
Seahawks	50.0
Opponents	27.0

RECORD HOLDERS
INDIVIDUAL RECORDS—CAREER

Category	Name	Performance
Rushing (Yds.)	Shaun Alexander, 2000-05	7,817
Passing (Yds.)	Dave Krieg, 1980-1991	26,132
Passing (TDs)	Dave Krieg, 1980-1991	195
Receiving (No.)	Steve Largent, 1976-1989	819
Receiving (Yds.)	Steve Largent, 1976-1989	13,089
Interceptions	Dave Brown, 1976-1986	50
Punting (Avg.)	Rick Tuten, 1991-97	43.8
Punt Return (Avg.)	Charlie Rogers, 1999-2001	12.7
Kickoff Return (Avg.)	Steve Broussard, 1995-98	23.2
Field Goals	Norm Johnson, 1982-1990	159
Touchdowns (Tot.)	Steve Largent, 1976-1989	101
Points	Norm Johnson, 1982-1990	810

INDIVIDUAL RECORDS—SINGLE SEASON

Category	Name	Performance
Rushing (Yds.)	Shaun Alexander, 2005	1,880
Passing (Yds.)	Matt Hasselbeck, 2003	3,841
Passing (TDs)	Dave Krieg, 1984	32
Receiving (No.)	Darrell Jackson, 2004	87
Receiving (Yds.)	Steve Largent, 1985	1,287
Interceptions	John Harris, 1981	10
	Kenny Easley, 1984	10
Punting (Avg.)	Rick Tuten, 1995	45.0
Punt Return (Avg.)	Charlie Rogers, 1999	14.5
Kickoff Return (Avg.)	Charlie Rogers, 2000	24.9
Field Goals	Todd Peterson, 1999	34
Touchdowns (Tot.)	Shaun Alexander, 2005	*28
Points	Shaun Alexander, 2005	168

INDIVIDUAL RECORDS—SINGLE GAME

Category	Name	Performance
Rushing (Yds.)	Shaun Alexander, 11-11-01	266
Passing (Yds.)	Matt Hasselbeck, 12-29-02	449
Passing (TDs)	Dave Krieg, 12-2-84, 9-15-85, 11-28-88	5
	Warren Moon, 10-26-97	5
	Matt Hasselbeck, 11-23-03	5
Receiving (No.)	Steve Largent, 10-18-87	15
Receiving (Yds.)	Steve Largent, 10-18-87	261
Interceptions	Kenny Easley, 9-3-84	3
	Eugene Robinson, 12-6-92	3
	Darryl Williams, 9-21-97	3
Field Goals	Norm Johnson, 9-20-87, 12-18-88	5
Touchdowns (Tot.)	Shaun Alexander, 9-29-02	5
Points	Shaun Alexander, 9-29-02	30

*NFL Record

2006 VETERAN ROSTER

No.	Name	Pos.	Ht.	Wt.	Birthdate	NFL Exp.	College	Hometown	How Acq.	'05 Games/ Starts
37	Alexander, Shaun	RB	5-11	225	8/30/77	7	Alabama	Florence, Ky.	D1a-'00	16/16
68	Ashworth, Tom	T/G	6-6	305	10/10/77	4	Colorado	Centennial, Colo.	UFA(NE)-'06	14/11*
	Austin, Reggie	CB	5-9	185	1/21/77	4	Wake Forest	Atlanta, Ga.	FA-'06	0*
27	Babineaux, Jordan	CB	6-0	200	8/31/82	3	Southern Arkansas	Port Arthur, Texas	FA-'04	16/4
85	Bannister, Alex	WR	6-5	207	4/23/79	5	Eastern Kentucky	Cincinnati, Ohio	D5-'01	2/0
57	Bentley, Kevin	LB	6-0	245	12/29/79	5	Northwestern	Montclair, Calif.	UFA(Cle)-'05	15/3
99	Bernard, Rocky	DT	6-3	293	4/19/79	5	Texas A&M	Baytown, Texas	D5a-'02	16/7
28	Boulware, Michael	S	6-3	223	9/17/81	3	Florida State	Columbia, S.C.	D2-'04	16/16
3	Brown, Josh	K	6-0	202	4/29/79	4	Nebraska	Foyil, Okla.	D7a-'03	16/0
81	Burleson, Nate	WR	6-0	192	8/19/81	4	Nevada	Seattle, Wash.	RFA(Minn)-'06	12/9*
36	Carthon, Ran	FB	6-0	218	2/10/81	2	Florida	Miami, Fla.	FA-'06	6/0*
40	Celestin, Oliver	S	6-0	207	2/25/81	3	Texas Southern	New Orleans, La.	FA-'06	12/0*
92	Cooper, Chris	DE	6-5	285	12/27/77	5	Nebraska-Omaha	Rochester, Minn.	FA-'06	0*
91	Darby, Chuck	DT	6-0	270	10/22/75	6	South Carolina State	North, S.C.	UFA(TB)-'05	14/14
52	Darche, Jean-Philippe	LS	6-0	246	2/28/75	7	McGill	Montreal, Quebec, Canada	FA-'00	16/0
95	Davis, Russell	DT	6-4	306	3/28/75	8	North Carolina	Fayetteville, N.C.	UFA(Ariz)-'06	3/3*
84	Engram, Bobby	WR	5-10	188	1/7/73	11	Penn State	Camden, S.C.	UFA(Chi)-'01	13/13
94	Fisher, Bryce	DE	6-3	268	5/12/77	6	Air Force Academy	Renton, Wash.	UFA(StL)-'05	16/15
25	Frazier, Lance	CB	5-10	183	5/23/81	2	West Virginia	Boynton Beach, Fla.	FA-'06	0*
62	Gray, Chris	G	6-4	308	6/19/70	14	Auburn	Birmingham, Ala.	UFA(Chi)-'98	16/16
32 t-	Green, Mike	S	6-0	195	12/6/76	7	Northwestern State (La.)	Ruston, La.	T(Chi)-'06	16/3
	Greene, David	QB	6-3	226	6/22/82	2	Georgia	Snellville, Ga.	D3a-'05	0*
18	Hackett, D.J.	WR	6-2	199	7/3/81	2	Colorado	Ontario, Calif.	D5-'04	13/3
5	Hamdan, Gibran	QB	6-6	240	2/8/81	2	Indiana	San Diego, Calif.	FA-'06	0*
26	Hamlin, Ken	S	6-2	209	1/20/81	4	Arkansas	Memphis, Tenn.	D2-'03	6/6
42	Harts, Shaunard	S	6-0	210	8/4/78	5	Boise State	Pittsburg, Calif.	FA-'06	0*
8	Hasselbeck, Matt	QB	6-4	223	9/25/75	8	Boston College	Westwood, Mass.	T(GB)-'01	16/16
46	Heller, Will	TE	6-6	265	2/28/81	4	Georgia Tech	Dunwoody, Ga.	FA-'06	7/0*
31	Herndon, Kelly	CB	5-10	180	11/3/76	5	Toledo	Twinsburg, Ohio	RFA(Den)-'05	12/6
56	Hill, Leroy	LB	6-1	229	9/14/82	2	Clemson	Haddock, Ga.	D3b-'05	15/9
19	Howry, Keenan	WR	5-10	178	6/17/81	4	Oregon	Los Alamitos, Calif.	FA-'06	4/0*
	Hunter, Wayne	T	6-5	303	7/2/81	2	Hawaii	Honolulu, Hawaii	D3-'03	1/0
82	Jackson, Darrell	WR	6-0	201	12/6/78	7	Florida	Tampa, Fla.	D3-'00	6/6
71	Jones, Walter	T	6-5	315	1/19/74	10	Florida State	Aliceville, Ala.	D1b-'97	15/15
58	Kacyvenski, Isaiah	LB	6-1	252	10/3/77	7	Harvard	Endicott, N.Y.	D4b-'00	16/0
	Kashama, Alain	DE	6-4	262	12/8/79	2	Michigan	Montreal, Quebec, Canada	T(Chi)-'05	1/0
13	Kasper, Kevin	WR	6-1	193	12/23/77	5	Iowa	Hinsdale, Ill.	FA-'06	0*
53	Koutouvides, Niko	LB	6-2	238	3/25/81	3	Purdue	Plainville, Conn.	D4-'04	12/0
54	Lewis, D.D.	LB	6-1	241	1/8/79	4	Texas	Houston, Texas	FA-'02	12/12
75	Locklear, Sean	T	6-4	301	5/29/81	3	North Carolina State	Lumberton, N.C.	D3-'04	16/16
88	Mili, Itula	TE	6-4	260	4/20/73	8	Brigham Young	Laie, Hawaii	D6-'97	2/0
20	Morris, Maurice	RB	5-11	202	12/1/79	5	Oregon	Chester, S.C.	D2a-'02	16/2
44	Peterson, Julian	LB	6-3	235	7/28/78	7	Michigan State	Washington, D.C.	UFA(SF)-'06	15/14*
35	Pruitt, Etric	FS	6-0	196	8/16/81	3	Southern Mississippi	Theodore, Ala.	FA-'05	6/0
72	Rasmussen, Kemp	DE	6-3	265	5/25/79	5	Indiana	Hadley, Mich.	UFA(Car)-'06	15/0*
16	Rouen, Tom	P	6-3	225	6/9/68	14	Colorado	Littleton, Colo.	FA-'05	12/0
33	Scobey, Josh	RB	6-0	220	12/11/79	4	Kansas State	Oklahoma City, Okla.	W(Ariz)-'05	16/0
65	Spencer, Chris	C	6-3	309	3/28/82	2	Mississippi	Madison, Miss.	D1-'05	9/0
86	Stevens, Jerramy	TE	6-7	260	11/13/79	5	Washington	Olympia, Wash.	D1-'02	16/11
38	Strong, Mack	FB	6-0	245	9/11/71	13	Georgia	Columbus, Ga.	FA-'93	16/6
69	Tafoya, Joe	DE	6-4	265	9/6/78	5	Arizona	Pittsburg, Calif.	W(TB)-'05	15/1
51	Tatupu, Lofa	LB	6-0	238	11/15/82	2	Southern California	Wretham, Mass.	D2-'05	16/16
93	Terrill, Craig	DT	6-2	294	6/27/80	3	Purdue	Lebanon, Ind.	D6-'04	16/0
61	Tobeck, Robbie	C	6-4	297	3/6/70	13	Washington State	Tarpon Springs, Fla.	UFA(Atl)-'00	16/16
23	Trufant, Marcus	CB	5-11	199	12/25/80	4	Washington State	Tacoma, Wash.	D1-'03	15/15
90	Tubbs, Marcus	DT	6-3	324	5/16/81	3	Texas	DeSoto, Texas	D1-'04	13/11
89	Urban, Jerheme	WR	6-3	212	11/26/80	3	Trinity	Victoria, Texas	FA-'05	4/1
15	Wallace, Seneca	QB	5-11	196	8/6/80	2	Iowa State	Sacramento, Calif.	D4a-'03	6/0
10	Wallace, Taco	WR	6-1	190	4/14/81	2	Kansas State	Los Angeles, Calif.	FA-'06	1/0*
83	Warrick, Peter	WR	5-11	195	6/19/77	7	Florida State	Bradenton, Fla.	FA-'05	13/5
43	Weaver, Leonard	FB	6-0	251	9/23/82	2	Carson-Newman	Melbourne, Fla.	FA-'05	16/0
22	Williams, Jimmy	CB	5-11	190	3/10/79	6	Vanderbilt	Baton Rouge, La.	FA-'05	14/1
74	Willis, Ray	T	6-6	327	8/13/82	2	Florida State	Angleton, Texas	D4-'05	6/0
98	Wistrom, Grant	DE	6-4	272	7/3/76	9	Nebraska	Webb City, Mo.	UFA(StL)-'04	16/16
77	Womack, Floyd	T/G	6-4	333	11/15/78	6	Mississippi State	Cleveland, Miss.	D4c-'01	11/0
50	Wortham, Cornelius	LB	6-1	236	1/25/82	2	Alabama	Calhoun City, Miss.	D7b-'05	8/0

* Ashworth played 14 games with New England in '05; Austin last active with Chicago in '02; Burleson played 12 games with Minnesota; Carthon played 6 games with Indianapolis; Celestin played 12 games with N.Y. Jets; Cooper missed '05 season with San Francisco because of injury; Davis played 3 games with Arizona; Frazier last active with Dallas in '04; Greene inactive for 16 games; Hamdan last active with Washington in '03; Harts last active with Kansas City in '04; Heller played 7 games with Tampa Bay; Howry played 4 games with Minnesota; Kasper last active with New England in '04; Peterson played 15 games with San Francisco; Rasmussen played 15 games with Carolina; T. Wallace played 1 game with Green Bay.

t- Seahawks traded for Green (Chi).

Players lost through free agency (5): DE Rodney Bailey (Pitt; 8 games in '05), TE Ryan Hannam (Dall; 16), Steve Hutchinson (Minn; 16), WR Joe Jurevicius (Cle, 16), S Marquand Manuel (GB; 16).

Also played with Seahawks in '05—P Leo Araguz (4 games), CB Andre Dyson (10), CB Michael Harden (4), CB/S John Howell (10), LB Jamie Sharper (8).

2006 FIRST-YEAR ROSTER

Name	Pos.	Ht.	Wt.	Birthdate	College	Hometown	How Acq.
Benjamin, Evan	LB	6-0	225	1/29/83	Washington	Redmond, Wash.	FA
Brown, Tony (1)	WR	6-2	199	5/29/81	Tennessee	Lauderdale Lakes, Fla.	FA-'05
Dixon, Jimmy (1)	RB	6-1	230	4/26/82	Georgia Tech	Arlington, Texas	FA
Edwards, Brock (1)	TE	6-4	255	11/13/81	Texas	Fort Worth, Texas	FA
Fulton, Skyler (1)	WR	6-0	200	6/17/82	Arizona State	Olympia, Wash.	FA
Gomez, Mike (1)	TE	6-6	240	4/23/82	Illinois	Miami, Fla.	FA
Haw, Brandon (1)	CB	6-0	195	9/24/80	Rutgers	Cheverly, Md.	FA-'05
Henry, William (1)	G	6-4	295	10/16/81	Clemson	Greenville, S.C.	FA-'05
Henshaw, Matt	TE	6-4	248	3/17/83	Florida State	Brentwood, Tenn.	FA
Hobbs, Kevin	CB	6-0	195	4/30/83	Auburn	Tampa, Fla.	FA
Huckeba, Jeb (1)	DE	6-4	252	5/20/82	Arkansas	Searcy, Ark.	D5-'05
Jennings, Kelly	CB	5-11	178	11/30/82	Miami	Live Oak, Fla.	D1
Jones, C.J. (1)	WR	5-11	195	9/20/80	Iowa	Boynton Beach, Fla.	FA
Killeen, Ryan (1)	K	5-11	185	7/11/83	Southern California	Norco, Calif.	FA
Kirtman, David	FB	6-0	232	2/12/83	Southern California	Mercer Island, Wash.	D5
Laury, Lance	LB	6-2	233	1/17/82	South Carolina	Hopkins, S.C.	FA
Lindstrom, Gabe (1)	P	6-4	220	5/25/76	Toledo	Bisbee, Ariz.	FA
Lulay, Travis	QB	6-2	216	9/27/83	Montana State	Aumsville, Ore.	FA
Mann, Maurice (1)	WR	6-1	190	9/14/82	Nevada	Seaside, Calif.	FA-'05
McIntyre, Garrett	DT	6-3	262	11/26/84	Fresno State	S. Lake Tahoe, Calif.	FA
Moses, Renaldo	DE	6-4	208	6/25/82	North Carolina State	Rockingham, N.C.	FA
Obomanu, Ben	WR	6-0	203	10/30/83	Auburn	Selma, Ala.	D7b
Plackemeier, Ryan	P	6-3	248	3/5/84	Wake Forest	Bonsall, Calif.	D7a
Pollard, Robert (1)	DE	6-2	278	6/28/81	Texas Christian	Beaumont, Texas	FA-'05
Ralph, Kyle	G	6-3	307	9/30/84	North Carolina	Cleves, Ohio	FA
Reynolds, Lance	C	6-2	305	6/17/80	Brigham Young	Provo, Utah	FA
Ross, Gerard	CB	6-1	200	12/27/82	Florida State	Jacksonville, Fla.	FA
Ross, Pat	C	6-3	301	3/16/83	Boston College	Reading, Ohio	FA
Sims, Rob	G	6-3	307	12/6/83	Ohio State	Macedonia, Ohio	D4
Syptak, John	DE	6-1	253	3/16/84	Rice	Bellville, Texas	FA
Tapp, Darryl	DE	6-1	265	9/13/84	Virginia Tech	Chesapeake, Va.	D2
Weeks, Marquis (1)	RB	5-10	216	10/2/80	Virginia	Norristown, Pa.	FA-'05
Willis, Keith (1)	TE	6-6	264	12/14/80	Virginia Tech	Norfolk, Va.	FA

The term NFL Rookie is defined as a player who is in his first season of professional football and has not been on the roster of another professional football team for any regular-season or postseason games. A Rookie is designated by an "R" on NFL rosters. Players who have been active in another professional football league or players who have NFL experience, including either preseason training camp or being on an Active List or Inactive List, or on Reserve/Injured or Reserve/Physically Unable to Perform for fewer than six regular-season games, are termed NFL First-Year Players. An NFL First-Year Player is designated by a "1" on NFL rosters. Thereafter, a player is credited with an additional year of experience for each season in which he accumulates six games on the Active List or Inactive List, or on Reserve/Injured or Reserve/Physically Unable to Perform.

Log on to www.seahawks.com for an up-to-date roster.

SEATTLE SEAHAWKS

COACHING STAFF

**Executive Vice President of Football Operations/Head Coach,
Mike Holmgren**

Pro Career: Named as the Seahawks' sixth head coach on January 8, 1999. In 2004, the Seahawks won their first NFC West crown and third-ever division title. Under Holmgren's tutelage in 2003, the Seahawks posted their first double-digit victory total since 1986. In his first season, 1999, Holmgren guided the Seahawks to their first postseason appearance since 1988. Last season, led them to a franchise-best record 13-3 finish, and their first-ever Super Bowl appearance. Holmgren joined Seattle after serving as the head coach of the Green Bay Packers (1992-98). By winning at least one game in five consecutive postseasons (1993-97) Holmgren and John Madden (1973-77) as the only coaches in league history to accomplish that feat. In 20 NFL seasons (1999-2005 head coach Seattle, 1992-98 head coach Green Bay, 1986-1991 assistant coach San Francisco) Holmgren's teams have a 209-109-1 (.657) record, posted double-digit win totals 12 times, made the postseason 15 times, won three Super Bowls (XXIII, XXIV, and XXXI), and reached two others (XXXII and XL). Career record: 149-95.

Background: Quarterback at Southern California (1966-69) and was drafted by the St. Louis Cardinals in the eighth round of the 1970 NFL Draft. He served as an assistant coach at San Francisco State (1981) and Brigham Young (1982-85). Earned his bachelor degree in business finance at Southern California.

Personal: Born June 15, 1948, in San Francisco. He and his wife, Kathy, have four daughters—Calla, Jenny, Emily, and Gretchen.

ASSISTANT COACHES

Teryl Austin, defensive backs; born March 3, 1965, Sharon, Pa. Defensive back Pittsburgh 1984-87. Pro defensive back Montreal Machine (WLAF) 1991. College coach: Penn State 1991-92, Wake Forest 1993-95, Syracuse 1996-98, Michigan 1999-2002. Pro coach: Joined Seahawks in 2003.

Dwaine Board, defensive line; born November 29, 1956, Rocky Mount, Va. Defensive lineman North Carolina A&T 1974-77. Pro defensive lineman San Francisco 49ers 1979-1987, New Orleans Saints 1988. Pro coach: San Francisco 49ers 1990-2002, joined Seahawks in 2003.

Bob Casullo, special teams; born March 21, 1951, Little Falls, N.Y. Running back Brockport (N.Y.) State College 1970-73. No pro playing experience. College coach: Syracuse 1985-1994, Georgia Tech 1995-98, Michigan State 1999. Pro coach: Oakland Raiders 2000-03, New York Jets 2004, joined Seahawks in 2005.

Mike Clark, strength and conditioning; born August 22, 1954, Wichita, Kan. Linebacker Ottawa College 1973-76. No pro playing experience. College coach: Kansas 1977-78, 1982, Wyoming 1981, Oregon 1983-87, Southern California 1988-89, Texas A&M 2000-2003, joined Seahawks in 2004.

Nolan Cromwell, wide receivers; born January 30, 1955, Smith Center, Kan. Quarterback/safety Kansas 1973-76. Pro defensive back Los Angeles Rams 1977-1987. Pro coach: Los Angeles Rams 1991, Green Bay Packers 1992-98, joined Seahawks in 1999.

Keith Gilbertson, offensive consultant; born May 15, 1948, Snohomish, Wash. Defensive line Central Washington 1967, Columbia Basin (Wash.) J.C. 1968, Hawaii 1969-1970. No pro playing experience. College coach: Idaho State 1971-74, Western Washington 1975, Washington 1976, Utah State 1977-1981, Idaho 1982, 1986-88, Washington 1989-1991, California 1992-95, Washington 1999-2004. Pro coach: L.A. Express (USFL) 1983-85, Seattle Seahawks 1996-98, re-joined Seahawks in 2005.

Gil Haskell, offensive coordinator; born September 24, 1943, San Francisco. Defensive back San Francisco State 1961, 1963-65. No pro playing experience. College coach: Southern California 1978-1982. Pro coach: Los Angeles Rams 1983-1991, Green Bay Packers 1992-97, Carolina Panthers 1998-99, joined Seahawks in 2000.

Tom Headlee, quality control/defense; born November 6, 1976, Bothell, Wash. Attended Washington State. No college or pro playing experience. Pro coach: Joined Seahawks in 2006.

John Jamison, special teams assistant; born May 26, 1948, San Francisco. Wide receiver California 1968. No pro playing experience. Pro coach: Joined Seahawks in 2005.

Darren Krein, asst. strength & conditioning; born July 7, 1971, Aurora, Colo. Linebacker/defensive end Miami 1989-1993. Pro linebacker San Diego Chargers 1994, Barcelona Dragons (NFLE) 1996. Pro coach: Seattle 1997-98, re-joined Seahawks in 2002.

Bill Laveroni, offensive line; born July 20, 1948, San Francisco. Center California 1967-69. No pro playing experience. College coach: California 1970, 1978, 1983-89, San Francisco 1971, Utah State 1979-1982, San Jose State 1990-94, Rutgers 1996-2000, Vanderbilt 2001. Pro coach: San Jose Sabercats (AFL) 1995, joined Seahawks in 2002.

Jim Lind, tight ends; born Novemeber 11, 1947, Isle, Minn. Linebacker Bethel College 1965-66, defensive back Bemidji State 1971-72. No pro playing experience. College coach: St. Cloud State 1977-78, St. John's (Minn.) 1979-1980, Brigham Young 1981-82, Minnesota-

Morris 1983-86 (head coach), Wisconsin-Eau Claire 1987-1991 (head coach). Pro coach: Green Bay Packers 1992-98, joined Seahawks in 1999.

Larry Marmie, defensive assistant/secondary; born October 17, 1942, Berea, Kent. Quarterback Eastern Kentucky 1962-65. No pro playing experience. College coach: Morehead State 1968-1971, Eastern Kentucky 1972-76, Tulsa 1977-78, North Carolina 1979-1982, Tennessee 1983-84, Arizona State 1985-1991 (head coach 1988-1991), Tennessee 1992-94, UCLA 1995. Pro coach: Arizona Cardinals 1996-2003, St. Louis Rams 2004-05, joined Seahawks in 2006.

John Marshall, defensive coordinator; born October 2, 1945, Arroyo Grande, Calif. Linebacker Washington State 1964. No pro playing experience. College coach: Oregon 1970-76, Southern California 1977-79. Pro coach: Green Bay Packers 1980-82, Indianapolis Colts 1986-88, San Francisco 49ers 1989-1998, Carolina Panthers 1999-2001, Detroit Lions 2002, joined Seahawks in 2003.

Stump Mitchell, running backs; born March 15, 1959, St. Mary's, Ga. Tailback The Citadel 1977-1980. Running back St. Louis/Phoenix Cardinals 1981-89. College coach: Morgan State 1995-98 (head coach 1996-98). Pro coach: San Antonio Rough Riders (WLAF) 1991, joined Seahawks in 1999.

Gary Reynolds, offensive assistant/quality control; born October 15, 1966, Boston. Attended Texas A&M. No college or pro playing experience. College coach: Texas A&M 1991, Tennessee 1992. Pro coach: Green Bay Packers 1996-98, joined Seahawks in 1999.

Ray Rhodes, special projects/defense; born October 20, 1950, Mexia, Texas. Running back Texas Christian 1969-1970, wide receiver/defensive back/kick returner Tulsa 1972-73. Pro wide receiver/defensive back New York Giants 1974-79, San Francisco 49ers 1980. Pro coach: San Francisco 49ers 1981-1991, 1994, Green Bay Packers 1992-93, 1999 (head coach 1999), Philadelphia Eagles 1995-98 (head coach), Washington Redskins 2000, Denver Broncos 2001-02, joined Seahawks in 2003.

Zerick Rollins, linebackers; born June 20, 1975, Houston. Defensive end Texas A&M 1995-97. No pro playing experience. Graduate assistant Texas A&M 1997-2000. Pro coach: Joined Seahawks in 2001.

Jim Zorn, quarterbacks; born May 10, 1953, Whittier, Calif. Quarterback Cal Poly-Pomona 1973-75. Pro quarterback Seattle Seahawks 1975-1984, Green Bay Packers 1985, Winnipeg Blue Bombers (CFL) 1986, Tampa Bay Buccaneers 1987. College coach: Boise State 1989-1991, Utah State 1992-94, Minnesota 1995-96. Pro coach: Seattle Seahawks 1997, Detroit Lions 1998-2000, re-joined Seahawks in 2001.

**National Football Conference
South Division**
Team Colors: Buccaneer Red, Pewter,
Black, and Orange
One Buccaneer Place
Tampa, Florida 33607
Telephone: (813) 870-2700

2006 SCHEDULE
PRESEASON
Aug. 11 **New York Jets** 7:30
Aug. 19 **Miami** 7:30
Aug. 26 at Jacksonville 8:00
Aug. 31 at Houston 7:00

REGULAR SEASON
Sept. 10 **Baltimore**.........................1:00
Sept. 17 at Atlanta..........................1:00
Sept. 24 **Carolina**...........................1:00
Oct. 1   Open Date
Oct. 8   at New Orleans................12:00
Oct. 15 **Cincinnati** 1:00
Oct. 22 **Philadelphia** 1:00
Oct. 29 at N.Y. Giants.....................1:00
Nov. 5   **New Orleans**......................1:00
Nov. 13 at Carolina (Mon.) 8:30
Nov. 19 **Washington** 1:00
Nov. 23 at Dallas (Thu.) 3:15
Dec. 3   at Pittsburgh......................1:00
Dec. 10 **Atlanta**.............................1:00
Dec. 17 at Chicago.......................12:00
Dec. 24 at Cleveland 1:00
Dec. 31 **Seattle**.............................1:00

Stadium: Raymond James Stadium
(opened in 1998)
  • **Capacity:** 65,657
  Tampa, Florida 33607
Playing Surface: Grass
Training Camp: Disney's Wide World of
Sports
Lake Buena Vista, Florida
92830

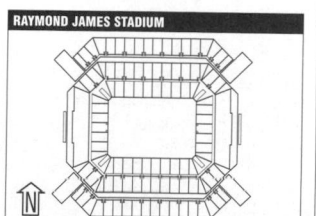

RAYMOND JAMES STADIUM

CLUB OFFICIALS
Owner/President: Malcolm Glazer
Executive Vice President: Bryan Glazer
Executive Vice President: Joel Glazer
Executive Vice President: Edward Glazer
General Manager: Bruce Allen
Chief Operating Officer: Eric Land
Director of Football Operations:
  Mark Arteaga
Director of College Scouting:
  Dennis Hickey
Director of Pro Personnel: Mark Dominik
Personnel Executive: Doug Williams
General Counsel: Roxanne Kosarzycki
Director of Player Development:
  Eric Vance
College Scouts: Jim, Abrams,
  Reggie Cobb, Frank Dorazio,
  Brian Gardner, Seth Turner
National Combine Scout: Mike Martin
Director of Accounting: Nick Reader
Director of Game Day and Video
  Production: Chris Kartzmark
Director of Information Technology:
  Scott Burgin
Director of Marketing and Business
  Development: Jeff Ajluni
Director of Public Relations: Jeff Kamis
Director of Sales: Kristin Bold
Director of Security/Facilities:
  Andre Trescastro
Director of Team Services: Tom Szubka
Director of Ticketing and Business
  Administration: Jason Layton
Broadcasting Operations Manager:
  Jeff Ryan
Internet Manager: Scott Smith
Public Relations Manager: Jason Wahlers
Trainer: Todd Toriscelli
Director of Rehabilitation:
  Shannon Merrick
Equipment Manager: Tim Sain
Assistant Equipment Manager:
  Mark Meschede
Video Director: Dave Levy

COACHING HISTORY
(189-292-1)
Records include postseason games
1976-1984 John McKay.................45-91-1
1985-86   Leeman Bennett 4-28-0
1987-1990 Ray Perkins*................19-41-0
1990-91   Richard Williamson 4-15-0
1992-95   Sam Wyche 23-41-0
1996-2001 Tony Dungy.................56-46-0
2002-05   Jon Gruden 38-30-0
*Released after 13 games in 1990

ATTENDANCE
Home 507,346   Away 519,389
Total 1,026,735
Single-game home record,
  73,523 (12/7/97)
Single-season home record,
  545,980 (1979)

2006 DRAFT CHOICES
Round	Name	Pos.	College
1	Davin Joseph	G/T	Oklahoma
2	Jeremy Trueblood	T	Boston College
3	Maurice Stovall	WR	Notre Dame
4	Alan Zemaitis	DB	Penn State
5	Julian Jenkins	DE/DT	Stanford
6	Bruce Gradkowski	QB	Toledo
	T.J. Williams	TE	North Carolina St.
7	Justin Phinisee	DB	Oregon
	Charles Bennett	DE	Clemson
	Tim Massaquoi	TE	Michigan

2005 TEAM RECORD

PRESEASON (2-2)

Date	Result	Opponent
8/12	W 20-17	at Tennessee
8/20	L 17-20	Jacksonville
8/27	L 14-17	at Miami
9/1	W 38-14	Houston

REGULAR SEASON (11-5)

Date	Result	Opponent	Att.
9/11	W 24-13	at Minnesota	63,939
9/18	W 19-3	Buffalo	64,777
9/25	W 17-16	at Green Bay	70,518
10/2	W 17-13	Detroit	64,994
10/9	L 12-14	at N.Y. Jets	77,852
10/16	W 27-13	Miami	65,168
10/30	L 10-15	at San Francisco	63,358
11/6	L 14-34	Carolina	65,014
11/13	W 36-35	Washington	65,421
11/20	W 30-27	at Atlanta	70,794
11/27	L 10-13	Chicago	65,506
12/4	W 10-3	at New Orleans	34,411
12/11	W 20-10	at Carolina	73,467
12/17	L 0-28	at New England	68,756
12/24	W 27-24	Atlanta (OT)	65,482
1/1	W 27-13	New Orleans	65,379

(OT) Overtime

POSTSEASON (0-1)

Date	Result	Opponent	
1/7	L 10-17	Washington	65,514

SCORE BY PERIODS

Buccaneers	64	103	48	82	3	—	300
Opponents	50	100	57	67	0	—	274

2005 TEAM STATISTICS

	Buccaneers	Opp.
Total First Downs	268	254
Rushing	83	75
Passing	161	148
Penalty	24	31
3rd Down: Made/Att	87/221	75/214
3rd Down Pct.	39.4	35.0
4th Down: Made/Att	4/7	7/18
4th Down Pct.	57.1	38.9
Possession Avg.	30:45	29:15
Total Net Yards	4,716	4,444
Avg. Per Game	294.8	277.8
Total Plays	985	950
Avg. Per Play	4.8	4.7
Net Yards Rushing	1,826	1,515
Avg. Per Game	114.1	94.7
Total Rushes	457	438
Net Yards Passing	2,890	2,929
Avg. Per Game	180.6	183.1
Sacked/Yards Lost	41/281	36/229
Gross Yards	3171	3158
Att./Completions	487/303	476/275
Completion Pct.	62.2	57.8
Had Intercepted	14	17
Punts/Average	90/45.6	80/43.9
Net Punting Avg.	90/37.5	80/36.7
Penalties/Yards	131/1085	108/830
Fumbles/Ball Lost	16/9	25/13
Touchdowns	33	28
Rushing	13	10
Passing	17	15
Returns	3	3

2005 INDIVIDUAL STATISTICS

PASSING

PASSING	Att.	Comp.	Yds.	Pct.	TD	Int.	Tkld.	Rate
Simms	313	191	2,035	61.0	10	7	29/205	81.4
Griese	174	112	1,136	64.4	7	7	12/76	79.6
Buccaneers	487	303	3,171	62.2	17	14	41/281	80.7
Opponents	476	275	3,158	57.8	15	17	36/229	73.5

SCORING

SCORING	TD R	TD P	TD Rt	PAT	FG	Saf	PTS
M. Bryant	0	0	0	31/31	21/25	0	94
Galloway	0	10	0	0/0	0/0	0	60
Alstott	6	1	0	0/0	0/0	0	44
Williams	6	0	0	0/0	0/0	0	36
Pittman	1	1	0	0/0	0/0	0	12
Smith	0	2	0	0/0	0/0	0	12
Allen	0	0	1	0/0	0/0	0	6
Cook	0	1	0	0/0	0/0	0	6
Hilliard	0	1	0	0/0	0/0	0	6
McFarland	0	0	1	0/0	0/0	0	6
Shepherd	0	1	0	0/0	0/0	0	6
D. White	0	0	1	0/0	0/0	0	6
France	0	0	0	1/1	1/2	0	4
Quarles	0	0	0	0/0	0/0	1	2
Buccaneers	13	17	3	32/32	22/27	1	300
Opponents	10	15	3	26/27	26/33	0	274

2-Pt. Conversions: Alstott.
Buccaneers 1-1, Opponents 1-1.

RUSHING

RUSHING	No.	Yds	Avg	LG	TD
Williams	290	1,178	4.1	71t	6
Pittman	70	436	6.2	64	1
Graham	28	83	3.0	16	0
Alstott	34	80	2.4	9	6
Simms	19	31	1.6	10	0
Griese	13	12	0.9	7	0
Galloway	2	4	2.0	4	0
Clayton	1	2	2.0	2	0
Buccaneers	457	1,826	4.0	71t	13
Opponents	438	1,515	3.5	31	10

RECEIVING

RECEIVING	No.	Yds	Avg	LG	TD
Galloway	83	1,287	15.5	80t	10
Smith	41	367	9.0	24	2
Pittman	36	300	8.3	41t	1
Hilliard	35	282	8.1	22	1
Clayton	32	372	11.6	41	0
Alstott	25	222	8.9	24	1
Williams	20	81	4.1	15	0
Becht	16	112	7.0	17	0
Cook	7	43	6.1	11	1
Shepherd	6	103	17.2	46	1
Moore	1	5	5.0	5	0
Simms	1	-3	-3.0	-3	0
Buccaneers	303	3,171	10.5	80t	17
Opponents	275	3,158	11.5	62	15

INTERCEPTIONS

INTERCEPTIONS	No.	Yds	Avg	LG	TD
Barber	5	105	21.0	42	0
Kelly	4	19	4.8	14	0
Allen	3	26	8.7	26	0
Bolden	2	46	23.0	28	0
D. Jackson	1	21	21.0	21	0
Rice	1	6	6.0	6	0
Brooks	1	0	0.0	0	0
Buccaneers	17	223	13.1	42	0
Opponents	14	480	34.3	88t	2

PUNTING

PUNTING	No.	Yds.	Avg.	In 20	LG
Bidwell	90	4,101	45.6	24	61
Buccaneers	90	4,101	45.6	24	61
Opponents	80	3,509	43.9	18	62

PUNT RETURNS

PUNT RETURNS	Ret	FC	Yds	Avg	LG	TD
Jones	51	18	492	9.6	31	0
Buccaneers	51	18	492	9.6	31	0
Opponents	49	16	466	9.5	44	0

KICKOFF RETURNS

KICKOFF RETURNS	No.	Yds	Avg	LG	TD
Cox	24	464	19.3	30	0
Shepherd	20	414	20.7	30	0
Jones	5	95	19.0	24	0
Graham	4	74	18.5	22	0
Pittman	3	85	28.3	37	0
Smith	1	12	12.0	12	0
Alstott	1	2	2.0	2	0
Bradley	1	2	2.0	2	0
Buccaneers	59	1,148	19.5	37	0
Opponents	63	1,368	21.7	94t	1

FIELD GOALS

FIELD GOALS	1-19	20-29	30-39	40-49	50+
M. Bryant	0/0	2/4	8/8	10/11	1/2
France	0/0	1/1	0/0	0/1	0/0
Buccaneers	0/0	3/5	8/8	10/12	1/2
Opponents	0/0	9/10	7/8	8/12	2/3

SACKS

SACKS	No.
Rice	14.0
Spires	4.0
Brooks	3.0
D. White	3.0
Barber	2.0
McFarland	2.0
Nece	2.0
Wyms	2.0
D. Jackson	1.0
Kelly	1.0
Quarles	1.0
TEAM	1.0
Buccaneers	36.0
Opponents	41.0

RECORD HOLDERS
INDIVIDUAL RECORDS—CAREER

Category	Name	Performance
Rushing (Yds.)	James Wilder, 1981-89	5,957
Passing (Yds.)	Vinny Testaverde, 1987-1992	14,820
Passing (TDs)	Vinny Testaverde, 1987-1992	77
Receiving (No.)	James Wilder, 1981-89	430
Receiving (Yds.)	Mark Carrier, 1987-1992	5,018
Interceptions	Donnie Abraham, 1996-2001	31
Punting (Avg.)	Josh Bidwell, 2004-05	44.0
Punt Return (Avg.)	Jacquez Green, 1998-2001	12.0
Kickoff Return (Avg.)	Aaron Stecker, 2000-03	23.8
Field Goals	Martín Gramatica, 1999-2004	137
Touchdowns (Tot.)	Mike Alstott, 1996-2005	68
Points	Martín Gramatica, 1999-2004	592

INDIVIDUAL RECORDS—SINGLE SEASON

Category	Name	Performance
Rushing (Yds.)	James Wilder, 1984	1,544
Passing (Yds.)	Brad Johnson, 2003	3,811
Passing (TDs)	Brad Johnson, 2003	26
Receiving (No.)	Keyshawn Johnson, 2001	106
Receiving (Yds.)	Mark Carrier, 1989	1,422
Interceptions	Ronde Barber, 2001	10
Punting (Avg.)	Josh Bidwell, 2005	45.6
Punt Return (Avg.)	Karl Williams, 1996	21.1
Kickoff Return (Avg.)	Karl Williams, 1996	27.4
Field Goals	Martín Gramatica, 2002	32
Touchdowns (Tot.)	James Wilder, 1984	13
Points	Martín Gramatica, 2002	128

INDIVIDUAL RECORDS—SINGLE GAME

Category	Name	Performance
Rushing (Yds.)	James Wilder, 11-6-83	219
Passing (Yds.)	Doug Williams, 11-16-80	486
Passing (TDs)	Steve DeBerg, 9-13-87	5
	Brad Johnson, 11-3-02	5
Receiving (No.)	James Wilder, 9-15-85	13
Receiving (Yds.)	Mark Carrier, 12-6-87	212
Interceptions	Ronde Barber, 12-23-01, 12-4-05	3
Field Goals	Martín Gramatica, 12-29-02	5
Touchdowns (Tot.)	Jimmie Giles, 10-20-85	4
Points	Jimmie Giles, 10-20-85	24

2006 VETERAN ROSTER

No.	Name	Pos.	Ht.	Wt.	Birthdate	NFL Exp.	College	Hometown	How Acq.	'05 Games/ Starts
46	Adams, Blue	CB	5-10	184	10/15/79	3	Cincinnati	Miami, Fla.	FA-'05	13/0
26	Allen, Will	S	6-1	200	6/17/82	3	Ohio State	Dayton, Ohio	D4-'04	13/8
40	Alstott, Mike	FB	6-1	248	12/21/73	11	Purdue	Joliet, Ill.	D2-'96	16/7
49	Anelli, Mark	TE/LS	6-3	265	6/5/79	2	Wisconsin	Addison, Ill.	FA-'06	0*
20	Barber, Ronde	CB	5-10	184	4/7/75	10	Virginia	Roanoke, Va.	D3b-'97	16/16
88	Becht, Anthony	TE	6-5	272	8/8/77	7	West Virginia	Drexel Hill, Pa.	UFA(NYJ)-'05	16/16
9	Bidwell, Josh	P	6-3	220	3/13/76	7	Oregon	Winston, Ore.	UFA(GB)-'04	16/0
68	Bogle, Phil	G	6-2	322	9/27/79	2	New Haven	Spring Valley, N.Y.	FA-'06	0*
21	Bolden, Juran	CB	6-3	210	6/27/74	9	Mississippi Delta	Tampa, Fla.	FA-'05	16/2
91	Bradley, Jon	DT	6-0	301	1/13/81	3	Arkansas State	West Helena, Ark.	FA-'04	13/0
55	Brooks, Derrick	LB	6-0	235	4/18/73	12	Florida State	Pensacola, Fla.	D1b-'95	16/16
64	Bryant, Anthony	DT	6-3	336	11/6/81	2	Alabama	Newbern, Ala.	D6-'05	4/0
3	Bryant, Matt	K	5-9	200	5/29/75	5	Baylor	Orange, Texas	FA-05	15/0
72	Buenning, Dan	G	6-4	320	10/26/81	2	Wisconsin	Green Bay, Wis.	D4-'05	16/16
	Carter, Jonathan	WR	6-0	180	3/20/79	4	Troy State	Lineville, Ala.	FA-'06	0*
80	Clayton, Michael	WR	6-4	215	10/13/82	3	Louisiana State	Baton Rouge, La.	D1-'04	14/10
61	Colmer, Chris	T	6-5	310	11/21/80	2	North Carolina State	Port Jefferson, N.Y.	D3b-'05	0*
58	Cooper, Marquis	LB	6-3	213	3/11/82	3	Washington	Gilbert, Ariz.	D3-'04	12/0
27	Cox, Torrie	CB	5-10	181	10/29/80	4	Pittsburgh	Miami, Fla.	D6-'03	15/0
69	Davis, Anthony	T	6-4	322	3/27/80	3	Virginia Tech	Victoria, Va.	FA-'03	16/16
78	Fonoti, Toniu	G	6-4	350	11/26/81	5	Nebraska	Hauula, Hawaii	UFA(Minn)-'06	3/3*
84	Galloway, Joey	WR	5-11	197	11/20/71	12	Ohio State	Bellaire, Ohio	T(Dall)-'04	16/16
34	Graham, Earnest	RB	5-9	225	1/15/80	3	Florida	Ft. Myers, Fla.	FA-'03	16/0
19	Hilliard, Ike	WR	5-11	210	4/5/76	10	Florida	Patterson, La.	FA-'05	16/2
95	Hovan, Chris	DT	6-2	296	5/12/78	7	Boston College	Rocky River, Ohio	FA-'05	16/16
74	Jackson, Scott	C	6-4	300	1/19/79	2	Brigham Young	Ranch Palos Verdes, Calif.	FA-'04	0*
11	Johnson, B.J.	WR	5-11	207	8/4/82	2	Texas	Grand Prairie, Texas	FA-'06	0*
89	Jones, Mark	WR	5-9	185	11/3/80	3	Tennessee	Wallingford, Pa.	FA-'05	16/0
25	Kelly, Brian	CB	5-11	193	1/14/76	9	Southern California	Aurora, Colo.	D2b-'98	16/16
79	Mahan, Sean	G/C	6-3	301	5/28/80	4	Notre Dame	Jenks, Okla.	D5-'03	16/16
54	Mallard, Wesly	LB	6-1	230	11/21/78	5	Oregon	Columbus, Ga.	FA-'05	9/0*
12	McCown, Luke	QB	6-3	212	7/12/81	3	Louisiana Tech	Jacksonville, Texas	T(Cle)-'05	0*
92	McFarland, Anthony	DT	6-0	300	12/18/77	8	Louisiana State	Winnsboro, La.	D1-'99	15/15
83	Moore, Dave	TE	6-2	250	11/11/69	15	Pittsburgh	Succasunna, N.J.	FA-'04	16/1
56	Nece, Ryan	LB	6-3	224	2/24/79	5	UCLA	San Bernardino, Calif.	FA-'02	16/14
28	Nicholson, Donte	S	6-1	216	12/18/81	2	Oklahoma	Diamond Bay, Calif.	D5a-'05	9/0
39	Pearson, Kalvin	CB/S	5-10	190	10/22/78	2	Grambling State	Town Creek, Ala.	FA-'04	14/1
23	Phillips, Jermaine	S	6-1	214	3/27/79	5	Georgia	Roswell, Ga.	D5-'02	13/13
32	Pittman, Michael	RB	6-0	228	8/14/75	9	Fresno State	San Diego, Calif.	UFA(Ariz)-'02	16/4
53	Quarles, Shelton	LB	6-1	225	9/11/71	10	Vanderbilt	Whites Creek, Tenn.	FA-'97	16/16
13	Rattay, Tim	QB	6-0	200	3/15/77	7	Louisiana Tech	Elyria, Ohio	T(SF)-'05	4/4*
44	Razzano, Rick	FB	5-11	250	1/28/81	2	Miississippi	Milford, Ohio	D6a-'05	1/0
97	Rice, Simeon	DE	6-5	268	2/24/74	11	Illinois	Chicago, Ill.	UFA(Ariz)-'01	15/15
87	Russell, J.R.	WR	6-3	206	12/5/81	2	Louisville	Tampa, Fla.	D7d-'05	0*
51	Ruud, Barrett	LB	6-0	241	5/20/83	2	Nebraska	Lincoln, Neb.	D2-'05	16/0
86	Shepherd, Edell	WR	6-1	175	5/18/80	3	San Jose State	Los Angeles, Calif.	FA-'03	16/0
2	Simms, Chris	QB	6-4	220	8/29/80	4	Texas	Ramapo, N.J.	D3-'03	11/10
81	Smith, Alex	TE	6-4	258	5/22/82	2	Stanford	Denver, Colo.	D3a-'05	16/10
33	Sowell, Jerald	FB	6-0	237	1/21/74	10	Tulane	Baker, La.	FA-'06	16/16*
94	Spires, Greg	DE	6-1	265	8/12/74	9	Florida State	Cape Coral, Fla.	UFA(Cle)-'02	16/16
77	Terry, Jeb	G	6-5	311	4/10/81	3	North Carolina	Dallas, Texas	D5-'04	16/0
68	Tucker, Torrin	T	6-6	315	12/25/79	4	Southern Mississippi	Meridian, Miss.	FA-'06	16/10*
76	Wade, John	C	6-5	299	1/25/75	9	Marshall	Harrisonburg, Va.	UFA(Jax)-'03	16/16
67	Walker, Kenyatta	T	6-5	302	2/1/79	6	Florida	Meridian, Miss.	D1-'01	16/16
82	Warren, Paris	WR	6-0	213	9/6/82	2	Utah	Sacramento, Calif.	D7b-'05	0*
90	White, Dewayne	DE	6-2	273	10/19/79	4	Louisville	Marbury, Ala.	D2-'03	16/1
98	Williams, Andrew	DE	6-2	280	4/18/79	3	Miami	Tampa, Fla.	W(SF)-'05	0*
24	Williams, Carnell	RB	5-11	217	4/21/82	2	Auburn	Attalla, Ala.	D1-'05	14/14
71	Williams, Todd	T	6-5	325	9/4/78	3	Florida State	Bradenton, Fla.	FA-'06	0*
50	Winborn, Jamie	LB	5-11	242	5/14/79	6	Vanderbilt	Wetumpka, Ala.	UFA(Jax)-'06	8/2*
	Wright, Keith	DT	6-2	275	6/8/80	2	Missouri	Sacramento, Calif.	FA-'06	0*
96	Wyms, Ellis	DT/DE	6-3	290	4/12/79	6	Mississippi State	Indianola, Miss.	D6b-'01	16/1

* Anelli last active with San Francisco in '02; Bogle last active with San Diego in '04; Carter last active with N.Y. Jets in '04; Colmer inactive for 16 games; Fonoti played 2 games with San Diego and 1 game with Minnesota; Jackson did not play in 2 games; Johnson missed '04 season with Denver because of injury; Mallard played 3 games with New England and 6 games with Tampa Bay; McCown did not play in 10 games with Cleveland; Rattay played 4 games with San Francisco; Russell inactive for 11 games; Sowell played 16 games with N.Y. Jets; Tucker played 16 games with Dallas; Warren inactive for 5 games; A. Williams last active with San Francisco in '04; T. Williams last active with Tennessee in '05; Winborn played 3 games with San Francisco and 5 games with Jacksonville; Wright last active with Tampa Bay in '04.

Players lost through free agency (3): FB Jameel Cook (Hou; 16 games in '05), S Dexter Jackson (Cin; 11), T Todd Steussie (StL; 15).

Also played with Buccaneers in '05—K Todd France (1 game), QB Brian Griese (6), TE Nate Lawrie (5).

2006 FIRST-YEAR ROSTER

Name	Pos.	Ht.	Wt.	Birthdate	College	Hometown	How Acq.
Abdullah, Hamza	S	6-2	213	8/20/83	Washington State	Pomona, Calif.	FA
Addae, Jahmile	S	6-0	205	5/30/82	West Virginia	Riverview, Fla.	FA
Allen, Jared (1)	QB	6-3	215	8/26/81	Florida Atlantic	Edmond, Okla.	FA-'05
Beitia, Xavier (1)	K	5-10	198	11/23/82	Florida State	Tampa, Fla.	FA
Bennett, Charles	DE	6-3	254	4/4/83	Clemson	Camden, S.C.	D7b
Brackins, Larry (1)	WR	6-4	205	11/5/82	Pearl River (Miss.) J.C.	Dothan, Ala.	D5b-'05
Cargile, Steve (1)	S	6-1	201	6/2/82	Columbia	Cleveland, Ohio	FA
Cash, Antoine (1)	LB	6-1	223	3/5/82	Southern Mississippi	Anguilla, Miss.	FA-'05
Clinkscale, Jonathan (1)	G/C	6-2	315	4/17/82	Wisconsin	Altadena, Calif.	FA-'05
Davis, Carey (1)	FB	5-10	225	3/27/81	Illinois	St. Louis, Mo.	FA
Douglas, Robert (1)	FB	6-2	240	7/25/82	Memphis	St. Louis, Mo.	FA
Ellick, Dwight (1)	CB	5-10	182	9/30/82	Notre Dame	Tampa, Fla.	FA
Gessner, Chas (1)	WR	6-4	215	8/17/81	Brown	Good Counsel, Md.	FA
Gradkowski, Bruce	QB	6-1	220	1/27/83	Toledo	Pittsburgh, Pa.	D6a
Hall, Andre	RB	5-10	205	8/20/82	South Florida	St. Petersburg, Fla.	FA
Houston, Reuben	CB	6-0	190	10/30/82	Georgia Tech	Peachtree City, Ga.	FA
Jenkins, Julian	DT/DE	6-3	273	10/25/83	Stanford	Atlanta, Ga.	D5
Joseph, Davin	G/T	6-3	313	11/22/83	Oklahoma	Hallandale, Fla.	D1
Lewis, Jacque (1)	RB	5-10	192	3/10/82	North Carolina	Winston-Salem, N.C.	FA
Lightbody, Sam (1)	T	6-9	325	4/22/81	Washington State	Huntington Beach, Calif.	FA
Massaquoi, Tim	TE	6-3	255	7/8/82	Michigan	Allentown, Pa.	D7c
McCoy, Derek (1)	WR	6-3	210	11/13/80	Colorado	Thornton, Colo.	FA
McGruder, Lynn (1)	DT	6-2	302	2/13/82	Oklahoma	Las Vegas, Nev.	FA-'05
Nerys, Jason (1)	G	6-4	310	6/16/81	Delaware	Waldwick, N.J.	FA
Patrick, James (1)	CB	5-11	175	6/4/82	Stillman College	Tuskegee, Ala.	FA-'05
Phinisee, Justin	CB	5-11	200	1/1/83	Oregon	Compton, Calif.	D7a
Rodgers, Stefan (1)	T	6-4	305	11/3/81	Lambuth	Little Rock, Ark.	FA-'05
Simjanovski, Brian (1)	P	6-3	205	5/29/81	San Diego State	Escondido, Calif.	FA-'05
Stovall, Maurice	WR	6-5	220	2/21/85	Notre Dame	Philadelphia, Pa.	D3
Stubbs, Terrence (1)	WR	5-11	190	3/25/80	Temple	Chesapeake, Va.	FA
Stutz, Boone	TE/LS	6-6	260	11/4/82	Texas A&M	Arlington, Texas	FA
Taylor, Jermaine (1)	LB	6-0	220	11/29/81	Bridgewater	Miramar, Fla.	FA-'05
Trucks, Anthony	LB	6-1	230	12/1/83	Oregon	Antioch, Calif.	FA
Trueblood, Jeremy	T	6-8	320	5/10/83	Boston College	Indianapolis, Ind.	D2
Watson, Derek (1)	RB	6-0	212	5/1/81	South Carolina State	Williamson, S.C.	FA-'05
Williams, T.J.	TE	6-3	258	9/24/82	North Carolina State	Tarboro, N.C.	D6b
Zemaitis, Alan	CB	6-2	200	8/24/82	Penn State	Rochester, N.Y.	D4

The term NFL Rookie is defined as a player who is in his first season of professional football and has not been on the roster of another professional football team for any regular-season or postseason games. A Rookie is designated by an "R" on NFL rosters. Players who have been active in another professional football league or players who have NFL experience, including either preseason training camp or being on an Active List or Inactive List, or on Reserve/Injured or Reserve/Physically Unable to Perform for fewer than six regular-season games, are termed NFL First-Year Players. An NFL First-Year Player is designated by a "1" on NFL rosters. Thereafter, a player is credited with an additional year of experience for each season in which he accumulates six games on the Active List or Inactive List, or on Reserve/Injured or Reserve/Physically Unable to Perform.

Log on to www.buccaneers.com for an up-to-date roster.

COACHING STAFF

Head Coach,
Jon Gruden

Pro Career: Gruden was named the seventh head coach in Buccaneers history on February 18, 2002, when he signed a five-year contract. Gruden led Tampa Bay to its first Super Bowl title in his first season as head coach in 2002. Gruden set two NFL records—he became the youngest head coach (39) to win a Super Bowl, and was the first veteran head coach to lead his team to the Super Bowl in his first season with a new team. Last season, the Buccaneers won the NFC South for the second time in four seasons. Prior to joining the Buccaneers, Gruden guided the Oakland Raiders to division titles in each of his final two seasons. He steered the Raiders to a 40-28 mark in four seasons (1998-2001), with postseason appearances in 2000 and 2001. Under Gruden, the Raiders advanced to the AFC title game in 2000 and in 2001 lost a divisional playoff game to eventual Super Bowl champion New England. Prior to his four seasons in Oakland, Gruden spent 1995-97 as offensive coordinator for the Philadelphia Eagles and three years (1992-94) as wide receivers coach for Green Bay Packers. He worked as offensive assistant for the San Francisco 49ers in 1990. Career record: 78-58.

Background: Quarterback at Dayton (1982-84), graduating with a degree in communications. The Flyers had a 24-7 record in Gruden's three varsity seasons. Coach collegiately at Tennessee (1986-87), Southeast Missouri State (1988), Pacific (1989), and Pittsburgh (1991).

Personal: Born August 17, 1963 in Sandusky, Ohio. Jon and his wife Cindy, have three sons, Jon II, Michael, and Jayson.

ASSISTANT COACHES

Joe Barry, linebackers; born July 5, 1970, Boulder, Colo. Linebacker Southern California 1991-93. No pro playing experience. College coach: Southern California 1994-95, Northern Arizona 1996-98, Nevada-Las Vegas 1999. Pro coach: San Francisco 49ers 2000, joined Buccaneers in 2001.

Tim Berbenich, offensive quality control; born December 19, 1979, Huntington, N.Y. Wide receiver Hamilton College 1998-2001. No pro playing experience. Pro coach: New York Jets 2003-05, joined Buccaneers in 2006.

Richard Bisaccia, special teams coordinator; born June 3, 1960, Yonkers, N.Y. Defensive back Yankton College 1979-1982, Philadelphia Stars (USFL) 1983. College coach: Wayne State College 1983-87, South Carolina 1988-1993, Clemson 1994-98, Mississippi 1999-2001. Pro coach: Joined Buccaneers in 2002.

Casey Bradley, defensive quality control; born July 5, 1966, Zumbrota, Minn. Safety/punter North Dakota State 1984-1988. No pro playing experience. College coach: North Dakota State 1990-1991, 1996-2005, Fort Lewis College 1992-1996. Pro coach: Joined Buccaneers in 2006.

Greg Burns, defensive backs; born November 9, 1972, Brooklyn, N.Y. Defensive back Washington State 1991-93, 1995. No pro playing experience. College coach: Idaho 1997, Louisville 1998-2001, Southern California 2002-05. Pro coach: Joined Buccaneers in 2006.

Jethro Franklin, defensive line; born October 25, 1965, St. Lazaire, France. Defensive lineman San Jose (Calif.) C.C. 1984-85, Fresno State 1986-87. Pro defensive lineman Houston Oilers 1988, Seattle Seahawks 1989-1990. College coach: Fresno State 1991-98, UCLA 1999, Southern California 2005. Pro coach: Green Bay Packers 2000-04, joined Buccaneers in 2006.

Jay Gruden, offensive assistant; born March 4, 1967. Quarterback Louisville 1985-88. Pro quarterback Tampa Bay Storm (AFL) 1991-96, Orlando Predators (AFL) 2002-03. Pro coach: Nashville Kats (AFL) 1997, Orlando Predators (AFL) 1998-2001, 2004-06, joined Buccaneers in 2002.

Nathaniel Hackett, offensive quality control; born December 19, 1979, Fullerton, Calif. Linebacker Cal-Davis 1999-2002. No pro playing experience. College coach: Stanford 2003-05. Pro coach: Joined Buccaneers in 2006.

Paul Hackett, quarterbacks; born July 5, 1947, Burlington, Vt. Quarterback Cal-Davis 1965-68. No pro playing experience. College coach: Cal-Davis 1969-1971, California 1972-75, Southern California 1976-1980, 1998-2000 (head coach 1998-2000), Pittsburgh 1989-1992 (head coach 1990-92). Pro coach: Cleveland Browns 1981-82, San Francisco 49ers 1983-85, Dallas Cowboys 1986-88, Kansas City Chiefs 1993-97, New York Jets 2001-04, joined Buccaneers in 2005.

Monte Kiffin, defensive coordinator; born February 29, 1940, Lexington, Neb. Offensive/defensive tackle Nebraska 1959-1963. Pro defensive end Winnipeg Blue Bombers (CFL) 1965. College coach: Nebraska 1966-1976, Arkansas 1977-79, North Carolina State 1980-82 (head coach). Pro coach: Green Bay Packers 1983, Buffalo Bills 1984-85, Minnesota Vikings 1986-89, 1991-94, New York Jets 1990, New Orleans Saints 1995, joined Buccaneers in 1996.

Aaron Kromer, senior assistant/offensive line; born April 30, 1967, Sandusky, Ohio. Offensive tackle Miami (Ohio) 1986-89. No pro playing experience. College coach: Miami (Ohio) 1990-98, Northwestern 1999-2000. Pro coach: Oakland Raiders

2001-04, joined Buccaneers in 2005.

Jimmy Lake, asst. defensive backs; born December 17, 1976, San Francisco. Safety Eastern Washington 1995-98. No pro playing experience. College coach: Eastern Washington 1999-2003, Washington 2004, Montana State 2005. Pro coach: Joined Buccaneers in 2006.

Richard Mann, wide receivers; born April 20, 1947, Aliquippa, Pa. Wide receiver Arizona State 1966-68. No pro playing experience. College coach: Arizona State 1974-79, Louisville 1980-81. Pro coach: Baltimore/Indianapolis Colts 1982-84, Cleveland Browns 1985-1993, New York Jets 1994-96, Baltimore Ravens 1997-98, Kansas City Chiefs 1999-2000, Washington Redskins 2001, joined Buccaneers in 2002.

Ron Middleton, tight ends/asst. special teams; born July 17, 1965, Atmore, Ala. Tight end Auburn 1982-85. Pro tight end Atlanta Falcons 1986-87, Washington Redskins 1988, 1990-93, Cleveland Browns 1989, Los Angeles Rams 1994, San Diego Chargers 1995. College coach: Troy State 1997-98, Mississippi 1999-2003. Pro coach: Joined Buccaneers in 2004.

Mike Morris, head strength and conditioning; born May 7, 1964, Ayer, Mass. Wide receiver Syracuse 1981-85. No pro playing experience. Pro coach: New England Patriots 1997-99, joined Buccaneers in 2002.

Bill Muir, offensive coordinator/offensive line; born October 26, 1942, Pittsburgh. Tackle Susquehanna 1962-64. No pro playing experience. College coach: Susquehanna 1965, Delaware Valley 1966-67, Rhode Island 1970-71, Idaho State 1972-73, Southern Methodist 1976-77. Pro coach: Orlando (Continental Football League) 1968-69, Houston Shreveport Steamer (WFL) 1975, New England Patriots 1982-88, Indianapolis Colts 1989-1991, Philadelphia Eagles 1992-94, New York Jets 1995-2001, joined Buccaneers in 2002.

Kurt Shultz, asst. strength and conditioning; born March 10, 1972, Baltimore. Attended Maryland. No college or pro playing experience. College coach: Loyola (Md.) 1995-98, Maryland and Johns Hopkins 1999-2002. Pro coach: Cincinnati Bengals 2003, Minnesota Vikings 2004-05, joined Buccaneers in 2006.

Art Valero, asst. head coach/running backs; born May 12, 1958, Whittier, Calif. Offensive lineman Boise State 1979-1980. No pro playing experience. College coach: Boise State 1981-82, Iowa State 1983, Long Beach State 1984-86, New Mexico 1987-89, Idaho 1990-94, Louisville 1998-2001. Pro coach: Kansas City Chiefs 1994, Buffalo Bills 1996, joined Buccaneers in 2002.

**National Football Conference
East Division
Team Colors:** Burgundy and Gold
**Redskins Park
21300 Redskins Park Drive
Ashburn, Virginia 20147
Telephone:** (703) 726-7000

2006 SCHEDULE
PRESEASON
Aug. 13	at Cincinnati	8:00
Aug. 19	**New York Jets**	8:00
Aug. 26	at New England	8:00
Aug. 31	**Baltimore**	8:00

REGULAR SEASON
Sept. 11	**Minnesota** (Mon.)	7:00
Sept. 17	at Dallas	7:15
Sept. 24	at Houston	12:00
Oct. 1	**Jacksonville**	4:15
Oct. 8	at N.Y. Giants	1:00
Oct. 15	**Tennessee**	1:00
Oct. 22	at Indianapolis	4:15
Oct. 29	Open Date	
Nov. 5	**Dallas**	1:00
Nov. 12	at Philadelphia	1:00
Nov. 19	at Tampa Bay	1:00
Nov. 26	**Carolina**	1:00
Dec. 3	**Atlanta**	1:00
Dec. 10	**Philadelphia**	1:00
Dec. 17	at New Orleans	12:00
Dec. 24	at St. Louis	12:00
Dec. 30	**N.Y. Giants** (Sat.)	8:00

Stadium: FedExField (opened in 1997)
 •**Capacity:** 91,704
 1600 FedEx Way
 Landover, Maryland 20785
Playing Surface: Natural Grass
Training Camp: Redskins Park
 Ashburn, Virginia 20147

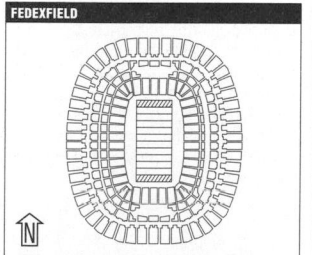

FEDEXFIELD

CLUB OFFICIALS
Owner: Daniel M. Snyder
Chief Operating Officer: Mitch Gershman
Chief Financial Officer: Jay Sloan
General Counsel: Dave Donovan
Senior Vice President: Karl Swanson
Senior Vice President, Marketing:
 Mike Stevens
Senior Vice President, Stadium
 Operations: Michael Dillow
Director of Ticket Operations: Jeff Ritter
Vice President, Football Operations:
 Vinny Cerrato
Director of Pro Personnel: Louis Riddick
Director of College Scouting:
 Scott Campbell
Pro Scouts: Terry Ray, Donnie Warren
College Scouts: Mike Faulkiner,
 Tim Gribble, Shemy Schembechler,
 Jim Zeches
National Scout: Russ Bolinger,
 Joel Patten
Director of Football Administration:
 Eric Schaffer
Director of Player Development:
 John "JJ" Jefferson
Director of Public Relations:
 Patrick Wixted
Leadership Council/Community Affairs:
 Charlene Lefkowitz
Director of Team Administration:
 Derrick Crawford
Video Director: Mike Bracken
Video Department: Tom Long, Matt Shea
Director of Sports Medicine: Bubba Tyer
Head Athletic Trainer: John Burrell
Assistant Athletic Trainers: Eric Steward,
 Larry Hess
Equipment Manager: Brad Berlin
Assistant Equipment Manager:
 Anders Beutel

COACHING HISTORY
**Boston 1932-36
(538-484-27)**
Records include postseason games
1932	Lud Wray	4-4-2
1933-34	William (Lone Star) Dietz	11-11-2
1935	Eddie Casey	2-8-1
1936-1942	Ray Flaherty	56-23-3
1943	Arthur (Dutch) Bergman	7-4-1
1944-45	Dudley DeGroot	14-6-1
1946-48	Glen (Turk) Edwards	16-18-1
1949	John Whelchel*	3-3-1
1949-1951	Herman Ball**	4-16-0
1951	Dick Todd	5-4-0
1952-53	Earl (Curly) Lambeau	10-13-1
1954-58	Joe Kuharich	26-32-2
1959-1960	Mike Nixon	4-18-2
1961-65	Bill McPeak	21-46-3
1966-68	Otto Graham	17-22-3
1969	Vince Lombardi	7-5-2
1970	Bill Austin	6-8-0
1971-77	George Allen	69-35-1
1978-1980	Jack Pardee	24-24-0
1981-1992	Joe Gibbs	140-65-0
1993	Richie Petitbon	4-12-0
1994-2000	Norv Turner***	50-60-1
2000	Terry Robiskie	1-2-0
2001	Marty Schottenheimer	8-8-0
2002-03	Steve Spurrier	12-20-0
2004-05	Joe Gibbs	17-17-0

*Released after seven games in 1949
**Released after three games in 1951
***Released after 13 games in 2000

ATTENDANCE
Home 707,614   Away 532,609
Total 1,240,223
Single-game home record,
 88,678 (9/27/04)
Single-season home record,
 707,614 (2004)

2006 DRAFT CHOICES
Round	Name	Pos.	College
2	Rocky McIntosh	LB	Miami
5	Anthony Montgomery	DT	Minnesota
6	Reed Doughty	DB	Northern Colorado
	Kedric Golston	DT	Georgia
7	Kili Lefotu	G	Arizona
	Kevin Simon	LB	Tennessee

2005 TEAM RECORD
PRESEASON (3-1)

Date	Result		Opponent
8/13	L	10-28	at Carolina
8/19	L	17-24	Cincinnati
8/26	W	17-10	Pittsburgh
9/1	L	20-26	at Baltimore

REGULAR SEASON (10-6)

Date	Result		Opponent	Att.
9/11	W	9-7	Chicago	90,138
9/19	W	14-13	at Dallas	65,207
10/2	W	20-17	Seattle (OT)	90,215
10/9	L	19-21	at Denver	75,880
10/16	L	21-28	at Kansas City	78,083
10/23	W	52-17	San Francisco	90,224
10/30	L	0-36	at N.Y. Giants	78,630
11/6	W	17-10	Philadelphia	90,298
11/13	L	35-36	at Tampa Bay	65,421
11/20	L	13-16	Oakland	90,129
11/27	L	17-23	San Diego (OT)	84,930
12/4	W	24-9	at St. Louis	65,701
12/11	W	17-13	at Arizona	46,654
12/18	W	35-7	Dallas	90,588
12/24	W	35-20	N.Y. Giants	90,477
1/1	W	31-20	at Philadelphia	67,700

REGULAR SEASON (1-1)

Date	Result		Opponent	Att.
1/7	W	17-10	at Tampa Bay	65,514
1/14	L	10-20	at Seattle	67,551

SCORE BY PERIODS

Redskins	69	114	101	72	3	—	359
Opponents	63	78	86	60	6	—	293

2005 TEAM STATISTICS

	Redskins	Opp.
Total First Downs	301	258
Rushing	114	74
Passing	166	158
Penalty	21	26
3rd Down: Made/Att	97/230	81/222
3rd Down Pct.	42.2	36.5
4th Down: Made/Att	6/11	5/13
4th Down Pct.	54.5	38.5
Possession Avg.	31:33	28:27
Total Net Yards	5,289	4,767
Avg. Per Game	330.6	297.9
Total Plays	1,037	981
Avg. Per Play	5.1	4.9
Net Yards Rushing	2183	1686
Avg. Per Game	136.4	105.4
Total Rushes	525	411
Net Yards Passing	3,106	3,081
Avg. Per Game	194.1	192.6
Sacked/Yards Lost	31/240	35/237
Gross Yards	3,346	3,318
Att./Completions	481/278	535/291
Completion Pct.	57.8	54.4
Had Intercepted	11	16
Punts/Average	87/40.3	88/41.3
Net Punting Avg.	87/36.5	88/37.7
Penalties/Yards	108/925	105/879
Fumbles/Ball Lost	29/16	32/12
Touchdowns	44	32
Rushing	15	15
Passing	25	15
Returns	4	2

2005 INDIVIDUAL STATISTICS

PASSING	Att.	Comp.	Yds.	Pct.	TD	Int.	Tkld.	Rate
Brunell	454	262	3,050	57.7	23	10	27/213	85.9
Ramsey	25	15	279	60.0	1	1	4/27	95.3
Portis	2	1	17	50.0	1	0	0/0	118.8
Redskins	481	278	3,346	57.8	25	11	31/240	87.0
Opponents	535	291	3,318	54.4	15	16	35/237	70.1

SCORING	TD R	TD P	TD Rt	PAT	FG	Saf	PTS
Portis	11	0	0	0/0	0/0	0	68
Hall	0	0	0	27/27	12/14	0	63
Moss	0	9	0	0/0	0/0	0	54
Sellers	1	7	0	0/0	0/0	0	48
Cooley	0	7	0	0/0	0/0	0	42
Novak	0	0	0	15/15	5/7	0	30
Betts	1	1	1	0/0	0/0	0	18
Cartwright	2	0	0	0/0	0/0	0	12
A. Brown	0	0	1	0/0	0/0	0	6
Marshall	0	0	1	0/0	0/0	0	6
Royal	0	1	0	0/0	0/0	0	6
Taylor	0	0	1	0/0	0/0	0	6
Redskins	15	25	4	42/42	17/21	0	359
Opponents	15	15	2	29/29	22/31	1	293

2-Pt. Conversions: Portis.
Redskins 1-2, Opponents 2-2.

RUSHING	No.	Yds	Avg	LG	TD
Portis	352	1,516	4.3	47t	11
Betts	89	338	3.8	22	1
Cartwright	27	199	7.4	52	2
Brunell	42	111	2.6	25	0
Thrash	1	8	8.0	8	0
A. Brown	2	7	3.5	4	0
Broughton	1	3	3.0	3	0
Ramsey	7	3	0.4	5	0
Sellers	1	1	1.0	1t	1
Moss	3	-3	-1.0	3	0
Redskins	525	2,183	4.2	52	15
Opponents	411	1,686	4.1	72t	15

RECEIVING	No.	Yds	Avg	LG	TD
Moss	84	1,483	17.7	78t	9
Cooley	71	774	10.9	32	7
Portis	30	216	7.2	23	0
Patten	22	217	9.9	32	0
Royal	18	131	7.3	29	1
Thrash	14	194	13.9	41	0
Sellers	12	72	6.0	19t	7
Jacobs	11	100	9.1	24	0
Betts	10	78	7.8	26	1
Kozlowski	2	26	13.0	18	0
Cartwright	2	23	11.5	17	0
Farris	1	18	18.0	18	0
Johnson	1	14	14.0	14	0
Redskins	278	3,346	12.0	78t	25
Opponents	291	3,318	11.4	70t	15

INTERCEPTIONS	No.	Yds	Avg	LG	TD
Marshall	4	55	13.8	27	1
Clark	3	10	3.3	6	0
Taylor	2	34	17.0	32	0
Rogers	2	14	7.0	14	0
Washington	1	41	41.0	41	0
Patterson	1	20	20.0	20	0
Springs	1	2	2.0	2	0
Griffin	1	0	0.0	0	0
Harris	1	0	0.0	0	0
Redskins	16	176	11.0	41	1
Opponents	11	183	16.6	36	1

PUNTING	No.	Yds.	Avg.	In 20	LG
Frost	76	3,074	40.4	23	55
Groom	11	429	39.0	2	57
Redskins	87	3,503	40.3	25	57
Opponents	88	3,636	41.3	26	65

PUNT RETURNS	Ret	FC	Yds	Avg	LG	TD
A. Brown	13	12	63	4.8	16	0
Thrash	10	15	77	7.7	18	0
Moss	7	1	40	5.7	14	0
Redskins	30	28	180	6.0	18	0
Opponents	40	18	189	4.7	19	0

KICKOFF RETURNS	No.	Yds	Avg	LG	TD
Betts	24	621	25.9	94t	1
A. Brown	19	439	23.1	91t	1
Thrash	7	170	24.3	31	0
Cartwright	4	82	20.5	25	0
Parson	3	71	23.7	35	0
Sellers	3	50	16.7	20	0
Broughton	1	5	5.0	5	0
Evans	1	0	0.0	0	0
Redskins	62	1438	23.2	94t	2
Opponents	72	1503	20.9	49	0

FIELD GOALS	1-19	20-29	30-39	40-49	50+
Hall	1/1	3/3	3/3	5/6	0/1
Novak	0/0	1/1	3/5	1/1	0/0
Redskins	1/1	4/4	6/8	6/7	0/1
Opponents	1/1	3/4	9/10	7/13	2/3

SACKS	No.
Daniels	8.0
Washington	7.5
Griffin	4.0
Evans	3.0
Prioleau	3.0
TEAM	3.0
C. Clemons	2.0
Marshall	2.0
Taylor	1.0
Clark	0.5
Salave'a	0.5
Wynn	0.5
Redskins	35.0
Opponents	31.0

RECORD HOLDERS
INDIVIDUAL RECORDS—CAREER

Category	Name	Performance
Rushing (Yds.)	John Riggins, 1976-79, 1981-85	7,472
Passing (Yds.)	Joe Theismann, 1974-1985	25,206
Passing (TDs)	Sammy Baugh, 1937-1952	187
Receiving (No.)	Art Monk, 1980-1993	888
Receiving (Yds.)	Art Monk, 1980-1993	12,028
Interceptions	Darrell Green, 1983-2001	54
Punting (Avg.)	Sammy Baugh, 1937-1952	45.1
Punt Return (Avg.)	Johnny Williams, 1952-53	12.8
Kickoff Return (Avg.)	Bobby Mitchell, 1962-68	28.5
Field Goals	Mark Moseley, 1974-1986	263
Touchdowns (Tot.)	Charley Taylor, 1964-1977	90
Points	Mark Moseley, 1974-1986	1,206

INDIVIDUAL RECORDS—SINGLE SEASON

Category	Name	Performance
Rushing (Yds.)	Clinton Portis, 2005	1,516
Passing (Yds.)	Jay Schroeder, 1986	4,109
Passing (TDs)	Sonny Jurgensen, 1967	31
Receiving (No.)	Art Monk, 1984	106
Receiving (Yds.)	Santana Moss, 2005	1,483
Interceptions	Dan Sandifer, 1948	13
Punting (Avg.)	Sammy Baugh, 1940	*51.4
Punt Return (Avg.)	Johnny Williams, 1952	15.3
Kickoff Return (Avg.)	Mike Nelms, 1981	29.7
Field Goals	Mark Moseley, 1983	33
Touchdowns (Tot.)	John Riggins, 1983	24
Points	Mark Moseley, 1983	161

INDIVIDUAL RECORDS—SINGLE GAME

Category	Name	Performance
Rushing (Yds.)	Gerald Riggs, 9-17-89	221
Passing (Yds.)	Sammy Baugh, 10-31-43	446
Passing (TDs)	Sammy Baugh, 10-31-43, 11-23-47	6
	Mark Rypien, 11-10-91	6
Receiving (No.)	Art Monk, 12-15-85, 11-4-90	13
	Kelvin Bryant, 12-7-86	13
Receiving (Yds.)	Anthony Allen, 10-4-87	255
Interceptions	Sammy Baugh, 11-14-43	*4
	Dan Sandifer, 10-31-48	*4
Field Goals	Many times	5
	Last time by Chip Lohmiller, 10-25-92	
Touchdowns (Tot.)	Dick James, 12-17-61	4
	Larry Brown, 12-16-73	4
Points	Dick James, 12-17-61	24
	Larry Brown, 12-16-73	24

*NFL Record

2006 VETERAN ROSTER

No.	Name	Pos.	Ht.	Wt.	Birthdate	NFL Exp.	College	Hometown	How Acq.	'05 Games/ Starts
71	Albright, Ethan	LS	6-5	265	5/1/71	12	North Carolina	Greensboro, N.C.	UFA(Buff)-'01	16/0
40	Archuleta, Adam	S	6-0	223	11/27/77	6	Arizona State	Chandler, Ariz.	UFA(StL)-'06	14/14*
46	Betts, Ladell	RB	5-10	223	8/27/79	5	Iowa	Blue Springs, Mo.	D2-'02	12/0
73	Boschetti, Ryan	DT/DE	6-4	305	10/7/81	3	UCLA	Belmont, Calif.	FA-'04	13/1
5	Bramlet, Casey	QB	6-4	220	4/2/81	2	Wyoming	Wheatland, Wyo.	FA-'06	0*
30	Broughton, Nehemiah	FB	5-11	255	11/4/81	2	The Citadel	North Charleston, S.C.	D7-'05	4/0
8	Brunell, Mark	QB	6-1	217	9/17/70	14	Washington	Santa Maria, Calif.	T(Jax)-'04	16/15
17	Campbell, Jason	QB	6-4	230	12/31/81	2	Auburn	Taylorsville, Miss.	D1-'05	0*
50	Campbell, Khary	LB	6-3	232	4/4/79	5	Bowling Green	Toledo, Ohio	FA-'04	14/0
99	Carter, Andre	DE	6-4	265	12/19/80	6	Stanford	Denver, Colo.	UFA(SF)-'06	16/14*
39	Carter, Kerry	RB	6-2	237	5/12/79	3	California	Vaughn, Ontario, Canada	FA-'06	0*
31	Cartwright, Rock	FB	5-7	215	12/3/79	5	Kansas State	Conroe, Texas	D6-'02	16/0
13	Cash, Ataveus	WR	6-2	203	5/2/79	2	Hampton	Washington, D.C.	FA-'06	0*
58	Clemons, Chris	LB	6-3	240	10/30/81	3	Georgia	Griffin, Ga.	FA-'03	13/1
90	Clemons, Nic	DT/DE	6-6	298	2/3/80	2	Georgia	Griffin, Ga.	FA-'03	8/0
15	Collins, Todd	QB	6-4	228	11/5/71	11	Michigan	Walpole, Mass.	UFA(KC)-'06	1/0*
47	Cooley, Chris	TE	6-3	250	7/11/82	3	Utah State	Powell, Utah	D3-'04	16/16
93	Daniels, Phillip	DE/DT	6-3	290	3/4/73	11	Georgia	Donalson, Ga.	UFA(Chi)-'04	16/16
66	Dockery, Derrick	G/T	6-6	335	9/7/80	4	Texas	Lakeview, Texas	D3-'03	16/16
92	Evans, Demetric	DT/DE	6-3	285	3/3/79	5	Georgia	Haynesville, La.	FA-'04	16/3
86	Farris, Jimmy	WR	6-0	200	4/13/78	4	Montana	Lewiston, Idaho	FA-'05	4/0
88	Fauria, Christian	TE	6-4	250	9/22/71	12	Colorado	Northridge, Calif.	UFA(NE)-'06	16/10*
4	Frost, Derrick	P	6-2	202	11/25/80	3	Northern Iowa	St. Louis, Mo.	FA-'05	14/0
96	Griffin, Cornelius	DT	6-3	310	12/3/76	7	Alabama	Brundidge, Ala.	UFA(NYG)-'04	13/12
10	Hall, John	K	6-3	240	3/17/74	10	Wisconsin	Port Charlotte, Fla.	UFA(NYJ)-'03	10/0
57	Holdman, Warrick	LB	6-1	243	11/22/75	8	Texas A&M	Alief, Texas	UFA(Cle)-'05	14/7
84	Jacobs, Taylor	WR	6-0	202	5/30/81	4	Florida	Tallahassee, Fla.	D2-'03	15/3
76	Jansen, Jon	T	6-6	308	1/28/76	7	Michigan	Clawson, Mich.	D2-'99	16/16
32	Jimoh, Ade	CB/S	6-1	195	4/18/80	4	Utah State	Woodland Hills, Calif.	FA-'03	16/0
87	Johnson, Robert	TE	6-6	278	6/20/80	2	Auburn	Montgomery, Ala.	FA-'05	2/0
18	Johnson, Ron	WR	6-3	226	9/11/82	3	Minnesota	Detroit, Mich.	FA-'06	0*
91	Killings, Cedric	DT/DE	6-2	310	12/14/77	4	Carson-Newman	Miami, Fla.	FA-'04	10/1
85 t-	Lloyd, Brandon	WR	6-0	192	7/5/81	4	Illinois	Kansas City, Mo.	T(SF)-'06	16/15*
98	Marshall, Lemar	LB	6-2	232	12/17/76	5	Michigan State	Cincinnati, Ohio	FA-'01	16/16
59	McCune, Robert	LB	6-0	240	3/9/79	2	Louisville	Mobile, Ala.	D5-'05	5/0
69	Molinaro, Jim	G/T	6-6	310	4/27/81	3	Notre Dame	Bethlehem, Pa.	D6-'04	3/0
35	Morton, Christian	CB/S	6-0	181	4/28/81	2	Illinois	St. Louis, Mo.	FA-'05	5/1*
89	Moss, Santana	WR	5-10	190	6/1/79	6	Miami	Miami, Fla.	T(NYJ)-'05	16/16
80	Patten, David	WR	5-10	190	8/19/74	10	Western Carolina	Columbia, S.C.	UFA(NE)-'05	9/7
34	Patterson, Dimitri	CB/S	5-10	193	6/18/83	2	Tuskegee	Miami, Fla.	FA-'05	3/0
26	Portis, Clinton	RB	5-11	212	9/1/81	5	Miami	Gainesville, Fla.	T(Den)-'04	16/16
20	Prioleau, Pierson	CB/S	5-11	185	8/6/77	8	Virginia Tech	Alvin, S.C.	UFA(Buff)-'05	15/6
62	Pucillo, Mike	G/T	6-4	311	7/14/79	4	Auburn	Cleveland, Ohio	UFA(Cle)-'06	10/6*
61	Rabach, Casey	C/G	6-4	295	9/24/77	5	Wisconsin	Sturgeon Bay, Wis.	UFA(Balt)-'05	16/16
82	Randle El, Antwaan	WR	5-10	192	8/17/79	5	Indiana	Riverdale, Ill.	UFA(Pitt)-'06	16/15*
75	Riley, Karon	DE	6-2	256	8/23/78	4	Minnesota	Detroit, Mich.	UFA(Atl)-'06	0*
22	Rogers, Carlos	CB	6-0	195	7/2/81	2	Auburn	Augusta, Ga.	D1-'05	12/5
95	Salave'a, Joe	DT/DE	6-3	317	7/28/77	8	Arizona	Leone, American Samoa	FA-'04	14/13
60	Samuels, Chris	T	6-5	310	7/28/77	7	Alabama	Mobile, Ala.	D1-'00	16/16
45	Sellers, Mike	FB	6-3	278	7/21/75	7	Walla Walla (Wash.) C.C.	North Thurston, Wash.	FA-'04	15/6
24	Springs, Shawn	CB	6-0	200	3/11/75	10	Ohio State	Silver Spring, Md.	UFA(Sea)-'04	15/15
21	Taylor, Sean	S	6-2	232	4/1/83	3	Miami	Miami, Fla.	D1-'04	15/15
77	Thomas, Randy	G	6-5	310	1/19/76	8	Mississippi State	East Point, Ga.	UFA(NYJ)-'03	14/14
83	Thrash, James	WR	6-0	205	4/28/75	10	Missouri State	Wewoka, Okla.	T(Phil)-'04	12/2
72	Walter, Tyson	G/T	6-4	303	3/17/78	4	Ohio State	Kenston, Ohio	UFA(Hou)-'06	0*
53	Washington, Marcus	LB	6-3	250	10/17/76	7	Auburn	Auburn, Ala.	UFA(Ind)-'04	16/16
48	White, Manuel	FB	6-2	245	7/2/82	2	UCLA	Canyon Country, Calif.	D4-'05	0*
25	Wright, Kenny	CB	6-1	207	9/14/77	8	Northwestern State	Ruston, La.	UFA(Jax)-'06	16/16*
97	Wynn, Renaldo	DE/DT	6-3	285	9/3/74	10	Notre Dame	Chicago, Ill.	UFA(Jax)-'02	16/15

* Archuleta played 14 games with St. Louis in '05; Bramlet last active with Cincinnati in '04; J. Campbell inactive for 16 games; A. Carter played 16 games with San Francisco; K. Carter last active with Seattle in '04; Cash last active with N.Y. Giants in '03; Collins played 1 game with Kansas City; Fauria played 16 games with New England; Ron Johnson last active with Baltimore in '03; Lloyd played 16 games with San Francisco; Morton played 4 games with Atlanta and 1 game with Washington; Pucillo played 10 games with Cleveland; Randle El played 16 games with Pittsburgh; Riley last active with Atlanta in '04; Walter inactive for 7 games with Houston; White missed '05 season because of injury; Wright played 16 games with Jacksonville.

t - Redskins traded for Lloyd (SF).

Traded—QB Patrick Ramsey (4 games in '05) to N.Y. Jets.

Players lost through free agency (4): LB LaVar Arrington (NYG; 13 games in '05), S Ryan Clark (Pitt; 13), TE Robert Royal (Buff, 15), S Omar Stoutmire (NYJ; 10).

Also played with Redskins in '05—S Matt Bowen (13 games), WR/KR Antonio Brown (7), G/T Ray Brown (15), G/T Lennie Friedman (10), P Andy Groom (2), CB Walt Harris (13), DT/DE Aki Jones (4), LB Zak Keasey (1), TE Brian Kozlowski (16), K Nick Novak (5), WR Rich Parson (1), C/G Cory Raymer (3).

2006 FIRST-YEAR ROSTER

Name	Pos.	Ht.	Wt.	Birthdate	College	Hometown	How Acq.
Alston, Jon (1)	G/T	6-5	310	9/4/82	South Carolina	Ladson, S.C.	FA-'05
Brown, Manaia	DE/DT	6-4	313	7/17/81	Brigham Young	West Valley City, Utah	FA
Burns, Curry (1)	S	6-0	203	2/12/81	Louisville	Miami, Fla.	FA-'05
Combs, Jonathan (1)	RB	5-9	227	2/28/82	Texas College	Houston, Texas	FA-'05
Doughty, Reed	S	6-1	210	11/4/82	Northern Colorado	Johnstown, Colo.	D6
Espy, Mike	WR	5-11	195	11/29/82	Mississippi	Madison, Miss.	FA
Eubanks, John	CB	5-10	173	7/13/83	Southern Mississippi	Mound Bayou, Miss.	FA
Fenner, Derrick	WR	6-0	193	12/25/82	Maryland	Hampton, Va.	FA
Golston, Kedric	DT	6-4	292	5/30/83	Georgia	Tyrone, Ga.	D6
Harris, Steven (1)	WR	5-10	183	11/10/81	Arkansas	Jonesboro, Ark.	FA-'05
Harvey, Jasper	G/T	6-3	305	4/8/83	San Diego State	Marrero, La.	FA
Havner, Spencer	LB	6-2	245	2/2/83	UCLA	Nevada City, Calif.	FA
Hawkins, Chris	CB/S	5-10	184	8/14/82	Marshall	Kinston, N.C.	FA
Jones, Jim (1)	G/T	6-3	319	1/27/78	Notre Dame	Oak Lawn, Ill.	FA-'05
Jones, Tyler (1)	K	6-1	201	2/25/80	Boise State	Boise, Idaho	FA
Lefotu, Kili	G/T	6-5	315	11/23/83	Arizona	Honolulu, Hawaii	D7
Lonie, David	P	6-6	220	5/6/79	California	Palm Beach, Australia	FA
Lumsden, Jesse (1)	RB	6-2	219	8/3/82	McMasters (Canada)	Burlington, Ontario, Canada	FA
Manupuna, Vaka	DT	6-0	300	6/30/82	Colorado	Honolulu, Hawaii	FA
McIntosh, Rocky	LB	6-2	231	11/15/82	Miami	Gaffney, S.C.	D2
Mineo, Chris	DT	6-2	205	11/9/82	Texas-El Paso	Odessa, Texas	FA
Montgomery, Anthony	DT	6-5	305	3/8/84	Minnesota	Cleveland, Ohio	D5
Ndukwe, Ikechuku (1)	G/T	6-4	338	7/17/82	Northwestern	Morgantown, W. Va.	FA-'05
Onyenegecha, Chijioke	CB/S	6-1	202	3/15/83	Oklahoma	Richmond, Calif.	FA
Ortega, Buck	TE	6-4	227	11/22/81	Miami	Miami, Fla.	FA
Pino, Chris	G/T	6-5	315	8/18/82	San Diego State	Oceanside, Calif.	FA
Powell, Calen (1)	TE	6-5	257	2/16/81	Duke	Bellevue, Wash.	FA
Simon, Kevin	LB	5-11	234	6/12/83	Tennessee	Walnut Creek, Calif.	D7
Smith, Richard (1)	WR	5-10	191	7/16/80	Arkansas	Independence, Mo.	FA
Stull, Justin	LB	6-1	235	9/20/83	Princeton	Lititz, Pa.	FA
Sykes, Joe	LB	6-2	266	11/22/82	Southern A&M	Grenada, Miss.	FA
Williams, Aric (1)	CB/S	5-11	187	3/21/82	Oregon State	Los Angeles, Calif.	FA
Woodard, Jonta (1)	G/T	6-5	325	7/22/78	Louisville	Stockton, Calif.	FA

The term NFL Rookie is defined as a player who is in his first season of professional football and has not been on the roster of another professional football team for any regular-season or postseason games. A Rookie is designated by an "R" on NFL rosters. Players who have been active in another professional football league or players who have NFL experience, including either preseason training camp or being on an Active List or Inactive List, or on Reserve/Injured or Reserve/Physically Unable to Perform for fewer than six regular-season games, are termed NFL First-Year Players. An NFL First-Year Player is designated by a "1" on NFL rosters. Thereafter, a player is credited with an additional year of experience for each season in which he accumulates six games on the Active List or Inactive List, or on Reserve/Injured or Reserve/Physically Unable to Perform.

Log on to www.redskins.com for an up-to-date roster.

COACHING STAFF
Head Coach,
Joe Gibbs
Pro Career: On January 7, 2004, Joe Gibbs made his return to the Washington Redskins as head coach and team president. The most successful coach in Redskins history, Gibbs, who coached the team from 1981-1992, led the Redskins to four Super Bowls (XVI, XVII, XXII, and XXVI). He is the only coach to win three Super Bowls with three different quarterbacks. His 157 wins ranks 12th in NFL history, and his .657 win percentage is third among all NFL coaches with more than 125 wins. Gibbs coached with the St. Louis Cardinals (1973-1977), Tampa Bay Buccaneers (1978), and San Diego Chargers (1979-1980), before joining the Redskins in 1981. Career record: 157-82.
Background: Played tight end, offensive guard and linebacker at San Diego State. Coached at San Diego State (1964-66), Florida State (1967-1968), USC (1969-1970), and Arkansas (1971-1972).
Personal: Born November 25, 1940 in Mocksville, N.C,. lives in Charlotte, with wife Pat. They have two sons: J.D. and Coy.

ASSISTANT COACHES
Greg Blache, defensive coordinator-defensive line; born March 9, 1949, New Orleans. Attended Notre Dame. No college or pro playing experience. College coach: Notre Dame 1972-75, 1981-83, Tulane 1976-1980, Southern 1986, Kansas 1987. Pro coach: Jacksonville Bulls (USFL) 1984-85, Green Bay Packers 1988-1993, Indianapolis Colts 1994-98, Chicago Bears 1999-2003, joined Redskins in 2004.
Don Breaux, offensive coordinator; born August 3, 1940, Jennings, La. Quarterback McNeese State 1958-1961. Pro quarterback Denver Broncos 1963, San Diego Chargers 1964-65. College coach: Florida State 1966-67, Arkansas 1968-1971, 1977-1980, Florida 1973-74, Texas 1975-76. Pro coach: Houston Oilers 1972, Washington Redskins 1981-1993, New York Jets 1994, Carolina Panthers 1995-2001, re-joined Redskins in 2004.
Joe Bugel, asst. head coach-offense; born March 10, 1940, Pittsburgh. Guard/linebacker Western Kentucky 1960-63. No pro playing experience. College coach: Western Kentucky 1964-1968, Navy 1969-1972, Iowa State 1973, Ohio State 1974. Pro coach: Detroit Lions 1975-76, Houston Oilers 1977-1980, Washington Redskins 1981-89, Phoenix Cardinals 1990-1993 (head coach), Oakland Raiders 1995-97 (head coach 1997), San Diego Chargers 1998-2001, re-joined Redskins in 2004.
Jack Burns, offensive assistant; born January 3, 1949, Tampa. Safety Florida 1967-1970. No pro playing experience.

College coach: Florida 1971-73, 1975, Louisville 1974, 1985-88, Texas 1976, Vanderbilt 1977-78, Auburn 1979-1980. Pro coach: Tampa Bay Bandits (USFL) 1983, Washington Redskins 1989-1991, Minnesota Vikings 1992-93, Atlanta Falcons 1997-2003, re-joined Redskins in 2004.
Earnest Byner, running backs; born September 15, 1962, Milledgeville, Ga. Running back East Carolina 1980-83. Pro running back Cleveland Browns 1984-88, 1994-95, Washington Redskins 1989-1993, Baltimore Ravens 1996-97. Pro coach: Joined Redskins in 2004.
Bobby Crumpler, strength and conditioning; born April 23, 1965, Newton Grove, N.C. Running back North Carolina State 1983-87. No pro playing experience. College coach: North Carolina State 1989, 1992-96, 2000-01, Kansas 2002. Pro coach: Joined Redskins in 2003.
Coy Gibbs, quality control-offense; born December 9, 1972, Little Rock, Ark. Linebacker Stanford 1991-94. No pro playing experience. Pro coach: Joined Redskins in 2004.
Jerry Gray, secondary-cornerbacks; born December 16, 1962, Lubbock, Texas. Safety Texas 1981-84. Pro defensive back Los Angeles Rams 1985-1991, Houston Oilers 1992, Tampa Bay Buccaneers 1993. College coach: Southern Methodist 1995-96. Pro coach: Tennessee Titans 1997-2000, Buffalo Bills 2001-05, joined Redskins in 2006.
John Hastings, strength and conditioning; born July 5, 1964, Newport News, Va. Attended Ohio University. No college or pro playing experience. Pro coach: San Diego Chargers 1990-2001, joined Redskins in 2002.
Stan Hixon, wide receivers; born July 24, 1957, Lakeland, Fla. Wide receiver Iowa State 1975-78. No pro playing experience. College coach: Morehead State 1980-82, Appalachian State 1983-88, South Carolina 1989-1992, Wake Forest 1993-94, Georgia Tech 1995-99, Louisiana State 2000-03. Pro coach: Joined Redskins in 2004.
Steve Jackson, passing game-safeties; born April 8, 1969, Houston. Defensive back Purdue 1987-1990. Pro defensive back Houston Oilers/Tennessee Titans 1991-1999. Pro coach: Buffalo Bills 2001-03, joined Redskins in 2004.
Bill Lazor, quarterbacks; born June 14, 1972, Scranton, Pa. Quarterback Cornell 1991-93. No pro playing experience. College coach: Cornell 1994-2000, Buffalo 2001-02. Pro coach: Atlanta Falcons 2003, joined Redskins in 2004.
Dale Lindsey, linebackers; born January 18, 1943, Bedford, Ind. Linebacker Western Kentucky 1961-64. Pro linebacker Cleveland Browns 1965-1973. College coach: Southern Methodist 1988-89. Pro coach: Green Bay Packers 1986-87, New England Patriots 1990, Tampa

Bay Buccaneers 1991, San Diego Chargers 1992-96, 2002-03, Washington Redskins 1997-98, Chicago Bears 1999-2001, re-joined Redskins in 2004.
Kirk Olivadotti, defensive line/special teams; born January 1, 1974, Wilmington, Del. Wide receiver Purdue 1992-1996. No pro playing experience. College coach: Maine Maritime Academy 1997, Indiana State 1998-99. Pro coach: Joined Redskins in 2000.
Al Saunders, associate head coach-offense; born February 1, 1947, London, England. Wide receiver/defensive back San Jose State 1966-68. No pro playing experience. College coach: Southern California 1970-71, Missouri 1972, Utah State 1973-75, California 1976-1981, Tennessee 1982. Pro coach: San Diego Chargers 1983-88 (head coach 1986-88), Kansas City Chiefs 1989-1998, 2001-05, St. Louis Rams 1999-2000, joined Redskins in 2006.
Bob Saunders, assistant coach/special projects; born November 21, 1976, Walnut Creek, Calif. Wide receiver/defensive back Southern Methodist 1995. No pro playing experience. Pro coach: Kansas City Chiefs 2002-05, joined Redskins in 2006.
Warren (Rennie) Simmons, tight end; born February 25, 1942, Poughkeepsie, N.Y. Center San Diego State 1961-65. No pro playing experience. College coach: Cal State-Fullerton 1974-78, Cerritos (Calif.) J.C. 1978-1980, Vanderbilt 1995. Pro coach: Washington Redskins 1981-1993, Los Angeles Rams 1994, Houston Oilers 1996, Atlanta Falcons 1997-2003, re-joined Redskins in 2004.
Danny Smith, special teams; born September 7, 1953, Pittsburgh. Defensive back Edinboro State 1972-75. No pro playing experience. College coach: Edinboro State 1976, Clemson 1979, William & Mary 1980-83, The Citadel 1984-86, Georgia Tech 1987-1994. Pro coach: Philadelphia Eagles 1995-98, Detroit Lions 1999-2000, Buffalo Bills 2001-03, joined Redskins in 2004.
Gregg Williams, asst. head coach-defense; born July 15, 1958, Excelsior Springs, Mo. Quarterback Northeast Missouri State 1976-79. No pro playing experience. College coach: Houston 1988-89. Pro coach: Houston Oilers/Tennessee Titans 1990-2000, Buffalo Bills 2001-03 (head coach), joined Redskins in 2004.

2005 Season in Review

2005 TRADES

Defensive tackle **Gerard Warren** from Cleveland to Denver for a fourth-round selection in 2005 (#126). (3/3)

Wide receiver **Randy Moss** from Minnesota to Oakland for linebacker **Napoleon Harris** and the Raiders' first-round selection in 2005 (WR **Troy Williamson**) and seventh-round selection in 2005 (DB **Adrian Ward**). (3/3)

Cornerback **Duane Starks** and the Cardinals' fifth-round selection in 2005 (#145) from Arizona to New England for the Patriots' third-round selection in 2005 (LB **Darryl Blackstock**) and fifth-round selection in 2005 (LB **Lance Mitchell**). (3/4)

Quarterback **Trent Dilfer** from Seattle to Cleveland for the Broncos' fourth-round selection in 2005 (#126). (3/7)

Wide receiver **Santana Moss** from New York Jets to Washington for wide receiver **Laveranues Coles**. (3/7)

Linebacker **Sam Cowart** from New York Jets to Minnesota for the Vikings' seventh-round selection in 2005 (#230). (3/18)

Defensive end **Ebenezer Ekuban** and defensive tackle **Michael Myers** from Cleveland to Denver for running back **Rueben Droughns**. (3/18)

Defensive end **Carlos Hall** from Tennessee to Minnesota for the Vikings' seventh-round selection in 2005 (#230). (3/18)

Denver's first-round selection in 2005 (QB **Jason Campbell**) from Denver to Washington for the Redskins' third-round selection in 2005 (DB **Karl Paymah**) and unannounced future selection choice. (4/20)

Defensive back **Phillip Buchanon** from Oakland to Houston for the Texans' second-round selection in 2005 (#47) and third-round selection in 2005 (LB **Kirk Morrison**). (4/21)

Tight end **Doug Jolley** and the Texans' second-round selection in 2005 (K **Mike Nugent**), the Cardinals' sixth-round selection in 2005 (RB **Cedric Houston**) and the Cowboys' sixth-round selection in 2005 (#185) from Oakland to New York Jets for the Jets' first-round selection in 2005 (#26) and the Vikings' sixth-round selection in 2005 (#230). (4/21)

Defensive back **Patrick Surtain** and the Dolphins' fifth-round selection in 2005 (LB **Boomer Grigsby**) from Miami to Kansas City for the Chiefs' second-round selection in 2005 (#46) and the Packers' fifth-round selection in 2005 (T **Anthony Alabi**). (4/23)

Houston's first-round selection in 2005 (T **Jammal Brown**) from Houston to New Orleans for the Saints' first-round selection in 2005 (DE **Travis Johnson**) and third-round selection in 2006. (4/23)

New York Jets' first-round selection in 2005 (C **Chris Spencer**) and fourth-round selection in 2005 (T **Ray Willis**) from Oakland to Seattle for the Seahawks' first-round selection in 2005 (DB **Fabian Washington**). (4/21)

Detroit's second-round selection in 2005 (T **Michael Roos**) and fourth-round selection in 2005 (T **David Stewart)** from Detroit to Tennessee for the Titans' second-round selection in 2005 (DT **Shaun Cody**). (4/23)

Carolina's second-round selection in 2005 (LB **Lofa Tatupu**) from Carolina to Seattle for the Seahawks' second-round selection in 2005 (RB **Eric Shelton**), Seahawks' fourth-round selection (QB **Stefan LeFors**) and Broncos' fourth-round selection in 2005 (#126). (4/23)

Baltimore's third-round selection in 2005 (DB **Ellis Hobbs**), the Ravens' sixth-round selection in 2005 (#195), and the Ravens' third-round selection in 2006 (#75) from Baltimore to New England for the Patriots' second-round selection in 2005 (T **Adam Terry**). (4/23)

Carolina's fourth-round selection in 2005 (DB **Marviel Underwood**) and the Broncos' fourth-round selection in 2005 (#126) from Carolina to Green Bay for the Packers' third-round selection in 2005 (DT **Atiyyah Ellison**). (4/23)

Philadelphia's third-round selection in 2005 (T **Adam Snyder**) from Philadelphia to San Francisco for the 49ers' fourth-round selection in 2005 (DB **Sean Considine**) and sixth-round selection in 2005 (#175). (4/23)

Minnesota's fourth-round selection in 2005 (RB **Manuel White**) and fifth-round selection in 2005 (LB **Robert McCune**) from Minnesota to Washington for the Redskins' fourth-round selection in 2005 (RB **Ciatrick Fason**). (4/24)

Quarterback **Luke McCown** from Cleveland to Tampa Bay for the Chargers' sixth-round selection in 2005 (DE **Andrew Hoffman**). (4/24)

Jacksonville's fourth-round selection in 2005 (DB **Kerry Rhodes**) from Jacksonville to New York Jets for the Jets' fourth-round selection in 2005 (RB **Alvin Pearman**) and the Cowboys' sixth-round selection in 2005 (KR **Chad Owens**). (4/24)

Denver's fourth-round selection in 2005 (T **Todd Herremans**) from Green Bay to Philadelphia for the Eagles' fifth-round selection in 2005 (DB **Michael Hawkins**), the 49ers' sixth-round selection in 2005 (#175) and seventh-round selection in 2005 (DB **Kurt Campbell**). (4/24)

Dallas' fifth-round selection in 2005 (#148) and fourth-round selection in 2006 (#116) from Dallas to Philadelphia for the Eagles' fourth-round selection in 2005 (DE **Chris Canty**) and sixth-round selection in 2006 (DT **Montavious Stanley**). (4/24)

St. Louis' fifth-round selection in 2005 (WR **Larry Brackins**) and the Rams' seventh-round selection in 2005 (DB **Hamza Abdullah**) from St. Louis to Tampa Bay for the Giants' fifth-round selection in 2005 (TE **Jerome Collins**). (4/24)

Detroit's fourth-round selection in 2006 (RB **Garrett Mills**) from Detroit to New England for the Cardinals' fifth-round selection in 2005 (QB **Dan Orlovsky**) and sixth-round selection in 2005 (LB

Johnathan Goddard). (4/24)

Indianapolis' fourth-round selection in 2006 (#127) from Indianapolis to Philadelphia for the Cowboys' fifth-round selection in 2005 (DE **Jonathan Welsh**). (4/24)

San Francisco's sixth-round selection in 2005 (#175) from Green Bay to New England for the Ravens' sixth-round selection in 2005 (WR **Craig Bragg**) and the Patriots' seventh-round selection in 2005 (G **William Whitticker**). (4/24)

San Francisco's sixth-round selection in 2005 (DT **Anttaj Hawthorne**) from New England to Oakland for the Vikings' seventh-round selection in 2005 (QB **Matt Cassel**) and Raiders' fifth-round selection in 2006 (T **Ryan O'Callaghan**). (4/24)

Punter **Todd Sauerbrun** from Carolina to Denver for punter **Jason Baker** and the Broncos' seventh-round selection in 2006 (DE **Stanley McClover**). (5/19)

Defensive back **Pete Hunter** from Dallas to the New York Jets for the Jets' seventh-round selection in 2006 (T **Pat McQuistan**). (7/14)

Defensive back **Willie Middlebrooks** from Denver to San Francisco for defensive end **John Engelberger**. (7/15)

Running back **Travis Henry** from Buffalo to Tennessee for the Titans' third-round selection in 2006 (DB **Ashton Youboty**). (7/19)

Wide receiver **Rod Gardner** from Washington to Carolina for the Panthers' sixth-round selection in 2006 (DT **Kedric Golston**). (7/28)

Defensive back **Ron Flemons** from Miami to Seattle for defensive back **Kris Richard**. (8/4)

Defensive back **Jon McGraw** from the New York Jets to Detroit for an unannounced selection choice. (8/10)

Guard **Sam Wilder** from Dallas to Tampa Bay for an unannounced selection choice. (8/17)

Wide receiver **Andre Davis** from Cleveland to New England for the Patriots' fifth-round selection in 2006 (DB **DeMario Minter**). (8/22)

Kicker **Seth Marler** from Jacksonville to Dallas for an unannounced selection choice. (8/26)

Defensive end **Alain Kashama** from Chicago to Seattle for the Seahawks' sixth-round selection in 2006 (G **Tyler Reed**). (8/29)

Tight end **John Owens** from Chicago to Miami for linebacker **Brendon Ayanbadejo**. (8/29)

Center **Melvin Fowler** from Cleveland to Minnesota for tackle **Nat Dorsey**. (9/3)

Defensive back **Chris Johnson** from Green Bay to St. Louis for linebacker **Robert Thomas**. (9/3)

Tackle **Steve Morley** from Green Bay to the New York Jets for an unannounced selection choice. (9/3)

Linebacker **Scott Fujita** from Kansas City to Dallas for the Cowboys' sixth-round selection in 2006 (G **Tre' Stallings**). (9/3)

Linebacker **Rocky Calmus** from Tennessee to Indianapolis for an unannounced selection choice. (9/3)

Linebacker **Jamie Winborn** from San Francisco to Jacksonville for an unannounced selection choice. (10/6)

Running back **Jesse Chatman** from Miami to New Orleans for an unannounced selection choice. (10/11)

Quarterback **A. J. Feeley** and the Dolphins' sixth-round selection in 2006 (K **Kurt Smith**) from Miami to San Diego for quarterback **Cleo Lemon**. (10/18)

Guard **Toniu Fonoti** from San Diego to Minnesota for the Vikings' seventh-round selection in 2006 (T **Jimmy Martin**). (10/18)

Quarterback **Tim Rattay** from San Francisco to Tampa Bay for the Buccaneers' selection in 2006 (DB **Marcus Hudson**). (10/18)

 * *Draft choice number is listed if club later traded the pick.*

2006 TRADES

Wide receiver **Brandon Lloyd** from San Francisco to Washington for the Redskins' third-round selection in 2006 (WR **Brandon Williams**) and an unannounced selection choice. (3/13)

Quarterback **Daunte Culpepper** from Minnesota to Miami for the Dolphins' second-round selection in 2006 (C **Ryan Cook**). (3/15)

Quarterback **Patrick Ramsey** from Washington to New York Jets for the Jets' sixth-round selection in 2006 (DB **Reed Doughty**). (3/17)

Defensive back **Chris Crocker** from Cleveland to Atlanta for the Falcons' fourth-round selection in 2006 (G **Isaac Sowells**). (3/20)

Defensive end **John Abraham** from New York Jets to Atlanta. Atlanta's first-round selection in 2006 (#15) from Atlanta to Denver. Denver's first-round selection in 2006 (C **Nick Mangold**) from Denver to New York Jets. Denver's third-round selection in 2006 (#93) and an unannounced selection from Denver to Atlanta. (3/22)

Defensive back **Bryan Scott** from Atlanta to New Orleans for tackle **Wayne Gandy**. (4/6)

Wide receiver **Eric Moulds** from Buffalo to Houston for the Texans' fifth-round selection in 2006 (DT **Kyle Williams**). (4/6)

Defensive back **Sammy Davis** from San Diego to San Francisco for wide receiver **Rashaun Woods**. (4/13)

Denver's first-round selection in 2006 (DE **Manny Lawson**) from Denver to San Francisco for the 49ers' second-round selection in 2006 (#37) and third-round selection in 2006 (#68). (4/19)

Defensive back **Mike Green** from Chicago to Seattle for the Seahawks' sixth-round selection in 2006 (G **Tyler Reed**). (4/25)

Atlanta's first-round selection in 2006 (DB **Tye Hill**) and San Francisco's third-round selection in 2006 (DT **Claude Wroten**) from Denver to St. Louis for the Rams' first-round selection in 2006 (QB **Jay Cutler**). (4/29)

Baltimore's first-round selection in

2006 (DE **Kamerion Wimbley**) and sixth-round selection in 2006 (DT **Babatunde Oshinowo**) from Baltimore to Cleveland for the Browns' first-round selection in 2006 (DT **Haloti Ngata**). (4/29)

N.Y. Giants' first-round selection in 2006 (WR **Santonio Holmes**) from Giants to Pittsburgh for the Steelers' first-round selection in 2006 (DE **Mathias Kiwanuka**), third-round selection in 2006 (LB **Gerris Wilkinson**), and fourth-round selection in 2006 (T **Guy Whimper**). (4/29)

Buffalo's second-round selection in 2006 (DB **Danieal Manning**) and third-round selection in 2006 (DT **Dusty Dvoracek**) from Buffalo to Chicago for the Bears' first-round selection in 2006 (DT **John McCargo**). (4/29)

Center **Jeff Faine** and the Browns' second-round selection in 2006 (DB **Roman Harper**) from Cleveland to New Orleans for the Saints' second-round selection (LB **D'Qwell Jackson**). (4/29)

N.Y. Jets' second-round selection in 2006 (LB **Rocky McIntosh**) from the Jets to Washington for the Redskins' second-round selection in 2006 (#53), sixth-round selection in 2006 (DB **Drew Coleman**), and second-round selection in 2007. (4/29)

Green Bay's second-round selection in 2006 (WR **Chad Jackson**) from Green Bay to New England for the Redskins' second-round selection in 2006 (WR **Greg Jennings**) and the Ravens' third-round selection in 2006 (G **Jason Spitz**). (4/29)

Wide receiver **Javon Walker** from Green Bay to Denver for the 49ers' second-round selection in 2006 (#37). (4/29)

Atlanta's second-round selection in 2006 (T **Daryn Colledge**), the Broncos' third-round selection in 2006 (#93), and the Falcons' fifth-round selection in 2006 (QB **Ingle Martin**) from Atlanta to Green Bay for the 49ers' second-round selection in 2006 (DB **Jimmy Williams**) and the Packers' fifth-round selection in 2006 (T **Quinn Ojinnaka**). (4/29)

Philadelphia's second-round selection in 2006 (#45) and the Cowboys' fourth-round selection in 2006 (LB **Stephen Tulloch**) from Philadelphia to Tennessee for the Titans' second-round selection in 2006 (T **Winston Justice**). (4/29)

Baltimore's second-round selection in 2006 (WR **Sinorice Moss**) from Baltimore to the N.Y. Giants for the Giants' second-round selection in 2006 (C **Chris Chester**) and third-round selection in 2006 (DB **David Pittman**). (4/29)

Dallas' second-round selection in 2006 (#49) from Dallas to the N.Y. Jets for the Redskins' second-round selection in 2006 (TE **Anthony Fasano**), the Redskins' sixth-round selection in 2006 (#189), and the Jets' seventh-round selection in 2006 (T **Pat McQuistan**). (4/29)

Minnesota's third-round selection in 2006 (DB **Anthony Smith**) and the Seahawks' third-round selection in 2006 (WR

Willie Reid) from Minnesota to Pittsburgh for the Steelers' second-round selection in 2006 (QB **Tarvaris Jackson**). (4/29)

N.Y. Jets' third-round selection in 2006 (LB **Chris Gocong**) from the Jets to Philadelphia for the Eagles' third-round selection in 2006 (LB **Anthony Schlegel**) and seventh-round selection in 2006 (DE **Titus Adams**). (4/29)

Dallas' third-round selection in 2006 (LB **Clint Ingram**) from Dallas to Jacksonville for the Jaguars' third-round selection in 2006 (DE **Jason Hatcher**) and fourth-round selection in 2006 (KR **Skyler Green**). (4/29)

Denver's third-round selection in 2006 (TE **Dominique Byrd**) from Green Bay to St. Louis for the Rams' fourth-round selection in 2006 (#109) and sixth-round selection in 2006 (DT **Johnny Jolly**). (4/29)

Defensive tackle **Hollis Thomas** and Philadelphia's fourth-round selection in 2006 (T **Jahri Evans**) from Philadelphia to New Orleans for the Saints' fourth-round selection in 2006 (G **Max Jean-Gilles**). (4/30)

Guard **Artis Hicks** and Indianapolis' fourth-round selection in 2006 (DE **Ray Edwards**) from Philadelphia to Minnesota for the Vikings' fourth-round selection in 2006 (#115) and sixth-round selection in 2006 (#185). (4/30)

Tight end **Brandon Manumaleuna** from St. Louis to San Diego for the Chargers' fourth-round selection in 2006 (DE **Victor Adeyanju**). (4/30)

St. Louis' fourth-round selection in 2006 (WR **Jason Avant**) from Green Bay to Philadelphia for the Vikings' fourth-round selection in 2006 (DB **Will Blackmon**) and the Vikings' sixth-round selection in 2006 (DB **Tyrone Culver**). (4/30)

Dallas' fifth-round selection in 2006 (TE **Jason Pociask**) and the Redskins' sixth-round selection in 2006 (DB **Drew Coleman**) from Dallas to the N.Y. Jets for the Jets' fifth-round selection in 2006 (DB **Pat Watkins**). (4/30)

Jacksonville's sixth-round selection in 2006 (DE **Melvin Oliver**) from Jacksonville to San Francisco for the 49ers' seventh-round selection in 2006 (DE **James Wyche**) and the Jaguars' seventh-round selection in 2006 (DB **Dee Webb**). (4/30)

Indianapolis' sixth-round selection in 2007 from Indianapolis to Tennessee for the Colts' seventh-round selection in 2006 (DB **T.J. Rushing**). (4/30)

Quarterback **Trent Dilfer** from Cleveland to San Francisco for quarterback **Ken Dorsey** and an unannounced selection. (5/8)

Quarterback **Joey Harrington** from Detroit to Miami for an unannounced selection. (5/15)

 * *Draft choice number is listed if club later traded the pick.*

PRESEASON STANDINGS
AMERICAN FOOTBALL CONFERENCE
East Division

	W	L	T	Pct.	Pts.	OP
N.Y. Jets	3	1	0	.750	89	53
Buffalo	2	2	0	.500	63	54
New England	2	2	0	.500	80	80
Miami	1	4	0	.200	78	105

North Division

	W	L	T	Pct.	Pts.	OP
Cleveland	3	1	0	.750	74	56
Pittsburgh	3	1	0	.750	86	68
Baltimore	2	2	0	.500	64	62
Cincinnati	2	2	0	.500	92	67

South Division

	W	L	T	Pct.	Pts.	OP
Jacksonville	2	2	0	.500	74	84
Houston	1	3	0	.250	56	96
Tennessee	1	3	0	.250	71	78
Indianapolis	0	5	0	.000	72	143

West Division

	W	L	T	Pct.	Pts.	OP
Denver	4	0	0	1.000	113	80
San Diego	2	2	0	.500	87	74
Oakland	1	3	0	.250	59	63
Kansas City	0	4	0	.000	73	101

AFC PRESEASON RECORDS—TEAM BY TEAM

East Division
BUFFALO (2-2)

17	at Indianapolis	10
27	GREEN BAY	7
12	at Chicago	16
7	DETROIT	21
63		54

MIAMI (1-4)

24	Chicago (b)	27
17	at Jacksonville	27
3	at Pittsburgh	17
17	TAMPA BAY	14
17	ATLANTA	20
78		105

NEW ENGLAND (2-2)

23	at Cincinnati	13
27	NEW ORLEANS	37
27	at Green Bay	3
3	NEW YORK GIANTS	27
80		80

N.Y. JETS (3-1)

10	DETROIT	3
28	MINNESOTA	21
14	at New York Giants	15
37	at Philadelphia	14
89		53

North Division
BALTIMORE (2-2)

3	at Atlanta	16
14	PHILADELPHIA	20
21	at New Orleans	6
26	WASHINGTON	20
64		62

CINCINNATI (2-2)

13	NEW ENGLAND	23
24	at Washington	17
17	at Philadelphia	27
38	INDIANAPOLIS	0
92		67

CLEVELAND (3-1)

17	NEW YORK GIANTS	14
21	at Detroit	13
20	CAROLINA	23
16	at Chicago	6
74		56

PITTSBURGH (3-1)

38	PHILADELPHIA	31
17	MIAMI	3
10	at Washington	17
21	at Carolina	17
86		68

South Division
HOUSTON (1-3)

14	DENVER	20
19	OAKLAND	17
9	at Dallas	21
14	at Tampa Bay	38
56		96

INDIANAPOLIS (0-5)

21	Atlanta (a)	27
10	BUFFALO	17
17	CHICAGO	24
24	at Denver	37
0	at Cincinnati	38
72		143

JACKSONVILLE (2-2)

27	MIAMI	17
20	at Tampa Bay	17
7	ATLANTA	23
20	at Dallas	27
74		84

TENNESSEE (1-3)

17	TAMPA BAY	20
24	at Atlanta	21
13	at San Francisco	16
17	GREEN BAY	21
71		78

West Division
DENVER (4-0)

20	at Houston	14
26	SAN FRANCISCO	21
37	INDIANAPOLIS	24
30	at Arizona	21
113		80

KANSAS CITY (0-4)

16	at Minnesota	27
17	ARIZONA	24
17	SEATTLE	23
23	at St. Louis	27
73		101

OAKLAND (1-3)

13	at San Francisco	21
17	at Houston	19
16	ARIZONA	17
13	NEW ORLEANS	6
59		63

SAN DIEGO (2-2)

7	at Green Bay	10
36	ST. LOUIS	21
16	at Minnesota	19
28	SAN FRANCISCO	24
87		74

(a) American Bowl at Tokyo, Japan
(b) Pro Football Hall of Fame Game at Canton, Ohio

NFC PRESEASON RECORDS—TEAM BY TEAM

East Division

DALLAS (3-1)

11	at Arizona	13
18	at Seattle	10
21	HOUSTON	9
27	JACKSONVILLE	20
77		52

N.Y. GIANTS (3-1)

14	at Cleveland	17
27	CAROLINA	21
15	NEW YORK JETS	14
27	at New England	3
83		55

PHILADELPHIA (2-2)

31	at Pittsburgh	38
20	at Baltimore	14
27	CINCINNATI	17
14	NEW YORK JETS	37
92		106

WASHINGTON (1-3)

10	at Carolina	28
17	CINCINNATI	24
17	PITTSBURGH	10
20	at Baltimore	26
64		88

North Division

CHICAGO (3-2)

27	Miami (b)	24
13	at St. Louis	17
24	at Indianapolis	17
16	BUFFALO	12
6	CLEVELAND	16
86		86

DETROIT (1-3

3	at New York Jets	10
13	CLEVELAND	21
13	ST. LOUIS	37
21	at Buffalo	7
50		75

GREEN BAY (2-2)

10	SAN DIEGO	7
7	at Buffalo	27
3	NEW ENGLAND	27
21	at Tennessee	17
41		78

MINNESOTA (3-1)

27	KANSAS CITY	16
21	at New York Jets	28
19	SAN DIEGO	16
23	at Seattle	21
90		81

South Division

ATLANTA (4-1)

27	Indianapolis (a)	21
16	BALTIMORE	3
21	TENNESSEE	24
23	at Jacksonville	7
20	at Miami	17
107		72

CAROLINA (2-2)

28	WASHINGTON	10
21	at New York Giants	27
23	at Cleveland	20
17	PITTSBURGH	21
89		78

NEW ORLEANS (1-3)

15	SEATTLE	34
37	at New England	27
6	BALTIMORE	21
6	at Oakland	13
64		95

TAMPA BAY (2-2)

20	at Tennessee	17
17	JACKSONVILLE	20
14	at Miami	17
38	HOUSTON	14
89		68

West Division

ARIZONA (3-1)

13	DALLAS	11
24	at Kansas City	17
17	at Oakland	16
21	DENVER	30
75		74

ST. LOUIS (3-1)

17	CHICAGO	13
21	at San Diego	36
37	at Detroit	13
27	KANSAS CITY	23
102		85

SAN FRANCISCO (2-2)

21	OAKLAND	13
21	at Denver	26
16	TENNESSEE	13
24	at San Diego	28
82		80

SEATTLE (2-2)

34	at New Orleans	15
10	DALLAS	18
23	at Kansas City	17
21	MINNESOTA	23
88		73

PRESEASON STANDINGS
NATIONAL FOOTBALL CONFERENCE

East Division

	W	L	T	Pct.	Pts.	OP
Dallas	3	1	0	.750	77	52
N.Y. Giants	3	1	0	.750	83	55
Philadelphia	2	2	0	.500	92	106
Washington	1	3	0	.250	64	88

North Division

	W	L	T	Pct.	Pts.	OP
Minnesota	3	1	0	.750	90	81
Chicago	3	2	0	.600	86	86
Green Bay	2	2	0	.500	41	78
Detroit	1	3	0	.250	50	75

South Division

	W	L	T	Pct.	Pts.	OP
Atlanta	4	1	0	.800	107	72
Carolina	2	2	0	.500	89	78
Tampa Bay	2	2	0	.500	89	68
New Orleans	1	3	0	.250	64	95

West Division

	W	L	T	Pct.	Pts.	OP
Arizona	3	1	0	.750	75	74
St. Louis	3	1	0	.750	102	85
San Francisco	2	2	0	.500	82	80
Seattle	2	2	0	.500	88	73

(a) American Bowl at Tokyo, Japan
(b) Pro Football Hall of Fame Game at Canton, Ohio

AMERICAN FOOTBALL CONFERENCE

BALTIMORE (6-10)
7	INDIANAPOLIS	24
10	at Tennessee	25
13	NEW YORK JETS	3
17	at Detroit	35
16	CLEVELAND	3
6	at Chicago	10
19	at Pittsburgh	20
9	CINCINNATI	21
3	at Jacksonville	30
16	PITTSBURGH (OT)	13
29	at Cincinnati	42
16	HOUSTON	15
10	at Denver	12
48	GREEN BAY	3
30	MINNESOTA	23
16	at Cleveland	20
265		**299**

BUFFALO (5-11)
22	HOUSTON	7
3	at Tampa Bay	19
16	ATLANTA	24
7	at New Orleans	19
20	MIAMI	14
27	NEW YORK JETS	17
17	at Oakland	38
16	at New England	21
14	KANSAS CITY	3
10	at San Diego	48
9	CAROLINA	13
23	at Miami	24
7	NEW ENGLAND	35
17	DENVER	28
37	at Cincinnati	27
26	at New York Jets	30
271		**367**

CINCINNATI (11-5)
27	at Cleveland	13
37	MINNESOTA	8
24	at Chicago	7
16	HOUSTON	10
20	at Jacksonville	23
31	at Tennessee	23
13	PITTSBURGH	27
21	GREEN BAY	14
21	at Baltimore	9
37	INDIANAPOLIS	45
42	BALTIMORE	29
38	at Pittsburgh	31
23	CLEVELAND	20
41	at Detroit	17
27	BUFFALO	37
3	at Kansas City	37
421		**350**

CLEVELAND (6-10)
13	CINCINNATI	27
26	at Green Bay	24
6	at Indianapolis	13
20	CHICAGO	10
3	at Baltimore	16
10	DETROIT	13
16	at Houston	19
20	TENNESSEE	14
21	at Pittsburgh	34
22	MIAMI	0
12	at Minnesota	24
14	JACKSONVILLE	20
20	at Cincinnati	23
9	at Oakland	7
0	PITTSBURGH	41
20	BALTIMORE	16
232		**301**

DENVER (13-3)
10	at Miami	34
20	SAN DIEGO	17
30	KANSAS CITY	10
20	at Jacksonville	7
21	WASHINGTON	19
28	NEW ENGLAND	20
23	at New York Giants	24
49	PHILADELPHIA	21
31	at Oakland	17
27	NEW YORK JETS	0
24	at Dallas (OT)	21
27	at Kansas City	31
12	BALTIMORE	10
28	at Buffalo	17
22	OAKLAND	3
23	at San Diego	7
395		**258**

HOUSTON (2-14)
7	at Buffalo	22
7	PITTSBURGH	27
10	at Cincinnati	16
20	TENNESSEE	34
10	at Seattle	42
20	INDIANAPOLIS	38
19	CLEVELAND	16
14	at Jacksonville	21
17	at Indianapolis	31
17	KANSAS CITY	45
27	ST. LOUIS (OT)	33
15	at Baltimore	16
10	at Tennessee	13
30	ARIZONA	19
20	JACKSONVILLE	38
17	at San Francisco (OT)	20
260		**431**

INDIANAPOLIS (14-2)
24	at Baltimore	7
10	JACKSONVILLE	3
13	CLEVELAND	6
31	at Tennessee	10
28	at San Francisco	3
45	ST. LOUIS	28
38	at Houston	20
40	at New England	21
31	HOUSTON	17
45	at Cincinnati	37
26	PITTSBURGH	7
35	TENNESSEE	3
26	at Jacksonville	18
17	SAN DIEGO	26
13	at Seattle	28
17	ARIZONA	13
439		**247**

JACKSONVILLE (12-4)
26	SEATTLE	14
3	at Indianapolis	10
26	at New York Jets (OT)	20
7	DENVER	20
23	CINCINNATI	20
23	at Pittsburgh (OT)	17
21	at St. Louis	24
20	HOUSTON	14
30	BALTIMORE	3
31	at Tennessee	28
24	at Arizona	17
20	at Cleveland	14
18	INDIANAPOLIS	26
10	SAN FRANCISCO	9
38	at Houston	20
40	TENNESSEE	13
361		**269**

KANSAS CITY (10-6)
27	NEW YORK JETS	7
23	at Oakland	17
10	at Denver	30
31	PHILADELPHIA	37
28	WASHINGTON	21
30	at Miami	20
20	at San Diego	28
27	OAKLAND	23
3	at Buffalo	14
45	at Houston	17
26	NEW ENGLAND	16
31	DENVER	27
28	at Dallas	31
17	at New York Giants	27
20	SAN DIEGO	7
37	CINCINNATI	3
403		**325**

MIAMI (9-7)
34	DENVER	10
7	at New York Jets	17
27	CAROLINA	24
14	at Buffalo	20
13	at Tampa Bay	27
20	KANSAS CITY	30
21	at New Orleans	6
10	ATLANTA	17
16	NEW ENGLAND	23
0	at Cleveland	22
33	at Oakland	21
24	BUFFALO	23
23	at San Diego	21
24	NEW YORK JETS	20
24	TENNESSEE	10
28	at New England	26
318		**317**

NEW ENGLAND (10-6)
30	OAKLAND	20
17	at Carolina	27
23	at Pittsburgh	20
17	SAN DIEGO	41
31	at Atlanta	28
20	at Denver	28
21	BUFFALO	16
21	INDIANAPOLIS	40
23	at Miami	16
24	NEW ORLEANS	17
16	at Kansas City	26
16	NEW YORK JETS	3
35	at Buffalo	7
28	TAMPA BAY	0
31	at New York Jets	21
26	MIAMI	28
379		**338**

NEW YORK JETS (4-12)
7	at Kansas City	27
17	MIAMI	7
20	JACKSONVILLE (OT)	26
3	at Baltimore	13
14	TAMPA BAY	12
17	at Buffalo	27
14	at Atlanta	27
26	SAN DIEGO	31
3	at Carolina	30
0	at Denver	27
19	NEW ORLEANS	21
3	at New England	16
26	OAKLAND	10
20	at Miami	24
21	NEW ENGLAND	31
30	BUFFALO	26
240		**355**

OAKLAND (4-12)
20	at New England	30
17	KANSAS CITY	23
20	at Philadelphia	23
19	DALLAS	13
14	SAN DIEGO	27
38	BUFFALO	17
34	at Tennessee	25
23	at Kansas City	27
17	DENVER	31
16	at Washington	13
21	MIAMI	33
10	at San Diego	34
10	at New York Jets	26
7	CLEVELAND	9
3	at Denver	22
21	NEW YORK GIANTS	30
290		**383**

PITTSBURGH (11-5)
34	TENNESSEE	7
27	at Houston	7
20	NEW ENGLAND	23
24	at San Diego	22
17	JACKSONVILLE (OT)	23
27	at Cincinnati	13
20	BALTIMORE	19
20	at Green Bay	10
34	CLEVELAND	21
13	at Baltimore (OT)	16
7	at Indianapolis	26
31	CINCINNATI	38
21	CHICAGO	9
18	at Minnesota	3
41	at Cleveland	0
35	DETROIT	21
389		**258**

SAN DIEGO (9-7)
24	DALLAS	28
17	at Denver	20
45	NEW YORK GIANTS	23
41	at New England	17
22	PITTSBURGH	24
27	at Oakland	14
17	at Philadelphia	20
28	KANSAS CITY	20
31	at New York Jets	26
48	BUFFALO	10
23	at Washington (OT)	17
34	OAKLAND	10
21	MIAMI	23
26	at Indianapolis	17
7	at Kansas City	20
7	DENVER	23
418		**312**

TENNESSEE (4-12)
7	at Pittsburgh	34
25	BALTIMORE	10
27	at St. Louis	31
10	INDIANAPOLIS	31
34	at Houston	20
23	CINCINNATI	31
10	at Arizona	20
25	OAKLAND	34
14	at Cleveland	20
28	JACKSONVILLE	31
33	SAN FRANCISCO	22
3	at Indianapolis	35
13	HOUSTON	10
24	SEATTLE	28
10	at Miami	24
13	at Jacksonville	40
299		**421**

NATIONAL FOOTBALL CONFERENCE

ARIZONA (5-11)
19	at New York Giants	42
12	ST. LOUIS	17
12	at Seattle	37
31	SAN FRANCISCO	14
20	CAROLINA	24
20	TENNESSEE	10
13	at Dallas	34
19	SEATTLE	33
21	at Detroit	29
38	at St. Louis	28
17	JACKSONVILLE	24
17	at San Francisco	10
13	WASHINGTON	17
19	at Houston	30
27	PHILADELPHIA	21
13	at Indianapolis	17
311		**387**

ATLANTA (8-8)
14	PHILADELPHIA	10
18	at Seattle	21
24	at Buffalo	16
30	MINNESOTA	10
28	NEW ENGLAND	31
34	at New Orleans	31
27	NEW YORK JETS	14
17	at Miami	10
25	GREEN BAY	33
27	TAMPA BAY	30
27	at Detroit	7
6	at Carolina	24
36	NEW ORLEANS	17
3	at Chicago	16
24	at Tampa Bay (OT)	27
11	CAROLINA	44
351		**341**

CAROLINA (11-5)
20	NEW ORLEANS	23
27	NEW ENGLAND	17
24	at Miami	27
32	GREEN BAY	29
24	at Arizona	20
21	at Detroit	20
38	MINNESOTA	13
34	at Tampa Bay	14
30	NEW YORK JETS	3
3	at Chicago	13
13	at Buffalo	9
24	ATLANTA	6
10	TAMPA BAY	20
27	at New Orleans	10
20	DALLAS	24
44	at Atlanta	11
391		**259**

CHICAGO (11-5)
7	at Washington	9
38	DETROIT	6
7	CINCINNATI	24
10	at Cleveland	20
28	MINNESOTA	3
10	BALTIMORE	6
19	at Detroit (OT)	13
20	at New Orleans	17
17	SAN FRANCISCO	9
13	CAROLINA	3
13	at Tampa Bay	10
19	GREEN BAY	7
9	at Pittsburgh	21
16	ATLANTA	3
24	at Green Bay	17
10	at Minnesota	34
260		**202**

DALLAS (9-7)
28	at San Diego	24
13	WASHINGTON	14
34	at San Francisco	31
13	at Oakland	19
33	PHILADELPHIA	10
16	N.Y. GIANTS (OT)	13
10	at Seattle	13
34	ARIZONA	13
21	at Philadelphia	20
20	DETROIT	7
21	DENVER (OT)	24
10	at New York Giants	17
31	KANSAS CITY	28
7	at Washington	35
24	at Carolina	20
10	ST. LOUIS	20
325		**308**

DETROIT (5-11)
17	GREEN BAY	3
6	at Chicago	38
13	at Tampa Bay	17
35	BALTIMORE	17
20	CAROLINA	21
13	at Cleveland	10
13	CHICAGO (OT)	19
14	at Minnesota	27
29	ARIZONA	21
7	at Dallas	20
7	ATLANTA	27
16	MINNESOTA	21
13	at Green Bay (OT)	16
17	CINCINNATI	41
13	at New Orleans	12
21	at Pittsburgh	35
254		**345**

GREEN BAY (4-12)
3	at Detroit	17
24	CLEVELAND	26
16	TAMPA BAY	17
29	at Carolina	32
52	NEW ORLEANS	3
20	at Minnesota	23
14	at Cincinnati	21
10	PITTSBURGH	20
33	at Atlanta	25
17	MINNESOTA	20
14	at Philadelphia	19
7	at Chicago	19
16	DETROIT (OT)	13
3	at Baltimore	48
17	CHICAGO	24
23	SEATTLE	17
298		**344**

MINNESOTA (9-7)
13	TAMPA BAY	24
8	at Cincinnati	37
33	NEW ORLEANS	16
10	at Atlanta	30
3	at Chicago	28
23	GREEN BAY	20
13	at Carolina	38
27	DETROIT	14
24	at New York Giants	21
20	at Green Bay	17
24	CLEVELAND	12
21	at Detroit	16
27	ST. LOUIS	13
3	PITTSBURGH	18
23	at Baltimore	30
34	CHICAGO	10
306		**344**

NEW ORLEANS (3-13)
23	at Carolina	20
10	NEW YORK GIANTS	27
16	at Minnesota	33
19	BUFFALO	7
3	at Green Bay	52
31	ATLANTA	34
17	at St. Louis	28
6	MIAMI	21
17	CHICAGO	20
17	at New England	24
21	at N.Y. Jets	18
3	TAMPA BAY	10
17	at Atlanta	36
10	CAROLINA	27
12	DETROIT	13
13	at Tampa Bay	27
235		**398**

NEW YORK GIANTS (11-5)
42	ARIZONA	19
27	at New Orleans	10
23	at San Diego	45
44	ST .LOUIS	24
13	at Dallas (OT)	16
24	DENVER	23
36	WASHINGTON	0
24	at San Francisco	6
21	MINNESOTA	24
27	PHILADELPHIA	17
21	at Seattle (OT)	24
17	DALLAS	10
26	at Philadelphia (OT)	23
27	KANSAS CITY	17
20	at Washington	35
30	at Oakland	21
422		**314**

PHILADELPHIA (6-10)
10	at Atlanta	14
42	SAN FRANCISCO	3
23	OAKLAND	20
37	at Kansas City	31
10	at Dallas	33
20	SAN DIEGO	17
21	at Denver	49
10	at Washington	17
20	DALLAS	21
17	at New York Giants	27
19	GREEN BAY	14
0	SEATTLE	42
23	N.Y. GIANTS (OT)	26
17	at St. Louis	16
21	at Arizona	27
20	WASHINGTON	31
310		**388**

ST. LOUIS (6-10)
25	at San Francisco	28
17	at Arizona	12
31	TENNESSEE	27
24	at New York Giants	44
31	SEATTLE	37
28	at Indianapolis	45
28	NEW ORLEANS	17
24	JACKSONVILLE	21
16	at Seattle	31
28	ARIZONA	38
33	at Houston (OT)	27
9	WASHINGTON	24
13	at Minnesota	27
16	PHILADELPHIA	17
20	SAN FRANCISCO	24
20	at Dallas	10
363		**429**

SAN FRANCISCO (4-12)
28	ST. LOUIS	25
3	at Philadelphia	42
31	DALLAS	34
14	at Arizona	31
3	INDIANAPOLIS	28
17	at Washington	52
15	TAMPA BAY	10
6	NEW YORK GIANTS	24
9	at Chicago	17
25	SEATTLE	27
22	at Tennessee	33
10	ARIZONA	17
3	at Seattle	41
9	at Jacksonville	10
24	at St. Louis	20
20	HOUSTON (OT)	17
239		**428**

SEATTLE (13-3)
14	at Jacksonville	26
21	ATLANTA	18
37	ARIZONA	12
17	at Washington (OT)	20
37	at St. Louis	31
42	HOUSTON	10
13	DALLAS	10
33	at Arizona	19
31	ST. LOUIS	16
27	at San Francisco	25
24	N.Y. GIANTS (OT)	21
42	at Philadelphia	0
41	SAN FRANCISCO	3
28	at Tennessee	24
28	INDIANAPOLIS	13
17	at Green Bay	23
452		**271**

TAMPA BAY (11-5)
24	at Minnesota	13
19	BUFFALO	3
17	at Green Bay	16
17	DETROIT	13
12	at New York Jets	14
27	MIAMI	13
10	at San Francisco	15
14	CAROLINA	34
36	WASHINGTON	35
30	at Atlanta	27
10	CHICAGO	13
20	at Carolina	10
0	at New England	28
27	ATLANTA (OT)	24
27	NEW ORLEANS	13
300		**274**

WASHINGTON (10-6)
9	CHICAGO	7
14	at Dallas	13
20	SEATTLE (OT)	17
19	at Denver	21
21	at Kansas City	28
52	SAN FRANCISCO	17
0	at New York Giants	36
17	PHILADELPHIA	10
35	at Tampa Bay	36
13	OAKLAND	16
17	SAN DIEGO (OT)	23
24	at St. Louis	9
17	at Arizona	13
35	DALLAS	7
35	NEW YORK GIANTS	20
31	at Philadelphia	20
359		**293**

FINAL STANDINGS

AMERICAN FOOTBALL CONFERENCE

East Division	W	L	T	Pct.	Pts.	OP
New England	10	6	0	.625	379	338
Miami	9	7	0	.563	318	317
Buffalo	5	11	0	.313	271	367
New York Jets	4	12	0	.250	240	355
North Division						
Cincinnati	11	5	0	.688	421	350
* Pittsburgh	11	5	0	.688	389	258
Baltimore	6	10	0	.375	265	299
Cleveland	6	10	0	.375	232	301
South Division						
# Indianapolis	14	2	0	.875	439	247
* Jacksonville	12	4	0	.750	361	269
Tennessee	4	12	0	.250	299	421
Houston	2	14	0	.125	260	431
West Division						
Denver	13	3	0	.813	395	258
Kansas City	10	6	0	.625	403	325
San Diego	9	7	0	.563	418	312
Oakland	4	12	0	.250	290	383

NATIONAL FOOTBALL CONFERENCE

East Division	W	L	T	Pct.	Pts.	OP
New York Giants	11	5	0	.688	422	314
* Washington	10	6	0	.625	359	293
Dallas	9	7	0	.563	325	308
Philadelphia	6	10	0	.375	310	388
North Division						
Chicago	11	5	0	.688	260	202
Minnesota	9	7	0	.563	306	344
Detroit	5	11	0	.313	254	345
Green Bay	4	12	0	.250	298	344
South Division						
Tampa Bay	11	5	0	.688	300	274
* Carolina	11	5	0	.688	391	259
Atlanta	8	8	0	.500	351	341
New Orleans	3	13	0	.188	235	398
West Division						
# Seattle	13	3	0	.813	452	271
St. Louis	6	10	0	.375	363	429
Arizona	5	11	0	.313	311	387
San Francisco	4	12	0	.250	239	428

* Wild-Card qualifier for playoffs
# Top playoff seed in conference

Cincinnati finished ahead of Pittsburgh based on better division record (5-1 to 4-2). Baltimore finished ahead of Cleveland based on better division record (2-4 to 1-5). Tampa Bay finished ahead of Carolina based on better division record (5-1 to 4-2). Chicago finished ahead of Tampa Bay, and Tampa Bay finished ahead of the New York Giants, based on better conference record (Bears' 10-2 to Buccaneers' 9-3 to Giants' 8-4).

WILD-CARD PLAYOFFS

AFC
NEW ENGLAND 28, Jacksonville 3
Pittsburgh 31, CINCINNATI 17

NFC
Washington 17, TAMPA BAY 10
Carolina 23, NEW YORK GIANTS 0

DIVISIONAL PLAYOFFS

AFC
DENVER 27, New England 13
Pittsburgh 21, INDIANAPOLIS 18

NFC
SEATTLE 20, Washington 10
Carolina 29, CHICAGO 21

CHAMPIONSHIP GAMES

AFC
Pittsburgh 34, DENVER 17

NFC
SEATTLE 34, Carolina 14

SUPER BOWL XL

Pittsburgh (AFC) 21, Seattle (NFC) 10
at Ford Field, Detroit, Michigan

AFC-NFC PRO BOWL

NFC 23, AFC 17
at Aloha Stadium, Honolulu, Hawaii

Home teams in playoff games are indicated in CAPS.

FIRST WEEK SUMMARIES
American Football Conference

East Division	W	L	T	Pct.	Pts.	OP
Buffalo	1	0	0	1.000	22	7
Miami	1	0	0	1.000	34	10
New England	1	0	0	1.000	30	20
N.Y. Jets	0	1	0	.000	7	27

North Division	W	L	T	Pct.	Pts.	OP
Cincinnati	1	0	0	1.000	27	13
Pittsburgh	1	0	0	1.000	34	7
Baltimore	0	1	0	.000	7	24
Cleveland	0	1	0	.000	13	27

South Division	W	L	T	Pct.	Pts.	OP
Indianapolis	1	0	0	1.000	24	7
Jacksonville	1	0	0	1.000	26	14
Houston	0	1	0	.000	7	22
Tennessee	0	1	0	.000	7	34

West Division	W	L	T	Pct.	Pts.	OP
Kansas City	1	0	0	1.000	27	7
Denver	0	1	0	.000	10	34
Oakland	0	1	0	.000	20	30
San Diego	0	1	0	.000	24	28

National Football Conference

East Division	W	L	T	Pct.	Pts.	OP
Dallas	1	0	0	1.000	28	24
N.Y. Giants	1	0	0	1.000	42	19
Washington	1	0	0	1.000	9	7
Philadelphia	0	1	0	.000	10	14

North Division	W	L	T	Pct.	Pts.	OP
Detroit	1	0	0	1.000	17	3
Chicago	0	1	0	.000	7	9
Green Bay	0	1	0	.000	3	17
Minnesota	0	1	0	.000	13	24

South Division	W	L	T	Pct.	Pts.	OP
Atlanta	1	0	0	1.000	14	10
New Orleans	1	0	0	1.000	23	20
Tampa Bay	1	0	0	1.000	24	13
Carolina	0	1	0	.000	20	23

West Division	W	L	T	Pct.	Pts.	OP
San Francisco	1	0	0	1.000	28	25
Arizona	0	1	0	.000	19	42
St. Louis	0	1	0	.000	25	28
Seattle	0	1	0	.000	14	26

THURSDAY NIGHT, SEPTEMBER 8

NEW ENGLAND 30, OAKLAND 20—at Gillette Stadium, attendance 68,756. Tom Brady passed for 306 yards and 2 touchdowns, and Corey Dillon added 2 scoring runs, for the defending Super Bowl champions. The Patriots scored on three of their first four possessions to take a 17-14 lead. On seven consecutive possessions spanning the second and third quarters, the Raiders failed to cross midfield. An interception by Vince Wilfork at the Raiders' 20 led to Dillon's first touchdown to give New England a 23-14 lead with 5:05 left in the third quarter. Dillon's 2-yard run with 9:29 remaining capped a 6-play, 84-yard drive to extend the lead to 30-14. Randal Williams blocked Josh Miller's punt with 4:01 left to set up Kerry Collins' second touchdown pass to Courtney Anderson with 3:04 remaining. Collins' 2-point conversion pass attempt for Randy Moss fell incomplete, and Dillon gained a key first down to allow the Patriots to run out the clock. Brady was 24 of 38 for 306 yards and 2 touchdowns. Collins was 18 of 39 for 265 yards and 3 touchdowns, with 1 interception. Moss had 5 receptions for 130 yards.

Oakland	7	7	0	6	—	20
New England	10	7	6	7	—	30

Oak	—	C. Anderson 2 pass from K. Collins (Janikowski kick)
NE	—	FG Vinatieri 26
NE	—	Branch 18 pass from Brady (Vinatieri kick)
Oak	—	R. Moss 73 pass from K. Collins (Janikowski kick)
NE	—	Dwight 5 pass from Brady (Vinatieri kick)

NE	—	Dillon 8 run (kick blocked)
NE	—	Dillon 2 run (Vinatieri kick)
Oak	—	C. Anderson 5 pass from K. Collins (pass failed)

SUNDAY, SEPTEMBER 11

BUFFALO 22, HOUSTON 7—at Ralph Wilson Stadium, attendance 71,781. The Bills' defense allowed just 120 yards, forced 5 turnovers, and registered 5 sacks as the Bills were victorious in J.P. Losman's first career start. Losman guided the Bills on five consecutive scoring drives to begin the game, capped by his 1-yard touchdown pass to tackle-eligible Jason Peters, for a 19-7 lead with 29 seconds left in the half. In the fourth quarter, Takeo Spikes forced David Carr to fumble and Lawyer Milloy recovered at the Texans' 23 to set up Rian Lindell's fifth field goal for a 22-7 lead with 7:11 to play. Losman was 17 of 28 for 170 yards and 1 touchdown. Willis McGahee had 22 carries for 117 yards. Carr was 9 of 21 for 70 yards, with 3 interceptions.

Houston	0	7	0	0	—	7
Buffalo	6	13	0	3	—	22

Buff	—	FG Lindell 35
Buff	—	FG Lindell 21
Buff	—	FG Lindell 42
Buff	—	FG Lindell 39
Hou	—	Carr 1 run (K. Brown kick)
Buff	—	Peters 1 pass from Losman (Lindell kick)
Buff	—	FG Lindell 31

NEW ORLEANS 23, CAROLINA 20—at Bank of America Stadium, attendance 72,920. John Carney kicked a 47-yard field goal with three seconds remaining as the Saints posted an emotional victory. Playing their first regular-season game since Hurricane Katrina ravaged the Gulf Coast, the Saints drove into Panthers' territory on seven of their eight possessions. The Saints led 14-7 at halftime, and intercepted 2 passes deep in Panthers' territory early in the second half, but were only able to generate a field goal by Carney for a 17-7 lead. Trailing 20-17, the Panthers forced a punt with 2:50 left, and Jake Delhomme completed a key 11-yard pass to Nick Goings to set up John Kasay's tying 46-yard field goal with 1:04 remaining. Beginning from their own 22 yard line, Aaron Brooks completed passes of 11 and 25 yards to Joe Horn, followed by a 5-yard out-pattern to Donte' Stallworth and 3-yard dive by Deuce McAllister to set up Carney's winning kick. Brooks was 18 of 24 for 192 yards. Delhomme was 19 of 31 for 212 yards and 1 touchdown, with 2 interceptions. Smith had 8 receptions for 138 yards, and Kris Jenkins suffered a season-ending knee injury.

New Orleans	7	7	3	6	—	23
Carolina	7	0	7	6	—	20

NO	—	McAllister 4 run (Carney kick)
Car	—	S. Smith 33 pass from Delhomme (Kasay kick)
NO	—	McAllister 2 run (Carney kick)
NO	—	FG Carney 29
Car	—	S. Davis 1 run (Kasay kick)
NO	—	FG Carney 48
Car	—	FG Kasay 39
Car	—	FG Kasay 46
NO	—	FG Carney 47

CINCINNATI 27, CLEVELAND 13—at Cleveland Browns Stadium, attendance 73,013. Carson Palmer passed for 2 touchdowns as the Bengals won the season opener for just the second time since 1997. The Bengals scored on three consecutive first-half drives, capped by Kevin Walter's 20-yard touchdown catch to conclude a 91-yard drive with 45 seconds left in the half for a 17-10 lead. Cincinnati then marched 78 yards with the opening drive of the second half to take a 24-10 lead on Jeremi Johnson's touchdown catch.

Odell Thurman intercepted Trent Dilfer's pass two plays later to set up Shayne Graham's second field goal with 8:24 left in the third quarter. Palmer was 26 of 34 for 280 yards and 2 touchdowns, with 1 interception. Rudi Johnson had 26 carries for 126 yards. Dilfer was 26 of 43 for 278 yards and 1 touchdown, with 2 interceptions. Frisman Jackson had 8 catches for 128 yards.

Cincinnati	0	17	10	0	—	27
Cleveland	3	7	0	3	—	13

Cle	—	FG Dawson 29
Cin	—	R. Johnson 1 run (Graham kick)
Cin	—	FG Graham 32
Cle	—	Jackson 68 pass from Dilfer (Dawson kick)
Cin	—	Walter 20 pass from Palmer (Graham kick)
Cin	—	J. Johnson 18 pass from Palmer (Graham kick)
Cin	—	FG Graham 23
Cle	—	FG Dawson 34

DETROIT 17, GREEN BAY 3—at Ford Field, attendance 61,877. Joey Harrington passed for 2 touchdowns and the Lions' defense limited the Packers to their lowest point total since 1992. Trailing 7-3 at halftime, the Packers began the second half with the ball, but Brett Favre fumbled three plays into the half and Kalimba Edwards recovered at the Packers' 34 to set up Jason Hanson's 21-yard field goal. Kenoy Kennedy's interception midway through the fourth quarter, and Harrington's 31-yard pass to Charles Rogers, set up Mike Williams' first career touchdown catch on third-and-goal from the Packers' 3 with 4:13 to play for a 17-3 lead. Javon Walker suffered a season-ending knee injury on a third-quarter 55-yard pass play that was nullified by offensive pass interference. Harrington was 15 of 28 for 167 yards and 2 touchdowns. Favre was 27 of 44 for 201 yards, with 2 interceptions.

Green Bay	0	3	0	0	—	3
Detroit	7	0	3	7	—	17

Det	—	Pollard 9 pass from Harrington (Hanson kick)
GB	—	FG Longwell 50
Det	—	FG Hanson 21
Det	—	M. Williams 3 pass from Harrington (Hanson kick)

JACKSONVILLE 26, SEATTLE 14—at ALLTEL Stadium, attendance 65,204. Byron Leftwich passed for 2 touchdowns and the Jaguars' defense forced 5 turnovers en route to victory. Rashean Mathis recovered the Seahawks' fumble on the opening kickoff to set up the first of Josh Scobee's 4 field goals. Matt Hasselbeck's 9-yard touchdown pass to Darrell Jackson with 47 seconds left in the half gave the Seahawks a 14-13 halftime lead. Jacksonville began the second half with a 12-play, 78-yard drive capped by Jimmy Smith's second touchdown catch, from 7 yards, for a 20-14 lead. Daryl Smith's interception at the Seahawks' 15 midway through the fourth quarter led to Scobee's third field goal, and three plays later Akin Ayodele sacked Hasselbeck and forced him to fumble. Mike Peterson recovered and Scobee's 41-yard field goal with 1:55 remaining finished the scoring. Leftwich was 17 of 31 for 252 yards and 2 touchdowns, with 2 interceptions. Smith had 7 receptions for 130 yards. Hasselbeck was 21 of 37 for 246 yards and 2 touchdowns, with 2 interceptions.

Seattle	0	14	0	0	—	14
Jacksonville	6	7	7	6	—	26

Jax	—	FG Scobee 23
Jax	—	FG Scobee 41
Sea	—	Jurevicius 33 pass from Hasselbeck (J. Brown kick)
Jax	—	J. Smith 30 pass from Leftwich (Scobee kick)

Sea	—	Jackson 9 pass from Hasselbeck (J. Brown kick)
Jax	—	J. Smith 7 pass from Leftwich (Scobee kick)
Jax	—	FG Scobee 29
Jax	—	FG Scobee 41

KANSAS CITY 27, N.Y. JETS 7—at Arrowhead Stadium, attendance 78,014. The Chiefs rushed for 198 yards, and the defense forced 3 turnovers and recorded 3 sacks, as Kansas City came within 29 seconds of posting a shutout. The Chiefs marched 75 and 95 yards on their first two possessions to take a 14-0 lead. The Jets responded by driving to the Chiefs' 10, but Jared Allen sacked Chad Pennington and forced him to fumble. The Jets drove to the Chiefs' 10 early in the third quarter, only to have Eric Hicks block rookie kicker Mike Nugent's first-ever field-goal attempt, from 28 yards. The Jets twice were stopped on fourth down in Chiefs' territory, and only scored when Jay Fiedler entered the game and engineered an 11-play, 78-yard drive to pass to Chris Baker with 29 seconds left. Trent Green was 15 of 26 for 200 yards, with 1 interception. Larry Johnson had 9 carries for 110 yards. Pennington was 21 of 34 for 264 yards, with 1 interception, and Fiedler was 6 of 10 for 88 yards and 1 touchdown. Baker had 7 catches for 124 yards.

N.Y. Jets	0	0	0	7	—	7
Kansas City	14	3	3	7	—	27
KC	—	L. Johnson 35 run (Tynes kick)
KC	—	Holmes 3 run (Tynes kick)
KC	—	FG Tynes 41
KC	—	FG Tynes 38
KC	—	L. Johnson 4 run (Tynes kick)
NYJ	—	Baker 23 pass from Fiedler (Nugent kick)

MIAMI 34, DENVER 10—at Dolphins Stadium, attendance 72,324. Making his Dolphins' debut, Gus Frerotte passed for 275 yards and 2 touchdowns as Miami pulled away for Nick Saban's first NFL coaching victory. The Dolphins led 6-3 at halftime, quelling the Broncos' best scoring opportunity in the second quarter when Zach Thomas and Jason Taylor combined to stop Tatum Bell on fourth-and-goal from the Dolphins' 1. Denver cut the deficit to 20-10, but the ensuing kickoff sailed out of bounds and Frerotte connected on a 60-yard touchdown pass to Marty Booker on the next play for a 27-10 lead with 9:09 remaining. Taylor sacked Jake Plummer on the final play of the game, forced him to fumble, and returned the ball 85 yards for a touchdown. Taylor's fumble return was the fifth of his career, tying him with Jessie Tuggle for the most fumble returns for a touchdown in NFL history. Frerotte was 24 of 36 for 275 yards and 2 touchdowns, with 1 interception. Booker had 5 catches for 104 yards. Plummer was 22 of 48 for 251 yards and 1 touchdown, with 2 interceptions.

Denver	0	3	0	7	—	10
Miami	3	3	7	21	—	34
Mia	—	FG Mare 29
Mia	—	FG Mare 44
Den	—	FG Elam 28
Mia	—	McMichael 2 pass from Frerotte (Mare kick)
Mia	—	Morris 9 run (Mare kick)
Den	—	K. Johnson 2 pass from Plummer (Elam kick)
Mia	—	Booker 60 pass from Frerotte (Mare kick)
Mia	—	Taylor 85 fumble return (Mare kick)

TAMPA BAY 24, MINNESOTA 13—at Metrodome, attendance 63,939. Brian Griese passed for 2 touchdowns and the Buccaneers' defense held the Vikings without an offensive touchdown. Darren Sharper

returned an interception 88 yards for a touchdown, but. Griese responded with touchdown passes to Alex Smith to cap drives of 71 and 80 yards. Trailing 17-10 and faced with fourth-and-goal from the Buccaneers' 4 with 6:17 remaining, the Vikings opted for Paul Edinger's second field goal. Prior to each of Edinger's field goals, Jermaine Wiggins had touchdown catches nullified by an offensive penalty. The Vikings got the ball back and drove to the Buccaneers' 12, but Brian Kelly intercepted Daunte Culpepper's pass with 1:45 to play. On third-and-1, Williams ran through a hole on the left side and streaked 71 yards a touchdown to seal the victory. Griese was 18 of 29 for 213 yards and 2 touchdowns, with 2 interceptions. Williams had 27 carries for 148 yards. Culpepper was 22 of 33 for 233 yards, with 3 interceptions.

Tampa Bay	0	17	0	7	—	24
Minnesota	7	0	3	3	—	13
Minn	—	Sharper 88 interception return (Edinger kick)
TB	—	A. Smith 23 pass from Griese (Bryant kick)
TB	—	A. Smith 2 pass from Griese (Bryant kick)
TB	—	FG Bryant 41
Minn	—	FG Edinger 53
Minn	—	FG Edinger 22
TB	—	C. Williams 71 run (Bryant kick)

N.Y. GIANTS 42, ARIZONA 19—at Giants Stadium, attendance 78.387. Two special-team touchdowns allowed the Giants to pull away. Arizona led 13-7 at halftime, but the Giants drove 63 yards for a touchdown to begin the second half. Gibril Wilson intercepted Kurt Warner on the first play after the kickoff to set up Tiki Barber's 21-yard scoring run on the next play for 2 touchdowns in 25 seconds and a 21-13 lead. Arizona pulled within 21-19 on the ensuing drive, but Willie Ponder took the next kickoff 95 yards for a touchdown. Chad Morton finished the scoring with his 52-yard punt return. Eli Manning was 10 of 23 for 172 yards and 2 touchdowns, with 2 interceptions. Warner was 27 of 46 for 264 yards and 1 touchdown, with 1 interception. Larry Fitzgerald had 13 catches for 155 yards.

Arizona	0	13	6	0	—	19
N.Y. Giants	7	0	21	14	—	42
NYG	—	Shockey 20 pass from Manning (Feely kick)
Ariz	—	FG Rackers 24
Ariz	—	Dansby 18 interception return (Rackers kick)
Ariz	—	FG Rackers 42
NYG	—	Jacobs 5 run (Feely kick)
NYG	—	Barber 21 run (Feely kick)
Ariz	—	Fitzgerald 1 pass from Warner (pass failed)
NYG	—	Ponder 95 kickoff return (Feely kick)
NYG	—	Burress 13 pass from Manning (Feely kick)
NYG	—	Morton 52 punt return (Feely kick)

PITTSBURGH 34, TENNESSEE 7—at Heinz Field, attendance 62,931. Making his first NFL start, Willie Parker rushed for 161 yards and 1 touchdown as the Steelers throttled the Titans. Tennessee began the game with an 11-play, 61-yard touchdown drive, but failed to score again. The Titans had many opportunities, but in the first half missed a field goal and threw an interception in the red zone, and lost a fumble at the Steelers' 19 early in the fourth quarter. The Steelers scored on their first six possessions, four of which covered at least 74 yards and another being a 1-play drive that resulted in Ben Roethlisberger's 63-yard touchdown pass to Antwaan Randle El. Roethlisberger was 9 of 11 for 218 yards and 2 touchdowns. Park-

er, starting in place of injured running backs Duce Staley and Jerome Bettis, had 22 carries for 161 yards. Steve McNair was 18 of 26 for 219 yards and 1 touchdown, with 1 interception.

Tennessee	7	0	0	0	—	7
Pittsburgh	7	13	14	0	—	34
Tenn	—	Troupe 1 pass from McNair (Bironas kick)
Pitt	—	Miller 3 pass from Roethlisberger (Reed kick)
Pitt	—	FG Reed 44
Pitt	—	Randle El 63 pass from Roethlisberger (Reed kick)
Pitt	—	FG Reed 27
Pitt	—	Parker 11 run (Reed kick)
Pitt	—	Haynes 5 run (Reed kick)

DALLAS 28, SAN DIEGO 24—at Qualcomm Stadium, attendance 67,679. Aaron Glenn intercepted a pass in the end zone with 22 seconds left to secure the Cowboys' victory. Anthony Henry's interception in the second quarter set up Drew Bledsoe's 13-yard touchdown pass to give Dallas a 14-7 lead. Tied 14-14, the Chargers began the second half with a 49-yard kickoff return by Darren Sproles to set up Drew Brees' 17-yard touchdown pass to Keenan McCardell. The Chargers led 24-21 in the fourth quarter when Mike Scifres' 18-yard punt gave Dallas the ball at the Chargers' 44. Nine plays later, Keyshawn Johnson caught his second touchdown pass for a 28-24 lead with 3:06 left. Brees completed a 33-yard pass to Eric Parker on fourth-and-7 to reach the Cowboys' 7 with 47 seconds left. With one timeout left, Brees attempted four consecutive passes, the last of which was intercepted by Glenn. Bledsoe was 18 of 24 for 226 yards and 3 touchdowns. Brees was 18 of 35 for 209 yards and 2 touchdowns, with 2 interceptions. McCardell had 9 catches for 123 yards.

Dallas	0	14	7	7	—	28
San Diego	7	7	10	0	—	24
SD	—	Tomlinson 2 run (Kaeding kick)
Dall	—	Crayton 20 pass from Bledsoe (Cortez kick)
Dall	—	K. Johnson 13 pass from Bledsoe (Cortez kick)
SD	—	McCardell 20 pass from Brees (Kaeding kick)
SD	—	McCardell 17 pass from Brees (Kaeding kick)
Dall	—	J. Jones 5 run (Cortez kick)
SD	—	FG Kaeding 33
Dall	—	K. Johnson 2 pass from Bledsoe (Cortez kick)

SAN FRANCISCO 28, ST. LOUIS 25—at Monster Park, attendance 67,918. Mike Adams intercepted a pass at the 49ers' 24 with 52 seconds remaining to help coach Mike Nolan win his NFL debut. The 49ers won despite being outgained 405-217 yards, and losing the battle of the clock, 39:23-20:37. The Rams drove into the red zone five times, but settled for 4 field goals and 1 touchdown. Trailing 6-0, Tim Rattay completed a 35-yard touchdown pass to Brandon Lloyd. The 49ers' defense then forced a punt, and Otis Amey returned it 75 yards for a touchdown. Kevan Barlow's 9-yard run capped the opening drive of the second half for a 28-9 lead. The Rams scored on their next two possessions to cut the deficit to 28-18, and a 19-play, 78-yard drive, which included 3 fourth-down conversions, the last of which was Marc Bulger's 6-yard touchdown pass to Brandon Manumaleuna, pulled the Rams' within 28-25 with 2:13 to play. The Rams' defense forced a three-and-out, and Shaun McDonald's 13-yard punt return to the 49ers' 38 gave St. Louis great field position with 59 seconds left. Following an offside penalty, Adams intercepted Bulger's pass to secure the victory. Rattay was 11 of 16 for 165 yards and 2 touchdowns. Bryant Young had 3 of the 49ers' 7 sacks. Bulger was 34 of 56 for 362 yards and 2 touchdowns, with 1 interception.

St. Louis	3	6	3	13	—	25
San Francisco	0	21	7	0	—	28

StL	—	FG Wilkins 30
StL	—	FG Wilkins 41
SF	—	Lloyd 35 pass from Rattay (Nedney kick)
SF	—	Arney 75 punt return (Nedney kick)
SF	—	Battle 6 pass from Rattay (Nedney kick)
StL	—	FG Wilkins 33
SF	—	Barlow 9 run (Nedney kick)
StL	—	FG Wilkins 41
StL	—	Bruce 29 pass from Bulger (run failed)
StL	—	Manumaleuna 6 pass from Bulger (Wilkins kick)

WASHINGTON 9, CHICAGO 7—at FedExField, attendance 90,138. The Redskins' defense allowed 166 yards and forced 2 turnovers as Washington held off the Bears. Early in the second quarter, Lance Briggs sacked Patrick Ramsey and forced him to fumble away the ball at the Bears' 19. Ramsey injured his neck on the play, and Mark Brunell replaced him on the next series and guided the Redskins to consecutive field goals. The Bears failed to threaten in the first half, but Antonio Brown fumbled the second half's opening kickoff at the Redskins' 23 and Thomas Jones scored seven plays later for a 7-6 lead. Brunell responded with a 15-play, 63-yard drive, including a 1-yard sneak on fourth-and-1, to set up John Hall's third field goal. Lemar Marshall intercepted Kyle Orton's pass in the end zone on the next possession to quash the Bears' best drive, and with 1:32 to play Cornelius Griffin sacked Orton, forced him to fumble, and recovered the ball to clinch the victory. Ramsey was 6 of 11 for 105 yards, with 1 interception, and Brunell was 8 of 14 for 70 yards. Clinton Portis had 21 carries for 121 yards. Orton was 15 of 28 for 141 yards, with 1 interception.

Chicago	0	0	7	0	—	7
Washington	0	6	3	0	—	9

Wash	—	FG Hall 40
Wash	—	FG Hall 43
Chi	—	T. Jones 1 run (Brien kick)
Wash	—	FG Hall 19

SUNDAY NIGHT, SEPTEMBER 11
INDIANAPOLIS 24, BALTIMORE 7—at M&T Bank Stadium, attendance 70,501. The Colts' defense forced 4 turnovers and came within 13 seconds of their first shutout since 1997 to defeat the Ravens. Trailing 3-0, Matt Stover's 47-yard field-goal attempt sailed wide left. The Colts responded with a 63-yard touchdown drive, capped by Marvin Harrison's 28-yard touchdown catch. The Colts' defense then forced a three-and-out, and Peyton Manning needed just four plays to drive 71 yards for Ben Utecht's first career touchdown catch for a 17-0 lead with 4:08 left in the third quarter. Stover missed a third field goal early in the fourth quarter, and Gary Brackett and Cato June quelled other drives with interceptions, Brackett's occurring in the end zone while June returned his interception 30 yards for a touchdown with 2:39 to play. Manning was 21 of 36 for 254 yards and 2 touchdowns. Kyle Boller was 15 of 23 for 141 yards, with 1 interception, and Anthony Wright was 19 of 31 for 214 yards and 1 touchdown, with 2 interceptions.

Indianapolis	0	3	14	7	—	24
Baltimore	0	0	0	7	—	7

Ind	—	FG Vanderjagt 20
Ind	—	Harrison 28 pass from Manning (Vanderjagt kick)
Ind	—	Utecht 26 pass from Manning (Vanderjagt kick)
Ind	—	June 30 interception return (Vanderjagt kick)
Balt	—	Wilcox 17 pass from Wright (Stover kick)

MONDAY NIGHT, SEPTEMBER 12
ATLANTA 14, PHILADELPHIA 10—at Georgia Dome, attendance 70,806. Warrick Dunn rushed for 117 yards and the Falcons' defense slowed the Eagles as Atlanta defeated the team that knocked it out of the playoffs each of the previous two seasons. The Falcons drove 58 and 64 yards on consecutive possessions late in the first quarter, the second set up by Michael Vick's 58-yard pass to Michael Jenkins to the Eagles' 1, to take a 14-0 lead. The Eagles responded with a 78-yard scoring drive to cut the deficit to 14-7, but David Akers missed a 49-yard field goal just before halftime and Keith Brooking recovered Donovan McNabb's fumble at the Falcons' 31 early in the third quarter to maintain the seven-point lead. In the fourth quarter, Brian Dawkins forced Vick to fumble on third-and-goal and Michael Lewis recovered. Ten plays later, Akers kicked a 44-yard field goal to cut the deficit to 14-10 with 9:20 remaining. The Eagles had one last chance, but McNabb threw four consecutive incompletions from the Eagles' 49. Vick was 12 of 23 for 156 yards, with 1 interception, and rushed 11 times for 68 yards. Dunn rushed 21 times for 117 yards. McNabb was 24 of 45 for 257 yards and 1 touchdown, with 1 interception. Terrell Owens had 7 catches for 112 yards.

Philadelphia	0	7	0	3	—	10
Atlanta	14	0	0	0	—	14

Atl	—	Vick 7 run (Peterson kick)
Atl	—	Duckett 1 run (Peterson kick)
Phil	—	Westbrook 9 pass from McNabb (Akers kick)
Phil	—	FG Akers 44

SECOND WEEK SUMMARIES
American Football Conference

East Division	W	L	T	Pct.	Pts.	OP
Buffalo	1	1	0	.500	25	26
Miami	1	1	0	.500	41	27
New England	1	1	0	.500	47	47
N.Y. Jets	1	1	0	.500	24	34
North Division	W	L	T	Pct.	Pts.	OP
Cincinnati	2	0	0	1.000	64	21
Pittsburgh	2	0	0	1.000	61	14
Cleveland	1	1	0	.500	39	51
Baltimore	0	2	0	.000	17	49
South Division	W	L	T	Pct.	Pts.	OP
Indianapolis	2	0	0	1.000	34	10
Jacksonville	1	1	0	.500	29	24
Tennessee	1	1	0	.500	32	44
Houston	0	2	0	.000	14	49
West Division	W	L	T	Pct.	Pts.	OP
Kansas City	2	0	0	1.000	50	24
Denver	1	1	0	.500	30	51
Oakland	0	2	0	.000	37	53
San Diego	0	2	0	.000	41	48

National Football Conference

East Division	W	L	T	Pct.	Pts.	OP
N.Y. Giants	2	0	0	1.000	69	29
Washington	2	0	0	1.000	23	20
Dallas	1	1	0	.500	41	38
Philadelphia	1	1	0	.500	52	17
North Division	W	L	T	Pct.	Pts.	OP
Chicago	1	1	0	.500	45	15
Detroit	1	1	0	.500	23	41
Green Bay	0	2	0	.000	27	43
Minnesota	0	2	0	.000	21	61
South Division	W	L	T	Pct.	Pts.	OP
Tampa Bay	2	0	0	1.000	43	16
Atlanta	1	1	0	.500	32	31
Carolina	1	1	0	.500	47	40
New Orleans	1	1	0	.500	33	47

West Division	W	L	T	Pct.	Pts.	OP
St. Louis	1	1	0	.500	42	40
San Francisco	1	1	0	.500	31	67
Seattle	1	1	0	.500	35	44
Arizona	0	2	0	.000	31	59

SUNDAY, SEPTEMBER 18
ST. LOUIS 17, ARIZONA 12—at Sun Devil Stadium, attendance 45,160. A false start penalty with seven seconds remaining at the Rams' 10-yard line allowed St. Louis to hold off the Cardinals. Of the Rams' 10 non-touchdown possessions, just one generated more than 19 yards, which led to a field goal in the second quarter. Neil Rackers' fourth field goal, from 35 yards with 6:59 to play, cut the deficit to 17-12. The Cardinals' began their final drive from their own 14-yard line with 1:53 remaining. Kurt Warner completed six consecutive passes to reach the Rams' 5 with 27 seconds left. On first-and-goal, Adam Archuleta sacked Warner for a 5-yard loss. With no timeouts and the clock running, the Cardinals were flagged for a false start with seven seconds left. By rule, a 10-second runoff is enforced, which ended the game. Marc Bulger was 18 of 29 for 216 yards and 1 touchdown, with 1 interception. Warner was 29 of 42 for 327 yards, with 1 interception. Anquan Boldin had 8 receptions for 119 yards.

St. Louis	7	3	7	0	—	17
Arizona	3	3	3	3	—	12

StL	—	Holt 19 pass from Bulger (Wilkins kick)
Ariz	—	FG Rackers 29
Ariz	—	FG Rackers 26
StL	—	FG Wilkins 29
Ariz	—	FG Rackers 48
StL	—	Jackson 7 run (Wilkins kick)
Ariz	—	FG Rackers 35

CAROLINA 27, NEW ENGLAND 17—at Bank of America Stadium, attendance 73,528. Stephen Davis rushed for 77 yards and 3 touchdowns as the Panthers downed the defending Super Bowl champions. Following a field goal, the Panthers' defense forced a punt and Chris Gamble's 76-yard return led to Davis' second touchdown for 10 points in less than two minutes and a 17-7 lead. Adam Vinatieri cut the deficit to 20-10 in the third quarter, and Mike Vrabel intercepted a pass and returned it untouched 24 yards for a touchdown for 10 points in 17 seconds to pull within 20-17. Late in the third quarter, Mike Rucker stripped Tom Brady and forced him to fumble. Julius Peppers recovered the ball and Davis scored four plays later for a 27-17 lead. Gamble quelled the Patriots' final challenge, forcing Daniel Graham to fumble. Dan Morgan recovered with 2:17 remaining to clinch the victory. Jake Delhomme was 11 of 26 for 154 yards, with 1 interception. Brady was 23 of 44 for 270 yards and 1 touchdown, with 1 interception.

New England	7	0	10	0	—	17
Carolina	7	10	3	7	—	27

NE	—	Graham 1 pass from Brady (Vinatieri kick)
Car	—	S. Davis 1 run (Kasay kick)
Car	—	FG Kasay 51
Car	—	S. Davis 1 run (Kasay kick)
Car	—	FG Kasay 50
NE	—	FG Vinatieri 45
NE	—	Vrabel 24 interception return (Vinatieri kick)
Car	—	S. Davis 1 run (Kasay kick)

CHICAGO 38, DETROIT 6—at Soldier Field, attendance 62,019. Thomas Jones rushed for 139 yards and 2 touchdowns and the Bears' defense intercepted 5 passes to throttle the Lions. Leading 10-6 early in the second quarter, Bobby Wade returned a punt 73 yards down the left sideline for a touchdown. The Lions drove to the Bears' 12 on the next possession, but Nathan Vasher intercepted a pass in the end zone. The Bears needed just seven plays to drive 80 yards, capped by Muhsin Muhammad's 28-yard touchdown catch with 1:14 left in the half for a 24-6 lead. On the next play from scrimmage, Mike Brown intercepted a pass and returned it 41 yards for a touchdown and 31-6 halftime lead. The 31 first-half points marked the most points the Bears had scored in a game, let alone a half, since the final game of 2001. Kyle Orton was 14 of 21 for 150 yards and 1 touchdown. Jones had 20 carries for 139 yards. Harrington was 19 of 37 for 196 yards and 1 touchdown, with 5 interceptions.

Detroit	6	0	0	0	—	6
Chicago	10	21	0	7	—	38

Chi	—	T. Jones 3 run (Brien kick)
Det	—	R. Williams 51 pass from Harrington (kick blocked)
Chi	—	FG Brien 48
Chi	—	Wade 73 punt return (Brien kick)
Chi	—	Muhammad 28 pass from Orton (Brien kick)
Chi	—	Brown 41 interception return (Brien kick)
Chi	—	T. Jones 16 run (Brien kick)

CINCINNATI 37, MINNESOTA 8—at Paul Brown Stadium, attendance 65,763. Carson Palmer passed for 3 touchdowns and the defense forced 7 turnovers as the Bengals posted their first 2-0 start since 2001. The Bengals outgained the Vikings 504-304 yards and maintained possession for 38:40. The Bengals scored on five of their six first-half possessions, the last two scores set up by a fumble and interception in the final five minutes of the half, for a 27-0 halftime lead. Deltha O'Neal intercepted 2 passes to set up 10 quick points in the third quarter for a 37-0 lead, and the Vikings scored with 3:17 remaining. Palmer was 27 of 40 for 337 yards and 3 touchdowns, with 1 interception. Chad Johnson had 7 receptions for 139 yards. Culpepper was 21 of 37 for 236 yards, with 5 interceptions.

Minnesota	0	0	0	8	—	8
Cincinnati	14	13	7	3	—	37

Cin	—	C. Johnson 70 pass from Palmer (Graham kick)
Cin	—	Houshmandzadeh 12 pass from Palmer (Graham kick)
Cin	—	FG Graham 40
Cin	—	FG Graham 29
Cin	—	Schobel 8 pass from Palmer (Graham kick)
Cin	—	Houshmandzadeh 16 run (Graham kick)
Cin	—	FG Graham 30
Minn	—	Culpepper 5 run (Robinson pass from Culpepper)

DENVER 20, SAN DIEGO 17—at INVESCO Field at Mile High, attendance 75,310. Jason Elam kicked a 41-yard field goal with five seconds remaining to lift the Broncos past the Chargers. LaDainian Tomlinson's 16-yard scoring run with 12:13 left in the second quarter marked an NFL record fourteenth consecutive game in which he had a rushing touchdown. On the first play of the second half, Champ Bailey intercepted an errant pass and returned it untouched 25 yards for a touchdown to trim the Broncos' deficit to 14-10. Elam missed two 53-yard field-goal attempts in the third quarter, but the Broncos used a 37-yard punt return by Darrent Williams to set up Kyle Johnson's 3-yard touchdown run with 8:46 remaining for a 17-14 lead. The Chargers' responded with a 49-yard drive, capped by Nate Kaeding's 42-yard field goal with 5:21 to play. The Broncos answered with a 12-play, 57-yard drive, keyed by Ron Dayne's 10-yard run on fourth-and-2, to set up Elam's winning kick. Not counting the Chargers' three scoring drives, the Broncos' defense limited San Diego to 1 yard total in

its nine other possessions. Jake Plummer was 23 of 37 for 248 yards, with 1 interception. Drew Brees was 15 of 23 for 175 yards, with 1 interception.

San Diego	0	14	0	3	—	17
Denver	3	0	7	10	—	20

Den	—	FG Elam 45
SD	—	Tomlinson 16 run (Kaeding kick)
SD	—	Tomlinson 4 run (Kaeding kick)
Den	—	Bailey 25 interception return (Elam kick)
Den	—	K. Johnson 3 run (Elam kick)
SD	—	FG Kaeding 42
Den	—	FG Elam 41

CLEVELAND 26, GREEN BAY 24—at Lambeau Field, attendance 70,400. Trent Dilfer passed for 336 yards and 3 touchdowns for the Browns. Brett Favre's 17-yard pass to Ahman Green with 6:16 left in the second quarter allowed Favre to become the third player in NFL history with 50,000 passing yards, joining Dan Marino and John Elway. The Packers retired Reggie White's number at halftime, but were trailing 13-7 because Cleveland had scored on three of its first four possessions. Gary Baxter's interception in the end zone thwarted a drive late in the third quarter. Two plays later, Dilfer hit Braylon Edwards on a short, slant pattern, and Edwards raced 80 yards for a touchdown and 19-7 lead. The Packers drove 62 and 96 yards on their next two drives to trim the deficit to 19-17 with 3:40 remaining. On second-and-9 with 2:00 left, Dilfer completed a 62-yard touchdown pass to Steve Heiden for a 26-17 lead. Tony Fisher caught a scoring pass with four seconds left, but Brodney Pool recovered the ensuing onside kick to clinch the victory. Dilfer was 21 of 32 for 336 yards and 3 touchdowns. Heiden had 6 receptions for 104 yards, and Edwards had 3 catches for 107 yards. Favre was 32 of 44 for 342 yards and 3 touchdowns, with 2 interceptions. Donald Driver had 6 catches for 105 yards.

Cleveland	7	6	6	7	—	26
Green Bay	7	0	0	17	—	24

GB	—	Driver 42 pass from Favre (Longwell kick)
Cle	—	Heiden 1 pass from Dilfer (Dawson kick)
Cle	—	FG Dawson 21
Cle	—	FG Dawson 39
Cle	—	Edwards 80 pass from Dilfer (kick blocked)
GB	—	FG Longwell 34
GB	—	Ferguson 19 pass from Favre (Longwell kick)
Cle	—	Heiden 62 pass from Dilfer (Dawson kick)
GB	—	Fisher 4 pass from Favre (Longwell kick)

PITTSBURGH 27, HOUSTON 7—at Reliant Stadium, attendance 70,742. The Steelers recorded 8 sacks and Ben Roethlisberger improved to 15-0 as a starter as the Steelers handled the Texans. Not counting a three-play possession at the end of the first half, the Steelers scored on their first five drives. Four of the five possessions covered at least 60 yards. The Steelers outgained the Texans 273-66 in the first half en route to their 20-0 halftime lead. Roethlisberger was 14 of 21 for 254 yards and 2 touchdowns. Willie Parker rushed 25 times for 111 yards. Safety Troy Polamalu's 3 sacks tied an NFL record for most sacks by a defensive back. David Carr was 16 of 26 for 167 yards and 1 touchdown.

Pittsburgh	10	10	7	0	—	27
Houston	0	0	7	0	—	7

Pitt	—	FG Reed 37
Pitt	—	Ward 16 pass from Roethlisberger (Reed kick)
Pitt	—	Ward 14 pass from Roethlisberger (Reed kick)

Pitt	—	FG Reed 35
Hou	—	D. Davis 3 pass from Carr (K. Brown kick)
Pitt	—	Parker 10 run (Reed kick)

INDIANAPOLIS 10, JACKSONVILLE 3—at RCA Dome, attendance 56,460. Byron Leftwich's pass into the end zone was batted down by Bob Sanders and Nick Harper as time expired to allow the Colts to hold off the Jaguars. In the third quarter, Alvin Pearman returned a punt 33 yards to the Colts' 33 to set up JoshScobee's 28-yard field goal for a 3-0 lead. The Colts finally scored when they engineered a 17-play, 88-yard drive that took nearly nine minutes and was capped by Ran Carthon's 6-yard touchdown run on third-and-goal with 8:27 remaining. Mike Vanderjagt's 41-yard field goal on the ensuing possession stretched the lead to 10-3 with 1:50 left. Leftwich completed a 24-yard pass to Jimmy Smith on third-and-18 and a 25-yard pass to Ernest Wilford on third-and-15 to reach the Colts' 22. After spiking the ball to stop the clock with three seconds, Leftwich attempted to find Smith down the right side, but Sanders and Harper batted down the ball. Montae Reagor had 3 of the Colts' 6 sacks. Peyton Manning was 13 of 28 for 122 yards, with 1 interception. James rushed 27 times for 128 yards. Leftwich was 16 of 29 for 198 yards.

Jacksonville	0	0	3	0	—	3
Indianapolis	0	0	0	10	—	10

Jax	—	FG Scobee 28
Ind	—	Carthon 6 run (Vanderjagt kick)
Ind	—	FG Vanderjagt 41

N.Y. JETS 17, MIAMI 7—at The Meadowlands, attendance 77,918. Chad Pennington passed for 2 touchdowns as the Jets rebounded from their Week 1 defeat. The Dolphins crossed the Jets' 40 just once until the fourth quarter, when Randy McMichael's 4-yard scoring catch pulled the Dolphins within 10-7 with 14:13 remaining. The Jets, who had driven 80 yards to open the game, responded to McMichael's touchdown with a 10-play, 80-yard drive, highlighted by Pennington's 20-yard pass to Justin McCareins on third-and-12 at their own 18. Jerald Sowell's 1-yard scoring catch with 8:19 left gave the Jets a 17-7 lead. David Barrett's interception at the Jets' 15 with 2:44 remaining clinched the victory. Pennington was 19 of 30 for 190 yards and 2 touchdowns. Gus Frerotte was 20 of 43 for 177 yards and 1 touchdown, with 1 interception.

Miami	0	0	0	7	—	7
N.Y. Jets	7	3	0	7	—	17

NYJ	—	Coles 7 pass from Pennington (Nugent kick)
NYJ	—	FG Nugent 41
Mia	—	McMichael 4 pass from Frerotte (Mare kick)
NYJ	—	Sowell 1 pass from Pennington (Nugent kick)

PHILADELPHIA 42, SAN FRANCISCO 3—at Lincoln Financial Field, attendance 67,727. Donovan McNabb passed for 5 touchdowns as the Eagles rolled past the 49ers. McNabb's 68-yard touchdown pass to Terrell Owens three plays into the game served as omen for the Eagles. Drives of 70 and 91 yards increased the lead to 21-0, and Lito Sheppard's 34-yard interception return to the 49ers' 2 led to Brian Westbrook's touchdown catch and 28-0 lead with 11:22 left in the second quarter. The Eagles had advantages in first downs (30-8), total yards (583-142), and time of possession (37:57-22:03). McNabb was 23 of 29 for 342 yards and 5 touchdowns. L.J. Smith had 9 receptions for 119 yards, and Owens added 5 catches for 143 yards. Tim Rattay was 13 of 26 for 107 yards, with 3 interceptions, and first overall selection Alex Smith entered with 3:37 remaining and his lone pass attempt sailed incomplete.

| San Francisco | 0 | 0 | 3 | 0 | — | 3 |
| Philadelphia | 14 | 14 | 7 | 7 | — | 42 |

Phil — Owens 68 pass from McNabb (Akers kick)
Phil — L. Smith 6 pass from McNabb (Akers kick)
Phil — Owens 42 pass from McNabb (Akers kick)
Phil — Westbrook 2 pass from McNabb (Simoneau kick)
SF — FG Nedney 32
Phil — Lewis 6 pass from McNabb (Akers kick)
Phil — Gordon 6 run (Akers kick)

SEATTLE 21, ATLANTA 18—at Qwest Stadium, attendance 66,030. Shaun Alexander rushed for 144 yards and Matt Hasselbeck passed for 2 touchdowns as the Seahawks evened their record. The Seahawks' offense outgained the Falcons 428-223 total yards, and Atlanta gained just 3 first downs in six first-half possessions. The Seahawks, meanwhile, had strung together consecutive drives of 75, 68, and 80 yards in the second quarter to take a 21-0 lead. DeAngelo Hall's 27-yard punt return early in the third quarter sparked the Falcons. Atlanta scored on its first two drives of the half to pull within 21-10. Christian Morton recovered Bobby Engram's fumble near midfield with 6:56 remaining. Michael Vick scrambled for 32 yards on the next play, but tweaked his hamstring. Matt Schaub replaced Vick a few plays later, and T.J. Duckett scored on a 1-yard plunge with 3:58 left to cut the deficit to 21-18. The Falcons' defense forced a three-and-out, and Vick returned. However, Bryce Fisher's sack of Vick sent him back to the sideline. Schaub's fourth-and-14 pass with 1:35 left fell incomplete. Hasselbeck was 20 of 31 for 281 yards and 2 touchdowns. Alexander rushed 26 times for 144 yards. Darrell Jackson had 8 catches for 131 yards. Vick was 11 of 19 for 123 yards and 1 touchdown, while Schaub was 0 for 1.

| Atlanta | 0 | 0 | 10 | 8 | — | 18 |
| Seattle | 0 | 21 | 0 | 0 | — | 21 |

Sea — Jurevicius 6 pass from Hasselbeck (J. Brown kick)
Sea — Alexander 14 run (J. Brown kick)
Sea — Stevens 35 pass from Hasselbeck (J. Brown kick)
Atl — Finneran 5 pass from Vick (Peterson kick)
Atl — FG Peterson 30
Atl — Duckett 1 run (Crumpler pass from Schaub)

TAMPA BAY 19, BUFFALO 3—at Raymond James Stadium, attendance 64,777. Cardell Williams rushed for 128 yards and the Buccaneers' defense permitted just 147 yards to improve their record to 2-0. The Bills failed to gain a first down on their first five possessions, with the fifth drive ending with J.P. Losman inadvertently stepping on the backline of the end zone while scrambling away from Shelton Quarles. Tampa Bay responded to the safety with a 67-yard touchdown drive. Leading 9-3, Williams capped a 9-play, 80-yard third-quarter drive with a 3-yard scoring run, and Matt Bryant capped the scoring with a 40-yard field goal for a 19-3 lead with 9:22 to play. Brian Griese was 16 of 22 for 136 yards, and Williams had 24 carries for 128 yards. Losman was 11 of 28 for 113 yards.

| Buffalo | 0 | 3 | 0 | 0 | — | 3 |
| Tampa Bay | 0 | 9 | 7 | 3 | — | 19 |

TB — Safety, Losman sacked out of bounds in end zone by Quarles
TB — Alstott 1 run (Bryant kick)
Buff — FG Lindell 40
TB — Williams 3 run (Bryant kick)

TB — FG Bryant 40

TENNESSEE 25, BALTIMORE 10—at The Coliseum, attendance 69,149. The Titans' defense recorded 6 sacks and allowed just 182 yards for the Titans. The Titans' defense did not allow a first down in the first half. The one turnover they forced, a fumble by Jamal Lewis recovered by Kyle Vanden Bosch, led to Steve McNair's 2-yard touchdown pass to Troy Fleming. The Ravens cut the deficit to 13-3 with a field goal early in the third quarter. In the fourth quarter Brad Kassell intercepted Anthony Wright and returned it 21 yards for a touchdown and 23-3 lead with 11:53 to play. With 2:48 to play, the Ravens punted from their own 1-yard line. Robert Reynolds blocked David Zastudil's punt. Will Demps recovered the ball in the end zone and was tackled by Reynolds for a safety. McNair was 19 of 36 for 195 yards and 1 touchdown. Wright was 25 of 40 for 212 yards and 1 touchdown, with 1 interception.

| Baltimore | 0 | 0 | 3 | 7 | — | 10 |
| Tennessee | 7 | 6 | 3 | 9 | — | 25 |

Tenn — Fleming 2 pass from McNair (Bironas kick)
Tenn — FG Bironas 29
Tenn — FG Bironas 29
Balt — FG Stover 30
Tenn — FG Bironas 47
Tenn — Kassell 21 interception return (Bironas kick)
Balt — Mason 12 pass from Wright (Stover kick)
Tenn — Safety, Demps tackled in end zone by Reynolds

SUNDAY NIGHT, SEPTEMBER 18
KANSAS CITY 23, OAKLAND 17—at McAfee Coliseum, attendance 62,273. Sammy Knight knocked away Kerry Collins' fourth-and-goal pass in the end zone with 1:46 remaining to secure the Chiefs' 2-0 start. Gary Stills recovered a muffed punt at the Raiders' 17 four plays into the game to set up Priest Holmes' 1-yard leap-over-the-top touchdown. Trailing 17-10, Langston Walker blocked Lawrence Tynes' 46-yard field-goal attempt early in the third quarter. On the next play, Kerry Collins completed a 64-yard scoring pass to Randy Moss to tie the game. The Chiefs answered with a 15-play drive that consumed 9:18 and ended with a field goal. Leading 23-17 and with the ball, Charles Woodson forced Parker to fumble. Stuart Schwiegert recovered the ball near midfield with 4:52 to play. The Raiders reached the Chiefs' 13, but Collins completed just a 4-yard pass and had two incompletions to set up Knight knocking down a pass intended for Jerry Porter. Green was 18 of 28 for 237 yards. Collins was 21 of 35 for 263 yards and 1 touchdown. Moss had 5 catches for 127 yards.

| Kansas City | 7 | 10 | 3 | 3 | — | 23 |
| Oakland | 0 | 10 | 7 | 0 | — | 17 |

KC — Holmes 1 run (Tynes kick)
Oak — Jordan 1 run (Janikowski kick)
KC — L. Johnson 6 run (Tynes kick)
Oak — FG Janikowski 29
KC — FG Tynes 31
Oak — Moss 64 pass from Collins (Janikowski kick)
KC — FG Tynes 39
KC — FG Tynes 42

MONDAY NIGHT, SEPTEMBER 19
N.Y. GIANTS 27, NEW ORLEANS 10—at Giants Stadium, attendance 68,031. Tiki Barber scored 2 touchdowns and the Giants' defense forced 6 turnovers to outlast the Saints. The game, originally scheduled to be played in New Orleans, was moved to Giants Stadium as part of NFL Hurricane Relief Weekend to generate donations for Hurricane Katrina victims. The Saints outgained the Giants 422-257 in total yards,

but committed 4 turnovers in the second half, all inside Giants' territory. Chase Blackburn recovered Fred McAfee's fumble at the Saints' 10-yard line on the opening kickoff. Brandon Jacobs scored three plays later, and Eli Manning's 6-yard touchdown pass to Barber capped an 11-play, 76-yard drive on the ensuing possession for a 14-0 lead. Carlos Emmons' second-quarter interception at the Saints' 41 led to Barber's second touchdown. Fred Thomas recovered James Butler's muffed punt just before halftime to set up John Carney's field goal to cut the deficit to 21-10. William Joseph's fumble recovery at the Saints' 41 early in the third quarter led to Jay Feely's 39-yard field goal, and he added a 30-yard field goal with 6:37 to play. Joe Horn fumbled a ball out of the end zone with 3:40 remaining to quell the Saints' final threat. Manning was 13 of 24 for 165 yards and 1 touchdown. Brooks was 27 of 45 for 375 yards and 1 touchdown, with 3 interceptions. Horn had 9 receptions for 143 yards, and Donte' Stallworth added 8 catches for 141 yards.

| N.Y. Giants | 14 | 7 | 3 | 3 | — | 27 |
| New Orleans | 0 | 10 | 0 | 0 | — | 10 |

NYG — Jacobs 1 run (Feely kick)
NYG — Barber 6 pass from E.Manning (Feely kick)
NO — Horn 21 pass from Brooks (Carney kick)
NYG — Barber 12 run (Feely kick)
NO — FG Carney 21
NYG — FG Feely 39
NYG — FG Feely 30

WASHINGTON 14, DALLAS 13—at Texas Stadium, attendance 65,207. Mark Brunell completed 2 long touchdown passes to Santana Moss in the final four minutes as the Redskins rallied to surprise the Cowboys. The defeat marked Bill Parcells' first loss in 77 career games in which he had a 13-plus point lead in the fourth quarter. After the Cowboys honored Troy Aikman, Michael Irvin, and Emmitt Smith by enshrining them into the Ring of Honor, Drew Bledsoe and Terry Glenn hooked up on a 70-yard flea-flicker for a 10-0 lead early in the third quarter. José Cortez's second field goal increased the lead to 13-0 with 5:58 left. Faced with third-and-27, Brunell scrambled 25 yards, and then completed a 20-yard pass to James Thrash on fourth-and-2. Four plays later, on fourth-and-15, Brunell found Moss in the end zone on a perfectly placed 39-yard touchdown pass with 3:46 left. The Cowboys were forced to punt, and on the second play Brunell hit Moss in stride deep down the right side for a 14-13 lead, marking the duo's second touchdown within 1:11. Glenn was tackled a yard shy of a first down on fourth-and-4 with 1:47 remaining. The Cowboys got the ball back with 36 seconds left, but Glenn was tackled at the Redskins' 43 as time expired. Brunell was 20 of 34 for 291 yards and 2 touchdowns, with 1 interception. Moss had 5 catches for 159 yards. Bledsoe was 21 of 36 for 261 yards and 1 touchdown. Glenn had 6 catches for 157 yards.

| Washington | 0 | 0 | 0 | 14 | — | 14 |
| Dallas | 0 | 3 | 7 | 3 | — | 13 |

Dall — FG Cortez 33
Dall — Glenn 70 pass from Bledsoe (Cortez kick)
Dall — FG Cortez 41
Wash — S. Moss 39 pass from Brunell (Novak kick)
Wash — S. Moss 70 pass from Brunell (Novak kick)

THIRD WEEK SUMMARIES
American Football Conference

East Division	W	L	T	Pct.	Pts.	OP
Miami	2	1	0	.667	68	51
New England	2	1	0	.667	70	67
Buffalo	1	2	0	.333	41	50

N.Y. Jets	1	2	0	.333	44	60
North Division	**W**	**L**	**T**	**Pct.**	**Pts.**	**OP**
Cincinnati	3	0	0	1.000	88	28
Pittsburgh	2	1	0	.667	81	37
Cleveland	1	2	0	.333	45	64
Baltimore	0	2	0	.000	17	49
South Division	**W**	**L**	**T**	**Pct.**	**Pts.**	**OP**
Indianapolis	3	0	0	1.000	47	16
Jacksonville	2	1	0	.667	55	44
Tennessee	1	2	0	.333	59	75
Houston	0	2	0	.000	14	49
West Division	**W**	**L**	**T**	**Pct.**	**Pts.**	**OP**
Denver	2	1	0	.667	60	61
Kansas City	2	1	0	.667	60	54
San Diego	1	2	0	.333	86	71
Oakland	0	3	0	.000	57	76
National Football Conference						
East Division	**W**	**L**	**T**	**Pct.**	**Pts.**	**OP**
Washington	2	0	0	1.000	23	20
Dallas	2	1	0	.667	75	69
N.Y. Giants	2	1	0	.667	92	74
Philadelphia	2	1	0	.667	75	37
North Division	**W**	**L**	**T**	**Pct.**	**Pts.**	**OP**
Detroit	1	1	0	.500	23	41
Chicago	1	2	0	.333	52	39
Minnesota	1	2	0	.333	54	77
Green Bay	0	3	0	.000	43	60
South Division	**W**	**L**	**T**	**Pct.**	**Pts.**	**OP**
Tampa Bay	3	0	0	1.000	60	32
Atlanta	2	1	0	.667	56	47
Carolina	1	2	0	.333	71	67
New Orleans	1	2	0	.333	49	80
West Division	**W**	**L**	**T**	**Pct.**	**Pts.**	**OP**
St. Louis	2	1	0	.667	73	67
Seattle	2	1	0	.667	72	56
San Francisco	1	2	0	.333	62	101
Arizona	0	3	0	.000	43	96

SUNDAY, SEPTEMBER 25

ATLANTA 24, BUFFALO 16—at Ralph Wilson Stadium, attendance 72,032. The Falcons' defense allowed just 3 points on the final seven possessions for a hard-earned victory. With a steady rain falling, Todd Peterson kicked a 27-yard field goal as the half expired to stretch the lead to 17-13. Chris Kelsay intercepted Michael Vick's pass two plays into the second half to set up Rian Lindell's 30-yard field goal with 10:10 left in the third quarter. Early in the fourth quarter, faced with third-and-10 from the Bills' 39, Vick scrambled for 27 yards and T.J. Duckett scored on the next play to give Atlanta a 24-16 lead. Ryan Denney recovered DeAngelo Hall's muffed punt at the Bills' 44 with 5:01 left. Five plays later, on fourth-and-1 from the Falcons' 29, J.P. Losman was stopped short of a first down. On the Bills' final possession, Rod Coleman forced Losman to fumble and Patrick Kerney recovered. Atlanta outgained the Bills 403-208 total yards. Vick was 15 of 27 for 167 yards and 2 touchdowns, with 1 interception. Losman was 10 of 23 for 75 yards, with 1 interception. Willis McGahee rushed 27 times for 140 yards.

Atlanta	7	10	0	7	—	24
Buffalo	3	10	3	0	—	16
Buff	—	FG Lindell 36				
Atl	—	Blakley 9 pass from Vick (Peterson kick)				
Buff	—	FG Lindell 41				
Atl	—	Jenkins 15 pass from Vick (Peterson kick)				
Buff	—	McGahee 8 run (Lindell kick)				
Atl	—	FG Peterson 27				
Buff	—	FG Lindell 30				
Atl	—	Duckett 12 run (Peterson kick)				

CINCINNATI 24, CHICAGO 7—at Soldier Field, attendance 62,045. Carson Palmer passed for 3 touchdowns, two to Chad Johnson, and the Bengals' defense intercepted 5 passes to improve to 3-0 for the first time since 1990. The Bengals became the first team in 20 years to have a combined 10 interceptions in consecutive games. With a steady rain falling, Deltha O'Neal intercepted Kyle Orton at the Bears' 30 early in the third quarter. Seven plays later, Palmer threw a 36-yard touchdown pass to rookie Chris Henry for a 17-0 lead. Thomas Jones completed a 14-play, 70-yard drive with a 2-yard scoring run with 13:30 remaining, but three plays later Palmer hit Johnson with a 40-yard long pass down the left sideline for a 24-7 lead. Palmer was 16 of 23 for 169 yards and 3 touchdowns. Orton was 17 of 39 for 149 yards, with 5 interceptions. Jones had 27 carries for 106 yards.

Cincinnati	10	0	7	7	—	24
Chicago	0	0	0	7	—	7
Cin	—	C. Johnson 18 pass from Palmer (Graham kick)				
Cin	—	FG Graham 33				
Cin	—	Henry 36 pass from Palmer (Graham kick)				
Chi	—	T. Jones 2 run (Brien kick)				
Cin	—	C. Johnson 40 pass from Palmer (Graham kick)				

TAMPA BAY 17, GREEN BAY 16—at Lambeau Field, attendance 70,518. Carnell Williams rushed 37 times for 158 yards as the Buccaneers improved to 3-0 for the first time since 2000. Williams' 434 rushing yards marked the best three-game stretch to begin an NFL career. The Packers began the season 0-3 for the first time since 1988. The Buccaneers' defense forced 4 turnovers, including 2 interceptions by Will Allen. Tampa Bay led 17-6 early in the second quarter, with two of its three scores set up by a fumble recovery by Ronde Barber and an interception by Brian Kelly. Ryan Longwell, who missed an extra point in the first half because of a bad snap, missed a 42-yard field goal in the third quarter as the deficit remained 17-13. Ahmad Carroll's interception and 38-yard return to the Buccaneers' 32 led to Longwell's 32-yard field goal with 7:18 to play. With 5:03 left, Brett Favre attempted a long pass down the left sideline. Juran Bolden tipped the pass away from Robert Ferguson, and Allen intercepted it at the Buccaneers' 5. Williams carried the ball on seven of the next eight plays, highlighted by a 24-yard run just before the two-minute warning to clinch the victory. Brian Griese was 17 of 26 for 139 yards and 2 touchdowns, with 1 interceptions. Favre was 14 of 24 for 195 yards and 2 touchdowns, with 3 interceptions.

Tampa Bay	7	10	0	0	—	17
Green Bay	6	7	0	3	—	16
TB	—	Galloway 5 pass from Griese (Bryant kick)				
GB	—	Ferguson 37 pass from Favre (kick failed)				
TB	—	Galloway 10 pass from Griese (Bryant kick)				
TB	—	FG Bryant 42				
GB	—	Chatman 20 pass from Favre (Longwell kick)				
GB	—	FG Longwell 32				

INDIANAPOLIS 13, CLEVELAND 6—at RCA Dome, attendance 57,127. Edgerrin James rushed for 108 yards and the Colts' defense recorded 4 sacks, 3 by Dwight Freeney, to remain undefeated. Indianapolis became the sixth team since 1945 to hold its first three opponents to single digits. The Colts had scoring drives of 66 and 84 yards in the first half, and took nearly eight minutes off the clock to set up Mike Vanderjagt's field goal to begin the second half for a 13-3 lead. The Browns responded with a 19-play, 86-yard drive, but had to settle for Phil Dawson's field goal with 14:11 left. Cleveland got the ball back one last time, punted with 7:40 left, and the Colts ran out the clock. Peyton Manning became the second-fastest quarterback to reach 30,000 passing yards, in his 115th game, one more than Dan Marino. Manning and Marvin Harrison surpassed Jim Kelly-Andre Reed to become the most prolific duo in NFL history, breaking the mark of 9,538 yards. Manning was 19 of 23 for 228 yards, with 1 interception. James rushed 27 times for 108 yards. Trent Dilfer was 22 of 29 for 208 yards.

Cleveland	0	3	0	3	—	6
Indianapolis	7	3	3	0	—	13
Ind	—	James 2 run (Vanderjagt kick)				
Cle	—	FG Dawson 40				
Ind	—	FG Vanderjagt 20				
Ind	—	FG Vanderjagt 23				
Cle	—	FG Dawson 22				

MIAMI 27, CAROLINA 24—at Pro Player Stadium, attendance 72,288. Olindo Mare kicked a 32-yard field goal with four seconds remaining to knock off the Panthers. The Dolphins led 7-3 when Steve Smith muffed a punt at the Panthers' 16. Travares Tillman recovered the ball and Gus Frerotte completed an 18-yard scoring pass to Randy McMichael two plays later for a 14-3 lead. Smith responded with 2 touchdown catches in the second quarter, including a 3-yard grab with 54 seconds left in the half, to cut the deficit to 21-17. Olindo Mare's 27-yard field goal in the middle of the fourth quarter extended the Dolphins' lead to 24-17, but three plays later a 53-yard touchdown pass to Smith tied the game. Lance Schulters intercepted Jake Delhomme's pass at the Panthers' 38 returned the ball 37 yards to the Dolphins' 25 with 1:51 left to set up Mare's winning field. Frerotte was 14 of 33 for 171 yards and 2 touchdowns, with 1 interception. Ronnie Brown had 23 carries for 132 yards. Delhomme was 19 of 35 for 285 yards and 3 touchdowns, with 1 interception. Smith had 11 catches for 170 yards.

Carolina	3	14	0	7	—	24
Miami	14	7	0	6	—	27
Mia	—	Brown 1 run (Mare kick)				
Car	—	FG Kasay 52				
Mia	—	McMichael 18 pass from Frerotte (Mare kick)				
Car	—	S. Smith 1 pass from Delhomme (Kasay kick)				
Mia	—	Chambers 42 pass from Frerotte (Mare kick)				
Car	—	S. Smith 3 pass from Delhomme (Kasay kick)				
Mia	—	FG Mare 27				
Car	—	S. Smith 53 pass from Delhomme (Kasay kick)				
Mia	—	FG Mare 32				

MINNESOTA 33, NEW ORLEANS 16—at Metrodome, attendance 63,952. Daunte Culpepper passed for 300 yards and 3 touchdowns as the Vikings posted their first victory. The Vikings maintained possession for 38:13. Antoine Winfield recovered Aaron Stecker's fumble on the opening kickoff, and on the next play Culpepper fired a 24-yard touchdown pass to Travis Taylor for a 7-0 lead 13 seconds into the game. Keith Newman's interception later in the quarter set up Taylor's second touchdown catch for a 17-0 lead. The Saints scored 16 unanswered points, with Deuce McAllister capping a 64-yard drive with a 1-yard plunge with 11:40 remaining to pull within 24-16. The Vikings responded with a field goal, and Winfield intercepted a pass on the next play to set up Paul Edinger's third field goal with 4:29 remaining. Culpepper was 21 of 29 for 300 yards and 3 touchdowns. Mewelde Moore had 23 carries for 101 yards. Aaron Brooks was 12 of 32 for 199 yards and 1 touchdown, with 2 interceptions.

New Orleans	0	6	3	7	—	16
Minnesota	17	7	0	9	—	33
Minn	—	Taylor 24 pass from Culpepper (Edinger kick)				
Minn	—	FG Edinger 24				

Minn	—	Taylor 13 pass from Culpepper (Edinger kick)	
Minn	—	Williamson 53 pass from Culpepper (Edinger kick)	
NO	—	Conwell 13 pass from Brooks (pass failed)	
NO	—	FG Carney 22	
NO	—	McAllister 1 run (Carney kick)	
Minn	—	FG Edinger 28	
Minn	—	FG Edinger 48	
Minn	—	FG Edinger 34	

JACKSONVILLE 26, N.Y. JETS 20 (OT)—at The Meadowlands, attendance 77,422. Byron Leftwich completed a 36-yard touchdown pass to Jimmy Smith 6:05 into overtime as the Jaguars won on the road. The Jaguars' defense allowed just 168 yards and recorded 4 sacks, and Jacksonville had a 40:31-25:34 time of possession advantage. Early in the third quarter, John Abraham forced Leftwich to fumble. James Reed recovered the fumble and returned it 33 yards for a touchdown to take a 14-10 lead. The Jaguars responded with a field goal, and late in the quarter Justin Miller muffed a punt. Gerald Sensabaugh recovered the ball at the Jets' 16, and Fred Taylor scored four plays later for a 20-14 Jacksonville lead with 14:57 remaining. The Jets answered with a field goal, and David Barrett recovered Reggie Williams' fumble and returned it 30 yards to the Jaguars' 21 with 3:02 remaining. Six plays later, rookie Mike Nugent kicked a 25-yard field goal with 1:14 to play. In overtime, both teams recorded interceptions, including Kerry Rhodes at the Jets' 12. A holding penalty and sack by Paul Spicer pushed the Jets back to their own 1-yard line, and Ben Graham's 44-yard punt and Alvin Pearman's 11-yard return to the Jets' 34 led to Smith's winning catch. Leftwich was 16 of 23 for 177 yards and 2 touchdowns, with 1 interception. Taylor carried 37 times for 98 yards. Pennington was 9 of 19 for 76 yards, with 2 interceptions, and Jay Fiedler was 2 of 3 for 19 yards.

Jacksonville	3	7	3	6	—	26	
N.Y. Jets	0	7	7	6	—	20	
Jax	—	FG Scobee 32					
Jax	—	Wilford 21 pass from Leftwich (Scobee kick)					
NYJ	—	Sowell 1 run (Nugent kick)					
NYJ	—	Reed 33 fumble return (Nugent kick)					
Jax	—	FG Scobee 40					
Jax	—	Taylor 3 run (Scobee kick)					
NYJ	—	FG Nugent 35					
NYJ	—	FG Nugent 25					
Jax	—	J. Smith 36 pass from Leftwich					

PHILADELPHIA 23, OAKLAND 20—at Lincoln Financial Field, attendance 67,735. A gimpy David Akers kicked a 23-yard field goal with nine seconds remaining to lift the Eagles past the Raiders. Akers reinjured his non-kicking right hamstring on the opening kickoff. The Raiders only needed to drive 50 yards, capped by Kerry Collins' 8-yard pass to LaMont Jordan, for a 7-0 lead. The Eagles drove into Raiders' territory on four consecutive possessions before Brian Westbrook scored on an 18-yard run. With Akers ailing, linebacker Mark Simoneau's extra-point attempt was short, and the Raiders led 7-6. Trailing 20-10, the Raiders responded with a field goal, but Sebastian Janikowski missed his second field goal on the Raiders next drive and the Eagles maintained a 20-13 lead with 5:20 to play. The Raiders forced a punt, and Collins completed a 31-yard pass to Randy Moss on third-and-15 and a 17-yard pass to Courtney Anderson on third-and-10 to set up his 27-yard scoring toss to Doug Gabriel to tie the game with 2:17 to play. McNabb found Greg Lewis for 13 yards on third-and-9 and connected on a 14-yard pass to Terrell Owens to the Raiders' 17 before Akers kicked the winning

field goal before limping off the field. McNabb was 30 of 52 for 365 yards and 2 touchdowns, with 1 interception. Westbrook had 6 catches for 140 yards. Collins was 24 of 42 for 345 yards and 2 touchdowns. Anderson had 5 catches for 100 yards.

Oakland	7	3	0	10	—	20	
Philadelphia	0	6	14	3	—	23	
Oak	—	Jordan 8 pass from Collins (Janikowski kick)					
Phil	—	Westbrook 18 run (kick failed)					
Oak	—	FG Janikowski 28					
Phil	—	Owens 4 pass from McNabb (Akers kick)					
Phil	—	Westbrook 5 pass from McNabb (Akers kick)					
Oak	—	FG Janikowski 26					
Oak	—	Gabriel 27 pass from Collins (Janikowski kick)					
Phil	—	FG Akers 23					

NEW ENGLAND 23, PITTSBURGH 20—at Heinz Field, attendance 64,868. Adam Vinatieri kicked a 43-yard field goal with one second left as the Patriots rallied to win on the road. The loss marked the first regular-season defeat, after 15 victories, of Ben Roethlisberger's career. The Steelers led 10-7 and were driving for another score when Antwaan Randle El attempted to lateral to Hines Ward in the open field during a 49-yard play. Eugene Wilson recovered to thwart the rally. Trailing 13-7, Tim Dwight returned a punt 28 yards to set up Vinatieri's 48-yard field goal late in the third quarter. Brady completed all 5 of his pass attempts on their next drive to set up Corey Dillon's 7-yard run for a 17-13 lead with 10:37 to play. Vinatieri's 35-yard field goal with 3:19 to play gave the Patriots a 20-13 lead. A 23-yard pass interference penalty on fourth down led to Roethlisberger's 4-yard touchdown pass to Hines Ward with 1:21 remaining to tie the game. Brady completed all 3 of his pass attempts on the final drive, capped by Vinatieri's winning kick. Brady was 31 of 41 for 372 yards, with 1 interception. Givens had 9 catches for 130 yards. Roethlisberger was 12 of 28 for 216 yards and 2 touchdowns. Ward had 4 receptions for 110 yards.

New England	7	0	3	13	—	23	
Pittsburgh	10	0	3	7	—	20	
NE	—	Dillon 4 run (Vinatieri kick)					
Pitt	—	Ward 85 pass from Roethlisberger (Reed kick)					
Pitt	—	FG Reed 33					
Pitt	—	FG Reed 24					
NE	—	FG Vinatieri 48					
NE	—	Dillon 7 run (Vinatieri kick)					
NE	—	FG Vinatieri 35					
Pitt	—	Ward 4 pass from Roethlisberger (Reed kick)					
NE	—	FG Vinatieri 43					

ST. LOUIS 31, TENNESSEE 27—at Edward Jones Dome, attendance 65,835. Marc Bulger passed for 3 touchdowns as the Rams outlasted the Titans. The Titans led 10-0 and drove to the Rams' 20, but Adam Archuleta stepped in front of Steve McNair's swing pass and raced untouched 85 yards down the left sideline for a touchdown. Michael Hawthorne recovered a fumble on the next drive to set up Jeff Wilkins' field goal, and Hawthorne's interception on the ensuing possession led to Marshall Faulk's 13-yard touchdown catch and a 17-10 Rams lead. The Titans trailed 24-10 late in the third quarter before scoring 2 touchdowns in 45 seconds, capped by Antwan Odom's 25-yard fumble return, after Kyle Vanden Bosch sacked Bulger. The Rams retook the lead on the first play of the fourth quarter, but the Titans trimmed the deficit to three points following Peter Sirmon's fumble recovery and Rob Bironas' field goal with 6:02 to play. The Titans drove to the Rams' 28 on their final possession, but McNair's fourth-down pass sailed out of

bounds. Bulger was 21 of 28 for 292 yards and 3 touchdowns, with 1 interception. Holt had 9 receptions for 163 yards. McNair was 24 of 39 for 261 yards and 2 touchdowns, with 2 interceptions.

Tennessee	10	0	14	3	—	27	
St. Louis	0	17	7	7	—	31	
Tenn	—	Troupe 16 pass from McNair (Bironas kick)					
Tenn	—	FG Bironas 41					
StL	—	Archuleta 85 interception return (Wilkins kick)					
StL	—	FG Wilkins 46					
StL	—	M. Faulk 13 pass from Bulger (Wilkins kick)					
StL	—	Holt 32 pass from Bulger (Wilkins kick)					
Tenn	—	B. Jones 4 pass from McNair (Bironas kick)					
Tenn	—	Odom 25 fumble return (Bironas kick)					
StL	—	Curtis 10 pass from Bulger (Wilkins kick)					
Tenn	—	FG Bironas 39					

DALLAS 34, SAN FRANCISCO 31—at Monster Park, attendance 68,247. Drew Bledsoe completed a 14-yard touchdown pass to Keyshawn Johnson with 1:51 left as the Cowboys rallied to defeat the 49ers. Tony Parrish's 34-yard interception return for a touchdown in the middle of the second quarter gave the 49ers a 21-6 lead. Another interception by Parrish led to Tim Rattay's second touchdown pass to Brandon Lloyd for a 31-19 lead in the final minute of the third quarter. Bledsoe's 58-yard pass to Terry Glenn on the next possession set up Julius Jones' second scoring run nine seconds into the fourth quarter. The Cowboys began a drive on their own 24 with 6:05 left, and Bledsoe completed 4 consecutive passes, capped by a 44-yard pass to Glenn, to set up Johnson's 14-yard touchdown catch and conversion with 1:51 left. Dat Nguyen intercepted Rattay's pass at the 49ers' 43 with 54 seconds left to clinch the victory. Bledsoe was 24 of 38 for 363 yards and 2 touchdowns, with 2 interceptions. Glenn had 5 receptions for 137 yards. Rattay was 21 of 34 for 269 yards and 3 touchdowns, with 2 interceptions. Lloyd had 4 catches for 142 yards.

Dallas	0	12	7	15	—	34	
San Francisco	7	17	7	0	—	31	
SF	—	Battle 15 pass from Rattay (Nedney kick)					
Dall	—	Bledsoe 6 run (kick failed)					
SF	—	Lloyd 89 pass from Rattay (Nedney kick)					
SF	—	Parrish 34 interception return (Nedney kick)					
Dall	—	Witten 6 pass from Bledsoe (pass failed)					
SF	—	FG Nedney 20					
Dall	—	J. Jones 1 run (Cortez kick)					
SF	—	Lloyd 13 pass from Rattay (Nedney kick)					
Dall	—	J. Jones 1 run (Cortez kick)					
Dall	—	K. Johnson 14 pass from Bledsoe (K. Johnson pass from Bledsoe)					

SEATTLE 37, ARIZONA 12—at Qwest Field, attendance 64,843. Shaun Alexander rushed for 4 touchdowns as the Seahawks rolled up 447 yards of offense. The Cardinals kicked field goals on three of their first four possessions and trailed just 10-9 at halftime. Alexander capped an 80-yard drive to begin the second half with his second touchdown. Three plays later, Michael Boulware sacked Josh McCown and forced him to fumble. Rocky Bernard recovered at the Cardinals' 1 and Alexander scored on the next play for a 24-9 lead. After Neil Rackers' fourth field goal cut the deficit to 24-12 with 5:06 left in the third quarter, the Seahawks scored on their final three possessions, with Alexander's 1-yard scoring run to begin the fourth quarter capping his big day. Matt Hasselbeck was 20 of 31 for 242 yards. Alexander carried 22 times for 140 yards. Darrell Jackson had 8 receptions for 125 yards. Kurt Warner was 8 of 13 for 105 yards before leaving in the second quarter with an injured groin. McCown was 10 of 23 for 97 yards, with 1 interception.

Arizona	3	6	3	0 —	12
Seattle	7	3	14	13 —	37

Ariz	—	FG Rackers 54
Sea	—	Alexander 25 run (J. Brown kick)
Ariz	—	FG Rackers 39
Sea	—	FG J. Brown 33
Ariz	—	FG Rackers 50
Sea	—	Alexander 1 run (J. Brown kick)
Sea	—	Alexander 1 run (J. Brown kick)
Ariz	—	FG Rackers 39
Sea	—	Alexander 1 run (J. Brown kick)
Sea	—	FG J. Brown 23
Sea	—	FG J. Brown 47

SUNDAY NIGHT, SEPTEMBER 25

SAN DIEGO 45, N.Y. GIANTS 23—at Qualcomm Stadium, attendance 65,373. LaDainian Tomlinson rushed for 192 yards and 3 touchdowns, and passed for another score, as the Chargers pulled away. The Chargers scored on their first three possessions, driving 65, 85, and 62 yards, to take a 21-3 lead. The Giants scored on their last three drives of the half to pull within 21-20 at halftime. The Chargers need just four plays to score to begin the second half, with Tomlinson rolling right and tossing a 26-yard scoring pass to Keenan McCardell. A 77-yard scoring drive increased the lead to 35-20. Feely cut the deficit to 35-23, but Darren Sproles returned the ensuing kickoff 58 yards and Tomlinson scored six plays later for a 42-23 lead with 8:30 to play. The Chargers outgained the Giants, 485-424 total yards. Brees was 19 of 22 for 191 yards and 2 touchdowns. Tomlinson had 21 carries for 192 yards. Manning was 24 of 41 for 352 yards and 2 touchdowns. Jeremy Shockey had 6 receptions for 101 yards.

N.Y. Giants	3	17	0	3 —	23
San Diego	7	14	14	10 —	45

NYG	—	FG Feely 22
SD	—	Tomlinson 1 run (Kaeding kick)
SD	—	McCardell 15 pass from Brees (Kaeding kick)
SD	—	Tomlinson 3 run (Kaeding kick)
NYG	—	Burress 5 pass from Manning (Feely kick)
NYG	—	Tyree 4 pass from Manning (Feely kick)
NYG	—	FG Feely 40
SD	—	McCardell 26 pass from Tomlinson (Kaeding kick)
SD	—	Gates 14 pass from Brees (Kaeding kick)
NYG	—	FG Feely 28
SD	—	Tomlinson 5 run (Kaeding kick)
SD	—	FG Kaeding 44

MONDAY NIGHT, SEPTEMBER 26

DENVER 30, KANSAS CITY 10—at INVESCO Field at Mile High, attendance 76,381. Jake Plummer passed for a touchdown and ran for another as the Broncos scored on six of their first seven possessions, not counting a kneeldown before halftime. Denver drove 68 and 80 yards on its first two drives for a 10-0 lead. Ian Gold then recovered Larry Johnson's fumble and, on the next play, Plummer completed a 12-yard touchdown pass to Rod Smith for a 17-0 lead with left in the first quarter. Leading 20-3 at halftime, ncos drove 70 and 82 yards with their first two half possessions for a 30-3 lead. Plummer

was 13 of 18 for 152 yards and 1 touchdown. Trent Green was 23 of 44 for 221 yards and 1 touchdown. Eddie Kennison had 8 receptions for 112 yards.

Kansas City	0	3	0	7 —	10
Denver	17	3	7	3 —	30

Den	—	FG Elam 30
Den	—	Anderson 44 run (Elam kick)
Den	—	R. Smith 12 pass from Plummer (Elam kick)
Den	—	FG Elam 51
KC	—	FG Tynes 28
Den	—	Plummer 1 run (Elam kick)
Den	—	FG Elam 25
KC	—	Parker 21 pass from Green (Tynes kick)

FOURTH WEEK SUMMARIES
American Football Conference

East Division	W	L	T	Pct.	Pts.	OP
Miami	2	1	0	.667	68	51
New England	2	2	0	.500	87	108
Buffalo	1	3	0	.250	48	69
N.Y. Jets	1	3	0	.250	47	73
North Division	**W**	**L**	**T**	**Pct.**	**Pts.**	**OP**
Cincinnati	4	0	0	1.000	104	38
Pittsburgh	2	1	0	.667	81	37
Baltimore	1	2	0	.333	30	52
Cleveland	1	2	0	.333	45	64
South Division	**W**	**L**	**T**	**Pct.**	**Pts.**	**OP**
Indianapolis	4	0	0	1.000	78	26
Jacksonville	2	2	0	.500	62	64
Tennessee	1	3	0	.250	69	106
Houston	0	3	0	.000	24	65
West Division	**W**	**L**	**T**	**Pct.**	**Pts.**	**OP**
Denver	3	1	0	.750	80	68
Kansas City	2	2	0	.500	91	91
San Diego	2	2	0	.500	127	88
Oakland	1	3	0	.250	76	89

National Football Conference

East Division	W	L	T	Pct.	Pts.	OP
Washington	3	0	0	1.000	43	37
N.Y. Giants	3	1	0	.750	136	98
Philadelphia	3	1	0	.750	112	68
Dallas	2	2	0	.500	88	88
North Division	**W**	**L**	**T**	**Pct.**	**Pts.**	**OP**
Chicago	1	2	0	.333	52	39
Detroit	1	2	0	.333	36	58
Minnesota	1	3	0	.250	64	107
Green Bay	0	4	0	.000	72	92
South Division	**W**	**L**	**T**	**Pct.**	**Pts.**	**OP**
Tampa Bay	4	0	0	1.000	77	45
Atlanta	3	1	0	.750	86	57
Carolina	2	2	0	.500	103	96
New Orleans	2	2	0	.500	68	87
West Division	**W**	**L**	**T**	**Pct.**	**Pts.**	**OP**
St. Louis	2	2	0	.500	97	111
Seattle	2	2	0	.500	89	76
Arizona	1	3	0	.250	74	110
San Francisco	1	3	0	.333	76	132

SUNDAY, OCTOBER 2

ATLANTA 30, MINNESOTA 10—at Georgia Dome, attendance 69,552. The Falcons' defense recorded 9 sacks and forced 3 turnovers and the offense rushed for 274 yards to jump to a 27-0 lead and defeat the Vikings. Atlanta drove 78, 63, 69, and 61 yards in four of their five first-half drives to take a 24-0 lead. In the third quarter, Rod Coleman sacked Daunte Culpepper and forced him to fumble. Patrick Kerney recovered and Todd Peterson kicked a 26-yard field goal 12 plays later for a 27-0 lead with four seconds left in the third quarter. Michael Vick was 6 of 8 for 49 yards and 1 touchdown before spraining his knee when hit by Erasmus James while delivering an incomplete pass with the score 14-0 in the second quarter. Matt Schaub replaced Vick and was 5 of 14 for 39 yards. Warrick Dunn had 18 carries for 126 yards. Culpepper was 23 of 34 for 250 yards and 1 touchdown, with 2

interceptions.

Minnesota	0	0	0	10 —	10
Atlanta	14	10	3	3 —	30

Atl	—	Crumpler 5 pass from Vick (Peterson kick)
Atl	—	Duckett 1 run (Peterson kick)
Atl	—	Dunn 37 run (Peterson kick)
Atl	—	FG Peterson 38
Atl	—	FG Peterson 26
Minn	—	FG Edinger 43
Atl	—	FG Peterson 39
Minn	—	Williamson 16 pass from Culpepper (Edinger kick)

BALTIMORE 13, N.Y. JETS 3—at M&T Bank Stadium, attendance 70,479. The Ravens' defense recorded 5 sacks, allowed 8 first downs, and 152 yards. Baltimore led 6-0 at halftime, but Jamal Lewis fumbled on the second play of the second half. Victor Hobson recovered the fumble and returned it 43 yards to the Ravens' 1 where Todd Heap tackled him. The Ravens' defense protected the lead as Curtis Martin was stopped twice, and Brooks Bollinger was sacked by Ray Lewis, forcing the Jets to settle for a field goal. The Ravens' offense responded with a 13-play, 71-yard drive, highlighted by Anthony Wright's 2-yard sneak on fourth-and-1, and capped by Jamal Lewis' 1-yard run for a 13-3 lead late in the third quarter. The Jets failed to score inside the Ravens' 40 the remainder of the game. Wright was 15 of 21 for 144 yards, with 1 interception. Bollinger, making his first NFL start, was 14 of 28 for 149 yards.

N.Y. Jets	0	0	3	0 —	3
Baltimore	3	3	7	0 —	13

Balt	—	FG Stover 42
Balt	—	FG Stover 25
NYJ	—	FG Nugent 21
Balt	—	J. Lewis 1 run (Stover kick)

CINCINNATI 16, HOUSTON 10—at Paul Brown Stadium, attendance 65,714. Shayne Graham kicked 3 field goals and the Bengals' defense recorded 7 sacks to improve their record to 4-0 for the first time since 1988, when they made their last Super Bowl appearance. The Bengals had scoring drives of 84 and 85 yards in the first half, but Houston responded with a 90-yard drive to tie the game with 7:40 left in the third quarter. Graham missed a 42-yard field goal late in the third quarter, but made a 27-yard field goal to give Cincinnati a 13-10 lead with 5:04 left in the game. Six plays later, Justin Smith hit David Carr as he was throwing and forced him to fumble. John Thornton recovered the ball and Graham made a 46-yard field goal with 1:10 to play. Brian Simmons sacked Carr on his own 35 as time expired. Carson Palmer was 25 of 34 for 276 yards and 1 touchdown. T.J. Houshmandzadeh had 8 receptions for 105 yards. Carr was 17 of 26 for 174 yards and 1 touchdown.

Houston	0	3	7	0 —	10
Cincinnati	3	7	0	6 —	16

Cin	—	FG Graham 24
Hou	—	FG K. Brown 28
Cin	—	J. Johnson 1 pass from Palmer (Graham kick)
Hou	—	Norris 4 pass from Carr (K. Brown kick)
Cin	—	FG Graham 27
Cin	—	FG Graham 46

DENVER 20, JACKSONVILLE 7—at ALLTEL Stadium, attendance 66,045. The Broncos' defense forced 4 turnovers, including 3 in the fourth quarter, and held the Jaguars to a franchise-low 12 rushing yards. Denver strung together a 17-play, 80-yard drive, including a 1-yard run on fourth-and-1 by Mike Anderson, to set up Jake Plummer's 2-yard touchdown pass to former tight end and now tackle-eligible Dwayne Carswell. Following a Jaguars' punt, Carswell capped an

8-play, 64-yard drive with a 1-yard touchdown catch. Jimmy Smith caught a 45-yard touchdown pass to cap the Jaguars' opening drive of the second half and had the ball early in the fourth quarter, but Domonique Foxworth intercepted a pass to set up Jason Elam's 33-yard field goal and a 17-7 lead. Nick Ferguson intercepted Byron Leftwich's pass on the ensuing possession to set up another field goal with 2:42 to play. Plummer was 19 of 26 for 136 yards and 2 touchdowns. Anderson had 23 carries for 115 yards. Leftwich was 20 of 34 for 240 yards and 1 touchdown, with 2 interceptions. Smith had 5 catches for 109 yards.

Denver	0	14	0	6	—	20
Jacksonville	0	0	7	0	—	7
Den	—	Carswell 2 pass from Plummer (Elam kick)				
Den	—	Carswell 1 pass from Plummer (Elam kick)				
Jax	—	J. Smith 45 pass from Leftwich (Scobee kick)				
Den	—	FG Elam 33				
Den	—	FG Elam 42				

PHILADELPHIA 37, KANSAS CITY 31—at Arrowhead Stadium, attendance 78,742. The Eagles' defense forced 4 turnovers which led to 24 points as the Eagles scored 31 unanswered points to rally from a 17-point deficit and shock the Chiefs. Trailing 17-0, Sheldon Brown intercepted a Trent Green pass and returned it 40 yards for a touchdown. Dante Hall responded by returning the ensuing kickoff 96 yards for a touchdown and 24-6 lead with 4:27 left in the half. The Chiefs defense forced a punt and made the ball, but Larry Johnson fumbled and Sam Rayburn recovered at midfield with 2:40 left in the half. The Eagles responded by scoring on six of their next seven possessions, the last two scores set up by turnovers, to take a 37-24 lead with 3:22 to play. The Chiefs drove 75 yards and pulled within 37-31 on Hall's 15-yard touchdown catch with 1:24 remaining. Reno Mahe recovered the onside kick to clinch the victory. Donovan McNabb was 33 of 48 for 369 yards and 3 touchdowns, with 1 interception. Terrell Owens had 11 receptions for 171 yards. Green was 19 of 30 for 221 yards and 2 touchdowns, with 2 interceptions. Eddie Kennison had 7 catches for 109 yards.

Philadelphia	0	13	11	13	—	37
Kansas City	10	14	0	7	—	31
KC	—	Holmes 3 run (Tynes kick)				
KC	—	FG Tynes 38				
KC	—	Kennison 8 pass from Green (Tynes kick)				
Phil	—	Brown 40 interception return (pass failed)				
KC	—	Hall 96 kickoff return (Tynes kick)				
Phil	—	Owens 7 pass from McNabb (France kick)				
Phil	—	FG France 44				
Phil	—	Bartrum 3 pass from McNabb (Westbrook pass from McNabb)				
Phil	—	FG France 37				
Phil	—	L. Smith 1 pass from McNabb (France kick)				
Phil	—	FG France 26				
KC	—	Hall 15 pass from Green (Tynes kick)				

SAN DIEGO 41, NEW ENGLAND 17—at Gillette Stadium, attendance 68,756. LaDainian Tomlinson had 2 touchdown runs as the Chargers snapped the Patriots' 21-game home winning streak. Tomlinson's 8-yard touchdown run with 2:47 left in the first half extended his NFL record to 16 consecutive games with a rushing touchdown and gave the Chargers a 17-14 lead. With the score tied at the half, the Chargers' defense forced punts on the first three posses-

sions of the second half and the offense responded with drives of 80, 75, and 72 yards, consuming nearly 18 minutes of clock, to take a 34-17 lead with 4:44 to play. The key play of the three drives was Drew Brees' 28-yard touchdown pass to Reche Caldwell on third-and-8 late in the third quarter that gave San Diego a 31-17 lead. Leading 34-17, Donnie Edwards intercepted a pass, then lateraled to Clinton Hart who returned the ball 40 yards for a touchdown and 41-17 lead with 4:30 remaining. Brees was 19 of 24 for 248 yards and 2 touchdowns. Antonio Gates had 6 receptions for 108 yards. Tomlinson had 25 carries for 134 yards. Brady was 19 of 32 for 224 yards and 1 touchdown, with 1 interception.

San Diego	3	14	14	10	—	41
New England	7	10	0	0	—	17
SD	—	FG Kaeding 42				
NE	—	Dillon 1 run (Vinatieri kick)				
SD	—	McCardell 11 pass from Brees (Kaeding kick)				
NE	—	Dwight 30 pass from Brady (Vinatieri kick)				
SD	—	Tomlinson 8 run (Kaeding kick)				
NE	—	FG Vinatieri 24				
SD	—	Tomlinson 1 run (Kaeding kick)				
SD	—	Caldwell 28 pass from Brees (Kaeding kick)				
SD	—	FG Kaeding 21				
SD	—	Hart 40 interception return (Kaeding kick)				

NEW ORLEANS 19, BUFFALO 7—at Alamodome, attendance 58,688. Deuce McAllister rushed for 130 yards and John Carney kicked 4 field goals for the Saints. The game was the first of three scheduled to be played in San Antonio because of Hurricane Katrina. The Bills marched downfield on their opening drive, capped by Willis McGahee's 1-yard run, to take a 7-0 lead. Buffalo only drove inside the Saints' 30 one time the rest of the day, when Rian Lindell missed a 45-yard field goal. The Saints scored on three consecutive possessions in the second quarter, the second set up by Jason Craft's interception, and capped by Carney's 40-yard field goal just before halftime for a 13-7 lead. Carney added 2 field goals in the final five minutes to put the game out of reach. Aaron Brooks was 15 of 24 for 172 yards. McAllister had 27 carries for 130 yards. Donte' Stallworth had 8 catches for 129 yards. J.P. Losman was 7 of 15 for 75 yards, with 1 interception before being replaced in the fourth quarter by Kelly Holcomb, who was 3 of 6 for 28 yards.

Buffalo	7	0	0	0	—	7
New Orleans	0	13	0	6	—	19
Buff	—	McGahee 1 run (Lindell kick)				
NO	—	FG Carney 23				
NO	—	Brooks 4 run (Carney kick)				
NO	—	FG Carney 40				
NO	—	FG Carney 20				
NO	—	FG Carney 37				

N.Y. GIANTS 44, ST. LOUIS 24—at Giants Stadium, attendance 78,453. Eli Manning passed for 296 yards and 4 touchdowns, and Plaxico Burress had 10 catches for 204 yards, as the Giants overwhelmed the Rams. The Rams outgained the Giants 476-456 yards, but committed 5 turnovers which resulted in 20 points. The Giants scored on their first five possessions, with only the last one set up by a turnover, to take a 27-7 lead with 9:25 left in the first half. The Rams rallied to score twice on their next two possessions, and had a chance to pull within seven points but Jeff Wilkins' 48-yard field-goal attempt sailed wide left just before halftime. The Rams opened the second half by driving to the Giants' 6, but Shaun McDonald mishandled Steven Jackson's reverse lateral and Fred Robbins recovered. The Giants drove 87 yards on the ensuing possession, capped by Jeremy Shockey's

31-yard touchdown catch for a 34-17 lead with 5:19 left in the third quarter. Manning was 19 of 35 for 296 yards and 4 touchdowns. Burress had 10 catches for 204 yards, and Tiki Barber had 24 carries for 128 yards. Marc Bulger was 40 of 62 for 442 yards and 2 touchdowns, with 3 interceptions. McDonald had 9 receptions for 121 yards.

St. Louis	7	10	0	7	—	24
N.Y. Giants	17	10	7	10	—	44
NYG	—	Burress 31 pass from Manning (Feely kick)				
NYG	—	FG Feely 38				
StL	—	Jackson 13 pass from Bulger (Wilkins kick)				
NYG	—	Toomer 1 pass from Manning (Feely kick)				
NYG	—	Burress 17 pass from Manning (Feely kick)				
NYG	—	FG Feely 32				
StL	—	Jackson 1 run (Wilkins kick)				
StL	—	FG Wilkins 37				
NYG	—	Shockey 31 pass from Manning (Feely kick)				
NYG	—	FG Feely 23				
StL	—	Holt 22 pass from Bulger (Wilkins kick)				
NYG	—	Barber 16 run (Feely kick)				

OAKLAND 19, DALLAS 13—at McAfee Coliseum, attendance 62,400. Drew Bledsoe's fourth-down pass for Terry Glenn was incomplete at the goal line with 1:45 remaining as Oakland broke into the win column. The Raiders scored with their first two possessions of the game, and drove 75 yards to kick a field goal to begin the second half to take a 13-3 lead. Trailing 16-6, Bledsoe threw a 63-yard touchdown pass to Patrick Crayton with 8:51 to play. The Raiders responded with a 10-play drive for Sebastian Janikowski's fourth field goal with 4:29 to play. Glenn caught a 57-yard pass on third-and-13, and moments later the Cowboys' drive to the Raiders' 3. Faced with second-and-2, Julius Jones was dropped for a 2-yard loss, and Bledsoe's final two passes fell incomplete. Kerry Collins was 13 of 23 for 218 yards. Randy Moss had 4 receptions for 123 yards, and Jordan rushed 26 times for 126 yards. Bledsoe was 11 of 26 for 212 yards and 1 touchdown, with 1 interception.

Dallas	0	3	3	7	—	13
Oakland	10	0	3	6	—	19
Oak	—	FG Janikowski 30				
Oak	—	Jordan 2 run (Janikowski kick)				
Dall	—	FG Cortez 29				
Oak	—	FG Janikowski 23				
Dall	—	FG Cortez 30				
Oak	—	FG Janikowski 49				
Dall	—	Crayton 63 pass from Bledsoe (Cortez kick)				
Oak	—	FG Janikowski 43				

TAMPA BAY 17, DETROIT 13—at Raymond James Stadium, attendance 64,994. Brian Griese passed for 2 touchdowns and the Lions twice had receivers barely out of the end zone to deny a potential last-minute touchdown, giving the Buccaneers their first 4-0 start since 1997. In the second quarter, Teddy Lehman's 17-yard interception return set up Detroit's first touchdown. Griese responded with a swing pass to Michael Pittman that turned into a 41-yard touchdown for a 10-10 score with 1:12 left in the half. Three plays into the second half, Joey Galloway caught a long pass for an 80-yard touchdown. Terrence Holt's interception in the fourth quarter set up Jason Hanson's 23-yard field goal to pull within 17-13 with 7:29 to play. The Lions forced a punt with 5:14 to play. Joey Harrington connected with Kevin Johnson on an 8-yard pass on fourth-and-5 to keep alive the drive, and his 12-yard pass on the right corner of the end zone to Marcus Pollard appeared to give the Lions the lead, but replay ruled Pollard did not get both knees in bounds. On the next play, Mike Williams caught a pass on the left side of the end zone, but barely came down out of bounds. Harrington's fourth-down pass sailed incomplete as time expired. Griese was 22 of 39 for 302 yards and 2 touchdowns, with 3 interceptions. Galloway had 7 catches for 166 yards. Harrington was 15 of 27 for 137 yards.

| Detroit | 0 | 10 | 0 | 3 | — | 13 |
| Tampa Bay | 3 | 7 | 7 | 0 | — | 17 |

TB	—	FG Bryant 43
Det	—	FG Hanson 44
Det	—	K. Jones 8 run (Hanson kick)
TB	—	Pittman 41 pass from Griese (Bryant kick)
TB	—	Galloway 80 pass from Griese (Bryant kick)
Det	—	FG Hanson 23

INDIANAPOLIS 31, TENNESSEE 10—at The Coliseum, attendance 69,149. Peyton Manning passed for 4 touchdowns, 2 to Marvin Harrison, as the Colts improved their record to 4-0. The Colts nearly became just the second team since 1945 to hold their first four opponents to single digits, but the Titans scored on Bo Scaife's 6-yard touchdown catch with 4:31 to play. Harrison finished the game with 101 touchdown receptions, third all time to Jerry Rice (197) and Cris Carter (130). The Colts led 17-3 at halftime, drove 60 yards for a touchdown with their first possession of the second half, and following a missed 38-yard field goal the Colts drove 72 yards for another touchdown for a 31-3 lead with 13:09 to play. Manning was 20 of 27 for 264 yards and 4 touchdowns. Harrison had 9 catches for 109 yards. Steve McNair was 28 of 37 for 220 yards and 1 touchdown, with 1 interception.

| Indianapolis | 7 | 10 | 7 | 7 | — | 31 |
| Tennessee | 3 | 0 | 0 | 7 | — | 10 |

Ind	—	Wayne 25 pass from Manning (Vanderjagt kick)
Tenn	—	FG Bironas 34
Ind	—	FG Vanderjagt 20
Ind	—	Harrison 11 pass from Manning (Vanderjagt kick)
Ind	—	James 8 pass from Manning (Vanderjagt kick)
Ind	—	Harrison 24 pass from Manning (Vanderjagt kick)
Tenn	—	Scaife 6 pass from McNair (Bironas kick)

WASHINGTON 20, SEATTLE 17 (OT)—at FedExField, attendance 90,215. Nick Novak made a 39-yard field goal in overtime as the Redskins survived a Josh Brown missed field goal at the end of regulation to improve to 3-0 for the first time since 1991. Novak, playing for the injured John Hall, had his first NFL field-goal attempt blocked to conclude the opening drive of the game. The Redskins' 16-play, 85-yard second-quarter drive resulted in a touchdown and 7-3 halftime lead. Brown missed a 47-yard field-goal attempt to begin the second half, and the Redskins' responded with Mark Brunell's second touchdown for a 14-3 lead. Trailing 17-10 with 7:42 remaining, Matt Hasselbeck engineered a 14-play, 91-yard drive, capped by Darrell Jackson's 6-yard touchdown catch with 1:23 left to tie the game. Two plays later, Kelly Herndon intercepted a pass at the Redskins' 33 with 49 seconds left. Shaun Alexander gained a total of 4 yards on two plays to set up Brown's field-goal attempt, which hit the left upright as regulation ended. In overtime, the Redskins won the toss and converted 3 third-down situations, 2 on passes to Santana Moss and the other on a 18-yard scramble by Brunell, to set up Novak's winning kick. Brunell was 20 of 36 for 226 yards and 2 touchdowns, with 1 interception. Hasselbeck was 26 of 38 for 242 yards and 1 touchdown. Bobby Engram had 9

catches for 106 yards.

| Seattle | 3 | 0 | 7 | 7 | 0 | — | 17 |
| Washington | 0 | 7 | 10 | 0 | 3 | — | 20 |

Sea	—	FG J. Brown 53
Wash	—	Royal 1 pass from Brunell (Novak kick)
Wash	—	Sellers 4 pass from Brunell (Novak kick)
Sea	—	Alexander 3 run (J. Brown kick)
Wash	—	FG Novak 41
Sea	—	Jackson 6 pass from Hasselbeck (J. Brown kick)
Wash	—	FG Novak 39

SUNDAY NIGHT, OCTOBER 2
ARIZONA 31, SAN FRANCISCO 14—at Azteca Stadium, attendance 103,467. In the first regular-season game played outside the United States, Josh McCown passed for a career-high 385 yards and Neil Rackers kicked 6 field goals. The game was played in Mexico City before the largest regular-season crowd in NFL history. The Cardinals outgained the 49ers 463-168 total yards, maintained possession for 37:48-22:12, and had 24 first downs and allowed just 8. Arizona fumbled on two of their first three possessions, both of which resulted in touchdowns, to give San Francisco a 14-0 lead. The 49ers' failed to cross the Cardinals' 30 the entire game, but still led 14-12 at halftime. In the second half, Rackers made field goals to convert the Cardinals' first three possessions of the half, and Anquan Boldin's 27-yard touchdown catch with 8:29 to play gave the Cardinals a 28-14 lead. McCown was 32 of 46 for 385 yards and 2 touchdowns. Boldin had 8 catches for 116 yards, and Larry Fitzgerald had 7 receptions for 102 yards. Tim Rattay was 11 of 21 for 126 yards, with 1 interception, and Alex Smith entered in the fourth quarter and was 6 of 10 for 34 yards. Brandon Lloyd had 7 catches for 102 yards.

| San Francisco | 14 | 0 | 0 | 0 | — | 14 |
| Arizona | 0 | 12 | 6 | 13 | — | 31 |

SF	—	D. Smith fumble recovery in end zone (Nedney kick)
SF	—	D. Johnson 78 fumble return (Nedney kick)
Ariz	—	FG Rackers 40
Ariz	—	FG Rackers 45
Ariz	—	Fitzgerald 17 pass from McCown (pass failed)
Ariz	—	FG Rackers 48
Ariz	—	FG Rackers 23
Ariz	—	FG Rackers 43
Ariz	—	Boldin 27 pass from McCown (Rackers kick)
Ariz	—	FG Rackers 24

MONDAY NIGHT, OCTOBER 3
CAROLINA 32, GREEN BAY 29—at Bank of America Stadium, attendance 73,657. Jake Delhomme passed for 2 touchdowns but the Panthers had to hold off a late rally to defeat the Packers. The Panthers scored on four of their first five possessions, capped by Stephen Davis' 11-yard touchdown run that was set up by Ken Lucas' interception, to take a 23-7 lead with 3:19 left in the first half. Davis scored a second touchdown, but the Panthers missed a 2-point conversion attempt, to take a 32-13 lead with 14:44 to play. The Panthers then forced a punt, but three plays later Kabeer Gbaja-Biamila forced Delhomme to fumble. Cullen Jenkins recovered the ball, and Brett Favre fired a 16-yard touchdown pass to Donald Lee on the next play. Favre's 2-point conversion pass to David Martin trimmed the deficit to 32-21 with 11:49 to play. The Packers' defense forced a punt, and Favre engineered a 13-play, 90-yard drive capped by Antonio Chatman's 4-yard scoring grab with 3:07 left. Robert Ferguson's 2-point conversion catch cut the deficit to 32-29, and the Packers' defense forced a three-and-out

and Favre took over at the Panthers' 37 with 1:58 to play. A 15-yard strike to Donald Driver opened the drive, but on fourth-and-3 from the Panthers' 41 Favre's pass intended for Driver fell incomplete with 1:03 to play. Delhomme was 17 of 24 for 206 yards and 2 touchdowns. Favre was 28 of 47 for 303 yards and 4 touchdowns, with 1 interception.

| Green Bay | 7 | 0 | 6 | 16 | — | 29 |
| Carolina | 7 | 16 | 3 | 6 | — | 32 |

Car	—	Mangum 2 pass from Delhomme (Kasay kick)
GB	—	Martin 21 pass from Favre (Longwell kick)
Car	—	FG Kasay 32
Car	—	Gaines 19 pass from Delhomme (kick blocked)
Car	—	S. Davis 11 run (Kasay kick)
Car	—	FG Kasay 38
GB	—	Driver 26 pass from Favre (pass failed)
Car	—	S. Davis 1 run (pass failed)
GB	—	D. Lee 16 pass from Favre (Martin pass from Favre)
GB	—	Chatman 4 pass from Favre (Ferguson pass from Favre)

FIFTH WEEK SUMMARIES
American Football Conference

East Division	W	L	T	Pct.	Pts.	OP
New England	3	2	0	.600	118	136
Miami	2	2	0	.500	82	71
Buffalo	2	3	0	.400	68	83
N.Y. Jets	2	3	0	.400	61	85
North Division	**W**	**L**	**T**	**Pct.**	**Pts.**	**OP**
Cincinnati	4	1	0	.800	124	61
Pittsburgh	3	1	0	.750	105	59
Cleveland	2	2	0	.500	65	74
Baltimore	1	3	0	.250	47	87
South Division	**W**	**L**	**T**	**Pct.**	**Pts.**	**OP**
Indianapolis	5	0	0	1.000	106	29
Jacksonville	3	2	0	.600	85	84
Tennessee	2	3	0	.400	103	126
Houston	0	4	0	.000	44	99
West Division	**W**	**L**	**T**	**Pct.**	**Pts.**	**OP**
Denver	4	1	0	.800	101	87
Kansas City	2	2	0	.500	91	91
San Diego	2	3	0	.400	149	112
Oakland	1	3	0	.250	76	89

National Football Conference

East Division	W	L	T	Pct.	Pts.	OP
N.Y. Giants	3	1	0	.750	136	98
Washington	3	1	0	.750	62	58
Dallas	3	2	0	.600	121	98
Philadelphia	3	2	0	.600	122	101
North Division	**W**	**L**	**T**	**Pct.**	**Pts.**	**OP**
Detroit	2	2	0	.500	71	75
Chicago	1	3	0	.250	62	59
Minnesota	1	3	0	.250	64	107
Green Bay	1	4	0	.200	124	95
South Division	**W**	**L**	**T**	**Pct.**	**Pts.**	**OP**
Tampa Bay	4	1	0	.800	89	59
Atlanta	3	2	0	.600	114	88
Carolina	3	2	0	.600	127	116
New Orleans	2	3	0	.400	71	139
West Division	**W**	**L**	**T**	**Pct.**	**Pts.**	**OP**
Seattle	3	2	0	.600	126	107
St. Louis	2	3	0	.400	128	148
Arizona	1	4	0	.200	94	134
San Francisco	1	4	0	.200	79	160

SUNDAY, OCTOBER 9
CAROLINA 24, ARIZONA 20—at Sun Devil Stadium, attendance 38,809. Steve Smith caught 2 touchdown passes as the Panthers rallied to defeat the Cardinals. Tied 10-10 in the second quarter, the Cardinals drove 90 yards in six plays, capped by Anquan Boldin's catch and tremendous open field running for a 20-yard touchdown. Trailing 20-10 late in the third quar-

ter, Thomas Davis forced Boldin to fumble. Ken Lucas recovered the ball and ran 20 yards to the 5-yard line to set up Stephen Davis' 1-yard run with 14:57 to play. The Panthers' defense forced a punt, and the offense drove 94 yards, capped by Jake Delhomme's 4-yard touchdown pass to Smith, to take a 24-20 lead with 6:54 to play. On fourth-and-6 from the Panthers' 33 with 2:04 to play, Marlon McCree intercepted Josh McCown's pass. The Cardinals had one last chance, but McCown was tackled a yard shy of a first down on a fourth-and-10 scramble with 55 seconds left. Delhomme was 18 of 29 for 243 yards and 2 touchdowns,with 1 interception. Smith had 8 catches for 119 yards. McCown was 29 of 46 for 398 yards and 2 touchdowns, with 3 interceptions. Boldin had 10 catches for 162 yards and Larry Fitzgerald added 9 receptions for 136 yards.

Carolina	3	7	0	14	—	24
Arizona	0	17	3	0	—	20
Car	—	FG Kasay 46				
Ariz	—	Fitzgerald 26 pass from McCown (Rackers kick)				
Car	—	S. Smith 65 pass from Delhomme (Kasay kick)				
Ariz	—	FG Rackers 39				
Ariz	—	Boldin 20 pass from McCown (Rackers kick)				
Ariz	—	FG Rackers 49				
Car	—	S. Davis 1 run (Kasay kick)				
Car	—	S. Smith 4 pass from Delhomme (Kasay kick)				

NEW ENGLAND 31, ATLANTA 28—at Georgia Dome, attendance 71,079. Adam Vinatieri kicked a 29-yard field goal with 17 seconds remaining as the Patriots held off the Falcons. Late in the first quarter, Daniel Graham caught a screen pass and broke numerous tackles en route to a 45-yard touchdown and 14-0 lead. The Falcons, led by Matt Schaub, playing in place of Michael Vick, who had a knee injury, scored on their next three possessions to pull within 14-13 at halftime. Tom Brady needed just two plays to cover 78 yards to begin the second half, capped by Ben Watson's 33-yard scoring catch, for a 21-13 lead. Trailing 28-13, Demorrio Williams intercepted a pass near midfield late in the third quarter to set up Schaub's 25-yard touchdown pass to Alge Crumpler. Dez White's 14-yard touchdown catch, and Brian Finneran's two-point conversion catch, tied the game with 3:52 to play. Brady methodically led the Patriots down the field, highlighted by Brady's third-and-4 pass to Deion Branch for 9 yards to the Falcons' 29, to set up Vinatieri's winning kick. Brady was 22 of 27 for 350 yards and 3 touchdowns, with 1 interception. Deion Branch had 8 receptions for 107 yards, and Graham added 5 catches for 119 yards. Corey Dillon carried 23 times for 106 yards. Schaub was 18 of 34 for 298 yards and 3 touchdowns. Finneran had 5 catches for 103 yards.

New England	14	0	14	3	—	31
Atlanta	0	13	0	15	—	28
NE	—	Pass 6 run (Vinatieri kick)				
NE	—	Graham 45 pass from Brady (Vinatieri kick)				
Atl	—	Griffith 2 pass from Schaub (Peterson kick)				
Atl	—	FG Peterson 33				
Atl	—	FG Koenen 58				
NE	—	Watson 33 pass from Brady (Vinatieri kick)				
NE	—	B. Johnson 55 pass from Brady (Vinatieri kick)				
Atl	—	Crumpler 25 pass from Schaub (Peterson kick)				
Atl	—	D. White 14 pass from Schaub (Finneran pass from Schaub)				
NE	—	FG Vinatieri 29				

BUFFALO 20, MIAMI 14—at Ralph Wilson Stadium, attendance 72,160. The Bills' defense forced 5 turnovers to hold off the Dolphins. The Bills scored on their first three possessions, with drives of eight, 11, and 12 plays, to take a 17-0 lead with 8:08 left in the first half. Buffalo led 17-7 and had the ball with 9:39 left when Kelly Holcomb fumbled and Jeff Zgonina recovered at the Bills' 35. Three plays later, Randy McMichael caught a 30-yard touchdown to pull within 17-14. The Bills responded with Rian Lindell's 47-yard field goal with 4:35 to play. The Dolphins drove to the Bills' 25, but Ronnie Brown fumbled and Troy Vincent recovered at the Bills' 18 with 1:37 to play. Miami got the ball back and reached their own 46, but Ryan Denney sacked Gus Frerotte on the final play. Holcomb was 20 of 26 for 169 yards and 1 touchdown. Frerotte was 21 of 33 for 226 yards and 2 touchdowns, with 3 interceptions.

Miami	0	0	7	7	—	14
Buffalo	10	7	0	3	—	20
Buff	—	McGahee 1 run (Lindell kick)				
Buff	—	FG Lindell 24				
Buff	—	Moulds 2 pass from Holcomb (Lindell kick)				
Mia	—	Heller 1 pass from Frerotte (Mare kick)				
Mia	—	McMichael 30 pass from Frerotte (Mare kick)				
Buff	—	FG Lindell 47				

CLEVELAND 20, CHICAGO 10—at Cleveland Browns Stadium, attendance 73,079. Trent Dilfer threw 2 touchdown passes to Antonio Bryant 38 seconds apart in the waning moments as the Browns rallied to defeat the Bears. Dilfer's first touchdown pass to Bryant, with 3:02 left, gave the Browns a 13-10 lead. Three plays later Chris Crocker sacked Kyle Orton and forced him to fumble. Crocker recovered the ball, and Bryant caught his second touchdown two plays later to give the Browns a 20-10 lead with 2:24 to play. Dilfer was 23 of 34 for 218 yards and 2 touchdowns, with 2 interceptions. Orton was 16 of 26 for 117 yards and 1 touchdown. Thomas Jones rushed 24 times for 137 yards.

Chicago	0	3	7	0	—	10
Cleveland	3	3	0	14	—	20
Cle	—	FG Dawson 19				
Chi	—	FG Gould 44				
Cle	—	FG Dawson 44				
Chi	—	M. Edwards 8 pass from Orton (Gould kick)				
Cle	—	Bryant 33 pass from Dilfer (Dawson kick)				
Cle	—	Bryant 28 pass from Dilfer (Dawson kick)				

DALLAS 33, PHILADELPHIA 10—at Texas Stadium, attendance 63,199. Drew Bledsoe passed for 3 touchdowns as the Cowboys jumped to a 30-3 lead to catch the Eagles in the NFC East. The Cowboys had advantages in yards (456-129), first downs (28-6), and time of possession (40:43-19:17). The Cowboys scored on six of their first seven possessions, being stopped on the Eagles' 1 in their lone non-scoring drive, to jump to a 30-3 lead with 11:39 left in the third quarter. The Eagles drove 71 yards for a field goal in the second quarter, but gained just 58 yards on their other ten possessions. Bledsoe was 24 of 35 for 289 yards and 3 touchdowns. Terry Glenn had 7 receptions for 118 yards. Donovan McNabb was 13 of 26 for 131 yards.

Philadelphia	0	3	0	7	—	10
Dallas	17	10	3	3	—	33
Dall	—	Glenn 15 pass from Bledsoe (Cortez kick)				
Dall	—	Glenn 38 pass from Bledsoe (Cortez kick)				
Dall	—	FG Cortez 28				

Phil	—	FG France 23
Dall	—	Polite 12 pass from Bledsoe (Cortez kick)
Dall	—	FG Cortez 33
Dall	—	FG Cortez 37
Phil	—	S. Brown 80 fumble return (France kick)
Dall	—	FG Cortez 45

DENVER 21, WASHINGTON 19—at INVESCO Field at Mile High, attendance 75,880. Tatum Bell rushed for 2 touchdowns as the Broncos held off the Redskins. The Redskins dominated the numbers, with a 28-11 first-down advantage and gained almost 200 more yards (447-257). The Broncos led 14-10 in the third quarter when Trevor Pryce blocked Nick Novak's 38-yard field-goal attempt. Three plays later, Bell flew around right end on third-and-5 and scored on a 55-yard run to give the Broncos a 21-10 lead. Charlie Clemons blocked Todd Sauerbrun's punt in the fourth quarter to set up Novak's 36-yard field goal with 6:25 to play. The Redskins' defense forced a punt and Mark Brunell's 11-yard touchdown pass to Chris Cooley cut the deficit to 21-19 with 1:09 to play. Brunell's two-point conversion pass attempt to David Patten fell incomplete, and Ashley Lelie recovered the ensuing onside kick. Jake Plummer was 10 of 25 for 92 yards and 1 touchdown. Bell had 12 carries for 127 yards. Brunell was 30 of 53 for 322 yards and 2 touchdowns. Clinton Portis rushed 20 times for 103 yards and Santana Moss had 8 catches for 116 yards.

Washington	7	3	0	9	—	19
Denver	7	7	7	0	—	21
Den	—	Bell 34 run (Elam kick)				
Wash	—	Sellers 2 pass from Brunell (Novak kick)				
Den	—	Lelie 5 pass from Plummer (Elam kick)				
Wash	—	FG Novak 34				
Den	—	Bell 55 run (Elam kick)				
Wash	—	FG Novak 36				
Wash	—	Cooley 11 pass from Brunell (pass failed)				

DETROIT 35, BALTIMORE 17—at Ford Field, attendance 61,201. Kevin Jones scored 2 touchdowns as the Ravens committed 21 penalties in defeat. Leading 14-10 at halftime, the Lions drove 73 yards in 18 plays, capped by Artose Pinner's 1-yard run to take a 21-10 lead. The Lions' defense forced a punt and R.W. McQuarters' 49-yard return set up Casey FitzSimmons' 2-yard touchdown catch with 14:55 to play. Todd Heap's 6-yard touchdown catch cut the deficit to 28-17 with 8:59 to play, but Shawn Bryson outran the Ravens' defense and scored on a 77-yard run with 7:05 remaining. Joey Harrington was 10 of 23 for 97 yards and 1 touchdown, with 2 interceptions. Anthony Wright was 20 of 37 for 230 yards and 2 touchdowns, with 2 interceptions.

Baltimore	0	10	0	7	—	17
Detroit	14	0	7	14	—	35
Det	—	K. Jones 14 run (Hanson kick)				
Det	—	K. Jones 1 run (Hanson kick)				
Balt	—	J. Lewis 15 pass from Wright (Stover kick)				
Balt	—	FG Stover 46				
Det	—	Pinner 1 run (Hanson kick)				
Det	—	Fitzsimmons 2 pass from Harrington (Hanson kick)				
Balt	—	Heap 6 pass from Wright (Stover kick)				
Det	—	Bryson 77 run (Hanson kick)				

GREEN BAY 52, NEW ORLEANS 3—at Lambeau Field, attendance 70,500. Brett Favre passed for 3 touchdowns as the Packers scored 52 unanswered points for their first home victory. The Packers' defense forced 5 turnovers, the first of which was an interception returned 22 yards for a touchdown by Al Harris for a 14-3 lead. Harris intercepted another pass four plays later to set up the first of Najeh Davenport's 2 touchdown runs. Kenny Peterson recovered an Ernie Conwell fumble late in the first half to set up Favre's 1-yard touchdown pass to David Martin for a 35-3 lead with 24 seconds left in the half. Favre was 19 of 27 for 215 yards and 3 touchdowns. Aaron Brooks was 9 of 22 for 146 yards, with 2 interceptions, and Todd Bouman was 5 of 13 for 31 yards, with 1 interception.

New Orleans	3	0	0	0	—	3
Green Bay	14	21	10	7	—	52

NO	—	FG Carney 33
GB	—	Davenport 1 run (Longwell kick)
GB	—	Harris 22 interception return (Longwell kick)
GB	—	Davenport 4 run (Longwell kick)
GB	—	Ferguson 25 pass from Favre (Longwell kick)
GB	—	Martin 1 pass from Favre (Longwell kick)
GB	—	D. Lee 26 pass from Favre (Longwell kick)
GB	—	FG Longwell 26
GB	—	Barnett 95 interception return (Longwell kick)

TENNESSEE 34, HOUSTON 20—at Reliant Stadium, attendance 70,430. Steve McNair passed for 2 touchdowns and ran for another as the Titans pulled away from Houston. The Titans led 10-9 in the third quarter when Jarrod Payton scored his first NFL touchdown to cap a 76-yard drive and give the Titans a 17-9 lead. The Titans scored on their next three possessions as well, highlighted by Adam Jones' 71-yard kickoff return to set up Steve McNair's 1-yard run for a 34-12 lead with 7:45 to play. McNair was 22 of 31 for 220 yards and 2 touchdowns. David Carr was 18 of 27 for 131 yards and 1 touchdown, with 1 interception. Domanick Davis had 19 carries for 130 yards.

Tennessee	7	3	14	10	—	34
Houston	0	6	3	11	—	20

Tenn	—	Troupe 10 pass from McNair (Bironas kick)
Hou	—	FG K. Brown 32
Hou	—	FG K. Brown 38
Tenn	—	FG Bironas 52
Hou	—	FG K. Brown 43
Tenn	—	Payton 5 run (Bironas kick)
Tenn	—	Bennett 16 pass from McNair (Bironas kick)
Tenn	—	FG Bironas 49
Hou	—	FG K. Brown 47
Tenn	—	McNair 1 run (Bironas kick)
Hou	—	Bradford 3 pass from Carr (Bradford pass from Carr)

N.Y. JETS 14, TAMPA BAY 12—at The Meadowlands, attendance 77,852. Curtis Martin rushed for 2 touchdowns as the Jets held off the Buccaneers. Trailing 6-0 in the second quarter, Ty Law intercepted a pass and returned it 43 yards to the Buccaneers' 8 to set up Martin's first touchdown. Martin capped the opening drive of the second half by scoring on fourth-and-goal from the Buccaneers' 1 for a 14-9 lead. Ronde Barber's interception led to Bryant's fourth field goal to pull within 14-12 with 4:00 to play. On their final drive, the Buccaneers reached their own 40, but Joey Galloway caught a pass over the middle and was tackled at the Jets' 34 as time expired. Vinny Testaverde was 13 of 19 for 163 yards, with 1 interception. Brian Griese was 27 of 42 for 226 yards, with 1 interception.

Tampa Bay	3	6	0	3	—	12
N.Y. Jets	0	7	7	0	—	14

TB	—	FG Bryant 35
TB	—	FG Bryant 36
NYJ	—	Martin 2 run (Nugent kick)
TB	—	FG Bryant 43
NYJ	—	Martin 1 run (Nugent kick)
TB	—	FG Bryant 30

SEATTLE 37, ST. LOUIS 31—at Edward Jones Dome, attendance 65,707. Shaun Alexander scored 2 touchdowns and the Seahawks gained 433 yards to outlast the Rams. Marc Bulger's 26-yard touchdown pass to Torry Holt tied the game with 2:02 left in the half, but the Seahawks responded by driving 60 yards, capped by Josh Brown's 34-yard field goal as the half expired. In the third quarter, Brown kicked his second field goal, and three plays later Lofa Tatupu intercepted a pass to set up Alexander's 18-yard run to give Seattle a 34-21 lead. The Rams answered with a 12-play, 80-yard drive capped by Steven Jackson's 4-yard run. Brown's 28-yard field goal with 7:32 to play increased the lead to 37-28. The Rams cut the deficit to 37-31 and then forced a punt, but Shaun McDonald fumbled and Jean-Philippe Darche recovered the ball at 2:51 to play. Matt Hasselbeck was 27 of 38 for 316 yards and 2 touchdowns. Joe Jurevicius had 9 catches for 137 yards, and Alexander had 25 carries for 119 yards. Bulger was 24 of 40 for 336 yards and 2 touchdowns, with 1 interception. Holt had 8 catches for 126 yards.

Seattle	14	10	10	3	—	37
St. Louis	7	14	7	3	—	31

StL	—	C. Johnson 99 kickoff return (Wilkins kick)
Sea	—	Alexander 1 run (J. Brown kick)
Sea	—	Stevens 29 pass from Hasselbeck (J. Brown kick)
StL	—	Curtis 25 pass from Bulger (Wilkins kick)
Sea	—	Jurevicius 24 pass from Hasselbeck (J. Brown kick)
StL	—	Holt 26 pass from Bulger (Wilkins kick)
Sea	—	FG J. Brown 34
Sea	—	FG J. Brown 44
Sea	—	Alexander 18 run (J. Brown kick)
StL	—	Jackson 4 run (Wilkins kick)
Sea	—	FG J. Brown 28
StL	—	FG Wilkins 40

INDIANAPOLIS 28, SAN FRANCISCO 3—at Monster Park, attendance 68,084. The Colts' defense intercepted 4 passes and registered 5 sacks as Alex Smith lost his first NFL start. The Colts outgained the 49ers 365-177. Cato June's 24-yard interception return for a touchdown in the second quarter increased the lead to 14-0. The Colts attempted an onside kick to begin the second half, but Terry Jackson recovered to set up Joe Nedney's field goal. Bruce Thornton intercepted Peyton Manning's pass two plays later to give the 49ers the ball back, but June's second interception stopped the 49ers. Twelve plays later, Edgerrin James scored from the 4-yard line, and on the next drive Troy Walters scored on an 18-yard pass with 5:58 to play. Manning was 23 of 31 for 255 yards and 1 touchdown, with 2 interceptions. James had 21 carries for 105 yards. Smith was 9 of 23 for 74 yards, with 4 interceptions.

Indianapolis	7	7	0	13	—	28
San Francisco	0	0	3	0	—	3

Ind	—	Rhodes 6 run (Vanderjagt kick)
Ind	—	June 24 interception return (Vanderjagt kick)
SF	—	FG Nedney 30
Ind	—	James 4 run (Vanderjagt kick)
Ind	—	Walters 18 pass from Manning (Vanderjagt kick)

SUNDAY NIGHT, OCTOBER 9
JACKSONVILLE 23, CINCINNATI 20—at ALLTEL Stadium, attendance 66,137. Fred Taylor rushed for 132

yards and Byron Leftwich passed for 2 touchdowns to hand the Bengals their first defeat. The Jaguars scored on three of their first four possessions, the second set up by Derrick Wimbush's blocked punt, to take a 13-0 lead. Wimbush's 36-yard kickoff return to begin the second half led to Leftwich's 11-yard touchdown pass to Ernest Wilford for a 20-7 lead early in the third quarter. Rudi Johnson was stopped on fourth-and-1 from the Bengals' 39 early in the fourth quarter, and Josh Scobee kicked a 53-yard field goal with 9:45 to play to give the Jaguars a 23-13 lead. Carson Palmer connected on a 47-yard pass with Chris Henry and, two plays later, a 25-yard touchdown pass to Henry, to cut the deficit to 23-20 with 5:16 remaining. The Bengals got the ball back and reached the Jaguars' 45 but Palmer fumbled in the pocket and Akin Ayodele recovered. Greg Jones gained 2 first downs in the final 1:16 to clinch the victory. Leftwich was 10 of 24 for 161 yards and 2 touchdowns. Palmer was 22 of 33 for 239 yards and 2 touchdowns.

Cincinnati	0	7	6	7	—	20
Jacksonville	10	3	7	3	—	23

Jax	—	Wrighster 26 pass from Leftwich (Scobee kick)
Jax	—	FG Scobee 32
Jax	—	FG Scobee 51
Cin	—	C. Johnson 14 pass from Palmer (Graham kick)
Jax	—	Wilford 11 pass from Leftwich (Scobee kick)
Cin	—	FG Graham 31
Cin	—	FG Graham 48
Jax	—	FG Scobee 53
Cin	—	Henry 25 pass from Palmer (Graham kick)

MONDAY NIGHT, OCTOBER 10
PITTSBURGH 24, SAN DIEGO 22—at Qualcomm Stadium, attendance 68,537. Jeff Reed kicked a 40-yard field goal with six seconds left as the Chargers blew a fourth-quarter lead for the third time in their three losses. James Harrison's interception at the Chargers' 41 led to Jerome Bettis' 1-yard run and a 14-0 Steelers' lead. Down 14-7 at halftime, the Chargers drove inside the Steelers' 25 on three consecutive possessions, but settled for 3 field goals, the last of which gave the Chargers a 16-14 lead with 11:41 left. Ben Roethlisberger needed just three plays, all passes, to retake the lead on Heath Miller's 16-yard scoring grab with 10:30 left. The Chargers answered, capped by LaDainian Tomlinson's 2-yard run, for a 22-21 lead with 4:42 to play. Tomlinson tried a 2-point conversion rush attempt, but failed. On the ensuing possession, Bettis converted two third-and-1 opportunities to set up Reed's winning kick. Roethlisberger was 17 of 26 for 225 yards and 1 touchdown. Brees was 20 of 35 for 219 yards and 1 touchdown, with 1 interception.

Pittsburgh	0	14	0	10	—	24
San Diego	0	7	6	9	—	22

Pitt	—	Roethlisberger 7 run (Reed kick)
Pitt	—	Bettis 1 run (Reed kick)
SD	—	Gates 11 pass from Brees (Kaeding kick)
SD	—	FG Kaeding 34
SD	—	FG Kaeding 32
SD	—	FG Kaeding 41
Pitt	—	Miller 16 pass from Roethlisberger (Reed kick)
SD	—	Tomlinson 4 run (run failed)
Pitt	—	FG Reed 40

SIXTH WEEK SUMMARIES
American Football Conference

East Division	W	L	T	Pct.	Pts.	OP
Buffalo	3	3	0	.500	95	100

	W	L	T	Pct.	Pts.	OP
New England	3	3	0	.500	138	164
Miami	2	3	0	.400	95	98
N.Y. Jets	2	4	0	.333	78	112
North Division	**W**	**L**	**T**	**Pct.**	**Pts.**	**OP**
Cincinnati	5	1	0	.833	155	84
Pittsburgh	3	2	0	.600	122	82
Baltimore	2	3	0	.400	63	90
Cleveland	2	3	0	.400	68	90
South Division	**W**	**L**	**T**	**Pct.**	**Pts.**	**OP**
Indianapolis	6	0	0	1.000	151	57
Jacksonville	4	2	0	.667	108	101
Tennessee	2	4	0	.333	126	157
Houston	0	5	0	.000	54	141
West Division	**W**	**L**	**T**	**Pct.**	**Pts.**	**OP**
Denver	5	1	0	.833	129	107
Kansas City	3	2	0	.600	119	112
San Diego	3	3	0	.500	176	126
Oakland	1	4	0	.200	90	116

National Football Conference

East Division	**W**	**L**	**T**	**Pct.**	**Pts.**	**OP**
Dallas	4	2	0	.667	137	111
N.Y. Giants	3	2	0	.600	149	114
Philadelphia	3	2	0	.600	122	101
Washington	3	2	0	.600	83	86
North Division	**W**	**L**	**T**	**Pct.**	**Pts.**	**OP**
Chicago	2	3	0	.400	90	62
Detroit	2	3	0	.400	91	96
Green Bay	1	4	0	.200	124	95
Minnesota	1	4	0	.200	67	135
South Division	**W**	**L**	**T**	**Pct.**	**Pts.**	**OP**
Tampa Bay	5	1	0	.833	116	72
Atlanta	4	2	0	.667	148	119
Carolina	4	2	0	.667	148	136
New Orleans	2	4	0	.333	102	173
West Division	**W**	**L**	**T**	**Pct.**	**Pts.**	**OP**
Seattle	4	2	0	.667	168	117
St. Louis	2	4	0	.333	156	193
Arizona	1	4	0	.200	94	134
San Francisco	1	4	0	.200	79	160

SUNDAY, OCTOBER 16

BALTIMORE 16, CLEVELAND 3—at M&T Bank Stadium, attendance 70,196. Matt Stover kicked 3 field goals and Todd Heap caught a touchdown pass for the Ravens. The Ravens' defense allowed the Browns to drive inside the Ravens' 45 just one time. That 13-play drive led to Phil Dawson's third-quarter field goal, by which time the Ravens already had claimed a 16-0 lead. In the first quarter, Ray Lewis recovered a fumble at the Browns' 20 to set up Todd Heap's 3-yard touchdown catch. Stover kicked field goals to conclude three of the next four possessions. Anthony Wright was 23 of 31 for 213 yards and 1 touchdown, with 1 interception. Trent Dilfer was 16 of 30 for 147 yards, with 1 interception.

Cleveland	0	0	3	0	—	3
Baltimore	10	6	0	0	—	16
Balt	—	Heap 3 pass from Wright (Stover kick)				
Balt	—	FG Stover 39				
Balt	—	FG Stover 27				
Balt	—	FG Stover 38				
Cle	—	FG Dawson 24				

BUFFALO 27, N.Y. JETS 17—at Ralph Wilson Stadium, attendance 72,045. Kelly Holcomb passed for 2 touchdowns and the Bills' defense recorded 5 sacks to defeat the Jets. The Bills led 14-3 late in the first half when Ty Law intercepted a pass at the Jets' 9 to stop a drive. Seven plays later, Martin scored on a 1-yard run to pull within 14-10 with 30 seconds left in the half. Terrence McGee returned the ensuing kickoff 42 yards to set up Rian Lindell's 50-yard field goal as the half expired. Angelo Crowell intercepted a pass at the Bills' 9 early in the second half, and Willis McGahee scored 10 plays later for a 24-10 lead. Later in the quarter, Mark Brown intercepted a pass and returned it to the Bills' 2 to set up Vinny Testaverde's sneak to

pull within 24-17. The Bills led 27-17 in the fourth quarter and the Jets had two final possessions, but London Fletcher recovered a fumble and McGee intercepted a pass at the Bills' 1 with 3:01 left to clinch the victory. Holcomb was 18 of 26 for 172 yards and 2 touchdowns, with 2 interceptions. McGahee rushed 29 times for 143 yards. Testaverde was 12 of 26 for 161 yards, with 2 interceptions. Curtis Martin rushed 18 times for 148 yards. Justin McCareins had 5 catches for 116 yards.

N.Y. Jets	0	10	7	0	—	17
Buffalo	7	10	7	3	—	27
Buff	—	J. Smith 8 pass from Holcomb (Lindell kick)				
Buff	—	Moulds 15 pass from Holcomb (Lindell kick)				
NYJ	—	FG Nugent 44				
NYJ	—	Martin 1 run (Nugent kick)				
Buff	—	FG Lindell 50				
Buff	—	McGahee 1 run (Lindell kick)				
NYJ	—	Testaverde 1 run (Nugent kick)				
Buff	—	FG Lindell 38				

CHICAGO 28, MINNESOTA 3—at Soldier Field, attendance 62,143. Thomas Jones rushed for 2 touchdowns and Kyle Orton passed for 2 scores as the Bears overwhelmed the Vikings. The Vikings drove into Bears' territory five times in the first half, but had 1 punt, 2 missed field goals, and were stopped once on downs. Leading 7-3 in the third quarter, Charles Tillman intercepted a pass and returned it 55 yards to the Vikings' 3. Two plays later, Desmond Clark's second touchdown catch gave Chicago a 14-3 lead. Jones scored twice in the fourth quarter to seal the victory. Orton was 16 of 25 for 117 yards and 2 touchdowns, with 1 interception. Daunte Culpepper was 26 of 48 for 237 yards, with 2 interceptions. Jermaine Wiggins had 10 catches for 68 yards.

Minnesota	0	3	0	0	—	3
Chicago	0	7	7	14	—	28
Minn	—	FG Edinger 23				
Chi	—	Clark 3 pass from Orton (Gould kick)				
Chi	—	Clark 2 pass from Orton (Gould kick)				
Chi	—	T. Jones 24 run (Gould kick)				
Chi	—	T. Jones 1 run (Gould kick)				

DALLAS 16, N.Y. GIANTS 13 (OT)—at Texas Stadium, attendance 62,278. José Cortez kicked a 45-yard field goal to allow the Cowboys to remain in first place. Both teams committed 4 turnovers, with all four of the Giants' coming in the second half. Dallas took a 13-6 lead on Cortez's second field goal with 4:40 to play. Roy Williams recovered a Brandon Jacobs fumble at the Cowboys' 1 with 1:18 to play. The Giants forced a punt and regained possession at the Giants' 48 with 52 seconds to play. Eli Manning completed a 28-yard pass to Plaxico Burress on first down, and on the next play Manning hit Jeremy Shockey with a 24-yard pass for a touchdown to tie the game with 19 seconds left. The Cowboys won the coin toss, and Drew Bledsoe completed passes on the first three plays, capped by Jason Witten's 26-yard catch at the Giants' 28, to set up Cortez's winning kick. Bledsoe was 26 of 37 for 312 yards and 1 touchdown, with 1 interception. Keyshawn Johnson had 8 catches for 120 yards. Manning was 14 of 29 for 215 yards and 1 touchdown, with 1 interception. Shockey had 5 catches for 129 yards.

N.Y. Giants	3	3	0	7	0	—	13
Dallas	0	7	0	6	3	—	16
NYG	—	FG Feely 50					
NYG	—	FG Feely 45					
Dall	—	Witten 2 pass from Bledsoe (Cortez kick)					
Dall	—	FG Cortez 29					
Dall	—	FG Cortez 28					

NYG	—	Shockey 24 pass from Manning (Feely kick)				
Dall	—	FG Cortez 45				

DENVER 28, NEW ENGLAND 20—at INVESCO Field at Mile High, attendance 76,571. Jake Plummer passed for 2 touchdowns as the Broncos rattled off 28 unanswered points before holding off the Patriots. Trailing 3-0, the Broncos had three touchdown drives, each of which had at least one big play. The first drive was highlighted by Plummer's 72-yard pass to Rod Smith, the second by his 55-yard pass to Ashley Lelie, and the third by Tatum Bell's 68-yard run. The Broncos took the opening kickoff of the second half and drove 74 yards to set up Mike Anderson's 2-yard scoring run for a 28-3 lead. The Patriots scored on three consecutive possessions, capped by Tom Brady's 8-yard touchdown pass to David Givens with 8:01 left, to pull within 28-20. The Patriots had one possession deep in Broncos territory, punted, and the Broncos ran out the final 3:36, capped by Plummer's 8-yard pass to Rod Smith on second-and-7 to run out the clock. Plummer was 17 of 24 for 262 yards and 2 touchdowns. Smith had 6 catches for 123 yards. Bell had 13 carries for 114 yards. Brady was 24 of 46 for 299 yards and 1 touchdown.

New England	3	0	3	14	—	20
Denver	0	21	7	0	—	28
NE	—	FG Vinatieri 39				
Den	—	Bell 3 run (Elam kick)				
Den	—	R. Smith 6 pass from Plummer (Elam kick)				
Den	—	K. Johnson 1 pass from Plummer (Elam kick)				
Den	—	Anderson 2 run (Elam kick)				
NE	—	FG Vinatieri 38				
NE	—	Pass 8 run (Vinatieri kick)				
NE	—	Givens 8 pass from Brady (Vinatieri kick)				

CAROLINA 21, DETROIT 20—at Ford Field, attendance 61,083. Chris Weinke, making his first appearance since 2002, completed a 3-yard touchdown pass to Ricky Proehl with 32 seconds left as the Panthers fought off the Lions. Weinke came off the bench to replace an injured Jake Delhomme on the final drive and culminated the possession with the winning pass. In the third quarter, Jason Hanson kicked a 52-yard field goal to give Detroit a 17-14 lead. The Panthers drove to the Lions' 4, but Delhomme was stopped for no gain on fourth-and-1 to turn the ball over on downs. Joey Harrington completed an 86-yard pass to Marcus Pollard to set up Hanson's 25-yard field goal for a 20-14 lead with 5:08 to play. With 3:13 remaining, the Panthers started on their own 21. Two plays into the drive, Delhomme was injured on a 5-yard scramble. Weinke entered the game and completed his first three passes. Of his five completions, four went to Proehl, capped by his 3-yard catch with 32 seconds left. R.W. McQuarters returned the ensuing kickoff 43 yards to put the ball at the Lions' 49 with 24 seconds left, but Harrington threw 4 consecutive incompletions. Delhomme was 15 of 25 for 236 yards and 2 touchdowns, with 3 interceptions. Weinke was 5 of 7 for 47 yards and 1 touchdown. Steve Smith had 6 receptions for 123 yards. Harrington was 17 of 28 for 201 yards, with 1 interception.

Carolina	7	7	0	7	—	21
Detroit	0	14	3	3	—	20
Car	—	Gardner 4 pass from Delhomme (Kasay kick)				
Det	—	Bailey 34 interception return (Hanson kick)				
Car	—	S. Smith 80 pass from Delhomme (Kasay kick)				
Det	—	Kennedy 64 interception return (Hanson kick)				
Det	—	FG Hanson 52				

Det	—	FG Hanson 25
Car	—	Proehl 3 pass from Weinke (Kasay kick)

KANSAS CITY 28, WASHINGTON 21—at Arrowhead Stadium, attendance 78,083. Priest Holmes went across the field 60 yards with a screen pass for the winning touchdown early in the fourth quarter. The Chiefs trailed 7-6 at halftime, but Holmes capped the opening drive of the second half with a touchdown for a 14-7 lead. Two plays later, Santana Moss took a screen pass and raced 78 yards for a touchdown to tie the game. Later in the third quarter, Carlos Hall forced Rock Cartwright to fumble. Sammy Knight picked up the ball and went 80 yards for a touchdown. The Redskins responded with a 12-play, 67-yard touchdown drive to tie the game, but Holmes scored four plays later for a 28-21 lead with 13:21 to play. The Redskins reached the Chiefs' 33 with 38 seconds left, but Mark Brunell threw four consecutive incompletions. Trent Green was 15 of 25 for 181 yards and 1 touchdown. Holmes had 5 catches for 100 yards. Brunell was 25 of 41 for 331 yards and 3 touchdowns. Moss had 10 receptions for 173 yards.

Washington	0	7	14	0	—	21
Kansas City	3	3	15	7	—	28

KC	—	FG Tynes 20
Wash	—	S. Moss 4 pass from Brunell (Novak kick)
KC	—	FG Tynes 38
KC	—	Holmes 6 run (Boerigter pass from Green)
Wash	—	S. Moss 78 pass from Brunell (Novak kick)
KC	—	Knight 80 fumble return (Tynes kick)
Wash	—	Cooley 11 pass from Brunell (Novak kick)
KC	—	Holmes 60 pass from Green (Tynes kick)

ATLANTA 34, NEW ORLEANS 31—at Alamodome, attendance 65,562. Todd Peterson's second-chance 36-yard field goal as time expired lifted the Falcons to their best start since 1998. DeAngelo Hall returned a fumble 66 yards for a touchdown in the second qurter to tie the game 10-10. The Saints then drove to the Falcons' 29 with four seconds left in the half, but Michael Boley, who moments earlier had forced AntowainSmith's fumble, blocked John Carney's 47-yard field goal attempt. Demorrio Williams recovered the loose ball and returned it 59 yards for a touchdown and 17-10 halftime lead for the Falcons. The Saints scored touchdowns with their first two drives of the second half, sandwiched around an 18-play, 82-yard touchdown drive by the Falcons, to tie the game 24-24 with 6:56 to play. The Saints' defense forced a punt, but Keith Brooking intercepted Aaron Brooks' pass and Warrick Dunn scored on the next play for a 31-24 lead with 4:37 left. Brooks' 15-yard touchdown pass to Devery Henderson capped an 85-yard drive and tied the game with 46 seconds remaining. Michael Vick completed 3 passes to Alge Crumpler to set up Peterson's 41-yard field goal attempt with six seconds left. The kick sailed wide left, but the Falcons were called for defensive holding. After the penalty, Peterson redeemed himself with a 36-yard field goal. Vick was 11 of 23 for 112 yards and 1 touchdown, with 1 interception. Dunn had 22 carries for 100 yards. Brooks was 22 of 33 for 259 yards and 2 touchdowns, with 1 interception.

Atlanta	3	14	0	17	—	34
New Orleans	7	3	14	7	—	31

Atl	—	FG Peterson 37
NO	—	A. Smith 24 run (Carney kick)
NO	—	FG Carney 19
Atl	—	Hall 66 fumble return (Peterson kick)
Atl	—	D. Williams 59 blocked field goal return (Peterson kick)
NO	—	A. Smith 1 run (Carney kick)
Atl	—	Griffith 12 pass from Vick (Peterson kick)
NO	—	Stallworth 27 pass from Brooks (Carney kick)
Atl	—	Dunn 21 run (Peterson kick)
NO	—	Henderson 15 pass from Brooks (Carney kick)
Atl	—	FG Peterson 36

SAN DIEGO 27, OAKLAND 14—at McAfee Coliseum, attendance 52,666. LaDainian Tomlinson became the fifth player since 1966 to score a touchdown via rushing, receiving, and passing in the same game. The Chargers posted their fourth consecutive win against the Raiders, marking their longest stretch of success against the club since 1962. Tomlinson's 35-yard scoring catch was the 18th consecutive game with a touchdown, which equaled Lenny Moore's NFL record, and with his 7-yard touchdown run he became the first player in NFL history to have at least 10 rushing touchdowns in each of his first five seasons. San Diego scored on consecutive drives of 70, 55, 59, and 84 yards in the first half, capped by Tomlinson's 4-yard halfback-option touchdown pass to Justin Peelle with 2:39 left in the half for a 24-7 lead. The Raiders pulled within 13 points and drove to the Chargers' 9, but Kerry Collins' fourth-down pass fell incomplete with 4:58 remaining. Drew Brees was 14 of 20 for 164 yards and 1 touchdown. Tomlinson had 31 carries for 140 yards. Collins was 24 of 48 for 292 yards, with 1 interception.

San Diego	14	10	3	0	—	27
Oakland	7	0	7	0	—	14

SD	—	Tomlinson 35 pass from Brees (Kaeding kick)
SD	—	Tomlinson 7 run (Kaeding kick)
Oak	—	Jordan 4 run (Janikowski kick)
SD	—	FG Kaeding 24
SD	—	Peelle 4 pass from Tomlinson (Kaeding kick)
SD	—	FG Kaeding 33
Oak	—	Jordan 1 run (Janikowski kick)

JACKSONVILLE 23, PITTSBURGH 17 (OT)—at Heinz Field, attendance 63,891. Rashean Mathis returned an interception 41 yards for a touchdown 3:36 into overtime as the Jaguars forced 4 turnovers to defeat the Steelers. With Ben Roethlisberger injured, Tommy Maddox started for the Steelers and was intercepted on two of his first three possessions. The latter, by Mike Peterson, was followed one play later by Greg Jones' 7-yard touchdown run. The Steelers answered with Maddox's 15-yard touchdown pass to Heath Miller and three plays later Antwaan Randle El returned a punt 72 yards for a score to give Pittsburgh a 14-7 lead. Byron Leftwich's 10-yard touchdown pass to Matt Jones capped the opening drive of the second half for a 17-14 lead. Jeff Reed tied the game with a 29-yard field goal with 9:38 left, but his 46-yard attempt on the next possession sailed wide right with 3:28 remaining. The Jaguars drove to the Steelers' 32, but Bryant McFadden intercepted Leftwich's pass for a touchback with 19 seconds left to force overtime. The Steelers won the toss, and Quincy Morgan returned the kickoff 74 yards to the Jaguars' 26, but on third-and-11, Maddox dropped the snap and Reggie Hayward recovered the ball. The Steelers' defense forced a punt, but two plays later Mathis stepped in front of Maddox's pass in the flat and returned it untouched 41 yards for the game-ending touchdown. Leftwich was 19 of 35 for 177 yards and 1 touchdown, with 1 interception. Maddox was 11 of 28 for 154 yards and 1 touchdown, with 3 interceptions.

Jacksonville	7	3	7	0	6	—	23
Pittsburgh	0	14	0	3	0	—	17

Jax	—	G. Jones 7 run (Scobee kick)
Pitt	—	Miller 15 pass from Maddox (Reed kick)
Pitt	—	Randle El 72 punt return (Reed kick)
Jax	—	FG Scobee 23
Jax	—	M. Jones 10 pass from Leftwich (Scobee kick)
Pitt	—	FG Reed 29
Jax	—	Mathis 41 interception return

TAMPA BAY 27, MIAMI 13—at Raymond James Stadium, attendance 65,168. Tampa Bay, playing without injured Carnell Williams, overcame a season-ending injury to Brian Griese to defeat the Dolphins. The Buccaneers scored on their first two drives for a 10-3 lead. Leading 13-3, Michael Pittman took a pitch and ran 57 yards for a touchdown on a 20-6 lead with 1:32 left in the third quarter. Three plays later, Greg Spires sacked Gus Frerotte, forced him to fumble, and Will Allen recovered the ball and ran 33 yards for a touchdown to cap a 17-0 run in a span of 4:26 to pull away. Griese was 12 of 16 for 120 yards and 1 touchdown. Griese was injured late in the second quarter, and Chris Simms was 6 of 10 for 69 yards. Pittman carried 15 times for 127 yards. Frerotte was 21 of 43 for 267 yards.

Miami	3	0	3	7	—	13
Tampa Bay	10	0	17	0	—	27

TB	—	Galloway 7 pass from Griese (Bryant kick)
Mia	—	FG Mare 47
TB	—	FG Bryant 36
Mia	—	FG Mare 53
TB	—	FG Bryant 32
TB	—	Pittman 57 run (Bryant kick)
TB	—	Allen 33 fumble return (Bryant kick)
Mia	—	R. Brown 8 run (Mare kick)

CINCINNATI 31, TENNESSEE 23—at The Coliseum, attendance 69,149. The Bengals used two key second-half turnovers to rally and match their best start since 1988. Tennessee scored on three consecutive possessions, minus a 1-play kneel down at the end of the half, capped by Chris Brown's 9-yard run for a 17-10 lead with 4:32 left in the third quarter. The Titans' defense then forced a punt, but two plays later Odell Thurman intercepted a pass and returned it 30 yards for a touchdown to tie the game. Rob Bironas gave Tennessee a 20-17 lead with a 29-yard field goal 4:54 to play, but three plays later Chad Johnson caught a 15-yard touchdown pass to give Cincinnati a 24-20 lead with 4:19 remaining. Four plays later, Kevin Kaesviharn intercepted a pass near midfield to stop one drive, and after a punt, Tory James recovered Brown's fumble and returned it to the Titans' 1 to set up Rudi Johnson's touchdown run with 2:26 to play. Bironas added a 47-yard field goal with 32 seconds left to pull within eight points, but Kevin Walter recovered the onside kick to secure the victory. Carson Palmer was 27 of 33 for 272 yards and 2 touchdowns. Chad Johnson had 8 catches for 135 yards. Steve McNair was 26 of 41 for 259 yards, with 2 interceptions.

Cincinnati	0	7	10	14	—	31
Tennessee	0	10	7	6	—	23

Tenn	—	C. Brown 4 run (Bironas kick)
Tenn	—	FG Bironas 24
Cin	—	C. Perry 1 pass from Palmer (Graham kick)
Cin	—	FG Graham 21
Tenn	—	C. Brown 9 run (Bironas kick)
Cin	—	Thurman 30 interception return (Graham kick)
Tenn	—	FG Bironas 29
Cin	—	C. Johnson 15 pass from Palmer (Graham kick)

Cin	—	R. Johnson 1 run (Graham kick)
Tenn	—	FG Bironas 47

SUNDAY NIGHT, OCTOBER 16
SEATTLE 42, HOUSTON 10—at Qwest Field, attendance 66,196. Shaun Alexander rushed for 4 touchdowns as the Seahawks established a franchise record with 320 rushing yards. Seattle scored touchdowns on three of their first four possessions for a 21-3 halftime lead. Seattle began the second half with scoring drives of 70, 76, and 88 yards, which all resulted in touchdowns, capped by Maurice Morris' 11-yard run with 5:14 to play. Matt Hasselbeck was 14 of 20 for 168 yards and 1 touchdown, with 1 interception. Alexander had 22 carries for 141 yards, and Morris added 8 carries for 104 yards. It was the third time in franchise history two running backs had at least 100 yards in the same game. David Carr was 19 of 33 for 179 yards and 1 touchdown. Jabar Gaffney had 10 catches for 87 yards.

Houston	0	3	7	0	—	10
Seattle	14	7	7	14	—	42

Sea	—	Alexander 4 run (J. Brown kick)
Sea	—	Alexander 5 run (J. Brown kick)
Hou	—	FG K. Brown 39
Sea	—	Jurevicius 3 pass from Hasselbeck (J. Brown kick)
Sea	—	Alexander 1 run (J. Brown kick)
Hou	—	Davis 27 pass from Carr (K. Brown kick)
Sea	—	Alexander 23 run (J. Brown kick)
Sea	—	Morris 11 run (J. Brown kick)

MONDAY NIGHT, OCTOBER 17
INDIANAPOLIS 45, ST. LOUIS 28—at RCA Dome, attendance 57,307. Edgerrin James rushed for 143 yards and 3 touchdowns as the Colts overcame a 17-point deficit to remain undefeated. The Rams scored on their first three possessions to take a 17-0 lead with 3:31 left in the first quarter. In the second quarter, Cato June intercepted Marc Bulger's pass. Bulger was injured during the return, and James scored six plays later. Jamie Martin entered for the Rams, who failed to drive inside the Colts' 30 until their final possession. The Colts' offense, after Vanderjagt's miss, scored on seven of their next eight possessions. Three of the Colts' four second-half touchdowns followed turnovers, on drives of 35, 14, and 19 yards. Peyton Manning was 22 of 32 for 191 yards and 2 touchdowns. James rushed 23 times for 143 yards. Bulger was 6 of 8 for 121 yards and 1 touchdown, with 1 interception. Martin was 17 of 21 for 134 yards and 1 touchdown, with 2 interceptions.

St. Louis	17	3	0	8	—	28
Indianapolis	0	14	10	21	—	45

StL	—	S. Jackson 21 run (Wilkins kick)
StL	—	FG Wilkins 29
StL	—	Curtis 57 pass from Bulger (Wilkins kick)
Ind	—	James 1 run (Vanderjagt kick)
Ind	—	Wayne 3 pass from Manning (Vanderjagt kick)
StL	—	FG Wilkins 49
Ind	—	FG Vanderjagt 22
Ind	—	James 8 run (Vanderjagt kick)
Ind	—	Rhodes 1 run (Vanderjagt kick)
Ind	—	Harrison 6 pass from Manning (Vanderjagt kick)
Ind	—	James 1 run (Vanderjagt kick)
StL	—	Cleeland 9 pass from Martin (Faulk run)

SEVENTH WEEK SUMMARIES
American Football Conference

East Division	W	L	T	Pct.	Pts.	OP
New England	3	3	0	.500	138	164
Buffalo	3	4	0	.429	112	138
Miami	2	4	0	.333	105	128

N.Y. Jets	2	5	0	.286	92	139
North Division	W	L	T	Pct.	Pts.	OP
Cincinnati	5	2	0	.714	168	111
Pittsburgh	4	2	0	.667	149	95
Baltimore	2	4	0	.333	69	100
Cleveland	2	4	0	.333	78	103
South Division	W	L	T	Pct.	Pts.	OP
Indianapolis	7	0	0	1.000	189	77
Jacksonville	4	2	0	.667	108	101
Tennessee	2	5	0	.286	136	177
Houston	0	6	0	.000	74	179
West Division	W	L	T	Pct.	Pts.	OP
Denver	5	2	0	.714	152	131
Kansas City	4	2	0	.667	149	132
San Diego	3	4	0	.429	193	146
Oakland	2	4	0	.333	128	133

National Football Conference

East Division	W	L	T	Pct.	Pts.	OP
N.Y. Giants	4	2	0	.667	173	137
Philadelphia	4	2	0	.667	142	118
Washington	4	2	0	.667	135	103
Dallas	4	3	0	.571	147	124
North Division	W	L	T	Pct.	Pts.	OP
Chicago	3	3	0	.500	100	68
Detroit	3	3	0	.500	104	106
Minnesota	2	4	0	.333	90	155
Green Bay	1	5	0	.167	144	118
South Division	W	L	T	Pct.	Pts.	OP
Tampa Bay	5	1	0	.833	116	72
Atlanta	5	2	0	.714	175	133
Carolina	4	2	0	.667	148	136
New Orleans	2	5	0	.286	119	201
West Division	W	L	T	Pct.	Pts.	OP
Seattle	5	2	0	.714	181	127
St. Louis	3	4	0	.429	184	210
Arizona	2	4	0	.333	114	144
San Francisco	1	5	0	.167	96	212

FRIDAY NIGHT, OCTOBER 21
KANSAS CITY 30, MIAMI 20—at Dolphins Stadium, attendance 68,350. Priest Holmes scored 2 touchdowns as the Chiefs tallied 462 yards of offense. The game was moved up two days to Friday to avoid incoming Hurricane Wilma. The decision was made less than 48 hours prior to game-time and forced the Chiefs to land in Miami less than six hours before kickoff. The Chiefs led 14-6 at halftime, but Ronnie Brown scored on a 65-yard touchdown run on the first play of the second half to pull the Dolphins within one point. The Chiefs responded immediately when Dante Hall's 40-yard kickoff return, a 24-yard pass to Jason Dunn, and Priest Holmes' 35-yard touchdown run just 1:01 later to take a 21-13 lead. The Chiefs added field goals on their next three possessions to pull away. Trent Green was 20 of 34 for 289 yards. Gus Frerotte was 11 of 29 for 125 yards, with 1 interception, and Sage Rosenfels entered in the fourth quarter and completed his lone pass for a 77-yard touchdown.

Kansas City	7	7	10	6	—	30
Miami	0	6	7	7	—	20

KC	—	Holmes 1 run (Tynes kick)
Mia	—	FG Mare 33
KC	—	L. Johnson 2 run (Tynes kick)
Mia	—	FG Mare 23
Mia	—	R. Brown 65 run (Mare kick)
KC	—	Holmes 35 run (Tynes kick)
KC	—	FG Tynes 30
KC	—	FG Tynes 51
KC	—	FG Tynes 52
Mia	—	Chambers 77 pass from Rosenfels (Mare kick)

SUNDAY, OCTOBER 23
ARIZONA 20, TENNESSEE 10—at Sun Devil Stadium, attendance 39,482. The Cardinals benefited from 17 points off turnovers to rally and defeat the Titans. Tennessee allowed just 173 total yards, but the offense committed 3 turnovers. The Titans scored on their first two drives to take a 10-0 lead, but drove inside the Cardinals' 30 just twice the rest of the game. Quentin Harris' fumble recovery in the second quarter led to Neil Rackers' 33-yard field goal, and moments later David Macklin returned an interception 60 yards to tie the game. Late in the third quarter, Rackers capped a 59-yard drive with a 24-yard field goal for a 13-10 lead. In the fourth quarter, Karlos Dansby sacked Billy Volek and forced him to fumble. Three plays later, on third-and-10, Josh McCown fired a 34-yard touchdown pass to Larry Fitzgerald with 5:20 remaining. McCown was 12 of 28 for 140 yards and 1 touchdown, with 1 interception. Playing without injured Steve McNair, Billy Volek started and was 18 of 32 for 198 yards and 1 touchdown, with 1 interception. Matt Mauck was 8 of 13 for 71 yards.

Tennessee	10	0	0	0	—	10
Arizona	0	10	3	7	—	20

Tenn	—	B. Jones 38 pass from Volek (Bironas kick)
Tenn	—	FG Bironas 53
Ariz	—	FG Rackers 33
Ariz	—	Macklin 60 interception return (Rackers kick)
Ariz	—	FG Rackers 24
Ariz	—	Fitzgerald 34 pass from McCown (Rackers kick)

CHICAGO 10, BALTIMORE 6—at Soldier Field, attendance 62,102. The Bears' defense allowed just 199 yards and registered 4 sacks to win a defensive battle. The Ravens scored on consecutive drives just before halftime to pull within 7-6, but the Ravens' offense did not cross the Bears' 44 in five second-half possessions. Robbie Gould's 23-yard field goal late in the third quarter gave Chicago a 10-6 lead, and Thomas Jones' 1-yard run on fourth-and-1 from the Ravens' 30 with 1:13 to play clinched the victory. Kyle Orton was 15 of 29 for 145 yards and 1 touchdown. Jones had 25 carries for 139 yards. Anthony Wright was 18 of 32 for 164 yards.

Baltimore	0	6	0	0	—	6
Chicago	7	0	3	0	—	10

Chi	—	Edwards 9 pass from Orton (Gould kick)
Balt	—	FG Stover 40
Balt	—	FG Stover 29
Chi	—	FG Gould 23

PITTSBURGH 27, CINCINNATI 13—at Paul Brown Stadium, attendance 66,104. Ben Roethlisberger, who had missed the previous week's game with an injured knee, passed for 2 touchdowns for the Steelers. The Bengals maintained possession for nearly 11 minutes in the first half, but made just two of three field goals and trailed 7-6 at halftime. Chris Hope's interception early in the second half, the first interception in 20 quarters for Carson Palmer, set up Jeff Reed's 27-yard field goal. Three plays later, Kimo von Oelhoffen tipped Palmer's pass and Aaron Smith intercepted the ball to set up Willie Parker's 37-yard touchdown run for a 17-6 lead. The Steelers scored on their next two drives as well, capped by Reed's 39-yard field goal for a 27-6 lead with 6:56 to play. Roethlisberger was 9 of 14 for 93 yards and 2 touchdowns, with 1 interception. Parker had 18 carries for 131 yards. Palmer was 21 of 36 for 227 yards, with 2 interceptions.

Pittsburgh	0	7	13	7	—	27
Cincinnati	3	3	0	7	—	13

Cin	—	FG Graham 26
Pitt	—	Miller 2 pass from Roethlisberger (Reed kick)
Cin	—	FG Graham 39
Pitt	—	FG Reed 27
Pitt	—	Parker 37 run (Reed kick)
Pitt	—	Ward 4 pass from Roethlisberger (Reed kick)

Pitt — FG Reed 39

Cin — Palmer 4 run (Graham kick)

DETROIT 13, CLEVELAND 10—at Cleveland Browns Stadium, attendance 72,923. The Lions' defense forced 3 turnovers as Detroit rallied on the road. The Lions sacked Trent Dilfer 4 times. Dré Bly's second-quarter interception set up Jeff Garcia's fourth-and-goal 1-yard touchdown run for a 7-3 lead. Josh Cribbs returned the ensuing kickoff 90 yards for a touchdown and 10-7 lead. Jason Hanson's second field goal, from 50 yards with 14:07 to play, gave Detroit a 13-10 advantage. Two penalties and a sack by Dan Wilkinson forced the Browns to punt on fourth-and-26 with 1:29 left, and Artose Pinner gained 2 yards on third-and-1 to clinch the victory. Garcia was 22 of 34 for 210 yards. Dilfer was 10 of 19 for 73 yards, with 3 interceptions. Reuben Droughns had 19 carries for 100 yards.

Detroit	0	7	3	3	—	13
Cleveland	3	7	0	0	—	10

Cle — FG Dawson 30

Det — Garcia 1 run (Hanson kick)

Cle — Cribbs 90 kickoff return (Dawson kick)

Det — FG Hanson 47

Det — FG Hanson 50

INDIANAPOLIS 38, HOUSTON 20—at Reliant Stadium, attendance 70,621. Edgerrin James rushed for 139 yards and scored the go-ahead 9-yard touchdown run in the third quarter to keep the Colts undefeated. The Colts outgained the Texans 437-139 total yards. In the second quarter, Dunta Robinson intercepted Peyton Manning's pass and David Carr completed an 8-yard touchdown pass to Jabar Gaffney with 30 seconds left in the half to tie the game at 14-14. James' 9-yard touchdown run capped the opening 77-yard second half drive. Indianapolis then drove 66 yards in 16 plays on their next possession, capped by Mike Vanderjagt's 36-yard field goal, for a 24-14 lead. Marvin Harrison's 7-yard touchdown catch capped the next possession, and six plays later Ron Mathis sacked Carr, forced him to fumble. Montae Reagor recovered and returned the ball 37 yards for a 38-14 lead with 8:07 to play. Manning was 21 of 27 for 237 yards and 2 touchdowns, with 1 interception. James had 21 carries for 139 yards. Carr was 6 of 9 for 48 yards and 1 touchdown, with 1 interception, and sacked 5 times.

Indianapolis	7	7	10	14	—	38
Houston	0	14	0	6	—	20

Ind — James 1 run (Vanderjagt kick)

Ind — Clark 31 pass from Manning (Vanderjagt kick)

Hou — Davis 8 run (K. Brown kick)

Hou — Gaffney 8 pass from Carr (K. Brown kick)

Ind — James 9 run (Vanderjagt kick)

Ind — FG Vanderjagt 36

Ind — Harrison 7 pass from Manning (Vanderjagt kick)

Ind — Reagor 37 fumble return (Vanderjagt kick)

Hou — Mathis 89 kickoff return (pass failed)

MINNESOTA 23, GREEN BAY 20—at Metrodome, attendance 64,278. Paul Edinger kicked a 56-yard field goal as time expired to lift the Vikings to a comeback victory. The Packers scored on their last three possessions of the first half, capped by Ryan Longwell's 53-yard field goal with 22 seconds left, for a 17-0 lead. The Vikings scored on all five of their second half possessions, the last of which culminated with Mewelde Moore's 14-yard touchdown catch with 3:10 to play to give Minnesota a 20-17 lead. The Packers responded with a 56-yard drive and tied the

game on Longwell's 39-yard kick with 24 seconds remaining. Koren Robinson returned the ensuing kickoff 25 yards to the Vikings' 36. Daunte Culpepper completed a 14-yard pass to Moore and 12-yard toss to Marcus Robinson with two seconds left to set up Edinger's winning kick. Culpepper was 23 of 31 for 280 yards and 2 touchdowns. Brett Favre was 28 of 36 for 315 yards and 2 touchdowns. Donald Driver had 8 catches for 114 yards.

Green Bay	0	17	0	3	—	20
Minnesota	0	0	10	13	—	23

GB — Driver 22 pass from Favre (Longwell kick)

GB — Chatman 4 pass from Favre (Longwell kick)

GB — FG Longwell 53

Minn — FG Edinger 27

Minn — M. Robinson 27 pass from Culpepper (Edinger kick)

Minn — FG Edinger 22

Minn — Moore 14 pass from Culpepper (Edinger kick)

GB — FG Longwell 39

Minn — FG Edinger 56

N.Y. GIANTS 24, DENVER 23—at Giants Stadium, attendance 78,516. Eli Manning completed a 2-yard touchdown pass to Amani Toomer with five seconds remaining to culminate the Giants' comeback. The Broncos scored on four of their first five possessions, with the one non-scoring drive being a 2-play drive at the end of the first half, to take a 20-10 lead with 13:26 left in the third quarter. Jason Elam's 27-yard field goal with 13:18 left increased the advantage to 23-10. Manning's 23-yard pass to Plaxico Burress set up Tiki Barber's 4-yard run with 9:07 to play. Elam missed a 49-yard field goal on their next possession, but Champ Bailey intercepted a pass with 4:46 remaining. However, the Giants forced a punt and Manning took over at the Giants' 17 with 3:29 remaining. Manning completed 2 third-down passes, including a 24-yard pass to Jeremy Shockey to the Broncos' 8, and capped the drive with his third-and-goal 2-yard toss to Toomer. Manning was 23 of 42 for 214 yards and 2 touchdowns, with 1 interception. Jake Plummer was 18 of 29 for 194 yards and 1 touchdown. Mike Anderson had 24 carries for 120 yards.

Denver	6	7	7	3	—	23
N.Y. Giants	3	0	14	7	—	24

Den — FG Elam 49

NYG — Burress 18 pass from Manning (Feely kick)

Den — FG Elam 42

Den — Anderson 2 run (Elam kick)

NYG — FG Feely 52

Den — K. Johnson 4 pass from Plummer (Elam kick)

Den — FG Elam 27

NYG — Barber 4 run (Feely kick)

NYG — Toomer 2 pass from Manning (Feely kick)

OAKLAND 38, BUFFALO 17—at McAfee Coliseum, attendance 42,779. LaMont Jordan scored 3 touchdowns to snap the Bills' two-game winning streak. The Raiders outgained the Bills 416-210 total yards, and had five scoring drives of at least 9 plays. The Bills began the game with a 14-play, 82-yard drive, but the Raiders took the lead for good as Jordan capped a 9-play, 60-yard drive with a 1-yard touchdown run with 40 seconds left in the half. The Raiders drove 80 yards for a touchdown to begin the second half, but Troy Vincent's fumble recovery led to Jake Reed's 9-yard touchdown catch on the first play of the fourth quarter to pull the Bills within 24-17. The Raiders responded with a 10-play, 77-yard touchdown drive and, following a punt, Zack Crockett capped a 15-play, 69-yard drive with a 2-yard touch-

down run in the final minute. Kerry Collins was 19 of 27 for 261 yards and 1 touchdown. Doug Gabriel had 5 catches for 101 yards, and Jordan had 28 carries for 122 yards. Kelly Holcomb was 19 of 27 for 159 yards and 2 touchdowns.

Buffalo	7	3	0	7	—	17
Oakland	0	17	7	14	—	38

Buff — Evans 5 pass from Holcomb (Lindell kick)

Oak — FG Janikowski 25

Oak — R. Moss 22 pass from Collins (Janikowski kick)

Buff — FG Lindell 41

Oak — Jordan 1 run (Janikowski kick)

Oak — Jordan 17 run (Janikowski kick)

Buff — Reed 9 pass from Holcomb (Lindell kick)

Oak — Jordan 7 run (Janikowski kick)

Oak — Crockett 2 run (Janikowski kick)

PHILADELPHIA 20, SAN DIEGO 17—at Lincoln Financial Field, attendance 67,747. Quintin Mikell blocked a field goal and Matt Ware returned it 65 yards for a touchdown with 2:25 remaining to lift the Eagles to victory. The Eagles' defense forced 3 turnovers and limited LaDainian Tomlinson to 7 yards on 17 carries. Trailing 10-0, the Chargers scored on three consecutive possessions, the last set up by Jamar Fletcher's interception to set up Nate Kaeding's 34-yard field goal, for a 17-10 lead with 9:21 left. The Chargers forced a punt and got the ball back, but Marc Simoneau hit Drew Brees as he was attempting to pass and Jeremiah Trotter intercepted the ball to set up Doug France's 40-yard field goal. The Eagles' defense forced a punt, but Donovan McNabb's fourth-and-1 pass fell incomplete with 3:29 remaining. Four plays later, Nate Kaeding lined up for a 40-yard field-goal attempt, but Mikell came around the end and blocked the kick. Ware caught the bouncing ball in stride and ran untouched 65 yards for a 20-17 lead. San Diego drove to the Eagles' 37, and Brees completed a 19-yard pass to Reché Caldwell, but Sheldon Brown caused Caldwell to fumble. Darwin Walker recovered the ball to clinch the victory. McNabb was 35 of 54 for 287 yards and 1 touchdown, with 2 interceptions. Brian Westbrook had 10 catches for 75 yards. Brees was 23 of 40 for 299 yards and 2 touchdowns, with 2 interceptions.

San Diego	0	0	7	10	—	17
Philadelphia	0	7	3	10	—	20

Phil — Owens 4 pass from McNabb (France kick)

Phil — FG France 23

SD — McCardell 19 pass from Brees (Kaeding kick)

SD — Gates 8 pass from Brees (Kaeding kick)

SD — FG Kaeding 34

Phil — FG France 40

Phil — Ware 65 blocked field goal return (France kick)

ST. LOUIS 28, NEW ORLEANS 17—at Edward Jones Dome, attendance 64,586. Mike Furrey returned an interception 67 yards for a touchdown with 1:55 remaining as the Rams rallied and then held off the Saints. New Orleans led 14-7 when holder Todd Bouman was tackled shy of a first down on a fourth-and-1 fake field-goal attempt late in the third quarter, but following a punt John Carney booted a 22-yard field goal for a 17-7 lead with 13:31 remaining. The Rams needed just 8 plays to score on Steven Jackson's 1-yard run, and two plays later Adam Archuleta recovered Donté Stallworth's fumble. Five plays later, Kevin Curtis scored on a reverse with 5:58 to play for a 21-17 lead. Following an exchange of punts, the Saints began on their own 26, and drove to the 42-yard line but Furrey made the interception and ran 67 yards for the game's final points. Jamie Martin, making his fourth career start in place of injured Marc Bulger, was 18 of 29 for 198 yards. Brooks was 18 of 39 for 230 yards and 2 touchdowns, with 1 interception. Az-Zahir Hakim had 6 catches for 100 yards.

New Orleans	14	0	3	—	17		
St. Louis	0	7	0	21	—	28	

NO	—	Stallworth 11 pass from Brooks (Carney kick)
NO	—	Hakim 17 pass from Brooks (Carney kick)
StL	—	S. Jackson 6 run (Wilkins kick)
NO	—	FG Carney 22
StL	—	S. Jackson 1 run (Wilkins kick)
StL	—	Curtis 5 run (Wilkins kick)
StL	—	Furrey 67 interception return (Wilkins kick)

SEATTLE 13, DALLAS 10—at Qwest Field, attendance 67,046. Jordan Babineaux's interception with five seconds set up Josh Brown's 50-yard field goal as time expired to lift the Seahawks to victory. Dallas led 7-0 and had the ball near midfield, but Michael Boulware intercepted Drew Bledsoe's pass with 1:43 left in the half to setup Brown's 55-yard field goal to pull within 7-3. A muffed punt gave Dallas a scoring chance early in the fourth quarter, but José Cortez missed a 29-yard field-goal attempt wide left. Roy Williams intercepted Matt Hasselbeck's pass at the Seahawks' 24 with 3:04 remaining to set up Cortez's 21-yard field goal with 2:06 left for a 10-3 lead. Hasselbeck responded by completing 22-yard passes to Jerheme Urban and Jerramy Stevens, and capped the 81-yard drive with a 1-yard touchdown pass to Ryan Hannam with 40 seconds left to tie the game. Tyson Thompson returned the ensuing kickoff 39 yards to the Cowboys' 41. Two plays later, on third-and-7, Bledsoe attempted a pass to Terry Glenn that was intercepted by Babineaux, who was knocked out of bounds at the Cowboys' 32 with five seconds left. Brown trotted onto the field and made the game-winning kick as time expired. Hasselbeck was 23 of 42 for 224 yards and 1 touchdown, with 2 interceptions. Bledsoe was 13 of 24 for 136 yards and 1 touchdown, with 2 interceptions.

Dallas	7	0	0	3	— 10
Seattle	0	3	0	10	— 13

Dall	—	K. Johnson 5 pass from Bledsoe (Cortez kick)
Sea	—	FG J. Brown 55
Dall	—	FG Cortez 21
Sea	—	Hannam 1 pass from Hasselbeck (J. Brown kick)
Sea	—	FG J. Brown 50

WASHINGTON 52, SAN FRANCISCO 17—at FedEx Field, attendance 90,224. Mark Brunell passed for 3 touchdowns and Clinton Portis scored 3 times en route to a 45-point blowout. Washington outgained the 49ers 457-194 total yards, and scored touchdowns on five of their first six possessions, the last set up by Phillip Daniels' fumble recovery, for a 35-7 halftime lead. The Redskins increased the lead to 52-7 with 9:26 left. Brunell was 13 of 20 for 252 yards and 3 touchdowns. Portis had 19 carries for 101 yards. Santana Moss had 5 catches for 112 yards. Alex Smith was 8 of 16 for 92 yards, with 1 interception.

San Francisco	7	0	0	10	— 17
Washington	14	21	10	7	— 52

Wash	—	Sellers 2 pass from Brunell (Novak kick)
Wash	—	Portis 1 run (Novak kick)
SF	—	Barlow 17 run (Nedney kick)
Wash	—	Portis 1 run (Novak kick)
Wash	—	S. Moss 32 pass from Brunell (Novak kick)
Wash	—	Sellers 19 pass from Brunell (Novak kick)

Wash	—	Portis 1 run (Novak kick)
Wash	—	FG Novak 27
Wash	—	Cartwright 4 run (Novak kick)
SF	—	FG Nedney 47
SF	—	Gore 72 run (Nedney kick)

MONDAY NIGHT, OCTOBER 24

ATLANTA 27, N.Y. JETS 14—at Georgia Dome, attendance 70,995. Michael Vick scored 2 touchdowns as the Falcons jumped to a 20-0 lead en route to victory. Vinny Testaverde fumbled 3 times in the first 18 minutes. The last fumble, caused by Rod Coleman's sack and returned 24 yards for a touchdown by Chauncey Davis, gave Atlanta a 17-0 lead with 12:23 left in the second quarter. Vick's 1-yard run capped a 13-play, 48-yard drive for a 27-7 lead with 6:35 left in the third quarter. With Brooks Bollinger at quarterback, the Jets pulled within 27-14 and drove to the Falcons' 11 with 3:39 left, but Bollinger's fourth-and-1 pass intended for Curtis Martin fell incomplete. Vick was 11 of 26 for 116 yards, with 3 interceptions. Warrick Dunn had 24 carries for 155 yards. Testaverde was 11 of 18 for 140 yards, with 1 interception. Bollinger entered late in the third quarter and was 12 of 22 for 94 yards.

N.Y. Jets	0	7	0	7	— 14
Atlanta	10	10	7	0	— 27

Atl	—	Vick 1 run (Peterson kick)
Atl	—	FG Peterson 22
Atl	—	Ch. Davis 24 fumble return (Peterson kick)
Atl	—	FG Peterson 41
NYJ	—	Testaverde 1 run (Nugent kick)
Atl	—	Vick 1 run (Peterson kick)
NYJ	—	Martin 1 run (Nugent kick)

EIGHTH WEEK SUMMARIES

American Football Conference

East Division	W	L	T	Pct.	Pts.	OP
New England	4	3	0	.571	159	180
Miami	3	4	0	.429	136	134
Buffalo	3	5	0	.375	128	159
N.Y. Jets	2	5	0	.286	92	139
North Division	**W**	**L**	**T**	**Pct.**	**Pts.**	**OP**
Cincinnati	6	2	0	.750	189	125
Pittsburgh	5	2	0	.714	169	114
Baltimore	2	5	0	.286	88	120
Cleveland	2	5	0	.286	94	122
South Division	**W**	**L**	**T**	**Pct.**	**Pts.**	**OP**
Indianapolis	7	0	0	1.000	189	77
Jacksonville	4	3	0	.571	129	125
Tennessee	2	6	0	.250	161	211
Houston	1	6	0	.143	93	195
West Division	**W**	**L**	**T**	**Pct.**	**Pts.**	**OP**
Denver	6	2	0	.750	201	152
Kansas City	4	3	0	.571	169	160
San Diego	4	4	0	.500	221	166
Oakland	3	4	0	.429	162	158

National Football Conference

East Division	W	L	T	Pct.	Pts.	OP
N.Y. Giants	5	2	0	.714	209	137
Dallas	5	3	0	.625	181	137
Philadelphia	4	3	0	.571	163	167
Washington	4	3	0	.571	135	139
North Division	**W**	**L**	**T**	**Pct.**	**Pts.**	**OP**
Chicago	4	3	0	.571	119	81
Detroit	3	4	0	.429	117	125
Minnesota	2	5	0	.286	103	193
Green Bay	1	6	0	.143	158	139
South Division	**W**	**L**	**T**	**Pct.**	**Pts.**	**OP**
Atlanta	5	2	0	.714	175	133
Carolina	5	2	0	.714	186	149
Tampa Bay	5	2	0	.714	126	87
New Orleans	2	6	0	.250	125	222
West Division	**W**	**L**	**T**	**Pct.**	**Pts.**	**OP**
Seattle	5	2	0	.714	181	127
St. Louis	4	4	0	.500	208	231
Arizona	2	5	0	.286	127	178
San Francisco	2	5	0	.286	111	222

SUNDAY, OCTOBER 30

CAROLINA 38, MINNESOTA 13—at Bank of America Stadium, attendance 73,502. Steve Smith set a club record with 201 receiving yards as the Panthers won their fourth consecutive game. Daunte Culpepper suffered a season-ending knee injury on the last play of the first quarter. Paul Edinger missed a 33-yard field goal after the injury, and the Panthers scored on their next four possessions en route to a 31-7 lead with 7:25 left in the third quarter. Carolina had touchdown drives of 68, 80, 63, 76, and 79 yards in the game. Jake Delhomme was 21 of 30 for 341 yards and 3 touchdowns. Smith had 11 catches for 201 yards. Culpepper was 3 of 4 for 28 yards, and Brad Johnson was 13 of 28 for 162 yards and 1 touchdown.

Minnesota	0	0	7	6	— 13
Carolina	7	17	7	7	— 38

Car	—	S. Davis 7 run (Kasay kick)
Car	—	FG Kasay 44
Car	—	S. Davis 1 run (Kasay kick)
Car	—	S. Smith 13 pass from Delhomme (Kasay kick)
Minn	—	M. Moore 4 run (Edinger kick)
Car	—	Mangum 1 pass from Delhomme (Kasay kick)
Car	—	Colbert 25 pass from Delhomme (Kasay kick)
Minn	—	M. Robinson 5 pass from B. Johnson (run failed)

CINCINNATI 21, GREEN BAY 14—at Paul Brown Stadium, attendance 65,940. Carson Palmer passed for 3 touchdowns and the Bengals intercepted 5 passes to hold off the Packers. The Bengals jumped to a 14-7 lead early in the second quarter and then ended five of the Packers' next six drives with an interception. However, the Bengals' offense did not score until the last interception, by Odell Thurman, which was followed one play later by Jeremi Johnson's 27-yard touchdown catch for a 21-7 lead with 13:17 to play. Ahmad Carroll intercepted a pass midway through the fourth quarter to spark an 88-yard drive capped by Brett Favre's 1-yard toss to Bubba Franks with 3:11 to play. The Packers got the ball on their own 10 with 56 seconds left and drove to the Bengals' 30. But on the final play Favre was penalized for crossing the line of scrimmage before attempting his pass. Palmer was 22 of 34 for 237 yards and 3 touchdowns, with 1 interception. Favre was 27 of 40 for 290 yards and 1 touchdown, with 5 interceptions.

Green Bay	0	7	0	7	— 14
Cincinnati	7	7	0	7	— 21

Cin	—	Perry 4 pass from Palmer (Graham kick)
GB	—	Fisher 1 run (Longwell kick)
Cin	—	Houshmandzadeh 8 pass from Palmer (Graham kick)
Cin	—	J. Johnson 27 pass from Palmer (Graham kick)
GB	—	Franks 1 pass from Favre (Longwell kick)

DALLAS 34, ARIZONA 13—at Texas Stadium, attendance 62,068. Rookie Marion Barber rushed for 127 yards and 2 touchdowns in his first NFL start. The Cowboys scored on four of their five first-half possessions for a 24-10 halftime lead. The Cardinals trailed 27-13 and had the ball near midfield, but Anthony Henry intercepted a pass and returned it 58 yards for a game-clinching touchdown. Drew Bledsoe was 19 of 24 for 220 yards and 1 touchdown. Barber had 27 carries for 127 yards. Josh McCown was 16 of 33 for 161 yards and 1 touchdown, with 2 interceptions.

Arizona	3	7	3	0	— 13
Dallas	10	14	3	7	— 34

Ariz	—	FG Rackers 52

Dall	—	Barber 28 run (Suisham kick)
Dall	—	FG Suisham 21
Ariz	—	Boldin 44 pass from McCown (Rackers kick)
Dall	—	K. Johnson 5 pass from Bledsoe (Suisham kick)
Dall	—	Barber 10 run (Suisham kick)
Ariz	—	FG Rackers 47
Dall	—	FG Suisham 21
Dall	—	Henry 58 interception return (Suisham kick)

DENVER 49, PHILADELPHIA 21—at INVESCO Field at Mile High, attendance 76,530. Jake Plummer passed for 4 touchdowns as the Broncos jumped to a big lead, withstood a rally, then pulled away from the Eagles. The Broncos took a 28-0 lead on Plummer's 3-yard touchdown pass to Stephen Alexander with 7:47 left in the first half. Trailing 28-7, Terrell Owens turned a short pass into a 91-yard touchdown,and Owens' 46-yard catch a few possessions later set up Brian Westbrook's 14-yard scoring catch to trim the deficit to 28-21 with 1:33 left in the third quarter. The Eagles forced another punt, and drove to the Broncos' 24, but Domonique Foxworth intercepted Donovan McNabb's pass in the end zone for a touchback. Five plays later, Devoe took a short pass and broke free for a 44-yard touchdown on a 35-21 lead with 9:53 remaining. Tatum Bell ran for 2 touchdowns in the final 6:31 to complete the scoring. Plummer was 22 of 35 for 309 yards and 4 touchdowns. Mike Anderson had 21 carries for 126 yards and Bell had 14 rushes for 107 yards. McNabb was 12 of 34 for 283 yards and 3 touchdowns, with 2 interceptions.

Philadelphia	0	7	14	0	—	21
Denver	14	14	0	21	—	49

Den	—	M. Anderson 2 run (Elam kick)
Den	—	K. Johnson 6 pass from Plummer (Elam kick)
Den	—	R. Smith 2 pass from Plummer (Elam kick)
Den	—	Alexander 3 pass from Plummer (Elam kick)
Phil	—	L. Smith 1 pass from McNabb (Cortez kick)
Phil	—	Owens 91 pass from McNabb (Cortez kick)
Phil	—	Westbrook 14 pass from McNabb (Cortez kick)
Den	—	Devoe 44 pass from Plummer (Elam kick)
Den	—	Bell 67 run (Elam kick)
Den	—	Bell 6 run (Elam kick)

CHICAGO 19, DETROIT 13 (OT)—at Ford Field, attendance 61,814. Charles Tillman intercepted a pass and returned it 22 yards for a touchdown in overtime to propel the Bears into first place in the NFC North. The Bears scored on three consecutive first-half possessions, highlighted by a 10-play, 99-yard scoring drive, and capped by Robbie Gould's 20-yard field goal with 17 seconds left in the half for a 13-3 lead. Jason Hanson tied the game with a 39-yard field goal with 13:20 remaining. Kalimba Edwards recovered Thomas Jones' fumble at the Lions' 28 with 9:40 to play to quell the final scoring threat of regulation. In overtime, following a pair of punts, Jeff Garcia's third-and-5 across-the-field pass was picked off by Tillman, who returned it untouched for 22 yards 6:17 into overtime. Kyle Orton was 17 of 31 for 230 yards and 1 touchdown. Garcia was 23 of 35 for 197 yards, with 1 interception.

Chicago	0	13	0	0	6	— 19
Detroit	3	0	7	3	0	— 13

Det	—	FG Hanson 32
Chi	—	Muhammad 23 pass from Orton (Gould kick)
Chi	—	FG Gould 38
Chi	—	FG Gould 20
Det	—	K. Jones 6 run (Hanson kick)
Det	—	FG Hanson 30
Chi	—	Tillman 22 interception return

HOUSTON 19, CLEVELAND 16—at Reliant Stadium, attendance 70,064. Kris Brown kicked a 40-yard field goal with 2:54 remaining, and Jerome Mathis caught a touchdown pass and averaged 35.4 yards per kick-off return, as Houston posted its first victory. Robaire Smith's fumble recovery in the third quarter led to Brown's second field goal, and Antwan Peek's fumble recovery on the next drive led to Brown's go-ahead 35-yard field goal with 14:08 to play. Phil Dawson kicked a 37-yard field goal with 5:06 remaining, but Mathis' 63-yard kickoff return set up Brown's winning kick with 2:45 to play. The Browns fell short of a comeback as Trent Dilfer's fourth-and-17 pass from the Texans' 46 fell incomplete with 43 seconds to play. David Carr was 10 of 20 for 138 yards and 1 touchdown, with 1 interception. Dilfer was 12 of 25 for 185 yards and 1 touchdown.

Cleveland	10	3	0	3	— 16
Houston	7	3	3	6	— 19

Hou	—	Mathis 34 pass from Carr (K. Brown kick)
Cle	—	Shea 8 pass from Dilfer (Dawson kick)
Cle	—	FG Dawson 28
Cle	—	FG Dawson 29
Hou	—	FG K. Brown 38
Hou	—	FG K. Brown 37
Hou	—	FG K. Brown 35
Cle	—	FG Dawson 37
Hou	—	FG K. Brown 40

MIAMI 21, NEW ORLEANS 6—at Tiger Stadium, attendance 61,643. The Dolphins' defense registered 6 sacks and Kevin Carter recorded a safety as the Dolphins snapped a three-game losing streak. The game was played in Baton Rouge, and was the first game in Louisiana for the Saints following Hurricane Katrina. The game was also a welcome home for Miami coach Nick Saban, who had coached at Louisiana State the previous five seasons. John Carney cut the deficit to 9-6 with a 49-yard field goal with 3:37 left in the third quarter, and the Saints forced a three-and-out to regain possession. But on third-and-17 from their own 8-yard line, Carter sacked Aaron Brooks for a safety. Five plays later, Chris Chambers caught a 12-yard touchdown pass for a 18-6 lead with 11:09 to play. Gus Frerotte was 16 of 28 for 168 yards and 1 touchdown, with 1 interception. Ronnie Brown had 23 carries for 106 yards. Brooks was 14 of 31 for 181 yards, with 1 interception.

Miami	3	6	2	10	— 21
New Orleans	3	0	3	0	— 6

NO	—	FG Carney 26
Mia	—	FG Mare 37
Mia	—	FG Mare 36
Mia	—	FG Mare 41
NO	—	FG Carney 49
Mia	—	Safety, Carter sacked Brooks in end zone
Mia	—	Chambers 12 pass from Frerotte (Mare kick)
Mia	—	FG Mare 46

N.Y. GIANTS 36, WASHINGTON 0—at Giants Stadium, attendance 78,630. Tiki Barber rushed for a career-high 206 yards, in just three quarters, as the Giants moved into first place in the NFC East with an emotional victory five days after the death of 89-year-old owner Wellington Mara. The Giants had more first downs (19-7), total yards (386-125), and time of possession (39:21-20:39). The Giants forced 8 punts and 3 turnovers on the Redskins' first 11 possessions. Barber's final carry of the day was his 4-yard

scoring run, six plays after Osi Umenyiora's fumble recovery, which gave the Giants a 36-0 lead with 1:07 remaining in the third quarter. Eli Manning was 12 of 31 for 146 yards and 1 touchdown, with 1 interception. Barber had 24 carries for 206 yards. Mark Brunell was 11 of 28 for 65 yards, with 1 interception before replaced by Patrick Ramsey, who was 3 of 6 for 62 yards.

Washington	0	0	0	0	—	0
N.Y. Giants	6	13	17	0	—	36

NYG	—	FG Feely 39
NYG	—	FG Feely 50
NYG	—	Jacobs 3 run (Feely kick)
NYG	—	FG Feely 33
NYG	—	FG Feely 39
NYG	—	Shockey 10 pass from Manning (Feely kick)
NYG	—	FG Feely 44
NYG	—	Barber 4 run (Feely kick)

ST. LOUIS 24, JACKSONVILLE 21—at Edward Jones Dome, attendance 65,251. Steven Jackson rushed for 179 yards and caught the go-ahead touchdown pass early in the fourth quarter as the Rams won for the second time in three games with Joe Vitt as head coach. Playing without injured Marc Bulger, Torry Holt, and Isaac Bruce, the Rams scored just over two minutes into the game as Drew Wahlroos blocked a punt that Brandon Chillar returned 29 yards for a touchdown. Fred Taylor scored on a 71-yard run two plays later, but Kevin Curtis caught an 83-yard touchdown pass three plays after that for a 14-7 lead just 4:06 into the game. The Jaguars took a 21-17 lead into the fourth quarter, but Mike Furrey's interception and 37-yard return set up Jackson's 19-yard touchdown catch with 12:45 to play. The Jaguars drove to the Rams' 26, but Josh Scobee pushed a 44-yard field goal wide right with 9:25 remaining. Jamie Martin was 13 of 21 for 200 yards and 2 touchdowns, with 3 interceptions. Jackson carried 25 times for 179 yards, and Curtis had 3 catches for 105 yards. Leftwich was 18 of 31 for 213 yards and 2 touchdowns, with 1 interception. Taylor had 22 carries for 165 yards, and Ernest Wilford had 6 receptions for 145 yards.

Jacksonville	7	7	7	0	— 21
St. Louis	14	3	0	7	— 24

StL	—	Chillar 29 blocked punt return (Wilkins kick)
Jax	—	Taylor 71 run (Scobee kick)
StL	—	Curtis 83 pass from Martin (Wilkins kick)
Jax	—	Wilford 20 pass from Leftwich (Scobee kick)
StL	—	FG Wilkins 41
Jax	—	M. Jones 15 pass from Leftwich (Scobee kick)
StL	—	Jackson 19 pass from Martin (Wilkins kick)

SAN DIEGO 28, KANSAS CITY 20—at Qualcomm Stadium, attendance 65,750. Antonio Gates caught 3 touchdown passes and Drew Brees passed for 324 yards as the Chargers held off the Chiefs. The Chiefs pulled with 21-10 late in the third quarter and drove to the Chargers' 13, but Shawne Merriman sacked Trent Green and forced him to fumble. Shaun Phillips recovered the ball to quell that drive, but Lawrence Tynes' 20-yard field goal pulled Kansas City within 21-13 with 12:00 remaining. Five plays later, Gates caught a 35-yard touchdown on third-and-4 with 9:10 to play. Eddie Kennison caught a 7-yard touchdown pass with 2:12 remaining. Kassim Osgood recovered the ensuing onside kick, and the Chiefs got the ball with 22 seconds left and did not threaten. Brees was 25 of 43 for 324 yards and 3 touchdowns, with 1 interception. Gates set career highs with 10 catches for 145 yards. Trent Green was 31 of 43 for 347 yards and 2 touchdowns. Kennison had 7 catches for 115 yards.

Kansas City	0	3	7	10	—	20
San Diego	7	14	0	7	—	28

SD — Gates 19 pass from Brees (Kaeding kick)
SD — Parker 17 pass from Tomlinson (Kaeding kick)
KC — FG Tynes 34
SD — Gates 20 pass from Brees (Kaeding kick)
KC — Gonzalez 16 pass from Green (Tynes kick)
KC — FG Tynes 20
SD — Gates 35 pass from Brees (Kaeding kick)
KC — Kennison 7 pass from Green (Tynes kick)

SAN FRANCISCO 15, TAMPA BAY 10—at Monster Park, attendance 63,358. Joe Nedney kicked 5 field goals as the 49ers surprised the first-place Buccaneers. The 49ers gained just 208 yards, but 2 of their 5 field goals were set up by interceptions. Shawntae Spencer's 24-yard interception return to the Buccaneers' 27 set up Nedney's third field goal, and Brandon Moore's 12-yard interception return to the Buccaneers' 35 four plays later led to Nedney's 46-yard boot for a 12-3 lead with 2:45 left in the third quarter. Joey Galloway's 78-yard scoring catch trimmed the deficit to 12-10 with 10:33 left. Cody Pickett replaced an injured Ken Dorsey, and Pickett's lone pass was a 10-yard completion to Brandon Lloyd for a first down to help set up Nedney's final field goal with 1:56 remaining. On the next play, Bryant Young sacked Chris Simms and Julian Peterson recovered. Dorsey was 7 of 18 for 40 yards, and Pickett, who also played special teams and had a tackle 32 seconds before taking his first snap, was 1 for 1 for 10 yards. Kevan Barlow had 26 carries for 101 yards. Simms was 21 of 34 for 264 yards and 1 touchdown, with 2 interceptions. Galloway had 8 catches for 149 yards.

Tampa Bay	0	3	0	7	—	10
San Francisco	0	6	6	3	—	15

SF — FG Nedney 45
TB — FG Bryant 47
SF — FG Nedney 47
SF — FG Nedney 41
SF — FG Nedney 46
TB — Galloway 78 pass from Simms (Bryant kick)
SF — FG Nedney 28

OAKLAND 34, TENNESSEE 25—at The Coliseum, attendance 69,149. Kerry Collins had 3 touchdown passes, including 2 to Jerry Porter, as the Raiders won for the third time in four games. The Raiders jumped to a 17-0 lead, but the Titans scored on their next two possessions. Adam Jones returned the ensuing punt 82 yards for a touchdown, but a penalty nullified the return. Three plays later, Warren Sapp sacked Steve McNair and forced him to fumble. Jarrod Cooper recovered the ball for a touchdown and 24-12 lead. The Titans trailed 24-15 when Reynaldo Hill returned an interception 52 yards for a touchdown with just 12 seconds left in the half. The Titans pulled with 27-25 with 7:48 to play, but on third-and-10 Collins connected with Porter on a 44-yard touchdown for a 34-25 lead with 4:37 remaining. McNair was 26 of 40 for 229 yards and 1 touchdown. Collins was 17 of 29 for 238 yards and 3 touchdowns, with 1 interception. Porter had 6 catches for 123 yards.

Oakland	17	7	3	7	—	34
Tennessee	0	22	0	3	—	25

Oak — Porter 26 pass from Collins (Janikowski kick)
Oak — FG Janikowski 22
Oak — Jordan 18 pass from Collins (Janikowski kick)

Tenn — Roby 19 pass from McNair (kick failed)
Tenn — Brown 38 run (pass failed)
Oak — Cooper fumble recovery in end zone (Janikowski kick)
Tenn — FG Bironas 39
Tenn — Hill 52 interception return (Bironas kick)
Oak — FG Janikowski 32
Tenn — FG Bironas 24
Oak — Porter 44 pass from Collins (Janikowski kick)

SUNDAY NIGHT, OCTOBER 30
NEW ENGLAND 21, BUFFALO 16—at Gillette Stadium, attendance 68,756. Corey Dillon scored 2 fourth-quarter touchdowns as the Patriots were victorious on the night Tedy Bruschi returned to the lineup. Bruschi, who had 7 tackles, had missed the first six games while recovering from a stroke suffered three days after the Pro Bowl. Rian Lindell's 35-yard field goal gave the Bills a 13-7 lead, and on the next play Aaron Schobel sacked Tom Brady and forced him to fumble. Lauvale Sape recovered the fumble and Lindell's 41-yard field goal seven plays later gave Buffalo a 16-7 lead with 10:07 remaining. Deion Branch's 37-yard catch sparked a 61-yard drive, capped by Dillon's first touchdown. Two plays later, Rosevelt Colvin sacked Kelly Holcomb, forced him to fumble, and recovered the ball at the Bills' 23. Branch's 22-yard catch led to Dillon's second touchdown in less than two minutes for a 21-16 lead with 5:32 to play. Brady was 14 of 21 for 199 yards and 1 touchdown. Holcomb was 20 of 33 for 263 yards and 1 touchdown, with 1 interception. Eric Moulds had 9 catches for 125 yards and Willis McGahee rushed 31 times for 136 yards.

Buffalo	0	3	7	6	—	16
New England	0	0	7	14	—	21

Buff — FG Lindell 23
NE — Branch 33 pass from Brady (Vinatieri kick)
Buff — Moulds 55 pass from Holcomb (Lindell kick)
Buff — FG Lindell 35
Buff — FG Lindell 41
NE — Dillon 1 run (Vinatieri kick)
NE — Dillon 1 run (Vinatieri kick)

MONDAY NIGHT, OCTOBER 31
PITTSBURGH 20, BALTIMORE 19—at Heinz Field, attendance 64,178. Jeff Reed kicked a 37-yard field goal with 1:36 to play as the Steelers rallied to hold off the Ravens. Chris Hope intercepted Anthony Wright's flea-flicker pass early in the second half to spark a 10-play, 64-yard drive, highlighted by Ben Roethlisberger's 2 third-down conversion passes, and capped by Heath Miller's 8-yard touchdown catch with 7:47 left in the third quarter for a 17-10 lead. The Ravens pulled within 17-16 and forced a punt with 5:48 to play. However, Greg Warren's snap was high. Chris Gardocki pulled down the snap, but was unable to punt and threw an incomplete pass. Six plays later, Matt Stover's fourth field goal gave Baltimore a 19-17 lead with 3:21 remaining. Quincy Morgan's 23-yard catch and Jerome Bettis' 11-yard run set up Jeff Reed's 37-yard field goal with 1:36 to play. Wright's fourth-and-6 pass from the Ravens' 47 fell incomplete with 20 seconds to play to clinch the victory. Roethlisberger was 18 of 30 for 177 yards and 2 touchdowns, with 1 interception. Wright was 25 of 44 for 252 yards and 1 touchdown, with 2 interceptions.

Baltimore	7	3	0	9	—	19
Pittsburgh	7	3	7	3	—	20

Pitt — Miller 4 pass from Roethlisberger (Reed kick)
Balt — Taylor 13 pass from Wright (Stover kick)
Pitt — FG Reed 42

Balt — FG Stover 22
Pitt — Miller 8 pass from Roethlisberger (Reed kick)
Balt — FG Stover 40
Balt — FG Stover 49
Balt — FG Stover 47
Pitt — FG Reed 37

NINTH WEEK SUMMARIES
American Football Conference

East Division	W	L	T	Pct.	Pts.	OP
New England	4	4	0	.500	180	220
Buffalo	3	5	0	.375	128	159
Miami	3	5	0	.375	146	151
N.Y. Jets	2	6	0	.250	118	170
North Division	**W**	**L**	**T**	**Pct.**	**Pts.**	**OP**
Cincinnati	7	2	0	.778	210	134
Pittsburgh	6	2	0	.750	189	124
Cleveland	3	5	0	.375	114	136
Baltimore	2	6	0	.250	97	141
South Division	**W**	**L**	**T**	**Pct.**	**Pts.**	**OP**
Indianapolis	8	0	0	1.000	229	98
Jacksonville	5	3	0	.625	150	139
Tennessee	2	7	0	.222	175	231
Houston	1	7	0	.125	107	216
West Division	**W**	**L**	**T**	**Pct.**	**Pts.**	**OP**
Denver	6	2	0	.750	201	152
Kansas City	5	3	0	.625	196	183
San Diego	5	4	0	.556	252	192
Oakland	3	5	0	.375	185	185

National Football Conference

East Division	W	L	T	Pct.	Pts.	OP
N.Y. Giants	6	2	0	.750	233	143
Dallas	5	3	0	.625	181	137
Washington	5	3	0	.625	152	149
Philadelphia	4	4	0	.500	173	184
North Division	**W**	**L**	**T**	**Pct.**	**Pts.**	**OP**
Chicago	5	3	0	.625	139	98
Detroit	3	5	0	.375	131	152
Minnesota	3	5	0	.375	130	207
Green Bay	1	7	0	.125	168	159
South Division	**W**	**L**	**T**	**Pct.**	**Pts.**	**OP**
Atlanta	6	2	0	.750	192	143
Carolina	6	2	0	.750	220	163
Tampa Bay	5	3	0	.625	140	121
New Orleans	2	7	0	.222	142	242
West Division	**W**	**L**	**T**	**Pct.**	**Pts.**	**OP**
Seattle	6	2	0	.750	214	146
St. Louis	4	4	0	.500	208	231
Arizona	2	6	0	.250	146	211
San Francisco	2	6	0	.250	117	246

SUNDAY, NOVEMBER 6
SEATTLE 33, ARIZONA 19—at Sun Devil Stadium, attendance 43,542. Shaun Alexander rushed for 173 yards and 2 touchdowns as the Seahawks won their fourth consecutive game. Alexander raced 88 yards for a touchdown on the first play of the second half for a 24-6 lead. Arizona put together a 14-play, 80-yard drive in the third quarter, capped by Bryant Johnson's 6-yard touchdown catch. The Cardinals' defense forced a punt and Neil Rackers added his fourth field goal that trimmed the deficit to 27-19 with 12:09 remaining. Seattle responded with a 12-play, 93-yard drive, capped by Alexander's 14-yard run with 5:19 to play. Hasselbeck was 13 of 20 for 158 yards and 1 touchdown. Alexander rushed 23 times for 173 yards. Kurt Warner, making his first start since returning from an injury in week three, was 29 of 48 for 334 yards and 1 touchdown, with 3 interceptions. Larry Fitzgerald had 8 receptions for 102 yards.

Seattle	3	14	10	6	—	33
Arizona	3	3	10	3	—	19

Ariz — FG Rackers 23
Sea — FG J. Brown 26
Sea — Jurevicius 4 pass from Hasselbeck (J. Brown kick)
Ariz — FG Rackers 31

Sea	—	Hasselbeck 1 run
		(J. Brown kick)
Sea	—	Alexander 88 run (J. Brown kick)
Ariz	—	FG Rackers 50
Sea	—	FG J. Brown 28
Ariz	—	B. Johnson 6 pass from Warner
		(Rackers kick)
Ariz	—	FG Rackers 44
Sea	—	Alexander 14 run (kick blocked)

CINCINNATI 21, BALTIMORE 9—at M&T Bank Stadium, attendance 70,196. Carson Palmer passed for 2 touchdowns for the Bengals. Matt Stover's third field goal cut the deficit to 14-9 with 12:46 to play, but the Bengals answered with a 12-play, 91-yard drive, highlighted by 2 third-and-9 conversions by Palmer, and capped by Chris Henry's 3-yard touchdown catch on third-and-goal with 6:05 to play. Palmer was 19 of 26 for 248 yards and 2 touchdowns. Anthony Wright was 19 of 30 for 153 yards.

Cincinnati	0	14	0	7	—	21
Baltimore	3	3	0	3	—	9
Balt	—	FG Stover 34
Cin	—	R. Johnson 1 run (Graham kick)
Cin	—	T. Perry 8 pass from Palmer
		(Graham kick)
Balt	—	FG Stover 32
Balt	—	FG Stover 31
Cin	—	Henry 3 pass from Palmer
		(Graham kick)

CLEVELAND 20, TENNESSEE 14—at Cleveland Browns Stadium, attendance 72,594. Brodney Pool intercepted a pass near the goal line as time expired as the Browns survived a game played amidst winds gusting to 40 miles per hour. With the score tied 7-7 at halftime, the Browns scored on their first two possessions of the second half to take a 17-7 lead. The second score, a 6-yard touchdown run by Jason Wright, was the Browns' first rushing touchdown in 13 games. A failed fake punt by the Titans set up Phil Dawson's second field goal for a 20-7 lead with 13:35 remaining. Chris Brown's 15-yard touchdown run capped a 73-yard drive to pull within 20-14 with 7:13 to play. The Browns had a chance to clinch with 39 seconds left but Dawson's 29-yard field goal was nullified by a holding penalty. His follow up 39-yard field-goal attempt, into the wind, was pushed wide right. McNair completed passes of 13 and 29 yards to reach the Browns' 28 with two seconds left, but Pool intercepted McNair's desperation pass as time expired. Trent Dilfer was 18 of 34 for 272 yards and 1 touchdown, with 1 interception. Reuben Droughns rushed 20 times for 116 yards. McNair was 18 of 41 for 235 yards and 1 touchdown, with 1 interception.

Tennessee	0	7	0	7	—	14
Cleveland	7	0	10	3	—	20
Cle	—	Northcutt 58 pass from Dilfer
		(Dawson kick)
Tenn	—	Kinney 24 pass from McNair
		(Bironas kick)
Cle	—	FG Dawson 37
Cle	—	Wright 6 run (Dawson kick)
Cle	—	FG Dawson 19
Tenn	—	C. Brown 15 run (Bironas kick)

PITTSBURGH 20, GREEN BAY 10—at Lambeau Field, attendance 70,607. The Steelers' defense forced 3 turnovers and Troy Polamalu returned a fumble for a touchdown as the Steelers won their eleventh consecutive road game. The Packers trailed 6-3 and drove to the Steelers' 12 early in the second quarter. On third-and-goal, Bryant McFadden blitzed and forced Brett Favre to fumble. Polamalu picked up the ball and raced 77 yards for a touchdown and 13-3 lead. Ryan Longwell missed a 31-yard field-goal attempt just before halftime, but the Packers regrouped and used up the first half of the third quar-

ter on a 65-yard drive, capped by Samkon Gado's first NFL touchdown. In the fourth quarter, Tyrone Carter intercepted a pass at the Packers' 20, and Duce Staley scored four plays later on a 20-10 lead with 6:16 to play. Favre twice threw incompletions from near the Steelers' 30 in the final moments. Charlie Batch, making his first start in place of injured Ben Roethlisberger, was 9 of 16 for 65 yards, with 1 interception. Favre was 20 of 35 for 214 yards, with 1 interception.

Pittsburgh	6	7	0	7	—	20
Green Bay	3	0	7	0	—	10
Pitt	—	FG Reed 32
Pitt	—	FG Reed 24
GB	—	FG Longwell 40
Pitt	—	Polamalu 77 fumble return
		(Reed kick)
GB	—	Gado 1 run (Longwell kick)
Pitt	—	Staley 3 run (Reed kick)

JACKSONVILLE 21, HOUSTON 14—at ALLTEL Stadium, attendance 64,613. Greg Jones, playing in place of injured Fred Taylor, scored on a 12-yard touchdown run with 2:53 left as the Jaguars rallied for a victory. Trailing 14-7, Jacksonville answered with drives of 80 and 82 yards, the latter drive highlighted by Jimmy Smith's 17-yard catch, to set up Jones' run. Houston drove to the Jaguars' 42 with 54 seconds left, but Carr's fourth-and-9 pass down the sideline could not be caught by Corey Bradford. Byron Leftwich was 19 of 25 for 218 yards and 1 touchdown. Carr was 22 of 30 for 219 yards and 1 touchdown.

Houston	0	7	0	7	—	14
Jacksonville	0	0	7	14	—	21
Tenn	—	Bradford 31 pass from Carr
		(K. Brown kick)
Jax	—	Wilford 12 pass from Leftwich
		(Scobee kick)
Tenn	—	Wells 7 run (K. Brown kick)
Jax	—	Leftwich 8 run (Scobee kick)
Jax	—	G. Jones 12 run (Scobee kick)

KANSAS CITY 27, OAKLAND 23—at Arrowhead Stadium, attendance 79,033. Larry Johnson scored on a 1-yard run as time expired to lift the Chiefs. The Raiders led 9-6 late in the third quarter when the Chiefs drove 72 yards, highlighted by 3 third-down conversions, and capped by Trent Green's 6-yard touchdown pass to Tony Richardson. Greg Wesley intercepted Kerry Collins' pass on the next play and Johnson scored on a 15-yard run five plays later for a 20-9 lead with 12:56 to play. Oakland drove 71 and 84 yards on its next two possessions, with Randy Moss' lone reception, a 7-yard touchdown catch on third-and-3 with 1:45 remaining, giving the Raiders a 23-20 lead. The Chiefs drove to the Raiders' 37 with 19 seconds left. Green dumped a short pass to Johnson who raced down the middle of the field before being tackled at the Raiders' 1 with five seconds left. The Chiefs used their final timeout and eschewed the tying field goal and instead handed to Johnson, who went over right guard for the victory. Green was 22 of 35 for 235 yards and 1 touchdown. Johnson had 22 carries for 107 yards. Collins was 21 of 40 for 175 yard and 2 touchdowns, with 1 interception.

Oakland	3	6	0	14	—	23
Kansas City	0	6	7	14	—	27
Oak	—	FG Janikowski 32
Oak	—	FG Janikowski 49
KC	—	FG Tynes 27
KC	—	FG Tynes 47
Oak	—	FG Janikowski 48
KC	—	Richardson 6 pass from Green
		(Tynes kick)
KC	—	L. Johnson 15 run (Tynes kick)
Oak	—	Porter 4 pass from Collins
		(pass failed)
Oak	—	R. Moss 7 pass from Collins
		(Jordan run)

| KC | — | L. Johnson 1 run (Tynes kick) |

ATLANTA 17, MIAMI 10—at Dolphins Stadium, attendance 72,187. Keion Carpenter intercepted a pass at the Falcons' 5 with 2:41 remaining as the Falcons held off the Dolphins. The Falcons held the ball for 36:15, and had four drives in excess of 70 yards, but led just 17-10 and punted to the Dolphins with 6:38 to play. Starting from their own 42, Reggie Brown gained 5 yards on fourth-and-1 to help the Dolphins reach the Falcons' 8. On third-and-2, Carpenter intercepted Gus Frerotte's pass intended for Chris Chambers, and the Falcons ran out the clock. Michael Vick was 22 of 31 for 228 yards and 1 touchdown. Frerotte was 13 of 22 for 103 yards, with 1 interception.

Atlanta	7	7	3	0	—	17
Miami	0	10	0	0	—	10
Atl	—	Dunn 1 run (Peterson kick)
Mia	—	R. Williams 23 run (Mare kick)
Atl	—	Finneran 11 pass from Vick
		(Peterson kick)
Mia	—	FG Mare 28
Atl	—	FG Peterson 21

MINNESOTA 27, DETROIT 14—at Metrodome, attendance 63,813. Brad Johnson, making his first start in place of injured Daunte Culpepper, passed for 2 touchdowns as the Vikings caught the Lions in the NFC North. The Vikings scored 21 points in the span of 3:24 of the second quarter to take a 24-0 lead. Michael Bennett capped a 5-yard scoring pass from Johnson for a 10-0 lead. Three plays later, Joey Harrington was sacked by Brian Williams and fumbled. Kevin Williams recovered at the Lions' 14 and Ciatrick Fason scored three plays later. Two plays after the ensuing kickoff, Antoine Winfield intercepted a pass at the Lions' 11 and Nate Burleson caught a touchdown pass three plays later for a 24-0 lead with 4:02 left in the first half. Johnson was 15 of 22 for 136 yards and 2 touchdowns. Bennett rushed 18 times for 106 yards. Harrington was 28 of 48 for 263 yards and 1 touchdown, with 2 interceptions. Scottie Vines had 9 receptions for 109 yards.

Detroit	0	7	0	7	—	14
Minnesota	3	21	0	3	—	27
Minn	—	FG Edinger 21
Minn	—	Bennett 4 pass from B. Johnson
		(Edinger kick)
Minn	—	Fason 3 run (Edinger kick)
Minn	—	Burleson 15 pass from
		B. Johnson (Edinger kick)
Det	—	Pinner 1 run (Hanson kick)
Det	—	Pollard 23 pass from
		Harrington (Hanson kick)
Minn	—	FG Edinger 40

CHICAGO 20, NEW ORLEANS 17—at Tiger Stadium, attendance 32,637. In a game played in Baton Rouge because of Hurricane Katrina, Robbie Gould kicked a 28-yard field goal with six seconds left to hand the Saints their fifth consecutive loss. The Bears committed 3 first-half turnovers, but the Saints were unable to capitalize on any of them and the score was 10-10 at halftime. Adrian Peterson's 6-yard touchdown run gave Chicago a 17-10 lead. The Saints drove 80 yards in the fourth quarter, capped by Aaron Brooks' 1-yard run to tie the game with 7:44 to play. Following an exchange of punts, the Bears began the final drive from their own 25 with 4:08 to play. Cedric Benson gained 27 yards on the first play, and Kyle Orton completed a 22-yard pass to Muhsin Muhammad on third-and-5 to reach the Saints' 10 to set up Gould's winning kick. Orton was 12 of 26 for 137 yards and 1 touchdown, with 2 interceptions. Brooks was 16 of 26 for 170 yards and 1 touchdown, with 2 interceptions. Antowain Smith had 17 carries for 110 yards.

| Chicago | 7 | 3 | 3 | 7 | — | 20 |
| New Orleans | 3 | 7 | 0 | 7 | — | 17 |

NO	—	FG Carney 22
Chi	—	Gage 4 pass from Orton (Gould kick)
NO	—	Stallworth 15 pass from Brooks (Carney kick)
Chi	—	FG Gould 35
Chi	—	Peterson 6 run (Gould kick)
NO	—	Brooks 1 run (Carney kick)
Chi	—	FG Gould 28

SAN DIEGO 31, N.Y. JETS 26—at The Meadowlands, attendance 77,662. LaDainian Tomlinson scored 4 touchdowns and Quentin Jammer knocked down a fourth-and-goal pass in the end zone with 53 seconds left as the Chargers won a close game. David Barrett intercepted a Drew Brees pass at the Jets' 4 with 38 seconds left in the half to keep the Jets within 21-10. Tomlinson's fourth touchdown gave San Diego a 28-13 lead with 3:51 left in the third quarter. Vinny Testaverde, who re-injured a calf muscle on the previous drive, was replaced by Brooks Bollinger, who guided a 13-play, 75-yard scoring drive. The Chargers answered by driving to the Jets' 1, but settled for a Nate Kaeding field goal for a 31-20 lead with 8:35 remaining. Justin Miller returned the ensuing kickoff 45 yards and Bollinger completed an 8-yard scoring pass to Laveranues Coles' with 6:14 to play. Bollinger's 2-point conversion pass attempt to Wayne Chrebet was incomplete, maintaining the five-point deficit at 31-26. A few plays later, John Abraham sacked Brees and forced him to fumble. Jonathan Vilma recovered the ball at the Chargers' 30 with 3:06 left. The Jets drove to the Chargers' 3, but Curtis Martin was stopped for no gain, and Bollinger attempted 2 incompletions before Jammer knocked down a pass intended for Justin McCareins in the back right corner of the end zone. Brees was 20 of 27 for 270 yards and 1 touchdown, with 1 interception. Tomlinson carried 25 times for 107 yards. Antonio Gates had 8 catches for 132 yards. Testaverde was 6 of 11 for 98 yards. Bollinger was 11 of 20 for 106 yards and 2 touchdowns.

San Diego	14	7	7	3	—	31
N.Y. Jets	0	10	3	13	—	26

SD	—	Tomlinson 4 run (Kaeding kick)
SD	—	Tomlinson 25 pass from Brees (Kaeding kick)
NYJ	—	Martin 1 run (Nugent kick)
SD	—	Tomlinson 1 run (Kaeding kick)
NYJ	—	FG Nugent 35
NYJ	—	FG Nugent 22
SD	—	Tomlinson 1 run (Kaeding kick)
NYJ	—	Sowell 5 pass from Bollinger (Nugent kick)
SD	—	FG Kaeding 18
NYJ	—	Coles 8 pass from Bollinger (pass failed)

N.Y. GIANTS 24, SAN FRANCISCO 6—at Monster Park, attendance 63,820. The Giants' defense permitted just 138 yards as the Giants pulled away from the 49ers. The 49ers trailed just 3-0 and were faced with third-and-33 from their own 47 with 1:03 left in the half. Instead of running, Cody Pickett, making his first NFL start, attempted a pass that was intercepted by Brent Alexander, who lateraled to Will Allen to get to the 49ers' 41 with 52 seconds left. On fourth-and-1, Eli Manning completed a 32-yard touchdown pass to Jeremy Shockey for a 10-0 lead with just 13 seconds left in the half. The 49ers kicked field goals in their first two second-half possessions to pull within 10-6, but Manning completed a 50-yard pass to Plaxico Burress to set up Brandon Jacobs' 1-yard plunge with 13:19 left. The Giants forced a punt, and Jacobs scored 10 plays later for a 24-6 lead with 6:10 to play. Manning was 18 of 33 for 251 yards and 1 touchdown. Pickett was 12 of 21 for 102 yards, with 1 interception.

N.Y. Giants	3	7	0	14	—	24
San Francisco	0	0	6	0	—	6

NYG	—	FG Feely 22
NYG	—	Shockey 32 pass from Manning (Feely kick)
SF	—	FG Nedney 48
SF	—	FG Nedney 52
NYG	—	Jacobs 1 run (Feely kick)
NYG	—	Jacobs 1 run (Feely kick)

CAROLINA 34, TAMPA BAY 14—at Raymond James Stadium, attendance 65,014. The Panthers' defense forced 4 interceptions and registered 5 sacks as Carolina moved past Tampa Bay in the NFC South. Four plays into the second half, Chris Gamble intercepted a pass and returned it 61 yards for a touchdown and 24-7 lead. Later in the third quarter, Mike Rucker sacked Chris Simms and forced him to fumble. Brentson Buckner recovered to set up John Kasay's field goal for a 27-7 lead. Jake Delhomme was 11 of 18 for 216 yards and 1 touchdown. Steve Smith had 5 catches for 106 yards. Simms was 25 of 42 for 259 yards and 1 touchdown, with 2 interceptions.

Carolina	10	7	10	7	—	34
Tampa Bay	0	7	0	7	—	14

Car	—	FG Kasay 30
Car	—	S. Davis 4 run (Kasay kick)
TB	—	Galloway 50 pass from Simms (Bryant kick)
Car	—	S. Davis 1 run (Kasay kick)
Car	—	Gamble 61 interception return (Kasay kick)
Car	—	FG Kasay 20
Car	—	S. Smith 35 pass from Delhomme (Kasay kick)
TB	—	Alstott 1 run (Bryant kick)

SUNDAY NIGHT, NOVEMBER 6
WASHINGTON 17, PHILADELPHIA 10—at FedEx Field, attendance 90,298. Ryan Clark intercepted a pass at the Redskins' 3 with 1:32 remaining to drop the Eagles into last place in the NFC East. Trailing 10-7, the Eagles tied the game with David Akers' 34-yard field goal, but the Redskins used a 40-yard kickoff return by Ladell Betts to set up Clinton Portis' 6-yard touchdown run with 2:47 left in the third quarter. The Eagles did not threaten until their final possession. Beginning from their own 15 with 2:41 left, Donovan McNabb completed a 26-yard pass to Brown and 27-yard pass to Westbrook. The Eagles reached the Redskins' 7 and had second-and-4, but McNabb threw 2 incompletions before Clark stepped in front of his fourth-down pass to clinch the victory. Brunell was 21 of 29 for 224 yards. McNabb was 22 of 35 for 304 yards and 1 touchdown, with 1 interception.

Philadelphia	7	0	3	0	—	10
Washington	0	10	7	0	—	17

Phil	—	R. Brown 56 pass from McNabb (Akers kick)
Wash	—	FG Hall 24
Wash	—	Sellers 1 run (Hall kick)
Phil	—	FG Akers 34
Wash	—	Portis 6 run (Hall kick)

MONDAY NIGHT, NOVEMBER 7
INDIANAPOLIS 40, NEW ENGLAND 21—at Gillette Stadium, attendance 68,756. The Colts scored on seven of their first eight possessions en route to winning in Foxborough for the first time since 1995. The Patriots trailed just 14-7 in the second quarter when Mike Vrabel intercepted Peyton Manning's pass. Six plays later, Corey Dillon fumbled at the Colts' 18 and Jason David recovered. Manning engineered a 9-play, 73-yard drive, capped by Reggie Wayne's 10-yard touchdown catch with nine seconds left in the half for a 21-7 lead. Daniel Graham caught a 31-yard touchdown pass with 5:46 left in the third quarter to cut the

deficit to 28-14. The Patriots then attempted an onside kick, but Joseph Jefferson recovered to set up Mike Vanderjagt's 35-yard field goal. The Patriots pulled within 13 points, but the Colts needed just seven plays, capped by Marvin Harrison's 30-yard touchdown catch with 5:53 to play, to finish the scoring. Manning was 28 of 37 for 321 yards and 3 touchdowns, with 1 interception. Edgerrin James had 34 carries for 104 yards. Harrison had 9 catches for 128 yards. Wayne had 9 catches for 124 yards. Tom Brady was 22 of 34 for 265 yards and 3 touchdowns.

Indianapolis	7	14	10	9	—	40
New England	7	0	7	7	—	21

Ind	—	Harrison 1 pass from Manning (Vanderjagt kick)
NE	—	Branch 16 pass from Brady (Vinatieri kick)
Ind	—	James 2 run (Vanderjagt kick)
Ind	—	Wayne 10 pass from Manning (Vanderjagt kick)
Ind	—	Rhodes 4 run (Vanderjagt kick)
NE	—	Graham 31 pass from Brady (Vinatieri kick)
Ind	—	FG Vanderjagt 35
Ind	—	FG Vanderjagt 20
NE	—	T. Brown 19 pass from Brady (Vinatieri kick)
Ind	—	Harrison 30 pass from Manning (pass failed)

TENTH WEEK SUMMARIES
American Football Conference

East Division	W	L	T	Pct.	Pts.	OP
New England	5	4	0	.556	203	236
Buffalo	4	5	0	.444	142	162
Miami	3	6	0	.333	162	174
N.Y. Jets	2	7	0	.222	121	200
North Division	**W**	**L**	**T**	**Pct.**	**Pts.**	**OP**
Cincinnati	7	2	0	.778	210	134
Pittsburgh	7	2	0	.778	223	145
Cleveland	3	6	0	.333	135	170
Baltimore	2	7	0	.222	100	171
South Division	**W**	**L**	**T**	**Pct.**	**Pts.**	**OP**
Indianapolis	9	0	0	1.000	260	115
Jacksonville	6	3	0	.667	180	142
Tennessee	2	7	0	.222	175	231
Houston	1	8	0	.111	124	247
West Division	**W**	**L**	**T**	**Pct.**	**Pts.**	**OP**
Denver	7	2	0	.778	232	169
Kansas City	5	4	0	.556	199	197
San Diego	5	4	0	.556	252	192
Oakland	3	6	0	.333	202	216

National Football Conference

East Division	W	L	T	Pct.	Pts.	OP
Dallas	6	3	0	.667	202	157
N.Y. Giants	6	3	0	.667	254	167
Washington	5	4	0	.556	187	185
Philadelphia	4	5	0	.444	193	205
North Division	**W**	**L**	**T**	**Pct.**	**Pts.**	**OP**
Chicago	6	3	0	.667	156	107
Detroit	4	5	0	.444	160	173
Minnesota	4	5	0	.444	154	228
Green Bay	2	7	0	.222	201	184
South Division	**W**	**L**	**T**	**Pct.**	**Pts.**	**OP**
Carolina	7	2	0	.778	250	166
Atlanta	6	3	0	.667	217	176
Tampa Bay	6	3	0	.667	176	156
New Orleans	2	7	0	.222	142	242
West Division	**W**	**L**	**T**	**Pct.**	**Pts.**	**OP**
Seattle	7	2	0	.778	245	162
St. Louis	4	5	0	.444	224	262
Arizona	2	7	0	.222	167	240
San Francisco	2	7	0	.222	126	263

SUNDAY, NOVEMBER 13
GREEN BAY 33, ATLANTA 25—at Georgia Dome, attendance 71,001. Samkon Gado, making his first NFL start, rushed for 103 yards and scored 3 touch-

downs as the Packers surprised the Falcons. The Packers led 14-0 after just 7:10, the second touchdown set up by Mark Roman's fumble recovery, and led 23-14 entering the fourth quarter. The Falcons trailed 26-17 with 4:40 to play when Roddy White fumbled and Nick Barnett recovered and returned the ball 20 yards to the Falcons' 2. Gado scored on the next play to extend the lead to 33-17. White caught his first NFL touchdown with 1:43 left, but Nick Collins recovered the ensuing onside kick. Favre was 26 of 39 for 252 yards and 1 touchdown, with 1 interception. Donald Driver had 10 catches for 114 yards. Gado rushed 25 times for 103 yards. Michael Vick was 20 of 30 for 209 yards and 2 touchdowns.

Green Bay	14	3	6	10	—	33
Atlanta	0	14	0	11	—	25
GB	—	Gado 9 run (Longwell kick)				
GB	—	Gado 1 run (Longwell kick)				
Atl	—	Dunn 21 pass from Vick (Peterson kick)				
Atl	—	Vick 1 run (Peterson kick)				
GB	—	FG Longwell 46				
GB	—	FG Longwell 23				
GB	—	FG Longwell 53				
Atl	—	FG Peterson 37				
GB	—	FG Longwell 51				
GB	—	Gado 2 run (Longwell kick)				
Atl	—	White 19 pass from Vick (Finneran pass from Vick)				

BUFFALO 14, KANSAS CITY 3—at Ralph Wilson Stadium, attendance 72,093. J.P. Losman replaced an injured Kelly Holcomb and passed for 2 touchdowns, and the Bills' defense intercepted 3 passes, as Buffalo improved to 4-1 at home. The Chiefs drove inside the Bills' 30 four times, but Lawrence Tynes made just 1 field goal. He missed 2 field goals and James Posey recovered Trent Green's fumble on the other possession. Losman's 29-yard touchdown pass came two plays after Rashad Baker's interception. Justin Bannan sacked Green at the Bills' 33 on fourth down with 1:26 to play. Will Shields became the fourth player since 1970 to start 200 consecutive games, and Tony Gonzalez became the club's all-time leader in receiving yards with 7,362, surpassing Otis Taylor. Holcomb was 4 of 6 for 25 yards. Losman replaced him in the second quarter and was 9 of 16 for 137 yards and 2 touchdowns. Green was 23 of 40 for 220 yards, with 3 interceptions.

Kansas City	3	0	0	0	—	3
Buffalo	0	7	7	0	—	14
KC	—	FG Tynes 35				
Buff	—	Evans 33 pass from Losman (Lindell kick)				
Buff	—	Evans 29 pass from Losman (Lindell kick)				

CAROLINA 30, N.Y. JETS 3—at Bank of America Stadium, attendance 73,529. The Panthers' defense forced 6 turnovers as Carolina pulled away from the Jets. The Panthers led 10-3 at halftime before the defense forced turnovers on five consecutive possessions of the second half. Ken Lucas' interception led to Stephen Davis' 1-yard run with 13:25 to play. Chris Gamble recovered a fumble on the ensuing kickoff to set up a field goal, and Gamble's interception on the next play led to John Kasay's 28-yard field goal for a 23-3 lead. Four plays later, Will Witherspoon intercepted a pass and returned it 35 yards for a touchdown with 5:30 to play. Jake Delhomme was 10 of 20 for 119 yards and 1 touchdown, with 2 interceptions. Brooks Bollinger was 11 of 21 for 98 yards, with 4 interceptions.

N.Y. Jets	0	3	0	0	—	3
Carolina	7	3	0	20	—	30
Car	—	Colbert 19 pass from Delhomme (Kasay kick)				
NYJ	—	FG Nugent 22				

Car	—	FG Kasay 23				
Car	—	S. Davis 1 run (Kasay kick)				
Car	—	FG Kasay 42				
Car	—	FG Kasay 28				
Car	—	Witherspoon 35 interception return (Kasay kick)				

CHICAGO 17, SAN FRANCISCO 9—at Soldier Field, attendance 62,153. Nathan Vasher set an NFL record with a 108-yard missed field goal return to propel the Bears to their fifth consecutive victory. Chicago trailed 3-0 as Joe Nedney attempted a 52-yard field goal with three seconds left in the half. The kick was short and Vasher caught it, hesitated, ran to the Bears' 15, then cut across field and up the sideline for a 108-yard return. The Bears' defense allowed just 1 completion, a 28-yard pass to Brandon Lloyd three plays into the second half. Lloyd's catch led to Nedney's second field goal, but Adrian Peterson's 34-yard run led to his 7-yard touchdown run with 14:33 to play for a 14-6 lead. The Chiefs' third field goal with 10:54 to play. The 49ers then forced a punt, but Rasheed Marshall muffed the punt and Chris Thompson recovered to set up Robbie Gould's 37-yard field goal with 7:40 remaining. Kyle Orton was 8 of 13 for 67 yards, with 1 interception. Peterson had 24 carries for 120 yards. Cody Pickett was 1 of 13 for 28 yards, with 1 interception.

San Francisco	0	3	3	3	—	9
Chicago	0	7	0	10	—	17
SF	—	FG Nedney 30				
Chi	—	Vasher 108 field goal return (Gould kick)				
SF	—	FG Nedney 34				
Chi	—	Peterson 7 run (Gould kick)				
SF	—	FG Nedney 29				
Chi	—	FG Gould 37				

DETROIT 29, ARIZONA 21—at Ford Field, attendance 61,091. Joey Harrington passed for 3 touchdowns, all to Roy Williams, as the Lions snapped a 2-game losing streak. The Lions led 16-0 less than 19 minutes into the game. and Williams' 29-yard touchdown catch stretched the lead to 26-11. Kurt Warner's 8-yard scoring pass to Larry Fitzgerald cut the deficit to 29-21 with 2:24 to play, and the Cardinals got the ball back on their own 18 with 1:01 left, but Warner's fourth-and-2 pass was incomplete. Harrington was 22 of 32 for 231 yards and 3 touchdowns. Williams had 7 receptions for 117 yards. Warner was 29 of 45 for 359 yards and 1 touchdown. Fitzgerald had 9 catches for 141 yards.

Arizona	0	3	8	10	—	21
Detroit	9	10	7	3	—	29
Det	—	R. Williams 7 pass from Harrington (Hanson kick)				
Det	—	Safety, Wilkinson tackled Ayanbadejo in end zone				
Det	—	R. Williams 21 pass from Harrington (Hanson kick)				
Ariz	—	FG Rackers 51				
Det	—	FG Hanson 26				
Ariz	—	Arrington 1 run (Ayanbadejo run)				
Det	—	R. Williams 29 pass from Harrington (Hanson kick)				
Ariz	—	FG Rackers 28				
Det	—	FG Hanson 20				
Ariz	—	Fitzgerald 8 pass from Warner (Rackers kick)				

INDIANAPOLIS 31, HOUSTON 17—at RCA Dome, attendance 57,209. Peyton Manning passed for 297 yards and 3 touchdowns as the Colts improved their record to 9-0. The Colts outgained the Texans 419-209 total yards, and scored on three consecutive first-half possessions to take a 21-0 lead. A muffed punt led to Houston's first touchdown, and the Texans scored early in the second half to cut the deficit to 24-

14. Manning responded by completing all 4 pass attempts on a 5-play, 75-yard drive capped by Marvin Harrison's 30-yard touchdown catch with 5:54 left in the third quarter. Manning was 26 of 35 for 297 yards and 3 touchdowns. Edgerrin James rushed 26 times for 122 yards. Harrison had 7 catches for 108 yards. James and Harrison each had 100 yards in the same game for the 21st time, surpassing the NFL record previously held by Emmitt Smith and Michael Irvin. Carr was 16 of 25 for 138 yards and 1 touchdown.

Houston	0	7	10	0	—	17
Indianapolis	7	14	7	3	—	31
Ind	—	Clark 14 pass from Manning (Vanderjagt kick)				
Ind	—	James 5 run (Vanderjagt kick)				
Ind	—	Stokley 21 pass from Manning (Vanderjagt kick)				
Hou	—	Wells 14 run (K. Brown kick)				
Hou	—	Gaffney 13 pass from Carr (K. Brown kick)				
Ind	—	Harrison 30 pass from Manning (Vanderjagt kick)				
Hou	—	FG K. Brown 24				
Ind	—	FG Vanderjagt 45				

JACKSONVILLE 30, BALTIMORE 3—at ALLTEL Stadium, attendance 66,107. Greg Jones rushed for a career-high 106 yards and 1 touchdown as the Jaguars broke their NFL-record-tying mark of 58 games of not scoring at least 30 points. After 2 field goals, Mike Peterson intercepted a pass and returned it 26 yards for a touchdown with 2:01 to cap the scoring. Byron Leftwich was 16 of 30 for 211 yards and 1 touchdown. Jones had 25 carries for 106 yards, and Matt Jones had 5 catches for 117 yards. Kyle Boller was 19 of 33 for 142 yards, with 3 interceptions.

Baltimore	3	0	0	0	—	3
Jacksonville	0	10	7	13	—	30
Balt	—	FG Stover 41				
Jax	—	M. Jones 32 pass from Leftwich (Scobee kick)				
Jax	—	FG Scobee 48				
Jax	—	G. Jones 1 run (Scobee kick)				
Jax	—	FG Scobee 33				
Jax	—	FG Scobee 26				
Jax	—	Peterson 26 interception return (Scobee kick)				

NEW ENGLAND 23, MIAMI 16—at Dolphins Stadium, attendance 73,405. Tom Brady passed for 2 second-half touchdowns as the Patriots handed the Dolphins their fifth loss in six games. Playing with four offensive starters inactive, and a fifth, Corey Dillon, injured after 2 plays, New England turned to Brady and running back Heath Evans, who had been released by the Dolphins less than three weeks earlier. Evans surpassed his 4-year career totals by rushing 17 times for 84 yards. Adam Vinatieri's third field goal gave the Patriots a 15-7 lead with 12:24 to play, but Olindo Mare answered with a 36-yard field goal and Yeremiah Bell intercepted a pass with 5:09 left. Six plays later, Chris Chambers caught a 15-yard touchdown pass for a 16-15 lead with 2:59 to play. On the next play, Brady connected with Tim Dwight on a 59-yard pass play and Ben Watson caught a 17-yard touchdown on the next play for a 21-16 lead. Evans tacked on the 2-point conversion run with 2:16 to play, but the Dolphins drove to the Patriots 5 with 58 seconds left. On fourth-and-goal from the 10, Gus Frerotte's pass sailed out of Chambers' reach in the end zone with 36 seconds to play. Brady was 21 of 36 for 275 yards and 2 touchdowns, with 2 interceptions. Frerotte was 25 of 47 for 360 yards and 2 touchdowns, with 1 interception. Marty Booker had 5 catches for 102 yards.

| New England | 0 | 3 | 9 | 11 | — | 23 |
| Miami | 0 | 7 | 0 | 9 | — | 16 |

Mia	—	Chambers 3 pass from Frerotte (Mare kick)
NE	—	FG Vinatieri 35
NE	—	FG Vinatieri 32
NE	—	Watson 16 pass from Brady (pass failed)
NE	—	FG Vinatieri 33
Mia	—	FG Mare 36
Mia	—	Chambers 15 pass from Frerotte (pass failed)
NE	—	Watson 17 pass from Brady (Evans run)

MINNESOTA 24, N.Y. GIANTS 21—at Giants Stadium, attendance 78,637. The Vikings became the first team in NFL history to score on an interception, kickoff, and punt return in the same game, but needed Paul Edinger's 48-yard field goal with 10 seconds remaining to defeat the Giants. The Giants tallied 405 yards of offense, but committed 5 turnovers. The Giants' defense permitted just 137 yards, including only 6 in the first half, but Darren Sharper's 92-yard interception return gave Minnesota a 7-6 halftime lead. Koren Robinson returned the opening kickoff of the second half 86 yards for a touchdown. The Giants responded with Amani Toomer's 23-yard scoring catch, but the Vikings increased their lead to 21-13 with 5:27 left in the third quarter on Mewelde Moore's 71-yard punt return. Sharper's second interception, in the end zone, thwarted a drive with 3:48 to play in the game, but the Giants got the ball back and drove 67 yards, capped by Tiki Barber's 3-yard run with 1:21 remaining. Barber added the 2-point conversion run to tie the game, but Brad Johnson fired a 21-yard pass to Jermaine Wiggins and matching 11-yard passes to Marcus Robinson and Travis Taylor to set up Edinger's winning kick. Johnson was 17 of 30 for 144 yards. Eli Manning was 23 of 48 for 291 yards and 1 touchdown, with 4 interceptions. Barber had 8 catches for 111 yards.

| Minnesota | 0 | 7 | 14 | 3 | — | 24 |
| N.Y. Giants | 0 | 6 | 7 | 8 | — | 21 |

Minn	—	Sharper 92 interception return (Edinger kick)
NYG	—	FG Feely 35
NYG	—	FG Feely 48
Minn	—	K. Robinson 86 kickoff return (Edinger kick)
NYG	—	Toomer 23 pass from E. Manning (Feely kick)
Minn	—	Moore 71 punt return (Edinger kick)
NYG	—	Barber 3 run (Barber run)
Minn	—	FG Edinger 48

DENVER 31, OAKLAND 17—at McAfee Coliseum, attendance 62,279. Darrent Williams had a 52-yard punt return to set up a touchdown and added an 80-yard interception return for a score in the fourth quarter for the Broncos. Denver scored on five consecutive possessions to take a 23-0 lead late in the third quarter. Trailing 23-10, Jarrod Cooper recovered Tatum Bell's fumble at the Broncos' 33 with 8:34 to play, but five plays later Williams intercepted Kerry Collins' pass and returned it 80 yards for the decisive touchdown. Jake Plummer was 16 of 22 for 205 yards and 1 touchdown. Collins was 26 of 50 for 310 yards and 2 touchdowns, with 3 interceptions.

| Denver | 0 | 13 | 10 | 8 | — | 31 |
| Oakland | 0 | 0 | 0 | 17 | — | 17 |

Den	—	R. Smith 27 pass from Plummer (Elam kick)
Den	—	FG Elam 22
Den	—	FG Elam 38
Den	—	Anderson 1 run (Elam kick)
Den	—	FG Elam 25
Oak	—	R. Moss 29 pass from Collins (Janikowski kick)

Oak	—	FG Janikowski 40
Den	—	Da. Williams 80 interception return (Putzier pass from Plummer)
Oak	—	Gabriel 14 pass from Collins (Janikowski kick)

SEATTLE 31, ST. LOUIS 16—at Qwest Field, attendance 67,192. Shaun Alexander scored 3 touchdowns as the Seahawks increased their lead over the Rams to three games in the NFC West. The Rams led 3-0 and lined up for a 26-yard field goal but holder Dane Looker lateraled to kicker Jeff Wilkins, who rolled out but was tackled by Marcus Trufant to quell the fake field-goal attempt. Dexter Coakley intercepted a pass to begin the second half to set up Wilkins' second field goal, but Seattle answered with touchdowns on its next two possessions for a 24-6 lead. Marc Bulger's 14-yard touchdown pass to Torry Holt on fourth-and-11 with 7:00 remaining cut the deficit to 24-16. The Seahawks marched 12 plays in 69 yards, converting 4 third downs, capped by Alexander's 17-yard run with 1:12 to play to finish the scoring. Matt Hasselbeck was 17 of 29 for 243 yards and 1 touchdown, with 2 interceptions. Alexander rushed 33 times for 165 yards. Bulger was 28 of 40 for 304 yards and 1 touchdown, with 1 interception.

| St. Louis | 3 | 0 | 6 | 7 | — | 16 |
| Seattle | 0 | 10 | 14 | 7 | — | 31 |

StL	—	FG Wilkins 31
Sea	—	Alexander 6 run (J. Brown kick)
Sea	—	FG J. Brown 31
StL	—	FG Wilkins 36
Sea	—	Alexander 4 run (J. Brown kick)
Sea	—	Hackett 31 pass from Hasselbeck (J. Brown kick)
StL	—	FG Wilkins 39
StL	—	Holt 14 pass from Bulger (Wilkins kick)
Sea	—	Alexander 17 run (J. Brown kick)

TAMPA BAY 36, WASHINGTON 35—at Raymond James Stadium, attendance 65,421. Mike Alstott scored on a 2-point conversion run with 58 seconds left as the Buccaneers surpassed their victory total from 2004. The Redskins used a 16-play, 76-yard drive to take a 35-28 lead with 8:19 to play. The Buccaneers forced a punt with 1:52 left, and five plays later Chris Simms completed a 30-yard touchdown pass to Edell Shepherd to pull within 35-34. Walt Harris blocked the potential game-tying extra point, but the Redskins were offsides. With the ball on the 1-yard line, Tampa Bay went for the 2-point conversion, and Alstott was hit at the line before twisting just over the plain with 58 seconds left. The Redskins reached their own 46 but were stopped on downs. Simms was 15 of 29 for 279 yards and 3 touchdowns. Joey Galloway had 7 catches for 131 yards. Mark Brunell was 23 of 35 for 226 yards and 2 touchdowns, with 2 interceptions. Portis had 23 carries for 144 yards.

| Washington | 3 | 10 | 15 | 7 | — | 35 |
| Tampa Bay | 7 | 14 | 7 | 8 | — | 36 |

TB	—	Alstott 2 run (Bryant kick)
Wash	—	FG Hall 33
TB	—	Alstott 1 run (Bryant kick)
Wash	—	Betts 94 kickoff return (Hall kick)
TB	—	Galloway 24 pass from Simms (Bryant kick)
Wash	—	FG Hall 40
Wash	—	Sellers 7 pass from Brunell (Portis pass from Brunell)
Wash	—	Betts 17 pass from Brunell (Hall kick)
TB	—	Hilliard 4 pass from Simms (Bryant kick)
Wash	—	Portis 8 run (Hall kick)
TB	—	Shepherd 30 pass from Simms (Alstott run)

SUNDAY NIGHT, NOVEMBER 13
PITTSBURGH 34, CLEVELAND 21—at Heinz Field, attendance 63,491. Charlie Batch ran for a touchdown and Antwaan Randle El passed for a score as the Steelers stayed even with Cincinnati in the AFC North. Charlie Batch, starting for injured Ben Roethlisberger, engineered 3 consecutive scoring drives, capped by his 1-yard run with six seconds left in the half for a 17-7 lead. Batch was injured prior to his touchdown run, and did not play in the second half. Tommy Maddox came in, and on the third quarter's third play, Randle El took a reverse handoff from Duce Staley and fired a 51-yard touchdown pass to Hines Ward for a 24-7 lead. The Steelers led by at least 13 the remainder of the game. Batch was 13 of 19 for 150 yards. Maddox was 4 of 7 for 22 yards. Ward had 8 catches for 124 yards and surpassed John Stallworth to become the club's all time leader in receptions. Trent Dilfer was 17 of 34 for 253 yards and 1 touchdown, with 1 interception.

| Cleveland | 7 | 0 | 0 | 14 | — | 21 |
| Pittsburgh | 0 | 17 | 7 | 10 | — | 34 |

Cle	—	Droughns 5 run (Dawson kick)
Pitt	—	Bettis 1 run (Reed kick)
Pitt	—	FG Reed 42
Pitt	—	Batch 1 run (Reed kick)
Pitt	—	Ward 51 pass from Randle El (Reed kick)
Pitt	—	FG Reed 33
Cle	—	Bodden 59 return of blocked field goal (Dawson kick)
Pitt	—	Haynes 10 run (Reed kick)
Cle	—	Bryant 9 pass from Dilfer (Dawson kick)

MONDAY NIGHT, NOVEMBER 14
DALLAS 21, PHILADELPHIA 20—at Lincoln Financial Field, attendance 67,739. Roy Williams returned an interception 46 yards for a touchdown as the Cowboys overcame a 13-point deficit in the final four minutes. David Akers' second field goal gave the Eagles a 20-7 lead with 9:12 to play. After an exchange of punts, the Cowboys got the ball on their own 28 with 3:44 to play. Drew Bledsoe completed a 15-yard pass to Keyshawn Johnson and 11-yard to Terry Glenn, followed by a 26-yard run on a draw play by Marion Barber to set up Glenn's 20-yard touchdown catch with 3:04 remaining. Two plays later, Donovan McNabb underthrew his pass and Williams intercepted the ball and returned it down the left sideline 46 yards for a touchdown with 2:43 left, giving Dallas 14 points in 21 seconds. McNabb was injured on the return, and Mike McMahon, after an exchange of punts, scrambled 9 yards to the Cowboys' 42 with four seconds left to give Akers a 60-yard field-goal attempt, which fell short. Bledsoe was 17 of 24 for 196 yards and 1 touchdown, with 1 interception. McNabb was 19 of 34 for 169 yards, with 1 interception.

| Dallas | 7 | 0 | 0 | 14 | — | 21 |
| Philadelphia | 7 | 7 | 3 | 3 | — | 20 |

Phil	—	Westbrook 15 run (Akers kick)
Dall	—	M. Barber 1 run (Suisham kick)
Phil	—	McNabb 2 run (Akers kick)
Phil	—	FG Akers 48
Phil	—	FG Akers 20
Dall	—	T. Glenn 20 pass from Bledsoe (Suisham kick)
Dall	—	R. Williams 46 interception return (Suisham kick)

ELEVENTH WEEK SUMMARIES
American Football Conference

East Division	W	L	T	Pct.	Pts.	OP
New England	6	4	0	.600	227	253
Buffalo	4	6	0	.400	152	210
Miami	3	7	0	.300	162	196
N.Y. Jets	2	8	0	.200	121	227

North Division	W	L	T	Pct.	Pts.	OP
Cincinnati	7	3	0	.700	247	179
Pittsburgh	7	3	0	.700	236	161
Cleveland	4	6	0	.400	157	170
Baltimore	3	7	0	.300	116	184
South Division	**W**	**L**	**T**	**Pct.**	**Pts.**	**OP**
Indianapolis	10	0	0	1.000	305	152
Jacksonville	7	3	0	.700	211	170
Tennessee	2	8	0	.200	203	262
Houston	1	9	0	.100	141	292
West Division	**W**	**L**	**T**	**Pct.**	**Pts.**	**OP**
Denver	8	2	0	.800	259	169
Kansas City	6	4	0	.600	244	214
San Diego	6	4	0	.600	300	202
Oakland	4	6	0	.400	218	229

National Football Conference

East Division	W	L	T	Pct.	Pts.	OP
Dallas	7	3	0	.700	222	164
N.Y. Giants	7	3	0	.700	281	184
Washington	5	5	0	.500	200	201
Philadelphia	4	6	0	.400	210	232
North Division	**W**	**L**	**T**	**Pct.**	**Pts.**	**OP**
Chicago	7	3	0	.700	169	110
Minnesota	5	5	0	.500	174	245
Detroit	4	6	0	.400	167	193
Green Bay	2	8	0	.200	218	204
South Division	**W**	**L**	**T**	**Pct.**	**Pts.**	**OP**
Carolina	7	3	0	.700	253	179
Tampa Bay	7	3	0	.700	206	183
Atlanta	6	4	0	.600	244	206
New Orleans	2	8	0	.200	159	264
West Division	**W**	**L**	**T**	**Pct.**	**Pts.**	**OP**
Seattle	8	2	0	.800	272	187
St. Louis	4	6	0	.400	252	300
Arizona	3	7	0	.300	205	268
San Francisco	2	8	0	.200	151	290

SUNDAY, NOVEMBER 20

TAMPA BAY 30, ATLANTA 27—at Georgia Dome, attendance 70,794. Matt Bryant kicked a 45-yard field goal with 42 seconds left as the Buccaneers scored the final 10 points in the last two minutes to knock off the Falcons. With the score 20-20 early in the fourth quarter, Keith Brooking intercepted a pass and Michael Jenkins caught a 10-yard touchdown pass with 7:36 remaining to give Atlanta 27-20 lead. Chris Simms answered with an 11-play, 71-yard drive, highlighted by his 8-yard pass to Carnell Williams on third-and-6, and capped by Williams' 9-yard run with 1:55 to play to tie the game. Three plays later, Derrick Brooks sacked Michael Vick and forced him to fumble. Shelton Quarles recovered at the Falcons' 34 with 1:07 remaining and Bryant kicked a 45-yard field goal with 42 seconds left. The Falcons drove to the Buccaneers' 37 with five seconds left, and punter Michael Koenen's 55-yard field-goal attempt was wide right as time expired. Simms was 11 of 19 for 118 yards, with 1 interception. Williams rushed 19 times for 116 yards. Vick was 21 of 38 for 306 yards and 2 touchdowns.

Tampa Bay	10	3	7	10	—	30
Atlanta	0	10	7	10	—	27

TB	—	FG Bryant 31
TB	—	McFarland recovered fumble in end zone (Bryant kick)
TB	—	FG Bryant 45
Atl	—	FG Peterson 31
Atl	—	Duckett 1 run (Peterson kick)
Atl	—	Crumpler 4 pass from Vick (Peterson kick)
TB	—	Alstott 1 run (Bryant kick)
Atl	—	FG Peterson 20
Atl	—	Jenkins 10 pass from Vick (Peterson kick)
TB	—	Williams 9 run (Bryant kick)
TB	—	FG Bryant 45

BALTIMORE 16, PITTSBURGH 13 (OT)—at M&T Bank Stadium, attendance 70,601. Matt Stover kicked a 44-yard field goal in overtime as the Ravens snapped the Steelers' 11-game road winning streak, which equaled the second longest in NFL history. Stover's 25-yard field goal just before halftime increased the Ravens' advantage to 13-6. In 5 second-half possessions, the Steelers' defense did not allow the Ravens to cross the Pittsburgh 48-yard line, and Willie Parker's 11-yard run, keyed by 2 Antwaan Randle El catches, capped an 85-yard drive and tied the game with 5:15 to play. In overtime, the Steelers won the toss, but after a combined 3 punts, the Ravens began from their own 44-yard line and Kyle Boller completed a 12-yard pass to Randy Hymes and 6-yard pass to Todd Heap to set up Stover's winning kick. Boller was 21 of 36 for 163 yards and 1 touchdown, with 1 interception. Tommy Maddox, playing for the injured Ben Roethlisberger, was 19 of 36 for 230 yards and 1 touchdown, with 1 interception.

Pittsburgh	0	6	0	7	0	—	13
Baltimore	0	13	0	0	3	—	16

Balt	—	FG Stover 47
Pitt	—	FG Reed 44
Balt	—	Hymes 3 pass from Boller (Stover kick)
Pitt	—	FG Reed 37
Balt	—	FG Stover 25
Pitt	—	Parker 11 pass from Maddox (Reed kick)
Balt	—	FG Stover 44

CHICAGO 13, CAROLINA 3—at Soldier Field, attendance 62,156. The Bears' defense registered 8 sacks and Nathan Vasher's interceptions set up 10 of the club's 13 points as Chicago posted its sixth consecutive victory. John Kasay kicked a 38-yard field goal in the fourth quarter, and the Panthers drove to the Bears' 18 in the final minute before Adewale Ogunleye sacked Delhomme on fourth down to quell the threat. Kyle Orton was 15 of 26 for 136 yards. Delhomme was 22 of 38 for 235 yards, with 2 interceptions. Steve Smith had 14 catches for 169 yards.

Carolina	0	0	0	3	—	3
Chicago	10	3	0	0	—	13

Chi	—	Muhammad 3 pass from Orton (Gould kick)
Chi	—	FG Gould 33
Chi	—	FG Gould 39
Car	—	FG Kasay 38

INDIANAPOLIS 45, CINCINNATI 37—at Paul Brown Stadium, attendance 65,995. Peyton Manning passed for 3 touchdowns as the Colts held off the Bengals to remain undefeated. The Colts scored touchdowns on their first five possessions to take a 35-17 lead with 3:41 left in the second quarter. Shayne Graham's 41-yard field goal with 1:29 left cut the deficit to 35-20, and Keiwan Ratliff intercepted Manning's pass and returned it 35 yards to the Bengals' 14 to set up Rudi Johnson's 1-yard run with 12 seconds left in the half to pull within 35-27. The 62 first-half points equaled the second-most in NFL history. Tab Perry began the second half with a 39-yard kickoff return and Carson Palmer's 15-yard touchdown pass to Chris Henry capped a 17-point run by the Bengals in a span of 3:37 to trail by a point. The Colts used a 15-play, 77-yard drive that fininshed with Edgerrin James' 2-yard touchdown run. Manning was 24 of 40 for 365 yards and 3 touchdowns, with 1 interception. Dallas Clark had 6 catches for 125 yards and Wayne added 5 receptions for 117 yards. Palmer was 25 of 38 for 335 yards and 2 touchdowns, with 1 interception. Chad Johnson had 8 catches for 189 yards.

Indianapolis	14	21	7	3	—	45
Cincinnati	10	17	7	3	—	37

Ind	—	Rhodes 4 run (Vanderjagt kick)
Cin	—	FG Graham 43
Ind	—	Wayne 66 pass from Manning (Vanderjagt kick)
Cin	—	C. Johnson 68 pass from Palmer (Graham kick)
Ind	—	Fletcher 9 pass from Manning (Vanderjagt kick)
Cin	—	R. Johnson 1 run (Graham kick)
Ind	—	James 1 run (Vanderjagt kick)
Ind	—	Clark 21 pass from Manning (Vanderjagt kick)
Cin	—	FG Graham 41
Cin	—	R. Johnson 1 run (Graham kick)
Cin	—	Henry 15 pass from Palmer (Graham kick)
Ind	—	James 2 run (Vanderjagt kick)
Ind	—	FG Vanderjagt 19
Cin	—	FG Graham 44

CLEVELAND 22, MIAMI 0—at Cleveland Browns Stadium, attendance 72,773. The Browns' defense allowed just 55 passing yards and Reuben Droughns rushed for 166 yards as the Browns posted their first shutout since 2001. Droughns had a 75-yard touchdown run on the Browns' first play from scrimmage. The Browns scored on two of their first three drives of the second half, the latter set up by Chris Crocker's interception, for a 22-0 lead with 1:35 left in the third quarter. Trent Dilfer was 11 of 28 for 137 yards and 1 touchdown, and Charlie Frye made his first NFL appearance and was 6 of 11 for 58 yards, with 1 interception. Droughns rushed 30 times for 166 yards. Sage Rosenfels was 5 of 10 for 14 yards, with 2 interceptions, and Gus Frerotte was 4 of 18 for 53 yards.

Miami	0	0	0	0	—	0
Cleveland	9	3	10	0	—	22

Cle	—	Droughns 75 run (kick failed)
Cle	—	FG Dawson 23
Cle	—	FG Dawson 40
Cle	—	Smith 6 pass from Dilfer (Dawson kick)
Cle	—	FG Dawson 24

DALLAS 20, DETROIT 7—at Texas Stadium, attendance 62,670. Marion Barber rushed for 2 touchdowns and Billy Cundiff kicked a club-record 56-yard field goal as the Cowboys posted their third consecutive victory. The Lions had possession just once in the final 11 minutes, and Dat Nguyen recovered Joey Harrington's fumble, caused by Greg Ellis, with 4:17 remaining to end their final drive. Detroit committed 17 penalties for 129 yards. Drew Bledsoe was 12 of 23 for 110 yards. Harrington was 17 of 25 for 169 yards.

Detroit	0	7	0	0	—	7
Dallas	7	6	7	0	—	20

Dall	—	Barber 6 run (Cundiff kick)
Dall	—	FG Cundiff 19
Det	—	K. Jones 2 run (Hanson kick)
Dall	—	FG Cundiff 56
Dall	—	Barber 4 run (Cundiff kick)

DENVER 27, N.Y. JETS 0—at INVESCO Field at Mile High, attendance 76,255. Mike Anderson rushed for 113 yards and 3 touchdowns as the Broncos defense allowed just 195 yards, forced 5 turnovers, and registered 4 sacks to post their first shutout since 1997. Anderson's 3-yard touchdown run capped a 13-play, 60-yard drive with 1:56 remaining for a 27-0 lead. Jake Plummer was 18 of 26 for 225 yards. Anderson carried 26 times for 113 yards. Vinny Testaverde was 15 of 25 for 152 yards, with 2 interceptions. The Jets carried the ball just 7 times for 22 yards.

N.Y. Jets	0	0	0	0	—	0
Denver	7	10	0	10	—	27

Den	—	Anderson 1 run (Elam kick)
Den	—	FG Elam 26
Den	—	Anderson 1 run (Elam kick)
Den	—	FG Elam 47

Den — Anderson 3 run (Elam kick)

NEW ENGLAND 24, NEW ORLEANS 17—at Gillette Stadium, attendance 68,756. Tom Brady passed for 3 touchdowns and Eugene Wilson intercepted a pass in the end zone as time expired to give the Patriots consecutive victories for the first time in 2005. Adam Vinatieri capped an 11-play drive with a 37-yard field goal with 7:52 left for a 24-7 lead. The Saints scored on their next two drives, with Carney's 46-yard field goal cutting the lead to 24-17 with 2:20 remaining. The Saints' defense forced a three-and-out and got the ball back on their own 22 with 1:46 left. Aaron Brooks completed 3 consecutive passes, and then scrambled 20 yards to reach the Patriots' 22. On third-and-10 with nine seconds left, Brooks threw a pass into the end zone intended for Joe Horn but Wilson intercepted the pass as time expired. Brady was 15 of 29 for 22 yards and 3 touchdowns. Brooks was 27 of 50 for 343 yards and 2 touchdowns, with 1 interception.

New Orleans	0	7	0	10	—	17
New England	7	7	7	3	—	24

NE	—	Branch 2 pass from Brady (Vinatieri kick)
NE	—	Vrabel 1 pass from Brady (Vinatieri kick)
NO	—	Stallworth 7 pass from Brooks (Carney kick)
NE	—	Davis 60 pass from Brady (Vinatieri kick)
NE	—	FG Vinatieri 37
NO	—	Stallworth 12 pass from Brooks (Carney kick)
NO	—	FG Carney 46

N.Y. GIANTS 27, PHILADELPHIA 17—at Giants Stadium, attendance 75,626. Eli Manning passed for 3 touchdowns as the Giants surpassed their 2004 victory total. With Donovan McNabb out for the season, Mike McMahon made his first start and the Eagles were forced to punt on their first six possessions. Manning engineered a 69-yard touchdown drive to increase the lead to 20-10, but McMahon came right back with a 1-yard scoring sneak with 7:33 remaining. On third-and-2, Manning found Plaxico Burress with a 61-yard touchdown pass for a 27-17 lead with 5:24 to play. David Akers missed a 38-yard field goal with 19 seconds left to end the Eagles' last scoring chance. Manning was 17 of 26 for 218 yards and 3 touchdowns. Burress had 6 catches for 113 yards. McMahon was 18 of 39 for 298 yards and 1 touchdown, with 1 interception.

Philadelphia	0	0	10	7	—	17
N.Y. Giants	0	10	3	14	—	27

NYG	—	FG Feely 26
NYG	—	Toomer 1 pass from Manning (Feely kick)
Phil	—	R. Brown 22 pass from McMahon (Akers kick)
NYG	—	FG Feely 27
Phil	—	FG Akers 20
NYG	—	Shockey 1 pass from Manning (Feely kick)
Phil	—	McMahon 1 run (Akers kick)
NYG	—	Burress 61 pass from Manning (Feely kick)

ARIZONA 38, ST. LOUIS 28—at Edward Jones Dome, attendance 65,750. Kurt Warner passed for 3 touchdowns, including 2 in the fourth quarter as the Cardinals rallied to victory. Reggie Swinton's 90-yard kickoff return set up Larry Fitzgerald's 7-yard touchdown catch for a 31-20 lead with 3:11 to play. Darryl Blackstock sacked Jamie Martin on the next play from scrimmage and forced him to fumble. Adrian Wilson recovered and J.J. Arrington scored with 1:54 left. Warner was 27 of 39 for 285 yards and 3 touch-

downs. Fitzgerald had 9 catches for 104 yards, and Boldin added 8 receptions for 105 yards. Wilson had 3 sacks, 1 forced fumble, and recovered a fumble. Marc Bulger was 19 of 24 for 224 yards and 2 touchdowns before suffering a season-ending shoulder injury late in the third quarter. Jamie Martin was 14 of 19 for 161 yards and 1 touchdown. Torry Holt had 11 catches for 129 yards.

Arizona	3	10	3	22	—	38
St. Louis	3	7	7	11	—	28

StL	—	FG Wilkins 27
Ariz	—	FG Rackers 32
StL	—	Holt 22 pass from Bulger (Wilkins kick)
Ariz	—	Boldin 13 pass from Warner (Rackers kick)
Ariz	—	FG Rackers 33
Ariz	—	FG Rackers 51
StL	—	Bruce 46 pass from Bulger (Wilkins kick)
Ariz	—	Bergen 9 pass from Warner (Boldin pass from Warner)
StL	—	FG Wilkins 32
Ariz	—	Fitzgerald 7 pass from Warner (Rackers kick)
Ariz	—	Arrington 7 run (Rackers kick)
StL	—	Curtis 26 pass from Martin (Harris pass from Martin)

SAN DIEGO 48, BUFFALO 10—at Qualcomm Stadium, attendance 65,602. Drew Brees had nearly as many touchdown passes (4) as incompletions (5) as the Chargers overwhelmed the Bills. On the day the Chargers retired Lance Alworth's number 19, the Chargers scored on five of their six first-half possessions, with drives of 75, 72, 70, 22, and 83 yards, capped by Keenan McCardell's 29-yard touchdown catch with 37 seconds left in the half for a 35-10 lead. The Chargers scored on their first three drives of the second half as well, and of their 11 possessions for the game, San Diego scored eight times, punted once, and had two 1-play kneel downs, one at the end of the half and the other at the end of the game. Brees was 28 of 33 for 339 yards and 4 touchdowns. J.P. Losman was 20 of 36 for 18 yards and 1 touchdown, with 1 interception.

Buffalo	3	7	0	0	—	10
San Diego	14	21	3	10	—	48

SD	—	Tomlinson 1 run (Kaeding kick)
Buff	—	FG Lindell 53
SD	—	Gates 27 pass from Brees (Kaeding kick)
SD	—	Parker 23 pass from Brees (Kaeding kick)
SD	—	Neal 2 pass from Brees (Kaeding kick)
Buff	—	Shelton 3 pass from Losman (Lindell kick)
SD	—	McCardell 29 pass from Brees (Kaeding kick)
SD	—	FG Kaeding 28
SD	—	FG Kaeding 38
SD	—	Turner 8 run (Kaeding kick)

SEATTLE 27, SAN FRANCISCO 25—at Monster Park, attendance 63,590. The Seahawks survived a failed 2-point conversion attempt with 28 seconds left to escape San Francisco with their sixth consecutive victory. Josh Scobee recovered a kickoff to set up Josh Brown's second field goal for a 27-12 lead with 2:23 remaining in the third quarter. The 49ers bounced back on the ensuing drive with Ken Dorsey's 22-yard scoring pass to Brandon Lloyd. The Seahawks failed to get a first down on three fourth-quarter possessions, and the 49ers drove 76 yards, highlighted by 2 key third-down passes by Dorsey, and capped by Maurice Hicks' 1-yard run with 28 seconds left. However, Dorsey's 2-point conversion pass short-hopped

Johnnie Morton, and Marquand Manuel recovered the onside kick. Matt Hasselbeck was 19 of 31 for 233 yards and 1 touchdown. Shaun Alexander rushed 24 times for 115 yards. Dorsey was 18 of 29 for 249 yards and 1 touchdown. Lloyd had 7 catches for 119 yards.

Seattle	3	14	10	0	—	27
San Francisco	3	6	13	3	—	25

Sea	—	FG J. Brown 21
SF	—	FG Nedney 33
Sea	—	Alexander 8 run (J. Brown kick)
SF	—	FG Nedney 31
Sea	—	Hackett 12 pass from Hasselbeck (J. Brown kick)
SF	—	FG Nedney 40
SF	—	FG Nedney 22
Sea	—	Alexander 1 run (J. Brown kick)
Sea	—	FG J. Brown 47
SF	—	Lloyd 22 pass from Dorsey (Nedney kick)
SF	—	Hicks 1 run (pass failed)

JACKSONVILLE 31, TENNESSEE 28—at The Coliseum, attendance 69,149. Byron Leftwich passed for 3 touchdowns and ran for another as Jacksonville rallied to victory to post its best 10-game start since 1999. Leftwich engineered touchdown drives of 79 and 89 yards to take a 28-21 lead with 9:21 left. The Titans punted with 4:30 left, but the Jaguars converted 2 key third-down situations and Josh Scobee kicked a 31-yard field goal with 1:52 to play. Roydell Williams caught an 8-yard touchdown pass with 10 seconds left, but the onside kick skipped out of bounds. Leftwich was 22 of 38 for 258 yards and 3 touchdowns. Steve McNair was 20 of 30 for 208 yards and 2 touchdowns, with 1 interception.

Jacksonville	0	7	14	10	—	31
Tennessee	0	14	7	7	—	28

Tenn	—	C. Brown 15 pass from McNair (Bironas kick)
Jax	—	Brady 1 pass from Leftwich (Scobee kick)
Tenn	—	C. Brown 1 run (Bironas kick)
Jax	—	Leftwich 2 run (Scobee kick)
Tenn	—	Odom 27 fumble return (Bironas kick)
Jax	—	Wilford 18 pass from Leftwich (Scobee kick)
Jax	—	M. Jones 7 pass from Leftwich (Scobee kick)
Jax	—	FG Scobee 31
Tenn	—	R. Williams 8 pass from McNair (Bironas kick)

OAKLAND 16, WASHINGTON 13—at FedExField, attendance 90,129. Sebastian Janikowski made a 19-yard field goal with 1:08 remaining to lift the Raiders. Kerry Collins connected with Jerry Porter on a 49-yard touchdown pass just four plays into the second half, and Janikowski capped an 87-yard drive with a 25-yard game-tying field goal with 7:56 remaining. Collins completed 2 key passes to LaMont Jordan to set up Janikowski's 19-yard kick with 1:08 to play. The Redskins reached the Raiders' 43 with 17 seconds left, but Derrick Burgess sacked Mark Brunell, forced him to fumble, and recovered the ball. Collins was 19 of 36 for 289 yards and 1 touchdown, with 1 interception. Jerry Porter had 6 catches for 142 yards. Brunell was 14 of 32 for 155 yards.

Oakland	3	0	7	6	—	16
Washington	7	6	0	0	—	13

Wash	—	Marshall 17 interception return (Hall kick)
Oak	—	FG Janikowski 30
Wash	—	FG Hall 24
Wash	—	FG Hall 45
Oak	—	Porter 49 pass from Collins (Janikowski kick)

Oak — FG Janikowski 25
Oak — FG Janikowski 19

SUNDAY NIGHT, NOVEMBER 20
KANSAS CITY 45, HOUSTON 17—at Reliant Stadium, attendance 70,481. Larry Johnson rushed for 211 yards and 2 touchdowns and Trent Green passed for 3 scores as the Chiefs overwhelmed the Texans. Eric Warfield returned an interception 57 yards for a touchdown with three seconds left in the half to give the Chiefs a 31-7 halftime lead. The Texans scored on consecutive possessions in the third quarter to trim the deficit to 31-17, but the Chiefs scored touchdowns on their next two drives to pull away. Green was 19 of 29 for 220 yards and 3 touchdowns, with 1 interception. Johnson had 36 carries for 211 yards. David Carr was 19 of 36 for 182 yards, with 1 interception.

Kansas City	10	21	0	14 —	45
Houston	7	0	10	0 —	17

KC — FG Tynes 35
KC — L. Johnson 23 run (Tynes kick)
Hou — Mathis 99 kickoff return (K. Brown kick)
KC — Kennison 26 pas from Green (Tynes kick)
KC — L. Johnson 1 run (Tynes kick)
KC — Warfield 57 interception return (Tynes kick)
Hou — Davis 3 run (K. Brown kick)
Hou — FG K. Brown 22
KC — Kennison 7 pass from Green (Tynes kick)
KC — Parker 6 pass from Green (Tynes kick)

MONDAY NIGHT, NOVEMBER 21
MINNESOTA 20, GREEN BAY 17—at Lambeau Field, attendance 70,610. Paul Edinger kicked a 27-yard field goal as time expired to give the Vikings their third consecutive victory. Ryan Longwell tied the game at 17-17 with a 46-yard field goal with 3:03 remaining, but Brad Johnson connected with Koren Robinson on a 35-yard pass to the Packers' 6. Edinger made the game-winning kick as time expired. Brad Johnson was 18 of 30 for 196 yards, with 1 interception. Mewelde Moore had 22 carries for 122 yards. Favre was 30 of 33 for 227 yards and 2 touchdowns, with 2 interceptions.

Minnesota	0	7	7	6 —	20
Green Bay	7	7	0	3 —	17

GB — Driver 15 pass from Favre (Longwell kick)
Minn — Edwards 51 interception return (Edinger kick)
GB — Driver 53 pass from Favre (Longwell kick)
Minn — Fason 1 run (Edinger kick)
Minn — FG Edinger 24
GB — FG Longwell 46
Minn — FG Edinger 27

TWELFTH WEEK SUMMARIES
American Football Conference

East Division	W	L	T	Pct.	Pts.	OP
New England	6	5	0	.545	243	279
Buffalo	4	7	0	.364	161	223
Miami	4	7	0	.364	195	217
N.Y. Jets	2	9	0	.182	140	248
North Division	**W**	**L**	**T**	**Pct.**	**Pts.**	**OP**
Cincinnati	8	3	0	.727	289	208
Pittsburgh	7	4	0	.636	243	187
Cleveland	4	7	0	.364	169	194
Baltimore	3	8	0	.273	145	228
South Division	**W**	**L**	**T**	**Pct.**	**Pts.**	**OP**
Indianapolis	11	0	0	1.000	331	159
Jacksonville	8	3	0	.727	235	187
Tennessee	3	8	0	.273	236	284

Houston	1	10	0	.091	168	325
West Division	**W**	**L**	**T**	**Pct.**	**Pts.**	**OP**
Denver	9	2	0	.818	283	190
Kansas City	7	4	0	.636	270	230
San Diego	7	4	0	.636	323	219
Oakland	4	7	0	.364	239	262

National Football Conference

East Division	W	L	T	Pct.	Pts.	OP
Dallas	7	4	0	.636	243	188
N.Y. Giants	7	4	0	.636	302	208
Philadelphia	5	6	0	.455	229	246
Washington	5	6	0	.455	217	224
North Division	**W**	**L**	**T**	**Pct.**	**Pts.**	**OP**
Chicago	8	3	0	.727	182	120
Minnesota	6	5	0	.545	198	257
Detroit	4	7	0	.364	174	220
Green Bay	2	9	0	.182	232	223
South Division	**W**	**L**	**T**	**Pct.**	**Pts.**	**OP**
Carolina	8	3	0	.727	266	188
Atlanta	7	4	0	.636	271	213
Tampa Bay	7	4	0	.636	216	196
New Orleans	3	8	0	.273	180	285
West Division	**W**	**L**	**T**	**Pct.**	**Pts.**	**OP**
Seattle	9	2	0	.818	296	208
St. Louis	5	6	0	.455	285	327
Arizona	3	8	0	.273	222	292
San Francisco	2	9	0	.182	173	323

THURSDAY, NOVEMBER 24
ATLANTA 27, DETROIT 7—at Ford Field, attendance 62,390. Alge Crumpler had 2 touchdown catches as the Falcons' defense forced 4 turnovers in Steve Mariucci's last game as Lions' coach. Chauncey Davis recovered Shawn Bryson's fumble to set up T.J. Duckett's 1-yard run for a 10-0 lead. The Falcons forced a punt and Michael Vick scrambled 19 yards on third-and-10 that led to Crumpler's 6-yard touchdown catch for a 17-0 lead with 10:44 left in the second quarter. The Falcons forced a three-and-out to begin the second half and Allen Rossum's 29-yard punt return led to Crumpler's 32-yard catch. Jason Webster's interception three plays later set up Todd Peterson's 23-yard field goal with 5:11 to play in the third quarter for a 27-0 lead. Vick was 12 of 22 for 146 yards and 2 touchdowns, with 1 interception. Joey Harrington was 6 of 13 for 61 yards, with 1 interception. Jeff Garcia was 14 of 24 for 154 yards and 1 touchdown, with 1 interception. Dan Orlovsky was 5 of 11 for 43 yards.

Atlanta	10	7	10	0 —	27
Detroit	0	0	0	7 —	7

Atl — FG Peterson 21
Atl — Duckett 1 run (Peterson kick)
Atl — Crumpler 6 pass from Vick (Peterson kick)
Atl — Crumpler 32 pass from Vick (Peterson kick)
Atl — FG Peterson 23
Det — R. Williams 31 pass from Garcia (Hanson kick)

DENVER 24, DALLAS 21 (OT)—at Texas Stadium, attendance 63,273. Ron Dayne scored a touchdown and his 55-yard run set up Jason Elam's field goal just 1:11 into overtime to give the Broncos their fourth consecutive victory. Late in the third quarter Keith Davis downed Mat McBriar's punt at the Broncos' 1. Two plays later, Roy Williams forced Mike Anderson to fumble and Terence Newman recovered the ball at the Broncos' 10. Jason Witten's 4-yard touchdown catch on third-and-goal tied the game with 13:36 to play. The Cowboys forced a punt and drove to the Broncos' 15, but Billy Cundiff missed his 34-yard field goal wide left. In overtime, the Broncos won the toss and on the second play of scrimmage Dayne's 55-yard run to the Cowboys' 6 led to Elam's winning kick. Jake Plummer was 15 of 24 for 162 yards and 1 touchdown, with 1 interception. Drew Bledsoe was 29

of 44 for 232 yards and 2 touchdowns, with 2 interceptions.

Denver	7	7	7	0	3 —	24
Dallas	7	7	0	7	0 —	21

Den — Bailey 65 interception return (Elam kick)
Dall — K. Johnson 14 pass from Bledsoe (Cundiff kick)
Den — R. Smith 20 pass from Plummer (Elam kick)
Dall — Bledsoe 1 run (Cundiff kick)
Den — Dayne 16 run (Elam kick)
Dall — Witten 4 pass from Bledsoe (Cundiff kick)
Den — FG Elam 24

SUNDAY, NOVEMBER 27
JACKSONVILLE 24, ARIZONA 17—at Sun Devil Stadium, attendance 39,198. The Jaguars overcame the loss of Byron Leftwich to win their fourth consecutive game. Leftwich was injured in the first quarter, and David Garrard replaced him and capped the 67-yard drive with a 16-yard touchdown run for a 7-0 lead. Derrick Wimbush returned a kickoff 91 yards for a touchdown for a 17-3 third-quarter lead. Greg Jones scored for a 24-10 lead with 4:20 left. The Cardinals needed just four plays to score another touchdown, forced a punt, and drove to the Jaguars' 36 with 32 seconds left. Kurt Warner rolled right and was sacked by Akin Ayodele. Rob Meier recovered the fumble to end the scoring threat. Garrard was 12 of 26 for 115 yards. Warner was 29 of 46 for 315 yards and 2 touchdowns, with 1 interception. Anquan Boldin had 10 catches for 115 yards.

Jacksonville	7	3	7	7 —	24
Arizona	0	0	3	14 —	17

Jax — Garrard 16 run (Scobee kick)
Jax — FG Scobee 30
Ariz — FG Rackers 42
Jax — Wimbush 91 kickoff return (Scobee kick)
Ariz — Edwards 1 pass from Warner (Rackers kick)
Jax — G. Jones 25 run (Scobee kick)
Ariz — Fitzgerald 5 pass from Warner (Rackers kick)

CAROLINA 13, BUFFALO 9—at Ralph Wilson Stadium, attendance 71,440. Jake Delhomme completed a 3-yard touchdown pass to Michael Gaines with 2:16 remaining as the Panthers pulled into first place in the NFC South. Gaines' touchdown catch came on third-and-goal with 2:16 to play. The Bills drove to the Panthers' 43 with 47 seconds left, but Chris Gamble intercepted J.P. Losman's pass to clinch the victory. Delhomme was 20 of 27 for 191 yards and 1 touchdown. Losman was 16 of 29 for 197 yards, with 1 interception.

Carolina	0	3	3	7 —	13
Buffalo	0	6	0	3 —	9

Car — FG Kasay 25
Buff — FG Lindell 31
Buff — FG Lindell 45
Car — FG Kasay 25
Buff — FG Lindell 33
Car — Gaines 3 pass from Delhomme (Kasay kick)

CINCINNATI 42, BALTIMORE 29—at Paul Brown Stadium, attendance 65,680. Carson Palmer passed for 3 touchdowns as the Bengals jumped to a 34-0 lead before holding off the Ravens. The Ravens scored 3 consecutive touchdowns, the latter two scores set up by B.J. Ward's fumble recovery and Deion Sanders' interception, to pull within 34-21 with 11:58 to play. Palmer completed a third-and-9 pass to T.J. Houshmandzadeh that led to Rudi Johnson's 3-yard run with 6:03 left. Palmer was 22 of 30 for 302 yards and 3 touchdowns, with 1 interception. Johnson had 27 carries for 114 yards. Houshmandzadeh had 9 catches for 147 yards. Boller was 18 of 32 for 211 yards and 3 touchdowns, with 2 interceptions. Jamal Lewis had 23 carries for 113 yards.

Baltimore	0	0	14	15	—	29
Cincinnati	3	14	17	8	—	42

Cin	—	FG Graham 26
Cin	—	R. Johnson 6 run (Graham kick)
Cin	—	C. Johnson 54 pass from Palmer (Graham kick)
Cin	—	Houshmandzadeh 30 pass from Palmer (Graham kick)
Cin	—	Henry 27 pass from Palmer (Graham kick)
Cin	—	FG Graham 31
Balt	—	Mason 28 pass from Boller (Stover kick)
Balt	—	Heap 34 pass from Boller (Stover kick)
Balt	—	J. Lewis 5 run (Stover kick)
Cin	—	R. Johnson 3 run (Schobel pass from Palmer)
Balt	—	Heap 17 pass from Boller (Green run)

ST. LOUIS 33, HOUSTON 27 (OT)—at Reliant Stadium, attendance 70,010. Ryan Fitzpatrick made his first NFL appearance and engineered a 10-point rally in the final 26 seconds of regulation to propel the Rams to victory. Fitzpatrick was playing in place of Jamie Martin, who was injured on a first-quarter sack by DaShon Polk. Trailing 24-3, Fitzpatrick engineered a 13-play, 77-yard scoring drive to pull within 24-17 with 6:37 remaining. Brown made a 35-yard field goal with 2:49 left to increase the advantage to 27-17. Fitzpatrick completed a fourth-and-1 pass to Torry Holt for a first down, and moments later on fourth-and-6, he scrambled in the pocket before launching a 43-yard touchdown pass to Isaac Bruce with 26 seconds left. Holt then recovered the onside kick and caught a 19-yard pass to set up Jeff Wilkins' 47-yard field goal as regulation expired. In overtime, the Rams' defense forced a punt and six plays later Kevin Curtis took a screen pass and raced 56 yards up the left sideline for the game-ending touchdown. Martin was 2 of 3 for 14 yards. Fitzpatrick was 19 of 30 for 310 yards and 3 touchdowns, with 1 interception. Holt had 10 catches for 130 yards. Jackson carried 25 times for 110 yards. Carr was 25 of 34 for 293 yards and 3 touchdowns, with 1 interception.

St. Louis	0	3	7	17	6	—	33
Houston	7	17	0	3	0	—	27

Hou	—	A. Johnson 5 pass from Carr (K. Brown kick)
Hou	—	Davis 30 pass from Carr (K. Brown kick)
Hou	—	FG K. Brown 39
StL	—	FG Wilkins 37
Hou	—	Bradford 10 pass from Carr (K. Brown kick)
StL	—	Holt 19 pass from Fitzpatrick (Wilkins kick)
StL	—	Jackson 1 run (Wilkins kick)
Hou	—	FG K. Brown 35
StL	—	Bruce 43 pass from Fitzpatrick (Wilkins kick)
StL	—	FG Wilkins 47
StL	—	Curtis 56 pass from Fitzpatrick

KANSAS CITY 26, NEW ENGLAND 16—at Arrowhead Stadium, attendance 78,025. Greg Wesley intercepted 3 passes and Lawrence Tynes equalled an NFL record with 4 field goals in a quarter as the Chiefs held off the Patriots. Trent Green completed a long 52-yard touchdown pass to Dante Hall for a 26-3 lead. The Patriots drove 69 and 78 yards on their next two possessions, but were unable to complete a 2-point conversion and

trailed 26-16 with 10:03 to play. The Patriots forced a punt and drove near midfield, but Wesley intercepted his third pass at 3:43 remaining, and Sammy Knight intercepted a bobbled pass with 1:56 left to clinch the victory. Green was 19 of 26 for 323 yards and 1 touchdown. Larry Johnson had 31 carries for 119 yards. Tom Brady was 22 of 40 for 248 yards and 1 touchdown, with 4 interceptions.

New England	0	3	7	6	—	16
Kansas City	7	12	7	0	—	26

KC	—	L. Johnson 1 run (Tynes kick)
KC	—	FG Tynes 25
KC	—	FG Tynes 20
NE	—	FG Vinatieri 29
KC	—	FG Tynes 33
KC	—	FG Tynes 47
KC	—	Hall 52 pass from Green (Tynes kick)
NE	—	Pass 1 run (Vinatieri kick)
NE	—	Fauria 1 pass from Brady (pass failed)

MINNESOTA 24, CLEVELAND 12—at Metrodome, attendance 63,814. Marcus Robinson had 3 touchdown catches and Darren Sharper intercepted 2 passes as the Vikings won their fourth consecutive game. In the third quarter, Keith Newman sacked Trent Dilfer and forced him to fumble. E.J. Henderson recovered at the Browns' 17 that set up Robinson's second scoring catch to give Minnesota a 17-3 lead. Sharper's interception and 18-yard return to the Browns' 32 was followed four plays later by Robinson's catch for a 24-6 lead. Brad Johnson was 19 of 28 for 207 yards and 3 touchdowns, with 1 interception. Dilfer was 23 of 35 for 214 yards and 1 touchdown, with 2 interceptions.

Cleveland	0	3	3	6	—	12
Minnesota	3	7	7	7	—	24

Minn	—	FG Edinger 43
Minn	—	M. Robinson 15 pass from B. Johnson (Edinger kick)
Cle	—	FG Dawson 32
Minn	—	M. Robinson 15 pass from B. Johnson (Edinger kick)
Cle	—	FG Dawson 38
Minn	—	M. Robinson 2 pass from B. Johnson (Edinger kick)
Cle	—	Northcutt 9 pass from Dilfer (run failed)

MIAMI 33, OAKLAND 21—at McAfee Coliseum, attendance 49,097. Gus Frerotte passed for 2 touchdowns as the Dolphins' defense registered 7 sacks and forced 3 turnovers to snap a three-game losing streak. Trailing 23-21, the Raiders got the ball back, but on fourth-and-1 from their own 44 with 6:20 left, Oakland punted. Seven plays later, Ricky Williams scored on a 34-yard run to take a 30-21 lead. Holliday sacked Collins late in the fourth quarter and forced him to fumble. Taylor recovered and Olindo Mare booted a 27-yard field goal with 1:10 to play. Gus Frerotte was 18 of 31 for 261 yards and 2 touchdowns, with 1 interception. Chris Chambers had 6 catches for 101 yards. Collins was 21 of 37 for 226 yards, with 2 interceptions.

Miami	7	7	9	10	—	33
Oakland	0	7	7	7	—	21

Mia	—	Gilmore 44 pass from Frerotte (Mare kick)
Oak	—	Jordan 1 run (Janikowski kick)
Mia	—	R. Brown 1 run (Mare kick)
Mia	—	Safety, Taylor sacked Collins in end zone
Oak	—	Jordan 8 run (Janikowski kick)
Mia	—	McMichael 25 pass from Frerotte (Mare kick)
Oak	—	Collins 18 run (Janikowski kick)
Mia	—	Williams 34 run (Mare kick)

Mia	—	FG Mare 27

PHILADELPHIA 19, GREEN BAY 14—at Lincoln Financial Field, attendance 67,665. Roderick Hood intercepted a pass in the end zone with 38 seconds left as the Eagles forced 5 turnovers and snapped a four-game losing streak. Ryan Moats recovered Andrae Thurman's fumbled kickoff to set up David Akers' fourth field goal with 1:49 remaining. Favre led the Packers to midfield, but his deep pass into double coverage intended for Robert Ferguson was intercepted by Hood. Mike McMahon was 12 of 28 for 91 yards. Brian Westbrook had 20 carries for 120 yards. Favre was 15 of 33 for 171 yards and 1 touchdown, with 2 interceptions. Samkon Gado carried 26 times for 111 yards.

Green Bay	7	7	0	0	—	14
Philadelphia	10	0	3	6	—	19

Phil	—	FG Akers 44
Phil	—	Westbrook 27 run (Akers kick)
GB	—	Gado 33 run (Longwell kick)
GB	—	Martin 13 pass from Favre (Longwell kick)
Phil	—	FG Akers 38
Phil	—	FG Akers 37
Phil	—	FG Akers 33

SEATTLE 24, N.Y. GIANTS 21 (OT)—at Qwest Field, attendance 67,102. Josh Brown made a 36-yard field goal with just 2:45 left in overtime as the Seahawks survived 3 missed field-goal attempts by Jay Feely to win their seventh consecutive game. Giants' punter Jeff Feagles set an NFL record by playing in his 283rd consecutive game. Seattle's only fourth-down run, on fourth-and-1, with 4:33 to play capped a 13-play, 80-yard drive and gave Seattle a 21-13 lead. Eli Manning lofted an 18-yard touchdown pass to Amani Toomer, who barely got two feet down in the back of the end zone, and then connected with Jeremy Shockey on a 2-point conversion catch with 1:59 remaining. The Giants got the ball back, but Feely's 40-yard field-goal attempt sailed just wide left as time expired in regulation. In overtime, Feely was short from 54 yards and 45 yards before Alexander's 13-yard run set up Josh Brown's game-winning field goal. Matt Hasselbeck was 21 of 37 for 249 yards and 2 touchdowns, with 1 interception. Joe Jurevicius had 8 catches for 137 yards. Alexander rushed 31 times for 110 yards. Manning was 29 of 53 for 344 yards and 2 touchdowns, with 1 interception. Shockey had 10 catches for 127 yards and Plaxico Burress had 6 receptions for 109 yards. Tiki Barber rushed 26 times for 151 yards.

N.Y. Giants	0	10	3	8	0	—	21
Seattle	7	0	7	7	3	—	24

Sea	—	Jurevicius 35 pass from Hasselbeck (J. Brown kick)
NYG	—	FG Feely 39
NYG	—	Shockey 7 pass from E. Manning (Feely kick)
NYG	—	FG Feely 43
Sea	—	Jurevicius 16 pass from Hasselbeck (J. Brown kick)
Sea	—	Alexander 4 run (J. Brown kick)
NYG	—	Toomer 18 pass from E. Manning (Shockey pass from E. Manning)
Sea	—	FG J. Brown 36

CHICAGO 13, TAMPA BAY 10—at Raymond James Stadium, attendance 65,506. The Bears' defense registered 4 sacks as Chicago won its seventh consecutive game. The seven-game winning streak matched the club's longest in 19 years. Trailing 13-3, Mike Alstott capped a 50-yard drive with a 2-yard plunge with 7:00 remaining. The Buccaneers forced a punt and drove to the Bears' 11, but Matt Bryant pushed his 29-yard field-goal attempt with 2:47 left. Simms was 19 of 30 for 202 yards. Joey Galloway had 7 catches for 138 yards. Kyle Orton was 14 of 28 for 134 yards and 1 touchdown, with 1 interception.

Chicago	7	3	3	0	—	13
Tampa Bay	3	0	0	7	—	10

Chi	—	Gilmore 1 pass from Orton (Gould kick)
TB	—	FG Bryant 27
Chi	—	FG Gould 25
Chi	—	FG Gould 36
TB	—	Alstott 2 run (Bryant kick)

TENNESSEE 33, SAN FRANCISCO 22—at The Coliseum, attendance 69,149. Steve McNair passed for 3 touchdowns, all in the third quarter, as the Titans snapped a five-game losing streak. Roydell Williams caught a 50-yard scoring pass from Steve McNair for a 23-14 lead. Following another three-and-out, McNair capped a 68-yard drive with a 4-yard scoring pass to Erron Kinney for a 30-14 lead with 4:54 left in the third quarter. The 49ers pulled with 11 points with 1:15 left, and Derrick Johnson recovered the onside kick, but Kyle Vanden Bosch sacked Ken Dorsey, forced him to fumble, and Andre Woolfolk recovered at the Titans' 40 with five seconds left. McNair was 23 of 41 for 343 yards and 3 touchdowns, with 1 interception. Dorsey was 23 of 43 for 192 yards and 1 touchdown, with 2 interceptions.

San Francisco	0	14	0	8	—	22
Tennessee	3	6	21	3	—	33

Tenn	—	FG Bironas 36
SF	—	Barlow 1 run (Cortez kick)
Tenn	—	FG Bironas 41
Tenn	—	FG Bironas 21
SF	—	Spencer 61 interception return (Cortez kick)
Tenn	—	C. Brown 41 pass from McNair (Bironas kick)
Tenn	—	R. Williams 50 pass from McNair (Bironas kick)
Tenn	—	Kinney 4 pass from McNair (Bironas kick)
Tenn	—	FG Bironas 22
SF	—	Battle 17 pass from Dorsey (T. Jackson pass from Dorsey)

SAN DIEGO 23, WASHINGTON 17 (OT)—at FedEx Field, attendance 84,930. LaDainian Tomlinson rushed for 184 yards and scored on a 41-yard run on the second play of overtime to lift the Chargers to their fourth consecutive victory. Tomlinson scored on a 22-yard run with 3:29 left to tie the game. The Chargers regained possession, but Marcus Washington tipped a pass and Shawn Springs intercepted it at the Chargers' 31 with 1:04 remaining. A holding penalty pushed the Redskins back to the Chargers' 35, and John Hall missed a 52-yard field-goal attempt wide right with 30 seconds left. Walt Harris intercepted Drew Brees' Hail Mary pass in the end zone to end regulation. The Chargers, however, won the overtime coin toss. On first down, Antonio Gates caught a 24-yard pass, and Tomlinson broke free over left tackle for a 41-yard run on the next play with 34 seconds elapsed for the sixth-fastest overtime finish in NFL history. Brees was 22 of 44 for 215 yards, with 3 interceptions. Tomlinson had 25 carries for 184 yards. Mark Brunell was 17 of 27 for 194 yards and 1 touchdown.

San Diego	0	7	0	10	6	—	23
Washington	3	7	7	0	0	—	17

Wash	—	FG Hall 38
SD	—	Tomlinson 1 run (Kaeding kick)
Wash	—	S. Moss 22 pas from Brunell (Hall kick)
Wash	—	Cartwright 13 run (Hall kick)
SD	—	FG Kaeding 48
SD	—	Tomlinson 32 run (Kaeding kick)
SD	—	Tomlinson 41 run

SUNDAY NIGHT, NOVEMBER 27

NEW ORLEANS 21, N.Y. JETS 19—at The Meadowlands, attendance 77,152. Aaron Brooks passed for 3 touchdowns as the Saints held off the Jets and snapped their six-game losing streak. Devery Henderson's 30-yard touchdown catch with 8:32 remaining gave the Saints a 21-19 lead. The Jets' final chance began from their own 46-yard line with 1:37 left. Brooks Bollinger completed a 21-yard pass to Doug Jolley and reached the Saints' 34, but Nugent's 53-yard field-goal attempt fell just short with 11 seconds remaining. Brooks was 17 of 23 for 181 yards and 3 touchdowns. Bollinger was 19 of 28 for 251 yards and 1 touchdown.

New Orleans	0	14	0	7	—	21
N.Y. Jets	3	6	7	3	—	19

NYJ	—	FG Nugent 29
NO	—	Stallworth 21 pass from Brooks (Carney kick)
NYJ	—	FG Nugent 45
NO	—	Hilton 15 pass from Brooks (Carney kick)
NYJ	—	FG Nugent 41
NYJ	—	McCareins 27 pass from Bollinger (Nugent kick)
NYJ	—	FG Nugent 38
NO	—	Henderson 30 pass from Brooks (Stallworth pass from Brooks)

MONDAY NIGHT, NOVEMBER 28

INDIANAPOLIS 26, PITTSBURGH 7—at RCA Dome, attendance 57,442. Peyton Manning fired an 80-yard touchdown to Marvin Harrison on a play-action pass on the Colts' first play from scrimmage as Indianapolis improved to 11-0. The Colts' defense registered 3 sacks and allowed just 197 yards. Troy Polamalu's 36-yard interception return late in the first quarter set up Hines Ward's 12-yard touchdown catch on third-and-goal to cut the deficit to 10-7. The Steelers then forced a punt and drove to the Colts' 23, but Jeff Reed missed a 41-yard attempt. Leading 13-7, Mike Doss intercepted a pass with 15 seconds left in the half. Manning completed a 14-yard pass to Harrison, and Edgerrin James had a 5-yard run to set up Mike Vanderjagt's 44-yard field goal as the half expired for a 16-7 lead. The Steelers attempted an onside kick to begin the second half, but Matt Giordano recovered the ball and seven plays later Bryan Fletcher caught his first touchdown pass for a 23-7 lead. Manning was 15 of 25 for 245 yards and 2 touchdowns, with 1 interception. Harrison had 4 catches for 128 yards. James had 29 carries for 124 yards. Ben Roethlisberger was 17 of 26 for 133 yards and 1 touchdown, with 2 interceptions.

Pittsburgh	7	0	0	0	—	7
Indianapolis	10	6	7	3	—	26

Ind	—	Harrison 80 pass from P. Manning (Vanderjagt kick)
Ind	—	FG Vanderjagt 29
Pitt	—	Ward 12 pass from Roethlisberger (Reed kick)
Ind	—	FG Vanderjagt 48
Ind	—	FG Vanderjagt 44
Ind	—	Fletcher 12 pass from P. Manning (Vanderjagt kick)
Ind	—	FG Vanderjagt 28

THIRTEENTH WEEK SUMMARIES
American Football Conference

East Division	W	L	T	Pct.	Pts.	OP
New England	7	5	0	.583	259	282
Miami	5	7	0	.417	219	240
Buffalo	4	8	0	.333	184	247
N.Y. Jets	2	10	0	.167	143	264
North Division	**W**	**L**	**T**	**Pct.**	**Pts.**	**OP**
Cincinnati	9	3	0	.750	327	239
Pittsburgh	7	5	0	.583	274	225
Baltimore	4	8	0	.333	161	241

Cleveland	4	8	0	.333	183	214
South Division	**W**	**L**	**T**	**Pct.**	**Pts.**	**OP**
Indianapolis#	12	0	0	1.000	366	162
Jacksonville	9	3	0	.750	255	201
Tennessee	3	9	0	.250	239	319
Houston	1	11	0	.083	183	341
West Division	**W**	**L**	**T**	**Pct.**	**Pts.**	**OP**
Denver	9	3	0	.750	310	221
Kansas City	8	4	0	.667	301	257
San Diego	8	4	0	.667	357	229
Oakland	4	8	0	.333	249	296

National Football Conference

East Division	W	L	T	Pct.	Pts.	OP
N.Y. Giants	8	4	0	.667	319	218
Dallas	7	5	0	.583	253	205
Washington	6	6	0	.500	241	233
Philadelphia	5	7	0	.417	229	288
North Division	**W**	**L**	**T**	**Pct.**	**Pts.**	**OP**
Chicago	9	3	0	.750	201	127
Minnesota	7	5	0	.583	219	273
Detroit	4	8	0	.333	190	241
Green Bay	2	10	0	.167	239	242
South Division	**W**	**L**	**T**	**Pct.**	**Pts.**	**OP**
Carolina	9	3	0	.750	290	194
Tampa Bay	8	4	0	.667	226	199
Atlanta	7	5	0	.583	277	237
New Orleans	3	9	0	.250	183	295
West Division	**W**	**L**	**T**	**Pct.**	**Pts.**	**OP**
Seattle*	10	2	0	.833	338	208
St. Louis	5	7	0	.417	294	351
Arizona	4	8	0	.333	239	302
San Francisco	2	10	0	.167	183	340

*Clinched division title
#Clinched playoff berth

SUNDAY, DECEMBER 4

BALTIMORE 16, HOUSTON 15—at M&T Bank Stadium, attendance 69,909. Matt Stover kicked a 38-yard field goal with six seconds left as the Ravens rallied twice in the fourth quarter for the victory. Kris Brown's fourth field goal cut the deficit to one point with 3:31 remaining, and after forcing a three-and-out, Domanick Davis returned the punt 21 yards to the Ravens' 29 to set up Brown's 39-yard field goal with 1:08 to play. Kyle Boller responded by completing a 24-yard pass to Todd Heap on third down, and his 35-yard pass to Mark Clayton led to Stover's winning kick. Boller was 17 of 33 for 198 yards, with 1 interception. Carr was 17 of 37 for 165 yards, with 1 interception. Davis had 29 carries for 155 yards.

Houston	3	3	0	9	—	15
Baltimore	0	7	0	9	—	16

Hou	—	FG K. Brown 39
Balt	—	Boller 6 run (Stover kick)
Hou	—	FG K. Brown 26
Hou	—	FG K. Brown 22
Balt	—	Thomas 20 interception return (pass failed)
Hou	—	FG K. Brown 29
Hou	—	FG K. Brown 39
Balt	—	FG Stover 38

CAROLINA 24, ATLANTA 6—at Bank of America Stadium, attendance 73,661. DeShaun Foster rushed for 131 yards and scored 2 touchdowns as the Panthers defeated Michael Vick for the first time in six games. Ricky Manning Jr. intercepted a pass and returned it 10 yards to the Falcons' 11 with 3:57 remaining that led to Foster's 6-yard run with 2:19 to play. Jake Delhomme was 17 of 27 for 164 yards and 2 touchdowns, with 1 interception. Vick was 17 of 35 for 171 yards, with 2 interceptions.

Atlanta	3	3	0	0	—	6
Carolina	7	7	0	10	—	24

Atl	—	FG Peterson 36
Car	—	Foster 18 pass from Delhomme (Kasay kick)
Atl	—	FG Peterson 43

Car — S. Smith 18 pass from
Delhomme (Kasay kick)
Car — FG Kasay 20
Car — Foster 6 run (Kasay kick)

CHICAGO 19, GREEN BAY 7—at Soldier Field, attendance 62,177. Robbie Gould kicked 4 field goals and the defense had 2 key interceptions as the Bears snapped an 12-game losing streak at home to Green Bay. The Packers led 7-6 and drove to the Bears' 7 with 24 seconds left, but Charles Tillman intercepted Brett Favre's pass and returned it 95 yards to set up Gould's third field goal for a 9-7 lead as the half expired. The Packers trailed 12-7 and had the ball near midfield with 3:06 to play only to have Nathan Vasher intercept a pass and return it 45 yards for a touchdown. Kyle Orton was 6 of 17 for 68 yards, with 1 interception. Favre was 31 of 58 for 277 yards, with 2 interceptions.

Green Bay	0	7	0	0	—	7
Chicago	0	9	0	10	—	19

Chi — FG Gould 21
GB — Gado 2 run (Longwell kick)
Chi — FG Gould 40
Chi — FG Gould 25
Chi — FG Gould 35
Chi — Vasher 45 interception return
(Gould kick)

JACKSONVILLE 20, CLEVELAND 14—at Cleveland Browns Stadium, attendance 70,941. David Garrard passed for 2 second-half touchdowns as the Jaguars won their fifth consecutive game. Charlie Frye made his first start and completed 2 touchdown passes to Braylon Edwards in the second quarter for a 14-3 halftime lead. The Jaguars took a 20-14 lead, but faced third-and-19 from the Jaguars' 35 when Garrard scrambled 28 yards to clinch the victory. Garrard was 11 of 20 for 116 yards and 2 touchdowns, with 1 interception. Frye was 13 of 20 for 226 yards and 2 touchdowns.

Jacksonville	3	0	17	0	—	20
Cleveland	0	14	0	0	—	14

Jax — FG Scobee 24
Cle — Edwards 34 pass from Frye
(Dawson kick)
Cle — Edwards 17 pass from Frye
(Dawson kick)
Jax — FG Scobee 29
Jax — Wrighster 9 pass from Garrard
(Scobee kick)
Jax — J. Smith 12 pass from Garrard
(Scobee kick)

MINNESOTA 21, DETROIT 16—at Ford Field, attendance 61,375. Michael Bennett scored twice as the Vikings won their fourth consecutive game to spoil Dick Jauron's first game as interim head coach. Brad Johnson completed an 80-yard touchdown pass to Koren Robinson on the Vikings' first play from scrimmage. Detroit trailed 21-16 but got the ball on their own 7-yard line with 2:46 left. Detroit drove to the Vikings' 46 with 52 seconds left only to have Corey Chavous intercept a pass to secure the victory. Johnson was 17 of 23 for 256 yards and 2 touchdowns. Robinson had 4 catches for 148 yards. Jeff Garcia was 17 of 35 for 126 yards, with 1 interception.

Minnesota	7	7	7	0	—	21
Detroit	3	3	3	7	—	16

Det — FG FG Hanson 45
Minn — K. Robinson 80 pass from
B. Johnson (Edinger kick)
Minn — Bennett 7 run (Edinger kick)
Det — FG Hanson 26
Minn — Bennett 5 pass from B. Johnson
(Edinger kick)
Det — FG Hanson 28
Det — Pinner 6 run (Hanson kick)

INDIANAPOLIS 35, TENNESSEE 3—at RCA Dome, attendance 57,228. Peyton Manning passed for 3 touchdowns as the Colts became just the fifth team to begin a season with a 12-0 record. The Titans drove into Colts' territory four times in the second half but were stopped on downs three times. On the other possession Dwight Freeney's sack forced a fumble that Larry Tripplett returned 60 yards for a touchdown with 11:44 left to finish the scoring. Manning was 13 of 17 for 187 yards and 3 touchdowns. Edgerrin James carried 28 times for 107 yards. Steve McNair was 22 of 33 for 220 yards.

Tennessee	0	3	0	0	—	3
Indianapolis	7	7	14	7	—	35

Ind — Harrison 10 pass from Manning
(Vanderjagt kick)
Ind — Fletcher 13 pass from Manning
(Vanderjagt kick)
Tenn — FG Bironas 24
Ind — Wayne 27 pass from Manning
(Vanderjagt kick)
Ind — James 2 run (Vanderjagt kick)
Ind — Tripplett 60 fumble return
(Vanderjagt kick)

KANSAS CITY 31, DENVER 27—at Arrowhead Stadium, attendance 78,261. Larry Johnson rushed for 140 yards and scored the game-winning touchdown as the Chiefs snapped the Broncos' four-game winning streak. The score was tied 24-24 late in the third quarter when Darrent Williams' interception set up Jason Elam's go-ahead field goal with 13:31 to play. The Chiefs responded with a 70-yard drive, highlighted by Johnson's 30-yard run and capped by his 4-yard scoring jaunt with 9:58 remaining. After an exchange of punts, the Broncos regained possession and eschewed the punt on fourth-and-1 from their own 47 with 2:01 to play. Mike Anderson ran up the middle and was spotted a first down. The Chiefs challenged the spot and the call was overturned. The Chiefs ran off all but the game's final three seconds to clinch the victory and pull within one game of first place. Trent Green was 16 of 23 for 253 yards and 2 touchdowns, with 2 interceptions. Eddie Kennison had 4 receptions for 108 yards. Johnson carried 30 times for 140 yards. Jake Plummer was 18 of 29 for 278 yards and 1 touchdown, with 2 interceptions.

Denver	7	14	3	3	—	27
Kansas City	7	14	3	7	—	31

Den — Anderson 66 pass from
Plummer (Elam kick)
KC — Hall 41 pass from Green
(Tynes kick)
Den — L. Johnson 1 run (Tynes kick)
KC — Anderson 1 run (Elam kick)
KC — Gonzalez 25 pass from Green
(Tynes kick)
Den — Van Pelt 7 run (Elam kick)
Den — FG Tynes 34
KC — FG Elam 22
Den — FG Elam 40
KC — L. Johnson 4 run (Tynes kick)

MIAMI 24, BUFFALO 23—at Dolphins Stadium, attendance 72,051. Chris Chambers set club records with 15 catches for 238 yards, including the game-winning leaping 4-yard touchdown catch on fourth-and-goal with six seconds left, to help the Dolphins rally from a 23-3 fourth-quarter deficit to shock the Bills. Lee Evans caught 3 touchdown passes in the first 12:46 of the game to give Buffalo a 21-0 lead. Trailing 23-3 late in the third quarter, Sam Madison intercepted J.P. Losman's pass to keep Miami in the game. Sage Rosenfels entered the game for the injured Gus Frerotte, who got hurt on a safety on the previous possession. Rosenfels proceeded to engineer scoring drives of 70 and 49 yards to pull within 23-17 with 7:35 to play. With 1:51 left the Dolphins regained posses-

sion on their own 27. On third-and-10, Rosenfels completed a 57-yard pass to Chambers. On fourth-and-goal with six seconds left, Rosenfels lofted a pass to the right side of the end zone. Chambers outleaped Jabari Greer for the victory. The Dolphins attempted a club record 65 passes en route to victory. Frerotte was 12 of 28 for 115 yards, and Rosenfels was 22 of 37 for 272 yards and 2 touchdowns, with 1 interception. Losman was 13 of 26 for 224 yards and 3 touchdowns, with 1 interception. Evans had 5 catches for 117 yards.

Buffalo	21	0	2	0	—	23
Miami	0	3	0	21	—	24

Buff — Evans 46 pass from Losman
(Lindell kick)
Buff — Evans 56 pass from Losman
(Lindell kick)
Buff — Evans 4 pass from Losman
(Lindell kick)
Mia — FG Mare 23
Buff — Safety, Fletcher sacked Frerotte
in end zone
Mia — Williams 5 run (Mare kick)
Mia — Brown 23 pass from Rosenfels
(Mare kick)
Mia — Chambers 4 pass from
Rosenfels (Mare kick)

NEW ENGLAND 16, N.Y. JETS 3—at Gillette Stadium, attendance 68,756. Adam Vinatieri kicked 3 field goals and the Patriots' defense allowed just 164 yards as they maintained a two-game lead in the AFC East. The Jets drove to the Patriots' 19 with 7:46 remaining, but Brooks Bollinger's third- and fourth-down passes fell incomplete. With 4:04 to play, Ellis Hobbs intercepted a pass at the Patriots' 40 to thwart the Jets' final threat. Tom Brady was 27 of 37 for 271 yards. Bollinger was 15 of 37 for 135 yards, with 1 interception.

N.Y. Jets	0	3	0	0	—	3
New England	0	6	7	3	—	16

NE — FG Vinatieri 21
NYJ — FG Nugent 38
NE — FG Vinatieri 34
NE — Dillon 1 run (Vinatieri kick)
NE — FG Vinatieri 22

TAMPA BAY 10, NEW ORLEANS 3—at Tiger Stadium, attendance 34,411. Ronde Barber intercepted 3 passes, including the game-clincher in the end zone with 1:20 to play, for the Buccaneers in Baton Rouge. Chris Simms' 30-yard touchdown pass to Joey Galloway came five plays after Barber's second interception and gave Tampa Bay a 7-0 lead. Trailing 7-3, the Saints took over eight minutes to drive to the Buccaneers' 30 to begin the second half, but Dexter Jackson intercepted Aaron Brooks' fourth-and-6 pass. Tampa Bay increased the lead to 10-3, but the Saints drove to the Buccaneers' 20 with 1:33 to play. After an illegal motion penalty, Brooks attempted to connect with Joe Horn in the end zone only to have Barber snare his third interception, which allowed Tampa Bay to kneel down three times to run out the clock. Simms was 12 of 21 for 123 yards and 1 touchdown. Brooks was 18 of 34 for 215 yards, with 4 interceptions.

Tampa Bay	0	7	0	3	—	10
New Orleans	0	3	0	0	—	3

TB — Galloway 30 pass from Simms
(France kick)
NO — FG Carney 26
TB — FG France 28

N.Y. GIANTS 17, DALLAS 10—at Giants Stadium, attendance 78,645. The Giants' defense forced 4 turnovers and registered 4 sacks to defeat the Cowboys. Trailing 10-0 at halftime, the Cowboys fumbled on the first play of the second half when Kendrick Clancy pulled on Drew Bledsoe's arm as he attempted a handoff to Julius Jones. Antonio Pierce picked up the fumble and returned it 12 yards for a touchdown. The Cowboys responded with a field goal and, Aaron Glenn intercepted a pass and one play later Terry Glenn scored to pull within 17-10. Jay Feely missed a 33-yard field goal with 5:18 to play, but the Giants held on and clinched the game with Brent Alexander's interception with 1:47 remaining. Eli Manning was 12 of 31 for 152 yards, with 2 interceptions. Tlki Barber had 30 carries for 115 yards. Bledsoe was 15 of 39 for 146 yards and 1 touchdown, with 2 interceptions.

Dallas	0	0	10	0	—	10
N.Y. Giants	0	10	7	0	—	17

NYG	—	Jacobs 1 run (Feely kick)
NYG	—	FG Feely 27
NYG	—	Pierce 12 fumble return (Feely kick)
Dall	—	FG Cundiff 34
Dall	—	Glenn 7 pass from Bledsoe (Cundiff kick)

CINCINNATI 38, PITTSBURGH 31—at Heinz Field, attendance 63,044. Carson Palmer passed for 3 touchdowns and Rudi Johnson ran for 2 scores as the Bengals took a two-game lead in the AFC North. Tied 24-24, Tab Perry returned s kickoff 94 yards to the Steelers' 3 that led to Johnson's first touchdown. In the fourth quarter, Odell Thurman intercepted a pass near midfield and six plays later Johnson scored from 14 yards to give the Bengals a 38-24 lead with 6:09 to play. Hines Ward's second touchdown cut the deficit to seven points with 2:59 remaining, and the Steelers forced a punt, but the Bengals stopped Pittsburgh on downs, capped by Justin Smith's sack with 1:23 to play. Palmer was 22 of 38 for 227 yards and 2 touchdowns. Ben Roethlisberger was 29 of 41 for 386 yards and 3 touchdowns, with 3 interceptions. Ward had 9 receptions for 135 yards.

Cincinnati	7	14	10	7	—	38
Pittsburgh	14	3	7	7	—	31

Pitt	—	Bettis 1 run (Reed kick)
Cin	—	Houshmandzadeh 43 pass from Palmer (Graham kick)
Pitt	—	Morgan 25 pass from Roethlisberger (Reed kick)
Cin	—	Kelly 1 pass from Palmer (Graham kick)
Cin	—	Houshmandzadeh 6 pass from Palmer (Graham kick)
Pltt	—	FG Reed 23
Cin	—	FG Graham 30
Pitt	—	Ward 20 pass from Roethlisberger (Reed kick)
Cin	—	R. Johnson 1 run (Graham kick)
Cin	—	R. Johnson 14 run (Graham kick)
Pitt	—	Ward 6 pass from Roethlisberger (Reed kick)

WASHINGTON 24, ST. LOUIS 9—at Edward Jones Dome, attendance 65,701. The Redskins rushed for 257 yards, highlighted by 2 touchdowns by Clinton Portis, to snap a three-game losing streak. A safety cut the deficit to 17-9 with 11:55 left and the Rams got the ball following the free kick, but Ryan Fitzpatrick fumbled a snap two plays later and Renaldo Wynn recovered. Chris Cooley's 4-yard touchdown catch on third-and-goal with 5:50 left increased the lead to 24-9, and Carlos Rogers intercepted a pass at the Redskins' 8 with 2:47 to play to clinch the victory. Mark Brunell was 14 of 21 for 156 yards and 1 touchdown. Portis had 27 carries for 136 yards, and Rock Cartwright added 6 carries for 118 yards. Fitzpatrick, making his first NFL start, was 21 of 36 for 163 yards, with 1 interception.

Washington	7	3	0	14	—	24
St. Louis	0	7	0	2	—	9

Wash	—	Portis 47 run (Hall kick)

StL	—	Fitzpatrick 7 run (Wilkins kick)
Wash	—	FG Hall 38
Wash	—	Portis 1 run (Hall kick)
StL	—	Safety, Brunell fumble out of bounds in end zone
Wash	—	Cooley 4 pass from Brunell (Hall kick)

ARIZONA 17, SAN FRANCISCO 10—at Monster Park, attendance 60,439. Kurt Warner passed for 354 yards and the game-winning touchdown in the fourth quarter as the Cardinals swept the season series from the 49ers. Darnell Dockett forced Gore to fumble early in the fourth quarter and Adrian Wilson recovered. Three plays later Warner fired a short pass to Anquan Boldin, who rumbled for a 54-yard touchdown, along with a 2-point conversion run by Obafemi Ayanbadejo, for a 17-10 lead with 10:45 to play. Eric Green intercepted a pass at the 49ers' 42 with 1:42 remaining to clinch the victory. Warner was 29 of 45 for 354 yards and 1 touchdown, with 2 interceptions. Boldin had 11 receptions for 156 yards and Larry Fitzgerald added 8 catches for 129 yards. Alex Smith was 16 of 24 for 185 yards, with 3 interceptions.

Arizona	3	0	6	8	—	17
San Francisco	0	7	3	0	—	10

Ariz	—	FG Novak 30
SF	—	Hicks 1 run (Nedney kick)
Ariz	—	FG Novak 35
Ariz	—	FG Novak 19
SF	—	FG Nedney 48
Ariz	—	Boldin 54 pass from Warner (Ayanbadejo run)

SUNDAY NIGHT, DECEMBER 4

SAN DIEGO 34, OAKLAND 10—at Qualcomm Stadium, attendance 66,436. Drew Brees passed for 2 touchdowns as the Chargers won their fifth consecutive game. The Chargers took a 27-10 lead in the fourth quarter, and Hart iced the game by returning an interception 70 yards for a touchdown with 6:29 remaining. Brees was 17 of 22 for 160 yards and 2 touchdowns. Kerry Collins was 22 of 40 for 236 yards and 1 touchdown, with 1 interception.

Oakland	3	7	0	0	—	10
San Diego	3	14	7	10	—	34

Oak	—	FG Janikowski 37
SD	—	FG Kaeding 41
SD	—	Gates 6 pass from Brees (Kaeding kick)
Oak	—	C. Anderson 16 pass from Collins (Janikowski kick)
SD	—	Turner 2 run (Kaeding kick)
SD	—	Parker 1 pass from Brees (Kaeding kick)
SD	—	FG Kaeding 32
SD	—	Hart 70 interception return (Kaeding kick)

MONDAY NIGHT, DECEMBER 5

SEATTLE 42, PHILADELPHIA 0—at Lincoln Financial Field, attendance 67,637. The Seahawks, which had clinched the NFC West because of the Rams' loss the previous day, scored 3 defensive touchdowns by Andre Dyson, to win their eighth consecutive game. With a 25 degree wind chill, neither team had 200 yards of offense, but the Seahawks forced 6 turnovers while committing none. The Eagles, which retired Reggie White's number 92 at halftime, suffered their worst home loss in 43 seasons. Seattle began the game with a 16-play, 65-yard drive that consumed 8:10 to take a 7-0 lead. Dyson returned an interception 72 yards for a touchdown on the next possession, and Lofa Tatupu added a 38-yard interception return with 11:31 left in the second quarter. Tatupu tipped a pass later in the quarter that Michael Boulware intercepted and returned 32 yards to set up Shaun Alexander's scoring run, and D.J. Hackett's

42-yard catch set up a touchdown for a 35-0 lead. Matt Hasselbeck was 8 of 15 for 98 yards and 1 touchdown. Mike McMahon started and was 4 of 10 for 61 yards, with 2 interceptions. Koy Detmer came in trailing 21-0, and was 13 of 29 for 84 yards ,with 2 interceptions.

Seattle	14	21	7	0	—	42
Philadelphia	0	0	0	0	—	0

Sea	—	Engram 11 pass from Hasselbeck (J. Brown kick)
Sea	—	Dyson 72 interception return (J. Brown kick)
Sea	—	Tatupu 38 interception return (J. Brown kick)
Sea	—	Alexander 2 run (J. Brown kick)
Sea	—	Alexander 1 run (J. Brown kick)
Sea	—	Dyson 25 fumble return (J. Brown kick)

FOURTEENTH WEEK SUMMARIES

American Football Conference

East Division	W	L	T	Pct.	Pts.	OP
New England	8	5	0	.615	294	289
Miami	6	7	0	.462	242	261
Buffalo	4	9	0	.308	191	282
N.Y. Jets	3	10	0	.231	169	274
North Division	**W**	**L**	**T**	**Pct.**	**Pts.**	**OP**
Cincinnati	10	3	0	.769	350	259
Pittsburgh	8	5	0	.615	295	234
Baltimore	4	9	0	.308	171	253
Cincinnati	4	9	0	.308	203	237
South Division	**W**	**L**	**T**	**Pct.**	**Pts.**	**OP**
Indianapolis*	13	0	0	1.000	392	180
Jacksonville	9	4	0	.692	273	227
Tennessee	4	9	0	.308	252	329
Houston	1	12	0	.077	193	354
West Division	**W**	**L**	**T**	**Pct.**	**Pts.**	**OP**
Denver	10	3	0	.769	322	231
Kansas City	8	5	0	.615	329	288
San Diego	8	5	0	.615	378	252
Oakland	4	9	0	.308	259	322

National Football Conference

East Division	W	L	T	Pct.	Pts.	OP
N.Y. Giants	9	4	0	.692	345	241
Dallas	8	5	0	.615	284	233
Washington	7	6	0	.538	258	246
Philadelphia	5	8	0	.385	252	314
North Division	**W**	**L**	**T**	**Pct.**	**Pts.**	**OP**
Chicago	9	4	0	.692	210	148
Minnesota	8	5	0	.615	246	286
Detroit	4	9	0	.308	203	257
Green Bay	3	10	0	.231	255	255
South Division	**W**	**L**	**T**	**Pct.**	**Pts.**	**OP**
Carolina	9	4	0	.692	300	214
Tampa Bay	9	4	0	.692	246	209
Atlanta	8	5	0	.615	313	254
New Orleans	3	10	0	.231	200	331
West Division	**W**	**L**	**T**	**Pct.**	**Pts.**	**OP**
Seattle*	11	2	0	.846	379	211
St. Louis	5	8	0	.385	307	318
Arizona	4	9	0	.308	252	319
San Francisco	2	11	0	.154	186	381

*Clinched division title

SUNDAY, DECEMBER 11

WASHINGTON 17, ARIZONA 13—at Sun Devil Stadium, attendance 46,654. Clinton Portis rushed for 105 yards and Antonio Brown returned a kickoff 91 yards for a touchdown as the Redskins kept their playoff hopes alive. The Cardinals drove to the Redskins' 29 with 1:59 left, but Sean Taylor stopped J.J. Arrington for 1 yard on fourth-and-2, and Portis gained 7 yards on third-and-6 with 1:45 to play to clinch the victory. Brunell was 18 of 28 for 122 yards, with 3 interceptions. Portis carried 26 times for 105 yards. Kurt Warner was 25 of 41 for 255 yards and 1 touchdown, with 1 interception. Anquan Boldin had 9 receptions for 114 yards.

Washington	0	3	14	0	—	17
Arizona	0	10	3	0	—	13

Wash	—	FG Hall 41
Ariz	—	McCoy 2 pass from Warner (Rackers kick)
Ariz	—	FG Rackers 44
Wash	—	Portis 15 run (Hall kick)
Ariz	—	FG Rackers 20
Wash	—	A. Brown 91 kickoff return (Hall kick)

NEW ENGLAND 35, BUFFALO 7—at Ralph Wilson Stadium, attendance 71,810. Tom Brady passed for 2 touchdowns, ran for another, and the Patriots' defense allowed just 183 yards to hand the Bills their fourth consecutive defeat. The Patriots set a franchise record with 32 first downs, while also maintaining possession for 41:59 and outgaining the Bills 494-183 total yards. James Sanders returned an interception 39 yards with 2:43 left to take a 35-0 lead. Brady was 29 of 38 for 329 yards and 2 touchdowns, with 2 interceptions. J.P. Losman was 10 of 27 for 181 yards and 1 touchdown, with 3 interceptions.

New England	7	7	7	14	—	35
Buffalo	0	0	0	7	—	7

NE	—	Brady 3 run (Vinatieri kick)
NE	—	Dillon 12 run (Vinatieri kick)
NE	—	T. Brown 5 pass from Brady (Vinatieri kick)
NE	—	Faulk 2 pass from Brady (Vinatieri kick)
NE	—	Sanders 39 interception return (Vinatieri kick)
Buff	—	Reed 51 pass from Losman (Lindell kick)

TAMPA BAY 20, CAROLINA 10—at Bank of America Stadium, attendance 73,467. Carnell Williams rushed for 112 yards and 2 touchdowns for the Buccaneers. Carolina cut the deficit to 13-3 and drove to the Buccaneers' 12, but Ronde Barber intercepted Jake Delhomme's pass with 11:38 to play. Barber's 35-yard return set up Williams' second touchdown for a 20-3 lead with 5:39 left. Barber's sack of Delhomme with 4:25 to play allowed him to post 20 sacks and intercept 20 passes. Chris Simms was 20 of 27 for 138 yards. Delhomme was 21 of 33 for 220 yards and 1 touchdown, with 1 interception. Steve Smith had 5 catches for 103 yards.

Tampa Bay	7	3	3	7	—	20
Carolina	0	0	3	7	—	10

TB	—	Williams 14 run (Bryant kick)
TB	—	FG Bryant 34
TB	—	FG Bryant 36
Car	—	FG Kasay 39
TB	—	Williams 10 run (Bryant kick)
Car	—	Proehl 10 pass from Delhomme (Kasay kick)

CINCINNATI 23, CLEVELAND 20—at Paul Brown Stadium, attendance 65,788. Shayne Graham kicked a 37-yard field goal as time expired as the Bengals reached 10 victories for the first time since 1988. With winds gusting up to 30 miles per hour, Deltha O'Neal's franchise record-tying ninth interception led to Carson Palmer's 8-yard touchdown pass to T.J. Houshmandzadeh for a 20-17 lead. Phil Dawson tied the game with a 29-yard field goal with 4:19 to play. The Bengals benefited for 2 third-down defensive penalties to keep their final drive alive, and Graham knocked in the 37-yard field goal as time expired. Palmer was 13 of 27 for 93 yards and 1 touchdown, with 1 interception. Rudi Johnson had 30 carries for 169 yards. Charlie Frye, making his first road start, was 16 of 24 for 138 yards and 1 touchdown, with 1 interception.

Cleveland	7	3	7	3	—	20
Cincinnati	7	6	7	3	—	23

Cle	—	Frye 3 run (Dawson kick)
Cin	—	R. Johnson 8 run (Graham kick)
Cle	—	Heiden 2 pass from Frye (Dawson kick)
Cin	—	FG Graham 21
Cin	—	FG Graham 27
Cle	—	FG Dawson 41
Cin	—	Houshmandzadeh 4 pass from Palmer (Graham kick)
Cle	—	FG Dawson 29
Cin	—	FG Graham 37

DALLAS 31, KANSAS CITY 28—at Texas Stadium, attendance 63,432. Dan Campbell caught a 1-yard touchdown pass with 22 seconds left and Lawrence Tynes missed a 41-yard field goal as time expired to allow the Cowboys to snap their two-game losing streak. Terry Glenn scored his first career rushing touchdown on a 6-yard end around for a 24-21 lead with 13:07 remaining. Eddie Kennison's 47-yard touchdown catch gave the Chiefs a 28-24 lead with 3:55 to play. Campbell's touchdown catch capped a 14-play, 68-yard drive to take a 31-28 lead. With 16 seconds left, Green completed a 14-yard pass to Samie Parker and 34-yard pass to Dante Hall to set up Tynes' 41-yard attempt, which sailed wide right. Bledsoe was 22 of 34 for 332 yards and 3 touchdowns. Glenn had 6 catches for 138 yards. Green was 20 of 32 for 340 yards and 1 touchdown. Larry Johnson had 26 carries for 143 yards.

Kansas City	7	7	7	7	—	28
Dallas	0	17	0	14	—	31

KC	—	L. Johnson 11 run (Tynes kick)
Dall	—	FG Cundiff 34
KC	—	L. Johnson 1 run (Tynes kick)
Dall	—	Glenn 71 pass from Bledsoe (Cundiff kick)
Dall	—	Witten 26 pass from Bledsoe (Cundiff kick)
KC	—	L. Johnson 21 run (Tynes kick)
Dall	—	Glenn 6 run (Cundiff kick)
KC	—	Kennison 47 pass from Green (Tynes kick)
Dall	—	Campbell 1 pass from Bledsoe (Cundiff kick)

DENVER 12, BALTIMORE 10—at INVESCO Field at Mile High, attendance 75,651. The Broncos' defense forced 4 turnovers as Denver increased its lead in the AFC West to two games. The Ravens twice drove into the red zone, but Champ Bailey intercepted a pass at the Broncos' 6 late in the third quarter and Taylor was dropped for a 4-yard loss on fourth-and-goal from the Broncos' 1 with 9:54 to play. Mark Clayton caught a 39-yard scoring pass with 1:52 remaining, but Ashley Lelie's 8-yard catch on second-and-8 with 1:29 left clinched the victory. Jake Plummer was 19 of 33 for 236 yards and 1 touchdown. Kyle Boller was 23 of 39 for 251 yards and 1 touchdown, with 2 interceptions. Clayton had 7 catches for 105 yards.

Baltimore	3	0	0	7	—	10
Denver	3	3	6	0	—	12

Balt	—	FG Stover 29
Den	—	FG Elam 47
Den	—	FG Elam 48
Den	—	K. Johnson 7 pass from Plummer (kick failed)
Balt	—	Clayton 39 pass from Boller (Stover kick)

INDIANAPOLIS 26, JACKSONVILLE 18—at ALLTEL Stadium, attendance 67,164. Marvin Harrison scored 2 touchdowns and Mike Vanderjagt added 4 field goals as the Colts became the fourth team to begin a season 13-0 and clinched home-field advantage through the playoffs. Trailing 26-3, David Garrard scored on a 5-yard run with 4:08 to play, and Rashean Mathis recovered the onside kick to set up Jimmy

Smith's 1-yard touchdown catch with 1:54 left. Garrard's 2-point conversion run pulled the Jaguars within 26-18. With all three timeouts in their possession, the Jaguars kicked deep and stopped Edgerrin James twice before Peyton Manning completed a 12-yard pass to Dallas Clark on third-and-7 with 1:39 to play to clinch the victory. Manning was 24 of 36 for 324 yards and 2 touchdowns. Harrison had 6 receptions for 137 yards. Garrard was 26 of 35 for 250 yards and 1 touchdown. Smith had 8 catches for 102 yards.

Indianapolis	7	10	6	3	—	26
Jacksonville	0	3	0	15	—	18

Ind	—	Harrison 9 pass from Manning (Vanderjagt kick)
Jax	—	FG Scobee 27
Ind	—	Harrison 65 pass from Manning (Vanderjagt kick)
Ind	—	FG Vanderjagt 40
Ind	—	FG Vanderjagt 34
Ind	—	FG Vanderjagt 38
Ind	—	FG Vanderjagt 46
Jax	—	Garrard 5 run (Scobee kick)
Jax	—	J. Smith 1 pass from Garrard (Garrard run)

MINNESOTA 27, ST. LOUIS 13—at Metrodome, attendance 64,005. The Vikings' defense forced 6 turnovers as Minnesota won its sixth consecutive game and pulled within one game of first place. Leading 20-13, Brian Williams intercepted a pass on the and returned the ball 31 yards to the Rams' 21 to set up Ciatrick Fason's 1-yard touchdown run with 3:11 left in the third quarter. Fred Smoot's interception in the end zone with 9:42 to play stopped one drive, and Ryan Fitzpatrick's fourth-and-goal pass from the 4-yard line was incomplete with 2:42 left. Darren Sharper clinched the victory with an interception for a touchback with 20 seconds left. Brad Johnson was 16 of 25 for 146 yards. Fitzpatrick was 26 of 45 for 235 yards, with 5 interceptions. Torry Holt had 10 catches for 95 yards. Marshall Faulk had 4 catches for 32 yards, and moved into first place among running backs with 6,801 receiving yards, surpassing the previous mark set by Larry Centers.

St. Louis	0	6	7	0	—	13
Minnesota	7	6	14	0	—	27

Minn	—	K. Robinson 13 run (Edinger kick)
StL	—	FG Wilkins 51
Minn	—	FG Edinger 37
Minn	—	FG Edinger 44
StL	—	FG Wilkins 23
StL	—	Fitzpatrick 14 run (Wilkins kick)
Minn	—	Bennett 7 run (Edinger kick)
Minn	—	Fason 1 run (Edinger kick)

N.Y. JETS 26, OAKLAND 10—at The Meadowlands, attendance 77,561. The Jets' defense forced 4 turnovers and registered 6 sacks to snap a seven-game losing streak. Curtis Martin missed the game with an injured knee, snapping his consecutive game streak at 119 games. John Abraham forced 2 fumbles to set up field goals to give the Jets a 19-3 lead with 14:54 to play. Brooks Bollinger was 14 of 26 for 119 yards and 1 touchdown. Marques Tuiasosopo, making his first start of the season, was 14 of 26 for 124 yards and 1 touchdown, with 2 interceptions.

Oakland	0	3	0	7	—	10
N.Y. Jets	3	3	6	14	—	26

NYJ	—	FG Nugent 33
NYJ	—	FG Nugent 20
Oak	—	FG Janikowski 42
NYJ	—	FG Nugent 35
NYJ	—	FG Nugent 21
NYJ	—	McCareins 4 pass from Bollinger (Nugent kick)
Oak	—	Porter 20 pass from Tuiasosopo (Janikowski kick)

NYJ — Houston 2 run (Nugent kick)

N.Y. GIANTS 26, PHILADELPHIA 23 (OT)—at Lincoln Financial Field, attendance 67,443. Jay Feely kicked a 36-yard field goal with 3:55 left in overtime for the Giants. Sheldon Brown then intercepted Eli Manning's pass at the Eagles' 43 to set up David Akers' game-tying 50-yard field goal. Michael Lewis intercepted Manning near the end of regulation to force overtime, and Brian Dawkins intercepted a pass at the Eagles' 37 in overtime. Osi Umenyiora sacked Mike McMahon and forced him to fumble. Kenderick Allen recovered at the Eagles' 27 to set up Feely's winning kick. Manning was 28 of 44 for 312 yards and 1 touchdown, with 3 interceptions. Jeremy Shockey had 10 catches for 107 yards, and Tiki Barber rushed 32 times for 124 yards. McMahon was 14 of 32 for 190 yards. Ryan Moats added 11 carries for 114 yards.

N.Y. Giants	7	10	3	3	3	—	26
Philadelphia	7	10	0	6	0	—	23
NYG	—	Barber 4 pass from Manning (Feely kick)					
Phil	—	Moats 40 run (Akers kick)					
NYG	—	Manning 1 run (Feely kick)					
NYG	—	FG Feely 24					
Phil	—	Moats 18 run (Akers kick)					
Phil	—	FG Akers 42					
NYG	—	FG Feely 21					
NYG	—	FG Feely 27					
Phil	—	FG Akers 36					
Phil	—	FG Akers 50					
NYG	—	FG Feely 36					

PITTSBURGH 21, CHICAGO 9—at Heinz Field, attendance 61,237. Jerome Bettis rushed for 101 yards and 2 touchdowns as the Steelers broke their own three-game losing skid and snapped the Bears' eight-game winning streak. The Steelers maintained possession for 37:19 against the NFL's number-one ranked defense. The Steelers had touchdown drives of 66 and 73 yards in two of their first three possessions to take a 14-3 lead. With heavy snow falling in the second half, Bettis dragged three players into the end zone to complete a 12-play drive to take a 21-3 lead. Ben Roethlisberger was 13 of 20 for 173 yards and 1 touchdown. Bettis carried 17 times for 101 yards. Kyle Orton was 17 of 35 for 207 yards.

Chicago	3	0	0	6	—	9
Pittsburgh	7	7	7	0	—	21
Pitt	—	Ward 14 pass from Roethlisberger (Reed kick)				
Chi	—	FG Gould 29				
Pitt	—	Bettis 1 run (Reed kick)				
Pitt	—	Bettis 5 run (Reed kick)				
Chi	—	T. Jones 1 run (kick failed)				

MIAMI 23, SAN DIEGO 21—at Qualcomm Stadium, attendance 65,026. Gus Frerotte passed for 229 yards and 2 touchdown passes to Chris Chambers as the Dolphins snapped the Chargers' five-game winning streak. Chambers caught a 35-yard touchdown to give Miami a 20-7 lead. Drew Brees' 4-yard quarterback draw cut the deficit to 20-14 with 10:34 to play. On Miami's next drive, Ronnie Brown fumbled at the Chargers' 1, and Clinton Hart recovered. Yeremiah Bell forced Brees to fumble on the next possession, and Kevin Carter recovered at the Chargers' 23 to set up Olindo Mare's 20-yard field goal with 1:11 to play. The Chargers scored with 14 seconds left, but Randy McMichael recovered the onside kick. Frerotte was 14 of 22 for 229 yards and 2 touchdowns. Chambers had 8 receptions for 121 yards. Brees was 35 of 52 for 279 yards and 2 touchdowns. Antonio Gates had 13 receptions for 123 yards.

Miami	0	3	17	3	—	23
San Diego	7	0	14	0	—	21
SD	—	McCardell 8 pass from Brees (Kaeding kick)				

Mia	—	FG Mare 29				
Mia	—	FG Mare 39				
Mia	—	Chambers 8 pass from Frerotte (Mare kick)				
Mia	—	Chambers 35 pass from Frerotte (Mare kick)				
SD	—	Brees 4 run (Kaeding kick)				
Mia	—	FG Mare 20				
SD	—	Gates 8 pass from Brees (Kaeding kick)				

SEATTLE 41, SAN FRANCISCO 3—at Qwest Field, attendance 66,690. Matt Hasselbeck passed for 4 touchdowns and the Seahawks' defense set a club record by allowing just 113 total yards to post their club-record ninth consecutive victory. The Seahawks scored 14 points in 18 seconds of the second quarter, the second set up by Lofa Tatupu's fumble recovery, to take a 21-3 lead. Moments later, Tatupu intercepted a pass at the 49ers' 46 that led to Josh Brown's 52-yard field goal to take a 24-3 lead with 7:28 left before halftime. The Seahawks' defense did not allow the 49ers to cross midfield the remainder of the game. Hasselbeck was 21 of 25 for 226 yards and 4 touchdowns, with 1 interception. Shaun Alexander had 21 carries for 108 yards. Alex Smith was 9 of 22 for 77 yards, with 1 interception.

San Francisco	3	0	0	0	—	3
Seattle	7	17	14	3	—	41
Sea	—	Engram 28 pass from Hasselbeck (J. Brown kick)				
SF	—	FG Nedney 39				
Sea	—	Stevens 8 pass from Hasselbeck (J. Brown kick)				
Sea	—	Jurevicius 21 pass from Hasselbeck (J. Brown kick)				
Sea	—	FG J. Brown 52				
Sea	—	Engram 7 pass from Hasselbeck (J. Brown kick)				
Sea	—	Alexander 3 run (J. Brown kick)				
Sea	—	FG J. Brown 52				

TENNESSEE 13, HOUSTON 10—at The Coliseum, attendance 69,149. Kris Brown missed a 31-yard field goal with no time remaining as the Titans held off the Texans. Trailing 10-3 late in the third quarter, Adam Jones returned a punt 52 yards for a touchdown. With 5:58 to play, the Texans converted a fake field goal as Kris Brown ran 4 yards for a first down. Four plays later, Brown attempted a 37-yard field goal and it was blocked by Tank Williams. The Titans drove 70 yards in 10 plays capped by Rob Bironas' 21-yard field goal with 10 seconds to play. On the ensuing kickoff, Todd Washington picked up the bouncing ball and lateraled to Jerome Mathis, who returned the kick 50 yards and was tackled via the facemask with no time left. The defensive penalty allowed Brown to attempt a 31-yard field goal with no time remaining, but it went wide left. Steve McNair was 18 of 30 for 208 yards. David Carr was 17 of 26 for 116 yards and 1 touchdown. Domanick Davis had 22 carries for 139 yards.

Houston	3	7	0	0	—	10
Tennessee	0	3	7	3	—	13
Hou	—	FG K. Brown 30				
Tenn	—	FG Bironas 23				
Hou	—	Davis 3 pass from Carr (K. Brown kick)				
Tenn	—	A. Jones 52 punt return (Bironas kick)				
Tenn	—	FG Bironas 21				

SUNDAY NIGHT, DECEMBER 11
GREEN BAY 16, DETROIT 13 (OT)—at Lambeau Field, attendance 70,019. Ryan Longwell kicked a 28-yard field goal in overtime as the Packers defeated the Lions in Wisconsin for the thirteenth consecutive season. Longwell's 39-yard field goal tied the game with 14:22 to play. The Lions responded by driving to

the Packers' 1. Artose Pinner was stopped for no gain on second- and third-and-goal, and after a timeout, Jeff Garcia was stopped by Na'il Diggs on fourth-and-goal. The Packers won the overtime coin toss and drove 56 yards, highlighted by Brett Favre's 8-yard pass to William Henderson on third-and-7, to set up Longwell's winning kick. Favre was 21 of 31 for 170 yards, with 1 interception. Samkon Gado had 29 carries for 171 yards. Garcia was 13 of 24 for 112 yards and 1 touchdown.

Detroit	13	0	0	0	0	—	13
Green Bay	3	7	0	3	3	—	16
Det	—	FG Hanson 19					
Det	—	FG Hanson 23					
GB	—	FG Longwell 36					
Det	—	R. Williams 4 pass from Garcia (Hanson kick)					
GB	—	Gado 64 run (Longwell kick)					
GB	—	FG Longwell 39					
GB	—	FG Longwell 28					

MONDAY NIGHT, DECEMBER 12
ATLANTA 36, NEW ORLEANS 17—at Georgia Dome, attendance 70,083. Michael Vick passed for 1 touchdown and ran for 2 more scores as the Falcons pulled away. Vick's 17-yard scamper in the third quarter gave Atlanta a 30-17 lead. Antwan Lake sacked Brooks for a safety late in the third quarter, and Todd Peterson added 2 field goals. Vick was 12 of 23 for 231 yards and 1 touchdown, with 1 interception. Brooks was 27 of 46 for 219 yards and 1 touchdown.

New Orleans	3	14	0	0	—	17
Atlanta	7	14	9	6	—	36
Atl	—	Duckett 1 run (Peterson kick)				
NO	—	FG Carney 47				
NO	—	A. Smith 6 run (Carney kick)				
Atl	—	Vick 2 run (Peterson kick)				
Atl	—	White 54 pass from Vick (Peterson kick)				
NO	—	Hakim 9 pass from Brooks (Carney kick)				
Atl	—	Vick 17 run (Peterson kick)				
Atl	—	Safety, Lake sacked Brooks in end zone				
Atl	—	FG Peterson 43				
Atl	—	FG Peterson 20				

FIFTEENTH WEEK SUMMARIES
American Football Conference

East Division	W	L	T	Pct.	Pts.	OP
New England*	9	5	0	.643	322	289
Miami	7	7	0	.500	266	281
Buffalo	4	10	0	.286	208	310
N.Y. Jets	3	11	0	.214	199	298
North Division	**W**	**L**	**T**	**Pct.**	**Pts.**	**OP**
Cincinnati*	11	3	0	.786	391	276
Pittsburgh	9	5	0	.643	313	237
Baltimore	5	9	0	.357	219	256
Cleveland	5	9	0	.357	212	244
South Division	**W**	**L**	**T**	**Pct.**	**Pts.**	**OP**
Indianapolis*	13	1	0	.929	409	206
Jacksonville	10	4	0	.714	283	236
Tennessee	4	10	0	.286	276	357
Houston	2	12	0	.143	223	373
West Division	**W**	**L**	**T**	**Pct.**	**Pts.**	**OP**
Denver#	11	3	0	.786	350	248
San Diego	9	5	0	.643	404	269
Kansas City	8	6	0	.571	346	315
Oakland	4	10	0	.286	266	331

National Football Conference

East Division	W	L	T	Pct.	Pts.	OP
N.Y. Giants	10	4	0	.714	372	258
Dallas	8	6	0	.571	291	268
Washington	8	6	0	.571	293	253
Philadelphia	6	8	0	.429	269	330
North Division	**W**	**L**	**T**	**Pct.**	**Pts.**	**OP**
Chicago	10	4	0	.714	226	151
Minnesota	8	6	0	.571	249	304

Detroit	4	10	0	.286	220	298
Green Bay	3	11	0	.214	258	303
South Division	**W**	**L**	**T**	**Pct.**	**Pts.**	**OP**
Carolina	10	4	0	.714	327	224
Tampa Bay	9	5	0	.643	246	237
Atlanta	8	6	0	.571	316	270
New Orleans	3	11	0	.214	210	358
West Division	**W**	**L**	**T**	**Pct.**	**Pts.**	**OP**
Seattle*	12	2	0	.857	407	235
St. Louis	5	9	0	.357	323	395
Arizona	4	10	0	.286	271	349
San Francisco	2	12	0	.143	195	391

*Clinched division title
#Clinched playoff berth

SATURDAY, DECEMBER 17

NEW ENGLAND 28, TAMPA BAY 0—at Gillette Stadium, attendance 68,756. Tom Brady passed for 3 touchdowns as the Patriots clinched the AFC East. The Patriots outgained the Buccaneers 336-138 total yards, marking the third consecutive game the Patriots held an opponent under 200 yards, and registered 7 sacks. Leading 14-0, Mike Vrabel sacked Chris Simms and forced him to fumble. Willie McGinest recovered the ball and returned it 19 yards to set up David Givens' 16-yard touchdown catch with 27 seconds left in the half for a 21-0 lead. Tampa Bay did not run a play inside the Patriots' 30, and had an 81-yard scoring punt return by Mark Jones nullified by a penalty. Brady was 20 of 31 for 258 yards and 3 touchdowns. Givens had 6 catches for 137 yards. Simms was 21 of 34 for 155 yards.

Tampa Bay	0	0	0	0 — 0
New England	7	14	0	7 — 28

NE	—	Ashworth 1 pass from Brady (Vinatieri kick)
NE	—	Dillon 3 run (Vinatieri kick)
NE	—	Givens 16 pass from Brady (Vinatieri kick)
NE	—	Dillon 2 pass from Brady (Vinatieri kick)

N.Y. GIANTS 27, KANSAS CITY 17—at Giants Stadium, attendance 78,625. Tiki Barber rushed for a club-record 220 yards and scored 2 touchdowns as the Giants overran the Chiefs. Kansas City had not allowed a 100-yard rusher in its previous 20 games. With the score tied 10-10 late in the third quarter, Feely added a second field goal and, after a three-and-out, Eli Manning fired a 31-yard scoring pass to Amani Toomer. The Chiefs drove 69 yards, capped by Larry Johnson's second touchdown, to pull within 27-24 with 8:29 left, but Barber carried 6 times on the ensuing 10-play drive, scoring from 20 yards with 2:48 left. James Butler intercepted a pass with 2:04 remaining and, after a punt, Nick Greisen recovered a fumble with 43 seconds left to clinch the victory. Manning was 17 of 32 for 186 yards and 1 touchdown, with 1 interception. Barber carried 29 times for 220 yards. Trent Green was 15 of 28 for 176 yards, with 1 interception.

Kansas City	0	3	7	7 — 17
N.Y. Giants	0	10	3	14 — 27

KC	—	FG Tynes 19
NYG	—	Barber 41 run (Feely kick)
NYG	—	FG Feely 41
KC	—	L. Johnson 14 run (Tynes kick)
NYG	—	FG Feely 35
NYG	—	Toomer 31 pass from Manning (Feely kick)
KC	—	L. Johnson 1 run (Tynes kick)
NYG	—	Barber 20 run (Feely kick)

SATURDAY NIGHT, DECEMBER 17

DENVER 28, BUFFALO 8—at Ralph Wilson Stadium, attendance 71,887. Mike Anderson scored 2 second-half touchdowns and Jake Plummer passed for 2 scores as the Broncos clinched a postseason berth.

Following a Rian Lindell field goal, the Broncos drove 70 yards, capped by Anderson's 11-yard run for a 21-10 lead. The Broncos forced a punt, and then drove 71 yards in 15 plays, capped by Anderson's second scoring run with 5:49 to play. Plummer was 20 of 37 for 259 yards and 2 touchdowns. Rod Smith had 11 catches for 137 yards. Kelly Holcomb was 22 of 35 for 202 yards and 1 touchdown. Eric Moulds had 9 receptions for 110 yards.

Denver	0	7	14	7 — 28
Buffalo	7	0	3	7 — 17

Buff	—	McGahee 1 run (Lindell kick)
Den	—	R. Smith 3 pass from Plummer (Elam kick)
Den	—	Duke 1 pass from Plummer (Elam kick)
Buff	—	FG Lindell 31
Den	—	Anderson 11 run (Elam kick)
Den	—	Anderson 6 run (Elam kick)
Buff	—	Burns 19 pass from Holcomb (Lindell kick)

SUNDAY, DECEMBER 18

CINCINNATI 41, DETROIT 17—at Ford Field, attendance 61,749. Carson Palmer passed for 3 touchdowns as the Bengals won their first division title in 15 seasons. Cincinnati drove 64 yards on the opening drive of the second half for a 31-7 lead. Palmer was 28 of 39 for 274 yards and 3 touchdowns, with 2 interceptions. Chad Johnson had 11 catches for 99 yards, and Rudi Johnson carried 24 times for 117 yards. Jeff Garcia was 13 of 21 for 138 yards and 1 touchdown, with 3 interceptions.

Cincinnati	17	7	7	10 — 41
Detroit	0	7	3	7 — 17

Cin	—	FG Graham 28
Cin	—	Washington 18 pass from Palmer (Graham kick)
Cin	—	C. Johnson 1 pass from Palmer (Graham kick)
Det	—	R. Williams 5 pass from Garcia (Hanson kick)
Cin	—	Houshmandzadeh 7 pass from Palmer (Graham kick)
Cin	—	R. Johnson 4 run (Graham kick)
Det	—	FG Hanson 45
Det	—	R. Johnson 16 run (Graham kick)
Det	—	Rogers 35 pass from Harrington (Hanson kick)
Cin	—	FG Graham 33

HOUSTON 30, ARIZONA 19—at Reliant Stadium, attendance 70,024. The Texans' defense forced 4 turnovers and registered 6 sacks as Houston snapped its six-game losing streak. The Texans scored on five consecutive possessions, to take a 27-10 lead with 12:13 left in the third quarter. Karlos Dansby's fumble recovery, which was set up by Ross Kolodziej's sack, led to Larry Fitzgerald's 12-yard touchdown catch to trim the deficit to 27-19 with 5:32 to play. The Cardinals' defense forced a punt, but a few plays later Obafemi Ayanbadejo fumbled and Jason Simmons recovered to set up Kris Brown's field goal with 27 seconds left. David Carr was 22 of 33 for 150 yards, with 1 interception. Kurt Warner was 10 of 10 for 115 yards and 1 touchdown before suffering a season-ending knee injury in the first half. John Navarre was 14 of 24 for 174 yards and 1 touchdown, with 1 interception. Anquan Boldin had 8 catches for 134 yards.

Arizona	3	7	0	9 — 19
Houston	0	24	3	3 — 30

Ariz	—	FG Rackers 26
Hou	—	Wells 7 run (K. Brown kick)
Ariz	—	Boldin 20 pass from Warner (Rackers kick)
Hou	—	Morency 25 run (K. Brown kick)
Hou	—	Wells 3 run (K. Brown kick)
Hou	—	FG K. Brown 27
Hou	—	FG K. Brown 41
Ariz	—	FG Rackers 42
Ariz	—	Fitzgerald 12 pass from Navarre (bad snap)
Hou	—	FG K. Brown 26

SAN DIEGO 26, INDIANAPOLIS 17—at RCA Dome, attendance 57,389. Michael Turner scored on an 83-yard run with 2:09 to play as the Colts lost their first game. The Chargers' defense held Edgerrin James to 25 yards, the second-lowest total of his career, and Peyton Manning was sacked 4 times after having been sacked just 12 times in his first 13 games. Trailing 16-0, the Colts responded by scoring 17 points in a span of 6:01, the latter two scores set up by Gary Brackett's interception and Montae Reagor's fumble recovery at the Chargers' 4, to give the Colts a 17-16 lead with 40 seconds left in the third quarter. In the fourth quarter, Drew Brees fired a 54-yard pass to Keenan McCardell to set up Nate Kaeding's 49-yard field goal with 6:36 to play. The Colts drove to the Chargers' 23, but Peyton Manning's 12-yard intentional grounding penalty and Luis Castillo's sack forced Indianapolis to punt with 2:28 to play. Two plays later, with LaDainian Tomlinson sidelined with a rib injury, Turner raced 83 yards down the right sideline for a touchdown with 2:09 remaining. Quentin Jammer intercepted a pass with 1:35 to play to clinch the victory. Brees was 22 of 33 for 255 yards and 1 touchdown, with 2 interceptions. Turner carried 8 times for 113 yards. Manning was 26 of 45 for 336 yards and 1 touchdown, with 2 interceptions. Reggie Wayne had 10 catches for 91 yards, and Marvin Harrison had 8 receptions for 135 yards.

San Diego	10	3	3	10 — 26
Indianapolis	0	0	17	0 — 17

SD	—	McCardell 29 pass from Brees (Kaeding kick)
SD	—	FG Kaeding 36
SD	—	FG Kaeding 20
SD	—	FG Kaeding 48
Ind	—	FG Vanderjagt 32
Ind	—	James 1 run (Vanderjagt kick)
Ind	—	Clark 1 pass from Manning (Vanderjagt kick)
SD	—	FG Kaeding 49
SD	—	Turner 83 run (Kaeding kick)

JACKSONVILLE 10, SAN FRANCISCO 9—at ALLTEL Stadium, attendance 64,105. David Garrard ran for a touchdown as the Jaguars rallied to defeat the 49ers. Alex Smith's 28-yard pass to Johnnie Morton set up Nedney's go-ahead field goal with 14:56 to play. Jimmy Smith's 13-yard catch on third-and-8 kept alive the ensuing drive and set up Scobee's 32-yard field goal for a 10-9 lead with 9:41 remaining. The 49ers failed to generate a first down on their final four possessions. Garrard was 21 of 40 for 216 yards. Smith was 8 of 24 for 123 yards, with 1 interception.

San Francisco	3	3	0	3 — 9
Jacksonville	0	7	0	3 — 10

SF	—	FG Nedney 35
Jax	—	Garrard 13 run (Scobee kick)
SF	—	FG Nedney 47
SF	—	FG Nedney 33
Jax	—	FG Scobee 32

MIAMI 24, N.Y. JETS 20—at Dolphins Stadium, attendance 64,900. The Dolphins' defense forced 3 turnovers and registered 6 sacks as Miami won its fourth consecutive game. Sage Rosenfels fired a 50-yard touchdown pass to Marty Booker for a 24-17 lead with 10:55 remaining. The Jets drove to the Dolphins' 15, and David Bowens sacked Brooks Bollinger on third down to force New York to settle for Mike Nugent's field goal with 4:32 to play. The Jets forced a punt and drove to the Dolphins' 14 with 1:09

remaining, but Bollinger threw 4 consecutive incomplete passes. Gus Frerotte played the first half before he injured his throwing hand. Frerotte was 8 of 16 for 76 yards and 1 touchdown, with 1 interception. Rosenfels was 6 of 13 for 99 yards, and 1 touchdown. Bollinger was 28 of 42 for 327 yards and 2 touchdowns. Doug Jolley had 9 catches for 102 yards.

| N.Y. Jets | 0 | 10 | 7 | 3 | — | 20 |
| Miami | 7 | 3 | 0 | 14 | — | 24 |

Mia	—	Chambers 8 pass from Frerotte (Mare kick)
Mia	—	FG Mare 32
NYJ	—	Coles 4 pass from Bollinger (Nugent kick)
NYJ	—	FG Nugent 42
NYJ	—	Jolley 60 pass from Bollinger (Nugent kick)
Mia	—	Williams 23 run (Mare kick)
Mia	—	Booker 50 pass from Rosenfels (Mare kick)
NYJ	—	FG Nugent 42

PITTSBURGH 18, MINNESOTA 3—at Metrodome, attendance 64,136. The Steelers' defense forced 3 turnovers and allowed just 185 yards to snap the Vikings' six-game winning streak. Just before half-time, Deshea Townsend intercepted a pass in the end zone for a touchback, and Paul Edinger's 32-yard field-goal attempt was blocked by Kimo von Oelhoffen early in the third quarter. The Steelers answered with a field goal by Jeff Reed and Tyrone Carter recovered a fumble on the kickoff to set up Reed's 26-yard field goal with 36 seconds left in the third quarter for a 16-3 lead, and the Vikings never threatened. Ben Roethlisberger was 10 of 15 for 149 yards. Brad Johnson was 16 of 30 for 143 yards, with 2 interceptions.

| Pittsburgh | 3 | 7 | 6 | 2 | — | 18 |
| Minnesota | 3 | 0 | 0 | 0 | — | 3 |

Pitt	—	FG Reed 21
Minn	—	FG Edinger 20
Pitt	—	Roethlisberger 3 run (Reed kick)
Pitt	—	FG Reed 41
Pitt	—	FG Reed 26
Pitt	—	Safety, Foote and Porter tackled Bennett in end zone

CAROLINA 27, NEW ORLEANS 10—at Tiger Stadium, attendance 32,551. Steve Smith ran for a touchdown and caught another as the Panthers moved back into first place in the NFC South. In their fourth and final game played in Baton Rouge because of Hurricane Katrina, the Saints drove 80 yards to tie the game in the first quarter. However, the Panthers forced 6 turnovers, including 2 in the second quarter, capped by Jake Delhomme's 2-yard run with 41 seconds left in the half for a 17-7 lead. Smith's 33-yard catch late in the third quarter set up his 15-yard touchdown catch for a 24-7 lead. John Carney's 44-yard field goal, following T.J. Slaughter's interception, trimmed the deficit to 24-10 with 5:47 to play. The Saints then forced a punt, but Az-Zahir Hakim muffed the punt and David Wesley recovered with 4:29 remaining to set up John Kasay's second field goal to clinch the victory. Delhomme was 13 of 21 for 176 yards and 1 touchdown, with 1 interception. Todd Bouman, making his first start of the season, was 17 of 34 for 193 yards and 1 touchdown, with 4 interceptions. Donte' Stallworth had 5 receptions for 102 yards.

| Carolina | 7 | 10 | 7 | 3 | — | 27 |
| New Orleans | 7 | 0 | 0 | 3 | — | 10 |

Car	—	Smith 20 run (Kasay kick)
NO	—	Stallworth 23 pass from Bouman (Carney kick)
Car	—	FG Kasay 32
Car	—	Delhomme 2 run (Kasay kick)
Car	—	Smith 15 pass from Delhomme (Kasay kick)
NO	—	FG Carney 44

| Car | — | FG Kasay 29 |

CLEVELAND 9, OAKLAND 7—at McAfee Coliseum, attendance 60,147. Phil Dawson kicked a 37-yard field goal as time expired to snap the Browns' three-game losing streak. Playing in the rain and on a wet field, Leigh Bodden's interception near midfield led to Dawson's 24-yard field goal with 1:48 left in the third quarter. The Raiders had a chance to extend their 7-6 lead with 3:15 to play, but Sebastian Janikowski's 46-yard field-goal attempt was blocked by Alvin McKinley. The Browns drove 43 yards, aided by a 15-yard facemask penalty, to set up Dawson's winning kick. Charlie Frye was 21 of 32 for 198 yards, with 1 interception to post his first NFL victory. Kerry Collins was 14 of 30 for 132 yards and 1 touchdown, with 1 interception. LaMont Jordan had 25 carries for 132 yards.

| Cleveland | 0 | 3 | 3 | 3 | — | 9 |
| Oakland | 0 | 7 | 0 | 0 | — | 7 |

Oak	—	Moss 28 pass from Collins (Janikowski kick)
Cle	—	FG Dawson 44
Cle	—	FG Dawson 24
Cle	—	FG Dawson 37

PHILADELPHIA 17, ST. LOUIS 16—at Edward Jones Dome, attendance 65,832. Mike Bartrum caught a 3-yard touchdown pass on the first play of the fourth quarter as the Rams lost for the fifth time in six games. Reno Mahe's 13-yard punt return and 10-yard run sparked the Eagles to set up David Akers' 31-yard field goal with 3:10 left in the third quarter to pull within 16-10. Three plays later, Brian Dawkins intercepted Ryan Fitzpatrick's pass, and on third-and-2 from the Rams' 3 Mike McMahon rolled right and hit Bartrum with a scoring pass with 14:52 to play. McMahon was 15 of 28 for 97 yards and 1 touchdown, with 3 interceptions. Fitzpatrick was 10 of 24 for 69 yards and 1 touchdown, with 1 interception, and Jamie Martin was 8 of 11 for 58 yards.

| Philadelphia | 7 | 0 | 3 | 7 | — | 17 |
| St. Louis | 3 | 10 | 3 | 0 | — | 16 |

StL	—	FG Wilkins 26
Phil	—	Moats 59 run (Akers kick)
StL	—	Holt 5 pass from Fitzpatrick (Wilkins kick)
StL	—	FG Wilkins 53
StL	—	FG Wilkins 28
Phil	—	FG Akers 31
Phil	—	Bartrum 3 pass from McMahon (Akers kick)

SEATTLE 28, TENNESSEE 24—at The Coliseum, attendance 69,149. Matt Hasselbeck passed for 3 touchdowns as the Seahawks rallied to win their tenth consecutive game and clinch a first-round bye. The Titans held a 24-14 lead with 6:14 left in the fourth quarter. On the next play from scrimmage, Hasselbeck completed a 56-yard pass to Bobby Engram and cut the deficit to 24-21 on Joe Jurevicius' 4-yard scoring grab. The Titans drove to the Seahawks' 6, but on fourth-and-1, Michael Boulware and Grant Wistrom stopped Chris Brown for a 1-yard loss. Seattle answered with a 13-play, 93-yard drive, capped by Darrell Jackson's 2-yard touchdown catch with 8:59 to play for a 28-24 lead. The Titans drove to the Seahawks' 34, but Steve McNair's fourth-and-2 pass fell incomplete with 5:03 left, and Shaun Alexander got 1 yard on third-and-1 with 2:28 to play to clinch the victory. Hasselbeck was 21 of 27 for 285 yards and 3 touchdowns. Alexander had 26 carries for 172 yards. McNair was 23 of 38 for 310 yards and 2 touchdowns. Ben Troupe had 6 receptions for 116 yards.

| Seattle | 14 | 0 | 7 | 7 | — | 28 |
| Tennessee | 0 | 14 | 10 | 0 | — | 24 |

| Sea | — | Stevens 22 pass from Hasselbeck (J. Brown kick) |
| Sea | — | Alexander 1 run (J. Brown kick) |

Tenn	—	Payton 3 run (Bironas kick)
Tenn	—	D. Bennett 4 pass from McNair (Bironas kick)
Tenn	—	D. Bennett 14 pass from McNair (Bironas kick)
Tenn	—	FG Bironas 38
Sea	—	Jurevicius 4 pass from Hasselbeck (J. Brown kick)
Sea	—	Jackson 2 pass from Hasselbeck (J. Brown kick)

WASHINGTON 35, DALLAS 7—at FedExField, attendance 90,588. Mark Brunell passed for 4 touchdowns as the Redskins swept Dallas for the first time in 10 years and posted their largest margin of victory in the 90th game between the clubs. Mike Sellers' 3-yard touchdown catch with 1:25 left in the half gave the Redskins a 21-0 lead, and four plays later, Marcus Washington intercepted a pass and returned it 41 yards to set up Chris Cooley's 30-yard catch with 12 seconds remaining for a 28-0 lead. Three plays into the second half, Washington sacked Drew Bledsoe and forced him to fumble. Phillip Daniels recovered and six plays later Ladell Betts scored for a 35-0 lead with 10:15 left in the third quarter. Brunell was 12 of 20 for 163 yards and 4 touchdowns. Portis had 23 carries for 112 yards. Bledsoe was 16 of 29 for 153 yards and 1 touchdown, with 3 interceptions.

| Dallas | 0 | 0 | 0 | 7 | — | 7 |
| Washington | 7 | 21 | 7 | 0 | — | 35 |

Wash	—	Cooley 8 pass from Brunell (Hall kick)
Wash	—	Cooley 2 pass from Brunell (Hall kick)
Wash	—	Sellers 3 pass from Brunell (Hall kick)
Wash	—	Cooley 30 pass from Brunell (Hall kick)
Wash	—	Betts 1 run (Hall kick)
Dall	—	Witten 2 pass from Bledsoe (Cundiff kick)

SUNDAY NIGHT, DECEMBER 18

CHICAGO 16, ATLANTA 3—at Soldier Field, attendance 62,170. The Bears forced 3 turnovers as Chicago won in 12 degree weather, with a wind chill of minus-3. Kyle Orton guided the Bears to 2 scoring drives in the first half for a 6-3 halftime lead, but Rex Grossman, who was injured in the preseason, was put into the lineup for the second half. Grossman guided the club to the Falcons' 8 where Keion Carpenter intercepted his pass. However, Carpenter fumbled and Justin Gage recovered to set up Thomas Jones' 1-yard scoring run. Chicago drove 50 yards with its next drive for Robbie Gould's third field goal for a 16-3 lead with 53 seconds left in the third quarter. Orton was 2 of 10 for 12 yards in the first half before replaced by Grossman, who was 9 of 16 for 93 yards, with 1 interception. Michael Vick was 13 of 32 for 122 yards, with 2 interceptions.

| Atlanta | 0 | 3 | 0 | 0 | — | 3 |
| Chicago | 0 | 6 | 10 | 0 | — | 16 |

Atl	—	FG Peterson 30
Chi	—	FG Gould 35
Chi	—	FG Gould 29
Chi	—	T. Jones 1 run (Gould kick)
Chi	—	FG Gould 39

MONDAY NIGHT, DECEMBER 19

BALTIMORE 48, GREEN BAY 3—at M&T Bank Stadium, attendance 70,604. Kyle Boller passed for 3 touchdowns and the Ravens' defense forced 5 turnovers en route to the biggest rout in *Monday Night Football* history. The Ravens also set a club record for points in a game. A 49-yard punt return by B.J. Sams to the Packers' 18 set up Boller's first touchdown pass less than four minutes into the game. Baltimore scored on four of its next five possessions, on drives of 75, 96, 63, and 72 yards to take a 31-3 lead with 9:43 left in the third quarter. Boller was 19 of 27 for 253 yards and 3 touchdowns. Todd Heap had 9 receptions for 110 yards. Lewis added 22 carries for 105 yards. Brett Favre was 14 of 29 for 144 yards, with 2 interceptions. Aaron Rodgers was 8 of 15 for 65 yards, with 1 interception and 2 lost fumbles.

Green Bay	3	0	0	0	—	3
Baltimore	14	10	10	14	—	48

Balt	—	Heap 2 pass from Boller (Stover kick)
Balt	—	Clayton 11 run (Stover kick)
GB	—	FG Longwell 27
Balt	—	Hymes 13 pass from Boller (Stover kick)
Balt	—	FG Stover 23
Balt	—	Heap 27 pass from Boller (Stover kick)
Balt	—	FG Stover 40
Balt	—	J. Lewis 3 run (Stover kick)
Balt	—	A. Thomas 35 fumble return (Stover kick)

SIXTEENTH WEEK SUMMARIES
American Football Conference

East Division	W	L	T	Pct.	Pts.	OP
New England*	10	5	0	.667	353	310
Miami	8	7	0	.533	290	291
Buffalo	5	10	0	.333	245	337
N.Y. Jets	3	12	0	.200	210	329
North Division	**W**	**L**	**T**	**Pct.**	**Pts.**	**OP**
Cincinnati*	11	4	0	.733	418	313
Pittsburgh	10	5	0	.667	354	237
Baltimore	6	9	0	.400	249	279
Cleveland	5	10	0	.333	212	285
South Division	**W**	**L**	**T**	**Pct.**	**Pts.**	**OP**
Indianapolis*	13	2	0	.867	422	234
Jacksonville#	11	4	0	.733	321	256
Tennessee	4	11	0	.267	286	381
Houston	2	13	0	.133	243	411
West Division	**W**	**L**	**T**	**Pts.**	**Pts.**	**OP**
Denver*	12	3	0	.800	372	251
Kansas City	9	6	0	.600	366	322
San Diego	9	6	0	.600	411	289
Oakland	4	11	0	.267	269	353

National Football Conference

East Division	W	L	T	Pct.	Pts.	OP
N.Y. Giants#	10	5	0	.667	392	293
Dallas	9	6	0	.600	315	288
Washington	9	6	0	.600	315	288
Philadelphia	6	9	0	.400	290	357
North Division	**W**	**L**	**T**	**Pct.**	**Pts.**	**OP**
Chicago*	11	4	0	.733	250	168
Minnesota	8	7	0	.533	272	334
Detroit	5	10	0	.333	233	310
Green Bay	3	12	0	.200	275	327
South Division	**W**	**L**	**T**	**Pct.**	**Pts.**	**OP**
Carolina	10	5	0	.667	347	248
Tampa Bay	10	5	0	.667	273	261
Atlanta	8	7	0	.533	340	297
New Orleans	3	12	0	.200	222	371
West Division	**W**	**L**	**T**	**Pct.**	**Pts.**	**OP**
Seattle*	13	2	0	.867	435	248
Arizona	5	10	0	.333	298	370
St. Louis	5	10	0	.333	343	419
San Francisco	3	12	0	.200	219	411

*Clinched division title
#Clinched playoff berth

SATURDAY, DECEMBER 24

ARIZONA 27, PHILADELPHIA 21—at Sun Devil Stadium, attendance 44,723. Josh McCown passed for 2 touchdowns as the Cardinals won their final game played after 18 seasons at Sun Devil Stadium. Anquan Boldin's 20-yard scoring reception gave the Cardinals a 27-7 lead with 11:25 remaining. Mike McMahon's second scoring sneak, with 26 seconds left, cut the deficit to 27-21, but Eric Green recovered the onside kick to ensure the victory. McCown was 27 of 38 for 294 yards and 2 touchdowns, with 1 interception. McMahon was 12 of 33 for 151 yards and 1 touchdown, with 1 interception.

Philadelphia	0	7	0	14	—	21
Arizona	6	7	7	7	—	27

Ariz	—	FG Rackers 32
Ariz	—	FG Rackers 32
Ariz	—	Dansby 11 interception return (Rackers kick)
Phil	—	McMahon 1 run (Akers kick)
Ariz	—	Fitzgerald 25 pass from McCown (Rackers kick)
Ariz	—	Boldin 20 pass from McCown (Rackers kick)
Phil	—	McMullen 21 pass from McMahon (Akers kick)
Phil	—	McMahon 1 run (Akers kick)

DALLAS 24, CAROLINA 20—at Bank of America Stadium, attendance 69,987. The Cowboys took advantage of a roughing the kicker penalty to score the winning touchdown with 24 seconds left and keep their playoff hopes alive. Dallas held the 17-13 lead late in the fourth quarter, but Jake Delhomme completed a 35-yard touchdown pass to Ricky Proehl for a 20-17 lead with 2:32 remaining. Tyson Thompson returned the ensuing kickoff 40 yards to help the Cowboys reach the Panthers' 15. With 1:08 left, Billy Cundiff attempted to tie the game with a 33-yard attempt. The kick sailed wide right, but Ken Lucas and Julius Peppers just missed blocking the attempt, and Peppers was flagged for running into the kicker. Two plays later, Drew Bledsoe found Terry Glenn open for a touchdown with 24 seconds left. Bledsoe was 15 of 23 for 209 yards and 1 touchdown, with 1 interception. Jones had 34 carries for 194 yards. Delhomme was 14 of 31 for 260 yards and 2 touchdowns, with 1 interception. Proehl had 2 catches for 104 yards.

Dallas	7	3	7	7	—	24
Carolina	10	3	0	7	—	20

Car	—	FG Kasay 24
Car	—	Carter 32 pass from Delhomme (Kasay kick)
Dall	—	J. Jones 8 run (Cundiff kick)
Dall	—	FG Cundiff 24
Car	—	FG Kasay 47
Dall	—	J. Jones 43 run (Cundiff kick)
Car	—	Proehl 35 pass from Delhomme (Kasay kick)
Dall	—	Glenn 2 pass from Bledsoe (Cundiff kick)

BUFFALO 37, CINCINNATI 27—at Paul Brown Stadium, attendance 65,485. Terrence McGee became the first player in NFL history to return an interception and kickoff for a touchdown in the same game as the Bills posted their only road victory of the season. Shayne Graham's field goal capped the next drive and increased Cincinnati's lead to 17-13, only to have McGee return the kickoff down the left sideline 99 yards for a touchdown. After an exchange of touchdowns, Graham tied the game with a 27-yard field goal with 7:27 to play. The Bengals' defense used a goal-line stand to limit the Bills to Rian Lindell's go-ahead 22-yard field goal with 58 seconds left, but two plays later McGee stepped in front of Carson Palmer's pass in the left flat and returned the ball untouched 46 yards for the game-clinching touchdown. Kelly Holcomb was 24 of 31 for 308 yards and 1 touchdown, with 1 interception. Eric Moulds had 10 catches for 99 yards, and Lee Evans had 5 receptions for 107 yards. Palmer was 25 of 36 for 266 yards and 2 touchdowns, with 2 interceptions. Johnson had 9 catches for 117 yards.

Buffalo	6	7	7	17	—	37
Cincinnati	0	14	10	3	—	27

Buff	—	FG Lindell 21
Buff	—	FG Lindell 24
Cin	—	T. Perry 2 run (Graham kick)
Buff	—	Evans 3 pass from Holcomb (Lindell kick)
Cin	—	C. Johnson 41 pass from Palmer (Graham kick)
Cin	—	FG Graham 31
Buff	—	McGee 99 kickoff return (Lindell kick)
Cin	—	Henry 27 pass from Palmer (Graham kick)
Buff	—	Holcomb 1 run (Lindell kick)
Cin	—	FG Graham 27
Buff	—	FG Lindell 22
Buff	—	McGee 46 interception return (Lindell kick)

PITTSBURGH 41, CLEVELAND 0—at Cleveland Browns Stadium, attendance 73,136. The Steelers' defense registered 8 sacks, 3 by Joey Porter, and permitted just 178 yards as the Steelers remained in control of their playoff destiny. The Steelers, who rolled up 457 yards, led 17-0 before the Browns had a first down, and Willie Parker's 80-yard touchdown run with 9:02 left in the third quarter extended the lead to 27-0. Ben Roethlisberger was 13 of 20 for 226 yards and 1 touchdown, and Charlie Batch completed his lone pass attempt for a 31-yard touchdown. Parker had 17 carries for 130 yards. Hines Ward had 7 catches for 105 yards. Charlie Frye was 20 of 39 for 183 yards.

Pittsburgh	14	6	14	7	—	41
Cleveland	0	0	0	0	—	0

Pitt	—	Bettis 2 run (Reed kick)
Pitt	—	Ward 7 pass from Roethlisberger (Reed kick)
Pitt	—	FG Reed 26
Pitt	—	FG Reed 31
Pitt	—	Parker 80 run (Reed kick)
Pitt	—	Haynes 15 run (Reed kick)
Pitt	—	Morgan 31 pass from Batch (Reed kick)

DENVER 22, OAKLAND 3—at INVESCO Field at Mile High, attendance 76,212. Jake Plummer passed for 268 yards as the Broncos claimed the second-seed in the AFC. Trailing 16-0 in the second quarter, the Raiders drove 64 yards to the Broncos' 4 in the final minute of the half, only to have Nick Ferguson intercept Kerry Collins' pass attempt for a touchback. Two Jason Elam field goals on the opening two drives of the second half gave Denver a 22-0 lead. Plummer was 19 of 29 for 268 yards, with 1 interception. Ashley Lelie had 6 catches for 110 yards. Collins was 17 of 41 for 178 yards, with 1 interception.

Oakland	0	0	0	3	—	3
Denver	10	6	6	0	—	22

Den	—	FG Elam 29
Den	—	Plummer 1 run (Elam kick)
Den	—	Anderson 2 run (bad hold)
Den	—	FG Elam 33
Den	—	FG Elam 34
Oak	—	FG Janikowski 43

JACKSONVILLE 38, HOUSTON 20—at Reliant Stadium, attendance 70,025. The Jaguars made their sixth second-half comeback to clinch their first postseason berth since 1999. David Carr lofted a 53-yard touchdown pass to Andre Johnson to give the Texans a 20-17 advantage with 12:15 left. The Jaguars responded with a 66-yard touchdown drive, and after Kris Brown missed a 48-yard field-goal attempt, David Garrard completed a 36-yard touchdown pass to Ernest Wilford with 2:37 to play. Terry Cousin's interception two plays later set up Toefield's final touchdown. Garrard was 18 of 31 for 292 yards and 1 touchdown. Wilford had 4 catches for 118 yards. Fred Taylor had 22 carries for 101 yards. Carr was 19 of 29 for 295 yards and 2 touchdowns, with 1 interception. Johnson had 7 catches for 119 yards, and Corey Bradford added 4 receptions for 101 yards.

Jacksonville	7	3	7	21	—	38
Houston	3	10	0	7	—	20

Jax	—	Toefield 1 run (Scobee kick)
Hou	—	FG K. Brown 37
Hou	—	Bradford 50 pass from Carr (K. Brown kick)
Jax	—	FG Scobee 26
Hou	—	FG K. Brown 53
Jax	—	Toefield 2 run (Scobee kick)
Hou	—	A. Johnson 53 pass from Carr (K. Brown kick)
Jax	—	Taylor 1 run (Scobee kick)
Jax	—	Wilford 36 pass from Garrard (Scobee kick)
Jax	—	Toefield 17 run (Scobee kick)

KANSAS CITY 20, SAN DIEGO 7—at Arrowhead Stadium, attendance 75,956. Larry Johnson scored 2 touchdowns and the Chiefs' defense permitted just 233 yards as Kansas City remained in the playoff chase. The loss eliminated the Chargers from postseason consideration. Playing in the rain, the Chargers had just three drives of more than 20 yards. The Chargers drove to the Chiefs' 17 to begin the second half, but Drew Brees' pass went through LaDainian Tomlinson's hands and was intercepted by Patrick Surtain. San Diego's lone other scoring threat came with 3:37 left, but Brees' fourth-down pass from the Chiefs' 22 fell incomplete. Trent Green was 19 of 35 for 207 yards and 2 touchdowns. Johnson had 32 carries for 131 yards. Brees was 18 of 33 for 161 yards and 1 touchdown, with 1 interception.

San Diego	7	0	0	0	—	7
Kansas City	7	13	0	0	—	20

KC	—	L. Johnson 4 run (Tynes kick)
SD	—	Gates 18 pass from Brees (Kaeding kick)
KC	—	Parker 42 pass from Green (Tynes kick)
KC	—	L. Johnson 28 pass from Green (kick failed)

MIAMI 24, TENNESSEE 10—at Dolphins Stadium, attendance 72,001. Ricky Williams rushed for a season-high 172 yards and 1 touchdown as the Dolphins won their fifth consecutive game. Chris Chambers capped the first half with a 7-yard touchdown catch with 27 seconds remaining for a 17-3 halftime lead. Billy Volek replaced an injured Steve McNair and fired a 55-yard touchdown pass to Drew Bennett with 12:20 remaining in the game. With the Titans trying to get the ball back for a final chance, Williams had a 35-yard run with 2:16 remaining and capped the possession with a 19-yard touchdown run with 1:48 to play. Gus Frerotte was 14 of 30 for 151 yards and 2 touchdowns, with 1 interception. Williams carried 26 times for 172 yards. McNair was 5 of 13 for 34 yards, with 2 interceptions, and Volek was 14 of 24 for 132 yards and 1 touchdown.

Tennessee	3	0	0	7	—	10
Miami	0	17	0	7	—	24

Tenn	—	FG Bironas 24
Mia	—	FG Mare 25
Mia	—	Chambers 11 pass from Frerotte (Mare kick)
Mia	—	Chambers 7 pass from Frerotte (Mare kick)
Tenn	—	Bennett 55 pass from Volek (Bironas kick)
Mia	—	R. Williams 19 run (Mare kick)

DETROIT 13, NEW ORLEANS 12—at Alamodome, attendance 63,747. Jason Hanson kicked a 39-yard field goal as time expired to lift the Lions to victory in San Antonio. The game's lone touchdown came on

defense in the second quarter, when James Hall forced Aaron Stecker to fumble and Shaun Rogers returned the ball 21 yards for a touchdown with 5:45 left in the half. John Carney kicked field goals on the Saints next three possessions for a 9-7 lead. The Lions reached the Saints' 1 midway through the fourth quarter, but held the Lions to a field goal and then completed a 17-play, 70-yard drive with Carney's fourth field goal for a 12-10 lead with 1:52 left. Joey Harrington completed a 40-yard pass to Roy Williams to reach the Saints' 36. With 23 seconds left, Williams caught a 15-yard pass over the middle. With no timeouts, the Lions rushed the special-teams unit onto the field, and Hanson kicked a low liner over the crossbar as time expired. Harrington was 17 of 30 for 210 yards, with 1 interception. Williams had 4 catches for 111 yards. Todd Bouman was 21 of 38 for 233 yards.

Detroit	0	7	0	6	—	13
New Orleans	0	3	6	3	—	12

Det	—	S. Rogers 21 fumble return (Hanson kick)
NO	—	FG Carney 35
NO	—	FG Carney 47
NO	—	FG Carney 33
Det	—	FG Hanson 21
NO	—	FG Carney 20
Det	—	FG Hanson 39

SAN FRANCISCO 24, ST. LOUIS 20—at Edward Jones Dome, attendance 65,473. The 49ers used 2 long touchdown runs to snap a seven-game losing streak and sweep the Rams for the first time since 1998. Alex Smith completed a 22-yard pass to Jason McAddley that set up Joe Nedney's 56-yard field goal as the half expired to pull within 20-17. Frank Gore's 30-yard scoring run capped a 77-yard drive and gave the 49ers a 24-20 lead with 4:05 remaining. The Rams drove to the 49ers' 31, but Ben Emanuel intercepted Jamie Martin's pass with 59 seconds left. Smith was 12 of 16 for 131 yards. Maurice Hicks ran 10 carries for 109 yards. Martin was 33 of 41 for 354 yards and 1 touchdown, with 2 interceptions. Torry Holt had 10 catches for 163 yards.

San Francisco	7	10	0	7	—	24
St. Louis	3	17	0	0	—	20

SF	—	Hicks 73 run (Nedney kick)
StL	—	FG Wilkins 50
StL	—	Jackson 3 run (Wilkins kick)
StL	—	Holt 40 pass from Martin (Wilkins kick)
StL	—	FG Wilkins 51
SF	—	Gore 10 run (Nedney kick)
SF	—	FG Nedney 56
SF	—	Gore 30 run (Nedney kick)

SEATTLE 28, INDIANAPOLIS 13—at Qwest Field, attendance 67,855. Shaun Alexander scored 3 touchdowns as the Seahawks won their eleventh consecutive game and clinched NFC home-field advantage throughout the postseason. The Colts, who had clinched AFC home-field advantage two weeks earlier, played without coach Tony Dungy, whose son passed away two days earlier. The Seahawks scored on three of their first five possessions, capped by Alexander's 6-yard touchdown catch to culminate a 67-yard drive to begin the second half for a 21-6 lead. Craig Terrill's fumble recovery and 18-yard return to the Colts' 17 set up Alexander's NFL record-tying 27th touchdown with 3:58 to play. Matt Hasselbeck was 17 of 21 for 168 yards and 2 touchdowns. Alexander had 21 carries for 139 yards. Peyton Manning was 9 of 12 for 116 yards before replaced by Jim Sorgi, who was 22 of 31 for 237 yards and 1 touchdown. Brandon Stokley had 5 catches for 122 yards.

Indianapolis	3	3	0	7	—	13
Seattle	7	7	7	7	—	28

Ind	—	FG Vanderjagt 24
Sea	—	Alexander 2 run (J. Brown kick)

Sea	—	Stevens 15 pass from Hasselbeck (J. Brown kick)
Ind	—	FG Vanderjagt 32
Sea	—	Alexander 6 pass from Hasselbeck (J. Brown kick)
Sea	—	Alexander 1 run (J. Brown kick)
Ind	—	Walters 6 pass from Sorgi (Vanderjagt kick)

TAMPA BAY 27, ATLANTA 24 (OT)—at Raymond James Stadium, attendance 65,482. Matt Bryant's 41-yard field goal with just 15 seconds left in overtime kept the Buccaneers alive in the playoff chase while dashing the Falcons' postseason chances. Bryant tied the game with a 50-yard field goal with 9:01 left, but the Falcons answered with a 79-yard drive, highlighted by Jenkins' 37-yard catch to the Buccaneers' 2, to take a 24-17 lead with 4:18 to play. Tampa Bay drove downfield and on fourth-and-1 from the Falcons' 6, Carnell Williams ran around the left side for a game-tying touchdown with 25 seconds left. Tampa Bay won the overtime coin toss, but fumbled the kickoff and Ronnie Heard recovered at the Buccaneers' 18. Two plays later, on third-and-2, Todd Peterson attempted a game-winning field goal but Dewayne White blocked the kick. The Buccaneers' marched to the Falcons' 9, but Bryant missed a 27-yard attempt wide left. The Buccaneers forced a punt with 1:08 left, and Mark Jones returned the punt 28 yards to the Falcons' 49. Chris Simms completed passes of 15 yards to Alex Smith and 11 yards to Anthony Becht to set up Bryant's game-winning kick. Simms was 29 of 42 for 285 yards and 2 touchdowns, with 2 interceptions. Williams carried 31 times for 150 yards. Michael Vick was 16 of 26 for 161 yards and 2 touchdowns.

Atlanta	7	10	0	7	0	—	24
Tampa Bay	7	7	0	10	3	—	27

Atl	—	Griffith 4 pass from Vick (Peterson kick)
TB	—	Cook 5 pass from Simms (Bryant kick)
TB	—	Alstott 13 pass from Simms (Bryant kick)
Atl	—	Jenkins 8 pass from Vick (Peterson kick)
Atl	—	FG Peterson 31
TB	—	FG Bryant 50
Atl	—	Duckett 2 run (Peterson kick)
TB	—	Williams 6 run (Bryant kick)
TB	—	FG Bryant 41

WASHINGTON 35, N.Y. GIANTS 20—at FedExField, attendance 90,477. Santana Moss had 160 receiving yards and 3 touchdown catches as the Redskins won their fourth consecutive game and remained in control of their own postseason destiny. The Giants claimed a postseason berth the next day when the Vikings lost to Baltimore. Leading 21-17, Renaldo Wynn blocked Jay Feely's 29-yard field goal attempt in the third quarter, and five plays later Moss caught a 20-yard pass, broke a tackle and raced into the end zone for a 72-yard touchdown to give the Redskins a 28-17 lead. The Giants responded with a field goal, but Clinton Portis capped a 79-yard drive on the next possession with a 19-yard scamper for a 35-20 lead with 12:43 to play. Mark Brunell was 7 of 11 for 112 yards and 2 touchdowns, with 1 interception, before injuring his knee early in the second half. Patrick Ramsey replaced Brunell and was 5 of 7 for 104 yards and 1 touchdown. Moss had 5 catches for 160 yards, and Portis had 27 carries for 108 yards. Eli Manning was 23 of 41 for 244 yards and 1 touchdown, with 1 interception.

N.Y. Giants	10	7	3	0	—	20
Washington	14	7	7	7	—	35

Wash	—	S. Moss 17 pass from Brunell (Hall kick)

NYG — FG Feely 47
NYG — Blackburn 31 interception return
(Feely kick)
Wash — S. Moss 59 pass from Brunell
(Hall kick)
Wash — Cooley 17 pass from Portis
(Hall kick)
NYG — Toomer 25 pass from Manning
(Feely kick)
Wash — S. Moss 72 pass from Ramsey
(Hall kick)
NYG — FG Feely 38
Wash — Portis 19 run (Hall kick)

SUNDAY, DECEMBER 25

CHICAGO 24, GREEN BAY 17—at Lambeau Field, attendance 69,757. The Bears' defense intercepted 4 passes as Chicago won the NFC North, clinched a first-round bye, and swept the Packers for the first time since 1991. Rex Grossman, making his first start of the season, guided the Bears to touchdown drives of 68 and 72 yards on two of their first three possessions for a 14-7 lead. Trailing 24-7, Antonio Chatman returned a punt 85 yards for a touchdown with 7:54 to play, and following a punt, the Packers drove 65 yards in less than two minutes and kicked a 26-yard field goal with 1:54 to play. Nathan Vasher recovered the onside kick, but the Packers stopped the Bears and got the ball at their own 9-yard line with 1:26 left and no timeouts. On the first play, Brett Favre completed a post pass to Donald Driver for 56 yards to the Bears' 35. After a spike, Favre was sacked on successive plays by Tank Johnson and Alex Brown before Chris Harris intercepted his fourth-and-27 pass as time expired. Grossman was 11 of 23 for 166 yards and 1 touchdown, with 1 interception. Thomas Jones had 25 carries for 150 yards. Favre was 30 of 51 for 317 yards, with 4 interceptions. Driver had 6 catches for 107 yards.

Chicago	7	7	10	0 —	24
Green Bay	0	7	0	10 —	17

Chi — Muhammad 12 pass from Grossman (Gould kick)
GB — Herron 1 run (Longwell kick)
Chi — T. Jones 2 run (Gould kick)
Chi — FG Gould 45
Chi — Briggs 10 interception return (Gould kick)
GB — Chatman 85 punt return (Longwell kick)
GB — FG Longwell 26

SUNDAY NIGHT, DECEMBER 25

BALTIMORE 30, MINNESOTA 23—at M&T Bank Stadium, attendance 70,246. Kyle Boller passed for 3 touchdowns as the Vikings were knocked out of the playoff picture. The Ravens had scoring drives of 75 and 79 yards to take a 24-20 lead with 14:47 to play. Stover booted a 38-yard field goal with 1:55 left to extend the lead to 27-20. Two plays later, Adalius Thomas forced Brad Johnson to fumble and Anthony Weaver recovered at the Vikings' 10 to set up Stover's 19-yard field goal with 1:03 remaining. The Vikings reached the Ravens' 28 with 20 seconds left and chose to kick a field goal, which Edinger made from 46 yards, but Chad Williams recovered the onside kick to clinch the victory. Boller was 24 of 34 for 289 yards and 3 touchdowns, with 1 interception. Derrick Mason had 9 catches for 103 yards. Johnson was 25 of 36 for 248 yards and 2 touchdowns.

Minnesota	7	7	6	3 —	23
Baltimore	7	3	7	13 —	30

Minn — Taylor 13 pass from B. Johnson (Edinger kick)
Balt — Heap 6 pass from Boller (Stover kick)
Minn — Wiggins 5 pass from B. Johnson (Edinger kick)

Balt — FG Stover 37
Minn — FG Edinger 36
Balt — Clayton 47 pass from Boller (Stover kick)
Minn — FG Edinger 40
Balt — Mason 39 pass from Boller (Stover kick)
Balt — FG Stover 38
Balt — FG Stover 19
Minn — FG Edinger 46

MONDAY NIGHT, DECEMBER 26

NEW ENGLAND 31, N.Y. JETS 21—at The Meadowlands, attendance 77,569. Linebacker Mike Vrabel became the first player in 23 years with 2 touchdown catches and a sack in the same game as the Patriots won the final ABC *Monday Night Football* game. The Patriots used a dominating defensive performance to jump to a 28-7 lead. The Jets' lone first-half touchdown came on an interception return by Ty Law, and the Patriots did not allow a first down until there was 5:17 left in the third quarter, at which point the Patriots had run 63 plays compared to the Jets' 13. Tom Brady was 18 of 29 for 185 yards and 2 touchdowns, with 1 interception. Brooks Bollinger was 11 of 19 for 100 yards and 1 touchdown, with 1 interception. Vinny Testaverde was 3 of 7 for 63 yards, and his 27-yard scoring pass to Laveranues Coles with 2:10 remaining allowed him to become the first player in NFL history to complete a touchdown pass in 19 consecutive seasons.

New England	7	14	7	3 —	31
N.Y. Jets	7	0	0	14 —	21

NE — Vrabel 1 pass from Brady (Vinatieri kick)
NYJ — Law 74 interception return (Nugent kick)
NE — Vrabel 2 pass from Brady (Vinatieri kick)
NE — Dillon 1 run (Vinatieri kick)
NE — Dillon 5 run (Vinatieri kick)
NYJ — Coles 11 pass from Bollinger (Nugent kick)
NE — FG Vinatieri 26
NYJ — Coles 27 pass from Testaverde (Nugent kick)

SEVENTEENTH WEEK SUMMARIES

American Football Conference

East Division	W	L	T	Pct.	Pts.	OP
New England*	10	6	0	.625	379	338
Miami	9	7	0	.562	318	317
Buffalo	5	11	0	.312	271	367
N.Y. Jets	4	12	0	.250	240	355
North Division	**W**	**L**	**T**	**Pct.**	**Pts.**	**OP**
Cincinnati*	11	5	0	.688	421	350
Pittsburgh#	11	5	0	.688	389	258
Baltimore	6	10	0	.375	265	299
Cleveland	6	10	0	.375	232	301
South Division	**W**	**L**	**T**	**Pct.**	**Pts.**	**OP**
Indianapolis*	14	2	0	.875	439	247
Jacksonville#	12	4	0	.750	361	269
Tennessee	4	12	0	.250	299	421
Houston	2	14	0	.125	260	431
West Division	**W**	**L**	**T**	**Pct.**	**Pts.**	**OP**
Denver*	13	3	0	.812	395	258
Kansas City	10	6	0	.625	403	325
San Diego	9	7	0	.562	418	312
Oakland	4	12	0	.250	290	383

National Football Conference

East Division	W	L	T	Pct.	Pts.	OP
N.Y. Giants*	11	5	0	.688	422	314
Washington#	10	6	0	.625	359	293
Dallas	9	7	0	.562	325	308
Philadelphia	6	10	0	.375	310	388
North Division	**W**	**L**	**T**	**Pct.**	**Pts.**	**OP**
Chicago*	11	5	0	.688	260	202
Minnesota	9	7	0	.562	306	344
Detroit	5	11	0	.312	254	345
Green Bay	4	12	0	.250	298	344
South Division	**W**	**L**	**T**	**Pct.**	**Pts.**	**OP**
Tampa Bay*	11	5	0	.688	300	274
Carolina#	11	5	0	.688	391	259
Atlanta	8	8	0	.500	351	341
New Orleans	3	13	0	.188	235	398
West Division	**W**	**L**	**T**	**Pct.**	**Pts.**	**OP**
Seattle*	13	3	0	.867	435	248
St. Louis	6	10	0	.375	363	429
Arizona	5	11	0	.312	311	387
San Francisco	4	12	0	.250	239	428

*Clinched division title
#Clinched playoff berth

SATURDAY, DECEMBER 31

DENVER 23, SAN DIEGO 7—at Qualcomm Stadium, attendance 65,513. John Lynch had 2 sacks that led directly to nine points, and Tatum Bell scored 3 touchdowns, to propel the Broncos to victory. The Broncos led 7-0 late in the first half when Lynch sacked Drew Brees near the goal line and forced him to fumble. Sam Brandon recovered the ball at the Chargers' 1, and Bell scored on the next play for a 14-0 lead. Brees was injured during the fumble recovery, and Philip Rivers entered the game and engineered a 10-play, 69-yard scoring drive just before halftime. In the third quarter, Lynch sacked Rivers in the end zone and forced him to fumble. Tackle Shane Olivea recovered the ball in the end zone and was downed by Demetrin Veal for a safety and 16-7 lead. Curome Cox intercepted a pass in the fourth quarter and Bell scored from 19 yards out on the next play with 4:32 remaining to finish the scoring. Jake Plummer was 8 of 14 for 91 yards, and Bradlee Van Pelt was 2 of 8 for 7 yards. Brees was 8 of 14 for 68 yards, and Rivers was 12 of 22 for 115 yards, with 1 interception.

Denver	0	14	2	7 —	23
San Diego	0	7	0	0 —	7

Den — Bell 6 run (Elam kick)
Den — Bell 1 run (Elam kick)
SD — Tomlinson 6 run (Kaeding kick)
Den — Safety, Veal tackled Olivea in end zone
Den — Bell 19 run (Elam kick)

SATURDAY NIGHT, DECEMBER 31

N.Y. GIANTS 30, OAKLAND 21—at McAfee Coliseum, attendance 44,594. Tiki Barber had a club-record 95-yard touchdown run and became just the third player in NFL history with three 200-yard rushing games in a season as the Giants clinched the NFC East. Barber's 95-yard run sparked the Giants, who scored on their next three possessions as well, to take a 20-7 lead. Late in the third quarter, Chad Morton's 58-yard punt return to the Raiders' 3 set up Brandon Jacobs' 1-yard run, but Randy Moss caught a 44-yard touchdown pass down the right sideline two plays later to pull within 27-21. The Giants responded with a field goal, and the Raiders did not threaten again until they reached the Giants' 1 with 3:44 to play. Zack Crockett was stopped for no gain on three consecutive plays, and Kerry Collins was stopped on a quarterback sneak attempt on fourth-and-goal with 2:31 to play. Eli Manning was 12 of 24 for 204 yards and 1 touchdown. Barber had 28 carries for 203 yards. Collins was 26 of 48 for 331 yards and 3 touchdowns.

N.Y. Giants	7	13	7	3 —	30
Oakland	7	7	7	0 —	21

NYG — Barber 95 run (Feely kick)
Oak — R. Moss 15 pass from Collins (Janikowski kick)
NYG — FG Feely 25
NYG — Burress 78 pass from Manning (Feely kick)
NYG — FG Feely 38
Oak — Gabriel 8 pass from Collins (Janikowski kick)

NYG — Jacobs 1 run (Feely kick)
Oak — R. Moss 44 pass from Collins
(Janikowski kick)
NYG — FG Feely 46

SUNDAY, JANUARY 1, 2006
CAROLINA 44, ATLANTA 11—at Georgia Dome, attendance 70,796. The Panthers' defense registered 5 sacks and had 4 takeaways as the Panthers clinched a playoff berth. The 33-point margin of victory was the biggest in the Panthers' 11-year history. Carolina scored on their first six possessions. Jake Delhomme was 14 of 20 for 163 yards and 2 touchdowns, and Chris Weinke was 2 of 5 for 17 yards. DeShaun Foster had 18 carries for 165 yards. Steve Smith had 9 catches for 131 yards. Michael Vick was 15 of 24 for 115 yards, with 1 interception. Matt Schaub was 9 of 13 for 110 yards and 1 touchdown.

Carolina	14	13	10	7	—	44
Atlanta	3	0	0	8	—	11

Car — Proehl 12 pass from Delhomme (Kasay kick)
Atl — FG Peterson 29
Car — Foster 70 run (Kasay kick)
Car — FG Kasay 19
Car — S. Smith 42 pass from Delhomme (Kasay kick)
Car — FG Kasay 41
Car — Robertson 1 run (Kasay kick)
Car — FG Kasay 34
Car — Manning 8 fumble return (Kasay kick)
Atl — White 14 pass from Schaub (Finneran pass from Schaub)

CLEVELAND 20, BALTIMORE 16—at Cleveland Browns Stadium, attendance 69,871. Dennis Northcutt returned a punt 62 yards for a touchdown as the Browns rallied to victory. In the third quarter, Josh Cribbs returned a kickoff 54 yards, fumbled, but Sean Jones scooped up the ball for the Browns and ran another 11 yards to the Ravens' 24. Antonio Bryant scored three plays later to pull within 16-13, and after a three-and-out, Northcutt fielded a punt, ran left, then cut all the way across the field for a 62-yard return. Brian Russell intercepted a pass at the Browns' 18 on fourth down with 58 seconds left to secure the victory. Charlie Frye was 22 of 37 for 199 yards and 1 touchdown, with 1 interception. Bryant had 9 catches for 123 yards. Kyle Boller was 15 of 36 for 151 yards, with 2 interceptions.

Baltimore	0	13	3	0	—	16
Cleveland	0	6	14	0	—	20

Balt — FG Stover 21
Balt — FG Stover 43
Balt — Thomas 9 fumble return (Stover kick)
Cle — FG Dawson 21
Cle — FG Dawson 39
Balt — FG Stover 31
Cle — Bryant 6 pass from Frye (Dawson kick)
Cle — Northcutt 62 punt return (Dawson kick)

GREEN BAY 23, SEATTLE 17—at Lambeau Field, attendance 69,928. Brett Favre completed the go-ahead touchdown pass as the Packers ended the Seahawks' 11-game winning streak. Shaun Alexander scored on a 1-yard run in the second quarter to set the NFL single-season record with 28 touchdowns, and his 73 rushing yards allowed him to pass Tiki Barber for the NFL rushing title. Seneca Wallace engineered a 71-yard scoring drive to begin the second half, capped by his first NFL touchdown pass, of 5 yards to Joe Jurevicius for a 14-13 lead. Al Harris' interception later in the quarter set up Favre's 9-yard scoring pass to Antonio Chatman on third-and-goal

for a 20-14 lead with 3:41 left in the third quarter. Josh Brown kicked a 44-yard field goal with 1:38 to play, but Nick Collins recovered the ensuing onside kick to secure the victory. Favre was 21 of 37 for 259 yards and 1 touchdown, with 1 interception. Donald Driver had 6 catches for 118 yards. Matt Hasselbeck was 6 of 8 for 76 yards. With Seattle having secured home-field advantage, Wallace was 9 of 17 for 98 yards and 1 touchdown, with 1 interception.

Seattle	0	7	7	3	—	17
Green Bay	6	7	7	3	—	23

GB — FG Longwell 26
GB — FG Longwell 32
Sea — Alexander 1 run (J. Brown kick)
GB — Herron 11 run (Longwell kick)
Sea — Jurevicius 5 pass from Wallace (J. Brown kick)
GB — Chatman 9 pass from Favre (Longwell kick)
GB — FG Longwell 28
Sea — FG J. Brown 44

INDIANAPOLIS 17, ARIZONA 13—at RCA Dome, attendance 57,211. Rob Morris recovered Josh McCown's fumble at the goal line with 13 seconds left as the Colts set a franchise record for victories in a season. Tony Dungy returned to the sidelines after having missed one game following the death of his son. Neil Rackers kicked 2 field goals, giving him an NFL-record 40 for the season, and Anquan Boldin and Larry Fitzgerald became just the third pair of teammates to each have 100 receptions in the same season. The Cardinals committed 2 turnovers in the red zone. The first was an interception by Gilbert Gardner at the Colts' 1 in the second quarter. Leading 10-3, Jim Sorgi, who replaced Peyton Manning in the first quarter since the Colts' top1 seed in the AFC was secure, engineered a 52-yard drive to begin the second half for a 17-3 lead. The Cardinals scored on their next two drives to pull within 17-13 with 10:59 to play, and Arizona forced a punt and drove to the Colts' 2 with 1:18 left. Marcel Shipp gained 1 yard before McCown tried a quarterback sneak on fourth-and-goal. Larry Tripplett forced McCown to fumble and Morris recovered. Manning was 1 of 2 for 5 yards. Sorgi was 20 of 31 for 207 yards and 2 touchdowns, with 1 interception. McCown was 31 of 42 for 297 yards and 1 touchdown, with 1 interception.

Arizona	0	3	7	3	—	13
Indianapolis	7	3	7	0	—	17

Ind — Utecht 14 pass from Sorgi (Vanderjagt kick)
Ariz — FG Rackers 28
Ind — FG Vanderjagt 44
Ind — Walters 18 pass from Sorgi (Vanderjagt kick)
Ariz — Fitzgerald 25 pass from McCown (Rackers kick)
Ariz — FG Rackers 42

JACKSONVILLE 40, TENNESSEE 13—at ALLTEL Stadium, attendance 70,255. With their fifth seed in the AFC locked into place, the Jaguars jumped to a 40-0 lead to finish the season strong. The Jaguars' defense allowed just 6 first downs in the first three quarters and did not allow a play inside their own 35. David Garrard was 10 of 16 for 128 yards, and Quinn Gray was 8 of 14 for 100 yards and 2 touchdowns. LaBrandon Toefield had 25 carries for 102 yards. Matt Mauck, in his first NFL start, was 7 of 14 for 65 yards, with 1 interception, and Billy Volek was 14 of 25 for 114 yards and 2 touchdowns.

Tennessee	0	0	0	13	—	13
Jacksonville	17	10	13	0	—	40

Jax — Pearman 6 run (Scobee kick)
Jax — Toefield 32 run (Scobee kick)
Jax — FG Scobee 46
Jax — FG Scobee 38

Jax — Wimbush 6 run (Scobee kick)
Jax — M. Jones 10 pass from Gray (Scobee kick)
Jax — Wilford 14 pass from Gray (kick failed)
Tenn — Troupe 4 pass from Volek (Bironas kick)
Tenn — Scaife 10 pass from Volek (kick failed)

KANSAS CITY 37, CINCINNATI 3—at Arrowhead Stadium, attendance 77,211. Larry Johnson rushed for 201 yards and 3 touchdowns as the Chiefs won Dick Vermeil's final game. Vermeil had informed his team the previous evening that he would retire, and the Chiefs outgained the Bengals 537-161, but Pittsburgh's victory over Detroit in a game played at the same time eliminated the Chiefs from postseason consideration. Sammy Knight intercepted Jon Kitna's pass late in the first half and Johnson scored two plays later for a 20-3 halftime lead. Johnson's 20-yard run around left end capped the opening drive of the second half for a 27-3 lead with 12:41 left in the third quarter. Trent Green was 23 of 29 for 344 yards and 1 touchdown. Johnson had 26 carries for 201 yards, and Eddie Kennison had 7 catches for 151 yards. Carson Palmer was 5 of 8 for 54 yards. With a playoff berth secure, Kitna replaced him and was 13 of 24 for 76 yards, with 2 interceptions.

Cincinnati	3	0	0	0	—	3
Kansas City	3	17	10	7	—	37

KC — FG Tynes 39
Cin — FG Graham 49
KC — FG Tynes 24
KC — L. Johnson 49 run (Tynes kick)
KC — L. Johnson 14 run (Tynes kick)
KC — L. Johnson 20 run (Tynes kick)
KC — FG Tynes 23
KC — D. Brown 8 pass from Green (Tynes kick)

MINNESOTA 34, CHICAGO 10—at Metrodome, attendance 64,023. Brad Johnson passed for 2 touchdowns as the Vikings scored on four consecutive second-half possessions to pull away. The Bears, with their second seed in the NFC secure, drove 63 yards with their first possession for a field goal, but did not threaten again until the fourth quarter. The Vikings posted touchdown drives of 90, 69, 82, and 80 yards against the Bears, capped by Michael Bennett's 61-yard touchdown run with 5:10 to play. Johnson was 27 of 40 for 247 yards and 2 touchdowns. Kyle Orton was 6 of 14 for 59 yards, and Jeff Blake was 7 of 8 for 44 yards and 1 touchdown.

Chicago	3	0	0	7	—	10
Minnesota	0	17	7	10	—	34

Chi — FG Gould 22
Minn — FG Edinger 54
Minn — Fason 2 run (Edinger kick)
Minn — Taylor 17 pass from B. Johnson (Edinger kick)
Minn — Moore 7 pass from B. Johnson (Edinger kick)
Minn — FG Edinger 27
Chi — Gage 4 pass from Blake (Gould kick)
Minn — Bennett 61 run (Edinger kick)

MIAMI 28, NEW ENGLAND 26—at Gillette Stadium, attendance 68,756. Matt Cassel's 2-point conversion pass fell incomplete with no time on the clock as the Dolphins held on for their sixth consecutive victory. In the fourth quarter, Doug Flutie became the first player since 1941 to dropkick an extra point. Cassel, playing because the Patriots had clinched the division title, completed his first career touchdown pass, a 9-yarder to Tim Dwight with 6:10 to play. Flutie's drop-kicked extra point cut the deficit to 25-20. Following an Olindo Mare field goal, Cassel engineered an 11-play, 62-yard drive capped by Ben Watson's 9-yard touchdown catch as time expired. But his 2-point conversion pass fell incomplete. Gus Frerotte was 22 of 35 for 239 yards and 1 touchdown. Ricky Williams had 28 carries for 108 yards. Tom Brady was 3 of 8 for 37 yards and 1 touchdown, with 1 interception, and Cassel was 11 of 20 for 168 yards and 2 touchdowns.

Miami	7	6	5	10	—	28
New England	7	3	3	13	—	26
Mia	—	R. Williams 2 run (Mare kick)
NE	—	Branch 11 pass from Brady (Vinatieri kick)
Mia	—	FG Mare 36
Mia	—	FG Mare 38
NE	—	FG Vinatieri 49
Mia	—	FG Mare 41
NE	—	FG Vinatieri 33
Mia	—	Safety, R. Howard forced Cassel to fumble out of end zone
Mia	—	Booker 15 pass from Frerotte (Mare kick)
NE	—	Dwight 9 pass from Cassel (Flutie kick)
Mia	—	FG Mare 42
NE	—	Watson 9 pass from Cassel (pass failed)

N.Y. JETS 30, BUFFALO 26—at The Meadowlands, attendance 76,822. The Jets' defense forced 4 turnovers and Justin Miller returned a kickoff 95 yards for the game-deciding touchdown as the Jets snapped a two-game losing streak. The Bills scored on their first two drives of the second half, capped by Roscoe Parrish's 3-yard grab, for a 23-20 lead in the final minute of the third quarter. After an exchange of field goals, Miller returned the ensuing kickoff 95 yards for a touchdown and 30-26 lead with 5:58 to play. The Bills drove to the Jets' 34, but John Abraham sacked Kelly Holcomb on fourth down with 2:46 remaining. The Bills got the ball on their own 20-yard line with 54 seconds left, but Ty Law's third interception of the game clinched the victory. Brooks Bollinger was 11 of 20 for 153 yards. Holcomb was 23 of 37 for 184 yards and 2 touchdowns, with 4 interceptions. Willis McGahee had 22 carries for 113 yards.

Buffalo	3	10	10	3	—	26
N.Y. Jets	3	14	3	10	—	30
Buff	—	FG Lindell 21
NYJ	—	FG Nugent 49
Buff	—	FG Lindell 24
NYJ	—	Houston 3 run (Nugent kick)
NYJ	—	M. Brown 33 interception return (Nugent kick)
Buff	—	Moulds 22 pass from Holcomb (Lindell kick)
Buff	—	FG Lindell 52
NYJ	—	FG Nugent 25
Buff	—	Parrish 3 pass from Holcomb (Lindell kick)
NYJ	—	FG Nugent 34
Buff	—	FG Lindell 36
NYJ	—	J. Miller 95 kickoff return (Nugent kick)

WASHINGTON 31, PHILADELPHIA 20—at Lincoln Financial Field, attendance 67,700. Clinton Portis rushed for 2 touchdowns as the Redskins rallied to secure their first postseason appearance since 1999. Santana Moss' 54-yard catch set up Portis' 2-yard touchdown run to tie the game with 11:46 left in the third quarter. The Eagles led 20-17 and had the ball in the fourth quarter, but Lemar Marshall intercepted Mike McMahon's pass and Portis scored on a 22-yard run on the next play to give the Redskins a 24-20 lead with 12:19 remaining. The Eagles had the ball late, but Phillip Daniels sacked Koy Detmer and forced him to fumble. Sean Taylor returned the ball 39 yards

for the game-clinching touchdown with 2:16 to play. Mark Brunell was 9 of 25 for 141 yards and 1 touchdown, with 1 interception. McMahon was 16 of 31 for 234 yards and 2 touchdowns, with 1 interception. Detmer entered in the fourth quarter and was 5 of 11 for 27 yards, with 1 interception.

Washington	7	3	14	—	31
Philadelphia	10	7	3	0	—	20
Phil	—	FG Akers 49
Wash	—	Sellers 4 pass from Brunell (Hall kick)
Phil	—	R. Brown 33 pass from McMahon (Akers kick)
Phil	—	R. Brown 8 pass from McMahon (Akers kick)
Wash	—	FG Hall 25
Wash	—	Portis 2 run (Hall kick)
Phil	—	FG Akers 35
Wash	—	Portis 22 run (Hall kick)
Wash	—	Taylor 39 fumble return (Hall kick)

PITTSBURGH 35, DETROIT 21—at Heinz Field, attendance 63,794. Jerome Bettis rushed for 3 touchdowns as the Steelers clinched the final AFC postseason berth. Needing a victory to ensure a spot in the playoffs, Antwaan Randle El returned a punt 81 yards for a touchdown just 1:17 into the game. However, the Lions had consecutive scoring drives of 59 and 81 yards to take a 14-7 lead. With the score 14-14, punt returner Eddie Drummond fumbled and Brett Keisel recovered at the Lions' 37. Four plays later, Bettis scored from the 5-yard line for a 21-14 lead just 1:11 before halftime. Bettis' 4-yard scoring run to cap the opening 77-yard drive of the second half, set up by Hines Ward's 40-yard reception, gave the Steelers a 28-14 lead. The Lions responded with a 12-play touchdown drive, but Heath Miller's 43-yard catch led to Ben Roethlisberger's 7-yard touchdown run with 42 seconds left in the third quarter. Roethlisberger was 7 of 16 for 135 yards, with 2 interceptions. Willie Parker had 26 carries for 135 yards. Joey Harrington was 17 of 33 for 212 yards and 3 touchdowns.

Detroit	14	0	7	0	—	21
Pittsburgh	14	7	14	0	—	35
Pitt	—	Randle El 81 punt return (Reed kick)
Det	—	Pollard 11 pass from Harrington (Hanson kick)
Det	—	Schlesinger 1 pass from Harrington (Hanson kick)
Pitt	—	Bettis 1 run (Reed kick)
Pitt	—	Bettis 5 run (Reed kick)
Pitt	—	Bettis 4 run (Reed kick)
Det	—	R. Williams 15 pass from Harrington (Hanson kick)
Pitt	—	Roethlisberger 7 run (Reed kick)

SAN FRANCISCO 20, HOUSTON 17 (OT)—at Monster Park, attendance 67,970. Mike Adams intercepted 2 passes, one returned for a game-tying touchdown and the second set up the game-winning field goal, as the 49ers won their second consecutive game. The defeat saddled the Texans with the first pick in the 2006 NFL Draft. Adams intercepted a pass late in the third quarter and returned it 40 yards to tie the game 17-17. The wind pushed Kris Brown's 31-yard field goal-attempt wide right with 6:07 to play. In overtime, Adams intercepted Tony Banks' pass intended for Bradford. Adams lateraled to Ben Emanuel, who returned the ball 35 yards to the Texans' 21. Joe Nedney made a 33-yard field goal three plays later to cap the comeback. Alex Smith was 16 of 29 for 159 yards and 1 touchdown, with 1 interception. Frank Gore carried 25 times for 108 yards. David Carr was 4 of 11 for 23 yards, before suffering an injury in the second quarter. Banks was 14 of 25 for 173 yards and 1 touchdown, with 2 interceptions.

Houston	10	0	7	0	0	—	17
San Francisco	0	7	10	0	3	—	20
Hou	—	FG K. Brown 21
Hou	—	Morency 3 run (K. Brown kick)
SF	—	Lloyd 14 pass from A. Smith (Nedney kick)
SF	—	FG Nedney 42
Hou	—	Bradford 25 pass from Banks (K. Brown kick)
SF	—	Adams 40 interception return (Nedney kick)
SF	—	FG Nedney 33

TAMPA BAY 27, NEW ORLEANS 13—at Raymond James Stadium, attendance 65,379. Dewayne White sacked Todd Bouman, forced him to fumble, and returned the ball 34 yards for a touchdown with 1:43 left to clinch the NFC South for the Buccaneers. Tampa Bay, who had clinched a playoff berth with the Giants' victory the previous night but needed a victory to clinch the division, scored on its first two drives for a 14-3 lead. The Saints trailed 20-13 but got the ball back on their own 25 with 2:11 to play. Bouman completed a 21-yard pass to Zachary Hilton to reach their own 46, but two plays later White stripped Bouman of the ball and returned it for the game-clinching score. Chris Simms was 12 of 25 for 143 yards and 2 touchdowns. Bouman was 25 of 37 for 265 yards and 1 touchdown, with 2 interceptions.

New Orleans	0	10	0	3	—	13
Tampa Bay	7	10	0	10	—	27
TB	—	Galloway 7 pass from Simms (Bryant kick)
NO	—	FG Carney 25
TB	—	Galloway 4 pass from Simms (Bryant kick)
NO	—	Henderson 24 pass from Bouman (Carney kick)
TB	—	FG Bryant 46
NO	—	FG Carney 24
TB	—	FG Bryant 26
TB	—	White 34 fumble return (Bryant kick)

SUNDAY NIGHT, JANUARY 1, 2006

ST. LOUIS 20, DALLAS 10—at Texas Stadium, attendance 73,656. The Rams' defense forced 4 turnovers, all in the second half, en route to victory. The Cowboys entered the day with playoff hopes, but once the New York Giants, Carolina, and Washington had all won in the previous 24 hours, Dallas was eliminated prior to taking the field. Tied 10-10, Pisa Tinoisamoa sacked Drew Bledsoe and forced him to fumble. Anthony Hargrove recovered at the Cowboys' 40, and Jamie Martin connected on a 29-yard pass to Brandon Manumaleuna to set up Arlen Harris' 1-yard run with 11:57 to play. Oshiomogho Atogwe intercepted Bledsoe later in the fourth quarter and returned the ball 42 yards to the Cowboys' 3 to set up Jeff Wilkins' 20-yard field goal with 1:05 to play. Martin was 19 of 32 for 158 yards. Bledsoe was 18 of 39 for 242 yards and 1 touchdown, with 2 interceptions.

St. Louis	0	10	0	10	—	20
Dallas	7	3	0	0	—	10
Dall	—	Witten 19 pass from Bledsoe (Suisham kick)
StL	—	FG Wilkins 49
StL	—	Cason 8 run (Wilkins kick)
Dall	—	FG Suisham 22
StL	—	Harris 1 run (Wilkins kick)
StL	—	FG Wilkins 20

2005 PRO FOOTBALL AWARDS

ASSOCIATED PRESS
Most Valuable Player	Shaun Alexander
Offensive Player of the Year	Shaun Alexander
Defensive Player of the Year	Brian Urlacher
Offensive Rookie of the Year	Carnell Williams
Defensive Rookie of the Year	Shawne Merriman
Coach of the Year	Lovie Smith
Comeback Player of the Year	Steve Smith/ Tedy Bruschi

THE SPORTING NEWS
Player of the Year	Shaun Alexander
Rookie of the Year	Shawne Merriman
Coach of the Year	Tony Dungy

PRO FOOTBALL WEEKLY/PFWA
Executive of the Year	Bill Polian
Most Valuable Player	Shaun Alexander
Defensive Most Valuable Player	Brian Urlacher
Offensive Rookie of the Year	Carnell Williams
Defensive Rookie of the Year	Shawne Merriman
Coach of the Year	Lovie Smith
Assistant Coach of the Year	Ron Rivera
Golden Toe	Neil Rackers
Comeback Player of the Year	Steve Smith
Most Improved Player of the Year	Osi Umenyiora

SPORTS ILLUSTRATED
Player of the Year	Tiki Barber
Rookie of the Year	Carnell Williams
Coach of the Year	Tony Dungy

MAXWELL CLUB PLAYER OF THE YEAR
(Bert Bell Trophy)	Shaun Alexander

MAXWELL CLUB COACH OF THE YEAR
(Earle "Greasy" Neale Trophy)	Tony Dungy

DIET PEPSI ROOKIE OF THE YEAR
Rookie of the Year	Carnell Williams

FEDEX AIR & GROUND NFL PLAYERS OF THE YEAR
FedEx Express NFL Player of the Year	Carson Palmer
FedEx Ground NFL Player of the Year	Shaun Alexander

WALTER PAYTON/ NFL MAN OF THE YEAR
Man of the Year	Peyton Manning

SUPER BOWL XL MOST VALUABLE PLAYER
Pete Rozelle Trophy	Hines Ward

AFC-NFC 2006 PRO BOWL PLAYER OF THE GAME
Dan McGuire Award	Derrick Brooks

2005 ALL-PRO TEAMS

2005 PFW/PFWA ALL-PRO TEAM
Selected by *Pro Football Weekly* and the Professional Football Writers of America

Offense:
Peyton Manning, Indianapolis	Quarterback
Shaun Alexander, Seattle	Running Back
Tiki Barber, New York Giants	Running Back
Antonio Gates, San Diego	Tight End
Steve Smith, Carolina	Wide Receiver
Chad Johnson, Cincinnati	Wide Receiver
Walter Jones, Seattle	Tackle
Willie Anderson, Cincinnati	Tackle
Steve Hutchinson, Seattle	Guard
Alan Faneca, Pittsburgh	Guard
Olin Kreutz, Chicago	Center

Defense:
Dwight Freeney, Indianapolis	End
Osi Umenyiora, New York Giants	End
Richard Seymour, New England	Tackle
Rod Coleman, Atlanta	Tackle
Lance Briggs, Chicago	Outside Linebacker
Cato June, Indianapolis	Outside Linebacker
Brian Urlacher, Chicago	Middle Linebacker
Champ Bailey, Denver	Cornerback
Nathan Vasher, Chicago	Cornerback
Troy Polamalu, Pittsburgh	Safety
Darren Sharper, Minnesota	Safety

Special Teams:
Neil Rackers, Arizona	Kicker
Brian Moorman, Buffalo	Punter
Jerome Mathis, Houston	Kick Returner
Antwaan Randle El, Pittsburgh	Punt Returner
David Tyree, New York Giants	Special Teams Player

2005 ASSOCIATED PRESS ALL-PRO TEAM
Selected by the *Associated Press*

Offense:
Peyton Manning, Indianapolis	Quarterback
Shaun Alexander, Seattle	Running Back
Tiki Barber, New York Giants	Running Back
Mack Strong, Seattle	Fullback
Antonio Gates, San Diego	Tight End
Steve Smith, Carolina	Wide Receiver
Chad Johnson, Cincinnati	Wide Receiver
Walter Jones, Seattle	Tackle
Willie Anderson, Cincinnati	Tackle
Steve Hutchinson, Seattle	Guard
Alan Faneca, Pittsburgh	Guard
Brian Waters, Kansas City	Guard
Jeff Saturday, Indianapolis	Center

Defense:
Dwight Freeney, Indianapolis	End
Osi Umenyiora, New York Giants	End
Jamal Williams, San Diego	Tackle
Richard Seymour, New England	Tackle
Lance Briggs, Chicago	Outside Linebacker
Derrick Brooks, Tampa Bay	Outside Linebacker
Brian Urlacher, Chicago	Inside Linebacker
Al Wilson, Denver	Inside Linebacker
Ronde Barber, Tampa Bay	Cornerback
Champ Bailey, Denver	Cornerback
Troy Polamalu, Pittsburgh	Safety
Bob Sanders, Indianapolis	Safety

Specialists:
Neil Rackers, Arizona	Kicker
Brian Moorman, Buffalo	Punter
Jerome Mathis, Houston	Kick Returner

2005 ALL-NFL TEAM

Selected by the *Associated Press, Pro Football Weekly,* and the Professional Football Writers of America

Offense:

Peyton Manning, Indianapolis (AP, PFW)	Quarterback
Shaun Alexander, Seattle (AP, PFW)	Running Back
Tiki Barber, New York Giants (AP, PFW)	Running Back
Mack Strong, Seattle (AP)	Fullback
Antonio Gates, San Diego (AP, PFW)	Tight End
Steve Smith, Carolina (AP, PFW)	Wide Receiver
Chad Johnson, Cincinnati (AP, PFW)	Wide Receiver
Walter Jones, Seattle (AP, PFW)	Tackle
Willie Anderson, Cincinnati (AP, PFW)	Tackle
Steve Hutchinson, Seattle (AP, PFW)	Guard
Alan Faneca, Pittsburgh (AP, PFW)	Guard
Brian Waters, Kansas City (AP)	Guard
Olin Kreutz, Chicago (PFW)	Center
Jeff Saturday, Indianapolis (AP)	Center

Defense:

Dwight Freeney, Indianapolis (AP, PFW)	End
Osi Umenyiora, New York Giants (AP, PFW)	End
Richard Seymour, New England (AP, PFW)	Tackle
Rod Coleman, Atlanta (PFW)	Tackle
Jamal Williams, San Diego (AP)	Tackle
Lance Briggs, Chicago (AP, PFW)	Outside Linebacker
Derrick Brooks, Tampa Bay (AP)	Outside Linebacker
Cato June, Indianapolis (PFW)	Outside Linebacker
Brian Urlacher, Chicago (AP, PFW)	Middle/Inside Linebacker
Al Wilson, Denver (AP)	Inside Linebacker
Champ Bailey, Denver (AP, PFW)	Cornerback
Ronde Barber, Tampa Bay (AP)	Cornerback
Nathan Vasher, Chicago (PFW)	Cornerback
Troy Polamalu, Pittsburgh (AP, PFW)	Safety
Bob Sanders, Indianapolis (AP)	Safety
Darren Sharper, Minnesota (PFW)	Safety

Specialists:

Neil Rackers, Arizona (AP, PFW)	Kicker
Brian Moorman, Buffalo (AP, PFW)	Punter
Jerome Mathis, Houston (AP, PFW)	Kick Returner
Antwaan Randle El, Pittsburgh (PFW)	Punt Returner
David Tyree, New York Giants (PFW)	Special Teams Player

2005 PFW/PFWA ALL-ROOKIE TEAM

Selected by *Pro Football Weekly* and the Professional Football Writers of America

Offense:

Kyle Orton, Chicago	Quarterback
Carnell Williams, Tampa Bay	Running Back
Ronnie Brown, Miami	Running Back
Heath Miller, Pittsburgh	Tight End
Mark Clayton, Baltimore	Wide Receiver
Chris Henry, Cincinnati	Wide Receiver
Jammal Brown, New Orleans	Tackle
Khalif Barnes, Jacksonville	Tackle
Logan Mankins, New England	Guard
Dan Buenning, Tampa Bay	Guard
Chris Spencer, Seattle	Center

Defense:

Marcus Spears, Dallas	End
Trent Cole, Philadelphia	End
Luis Castillo, San Diego	Tackle
Mike Patterson, Philadelphia	Tackle
Shawne Merriman, San Diego	Linebacker
Odell Thurman, Cincinnati	Linebacker
Lofa Tatupu, Seattle	Linebacker
Darrent Williams, Denver	Cornerback
Ellis Hobbs, New England	Cornerback
Nick Collins, Green Bay	Safety
Kerry Rhodes, New York Jets	Safety

Special Teams:

Mike Nugent, New York Jets	Kicker
Chris Kluwe, Minnesota	Punter
Jerome Mathis, Houston	Kickoff Returner
Pacman Jones, Tennessee	Punt Returner
Michael Boley, Atlanta	Special Teams Player

2005 AFC PLAYERS OF THE WEEK

	Offense		Defense		Special Teams	
Week 1	RB	Willie Parker, Pittsburgh	LB	Gary Brackett, Indianapolis	K	Josh Scobee, Jacksonville
Week 2	QB	Trent Dilfer, Cleveland	CB	Deltha O'Neal, Cincinnati	P	Hunter Smith, Indianapolis
Week 3	RB	LaDainian Tomlinson, San Diego	S	Lance Schulters, Miami	K	Adam Vinatieri, New England
Week 4	QB	Drew Brees, San Diego	LB	Al Wilson, Denver	K	Sebastian Janikowski, Oakland
Week 5	QB	Tom Brady, New England	DT	Dewayne Robertson, N.Y. Jets	K	Josh Scobee, Jacksonville
Week 6	RB	LaDainian Tomlinson, San Diego	DE	Jared Allen, Kansas City	P	Todd Sauerbrun, Denver
Week 7	RB	LaMont Jordan, Oakland	DE	Robert Mathis, Indianapolis	K	Lawrence Tynes, Kansas City
Week 8	QB	Jake Plummer, Denver	LB	Tedy Bruschi, New England	KR-WR	Jerome Mathis, Houston
Week 9	QB	Peyton Manning, Indianapolis	LB	Brian Simmons, Cincinnati	P	Kyle Richardson, Cleveland
Week 10	WR	Hines Ward, Pittsburgh	LB	Mike Peterson, Jacksonville	P	Brian Moorman, Buffalo
Week 11	RB	Larry Johnson, Kansas City	LB	Andra Davis, Cleveland	K	Matt Stover, Baltimore
Week 12	RB	LaDainian Tomlinson, San Diego	DE	Jason Taylor, Miami	KR-RB	Derrick Wimbush, Jacksonville
Week 13	WR	Chris Chambers, Miami	LB	Terrell Suggs, Baltimore	KR-WR	Tab Perry, Cincinnati
Week 14	RB	Jerome Bettis, Pittsburgh	LB	Zach Thomas, Miami	KR-PR-CB	Pacman Jones, Tennessee
Week 15	WR	Rod Smith, Denver	LB	Shawne Merriman, San Diego	K	Phil Dawson, Cleveland
Week 16	RB	Larry Johnson, Kansas City	LB	Joey Porter, Pittsburgh	KR-CB	Terrence McGee, Buffalo
Week 17	RB	Larry Johnson, Kansas City	S	John Lynch, Denver	QB-K	Doug Flutie, New England

2005 AFC PLAYERS OF THE MONTH

	Offense		Defense		Special Teams	
September	QB	Carson Palmer, Cincinnati	DE	Dwight Freeney, Indianapolis	P	Chris Hanson, Jacksonville
October	RB	Edgerrin James, Indianapolis	DE	Derrick Burgess, Oakland	P	Todd Sauerbrun, Denver
November	RB	Larry Johnson, Kansas City	CB	Champ Bailey, Denver	P	Brian Moorman, Buffalo
December	RB	Larry Johnson, Kansas City	LB	Mike Peterson, Jacksonville	P	Hunter Smith, Indianapolis

2005 NFC PLAYERS OF THE WEEK

	Offense		Defense		Special Teams	
Week 1	QB	Drew Bledsoe, Dallas	DT	Bryant Young, San Francisco	K	John Carney, New Orleans
Week 2	WR	Santana Moss, Washington	LB	Shelton Quarles, Tampa Bay	PR	Bobby Wade, Chicago
Week 3	RB	Shaun Alexander, Seattle	DT	Rod Coleman, Atlanta	P	Josh Bidwell, Tampa Bay
Week 4	WR	Plaxico Burress, N.Y. Giants	DE	Darren Howard, New Orleans	K	Neil Rackers, Arizona
Week 5	QB	Matt Hasselbeck, Seattle	CB	Al Harris, Green Bay	PR	R.W. McQuarters, Detroit
Week 6	RB	Shaun Alexander, Seattle	CB	Anthony Henry, Dallas	P	Josh Bidwell, Tampa Bay
Week 7	QB	Daunte Culpepper, Minnesota	LB	Jeremiah Trotter, Philadelphia	K	Josh Brown, Seattle
Week 8	RB	Tiki Barber, N.Y. Giants	CB	Charles Tillman, Chicago	K	Joe Nedney, San Francisco
Week 9	RB	Shaun Alexander, Seattle	DE	Mike Rucker, Carolina	K	Robbie Gould, Chicago
Week 10	RB	Samkon Gado, Green Bay	S	Darren Sharper, Minnesota	CB	Nathan Vasher, Chicago
Week 11	QB	Kurt Warner, Arizona	CB	Nathan Vasher, Chicago	WR	David Tyree, N.Y. Giants
Week 12	QB	Ryan Fitzpatrick, St. Louis	DE	Alex Brown, Chicago	K	David Akers, Philadelphia
Week 13	RB	DeShaun Foster, Carolina	CB	Andre Dyson, Seattle	P	Jeff Feagles, N.Y. Giants
Week 14	QB	Drew Bledsoe, Dallas	CB	Ronde Barber, Tampa Bay	KR	Antonio Brown, Washington
Week 15	RB	Tiki Barber, N.Y. Giants	DE	Phillip Daniels, Washington	PR	Bernard Berrian, Chicago
Week 16	WR	Santana Moss, Washington	LB	DeMarcus Ware, Dallas	DE	Dewayne White, Tampa Bay
Week 17	RB	Tiki Barber, N.Y. Giants	DE	Simeon Rice, Tampa Bay	TE	Mike Sellers, Washington

2005 NFC PLAYERS OF THE MONTH

	Offense		Defense		Special Teams	
September	QB	Donovan McNabb, Philadelphia	S	Adam Archuleta, St. Louis	P	Chris Kluwe, Minnesota
October	WR	Steve Smith, Carolina	DT	Rod Coleman, Atlanta	K	Neil Rackers, Arizona
November	RB	Shaun Alexander, Seattle	S	Darren Sharper, Minnesota	P	Josh Bidwell, Tampa Bay
December	RB	Tiki Barber, N.Y. Giants	LB	Marcus Washington, Washington	K	Neil Rackers, Arizona

2005 NFL ROOKIES OF THE MONTH

	Offense (College)		Defense (College)	
September	RB	Carnell Williams, Tampa Bay (Auburn)	LB	Odell Thurman, Cincinnati (Georgia)
October	TE	Heath Miller, Pittsburgh (Virginia)	LB	DeMarcus Ware, Dallas (Troy)
November	RB	Samkon Gado, Green Bay (Liberty)	DE	Trent Cole, Philadelphia (Cincinnati)
December	RB	Carnell Williams, Tampa Bay (Auburn)	LB	Lofa Tatupu, Seattle (Southern California)

TEN BEST RUSHING PERFORMANCES, 2005

		Att.	Yards	TD
1.	Tiki Barber	29	220	2
	New York Giants vs. Kansas City, Dec. 17			
2.	Larry Johnson	36	211	2
	Kansas City vs. Houston, Nov. 20			
3.	Tiki Barber	24	206	1
	New York Giants vs. Washington, Oct. 30			
4.	Tiki Barber	28	203	1
	New York Giants vs. Oakland, Dec. 31			
5.	Larry Johnson	26	201	3
	Kansas City vs. Cincinnati, Jan. 1			
6.	Julius Jones	34	194	2
	Dallas vs. Carolina, Dec. 24			
7.	LaDainian Tomlinson	21	192	3
	San Diego vs. New York Giants, Sept. 25			
8.	LaDainian Tomlinson	25	184	3
	San Diego vs. Washington, Nov. 27			
9.	Steven Jackson	25	179	0
	St. Louis vs. Jacksonville, Oct. 30			
10.	Shaun Alexander	23	173	2
	Seattle vs. Arizona, Nov. 6			

100-YARD RUSHING PERFORMANCES, 2005

First Week

Willie Parker, Pittsburgh	161 yards vs. Tennessee
Carnell Williams, Tampa Bay	148 yards vs. Minnesota
Rudi Johnson, Cincinnati	126 yards vs. Cleveland
Clinton Portis, Washington	121 yards vs. Chicago
Warrick Dunn, Atlanta	117 yards vs. Philadelphia
Willis McGahee, Buffalo	117 yards vs. Houston
Larry Johnson, Kansas City	110 yards vs. New York Jets

Second Week

Shaun Alexander, Seattle	144 yards vs. Atlanta
Thomas Jones, Chicago	139 yards vs. Detroit
Edgerrin James, Indianapolis	128 yards vs. Jacksonville
Carnell Williams, Tampa Bay	128 yards vs. Buffalo
Willie Parker, Pittsburgh	111 yards vs. Houston

Third Week

LaDainian Tomlinson, San Diego	192 yards vs. New York Giants
Carnell Williams, Tampa Bay	158 yards vs. Green Bay
Shaun Alexander, Seattle	140 yards vs. Arizona
Willis McGahee, Buffalo	140 yards vs. Atlanta
Ronnie Brown, Miami	132 yards vs. Carolina
Edgerrin James, Indianapolis	108 yards vs. Cleveland
Thomas Jones, Chicago	106 yards vs. Cincinnati
Mewelde Moore, Minnesota	101 yards vs. New Orleans

Fourth Week

LaDainian Tomlinson, San Diego	134 yards vs. New England
Deuce McAllister, New Orleans	130 yards vs. Buffalo
Tiki Barber, New York Giants	128 yards vs. St. Louis
Warrick Dunn, Atlanta	126 yards vs. Minnesota
LaMont Jordan, Oakland	126 yards vs. Dallas
Mike Anderson, Denver	115 yards vs. Jacksonville

Fifth Week

Thomas Jones, Chicago	137 yards vs. Cleveland
Fred Taylor, Jacksonville	132 yards vs. Cincinnati
Domanick Davis, Houston	130 yards vs. Tennessee
Tatum Bell, Denver	127 yards vs. Washington
Shaun Alexander, Seattle	119 yards vs. St. Louis
Corey Dillon, New England	106 yards vs. Atlanta
Edgerrin James, Indianapolis	105 yards vs. San Francisco
Clinton Portis, Washington	103 yards vs. Denver

Sixth Week

Curtis Martin, New York Jets	148 yards vs. Buffalo
Edgerrin James, Indianapolis	143 yards vs. St. Louis
Willis McGahee, Buffalo	143 yards vs. New York Jets
Shaun Alexander, Seattle	141 yards vs. Houston
LaDainian Tomlinson, San Diego	140 yards vs. Oakland

Michael Pittman, Tampa Bay	127 yards vs. Miami
Tatum Bell, Denver	114 yards vs. New England
Maurice Morris, Seattle	104 yards vs. Houston
Warrick Dunn, Atlanta	100 yards vs. New Orleans

Seventh Week

Warrick Dunn, Atlanta	155 yards vs. New York Jets
Edgerrin James, Indianapolis	139 yards vs. Houston
Thomas Jones, Chicago	139 yards vs. Baltimore
Willie Parker, Pittsburgh	131 yards vs. Cincinnati
LaMont Jordan, Oakland	122 yards vs. Buffalo
Mike Anderson, Denver	120 yards vs. New York Giants
Clinton Portis, Washington	101 yards vs. San Francisco
Reuben Droughns, Cleveland	100 yards vs. Detroit

Eighth Week

Tiki Barber, New York Giants	206 yards vs. Washington
Steven Jackson, St. Louis	179 yards vs. Jacksonville
Fred Taylor, Jacksonville	165 yards vs. St. Louis
Willis McGahee, Buffalo	136 yards vs. New England
Marion Barber, Dallas	127 yards vs. Arizona
Mike Anderson, Denver	126 yards vs. Philadelphia
Tatum Bell, Denver	107 yards vs. Philadelphia
Ronnie Brown, Miami	106 yards vs. New Orleans
Kevan Barlow, San Francisco	101 yards vs. Tampa Bay

Ninth Week

Shaun Alexander, Seattle	173 yards vs. Arizona
Reuben Droughns, Cleveland	116 yards vs. Tennessee
Antowain Smith, New Orleans	110 yards vs. Chicago
Larry Johnson, Kansas City	107 yards vs. Oakland
LaDainian Tomlinson, San Diego	107 yards vs. New York Jets
Michael Bennett, Minnesota	106 yards vs. Detroit
Edgerrin James, Indianapolis	104 yards vs. New England

Tenth Week

Shaun Alexander, Seattle	165 yards vs. St. Louis
Clinton Portis, Washington	144 yards vs. Tampa Bay
Larry Johnson, Kansas City	132 yards vs. Buffalo
Edgerrin James, Indianapolis	122 yards vs. Houston
Adrian Peterson, Chicago	120 yards vs. San Francisco
Greg Jones, Jacksonville	106 yards vs. Baltimore
Samkon Gado, Green Bay	103 yards vs. Atlanta

Eleventh Week

Larry Johnson, Kansas City	211 yards vs. Houston
Reuben Droughns, Cleveland	166 yards vs. Miami
Mewelde Moore, Minnesota	122 yards vs. Green Bay
Carnell Williams, Tampa Bay	116 yards vs. Atlanta
Shaun Alexander, Seattle	115 yards vs. San Francisco
Mike Anderson, Denver	113 yards vs. New York Jets
Tiki Barber, New York Giants	112 yards vs. Philadelphia

Twelfth Week

LaDainian Tomlinson, San Diego	184 yards vs. Washington
Tiki Barber, New York Giants	151 yards vs. Seattle
Edgerrin James, Indianapolis	124 yards vs. Pittsburgh
Brian Westbrook, Philadelphia	120 yards vs. Green Bay
Larry Johnson, Kansas City	119 yards vs. New England
Warrick Dunn, Atlanta	116 yards vs. Detroit
Rudi Johnson, Cincinnati	114 yards vs. Baltimore
Jamal Lewis, Baltimore	113 yards vs. Cincinnati
Samkon Gado, Green Bay	111 yards vs. Philadelphia
Shaun Alexander, Seattle	110 yards vs. New York Giants
Steven Jackson, St. Louis	110 yards vs. Houston

Thirteenth Week

Domanick Davis, Houston	155 yards vs. Baltimore
Larry Johnson, Kansas City	140 yards vs. Denver
Clinton Portis, Washington	136 yards vs. St. Louis
DeShaun Foster, Carolina	131 yards vs. Atlanta
Rock Cartwright, Washington	118 yards vs. St. Louis
Tiki Barber, New York Giants	115 yards vs. Dallas
Edgerrin James, Indianapolis	107 yards vs. Tennessee
Greg Jones, Jacksonville	103 yards vs. Cleveland

Fourteenth Week

Samkon Gado, Green Bay	171 yards vs. Detroit

Rudi Johnson, Cincinnati	169 yards vs. Cleveland
Larry Johnson, Kansas City	143 yards vs. Dallas
Domanick Davis, Houston	139 yards vs. Tennessee
Tiki Barber, New York Giants	124 yards vs. Philadelphia
Ryan Moats, Philadelphia	114 yards vs. New York Giants
Carnell Williams, Tampa Bay	112 yards vs. Carolina
Shaun Alexander, Seattle	108 yards vs. San Francisco
Clinton Portis, Washington	105 yards vs. Arizona
Corey Dillon, New England	102 yards vs. Buffalo
Jerome Bettis, Pittsburgh	101 yards vs. Chicago

Fifteenth Week

Tiki Barber, New York Giants	220 yards vs. Kansas City
Shaun Alexander, Seattle	172 yards vs. Tennessee
Larry Johnson, Kansas City	167 yards vs. New York Giants
LaMont Jordan, Oakland	132 yards vs. Cleveland
Rudi Johnson, Cincinnati	117 yards vs. Detroit
Michael Turner, San Diego	113 yards vs. Indianapolis
Clinton Portis, Washington	112 yards vs. Dallas
Jamal Lewis, Baltimore	105 yards vs. Green Bay

Sixteenth Week

Julius Jones, Dallas	194 yards vs. Carolina
Ricky Williams, Miami	172 yards vs. Tennessee
Carnell Williams, Tampa Bay	150 yards vs. Atlanta
Shaun Alexander, Seattle	139 yards vs. Indianapolis
Larry Johnson, Kansas City	131 yards vs. San Diego
Willie Parker, Pittsburgh	130 yards vs. Cleveland
Maurice Hicks, San Francisco	109 yards vs. St. Louis
Clinton Portis, Washington	108 yards vs. New York Giants
Thomas Jones, Chicago	105 yards vs. Green Bay
Fred Taylor, Jacksonville	101 yards vs. Houston

Seventeenth Week

Tiki Barber, New York Giants	203 yards vs. Oakland
Larry Johnson, Kansas City	201 yards vs. Cincinnati
DeShaun Foster, Carolina	165 yards vs. Atlanta
Willie Parker, Pittsburgh	135 yards vs. Detroit
Willis McGahee, Buffalo	113 yards vs. New York Jets
Clinton Portis, Washington	112 yards vs. Philadelphia
Frank Gore, San Francisco	108 yards vs. Houston
Ricky Williams, Miami	108 yards vs. New England
LaBrandon Toefield, Jacksonville	102 yards vs. Tennessee

Times 100 or More (138)
Alexander, 11; L. Johnson, 10; James, Portis, 9;
T. Barber, 8; C. Williams, 6; Dunn, T. Jones, McGahee,
Parker, Tomlinson, 5; M. Anderson, R. Johnson, 4; Bell,
Davis, Droughns, Gado, Jordan, Taylor, 3; Brown, Dillon,
Foster, Jackson, G. Jones, Lewis, Moore, R. Williams, 2.

TEN BEST PASSING PERFORMANCES, 2005

	Att.	Comp.	Yards	TD
1. Marc Bulger	62	40	442	2
St. Louis vs. New York Giants, Oct. 2				
2. Josh McCown	46	29	398	2
Arizona vs. Carolina, Oct. 9				
3. Ben Roethlisberger	41	29	386	3
Pittsburgh vs. Cincinnati, Dec. 4				
4. Josh McCown	46	32	385	2
Arizona vs. San Francisco, Oct. 2				
5. Aaron Brooks	45	27	375	1
New Orleans vs. New York Giants, Sept. 19				
6. Tom Brady	41	31	372	0
New England vs. Pittsburgh, Sept. 25				
7. Donovan McNabb	48	33	369	3
Philadelphia vs. Kansas City, Oct. 2				
8. Peyton Manning	40	24	365	3
Indianapolis vs. Cincinnati, Nov. 20				
Donovan McNabb	52	30	365	2
Philadelphia vs. Oakland, Sept. 25				
10. Drew Bledsoe	38	24	363	2
Dallas vs. Arizona, Sept. 25				

300-YARD PASSING PERFORMANCES, 2005

First Week

Marc Bulger, St. Louis	362 yards vs. San Francisco
Tom Brady, New England	306 yards vs. Oakland

Second Week

Aaron Brooks, New Orleans	375 yards vs. New York Giants
Brett Favre, Green Bay	342 yards vs. Cleveland
Donovan McNabb, Philadelphia	342 yards vs. San Francisco
Carson Palmer, Cincinnati	337 yards vs. Minnesota
Trent Dilfer, Cleveland	336 yards vs. Green Bay
Kurt Warner, Arizona	327 yards vs. St. Louis

Third Week

Tom Brady, New England	375 yards vs. Pittsburgh
Donovan McNabb, Philadelphia	365 yards vs. Oakland
Drew Bledsoe, Dallas	363 yards vs. Arizona
Eli Manning, New York Giants	352 yards vs. San Diego
Kerry Collins, Oakland	345 yards vs. Philadelphia
Daunte Culpepper, Minnesota	300 yards vs. New Orleans

Fourth Week

Marc Bulger, St. Louis	442 yards vs. New York Giants
Josh McCown, Arizona	385 yards vs. San Francisco
Donovan McNabb, Philadelphia	369 yards vs. Kansas City
Brett Favre, Green Bay	303 yards vs. Carolina
Brian Griese, Tampa Bay	302 yards vs. Detroit

Fifth Week

Josh McCown, Arizona	398 yards vs. Carolina
Tom Brady, New England	350 yards vs. Atlanta
Marc Bulger, St. Louis	336 yards vs. Seattle
Mark Brunell, Washington	322 yards vs. Denver
Matt Hasselbeck, Seattle	316 yards vs. St. Louis

Sixth Week

Mark Brunell, Washington	331 yards vs. Kansas City
Drew Bledsoe, Dallas	312 yards vs. New York Giants

Seventh Week

Brett Favre, Green Bay	315 yards vs. Minnesota

Eighth Week

Trent Green, Kansas City	347 yards vs. San Diego
Jake Delhomme, Carolina	341 yards vs. Minnesota
Drew Brees, San Diego	324 yards vs. Kansas City
Jake Plummer, Denver	309 yards vs. Philadelphia

Ninth Week

Kurt Warner, Arizona	334 yards vs. Seattle
Peyton Manning, Indianapolis	321 yards vs. New England
Donovan McNabb, Philadelphia	304 yards vs. Washington

Tenth Week

Gus Frerotte, Miami	360 yards vs. New England

Kurt Warner, Arizona — 359 yards vs. Detroit
Kerry Collins, Oakland — 310 yards vs. Denver
Marc Bulger, St. Louis — 304 yards vs. Seattle

Eleventh Week
Peyton Manning, Indianapolis — 365 yards vs. Cincinnati
Aaron Brooks, New Orleans — 343 yards vs. New England
Drew Brees, San Diego — 339 yards vs. Buffalo
Carson Palmer, Cincinnati — 335 yards vs. Indianapolis
Michael Vick, Atlanta — 306 yards vs. Tampa Bay

Twelfth Week
Eli Manning, New York Giants — 344 yards vs. Seattle
Steve McNair, Tennessee — 343 yards vs. San Francisco
Trent Green, Kansas City — 323 yards vs. New England
Kurt Warner, Arizona — 315 yards vs. Jacksonville
Ryan Fitzpatrick, St. Louis — 310 yards vs. Houston
Carson Palmer, Cincinnati — 302 yards vs. Baltimore

Thirteenth Week
Ben Roethlisberger, Pittsburgh — 386 yards vs. Cincinnati
Kurt Warner, Arizona — 354 yards vs. San Francisco

Fourteenth Week
Trent Green, Kansas City — 340 yards vs. Dallas
Drew Bledsoe, Dallas — 332 yards vs. Kansas City
Tom Brady, New England — 329 yards vs. Buffalo
Peyton Manning, Indianapolis — 324 yards vs. Jacksonville
Eli Manning, New York Giants — 312 yards vs. Philadelphia

Fifteenth Week
Peyton Manning, Indianapolis — 336 yards vs. San Diego
Brooks Bollinger, New York Jets — 327 yards vs. Miami
Steve McNair, Tennessee — 310 yards vs. Seattle

Sixteenth Week
Jamie Martin, St. Louis — 354 yards vs. San Francisco
Brett Favre, Green Bay — 317 yards vs. Chicago
Kelly Holcomb, Buffalo — 308 yards vs. Cincinnati

Seventeenth Week
Trent Green, Kansas City — 344 yards vs. Cincinnati
Kerry Collins, Oakland — 331 yards vs. New York Giants
Jake Delhomme, Carolina — 307 yards vs. New Orleans

Times 300 or more (64)
Warner, 5; Brady, Bulger, Favre, Green, P. Manning,
McNabb, 4; Bledsoe, Collins, E. Manning, Palmer 3;
Brees, Brooks, Brunell, McCown, McNair, 2.

TEN BEST RECEIVING PERFORMANCES, 2005

	No.	Yards	TD
1. Chris Chambers	15	238	1
Miami vs. Buffalo, Dec. 4			
2. Plaxico Burress	10	204	2
New York Giants vs. St. Louis, Oct. 2			
3. Steve Smith	11	201	1
Carolina vs. Minnesota, Oct. 30			
4. Chad Johnson	8	189	1
Cincinnati vs. Indianapolis, Nov. 20			
5. Santana Moss	10	173	2
Washington vs. Kansas City, Oct. 16			
6. Terrell Owens	11	171	1
Philadelphia vs. Kansas City, Oct. 2			
7. Steve Smith	11	170	3
Carolina vs. Miami, Sept. 25			
8. Steve Smith	14	169	0
Carolina vs. Chicago, Nov. 20			
9. Joey Galloway	7	166	1
Tampa Bay vs. Detroit, Oct. 2			
10. Torry Holt	9	163	1
St. Louis vs. Tennessee, Sept. 25			
Torry Holt	10	163	1
St. Louis vs. San Francisco, Dec. 24			

100-YARD RECEIVING PERFORMANCES, 2005

First Week
Larry Fitzgerald, Arizona — 155 yards vs. New York Giants
Steve Smith, Carolina — 138 yards vs. New Orleans
Randy Moss, Oakland — 130 yards vs. New England
Jimmy Smith, Jacksonville — 130 yards vs. Seattle
Frisman Jackson, Cleveland — 128 yards vs. Cincinnati
Torry Holt, St. Louis — 125 yards vs. San Francisco
Chris Baker, New York Jets — 124 yards vs. Kansas City
Keenan McCardell, San Diego — 123 yards vs. Dallas
Terrell Owens, Philadelphia — 112 yards vs. Atlanta
Marty Booker, Miami — 104 yards vs. Denver

Second Week
Santana Moss, Washington — 159 yards vs. Dallas
Terry Glenn, Dallas — 157 yards vs. Washington
Joe Horn, New Orleans — 143 yards vs. New York Giants
Terrell Owens, Philadelphia — 143 yards vs. San Francisco
Donte' Stallworth, New Orleans — 141 yards vs. New York Giants
Randy Moss, Oakland — 127 yards vs. Kansas City
Chad Johnson, Cincinnati — 139 yards vs. Minnesota
Darrell Jackson, Seattle — 131 yards vs. Atlanta
Anquan Boldin, Arizona — 119 yards vs. St. Louis
L.J. Smith, Philadelphia — 119 yards vs. San Francisco
Braylon Edwards, Cleveland — 107 yards vs. Green Bay
Donald Driver, Green Bay — 105 yards vs. Cleveland
Steve Heiden, Cleveland — 104 yards vs. Green Bay

Third Week
Steve Smith, Carolina — 170 yards vs. Miami
Torry Holt, St. Louis — 163 yards vs. Tennessee
Brandon Lloyd, San Francisco — 142 yards vs. Dallas
Brian Westbrook, Philadelphia — 140 yards vs. Oakland
Terry Glenn, Dallas — 137 yards vs. San Francisco
David Givens, New England — 130 yards vs. Pittsburgh
Darrell Jackson, Seattle — 125 yards vs. Arizona
Eddie Kennison, Kansas City — 112 yards vs. Denver
Hines Ward, Pittsburgh — 110 yards vs. New England
Jeremy Shockey, New York Giants — 101 yards vs. San Diego
Courtney Anderson, Oakland — 100 yards vs. Philadelphia

Fourth Week
Plaxico Burress, New York Giants — 203 yards vs. St. Louis
Terrell Owens, Philadelphia — 171 yards vs. Kansas City
Joey Galloway, Tampa Bay — 166 yards vs. Detroit
Donte' Stallworth, New Orleans — 129 yards vs. Buffalo
Randy Moss, Oakland — 123 yards vs. Dallas
Shaun McDonald, St. Louis — 121 yards vs. New York Giants
Anquan Boldin, Arizona — 116 yards vs. San Francisco
Marvin Harrison, Indianapolis — 109 yards vs. Tennessee
Eddie Kennison, Kansas City — 109 yards vs. Philadelphia
Jimmy Smith, Jacksonville — 109 yards vs. Denver
Antonio Gates, San Diego — 108 yards vs. New England
Bobby Engram, Seattle — 106 yards vs. Washington
T.J. Houshmandzadeh, Cincinnati — 105 yards vs. Houston
Larry Fitzgerald, Arizona — 102 yards vs. San Francisco
Brandon Lloyd, San Francisco — 102 yards vs. Arizona

Fifth Week
Anquan Boldin, Arizona — 162 yards vs. Carolina
Joe Jurevicius, Seattle — 137 yards vs. St. Louis
Larry Fitzgerald, Arizona — 136 yards vs. Carolina
Torry Holt, St. Louis — 126 yards vs. Seattle
Daniel Graham, New England — 119 yards vs. Atlanta
Steve Smith, Carolina — 119 yards vs. Arizona
Terry Glenn, Dallas — 118 yards vs. Philadelphia
Santana Moss, Washington — 116 yards vs. Denver
Az-Zahir Hakim, New Orleans — 108 yards vs. Green Bay
Deion Branch, New England — 107 yards vs. Atlanta
Brian Finneran, Atlanta — 103 yards vs. New England

Sixth Week
Santana Moss, Washington — 173 yards vs. Kansas City
Chad Johnson, Cincinnati — 135 yards vs. Tennessee

Jeremy Shockey, New York Giants	129 yards vs. Dallas	Lee Evans, Buffalo	117 yards vs. Miami
Rod Smith, Denver	123 yards vs. New England	Eddie Kennison, Kansas City	108 yards vs. Denver
Steve Smith, Carolina	123 yards vs. Detroit		

Fourteenth Week

Keyshawn Johnson, Dallas	120 yards vs. New York Giants	Terry Glenn, Dallas	138 yards vs. Kansas City
Justin McCareins, New York Jets	116 yards vs. Buffalo	Marvin Harrison, Indianapolis	137 yards vs. Jacksonville
Marcus Pollard, Detroit	105 yards vs. Carolina	Antonio Gates, San Diego	123 yards vs. Miami
Priest Holmes, Kansas City	100 yards vs. Washington	Chris Chambers, Miami	121 yards vs. San Diego

Seventh Week / Anquan Boldin, Arizona 114 yards vs. Washington

Donald Driver, Green Bay	114 yards vs. Minnesota	Jeremy Shockey, New York Giants	107 yards vs. Philadelphia
Santana Moss, Washington	112 yards vs. San Francisco	Mark Clayton, Baltimore	105 yards vs. Denver
Doug Garbriel, Oakland	101 yards vs. Buffalo	Steve Smith, Carolina	103 yards vs. Tampa Bay
Az-Zahir Hakim, New Orleans	100 yards vs. St. Louis	Jimmy Smith, Jacksonville	102 yards vs. Indianapolis

Eighth Week / **Fifteenth Week**

Steve Smith, Carolina	201 yards vs. Minnesota	David Givens, New England	137 yards vs. Tampa Bay
Terrell Owens, Philadelphia	154 yards vs. Denver	Rod Smith, Denver	137 yards vs. Buffalo
Joey Galloway, Tampa Bay	149 yards vs. San Francisco	Marvin Harrison, Indianapolis	135 yards vs. San Diego
Antonio Gates, San Diego	145 yards vs. Kansas City	Anquan Boldin, Arizona	134 yards vs. Houston
Ernest Wilford, Jacksonville	145 yards vs. St. Louis	Ben Troupe, Tennessee	116 yards vs. Seattle
Eric Moulds, Buffalo	125 yards vs. New England	Todd Heap, Baltimore	110 yards vs. Green Bay
Jerry Porter, Oakland	123 yards vs. Tennessee	Eric Moulds, Buffalo	110 yards vs. Denver
Eddie Kennison, Kansas City	115 yards vs. San Diego	Doug Jolley, New York Jets	102 yards vs. Miami
Kevin Curtis, St. Louis	105 yards vs. Jacksonville	Donte' Stallworth, New Orleans	102 yards vs. Carolina

Ninth Week / **Sixteenth Week**

Antonio Gates, San Diego	132 yards vs. New York Jets	Torry Holt, St. Louis	163 yards vs. San Francisco
Marvin Harrison, Indianapolis	128 yards vs. New England	Santana Moss, Washington	160 yards vs. New York Giants
Reggie Wayne, Indianapolis	124 yards vs. New England	Brandon Stokley, Indianapolis	122 yards vs. Seattle
Scottie Vines, Detroit	109 yards vs. Minnesota	Andre Johnson, Houston	119 yards vs. Jacksonville
Steve Smith, Carolina	106 yards vs. Tampa Bay	Ernest Wilford, Jacksonville	118 yards vs. Houston
Larry Fitzgerald, Arizona	102 yards vs. Seattle	Chad Johnson, Cincinnati	117 yards vs. Buffalo

Tenth Week / Roy Williams, Detroit 111 yards vs. New Orleans

Larry Fitzgerald, Arizona	141 yards vs. Detroit	Ashley Lelie, Denver	110 yards vs. Oakland
Joey Galloway, Tampa Bay	131 yards vs. Washington	Donald Driver, Green Bay	107 yards vs. Chicago
Hines Ward, Pittsburgh	124 yards vs. Cleveland	Lee Evans, Buffalo	107 yards vs. Cincinnati
Matt Jones, Jacksonville	117 yards vs. Baltimore	Hines Ward, Pittsburgh	105 yards vs. Cleveland
Roy Williams, Detroit	117 yards vs. Arizona	Ricky Proehl, Carolina	104 yards vs. Dallas
Donald Driver, Green Bay	114 yards vs. Atlanta	Derrick Mason, Baltimore	103 yards vs. Minnesota
Tiki Barber, New York Giants	111 yards vs. Minnesota	Corey Bradford, Houston	101 yards vs. Jacksonville
Marvin Harrison, Indianapolis	108 yards vs. Houston		

Marty Booker, Miami 102 yards vs. New England / **Seventeenth Week**

		Eddie Kennison, Kansas City	151 yards vs. Cincinnati
		Steve Smith, Carolina	131 yards vs. Atlanta

Eleventh Week

Chad Johnson, Cincinnati	189 yards vs. Indianapolis	Plaxico Burress, New York Giants	128 yards vs. Oakland
Steve Smith, Carolina	169 yards vs. Chicago	Antonio Bryant, Cleveland	123 yards vs. Baltimore
Jerry Porter, Oakland	142 yards vs. Washington	Donald Driver, Green Bay	118 yards vs. Seattle
Torry Holt, St. Louis	129 yards vs. Arizona	Randy Moss, Oakland	116 yards vs. New York Giants
Dallas Clark, Indianapolis	125 yards vs. Cincinnati	Doug Gabriel, Oakland	100 yards vs. New York Giants
Brandon Lloyd, San Francisco	119 yards vs. Seattle		
Reggie Wayne, Indianapolis	117 yards vs. Cincinnati		
Plaxico Burress, New York Giants	113 yards vs. Philadelphia		
Roddy White, Atlanta	108 yards vs. Tampa Bay		
Anquan Boldin, Arizona	105 yards vs. St. Louis		
Larry Fitzgerald, Arizona	104 yards vs. St. Louis		

Times 100 or more (166)

S. Smith, 9; Boldin, 8; Fitzgerald, 7; Harrison, Holt, 6; Driver, Kennison, S. Moss, 5; Burress, Galloway, Gates, Glenn, C. Johnson, R. Moss, Owens, Shockey, Ward, 4; Chambers, Lloyd, J. Smith, Stallworth, 3; Booker, Evans, Gabriel, Givens, Hakim, Houshmandzadeh, D. Jackson, A. Johnson, Jurevicius, Moulds, Porter, R. Smith, Wayne, Wilford, R. Williams, 2.

Twelfth Week

Andre Johnson, Houston	159 yards vs. St. Louis
T.J. Houshmandzadeh, Cincinnati	147 yards vs. Baltimore
Joey Galloway, Tampa Bay	138 yards vs. Chicago
Joe Jurevicius, Seattle	137 yards vs. New York Giants
Torry Holt, St. Louis	130 yards vs. Houston
Marvin Harrison, Indianapolis	128 yards vs. Pittsburgh
Jeremy Shockey, New York Giatns	127 yards vs. Seattle
Anquan Boldin, Arizona	115 yards vs. Jacksonville
Plaxico Burress, New York Giants	109 yards vs. Seattle
Chris Brown, Tennessee	105 yards vs. San Francisco
Alge Crumpler, Atlanta	104 yards vs. Detroit
Chris Chambers, Miami	101 yards vs. Oakland

Thirteenth Week

Chris Chambers, Miami	238 yards vs. Buffalo
Anquan Boldin, Arizona	156 yards vs. San Francisco
Koren Robinson, Minnesota	148 yards vs. Detroit
Hines Ward, Pittsburgh	135 yards vs. Cincinnati
Larry Fitzgerald, Arizona	129 yards vs. San Francisco

TOP QUARTERBACK SACK PERFORMANCES, 2005
(3.0 or More Sacks Per Game Needed to Qualify)

First Week
Bryant Young, San Francisco .... 3.0 vs. St. Louis
Second Week
Troy Polamalu, Pittsburgh .... 3.0 vs. Houston
Montae Reagor, Indianapolis .... 3.0 vs. Jacksonville
Kyle Vanden Bosch, Tennessee .... 3.0 vs. Baltimore
Third Week
Dwight Freeney, Indianapolis .... 3.0 vs. Cleveland
Paul Spicer, Jacksonville .... 3.0 vs. New York Jets
Fourth Week
None
Fifth Week
None
Sixth Week
Jared Allen, Kansas City .... 3.0 vs. Washington
Seventh Week
None
Eighth Week
Warren Sapp, Oakland .... 3.0 vs. Tennessee
Ninth Week
Tommy Kelly, Oakland .... 3.0 vs. Kansas City
Julius Peppers, Carolina .... 3.0 vs. Tampa Bay
Tenth Week
None
Eleventh Week
Aaron Kampman, Green Bay .... 3.0 vs. Minnesota
Adewale Ogunleye, Chicago .... 3.0 vs. Carolina
Adrian Wilson, Arizona .... 3.0 vs. St. Louis
Twelfth Week
Jason Taylor, Miami .... 3.0 vs. Oakland
Thirteenth Week
Shantee Orr, Houston .... 3.0 vs. Baltimore
Terrell Suggs, Baltimore .... 3.0 vs. Houston
Fourteenth Week
None
Fifteenth Week
Phillip Daniels, Washington .... 4.0 vs. Dallas
Jason Taylor, Miami .... 3.0 vs. New York Jets
Sixteenth Week
Julius Peppers, Carolina .... 3.0 vs. Dallas
Joey Porter, Pittsburgh .... 3.0 vs. Cleveland
DeMarcus Ware, Dallas .... 3.0 vs. Carolina
Seventeenth Week
None

2006 PLAYER RANKINGS AND PROJECTIONS

The *NFL.com 2006 Fantasy Football Preview*, available at newsstands now, contains 160 pages of fantasy football facts, tips, and projections for the upcoming season. The following eight pages display the projections for the running backs, wide receivers, quarterbacks, tight ends, and kickers for the 2006 season, as devised by the magazine's experts. Page 297 provides the statistical average for each team's defense over the past three seasons, allowing you a comprehensive look at which team defense can consistently help lead your fantasy team to the title. Pick up a copy of the *NFL.com 2006 Fantasy Football Preview* today.

RUNNING BACKS	Rushing Yards	Rushing Touchdowns	Receiving	Receiving Yards	Receiving Touchdowns	Total Touchdowns
1. LaDainian Tomlinson, San Diego	1300	15	45	425	1	16
2. Larry Johnson, Kansas City	1600	13	35	300	1	14
3. Shaun Alexander, Seattle.	1525	15	25	150	2	17
4. Ronnie Brown, Miami	1400	12	30	300	1	13
5. Tiki Barber, N.Y. Giants	1350	8	45	400	2	10
6. Steven Jackson, St. Louis	1300	12	30	250	1	13
7. Rudi Johnson, Cincinnati	1375	13	25	100	0	13
8. Clinton Portis, Washington	1450	9	30	250	1	10
9. Willis McGahee, Buffalo	1450	10	25	125	1	11
10. LaMont Jordan, Oakland	1175	11	50	350	0	11
11. Edgerrin James, Arizona	1100	6	35	425	3	9
12. DeShaun Foster, Carolina	1200	10	30	225	1	11
13. Julius Jones, Dallas	1100	8	32	250	1	9
14. Carnell Williams, Tampa Bay	1250	9	25	125	0	9
15. Kevin Jones, Detroit	1200	9	25	150	1	10
16. Brian Westbrook, Philadelphia	925	6	55	525	4	10
17. Reuben Droughns, Cleveland	1175	6	35	375	1	7
18. Jamal Lewis, Baltimore	1150	7	30	250	1	8
19. Deuce McAllister, New Orleans	1150	10	35	250	1	11
20. Domanick Davis, Houston	1075	6	35	350	2	8
21. Frank Gore, San Francisco	1100	7	25	250	2	9
22. Ahman Green, Green Bay	1050	8	30	250	0	8
23. Chris Brown, Tennessee	1000	7	20	275	1	8
24. Tatum Bell, Denver	1100	5	25	225	2	7
25. Corey Dillon, New England	1075	8	15	100	0	8
26. Warrick Dunn, Atlanta	975	5	25	200	1	6
27. Chester Taylor, Minnesota	950	5	30	225	0	5
28. Dominic Rhodes, Indianapolis	950	5	20	150	2	7
29. Willie Parker, Pittsburgh	1050	3	20	225	0	3
30. Cedric Benson, Chicago	825	7	15	125	0	7
31. Ron Dayne, Denver	775	8	10	100	0	8
32. Greg Jones, Jacksonville	950	6	20	125	0	6
33. Thomas Jones, Chicago	775	5	30	200	1	6
34. Cedric Houston, N.Y. Jets.	850	6	25	175	0	6
35. Chris Perry, Cincinnati	500	3	45	375	1	4
36. T.J. Duckett, Atlanta	625	7	12	100	0	7
37. Fred Taylor, Jacksonville	675	4	20	125	0	4
38. Duce Staley, Pittsburgh	525	7	10	100	0	7
39. Michael Pittman, Tampa Bay	375	2	35	350	2	4
40. Curtis Martin, N.Y. Jets	550	3	15	150	0	3
41. Travis Henry, Tennessee	450	3	15	100	1	4
42. Mike Anderson, Baltimore	450	2	15	150	0	2
43. Mewelde Moore, Minnesota	475	3	25	275	0	3
44. Kevan Barlow, San Francisco	400	2	20	175	2	4
45. Marion Barber, Dallas	375	2	10	100	0	2
46. Brandon Jacobs, N.Y. Giants	200	6	5	50	0	6
47. Michael Bennett, New Orleans	350	2	20	200	1	3
48. Eric Shelton, Carolina	350	4	10	125	0	4
49. Reggie Bush, New Orleans	*645*	*2*	*45*	*610*	*4*	*6*
50. Joseph Addai, Indianapolis	*920*	*6*	*30*	*325*	*1*	*7*
51. LenDale White, Tennessee	*425*	*8*	*10*	*110*	*0*	*8*
52. Ryan Moats, Philadelphia	425	3	10	50	0	3
53. Marshall Faulk, St. Louis	175	1	36	300	2	3
54. Najeh Davenport, Green Bay	400	2	5	35	0	5
55. DeAngelo Williams, Carolina	*550*	*1*	*15*	*145*	*0*	*1*
56. Laurence Maroney, New England	*275*	*1*	*20*	*245*	*1*	*2*
57. Priest Holmes, Kansas City	145	2	15	165	2	4
58. Verron Haynes, Pittsburgh	250	2	12	100	1	3

		Rushing Yards	Rushing Touchdowns	Receiving	Receiving Yards	Receiving Touchdowns	Total Touchdowns
59.	J.J. Arrington, Arizona	300	2	15	100	0	2
60.	Michael Turner, San Diego	350	2	5	45	0	2
61.	Kevin Faulk, New England	200	1	30	250	0	1
62.	Aaron Stecker, New Orleans	200	0	20	250	1	1
63.	Artose Pinner, Detroit	300	2	10	55	0	2
64.	Shaud Williams, Buffalo	225	2	10	125	0	2
65.	Nick Goings, Carolina	225	1	20	175	0	1
66.	Quentin Griffin, Kansas City	250	2	5	50	0	2
67.	*Maurice Jones-Drew, Jacksonville*	*140*	*1*	*30*	*225*	*1*	*2*
68.	Samkon Gado, Green Bay	200	1	15	100	1	2
69.	Maurice Morris, Seattle	250	2	5	40	0	2
70.	Patrick Pass, New England	225	2	20	75	0	2
71.	Mike Alstott, Tampa Bay	100	3	15	125	0	3
72.	Dee Brown, Kansas City	175	2	5	60	0	2
73.	Lee Suggs, Cleveland	175	1	13	100	1	2
74.	Sammy Morris, Miami	200	1	10	55	0	1
75.	Adrian Peterson, Chicago	200	1	5	35	0	1
76.	Antowain Smith, Houston	175	1	5	40	0	1
77.	Ladell Betts, Washington	100	1	15	145	0	1
78.	Maurice Hicks, San Francisco	200	1	5	30	0	1
79.	Correll Buckhalter, Philadelphia	150	1	5	75	0	1
80.	Zack Crockett, Oakland	75	2	10	75	0	2
81.	Tony Fisher, St. Louis	125	0	20	140	0	0
82.	James Mungro, Indianapolis	125	1	8	75	0	1
83.	LaBrandon Toefield, Jacksonville	125	1	5	50	0	1
84.	Justin Griffith, Atlanta	50	0	10	50	2	2
85.	Heath Evans, New England	100	1	5	50	0	1
86.	William Henderson, Green Bay	0	0	25	200	0	0
87.	Rock Cartwright, Washington	125	1	2	20	0	1
88.	Derrick Ward, N.Y. Giants	125	1	3	25	0	1
89.	Lorenzo Neal, San Diego	50	1	20	90	0	1
90.	Kyle Johnson, Denver	10	0	15	125	1	1
91.	Jamal Robertson, Carolina	125	0	5	50	0	0
92.	Shawn Bryson, Detroit	75	0	12	100	0	0
93.	Ciatrick Fason, Minnesota	100	1	0	0	0	1
94.	Jarrett Payton, Tennessee	125	0	5	40	0	0
95.	Jeremi Johnson, Cincinnati	25	0	10	75	1	1
96.	Obafemi Ayanbadejo, Arizona	25	0	15	125	0	0
97.	Marcel Shipp, Arizona	100	0	5	40	0	0
98.	Mack Strong, Seattle	50	0	15	90	0	0
99.	Darren Sproles, San Diego	10	0	20	175	0	0
100.	Dan Kreider, Pittsburgh	35	0	5	45	0	0

Players in bold/italics are rookies who could have significantly higher value.

For more in-depth analysis, pick up a copy of the NFL.com 2006 Fantasy Football Preview, *available at newsstands today.*

WIDE RECEIVERS	Receiving	Yards	Touchdowns
1. Randy Moss, Oakland	90	1400	13
2. Chad Johnson, Cincinnati	100	1325	12
3. Terrell Owens, Dallas	90	1375	11
4. Steve Smith, Carolina	88	1350	10
5. Reggie Wayne, Indianapolis	95	1300	11
6. Anquan Boldin, Arizona	90	1400	9
7. Larry Fitzgerald, Arizona	88	1275	10
8. Darrell Jackson, Seattle	85	1200	11
9. Torry Holt, St. Louis	90	1175	11
10. Roy Williams, Detroit	80	1250	10
11. Deion Branch, New England	90	1200	11
12. Chris Chambers, Miami	80	1175	10
13. Marvin Harrison, Indianapolis	75	1125	9
14. Andre Johnson, Houston	80	1100	9
15. Hines Ward, Pittsburgh	75	1150	8
16. Joe Horn, New Orleans	85	1150	8
17. Derrick Mason, Baltimore	90	1150	8
18. Santana Moss, Washington	75	1200	7
19. Plaxico Burress, N.Y. Giants	72	1050	8
20. Braylon Edwards, Cleveland	70	1100	7
21. Laveranues Coles, N.Y. Jets	80	1100	7
22. Javon Walker, Denver	72	1100	7
23. Ashley Lelie, Denver	65	1050	8
24. Mike Williams, Detroit	64	925	7
25. Lee Evans, Buffalo	68	1000	6
26. Troy Williamson, Minnesota	55	950	7
27. Matt Jones, Jacksonville	64	925	8
28. Reggie Brown, Philadelphia	72	925	8
29. Michael Clayton, Tampa Bay	72	850	7
30. Samie Parker, Kansas City	60	900	6
31. Jerry Porter, Oakland	68	825	6
32. Rod Smith, Denver	78	875	5
33. Nate Burleson, Seattle	68	850	5
34. T.J. Houshmandzadeh, Cincinnati	70	850	6
35. Antonio Bryant, San Francisco	74	875	5
36. Bernard Berrian, Chicago	56	850	6
37. Mark Clayton, Baltimore	60	825	5
38. Joey Galloway, Tampa Bay	64	825	5
39. Donte' Stallworth, New Orleans	64	800	5
40. Donald Driver, Green Bay	64	800	5
41. Roydell Williams, Tennessee	68	800	5
42. Keenan McCardell, San Diego	64	775	5
43. Roddy White, Atlanta	50	725	6
44. Koren Robinson, Minnesota	64	725	5
45. Amani Toomer, N.Y. Giants	60	700	5
46. Ernest Wilford, Jacksonville	48	725	4
47. Justin McCareins, N.Y. Jets	50	725	4
48. Kevin Curtis, St. Louis	56	700	4
49. Terry Glenn, Dallas	48	700	4
50. Cedrick Wilson, Pittsburgh	48	700	4
51. Eric Moulds, Houston	60	650	4
52. David Givens, Tennessee	58	700	3
53. Reche Caldwell, New England	55	700	3
54. Eric Parker, San Diego	54	700	3
55. Jabar Gaffney, Philadelphia	60	700	3
56. Shaun McDonald, St. Louis	54	625	4
57. Michael Jenkins, Atlanta	45	625	4
58. Brandon Stokley, Indianapolis	55	625	4
59. Eddie Kennison, Kansas City	48	650	3
60. Keyshawn Johnson, Carolina	55	575	4
61. Brandon Lloyd, Washington	45	625	3
62. Joe Jurevicius, Cleveland	48	575	3
63. Muhsin Muhammad, Chicago	56	600	2
64. Chris Henry, Cincinnati	44	500	3
65. Chad Jackson, New England	*38*	*525*	*3*
66. Santonio Holmes, Pittsburgh	*30*	*515*	*4*
67. Sinorice Moss, N.Y. Giants	*40*	*575*	*1*
68. Andre' Davis, Buffalo	42	495	3
69. Marty Booker, Miami	38	525	1

WIDE RECEIVERS	Receiving	Yards	Touchdowns
70. Bobby Engram, Seattle	51	525	2
71. Josh Reed, Buffalo	32	450	3
72. Devery Henderson, New Orleans	35	440	3
73. Travis Taylor, Minnesota	40	495	2
74. Mark Bradley, Chicago	37	480	2
75. Dennis Northcutt, Cleveland	37	425	3
76. Peerless Price, Buffalo	48	480	3
77. Scott Vines, Detroit	30	400	3
78. Bryant Johnson, Atlanta	30	395	3
79. Jason McAddley, San Francisco	34	450	2
80. Marcus Robinson, Minnesota	29	380	3
81. Doug Gabriel, Oakland	32	405	2
82. Drew Bennett, Tennessee	40	400	2
83. Robert Ferguson, Green Bay	32	400	2
84. Greg Lewis, Philadelphia	35	400	2
85. Dante Hall, Kansas City	33	400	2
86. Jerricho Cotchery, N.Y. Jets	25	385	2
87. Kevin Walter, Houston	26	380	2
88. Keary Colbert, Carolina	30	375	2
89. Tim Carter, N.Y. Giants	30	375	2
90. Dane Looker, St. Louis	25	350	2
91. Brandon Williams, San Francisco	*28*	*340*	*2*
92. Darius Watts, Denver	27	325	2
93. D.J. Hackett, Seattle	30	380	1
94. Edell Shepherd, Tampa Bay	16	280	3
95. Frisman Jackson, Cleveland	20	315	2
96. Troy Brown, New England	35	375	1
97. Brandon Jones, Tennessee	22	305	2
98. Roscoe Parrish, Buffalo	22	295	2
99. Charlie Adams, Denver	25	350	1
100. Charles Rogers, Detroit	25	275	2

Players in bold/italics are rookies who could have significantly higher value.

For more in-depth analysis, pick up a copy of the NFL.com 2006 Fantasy Football Preview, *available at newsstands today.*

QUARTERBACKS	Passing Yards	Passing Touchdowns	Rushing Yards	Rushing Touchdowns
1. Peyton Manning, Indianapolis	4150	33	25	0
2. Matt Hasselbeck, Seattle	4100	27	100	0
3. Tom Brady, New England	3850	24	100	0
4. Donovan McNabb, Philadelphia	3550	25	150	2
5. Carson Palmer, Cincinnati	3575	25	50	0
6. Daunte Culpepper, Miami	3325	23	150	4
7. Eli Manning, N.Y. Giants	3550	25	75	1
8. Drew Bledsoe, Dallas	3700	24	25	1
9. David Carr, Houston	3450	23	175	2
10. Marc Bulger, St. Louis	3400	23	75	1
11. Michael Vick, Atlanta	2850	15	425	5
12. Jake Delhomme, Carolina	3300	22	75	1
13. Jake Plummer, Denver	3400	20	200	2
14. Aaron Brooks, Oakland	3300	22	200	1
15. Trent Green, Kansas City	3500	22	75	0
16. Ben Roethlisberger, Pittsburgh	3350	21	50	3
17. Brett Favre, Green Bay	3200	16	75	1
18. Philip Rivers, San Diego	3175	21	100	0
19. Drew Brees, New Orleans	3275	20	75	0
20. Billy Volek, Tennessee	3050	19	100	1
21. Kurt Warner, Arizona	2900	16	50	0
22. Kyle Boller, Baltimore	3000	20	100	0
23. Byron Leftwich, Jacksonville	2750	15	125	1
24. Jon Kitna, Detroit	3025	19	60	0
25. Alex Smith, San Francisco	2450	16	175	3
26. J.P. Losman, Buffalo	2400	14	175	2
27. Chris Simms, Tampa Bay	2700	17	75	0
28. Mark Brunell, Washington	2550	15	75	0
29. Chad Pennington, N.Y. Jets	2600	12	75	0
30. Charlie Frye, Cleveland	1800	10	150	3
31. Brad Johnson, Minnesota	2200	12	45	0
32. Rex Grossman, Chicago	2175	12	75	0
33. John Navarre, Arizona	1075	7	25	0
34. Trent Dilfer, San Francisco	1275	4	25	0
35. Jim Sorgi, Indianapolis	375	4	50	1
36. Josh McCown, Detroit	625	5	50	1
37. Jason Campbell, Washington	650	4	100	1
38. David Garrard, Jacksonville	350	3	100	2
39. Patrick Ramsey, N.Y. Jets	575	4	25	0
40. Gus Frerotte, St. Louis	575	2	35	0
41. Brian Griese, Chicago	500	4	10	0
42. Steve McNair, Tennessee	600	3	15	0
43. A.J. Feeley, San Diego	600	3	25	0
44. Matt Schaub, Atlanta	350	4	20	0
45. Mike McMahon, Minnesota	550	2	50	0
46. Kelly Holcomb, Buffalo	550	2	20	0
47. Ken Dorsey, Cleveland	550	1	20	0
48. Jeff Garcia, Philadelphia	250	2	30	0
49. Tim Rattay, Tampa Bay	225	2	10	0
50. Matt Leinart, Arizona	*220*	*2*	*10*	*0*
51. Craig Nall, Buffalo	350	1	10	0
52. Jamie Martin, New Orleans	225	2	10	0
53. Anthony Wright, Cincinnati	200	1	50	0
54. Marques Tuiasosopo, Oakland	150	2	15	0
55. Drew Henson, Dallas	250	1	20	0
56. Aaron Rodgers, Green Bay	250	1	5	0
57. Joey Harrington, Miami	150	1	25	0
58. Craig Krenzel, Cincinnati	200	1	5	0
59. Charlie Batch, Pittsburgh	175	1	5	0
60. Matt Cassel, New England	150	1	5	0

Players in bold/italics are rookies who could have significantly higher value.

TIGHT ENDS	Receiving	Yards	Touchdowns
1. Antonio Gates, San Diego	80	975	9
2. Tony Gonzalez, Kansas City	75	800	7
3. Jason Witten, Dallas	72	825	5
4. Alge Crumpler, Atlanta	62	800	5
5. Heath Miller, Pittsburgh	50	625	7
6. Jeremy Shockey, N.Y. Giants	60	725	5
7. Ben Watson, New England	48	675	6
8. Todd Heap, Baltimore	65	675	6
9. Eric Johnson, San Francisco	65	700	6
10. Randy McMichael, Miami	65	625	5
11. L.J. Smith, Philadelphia	60	600	5
12. Dallas Clark, Indianapolis	46	525	6
13. Ben Troupe, Tennessee	60	625	6
14. Chris Cooley, Washington	50	550	4
15. Jeb Putzier, Houston	44	525	4
16. Jerramy Stevens, Seattle	50	575	4
17. Zachary Hilton, New Orleans	45	525	4
18. Alex Smith, Tampa Bay	44	450	4
19. Kellen Winslow, Cleveland	32	400	4
20. Kevin Everett, Buffalo	42	525	3
21. Jermaine Wiggins, Minnesota	50	450	2
22. Bo Scaife, Tennessee	35	350	3
23. Adam Bergen, Arizona	30	300	2
24. Vernon Davis, San Francisco	*30*	*250*	*3*
25. Wesley Duke, Denver	24	300	2
26. Marcus Pollard, Detroit	40	350	2
27. Brandon Manumaleuna, San Diego	25	350	2
28. Michael Gaines, Carolina	15	250	3
29. Steve Heiden, Cleveland	35	300	2
30. Mark Campbell, New Orleans	30	275	2
31. Tony Stewart, Cincinnati	25	250	2
32. George Wrighster, Jacksonville	15	225	2
33. Bubba Franks, Green Bay	20	225	2
34. Doug Jolley, N.Y. Jets	25	275	1
35. Stephen Alexander, Denver	20	200	2
36. Erron Kinney, Tennessee	35	250	1
37. Desmond Clark, Chicago	18	250	1
38. Courtney Anderson, Oakland	17	225	1
39. Daniel Graham, New England	15	200	1
40. Bryan Fletcher, Indianapolis	15	200	1
41. Mike Sellers, Washington	12	75	3
42. Reggie Kelly, Cincinnati	20	175	1
43. Matt Schobel, Philadelphia	15	150	1
44. Kris Mangum, Carolina	16	140	1
45. Aaron Shea, San Diego	15	130	1
46. Jim Kleinsasser, Minnesota	15	125	1
47. Daniel Wilcox, Baltimore	10	125	1
48. Kyle Brady, Jacksonville	14	100	1
49. Donald Lee, Green Bay	15	75	1
50. Marcedes Lewis, Jacksonville	*13*	*80*	*1*

Players in bold/italics are rookies who could have significantly higher value.

For more in-depth analysis, pick up a copy of the NFL.com 2006 Fantasy Football Preview, available at newsstands today.

KICKERS		PTS	XP/XPA	FG/FGA
1.	David Akers, Philadelphia	132	42/42	30/34
2.	Neil Rackers, Arizona	128	35/36	31/36
3.	Adam Vinatieri, Indianapolis	133	49/49	28/30
4.	Jeff Reed, Pittsburgh	124	40/40	28/34
5.	Shayne Graham, Cincinnati	124	46/46	26/29
6.	Ryan Longwell, Minnesota	120	30/30	30/33
7.	Mike Vanderjagt, Dallas	114	39/39	25/30
8.	Sebastian Janikowski, Oakland	119	38/38	27/30
9.	John Kasay, Carolina	124	37/37	29/33
10.	Nate Kaeding, San Diego	117	42/43	25/31
11.	Josh Brown, Seattle	115	46/47	23/27
12.	Lawrence Tynes, Kansas City	114	39/40	25/32
13.	Josh Scobee, Jacksonville	112	34/34	26/32
14.	Jay Feely, N.Y. Giants	112	40/41	24/32
15.	Jason Elam, Denver	109	40/40	23/28
16.	Rian Lindell, Buffalo	109	34/34	25/29
17.	Jason Hanson, Detroit	109	40/40	23/26
18.	Matt Stover, Baltimore	108	36/36	24/29
19.	Olindo Mare, Miami	106	40/40	22/27
20.	Kris Brown, Houston	105	36/37	23/30
21.	John Hall, Washington	104	35/36	23/28
22.	Jeff Wilkins, St. Louis	102	36/37	22/29
23.	Rob Bironas, Tennessee	103	40/41	21/25
24.	Joe Nedney, San Francisco	102	33/33	23/29
25.	Matt Bryant, Tampa Bay	102	36/36	22/28
26.	John Carney, New Orleans	99	36/36	21/27
27.	Mike Nugent, N.Y. Jets	97	28/29	23/27
28.	Martín Gramatica, New England	95	41/42	18/25
29.	Phil Dawson, Cleveland	93	27/27	22/27
30.	Robbie Gould, Chicago	93	24/24	23/30

DEFENSE/ SPECIAL TEAMS*	Yards Per Game	Points Per Game	Takeaways	Sacks	Safeties	Touchdowns DEF/RET
1. Bears	309.3	18.3	27.7	31.3	1.0	5.7
2. Ravens	285.3	17.7	33.7	42.7	0.0	6.3
3. Panthers	304.8	18.8	35.3	39.7	0.3	3.7
4. Bills	292.5	19.4	29.0	40.3	1.7	5.0
5. Buccaneers	280.5	17.5	30.0	39.0	0.7	3.7
6. Steelers	280.4	17.4	29.0	41.0	0.7	4.0
7. Dolphins	307.5	19.4	30.7	43.0	1.7	2.3
8. Bengals	341.8	23.1	34.7	31.7	0.0	2.7
9. Giants	328.1	21.8	29.0	42.0	0.0	4.0
10. Chiefs	354.0	22.8	29.7	35.3	0.0	4.7
11. Colts	325.7	19.4	32.3	40.7	0.0	4.0
12. Eagles	325.6	19.5	27.0	38.0	0.3	2.7
13. Cowboys	294.9	20.3	24.3	34.0	1.0	1.7
14. Falcons	344.1	22.9	30.7	40.3	0.3	4.3
15. Seahawks	331.8	20.2	30.0	42.0	0.3	3.3
16. Patriots	310.9	17.4	31.7	39.7	0.3	4.7
17. Vikings	342.3	22.8	30.7	36.7	0.7	4.0
18. Jaguars	301.0	18.3	27.7	36.0	0.7	1.3
19. Broncos	289.6	18.0	25.3	34.0	0.7	2.7
20. Redskins	301.3	19.4	28.0	34.0	0.3	2.3
21. Titans	327.8	24.7	28.0	37.0	0.7	4.7
22. Jets	315.4	19.1	27.0	34.0	0.3	3.0
23. 49ers	347.3	25.4	28.0	33.0	0.7	4.0
24. Chargers	331.3	22.2	24.3	35.0	0.3	1.7
25. Browns	317.5	21.1	24.3	30.0	0.0	2.3
26. Cardinals	320.3	24.2	26.3	32.0	0.3	2.3
27. Texans	361.7	24.0	22.7	26.7	0.0	2.7
28. Lions	331.7	22.4	27.7	32.3	0.7	5.3
29. Rams	333.5	23.9	29.3	39.0	0.7	4.0
30. Raiders	356.9	25.1	20.7	28.7	0.7	2.3
31. Packers	319.4	21.5	22.7	36.3	0.0	3.7
32. Saints	341.0	23.5	26.3	31.3	0.7	2.3

*Defense/Special Team statistics reflect an average of the past three seasons (2003-05); clubs are ranked in projected order.

For more in-depth analysis, pick up a copy of the NFL.com 2006 Fantasy Football Preview, available at newsstands today.

AMERICAN FOOTBALL CONFERENCE OFFENSE

	Balt.	Buff.	Cin.	Cle.	Den.	Hou.	Ind.	Jax.	KC	Mia.	NE	NYJ	Oak.	Pitt.	SD	Tenn.
First Downs	286	259	342	241	330	243	363	301	347	274	334	251	294	297	337	279
Rushing	97	96	109	76	145	89	116	97	138	93	101	74	80	120	116	72
Passing	163	129	203	149	162	142	217	170	182	159	204	146	189	144	191	191
Penalty	26	34	30	16	23	12	30	34	27	22	29	31	25	33	30	16
Rushes	452	428	459	395	542	437	465	502	520	444	439	384	361	549	465	397
Net Yds. Gained	1605	1607	1910	1503	2539	1816	1703	1959	2382	1898	1512	1328	1369	2223	2072	1525
Avg. Gain	3.6	3.8	4.2	3.8	4.7	4.2	3.7	3.9	4.6	4.3	3.4	3.5	3.8	4.0	4.5	3.8
Avg. Yds. per Game	100.3	100.4	119.4	93.9	158.7	113.5	106.4	122.4	148.9	118.6	94.5	83.0	85.6	138.9	129.5	95.3
Passes Attempted	562	459	538	497	465	449	515	487	507	556	564	470	591	379	526	594
Completed	335	269	362	297	279	270	347	283	317	291	352	268	316	228	338	358
% Completed	59.6	58.6	67.3	59.8	60.0	60.1	67.4	58.1	62.5	52.3	62.4	57.0	53.5	60.2	64.3	60.3
Total Yds. Gained	3381	2852	3935	3323	3373	2661	4191	3352	4014	3458	4322	2989	3883	3104	3738	3797
Times Sacked	42	43	21	46	23	68	20	32	32	26	28	53	45	32	31	31
Yds. Lost	293	337	115	276	146	424	95	162	204	158	202	347	301	178	243	200
Net Yds. Gained	3088	2515	3820	3047	3227	2237	4096	3190	3810	3300	4120	2642	3582	2926	3495	3597
Avg. Yds. per Game	193.0	157.2	238.8	190.4	201.7	139.8	256.0	199.4	238.1	206.3	257.5	165.1	223.9	182.9	218.4	224.8
Net Yds. per Pass Play	5.11	5.01	6.83	5.61	6.61	4.33	7.66	6.15	7.07	5.67	6.96	5.05	5.63	7.12	6.27	5.76
Yds. Gained per Comp.	10.09	10.60	10.87	11.19	12.09	9.86	12.08	11.84	12.66	11.88	12.28	11.15	12.29	13.61	11.06	10.61
Combined Net																
Yds. Gained	4693	4122	5730	4550	5766	4053	5799	5149	6192	5198	5632	3970	4951	5149	5567	5122
% Total Yds. Rushing	34.2	39.0	33.3	33.0	44.0	44.8	29.4	38.0	38.5	36.5	26.8	33.5	27.7	43.2	37.2	29.8
% Total Yds. Passing	65.8	61.0	66.7	67.0	56.0	55.2	70.6	62.0	61.5	63.5	73.2	66.5	72.3	56.8	62.8	70.2
Avg. Yds. per Game	293.3	257.6	358.1	284.4	360.4	253.3	362.4	321.8	387.0	324.9	352.0	248.1	309.4	321.8	347.9	320.1
Ball Control Plays	1056	930	1018	938	1030	954	1000	1021	1059	1026	1031	907	997	960	1022	1022
Avg. Yds. per Play	4.4	4.4	5.6	4.9	5.6	4.2	5.8	5.0	5.8	5.1	5.5	4.4	5.0	5.4	5.4	5.0
Avg. Time of Poss.	30:22	29:04	30:52	28:00	32:37	28:10	30:22	31:33	32:09	27:25	30:19	26:37	28:07	31:16	31:34	31:13
Third Down Efficiency	39.1	36.8	42.9	33.0	36.2	34.2	48.7	41.3	42.7	35.1	42.1	35.3	39.7	35.4	42.3	34.4
Had Intercepted	21	16	14	17	7	13	11	6	10	16	15	15	14	14	16	14
Yds. Opp. Returned	256	209	247	215	43	225	136	90	196	127	188	147	336	194	230	293
Ret. by Opp. for TD	3	2	1	0	0	3	0	0	1	0	2	1	4	1	1	4
Punts	86	71	61	80	73	77	52	83	65	89	77	75	82	69	71	78
Yds. Punted	3685	3242	2591	3234	3157	2990	2301	3517	2564	3835	3431	3251	3744	2875	3104	3371
Avg. Yds. per Punt	42.8	45.7	42.5	40.4	43.2	38.8	44.3	42.4	39.4	43.1	44.6	43.3	45.7	41.7	43.7	43.2
Punt Returns	39	28	28	37	33	30	24	53	43	43	40	34	37	46	39	45
Yds. Returned	431	279	157	373	281	223	182	415	293	390	314	219	206	470	245	418
Avg. Yds. per Return	11.1	10.0	5.6	10.1	8.5	7.4	7.6	7.8	6.8	9.1	7.9	6.4	5.6	10.2	6.3	9.3
Returned for TD	0	0	0	1	0	0	0	0	0	0	0	0	0	2	0	1
Kickoff Returns	60	75	67	68	47	84	51	50	68	68	70	71	80	56	69	70
Yds. Returned	1289	1992	1580	1506	975	2173	1017	1197	1591	1501	1555	1728	1832	1208	1667	1697
Avg. Yds. per Return	21.5	26.6	23.6	22.1	20.7	25.9	19.9	23.9	23.4	22.1	22.2	24.3	22.9	21.6	24.2	24.2
Returned for TD	0	1	0	1	0	2	0	1	0	0	0	1	0	0	0	0
Fumbles	28	26	18	27	19	30	14	27	23	31	19	36	26	22	22	27
Lost	15	10	6	13	9	11	8	11	13	14	9	19	9	9	12	12
Out of Bounds	0	4	3	0	2	2	1	2	0	1	1	1	3	0	1	3
Own Rec. for TD	0	0	0	0	0	0	0	0	0	0	0	0	0	0	0	0
Opp. Rec. by	15	13	13	8	16	9	13	9	15	17	8	7	14	15	10	11
Opp. Rec. for TD	2	0	0	0	0	0	2	0	1	1	0	1	1	1	0	2
Penalties	139	120	110	99	97	106	94	121	115	132	110	98	147	99	110	125
Yds. Penalized	1067	897	920	770	756	854	690	1006	890	1055	921	801	1132	876	890	1002
Total Points Scored	265	271	421	232	395	260	439	361	403	318	379	240	290	389	418	299
Total TDs	25	26	48	22	46	26	53	42	46	34	46	25	33	45	51	33
TDs Rushing	5	6	15	4	25	9	18	18	26	11	16	10	11	21	22	8
TDs Passing	17	18	32	15	18	15	31	21	17	22	28	11	21	21	27	20
TDs on Ret. and Rec.	3	2	1	3	3	2	4	3	3	1	2	4	1	3	2	5
Extra Point Kicks	23	26	47	19	43	24	52	38	44	33	41	24	30	45	49	30
Extra Point Kicks Att.	23	26	47	21	44	24	52	39	45	33	42	24	30	45	49	32
2Pt Conversions	1	0	1	0	1	1	0	1	1	0	1	0	1	0	0	0
2Pt Conversions Att.	2	0	1	1	2	2	1	1	1	1	4	1	3	0	1	1
Safeties	0	1	0	0	1	0	0	0	0	3	0	0	0	1	0	0
Field Goals Made	30	29	28	27	24	26	23	23	27	25	20	22	20	24	21	23
Field Goals Attempted	35	35	32	29	32	34	26	30	33	30	25	28	30	29	24	29
% Successful	85.7	82.9	87.5	93.1	75.0	76.5	88.5	76.7	81.8	83.3	80.0	78.6	66.7	82.8	87.5	79.3

AMERICAN FOOTBALL CONFERENCE DEFENSE

	Balt.	Buff.	Cin.	Cle.	Den.	Hou.	Ind.	Jax.	KC	Mia.	NE	NYJ	Oak.	Pitt.	SD	Tenn.
First Downs	277	343	321	292	295	348	269	273	292	319	306	321	299	275	306	294
Rushing	79	146	109	116	82	123	91	79	84	94	94	136	100	75	90	89
Passing	161	169	185	161	183	188	163	158	189	183	179	151	165	179	189	180
Penalty	37	28	27	15	30	37	15	36	19	42	33	34	34	21	27	25
Rushes	431	489	429	527	344	506	398	434	383	480	437	554	507	402	386	449
Net Yds. Gained	1591	2205	1850	2202	1363	2303	1762	1709	1570	1771	1580	2185	2049	1376	1349	1894
Avg. Gain	3.7	4.5	4.3	4.2	4.0	4.6	4.4	3.9	4.1	3.7	3.6	3.9	4.0	3.4	3.5	4.2
Avg. Yds. per Game	99.4	137.8	115.6	137.6	85.2	143.9	110.1	106.8	98.1	110.7	98.8	136.6	128.1	86.0	84.3	118.4
Passes Attempted	525	503	519	471	613	469	509	482	559	549	527	463	486	549	567	470
Completed	296	314	324	279	344	304	343	285	325	323	296	284	296	315	338	296
% Completed	56.4	62.4	62.4	59.2	56.1	64.8	67.4	59.1	58.1	58.8	56.2	61.3	60.9	57.4	59.6	63.0
Total Yds. Gained	3228	3560	3749	3009	3833	3727	3469	3223	3862	3682	3926	2948	3481	3480	3888	3462
Times Sacked	42	38	28	23	28	37	46	47	29	49	33	30	36	47	46	41
Yds. Lost	270	269	180	142	190	206	318	277	183	375	223	193	238	312	289	246
Net Yds. Gained	2958	3291	3569	2867	3643	3521	3151	2946	3679	3307	3703	2755	3243	3168	3599	3216
Avg. Yds. per Game	184.9	205.7	223.1	179.2	227.7	220.1	196.9	184.1	229.9	206.7	231.4	172.2	202.7	198.0	224.9	201.0
Net Yds. per Pass Play	5.22	6.08	6.52	5.80	5.68	6.96	5.68	5.57	6.26	5.53	6.61	5.59	6.21	5.32	5.87	6.29
Yds. Gained per Comp.	10.91	11.34	11.57	10.78	11.14	12.26	10.11	11.31	11.88	11.40	13.26	10.38	11.76	11.05	11.50	11.70
Combined Net Yds. Gained	4549	5496	5419	5069	5006	5824	4913	4655	5249	5078	5283	4940	5292	4544	4948	5110
% Total Yds. Rushing	35.0	40.1	34.1	43.4	27.2	39.5	35.9	36.7	29.9	34.9	29.9	44.2	38.7	30.3	27.3	37.1
% Total Yds. Passing	65.0	59.9	65.9	56.6	72.8	60.5	64.1	63.3	70.1	65.1	70.1	55.8	61.3	69.7	72.7	62.9
Avg. Yds. per Game	284.3	343.5	338.7	316.8	312.9	364.0	307.1	290.9	328.1	317.4	330.2	308.8	330.8	284.0	309.3	319.4
Ball Control Plays	998	1030	976	1021	985	1012	953	963	971	1078	997	1047	1029	998	999	960
Avg. Yds. per Play	4.6	5.3	5.6	5.0	5.1	5.8	5.2	4.8	5.4	4.7	5.3	4.7	5.1	4.6	5.0	5.3
Avg. Time of Poss.	29:38	30:56	29:09	32:00	27:23	31:50	29:38	28:27	27:51	32:35	29:41	33:23	31:53	28:44	28:26	28:47
Third Down Efficiency	36.1	46.5	42.6	40.5	36.7	38.3	36.7	32.7	37.9	40.3	42.0	41.5	40.7	39.7	37.3	35.5
Intercepted By	11	17	31	15	20	7	18	19	16	14	10	21	5	15	10	9
Yds. Returned By	191	233	260	130	379	46	259	184	232	136	85	279	38	179	205	129
Returned for TD	1	1	1	0	3	0	2	2	1	0	2	2	0	0	2	2
Punts	89	62	50	72	81	63	67	88	69	92	81	62	76	80	78	85
Yds. Punted	3605	2492	2106	3058	3633	2528	2791	3763	3155	3957	3537	2787	3156	3463	3274	3746
Avg. Yds. per Punt	40.5	40.2	42.1	42.5	44.9	40.1	41.7	42.8	45.7	43.0	43.7	45.0	41.5	43.3	42.0	44.1
Punt Returns	55	42	32	36	36	33	25	29	23	46	42	36	39	37	26	32
Yds. Returned	481	285	260	347	266	219	272	236	179	227	405	305	460	336	244	144
Avg. Yds. per Return	8.7	6.8	8.1	9.6	7.4	6.6	10.9	8.1	7.8	4.9	9.6	8.5	11.8	9.1	9.4	4.5
Returned for TD	1	0	0	0	0	0	1	0	0	0	0	0	0	0	0	0
Kickoff Returns	62	64	85	56	67	55	89	56	83	56	68	60	56	77	83	57
Yds. Returned	1352	1308	1787	1182	1696	1194	1978	1327	2053	1425	1487	1250	1369	1685	1856	1290
Avg. Yds. per Return	21.8	20.4	21.0	21.1	25.3	21.7	22.2	23.7	24.7	25.4	21.9	20.8	24.4	21.9	22.4	22.6
Returned for TD	0	1	1	0	0	0	1	0	1	0	0	0	0	0	0	0
Fumbles	28	24	31	21	29	24	32	21	33	35	13	24	22	30	23	20
Lost	15	13	13	8	16	9	13	9	15	17	8	7	14	15	10	11
Out of Bounds	0	1	2	2	3	3	1	1	2	4	1	1	0	0	3	1
Own Rec. for TD	0	0	0	0	0	0	0	0	0	0	0	0	0	0	0	0
Opp. Rec. by	15	10	6	13	9	11	8	11	13	14	9	19	9	9	12	12
Opp. Rec. for TD	0	0	0	1	1	0	1	0	2	0	1	0	1	0	0	0
Penalties	110	124	110	97	139	105	119	130	90	105	132	115	101	120	110	95
Yds. Penalized	844	904	985	716	989	846	857	1055	805	827	1068	981	825	1031	831	718
Total Points Scored	299	367	350	301	258	431	247	269	325	317	338	355	383	258	312	421
Total TDs	30	44	39	31	31	50	27	30	38	35	38	38	40	27	36	51
TDs Rushing	8	22	16	11	10	21	9	4	11	11	11	19	18	10	14	12
TDs Passing	18	19	21	19	20	24	17	22	25	23	25	17	18	15	20	33
TDs on Ret. and Rec.	4	3	2	1	1	5	1	4	2	1	2	2	4	2	2	6
Extra Point Kicks	28	44	37	31	30	47	24	29	33	31	34	37	34	24	34	48
Extra Point Kicks Att.	29	44	37	31	30	47	24	30	33	32	34	37	37	25	35	49
2Pt Conversions	1	0	2	0	0	0	2	0	2	1	1	0	1	0	0	2
2Pt Conversions Att.	1	0	2	0	1	2	3	0	5	3	4	0	3	1	1	2
Safeties	1	1	0	0	0	0	0	0	0	1	1	0	1	0	1	0
Field Goals Made	29	19	25	28	14	28	19	20	20	24	24	30	35	24	20	21
Field Goals Attempted	31	25	28	35	18	32	27	27	26	24	30	35	38	30	29	27
% Successful	93.5	76.0	89.3	80.0	77.8	87.5	70.4	74.1	76.9	100.0	80.0	85.7	92.1	80.0	69.0	77.8

NATIONAL FOOTBALL CONFERENCE OFFENSE

	Ariz.	Atl.	Car.	Chi.	Dall.	Det.	GB	Minn.	NO	NYG	Phil.	StL	SF	Sea.	TB	Wash.
First Downs	304	313	278	233	318	258	318	285	312	312	282	314	191	361	268	301
Rushing	58	139	82	99	97	69	76	83	89	106	73	82	70	142	83	114
Passing	224	149	157	111	177	151	206	169	182	172	182	209	96	192	161	166
Penalty	22	25	39	23	44	38	36	33	41	34	27	23	25	27	24	21
Rushes	360	531	487	488	521	404	398	381	423	469	365	380	428	519	457	525
Net Yds. Gained	1138	2546	1679	2099	1861	1471	1352	1467	1688	2209	1432	1535	1689	2457	1826	2183
Avg. Gain	3.2	4.8	3.4	4.3	3.6	3.6	3.4	3.9	4.0	4.7	3.9	4.0	3.9	4.7	4.0	4.2
Avg. Yds. per Game	71.1	159.1	104.9	131.2	116.3	91.9	84.5	91.7	105.5	138.1	89.5	95.9	105.6	153.6	114.1	136.4
Passes Attempted	670	451	449	418	500	520	626	510	553	558	620	599	389	474	487	481
Completed	419	247	269	219	300	297	383	323	308	294	337	392	204	307	303	278
% Completed	62.5	54.8	59.9	52.4	60.0	57.1	61.2	63.3	55.7	52.7	54.4	65.4	52.4	64.8	62.2	57.8
Total Yds. Gained	4723	2907	3485	2201	3639	3021	3964	3449	3604	3762	3903	4351	2190	3632	3171	3346
Times Sacked	45	39	28	31	50	31	27	54	41	28	42	46	48	27	41	31
Yds. Lost	286	228	214	199	298	173	198	303	261	184	226	315	292	174	281	240
Net Yds. Gained	4437	2679	3271	2002	3341	2848	3766	3146	3343	3578	3677	4036	1898	3458	2890	3106
Avg. Yds. per Game	277.3	167.4	204.4	125.1	208.8	178.0	235.4	196.6	208.9	223.6	229.8	252.3	118.6	216.1	180.6	194.1
Net Yds. per Pass Play	6.21	5.47	6.86	4.46	6.07	5.17	5.77	5.58	5.63	6.11	5.55	6.26	4.34	6.90	5.47	6.07
Yds. Gained per Comp.	11.27	11.77	12.96	10.05	12.13	10.17	10.35	10.68	11.70	12.80	11.58	11.10	10.74	11.83	10.47	12.04
Combined Net Yds. Gained	5575	5225	4950	4101	5202	4319	5118	4613	5031	5787	5109	5571	3587	5915	4716	5289
% Total Yds. Rushing	20.4	48.7	33.9	51.2	35.8	34.1	26.4	31.8	33.6	38.2	28.0	27.6	47.1	41.5	38.7	41.3
% Total Yds. Passing	79.6	51.3	66.1	48.8	64.2	65.9	73.6	68.2	66.4	61.8	72.0	72.4	52.9	58.5	61.3	58.7
Avg. Yds. per Game	348.4	326.6	309.4	256.3	325.1	269.9	319.9	288.3	314.4	361.7	319.3	348.2	224.2	369.7	294.8	330.6
Ball Control Plays	1075	1021	964	937	1071	955	1051	945	1017	1055	1027	1025	865	1020	985	1037
Avg. Yds. per Play	5.2	5.1	5.1	4.4	4.9	4.5	4.9	4.9	4.9	5.5	5.0	5.4	4.1	5.8	4.8	5.1
Avg. Time of Poss.	31:20	29:58	30:48	28:41	32:24	29:13	30:48	28:46	30:32	30:26	28:22	30:14	27:18	29:17	30:45	31:33
Third Down Efficiency	38.1	42.9	42.2	28.8	40.5	38.8	41.2	32.7	38.9	39.6	32.7	36.5	24.0	39.6	39.4	42.2
Had Intercepted	21	13	16	15	17	18	30	16	24	17	20	24	21	10	14	11
Yds. Opp Returned	334	163	335	66	326	271	370	220	456	302	339	268	265	93	480	183
Ret. by Opp. for TD	1	0	3	0	2	2	3	0	3	2	4	0	1	0	2	1
Punts	74	78	73	98	82	84	70	81	71	73	100	73	108	80	90	87
Yds. Punted	3206	3300	3154	3965	3474	3656	2726	3505	3066	3070	4072	3008	4447	3282	4101	3503
Avg. Yds. per Punt	43.3	42.3	43.2	40.5	42.4	43.5	38.9	43.3	43.2	42.1	40.7	41.2	41.2	41.0	45.6	40.3
Punt Returns	50	31	41	46	45	36	45	41	46	49	53	30	28	31	51	30
Yds. Returned	383	261	444	417	284	274	381	344	320	453	448	175	212	177	492	180
Avg. Yds. per Return	7.7	8.4	10.8	9.1	6.3	7.6	8.5	8.4	7.0	9.2	8.5	5.8	7.6	5.7	9.6	6.0
Returned for TD	0	0	0	1	0	0	1	1	0	1	0	0	1	0	0	0
Kickoff Returns	76	70	53	55	64	73	75	71	75	63	71	74	81	61	59	62
Yds. Returned	1719	1482	1083	1092	1523	1576	1418	1549	1516	1529	1578	1580	1540	1347	1148	1438
Avg. Yds. per Return	22.6	21.2	20.4	19.9	23.8	21.6	18.9	21.8	20.2	24.3	22.2	21.4	19.0	22.1	19.5	23.2
Returned for TD	0	0	0	0	0	0	0	1	0	1	0	1	0	0	0	2
Fumbles	26	26	23	32	36	21	31	25	23	17	34	24	31	18	16	29
Lost	16	16	10	13	14	12	15	14	19	8	14	13	14	7	9	16
Out of Bounds	0	4	2	1	2	0	1	2	2	1	3	2	0	2	1	3
Own Rec. for TD	0	0	0	0	0	0	0	0	0	0	0	1	0	0	0	0
Opp. Rec. by	11	13	19	10	11	12	11	11	9	19	10	14	10	11	13	12
Opp. Rec. for TD	0	2	1	0	0	1	0	0	0	1	1	0	1	1	3	1
Penalties	145	114	91	105	99	115	119	128	135	143	134	131	106	94	131	108
Yds. Penalized	1184	1043	732	850	739	838	918	1013	1130	1115	1130	941	780	846	1085	925
Total Points Scored	311	351	391	260	325	254	298	306	235	422	310	363	239	452	300	359
Total TDs	26	39	45	28	38	28	34	33	23	45	35	40	23	57	33	44
TDs Rushing	2	17	17	11	13	10	11	10	8	17	11	13	9	29	13	15
TDs Passing	21	19	25	11	23	15	20	18	15	24	21	23	8	25	17	25
TDs on Ret. and Rec.	3	3	3	6	2	3	3	5	0	4	3	4	6	3	3	4
Extra Point Kicks	20	35	43	26	35	27	30	31	22	43	32	36	21	56	32	42
Extra Point Kicks Att.	20	35	44	27	36	28	31	31	22	43	33	36	21	57	32	42
2Pt Conversions	3	4	0	0	1	0	2	1	0	2	1	2	1	0	1	1
2Pt Conversions Att.	6	4	1	0	2	0	3	2	1	2	2	3	2	0	1	2
Safeties	0	1	0	0	0	1	0	0	0	0	0	1	0	0	0	0
Field Goals Made	43	24	26	22	20	19	20	25	25	35	22	27	26	18	22	17
Field Goals Attempted	45	27	34	31	28	24	27	34	32	42	29	31	29	25	27	21
% Successful	95.6	88.9	76.5	71.0	71.4	79.2	74.1	73.5	78.1	83.3	75.9	87.1	89.7	72.0	81.5	81.0

NATIONAL FOOTBALL CONFERENCE DEFENSE

	Ariz.	Atl.	Car.	Chi.	Dall.	Det.	GB	Minn.	NO	NYG	Phil.	StL	SF	Sea.	TB	Wash.
First Downs	272	319	262	259	256	308	280	304	281	302	290	321	335	295	254	258
Rushing	83	122	72	83	87	109	107	96	103	83	91	116	115	78	75	74
Passing	158	167	160	153	150	166	143	177	145	189	171	178	205	194	148	158
Penalty	31	30	30	23	19	33	30	31	33	30	28	27	15	23	31	26
Rushes	411	438	408	443	414	488	504	462	503	428	506	459	486	420	438	411
Net Yds. Gained	1632	2063	1465	1637	1731	2040	2010	1841	2145	1656	1883	2178	1832	1510	1515	1686
Avg. Gain	4.0	4.7	3.6	3.7	4.2	4.2	4.0	4.0	4.3	3.9	3.7	4.7	3.8	3.6	3.5	4.1
Avg. Yds. per Game	102.0	128.9	91.6	102.3	108.2	127.5	125.6	115.1	134.1	103.5	117.7	136.1	114.5	94.4	94.7	105.4
Passes Attempted	488	526	528	550	495	487	430	533	418	580	503	507	576	571	476	535
Completed	301	320	305	313	271	295	252	319	241	329	297	314	374	331	275	291
% Completed	61.7	60.8	57.8	56.9	54.7	60.6	58.6	59.8	57.7	56.7	59.0	61.9	64.9	58.0	57.8	54.4
Total Yds. Gained	3314	3394	3351	3147	3319	3305	2876	3539	3014	3852	3507	3619	4620	3861	3158	3318
Times Sacked	37	37	45	41	37	31	35	34	25	41	29	41	28	50	36	35
Yds. Lost	217	257	294	275	236	187	196	207	165	268	184	195	193	302	229	237
Net Yds. Gained	3097	3137	3057	2872	3083	3118	2680	3332	2849	3584	3323	3424	4427	3559	2929	3081
Avg. Yds. per Game	193.6	196.1	191.1	179.5	192.7	194.9	167.5	208.3	178.1	224.0	207.7	214.0	276.7	222.4	183.1	192.6
Net Yds. per Pass Play	5.90	5.57	5.34	4.86	5.80	6.02	5.76	5.88	6.43	5.77	6.25	6.25	7.33	5.73	5.72	5.41
Yds. Gained per Comp.	11.01	10.61	10.99	10.05	12.25	11.20	11.41	11.09	12.51	11.71	11.81	11.53	12.35	11.66	11.48	11.40
Combined Net																
Yds. Gained	4729	5200	4522	4509	4814	5158	4690	5173	4994	5240	5206	5602	6259	5069	4444	4767
% Total Yds. Rushing	34.5	39.7	32.4	36.3	36.0	39.6	42.9	35.6	43.0	31.6	36.2	38.9	29.3	29.8	34.1	35.4
% Total Yds. Passing	65.5	60.3	67.6	63.7	64.0	60.4	57.1	64.4	57.0	68.4	63.8	61.1	70.7	70.2	65.9	64.6
Avg. Yds. per Game	295.6	325.0	282.6	281.8	300.9	322.4	293.1	323.3	312.1	327.5	325.4	350.1	391.2	316.8	277.8	297.9
Ball Control Plays	936	1001	981	1034	946	1006	969	1029	946	1049	1038	1007	1090	1041	950	981
Avg. Yds. per Play	5.1	5.2	4.6	4.4	5.1	5.1	4.8	5.0	5.3	5.0	5.0	5.6	5.7	4.9	4.7	4.9
Avg. Time of Poss.	28:40	30:02	29:12	31:19	27:36	30:47	29:12	31:14	29:28	29:34	31:38	29:46	32:42	30:43	29:15	28:27
Third Down Efficiency	34.2	30.2	40.7	31.9	34.6	39.4	35.9	43.0	40.5	39.8	34.3	40.2	38.5	38.0	35.0	36.5
Intercepted By	15	16	23	24	15	19	10	24	10	17	17	13	16	16	17	16
Yds. Returned By	285	268	440	524	187	308	205	392	182	354	195	364	220	315	223	176
Returned for TD	3	0	2	4	2	2	2	3	0	1	1	2	3	2	0	1
Punts	85	79	79	97	95	72	85	72	76	88	104	68	71	77	80	88
Yds. Punted	3752	3401	3562	3982	3892	2899	3597	3013	3462	3651	4361	2722	2846	3091	3509	3636
Avg. Yds. per Punt	44.1	43.1	45.1	41.1	41.0	40.3	42.3	41.8	45.6	41.5	41.9	40.0	40.1	40.1	43.9	41.3
Punt Returns	39	35	36	39	33	50	49	45	33	36	57	39	62	41	49	40
Yds. Returned	328	238	235	312	250	520	339	495	260	309	310	410	471	343	466	189
Avg. Yds. per Return	8.4	6.8	6.5	8.0	7.6	10.4	6.9	11.0	7.9	8.6	5.4	10.5	7.6	8.4	9.5	4.7
Returned for TD	1	0	0	1	0	2	0	0	0	1	0	1	0	0	0	0
Kickoff Returns	60	59	80	63	66	55	65	67	61	85	67	70	48	82	63	72
Yds. Returned	1700	1138	1702	1255	1432	1239	1404	1416	1404	1867	1416	1781	960	1802	1368	1503
Avg. Yds. per Return	28.3	19.3	21.3	19.9	21.7	22.5	21.6	21.1	23.0	22.0	21.1	25.4	20.0	22.0	21.7	20.9
Returned for TD	3	0	0	0	0	1	0	0	0	1	1	0	0	1	1	0
Fumbles	24	22	25	26	21	24	33	22	19	29	25	27	18	25	25	32
Lost	11	13	19	10	11	12	11	11	9	20	10	14	10	11	13	12
Out of Bounds	0	2	1	1	1	2	1	3	1	1	3	3	0	2	1	3
Own Rec. for TD	1	0	0	0	0	0	0	0	0	0	0	0	0	0	0	0
Opp. Rec. by	16	16	10	13	14	12	15	14	18	8	14	13	14	7	9	16
Opp. Rec. for TD	1	2	0	0	2	0	2	0	3	0	2	1	0	0	0	1
Penalties	103	114	128	118	142	130	98	137	127	136	112	117	120	123	108	105
Yds. Penalized	819	981	1045	1016	1015	953	975	990	985	1180	910	1066	961	909	830	879
Total Points Scored	387	341	259	202	308	345	344	344	398	314	388	429	428	271	274	293
Total TDs	46	38	27	20	35	39	37	37	43	36	46	50	49	24	28	32
TDs Rushing	22	18	9	9	13	15	10	14	16	12	15	22	19	5	10	15
TDs Passing	17	18	15	10	18	19	22	23	20	20	24	26	28	18	15	15
TDs on Ret. and Rec.	7	2	3	1	4	5	5	0	7	4	7	2	2	1	3	2
Extra Point Kicks	44	38	22	19	35	37	33	34	43	35	46	49	43	21	26	29
Extra Point Kicks Att.	45	38	22	20	35	37	35	34	43	35	46	49	44	21	27	29
2Pt Conversions	1	0	3	0	0	1	1	1	0	0	0	1	2	2	1	2
2Pt Conversions Att.	1	0	5	0	0	1	2	3	0	1	0	1	5	3	1	2
Safeties	1	0	0	0	0	0	0	1	2	0	0	0	0	0	0	1
Field Goals Made	21	25	23	21	21	24	29	28	31	21	22	26	29	34	26	22
Field Goals Attempted	24	30	27	29	27	30	34	33	39	30	27	33	36	42	33	31
% Successful	87.5	83.3	85.2	72.4	77.8	80.0	85.3	84.8	79.5	70.0	81.5	78.8	80.6	81.0	78.8	71.0

AFC, NFC, AND NFL SUMMARY

	AFC Offense Total	AFC Offense Average	AFC Defense Total	AFC Defense Average	NFC Offense Total	NFC Offense Average	NFC Defense Total	NFC Defense Average	NFL Total	NFL Average
First Downs	4778	298.6	4830	301.9	4648	290.5	4596	287.3	9426	294.6
Rushing	1619	101.2	1587	99.2	1462	91.4	1494	93.4	3081	96.3
Passing	2741	171.3	2783	173.9	2704	169.0	2662	166.4	5445	170.2
Penalty	418	26.1	460	28.8	482	30.1	440	27.5	900	28.1
Rushes	7239	452.4	7156	447.3	7136	446.0	7219	451.2	14375	449.2
Net Yds. Gained	28951	1809.4	28759	1797.4	28632	1789.5	28824	1801.5	57583	1799.5
Avg. Gain	—	4.0	—	4.0	—	4.0	—	4.0	—	4.0
Avg. Yds. per Game	—	113.1	—	112.3	—	111.8	—	112.6	—	112.5
Passes Attempted	8159	509.9	8261	516.3	8305	519.1	8203	512.7	16464	514.5
Completed	4910	306.9	4962	310.1	4880	305.0	4828	301.8	9790	305.9
% Completed	—	60.2	—	60.1	—	58.8	—	58.9	—	59.5
Total Yds. Gained	56373	3523.3	56527	3532.9	55348	3459.3	55194	3449.6	111721	3491.3
Times Sacked	573	35.8	600	37.5	609	38.1	582	36.4	1182	36.9
Yds. Lost	3681	230.1	3911	244.4	3872	242.0	3642	227.6	7553	236.0
Net Yds. Gained	52692	3293.3	52616	3288.5	51476	3217.3	51552	3222.0	104168	3255.3
Avg. Yds. per Game	—	205.8	—	205.5	—	201.1	—	201.4	—	203.5
Net Yds. per Pass Play	—	6.03	—	5.94	—	5.77	—	5.87	—	5.90
Yds. Gained per Comp.	—	11.48	—	11.39	—	11.34	—	11.43	—	11.41
Combined Net Yds. Gained	81643	5102.7	81375	5085.9	80108	5006.8	80376	5023.5	161751	5054.7
% Total Yds. Rushing	—	35.5	—	35.3	—	35.7	—	35.9	—	35.6
% Total Yds. Passing	—	64.5	—	64.7	—	64.3	—	64.1	—	64.4
Avg. Yds. per Game	—	318.9	—	317.9	—	312.9	—	314.0	—	315.9
Ball Control Plays	15971	998.2	16017	1001.1	16050	1003.1	16004	1000.3	32021	1000.7
Avg. Yds. per Play	—	5.1	—	5.1	—	5.0	—	5.0	—	5.1
Third Down Efficiency	—	38.7	—	39.1	—	37.5	—	37.1	—	38.1
Interceptions	219	13.7	238	14.9	287	17.9	268	16.8	506	15.8
Yds. Returned	3132	195.8	2965	185.3	4471	279.4	4638	289.9	7603	237.6
Returned for TD	23	1.4	19	1.2	24	1.5	28	1.8	47	1.5
Punts	1189	74.3	1195	74.7	1322	82.6	1316	82.3	2511	78.5
Yds. Punted	50892	3180.8	51051	3190.7	55535	3470.9	55376	3461.0	106427	3325.8
Avg. Yds. per Punt	—	42.8	—	42.7	—	42.0	—	42.1	—	42.4
Punt Returns	599	37.4	569	35.6	653	40.8	683	42.7	1252	39.1
Yds. Returned	4896	306.0	4666	291.6	5245	327.8	5475	342.2	10141	316.9
Avg. Yds. per Return	—	8.2	—	8.2	—	8.0	—	8.0	—	8.1
Returned for TD	4	0.3	3	0.2	5	0.3	6	0.4	9	0.3
Kickoff Returns	1054	65.9	1074	67.1	1083	67.7	1063	66.4	2137	66.8
Yds. Returned	24508	1531.8	24239	1514.9	23118	1444.9	23387	1461.7	47626	1488.3
Avg. Yds. per Return	—	23.3	—	22.6	—	21.3	—	22.0	—	22.3
Returned for TD	7	0.4	4	0.3	5	0.3	8	0.5	12	0.4
Fumbles	395	24.7	410	25.6	412	25.8	397	24.8	807	25.2
Lost	180	11.3	193	12.1	210	13.1	197	12.3	390	12.2
Out of Bounds	24	1.5	25	1.6	26	1.6	25	1.6	50	1.6
Own Rec. for TD	0	0.0	0	0.0	1	0.1	1	0.1	1	0.0
Opp. Rec.	193	12.1	180	11.3	196	12.3	209	13.1	389	12.2
Opp. Rec. for TD	11	0.7	9	0.6	12	0.8	14	0.9	23	0.7
Penalties	1822	113.9	1802	112.6	1898	118.6	1918	119.9	3720	116.3
Yds. Penalized	14527	907.9	14282	892.6	15269	954.3	15514	969.6	29796	931.1
Total Points Scored	5380	336.3	5231	326.9	5176	323.5	5325	332.8	10556	329.9
Total TDs	601	37.6	585	36.6	571	35.7	587	36.7	1172	36.6
TDs Rushing	225	14.1	207	12.9	206	12.9	224	14.0	431	13.5
TDs Passing	334	20.9	336	21.0	310	19.4	308	19.3	644	20.1
TDs on Ret. and Rec.	42	2.6	42	2.6	55	3.4	55	3.4	97	3.0
Extra Point Kicks	568	35.5	545	34.1	531	33.2	554	34.6	1099	34.3
Extra Point Kicks Att.	576	36.0	554	34.6	538	33.6	560	35.0	1114	34.8
2Pt Conversions	8	0.5	12	0.8	19	1.2	15	0.9	27	0.8
2Pt Conversions Att.	22	1.4	28	1.8	31	1.9	25	1.6	53	1.7
Safeties	7	0.4	6	0.4	4	0.3	5	0.3	11	0.3
Field Goals Made	392	24.5	380	23.8	391	24.4	403	25.2	783	24.5
Field Goals Attempted	481	30.1	462	28.9	486	30.4	505	31.6	967	30.2
% Successful	—	81.5	—	82.3	—	80.5	—	79.8	—	81.0

CLUB LEADERS

	Offense	Defense
First Downs	Indianapolis 363	Tampa Bay 254
Rushing	Denver 145	Carolina 72
Passing	Arizona 224	Green Bay 143
Penalty	Dallas 44	Cleveland
		& Indianapolis
		& San Francisco 15
Rushes	Pittsburgh 549	Denver 344
Net Yds. Gained	Atlanta 2546	San Diego 1349
Avg. Gain	Atlanta 4.8	Pittsburgh 3.4
Passes Attempted	Arizona 670	New Orleans 418
Completed	Arizona 419	New Orleans 241
% Completed	Indianapolis 67.4	Washington 54.4
Total Yds. Gained	Arizona 4723	Green Bay 2876
Times Sacked	Indianapolis 20	Seattle 50
Yds. Lost	Indianapolis 95	Miami 375
Net Yds. Gained	Arizona 4437	Green Bay 2680
Net Yds. per Pass Play	Indianapolis 7.7	Chicago 4.9
Yds. Gained per Comp.	Pittsburgh 13.6	Chicago 10.1
Combined Net Yds. Gained	Kansas City 6192	Tampa Bay 4444
% Total Yds. Rushing	Chicago 51.2	Denver 27.2
% Total Yds. Passing	Arizona 79.6	N.Y. Jets 55.8
Ball Control Plays	Arizona 1075	Arizona 936
Avg. Yds. per Play	Kansas City 5.8	Chicago 4.4
Avg. Time of Poss.	Denver 32:37	—
Third Down Efficiency	Indianapolis 48.7	Atlanta 30.2
Interceptions	—	Cincinnati 31
Yds. Returned	—	Chicago 524
Returned for TD	—	Chicago 4
Punts	San Francisco 108	—
Yds. Punted	San Francisco 4447	—
Avg. Yds. per Punt	Buffalo 45.7	—
Punt Returns	Jacksonville	
	& Philadelphia 53	Kansas City 23
Yds. Returned	Tampa Bay 492	Tennessee 144
Avg. Yds. per Return	Baltimore 11.1	Tennessee 4.5
Returned for TD	Pittsburgh 2	
Kickoff Returns	Houston 84	San Francisco 48
Yds. Returned	Houston 2173	San Francisco 960
Avg. Yds. per Return	Buffalo 26.6	Atlanta 19.3
Returned for TD	Houston	
	& Washington 2	—
Total Points Scored	Seattle 452	Chicago 202
Total TDs	Seattle 57	Chicago 20
TDs Rushing	Seattle 29	Jacksonville 4
TDs Passing	Cincinnati 32	Chicago 10
TDs on Ret. and Rec.	Chicago	
	& San Francisco 6	Minnesota 0
Extra Point Kicks	Seattle 56	Chicago 19
2-Point Conversions	Atlanta 4	—
Safeties	Miami 3	—
Field Goals Made	Arizona 43	Denver 14
Field Goals Attempted	Arizona 45	Denver 18
% Successful	Arizona 95.6	San Diego 69.0

NFL CLUB RANKINGS BY YARDS

	Offense			Defense		
	Total	Rush	Pass	Total	Rush	Pass
Arizona	8	32	*1	8	10	12
Atlanta	12	*1	27	22	26	14
Baltimore	24	21	22	5	9	8
Buffalo	28	20	29	29	31	19
Carolina	22	19	17	3	4	9
Chicago	29	8	31	2	11	5
Cincinnati	6	11	5	28	20	26
Cleveland	26	25	23	16T	30	4
Dallas	13	13	15	10	15	11
Denver	5	2	18	15	2	29
Detroit	27	26	26	20	24	13
Green Bay	18	30	7	7	23	*1
Houston	30	15	30	31	32	24
Indianapolis	3	16	3	11	16	15
Jacksonville	15T	10	19	6	14	7
Kansas City	*1	4	6	25	7	30
Miami	14	12	16	18	17	20
Minnesota	25	27	20	21	19	22
New England	7	24	2	26	8	31
New Orleans	20	18	14	14	27	3
New York Giants	4	6	11	24	12	27
New York Jets	31	31	28	12	29	2
Oakland	21	29	10	27	25	18
Philadelphia	19	28	8	23	21	21
Pittsburgh	15T	5	24	4	3	16
St. Louis	9	22	4	30	28	23
San Diego	10	9	12	13	*1	28
San Francisco	32	17	32	32	18	32
Seattle	2	3	13	16T	5	25
Tampa Bay	23	14	25	*1	6	6
Tennessee	17	23	9	19	22	17
Washington	11	7	21	9	13	10

T = Tied for position   * = League Leader

AFC TAKEAWAYS/GIVEAWAYS

	Takeaways			Giveaways			Net
	Int	Fum	Total	Int	Fum	Total	Diff.
Cincinnati	31	13	44	14	6	20	+24
Denver	20	16	36	7	9	16	+20
Indianapolis	18	13	31	11	8	19	+12
Jacksonville	19	9	28	6	11	17	+11
Kansas City	16	15	31	10	13	23	+8
Pittsburgh	15	15	30	14	9	23	+7
Buffalo	17	13	30	16	10	26	+4
Miami	14	17	31	16	14	30	+1
Oakland	5	14	19	14	9	23	-4
New England	10	8	18	15	9	24	-6
N.Y. Jets	21	7	28	15	19	34	-6
Tennessee	9	11	20	14	12	26	-6
Cleveland	15	8	23	17	13	30	-7
Houston	7	9	16	13	11	24	-8
San Diego	10	10	20	16	12	28	-8
Baltimore	11	15	26	21	15	36	-10
AFC Totals	238	193	431	219	180	399	+32

NFC TAKEAWAYS/GIVEAWAYS

	Takeaways			Giveaways			Net
	Int	Fum	Total	Int	Fum	Total	Diff.
Carolina	23	19	42	16	10	26	+16
N.Y. Giants	17	20	37	17	8	25	+12
Seattle	16	11	27	10	7	17	+10
Tampa Bay	17	13	30	14	9	23	+7
Chicago	24	10	34	15	13	28	+6
Minnesota	24	11	35	16	14	30	+5
Detroit	19	12	31	18	12	30	+1
Washington	16	12	28	11	16	27	+1
Atlanta	16	13	29	13	16	29	0
Dallas	15	11	26	17	14	31	-5
Philadelphia	17	10	27	20	14	34	-7
San Francisco	16	10	26	21	14	35	-9
St. Louis	13	14	27	24	13	37	-10
Arizona	15	11	26	21	16	37	-11
Green Bay	10	11	21	30	15	45	-24
New Orleans	10	9	19	24	19	43	-24
NFC Totals	268	197	465	287	210	497	-32

SCORING

POINTS
NFC:	168	Shaun Alexander, Seattle
AFC:	131	Shayne Graham, Cincinnati

TOUCHDOWNS
NFC:	28	Shaun Alexander, Seattle
AFC:	21	Larry Johnson, Kansas City

EXTRA POINT KICKS
NFC:	56	Josh Brown, Seattle
AFC:	52	Mike Vanderjagt, Indianapolis

TWO-POINT EXTRA POINT PLAYS
NFC:	3	Brian Finneran, Atlanta
AFC:	1	Marc Boerigter, Kansas City
	1	Corey Bradford, Houston
	1	Heath Evans, Miami-New England
	1	David Garrard, Jacksonville
	1	* Justin Green, Baltimore
	1	LaMont Jordan, Oakland
	1	Jeb Putzier, Denver
	1	Matt Schobel, Cincinnati

FIELD GOALS
NFC:	40	Neil Rackers, Arizona
AFC:	30	Matt Stover, Baltimore

FIELD GOAL ATTEMPTS
NFC:	42	Jay Feely, N.Y. Giants
	42	Neil Rackers, Arizona
AFC:	35	Rian Lindell, Buffalo

LONGEST FIELD GOAL
NFC:	58	* Michael Koenen, Atlanta vs. New England, October 9
AFC:	53	Josh Scobee, Jacksonville vs. Cincinnati, October 9
	53	Olindo Mare, Miami at Tampa Bay, October 16
	53	Rob Bironas, Tennessee at Arizona, October 23
	53	Rian Lindell, Buffalo at San Diego, November 20
	53	Kris Brown, Houston vs. Jacksonville, December 24

MOST POINTS, GAME
AFC:	24	LaDainian Tomlinson, San Diego at N.Y. Jets, November 6 (4 TD)
NFC:	24	Shaun Alexander, Seattle vs. Arizona, September 25 (4 TD)
	24	Shaun Alexander, Seattle vs. Houston, October 16 (4 TD)

TEAM LEADERS, POINTS
AFC: BALTIMORE, 113, Matt Stover; BUFFALO, 113, Rian Lindell; CINCINNATI, 131, Shayne Graham; CLEVELAND, 100, Phil Dawson; DENVER, 115, Jason Elam; HOUSTON, 102, Kris Brown; INDIANAPOLIS, 121, Mike Vanderjagt; JACKSONVILLE, 107, Josh Scobee; KANSAS CITY, 126, Larry Johnson; MIAMI, 108, Olindo Mare; NEW ENGLAND, 100, Adam Vinatieri; N.Y. JETS, 90, *Mike Nugent; OAKLAND, 90, Sebastian Janikowski; PITTSBURGH, 117, Jeff Reed; SAN DIEGO, 120, LaDainian Tomlinson; TENNESSEE, 99, Rob Bironas

NFC: ARIZONA, 140, Neil Rackers; ATLANTA, 104, Todd Peterson; CAROLINA, 121, John Kasay; CHICAGO, 82, *Robbie Gould; DALLAS, 49, Jose Cortez; DETROIT, 84, Jason Hanson; GREEN BAY, 90, Ryan Longwell; MINNESOTA, 106, Paul Edinger; NEW ORLEANS, 97, John Carney; N.Y. GIANTS, 148, Jay Feely; PHILADELPHIA, 71, David Akers; ST. LOUIS, 117, Jeff Wilkins; SAN FRANCISCO, 97, Joe Nedney; SEATTLE, 168, Shaun Alexander; TAMPA BAY, 94, Matt Bryant; WASHINGTON, 68, Clinton Portis

TEAM CHAMPION
NFC:	452	Seattle
AFC:	439	Indianapolis

NFL TOP TEN SCORERS—KICKERS
	XP	XPA	FG	FGA	PTS
Feely, Jay, NY-G	43	43	35	42	148
Rackers, Neil, Ariz	20	20	40	42	140
Graham, Shayne, Cin.	47	47	28	32	131
Tynes, Lawrence, K.C.	44	45	27	33	125
Kasay, John, Car.	43	44	26	34	121
Vanderjagt, Mike, Ind.	52	52	23	25	121
Reed, Jeff, Pit.	45	45	24	29	117
Wilkins, Jeff, St.L	36	36	27	31	117
Elam, Jason, Den.	43	44	24	32	115
Lindell, Rian, Buf.	26	26	29	35	113
Stover, Matt, Bal.	23	23	30	34	113

NFL TOP TEN SCORERS—NONKICKERS
	TD	TDR	TDP	TDM	2-PT.	PTS
Alexander, Shaun, Sea.	28	27	1	0	0	168
Johnson, Larry, K.C.	21	20	1	0	0	126
Tomlinson, LaDainian, S.D.	20	18	2	0	0	120
James, Edgerrin, Ind.	14	13	1	0	0	84
Anderson, Mike, Den.	13	12	1	0	0	78
Dillon, Corey, N.E.	13	12	1	0	0	78
Smith, Steve, Car.	13	1	12	0	0	78
Davis, Stephen, Car.	12	12	0	0	0	72
Harrison, Marvin, Ind.	12	0	12	0	0	72
Johnson, Rudi, Cin.	12	12	0	0	0	72

AFC—INDIVIDUAL SCORERS
KICKERS
	XP	XPA	FG	FGA	PTS
Graham, Shayne, Cin.	47	47	28	32	131
Tynes, Lawrence, K.C.	44	45	27	33	125
Vanderjagt, Mike, Ind.	52	52	23	25	121
Reed, Jeff, Pit.	45	45	24	29	117
Elam, Jason, Den.	43	44	24	32	115
Lindell, Rian, Buf.	26	26	29	35	113
Stover, Matt, Bal.	23	23	30	34	113
Kaeding, Nate, S.D.	49	49	21	24	112
Mare, Olindo, Mia.	33	33	25	30	108
Scobee, Josh, Jac.	38	39	23	30	107
Brown, Kris, Hou.	24	24	26	34	102
Dawson, Phil, Cle.	19	21	27	29	100
Vinatieri, Adam, N.E.	40	41	20	25	100
Bironas, Rob, Ten.	30	32	23	29	99
Janikowski, Sebastian, Oak.	30	30	20	30	90
* Nugent, Mike, NYJ	24	24	22	28	90
Flutie, Doug, N.E.	1	1	0	0	1
Elling, Aaron, Bal.	0	0	0	1	0
* Rayner, Dave, Ind.	0	0	0	1	0

NONKICKERS
	TD	TDR	TDP	TDM	2-PT.	PTS
Johnson, Larry, K.C.	21	20	1	0	0	126
Tomlinson, LaDainian, S.D.	20	18	2	0	0	120
James, Edgerrin, Ind.	14	13	1	0	0	84
Anderson, Mike, Den.	13	12	1	0	0	78

	TD	TDR	TDP	TDM	2-PT.	PTS
Dillon, Corey, N.E.	13	12	1	0	0	78
Harrison, Marvin, Ind.	12	0	12	0	0	72
Johnson, Rudi, Cin.	12	12	0	0	0	72
Jordan, LaMont, Oak.	11	9	2	0	1	68
Chambers, Chris, Mia.	11	0	11	0	0	66
Ward, Hines, Pit.	11	0	11	0	0	66
Gates, Antonio, S.D.	10	0	10	0	0	60
Bettis, Jerome, Pit.	9	9	0	0	0	54
Johnson, Chad, Cin.	9	0	9	0	0	54
McCardell, Keenan, S.D.	9	0	9	0	0	54
Bell, Tatum, Den.	8	8	0	0	0	48
Houshmandzadeh, T.J., Cin.	8	1	7	0	0	48
Moss, Randy, Oak.	8	0	8	0	0	48
Brown, Chris, Ten.	7	5	2	0	0	42
Evans, Lee, Buf.	7	0	7	0	0	42
Heap, Todd, Bal.	7	0	7	0	0	42
Holmes, Priest, K.C.	7	6	1	0	0	42
Wilford, Ernest, Jac.	7	0	7	0	0	42
Davis, Domanick, Hou.	6	2	4	0	0	36
* Henry, Chris, Cin.	6	0	6	0	0	36
Johnson, Kyle, Den.	6	1	5	0	0	36
* Miller, Heath, Pit.	6	0	6	0	0	36
Smith, Jimmy, Jac.	6	0	6	0	0	36
Smith, Rod, Den.	6	0	6	0	0	36
Williams, Ricky, Mia.	6	6	0	0	0	36
Bradford, Corey, Hou.	5	0	5	0	1	32
Branch, Deion, N.E.	5	0	5	0	0	30
* Brown, Ronnie, Mia.	5	4	1	0	0	30
Coles, Laveranues, NYJ	5	0	5	0	0	30
* Jones, Matt, Jac.	5	0	5	0	0	30
Kennison, Eddie, K.C.	5	0	5	0	0	30
Martin, Curtis, NYJ	5	5	0	0	0	30
McGahee, Willis, Buf.	5	5	0	0	0	30
McMichael, Randy, Mia.	5	0	5	0	0	30
Parker, Willie, Pit.	5	4	1	0	0	30
Porter, Jerry, Oak.	5	0	5	0	0	30
Wayne, Reggie, Ind.	5	0	5	0	0	30
Bennett, Drew, Ten.	4	0	4	0	0	24
Bryant, Antonio, Cle.	4	0	4	0	0	24
Clark, Dallas, Ind.	4	0	4	0	0	24
Hall, Dante, K.C.	4	0	3	1	0	24
Jones, Greg, Jac.	4	4	0	0	0	24
Lewis, Jamal, Bal.	4	3	1	0	0	24
Moulds, Eric, Buf.	4	0	4	0	0	24
Rhodes, Dominic, Ind.	4	4	0	0	0	24
Toefield, LaBrandon, Jac.	4	4	0	0	0	24
Troupe, Ben, Ten.	4	0	4	0	0	24
Vrabel, Mike, N.E.	4	0	3	1	0	24
Watson, Ben, N.E.	4	0	4	0	0	24
Wells, Jonathan, Hou.	4	4	0	0	0	24
Garrard, David, Jac.	3	3	0	0	1	20
Anderson, Courtney, Oak.	3	0	3	0	0	18
Booker, Marty, Mia.	3	0	3	0	0	18
* Clayton, Mark, Bal.	3	1	2	0	0	18
Dwight, Tim, N.E.	3	0	3	0	0	18
* Edwards, Braylon, Cle.	3	0	3	0	0	18
Fletcher, Bryan, Ind.	3	0	3	0	0	18
Gabriel, Doug, Oak.	3	0	3	0	0	18
Graham, Daniel, N.E.	3	0	3	0	0	18
Haynes, Verron, Pit.	3	3	0	0	0	18
Heiden, Steve, Cle.	3	0	3	0	0	18
Johnson, Jeremi, Cin.	3	0	3	0	0	18
Mason, Derrick, Bal.	3	0	3	0	0	18
* Mathis, Jerome, Hou.	3	0	1	2	0	18
Northcutt, Dennis, Cle.	3	0	2	1	0	18
Parker, Eric, S.D.	3	0	3	0	0	18
Parker, Samie, K.C.	3	0	3	0	0	18
Pass, Patrick, N.E.	3	3	0	0	0	18
Randle El, Antwaan, Pit.	3	0	1	2	0	18
Roethlisberger, Ben, Pit.	3	3	0	0	0	18
Sowell, Jerald, NYJ	3	1	2	0	0	18
Taylor, Fred, Jac.	3	3	0	0	0	18
Thomas, Adalius, Bal.	3	0	0	3	0	18
Turner, Michael, S.D.	3	3	0	0	0	18
Walters, Troy, Ind.	3	0	3	0	0	18
Bailey, Champ, Den.	2	0	0	2	0	12
Brown, Troy, N.E.	2	0	2	0	0	12
Carswell, Dwayne, Den.	2	0	2	0	0	12
Droughns, Reuben, Cle.	2	2	0	0	0	12
Fauria, Christian, N.E.	2	0	2	0	0	12
Gaffney, Jabar, Hou.	2	0	2	0	0	12
Givens, David, N.E.	2	0	2	0	0	12
Gonzalez, Tony, K.C.	2	0	2	0	0	12
Hart, Clinton, S.D.	2	0	0	2	0	12
* Houston, Cedric, NYJ	2	2	0	0	0	12
Hymes, Randy, Bal.	2	0	2	0	0	12
Johnson, Andre, Hou.	2	0	2	0	0	12
* Jones, Brandon, Ten.	2	0	2	0	0	12
June, Cato, Ind.	2	0	0	2	0	12
Kinney, Erron, Ten.	2	0	2	0	0	12
Leftwich, Byron, Jac.	2	2	0	0	0	12
McCareins, Justin, NYJ	2	0	2	0	0	12
McGee, Terrence, Buf.	2	0	0	2	0	12
* Morency, Vernand, Hou.	2	2	0	0	0	12
Morgan, Quincy, Pit.	2	0	2	0	0	12
Odom, Antwan, Ten.	2	0	0	2	0	12
* Payton, Jarrett, Ten.	2	2	0	0	0	12
Perry, Chris, Cin.	2	0	2	0	0	12
* Perry, Tab, Cin.	2	1	1	0	0	12
Plummer, Jake, Den.	2	2	0	0	0	12
Reed, Josh, Buf.	2	0	2	0	0	12
* Scaife, Bo, Ten.	2	0	2	0	0	12
Testaverde, Vinny, NYJ	2	2	0	0	0	12
Utecht, Ben, Ind.	2	0	2	0	0	12
* Williams, Roydell, Ten.	2	0	2	0	0	12
* Wimbush, Derrick, Jac.	2	1	0	1	0	12
Wrighster, George, Jac.	2	0	2	0	0	12
Schobel, Matt, Cin.	1	0	1	0	1	8
Taylor, Jason, Mia.	1	0	0	1	0	^8
Alexander, Stephen, Den.	1	0	1	0	0	6
Ashworth, Tom, N.E.	1	0	1	0	0	6
Baker, Chris, NYJ	1	0	1	0	0	6
Batch, Charlie, Pit.	1	1	0	0	0	6
Bodden, Leigh, Cle.	1	0	1	0	0	6
Boller, Kyle, Bal.	1	1	0	0	0	6
Brady, Kyle, Jac.	1	0	1	0	0	6
Brady, Tom, N.E.	1	1	0	0	0	6
Brees, Drew, S.D.	1	1	0	0	0	6
Brown, Dee, K.C.	1	0	1	0	0	6
Brown, Mark, NYJ	1	0	0	1	0	6
Burns, Joe, Buf.	1	0	1	0	0	6
Caldwell, Reche, S.D.	1	0	1	0	0	6
Carr, David, Hou.	1	1	0	0	0	6
Carthon, Ran, Ind.	1	1	0	0	0	6
Collins, Kerry, Oak.	1	1	0	0	0	6
Cooper, Jarrod, Oak.	1	0	0	1	0	6
* Cribbs, Josh, Cle.	1	0	0	1	0	6
Crockett, Zack, Oak.	1	1	0	0	0	6
Davis, Andre, N.E.	1	0	1	0	0	6
Dayne, Ron, Den.	1	1	0	0	0	6
Devoe, Todd, Den.	1	0	1	0	0	6
Duke, Wesley, Den.	1	0	1	0	0	6
Fleming, Troy, Ten.	1	0	1	0	0	6
* Frye, Charlie, Cle.	1	1	0	0	0	6
Gilmore, Bryan, Mia.	1	0	1	0	0	6
Heller, Will, Mia.	1	0	1	0	0	6

	TD	TDR	TDP	TDM	2-PT.	PTS
* Hill, Reynaldo, Ten.	1	0	0	1	0	6
Holcomb, Kelly, Buf.	1	1	0	0	0	6
Jackson, Frisman, Cle.	1	0	1	0	0	6
Johnson, Bethel, N.E.	1	0	1	0	0	6
Jolley, Doug, NYJ	1	0	1	0	0	6
* Jones, Pacman, Ten.	1	0	0	1	0	6
Kassell, Brad, Ten.	1	0	0	1	0	6
Kelly, Reggie, Cin.	1	0	1	0	0	6
Knight, Sammy, K.C.	1	0	0	1	0	6
Law, Ty, NYJ	1	0	0	1	0	6
Lelie, Ashley, Den.	1	0	1	0	0	6
Mathis, Rashean, Jac.	1	0	0	1	0	6
McNair, Steve, Ten.	1	1	0	0	0	6
* Miller, Justin, NYJ	1	0	0	1	0	6
Morris, Sammy, Mia.	1	1	0	0	0	6
Neal, Lorenzo, S.D.	1	0	1	0	0	6
Norris, Moran, Hou.	1	0	1	0	0	6
Palmer, Carson, Cin.	1	1	0	0	0	6
* Parrish, Roscoe, Buf.	1	0	1	0	0	6
* Pearman, Alvin, Jac.	1	1	0	0	0	6
Peelle, Justin, S.D.	1	0	1	0	0	6
Peters, Jason, Buf.	1	0	1	0	0	6
Peterson, Mike, Jac.	1	0	0	1	0	6
Polamalu, Troy, Pit.	1	0	0	1	0	6
Reagor, Montae, Ind.	1	0	0	1	0	6
Reed, James, NYJ	1	0	0	1	0	6
Richardson, Tony, K.C.	1	0	1	0	0	6
* Roby, Courtney, Ten.	1	0	1	0	0	6
* Sanders, James, N.E.	1	0	0	1	0	6
Shea, Aaron, Cle.	1	0	1	0	0	6
Shelton, Daimon, Buf.	1	0	1	0	0	6
Smith, Jonathan, Buf.	1	0	1	0	0	6
Smith, Terrelle, Cle.	1	0	1	0	0	6
Staley, Duce, Pit.	1	1	0	0	0	6
Stokley, Brandon, Ind.	1	0	1	0	0	6
Taylor, Chester, Bal.	1	0	1	0	0	6
* Thurman, Odell, Cin.	1	0	0	1	0	6
Tripplett, Larry, Ind.	1	0	0	1	0	6
Van Pelt, Bradlee, Den.	1	1	0	0	0	6
Walter, Kevin, Cin.	1	0	1	0	0	6
Warfield, Eric, K.C.	1	0	0	1	0	6
Washington, Kelley, Cin.	1	0	1	0	0	6
Wilcox, Daniel, Bal.	1	0	1	0	0	6
* Williams, Darrent, Den.	1	0	0	1	0	6
Wright, Jason, Cle.	1	1	0	0	0	6
Boerigter, Marc, K.C.	0	0	0	0	1	2
Carter, Kevin, Mia.	0	0	0	0	0	^2
Evans, Heath, N.E.	0	0	0	0	1	2
Fletcher, London, Buf.	0	0	0	0	0	^2
Foote, Larry, Pit.	0	0	0	0	0	^2
* Green, Justin, Bal.	0	0	0	0	1	2
Howard, Reggie, Mia.	0	0	0	0	0	^2
Putzier, Jeb, Den.	0	0	0	0	1	2
Reynolds, Rob, Ten.	0	0	0	0	0	^2
Veal, Demetrin, Den.	0	0	0	0	0	^2
Flutie, Doug, N.E.	0	0	0	0	0	#1

^ *Safety*
# *Scored kicking extra point*
* *Player that was a rookie in 2005*

NFC—INDIVIDUAL SCORERS
KICKERS

	XP	XPA	FG	FGA	PTS
Feely, Jay, NY-G	43	43	35	42	148
Rackers, Neil, Ariz	20	20	40	42	140
Kasay, John, Car.	43	44	26	34	121
Wilkins, Jeff, St.L	36	36	27	31	117

	XP	XPA	FG	FGA	PTS
Brown, Josh, Sea.	56	57	18	25	110
Edinger, Paul, Min.	31	31	25	34	106
Peterson, Todd, Atl.	35	35	23	25	104
Carney, John, N.O.	22	22	25	32	97
Nedney, Joe, S.F.	19	19	26	28	97
Bryant, Matt, T.B.	31	31	21	25	94
Longwell, Ryan, G.B.	30	31	20	27	90
Hanson, Jason, Det.	27	27	19	24	84
* Gould, Robbie, Chi.	19	20	21	27	82
Akers, David, Phi.	23	23	16	22	71
Hall, John, Was.	27	27	12	14	63
Cortez, Jose, Dal.-Phi.-S.F.	18	19	12	17	54
* Novak, Nick, Was.-Ariz	15	15	8	10	39
Cundiff, Billy, Dal.	14	14	5	8	29
France, Todd, Phi.-T.B.	6	6	7	9	27
* Suisham, Shaun, Dal.	8	8	3	4	17
Brien, Doug, Chi.	7	7	1	4	10
* Koenen, Michael, Atl.	0	0	1	2	3
Simoneau, Mark, Phi.	1	2	0	0	1
Hamilton, Remy, Det.	0	1	0	0	0

NONKICKERS

	TD	TDR	TDP	TDM	2-PT.	PTS
Alexander, Shaun, Sea.	28	27	1	0	0	168
Smith, Steve, Car.	13	1	12	0	0	78
Davis, Stephen, Car.	12	12	0	0	0	72
Barber, Tiki, NY-G	11	9	2	0	1	68
Portis, Clinton, Was.	11	11	0	0	1	68
Fitzgerald, Larry, Ariz	10	0	10	0	0	60
Galloway, Joey, T.B.	10	0	10	0	0	60
Jackson, Steven, St.L	10	8	2	0	0	60
Jurevicius, Joe, Sea.	10	0	10	0	0	60
Holt, Torry, St.L	9	0	9	0	0	54
Jones, Thomas, Chi.	9	9	0	0	0	54
Moss, Santana, Was.	9	0	9	0	0	54
Duckett, T.J., Atl.	8	8	0	0	0	48
Glenn, Terry, Dal.	8	1	7	0	0	48
Sellers, Mike, Was.	8	1	7	0	0	48
Williams, Roy, Det.	8	0	8	0	0	48
Alstott, Mike, T.B.	7	6	1	0	1	44
Boldin, Anquan, Ariz	7	0	7	0	1	44
Shockey, Jeremy, NY-G	7	0	7	0	1	44
Westbrook, Brian, Phi.	7	3	4	0	1	44
Burress, Plaxico, NY-G	7	0	7	0	0	42
Cooley, Chris, Was.	7	0	7	0	0	42
Curtis, Kevin, St.L	7	1	6	0	0	42
* Gado, Samkon, G.B.	7	6	1	0	0	42
* Jacobs, Brandon, NY-G	7	7	0	0	0	42
Stallworth, Donte', N.O.	7	0	7	0	0	42
Toomer, Amani, NY-G	7	0	7	0	0	42
Johnson, Keyshawn, Dal.	6	0	6	0	1	38
Owens, Terrell, Phi.	6	0	6	0	0	36
Vick, Michael, Atl.	6	6	0	0	0	36
* Williams, Carnell, T.B.	6	6	0	0	0	36
Witten, Jason, Dal.	6	0	6	0	0	36
Crumpler, Alge, Atl.	5	0	5	0	1	32
Robinson, Marcus, Min.	5	0	5	0	1	32
* Barber, Marion, Dal.	5	5	0	0	0	30
Bennett, Michael, Min.	5	3	2	0	0	30
Chatman, Antonio, G.B.	5	0	4	1	0	30
Driver, Donald, G.B.	5	0	5	0	0	30
Jones, Julius, Dal.	5	5	0	0	0	30
Jones, Kevin, Det.	5	5	0	0	0	30
Lloyd, Brandon, S.F.	5	0	5	0	0	30
Stevens, Jerramy, Sea.	5	0	5	0	0	30
* Brown, Reggie, Phi.	4	0	4	0	0	24
Dunn, Warrick, Atl.	4	3	1	0	0	24
* Fason, Ciatrick, Min.	4	4	0	0	0	24

Player	TD	TDR	TDP	TDM	2-PT.	PTS
Moore, Mewelde, Min.	4	1	2	1	0	24
Muhammad, Muhsin, Chi.	4	0	4	0	0	24
Proehl, Ricky, Car.	4	0	4	0	0	24
Taylor, Travis, Min.	4	0	4	0	0	24
Ferguson, Robert, G.B.	3	0	3	0	1	20
Martin, David, G.B.	3	0	3	0	1	20
Barlow, Kevan, S.F.	3	3	0	0	0	18
Battle, Arnaz, S.F.	3	0	3	0	0	18
Betts, Ladell, Was.	3	1	1	1	0	18
Bruce, Isaac, St.L	3	0	3	0	0	18
Engram, Bobby, Sea.	3	0	3	0	0	10
Finneran, Brian, Atl.	2	0	2	0	3	18
Foster, DeShaun, Car.	3	2	1	0	0	18
* Gore, Frank, S.F.	3	3	0	0	0	18
Griffith, Justin, Atl.	3	0	3	0	0	18
Henderson, Devery, N.O.	3	0	3	0	0	18
Hicks, Maurice, S.F.	3	3	0	0	0	18
Jackson, Darrell, Sea.	3	0	3	0	0	18
Jenkins, Michael, Atl.	3	0	3	0	0	18
McAllister, Deuce, N.O.	3	3	0	0	0	18
McMahon, Mike, Phi.	3	3	0	0	0	18
* Moats, Ryan, Phi.	3	3	0	0	0	18
Pinner, Artose, Det.	3	3	0	0	0	18
Pollard, Marcus, Det.	3	0	3	0	0	18
Robinson, Koren, Min.	3	1	1	1	0	18
Smith, Antowain, N.O.	3	3	0	0	0	18
Smith, L.J., Phi.	3	0	3	0	0	18
* White, Roddy, Atl.	3	0	3	0	0	18
* Arrington, J.J., Ariz	2	2	0	0	0	12
Bartrum, Mike, Phi.	2	0	2	0	0	12
Bledsoe, Drew, Dal.	2	2	0	0	0	12
Brooks, Aaron, N.O.	2	2	0	0	0	12
Brown, Sheldon, Phi.	2	0	0	2	0	12
Cartwright, Rock, Was.	2	2	0	0	0	12
Clark, Desmond, Chi.	2	0	2	0	0	12
Colbert, Keary, Car.	2	0	2	0	0	12
Crayton, Patrick, Dal.	2	0	2	0	0	12
Dansby, Karlos, Ariz	2	0	0	2	0	12
Davenport, Najeh, G.B.	2	2	0	0	0	12
Dyson, Andre, Sea.	2	0	0	2	0	12
Edwards, Marc, Chi	2	0	2	0	0	12
Fisher, Tony, G.B.	2	1	1	0	0	12
* Fitzpatrick, Ryan, St.L	2	2	0	0	0	12
Gage, Justin, Chi.	2	0	2	0	0	12
Gaines, Michael, Car.	2	0	2	0	0	12
Hackett, D.J., Sea.	2	0	2	0	0	12
Hakim, Az-Zahir, N.O.	2	0	2	0	0	12
* Herron, Noah, G.B.	2	2	0	0	0	12
Lee, Donald, G.B.	2	0	2	0	0	12
Mangum, Kris, Car.	2	0	2	0	0	12
Peterson, Adrian, Chi.	2	2	0	0	0	12
Pittman, Michael, T.B.	2	1	1	0	0	12
Sharper, Darren, Min.	2	0	0	2	0	12
* Smith, Alex, T.B.	2	0	2	0	0	12
Vasher, Nathan, Chi.	2	0	0	2	0	12
* Williamson, Troy, Min.	2	0	2	0	0	12
Faulk, Marshall, St.L	1	0	1	0	1	8
Harris, Arlen, St.L	1	1	0	0	1	8
Adams, Mike, S.F.	1	0	0	1	0	6
Allen, Will, T.B.	1	0	0	1	0	6
* Amey, Otis, S.F.	1	0	0	1	0	6
Archuleta, Adam, St.L	1	0	0	1	0	6
Bailey, Boss, Det.	1	0	0	1	0	6
Barnett, Nick, G.B.	1	0	0	1	0	6
* Bergen, Adam, Ariz	1	0	1	0	0	6
* Blackburn, Chase, NY-G	1	0	0	1	0	6
Blakley, Dwayne, Atl.	1	0	1	0	0	6
Briggs, Lance, Chi.	1	0	0	1	0	6
Brown, Antonio, Was.	1	0	0	1	0	6
Brown, Mike, Chi.	1	0	0	1	0	6
Bryson, Shawn, Det.	1	1	0	0	0	6
Burleson, Nate, Min.	1	0	1	0	0	6
Campbell, Dan, Dal.	1	0	1	0	0	6
Carter, Drew, Car.	1	0	1	0	0	6
Cason, Aveion, St.L	1	1	0	0	0	6
Chillar, Brandon, St.L	1	0	0	1	0	6
Cleeland, Cameron, St.L	1	0	1	0	0	6
Conwell, Ernie, N.O.	1	0	1	0	0	6
Cook, Jameel, T.B.	1	0	1	0	0	6
Culpepper, Daunte, Min.	1	1	0	0	0	6
* Davis, Chauncey, Atl.	1	0	0	1	0	6
Delhomme, Jake, Car.	1	1	0	0	0	6
* Edwards, Dovonte, Min.	1	0	0	1	0	6
Edwards, Eric, Ariz	1	0	1	0	0	6
Fitzsimmons, Casey, Det.	1	0	1	0	0	6
Franks, Bubba, G.B.	1	0	1	0	0	6
Furrey, Mike, St.L	1	0	0	1	0	6
Gamble, Chris, Car.	1	0	0	1	0	6
Garcia, Jeff, Det.	1	1	0	0	0	6
Gardner, Rod, Car.	1	0	1	0	0	6
Gilmore, John, Chi.	1	0	1	0	0	6
Gordon, Lamar, Phi.	1	1	0	0	0	6
Hall, DeAngelo, Atl.	1	0	0	1	0	6
Hannam, Ryan, Sea.	1	0	1	0	0	6
Harris, Al, G.B.	1	0	0	1	0	6
Hasselbeck, Matt, Sea.	1	1	0	0	0	6
Henry, Anthony, Dal.	1	0	0	1	0	6
Hilliard, Ike, T.B.	1	0	1	0	0	6
Hilton, Zach, N.O.	1	0	1	0	0	6
Horn, Joe, N.O.	1	0	1	0	0	6
Johnson, Bryant, Ariz	1	0	1	0	0	6
Johnson, Chris, St.L	1	0	0	1	0	6
* Johnson, Derrick, S.F.	1	0	0	1	0	6
Kennedy, Kenoy, Det.	1	0	0	1	0	6
Lewis, Greg, Phi.	1	0	1	0	0	6
Macklin, David, Ariz	1	0	0	1	0	6
Manning, Eli, NY-G	1	1	0	0	0	6
Manning, Ricky, Car.	1	0	0	1	0	6
Manumaleuna, Brandon, St.L	1	0	1	0	0	6
Marshall, Lemar, Was.	1	0	0	1	0	6
* McCoy, LeRon, Ariz	1	0	1	0	0	6
McFarland, Anthony, T.B.	1	0	0	1	0	6
McMullen, Billy, Phi.	1	0	1	0	0	6
McNabb, Donovan, Phi.	1	1	0	0	0	6
Morris, Maurice, Sea.	1	1	0	0	0	6
Morton, Chad, NY-G	1	0	0	1	0	6
Parrish, Tony, S.F.	1	0	0	1	0	6
Pierce, Antonio, NY-G	1	0	0	1	0	6
Polite, Lousaka, Dal.	1	0	1	0	0	6
Ponder, Willie, NY-G	1	0	0	1	0	6
Robertson, Jamal, Car.	1	1	0	0	0	6
Rogers, Charles, Det.	1	0	1	0	0	6
Rogers, Shaun, Det.	1	0	0	1	0	6
Royal, Robert, Was.	1	0	1	0	0	6
Schlesinger, Cory, Det.	1	0	1	0	0	6
Shepherd, Edell, T.B.	1	0	1	0	0	6
Smith, Derek M., S.F.	1	0	0	1	0	6
Spencer, Shawntae, S.F.	1	0	0	1	0	6
* Tatupu, Lofa, Sea.	1	0	0	1	0	6
Taylor, Sean, Was.	1	0	0	1	0	6
Tillman, Charles, Chi.	1	0	0	1	0	6
Tyree, David, NY-G	1	0	1	0	0	6
Wade, Bobby, Chi.	1	0	1	0	0	6
Ware, Matt, Phi.	1	0	0	1	0	6
White, Dewayne, T.B.	1	0	0	1	0	6
White, Dez, Atl.	1	0	1	0	0	6

	TD	TDR	TDP	TDM	2-PT.	PTS.		TD	TDR	TDP	TDM	2-PT.	PTS.
Wiggins, Jermaine, Min.	1	0	1	0	0	6	Quarles, Shelton, T.B.	0	0	0	0	0	^2
Williams, Demorrio, Atl.	1	0	0	1	0	6	Wilkinson, Dan, Det.	0	0	0	0	0	^2
* Williams, Mike, Det.	1	0	1	0	0	6	Simoneau, Mark, Phi.	0	0	0	0	0	#1
Williams, Roy, Dal.	1	0	0	1	0	6							
Witherspoon, Will, Car.	1	0	0	1	0	6	* Player that was a rookie in 2005						
Ayanbadejo, Obafemi, Ariz	0	0	0	0	2	4	^ Safety						
* Koenen, Michael, Atl.	0	0	0	0	0	3	Team safety credited to St. Louis						
Jackson, Terry, S.F.	0	0	0	0	1	2	# Scored kicking extra point						
Lake, Antwan, Atl.	0	0	0	0	0	^2							

AMERICAN FOOTBALL CONFERENCE—SCORING

	TD	TDR	TDP	TDM	XKG	XKAtt	X2G	X2Att	FG	FGA	SAF	POINTS
Indianapolis	53	18	31	4	52	52	0	1	23	26	0	439
Cincinnati	48	15	32	1	47	47	1	1	28	32	0	421
San Diego	51	22	27	2	49	49	0	1	21	24	0	418
Kansas City	46	26	17	3	44	45	1	1	27	33	0	403
Denver	46	25	18	3	43	44	1	2	24	32	1	395
Pittsburgh	45	21	21	3	45	45	0	0	24	29	1	389
New England	46	16	28	2	41	42	1	4	20	25	0	379
Jacksonville	42	18	21	3	38	39	1	1	23	30	0	361
Miami	34	11	22	1	33	33	0	1	25	30	3	318
Tennessee	33	8	20	5	30	32	0	1	23	29	1	299
Oakland	33	11	21	1	30	30	1	3	20	30	0	290
Buffalo	26	6	18	2	26	26	0	1	29	35	1	271
Baltimore	25	5	17	3	23	23	1	2	30	35	0	265
Houston	26	9	15	2	24	24	1	2	26	34	0	260
N.Y. Jets	25	10	11	4	24	24	0	1	22	28	0	240
Cleveland	22	4	15	3	19	21	0	1	27	29	0	232
AFC Total	601	225	334	42	568	576	8	22	392	481	7	5380
AFC Average	37.6	14.1	20.9	2.6	35.5	36.0	0.5	1.4	24.5	30.1	0.4	336.3

NATIONAL FOOTBALL CONFERENCE—SCORING

	TD	TDR	TDP	TDM	XKG	XKAtt	X2G	X2Att	FG	FGA	SAF	POINTS
Seattle	57	29	25	3	56	57	0	0	18	25	0	452
N.Y. Giants	45	17	24	4	43	43	2	2	35	42	0	422
Carolina	45	17	25	3	43	44	0	1	26	34	0	391
St. Louis	40	13	23	4	36	36	2	3	27	31	1	363
Washington	44	15	25	4	42	42	1	2	17	21	0	359
Atlanta	39	17	19	3	35	35	4	4	24	27	1	351
Dallas	38	13	23	2	35	36	1	2	20	28	0	325
Arizona	26	2	21	3	20	20	3	6	43	45	0	311
Philadelphia	35	11	21	3	32	33	1	2	22	29	0	310
Minnesota	33	10	18	5	31	31	1	2	25	34	0	306
Tampa Bay	33	13	17	3	32	32	1	1	22	27	1	300
Green Bay	34	11	20	3	30	31	2	3	20	27	0	298
Chicago	28	11	11	6	26	27	0	0	22	31	0	260
Detroit	28	10	15	3	27	28	0	0	19	24	1	254
San Francisco	23	9	8	6	21	21	1	2	26	29	0	239
New Orleans	23	8	15	0	22	22	0	1	25	32	0	235
NFC Total	571	206	310	55	531	538	19	31	391	486	4	5176
NFC Average	35.7	12.9	19.4	3.4	33.2	33.6	1.2	1.9	24.4	30.4	0.3	323.5
NFL Total	1172	431	644	97	1099	1114	27	53	783	967	11	10556
NFL Average	36.6	13.5	20.1	3.0	34.3	34.8	0.8	1.7	24.5	30.2	0.3	329.9

FIELD GOALS

FIELD GOAL PERCENTAGE
NFC: .952 Neil Rackers, Arizona
AFC: .931 Phil Dawson, Cleveland

FIELD GOALS
NFC: 40 Neil Rackers, Arizona
AFC: 30 Matt Stover, Baltimore

FIELD GOAL ATTEMPTS
NFC: 42 Jay Feely, N.Y. Giants
42 Neil Rackers, Arizona
AFC: 35 Rian Lindell, Buffalo

FIELD GOALS, GAME
NFC: 6 Neil Rackers, Arizona vs. San Francisco,
October 2 (6 attempts)
AFC: 5 Rian Lindell, Buffalo vs. Houston,
September 11 (5 attempts)
5 Kris Brown, Houston at Baltimore,
December 4 (5 attempts)

LONGEST FIELD GOAL
NFC: 58 * Michael Koenen, Atlanta vs. New England,
October 9
AFC: 53 Josh Scobee, Jacksonville vs. Cincinnati,
October 9
53 Olindo Mare, Miami at Tampa Bay,
October 16
53 Rob Bironas, Tennessee at Arizona,
October 23
53 Rian Lindell, Buffalo at San Diego,
November 20
53 Kris Brown, Houston vs. Jacksonville,
December 24

AVERAGE YARDS MADE
NFC: 39.1 Josh Brown, Seattle
AFC: 35.5 Nate Kaeding, San Diego

* Player that was a rookie in 2005

AMERICAN FOOTBALL CONFERENCE—FIELD GOALS

	FG	FGA	Pct	Long
Cleveland	27	29	.931	44
Indianapolis	23	26	.885	48
Cincinnati	28	32	.875	49
San Diego	21	24	.875	49
Baltimore	30	35	.857	49
Miami	25	30	.833	53
Buffalo	29	35	.829	53
Pittsburgh	24	29	.828	44
Kansas City	27	33	.818	52
New England	20	25	.800	49
Tennessee	23	29	.793	53
N.Y. Jets	22	28	.786	49
Jacksonville	23	30	.767	53
Houston	26	34	.765	53
Denver	24	32	.750	51
Oakland	20	30	.667	49
AFC Total	392	481	—	53
AFC Average	24.5	30.1	.815	—

NATIONAL FOOTBALL CONFERENCE—FIELD GOALS

	FG	FGA	Pct	Long
Arizona	43	45	.956	54
San Francisco	26	29	.897	56
Atlanta	24	27	.889	58
St. Louis	27	31	.871	53
N.Y. Giants	35	42	.833	52
Tampa Bay	22	27	.815	50
Washington	17	21	.810	45
Detroit	19	24	.792	52
New Orleans	25	32	.781	49
Carolina	26	34	.765	52
Philadelphia	22	29	.759	50
Green Bay	20	27	.741	53
Minnesota	25	34	.735	56
Seattle	18	25	.720	55
Dallas	20	28	.714	56
Chicago	22	31	.710	48
NFC Total	391	486	—	58
NFC Average	24.4	30.4	.805	—
League Total	783	967	—	58
League Average	24.5	30.2	.810	—

AFC—INDIVIDUAL FIELD GOALS

	1-19 Yards	20-29 Yards	30-39 Yards	40-49 Yards	50 or Longer	Totals	Avg Yds Att	Avg Yds Made	Avg Yds Miss	Long
Dawson, Phil, Cle.	2-2 1.000	11-11 1.000	9-11 .818	5-5 1.000	0-0 —	27-29 .931	31.6	31.3	36.5	44
Vanderjagt, Mike, Ind.	1-1 1.000	9-9 1.000	6-7 .857	7-8 .875	0-0 —	23-25 .920	32.8	32.2	39.5	48
Stover, Matt, Bal.	1-1 1.000	8-8 1.000	10-11 .909	11-14 .786	0-0 —	30-34 .882	35.9	34.9	43.3	49
Graham, Shayne, Cin.	0-0 —	11-11 1.000	10-11 .909	7-9 .778	0-1 .000	28-32 .875	34.0	32.8	43.0	49
Kaeding, Nate, S.D.	1-1 1.000	3-3 1.000	9-9 1.000	8-11 .727	0-0 —	21-24 .875	36.4	35.5	42.7	49
Mare, Olindo, Mia.	0-0 —	9-10 .900	9-12 .750	6-6 1.000	1-2 .500	25-30 .833	34.8	34.6	35.8	53
Lindell, Rian, Buf.	0-0 —	8-9 .889	11-13 .846	7-10 .700	3-3 1.000	29-35 .829	35.3	34.7	38.3	53
Reed, Jeff, Pit.	0-0 —	9-9 1.000	9-9 1.000	6-9 .667	0-2 .000	24-29 .828	35.4	33.1	46.8	44
Tynes, Lawrence, K.C.	1-1 1.000	8-8 1.000	12-13 .923	4-8 .500	2-3 .667	27-33 .818	35.4	33.7	43.0	52
Vinatieri, Adam, N.E.	0-0 —	7-7 1.000	9-10 .900	4-6 .667	0-2 .000	20-25 .800	36.4	33.9	46.4	49
Bironas, Rob, Ten.	0-0 —	10-10 1.000	6-7 .857	5-7 .714	2-5 .400	23-29 .793	37.4	34.6	48.3	53
* Nugent, Mike, NYJ	0-0 —	8-9 .889	7-7 1.000	7-10 .700	0-2 .000	22-28 .786	35.7	33.5	43.8	49
Scobee, Josh, Jac.	0-0 —	9-9 1.000	7-8 .875	5-10 .500	2-3 .667	23-30 .767	36.4	34.0	44.0	53
Brown, Kris, Hou.	0-0 —	9-9 1.000	12-17 .706	4-6 .667	1-2 .500	26-34 .765	35.6	34.1	40.6	53
Elam, Jason, Den.	0-0 —	9-10 .900	5-5 1.000	9-13 .692	1-4 .250	24-32 .750	38.0	35.3	46.0	51
Janikowski, Sebastian, Oak.	1-1 1.000	7-8 .875	5-6 .833	7-12 .583	0-3 .000	20-30 .667	37.6	33.6	45.6	49
(Nonqualifiers)										
Elling, Aaron, Bal.	0-0 —	0-0 —	0-0 —	0-0 —	0-1 .000	0-1 .000	54.0	—	54.0	0
* Rayner, Dave, Ind.	0-0 —	0-0 —	0-0 —	0-0 —	0-1 .000	0-1 .000	59.0	—	59.0	0
AFC Totals	7-7 1.000	135-140 .964	136-156 .872	102-144 .708	12-34 .353	392-481 .815	35.7	33.8	43.6	53
NFL Totals	13-13 1.000	259-272 .952	255-299 .853	208-291 .715	48-92 .522	783-967 .810	36.3	34.6	43.4	58

* Player that was a rookie in 2005
Leader based on overall percentage, minimum 16 field goals

NFC—INDIVIDUAL FIELD GOALS

	1-19 Yards	20-29 Yards	30-39 Yards	40-49 Yards	50 or Longer	Totals	Avg Yds Att	Avg Yds Made	Avg Yds Miss	Long
Rackers, Neil, Ariz	0-0 —	11-11 1.000	10-10 1.000	13-14 .929	6-7 .857	40-42 .952	38.1	37.6	48.5	54
Nedney, Joe, S.F.	0-0 —	4-4 1.000	10-11 .909	10-10 1.000	2-3 .667	26-28 .929	38.5	38.0	45.5	56
Peterson, Todd, Atl.	0-0 —	9-10 .900	11-11 1.000	3-4 .750	0-0 —	23-25 .920	31.6	31.0	38.5	43
Wilkins, Jeff, St.L	0-0 —	6-7 .857	8-8 1.000	9-11 .818	4-5 .800	27-31 .871	39.1	38.4	44.0	53
Bryant, Matt, T.B.	0-0 —	2-4 .500	8-8 1.000	10-11 .909	1-2 .500	21-25 .840	38.4	38.4	38.5	50
Feely, Jay, NY-G	0-0 —	11-13 .846	13-14 .929	8-10 .800	3-5 .600	35-42 .833	36.4	35.7	40.0	52
Hanson, Jason, Det.	1-1 1.000	9-9 1.000	3-3 1.000	4-7 .571	2-4 .500	19-24 .792	35.7	32.4	48.2	52
Carney, John, N.O.	1-1 1.000	12-13 .923	4-6 .667	8-12 .667	0-0 —	25-32 .781	33.6	32.2	38.4	49
* Gould, Robbie, Chi.	0-0 —	9-9 1.000	9-10 .900	3-8 .375	0-0 —	21-27 .778	35.0	32.3	44.7	45
Kasay, John, Car.	1-1 1.000	8-8 1.000	8-8 1.000	6-9 .667	3-8 .375	26-34 .765	38.9	35.2	50.8	52
Longwell, Ryan, G.B.	0-0 —	7-7 1.000	6-10 .600	3-5 .600	4-5 .800	20-27 .741	37.7	36.8	40.4	53
Edinger, Paul, Min.	0-0 —	11-11 1.000	3-8 .375	8-10 .800	3-5 .600	25-34 .735	36.5	35.5	39.4	56
Akers, David, Phi.	0-0 —	3-3 1.000	7-8 .875	5-9 .556	1-2 .500	16-22 .727	39.6	36.5	48.0	50
Brown, Josh, Sea.	0-0 —	5-5 1.000	4-5 .800	4-7 .571	5-8 .625	18-25 .720	41.3	39.1	46.9	55
Cortez, Jose, Dal.-S.F.	0-0 —	5-6 .833	4-5 .800	3-6 .500	0-0 —	12-17 .706	35.3	33.3	40.2	45
(Nonqualifiers)										
Hall, John, Was.	1-1 1.000	3-3 1.000	3-3 1.000	5-6 .833	0-1 .000	12-14 .857	36.3	34.2	49.0	45
* Novak, Nick, Was.-Ariz	1-1 1.000	1-1 1.000	5-7 .714	1-1 1.000	0-0 —	8-10 .800	33.7	32.5	38.5	40
France, Todd, Phi.-T.B.	0-0 —	4-4 1.000	1-1 1.000	2-4 .500	0-0 —	7-9 .778	33.8	31.6	41.5	44
Cundiff, Billy, Dal.	1-1 1.000	1-1 1.000	2-5 .400	0-0 —	1-1 1.000	5-8 .625	33.9	33.4	34.7	56
Brien, Doug, Chi.	0-0 —	0-0 —	0-2 .000	1-2 .500	0-0 —	1-4 .250	42.8	48.0	41.0	48
* Suisham, Shaun, Dal.	0-0 —	3-3 1.000	0-0 —	0-1 .000	0-0 —	3-4 .750	27.8	21.3	47.0	22
* Koenen, Michael, Atl.	0-0 —	0-0 —	0-0 —	0-0 —	1-2 .500	1-2 .500	56.5	58.0	55.0	58
NFC Totals	6-6 1.000	124-132 .939	119-143 .832	106-147 .721	36-58 .621	391-486 .805	36.9	35.4	43.2	58
NFL Totals	13-13 1.000	259-272 .952	255-299 .853	208-291 .715	48-92 .522	783-967 .810	36.3	34.6	43.4	58

* Player that was a rookie in 2005
Leader based on overall percentage, minimum 16 field goals

RUSHING

YARDS
NFC:	1880	Shaun Alexander, Seattle
AFC:	1750	Larry Johnson, Kansas City

YARDS, GAME
NFC:	220	Tiki Barber, N.Y. Giants vs. Kansas City, December 17 (29 attempts, 2 TD)
AFC:	211	Larry Johnson, Kansas City at Houston, November 20 (36 attempts, 2 TD)

LONGEST
NFC:	95	Tiki Barber, N.Y. Giants at Oakland, December 31 - TD
AFC:	83	Michael Turner, San Diego at Indianapolis, December 18 - TD

ATTEMPTS
NFC:	370	Shaun Alexander, Seattle
AFC:	360	Edgerrin James, Indianapolis

ATTEMPTS, GAME
AFC:	37	Fred Taylor, Jacksonville at N.Y. Jets, September 25 (98 yards, 1 TD) - (OT)
NFC:	37	* Carnell Williams, Tampa Bay at Green Bay, September 25 (158 yards, 0 TD)

YARDS PER ATTEMPT
NFC:	5.9	Michael Vick, Atlanta
AFC:	5.3	Tatum Bell, Denver

TOUCHDOWNS
NFC:	27	Shaun Alexander, Seattle
AFC:	20	Larry Johnson, Kansas City

TEAM LEADERS, YARDS

AFC: BALTIMORE, 906, Jamal Lewis; BUFFALO, 1247, Willis McGahee; CINCINNATI, 1458, Rudi Johnson; CLEVELAND, 1232, Reuben Droughns; DENVER, 1014, Mike Anderson; HOUSTON, 976, Domanick Davis; INDIANAPOLIS, 1506, Edgerrin James; JACKSONVILLE, 787, Fred Taylor; KANSAS CITY, 1750, Larry Johnson; MIAMI, 907, *Ronnie Brown; NEW ENGLAND, 733, Corey Dillon; N.Y. JETS, 735, Curtis Martin; OAKLAND, 1025, LaMont Jordan; PITTSBURGH, 1202, Willie Parker; SAN DIEGO, 1462, LaDainian Tomlinson; TENNESSEE, 851, Chris Brown;

NFC: ARIZONA, 451, Marcel Shipp; ATLANTA, 1416, Warrick Dunn; CAROLINA, 879, DeShaun Foster; CHICAGO, 1335, Thomas Jones; DALLAS, 993, Julius Jones; DETROIT, 664, Kevin Jones; GREEN BAY, 582, *Samkon Gado; MINNESOTA, 662, Mewelde Moore; NEW ORLEANS, 659, Antowain Smith; N.Y. GIANTS, 1860, Tiki Barber; PHILADELPHIA, 617, Brian Westbrook; ST. LOUIS, 1046, Steven Jackson; SAN FRANCISCO, 608, *Frank Gore; SEATTLE, 1880, Shaun Alexander; TAMPA BAY, 1178, *Carnell Williams; WASHINGTON, 1516, Clinton Portis

TEAM CHAMPION
NFC:	2546	Atlanta
AFC:	2539	Denver

*Player that was a rookie in 2005

NFL TOP TEN RUSHERS

	Att	Yards	Avg	Long	TD
Alexander, Shaun, Sea.	370	1880	5.1	88t	27
Barber, Tiki, NY-G	357	1860	5.2	95t	9
Johnson, Larry, K.C.	336	1750	5.2	49t	20
Portis, Clinton, Was.	352	1516	4.3	47t	11
James, Edgerrin, Ind.	360	1506	4.2	33	13
Tomlinson, LaDainian, S.D.	339	1462	4.3	62	18
Johnson, Rudi, Cin.	337	1458	4.3	33	12
Dunn, Warrick, Atl.	280	1416	5.1	65	3
Jones, Thomas, Chi.	314	1335	4.3	42	9
McGahee, Willis, Buf.	325	1247	3.8	27	5

AFC—INDIVIDUAL RUSHERS

	Att	Yards	Avg	Long	TD
Johnson, Larry, K.C.	336	1750	5.2	49t	20
James, Edgerrin, Ind.	360	1506	4.2	33	13
Tomlinson, LaDainian, S.D.	339	1462	4.3	62	18
Johnson, Rudi, Cin.	337	1458	4.3	33	12
McGahee, Willis, Buf.	325	1247	3.8	27	5
Droughns, Reuben, Cle.	309	1232	4.0	75t	2
Parker, Willie, Pit.	255	1202	4.7	80t	4
Jordan, LaMont, Oak.	272	1025	3.8	26	9
Anderson, Mike, Den.	239	1014	4.2	44t	12
Davis, Domanick, Hou.	230	976	4.2	44	2
Bell, Tatum, Den.	173	921	5.3	68	8
* Brown, Ronnie, Mia.	207	907	4.4	65t	4
Lewis, Jamal, Bal.	269	906	3.4	25	3
Brown, Chris, Ten.	224	851	3.8	38t	5
Taylor, Fred, Jac.	194	787	4.1	71t	3
Williams, Ricky, Mia.	168	743	4.4	35	6
Martin, Curtis, NYJ	220	735	3.3	49	5
Dillon, Corey, N.E.	209	733	3.5	29	12
Jones, Greg, Jac.	151	575	3.8	27	4
Taylor, Chester, Bal.	117	487	4.2	52	0
Holmes, Priest, K.C.	119	451	3.8	35t	6
Bettis, Jerome, Pit.	110	368	3.3	39	9
Henry, Travis, Ten.	88	335	3.8	29	0
Turner, Michael, S.D.	57	335	5.9	83t	3
Wells, Jonathan, Hou.	90	325	3.6	14t	4
Carr, David, Hou.	56	308	5.5	20	1
* Houston, Cedric, NYJ	81	302	3.7	17	2
Perry, Chris, Cin.	61	279	4.6	30	0
Haynes, Verron, Pit.	74	274	3.7	20	3
Dayne, Ron, Den.	53	270	5.1	55	1
Pass, Patrick, N.E.	54	245	4.5	31	3
Crockett, Zack, Oak.	60	208	3.5	24	1
Evans, Heath, Mia.-N.E.	52	192	3.7	21	0
* Morency, Vernand, Hou.	46	184	4.0	25t	2
Garrard, David, Jac.	31	172	5.5	28	3
Williams, Shaud, Buf.	45	161	3.6	28	0
Losman, J.P., Buf.	31	154	5.0	30	0
Plummer, Jake, Den.	46	151	3.3	22	2
* Pearman, Alvin, Jac.	39	149	3.8	45	1
Staley, Duce, Pit.	38	148	3.9	17	1
Faulk, Kevin, N.E.	51	145	2.8	13	0
Toefield, LaBrandon, Jac.	36	142	3.9	32t	4
McNair, Steve, Ten.	32	139	4.3	19	1
Bollinger, Brooks, NYJ	35	135	3.9	15	0
Rhodes, Dominic, Ind.	40	118	3.0	24	4
* Payton, Jarrett, Ten.	33	105	3.2	15	2
Neal, Lorenzo, S.D.	29	98	3.4	9	0
Chambers, Chris, Mia.	12	92	7.7	61	0
Brady, Tom, N.E.	27	89	3.3	15	1
Lelie, Ashley, Den.	5	84	16.8	39	0
Green, Trent, K.C.	35	82	2.3	13	0
Green, William, Cle.	20	78	3.9	17	0
Randle El, Antwaan, Pit.	12	73	6.1	43	0
Roethlisberger, Ben, Pit.	31	69	2.2	13	3
Wright, Anthony, Bal.	18	68	3.8	22	0

	Att	Yards	Avg	Long	TD
Leftwich, Byron, Jac.	31	67	2.2	9	2
Boller, Kyle, Bal.	23	66	2.9	9	1
Houshmandzadeh, T.J., Cin.	8	62	7.8	17	1
Frerotte, Gus, Mia.	27	61	2.3	14	0
* Frye, Charlie, Cle.	18	60	3.3	16	1
Askew, B.J., NYJ	13	59	4.5	14	0
Morris, Sammy, Mia.	16	58	3.6	9t	1
Parker, Eric, S.D.	4	55	13.8	30	0
Blaylock, Derrick, NYJ	17	53	3.1	11	0
* Jones, Matt, Jac.	12	51	4.3	25	0
Whitted, Alvis, Oak.	2	51	25.5	27	0
* Sproles, Darren, S.D.	8	50	6.3	21	0
Brees, Drew, S.D.	21	49	2.3	9	1
Van Pelt, Bradlee, Den.	11	48	4.4	11	1
Dilfer, Trent, Cle.	20	46	2.3	12	0
Manning, Peyton, Ind.	33	45	1.4	12	0
Kennison, Eddie, K.C.	7	43	6.1	23	0
Palmer, Carson, Cin.	34	41	1.2	14	1
Collins, Kerry, Oak.	17	39	2.3	18t	1
Mauck, Matt, Ten.	7	39	5.6	12	0
Evans, Lee, Buf.	4	38	9.5	39	0
* Clayton, Mark, Bal.	8	33	4.1	11t	1
Johnson, Chad, Cin.	5	33	6.6	11	0
Northcutt, Dennis, Cle.	2	33	16.5	31	0
* Nash, Damien, Ten.	6	32	5.3	8	0
Batch, Charlie, Pit.	11	30	2.7	15	1
Fargas, Justin, Oak.	5	28	5.6	15	0
Pennington, Chad, NYJ	6	27	4.5	14	0
Wright, Jason, Cle.	11	27	2.5	6t	1
Maddox, Tommy, Pit.	8	26	3.3	16	0
Stewart, Kordell, Bal.	4	24	6.0	13	0
Brown, Dee, K.C.	7	21	3.0	7	0
Kreider, Dan, Pit.	3	21	7.0	12	0
Sapp, Cecil, Den.	5	21	4.2	10	0
Richardson, Tony, K.C.	6	20	3.3	8	0
Tuiasosopo, Marques, Oak.	2	19	9.5	10	0
Carthon, Ran, Ind.	13	18	1.4	7	1
Minor, Travis, Mia.	5	17	3.4	9	0
White, Jamel, Bal.	6	17	2.8	5	0
* Roby, Courtney, Ten.	2	16	8.0	11	0
Mungro, James, Ind.	7	15	2.1	7	0
Rosenfels, Sage, Mia.	6	15	2.5	12	0
Suggs, Lee, Cle.	8	15	1.9	7	0
Adams, Charlie, Den.	5	14	2.8	13	0
Johnson, Jeremi, Cin.	8	14	1.8	5	0
Kitna, Jon, Cin.	2	14	7.0	11	0
Zereoue, Amos, N.E.	7	14	2.0	12	0
Gaffney, Jabar, Hou.	4	13	3.3	10	0
Givens, David, N.E.	2	13	6.5	9	0
* Cassel, Matt, N.E.	6	12	2.0	9	0
* Wimbush, Derrick, Jac.	3	12	4.0	7	1
Dwight, Tim, N.E.	4	11	2.8	12	0
Hall, Dante, K.C.	7	11	1.6	7	0
Holcomb, Kelly, Buf.	18	11	0.6	8	1
Caldwell, Reche, S.D.	2	10	5.0	7	0
Johnson, Andre, Hou.	6	10	1.7	5	0
Ward, Hines, Pit.	3	10	3.3	7	0
Johnson, Kyle, Den.	4	9	2.3	4	1
* Perry, Tab, Cin.	3	9	3.0	7	1
Smith, Terrelle, Cle.	6	9	1.5	4	0
McCareins, Justin, NYJ	1	8	8.0	8	0
Smith, Rod, Den.	1	7	7.0	7	0
McCardell, Keenan, S.D.	2	6	3.0	3	0
Wilson, Kris, K.C.	1	6	6.0	6	0
Gabriel, Doug, Oak.	1	5	5.0	5	0
Welker, Wes, Mia.	1	5	5.0	5	0
Brown, Kris, Hou.	1	4	4.0	4	0
Cotchery, Jerricho, NYJ	1	4	4.0	4	0

	Att	Yards	Avg	Long	TD
* Green, Justin, Bal.	5	4	0.8	4	0
Osgood, Kassim, S.D.	1	4	4.0	4	0
Pinnock, Andrew, S.D.	1	4	4.0	4	0
Testaverde, Vinny, NYJ	7	4	0.6	2	2
Bennett, Drew, Ten.	1	3	3.0	3	0
Bryant, Antonio, Cle.	1	3	3.0	3	0
Volek, Billy, Ten.	1	3	3.0	3	0
Williams, Reggie, Jac.	2	3	1.5	10	0
Lechler, Shane, Oak.	1	2	2.0	2	0
Gray, Quinn, Jac.	3	1	0.3	3	0
* Jones, Brandon, Ten.	1	1	1.0	1	0
Smith, Jonathan, Buf.	1	1	1.0	1	0
Sorgi, Jim, Ind.	12	1	0.1	6	0
Sowell, Jerald, NYJ	1	1	1.0	1t	1
Wade, Bobby, Ten.	1	1	1.0	1	0
Fiedler, Jay, NYJ	1	0	0.0	0	0
* Graham, Ben, NYJ	1	0	0.0	0	0
Hentrich, Craig, Ten.	1	0	0.0	0	0
Jones, Donnie, Mia.	1	0	0.0	0	0
Luchey, Nicolas, Cin.	1	0	0.0	0	0
Sanders, Deion, Bal.	1	0	0.0	0	0
Shelton, Daimon, Buf.	1	0	0.0	0	0
Stanley, Chad, Hou.	1	0	0.0	0	0
Wilson, Cedrick, Pit.	1	0	0.0	0	0
Zastudil, Dave, Bal.	1	0	0.0	0	0
Flutie, Doug, N.E.	5	-1	-0.2	2	0
Rivers, Philip, S.D.	1	-1	-1.0	-1	0
Banks, Tony, Hou.	2	-2	-1.0	-1	0
Bradford, Corey, Hou.	1	-2	-2.0	-2	0
Collins, Todd, K.C.	2	-2	-1.0	-1	0
* Parrish, Roscoe, Buf.	2	-2	-1.0	4	0
Reed, Josh, Buf.	1	-3	-3.0	-3	0
Porter, Jerry, Oak.	1	-8	-8.0	-8	0

*t = Touchdown; * Player that was a rookie in 2005*
Leader based on most yards gained

NFC—INDIVIDUAL RUSHERS

	Att	Yards	Avg	Long	TD
Alexander, Shaun, Sea.	370	1880	5.1	88t	27
Barber, Tiki, NY-G	357	1860	5.2	95t	9
Portis, Clinton, Was.	352	1516	4.3	47t	11
Dunn, Warrick, Atl.	280	1416	5.1	65	3
Jones, Thomas, Chi.	314	1335	4.3	42	9
* Williams, Carnell, T.B.	290	1178	4.1	71t	6
Jackson, Steven, St.L	254	1046	4.1	51	8
Jones, Julius, Dal.	257	993	3.9	51	5
Foster, DeShaun, Car.	205	879	4.3	70t	2
Jones, Kevin, Det.	186	664	3.6	40	5
Moore, Mewelde, Min.	155	662	4.3	33	1
Smith, Antowain, N.O.	166	659	4.0	42	3
Westbrook, Brian, Phi.	156	617	4.0	31	3
* Gore, Frank, S.F.	127	608	4.8	72t	3
Vick, Michael, Atl.	102	597	5.9	32	6
* Gado, Samkon, G.B.	143	582	4.1	64t	6
Barlow, Kevan, S.F.	176	581	3.3	29	3
Davis, Stephen, Car.	180	549	3.1	39	12
* Barber, Marion, Dal.	138	538	3.9	28t	5
Bennett, Michael, Min.	126	473	3.8	61t	3
Shipp, Marcel, Ariz	157	451	2.9	19	0
Pittman, Michael, T.B.	70	436	6.2	64	1
Peterson, Adrian, Chi.	76	391	5.1	36	2
Duckett, T.J., Atl.	121	380	3.1	25	8
* Arrington, J.J., Ariz	112	370	3.3	32	2
Stecker, Aaron, N.O.	95	363	3.8	32	0
Pinner, Artose, Det.	106	349	3.3	19	3
Betts, Ladell, Was.	89	338	3.8	22	1

	Att	Yards	Avg	Long	TD
McAllister, Deuce, N.O.	93	335	3.6	26	3
Hicks, Maurice, S.F.	59	308	5.2	73t	3
Bryson, Shawn, Det.	64	306	4.8	77t	1
Faulk, Marshall, St.L	65	292	4.5	20	0
Morris, Maurice, Sea.	71	288	4.1	49	1
Brooks, Aaron, N.O.	45	281	6.2	22	2
* Moats, Ryan, Phi.	55	278	5.1	59t	3
* Benson, Cedric, Chi.	67	272	4.1	36	0
Green, Ahman, G.B.	77	255	3.3	13	0
Cartwright, Rock, Was.	27	199	7.4	52	2
Gordon, Lamar, Phi.	54	182	3.4	11	1
* Thompson, Tyson, Dal.	46	182	4.0	16	0
Fisher, Tony, G.B.	60	173	2.9	17	1
Culpepper, Daunte, Min.	24	147	6.1	18	1
McCown, Josh, Ariz	29	139	4.8	12	0
Goings, Nick, Car.	37	133	3.6	17	0
Hasselbeck, Matt, Sea.	36	124	3.4	23	1
* Herron, Noah, Pit.-G.B.	48	123	2.6	17	2
Ward, Derrick, NY-G	35	123	3.5	12	0
McMahon, Mike, Phi.	34	118	3.5	19	3
Brunell, Mark, Was.	42	111	2.6	25	0
Davenport, Najeh, G.B.	30	105	3.5	24	2
* Smith, Alex, S.F.	30	103	3.4	19	0
* Jacobs, Brandon, NY-G	38	99	2.6	21	7
Thomas, Anthony, Dal.-N.O.	43	92	2.1	12	0
Mahe, Reno, Phi.	20	87	4.4	13	0
Graham, Earnest, T.B.	28	83	3.0	16	0
Alstott, Mike, T.B.	34	80	2.4	9	6
Harrington, Joey, Det.	24	80	3.3	15	0
Manning, Eli, NY-G	29	80	2.8	14	1
* Weaver, Leonard, Sea.	17	80	4.7	24	0
Strong, Mack, Sea.	17	78	4.6	16	0
Schaub, Matt, Atl.	9	76	8.4	23	0
Perry, Bruce, Phi.	16	74	4.6	11	0
Cason, Aveion, St.L	10	65	6.5	14	1
Griffith, Justin, Atl.	15	65	4.3	19	0
* Fitzpatrick, Ryan, St.L	14	64	4.6	14t	2
* Fason, Ciatrick, Min.	32	62	1.9	15	4
Favre, Brett, G.B.	18	62	3.4	20	0
Cloud, Mike, N.E.-NY-G	24	59	2.5	15	0
McNabb, Donovan, Phi.	25	55	2.2	11	1
Johnson, Brad, Min.	18	53	2.9	16	0
Garcia, Jeff, Det.	17	51	3.0	14	1
Bledsoe, Drew, Dal.	34	50	1.5	9	2
Ayanbadejo, Obafemi, Ariz	22	46	2.1	11	0
Carter, Tim, NY-G	6	46	7.7	22	0
Boldin, Anquan, Ariz	12	45	3.8	11	0
* Orton, Kyle, Chi.	24	44	1.8	15	0
Pickett, Cody, S.F.	13	42	3.2	12	0
Fitzgerald, Larry, Ariz	8	41	5.1	15	0
Robertson, Jamal, Car.	14	41	2.9	11	1
Chatman, Antonio, G.B.	8	34	4.3	11	0
Berrian, Bernard, Chi.	2	31	15.5	37	0
Delhomme, Jake, Car.	24	31	1.3	12	1
Simms, Chris, T.B.	19	31	1.6	10	0
Bulger, Marc, St.L	9	29	3.2	9	0
Warner, Kurt, Ariz	13	28	2.2	13	0
* Williamson, Troy, Min.	3	28	9.3	11	0
Robinson, Koren, Min.	4	27	6.8	13t	1
Smith, Steve, Car.	4	25	6.3	20t	0
Hoover, Brad, Car.	10	22	2.2	4	0
McKie, Jason, Chi.	3	22	7.3	13	0
Harris, Arlen, St.L	13	21	1.6	10	1
Williams, Moe, Min.	13	20	1.5	9	0
Rattay, Tim, S.F.	7	18	2.6	13	0
Lee, ReShard, G.B.	11	16	1.5	4	0
Smith, Paul, Det.	4	16	4.0	6	0
Bouman, Todd, N.O.	8	15	1.9	6	0
Driver, Donald, G.B.	2	13	6.5	9	0
Lewis, Greg, Phi.	2	13	6.5	8	0
Griese, Brian, T.B.	13	12	0.9	7	0
Karney, Mike, N.O.	6	12	2.0	3	0
* White, Roddy, Atl.	4	12	3.0	16	0
Battle, Arnaz, S.F.	8	11	1.4	9	0
Dorsey, Ken, S.F.	4	11	2.8	6	0
Jackson, James, Ariz	4	11	2.8	3	0
Jackson, Terry, S.F.	2	11	5.5	11	0
Henderson, Devery, N.O.	1	9	9.0	9	0
Price, Peerless, Dal.	1	9	9.0	9	0
Polite, Lousaka, Dal.	2	8	4.0	6	0
Thrash, James, Was.	1	8	8.0	8	0
Anderson, Damien, Ariz	2	7	3.5	6	0
Brown, Antonio, Was.	2	7	3.5	4	0
Jackson, Darrell, Sea.	1	7	7.0	7	0
McDonald, Shaun, St.L	1	7	7.0	7	0
* Rodgers, Aaron, G.B.	2	7	3.5	8	0
Vines, Scott, Det.	1	7	7.0	7	0
Colbert, Keary, Car.	1	6	6.0	6	0
Martin, Jamie, St.L	9	6	0.7	9	0
Smart, Rod, Car.	3	6	2.0	6	0
* Brown, Reggie, Phi.	1	5	5.0	5	0
Curtis, Kevin, St.L	1	5	5.0	5t	1
Johnson, Bryan, Chi.	1	5	5.0	5	0
Warrick, Peter, Sea.	1	5	5.0	5	0
Galloway, Joey, T.B.	2	4	2.0	4	0
Newman, Terence, Dal.	1	4	4.0	4	0
Ponder, Willie, NY-G	1	4	4.0	4	0
* Broughton, Nehemiah, Was.	1	3	3.0	3	0
Hetherington, Chris, S.F.	1	3	3.0	3	0
Johnson, Keyshawn, Dal.	1	3	3.0	3	0
Ramsey, Patrick, Was.	7	3	0.4	5	0
Taylor, Travis, Min.	2	3	1.5	5	0
Clayton, Michael, T.B.	1	2	2.0	2	0
Holt, Torry, St.L	1	2	2.0	2	0
Manumaleuna, Brandon, St.L	1	2	2.0	2	0
Owens, Terrell, Phi.	1	2	2.0	2	0
Stallworth, Donte', N.O.	2	2	1.0	3	0
Detmer, Koy, Phi.	1	1	1.0	1	0
Schlesinger, Cory, Det.	1	1	1.0	1	0
Sellers, Mike, Was.	1	1	1.0	1t	1
Crayton, Patrick, Dal.	1	0	0.0	0	0
* Hedgecock, Madison, St.L	1	0	0.0	0	0
Johnson, Bryant, Ariz	1	0	0.0	0	0
Blake, Jeff, Chi.	1	-1	-1.0	-1	0
Hill, Shaun, Min.	2	-2	-1.0	-1	0
Romo, Tony, Dal.	2	-2	-1.0	-1	0
Drummond, Eddie, Det.	1	-3	-3.0	-3	0
Hasselbeck, Tim, NY-G	2	-3	-1.5	-1	0
Moss, Santana, Was.	3	-3	-1.0	3	0
Glenn, Terry, Dal.	2	-4	-2.0	6t	1
Wilkins, Jeff, St.L	1	-4	-4.0	-4	0
Henderson, William, G.B.	1	-5	-5.0	-5	0
Wallace, Seneca, Sea.	6	-5	-0.8	0	0
Weinke, Chris, Car.	8	-5	-0.6	1	0
Burleson, Nate, Min.	2	-6	-3.0	-2	0
* Marshall, Rasheed, S.F.	1	-7	-7.0	-7	0
Proehl, Ricky, Car.	1	-8	-8.0	-8	0
Sander, B.J., G.B.	1	-11	-11.0	-11	0

*t = Touchdown; * Player that was a rookie in 2005*
Leader based on most yards gained

AMERICAN FOOTBALL CONFERENCE—RUSHING

	Att	Yards	Avg	Long	TD
Denver	542	2539	4.7	68	25
Kansas City	520	2382	4.6	49t	26
Pittsburgh	549	2223	4.0	80t	21
San Diego	465	2072	4.5	83t	22
Jacksonville	502	1959	3.9	71t	18
Cincinnati	459	1910	4.2	33	15
Miami	444	1898	4.3	65t	11
Houston	437	1816	4.2	44	9
Indianapolis	465	1703	3.7	33	18
Buffalo	428	1607	3.8	39	6
Baltimore	452	1605	3.6	52	5
Tennessee	397	1525	3.8	38t	8
New England	439	1512	3.4	31	16
Cleveland	395	1503	3.8	75t	4
Oakland	361	1369	3.8	27	11
N.Y. Jets	384	1328	3.5	49	10
AFC Total	7239	28951	4.0	83t	225
AFC Average	452.4	1809.4	4.0	—	14.1

NATIONAL FOOTBALL CONFERENCE—RUSHING

	Att	Yards	Avg	Long	TD
Atlanta	531	2546	4.8	65	17
Seattle	519	2457	4.7	88t	29
N.Y. Giants	469	2209	4.7	95t	17
Washington	525	2183	4.2	52	15
Chicago	488	2099	4.3	42	11
Dallas	521	1861	3.6	51	13
Tampa Bay	457	1826	4.0	71t	13
San Francisco	428	1689	3.9	73t	9
New Orleans	423	1688	4.0	42	8
Carolina	487	1679	3.4	70t	17
St. Louis	380	1535	4.0	51	13
Detroit	404	1471	3.6	77t	10
Minnesota	381	1467	3.9	61t	10
Philadelphia	365	1432	3.9	59t	11
Green Bay	398	1352	3.4	64t	11
Arizona	360	1138	3.2	32	2
NFC Total	7136	28632	4.0	95t	206
NFC Average	446.0	1789.5	4.0	—	12.9
League Total	14375	57583	—	95t	431
League Average	449.2	1799.5	4.0	—	13.5

PASSING

HIGHEST RATING
AFC: 104.1   Peyton Manning, Indianapolis
NFC: 98.2   Matt Hasselbeck, Seattle

COMPLETION PERCENTAGE
AFC: 67.8   Carson Palmer, Cincinnati
NFC: 66.9   Marc Bulger, St. Louis

ATTEMPTS
NFC: 607   Brett Favre, Green Bay
AFC: 565   Kerry Collins, Oakland

COMPLETIONS
NFC: 372   Brett Favre, Green Bay
AFC: 345   Carson Palmer, Cincinnati

YARDS
AFC: 4110   Tom Brady, New England
NFC: 3881   Brett Favre, Green Bay

YARDS, GAME
NFC: 442   Marc Bulger, St. Louis at N.Y. Giants,
                 October 2 (40-62, 2 TD)
AFC: 386   Ben Roethlisberger, Pittsburgh vs.
                 Cincinnati, December 4 (29-41, 3 TD)

LONGEST
NFC: 91   Donovan McNabb (to Terrell Owens),
                 Philadelphia at Denver, October 30 - TD
AFC: 85   Ben Roethlisberger (to Hines Ward),
                 Pittsburgh vs. New England,
                 September 25 - TD

YARDS PER ATTEMPT
AFC: 8.90   Ben Roethlisberger, Pittsburgh
NFC: 8.00   Marc Bulger, St. Louis

TOUCHDOWN PASSES
AFC: 32   Carson Palmer, Cincinnati
NFC: 24   Jake Delhomme, Carolina
        24   Matt Hasselbeck, Seattle
        24   Eli Manning, N.Y. Giants

TOUCHDOWN PASSES, GAME
NFC: 5   Donovan McNabb, Philadelphia vs.
                 San Francisco, September 18
                 (23-29, 342 yards)
AFC: 4   Peyton Manning, Indianapolis at Tennessee,
                 October 2 (20-27, 264 yards)
        4   Jake Plummer, Denver vs. Philadelphia,
                 October 30 (22-35, 309 yards)
        4   Drew Brees, San Diego vs. Buffalo,
                 November 20 (28-33, 339 yards)

LOWEST INTERCEPTION PERCENTAGE
AFC: 1.5   Jake Plummer, Denver
NFC: 1.4   Brad Johnson, Minnesota

TEAM CHAMPION (MOST NET YARDS)
NFC: 4437   Arizona
AFC: 4120   New England

NFL TOP TEN PASSERS

	Att	Comp	Pct Comp	Yds	Avg Gain	TD	Pct TD	Long	Int	Pct Int	Sack	Yds Lost	Rating Points
Manning, Peyton, Ind.	453	305	67.3	3747	8.27	28	6.2	80t	10	2.2	17	81	104.1
Palmer, Carson, Cin.	509	345	67.8	3836	7.54	32	6.3	70t	12	2.4	19	105	101.1
Roethlisberger, Ben, Pit.	268	168	62.7	2385	8.90	17	6.3	85t	9	3.4	23	129	98.6
Hasselbeck, Matt, Sea.	449	294	65.5	3459	7.70	24	5.3	56	9	2.0	24	154	98.2
Bulger, Marc, St.L	287	192	66.9	2297	8.00	14	4.9	57t	9	3.1	26	188	94.4
Brady, Tom, N.E.	530	334	63.0	4110	7.75	26	4.9	71	14	2.6	26	188	92.3
Plummer, Jake, Den.	456	277	60.7	3366	7.38	18	3.9	72	7	1.5	22	135	90.2
Green, Trent, K.C.	507	317	62.5	4014	7.92	17	3.4	60t	10	2.0	32	204	90.1
Leftwich, Byron, Jac.	302	175	57.9	2123	7.03	15	5.0	45t	5	1.7	23	110	89.3
Brees, Drew, S.D.	500	323	64.6	3576	7.15	24	4.8	54	15	3.0	27	223	89.2

*Player that was a rookie in 2005

AMERICAN FOOTBALL CONFERENCE—PASSING

	Att	Comp	Pct Comp	Gross Yards	Sacked	Yds Lost	Net Yards	Yds/ Att	Yards/ Comp	TD	Pct TD	Long	Int	Pct Int
New England	564	352	62.4	4322	28	202	4120	7.66	12.28	28	4.96	71	15	2.7
Indianapolis	515	347	67.4	4191	20	95	4096	8.14	12.08	31	6.02	80t	11	2.1
Kansas City	507	317	62.5	4014	32	204	3810	7.92	12.66	17	3.35	60t	10	2.0
Cincinnati	538	362	67.3	3935	21	115	3820	7.31	10.87	32	5.95	70t	14	2.6
Oakland	591	316	53.5	3883	45	301	3582	6.57	12.29	21	3.55	79	14	2.4
Tennessee	594	358	60.3	3797	31	200	3597	6.39	10.61	20	3.37	57	14	2.4
San Diego	526	338	64.3	3738	31	243	3495	7.11	11.06	27	5.13	54	16	3.0
Miami	556	291	52.3	3458	26	158	3300	6.22	11.88	22	3.96	77t	16	2.9
Baltimore	562	335	59.6	3381	42	293	3088	6.02	10.09	17	3.02	48	21	3.7
Denver	465	279	60.0	3373	23	146	3227	7.25	12.09	18	3.87	72	7	1.5
Jacksonville	487	283	58.1	3352	32	162	3190	6.88	11.84	21	4.31	45t	6	1.2
Cleveland	497	297	59.8	3323	46	276	3047	6.69	11.19	15	3.02	80t	17	3.4
Pittsburgh	379	228	60.2	3104	32	178	2926	8.19	13.61	21	5.54	85t	14	3.7
N.Y. Jets	470	268	57.0	2989	53	347	2642	6.36	11.15	11	2.34	60t	15	3.2
Buffalo	459	269	58.6	2852	43	337	2515	6.21	10.60	18	3.92	65	16	3.5
Houston	449	270	60.1	2661	68	424	2237	5.93	9.86	15	3.34	53t	13	2.9
AFC Total	8159	4910	—	56373	573	3681	52692	—	—	334	—	85t	219	—
AFC Average	509.9	306.9	60.2	3523.3	35.8	230.1	3293.3	6.91	11.48	20.9	4.1	—	13.7	2.7

NATIONAL FOOTBALL CONFERENCE—PASSING

	Att	Comp	Pct Comp	Gross Yards	Sacked	Yds Lost	Net Yards	Yds/ Att	Yards/ Comp	TD	Pct TD	Long	Int	Pct Int
Arizona	670	419	62.5	4723	45	286	4437	7.05	11.27	21	3.13	63	21	3.1
St. Louis	599	392	65.4	4351	46	315	4036	7.26	11.10	23	3.84	83t	24	4.0
Green Bay	626	383	61.2	3964	27	198	3766	6.33	10.35	20	3.19	59	30	4.8
Philadelphia	620	337	54.4	3903	42	226	3677	6.30	11.58	21	3.39	91t	20	3.2
N.Y. Giants	558	294	52.7	3762	28	184	3578	6.74	12.80	24	4.30	78t	17	3.0
Dallas	500	300	60.0	3639	50	298	3341	7.28	12.13	23	4.60	71t	17	3.4
Seattle	474	307	64.8	3632	27	174	3458	7.66	11.83	25	5.27	56	10	2.1
New Orleans	553	308	55.7	3604	41	261	3343	6.52	11.70	15	2.71	66	24	4.3
Carolina	449	269	59.9	3485	28	214	3271	7.76	12.96	25	5.57	80t	16	3.6
Minnesota	510	323	63.3	3449	54	303	3146	6.76	10.68	18	3.53	80t	16	3.1
Washington	481	278	57.8	3346	31	240	3106	6.96	12.04	25	5.20	78t	11	2.3
Tampa Bay	487	303	62.2	3171	41	281	2890	6.51	10.47	17	3.49	80t	14	2.9
Detroit	520	297	57.1	3021	31	173	2848	5.81	10.17	15	2.88	86	18	3.5
Atlanta	451	247	54.8	2907	39	228	2679	6.45	11.77	19	4.21	58	13	2.9
Chicago	418	219	52.4	2201	31	199	2002	5.27	10.05	11	2.63	54	15	3.6
San Francisco	389	204	52.4	2190	48	292	1898	5.63	10.74	8	2.06	89t	21	5.4
NFC Total	8305	4880	—	55348	609	3872	51476	—	—	310	—	91t	287	—
NFC Average	519.1	305.0	58.8	3459.3	38.1	242.0	3217.3	6.66	11.34	19.4	3.7	—	17.9	3.5
League Total	16464	9790	—	111721	1182	7553	104168	—	—	644	—	91t	506	—
League Average	514.5	305.9	59.5	3491.3	36.9	236.0	3255.3	6.79	11.41	20.1	3.9	—	15.8	3.1

AFC—INDIVIDUAL PASSERS

	Att	Comp	Pct Comp	Yds	Avg Gain	TD	Pct TD	Long	Int	Pct Int	Sack	Yds Lost	Rating Points
Manning, Peyton, Ind.	453	305	67.3	3747	8.27	28	6.2	80t	10	2.2	17	81	104.1
Palmer, Carson, Cin.	509	345	67.8	3836	7.54	32	6.3	70t	12	2.4	19	105	101.1
Roethlisberger, Ben, Pit.	268	168	62.7	2385	8.90	17	6.3	85t	9	3.4	23	129	98.6
Brady, Tom, N.E.	530	334	63.0	4110	7.75	26	4.9	71	14	2.6	26	188	92.3
Plummer, Jake, Den.	456	277	60.7	3366	7.38	18	3.9	72	7	1.5	22	135	90.2
Green, Trent, K.C.	507	317	62.5	4014	7.92	17	3.4	60t	10	2.0	32	204	90.1
Leftwich, Byron, Jac.	302	175	57.9	2123	7.03	15	5.0	45t	5	1.7	23	110	89.3
Brees, Drew, S.D.	500	323	64.6	3576	7.15	24	4.8	54	15	3.0	27	223	89.2
Holcomb, Kelly, Buf.	230	155	67.4	1509	6.56	10	4.3	65	8	3.5	17	140	85.6
McNair, Steve, Ten.	476	292	61.3	3161	6.64	16	3.4	57	11	2.3	20	134	82.4
Collins, Kerry, Oak.	565	302	53.5	3759	6.65	20	3.5	79	12	2.1	39	261	77.3
Carr, David, Hou.	423	256	60.5	2488	5.88	14	3.3	53t	11	2.6	68	424	77.2
Dilfer, Trent, Cle.	333	199	59.8	2321	6.97	11	3.3	80t	12	3.6	23	139	76.9
Bollinger, Brooks, NYJ	266	150	56.4	1558	5.86	7	2.6	60t	6	2.3	32	193	72.9
Frerotte, Gus, Mia.	494	257	52.0	2996	6.06	18	3.6	60t	13	2.6	26	158	71.9
Boller, Kyle, Bal.	293	171	58.4	1799	6.14	11	3.8	47t	12	4.1	23	146	71.8
Wright, Anthony, Bal.	266	164	61.7	1582	5.95	6	2.3	48	9	3.4	19	147	71.7
Losman, J.P., Buf.	228	113	49.6	1340	5.88	8	3.5	58	8	3.5	26	197	64.9
(Nonqualifiers)													
Gray, Quinn, Jac.	14	8	57.1	100	7.14	2	14.3	26	0	0.0	1	7	119.0
Fiedler, Jay, NYJ	13	8	61.5	107	8.23	1	7.7	23t	0	0.0	0	0	113.3
Sorgi, Jim, Ind.	61	42	68.9	444	7.28	3	4.9	45	1	1.6	3	14	99.4
* Cassel, Matt, N.E.	24	13	54.2	183	7.63	2	8.3	36	1	4.2	1	1	89.4
Garrard, David, Jac.	168	98	58.3	1117	6.65	4	2.4	37	1	0.6	8	45	83.9
Batch, Charlie, Pit.	36	23	63.9	246	6.83	1	2.8	43	1	2.8	1	6	81.5
Rosenfels, Sage, Mia.	61	34	55.7	462	7.57	4	6.6	77t	3	4.9	0	0	81.5
Volek, Billy, Ten.	88	50	56.8	474	5.39	4	4.5	55t	2	2.3	9	45	77.7
* Frye, Charlie, Cle.	164	98	59.8	1002	6.11	4	2.4	45	5	3.0	22	135	72.8
Pennington, Chad, NYJ	83	49	59.0	530	6.39	2	2.4	37	3	3.6	9	52	70.9
Testaverde, Vinny, NYJ	106	60	56.6	777	7.33	1	0.9	47	6	5.7	12	102	59.4
Banks, Tony, Hou.	25	14	56.0	173	6.92	1	4.0	31	2	8.0	0	0	57.6
Flutie, Doug, N.E.	10	5	50.0	29	2.90	0	0.0	13	0	0.0	1	13	56.3
Mauck, Matt, Ten.	27	15	55.6	136	5.04	0	0.0	17	1	3.7	1	8	53.9
Maddox, Tommy, Pit.	71	34	47.9	406	5.72	2	2.8	32	4	5.6	8	43	51.7
Rivers, Philip, S.D.	22	12	54.5	115	5.23	0	0.0	22	1	4.5	3	16	50.4
Tuiasosopo, Marques, Oak.	26	14	53.8	124	4.77	1	3.8	20t	2	7.7	6	40	47.6
Kitna, Jon, Cin.	29	17	58.6	99	3.41	0	0.0	16	2	6.9	2	10	36.4
(Fewer than 10 attempts)													
Bennett, Drew, Ten.	1	0	0.0	0	0.00	0	0.0	0	0	0.0	0	0	39.6
Booker, Marty, Mia.	1	0	0.0	0	0.00	0	0.0	0	0	0.0	0	0	39.6
* Clayton, Mark, Bal.	1	0	0.0	0	0.00	0	0.0	0	0	0.0	0	0	39.6
Davis, Domanick, Hou.	1	0	0.0	0	0.00	0	0.0	0	0	0.0	0	0	39.6
Gardocki, Chris, Pit.	1	0	0.0	0	0.00	0	0.0	0	0	0.0	0	0	39.6
Hentrich, Craig, Ten.	2	1	50.0	26	13.00	0	0.0	26	0	0.0	0	0	95.8
Hymes, Randy, Bal.	2	0	0.0	0	0.00	0	0.0	0	0	0.0	0	0	39.6
Jackson, Frisman, Cle.	0	0	—	0	—	0	—	—	0	—	1	2	—
* Jones, Matt, Jac.	3	2	66.7	12	4.00	0	0.0	6	0	0.0	0	0	74.3
* Jones, Pacman, Ten.	0	0	—	0	—	0	—	—	0	—	1	13	—
Kingsbury, Kliff, NYJ	2	1	50.0	17	8.50	0	0.0	17	0	0.0	0	0	79.2
McCardell, Keenan, S.D.	0	0	—	0	—	0	—	—	0	—	1	4	—
* Parrish, Roscoe, Buf.	1	1	100.0	3	3.00	0	0.0	3	0	0.0	0	0	79.2
Randle El, Antwaan, Pit.	3	3	100.0	67	22.33	1	33.3	51t	0	0.0	0	0	158.3
Smith, Hunter, Ind.	1	0	0.0	0	0.00	0	0.0	0	0	0.0	0	0	39.6
Smith, Rod, Den.	1	0	0.0	0	0.00	0	0.0	0	0	0.0	1	11	39.6
Tomlinson, LaDainian, S.D.	4	3	75.0	47	11.75	3	75.0	26t	0	0.0	0	0	153.1
Van Pelt, Bradlee, Den.	8	2	25.0	7	0.88	0	0.0	5	0	0.0	0	0	39.6

*t = Touchdown; * Player that was a rookie in 2005*
Leader based on rating points, minimum 224 attempts

NFC—INDIVIDUAL PASSERS

	Att	Comp	Pct Comp	Yds	Avg Gain	TD	Pct TD	Long	Int	Pct Int	Sack	Yds Lost	Rating Points
Hasselbeck, Matt, Sea.	449	294	65.5	3459	7.70	24	5.3	56	9	2.0	24	154	98.2
Bulger, Marc, St.L	287	192	66.9	2297	8.00	14	4.9	57t	9	3.1	26	188	94.4
Johnson, Brad, Min.	294	184	62.6	1885	6.41	12	4.1	80t	4	1.4	23	134	88.9
Delhomme, Jake, Car.	435	262	60.2	3421	7.86	24	5.5	80t	16	3.7	28	214	88.1
Brunell, Mark, Was.	454	262	57.7	3050	6.72	23	5.1	78t	10	2.2	27	213	85.9
Warner, Kurt, Ariz	375	242	64.5	2713	7.23	11	2.9	63	9	2.4	23	158	85.8
McNabb, Donovan, Phi.	357	211	59.1	2507	7.02	16	4.5	91t	9	2.5	19	112	85.0
Bledsoe, Drew, Dal.	499	300	60.1	3639	7.29	23	4.6	71t	17	3.4	49	295	83.7
Simms, Chris, T.B.	313	191	61.0	2035	6.50	10	3.2	78t	7	2.2	29	205	81.4
Manning, Eli, NY-G	557	294	52.8	3762	6.75	24	4.3	78t	17	3.1	28	184	75.9
McCown, Josh, Ariz	270	163	60.4	1836	6.80	9	3.3	49	11	4.1	18	101	74.9
Vick, Michael, Atl.	387	214	55.3	2412	6.23	15	3.9	58	13	3.4	33	201	73.1
Harrington, Joey, Det.	330	188	57.0	2021	6.12	12	3.6	86	12	3.6	24	136	72.0
Favre, Brett, G.B.	607	372	61.3	3881	6.39	20	3.3	59	29	4.8	24	170	70.9
Brooks, Aaron, N.O.	431	240	55.7	2882	6.69	13	3.0	66	17	3.9	33	202	70.0
* Orton, Kyle, Chi.	368	190	51.6	1869	5.08	9	2.4	54	13	3.5	30	190	59.7
(Nonqualifiers)													
Schaub, Matt, Atl.	64	33	51.6	495	7.73	4	6.3	53	0	0.0	6	27	98.1
Ramsey, Patrick, Was.	25	15	60.0	279	11.16	1	4.0	72t	1	4.0	4	27	95.3
Weinke, Chris, Car.	13	7	53.8	64	4.92	1	7.7	18	0	0.0	0	0	93.1
Martin, Jamie, St.L	177	124	70.1	1277	7.21	5	2.8	83t	7	4.0	11	78	83.5
Griese, Brian, T.B.	174	112	64.4	1136	6.53	7	4.0	80t	7	4.0	12	76	79.6
Navarre, John, Ariz	24	14	58.3	174	7.25	1	4.2	43	1	4.2	4	27	77.4
Culpepper, Daunte, Min.	216	139	64.4	1564	7.24	6	2.8	68	12	5.6	31	169	72.0
Wallace, Seneca, Sea.	25	13	52.0	173	6.92	1	4.0	42	1	4.0	3	20	70.9
Rattay, Tim, S.F.	97	56	57.7	667	6.88	5	5.2	89t	6	6.2	10	63	70.3
Dorsey, Ken, S.F.	90	48	53.3	481	5.34	2	2.2	44	2	2.2	6	28	66.9
Garcia, Jeff, Det.	173	102	59.0	937	5.42	3	1.7	49	6	3.5	6	34	65.1
Grossman, Rex, Chi.	39	20	51.3	259	6.64	1	2.6	54	2	5.1	1	9	59.7
* Fitzpatrick, Ryan, St.L	135	76	56.3	777	5.76	4	3.0	56t	8	5.9	9	49	58.2
McMahon, Mike, Phi.	207	94	45.4	1158	5.59	5	2.4	48	8	3.9	19	96	55.2
Bouman, Todd, N.O.	122	68	55.7	722	5.92	2	1.6	43	7	5.7	8	59	54.7
* Orlovsky, Dan, Det.	17	7	41.2	63	3.71	0	0.0	20	0	0.0	1	3	51.8
Detmer, Koy, Phi.	56	32	57.1	238	4.25	0	0.0	24	3	5.4	3	15	45.1
* Smith, Alex, S.F.	165	84	50.9	875	5.30	1	0.6	47	11	6.7	29	185	40.8
* Rodgers, Aaron, G.B.	16	9	56.3	65	4.06	0	0.0	16	1	6.3	3	28	39.8
Pickett, Cody, S.F.	35	14	40.0	140	4.00	0	0.0	28	2	5.7	3	16	28.3
(Fewer than 10 attempts)													
* Barber, Marion, Dal.	0	0	—	0	—	0	—	—	0	—	1	3	—
Barber, Tiki, NY-G	1	0	0.0	0	0.00	0	0.0	0	0	0.0	0	0	39.6
Battle, Arnaz, S.F.	2	2	100.0	27	13.50	0	0.0	24	0	0.0	0	0	118.8
Blake, Jeff, Chi.	9	8	88.9	55	6.11	1	11.1	17	0	0.0	0	0	129.2
Boldin, Anquan, Ariz	1	0	0.0	0	0.00	0	0.0	0	0	0.0	0	0	39.6
Fisher, Tony, G.B.	1	1	100.0	14	14.00	0	0.0	14	0	0.0	0	0	118.8
Foster, DeShaun, Car.	1	0	0.0	0	0.00	0	0.0	0	0	0.0	0	0	39.6
* Gado, Samkon, G.B.	1	0	0.0	0	0.00	0	0.0	0	0	0.0	0	0	39.6
Johnson, Keyshawn, Dal.	1	0	0.0	0	0.00	0	0.0	0	0	0.0	0	0	39.6
Maynard, Brad, Chi.	2	1	50.0	18	9.00	0	0.0	18	0	0.0	0	0	81.3
Portis, Clinton, Was.	2	1	50.0	17	8.50	1	50.0	17t	0	0.0	0	0	118.8
Sander, B.J., G.B.	1	1	100.0	4	4.00	0	0.0	4	0	0.0	0	0	83.3
Westbrook, Brian, Phi.	0	0	—	0	—	0	—	—	0	—	1	3	—

*t = Touchdown; * Player that was a rookie in 2005*
Leader based on rating points, minimum 224 attempts

PASS RECEIVING

RECEPTIONS
NFC:	103	Larry Fitzgerald, Arizona
	103	Steve Smith, Carolina
AFC:	97	Chad Johnson, Cincinnati

RECEPTIONS, GAME
AFC:	15	Chris Chambers, Miami vs. Buffalo, December 4 (238 yards, 1 TD)
NFC:	14	Steve Smith, Carolina at Chicago, November 20 (169 yards, 0 TD)

YARDS
NFC:	1563	Steve Smith, Carolina
AFC:	1432	Chad Johnson, Cincinnati

YARDS, GAME
AFC:	238	Chris Chambers, Miami vs. Buffalo, December 4 (15 receptions, 1 TD)
NFC:	204	Plaxico Burress, N.Y. Giants vs. St. Louis, October 2 (10 receptions, 2 TD)

LONGEST
NFC:	91	Terrell Owens (from Donovan McNabb), Philadelphia at Denver, October 30 - TD
AFC:	85	Hines Ward (from Ben Roethlisberger), Pittsburgh vs. New England, September 25 - TD

YARDS PER RECEPTION
AFC:	18.3	Ashley Lelie, Denver
NFC:	18.3	Terry Glenn, Dallas

TOUCHDOWNS
AFC:	12	Marvin Harrison, Indianapolis
NFC:	12	Steve Smith, Carolina

TEAM LEADERS, RECEPTIONS
AFC: BALTIMORE, 86, Derrick Mason; BUFFALO, 81, Eric Moulds; CINCINNATI, 97, Chad Johnson; CLEVELAND, 69, Antonio Bryant; DENVER, 85, Rod Smith; HOUSTON, 63, Andre Johnson; INDIANAPOLIS, 83, Reggie Wayne; JACKSONVILLE, 70, Jimmy Smith; KANSAS CITY, 78, Tony Gonzalez; MIAMI, 82, Chris Chambers; NEW ENGLAND, 78, Deion Branch; N.Y. JETS, 73, Laveranues Coles; OAKLAND, 76, Jerry Porter; PITTSBURGH, 69, Hines Ward; SAN DIEGO, 89, Antonio Gates; TENNESSEE, 58, Drew Bennett

NFC: ARIZONA, 103, Larry Fitzgerald; ATLANTA, 65, Alge Crumpler; CAROLINA, 103, Steve Smith; CHICAGO, 64, Muhsin Muhammad; DALLAS, 71, Keyshawn Johnson; DETROIT, 46, Marcus Pollard; GREEN BAY, 86, Donald Driver; MINNESOTA, 69, Jermaine Wiggins; NEW ORLEANS, 70, Donte' Stallworth; N.Y. GIANTS, 76, Plaxico Burress; PHILADELPHIA, 61, L.J. Smith, Brian Westbrook; ST. LOUIS, 102, Torry Holt; SAN FRANCISCO, 48, Brandon Lloyd; SEATTLE, 67, Bobby Engram; TAMPA BAY, 83, Joey Galloway; WASHINGTON, 84, Santana Moss

Player that was a rookie in 2005

NFL TOP TEN PASS RECEIVERS
	No	Yards	Avg	Long	TD
Fitzgerald, Larry, Ariz	103	1409	13.7	47	10
Smith, Steve, Car.	103	1563	15.2	80t	12
Boldin, Anquan, Ariz	102	1402	13.7	54t	7
Holt, Torry, St.L	102	1331	13.0	44	9
Johnson, Chad, Cin.	97	1432	14.8	70t	9
Gates, Antonio, S.D.	89	1101	12.4	38	10
Driver, Donald, G.B.	86	1221	14.2	59	5
Mason, Derrick, Bal.	86	1073	12.5	39t	3
Smith, Rod, Den.	85	1105	13.0	72	6
Moss, Santana, Was.	84	1483	17.7	78t	9

NFL TOP TEN RECEIVERS BY YARDS
	Yards	No	Avg	Long	TD
Smith, Steve, Car.	1563	103	15.2	80t	12
Moss, Santana, Was.	1483	84	17.7	78t	9
Johnson, Chad, Cin.	1432	97	14.8	70t	9
Fitzgerald, Larry, Ariz	1409	103	13.7	47	10
Boldin, Anquan, Ariz	1402	102	13.7	54t	7
Holt, Torry, St.L	1331	102	13.0	44	9
Galloway, Joey, T.B.	1287	83	15.5	80t	10
Driver, Donald, G.B.	1221	86	14.2	59	5
Burress, Plaxico, NY-G	1214	76	16.0	78t	7
Harrison, Marvin, Ind.	1146	82	14.0	80t	12

AFC—INDIVIDUAL RECEIVERS
	No	Yards	Avg	Long	TD
Johnson, Chad, Cin.	97	1432	14.8	70t	9
Gates, Antonio, S.D.	89	1101	12.4	38	10
Mason, Derrick, Bal.	86	1073	12.5	39t	3
Smith, Rod, Den.	85	1105	13.0	72	6
Wayne, Reggie, Ind.	83	1055	12.7	66t	5
Harrison, Marvin, Ind.	82	1146	14.0	80t	12
Chambers, Chris, Mia.	82	1118	13.6	77t	11
Moulds, Eric, Buf.	81	816	10.1	55t	4
Branch, Deion, N.E.	78	998	12.8	51	5
Houshmandzadeh, T.J., Cin.	78	956	12.3	43t	7
Gonzalez, Tony, K.C.	78	905	11.6	39	2
Porter, Jerry, Oak.	76	942	12.4	49t	5
Heap, Todd, Bal.	75	855	11.4	48	7
Coles, Laveranues, NYJ	73	845	11.6	43	5
Smith, Jimmy, Jac.	70	1023	14.6	45t	6
McCardell, Keenan, S.D.	70	917	13.1	54	9
Jordan, LaMont, Oak.	70	563	8.0	28	2
Bryant, Antonio, Cle.	69	1009	14.6	54	4
Ward, Hines, Pit.	69	975	14.1	85t	11
Kennison, Eddie, K.C.	68	1102	16.2	55	5
Johnson, Andre, Hou.	63	688	10.9	53t	2
Moss, Randy, Oak.	60	1005	16.8	79	8
McMichael, Randy, Mia.	60	582	9.7	30t	5
Givens, David, N.E.	59	738	12.5	40	1
Bennett, Drew, Ten.	58	738	12.7	55t	4
Parker, Eric, S.D.	57	725	12.7	49	3
Kinney, Erron, Ten.	55	543	9.9	27	2
Troupe, Ben, Ten.	55	530	9.6	35	4
Gaffney, Jabar, Hou.	55	492	8.9	29	2
Tomlinson, LaDainian, S.D.	51	370	7.3	41	2
Perry, Chris, Cin.	51	328	6.4	28	2
Evans, Lee, Buf.	48	743	15.5	65	7
* Clayton, Mark, Bal.	44	471	10.7	47t	2
James, Edgerrin, Ind.	44	337	7.7	20	1
McCareins, Justin, NYJ	43	713	16.6	45	2
Heiden, Steve, Cle.	43	401	9.3	62t	3
Lelie, Ashley, Den.	42	770	18.3	56	1
Northcutt, Dennis, Cle.	42	441	10.5	58t	2
Wilford, Ernest, Jac.	41	681	16.6	39	7
Stokley, Brandon, Ind.	41	543	13.2	45	1
Taylor, Chester, Bal.	41	292	7.1	20	1
Booker, Marty, Mia.	39	686	17.6	60t	3

Player	No	Yards	Avg	Long	TD
Brown, Troy, N.E.	39	466	11.9	71	2
* Miller, Heath, Pit.	39	459	11.8	50	6
Droughns, Reuben, Cle.	39	369	9.5	51	0
Davis, Domanick, Hou.	39	337	8.6	33	4
Gabriel, Doug, Oak.	37	554	15.0	38	3
Clark, Dallas, Ind.	37	488	13.2	56	4
Putzier, Jeb, Den.	37	481	13.0	32	0
* Scaife, Bo, Ten.	37	273	7.4	19	2
Parker, Samie, K.C.	36	533	14.8	49	3
* Jones, Matt, Jac.	36	432	12.0	42	5
Randle El, Antwaan, Pit.	35	558	15.9	63t	1
Williams, Reggie, Jac.	35	445	12.7	41	0
Bradford, Corey, Hou.	34	436	12.8	50t	5
Hall, Dante, K.C.	34	436	12.8	52t	3
Johnson, Larry, K.C.	33	343	10.4	36	1
* Edwards, Braylon, Cle.	32	512	16.0	80t	3
Reed, Josh, Buf.	32	449	14.0	51t	2
* Pearman, Alvin, Jac.	32	240	7.5	19	0
* Brown, Ronnie, Mia.	32	232	7.3	38	1
Lewis, Jamal, Bal.	32	191	6.0	15t	1
* Henry, Chris, Cin.	31	422	13.6	47	6
Watson, Ben, N.E.	29	441	15.2	35	4
Welker, Wes, Mia.	29	434	15.0	47	0
Jolley, Doug, NYJ	29	324	11.2	60t	1
Faulk, Kevin, N.E.	29	260	9.0	23	0
Caldwell, Reche, S.D.	28	352	12.6	43	1
McGahee, Willis, Buf.	28	178	6.4	19	0
Sowell, Jerald, NYJ	28	155	5.5	28	2
Wilson, Cedrick, Pit.	26	451	17.3	46	0
Brown, Chris, Ten.	25	327	13.1	57	2
Anderson, Courtney, Oak.	24	303	12.6	36	3
Jackson, Frisman, Cle.	24	287	12.0	68t	1
Rivers, Marcellus, Hou.	24	168	7.0	20	0
Neal, Lorenzo, S.D.	24	145	6.0	21	1
Martin, Curtis, NYJ	24	118	4.9	14	0
* Jones, Brandon, Ten.	23	299	13.0	38t	2
Johnson, Rudi, Cin.	23	90	3.9	15	0
Pass, Patrick, N.E.	22	227	10.3	39	0
Calico, Tyrone, Ten.	22	191	8.7	18	0
Dillon, Corey, N.E.	22	181	8.2	25	1
Wells, Jonathan, Hou.	22	179	8.1	20	0
* Williams, Roydell, Ten.	21	299	14.2	50t	2
* Roby, Courtney, Ten.	21	289	13.8	32	1
Adams, Charlie, Den.	21	203	9.7	21	0
Holmes, Priest, K.C.	21	197	9.4	60t	1
Alexander, Stephen, Den.	21	170	8.1	15	1
Wilcox, Daniel, Bal.	20	154	7.7	17t	1
Dwight, Tim, N.E.	19	332	17.5	59	3
Cotchery, Jerricho, NYJ	19	251	13.2	45	0
Walter, Kevin, Cin.	19	211	11.1	33	1
Campbell, Mark, Buf.	19	139	7.3	27	0
Baker, Tyrone, NYJ	18	269	14.9	47	1
Parker, Willie, Pit.	18	218	12.1	48	1
Anderson, Mike, Den.	18	212	11.8	66t	1
Fletcher, Bryan, Ind.	18	202	11.2	23	3
Schobel, Matt, Cin.	18	193	10.7	28	1
Horn, Chris, K.C.	18	187	10.4	50	0
Brady, Kyle, Jac.	18	157	8.7	33	1
Shea, Aaron, Cle.	18	153	8.5	27	1
Bell, Tatum, Den.	18	104	5.8	14	0
Johnson, Kyle, Den.	17	160	9.4	33	5
Williams, Shaud, Buf.	17	118	6.9	23	0
Williams, Ricky, Mia.	17	93	5.5	19	0
Graham, Daniel, N.E.	16	235	14.7	45t	3
Chrebet, Wayne, NYJ	15	153	10.2	20	0
* Parrish, Roscoe, Buf.	15	148	9.9	28	1
Kelly, Reggie, Cin.	15	90	6.0	16	1
Whitted, Alvis, Oak.	14	183	13.1	26	0
Walters, Troy, Ind.	14	152	10.9	39	3
Wade, Bobby, Chi.-Ten.	14	120	8.6	17	0
Evans, Heath, Mia.-N.E.	14	105	7.5	19	0
Williams, Randal, Oak.	13	164	12.6	34	0
Wrighster, George, Jac.	13	120	9.2	27	2
Henry, Travis, Ten.	13	117	9.0	42	0
Crockett, Zack, Oak.	13	111	8.5	23	0
Shelton, Daimon, Buf.	13	98	7.5	21	1
Taylor, Fred, Jac.	13	83	6.4	13	0
Rhodes, Dominic, Ind.	12	88	7.3	15	0
Johnson, Jeremi, Cin.	12	65	5.4	27t	3
Smith, Terrelle, Cle.	12	58	4.8	9	1
Hymes, Randy, Bal.	11	132	12.0	21	2
Haynes, Verron, Pit.	11	113	10.3	18	0
Peelle, Justin, S.D.	11	38	3.5	11	1
Washington, Kelley, Cin.	10	101	10.1	18t	1
* Morency, Vernand, Hou.	10	87	8.7	16	0
Fleming, Troy, Ten.	10	69	6.9	18	1
Jones, Greg, Jac.	10	65	6.5	10	0
Davis, Andre, N.E.	9	190	21.1	60t	1
Morgan, Quincy, Pit.	9	150	16.7	31t	2
Armstrong, Derick, Hou.	9	115	12.8	28	0
Devoe, Todd, Den.	9	87	9.7	44t	1
Richardson, Tony, K.C.	9	68	7.6	22	1
Boerigter, Marc, K.C.	8	119	14.9	38	0
* Houston, Cedric, NYJ	8	66	8.3	16	0
Fauria, Christian, N.E.	8	57	7.1	18	2
Diamond, Lorenzo, Mia.	8	54	6.8	18	0
Morris, Sammy, Mia.	8	54	6.8	18	0
Moorehead, Aaron, Ind.	7	75	10.7	24	0
Kreider, Dan, Pit.	7	43	6.1	9	0
* Green, Justin, Bal.	7	32	4.6	8	0
Dinkins, Darnell, Bal.	6	55	9.2	15	0
Foschi, John Paul, Oak.	6	37	6.2	11	0
Staley, Duce, Pit.	6	34	5.7	9	0
* Payton, Jarrett, Ten.	6	30	5.0	9	0
Suggs, Lee, Cle.	6	26	4.3	8	0
Gilmore, Bryan, Mia.	5	105	21.0	44t	1
* Mathis, Jerome, Hou.	5	65	13.0	34t	1
Smith, Jonathan, Buf.	5	56	11.2	19	1
Dunn, Jason, K.C.	5	53	10.6	24	0
* Dreessen, Joel, NYJ	5	41	8.2	17	0
Green, William, Cle.	5	30	6.0	14	0
* Wimbush, Derrick, Jac.	5	26	5.2	6	0
Boston, David, Mia.	4	80	20.0	54	0
Johnson, Bethel, N.E.	4	67	16.8	55t	1
Aiken, Sam, Buf.	4	57	14.3	22	0
Morgan, Donovan, Hou.	4	42	10.5	14	0
Bettis, Jerome, Pit.	4	40	10.0	16	0
Stewart, Tony, Cin.	4	26	6.5	10	0
* Perry, Tab, Cin.	4	21	5.3	13	1
* Jackson, Vincent, S.D.	3	59	19.7	21	0
Moore, Clarence, Bal.	3	59	19.7	24	0
Utecht, Ben, Ind.	3	59	19.7	26t	2
Tuman, Jerame, Pit.	3	57	19.0	27	0
Jones, Brian, Jac.	3	49	16.3	41	0
Wilson, Kris, K.C.	3	33	11.0	16	0
* Childress, Brandon, N.E.	3	32	10.7	21	0
Mungro, James, Ind.	3	28	9.3	17	0
Brown, Dee, K.C.	3	23	7.7	9	1
Blaylock, Derrick, NYJ	3	17	5.7	10	0
Dayne, Ron, Den.	3	17	5.7	7	0
Euhus, Tim, Buf.	3	17	5.7	9	0
Toefield, LaBrandon, Jac.	3	17	5.7	11	0
Hankton, Cortez, Jac.	3	15	5.0	8	0
Wright, Jason, Cle.	3	15	5.0	15	0
* Nash, Damien, Ten.	3	14	4.7	7	0
Mughelli, Ovie, Bal.	3	13	4.3	6	0

	No	Yards	Avg	Long	TD
* Sproles, Darren, S.D.	3	10	3.3	6	0
Smith, Musa, Bal.	3	5	1.7	4	0
Vrabel, Mike, N.E.	3	4	1.3	2t	3
Johnson, Pat, Bal.	2	31	15.5	19	0
Murphy, Matt, Hou.	2	26	13.0	14	0
* Ridgeway, Dante, NYJ	2	26	13.0	17	0
Bruener, Mark, Hou.	2	22	11.0	19	0
Duke, Wesley, Den.	2	22	11.0	21	1
Watts, Darius, Den.	2	22	11.0	12	0
Osgood, Kassim, S.D.	2	21	10.5	15	0
Ricard, Alan, Bal.	2	18	9.0	11	0
Sapp, Cecil, Den.	2	17	8.5	12	0
* Irons, Paul, Cle.	2	16	8.0	14	0
* Guenther, Gregg, Ten.	2	13	6.5	8	0
Curry, Ronald, Oak.	2	12	6.0	8	0
Hartsock, Ben, Ind.	2	8	4.0	7	0
Peters, Jason, Buf.	2	5	2.5	4	1
Carswell, Dwayne, Den.	2	3	1.5	2t	2
Nickey, Donnie, Ten.	1	26	26.0	26	0
Burns, Joe, Buf.	1	19	19.0	19t	1
Cruz, Ronnie, K.C.	1	15	15.0	15	0
Askew, B.J., NYJ	1	11	11.0	11	0
Carthon, Ran, Ind.	1	10	10.0	10	0
Fargas, Justin, Oak.	1	9	9.0	9	0
Neufeld, Ryan, Buf.	1	9	9.0	9	0
* Cribbs, Josh, Cle.	1	7	7.0	7	0
Kranchick, Matt, Pit.	1	6	6.0	6	0
* Small, O.J., Ten.	1	6	6.0	6	0
Zereoue, Amos, N.E.	1	5	5.0	5	0
Norris, Moran, Hou.	1	4	4.0	4t	1
* Holmes, Alex, Mia.	1	2	2.0	2	0
Ashworth, Tom, N.E.	1	1	1.0	1t	1
Heller, Will, Mia.	1	1	1.0	1t	1
Minor, Travis, Mia.	1	0	0.0	0	0
Faine, Jeff, Cle.	1	-1	-1.0	-1	0
Manuwai, Vince, Jac.	1	-1	-1.0	-1	0
* Roos, Michael, Ten.	1	-7	-7.0	-7	0

t = Touchdown; * Player that was a rookie in 2005
Leader based on receptions

NFC—INDIVIDUAL RECEIVERS

	No	Yards	Avg	Long	TD
Smith, Steve, Car.	103	1563	15.2	80t	12
Fitzgerald, Larry, Ariz	103	1409	13.7	47	10
Boldin, Anquan, Ariz	102	1402	13.7	54t	7
Holt, Torry, St.L	102	1331	13.0	44	9
Driver, Donald, G.B.	86	1221	14.2	59	5
Moss, Santana, Was.	84	1483	17.7	78t	9
Galloway, Joey, T.B.	83	1287	15.5	80t	10
Burress, Plaxico, NY-G	76	1214	16.0	78t	7
Johnson, Keyshawn, Dal.	71	839	11.8	34	6
Cooley, Chris, Was.	71	774	10.9	32	7
Stallworth, Donte', N.O.	70	945	13.5	43	7
Wiggins, Jermaine, Min.	69	568	8.2	24	1
Engram, Bobby, Sea.	67	778	11.6	56	3
Witten, Jason, Dal.	66	757	11.5	34	6
Shockey, Jeremy, NY-G	65	891	13.7	59	7
Crumpler, Alge, Atl.	65	877	13.5	48	5
Muhammad, Muhsin, Chi.	64	750	11.7	33	4
Glenn, Terry, Dal.	62	1136	18.3	71t	7
Smith, L.J., Phi.	61	682	11.2	48	3
Westbrook, Brian, Phi.	61	616	10.1	62	4
Curtis, Kevin, St.L	60	801	13.4	83t	6
Toomer, Amani, NY-G	60	684	11.4	37	7
Jurevicius, Joe, Sea.	55	694	12.6	52	10
Barber, Tiki, NY-G	54	530	9.8	48	2
Finneran, Brian, Atl.	50	611	12.2	53	2

	No	Yards	Avg	Long	TD
Taylor, Travis, Min.	50	604	12.1	31	4
Horn, Joe, N.O.	49	654	13.3	30	1
Chatman, Antonio, G.B.	49	549	11.2	25	4
Lloyd, Brandon, S.F.	48	733	15.3	89t	5
Lewis, Greg, Phi.	48	561	11.7	34	1
Fisher, Tony, G.B.	48	347	7.2	15	1
Owens, Terrell, Phi.	47	763	16.2	91t	6
McDonald, Shaun, St.L	46	523	11.4	31	0
Pollard, Marcus, Det.	46	516	11.2	86	3
Williams, Roy, Det.	45	687	15.3	51t	8
Stevens, Jerramy, Sea.	45	554	12.3	35t	5
Faulk, Marshall, St.L	44	291	6.6	18	1
* Brown, Reggie, Phi.	43	571	13.3	56t	4
Jackson, Steven, St.L	43	320	7.4	27	2
* Smith, Alex, T.B.	41	367	9.0	24	2
Johnson, Bryant, Ariz	40	432	10.8	41	1
Vines, Scott, Det.	40	417	10.4	40	0
Jackson, Darrell, Sea.	38	482	12.7	48	3
Moore, Mewelde, Min.	37	339	9.2	29	2
Bryson, Shawn, Det.	37	284	7.7	63	0
Bruce, Isaac, St.L	36	525	14.6	46t	3
Jenkins, Michael, Atl.	36	508	14.1	58	3
Pittman, Michael, T.B.	36	300	8.3	41t	1
Hilton, Zach, N.O.	35	396	11.3	29	1
Hilliard, Ike, T.B.	35	282	8.1	22	1
Stecker, Aaron, N.O.	35	281	8.0	41	0
Shipp, Marcel, Ariz	35	255	7.3	28	0
Jones, Julius, Dal.	35	218	6.2	26	0
Hakim, Az-Zahir, N.O.	34	489	14.4	42	2
Foster, DeShaun, Car.	34	372	10.9	47	1
Ayanbadejo, Obafemi, Ariz	34	231	6.8	18	0
Lee, Donald, G.B.	33	294	8.9	27	2
Clayton, Michael, T.B.	32	372	11.6	41	0
Battle, Arnaz, S.F.	32	363	11.3	39	3
Robinson, Marcus, Min.	31	515	16.6	68	5
Gage, Justin, Chi.	31	346	11.2	25	2
Barlow, Kevan, S.F.	31	241	7.8	24	0
Burleson, Nate, Min.	30	328	10.9	20	1
Henderson, William, G.B.	30	264	8.8	32	0
Portis, Clinton, Was.	30	216	7.2	23	0
* White, Roddy, Atl.	29	446	15.4	54t	3
* Williams, Mike, Det.	29	350	12.1	49	1
Dunn, Warrick, Atl.	29	220	7.6	24	1
Hackett, D.J., Sea.	28	400	14.3	47	2
* Bergen, Adam, Ariz	28	270	9.6	32	1
Ferguson, Robert, G.B.	27	366	13.6	51	3
Martin, David, G.B.	27	224	8.3	21t	3
Bennett, Michael, Min.	27	124	4.6	20	2
Jones, Thomas, Chi.	26	143	5.5	41	0
Proehl, Ricky, Car.	25	441	17.6	69	4
Colbert, Keary, Car.	25	282	11.3	42	2
Alstott, Mike, T.B.	25	222	8.9	24	1
Franks, Bubba, G.B.	25	207	8.3	24	1
* Arrington, J.J., Ariz	25	139	5.6	15	0
* Williamson, Troy, Min.	24	372	15.5	56	2
Clark, Desmond, Chi.	24	229	9.5	31	2
Looker, Dane, St.L	23	237	10.3	23	0
Mangum, Kris, Car.	23	202	8.8	24	2
Robinson, Koren, Min.	22	347	15.8	80t	1
Henderson, Devery, N.O.	22	343	15.6	66	3
Crayton, Patrick, Dal.	22	341	15.5	63t	2
Patten, David, Was.	22	217	9.9	32	0
Kleinsasser, Jimmy, Min.	22	171	7.8	15	0
Strong, Mack, Sea.	22	166	7.5	27	0
Morton, Johnnie, S.F.	21	288	13.7	30	0
Pinner, Artose, Det.	21	181	8.6	24	0
Griffith, Justin, Atl.	21	111	5.3	17	3
Jones, Kevin, Det.	20	109	5.5	28	0

	No	Yards	Avg	Long	TD		No	Yards	Avg	Long	TD
* Williams, Carnell, T.B.	20	81	4.1	15	0	Johnson, Bryan, Chi.	5	15	3.0	7	0
Green, Ahman, G.B.	19	147	7.7	20	0	Newhouse, Reggie, Ariz	4	45	11.3	17	0
McMullen, Billy, Phi.	18	268	14.9	38	1	Harris, Arlen, St.L	4	34	8.5	17	0
* Bradley, Mark, Chi.	18	230	12.8	54	0	Blakley, Dwayne, Atl.	4	30	7.5	10	1
* McCoy, LeRon, Ariz	18	191	10.6	24	1	Walker, Javon, G.B.	4	27	6.8	9	0
Royal, Robert, Was.	18	131	7.3	29	1	McKie, Jason, Chi.	4	15	3.8	11	0
* Barber, Marion, Dal.	18	115	6.4	21	0	Thomas, Anthony, Dal.-N.O.	4	13	3.3	6	0
Johnson, Kevin, Det.	17	133	7.8	25	0	* Moats, Ryan, Phi.	4	7	1.8	9	0
McAllister, Deuce, N.O.	17	117	6.9	22	0	Poole, Nate, N.O.	3	63	21.0	42	0
Becht, Anthony, T.B.	16	112	7.0	17	0	Johnson, Teyo, Ariz	3	29	9.7	13	0
* Gore, Frank, S.F.	15	131	8.7	47	0	Campbell, Dan, Dal.	3	24	8.0	18	1
Alexander, Shaun, Sea.	15	78	5.2	9	1	Bush, Steve, S.F.	3	21	7.0	10	0
Rogers, Charles, Det.	14	197	14.1	35t	1	Williams, Roland, St.L	3	21	7.0	12	0
Thrash, James, Was.	14	194	13.9	41	0	Reid, Gabe, Chi.	3	20	6.7	10	0
Goings, Nick, Car.	14	151	10.8	30	0	* Thompson, Tyson, Dal.	3	16	5.3	8	0
Hoover, Brad, Car.	14	87	6.2	12	0	McCrary, Fred, Atl.	3	12	4.0	11	0
Berrian, Bernard, Chi.	13	246	18.9	54	0	Smith, Trent, S.F.	3	7	2.3	6	0
Conwell, Ernie, N.O.	13	165	12.7	31	1	Jackson, James, Ariz	2	31	15.5	19	0
Gardner, Rod, Car.-G.B.	13	151	11.6	33	1	Kozlowski, Brian, Was.	2	26	13.0	18	0
Manumaleuna, Brandon, St.L	13	129	9.9	33	1	White, Dez, Atl.	2	25	12.5	14t	1
Finn, Jim, NY-G	13	98	7.5	15	0	Cartwright, Rock, Was.	2	23	11.5	17	0
Hannam, Ryan, Sea.	13	89	6.8	20	1	Owens, Richard, Min.	2	18	9.0	12	0
Parry, Josh, Phi.	13	89	6.8	13	0	Edwards, Troy, Det.	2	15	7.5	8	0
Gaines, Michael, Car.	12	155	12.9	38	2	Pierce, Brett, Dal.	2	15	7.5	10	0
Edwards, Eric, Ariz	12	133	11.1	63	1	Ward, Derrick, NY-G	2	13	6.5	8	0
Sellers, Mike, Was.	12	72	6.0	19t	7	Beasley, Fred, S.F.	2	12	6.0	6	0
Mahe, Reno, Phi.	12	68	5.7	12	0	Berlin, Eddie, Chi.	2	9	4.5	9	0
Hicks, Maurice, S.F.	12	47	3.9	11	0	Bartrum, Mike, Phi.	2	6	3.0	3t	2
Smith, Antowain, N.O.	12	46	3.8	8	0	Davenport, Najeh, G.B.	2	3	1.5	2	0
Warrick, Peter, Sea.	11	180	16.4	42	0	Robinson, Jeff, St.L	1	28	28.0	28	0
Lee, Charles, Ariz	11	152	13.8	49	0	Williams, Walter, G.B.	1	19	19.0	19	0
Jacobs, Taylor, Was.	11	100	9.1	24	0	Farris, Jimmy, Was.	1	18	18.0	18	0
Gordon, Lamar, Phi.	11	79	7.2	18	0	Pathon, Jerome, Atl.	1	18	18.0	18	0
Carter, Tim, NY-G	10	186	18.6	44	0	Johnson, Robert, Was.	1	14	14.0	14	0
Betts, Ladell, Was.	10	78	7.8	26	1	* Thompson, Dominique, St.L	1	13	13.0	13	0
* Gado, Samkon, G.B.	10	77	7.7	30	1	* Weaver, Leonard, Sea.	1	12	12.0	12	0
Jackson, Terry, S.F.	10	67	6.7	12	0	Angulo, Richard, Min.	1	11	11.0	11	0
Edwards, Marc, Chi.	10	66	6.6	13	2	Cason, Aveion, St.L	1	11	11.0	11	0
Karney, Mike, N.O.	10	61	6.1	10	0	Martinez, Glenn, Det.	1	11	11.0	11	0
Fitzsimmons, Casey, Det.	10	45	4.5	11	1	Copper, Terrance, Dal.	1	5	5.0	5	0
Jones, Terry, S.F.	9	76	8.4	21	0	Lee, ReShard, G.B.	1	5	5.0	5	0
Polite, Lousaka, Dal.	9	72	8.0	15	1	Moore, Dave, T.B.	1	5	5.0	5	0
* Hedgecock, Madison, St.L	9	69	7.7	15	0	Baxter, Jarrod, Ariz	1	4	4.0	4	0
Shiancoe, Visanthe, NY-G	8	91	11.4	17	0	* Benson, Cedric, Chi.	1	3	3.0	3	0
Williams, Moe, Min.	8	52	6.5	25	0	Berton, Sean, NY-G	1	3	3.0	3	0
Schlesinger, Cory, Det.	8	31	3.9	8	1	Bulger, Marc, St.L	1	1	1.0	1	0
Urban, Jerheme, Sea.	7	151	21.6	46	0	Gilmore, John, Chi.	1	1	1.0	1t	1
McAddley, Jason, S.F.	7	125	17.9	38	0	Warner, Kurt, Ariz	1	0	0.0	0	0
Thurman, Andrae, G.B.	7	92	13.1	33	0	* Marshall, Rasheed, S.F.	1	-1	-1.0	0	0
Peterson, Adrian, Chi.	7	48	6.9	18	0	Simms, Chris, T.B.	1	-3	-3.0	-3	0
Cook, Jameel, T.B.	7	43	6.1	11	1	Harrington, Joey, Det.	1	-4	-4.0	-4	0
* Spach, Stephen, Phi.	7	42	6.0	8	0	Vick, Michael, Atl.	1	-14	-14.0	-14	0
Shepherd, Edell, T.B.	6	103	17.2	46	1						
Price, Peerless, Dal.	6	96	16.0	58	0	*t = Touchdown; * Player that was a rookie in 2005*					
Duckett, T.J., Atl.	6	63	10.5	19	0	*Leader based on receptions*					
Smith, Paul, Det.	6	49	8.2	11	0						
Hall, Lamont, N.O.	6	36	6.0	8	0						
Carter, Drew, Car.	5	103	20.6	40	1						
McCants, Darnerien, Phi.	5	87	17.4	22	0						
Lewis, Chad, Phi.	5	64	12.8	17	0						
* Bajema, Billy, S.F.	5	54	10.8	24	0						
Tyree, David, NY-G	5	52	10.4	18	1						
Morris, Maurice, Sea.	5	48	9.6	20	0						
Davis, Stephen, Car.	5	45	9.0	21	0						
* Murphy, Terrence, G.B.	5	36	7.2	12	0						
Hetherington, Chris, S.F.	5	26	5.2	11	0						
Leach, Vonta, G.B.	5	19	3.8	9	0						
Cleeland, Cameron, St.L	5	17	3.4	9t	1						

INTERCEPTIONS

INTERCEPTIONS

AFC:	10	Ty Law, N.Y. Jets
	10	Deltha O'Neal, Cincinnati
NFC:	9	Darren Sharper, Minnesota

INTERCEPTIONS, GAME

AFC:	3	Deltha O'Neal, Cincinnati vs. Minnesota, September 18 (27 yards, 0 TD)
	3	Greg Wesley, Kansas City vs. New England, November 27 (26 yards, 0 TD)
	3	Ty Law, N.Y. Jets vs. Buffalo, January 1 (56 yards, 0 TD)
NFC:	3	Darren Sharper, Minnesota at N.Y. Giants, November 13 (123 yards, 1 TD)
	3	Ronde Barber, Tampa Bay at New Orleans, December 4 (70 yards, 0 TD)

*Player that was a rookie in 2005

YARDS

NFC:	276	Darren Sharper, Minnesota
AFC:	195	Ty Law, N.Y. Jets

LONGEST

NFC:	95	Nick Barnett, Green Bay vs. New Orleans, October 9 - TD
	95	Charles Tillman, Chicago vs. Green Bay, December 4
AFC:	80	* Darrent Williams, Denver at Oakland, November 13 - TD

TOUCHDOWNS

AFC:	2	Champ Bailey, Denver
	2	Clinton Hart, San Diego
	2	Cato June, Indianapolis
NFC:	2	Karlos Dansby, Arizona
	2	Darren Sharper, Minnesota

TEAM LEADERS, INTERCEPTIONS;

AFC: BALTIMORE, 2, Deion Sanders, Terrell Suggs, Adalius Thomas; BUFFALO, 4, Terrence McGee, Troy Vincent; CINCINNATI, 10, Deltha O'Neal; CLEVELAND, 3, Leigh Bodden, Brian Russell; DENVER, 8, Champ Bailey; HOUSTON, 2, Glenn Earl; INDIANAPOLIS, 5, Cato June; JACKSONVILLE, 5, Rashean Mathis; KANSAS CITY, 6, Greg Wesley; MIAMI, 4, Lance Schulters; NEW ENGLAND, 3, *Ellis Hobbs, Asante Samuel; N.Y. JETS, 10, Ty Law; OAKLAND, 2, Stuart Schweigert; PITTSBURGH, 3, Chris Hope; SAN DIEGO, 3, Bhawoh Jue; TENNESSEE, 3, *Reynaldo Hill

NFC: ARIZONA, 3, Karlos Dansby; ATLANTA, 6, DeAngelo Hall; CAROLINA, 7, Chris Gamble; CHICAGO, 8, Nathan Vasher; DALLAS, 4, Aaron Glenn; DETROIT, 6, Dre' Bly; GREEN BAY, 3, Al Harris; MINNESOTA, 9, Darren Sharper; NEW ORLEANS, 3, Jason Craft; N.Y. GIANTS, 4, Brent Alexander; PHILADELPHIA, 4, Sheldon Brown; ST. LOUIS, 4, Mike Furrey; SAN FRANCISCO, 4, Mike Adams, Shawntae Spencer; SEATTLE, 4, Michael Boulware; TAMPA BAY, 5, Ronde Barber; WASHINGTON, 4, Lemar Marshall

TEAM CHAMPION

AFC:	31	Cincinnati
NFC:	24	Chicago
	24	Minnesota

NFL TOP TEN INTERCEPTORS

	No	Yards	Avg	Long	TD
Law, Ty, NYJ	10	195	19.5	74t	1
O'Neal, Deltha, Cin.	10	103	10.3	37	0
Sharper, Darren, Min.	9	276	30.7	92t	2
Bailey, Champ, Den.	8	139	17.4	65t	2
Vasher, Nathan, Chi.	8	145	18.1	46	1
Gamble, Chris, Car.	7	157	22.4	61t	1
Bly, Dre', Det.	6	54	9.0	28	0
Hall, DeAngelo, Atl.	6	177	29.5	65	0
Lucas, Ken, Car.	6	70	11.7	32	0
Wesley, Greg, K.C.	6	106	17.7	51	0

AFC—INDIVIDUAL INTERCEPTORS

	No	Yards	Avg	Long	TD
Law, Ty, NYJ	10	195	19.5	74t	1
O'Neal, Deltha, Cin.	10	103	10.3	37	0
Bailey, Champ, Den.	8	139	17.4	65t	2
Wesley, Greg, K.C.	6	106	17.7	51	0
June, Cato, Ind.	5	115	23.0	36	2
Mathis, Rashean, Jac.	5	79	15.8	41t	1
Ferguson, Nick, Den.	5	59	11.8	30	0
* Thurman, Odell, Cin.	5	59	11.8	30t	1
Barrett, David, NYJ	5	28	5.6	13	0
James, Tory, Cin.	5	5	1.0	5	0
McGee, Terrence, Buf.	4	97	24.3	46t	1
Schulters, Lance, Mia.	4	78	19.5	37	0
Vincent, Troy, Buf.	4	78	19.5	42	0
Surtain, Patrick, K.C.	4	57	14.3	53	0
Cousin, Terry, Jac.	4	18	4.5	14	0
* Hill, Reynaldo, Ten.	3	88	29.3	52t	1
Hope, Chris, Pit.	3	60	20.0	55	0
Peterson, Mike, Jac.	3	54	18.0	26t	1
Ratliff, Keiwan, Cin.	3	52	17.3	35	0
Brackett, Gary, Ind.	3	50	16.7	31	0
Russell, Brian, Cle.	3	50	16.7	37	0
Harper, Nick, Ind.	3	41	13.7	21	0
Tillman, Travares, Mia.	3	38	12.7	22	0
Grant, Deon, Jac.	3	29	9.7	29	0
Jue, Bhawoh, S.D.	3	28	9.3	20	0
Samuel, Asante, N.E.	3	15	5.0	15	0
Kaesviharn, Kevin, Cin.	3	9	3.0	6	0
* Hobbs, Ellis, N.E.	3	8	2.7	8	0
Bodden, Leigh, Cle.	3	6	2.0	6	0
* Williams, Darrent, Den.	2	108	54.0	80t	1
Sanders, Deion, Bal.	2	57	28.5	33	0
Brown, Mark, NYJ	2	51	25.5	33t	1
Thomas, Adalius, Bal.	2	48	24.0	28	1
Polamalu, Troy, Pit.	2	42	21.0	36	0
Suggs, Terrell, Bal.	2	38	19.0	38	0
Crocker, Chris, Cle.	2	35	17.5	24	0
Schweigert, Stuart, Oak.	2	35	17.5	33	0
Townsend, Deshea, Pit.	2	26	13.0	26	0
* Foxworth, Domonique, Den.	2	23	11.5	23	0
Vrabel, Mike, N.E.	2	23	11.5	24t	1
Bulluck, Keith, Ten.	2	16	8.0	16	0
Edwards, Donnie, S.D.	2	15	7.5	14	0
Simmons, Brian, Cin.	2	15	7.5	16	0
McCutcheon, Daylon, Cle.	2	14	7.0	14	0
David, Jason, Ind.	2	13	6.5	13	0
Knight, Sammy, K.C.	2	12	6.0	12	0
Madison, Sam, Mia.	2	11	5.5	11	0
Baxter, Gary, Cle.	2	10	5.0	10	0
Porter, Joey, Pit.	2	9	4.5	9	0
Doss, Mike, Ind.	2	8	4.0	8	0
Coleman, Erik, NYJ	2	4	2.0	4	0
Wright, Kenny, Jac.	2	4	2.0	4	0
Crowell, Angelo, Buf.	2	3	1.5	2	0
Earl, Glenn, Hou.	2	2	1.0	2	0
Lynch, John, Den.	2	2	1.0	1	0

	No	Yards	Avg	Long	TD		No	Yards	Avg	Long	TD
Clements, Nate, Buf.	2	0	0.0	0	0	Bly, Dre', Det.	6	54	9.0	28	0
McCleon, Dexter, K.C.	2	0	0.0	0	0	Tillman, Charles, Chi.	5	172	34.4	95	1
Hart, Clinton, S.D.	1	110	110.0	70t	2	Barber, Ronde, T.B.	5	105	21.0	42	0
Warfield, Eric, K.C.	1	57	57.0	57t	1	Furrey, Mike, St.L	4	143	35.8	67t	1
Cox, Curome, Den.	1	48	48.0	48	0	Boulware, Michael, Sea.	4	107	26.8	40	0
* Sanders, James, N.E.	1	39	39.0	39t	1	Spencer, Shawntae, S.F.	4	85	21.3	61t	1
Sanders, Lewis, Hou.	1	29	29.0	29	0	Brown, Sheldon, Phi.	4	67	16.8	40t	1
Harrison, James, Pit.	1	25	25.0	25	0	Williams, Brian, Min.	4	59	14.8	31	0
Reed, Ed, Bal.	1	23	23.0	23	0	Marshall, Lemar, Was.	4	55	13.8	27	1
Kassell, Brad, Ten.	1	21	21.0	21t	1	Brooking, Keith, Atl.	4	50	12.5	22	0
Fletcher, London, Buf.	1	20	20.0	20	0	Alexander, Brent, NY-G	4	45	11.3	24	0
Fletcher, Jamar, S.D.	1	19	19.0	19	0	Adams, Mike, S.F.	4	36	9.0	40t	1
Baker, Rashad, Buf.	1	18	18.0	18	0	Kelly, Brian, T.B.	4	19	4.8	14	0
Kelsay, Chris, Buf.	1	17	17.0	17	0	Glenn, Aaron, Dal.	4	10	2.5	10	0
Gardner, Gilbert, Ind.	1	16	16.0	16	0	Winfield, Antoine, Min.	4	5	1.3	4	0
* Jackson, Marlin, Ind.	1	16	16.0	16	0	Brown, Mike, Chi.	3	116	38.7	72	1
Ohalete, Ifeanyi, Cin.	1	15	15.0	15	0	Henry, Anthony, Dal.	3	102	34.0	58t	1
Colclough, Ricardo, Pit.	1	14	14.0	14	0	McCree, Marlon, Car.	3	73	24.3	46	0
Davis, Andra, Cle.	1	14	14.0	14	0	Sheppard, Lito, Phi.	3	72	24.0	34	0
Jammer, Quentin, S.D.	1	14	14.0	14	0	Craft, Jason, N.O.	3	63	21.0	39	0
Williams, Chad, Bal.	1	14	14.0	14	0	Babineaux, Jordan, Sea.	3	56	18.7	25	0
Rolle, Samari, Bal.	1	11	11.0	11	0	* Tatupu, Lofa, Sea.	3	55	18.3	38t	1
Wilhelm, Matt, S.D.	1	10	10.0	10	0	Williams, Roy, Dal.	3	52	17.3	46t	1
Florence, Drayton, S.D.	1	9	9.0	9	0	* Harris, Chris, Chi.	3	44	14.7	44	0
Coleman, Marcus, Hou.	1	6	6.0	6	0	Dansby, Karlos, Ariz	3	31	10.3	18t	2
* Brown, C.C., Hou.	1	5	5.0	5	0	Harris, Al, G.B.	3	30	10.0	22t	1
Howard, Reggie, Mia.	1	5	5.0	5	0	Allen, Will, T.B.	3	26	8.7	26	0
* Daniels, Travis, Mia.	1	4	4.0	4	0	Dawkins, Brian, Phi.	3	24	8.0	24	0
Carter, Tyrone, Pit.	1	3	3.0	3	0	Goodman, Andre', Det.	3	17	5.7	21	0
Evans, Troy, Hou.	1	3	3.0	3	0	Hood, Roderick, Phi.	3	17	5.7	17	0
Sapp, Warren, Oak.	1	3	3.0	3	0	Newman, Terence, Dal.	3	16	5.3	12	0
Woolfolk, Andre, Ten.	1	3	3.0	3	0	Clark, Ryan, Was.	3	10	3.3	6	0
Williams, Madieu, Cin.	1	2	2.0	2	0	Macklin, David, Ariz	2	79	39.5	60t	1
* Pool, Brodney, Cle.	1	1	1.0	1	0	Kennedy, Kenoy, Det.	2	64	32.0	64t	1
Robinson, Dunta, Hou.	1	1	1.0	1	0	Smith, Dwight, N.O.	2	53	26.5	28	0
Vilma, Jonathan, NYJ	1	1	1.0	1	0	Holt, Terrence, Det.	2	51	25.5	51	0
Williams, Tank, Ten.	1	1	1.0	1	0	Tate, Robert, Ariz	2	47	23.5	25	0
Bell, Yeremiah, Mia.	1	0	0.0	0	0	Bolden, Juran, T.B.	2	46	23.0	28	0
Cooper, Deke, Jac.	1	0	0.0	0	0	Pierce, Antonio, NY-G	2	41	20.5	24	0
Hill, Renaldo, Oak.	1	0	0.0	0	0	Carroll, Ahmad, G.B.	2	38	19.0	38	0
Lewis, Ray, Bal.	1	0	0.0	0	0	Wallace, Al, Car.	2	38	19.0	38	0
McAlister, Chris, Bal.	1	0	0.0	0	0	Wilson, Gibril, NY-G	2	36	18.0	19	0
* McFadden, Bryant, Pit.	1	0	0.0	0	0	Tinoisamoa, Pisa, St.L	2	35	17.5	20	0
Milloy, Lawyer, Buf.	1	0	0.0	0	0	Witherspoon, Will, Car.	2	35	17.5	35t	1
Mitchell, Kawika, K.C.	1	0	0.0	0	0	Parrish, Tony, S.F.	2	34	17.0	34t	1
* Rhodes, Kerry, NYJ	1	0	0.0	0	0	Taylor, Sean, Was.	2	34	17.0	32	0
Sanders, Bob, Ind.	1	0	0.0	0	0	Williams, Shaun, NY-G	2	34	17.0	34	0
Schobel, Aaron, Buf.	1	0	0.0	0	0	Briggs, Lance, Chi.	2	30	15.0	20	1
Smith, Aaron, Pit.	1	0	0.0	0	0	McQuarters, R.W., Det.	2	25	12.5	19	0
Smith, Daryl, Jac.	1	0	0.0	0	0	Darling, James, Ariz	2	22	11.0	15	0
Spragan, Donnie, Mia.	1	0	0.0	0	0	Manning, Ricky, Car.	2	20	10.0	10	0
Stewart, Matt, Cle.	1	0	0.0	0	0	Roman, Mark, G.B.	2	18	9.0	12	0
Taylor, Ike, Pit.	1	0	0.0	0	0	* Butler, James, NY-G	2	16	8.0	16	0
Thomas, Zach, Mia.	1	0	0.0	0	0	* Rogers, Carlos, Was.	2	14	7.0	14	0
Thompson, Lamont, Ten.	1	0	0.0	0	0	Lewis, Michael, Phi.	2	13	6.5	13	0
Thornton, John, Cin.	1	0	0.0	0	0	Herndon, Kelly, Sea.	2	12	6.0	10	0
Wilson, Eugene, N.E.	1	0	0.0	0	0	Williams, Demorrio, Atl.	2	6	3.0	6	0
Woodson, Charles, Oak.	1	0	0.0	0	0	Williams, Jimmy, Sea.	2	6	3.0	6	0
						Thomas, Fred, N.O.	2	4	2.0	4	0
						Carpenter, Keion, Atl.	2	1	0.5	1	0
						Chavous, Corey, Min.	2	0	0.0	0	0
						Groce, DeJuan, St.L	2	0	0.0	0	0

*t = Touchdown; * Player that was a rookie in 2005*
Leader based on interceptions

	No	Yards	Avg	Long	TD
Smoot, Fred, Min.	2	0	0.0	0	0
Thornton, Bruce, S.F.	2	0	0.0	0	0

NFC—INDIVIDUAL INTERCEPTORS

	No	Yards	Avg	Long	TD		No	Yards	Avg	Long	TD
Sharper, Darren, Min.	9	276	30.7	92t	2	Barnett, Nick, G.B.	1	95	95.0	95t	1
Vasher, Nathan, Chi.	8	145	18.1	46	1	Archuleta, Adam, St.L	1	85	85.0	85t	1
Gamble, Chris, Car.	7	157	22.4	61t	1	Dyson, Andre, Sea.	1	72	72.0	72t	1
Hall, DeAngelo, Atl.	6	177	29.5	65	0	Walker, Frank, NY-G	1	71	71.0	71	0
Lucas, Ken, Car.	6	70	11.7	32	0	* Bullocks, Josh, N.O.	1	51	51.0	51	0

	No	Yards	Avg	Long	TD
* Edwards, Dovonte, Min.	1	51	51.0	51t	1
Minter, Mike, Car.	1	47	47.0	47	0
* Atogwe, O.J., St.L	1	42	42.0	42	0
Washington, Marcus, Was.	1	41	41.0	41	0
* Emanuel, Ben, S.F.	1	38	38.0	35	0
Torbor, Reggie, NY-G	1	37	37.0	37	0
Wilson, Adrian, Ariz	1	36	36.0	36	0
Bailey, Boss, Det.	1	34	34.0	34t	1
* Blackburn, Chase, NY-G	1	31	31.0	31t	1
* Rolle, Antrel, Ariz	1	29	29.0	29	0
Hawthorne, Michael, St.L	1	24	24.0	24	0
Thomas, Robert, G.B.	1	24	24.0	24	0
Walker, Bracy, Det.	1	22	22.0	22	0
Jackson, Dexter, T.B.	1	21	21.0	21	0
Lehman, Teddy, Det.	1	21	21.0	17	0
Deloatch, Curtis, NY-G	1	20	20.0	20	0
* Patterson, Dimitri, Was.	1	20	20.0	20	0
Wayne, Nate, Det.	1	20	20.0	20	0
Ivy, Corey, St.L	1	19	19.0	19	0
Webster, Jason, Atl.	1	19	19.0	19	0
Coakley, Dexter, St.L	1	16	16.0	16	0
Scott, Bryan, Atl.	1	15	15.0	15	0
Dockett, Darnell, Ariz	1	14	14.0	14	0
Green, Michael, Chi.	1	14	14.0	14	0
* Green, Eric, Ariz	1	13	13.0	13	0
Smith, Derek M., S.F.	1	13	13.0	13	0
Moore, Brandon, S.F.	1	12	12.0	12	0
Griffith, Robert, Ariz	1	11	11.0	11	0
McKenzie, Mike, N.O.	1	11	11.0	11	0
Nguyen, Dat, Dal.	1	7	7.0	7	0
Trufant, Marcus, Sea.	1	7	7.0	7	0
Emmons, Carlos, NY-G	1	6	6.0	6	0
Rice, Simeon, T.B.	1	6	6.0	6	0
Huff, Orlando, Ariz	1	3	3.0	3	0
Scott, Ian, Chi.	1	3	3.0	3	0
Lewis, Keith, S.F.	1	2	2.0	2	0
Springs, Shawn, Was.	1	2	2.0	2	0
Trotter, Jeremiah, Phi.	1	2	2.0	2	0
Newman, Keith, Min.	1	1	1.0	1	0
Brooks, Derrick, T.B.	1	0	0.0	0	0
* Collins, Nick, G.B.	1	0	0.0	0	0
Griffin, Cornelius, Was.	1	0	0.0	0	0
Harris, Walt, Was.	1	0	0.0	0	0
Hillenmeyer, Hunter, Chi.	1	0	0.0	0	0
Jones, Dhani, Phi.	1	0	0.0	0	0
Offord, Willie, Min.	1	0	0.0	0	0
Singleton, Alshermond, Dal.	1	0	0.0	0	0
Slaughter, T.J., N.O.	1	0	0.0	0	0
Allen, Will, NY-G	0	17	—	17	0

t = Touchdown; * Player that was a rookie in 2005
Leader based on interceptions

AMERICAN FOOTBALL CONFERENCE—INTERCEPTIONS

	No	Yards	Avg	Long	TD
Cincinnati	31	260	8.4	37	1
N.Y. Jets	21	279	13.3	74t	2
Denver	20	379	19.0	80t	3
Jacksonville	19	184	9.7	41t	2
Indianapolis	18	259	14.4	36	2
Buffalo	17	233	13.7	46t	1
Kansas City	16	232	14.5	57t	1
Cleveland	15	130	8.7	37	0
Pittsburgh	15	179	11.9	55	0
Miami	14	136	9.7	37	0
Baltimore	11	191	17.4	48	1
New England	10	85	8.5	39t	2
San Diego	10	205	20.5	70t	2
Tennessee	9	129	14.3	52t	2
Houston	7	46	6.6	29	0
Oakland	5	38	7.6	33	0
AFC Total	238	2965	12.5	80t	19
AFC Average	14.9	185.3	12.5	—	1.2

NATIONAL FOOTBALL CONFERENCE—INTERCEPTIONS

	No	Yards	Avg	Long	TD
Chicago	24	524	21.8	95	4
Minnesota	24	392	16.3	92t	3
Carolina	23	440	19.1	61t	2
Detroit	19	308	16.2	64t	2
N.Y. Giants	17	354	20.8	71	1
Philadelphia	17	195	11.5	40t	1
Tampa Bay	17	223	13.1	42	0
Atlanta	16	268	16.8	65	0
San Francisco	16	220	13.8	61t	3
Seattle	16	315	19.7	72t	2
Washington	16	176	11.0	41	1
Arizona	15	285	19.0	60t	3
Dallas	15	187	12.5	58t	2
St. Louis	13	364	28.0	85t	2
Green Bay	10	205	20.5	95t	2
New Orleans	10	182	18.2	51	0
NFC Total	268	4638	17.3	95	28
NFC Average	16.8	289.9	17.3	—	1.8
League Total	506	7603	—	95	47
League Average	15.8	237.6	15.0	—	1.5

KICKOFF RETURNS

YARDS PER RETURN
AFC:	30.2	Terrence McGee, Buffalo
NFC:	26.0	Koren Robinson, Minnesota

YARDS
AFC:	1752	* Chris Carr, Oakland
NFC:	1456	Reggie Swinton, Arizona

YARDS, GAME
AFC:	266	* Jerome Mathis, Houston vs. Indianapolis, October 23 (7 returns, 1 TD)
	266	* Jerome Mathis, Houston vs. Kansas City, November 20 (7 returns, 1 TD)
NFC:	202	Chris Johnson, St. Louis vs. Seattle, October 9 (6 returns, 1 TD)

LONGEST
AFC:	99	* Jerome Mathis, Houston vs. Kansas City, November 20 - TD
	99	Terrence McGee, Buffalo at Cincinnati, December 24 - TD
NFC:	99	Chris Johnson, St. Louis vs. Seattle, October 9 - TD

RETURNS
AFC:	73	* Chris Carr, Oakland
NFC:	63	Reggie Swinton, Arizona

RETURNS, GAME
AFC:	8	Dante Hall, Kansas City vs. Philadelphia, October 2 (234 yards, 1 TD)
	8	* Tab Perry, Cincinnati vs. Indianapolis, November 20 (181 yards, 0 TD)
	8	B.J. Sams, Baltimore at Cincinnati, November 27 (145 yards, 0 TD)
NFC:	8	Chris Johnson, St. Louis at Indianapolis, October 17 (151 yards, 0 TD)
	8	Maurice Hicks, San Francisco at Washington, October 23 (133 yards, 0 TD)
	8	Allen Rossum, Atlanta vs. Green Bay, November 13 (156 yards, 0 TD)
	8	* DeAndra Cobb, Atlanta vs. Carolina, January 1 (181 yards, 0 TD)

TOUCHDOWNS
AFC:	2	* Jerome Mathis, Houston
NFC:	1	Ladell Betts, Washington
	1	Antonio Brown, Washington
	1	Chris Johnson, St. Louis
	1	Willie Ponder, N.Y. Giants
	1	Koren Robinson, Minnesota

TEAM CHAMPION
AFC:	26.6	Buffalo
NFC:	24.3	N.Y. Giants

NFL TOP TEN KICKOFF RETURNERS
	No	Yards	Avg	Long	TD
McGee, Terrence, Buf.	46	1391	30.2	99t	1
* Mathis, Jerome, Hou.	54	1542	28.6	99t	2
* Miller, Justin, NYJ	60	1577	26.3	95t	1
* Jones, Pacman, Ten.	43	1127	26.2	85	0
Robinson, Koren, Min.	47	1221	26.0	86t	1
Betts, Ladell, Was.	24	621	25.9	94t	1
Ponder, Willie, NY-G	35	905	25.9	95t	1
Morgan, Quincy, Pit.	23	583	25.3	74	0
* Thompson, Tyson, Dal.	57	1399	24.5	49	0
* Wimbush, Derrick, Jac.	39	955	24.5	91t	1

AFC—INDIVIDUAL KICKOFF RETURNERS
	No	Yards	Avg	Long	TD
McGee, Terrence, Buf.	46	1391	30.2	99t	1
* Mathis, Jerome, Hou.	54	1542	28.6	99t	2
* Miller, Justin, NYJ	60	1577	26.3	95t	1
* Jones, Pacman, Ten.	43	1127	26.2	85	0
Morgan, Quincy, Pit.	23	583	25.3	74	0
* Wimbush, Derrick, Jac.	39	955	24.5	91t	1
* Perry, Tab, Cin.	64	1562	24.4	94	0
* Cribbs, Josh, Cle.	45	1094	24.3	90t	1
* Sproles, Darren, S.D.	63	1528	24.3	58	0
* Carr, Chris, Oak.	73	1752	24.0	62	0
Hall, Dante, K.C.	65	1560	24.0	96t	1
Sams, B.J., Bal.	44f	998	22.7	87	0
Welker, Wes, Mia.	61	1379	22.6	46	0
* Roby, Courtney, Ten.	22	495	22.5	59	0
Johnson, Bethel, N.E.	31	694	22.4	54	0
* Morency, Vernand, Hou.	20	437	21.9	31	0
Colclough, Ricardo, Pit.	22	473	21.5	63	0
Rhodes, Dominic, Ind.	41	855	20.9	39	0
(Nonqualifiers)					
* Williams, Darrent, Den.	18	431	23.9	36	0
* Hobbs, Ellis, N.E.	15	361	24.1	37	0
Alexander, Roc, Den.	12	261	21.8	31	0
Taylor, Chester, Bal.	12	253	21.1	45	0
* Parrish, Roscoe, Buf.	10	261	26.1	45	0
Dwight, Tim, N.E.	10	250	25.0	38	0
Adams, Charlie, Den.	10	218	21.8	32	0
* Pearman, Alvin, Jac.	8	187	23.4	34	0
Smith, Jonathan, Buf.	5	124	24.8	44	0
Droughns, Reuben, Cle.	5	119	23.8	35	0
Wells, Jonathan, Hou.	5	106	21.2	40	0
Carthon, Ran, Ind.	5	92	18.4	25	0
Green, William, Cle.	5	79	15.8	22	0
Cotchery, Jerricho, NYJ	4	105	26.3	30	0
Faulk, Kevin, N.E.	4	81	20.3	26	0
Reed, Josh, Buf.	4	69	17.3	24	0
Gabriel, Doug, Oak.	4	64	16.0	21	0
Davis, Andre, N.E.	3	108	36.0	65	0
Caldwell, Reche, S.D.	3	99	33.0	60	0
Gilmore, Bryan, Mia.	3	84	28.0	29	0
* Perkins, Antonio, Cle.	3	82	27.3	35	0
Taylor, Ike, Pit.	3	59	19.7	24	0
Wilson, Cedrick, Pit.	3	53	17.7	29	0
McIntyre, Corey, Cle.	3	47	15.7	17	0
Burns, Joe, Buf.	3	46	15.3	19	0
Neufeld, Ryan, Buf.	3	39	13.0	23	0
Horn, Chris, K.C.	3	31	10.3	11	0
Shea, Aaron, Cle.	3	29	9.7	13	0
Hollings, Tony, Hou.	2	46	23.0	28	0
Mungro, James, Ind.	2	39	19.5	22	0
Pass, Patrick, N.E.	2	31	15.5	21	0
Sapp, Cecil, Den.	2	28	14.0	20	0
Shelton, Daimon, Buf.	2	26	13.0	16	0
* Payton, Jarrett, Ten.	2	24	12.0	24	0
Smith, Terrelle, Cle.	2	24	12.0	13	0
Keisel, Brett, Pit.	2	23	11.5	12	0
Minor, Travis, Mia.	2	22	11.0	19	0
* Houston, Cedric, NYJ	2	18	9.0	18	0
White, Jamel, Bal.	2	18	9.0	9	0
Flemister, Zeron, Oak.	2	16	8.0	8	0
Baker, Chris, NYJ	2	11	5.5	11	0
Schobel, Matt, Cin.	2	4	2.0	4	0
* Leonhard, Jim, Buf.	1	36	36.0	36	0
Alexis, Rich, Jac.	1	31	31.0	31	0
Davis, Domanick, Hou.	1	29	29.0	29	0
Brady, Kyle, Jac.	1	24	24.0	24	0
Pinnock, Andrew, S.D.	1	24	24.0	24	0
Anderson, Mike, Den.	1	18	18.0	18	0
Blaylock, Derrick, NYJ	1	17	17.0	17	0

2005 INDIVIDUAL STATISTICS—KICKOFF RETURNS

	No	Yards	Avg	Long	TD
Wright, Jason, Cle.	1	17	17.0	17	0
Parker, Eric, S.D.	1	16	16.0	16	0
Randle El, Antwaan, Pit.	1	16	16.0	16	0
Cloud, Mike, N.E.	1	15	15.0	15	0
Jackson, Frisman, Cle.	1	15	15.0	15	0
Banta-Cain, Tully, N.E.	1	14	14.0	14	0
O'Neal, Deltha, Cin.	1	14	14.0	14	0
Walters, Troy, Ind.	1	13	13.0	13	0
Bruener, Mark, Hou.	1	11	11.0	11	0
Heller, Will, Mia.	1	11	11.0	11	0
Jefferson, Joseph, Ind.	1	11	11.0	11	0
Dinkins, Darnell, Bal.	1f	10	10.0	10	0
* Green, Justin, Bal.	1	10	10.0	10	0
Fleming, Troy, Ten.	1	9	9.0	9	0
Johnson, Kyle, Den.	1	8	8.0	8	0
Utecht, Ben, Ind.	1	7	7.0	7	0
Veal, Demetrin, Den.	1	6	6.0	6	0
Bowens, David, Mia.	1	5	5.0	5	0
Engelberger, John, Den.	1f	5	5.0	5	0
Kreider, Dan, Pit.	1	3	3.0	3	0
Norris, Moran, Hou.	1	2	2.0	2	0
Watson, Ben, N.E.	1	1	1.0	1	0
Barrett, David, NYJ	1	0	0.0	0	0
Carswell, Dwayne, Den.	1	0	0.0	0	0
Euhus, Tim, Buf.	1	0	0.0	0	0
Hulsey, Corey, Oak.	1	0	0.0	0	0
Izzo, Larry, N.E.	1	0	0.0	0	0
Jones, Greg, Jac.	1	0	0.0	0	0
Lawton, Luke, NYJ	1	0	0.0	0	0
Stone, Michael, N.E.	1	0	0.0	0	0
Turner, Michael, S.D.	1	0	0.0	0	0
Harrison, James, Pit.	1	-2	-2.0	-2	0
McCareins, Justin, NYJ	0f	0	—	—	0

t = Touchdown; * Player that was a rookie in 2005
f = Fair Catch
Leader based on average return, minimum 20 returns

NFC—INDIVIDUAL KICKOFF RETURNERS

	No	Yards	Avg	Long	TD
Robinson, Koren, Min.	47	1221	26.0	86t	1
Betts, Ladell, Was.	24	621	25.9	94t	1
Ponder, Willie, NY-G	35	905	25.9	95t	1
* Thompson, Tyson, Dal.	57	1399	24.5	49	0
Hood, Roderick, Phi.	38	900	23.7	53	0
Morton, Chad, NY-G	24	559	23.3	41	0
Swinton, Reggie, Ariz	63	1456	23.1	90	0
Rossum, Allen, Atl.	31	702	22.6	47	0
Johnson, Chris, St.L	38	857	22.6	99t	1
Scobey, Josh, Sea.	59	1326	22.5	53	0
McAfee, Fred, N.O.	22	485	22.0	34	0
Azumah, Jerry, Chi.	32	705	22.0	40	0
Drummond, Eddie, Det.	49	1077	22.0	48	0
Stecker, Aaron, N.O.	31	672	21.7	46	0
Smart, Rod, Car.	29	615	21.2	60	0
Shepherd, Edell, T.B.	20	414	20.7	30	0
Allen, David, St.L	23	472	20.5	32	0
Hicks, Maurice, S.F.	34	689	20.3	40	0
Cox, Torrie, T.B.	24	464	19.3	30	0
* Marshall, Rasheed, S.F.	26	488	18.8	29	0
(Nonqualifiers)					
Brown, Antonio, Was.	19	439	23.1	91t	1
Carroll, Ahmad, G.B.	19	390	20.5	57	0
McQuarters, R.W., Det.	16	381	23.8	73	0
* Cobb, DeAndra, Atl.	16	359	22.4	39	0
Robertson, Jamal, Car.	16	343	21.4	42	0
Wynn, Dexter, Phi.	16	284	17.8	27	0
Lee, ReShard, G.B.	15	319	21.3	35	0
* Amey, Otis, S.F.	14	241	17.2	25	0

	No	Yards	Avg	Long	TD
* Williamson, Troy, Min.	12	192	16.0	28	0
* Davis, Rashied, Chi.	11	251	22.8	34	0
Perry, Bruce, Phi.	10	273	27.3	49	0
Davenport, Najeh, G.B.	10	189	18.9	27	0
Fair, Terry, St.L	10	182	18.2	35	0
Thurman, Andrae, Ten.-G.B.	10	178	17.8	25	0
Hakim, Az-Zahir, N.O.	9	171	19.0	29	0
Griffith, Justin, Atl.	8	149	18.6	23	0
Bryant, Romby, Atl.	8	137	17.1	23	0
Lewis, Michael, N.O.	8	137	17.1	20	0
Moses, J.J., Ariz	7	177	25.3	35	0
Thrash, James, Was.	7	170	24.3	31	0
McAddley, Jason, S.F.	7	122	17.4	22	0
Jones, Greg, T.B.	5	95	19.0	24	0
Chatman, Antonio, G.B.	5	91	18.2	33	0
* Murphy, Terrence, G.B.	5	91	18.2	29	0
Cartwright, Rock, Was.	4	82	20.5	25	0
Jones, Jamal, G.B.	4	80	20.0	25	0
Graham, Earnest, T.B.	4	74	18.5	22	0
Moore, Mewelde, Min.	4	72	18.0	27	0
* Bradley, Mark, Chi.	4	70	17.5	23	0
Bryson, Shawn, Det.	4	55	13.8	25	0
Pittman, Michael, T.B.	3	85	28.3	37	0
* Parson, Rich, Was.	3	71	23.7	35	0
Gordon, Lamar, Phi.	3	64	21.3	25	0
Smith, Steve, Car.	3	61	20.3	33	0
* Barber, Marion, Dal.	3	58	19.3	21	0
Pathon, Jerome, Atl.	3	54	18.0	21	0
Sellers, Mike, Was.	3	50	16.7	20	0
Leach, Vonta, G.B.	3	39	13.0	20	0
McKie, Jason, Chi.	3	29	9.7	17	0
Owens, Richard, Min.	3	25	8.3	16	0
* Jacobs, Brandon, NY-G	2	58	29.0	33	0
Cason, Aveion, St.L	2	48	24.0	29	0
Hall, DeAngelo, Atl.	2	45	22.5	23	0
Johnson, Bryant, Ariz	2	45	22.5	24	0
Ferguson, Robert, G.B.	2	44	22.0	22	0
Martinez, Glenn, Det.	2	42	21.0	24	0
Duckett, T.J., Atl.	2	36	18.0	18	0
Copper, Terrance, Dal.	2	32	16.0	21	0
Peterson, Adrian, Chi.	2	32	16.0	19	0
* Moats, Ryan, Phi.	2	26	13.0	15	0
Gaines, Michael, Car.	2	24	12.0	13	0
Henderson, William, G.B.	2	20	10.0	10	0
Whitehead, Willie, N.O.	2	12	6.0	12	0
Hall, Lamont, N.O.	2	9	4.5	5	0
* Fason, Ciatrick, Min.	2	4	2.0	4	0
Smith, Antowain, N.O.	1	30	30.0	30	0
Goings, Nick, Car.	1	21	21.0	21	0
Harris, Arlen, St.L	1	21	21.0	21	0
Morris, Maurice, Sea.	1	21	21.0	21	0
Glenn, Aaron, Dal.	1	20	20.0	20	0
Mahe, Reno, Phi.	1	19	19.0	19	0
Ayanbadejo, Obafemi, Ariz	1	16	16.0	16	0
Williams, Moe, Min.	1	16	16.0	16	0
Campbell, Dan, Dal.	1	14	14.0	14	0
Jackson, James, Ariz	1	14	14.0	14	0
Johnson, Kevin, Det.	1	14	14.0	14	0
Williams, Corey, G.B.	1	14	14.0	14	0
Henderson, E.J., Min.	1	13	13.0	13	0
* Patterson, Mike, Phi.	1	12	12.0	12	0
* Smith, Alex, T.B.	1	12	12.0	12	0
Hoover, Brad, Car.	1	10	10.0	10	0
Mangum, Kris, Car.	1	9	9.0	9	0
Anderson, Damien, Ariz	1	7	7.0	7	0
DeVries, Jared, Det.	1	7	7.0	7	0
Herrera, Anthony, Min.	1	6	6.0	6	0
* Broughton, Nehemiah, Was.	1	5	5.0	5	0
Gilmore, John, Chi.	1	5	5.0	5	0

	No	Yards	Avg	Long	TD
Peterson, Kenny, G.B.	1	5	5.0	5	0
Shiancoe, Visanthe, NY-G	1	5	5.0	5	0
* Green, Eric, Ariz	1	4	4.0	4	0
Allen, Kenderick, NY-G	1	2	2.0	2	0
Alstott, Mike, T.B.	1	2	2.0	2	0
Bradley, Jon, T.B.	1	2	2.0	2	0
Evans, Demetric, Was.	1	0	0.0	0	0
Idonije, Israel, Chi.	1	0	0.0	0	0
Tafoya, Joe, Sea.	1	0	0.0	0	0
Vasher, Nathan, Chi.	1	0	0.0	0	0
Hannam, Ryan, Sea.	0f	0	—	—	0

t = Touchdown; * Player that was a rookie in 2005
f = Fair Catch
Leader based on average return, minimum 20 returns

AMERICAN FOOTBALL CONFERENCE—KICKOFF RETURNS

	No	Yards	Avg	Long	TD
Buffalo	75	1992	26.6	99t	1
Houston	84	2173	25.9	99t	2
N.Y. Jets	71	1728	24.3	95t	1
Tennessee	70	1697	24.2	85	0
San Diego	69	1667	24.2	60	0
Jacksonville	50	1197	23.9	91t	1
Cincinnati	67	1580	23.6	94	0
Kansas City	68	1591	23.4	96t	1
Oakland	80	1832	22.9	62	0
New England	70	1555	22.2	65	0
Cleveland	68	1506	22.1	90t	1
Miami	68	1501	22.1	46	0
Pittsburgh	56	1208	21.6	74	0
Baltimore	60	1289	21.5	87	0
Denver	47	975	20.7	36	0
Indianapolls	51	1017	19.9	39	0
AFC Total	1054	24508	23.3	99t	7
AFC Average	65.9	1531.8	23.3	—	0.4

NATIONAL FOOTBALL CONFERENCE—KICKOFF RETURNS

	No	Yards	Avg	Long	TD
N.Y. Giants	63	1529	24.3	95t	1
Dallas	64	1523	23.8	49	0
Washington	62	1438	23.2	94t	2
Arizona	76	1719	22.6	90	0
Philadelphia	71	1578	22.2	53	0
Seattle	61	1347	22.1	53	0
Minnesota	71	1549	21.8	86t	1
Detroit	73	1576	21.6	73	0
St. Louis	74	1580	21.4	99t	1
Atlanta	70	1482	21.2	47	0
Carolina	53	1083	20.4	60	0
New Orleans	75	1516	20.2	46	0
Chicago	55	1092	19.9	40	0
Tampa Bay	59	1148	19.5	37	0
San Francisco	81	1540	19.0	40	0
Green Bay	75	1418	18.9	57	0
NFC Total	1083	23118	21.3	99t	5
NFC Average	67.7	1444.9	21.3	—	0.3
League Total	2137	47626	—	99t	12
League Average	66.8	1488.3	22.3	—	0.4

2005 INDIVIDUAL STATISTICS—PUNTING

PUNTING

AVERAGE YARDS PER PUNT
AFC: 45.7 Brian Moorman, Buffalo
NFC: 45.6 Josh Bidwell, Tampa Bay

NET AVERAGE YARDS PER PUNT
AFC: 39.3 Donnie Jones, Miami
NFC: 38.9 Jason Baker, Carolina

LONGEST
AFC: 75 Kyle Larson, Cincinnati at Jacksonville, October 9
NFC: 69 Mitch Berger, New Orleans vs. Carolina, December 18

PUNTS
NFC: 107 Andy Lee, San Francisco
AFC: 88 Donnie Jones, Miami

PUNTS, GAME
NFC: 10 Scott Player, Arizona vs. Tennessee, October 23 (496 yards)
10 Sean Landeta, Philadelphia at Arizona, December 24 (500 yards)
10 Derrick Frost, Washington at Philadelphia, January 1 (410 yards)

AFC: 9 Dave Zastudil, Baltimore at Tennessee, September 18 (379 yards)
9 Kyle Larson, Cincinnati at Chicago, September 25 (360 yards)
9 * Ben Graham, N.Y. Jets at Baltimore, October 2 (380 yards)
9 Chris Hanson, Jacksonville at Pittsburgh, October 16 (422 yards) - (OT)
9 Dave Zastudil, Baltimore at Chicago, October 23 (397 yards)
9 Chad Stanley, Houston at Tennessee, December 11 (322 yards)
9 Craig Hentrich, Tennessee at Miami, December 24 (382 yards)
9 Donnie Jones, Miami vs. Tennessee, December 24 (400 yards)
9 Shane Lechler, Oakland vs. N.Y. Giants, December 31 (421 yards)

TEAM CHAMPION
AFC: 45.7 Buffalo
NFC: 45.6 Tampa Bay

Player that was a rookie in 2005

AMERICAN FOOTBALL CONFERENCE—PUNTING

	Total Punts	Yards	Long	Avg	TB	Blk	Opp Ret	Return Yards	In 20	Net Avg
Buffalo	71	3242	68	45.7	9	0	42	285	22	39.1
Oakland	82	3744	64	45.7	9	0	39	460	26	37.9
New England	77	3431	59	44.6	4	1	42	405	22	38.3
Indianapolis	52	2301	58	44.3	5	0	25	272	23	37.1
San Diego	71	3104	71	43.7	8	0	26	244	25	38.0
N.Y. Jets	75	3251	59	43.3	6	0	36	305	19	37.7
Denver	73	3157	66	43.2	6	1	36	266	24	38.0
Tennessee	78	3371	59	43.2	14	0	32	144	21	37.8
Miami	89	3835	63	43.1	7	0	46	227	31	39.0
Baltimore	86	3685	60	42.8	7	1	55	481	12	35.6
Cincinnati	61	2591	75	42.5	8	1	32	260	13	35.6
Jacksonville	83	3517	74	42.4	11	1	29	236	33	36.9
Pittsburgh	69	2875	65	41.7	8	0	37	336	23	34.5
Cleveland	80	3234	61	40.4	9	0	36	347	24	33.8
Kansas City	65	2564	62	39.4	5	0	23	179	27	35.2
Houston	77	2990	61	38.8	1	0	33	219	29	35.7
AFC Total	1189	50892	75	—	117	5	569	4666	374	—
AFC Average	74.3	3180.8	--	42.8	7.3	0.3	35.6	291.6	23.4	36.9

NATIONAL FOOTBALL CONFERENCE—PUNTING

	Total Punts	Yards	Long	Avg	TB	Blk	Opp Ret	Return Yards	In 20	Net Avg
Tampa Bay	90	4101	61	45.6	13	0	49	466	24	37.5
Detroit	84	3656	60	43.5	2	0	50	520	34	36.9
Arizona	74	3206	60	43.3	7	1	39	328	18	37.0
Minnesota	81	3505	62	43.3	6	0	45	495	19	35.7
Carolina	73	3154	59	43.2	5	0	36	235	23	38.6
New Orleans	71	3066	69	43.2	3	0	33	260	28	38.7
Dallas	82	3474	63	42.4	10	0	33	250	28	36.9
Atlanta	78	3300	67	42.3	9	0	35	238	23	36.9
N.Y. Giants	73	3070	56	42.1	3	0	36	309	26	37.0
St. Louis	73	3008	63	41.2	6	0	39	410	16	33.9
San Francisco	108	4447	58	41.2	3	1	62	471	15	36.3
Seattle	80	3282	62	41.0	8	0	41	343	25	34.7
Philadelphia	100	4072	59	40.7	3	1	57	310	25	37.0
Chicago	98	3965	63	40.5	11	1	39	312	24	35.0
Washington	87	3503	57	40.3	7	0	40	189	25	36.5
Green Bay	70	2726	53	38.9	2	0	49	339	11	33.5
NFC Total	1322	55535	69	—	98	4	683	5475	364	—
NFC Average	82.6	3470.9	—	42.0	6.1	0.3	42.7	342.2	22.8	36.4
NFL Total	2511	106427	75	—	215	9	1252	10141	738	—
NFL Average	78.5	3325.8	—	42.4	6.7	0.3	39.1	316.9	23.1	36.6

NFL TOP TEN PUNTERS

	No	Yards	Long	Avg	Total Punts	TB	Blk	Opp Ret	Return Yards	In 20	Net Avg
Moorman, Brian, Buf.	71	3242	68	45.7	71	9	0	42	285	22	39.1
Lechler, Shane, Oak.	82	3744	64	45.7	82	9	0	39	460	26	37.9
Bidwell, Josh, T.B.	90	4101	61	45.6	90	13	0	49	466	24	37.5
Miller, Josh, N.E.	76	3431	59	45.1	77	4	1	42	405	22	38.3
Smith, Hunter, Ind.	52	2301	58	44.3	52	5	0	25	272	23	37.1
* Kluwe, Chris, Min.	71	3130	62	44.1	71	6	0	41	470	17	35.8
Player, Scott, Ariz	73	3206	60	43.9	74	7	1	39	328	18	37.0
Sauerbrun, Todd, Den.	72	3157	66	43.8	73	6	1	36	266	24	38.0
Scifres, Mike, S.D.	71	3104	71	43.7	71	8	0	26	244	25	38.0
* Graham, Ben, NYJ	74	3233	59	43.7	74	6	0	36	305	18	37.9

AFC—INDIVIDUAL PUNTERS

	No	Yards	Long	Avg	Total Punts	TB	Blk	Opp Ret	Return Yards	In 20	Net Avg
Moorman, Brian, Buf.	71	3242	68	45.7	71	9	0	42	285	22	39.1
Lechler, Shane, Oak.	82	3744	64	45.7	82	9	0	39	460	26	37.9
Miller, Josh, N.E.	76	3431	59	45.1	77	4	1	42	405	22	38.3
Smith, Hunter, Ind.	52	2301	58	44.3	52	5	0	25	272	23	37.1
Sauerbrun, Todd, Den.	72	3157	66	43.8	73	6	1	36	266	24	38.0
Scifres, Mike, S.D.	71	3104	71	43.7	71	8	0	26	244	25	38.0
* Graham, Ben, NYJ	74	3233	59	43.7	74	6	0	36	305	18	37.9
Jones, Donnie, Mia.	88	3827	63	43.5	88	7	0	46	227	31	39.3
Zastudil, Dave, Bal.	84	3653	60	43.5	85	7	1	55	481	11	35.7
Hentrich, Craig, Ten.	78	3371	59	43.2	78	14	0	32	144	21	37.8
Larson, Kyle, Cin.	60	2591	75	43.2	61	8	1	32	260	13	35.6
Hanson, Chris, Jac.	82	3517	74	42.9	83	11	1	29	236	33	36.9
Gardocki, Chris, Pit.	67	2803	65	41.8	67	7	0	37	336	22	34.7
Richardson, Kyle, Cle.	78	3181	61	40.8	78	9	0	36	347	22	34.0
* Colquitt, Dustin, K.C.	65	2564	62	39.4	65	5	0	23	179	27	35.2
Stanley, Chad, Hou.	77	2990	61	38.8	77	1	0	33	219	29	35.7
(Nonqualifiers)											
Roethlisberger, Ben, Pit.	2	72	39	36.0	2	1	0	0	0	1	26.0
Dawson, Phil, Cle.	2	53	31	26.5	2	0	0	0	0	2	26.5
Elling, Aaron, Bal.	1	32	32	32.0	1	0	0	0	0	1	32.0
* Nugent, Mike, NYJ	1	18	18	18.0	1	0	0	0	0	1	18.0
Mare, Olindo, Mia.	1	8	8	8.0	1	0	0	0	0	1	8.0

NFC—INDIVIDUAL PUNTERS

	No	Yards	Long	Avg	Total Punts	TB	Blk	Opp Ret	Return Yards	In 20	Net Avg
Bidwell, Josh, T.B.	90	4101	61	45.6	90	13	0	49	466	24	37.5
* Kluwe, Chris, Min.	71	3130	62	44.1	71	6	0	41	470	17	35.8
Player, Scott, Ariz	73	3206	60	43.9	74	7	1	39	328	18	37.0
Harris, Nick, Det.	84	3656	60	43.5	84	2	0	50	520	34	36.0
Baker, Jason, Car.	72	3118	59	43.3	72	4	0	36	235	23	38.9
Berger, Mitch, N.O.	71	3066	69	43.2	71	3	0	33	260	28	38.7
Barker, Bryan, St.L	50	2137	63	42.7	50	4	0	31	277	13	35.6
McBriar, Mat, Dal.	81	3439	63	42.5	81	9	0	33	250	28	37.1
* Koenen, Michael, Atl.	78	3300	67	42.3	78	9	0	35	238	23	36.9
Feagles, Jeff, NY-G	73	3070	56	42.1	73	3	0	36	309	26	37.0
Rouen, Tom, Sea.	61	2539	62	41.6	61	7	0	33	265	20	35.0
Lee, Andy, S.F.	107	4447	58	41.6	108	3	1	62	471	15	36.3
Maynard, Brad, Chi.	96	3937	63	41.0	97	11	1	38	293	24	35.3
Frost, Derrick, Was.	76	3074	55	40.4	76	6	0	34	163	23	36.7
Sander, B.J., G.B.	64	2508	53	39.2	64	2	0	45	297	11	33.9
* Hodges, Reggie, St.L-Phi.	41	1535	55	37.4	42	2	1	13	142	9	32.2
(Nonqualifiers)											
Johnson, Dirk, Phi.	39	1615	59	41.4	39	0	0	25	119	11	38.4
Landeta, Sean, Phi.	34	1483	56	43.6	34	2	0	22	143	7	38.2
Araguz, Leo, Sea.	18	723	53	40.2	18	1	0	8	78	4	34.7
Groom, Andy, Was.	11	429	57	39.0	11	1	0	6	26	2	34.8
Bennett, Darren, Min.	8	300	53	37.5	8	0	0	4	25	1	34.4
Murphy, Nick, Phi.	7	275	44	39.3	7	0	0	5	39	1	33.7
Flinn, Ryan, G.B.	6	218	42	36.3	6	0	0	4	42	0	29.3
Edinger, Paul, Min.	2	75	40	37.5	2	0	0	0	0	1	37.5
Kasay, John, Car.	1	36	36	36.0	1	1	0	0	0	0	16.0
Cundiff, Billy, Dal.	1	35	35	35.0	1	1	0	0	0	0	15.0
Wilkins, Jeff, St.L	1	35	35	35.0	1	1	0	0	0	0	15.0
* Gould, Robbie, Chi.	1	28	28	28.0	1	0	0	1	19	0	9.0
Brown, Josh, Sea.	1	20	20	20.0	1	0	0	0	0	1	20.0

Player that was a rookie in 2005
Leader based on average, minimum 40 punts

PUNT RETURNS

YARDS PER RETURN
NFC: 12.8 Reno Mahe, Philadelphia
AFC: 12.2 B.J. Sams, Baltimore

YARDS
NFC: 492 Mark Jones, Tampa Bay
AFC: 448 Antwaan Randle El, Pittsburgh

YARDS, GAME
NFC: 108 Reno Mahe, Philadelphia vs. Seattle, December 5 (7 returns, 0 TD)
AFC: 94 Antwaan Randle El, Pittsburgh vs. Jacksonville, October 16 (5 returns, 1 TD) - (OT)

LONGEST
NFC: 85 Antonio Chatman, Green Bay vs. Chicago, December 25 - TD
AFC: 81 Antwaan Randle El, Pittsburgh vs. Detroit, January 1 - TD

RETURNS
NFC: 51 Mark Jones, Tampa Bay
AFC: 49 * Alvin Pearman, Jacksonville

RETURNS, GAME
NFC: 9 Reggie Swinton, Arizona vs. Philadelphia, December 24 (57 yards, 0 TD)
AFC: 8 * Pacman Jones, Tennessee at Miami, December 24 (25 yards, 0 TD)

FAIR CATCHES
AFC: 25 Troy Walters, Indianapolis
NFC: 22 Jimmy Williams, Seattle

TOUCHDOWNS
AFC: 2 Antwaan Randle El, Pittsburgh
NFC: 1 * Otis Amey, San Francisco
1 Antonio Chatman, Green Bay
1 Mewelde Moore, Minnesota
1 Chad Morton, N.Y. Giants
1 Bobby Wade, Chicago

TEAM CHAMPION
AFC: 11.1 Baltimore
NFC: 10.8 Carolina

NFL TOP TEN PUNT RETURNERS

	No	FC	Yards	Avg	Long	TD
Mahe, Reno, Phi.	21	9	269	12.8	44	0
Sams, B.J., Bal.	33	10	401	12.2	51	0
Moore, Mewelde, Min.	21	9	245	11.7	71t	1
Smith, Steve, Car.	27	6	286	10.6	44	0
Northcutt, Dennis, Cle.	35	13	368	10.5	62t	1
Randle El, Antwaan, Pit.	44	12	448	10.2	81t	2
Jones, Mark, T.B.	51	18	492	9.6	31	0
Morton, Chad, NY-G	47	16	453	9.6	58	1
Wade, Bobby, Chi.	33	9	317	9.6	73t	1
* Jones, Pacman, Ten.	29	8	272	9.4	52t	1

AFC—INDIVIDUAL PUNT RETURNERS

	No	FC	Yards	Avg	Long	TD
Sams, B.J., Bal.	33	10	401	12.2	51	0
Northcutt, Dennis, Cle.	35	13	368	10.5	62t	1
Randle El, Antwaan, Pit.	44	12	448	10.2	81t	2
* Jones, Pacman, Ten.	29	8	272	9.4	52t	1
Welker, Wes, Mia.	43	23	390	9.1	47	0
Dwight, Tim, N.E.	32	13	273	8.5	29	0
* Pearman, Alvin, Jac.	49	15	410	8.4	24	0
Walters, Troy, Ind.	21	25	172	8.2	29	0
Cotchery, Jerricho, NYJ	23	7	182	7.9	18	0
Hall, Dante, K.C.	42	6	276	6.6	52	0
Ratliff, Keiwan, Cin.	28	14	157	5.6	13	0
* Carr, Chris, Oak.	34	7	186	5.5	34	0
(Nonqualifiers)						
* Sproles, Darren, S.D.	18	5	108	6.0	23	0
Parker, Eric, S.D.	18	9	106	5.9	15	0
* Williams, Darrent, Den.	17	12	148	8.7	52	0
Adams, Charlie, Den.	16	5	133	8.3	32	0
* Parrish, Roscoe, Buf.	14	9	186	13.3	43	0
Buchanon, Phillip, Hou.	12	6	101	8.4	37	0
* Mathis, Jerome, Hou.	12	0	68	5.7	19	0
Thurman, Andre, Ten.	9	5	31	3.4	11	0
Clements, Nate, Buf.	8	3	52	6.5	13	0
Brown, Troy, N.E.	7	5	30	4.3	7	0
Smith, Jonathan, Buf.	6	5	41	6.8	17	0
* Clayton, Mark, Bal.	6	2	30	5.0	10	0
* Miller, Justin, NYJ	6	1	9	1.5	12	0
* Jones, Brandon, Ten.	5	0	75	15.0	32	0
McCareins, Justin, NYJ	5	4	28	5.6	12	0
McCardell, Keenan, S.D.	3	3	31	10.3	14	0
Morgan, Donovan, Hou.	3	0	30	10.0	23	0
Davis, Domanick, Hou.	3	1	24	8.0	21	0
Woodson, Charles, Oak.	3	0	20	6.7	15	0
* Owens, Chad, Jac.	3	0	6	2.0	6	0
Thompson, Lamont, Ten.	1	0	31	31.0	31	0
Taylor, Ike, Pit.	1	0	19	19.0	19	0
Kennison, Eddie, K.C.	1	1	17	17.0	17	0
Johnson, Bethel, N.E.	1	0	11	11.0	11	0
Harrison, Marvin, Ind.	1	0	10	10.0	10	0
Williams, Tank, Ten.	1	0	9	9.0	9	0
* Cribbs, Josh, Cle.	1	0	5	5.0	5	0
Iwuoma, Chidi, Pit.	1	0	3	3.0	3	0
David, Jason, Ind.	1	0	0	0.0	0	0
* Jackson, Marlin, Ind.	1	0	0	0.0	0	0
Jones, Sean, Cle.	1	0	0	0.0	0	0
Mathis, Rashean, Jac.	1	0	-1	-1.0	-1	0
Harrison, James, Pit.	0	1	0	—	—	0
Sanders, Deion, Bal.	0	1	0	—	—	0

*t = Touchdown; * Player that was a rookie in 2005*
Leader based on average return, minimum 20 returns

NFC—INDIVIDUAL PUNT RETURNERS

	No	FC	Yards	Avg	Long	TD
Mahe, Reno, Phi.	21	9	269	12.8	44	0
Moore, Mewelde, Min.	21	9	245	11.7	71t	1
Smith, Steve, Car.	27	6	286	10.6	44	0
Jones, Mark, T.B.	51	18	492	9.6	31	0
Morton, Chad, NY-G	47	16	453	9.6	58	1
Wade, Bobby, Chi.	33	9	317	9.6	73t	1
Chatman, Antonio, G.B.	45	18	381	8.5	85t	1
Swinton, Reggie, Ariz	42	14	334	8.0	32	0
Hakim, Az-Zahir, N.O.	34	4	260	7.6	42	0
Crayton, Patrick, Dal.	23	9	166	7.2	25	0
Drummond, Eddie, Det.	26	11	157	6.0	38	0
Williams, Jimmy, Sea.	24	22	139	5.8	24	0
Wynn, Dexter, Phi.	22	10	110	5.0	27	0
(Nonqualifiers)						
Rossum, Allen, Atl.	17	12	145	8.5	29	0
* Marshall, Rasheed, S.F.	17	10	87	5.1	13	0
Gamble, Chris, Car.	14	5	158	11.3	76	0
Brown, Antonio, Was.	13	12	63	4.8	16	0
Howry, Keenan, Min.	12	5	78	6.5	19	0
Price, Peerless, Dal.	12	6	63	5.3	11	0
* Amey, Otis, S.F.	11	2	125	11.4	75t	1
McQuarters, R.W., Det.	10	2	117	11.7	49	0
Thrash, James, Was.	10	15	77	7.7	18	0
Newman, Terence, Dal.	10	6	55	5.5	26	0
Hall, DeAngelo, Atl.	8	2	82	10.3	27	0
Berrian, Bernard, Chi.	8	3	69	8.6	24	0
Looker, Dane, St.L	8	2	69	8.6	17	0
Westbrook, Brian, Phi.	8	2	60	7.5	23	0
McDonald, Shaun, St.L	8	6	33	4.1	14	0
Stallworth, Donte', N.O.	7	1	52	7.4	27	0
Moses, J.J., Ariz	7	0	40	5.7	12	0
Moss, Santana, Was.	7	1	40	5.7	14	0
Allen, David, St.L	7	6	38	5.4	12	0
Warrick, Peter, Sea.	6	0	29	4.8	10	0
* Davis, Rashied, Chi.	5	1	31	6.2	21	0
Burleson, Nate, Min.	5	0	21	4.2	10	0
Furrey, Mike, St.L	4	2	28	7.0	13	0
Lewis, Michael, N.O.	4	0	8	2.0	5	0
Jenkins, Michael, Atl.	3	0	19	6.3	15	0
Fair, Terry, St.L	3	6	7	2.3	8	0
Sheppard, Lito, Phi.	2	3	9	4.5	8	0
Finneran, Brian, Atl.	2	8	7	3.5	5	0
Robinson, Koren, Min.	2	0	0	0.0	0	0
Engram, Bobby, Sea.	1	1	9	9.0	9	0
Johnson, Bryant, Ariz	1	2	9	9.0	9	0
* Cobb, DeAndra, Atl.	1	0	8	8.0	8	0
* Blackburn, Chase, NY-G	1	0	0	0.0	0	0
* Butler, James, NY-G	1	0	0	0.0	0	0
Taylor, Travis, Min.	1	0	0	0.0	0	0
Thomas, Fred, N.O.	1	0	0	0.0	0	0
* Atogwe, O.J., St.L	0	1	0	—	—	0
* Torrence, Leigh, Atl.	0	1	0	—	—	0

*t = Touchdown; * Player that was a rookie in 2005*
Leader based on average return, minimum 20 returns

AMERICAN FOOTBALL CONFERENCE—PUNT RETURNS

	No	FC	Yards	Avg	Long	TD
Baltimore	39	13	431	11.1	51	0
Pittsburgh	46	13	470	10.2	81t	2
Cleveland	37	13	373	10.1	62t	1
Buffalo	28	17	279	10.0	43	0
Tennessee	45	13	418	9.3	52t	1
Miami	43	23	390	9.1	47	0
Denver	33	17	281	8.5	52	0
New England	40	18	314	7.9	29	0
Jacksonville	53	15	415	7.8	24	0
Indianapolis	24	25	182	7.6	29	0
Houston	30	7	223	7.4	37	0
Kansas City	43	7	293	6.8	52	0
N.Y. Jets	34	12	219	6.4	18	0
San Diego	39	17	245	6.3	23	0
Cincinnati	28	14	157	5.6	13	0
Oakland	37	7	206	5.6	34	0
AFC Total	599	231	4896	8.2	81t	4
AFC Average	37.4	14.4	306.0	8.2	—	0.3

NATIONAL FOOTBALL CONFERENCE—PUNT RETURNS

	No	FC	Yards	Avg	Long	TD
Carolina	41	11	444	10.8	76	0
Tampa Bay	51	18	492	9.6	31	0
N.Y. Giants	49	16	453	9.2	58	1
Chicago	46	13	417	9.1	73t	1
Green Bay	45	18	381	8.5	85t	1
Philadelphia	53	24	448	8.5	44	0
Atlanta	31	23	261	8.4	29	0
Minnesota	41	14	344	8.4	71t	1
Arizona	50	16	383	7.7	32	0
Detroit	36	13	274	7.6	49	0
San Francisco	28	12	212	7.6	75t	1
New Orleans	46	5	320	7.0	42	0
Dallas	45	21	284	6.3	26	0
Washington	30	28	180	6.0	18	0
St. Louis	30	23	175	5.8	17	0
Seattle	31	23	177	5.7	24	0
NFC Total	653	278	5245	8.0	85t	5
NFC Average	40.8	17.4	327.8	8.0	—	0.3
League Total	1252	509	10141	—	85t	9
League Average	39.1	15.9	316.9	8.1	—	0.3

FUMBLES

MOST FUMBLES
AFC:	17	David Carr, Houston
NFC:	17	Drew Bledsoe, Dallas

MOST FUMBLES, GAME
AFC:	6	Chad Pennington, N.Y. Jets at Kansas City, September 11
NFC:	4	Bobby Wade, Chicago vs. San Francisco, November 13

OWN FUMBLES RECOVERED
AFC:	6	David Carr, Houston
NFC:	6	* Alex Smith, San Francisco

OWN FUMBLES RECOVERED, GAME
AFC:	3	Chad Pennington, N.Y. Jets at Kansas City, September 11 (0 yards, 0 TD)
NFC:	3	Drew Bledsoe, Dallas vs. Washington, September 19 (0 yards, 0 TD)
	3	Mike McMahon, Philadelphia at N.Y. Giants, November 20 (0 yards, 0 TD)

OPPONENTS' FUMBLES RECOVERED
AFC:	4	Randall Godfrey, San Diego
	4	Montae Reagor, Indianapolis
NFC:	3	Nick Barnett, Green Bay
	3	Kalimba Edwards, Detroit
	3	Kabeer Gbaja-Biamila, Green Bay
	3	Nick Greisen, N.Y. Giants
	3	Patrick Kerney, Atlanta
	3	Ricky Manning, Carolina
	3	Dewayne White, Tampa Bay

OPPONENTS' FUMBLES RECOVERED, GAME
AFC:	2	Jared Allen, Kansas City vs. Washington, October 16 (0 yards, 0 TD)
	2	Troy Polamalu, Pittsburgh at Green Bay, November 6 (78 yards, 1 TD)
NFC:	2	Nick Barnett, Green Bay at Atlanta, November 13 (18 yards, 0 TD)
	2	Ricky Manning, Carolina at Atlanta, January 1 (11 yards, 1 TD)

YARDS
NFC:	86	DeAngelo Hall, Atlanta
AFC:	85	Jason Taylor, Miami

LONGEST
AFC:	85	Jason Taylor, Miami vs. Denver, September 11 - TD
NFC:	80	Sheldon Brown, Philadelphia at Dallas, October 9 - TD

AFC—TOUCHDOWNS ON FUMBLE RECOVERIES
Odom, Antwan, Ten.	2
Thomas, Adalius, Bal.	2
Cooper, Jarrod, Oak.	1
Knight, Sammy, K.C.	1
Polamalu, Troy, Pit.	1
Reagor, Montae, Ind.	1
Reed, James, NYJ	1
Taylor, Jason, Mia.	1
Tripplett, Larry, Ind.	1

NFC—TOUCHDOWNS ON FUMBLE RECOVERIES
Allen, Will, T.B.	1
Brown, Sheldon, Phi.	1
* Davis, Chauncey, Atl.	1
Dyson, Andre, Sea.	1

Hall, DeAngelo, Atl.	1
* Johnson, Derrick, S.F.	1
Manning, Ricky, Car.	1
McFarland, Anthony, T.B.	1
Pierce, Antonio, NY-G	1
Rogers, Shaun, Det.	1
Smith, Derek M., S.F.	1
Taylor, Sean, Was.	1
White, Dewayne, T.B.	1

AFC FUMBLES—INDIVIDUAL

	Fum	Own Rec	Opp Rec	Yards	Tot Rec
Abraham, John, NYJ	0	0	1	0	1
Adams, Charlie, Den.	4	0	0	0	0
Aiken, Sam, Buf.	0	0	1	0	1
Alexander, Roc, Den.	0	0	1	0	1
Allen, Jared, K.C.	0	0	2	0	2
Anderson, Bennie, Buf.	0	1	0	0	1
Anderson, Charlie, Hou.	0	0	1	0	1
Anderson, Courtney, Oak.	1	0	0	0	0
Anderson, Mike, Den.	2	0	0	0	0
Ashworth, Tom, N.E.	0	1	0	0	1
Ayodele, Akin, Jac.	0	0	1	0	1
Badger, Brad, Oak.	0	2	0	0	2
Baker, Chris, NYJ	1	0	0	0	0
Barrett, David, NYJ	1	0	1	30	1
Batch, Charlie, Pit.	1	2	0	0	2
Bell, Tatum, Den.	3	1	0	0	1
Bell, Yeremiah, Mia.	0	0	2	12	2
Bironas, Rob, Ten.	0	1	0	0	1
Bober, Chris, K.C.	0	1	0	0	1
Boller, Kyle, Bal.	8	4	0	0	4
Bollinger, Brooks, NYJ	3	2	0	-3	2
Brady, Kyle, Jac.	3	1	0	0	1
Brady, Tom, N.E.	4	0	0	0	0
Brandon, Sam, Den.	0	0	1	0	1
Brees, Drew, S.D.	8	0	0	0	0
Brock, Raheem, Ind.	0	0	1	15	1
Brown, Chris, Ten.	4	0	0	0	0
Brown, Courtney, Den.	0	0	2	0	2
Brown, Mark, NYJ	0	1	0	0	1
* Brown, Ronnie, Mia.	4	2	0	0	2
Bruener, Mark, Hou.	0	2	0	0	2
Bryant, Antonio, Cle.	1	1	0	0	1
Buchanon, Phillip, Hou.	2	2	0	0	2
Bulluck, Keith, Ten.	0	0	1	0	1
Burgess, Derrick, Oak.	0	0	2	0	2
Burns, Keith, Den.	0	1	0	0	1
Caldwell, Reche, S.D.	2	0	0	0	0
Calico, Tyrone, Ten.	1	0	0	0	0
Carey, Vernon, Mia.	0	0	1	0	1
Carlisle, Cooper, Den.	0	2	0	0	2
* Carr, Chris, Oak.	5	3	0	-1	3
Carr, David, Hou.	17	6	0	-7	6
Carter, Kevin, Mia.	0	0	1	0	1
Carter, Tyrone, Pit.	0	0	1	0	1
Carthon, Ran, Ind.	1	0	0	0	0
* Cassel, Matt, N.E.	2	0	0	-1	1
Chambers, Chris, Mia.	5	2	0	-2	2
Clements, Nate, Buf.	0	0	1	0	1
Clemons, Duane, Cin.	0	0	1	0	1
Colclough, Ricardo, Pit.	1	0	0	0	0
Coleman, Marcus, Hou.	1	0	0	0	0
Coles, Laveranues, NYJ	1	0	0	0	0
Collins, Kerry, Oak.	13	1	0	-16	1
Colvin, Rosevelt, N.E.	0	0	1	0	1
Cooper, Deke, Jac.	0	1	0	0	1
Cooper, Jarrod, Oak.	0	0	2	0	2
Cotchery, Jerricho, NYJ	2	1	0	0	1

	Fum	Own Rec	Opp Rec	Yards	Tot Rec		Fum	Own Rec	Opp Rec	Yards	Tot Rec
Cousin, Terry, Jac.	0	1	0	0	1	Howard, Reggie, Mia.	0	1	0	0	1
* Cribbs, Josh, Cle.	4	0	0	0	0	Iwuoma, Chidi, Pit.	0	0	1	0	1
Crocker, Chris, Cle.	0	0	1	0	1	Jackson, Eddie, Mia.	0	0	1	0	1
Crockett, Zack, Oak.	1	1	0	0	1	* Jackson, Marlin, Ind.	1	0	0	0	0
* Crowder, Channing, Mia.	0	0	2	0	2	James, Edgerrin, Ind.	2	1	0	0	1
* Daniels, Travis, Mia.	0	0	1	0	1	James, Tory, Cin.	0	0	1	26	1
David, Jason, Ind.	1	0	2	5	2	Johnson, Andre, Hou.	1	0	0	0	0
Davis, Domanick, Hou.	2	1	0	0	1	Johnson, Bethel, N.E.	1	1	0	0	1
Dayne, Ron, Den.	1	0	0	0	0	Johnson, Chad, Cin.	1	0	0	0	0
Demps, Will, Bal.	0	0	2	22	2	* Johnson, Derrick, K.C.	0	0	1	0	1
* Denney, John, Mia.	1	0	0	-12	0	Johnson, Jeremi, Cin.	2	1	0	0	1
Denney, Ryan, Buf.	0	0	1	0	1	Johnson, Larry, K.C.	5	3	0	0	3
Devoe, Todd, Den.	0	0	2	0	2	Johnson, Rudi, Cin.	1	2	0	0	2
Dilfer, Trent, Cle.	9	0	0	-14	0	Jolley, Doug, NYJ	1	0	0	0	0
Dillon, Corey, N.E.	1	0	0	0	0	Jones, Levi, Cin.	0	1	0	0	1
Dinkins, Darnell, Bal.	0	1	0	0	1	* Jones, Matt, Jac.	2	2	0	0	2
Droughns, Reuben, Cle.	6	5	0	0	5	* Jones, Pacman, Ten.	5	1	0	0	1
Dwight, Tim, N.E.	1	1	0	0	1	Jones, Sean, Cle.	0	1	0	11	1
Ekuban, Ebenezer, Den.	0	0	1	0	1	Jordan, LaMont, Oak.	2	0	0	0	0
Evans, Troy, Hou.	0	1	0	0	1	Jordan, Leander, S.D.	0	1	0	0	1
Faneca, Alan, Pit.	0	2	0	0	2	Kaesviharn, Kevin, Cin.	0	0	3	0	3
Farrior, James, Pit.	0	0	1	0	1	Kassell, Brad, Ten.	0	0	3	0	3
Faulk, Kevin, N.E.	3	1	0	0	1	* Katula, Matt, Bal.	1	0	0	-10	0
Ferguson, Nick, Den.	0	0	1	0	1	Keisel, Brett, Pit.	0	0	1	0	1
Fiedler, Jay, NYJ	1	1	0	-5	1	Kelly, Reggie, Cin.	1	1	0	0	1
Fleming, Troy, Ten.	0	1	0	0	1	Kelsay, Chris, Buf.	0	0	1	2	1
Fletcher, London, Buf.	0	0	2	0	2	Kemoeatu, Maake, Bal.	0	0	1	0	1
Florence, Drayton, S.D.	1	0	0	0	0	Kennison, Eddie, K.C.	1	0	0	0	0
Flutie, Doug, N.E.	2	1	0	-9	1	Kiel, Terrence, S.D.	0	0	1	0	1
Foote, Larry, Pit.	0	0	1	27	1	Kirschke, Travis, Pit.	0	0	1	0	1
* Foxworth, Domonique, Den.	0	1	1	9	2	Knight, Sammy, K.C.	0	0	2	80	2
Frerotte, Gus, Mia.	13	4	0	-36	4	LaBoy, Travis, Ten.	0	0	1	0	1
* Frye, Charlie, Cle.	7	2	0	-11	2	Law, Ty, NYJ	1	1	0	0	1
Garrard, David, Jac.	4	1	0	0	1	Leber, Ben, S.D.	0	0	1	0	1
Gibson, Derrick, Oak.	0	0	1	0	1	Leftwich, Byron, Jac.	8	1	0	0	1
Gilbert, Tony, Jac.	0	0	1	0	1	Lewis, Jamal, Bal.	5	0	0	0	0
Godfrey, Randall, S.D.	0	0	4	35	4	Lewis, Ray, Bal.	0	0	1	0	1
Gold, Ian, Den.	0	0	2	0	2	Lilja, Ryan, Ind.	0	1	0	0	1
Gonzalez, Tony, K.C.	0	1	0	0	1	Losman, J.P., Buf.	7	3	0	-2	3
* Graham, Ben, NYJ	1	0	0	-9	0	Maddox, Tommy, Pit.	2	0	0	-9	0
Graham, Daniel, N.E.	1	1	0	0	1	* Mankins, Logan, N.E.	0	1	0	0	1
Gray, Quinn, Jac.	1	0	0	0	0	Manning, Peyton, Ind.	5	0	0	-1	0
Green, Roderick, Bal.	0	0	1	0	1	Manuwai, Vince, Jac.	0	2	0	0	2
Green, Trent, K.C.	8	1	0	-10	1	Mare, Olindo, Mia.	0	0	1	0	1
Greenwood, Morlon, Hou.	0	0	2	0	2	Martin, Curtis, NYJ	2	2	0	0	2
* Griffin, Kris, K.C.	0	0	1	0	1	Mason, Derrick, Bal.	1	0	0	0	0
Hall, Carlos, K.C.	0	0	1	0	1	* Mathis, Jerome, Hou.	3	1	0	0	1
Hall, Dante, K.C.	5	2	0	0	2	Mathis, Rashean, Jac.	0	0	1	0	1
Hamilton, Bobby, Oak.	0	0	2	8	2	Mauck, Matt, Ten.	1	0	0	0	0
Harper, Nick, Ind.	0	0	1	7	1	McCray, Bobby, Jac.	0	0	1	0	1
Harrison, James, Pit.	0	1	0	0	1	McDougle, Stockar, Mia.	0	1	0	0	1
Hart, Clinton, S.D.	0	0	2	-1	2	* McFadden, Bryant, Pit.	0	0	1	9	1
Hartings, Jeff, Pit.	1	0	0	-9	0	McGahee, Willis, Buf.	1	0	0	0	0
Haynes, Verron, Pit.	2	1	0	0	1	McGee, Terrence, Buf.	1	1	1	0	2
Hayward, Reggie, Jac.	0	0	1	0	1	McGinest, Willie, N.E.	0	0	1	19	1
Heap, Todd, Bal.	2	1	0	0	1	McKinney, Steve, Hou.	1	0	0	-1	0
* Henry, Chris, Cin.	2	0	0	0	0	McMichael, Randy, Mia.	1	0	0	0	0
Henry, Travis, Ten.	2	1	0	0	1	McNair, Steve, Ten.	7	2	0	-1	2
Hentrich, Craig, Ten.	1	0	0	-3	0	Meier, Rob, Jac.	0	0	1	0	1
* Hobbs, Ellis, N.E.	1	1	1	7	2	Mickens, Ray, Cle.	0	0	1	13	1
Hobson, Victor, NYJ	0	0	1	43	1	Miller, Caleb, Cin.	0	0	1	0	1
Holcomb, Kelly, Buf.	13	3	0	-31	3	* Miller, Heath, Pit.	0	1	0	0	1
Holliday, Vonnie, Mia.	0	0	2	12	2	* Miller, Justin, NYJ	3	0	0	0	0
Holmes, Priest, K.C.	1	0	0	0	0	Milloy, Lawyer, Buf.	0	0	1	0	1
Hope, Chris, Pit.	0	0	1	6	1	Mitchell, Kawika, K.C.	0	1	1	0	2
Hopkins, Brad, Ten.	0	1	0	0	1	* Morency, Vernand, Hou.	1	0	1	0	1
Houshmandzadeh, T.J., Cin.	1	0	0	0	0	Morey, Sean, Pit.	0	1	0	0	1
* Houston, Cedric, NYJ	1	0	0	0	0	Morgan, Quincy, Pit.	1	0	0	0	0

	Fum	Own Rec	Opp Rec	Yards	Tot Rec
Morris, Rob, Ind.	0	0	1	0	1
* Morrison, Kirk, Oak.	0	0	2	0	2
Moss, Randy, Oak.	0	1	0	0	1
Mughelli, Ovie, Bal.	1	0	0	0	0
Myers, Michael, Den.	0	0	1	0	1
Naeole, Chris, Jac.	0	1	0	0	1
Navies, Hannibal, Cin.	0	0	1	0	1
Neal, Lorenzo, S.D.	0	1	0	0	1
Nickey, Donnie, Ten.	0	1	0	0	1
Oben, Roman, S.D.	0	1	0	0	1
Odom, Antwan, Ten.	0	0	2	52	2
Ogden, Jonathan, Bal.	0	2	0	0	2
Olivea, Shane, S.D.	0	2	0	0	2
Olson, Benji, Ten.	0	1	0	0	1
O'Neal, Deltha, Cin.	0	0	1	26	1
* Owens, Chad, Jac.	2	1	0	0	1
Palmer, Carson, Cin.	5	1	0	-2	1
Parker, Eric, S.D.	2	1	0	0	1
* Parker, J'Vonne, Cle.	0	0	1	0	1
Parker, Samie, K.C.	2	0	0	0	0
Parker, Willie, Pit.	4	2	0	0	2
* Parrish, Roscoe, Buf.	2	1	0	0	1
Pass, Patrick, N.E.	2	0	0	0	0
* Payton, Jarrett, Ten.	0	1	0	0	1
* Pearman, Alvin, Jac.	4	1	0	0	1
Peek, Antwan, Hou.	0	0	2	0	2
Pennington, Chad, NYJ	8	4	0	-22	4
Perry, Chris, Cin.	2	1	0	0	1
* Perry, Tab, Cin.	1	1	1	0	2
Peterson, Mike, Jac.	0	0	1	0	1
Phillips, Shaun, S.D.	0	0	1	0	1
Plummer, Jake, Den.	4	1	0	-10	1
Polamalu, Troy, Pit.	0	0	2	78	2
* Pollack, David, Cin.	0	0	1	6	1
Polley, Tommy, Bal.	0	0	1	2	1
* Pool, Brodney, Cle.	0	1	1	0	2
Porter, Jerry, Oak.	1	1	0	0	1
Porter, Joey, Pit.	0	0	1	0	1
Posey, Jeff, Buf.	0	0	1	46	1
Pucillo, Mike, Cle.	0	1	0	0	1
Putzier, Jeb, Den.	1	1	0	0	1
* Randall, Marcus, Ten.	0	1	0	0	1
Randle El, Antwaan, Pit.	4	0	0	0	0
Ratliff, Keiwan, Cin.	0	0	1	0	1
Reagor, Montae, Ind.	0	0	4	37	4
Reed, James, NYJ	0	0	2	33	2
Reid, Dexter, Ind.	0	1	0	0	1
Reynolds, Rob, Ten.	0	1	0	0	1
Rhodes, Dominic, Ind.	2	0	0	0	0
Rivers, Marcellus, Hou.	0	1	0	0	1
Rivers, Philip, S.D.	2	0	0	0	0
Robinson, Dunta, Hou.	0	1	0	0	1
* Roby, Courtney, Ten.	1	0	0	0	0
Roethlisberger, Ben, Pit.	2	1	0	-1	1
Rosenfels, Sage, Mia.	1	1	0	-11	1
* Roth, Matt, Mia.	0	0	1	0	1
Roye, Orpheus, Cle.	0	0	1	0	1
Ruff, Orlando, Cle.	0	0	1	6	1
Sanders, Bob, Ind.	0	0	1	0	1
Sanders, Deion, Bal.	1	0	0	0	0
* Sanders, James, N.E.	0	0	1	0	1
Sands, Terdell, Oak.	0	0	1	0	1
Sape, Lauvale, Buf.	0	0	1	0	1
Sapp, Cecil, Den.	0	1	1	0	2
Saturday, Jeff, Ind.	0	1	1	0	2
Schobel, Aaron, Buf.	0	0	1	0	1
Schobel, Matt, Cin.	1	0	0	0	0
Schweigert, Stuart, Oak.	0	0	3	3	3
Scifres, Mike, S.D.	1	1	0	0	1
Scott, Bart, Bal.	0	0	2	11	2
* Sensabaugh, Gerald, Jac.	0	0	1	0	1
Seymour, Richard, N.E.	0	0	1	0	1
Shelton, Daimon, Buf.	1	0	0	0	0
Siavii, Junior, K.C.	0	0	1	0	1
Simmons, Brian, Cin.	1	0	0	0	0
Simmons, Jason, Hou.	0	0	1	0	1
Sims, Barry, Oak.	0	2	0	0	2
Sirmon, Peter, Ten.	0	0	1	41	1
Slaughter, Chad, Oak.	0	1	0	0	1
Smith, Aaron, Pit.	0	0	1	0	1
Smith, Jonathan, Buf.	1	1	0	0	1
Smith, Justin, Cin.	0	0	1	0	1
Smith, Robaire, Hou.	0	0	1	3	1
Smith, Rod, Den.	2	0	0	0	0
Smith, Terrelle, Cle.	0	1	0	0	1
Sorgi, Jim, Ind.	1	0	0	0	0
Sowell, Jerald, NYJ	1	3	0	0	3
* Speegle, Nick, Cle.	0	0	1	0	1
Spicer, Paul, Jac.	0	0	1	0	1
* Sproles, Darren, S.D.	3	1	0	0	1
Staley, Duce, Pit.	1	1	0	0	1
Stanley, Chad, Hou.	1	0	0	-9	0
Stills, Gary, K.C.	0	0	1	0	1
Stone, Ron, Oak.	0	2	0	0	2
Strait, Derrick, NYJ	0	0	1	0	1
Suggs, Terrell, Bal.	0	0	1	0	1
Surtain, Patrick, K.C.	1	0	1	2	1
Taylor, Chester, Bal.	3	0	0	0	0
Taylor, Fred, Jac.	0	1	0	0	1
Taylor, Ike, Pit.	0	0	2	8	2
Taylor, Jason, Mia.	0	0	2	85	2
Teague, Trey, Buf.	0	1	0	0	1
* Terry, Adam, Bal.	0	1	0	0	1
Testaverde, Vinny, NYJ	8	1	0	-11	1
Thomas, Adalius, Bal.	0	1	3	44	4
Thomas, Zach, Mia.	0	0	1	0	1
Thompson, Chaun, Cle.	0	0	1	0	1
Thornton, John, Cin.	0	0	1	0	1
* Thurman, Odell, Cin.	0	1	0	23	1
Tillman, Travares, Mia.	0	0	1	0	1
Tomlinson, LaDainian, S.D.	3	1	0	0	1
Townsend, Deshea, Pit.	0	0	1	2	1
Tripplett, Larry, Ind.	0	0	2	60	2
Troupe, Ben, Ten.	2	0	0	0	0
Tuiasosopo, Marques, Oak.	2	0	0	0	0
Unck, Mason, Cle.	0	2	0	0	2
Vanden Bosch, Kyle, Ten.	0	0	1	0	1
Veal, Demetrin, Den.	0	0	1	0	1
Vilma, Jonathan, NYJ	1	0	1	4	1
Vincent, Troy, Buf.	0	0	2	0	2
Volek, Billy, Ten.	3	0	0	0	0
Wade, Todd, Hou.	0	1	0	0	1
Walker, Ramon, Hou.	0	0	1	0	1
* Ward, B.J., Bal.	0	0	1	11	1
Ward, Hines, Pit.	1	0	0	0	0
Warfield, Eric, K.C.	0	0	2	0	2
* Warren, Greg, Pit.	1	0	0	0	0
Warren, Ty, N.E.	0	0	1	5	1
Washington, Dewayne, K.C.	0	0	1	0	1
* Washington, Fabian, Oak.	0	0	1	0	1
Waters, Brian, K.C.	0	1	0	0	1
Watson, Ben, N.E.	1	0	0	0	0
Wayne, Reggie, Ind.	1	1	0	0	1
Weary, Fred, Hou.	0	1	0	0	1
Weaver, Anthony, Bal.	0	0	1	0	1
Welker, Wes, Mia.	5	4	0	0	4

	Fum	Own Rec	Opp Rec	Yards	Tot Rec
Wells, Jonathan, Hou.	1	0	0	0	0
Wilcox, Daniel, Bal.	0	0	1	0	1
Wilfork, Vince, N.E.	0	0	1	0	1
Wilkerson, Jimmy, K.C.	0	0	1	0	1
* Williams, Darrent, Den.	2	0	1	0	1
Williams, Jamal, S.D.	0	0	1	0	1
Williams, Maurice, Jac.	0	1	0	0	1
Williams, Reggie, Jac.	2	0	0	0	0
Williams, Ricky, Mia.	1	1	0	0	1
Williams, Shaud, Buf.	0	1	0	0	1
Williams, Tank, Ten.	0	0	1	5	1
Wilson, Al, Den.	0	0	1	0	1
Wilson, Cedrick, Pit.	1	1	0	0	1
Wilson, Eugene, N.E.	0	0	1	0	1
* Wimbush, Derrick, Jac.	1	0	0	0	0
Woodson, Charles, Oak.	1	0	0	0	0
Woolfolk, Andre, Ten.	0	0	1	8	1
Wright, Anthony, Bal.	5	2	0	-8	2
Zastudil, Dave, Bal.	1	1	0	-2	1
Zgonina, Jeff, Mia.	0	0	1	0	1

*Player that was a rookie in 2005
Yards includes aborted plays, own recoveries, and opponents' recoveries.

NFC FUMBLES—INDIVIDUAL

	Fum	Own Rec	Opp Rec	Yards	Tot Rec
Adams, Mike, S.F.	0	0	1	0	1
Alexander, Brent, NY-G	0	0	1	9	1
Alexander, Shaun, Sea.	5	0	0	0	0
Allen, David, St.L	1	0	0	0	0
Allen, Kenderick, NY-G	0	0	2	2	2
Allen, Larry, Dal.	0	1	0	0	1
Allen, Will, T.B.	0	0	1	33	1
Allen, Will, NY-G	0	0	1	0	1
* Amey, Otis, S.F.	1	0	0	0	0
Archuleta, Adam, St.L	0	0	1	0	1
* Arrington, J.J., Ariz	1	1	0	0	1
* Atogwe, O.J., St.L	0	0	1	0	1
Ayanbadejo, Brendon, Chi.	0	1	0	0	1
Ayanbadejo, Obafemi, Ariz	1	0	0	0	0
* Babineaux, Jonathan, Atl.	0	0	1	0	1
Babineaux, Jordan, Sea.	0	0	1	0	1
Bailey, Rodney, Sea.	0	0	1	0	1
* Bajema, Billy, S.F.	0	1	0	0	1
* Barber, Marion, Dal.	3	3	0	-5	3
Barber, Ronde, T.B.	0	0	1	4	1
Barber, Tiki, NY-G	1	1	0	0	1
Barlow, Kevan, S.F.	2	0	0	0	0
Barnett, Nick, G.B.	0	0	3	17	3
* Barron, Alex, St.L	0	1	0	0	1
Battle, Arnaz, S.F.	1	0	0	0	0
Bennett, Michael, Min.	5	1	0	0	1
* Benson, Cedric, Chi.	1	1	0	0	1
* Bergen, Adam, Ariz	0	1	0	0	1
Bernard, Rocky, Sea.	0	0	2	5	2
Berrian, Bernard, Chi.	1	0	0	0	0
Berry, Bertrand, Ariz	0	0	1	0	1
Betts, Ladell, Was.	3	0	0	0	0
* Blackburn, Chase, NY-G	0	0	1	0	1
Bledsoe, Drew, Dal.	17	3	0	-12	3
Bly, Dre', Det.	1	0	1	0	1
Bockwoldt, Colby, N.O.	0	0	1	0	1
Boldin, Anquan, Ariz	2	0	0	0	0
Bouman, Todd, N.O.	4	0	0	0	0
* Bradley, Mark, Chi.	1	0	0	0	0
Briggs, Lance, Chi.	0	0	2	0	2
Brooking, Keith, Atl.	0	0	1	0	1
Brooks, Aaron, N.O.	4	2	0	-12	2
Brown, Antonio, Was.	2	1	0	0	1
* Brown, Reggie, Phi.	1	0	0	0	0
Brown, Sheldon, Phi.	0	0	1	80	1
Brunell, Mark, Was.	11	1	0	-17	1
Bryant, Tony, N.O.	0	0	1	5	1
Bryson, Shawn, Det.	1	1	0	0	1
Buckner, Brentson, Car.	0	0	1	0	1
Bulger, Marc, St.L	4	1	0	-8	1
Burleson, Nate, Min.	0	2	0	0	2
Burress, Plaxico, NY-G	1	0	0	0	0
* Butler, James, NY-G	1	0	1	5	1
Butler, Kelly, Det.	0	2	0	0	2
Carpenter, Keion, Atl.	1	0	0	0	0
Carroll, Ahmad, G.B.	1	0	0	0	0
Cartwright, Rock, Was.	1	0	0	0	0
Chavous, Corey, Min.	0	0	1	0	1
Chillar, Brandon, St.L	0	0	1	8	1
Clancy, Kendrick, NY-G	0	0	1	0	1
Clarke, Adrien, Phi.	0	1	0	0	1
Clayton, Michael, T.B.	1	0	0	0	0
Clement, Anthony, S.F.	0	1	0	0	1
* Cody, Shaun, Det.	0	0	1	0	1
Colbert, Keary, Car.	1	0	0	0	0
Conwell, Ernie, N.O.	1	0	0	0	0
Cooley, Chris, Was.	3	0	0	0	0
Crayton, Patrick, Dal.	3	2	0	0	2
Crumpler, Alge, Atl.	1	0	0	0	0
Culpepper, Daunte, Min.	5	0	0	-4	0
Curtis, Kevin, St.L	2	0	0	0	0
Daniels, Phillip, Was.	0	0	2	0	2
Dansby, Karlos, Ariz	0	0	2	0	2
Darche, J.P., Sea.	0	0	1	0	1
Davenport, Najeh, G.B.	1	1	0	0	1
* Davis, Chauncey, Atl.	0	0	2	24	2
Davis, James, Det.	0	0	1	0	1
Davis, Keith, Dal.	0	0	1	5	1
* Davis, Rashied, Chi.	2	1	0	0	1
Davis, Stephen, Car.	2	0	0	0	0
Dawkins, Brian, Phi.	0	0	1	0	1
Delhomme, Jake, Car.	12	3	0	-4	3
Detmer, Koy, Phi.	2	0	0	0	0
DeVries, Jared, Det.	0	0	2	0	2
Diehl, David, NY-G	0	2	0	0	2
Diggs, Na'il, G.B.	0	0	1	0	1
Dockery, Derrick, Was.	0	2	0	0	2
Dorsey, Ken, S.F.	2	0	0	0	0
Douglas, Marques, S.F.	0	0	2	0	2
Draft, Chris, Car.	0	1	1	0	2
Drummond, Eddie, Det.	1	0	0	0	0
Duckett, T.J., Atl.	2	0	0	0	0
Dunn, Warrick, Atl.	3	2	0	1	2
Dyson, Andre, Sea.	0	0	1	25	1
Edwards, Kalimba, Det.	0	0	3	10	3
Ellis, Greg, Dal.	0	0	2	37	2
* Emanuel, Ben, S.F.	0	1	0	0	1
Engram, Bobby, Sea.	2	0	0	0	0
Evans, Demetric, Was.	0	0	1	0	1
* Fason, Ciatrick, Min.	1	0	0	0	0
Faulk, Marshall, St.L	2	1	0	0	1
Favre, Brett, G.B.	10	2	0	-1	2
Ferguson, Jason, Dal.	0	0	1	0	1
Finn, Jim, NY-G	1	0	0	0	0
Fisher, Tony, G.B.	2	2	0	0	2
Fisher, Travis, St.L	0	0	1	0	1

2005 INDIVIDUAL STATISTICS—FUMBLES

	Fum	Own Rec	Opp Rec	Yards	Tot Rec		Fum	Own Rec	Opp Rec	Yards	Tot Rec
* Fitzpatrick, Ryan, St.L	3	1	0	-3	1	Jurevicius, Joe, Sea.	1	0	0	0	0
Flanagan, Mike, G.B.	2	1	0	-15	1	Kennedy, Kenoy, Det.	1	0	0	0	0
Foster, DeShaun, Car.	2	0	0	0	0	Kerney, Patrick, Atl.	0	0	3	2	3
Fowler, Ryan, Dal.	0	0	1	9	1	Kleinsasser, Jimmy, Min.	1	0	0	0	0
Furrey, Mike, St.L	0	1	2	0	3	Kolodziej, Ross, Ariz	0	0	2	0	2
* Gado, Samkon, G.B.	4	0	0	0	0	Kreutz, Olin, Chi.	0	1	0	0	1
Gage, Justin, Chi.	0	0	1	0	1	Leach, Vonta, G.B.	0	2	0	0	2
Gamble, Chris, Car.	0	0	1	0	1	Leckey, Nick, Ariz	0	1	0	0	1
Garcia, Jeff, Det.	1	0	0	-3	0	Lee, ReShard, G.B.	2	0	0	0	0
Gbaja-Biamila, Kabeer, G.B.	0	0	3	0	3	Lewis, Damione, St.L	0	0	1	0	1
Goings, Nick, Car.	1	0	0	0	0	Lewis, Michael, N.O.	1	0	0	0	0
Goodman, Andre', Det.	0	1	0	15	1	Lewis, Michael, Phi.	0	0	1	0	1
Gordon, Lamar, Phi.	3	1	0	1	1	Little, Leonard, St.L	0	0	2	0	2
* Gore, Frank, S.F.	2	1	0	0	1	Lloyd, Brandon, S.F.	1	0	0	0	0
Graham, Earnest, T.B.	1	0	0	0	0	Locklear, Sean, Sea.	0	2	0	0	2
Grant, Charles, N.O.	0	0	1	23	1	Lucas, Ken, Car.	0	0	1	24	1
Green, Ahman, G.B.	1	0	0	0	0	Mahan, Sean, T.B.	0	1	0	0	1
* Green, Eric, Ariz	0	0	1	0	1	Mahe, Reno, Phi.	2	2	1	0	3
Green, Michael, Chi.	0	0	1	0	1	Manning, Eli, NY-G	9	0	0	0	0
Greisen, Nick, NY-G	0	0	3	28	3	Manning, Ricky, Car.	0	0	3	11	3
Griese, Brian, T.B.	2	1	0	0	1	Manuel, Marquand, Sea.	0	0	1	0	1
Griffin, Cornelius, Was.	0	0	1	0	1	Manumaleuna, Brandon, St.L	2	0	0	0	0
Griffith, Justin, Atl.	1	0	0	0	0	* Marshall, Rasheed, S.F.	4	1	0	0	1
Gross, Jordan, Car.	0	2	1	0	3	Martin, Jamie, St.L	2	0	0	0	0
Hakim, Az-Zahir, N.O.	1	0	0	0	0	Maxwell, Jim, S.F.	0	0	1	0	1
Hall, DeAngelo, Atl.	2	1	2	86	3	Maynard, Brad, Chi.	1	1	0	0	1
Hankton, Karl, Car.	0	1	0	11	1	McAddley, Jason, S.F.	0	0	1	0	1
Hargrove, Anthony, St.L	0	0	2	0	2	McAfee, Fred, N.O.	2	0	0	0	0
Harrington, Joey, Det.	7	1	0	-3	1	McClure, Todd, Atl.	0	1	0	0	1
Harris, Arlen, St.L	0	1	0	0	1	McCown, Josh, Ariz	5	0	0	0	0
* Harris, Chris, Chi.	0	1	1	49	2	McCree, Marlon, Car.	0	0	1	4	1
Harris, Quentin, Ariz	0	0	2	0	2	McDonald, Shaun, St.L	1	0	0	0	0
Harris, Tommie, Chi.	0	0	2	0	2	McFarland, Anthony, T.B.	0	0	2	0	2
Hasselbeck, Matt, Sea.	4	0	0	0	0	McGraw, Jon, Det.	0	0	1	0	1
Hawthorne, Michael, St.L	0	0	1	0	1	McKenzie, Kareem, NY-G	0	2	0	0	2
Heard, Ronnie, Atl.	0	0	1	0	1	McKenzie, Mike, N.O.	1	0	0	0	0
Heitmann, Eric, S.F.	0	1	1	0	2	McKie, Jason, Chi.	0	1	0	0	1
Henderson, E.J., Min.	0	0	1	0	1	McKinnie, Bryant, Min.	0	1	0	0	1
Henderson, William, G.B.	1	0	0	0	0	McMahon, Mike, Phi.	8	3	0	-8	3
Holdman, Warrick, Was.	0	0	1	0	1	McMullen, Billy, Phi.	1	0	0	0	0
Holland, Montrae, N.O.	0	1	0	0	1	McNabb, Donovan, Phi.	8	3	0	-18	3
Holt, Terrence, Det.	0	1	1	38	2	McQuarters, R.W., Det.	2	1	0	0	1
Holt, Torry, St.L	2	1	0	0	1	* Moats, Ryan, Phi.	3	1	1	0	2
Hood, Roderick, Phi.	1	0	0	0	0	Moore, Brandon, S.F.	1	0	1	9	1
Hoover, Brad, Car.	0	1	0	0	1	Moore, Mewelde, Min.	2	2	0	0	2
Horn, Joe, N.O.	2	0	0	0	0	Moorehead, Kindal, Car.	0	0	2	0	2
Hovan, Chris, T.B.	0	0	2	0	2	Morgan, Dan, Car.	0	0	1	0	1
Howard, Darren, N.O.	0	0	2	-2	2	Morris, Maurice, Sea.	0	1	0	-1	1
Idonije, Israel, Chi.	1	1	0	0	1	Morton, Chad, NY-G	1	1	0	0	1
Jackson, Steven, St.L	3	0	1	-7	1	Morton, Christian, Atl.	0	0	1	14	1
* Jacobs, Brandon, NY-G	1	0	0	0	0	Moss, Santana, Was.	3	1	0	0	1
Jansen, Jon, Was.	0	2	0	0	2	Navarre, John, Ariz	1	1	0	0	1
Jenkins, Cullen, G.B.	0	0	1	-2	1	Newman, Keith, Min.	0	0	1	0	1
Jenkins, Michael, Atl.	1	0	0	0	0	Newman, Terence, Dal.	3	3	1	0	4
Jennings, Brian, S.F.	0	0	1	0	1	Nguyen, Dat, Dal.	0	0	2	0	2
Johnson, Al, Dal.	1	1	0	0	1	Odom, Joe, Chi.	0	0	1	0	1
Johnson, Brad, Min.	5	1	0	-1	1	Ogunleye, Adewale, Chi.	0	0	1	0	1
Johnson, Bryan, Chi.	0	1	0	0	1	* Orlovsky, Dan, Det.	1	0	0	0	0
Johnson, Chris, St.L	2	1	0	0	1	* Orton, Kyle, Chi.	12	3	0	-13	3
* Johnson, Derrick, S.F.	0	0	1	78	1	Owens, Richard, Min.	0	0	1	0	1
Johnson, Keyshawn, Dal.	3	0	0	0	0	Pace, Calvin, Ariz	1	0	1	0	1
Jones, Jamal, G.B.	1	0	0	0	0	Pace, Orlando, St.L	0	1	1	0	2
Jones, Julius, Dal.	4	1	0	0	1	Parry, Josh, Phi.	0	1	0	0	1
Jones, Kevin, Det.	2	2	0	23	2	Pearson, Kalvin, T.B.	0	0	1	0	1
Jones, Mark, T.B.	1	1	0	0	1	Peppers, Julius, Car.	0	0	1	10	1
Jones, Thomas, Chi.	2	0	0	0	0	Peterson, Adrian, Chi.	1	1	0	0	1
Jones, Walter, Sea.	0	1	0	0	1	Peterson, Julian, S.F.	0	0	1	0	1
Joseph, William, NY-G	0	0	1	5	1	Peterson, Kenny, G.B.	0	1	1	18	2

	Fum	Own Rec	Opp Rec	Yards	Tot Rec
Pickett, Cody, S.F.	3	1	0	-12	1
Pierce, Antonio, NY-G	0	0	2	12	2
Pierce, Brett, Dal.	0	1	0	0	1
Pittman, Michael, T.B.	1	1	0	0	1
Polite, Lousaka, Dal.	0	2	0	0	2
Pollard, Marcus, Det.	1	0	0	0	0
Ponder, Willie, NY-G	1	0	1	0	1
Portis, Clinton, Was.	3	2	0	0	2
Prioleau, Pierson, Was.	0	1	1	4	2
Quarles, Shelton, T.B.	0	0	1	0	1
Ramsey, Patrick, Was.	2	0	0	0	0
Rasmussen, Kemp, Car.	0	0	1	0	1
Rattay, Tim, S.F.	3	1	0	-2	1
Rayburn, Sam, Phi.	0	0	1	0	1
Redding, Cory, Det.	0	0	1	0	1
Reeves, Jacques, Dal.	0	0	1	0	1
Robbins, Fred, NY-G	0	0	1	0	1
Robertson, Jamal, Car.	1	0	0	0	0
Robinson, Koren, Min.	2	0	0	0	0
* Rodgers, Aaron, G.B.	2	0	0	0	0
Rogers, Shaun, Det.	0	0	1	21	1
Roman, Mark, G.B.	0	0	2	0	2
Ross, Oliver, Ariz	0	1	0	0	1
Rossum, Allen, Atl.	2	1	0	0	1
Rucker, Mike, Car.	0	0	2	11	2
Runyan, Jon, Phi.	0	2	0	1	2
* Ruud, Barrett, T.B.	0	0	1	0	1
Salave'a, Joe, Was.	0	0	1	0	1
Sander, B.J., G.B.	1	1	0	0	1
Schaub, Matt, Atl.	1	0	0	0	0
Scobey, Josh, Sea.	2	0	1	0	1
Scott, Bryan, Atl.	0	0	1	0	1
Scott, Darrion, Min.	0	0	1	1	1
Seidman, Mike, Car.	1	0	0	0	0
Sellers, Mike, Was.	0	0	1	0	1
Sharper, Darren, Min.	1	0	1	14	1
Shepherd, Edell, T.B.	1	0	0	0	0
Shipp, Marcel, Ariz	4	1	0	0	1
Simms, Chris, T.B.	6	1	0	-1	1
Smart, Rod, Car	1	0	0	0	0
* Smith, Alex, S.F.	11	6	0	-10	6
Smith, Antowain, N.O.	2	0	0	0	0
Smith, Derek M., S.F.	0	1	0	0	1
Smith, Dwight, N.O.	1	0	0	0	0
Smith, L.J., Phi.	1	0	0	0	0
Smith, Paul, Det.	1	0	0	0	0
Smith, Raonall, Min.	0	0	2	0	2
Smith, Steve, Car.	2	2	0	5	2
Smith, Will, N.O.	0	0	1	-2	1
Snee, Chris, NY-G	0	1	0	0	1
* Snyder, Adam, S.F.	0	2	0	0	2
* Spears, Marcus, Dal.	0	0	1	59	1
Stallworth, Donte', N.O.	1	0	0	0	0
Stecker, Aaron, N.O.	3	0	0	0	0
Stevens, Jerramy, Sea.	0	2	0	0	2
Stokes, Barry, Atl.	0	1	0	0	1
Strahan, Michael, NY-G	0	0	1	0	1
Swinton, Reggie, Ariz	2	1	0	0	1
Tafoya, Joe, Sea.	0	1	0	0	1
* Tatupu, Lofa, Sea.	0	0	1	0	1
Tauscher, Mark, G.B.	0	1	0	0	1
Taylor, Sean, Was.	0	0	1	39	1
Taylor, Travis, Min.	1	0	0	0	0
Terrill, Craig, Sea.	0	0	1	18	1
Thomas, Anthony, Dal.	0	1	0	0	1
Thomas, Fred, N.O.	0	0	2	0	2
Thomas, Juqua, Phi.	0	0	1	16	1
Thompson, Chris, Chi.	0	0	1	0	1

	Fum	Own Rec	Opp Rec	Yards	Tot Rec
* Thompson, Tyson, Dal.	2	1	0	0	1
Thrash, James, Was.	1	0	0	0	0
Thurman, Andrae, G.B.	1	1	0	0	1
Tillman, Charles, Chi.	0	1	0	0	1
Torbor, Reggie, NY-G	0	0	1	0	1
Tubbs, Marcus, Sea.	0	0	1	0	1
Tucker, Torrin, Dal.	0	1	0	0	1
Tufts, Sean, Car.	0	0	1	0	1
Tyree, David, NY-G	1	1	0	0	1
Umenyiora, Osi, NY-G	0	0	2	0	2
Vick, Michael, Atl.	11	0	0	-6	0
Wade, Bobby, Chi.	10	4	0	0	4
Wahle, Mike, Car.	0	1	0	0	1
Walker, Darwin, Phi.	0	0	2	18	2
Wallace, Al, Car.	0	0	1	6	1
Wallace, Seneca, Sea.	2	1	0	-4	1
Ware, Matt, Phi.	0	0	1	0	1
Warner, Kurt, Ariz	9	3	0	-9	3
Washington, Marcus, Was.	0	0	2	-1	2
Wells, Scott, G.B.	2	2	0	-20	2
Wesley, Dante, Car.	0	0	1	0	1
White, Dewayne, T.B.	0	0	3	52	3
* White, Roddy, Atl.	1	0	0	0	0
Whitehead, Willie, N.O.	0	0	1	0	1
* Whitticker, Will, G.B.	0	1	0	0	1
Williams, Brian, Min.	1	0	0	0	0
* Williams, Carnell, T.B.	3	1	0	0	1
Williams, Demorrio, Atl.	0	0	1	0	1
Williams, Jimmy, Sea.	2	1	0	0	1
Williams, Kevin, Min.	0	0	1	6	1
* Williams, Mike, Det.	2	0	0	0	0
Williams, Moe, Min.	1	1	0	0	1
Williams, Pat, Min.	0	1	0	0	1
Williams, Roy, Dal.	0	0	1	0	1
Wilson, Adrian, Ariz	0	0	2	0	2
Winfield, Antoine, Min.	0	0	2	0	2
Wyms, Ellis, T.B.	0	0	1	0	1
Wynn, Dexter, Phi.	4	3	0	0	3
Wynn, Renaldo, Was.	0	0	1	0	1

* Player that was a rookie in 2005
Yards includes aborted plays, own recoveries, and opponents' recoveries.

AMERICAN FOOTBALL CONFERENCE—FUMBLES

	Fum	Own Rec	Fum OB	TD	Opp Rec	Fum TD	Yards	Tot Rec
Indianapolis	14	5	1	0	13	2	123	18
Cincinnati	18	9	3	0	13	0	79	22
Denver	19	8	2	0	16	0	-1	24
New England	19	9	1	0	8	0	21	17
Pittsburgh	22	13	0	0	15	1	111	28
San Diego	22	9	1	0	10	0	34	19
Kansas City	23	10	0	0	15	1	72	25
Buffalo	26	12	4	0	13	0	15	25
Oakland	26	14	3	0	14	1	-6	28
Cleveland	27	14	0	0	8	0	5	22
Jacksonville	27	14	2	0	9	0	0	23
Tennessee	27	12	3	0	11	2	102	23
Baltimore	28	13	0	0	15	2	70	28
Houston	30	17	2	0	9	0	-14	26
Miami	31	16	1	0	17	1	48	33
N.Y. Jets	36	16	1	0	7	1	60	23
AFC Total	395	191	24	0	193	11	719	384
AFC Average	24.7	11.9	1.5	0.0	12.1	0.7	44.9	24.0

NATIONAL FOOTBALL CONFERENCE—FUMBLES

	Fum	Own Rec	Fum OB	TD	Opp Rec	Fum TD	Yards	Tot Rec
Tampa Bay	16	6	1	0	13	3	88	19
N.Y. Giants	17	8	1	0	19	1	61	27
Seattle	18	9	2	0	11	1	43	20
Detroit	21	9	0	0	12	1	101	21
Carolina	23	11	2	0	19	1	78	30
New Orleans	23	3	2	0	9	0	12	12
St. Louis	24	9	2	0	14	0	-10	23
Minnesota	25	9	2	0	11	0	16	20
Arizona	26	10	0	0	11	0	-9	21
Atlanta	26	6	4	0	13	2	121	19
Washington	29	10	3	0	12	1	25	22
Green Bay	31	15	1	0	11	0	-3	26
San Francisco	31	17	0	1	10	1	63	27
Chicago	32	18	1	0	10	0	36	28
Philadelphia	34	17	3	0	10	1	90	27
Dallas	36	20	2	0	11	0	93	31
NFC Total	412	177	26	1	196	12	805	373
NFC Average	25.8	11.1	1.6	0.1	12.3	0.8	50.3	23.3
NFL Total	807	368	50	1	389	23	1524	757
NFL Average	25.2	11.5	1.6	0.0	12.2	0.7	47.6	23.7

SACKS

MOST SACKS

AFC: 16.0 Derrick Burgess, Oakland
NFC: 14.5 Osi Umenyiora, N.Y. Giants

MOST SACKS, GAME

NFC: 4.0 Phillip Daniels, Washington vs. Dallas, December 18

AFC: 3.0 Kyle Vanden Bosch, Tennessee vs. Baltimore, September 18

3.0 Montae Reagor, Indianapolis vs. Jacksonville, September 18

3.0 Troy Polamalu, Pittsburgh at Houston, September 18

3.0 Dwight Freeney, Indianapolis vs. Cleveland, September 25

3.0 Paul Spicer, Jacksonville at N.Y. Jets, September 25 - (OT)

3.0 Jared Allen, Kansas City vs. Washington, October 16

3.0 Warren Sapp, Oakland at Tennessee, October 30

3.0 Tommy Kelly, Oakland at Kansas City, November 6

3.0 Jason Taylor, Miami at Oakland, November 27

3.0 Shantee Orr, Houston at Baltimore, December 4

3.0 Terrell Suggs, Baltimore vs. Houston, December 4

3.0 Jason Taylor, Miami vs. N.Y. Jets, December 18

3.0 Joey Porter, Pittsburgh at Cleveland, December 24

TEAM LEADERS, SACKS

AFC: BALTIMORE, 9.0, Adalius Thomas; BUFFALO, 12.0, Aaron Schobel; CINCINNATI, 6.0, Justin Smith; CLEVELAND, 5.0, Alvin McKinley, Chaun Thompson; DENVER, 4.0, Ebenezer Ekuban, John Lynch, Trevor Pryce; HOUSTON, 7.0, Shantee Orr; INDIANAPOLIS, 11.5, Robert Mathis; JACKSONVILLE, 8.5, Reggie Hayward; KANSAS CITY, 11.0, Jared Allen; MIAMI, 12.0, Jason Taylor; NEW ENGLAND, 7.0, Rosevelt Colvin; N.Y. JETS, 10.5, John Abraham; OAKLAND, 16.0, Derrick Burgess; PITTSBURGH, 10.5, Joey Porter; SAN DIEGO, 10.0, *Shawne Merriman; TENNESSEE, 12.5, Kyle Vanden Bosch

NFC: ARIZONA, 8.0, Adrian Wilson; ATLANTA, 10.5, Rod Coleman; CAROLINA, 10.5, Julius Peppers; CHICAGO, 10.0, Adewale Ogunleye; DALLAS, 8.0, Greg Ellis, *DeMarcus Ware; DETROIT, 7.0, Kalimba Edwards; GREEN BAY, 8.0, Kabeer Gbaja-Biamila; MINNESOTA, 7.5, Lance Johnstone; NEW ORLEANS, 8.5, Will Smith; N.Y. GIANTS, 14.5, Osi Umenyiora; PHILADELPHIA, 7.5, Jevon Kearse; ST. LOUIS, 9.5, Leonard Little; SAN FRANCISCO, 8.0, Bryant Young; SEATTLE, 9.0, Bryce Fisher; TAMPA BAY, 14.0, Simeon Rice; WASHINGTON, 8.0, Phillip Daniels

TEAM CHAMPION

NFC: 50.0 Seattle
AFC: 49.0 Miami

NFL TOP TEN LEADERS—SACKS

	Sacks
Burgess, Derrick, Oak.	16.0
Umenyiora, Osi, NY-G	14.5
Rice, Simeon, T.B.	14.0
Vanden Bosch, Kyle, Ten.	12.5
Schobel, Aaron, Buf.	12.0
Taylor, Jason, Mia.	12.0
Mathis, Robert, Ind.	11.5
Strahan, Michael, NY-G	11.5
Allen, Jared, K.C.	11.0
Freeney, Dwight, Ind.	11.0

AMERICAN FOOTBALL CONFERENCE—SACKS

	Sacks	Yards
Miami	49	375
Jacksonville	47	277
Pittsburgh	47	312
Indianapolis	46	318
San Diego	46	289
Baltimore	42	270
Tennessee	41	246
Buffalo	38	269
Houston	37	206
Oakland	36	238
New England	33	223
N.Y. Jets	30	193
Kansas City	29	183
Cincinnati	28	180
Denver	28	190
Cleveland	23	142
AFC Total	600	3911
AFC Average	37.5	244.4

NATIONAL FOOTBALL CONFERENCE—SACKS

	Sacks	Yards
Seattle	50	302
Carolina	45	294
Chicago	41	275
N.Y. Giants	41	268
St. Louis	41	195
Arizona	37	217
Atlanta	37	257
Dallas	37	236
Tampa Bay	36	229
Green Bay	35	196
Washington	35	237
Minnesota	34	207
Detroit	31	187
Philadelphia	29	184
San Francisco	28	193
New Orleans	25	165
NFC Total	582	3642
NFC Average	36.4	227.6
League Total	1182	7553
League Average	36.9	236.0

AFC—INDIVIDUAL SACKS

	Sacks
Burgess, Derrick, Oak.	16.0
Vanden Bosch, Kyle, Ten.	12.5
Schobel, Aaron, Buf.	12.0
Taylor, Jason, Mia.	12.0
Mathis, Robert, Ind.	11.5
Allen, Jared, K.C.	11.0
Freeney, Dwight, Ind.	11.0
Abraham, John, NYJ	10.5
Porter, Joey, Pit.	10.5
* Merriman, Shawne, S.D.	10.0
Haggans, Clark, Pit.	9.0
Thomas, Adalius, Bal.	9.0
Hayward, Reggie, Jac.	8.5
Suggs, Terrell, Bal.	8.0
Spicer, Paul, Jac.	7.5
Colvin, Rosevelt, N.E.	7.0
Orr, Shantee, Hou.	7.0
Phillips, Shaun, S.D.	7.0
Brock, Raheem, Ind.	6.5
LaBoy, Travis, Ten.	6.5
Bowens, David, Mia.	6.0
Carter, Kevin, Mia.	6.0
McGinest, Willie, N.E.	6.0
Meier, Rob, Jac.	6.0
Peek, Antwan, Hou.	6.0
Peterson, Mike, Jac.	6.0
Smith, Justin, Cin.	6.0
McCray, Bobby, Jac.	5.5
Reagor, Montae, Ind.	5.5
Bulluck, Keith, Ten.	5.0
Holliday, Vonnie, Mia.	5.0
McKinley, Alvin, Cle.	5.0
Sapp, Warren, Oak.	5.0
Thompson, Chaun, Cle.	5.0
Foley, Steve, S.D.	4.5
Kelly, Tommy, Oak.	4.5
* Pollack, David, Cin.	4.5
Scott, DeQuincy, S.D.	4.5
Vrabel, Mike, N.E.	4.5
Babin, Jason, Hou.	4.0
Denney, Ryan, Buf.	4.0
Ekuban, Ebenezer, Den.	4.0
Fletcher, London, Buf.	4.0
Hicks, Eric, K.C.	4.0
Lynch, John, Den.	4.0
Payne, Seth, Hou.	4.0
Polley, Tommy, Bal.	4.0
Pryce, Trevor, Den.	4.0
Scott, Bart, Bal.	4.0
Seymour, Richard, N.E.	4.0
Simmons, Brian, Cin.	4.0
Smith, Daryl, Jac.	4.0
Tripplett, Larry, Ind.	4.0
* Castillo, Luis, S.D.	3.5
Long, Rien, Ten.	3.5
Polk, DaShon, Hou.	3.5
Robertson, Dewayne, NYJ	3.5
Thomas, Bryan, NYJ	3.5
von Oelhoffen, Kimo, Pit.	3.5
Adams, Sam, Buf.	3.0
Bell, Yeremiah, Mia.	3.0
Crowell, Angelo, Buf.	3.0
Edwards, Donnie, S.D.	3.0
Foote, Larry, Pit.	3.0
Geathers, Robert, Cin.	3.0
Gold, Ian, Den.	3.0
Harrison, James, Pit.	3.0
Haynesworth, Albert, Ten.	3.0

	Sacks
Henderson, John, Jac.	3.0
Keisel, Brett, Pit.	3.0
Legree, Lance, NYJ	3.0
Olshansky, Igor, S.D.	3.0
Polamalu, Troy, Pit.	3.0
Posey, Jeff, Buf.	3.0
Roye, Orpheus, Cle.	3.0
Starks, Randy, Ten.	3.0
Thomas, Josh, Ind.	3.0
Townsend, Deshea, Pit.	3.0
Warren, Gerard, Den.	3.0
Wilson, Al, Den.	3.0
Ayodele, Akin, Jac.	2.5
Boulware, Peter, Bal.	2.5
Ellis, Shaun, NYJ	2.5
Green, Jarvis, N.E.	2.5
Gregg, Kelly, Bal.	2.5
Kelsay, Chris, Buf.	2.5
Sapp, Benny, K.C.	2.5
Sirmon, Peter, Ten.	2.5
Brown, Courtney, Den.	2.0
Browning, John, K.C.	2.0
Bruschi, Tedy, N.E.	2.0
Clemons, Duane, Cin.	2.0
Crocker, Chris, Cle.	2.0
Davis, Andra, Cle.	2.0
Eason, Nick, Cle.	2.0
Farrior, James, Pit.	2.0
Green, Roderick, Bal.	2.0
Greenwood, Morlon, Hou.	2.0
Hamilton, Bobby, Oak.	2.0
Howard, Reggie, Mia.	2.0
Jasper, Ed, Oak.	2.0
* Johnson, Derrick, K.C.	2.0
Jones, Tebucky, Mia.	2.0
Knight, Sammy, K.C.	2.0
Lang, Kenard, Cle.	2.0
Leber, Ben, S.D.	2.0
Mitchell, Kawika, K.C.	2.0
Odom, Antwan, Ten.	2.0
Reed, James, NYJ	2.0
Schulters, Lance, Mia.	2.0
Smith, Aaron, Pit.	2.0
Thomas, Zach, Mia.	2.0
Thornton, David, Ind.	2.0
Thornton, John, Cin.	2.0
Traylor, Keith, Mia.	2.0
Weaver, Anthony, Bal.	2.0
Zgonina, Jeff, Mia.	2.0
Bannan, Justin, Buf.	1.5
Bell, Kendrell, K.C.	1.5
Brown, Mark, NYJ	1.5
Cooper, Stephen, S.D.	1.5
Grant, Deon, Jac.	1.5
Johnson, Jarret, Bal.	1.5
Smith, Robaire, Hou.	1.5
* Thurman, Odell, Cin.	1.5
Warren, Ty, N.E.	1.5
Williams, Chad, Bal.	1.5
Anderson, Charlie, Hou.	1.0
Anderson, Tim, Buf.	1.0
Baker, Rashad, Buf.	1.0
Beisel, Monty, N.E.	1.0
Brackett, Gary, Ind.	1.0
Brayton, Tyler, Oak.	1.0
Carter, Tyrone, Pit.	1.0
Cesaire, Jacques, S.D.	1.0
Chatham, Matt, N.E.	1.0
Clark, Danny, Oak.	1.0

	Sacks
Colclough, Ricardo, Pit.	1.0
Coleman, Marco, Den.	1.0
Dalton, Lional, K.C.	1.0
Davis, Sammy, S.D.	1.0
DeLoach, Jerry, Hou.	1.0
Fletcher, Jamar, S.D.	1.0
Franklin, Aubrayo, Bal.	1.0
* Frazier, Andre, Pit.	1.0
Gardner, Gilbert, Ind.	1.0
Gibson, Derrick, Oak.	1.0
Godfrey, Randall, S.D.	1.0
Grant, DeLawrence, Oak.	1.0
Greer, Jabari, Buf.	1.0
Hall, Carlos, K.C.	1.0
* Harris, Marques, S.D.	1.0
Hawkins, Artrell, N.E.	1.0
Hobson, Victor, NYJ	1.0
* Johnson, Travis, Hou.	1.0
Kaesviharn, Kevin, Cin.	1.0
Kelley, Ethan, Cle.	1.0
Kemoeatu, Maake, Bal.	1.0
Kiel, Terrence, S.D.	1.0
Kirschke, Travis, Pit.	1.0
Lewis, Ray, Bal.	1.0
Maddox, Anthony, Jac.	1.0
* Malone, Alfred, Hou.	1.0
* McFadden, Bryant, Pit.	1.0
* McKenzie, Chris, Hou.	1.0
Milloy, Lawyer, Buf.	1.0
Mitchell, Anthony, Cin.	1.0
Myers, Michael, Den.	1.0
* Pool, Brodney, Cle.	1.0
Poteat, Hank, N.E.	1.0
Powell, Carl, Cin.	1.0
* Rhodes, Kerry, NYJ	1.0
Robinson, Dunta, Hou.	1.0
* Roth, Matt, Mia.	1.0
* Routt, Stanford, Oak.	1.0
Sands, Terdell, Oak.	1.0
Schobel, Bo, Ten.	1.0
Seau, Junior, Mia.	1.0
Simmons, Jason, Hou.	1.0
Spikes, Takeo, Buf.	1.0
Spragan, Donnie, Mia.	1.0
Stroud, Marcus, Jac.	1.0
Thompson, Lamont, Ten.	1.0
Veal, Demetrin, Den.	1.0
Walker, Gary, Hou.	1.0
Washington, Rashad, NYJ	1.0
Wilhelm, Matt, S.D.	1.0
* Williams, Darrent, Den.	1.0
Wong, Kailee, Hou.	1.0
* Wright, Manuel, Mia.	1.0
Banta-Cain, Tully, N.E.	0.5
Clauss, Jared, Ten.	0.5
Cooper, Jarrod, Oak.	0.5
Cousin, Terry, Jac.	0.5
Klecko, Dan, N.E.	0.5
Labinjo, Mike, Ind.	0.5
Vilma, Jonathan, NYJ	0.5
Waddell, Michael, Ten.	0.5
Wilfork, Vince, N.E.	0.5

*Player that was a rookie in 2005

NFC—INDIVIDUAL SACKS

	Sacks
Umenyiora, Osi, NY-G	14.5
Rice, Simeon, T.B.	14.0
Strahan, Michael, NY-G	11.5
Coleman, Rod, Atl.	10.5
Peppers, Julius, Car.	10.5
Ogunleye, Adewale, Chi.	10.0
Little, Leonard, St.L	9.5
Fisher, Bryce, Sea.	9.0
Bernard, Rocky, Sea.	8.5
Smith, Will, N.O.	8.5
Daniels, Phillip, Was.	8.0
Ellis, Greg, Dal.	8.0
Gbaja-Biamila, Kabeer, G.B.	8.0
* Ware, DeMarcus, Dal.	8.0
Wilson, Adrian, Ariz	8.0
Young, Bryant, S.F.	8.0
* Hill, Leroy, Sea.	7.5
Johnstone, Lance, Min.	7.5
Kearse, Jevon, Phi.	7.5
Okeafor, Chike, Ariz	7.5
Rucker, Mike, Car.	7.5
Washington, Marcus, Was.	7.5
Edwards, Kalimba, Det.	7.0
Hargrove, Anthony, St.L	6.5
Kampman, Aaron, G.B.	6.5
Kerney, Patrick, Atl.	6.5
Berry, Bertrand, Ariz	6.0
Brown, Alex, Chi.	6.0
Urlacher, Brian, Chi.	6.0
Rogers, Shaun, Det.	5.5
Tubbs, Marcus, Sea.	5.5
* Cole, Trent, Phi.	5.0
Hall, James, Det.	5.0
Johnson, Tank, Chi.	5.0
Moore, Brandon, S.F.	5.0
Moorehead, Kindal, Car.	5.0
Wallace, Al, Car.	5.0
Carter, Andre, S.F.	4.5
Bryant, Tony, N.O.	4.0
Carstens, Jordan, Car.	4.0
Dansby, Karlos, Ariz	4.0
Griffin, Cornelius, Was.	4.0
* James, Erasmus, Min.	4.0
Scott, Darrion, Min.	4.0
Spires, Greg, T.B.	4.0
* Tatupu, Lofa, Sea.	4.0
Williams, Kevin, Min.	4.0
Wistrom, Grant, Sea.	4.0
Archuleta, Adam, St.L	3.5
Brooking, Keith, Atl.	3.5
Dawkins, Brian, Phi.	3.5
Howard, Darren, N.O.	3.5
Lake, Antwan, Atl.	3.5
* Patterson, Mike, Phi.	3.5
Brooks, Derrick, T.B.	3.0
DeVries, Jared, Det.	3.0
Evans, Demetric, Was.	3.0
Glover, La'Roi, Dal.	3.0
* Green, Brandon, St.L	3.0
Harris, Al, G.B.	3.0
Harris, Tommie, Chi.	3.0
Jenkins, Cullen, G.B.	3.0
Kennedy, Jimmy, St.L	3.0
Kolodziej, Ross, Ariz	3.0
Morgan, Dan, Car.	3.0
* Mosley, C.J., Min.	3.0
Newman, Keith, Min.	3.0
Peterson, Kenny, G.B.	3.0

	Sacks
Peterson, Julian, S.F.	3.0
Prioleau, Pierson, Was.	3.0
Smith, Antonio, Ariz	3.0
Smith, Brady, Atl.	3.0
Thomas, Fred, N.O.	3.0
White, Dewayne, T.B.	3.0
Wilkinson, Dan, Det.	3.0
Williams, Demorrio, Atl.	3.0
Wilson, Gibril, NY-G	3.0
Adams, Anthony, S.F.	2.5
* Canty, Chris, Dal.	2.5
Darby, Chartric, Sea.	2.5
Grant, Charles, N.O.	2.5
Jackson, Tyoka, St.L	2.5
James, Bradie, Dal.	2.5
Lavalais, Chad, Atl.	2.5
Pierce, Antonio, NY-G	2.5
Walker, Darwin, Phi.	2.5
Williams, Roy, Dal.	2.5
Witherspoon, Will, Car.	2.5
Allen, Kenderick, NY-G	2.0
Barber, Ronde, T.B.	2.0
Boulware, Michael, Sea.	2.0
Briggs, Lance, Chi.	2.0
Clancy, Kendrick, NY-G	2.0
Clemons, Chris, Was.	2.0
Coakley, Dexter, St.L	2.0
Cole, Colin, G.B.	2.0
Cowart, Sam, Min.	2.0
Draft, Chris, Car.	2.0
Fujita, Scott, Dal.	2.0
Ivy, Corey, St.L	2.0
Joseph, William, NY-G	2.0
Kalu, N. D., Phi.	2.0
Marshall, Lemar, Was.	2.0
McFarland, Anthony, T.B.	2.0
Nece, Ryan, T.B.	2.0
Pickett, Ryan, St.L	2.0
* Poppinga, Brady, G.B.	2.0
* Shropshire, Darrell, Atl.	2.0
Terrill, Craig, Sea.	2.0
Williams, Corey, G.B.	2.0
Wyms, Ellis, T.B.	2.0
Boone, Alfonso, Chi.	1.5
* Cody, Shaun, Det.	1.5
* Davis, Thomas, Car.	1.5
Haynes, Michael, Chi.	1.5
Lenon, Paris, G.B.	1.5
Minter, Mike, Car.	1.5
Robbins, Fred, NY-G	1.5
Shanle, Scott, Dal.	1.5
* Spears, Marcus, Dal.	1.5
Tinoisamoa, Pisa, St.L	1.5
Williams, Pat, Min.	1.5
Adams, Mike, S.F.	1.5
* Atogwe, O.J., St.L	1.0
Azumah, Jerry, Chi.	1.0
Bailey, Boss, Det.	1.0
Barnett, Nick, G.B.	1.0
* Blackstock, Darryl, Ariz	1.0
Brown, Mike, Chi.	1.0
Brown, Sheldon, Phi.	1.0
Buckner, Brentson, Car.	1.0
* Burnett, Kevin, Dal.	1.0
Craft, Jason, N.O.	1.0
Darling, James, Ariz	1.0
* Davis, Chauncey, Atl.	1.0
Douglas, Marques, S.F.	1.0
Ferguson, Jason, Dal.	1.0

	Sacks
Greisen, Nick, NY-G	1.0
* Harris, Chris, Chi.	1.0
Harris, Napoleon, Min.	1.0
Henderson, E.J., Min.	1.0
Hillenmeyer, Hunter, Chi.	1.0
Huff, Orlando, Ariz	1.0
Idonije, Israel, Chi.	1.0
Jackson, Dexter, T.B.	1.0
Jackson, Grady, G.B.	1.0
* Johnson, Derrick, S.F.	1.0
Kelly, Brian, T.B.	1.0
Lewis, Damione, St.L	1.0
Lewis, Michael, Phi.	1.0
* Montgomery, Mike, G.B.	1.0
Moore, Langston, Ariz	1.0
Newman, Terence, Dal.	1.0
Nguyen, Dat, Dal.	1.0
Pace, Calvin, Ariz	1.0
Quarles, Shelton, T.B.	1.0
* Ratliff, Jay, Dal.	1.0
Rayburn, Sam, Phi.	1.0
Redding, Cory, Det.	1.0
Scott, Bryan, Atl.	1.0
Sheppard, Lito, Phi.	1.0
Smith, Dwight, N.O.	1.0
Smith, Keith, Det.	1.0
Smith, Raonall, Min.	1.0
Tafoya, Joe, Sea.	1.0
Taylor, Sean, Was.	1.0
Tillman, Charles, Chi.	1.0
Trotter, Jeremiah, Phi.	1.0
Trufant, Marcus, Sea.	1.0
* Tuck, Justin, NY-G	1.0
Udeze, Kenechi, Min.	1.0
Watson, Courtney, N.O.	1.0
Williams, Brian, Min.	1.0
Woods, LeVar, Det.	1.0
* Babineaux, Jonathan, Atl.	0.5
Claiborne, Chris, St.L	0.5
Clark, Ryan, Was.	0.5
Coleman, Kenyon, Dal.	0.5
Dockett, Darnell, Ariz	0.5
* Emanuel, Ben, S.F.	0.5
Hall, Travis, S.F.	0.5
Salave'a, Joe, Was.	0.5
Short, Brandon, Car.	0.5
Whitehead, Willie, N.O.	0.5
Wynn, Renaldo, Was.	0.5

*Player that was a rookie in 2005

2005 NFL PAID ATTENDANCE BREAKDOWN

	Games	Attendance	Average
NFL Preseason Total	66	3,977,388	60,263
NFL Regular-Season Total	256	17,012,453	66,455
NFL Postseason Total	12	802,255	66,855
NFL All Games	334	21,792,096	65,246

1.1-MILLION CLUB

During the 2005 season, eight teams drew more than 1.1 million paid attendance home and away during the regular season. For the sixth consecutive year, the Washington Redskins led the league in regular-season paid attendance (1,240,233) and home paid attendance (707,614).

Team	Total Paid Home Attendance	Total Paid Visiting Attendance	Total Paid Attendance
Washington	707,614	532,609	1,240,223
New York Jets	619,842	577,382	1,197,224
Kansas City	625,081	552,499	1,177,580
New York Giants	628,527	524,145	1,152,672
Denver	595,671	551,594	1,147,265
New England	567,714	579,133	1,146,847
San Diego	547,937	560,903	1,108,840
Miami	575,256	529,767	1,105,023

For complete year-by-year attendance records, see pages 614-615.

Inside the Numbers

GREATEST COMEBACKS IN NFL HISTORY
(Most Points Overcome To Win Game)

REGULAR SEASON GAMES

FROM 28 POINTS BEHIND TO WIN:
December 7, 1980, at San Francisco

New Orleans	14	21	0	0	0	— 35
San Francisco	0	7	14	14	3	— 38

- NO — Harris 33 pass from Manning (Ricardo kick)
- NO — Childs 21 pass from Manning (Ricardo kick)
- NO — Holmes 1 run (Ricardo kick)
- SF — Solomon 57 punt return (Wersching kick)
- NO — Holmes 1 run (Ricardo kick)
- NO — Harris 41 pass from Manning (Ricardo kick)
- SF — Montana 1 run (Wersching kick)
- SF — Clark 71 pass from Montana (Wersching kick)
- SF — Solomon 14 pass from Montana (Wersching kick)
- SF — Elliott 7 run (Wersching kick)
- SF — FG Wersching 36

FROM 26 POINTS BEHIND TO WIN:
September 21, 1997, at Buffalo

Indianapolis	14	12	0	9	— 35
Buffalo	0	10	6	21	— 37

- Ind — Bailey 10 pass from Harbaugh (Blanchard kick)
- Ind — Faulk 10 run (Blanchard kick)
- Ind — FG Blanchard 39
- Ind — FG Blanchard 36
- Ind — FG Blanchard 49
- Ind — FG Blanchard 22
- Buff — Johnson 16 pass from Collins (Christie kick)
- Buff — FG Christie 27
- Buff — A. Smith 15 run (2-pt attempt failed)
- Ind — FG Blanchard 25
- Buff — Early 4 pass from Collins (Christie kick)
- Buff — A. Smith 1 run (Christie kick)
- Buff — A. Smith 54 run (Christie kick)
- Ind — Harrison 2 pass from Justin (2-pt attempt failed)

FROM 25 POINTS BEHIND TO WIN:
November 8, 1987, at St. Louis

Tampa Bay	7	7	14	0	— 28
St. Louis	0	3	0	28	— 31

- TB — Carrier 5 pass from DeBerg (Igwebuike kick)
- TB — Carter 3 pass from DeBerg (Igwebuike kick)
- StL — FG Gallery 31
- TB — Smith 34 pass from DeBerg (Igwebuike kick)
- TB — Smith 3 run (Igwebuike kick)

- StL — Awalt 4 pass from Lomax (Gallery kick)
- StL — Noga 23 fumble recovery (Gallery kick)
- StL — J. Smith 11 pass from Lomax (Gallery kick)
- StL — J. Smith 17 pass from Lomax (Gallery kick)

FROM 24 POINTS BEHIND TO WIN:
October 27, 1946, at Washington

Philadelphia	0	0	14	14	— 28
Washington	10	14	0	0	— 24

- Wash — Rosato 2 run (Poillon kick)
- Wash — FG Poillon 28
- Wash — Rosato 4 run (Poillon kick)
- Wash — Lapka recovered fumble in end zone (Poillon kick)
- Phil — Steele 1 run (Lio kick)
- Phil — Pritchard 45 pass from Thompson (Lio kick)
- Phil — Steinke 7 pass from Thompson (Lio kick)
- Phil — Ferrante 30 pass from Thompson (Lio kick)

FROM 24 POINTS BEHIND TO WIN:
October 20, 1957, at Detroit

Baltimore	7	14	6	0	— 27
Detroit	0	3	7	21	— 31

- Balt — Mutscheller 15 pass from Unitas (Rechichar kick)
- Det — FG Martin 47
- Balt — Moore 72 pass from Unitas (Rechichar kick)
- Balt — Mutscheller 52 pass from Unitas (Rechichar kick)
- Balt — Moore 4 pass from Unitas (kick failed)
- Det — Junker 14 pass from Rote (Layne kick)
- Det — Cassady 26 pass from Layne (Layne kick)
- Det — Johnson 1 run (Layne kick)
- Det — Cassady 29 pass from Layne (Layne kick)

FROM 24 POINTS BEHIND TO WIN:
October 25, 1959, at Minneapolis

Philadelphia	0	0	21	7	— 28
Chicago Cardinals	7	10	7	0	— 24

- Cardinals — Crow 10 pass from Roach (Conrad kick)
- Cardinals — J. Hill 77 blocked field goal return (Conrad kick)
- Cardinals — FG Conrad 15
- Cardinals — Lane 37 interception return (Conrad kick)
- Phil — Barnes 1 run (Walston kick)
- Phil — McDonald 29 pass from Van Brocklin (Walston kick)
- Phil — Barnes 2 run (Walston kick)
- Phil — McDonald 22 pass from Van Brocklin (Walston kick)

FROM 24 POINTS BEHIND TO WIN:
October 23, 1960, at Denver

Boston	10	7	7	0	— 24
Denver	0	0	14	17	— 31

- Bos — FG Cappelletti 12

- Bos — Colclough 10 pass from Songin (Cappelletti kick)
- Bos — Wells 6 pass from Songin (Cappelletti kick)
- Bos — Miller 47 pass from Songin (Cappelletti kick)
- Den — Carmichael 21 pass from Tripucka (Mingo kick)
- Den — Jessup 19 pass from Tripucka (Mingo kick)
- Den — Carmichael 35 lateral from Taylor, pass from Tripucka (Mingo kick)
- Den — Taylor 8 pass from Tripucka (Mingo kick)
- Den — FG Mingo 9

FROM 24 POINTS BEHIND TO WIN:
December 15, 1974, at Miami

New England	21	3	0	3	— 27
Miami	0	17	7	10	— 34

- NE — Hannah recovered fumble in end zone (J. Smith kick)
- NE — Sanders 23 interception return (J. Smith kick)
- NE — Herron 4 pass from Plunkett (J. Smith kick)
- NE — FG J. Smith 46
- Mia — Nottingham 1 run (Yepremian kick)
- Mia — Baker 37 pass from Morrall (Yepremian kick)
- Mia — FG Yepremian 28
- Mia — Baker 46 pass from Morrall (Yepremian kick)
- NE — FG J. Smith 34
- Mia — Nottingham 2 run (Yepremian kick)
- Mia — FG Yepremian 40

FROM 24 POINTS BEHIND TO WIN:
December 4, 1977, at Minnesota

San Francisco	0	10	14	3	— 27
Minnesota	0	0	7	21	— 28

- SF — Delvin Williams 2 run (Wersching kick)
- SF — FG Wersching 31
- SF — Dave Williams 80 kickoff return (Wersching kick)
- SF — Delvin Williams 5 run (Wersching kick)
- Minn — McClanahan 15 pass from Lee (Cox kick)
- Minn — Rashad 8 pass from Kramer (Cox kick)
- Minn — Tucker 9 pass from Kramer (Cox kick)
- SF — FG Wersching 31
- Minn — S. White 69 pass from Kramer (Cox kick)

FROM 24 POINTS BEHIND TO WIN:
September 23, 1979, at Denver

Seattle	10	10	14	0	— 34
Denver	0	10	21	6	— 37

- Sea — FG Herrera 28
- Sea — Doornink 5 run (Herrera kick)
- Den — FG Turner 27

Sea — Doornink 5 run
    (Herrera kick)
Den — Armstrong 2 run
    (Turner kick)
Sea — FG Herrera 22
Sea — McCullum 13 pass from
    Zorn (Herrera kick)
Sea — Smith 1 run (Herrera kick)
Den — Studdard 2 pass from
    Morton (Turner kick)
Den — Moses 11 pass from
    Morton (Turner kick)
Den — Upchurch 35 pass from
    Morton (Turner kick)
Den — Lytle 1 run (kick failed)

FROM 24 POINTS BEHIND TO WIN:
September 23, 1979, at Cincinnati

Houston	0	10	17	0	3 —	30
Cincinnati	14	10	0	3	0 —	27

Cin — Johnson 1 run (Bahr kick)
Cin — Alexander 2 run (Bahr kick)
Cin — Johnson 1 run (Bahr kick)
Cin — FG Bahr 52
Hou — Burrough 35 pass from
    Pastorini (Fritsch kick)
Hou — FG Fritsch 33
Hou — Campbell 8 run
    (Fritsch kick)
Hou — Caster 22 pass from
    Pastorini (Fritsch kick)
Hou — FG Fritsch 47
Cin — FG Bahr 55
Hou — FG Fritsch 29

FROM 24 POINTS BEHIND TO WIN:
November 22, 1982, at Los Angeles

San Diego	10	14	0	0 —	24
L.A. Raiders	0	7	14	7 —	28

SD — FG Benirschke 19
SD — Scales 29 pass from Fouts
    (Benirschke kick)
SD — Muncie 2 run
    (Benirschke kick)
SD — Muncie 1 run
    (Benirschke kick)
Raiders — Christensen 1 pass from
    Plunkett (Bahr kick)
Raiders — Allen 3 run (Bahr kick)
Raiders — Allen 6 run (Bahr kick)
Raiders — Hawkins 1 run (Bahr kick)

FROM 24 POINTS BEHIND TO WIN:
September 26, 1988, at Denver

L.A. Raiders	0	0	14	13	3 —	30
Denver	7	17	0	3	0 —	27

Den — Dorsett 1 run (Karlis kick)
Den — Dorsett 1 run (Karlis kick)
Den — Sewell 7 pass from Elway
    (Karlis kick)
Den — FG Karlis 39
Raiders — Smith 40 pass from
    Schroeder (Bahr kick)
Raiders — Smith 42 pass from
    Schroeder (Bahr kick)
Raiders — FG Bahr 28
Raiders — Allen 4 run (Bahr kick)
Den — FG Karlis 25
Raiders — FG Bahr 44
Raiders — FG Bahr 35

FROM 24 POINTS BEHIND TO WIN:
December 6, 1992, at Tampa

L.A. Rams	0	3	21	7 —	31
Tampa Bay	6	21	0	0 —	27

TB — FG Murray 34
TB — FG Murray 47
TB — Armstrong 81 pass from
    Testaverde (Murray kick)
TB — Jones 26 fumble recovery
    (Murray kick)
Rams — FG Zendejas 18
TB — Carrier 10 pass from
    Testaverde (Murray kick)
Rams — Anderson 40 pass from
    Everett (Zendejas kick)
Rams — Chadwick 27 pass from
    Everett (Zendejas kick)
Rams — Lang 1 run (Zendejas kick)
Rams — Carter 8 pass from Everett
    (Zendejas kick)

POSTSEASON GAMES

FROM 32 POINTS BEHIND TO WIN:
AFC First-Round Playoff Game
January 3, 1993, at Buffalo

Houston	7	21	7	3	0 —	38
Buffalo	3	0	28	7	3 —	41

Hou — Jeffires 3 pass from Moon
    (Del Greco kick)
Buff — FG Christie 36
Hou — Slaughter 7 pass from Moon
    (Del Greco kick)
Hou — Duncan 26 pass from Moon
    (Del Greco kick)
Hou — Jeffires 27 pass from Moon
    (Del Greco kick)
Hou — McDowell 58 interception
    return (Del Greco kick)
Buff — Davis 1 run (Christie kick)
Buff — Beebe 38 pass from Reich
    (Christie kick)
Buff — Reed 26 pass from Reich
    (Christie kick)
Buff — Reed 18 pass from Reich
    (Christie kick)
Buff — Reed 17 pass from Reich
    (Christie kick)
Hou — FG Del Greco 26
Buff — FG Christie 32

FROM 24 POINTS BEHIND TO WIN:
NFC First-Round Playoff Game
January 5, 2003, at San Francisco

N.Y. Giants	7	21	10	0 —	38
San Francisco	7	7	8	17 —	39

SF — Owens 76 pass from Garcia
    (Chandler kick)
NYG — Toomer 12 pass from
    Collins (Bryant kick)
NYG — Shockey 2 pass from
    Collins (Bryant kick)
SF — Barlow 1 run (Chandler
    kick)
NYG — Toomer 8 pass from Collins
    (Bryant kick)
NYG — Toomer 24 pass from
    Collins (Bryant kick)
NYG — Barber 6 run (Bryant kick)
NYG — FG Bryant 21

SF — Owens 26 pass from Garcia
    (Owens from Garcia)
SF — Garcia 14 run
    (Owens from Garcia)
SF — Garcia 14 run
    (Owens from Garcia)
SF — FG Chandler 25
SF — Streets 13 pass from Garcia
    (2-pt attempt failed)

FROM 20 POINTS BEHIND TO WIN:
Western Conference Playoff Game
December 22, 1957, at San Francisco

Detroit	0	7	14	10 —	31
San Francisco	14	10	3	0 —	27

SF — Owens 34 pass from Tittle
    (Soltau kick)
SF — McElhenny 47 pass from
    Tittle (Soltau kick)
Det — Junker 4 pass from Rote
    (Martin kick)
SF — Wilson 12 pass from Tittle
    (Soltau kick)
SF — FG Soltau 25
SF — FG Soltau 10
Det — Tracy 2 run (Martin kick)
Det — Tracy 58 run (Martin kick)
Det — Gedman 3 run (Martin kick)
Det — FG Martin 14

FROM 18 POINTS BEHIND TO WIN:
NFC Divisional Playoff Game
December 23, 1972, at San Francisco

Dallas	3	10	0	17 —	30
San Francisco	7	14	7	0 —	28

SF — Washington 97 kickoff
    return (Gossett kick)
Dall — FG Fritsch 37
SF — Schreiber 1 run
    (Gossett kick)
SF — Schreiber 1 run
    (Gossett kick)
Dall — FG Fritsch 45
Dall — Alworth 28 pass from
    Morton (Fritsch kick)
SF — Schreiber 1 run
    (Gossett kick)
Dall — FG Fritsch 27
Dall — Parks 20 pass from
    Staubach (Fritsch kick)
Dall — Sellers 10 pass from
    Staubach (Fritsch kick)

FROM 18 POINTS BEHIND TO WIN:
AFC Divisional Playoff Game
January 4, 1986, at Miami

Cleveland	7	7	7	0 —	21
Miami	3	0	14	7 —	24

Mia — FG Reveiz 51
Cle — Newsome 16 pass from
    Kosar (Bahr kick)
Cle — Byner 21 run (Bahr kick)
Cle — Byner 66 run (Bahr kick)
Mia — Moore 6 pass from Marino
    (Reveiz kick)
Mia — Davenport 31 run
    (Reveiz kick)
Mia — Davenport 1 run
    (Reveiz kick)

RECORDS FOR NFL TEAMS FOR MOST POINTS IN A GAME (REGULAR SEASON ONLY)

Note: When the record has been achieved more than once, only the most recent game is shown; summaries are listed in alphabetical order by conference. Bold face indicates team holding record.

BALTIMORE RAVENS

December 19, 2005, at Baltimore

Green Bay	3	0	0	0	— 3
Baltimore	14	10	10	14	— 48

TD: Balt—Todd Heap 2, Mark Clayton, Randy Hymes, Jamal Lewis, Adalius Thomas. TD Passes: Balt—Kyle Boller 3. FG: Balt—Matt Stover 2; GB—Ryan Longwell.

BUFFALO BILLS

September 18, 1966, at Buffalo

Miami	3	7	0	14	— 24
Buffalo	21	27	3	7	— 58

TD: Buff—Bobby Burnett 2, Butch Byrd 2, Jack Spikes 2, Bobby Crockett, Jack Kemp; Mia—Dave Kocourek, Bo Roberson, John Roderick. TD Passes: Buff—Jack Kemp, Daryle Lamonica; Mia—George Wilson 3. FG: Buff—Booth Lusteg; Mia—Gene Mingo.

CINCINNATI BENGALS

December 17, 1989, at Cincinnati

Houston	0	0	0	7	— 7
Cincinnati	21	10	21	9	— 61

TD: Cin—Eddie Brown 2, Eric Ball, James Brooks, Ira Hillary, Rodney Holman, Tim McGee, Craig Taylor; Hou—Lorenzo White. TD Passes: Cin—Boomer Esiason 4, Erik Wilhelm. FG: Cin—Jim Breech 2.

CLEVELAND BROWNS

November 7, 1954, at Cleveland

Washington	0	3	0	0	— 3
Cleveland	13	14	21	14	— 62

TD: Cle—Darrell Brewster 2, Mo Bassett, Ken Gorgal, Otto Graham, Dub Jones, Dante Lavelli, Curley Morrison. TD Passes: Cle—George Ratterman 3, Otto Graham. FG: Cle—Lou Groza 2; Wash—Vic Janowicz.

DENVER BRONCOS

October 6, 1963, at Denver

San Diego	13	7	0	14	— 34
Denver	3	14	9	24	— 50

TD: Den—Lionel Taylor 2, Goose Gonsoulin, Gene Prebola, Donnie Stone; SD—Keith Lincoln 2, Lance Alworth, Paul Lowe, Jacque MacKinnon. TD Passes: Den—John McCormick 3; SD—Tobin Rote 3, John Hadl 2. FG: Den—Gene Mingo 5.

HOUSTON TEXANS

November 28, 2004 at Houston

Tennessee	14	7	0	0	— 21
Houston	3	7	14	7	— 31

TD: Tenn—Erron Kinney 2, Derrick Mason; Hou—Domanick Davis, Andre Johnson, Billy Miller, Jonathan Wells. TD Passes: Tenn—Steve McNair 3; Hou—David Carr 2. FG: Hou—Kris Brown.

INDIANAPOLIS COLTS

December 12, 1976, at Baltimore

Buffalo	3	3	7	7	— 20
Baltimore Colts	7	13	28	10	— 58

TD: Balt—Roger Carr, Raymond Chester, Glenn Doughty, Roosevelt Leaks, Derrel Luce, Lydell Mitchell, Howard Stevens; Buff—Bob Chandler, O.J. Simpson. TD Passes: Balt—Bert Jones 3; Buff—Gary Marangi. FG: Balt—Toni Linhart 3; Buff—George Jakowenko 2.

JACKSONVILLE JAGUARS

December 3, 2000, at Jacksonville

Cleveland	0	0	0	0	— 0
Jacksonville	3	17	21	7	— 48

TD: Jax—Fred Taylor 3, Keenan McCardell, Mark Brunell, Shyrone Stith. TD Passes: Jax—Mark Brunell. FG: Jax—Mike Hollis 2.

KANSAS CITY CHIEFS

September 7, 1963, at Denver

Kansas City	14	14	21	10	— 59
Denver	0	7	0	0	— 7

TD: KC—Chris Burford 2, Frank Jackson 2, Dave Grayson, Abner Haynes, Sherrill Headrick, Curtis McClinton; Den—Lionel Taylor. TD Passes: KC—Len Dawson 4, Curtis McClinton; Den—Mickey Slaughter. FG: KC—Tommy Brooker.

MIAMI DOLPHINS

November 24, 1977, at St. Louis

Miami	14	14	20	7	— 55
St. Louis Cardinals	7	0	0	7	— 14

TD: Mia—Nat Moore 3, Gary Davis, Duriel Harris, Leroy Harris, Benny Malone, Andre Tillman; StL—Ike Harris, Terry Metcalf. TD Passes: Mia—Bob Griese 6; StL—Jim Hart.

NEW ENGLAND PATRIOTS

September 9, 1979, at New England

New York Jets	3	0	0	0	— 3
New England	14	21	7	14	— 56

TD: NE—Harold Jackson 3, Stanley Morgan 2, Allan Clark, Andy Johnson, Don Westbrook. TD Passes: NE—Steve Grogan 5, Tom Owen. FG: NYJ—Pat Leahy.

NEW YORK JETS

November 17, 1985, at New York

Tampa Bay	14	7	0	0	— 28
New York Jets	17	24	14	7	— 62

TD: NYJ—Mickey Shuler 3, Johnny Hector 2, Tony Paige, Al Toon, Wesley Walker; TB—James Wilder 2, Kevin House, Calvin Magee. TD Passes: NYJ—Ken O'Brien 5; TB—Steve DeBerg 3. FG: NYJ—Pat Leahy 2.

OAKLAND RAIDERS

September 29, 2002 at Oakland

Tennessee	7	0	12	6	— 25
Oakland	21	10	7	14	— 52

TD: Oak—Tim Brown, Phillip Buchanon, Charlie Garner, Terry Kirby, Jerry Porter, Jim Rice, Rod Woodson; Tenn—Drew Bennett, Eddie George, Justin McCareins, John Simon. TD Passes: Oak—Rich Gannon 4; Tenn—Steve McNair 2. FG: Oak—Sebastian Janikowski.

PITTSBURGH STEELERS

November 30, 1952, at Pittsburgh

New York Giants	0	0	7	0	— 7
Pittsburgh	14	14	7	28	— 63

TD: Pitt—Lynn Chandnois 2, Dick Hensley 2, Jack Butler, George Hays, Ray Mathews, Ed Modzelewski, Elbie Nickel; NYG—Bill Stribling. TD Passes: Pitt—Jim Finks 4, Gary Kerkorian; NYG—Tom Landry.

SAN DIEGO CHARGERS

December 22, 1963, at San Diego

Denver	7	10	3	0	— 20
San Diego	10	16	10	22	— 58

TD: SD—Paul Lowe 2, Chuck Allen, Bobby Jackson, Dave Kocourek, Keith Lincoln, Jacque MacKinnon; Den—Billy Joe, Donnie Stone. TD Passes: SD—John Hadl, Tobin Rote; Den—Don Breaux. FG: SD—George Blair 3; Den—Gene Mingo 2.

TENNESSEE TITANS

December 9, 1990, at Houston

Cleveland	0	7	7	0	— 14
Houston Oilers	14	31	7	6	— 58

TD: Hou—Lorenzo White 4, Ernest Givins, Leonard Harris, Tony Jones, Terry Kinard; Cle—Eric Metcalf 2. TD Passes: Hou—Warren Moon 2, Cody Carlson; Cle—Bernie Kosar. FG: Hou—Teddy Garcia.

ARIZONA CARDINALS
November 13, 1949, at New York

Chicago Cardinals	7	31	14	13	— 65
New York Bulldogs	7	0	6	7	— 20

TD: Chi—Red Cochran 2, Pat Harder 2, Bill Dewell, Mel Kutner, Bob Ravensburg, Vic Schwall, Charlie Trippi; NY—Joe Golding, Frank Muehlheuser, Johnny Rauch. TD Passes: Chi—Paul Christman 3, Jim Hardy 3; NY—Bobby Layne. FG: Chi—Pat Harder.

ATLANTA FALCONS
September 16, 1973, at New Orleans

Atlanta	0	24	21	17	— 62
New Orleans	0	0	7	0	— 7

TD: Atl—Ken Burrow 2, Eddie Ray 2, Wes Chesson, Tom Hayes, Art Malone, Joe Profit; NO—Bill Butler. TD Passes: Atl—Dick Shiner 3, Bob Lee; NO—Archie Manning. FG: Atl—Nick Mike-Mayer 2.

CAROLINA PANTHERS
December 8, 2002, at Carolina

Cincinnati	7	10	14	0	— 31
Carolina	9	7	21	15	— 52

TD: Car—Steve Smith 3, Dee Brown, Muhsin Muhammad, Al Wallace, Wesley Walls; Cin—Peter Warrick 2, Jon Kitna, Takeo Spikes. TD Passes: Car—Rodney Peete 3; Cin—Jon Kitna 2. FG: Cin—Neil Rackers.

CHICAGO BEARS
December 7, 1980, at Chicago

Green Bay	0	7	0	0	— 7
Chicago	0	28	13	20	— 61

TD: Chi—Walter Payton 3, Brian Baschnagel, Robin Earl, Roland Harper, Willie McClendon, Len Walterscheid, Rickey Watts; GB—James Lofton. TD Passes: Chi—Vince Evans 3; GB—Lynn Dickey.

DALLAS COWBOYS
October 12, 1980, at Dallas

San Francisco	0	7	0	7	— 14
Dallas	14	24	14	7	— 59

TD: Dall—Drew Pearson 3, Ron Springs 2, Tony Dorsett, Billy Joe DuPrce, Robert Newhouse, SF—Dwight Clark 2. TD Passes: Dall—Danny White 4; SF—Steve DeBerg 2. FG: Dall—Rafael Septien.

DETROIT LIONS
November 27, 1997, at Detroit

Chicago	14	6	0	0	— 20
Detroit	3	14	17	21	— 55

TD: Det—Herman Moore, Johnnie Morton, Ron Rivers, Barry Sanders 3, Tracy Scroggins; Chi—Raymont Harris, Ricky Proehl. TD Passes: Det—Scott Mitchell 2; Chi—Erik Kramer. FG: Det—Jason Hanson 2; Chi—Jeff Jaeger 2.

GREEN BAY PACKERS
October 7, 1945, at Milwaukee

Detroit	0	7	7	7	— 21
Green Bay	0	41	9	7	— 57

TD: GB—Don Hutson 4, Charley Brock, Irv Comp, Ted Fritsch, Clyde Goodnight; Det—Chuck Fenenbock, John Greene, Bob Westfall. TD Passes: GB—Tex McKay 4, Lou Brock, Irv Comp; Det—Dave Ryan.

MINNESOTA VIKINGS
October 18, 1970, at Minnesota

Dallas	3	3	0	7	— 13
Minnesota	14	20	17	3	— 54

TD: Minn—Clint Jones 2, Ed Sharockman 2, John Beasley, Dave Osborn; Dall—Calvin Hill. TD Pass: Minn—Gary Cuozzo. FG: Minn—Fred Cox 4; Dall—Mike Clark 2.

NEW ORLEANS SAINTS
November 21, 1976, at Seattle

New Orleans	3	17	28	3	— 51
Seattle	6	0	7	14	— 27

TD: NO—Bobby Douglass 2, Tony Galbreath, Chuck Muncie, Tom Myers, Elex Price; Sea—Sherman Smith 2, Steve Largent, Jim Zorn. TD Pass: Sea—Bill Munson. FG: NO—Rich Szaro 3.

NEW YORK GIANTS
November 26, 1972, at New York

Philadelphia	3	7	0	0	— 10
New York Giants	14	24	10	14	— 62

TD: NYG—Don Herrmann 2, Ron Johnson 2, Bob Tucker 2, Randy Johnson; Phil—Harold Jackson. TD Passes: NYG—Norm Snead 3, Randy Johnson 2; Phil—John Reaves. FG: NYG—Pete Gogolak 2; Phil—Tom Dempsey.

PHILADELPHIA EAGLES
November 6, 1934, at Philadelphia

Cincinnati Reds	0	0	0	0	— 0
Philadelphia	26	6	12	20	— 64

TD: Phil—Joe Carter 3, Swede Hanson 3, Marvin Ellstrom, Roger Kirkman, Ed Matesic, Ed Storm. TD Passes: Phil—Ed Matesic 2, Albert Weiner 2, Marvin Elstrom.

ST. LOUIS RAMS
October 22, 1950, at Los Angeles

Baltimore	13	0	7	7	— 27
Los Angeles Rams	21	14	14	21	— 70

TD: LA—Bob Boyd 2, Vitamin T. Smith 2, Tom Fears, Elroy (Crazylegs) Hirsch, Dick Hoerner, Ralph Pasquariello, Dan Towler, Bob Waterfield; Balt—Chet Mutryn 2, Adrian Burk, Billy Stone. TD Passes: LA—Norm Van Brocklin 2, Bob Waterfield 2, Glenn Davis; Balt—Adrian Burk 3.

SAN FRANCISCO 49ERS
October 18, 1992, at San Francisco

Atlanta	7	3	0	7	— 17
San Francisco	21	21	14	0	— 56

TD: SF—Jerry Rice 3, Ricky Watters 3, Brent Jones, Tom Rathman; Atl—Michael Haynes, Jason Phillips. TD Passes: SF—Steve Young 3; Atl—Chris Miller, Wade Wilson. FG: Atl—Norm Johnson.

SEATTLE SEAHAWKS
October 30, 1977, at Seattle

Buffalo	3	0	7	7	— 17
Seattle	14	28	7	7	— 56

TD: Sea—Steve Largent 2, Duke Fergerson, Al Hunter, David Sims, Sherman Smith, Don Testerman, Jim Zorn; Buff—Joe Ferguson, John Kimbrough. TD Passes: Sea—Jim Zorn 4; Buff—Joe Ferguson. FG: Buff—Carson Long.

TAMPA BAY BUCCANEERS
December 23, 2001, at Tampa Bay

New Orleans	0	0	7	14	— 21
Tampa Bay	17	13	3	15	— 48

TD: TB—Mike Alstott, Ronde Barber, Warrick Dunn, Dave Moore, Karl Williams; NO—Joe Horn 2, Eddie Williams. TD Passes: TB—Brad Johnson 3; NO—Aaron Brooks 3. FG: TB—Martin Gramatica 4.

WASHINGTON REDSKINS
November 27, 1966, at Washington

New York Giants	0	14	14	13	— 41
Washington	13	21	14	24	— 72

TD: Wash—A.D. Whitfield 3, Brig Owens 2, Charley Taylor 2, Rickie Harris, Joe Don Looney, Bobby Mitchell; NYG—Allen Jacobs, Homer Jones, Dan Lewis, Joe Morrison, Aaron Thomas, Gary Wood. TD Passes: Wash—Sonny Jurgensen 3; NYG—Gary Wood 2, Tom Kennedy. FG: Wash—Charlie Gogolak.

INSIDE THE NUMBERS

RECORDS OF NFL TEAMS SINCE 1970 AFL-NFL MERGER

AFC	W	L	T	Pct.	Division Titles	Playoff Berths	Postseason Record	Super Bowl Record
Miami	347	203	2	.631	12	21	20-19	2-3
Pittsburgh	333	217	2	.605	17	22	28-17	5-1
Denver	323	223	6	.591	10	17	17-15	2-4
Oakland	317	229	6	.580	12	18	22-15	3-1
Jacksonville**	94	82	0	.534	2	5	4-5	0-0
Kansas City	279	266	7	.512	5	10	3-10	0-0
New England	275	277	0	.498	8	13	16-10	3-2
Baltimore***	78	81	1	.491	1	3	5-2	1-0
Buffalo	262	288	2	.476	7	13	12-13	0-4
Tennessee	262	288	2	.476	4	14	12-14	0-1
Indianapolis	257	293	2	.467	9	14	9-13	1-0
Cleveland+	230	271	3	.459	6	11	4-11	0-0
Cincinnati	246	306	0	.446	6	8	5-8	0-2
San Diego	243	304	5	.444	6	8	6-8	0-1
N.Y. Jets	239	311	2	.435	2	9	6-9	0-0
Houston****	18	46	0	.281	0	0	0-0	0-0

NFC	W	L	T	Pct.	Division Titles	Playoff Berths	Postseason Record	Super Bowl Record
Dallas	325	227	0	.589	15	23	31-18	5-3
Minnesota	319	231	2	.580	14	22	16-22	0-3
San Francisco	318	231	3	.579	17	21	25-16	5-0
Washington	311	239	2	.565	6	15	20-12	3-2
St. Louis	299	249	4	.545	11	19	16-18	1-2
Philadelphia	277	268	7	.508	6	15	12-15	0-2
Green Bay	272	272	8	.500	7	12	12-11	1-1
Chicago	270	281	1	.490	8	12	7-11	1-0
Seattle*	227	241	0	.485	4	8	5-8	0-1
N.Y. Giants	264	285	3	.481	6	11	12-9	2-1
Carolina**	82	94	0	.466	2	3	6-3	0-1
Detroit	236	312	4	.431	3	9	1-9	0-0
Atlanta	233	314	5	.426	3	8	6-8	0-1
New Orleans	225	323	4	.411	2	5	1-5	0-0
Arizona	219	327	6	.402	2	4	1-4	0-0
Tampa Bay*	183	284	1	.392	5	9	6-8	1-0

*Entered NFL in 1976.
**Entered NFL in 1995.
***Entered NFL in 1996.
****Entered NFL in 2002.
+Did not play 1996-98.
Oakland totals include L.A. Raiders, 1982-1994.
Tennessee totals include Houston, 1970-1996.
Indianapolis totals include Baltimore, 1970-1983.
St. Louis totals include L.A. Rams, 1970-1994.
Arizona totals include St. Louis, 1970-1987, and Phoenix, 1988-1993.
Tie games before 1972 are not calculated in won-lost percentage.

HOME RECORDS OF NFL TEAMS SINCE 1970 AFL-NFL MERGER

AFC	W	L	T	Pct.
Miami	199	75	1	.725
Denver	198	75	4	.724
Pittsburgh	198	77	1	.719
Oakland	176	98	2	.642
Baltimore***	50	29	1	.631
Jacksonville**	55	33	0	.625
Kansas City	170	102	3	.625
New England	160	116	0	.580
Buffalo	155	121	1	.561
Tennessee	151	124	1	.549
Cincinnati	151	125	0	.547
Cleveland+	127	122	2	.510
San Diego	139	134	2	.509
Indianapolis	136	138	2	.496
N.Y. Jets	129	145	1	.471
Houston****	10	22	0	.313

NFC	W	L	T	Pct.
Dallas	188	88	0	.681
Minnesota	188	88	0	.681
Washington	177	96	2	.648
San Francisco	171	103	2	.624
Green Bay	165	106	5	.607
St. Louis	166	108	2	.606
Chicago	161	114	1	.585
Seattle*	135	100	0	.574
Philadelphia	156	118	3	.569
Detroit	153	122	1	.556
N.Y. Giants	148	128	1	.536
Carolina**	45	43	0	.511
Atlanta	140	136	1	.507
Tampa Bay*	113	120	1	.485
Arizona	130	142	3	.478
New Orleans	121	154	1	.440

*Entered NFL in 1976.
**Entered NFL in 1995.
***Entered NFL in 1996.
****Entered NFL in 2002.
+Did not play 1996-98.
Oakland totals include L.A. Raiders, 1982-1994.
Tennessee totals include Houston, 1970-1996.
Indianapolis totals include Baltimore, 1970-1983.
St. Louis totals include L.A. Rams, 1970-1994.
Arizona totals include St. Louis, 1970-1987, and Phoenix, 1988-1993.
Tie games before 1972 are not calculated in won-lost percentage.

ROAD RECORDS OF NFL TEAMS SINCE 1970 AFL-NFL MERGER

AFC	W	L	T	Pct.
Miami	148	128	1	.536
Oakland	141	131	4	.518
Pittsburgh	135	140	1	.491
Denver	125	148	2	.458
Jacksonville**	39	49	0	.443
Indianapolis	121	155	0	.438
New England	115	161	0	.417
Cleveland+	103	149	1	.409
Tennessee	111	164	1	.404
Kansas City	109	164	4	.400
N.Y. Jets	110	166	1	.399
Buffalo	107	167	1	.391
San Diego	104	170	3	.380
Baltimore***	28	52	0	.350
Cincinnati	95	181	0	.344
Houston****	8	24	0	.250

NFC	W	L	T	Pct.
San Francisco	147	128	1	.534
Dallas	137	139	0	.496
St. Louis	133	141	2	.486
Washington	134	143	0	.484
Minnesota	131	143	1	.478
Philadelphia	121	150	4	.447
N.Y. Giants	116	157	2	.425
Carolina**	37	51	0	.420
Chicago	109	167	0	.395
Seattle*	92	141	0	.395
Green Bay	107	166	3	.393
New Orleans	104	169	3	.381
Atlanta	93	178	4	.344
Arizona	89	185	3	.326
Detroit	83	190	3	.305
Tampa Bay*	70	164	0	.299

*Entered NFL in 1976.
**Entered NFL in 1995.
***Entered NFL in 1996.
****Entered NFL in 2002.
+Did not play 1996-98.
Oakland totals include L.A. Raiders, 1982-1994.
Tennessee totals include Houston, 1970-1996.
Indianapolis totals include Baltimore, 1970-1983.
St. Louis totals include L.A. Rams, 1970-1994.
Arizona totals include St. Louis, 1970-1987, and Phoenix, 1988-1993.
Tie games before 1972 are not calculated in won-lost percentage.

RECORDS OF TEAMS ON OPENING DAY

AFC	W	L	T	Pct.	Longest W Strk.	Longest L Strk.	Current Streak
Jacksonville	8	3	0	.727	6	2	W-2
Denver	29	16	1	.644	4	4	L-1
Miami	23	16	1	.590	11	5	W-1
Kansas City	26	20	0	.565	7	4	W-1
San Diego	26	20	0	.565	6	6	L-1
Pittsburgh	35	32	4	.522	4	3	W-3
Tennessee	24	22	0	.522	4	3	L-1
Oakland	24	22	0	.522	5	5	L-3
Cleveland	27	26	0	.509	5	6	L-1
Indianapolis	31	30	1	.508	8	8	W-1
Houston	2	2	0	.500	2	2	L-2
New England	22	24	0	.478	6	3	W-2
Cincinnati	17	21	0	.447	4	4	W-1
Buffalo	19	27	0	.413	6	5	W-1
N.Y. Jets	19	27	0	.413	3	5	L-1
Baltimore	3	7	0	.300	2	4	L-4

NFC	W	L	T	Pct.	Longest W Strk.	Longest L Strk.	Current Streak
Dallas	31	14	1	.689	17	5	W-1
N.Y. Giants	46	30	5	.605	4	3	W-1
Chicago	48	33	5	.593	9	6	L-3
Green Bay	47	35	3	.573	5	6	L-1
Minnesota	25	19	1	.568	5	3	L-1
Detroit	41	33	2	.554	10	4	W-3
St. Louis	37	31	0	.544	5	6	L-1
San Francisco	29	26	1	.527	5	3	W-1
Atlanta	21	19	0	.525	5	3	W-3
Washington	36	34	4	.514	6	5	W-4
Tampa Bay	13	17	0	.433	3	5	W-1
Arizona	33	50	2	.398	6	7	L-6
Philadelphia	28	43	1	.394	5	9	L-1
Carolina	4	7	0	.364	3	4	L 2
New Orleans	12	27	0	.308	2	6	W-1
Seattle	9	21	0	.300	3	8	L-1

Kansas City totals include Dallas Texans, 1960-62.
Oakland totals include L.A. Raiders, 1982-1994.
San Diego totals include L.A. Chargers, 1960.
Indianapolis totals include Baltimore, 1953-1983.
Tennessee totals include Houston, 1960-1996.
New England totals include Boston, 1960-1970.
St. Louis totals include Cleveland, 1937-1942 and 1944-45, and L.A. Rams, 1946-1994.
Detroit totals include Portsmouth, 1930-33.
Arizona totals include Chi. Cardinals, 1920-1959, St. Louis, 1960-1987, and Phoenix, 1988-1993.
Chicago totals include Decatur, 1920.
Washington totals include Boston Braves, 1932 and Boston Redskins, 1933-36.
NOTE: All tied games occurred prior to 1972, when calculation of ties in percentages as half-win, half-loss was begun.

RECORDS OF NFL TEAMS, 1996-2005

AFC	W	L	T	Pct.	Division Titles	Playoff Berths	Postseason Record	Super Bowl Record
Denver	106	54	0	.663	3	7	8-5	2-0
New England	101	59	0	.631	6	7	13-4	3-1
Pittsburgh	98	61	1	.616	5	6	9-5	1-0
Indianapolis	92	68	0	.575	4	7	3-7	0-0
Jacksonville	90	70	0	.563	2	5	4-5	0-0
Miami	90	70	0	.563	1	5	3-5	0-0
Kansas City	89	71	0	.556	2	2	0-2	0-0
Tennessee	89	71	0	.556	2	4	5-4	0-1
Baltimore	78	81	1	.491	1	3	5-2	1-0
N.Y. Jets	78	82	0	.488	2	4	3-4	0-0
Buffalo	76	84	0	.475	0	3	0-3	0-0
Oakland	73	87	0	.456	3	3	4-3	0-1
San Diego	64	96	0	.400	1	1	0-1	0-0
Cincinnati	61	99	0	.381	1	1	0-1	0-0
Cleveland	36	76	0	.321	0	1	0-1	0-0
Houston	18	46	0	.281	0	0	0-0	0-0

Cleveland did not play from 1996-98.
Houston entered the NFL in 2002.
Tennessee totals include Houston, 1995.

NFC	W	L	T	Pct.	Division Titles	Playoff Berths	Postseason Record	Super Bowl Record
Green Bay	102	58	0	.638	5	7	7-6	1-1
Minnesota	91	69	0	.569	2	6	5-6	0-0
Philadelphia	89	70	1	.559	4	6	7-6	0-1
Tampa Bay	89	71	0	.556	3	6	5-5	1-0
Seattle	86	74	0	.538	3	4	2-4	0-1
St. Louis	85	75	0	.531	3	5	6-4	1-1
San Francisco	82	78	0	.513	2	5	4-5	0-0
N.Y. Giants	81	78	1	.509	3	4	2-4	0-1
Washington	77	82	1	.484	1	2	2-2	0-0
Carolina	75	85	0	.469	2	3	6-3	0-1
Dallas	74	86	0	.463	2	4	1-4	0-0
Atlanta	73	86	1	.459	2	3	4-3	0-1
Chicago	66	94	0	.413	2	2	0-2	0-0
New Orleans	63	97	0	.394	1	1	1-1	0-0
Detroit	57	103	0	.356	0	2	0-2	0-0
Arizona	56	104	0	.350	0	1	1-1	0-0

Seattle was in the AFC from 1996-2001.

HOME RECORDS, 1996-2005

AFC	W - L - T	Pct.
Denver	64-16-0	.800
New England	58-22-0	.725
Kansas City	57-23-0	.713
Pittsburgh	54-25-1	.681
Jacksonville	53-27-0	.663
Miami	53-27-0	.663
Indianapolis	51-29-0	.638
Baltimore	50-29-1	.631
Buffalo	47-33-0	.588
Tennessee	47-33-0	.588
N.Y. Jets	43-37-0	.538
Oakland	42-38-0	.525
Cincinnati	38-42-0	.475
San Diego	38-42-0	.475
Cleveland	18-38-0	.321
Houston	10-22-0	.313

NFC	W - L - T	Pct.
Green Bay	61-19-0	.763
Minnesota	57-23-0	.713
Tampa Bay	53-27-0	.663
Seattle	52-28-0	.650
San Francisco	51-29-0	.638
Dallas	50-30-0	.625
Philadelphia	50-30-0	.625
St. Louis	50-30-0	.625
Washington	45-34-1	.569
N.Y. Giants	44-36-0	.550
Chicago	42-38-0	.525
Atlanta	41-39-0	.513
Carolina	40-40-0	.500
Detroit	40-40-0	.500
Arizona	38-42-0	.475
New Orleans	31-49-0	.388

Cleveland did not play from 1996-98.
Houston entered the NFL in 2002.
Tennessee totals include Houston, 1996.
Seattle was in the AFC from 1996-2001.

ROAD RECORDS, 1996-2005

AFC	W-L-T	Pct.
Pittsburgh	44-36-0	.550
New England	43-37-0	.538
Denver	42-38-0	.525
Tennessee	42-38-0	.525
Indianapolis	41-39-0	.513
Jacksonville	37-43-0	.463
Miami	37-43-0	.463
N.Y. Jets	35-45-0	.438
Kansas City	32-48-0	.400
Oakland	31-49-0	.388
Buffalo	29-51-0	.363
Baltimore	28-52-0	.350
San Diego	26-54-0	.325
Cleveland	18-38-0	.321
Cincinnati	23-57-0	.288
Houston	8-24-0	.250

NFC	W-L-T	Pct.
Green Bay	41-39-0	.513
Philadelphia	39-40-1	.494
N.Y. Giants	37-42-1	.469
Tampa Bay	36-44-0	.450
Carolina	35-45-0	.438
St. Louis	35-45-0	.438
Minnesota	34-46-0	.425
Seattle	34-46-0	.425
Atlanta	32-47-1	.406
New Orleans	32-48-0	.400
Washington	32-48-0	.400
San Francisco	31-49-0	.388
Chicago	24-56-0	.300
Dallas	24-56-0	.300
Arizona	18-62-0	.225
Detroit	17-63-0	.213

Cleveland did not play from 1996-98.
Houston entered the NFL in 2002.
Tennessee totals include Houston, 1996.
Seattle was in the AFC from 1996-2001.

RECORDS BY MONTHS, 1996-2005

AFC	Sept. W-L-T	Oct. W-L-T	Nov. W-L-T	Dec. W-L-T	Total W-L-T	Pct.
Denver	28-10-0	25-15-0	29-9-0	24-20-0	106-54-0	.663
New England	21-13-0	23-18-0	27-15-0	30-13-0	101-59-0	.631
Pittsburgh	18-15-0	30-9-0	23-19-1	27-18-0	98-61-1	.616
Indianapolis	21-13-0	20-18-0	23-20-0	28-17-0	92-68-0	.575
Jacksonville	22-14-0	15-24-0	26-14-0	27-18-0	90-70-0	.563
Miami	22-11-0	22-17-0	23-20-0	23-22-0	90-70-0	.563
Kansas City	24-14-0	21-16-0	19-23-0	25-18-0	89-71-0	.556
Tennessee	15-19-0	26-15-0	22-17-0	26-20-0	89-71-0	.556
Baltimore	18-17-0	15-24-0	21-21-1	24-19-0	78-81-1	.491
N.Y. Jets	13-22-0	19-19-0	24-17-0	22-24-0	78-82-0	.488
Buffalo	14-19-0	23-20-0	20-20-0	19-25-0	76-84-0	.475
Oakland	19-18-0	20-17-0	18-23-0	16-29-0	73-87-0	.456
San Diego	18-19-0	18-21-0	14-26-0	14-30-0	64-96-0	.400
Cincinnati	10-25-0	13-27-0	17-24-0	21-23-0	61-99-0	.381
Cleveland	9-15-0	10-19-0	9-18-0	8-24-0	36-76-0	.321
Houston	4-9-0	5-10-0	5-12-0	4-15-0	18-46-0	.281

Clevland did not play from 1996-98.
Houston entered the NFL in 2002.
Tennessee totals include Houston, 1996.
September totals include August; December totals include January.

NFC	Sept. W-L-T	Oct. W-L-T	Nov. W-L-T	Dec. W-L-T	Total W-L-T	Pct.
Green Bay	24-14-0	19-15-0	24-18-0	35-11-0	102-58-0	.638
Minnesota	23-14-0	24-13-0	23-18-0	21-24-0	91-69-0	.569
Philadelphia	17-19-0	24-14-0	25-18-1	23-19-0	89-70-1	.559
Tampa Bay	20-16-0	16-21-0	26-16-0	27-18-0	89-71-0	.556
Seattle	20-17-0	17-18-0	24-19-0	25-20-0	86-74-0	.538
St. Louis	18-18-0	22-16-0	18-23-0	27-18-0	85-75-0	.531
San Francisco	18-16-0	21-19-0	20-21-0	23-22-0	82-78-0	.513
N.Y. Giants	20-17-0	22-16-0	14-26-1	25-19-0	81-78-1	.509
Washington	18-17-0	18-21-0	17-25-1	24-19-0	77-82-1	.484
Carolina	16-17-0	14-27-0	20-22-0	25-19-0	75-85-0	.469
Dallas	18-17-0	20-19-0	20-23-0	16-27-0	74-86-0	.463
Atlanta	13-22-0	17-23-0	23-17-1	20-24-0	73-86-1	.459
Chicago	8-28-0	18-20-0	20-22-0	20-24-0	66-94-0	.413
New Orleans	14-21-0	18-23-0	15-24-0	16-29-0	63-97-0	.394
Detroit	17-19-0	13-23-0	17-29-0	10-32-0	57-103-0	.356
Arizona	10-25-0	13-24-0	18-25-0	15-30-0	56-104-0	.350

Seattle was in the AFC from 1996-2001.
September totals include August; December totals include January.

TAKEAWAYS/GIVEAWAYS, 1996-2005

AFC	Takeaways Int.	Fum.	Total	Giveaways Int.	Fum.	Total	Net.Diff.
Kansas City	176	138	314	148	94	242	72
New England	191	119	310	154	104	258	52
Jacksonville	147	133	280	124	105	229	51
Denver	174	124	298	156	93	249	49
Pittsburgh	173	144	317	164	109	273	44
N.Y. Jets	181	113	294	162	102	264	30
Tennessee	150	134	284	141	117	258	26
Miami	194	124	318	172	134	306	12
Cincinnati	168	119	287	168	114	282	5
Baltimore	190	123	313	175	143	318	- 5
Oakland	155	115	270	148	127	275	- 5
Indianapolis	134	127	261	161	107	268	- 7
Houston	53	36	89	60	45	105	-16
Cleveland	115	74	189	133	93	226	-37
Buffalo	147	109	256	174	128	302	-46
San Diego	170	99	269	207	126	333	-64

Cleveland did not play from 1996-98.
Houston entered the NFL in 2002.
Tennessee totals include Houston, 1996.

NFC	Takeaways Int.	Fum.	Total	Giveaways Int.	Fum.	Total	Net.Diff.
Tampa Bay	200	120	320	155	125	280	40
San Francisco	183	111	294	150	111	261	33
Seattle	186	129	315	165	123	288	27
N.Y. Giants	172	128	300	161	115	276	24
Philadelphia	165	138	303	152	132	284	19
Washington	179	116	295	159	125	284	11
Carolina	190	145	335	178	148	326	9
Atlanta	162	137	299	174	129	303	- 4
Green Bay	190	125	315	192	128	320	- 5
Detroit	155	113	268	188	91	279	-11
Minnesota	160	117	277	177	120	297	-20
Dallas	149	115	264	165	129	294	-30
Chicago	154	133	287	176	145	321	-34
New Orleans	160	141	301	199	153	352	-51
St. Louis	191	119	310	212	165	377	-67
Arizona	150	109	259	214	147	361	-102

Seattle was in the AFC from 1996-2001.

BEST TAKEAWAY/GIVEAWAY DIFFERENTIAL, SEASON
+43   Washington, 1983
+26   Kansas City, 1990
+25   N.Y. Giants, 1997

HIGH AND LOW SINGLE-GAME YARDAGE TOTALS, 1996-2005
Most Total Yards, Game
645   Pittsburgh vs. Atlanta, Nov. 10, 2002 (OT)
615   Arizona at Washington, Nov. 10, 1996 (OT)
614   St. Louis vs. San Diego, Oct. 1, 2000
605   Minnesota at New Orleans, Oct. 17, 2004
591   Seattle at San Diego, Dec. 29, 2002 (OT)
Fewest Total Yards, Game
26   Cleveland at Buffalo, Dec. 12, 2004
40   Cleveland vs. Pittsburgh, Sept. 12, 1999
47   Houston at Pittsburgh, Dec. 8, 2002
53   Cleveland at Jacksonville, Dec. 3, 2000
93   Oakland at Kansas City, Dec. 7, 1997
Most Yards Rushing, Game
407   Cincinnati vs. Denver, Oct. 22, 2000
343   Baltimore vs. Cleveland, Sept. 14, 2003
337   St. Louis vs. Carolina, Nov. 11, 2001
328   San Francisco vs. Detroit, Dec. 14, 1998
320   Seattle vs. Houston, Oct. 16, 2005
Fewest Yards Rushing, Game
4   Buffalo at Tennessee, Nov. 23, 1997
    Cincinnati at Baltimore, Sept. 24, 2000
5   New England at Pittsburgh, Oct. 31, 2004

8   St. Louis vs. Arizona, Nov. 20, 2005
6   Dallas at New Orleans, Dec. 6, 1998
Most Yards Passing, Game
507   Arizona at Washington, Nov. 10, 1996 (OT)
499   Denver vs. Atlanta, Oct. 31, 2004
474   Kansas City at Oakland, Nov. 5, 2000
473   N.Y. Jets at Baltimore, Dec. 24, 2000
472   Indianapolis at Kansas City, Oct. 31, 2004
Fewest Yards Passing, Game
-19   San Diego at Kansas City, Sept. 20, 1998
-9   Cleveland at Jacksonville, Dec. 3, 2000
-3   Cleveland at Buffalo, Dec. 12, 2004
0   Oakland at San Diego, Dec. 28, 2003
6   Houston vs. Indianapolis, Oct. 23, 2005

NFL INDIVIDUAL LEADERS, 1996-2005

Points
Jason Elam	1,187
Adam Vinatieri	1,158
Jeff Wilkins	1,125
Matt Stover	1,114
Ryan Longwell	1,054

Passing Yards
Brett Favre	38,790
Peyton Manning	33,189
Drew Bledsoe	32,891
Kerry Collins	30,920
Mark Brunell	27,774

Touchdowns
Marshall Faulk	110
Marvin Harrison	110
Terrell Owens	103
Shaun Alexander	100
Randy Moss	99

TD Passes
Brett Favre	288
Peyton Manning	244
Drew Bledsoe	191
Mark Brunell	159
Kerry Collins	159

Field Goals
Matt Stover	272
Adam Vinatieri	263
Jason Elam	254
Jeff Wilkins	239
John Carney	238

Receptions
Marvin Harrison	927
Jimmy Smith	840
Rod Smith	791
Keenan McCardell	745
Keyshawn Johnson	744

Rushes
Curtis Martin	3,150
Eddie George	2,865
Jerome Bettis	2,683
Corey Dillon	2,419
Emmitt Smith	2,402

Reception Yards
Marvin Harrison	12,331
Jimmy Smith	11,999
Rod Smith	10,725
Terrell Owens	10,535
Isaac Bruce	10,225

Rushing Yards
Curtis Martin	12,614
Jerome Bettis	10,571
Eddie George	10,441
Corey Dillon	10,429
Marshall Faulk	9,919

Receiving TDs
Marvin Harrison	110
Terrell Owens	101
Randy Moss	98
Three tied	64

Rushing TDs
Shaun Alexander	89
Priest Holmes	86
Jerome Bettis	78
Marshall Faulk	78
Curtis Martin	76

Interceptions
Darren Sharper	45
Ty Law	43
Terrell Buckley	39
Rod Woodson	39
Two tied	38

Pass Attempts
Brett Favre	5,461
Drew Bledsoe	4,792
Kerry Collins	4,649
Peyton Manning	4,333
Jake Plummer	4,033

Sacks
Simeon Rice	119.0
Michael Strahan	116.5
Jason Taylor	92.5
Kevin Carter	86.0
Warren Sapp	81.5

Completions
Brett Favre	3,336
Drew Bledsoe	2,812
Peyton Manning	2,769
Kerry Collins	2,612
Mark Brunell	2,363

NFL GAMES IN WHICH A TEAM HAS SCORED 60 OR MORE POINTS

(Home team in capitals)

Regular Season

WASHINGTON 72, New York Giants 41	November 27, 1966
LOS ANGELES RAMS 70, Baltimore 27	October 22, 1950
Chicago Cardinals 65, NEW YORK BULLDOGS 20	November 13, 1949
LOS ANGELES RAMS 65, Detroit 24	October 29, 1950
PHILADELPHIA 64, Cincinnati 0	November 6, 1934
CHICAGO CARDINALS 63, New York Giants 35	October 17, 1948
AKRON 62, Oorang 0	October 29, 1922
PITTSBURGH 62, New York Giants 7	November 30, 1952
CLEVELAND 62, New York Giants 14	December 6, 1953
CLEVELAND 62, Washington 3	November 7, 1954
NEW YORK GIANTS 62, Philadelphia 10	November 26, 1972
Atlanta 62, NEW ORLEANS 7	September 16, 1973
NEW YORK JETS 62, Tampa Bay 28	November 17, 1985
CHICAGO 61, San Francisco 20	December 12, 1965
Cincinnati 61, HOUSTON 17	December 17, 1972
CHICAGO 61, Green Bay 7	December 7, 1980
CINCINNATI 61, Houston 7	December 17, 1989
ROCK ISLAND 60, Evansville 0	October 15, 1922
CHICAGO CARDINALS 60, Rochester 0	October 7, 1923

Postseason

Chicago Bears 73, WASHINGTON 0	December 8, 1940
JACKSONVILLE 62, Miami 7	January 15, 2000

YOUNGEST AND OLDEST PLAYERS IN NFL IN 2005

10 Youngest Players

	Birthdate	Games	Starts	Position
Shawne Merriman, San Diego	5/25/1984	15	10	LB
Brodney Pool, Cleveland	5/24/1984	13	0	DB
Alex Smith, San Francisco	5/7/1984	9	7	QB
Dante Ridgeway, N.Y. Jets	4/18/1984	7	0	WR
Manuel Wright, Miami	4/13/1984	3	0	DT
Justin Miller, N.Y. Jets	2/14/1984	16	8	CB
Mike Williams, Detroit	1/4/1984	14	4	WR
Paul Irons, Cleveland	12/23/1983	2	1	TE
Randy Starks, Tennessee	12/14/1983	16	16	DT
Channing Crowder, Miami	12/2/1983	16	13	LB
Aaron Rodgers, Green Bay	12/2/1983	3	0	QB

10 Oldest Players

	Birthdate	Games	Starts	Position
Sean Landeta, Philadelphia	1/6/1962	5	0	P
Doug Flutie, New England	10/23/1962	5	0	QB
Ray Brown, Washington	12/12/1962	15	2	T
Vinny Testaverde, N.Y. Jets	11/13/1963	6	4	QB
John Carney, New Orleans	4/20/1964	16	0	K
Bryan Barker, St. Louis	6/28/1964	11	0	P
Darren Bennett, Minnesota	1/9/1965	1	0	P
Jeff Feagles, N.Y. Giants	3/7/1966	16	0	P
Deion Sanders, Baltimore	8/9/1967	16	4	CB
Matt Stover, Baltimore	1/27/1968	16	0	K

YOUNGEST AND OLDEST REGULAR STARTERS BY POSITION IN 2005

Minimum: 8 Games Started

	Youngest		Oldest	
QB	11/14/1982	Kyle Orton, Chi.	9/13/1968	Brad Johnson, Min.
RB	7/22/1983	Steven Jackson, St.L	12/27/1970	Lorenzo Neal, SD
WR	8/31/1983	Larry Fitzgerald, Ariz	2/9/1969	Jimmy Smith, Jac.
TE	9/3/1983	Adam Bergen, Ariz	9/22/1971	Christian Fauria, NE
T	10/5/1982	Michael Roos, Ten.	4/18/1970	Willie Roaf, KC
G	12/25/1982	Shawn Andrews, Phi.	6/19/1970	Chris Gray, Sea.
C	3/12/1982	Nick Leckey, Ariz	3/6/1970	Robbie Tobeck, Sea.
DE	8/11/1983	Robert Geathers, Cin.	1/30/1971	Kimo von Oelhoffen, Pit.
DT	12/14/1983	Randy Starks, Ten.	4/13/1968	Ted Washington, Oak.
LB	5/25/1984	Shawne Merriman, S.D.	9/11/1971	Shelton Quarles, TB
CB	2/14/1984	Justin Miller, NYJ	5/18/1973	Tory James, Cin.
S	8/16/1983	Nick Collins, GB	11/30/1970	Robert Griffith, Ariz

OLDEST INDIVIDUAL SINGLE-SEASON OR SINGLE-GAME RECORDS IN NFL RECORD & FACT BOOK

Most Points, Game—40, Ernie Nevers, Chi. Cardinals vs. Chi. Bears, Nov. 28, 1929 (6-td, 4-pat)

Most Touchdowns Rushing, Game—6, Ernie Nevers, Chi. Cardinals vs. Chi. Bears, Nov. 28, 1929

Highest Rushing Average Gain, Season (Qualifiers)—8.44, Beattie Feathers, Chi. Bears, 1934 (119-1,004)

Highest Punting Average, Season (Qualifiers)—51.40, Sammy Baugh, Washington, 1940 (35-1,799)

Highest Punting Average, Rookie, Season (Qualifiers)—45.92, Frank Sinkwich, Detroit, 1943 (12-551)

Highest Punting Average, Game (minimum: 4 punts)—61.75, Bob Cifers, Detroit vs. Chi. Bears, Nov. 24, 1946 (4-247)

Highest Average Gain, Pass Receptions, Season (minimum: 24 receptions)—32.58, Don Currivan, Boston, 1947 (24-782)

Highest Average Gain, Passing, Game (minimum: 20 passes)—18.58, Sammy Baugh, Washington vs. Boston, Oct. 31, 1948 (24-446)

Most Touchdowns, Fumble Recoveries, Game—2, Fred (Dippy) Evans, Chi. Bears vs. Washington, Nov. 28, 1948

Most Yards Gained, Intercepted Passes, Rookie, Season—301, Don Doll, Detroit, 1949

Most Passes Had Intercepted, Game—8, Jim Hardy, Chi. Cardinals vs. Philadelphia, Sept. 24, 1950

Highest Kickoff Return Average, Game (minimum: 3 returns)—73.50, Wally Triplett, Detroit vs. Los Angeles, Oct. 29, 1950 (4-294)

Highest Punt Return Average, Season (Qualifiers)—23.00, Herb Rich, Baltimore, 1950 (12-276)

Highest Punt Return Average, Rookie, Season (Qualifiers)—23.00, Herb Rich, Baltimore, 1950 (12-276)

Most Yards Passing, Game—554, Norm Van Brocklin, Los Angeles vs. N.Y. Yanks, Sept. 28, 1951

Most Touchdowns, Punt Returns, Rookie, Season—4, Jack Christiansen, Detroit, 1951

Most Interceptions By, Season—14, Dick (Night Train) Lane, Los Angeles, 1952

Most Interceptions By, Rookie, Season—14, Dick (Night Train) Lane, Los Angeles, 1952

Highest Average Gain, Passing, Season (Qualifiers)—11.17, Tommy O'Connell, Cleveland, 1957 (110-1,229)

Most Points, Season—176, Paul Hornung, Green Bay, 1960 (15-td, 41-pat,15-fg)

Most Yards Gained, Pass Receptions, Rookie, Season—1,473, Bill Groman, Houston, 1960

NFL INDIVIDUAL LEADERS OVER RECENT SEASONS

Last 2 Seasons		Last 3 Seasons		Last 4 Seasons	
Points					
288	Shaun Alexander	397	Mike Vanderjagt	500	Mike Vanderjagt
253	Shayne Graham	384	Shaun Alexander	492	Shaun Alexander
244	Jason Elam	369	Jeff Wilkins	484	Jason Elam
242	Jay Feely	364	Jason Elam	470	Adam Vinatieri
241	Two tied	364	Matt Stover	469	Jay Feely
Touchdowns					
48	Shaun Alexander	64	Shaun Alexander	82	Shaun Alexander
38	LaDainian Tomlinson	55	LaDainian Tomlinson	73	Priest Holmes
32	Larry Johnson	49	Priest Holmes	70	LaDainian Tomlinson
27	Marvin Harrison	38	Randy Moss	49	Clinton Portis
26	Two tied	37	Marvin Harrison	48	Marvin Harrison
Field Goals					
62	Neil Rackers	92	Matt Stover	97	David Akers
59	Matt Stover	85	Jeff Wilkins	95	Ryan Longwell
55	Shayne Graham	80	Jason Elam	93	Sebastian Janikowski
53	Three tied	80	Mike Vanderjagt	93	Rian Lindell
		77	Two tied	92	Jeff Reed
Rushes					
723	Shaun Alexander	1,049	Shaun Alexander	1,363	LaDainian Tomlinson
698	Rudi Johnson	1,004	Edgerrin James	1,344	Shaun Alexander
695	Clinton Portis	991	LaDainian Tomlinson	1,281	Edgerrin James
694	Edgerrin James	985	Clinton Portis	1,261	Tiki Barber
679	Tiki Barber	957	Tiki Barber	1,258	Clinton Portis
Rushing Yards					
3,576	Shaun Alexander	5,011	Shaun Alexander	6,186	Shaun Alexander
3,378	Tiki Barber	4,594	Tiki Barber	6,125	LaDainian Tomlinson
3,054	Edgerrin James	4,442	LaDainian Tomlinson	5,981	Tiki Barber
2,912	Rudi Johnson	4,422	Clinton Portis	5,930	Clinton Portis
2,831	Clinton Portis	4,313	Edgerrin James	5,305	Jamal Lewis
Rushing Touchdowns					
43	Shaun Alexander	57	Shaun Alexander	73	Shaun Alexander
35	LaDainian Tomlinson	48	LaDainian Tomlinson	68	Priest Holmes
29	Larry Johnson	47	Priest Holmes	62	LaDainian Tomlinson
24	Corey Dillon	33	Edgerrin James	45	Clinton Portis
24	Rudi Johnson	33	Rudi Johnson	38	Jerome Bettis
Passes					
1,147	Brett Favre	1,618	Brett Favre	2,169	Brett Favre
1,078	Kerry Collins	1,586	Trent Green	2,132	Tom Brady
1,063	Trent Green	1,578	Kerry Collins	2,123	Kerry Collins
1,004	Tom Brady	1,531	Tom Brady	2,107	Peyton Manning
977	Jake Plummer	1,516	Peyton Manning	2,056	Trent Green
Completions					
718	Brett Favre	1,026	Brett Favre	1,412	Peyton Manning
686	Trent Green	1,020	Peyton Manning	1,367	Brett Favre
641	Peyton Manning	1,016	Trent Green	1,312	Tom Brady
622	Tom Brady	939	Tom Brady	1,303	Trent Green
608	Carson Palmer	886	Matt Hasselbeck	1,210	Kerry Collins
Passing Yards					
8,605	Trent Green	12,644	Trent Green	16,771	Peyton Manning
8,304	Peyton Manning	12,571	Peyton Manning	16,334	Trent Green
7,969	Brett Favre	11,422	Tom Brady	15,186	Tom Brady
7,802	Tom Brady	11,330	Brett Favre	14,988	Brett Favre
7,455	Jake Plummer	10,682	Matt Hasselbeck	14,437	Kerry Collins

Last 2 Seasons		Last 3 Seasons		Last 4 Seasons	
Touchdown Passes					
77	Peyton Manning	106	Peyton Manning	133	Peyton Manning
54	Tom Brady	82	Brett Favre	109	Brett Favre
53	Jake Delhomme	77	Tom Brady	105	Tom Brady
51	Drew Brees	72	Jake Delhomme	94	Trent Green
50	Two tied	72	Matt Hasselbeck	88	Daunte Culpepper
Receptions					
196	Torry Holt	313	Torry Holt	405	Marvin Harrison
192	Chad Johnson	282	Chad Johnson	404	Torry Holt
182	Derrick Mason	277	Derrick Mason	356	Derrick Mason
180	Tony Gonzalez	262	Marvin Harrison	356	Hines Ward
170	Two tied	259	Anquan Boldin	351	Chad Johnson
Reception Yards					
2,706	Chad Johnson	4,399	Torry Holt	5,701	Torry Holt
2,703	Torry Holt	4,061	Chad Johnson	5,253	Marvin Harrison
2,429	Donald Driver	3,544	Derrick Mason	5,227	Chad Johnson
2,321	Santana Moss	3,531	Marvin Harrison	4,751	Randy Moss
2,265	Reggie Wayne	3,426	Santana Moss	4,556	Derrick Mason
Receiving Touchdowns					
27	Marvin Harrison	38	Randy Moss	48	Marvin Harrison
23	Antonio Gates	37	Marvin Harrison	45	Randy Moss
21	Randy Moss	31	Torry Holt	42	Terrell Owens
20	Muhsin Muhammad	29	Chris Chambers	37	Hines Ward
20	Terrell Owens	29	Terrell Owens	35	Torry Holt
Interceptions					
14	Deltha O'Neal	18	Darren Sharper	25	Darren Sharper
13	Chris Gamble	17	Tory James	22	Tony Parrish
13	Tory James	17	Ty Law	22	Ed Reed
13	Darren Sharper	17	Ed Reed	22	Greg Wesley
13	Nathan Vasher	16	Two tied	21	Three tied
Sacks					
27.0	Dwight Freeney	41.0	Simeon Rice	56.5	Simeon Rice
26.0	Simeon Rice	38.0	Dwight Freeney	53.0	Jason Taylor
22.0	Rod Coleman	34.5	Jason Taylor	51.0	Dwight Freeney
22.0	Robert Mathis	34.0	Michael Strahan	45.0	Michael Strahan
21.5	Four tied	32.0	Bertrand Berry	43.5	Kabeer Gbaja-Biamila

NFL TEAM LEADERS OVER RECENT SEASONS

Highest Won-Lost Percentage

.813	Indianapolis	.792	Indianapolis	.750	Indianapolis
.813	Pittsburgh	.792	New England	.734	New England
.750	New England	.688	Denver	.672	Philadelphia
.719	Denver	.667	Pittsburgh	.664	Pittsburgh
.688	Seattle	.667	Seattle	.656	Denver

Most Points

961	Indianapolis	1,408	Indianapolis	1,837	Kansas City
886	Kansas City	1,370	Kansas City	1,757	Indianapolis
864	San Diego	1,227	Seattle	1,582	Seattle
823	Seattle	1,177	San Diego	1,562	Green Bay
816	New England	1,164	Two tied	1,549	Denver

Most Total Yards

12,887	Kansas City	18,797	Kansas City	24,797	Kansas City
12,274	Indianapolis	18,148	Indianapolis	23,786	Denver
12,098	Denver	17,696	Denver	23,764	Indianapolis
11,549	Seattle	17,273	Green Bay	23,438	Minnesota
11,475	Green Bay	17,246	Minnesota	22,994	Seattle

INSIDE THE NUMBERS

Last 2 Seasons	Last 3 Seasons	Last 4 Seasons

Most Rushing Yards

5,218	Atlanta	7,501	Denver	9,767	Denver
4,872	Denver	7,167	Atlanta	9,535	Atlanta
4,687	Pittsburgh	6,600	Kansas City	8,978	Kansas City
4,671	Kansas City	6,561	Seattle	8,540	San Diego
4,552	Seattle	6,403	San Diego	8,301	Seattle

Most Passing Yards

8,719	Indianapolis	12,898	Indianapolis	16,953	Indianapolis
8,289	St. Louis	12,250	St. Louis	16,404	St. Louis
8,216	Kansas City	12,197	Kansas City	15,819	Kansas City
8,215	Green Bay	11,613	Minnesota	15,298	Minnesota
7,708	New England	11,455	Green Bay	15,082	Green Bay

Fewest Turnovers

36	Indianapolis	56	Indianapolis	83	Kansas City
39	Jacksonville	68	Kansas City	85	Jacksonville
44	Pittsburgh	69	Denver	88	Indianapolis
44	Seattle	70	Jacksonville	89	N.Y. Jets
45	Denver	70	N.Y. Jets	96	Denver

Fewest Points Allowed

509	Pittsburgh	836	New England	1,038	Tampa Bay
533	Chicago	836	Pittsburgh	1,176	Philadelphia
549	Jacksonville	842	Tampa Bay	1,181	Pittsburgh
558	Washington	848	Baltimore	1,182	New England
562	Denver	863	Denver	1,195	Jacksonville

Fewest Total Yards Allowed

8,678	Pittsburgh	13,461	Pittsburgh	17,506	Tampa Bay
8,996	Tampa Bay	13,462	Tampa Bay	18,296	Pittsburgh
9,048	Washington	13,693	Baltimore	18,724	Denver
9,352	Baltimore	13,898	Denver	19,046	Baltimore
9,465	Denver	14,037	Buffalo	19,226	Buffalo

Fewest Rushing Yards Allowed

2,656	San Diego	4,416	Pittsburgh	5,791	Pittsburgh
2,675	Pittsburgh	4,480	Denver	5,969	Denver
2,875	Denver	4,586	New England	6,530	Tennessee
2,990	Washington	4,808	Baltimore	6,570	Baltimore
3,152	New England	4,874	San Diego	6,613	San Diego

Fewest Passing Yards Allowed

5,508	Tampa Bay	8,218	Tampa Bay	10,708	Tampa Bay
5,768	Cleveland	8,614	Cleveland	11,689	Buffalo
5,899	Miami	8,622	Buffalo	11,883	Cleveland
5,915	Buffalo	8,885	Baltimore	12,286	Washington
6,003	Pittsburgh	9,045	Pittsburgh	12,336	Miami

Most Opponents' Turnovers

80	Carolina	106	Carolina	139	Carolina
80	Cincinnati	104	Cincinnati	132	Baltimore
69	Buffalo	101	Baltimore	131	Atlanta
67	Indianapolis	97	Indianapolis	128	Tampa Bay
65	N.Y. Giants	95	New England	124	Three tied

CURTIS MARTIN'S CAREER RUSHING VS. EACH OPPONENT

Opponent	Games	Rushes	Yards	Yards Per Rush	Yards Per Game	TD
Arizona	3	89	322	3.6	107.3	1
Atlanta	3	53	173	3.3	57.7	3
Baltimore	5	102	306	3.0	61.2	2
Buffalo	21	455	1,779	3.9	84.7	10
Carolina	4	91	429	4.7	107.3	4
Chicago	3	52	235	4.5	78.3	1
Cincinnati	2	53	274	5.2	137.0	1
Cleveland	3	54	255	4.7	85.0	1
Dallas	3	67	268	4.0	89.3	0
Denver	7	95	317	3.3	45.3	4
Detroit	2	38	164	4.3	82.0	1
Green Bay	3	66	258	3.9	86.0	2
Houston	2	40	222	5.6	111.0	1
Indianapolis	15	345	1,645	4.8	109.7	7
Jacksonville	5	88	321	3.6	64.2	1
Kansas City	5	104	362	3.5	72.4	4
Miami	20	409	1,507	3.7	75.4	13
Minnesota	2	42	174	4.1	87.0	1
New England	15	311	1,218	3.9	81.2	5
New Orleans	3	76	269	3.5	89.7	2
N.Y. Giants	3	42	121	2.9	40.3	0
N.Y. Jets	6	163	737	4.5	122.8	7
Oakland	5	89	271	3.0	54.2	0
Philadelphia	1	20	110	5.5	110.0	0
Pittsburgh	5	107	483	4.5	96.6	0
St. Louis	2	42	216	5.1	108.0	0
San Diego	5	107	366	3.4	73.2	4
San Francisco	4	91	308	3.4	77.0	4
Seattle	3	75	329	4.4	109.7	4
Tampa Bay	3	49	175	3.6	58.3	2
Tennessee	2	51	190	3.7	95.0	2
Washington	3	52	297	5.7	99.0	3
Totals	168	3,518	14,101	4.0	83.9	90

Arizona totals include eight games vs. Phoenx
Oakland totals include one game vs. L.A. Raiders
St. Louis totals include two games vs. L.A. Rams
Tennessee totals include two games vs. Houston

MARSHALL FAULK'S CAREER RUSHING VS. EACH OPPONENT

Opponent	Games	Rushes	Yards	Yards Per Rush	Yards Per Game	TD
Arizona	8	107	528	4.9	66.0	2
Atlanta	8	143	906	6.3	113.3	5
Baltimore	4	75	338	4.5	84.5	4
Buffalo	11	207	696	3.4	63.3	5
Carolina	7	136	795	5.8	113.6	5
Chicago	2	30	157	5.2	78.5	0
Cincinnati	7	125	471	3.8	67.3	4
Cleveland	3	62	296	4.8	98.7	2
Dallas	2	29	98	3.4	49.0	0
Denver	2	24	97	4.0	48.5	2
Detroit	4	49	159	3.2	39.8	2
Green Bay	2	24	123	5.1	61.5	0
Houston	1	1	5	5.0	5.0	0
Indianapolis	2	29	135	4.7	67.5	3
Jacksonville	2	28	77	2.8	38.5	1
Kansas City	3	47	151	3.2	50.3	1
Miami	11	193	737	3.8	67.0	4
Minnesota	4	70	370	5.3	92.5	9
New England	11	166	603	3.6	54.8	1
New Orleans	9	167	769	4.6	85.4	7
N.Y. Giants	5	50	224	4.5	44.8	2
N.Y. Jets	11	193	725	3.8	65.9	5
Oakland	2	40	199	5.0	99.5	2
Philadelphia	6	84	422	5.0	70.3	4
Pittsburgh	2	35	116	3.3	58.0	0
St. Louis	1	19	177	9.3	177.0	3

(Curtis Martin continued)

Opponent	Games	Rushes	Yards	Yards Per Rush	Yards Per Game	TD
San Diego	6	82	237	2.9	39.5	1
San Francisco	14	228	1,017	4.5	72.6	8
Seattle	13	216	866	4.0	66.6	8
Tampa Bay	6	87	327	3.8	54.5	6
Tennessee	3	45	283	6.3	94.3	3
Washington	4	45	175	3.9	43.8	1
Totals	176	2,836	12,279	4.3	69.8	100

Tennessee totals include one game vs. Houston

COREY DILLON'S CAREER RUSHING VS. EACH OPPONENT

Opponent	Games	Rushes	Yards	Yards Per Rush	Yards Per Game	TD
Arizona	4	74	379	5.1	94.8	1
Atlanta	2	41	172	4.2	86.0	0
Baltimore	15	260	907	3.5	60.5	3
Buffalo	6	109	500	4.6	83.3	5
Carolina	3	52	204	3.9	68.0	0
Chicago	1	16	30	1.9	30.0	0
Cincinnati	1	22	88	4.0	88.0	1
Cleveland	11	217	1,111	5.1	101.0	7
Dallas	2	46	221	4.8	110.5	1
Denver	4	76	480	6.3	120.0	2
Detroit	2	44	261	5.9	130.5	3
Green Bay	1	16	28	1.8	28.0	0
Houston	1	22	92	4.2	92.0	0
Indianapolis	6	87	423	4.9	70.5	3
Jacksonville	10	175	625	3.6	62.5	3
Kansas City	2	32	119	3.7	59.5	2
Miami	4	66	325	4.9	81.3	1
Minnesota	1	21	66	3.1	66.0	0
New England	2	52	183	3.5	91.5	1
New Orleans	1	18	126	7.0	126.0	0
N.Y. Giants	1	5	8	1.6	8.0	1
N.Y. Jets	6	124	479	3.9	79.8	5
Oakland	3	55	206	3.7	68.7	3
Philadelphia	2	35	153	4.4	76.5	0
Pittsburgh	14	239	954	4.0	68.1	7
St. Louis	3	47	188	4.0	62.7	1
San Diego	6	87	387	4.4	64.5	2
San Francisco	3	48	273	5.7	91.0	2
Seattle	2	39	186	4.8	93.0	2
Tampa Bay	4	77	256	3.3	64.0	1
Tennessee	11	217	999	4.6	90.8	12
Totals	134	2,419	10,429	4.3	77.8	69

EDGERRIN JAMES'S CAREER RUSHING VS. EACH OPPONENT

Opponent	Games	Rushes	Yards	Yards Per Rush	Yards Per Game	TD
Atlanta	1	20	126	6.3	126.0	0
Baltimore	3	62	200	3.2	66.7	1
Buffalo	6	141	552	3.9	92.0	7
Chicago	2	40	272	6.8	136.0	2
Cincinnati	3	72	201	2.8	67.0	5
Cleveland	4	80	320	4.0	80.0	4
Dallas	2	51	223	4.4	111.5	1
Denver	3	37	124	3.4	41.3	2
Detroit	2	54	244	4.5	122.0	1
Green Bay	2	38	133	3.5	66.5	1
Houston	8	190	879	4.6	109.9	4
Jacksonville	9	199	785	3.9	87.2	2
Kansas City	4	85	369	4.3	92.3	1
Miami	6	159	668	4.2	111.3	3
Minnesota	2	52	251	4.8	125.5	0
New England	9	232	950	4.1	105.6	3
N.Y. Giants	2	26	121	4.7	60.5	0
N.Y. Jets	6	156	627	4.0	104.5	6
Oakland	3	76	343	4.5	114.3	2
Philadelphia	1	22	152	6.9	152.0	2

Opponent	Games	Rushes	Yards	Yards Per Rush	Yards Per Game	TD
Pittsburgh	2	49	186	3.8	93.0	0
St. Louis	1	23	143	6.2	143.0	2
San Diego	3	52	157	3.0	52.3	1
San Francisco	1	21	105	5.0	105.0	1
Seattle	2	51	260	5.1	130.0	3
Tennessee	7	164	713	4.3	101.9	8
Washington	2	36	122	3.4	61.0	1
Totals	96	2,188	9,226	4.2	96.1	64

MARVIN HARRISON'S CAREER RECEIVING VS. EACH OPPONENT

Opponent	Games	Rec.	Yards	Yards/ Rec.	Yards/ Game	TD
Arizona	2	8	104	13.0	52.0	1
Atlanta	2	12	183	15.3	91.5	2
Baltimore	6	31	436	14.1	72.7	3
Buffalo	13	59	810	13.7	62.3	9
Carolina	1	8	119	14.9	119.0	0
Chicago	2	10	91	9.1	45.5	1
Cincinnati	5	36	511	14.2	102.2	3
Cleveland	4	38	407	10.7	101.8	2
Dallas	3	23	239	10.4	79.7	3
Denver	4	31	353	11.4	88.3	3
Detroit	3	24	266	11.1	88.7	5
Green Bay	3	15	191	12.7	63.7	2
Houston	8	46	566	12.3	70.8	3
Jacksonville	9	35	514	14.7	57.1	8
Kansas City	5	35	528	15.1	105.6	6
Miami	14	79	1,059	13.4	75.6	8
Minnesota	3	25	255	10.2	85.0	4
New England	15	94	1,313	14.0	87.5	12
New Orleans	3	19	308	16.2	102.7	3
N.Y. Giants	2	16	237	14.8	118.5	3
N.Y. Jets	12	66	747	11.3	62.3	5
Oakland	3	21	245	11.7	81.7	3
Philadelphia	3	17	303	17.8	101.0	4
Pittsburgh	3	15	256	17.1	85.3	2
St. Louis	2	9	135	15.0	67.5	1
San Diego	6	37	563	15.2	93.8	2
San Francisco	3	16	243	15.2	81.0	4
Seattle	2	11	172	15.6	86.0	0
Tampa Bay	2	14	233	16.6	116.5	2
Tennessee	8	60	732	12.2	91.5	6
Washington	3	17	212	12.5	70.7	0
Totals	154	927	12,331	13.3	80.1	110

KEENAN McCARDELL'S CAREER RECEIVING VS. EACH OPPONENT

Opponent	Games	Rec.	Yards	Yards/ Rec.	Yards/ Game	TD
Arizona	2	3	65	21.7	32.5	1
Atlanta	6	33	404	12.2	67.3	4
Baltimore	13	82	941	11.5	72.4	1
Buffalo	5	27	314	11.6	62.8	1
Carolina	6	28	381	13.6	63.5	3
Chicago	3	18	176	9.8	58.7	1
Cincinnati	17	71	948	13.4	55.8	10
Cleveland	7	38	418	11.0	59.7	2
Dallas	5	25	330	13.2	66.0	3
Denver	6	25	281	11.2	46.8	0
Detroit	3	7	123	17.6	41.0	1
Green Bay	4	19	256	13.5	64.0	1
Houston	1	5	59	11.8	59.0	0
Indianapolis	4	12	260	21.7	65.0	3
Jacksonville	3	16	161	10.1	53.7	0
Kansas City	8	30	433	14.4	54.1	1
Miami	2	10	144	14.4	72.0	3
Minnesota	3	7	58	8.3	19.3	1
New England	6	23	335	14.6	55.8	5
New Orleans	7	44	519	11.8	74.1	3

Opponent	Games	Rec.	Yards	Yards/ Rec.	Yards/ Game	TD
N.Y. Giants	4	28	365	13.0	91.3	2
N.Y. Jets	4	11	136	12.4	34.0	0
Oakland	6	28	414	14.8	69.0	2
Philadelphia	5	17	215	12.6	43.0	1
Pittsburgh	19	68	848	12.5	44.6	3
St. Louis	3	23	332	14.4	110.7	2
San Diego	1	9	97	10.8	97.0	0
San Francisco	3	11	197	17.9	65.7	1
Seattle	4	18	312	17.3	78.0	1
Tampa Bay	3	11	143	13.0	47.7	2
Tennessee	18	61	805	13.2	44.7	4
Washington	4	17	210	12.4	52.5	0
Totals	185	825	10,680	12.9	57.7	62

St. Louis totals include one game vs. L.A. Rams
Tennessee totals include seven games vs. Houston

ISAAC BRUCE'S CAREER RECEIVING VS. EACH OPPONENT

Opponent	Games	Rec.	Yards	Yards/ Rec.	Yards/ Game	TD
Arizona	10	42	630	15.0	63.0	5
Atlanta	16	71	1,283	18.1	80.2	10
Baltimore	3	21	334	15.9	111.3	2
Buffalo	2	12	194	16.2	97.0	1
Carolina	13	61	790	13.0	60.8	4
Chicago	6	34	456	13.4	76.0	1
Cincinnati	2	10	192	19.2	96.0	0
Cleveland	2	7	75	10.7	37.5	2
Dallas	2	4	60	15.0	30.0	1
Denver	4	11	140	12.7	35.0	0
Detroit	3	8	100	12.5	33.3	0
Green Bay	6	33	462	14.0	77.0	3
Houston	1	4	94	23.5	94.0	1
Indianapolis	2	13	256	19.7	128.0	2
Jacksonville	1	2	30	15.0	30.0	0
Kansas City	4	19	282	14.8	70.5	4
Miami	4	29	416	14.3	104.0	1
Minnesota	4	26	381	14.7	95.3	2
New England	2	11	189	17.2	94.5	1
New Orleans	14	79	1,397	17.7	99.8	11
N.Y. Giants	6	27	381	14.1	63.5	2
N.Y. Jets	4	18	254	14.1	63.5	3
Oakland	2	9	118	13.1	59.0	1
Philadelphia	6	28	382	13.6	63.7	2
Pittsburgh	2	10	181	18.1	90.5	0
San Diego	3	20	343	17.2	114.3	5
San Francisco	22	104	1,586	15.3	72.1	10
Seattle	9	41	587	14.3	65.2	2
Tampa Bay	4	11	163	14.8	40.8	0
Tennessee	2	7	64	9.1	32.0	1
Washington	6	41	458	11.2	76.3	0
Totals	167	813	12,278	15.1	73.5	77

ROD SMITH'S CAREER RECEIVING VS. EACH OPPONENT

Opponent	Games	Rec.	Yards	Yards/ Rec.	Yards/ Game	TD
Arizona	3	19	224	11.8	74.7	3
Atlanta	3	19	353	18.6	117.7	3
Baltimore	5	20	266	13.3	53.2	0
Buffalo	4	21	266	12.7	66.5	2
Carolina	2	8	00	12.5	50.0	1
Chicago	2	10	100	10.0	50.0	1
Cincinnati	5	25	02	12.1	60.4	4
Cleveland	2	9	152	16.9	76.0	3
Dallas	4	16	214	13.4	53.5	1
Detroit	2	9	85	9.4	42.5	0
Green Bay	2	5	63	12.6	31.5	0
Houston	1	3	29	9.7	29.0	1
Indianapolis	4	23	283	12.3	70.8	2

Opponent	Games	Rec.	Yards	Yards/Rec.	Yards/Game	TD
Jacksonville	5	22	259	11.8	51.8	1
Kansas City	20	117	1,734	14.8	86.7	4
Miami	5	27	329	12.2	65.8	0
Minnesota	3	10	141	14.1	47.0	0
New England	10	50	785	15.7	78.5	3
New Orleans	2	5	51	10.2	25.5	0
N.Y. Giants	3	16	217	13.6	72.3	1
N.Y. Jets	4	19	319	16.8	79.8	0
Oakland	22	99	1,291	13.0	58.7	10
Philadelphia	3	12	171	14.3	57.0	3
Pittsburgh	2	8	185	23.1	92.5	3
St. Louis	3	12	261	21.8	87.0	4
San Diego	21	108	1,355	12.5	64.5	6
San Francisco	3	16	175	10.9	58.3	0
Seattle	14	68	925	13.6	66.1	6
Tampa Bay	2	6	56	9.3	28.0	0
Tennessee	2	7	82	11.7	41.0	1
Washington	4	8	104	13.0	26.0	2
Totals	167	797	10,877	13.6	65.1	65

Tennessee totals include one game vs. Houston

Opponent	Games	FG	FGA	FG%	Long FG	XP	XPA	Pts.
San Francisco	6	12	14	85.7	50	10	10	46
Seattle	23	49	57	86.0	54	35	36	182
Tampa Bay	13	17	21	81.0	48	28	29	79
Tennessee	4	9	10	90.0	48	2	2	29
Washington	4	9	13	69.2	41	8	8	35
Totals	245	390	480	81.3	54	464	470	1,634

Arizona totals include one game vs. Phoenix
Oakland totals include ten games vs. L.A. Raiders
St. Louis totals include two games vs. L.A. Rams
Tennessee totals include two games vs. Houston

MATT STOVER'S CAREER KICKING VS. EACH OPPONENT

Opponent	Games	FG	FGA	FG%	Long FG	XP	XPA	Pts.
Arizona	4	9	9	100.0	46	7	7	34
Atlanta	3	3	5	60.0	38	5	5	14
Buffalo	3	7	10	70.0	47	4	4	25
Carolina	2	3	4	75.0	46	2	2	11
Chicago	4	6	9	66.7	43	5	5	23
Cincinnati	30	57	64	89.1	50	74	74	245
Cleveland	14	33	36	91.7	45	28	28	127
Dallas	4	7	9	77.8	50	9	9	30
Denver	9	13	15	86.7	45	14	14	53
Detroit	4	4	4	100.0	46	8	8	20
Green Bay	5	7	8	87.5	46	13	13	34
Houston	2	4	4	100.0	47	3	3	15
Indianapolis	10	13	21	61.9	51	21	21	60
Jacksonville	17	30	34	88.2	49	27	27	117
Kansas City	6	4	6	66.7	50	12	12	24
Miami	7	10	12	83.3	45	9	10	39
Minnesota	5	10	10	100.0	38	7	7	37
New England	8	11	14	78.6	41	10	10	43
New Orleans	4	4	6	66.7	43	10	10	22
N.Y. Giants	4	7	7	100.0	46	9	9	30
N.Y. Jets	7	11	13	84.6	45	15	15	48
Oakland	5	7	10	70.0	37	8	8	29
Philadelphia	4	7	8	87.5	50	7	8	28
Pittsburgh	30	42	51	82.4	51	48	48	174
St. Louis	4	5	9	55.6	50	10	11	25
San Diego	7	12	12	100.0	49	12	12	48
San Francisco	3	8	8	100.0	47	9	9	33
Seattle	4	5	7	71.4	42	14	14	29
Tampa Bay	2	4	4	100.0	43	2	2	14
Tennessee	24	32	42	76.2	55	46	46	142
Washington	4	5	6	83.3	51	6	6	21
Totals	239	380	457	83.2	55	454	457	1,594

Oakland totals include two games vs. L.A. Raiders
St. Louis totals include one game vs. L.A. Rams
Tennessee totals include twelve games vs. Houston

JOHN CARNEY'S CAREER KICKING VS. EACH OPPONENT

Opponent	Games	FG	FGA	FG%	Long FG	XP	XPA	Pts.
Arizona	4	5	5	100.0	50	9	9	24
Atlanta	13	19	27	70.4	50	30	30	87
Baltimore	3	4	4	100.0	47	6	6	18
Buffalo	5	10	12	83.3	54	9	9	39
Carolina	12	16	19	84.2	48	25	25	73
Chicago	6	7	13	53.8	50	12	12	33
Cincinnati	5	12	13	92.3	48	12	12	48
Cleveland	5	8	10	80.0	48	11	11	35
Dallas	3	4	4	100.0	44	5	5	17
Denver	21	37	43	86.0	50	31	32	142
Detroit	6	8	10	80.0	47	9	9	33
Green Bay	5	5	9	55.6	47	7	7	22
Houston	1	1	1	100.0	39	4	4	7
Indianapolis	9	17	20	85.0	50	23	23	74
Jacksonville	1	2	2	100.0	38	1	2	7
Kansas City	21	21	28	75.0	54	42	42	105
Miami	6	9	12	75.0	49	12	12	39
Minnesota	6	13	14	92.9	50	14	15	53
New England	6	3	8	37.5	46	9	9	18
New Orleans	4	10	10	100.0	49	11	11	41
N.Y. Giants	5	9	11	81.8	46	12	12	39
N.Y. Jets	6	5	6	83.3	53	16	16	31
Oakland	21	34	42	81.0	48	33	34	135
Philadelphia	4	4	5	80.0	35	6	6	18
Pittsburgh	9	14	16	87.5	48	14	14	56
St. Louis	7	16	19	84.2	53	16	16	64
San Diego	1	1	2	50.0	37	2	2	5

BRETT FAVRE'S CAREER PASSING VS. EACH OPPONENT

Opponent	Games	Att.	Cmp.	Pct.	Yards	Avg. Gain	TD	Int.	Sacked
Arizona	3	98	61	62.2	833	8.50	4	2	3/21
Atlanta	5	191	129	67.5	1,395	7.30	8	6	9/68
Baltimore	3	104	63	60.6	741	7.13	5	4	3/14
Buffalo	4	126	74	58.7	753	5.98	8	3	7/54
Carolina	8	308	188	61.0	2,167	7.04	20	12	17/130
Chicago	28	933	582	62.4	6,730	7.21	51	31	42/281
Cincinnati	4	156	102	65.4	1,181	7.57	7	7	10/70
Cleveland	4	133	93	69.9	914	6.87	9	2	5/28
Dallas	7	269	161	59.9	1,641	6.10	13	4	13/97
Denver	4	114	59	51.8	751	6.59	6	9	4/26
Detroit	28	1,002	624	62.3	7,260	7.25	46	34	54/349
Houston	1	50	33	66.0	383	7.66	1	2	0/0

Opponent	Games	Att.	Cmp.	Pct.	Yards	Avg. Gain	TD	Int.	Sacked
Indianapolis	3	105	71	67.6	1,024	9.75	9	3	6/52
Jacksonville	3	116	74	63.8	931	8.03	7	4	5/36
Kansas City	3	119	72	60.5	799	6.71	5	5	11/65
Miami	4	147	92	62.6	996	6.78	5	3	9/42
Minnesota	27	891	551	61.8	6,052	6.79	47	31	48/317
New England	3	108	65	60.2	680	6.30	7	2	6/46
New Orleans	4	133	87	65.4	943	7.09	10	1	9/47
N.Y. Giants	5	150	89	59.3	1,112	7.41	7	4	7/44
N.Y. Jets	3	95	50	52.6	507	5.34	4	2	3/21
Oakland	3	105	64	61.0	922	8.78	9	3	6/31
Philadelphia	10	324	176	54.3	2,127	6.56	12	17	24/160
Pittsburgh	4	125	79	63.2	959	7.67	4	2	8/55
St. Louis	9	278	171	61.5	1,954	7.03	15	11	16/136
San Diego	4	111	70	63.1	828	7.46	10	4	5/56
San Francisco	6	199	122	61.3	1,515	7.61	10	8	9/54
Seattle	4	131	74	56.5	833	6.36	8	5	9/49
Tampa Bay	23	774	474	61.2	5,125	6.62	37	23	44/245
Tennessee	4	134	77	57.5	945	7.05	8	5	7/18
Washington	4	81	51	63.0	614	7.58	4	6	4/49
Totals	225	7,610	4,678	61.5	53,615	7.05	396	255	403/2,661

Oakland totals include one game vs. L.A. Raiders
St. Louis totals include four games vs. L.A. Rams
Tennessee totals include one game vs. Houston

DREW BLEDSOE'S CAREER PASSING VS. EACH OPPONENT

Opponent	Games	Att.	Cmp.	Pct.	Yards	Avg. Gain	TD	Int.	Sacked
Arizona	5	115	70	60.9	883	7.68	11	0	12/73
Atlanta	1	34	19	55.9	229	6.74	1	1	5/48
Baltimore	3	101	60	59.4	621	6.15	5	5	6/24
Buffalo	16	504	280	55.6	3,327	6.60	22	10	37/261
Carolina	2	67	37	55.2	437	6.52	1	1	5/29
Chicago	4	157	100	63.7	1,131	7.20	9	2	9/72
Cincinnati	7	242	142	58.7	1,595	6.59	7	3	13/77
Cleveland	6	242	131	54.1	1,383	5.71	4	7	12/78
Dallas	3	99	51	51.5	458	4.63	0	5	4/19
Denver	8	304	173	56.9	1,983	6.52	11	5	22/155
Detroit	5	173	99	57.2	1,050	6.07	3	3	10/58
Green Bay	3	125	67	53.6	781	6.25	3	6	10/72
Houston	2	59	34	57.6	438	7.42	2	0	7/55
Indianapolis	16	518	315	60.8	3,622	6.99	25	11	25/185
Jacksonville	4	130	89	68.5	956	7.35	6	1	7/38
Kansas City	7	270	167	61.9	1,789	6.63	13	7	18/123
Miami	22	765	412	53.9	5,397	7.05	30	29	50/324
Minnesota	4	196	128	65.3	1,392	7.10	9	2	9/72
New England	6	202	115	56.9	1,266	6.27	5	11	19/127
New Orleans	2	66	39	59.1	514	7.79	1	5	5/32
N.Y. Giants	5	180	111	61.7	1,244	6.91	6	5	13/85
N.Y. Jets	22	734	409	55.7	4,544	6.19	21	29	56/404
Oakland	4	158	79	50.0	1,148	7.27	6	8	19/105
Philadelphia	4	151	91	60.3	1,112	7.36	5	5	10/65
Pittsburgh	5	208	115	55.3	1,359	6.53	8	12	7/55
St. Louis	3	98	44	44.9	603	6.15	5	4	10/68
San Diego	5	161	95	59.0	1,129	7.01	12	2	9/50
San Francisco	3	121	66	54.5	776	6.41	3	5	7/38
Seattle	3	105	58	55.2	649	6.18	3	7	7/43
Tampa Bay	2	64	39	60.9	333	5.20	1	2	11/84
Tennessee	2	60	35	58.3	418	6.97	3	0	7/38
Washington	4	139	79	56.8	880	6.33	3	5	10/71
Totals	188	6,548	3,749	57.3	43,447	6.64	244	198	451/3,028

Arizona totals include one game vs. Phoenix
Oakland totals include one game vs. L.A. Raiders

PEYTON MANNING'S CAREER PASSING VS. EACH OPPONENT

Opponent	Games	Att.	Cmp.	Pct.	Yards	Avg. Gain	TD	Int.	Sacked
Arizona	1	2	1	50.0	5	2.50	0	0	1/0
Atlanta	3	92	67	72.8	774	8.41	10	3	1/9
Baltimore	5	199	125	62.8	1,454	7.31	9	3	10/87
Buffalo	9	281	168	59.8	2,014	7.17	12	9	9/66
Carolina	2	68	40	58.8	518	7.62	2	3	5/18
Chicago	2	67	43	64.2	513	7.66	6	2	2/21
Cincinnati	4	133	79	59.4	1,083	8.14	10	3	2/12
Cleveland	4	143	93	65.0	992	6.94	2	4	2/10
Dallas	2	72	51	70.8	565	7.85	3	1	1/13
Denver	4	99	56	56.6	572	5.78	2	2	5/30
Detroit	2	61	45	73.8	524	8.59	9	2	1/7
Green Bay	2	84	53	63.1	687	8.18	8	1	4/27
Houston	8	246	175	71.1	2,103	8.55	19	4	10/64
Jacksonville	9	305	195	63.9	2,394	7.85	19	5	5/41
Kansas City	4	139	87	62.6	1,236	8.89	9	3	7/62
Miami	10	341	208	61.0	2,372	6.96	14	18	17/126
Minnesota	2	65	48	73.8	551	8.48	8	1	1/4
New England	11	398	246	61.8	2,863	7.19	23	16	14/88
New Orleans	3	85	57	67.1	885	10.41	8	4	5/26
N.Y. Giants	2	81	50	61.7	602	7.43	5	3	2/16
N.Y. Jets	9	343	212	61.8	2,286	6.66	12	11	11/60
Oakland	3	115	75	65.2	806	7.01	8	5	4/33
Philadelphia	2	49	34	69.4	554	11.31	6	0	1/8
Pittsburgh	2	73	47	64.4	549	7.52	3	4	4/15
St. Louis	2	60	37	61.7	386	6.43	2	1	4/21
San Diego	4	166	94	56.6	1,260	7.59	6	5	8/45
San Francisco	3	112	72	64.3	856	7.64	5	6	3/16
Seattle	3	81	52	64.2	732	9.04	2	1	3/6
Tampa Bay	1	47	34	72.3	386	8.21	2	1	1/5
Tennessee	8	257	181	70.4	2,155	8.39	16	6	9/60
Washington	2	69	44	63.8	512	7.42	4	3	4/26
Totals	128	4,333	2,769	63.9	33,189	7.66	244	130	156/1,022

STEVE McNAIR'S CAREER PASSING VS. EACH OPPONENT

Opponent	Games	Att.	Cmp.	Pct.	Yards	Avg. Gain	TD	Int.	Sacked
Arizona	1	17	9	52.9	146	8.59	2	0	2/13
Atlanta	3	50	29	58.0	369	7.38	3	0	3/18
Baltimore	13	437	248	56.8	2,599	5.95	7	11	26/153
Buffalo	3	81	44	54.3	487	6.01	2	1	7/45
Carolina	2	39	22	56.4	281	7.21	1	1	4/31
Chicago	1	29	18	62.1	187	6.45	1	1	4/11
Cincinnati	13	332	199	59.9	2,551	7.68	20	5	17/115
Cleveland	8	185	104	56.2	1,322	7.15	8	6	9/62
Dallas	3	78	46	59.0	495	6.35	3	3	3/24
Detroit	2	62	31	50.0	419	6.76	2	3	3/25
Green Bay	3	110	69	62.7	752	6.84	7	1	5/28
Houston	8	242	137	56.6	1,811	7.48	13	8	5/23
Indianapolis	7	213	145	68.1	1,405	6.60	6	2	13/104
Jacksonville	16	457	286	62.6	3,359	7.35	20	13	29/167
Kansas City	1	18	11	61.1	93	5.17	0	2	2/5
Miami	6	125	67	53.6	740	5.92	4	7	7/36
Minnesota	3	71	43	60.6	565	7.96	2	0	6/52
New England	3	107	62	57.9	698	6.52	1	4	6/36
New Orleans	1	33	22	66.7	252	7.64	2	0	2/1
N.Y. Giants	3	101	67	66.3	810	8.02	6	1	4/19
N.Y. Jets	4	103	53	51.5	749	7.27	5	2	7/52
Oakland	6	196	123	62.8	1,370	6.99	7	9	17/113
Philadelphia	2	71	47	66.2	479	6.75	2	1	3/13
Pittsburgh	13	327	198	60.6	2,453	7.50	17	11	23/131
St. Louis	2	68	37	54.4	447	6.57	4	2	3/21
San Diego	1	34	20	58.8	193	5.68	1	0	3/19
San Francisco	2	50	28	56.0	388	7.76	3	2	1/10
Seattle	4	118	65	55.1	835	7.08	4	3	5/24
Tampa Bay	2	39	24	61.5	353	9.05	1	1	3/22
Washington	3	78	51	65.4	533	6.83	2	3	7/25
Totals	139	3,871	2,305	59.5	27,141	7.01	156	103	229/1,398

The NFL rates its passers for statistical purposes against a fixed performance standard based on statistical achievements of all qualified pro passers since 1960. The current system replaced one that rated passers in relation to their position in a total group based on various criteria. The current system, which was adopted in 1973, removes inequities that existed in the former method and, at the same time, provides a means of comparing passing performances from one season to the next.

It is important to remember that the system is used to rate passers, not quarterbacks. Statistics do not reflect leadership, play-calling, and other intangible factors that go into making a successful professional quarterback. Four categories are used as a basis for compiling a rating:

—Percentage of completions per attempt
—Average yards gained per attempt
—Percentage of touchdown passes per attempt
—Percentage of interceptions per attempt

The average standard is 1.000. The bottom is .000. To earn a 2.000 rating, a passer must perform at exceptional levels, i.e., 70 percent in completions, 10 percent in touchdowns, 1.5 percent in interceptions, and 11 yards average gain per pass attempt. The maximum passer can receive in any category is 2.375.

For example, to gain a 2.375 in completion percentage, a passer would have to complete 77.5 percent of his passes. The NFL record is 70.55 by Ken Anderson (Cincinnati, 1982). To earn a 2.375 in percentage of touchdowns, a passer would have to achieve a percentage of 11.9. The record is 13.9 by Sid Luckman (Chicago, 1943). To gain 2.375 in percentage of interceptions, a passer would have to go the entire season without an interception. The 2.375 figure in average yards is 12.50, compared with the NFL record of 11.17 by Tommy O'Connell (Cleveland, 1957).

In order to make the rating more understandable, the point rating is then converted into a scale of 100, with 158.3 being the highest rating a passer can achieve. In cases where statistical performance has been superior, it is possible for a passer to surpass a 100 rating. For example, take Steve Young's record-setting season in 1994 when he completed 324 of 461 passes for 3,969 yards, 35 touchdowns, and 10 interceptions. The four calculations would be:

—Percentage of Completions—324 of 461 is 70.28 percent. Subtract 30 from the completion percentage (40.28) and multiply the result by 0.05. The result is a point rating of 2.014. Note: If the result is less than zero (Comp. Pct. less than 30.0), award zero points. If the results are greater than 2.375 (Comp. Pct. greater than 77.5), award 2.375.

—Average Yards Gained Per Attempt—3,969 yards divided by 461 attempts is 8.61. Subtract three yards from yards-per-attempt (5.61) and multiply the result by 0.25. The result is 1.403. Note: If the result is less than zero (yards per attempt less than 3.0), award zero points. If the result is greater than 2.375 (yards per attempt greater than 12.5), award 2.375 points.

—Percentage of Touchdown Passes—35 touchdowns in 461 attempts is 7.59 percent. Multiply the touchdown percentage by 0.2. The result is 1.518. Note: If the result is greater than 2.375 (touchdown percentage greater than 11.875), award 2.375.

—Percentage of Interceptions—10 interceptions in 461 attempts is 2.17 percent. Multiply the interception percentage by 0.25 (0.542) and subtract the number from 2.375. The result is 1.833. Note: If the result is less than zero (interception percentage greater than 9.5), award zero points.

The sum of the four steps is (2.014 + 1.403 + 1.518 + 1.833) 6.768. The sum is then divided by six (1.128) and multiplied by 100. In this case, the result is 112.8. This same formula can be used to determine a passer rating for any player who attempts at least one pass.

The following is a list of the 38 qualifying passers who had a single-season passer rating of 100 or higher:

Player, Team	Season	Rating	Att.	Comp.	Pct.	Yds.	Avg.	TD	TD Pct.	Int.	Int. Pct.
Peyton Manning, Indianapolis	2004	121.1	497	336	67.6	4,557	9.17	49	9.9	10	2.0
Steve Young, San Francisco	1994	112.8	461	324	70.2	3,969	8.61	35	7.6	10	2.2
Joe Montana, San Francisco	1989	112.4	386	271	70.2	3,521	9.12	26	6.7	8	2.1
Daunte Culpepper, Minnesota	2004	110.9	548	379	69.2	4,717	8.61	39	7.1	11	2.0
Milt Plum, Cleveland	1960	110.4	250	151	60.4	2,297	9.19	21	8.4	5	2.0
Sammy Baugh, Washington	1945	109.9	182	128	70.3	1,669	9.17	11	6.0	4	2.2
Kurt Warner, St. Louis	1999	109.2	499	325	65.1	4,353	8.72	41	8.2	13	2.6
Dan Marino, Miami	1984	108.9	564	362	64.2	5,084	9.01	48	8.5	17	3.0
Sid Luckman, Chicago Bears	1943	107.5	202	110	54.5	2,194	10.86	28	13.9	12	5.9
Steve Young, San Francisco	1992	107.0	402	268	66.7	3,465	8.62	25	6.2	7	1.7
Randall Cunningham, Minnesota	1998	106.0	425	259	60.9	3,704	8.72	34	8.0	10	2.4
Bart Starr, Green Bay	1966	105.0	251	156	62.2	2,257	8.99	14	5.6	3	1.2
Drew Brees, San Diego	2004	104.8	400	262	65.5	3,159	7.90	27	6.8	7	1.8
Roger Staubach, Dallas	1971	104.8	211	126	59.7	1,882	8.92	15	7.1	4	1.9
Y.A. Tittle, N.Y. Giants	1963	104.8	367	221	60.2	3,145	8.57	36	9.8	14	3.8
Donovan McNabb, Philadelphia	2004	104.7	469	300	64.0	3,875	8.06	31	6.6	8	1.7
Steve Young, San Francisco	1997	104.7	356	241	67.7	3,029	8.51	19	5.3	6	1.7
Bart Starr, Green Bay	1968	104.3	171	109	63.7	1,617	9.46	15	8.8	8	4.7
Chad Pennington, N.Y. Jets	2002	104.2	399	275	68.9	3,120	7.82	22	5.5	6	1.5
Peyton Manning, Indianapolis	2005	104.1	453	305	67.3	3,747	8.27	28	6.2	10	2.2
Ken Stabler, Oakland	1976	103.4	291	194	66.7	2,737	9.41	27	9.3	17	5.8
Brian Griese, Denver	2000	102.9	336	216	64.3	2,688	8.00	19	5.7	4	1.2
Joe Montana, San Francisco	1984	102.9	432	279	64.6	3,630	8.40	28	6.5	10	2.3
Charlie Conerly, N.Y. Giants	1959	102.7	194	113	58.2	1,706	8.79	14	7.2	4	2.1
Bert Jones, Baltimore	1976	102.5	343	207	60.3	3,104	9.05	24	7.0	9	2.6
Joe Montana, San Francisco	1987	102.1	398	266	66.8	3,054	7.67	31	7.8	13	3.3
Trent Green, St. Louis	2000	101.8	240	145	60.4	2,063	8.60	16	6.7	5	2.1
Steve Young, San Francisco	1991	101.8	279	180	64.5	2,517	9.02	17	6.1	8	2.9
Len Dawson, Kansas City	1966	101.7	284	159	56.0	2,527	8.90	26	9.2	10	3.5
Vinny Testaverde, N.Y. Jets	1998	101.6	421	259	61.5	3,256	7.73	29	6.9	7	1.7
Steve Young, San Francisco	1993	101.5	462	314	68.0	4,023	8.71	29	6.3	16	3.5
Kurt Warner, St. Louis	2001	101.4	546	375	68.7	4,830	8.85	36	6.6	22	4.0
Jim Kelly, Buffalo	1990	101.2	346	219	63.3	2,829	8.18	24	6.9	9	2.6
Carson Palmer, Cincinnati	2005	101.1	509	345	67.8	3,836	7.54	32	6.3	12	2.4
Steve Young, San Francisco	1998	101.1	517	322	62.3	4,170	8.07	36	7.0	12	2.3
Chris Chandler, Atlanta	1998	100.9	327	190	58.1	3,154	9.65	25	7.6	12	3.7
Jim Harbaugh, Indianapolis	1995	100.7	314	200	63.7	2,575	8.20	17	5.4	5	1.6
Steve McNair, Tennessee	2003	100.4	400	250	62.5	3,215	8.04	24	6.0	7	1.8

HIGHEST NFL POSTSEASON PASSER RATINGS (MINIMUM: 150 ATTEMPTS)

Player	Games	Att.	Cmp.	Pct.	Yards	Avg. Gain	TD	Int.	Rating
Bart Starr	10	213	130	61.0	1,753	8.23	15	3	104.8
Joe Montana	23	734	460	62.7	5,772	7.86	45	21	95.6
Jake Delhomme	7	192	113	58.9	1,642	8.55	11	5	95.0
Ken Anderson	6	166	110	66.3	1,321	7.96	9	6	93.5
Kurt Warner	7	268	169	63.1	2,221	8.29	15	10	92.3
Joe Theismann	10	211	128	60.7	1,782	8.45	11	7	91.4
Tom Brady	11	367	225	61.3	2,493	6.79	15	5	89.4
Peyton Manning	9	321	193	60.1	2,462	7.67	15	8	89.3
Troy Aikman	16	502	320	63.7	3,849	7.67	23	17	88.3
Steve Young	22	471	292	62.0	3,326	7.06	20	13	85.8

HIGHEST NFL POSTSEASON PASSER RATINGS, ACTIVE PLAYERS (MINIMUM: 100 ATTEMPTS)

Player	Games	Att.	Cmp.	Pct.	Yards	Avg. Gain	TD	Int.	Rating
Jake Delhomme	7	192	113	58.9	1,642	8.55	11	5	95.0
Kurt Warner	7	268	169	63.1	2,221	8.29	15	10	92.3
Tom Brady	11	367	225	61.3	2,493	6.79	15	5	89.4
Peyton Manning	9	321	193	60.1	2,462	7.67	15	8	89.3
Matt Hasselbeck	5	191	114	59.7	1,353	7.08	6	3	85.3
Brett Favre	20	663	401	60.5	4,902	7.39	34	26	84.0
Vinny Testaverde	5	189	114	60.3	1,320	6.98	6	5	81.0
Donovan McNabb	12	419	249	59.4	2,630	6.28	18	12	80.1
Kerry Collins	6	199	115	57.8	1,275	6.41	12	10	76.1
Jake Plummer	6	197	122	61.9	1,340	6.80	7	10	72.7

ALL-TIME RANKINGS OF PLAYERS IN FOUR CATEGORIES THAT DETERMINE NFL PASSER RATING
Minimum: 1,500 Attempts

COMPLETION PERCENTAGE	Pct.	Att.	Comp.
Kurt Warner	65.68	2,340	1,537
Marc Bulger	65.02	1,518	987
Daunte Culpepper	64.37	2,607	1,678
Steve Young	64.28	4,149	2,667
Peyton Manning	63.90	4,333	2,769
Joe Montana	63.24	5,391	3,409
Brian Griese	63.11	2,318	1,463
Drew Brees	62.19	1,809	1,125
Tom Brady	61.89	2,548	1,577
Brad Johnson	61.87	3,798	2,350

TOUCHDOWN PERCENTAGE	Pct.	Att.	TD
Sid Luckman	7.86	1,744	137
Frank Ryan	6.99	2,133	149
Len Dawson	6.39	3,741	239
Daryle Lamonica	6.31	2,601	164
Sammy Baugh	6.24	2,995	187
Charley Conerly	6.11	2,833	173
Bob Waterfield	6.00	1,617	97
Earl Morrall	5.99	2,689	161
Sonny Jurgensen	5.98	4,262	255
Norm Van Brocklin	5.98	2,895	173

AVERAGE YARDS PER PASS	Avg.	Att.	Yards
Otto Graham	8.63	1,565	13,499
Sid Luckman	8.42	1,744	14,686
Kurt Warner	8.21	2,340	19,214
Norm Van Brocklin	8.16	2,895	23,611
Steve Young	7.98	4,149	33,124
Marc Bulger	7.86	1,518	11,932
Ed Brown	7.85	1,987	15,600
Bart Starr	7.85	3,149	24,718
Johnny Unitas	7.76	5,186	40,239
Earl Morrall	7.74	2,689	20,809

INTERCEPTION PERCENTAGE	Pct.	Att.	Int.
Neil O'Donnell	2.11	3,229	68
Donovan McNabb	2.24	2,943	66
Mark Brunell	2.35	4,334	102
Steve Bono	2.47	1,701	42
Rich Gannon	2.47	4,206	104
Jeff Garcia	2.55	2,785	71
Joe Montana	2.58	5,391	139
Steve Young	2.58	4,149	107
Matt Hasselbeck	2.59	2,205	57
Bernie Kosar	2.59	3,365	87

STARTING RECORDS OF ACTIVE NFL QUARTERBACKS

Minimum: 10 starts

	W - L - T	Pct.
Ben Roethlisberger	22- 3-0	.880
Tom Brady	58-20-0	.744
Donovan McNabb	60-28-0	.682
Kyle Orton	10- 5-0	.667
Marc Bulger	28-16-0	.636
Brett Favre	139-82-0	.629
Peyton Manning	80-48-0	.625
Michael Vick	31-19-1	.618
Jay Fiedler	37-23-0	.617
Kurt Warner	42-27-0	.609
Brad Johnson	65-43-0	.602
Jake Delhomme	29-20-0	.592
Matt Hasselbeck	40-28-0	.588
Carson Palmer	17-12-0	.586
Chris Simms	7- 5-0	.583
Steve McNair	76-55-0	.580
Chad Pennington	21-16-0	.568
Byron Leftwich	21-17-0	.553
Brian Griese	39-33-0	.542
A.J. Feeley	7- 6-0	.538
Trent Dilfer	57-50-0	.533
Mark Brunell	75-66-0	.532
Kyle Boller	18-16-0	.529
Trent Green	52-47-0	.525
Eli Manning	12-11-0	.522
Drew Brees	30-28-0	.517
Drew Bledsoe	95-92-0	.508
Shane Matthews	11-11-0	.500
Jake Plummer	62-63-0	.496
Daunte Culpepper	38-42-0	.475
Aaron Brooks	38-44-0	.463
Gus Frerotte	36-42-1	.462
Jon Kitna	36-43-0	.456
Kerry Collins	66-79-0	.455
Josh McCown	10-12-0	.455
Jeff Garcia	39-47-0	.453
Tony Banks	35-43-0	.449
Ty Detmer	11-14-0	.440
Charlie Batch	21-27-0	.438
Tommy Maddox	15-20-1	.431
Vinny Testaverde	88-119-1	.425
Anthony Wright	8-11-0	.421
Patrick Ramsey	10-14-0	.417
Todd Collins	7-10-0	.412
Jeff Blake	39-61-0	.390
Kelly Holcomb	8-13-0	.381
Joey Harrington	18-37-0	.327
Billy Volek	3- 7-0	.300
David Carr	16-43-0	.271
Tim Rattay	4-12-0	.250
Mike McMahon	3-11-0	.214
Ken Dorsey	2- 8-0	.200
Chris Weinke	1-15-0	.063

TEAMS THAT FINISHED IN FIRST PLACE IN THEIR DIVISION THE SEASON AFTER FINISHING IN LAST PLACE

Season	Team	Record	Prior Season
1967	Houston	9-4-1	*3-11-0
1968	Minnesota	8-6-0	3- 8-3
1970	Cincinnati	8-6-0	4- 9-1
1970	San Francisco	10-3-1	4- 8-2
1972	Green Bay	10-4-0	4- 8-2
1975	Baltimore	10-4-0	2-12-0
1979	Tampa Bay	10-6-0	5-11-0
1981	Cincinnati	12-4-0	6-10-0
1987	Indianapolis	9-6-0	3-13-0
1988	Cincinnati	12-4-0	4-11-0
1990	Cincinnati	9-7-0	8- 8-0
1991	Denver	12-4-0	5-11-0

1992	San Diego	11-5-0	4-12-0
1993	Detroit	10-6-0	5-11-0
1997	N.Y. Giants	10-5-1	6-10-0
1999	Indianapolis	13-3-0	3-13-0
1999	St. Louis	13-3-0	4-12-0
2000	New Orleans	10-6-0	3-13-0
2001	Chicago	13-3-0	5-11-0
2001	New England	11-5-0	5-11-0
2003	Carolina	11-5-0	7- 9-0
2003	Kansas City	13-3-0	*8- 8-0
2004	Atlanta	11-5-0	5-11-0
2004	San Diego	12-4-0	*4-12-0
2005	Chicago	11-5-0	5-11-0
2005	Tampa Bay	11-5-0	5-11-0

tied for last place

LONGEST WINNING STREAKS SINCE 1970

18	New England, 2003-04	(12 in 2003, 6 in 2004)
16	Miami, 1971-73	(1 in 1971, 14 in 1972, 1 in 1973)
16	Miami, 1983-84	(5 in 1983, 11 in 1984)
16	Pittsburgh, 2004-05	(14 in 2004, 2 in 2005)
15	San Francisco, 1989-90	(5 in 1989, 10 in 1990)
14	Oakland, 1976-77	(10 in 1976, 4 in 1977)
14	Denver, 1997-98	(1 in 1997, 13 in 1998)
13	Minnesota, 1974-75	(3 in 1974, 10 in 1975)
13	Chicago, 1984-85	(1 in 1984, 12 in 1985)
13	N.Y. Giants, 1989-90	(3 in 1989, 10 in 1990)
13	Indianapolis, 2005	
12	Washington, 1990-91	(1 in 1990, 11 in 1991)
11	Pittsburgh, 1975	
11	Baltimore, 1975-76	(9 in 1975, 2 in 1976)
11	Chicago, 1986-87	(7 in 1986, 4 in 1987)
11	Houston, 1993	
11	San Francisco, 1997	
11	Jacksonville, 1999	
11	Indianapolis, 1999	
11	Seattle, 2005	
10	Miami, 1973	
10	Pittsburgh, 1976-77	(9 in 1976, 1 in 1977)
10	Denver, 1984	
10	San Francisco, 1994	
10	Minnesota, 1999-00	(3 in 1999, 7 in 2000)

NFL PLAYOFF APPEARANCES BY SEASONS

Team	Number of Seasons in Playoffs
Dallas	27
N.Y. Giants	27
St. Louis	27
Cleveland	24
Minnesota	24
Chicago	23
Green Bay	23
Pittsburgh	23
San Francisco	22
Miami	21
Oakland	21
Washington	21
Indianapolis	19
Philadelphia	19
Tennessee	19
Buffalo	17
Denver	17
Detroit	14
Kansas City	14
New England	14
San Diego	13
N.Y. Jets	11
Tampa Bay	9
Atlanta	8
Cincinnati	8
Seattle	8

Arizona	6			
Jacksonville	5			
New Orleans	5			
Baltimore	3			
Carolina	3			

2000	110	138	0	.444
2001	112	136	0	.452
2002	107	148	1	.420
2003	99	157	0	.387
2004	111	145	0	.434
2005	105	151	0	.410

TEAMS IN SUPER BOWL CONTENTION (1978-2005)

	With 3 Weeks to Play	With 2 Weeks to Play	With 1 Week to Play
2005	18	17	14
2004	*27	*26	17
2003	22	17	14
2002	21	21	*19
2001	23	16	13
2000	19	17	16
1999	23	20	16
1998	22	19	14
1997	22	18	14
1996	23	21	13
1995	*27	21	18
1994	25	22	15
1993	20	18	16
1992	20	16	14
1991	20	18	13
1990	23	20	15
1989	21	18	17
1988	21	18	15
1987	19	19	15
1986	19	17	14
1985	21	18	13
1984	18	14	13
1983	24	19	15
1982	20	17	16
1981	21	20	16
1980	20	14	12
1979	19	15	13
1978	20	17	12

RECORD OF TEAMS ON THE ROAD (1970-2005)

Year	W	L	T	Pct
1970	72	101	9	.420
1971	74	100	8	.429
1972	87	90	5	.492
1973	66	109	7	.382
1974	82	99	1	.453
1975	81	101	0	.445
1976	83	112	1	.426
1977	83	113	0	.423
1978	93	130	1	.417
1979	92	132	0	.411
1980	101	122	1	.453
1981	84	139	1	.377
1982	57	68	1	.456
1983	104	119	1	.467
1984	94	129	1	.422
1985	80	144	0	.357
1986	104	118	2	.469
1987	95	114	1	.455
1988	92	131	1	.413
1989	95	128	1	.426
1990	93	131	0	.415
1991	92	132	0	.411
1992	88	136	0	.393
1993	101	123	0	.451
1994	96	128	0	.429
1995	96	144	0	.400
1996	91	149	0	.379
1997	93	145	2	.392
1998	89	151	0	.371
1999	100	148	0	.403

GAMES DECIDED BY 7 POINTS OR LESS AND 3 POINTS OR LESS (1970-2005)

	Games Decided by 7 Points or Less	Games Decided by 3 Points or Less
1970	59 of 182 (32.4%)	34 of 182 (18.7%)
1971	76 of 182 (41.8%)	35 of 182 (19.2%)
1972	71 of 182 (39.0%)	38 of 182 (20.9%)
1973	60 of 182 (32.9%)	28 of 182 (15.4%)
1974	91 of 182 (50.0%)	37 of 182 (20.3%)
1975	62 of 182 (34.1%)	35 of 182 (19.2%)
1976	73 of 196 (37.2%)	38 of 196 (19.4%)
1977	85 of 196 (43.4%)	36 of 196 (18.4%)
1978	108 of 224 (48.2%)	49 of 224 (21.9%)
1979	104 of 224 (46.4%)	51 of 224 (22.8%)
1980	108 of 224 (48.2%)	58 of 224 (25.9%)
1981	91 of 224 (40.6%)	60 of 224 (26.8%)
1982	61 of 126 (48.4%)	33 of 126 (26.2%)
1983	106 of 224 (47.3%)	54 of 224 (24.1%)
1984	95 of 224 (42.4%)	58 of 224 (25.9%)
1985	87 of 224 (38.8%)	38 of 224 (17.0%)
1986	106 of 224 (47.3%)	48 of 224 (21.4%)
1987	99 of 210 (47.1%)	40 of 210 (19.0%)
1988	113 of 224 (50.4%)	62 of 224 (27.7%)
1989	107 of 224 (47.8%)	55 of 224 (24.6%)
1990	97 of 224 (43.3%)	54 of 224 (24.1%)
1991	112 of 224 (50.0%)	57 of 224 (25.4%)
1992	88 of 224 (39.3%)	48 of 224 (21.4%)
1993	*105 of 224 (46.9%)	53 of 224 (23.7%)
1994	115 of 224 (51.3%)	60 of 224 (26.8%)
1995	115 of 240 (47.9%)	61 of 240 (25.4%)
1996	109 of 240 (45.4%)	47 of 240 (19.6%)
1997	111 of 240 (46.3%)	67 of 240 (27.9%)
1998	113 of 240 (47.1%)	50 of 240 (20.8%)
1999	115 of 248 (46.4%)	**64 of 248 (25.8%)
2000	109 of 248 (44.0%)	61 of 248 (24.6%)
2001	121 of 248 (48.8%)	62 of 248 (25.0%)
2002	126 of 256 (49.2%)	63 of 256 (24.6%)
2003	124 of 256 (48.4%)	60 of 256 (23.4%)
2004	116 of 256 (45.3%)	61 of 256 (23.8%)
2005	114 of 256 (44.5%)	60 of 256 (23.4%)

*Week record: Dec. 11-13, 1993 (Week 15), 12 of 14 games (86%) decided by 7 points or less.
**Week record: Oct. 10-11, 1999 (Week 5), 10 of 14 games (71%) decided by 3 points or less.

GAMES DECIDED BY 8 PTS. OR LESS (1994-2005)

1994	121 of 224 (54.0%)	2000	119 of 248 (48.0%)
1995	123 of 240 (51.3%)	2001	128 of 248 (51.6%)
1996	115 of 240 (47.9%)	2002	137 of 256 (53.5%)
1997	120 of 240 (50.0%)	2003	132 of 256 (51.6%)
1998	120 of 240 (50.0%)	2004	121 of 256 (47.3%)
1999	124 of 248 (50.0%)	2005	123 of 256 (48.0%)

TWO-POINT CONVERSION RESULTS (1994-2005)

1994	59 of 116 (50.9%)	2000	35 of 85 (41.2%)
1995	40 of 104 (38.5%)	2001	40 of 90 (44.4%)
1996	44 of 92 (47.8%)	2002	47 of 98 (48.0%)
1997	47 of 109 (43.1%)	2003	29 of 66 (43.9%)
1998	41 of 105 (39.1%)	2004	37 of 76 (48.7%)
1999	31 of 84 (36.9%)	2005	27 of 53 (50.9%)

RECORDS AFTER BYE WEEKS (1990-2005)

AFC		NFC	
Baltimore	6-4	Arizona	9-8
Buffalo	11-6	Atlanta	9-8
Cincinnati	4-13	Carolina	4-7
Cleveland	4-8	Chicago	10-7
Denver	13-4	Dallas	12-5
Houston	1-3	Detroit	7-10
Indianapolis	8-9	Green Bay	9-8
Jacksonville	6-5	Minnesota	13-4
Kansas City	11-6	New Orleans	8-9
Miami	10-7	N.Y. Giants	3-14
New England	8-9	Philadelphia	13-4
N.Y. Jets	8-9	St. Louis	9-8
Oakland	9-8	San Francisco	8-9
Pittsburgh	10-7	Seattle	4-13
San Diego	8-8	Tampa Bay	6-11
Tennessee	9-8	Washington	9-8

2005 RECORDS OF TEAMS IN CLOSE GAMES

AFC	Overall Record	Decided by 8 Pts. or Less	Decided By 3 Pts. or Less
Baltimore	6-10	3-4	2-2
Buffalo	5-11	1-5	0-1
Cincinnati	11-5	5-2	1-1
Cleveland	6-10	4-5	2-3
Denver	13-3	5-2	4-1
Houston	2-14	1-6	1-3
Indianapolis	14-2	5-0	0-0
Jacksonville	12-4	8-3	3-1
Kansas City	10-6	4-3	0-1
Miami	9-7	5-3	4-0
New England	10-6	5-2	2-1
N.Y. Jets	4-12	2-4	1-1
Oakland	4-12	2-4	1-2
Pittsburgh	11-5	2-4	2-2
San Diego	9-7	3-5	0-4
Tennessee	4-12	1-5	1-1

NFC	Overall Record	Decided by 8 Pts. or Less	Decided By 3 Pts. or Less
Arizona	5-11	2-6	0-0
Atlanta	8-8	4-5	1-4
Carolina	11-5	4-3	2-2
Chicago	11-5	6-1	2-1
Dallas	9-7	6-5	4-3
Detroit	5-11	3-5	2-2
Green Bay	4-12	3-8	1-5
Minnesota	9-7	4-1	3-0
New Orleans	3-13	2-5	2-3
N.Y. Giants	11-5	3-3	2-3
Philadelphia	6-10	5-5	3-2
St. Louis	6-10	4-4	1-2
San Francisco	4-12	4-5	2-3
Seattle	13-3	6-2	4-1
Tampa Bay	11-5	6-3	4-2
Washington	10-6	5-5	3-3

SUPER BOWL CHAMPIONS THAT DID NOT MAKE PLAYOFFS THE FOLLOWING YEAR

Tampa Bay—Super Bowl XXXVII champions did not make playoffs in 2003 season.

New England—Super Bowl XXXVI champions did not make playoffs in the 2002 season.

Denver—Super Bowl XXXIII champions did not make playoffs in the 1999 season.

N.Y. Giants—Super Bowl XXV champions did not make playoffs in the 1991 season.

Washington—Super Bowl XXII champions did not make playoffs in the 1988 season.

N.Y. Giants—Super Bowl XXI champions did not make playoffs in the 1987 season.

San Francisco—Super Bowl XVI champions did not make playoffs in the 1982 season.

Oakland—Super Bowl XV champions did not make playoffs in the 1981 season.

Pittsburgh—Super Bowl XIV champions did not make playoffs in the 1980 season.

Kansas City—Super Bowl IV champions did not make playoffs in the 1970 season.

Green Bay—Super Bowl II champions did not make playoffs in the 1968 season.

NON-DIVISION WINNERS THAT PLAYED IN SUPER BOWL

2005	Pittsburgh Steelers	Super Bowl XL
	(Defeated Seattle, 21-10)	
2000	Baltimore Ravens	Super Bowl XXXV
	(Defeated N.Y. Giants, 34-7)	
1999	Tennessee Titans	Super Bowl XXXIV
	(Lost to St. Louis, 23-16)	
1997	Denver Broncos	Super Bowl XXXII
	(Defeated Green Bay, 31-24)	
1992	Buffalo Bills	Super Bowl XXVII
	(Lost to Dallas, 52-17)	
1985	New England Patriots	Super Bowl XX
	(Lost to Chicago, 46-10)	
1980	Oakland Raiders	Super Bowl XV
	(Defeated Philadelphia, 27-10)	
1975	Dallas Cowboys	Super Bowl X
	(Lost to Pittsburgh, 21-17)	
1969	Kansas City Chiefs	Super Bowl IV
	(Defeated Minnesota, 23-7)	

TEAMS AT OR UNDER .500 IN POSTSEASON PLAY

2004	Minnesota Vikings	8-8
2004	St. Louis Rams	8-8
1999	Dallas Cowboys	8-8
1999	Detroit Lions	8-8
1991	New York Jets	8-8
1990	New Orleans Saints	8-8
1985	Cleveland Browns	8-8
1982	Cleveland Browns	4-5
1982	Detroit Lions	4-5
1969	Houston Oilers	6-6-2

COLDEST NFL GAMES ON RECORD

-13 degrees (-48 degree wind chill)—December 31, 1967, Lambeau Field, Green Bay, Wisconsin, NFL Championship (Green Bay 21, Dallas 17)

-9 degrees (-59 degree wind chill)—January 10, 1982, Riverfront Stadium, Cincinnati, Ohio, AFC Championship (Cincinnati 27, San Diego 7)

0 degrees (-32 degree wind chill)—January 15, 1994, Rich Stadium, Orchard Park, New York, AFC Divisional Playoff (Buffalo 29, Los Angeles Raiders 23)

TEAM LEADERS

Offense	Most Scored		Fewest Scored	
1st Quarter	99	Pittsburgh	23	N.Y. Jets
2nd Quarter	148	Seattle	65	Cleveland
3rd Quarter	121	Seattle	22	New Orleans
4th Quarter	139	Miami	45	Houston

Defense	Most Allowed		Fewest Allowed	
1st Quarter	113	Philadelphia	30	Jacksonville
2nd Quarter	150	San Francisco	49	Pittsburgh
3rd Quarter	108	Tennessee	34	Chicago
4th Quarter	140	Houston	50	Detroit

2005 NFL SCORE BY QUARTERS

AFC Offense	1	2	3	4	OT	PTS
Indianapolis	90	122	119	108	0	439
Cincinnati	84	147	98	92	0	421
San Diego	93	139	74	106	6	418
Kansas City	85	136	79	103	0	403
Denver	81	143	83	85	3	395
Pittsburgh	99	121	103	66	0	389
New England	90	74	97	118	0	379
Jacksonville	67	70	113	99	12	361
Miami	44	78	57	139	0	318
Tennessee	50	88	83	78	0	299
Oakland	64	81	48	97	0	290
Buffalo	80	86	46	59	0	271
Baltimore	50	77	44	91	3	265
Houston	40	111	64	45	0	260
N.Y. Jets	23	83	50	84	0	240
Cleveland	56	65	52	59	0	232

NFC Offense	1	2	3	4	OT	PTS
Seattle	93	148	121	87	3	452
N.Y. Giants	84	136	84	115	3	422
Carolina	96	117	53	125	0	391
St. Louis	67	123	54	113	6	363
Washington	69	114	101	72	3	359
Atlanta	78	132	49	92	0	351
Dallas	69	99	54	100	3	325
Arizona	27	111	74	99	0	311
Philadelphia	62	88	81	79	0	310
Minnesota	54	89	82	81	0	306
Tampa Bay	64	103	48	82	3	300
Green Bay	77	100	36	82	3	298
Chicago	54	82	54	64	6	260
Detroit	69	72	43	70	0	254
San Francisco	44	94	51	47	3	239
New Orleans	47	97	22	69	0	235

AFC Defense	1	2	3	4	OT	PTS
Indianapolis	61	63	47	76	0	247
Denver	44	61	37	116	0	258
Pittsburgh	78	49	54	68	9	258
Jacksonville	30	117	36	86	0	269
Baltimore	54	75	90	80	0	299
Cleveland	58	102	81	60	0	301
San Diego	36	126	77	73	0	312
Miami	94	67	71	85	0	317
Kansas City	51	110	76	88	0	325
New England	55	117	56	110	0	338
Cincinnati	60	102	89	99	0	350
N.Y. Jets	85	109	58	97	6	355
Buffalo	34	135	75	123	0	367
Oakland	75	132	84	92	0	383
Tennessee	79	132	108	102	0	421
Houston	84	115	83	140	9	431

NFC Defense	1	2	3	4	OT	PTS
Chicago	35	69	34	64	0	202
Carolina	72	73	42	72	0	259
Seattle	44	80	83	61	3	271
Tampa Bay	50	100	57	67	0	274
Washington	63	78	86	60	6	293
Dallas	68	112	61	64	3	308
N.Y. Giants	55	95	95	63	6	314
Atlanta	79	111	57	91	3	341
Green Bay	88	100	59	97	0	344
Minnesota	51	136	60	97	0	344
Detroit	84	136	66	50	9	345
Arizona	87	105	103	92	0	387
Philadelphia	113	119	50	103	3	388
New Orleans	103	126	59	110	0	398
San Francisco	70	150	91	117	0	428
St. Louis	110	124	92	103	0	429
NFL Totals	**2,150**	**3,326**	**2,217**	**2,806**	**57**	**10,556**

LARGEST TRADES IN NFL HISTORY
(Based on number of players or draft choices involved)

18—October 13, 1989—RB Herschel Walker from the Dallas Cowboys to Minnesota. Dallas also traded its third-round choice in 1990, its tenth-round choice in 1990, and its third-round choice in 1991 to Minnesota. Minnesota traded LB Jesse Solomon, LB David Howard, CB Issiac Holt, and DE Alex Stewart along with its first-round choice in 1990, its second-round choice in 1990, its sixth-round choice in 1990, its first-round choice in 1991, its second-round choice in 1991, its first-round choice in 1992, its second-round choice in 1992, and its third-round choice in 1992 to Dallas. Minnesota traded RB Darrin Nelson to Dallas, which traded Nelson to San Diego for the Chargers' fifth-round choice in 1990, which Dallas then sent to Minnesota.

15—March 26, 1953—T Mike McCormack, DT Don Colo, LB Tom Catlin, DB John Petitbon, and G Herschell Forester to Cleveland for DB Don Shula, DB Bert Rechichar, DB Carl Taseff, LB Ed Sharkey, E Gern Nagler, QB Harry Agganis, T Dick Batten, T Stu Sheets, G Art Spinney, and G Elmer Willhoite.

15—January 28, 1971—LB Marlin McKeever, first- and third-round choices in 1971, and third-, fourth-, fifth-, sixth-, and seventh-round choices in 1972 from Washington to the Los Angeles Rams for LB Maxie Baughan, LB Jack Pardee, LB Myron Pottios, RB Jeff Jordan, G John Wilbur, DT Diron Talbert, and a fifth-round choice in 1971.

12—June 13, 1952—Selection rights to Les Richter from the Dallas Texans to the Los Angeles Rams for RB Dick Hoerner, DB Tom Keane, DB George Sims, C Joe Reid, HB Billy Baggett, T Jack Halliday, FB Dick McKissack, LB Vic Vasicek, E Richard Wilkins, C Aubrey Phillips, and RB Dave Anderson.

10—March 23, 1959—HB Ollie Matson from the Chicago Cardinals to the Los Angeles Rams for T Frank Fuller, DE Glenn Holtzman, T Ken Panfil, DT Art Hauser, E John Tracey, FB Larry Hickman, HB Don Brown, the Rams second-round choice in 1960, and a player to be delivered during the 1959 training camp.

10—October 31, 1987—RB Eric Dickerson from the Los Angeles Rams to Indianapolis. The rights to LB Cornelius Bennett from Indianapolis to Buffalo. Indianapolis running back Owen Gill and the Colts' first- and second-round choices in 1988 and second-round choice in 1989, plus Bills running back Greg Bell and Buffalo's first-round choice in 1988 and first- and second-round choices in 1989 to the Rams.

2006 TOP 100 TELEVISION MARKETS
(NFL TEAM MARKETS IN BOLD)

RANK	MARKET	TV HOUSEHOLDS	% of U.S.
1	**New York**	**7,375,530**	**6.692**
2	Los Angeles	5,536,430	5.023
3	**Chicago**	**3,430,790**	**3.113**
4	**Philadelphia**	**2,925,560**	**2.654**
5	**Boston (Manchester)**	**2,375,310**	**2.155**
6	**San Francisco-Oakland-San Jose**	**2,355,740**	**2.137**
7	**Dallas-Ft. Worth**	**2,336,140**	**2.120**
8	**Washington, DC (Hagerstown)**	**2,252,550**	**2.044**
9	**Atlanta**	**2,097,220**	**1.903**
10	**Houston**	**1,938,670**	**1.759**
11	**Detroit**	**1,936,350**	**1.757**
12	**Tampa-St. Petersburg (Sarasota)**	**1,710,400**	**1.552**
13	**Seattle-Tacoma**	**1,701,950**	**1.544**
14	**Phoenix (Prescott)**	**1,660,430**	**1.507**
15	**Minneapolis-St. Paul**	**1,652,940**	**1.500**
16	**Cleveland-Akron (Canton)**	**1,541,780**	**1.399**
17	**Miami-Ft. Lauderdale**	**1,522,960**	**1.382**
18	**Denver**	**1,415,180**	**1.284**
19	Sacramnto-Stockton-Modesto	1,345,820	1.221
20	Orlando-Daytona Beach-Melbourne	1,345,700	1.221
21	**St. Louis**	**1,222,380**	**1.109**
22	**Pittsburgh**	**1,169,800**	**1.061**
23	Portland, OR	1,099,890	0.998
24	**Baltimore**	**1,089,220**	**0.988**
25	**Indianapolis**	**1,053,750**	**0.956**
26	**San Diego**	**1,026,160**	**0.931**
27	**Charlotte**	**1,020,130**	**0.926**
28	Hartford & New Haven	1,013,350	0.919
29	Raleigh-Durham (Fayeteville)	985,200	0.894
30	**Nashville**	**927,500**	**0.842**
31	**Kansas City**	**903,540**	**0.820**
32	Columbus, OH	890,770	0.808
33	Milwaukee	880,390	0.799
34	**Cincinnati**	**880,190**	**0.799**
35	Greenville-Spartanburg-Asheville-Anderson	815,460	0.740
36	Salt Lake City	810,830	0.736
37	San Antonio	760,410	0.690
38	West Palm Beach-Ft. Pierce	751,930	0.682
39	Grand Rapids-Kalamazoo-Battle Creek	731,630	0.664
40	Birmingham (Anniston, Tuscaloosa)	716,520	0.650
41	Harrisburg-Lancaster-Lebanon-York	707,010	0.641
42	Norfolk-Portsmouth-Newport News	704,810	0.640
43	**New Orleans**	**672,150**	**0.610**
44	Memphis	657,670	0.597
45	Oklahoma City	655,400	0.595
46	Albuquerque-Santa Fe	653,680	0.593
47	Greensboro-High Point-Winston Salem	652,020	0.592
48	Las Vegas	651,110	0.591
49	**Buffalo**	**644,430**	**0.585**
50	Louisville	643,290	0.584

2006 TOP 100 TELEVISION MARKETS
(NFL TEAM MARKETS IN BOLD)

RANK	MARKET	TV HOUSEHOLDS	% of U.S.
51	Providence-New Bedford	639,590	0.580
52	**Jacksonville**	**624,220**	**0.566**
53	Austin	589,360	0.535
54	Wilkes Barre-Scranton	588,540	0.534
55	Albany-Schenectady-Troy	552,250	0.501
56	Fresno-Visalia	546,210	0.496
57	Little Rock-Pine Bluff	531,470	0.482
58	Knoxville	516,180	0.468
59	Dayton	513,610	0.466
60	Richmond-Petersburg	510,770	0.463
61	Tulsa	510,480	0.463
62	Mobile-Pensacola (Ft. Walton Beach)	501,130	0.455
63	Lexington	478,560	0.434
64	Charleston-Huntington	477,890	0.434
65	Flint-Saginaw-Bay City	475,500	0.431
66	Ft. Myers-Naples	461,920	0.419
67	Wichita-Hutchinson Plus	446,820	0.405
68	Roanoke-Lynchburg	440,390	0.400
69	**Green Bay-Appleton**	**432,810**	**0.393**
70	Toledo	426,520	0.387
71	Tucson (Sierra Vista)	422,480	0.383
72	Honolulu	414,960	0.377
73	Des Moines-Ames	413,590	0.375
74	Portland-Auburn	407,050	0.369
75	Omaha	399,830	0.363
76	Syracuse	398,240	0.361
77	Springfield, MO	395,820	0.359
78	Spokane	389,630	0.354
79	Rochester, NY	385,460	0.350
80	Paducah-Cape Girardeau-Harrisburg	383,330	0.348
81	Shreveport	382,080	0.347
82	Champaign & Springfield-Decatur	378,100	0.343
83	Columbia, SC	373,260	0.339
84	Huntsville-Decatur (Florence)	370,820	0.336
85	Madison	365,550	0.332
86	Chattanooga	354,230	0.321
87	South Bend-Elkhart	333,190	0.302
88	Cedar Rapids-Waterloo-IWC&Dubuque	331,480	0.301
89	Jackson, MS	328,350	0.298
90	Burlington-Plattsburgh	325,720	0.296
91	Tri-Cities, TN-VA	323,690	0.294
92	Harlingen-Weslaco-Brownsville-McAllen	318,800	0.289
93	Colorado Springs-Pueblo	315,010	0.286
94	Waco-Temple-Bryan	310,960	0.282
95	Davenport-Rock Island-Moline	308,380	0.280
96	Baton Rouge	305,810	0.277
97	Savannah	296,100	0.269
98	Johnstown-Altoona	294,810	0.267
99	El Paso (Las Cruces)	290,540	0.264
100	Evansville	288,800	0.262
	TOTAL NFL MARKETS	**51,895,780**	**47.086**
	TOTAL TOP 100 MARKETS	**94,718,360**	**85.940**
	TOTAL MARKETS	**110,213,910**	**100.000**

RETIRED UNIFORM NUMBERS IN NFL

AFC

Baltimore	None	
Buffalo	Jim Kelly	12
Cincinnati	Bob Johnson	54
Cleveland	Otto Graham	14
	Jim Brown	32
	Ernie Davis	45
	Don Fleming	46
	Lou Groza	76
Denver	John Elway	7
	Frank Tripucka	18
	Floyd Little	44
Houston	None	
Indianapolis	Johnny Unitas	19
	Buddy Young	22
	Lenny Moore	24
	Art Donovan	70
	Jim Parker	77
	Raymond Berry	82
	Gino Marchetti	89
Jacksonville	None	
Kansas City	Jan Stenerud	3
	Len Dawson	16
	Abner Haynes	28
	Stone Johnson	33
	Mack Lee Hill	36
	Willie Lanier	63
	Bobby Bell	78
	Buck Buchanan	86
Miami	Bob Griese	12
	Dan Marino	13
	Larry Csonka	39
New England	Bruce Armstrong	78
	Gino Cappelletti	20
	Mike Haynes	40
	Steve Nelson	57
	John Hannah	73
	Jim Lee Hunt	79
	Bob Dee	89
New York Jets	Joe Namath	12
	Don Maynard	13
	Joe Klecko	73
Oakland	None	
Pittsburgh	Ernie Stautner	70
San Diego	Dan Fouts	14
	Lance Alworth	19
Tennessee	Earl Campbell	34
	Jim Norton	43
	Mike Munchak	63
	Elvin Bethea	65
	Bruce Matthews	74

NFC

Arizona	Larry Wilson	8
	Pat Tillman	40
	Stan Mauldin	77
	J.V. Cain	88
	Marshall Goldberg	99
Atlanta	Steve Bartkowski	10
	William Andrews	31
	Jeff Van Note	57
	Tommy Nobis	60
Carolina	Sam Mills	51
Chicago	Bronko Nagurski	3
	George McAfee	5
	George Halas	7
	Willie Galimore	28
	Walter Payton	34
	Gale Sayers	40
	Brian Piccolo	41
	Sid Luckman	42
	Dick Butkus	51
	Bill Hewitt	56
	Bill George	61
	Bulldog Turner	66
	Red Grange	77
Dallas	None	
Detroit	Dutch Clark	7
	Bobby Layne	22
	Doak Walker	37
	Joe Schmidt	56
	Chuck Hughes	85
Green Bay	Tony Canadeo	3
	Don Hutson	14
	Bart Starr	15
	Ray Nitschke	66
	Reggie White	92
Minnesota	Fran Tarkenton	10
	Mick Tingelhoff	53
	Jim Marshall	70
	Korey Stringer	77
	Cris Carter	80
	Alan Page	88
New Orleans	Jim Taylor	31
	Doug Atkins	81
New York Giants	Ray Flaherty	1
	Tuffy Leemans	4
	Mel Hein	7
	Phil Simms	11
	Y.A. Tittle	14
	Frank Gifford	16
	Al Blozis	32
	Joe Morrison	40
	Charlie Conerly	42
	Ken Strong	50
	Lawrence Taylor	56
Philadelphia	Steve Van Buren	15
	Tom Brookshier	40
	Pete Retzlaff	44
	Chuck Bednarik	60
	Al Wistert	70
	Reggie White	92
	Jerome Brown	99
St. Louis	Bob Waterfield	7
	Eric Dickerson	29
	Merlin Olsen	74
	Jackie Slater	78
	Jack Youngblood	85
San Francisco	John Brodie	12
	Joe Montana	16
	Joe Perry	34
	Jimmy Johnson	37
	Hugh McElhenny	39
	Ronnie Lott	42
	Charlie Krueger	70
	Leo Nomellini	73
	Bob St. Clair	79
	Dwight Clark	87
Seattle	"Fans/the twelfth man"	12
	Steve Largent	80
Tampa Bay	Lee Roy Selmon	63
Washington	Sammy Baugh	33

ALL-TIME REGULAR-SEASON RECORDS OF CURRENT NFL TEAMS

AFC
BALTIMORE RAVENS

Season	All Games			Home Games			Road Games		
	W	L	T	W	L	T	W	L	T
1996	4	12		4	4		0	8	
1997	6	9	1	3	4	1	3	5	
1998	6	10		4	4		2	6	
1999	8	8		4	4		4	4	
2000	12	4		6	2		6	2	
2001	10	6		6	2		4	4	
2002	7	9		4	4		3	5	
2003	10	6		7	1		3	5	
2004	9	7		6	2		3	5	
2005	6	10		6	2		0	8	
	78	81	1	50	29	1	28	52	

BUFFALO BILLS

Season	All Games			Home Games			Road Games		
	W	L	T	W	L	T	W	L	T
1960	5	8	1	3	4		2	4	1
1961	6	8		2	5		4	3	
1962	7	6	1	3	3	1	4	3	
1963	7	6	1	4	2	1	3	4	
1964	12	2		6	1		6	1	
1965	10	3	1	5	2		5	1	1
1966	9	4	1	4	2	1	5	2	
1967	4	10		2	5		2	5	
1968	1	12	1	1	6		0	6	1
1969	4	10		4	3		0	7	
1970	3	10	1	1	6		2	4	1
1971	1	13		1	6		0	7	
1972	4	9	1	2	4	1	2	5	
1973	9	5		5	2		4	3	
1974	9	5		5	2		4	3	
1975	8	6		3	4		5	2	
1976	2	12		1	6		1	6	
1977	3	11		1	6		2	5	
1978	5	11		4	4		1	7	
1979	7	9		3	5		4	4	
1980	11	5		6	2		5	3	
1981	10	6		7	1		3	5	
1982	4	5		4	1		0	4	
1983	8	8		3	5		5	3	
1984	2	14		2	6		0	8	
1985	2	14		2	6		0	8	
1986	4	12		3	5		1	7	
1987	7	8		4	4		3	4	
1988	12	4		8	0		4	4	
1989	9	7		6	2		3	5	
1990	13	3		8	0		5	3	
1991	13	3		7	1		6	2	
1992	11	5		6	2		5	3	
1993	12	4		6	2		6	2	
1994	7	9		4	4		3	5	
1995	10	6		6	2		4	4	
1996	10	6		7	1		3	5	
1997	6	10		4	4		2	6	
1998	10	6		6	2		4	4	
1999	11	5		6	2		5	3	
2000	8	8		5	3		3	5	
2001	3	13		1	7		2	6	
2002	8	8		5	3		3	5	
2003	6	10		4	4		2	6	
2004	9	7		5	3		4	4	
2005	5	11		4	4		1	7	
	327	357	8	189	154	4	138	203	4

CINCINNATI BENGALS

Season	All Games			Home Games			Road Games		
	W	L	T	W	L	T	W	L	T
1968	3	11		2	5		1	6	
1969	4	9	1	4	3		0	6	1
1970	8	6		5	2		3	4	
1971	4	10		3	4		1	6	
1972	8	6		4	3		4	3	
1973	10	4		7	0		3	4	
1974	7	7		4	3		3	4	
1975	11	3		6	1		5	2	
1976	10	4		6	l		4	3	
1977	8	6		5	2		3	4	
1978	4	12		3	5		1	7	
1979	4	12		4	4		0	8	
1980	6	10		3	5		3	5	
1981	12	4		6	2		6	2	
1982	7	2		4	0		3	2	
1983	7	9		4	4		3	5	
1984	8	8		5	3		3	5	
1985	7	9		5	3		2	6	
1986	10	6		6	2		4	4	
1987	4	11		1	7		3	4	
1988	12	4		8	0		4	4	
1989	8	8		5	3		3	5	
1990	9	7		5	3		4	4	
1991	3	13		3	5		0	8	
1992	5	11		3	5		2	6	
1993	3	13		3	5		0	8	
1994	3	13		2	6		1	7	
1995	7	9		3	5		4	4	
1996	8	8		6	2		2	6	
1997	7	9		6	2		1	7	
1998	3	13		1	7		2	6	
1999	4	12		2	6		2	6	
2000	4	12		3	5		1	7	
2001	6	10		4	4		2	6	
2002	2	14		1	7		1	7	
2003	8	8		5	3		3	5	
2004	8	8		5	3		3	5	
2005	11	5		5	3		6	2	
	253	326	1	157	133		96	193	1

CLEVELAND BROWNS*

Season	All Games			Home Games			Road Games		
	W	L	T	W	L	T	W	L	T
1950	10	2		5	1		5	1	
1951	11	1		6	0		5	1	
1952	8	4		4	2		4	2	
1953	11	1		6	0		5	1	
1954	9	3		5	1		4	2	
1955	9	2	1	5	1		4	1	1
1956	5	7		1	5		4	2	
1957	9	2	1	6	0		3	2	1
1958	9	3		4	2		5	1	
1959	7	5		3	3		4	2	
1960	8	3	1	4	2		4	1	1
1961	8	5	1	4	3		4	2	1
1962	7	6	1	4	2	1	3	4	
1963	10	4		5	2		5	2	
1964	10	3	1	5	1	1	5	2	
1965	11	3		5	2		6	1	
1966	9	5		5	2		4	3	
1967	9	5		6	1		3	4	
1968	10	4		5	2		5	2	
1969	10	3	1	5	1	1	5	2	
1970	7	7		4	3		3	4	
1971	9	5		4	3		5	2	
1972	10	4		4	3		6	1	
1973	7	5	2	5	1	1	2	4	1

Season	All Games W	L	T	Home Games W	L	T	Road Games W	L	T
1974	4	10		3	4		1	6	
1975	3	11		3	4		0	7	
1976	9	5		6	1		3	4	
1977	6	8		2	5		4	3	
1978	8	8		5	3		3	5	
1979	9	7		5	3		4	4	
1980	11	5		6	2		5	3	
1981	5	11		3	5		2	6	
1982	4	5		2	2		2	3	
1983	9	7		6	2		3	5	
1984	5	11		2	6		3	5	
1985	8	8		5	3		3	5	
1986	12	4		6	2		6	2	
1987	10	5		5	2		5	3	
1988	10	6		6	2		4	4	
1989	9	6	1	5	2	1	4	4	
1990	3	13		2	6		1	7	
1991	6	10		3	5		3	5	
1992	7	9		4	4		3	5	
1993	7	9		4	4		3	5	
1994	11	5		6	2		5	3	
1995	5	11		3	5		2	6	
1999	2	14		0	8		2	6	
2000	3	13		2	6		1	7	
2001	7	9		4	4		3	5	
2002	9	7		3	5		6	2	
2003	5	11		2	6		3	5	
2004	4	12		3	5		1	7	
2005	6	10		4	4		2	6	
	410	342	10	220	155	5	190	187	5

Did not play from 1996-98.

DENVER BRONCOS

Season	All Games W	L	T	Home Games W	L	T	Road Games W	L	T
1960	4	9	1	2	4	1	2	5	
1961	3	11		2	5		1	6	
1962	7	7		3	4		4	3	
1963	2	11	1	2	5		0	6	1
1964	2	11	1	2	4	1	0	7	
1965	4	10		2	5		2	5	
1966	4	10		3	4		1	6	
1967	3	11		1	6		2	5	
1968	5	9		3	4		2	5	
1969	5	8	1	4	2	1	1	6	
1970	5	8	1	3	3	1	2	5	
1971	4	9	1	2	4	1	2	5	
1972	5	9		3	4		2	5	
1973	7	5	2	3	3	1	4	2	1
1974	7	6	1	3	3	1	4	3	
1975	6	8		5	2		1	6	
1976	9	5		6	1		3	4	
1977	12	2		6	1		6	1	
1978	10	6		6	2		4	4	
1979	10	6		6	2		4	4	
1980	8	8		4	4		4	4	
1981	10	6		8	0		2	6	
1982	2	7		1	4		1	3	
1983	9	7		6	2		3	5	
1984	13	3		7	1		6	2	
1985	11	5		6	2		5	3	
1986	11	5		7	1		4	4	
1987	10	4	1	7	1		3	3	1
1988	8	8		6	2		2	6	
1989	11	5		6	2		5	3	
1990	5	11		4	4		1	7	
1991	12	4		7	1		5	3	
1992	8	8		7	1		1	7	

Season	All Games W	L	T	Home Games W	L	T	Road Games W	L	T
1993	9	7		5	3		4	4	
1994	7	9		4	4		3	5	
1995	8	8		6	2		2	6	
1996	13	3		8	0		5	3	
1997	12	4		8	0		4	4	
1998	14	2		8	0		6	2	
1999	6	10		3	5		3	5	
2000	11	5		6	2		5	3	
2001	8	8		6	2		2	6	
2002	9	7		5	3		4	4	
2003	10	6		6	2		4	4	
2004	10	6		6	2		4	4	
2005	13	3		8	0		5	3	
	362	320	10	222	118	7	140	202	3

HOUSTON TEXANS

Season	All Games W	L	T	Home Games W	L	T	Road Games W	L	T
2002	4	12		2	6		2	6	
2003	5	11		3	5		2	6	
2004	7	9		3	5		4	4	
2005	2	14		2	6		0	8	
	18	46		10	22		8	24	

INDIANAPOLIS COLTS*

Season	All Games W	L	T	Home Games W	L	T	Road Games W	L	T
1953	3	9		2	4		1	5	
1954	3	9		2	4		1	5	
1955	5	6	1	4	1	1	1	5	
1956	5	7		4	2		1	5	
1957	7	5		4	2		3	3	
1958	9	3		6	0		3	3	
1959	9	3		4	2		5	1	
1960	6	6		4	2		2	4	
1961	8	6		5	2		3	4	
1962	7	7		3	4		4	3	
1963	8	6		4	3		4	3	
1964	12	2		7	1		5	1	
1965	10	3	1	5	2		5	1	1
1966	9	5		5	2		4	3	
1967	11	1	2	6	0	1	5	1	1
1968	13	1		6	1		7	0	
1969	8	5	1	4	2	1	4	3	
1970	11	2	1	5	1	1	6	1	
1971	10	4		5	2		5	2	
1972	5	9		2	5		3	4	
1973	4	10		3	4		1	6	
1974	2	12		0	7		2	5	
1975	10	4		5	2		5	2	
1976	11	3		6	1		5	2	
1977	10	4		6	1		4	3	
1978	5	11		2	6		3	5	
1979	5	11		3	5		2	6	
1980	7	9		2	6		5	3	
1981	2	14		1	7		1	7	
1982	0	8	1	0	3	1	0	5	
1983	7	9		3	5		4	4	
1984	4	12		2	6		2	6	
1985	5	11		4	4		1	7	
1986	3	13		1	7		2	6	
1987	9	6		4	4		5	2	
1988	9	7		6	2		3	5	
1989	8	8		6	2		2	6	
1990	7	9		3	5		4	4	
1991	1	15		0	8		1	7	
1992	9	7		4	4		5	3	
1993	4	12		2	6		2	6	

Season	All Games W	L	T	Home Games W	L	T	Road Games W	L	T
1994	8	8		5	3		3	5	
1995	9	7		5	3		4	4	
1996	9	7		6	2		3	5	
1997	3	13		2	6		1	7	
1998	3	13		3	5		0	8	
1999	13	3		7	1		6	2	
2000	10	6		6	2		4	4	
2001	6	10		3	5		3	5	
2002	10	6		5	3		5	3	
2003	12	4		5	3		7	1	
2004	12	4		7	1		5	3	
2005	14	2		7	1		7	1	
	390	377	7	211	172	5	179	205	2

*includes Baltimore Colts (1953-1983).

JACKSONVILLE JAGUARS

Season	All Games W	L	T	Home Games W	L	T	Road Games W	L	T
1995	4	12		2	6		2	6	
1996	9	7		7	1		2	6	
1997	11	5		7	1		4	4	
1998	11	5		7	1		4	4	
1999	14	2		7	1		7	1	
2000	7	9		4	4		3	5	
2001	6	10		3	5		3	5	
2002	6	10		3	5		3	5	
2003	5	11		5	3		0	8	
2004	9	7		4	4		5	3	
2005	12	4		6	2		6	2	
	94	82		55	33		39	49	

KANSAS CITY CHIEFS*

Season	All Games W	L	T	Home Games W	L	T	Road Games W	L	T
1960	8	6		5	2		3	4	
1961	6	8		4	3		2	5	
1962	11	3		6	1		5	2	
1963	5	7	2	4	3		1	4	2
1964	7	7		4	3		3	4	
1965	7	5	2	5	2		2	3	2
1966	11	2	1	4	2	1	7	0	
1967	9	5		4	3		5	2	
1968	12	2		6	1		6	1	
1969	11	3		6	1		5	2	
1970	7	5	2	4	1	2	3	4	
1971	10	3	1	7	0		3	3	1
1972	8	6		3	4		5	2	
1973	7	5	2	5	1	1	2	4	1
1974	5	9		1	6		4	3	
1975	5	9		3	4		2	5	
1976	5	9		1	6		4	3	
1977	2	12		1	6		1	6	
1978	4	12		3	5		1	7	
1979	7	9		3	5		4	4	
1980	8	8		3	5		5	3	
1981	9	7		5	3		4	4	
1982	3	6		2	2		1	4	
1983	6	10		5	3		1	7	
1984	8	8		5	3		3	5	
1985	6	10		5	3		1	7	
1986	10	6		6	2		4	4	
1987	4	11		3	4		1	7	
1988	4	11	1	4	4		0	7	1
1989	8	7	1	5	3		3	4	1
1990	11	5		6	2		5	3	
1991	10	6		6	2		4	4	
1992	10	6		7	1		3	5	
1993	11	5		7	1		4	4	

Season	All Games W	L	T	Home Games W	L	T	Road Games W	L	T
1994	9	7		5	3		4	4	
1995	13	3		8	0		5	3	
1996	9	7		5	3		4	4	
1997	13	3		8	0		5	3	
1998	7	9		5	3		2	6	
1999	9	7		6	2		3	5	
2000	7	9		5	3		2	6	
2001	6	10		3	5		3	5	
2002	8	8		6	2		2	6	
2003	13	3		8	0		5	3	
2004	7	9		4	4		3	5	
2005	10	6		7	1		3	5	
	366	314	12	218	123	4	148	191	8

*includes Dallas Texans (1960-62).

MIAMI DOLPHINS

Season	All Games W	L	T	Home Games W	L	T	Road Games W	L	T
1966	3	11		2	5		1	6	
1967	4	10		4	3		0	7	
1968	5	8	1	1	5	1	4	3	
1969	3	10	1	2	4	1	1	6	
1970	10	4		6	1		4	3	
1971	10	3	1	6	1		4	2	1
1972	14	0		7	0		7	0	
1973	12	2		7	0		5	2	
1974	11	3		7	0		4	3	
1975	10	4		5	2		5	2	
1976	6	8		3	4		3	4	
1977	10	4		6	1		4	3	
1978	11	5		7	1		4	4	
1979	10	6		6	2		4	4	
1980	8	8		5	3		3	5	
1981	11	4	1	6	1	1	5	3	
1982	7	2		4	0		3	2	
1983	12	4		7	1		5	3	
1984	14	2		7	1		7	1	
1985	12	4		8	0		4	4	
1986	8	8		4	4		4	4	
1987	8	7		4	3		4	4	
1988	6	10		4	4		2	6	
1989	8	8		4	4		4	4	
1990	12	4		7	1		5	3	
1991	8	8		5	3		3	5	
1992	11	5		6	2		5	3	
1993	9	7		4	4		5	3	
1994	10	6		6	2		4	4	
1995	9	7		5	3		4	4	
1996	8	8		4	4		4	4	
1997	9	7		6	2		3	5	
1998	10	6		7	1		3	5	
1999	9	7		5	3		4	4	
2000	11	5		5	3		6	2	
2001	11	5		7	1		4	4	
2002	9	7		7	1		2	6	
2003	10	6		4	4		6	2	
2004	4	12		3	5		1	7	
2005	9	7		5	3		4	4	
	362	242	4	208	92	3	154	150	1

NEW ENGLAND PATRIOTS*

Season	All Games W	L	T	Home Games W	L	T	Road Games W	L	T
1960	5	9		3	4		2	5	
1961	9	4	1	4	2	1	5	2	
1962	9	4	1	6	1		3	3	1
1963	7	6	1	5	1	1	2	5	
1964	10	3	1	4	2	1	6	1	

Season	All Games W	L	T	Home Games W	L	T	Road Games W	L	T
1965	4	8	2	1	4	2	3	4	
1966	8	4	2	4	2	1	4	2	1
1967	3	10	1	2	4		1	6	1
1968	4	10		2	5		2	5	
1969	4	10		2	5		2	5	
1970	2	12		1	6		1	6	
1971	6	8		5	2		1	6	
1972	3	11		2	5		1	6	
1973	5	9		3	4		2	5	
1974	7	7		3	4		4	3	
1975	3	11		2	5		1	6	
1976	11	3		6	1		5	2	
1977	9	5		6	1		3	4	
1978	11	5		5	3		6	2	
1979	9	7		6	2		3	5	
1980	10	6		6	2		4	4	
1981	2	14		2	6		0	8	
1982	5	4		3	1		2	3	
1983	8	8		5	3		3	5	
1984	9	7		5	3		4	4	
1985	11	5		7	1		4	4	
1986	11	5		4	4		7	1	
1987	8	7		5	3		3	4	
1988	9	7		7	1		2	6	
1989	5	11		3	5		2	6	
1990	1	15		0	8		1	7	
1991	6	10		4	4		2	6	
1992	2	14		1	7		1	7	
1993	5	11		3	5		2	6	
1994	10	6		5	3		5	3	
1995	6	10		3	5		3	5	
1996	11	5		6	2		5	3	
1997	10	6		6	2		4	4	
1998	9	7		6	2		3	5	
1999	8	8		5	3		3	5	
2000	5	11		3	5		2	6	
2001	11	5		6	2		5	3	
2002	9	7		5	3		4	4	
2003	14	2		8	0		6	2	
2004	14	2		8	0		6	2	
2005	10	6		5	3		5	3	
	338	345	9	193	146	6	145	199	3

*includes Boston Patriots (1960-1970).

NEW YORK JETS*

Season	All Games W	L	T	Home Games W	L	T	Road Games W	L	T
1960	7	7		3	4		4	3	
1961	7	7		5	2		2	5	
1962	5	9		2	5		3	4	
1963	5	8	1	4	2	1	1	6	
1964	5	8	1	5	1	1	0	7	
1965	5	8	1	3	3	1	2	5	
1966	6	6	2	4	3		2	3	2
1967	8	5	1	4	2	1	4	3	
1968	11	3		6	1		5	2	
1969	10	4		5	2		5	2	
1970	4	10		2	5		2	5	
1971	6	8		4	3		2	5	
1972	7	7		4	3		3	4	
1973	4	10		2	4		2	6	
1974	7	7		3	4		4	3	
1975	3	11		1	6		2	5	
1976	3	11		2	5		1	6	
1977	3	11		1	6		2	5	
1978	8	8		4	4		4	4	
1979	8	8		6	2		2	6	
1980	4	12		2	6		2	6	
1981	10	5	1	6	2		4	3	1
1982	6	3		3	1		3	2	
1983	7	9		2	6		5	3	
1984	7	9		3	5		4	4	
1985	11	5		7	1		4	4	
1986	10	6		5	3		5	3	
1987	6	9		4	4		2	5	
1988	8	7	1	5	2	1	3	5	
1989	4	12		1	7		3	5	
1990	6	10		3	5		3	5	
1991	8	8		4	4		4	4	
1992	4	12		3	5		1	7	
1993	8	8		3	5		5	3	
1994	6	10		4	4		2	6	
1995	3	13		2	6		1	7	
1996	1	15		0	8		1	7	
1997	9	7		5	3		4	4	
1998	12	4		7	1		5	3	
1999	8	8		4	4		4	4	
2000	9	7		5	3		4	4	
2001	10	6		3	5		7	1	
2002	9	7		5	3		4	4	
2003	6	10		4	4		2	6	
2004	10	6		6	2		4	4	
2005	4	12		4	4		0	8	
	308	376	8	170	170	5	138	206	3

*includes New York Titans (1960-62).

OAKLAND RAIDERS*

Season	All Games W	L	T	Home Games W	L	T	Road Games W	L	T
1960	6	8		3	4		3	4	
1961	2	12		1	6		1	6	
1962	1	13		1	6		0	7	
1963	10	4		6	1		4	3	
1964	5	7	2	5	2		0	5	2
1965	8	5	1	5	2		3	3	1
1966	8	5	1	3	3	1	5	2	
1967	13	1		7	0		6	1	
1968	12	2		6	1		6	1	
1969	12	1	1	7	0		5	1	1
1970	8	4	2	6	1		2	3	2
1971	8	4	2	5	1	1	3	3	1
1972	10	3	1	5	1	1	5	2	
1973	9	4	1	5	2		4	2	1
1974	12	2		6	1		6	1	
1975	11	3		6	1		5	2	
1976	13	1		7	0		6	1	
1977	11	3		6	1		5	2	
1978	9	7		4	4		5	3	
1979	9	7		6	2		3	5	
1980	11	5		6	2		5	3	
1981	7	9		4	4		3	5	
1982	8	1		4	0		4	1	
1983	12	4		6	2		6	2	
1984	11	5		6	2		5	3	
1985	12	4		7	1		5	3	
1986	8	8		3	5		5	3	
1987	5	10		3	5		2	5	
1988	7	9		3	5		4	4	
1989	8	8		7	1		1	7	
1990	12	4		6	2		6	2	
1991	9	7		5	3		4	4	
1992	7	9		5	3		2	6	
1993	10	6		5	3		5	3	
1994	9	7		4	4		5	3	
1995	8	8		4	4		4	4	
1996	7	9		4	4		3	5	

Season	All Games W	L	T	Home Games W	L	T	Road Games W	L	T
1997	4	12		2	6		2	6	
1998	8	8		4	4		4	4	
1999	8	8		5	3		3	5	
2000	12	4		7	1		5	3	
2001	10	6		5	3		5	3	
2002	11	5		6	2		5	3	
2003	4	12		4	4		0	8	
2004	5	11		3	5		2	6	
2005	4	12		2	6		2	6	
	394	287	11	220	123	3	174	164	8

includes Los Angeles Raiders (1982-1994).

PITTSBURGH STEELERS*

Season	All Games W	L	T	Home Games W	L	T	Road Games W	L	T
1933	3	6	2	2	3		1	3	2
1934	2	10		1	5		1	5	
1935	4	8		2	5		2	3	
1936	6	6		4	1		2	5	
1937	4	7		2	4		2	3	
1938	2	9		0	5		2	4	
1939	1	9	1	1	4		0	5	1
1940	2	7	2	1	2	2	1	5	
1941	1	9	1	1	4		0	5	1
1942	7	4		3	2		4	2	
1945	2	8		1	4		1	4	
1946	5	5	1	4	1		1	4	1
1947	8	4		5	1		3	3	
1948	4	8		4	2		0	6	
1949	6	5	1	3	2	1	3	3	
1950	6	6		2	4		4	2	
1951	4	7	1	1	4	1	3	3	
1952	5	7		2	4		3	3	
1953	6	6		3	3		3	3	
1954	5	7		4	2		1	5	
1955	4	8		3	2		1	6	
1956	5	7		3	3		2	4	
1957	6	6		4	2		2	4	
1958	7	4	1	5	1		2	3	1
1959	6	5	1	3	2	1	3	3	
1960	5	6	1	4	2		1	4	1
1961	6	8		4	3		2	5	
1962	9	5		4	3		5	2	
1963	7	4	3	5	0	2	2	4	1
1964	5	9		2	5		3	4	
1965	2	12		1	6		1	6	
1966	5	8	1	3	3	1	2	5	
1967	4	9	1	1	6		3	3	1
1968	2	11	1	1	6		1	5	1
1969	1	13		1	6		0	7	
1970	5	9		4	3		1	6	
1971	6	8		5	2		1	6	
1972	11	3		7	0		4	3	
1973	10	4		7	1		3	3	
1974	10	3	1	5	2		5	1	1
1975	12	2		6	1		6	1	
1976	10	4		6	1		4	3	
1977	9	5		6	1		3	4	
1978	14	2		7	1		7	1	
1979	12	4		8	0		4	4	
1980	9	7		6	2		3	5	
1981	8	8		5	3		3	5	
1982	6	3		4	0		2	3	
1983	10	6		4	4		6	2	
1984	9	7		6	2		3	5	
1985	7	9		5	3		2	6	
1986	6	10		4	4		2	6	
1987	8	7		4	3		4	4	
1988	5	11		4	4		1	7	
1989	9	7		4	4		5	3	
1990	9	7		6	2		3	5	
1991	7	9		5	3		2	6	
1992	11	5		7	1		4	4	
1993	9	7		6	2		3	5	
1994	12	4		7	1		5	3	
1995	11	5		6	2		5	3	
1996	10	6		7	1		3	5	
1997	11	5		7	1		4	4	
1998	7	9		5	3		2	6	
1999	6	10		2	6		4	4	
2000	9	7		4	4		5	3	
2001	13	3		7	1		6	2	
2002	10	5	1	5	2	1	5	3	
2003	6	10		4	4		2	6	
2004	15	1		8	0		7	1	
2005	11	5		5	3		6	2	
	490	470	20	288	189	9	202	281	11

includes Pittsburgh Pirates (1933-1940).

SAN DIEGO CHARGERS*

Season	All Games W	L	T	Home Games W	L	T	Road Games W	L	T
1960	10	4		5	2		5	2	
1961	12	2		6	1		6	1	
1962	4	10		3	4		1	6	
1963	11	3		6	1		5	2	
1964	8	5	1	4	3		4	2	1
1965	9	2	3	4	1	2	5	1	1
1966	7	6	1	5	2		2	4	1
1967	8	5	1	5	2	1	3	3	
1968	9	5		4	3		5	2	
1969	8	6		5	2		3	4	
1970	5	6	3	2	3	2	3	3	1
1971	6	8		6	1		0	7	
1972	4	9	1	2	5		2	4	1
1973	2	11	1	2	5		0	6	1
1974	5	9		3	4		2	5	
1975	2	12		1	6		1	6	
1976	6	8		3	4		3	4	
1977	7	7		3	4		4	3	
1978	9	7		5	3		4	4	
1979	12	4		7	1		5	3	
1980	11	5		6	2		5	3	
1981	10	6		5	3		5	3	
1982	6	3		3	1		3	2	
1983	6	10		4	4		2	6	
1984	7	9		4	4		3	5	
1985	8	8		6	2		2	6	
1986	4	12		2	6		2	6	
1987	8	7		4	3		4	4	
1988	6	10		3	5		3	5	
1989	6	10		4	4		2	6	
1990	6	10		3	5		3	5	
1991	4	12		3	5		1	7	
1992	11	5		6	2		5	3	
1993	8	8		4	4		4	4	
1994	11	5		5	3		6	2	
1995	9	7		5	3		4	4	
1996	8	8		5	3		3	5	
1997	4	12		2	6		2	6	
1998	5	11		4	4		1	7	
1999	8	8		4	4		4	4	
2000	1	15		1	7		0	8	
2001	5	11		4	4		1	7	
2002	8	8		5	3		3	5	
2003	4	12		2	6		2	6	

Season	All Games W	L	T	Home Games W	L	T	Road Games W	L	T
2004	12	4		7	1		5	3	
2005	9	7		4	4		5	3	
	329	352	11	186	155	5	143	197	6

*includes Los Angeles Chargers (1960).

TENNESSEE TITANS*

Season	All Games W	L	T	Home Games W	L	T	Road Games W	L	T
1960	10	4		6	1		4	3	
1961	10	3	1	6	1		4	2	1
1962	11	3		6	1		5	2	
1963	6	8		4	3		2	5	
1964	4	10		3	4		1	6	
1965	4	10		3	4		1	6	
1966	3	11		3	4		0	7	
1967	9	4	1	5	2		4	2	1
1968	7	7		3	4		4	3	
1969	6	6	2	4	2	1	2	4	1
1970	3	10	1	1	6		2	4	1
1971	4	9	1	3	3	1	1	6	
1972	1	13		1	6		0	7	
1973	1	13		0	7		1	6	
1974	7	7		3	4		4	3	
1975	10	4		5	2		5	2	
1976	5	9		3	4		2	5	
1977	8	6		5	2		3	4	
1978	10	6		5	3		5	3	
1979	11	5		6	2		5	3	
1980	11	5		6	2		5	3	
1981	7	9		5	3		2	6	
1982	1	8		1	4		0	4	
1983	2	14		2	6		0	8	
1984	3	13		2	6		1	7	
1985	5	11		4	4		1	7	
1986	5	11		4	4		1	7	
1987	9	6		5	2		4	4	
1988	10	6		7	1		3	5	
1989	9	7		6	2		3	5	
1990	9	7		6	2		3	5	
1991	11	5		7	1		4	4	
1992	10	6		5	3		5	3	
1993	12	4		7	1		5	3	
1994	2	14		2	6		0	8	
1995	7	9		3	5		4	4	
1996	8	8		2	6		6	2	
1997	8	8		6	2		2	6	
1998	8	8		3	5		5	3	
1999	13	3		8	0		5	3	
2000	13	3		7	1		6	2	
2001	7	9		3	5		4	4	
2002	11	5		6	2		5	3	
2003	12	4		7	1		5	3	
2004	5	11		2	6		3	5	
2005	4	12		3	5		1	7	
	332	354	6	194	150	2	138	204	4

*includes Houston Oilers (1960-1996) and Tennessee Oilers (1997-98).

NFC
ARIZONA CARDINALS*

Season	All Games W	L	T	Home Games W	L	T	Road Games W	L	T
1920	6	2	2	5	1	1	1	1	1
1921	3	3	2	3	3	1	0	0	1
1922	8	3		8	3		0	0	
1923	8	4		8	3		0	1	
1924	5	4	1	5	3	1	0	1	
1925	11	2	1	11	2		0	0	1
1926	5	6	1	3	3		2	3	1
1927	3	7	1	2	3	1	1	4	
1928	1	5		1	1		0	4	
1929	6	6	1	3	2		3	4	1
1930	5	6	2	3	2		2	4	2
1931	5	4		3	0		2	4	
1932	2	6	2	1	2	1	1	4	1
1933	1	9	1	0	4	1	1	5	
1934	5	6		2	2		3	4	
1935	6	4	2	2	2		4	2	2
1936	3	8	1	3	1	1	0	7	
1937	5	5	1	1	3		4	2	1
1938	2	9		1	4		1	5	
1939	1	10		0	4		1	6	
1940	2	7	2	2	1	1	0	6	1
1941	3	7	1	0	3	1	3	4	
1942	3	8		2	2		1	6	
1943	0	10		0	3		0	7	
1945	1	9		0	3		1	6	
1946	6	5		2	2		4	3	
1947	9	3		5	0		4	3	
1948	11	1		5	1		6	0	
1949	6	5	1	2	3	1	4	2	
1950	5	7		3	3		2	4	
1951	3	9		1	5		2	4	
1952	4	8		2	4		2	4	
1953	1	10	1	0	5	1	1	5	
1954	2	10		2	4		0	6	
1955	4	7	1	3	2	1	1	5	
1956	7	5		4	2		3	3	
1957	3	9		0	6		3	3	
1958	2	9	1	1	4	1	1	5	
1959	2	10		2	4		0	6	
1960	6	5	1	3	2	1	3	3	
1961	7	7		3	4		4	3	
1962	4	9	1	2	4	1	2	5	
1963	9	5		3	4		6	1	
1964	9	3	2	4	1	1	5	2	1
1965	5	9		2	5		3	4	
1966	8	5	1	5	1	1	3	4	
1967	6	7	1	3	3	1	3	4	
1968	9	4	1	4	2	1	5	2	
1969	4	9	1	3	4		1	5	1
1970	8	5	1	6	1		2	4	1
1971	4	9	1	1	5	1	3	4	
1972	4	9	1	2	5		2	4	1
1973	4	9	1	2	4	1	2	5	
1974	10	4		5	2		5	2	
1975	11	3		6	1		5	2	
1976	10	4		6	1		4	3	
1977	7	7		4	3		3	4	
1978	6	10		3	5		3	5	
1979	5	11		3	5		2	6	
1980	5	11		2	6		3	5	
1981	7	9		5	3		2	6	
1982	5	4		1	3		4	1	
1983	8	7	1	4	3	1	4	4	
1984	9	7		5	3		4	4	
1985	5	11		4	4		1	7	
1986	4	11	1	3	5		1	6	1
1987	7	8		4	3		3	5	
1988	7	9		4	4		3	5	
1989	5	11		2	6		3	5	
1990	5	11		3	5		2	6	
1991	4	12		2	6		2	6	
1992	4	12		3	5		1	7	
1993	7	9		4	4		3	5	
1994	8	8		5	3		3	5	

Season	All Games W	L	T	Home Games W	L	T	Road Games W	L	T
1995	4	12		3	5		1	7	
1996	7	9		5	3		2	6	
1997	4	12		3	5		1	7	
1998	9	7		5	3		4	4	
1999	6	10		4	4		2	6	
2000	3	13		3	5		0	8	
2001	7	9		3	5		4	4	
2002	5	11		3	5		2	6	
2003	4	12		4	4		0	8	
2004	6	10		5	3		1	7	
2005	5	11		3	5		2	6	
	451	638	39	263	277	22	188	361	17

includes Chicago Cardinals (1920-1959), St. Louis Cardinals (1960-1987), and Phoenix Cardinals (1988-1993).

ATLANTA FALCONS

Season	All Games W	L	T	Home Games W	L	T	Road Games W	L	T
1966	3	11		1	6		2	5	
1967	1	12	1	1	5	1	0	7	
1968	2	12		1	6		1	6	
1969	6	8		4	3		2	5	
1970	4	8	2	3	4		1	4	2
1971	7	6	1	4	3		3	3	1
1972	7	7		4	3		3	4	
1973	9	5		4	3		5	2	
1974	3	11		2	5		1	6	
1975	4	10		3	4		1	6	
1976	4	10		3	4		1	6	
1977	7	7		4	3		3	4	
1978	9	7		7	1		2	6	
1979	6	10		3	5		3	5	
1980	12	4		6	2		6	2	
1981	7	9		4	4		3	5	
1982	5	4		2	3		3	1	
1983	7	9		4	4		3	5	
1984	4	12		2	6		2	6	
1985	4	12		3	5		1	7	
1986	7	8	1	2	5	1	5	3	
1987	3	12		2	6		1	6	
1988	5	11		2	6		3	5	
1989	3	13		3	5		0	8	
1990	5	11		5	3		0	8	
1991	10	6		6	2		4	4	
1992	6	10		5	3		1	7	
1993	6	10		4	4		2	6	
1994	7	9		5	3		2	6	
1995	9	7		7	1		2	6	
1996	3	13		2	6		1	7	
1997	7	9		3	5		4	4	
1998	14	2		8	0		6	2	
1999	5	11		4	4		1	7	
2000	4	12		3	5		1	7	
2001	7	9		3	5		4	4	
2002	9	6	1	5	3		4	3	1
2003	5	11		2	6		3	5	
2004	11	5		7	1		4	4	
2005	8	8		4	4		4	4	
	245	357	6	147	156	2	98	201	4

CAROLINA PANTHERS

Season	All Games W	L	T	Home Games W	L	T	Road Games W	L	T
1995	7	9		5	3		2	6	
1996	12	4		8	0		4	4	
1997	7	9		2	6		5	3	
1998	4	12		2	6		2	6	
1999	8	8		5	3		3	5	

Season	All Games W	L	T	Home Games W	L	T	Road Games W	L	T
2000	7	9		5	3		2	6	
2001	1	15		0	8		1	7	
2002	7	9		4	4		3	5	
2003	11	5		6	2		5	3	
2004	7	9		3	5		4	4	
2005	11	5		5	3		6	2	
	82	94		45	43		37	51	

CHICAGO BEARS*

Season	All Games W	L	T	Home Games W	L	T	Road Games W	L	T
1920	10	1	2	6	0	1	4	1	1
1921	9	1	1	9	1	1	0	0	
1922	9	3		7	1		2	2	
1923	9	2	1	7	1	1	2	1	
1924	6	1	4	5	0	3	1	1	1
1925	9	5	3	7	1	1	2	4	2
1926	12	1	3	10	0	2	2	1	1
1927	9	3	2	7	1	1	2	2	1
1928	7	5	1	6	3		1	2	1
1929	4	9	2	1	5	2	3	4	
1930	9	4	1	5	2	1	4	2	
1931	8	5		6	3		2	2	
1932	7	1	6	6	1	1	1	0	5
1933	10	2	1	6	0		4	2	1
1934	13	0		5	0		8	0	
1935	6	4	2	1	2	2	5	2	
1936	9	3		3	1		6	2	
1937	9	1	1	4	1		5	0	1
1938	6	5		2	3		4	2	
1939	8	3		4	1		4	2	
1940	8	3		5	0		3	3	
1941	10	1		5	1		5	0	
1942	11	0		6	0		5	0	
1943	8	1	1	5	0		3	1	1
1944	6	3	1	4	0	1	2	3	
1945	3	7		2	3		1	4	
1946	8	2	1	4	1	1	4	1	
1947	8	4		4	2		4	2	
1948	10	2		5	1		5	1	
1949	9	3		5	1		4	2	
1950	9	3		6	0		3	3	
1951	7	5		3	3		4	2	
1952	5	7		3	3		2	4	
1953	3	8	1	1	4	1	2	4	
1954	8	4		4	2		4	2	
1955	8	4		5	1		3	3	
1956	9	2	1	6	0		3	2	1
1957	5	7		2	4		3	3	
1958	8	4		5	1		3	3	
1959	8	4		4	2		4	2	
1960	5	6	1	4	2		1	4	1
1961	8	6		5	2		3	4	
1962	9	5		4	3		5	2	
1963	11	1	2	6	0	1	5	1	1
1964	5	9		2	5		3	4	
1965	9	5		5	2		4	3	
1966	5	7	2	4	1	2	1	6	
1967	7	6	1	3	3	1	4	3	
1968	7	7		2	5		5	2	
1969	1	13		1	6		0	7	
1970	6	8		3	4		3	4	
1971	6	8		4	3		2	5	
1972	4	9	1	1	5	1	3	4	
1973	3	11		1	6		2	5	
1974	4	10		4	3		0	7	
1975	4	10		3	4		1	6	
1976	7	7		4	3		3	4	

Season	All Games W	L	T	Home Games W	L	T	Road Games W	L	T
1977	9	5		5	2		4	3	
1978	7	9		4	4		3	5	
1979	10	6		6	2		4	4	
1980	7	9		5	3		2	6	
1981	6	10		4	4		2	6	
1982	3	6		2	2		1	4	
1983	8	8		5	3		3	5	
1984	10	6		6	2		4	4	
1985	15	1		8	0		7	1	
1986	14	2		7	1		7	1	
1987	11	4		6	2		5	2	
1988	12	4		7	1		5	3	
1989	6	10		4	4		2	6	
1990	11	5		7	1		4	4	
1991	11	5		6	2		5	3	
1992	5	11		4	4		1	7	
1993	7	9		3	5		4	4	
1994	9	7		5	3		4	4	
1995	9	7		5	3		4	4	
1996	7	9		6	2		1	7	
1997	4	12		2	6		2	6	
1998	4	12		3	5		1	7	
1999	6	10		3	5		3	5	
2000	5	11		3	5		2	6	
2001	13	3		7	1		6	2	
2002	4	12		3	5		1	7	
2003	7	9		6	2		1	7	
2004	5	11		2	6		3	5	
2005	11	5		7	1		4	4	
	657	479	42	388	199	24	269	280	18

*includes Decatur Staleys (1920) and Chicago Staleys (1921).

Season	All Games W	L	T	Home Games W	L	T	Road Games W	L	T
1993	12	4		6	2		6	2	
1994	12	4		6	2		6	2	
1995	12	4		6	2		6	2	
1996	10	6		6	2		4	4	
1997	6	10		5	3		1	7	
1998	10	6		6	2		4	4	
1999	8	8		7	1		1	7	
2000	5	11		3	5		2	6	
2001	5	11		4	4		1	7	
2002	5	11		4	4		1	7	
2003	10	6		6	2		4	4	
2004	6	10		4	4		2	6	
2005	9	7		5	3		4	4	
	392	292	6	224	117	4	168	175	2

DETROIT LIONS*

Season	All Games W	L	T	Home Games W	L	T	Road Games W	L	T
1930	5	6	3	5	1	2	0	5	1
1931	11	3		8	0		3	3	
1932	6	2	4	3	0	2	3	2	2
1933	6	5		4	1		2	4	
1934	10	3		6	2		4	1	
1935	7	3	2	5	0	1	2	3	1
1936	8	4		5	1		3	3	
1937	7	4		4	2		3	2	
1938	7	4		4	3		3	1	
1939	6	5		4	2		2	3	
1940	5	5	1	3	3		2	2	1
1941	4	6	1	3	2		1	4	1
1942	0	11		0	7		0	4	
1943	3	6	1	2	2	1	1	4	
1944	6	3	1	4	2		2	1	1
1945	7	3		4	1		3	2	
1946	1	10		1	5		0	5	
1947	3	9		2	4		1	5	
1948	2	10		2	4		0	6	
1949	4	8		2	4		2	4	
1950	6	6		4	2		2	4	
1951	7	4	1	3	3	1	4	1	
1952	9	3		6	1		3	2	
1953	10	2		5	1		5	1	
1954	9	2	1	5	0	1	4	2	
1955	3	9		3	4		0	5	
1956	9	3		5	1		4	2	
1957	8	4		5	1		3	3	
1958	4	7	1	2	4		2	3	1
1959	3	8	1	2	4		1	4	1
1960	7	5		5	1		2	4	
1961	8	5	1	2	5		6	0	1
1962	11	3		7	0		4	3	
1963	5	8	1	3	3	1	2	5	
1964	7	5	2	3	3	1	4	2	1
1965	6	7	1	2	4	1	4	3	
1966	4	9	1	3	4		1	5	1
1967	5	7	2	3	4		2	3	2
1968	4	8	2	1	4	2	3	4	
1969	9	4	1	5	2		4	2	1
1970	10	4		6	1		4	3	
1971	7	6	1	3	4		4	2	1
1972	8	5	1	5	2		3	3	1
1973	6	7	1	4	3		2	4	1
1974	7	7		5	2		2	5	
1975	7	7		4	3		3	4	
1976	6	8		5	2		1	6	
1977	6	8		5	2		1	6	
1978	7	9		5	3		2	6	
1979	2	14		2	6		0	8	

DALLAS COWBOYS

Season	All Games W	L	T	Home Games W	L	T	Road Games W	L	T
1960	0	11	1	0	6		0	5	1
1961	4	9	1	2	4	1	2	5	
1962	5	8	1	2	4	1	3	4	
1963	4	10		3	4		1	6	
1964	5	8	1	2	4	1	3	4	
1965	7	7		5	2		2	5	
1966	10	3	1	6	1		4	2	1
1967	9	5		5	2		4	3	
1968	12	2		5	2		7	0	
1969	11	2	1	6	0	1	5	2	
1970	10	4		6	1		4	3	
1971	11	3		6	1		5	2	
1972	10	4		5	2		5	2	
1973	10	4		6	1		4	3	
1974	8	6		5	2		3	4	
1975	10	4		5	2		5	2	
1976	11	3		6	1		5	2	
1977	12	2		6	1		6	1	
1978	12	4		7	1		5	3	
1979	11	5		6	2		5	3	
1980	12	4		8	0		4	4	
1981	12	4		8	0		4	4	
1982	6	3		3	2		3	1	
1983	12	4		6	2		6	2	
1984	9	7		5	3		4	4	
1985	10	6		7	1		3	5	
1986	7	9		3	5		4	4	
1987	7	8		3	4		4	4	
1988	3	13		1	7		2	6	
1989	1	15		0	8		1	7	
1990	7	9		5	3		2	6	
1991	11	5		6	2		5	3	
1992	13	3		7	1		6	2	

Season	All Games W	L	T	Home Games W	L	T	Road Games W	L	T
1980	9	7		6	2		3	5	
1981	8	8		7	1		1	7	
1982	4	5		2	3		2	2	
1983	9	7		6	2		3	5	
1984	4	11	1	2	5	1	2	6	
1985	7	9		6	2		1	7	
1986	5	11		1	7		4	4	
1987	4	11		1	6		3	5	
1988	4	12		2	6		2	6	
1989	7	9		4	4		3	5	
1990	6	10		3	5		3	5	
1991	12	4		8	0		4	4	
1992	5	11		3	5		2	6	
1993	10	6		5	3		5	3	
1994	9	7		6	2		3	5	
1995	10	6		7	1		3	5	
1996	5	11		4	4		1	7	
1997	9	7		6	2		3	5	
1998	5	11		4	4		1	7	
1999	8	8		6	2		2	6	
2000	9	7		4	4		5	3	
2001	2	14		2	6		0	8	
2002	3	13		3	5		0	8	
2003	5	11		5	3		0	8	
2004	6	10		3	5		3	5	
2005	5	11		3	5		2	6	
	478	531	32	298	219	14	180	312	18

includes Portsmouth Spartans (1930-33).

Season	All Games W	L	T	Home Games W	L	T	Road Games W	L	T
1957	3	9		1	5		2	4	
1958	1	10	1	1	4	1	0	6	
1959	7	5		4	2		3	3	
1960	8	4		4	2		4	2	
1961	11	3		6	1		5	2	
1962	13	1		7	0		6	1	
1963	11	2	1	6	1		5	1	1
1964	8	5	1	4	3		4	2	1
1965	10	3	1	6	1		4	2	1
1966	12	2		6	1		6	1	
1967	9	4	1	4	2	1	5	2	
1968	6	7	1	2	5		4	2	1
1969	8	6		5	2		3	4	
1970	6	8		4	3		2	5	
1971	4	8	2	3	3	1	1	5	1
1972	10	4		4	3		6	1	
1973	5	7	2	3	2	2	2	5	
1974	6	8		4	3		2	5	
1975	4	10		3	4		1	6	
1976	5	9		4	3		1	6	
1977	4	10		2	5		2	5	
1978	8	7	1	5	2	1	3	5	
1979	5	11		4	4		1	7	
1980	5	10	1	4	4		1	6	1
1981	8	8		4	4		4	4	
1982	5	3	1	3	1		2	2	1
1983	8	8		5	3		3	5	
1984	8	8		5	3		3	5	
1985	8	8		5	3		3	5	
1986	4	12		1	7		3	5	
1987	5	9	1	2	5	1	3	4	
1988	4	12		2	6		2	6	
1989	10	6		6	2		4	4	
1990	6	10		3	5		3	5	
1991	4	12		2	6		2	6	
1992	9	7		6	2		3	5	
1993	9	7		6	2		3	5	
1994	9	7		7	1		2	6	
1995	11	5		7	1		4	4	
1996	13	3		8	0		5	3	
1997	13	3		8	0		5	3	
1998	11	5		7	1		4	4	
1999	8	8		5	3		3	5	
2000	9	7		6	2		3	5	
2001	12	4		7	1		5	3	
2002	12	4		8	0		4	4	
2003	10	6		5	3		5	3	
2004	10	6		4	4		6	2	
2005	4	12		3	5		1	7	
	616	492	36	356	199	16	260	293	20

GREEN BAY PACKERS

Season	All Games W	L	T	Home Games W	L	T	Road Games W	L	T
1921	3	2	1	2	1		1	1	1
1922	4	3	3	4	1	1	0	2	2
1923	7	2	1	4	2	1	3	0	
1924	7	4		5	0		2	4	
1925	8	5		6	0		2	5	
1926	7	3	3	4	1	2	3	2	1
1927	7	2	1	6	1		1	1	1
1928	6	4	3	2	2	2	4	2	1
1929	12	0	1	5	0		7	0	1
1930	10	3	1	6	0		4	3	1
1931	12	2		8	0		4	2	
1932	10	3	1	5	0	1	5	3	
1933	5	7	1	3	2	1	2	5	
1934	7	6		4	2		3	4	
1935	8	4		5	2		3	2	
1936	10	1	1	5	1		5	0	1
1937	7	4		3	2		4	2	
1938	8	3		4	2		4	1	
1939	9	2		4	1		5	1	
1940	6	4	1	4	2		2	2	1
1941	10	1		4	1		6	0	
1942	8	2	1	4	1		4	1	1
1943	7	2	1	2	1	1	5	1	
1944	8	2		5	0		3	2	
1945	6	4		4	1		2	3	
1946	6	5		2	3		4	2	
1947	6	5	1	4	2		2	3	1
1948	3	9		2	4		1	5	
1949	2	10		1	5		1	5	
1950	3	9		3	3		0	6	
1951	3	9		2	4		1	5	
1952	6	6		3	3		3	3	
1953	2	9	1	1	5		1	4	1
1954	4	8		2	4		2	4	
1955	6	6		5	1		1	5	
1956	4	8		2	4		2	4	

MINNESOTA VIKINGS

Season	All Games W	L	T	Home Games W	L	T	Road Games W	L	T
1961	3	11		3	4		0	7	
1962	2	11	1	1	5	1	1	6	
1963	5	8	1	3	4		2	4	1
1964	8	5	1	4	3		4	2	1
1965	7	7		2	5		5	2	
1966	4	9	1	2	5		2	4	1
1967	3	8	3	1	4	2	2	4	1
1968	8	6		4	3		4	3	
1969	12	2		7	0		5	2	
1970	12	2		7	0		5	2	
1971	11	3		5	2		6	1	
1972	7	7		3	4		4	3	
1973	12	2		7	0		5	2	
1974	10	4		4	3		6	1	

Season	All Games W	L	T	Home Games W	L	T	Road Games W	L	T
1975	12	2		7	0		5	2	
1976	11	2	1	6	0	1	5	2	
1977	9	5		5	2		4	3	
1978	8	7	1	5	3		3	4	1
1979	7	9		5	3		2	6	
1980	9	7		5	3		4	4	
1981	7	9		5	3		2	6	
1982	5	4		4	1		1	3	
1983	8	8		3	5		5	3	
1984	3	13		2	6		1	7	
1985	7	9		4	4		3	5	
1986	9	7		5	3		4	4	
1987	8	7		5	3		3	4	
1988	11	5		7	1		4	4	
1989	10	6		8	0		2	6	
1990	6	10		4	4		2	6	
1991	8	8		4	4		4	4	
1992	11	5		5	3		6	2	
1993	9	7		4	4		5	3	
1994	10	6		6	2		4	4	
1995	8	8		6	2		2	6	
1996	9	7		5	3		4	4	
1997	9	7		5	3		4	4	
1998	15	1		8	0		7	1	
1999	10	6		6	2		4	4	
2000	11	5		7	1		4	4	
2001	5	11		5	3		0	8	
2002	6	10		4	4		2	6	
2003	9	7		6	2		3	5	
2004	8	8		5	3		3	5	
2005	9	7		6	2		3	5	
	371	298	9	215	121	4	156	177	5

NEW ORLEANS SAINTS

Season	All Games W	L	T	Home Games W	L	T	Road Games W	L	T
1967	3	11		2	5		1	6	
1968	4	9	1	3	4		1	5	1
1969	5	9		3	4		2	5	
1970	2	11	1	2	5		0	6	1
1971	4	8	2	2	4	1	2	4	1
1972	2	11	1	2	5		0	6	1
1973	5	9		5	2		0	7	
1974	5	9		4	3		1	6	
1975	2	12		2	5		0	7	
1976	4	10		2	5		2	5	
1977	3	11		2	5		1	6	
1978	7	9		3	5		4	4	
1979	8	8		3	5		5	3	
1980	1	15		0	8		1	7	
1981	4	12		2	6		2	6	
1982	4	5		2	3		2	2	
1983	8	8		5	3		3	5	
1984	7	9		3	5		4	4	
1985	5	11		3	5		2	6	
1986	7	9		4	4		3	5	
1987	12	3		6	1		6	2	
1988	10	6		5	3		5	3	
1989	9	7		5	3		4	4	
1990	8	8		5	3		3	5	
1991	11	5		6	2		5	3	
1992	12	4		6	2		6	2	
1993	8	8		4	4		4	4	
1994	7	9		3	5		4	4	
1995	7	9		4	4		3	5	
1996	3	13		2	6		1	7	
1997	6	10		3	5		3	5	
1998	6	10		4	4		2	6	

Season	All Games W	L	T	Home Games W	L	T	Road Games W	L	T
1999	3	13		3	5		0	8	
2000	10	6		3	5		7	1	
2001	7	9		3	5		4	4	
2002	9	7		4	4		5	3	
2003	8	8		5	3		3	5	
2004	8	8		3	5		5	3	
2005	3	13		1	7		2	6	
	237	352	5	129	167	1	108	185	4

NEW YORK GIANTS

Season	All Games W	L	T	Home Games W	L	T	Road Games W	L	T
1925	8	4		7	2		1	2	
1926	8	4	1	5	2	1	3	2	
1927	11	1	1	7	1		4	0	1
1928	4	7	2	1	2	2	3	5	
1929	13	1	1	7	1		6	0	1
1930	13	4		6	2		7	2	
1931	7	6	1	4	2	1	3	4	
1932	4	6	2	3	2	1	1	4	1
1933	11	3		7	0		4	3	
1934	8	5		5	1		3	4	
1935	9	3		4	2		5	1	
1936	5	6	1	3	3	1	2	3	
1937	6	3	2	4	2	1	2	1	1
1938	8	2	1	6	1		2	1	1
1939	9	1	1	6	0		3	1	1
1940	6	4	1	4	3		2	1	1
1941	8	3		5	2		3	1	
1942	5	5	1	3	2	1	2	3	
1943	6	3	1	4	2		2	1	1
1944	8	1	1	5	1		3	0	1
1945	3	6	1	2	4		1	2	1
1946	7	3	1	5	1	1	2	2	
1947	2	8	2	2	3	1	0	5	1
1948	4	8		2	4		2	4	
1949	6	6		2	4		4	2	
1950	10	2		5	1		5	1	
1951	9	2	1	5	1		4	1	1
1952	7	5		2	4		5	1	
1953	3	9		2	4		1	5	
1954	7	5		4	2		3	3	
1955	6	5	1	4	1	1	2	4	
1956	8	3	1	4	1	1	4	2	
1957	7	5		3	3		4	2	
1958	9	3		5	1		4	2	
1959	10	2		5	1		5	1	
1960	6	4	2	1	3	2	5	1	
1961	10	3	1	4	2	1	6	1	
1962	12	2		6	1		6	1	
1963	11	3		5	2		6	1	
1964	2	10	2	2	5		0	5	2
1965	7	7		3	4		4	3	
1966	1	12	1	1	6		0	6	1
1967	7	7		5	2		2	5	
1968	7	7		3	4		4	3	
1969	6	8		5	2		1	6	
1970	9	5		5	2		4	3	
1971	4	10		1	6		3	4	
1972	8	6		4	3		4	3	
1973	2	11	1	2	4	1	0	7	
1974	2	12		0	7		2	5	
1975	5	9		2	5		3	4	
1976	3	11		3	4		0	7	
1977	5	9		3	4		2	5	
1978	6	10		5	3		1	7	
1979	6	10		4	4		2	6	
1980	4	12		2	6		2	6	

Season	All Games W	L	T	Home Games W	L	T	Road Games W	L	T
1981	9	7		4	4		5	3	
1982	4	5		2	3		2	2	
1983	3	12	1	1	7		2	5	1
1984	9	7		6	2		3	5	
1985	10	6		6	2		4	4	
1986	14	2		8	0		6	2	
1987	6	9		5	3		1	6	
1988	10	6		5	3		5	3	
1989	12	4		7	1		5	3	
1990	13	3		7	1		6	2	
1991	8	8		5	3		3	5	
1992	6	10		4	4		2	6	
1993	11	5		6	2		5	3	
1994	9	7		4	4		5	3	
1995	5	11		3	5		2	6	
1996	6	10		3	5		3	5	
1997	10	5	1	6	2		4	3	1
1998	8	8		5	3		3	5	
1999	7	9		4	4		3	5	
2000	12	4		5	3		7	1	
2001	7	9		5	3		2	6	
2002	10	6		5	3		5	3	
2003	4	12		1	7		3	5	
2004	6	10		3	5		3	5	
2005	11	5		7	1		4	4	
	588	492	33	331	227	16	257	265	17

PHILADELPHIA EAGLES

Season	All Games W	L	T	Home Games W	L	T	Road Games W	L	T
1933	3	5	1	2	3	1	1	2	
1934	4	7		2	4		2	3	
1935	2	9		0	5		2	4	
1936	1	11		1	6		0	5	
1937	2	8	1	0	5	1	2	3	
1938	5	6		2	3		3	3	
1939	1	9	1	1	3	1	0	6	
1940	1	10		1	4		0	6	
1941	2	8	1	1	4	1	1	4	
1942	2	9		0	5		2	4	
1944	7	1	2	3	1	2	4	0	
1945	7	3		6	0		1	3	
1946	6	5		3	2		3	3	
1947	8	4		6	1		2	3	
1948	9	2	1	6	0		3	2	1
1949	11	1		6	0		5	1	
1950	6	6		2	4		4	2	
1951	4	8		1	5		3	3	
1952	7	5		4	2		3	3	
1953	7	4	1	5	0	1	2	4	
1954	7	4	1	5	1		2	3	1
1955	4	7	1	4	2		0	5	1
1956	3	8	1	2	3	1	1	5	
1957	4	8		3	3		1	5	
1958	2	9	1	2	4		0	5	1
1959	7	5		5	1		2	4	
1960	10	2		5	1		5	1	
1961	10	4		5	2		5	2	
1962	3	10	1	2	5		1	5	1
1963	2	10	2	1	5	1	1	5	1
1964	6	8		3	4		3	4	
1965	5	9		2	5		3	4	
1966	9	5		5	2		4	3	
1967	6	7	1	5	2		1	5	1
1968	2	12		1	6		1	6	
1969	4	9	1	2	5		2	4	1
1970	3	10	1	3	3	1	0	7	
1971	6	7	1	3	4		3	3	1

Season	All Games W	L	T	Home Games W	L	T	Road Games W	L	T
1972	2	11	1	0	6	1	2	5	
1973	5	8	1	4	3		1	5	1
1974	7	7		5	2		2	5	
1975	4	10		2	5		2	5	
1976	4	10		2	5		2	5	
1977	5	9		4	3		1	6	
1978	9	7		5	3		4	4	
1979	11	5		5	3		6	2	
1980	12	4		7	1		5	3	
1981	10	6		6	2		4	4	
1982	3	6		1	4		2	2	
1983	5	11		1	7		4	4	
1984	6	9	1	5	3		1	6	1
1985	7	9		4	4		3	5	
1986	5	10	1	2	5	1	3	5	
1987	7	8		4	4		3	4	
1988	10	6		5	3		5	3	
1989	11	5		6	2		5	3	
1990	10	6		6	2		4	4	
1991	10	6		4	4		6	2	
1992	11	5		8	0		3	5	
1993	8	8		3	5		5	3	
1994	7	9		5	3		2	6	
1995	10	6		6	2		4	4	
1996	10	6		5	3		5	3	
1997	6	9	1	6	2		0	7	1
1998	3	13		3	5		0	8	
1999	5	11		4	4		1	7	
2000	11	5		5	3		6	2	
2001	11	5		4	4		7	1	
2002	12	4		7	1		5	3	
2003	12	4		5	3		7	1	
2004	13	3		7	1		6	2	
2005	6	10		4	4		2	6	
	456	506	24	260	226	12	196	280	12

ST. LOUIS RAMS*

Season	All Games W	L	T	Home Games W	L	T	Road Games W	L	T
1937	1	10		0	5		1	5	
1938	4	7		2	2		2	5	
1939	5	5	1	3	2	1	2	3	
1940	4	6	1	3	1	1	1	5	
1941	2	9		1	4		1	5	
1942	5	6		3	2		2	4	
1944	4	6		1	2		3	4	
1945	9	1		4	0		5	1	
1946	6	4	1	3	2		3	2	1
1947	6	6		3	3		3	3	
1948	6	5	1	3	2	1	3	3	
1949	8	2	2	5	1		3	1	2
1950	9	3		5	1		4	2	
1951	8	4		5	2		3	2	
1952	9	3		5	1		4	2	
1953	8	3	1	5	1		3	2	1
1954	6	5	1	3	2	1	3	3	
1955	8	3	1	5	1		3	2	1
1956	4	8		4	2		0	6	
1957	6	6		5	1		1	5	
1958	8	4		4	2		4	2	
1959	2	10		0	6		2	4	
1960	4	7	1	2	3	1	2	4	
1961	4	10		4	3		0	7	
1962	1	12	1	0	7		1	5	1
1963	5	9		3	4		2	5	
1964	5	7	2	3	2	2	2	5	
1965	4	10		3	4		1	6	
1966	8	6		5	2		3	4	

Season	All Games W	L	T	Home Games W	L	T	Road Games W	L	T
1967	11	1	2	5	1	1	6	0	1
1968	10	3	1	5	2		5	1	1
1969	11	3		5	2		6	1	
1970	9	4	1	3	3	1	6	1	
1971	8	5	1	4	2	1	4	3	
1972	6	7	1	4	3		2	4	1
1973	12	2		7	0		5	2	
1974	10	4		6	1		4	3	
1975	12	2		6	1		6	1	
1976	10	3	1	5	2		5	1	1
1977	10	4		7	0		3	4	
1978	12	4		6	2		6	2	
1979	9	7		4	4		5	3	
1980	11	5		6	2		5	3	
1981	6	10		4	4		2	6	
1982	2	7		1	4		1	3	
1983	9	7		5	3		4	4	
1984	10	6		5	3		5	3	
1985	11	5		6	2		5	3	
1986	10	6		6	2		4	4	
1987	6	9		3	4		3	5	
1988	10	6		4	4		6	2	
1989	11	5		6	2		5	3	
1990	5	11		2	6		3	5	
1991	3	13		2	6		1	7	
1992	6	10		4	4		2	6	
1993	5	11		3	5		2	6	
1994	4	12		3	5		1	7	
1995	7	9		4	4		3	5	
1996	6	10		4	4		2	6	
1997	5	11		2	6		3	5	
1998	4	12		2	6		2	6	
1999	13	3		8	0		5	3	
2000	10	6		5	3		5	3	
2001	14	2		6	2		8	0	
2002	7	9		6	2		1	7	
2003	12	4		8	0		4	4	
2004	8	8		6	2		2	6	
2005	6	10		3	5		3	5	
	490	433	20	273	183	10	217	250	10

*includes Cleveland Rams (1937-1942, 1944-45) and Los Angeles Rams (1946-1994).

SAN FRANCISCO 49ERS

Season	All Games W	L	T	Home Games W	L	T	Road Games W	L	T
1950	3	9		3	3		0	6	
1951	7	4	1	5	1		2	3	1
1952	7	5		3	3		4	2	
1953	9	3		5	1		4	2	
1954	7	4	1	4	2		3	2	1
1955	4	8		2	4		2	4	
1956	5	6	1	3	3		2	3	1
1957	8	4		5	1		3	3	
1958	6	6		4	2		2	4	
1959	7	5		4	2		3	3	
1960	7	5		3	3		4	2	
1961	7	6	1	5	1	1	2	5	
1962	6	8		1	6		5	2	
1963	2	12		2	5		0	7	
1964	4	10		3	4		1	6	
1965	7	6	1	4	2	1	3	4	
1966	6	6	2	4	2	1	2	4	1
1967	7	7		3	4		4	3	
1968	7	6	1	3	3	1	4	3	
1969	4	8	2	3	3	1	1	5	1
1970	10	3	1	5	1	1	5	2	
1971	9	5		4	3		5	2	

Season	All Games W	L	T	Home Games W	L	T	Road Games W	L	T
1972	8	5	1	4	2	1	4	3	
1973	5	9		3	4		2	5	
1974	6	8		3	4		3	4	
1975	5	9		2	5		3	4	
1976	8	6		4	3		4	3	
1977	5	9		3	4		2	5	
1978	2	14		2	6		0	8	
1979	2	14		2	6		0	8	
1980	6	10		4	4		2	6	
1981	13	3		7	1		6	2	
1982	3	6		0	5		3	1	
1983	10	6		4	4		6	2	
1984	15	1		7	1		8	0	
1985	10	6		5	3		5	3	
1986	10	5	1	6	2		4	3	1
1987	13	2		6	1		7	1	
1988	10	6		4	4		6	2	
1989	14	2		6	2		8	0	
1990	14	2		6	2		8	0	
1991	10	6		7	1		3	5	
1992	14	2		7	1		7	1	
1993	10	6		6	2		4	4	
1994	13	3		7	1		6	2	
1995	11	5		6	2		5	3	
1996	12	4		6	2		6	2	
1997	13	3		8	0		5	3	
1998	12	4		8	0		4	4	
1999	4	12		3	5		1	7	
2000	6	10		4	4		2	6	
2001	12	4		7	1		5	3	
2002	10	6		5	3		5	3	
2003	7	9		6	2		1	7	
2004	2	14		1	7		1	7	
2005	4	12		3	5		1	7	
	438	359	13	240	158	7	198	201	6

SEATTLE SEAHAWKS

Season	All Games W	L	T	Home Games W	L	T	Road Games W	L	T
1976	2	12		1	6		1	6	
1977	5	9		3	4		2	5	
1978	9	7		5	3		4	4	
1979	9	7		5	3		4	4	
1980	4	12		0	8		4	4	
1981	6	10		5	3		1	7	
1982	4	5		3	2		1	3	
1983	9	7		5	3		4	4	
1984	12	4		7	1		5	3	
1985	8	8		5	3		3	5	
1986	10	6		7	1		3	5	
1987	9	6		6	2		3	4	
1988	9	7		5	3		4	4	
1989	7	9		3	5		4	4	
1990	9	7		5	3		4	4	
1991	7	9		5	3		2	6	
1992	2	14		1	7		1	7	
1993	6	10		4	4		2	6	
1994	6	10		3	5		3	5	
1995	8	8		5	3		3	5	
1996	7	9		4	4		3	5	
1997	8	8		4	4		4	4	
1998	8	8		6	2		2	6	
1999	9	7		5	3		4	4	
2000	6	10		3	5		3	5	
2001	9	7		6	2		3	5	
2002	7	9		3	5		4	4	
2003	10	6		8	0		2	6	
2004	9	7		5	3		4	4	

Season	All Games W	L	T	Home Games W	L	T	Road Games W	L	T
2005	13	3		8	0		5	3	
	227	241		135	100		92	141	

TAMPA BAY BUCCANEERS

Season	All Games W	L	T	Home Games W	L	T	Road Games W	L	T
1976	0	14		0	7		0	7	
1977	2	12		1	6		1	6	
1978	5	11		3	5		2	6	
1979	10	6		5	3		5	3	
1980	5	10	1	2	5	1	3	5	
1981	9	7		6	2		3	5	
1982	5	4		4	1		1	3	
1983	2	14		1	7		1	7	
1984	6	10		6	2		0	8	
1985	2	14		2	6		0	8	
1986	2	14		1	7		1	7	
1987	4	11		2	5		2	6	
1988	5	11		3	5		2	6	
1989	5	11		2	6		3	5	
1990	6	10		4	4		2	6	
1991	3	13		3	5		0	8	
1992	5	11		3	5		2	6	
1993	5	11		3	5		2	6	
1994	6	10		4	4		2	6	
1995	7	9		5	3		2	6	
1996	6	10		5	3		1	7	
1997	10	6		5	3		5	3	
1998	8	8		6	2		2	6	
1999	11	5		7	1		4	4	
2000	10	6		6	2		4	4	
2001	9	7		5	3		4	4	
2002	12	4		6	2		6	2	
2003	7	9		3	5		4	4	
2004	5	11		4	4		1	7	
2005	11	5		6	2		5	3	
	183	284	1	113	120	1	70	164	

WASHINGTON REDSKINS*

Season	All Games W	L	T	Home Games W	L	T	Road Games W	L	T
1932	4	4	2	2	3	1	2	1	1
1933	5	5	2	4	2		1	3	2
1934	6	6		4	3		2	3	
1935	2	8	1	2	5		0	3	1
1936	7	5		4	3		3	2	
1937	8	3		4	2		4	1	
1938	6	3	2	3	1	1	3	2	1
1939	8	2	1	5	0	1	3	2	
1940	9	2		6	0		3	2	
1941	6	5		4	2		2	3	
1942	10	1		5	1		5	0	
1943	6	3	1	4	2		2	1	1
1944	6	3	1	4	2		2	1	1
1945	8	2		6	0		2	2	
1946	5	5	1	3	2	1	2	3	
1947	4	8		4	2		0	6	
1948	7	5		4	2		3	3	
1949	4	7	1	3	3		1	4	1
1950	3	9		1	5		2	4	
1951	5	7		2	4		3	3	
1952	4	8		1	5		3	3	
1953	6	5	1	3	3		3	2	1
1954	3	9		3	3		0	6	
1955	8	4		3	3		5	1	
1956	6	6		4	2		2	4	
1957	5	6	1	2	3	1	3	3	
1958	4	7	1	3	2	1	1	5	
1959	3	9		2	4		1	5	
1960	1	9	2	1	4	1	0	5	1
1961	1	12	1	1	6		0	6	1
1962	5	7	2	3	4		2	3	2
1963	3	11		1	6		2	5	
1964	6	8		4	3		2	5	
1965	6	8		3	4		3	4	
1966	7	7		4	3		3	4	
1967	5	6	3	2	4	1	3	2	2
1968	5	9		3	4		2	5	
1969	7	5	2	4	2	1	3	3	1
1970	6	8		4	3		2	5	
1971	9	4	1	4	2	1	5	2	
1972	11	3		6	1		5	2	
1973	10	4		7	0		3	4	
1974	10	4		6	1		4	3	
1975	8	6		5	2		3	4	
1976	10	4		5	2		5	2	
1977	9	5		5	2		4	3	
1978	8	8		5	3		3	5	
1979	10	6		6	2		4	4	
1980	6	10		4	4		2	6	
1981	8	8		5	3		3	5	
1982	8	1		3	1		5	0	
1983	14	2		7	1		7	1	
1984	11	5		7	1		4	4	
1985	10	6		5	3		5	3	
1986	12	4		7	1		5	3	
1987	11	4		6	1		5	3	
1988	7	9		4	4		3	5	
1989	10	6		4	4		6	2	
1990	10	6		7	1		3	5	
1991	14	2		7	1		7	1	
1992	9	7		6	2		3	5	
1993	4	12		3	5		1	7	
1994	3	13		0	8		3	5	
1995	6	10		4	4		2	6	
1996	9	7		5	3		4	4	
1997	8	7	1	5	2	1	3	5	
1998	6	10		4	4		2	6	
1999	10	6		6	2		4	4	
2000	8	8		4	4		4	4	
2001	8	8		4	4		4	4	
2002	7	9		5	3		2	6	
2003	5	11		3	5		2	6	
2004	6	10		3	5		3	5	
2005	10	6		6	2		4	4	
	515	468	27	298	205	11	217	263	16

*includes Boston Braves (1932) and Boston Redskins (1933-36).

ALL-TIME RECORDS OF NFL TEAMS

AFC	W	L	T	Pct.
Miami	362	242	4	.599
Oakland	394	287	11	.578
Cleveland	410	342	10	.545
Kansas City	366	314	12	.538
Jacksonville	94	82	0	.534
Denver	362	320	10	.531
Pittsburgh	490	470	20	.510
Indianapolis	390	377	7	.508
New England	338	345	9	.495
Baltimore	78	81	1	.491
Tennessee	332	354	6	.484
San Diego	329	352	11	.483
Buffalo	327	357	8	.478
N.Y. Jets	308	376	8	.450
Cincinnati	253	326	1	.437
Houston	18	46	0	.281

NFC	W	L	T	Pct.
Chicago	657	479	42	.578
Dallas	392	292	6	.573
Green Bay	616	492	36	.556
Minnesota	371	298	9	.554
San Francisco	438	359	13	.549
N.Y. Giants	588	492	33	.544
St. Louis	490	433	20	.531
Washington	515	468	27	.524
Seattle	227	241	0	.485
Philadelphia	456	506	24	.474
Detroit	478	531	32	.474
Carolina	82	94	0	.466
Arizona	451	638	39	.414
Atlanta	245	357	6	.407
New Orleans	237	352	5	.403
Tampa Bay	183	284	1	.392

History

The Professional Football Hall of Fame is located in Canton, Ohio, site of the organizational meeting on September 17, 1920, from which the National Football League evolved. The NFL recognized Canton as the Hall of Fame site on April 27, 1961. Canton area individuals, foundations, and companies donated almost $400,000 in cash and services to provide funds for the construction of the original two-building complex, which was dedicated on September 7, 1963. Since that time, the Hall added three buildings with major expansion projects in 1971, 1978, and 1995. The Hall's largest-ever expansion, a $9.2 million project, was completed in early fall 1995. With the new fifth building, the Hall's size is now 82,307 square feet, more than four times its original size.

The expanded Hall represents the sport of pro football in many ways—through (1) GameDay Stadium, a dynamic two-part turntable theater featuring NFL action in Cinemascope for the first time, (2) a standard theater showing NFL films hourly, (3) six large exhibition areas where the history of pro football is detailed in memento, picture, and story form, (4) an extensive archive and information center, and (5) a new and enlarged museum store.

Throughout the years, the Pro Football Hall of Fame has become an extremely popular tourist attraction. At the end of 2005, a total of 7,776,901 fans had visited the Hall of Fame.

New members of the Pro Football Hall of Fame are elected annually by a 39-member National Board of Selectors, made up of media representatives from every league city, six at-large representatives, and a representative of the Pro Football Writers of America. Between three and six new members are elected each year. An affirmative vote of approximately 80 percent is needed for election.

Any fan may nominate any eligible player or contributor simply by writing to the Pro Football Hall of Fame. Players must be retired five years to be eligible, while a coach needs only to be retired with no time limit specified. Contributors (administrators, owners, *et al.*) may be elected while they are still active.

The charter class of 17 enshrinees was elected in 1963 and the honor roll now stands at 235 (145 living as of May 20, 2006) with the election of a six-man class in 2006. That class consists of Troy Aikman, Harry Carson, John Madden, Warren Moon, Reggie White, and Rayfield Wright.

ROSTER OF MEMBERS

HERB ADDERLEY
Cornerback. 6-0, 205. Born in Philadelphia, Pennsylvania, June 8, 1939. Michigan State. Inducted in 1980. 1961-69 Green Bay Packers, 1970-72 Dallas Cowboys. **Highlights:** 48 interceptions, 7 touchdowns. Played in four Super Bowls, five Pro Bowls.

TROY AIKMAN
Quarterback. 6-4, 219. Born in West Covina, California, November 21, 1966. Oklahoma, UCLA. Inducted in 2006. 1989-2000 Dallas Cowboys. **Highlights:** His 90 wins in 1990s make him winningest quarterback of any decade. Led Cowboys to three Super Bowl wins. Passed for 32,942 yards, 165 touchdowns. Named to six Pro Bowls.

GEORGE ALLEN
Coach. Born in Detroit, Michigan, April 29, 1918. Died December 31, 1990. Alma College, Eastern Michigan, Marquette, Michigan. Inducted in 2002. 1966-1970 Los Angeles Rams, 1971-77 Washington Redskins. **Highlights:** 118-54-5 overall record. Never suffered a losing season, and ranked tenth in coaching victories at time of retirement.

MARCUS ALLEN
Running back. 6-2, 210. Born in San Diego, California, March 26, 1960. Southern California. Inducted in 2003. 1982-1992 Los Angeles Raiders, 1993-1997 Kansas City Chiefs. **Highlights:** First player in NFL history to tally 10,000 rushing yards and 5,000 receiving yards. MVP, Super Bowl XVIII.

LANCE ALWORTH
Wide receiver. 6-0, 184. Born in Houston, Texas, August 3, 1940. Arkansas. Inducted in 1978. 1962-1970 San Diego Chargers, 1971-72 Dallas Cowboys. **Highlights:** 542 receptions for 10,266 yards, 85 touchdowns. All-AFL seven times, seven All-Star games.

DOUG ATKINS
Defensive end. 6-8, 275. Born in Humboldt, Tennessee, May 8, 1930. Tennessee. Inducted in 1982. 1953-54 Cleveland Browns, 1955-1966 Chicago Bears, 1967-69 New Orleans Saints. **Highlights:** Eight Pro Bowls, All-NFL four times. Played for 17 years, 205 games.

MORRIS (RED) BADGRO
End. 6-0, 190. Born in Orillia, Washington, December 1, 1902. Died July 13, 1998. Southern California. Inducted in 1981. 1927-28 New York Yankees, 1930-35 New York Giants, 1936 Brooklyn Dodgers. **Highlights:** First- or second-team All-NFL four times. Scored first touchdown in NFL Championship Game series.

LEM BARNEY
Cornerback. 6-0, 190. Born in Gulfport, Mississippi, September 8, 1945. Jackson State. Inducted in 1992. 1967-1977 Detroit Lions. **Highlights:** 56 interceptions for 1,077 yards, 11 touchdowns (7 defensive, 4 special teams). Seven Pro Bowls, All-NFL/NFC four times.

CLIFF BATTLES
Halfback. 6-1, 195. Born in Akron, Ohio, May 1, 1910. Died April 28, 1981. West Virginia Wesleyan. Inducted in 1968. 1932 Boston Braves, 1933-36 Boston Redskins, 1937 Washington Redskins. **Highlights:** NFL rushing champion 1932, 1937. First to gain more than 200 yards in a game, 1933.

LANCE ALWORTH

SAMMY BAUGH
Quarterback. 6-2, 180. Born in Temple, Texas, March 17, 1914. Texas Christian. Inducted in 1963. 1937-1952 Washington Redskins. **Highlights:** Charter enshrinee. Six-time NFL passing leader. NFL passing, punting, interception champ, 1943.

CHUCK BEDNARIK
Center-linebacker. 6-3, 230. Born in Bethlehem, Pennsylvania, May 1, 1925. Pennsylvania. Inducted in 1967. 1949-1962 Philadelphia Eagles. **Highlights:** Eight Pro Bowls. Missed three games in 14 years. Named NFL all-time center, 1969.

BERT BELL
Team owner. Commissioner. Born in Philadelphia, Pennsylvania, February 25, 1895. Died October 11, 1959. Pennsylvania. Inducted in 1963. 1933-1940 Philadelphia Eagles, 1941-42 Pittsburgh Steelers, 1943 Phil-Pitt, 1944 Card-Pitt, 1945-46 Pittsburgh Steelers. Commissioner, 1946-1959. **Highlights:** Charter enshrinee. Built NFL image as commissioner, 1946-1959. Set up long-term television policies.

BOBBY BELL
Linebacker. 6-4, 225. Born in Shelby, North Carolina, June 17, 1940. Minnesota. Inducted in 1983. 1963-1974 Kansas City Chiefs. **Highlights:** 26 interceptions. All-AFL/AFC eight times. Nine career touchdowns, 1 on onside kick return.

RAYMOND BERRY
End. 6-2, 187. Born in Corpus Christi, Texas, February 27, 1933. Southern Methodist. Inducted in 1973. 1955-1967 Baltimore Colts. **Highlights:** 631 receptions for 9,275 yards, 68 touchdowns. Set NFL title game mark with 12 catches for 178 yards, 1958.

ELVIN BETHEA
Defensive end. 6-2, 260. Born in Trenton, New Jersey, March 1, 1946. North Carolina A&T. Inducted in 2003. 1968-1983 Houston Oilers. **Highlights:** Led team in sacks six times. Elected to eight Pro Bowls. Played for 16 years, 210 games.

CHARLES W. BIDWILL SR.
Team owner. Born in Chicago, Illinois, September 16, 1895. Died April 19, 1947. Loyola of Chicago. Inducted in 1967. 1933-1943 Chicago Cardinals, 1944 Card-Pitt, 1945-47 Chicago Cardinals. **Highlights:** Guiding light for NFL during depression years. Built famous "Dream Backfield."

FRED BILETNIKOFF
Wide receiver. 6-1, 190. Born in Erie, Pennsylvania, February 23, 1943. Florida State. Inducted in 1988. 1965-1978 Oakland Raiders. **Highlights:** 589 receptions for 8,974 yards, 76 touchdowns. 40 catches 10 straight years. MVP, Super Bowl XI.

GEORGE BLANDA
Quarterback-kicker. 6-2, 215. Born in Youngwood, Pennsylvania, September 17, 1927. Kentucky. Inducted in 1981. 1949-1958 Chicago Bears, 1950 Baltimore Colts, 1960-66 Houston Oilers, 1967-1975 Oakland Raiders. **Highlights:** 2,002 career points. 26-season, 340-game career longest in NFL history.

MEL BLOUNT
Cornerback. 6-3, 205. Born in Vidalia, Georgia, April 10, 1948. Southern University. Inducted in 1989. 1970-1983 Pittsburgh Steelers. **Highlights:** 57 interceptions for 736 yards. NFL defensive MVP, 1975. Played in five Pro Bowls.

TERRY BRADSHAW
Quarterback. 6-3, 210. Born in Shreveport, Louisiana, September 2, 1948. Louisiana Tech. Inducted in 1989. 1970-1983 Pittsburgh Steelers. **Highlights:** 27,989 yards passing, 212 touchdowns. MVP in Super Bowls XIII, XIV.

BOB (BOOMER) BROWN
Tackle. 6-4, 280. Born in Cleveland, Ohio, December 8, 1941. Nebraska. Inducted in 2004. 1964-68 Philadelphia Eagles, 1969-1970 Los Angeles Rams, 1971-73 Oakland Raiders. **Highlights:** All-NFL seven of 10 seasons, six Pro Bowls. Named to 1960s All-Decade Team.

JIM BROWN
Fullback. 6-2, 228. Born in St. Simons, Georgia, February 17, 1936. Syracuse. Inducted in 1971. 1957-1965 Cleveland Browns. **Highlights:** 12,312 yards rushing, 756 points. Led NFL rushers eight years. Nine consecutive Pro Bowls.

PAUL BROWN
Coach. Born in Norwalk, Ohio, September 7, 1908. Died August 5, 1991. Miami (Ohio). Inducted in 1967. 1946-49 Cleveland Browns (AAFC), 1950-1962 Cleveland Browns. **Highlights:** Built Cleveland dynasty with 167-53-8 record, four AAFC titles, three NFL crowns. Returned to coaching with Cincinnati Bengals after induction, 1968-1975.

ROOSEVELT BROWN
Tackle. 6-3, 255. Born in Charlottesville, Virginia, October 20, 1932. Died June 9, 2004. Morgan State. Inducted in 1975. 1953-1965 New York Giants. **Highlights:** All-NFL eight consecutive years, nine Pro Bowls. NFL's lineman of year, 1956.

WILLIE BROWN
Cornerback. 6-1, 210. Born in Yazoo City, Mississippi, December 2, 1940. Grambling. Inducted in 1984. 1963-66 Denver Broncos, 1967-1978 Oakland Raiders. **Highlights:** 54 interceptions for 472 yards. Scored on 75-yard interception in Super Bowl XI.

BUCK BUCHANAN
Defensive tackle. 6-7, 274. Born in Gainesville, Alabama, September 10, 1940. Died July 16, 1992. Grambling. Inducted in 1990. 1963-1975 Kansas City Chiefs. **Highlights:** Led Chiefs defensive efforts in Super Bowl I, IV. Did not miss a game in 13 years.

NICK BUONICONTI
Linebacker. 5-11, 220. Born in Springfield, Massachusetts, December 15, 1940. Notre Dame. Inducted in 2001. 1962-68 Boston Patriots, 1969-1974, 1976 Miami Dolphins. **Highlights:** All-AFL/AFC eight times. Named to AFL's All-Time Team.

DICK BUTKUS
Linebacker. 6-3, 245. Born in Chicago, Illinois, December 9, 1942. Illinois. Inducted in 1979. 1965-1973 Chicago Bears. **Highlights:** All-NFL six years, eight consecutive Pro Bowls. 27 fumble recoveries.

EARL CAMPBELL
Running back. 5-11, 233. Born in Tyler, Texas, March 29, 1955. Texas. Inducted in 1991. 1978-1984 Houston Oilers, 1984-85 New Orleans Saints. **Highlights:** 9,407 yards rushing, 74 touchdowns. 1,934 yards rushing in 1980, including four games with at least 200 yards.

TONY CANADEO
Halfback. 5-11, 195. Born in Chicago, Illinois, May 5, 1919. Died November 29, 2003. Gonzaga. Inducted in 1974. 1941-44, 1946-1952 Green Bay Packers. **Highlights:** Two-way player. Third player to rush for 1,000 yards in single season, 1949.

JOE CARR
NFL president. Born in Columbus, Ohio, October 23, 1879. Died May 20, 1939. Did not attend college. Inducted in 1963. President, 1921-1939 National Football League. **Highlights:** Charter enshrinee. NFL co-organizer, 1920. Introduced standard player contract.

HARRY CARSON
Linebacker. 6-2, 237. Born in Florence, South Carolina, November 26, 1953. South Carolina State. Inducted in 2006. 1976-1988 New York Giants. **Highlights:** 11 career interceptions. Named to nine Pro Bowls. Named first- or second-team All-NFL six times.

DAVE CASPER
Tight end. 6-4, 240. Born in Bemidji, Minnesota, February 2, 1952. Notre Dame. Inducted in 2002. 1974-1980 Oakland Raiders, 1980-83 Houston Oilers, 1983 Minnesota Vikings, 1984 Los Angeles Raiders. **Highlights:** 378 receptions for 5,216 yards, 52 touchdowns. Five consecutive Pro Bowls.

GUY CHAMBERLIN
End. Coach. 6-2, 196. Born in Blue Springs, Nebraska, January 16, 1894. Died April 4, 1967. Nebraska. Inducted in 1965. 1919 Canton Bulldogs, 1920-21 Decatur Staleys/Chicago Staleys, player-coach 1922-23 Canton Bulldogs, 1924 Cleveland Bulldogs, 1925-26 Frankford Yellowjackets, 1927-28 Chicago Cardinals. **Highlights:** Player-coach of four NFL championship teams. Six-year coaching record of 58-16-7.

JACK CHRISTIANSEN
Safety. 6-1, 185. Born in Sublette, Kansas, December 20, 1928. Died June 29, 1986. Colorado State. Inducted in 1970. 1951-58 Detroit Lions. **Highlights:** 46 interceptions. NFL interception leader, 1953, 1957. Eight punt returns for touchdowns.

EARL (DUTCH) CLARK
Quarterback. 6-0, 185. Born in Fowler, Colorado, October 11, 1906. Died August 5, 1978. Colorado College. Inducted in 1963. 1931-32 Portsmouth Spartans, 1934-38 Detroit Lions. **Highlights:** Charter enshrinee. NFL scoring champion three years. Led Lions to 1935 NFL title.

GEORGE CONNOR
Tackle-linebacker. 6-3, 240. Born in Chicago, Illinois, January 21, 1925. Died March 31, 2003. Holy Cross, Notre Dame. Inducted in 1975. 1948-1955 Chicago Bears. **Highlights:** All-NFL at three positions—T, DT, LB. All-NFL five years. Played in first four Pro Bowls.

PRO FOOTBALL HALL OF FAME

JIMMY CONZELMAN
Quarterback. Coach. Team owner. 6-0, 180. Born in St. Louis, Missouri, March 6, 1898. Died July 31, 1970. Washington of St. Louis. Inducted in 1964. 1920 Decatur Staleys, 1921-22 Rock Island Independents, 1922-24 Milwaukee Badgers; owner-coach 1925-26 Detroit Panthers; player-coach 1927-29, coach 1930 Providence Steam Roller; coach 1940-42, 1946-48 Chicago Cardinals. **Highlights:** Player-coach of four NFL teams in 1920's. Coached Cardinals to 1947 NFL crown.

LOU CREEKMUR
Tackle-guard. 6-4, 255. Born in Hopelawn, New Jersey. January 22, 1927. William & Mary. Inducted in 1996. 1950-59 Detroit Lions. **Highlights:** All-NFL six times, twice at guard and four times at tackle. Selected to eight Pro Bowls and played on three NFL championship teams.

LARRY CSONKA
Running back. 6-3, 235. Born in Stow, Ohio, December 25, 1946. Syracuse. Inducted in 1987. 1968-1974, 1979 Miami Dolphins, 1976-78 New York Giants. **Highlights:** 8,081 yards rushing, 68 touchdowns. MVP Super Bowl VIII. Only 21 fumbles in 1,891 carries and 106 receptions.

AL DAVIS
Team, League Administrator. Born in Brockton, Massachusetts, July 4, 1929. Wittenberg, Syracuse. Inducted in 1992. 1963-1981, 1995-present Oakland Raiders, 1982-1994 Los Angeles Raiders, 1966 American Football League. **Highlights:** Only person to serve in pros as personnel assistant, scout, assistant coach, head coach, general manager, commissioner, team owner/CEO.

WILLIE DAVIS
Defensive end. 6-3, 245. Born in Lisbon, Louisiana, July 24, 1934. Grambling. Inducted in 1981. 1958-59 Cleveland Browns, 1960-69 Green Bay Packers. **Highlights:** All-NFL five seasons, five Pro Bowls. Did not miss game in 12-year career.

LEN DAWSON
Quarterback. 6-0, 190. Born in Alliance, Ohio, June 20, 1935. Purdue. Inducted in 1987. 1957-59 Pittsburgh Steelers, 1960-61 Cleveland Browns, 1962 Dallas Texans, 1963-1975 Kansas City Chiefs. **Highlights:** 28,711 yards passing, 239 touchdowns. Four AFL passing crowns. MVP, Super Bowl IV.

JOE DeLAMIELLEURE
Guard. 6-3, 254. Born in Detroit, Michigan, March 16, 1951. Michigan State. Inducted in 2003. 1973-1979, 1985 Buffalo Bills, 1980-1984 Cleveland Browns. **Highlights:** Selected All-Pro and All-AFC six consecutive times, 1975-1980. Named to six Pro Bowls. Played 13 years, 185 games.

ERIC DICKERSON
Running back. 6-3, 220. Born in Sealy, Texas, September 2, 1960. Southern Methodist. Inducted in 1999. 1983-87 Los Angeles Rams, 1987-1991 Indianapolis Colts, 1992 Los Angeles Raiders, 1993 Atlanta Falcons. **Highlights:** Rushed for 13,259 career yards, including an NFL record 2,105 yards in 1984. All-Pro five times, six Pro Bowls.

DAN DIERDORF
Tackle. 6-3, 290. Born in Canton, Ohio, June 29, 1949. Michigan. Inducted in 1996. 1971-1983 St. Louis Cardinals. **Highlights:** All-Pro five times, played in six Pro Bowls, named NFL's best blocker three times.

MIKE DITKA
Tight end. 6-3, 225. Born in Carnegie, Pennsylvania, October 18, 1939. Pittsburgh. Inducted in 1988. 1961-66 Chicago Bears, 1967-68 Philadelphia Eagles, 1969-1972 Dallas Cowboys. **Highlights:** 427 receptions for 5,812 yards, 43 touchdowns. First tight end selected to Hall of Fame. Five consecutive Pro Bowls.

ART DONOVAN
Defensive tackle. 6-3, 265. Born in Bronx, New York, June 5, 1925. Boston College. Inducted in 1968. 1950 Baltimore Colts, 1951 New York Yanks, 1952 Dallas Texans, 1953-1961 Baltimore Colts. **Highlights:** Five Pro Bowls. Vital part of Baltimore's climb to powerhouse status in 1950s.

TONY DORSETT
Running back. 5-11, 184. Born in Rochester, Pennsylvania, April 7, 1954. Pittsburgh. Inducted in 1994. 1977-1987 Dallas Cowboys, 1988 Denver Broncos. **Highlights:** 12,739 yards rushing, 398 receptions, 91 touchdowns. Ran record 99 yards for touchdown vs. Minnesota, January, 1983.

JOHN (PADDY) DRISCOLL
Quarterback. 5-11, 160. Born in Evanston, Illinois, January 11, 1896. Died June 29, 1968. Northwestern. Inducted in 1965. 1919 Hammond Pros, 1920 Decatur Staleys, 1920-25 Chicago Cardinals, 1926-29 Chicago Bears. **Highlights:** All-NFL seven times. Dropkicked record 4 field goals in one game, 1925.

BILL DUDLEY
Halfback. 5-10, 182. Born in Bluefield, Virginia, December 24, 1921. Virginia. Inducted in 1966. 1942, 1945-46 Pittsburgh Steelers, 1947-49 Detroit Lions, 1950-51, 1953 Washington Redskins. **Highlights:** Won NFL rushing, interception, punt return titles, 1946. All-NFL 1942, 1946, and 1947.

ALBERT GLEN (TURK) EDWARDS
Tackle. 6-2, 260. Born in Mold, Washington, September 28, 1907. Died January 12, 1973. Washington State. Inducted in 1969. 1932 Boston Braves, 1933-36 Boston Redskins, 1937-1940 Washington Redskins. **Highlights:** All-NFL 1932-34, 1936, 1937. Steamrolling blocker, smothering tackler.

CARL ELLER
Defensive end. 6-6, 247. Born in Winston-Salem, North Carolina, January 25, 1942. Minnesota. Inducted in 2004. 1964-1978 Minnesota Vikings, 1979 Seattle Seahawks. **Highlights:** Fixture on Vikings' "Purple People Eaters" defensive line, All-Pro five time, elected to six Pro Bowls.

JOHN ELWAY
Quarterback. 6-3, 215. Born in Port Angeles, Washington, June 28, 1960. Stanford. Inducted in 2004. 1983-1998 Denver Broncos. **Highlights:** Passed for 51,475 yards, 300 touchdowns. Named to nine Pro Bowls. NFL MVP, 1987; MVP, Super Bowl XXXIII.

WEEB EWBANK
Coach. Born in Richmond, Indiana, May 6, 1907. Died November 17, 1998. Miami (Ohio). Inducted in 1978. 1954-1962 Baltimore Colts, 1963-1973 New York Jets. **Highlights:** Only coach to win championships in both NFL, AFL. Led both Colts (1958 and 1959) and Jets (1968) to championships.

TOM FEARS
End. 6-2, 215. Born in Guadalajara, Mexico, December 3, 1923. Died January 4, 2000. Santa Clara, UCLA. Inducted in 1970. 1948-1956 Los Angeles Rams. **Highlights:** 400 receptions for 5,397 yards, 38 touchdowns. Led NFL receivers first three seasons. Had then-record 18 receptions in single game.

JIM FINKS
Administrator. Born in St. Louis, Missouri, August 31, 1927. Died May 8, 1994. Tulsa. Inducted 1995. 1964-1973 Minnesota Vikings, 1974-1982 Chicago Bears, 1986-1993 New Orleans Saints. **Highlights:** Developed Vikings, Bears, Saints—all teams with losing records—into winners.

RAY FLAHERTY
Coach. Born in Spokane, Washington, September 1, 1903. Died July 19, 1994. Gonzaga. Inducted in 1976. 1936-1942 Boston/Washington Redskins, 1946-48 New York Yankees (AAFC), 1949 Chicago Hornets (AAFC). **Highlights:** 82-41-5 coaching record. Introduced screen pass in 1937 title game and platoon system.

LEN FORD
Defensive end. 6-4, 260. Born in Washington, D.C., February 18, 1926. Died March 14, 1972. Morgan State, Michigan. Inducted in 1976. 1948-49 Los Angeles Dons (AAFC), 1950-57 Cleveland Browns, 1958 Green Bay Packers. **Highlights:** All-NFL five times, four Pro Bowls. Recovered 20 opponents' fumbles.

DAN FORTMANN
Guard. 6-0, 210. Born in Pearl River, New York, April 11, 1916. Died May 23, 1995. Colgate. Inducted in 1965. 1936-1943 Chicago Bears. **Highlights:** At 20, became youngest starter in NFL. First- or second-team All-NFL every season of career.

DAN FOUTS
Quarterback. 6-3, 210. Born in San Francisco, California, June 10, 1951. Oregon. Inducted in 1993. 1973-1987 San Diego Chargers. **Highlights:** 43,040 passing yards, 254 touchdowns. Six Pro Bowls, NFL MVP, 1982.

BENNY FRIEDMAN
Quarterback. 5-10, 183. Born in Cleveland, Ohio, March 18, 1905. Died November 23, 1982. Michigan. Inducted in 2005. 1927 Cleveland Bulldogs, 1928 Detroit Wolverines, 1929-1931 New York Giants, 1932-34 Brooklyn Dodgers. **Highlights:** NFL's first great passer. Set league mark for touchdowns with 20 in 1929. Led NFL in touchdown passes each of his first four seasons.

FRANK GATSKI
Center. 6-3, 240. Born in Farmington, West Virginia, March 18, 1919. Marshall, Auburn. Died November 22, 2005. Inducted in 1985. 1946-49 Cleveland Browns (AAFC), 1950-56 Cleveland Browns, 1957 Detroit Lions. **Highlights:** Never missed game in high school, college, or pro football. Played 11 championship games, winning eight.

BILL GEORGE
Linebacker. 6-2, 230. Born in Waynesburg, Pennsylvania, October 27, 1930. Died September 30, 1982. Wake Forest. Inducted in 1974. 1952-1965 Chicago Bears, 1966 Los Angeles Rams. **Highlights:** All-NFL eight years, eight consecutive Pro Bowls. 14 years of service, longest of any Bears player.

JOE GIBBS
Coach. Born in Mocksville, North Carolina, November 25, 1940. Cerritos (Calif.) J.C., San Diego State. Inducted in 1996. 1981-1992 Washington Redskins. **Highlights:** 124-60-0 record in regular season, 16-5 in postseason, including four Super Bowl appearances—winning three. Won 10 or more games eight times.

FRANK GIFFORD
Halfback. 6-1, 195. Born in Santa Monica, California, August 16, 1930. Southern California. Inducted in 1977. 1952-1960, 1962-64 New York Giants. **Highlights:** Starred on both offense and defense. Seven Pro Bowls, 1956 NFL player of the year.

SID GILLMAN
Coach. Born in Minneapolis, Minnesota, October 26, 1911. Died January 3, 2003. Ohio State. Inducted in 1983. 1955-59 Los Angeles Rams, 1960-69, 1971 Los Angeles/San Diego Chargers, 1973-74 Houston Oilers. **Highlights:** 123-104-7 coaching record. First to win division titles in both NFL, AFL.

OTTO GRAHAM
Quarterback. 6-1, 195. Born in Waukegan, Illinois, December 6, 1921. Died December 17, 2003. Northwestern. Inducted in 1965. 1946-49 Cleveland Browns (AAFC), 1950-55 Cleveland Browns. **Highlights:** 23,584 passing yards, 174 touchdowns. Guided Browns to 10 division or league crowns in 10 years.

HAROLD (RED) GRANGE
Halfback. 6-0, 185. Born in Forksville, Pennsylvania, June 13, 1903. Died January 28, 1991. Illinois. Inducted in 1963. 1925 Chicago Bears, 1926 New York Yankees (AFL), 1927 New York Yankees, 1929-1934 Chicago Bears. **Highlights:** Charter enshrinee. Nicknamed "Galloping Ghost." Name produced first huge pro football crowds.

BUD GRANT
Coach. Born in Superior, Wisconsin, May 20, 1927. Minnesota. Inducted in 1994. 1967-1983, 1985 Minnesota Vikings. **Highlights:** 168-108-5 coaching record. Led Vikings to 11 division championships, four Super Bowls.

JOE GREENE
Defensive tackle. 6-4, 260. Born in Temple, Texas, September 24, 1946. North Texas State. Inducted in 1987. 1969-1981 Pittsburgh Steelers. **Highlights:** NFL defensive player of the year, 1972, 1974. Four-time Super Bowl champion, 10 Pro Bowls.

FORREST GREGG
Tackle. 6-4, 250. Born in Birthright, Texas, October 18, 1933. Southern Methodist. Inducted in 1977. 1956, 1958-1970 Green Bay Packers, 1971 Dallas Cowboys. **Highlights:** Played 188 consecutive games. Nine Pro Bowls. Played on six NFL championship teams, three Super Bowl winners.

BOB GRIESE
Quarterback. 6-1, 190. Born in Evansville, Indiana, February 3, 1945. Purdue. Inducted in 1990. 1967-1980 Miami Dolphins. **Highlights:** 25,092 passing yards, 192 touchdowns. Led Miami to three AFC titles, Super Bowl VII, VIII wins.

LOU GROZA
Tackle-kicker. 6-3, 250. Born in Martins Ferry, Ohio, January 25, 1924. Died November 29, 2000. Ohio State. Inducted in 1974. 1946-49 Cleveland Browns (AAFC), 1950-59, 1961-67 Cleveland Browns. **Highlights:** 1,608 points in 21 years. Nine Pro Bowls, All-NFL six years. NFL player of the year, 1954.

JOE GUYON
Halfback. 6-1, 180. Born on White Earth Indian Reservation, Minnesota, November 26, 1892. Died November 27, 1971. Carlisle, Georgia Tech. Inducted in 1966. 1919-1920 Canton Bulldogs, 1921 Cleveland Indians, 1922-23 Oorang Indians, 1924 Rock Island Independents, 1924-25 Kansas City Cowboys, 1927 New York Giants. **Highlights:** Touchdown pass gave Giants victory over Bears to win 1927 championship.

GEORGE HALAS
End. Coach. Team owner. Born in Chicago, Illinois, February 2, 1895. Died October 31, 1983. Illinois. Inducted in 1963. Player-coach 1920 Decatur Staleys, 1921 Chicago Staleys, 1922-29 Chicago Bears; coach 1933-1942, 1946-1955, 1958-1967 Chicago Bears. **Highlights:** Charter enshrinee. 324 coaching wins. Only person associated with NFL throughout first 50 years. Coached Bears 40 seasons, won six NFL titles.

JACK HAM
Linebacker. 6-1, 225. Born in Johnstown, Pennsylvania, December 23, 1948. Penn State. Inducted in 1988. 1971-1982 Pittsburgh Steelers. **Highlights:** Won four Super Bowls, 21 opponents' fumbles recovered, 32 interceptions. Eight consecutive Pro Bowls.

DAN HAMPTON
Defensive tackle-defensive end. 6-5, 264. Born in Oklahoma City, Oklahoma, September 19, 1957. Arkansas. Inducted in 2002. 1979-1990 Chicago Bears. **Highlights:** A versatile player, he earned all-pro honors at both defensive tackle and defensive end. Named to four Pro Bowls.

JOHN HANNAH
Guard. 6-3, 265. Born in Canton, Georgia, April 4, 1951. Alabama. Inducted in 1991. 1973-1985 New England Patriots. **Highlights:** Renowned as premier guard of era. All-Pro 10 years, nine Pro Bowls.

FRANCO HARRIS
Running back. 6-2, 225. Born in Fort Dix, New Jersey, March 7, 1950. Penn State. Inducted in 1990. 1972-1983 Pittsburgh Steelers, 1984 Seattle Seahawks. **Highlights:** 12,120 rushing yards, 100 total touchdowns. 1,556 rushing yards in 19 postseason games. MVP in Super Bowl IX.

MIKE HAYNES
Cornerback. 6-2, 195. Born in Denison, Texas, July 1, 1953. Arizona State. Inducted in 1997. 1976-1982 New England Patriots, 1983-89 Los Angeles Raiders. **Highlights:** Defensive rookie of the year. Selected to nine Pro Bowls and intercepted 46 passes, plus one pick in Super Bowl XVIII.

ED HEALEY
Tackle. 6-3, 220. Born in Indian Orchard, Massachusetts, December 28, 1894. Died December 9, 1978. Dartmouth. Inducted in 1964. 1920-22 Rock Island Independents, 1922-27 Chicago Bears. **Highlights:** Two-way star. Perennial all-pro with Bears.

MEL HEIN
Center. 6-2, 225. Born in Redding, California, August 22, 1909. Died January 31, 1992. Washington State. Inducted in 1963. 1931-1945 New York Giants. **Highlights:** Charter enshrinee. 60-minute regular for 15 years. All-NFL eight consecutive years.

TED HENDRICKS
Linebacker. 6-7, 235. Born in Guatemala City, Guatemala, November 1, 1947. Miami. Inducted in 1990. 1969-1973 Baltimore Colts, 1974 Green Bay Packers, 1975-1981 Oakland Raiders, 1982-83 Los Angeles Raiders. **Highlights:** 25 blocked field goals, extra points, and punts, 26 interceptions. Played in 215 consecutive games.

WILBUR (PETE) HENRY
Tackle. 6-0, 250. Born in Mansfield, Ohio, October 31, 1897. Died February 7, 1952. Washington & Jefferson. Inducted in 1963. 1920-23, 1925-26 Canton Bulldogs, 1927 New York Giants, 1927-28 Pottsville Maroons. **Highlights:** Charter enshrinee. Largest player of his time at 250 pounds. Bulwark of Canton's championship lines.

ARNIE HERBER
Quarterback. 6-0, 200. Born in Green Bay, Wisconsin, April 2, 1910. Died October 14, 1969. Wisconsin, Regis College. Inducted in 1966. 1930-1940 Green Bay Packers, 1944-45 New York Giants. **Highlights:** NFL passing leader 1932, 1934, 1936. Came out of retirement to lead 1944 Giants to NFL Eastern crown.

BILL HEWITT
End. 5-11, 191. Born in Bay City, Michigan, October 8, 1909. Died January 14, 1947. Michigan. Inducted in 1971. 1932-36 Chicago Bears, 1937-39 Philadelphia Eagles, 1943 Phil-Pitt. **Highlights:** First to be named all-NFL with two teams—1933, 1934, 1936 Bears; 1937 Eagles.

CLARKE HINKLE
Fullback. 5-11, 201. Born in Toronto, Ohio, April 10, 1909. Died November 9, 1988. Bucknell. Inducted in 1964. 1932-1941 Green Bay Packers. **Highlights:** 3,860 yards rushing, 379 points. Fullback on offense, linebacker on defense.

ELROY (CRAZYLEGS) HIRSCH
Halfback-end. 6-2, 190. Born in Wausau, Wisconsin, June 17, 1923. Died January 28, 2004. Wisconsin, Michigan. Inducted in 1968. 1946-48 Chicago Rockets (AAFC), 1949-1957 Los Angeles Rams. **Highlights:** 387 receptions for 7,029 yards, 60 touchdowns. Key part of Rams' revolutionary "three end" offense, 1949.

PAUL HORNUNG
Halfback. 6-2, 220. Born in Louisville, Kentucky, December 23, 1935. Notre Dame. Inducted in 1986. 1957-1962, 1964-66 Green Bay Packers. **Highlights:** 760 points. Led NFL scorers three years, including record 176 points, 1960. Record 19 points scored in 1961 NFL title game.

KEN HOUSTON
Safety. 6-3, 198. Born in Lufkin, Texas, November 12, 1944. Prairie View A&M. Inducted in 1986. 1967-1972 Houston Oilers, 1973-1980 Washington Redskins. **Highlights:** 49 interceptions, 898 yards, 9 touchdowns. NFL's premier strong safety of 1970s. 12 Pro Bowls.

ROBERT (CAL) HUBBARD
Tackle. 6-5, 250. Born in Keytesville, Missouri, October 31, 1900. Died October 17, 1977. Centenary, Geneva. Inducted in 1963. 1927-28 New York Giants, 1929-1933, 1935 Green Bay Packers, 1936 New York Giants, 1936 Pittsburgh Pirates. **Highlights:** Charter enshrinee. Most feared lineman of his time. All-NFL six years, 1927-29, 1931-33.

SAM HUFF
Linebacker. 6-1, 230. Born in Morgantown, West Virginia, October 4, 1934. West Virginia. Inducted in 1982. 1956-1963 New York Giants, 1964-67, 1969 Washington Redskins. **Highlights:** 30 interceptions. Played in six NFL title games, five Pro Bowls. Redskins player-coach, 1969.

LAMAR HUNT
Team owner. Born in El Dorado, Arkansas, August 2, 1932. Southern Methodist. Inducted in 1972. 1959-present Dallas Texans/Kansas City Chiefs. **Highlights:** Driving force behind organization of AFL. Spearheaded merger negotiations with NFL, 1966.

DON HUTSON
End. 6-1, 180. Born in Pine Bluff, Arkansas, January 31, 1913. Died June 26, 1997. Alabama. Inducted in 1963. 1935-1945 Green Bay Packers. **Highlights:** Charter enshrinee. 488 receptions for 7,991 yards, 99 touchdowns. NFL receiving champion eight years. NFL MVP, 1941, 1942.

JIMMY JOHNSON
Cornerback. 6-2, 187. Born in Dallas, Texas, March 31, 1938. UCLA. Inducted in 1994. 1961-1976 San Francisco 49ers. **Highlights:** 47 interceptions for 615 yards. Five Pro Bowls. Opposing passers avoided throwing in his area.

JOHN HENRY JOHNSON
Fullback. 6-2, 225. Born in Waterproof, Louisiana, November 24, 1929. St. Mary's, Arizona State. Inducted in 1987. 1954-56 San Francisco 49ers, 1957-59 Detroit Lions, 1960-65 Pittsburgh Steelers, 1966 Houston Oilers. **Highlights:** 6,803 yards rushing, 55 total touchdowns. Member of San Francisco's "Million-Dollar" backfield.

CHARLIE JOINER
Wide receiver. 5-11, 180. Born in Many, Louisiana, October 14, 1947. Grambling. Inducted in 1996. 1969-1972 Houston Oilers, 1972-75 Cincinnati Bengals, 1976-1986 San Diego Chargers. **Highlights:** 750 receptions for 12,146 yards and 65 touchdowns. Played 18 seasons, 239 games, most ever for wide receiver at time of retirement.

DAVID (DEACON) JONES
Defensive end. 6-5, 260. Born in Eatonville, Florida, December 9, 1938. South Carolina State, Mississippi Vocational. Inducted in 1980. 1961-1971 Los Angeles Rams, 1972-73 San Diego Chargers, 1974 Washington Redskins. **Highlights:** Specialized in quarterback "sacks," a term he invented. Unanimous all-league five consecutive years.

STAN JONES
Guard-defensive tackle. 6-1, 250. Born in Altoona, Pennsylvania, November 24, 1931. Maryland. Inducted in 1991. 1954-1965 Chicago Bears, 1966 Washington Redskins. **Highlights:** Seven consecutive Pro Bowls. First to rely on weightlifting for football preparation.

HENRY JORDAN
Defensive tackle, 6-3, 240. Born in Emporia, Virginia, January 26, 1935. Died February 21, 1977. Virginia. Inducted in 1995. 1957-58 Cleveland Browns, 1959-1969 Green Bay Packers. **Highlights:** Fixture at DT during Packers' dynasty. Played in four Pro Bowls, seven NFL title games, Super Bowls I, II.

SONNY JURGENSEN
Quarterback. 6-0, 203. Born in Wilmington, North Carolina, August 23, 1934. Duke. Inducted in 1983. 1957-1963 Philadelphia Eagles, 1964-1974 Washington Redskins. **Highlights:** 32,224 yards passing, 255 touchdowns, 82.63 passer rating. Surpassed 3,000 yards passing in five seasons.

JIM KELLY
Quarterback. 6-3, 225. Born in Pittsburgh, Pennsylvania, February 14, 1960. Miami. Inducted in 2002. 1986-1996 Buffalo Bills. **Highlights:** Passed for more than 3,000 yards eight times. Mastered the no-huddle offense that propelled Bills to four consecutive Super Bowls.

LEROY KELLY
Running back. 6-0, 205. Born in Philadelphia, Pennsylvania, May 20, 1942. Morgan State. Inducted in 1994. 1964-1973 Cleveland Browns. **Highlights:** 7,274 yards rushing, 90 total touchdowns, 1,000-yard rusher first three years as starter. Punt return champion, 1965.

WALT KIESLING
Guard. Coach. 6-2, 245. Born in St. Paul, Minnesota, March 27, 1903. Died March 2, 1962. St. Thomas (Minnesota). Inducted in 1966. 1926-27 Duluth Eskimos, 1928 Pottsville Maroons, 1929-1933 Chicago Cardinals, 1934 Chicago Bears, 1935-36 Green Bay Packers, 1937-38 Pittsburgh Pirates; coach, 1939 Pittsburgh Pirates, 1940-42 Pittsburgh Steelers; co-coach, 1943 Phil-Pitt, 1944 Card-Pitt; coach, 1954-56 Pittsburgh Steelers. **Highlights:** 34-year career as pro player, assistant coach, head coach. Led Steelers to first winning season, 1942.

FRANK (BRUISER) KINARD
Tackle. 6-1, 210. Born in Pelahatchie, Mississippi, October 23, 1914. Died September 7, 1985. Mississippi. Inducted in 1971. 1938-1943 Brooklyn Dodgers, 1944 Brooklyn Tigers, 1946-47 New York Yankees (AAFC). **Highlights:** First man to earn both All-NFL, All-AAFC honors. Out because of injury only once.

PAUL KRAUSE
Safety. 6-3, 200. Born in Flint, Michigan, February 19, 1942. Iowa. Inducted in 1998. 1964-67 Washington Redskins, 1968-1979 Minnesota Vikings. **Highlights:** NFL all-time leader with 81 interceptions. Played in eight Pro Bowls. Starting safety in four Super Bowls.

EARL (CURLY) LAMBEAU
Coach. Born in Green Bay, Wisconsin, April 9, 1898. Died June 1, 1965. Notre Dame. Inducted in 1963. 1919-1949 Green Bay Packers, 1950-51 Chicago Cardinals, 1952-53 Washington Redskins. **Highlights:** Charter enshrinee. 229-134-22 coaching record with six NFL championships. Founded pre-NFL Packers, 1919.

JACK LAMBERT
Linebacker. 6-4, 220. Born in Mantua, Ohio, July 8, 1952. Kent State. Inducted in 1990. 1974-1984 Pittsburgh Steelers. **Highlights:** Leader of 'Steel Curtain.' NFL defensive player of year in 1976, nine Pro Bowls.

TOM LANDRY
Coach. Born in Mission, Texas, September 11, 1924. Died February 12, 2000. Texas. Inducted in 1990. 1960-1988 Dallas Cowboys. **Highlights:** 270-178-6 coaching record. 20 consecutive winning seasons. Innovator on offense and defense.

DICK (NIGHT TRAIN) LANE
Cornerback. 6-2, 210. Born in Austin, Texas, April 16, 1928. Died January 29, 2002. Scottsbluff Junior College. Inducted in 1974. 1952-53 Los Angeles Rams, 1954-59 Chicago Cardinals, 1960-65 Detroit Lions. **Highlights:** 68 interceptions for 1,207 yards, 5 touchdowns. Record 14 interceptions as rookie. Seven Pro Bowls.

JIM LANGER
Center. 6-2, 255. Born in Little Falls, Minnesota, May 16, 1948. South Dakota State. Inducted in 1987. 1970-79 Miami Dolphins, 1980-81 Minnesota Vikings. **Highlights:** Played every offensive down in Dolphins' perfect 1972 season. Six Pro Bowls.

WILLIE LANIER
Linebacker. 6-1, 245. Born in Clover, Virginia, August 21, 1945. Morgan State. Inducted in 1986. 1967-1977 Kansas City Chiefs. **Highlights:** 27 interceptions. Defensive star in Super Bowl IV upset. Nicknamed 'Contact' for ferocious tackling.

STEVE LARGENT
Wide receiver. 5-11, 191. Born in Tulsa, Oklahoma, September 28, 1954. Tulsa. Inducted in 1995. 1976-1989 Seattle Seahawks. **Highlights:** 819 receptions for 13,089 yards, 100 touchdowns. Receptions in 177 consecutive games.

YALE LARY
Defensive back-punter. 5-11, 189. Born in Fort Worth, Texas, November 24, 1930. Texas A&M. Inducted in 1979. 1952-53, 1956-1964 Detroit Lions. **Highlights:** 50 interceptions. Three NFL punting crowns, three touchdowns on punt returns. Nine Pro Bowls.

DANTE LAVELLI
End. 6-0, 199. Born in Hudson, Ohio, February 23, 1923. Ohio State. Inducted in 1975. 1946-49 Cleveland Browns (AAFC), 1950-56 Cleveland Browns. **Highlights:** 386 receptions for 6,488 yards, 62 touchdowns. 24 catches in six NFL title games.

BOBBY LAYNE
Quarterback. 6-2, 190. Born in Santa Anna, Texas, December 19, 1926. Died December 1, 1986. Texas. Inducted in 1967. 1948 Chicago Bears, 1949 New York Bulldogs, 1950-58 Detroit Lions, 1958-1962 Pittsburgh Steelers. **Highlights:** 26,768 yards passing, 196 touchdowns, 2,451 yards rushing. Late touchdown pass won 1953 NFL title game.

ALPHONSE (TUFFY) LEEMANS
Fullback. 6-0, 200. Born in Superior, Wisconsin, November 12, 1912. Died January 19, 1979. Oregon, George Washington. Inducted in 1978. 1936-1943 New York Giants. **Highlights:** 3,132 yards rushing, 2,318 yards passing, 422 yards receiving. Led NFL rushers as rookie, 1936.

MARV LEVY
Coach. Born in Chicago, Illinois, August 3, 1925. Wyoming, Coe College, Harvard. Inducted in 2001. 1978-1982 Kansas City Chiefs, 1986-1997 Buffalo Bills. **Highlights:** Led Bills to unprecedented four consecutive Super Bowls. Had 154-120 record. Coaching victories ranked 10th when retired.

BOB LILLY
Defensive tackle. 6-5, 260. Born in Olney, Texas, July 26, 1939. Texas Christian. Inducted in 1980. 1961-1974 Dallas Cowboys. **Highlights:** Eleven Pro Bowls. Played 196 consecutive games. Foundation of great Dallas defensive units.

LARRY LITTLE
Guard. 6-1, 265. Born in Groveland, Georgia, November 2, 1945. Bethune-Cookman. Inducted in 1993. 1967-68 San Diego Chargers, 1969-1980 Miami Dolphins. **Highlights:** Five Pro Bowls, started in three Super Bowls. Epitome of powerful Dolphins rushing game of 1970s.

JAMES LOFTON
Wide receiver. 6-3, 192. Born in Fort Ord, California, July 5, 1956. Stanford. Inducted in 2003. 1978-1986 Green Bay Packers, 1987-88 Los Angeles Raiders, 1989-1992 Buffalo Bills, 1993 Los Angeles Rams, 1993 Philadelphia Eagles. **Highlights:** Played 16 seasons, 233 games. Caught 764 passes for 75 touchdowns and a then-record 14,004 yards. All-Pro four times, eight Pro Bowls.

VINCE LOMBARDI
Coach. Born in Brooklyn, New York, June 11, 1913. Died September 3, 1970. Fordham. Inducted in 1971. 1959-1967 Green Bay Packers, 1969 Washington Redskins. **Highlights:** 105-35-6 coaching record in 10 years, including five NFL titles and victories in Super Bowls I and II.

HOWIE LONG
Defensive end. 6-5, 268. Born in Somerville, Massachusetts, January 6, 1960. Villanova. Inducted in 2000. 1981-1993 Oakland/Los Angeles Raiders. **Highlights:** All-Pro 1983, 1984, 1985. Named All-AFC four times, 1983-1986. Eight Pro Bowls.

RONNIE LOTT
Cornerback-safety. 6-0, 203. Born in Albuquerque, New Mexico, May 8, 1959. Southern California. Inducted in 2000. 1981-1990 San Francisco 49ers, 1991-92 Los Angeles Raiders, 1993-94 New York Jets. **Highlights:** Ten Pro Bowls, 63 career interceptions, and was named to the NFL's 75th Anniversary Team.

SID LUCKMAN
Quarterback. 6-0, 195. Born in Brooklyn, New York, November 21, 1916. Died July 5, 1998. Columbia. Inducted in 1965. 1939-1950 Chicago Bears. **Highlights:** 137 touchdown passes. All-NFL five times. League MVP in 1943.

WILLIAM ROY (LINK) LYMAN
Tackle. 6-2, 252. Born in Table Rock, Nebraska, November 30, 1898. Died December 28, 1972. Nebraska. Inducted in 1964. 1922-23, 1925 Canton Bulldogs, 1924 Cleveland Bulldogs, 1925 Frankford Yellowjackets, 1926-28, 1930-31, 1933-34 Chicago Bears. **Highlights:** Played for four NFL champions. In 16 seasons of college and pro football, played on one losing team.

TOM MACK
Guard. 6-3, 250. Born in Cleveland, Ohio, November 1, 1943. Michigan. Inducted in 1999. 1966-1978 Los Angeles Rams. **Highlights:** Never missed a game in entire 184-game career. Elected to 11 Pro Bowls.

JOHN MACKEY
Tight end. 6-2, 224. Born in New York, New York, September 24, 1941. Syracuse. Inducted in 1992. 1963-1971 Baltimore Colts, 1972 San Diego Chargers. **Highlights:** 331 receptions for 5,236 yards, 38 touchdowns. Second tight end to enter Hall of Fame.

JOHN MADDEN
Coach. Born in Austin, Minnesota, April 10, 1936. San Mateo Junior College, California Polytechnic College at San Luis Obispo. Inducted in 2006. 1969-1978 Oakland Raiders. **Highlights:** Became one of youngest coaches in history when hired at age 32. 112-39-7 overall record. Owns best regular season winning percentage among coaches with 100 wins.

TIM MARA
Team owner. Born in New York, New York, July 29, 1887. Died February 16, 1959. Did not attend college. Inducted in 1963. 1925-1959 New York Giants. **Highlights:** Charter enshrinee. Founder of New York Giants. Built team into powerhouse winning four NFL titles, 10 division titles.

WELLINGTON MARA
Team owner. Born in New York, New York, August 14, 1916. Died October 25, 2005. Fordham. Inducted in 1997. 1937-2005 New York Giants. **Highlights:** Lifetime contributor to NFL and New York Giants. Worked as Giants' ballboy, secretary, vice-president, president and co-CEO, NFC president 1984-present.

GINO MARCHETTI
Defensive end. 6-4, 245. Born in Smithers, West Virginia, January 2, 1927. San Francisco. Inducted in 1972. 1952 Dallas Texans, 1953-1964, 1966 Baltimore Colts. **Highlights:** Named top defensive end of NFL's first 50 years. 10 consecutive Pro Bowls. All-NFL seven times.

DAN MARINO
Quarterback. 6-4, 218. Born in Pittsburgh, Pennsylvania, September 15, 1961. Pittsburgh. Inducted in 2005. 1983-1999 Miami Dolphins. **Highlights:** Holds NFL records for career passing yardage (61,361), completions (4,967), attempts (8,358), and touchdowns (420). Voted to nine Pro Bowls.

GEORGE PRESTON MARSHALL
Team owner. Born in Grafton, West Virginia, October 11, 1896. Died August 9, 1969. Randolph-Macon. Inducted in 1963. 1932 Boston Braves, 1933-36 Boston Redskins, 1937-1969 Washington Redskins. **Highlights:** Charter enshrinee. Sponsored progressive rules changes. Organized first team band, pioneered halftime shows.

OLLIE MATSON
Halfback. 6-2, 220. Born in Trinity, Texas, May 1, 1930. San Francisco. Inducted in 1972. 1952, 1954-58 Chicago Cardinals, 1959-1962 Los Angeles Rams, 1963 Detroit Lions, 1964-66 Philadelphia Eagles. **Highlights:** Nine touchdowns on kickoff, punt returns. Traded for nine players in 1959.

DON MAYNARD
Wide receiver. 6-1, 185. Born in Crosbyton, Texas, January 25, 1935. Texas Western. Inducted in 1987. 1958 New York Giants, 1960-62 New York Titans, 1963-1972 New York Jets, 1973 St. Louis Cardinals. **Highlights:** 633 receptions for 11,834 yards, 88 touchdowns. At least 50 catches and 1,000 yards in five different seasons.

GEORGE McAFEE
Halfback. 6-0, 177. Born in Corbin, Kentucky, March 13, 1918. Duke. Inducted in 1966. 1940-41, 1945-1950 Chicago Bears. **Highlights:** Two-way star. 25 interceptions, 234 points. Career punt-return average of 12.78 yards per return.

MIKE McCORMACK
Tackle. 6-4, 250. Born in Chicago, Illinois, June 21, 1930. Kansas. Inducted in 1984. 1951 New York Yanks, 1954-1962 Cleveland Browns. **Highlights:** Excelled as offensive right tackle for eight years. Six Pro Bowls.

TOMMY McDONALD
Wide receiver. 5-9, 175. Born in Roy, New Mexico, July 26, 1934. Oklahoma. Inducted in 1998. 1957-1963 Philadelphia Eagles, 1964 Dallas Cowboys, 1965-66 Los Angeles Rams, 1967 Atlanta Falcons, 1968 Cleveland Browns. **Highlights:** Recorded 495 receptions for 8,410 yards, 84 touchdowns.

HUGH McELHENNY
Halfback. 6-1, 198. Born in Los Angeles, California, December 31, 1928. Washington. Inducted in 1970. 1952-1960 San Francisco 49ers, 1961-62 Minnesota Vikings, 1963 New York Giants, 1964 Detroit Lions. **Highlights:** 5,281 rushing yards, 360 points. Totaled 11,369 yards rushing, receiving, and returning kicks.

JOHNNY (BLOOD) McNALLY
Halfback. 6-0, 185. Born in New Richmond, Wisconsin, November 27, 1903. Died November 28, 1985. Notre Dame, St. John's (Minnesota). Inducted in 1963. 1925-26 Milwaukee Badgers, 1926-27 Duluth Eskimos, 1928 Pottsville Maroons, 1929-1933, 1935-36 Green Bay Packers, 1934 Pittsburgh Pirates; player-coach, 1937-38 Pittsburgh Pirates. **Highlights:** Charter enshrinee. 49 touchdowns, 297 points in 14 seasons with five teams.

MIKE MICHALSKE
Guard. 6-0, 209. Born in Cleveland, Ohio, April 24, 1903. Died October 26, 1983. Penn State. Inducted in 1964. 1926 New York Yankees (AFL), 1927-28 New York Yankees, 1929-1935, 1937 Green Bay Packers. **Highlights:** Anchored Packers' championship lines, 1929-1931. First guard enshrined in Canton.

WAYNE MILLNER
End. 6-0, 191. Born in Roxbury, Massachusetts, January 31, 1913. Died November 19, 1976. Notre Dame. Inducted in 1968. 1936 Boston Redskins, 1937-1941, 1945 Washington Redskins. **Highlights:** Redskins' all-time leader with 124 catches when retired. 55- and 78-yard touchdown receptions in 1937 NFL Championship Game.

BOBBY MITCHELL
Running back-wide receiver. 6-0, 195. Born in Hot Springs, Arkansas, June 6, 1935. Illinois. Inducted in 1983. 1958-1961 Cleveland Browns, 1962-68 Washington Redskins. **Highlights:** 91 touchdowns, including 8 on kickoff and punt returns. 14,078 combined yards.

RON MIX
Tackle. 6-4, 255. Born in Los Angeles, California, March 10, 1938. Southern California. Inducted in 1979. 1960 Los Angeles Chargers, 1961-69 San Diego Chargers, 1971 Oakland Raiders. **Highlights:** All-AFL nine times. Only two holding penalties in 10 years with the Chargers.

JOE MONTANA
Quarterback. 6-2, 200. Born in New Eagle, Pennsylvania, June, 11, 1956. Notre Dame. Inducted in 2000. 1979-1992 San Francisco 49ers, 1993-94 Kansas City Chiefs. **Highlights:** MVP in Super Bowl's XVI, XIX, and XXIV. Eight Pro Bowls and All-NFL three times.

WARREN MOON
Quarterback. 6-3, 212. Born in Los Angeles, California, November 18, 1956. West Los Angeles Junior College, Washington. Inducted in 2006. 1984-1993 Houston Oilers, 1994-1996 Minnesota Vikings, 1997-1998 Seattle Seahawks, 1999-2000 Kansas City Chiefs. **Highlights:** Passed for 49,325 yards and 291 touchdowns in 17 NFL seasons. Elected to nine Pro Bowls including eight straight. Threw for 3,000 yards in nine seasons.

LENNY MOORE
Flanker-running back. 6-1, 198. Born in Reading, Pennsylvania, November 25, 1933. Penn State. Inducted in 1975. 1956-1967 Baltimore Colts. **Highlights:** From 1963-65, scored touchdowns in record 18 consecutive games. 113 career touchdowns, 12,451 combined net yards.

MARION MOTLEY
Fullback. 6-1, 238. Born in Leesburg, Georgia, June 5, 1920. Died June 27, 1999. South Carolina State, Nevada. Inducted in 1968. 1946-49 Cleveland Browns (AAFC), 1950-53 Cleveland Browns, 1955 Pittsburgh Steelers. **Highlights:** AAFC's all-time rushing champion. Led league in rushing in first NFL season.

MIKE MUNCHAK
Guard. 6-3, 281. Born in Scranton, Pennsylvania, March 5, 1960. Penn State. Inducted in 2001. 1982-1993 Houston Oilers. **Highlights:** Devastating blocker, All-AFC seven times, elected to nine Pro Bowls.

ANTHONY MUÑOZ
Tackle. 6-6, 278. Born in Ontario, California, August 19, 1958. Southern California. Inducted in 1998. 1980-1992 Cincinnati Bengals. **Highlights:** All-Pro choice 11 consecutive years, 1981-1991. Selected to 11 straight Pro Bowls.

GEORGE MUSSO
Guard-tackle. 6-2, 270. Born in Collinsville, Illinois. April 8, 1910. Died September 5, 2000. Millikin. Inducted in 1982. 1933-1944 Chicago Bears. **Highlights:** First player to achieve All-NFL status at two positions—tackle in 1935 and guard in 1937.

BRONKO NAGURSKI
Fullback. 6-2, 225. Born in Rainy River, Ontario, Canada, November 3, 1908. Died January 7, 1990. Minnesota. Inducted in 1963. 1930-37, 1943 Chicago Bears. **Highlights:** Charter enshrinee. 2,778 rushing yards in nine seasons. All-NFL five times.

JOE NAMATH
Quarterback. 6-2, 200. Born in Beaver Falls, Pennsylvania, May 31, 1943. Alabama. Inducted in 1985. 1965-1976 New York Jets, 1977 Los Angeles Rams. **Highlights:** First quarterback to pass for more than 4,000 yards in season, 1967. Guaranteed, delivered victory over Colts in Super Bowl III.

EARLE (GREASY) NEALE
Coach. Born in Parkersburg, West Virginia, November 5, 1891. Died November 2, 1973. West Virginia Wesleyan. Inducted in 1969. 1941-42, 1944-1950 Philadelphia Eagles; co-coach, 1943 Phil-Pitt. **Highlights:** Turned Eagles into winners with three consecutive division crowns, NFL championships in 1948 and 1949.

ERNIE NEVERS
Fullback. 6-1, 205. Born in Willow River, Minnesota, June 11, 1903. Died May 3, 1976. Stanford. Inducted in 1963. 1926-27 Duluth Eskimos, 1929-1931 Chicago Cardinals. **Highlights:** Charter enshrinee. Holds NFL's longest-standing record, 40 points in one game in 1929.

OZZIE NEWSOME
Tight end. 6-2, 232. Born in Muscle Shoals, Alabama, March 16, 1956. Alabama. Inducted in 1999. 1978-1990 Cleveland Browns. **Highlights:** Finished career as all-time leader among tight ends with 662 receptions for 7,980 yards.

RAY NITSCHKE
Linebacker. 6-3, 235. Born in Elmwood Park, Illinois, December 29, 1936. Died March 8, 1998. Illinois. Inducted in 1978. 1958-1972 Green Bay Packers. **Highlights:** MVP of 1962 title game. Named NFL's all-time linebacker in 1969.

CHUCK NOLL
Coach. Born in Cleveland, Ohio, January 5, 1932. Dayton. Inducted in 1993. 1969-1991 Pittsburgh Steelers. **Highlights:** Coached for 23 years. Only coach to win four Super Bowl titles (IX, X, XIII, XIV).

LEO NOMELLINI
Defensive tackle. 6-3, 264. Born in Lucca, Italy, June 19, 1924. Died October 17, 2000. Minnesota. Inducted in 1969. 1950-1963 San Francisco 49ers. **Highlights:** Played every 49ers game for 14 seasons. 10 Pro Bowls.

MERLIN OLSEN
Defensive tackle. 6-5, 270. Born in Logan, Utah, September 15, 1940. Utah State. Inducted in 1982. 1962-1976 Los Angeles Rams. **Highlights:** Member of the Fearsome "Foursome. Named" to 14 consecutive Pro Bowls, Rams' all-time team.

JIM OTTO
Center. 6-2, 255. Born in Wausau, Wisconsin, January 5, 1938. Miami. Inducted in 1980. 1960-1974 Oakland Raiders. **Highlights:** Named AFL's all-time center. Played in 210 games, 12 AFL All-Star Games or Pro Bowls, six AFL/AFC title games.

STEVE OWEN
Tackle. Coach. 6-2, 235. Born in Cleo Springs, Oklahoma, April 21, 1898. Died May 17, 1964. Phillips. Inducted in 1966. 1924-25 Kansas City Cowboys, 1925 Cleveland Bulldogs, 1926-1931, 1933 New York Giants; coach, 1930-1953 New York Giants. **Highlights:** Both player and coach. Coached Giants to record of 155-108-17, eight divisional titles, two NFL championships.

ALAN PAGE
Defensive tackle. 6-4, 225. Born in Canton, Ohio, August 7, 1945. Notre Dame. Inducted in 1988. 1967-1978 Minnesota Vikings, 1978-1981 Chicago Bears. **Highlights:** Dominating defensive tackle played in 218 consecutive games, four Super Bowls. Won league MVP honors in 1971.

CLARENCE (ACE) PARKER
Quarterback. 5-11, 168. Born in Portsmouth, Virginia, May 17, 1912. Duke. Inducted in 1972. 1937-1941 Brooklyn Dodgers, 1945 Boston Yanks, 1946 New York Yankees (AAFC). **Highlights:** Two-way threat. Two-time All-NFL performer, league MVP in 1940.

JIM PARKER
Guard-tackle. 6-3, 273. Born in Macon, Georgia, April 3, 1934. Died July 18, 2005. Ohio State. Inducted in 1973. 1957-1967 Baltimore Colts. **Highlights:** First full-time offensive lineman elected to Hall of Fame. All-NFL eight consecutive years, eight Pro Bowls.

WALTER PAYTON
Running back. 5-10, 202. Born in Columbia, Mississippi, July 25, 1954. Died November 1, 1999. Jackson State. Inducted in 1993. 1975-1987 Chicago Bears. **Highlights:** NFL's all-time leading rusher with 16,726 yards and combined net yardage with 21,803 at time of retirement.

JOE PERRY
Fullback. 6-0, 200. Born in Stevens, Arkansas, January 22, 1927. Compton Junior College. Inducted in 1969. 1948-49 San Francisco 49ers (AAFC), 1950-1960, 1963 San Francisco 49ers, 1961-62 Baltimore Colts. **Highlights:** First player in NFL history to gain 1,000 yards two consecutive seasons. 12,532 combined yards.

PETE PIHOS
End. 6-1, 210. Born in Orlando, Florida, October 22, 1923. Indiana. Inducted in 1970. 1947-1955 Philadelphia Eagles. **Highlights:** Three-time NFL receiving champion. Caught winning touchdown in 1949 NFL Championship Game.

FRITZ POLLARD
Halfback-Coach. 5-9, 165. Born in Chicago, Illinois, January 27, 1894. Died May 11, 1986. Brown. Inducted in 2005. 1919-1921, 1925-26 Akron Pros/Indians, 1922 Milwaukee Badgers, 1923, 1925 Hammond Pros, 1925 Providence Steam Roller. **Highlights:** True pioneer as one of two African American players in the NFL in 1920 and helped lead Akron to league title that season. In 1921, became the league's first black head coach.

HUGH (SHORTY) RAY
Supervisor of officials 1938-1952. Born in Highland Park, Illinois, September 21, 1884. Died September 16, 1956. Illinois. Inducted in 1966. **Highlights:** Supervisor of Officials, 1938-1952. Streamlined rules to improve game tempo, player safety.

DAN REEVES
Team owner. Born in New York, New York, June 30, 1912. Died April 15, 1971. Georgetown. Inducted in 1967. 1941-45 Cleveland Rams, 1946-1971 Los Angeles Rams. **Highlights:** Moved Rams to Los Angeles in 1946 and opened up West Coast to pro football. First postwar owner to sign African-American player.

MEL RENFRO
Cornerback-safety. 6-0, 192. Born in Houston, Texas, December 30, 1941. Oregon. Inducted in 1996. 1964-1977 Dallas Cowboys. **Highlights:** 52 interceptions for 626 yards and 3 touchdowns. Also added 842 yards on punt returns, 2,246 yards on kickoff returns. Elected to Pro Bowl first 10 seasons.

JOHN RIGGINS
Running back. 6-2, 240. Born in Seneca, Kansas, August 4, 1949. Kansas. Inducted in 1992. 1971-75 New York Jets, 1976-79, 1981-85 Washington Redskins. **Highlights:** 11,352 rushing yards, 116 total touchdowns. MVP of Super Bowl XVII with 166 rushing yards including game-winning 43-yard touchdown.

JIM RINGO
Center. 6-2, 230. Born in Orange, New Jersey, November 21, 1931. Syracuse. Inducted in 1981. 1953-1963 Green Bay Packers, 1964-67 Philadelphia Eagles. **Highlights:** Ten-time Pro Bowl selection, seven-time All-NFL selection. Started in then-record 182 consecutive games.

ANDY ROBUSTELLI
Defensive end. 6-0, 230. Born in Stamford, Connecticut, December 6, 1925. Arnold College. Inducted in 1971. 1951-55 Los Angeles Rams, 1956-1964 New York Giants. **Highlights:** Anchored defense in eight championship games. Named NFL's top player in 1962.

ART ROONEY
Team owner. Born in Coulterville, Pennsylvania, January 27, 1901. Died August 25, 1988. Georgetown, Duquesne. Inducted in 1964. 1933-39 Pittsburgh Pirates, 1940-42, 1945-1988 Pittsburgh Steelers, 1943 Phil-Pitt, 1944 Card-Pitt. **Highlights:** Founded Pittsburgh Pirates in 1933 and renamed them Steelers in 1940. Team won four Super Bowls in 1970s.

DAN ROONEY
Team owner. Born in Pittsburgh, Pennsylvania, July, 20, 1932. Duquesne. Inducted in 2000. 1955-present Pittsburgh Steelers. **Highlights:** Has been on the board of directors for the NFL Trust Fund, NFL Films, and Scheduling Committee. Played a key role in the labor agreement reached in 1993 between the NFL owners and players.

PETE ROZELLE
Commissioner. Born in South Gate, California, March 1, 1926. Died December 6, 1996. Compton Junior College, San Francisco. Inducted in 1985. Commissioner, 1960-1989. **Highlights:** Negotiated first league-wide television contract in 1962. Generally recognized as premiere commissioner in all of sports. Credited with making NFL the nation's most popular sport.

BOB ST. CLAIR
Tackle. 6-9, 265. Born in San Francisco, California, February 18, 1931. San Francisco, Tulsa. Inducted in 1990. 1953-1963 San Francisco 49ers. **Highlights:** Exceptional offensive lineman. Also played goal-line defense and had 10 blocked field goals, 1956.

BARRY SANDERS
Running back. 5-8, 203. Born in Wichita, Kansas, July 16, 1968. Oklahoma State. Inducted in 2004. 1989-1998 Detroit Lions. **Highlights:** 15,269 rushing yards, 99 touchdowns. Rushed for 1,000 yards in each of 10 seasons. NFL co-MVP, 1997. Selected to 10 Pro Bowls.

GALE SAYERS
Running back. 6-0, 200. Born in Wichita, Kansas, May 30, 1943. Kansas. Inducted in 1977. 1965-1971 Chicago Bears. **Highlights:** Broke into league by scoring rookie-record 22 touchdowns. Led league in rushing in 1966, 1969. MVP of three Pro Bowls.

JOE SCHMIDT
Linebacker. 6-0, 222. Born in Pittsburgh, Pennsylvania, January 18, 1932. Pittsburgh. Inducted in 1973. 1953-1965 Detroit Lions. **Highlights:** 24 interceptions. Lions' team captain for nine years. Mastered middle linebacker position that evolved in 1950s.

TEX SCHRAMM
Team president-general manager. Born in San Gabriel, California, June 2, 1920. Died July 15, 2003. Texas. Inducted in 1991. 1947-1956 Los Angeles Rams. 1960-1989 Dallas Cowboys. **Highlights:** Played prominent role in AFL-NFL merger. Chairman of Competition Committee from 1966-1988.

LEE ROY SELMON
Defensive end. 6-3, 250. Born in Eufaula, Oklahoma, October 20, 1954. Oklahoma. Inducted in 1995. 1976-1984 Tampa Bay Buccaneers. **Highlights:** 78½ sacks, 380 quarterback pressures, forced 28 fumbles. Six consecutive Pro Bowl selections.

BILLY SHAW
Guard. 6-2, 258. Born in Natchez, Mississippi, December 15, 1938. Georgia Tech. Inducted in 1999. 1961-69 Buffalo Bills. **Highlights:** First player who played entire career in AFL to be elected to Hall of Fame. Named to AFL's all-time team.

ART SHELL
Tackle. 6-5, 285. Born in Charleston, South Carolina, November 26, 1946. Maryland State-Eastern Shore. Inducted in 1989. 1968-82 Oakland/Los Angeles Raiders. **Highlights:** Cornerstone of Raiders' offensive line in 1970s. 207 regular-season games, 23 postseason games, eight Pro Bowls.

DON SHULA
Coach. Born in Grand River, Ohio, January 4, 1930. John Carroll. Inducted in 1997. 1963-69 Baltimore Colts, 1970-1995 Miami Dolphins. **Highlights:** Won more games (347) than any coach in NFL history. Won two Super Bowl titles, including Super Bowl VII when Dolphins recorded NFL's only perfect season (17-0).

O.J. SIMPSON
Running back. 6-1, 212. Born in San Francisco, California, July 9, 1947. City College (San Francisco), Southern California. Inducted in 1985. 1969-1977 Buffalo Bills, 1978-79 San Francisco 49ers. **Highlights:** In 1973, became first player to rush for 2,000 yards in season. Finished career with four rushing titles, 11,236 yards.

MIKE SINGLETARY
Linebacker. 6-0, 230. Born in Houston, Texas, October 9, 1958. Baylor. Inducted in 1998. 1981-1992 Chicago Bears. **Highlights:** All-Pro choice eight times and All-NFC nine consecutive seasons. Selected to 10 Pro Bowls.

JACKIE SLATER
Tackle. 6-4, 277. Born in Jackson, Mississippi, May 27, 1954. Jackson State. Inducted in 2001. 1976-1995 Los Angeles/St. Louis Rams. **Highlights:** Played 20 seasons, 259 games. Blocked for seven different 1,000-yard rushers. Seven Pro Bowls.

JACKIE SMITH
Tight end. 6-4, 232. Born in Columbia, Mississippi, February 23, 1940. Northwestern State (Louisiana). Inducted in 1994. 1963-1977 St. Louis Cardinals, 1978 Dallas Cowboys. **Highlights:** 480 receptions for 7,918 yards, 40 touchdowns. Third tight end to be elected to Hall of Fame.

JOHN STALLWORTH
Wide receiver. 6-2, 191. Born in Tuscaloosa, Alabama, July 15, 1952. Alabama A&M. Inducted in 2002. 1974-1987 Pittsburgh Steelers. **Highlights:** 537 receptions for 8,723 yards, 63 touchdowns. Scored go-ahead touchdown in Super Bowl XIV on 73-yard reception.

BART STARR
Quarterback. 6-1, 200. Born in Montgomery, Alabama, January 9, 1934. Alabama. Inducted in 1977. 1956-1971 Green Bay Packers. **Highlights:** Quarterbacked Packers to six division titles, five NFL titles, and first two Super Bowls in which he was MVP.

ROGER STAUBACH
Quarterback. 6-3, 202. Born in Cincinnati, Ohio, February 5, 1942. New Mexico Military Institute, Navy. Inducted in 1985. 1969-1979 Dallas Cowboys. **Highlights:** Led Cowboys to four NFC titles and victories in Super Bowls VI, XII. When retired, 83.4 career passer rating was best of all time.

ERNIE STAUTNER
Defensive tackle. 6-2, 235. Born in Prinzing-by-Cham, Bavaria, April 20, 1925. Died February 16, 2006. Boston College. Inducted in 1969. 1950-1963 Pittsburgh Steelers. **Highlights:** Played in nine Pro Bowls and won the best lineman award in 1957. Recorded 3 safeties.

JAN STENERUD
Kicker. 6-2, 190. Born in Fetsund, Norway, November 26, 1942. Montana State. Inducted in 1991. 1967-1979 Kansas City Chiefs, 1980-83 Green Bay Packers, 1984-85 Minnesota Vikings. **Highlights:** 1,699 points on 580 extra points, 373 field goals. First pure placekicker to enter Hall of Fame.

DWIGHT STEPHENSON
Center. 6-2, 255. Born in Murfreesboro, North Carolina, November 20, 1957. Alabama. Inducted in 1998. 1980-87 Miami Dolphins. **Highlights:** Recognized as premier center of his time. All-Pro, All-AFC five straight years. Selected to five Pro Bowls.

HANK STRAM
Coach. Born in Chicago, Illinois, January 3, 1923. Died July 4, 2005. Purdue. Inducted in 2003. 1960-1974 Dallas Texans/Kansas City Chiefs, 1976-1977 New Orleans Saints. **Highlights:** Overall record of 136-100-10. Recorded most wins in AFL history. Guided teams to titles in 1962, 1966, and 1969. Led Chiefs to AFL win in Super Bowl IV.

KEN STRONG
Halfback. 5-11, 210. Born in West Haven, Connecticut, April 21, 1906. Died October 5, 1979. New York University. Inducted in 1967. 1929-1932 Staton Island Stapletons, 1933-35, 1939, 1944-47 New York Giants, 1936-37 New York Yanks (AFL). **Highlights:** Scored 17 points to lead Giants to victory in 1934 'Sneakers' game, led NFL with 64 points, 1933.

JOE STYDAHAR
Tackle. 6-4, 230. Born in Kaylor, Pennsylvania, March 17, 1912. Died March 23, 1977. West Virginia. Inducted in 1967. 1936-1942, 1945-46 Chicago Bears. **Highlights:** One of stalwarts of Bears' 'Monsters of the Midway.' Played on five divisional, three NFL championship teams.

LYNN SWANN
Wide receiver. 5-11, 180. Born in Alcoa, Tennessee, March 7, 1952. Southern California. Inducted in 2001. 1974-1982 Pittsburgh Steelers. **Highlights:** All-AFC three times. Selected to three Pro Bowls. MVP, Super Bowl X.

FRAN TARKENTON
Quarterback. 6-0, 185. Born in Richmond, Virginia, February 3, 1940. Georgia. Inducted in 1986. 1961-66, 1972-78 Minnesota Vikings, 1967-1971 New York Giants. **Highlights:** At retirement, held NFL records for attempts (6,467), completions (3,686), yards (47,003), and touchdowns (342). Four touchdown passes in first NFL game.

CHARLEY TAYLOR
Running back-wide receiver. 6-3, 210. Born in Grand Prairie, Texas, September 28, 1941. Arizona State. Inducted in 1984. 1964-1975, 1977 Washington Redskins. **Highlights:** Won rookie of year honors as running back. Switched to wide receiver and won receiving titles in 1966, 1967.

JIM TAYLOR
Fullback. 6-0, 216. Born in Baton Rouge, Louisiana, September 20, 1935. Louisiana State. Inducted in 1976. 1958-1966 Green Bay Packers, 1967 New Orleans Saints. **Highlights:** 8,597 rushing yards, 558 points. In 1962, led league in rushing and scoring with 19 touchdowns.

LAWRENCE TAYLOR
Linebacker. 6-3, 237. Born in Williamsburg, Virginia, February 4, 1959. North Carolina. Inducted in 1999. 1981-1993 New York Giants. **Highlights:** Redefined the position of outside linebacker. All-Pro nine times, 10 Pro Bowls. NFL MVP in 1986.

JIM THORPE
Halfback. 6-1, 190. Born in Prague, Oklahoma, May 28, 1888. Died March 28, 1953. Carlisle. Inducted in 1963. 1915-17, 1919-1920, 1926 Canton Bulldogs, 1921 Cleveland Indians, 1922-23 Oorang Indians, 1924 Rock Island Independents, 1925 New York Giants, 1928 Chicago Cardinals. **Highlights:** Charter enshrinee. First president of American Professional Football Association, 1920. Played for 12 seasons.

Y.A. TITTLE
Quarterback. 6-0, 200. Born in Marshall, Texas, October 24, 1926. Louisiana State. Inducted in 1971. 1948-49 Baltimore Colts (AAFC), 1950 Baltimore Colts, 1951-1960 San Francisco 49ers, 1961-64 New York Giants. **Highlights:** 33,070 yards, 242 touchdowns. 33 touchdown passes in 1962 and 36 in 1963. Two-time league MVP.

GEORGE TRAFTON
Center. 6-2, 235. Born in Chicago, Illinois, December 6, 1896. Died September 5, 1971. Notre Dame. Inducted in 1964. 1920-1932 Decatur Staleys/Chicago Staleys/Chicago Bears. **Highlights:** First center to snap with one hand. Named top NFL center of 1920s.

CHARLEY TRIPPI
Halfback-quarterback. 6-0, 185. Born in Pittston, Pennsylvania, December 14, 1922. Georgia. Inducted in 1968. 1947-1955 Chicago Cardinals. **Highlights:** One of football's most versatile performers. Played halfback five years, quarterback for two, defense for two.

EMLEN TUNNELL
Safety. 6-1, 200. Born in Bryn Mawr, Pennsylvania, March 29, 1925. Died July 22, 1975. Toledo, Iowa. Inducted in 1967. 1948-1958 New York Giants, 1959-1961 Green Bay Packers. **Highlights:** 79 interceptions. Gained more yards on kickoff, punt, and interception returns (924) in 1952 than that season's NFL rushing leader.

CLYDE (BULLDOG) TURNER
Center. 6-2, 235. Born in Plains, Texas, March 10, 1919. Died October 30, 1998. Hardin-Simmons. Inducted in 1966. 1940-1952 Chicago Bears. **Highlights:** Anchored defense for four NFL championship teams, including 4 interceptions in five title games.

JOHNNY UNITAS
Quarterback. 6-1, 195. Born in Pittsburgh, Pennsylvania, May 7, 1933. Died September 11, 2002. Louisville. Inducted in 1979. 1956-1972 Baltimore Colts, 1973 San Diego Chargers. **Highlights:** 40,239 passing yards, 290 touchdowns. Led Colts to two NFL championships. Passed for at least one touchdown in 47 consecutive games.

GENE UPSHAW
Guard. 6-5, 255. Born in Robstown, Texas, August 15, 1945. Texas A & I. Inducted in 1987. 1967-1981 Oakland Raiders. **Highlights:** Premier guard of his era played in 10 AFL/AFC Championship Games, three Super Bowls, seven Pro Bowls.

NORM VAN BROCKLIN
Quarterback. 6-1, 190. Born in Eagle Butte, South Dakota, March 15, 1926. Died May 2, 1983. Oregon. Inducted in 1971. 1949-1957 Los Angeles Rams, 1958-1960 Philadelphia Eagles. **Highlights:** NFL-record 554 yards passing in 1951 season opener. Guided Eagles to NFL crown as league MVP in 1960.

STEVE VAN BUREN
Halfback. 6-1, 200. Born in La Ceiba, Honduras, December 28, 1920. Louisiana State. Inducted in 1965. 1944-1951 Philadelphia Eagles. **Highlights:** Four-time rushing champion. Won 1944 punt-return title and was 1945 kickoff-return champion.

DOAK WALKER
Halfback. 5-11, 173. Born in Dallas, Texas, January 1, 1927. Died September 27, 1998. Southern Methodist. Inducted in 1986. 1950-55 Detroit Lions. **Highlights:** 534 points. Won two NFL scoring titles. Had winning 67-yard scoring run in 1952 title game.

BILL WALSH
Coach. Born in Los Angeles, California, November 30, 1931. San Jose State. Inducted in 1993. 1979-1988 San Francisco 49ers. **Highlights:** 102-63-1 coaching record. Guided 49ers to three Super Bowl titles (XVI, XIX, XXIII) in 10 years.

PAUL WARFIELD
Wide receiver. 6-0, 188. Born in Warren, Ohio, November 28, 1942. Ohio State. Inducted in 1983. 1964-69, 1976-77 Cleveland Browns, 1970-74 Miami Dolphins. **Highlights:** 8,565 yards receiving, 85 touchdowns. Eight-time Pro Bowl player. Key to both Cleveland and Miami offenses.

BOB WATERFIELD
Quarterback. 6-2, 200. Born in Elmira, New York, July 26, 1920. Died March 25, 1983. UCLA. Inducted in 1965. 1945 Cleveland Rams, 1946-1952 Los Angeles Rams. **Highlights:** NFL MVP as rookie in 1945 and led Rams to NFL title. Grabbed 20 interceptions in limited defensive duties.

MIKE WEBSTER
Center. 6-2, 260. Born in Tomahawk, Wisconsin, March 18, 1952. Died September 24, 2002. Wisconsin. Inducted in 1997. 1974-1988 Pittsburgh Steelers, 1989-1990 Kansas City Chiefs. **Highlights:** Played in 245 games, nine Pro Bowls, and won four Super Bowls during 17-year career.

ARNIE WEINMEISTER
Defensive tackle. 6-4, 235. Born in Rhein, Saskatchewan, Canada, March 23, 1923. Died June 29, 2000. Washington. Inducted in 1984. 1948-49 New York Yankees (AAFC), 1950-53 New York Giants. **Highlights:** Dominant defensive tackle of his time. Four-time All-NFL selection, four Pro Bowls.

RANDY WHITE
Defensive tackle. 6-4, 265. Born in Pittsburgh, Pennsylvania, January 15, 1953. Maryland. Inducted in 1994. 1975-1988 Dallas Cowboys. **Highlights:** Missed only one game in 14 seasons. Co-MVP of Super Bowl XII. Nine-time Pro Bowl selection.

REGGIE WHITE
Defensive tackle-defensive end. 6-5, 291. Born in Chattanooga, Tennessee, December 19, 1961. Died December 26, 2004. Tennessee. Inducted in 2006. 1985-1992 Philadelphia Eagles, 1993-1998 Green Bay Packers, 2000 Carolina Panthers. **Highlights:** Retired as all-time sack leader with 198. Named All-Pro 13 of 15 seasons including 10 as first-team selection. Named to 13 straight Pro Bowls.

DAVE WILCOX
Linebacker. 6-3, 241. Born in Ontario, Oregon, September, 29, 1942. Boise State, Oregon. Inducted in 2000. 1964-1974 San Francisco 49ers. **Highlights:** Seven Pro Bowls, All-NFL five times. Missed only one game because of injury.

BILL WILLIS
Guard. 6-2, 215. Born in Columbus, Ohio, October 5, 1921. Ohio State. Inducted in 1977. 1946-1953 Cleveland Browns (AAFC/NFL). **Highlights:** Two-way player who excelled on defense. Four-time All-NFL player, played in three Pro Bowls.

LARRY WILSON
Safety. 6-0, 190. Born in Rigby, Idaho, March 24, 1938. Utah. Inducted in 1978. 1960-1972 St. Louis Cardinals. **Highlights:** 52 interceptions. Had interception in seven consecutive games in 1966. Made "safety blitz" famous.

KELLEN WINSLOW
Tight end. 6-5, 250. Born in St. Louis, Missouri, November 5, 1957. Missouri. Inducted in 1995. 1979-1987 San Diego Chargers **Highlights:** 541 receptions for 6,741 yards, 45 touchdowns. 13 catches, blocked field goal in 1981 playoff win over Miami.

ALEX WOJCIECHOWICZ
Center. 6-0, 235. Born in South River, New Jersey, August 12, 1915. Died July 13, 1992. Fordham. Inducted in 1968. 1938-1946 Detroit Lions, 1946-1950 Philadelphia Eagles. **Highlights:** One of league's first iron men. Played both ways for eight years with Lions.

WILLIE WOOD
Safety. 5-10, 190. Born in Washington, D.C., December 23, 1936. Southern California. Inducted in 1989. 1960-1971 Green Bay Packers. **Highlights:** 48 interceptions. Competed in six NFL Championship Games and Super Bowls I and II.

RAYFIELD WRIGHT
Tackle. 6-6, 255. Born in Griffin, Georgia, August 23, 1945. Fort Valley State. Inducted in 2006. 1967-1979 Dallas Cowboys. **Highlights:** Named first- or second-team All-Pro and voted to Pro Bowl six straight seasons, 1971-76. Played in six NFC championship games and five Super Bowls. Named to NFL's All-Decade Team of 1970s.

RON YARY
Tackle. 6-5, 255. Born in Chicago, Illinois, July 16, 1946. Cerritos (Calif.) J.C., Southern California. Inducted in 2001. 1968-1981 Minnesota Vikings, 1982 Los Angeles Rams. **Highlights:** All-Pro six consecutive seasons, All-NFC eight consecutive years. Named to seven Pro Bowls. Started in four Super Bowls and five NFL/NFC Championship Games.

STEVE YOUNG
Quarterback. 6-2, 205. Born in Salt Lake City, Utah, October 11, 1961. Brigham Young. Inducted in 2005. 1985-86 Tampa Bay Buccaneers, 1987-1999 San Francisco 49ers. **Highlights:** Led the NFL in passing a record-tying six times. Passed for more than 33,000 yards and 232 touchdowns in career. MVP of Super Bowl XXIX. Elected to seven Pro Bowls.

JACK YOUNGBLOOD
Defensive end. 6-4, 247. Born in Jacksonville, Florida, January 26, 1950. Florida. Inducted in 2001. 1971-1984 Los Angeles Rams. **Highlights:** Played in club-record 201 consecutive games. Played in five NFC Championship Games, one Super Bowl. Named All-Pro five times, All-NFC seven times. Elected to seven consecutive Pro Bowls.

ENSHRINEES BY YEAR OF INDUCTION
*Deceased
(Date of enshrinement in parentheses)

1963 CHARTER CLASS
(September 7, 1963)
Sammy Baugh
Bert Bell*
Joe Carr*
Earl (Dutch) Clark*
Harold (Red) Grange*
George Halas*
Mel Hein*
Wilbur (Pete) Henry*
Robert (Cal) Hubbard*
Don Hutson*
Earl (Curly) Lambeau*
Tim Mara*
George Preston Marshall*
John (Blood) McNally*
Bronko Nagurski*
Ernie Nevers*
Jim Thorpe*

CLASS OF 1964
(September 6, 1964)
Jimmy Conzelman*
Ed Healey*
Clarke Hinkle*
William Roy (Link) Lyman*
Mike Michalske*
Art Rooney*
George Trafton*

CLASS OF 1965
(September 12, 1965)
Guy Chamberlin*
John (Paddy) Driscoll*
Dan Fortmann*
Otto Graham*
Sid Luckman*
Steve Van Buren*
Bob Waterfield*

CLASS OF 1966
(September 17, 1966)
Bill Dudley
Joe Guyon*
Arnie Herber*
Walt Kiesling*
George McAfee*
Steve Owen*
Hugh (Shorty) Ray*
Clyde (Bulldog) Turner*

CLASS OF 1967
(August 5, 1967)
Chuck Bednarik
Charles W. Bidwill Sr.*
Paul Brown*
Bobby Layne*
Dan Reeves*
Ken Strong*
Joe Stydahar*
Emlen Tunnell*

CLASS OF 1968
(August 3, 1968)
Cliff Battles*
Art Donovan
Elroy (Crazylegs) Hirsch*
Wayne Millner*
Marion Motley*
Charley Trippi*
Alex Wojciechowicz*

CLASS OF 1969
(September 13, 1969)
Albert Glen (Turk) Edwards*
Earle (Greasy) Neale*
Leo Nomellini*
Joe Perry
Ernie Stautner*

CLASS OF 1970
(August 8, 1970)
Jack Christiansen*
Tom Fears*
Hugh McElhenny
Pete Pihos

CLASS OF 1971
(July 31, 1971)
Jim Brown
Bill Hewitt*
Frank (Bruiser) Kinard*
Vince Lombardi*
Andy Robustelli
Y. A. Tittle
Norm Van Brocklin*

CLASS OF 1972
(July 29, 1972)
Lamar Hunt
Gino Marchetti
Ollie Matson
Clarence (Ace) Parker

CLASS OF 1973
(July 28, 1973)
Raymond Berry
Jim Parker*
Joe Schmidt

CLASS OF 1974
(July 27, 1974)
Tony Canadeo*
Bill George*
Lou Groza*
Dick (Night Train) Lane*

CLASS OF 1975
(August 2, 1975)
Roosevelt Brown*
George Connor*
Dante Lavelli
Lenny Moore

CLASS OF 1976
(July 24, 1976)
Ray Flaherty*
Len Ford*
Jim Taylor

CLASS OF 1977
(July 30, 1977)
Frank Gifford
Forrest Gregg
Gale Sayers
Bart Starr
Bill Willis

CLASS OF 1978
(July 29, 1978)
Lance Alworth
Weeb Ewbank*
Alphonse (Tuffy) Leemans*
Ray Nitschke*
Larry Wilson

CLASS OF 1979
(July 28, 1979)
Dick Butkus
Yale Lary
Ron Mix
Johnny Unitas*

CLASS OF 1980
(August 2, 1980)
Herb Adderley
David (Deacon) Jones
Bob Lilly
Jim Otto

CLASS OF 1981
(August 1, 1981)
Morris (Red) Badgro*
George Blanda
Willie Davis
Jim Ringo

CLASS OF 1982
(August 7, 1982)
Doug Atkins
Sam Huff
George Musso*
Merlin Olsen

CLASS OF 1983
(July 30, 1983)
Bobby Bell
Sid Gillman*
Sonny Jurgensen
Bobby Mitchell
Paul Warfield

CLASS OF 1984
(July 28, 1984)
Willie Brown
Mike McCormack
Charley Taylor
Arnie Weinmeister*

CLASS OF 1985
(August 3, 1985)
Frank Gatski*
Joe Namath
Pete Rozelle*
O. J. Simpson
Roger Staubach

CLASS OF 1986
(August 2, 1986)
Paul Hornung
Ken Houston
Willie Lanier
Fran Tarkenton
Doak Walker*

CLASS OF 1987
(August 8, 1987)
Larry Csonka
Len Dawson
Joe Greene
John Henry Johnson
Jim Langer
Don Maynard
Gene Upshaw

CLASS OF 1988
(July 30, 1988)
Fred Biletnikoff
Mike Ditka
Jack Ham
Alan Page

CLASS OF 1989
(August 5, 1989)
Mel Blount
Terry Bradshaw
Art Shell
Willie Wood

CLASS OF 1990
(August 4, 1990)
Buck Buchanan*
Bob Griese
Franco Harris
Ted Hendricks
Jack Lambert
Tom Landry*
Bob St. Clair

CLASS OF 1991
(July 27, 1991)
Earl Campbell
John Hannah
Stan Jones
Tex Schramm*
Jan Stenerud

CLASS OF 1992
(August 1, 1992)
Lem Barney
Al Davis
John Mackey
John Riggins

CLASS OF 1993
(July 31, 1993)
Dan Fouts
Larry Little
Chuck Noll
Walter Payton*
Bill Walsh

CLASS OF 1994
(July 30, 1994)
Tony Dorsett
Bud Grant
Jimmy Johnson
Leroy Kelly
Jackie Smith
Randy White

CLASS OF 1995
(July 29, 1995)
Jim Finks*
Henry Jordan*
Steve Largent
Lee Roy Selmon
Kellen Winslow

CLASS OF 1996
(July 27, 1996)
Lou Creekmur
Dan Dierdorf
Joe Gibbs
Charlie Joiner
Mel Renfro

CLASS OF 1997
(July 26, 1997)
Mike Haynes
Wellington Mara*
Don Shula
Mike Webster*

CLASS OF 1998
(August 1, 1998)
Paul Krause
Tommy McDonald
Anthony Muñoz
Mike Singletary
Dwight Stephenson

CLASS OF 1999
(August 7, 1999)
Eric Dickerson
Tom Mack
Ozzie Newsome
Billy Shaw
Lawrence Taylor

CLASS OF 2000
(July 29, 2000)
Howie Long
Ronnie Lott
Joe Montana
Dan Rooney
Dave Wilcox

CLASS OF 2001
(August 4, 2001)
Nick Buoniconti
Marv Levy
Mike Munchak
Jackie Slater
Lynn Swann
Ron Yary
Jack Youngblood

CLASS OF 2002
(August 3, 2002)
George Allen*
Dave Casper
Dan Hampton
Jim Kelly
John Stallworth

CLASS OF 2003
(August 3, 2003)
Marcus Allen
Elvin Bethea
Joe DeLamielleure
James Lofton
Hank Stram*

CLASS OF 2004
(August 8, 2004)
Bob (Boomer) Brown
Carl Eller
John Elway
Barry Sanders

CLASS OF 2005
(August 7, 2005)
Benny Friedman*
Dan Marino
Fritz Pollard*
Steve Young

CLASS OF 2006
(August 6, 2006)
Troy Aikman
Harry Carson
John Madden
Warren Moon
Reggie White*
Rayfield Wright

PRO FOOTBALL HALL OF FAME GAME (43)

Date	Winner	Loser	Attendance
August 11, 1962	New York Giants 21	St. Louis Cardinals 21	14,000
September 8, 1963	Pittsburgh Steelers 16	Cleveland Browns 7	18,462
September 6, 1964	Baltimore Colts 48	Pittsburgh Steelers 17	11,479
September 12, 1965	Washington Redskins 20	Detroit Lions 3	14,416
1966	No game was played		
August 5, 1967	Philadelphia Eagles 28	Cleveland Browns 13	17,304
August 3, 1968	Chicago Bears 30	Dallas Cowboys 24	14,578
September 13, 1969	Green Bay Packers 38	Atlanta Falcons 24	17,411
August 8, 1970	New Orleans Saints 14	Minnesota Vikings 13	17,932
July 31, 1971	Los Angeles Rams (NFC) 17	Houston Oilers (AFC) 6	19,384
July 29, 1972	Kansas City Chiefs (AFC) 23	New York Giants (NFC) 17	19,304
July 28, 1973	San Francisco 49ers (NFC) 20	New England Patriots (AFC) 7	19,685
July 27, 1974	St. Louis Cardinals (NFC) 21	Buffalo Bills (AFC) 13	17,286
August 2, 1975	Washington Redskins (NFC) 17	Cincinnati Bengals (AFC) 9	19,360
July 24, 1976	Denver Broncos (AFC) 10	Detroit Lions (NFC) 7	17,639
July 30, 1977	Chicago Bears (NFC) 20	New York Jets (AFC) 6	19,057
July 29, 1978	Philadelphia Eagles (NFC) 17	Miami Dolphins (AFC) 3	19,255
July 28, 1979	Oakland Raiders (AFC) 20	Dallas Cowboys (NFC) 13	20,648
August 2, 1980*	San Diego Chargers (AFC) 0	Green Bay Packers (NFC) 0	19,972
August 1, 1981	Cleveland Browns (AFC) 24	Atlanta Falcons (NFC) 10	23,921
August 7, 1982	Minnesota Vikings (NFC) 30	Baltimore Colts (AFC) 14	23,379
July 30, 1983	Pittsburgh Steelers (AFC) 27	New Orleans Saints (NFC) 14	23,909
July 28, 1984	Seattle Seahawks (AFC) 38	Tampa Bay Buccaneers (NFC) 0	22,250
August 3, 1985	New York Giants (NFC) 21	Houston Oilers (AFC) 20	23,940
August 2, 1986	New England Patriots (AFC) 21	St. Louis Cardinals (NFC) 16	22,739
August 8, 1987	San Francisco 49ers (NFC) 20	Kansas City Chiefs (AFC) 7	23,826
July 30, 1988	Cincinnati Bengals (AFC) 14	Los Angeles Rams (NFC) 7	23,801
August 5, 1989	Washington Redskins (NFC) 31	Buffalo Bills (AFC) 6	23,948
August 4, 1990	Chicago Bears (NFC) 13	Cleveland Browns (AFC) 0	23,952
July 27, 1991	Detroit Lions (NFC) 14	Denver Broncos (AFC) 3	23,815
August 1, 1992	New York Jets (AFC) 41	Philadelphia Eagles (NFC) 14	23,853
July 31, 1993	Los Angeles Raiders (AFC) 19	Green Bay Packers (NFC) 3	23,863
July 30, 1994	Atlanta Falcons (NFC) 21	San Diego Chargers (AFC) 17	23,185
July 29, 1995	Carolina Panthers (NFC) 20	Jacksonville Jaguars (AFC) 14	24,625
July 27, 1996	Indianapolis Colts (AFC) 10	New Orleans Saints (NFC) 3	23,376
July 26, 1997	Minnesota Vikings (NFC) 28	Seattle Seahawks (AFC) 26	23,846
August 1, 1998	Tampa Bay Buccaneers (NFC) 30	Pittsburgh Steelers (AFC) 6	23,875
August 9, 1999	Cleveland Browns (AFC) 20	Dallas Cowboys (NFC) 17 (OT)	25,156
July 31, 2000	New England Patriots (AFC) 20	San Francisco 49ers (NFC) 0	22,840
August 6, 2001	St. Louis Rams (NFC) 17	Miami Dolphins (AFC) 10	22,736
August 5, 2002	New York Giants (NFC) 34	Houston Texans (AFC) 17	22,461
August 4, 2003**	Kansas City Chiefs (AFC) 9	Green Bay Packers (NFC) 0	22,385
August 9, 2004	Washington Redskins (NFC) 20	Denver Broncos (AFC) 17	22,177
August 8, 2005	Chicago Bears (NFC) 27	Miami Dolphins (AFC) 24	22,292

*Game called with 5:29 remaining because of severe thunder and lightning.
**Game called with 5:49 remaining in the third quarter because of lightning and torrential rain.

1869

Rutgers and Princeton played a college soccer football game, the first ever, November 6. The game used modified London Football Association rules. During the next seven years, rugby gained favor with the major eastern schools over soccer, and modern football began to develop from rugby.

1876

At the Massasoit convention, the first rules for American football were written. Walter Camp, who would become known as the father of American football, first became involved with the game.

1892

In an era in which football was a major attraction of local athletic clubs, an intense competition between two Pittsburgh-area clubs, the Allegheny Athletic Association (AAA) and the Pittsburgh Athletic Club (PAC), led to the making of the first professional football player. Former Yale All-America guard William (Pudge) Heffelfinger was paid $500 by the AAA to play in a game against the PAC, becoming the first person to be paid to play football, November 12. The AAA won the game 4-0 when Heffelfinger picked up a PAC fumble and ran 35 yards for a touchdown.

1893

The Pittsburgh Athletic Club signed one of its players, probably halfback Grant Dibert, to the first known pro football contract, which covered all of the PAC's games for the year.

1895

John Brallier became the first football player to openly turn pro, accepting $10 and expenses to play for the Latrobe YMCA against the Jeannette Athletic Club.

1896

The Allegheny Athletic Association team fielded the first completely professional team for its abbreviated two-game season.

1897

The Latrobe Athletic Association football team went entire-ly professional, becoming the first team to play a full season with only professionals.

1898

A touchdown was changed from four points to five.

1899

Chris O'Brien formed a neighborhood team, which played under the name the Morgan Athletic Club, on the south side of Chicago. The team later became known as the Normals, then the Racine (for a street in Chicago) Cardinals, the Chicago Cardinals, the St. Louis Cardinals, the Phoenix Cardinals, and, in 1994, the Arizona Cardinals. The team remains the oldest continuing operation in pro football.

1900

William C. Temple took over the team payments for the Duquesne Country and Athletic Club, becoming the first known individual club owner.

1902

Baseball's Philadelphia Athletics, managed by Connie Mack, and the Philadelphia Phillies formed professional football teams, joining the Pittsburgh Stars in the first attempt at a pro football league, named the National Football League. The Athletics won the first night football game ever played, 39-0 over Kanaweola AC at Elmira, New York, November 21.

All three teams claimed the pro championship for the year, but the league president, Dave Berry, named the Stars the champions. Pitcher Rube Waddell was with the Athletics, and pitcher Christy Mathewson a fullback for Pittsburgh.

The first World Series of pro football, actually a five-team tournament, was played among a team made up of players from both the Athletics and the Phillies, but simply named New York; the New York Knickerbockers; the Syracuse AC; the Warlow AC; and the Orange (New Jersey) AC at New York's original Madison Square Garden. New York and Syracuse played the first indoor football game before 3,000, December 28. Syracuse, with Glen (Pop) Warner at guard, won 6-0 and

went on to win the tournament.

1903

The Franklin (Pa.) Athletic Club won the second and last World Series of pro football over the Oreos AC of Asbury Park, New Jersey; the Watertown Red and Blacks; and the Orange AC.

Pro football was popularized in Ohio when the Massillon Tigers, a strong amateur team, hired four Pittsburgh pros to play in the season-ending game against Akron. At the same time, pro football declined in the Pittsburgh area, and the emphasis on the pro game moved west from Pennsylvania to Ohio.

1904

A field goal was changed from five points to four.

Ohio had at least seven pro teams, with Massillon winning the Ohio Independent Championship, that is, the pro title. Talk surfaced about forming a state-wide league to end spiraling salaries brought about by constant bidding for players and to write universal rules for the game. The feeble attempt to start the league failed.

Halfback Charles Follis signed a contract with the Shelby (Ohio) AC, making him the first known black pro football player.

1905

The Canton AC, later to become known as the Bulldogs, became a professional team. Massillon again won the Ohio League championship.

1906

The forward pass was legalized. The first authenticated pass completion in a pro game came on October 27, when George (Peggy) Parratt of Massillon threw a completion to Dan (Bullet) Riley in a victory over a combined Benwood-Moundsville team.

Arch-rivals Canton and Massillon, the two best pro teams in America, played twice, with Canton winning the first game but Massillon winning the second and the Ohio League championship. A betting scandal and the financial disaster wrought upon the two clubs by paying huge salaries

caused a temporary decline in interest in pro football in the two cities and, somewhat, throughout Ohio.

1909

A field goal dropped from four points to three.

1912

A touchdown was increased from five points to six.

Jack Cusack revived a strong pro team in Canton.

1913

Jim Thorpe, a former football and track star at the Carlisle Indian School (Pa.) and a double gold medal winner at the 1912 Olympics in Stockholm, played for the Pine Village Pros in Indiana.

1915

Massillon again fielded a major team, reviving the old rivalry with Canton. Cusack signed Thorpe to play for Canton for $250 a game.

1916

With Thorpe and former Carlisle teammate Pete Calac starring, Canton went 9-0-1, won the Ohio League championship, and was acclaimed the pro football champion.

1917

Despite an upset by Massillon, Canton again won the Ohio League championship.

1919

Canton again won the Ohio League championship, despite the team having been turned over from Cusack to Ralph Hay. Thorpe and Calac were joined in the backfield by Joe Guyon.

Earl (Curly) Lambeau and George Calhoun organized the Green Bay Packers. Lambeau's employer at the Indian Packing Company provided $500 for equipment and allowed the team to use the company field for practices. The Packers went 10-1.

1920

Pro football was in a state of confusion due to three major problems: dramatically rising salaries; players continually jumping from one team to another following the highest offer; and the use of college players still enrolled in school.

A league in which all the members would follow the same rules seemed the answer. An organizational meeting, at which the Akron Pros, Canton Bulldogs, Cleveland Indians, and Dayton Triangles were represented, was held at the Jordan and Hupmobile auto showroom in Canton, Ohio, August 20. This meeting resulted in the formation of the American Professional Football Conference.

A second organizational meeting was held in Canton, September 17. The teams were from four states—Akron, Canton, Cleveland, and Dayton from Ohio; the Hammond Pros and Muncie Flyers from Indiana; the Rochester Jeffersons from New York; and the Rock Island Independents, Decatur Staleys, and Racine Cardinals from Illinois. The name of the league was changed to the American Professional Football Association. Hoping to capitalize on his fame, the members elected Thorpe president; Stanley Cofall of Cleveland was elected vice president. A membership fee of $100 per team was charged to give an appearance of respectability, but no team ever paid it. Scheduling was left up to the teams, and there were wide variations, both in the overall number of games played and in the number played against APFA member teams.

Four other teams—the Buffalo All-Americans, Chicago Tigers, Columbus Panhandles, and Detroit Heralds—joined the league sometime during the year. On September 26, the first game featuring an APFA team was played at Rock Island's Douglas Park. A crowd of 800 watched the Independents defeat the St. Paul Ideals 48-0. A week later, October 3, the first game matching two APFA teams was held. At Triangle Park, Dayton defeated Columbus 14-0, with Lou Partlow of Dayton scoring the first touchdown in a game between Association teams. The same day, Rock Island defeated Muncie 45-0.

By the beginning of December, most of the teams in the APFA had abandoned their hopes for a championship, and some of them, including the Chicago Tigers and the Detroit Heralds, had finished their seasons, disbanded, and had their franchises canceled by the Association. Four teams—Akron, Buffalo, Canton, and Decatur—still had championship as-pirations, but a series of late-season games among them left Akron as the only undefeated team in the Association. At one of these games, Akron sold tackle Bob Nash to Buffalo for $300 and five percent of the gate receipts—the first APFA player deal.

1921

At the league meeting in Akron, April 30, the championship of the 1920 season was awarded to the Akron Pros. The APFA was reorganized, with Joe Carr of the Columbus Panhandles named president and Carl Storck of Dayton secretary-treasurer. Carr moved the Association's headquarters to Columbus, drafted a league constitution and by-laws, gave teams territorial rights, restricted player movements, developed membership criteria for the franchises, and issued standings for the first time, so that the APFA would have a clear champion.

The Association's membership increased to 22 teams, including the Green Bay Packers, who were awarded to John Clair of the Acme Packing Company.

Thorpe moved from Canton to the Cleveland Indians, but he was hurt early in the season and played very little.

A.E. Staley turned the Decatur Staleys over to player-coach George Halas, who moved the team to Cubs Park in Chicago. Staley paid Halas $5,000 to keep the name Staleys for one more year. Halas made halfback Ed (Dutch) Sternaman his partner.

Player-coach Fritz Pollard of the Akron Pros became the first black head coach.

The Staleys claimed the APFA championship with a 9-1-1 record, as did Buffalo at 9-1-2. Carr ruled in favor of the Staleys, giving Halas his first championship.

1922

After admitting the use of players who had college eligi-bility remaining during the 1921 season, Clair and the Green Bay management withdrew from the APFA, January 28. Curly Lambeau promised to obey league rules and then used $50 of his own money to buy back the franchise. Bad weather and low attendance plagued the Packers, and Lambeau went broke, but local merchants arranged a $2,500 loan for the club. A public nonprofit corporation was set up to operate the team, with Lambeau as head coach and manager.

The American Professional Football Association changed its name to the National Football League, June 24. The Chicago Staleys became the Chicago Bears.

The NFL fielded 18 teams, including the new Oorang Indians of Marion, Ohio, an all-Indian team featuring Thorpe, Joe Guyon, and Pete Calac, and sponsored by the Oorang dog kennels.

Canton, led by player-coach Guy Chamberlin and tackles Link Lyman and Wilbur (Pete) Henry, emerged as the league's first true powerhouse, going 10-0-2.

1923

For the first time, all of the franchises considered to be part of the NFL fielded teams. Thorpe played his second and final season for the Oorang Indians. Against the Bears, Thorpe fumbled, and Halas picked up the ball and ran it 98 yards for a touchdown, a record that would last until 1972.

Canton had its second consecutive undefeated season, going 11-0-1 for the NFL title.

1924

The league had 18 franchises, including new ones in Kansas City, Kenosha, and Frankford, a section of Philadelphia. League champion Canton, successful on the field but not at the box office, was purchased by the owner of the Cleveland franchise, who kept the Canton franchise inactive, while using the best players for his Cleveland team, which he renamed the Bulldogs. Cleveland won the title with a 7-1-1 record.

1925

Five new franchises were admitted to the NFL—the New York Giants, who were awarded to Tim Mara and Billy Gibson for $500; the Detroit Panthers, featuring Jimmy Conzelman as owner, coach, and tailback; the Providence Steam Roller; a new Canton Bulldogs team; and the Pottsville Maroons, who had been perhaps the most successful independent pro team. The NFL established its first player limit, at 16 players.

Late in the season, the NFL made its greatest coup in gaining national recognition. Shortly after the University of Illinois season ended in November, All-America halfback Harold (Red) Grange signed a contract to play with the Chicago Bears. On Thanksgiving Day, a crowd of 36,000—the largest in pro football history—watched Grange and the Bears play the Chicago Cardinals to a scoreless tie at Wrigley Field. At the beginning of December, the Bears left on a barnstorming tour that saw them play eight games in 12 days, in St. Louis, Philadelphia, New York City, Washington, Boston, Pittsburgh, Detroit, and Chicago. A crowd of 73,000 watched the game against the Giants at the Polo Grounds, helping assure the future of the troubled NFL franchise in New York. The Bears then played nine more games in the South and West, including a game in Los Angeles, in which 75,000 fans watched them defeat the Los Angeles Tigers in the Los Angeles Memorial Coliseum.

Pottsville and the Chicago Cardinals were the top contenders for the league title, with Pottsville winning a late-season meeting 21-7. Pottsville scheduled a game against a team of former Notre Dame players for Shibe Park in Philadelphia. Frankford lodged a protest not only because the game was in Frankford's protected territory, but because it was being played the same day as a Yellow Jackets home game. Carr gave three different notices forbidding Pottsville to play the game, but Pottsville played anyway, December 12. That day, Carr fined the club, suspended it from all rights and privileges (including the right to play for the NFL championship), and re-turned its franchise to the league. The Cardinals, who ended the season with the best record in the league, were named the 1925 champions.

1926
Grange's manager, C.C. Pyle, told the Bears that Grange wouldn't play for them unless he was paid a five-figure salary and given one-third ownership of the team. The Bears refused. Pyle leased Yankee Stadium in New York City, then petitioned for an NFL franchise. After he was refused, he started the first American Football League. It lasted one season and included Grange's New York Yankees and eight other teams. The AFL champion Philadelphia Quakers played a December game against the New York Giants, seventh in the NFL, and the Giants won 31-0. At the end of the season, the AFL folded.

Halas pushed through a rule that prohibited any team from signing a player whose college class had not graduated.

The NFL grew to 22 teams, including the Duluth Eskimos, who signed All-America fullback Ernie Nevers of Stanford, giving the league a gate attraction to rival Grange. The 15-member Eskimos, dubbed the Iron Men of the North, played 29 exhibition and league games, 28 on the road, and Nevers played in all but 29 minutes of them.

Frankford edged the Bears for the championship, despite Halas having obtained John (Paddy) Driscoll from the Cardinals. On December 4, the Yellow Jackets scored in the final two minutes to defeat the Bears 7-6 and move ahead of them in the standings.

1927
At a special meeting in Cleveland, April 23, Carr decided to secure the NFL's future by eliminating the financially weaker teams and consolidating the quality players onto a limited number of more successful teams. The new-look NFL dropped to 12 teams, and the center of gravity of the league left the Midwest, where

the NFL had started, and began to emerge in the large cities of the East. One of the new teams was Grange's New York Yankees, but Grange suffered a knee injury and the Yankees finished in the middle of the pack. The NFL championship was won by the cross-town rival New York Giants, who posted 10 shutouts in 13 games.

1928
Grange and Nevers both retired from pro football, and Duluth disbanded, as the NFL was reduced to only 10 teams. The Providence Steam Roller of Jimmy Conzelman and Pearce Johnson won the championship, playing in the Cycledrome, a 10,000-seat oval that had been built for bicycle races.

1929
Chris O'Brien sold the Chicago Cardinals to David Jones, July 27.

The NFL added a fourth official, the field judge, July 28.

Grange and Nevers returned to the NFL. Nevers scored six rushing touchdowns and four extra points as the Cardinals beat Grange's Bears 40-6, November 28. The 40 points set a record that remains the NFL's oldest.

Providence became the first NFL team to host a game at night under floodlights, against the Cardinals, November 6.

The Packers added back Johnny Blood (McNally), tackle Cal Hubbard, and guard Mike Michalske, and won their first NFL championship, edging the Giants, who featured quarterback Benny Friedman.

1930
Dayton, the last of the NFL's original franchises, was purchased by William B. Dwyer and John C. Depler, moved to Brooklyn, and renamed the Dodgers. The Portsmouth, Ohio, Spartans entered the league.

The Packers edged the Giants for the title, but the most improved team was the Bears. Halas retired as a player and replaced himself as coach of the Bears with Ralph Jones, who refined the T-formation by introducing wide

ends and a halfback in motion. Jones also introduced rookie All-America fullback-tackle Bronko Nagurski.

The Giants defeated a team of former Notre Dame players coached by Knute Rockne 22-0 before 55,000 at the Polo Grounds, December 14. The proceeds went to the New York Unemployment Fund to help those suffering because of the Great Depression, and the easy victory helped give the NFL credibility with the press and the public.

1931
The NFL decreased to 10 teams, and halfway through the season the Frankford franchise folded. Carr fined the Bears, Packers, and Portsmouth $1,000 each for using players whose college classes had not graduated.

The Packers won an unprecedented third consecutive title, beating out the Spartans, who were led by rookie backs Earl (Dutch) Clark and Glenn Presnell.

1932
George Preston Marshall, Vincent Bendix, Jay O'Brien, and M. Dorland Doyle were awarded a franchise for Boston, July 9. Despite the presence of two rookies—halfback Cliff Battles and tackle Glen (Turk) Edwards—the new team, named the Braves, lost money and Marshall was left as the sole owner at the end of the year.

NFL membership dropped to eight teams, the lowest in history. Official statistics were kept for the first time. The Bears and the Spartans finished the season in the first-ever tie for first place. After the season finale, the league office arranged for an additional regular-season game to determine the league champion. The game was moved indoors to Chicago Stadium because of bitter cold and heavy snow. The arena allowed only an 80-yard field that came right to the walls. The goal posts were moved from the end lines to the goal lines and, for safety, inbounds lines or hashmarks where the ball would be put in play were drawn 10 yards from the walls that butted against the sidelines. The Bears won 9-0, December 18, scoring the

winning touchdown on a two-yard pass from Nagurski to Grange. The Spartans claimed Nagurski's pass was thrown from less than five yards behind the line of scrimmage, violating the existing passing rule, but the play stood.

1933
The NFL, which long had followed the rules of college football, made a number of significant changes from the college game for the first time and began to develop rules serving its needs and the style of play it preferred. The innovations from the 1932 championship game—inbounds line or hashmarks and goal posts on the goal lines—were adopted. Also the forward pass was legalized from anywhere behind the line of scrimmage, February 25.

Marshall and Halas pushed through a proposal that divided the NFL into two divisions, with the winners to meet in an annual championship game, July 8.

Three new franchises joined the league—the Pittsburgh Pirates of Art Rooney, the Philadelphia Eagles of Bert Bell and Lud Wray, and the Cincinnati Reds. The Staten Island Stapletons suspended operations for a year, but never returned to the league.

Halas bought out Sternaman, became sole owner of the Bears, and reinstated himself as head coach. Marshall changed the name of the Boston Braves to the Redskins. David Jones sold the Chicago Cardinals to Charles W. Bidwill.

In the first NFL Championship Game scheduled before the season, the Western Division champion Bears defeated the Eastern Division champion Giants 23-21 at Wrigley Field, December 17.

1934
G.A. (Dick) Richards purchased the Portsmouth Spartans, moved them to Detroit, and renamed them the Lions.

Professional football gained new prestige when the Bears were matched against the best college football players in the first Chicago College All-Star Game, August 31. The game ended in a scoreless tie before 79,432 at Soldier Field.

The Cincinnati Reds lost their first eight games, then were suspended from the league for defaulting on payments. The St. Louis Gunners, an independent team, joined the NFL by buying the Cincinnati franchise and went 1-2 the last three weeks.

Rookie Beattie Feathers of the Bears became the NFL's first 1,000-yard rusher, gaining 1,004 on 101 carries. The Thanksgiving Day game between the Bears and the Lions became the first NFL game broadcast nationally, with Graham McNamee the announcer for NBC radio.

In the championship game, on an extremely cold and icy day at the Polo Grounds, the Giants trailed the Bears 13-3 in the third quarter before changing to basketball shoes for better footing. The Giants won 30-13 in what has come to be known as the Sneakers Game, December 9.

The player waiver rule was adopted, December 10.

1935

The NFL adopted Bert Bell's proposal to hold an annual draft of college players, to begin in 1936, with teams selecting in an inverse order of finish, May 19. The inbounds line or hashmarks were moved nearer the center of the field, 15 yards from the sidelines.

All-America end Don Hutson of Alabama joined Green Bay. The Lions defeated the Giants 26-7 in the NFL Championship Game, December 15.

1936

There were no franchise transactions for the first year since the formation of the NFL. It also was the first year in which all member teams played the same number of games.

The Eagles made University of Chicago halfback and Heisman Trophy winner Jay Berwanger the first player ever selected in the NFL draft, February 8. The Eagles traded his rights to the Bears, but Berwanger never played pro football. The first player selected to actually sign was the number-two pick, Riley Smith of Alabama, who was selected by Boston.

A rival league was formed, and it became the second to

call itself the American Football League. The Boston Shamrocks were its champions.

Because of poor attendance, Marshall, the owner of the host team, moved the Championship Game from Boston to the Polo Grounds in New York. Green Bay defeated the Redskins 21-6, December 13.

1937

Homer Marshman was granted a Cleveland franchise, named the Rams, February 12. Marshall moved the Redskins to Washington, D.C., February 13. The Redskins signed TCU All-America tailback Sammy Baugh, who led them to a 28-21 victory over the Bears in the NFL Championship Game, December 12.

The Los Angeles Bulldogs had an 8-0 record to win the AFL title, but then the 2-year-old league folded.

1938

At the suggestion of Halas, Hugh (Shorty) Ray became a technical advisor on rules and officiating to the NFL. A new rule called for a 15-yard penalty for roughing the passer.

Rookie Byron (Whizzer) White of the Pittsburgh Pirates led the NFL in rushing. The Giants defeated the Packers 23-17 for the NFL title, December 11.

Marshall, *Los Angeles Times* sports editor Bill Henry, and promoter Tom Gallery established the Pro Bowl game between the NFL champion and a team of pro all-stars.

1939

The New York Giants defeated the Pro All-Stars 13-10 in the first Pro Bowl, at Wrigley Field, Los Angeles, January 15.

Carr, NFL president since 1921, died in Columbus, May 20. Carl Storck was named acting president, May 25.

An NFL game was televised for the first time when NBC broadcast the Brooklyn Dodgers-Philadelphia Eagles game from Ebbets Field to the approximately 1,000 sets then in New York, October 22.

Green Bay defeated New York 27-0 in the NFL Championship Game, December 10 at Milwaukee. NFL attendance

exceeded 1 million in a season for the first time, reaching 1,071,200.

1940

A six-team rival league, the third to call itself the American Football League, was formed, and the Columbus Bullies won its championship.

Halas' Bears, with additional coaching by Clark Shaughnessy of Stanford, defeated the Redskins 73-0 in the NFL Championship Game, December 8. The game, which was the most decisive victory in NFL history, popularized the Bears' T-formation with a man-in-motion. It was the first championship carried on network radio, broadcast by Red Barber to 120 stations of the Mutual Broadcasting System, which paid $2,500 for the rights.

Art Rooney sold the Pittsburgh franchise to Alexis Thompson, December 9, then bought part interest in the Philadelphia Eagles.

1941

Elmer Layden was named the first Commissioner of the NFL, March 1; Storck, the acting president, resigned, April 5. NFL headquarters were moved to Chicago.

Bell and Rooney traded the Eagles to Thompson for the Pirates, then re-named their new team the Steelers. Homer Marshman sold the Rams to Daniel F. Reeves and Fred Levy, Jr.

The league by-laws were revised to provide for playoffs in case there were ties in division races, and sudden-death overtimes in case a playoff game was tied after four quarters. An official *NFL Record Manual* was published for the first time.

Columbus again won the championship of the AFL, but the two-year-old league then folded.

The Bears and the Packers finished in a tie for the Western Division championship, setting up the first divisional playoff game in league history. The Bears won 33-14, then defeated the Giants 37-9 for the NFL championship, December 21.

1942

Players departing for service

in World War II depleted the rosters of NFL teams. Halas left the Bears in midseason to join the Navy, and Luke Johnsos and Heartley (Hunk) Anderson served as co-coaches as the Bears went 11-0 in the regular season. The Redskins defeated the Bears 14-6 in the NFL Championship Game, December 13.

1943

The Cleveland Rams, with co-owners Reeves and Levy in the service, were granted permission to suspend operations for one season, April 6. Levy transferred his stock in the team to Reeves, April 16.

The NFL adopted free substitution, April 7. The league also made the wearing of helmets mandatory and approved a 10-game schedule for all teams.

Philadelphia and Pittsburgh were granted permission to merge for one season, June 19. The team, known as Phil-Pitt (and called the Steagles by fans), divided home games between the two cities, and Earle (Greasy) Neale of Philadelphia and Walt Kiesling of Pittsburgh served as co-coaches. The merger automatically dissolved the last day of the season, December 5.

Ted Collins was granted a franchise for Boston, to become active in 1944.

Sammy Baugh led the league in passing, punting, and interceptions. He led the Redskins to a tie with the Giants for the Eastern Division title, and then to a 28-0 victory in a divisional playoff game. The Bears beat the Redskins 41-21 in the NFL Championship Game, December 26.

1944

Collins, who had wanted a franchise in Yankee Stadium in New York, named his new team in Boston the Yanks. Cleveland resumed operations. The Brooklyn Dodgers changed their name to the Tigers.

Coaching from the bench was legalized, April 20.

The Cardinals and the Steelers were granted permission to merge for one year under the name Card-Pitt, April 21. Phil Handler of the Cardinals and Walt Kiesling of the Steelers served as co-coaches. The merger automatically dissolved the last day of the season, December 3.

In the NFL Championship Game, Green Bay defeated the New York Giants 14-7, December 17.

1945

The inbounds lines or hashmarks were moved from 15 yards away from the sidelines to nearer the center of the field—20 yards from the sidelines.

Brooklyn and Boston merged into a team that played home games in both cities and was known simply as The Yanks. The team was coached by former Boston head coach Herb Kopf. In December, the Brooklyn franchise withdrew from the NFL to join the new All-America Football Conference; all the players on its active and reserve lists were assigned to The Yanks, who once again became the Boston Yanks.

Halas rejoined the Bears late in the season after service with the U.S. Navy. Although Halas took over much of the coaching duties, Anderson and Johnsos remained the coaches of record throughout the season.

Steve Van Buren of Philadelphia led the NFL in rushing, kickoff returns, and scoring.

After the Japanese surrendered ending World War II, a count showed that the NFL service roster, limited to men who had played in league games, totaled 638, 21 of whom had died in action.

Rookie quarterback Bob Waterfield led Cleveland to a 15-14 victory over Washington in the NFL Championship Game, December 16.

1946

The contract of Commissioner Layden was not renewed, and Bert Bell, the co-owner of the Steelers, replaced him, January 11. Bell moved the league headquarters from Chicago to the Philadelphia suburb of Bala-Cynwyd.

Free substitution was withdrawn and substitutions were limited to no more than three men at a time. Forward passes were made automatically incomplete upon striking the goal posts, January 11.

The NFL took on a truly national appearance for the first time when Reeves was granted permission by the league to move his NFL champion Rams to Los Angeles.

Halfback Kenny Washington (March 21) and end Woody Strode (May 7) signed with the Los Angeles Rams to become the first African-Americans to play in the NFL in the modern era. Guard Bill Willis (August 6) and running back Marion Motley (August 9) joined the AAFC with the Cleveland Browns.

The rival All-America Football Conference began play with eight teams. The Cleveland Browns, coached by Paul Brown, won the AAFC's first championship, defeating the New York Yankees 14-9.

Bill Dudley of the Steelers led the NFL in rushing, interceptions, and punt returns, and won the league's most valuable player award.

Backs Frank Filchock and Merle Hapes of the Giants were questioned about an attempt by a New York man to fix the championship game with the Bears. Bell suspended Hapes but allowed Filchock to play; he played well, but Chicago won 24-14, December 15.

1947

The NFL added a fifth official, the back judge.

A bonus choice was made for the first time in the NFL draft. One team each year would select the special choice before the first round began. The Chicago Bears won a lottery and the rights to the first choice and drafted back Bob Fenimore of Oklahoma A&M.

The Cleveland Browns again won the AAFC title, defeating the New York Yankees 14-3.

Charles Bidwill, Sr., owner of the Cardinals, died April 19, but his wife and sons retained ownership of the team. On December 28, the Cardinals won the NFL Championship Game 28-21 over the Philadelphia Eagles, who had beaten Pittsburgh 21-0 in a playoff.

1948

Plastic helmets were prohibited. A flexible artificial tee was permitted at the kickoff. Officials other than the referee

were equipped with whistles, not horns, January 14.

Fred Mandel sold the Detroit Lions to a syndicate headed by D. Lyle Fife, January 15.

Halfback Fred Gehrke of the Los Angeles Rams painted horns on the Rams' helmets, the first modern helmet emblems in pro football.

The Cleveland Browns won their third straight championship in the AAFC, going 14-0 and then defeating the Buffalo Bills 49-7.

In a blizzard, the Eagles defeated the Cardinals 7-0 in the NFL Championship Game, December 19.

1949

Alexis Thompson sold the champion Eagles to a syndicate headed by James P. Clark, January 15. The Boston Yanks became the New York Bulldogs, sharing the Polo Grounds with the Giants.

Free substitution was adopted for one year, January 20.

The NFL had two 1,000-yard rushers in the same season for the first time—Steve Van Buren of Philadelphia and Tony Canadeo of Green Bay.

The AAFC played its season with a one-division, seven-team format. On December 9, Bell announced a merger agreement in which three AAFC franchises—Cleveland, San Francisco, and Baltimore—would join the NFL in 1950. The Browns won their fourth consecutive AAFC title, defeating the 49ers 21-7, December 11.

In a heavy rain, the Eagles defeated the Rams 14-0 in the NFL Championship Game, December 18.

1950

Unlimited free substitution was restored, opening the way for the era of two platoons and specialization in pro football, January 20.

Curly Lambeau, founder of the franchise and Green Bay's head coach since 1921, resigned under fire, February 1.

The name National Football League was restored after about three months of the National-American Football League. The American and National conferences were created to replace the Eastern

and Western divisions, March 3.

The New York Bulldogs became the Yanks and divided the players of the former AAFC Yankees with the Giants. A special allocation draft was held in which the 13 teams drafted the remaining AAFC players, with special consideration for Baltimore, which received 15 choices compared to 10 for other teams.

The Los Angeles Rams became the first NFL team to have all of its games—both home and away—televised. The Washington Redskins followed the Rams in arranging to televise their games; other teams made deals to put selected games on television.

In the first game of the season, former AAFC champion Cleveland defeated NFL champion Philadelphia 35-10. For the first time, deadlocks occurred in both conferences and playoffs were necessary. The Browns defeated the Giants in the American and the Rams defeated the Bears in the National. Cleveland defeated Los Angeles 30-28 in the NFL Championship Game, December 24.

1951

The Pro Bowl game, dormant since 1942, was revived under a new format matching the all-stars of each conference at the Los Angeles Memorial Coliseum. The American Conference defeated the National Conference 28-27, January 14.

Abraham Watner returned the Baltimore franchise and its player contracts back to the NFL for $50,000. Baltimore's former players were made available for drafting at the same time as college players, January 18.

A rule was passed that no tackle, guard, or center would be eligible to catch a forward pass, January 18.

The Rams reversed their television policy and televised only road games.

The NFL Championship Game was televised coast-to-coast for the first time, December 23. The DuMont Network paid $75,000 for the rights to the game, in which the Rams defeated the Browns 24-17.

1952

Ted Collins sold the New York Yanks' franchise back to the NFL, January 19. A new franchise was awarded to a group in Dallas after it purchased the assets of the Yanks, January 24. The new Texans went 1-11, with the owners turning the franchise back to the league in midseason. For the last five games of the season, the commissioner's office operated the Texans as a road team, using Hershey, Pennsylvania, as a home base. At the end of the season the franchise was canceled, the last time an NFL team failed.

The Pittsburgh Steelers abandoned the Single-Wing for the T-formation, the last pro team to do so.

The Detroit Lions won their first NFL championship in 17 years, defeating the Browns 17-7 in the title game, December 28.

1953

A Baltimore group headed by Carroll Rosenbloom was granted a franchise and was awarded the holdings of the defunct Dallas organization, January 23. The team, named the Colts, put together the largest trade in league history, acquiring 10 players from Cleveland in exchange for five.

The names of the American and National conferences were changed to the Eastern and Western conferences, January 24.

Jim Thorpe died, March 28.

Mickey McBride, founder of the Cleveland Browns, sold the franchise to a syndicate headed by Dave R. Jones, June 10.

The NFL policy of blacking out home games was upheld by Judge Allan K. Grim of the U.S. District Court in Philadelphia, November 12.

The Lions again defeated the Browns in the NFL Championship Game, winning 17-16, December 27.

1954

The Canadian Football League began a series of raids on NFL teams, signing quarterback Eddie LeBaron and defensive end Gene Brito of Washington and defensive tackle Arnie Weinmeister of the Giants, among others.

Fullback Joe Perry of the 49ers became the first player in league history to gain 1,000 yards rushing in consecutive seasons.

Cleveland defeated Detroit 56-10 in the NFL Championship Game, December 26.

1955

The sudden-death overtime rule was used for the first time in a preseason game between the Rams and Giants at Portland, Oregon, August 28. The Rams won 23-17 three minutes into overtime.

A rule change declared the ball dead immediately if the ball carrier touched the ground with any part of his body except his hands or feet while in the grasp of an opponent.

The Baltimore Colts made an 80-cent phone call to Johnny Unitas and signed him as a free agent. Another quarterback, Otto Graham, played his last game as the Browns defeated the Rams 38-14 in the NFL Championship Game, December 26. Graham had quarterbacked the Browns to 10 championship-game appearances in 10 years.

NBC replaced DuMont as the network for the title game, paying a rights fee of $100,000.

1956

The NFL Players Association was founded.

Grabbing an opponent's facemask (other than the ball carrier) was made illegal. Using radio receivers to communicate with players on the field was prohibited. A natural leather ball with white end stripes replaced the white ball with black stripes for night games.

The Giants moved from the Polo Grounds to Yankee Stadium.

Halas retired as coach of the Bears, and was replaced by Paddy Driscoll.

CBS became the first network to broadcast some NFL regular-season games to selected television markets across the nation.

The Giants routed the Bears 47-7 in the NFL Championship Game, December 30.

1957

Pete Rozelle was named general manager of the Rams. Anthony J. Morabito, founder and co-owner of the 49ers, died of a heart attack during a game against the Bears at Kezar Stadium, October 28. An NFL-record crowd of 102,368 saw the 49ers-Rams game at the Los Angeles Memorial Coliseum, November 10.

The Lions came from 20 points down to post a 31-27 playoff victory over the 49ers, December 22. Detroit defeated Cleveland 59-14 in the NFL Championship Game, December 29.

1958

The bonus selection in the draft was eliminated, January 29. The last selection was quarterback King Hill of Rice by the Chicago Cardinals.

Halas reinstated himself as coach of the Bears.

Jim Brown of Cleveland gained an NFL-record 1,527 yards rushing. In a divisional playoff game, the Giants held Brown to eight yards and defeated Cleveland 10-0.

Baltimore, coached by Weeb Ewbank, defeated the Giants 23-17 in the first sudden-death overtime in an NFL Championship Game, December 28. The game ended when Colts fullback Alan Ameche scored on a one-yard touchdown run after 8:15 of overtime.

1959

Vince Lombardi was named head coach of the Green Bay Packers, January 28. Tim Mara, the co-founder of the Giants, died, February 17.

Lamar Hunt of Dallas announced his intentions to form a second pro football league. The first meeting was held in Chicago, August 14, and consisted of Hunt representing Dallas; Bob Howsam, Denver; K.S. (Bud) Adams, Houston; Barron Hilton, Los Angeles; Max Winter and Bill Boyer, Minneapolis; and Harry Wismer, New York City. They made plans to begin play in 1960.

The new league was named the American Football League, August 22. Buffalo, owned by Ralph Wilson, became the seventh franchise, October 28. Boston, owned by William H. Sullivan, became the eighth team, November 22. The first AFL draft, lasting 33 rounds, was held, November 22. Joe Foss was named AFL Commissioner, November 30. An additional draft of 20 rounds was held by the AFL, December 2.

NFL Commissioner Bert Bell died of a heart attack suffered at Franklin Field, Philadelphia, during the last two minutes of a game between the Eagles and the Steelers, October 11. Treasurer Austin Gunsel was named president in the office of the commissioner, October 14.

The Colts again defeated the Giants in the NFL Championship Game, 31-16, December 27.

1960

Pete Rozelle was elected NFL Commissioner as a compromise choice on the twenty-third ballot, January 26. Rozelle moved the league offices to New York City.

Hunt was elected AFL president for 1960, January 26. Minneapolis withdrew from the AFL, January 27, and the same ownership was given an NFL franchise for Minnesota (to start in 1961), January 28. Dallas received an NFL franchise for 1960, January 28. Oakland received an AFL franchise, January 30.

The AFL adopted the two-point option on points after touchdown, January 28. A no-tampering verbal pact, relative to players' contracts, was agreed to between the NFL and AFL, February 9.

The NFL owners voted to allow the transfer of the Chicago Cardinals to St. Louis, March 13.

The AFL signed a five-year television contract with ABC, June 9.

The Boston Patriots defeated the Buffalo Bills 28-7 before 16,000 at Buffalo in the first AFL preseason game, July 30. The Denver Broncos defeated the Patriots 13-10 before 21,597 at Boston in the first AFL regular-season game, September 9.

Philadelphia defeated Green Bay 17-13 in the NFL Championship Game, December 26.

1961

The Houston Oilers defeated the Los Angeles Chargers 24-16 before 32,183 in the first AFL Championship Game,

January 1.

Detroit defeated Cleveland 17-16 in the first Playoff Bowl, or Bert Bell Benefit Bowl, between second-place teams in each conference in Miami, January 7.

End Willard Dewveall of the Bears played out his option and joined the Oilers, becoming the first player to play out his contract and jump from the NFL to the AFL, January 14.

Ed McGah, Wayne Valley, and Robert Osborne bought out their partners in the ownership of the Raiders, January 17. The Chargers were transferred to San Diego, February 10. Dave R. Jones sold the Browns to a group headed by Arthur B. Modell, March 22. The Howsam brothers sold the Broncos to a group headed by Calvin Kunz and Gerry Phipps, May 26.

NBC was awarded a two-year contract for radio and television rights to the NFL Championship Game for $615,000 annually, $300,000 of which was to go directly into the NFL Player Benefit Plan, April 5.

Canton, Ohio, where the league that became the NFL was formed in 1920, was chosen as the site of the Pro Football Hall of Fame, April 27. Dick McCann, a former Redskins executive, was named executive director.

A bill legalizing single-network television contracts by professional sports leagues was introduced in Congress by Representative Emanuel Celler. It passed the House and Senate and was signed into law by President John F. Kennedy, September 30.

Houston defeated San Diego 10-3 for the AFL championship, December 24. Green Bay won its first NFL championship since 1944, defeating the New York Giants 37-0, December 31.

1962

The Western Division defeated the Eastern Division 47-27 in the first AFL All-Star Game, played before 20,973 in San Diego, January 7.

Both leagues prohibited grabbing any player's face-mask. The AFL voted to make the scoreboard clock the official timer of the game.

The NFL entered into a single-network agreement with CBS for telecasting all regular-season games for $4.65 million annually, January 10.

Judge Roszel Thompson of the U.S. District Court in Baltimore ruled against the AFL in its antitrust suit against the NFL, May 21. The AFL had charged the NFL with monopoly and conspiracy in areas of expansion, television, and player signings. The case lasted two and a half years, the trial two months.

McGah and Valley acquired controlling interest in the Raiders, May 24. The AFL assumed financial responsibility for the New York Titans, November 8. With Commissioner Rozelle as referee, Daniel F. Reeves regained the ownership of the Rams, outbidding his partners in sealed-envelope bidding for the team, November 27.

The Dallas Texans defeated the Oilers 20-17 for the AFL championship at Houston after 17 minutes, 54 seconds of overtime on a 25-yard field goal by Tommy Brooker, December 23. The game lasted a record 77 minutes, 54 seconds.

Judge Edward Weinfeld of the U.S. District Court in New York City upheld the legality of the NFL's television blackout within a 75-mile radius of home games and denied an injunction that would have forced the championship game between the Giants and the Packers to be televised in the New York City area, December 28. The Packers beat the Giants 16-7 for the NFL title, December 30.

1963

The Dallas Texans transferred to Kansas City, becoming the Chiefs, February 8. The New York Titans were sold to a five-man syndicate headed by David (Sonny) Werblin, March 28. Weeb Ewbank became the Titans' new head coach and the team's name was changed to the Jets, April 15. They began play in Shea Stadium.

NFL Properties, Inc., was founded to serve as the licensing arm of the NFL.

Rozelle indefinitely suspended Green Bay halfback Paul Hornung and Detroit defensive tackle Alex Karras for placing bets on their own teams and on other NFL games; he also fined five other Detroit players $2,000 each for betting on one game in which they did not participate, and the Detroit Lions Football Company $2,000 on each of two counts for failure to report information promptly and for lack of sideline supervision.

Paul Brown, head coach of the Browns since their inception, was fired and replaced by Blanton Collier. Don Shula replaced Weeb Ewbank as head coach of the Colts.

The AFL allowed the Jets and Raiders to select players from other franchises in hopes of giving the league more competitive balance, May 11.

NBC was awarded exclusive network broadcasting rights for the 1963 AFL Championship Game for $926,000, May 23.

The Pro Football Hall of Fame was dedicated at Canton, Ohio, September 7.

The U.S. Fourth Circuit Court of Appeals reaffirmed the lower court's finding for the NFL in the $10-million suit brought by the AFL, ending three and a half years of litigation, November 21.

Jim Brown of Cleveland rushed for an NFL single-season record 1,863 yards.

Boston defeated Buffalo 26-8 in the first divisional playoff game in AFL history, December 28.

The Bears defeated the Giants 14-10 in the NFL Championship Game, a record sixth and last title for Halas in his thirty-sixth season as the Bears' coach, December 29.

1964

The Chargers defeated the Patriots 51-10 in the AFL Championship Game, January 5.

William Clay Ford, the Lions' president since 1961, purchased the team, January 10. A group representing the late James P. Clark sold the Eagles to a group headed by Jerry Wolman, January 21. Carroll Rosenbloom, the majority owner of the Colts since 1953, acquired complete ownership of the team, January 23.

The AFL signed a five-year, $36-million television contract with NBC to begin with the 1965 season, January 29.

Hornung and Karras were reinstated by Rozelle, March 16.

CBS submitted the winning bid of $14.1 million per year for the NFL regular-season television rights for 1964 and 1965, January 24. CBS acquired the rights to the championship games for 1964 and 1965 for $1.8 million per game, April 17.

Pete Gogolak of Cornell signed a contract with Buffalo, becoming the first soccer-style kicker in pro football.

Buffalo defeated San Diego 20-7 in the AFL Championship Game, December 26. Cleveland defeated Baltimore 27-0 in the NFL Championship Game, December 27.

1965

The NFL teams pledged not to sign college seniors until completion of all their games, including bowl games, and empowered the Commissioner to discipline the clubs up to as much as the loss of an entire draft list for a violation of the pledge, February 15.

The NFL added a sixth official, the line judge, February 19. The color of the officials' penalty flags was changed from white to bright gold, April 5.

Commissioner Rozelle negotiated an agreement on behalf of the NFL clubs to purchase Ed Sabol's Blair Motion Pictures, which was renamed NFL Films, April.

Atlanta was awarded an NFL franchise for 1966, with Rankin Smith, Sr., as owner, June 30. Miami was awarded an AFL franchise for 1966, with Joe Robbie and Danny Thomas as owners, August 16.

Field Judge Burl Toler became the first black official in NFL history, September 19.

According to a Harris survey, sports fans chose professional football (41 percent) as their favorite sport, overtaking baseball (38 percent) for the first time, October.

Green Bay defeated Baltimore 13-10 in sudden-death overtime in a Western Conference playoff game. Don Chandler kicked a 25-yard field goal for the Packers after 13 minutes, 39 seconds of overtime, December 26. The Packers then defeated the Browns 23-12 in the NFL Championship Game, January 2.

In the AFL Championship Game, the Bills again defeated the Chargers, 23-0, December 26.

CBS acquired the rights to the NFL regular-season games in 1966 and 1967, with an option for 1968, for $18.8 million per year, December 29.

1966
The AFL-NFL war reached its peak, as the leagues spent a combined $7 million to sign their 1966 draft choices. The NFL signed 75 percent of its 232 draftees, the AFL 46 percent of its 181. Of the 111 common draft choices, 79 signed with the NFL, 28 with the AFL, and 4 went unsigned.

Buddy Young became the first African-American to work in the league office when Commissioner Rozelle named him director of player relations, February 1.

The rights to the 1966 and 1967 NFL Championship Games were sold to CBS for $2 million per game, February 14.

Foss resigned as AFL Commissioner, April 7. Al Davis, the head coach and general manager of the Raiders, was named to replace him, April 8.

Goal posts offset from the goal line, painted bright yellow, and with uprights 20 feet above the cross-bar were made standard in the NFL, May 16.

A series of secret meetings regarding a possible AFL-NFL merger were held in the spring between Hunt of Kansas City and Tex Schramm of Dallas. Rozelle announced the merger, June 8. Under the agreement, the two leagues would combine to form an expanded league with 24 teams, to be increased to 26 in 1968 and to 28 by 1970 or soon thereafter. All existing franchises would be retained, and no franchises would be transferred outside their metropolitan areas. While maintaining separate schedules through 1969, the leagues agreed to play an annual AFL-NFL World Championship Game beginning in January, 1967, and to hold a combined draft, also beginning in 1967. Preseason games would be held between teams of each league starting in 1967. Official regular-season play would start in 1970 when the two leagues would officially merge to form one league with two conferences. Rozelle was named Commissioner of the expanded league setup.

Davis rejoined the Raiders, and Milt Woodard was named president of the AFL, July 25.

The St. Louis Cardinals moved into newly constructed Busch Memorial Stadium.

Barron Hilton sold the Chargers to a group headed by Eugene Klein and Sam Schulman, August 25.

Congress approved the AFL-NFL merger, passing legislation exempting the agreement itself from antitrust action, October 21.

New Orleans was awarded an NFL franchise to begin play in 1967, November 1. John Mecom, Jr., of Houston was designated majority stockholder and president of the franchise, December 15.

The NFL was realigned for the 1967-69 seasons into the Capitol and Century Divisions in the Eastern Conference and the Central and Coastal Divisions in the Western Conference, December 2. New Orleans and the New York Giants agreed to switch divisions in 1968 and return to the 1967 alignment in 1969.

The rights to the Super Bowl for four years were sold to CBS and NBC for $9.5 million, December 13.

1967
Green Bay earned the right to represent the NFL in the first AFL-NFL World Championship Game by defeating Dallas 34-27, January 1. The same day, Kansas City defeated Buffalo 31-7 to represent the AFL. The Packers defeated the Chiefs 35-10 before 61,946 fans at the Los Angeles Memorial Coliseum in the first game between AFL and NFL teams, January 15. The winning players' share for the Packers was $15,000 each, and the losing players' share for the Chiefs was $7,500 each. The game was televised by both CBS and NBC.

The "sling-shot" goal post and a six-foot-wide border around the field were made standard in the NFL, February 22.

Baltimore made Bubba Smith, a Michigan State defensive lineman, the first choice in the first combined AFL-NFL draft, March 14.

The AFL awarded a franchise to begin play in 1968 to Cincinnati, May 24. A group with Paul Brown as part owner, general manager, and head coach, was awarded the Cincinnati franchise, September 27.

Arthur B. Modell, the president of the Cleveland Browns, was elected president of the NFL, May 28.

Defensive back Emlen Tunnell of the New York Giants became the first black player to enter the Pro Football Hall of Fame, August 5.

An AFL team defeated an NFL team for the first time, when Denver beat Detroit 13-7 in a preseason game, August 5.

Green Bay defeated Dallas 21-17 for the NFL championship on a last-minute 1-yard quarterback sneak by Bart Starr in 13-below-zero temperature at Green Bay, December 31. The same day, Oakland defeated Houston 40-7 for the AFL championship.

1968
Green Bay defeated Oakland 33-14 in Super Bowl II at Miami, January 14. The game had the first $3-million gate in pro football history.

Vince Lombardi resigned as head coach of the Packers, but remained as general manager, January 28.

Art McNally, a nine-year NFL game official, was named Supervisor of Officials, April 8. Werblin sold his shares in the Jets to his partners Don Lillis, Leon Hess, Townsend Martin, and Phil Iselin, May 21. Lillis assumed the presidency of the club, but then died July 23. Iselin was appointed president, August 6.

Halas retired for the fourth and last time as head coach of the Bears, May 27.

The Oilers left Rice Stadium for the Astrodome and became the first NFL team to play its home games in a domed stadium.

The movie *Heidi* became a footnote in sports history when NBC didn't show the last 50 seconds of the Jets-Raiders game in order to permit the children's special to begin on time. The Raiders scored two touchdowns in the last 42 seconds to win 43-32, November 17.

Ewbank became the first coach to win titles in both the NFL and AFL when his Jets defeated the Raiders 27-23 for the AFL championship, December 29. The same day, Baltimore defeated Cleveland 34-0.

1969
The AFL established a playoff format for the 1969 season, with the winner in one division playing the runner-up in the other, January 11.

An AFL team won the Super Bowl for the first time, as the Jets defeated the Colts 16-7 at Miami, January 12 in Super Bowl III. The title Super Bowl was recognized by the NFL for the first time.

Vince Lombardi became part owner, executive vice-president, and head coach of the Washington Redskins, February 7.

Wolman sold the Eagles to Leonard Tose, May 1.

Baltimore, Cleveland, and Pittsburgh agreed to join the AFL teams to form the 13-team American Football Conference of the NFL in 1970, May 17. The NFL also agreed on a playoff format that would include one "wild-card" team per conference—the second-place team with the best record.

The NFL announced a three-year agreement with ABC to televise *Monday Night Football*. The new series makes the NFL the first league with a regular series of national telecasts in prime time, May 26.

George Preston Marshall, president emeritus of the Redskins, died at 72, August 9.

The NFL marked its fiftieth year by the wearing of a special patch by each of the 16 teams.

1970
Kansas City defeated Minnesota 23-7 in Super Bowl IV at New Orleans, January 11. The gross receipts of approximately $3.8 million were the largest ever for a one-day sports event.

Four-year television contracts, under which CBS would televise all NFC games and NBC all AFC games

CHRONOLOGY OF PROFESSIONAL FOOTBALL

(except Monday night games) and the two would divide televising the Super Bowl and AFC-NFC Pro Bowl games, were announced, January 26.

Art Modell resigned as president of the NFL, March 12. Milt Woodard resigned as president of the AFL, March 13. Lamar Hunt was elected president of the AFC and George Halas was elected president of the NFC, March 19.

The merged 26-team league adopted rules changes putting names on the backs of players' jerseys, making a point after touchdown worth only one point, and making the scoreboard clock the official timing device of the game, March 18.

The Players Negotiating Committee and the NFL Players Association announced a four-year agreement guaranteeing approximately $4,535,000 annually to player pension and insurance benefits, August 3. The owners also agreed to contribute $250,000 annually to improve or implement items such as disability payments, widows' benefits, maternity benefits, and dental benefits. The agreement also provided for increased preseason game and per diem payments, averaging approximately $2.6 million annually.

The Pittsburgh Steelers moved into Three Rivers Stadium. The Cincinnati Bengals moved to Riverfront Stadium.

Vince Lombardi died of cancer at 57, September 3.

The Super Bowl trophy was renamed the Vince Lombardi trophy, September 10.

Tom Dempsey of New Orleans kicked a game-winning NFL-record 63-yard field goal against Detroit, November 8.

1971
Baltimore defeated Dallas 16-13 on Jim O'Brien's 32-yard field goal with five seconds to go in Super Bowl V at Miami, January 17. The NBC telecast was viewed in an estimated 23,980,000 homes, the largest audience ever for a one-day sports event.

The NFC defeated the AFC 27-6 in the first AFC-NFC Pro Bowl at Los Angeles, January 24.

The Boston Patriots changed their name to the New England Patriots, March 25. Their new stadium, Schaefer Stadium, was dedicated in a 20-14 preseason victory over the Giants.

The Philadelphia Eagles left Franklin Field and played their games at the new Veterans Stadium.

The San Francisco 49ers left Kezar Stadium and moved their games to Candlestick Park.

Daniel F. Reeves, the president and general manager of the Rams, died at 58, April 15.

The Dallas Cowboys moved from the Cotton Bowl into their new home, Texas Stadium, October 24.

Miami defeated Kansas City 27-24 in sudden-death overtime in an AFC Divisional Playoff Game, December 25. Garo Yepremian kicked a 37-yard field goal for the Dolphins after 22 minutes, 40 seconds of overtime, as the game lasted 82 minutes, 40 seconds overall, making it the longest game in history.

1972
Dallas defeated Miami 24-3 in Super Bowl VI at New Orleans, January 16. The CBS telecast was viewed in an estimated 27,450,000 homes, the top-rated one-day telecast ever.

The inbounds lines or hashmarks were moved nearer the center of the field, 23 yards, 1 foot, 9 inches from the sidelines, March 23. The method of determining won-lost percentage in standings changed. Tie games, previously not counted in the standings, were made equal to a half-game won and a half-game lost, May 24.

Robert Irsay purchased the Los Angeles Rams and transferred ownership of the club to Carroll Rosenbloom in exchange for the Baltimore Colts, July 13.

William V. Bidwill purchased the stock of his brother Charles (Stormy) Bidwill to become the sole owner of the St. Louis Cardinals, September 2.

The National District Attorneys Association endorsed the position of professional leagues in opposing proposed legalization of gambling on professional team sports,

September 28.

Franco Harris' "Immaculate Reception" gave the Steelers their first postseason win ever, 13-7 over the Raiders, December 23.

1973
Rozelle announced that all Super Bowl VII tickets were sold and that the game would be telecast in Los Angeles, the site of the game, on an experimental basis, January 3.

Miami defeated Washington 14-7 in Super Bowl VII at Los Angeles, completing a 17-0 season, the first perfect-record regular-season and postseason mark in NFL history, January 14. The NBC telecast was viewed by approximately 75 million people.

The AFC defeated the NFC 33-28 in the Pro Bowl in Dallas, the first time since 1942 that the game was played outside Los Angeles, January 21.

A jersey numbering system was adopted, April 5: 1-19 for quarterbacks and specialists, 20-49 for running backs and defensive backs, 50-59 for centers and linebackers, 60-79 for defensive linemen and interior offensive linemen other than centers, and 80-89 for wide receivers and tight ends. Players who had been in the NFL in 1972 could continue to use old numbers.

NFL Charities, a nonprofit organization, was created to derive an income from monies generated from NFL Properties' licensing of NFL trademarks and team names, June 26. NFL Charities was set up to support education and charitable activities and to supply economic support to persons formerly associated with professional football who were no longer able to support themselves.

Congress adopted experimental legislation (for three years) requiring any NFL game that had been declared a sell-out 72 hours prior to kickoff to be made available for local televising, September 14. The legislation provided for an annual review to be made by the Federal Communications Commission.

The Buffalo Bills moved their home games from War Memorial Stadium to Rich Stadium in nearby Orchard Park. The Giants tied the Eagles

23-23 in the final game in Yankee Stadium, September 23. The Giants played the rest of their home games at the Yale Bowl in New Haven, Connecticut.

A rival league, the World Football League, was formed and was reported in operation, October 2. It had plans to start play in 1974.

O.J. Simpson of Buffalo became the first player to rush for more than 2,000 yards in a season, gaining 2,003.

1974
Miami defeated Minnesota 24-7 in Super Bowl VIII at Houston, the second consecutive Super Bowl championship for the Dolphins, January 13. The CBS telecast was viewed by approximately 75 million people.

Rozelle was given a 10-year contract effective January 1, 1973, February 27.

Tampa Bay was awarded a franchise to begin operation in 1976, April 24.

Sweeping rules changes were adopted to add action and tempo to games: one sudden-death overtime period was added for preseason and regular-season games; the goal posts were moved from the goal line to the end lines; kickoffs were moved from the 40- to the 35-yard line; after missed field goals from beyond the 20, the ball was to be returned to the line of scrimmage; restrictions were placed on members of the punting team to open up return possibilities; roll-blocking and cutting of wide receivers was eliminated; the extent of downfield contact a defender could have with an eligible receiver was restricted; the penalties for offensive holding, illegal use of the hands, and tripping were reduced from 15 to 10 yards; wide receivers blocking back toward the ball within three yards of the line of scrimmage were prevented from blocking below the waist, April 25.

Seattle was awarded an NFL franchise to begin play in 1976, June 4. Lloyd W. Nordstrom, president of the Seattle Seahawks, and Hugh Culverhouse, president of the Tampa Bay Buccaneers, signed franchise agreements, December 5.

410　　　　　**2006 NFL Record & Fact Book**

The Birmingham Americans defeated the Florida Blazers 22-21 in the WFL World Bowl, winning the league championship, December 5.

1975

Pittsburgh defeated Minnesota 16-6 in Super Bowl IX at New Orleans, the Steelers' first championship since entering the NFL in 1933. The NBC telecast was viewed by approximately 78 million people.

The Memphis Southmen of the WFL signed Larry Csonka, Jim Kiick, and Paul Warfield of Miami, March 31.

The divisional winners with the highest won-loss percentage were made the home team for the divisional playoffs, and the surviving winners with the highest percentage made home teams for the championship games. Previously, the home sites were pre-determined by division on a rotating basis, June 26.

Referees were equipped with wireless microphones for all preseason, regular-season, and playoff games.

The Lions moved to the new Pontiac Silverdome. The Giants played their home games in Shea Stadium. The Saints moved into the Louisiana Superdome.

The World Football League folded, October 22.

1976

Pittsburgh defeated Dallas 21-17 in Super Bowl X in Miami. The Steelers joined Green Bay and Miami as the only teams to win two Super Bowls; the Cowboys became the first wild-card team to play in the Super Bowl. The CBS telecast was viewed by an estimated 80 million people, the largest television audience in history.

Lloyd Nordstrom, the president of the Seahawks, died at 66, January 20. His brother Elmer succeeded him as majority representative of the team.

The owners awarded Super Bowl XII, to be played on January 15, 1978, to New Orleans. They also adopted the use of two 30-second clocks for all games, visible to both players and fans to note the official time between the ready-for-play signal and snap

of the ball, March 16.

A veteran player allocation was held to stock the Seattle and Tampa Bay franchises with 39 players each, March 30-31. In the college draft, Seattle and Tampa Bay each received eight extra choices, April 8-9.

The Giants moved into new Giants Stadium in East Rutherford, New Jersey.

The Steelers defeated the College All-Stars in a storm-shortened Chicago College All-Star Game, the last of the series, July 23. St. Louis defeated San Diego 20-10 in a preseason game before 38,000 in Korakuen Stadium, Tokyo, in the first NFL game outside of North America, August 16.

1977

Oakland defeated Minnesota 32-14 in Super Bowl XI at Pasadena, January 9. The paid attendance was a pro record 103,438. The NBC telecast was viewed by 81.9 million people, the largest ever to view a sports event. The victory was the fifth consecutive for the AFC in the Super Bowl.

The NFL Players Association and the NFL Management Council ratified a collective bargaining agreement extending until 1982, covering five football seasons while continuing the pension plan—including years 1974, 1975, and 1976—with contributions totaling more than $55 million. The total cost of the agreement was estimated at $107 million. The agreement called for a college draft at least through 1986; contained a no-strike, no-suit clause; established a 43-man active player limit; reduced pension vesting to four years; provided for increases in minimum salaries and preseason and postseason pay; improved insurance, medical, and dental benefits; modified previous practices in player movement and control; and reaffirmed the NFL Commissioner's disciplinary authority. Additionally, the agreement called for the NFL member clubs to make payments totaling $16 million in the next 10 years to settle various legal disputes, February 25.

The San Francisco 49ers were sold to Edward J. DeBartolo, Jr., March 28.

A 16-game regular season, 4-game preseason was adopted to begin in 1978, March 29. A second wild-card team was adopted for the playoffs beginning in 1978, with the wild-card teams to play each other and the winners advancing to a round of eight postseason series.

The Seahawks were permanently aligned in the AFC Western Division and the Buccaneers in the NFC Central Division, March 31.

The owners awarded Super Bowl XIII, to be played on January 21, 1979, to Miami, to be played in the Orange Bowl; Super Bowl XIV, to be played January 20, 1980, was awarded to Pasadena, to be played in the Rose Bowl, June 14.

Rules changes were adopted to open up the passing game and to cut down on injuries. Defenders were permitted to make contact with eligible receivers only once; the head slap was outlawed; offensive linemen were prohibited from thrusting their hands to an opponent's neck, face, or head; and wide receivers were prohibited from clipping, even in the legal clipping zone.

Rozelle negotiated contracts with the three television networks to televise all NFL regular-season and postseason games, plus selected preseason games, for four years beginning with the 1978 season. ABC was awarded yearly rights to 16 Monday night games, four prime-time games, the AFC-NFC Pro Bowl, and the Hall of Fame games. CBS received the rights to all NFC regular-season and postseason games (except those in the ABC package) and to Super Bowls XIV and XVI. NBC received the rights to all AFC regular-season and postseason games (except those in the ABC package) and to Super Bowls XIII and XV. Industry sources considered it the largest single television package ever negotiated, October 12.

Chicago's Walter Payton set a single-game rushing record with 275 yards (40 carries) against Minnesota, November 20.

1978

Dallas defeated Denver 27-10 in Super Bowl XII, held indoors for the first time, at the Louisiana Superdome in New Orleans, January 15. The CBS telecast was viewed by more than 102 million people, meaning the game was watched by more viewers than any other show of any kind in the history of television. Dallas' victory was the first for the NFC in six years.

According to a Louis Harris Sports Survey, 70 percent of the nation's sports fans said they followed football, compared to 54 percent who followed baseball. Football increased its lead as the country's favorite, 26 percent to 16 percent for baseball, January 19.

A seventh official, the side judge, was added to the officiating crew, March 14.

The NFL continued a trend toward opening up the game. Rules changes permitted a defender to maintain contact with a receiver within five yards of the line of scrimmage, but restricted contact beyond that point. The pass-blocking rule was interpreted to permit the extending of arms and open hands, March 17.

A study on the use of instant replay as an officiating aid was made during seven nationally televised preseason games.

The NFL played for the first time in Mexico City, with the Saints defeating the Eagles 14-7 in a preseason game, August 5.

Bolstered by the expansion of the regular-season schedule from 14 to 16 weeks, NFL paid attendance exceeded 12 million (12,771,800) for the first time. The per-game average of 57,017 was the third-highest in league history and the most since 1973.

1979

Pittsburgh defeated Dallas 35-31 in Super Bowl XIII at Miami to become the first team ever to win three Super Bowls, January 21. The NBC telecast was viewed in 35,090,000 homes, by an estimated 96.6 million fans.

The owners awarded three future Super Bowl sites: Super Bowl XV to the Louisiana

Superdome in New Orleans, to be played on January 25, 1981; Super Bowl XVI to the Pontiac Silverdome in Pontiac, Michigan, to be played on January 24, 1982; and Super Bowl XVII to Pasadena's Rose Bowl, to be played on January 30, 1983, March 13.

NFL rules changes emphasized additional player safety. The changes prohibited players on the receiving team from blocking below the waist during kickoffs, punts, and field-goal attempts; prohibited the wearing of torn or altered equipment and exposed pads that could be hazardous; extended the zone in which there could be no crackback blocks; and instructed officials to quickly whistle a play dead when a quarterback was clearly in the grasp of a tackler, March 16.

Carroll Rosenbloom, the president of the Rams, drowned at 72, April 2. His widow, Georgia, assumed control of the club.

1980
Pittsburgh defeated the Los Angeles Rams 31-19 in Super Bowl XIV at Pasadena to become the first team to win four Super Bowls, January 20. The game was viewed in a record 35,330,000 homes.

The AFC-NFC Pro Bowl, won 37-27 by the NFC, was played before 48,060 fans at Aloha Stadium in Honolulu, Hawaii. It was the first time in the 30-year history of the Pro Bowl that the game was played in a non-NFL city.

Rules changes placed greater restrictions on contact in the area of the head, neck, and face. Under the heading of "personal foul," players were prohibited from directly striking, swinging, or clubbing on the head, neck, or face. Starting in 1980, a penalty could be called for such contact whether or not the initial contact was made below the neck area.

CBS, with a record bid of $12 million, won the national radio rights to 26 NFL regular-season games, including Monday Night Football, and all 10 postseason games for the 1980-83 seasons.

The Los Angeles Rams moved their home games to Anaheim Stadium in nearby Orange County, California.

The Oakland Raiders joined the Los Angeles Coliseum Commission's antitrust suit against the NFL. The suit contended the league violated antitrust laws in declining to approve a proposed move by the Raiders from Oakland to Los Angeles.

NFL regular-season attendance of nearly 13.4 million set a record for the third year in a row. The average paid attendance for the 224-game 1980 regular season was 59,787, the highest in the league's 61-year history. NFL games in 1980 were played before 92.4 percent of total stadium capacity.

Television ratings in 1980 were the second-best in NFL history, trailing only the combined ratings of the 1976 season. All three networks posted gains, and NBC's 15.0 rating was its best ever. CBS and ABC had their best ratings since 1977, with 15.3 and 20.8 ratings, respectively. CBS Radio reported a record audience of 7 million for Monday night and special games.

1981
Oakland defeated Philadelphia 27-10 in Super Bowl XV at the Louisiana Superdome in New Orleans, to become the first wild-card team to win a Super Bowl, January 25.

Edgar F. Kaiser, Jr., purchased the Denver Broncos from Gerald and Allan Phipps, February 26.

The owners adopted a disaster plan for re-stocking a team should the club be involved in a fatal accident, March 20.

The owners awarded Super Bowl XVIII to Tampa, to be played in Tampa Stadium on January 22, 1984, June 3.

A CBS-New York Times poll showed that 48 percent of sports fans preferred football to 31 percent for baseball.

The NFL teams hosted 167 representatives from 44 predominantly black colleges during training camps for a total of 289 days. The program was adopted for renewal during each training camp period.

NFL regular-season attendance—13.6 million for an average of 60,745—set a record for the fourth year in a row. It also was the first time the per-game average exceed-

ed 60,000. NFL games in 1981 were played before 93.8 percent of total stadium capacity.

ABC and CBS set all-time rating highs. ABC finished with a 21.7 rating and CBS with a 17.5 rating. NBC was down slightly to 13.9.

1982
San Francisco defeated Cincinnati 26-21 in Super Bowl XVI at the Pontiac Silverdome, in the first Super Bowl held in the North, January 24. The CBS telecast achieved the highest rating of any televised sports event ever, 49.1 with a 73.0 share. The game was viewed by a record 110.2 million fans. CBS Radio reported a record 14 million listeners for the game.

The NFL signed a five-year contract with the three television networks (ABC, CBS, and NBC) to televise all NFL regular-season and postseason games starting with the 1982 season.

A jury ruled against the NFL in the antitrust trial brought by the Los Angeles Coliseum Commission and the Oakland Raiders, May 7. The verdict cleared the way for the Raiders to move to Los Angeles, where they defeated Green Bay 24-3 in their first preseason game, August 29.

The 1982 season was reduced from a 16-game schedule to nine as the result of a 57-day players' strike. The strike was called by the NFLPA at midnight on Monday, September 20, following the Green Bay at New York Giants game. Play resumed November 21-22 following ratification of the Collective Bargaining Agreement by NFL owners, November 17 in New York.

Under the Collective Bargaining Agreement, which was to run through the 1986 season, the NFL draft was extended through 1992 and the veteran free-agent system was left basically unchanged. A minimum salary schedule for years of experience was established; training camp and postseason pay were increased; players' medical, insurance, and retirement benefits were increased; and a severance-pay system was introduced to aid in career

transition, a first in professional sports.

Despite the players' strike, the average paid attendance in 1982 was 58,472, the fifth-highest in league history.

The owners awarded the sites of two Super Bowls, December 14: Super Bowl XIX, to be played on January 20, 1985, to Stanford University Stadium in Stanford, California, with San Francisco as host team; and Super Bowl XX, to be played on January 26, 1986, to the Louisiana Superdome in New Orleans.

1983
Because of the shortened season, the NFL adopted a format of 16 teams competing in a Super Bowl Tournament for the 1982 playoffs. The NFC's number-one seed, Washington, defeated the AFC's number-two seed, Miami, 27-17 in Super Bowl XVII at the Rose Bowl in Pasadena, January 30.

Super Bowl XVII was the second-highest rated live television program of all time, giving the NFL a sweep of the top 10 live programs in television history. The game was viewed in more than 40 million homes, the largest ever for a live telecast.

George Halas, the owner of the Bears and the last surviving member of the NFL's second organizational meeting, died at 88, October 31.

1984
The Los Angeles Raiders defeated Washington 38-9 in Super Bowl XVIII at Tampa Stadium, January 22. The game achieved a 46.4 rating and 71.0 share.

An 11-man group headed by H.R. (Bum) Bright purchased the Dallas Cowboys from Clint Murchison, Jr., March 20. Club president Tex Schramm was designated as managing general partner.

Wellington Mara was named president of the NFC, March 20.

Patrick Bowlen purchased a majority interest in the Denver Broncos from Edgar Kaiser, Jr., March 21.

The Colts relocated to Indianapolis, March 28. Their new home became the Hoosier Dome.

The owners awarded two

Super Bowl sites at their May 23-25 meetings: Super Bowl XXI, to be played on January 25, 1987, to the Rose Bowl in Pasadena; and Super Bowl XXII, to be played on January 31, 1988, to San Diego Jack Murphy Stadium.

The New York Jets moved their home games to Giants Stadium in East Rutherford, New Jersey.

Alex G. Spanos purchased a majority interest in the San Diego Chargers from Eugene V. Klein, August 28.

Houston defeated Pittsburgh 23-20 to mark the one-hundredth overtime game in regular-season play since overtime was adopted in 1974, December 2.

On the field, many all-time records were set: Dan Marino of Miami passed for 5,084 yards and 48 touchdowns; Eric Dickerson of the Los Angeles Rams rushed for 2,105 yards; Art Monk of Washington caught 106 passes; and Walter Payton of Chicago broke Jim Brown's career rushing mark, finishing the season with 13,309 yards.

According to a CBS Sports/New York Times survey, 53 percent of the nation's sports fans said they most enjoyed watching football, compared to 18 percent for baseball, December 2-4.

NFL paid attendance exceeded 13 million for the fifth consecutive complete regular season when 13,398,112, an average of 59,813, attended games. The figure was the second-highest in league history. Teams averaged 42.4 points per game, the second-highest total since the 1970 merger.

1985

San Francisco defeated Miami 38-16 in Super Bowl XIX at Stanford Stadium in Stanford, California, January 20. The game was viewed on television by more people than any other live event in history. President Ronald Reagan, who took his second oath of office before tossing the coin for the game, was one of 115,936,000 viewers. The game drew a 46.4 rating and a 63.0 share. In addition, 6 million people watched the Super Bowl in the United Kingdom and a similar number in Italy.

Super Bowl XIX had a direct economic impact of $113.5 million on the San Francisco Bay area.

NBC Radio and the NFL entered into a two-year agreement granting NBC the radio rights to a 37-game package in each of the 1985-86 seasons, March 6. The package included 27 regular-season games and 10 postseason games.

Norman Braman, in partnership with Edward Leibowitz, bought the Philadelphia Eagles from Leonard Tose, April 29.

A group headed by Tom Benson, Jr., was approved to purchase the New Orleans Saints from John W. Mecom, Jr., June 3.

The NFL owners adopted a resolution calling for a series of overseas preseason games, beginning in 1986, with one game to be played in England/Europe and/or one game in Japan each year. The game would be a fifth preseason game for the clubs involved and all arrangements and selection of the clubs would be under the control of the Commissioner, May 23.

The league-wide conversion to videotape from movie film for coaching study was approved.

The NFL set a single-weekend paid attendance record when 902,657 tickets were sold for the weekend of October 27-28.

A Louis Harris poll in December revealed that pro football remained the sport most followed by Americans. Fifty-nine percent of those surveyed followed pro football, compared with 54 percent who followed baseball.

The Chicago-Miami Monday game had the highest rating, 29.6, and share, 46.0, of any prime-time game in NFL history, December 2. The game was viewed in more than 25 million homes.

The NFL showed a ratings increase on all three networks for the season, gaining 4 percent on NBC, 10 on CBS, and 16 on ABC.

1986

Chicago defeated New England 46-10 in Super Bowl XX at the Louisiana Superdome, January 26. The Patriots had

earned the right to play the Bears by becoming the first wild-card team to win three consecutive games on the road. The NBC telecast replaced the final episode of *M*A*S*H* as the most-viewed television program in history, with an audience of 127 million viewers, according to A.C. Nielsen figures. In addition to drawing a 48.3 rating and a 70 percent share in the United States, Super Bowl XX was televised to 59 foreign countries and beamed via satellite to the QE II. An estimated 300 million Chinese viewed a tape delay of the game in March. CBS Radio figures indicated an audience of 10 million for the game.

The owners adopted limited use of instant replay as an officiating aid, prohibited players from wearing or otherwise displaying equipment, apparel, or other items that carry commercial names, names of organizations, or personal messages of any type, March 11.

After an 11-week trial, a jury in U.S. District Court in New York awarded the United States Football League one dollar in its $1.7 billion antitrust suit against the NFL. The jury rejected all of the USFL's television-related claims, which were the self-proclaimed heart of the USFL's case. The jury deliberated five days, July 29.

Chicago defeated Dallas 17-6 at Wembley Stadium in London in the first American Bowl. The game drew a sellout crowd of 82,699 and the NBC national telecast in this country produced a 12.4 rating and 36 percent share, making it the highest daytime preseason television audience ever with 10.65-million viewers, August 3.

ABC's *NFL Monday Night Football*, in its seventeenth season, became the longest-running prime-time series in the history of the network.

1987

The New York Giants defeated Denver 39-20 in Super Bowl XXI and captured their first NFL title since 1956. The game, played in Pasadena's Rose Bowl, drew a sellout crowd of 101,063. According to A.C. Nielsen figures, the

CBS broadcast of the game was viewed in the U.S. on television by 122.64-million people, making the telecast the second most-watched television show of all-time behind Super Bowl XX. The game was watched live or on tape in 55 foreign countries and NBC Radio's broadcast of the game was heard by a record 10.1 million people.

New three-year TV contracts with ABC, CBS, and NBC were announced for 1987-89 at the NFL annual meeting in Maui, Hawaii, March 15. Commissioner Rozelle and Broadcast Committee Chairman Art Modell also announced a three-year contract with ESPN to televise 13 prime-time games each season. The ESPN contract was the first with a cable network. However, NFL games on ESPN also were scheduled for regular television in the city of the visiting team and in the home city if the game was sold out 72 hours in advance.

A special payment program was adopted to benefit nearly 1,000 former NFL players who participated in the League before the current Bert Bell NFL Pension Plan was created and made retroactive to the 1959 season. Players covered by the new program spent at least five years in the League and played all or part of their career prior to 1959. Each vested player would receive $60 per month for each year of service in the League for life.

NFL and CBS Radio jointly announced agreement granting CBS the radio rights to a 40-game package in each of the next three NFL seasons, 1987-89, April 7.

Over 400 former NFL players from the pre-1959 era received first payments from NFL owners, July 1.

The NFL's debut on ESPN produced the two highest-rated and most-watched sports programs in basic cable history. The Chicago at Miami game on August 16 drew an 8.9 rating in 3.81 million homes. Those records fell two weeks later when the Los Angeles Raiders at Dallas game achieved a 10.2 cable rating in 4.36 million homes.

The 1987 season was reduced from a 16-game season to 15 as the result of a 24-day players' strike. The strike was called by the NFLPA on Tuesday, September 22, following the New England at New York Jets game. Games scheduled for the third weekend were canceled but the games of weeks four, five, and six were played with replacement teams. Striking players returned for the seventh week of the season, October 25.

In a three-team deal involving 10 players and/or draft choices, the Los Angeles Rams traded running back Eric Dickerson to the Indianapolis Colts for six draft choices and two players. Buffalo obtained the rights to linebacker Cornelius Bennett from Indianapolis, sending Greg Bell and three draft choices to the Rams. The Colts added Owen Gill and three draft choices of their own to complete the deal with the Rams, October 31.

The Chicago at Minnesota game became the highest-rated and most-watched sports program in basic cable history when it drew a 14.4 cable rating in 6.5 million homes, December 6.

1988
Washington defeated Denver 42-10 in Super Bowl XXII to earn its second victory this decade in the NFL Championship Game. The game, played for the first time in San Diego Jack Murphy Stadium, drew a sellout crowd of 73,302. According to A.C. Nielsen figures, the ABC broadcast of the game was viewed in the U.S. on television by 115,000,000 people. The game was seen live or on tape in 60 foreign countries, including the People's Republic of China, and CBS's radio broadcast of the game was heard by 13.7 million people.

In a unanimous 3-0 decision, the 2nd Circuit Court of Appeals in New York upheld the verdict of the jury that in July, 1986, had awarded the United States Football League one dollar in its $1.7 billion antitrust suit against the NFL. In a 91-page opinion, Judge Ralph K. Winter said the USFL sought through court decree the success it failed to gain among football fans, March 10.

By a 23-5 margin, owners voted to continue the instant replay system for the third consecutive season with the Instant Replay Official to be assigned to a regular seven-man, on-the-field crew. At the NFL annual meeting in Phoenix, Arizona, a 45-second clock was also approved to replace the 30-second clock. For a normal sequence of plays, the interval between plays was changed to 45 seconds from the time the ball is signaled dead until it is snapped on the succeeding play.

NFL owners approved the transfer of the Cardinals' franchise from St. Louis to Phoenix; approved two supplemental drafts each year—one prior to training camp and one prior to the regular season; and voted to initiate an annual series of games in Japan/Asia as early as 1989 preseason, March 14-18.

The NFL Annual Selection Meeting returned to a separate two-day format and for the first time originated on a Sunday. ESPN drew a 3.6 rating during their seven-hour coverage of the draft, which was viewed in 1.6 million homes, April 24-25.

Art Rooney, founder and owner of the Steelers, died at 87, August 25.

Johnny Grier became the first African-American referee in NFL history, September 4.

Commissioner Rozelle announced that two teams would play a preseason game as part of the American Bowl series on August 6, 1989, in the Korakuen Tokyo Dome in Japan, December 16.

1989
San Francisco defeated Cincinnati 20-16 in Super Bowl XXIII. The game, played for the first time at Joe Robbie Stadium in Miami, was attended by a sellout crowd of 75,129. NBC's telecast of the game was watched by an estimated 110,780,000 viewers, according to A.C. Nielsen, making it the sixth most-watched program in television history. The game was seen live or on tape in 60 foreign countries, including an estimated 300 million in China. The CBS Radio broadcast of the game was heard by

11.2 million people.

Commissioner Rozelle announced his retirement, pending the naming of a successor, March 22 at the NFL annual meeting in Palm Desert, California.

Following the announcement, AFC president Lamar Hunt and NFC president Wellington Mara announced the formation of a six-man search committee composed of Art Modell, Robert Parins, Dan Rooney, and Ralph Wilson. Hunt and Mara served as co-chairmen.

By a 24-4 margin, owners voted to continue the instant replay system for the fourth straight season. A strengthened policy regarding anabolic steroids and masking agents was announced by Commissioner Rozelle. NFL clubs called for strong disciplinary measures in cases of feigned injuries and adopted a joint proposal by the Long-Range Planning and Finance committees regarding player personnel rules, March 19-23.

Two hundred twenty-nine unconditional free agents signed with new teams under management's Plan B system, April 1.

Jerry Jones purchased a majority interest in the Dallas Cowboys from H.R. (Bum) Bright, April 18.

Tex Schramm was named president of the new World League of American Football to work with a six-man committee of Dan Rooney, chairman; Norman Braman, Lamar Hunt, Victor Kiam, Mike Lynn, and Bill Walsh, April 18.

NFL and CBS Radio jointly announced agreement extending CBS's radio rights to an annual 40-game package through the 1994 season, April 18.

As of opening day, September 10, of the 229 Plan B free agents, 111 were active and 23 others were on teams' reserve lists. Ninety-two others were waived and three retired.

Art Shell was named head coach of the Los Angeles Raiders making him the NFL's first black head coach since Fritz Pollard coached the Akron Pros in 1921, October 3.

The site of the New England Patriots at San Francisco

49ers game scheduled for Candlestick Park on October 22 was switched to Stanford Stadium in the aftermath of the Bay Area Earthquake of October 17. The change was announced on October 19.

Paul Tagliabue became the seventh chief executive of the NFL on October 26 when he was chosen to succeed Commissioner Pete Rozelle on the sixth ballot of a three-day meeting in Cleveland, Ohio.

In all, 12 ballots were required to select Tagliabue. Two were conducted at a meeting in Chicago on July 6, and four at a meeting in Dallas on October 10-11. On the twelfth ballot, with Seattle absent, Tagliabue received more than the 19 affirmative votes required for election from among the 27 clubs present.

The transfer from Commissioner Rozelle to Commissioner Tagliabue took place at 12:01 A.M. on Sunday, November 5.

NFL Charities donated $1 million through United Way to benefit Bay Area earthquake victims, November 6.

NFL paid attendance of 17,399,538 was the highest total in league history. This included a total of 13,625,662 for an average of 60,829—both NFL records—for the 224-game regular season.

1990
San Francisco defeated Denver 55-10 in Super Bowl XXIV at the Louisiana Superdome, January 28. San Francisco joined Pittsburgh as the NFL's only teams to win four Super Bowls.

The NFL announced revisions in its 1990 draft eligibility rules. College juniors became eligible but must renounce their collegiate football eligibility before applying for the NFL Draft, February 16.

Commissioner Tagliabue announced NFL teams will play their 16-game schedule over 17 weeks in 1990 and 1991 and 16 games over 18 weeks in 1992 and 1993, February 27.

The NFL revised its playoff format to include two additional wild-card teams (one per conference), which raised the total to six wild-card teams.

Commissioner Tagliabue

and Broadcast Committee Chairman Art Modell announced a four-year contract with Turner Broadcasting to televise nine Sunday-night games.

New four-year TV agreements were ratified for 1990-93 for ABC, CBS, NBC, ESPN, and TNT at the NFL annual meeting in Orlando, Florida, March 12. The contracts totaled $3.6 billion, the largest in TV history.

The NFL announced plans to expand its American Bowl series of preseason games. In addition to games in London and Tokyo, American Bowl games were scheduled for Berlin, Germany, and Montreal, Canada, in 1990.

For the fifth straight year, NFL owners voted to continue a limited system of Instant Replay. Beginning in 1990, the replay official will have a two-minute time limit to make a decision. The vote was 21-7, March 12.

Commissioner Tagliabue announced the formation of a Committee on Expansion and Realignment, March 13. He also named a Player Advisory Council, comprised of 12 former NFL players, March 14.

One-hundred eighty-four Plan B unconditional free agents signed with new teams, April 2.

Commissioner Tagliabue appointed Dr. John Lombardo as the League's Drug Advisor for Anabolic Steroids, April 25 and named Dr. Lawrence Brown as the League's Advisor for Drugs of Abuse, May 17.

Commissioner Tagliabue named NFL referee Jerry Seeman as NFL Director of Officiating, replacing Art McNally, who announced his retirement after 31 years on the field and at the league office, July 12.

NFL International Week was celebrated with four preseason games in seven days in Tokyo, London, Berlin, and Montreal. More than 200,000 fans on three continents attended the four games, August 4-11.

Commissioner Tagliabue announced the NFL Teacher of the Month program in which the League furnishes grants and scholarships in recognition of teachers who provided a positive influence upon NFL

players in elementary and secondary schools, September 20.

For the first time since 1957, every NFL club won at least one of its first four games, October 1.

The Super Bowl Most Valuable Player trophy was renamed the Pete Rozelle trophy, October 8.

NFL total paid attendance of 17,665,671 was the highest total in League history. The regular-season total paid attendance of 13,959,896 was the highest ever, average of 62,321 for 224 games were the highest ever, surpassing the previous records set in the 1989 season.

1991

The New York Giants defeated Buffalo 20-19 in Super Bowl XXV to capture their second title in five years. The game was played before a sellout crowd of 73,813 at Tampa Stadium and became the first Super Bowl decided by one point, January 26. The ABC broadcast of the game was seen by more than 112-million people in the United States and was seen live or taped in 60 other countries.

NFL playoff games earned the top television rating spot of the week for each week of the month-long playoffs, January 29.

New York businessman Robert Tisch purchased a 50 percent interest in the New York Giants from Mrs. Helen Mara Nugent and her children, Tim Mara and Maura Mara Concannon, February 2.

NFL owners awarded Super Bowl XXVII to be played on January 31, 1993, to Pasadena, March 19.

NFL clubs voted to continue a limited system of Instant Replay for the sixth consecutive year. The vote was 21-7, March 19.

The NFL launched the World League of American Football, the first sports league to operate on a weekly basis on two separate continents, March 23.

NFL Charities presented a $250,000 donation to the United Service Organization. The donation was the second largest single grant ever by NFL Charities, April 5.

Commissioner Tagliabue

named Harold Henderson as Executive Vice President for Labor Relations and Chairman of the NFL Management Council Executive Committee, April 8.

NFL clubs approved a recommendation by the Expansion and Realignment Committee to add two teams for the 1994 season, resulting in six divisions of five teams each, May 22.

"NFL International Week" featured six 1990 playoff teams playing nationally televised games in London, Berlin, and Tokyo on July 28 and August 3-4. The games drew more than 150,000 fans.

Paul Brown, founder of the Cleveland Browns and Cincinnati Bengals, died at age 82, August 5.

NFL clubs approved a resolution establishing an international division. A three-year financial plan for the World League was approved by NFL clubs at a meeting in Dallas, October 23.

1992

The NFL agreed to provide a minimum of $2.5 million in financial support to the NFL Alumni Association and assistance to NFL Alumni-related programs. The agreement included contributions from NFL Charities to the Pre-59ers and Dire Need Programs for former players, January 25.

The Washington Redskins defeated the Buffalo Bills 37-24 in Super Bowl XXVI to capture their third world championship in 10 years, January 26. The game was played before a sellout crowd of 63,130 at the Hubert H. Humphrey Metrodome in Minneapolis and attracted the second largest television audience in Super Bowl history. The CBS broadcast was seen by more than 123 million people nationally, second only to the 127 million who viewed Super Bowl XX.

The use in officiating of a limited system of Instant Replay was not approved. The vote was 17-11 in favor of approval (21 votes were required). Instant Replay had been used for six consecutive years (1986-1991), March 18.

St. Louis businessman James Orthwein purchased

controlling interest in the New England Patriots from Victor Kiam, May 11.

In a Harris Poll taken during the NFL offseason, professional football again was declared the nation's most popular sport. Professional football finished atop similar surveys conducted by Harris in 1985 and 1989, May 23.

NFL clubs accepted the report of the Expansion Committee at a league meeting in Pasadena. The report names five cities as finalists for the two expansion teams—Baltimore, Charlotte, Jacksonville, Memphis, and St. Louis, May 19.

At a league meeting in Dallas, NFL clubs approved a proposal by the World League Board of Directors to restructure the World League and place future emphasis on its international success, September 17.

NFL teams played their 16-game regular-season schedule over 18 weeks for the only time in league history.

1993

The NFL and lawyers for the players announced a settlement of various lawsuits and an agreement on the terms of a seven-year deal that included a new player system to be in place through the 1999 season, January 6.

Commissioner Tagliabue announced the establishment of the "NFL World Partnership Program" to develop amateur football internationally through a series of clinics conducted by former NFL players and coaches, January 14.

As part of Super Bowl XXVII, the NFL announced the creation of the first NFL Youth Education Town, a facility located in south central Los Angeles for inner city youth, January 25.

The Dallas Cowboys defeated the Buffalo Bills 52-17 in Super Bowl XXVII to capture their first NFL title since 1978. The game was played before a crowd of 98,374 at the Rose Bowl in Pasadena, California. The NBC broadcast of the game was the most watched program in television history and was seen by 133,400,000 people in the United States. The rating for the game was 45.1, the tenth highest for any televised sports event. The game also was seen live or taped in 101 other countries, January 31.

The NFL and the NFL Players Association officially signed a 7-year Collective Bargaining Agreement in Washington, D.C., which guarantees more than $1 billion in pension, health, and post-career benefits for current and retired players—the most extensive benefits plan in pro sports. It was the NFL's first CBA since the 1982 agreement expired in 1987, June 29.

NFL Enterprises, a newly formed division of the NFL responsible for NFL Films, home video, and special domestic and international television programming was announced, August 19.

NFL announced plans to allow fans, for the first time ever, to join players and coaches in selecting the annual AFC and NFC Pro Bowl teams, October 12.

NFL clubs unanimously awarded the league's twenty-ninth franchise to the Carolina Panthers and owner Jerry Richardson at a meeting in Chicago, October 26.

At the same meeting in Chicago, NFL clubs approved a plan to form a European league with joint venture partners, October 27.

Don Shula became the winningest coach in NFL history when Miami beat Philadelphia to give Shula his 325th victory, one more than George Halas, November 14.

NFL clubs awarded the league's thirtieth franchise to the Jacksonville Jaguars and owner Wayne Weaver at a meeting in Chicago, November 30.

The NFL announced new 4-year television agreements with NBC, ABC, ESPN, TNT, and NFL newcomer FOX, which took over the NFC package from CBS, December 18.

The NFL completed its new TV agreements by announcing that NBC would retain the rights to the AFC package, December 20.

1994
The Dallas Cowboys defeated the Buffalo Bills 30-13 in Super Bowl XXVIII to become the fifth team to win back-to-

back Super Bowl titles. The game was viewed by the largest U.S. audience in television history—134.8 million people. The game's 45.5 rating was the highest for a Super Bowl since 1987 and the tenth highest-rated Super Bowl ever, January 30.

NFL clubs unanimously approved the transfer of the New England Patriots from James Orthwein to Robert Kraft at a meeting in Orlando, February 22.

In a move to increase offensive production, NFL clubs at the league's annual meeting in Orlando adopted a package of changes, including modifications in line play, chucking rules, and the roughing-the-passer rule, plus the adoption of the two-point conversion and moving the spot of the kickoff back to the 30-yard line, March 22.

NFL clubs approved the transfer of the majority interest in the Miami Dolphins from the Robbie family to H. Wayne Huizenga, March 23.

The NFL and FOX announced the formation of a joint venture to create a six-team World League to begin play in Europe in April, 1995, March 23.

The Carolina Panthers earned the right to select first in the 1995 NFL draft by winning a coin toss with the Jacksonville Jaguars. The Jaguars received the second selection in the 1995 draft, April 24.

NFL clubs approved the transfer of the Philadelphia Eagles from Norman Braman to Jeffrey Lurie, May 6.

The NFL launched "NFL Sunday Ticket," a new season subscription service for satellite television dish owners, June 1.

An all-time NFL record crowd of 112,376 attended the American Bowl game between Dallas and Houston in Mexico City. It concluded the biggest American Bowl series in NFL history with four games attracting a record 256,666 fans, August 15.

The NFL reached agreement on a new seven-year contract with its game officials, September 22.

The NFL Management Council and the NFL Players Association announced an agreement on the formulation

and implementation of the most comprehensive drug and alcohol policy in sports, October 28.

At an NFL meeting in Chicago, Commissioner Tagliabue slotted the two new expansion teams into the AFC Central (Jacksonville Jaguars) and NFC West (Carolina Panthers) for the 1995 season only. He also appointed a special committee on realignment to make recommendations on the 1996 season and beyond, November 2.

1995
The San Francisco 49ers became the first team to win five Super Bowls when they defeated the San Diego Chargers 49-26 in Super Bowl XXIX at Joe Robbie Stadium in Miami, January 29.

Carolina and Jacksonville stocked their expansion rosters with a total of 66 players from other NFL teams in a veteran player allocation draft in New York, February 16.

CBS Radio and the NFL agreed to a new four-year contract for an annual 53-game package of games, continuing a relationship that spanned 15 of the past 17 years, February 22.

NFL clubs approved the transfer of the Tampa Bay Buccaneers from the estate of the late Hugh Culverhouse to South Florida businessman Malcolm Glazer, March 13.

A series of safety-related rules changes were adopted at a league meeting in Phoenix, primarily related to the use of the helmet against defenseless players, March 14.

After a two-year hiatus, the World League of American Football returned to action with six teams in Europe, April 8.

The NFL became the first major sports league to establish a site on the Internet system of on-line computer communication, April 10.

The transfer of the Rams from Los Angeles to St. Louis was approved by a vote of the NFL clubs at a meeting in Dallas, April 12.

ABC's *NFL Monday Night Football* finished the 1994-95 television season as the fifth highest-rated show out of 146 with a 17.8 average rating, the highest finish in the 25-year history of the series, April 18.

In an ABC News Poll taken

during the NFL offseason, America's sports fans chose football as their favorite spectator sport by more than a 2-to-1 margin over basketball and baseball (35%-16%-12%), April 26.

The Frankfurt Galaxy defeated the Amsterdam Admirals 26-22 to win the 1995 World Bowl before a crowd of 23,847 in Amsterdam's Olympic Stadium, June 23.

Former NFL quarterback and Rhein Fire general manager Oliver Luck was named President of the World League, July 13.

The transfer of the Raiders from Los Angeles to Oakland was approved by a vote of the NFL clubs at a meeting in Chicago, July 22.

Jacksonville Municipal Stadium opened in Jacksonville, Florida before a sold-out crowd of more than 70,000 as the St. Louis Rams defeated the Jacksonville Jaguars 27-10 in their first preseason game, August 18.

NFL Charities and 50 NFL players donated $1 million to the United Negro College Fund in honor of the fiftieth anniversary of the UNCF and the integration of the modern NFL, September 15.

The Pro Football Hall of Fame in Canton, Ohio, completed an $8.9 million expansion including a $4 million contribution by the NFL clubs, October 14.

The Trans World Dome opened in St. Louis with a sold-out crowd of 65,598 as the Rams defeated the Carolina Panthers 28-17, November 12.

NFL paid attendance totaled 963,521 for 15 games in Week 12, the highest weekend total in the league's 76-year history, November 19-20.

On the field, many significant records and milestones were achieved: Miami's Dan Marino surpassed Pro Football Hall of Famer Fran Tarkenton in four major passing categories—attempts, completions, yards, and touchdowns—to become the NFL's all-time career leader. San Francisco's Jerry Rice became the all-time reception and receiving-yardage leader with career totals of 942 catches and 15,123 yards. Dallas' Emmitt Smith scored

25 touchdowns, breaking the season record of 24 set by Washington's John Riggins in 1983.

1996
The Dallas Cowboys won their third Super Bowl title in four years when they defeated the Pittsburgh Steelers 27-17 in Super Bowl XXX at Sun Devil Stadium in Tempe, Arizona. The game was viewed by the largest audience in U.S. television history—138.5 million people, January 28.

An agreement between the NFL and the city of Cleveland regarding the Cleveland Browns' relocation was approved by a vote of the NFL clubs, February 9. According to the agreement, the city of Cleveland retained the Browns' heritage and records, including the name, logo, colors, history, playing records, trophies, and memorabilia, and committed to building a new 72,000-seat stadium for a reactivated Browns' franchise to begin play there no later than 1999. Art Modell received approval to move his franchise to Baltimore and rename it.

NFL total paid attendance for all 1995 games reached a record level for the seventh consecutive year, exceeding 19 million for the first time (19,202,757), March 7.

The transfer of the Oilers from Houston to Nashville for the 1998 season was approved by a vote of the NFL clubs at a meeting in Atlanta, April 30.

The Scottish Claymores defeated the Frankfurt Galaxy 32-27 to win the 1996 World Bowl in front of 38,982 at Murrayfield Stadium in Edinburgh, Scotland, June 23.

The NFL returned to Baltimore when the new Baltimore Ravens defeated the Philadelphia Eagles 17-9 in a preseason game before a crowd of 63,804 at Memorial Stadium, August 3.

Ericsson Stadium opened in Charlotte, North Carolina with a crowd of 65,350 as the Carolina Panthers defeated the Chicago Bears 30-12 in a preseason game, August 3.

Points scored totaled 762 and NFL paid attendance totaled 964,079 for 15 games in Week 11, the highest week-

end totals in either category in the league's 77-year history, November 10-11.

Former NFL Commissioner Pete Rozelle died at his home in Rancho Santa Fe, California. Rozelle, regarded as the premiere commissioner in sports history, led the NFL for 29 years, from 1960-1989, December 6.

1997
Indianapolis Colts owner Robert Irsay died from complications related to a stroke he suffered in 1995. Irsay acquired the club in 1972 when he traded his Los Angeles Rams to Carrol Rosenbloom for the Colts. He later moved the Colts from Baltimore to Indianapolis in 1984, January 14.

The Green Bay Packers won their first NFL title in 29 years by defeating the New England Patriots 35-21 in Super Bowl XXXI at the Louisiana Superdome in New Orleans. The game was viewed by the fourth-largest audience in U.S. television history—128 million people, January 26.

The rules governing cross-ownership were modified, permitting NFL club owners to also own teams in other sports in their home market or markets without NFL teams. The vote was 24-5 (one abstention) in favor of approval, March 11.

Washington Redskins owner Jack Kent Cooke died at his home in Washington, D.C. Cooke became majority owner in 1974 and the Redskins won three Super Bowls under his leadership, April 6.

The Barcelona Dragons defeated the Rhein Fire 38-24 to win the 1997 World Bowl in front of 31,100 fans at Estadi Olimpic de Montjuic in Barcelona, Spain, June 22.

NFL clubs approved the transfer of the Seattle Seahawks from Ken Behring to Paul Allen, August 19.

Jack Kent Cooke Stadium opened in Raljon, Maryland with a crowd of 78,270 as the Washington Redskins defeated the Arizona Cardinals 19-13 in overtime, September 14.

The 10,000th regular-season game in NFL history was played when the Seattle Seahawks defeated the Tennessee Oilers 16-13 at the Kingdome in Seattle, October 5.

Atlanta Falcons owner Rankin Smith died of heart failure three days prior to his seventy-third birthday. Smith was the founder of the Falcons and was instrumental in bringing Super Bowls XXVIII and XXXIV to Atlanta, October 26.

NFL paid attendance totaled 999,778 for 15 games in Week 12, the highest weekend total in league history, November 16-17.

1998
The NFL reached agreement on record eight-year television contracts with four networks. ABC (*NFL Monday Night Football*) and FOX (NFC) retained their previous rights, CBS took over the AFC package from NBC, and ESPN won the right to broadcast the entire Sunday night cable package, January 13.

The World League was renamed the NFL Europe League, January 22.

The Denver Broncos won their first Super Bowl by defeating the defending champion Green Bay Packers 31-24 in Super Bowl XXXII at Qualcomm Stadium in San Diego. The game tied Super Bowl XXVII for the third-largest audience in U.S. television history with 133.4 million viewers, January 25.

The NFL clubs approved an extension of the Collective Bargaining Agreement through 2003. The extended CBA also created a $100 million fund for youth football, March 22.

The NFL clubs unanimously approved an expansion team for Cleveland to fulfill the commitment to return the Browns to the field in 1999, March 23.

A total of $25.1 million, the largest NFL postseason pool ever, was divided among 737 players who participated in the 1997 playoffs, March 24.

The Rhein Fire defeated the Frankfurt Galaxy 34-10 to win the 1998 World Bowl in front of 47,846 fans in Frankfurt's Waldstadion—the biggest crowd to witness a World Bowl since 1991, June 14.

NFL clubs approved the transfer of the Minnesota Vikings from a 10-man ownership group to Red McCombs, July 28.

The NFL Stadium at Camden Yards opened in Baltimore, Maryland before a

crowd of 65,938 as the Baltimore Ravens defeated the Chicago Bears 19-14 in a preseason game, August 8.

NFL paid attendance totaled 997,835 for 15 games in Week 1, the highest opening weekend total in league history and the second-highest total ever. In 1997, paid attendance totaled 999,778 for 15 games in Week 12, September 6-7.

Raymond James Stadium opened in Tampa, Florida before a crowd of 62,410 as the Tampa Bay Buccaneers defeated the Chicago Bears 27-15, September 20.

A Harris Poll says 55 percent of adults follow professional football, up 4 percent from 1997 and 6 percent from 1992, October 15.

Tennessee Oilers owner Bud Adams announced the team will change its name to the Tennessee Titans following the 1998 season. The NFL announced that the name Oilers will be retired—a first in league history, November 14.

1999
The Denver Broncos won their second consecutive Super Bowl title by defeating the NFC champion Atlanta Falcons 34-19 in Super Bowl XXXIII at Pro Player Stadium in Miami. The game was viewed by 127.5 million viewers, the sixth most-watched program in U.S. television history, January 31.

Jim Pyne, a center allocated by the Detroit Lions, was the first selection of the Cleveland Browns in the 1999 NFL Expansion Draft. The Browns eventually selected 37 players, February 9.

CBS Radio/Westwood One agreed to a 3-year extension of their exclusive national radio rights to NFL games, March 11.

NFL paid attendance of 19,741,493 for all games played during the 1998 season was the highest in league history, topping the 19,202,757 fans who paid to attend games in 1995. The 1998 regular-season total paid attendance of 15,364,873 for an average of 64,020 were also records, March 15.

By a vote of 28-3, the owners adopted an instant replay system as an officiating aid for the 1999 season, March 17.

New York Jets owner Leon Hess died from complications of a blood disease. Hess had been involved in the ownership of the Jets since 1963 and was sole owner of the club since 1984, May 9.

A group led by Washington area businessman Daniel Snyder is approved by NFL clubs as the new owner of the Washington Redskins at a league meeting in Atlanta, May 25.

The Frankfurt Galaxy became the first team in NFL Europe League history to win a second World Bowl by defeating the Barcelona Dragons 38-24 at Rheinstadion, in Düsseldorf, Germany, June 27.

The Cleveland Browns returned to the field for the first time since 1995 and defeated the Dallas Cowboys 20-17 in overtime in the annual Hall of Fame Game at Canton, Ohio, August 9.

Cleveland Browns Stadium opened in Cleveland, Ohio before a crowd of 71,398 as the Minnesota Vikings defeated the Browns in a preseason game, 24-17, August 21.

Adelphia Coliseum opened in Nashville, Tennessee before a crowd of 65,729 with the Tennessee Titans defeating the Atlanta Falcons 17-3 in a preseason game, August 26.

Houston, Texas and owner Robert McNair were awarded the NFL's thirty-second franchise in a vote of the NFL clubs at a league meeting in Atlanta. The team will begin play in 2002. The NFL clubs also voted to realign into eight divisions of four teams each for the 2002 season, October 6.

Walter Payton, the NFL's all-time leading rusher, died of liver cancer at the age of 45. Payton played for the Chicago Bears from 1975-1987 and rushed for an NFL-record 16,726 yards, November 1.

Former NFL Commissioner Pete Rozelle, who guided a still-developing league to its position today as America's most popular sport, was named by *The Sporting News* as the most powerful person in sports in the 20th Century, December 15.

2000

New York businessman Robert Wood Johnson IV was approved by NFL clubs as the new owner of the New York Jets at a league meeting, January 18.

The St. Louis Rams won their first Super Bowl by defeating the AFC champion Tennessee Titans 23-16 in Super Bowl XXXIV at the Georgia Dome in Atlanta. The game was viewed by 130.7 million viewers, the fifth most-watched program in U.S. television history, January 30.

For the first time in league history, paid attendance topped 16 million for the regular season and more than 65,000 per game, an increase of 1,300 per game over 1998. Paid attendance for all NFL games increased in 1999 for the third year in a row and was the highest ever in the 80-year history of the league. It marked the first time in league history that the 20-million paid attendance mark was reached for all games in a season, March 27.

The Rhein Fire won their second World Bowl in three years, defeating the Scottish Claymores 13-10 to win World Bowl 2000 in front of 35,680 at Frankfurt's Waldstadion, June 25.

More than 100 of the 136 living members of the Pro Football Hall of Fame gathered to celebrate Pro Football's Greatest Reunion in Canton, Ohio, July 28-31.

Paul Brown Stadium opened in Cincinnati, Ohio with a crowd of 56,180 as the Cincinnati Bengals defeated the Chicago Bears 24-20 in a preseason game, August 19.

Cincinnati's Corey Dillon set a single-game rushing record with 278 yards (22 carries) against Denver, breaking the previous record of 275 yards by Chicago's Walter Payton in 1977, October 22.

Minnesota's Gary Anderson converted a 21-yard field goal against Buffalo to pass George Blanda as the NFL's all-time scoring leader with 2,004 points, October 22.

The NFL named Mike Pereira as Director of Officiating and Larry Upson as Director of Officiating Operations to replace retiring Senior Director of Officiating Jerry Seeman,

December 1.

San Francisco's Terrell Owens set a single-game receiving record with 20 receptions (283 yards) against Chicago, surpassing the previous mark of 18 by Tom Fears of the Los Angeles Rams in 1950, December 17.

2001

NFL clubs approved additional league-wide revenue sharing at a special league meeting in Dallas. The teams agreed to pool the visiting team share of gate receipts for all preseason and regular-season games and divide the pool equally starting in 2002, January 17.

The Baltimore Ravens won their first Super Bowl by defeating the NFC champion New York Giants 34-7 in Super Bowl XXXV at Raymond James Stadium in Tampa. The game was witnessed by 131.2 million viewers, the fifth most-watched program in U.S. television history, January 28.

The *Sports Business Daily* named NFL Commissioner Paul Tagliabue the 2000 Sports Industrialist of the Year, February 28.

The NFL set an all-time paid attendance record in 2000 for the third consecutive year, reaching the 20-million paid attendance mark for only the second time in league history. Regular-season paid attendance of 16,387,289 for an average of 66,078 per game also was an all-time record for the third consecutive season. The Washington Redskins set an all-time NFL regular-season home paid attendance record with a total of 656,599 for eight games, breaking the record of 634,204 held by the 1980 Detroit Lions, March 26.

NFL owners unanimously approved a realignment plan for the league starting in 2002. With the addition of the Houston Texans, the league's 32 teams will be divided in eight four-team divisions. Seven clubs change divisions, and the Seattle Seahawks change conferences, moving from the AFC to the NFC. A new scheduling format ensures that every team meets every other team in the league at least once every four years, May 22.

The Berlin Thunder won their first World Bowl, defeat-

ing the Barcelona Dragons 24-17 to win World Bowl IX in front of 32,116 at Amsterdam ArenA, June 30.

Heinz Field opened in Pittsburgh, Pennsylvania before a crowd of 57,829 with the Pittsburgh Steelers defeating the Detroit Lions 20-7 in a preseason game; and INVESCO Field at Mile High opened in Denver, Colorado before a crowd of 74,063 with the Denver Broncos defeating the New Orleans Saints 31-24 in a preseason game, August 25.

President George W. Bush became the first United States President to be involved in an NFL regular-season pregame coin toss as he helped kick off the 2001 season from the White House. Via satellite, President Bush tossed the coin for the 10 regular-season games that started at 1:00 P.M. ET, September 9.

In the wake of the September 11 terrorist attacks, Commissioner Paul Tagliabue postponed the games scheduled for September 16-17, September 13.

The league's 16-game regular season was retained when the postponed Week 2 games were rescheduled for the weekend of January 6-7, September 18.

The NFL and its game officials agreed to a new six-year Collective Bargaining Agreement, ending a two-week lockout of the regular officials, who returned to work on September 23, September 19.

The NFL announced that the league's prohibition of anabolic steroids and related substances had been strengthened to include supplements containing ephedrine and other high-risk supplements, September 27.

The NFL announced that the Super Bowl would be rescheduled from January 27 to February 3 in order to retain the full playoff format for the 2002 season. It will be the first Super Bowl played in February, October 3.

President Bush designated Super Bowl XXXVI as a "National Special Security Event," allowing all security for the game to be coordinated by the Secret Service, November 26.

George Young, the NFL's senior vice president of football operations and former general manager of the New York Giants, died at the age of 71, December 8.

2002
The NFL and the NFL Players Association agreed to a fourth extension of the 1993 Collective Bargaining Agreement through 2007, January 7.

In an AFC Wild Card matchup, the Oakland Raiders defeated the New York Jets 38-24 in the NFL's first-ever prime-time playoff game, January 12.

In a special meeting in New Orleans, NFL owners voted unanimously to approve the purchase of the Atlanta Falcons to Home Depot co-founder Arthur Blank, February 2.

The New England Patriots won their first Super Bowl by defeating the NFC champion St. Louis Rams 20-17 in Super Bowl XXXVI at the Louisiana Superdome in New Orleans. The game marked the first time in Super Bowl history that the winning points came on the final play, a 48-yard field goal by Patriots kicker Adam Vinatieri. Super Bowl XXXVI was viewed by 131.7 million viewers, the fifth-most watched program in U.S. television history, February 3.

Tennessee Titans head coach Jeff Fisher was named co-chairman of the NFL Competition Committee, February 6.

Tony Boselli, a five-time Pro Bowl tackle allocated by the Jacksonville Jaguars, was the first selection of the Houston Texans in the 2002 NFL Expansion Draft. The Texans selected 19 players, February 18.

The NFL and Westwood One/CBS Radio Sports announced the renewal of a multiyear agreement for Westwood One/CBS Radio Sports to continue as the exclusive network radio home of the NFL, April 9.

NFL Europe kicked off its tenth season with a record 254 players allocated by NFL clubs, April 13-14.

The Berlin Thunder became the first team to win consecutive World Bowls, defeating the Rhein Fire 26-20 to win World Bowl X in front of 53,109 fans at Rheinstadion,

June 22.

Seahawks Stadium opened in Seattle, Washington with an attendance of 52,902 fans as the Indianapolis Colts defeated the Seattle Seahawks 28-10 in a preseason game, August 10.

Gillette Stadium opened in Foxboro, Massachusetts with a crowd of 68,436 fans as the New England Patriots defeated the Philadelphia Eagles 16-15 in a preseason game, August 17.

Reliant Stadium opened in Houston, Texas with 69,432 fans in attendance, the largest non-Super Bowl crowd to ever watch an NFL game in Houston as the Miami Dolphins defeated the Houston Texans 24-3 in a preseason game, August 24.

For the first time, the NFL season kicked off on a Thursday night in prime time as the San Francisco 49ers defeated the New York Giants 16-13 at Giants Stadium. The game was preceded by "NFL Kickoff Live From Times Square," presented by New York City and the NFL, a football and music festival honoring the resilient spirit of New York and America, September 5.

Week 1 of the 2002 season produced the highest-scoring and most competitive Kickoff Weekend in NFL history. The 16 games averaged 49.3 points per game. A total of 788 points and 89 touchdowns were scored, the most in league history for an opening weekend. Eleven of the 16 games were decided by one score (eight points or less), a Kickoff Weekend record, September 5-9.

Johnny Unitas, the legendary quarterback for the Baltimore Colts and a Pro Football Hall of Fame member, died at a heart attack at the age of 69, September 11.

Oakland Raiders wide receiver Jerry Rice became the all-time leader in yards from scrimmage, surpassing Pro Football Hall of Fame running back Walter Payton (21,281 yards), September 29.

Cleveland Browns owner Al Lerner, the NFL Finance Committee Chairman and Chairman and CEO of MBNA Corporation, died at the age of 69, October 23.

Dallas Cowboys running

back Emmitt Smith became the NFL's all-time rushing leader, surpassing Pro Football Hall of Fame running back Walter Payton (16,726 yards), October 27.

The NFL and NFLPA announced the creation of USA Football, the first national advocacy organization representing all levels of amateur football, December 5.

Indianapolis Colts wide receiver Marvin Harrison set the NFL single-season record for pass receptions with 143, surpassing Herman Moore (123), December 29.

The 2002 season concluded with 25 overtime games, the most in NFL history, December 30.

2003
The NFL announced the appointment of Steve Bornstein as executive vice president-media and president and chief executive officer of NFL Network, to be launched in 2003. The NFL Network will be the first television programming service fully dedicated to the NFL and the sport of football, January 16.

The Tampa Bay Buccaneers won their first Super Bowl by defeating the AFC champion Oakland Raiders 48-21 in Super Bowl XXXVII at Qualcomm Stadium in San Diego. The game was witnessed by 138.9 million viewers, making Super Bowl XXXVII the most-watched program in U.S. television history, January 26.

The NFL set an all-time paid attendance record in 2002 with 21,505,138, the first time paid attendance topped 21-million. Regular-season paid attendance of 16,833,310 was also an all-time record, March 26.

Chicago Bears chairman emeritus Edward W. McCaskey died at the age of 83, April 8.

The Frankfurt Galaxy became the first team to win three World Bowls, defeating the Rhein Fire 35-16 to win World Bowl XI in front of 28,138 fans at Hampden Park, June 14.

Tex Schramm, the legendary team president and general manager of the Dallas Cowboys and a member of the Pro Football Hall of Fame, died at the age of 83, July 15.

Lincoln Financial Field opened in Philadelphia, Pennsylvania with an attendance of 66,279 fans as the New England Patriots defeated the Philadelphia Eagles 24-12 in a preseason game, August 22.

A renovated Lambeau Field opened in Green Bay, Wisconsin with a crowd of 69,831 fans as the Carolina Panthers defeated the Green Bay Packers 20-7 in a preseason game, August 23.

A renovated Soldier Field opened in Chicago, Illinois with an attendance of 61,500 fans as the Green Bay Packers defeated the Chicago Bears 38-23 in a regular season game on ABC's *NFL Monday Night Football*, September 29.

NFL Network, the first 24-hour, year-round television channel dedicated to the NFL and the sport of football, launched on DirecTV, November 4.

Otto Graham, the legendary quarterback of the Cleveland Browns and a member of the Pro Football Hall of Fame, died at the age of 82, December 17.

NFL paid attendance totaled 1,106,818 for 16 games in Week 17, the highest weekend total in league history, December 27-28.

2004
The New England Patriots won their second Super Bowl in three years by defeating the NFC champion Carolina Panthers 32-29 in Super Bowl XXXVIII at Reliant Stadium in Houston. The game was witnessed by 144.4 million viewers, making Super Bowl XXXVIII the most-watched program in U.S. television history, February 1.

The NFL set an all-time paid attendance record in 2003 for the second consecutive year with a mark of 21,639,040. Regular-season paid attendance of 16,913,584 for an average of 66,328 per game were both all-time records, March 29.

By a vote of 29-3, NFL owners extended the instant replay system for another five seasons through 2008, March 30.

Steve Bisciotti took over as the controlling owner of the Baltimore Ravens, succeeding Art Modell, who operated the franchise for 43 years, April 8.

Former Arizona Cardinals safety Pat Tillman was killed in a firefight while on combat patrol with the U.S. Army Rangers in Afghanistan, April 22.

A federal appeals court formally ruled in favor of the NFL's draft eligibility rule in Maurice Clarett's lawsuit, citing federal labor policy in permitting the NFL and the Players Association to set rules for when players can enter the league, May 24.

The Berlin Thunder defeated the Frankfurt Galaxy 30-24 to win World Bowl XII in front of 35,413 fans at Arena Auf-Schalke, June 12.

The New England Patriots defeated the New York Jets 13-7 for their NFL-record 18th consecutive regular-season victory, October 24.

The NFL reached an agreement on six-year contract extensions with two of its network television partners—CBS and FOX—to run through the 2011 season, November 8.

The NFL and DirecTV announced a five-year extension on the NFL Sunday Ticket subscription television package to run through the 2010 season, November 8.

NFL Europe named the Hamburg Sea Devils as the league's newest team, November 24.

2005

Indianapolis Colts quarterback Peyton Manning set the NFL single-season record with 49 touchdown passes, January 2.

The New England Patriots became the second team in NFL history to win three Super Bowls in four seasons by defeating the Philadelphia Eagles 24-21 in Super Bowl XXXIX at ALLTEL Stadium in Jacksonville. The game was witnessed by 133.7 million viewers, making Super Bowl XXXIX the fifth-most watched program in U.S. television history, February 6.

The NFL set an all-time paid attendance record in 2004 for the third consecutive year with a mark of 21,708,624. Regular-season paid attendance increased to 17,000,811, the first time the NFL reached the 17-million mark. Average paid attendance of 66,409 was also an all-time high, March 21.

The Pat Tillman USO Center opened in Afghanistan. The NFL donated $250,000 to the USO to honor the memory of the former Arizona Cardinals player who died in Afghanistan while serving in the U.S. Army, April 1.

The NFL reached long-term agreements for its Sunday and Monday primetime TV packages. NBC returned to the NFL by acquiring the Sunday night package for six years (2006-2011). ESPN agreed on an eight-year deal to televise *Monday Night Football* from 2006-2013, April 18.

The NFL strengthened its steroids program by adopting the Olympic testosterone testing standard, tripling the number of times a player can be randomly tested during the offseason from two to six, adding substances to the list of banned substances, and putting new language in the policy to allow for testing of designer drugs and other substances that may have evaded detection, April 27.

NFL owners voted unanimously to approve the purchase of the Minnesota Vikings to real-estate developer Zygmunt Wilf, May 25.

NFL owners awarded Super Bowl XLIII, to be played on February 1, 2009 to Tampa, May 25.

The Amsterdam Admirals defeated the Berlin Thunder 27-21 to win World Bowl XIII in front of 35,134 fans at LTU Arean in Dússeldrof, Germany, June 11.

The NFL designated September 18-19 as "Hurricane Relief Weekend," which concluded with a telethon in conjunction with a Monday Night Football doubleheader on ABC and ESPN. The New York Giants-New Orleans Saints game, originally scheduled for the Louisiana Superdome, was moved to Giants Stadium following Hurricane Katrina. In total, the NFL, its owners, teams, players, and fans contributed $21 million to aid Hurricane Katrina rebuilding effort, September 19.

An NFL record 103,467 fans attended the Arizona Cardinals' 31-14 victory over the San Francisco 49ers at Mexi-co City's Azteca Stadium, the first-ever regular-season NFL game played outside the United States, October 2.

NFL owners, by a vote of 31-1, approved the business plan of the NFL Europe League through its 2010 season, October 6.

Wellington Mara, the New York Giants' president and co-chief executive officer, died at the age of 89, October 25.

Chicago Bears cornerback Nathan Vasher set an NFL record for the longest scoring play with a 108-yard touchdown return of an errant field goal by San Francico kicker Joe Nedney in Chicago, November 13.

Preston Robert Tisch, the Giants' chairman and co-chief executive officer, died at the age of 79, November 15.

Sports Illustrated named New England Patriots quarterback Tom Brady the 2005 Sportsman of the Year, December 5.

2006

Seattle Seahawks running back Shaun Alexander set the NFL single-season record for touchdowns with 28, January 1.

The NFL announced that NFL Network would begin airing a "Road To The Playoffs" package of eight primetime regular season NFL games starting in 2006, January 28.

The Pittsburgh Steelers won their fifth Super Bowl, defeating the Seattle Seahawks 21-10 in Super Bowl XL at Ford Field in Detroit, Michigan. The game was witnessed by 141.1 million viewers, making it the second-most watched program in U.S. ttelevision history, February 3.

The NFL clubs approved an extension of the Collective Bargaining Agreement through 2012. Owners also agreed on an expanded revenue sharing program that will redistribute $850 to $900 million over the course of the deal, March 8.

Commissioner Tagliabue announced his decision to retire by the end of July. The NFL enjoyed an era of unrivaled prosperity in the Tagliabue Era, including labor peace throughout his 17-year tenure, March 20.

The NFL set an all-time paid attendance record in 2005 for the fourth consecutive season. Attendance for all 2005 games was 21,792,096, an increase of nearly 84,000 over the previous record of 21,708,624 in 2004, March 27.

NFL clubs unanimously decided to return the name of the official game ball to "The Duke" in honor of the late New York Giants owner Wellington Mara, March 27.

NFL COMMISSIONERS AND PRESIDENTS*

1920....Jim Thorpe, President
1921-39..Joe Carr, President
1939-41.Carl Storck, President
1941-46 ....Elmer Layden, Commissioner
1946-1959 ....Bert Bell, Commissioner
1960-1989 ....Pete Rozelle, Commissioner
1989-present..Paul Tagliabue, Commissioner

*NFL treasurer Austin Gunsel served as president in the office of the commissioner following the death of Bert Bell (Oct. 11, 1959) until the election of Pete Rozelle (Jan. 26, 1960).

2005

AMERICAN CONFERENCE

East Division

	W	L	T	Pct.	Pts.	OP
New England	10	6	0	.625	379	338
Miami	9	7	0	.563	318	317
Buffalo	5	11	0	.313	271	367
N.Y. Jets	4	12	0	.250	240	355

North Division

	W	L	T	Pct.	Pts.	OP
Cincinnati	11	5	0	.688	421	350
Pittsburgh*	11	5	0	.688	389	258
Baltimore	6	10	0	.375	265	299
Cleveland	6	10	0	.375	232	301

South Division

	W	L	T	Pct.	Pts.	OP
Indianapolis#	14	2	0	.875	439	247
Jacksonville*	12	4	0	.750	361	269
Tennessee	4	12	0	.250	299	421
Houston	2	14	0	.125	260	431

West Division

	W	L	T	Pct.	Pts.	OP
Denver	13	3	0	.813	395	258
Kansas City	10	6	0	.625	403	325
San Diego	9	7	0	.563	418	312
Oakland	4	12	0	.250	290	383

NATIONAL CONFERENCE

East Division

	W	L	T	Pct.	Pts.	OP
N.Y. Giants	11	5	0	.688	422	314
Washington*	10	6	0	.625	359	293
Dallas	9	7	0	.563	325	308
Philadelphia	6	10	0	.375	310	388

North Division

	W	L	T	Pct.	Pts.	OP
Chicago	11	5	0	.688	260	202
Minnesota	9	7	0	.563	306	344
Detroit	5	11	0	.313	254	345
Green Bay	4	12	0	.250	298	344

South Division

	W	L	T	Pct.	Pts.	OP
Tampa Bay	11	5	0	.688	300	274
Carolina*	11	5	0	.688	391	259
Atlanta	8	8	0	.500	351	341
New Orleans	3	13	0	.188	235	398

West Division

	W	L	T	Pct.	Pts.	OP
Seattle#	13	3	0	.813	452	271
St. Louis	6	10	0	.375	363	429
Arizona	5	11	0	.313	311	387
San Francisco	4	12	0	.250	239	428

Wild Card qualifier for playoffs; #Top playoff seed in conference

Cincinnati finished ahead of Pittsburgh based on better division record (5-1 to 4-2). Baltimore finished ahead of Cleveland based on better division record (2-4 to 1-5). Tampa Bay finished ahead of Carolina based on better division record (5-1 to 4-2). Chicago finished ahead of Tampa Bay, and Tampa Bay finished ahead of the New York Giants, based on better conference record (Bears' 10-2 to Buccaneers' 9-3 to Giants' 8-4).

Wild Card playoff: NEW ENGLAND 28, Jacksonville 3

Pittsburgh 31, CINCINNATI 17

Divisional playoff: DENVER 27, New England 13

Pittsburgh 21, INDIANAPOLIS 18

AFC Championship: Pittsburgh 34, DENVER 17

Wild Card playoffs: Washington 17, TAMPA BAY 10

Carolina 23, NEW YORK GIANTS 0

Divisional playoff: SEATTLE 20, Washington 10

Carolina 29, CHICAGO 21

NFC Championship: SEATTLE 34, Carolina 14

Super Bowl XL: Pittsburgh (AFC) 21, Seattle (NFC) 10

at Ford Field, Detroit, Michigan

In Past Standings section, home teams in playoff games are indicated by capital letters.

Playoff Seeds

AFC	NFC
1. Indianapolis	**1. Seattle**
2. Denver	2. Chicago
3. Cincinnati	3. Tampa Bay
4. New England	4. New York Giants
5. Jacksonville	5. Carolina
6. Pittsburgh	6. Washington

2004

AMERICAN CONFERENCE

East Division

	W	L	T	Pct.	Pts.	OP
New England	14	2	0	.875	437	260
N.Y. Jets*	10	6	0	.625	333	261
Buffalo	9	7	0	.563	395	284
Miami	4	12	0	.250	275	354

North Division

	W	L	T	Pct.	Pts.	OP
Pittsburgh#	15	1	0	.938	372	251
Baltimore	9	7	0	.563	317	268
Cincinnati	8	8	0	.500	374	372
Cleveland	4	12	0	.250	276	390

South Division

	W	L	T	Pct.	Pts.	OP
Indianapolis	12	4	0	.750	522	351
Jacksonville	9	7	0	.563	261	280
Houston	7	9	0	.438	309	339
Tennessee	5	11	0	.313	344	439

West Division

	W	L	T	Pct.	Pts.	OP
San Diego	12	4	0	.750	446	313
Denver*	10	6	0	.625	381	304
Kansas City	7	9	0	.438	483	435
Oakland	5	11	0	.313	320	442

NATIONAL CONFERENCE

East Division

	W	L	T	Pct.	Pts.	OP
Philadelphia#	13	3	0	.813	386	260
N.Y. Giants	6	10	0	.375	303	347
Dallas	6	10	0	.375	293	405
Washington	6	10	0	.375	240	265

North Division

	W	L	T	Pct.	Pts.	OP
Green Bay	10	6	0	.625	424	380
Minnesota*	8	8	0	.500	405	395
Detroit	6	10	0	.375	296	350
Chicago	5	11	0	.313	231	331

South Division

	W	L	T	Pct.	Pts.	OP
Atlanta	11	5	0	.688	340	337
New Orleans	8	8	0	.500	348	405
Carolina	7	9	0	.438	355	339
Tampa Bay	5	11	0	.313	301	304

West Division

	W	L	T	Pct.	Pts.	OP
Seattle	9	7	0	.563	371	373
St. Louis*	8	8	0	.500	319	392
Arizona	6	10	0	.375	284	322
San Francisco	2	14	0	.125	259	452

Wild Card qualifier for playoffs; #Top playoff seed in conference

Indianapolis finished ahead of San Diego based on head-to-head victory. N.Y. Jets finished ahead of Denver based on better record vs. common opponents (5-0 to 3-2). St. Louis finished ahead of New Orleans and Minnesota based on best conference record (7-5 to Saints' 6-6 to Vikings' 5-7), and Minnesota finished ahead of New Orleans based on head-to-head victory. N.Y. Giants finished ahead of Dallas and Washington based on better head-to-head record (3-1 to Cowboys' 2-2 to Redskins' 1-3), and Dallas finished ahead of Washington based on head-to-head sweep (2-0).

Wild Card playoffs: N.Y. Jets 20, SAN DIEGO 17 (OT)

INDIANAPOLIS 49, Denver 24

Divisional playoffs: PITTSBURGH 20, N.Y. Jets 17 (OT)

NEW ENGLAND 20, Indianapolis 3

AFC Championship: New England 41, PITTSBURGH 27

Wild Card playoffs: St. Louis 27, SEATTLE 20

Minnesota 31, GREEN BAY 17

Divisional playoffs: ATLANTA 47, St. Louis 17

PHILADELPHIA 27, Minnesota 14

NFC Championship: PHILADELPHIA 27, Atlanta 10

Super Bowl XXXIX: New England (AFC) 24, Philadelphia (NFC) 21

at Alltel Stadium, Jacksonville, Florida

Playoff Seeds

AFC	NFC
1. Pittsburgh	**1. Philadelphia**
2. New England	2. Atlanta
3. Indianapolis	3. Green Bay
4. San Diego	4. Seattle
5. N.Y. Jets	5. St. Louis
6. Denver	6. Minnesota

2003

AMERICAN CONFERENCE

East Division

	W	L	T	Pct.	Pts.	OP
New England#	14	2	0	.875	348	238
Miami	10	6	0	.625	311	261
Buffalo	6	10	0	.375	243	279
N.Y. Jets	6	10	0	.375	283	299

North Division

	W	L	T	Pct.	Pts.	OP
Baltimore	10	6	0	.625	391	281
Cincinnati	8	8	0	.500	346	384
Pittsburgh	6	10	0	.375	300	327
Cleveland	5	11	0	.313	254	322

South Division

	W	L	T	Pct.	Pts.	OP
Indianapolis	12	4	0	.750	447	336
Tennessee*	12	4	0	.750	435	324
Jacksonville	5	11	0	.313	276	331
Houston	5	11	0	.313	255	380

West Division

	W	L	T	Pct.	Pts.	OP
Kansas City	13	3	0	.813	484	332
Denver*	10	6	0	.625	381	301
Oakland	4	12	0	.250	270	379
San Diego	4	12	0	.250	313	441

NATIONAL CONFERENCE

East Division

	W	L	T	Pct.	Pts.	OP
Philadelphia#	12	4	0	.750	374	287
Dallas*	10	6	0	.625	289	260
Washington	5	11	0	.313	287	372
N.Y. Giants	4	12	0	.250	243	387

North Division

	W	L	T	Pct.	Pts.	OP
Green Bay	10	6	0	.625	442	307
Minnesota	9	7	0	.563	416	353
Chicago	7	9	0	.438	283	346
Detroit	5	11	0	.313	270	379

South Division

	W	L	T	Pct.	Pts.	OP
Carolina	11	5	0	.688	325	304
New Orleans	8	8	0	.500	340	326
Tampa Bay	7	9	0	.438	301	264
Atlanta	5	11	0	.313	299	422

West Division

	W	L	T	Pct.	Pts.	OP
St. Louis	12	4	0	.750	447	328
Seattle*	10	6	0	.625	404	327
San Francisco	7	9	0	.438	384	337
Arizona	4	12	0	.250	225	452

*Wild Card qualifier for playoffs; #Top playoff seed in conference

Buffalo finished ahead of N.Y. Jets based on better division record (2-4 to Jets' 1-5). Indianapolis finished ahead of Tennessee based on head-to-head sweep (2-0). Jacksonville finished ahead of Houston based on better division record (2-4 to Texans' 1-5). Denver finished ahead of Miami based on better conference record (9-3 to Dolphins' 7-5). Oakland finished ahead of San Diego based on better conference record (3-9 to Chargers' 2-10). Philadelphia finished ahead of St. Louis based on better conference record (9-3 to Rams' 8-4). Seattle finished ahead of Dallas based on better strength of victory (65-95 to Cowboys' 62-98).

Wild Card playoffs: Tennessee 20, BALTIMORE 17; INDIANAPOLIS 41, Denver 10

Divisional playoffs: NEW ENGLAND 17, Tennessee 14; Indianapolis 38, KANSAS CITY 31

AFC Championship: NEW ENGLAND 24, Indianapolis 14

Wild Card playoffs: CAROLINA 29, Dallas 10; GREEN BAY 33, Seattle 27 (OT)

Divisional playoffs: Carolina 29, ST. LOUIS 23 (2OT); PHILADELPHIA 20, Green Bay 17 (OT)

NFC Championship: Carolina 14, PHILADELPHIA 3

Super Bowl XXXVIII: New England (AFC) 32, Carolina (NFC) 29 at Reliant Stadium, Houston, Texas

Playoff Seeds

AFC	NFC
1. New England	1. Philadelphia
2. Kansas City	2. St. Louis
3. Indianapolis	**3. Carolina**
4. Baltimore	4. Green Bay
5. Tennessee	5. Seattle
6. Denver	6. Dallas

2002

AMERICAN CONFERENCE

East Division

	W	L	T	Pct.	Pts.	OP
N.Y. Jets	9	7	0	.563	359	336
New England	9	7	0	.563	381	346
Miami	9	7	0	.563	378	301
Buffalo	8	8	0	.500	379	397

North Division

	W	L	T	Pct.	Pts.	OP
Pittsburgh	10	5	1	.656	390	345
Cleveland*	9	7	0	.563	344	320
Baltimore	7	9	0	.438	316	354
Cincinnati	2	14	0	.125	279	456

South Division

	W	L	T	Pct.	Pts.	OP
Tennessee	11	5	0	.688	367	324
Indianapolis*	10	6	0	.625	349	313
Jacksonville	6	10	0	.375	328	315
Houston	4	12	0	.250	213	356

West Division

	W	L	T	Pct.	Pts.	OP
Oakland#	11	5	0	.688	450	304
Denver	9	7	0	.563	392	344
San Diego	8	8	0	.500	333	367
Kansas City	8	8	0	.500	467	399

NATIONAL CONFERENCE

East Division

	W	L	T	Pct.	Pts.	OP
Philadelphia#	12	4	0	.750	415	241
N.Y. Giants*	10	6	0	.625	320	279
Washington	7	9	0	.438	307	365
Dallas	5	11	0	.313	217	329

North Division

	W	L	T	Pct.	Pts.	OP
Green Bay	12	4	0	.750	398	328
Minnesota	6	10	0	.375	390	442
Chicago	4	12	0	.250	281	379
Detroit	3	13	0	.188	306	451

South Division

	W	L	T	Pct.	Pts.	OP
Tampa Bay	12	4	0	.750	346	196
Atlanta*	9	6	1	.594	402	314
New Orleans	9	7	0	.563	432	388
Carolina	7	9	0	.438	258	302

West Division

	W	L	T	Pct.	Pts.	OP
San Francisco	10	6	0	.625	367	351
St. Louis	7	9	0	.438	316	369
Seattle	7	9	0	.438	355	369
Arizona	5	11	0	.313	262	417

*Wild Card qualifier for playoffs; #Top playoff seed in conference

New York Jets finished ahead of New England based on better record in common games (8-4 to Patriots' 7-5) and Miami based on better division record (4-2 to Dolphins' 2-4). New England finished ahead of Miami based on better division record (4-2 to Dolphins' 2-4). Cleveland finished ahead of Denver and New England based on better conference record (7-5 to Broncos' 5-7 and Patriots' 6-6). Oakland finished ahead of Tennessee based on better head-to-head record (1-0). San Diego finished ahead of Kansas City based on better division record (3-3 to Chiefs' 2-4). Philadelphia finished ahead of Green Bay and Tampa Bay based on better conference record (11-1 to Packers' 9-3 and Buccaneers' 9-3). Tampa Bay finished ahead of Green Bay based on better head-to-head record (1-0). St. Louis finished ahead of Seattle based on better division record (4-2 to Seahawks' 2-4).

Wild Card playoffs: N.Y. JETS 41, Indianapolis 0; PITTSBURGH 36, Cleveland 33

Divisional playoffs: TENNESSEE 34, Pittsburgh 31 (OT); OAKLAND 30, N.Y. Jets 10

AFC Championship: OAKLAND 41, Tennessee 24

Wild Card playoffs: Atlanta 27, GREEN BAY 7; SAN FRANCISCO 39, N.Y. Giants 38

Divisional playoffs: PHILADELPHIA 20, Atlanta 6; TAMPA BAY 31, San Francisco 6

NFC Championship: Tampa Bay 27, PHILADELPHIA 10

Super Bowl XXXVII: Tampa Bay (NFC) 48, Oakland (AFC) 21 at Qualcomm Stadium, San Diego, California

Playoff Seeds

AFC	NFC
1. Oakland	1. Philadelphia
2. Tennessee	**2. Tampa Bay**
3. Pittsburgh	3. Green Bay
4. N.Y. Jets	4. San Francisco
5. Indianapolis	5. N.Y. Giants
6. Cleveland	6. Atlanta

2001

AMERICAN CONFERENCE
Eastern Division
	W	L	T	Pct.	Pts.	OP
New England	11	5	0	.688	371	272
Miami*	11	5	0	.688	344	290
N.Y. Jets*	10	6	0	.625	308	295
Indianapolis	6	10	0	.375	413	486
Buffalo	3	13	0	.188	265	420

Central Division
	W	L	T	Pct.	Pts.	OP
Pittsburgh#	13	3	0	.813	352	212
Baltimore*	10	6	0	.625	303	265
Cleveland	7	9	0	.438	285	319
Tennessee	7	9	0	.438	336	388
Jacksonville	6	10	0	.375	294	286
Cincinnati	6	10	0	.375	226	309

Western Division
	W	L	T	Pct.	Pts.	OP
Oakland	10	6	0	.625	399	327
Seattle	9	7	0	.563	301	324
Denver	8	8	0	.500	340	339
Kansas City	6	10	0	.375	320	344
San Diego	5	11	0	.313	332	321

NATIONAL CONFERENCE
Eastern Division
	W	L	T	Pct.	Pts.	OP
Philadelphia	11	5	0	.688	343	208
Washington	8	8	0	.500	256	303
N.Y. Giants	7	9	0	.438	294	321
Arizona	7	9	0	.438	295	343
Dallas	5	11	0	.313	246	338

Central Division
	W	L	T	Pct.	Pts.	OP
Chicago	13	3	0	.813	338	203
Green Bay*	12	4	0	.750	390	266
Tampa Bay*	9	7	0	.563	324	280
Minnesota	5	11	0	.313	290	390
Detroit	2	14	0	.125	270	424

Western Division
	W	L	T	Pct.	Pts.	OP
St. Louis#	14	2	0	.875	503	273
San Francisco*	12	4	0	.750	409	282
New Orleans	7	9	0	.438	333	409
Atlanta	7	9	0	.438	291	377
Carolina	1	15	0	.063	253	410

Wild Card qualifier for playoffs; #Top playoff seed in conference
New England finished ahead of Miami based on better division record (6-2 to Dolphins' 5-3). Baltimore was second Wild Card ahead of N.Y. Jets based on better record against common opponents (3-2 to Jets' 2-2). Cleveland finished ahead of Tennessee based on better division record (5-5 to Titans' 3-7). Jacksonville finished ahead of Cincinnati based on head-to-head record (2-0). N.Y. Giants finished ahead of Arizona based on head-to-head record (2-0). Green Bay was first Wild Card ahead of San Francisco based on better conference record (9-3 to 49ers' 8-4). New Orleans finished ahead of Atlanta based on better division record (4-4 to Falcons' 3-5).
Wild Card playoffs: OAKLAND 38, N.Y. Jets 24;
  Baltimore 20, MIAMI 3
Divisional playoffs: NEW ENGLAND 16, Oakland 13 (OT);
  PITTSBURGH 27, Baltimore 10
AFC Championship: New England 24, PITTSBURGH 17
Wild Card playoffs: PHILADELPHIA 31, Tampa Bay 9;
  GREEN BAY 25, San Francisco 15
Divisional playoffs: Philadelphia 33, CHICAGO 19;
  ST. LOUIS 45, Green Bay 17
NFC Championship: ST. LOUIS 29, Philadelphia 24
Super Bowl XXXVI: New England (AFC) 20, St. Louis (NFC) 17
  at Louisiana Superdome, New Orleans, Louisiana

Playoff Seeds
AFC	NFC
1. Pittsburgh	1. St. Louis
2. New England	2. Chicago
3. Oakland	3. Philadelphia
4. Miami	4. Green Bay
5. Baltimore	5. San Francisco
6. N.Y. Jets	6. Tampa Bay

2000

AMERICAN CONFERENCE
Eastern Division
	W	L	T	Pct.	Pts.	OP
Miami	11	5	0	.688	323	226
Indianapolis*	10	6	0	.625	429	326
N.Y. Jets	9	7	0	.563	321	321
Buffalo	8	8	0	.500	315	350
New England	5	11	0	.313	276	338

Central Division
	W	L	T	Pct.	Pts.	OP
Tennessee#	13	3	0	.813	346	191
Baltimore*	12	4	0	.750	333	165
Pittsburgh	9	7	0	.563	321	255
Jacksonville	7	9	0	.438	367	327
Cincinnati	4	12	0	.250	185	359
Cleveland	3	13	0	.188	161	419

Western Division
	W	L	T	Pct.	Pts.	OP
Oakland	12	4	0	.750	479	299
Denver*	11	5	0	.688	485	369
Kansas City	7	9	0	.438	355	354
Seattle	6	10	0	.375	320	405
San Diego	1	15	0	.063	269	440

NATIONAL CONFERENCE
Eastern Division
	W	L	T	Pct.	Pts.	OP
N.Y. Giants#	12	4	0	.750	328	246
Philadelphia*	11	5	0	.688	351	245
Washington	8	8	0	.500	281	269
Dallas	5	11	0	.313	294	361
Arizona	3	13	0	.188	210	443

Central Division
	W	L	T	Pct.	Pts.	OP
Minnesota	11	5	0	.688	397	371
Tampa Bay*	10	6	0	.625	388	269
Green Bay	9	7	0	.563	353	323
Detroit	9	7	0	.563	307	307
Chicago	5	11	0	.313	216	355

Western Division
	W	L	T	Pct.	Pts.	OP
New Orleans	10	6	0	.625	354	305
St. Louis*	10	6	0	.625	540	471
Carolina	7	9	0	.438	310	310
San Francisco	6	10	0	.375	388	422
Atlanta	4	12	0	.250	252	413

Wild Card qualifier for playoffs; #Top playoff seed in conference
Green Bay finished ahead of Detroit based on better division record (5-3 to Lions' 3-5). New Orleans finished ahead of St. Louis based on better division record (7-1 to Rams' 5-3). Tampa Bay was second Wild Card based on head-to-head victory over St. Louis (1-0).
Wild Card playoffs: MIAMI 23, Indianapolis 17 (OT);
  BALTIMORE 21, Denver 3
Divisional playoffs: OAKLAND 27, Miami 0;
  Baltimore 24, TENNESSEE 10
AFC Championship: Baltimore 16, OAKLAND 3
Wild Card playoffs: NEW ORLEANS 31, St. Louis 28;
  PHILADELPHIA 21, Tampa Bay 3
Divisional playoffs: MINNESOTA 34, New Orleans 16;
  N.Y. GIANTS 20, Philadelphia 10
NFC Championship: N.Y. GIANTS 41, Minnesota 0
Super Bowl XXXV: Baltimore (AFC) 34, N.Y. Giants (NFC) 7
  at Raymond James Stadium, Tampa, Florida

Playoff Seeds
AFC	NFC
1. Tennessee	1. N.Y. Giants
2. Oakland	2. Minnesota
3. Miami	3. New Orleans
4. Baltimore	4. Philadelphia
5. Denver	5. Tampa Bay
6. Indianapolis	6. St. Louis

1999

AMERICAN CONFERENCE

Eastern Division

	W	L	T	Pct.	Pts.	OP
Indianapolis	13	3	0	.813	423	333
Buffalo*	11	5	0	.688	320	229
Miami*	9	7	0	.563	326	336
N.Y. Jets	8	8	0	.500	308	309
New England	8	8	0	.500	299	284

Central Division

	W	L	T	Pct.	Pts.	OP
Jacksonville#	14	2	0	.875	396	217
Tennessee*	13	3	0	.813	392	324
Baltimore	8	8	0	.500	324	277
Pittsburgh	6	10	0	.375	317	320
Cincinnati	4	12	0	.250	283	460
Cleveland	2	14	0	.125	217	437

Western Division

	W	L	T	Pct.	Pts.	OP
Seattle	9	7	0	.563	338	298
Kansas City	9	7	0	.563	390	322
San Diego	8	8	0	.500	269	316
Oakland	8	8	0	.500	390	329
Denver	6	10	0	.375	314	318

NATIONAL CONFERENCE

Eastern Division

	W	L	T	Pct.	Pts.	OP
Washington	10	6	0	.625	443	377
Dallas*	8	8	0	.500	352	276
N.Y. Giants	7	9	0	.438	299	358
Arizona	6	10	0	.375	245	382
Philadelphia	5	11	0	.313	272	357

Central Division

	W	L	T	Pct.	Pts.	OP
Tampa Bay	11	5	0	.688	270	235
Minnesota*	10	6	0	.625	399	335
Detroit*	8	8	0	.500	322	323
Green Bay	8	8	0	.500	357	341
Chicago	6	10	0	.375	272	341

Western Division

	W	L	T	Pct.	Pts.	OP
St. Louis#	13	3	0	.813	526	242
Carolina	8	8	0	.500	421	381
Atlanta	5	11	0	.313	285	380
San Francisco	4	12	0	.250	295	453
New Orleans	3	13	0	.188	260	434

*Wild Card qualifier for playoffs; #Top playoff seed in conference
Miami was third Wild Card ahead of Kansas City based on better
    record against common opponents (6-1 to Chiefs' 5-3). N.Y. Jets
    finished ahead of New England based on better division record
    (4-4 to Patriots' 2-6). Seattle finished ahead of Kansas City based
    on head-to-head sweep (2-0). San Diego finished ahead of
    Oakland based on better division record (5-3 to Raiders' 3-5).
    Dallas was second Wild Card based on better record against
    common opponents (3-2 to Lions' 3-3) and better conference
    record than Carolina (7-5 to Panthers' 6-6). Detroit was third
    Wild Card based on better conference record than Green Bay
    (7-5 to Packers' 6-6) and better conference record than Carolina
    (7-5 to Panthers' 6-6).
Wild Card playoffs: TENNESSEE 22, Buffalo 16;
    Miami 20, SEATTLE 17
Divisional playoffs: JACKSONVILLE 62, Miami 7;
    Tennessee 19, INDIANAPOLIS 16
AFC Championship: Tennessee 33, JACKSONVILLE 14
Wild Card playoffs: WASHINGTON 27, Detroit 13;
    MINNESOTA 27, Dallas 10
Divisional playoffs: TAMPA BAY 14, Washington 13;
    ST. LOUIS 49, Minnesota 37
NFC Championship: ST. LOUIS 11, Tampa Bay 6
Super Bowl XXXIV: St. Louis (NFC) 23, Tennessee (AFC) 16
    at Georgia Dome, Atlanta, Georgia

Playoff Seeds

AFC	NFC
1. Jacksonville	**1. St. Louis**
2. Indianapolis	2. Tampa Bay
3. Seattle	3. Washington
4. Tennessee	4. Minnesota
5. Buffalo	5. Dallas
6. Miami	6. Detroit

1998

AMERICAN CONFERENCE

Eastern Division

	W	L	T	Pct.	Pts.	OP
N.Y. Jets	12	4	0	.750	416	266
Miami*	10	6	0	.625	321	265
Buffalo*	10	6	0	.625	400	333
New England*	9	7	0	.563	337	329
Indianapolis	3	13	0	.188	310	444

Central Division

	W	L	T	Pct.	Pts.	OP
Jacksonville	11	5	0	.688	392	338
Tennessee	8	8	0	.500	330	320
Pittsburgh	7	9	0	.438	263	303
Baltimore	6	10	0	.375	269	335
Cincinnati	3	13	0	.188	268	452

Western Division

	W	L	T	Pct.	Pts.	OP
Denver#	14	2	0	.875	501	309
Oakland	8	8	0	.500	288	356
Seattle	8	8	0	.500	372	310
Kansas City	7	9	0	.438	327	363
San Diego	5	11	0	.313	241	342

NATIONAL CONFERENCE

Eastern Division

	W	L	T	Pct.	Pts.	OP
Dallas	10	6	0	.625	381	275
Arizona*	9	7	0	.563	325	378
N.Y. Giants	8	8	0	.500	287	309
Washington	6	10	0	.375	319	421
Philadelphia	3	13	0	.188	161	344

Central Division

	W	L	T	Pct.	Pts.	OP
Minnesota#	15	1	0	.938	556	296
Green Bay*	11	5	0	.688	408	319
Tampa Bay	8	8	0	.500	314	295
Detroit	5	11	0	.313	306	378
Chicago	4	12	0	.250	276	368

Western Division

	W	L	T	Pct.	Pts.	OP
Atlanta	14	2	0	.875	442	289
San Francisco*	12	4	0	.750	479	328
New Orleans	6	10	0	.375	305	359
Carolina	4	12	0	.250	336	413
St. Louis	4	12	0	.250	285	378

*Wild Card qualifier for playoffs; #Top playoff seed in conference
Miami finished ahead of Buffalo based on better net division points
    (6 to Bills' 0). Oakland finished ahead of Seattle based on head-
    to-head sweep (2-0). Carolina finished ahead of St. Louis based
    on head-to-head sweep (2-0).
Wild Card playoffs: MIAMI 24, Buffalo 17;
    JACKSONVILLE 25, New England 10
Divisional playoffs: DENVER 38, Miami 3;
    N.Y. JETS 34, Jacksonville 24
AFC Championship: DENVER 23, N.Y. Jets 10
Wild Card playoffs: Arizona 20, DALLAS 7;
    SAN FRANCISCO 30, Green Bay 27
Divisional playoffs: ATLANTA 20, San Francisco 18;
    MINNESOTA 41, Arizona 21
NFC Championship: Atlanta 30, MINNESOTA 27 (OT)
Super Bowl XXXIII: Denver (AFC) 34, Atlanta (NFC) 19,
    at Pro Player Stadium, Miami, Florida

Playoff Seeds

AFC	NFC
1. Denver	1. Minnesota
2. N.Y. Jets	**2. Atlanta**
3. Jacksonville	3. Dallas
4. Miami	4. San Francisco
5. Buffalo	5. Green Bay
6. New England	6. Arizona

1997

AMERICAN CONFERENCE
Eastern Division

	W	L	T	Pct.	Pts.	OP
New England	10	6	0	.625	369	289
Miami*	9	7	0	.563	339	327
N.Y. Jets	9	7	0	.563	348	287
Buffalo	6	10	0	.375	255	367
Indianapolis	3	13	0	.188	313	401

Central Division

	W	L	T	Pct.	Pts.	OP
Pittsburgh	11	5	0	.688	372	307
Jacksonville*	11	5	0	.688	394	318
Tennessee	8	8	0	.500	333	310
Cincinnati	7	9	0	.438	355	405
Baltimore	6	9	1	.406	326	345

Western Division

	W	L	T	Pct.	Pts.	OP
Kansas City#	13	3	0	.813	375	232
Denver*	12	4	0	.750	472	287
Seattle	8	8	0	.500	365	362
Oakland	4	12	0	.250	324	419
San Diego	4	12	0	.250	266	425

NATIONAL CONFERENCE
Eastern Division

	W	L	T	Pct.	Pts.	OP
N.Y. Giants	10	5	1	.656	307	265
Washington	8	7	1	.531	327	289
Philadelphia	6	9	1	.406	317	372
Dallas	6	10	0	.375	304	314
Arizona	4	12	0	.250	283	379

Central Division

	W	L	T	Pct.	Pts.	OP
Green Bay	13	3	0	.813	422	282
Tampa Bay*	10	6	0	.625	299	263
Detroit*	9	7	0	.563	379	306
Minnesota*	9	7	0	.563	354	359
Chicago	4	12	0	.250	263	421

Western Division

	W	L	T	Pct.	Pts.	OP
San Francisco#	13	3	0	.813	375	265
Carolina	7	9	0	.438	265	314
Atlanta	7	9	0	.438	320	361
New Orleans	6	10	0	.375	237	327
St. Louis	5	11	0	.313	299	359

*Wild Card qualifier for playoffs; #Top playoff seed in conference
Miami finished ahead of N.Y. Jets based on head-to-head sweep
(2-0). Pittsburgh finished ahead of Jacksonville based on better
net division points (78 to Jaguars' 23). Oakland finished ahead of
San Diego based on better division record (2-6 to Chargers' 1-7).
San Francisco was top playoff seed based on better conference
record than Green Bay (11-1 to Packers' 10-2). Detroit finished
ahead of Minnesota based on head-to-head sweep (2-0). Caroli-
na finished ahead of Atlanta based on head-to-head sweep (2-0).
Wild Card playoffs: DENVER 42, Jacksonville 17;
    NEW ENGLAND 17, Miami 3
Divisional playoffs: PITTSBURGH 7, New England 6;
    Denver 14, KANSAS CITY 10
AFC Championship: Denver 24, PITTSBURGH 21
Wild Card playoffs: Minnesota 23, N.Y. GIANTS 22;
    TAMPA BAY 20, Detroit 10
Divisional playoffs: SAN FRANCISCO 38, Minnesota 22;
    GREEN BAY 21, Tampa Bay 7
NFC Championship: Green Bay 23, SAN FRANCISCO 10
Super Bowl XXXII: Denver (AFC) 31, Green Bay (NFC) 24,
    at Qualcomm Stadium, San Diego, California

Playoff Seeds

AFC	NFC
1. Kansas City	1. San Francisco
2. Pittsburgh	**2. Green Bay**
3. New England	3. N.Y. Giants
4. Denver	4. Tampa Bay
5. Jacksonville	5. Detroit
6. Miami	6. Minnesota

1996

AMERICAN CONFERENCE
Eastern Division

	W	L	T	Pct.	Pts.	OP
New England	11	5	0	.688	418	313
Buffalo*	10	6	0	.625	319	266
Indianapolis*	9	7	0	.563	317	334
Miami	8	8	0	.500	339	325
N.Y. Jets	1	15	0	.063	279	454

Central Division

	W	L	T	Pct.	Pts.	OP
Pittsburgh	10	6	0	.625	344	257
Jacksonville*	9	7	0	.563	325	335
Cincinnati	8	8	0	.500	372	369
Houston	8	8	0	.500	345	319
Baltimore	4	12	0	.250	371	441

Western Division

	W	L	T	Pct.	Pts.	OP
Denver#	13	3	0	.813	391	275
Kansas City	9	7	0	.563	297	300
San Diego	8	8	0	.500	310	376
Oakland	7	9	0	.438	340	293
Seattle	7	9	0	.438	317	376

NATIONAL CONFERENCE
Eastern Division

	W	L	T	Pct.	Pts.	OP
Dallas	10	6	0	.625	286	250
Philadelphia*	10	6	0	.625	363	341
Washington	9	7	0	.563	364	312
Arizona	7	9	0	.438	300	397
N.Y. Giants	6	10	0	.375	242	297

Central Division

	W	L	T	Pct.	Pts.	OP
Green Bay#	13	3	0	.813	456	210
Minnesota*	9	7	0	.563	298	315
Chicago	7	9	0	.438	283	305
Tampa Bay	6	10	0	.375	221	293
Detroit	5	11	0	.313	302	368

Western Division

	W	L	T	Pct.	Pts.	OP
Carolina	12	4	0	.750	367	218
San Francisco*	12	4	0	.750	398	257
St. Louis	6	10	0	.375	303	409
Atlanta	3	13	0	.188	309	461
New Orleans	3	13	0	.188	229	339

*Wild Card qualifier for playoffs; #Top playoff seed in conference
Jacksonville was second Wild Card ahead of Indianapolis and
    Kansas City based on better conference record (7-5 to Colts' 6-6
    and Chiefs' 5-7). Indianapolis was third Wild Card based on
    head-to-head victory over Kansas City (1-0). Cincinnati finished
    ahead of Houston based on better net division points (19 to
    Oilers' 11). Oakland finished ahead of Seattle based on better
    division record (3-5 to Seahawks' 2-6). Dallas finished ahead of
    Philadelphia based on better record against common opponents
    (8-5 to Eagles' 7-6). Minnesota was third Wild Card based on
    better conference record than Washington (8-4 to Redskins'
    6-6). Carolina finished ahead of San Francisco based on head-to-
    head sweep (2-0). Atlanta finished ahead of New Orleans based
    on head-to-head sweep (2-0).
Wild Card playoffs: Jacksonville 30, BUFFALO 27;
    PITTSBURGH 42, Indianapolis 14
Divisional playoffs: Jacksonville 30, DENVER 27;
    NEW ENGLAND 28, Pittsburgh 3
AFC Championship: NEW ENGLAND 20, Jacksonville 6
Wild Card playoffs: DALLAS 40, Minnesota 15;
    SAN FRANCISCO 14, Philadelphia 0
Divisional playoffs: GREEN BAY 35, San Francisco 14;
    CAROLINA 26, Dallas 17
NFC Championship: GREEN BAY 30, Carolina 13
Super Bowl XXXI: Green Bay (NFC) 35, New England (AFC) 21,
    at Louisiana Superdome, New Orleans, Louisiana

Playoff Seeds

AFC	NFC
1. Denver	**1. Green Bay**
2. New England	2. Carolina
3. Pittsburgh	3. Dallas
4. Buffalo	4. San Francisco
5. Jacksonville	5. Philadelphia
6. Indianapolis	6. Minnesota

1995

AMERICAN CONFERENCE

Eastern Division

	W	L	T	Pct.	Pts.	OP
Buffalo	10	6	0	.625	350	335
Indianapolis*	9	7	0	.563	331	316
Miami*	9	7	0	.563	398	332
New England	6	10	0	.375	294	377
N.Y. Jets	3	13	0	.188	233	384

Central Division

	W	L	T	Pct.	Pts.	OP
Pittsburgh	11	5	0	.688	407	327
Cincinnati	7	9	0	.438	349	374
Houston	7	9	0	.438	348	324
Cleveland	5	11	0	.313	289	356
Jacksonville	4	12	0	.250	275	404

Western Division

	W	L	T	Pct.	Pts.	OP
Kansas City#	13	3	0	.813	358	241
San Diego*	9	7	0	.563	321	323
Seattle	8	8	0	.500	363	366
Denver	8	8	0	.500	388	345
Oakland	8	8	0	.500	348	332

NATIONAL CONFERENCE

Eastern Division

	W	L	T	Pct.	Pts.	OP
Dallas#	12	4	0	.750	435	291
Philadelphia*	10	6	0	.625	318	338
Washington	6	10	0	.375	326	359
N.Y. Giants	5	11	0	.313	290	340
Arizona	4	12	0	.250	275	422

Central Division

	W	L	T	Pct.	Pts.	OP
Green Bay	11	5	0	.688	404	314
Detroit*	10	6	0	.625	436	336
Chicago	9	7	0	.563	392	360
Minnesota	8	8	0	.500	412	385
Tampa Bay	7	9	0	.438	238	335

Western Division

	W	L	T	Pct.	Pts.	OP
San Francisco	11	5	0	.688	457	258
Atlanta*	9	7	0	.563	362	349
St. Louis	7	9	0	.438	309	418
Carolina	7	9	0	.438	289	325
New Orleans	7	9	0	.438	319	348

Wild Card qualifier for playoffs; #Top playoff seed in conference
Indianapolis finished ahead of Miami based on head-to-head sweep (2-0). San Diego was first Wild Card based on head-to-head victory over Indianapolis (1-0). Cincinnati finished ahead of Houston based on better division record (4-4 to Oilers' 3-5). Seattle finished ahead of Denver and Oakland based on best head-to-head record (3-1 to Broncos' 2-2 and Raiders' 1-3). Denver finished ahead of Oakland based on head-to-head sweep (2-0). Philadelphia was first Wild Card ahead of Detroit based on better conference record (9-3 to Lions' 7-5). San Francisco was second playoff seed ahead of Green Bay based on better conference record (8-4 to Packers' 7-5). Atlanta was third Wild Card ahead of Chicago based on better record against common opponents (4-2 to Bears' 3-3). St. Louis finished ahead of Carolina and New Orleans based on best head-to-head record (3-1 to Panthers' 1-3 and Saints' 2-2). Carolina finished ahead of New Orleans based on better conference record (4-8 to 3-9).

Wild Card playoffs: BUFFALO 37, Miami 22;
   Indianapolis 35, SAN DIEGO 20
Divisional playoffs: PITTSBURGH 40, Buffalo 21;
   Indianapolis 10, KANSAS CITY 7
AFC Championship: PITTSBURGH 20, Indianapolis 16
Wild Card playoffs: PHILADELPHIA 58, Detroit 37;
   GREEN BAY 37, Atlanta 20
Divisional playoffs: Green Bay 27, SAN FRANCISCO 17;
   DALLAS 30, Philadelphia 11
NFC Championship: DALLAS 38, Green Bay 27
Super Bowl XXX: Dallas (NFC) 27, Pittsburgh (AFC)17,
   at Sun Devil Stadium, Tempe, Arizona

Playoff Seeds

AFC	NFC
1. Kansas City	**1. Dallas**
2. Pittsburgh	2. San Francisco
3. Buffalo	3. Green Bay
4. San Diego	4. Philadelphia
5. Indianapolis	5. Detroit
6. Miami	6. Atlanta

1994

AMERICAN CONFERENCE

Eastern Division

	W	L	T	Pct.	Pts.	OP
Miami	10	6	0	.625	389	327
New England*	10	6	0	.625	351	312
Indianapolis	8	8	0	.500	307	320
Buffalo	7	9	0	.438	340	356
N.Y. Jets	6	10	0	.375	264	320

Central Division

	W	L	T	Pct.	Pts.	OP
Pittsburgh#	12	4	0	.750	316	234
Cleveland*	11	5	0	.688	340	204
Cincinnati	3	13	0	.188	276	406
Houston	2	14	0	.125	226	352

Western Division

	W	L	T	Pct.	Pts.	OP
San Diego	11	5	0	.688	381	306
Kansas City*	9	7	0	.563	319	298
L.A. Raiders	9	7	0	.563	303	327
Denver	7	9	0	.438	347	396
Seattle	6	10	0	.375	287	323

NATIONAL CONFERENCE

Eastern Division

	W	L	T	Pct.	Pts.	OP
Dallas	12	4	0	.750	414	248
N.Y. Giants	9	7	0	.563	279	305
Arizona	8	8	0	.500	235	267
Philadelphia	7	9	0	.438	308	308
Washington	3	13	0	.188	320	412

Central Division

	W	L	T	Pct.	Pts.	OP
Minnesota	10	6	0	.625	356	314
Green Bay*	9	7	0	.563	382	287
Detroit*	9	7	0	.563	357	342
Chicago*	9	7	0	.563	271	307
Tampa Bay	6	10	0	.375	251	351

Western Division

	W	L	T	Pct.	Pts.	OP
San Francisco#	13	3	0	.813	505	296
New Orleans	7	9	0	.438	348	407
Atlanta	7	9	0	.438	317	385
L.A. Rams	4	12	0	.250	286	365

Wild Card qualifier for playoffs; #Top playoff seed in conference
Miami finished ahead of New England based on head-to-head sweep (2-0). Kansas City finished ahead of L.A. Raiders based on head-to-head sweep (2-0). Green Bay was first Wild Card based on best head-to-head record (3-1) vs. Detroit (2-2) and Chicago (1-3) and better conference record (8-4) than N.Y. Giants (6-6). Detroit was second Wild Card based on better division record (4-4) than Chicago (3-5) and head-to-head victory over N.Y. Giants (1-0). Chicago was third Wild Card based on better record against common opponents (4-4) than N.Y. Giants (3-5). New Orleans finished ahead of Atlanta based on head-to-head sweep (2-0).

Wild Card playoffs: MIAMI 27, Kansas City 17;
   CLEVELAND 20, New England 13
Divisional playoffs: PITTSBURGH 29, Cleveland 9;
   SAN DIEGO 22, Miami 21
AFC Championship: San Diego 17, PITTSBURGH 13
Wild Card playoffs: GREEN BAY 16, Detroit 12;
   Chicago 35, MINNESOTA 18
Divisional playoffs: SAN FRANCISCO 44, Chicago 15;
   DALLAS 35, Green Bay 9
NFC Championship: SAN FRANCISCO 38, Dallas 28
Super Bowl XXIX: San Francisco (NFC) 49, San Diego (AFC) 26,
   at Joe Robbie Stadium, Miami, Florida

Playoff Seeds

AFC	NFC
1. Pittsburgh	**1. San Francisco**
2. San Diego	2. Dallas
3. Miami	3. Minnesota
4. Cleveland	4. Green Bay
5. New England	5. Detroit
6. Kansas City	6. Chicago

1993

AMERICAN CONFERENCE

Eastern Division

	W	L	T	Pct.	Pts.	OP
Buffalo#	12	4	0	.750	329	242
Miami	9	7	0	.563	349	351
N.Y. Jets	8	8	0	.500	270	247
New England	5	11	0	.313	238	286
Indianapolis	4	12	0	.250	189	378

Central Division

	W	L	T	Pct.	Pts.	OP
Houston	12	4	0	.750	368	238
Pittsburgh*	9	7	0	.563	308	281
Cleveland	7	9	0	.438	304	307
Cincinnati	3	13	0	.188	187	319

Western Division

	W	L	T	Pct.	Pts.	OP
Kansas City	11	5	0	.688	328	291
L.A. Raiders*	10	6	0	.625	306	326
Denver*	9	7	0	.563	373	284
San Diego	8	8	0	.500	322	290
Seattle	6	10	0	.375	280	314

NATIONAL CONFERENCE

Eastern Division

	W	L	T	Pct.	Pts.	OP
Dallas#	12	4	0	.750	376	229
N.Y. Giants*	11	5	0	.688	288	205
Philadelphia	8	8	0	.500	293	315
Phoenix	7	9	0	.438	326	269
Washington	4	12	0	.250	230	345

Central Division

	W	L	T	Pct.	Pts.	OP
Detroit	10	6	0	.625	298	292
Minnesota*	9	7	0	.563	277	290
Green Bay*	9	7	0	.563	340	282
Chicago	7	9	0	.438	234	230
Tampa Bay	5	11	0	.313	237	376

Western Division

	W	L	T	Pct.	Pts.	OP
San Francisco	10	6	0	.625	473	295
New Orleans	8	8	0	.500	317	343
Atlanta	6	10	0	.375	316	385
L.A. Rams	5	11	0	.313	221	367

*Wild Card qualifier for playoffs; #Top playoff seed in conference
Buffalo was top playoff seed based on head-to-head victory over Houston (1-0). Denver was second Wild Card, and Pittsburgh was third Wild Card ahead of Miami, based on better conference record (8-4 to Steelers' 7-5 to Dolphins' 6-6). San Francisco was second playoff seed based on head-to-head victory over Detroit (1-0). Minnesota finished ahead of Green Bay based on head-to-head sweep (2-0).

Wild Card playoffs: KANSAS CITY 27, Pittsburgh 24 (OT);
    L.A. RAIDERS 42, Denver 24
Divisional playoffs: BUFFALO 29, L.A. Raiders 23;
    Kansas City 28, HOUSTON 20
AFC Championship: BUFFALO 30, Kansas City 13
Wild Card playoffs: Green Bay 28, DETROIT 24;
    N.Y. GIANTS 17, Minnesota 10
Divisional playoffs: SAN FRANCISCO 44, N.Y. Giants 3;
    DALLAS 27, Green Bay 17
NFC Championship: DALLAS 38, San Francisco 21
Super Bowl XXVIII: Dallas (NFC) 30, Buffalo (AFC) 13,
    at Georgia Dome, Atlanta, Georgia

Playoff Seeds

AFC	NFC
1. **Buffalo**	1. **Dallas**
2. Houston	2. San Francisco
3. Kansas City	3. Detroit
4. L.A. Raiders	4. N.Y. Giants
5. Denver	5. Minnesota
6. Pittsburgh	6. Green Bay

1992

AMERICAN CONFERENCE

Eastern Division

	W	L	T	Pct.	Pts.	OP
Miami	11	5	0	.688	340	281
Buffalo*	11	5	0	.688	381	283
Indianapolis	9	7	0	.563	216	302
N.Y. Jets	4	12	0	.250	220	315
New England	2	14	0	.125	205	363

Central Division

	W	L	T	Pct.	Pts.	OP
Pittsburgh#	11	5	0	.688	299	225
Houston*	10	6	0	.625	352	258
Cleveland	7	9	0	.438	272	275
Cincinnati	5	11	0	.313	274	364

Western Division

	W	L	T	Pct.	Pts.	OP
San Diego	11	5	0	.688	335	241
Kansas City*	10	6	0	.625	348	282
Denver	8	8	0	.500	262	329
L.A. Raiders	7	9	0	.438	249	281
Seattle	2	14	0	.125	140	312

NATIONAL CONFERENCE

Eastern Division

	W	L	T	Pct.	Pts.	OP
Dallas	13	3	0	.813	409	243
Philadelphia*	11	5	0	.688	354	245
Washington*	9	7	0	.563	300	255
N.Y. Giants	6	10	0	.375	306	367
Phoenix	4	12	0	.250	243	332

Central Division

	W	L	T	Pct.	Pts.	OP
Minnesota	11	5	0	.688	374	249
Green Bay	9	7	0	.563	276	296
Tampa Bay	5	11	0	.313	267	365
Chicago	5	11	0	.313	295	361
Detroit	5	11	0	.313	273	332

Western Division

	W	L	T	Pct.	Pts.	OP
San Francisco#	14	2	0	.875	431	236
New Orleans*	12	4	0	.750	330	202
Atlanta	6	10	0	.375	327	414
L.A. Rams	6	10	0	.375	313	383

*Wild Card qualifier for playoffs; #Top playoff seed in conference
Pittsburgh was top playoff seed, and Miami was second playoff seed ahead of San Diego, based on conference record (10-2 to Dolphins' 9-3 to Chargers' 9-5). Miami finished ahead of Buffalo based on better conference record (9-3 to Bills' 7-5). Houston was second Wild Card based on head-to-head victory over Kansas City (1-0). Washington was third Wild Card based on better conference record than Green Bay (7-5 to Packers' 6-6). Tampa Bay finished ahead of Chicago and Detroit based on better conference record (5-9 to Bears' 4-8 and Lions' 3-9). Atlanta finished ahead of L.A. Rams based on better record against common opponents (5-7 to Rams' 4-8).

Wild Card playoffs: SAN DIEGO 17, Kansas City 0;
    BUFFALO 41, Houston 38 (OT)
Divisional playoffs: Buffalo 24, PITTSBURGH 3;
    MIAMI 31, San Diego 0
AFC Championship: Buffalo 29, MIAMI 10
Wild Card playoffs: Washington 24, MINNESOTA 7;
    Philadelphia 36, NEW ORLEANS 20
Divisional playoffs: SAN FRANCISCO 20, Washington 13;
    DALLAS 34, Philadelphia 10
NFC Championship: Dallas 30, SAN FRANCISCO 20
Super Bowl XXVII: Dallas (NFC) 52, Buffalo (AFC) 17,
    at Rose Bowl, Pasadena, California

Playoff Seeds

AFC	NFC
1. Pittsburgh	1. San Francisco
2. Miami	2. **Dallas**
3. San Diego	3. Minnesota
4. **Buffalo**	4. New Orleans
5. Houston	5. Philadelphia
6. Kansas City	6. Washington

1991

AMERICAN CONFERENCE

Eastern Division

	W	L	T	Pct.	Pts.	OP
Buffalo#	13	3	0	.813	458	318
N.Y. Jets*	8	8	0	.500	314	293
Miami	8	8	0	.500	343	349
New England	6	10	0	.375	211	305
Indianapolis	1	15	0	.063	143	381

Central Division

	W	L	T	Pct.	Pts.	OP
Houston	11	5	0	.688	386	251
Pittsburgh	7	9	0	.438	292	344
Cleveland	6	10	0	.375	293	298
Cincinnati	3	13	0	.188	263	435

Western Division

	W	L	T	Pct.	Pts.	OP
Denver	12	4	0	.750	304	235
Kansas City*	10	6	0	.625	322	252
L.A. Raiders*	9	7	0	.563	298	297
Seattle	7	9	0	.438	276	261
San Diego	4	12	0	.250	274	342

NATIONAL CONFERENCE

Eastern Division

	W	L	T	Pct.	Pts.	OP
Washington#	14	2	0	.875	485	224
Dallas*	11	5	0	.688	342	310
Philadelphia	10	6	0	.625	285	244
N.Y. Giants	8	8	0	.500	281	297
Phoenix	4	12	0	.250	196	344

Central Division

	W	L	T	Pct.	Pts.	OP
Detroit	12	4	0	.750	339	295
Chicago*	11	5	0	.688	299	269
Minnesota	8	8	0	.500	301	306
Green Bay	4	12	0	.250	273	313
Tampa Bay	3	13	0	.188	199	365

Western Division

	W	L	T	Pct.	Pts.	OP
New Orleans	11	5	0	.688	341	211
Atlanta*	10	6	0	.625	361	338
San Francisco	10	6	0	.625	393	239
L.A. Rams	3	13	0	.188	234	390

*Wild Card qualifier for playoffs; #Top playoff seed in conference
N.Y. Jets finished ahead of Miami based on head-to-head sweep (2-0). Chicago was first Wild Card based on better conference record than Dallas (9-3 to Cowboys' 8-4). Atlanta finished ahead of San Francisco based on head-to-head sweep (2-0), and was third Wild Card ahead of Philadelphia based on better conference record (7-5 to Eagles' 6-6).
Wild Card playoffs: KANSAS CITY 10, L.A. Raiders 6; HOUSTON 17, N.Y. Jets 10
Divisional playoffs: DENVER 26, Houston 24; BUFFALO 37, Kansas City 14
AFC Championship: BUFFALO 10, Denver 7
Wild Card playoffs: Atlanta 27, NEW ORLEANS 20; Dallas 17, CHICAGO 13
Divisional playoffs: WASHINGTON 24, Atlanta 7; DETROIT 38, Dallas 6
NFC Championship: WASHINGTON 41, Detroit 10
Super Bowl XXVI: Washington (NFC) 37, Buffalo (AFC) 24, at Hubert H. Humphrey Metrodome, Minneapolis, Minnesota

Playoff Seeds

AFC	NFC
1. Buffalo	1. Washington
2. Denver	2. Detroit
3. Houston	3. New Orleans
4. Kansas City	4. Chicago
5. L.A. Raiders	5. Dallas
6. N.Y. Jets	6. Atlanta

1990

AMERICAN CONFERENCE

Eastern Division

	W	L	T	Pct.	Pts.	OP
Buffalo#	13	3	0	.813	428	263
Miami*	12	4	0	.750	336	242
Indianapolis	7	9	0	.438	281	353
N.Y. Jets	6	10	0	.375	295	345
New England	1	15	0	.063	181	446

Central Division

	W	L	T	Pct.	Pts.	OP
Cincinnati	9	7	0	.563	360	352
Houston*	9	7	0	.563	405	307
Pittsburgh	9	7	0	.563	292	240
Cleveland	3	13	0	.188	228	462

Western Division

	W	L	T	Pct.	Pts.	OP
L.A. Raiders	12	4	0	.750	337	268
Kansas City*	11	5	0	.688	369	257
Seattle	9	7	0	.563	306	286
San Diego	6	10	0	.375	315	281
Denver	5	11	0	.313	331	374

NATIONAL CONFERENCE

Eastern Division

	W	L	T	Pct.	Pts.	OP
N.Y. Giants	13	3	0	.813	335	211
Philadelphia*	10	6	0	.625	396	299
Washington*	10	6	0	.625	381	301
Dallas	7	9	0	.438	244	308
Phoenix	5	11	0	.313	268	396

Central Division

	W	L	T	Pct.	Pts.	OP
Chicago	11	5	0	.688	348	280
Tampa Bay	6	10	0	.375	264	367
Detroit	6	10	0	.375	373	413
Green Bay	6	10	0	.375	271	347
Minnesota	6	10	0	.375	351	326

Western Division

	W	L	T	Pct.	Pts.	OP
San Francisco#	14	2	0	.875	353	239
New Orleans*	8	8	0	.500	274	275
L.A. Rams	5	11	0	.313	345	412
Atlanta	5	11	0	.313	348	365

*Wild Card qualifier for playoffs; #Top playoff seed in conference
Cincinnati finished ahead of Houston and Pittsburgh based on best head-to-head record (3-1 to Oilers' 2-2 to Steelers' 1-3). Houston was Wild Card based on better conference record (8-4) than Seattle (7-5) and Pittsburgh (6-6). Philadelphia finished ahead of Washington based on better division record (5-3 to Redskins' 4-4). Tampa Bay was second in NFC Central based on best head-to-head record (5-1) against Detroit (2-4), Green Bay (3-3), and Minnesota (2-4). Detroit finished third based on best net division points (minus 8) against Green Bay (minus 40). Green Bay finished ahead of Minnesota based on better conference record (5-7 to Vikings' 4-8). The L.A. Rams finished ahead of Atlanta based on net points in division (plus 1 to Falcons' minus 31).
Wild Card playoffs: MIAMI 17, Kansas City 16; CINCINNATI 41, Houston 14
Divisional playoffs: BUFFALO 44, Miami 34; L.A. RAIDERS 20, Cincinnati 10
AFC Championship: BUFFALO 51, L.A. Raiders 3
Wild Card playoffs: Washington 20, PHILADELPHIA 6; CHICAGO 16, New Orleans 6
Divisional playoffs: SAN FRANCISCO 28, Washington 10; N.Y. GIANTS 31, Chicago 3
NFC Championship: N.Y. Giants 15, SAN FRANCISCO 13
Super Bowl XXV: N.Y. Giants (NFC) 20, Buffalo (AFC) 19, at Tampa Stadium, Tampa, Florida

Playoff Seeds

AFC	NFC
1. Buffalo	1. San Francisco
2. L.A. Raiders	2. N.Y. Giants
3. Cincinnati	3. Chicago
4. Miami	4. Philadelphia
5. Kansas City	5. Washington
6. Houston	6. New Orleans

1989

AMERICAN CONFERENCE

Eastern Division

	W	L	T	Pct.	Pts.	OP
Buffalo	9	7	0	.563	409	317
Indianapolis	8	8	0	.500	298	301
Miami	8	8	0	.500	331	379
New England	5	11	0	.313	297	391
N.Y. Jets	4	12	0	.250	253	411

Central Division

	W	L	T	Pct.	Pts.	OP
Cleveland	9	6	1	.594	334	254
Houston*	9	7	0	.563	365	412
Pittsburgh*	9	7	0	.563	265	326
Cincinnati	8	8	0	.500	404	285

Western Division

	W	L	T	Pct.	Pts.	OP
Denver#	11	5	0	.688	362	226
Kansas City	8	7	1	.531	318	286
L.A. Raiders	8	8	0	.500	315	297
Seattle	7	9	0	.438	241	327
San Diego	6	10	0	.375	266	290

NATIONAL CONFERENCE

Eastern Division

	W	L	T	Pct.	Pts.	OP
N.Y. Giants	12	4	0	.750	348	252
Philadelphia*	11	5	0	.688	342	274
Washington	10	6	0	.625	386	308
Phoenix	5	11	0	.313	258	377
Dallas	1	15	0	.063	204	393

Central Division

	W	L	T	Pct.	Pts.	OP
Minnesota	10	6	0	.625	351	275
Green Bay	10	6	0	.625	362	356
Detroit	7	9	0	.438	312	364
Chicago	6	10	0	.375	358	377
Tampa Bay	5	11	0	.313	320	419

Western Division

	W	L	T	Pct.	Pts.	OP
San Francisco#	14	2	0	.875	442	253
L.A. Rams*	11	5	0	.688	426	344
New Orleans	9	7	0	.563	386	301
Atlanta	3	13	0	.188	279	437

*Wild Card qualifier for playoffs; #Top playoff seed in conference
Indianapolis finished ahead of Miami based on better conference record (7-5 vs. Dolphins' 6-8). Houston finished ahead of Pittsburgh based on head-to-head sweep (2-0). The L.A. Rams did not play San Francisco in the divisional playoffs because, from 1970-1989, two teams from the same division could not meet prior to the conference championship game. Philadelphia was first Wild Card ahead of L.A. Rams based on better record against common opponents (6-3 to Rams' 5-4). Minnesota finished ahead of Green Bay based on better division record (6-2 vs. Packers' 5-3).

Wild Card playoff: Pittsburgh 26, HOUSTON 23 (OT)
Divisional playoffs: CLEVELAND 34, Buffalo 30;
  DENVER 24, Pittsburgh 23
AFC Championship: DENVER 37, Cleveland 21
Wild Card playoff: L.A. Rams 21, PHILADELPHIA 7
Divisional playoffs: L.A. Rams 19, N.Y. GIANTS 13 (OT);
  SAN FRANCISCO 41, Minnesota 13
NFC Championship: SAN FRANCISCO 30, L.A. Rams 3
Super Bowl XXIV: San Francisco (NFC) 55, Denver (AFC) 10,
  at Louisiana Superdome, New Orleans, Louisiana

1988

AMERICAN CONFERENCE

Eastern Division

	W	L	T	Pct.	Pts.	OP
Buffalo	12	4	0	.750	329	237
Indianapolis	9	7	0	.563	354	315
New England	9	7	0	.563	250	284
N.Y. Jets	8	7	1	.531	372	354
Miami	6	10	0	.375	319	380

Central Division

	W	L	T	Pct.	Pts.	OP
Cincinnati#	12	4	0	.750	448	329
Cleveland*	10	6	0	.625	304	288
Houston*	10	6	0	.625	424	365
Pittsburgh	5	11	0	.313	336	421

Western Division

	W	L	T	Pct.	Pts.	OP
Seattle	9	7	0	.563	339	329
Denver	8	8	0	.500	327	352
L.A. Raiders	7	9	0	.438	325	369
San Diego	6	10	0	.375	231	332
Kansas City	4	11	1	.281	254	320

NATIONAL CONFERENCE

Eastern Division

	W	L	T	Pct.	Pts.	OP
Philadelphia	10	6	0	.625	379	319
N.Y. Giants	10	6	0	.625	359	304
Washington	7	9	0	.438	345	387
Phoenix	7	9	0	.438	344	398
Dallas	3	13	0	.188	265	381

Central Division

	W	L	T	Pct.	Pts.	OP
Chicago#	12	4	0	.750	312	215
Minnesota*	11	5	0	.688	406	233
Tampa Bay	5	11	0	.313	261	350
Detroit	4	12	0	.250	220	313
Green Bay	4	12	0	.250	240	315

Western Division

	W	L	T	Pct.	Pts.	OP
San Francisco	10	6	0	.625	369	294
L.A. Rams*	10	6	0	.625	407	293
New Orleans	10	6	0	.625	312	283
Atlanta	5	11	0	.313	244	315

*Wild Card qualifier for playoffs; #Top playoff seed in conference
Cincinnati was top playoff seed ahead of Buffalo based on head-to-head victory (1-0). Indianapolis finished ahead of New England based on better record against common opponents (7-5 to Patriots' 6-6). Cleveland finished ahead of Houston based on better division record (4-2 to Oilers' 3-3). Houston did not play Cincinnati, and Minnesota did not play Chicago in the divisional playoffs because, from 1970-1989, two teams from the same division could not meet prior to the conference championship game. Philadelphia finished first in NFC East based on head-to-head sweep of N.Y. Giants (2-0). Washington finished third in NFC East based on better division record (4-4) than Phoenix (3-5). Detroit finished fourth in NFC Central based on head-to-head sweep of Green Bay (2-0). San Francisco finished first in NFC West based on better head-to-head record (3-1) against L.A. Rams (2-2) and New Orleans (1-3). L.A. Rams finished second in NFC West based on better division record (4-2) than New Orleans (3-3) and earned Wild-Card position based on better conference record (8-4) than N.Y. Giants (9-5) and New Orleans (6-6).

Wild Card playoff: Houston 24, CLEVELAND 23
Divisional playoffs: CINCINNATI 21, Seattle 13;
  BUFFALO 17, Houston 10
AFC Championship: CINCINNATI 21, Buffalo 10
Wild Card playoff: MINNESOTA 28, L.A. Rams 17
Divisional playoffs: CHICAGO 20, Philadelphia 12;
  SAN FRANCISCO 34, Minnesota 9
NFC Championship: San Francisco 28, CHICAGO 3
Super Bowl XXIII: San Francisco (NFC) 20, Cincinnati (AFC) 16,
  at Joe Robbie Stadium, Miami, Florida

1987

AMERICAN CONFERENCE

Eastern Division

	W	L	T	Pct.	Pts.	OP
Indianapolis	9	6	0	.600	300	238
New England	8	7	0	.533	320	293
Miami	8	7	0	.533	362	335
Buffalo	7	8	0	.467	270	305
N.Y. Jets	6	9	0	.400	334	360

Central Division

	W	L	T	Pct.	Pts.	OP
Cleveland	10	5	0	.667	390	239
Houston*	9	6	0	.600	345	349
Pittsburgh	8	7	0	.533	285	299
Cincinnati	4	11	0	.267	285	370

Western Division

	W	L	T	Pct.	Pts.	OP
Denver#	10	4	1	.700	379	288
Seattle*	9	6	0	.600	371	314
San Diego	8	7	0	.533	253	317
L.A. Raiders	5	10	0	.333	301	289
Kansas City	4	11	0	.267	273	388

NATIONAL CONFERENCE

Eastern Division

	W	L	T	Pct.	Pts.	OP
Washington	11	4	0	.733	379	285
Dallas	7	8	0	.467	340	348
St. Louis	7	8	0	.467	362	368
Philadelphia	7	8	0	.467	337	380
N.Y. Giants	6	9	0	.400	280	312

Central Division

	W	L	T	Pct.	Pts.	OP
Chicago	11	4	0	.733	356	282
Minnesota*	8	7	0	.533	336	335
Green Bay	5	9	1	.367	255	300
Tampa Bay	4	11	0	.267	286	360
Detroit	4	11	0	.267	269	384

Western Division

	W	L	T	Pct.	Pts.	OP
San Francisco#	13	2	0	.867	459	253
New Orleans*	12	3	0	.800	422	283
L.A. Rams	6	9	0	.400	317	361
Atlanta	3	12	0	.200	205	436

*Wild Card qualifier for playoffs; #Top playoff seed in conference
New England finished ahead of Miami based on head-to-head sweep (2-0). Houston was first Wild Card ahead of Seattle based on better conference record (7-4 to Seahawks' 5-6). Chicago was second playoff seed ahead of Washington based on better conference record (9-2 to Redskins' 9-3). Dallas finished ahead of St. Louis and Philadelphia based on better division record (4-4 to Cardinals' 3-5 and Eagles' 3-5). St. Louis finished ahead of Philadelphia based on better conference record (7-7 to Eagles' 4-7). Tampa Bay finished ahead of Detroit based on better division record (3-4 to Lions' 2-5).
Wild Card playoff: HOUSTON 23, Seattle 20 (OT)
Divisional playoffs: CLEVELAND 38, Indianapolis 21; DENVER 34, Houston 10
AFC Championship: DENVER 38, Cleveland 33
Wild Card playoff: Minnesota 44, NEW ORLEANS 10
Divisional playoffs: Minnesota 36, SAN FRANCISCO 24; Washington 21, CHICAGO 17
NFC Championship: WASHINGTON 17, Minnesota 10
Super Bowl XXII: Washington (NFC) 42, Denver (AFC) 10, at San Diego Jack Murphy Stadium, San Diego, California
Note: 1987 regular season was reduced from 16 to 15 games for each team due to players' strike.

1986

AMERICAN CONFERENCE

Eastern Division

	W	L	T	Pct.	Pts.	OP
New England	11	5	0	.688	412	307
N.Y. Jets*	10	6	0	.625	364	386
Miami	8	8	0	.500	430	405
Buffalo	4	12	0	.250	287	348
Indianapolis	3	13	0	.188	229	400

Central Division

	W	L	T	Pct.	Pts.	OP
Cleveland#	12	4	0	.750	391	310
Cincinnati	10	6	0	.625	409	394
Pittsburgh	6	10	0	.375	307	336
Houston	5	11	0	.313	274	329

Western Division

	W	L	T	Pct.	Pts.	OP
Denver	11	5	0	.688	378	327
Kansas City*	10	6	0	.625	358	326
Seattle	10	6	0	.625	366	293
L.A. Raiders	8	8	0	.500	323	346
San Diego	4	12	0	.250	335	396

NATIONAL CONFERENCE

Eastern Division

	W	L	T	Pct.	Pts.	OP
N.Y. Giants#	14	2	0	.875	371	236
Washington*	12	4	0	.750	368	296
Dallas	7	9	0	.438	346	337
Philadelphia	5	10	1	.344	256	312
St. Louis	4	11	1	.281	218	351

Central Division

	W	L	T	Pct.	Pts.	OP
Chicago	14	2	0	.875	352	187
Minnesota	9	7	0	.563	398	273
Detroit	5	11	0	.313	277	326
Green Bay	4	12	0	.250	254	418
Tampa Bay	2	14	0	.125	239	473

Western Division

	W	L	T	Pct.	Pts.	OP
San Francisco	10	5	1	.656	374	247
L.A. Rams*	10	6	0	.625	309	267
Atlanta	7	8	1	.469	280	280
New Orleans	7	9	0	.438	288	287

*Wild Card qualifier for playoffs; #Top playoff seed in conference
Denver was second playoff seed ahead of New England based on head-to-head victory (1-0). N.Y. Jets were first Wild Card based on better conference record (8-4) than Kansas City (9-5), Seattle (7-5), and Cincinnati (7-5). Kansas City was second Wild Card based on better conference record (9-5) than Seattle (7-5) and Cincinnati (7-5). N.Y. Giants were top playoff seed based on better conference record than Chicago (11-1 to Bears' 10-2). Washington did not play the N.Y. Giants in the divisional playoffs because, from 1970-1989, two teams from the same division could not meet prior to the conference championship game.
Wild Card playoff: N.Y. JETS 35, Kansas City 15
Divisional playoffs: CLEVELAND 23, N.Y. Jets 20 (OT); DENVER 22, New England 17
AFC Championship: Denver 23, CLEVELAND 20 (OT)
Wild Card playoff: WASHINGTON 19, L.A. Rams 7
Divisional playoffs: Washington 27, CHICAGO 13 N.Y. GIANTS 49, San Francisco 3
NFC Championship: N.Y. GIANTS 17, Washington 0
Super Bowl XXI: N.Y. Giants (NFC) 39, Denver (AFC) 20, at Rose Bowl, Pasadena, California

1985

AMERICAN CONFERENCE

Eastern Division

	W	L	T	Pct.	Pts.	OP
Miami	12	4	0	.750	428	320
N.Y. Jets*	11	5	0	.688	393	264
New England*	11	5	0	.688	362	290
Indianapolis	5	11	0	.313	320	386
Buffalo	2	14	0	.125	200	381

Central Division

	W	L	T	Pct.	Pts.	OP
Cleveland	8	8	0	.500	287	294
Cincinnati	7	9	0	.438	441	437
Pittsburgh	7	9	0	.438	379	355
Houston	5	11	0	.313	284	412

Western Division

	W	L	T	Pct.	Pts.	OP
L.A. Raiders#	12	4	0	.750	354	308
Denver	11	5	0	.688	380	329
Seattle	8	8	0	.500	349	303
San Diego	8	8	0	.500	467	435
Kansas City	6	10	0	.375	317	360

NATIONAL CONFERENCE

Eastern Division

	W	L	T	Pct.	Pts.	OP
Dallas	10	6	0	.625	357	333
N.Y. Giants*	10	6	0	.625	399	283
Washington	10	6	0	.625	297	312
Philadelphia	7	9	0	.438	286	310
St. Louis	5	11	0	.313	278	414

Central Division

	W	L	T	Pct.	Pts.	OP
Chicago#	15	1	0	.938	456	198
Green Bay	8	8	0	.500	337	355
Minnesota	7	9	0	.438	346	359
Detroit	7	9	0	.438	307	366
Tampa Bay	2	14	0	.125	294	448

Western Division

	W	L	T	Pct.	Pts.	OP
L.A. Rams	11	5	0	.688	340	277
San Francisco*	10	6	0	.625	411	263
New Orleans	5	11	0	.313	294	401
Atlanta	4	12	0	.250	282	452

*Wild Card qualifier for playoffs; #Top playoff seed in conference
L.A. Raiders were top playoff seed ahead of Miami based on better record against common opponents (5-1 to 4-2). N.Y. Jets were first Wild Card based on better conference record (9-3) than New England (8-4) and Denver (8-4). New England was second Wild Card ahead of Denver based on better record against common opponents (4-2 to Broncos' 3-3). Cincinnati finished ahead of Pittsburgh based on head-to-head sweep (2-0). Seattle finished ahead of San Diego based on head-to-head sweep (2-0). Dallas finished ahead of N.Y. Giants and Washington based on better head-to-head record (4-0 to Giants' 1-3 and Redskins' 1-3). N.Y. Giants were first Wild Card based on better conference record (8-4) than San Francisco (7-5) and Washington (6-6). San Francisco was second Wild Card based on head-to-head victory over Washington (1-0). Minnesota finished ahead of Detroit based on better division record (3-5 to Lions' 2-6).
Wild Card playoff: New England 26, N.Y. JETS 14
Divisional playoffs: MIAMI 24, Cleveland 21;
New England 27, L.A. RAIDERS 20
AFC Championship: New England 31, MIAMI 14
Wild Card playoff: N.Y. GIANTS 17, San Francisco 3
Divisional playoffs: L.A. RAMS 20, Dallas 0;
CHICAGO 21, N.Y. Giants 0
NFC Championship: CHICAGO 24, L.A. Rams 0
Super Bowl XX: Chicago (NFC) 46, New England (AFC) 10,
at Louisiana Superdome, New Orleans, Louisiana

1984

AMERICAN CONFERENCE

Eastern Division

	W	L	T	Pct.	Pts.	OP
Miami#	14	2	0	.875	513	298
New England	9	7	0	.563	362	352
N.Y. Jets	7	9	0	.438	332	364
Indianapolis	4	12	0	.250	239	414
Buffalo	2	14	0	.125	250	454

Central Division

	W	L	T	Pct.	Pts.	OP
Pittsburgh	9	7	0	.563	387	310
Cincinnati	8	8	0	.500	339	339
Cleveland	5	11	0	.313	250	297
Houston	3	13	0	.188	240	437

Western Division

	W	L	T	Pct.	Pts.	OP
Denver	13	3	0	.813	353	241
Seattle*	12	4	0	.750	418	282
L.A. Raiders*	11	5	0	.688	368	278
Kansas City	8	8	0	.500	314	324
San Diego	7	9	0	.438	394	413

NATIONAL CONFERENCE

Eastern Division

	W	L	T	Pct.	Pts.	OP
Washington	11	5	0	.688	426	310
N.Y. Giants*	9	7	0	.563	299	301
St. Louis	9	7	0	.563	423	345
Dallas	9	7	0	.563	308	308
Philadelphia	6	9	1	.406	278	320

Central Division

	W	L	T	Pct.	Pts.	OP
Chicago	10	6	0	.625	325	248
Green Bay	8	8	0	.500	390	309
Tampa Bay	6	10	0	.375	335	380
Detroit	4	11	1	.281	283	408
Minnesota	3	13	0	.188	276	484

Western Division

	W	L	T	Pct.	Pts.	OP
San Francisco#	15	1	0	.938	475	227
L.A. Rams*	10	6	0	.625	346	316
New Orleans	7	9	0	.438	298	361
Atlanta	4	12	0	.250	281	382

*Wild Card qualifier for playoffs; #Top playoff seed in conference
N.Y. Giants finished ahead of St. Louis and Dallas based on best head-to-head record (3-1 to Cardinals' 2-2 and Cowboys' 1-3). St. Louis finished ahead of Dallas based on better division record (5-3 to Cowboys' 3-5).
Wild Card playoff: SEATTLE 13, L.A. Raiders 7
Divisional playoffs: MIAMI 31, Seattle 10;
Pittsburgh 24, DENVER 17
AFC Championship: MIAMI 45, Pittsburgh 28
Wild Card playoff: N.Y. Giants 16, L.A. RAMS 13
Divisional playoffs: SAN FRANCISCO 21, N.Y. Giants 10;
Chicago 23, WASHINGTON 19
NFC Championship: SAN FRANCISCO 23, Chicago 0
Super Bowl XIX: San Francisco (NFC) 38, Miami (AFC) 16,
at Stanford Stadium, Stanford, California

1983

AMERICAN CONFERENCE

Eastern Division

	W	L	T	Pct.	Pts.	OP
Miami	12	4	0	.750	389	250
New England	8	8	0	.500	274	289
Buffalo	8	8	0	.500	283	351
Baltimore	7	9	0	.438	264	354
N.Y. Jets	7	9	0	.438	313	331

Central Division

	W	L	T	Pct.	Pts.	OP
Pittsburgh	10	6	0	.625	355	303
Cleveland	9	7	0	.563	356	342
Cincinnati	7	9	0	.438	346	302
Houston	2	14	0	.125	288	460

Western Division

	W	L	T	Pct.	Pts.	OP
L.A. Raiders#	12	4	0	.750	442	338
Seattle*	9	7	0	.563	403	397
Denver*	9	7	0	.563	302	327
San Diego	6	10	0	.375	358	462
Kansas City	6	10	0	.375	386	367

NATIONAL CONFERENCE

Eastern Division

	W	L	T	Pct.	Pts.	OP
Washington#	14	2	0	.875	541	332
Dallas*	12	4	0	.750	479	360
St. Louis	8	7	1	.531	374	428
Philadelphia	5	11	0	.313	233	322
N.Y. Giants	3	12	1	.219	267	347

Central Division

	W	L	T	Pct.	Pts.	OP
Detroit	9	7	0	.563	347	286
Green Bay	8	8	0	.500	429	439
Chicago	8	8	0	.500	311	301
Minnesota	8	8	0	.500	316	348
Tampa Bay	2	14	0	.125	241	380

Western Division

	W	L	T	Pct.	Pts.	OP
San Francisco	10	6	0	.625	432	293
L.A. Rams*	9	7	0	.563	361	344
New Orleans	8	8	0	.500	319	337
Atlanta	7	9	0	.438	370	389

*Wild Card qualifier for playoffs; #Top playoff seed in conference

L.A. Raiders were top playoff seed ahead of Miami based on head-to-head victory (1-0). Seattle was second Wild Card ahead of Denver based on better division record (5-3 to Broncos' 3-5) after Cleveland was eliminated from three-way tie based on head-to-head record (Seattle and Denver 2-1 to Browns' 0-2). Seattle did not play the L.A. Raiders in the divisional playoffs because, from 1970-1989, two teams from the same division could not meet prior to the conference championship game. New England finished ahead of Buffalo based on head-to-head sweep (2-0). Baltimore finished ahead of N.Y. Jets based on better conference record (5-9 to Jets' 4-8). San Diego finished ahead of Kansas City based on head-to-head sweep (2-0). Green Bay finished ahead of Chicago based on better record against common opponents (5-5 to Bears' 4-6) after Minnesota was eliminated from three-way tie based on conference record (Chicago 7-7 and Green Bay 6-6 to Vikings' 4-8).

Wild Card playoff: SEATTLE 31, Denver 7
Divisional playoffs: Seattle 27, MIAMI 20;
   L.A. RAIDERS 38, Pittsburgh 10
AFC Championship: L.A. RAIDERS 30, Seattle 14
Wild Card playoff: L.A. Rams 24, DALLAS 17
Divisional playoffs: SAN FRANCISCO 24, Detroit 23;
   WASHINGTON 51, L.A. Rams 7
NFC Championship: WASHINGTON 24, San Francisco 21
Super Bowl XVIII: L.A. Raiders (AFC) 38, Washington (NFC) 9,
   at Tampa Stadium, Tampa, Florida

1982

AMERICAN CONFERENCE

	W	L	T	Pct.	Pts.	OP
L.A. Raiders#	8	1	0	.889	260	200
Miami	7	2	0	.778	198	131
Cincinnati	7	2	0	.778	232	177
Pittsburgh	6	3	0	.667	204	146
San Diego	6	3	0	.667	288	221
N.Y. Jets	6	3	0	.667	245	166
New England	5	4	0	.556	143	157
Cleveland	4	5	0	.444	140	182
Buffalo	4	5	0	.444	150	154
Seattle	4	5	0	.444	127	147
Kansas City	3	6	0	.333	176	184
Denver	2	7	0	.222	148	226
Houston	1	8	0	.111	136	245
Baltimore	0	8	1	.056	113	236

NATIONAL CONFERENCE

	W	L	T	Pct.	Pts.	OP
Washington#	8	1	0	.889	190	128
Dallas	6	3	0	.667	226	145
Green Bay	5	3	1	.611	226	169
Minnesota	5	4	0	.556	187	198
Atlanta	5	4	0	.556	183	199
St. Louis	5	4	0	.556	135	170
Tampa Bay	5	4	0	.556	158	178
Detroit	4	5	0	.444	181	176
New Orleans	4	5	0	.444	129	160
N.Y. Giants	4	5	0	.444	164	160
San Francisco	3	6	0	.333	209	206
Chicago	3	6	0	.333	141	174
Philadelphia	3	6	0	.333	191	195
L.A. Rams	2	7	0	.222	200	250

As the result of a 57-day players' strike, the 1982 NFL regular season schedule was reduced from 16 weeks to 9. At the conclusion of the regular season, the NFL conducted a 16-team postseason Super Bowl Tournament. Eight teams from each conference were seeded 1-8 based on their records during the season.

#Top playoff seed in conference

Miami finished ahead of Cincinnati based on better conference record (6-1 to Bengals' 6-2). Pittsburgh finished ahead of San Diego based on better record against common opponents (3-1 to Chargers' 2-1) after N.Y. Jets were eliminated from three-way tie based on conference record (Pittsburgh and San Diego 5-3 to Jets' 2-3). Cleveland finished ahead of Buffalo and Seattle based on better conference record (4-3 to Bills' 3-3 to Seahawks' 3-5). Buffalo finished ahead of Seattle based on better conference record (3-3 to Seahawks' 3-5). Minnesota (4-1), Atlanta (4-3), St. Louis (5-4), Tampa Bay (3-3) seeds were determined by best won-lost record in conference games. Detroit finished ahead of New Orleans and the N.Y. Giants based on best conference record (4-4 to Saints' 3-5 to Giants' 3-5). San Francisco finished ahead of Chicago, and Chicago finished ahead of Philadelphia, based on conference record (49ers' 2-3 to Bears' 2-5 to Eagles' 1-5).

First round playoff: MIAMI 28, New England 13;
   L.A. RAIDERS 27, Cleveland 10;
   N.Y. Jets 44, CINCINNATI 17;
   San Diego 31, PITTSBURGH 28
Second round playoff: N.Y. Jets 17, L.A. RAIDERS 14;
   MIAMI 34, San Diego 13
AFC Championship: MIAMI 14, N.Y. Jets 0
First round playoff: WASHINGTON 31, Detroit 7;
   GREEN BAY 41, St. Louis 16;
   MINNESOTA 30, Atlanta 24;
   DALLAS 30, Tampa Bay 17
Second round playoff: WASHINGTON 21, Minnesota 7;
   DALLAS 37, Green Bay 26
NFC Championship: WASHINGTON 31, Dallas 17
Super Bowl XVII: Washington (NFC) 27, Miami (AFC) 17,
   at Rose Bowl, Pasadena, California

1981

AMERICAN CONFERENCE

Eastern Division

	W	L	T	Pct.	Pts.	OP
Miami	11	4	1	.719	345	275
N.Y. Jets*	10	5	1	.656	355	287
Buffalo*	10	6	0	.625	311	276
Baltimore	2	14	0	.125	259	533
New England	2	14	0	.125	322	370

Central Division

	W	L	T	Pct.	Pts.	OP
Cincinnati#	12	4	0	.750	421	304
Pittsburgh	8	8	0	.500	356	297
Houston	7	9	0	.438	281	355
Cleveland	5	11	0	.313	276	375

Western Division

	W	L	T	Pct.	Pts.	OP
San Diego	10	6	0	.625	478	390
Denver	10	6	0	.625	321	289
Kansas City	9	7	0	.563	343	290
Oakland	7	9	0	.438	273	343
Seattle	6	10	0	.375	322	388

NATIONAL CONFERENCE

Eastern Division

	W	L	T	Pct.	Pts.	OP
Dallas	12	4	0	.750	367	277
Philadelphia*	10	6	0	.625	368	221
N.Y. Giants*	9	7	0	.563	295	257
Washington	8	8	0	.500	347	349
St. Louis	7	9	0	.438	315	408

Central Division

	W	L	T	Pct.	Pts.	OP
Tampa Bay	9	7	0	.563	315	268
Detroit	8	8	0	.500	397	322
Green Bay	8	8	0	.500	324	361
Minnesota	7	9	0	.438	325	369
Chicago	6	10	0	.375	253	324

Western Division

	W	L	T	Pct.	Pts.	OP
San Francisco#	13	3	0	.813	357	250
Atlanta	7	9	0	.438	426	355
Los Angeles	6	10	0	.375	303	351
New Orleans	4	12	0	.250	207	378

*Wild Card qualifier for playoffs; #Top playoff seed in conference
Baltimore finished ahead of New England based on head-to-head sweep (2-0). San Diego finished ahead of Denver based on better division record (6-2 to Broncos' 5-3). Buffalo was second Wild Card based on head-to-head victory over Denver (1-0). Detroit finished ahead of Green Bay based on better record against common opponents (5-5 to Packers' 4-6).
Wild Card playoff: Buffalo 31, N.Y. JETS 27
Divisional playoffs: San Diego 41, MIAMI 38 (OT); CINCINNATI 28, Buffalo 21
AFC Championship: CINCINNATI 27, San Diego 7
Wild Card playoff: N.Y. Giants 27, PHILADELPHIA 21
Divisional playoffs: DALLAS 38, Tampa Bay 0; SAN FRANCISCO 38, N.Y. Giants 24
NFC Championship: SAN FRANCISCO 28, Dallas 27
Super Bowl XVI: San Francisco (NFC) 26, Cincinnati (AFC) 21, at Silverdome, Pontiac, Michigan

1980

AMERICAN CONFERENCE

Eastern Division

	W	L	T	Pct.	Pts.	OP
Buffalo	11	5	0	.688	320	260
New England	10	6	0	.625	441	325
Miami	8	8	0	.500	266	305
Baltimore	7	9	0	.438	355	387
N.Y. Jets	4	12	0	.250	302	395

Central Division

	W	L	T	Pct.	Pts.	OP
Cleveland	11	5	0	.688	357	310
Houston*	11	5	0	.688	295	251
Pittsburgh	9	7	0	.563	352	313
Cincinnati	6	10	0	.375	244	312

Western Division

	W	L	T	Pct.	Pts.	OP
San Diego#	11	5	0	.688	418	327
Oakland*	11	5	0	.688	364	306
Kansas City	8	8	0	.500	319	336
Denver	8	8	0	.500	310	323
Seattle	4	12	0	.250	291	408

NATIONAL CONFERENCE

Eastern Division

	W	L	T	Pct.	Pts.	OP
Philadelphia	12	4	0	.750	384	222
Dallas*	12	4	0	.750	454	311
Washington	6	10	0	.375	261	293
St. Louis	5	11	0	.313	299	350
N.Y. Giants	4	12	0	.250	249	425

Central Division

	W	L	T	Pct.	Pts.	OP
Minnesota	9	7	0	.563	317	308
Detroit	9	7	0	.563	334	272
Chicago	7	9	0	.438	304	264
Tampa Bay	5	10	1	.344	271	341
Green Bay	5	10	1	.344	231	371

Western Division

	W	L	T	Pct.	Pts.	OP
Atlanta#	12	4	0	.750	405	272
Los Angeles*	11	5	0	.688	424	289
San Francisco	6	10	0	.375	320	415
New Orleans	1	15	0	.063	291	487

*Wild Card qualifier for playoffs; #Top playoff seed in conference
San Diego was top playoff seed based on better conference record than Cleveland and Buffalo (9-3 to Browns' 8-4 and Bills' 8-4). Cleveland was second playoff seed based on better record against common opponents (5-2 to Bills' 5-3). Cleveland finished ahead of Houston based on better conference record (8-4 to Oilers' 7-5). Oakland was first Wild Card based on better conference record than Houston (9-3 to Oilers' 7-5). San Diego finished ahead of Oakland based on better net points in division games (plus 60 net points to Raiders' plus 37). Oakland did not play San Diego in the divisional playoffs because, from 1970-1989, two teams from the same division could not meet prior to the conference championship game. Kansas City finished ahead of Denver based on head-to-head sweep (2-0). Atlanta was top playoff seed based on head-to-head victory over Philadelphia (1-0). Philadelphia finished ahead of Dallas based on better net points in division games (plus 84 net points to Cowboys' plus 50). Minnesota finished ahead of Detroit based on better conference record (8-4 to Lions' 9-3). Tampa Bay finished ahead of Green Bay based on better head-to-head record (1-0-1 to Packers' 0-1-1).
Wild Card playoff: OAKLAND 27, Houston 7
Divisional playoffs: SAN DIEGO 20, Buffalo 14; Oakland 14, CLEVELAND 12
AFC Championship: Oakland 34, SAN DIEGO 27
Wild Card playoff: DALLAS 34, Los Angeles 13
Divisional playoffs: PHILADELPHIA 31, Minnesota 16; Dallas 30, ATLANTA 27
NFC Championship: PHILADELPHIA 20, Dallas 7
Super Bowl XV: Oakland (AFC) 27, Philadelphia (NFC) 10, at Louisiana Superdome, New Orleans, Louisiana

1979

AMERICAN CONFERENCE

Eastern Division

	W	L	T	Pct.	Pts.	OP
Miami	10	6	0	.625	341	257
New England	9	7	0	.563	411	326
N.Y. Jets	8	8	0	.500	337	383
Buffalo	7	9	0	.438	268	279
Baltimore	5	11	0	.313	271	351

Central Division

	W	L	T	Pct.	Pts.	OP
Pittsburgh	12	4	0	.750	416	262
Houston*	11	5	0	.688	362	331
Cleveland	9	7	0	.563	359	352
Cincinnati	4	12	0	.250	337	421

Western Division

	W	L	T	Pct.	Pts.	OP
San Diego#	12	4	0	.750	411	246
Denver*	10	6	0	.625	289	262
Seattle	9	7	0	.563	378	372
Oakland	9	7	0	.563	365	337
Kansas City	7	9	0	.438	238	262

NATIONAL CONFERENCE

Eastern Division

	W	L	T	Pct.	Pts.	OP
Dallas#	11	5	0	.688	371	313
Philadelphia*	11	5	0	.688	339	282
Washington	10	6	0	.625	348	295
N.Y. Giants	6	10	0	.375	237	323
St. Louis	5	11	0	.313	307	358

Central Division

	W	L	T	Pct.	Pts.	OP
Tampa Bay	10	6	0	.625	273	237
Chicago*	10	6	0	.625	306	249
Minnesota	7	9	0	.438	259	337
Green Bay	5	11	0	.313	246	316
Detroit	2	14	0	.125	219	365

Western Division

	W	L	T	Pct.	Pts.	OP
Los Angeles	9	7	0	.563	323	309
New Orleans	8	8	0	.500	370	360
Atlanta	6	10	0	.375	300	388
San Francisco	2	14	0	.125	308	416

*Wild Card qualifier for playoffs; #Top playoff seed in conference
San Diego was top playoff seed based on head-to-head victory over Pittsburgh (1-0). Seattle finished ahead of Oakland based on head-to-head sweep (2-0). Dallas finished ahead of Philadelphia based on better conference record (10-2 to Eagles' 9-3). Philadelphia did not play Dallas in the divisional playoffs because, from 1970-1989, two teams from the same division could not meet prior to the conference championship game. Tampa Bay finished ahead of Chicago based on a better division record (6-2 to Bears' 5-3). Chicago was second Wild Card ahead of Washington based on better net points in all games (57 to Redskins' 53).
Wild Card playoff: HOUSTON 13, Denver 7
Divisional playoffs: Houston 17, SAN DIEGO 14;
  PITTSBURGH 34, Miami 14
AFC Championship: PITTSBURGH 27, Houston 13
Wild Card playoff: PHILADELPHIA 27, Chicago 17
Divisional playoffs: TAMPA BAY 24, Philadelphia 17;
  Los Angeles 21, DALLAS 19
NFC Championship: Los Angeles 9, TAMPA BAY 0
Super Bowl XIV: Pittsburgh (AFC) 31, Los Angeles (NFC) 19,
  at Rose Bowl, Pasadena, California

1978

AMERICAN CONFERENCE

Eastern Division

	W	L	T	Pct.	Pts.	OP
New England	11	5	0	.688	358	286
Miami*	11	5	0	.688	372	254
N.Y. Jets	8	8	0	.500	359	364
Buffalo	5	11	0	.313	302	354
Baltimore	5	11	0	.313	239	421

Central Division

	W	L	T	Pct.	Pts.	OP
Pittsburgh#	14	2	0	.875	356	195
Houston*	10	6	0	.625	283	298
Cleveland	8	8	0	.500	334	356
Cincinnati	4	12	0	.250	252	284

Western Division

	W	L	T	Pct.	Pts.	OP
Denver	10	6	0	.625	282	198
Oakland	9	7	0	.563	311	283
Seattle	9	7	0	.563	345	358
San Diego	9	7	0	.563	355	309
Kansas City	4	12	0	.250	243	327

NATIONAL CONFERENCE

Eastern Division

	W	L	T	Pct.	Pts.	OP
Dallas	12	4	0	.750	384	208
Philadelphia*	9	7	0	.563	270	250
Washington	8	8	0	.500	273	283
St. Louis	6	10	0	.375	248	296
N.Y. Giants	6	10	0	.375	264	298

Central Division

	W	L	T	Pct.	Pts.	OP
Minnesota	8	7	1	.531	294	306
Green Bay	8	7	1	.531	249	269
Detroit	7	9	0	.438	290	300
Chicago	7	9	0	.438	253	274
Tampa Bay	5	11	0	.313	241	259

Western Division

	W	L	T	Pct.	Pts.	OP
Los Angeles#	12	4	0	.750	316	245
Atlanta*	9	7	0	.563	240	290
New Orleans	7	9	0	.438	281	298
San Francisco	2	14	0	.125	219	350

*Wild Card qualifier for playoffs; #Top playoff seed in conference
New England finished ahead of Miami based on better division record (6-2 to Dolphins' 5-3). Buffalo finished ahead of Baltimore based on head-to-head sweep (2-0). Oakland finished ahead of Seattle and San Diego based on better record against common opponents (6-2 to Seahawks' 5-3 and Chargers' 4-4). Atlanta was first Wild Card based on better conference record than Philadelphia (8-4 to Eagles' 6-6). Houston did not play Pittsburgh, and Atlanta did not play Los Angeles in the divisional playoffs because, from 1970-1989, two teams from the same division could not meet prior to the conference championship game. St. Louis finished ahead of N.Y. Giants based on better division record (3-5 to Giants' 2-6). Minnesota finished ahead of Green Bay based on better head-to-head record (1-0-1). Detroit finished ahead of Chicago based on better division record (4-4 to Bears' 3-5).
Wild Card playoff: Houston 17, MIAMI 9
Divisional playoffs: Houston 31, NEW ENGLAND 14;
  PITTSBURGH 33, Denver 10
AFC Championship: PITTSBURGH 34, Houston 5
Wild Card playoff: ATLANTA 14, Philadelphia 13
Divisional playoffs: DALLAS 27, Atlanta 20;
  LOS ANGELES 34, Minnesota 10
NFC Championship: Dallas 28, LOS ANGELES 0
Super Bowl XIII: Pittsburgh (AFC) 35, Dallas (NFC) 31,
  at Orange Bowl, Miami, Florida

1977

AMERICAN CONFERENCE

Eastern Division

	W	L	T	Pct.	Pts.	OP
Baltimore	10	4	0	.714	295	221
Miami	10	4	0	.714	313	197
New England	9	5	0	.643	278	217
Buffalo	3	11	0	.214	160	313
N.Y. Jets	3	11	0	.214	191	300

Central Division

	W	L	T	Pct.	Pts.	OP
Pittsburgh	9	5	0	.643	283	243
Cincinnati	8	6	0	.571	238	235
Houston	8	6	0	.571	299	230
Cleveland	6	8	0	.429	269	267

Western Division

	W	L	T	Pct.	Pts.	OP
Denver#	12	2	0	.857	274	148
Oakland*	11	3	0	.786	351	230
San Diego	7	7	0	.500	222	205
Seattle	5	9	0	.357	282	373
Kansas City	2	12	0	.143	225	349

NATIONAL CONFERENCE

Eastern Division

	W	L	T	Pct.	Pts.	OP
Dallas#	12	2	0	.857	345	212
Washington	9	5	0	.643	196	189
St. Louis	7	7	0	.500	272	287
Philadelphia	5	9	0	.357	220	207
N.Y. Giants	5	9	0	.357	181	265

Central Division

	W	L	T	Pct.	Pts.	OP
Minnesota	9	5	0	.643	231	227
Chicago*	9	5	0	.643	255	253
Detroit	6	8	0	.429	183	252
Green Bay	4	10	0	.286	134	219
Tampa Bay	2	12	0	.143	103	223

Western Division

	W	L	T	Pct.	Pts.	OP
Los Angeles	10	4	0	.714	302	146
Atlanta	7	7	0	.500	179	129
San Francisco	5	9	0	.357	220	260
New Orleans	3	11	0	.214	232	336

*Wild Card qualifier for playoffs; #Top playoff seed in conference
Baltimore finished ahead of Miami based on better conference record (9-3 to Dolphins' 8-4). Buffalo finished ahead of N.Y. Jets based on better strength of schedule (.582 to Jets' .536). Cincinnati finished ahead of Houston based on better division record (6-3 to Oilers' 5-4). Oakland did not play Denver in the divisional playoffs because, from 1970-1989, two teams from the same division could not meet prior to the conference championship game. Minnesota finished ahead of Chicago based on fewer losses by common opponents (11 losses to 14 losses by the Bears' opponents). Chicago won Wild Card ahead of Washington based on better net points in conference games (48 to Redskins' 4). Philadelphia finished ahead of N.Y. Giants based on head-to-head sweep (2-0).
Divisional playoffs: DENVER 34, Pittsburgh 21; Oakland 37, BALTIMORE 31 (OT)
AFC Championship: DENVER 20, Oakland 17
Divisional playoffs: DALLAS 37, Chicago 7; Minnesota 14, LOS ANGELES 7
NFC Championship: DALLAS 23, Minnesota 6
Super Bowl XII: Dallas (NFC) 27, Denver (AFC) 10, at Louisiana Superdome, New Orleans, Louisiana

1976

AMERICAN CONFERENCE

Eastern Division

	W	L	T	Pct.	Pts.	OP
Baltimore	11	3	0	.786	417	246
New England*	11	3	0	.786	376	236
Miami	6	8	0	.429	263	264
N.Y. Jets	3	11	0	.214	169	383
Buffalo	2	12	0	.143	245	363

Central Division

	W	L	T	Pct.	Pts.	OP
Pittsburgh	10	4	0	.714	342	138
Cincinnati	10	4	0	.714	335	210
Cleveland	9	5	0	.643	267	287
Houston	5	9	0	.357	222	273

Western Division

	W	L	T	Pct.	Pts.	OP
Oakland#	13	1	0	.929	350	237
Denver	9	5	0	.643	315	206
San Diego	6	8	0	.429	248	285
Kansas City	5	9	0	.357	290	376
Tampa Bay	0	14	0	.000	125	412

NATIONAL CONFERENCE

Eastern Division

	W	L	T	Pct.	Pts.	OP
Dallas	11	3	0	.786	296	194
Washington*	10	4	0	.714	291	217
St. Louis	10	4	0	.714	309	267
Philadelphia	4	10	0	.286	165	286
N.Y. Giants	3	11	0	.214	170	250

Central Division

	W	L	T	Pct.	Pts.	OP
Minnesota#	11	2	1	.821	305	176
Chicago	7	7	0	.500	253	216
Detroit	6	8	0	.429	262	220
Green Bay	5	9	0	.357	218	299

Western Division

	W	L	T	Pct.	Pts.	OP
Los Angeles	10	3	1	.750	351	190
San Francisco	8	6	0	.571	270	190
Atlanta	4	10	0	.286	172	312
New Orleans	4	10	0	.286	253	346
Seattle	2	12	0	.143	229	429

*Wild Card qualifier for playoffs; #Top playoff seed in conference
Baltimore finished ahead of New England based on better division record (7-1 to Patriots' 6-2). Pittsburgh finished ahead of Cincinnati based on head-to-head sweep (2-0). Washington finished ahead of St. Louis based on head-to-head sweep (2-0). Atlanta finished ahead of New Orleans based on better division record (2-4 to Saints' 1-5).
Divisional playoffs: OAKLAND 24, New England 21; Pittsburgh 40, BALTIMORE 14
AFC Championship: OAKLAND 24, Pittsburgh 7
Divisional playoffs: MINNESOTA 35, Washington 20; Los Angeles 14, DALLAS 12
NFC Championship: MINNESOTA 24, Los Angeles 13
Super Bowl XI: Oakland (AFC) 32, Minnesota (NFC) 14, at Rose Bowl, Pasadena, California

1975

AMERICAN CONFERENCE
Eastern Division

	W	L	T	Pct.	Pts.	OP
Baltimore	10	4	0	.714	395	269
Miami	10	4	0	.714	357	222
Buffalo	8	6	0	.571	420	355
N.Y. Jets	3	11	0	.214	258	433
New England	3	11	0	.214	258	358

Central Division

	W	L	T	Pct.	Pts.	OP
Pittsburgh#	12	2	0	.857	373	162
Cincinnati*	11	3	0	.786	340	246
Houston	10	4	0	.714	293	226
Cleveland	3	11	0	.214	218	372

Western Division

	W	L	T	Pct.	Pts.	OP
Oakland	11	3	0	.786	375	255
Denver	6	8	0	.429	254	307
Kansas City	5	9	0	.357	282	341
San Diego	2	12	0	.143	189	345

NATIONAL CONFERENCE
Eastern Division

	W	L	T	Pct.	Pts.	OP
St. Louis	11	3	0	.786	356	276
Dallas*	10	4	0	.714	350	268
Washington	8	6	0	.571	325	276
N.Y. Giants	5	9	0	.357	216	306
Philadelphia	4	10	0	.286	225	302

Central Division

	W	L	T	Pct.	Pts.	OP
Minnesota#	12	2	0	.857	377	180
Detroit	7	7	0	.500	245	262
Chicago	4	10	0	.286	191	379
Green Bay	4	10	0	.286	226	285

Western Division

	W	L	T	Pct.	Pts.	OP
Los Angeles	12	2	0	.857	312	135
San Francisco	5	9	0	.357	255	286
Atlanta	4	10	0	.286	240	289
New Orleans	2	12	0	.143	165	360

Wild Card qualifier for playoffs; #Top playoff seed in conference
Baltimore finished ahead of Miami based on head-to-head sweep (2-0). Cincinnati did not play Pittsburgh in the divisional playoffs because, from 1970-1989, two teams from the same division could not meet prior to the conference championship game. N.Y. Jets finished ahead of New England based on head-to-head sweep (2-0). Minnesota was top playoff seed based on better Point Rating system than Los Angeles (3 to 6). Chicago finished ahead of Green Bay based on better division record (2-4 to Bears' 1-5).
Divisional playoffs: PITTSBURGH 28, Baltimore 10; OAKLAND 31, Cincinnati 28
AFC Championship: PITTSBURGH 16, Oakland 10
Divisional playoffs: LOS ANGELES 35, St. Louis 23; Dallas 17, MINNESOTA 14
NFC Championship: Dallas 37, LOS ANGELES 7
Super Bowl X: Pittsburgh (AFC) 21, Dallas (NFC) 17, at Orange Bowl, Miami, Florida

1974

AMERICAN CONFERENCE
Eastern Division

	W	L	T	Pct.	Pts.	OP
Miami	11	3	0	.786	327	216
Buffalo*	9	5	0	.643	264	244
New England	7	7	0	.500	348	289
N.Y. Jets	7	7	0	.500	279	300
Baltimore	2	12	0	.143	190	329

Central Division

	W	L	T	Pct.	Pts.	OP
Pittsburgh	10	3	1	.750	305	189
Houston	7	7	0	.500	236	282
Cincinnati	7	7	0	.500	283	259
Cleveland	4	10	0	.286	251	344

Western Division

	W	L	T	Pct.	Pts.	OP
Oakland	12	2	0	.857	355	228
Denver	7	6	1	.536	302	294
Kansas City	5	9	0	.357	233	293
San Diego	5	9	0	.357	212	285

NATIONAL CONFERENCE
Eastern Division

	W	L	T	Pct.	Pts.	OP
St. Louis	10	4	0	.714	285	218
Washington*	10	4	0	.714	320	196
Dallas	8	6	0	.571	297	235
Philadelphia	7	7	0	.500	242	217
N.Y. Giants	2	12	0	.143	195	299

Central Division

	W	L	T	Pct.	Pts.	OP
Minnesota	10	4	0	.714	310	195
Detroit	7	7	0	.500	256	270
Green Bay	6	8	0	.429	210	206
Chicago	4	10	0	.286	152	279

Western Division

	W	L	T	Pct.	Pts.	OP
Los Angeles	10	4	0	.714	263	181
San Francisco	6	8	0	.429	226	236
New Orleans	5	9	0	.357	166	263
Atlanta	3	11	0	.214	111	271

Wild Card qualifier for playoffs
New England finished ahead of N.Y. Jets based on better record against common opponents (5-4 to Jets' 4-5). Houston finished ahead of Cincinnati based on head-to-head sweep (2-0). Kansas City finished ahead of San Diego based on better record against common opponents (4-6 to Chargers' 3-7). St. Louis finished ahead of Washington based on head-to-head sweep (2-0).
Divisional playoffs: OAKLAND 28, Miami 26; PITTSBURGH 32, Buffalo 14
AFC Championship: Pittsburgh 24, OAKLAND 13
Divisional playoffs: MINNESOTA 30, St. Louis 14; LOS ANGELES 19, Washington 10
NFC Championship: MINNESOTA 14, Los Angeles 10
Super Bowl IX: Pittsburgh (AFC) 16, Minnesota (NFC) 6, at Tulane Stadium, New Orleans, Louisiana

From 1933-1974, sites for league/conference championship games alternated by division.

1973

AMERICAN CONFERENCE

Eastern Division

	W	L	T	Pct.	Pts.	OP
Miami	12	2	0	.857	343	150
Buffalo	9	5	0	.643	259	230
New England	5	9	0	.357	258	300
N.Y. Jets	4	10	0	.286	240	306
Baltimore	4	10	0	.286	226	341

Central Division

	W	L	T	Pct.	Pts.	OP
Cincinnati	10	4	0	.714	286	231
Pittsburgh*	10	4	0	.714	347	210
Cleveland	7	5	2	.571	234	255
Houston	1	13	0	.071	199	447

Western Division

	W	L	T	Pct.	Pts.	OP
Oakland	9	4	1	.679	292	175
Kansas City	7	5	2	.571	231	192
Denver	7	5	2	.571	354	296
San Diego	2	11	1	.179	188	386

NATIONAL CONFERENCE

Eastern Division

	W	L	T	Pct.	Pts.	OP
Dallas	10	4	0	.714	382	203
Washington*	10	4	0	.714	325	198
Philadelphia	5	8	1	.393	310	393
St. Louis	4	9	1	.321	286	365
N.Y. Giants	2	11	1	.179	226	362

Central Division

	W	L	T	Pct.	Pts.	OP
Minnesota	12	2	0	.857	296	168
Detroit	6	7	1	.464	271	247
Green Bay	5	7	2	.429	202	259
Chicago	3	11	0	.214	195	334

Western Division

	W	L	T	Pct.	Pts.	OP
Los Angeles	12	2	0	.857	388	178
Atlanta	9	5	0	.643	318	224
San Francisco	5	9	0	.357	262	319
New Orleans	5	9	0	.357	163	312

*Wild Card qualifier for playoffs

Cincinnati finished ahead of Pittsburgh based on better conference record (8-3 to Steelers' 7-4). N.Y. Jets finished ahead of Baltimore based on head-to-head sweep (2-0). Kansas City finished ahead of Denver based on better division record (4-2 to Broncos' 3-2-1). Dallas finished ahead of Washington based on better point differential in head-to-head games (13 points). San Francisco finished ahead of New Orleans based on better division record (2-4 to Saints' 1-5).

Divisional playoffs: OAKLAND 33, Pittsburgh 14; MIAMI 34, Cincinnati 16

AFC Championship: MIAMI 27, Oakland 10

Divisional playoffs: MINNESOTA 27, Washington 20; DALLAS 27, Los Angeles 16

NFC Championship: Minnesota 27, DALLAS 10

Super Bowl VIII: Miami (AFC) 24, Minnesota (NFC) 7, at Rice Stadium, Houston, Texas

1972

AMERICAN CONFERENCE

Eastern Division

	W	L	T	Pct.	Pts.	OP
Miami	14	0	0	1.000	385	171
N.Y. Jets	7	7	0	.500	367	324
Baltimore	5	9	0	.357	235	252
Buffalo	4	9	1	.321	257	377
New England	3	11	0	.214	192	446

Central Division

	W	L	T	Pct.	Pts.	OP
Pittsburgh	11	3	0	.786	343	175
Cleveland*	10	4	0	.714	268	249
Cincinnati	8	6	0	.571	299	229
Houston	1	13	0	.071	164	380

Western Division

	W	L	T	Pct.	Pts.	OP
Oakland	10	3	1	.750	365	248
Kansas City	8	6	0	.571	287	254
Denver	5	9	0	.357	325	350
San Diego	4	9	1	.321	264	344

NATIONAL CONFERENCE

Eastern Division

	W	L	T	Pct.	Pts.	OP
Washington	11	3	0	.786	336	218
Dallas*	10	4	0	.714	319	240
N.Y. Giants	8	6	0	.571	331	247
St. Louis	4	9	1	.321	193	303
Philadelphia	2	11	1	.179	145	352

Central Division

	W	L	T	Pct.	Pts.	OP
Green Bay	10	4	0	.714	304	226
Detroit	8	5	1	.607	339	290
Minnesota	7	7	0	.500	301	252
Chicago	4	9	1	.321	225	275

Western Division

	W	L	T	Pct.	Pts.	OP
San Francisco	8	5	1	.607	353	249
Atlanta	7	7	0	.500	269	274
Los Angeles	6	7	1	.464	291	286
New Orleans	2	11	1	.179	215	361

*Wild Card qualifier for playoffs

Dallas did not play Washington in the divisional playoffs because, from 1970-1989, two teams from the same division could not meet prior to the conference championship game.

Divisional playoffs: PITTSBURGH 13, Oakland 7; MIAMI 20, Cleveland 14

AFC Championship: Miami 21, PITTSBURGH 17

Divisional playoffs: Dallas 30, SAN FRANCISCO 28; WASHINGTON 16, Green Bay 3

NFC Championship: WASHINGTON 26, Dallas 3

Super Bowl VII: Miami (AFC) 14, Washington (NFC) 7, at Memorial Coliseum, Los Angeles, California

1971

AMERICAN CONFERENCE

Eastern Division

	W	L	T	Pct.	Pts.	OP
Miami	10	3	1	.769	315	174
Baltimore*	10	4	0	.714	313	140
New England	6	8	0	.429	238	325
N.Y. Jets	6	8	0	.429	212	299
Buffalo	1	13	0	.071	184	394

Central Division

	W	L	T	Pct.	Pts.	OP
Cleveland	9	5	0	.643	285	273
Pittsburgh	6	8	0	.429	246	292
Houston	4	9	1	.308	251	330
Cincinnati	4	10	0	.286	284	265

Western Division

	W	L	T	Pct.	Pts.	OP
Kansas City	10	3	1	.769	302	208
Oakland	8	4	2	.667	344	278
San Diego	6	8	0	.429	311	341
Denver	4	9	1	.308	203	275

NATIONAL CONFERENCE

Eastern Division

	W	L	T	Pct.	Pts.	OP
Dallas	11	3	0	.786	406	222
Washington*	9	4	1	.692	276	190
Philadelphia	6	7	1	.462	221	302
St. Louis	4	9	1	.308	231	279
N.Y. Giants	4	10	0	.286	228	362

Central Division

	W	L	T	Pct.	Pts.	OP
Minnesota	11	3	0	.786	245	139
Detroit	7	6	1	.538	341	286
Chicago	6	8	0	.429	185	276
Green Bay	4	8	2	.333	274	298

Western Division

	W	L	T	Pct.	Pts.	OP
San Francisco	9	5	0	.643	300	216
Los Angeles	8	5	1	.615	313	260
Atlanta	7	6	1	.538	274	277
New Orleans	4	8	2	.333	266	347

Wild Card qualifier for playoffs

New England finished ahead of N.Y. Jets based on better strength of schedule (.537 to Jets' .510).

Divisional playoffs: Miami 27, KANSAS CITY 24 (OT); Baltimore 20, CLEVELAND 3

AFC Championship: MIAMI 21, Baltimore 0

Divisional playoffs: Dallas 20, MINNESOTA 12; SAN FRANCISCO 24, Washington 20

NFC Championship: DALLAS 14, San Francisco 3

Super Bowl VI: Dallas (NFC) 24, Miami (AFC) 3, at Tulane Stadium, New Orleans, Louisiana

From 1920-1971, tie games were not included in winning percentage.

1970

AMERICAN CONFERENCE

Eastern Division

	W	L	T	Pct.	Pts.	OP
Baltimore	11	2	1	.846	321	234
Miami*	10	4	0	.714	297	228
N.Y. Jets	4	10	0	.286	255	286
Buffalo	3	10	1	.231	204	337
Boston Patriots	2	12	0	.143	149	361

Central Division

	W	L	T	Pct.	Pts.	OP
Cincinnati	8	6	0	.571	312	255
Cleveland	7	7	0	.500	286	265
Pittsburgh	5	9	0	.357	210	272
Houston	3	10	1	.231	217	352

Western Division

	W	L	T	Pct.	Pts.	OP
Oakland	8	4	2	.667	300	293
Kansas City	7	5	2	.583	272	244
San Diego	5	6	3	.455	282	278
Denver	5	8	1	.385	253	264

NATIONAL CONFERENCE

Eastern Division

	W	L	T	Pct.	Pts.	OP
Dallas	10	4	0	.714	299	221
N.Y. Giants	9	5	0	.643	301	270
St. Louis	8	5	1	.615	325	228
Washington	6	8	0	.429	297	314
Philadelphia	3	10	1	.231	241	332

Central Division

	W	L	T	Pct.	Pts.	OP
Minnesota	12	2	0	.857	335	143
Detroit*	10	4	0	.714	347	202
Green Bay	6	8	0	.429	196	293
Chicago	6	8	0	.429	256	261

Western Division

	W	L	T	Pct.	Pts.	OP
San Francisco	10	3	1	.769	352	267
Los Angeles	9	4	1	.692	325	202
Atlanta	4	8	2	.333	206	261
New Orleans	2	11	1	.154	172	347

Wild Card qualifier for playoffs

Miami did not play Baltimore, and Detroit did not play Minnesota, in the divisional playoffs because, from 1970-1989, two teams from the same division could not meet prior to the conference championship game. Green Bay finished ahead of Chicago based on better division record (2-4 to Bears' 1-5).

Divisional playoffs: BALTIMORE 17, Cincinnati 0; OAKLAND 21, Miami 14

AFC Championship: BALTIMORE 27, Oakland 17

Divisional playoffs: DALLAS 5, Detroit 0; San Francisco 17, MINNESOTA 14

NFC Championship: Dallas 17, SAN FRANCISCO 10

Super Bowl V: Baltimore (AFC) 16, Dallas (NFC) 13, at Orange Bowl, Miami, Florida

1969 NFL

EASTERN CONFERENCE
Capitol Division

	W	L	T	Pct.	Pts.	OP
Dallas	11	2	1	.846	369	223
Washington	7	5	2	.583	307	319
New Orleans	5	9	0	.357	311	393
Philadelphia	4	9	1	.308	279	377

Century Division

	W	L	T	Pct.	Pts.	OP
Cleveland	10	3	1	.769	351	300
N.Y. Giants	6	8	0	.429	264	298
St. Louis	4	9	1	.308	314	389
Pittsburgh	1	13	0	.071	218	404

WESTERN CONFERENCE
Coastal Division

	W	L	T	Pct.	Pts.	OP
Los Angeles	11	3	0	.786	320	243
Baltimore	8	5	1	.615	279	268
Atlanta	6	8	0	.429	276	268
San Francisco	4	8	2	.333	277	319

Central Division

	W	L	T	Pct.	Pts.	OP
Minnesota	12	2	0	.857	379	133
Detroit	9	4	1	.692	259	188
Green Bay	8	6	0	.571	269	221
Chicago	1	13	0	.071	210	339

Conference championships: Cleveland 38, DALLAS 14;
MINNESOTA 23, Los Angeles 20
NFL championship: MINNESOTA 27, Cleveland 7
Super Bowl IV: Kansas City (AFL) 23, Minnesota (NFL) 7,
at Tulane Stadium, New Orleans, Louisiana

1969 AFL

EASTERN DIVISION

	W	L	T	Pct.	Pts.	OP
N.Y. Jets	10	4	0	.714	353	269
Houston	6	6	2	.500	278	279
Boston Patriots	4	10	0	.286	266	316
Buffalo	4	10	0	.286	230	359
Miami	3	10	1	.231	233	332

WESTERN DIVISION

	W	L	T	Pct.	Pts.	OP
Oakland	12	1	1	.923	377	242
Kansas City	11	3	0	.786	359	177
San Diego	8	6	0	.571	288	276
Denver	5	8	1	.385	297	344
Cincinnati	4	9	1	.308	280	367

Divisional playoffs: Kansas City 13, N.Y. JETS 6;
OAKLAND 56, Houston 7
AFL championship: Kansas City 17, OAKLAND 7

1968 NFL

EASTERN CONFERENCE
Capitol Division

	W	L	T	Pct.	Pts.	OP
Dallas	12	2	0	.857	431	186
N.Y. Giants	7	7	0	.500	294	325
Washington	5	9	0	.357	249	358
Philadelphia	2	12	0	.143	202	351

Century Division

	W	L	T	Pct.	Pts.	OP
Cleveland	10	4	0	.714	394	273
St. Louis	9	4	1	.692	325	289
New Orleans	4	9	1	.308	246	327
Pittsburgh	2	11	1	.154	244	397

WESTERN CONFERENCE
Coastal Division

	W	L	T	Pct.	Pts.	OP
Baltimore	13	1	0	.929	402	144
Los Angeles	10	3	1	.769	312	200
San Francisco	7	6	1	.538	303	310
Atlanta	2	12	0	.143	170	389

Central Division

	W	L	T	Pct.	Pts.	OP
Minnesota	8	6	0	.571	282	242
Chicago	7	7	0	.500	250	333
Green Bay	6	7	1	.462	281	227
Detroit	4	8	2	.333	207	241

Conference championships: CLEVELAND 31, Dallas 20;
BALTIMORE 24, Minnesota 14
NFL championship: Baltimore 34, CLEVELAND 0
Super Bowl III: N.Y. Jets (AFL) 16, Baltimore (NFL) 7,
at Orange Bowl, Miami, Florida

1968 AFL

EASTERN DIVISION

	W	L	T	Pct.	Pts.	OP
N.Y. Jets	11	3	0	.786	419	280
Houston	7	7	0	.500	303	248
Miami	5	8	1	.385	276	355
Boston Patriots	4	10	0	.286	229	406
Buffalo	1	12	1	.077	199	367

WESTERN DIVISION

	W	L	T	Pct.	Pts.	OP
Oakland	12	2	0	.857	453	233
Kansas City	12	2	0	.857	371	170
San Diego	9	5	0	.643	382	310
Denver	5	9	0	.357	255	404
Cincinnati	3	11	0	.214	215	329

Western Division playoff: OAKLAND 41, Kansas City 6
AFL championship: N.Y. JETS 27, Oakland 23

1967 NFL

EASTERN CONFERENCE
Capitol Division

	W	L	T	Pct.	Pts.	OP
Dallas	9	5	0	.643	342	268
Philadelphia	6	7	1	.462	351	409
Washington	5	6	3	.455	347	353
New Orleans	3	11	0	.214	233	379

Century Division

	W	L	T	Pct.	Pts.	OP
Cleveland	9	5	0	.643	334	297
N.Y. Giants	7	7	0	.500	369	379
St. Louis	6	7	1	.462	333	356
Pittsburgh	4	9	1	.308	281	320

WESTERN CONFERENCE
Coastal Division

	W	L	T	Pct.	Pts.	OP
Los Angeles	11	1	2	.917	398	196
Baltimore	11	1	2	.917	394	198
San Francisco	7	7	0	.500	273	337
Atlanta	1	12	1	.077	175	422

Central Division

	W	L	T	Pct.	Pts.	OP
Green Bay	9	4	1	.692	332	209
Chicago	7	6	1	.538	239	218
Detroit	5	7	2	.417	260	259
Minnesota	3	8	3	.273	233	294

Los Angeles finished ahead of Baltimore based on better point differential in head-to-head games (net 24 points).
Conference championships: DALLAS 52, Cleveland 14;
GREEN BAY 28, Los Angeles 7
NFL championship: GREEN BAY 21, Dallas 17
Super Bowl II: Green Bay (NFL) 33, Oakland (AFL) 14,
at Orange Bowl, Miami, Florida

1967 AFL

EASTERN DIVISION

	W	L	T	Pct.	Pts.	OP
Houston	9	4	1	.692	258	199
N.Y. Jets	8	5	1	.615	371	329
Buffalo	4	10	0	.286	237	285
Miami	4	10	0	.286	219	407
Boston Patriots	3	10	1	.231	280	389

WESTERN DIVISION

	W	L	T	Pct.	Pts.	OP
Oakland	13	1	0	.929	468	233
Kansas City	9	5	0	.643	408	254
San Diego	8	5	1	.615	360	352
Denver	3	11	0	.214	256	409

AFL championship: OAKLAND 40, Houston 7

1966 NFL

EASTERN CONFERENCE

	W	L	T	Pct.	Pts.	OP
Dallas	10	3	1	.769	445	239
Cleveland	9	5	0	.643	403	259
Philadelphia	9	5	0	.643	326	340
St. Louis	8	5	1	.615	264	265
Washington	7	7	0	.500	351	355
Pittsburgh	5	8	1	.385	316	347
Atlanta	3	11	0	.214	204	437
N.Y. Giants	1	12	1	.077	263	501

WESTERN CONFERENCE

	W	L	T	Pct.	Pts.	OP
Green Bay	12	2	0	.857	335	163
Baltimore	9	5	0	.643	314	226
Los Angeles	8	6	0	.571	289	212
San Francisco	6	6	2	.500	320	325
Chicago	5	7	2	.417	234	272
Detroit	4	9	1	.308	206	317
Minnesota	4	9	1	.308	292	304

NFL championship: Green Bay 34, DALLAS 27
Super Bowl I: Green Bay (NFL) 35, Kansas City (AFL) 10,
at Memorial Coliseum, Los Angeles, California

1966 AFL

EASTERN DIVISION

	W	L	T	Pct.	Pts.	OP
Buffalo	9	4	1	.692	358	255
Boston Patriots	8	4	2	.677	315	283
N.Y. Jets	6	6	2	.500	322	312
Houston	3	11	0	.214	335	396
Miami	3	11	0	.214	213	362

WESTERN DIVISION

	W	L	T	Pct.	Pts.	OP
Kansas City	11	2	1	.846	448	276
Oakland	8	5	1	.615	315	288
San Diego	7	6	1	.538	335	284
Denver	4	10	0	.286	196	381

AFL championship: Kansas City 31, BUFFALO 7

1965 NFL

EASTERN CONFERENCE	W	L	T	Pct.	Pts.	OP	WESTERN CONFERENCE	W	L	T	Pct.	Pts.	OP
Cleveland	11	3	0	.786	363	325	Green Bay	10	3	1	.769	316	224
Dallas	7	7	0	.500	325	280	Baltimore	10	3	1	.769	389	284
N.Y. Giants	7	7	0	.500	270	338	Chicago	9	5	0	.643	409	275
Washington	6	8	0	.429	257	301	San Francisco	7	6	1	.538	421	402
Philadelphia	5	9	0	.357	363	359	Minnesota	7	7	0	.500	383	403
St. Louis	5	9	0	.357	296	309	Detroit	6	7	1	.462	257	295
Pittsburgh	2	12	0	.143	202	397	Los Angeles	4	10	0	.286	269	328

Western Conference playoff: GREEN BAY 13, Baltimore 10 (OT)
NFL championship: GREEN BAY 23, Cleveland 12

1965 AFL

EASTERN DIVISION	W	L	T	Pct.	Pts.	OP	WESTERN DIVISION	W	L	T	Pct.	Pts.	OP
Buffalo	10	3	1	.769	313	226	San Diego	9	2	3	.818	340	227
N.Y. Jets	5	8	1	.385	285	303	Oakland	8	5	1	.615	298	239
Boston Patriots	4	8	2	.333	244	302	Kansas City	7	5	2	.583	322	285
Houston	4	10	0	.286	298	429	Denver	4	10	0	.286	303	392

AFL championship: Buffalo 23, SAN DIEGO 0

1964 NFL

EASTERN CONFERENCE	W	L	T	Pct.	Pts.	OP	WESTERN CONFERENCE	W	L	T	Pct.	Pts.	OP
Cleveland	10	3	1	.769	415	293	Baltimore	12	2	0	.857	428	225
St. Louis	9	3	2	.750	357	331	Green Bay	8	5	1	.615	342	245
Philadelphia	6	8	0	.429	312	313	Minnesota	8	5	1	.615	355	296
Washington	6	8	0	.429	307	305	Detroit	7	5	2	.583	280	260
Dallas	5	8	1	.385	250	289	Los Angeles	5	7	2	.417	283	339
Pittsburgh	5	9	0	.357	253	315	Chicago	5	9	0	.357	260	379
N.Y. Giants	2	10	2	.167	241	399	San Francisco	4	10	0	.286	236	330

NFL championship: CLEVELAND 27, Baltimore 0

1964 AFL

EASTERN DIVISION	W	L	T	Pct.	Pts.	OP	WESTERN DIVISION	W	L	T	Pct.	Pts.	OP
Buffalo	12	2	0	.857	400	242	San Diego	8	5	1	.615	341	300
Boston Patriots	10	3	1	.769	365	297	Kansas City	7	7	0	.500	366	306
N.Y. Jets	5	8	1	.385	278	315	Oakland	5	7	2	.417	303	350
Houston	4	10	0	.286	310	355	Denver	2	11	1	.154	240	438

AFL championship: BUFFALO 20, San Diego 7

1963 NFL

EASTERN CONFERENCE	W	L	T	Pct.	Pts.	OP	WESTERN CONFERENCE	W	L	T	Pct.	Pts.	OP
N.Y. Giants	11	3	0	.786	448	280	Chicago	11	1	2	.917	301	144
Cleveland	10	4	0	.714	343	262	Green Bay	11	2	1	.846	369	206
St. Louis	9	5	0	.643	341	283	Baltimore	8	6	0	.571	316	285
Pittsburgh	7	4	3	.636	321	295	Detroit	5	8	1	.385	326	265
Dallas	4	10	0	.286	305	378	Minnesota	5	8	1	.385	309	390
Washington	3	11	0	.214	279	398	Los Angeles	5	9	0	.357	210	350
Philadelphia	2	10	2	.167	242	381	San Francisco	2	12	0	.143	198	391

NFL championship: CHICAGO 14, N.Y. Giants 10

1963 AFL

EASTERN DIVISION	W	L	T	Pct.	Pts.	OP	WESTERN DIVISION	W	L	T	Pct.	Pts.	OP
Boston Patriots	7	6	1	.538	327	257	San Diego	11	3	0	.786	399	255
Buffalo	7	6	1	.538	304	291	Oakland	10	4	0	.714	363	282
Houston	6	8	0	.429	302	372	Kansas City	5	7	2	.417	347	263
N.Y. Jets	5	8	1	.385	249	399	Denver	2	11	1	.154	301	473

Eastern Division playoff: Boston 26, BUFFALO 8
AFL championship: SAN DIEGO 51, Boston 10

1962 NFL

EASTERN CONFERENCE	W	L	T	Pct.	Pts.	OP	WESTERN CONFERENCE	W	L	T	Pct.	Pts.	OP
N.Y. Giants	12	2	0	.857	398	283	Green Bay	13	1	0	.929	415	148
Pittsburgh	9	5	0	.643	312	363	Detroit	11	3	0	.786	315	177
Cleveland	7	6	1	.538	291	257	Chicago	9	5	0	.643	321	287
Washington	5	7	2	.417	305	376	Baltimore	7	7	0	.500	293	288
Dallas Cowboys	5	8	1	.385	398	402	San Francisco	6	8	0	.429	282	331
St. Louis	4	9	1	.308	287	361	Minnesota	2	11	1	.154	254	410
Philadelphia	3	10	1	.231	282	356	Los Angeles	1	12	1	.077	220	334

NFL championship: Green Bay 16, N.Y. GIANTS 7

1962 AFL

EASTERN DIVISION	W	L	T	Pct.	Pts.	OP	WESTERN DIVISION	W	L	T	Pct.	Pts.	OP
Houston	11	3	0	.786	387	270	Dallas Texans	11	3	0	.786	389	233
Boston Patriots	9	4	1	.692	346	295	Denver	7	7	0	.500	353	334
Buffalo	7	6	1	.538	309	272	San Diego	4	10	0	.286	314	392
N.Y. Titans	5	9	0	.357	278	423	Oakland	1	13	0	.071	213	370

AFL championship: Dallas Texans 20, HOUSTON 17 (OT)

1961 NFL

EASTERN CONFERENCE	W	L	T	Pct.	Pts.	OP	WESTERN CONFERENCE	W	L	T	Pct.	Pts.	OP
N.Y. Giants	10	3	1	.769	368	220	Green Bay	11	3	0	.786	391	223
Philadelphia	10	4	0	.714	361	297	Detroit	8	5	1	.615	270	258
Cleveland	8	5	1	.615	319	270	Baltimore	8	6	0	.571	302	307
St. Louis	7	7	0	.500	279	267	Chicago	8	6	0	.571	326	302
Pittsburgh	6	8	0	.429	295	287	San Francisco	7	6	1	.538	346	272
Dallas Cowboys	4	9	1	.308	236	380	Los Angeles	4	10	0	.286	263	333
Washington	1	12	1	.077	174	392	Minnesota	3	11	0	.214	285	407

NFL championship: GREEN BAY 37, N.Y. Giants 0

1961 AFL

EASTERN DIVISION	W	L	T	Pct.	Pts.	OP	WESTERN DIVISION	W	L	T	Pct.	Pts.	OP
Houston	10	3	1	.769	513	242	San Diego	12	2	0	.857	396	219
Boston Patriots	9	4	1	.692	413	313	Dallas Texans	6	8	0	.429	334	343
N.Y. Titans	7	7	0	.500	301	390	Denver	3	11	0	.214	251	432
Buffalo	6	8	0	.429	294	342	Oakland	2	12	0	.143	237	458

AFL championship: Houston 10, SAN DIEGO 3

1960 NFL

EASTERN CONFERENCE	W	L	T	Pct.	Pts.	OP	WESTERN CONFERENCE	W	L	T	Pct.	Pts.	OP
Philadelphia	10	2	0	.833	321	246	Green Bay	8	4	0	.667	332	209
Cleveland	8	3	1	.727	362	217	Detroit	7	5	0	.583	239	212
N.Y. Giants	6	4	2	.600	271	261	San Francisco	7	5	0	.583	208	205
St. Louis	6	5	1	.545	288	230	Baltimore	6	6	0	.500	288	234
Pittsburgh	5	6	1	.455	240	275	Chicago	5	6	1	.455	194	299
Washington	1	9	2	.100	178	309	L.A. Rams	4	7	1	.364	265	297
							Dallas Cowboys	0	11	1	.000	177	369

NFL championship: PHILADELPHIA 17, Green Bay 13

1960 AFL

EASTERN CONFERENCE	W	L	T	Pct.	Pts.	OP	WESTERN CONFERENCE	W	L	T	Pct.	Pts.	OP
Houston	10	4	0	.714	379	285	L.A. Chargers	10	4	0	.714	373	336
N.Y. Titans	7	7	0	.500	382	399	Dallas Texans	8	6	0	.571	362	253
Buffalo	5	8	1	.385	296	303	Oakland	6	8	0	.429	319	388
Boston	5	9	0	.357	286	349	Denver	4	9	1	.308	309	393

AFL championship: HOUSTON 24, L.A. Chargers 16

1959

EASTERN CONFERENCE	W	L	T	Pct.	Pts.	OP	WESTERN CONFERENCE	W	L	T	Pct.	Pts.	OP
N.Y. Giants	10	2	0	.833	284	170	Baltimore	9	3	0	.750	374	251
Cleveland	7	5	0	.583	270	214	Chi. Bears	8	4	0	.667	252	196
Philadelphia	7	5	0	.583	268	278	Green Bay	7	5	0	.583	248	246
Pittsburgh	6	5	1	.545	257	216	San Francisco	7	5	0	.583	255	237
Washington	3	9	0	.250	185	350	Detroit	3	8	1	.273	203	275
Chi. Cardinals	2	10	0	.167	234	324	Los Angeles	2	10	0	.167	242	315

NFL championship: BALTIMORE 31, N.Y. Giants 16

1958

EASTERN CONFERENCE	W	L	T	Pct.	Pts.	OP	WESTERN CONFERENCE	W	L	T	Pct.	Pts.	OP
N.Y. Giants	9	3	0	.750	246	183	Baltimore	9	3	0	.750	381	203
Cleveland	9	3	0	.750	302	217	Chi. Bears	8	4	0	.667	298	230
Pittsburgh	7	4	1	.636	261	230	Los Angeles	8	4	0	.667	344	278
Washington	4	7	1	.364	214	268	San Francisco	6	6	0	.500	257	324
Chi. Cardinals	2	9	1	.182	261	356	Detroit	4	7	1	.364	261	276
Philadelphia	2	9	1	.182	235	306	Green Bay	1	10	1	.091	193	382

Eastern Conference playoff: N.Y. GIANTS 10, Cleveland 0
NFL championship: Baltimore 23, N.Y. GIANTS 17 (OT)

1957

EASTERN CONFERENCE	W	L	T	Pct.	Pts.	OP	WESTERN CONFERENCE	W	L	T	Pct.	Pts.	OP
Cleveland	9	2	1	.818	269	172	Detroit	8	4	0	.667	251	231
N.Y. Giants	7	5	0	.583	254	211	San Francisco	8	4	0	.667	260	264
Pittsburgh	6	6	0	.500	161	178	Baltimore	7	5	0	.583	303	235
Washington	5	6	1	.455	251	230	Los Angeles	6	6	0	.500	307	278
Philadelphia	4	8	0	.333	173	230	Chi. Bears	5	7	0	.417	203	211
Chi. Cardinals	3	9	0	.250	200	299	Green Bay	3	9	0	.250	218	311

Western Conference playoff: Detroit 31, SAN FRANCISCO 27
NFL championship: DETROIT 59, Cleveland 14

1956

EASTERN CONFERENCE	W	L	T	Pct.	Pts.	OP	WESTERN CONFERENCE	W	L	T	Pct.	Pts.	OP
N.Y. Giants	8	3	1	.727	264	197	Chi. Bears	9	2	1	.818	363	246
Chi. Cardinals	7	5	0	.583	240	182	Detroit	9	3	0	.750	300	188
Washington	6	6	0	.500	183	225	San Francisco	5	6	1	.455	233	284
Cleveland	5	7	0	.417	167	177	Baltimore	5	7	0	.417	270	322
Pittsburgh	5	7	0	.417	217	250	Green Bay	4	8	0	.333	264	342
Philadelphia	3	8	1	.273	143	215	Los Angeles	4	8	0	.333	291	307

NFL championship: N.Y. GIANTS 47, Chi. Bears 7

1955

EASTERN CONFERENCE	W	L	T	Pct.	Pts.	OP	WESTERN CONFERENCE	W	L	T	Pct.	Pts.	OP
Cleveland	9	2	1	.818	349	218	Los Angeles	8	3	1	.727	260	231
Washington	8	4	0	.667	246	222	Chi. Bears	8	4	0	.667	294	251
N.Y. Giants	6	5	1	.545	267	223	Green Bay	6	6	0	.500	258	276
Chi. Cardinals	4	7	1	.364	224	252	Detroit	5	6	1	.455	214	239
Philadelphia	4	7	1	.364	248	231	San Francisco	4	8	0	.333	216	298
Pittsburgh	4	8	0	.333	195	285	Detroit	3	9	0	.250	230	275

NFL championship: Cleveland 38, LOS ANGELES 14

1954

EASTERN CONFERENCE	W	L	T	Pct.	Pts.	OP	WESTERN CONFERENCE	W	L	T	Pct.	Pts.	OP
Cleveland	9	3	0	.750	336	162	Detroit	9	2	1	.818	337	189
Philadelphia	7	4	1	.636	284	230	Chi. Bears	8	4	0	.667	301	279
N.Y. Giants	7	5	0	.583	293	184	San Francisco	7	4	1	.636	313	251
Pittsburgh	5	7	0	.417	219	263	Los Angeles	6	5	1	.545	314	285
Washington	3	9	0	.250	207	432	Green Bay	4	8	0	.333	234	251
Chi. Cardinals	2	10	0	.167	183	347	Baltimore	3	9	0	.250	131	279

NFL championship: CLEVELAND 56, Detroit 10

1953

EASTERN CONFERENCE	W	L	T	Pct.	Pts.	OP	WESTERN CONFERENCE	W	L	T	Pct.	Pts.	OP
Cleveland	11	1	0	.917	348	162	Detroit	10	2	0	.833	271	205
Philadelphia	7	4	1	.636	352	215	San Francisco	9	3	0	.750	372	237
Washington	6	5	1	.545	208	215	Los Angeles	8	3	1	.727	366	236
Pittsburgh	6	6	0	.500	211	263	Chi. Bears	3	8	1	.273	218	262
N.Y. Giants	3	9	0	.250	179	277	Baltimore	3	9	0	.250	182	350
Chi. Cardinals	1	10	1	.091	190	337	Green Bay	2	9	1	.182	200	338

NFL championship: DETROIT 17, Cleveland 16

1952

AMERICAN CONFERENCE	W	L	T	Pct.	Pts.	OP	NATIONAL CONFERENCE	W	L	T	Pct.	Pts.	OP
Cleveland	8	4	0	.667	310	213	Detroit	9	3	0	.750	344	192
N.Y. Giants	7	5	0	.583	234	231	Los Angeles	9	3	0	.750	349	234
Philadelphia	7	5	0	.583	252	271	San Francisco	7	5	0	.583	285	221
Pittsburgh	5	7	0	.417	300	273	Green Bay	6	6	0	.500	295	312
Chi. Cardinals	4	8	0	.333	172	221	Chi. Bears	5	7	0	.417	245	326
Washington	4	8	0	.333	240	287	Dallas Texans	1	11	0	.083	182	427

National Conference playoff: DETROIT 31, Los Angeles 21
NFL championship: Detroit 17, CLEVELAND 7

1951

AMERICAN CONFERENCE	W	L	T	Pct.	Pts.	OP	NATIONAL CONFERENCE	W	L	T	Pct.	Pts.	OP
Cleveland	11	1	0	.917	331	152	Los Angeles	8	4	0	.667	392	261
N.Y. Giants	9	2	1	.818	254	161	Detroit	7	4	1	.636	336	259
Washington	5	7	0	.417	183	296	San Francisco	7	4	1	.636	255	205
Pittsburgh	4	7	1	.364	183	235	Chi. Bears	7	5	0	.583	286	282
Philadelphia	4	8	0	.333	234	264	Green Bay	3	9	0	.250	254	375
Chi. Cardinals	3	9	0	.250	210	287	N.Y. Yanks	1	9	2	.100	241	382

NFL championship: LOS ANGELES 24, Cleveland 17

1950

AMERICAN CONFERENCE	W	L	T	Pct.	Pts.	OP	NATIONAL CONFERENCE	W	L	T	Pct.	Pts.	OP
Cleveland	10	2	0	.833	310	144	Los Angeles	9	3	0	.750	466	309
N.Y. Giants	10	2	0	.833	268	150	Chi. Bears	9	3	0	.750	279	207
Philadelphia	6	6	0	.500	254	141	N.Y. Yanks	7	5	0	.583	366	367
Pittsburgh	6	6	0	.500	180	195	Detroit	6	6	0	.500	321	285
Chi. Cardinals	5	7	0	.417	233	287	Green Bay	3	9	0	.250	244	406
Washington	3	9	0	.250	232	326	San Francisco	3	9	0	.250	213	300
							Baltimore	1	11	0	.083	213	462

American Conference playoff: CLEVELAND 8, N.Y. Giants 3
National Conference playoff: LOS ANGELES 24, Chi. Bears 14
NFL championship: CLEVELAND 30, Los Angeles 28

1949

EASTERN DIVISION	W	L	T	Pct.	Pts.	OP	WESTERN DIVISION	W	L	T	Pct.	Pts.	OP
Philadelphia	11	1	0	.917	364	134	Los Angeles	8	2	2	.800	360	239
Pittsburgh	6	5	1	.545	224	214	Chi. Bears	9	3	0	.750	332	218
N.Y. Giants	6	6	0	.500	287	298	Chi. Cardinals	6	5	1	.545	360	301
Washington	4	7	1	.364	268	339	Detroit	4	8	0	.333	237	259
N.Y. Bulldogs	1	10	1	.091	153	368	Green Bay	2	10	0	.167	114	329

NFL championship: Philadelphia 14, LOS ANGELES 0

1948

EASTERN DIVISION	W	L	T	Pct.	Pts.	OP	WESTERN DIVISION	W	L	T	Pct.	Pts.	OP
Philadelphia	9	2	1	.818	376	156	Chi. Cardinals	11	1	0	.917	395	226
Washington	7	5	0	.583	291	287	Chi. Bears	10	2	0	.833	375	151
N.Y. Giants	4	8	0	.333	297	388	Los Angeles	6	5	1	.545	327	269
Pittsburgh	4	8	0	.333	200	243	Green Bay	3	9	0	.250	154	290
Boston	3	9	0	.250	174	372	Detroit	2	10	0	.167	200	407

NFL championship: PHILADELPHIA 7, Chi. Cardinals 0

1947

EASTERN DIVISION	W	L	T	Pct.	Pts.	OP	WESTERN DIVISION	W	L	T	Pct.	Pts.	OP
Philadelphia	8	4	0	.667	308	242	Chi. Cardinals	9	3	0	.750	306	231
Pittsburgh	8	4	0	.667	240	259	Chi. Bears	8	4	0	.667	363	241
Boston	4	7	1	.364	168	256	Green Bay	6	5	1	.545	274	210
Washington	4	8	0	.333	295	367	Los Angeles	6	6	0	.500	259	214
N.Y. Giants	2	8	2	.200	190	309	Detroit	3	9	0	.250	231	305

Eastern Division playoff: Philadelphia 21, PITTSBURGH 0
NFL championship: CHI. CARDINALS 28, Philadelphia 21

1946

EASTERN DIVISION	W	L	T	Pct.	Pts.	OP	WESTERN DIVISION	W	L	T	Pct.	Pts.	OP
N.Y. Giants	7	3	1	.700	236	162	Chi. Bears	8	2	1	.800	289	193
Philadelphia	6	5	0	.545	231	220	Los Angeles	6	4	1	.600	277	257
Washington	5	5	1	.500	171	191	Green Bay	6	5	0	.545	148	158
Pittsburgh	5	5	1	.500	136	117	Chi. Cardinals	6	5	0	.545	260	198
Boston	2	8	1	.200	189	273	Detroit	1	10	0	.091	142	310

NFL championship: Chi. Bears 24, N.Y. GIANTS 14

1945

EASTERN DIVISION	W	L	T	Pct.	Pts.	OP	WESTERN DIVISION	W	L	T	Pct.	Pts.	OP
Washington	8	2	0	.800	209	121	Cleveland	9	1	0	.900	244	136
Philadelphia	7	3	0	.700	272	133	Detroit	7	3	0	.700	195	194
N.Y. Giants	3	6	1	.333	179	198	Green Bay	6	4	0	.600	258	173
Boston	3	6	1	.333	123	211	Chi. Bears	3	7	0	.300	192	235
Pittsburgh	2	8	0	.200	79	220	Chi. Cardinals	1	9	0	.100	98	228

NFL championship: CLEVELAND 15, Washington 14

1944

EASTERN DIVISION	W	L	T	Pct.	Pts.	OP	WESTERN DIVISION	W	L	T	Pct.	Pts.	OP
N.Y. Giants	8	1	1	.889	206	75	Green Bay	8	2	0	.800	238	141
Philadelphia	7	1	2	.875	267	131	Chi. Bears	6	3	1	.667	258	172
Washington	6	3	1	.667	169	180	Detroit	6	3	1	.667	216	151
Boston	2	8	0	.200	82	233	Cleveland	4	6	0	.400	188	224
Brooklyn	0	10	0	.000	69	166	Card-Pitt	0	10	0	.000	108	328

NFL championship: Green Bay 14, N.Y. GIANTS 7

1943

EASTERN DIVISION	W	L	T	Pct.	Pts.	OP	WESTERN DIVISION	W	L	T	Pct.	Pts.	OP
Washington	6	3	1	.667	229	137	Chi. Bears	8	1	1	.889	303	157
N.Y. Giants	6	3	1	.667	197	170	Green Bay	7	2	1	.778	264	172
Phil-Pitt	5	4	1	.556	225	230	Detroit	3	6	1	.333	178	218
Brooklyn	2	8	0	.200	65	234	Chi. Cardinals	0	10	0	.000	95	238

Eastern Division playoff: Washington 28, N.Y. GIANTS 0
NFL championship: CHI. BEARS 41, Washington 21

1942

EASTERN DIVISION	W	L	T	Pct.	Pts.	OP	WESTERN DIVISION	W	L	T	Pct.	Pts.	OP
Washington	10	1	0	.909	227	102	Chi. Bears	11	0	0	1.000	376	84
Pittsburgh	7	4	0	.636	167	119	Green Bay	8	2	1	.800	300	215
N.Y. Giants	5	5	1	.500	155	139	Cleveland	5	6	0	.455	150	207
Brooklyn	3	8	0	.273	100	168	Chi. Cardinals	3	8	0	.273	98	209
Philadelphia	2	9	0	.182	134	239	Detroit	0	11	0	.000	38	263

NFL championship: WASHINGTON 14, Chi. Bears 6

1941

EASTERN DIVISION	W	L	T	Pct.	Pts.	OP	WESTERN DIVISION	W	L	T	Pct.	Pts.	OP
N.Y. Giants	8	3	0	.727	238	114	Chi. Bears	10	1	0	.909	396	147
Brooklyn	7	4	0	.636	158	127	Green Bay	10	1	0	.909	258	120
Washington	6	5	0	.545	176	174	Detroit	4	6	1	.400	121	195
Philadelphia	2	8	1	.200	119	218	Chi. Cardinals	3	7	1	.300	127	197
Pittsburgh	1	9	1	.100	103	276	Cleveland	2	9	0	.182	116	244

Western Division playoff: CHI. BEARS 33, Green Bay 14
NFL championship: CHI. BEARS 37, N.Y. Giants 9

1940

EASTERN DIVISION	W	L	T	Pct.	Pts.	OP	WESTERN DIVISION	W	L	T	Pct.	Pts.	OP
Washington	9	2	0	.818	245	142	Chi. Bears	8	3	0	.727	238	152
Brooklyn	8	3	0	.727	186	120	Green Bay	6	4	1	.600	238	155
N.Y. Giants	6	4	1	.600	131	133	Detroit	5	5	1	.500	138	153
Pittsburgh	2	7	2	.222	60	178	Cleveland	4	6	1	.400	171	191
Philadelphia	1	10	0	.091	111	211	Chi. Cardinals	2	7	2	.222	139	222

NFL championship: Chi. Bears 73, WASHINGTON 0

1939

EASTERN DIVISION	W	L	T	Pct.	Pts.	OP	WESTERN DIVISION	W	L	T	Pct.	Pts.	OP
N.Y. Giants	9	1	1	.900	168	85	Green Bay	9	2	0	.818	233	153
Washington	8	2	1	.800	242	94	Chi. Bears	8	3	0	.727	298	157
Brooklyn	4	6	1	.400	108	219	Detroit	6	5	0	.545	145	150
Philadelphia	1	9	1	.100	105	200	Cleveland	5	5	1	.500	195	164
Pittsburgh	1	9	1	.100	114	216	Chi. Cardinals	1	10	0	.091	84	254

NFL championship: GREEN BAY 27, N.Y. Giants 0

1938

EASTERN DIVISION	W	L	T	Pct.	Pts.	OP	WESTERN DIVISION	W	L	T	Pct.	Pts.	OP
N.Y. Giants	8	2	1	.800	194	79	Green Bay	8	3	0	.727	223	118
Washington	6	3	2	.667	148	154	Detroit	7	4	0	.636	119	108
Brooklyn	4	4	3	.500	131	161	Chi. Bears	6	5	0	.545	194	148
Philadelphia	5	6	0	.455	154	164	Cleveland	4	7	0	.364	131	215
Pittsburgh	2	9	0	.182	79	169	Chi. Cardinals	2	9	0	.182	111	168

NFL championship: N.Y. GIANTS 23, Green Bay 17

1937

EASTERN DIVISION	W	L	T	Pct.	Pts.	OP	WESTERN DIVISION	W	L	T	Pct.	Pts.	OP
Washington	8	3	0	.727	195	120	Chi. Bears	9	1	1	.900	201	100
N.Y. Giants	6	3	2	.667	128	109	Green Bay	7	4	0	.636	220	122
Pittsburgh	4	7	0	.364	122	145	Detroit	7	4	0	.636	180	105
Brooklyn	3	7	1	.300	82	174	Chi. Cardinals	5	5	1	.500	135	165
Philadelphia	2	8	1	.200	86	177	Cleveland	1	10	0	.091	75	207

NFL championship: Washington 28, CHI. BEARS 21

1936

EASTERN DIVISION	W	L	T	Pct.	Pts.	OP	WESTERN DIVISION	W	L	T	Pct.	Pts.	OP
Boston	7	5	0	.583	149	110	Green Bay	10	1	1	.909	248	118
Pittsburgh	6	6	0	.500	98	187	Chi. Bears	9	3	0	.750	222	94
N.Y. Giants	5	6	1	.455	115	163	Detroit	8	4	0	.667	235	102
Brooklyn	3	8	1	.273	92	161	Chi. Cardinals	3	8	1	.273	74	143
Philadelphia	1	11	0	.083	51	206							

NFL championship: Green Bay 21, Boston 6, at Polo Grounds, N.Y.

1935

EASTERN DIVISION	W	L	T	Pct.	Pts.	OP	WESTERN DIVISION	W	L	T	Pct.	Pts.	OP
N.Y. Giants	9	3	0	.750	180	96	Detroit	7	3	2	.700	191	111
Brooklyn	5	6	1	.455	90	141	Green Bay	8	4	0	.667	181	96
Pittsburgh	4	8	0	.333	100	209	Chi. Bears	6	4	2	.600	192	106
Boston	2	8	1	.200	65	123	Chi. Cardinals	6	4	2	.600	99	97
Philadelphia	2	9	0	.182	60	179							

NFL championship: DETROIT 26, N.Y. Giants 7
One game between Boston and Philadelphia was canceled.

1934

EASTERN DIVISION	W	L	T	Pct.	Pts.	OP	WESTERN DIVISION	W	L	T	Pct.	Pts.	OP
N.Y. Giants	8	5	0	.615	147	107	Chi. Bears	13	0	0	1.000	286	86
Boston	6	6	0	.500	107	94	Detroit	10	3	0	.769	238	59
Brooklyn	4	7	0	.364	61	153	Green Bay	7	6	0	.538	156	112
Philadelphia	4	7	0	.364	127	85	Chi. Cardinals	5	6	0	.455	80	84
Pittsburgh	2	10	0	.167	51	206	St. Louis	1	2	0	.333	27	61
							Cincinnati	0	8	0	.000	10	243

NFL championship: N.Y. GIANTS 30, Chi. Bears 13

1933

EASTERN DIVISION	W	L	T	Pct.	Pts.	OP	WESTERN DIVISION	W	L	T	Pct.	Pts.	OP
N.Y. Giants	11	3	0	.786	244	101	Chi. Bears	10	2	1	.833	133	82
Brooklyn	5	4	1	.556	93	54	Portsmouth	6	5	0	.545	128	87
Boston	5	5	2	.500	103	97	Green Bay	5	7	1	.417	170	107
Philadelphia	3	5	1	.375	77	158	Cincinnati	3	6	1	.333	38	110
Pittsburgh	3	6	2	.333	67	208	Chi. Cardinals	1	9	1	.100	52	101

NFL championship: CHI. BEARS 23, N.Y. Giants 21

1932

	W	L	T	Pct.
Chicago Bears	7	1	6	.875
Green Bay Packers	10	3	1	.769
Portsmouth Spartans	6	2	4	.750
Boston Braves	4	4	2	.500
New York Giants	4	6	2	.400
Brooklyn Dodgers	3	9	0	.250
Chicago Cardinals	2	6	2	.250
Staten Island Stapletons	2	7	3	.222

Chicago Bears and Portsmouth finished regularly scheduled games tied for first place. Bears won playoff game, which counted in standings, 9-0.

1931

	W	L	T	Pct.
Green Bay Packers	12	2	0	.857
Portsmouth Spartans	11	3	0	.786
Chicago Bears	8	5	0	.615
Chicago Cardinals	5	4	0	.556
New York Giants	7	6	1	.538
Providence Steam Roller	4	4	3	.500
Staten Island Stapletons	4	6	1	.400
Cleveland Indians	2	8	0	.200
Brooklyn Dodgers	2	12	0	.143
Frankford Yellow Jackets	1	6	1	.143

1930

	W	L	T	Pct.
Green Bay Packers	10	3	1	.769
New York Giants	13	4	0	.765
Chicago Bears	9	4	1	.692
Brooklyn Dodgers	7	4	1	.636
Providence Steam Roller	6	4	1	.600
Staten Island Stapletons	5	5	2	.500
Chicago Cardinals	5	6	2	.455
Portsmouth Spartans	5	6	3	.455
Frankford Yellow Jackets	4	13	1	.222
Minneapolis Red Jackets	1	7	1	.125
Newark Tornadoes	1	10	1	.091

1929

	W	L	T	Pct.
Green Bay Packers	12	0	1	1.000
New York Giants	13	1	1	.929
Frankford Yellow Jackets	10	4	5	.714
Chicago Cardinals	6	6	1	.500
Boston Bulldogs	4	4	0	.500
Staten Island Stapletons	3	4	3	.429
Providence Steam Roller	4	6	2	.400
Orange Tornadoes	3	5	4	.375
Chicago Bears	4	9	2	.308
Buffalo Bisons	1	7	1	.125
Minneapolis Red Jackets	1	9	0	.100
Dayton Triangles	0	6	0	.000

1928

	W	L	T	Pct.
Providence Steam Roller	8	1	2	.889
Frankford Yellow Jackets	11	3	2	.786
Detroit Wolverines	7	2	1	.778
Green Bay Packers	6	4	3	.600
Chicago Bears	7	5	1	.583
New York Giants	4	7	2	.364
New York Yankees	4	8	1	.333
Pottsville Maroons	2	8	0	.200
Chicago Cardinals	1	5	0	.167
Dayton Triangles	0	7	0	.000

1927

	W	L	T	Pct.
New York Giants	11	1	1	.917
Green Bay Packers	7	2	1	.778
Chicago Bears	9	3	2	.750
Cleveland Bulldogs	8	4	1	.667
Providence Steam Roller	8	5	1	.615
New York Yankees	7	8	1	.467
Frankford Yellow Jackets	6	9	3	.400
Pottsville Maroons	5	8	0	.385
Chicago Cardinals	3	7	1	.300
Dayton Triangles	1	6	1	.143
Duluth Eskimos	1	8	0	.111
Buffalo Bisons	0	5	0	.000

1926

	W	L	T	Pct.
Frankford Yellow Jackets	14	1	2	.933
Chicago Bears	12	1	3	.923
Pottsville Maroons	10	2	2	.833
Kansas City Cowboys	8	3	0	.727
Green Bay Packers	7	3	3	.700
Los Angeles Buccaneers	6	3	1	.667
New York Giants	8	4	1	.667
Duluth Eskimos	6	5	3	.545
Buffalo Rangers	4	4	2	.500
Chicago Cardinals	5	6	1	.455
Providence Steam Roller	5	7	1	.417
Detroit Panthers	4	6	2	.400
Hartford Blues	3	7	0	.300
Brooklyn Lions	3	8	0	.273
Milwaukee Badgers	2	7	0	.222
Akron Indians	1	4	3	.200
Dayton Triangles	1	4	1	.200
Racine Tornadoes	1	4	0	.200
Columbus Tigers	1	6	0	.143
Canton Bulldogs	1	9	3	.100
Hammond Pros	0	4	0	.000
Louisville Colonels	0	4	0	.000

1925

	W	L	T	Pct.
Chicago Cardinals	11	2	1	.846
Pottsville Maroons	10	2	0	.833
Detroit Panthers	8	2	2	.800
New York Giants	8	4	0	.667
Akron Indians	4	2	2	.667
Frankford Yellow Jackets	13	7	0	.650
Chicago Bears	9	5	3	.643
Rock Island Independents	5	3	3	.625
Green Bay Packers	8	5	0	.615
Providence Steam Roller	6	5	1	.545
Canton Bulldogs	4	4	0	.500
Cleveland Bulldogs	5	8	1	.385
Kansas City Cowboys	2	5	1	.286
Hammond Pros	1	4	0	.200
Buffalo Bisons	1	6	2	.143
Duluth Kelleys	0	3	0	.000
Rochester Jeffersons	0	6	1	.000
Milwaukee Badgers	0	6	0	.000
Dayton Triangles	0	7	1	.000
Columbus Tigers	0	9	0	.000

1924

	W	L	T	Pct.
Cleveland Bulldogs	7	1	1	.875
Chicago Bears	6	1	4	.857
Frankford Yellow Jackets	11	2	1	.846
Duluth Kelleys	5	1	0	.833
Rock Island Independents	5	2	2	.714
Green Bay Packers	7	4	0	.636
Racine Legion	4	3	3	.571
Chicago Cardinals	5	4	1	.556
Buffalo Bisons	6	5	0	.545
Columbus Tigers	4	4	0	.500
Hammond Pros	2	2	1	.500
Milwaukee Badgers	5	8	0	.385
Akron Indians	2	6	0	.250
Dayton Triangles	2	6	0	.250
Kansas City Blues	2	7	0	.222
Kenosha Maroons	0	4	1	.000
Minneapolis Marines	0	6	0	.000
Rochester Jeffersons	0	7	0	.000

1923

	W	L	T	Pct.
Canton Bulldogs	11	0	1	1.000
Chicago Bears	9	2	1	.818
Green Bay Packers	7	2	1	.778
Milwaukee Badgers	7	2	3	.778
Cleveland Indians	3	1	3	.750
Chicago Cardinals	8	4	0	.667
Duluth Kelleys	4	3	0	.571
Buffalo All-Americans	5	4	3	.556
Columbus Tigers	5	4	1	.556
Racine Legion	4	4	2	.500
Toledo Maroons	3	3	2	.500
Rock Island Independents	2	3	3	.400
Minneapolis Marines	2	5	2	.286
St. Louis All-Stars	1	4	2	.200
Hammond Pros	1	5	1	.167
Dayton Triangles	1	6	1	.143
Akron Indians	1	6	0	.143
Oorang Indians	1	10	0	.091
Louisville Brecks	0	3	0	.000
Rochester Jeffersons	0	4	0	.000

1922

	W	L	T	Pct.
Canton Bulldogs	10	0	2	1.000
Chicago Bears	9	3	0	.750
Chicago Cardinals	8	3	0	.727
Toledo Maroons	5	2	2	.714
Rock Island Independents	4	2	1	.667
Racine Legion	6	4	1	.600
Dayton Triangles	4	3	1	.571
Green Bay Packers	4	3	3	.571
Buffalo All-Americans	5	4	1	.556
Akron Pros	3	5	2	.375
Milwaukee Badgers	2	4	3	.333
Oorang Indians	3	6	0	.333
Minneapolis Marines	1	3	0	.250
Louisville Brecks	1	3	0	.250
Evansville Crimson Giants	0	3	0	.000
Rochester Jeffersons	0	4	1	.000
Hammond Pros	0	5	1	.000
Columbus Panhandles	0	8	0	.000

1921

	W	L	T	Pct.
Chicago Staleys	9	1	1	.900
Buffalo All-Americans	9	1	2	.900
Akron Pros	8	3	1	.727
Canton Bulldogs	5	2	3	.714
Rock Island Independents	4	2	1	.667
Evansville Crimson Giants	3	2	0	.600
Green Bay Packers	3	2	1	.600
Dayton Triangles	4	4	1	.500
Chicago Cardinals	3	3	2	.500
Rochester Jeffersons	2	3	0	.400
Cleveland Indians	3	5	0	.375
Washington Senators	1	2	0	.333
Cincinnati Celts	1	3	0	.250
Hammond Pros	1	3	1	.250
Minneapolis Marines	1	3	0	.250
Detroit Heralds	1	5	1	.167
Columbus Panhandles	1	8	0	.111
Tonawanda Kardex	0	1	0	.000
Muncie Flyers	0	2	0	.000
Louisville Brecks	0	2	0	.000
New York Giants	0	2	0	.000

1920*

	W	L	T	Pct.
Akron Pros	8	0	3	1.000
Decatur Staleys	10	1	2	.909
Buffalo All-Americans	9	1	1	.900
Chicago Cardinals	6	2	2	.750
Rock Island Independents	6	2	2	.750
Dayton Triangles	5	2	2	.714
Rochester Jeffersons	6	3	2	.667
Canton Bulldogs	7	4	2	.636
Detroit Heralds	2	3	3	.400
Cleveland Tigers	2	4	2	.333
Chicago Tigers	2	5	1	.286
Hammond Pros	2	5	0	.286
Columbus Panhandles	2	6	2	.250
Muncie Flyers	0	1	0	.000

*No official standings were maintained for the 1920 season, and the championship was awarded to the Akron Pros in a League meeting on April 30, 1921. Clubs played schedules that included games against nonleague opponents.

RS=REGULAR SEASON
PS=POSTSEASON
*ARIZONA vs. ATLANTA
RS: Cardinals lead series, 13-9
1966—Falcons, 16-10 (A)
1968—Cardinals, 17-12 (StL)
1971—Cardinals, 26-9 (A)
1973—Cardinals, 32-10 (A)
1975—Cardinals, 23-20 (StL)
1978—Cardinals, 42-21 (StL)
1980—Falcons, 33-27 (StL) OT
1981—Falcons, 41-20 (A)
1982—Cardinals, 23-20 (A)
1986—Falcons, 33-13 (A)
1987—Cardinals, 34-21 (A)
1989—Cardinals, 34-20 (P)
1990—Cardinals, 24-13 (A)
1991—Cardinals, 16-10 (P)
1992—Falcons, 20-17 (A)
1993—Cardinals, 27-10 (A)
1994—Falcons, 10-6 (Atl)
1995—Cardinals, 40-37 (Ariz) OT
1997—Cardinals, 29-26 (Ariz)
1999—Falcons, 37-14 (Atl)
2001—Falcons, 34-14 (Ariz)
2004—Falcons, 6-3 (Atl)
(RS Pts.—Cardinals 491, Falcons 459)
*Franchise known as Phoenix prior to
1994 and in St. Louis prior to 1988*
*ARIZONA vs. BALTIMORE
RS: Ravens lead series, 2-1
1997—Cardinals, 16-13 (B)
2000—Ravens, 13-7 (A)
2003—Ravens, 26-18 (A)
(RS Pts.—Ravens 52, Cardinals 41)
*ARIZONA vs. BUFFALO
RS: Bills lead series, 5-3
1971—Cardinals, 28-23 (B)
1975—Bills, 32-14 (StL)
1981—Cardinals, 24-0 (StL)
1984—Cardinals, 37-7 (StL)
1986—Bills, 17-10 (B)
1990—Bills, 45-14 (B)
1999—Bills, 31-21 (A)
2004—Bills, 38-14 (B)
(RS Pts.—Bills 193, Cardinals 162)
*Franchise known as Phoenix prior to
1994 and in St. Louis prior to 1988*
ARIZONA vs. CAROLINA
RS: Panthers lead series, 4-2
1995—Panthers, 27-7 (C)
2001—Cardinals, 30-7 (C)
2002—Cardinals, 16-13 (C)
2003—Panthers, 20-17 (A)
2004—Panthers, 35-10 (C)
2005—Panthers, 24-20 (A)
(RS Pts.—Panthers 126, Cardinals 100)
*ARIZONA vs. **CHICAGO
RS: Bears lead series, 54-26-6
(NP denotes Normal Park;
Wr denotes Wrigley Field;
Co denotes Comiskey Park;
So denotes Soldier Field;
all Chicago)
1920—Cardinals, 7-6 (NP)
        Staleys, 10-0 (Wr)
1921—Tie, 0-0 (Wr)
1922—Cardinals, 6-0 (Co)
        Cardinals, 9-0 (Co)
1923—Bears, 3-0 (Wr)

1924—Bears, 6-0 (Wr)
        Bears, 21-0 (Co)
1925—Cardinals, 9-0 (Co)
        Tie, 0-0 (Wr)
1926—Bears, 16-0 (Wr)
        Bears, 10-0 (So)
        Tie, 0-0 (Wr)
1927—Bears, 9-0 (NP)
        Cardinals, 3-0 (Wr)
1928—Bears, 15-0 (NP)
        Bears, 34-0 (Wr)
1929—Tie, 0-0 (Wr)
        Cardinals, 40-6 (Co)
1930—Bears, 32-6 (Co)
        Bears, 6-0 (Wr)
1931—Bears, 26-13 (Wr)
        Bears, 18-7 (Wr)
1932—Tie, 0-0 (Wr)
        Bears, 34-0 (Wr)
1933—Bears, 12-9 (Wr)
        Bears, 22-6 (Wr)
1934—Bears, 20-0 (Wr)
        Bears, 17-6 (Wr)
1935—Tie, 7-7 (Wr)
        Bears, 13-0 (Wr)
1936—Bears, 7-3 (Wr)
        Cardinals, 14-7 (Wr)
1937—Bears, 16-7 (Wr)
        Bears, 42-28 (Wr)
1938—Bears, 16-13 (So)
        Bears, 34-28 (Wr)
1939—Bears, 44-7 (Wr)
        Bears, 48-7 (Co)
1940—Cardinals, 21-7 (Co)
        Bears, 31-23 (Wr)
1941—Bears, 53-7 (Wr)
        Bears, 34-24 (Co)
1942—Bears, 41-14 (Wr)
        Bears, 21-7 (Co)
1943—Bears, 20-0 (Wr)
        Bears, 35-24 (Co)
1945—Cardinals, 16-7 (Wr)
        Bears, 28-20 (Co)
1946—Bears, 34-17 (Co)
        Cardinals, 35-28 (Wr)
1947—Cardinals, 31-7 (Co)
        Cardinals, 30-21 (Wr)
1948—Bears, 28-17 (Co)
        Cardinals, 24-21 (Wr)
1949—Bears, 17-7 (Co)
        Bears, 52-21 (Wr)
1950—Bears, 27-6 (Wr)
        Cardinals, 20-10 (Co)
1951—Cardinals, 28-14 (Co)
        Cardinals, 24-14 (Wr)
1952—Cardinals, 21-10 (Co)
        Bears, 10-7 (Wr)
1953—Cardinals, 24-17 (Wr)
1954—Bears, 29-7 (Co)
1955—Cardinals, 53-14 (Co)
1956—Bears, 10-3 (Wr)
1957—Bears, 14-6 (Co)
1958—Bears, 30-14 (Wr)
1959—Bears, 31-7 (So)
1965—Bears, 34-13 (Wr)
1966—Cardinals, 24-17 (StL)
1967—Bears, 30-3 (Wr)
1969—Cardinals, 20-17 (StL)
1972—Bears, 27-10 (StL)
1975—Cardinals, 34-20 (So)

1977—Cardinals, 16-13 (StL)
1978—Bears, 17-10 (So)
1979—Bears, 42-6 (So)
1982—Cardinals, 10-7 (So)
1984—Cardinals, 38-21 (StL)
1990—Bears, 31-21 (P)
1994—Bears, 19-16 (A) OT
1998—Cardinals, 20-7 (A)
2001—Bears, 20-13 (C)
2003—Bears, 28-3 (C)
(RS Pts.—Bears 1,622, Cardinals 1,050)
*Franchise known as Phoenix prior to
1994, in St. Louis prior to 1988, and in
Chicago prior to 1960*
**Franchise in Decatur prior to 1921 and
known as Staleys prior to 1922*
*ARIZONA vs. CINCINNATI
RS: Bengals lead series, 5-3
1973—Bengals, 42-24 (C)
1979—Bengals, 34-28 (C)
1985—Cardinals, 41-27 (StL)
1988—Bengals, 21-14 (C)
1994—Cardinals, 28-7 (A)
1997—Bengals, 24-21 (C)
2000—Bengals, 24-13 (C)
2003—Cardinals, 17-14 (A)
(RS Pts.—Bengals 193, Cardinals 186)
*Franchise known as Phoenix prior to
1994 and in St. Louis prior to 1988*
*ARIZONA vs. CLEVELAND
RS: Browns lead series, 33-11-3
1950—Browns, 34-24 (Cle)
        Browns, 10-7 (Chi)
1951—Browns, 34-17 (Chi)
        Browns, 49-28 (Cle)
1952—Browns, 28-13 (Cle)
        Browns, 10-0 (Chi)
1953—Browns, 27-7 (Chi)
        Browns, 27-16 (Cle)
1954—Browns, 31-7 (Cle)
        Browns, 35-3 (Chi)
1955—Browns, 26-20 (Chi)
        Browns, 35-24 (Cle)
1956—Cardinals, 9-7 (Chi)
        Cardinals, 24-7 (Cle)
1957—Browns, 17-7 (Chi)
        Browns, 31-0 (Cle)
1958—Browns, 35-28 (Cle)
        Browns, 38-24 (Chi)
1959—Browns, 34-7 (Chi)
        Browns, 17-7 (Cle)
1960—Browns, 28-27 (Cle)
        Tie, 17-17 (StL)
1961—Browns, 20-17 (Cle)
        Browns, 21-10 (StL)
1962—Browns, 34-7 (StL)
        Browns, 38-14 (Cle)
1963—Cardinals, 20-14 (Cle)
        Browns, 24-10 (StL)
1964—Tie, 33-33 (Cle)
        Cardinals, 28-19 (StL)
1965—Cardinals, 49-13 (Cle)
        Browns, 27-24 (StL)
1966—Cardinals, 34-28 (Cle)
        Browns, 38-10 (StL)
1967—Browns, 20-16 (Cle)
        Browns, 20-16 (StL)
1968—Cardinals, 27-21 (Cle)
        Cardinals, 27-16 (StL)
1969—Tie, 21-21 (Cle)

Browns, 27-21 (StL)
1974—Cardinals, 29-7 (StL)
1979—Browns, 38-20 (StL)
1985—Cardinals, 27-24 (Cle) OT
1988—Browns, 29-21 (P)
1994—Browns, 32-0 (Cle)
2000—Cardinals, 29-21 (A)
2003—Browns, 44-6 (Cle)
(RS Pts.—Browns 1,206, Cardinals 832)
*Franchise known as Phoenix prior to
1994, in St. Louis prior to 1988,
and in Chicago prior to 1960
ARIZONA vs. DALLAS
RS: Cowboys lead series, 54-27-1
PS: Cardinals lead series, 1-0
1960—Cardinals, 12-10 (StL)
1961—Cardinals, 31-17 (D)
Cardinals, 31-13 (StL)
1962—Cardinals, 28-24 (D)
Cardinals, 52-20 (StL)
1963—Cardinals, 34-7 (D)
Cowboys, 28-24 (StL)
1964—Cardinals, 16-6 (D)
Cowboys, 31-13 (StL)
1965—Cardinals, 20-13 (StL)
Cowboys, 27-13 (D)
1966—Tie, 10-10 (StL)
Cowboys, 31-17 (D)
1967—Cowboys, 46-21 (D)
1968—Cowboys, 27-10 (StL)
1969—Cowboys, 24-3 (D)
1970—Cardinals, 20-7 (StL)
Cardinals, 38-0 (D)
1971—Cowboys, 16-13 (StL)
Cowboys, 31-12 (D)
1972—Cowboys, 33-24 (D)
Cowboys, 27-6 (StL)
1973—Cowboys, 45-10 (D)
Cowboys, 30-3 (StL)
1974—Cardinals, 31-28 (StL)
Cowboys, 17-14 (D)
1975—Cowboys, 37-31 (D) OT
Cardinals, 31-17 (StL)
1976—Cardinals, 21-17 (StL)
Cowboys, 19-14 (D)
1977—Cowboys, 30-24 (StL)
Cardinals, 24-17 (D)
1978—Cowboys, 21-12 (D)
Cowboys, 24-21 (StL) OT
1979—Cowboys, 22-21 (StL)
Cowboys, 22-13 (D)
1980—Cowboys, 27-24 (StL)
Cowboys, 31-21 (D)
1981—Cowboys, 30-17 (D)
Cardinals, 20-17 (StL)
1982—Cowboys, 24-7 (StL)
1983—Cowboys, 34-17 (StL)
Cowboys, 35-17 (D)
1984—Cowboys, 31-20 (D)
Cowboys, 24-17 (StL)
1985—Cardinals, 21-10 (StL)
Cowboys, 35-17 (D)
1986—Cowboys, 31-7 (StL)
Cowboys, 37-6 (D)
1987—Cardinals, 24-13 (StL)
Cowboys, 21-16 (D)
1988—Cowboys, 17-14 (P)
Cardinals, 16-10 (D)
1989—Cardinals, 19-10 (D)
Cardinals, 24-20 (P)

1990—Cardinals, 20-3 (P)
Cowboys, 41-10 (D)
1991—Cowboys, 17-9 (P)
Cowboys, 27-7 (D)
1992—Cowboys, 31-20 (D)
Cowboys, 16-10 (P)
1993—Cowboys, 17-10 (P)
Cowboys, 20-15 (D)
1994—Cowboys, 38-3 (D)
Cowboys, 28-21 (A)
1995—Cowboys, 34-20 (D)
Cowboys, 37-13 (A)
1996—Cowboys, 17-3 (D)
Cowboys, 10-6 (A)
1997—Cardinals, 25-22 (A) OT
Cowboys, 24-6 (D)
1998—Cowboys, 38-10 (D)
Cowboys, 35-28 (A)
**Cardinals, 20-7 (D)
1999—Cowboys, 35-7 (D)
Cardinals, 13-9 (A)
2000—Cardinals, 32-31 (A)
Cowboys, 48-7 (D)
2001—Cowboys, 17-3 (D)
Cardinals, 17-10 (A)
2002—Cardinals, 9-6 (A) OT
2003—Cowboys, 24-7 (D)
2005—Cowboys, 34-13 (D)
(RS Pts.—Cowboys 1,909, Cardinals 1,397)
(PS Pts.—Cardinals 20, Cowboys 7)
*Franchise known as Phoenix prior to
1994 and in St. Louis prior to 1988
**NFC First-Round Playoff
ARIZONA vs. DENVER
RS: Broncos lead series, 6-0-1
1973—Tie, 17-17 (StL)
1977—Broncos, 7-0 (D)
1989—Broncos, 37-0 (P)
1991—Broncos, 24-19 (D)
1995—Broncos, 38-6 (D)
2001—Broncos, 38-17 (A)
2002—Broncos, 37-7 (D)
(RS Pts.—Broncos 198, Cardinals 66)
*Franchise known as Phoenix prior to
1994 and in St. Louis prior to 1988
ARIZONA vs. **DETROIT
RS: Lions lead series, 31-21-5
1930—Tie, 0-0 (Port)
Cardinals, 23-0 (C)
1931—Spartans, 13-3 (Port)
Cardinals, 20-19 (C)
1932—Tie, 7-7 (Port)
1933—Spartans, 7-6 (Port)
1934—Lions, 6-0 (D)
Lions, 17-13 (C)
1935—Tie, 10-10 (D)
Lions, 7-6 (C)
1936—Lions, 39-0 (D)
Lions, 14-7 (C)
1937—Lions, 16-7 (C)
Lions, 16-7 (D)
1938—Lions, 10-0 (D)
Lions, 7-3 (C)
1939—Lions, 21-3 (D)
Lions, 17-3 (C)
1940—Tie, 0-0 (Buffalo)
Lions, 43-14 (C)
1941—Tie, 14-14 (C)
Lions, 21-3 (D)
1942—Cardinals, 13-0 (C)

Cardinals, 7-0 (D)
1943—Lions, 35-17 (D)
Lions, 7-0 (Buffalo)
1945—Lions, 10-0 (Milwaukee)
Lions, 26-0 (D)
1946—Cardinals, 34-14 (C)
Cardinals, 36-14 (D)
1947—Cardinals, 45-21 (C)
Cardinals, 17-7 (D)
1948—Cardinals, 56-20 (C)
Cardinals, 28-14 (D)
1949—Lions, 24-7 (C)
Cardinals, 42-19 (D)
1959—Lions, 45-21 (D)
1961—Lions, 45-14 (StL)
1967—Cardinals, 38-28 (StL)
1969—Lions, 20-0 (D)
1970—Lions, 16-3 (D)
1973—Lions, 20-16 (StL)
1975—Cardinals, 24-13 (D)
1978—Cardinals, 21-14 (StL)
1980—Lions, 20-7 (D)
Cardinals, 24-23 (StL)
1989—Cardinals, 16-13 (D)
1993—Lions, 26-20 (D)
Lions, 21-14 (Phx)
1995—Cardinals, 20-17 (D)
1998—Cardinals, 17-15 (D)
1999—Cardinals, 23-19 (A)
2001—Cardinals, 45-38 (A)
2002—Cardinals, 23-20 (A) OT
2003—Lions, 42-24 (D)
2004—Lions, 26-12 (D)
2005—Lions, 29-21 (D)
(RS Pts.—Lions 1,038, Cardinals 864)
*Franchise known as Phoenix prior to
1994, in St. Louis prior to 1988,
and in Chicago prior to 1960
**Franchise in Portsmouth prior to 1934
and known as the Spartans
ARIZONA vs. GREEN BAY
RS: Packers lead series, 41-22-4
PS: Packers lead series, 1-0
1921—Tie, 3-3 (C)
1922—Cardinals, 16-3 (C)
1924—Cardinals, 3-0 (C)
1925—Cardinals, 9-6 (C)
1926—Cardinals, 13-7 (GB)
Packers, 3-0 (C)
1927—Packers, 13-0 (GB)
Tie, 6-6 (C)
1928—Packers, 20-0 (GB)
1929—Packers, 9-2 (GB)
Packers, 7-6 (C)
Packers, 12-0 (C)
1930—Packers, 14-0 (GB)
Cardinals, 13-6 (C)
1931—Packers, 26-7 (GB)
Cardinals, 21-13 (C)
1932—Packers, 15-7 (GB)
Packers, 19-9 (C)
1933—Packers, 14-6 (C)
1934—Packers, 15-0 (GB)
Cardinals, 9-0 (Mil)
Cardinals, 6-0 (C)
1935—Cardinals, 7-6 (GB)
Cardinals, 3-0 (Mil)
Cardinals, 9-7 (C)
1936—Packers, 10-7 (GB)
Packers, 24-0 (Mil)

Tie, 0-0 (C)
1937—Cardinals, 14-7 (GB)
Packers, 34-13 (Mil)
1938—Packers, 28-7 (Mil)
Packers, 24-22 (Buffalo)
1939—Packers, 14-10 (GB)
Packers, 27-20 (Mil)
1940—Packers, 31-6 (Mil)
Packers, 28-7 (C)
1941—Packers, 14-13 (Mil)
Packers, 17-9 (GB)
1942—Packers, 17-13 (C)
Packers, 55-24 (GB)
1943—Packers, 28-7 (C)
Packers, 35-14 (Mil)
1945—Packers, 33-14 (GB)
1946—Packers, 19-7 (C)
Cardinals, 24-6 (GB)
1947—Cardinals, 14-10 (GB)
Cardinals, 21-20 (C)
1948—Cardinals, 17-7 (Mil)
Cardinals, 42-7 (C)
1949—Cardinals, 39-17 (Mil)
Cardinals, 41-21 (C)
1955—Packers, 31-14 (GB)
1956—Packers, 24-21 (C)
1962—Packers, 17-0 (Mil)
1963—Packers, 30-7 (Mil)
1967—Packers, 31-23 (StL)
1969—Packers, 45-28 (GB)
1971—Tie, 16-16 (StL)
1973—Packers, 25-21 (GB)
1976—Cardinals, 29-0 (StL)
1982—**Packers, 41-16 (GB)
1984—Packers, 24-23 (GB)
1985—Cardinals, 43-28 (StL)
1988—Packers, 26-17 (P)
1990—Packers, 24-21 (P)
1999—Packers, 49-24 (GB)
2000—Packers, 29-3 (A)
2003—Cardinals, 20-13 (A)
(RS Pts.—Packers 1,169, Cardinals 870)
(PS Pts.—Packers 41, Cardinals 16)
*Franchise known as Phoenix prior to
1994, in St. Louis prior to 1988,
and in Chicago prior to 1960
**NFC First-Round Playoff

ARIZONA vs. HOUSTON
RS: Texans lead series, 1-0
2005—Texans, 30-19 (H)
(RS Pts.—Texans 30, Cardinals 19)
*ARIZONA vs. **INDIANAPOLIS
RS: Colts lead series, 7-6
1961—Colts, 16-0 (B)
1964—Colts, 47-27 (B)
1968—Colts, 27-0 (B)
1972—Cardinals, 10-3 (B)
1976—Cardinals, 24-17 (StL)
1978—Colts, 30-17 (StL)
1980—Cardinals, 17-10 (B)
1981—Cardinals, 35-24 (B)
1984—Cardinals, 34-33 (I)
1990—Cardinals, 20-17 (P)
1992—Colts, 16-13 (I)
1996—Colts, 20-13 (I)
2005—Colts, 17-13 (I)
(RS Pts.—Colts 277, Cardinals 223)
*Franchise known as Phoenix prior to
1994 and in St. Louis prior to 1988
**Franchise in Baltimore prior to 1984

ARIZONA vs. JACKSONVILLE
RS: Jaguars lead series, 2-0
2000—Jaguars, 44-10 (J)
2005—Jaguars, 24-17 (A)
(RS Pts.—Jaguars 68, Cardinals 27)
*ARIZONA vs. KANSAS CITY
RS: Chiefs lead series, 6-2-1
1970—Tie, 6-6 (KC)
1974—Chiefs, 17-13 (StL)
1980—Chiefs, 21-13 (StL)
1983—Chiefs, 38-14 (KC)
1986—Cardinals, 23-14 (StL)
1995—Chiefs, 24-3 (A)
1998—Chiefs, 34-24 (KC)
2001—Cardinals, 24-16 (A)
2002—Chiefs, 49-0 (KC)
(RS Pts.—Chiefs 219, Cardinals 120)
*Franchise known as Phoenix prior to
1994 and in St. Louis prior to 1988
*ARIZONA vs. MIAMI
RS: Dolphins lead series, 8-1
1972—Dolphins, 31-10 (M)
1977—Dolphins, 55-14 (StL)
1978—Dolphins, 24-10 (M)
1981—Dolphins, 20-7 (StL)
1984—Dolphins, 36-28 (StL)
1990—Dolphins, 23-3 (M)
1996—Dolphins, 38-10 (A)
1999—Dolphins, 19-16 (M)
2004—Cardinals, 24-23 (M)
(RS Pts.—Dolphins 269, Cardinals 122)
*Franchise known as Phoenix prior to
1994 and in St. Louis prior to 1988
*ARIZONA vs. MINNESOTA
RS: Cardinals lead series, 9-8
PS: Vikings lead series, 2-0
1963—Cardinals, 56-14 (M)
1967—Cardinals, 34-24 (M)
1969—Vikings, 27-10 (StL)
1972—Cardinals, 19-17 (M)
1974—Vikings, 28-24 (StL)
**Vikings, 30-14 (M)
1977—Cardinals, 27-7 (M)
1979—Cardinals, 37-7 (StL)
1981—Cardinals, 30-17 (StL)
1983—Cardinals, 41-31 (StL)
1991—Vikings, 34-7 (M)
Vikings, 28-0 (P)
1994—Cardinals, 17-7 (A)
1995—Vikings, 30-24 (A) OT
1996—Vikings, 41-17 (M)
1997—Vikings, 20-19 (A)
1998—**Vikings, 41-21 (M)
2000—Vikings, 31-14 (M)
2003—Cardinals, 18-17 (A)
(RS Pts.—Cardinals 394, Vikings 380)
(PS Pts.—Vikings 71, Cardinals 35)
*Franchise known as Phoenix prior to
1994 and in St. Louis prior to 1988
**NFC Divisional Playoff
*ARIZONA vs. **NEW ENGLAND
RS: Cardinals lead series, 6-5
1970—Cardinals, 31-0 (StL)
1975—Cardinals, 24-17 (StL)
1978—Patriots, 16-6 (StL)
1981—Cardinals, 27-20 (NE)
1984—Cardinals, 33-10 (NE)
1990—Cardinals, 34-14 (P)
1991—Cardinals, 24-10 (P)
1993—Patriots, 23-21 (P)

1996—Patriots, 31-0 (NE)
1999—Patriots, 27-3 (A)
2004—Patriots, 23-12 (A)
(RS Pts.—Cardinals 215, Patriots 191)
*Franchise known as Phoenix prior to
1994 and in St. Louis prior to 1988
**Franchise in Boston prior to 1971
*ARIZONA vs. NEW ORLEANS
RS: Cardinals lead series, 13-11
1967—Cardinals, 31-20 (StL)
1968—Cardinals, 21-20 (NO)
Cardinals, 31-17 (StL)
1969—Saints, 51-42 (StL)
1970—Cardinals, 24-17 (StL)
1974—Saints, 14-0 (NO)
1977—Cardinals, 49-31 (StL)
1980—Cardinals, 40-7 (NO)
1981—Cardinals, 30-3 (StL)
1982—Cardinals, 21-7 (NO)
1983—Saints, 28-17 (NO)
1984—Saints, 34-24 (NO)
1985—Cardinals, 28-16 (StL)
1986—Saints, 16-7 (StL)
1987—Cardinals, 24-19 (StL)
1990—Saints, 28-7 (NO)
1991—Saints, 27-3 (P)
1992—Saints, 30-21 (P)
1993—Saints, 20-17 (P)
1996—Cardinals, 28-14 (NO)
1997—Saints, 27-10 (NO)
1998—Cardinals, 19-17 (A)
2000—Saints, 21-10 (A)
2004—Saints, 34-10 (A)
(RS Pts.—Cardinals 538, Saints 494)
*Franchise known as Phoenix prior to
1994 and in St. Louis prior to 1988
*ARIZONA vs. N.Y. GIANTS
RS: Giants lead series, 78-41-2
1926—Giants, 20-0 (NY)
1927—Giants, 28-7 (NY)
1929—Giants, 24-21 (NY)
1930—Giants, 25-12 (NY)
Giants, 13-7 (C)
1935—Cardinals, 14-13 (NY)
1936—Giants, 14-6 (NY)
1938—Giants, 6-0 (NY)
1939—Giants, 17-7 (NY)
1941—Cardinals, 10-7 (NY)
1942—Giants, 21-7 (NY)
1943—Giants, 24-13 (NY)
1946—Giants, 28-24 (NY)
1947—Giants, 35-31 (NY)
1948—Cardinals, 63-35 (NY)
1949—Giants, 41-38 (C)
1950—Cardinals, 17-3 (C)
Giants, 51-21 (NY)
1951—Giants, 28-17 (NY)
Giants, 10-0 (C)
1952—Cardinals, 24-23 (NY)
Giants, 28-6 (C)
1953—Giants, 21-7 (NY)
Giants, 23-20 (C)
1954—Giants, 41-10 (C)
Giants, 31-17 (NY)
1955—Cardinals, 28-17 (C)
Giants, 10-0 (NY)
1956—Cardinals, 35-27 (C)
Giants, 23-10 (NY)
1957—Giants, 27-14 (NY)
Giants, 28-21 (C)

1958—Giants, 37-7 (Buffalo)
    Cardinals, 23-6 (NY)
1959—Giants, 9-3 (NY)
    Giants, 30-20 (Minn)
1960—Giants, 35-14 (StL)
    Cardinals, 20-13 (NY)
1961—Cardinals, 21-10 (NY)
    Giants, 24-9 (StL)
1962—Giants, 31-14 (StL)
    Giants, 31-28 (NY)
1963—Giants, 38-21 (StL)
    Cardinals, 24-17 (NY)
1964—Giants, 34-17 (NY)
    Tie, 10-10 (StL)
1965—Giants, 14-10 (NY)
    Giants, 28-15 (StL)
1966—Cardinals, 24-19 (StL)
    Cardinals, 20-17 (NY)
1967—Giants, 37-20 (StL)
    Giants, 37-14 (NY)
1968—Cardinals, 28-21 (NY)
1969—Cardinals, 42-17 (StL)
    Giants, 49-6 (NY)
1970—Giants, 35-17 (NY)
    Giants, 34-17 (StL)
1971—Giants, 21-20 (StL)
    Cardinals, 24-7 (NY)
1972—Giants, 27-21 (NY)
    Giants, 13-7 (StL)
1973—Cardinals, 35-27 (StL)
    Giants, 24-13 (New Haven)
1974—Cardinals, 23-21 (New Haven)
    Cardinals, 26-14 (StL)
1975—Cardinals, 26-14 (StL)
    Cardinals, 20-13 (NY)
1976—Cardinals, 27-21 (StL)
    Cardinals, 17-14 (NY)
1977—Cardinals, 28-0 (StL)
    Giants, 27-7 (NY)
1978—Cardinals, 20-10 (StL)
    Giants, 17-0 (NY)
1979—Cardinals, 27-14 (NY)
    Cardinals, 29-20 (StL)
1980—Giants, 41-35 (StL)
    Cardinals, 23-7 (NY)
1981—Giants, 34-14 (NY)
    Giants, 20-10 (StL)
1982—Cardinals, 24-21 (StL)
1983—Tie, 20-20 (StL) OT
    Cardinals, 10-6 (NY)
1984—Giants, 16-10 (NY)
    Cardinals, 31-21 (StL)
1985—Giants, 27-17 (NY)
    Giants, 34-3 (StL)
1986—Giants, 13-6 (StL)
    Giants, 27-7 (NY)
1987—Giants, 30-7 (NY)
    Cardinals, 27-24 (StL)
1988—Cardinals, 24-17 (P)
    Giants, 44-7 (NY)
1989—Giants, 35-7 (NY)
    Giants, 20-13 (P)
1990—Giants, 20-19 (NY)
    Giants, 24-21 (P)
1991—Giants, 20-9 (NY)
    Giants, 21-14 (P)
1992—Giants, 31-21 (NY)
    Cardinals, 19-0 (P)
1993—Giants, 19-17 (NY)
    Cardinals, 17-6 (P)

1994—Giants, 20-17 (A)
    Cardinals, 10-9 (NY)
1995—Giants, 27-21 (NY) OT
    Giants, 10-6 (A)
1996—Giants, 16-8 (NY)
    Cardinals, 31-23 (A)
1997—Giants, 27-13 (A)
    Giants, 19-10 (NY)
1998—Giants, 34-7 (NY)
    Giants, 23-19 (A)
1999—Cardinals, 14-3 (A)
    Cardinals, 34-24 (NY)
2000—Giants, 21-16 (NY)
    Giants, 31-7 (A)
2001—Giants, 17-10 (A)
    Giants, 17-13 (NY)
2002—Cardinals, 21-7 (A)
2004—Cardinals, 17-14 (A)
2005—Giants, 42-19 (NY)
(RS Pts.—Giants 2,661, Cardinals 2,046)
*Franchise known as Phoenix prior to
1994, in St. Louis prior to 1988,
and in Chicago prior to 1960*
*ARIZONA vs. N.Y. JETS
RS: Jets lead series, 4-2
1971—Cardinals, 17-10 (StL)
1975—Cardinals, 37-6 (NY)
1978—Jets, 23-10 (NY)
1996—Jets, 31-21 (A)
1999—Jets, 12-7 (NY)
2004—Jets, 13-3 (A)
(RS Pts.—Cardinals 95, Jets 95)
*Franchise known as Phoenix prior to
1994 and in St. Louis prior to 1988*
*ARIZONA vs. **OAKLAND
RS: Raiders lead series, 4-2
1973—Raiders, 17-10 (StL)
1983—Cardinals, 34-24 (LA)
1989—Raiders, 16-14 (LA)
1998—Raiders, 23-20 (A)
2001—Cardinals, 34-31 (O) OT
2002—Raiders, 41-20 (A)
(RS Pts.— Raiders 152, Cardinals 132)
*Franchise known as Phoenix prior to
1994 and in St. Louis prior to 1988
**Franchise in Los Angeles from
1982-1994*
*ARIZONA vs. PHILADELPHIA
RS: Cardinals lead series, 53-52-5
PS: Series tied, 1-1
1935—Cardinals, 12-3 (C)
1936—Cardinals, 13-0 (C)
1937—Tie, 6-6 (P)
1938—Eagles, 7-0 (Erie, Pa.)
1941—Eagles, 21-14 (P)
1945—Eagles, 21-6 (P)
1947—Cardinals, 45-21 (P)
    **Cardinals, 28-21 (C)
1948—Cardinals, 21-14 (C)
    **Eagles, 7-0 (P)
1949—Eagles, 28-3 (P)
1950—Eagles, 45-7 (C)
    Cardinals, 14-10 (P)
1951—Eagles, 17-14 (C)
1952—Eagles, 10-7 (P)
    Cardinals, 28-22 (C)
1953—Eagles, 56-17 (C)
    Eagles, 38-0 (P)
1954—Eagles, 35-16 (C)
    Eagles, 30-14 (P)

1955—Tie, 24-24 (C)
    Eagles, 27-3 (P)
1956—Cardinals, 20-6 (P)
    Cardinals, 28-17 (C)
1957—Eagles, 38-21 (C)
    Cardinals, 31-27 (P)
1958—Tie, 21-21 (C)
    Eagles, 49-21 (P)
1959—Eagles, 28-24 (Minn)
    Eagles, 27-17 (P)
1960—Eagles, 31-27 (P)
    Eagles, 20-6 (StL)
1961—Cardinals, 30-27 (P)
    Eagles, 20-7 (StL)
1962—Cardinals, 27-21 (P)
    Cardinals, 45-35 (StL)
1963—Cardinals, 28-24 (P)
    Cardinals, 38-14 (StL)
1964—Cardinals, 38-13 (P)
    Cardinals, 36-34 (StL)
1965—Eagles, 34-27 (P)
    Eagles, 28-24 (StL)
1966—Cardinals, 16-13 (StL)
    Cardinals, 41-10 (P)
1967—Eagles, 48-14 (StL)
1968—Cardinals, 45-17 (P)
1969—Eagles, 34-30 (StL)
1970—Cardinals, 35-20 (P)
    Cardinals, 23-14 (StL)
1971—Eagles, 37-20 (StL)
    Eagles, 19-7 (P)
1972—Tie, 6-6 (P)
    Cardinals, 24-23 (StL)
1973—Cardinals, 34-23 (P)
    Eagles, 27-24 (StL)
1974—Cardinals, 7-3 (StL)
    Cardinals, 13-3 (P)
1975—Cardinals, 31-20 (StL)
    Cardinals, 24-23 (P)
1976—Cardinals, 33-14 (StL)
    Cardinals, 17-14 (P)
1977—Cardinals, 21-17 (P)
    Cardinals, 21-16 (StL)
1978—Cardinals, 16-10 (P)
    Eagles, 14-10 (StL)
1979—Eagles, 24-20 (StL)
    Eagles, 16-13 (P)
1980—Cardinals, 24-14 (StL)
    Eagles, 17-3 (P)
1981—Eagles, 52-10 (StL)
    Eagles, 38-0 (P)
1982—Cardinals, 23-20 (P)
1983—Cardinals, 14-11 (P)
    Cardinals, 31-7 (StL)
1984—Cardinals, 34-14 (P)
    Cardinals, 17-16 (StL)
1985—Eagles, 30-7 (P)
    Eagles, 24-14 (StL)
1986—Cardinals, 13-10 (StL)
    Tie, 10-10 (P) OT
1987—Eagles, 28-23 (StL)
    Cardinals, 31-19 (P)
1988—Eagles, 31-21 (P)
    Eagles, 23-17 (Phx)
1989—Eagles, 17-5 (Phx)
    Eagles, 31-14 (P)
1990—Cardinals, 23-21 (P)
    Eagles, 23-21 (Phx)
1991—Cardinals, 26-10 (P)
    Eagles, 34-14 (Phx)

1992—Eagles, 31-14 (Phx)
Eagles, 7-3 (P)
1993—Eagles, 23-17 (P)
Cardinals, 16-3 (Phx)
1994—Eagles, 17-7 (P)
Cardinals, 12-6 (A)
1995—Eagles, 31-19 (A)
Eagles, 21-20 (P)
1996—Cardinals, 36-30 (A)
Eagles, 29-19 (P)
1997—Eagles, 13-10 (P) OT
Cardinals, 31-21 (A)
1998—Cardinals, 17-3 (A)
Cardinals, 20-17 (P) OT
1999—Cardinals, 25-24 (P)
Cardinals, 21-17 (A)
2000—Eagles, 33-14 (A)
Eagles, 34-9 (P)
2001—Cardinals, 21-20 (P)
Eagles, 21-7 (A)
2002—Eagles, 38-14 (P)
2005—Cardinals, 27-21 (A)
(RS Pts.—Eagles 2,340, Cardinals 2,133)
(PS Pts.—Eagles 28, Cardinals 28)
*Franchise known as Phoenix prior to
1994, in St. Louis prior to 1988,
and in Chicago prior to 1960
**NFL Championship
**ARIZONA vs. **PITTSBURGH*
RS: Steelers lead series, 31-22-3
1933—Pirates, 14-13 (C)
1935—Pirates, 17-13 (P)
1936—Cardinals, 14-6 (C)
1937—Cardinals, 13-7 (P)
1939—Cardinals, 10-0 (P)
1940—Tie, 7-7 (P)
1942—Steelers, 19-3 (P)
1945—Steelers, 23-0 (P)
1946—Steelers, 14-7 (P)
1948—Cardinals, 24-7 (P)
1950—Steelers, 28-17 (C)
Steelers, 28-7 (P)
1951—Steelers, 28-14 (C)
1952—Steelers, 34-28 (C)
Steelers, 17-14 (P)
1953—Steelers, 31-28 (P)
Steelers, 21-17 (C)
1954—Cardinals, 17-14 (C)
Steelers, 20-17 (P)
1955—Steelers, 14-7 (P)
Cardinals, 27-13 (C)
1956—Steelers, 14-7 (P)
Cardinals, 38-27 (C)
1957—Steelers, 29-20 (Phx)
Steelers, 27-2 (C)
1958—Steelers, 27-20 (C)
Steelers, 38-21 (P)
1959—Cardinals, 45-24 (C)
Steelers, 35-20 (P)
1960—Steelers, 27-14 (P)
Cardinals, 38-7 (StL)
1961—Steelers, 30-27 (P)
Cardinals, 20-0 (StL)
1962—Steelers, 26-17 (StL)
Steelers, 19-7 (P)
1963—Steelers, 23-10 (P)
Cardinals, 24-23 (StL)
1964—Cardinals, 34-30 (StL)
Cardinals, 21-20 (P)
1965—Cardinals, 20-7 (P)

Cardinals, 21-17 (StL)
1966—Steelers, 30-9 (P)
Cardinals, 6-3 (StL)
1967—Cardinals, 28-14 (P)
Tie, 14-14 (StL)
1968—Tie, 28-28 (StL)
Cardinals, 20-10 (P)
1969—Cardinals, 27-14 (P)
Cardinals, 47-10 (StL)
1972—Steelers, 25-19 (StL)
1979—Steelers, 24-21 (StL)
1985—Steelers, 23-10 (P)
1988—Cardinals, 31-14 (Phx)
1994—Cardinals, 20-17 (A) OT
1997—Steelers, 26-20 (A) OT
2003—Steelers, 28-15 (P)
(RS Pts.—Steelers 1,092, Cardinals 1,038)
*Franchise known as Phoenix prior to
1994, in St. Louis prior to 1988,
and in Chicago prior to 1960
**Steelers known as Pirates prior to 1941
**ARIZONA vs. **ST. LOUIS*
RS: Rams lead series, 29-23-2
PS: Rams lead series, 1-0
1937—Cardinals, 6-0 (Clev)
Cardinals, 13-7 (Chi)
1938—Cardinals, 7-6 (Clev)
Cardinals, 31-17 (Chi)
1939—Rams, 24-0 (Chi)
Rams, 14-0 (Clev)
1940—Rams, 26-14 (Clev)
Cardinals, 17-7 (Chi)
1941—Rams, 10-6 (Clev)
Cardinals, 7-0 (Chi)
1942—Cardinals, 7-0 (Buffalo)
Rams, 7-3 (Clev)
1945—Rams, 21-0 (Clev)
Rams, 35-21 (Chi)
1946—Cardinals, 34-10 (Chi)
Rams, 17-14 (LA)
1947—Rams, 27-7 (LA)
Cardinals, 17-10 (Chi)
1948—Cardinals, 27-22 (LA)
Cardinals, 27-24 (Chi)
1949—Tie, 28-28 (Chi)
Cardinals, 31-27 (LA)
1951—Rams, 45-21 (LA)
1953—Tie, 24-24 (Chi)
1954—Rams, 28-17 (LA)
1958—Rams, 20-14 (Chi)
1960—Cardinals, 43-21 (LA)
1965—Rams, 27-3 (StL)
1968—Rams, 24-13 (StL)
1970—Rams, 34-13 (LA)
1972—Cardinals, 24-14 (StL)
1975—***Rams, 35-23 (LA)
1976—Cardinals, 30-28 (LA)
1979—Rams, 21-0 (LA)
1980—Rams, 21-13 (StL)
1984—Rams, 16-13 (StL)
1985—Rams, 46-14 (LA)
1986—Rams, 16-10 (StL)
1987—Rams, 27-24 (StL)
1988—Cardinals, 41-27 (LA)
1989—Rams, 37-14 (LA)
1991—Cardinals, 24-14 (LA)
1992—Cardinals, 20-14 (LA)
1993—Cardinals, 38-10 (P)
1994—Rams, 14-12 (LA)
1996—Cardinals, 31-28 (A) OT

1998—Cardinals, 20-17 (StL)
2002—Rams, 27-14 (A)
Rams, 30-28 (StL)
2003—Rams, 37-13 (StL)
Rams, 30-27 (A) OT
2004—Rams, 17-10 (StL)
Cardinals, 31-7 (A)
2005—Rams, 17-12 (A)
Cardinals, 38-28 (StL)
(RS Pts.—Rams 1,105, Cardinals 966)
(PS Pts.—Rams 35, Cardinals 23)
*Franchise known as Phoenix prior to
1994, in St. Louis prior to 1988,
and in Chicago prior to 1960
**Franchise in Los Angeles prior to 1995
and in Cleveland prior to 1946
***NFC Divisional Playoff
**ARIZONA vs. SAN DIEGO*
RS: Chargers lead series, 7-3
1971—Chargers, 20-17 (SD)
1976—Chargers, 43-24 (SD)
1983—Cardinals, 44-14 (StL)
1987—Chargers, 28-24 (SD)
1989—Chargers, 24-13 (P)
1992—Chargers, 27-21 (P)
1995—Chargers, 28-25 (SD)
1998—Cardinals, 16-13 (A)
2001—Cardinals, 20-17 (SD)
2002—Chargers, 23-15 (A)
(RS Pts.—Chargers 237, Cardinals 219)
*Franchise known as Phoenix prior to
1994, in St. Louis prior to 1988,
**ARIZONA vs. SAN FRANCISCO*
RS: 49ers lead series, 17-12
1951—Cardinals, 27-21 (SF)
1957—Cardinals, 20-10 (SF)
1962—49ers, 24-17 (StL)
1964—Cardinals, 23-13 (SF)
1968—49ers, 35-17 (SF)
1971—49ers, 26-14 (StL)
1974—Cardinals, 34-9 (SF)
1976—Cardinals, 23-20 (StL) OT
1978—Cardinals, 16-10 (SF)
1979—Cardinals, 13-10 (StL)
1980—49ers, 24-21 (SF) OT
1982—49ers, 31-20 (StL)
1983—49ers, 42-27 (StL)
1986—49ers, 43-17 (SF)
1987—49ers, 34-28 (SF)
1988—Cardinals, 24-23 (P)
1991—49ers, 14-10 (SF)
1992—Cardinals, 24-14 (P)
1993—49ers, 28-14 (SF)
1999—49ers, 24-10 (A)
2000—49ers, 27-20 (SF)
2002—49ers, 38-28 (SF)
49ers, 17-14 (A)
2003—Cardinals, 16-13 (A) OT
49ers, 50-14 (SF)
2004—49ers, 31-28 (SF) OT
49ers, 31-28 (A) OT
2005—Cardinals, 31-14 (Mex. City)
Cardinals, 17-10 (SF)
(RS Pts.—49ers 686, Cardinals 595)
*Franchise known as Phoenix prior to
1994, in St. Louis prior to 1988,
and in Chicago prior to 1960
**ARIZONA vs. SEATTLE*
RS: Series tied, 7-7
1976—Cardinals, 30-24 (S)

1983—Cardinals, 33-28 (StL)
1989—Cardinals, 34-24 (S)
1993—Cardinals, 30-27 (S) OT
1995—Cardinals, 20-14 (A) OT
1998—Seahawks, 33-14 (S)
2002—Cardinals, 24-13 (S)
    Seahawks, 27-6 (A)
2003—Seahawks, 38-0 (A)
    Seahawks, 28-10 (S)
2004—Cardinals, 25-17 (A)
    Seahawks, 24-21 (S)
2005—Seahawks, 37-12 (S)
    Seahawks, 33-19 (A)
(RS Pts.—Seahawks 367, Cardinals 278)
*Franchise known as Phoenix prior to
1994 and in St. Louis prior to 1988*
*ARIZONA vs. TAMPA BAY
RS: Cardinals lead series, 8-7
1977—Buccaneers, 17-7 (TB)
1981—Buccaneers, 20-10 (TB)
1983—Cardinals, 34-27 (TB)
1985—Buccaneers, 16-0 (TB)
1986—Cardinals, 30-19 (TB)
    Cardinals, 21-17 (StL)
1987—Cardinals, 31-28 (StL)
    Cardinals, 31-14 (TB)
1988—Cardinals, 30-24 (TB)
1989—Buccaneers, 14-13 (P)
1992—Buccaneers, 23-7 (TB)
    Buccaneers, 7-3 (P)
1996—Cardinals, 13-9 (A)
1997—Buccaneers, 19-18 (TB)
2004—Cardinals, 12-7 (A)
(RS Pts.—Buccaneers 261, Cardinals 260)
*Franchise known as Phoenix prior to
1994 and in St. Louis prior to 1988*
*ARIZONA vs. **TENNESSEE
RS: Cardinals lead series, 5-3
1970—Cardinals, 44-0 (StL)
1974—Cardinals, 31-27 (H)
1979—Cardinals, 24-17 (H)
1985—Oilers, 20-10 (StL)
1988—Oilers, 38-20 (H)
1994—Cardinals, 30-12 (H)
1997—Oilers, 41-14 (H)
2005—Cardinals, 20-10 (A)
(RS Pts.—Cardinals 193, Titans 165)
*Franchise known as Phoenix prior to
1994 and in St. Louis prior to 1988*
**Franchise in Houston prior to 1997;
known as Oilers prior to 1999*
*ARIZONA vs. **WASHINGTON
RS: Redskins lead series, 71-44-2
1932—Cardinals, 9-0 (B)
    Braves, 8-6 (C)
1933—Redskins, 10-0 (C)
    Tie, 0-0 (B)
1934—Redskins, 9-0 (B)
1935—Cardinals, 6-0 (B)
1936—Redskins, 13-10 (B)
1937—Cardinals, 21-14 (W)
1939—Redskins, 28-7 (W)
1940—Redskins, 28-21 (W)
1942—Redskins, 28-0 (W)
1943—Redskins, 13-7 (W)
1945—Redskins, 24-21 (W)
1947—Redskins, 45-21 (W)
1949—Cardinals, 38-7 (C)
1950—Cardinals, 38-28 (W)
1951—Redskins, 7-3 (C)

    Redskins, 20-17 (W)
1952—Redskins, 23-7 (C)
    Cardinals, 17-6 (W)
1953—Redskins, 24-13 (C)
    Redskins, 28-17 (W)
1954—Cardinals, 38-16 (C)
    Redskins, 37-20 (W)
1955—Cardinals, 24-10 (W)
    Redskins, 31-0 (C)
1956—Cardinals, 31-3 (W)
    Redskins, 17-14 (C)
1957—Redskins, 37-14 (C)
    Cardinals, 44-14 (W)
1958—Cardinals, 37-10 (C)
    Redskins, 45-31 (W)
1959—Cardinals, 49-21 (C)
    Redskins, 23-14 (W)
1960—Cardinals, 44-7 (StL)
    Cardinals, 26-14 (W)
1961—Cardinals, 24-0 (W)
    Cardinals, 38-24 (StL)
1962—Redskins, 24-14 (W)
    Tie, 17-17 (StL)
1963—Cardinals, 21-7 (W)
    Cardinals, 24-20 (StL)
1964—Cardinals, 23-17 (W)
    Cardinals, 38-24 (StL)
1965—Cardinals, 37-16 (W)
    Redskins, 24-20 (StL)
1966—Cardinals, 23-7 (StL)
    Redskins, 26-20 (W)
1967—Cardinals, 27-21 (W)
1968—Cardinals, 41-14 (StL)
1969—Redskins, 33-17 (W)
1970—Cardinals, 27-17 (StL)
    Redskins, 28-27 (W)
1971—Redskins, 24-17 (StL)
    Redskins, 20-0 (W)
1972—Redskins, 24-10 (W)
    Redskins, 33-3 (StL)
1973—Cardinals, 34-27 (StL)
    Redskins, 31-13 (W)
1974—Cardinals, 17-10 (W)
    Cardinals, 23-20 (StL)
1975—Redskins, 27-17 (W)
    Cardinals, 20-17 (StL) OT
1976—Redskins, 20-10 (W)
    Redskins, 16-10 (StL)
1977—Redskins, 24-14 (W)
    Redskins, 26-20 (StL)
1978—Redskins, 28-10 (StL)
    Cardinals, 27-17 (W)
1979—Redskins, 17-7 (StL)
    Redskins, 30-28 (W)
1980—Redskins, 23-0 (W)
    Redskins, 31-7 (StL)
1981—Cardinals, 40-30 (StL)
    Redskins, 42-21 (W)
1982—Redskins, 12-7 (StL)
    Redskins, 28-0 (W)
1983—Redskins, 38-14 (StL)
    Redskins, 45-7 (W)
1984—Cardinals, 26-24 (StL)
    Redskins, 29-27 (W)
1985—Redskins, 27-10 (W)
    Redskins, 27-16 (StL)
1986—Redskins, 28-21 (W)
    Redskins, 20-17 (StL)
1987—Redskins, 28-21 (W)
    Redskins, 34-17 (StL)

1988—Cardinals, 30-21 (P)
    Redskins, 33-17 (W)
1989—Redskins, 30-28 (W)
    Redskins, 29-10 (P)
1990—Redskins, 31-0 (W)
    Redskins, 38-10 (P)
1991—Redskins, 34-0 (W)
    Redskins, 20-14 (P)
1992—Cardinals, 27-24 (P)
    Redskins, 41-3 (W)
1993—Cardinals, 17-10 (W)
    Cardinals, 36-6 (P)
1994—Cardinals, 19-16 (W) OT
    Cardinals, 17-15 (A)
1995—Redskins, 27-7 (W)
    Cardinals, 24-20 (A)
1996—Cardinals, 37-34 (W) OT
    Cardinals, 27-26 (A)
1997—Redskins, 19-13 (W) OT
    Redskins, 38-28 (A)
1998—Cardinals, 29-27 (A)
    Cardinals, 45-42 (W)
1999—Redskins, 24-10 (A)
    Redskins, 28-3 (W)
2000—Cardinals, 16-15 (A)
    Redskins, 20-3 (W)
2001—Redskins, 20-10 (A)
    Redskins, 20-17 (W)
2002—Redskins, 31-23 (W)
2005—Redskins, 17-13 (A)
(RS Pts.—Redskins 2,600, Cardinals 2,167)
*Franchise known as Phoenix prior to
1994, in St. Louis prior to 1988,
and in Chicago prior to 1960*
**Franchise in Boston prior to 1937 and
known as Braves prior to 1933*

ATLANTA vs. ARIZONA
RS: Cardinals lead series, 13-9;
See Arizona vs. Atlanta
ATLANTA vs. BALTIMORE
RS: Series tied, 1-1
1999—Ravens, 19-13 (A) OT
2002—Falcons, 20-17 (A)
(RS Pts.—Ravens 36, Falcons 33)
ATLANTA vs. BUFFALO
RS: Falcons lead series, 5-4
1973—Bills, 17-6 (A)
1977—Bills, 3-0 (B)
1980—Falcons, 30-14 (B)
1983—Falcons, 31-14 (A)
1989—Falcons, 30-28 (A)
1992—Bills, 41-14 (B)
1995—Bills, 23-17 (B)
2001—Falcons, 33-30 (A)
2005—Falcons, 24-16 (B)
(RS Pts.—Bills 186, Falcons 185)
ATLANTA vs. CAROLINA
RS: Falcons lead series, 14-8
1995—Falcons, 23-20 (A) OT
    Panthers, 21-17 (C)
1996—Panthers, 29-6 (C)
    Falcons, 20-17 (A)
1997—Panthers, 9-6 (A)
    Panthers, 21-12 (C)
1998—Falcons, 19-14 (A)
    Falcons, 51-23 (A)
1999—Falcons, 27-20 (A)
    Panthers, 34-28 (C)
2000—Falcons, 15-10 (C)

Falcons, 13-12 (A)
2001—Falcons, 24-16 (A)
Falcons, 10-7 (C)
2002—Falcons, 30-0 (A)
Falcons, 41-0 (C)
2003—Panthers, 23-3 (C)
Falcons, 20-14 (A) OT
2004—Falcons, 27-10 (A)
Falcons, 34-31 (A) OT
2005—Panthers, 24-6 (C)
Panthers, 44-11 (A)
(RS Pts.—Falcons 443, Panthers 399)

ATLANTA vs. CHICAGO
RS: Bears lead series, 12-10
1966—Bears, 23-6 (C)
1967—Bears, 23-14 (A)
1968—Falcons, 16-13 (C)
1969—Falcons, 48-31 (A)
1970—Bears, 23-14 (A)
1972—Falcons, 37-21 (C)
1973—Falcons, 46-6 (A)
1974—Falcons, 13-10 (A)
1976—Falcons, 10-0 (C)
1977—Falcons, 16-10 (C)
1978—Bears, 13-7 (C)
1980—Falcons, 28-17 (A)
1983—Falcons, 20-17 (C)
1985—Bears, 36-0 (A)
1986—Bears, 13-10 (A)
1990—Bears, 30-24 (C)
1992—Bears, 41-31 (C)
1993—Bears, 6-0 (C)
1998—Falcons, 20-13 (A)
2001—Bears, 31-3 (A)
2002—Bears, 14-13 (A)
2005—Bears, 16-3 (C)
(RS Pts.—Bears 407, Falcons 379)

ATLANTA vs. CINCINNATI
RS: Bengals lead series, 7-3
1971—Falcons, 9-6 (C)
1975—Bengals, 21-14 (A)
1978—Bengals, 37-7 (C)
1981—Bengals, 30-28 (A)
1984—Bengals, 35-14 (C)
1987—Bengals, 16-10 (A)
1990—Falcons, 38-17 (A)
1993—Bengals, 21-17 (C)
1996—Bengals, 41-31 (C)
2002—Falcons, 30-3 (A)
(RS Pts.—Bengals 227, Falcons 198)

ATLANTA vs. CLEVELAND
RS: Browns lead series, 9-2
1966—Browns, 49-17 (A)
1968—Browns, 30-7 (C)
1971—Falcons, 31-14 (C)
1976—Browns, 20-17 (A)
1978—Browns, 24-16 (A)
1981—Browns, 28-17 (C)
1984—Browns, 23-7 (A)
1987—Browns, 38-3 (C)
1990—Browns, 13-10 (C)
1993—Falcons, 17-14 (A)
2002—Browns, 24-16 (C)
(RS Pts.—Browns 277, Falcons 158)

ATLANTA vs. DALLAS
RS: Cowboys lead series, 12-8
PS: Cowboys lead series, 2-0
1966—Cowboys, 47-14 (A)
1967—Cowboys, 37-7 (D)
1969—Cowboys, 24-17 (A)

1970—Cowboys, 13-0 (D)
1974—Cowboys, 24-0 (A)
1976—Falcons, 17-10 (A)
1978—*Cowboys, 27-20 (D)
1980—*Cowboys, 30-27 (A)
1985—Cowboys, 24-10 (D)
1986—Falcons, 37-35 (D)
1987—Falcons, 21-10 (D)
1988—Cowboys, 26-20 (D)
1989—Falcons 27-21 (A)
1990—Falcons, 26-7 (A)
1991—Cowboys, 31-27 (D)
1992—Cowboys, 41-17 (A)
1993—Falcons, 27-14 (A)
1995—Cowboys, 28-13 (A)
1996—Cowboys, 32-28 (D)
1999—Cowboys, 24-7 (D)
2001—Falcons, 20-13 (A)
2003—Falcons, 27-13 (D)
(RS Pts.—Cowboys 474, Falcons 362)
(PS Pts.—Cowboys 57, Falcons 47)
NFC Divisional Playoff

ATLANTA vs. DENVER
RS: Broncos lead series, 7-4
PS: Broncos lead series, 1-0
1970—Broncos, 24-10 (D)
1972—Falcons, 23-20 (A)
1975—Falcons, 35-21 (A)
1979—Broncos, 20-17 (A) OT
1982—Falcons, 34-27 (D)
1985—Broncos, 44-28 (A)
1988—Broncos, 30-14 (D)
1994—Broncos, 32-28 (D)
1997—Broncos, 29-21 (A)
1998—*Broncos, 34-19 (Miami)
2000—Broncos, 42-14 (D)
2004—Falcons, 41-28 (D)
(RS Pts.—Broncos 317, Falcons 265)
(PS Pts.—Broncos 34, Falcons 19)
Super Bowl XXXIII

ATLANTA vs. DETROIT
RS: Lions lead series, 22-9
1966—Lions, 28-10 (D)
1967—Lions, 24-3 (D)
1968—Lions, 24-7 (A)
1969—Lions, 27-21 (D)
1971—Lions, 41-38 (D)
1972—Lions, 26-23 (A)
1973—Lions, 31-6 (D)
1975—Lions, 17-14 (A)
1976—Lions, 24-10 (D)
1977—Falcons, 17-6 (A)
1978—Falcons, 14-0 (A)
1979—Lions, 24-23 (D)
1980—Falcons, 43-28 (A)
1983—Falcons, 30-14 (D)
1984—Lions, 27-24 (A) OT
1985—Lions, 28-27 (A)
1986—Falcons, 20-6 (D)
1987—Lions, 30-13 (A)
1988—Lions, 31-17 (D)
1989—Lions, 31-24 (A)
1990—Lions, 21-14 (D)
1993—Lions, 30-13 (D)
1994—Lions, 31-28 (D) OT
1995—Falcons, 34-22 (A)
1996—Lions, 28-24 (D)
1997—Lions, 28-17 (D)
1998—Falcons, 24-17 (A)
2000—Lions, 13-10 (D)

2002—Falcons, 36-15 (A)
2004—Lions, 17-10 (A)
2005—Falcons, 27-7 (D)
(RS Pts.—Lions 696, Falcons 621)

ATLANTA vs. GREEN BAY
RS: Packers lead series, 12-10
PS: Series tied, 1-1
1966—Packers, 56-3 (Mil)
1967—Packers, 23-0 (Mil)
1968—Packers, 38-7 (A)
1969—Packers, 28-10 (GB)
1970—Packers, 27-24 (GB)
1971—Falcons, 28-21 (A)
1972—Falcons, 10-9 (Mil)
1974—Falcons, 10-3 (A)
1975—Packers, 22-13 (GB)
1976—Packers, 24-20 (A)
1979—Falcons, 25-7 (A)
1981—Falcons, 31-17 (GB)
1982—Packers, 38-7 (A)
1983—Falcons, 47-41 (A) OT
1988—Falcons, 20-0 (A)
1989—Packers, 23-21 (Mil)
1991—Falcons, 35-31 (A)
1992—Falcons, 24-10 (A)
1994—Packers, 21-17 (Mil)
1995—*Packers, 37-20 (GB)
2001—Falcons, 23-20 (GB)
2002—Packers, 37-34 (GB) OT
*Falcons, 27-7 (GB)
2005—Packers, 33-25 (A)
(RS Pts.—Packers 529, Falcons 434)
(PS Pts.—Falcons 47, Packers 44)
NFC First-Round Playoff

ATLANTA vs. HOUSTON
RS: Texans lead series, 1-0
2003—Texans, 17-13 (H)
(RS Pts.—Texans 17, Falcons 13)

ATLANTA vs. *INDIANAPOLIS
RS: Colts lead series, 12-1
1966—Colts, 19-7 (A)
1967—Colts, 38-31 (B)
Colts, 49-7 (A)
1968—Colts, 28-20 (A)
Colts, 44-0 (B)
1969—Colts, 21-14 (A)
Colts, 13-6 (B)
1974—Colts, 17-7 (A)
1986—Colts, 28-23 (A)
1989—Colts, 13-9 (I)
1998—Falcons, 28-21 (A)
2001—Colts, 41-27 (I)
2003—Colts, 38-7 (I)
(RS Pts.—Colts 370, Falcons 186)
Franchise in Baltimore prior to 1984

ATLANTA vs. JACKSONVILLE
RS: Jaguars lead series, 2-1
1996—Jaguars, 19-17 (J)
1999—Jaguars, 30-7 (A)
2003—Falcons, 21-14 (A)
(RS Pts.—Jaguars 63, Falcons 45)

ATLANTA vs. KANSAS CITY
RS: Chiefs lead series, 5-1
1972—Chiefs, 17-14 (A)
1985—Chiefs, 38-10 (KC)
1991—Chiefs, 14-3 (KC)
1994—Chiefs, 30-10 (A)
2000—Falcons, 29-13 (A)
2004—Chiefs, 56-10 (KC)
(RS Pts.—Chiefs 168, Falcons 76)

ATLANTA vs. MIAMI
RS: Dolphins lead series, 7-3
1970—Dolphins, 20-7 (A)
1974—Dolphins, 42-7 (M)
1980—Dolphins, 20-17 (A)
1983—Dolphins, 31-24 (M)
1986—Falcons, 20-14 (M)
1992—Dolphins, 21-17 (M)
1995—Dolphins, 21-20 (M)
1998—Falcons, 38-16 (A)
2001—Dolphins, 21-14 (M)
2005—Falcons, 17-10 (M)
(RS Pts.—Dolphins 216, Falcons 181)
ATLANTA vs. MINNESOTA
RS: Vikings lead series, 14-8
PS: Series tied, 1-1
1966—Falcons, 20-13 (M)
1967—Falcons, 21-20 (A)
1968—Vikings, 47-7 (M)
1969—Falcons, 10-3 (A)
1970—Vikings, 37-7 (A)
1971—Vikings, 24-7 (M)
1973—Falcons, 20-14 (A)
1974—Vikings, 23-10 (M)
1975—Vikings, 38-0 (M)
1977—Vikings, 14-7 (A)
1980—Vikings, 24-23 (M)
1981—Vikings, 31-30 (A)
1982—*Vikings, 30-24 (M)
1984—Vikings, 27-20 (M)
1985—Falcons, 14-13 (A)
1987—Vikings, 24-13 (M)
1989—Vikings, 43-17 (M)
1991—Vikings, 20-19 (A)
1996—Vikings, 23-17 (A)
1998—**Falcons, 30-27 (M) OT
1999—Vikings, 17-14 (A)
2002—Falcons, 30-24 (M) OT
2003—Vikings, 39-26 (A)
2005—Falcons, 30-10 (A)
(RS Pts.—Vikings 527, Falcons 363)
(PS Pts.—Vikings 57, Falcons 54)
*NFC First-Round Playoff
**NFC Championship
ATLANTA vs. NEW ENGLAND
RS: Falcons lead series, 6-5
1972—Patriots, 21-20 (NE)
1977—Patriots, 16-10 (A)
1980—Falcons, 37-21 (NE)
1983—Falcons, 24-13 (A)
1986—Patriots, 25-17 (NE)
1989—Falcons, 16-15 (A)
1992—Falcons, 34-0 (A)
1995—Falcons, 30-17 (A)
1998—Falcons, 41-10 (NE)
2001—Patriots, 24-10 (A)
2005—Patriots, 31-28 (A)
(RS Pts.—Falcons 267, Patriots 193)
ATLANTA vs. NEW ORLEANS
RS: Falcons lead series, 43-30
PS: Falcons lead series, 1-0
1967—Saints, 27-24 (NO)
1969—Falcons, 45-17 (A)
1970—Falcons, 14-3 (NO)
Falcons, 32-14 (A)
1971—Falcons, 28-6 (A)
Falcons, 24-20 (NO)
1972—Falcons, 21-14 (NO)
Falcons, 36-20 (A)
1973—Falcons, 62-7 (NO)

Falcons, 14-10 (A)
1974—Saints, 14-13 (NO)
Saints, 13-3 (A)
1975—Falcons, 14-7 (A)
Saints, 23-7 (NO)
1976—Saints, 30-0 (NO)
Falcons, 23-20 (A)
1977—Saints, 21-20 (NO)
Falcons, 35-7 (A)
1978—Falcons, 20-17 (NO)
Falcons, 20-17 (A)
1979—Falcons, 40-34 (NO) OT
Saints, 37-6 (A)
1980—Falcons, 41-14 (NO)
Falcons, 31-13 (A)
1981—Falcons, 27-0 (A)
Falcons, 41-10 (NO)
1982—Falcons, 35-0 (A)
Saints, 35-6 (NO)
1983—Saints, 19-17 (A)
Saints, 27-10 (NO)
1984—Falcons, 36-28 (NO)
Saints, 17-13 (A)
1985—Falcons, 31-24 (A)
Falcons, 16-10 (NO)
1986—Falcons, 31-10 (NO)
Saints, 14-9 (A)
1987—Saints, 38-0 (A)
1988—Saints, 29-21 (A)
Saints, 10-9 (NO)
1989—Saints, 20-13 (NO)
Saints, 26-17 (A)
1990—Falcons, 28-27 (A)
Saints, 10-7 (NO)
1991—Saints, 27-6 (A)
Falcons, 23-20 (NO) OT
*Falcons, 27-20 (NO)
1992—Falcons, 10-7 (A)
Saints, 22-14 (NO)
1993—Saints, 34-31 (A)
Falcons, 26-15 (NO)
1994—Saints, 33-32 (NO)
Saints, 29-20 (A)
1995—Falcons, 27-24 (NO) OT
Falcons, 19-14 (A)
1996—Falcons, 17-15 (A)
Falcons, 31-15 (NO)
1997—Falcons, 23-17 (NO)
Falcons, 20-3 (A)
1998—Falcons, 31-23 (A)
Falcons, 27-17 (NO)
1999—Falcons, 20-17 (NO)
Falcons, 35-12 (A)
2000—Saints, 21-19 (A)
Saints, 23-7 (NO)
2001—Falcons, 20-13 (NO)
Saints, 28-10 (A)
2002—Falcons, 37-35 (NO)
Falcons, 24-17 (A)
2003—Saints, 45-17 (A)
Saints, 23-20 (NO)
2004—Falcons, 24-21 (A)
Saints, 26-13 (NO)
2005—Falcons, 34-31 (San Antonio)
Falcons, 36-17 (A)
(RS Pts.—Falcons 1,610, Saints 1,406)
(PS Pts.—Falcons 27, Saints 20)
*NFC First-Round Playoff
ATLANTA vs. N.Y. GIANTS
RS: Falcons lead series, 10-7

1966—Falcons, 27-16 (NY)
1968—Falcons, 24-21 (A)
1971—Giants, 21-17 (A)
1974—Falcons, 14-7 (New Haven)
1977—Falcons, 17-3 (A)
1978—Falcons, 23-20 (A)
1979—Giants, 24-3 (NY)
1981—Giants, 27-24 (A) OT
1982—Falcons, 16-14 (NY)
1983—Giants, 16-13 (A) OT
1984—Giants, 19-7 (A)
1988—Giants, 23-16 (A)
1998—Falcons, 34-20 (NY)
2000—Giants, 13-6 (A)
2002—Falcons, 17-10 (NY)
2003—Falcons, 27-7 (NY)
2004—Falcons, 14-10 (NY)
(RS Pts.—Falcons 299, Giants 271)
ATLANTA vs. N.Y. JETS
RS: Falcons lead series, 5-4
1973—Falcons, 28-20 (NY)
1980—Jets, 14-7 (A)
1983—Falcons, 27-21 (NY)
1986—Jets, 28-14 (A)
1989—Jets, 27-7 (NY)
1992—Falcons, 20-17 (A)
1995—Falcons, 13-3 (NY)
1998—Jets, 28-3 (NY)
2005—Falcons, 27-14 (A)
(RS Pts.—Jets 172, Falcons 146)
ATLANTA vs. *OAKLAND
RS: Raiders lead series, 7-4
1971—Falcons, 24-13 (A)
1975—Raiders, 37-34 (O) OT
1979—Raiders, 50-19 (O)
1982—Falcons, 38-14 (A)
1985—Raiders, 34-24 (A)
1988—Falcons, 12-6 (LA)
1991—Falcons, 21-17 (A)
1994—Raiders, 30-17 (LA)
1997—Raiders, 36-31 (A)
2000—Raiders, 41-14 (O)
2004—Falcons, 35-10 (A)
(RS Pts.—Raiders 312, Falcons 245)
*Franchise in Los Angeles from 1982-1994
ATLANTA vs. PHILADELPHIA
RS: Eagles lead series, 11-10-1
PS: Eagles lead series, 2-1
1966—Eagles, 23-10 (P)
1967—Eagles, 38-7 (A)
1969—Falcons, 27-3 (P)
1970—Tie, 13-13 (P)
1973—Falcons, 44-27 (P)
1976—Eagles, 14-13 (A)
1978—*Falcons, 14-13 (A)
1979—Falcons, 14-10 (P)
1980—Falcons, 20-17 (P)
1981—Eagles, 16-13 (P)
1983—Eagles, 28-24 (A)
1984—Falcons, 26-10 (A)
1985—Eagles, 23-17 (P) OT
1986—Eagles, 16-0 (A)
1988—Falcons, 27-24 (P)
1990—Eagles, 24-23 (A)
1994—Falcons, 28-21 (A)
1996—Eagles, 33-18 (A)
1997—Falcons, 20-17 (A)
1998—Falcons, 17-12 (A)
2000—Eagles, 38-10 (P)
2002—**Eagles, 20-6 (P)

2003—Eagles, 23-16 (A)
2004—***Eagles, 27-10 (P)
2005—Falcons, 14-10 (A)
(RS Pts.—Eagles 440, Falcons 401)
(PS Pts.—Eagles 60, Falcons 30)
*NFC First-Round Playoff
**NFC Divisional Playoff
***NFC Championship

ATLANTA vs. PITTSBURGH
RS: Steelers lead series, 11-1-1
1966—Steelers, 57-33 (A)
1968—Steelers, 41-21 (A)
1970—Falcons, 27-16 (A)
1974—Steelers, 24-17 (P)
1978—Steelers, 31-7 (P)
1981—Steelers, 34-20 (A)
1984—Steelers, 35-10 (P)
1987—Steelers, 28-12 (A)
1990—Steelers, 21-9 (P)
1993—Steelers, 45-17 (A)
1996—Steelers, 20-17 (A)
1999—Steelers, 13-9 (P)
2002—Tie, 34-34 (P) OT
(RS Pts.—Steelers 399, Falcons 233)

ATLANTA vs. *ST. LOUIS
RS: Rams lead series, 46-24-2
PS: Falcons lead series, 1-0
1966—Rams, 19-14 (A)
1967—Rams, 31-3 (A)
Rams, 20-3 (LA)
1968—Rams, 27-14 (LA)
Rams, 17-10 (A)
1969—Rams, 17-7 (LA)
Rams, 38-6 (A)
1970—Tie, 10-10 (LA)
Rams, 17-7 (A)
1971—Tie, 20-20 (LA)
Rams, 24-16 (A)
1972—Falcons, 31-3 (A)
Rams, 20-7 (LA)
1973—Rams, 31-0 (LA)
Falcons, 15-13 (A)
1974—Rams, 21-0 (A)
Rams, 30-7 (A)
1975—Rams, 22-7 (LA)
Rams, 16-7 (A)
1976—Rams, 30-14 (A)
Rams, 59-0 (LA)
1977—Falcons, 17-6 (A)
Rams, 23-7 (LA)
1978—Rams, 10-0 (LA)
Falcons, 15-7 (A)
1979—Rams, 20-14 (LA)
Rams, 34-13 (A)
1980—Falcons, 13-10 (A)
Rams, 20-17 (LA) OT
1981—Rams, 37-35 (A)
Rams, 21-16 (LA)
1982—Falcons, 34-17 (A)
1983—Rams, 27-21 (LA)
Rams, 36-13 (A)
1984—Falcons, 30-28 (LA)
Rams, 24-10 (A)
1985—Rams, 17-6 (LA)
Falcons, 30-14 (A)
1986—Falcons, 26-14 (A)
Rams, 14-7 (LA)
1987—Falcons, 24-20 (A)
Rams, 33-0 (LA)
1988—Rams, 33-0 (A)

Rams, 22-7 (LA)
1989—Rams, 31-21 (A)
Rams, 26-14 (LA)
1990—Rams, 44-24 (LA)
Falcons, 20-13 (A)
1991—Falcons, 31-14 (A)
Falcons, 31-14 (LA)
1992—Falcons, 30-28 (A)
Rams, 38-27 (LA)
1993—Falcons, 30-24 (A)
Falcons, 13-0 (LA)
1994—Falcons, 31-13 (A)
Falcons, 8-5 (LA)
1995—Rams, 21-19 (StL)
Falcons, 31-6 (A)
1996—Rams, 59-16 (StL)
Rams, 34-27 (A)
1997—Falcons, 34-31 (A)
Falcons, 27-21 (StL)
1998—Falcons, 37-15 (A)
Falcons, 21-10 (StL)
1999—Rams, 35-7 (StL)
Rams, 41-13 (A)
2000—Rams, 41-20 (A)
Rams, 45-29 (StL)
2001—Rams, 35-6 (A)
Rams, 31-13 (StL)
2003—Rams, 36-0 (StL)
2004—Falcons, 34-17 (A)
**Falcons, 47-17 (A)
(RS Pts.—Rams 1,700, Falcons 1,167)
(PS Pts.—Falcons 47, Rams 17)
*Franchise in Los Angeles prior to 1995
**NFC Divisional Playoff

ATLANTA vs. SAN DIEGO
RS: Falcons lead series, 6-1
1973—Falcons, 41-0 (SD)
1979—Falcons, 28-26 (SD)
1988—Chargers, 10-7 (A)
1991—Falcons, 13-10 (SD)
1994—Falcons, 10-9 (A)
1997—Falcons, 14-3 (SD)
2004—Falcons, 21-20 (A)
(RS Pts.—Falcons 134, Chargers 78)

ATLANTA vs. SAN FRANCISCO
RS: 49ers lead series, 44-26-1
PS: Falcons lead series, 1-0
1966—49ers, 44-7 (A)
1967—49ers, 38-7 (SF)
49ers, 34-28 (A)
1968—49ers, 28-13 (SF)
49ers, 14-12 (A)
1969—Falcons, 24-12 (A)
Falcons, 21-7 (SF)
1970—Falcons, 21-20 (A)
49ers, 24-20 (SF)
1971—Falcons, 20-17 (A)
49ers, 24-3 (SF)
1972—49ers, 49-14 (A)
49ers, 20-0 (SF)
1973—49ers, 13-9 (A)
Falcons, 17-3 (SF)
1974—49ers, 16-10 (A)
49ers, 27-0 (SF)
1975—Falcons, 17-3 (SF)
Falcons, 31-9 (A)
1976—49ers, 15-0 (SF)
Falcons, 21-16 (A)
1977—Falcons, 7-0 (SF)
49ers, 10-3 (A)

1978—Falcons, 20-17 (SF)
Falcons, 21-10 (A)
1979—49ers, 20-15 (SF)
Falcons, 31-21 (A)
1980—Falcons, 20-17 (SF)
Falcons, 35-10 (A)
1981—Falcons, 34-17 (A)
49ers, 17-14 (SF)
1982—Falcons, 17-7 (SF)
1983—49ers, 24-20 (SF)
Falcons, 28-24 (A)
1984—49ers, 14-5 (SF)
49ers, 35-17 (A)
1985—49ers, 35-16 (SF)
49ers, 38-17 (A)
1986—Tie, 10-10 (A) OT
49ers, 20-0 (SF)
1987—49ers, 25-17 (A)
49ers, 35-7 (SF)
1988—49ers, 34-17 (SF)
49ers, 13-3 (A)
1989—49ers, 45-3 (SF)
49ers, 23-10 (A)
1990—49ers, 19-13 (SF)
49ers, 45-35 (A)
1991—Falcons, 39-34 (SF)
Falcons, 17-14 (A)
1992—49ers, 56-17 (SF)
49ers, 41-3 (A)
1993—49ers, 37-30 (A)
Falcons, 27-24 (A)
1994—49ers, 42-3 (A)
49ers, 50-14 (SF)
1995—49ers, 41-10 (SF)
Falcons, 28-27 (A)
1996—49ers, 39-17 (SF)
49ers, 34-10 (A)
1997—49ers, 34-7 (SF)
49ers, 35-28 (A)
1998—49ers, 31-20 (SF)
Falcons, 31-19 (A)
*Falcons, 20-18 (A)
1999—49ers, 26-7 (SF)
Falcons, 34-29 (A)
2000—Falcons, 36-28 (A)
49ers, 16-6 (SF)
2001—49ers, 16-13 (SF) OT
49ers, 37-31 (A) OT
2004—Falcons, 21-19 (SF)
(RS Pts.—49ers 1,730, Falcons 1,196)
(PS Pts.—Falcons 20, 49ers 18)
*NFC Divisional Playoff

ATLANTA vs. SEATTLE
RS: Seahawks lead series, 8-2
1976—Seahawks, 30-13 (S)
1979—Seahawks, 31-28 (A)
1985—Seahawks, 30-26 (S)
1988—Seahawks, 31-20 (A)
1991—Falcons, 26-13 (A)
1997—Falcons, 24-17 (S)
2000—Seahawks, 30-10 (A)
2002—Seahawks, 30-24 (A) OT
2004—Seahawks, 28-26 (S)
2005—Seahawks, 21-18 (S)
(RS Pts.—Seahawks 261, Falcons 215)

ATLANTA vs. TAMPA BAY
RS: Buccaneers lead series, 15-10
1977—Falcons, 17-0 (TB)
1978—Buccaneers, 14-9 (TB)
1979—Falcons, 17-14 (A)

ALL-TIME TEAM VS. TEAM RESULTS

1981—Buccaneers, 24-23 (TB)
1984—Buccaneers, 23-6 (TB)
1986—Falcons, 23-20 (TB) OT
1987—Buccaneers, 48-10 (TB)
1988—Falcons, 17-10 (A)
1990—Buccaneers, 23-17 (TB)
1991—Falcons, 43-7 (A)
1992—Falcons, 35-7 (TB)
1993—Buccaneers, 31-24 (A)
1994—Falcons, 34-13 (A)
1995—Falcons, 24-21 (TB)
1997—Buccaneers, 31-10 (A)
1999—Buccaneers, 19-10 (TB)
2000—Buccaneers, 27-14 (A)
2002—Buccaneers, 20-6 (A)
    Buccaneers, 34-10 (TB)
2003—Buccaneers, 31-10 (A)
    Falcons, 30-28 (TB)
2004—Falcons, 24-14 (A)
    Buccaneers, 27-0 (TB)
2005—Buccaneers, 30-27 (A)
    Buccaneers, 27-24 (TB) OT
(RS Pts.—Buccaneers 543, Falcons 464)
ATLANTA vs. *TENNESSEE
RS: Titans lead series, 6-5
1972—Falcons, 20-10 (A)
1976—Oilers, 20-14 (H)
1978—Falcons, 20-14 (A)
1981—Falcons, 31-27 (H)
1984—Falcons, 42-10 (A)
1987—Oilers, 37-33 (H)
1990—Falcons, 47-27 (A)
1993—Oilers, 33-17 (H)
1996—Oilers, 23-13 (A)
1999—Titans, 30-17 (T)
2003—Titans, 38-31 (A)
(RS Pts.—Falcons 285, Titans 269)
*Franchise in Houston prior to 1997;
known as Oilers prior to 1999
ATLANTA vs. WASHINGTON
RS: Redskins lead series, 14-4-1
PS: Redskins lead series, 1-0
1966—Redskins, 33-20 (W)
1967—Tie, 20-20 (A)
1969—Redskins, 27-20 (W)
1972—Redskins, 24-13 (W)
1975—Redskins, 30-27 (A)
1977—Redskins, 10-6 (W)
1978—Falcons, 20-17 (A)
1979—Redskins, 16-7 (A)
1980—Falcons, 10-6 (A)
1983—Redskins, 37-21 (W)
1984—Redskins, 27-14 (W)
1985—Redskins, 44-10 (A)
1987—Falcons, 21-20 (A)
1989—Redskins, 31-30 (A)
1991—Redskins, 56-17 (W)
    *Redskins, 24-7 (W)
1992—Redskins, 24-17 (W)
1993—Redskins, 30-17 (A)
1994—Falcons, 27-20 (W)
2003—Redskins, 33-31 (A)
(RS Pts.—Redskins 505, Falcons 348)
(PS Pts.—Redskins 24, Falcons 7)
*NFC Divisional Playoff

BALTIMORE vs. ARIZONA
RS: Ravens lead series, 2-1;
See Arizona vs. Baltimore

BALTIMORE vs. ATLANTA
RS: Series tied, 1-1;
See Atlanta vs. Baltimore
BALTIMORE vs. BUFFALO
RS: Series tied, 1-1
1999—Bills, 13-10 (Balt)
2004—Ravens, 20-6 (Balt)
(RS Pts.—Ravens 30, Bills 19)
BALTIMORE vs. CAROLINA
RS: Panthers lead series, 2-0
1996—Panthers, 27-16 (C)
2002—Panthers, 10-7 (C)
(RS Pts.—Panthers 37, Ravens 23)
BALTIMORE vs. CHICAGO
RS: Bears lead series, 2-1
1998—Bears, 24-3 (C)
2001—Ravens, 17-6 (B)
2005—Bears, 10-6 (C)
(RS Pts.—Bears 40, Ravens 26)
BALTIMORE vs. CINCINNATI
RS: Ravens lead series, 12-8
1996—Bengals, 24-21 (B)
    Bengals, 21-14 (C)
1997—Ravens, 23-10 (B)
    Bengals, 16-14 (C)
1998—Ravens, 31-24 (B)
    Ravens, 20-13 (C)
1999—Ravens, 34-31 (C)
    Ravens, 22-0 (B)
2000—Ravens, 37-0 (B)
    Ravens, 27-7 (C)
2001—Bengals, 21-10 (B)
    Ravens, 16-0 (B)
2002—Ravens, 38-27 (B)
    Ravens, 27-23 (C)
2003—Bengals, 34-26 (C)
    Ravens, 31-13 (B)
2004—Ravens, 23-9 (C)
    Bengals, 27-26 (B)
2005—Bengals, 21-9 (B)
    Bengals, 42-29 (C)
(RS Pts.—Ravens 478, Bengals 363)
BALTIMORE vs. CLEVELAND
RS: Ravens lead series, 9-5
1999—Ravens, 17-10 (B)
    Ravens, 41-9 (C)
2000—Ravens, 12-0 (C)
    Ravens, 44-7 (B)
2001—Browns, 24-14 (C)
    Browns, 27-17 (B)
2002—Ravens, 26-21 (C)
    Browns, 14-13 (B)
2003—Ravens, 33-13 (B)
    Ravens, 35-0 (C)
2004—Browns, 20-3 (C)
    Ravens, 27-13 (B)
2005—Ravens, 16-3 (B)
    Browns, 20-16 (C)
(RS Pts.—Ravens 314, Browns 181)
BALTIMORE vs. DALLAS
RS: Ravens lead series, 2-0
2000—Ravens, 27-0 (B)
2004—Ravens, 30-10 (B)
(RS Pts.—Ravens 57, Cowboys 10)
BALTIMORE vs. DENVER
RS: Ravens lead series, 3-2
PS: Ravens lead series, 1-0
1996—Broncos, 45-34 (D)
2000—*Ravens, 21-3 (B)
2001—Ravens, 20-13 (D)

2002—Ravens, 34-23 (B)
2003—Ravens, 26-6 (B)
2005—Broncos, 12-10 (D)
(RS Pts.—Ravens 124, Broncos 99)
(PS Pts.—Ravens 21, Broncos 3)
*AFC First-Round Playoff
BALTIMORE vs. DETROIT
RS: Series tied, 1-1
1998—Ravens, 19-10 (B)
2005—Lions, 35-17 (D)
(RS Pts.—Lions 45, Ravens 36)
BALTIMORE vs. GREEN BAY
RS: Packers lead series, 2-1
1998—Packers, 28-10 (GB)
2001—Packers, 31-23 (GB)
2005—Ravens, 48-3 (B)
(RS Pts.—Ravens 81, Packers 62)
BALTIMORE vs. HOUSTON
RS: Ravens lead series, 2-0
2002—Ravens, 23-19 (H)
2005—Ravens, 16-15 (H)
(RS Pts.—Ravens 39, Texans 34)
BALTIMORE vs. INDIANAPOLIS
RS: Colts lead series, 4-2
1996—Colts, 26-21 (I)
1998—Ravens, 38-31 (B)
2001—Ravens, 39-27 (B)
2002—Colts, 22-20 (I)
2004—Colts, 20-10 (I)
2005—Colts, 24-7 (B)
(RS Pts.—Colts 150, Ravens 135)
BALTIMORE vs. JACKSONVILLE
RS: Jaguars lead series, 9-6
1996—Jaguars, 30-27 (J)
    Jaguars, 28-25 (B) OT
1997—Jaguars, 28-27 (B)
    Jaguars, 29-27 (J)
1998—Jaguars, 24-10 (J)
    Jaguars, 45-19 (B)
1999—Jaguars, 6-3 (J)
    Jaguars, 30-23 (B)
2000—Ravens, 39-36 (B)
    Ravens, 15-10 (J)
2001—Ravens, 18-17 (B)
    Ravens, 24-21 (J)
2002—Ravens, 17-10 (B)
2003—Ravens, 24-17 (B)
2005—Jaguars, 30-3 (J)
(RS Pts.—Jaguars 361, Ravens 301)
BALTIMORE vs. KANSAS CITY
RS: Chiefs lead series, 3-0
1999—Chiefs, 35-8 (B)
2003—Chiefs, 17-10 (B)
2004—Chiefs, 27-24 (B)
(RS Pts.—Chiefs 79, Ravens 42)
BALTIMORE vs. MIAMI
RS: Dolphins lead series, 4-1
PS: Ravens lead series, 1-0
1997—Dolphins, 24-13 (B)
2000—Dolphins, 19-6 (M)
2001—*Ravens, 20-3 (M)
2002—Dolphins, 26-7 (M)
2003—Dolphins, 9-6 (M) OT
2004—Ravens, 30-23 (M)
(RS Pts.—Dolphins 101, Ravens 62)
(PS Pts.—Ravens 20, Dolphins 3)
*AFC First-Round Playoff
BALTIMORE vs. MINNESOTA
RS: Ravens lead series, 2-1
1998—Vikings, 38-28 (B)

2001—Ravens, 19-3 (B)
2005—Ravens, 30-23 (B)
(RS Pts.—Ravens 77, Vikings 64)
BALTIMORE vs. NEW ENGLAND
RS: Patriots lead series, 3-0
1996—Patriots, 46-38 (B)
1999—Patriots, 20-3 (NE)
2004—Patriots, 24-3 (NE)
(RS Pts.—Patriots 90, Ravens 44)
BALTIMORE vs. NEW ORLEANS
RS: Ravens lead series, 2-1
1996—Ravens, 17-10 (B)
1999—Ravens, 31-8 (B)
2002—Saints, 37-25 (B)
(RS Pts.—Ravens 73, Saints 55)
BALTIMORE vs. N.Y. GIANTS
RS: Ravens lead series, 2-0
PS: Ravens lead series, 1-0
1997—Ravens, 24-23 (NY)
2000—*Ravens, 34-7 (Tampa)
2004—Ravens, 37-14 (B)
(RS Pts.—Ravens 61, Giants 37)
(PS Pts.—Ravens 34, Giants 7)
*Super Bowl XXXV
BALTIMORE vs. N.Y. JETS
RS: Ravens lead series, 4-1
1997—Jets, 19-16 (NY) OT
1998—Ravens, 24-10 (NY)
2000—Ravens, 34-20 (B)
2004—Ravens, 20-17 (NY) OT
2005—Ravens, 13-3 (B)
(RS Pts.—Ravens 107, Jets 69)
BALTIMORE vs. OAKLAND
RS: Ravens lead series, 2-1
PS: Ravens lead series, 1-0
1996—Ravens, 19-14 (B)
1998—Ravens, 13-10 (B)
2000—*Ravens, 16-3 (O)
2003—Raiders, 20-12 (O)
(RS Pts.—Ravens 44, Raiders 44)
(PS Pts.—Ravens 16, Raiders 3)
*AFC Championship
BALTIMORE vs. PHILADELPHIA
RS: Eagles lead series, 1-0-1
1997—Tie, 10-10 (B) OT
2004—Eagles, 15-10 (P)
(RS Pts.—Eagles 25, Ravens 20)
BALTIMORE vs. PITTSBURGH
RS: Steelers lead series, 13-7
PS: Steelers lead series, 1-0
1996—Steelers, 31-17 (P)
      Ravens, 31-17 (B)
1997—Steelers, 42-34 (B)
      Steelers, 37-0 (P)
1998—Steelers, 20-13 (B)
      Steelers, 16-6 (P)
1999—Steelers, 23-20 (B)
      Ravens, 31-24 (P)
2000—Ravens, 16-0 (P)
      Steelers, 9-6 (B)
2001—Ravens, 13-10 (P)
      Steelers, 26-21 (B)
      *Steelers, 27-10 (P)
2002—Steelers, 31-18 (B)
      Steelers, 34-31 (P)
2003—Steelers, 34-15 (P)
      Ravens, 13-10 (B) OT
2004—Ravens, 30-13 (B)
      Steelers, 20-7 (P)
2005—Steelers, 20-19 (P)

Ravens, 16-13 (B) OT
(RS Pts.—Steelers 430, Ravens 357)
(PS Pts.—Steelers 27, Ravens 10)
*AFC Divisional Playoff
BALTIMORE vs. ST. LOUIS
RS: Rams lead series, 2-1
1996—Ravens, 37-31 (B) OT
1999—Rams, 27-10 (StL)
2003—Rams, 33-22 (StL)
(RS Pts.—Rams 91, Ravens 69)
BALTIMORE vs. SAN DIEGO
RS: Series tied, 2-2
1997—Chargers, 21-17 (SD)
1998—Chargers, 14-13 (SD)
2000—Ravens, 24-3 (B)
2003—Ravens, 24-10 (SD)
(RS Pts.—Ravens 78, Chargers 48)
BALTIMORE vs. SAN FRANCISCO
RS: Series tied, 1-1
1996—49ers, 38-20 (SF)
2003—Ravens, 44-6 (B)
(RS Pts.—Ravens 64, 49ers 44)
BALTIMORE vs. SEATTLE
RS: Ravens lead series, 2-0
1997—Ravens, 31-24 (B)
2003—Ravens, 44-41 (B) OT
(RS Pts.—Ravens 75, Seahawks 65)
BALTIMORE vs. TAMPA BAY
RS: Buccaneers lead series, 2-0
2001—Buccaneers, 22-10 (TB)
2002—Buccaneers, 25-0 (B)
(RS Pts.—Buccaneers 47, Ravens 10)
BALTIMORE vs. *TENNESSEE
RS: Series tied, 7-7
PS: Series tied, 1-1
1996—Oilers, 29-13 (H)
      Oilers, 24-21 (B)
1997—Ravens, 36-10 (T)
      Ravens, 21-19 (B)
1998—Oilers, 12-8 (B)
      Oilers, 16-14 (T)
1999—Titans, 14-11 (T)
      Ravens, 41-14 (B)
2000—Titans, 14-6 (B)
      Ravens, 24-23 (T)
      **Ravens, 24-10 (T)
2001—Ravens, 26-7 (B)
      Ravens, 16-10 (T)
2002—Ravens, 13-12 (B)
2003—***Titans, 20-17 (B)
2005—Titans, 25-10 (T)
(RS Pts.—Ravens 260, Titans 229)
(PS Pts.—Ravens 41, Titans 30)
*Franchise in Houston prior to 1997;
known as Oilers prior to 1999
**AFC Divisional Playoff
***AFC First-Round Playoff
BALTIMORE vs. WASHINGTON
RS: Ravens lead series, 2-1
1997—Ravens, 20-17 (W)
2000—Redskins, 10-3 (W)
2004—Ravens, 17-10 (W)
(RS Pts.—Ravens 40, Redskins 37)

BUFFALO vs. ARIZONA
RS: Bills lead series, 5-3;
See Arizona vs. Buffalo
BUFFALO vs. ATLANTA
RS: Falcons lead series, 5-4;
See Atlanta vs. Buffalo

BUFFALO vs. BALTIMORE
RS: Series tied, 1-1;
See Baltimore vs. Buffalo
BUFFALO vs. CAROLINA
RS: Bills lead series, 3-1
1995—Bills, 31-9 (B)
1998—Bills, 30-14 (C)
2001—Bills, 25-24 (B)
2005—Panthers, 13-9 (B)
(RS Pts.—Bills 95, Panthers 60)
BUFFALO vs. CHICAGO
RS: Bears lead series, 5-4
1970—Bears, 31-13 (C)
1974—Bills, 16-6 (B)
1979—Bears, 7-0 (B)
1988—Bears, 24-3 (C)
1991—Bills, 35-20 (B)
1994—Bears, 20-13 (B)
1997—Bears, 20-3 (C)
2000—Bills, 20-3 (B)
2002—Bills, 33-27 (B) OT
(RS Pts.—Bears 158, Bills 136)
BUFFALO vs. CINCINNATI
RS: Bills lead series, 13-9
PS: Bengals lead series, 2-0
1968—Bengals, 34-23 (C)
1969—Bills, 16-13 (B)
1970—Bengals, 43-14 (B)
1973—Bengals, 16-13 (B)
1975—Bengals, 33-24 (C)
1978—Bills, 5-0 (B)
1979—Bills, 51-24 (B)
1980—Bills, 14-0 (C)
1981—Bengals, 27-24 (C) OT
      *Bengals, 28-21 (C)
1983—Bills, 10-6 (C)
1984—Bengals, 52-21 (C)
1985—Bengals, 23-17 (B)
1986—Bengals, 36-33 (C) OT
1988—Bengals, 35-21 (C)
      **Bengals, 21-10 (C)
1989—Bills, 24-7 (B)
1991—Bills, 35-16 (B)
1996—Bills, 31-17 (B)
1998—Bills, 33-20 (C)
2002—Bills, 27-9 (B)
2003—Bills, 22-16 (B) OT
2004—Bills, 33-17 (C)
2005—Bills, 37-27 (C)
(RS Pts.—Bills 528, Bengals 471)
(PS Pts.—Bengals 49, Bills 31)
*AFC Divisional Playoff
**AFC Championship
BUFFALO vs. CLEVELAND
RS: Browns lead series, 7-5
PS: Browns lead series, 1-0
1972—Browns, 27-10 (C)
1974—Bills, 15-10 (C)
1977—Browns, 27-16 (B)
1978—Bills, 41-20 (C)
1981—Bills, 22-13 (B)
1984—Bills, 13-10 (B)
1985—Browns, 17-7 (C)
1986—Browns, 21-17 (B)
1987—Browns, 27-21 (C)
1989—*Browns, 34-30 (C)
1990—Bills, 42-0 (C)
1995—Bills, 22-19 (C)
2004—Bills, 37-7 (B)
(RS Pts.—Bills 239, Browns 222)

(PS Pts.—Browns 34, Bills 30)
AFC Divisional Playoff

BUFFALO vs. DALLAS
RS: Cowboys lead series, 4-3
PS: Cowboys lead series, 2-0
1971—Cowboys, 49-37 (B)
1976—Cowboys, 17-10 (D)
1981—Cowboys, 27-14 (D)
1984—Bills, 14-3 (B)
1992—*Cowboys, 52-17 (Pasadena)
1993—Bills, 13-10 (D)
    **Cowboys, 30-13 (Atlanta)
1996—Bills, 10-7 (B)
2003—Cowboys, 10-6 (D)
(RS Pts.—Cowboys 123, Bills 104)
(PS Pts.—Cowboys 82, Bills 30)
Super Bowl XXVII
**Super Bowl XXVIII*

BUFFALO vs. DENVER
RS: Bills lead series, 17-14-1
PS: Bills lead series, 1-0
1960—Broncos, 27-21 (B)
    Tie, 38-38 (D)
1961—Broncos, 22-10 (B)
    Bills, 23-10 (D)
1962—Broncos, 23-20 (B)
    Bills, 45-38 (D)
1963—Bills, 30-28 (D)
    Bills, 27-17 (B)
1964—Bills, 30-13 (B)
    Bills, 30-19 (D)
1965—Bills, 30-15 (B)
    Bills, 31-13 (D)
1966—Bills, 38-21 (B)
1967—Bills, 17-16 (D)
    Broncos, 21-20 (B)
1968—Broncos, 34-32 (D)
1969—Bills, 41-28 (D)
1970—Broncos, 25-10 (B)
1975—Bills, 38-14 (B)
1977—Broncos, 26-6 (D)
1979—Broncos, 19-16 (B)
1981—Bills, 9-7 (B)
1984—Broncos, 37-7 (B)
1987—Bills, 21-14 (B)
1989—Broncos, 28-14 (B)
1990—Bills, 29-28 (B)
1991—*Bills, 10-7 (B)
1992—Bills, 27-17 (B)
1994—Bills, 27-20 (B)
1995—Broncos, 22-7 (D)
1997—Broncos, 23-20 (B) OT
2002—Broncos, 28-23 (D)
2005—Broncos, 28-17 (B)
(RS Pts.—Bills 754, Broncos 719)
(PS Pts.—Bills 10, Broncos 7)
AFC Championship

BUFFALO vs. DETROIT
RS: Series tied, 3-3-1
1972—Tie, 21-21 (B)
1976—Lions, 27-14 (D)
1979—Bills, 20-17 (D)
1991—Lions, 17-14 (B) OT
1994—Lions, 35-21 (D)
1997—Bills, 22-13 (B)
2002—Bills, 24-17 (B)
(RS Pts.—Lions 147, Bills 136)

BUFFALO vs. GREEN BAY
RS: Bills lead series, 6-3
1974—Bills, 27-7 (GB)

1979—Bills, 19-12 (B)
1982—Packers, 33-21 (Mil)
1988—Bills, 28-0 (B)
1991—Bills, 34-24 (Mil)
1994—Bills 29-20 (B)
1997—Packers, 31-21 (GB)
2000—Bills 27-18 (B)
2002—Packers, 10-0 (GB)
(RS Pts.—Bills 206, Packers 155)

BUFFALO vs. HOUSTON
RS: Bills lead series, 2-1
2002—Bills, 31-24 (H)
2003—Texans, 12-10 (B)
2005—Bills, 22-7 (B)
(RS Pts.—Bills 63, Texans 43)

BUFFALO vs. *INDIANAPOLIS
RS: Bills lead series, 34-29-1
1970—Tie, 17-17 (Balt)
    Colts, 20-14 (Buff)
1971—Colts, 43-0 (Buff)
    Colts, 24-0 (Balt)
1972—Colts, 17-0 (Buff)
    Colts, 35-7 (Balt)
1973—Bills, 31-13 (Buff)
    Bills, 24-17 (Balt)
1974—Bills, 27-14 (Balt)
    Bills, 6-0 (Buff)
1975—Bills, 38-31 (Balt)
    Colts, 42-35 (Buff)
1976—Colts, 31-13 (Buff)
    Colts, 58-20 (Balt)
1977—Colts, 17-14 (Balt)
    Colts, 31-13 (Buff)
1978—Bills, 24-17 (Buff)
    Bills, 21-14 (Balt)
1979—Bills, 31-13 (Balt)
    Colts, 14-13 (Buff)
1980—Colts, 17-12 (Buff)
    Colts, 28-24 (Balt)
1981—Bills, 35-3 (Balt)
    Bills, 23-17 (Buff)
1982—Bills, 20-0 (Buff)
1983—Bills, 28-23 (Buff)
    Bills, 30-7 (Balt)
1984—Colts, 31-17 (I)
    Bills, 21-15 (Buff)
1985—Colts, 49-17 (I)
    Bills, 21-9 (Buff)
1986—Bills, 24-13 (Buff)
    Colts, 24-14 (I)
1987—Colts, 47-6 (Buff)
    Bills, 27-3 (I)
1988—Bills, 34-23 (Buff)
    Colts, 17-14 (I)
1989—Colts, 37-14 (I)
    Bills, 30-7 (Buff)
1990—Bills, 26-10 (Buff)
    Bills, 31-7 (I)
1991—Bills, 42-6 (Buff)
    Bills, 35-7 (I)
1992—Bills, 38-0 (Buff)
    Colts, 16-13 (I) OT
1993—Bills, 23-9 (Buff)
    Bills, 30-10 (I)
1994—Colts, 27-17 (Buff)
    Colts, 10-9 (I)
1995—Bills, 20-14 (Buff)
    Bills, 16-10 (I)
1996—Bills, 16-13 (Buff) OT
    Colts, 13-10 (I) OT

1997—Bills, 37-35 (B)
    Bills, 9-6 (I)
1998—Bills, 31-24 (I)
    Bills, 34-11 (B)
1999—Colts, 31-14 (I)
    Bills, 31-6 (B)
2000—Colts, 18-16 (B)
    Colts, 44-20 (I)
2001—Colts, 42-26 (I)
    Colts, 30-14 (B)
2003—Colts, 17-14 (B)
(RS Pts.—Bills 1,331, Colts 1,254)
Franchise in Baltimore prior to 1984

BUFFALO vs. JACKSONVILLE
RS: Bills lead series, 3-2
PS: Jaguars lead series, 1-0
1996—*Jaguars, 30-27 (B)
1997—Jaguars, 20-14 (B)
1998—Bills, 17-16 (B)
2001—Bills, 13-10 (J)
2003—Bills, 38-17 (J)
2004—Jaguars, 13-10 (B)
(RS Pts.—Bills 92, Jaguars 76)
(PS Pts.—Jaguars 30, Bills 27)
AFC First-Round Playoff

BUFFALO vs. *KANSAS CITY
RS: Bills lead series, 19-16-1
PS: Bills lead series, 2-1
1960—Texans, 45-28 (B)
    Texans, 24-7 (D)
1961—Bills, 27-24 (B)
    Bills, 30-20 (D)
1962—Texans, 41-21 (D)
    Bills, 23-14 (B)
1963—Tie, 27-27 (B)
    Bills, 35-26 (KC)
1964—Bills, 34-17 (B)
    Bills, 35-22 (KC)
1965—Bills, 23-7 (KC)
    Bills, 34-25 (B)
1966—Chiefs, 42-20 (B)
    Bills, 29-14 (KC)
    **Chiefs, 31-7 (B)
1967—Chiefs, 23-13 (KC)
1968—Chiefs, 18-7 (B)
1969—Chiefs, 29-7 (B)
    Chiefs, 22-19 (KC)
1971—Chiefs, 22-9 (KC)
1973—Bills, 23-14 (B)
1976—Bills, 50-17 (B)
1978—Bills, 28-13 (B)
    Chiefs, 14-10 (KC)
1982—Bills, 14-9 (B)
1983—Bills, 14-9 (KC)
1986—Chiefs, 20-17 (B)
    Bills, 17-14 (KC)
1991—Chiefs, 33-6 (KC)
    ***Bills, 37-14 (B)
1993—Chiefs, 23-7 (KC)
    ****Bills, 30-13 (B)
1994—Bills, 44-10 (B)
1996—Bills, 20-9 (B)
1997—Chiefs, 22-16 (KC)
2000—Bills, 21-17 (KC)
2002—Chiefs, 17-16 (KC)
2003—Chiefs, 38-5 (KC)
2005—Bills, 14-3 (B)
(RS Pts.—Bills 750, Chiefs 744)
(PS Pts.—Bills 74, Chiefs 58)
Franchise in Dallas prior to 1963 and

known as Texans
**AFL Championship*
***AFC Divisional Playoff*
****AFC Championship*
BUFFALO vs. MIAMI
RS: Dolphins lead series, 49-30-1
PS: Bills lead series, 3-1
1966—Bills, 58-24 (B)
      Bills, 29-0 (M)
1967—Bills, 35-13 (B)
      Dolphins, 17-14 (M)
1968—Tie, 14-14 (M)
      Dolphins, 21-17 (B)
1969—Dolphins, 24-6 (M)
      Bills, 28-3 (B)
1970—Dolphins, 33-14 (B)
      Dolphins, 45-7 (M)
1971—Dolphins, 29-14 (B)
      Dolphins, 34-0 (M)
1972—Dolphins, 24-23 (M)
      Dolphins, 30-16 (B)
1973—Dolphins, 27-6 (M)
      Dolphins, 17-0 (B)
1974—Dolphins, 24-16 (B)
      Dolphins, 35-28 (M)
1975—Dolphins, 35-30 (B)
      Dolphins, 31-21 (M)
1976—Dolphins, 30-21 (B)
      Dolphins, 45-27 (M)
1977—Dolphins, 13-0 (B)
      Dolphins, 31-14 (M)
1978—Dolphins, 31-24 (M)
      Dolphins, 25-24 (B)
1979—Dolphins, 9-7 (B)
      Dolphins, 17-7 (M)
1980—Bills, 17-7 (B)
      Dolphins, 17-14 (M)
1981—Bills, 31-21 (B)
      Dolphins, 16-6 (M)
1982—Dolphins, 9-7 (B)
      Dolphins, 27-10 (M)
1983—Dolphins, 12-0 (B)
      Bills, 38-35 (M) OT
1984—Dolphins, 21-17 (B)
      Dolphins, 38-7 (M)
1985—Dolphins, 23-14 (M)
      Dolphins, 28-0 (M)
1986—Dolphins, 27-14 (M)
      Dolphins, 34-24 (B)
1987—Bills, 34-31 (M) OT
      Bills, 27-0 (B)
1988—Bills, 9-6 (B)
      Bills, 31-6 (M)
1989—Bills, 27-24 (M)
      Bills, 31-17 (B)
1990—Dolphins, 30-7 (M)
      Bills, 24-14 (B)
      *Bills, 44-34 (B)
1991—Bills, 35-31 (B)
      Bills, 41-27 (M)
1992—Dolphins, 37-10 (B)
      Bills, 26-20 (M)
      **Bills, 29-10 (M)
1993—Dolphins, 22-13 (B)
      Bills, 47-34 (M)
1994—Bills, 21-11 (B)
      Bills, 42-31 (M)
1995—Dolphins, 23-6 (M)
      Bills, 23-20 (B)
      ***Bills, 37-22 (B)

1996—Dolphins, 21-7 (B)
      Dolphins, 16-14 (M)
1997—Bills, 9-6 (B)
      Dolphins, 30-13 (M)
1998—Dolphins, 13-7 (M)
      Bills, 30-24 (B)
      ***Dolphins, 24-17 (M)
1999—Bills, 23-18 (M)
      Bills, 23-3 (B)
2000—Dolphins, 22-13 (M)
      Dolphins, 33-6 (B)
2001—Dolphins, 34-27 (B)
      Dolphins, 34-7 (M)
2002—Bills, 23-10 (M)
      Bills, 38-21 (B)
2003—Dolphins, 17-7 (M)
      Dolphins, 20-3 (B)
2004—Bills, 20-13 (B)
      Bills, 42-32 (M)
2005—Bills, 20-14 (B)
      Dolphins, 24-23 (M)
(RS Pts.—Dolphins 1,785, Bills 1,508)
(PS Pts.—Bills 127, Dolphins 90)
AFC Divisional Playoff
**AFC Championship*
***AFC First-Round Playoff*
BUFFALO vs. MINNESOTA
RS: Vikings lead series, 7-3
1971—Vikings, 19-0 (M)
1975—Vikings, 35-13 (B)
1979—Vikings, 10-3 (M)
1982—Bills, 23-22 (B)
1985—Vikings, 27-20 (B)
1988—Bills, 13-10 (B)
1994—Vikings, 21-17 (B)
1997—Vikings, 34-13 (B)
2000—Vikings, 31-27 (M)
2002—Bills, 45-39 (M) OT
(RS Pts.—Vikings 248, Bills 174)
BUFFALO vs. *NEW ENGLAND
RS: Patriots lead series, 50-40-1
PS: Patriots lead series, 1-0
1960—Bills, 13-0 (Bos)
      Bills, 38-14 (Buff)
1961—Patriots, 23-21 (Buff)
      Patriots, 52-21 (Bos)
1962—Tie, 28-28 (Buff)
      Patriots, 21-10 (Bos)
1963—Bills, 28-21 (Buff)
      Patriots, 17-7 (Bos)
      **Patriots, 26-8 (Buff)
1964—Patriots, 36-28 (Buff)
      Bills, 24-14 (Bos)
1965—Bills, 24-7 (Buff)
      Bills, 23-7 (Bos)
1966—Patriots, 20-10 (Buff)
      Patriots, 14-3 (Bos)
1967—Patriots, 23-0 (Buff)
      Bills, 44-16 (Bos)
1968—Patriots, 16-7 (Buff)
      Patriots, 23-6 (Bos)
1969—Bills, 23-16 (Buff)
      Patriots, 35-21 (Bos)
1970—Bills, 45-10 (Bos)
      Patriots, 14-10 (Buff)
1971—Patriots, 38-33 (NE)
      Bills, 27-20 (Buff)
1972—Bills, 38-14 (Buff)
      Bills, 27-24 (NE)
1973—Bills, 31-13 (NE)

      Bills, 37-13 (Buff)
1974—Bills, 30-28 (Buff)
      Bills, 29-28 (NE)
1975—Bills, 45-31 (Buff)
      Bills, 34-14 (NE)
1976—Patriots, 26-22 (Buff)
      Patriots, 20-10 (NE)
1977—Bills, 24-14 (NE)
      Patriots, 20-7 (Buff)
1978—Patriots, 14-10 (Buff)
      Patriots, 26-24 (NE)
1979—Patriots, 26-6 (Buff)
      Bills, 16-13 (NE) OT
1980—Bills, 31-13 (Buff)
      Patriots, 24-2 (NE)
1981—Bills, 20-17 (Buff)
      Bills, 19-10 (NE)
1982—Patriots, 30-19 (NE)
1983—Patriots, 31-0 (Buff)
      Patriots, 21-7 (NE)
1984—Patriots, 21-17 (Buff)
      Patriots, 38-10 (NE)
1985—Patriots, 17-14 (Buff)
      Patriots, 14-3 (NE)
1986—Patriots, 23-3 (Buff)
      Patriots, 22-19 (NE)
1987—Patriots, 14-7 (NE)
      Patriots, 13-7 (Buff)
1988—Bills, 16-14 (NE)
      Bills, 23-20 (Buff)
1989—Bills, 31-10 (Buff)
      Patriots, 33-24 (NE)
1990—Bills, 27-10 (NE)
      Bills, 14-0 (Buff)
1991—Bills, 22-17 (Buff)
      Patriots, 16-13 (NE)
1992—Patriots, 41-7 (NE)
      Bills, 16-7 (Buff)
1993—Bills, 38-14 (Buff)
      Bills, 13-10 (NE) OT
1994—Bills, 38-35 (NE)
      Patriots, 41-17 (Buff)
1995—Patriots, 27-14 (NE)
      Patriots, 35-25 (Buff)
1996—Bills, 17-10 (Buff)
      Patriots, 28-25 (NE)
1997—Patriots, 33-6 (NE)
      Patriots, 31-10 (Buff)
1998—Bills, 13-10 (Buff)
      Patriots, 25-21 (NE)
1999—Bills, 17-7 (Buff)
      Bills, 13-10 (NE) OT
2000—Bills, 16-13 (NE) OT
      Patriots, 13-10 (Buff) OT
2001—Patriots, 21-11 (Buff)
      Patriots, 12-9 (Buff) OT
2002—Patriots, 38-7 (Buff)
      Patriots, 27-17 (NE)
2003—Bills, 31-0 (Buff)
      Patriots, 31-0 (NE)
2004—Patriots, 31-17 (Buff)
      Patriots, 29-6 (NE)
2005—Patriots, 21-16 (NE)
      Patriots, 35-7 (Buff)
(RS Pts.—Patriots 1,838, Bills 1,703)
(PS Pts.—Patriots 26, Bills 8)
Franchise in Boston prior to 1971
**Division Playoff*
BUFFALO vs. NEW ORLEANS
RS: Series tied, 4-4

1973—Saints, 13-0 (NO)
1980—Bills, 35-26 (NO)
1983—Bills, 27-21 (B)
1989—Saints, 22-19 (B)
1992—Bills, 20-16 (NO)
1998—Bills, 45-33 (NO)
2001—Saints, 24-6 (B)
2005—Saints, 19-7 (San Antonio)
(RS Pts.—Saints 174, Bills 159)

BUFFALO vs. N.Y. GIANTS
RS: Bills lead series, 6-3
PS: Giants lead series, 1-0
1970—Giants, 20-6 (NY)
1975—Giants, 17-14 (B)
1978—Bills, 41-17 (B)
1987—Bills, 6-3 (B) OT
1990—Bills, 17-13 (NY)
    *Giants, 20-19 (Tampa)
1993—Bills, 17-14 (B)
1996—Bills, 23-20 (NY) OT
1999—Giants, 19-17 (B)
2003—Bills, 24-7 (NY)
(RS Pts.—Bills 165, Giants 130)
(PS Pts.—Giants 20, Bills 19)
Super Bowl XXV

BUFFALO vs. *N.Y. JETS
RS: Bills lead series, 49-41
PS: Bills lead series, 1-0
1960—Titans, 27-3 (NY)
    Titans, 17-13 (B)
1961—Bills, 41-31 (B)
    Titans, 21-14 (NY)
1962—Titans, 17-6 (B)
    Bills, 20-3 (NY)
1963—Bills, 45-14 (B)
    Bills, 19-10 (NY)
1964—Bills, 34-24 (B)
    Bills, 20-7 (NY)
1965—Bills, 33-21 (B)
    Jets, 14-12 (NY)
1966—Bills, 33-23 (NY)
    Bills, 14-3 (B)
1967—Bills, 20-17 (B)
    Jets, 20-10 (NY)
1968—Bills, 37-35 (B)
    Jets, 25-21 (NY)
1969—Jets, 33-19 (B)
    Jets, 16-6 (NY)
1970—Bills, 34-31 (B)
    Bills, 10-6 (NY)
1971—Jets, 28-17 (NY)
    Jets, 20-7 (B)
1972—Jets, 41-24 (B)
    Jets, 41-3 (NY)
1973—Bills, 9-7 (B)
    Bills, 34-14 (NY)
1974—Bills, 16-12 (B)
    Jets, 20-10 (NY)
1975—Bills, 42-14 (B)
    Bills, 24-23 (NY)
1976—Jets, 17-14 (NY)
    Jets, 19-14 (B)
1977—Jets, 24-19 (B)
    Bills, 14-10 (NY)
1978—Jets, 21-20 (B)
    Jets, 45-14 (NY)
1979—Bills, 46-31 (B)
    Bills, 14-12 (NY)
1980—Bills, 20-10 (B)
    Bills, 31-24 (NY)

1981—Bills, 31-0 (B)
    Jets, 33-14 (NY)
    **Bills, 31-27 (NY)
1983—Jets, 34-10 (B)
    Bills, 24-17 (NY)
1984—Jets, 28-26 (B)
    Jets, 21-17 (NY)
1985—Jets, 42-3 (NY)
    Jets, 27-7 (B)
1986—Jets, 28-24 (B)
    Jets, 14-13 (NY)
1987—Jets, 31-28 (B)
    Bills, 17-14 (NY)
1988—Bills, 37-14 (NY)
    Bills, 9-6 (B) OT
1989—Bills, 34-3 (B)
    Bills, 37-0 (NY)
1990—Bills, 30-7 (NY)
    Bills, 30-27 (B)
1991—Bills, 23-20 (NY)
    Bills, 24-13 (B)
1992—Bills, 24-20 (NY)
    Jets, 24-17 (B)
1993—Bills, 19-10 (NY)
    Bills, 16-14 (B)
1994—Jets, 23-3 (B)
    Jets, 22-17 (NY)
1995—Bills, 29-10 (B)
    Bills, 28-26 (NY)
1996—Bills, 25-22 (NY)
    Bills, 35-10 (B)
1997—Bills, 28-22 (NY)
    Bills, 20-10 (B)
1998—Jets, 34-12 (NY)
    Jets, 17-10 (B)
1999—Bills, 17-3 (B)
    Jets, 17-7 (NY)
2000—Jets, 27-14 (NY)
    Bills, 23-20 (B)
2001—Jets, 42-36 (B)
    Bills, 14-9 (NY)
2002—Jets, 37-31 (B) OT
    Jets, 31-13 (NY)
2003—Jets, 30-3 (NY)
    Bills, 17-6 (B)
2004—Jets, 16-14 (NY)
    Bills, 22-17 (B)
2005—Bills, 27-17 (B)
    Jets, 30-26 (NY)
(RS Pts.—Bills 1,841, Jets 1,793)
(PS Pts.—Bills 31, Jets 27)
Jets known as Titans prior to 1963
**AFC First-Round Playoff*

BUFFALO vs. *OAKLAND
RS: Raiders lead series, 19-15
PS: Bills lead series, 2-0
1960—Bills, 38-9 (B)
    Raiders, 20-7 (O)
1961—Raiders, 31-22 (B)
    Bills, 26-21 (O)
1962—Bills, 14-6 (B)
    Bills, 10-6 (O)
1963—Raiders, 35-17 (O)
    Bills, 12-0 (B)
1964—Bills, 23-20 (B)
    Raiders, 16-13 (O)
1965—Bills, 17-12 (B)
    Bills, 17-14 (O)
1966—Bills, 31-10 (O)
1967—Raiders, 24-20 (B)

    Raiders, 28-21 (O)
1968—Raiders, 48-6 (B)
    Raiders, 13-10 (O)
1969—Raiders, 50-21 (O)
1972—Raiders, 28-16 (O)
1974—Bills, 21-20 (B)
1977—Raiders, 34-13 (O)
1980—Bills, 24-7 (B)
1983—Raiders, 27-24 (B)
1987—Raiders, 34-21 (LA)
1988—Bills, 37-21 (B)
1990—Bills, 38-24 (B)
    **Bills, 51-3 (B)
1991—Bills, 30-27 (LA) OT
1992—Raiders, 20-3 (LA)
1993—Raiders, 25-24 (B)
    ***Bills, 29-23 (B)
1998—Bills, 44-21 (B)
1999—Raiders, 20-14 (B)
2002—Raiders, 49-31 (B)
2004—Raiders, 13-10 (O)
2005—Raiders, 38-17 (O)
(RS Pts.—Raiders 771, Bills 692)
(PS Pts.—Bills 80, Raiders 26)
Franchise in Los Angeles from 1982-1994
**AFC Championship*
***AFC Divisional Playoff*

BUFFALO vs. PHILADELPHIA
RS: Bills lead series, 5-5
1973—Bills, 27-26 (B)
1981—Eagles, 20-14 (B)
1984—Eagles, 27-17 (B)
1985—Eagles, 21-17 (P)
1987—Eagles, 17-7 (P)
1990—Bills, 30-23 (B)
1993—Bills, 10-7 (P)
1996—Bills, 24-17 (P)
1999—Bills, 26-0 (B)
2003—Eagles, 23-13 (B)
(RS Pts.—Bills 185, Eagles 181)

BUFFALO vs. PITTSBURGH
RS: Steelers lead series, 10-8
PS: Steelers lead series, 2-1
1970—Steelers, 23-10 (P)
1972—Steelers, 38-21 (B)
1974—*Steelers, 32-14 (P)
1975—Bills, 30-21 (P)
1978—Steelers, 28-17 (B)
1979—Steelers, 28-0 (P)
1980—Bills, 28-13 (B)
1982—Bills, 13-0 (B)
1985—Steelers, 30-24 (P)
1986—Bills, 16-12 (B)
1988—Bills, 36-28 (B)
1991—Bills, 52-34 (B)
1992—Bills, 28-20 (B)
    *Bills, 24-3 (P)
1993—Steelers, 23-0 (P)
1994—Steelers, 23-10 (B)
1995—*Steelers, 40-21 (P)
1996—Steelers, 24-6 (P)
1999—Bills, 24-21 (B)
2001—Steelers, 20-3 (B)
2004—Steelers, 29-24 (B)
(RS Pts.—Steelers 415, Bills 342)
(PS Pts.—Steelers 75, Bills 59)
AFC Divisional Playoff

BUFFALO vs. *ST. LOUIS
RS: Bills lead series, 5-4
1970—Rams, 19-0 (B)

1974—Rams, 19-14 (LA)
1980—Bills, 10-7 (B) OT
1983—Rams, 41-17 (LA)
1989—Bills, 23-20 (B)
1992—Bills, 40-7 (B)
1995—Bills, 45-27 (StL)
1998—Rams, 34-33 (B)
2004—Bills, 37-17 (B)
(RS Pts.—Bills 219, Rams 191)
*Franchise in Los Angeles prior to 1995
BUFFALO vs. *SAN DIEGO
RS: Chargers lead series, 19-9-2
PS: Bills lead series, 2-1
1960—Chargers, 24-10 (B)
      Bills, 32-3 (LA)
1961—Chargers, 19-11 (B)
      Chargers, 28-10 (SD)
1962—Bills, 35-10 (B)
      Bills, 40-20 (SD)
1963—Chargers, 14-10 (SD)
      Chargers, 23-13 (B)
1964—Bills, 30-3 (B)
      Bills, 27-24 (SD)
      **Bills, 20-7 (B)
1965—Chargers, 34-3 (B)
      Tie, 20-20 (SD)
      **Bills, 23-0 (SD)
1966—Chargers, 27-7 (SD)
      Tie, 17-17 (B)
1967—Chargers, 37-17 (B)
1968—Chargers, 21-6 (B)
1969—Chargers, 45-6 (SD)
1971—Chargers, 20-3 (SD)
1973—Chargers, 34-7 (SD)
1976—Chargers, 34-13 (B)
1979—Chargers, 27-19 (SD)
1980—Bills, 26-24 (SD)
      ***Chargers, 20-14 (SD)
1981—Bills, 28-27 (SD)
1985—Chargers, 14-9 (B)
      Chargers, 40-7 (SD)
1998—Chargers, 16-11 (SD)
2000—Bills, 27-24 (B) OT
2001—Chargers, 27-24 (SD)
2002—Bills, 20-13 (B)
2005—Chargers, 48-10 (SD)
(RS Pts.—Chargers 717, Bills 501)
(PS Pts.—Bills 57, Chargers 27)
*Franchise in Los Angeles prior to 1961
**AFL Championship
***AFC Divisional Playoff
BUFFALO vs. SAN FRANCISCO
RS: Bills lead series, 5-4
1972—Bills, 27-20 (B)
1980—Bills, 18-13 (SF)
1983—49ers, 23-10 (B)
1989—49ers, 21-10 (SF)
1992—Bills, 34-31 (SF)
1995—49ers, 27-17 (SF)
1998—Bills, 26-21 (B)
2001—49ers, 35-0 (SF)
2004—Bills, 41-7 (SF)
(RS Pts.—49ers 198, Bills 183)
BUFFALO vs. SEATTLE
RS: Seahawks lead series, 6-4
1977—Seahawks, 56-17 (S)
1984—Seahawks, 31-28 (S)
1988—Bills, 13-3 (S)
1989—Seahawks, 17-16 (S)
1995—Bills, 27-21 (B)

1996—Seahawks, 26-18 (S)
1999—Seahawks, 26-16 (S)
2000—Bills, 42-23 (S)
2001—Seahawks, 23-20 (B)
2004—Bills, 38-9 (S)
(RS Pts.—Bills 235, Seahawks 235)
BUFFALO vs. TAMPA BAY
RS: Buccaneers lead series, 6-2
1976—Bills, 14-9 (TB)
1978—Buccaneers, 31-10 (TB)
1982—Buccaneers, 24-23 (TB)
1986—Buccaneers, 34-28 (TB)
1988—Buccaneers, 10-5 (TB)
1991—Bills, 17-10 (TB)
2000—Buccaneers, 31-17 (TB)
2005—Buccaneers, 19-3 (TB)
(RS Pts.—Buccaneers 168, Bills 117)
BUFFALO vs. *TENNESSEE
RS: Titans lead series, 23-14
PS: Bills lead series, 2-1
1960—Bills, 25-24 (B)
      Oilers, 31-23 (H)
1961—Bills, 22-12 (H)
      Oilers, 28-16 (B)
1962—Oilers, 28-23 (B)
      Oilers, 17-14 (H)
1963—Oilers, 31-20 (B)
      Oilers, 28-14 (H)
1964—Bills, 48-17 (H)
      Bills, 24-10 (B)
1965—Oilers, 19-17 (B)
      Bills, 29-18 (H)
1966—Bills, 27-20 (B)
      Bills, 42-20 (H)
1967—Oilers, 20-3 (B)
      Oilers, 10-3 (H)
1968—Oilers, 30-7 (B)
      Oilers, 35-6 (H)
1969—Oilers, 17-3 (B)
      Oilers, 28-14 (H)
1971—Oilers, 20-14 (B)
1974—Oilers, 21-9 (H)
1976—Oilers, 13-3 (B)
1978—Oilers, 17-10 (H)
1983—Bills, 30-13 (B)
1985—Bills, 20-0 (B)
1986—Oilers, 16-7 (H)
1987—Bills, 34-30 (B)
1988—**Bills, 17-10 (B)
1989—Bills, 47-41 (H) OT
1990—Oilers, 27-24 (H)
1992—Oilers, 27-3 (H)
      ***Bills, 41-38 (B) OT
1993—Bills, 35-7 (B)
1994—Bills, 15-7 (H)
1995—Oilers, 28-17 (B)
1997—Oilers, 31-14 (T)
1999—***Titans, 22-16 (T)
2000—Bills, 16-13 (B)
2003—Titans, 28-26 (T)
(RS Pts.—Titans 782, Bills 704)
(PS Pts.—Bills 74, Titans 70)
*Franchise in Houston prior to 1997;
known as Oilers prior to 1999
**AFC Divisional Playoff
***AFC First-Round Playoff
BUFFALO vs. WASHINGTON
RS: Bills lead series, 6-4
PS: Redskins lead series, 1-0
1972—Bills, 24-17 (W)

1977—Redskins, 10-0 (B)
1981—Bills, 21-14 (B)
1984—Redskins, 41-14 (W)
1987—Redskins, 27-7 (B)
1990—Redskins, 29-14 (W)
1991—*Redskins, 37-24 (Minneapolis)
1993—Bills, 24-10 (B)
1996—Bills, 38-13 (B)
1999—Bills, 34-17 (W)
2003—Bills, 24-7 (B)
(RS Pts.—Bills 200, Redskins 185)
(PS Pts.—Redskins 37, Bills 24)
*Super Bowl XXVI

CAROLINA vs. ARIZONA
RS: Panthers lead series, 4-2;
See Arizona vs. Carolina
CAROLINA vs. ATLANTA
RS: Falcons lead series, 14-8;
See Atlanta vs. Carolina
CAROLINA vs. BALTIMORE
RS: Panthers lead series, 2-0;
See Baltimore vs. Carolina
CAROLINA vs. BUFFALO
RS: Bills lead series, 3-1;
See Buffalo vs. Carolina
CAROLINA vs. CHICAGO
RS: Bears lead series, 2-1
PS: Panthers lead series, 1-0
1995—Bears, 31-27 (Chi)
2002—Panthers, 24-14 (Car)
2005—Bears, 13-3 (Chi)
      *Panthers, 29-21 (Chi)
(RS Pts.—Bears 58, Panthers 54)
(PS Pts.—Panthers 29, Bears 21)
*NFC Divisional Playoff
CAROLINA vs. CINCINNATI
RS: Panthers lead series, 2-0
1999—Panthers, 27-3 (Car)
2002—Panthers, 52-31 (Car)
(RS Pts.—Panthers 79, Bengals 34)
CAROLINA vs. CLEVELAND
RS: Panthers lead series, 2-0
1999—Panthers, 31-17 (Cle)
2002—Panthers, 13-6 (Cle)
(RS Pts.—Panthers 44, Browns 23)
CAROLINA vs. DALLAS
RS: Cowboys lead series, 5-1
PS: Panthers lead series, 2-0
1996—*Panthers, 26-17 (C)
1997—Panthers, 23-13 (D)
1998—Cowboys, 27-20 (D)
2000—Cowboys, 16-13 (C) OT
2002—Cowboys, 14-13 (D)
2003—Cowboys, 24-20 (D)
      **Panthers, 29-10 (C)
2005—Cowboys, 24-20 (C)
(RS Pts.—Cowboys 118, Panthers 109)
(PS Pts.—Panthers 55, Cowboys 27)
*NFC Divisional Playoff
*NFC First-Round Playoff
CAROLINA vs. DENVER
RS: Broncos lead series, 2-0
1997—Broncos, 34-0 (D)
2004—Broncos, 20-17 (D)
(RS Pts.—Broncos 54, Panthers 17)
CAROLINA vs. DETROIT
RS: Panthers lead series, 3-1
1999—Lions, 24-9 (C)
2002—Panthers, 31-7 (C)

2003—Panthers, 20-14 (C)
2005—Panthers, 21-20 (D)
(RS Pts.—Panthers 81, Lions 65)
CAROLINA vs. GREEN BAY
RS: Packers lead series, 5-3
PS: Packers lead series, 1-0
1996—*Packers, 30-13 (GB)
1997—Packers, 31-10 (C)
1998—Packers, 37-30 (C)
1999—Panthers, 33-31 (GB)
2000—Panthers, 31-14 (C)
2001—Packers, 28-7 (C)
2002—Packers, 17-14 (GB)
2004—Packers, 24-14 (C)
2005—Panthers, 32-29 (C)
(RS Pts.—Packers 211, Panthers 171)
(PS Pts.—Packers 30, Panthers 13)
*NFC Championship
CAROLINA vs. HOUSTON
RS: Texans lead series, 1-0
2003—Texans, 14-10 (H)
(RS Pts.—Texans 14, Panthers 10)
CAROLINA vs. INDIANAPOLIS
RS: Panthers lead series, 3-0
1995—Panthers, 13-10 (C)
1998—Panthers, 27-19 (I)
2003—Panthers, 23-20 (I) OT
(RS Pts.—Panthers 63, Colts 49)
CAROLINA vs. JACKSONVILLE
RS: Jaguars lead series, 2-1
1996—Jaguars, 24-14 (J)
1999—Jaguars, 22-20 (C)
2003—Panthers, 24-23 (C)
(RS Pts.—Jaguars 69, Panthers 58)
CAROLINA vs. KANSAS CITY
RS: Chiefs lead series, 2-1
1997—Chiefs, 35-14 (C)
2000—Chiefs, 15-14 (KC)
2004—Panthers, 28-17 (KC)
(RS Pts.—Chiefs 67, Panthers 56)
CAROLINA vs. MIAMI
RS: Dolphins lead series, 3-0
1998—Dolphins, 13-9 (C)
2001—Dolphins, 23-6 (M)
2005—Dolphins, 27-24 (M)
(RS Pts.—Dolphins 63, Panthers 39)
CAROLINA vs. MINNESOTA
RS: Series tied, 3-3
1996—Vikings, 14-12 (M)
1997—Vikings, 21-14 (M)
2000—Vikings, 31-17 (M)
2001—Panthers, 24-13 (M)
2002—Panthers, 21-14 (M)
2005—Panthers, 38-13 (C)
(RS Pts.—Panthers 126, Vikings 106)
CAROLINA vs. NEW ENGLAND
RS: Panthers lead series, 2-1
PS: Patriots lead series, 1-0
1995—Panthers, 20-17 (NE) OT
2001—Patriots, 38-6 (C)
2003—*Patriots, 32-29 (Houston)
2005—Patriots, 27-17 (C)
(RS Pts.—Patriots 72, Panthers 53)
(PS Pts.—Patriots 32, Panthers 29)
*Super Bowl XXXVIII
CAROLINA vs. NEW ORLEANS
RS: Series tied, 11-11
1995—Panthers, 20-3 (C)
Saints, 34-26 (NO)
1996—Panthers, 22-20 (NO)

Panthers, 19-7 (C)
1997—Panthers, 13-0 (NO)
Saints, 16-13 (C)
1998—Saints, 19-14 (NO)
Panthers, 31-17 (C)
1999—Saints, 19-10 (NO)
Panthers, 45-13 (C)
2000—Saints, 24-6 (NO)
Saints, 20-10 (C)
2001—Saints, 27-25 (C)
Saints, 27-23 (NO)
2002—Saints, 34-24 (C)
Panthers, 10-6 (NO)
2003—Panthers, 19-13 (C)
Panthers, 23-20 (NO) OT
2004—Panthers, 32-21 (NO)
Saints, 21-18 (C)
2005—Saints, 23-20 (C)
Panthers, 27-10 (Baton Rouge)
(RS Pts.—Panthers 450, Saints 394)
CAROLINA vs. N.Y. GIANTS
RS: Panthers lead series, 2-0
PS: Panthers lead series, 1-0
1996—Panthers, 27-17 (C)
2003—Panthers, 37-24 (NY)
2005—*Panthers, 23-0 (NY)
(RS Pts.—Panthers 64, Giants 41)
(PS Pts.—Panthers 23, Giants 0)
*NFC First-Round Playoff
CAROLINA vs. N.Y. JETS
RS: Series tied, 2-2
1995—Panthers, 26-15 (C)
1998—Jets, 48-21 (NY)
2001—Jets, 13-12 (C)
2005—Panthers, 30-3 (C)
(RS Pts.—Panthers 89, Jets 79)
CAROLINA vs. OAKLAND
RS: Raiders lead series, 2-1
1997—Panthers, 38-14 (C)
2000—Raiders, 52-9 (O)
2004—Raiders, 27-24 (C)
(RS Pts.— Raiders 93, Panthers 71)
CAROLINA vs. PHILADELPHIA
RS: Eagles lead series, 3-1
PS: Panthers lead series, 1-0
1996—Eagles, 20-9 (P)
1999—Panthers, 33-7 (C)
2003—Eagles, 25-16 (C)
*Panthers, 14-3 (P)
2004—Eagles, 30-8 (P)
(RS Pts.—Eagles 82, Panthers 66)
(PS Pts.—Panthers 14, Eagles 3)
*NFC Championship
CAROLINA vs. PITTSBURGH
RS: Steelers lead series, 2-1
1996—Panthers, 18-14 (C)
1999—Steelers, 30-20 (P)
2002—Steelers, 30-14 (P)
(RS Pts.—Steelers 74, Panthers 52)
CAROLINA vs. ST. LOUIS
RS: Panthers lead series, 8-7
PS: Panthers lead series, 1-0
1995—Panthers, 31-10 (C)
Rams, 28-17 (StL)
1996—Panthers, 45-13 (C)
Panthers, 20-10 (StL)
1997—Panthers, 16-10 (StL)
Rams, 30-18 (C)
1998—Panthers, 24-20 (StL)
Panthers, 20-13 (C)

1999—Rams, 35-10 (StL)
Rams, 34-21 (C)
2000—Panthers, 27-24 (StL)
Panthers, 16-3 (C)
2001—Rams, 48-14 (StL)
Rams, 38-32 (C)
2003—*Panthers, 29-23 (StL) 2OT
2004—Panthers, 20-7 (C)
(RS Pts.—Rams 344, Panthers 310)
(PS Pts.—Panthers 29, Rams 23)
*NFC Divisional Playoff
CAROLINA vs. SAN DIEGO
RS: Panthers lead series, 2-1
1997—Panthers, 26-7 (SD)
2000—Panthers, 30-22 (C)
2004—Chargers, 17-6 (C)
(RS Pts.—Panthers 62, Chargers 46)
CAROLINA vs. SAN FRANCISCO
RS: Panthers lead series, 8-7
1995—Panthers, 13-7 (C)
49ers, 31-10 (C)
1996—Panthers, 23-7 (C)
Panthers, 30-24 (SF)
1997—49ers, 34-21 (C)
49ers, 27-19 (SF)
1998—49ers, 25-23 (SF)
49ers, 31-28 (C) OT
1999—Panthers, 31-29 (SF)
Panthers, 41-24 (C)
2000—Panthers, 38-22 (SF)
Panthers, 34-16 (C)
2001—49ers, 24-14 (SF)
49ers, 25-22 (C) OT
2004—Panthers, 37-27 (SF)
(RS Pts.—Panthers 384, 49ers 353)
CAROLINA vs. SEATTLE
RS: Series tied, 1-1
PS: Seahawks lead series, 1-0
2000—Panthers, 26-3 (C)
2004—Seahawks, 23-17 (S)
2005—*Seahawks, 34-14 (S)
(RS Pts.—Panthers 43, Seahawks 26)
(PS Pts.—Seahawks 34, Panthers 14)
*NFC Championship
CAROLINA vs. TAMPA BAY
RS: Panthers lead series, 6-5
1995—Buccaneers, 20-13 (C)
1996—Panthers, 24-0 (C)
1998—Buccaneers, 16-13 (TB)
2002—Buccaneers, 12-9 (C)
Buccaneers, 23-10 (TB)
2003—Panthers, 12-9 (TB) OT
Panthers, 27-24 (C)
2004—Panthers, 21-14 (C)
Panthers, 37-20 (TB)
2005—Panthers, 34-14 (TB)
Buccaneers, 20-10 (C)
(RS Pts.—Panthers 210, Buccaneers 172)
CAROLINA vs. *TENNESSEE
RS: Series tied, 1-1
1996—Panthers, 31-6 (H)
2003—Titans, 37-17 (C)
(RS Pts.—Panthers 48, Titans 43)
*Franchise in Houston prior to 1997;
known as Oilers prior to 1999
CAROLINA vs. WASHINGTON
RS: Redskins lead series, 6-1
1995—Redskins, 20-17 (W)
1997—Redskins, 24-10 (C)
1998—Redskins, 28-25 (C)

1999—Redskins, 38-36 (W)
2000—Redskins, 20-17 (W)
2001—Redskins, 17-14 (W) OT
2003—Panthers, 20-17 (C)
(RS Pts.—Redskins 164, Panthers 139)

CHICAGO vs. ARIZONA
RS: Bears lead series, 54-26-6;
See Arizona vs. Chicago
CHICAGO vs. ATLANTA
RS: Bears lead series, 12-10;
See Atlanta vs. Chicago
CHICAGO vs. BALTIMORE
RS: Bears lead series, 2-1;
See Baltimore vs. Chicago
CHICAGO vs. BUFFALO
RS: Bears lead series, 5-4;
See Buffalo vs. Chicago
CHICAGO vs. CAROLINA
RS: Bears lead series, 2-1
PS: Panthers lead series, 1-0;
See Carolina vs. Chicago
CHICAGO vs. CINCINNATI
RS: Bengals lead series, 5-3
1972—Bengals, 13-3 (Chi)
1980—Bengals, 17-14 (Chi) OT
1986—Bears, 44-7 (Cin)
1989—Bears, 17-14 (Chi)
1992—Bengals, 31-28 (Chi) OT
1995—Bengals, 16-10 (Cin)
2001—Bears, 24-0 (Cin)
2005—Bengals, 24-7 (Chi)
(RS Pts.—Bears 147, Bengals 122)
CHICAGO vs. CLEVELAND
RS: Browns lead series, 9-4
1951—Browns, 42-21 (Cle)
1954—Browns, 39-10 (Chi)
1960—Browns, 42-0 (Cle)
1961—Bears, 17-14 (Chi)
1967—Browns, 24-0 (Cle)
1969—Browns, 28-24 (Chi)
1972—Bears, 17-0 (Cle)
1980—Browns, 27-21 (Cle)
1986—Bears, 41-31 (Chi)
1989—Browns, 27-7 (Cle)
1992—Browns, 27-14 (Cle)
2001—Bears, 27-21 (Chi) OT
2005—Browns, 20-10 (Cle)
(RS Pts.—Browns 342, Bears 209)
CHICAGO vs. DALLAS
RS: Cowboys lead series, 10-8
PS: Cowboys lead series, 2-0
1960—Bears, 17-7 (C)
1962—Bears, 34-33 (D)
1964—Cowboys, 24-10 (C)
1968—Cowboys, 34-3 (C)
1971—Bears, 23-19 (C)
1973—Cowboys, 20-17 (C)
1976—Cowboys, 31-21 (D)
1977—*Cowboys, 37-7 (D)
1979—Cowboys, 24-20 (D)
1981—Cowboys, 10-9 (D)
1984—Cowboys, 23-14 (C)
1985—Bears, 44-0 (D)
1986—Bears, 24-10 (D)
1988—Bears, 17-7 (C)
1991–**Cowboys, 17-13 (C)
1992—Cowboys, 27-14 (D)
1996—Bears, 22-6 (C)
1997—Cowboys, 27-3 (D)

1998—Bears, 13-12 (C)
2004—Cowboys, 21-7 (D)
(RS Pts.—Cowboys 335, Bears 312)
(PS Pts.—Cowboys 54, Bears 20)
*NFC Divisional Playoff
**NFC First-Round Playoff
CHICAGO vs. DENVER
RS: Series tied, 6-6
1971—Broncos, 6-3 (D)
1973—Bears, 33-14 (D)
1976—Broncos, 28-14 (C)
1978—Broncos, 16-7 (D)
1981—Bears, 35-24 (C)
1983—Bears, 31-14 (C)
1984—Bears, 27-0 (C)
1987—Broncos, 31-29 (D)
1990—Bears, 16-13 (D) OT
1993—Broncos, 13-3 (C)
1996—Broncos, 17-12 (D)
2003—Bears, 19-10 (D)
(RS Pts.—Bears 229, Broncos 186)
CHICAGO vs. *DETROIT
RS: Bears lead series, 85-62-5
1930—Spartans, 7-6 (P)
    Bears, 14-6 (C)
1931—Bears, 9-6 (C)
    Spartans, 3-0 (P)
1932—Tie, 13-13 (C)
    Tie, 7-7 (P)
    Bears, 9-0 (C)
1933—Bears, 17-14 (C)
    Bears, 17-7 (P)
1934—Bears, 19-16 (D)
    Bears, 10-7 (C)
1935—Tie, 20-20 (C)
    Lions, 14-2 (D)
1936—Bears, 12-10 (C)
    Lions, 13-7 (D)
1937—Bears, 28-20 (C)
    Bears, 13-0 (D)
1938—Lions, 13-7 (C)
    Lions, 14-7 (D)
1939—Lions, 10-0 (C)
    Bears, 23-13 (D)
1940—Bears, 7-0 (C)
    Lions, 17-14 (D)
1941—Bears, 49-0 (C)
    Bears, 24-7 (D)
1942—Bears, 16-0 (C)
    Bears, 42-0 (D)
1943—Bears, 27-21 (D)
    Bears, 35-14 (C)
1944—Tie, 21-21 (C)
    Lions, 41-21 (D)
1945—Lions, 16-10 (D)
    Lions, 35-28 (D)
1946—Bears, 42-6 (C)
    Bears, 45-24 (D)
1947—Bears, 33-24 (C)
    Bears, 34-14 (D)
1948—Bears, 28-0 (C)
    Bears, 42-14 (D)
1949—Bears, 27-24 (C)
    Bears, 28-7 (D)
1950—Bears, 35-21 (D)
    Bears, 6-3 (C)
1951—Bears, 28-23 (D)
    Lions, 41-28 (C)
1952—Bears, 24-23 (C)
    Lions, 45-21 (D)

1953—Lions, 20-16 (C)
    Lions, 13-7 (D)
1954—Lions, 48-23 (D)
    Bears, 28-24 (C)
1955—Bears, 24-14 (D)
    Bears, 21-20 (C)
1956—Lions, 42-10 (D)
    Bears, 38-21 (C)
1957—Bears, 27-7 (D)
    Lions, 21-13 (C)
1958—Bears, 20-7 (D)
    Bears, 21-16 (C)
1959—Bears, 24-14 (D)
    Bears, 25-14 (C)
1960—Bears, 28-7 (C)
    Lions, 36-0 (D)
1961—Bears, 31-17 (D)
    Lions, 16-15 (C)
1962—Lions, 11-3 (D)
    Bears, 3-0 (C)
1963—Bears, 37-21 (D)
    Bears, 24-14 (C)
1964—Lions, 10-0 (C)
    Bears, 27-24 (D)
1965—Bears, 38-10 (C)
    Bears, 17-10 (D)
1966—Lions, 14-3 (D)
    Tie, 10-10 (C)
1967—Bears, 14-3 (C)
    Bears, 27-13 (D)
1968—Lions, 42-0 (C)
    Bears, 28-10 (C)
1969—Lions, 13-7 (D)
    Lions, 20-3 (C)
1970—Lions, 28-14 (D)
    Lions, 16-10 (C)
1971—Bears, 28-23 (D)
    Lions, 28-3 (C)
1972—Lions, 38-24 (C)
    Lions, 14-0 (D)
1973—Lions, 30-7 (C)
    Lions, 40-7 (D)
1974—Bears, 17-9 (C)
    Lions, 34-17 (D)
1975—Lions, 27-7 (D)
    Bears, 25-21 (C)
1976—Bears, 10-3 (C)
    Lions, 14-10 (D)
1977—Bears, 30-20 (C)
    Bears, 31-14 (D)
1978—Bears, 19-0 (D)
    Lions, 21-17 (C)
1979—Bears, 35-7 (C)
    Lions, 20-0 (D)
1980—Bears, 24-7 (C)
    Bears, 23-17 (D) OT
1981—Lions, 48-17 (D)
    Lions, 23-7 (C)
1982—Lions, 17-10 (D)
    Bears, 20-17 (C)
1983—Bears, 31-17 (D)
    Lions, 38-17 (C)
1984—Bears, 16-14 (C)
    Bears, 30-13 (D)
1985—Bears, 24-3 (C)
    Bears, 37-17 (D)
1986—Bears, 13-7 (C)
    Bears, 16-13 (D)
1987—Bears, 30-10 (C)
    1988—Bears, 24-7 (D)

Bears, 13-12 (C)
1989—Bears, 47-27 (D)
Lions, 27-17 (C)
1990—Bears, 23-17 (C) OT
Lions, 38-21 (D)
1991—Bears, 20-10 (C)
Lions, 16-6 (D)
1992—Bears, 27-24 (C)
Lions, 16-3 (D)
1993—Bears, 10-6 (D)
Lions, 20-14 (C)
1994—Lions, 21-16 (D)
Bears, 20-10 (C)
1995—Lions, 24-17 (C)
Lions, 27-7 (D)
1996—Lions, 35-16 (D)
Bears, 31-14 (C)
1997—Lions, 32-7 (C)
Lions, 55-20 (D)
1998—Bears, 31-27 (C)
Lions, 26-3 (D)
1999—Lions, 21-17 (D)
Bears, 28-10 (C)
2000—Lions, 21-14 (C)
Bears, 23-20 (D)
2001—Bears, 13-10 (C)
Bears, 24-0 (D)
2002—Lions, 23-20 (D) OT
Bears, 20-17 (C) OT
2003—Bears, 24-16 (C)
Lions, 12-10 (D)
2004—Lions, 20-16 (D)
Lions, 19-13 (D)
2005—Bears, 38-6 (C)
Bears, 19-13 (D) OT
(RS Pts.—Bears 2,833, Lions 2,635)
*Franchise in Portsmouth prior to 1934
and known as the Spartans
CHICAGO vs. GREEN BAY
RS: Bears lead series, 86-78-6
PS: Bears lead series, 1-0
1921—Staleys, 20-0 (C)
1923—Bears, 3-0 (GB)
1924—Bears, 3-0 (C)
1925—Packers, 14-10 (GB)
Bears, 21-0 (C)
1926—Tie, 6-6 (GB)
Bears, 19-13 (C)
Tie, 3-3 (C)
1927—Bears, 7-6 (GB)
Bears, 14-6 (C)
1928—Tie, 12-12 (GB)
Packers, 16-6 (C)
Packers, 6-0 (C)
1929—Packers, 23-0 (GB)
Packers, 14-0 (C)
Packers, 25-0 (C)
1930—Packers, 7-0 (GB)
Packers, 13-12 (C)
Bears, 21-0 (C)
1931—Packers, 7-0 (GB)
Packers, 6-2 (C)
Bears, 7-6 (C)
1932—Tie, 0-0 (GB)
Packers, 2-0 (C)
Bears, 9-0 (C)
1933—Bears, 14-7 (GB)
Bears, 10-7 (C)
Bears, 7-6 (C)
1934—Bears, 24-10 (GB)

Bears, 27-14 (C)
1935—Packers, 7-0 (GB)
Packers, 17-14 (C)
1936—Bears, 30-3 (GB)
Packers, 21-10 (C)
1937—Bears, 14-2 (GB)
Packers, 24-14 (C)
1938—Bears, 2-0 (GB)
Packers, 24-17 (C)
1939—Packers, 21-16 (GB)
Bears, 30-27 (C)
1940—Bears, 41-10 (GB)
Bears, 14-7 (C)
1941—Bears, 25-17 (GB)
Packers, 16-14 (C)
**Bears, 33-14 (C)
1942—Bears, 44-28 (GB)
Bears, 38-7 (C)
1943—Tie, 21-21 (GB)
Bears, 21-7 (C)
1944—Packers, 42-28 (GB)
Bears, 21-0 (C)
1945—Packers, 31-21 (GB)
Bears, 28-24 (C)
1946—Bears, 30-7 (GB)
Bears, 10-7 (C)
1947—Packers, 29-20 (GB)
Bears, 20-17 (C)
1948—Bears, 45-7 (GB)
Bears, 7-6 (C)
1949—Bears, 17-0 (GB)
Bears, 24-3 (C)
1950—Packers, 31-21 (GB)
Bears, 28-14 (C)
1951—Bears, 31-20 (GB)
Bears, 24-13 (C)
1952—Bears, 24-14 (GB)
Packers, 41-28 (C)
1953—Bears, 17-13 (GB)
Tie, 21-21 (C)
1954—Bears, 10-3 (GB)
Bears, 28-23 (C)
1955—Packers, 24-3 (GB)
Bears, 52-31 (C)
1956—Bears, 37-21 (GB)
Bears, 38-14 (C)
1957—Packers, 21-17 (GB)
Bears, 21-14 (C)
1958—Bears, 34-20 (GB)
Bears, 24-10 (C)
1959—Packers, 9-6 (GB)
Bears, 28-17 (C)
1960—Bears, 17-14 (GB)
Packers, 41-13 (C)
1961—Packers, 24-0 (GB)
Packers, 31-28 (C)
1962—Packers, 49-0 (GB)
Packers, 38-7 (C)
1963—Bears, 10-3 (GB)
Bears, 26-7 (C)
1964—Packers, 23-12 (GB)
Packers, 17-3 (C)
1965—Packers, 23-14 (GB)
Bears, 31-10 (C)
1966—Packers, 17-0 (C)
Packers, 13-6 (GB)
1967—Packers, 13-10 (GB)
Packers, 17-13 (C)
1968—Bears, 13-10 (GB)
Packers, 28-27 (C)

1969—Packers, 17-0 (GB)
Packers, 21-3 (C)
1970—Packers, 20-19 (GB)
Bears, 35-17 (C)
1971—Packers, 17-14 (C)
Packers, 31-10 (GB)
1972—Packers, 20-17 (GB)
Packers, 23-17 (C)
1973—Bears, 31-17 (GB)
Packers, 21-0 (C)
1974—Bears, 10-9 (C)
Packers, 20-3 (Mil)
1975—Bears, 27-14 (C)
Packers, 28-7 (GB)
1976—Bears, 24-13 (C)
Bears, 16-10 (GB)
1977—Packers, 26-0 (GB)
Bears, 21-10 (C)
1978—Packers, 24-14 (GB)
Bears, 14-0 (C)
1979—Bears, 6-3 (C)
Bears, 15-14 (GB)
1980—Packers, 12-6 (GB) OT
Bears, 61-7 (C)
1981—Packers, 16-9 (C)
Packers, 21-17 (GB)
1983—Packers, 31-28 (GB)
Bears, 23-21 (C)
1984—Bears, 9-7 (GB)
Packers, 20-14 (C)
1985—Bears, 23-7 (C)
Bears, 16-10 (GB)
1986—Bears, 25-12 (GB)
Bears, 12-10 (C)
1987—Bears, 26-24 (GB)
Bears, 23-10 (C)
1988—Bears, 24-6 (GB)
Bears, 16-0 (C)
1989—Packers, 14-13 (GB)
Packers, 40-28 (C)
1990—Bears, 31-13 (GB)
Bears, 27-13 (C)
1991—Bears, 10-0 (GB)
Bears, 27-13 (C)
1992—Bears, 30-10 (GB)
Packers, 17-3 (C)
1993—Packers, 17-3 (GB)
Bears, 30-17 (C)
1994—Packers, 33-6 (C)
Packers, 40-3 (GB)
1995—Packers, 27-24 (C)
Packers, 35-28 (GB)
1996—Packers, 37-6 (C)
Packers, 28-17 (GB)
1997—Packers, 38-24 (GB)
Packers, 24-23 (C)
1998—Packers, 26-20 (GB)
Packers, 16-13 (C)
1999—Bears, 14-13 (GB)
Packers, 35-19 (C)
2000—Bears, 27-24 (GB)
Packers, 28-6 (C)
2001—Packers, 20-12 (C)
Packers, 17-7 (GB)
2002—Packers, 34-21 (C)
Packers, 30-20 (GB)
2003—Packers, 38-23 (C)
Packers, 34-21 (GB)
2004—Bears, 21-10 (GB)
Packers, 31-14 (C)

2005—Bears, 19-7 (C)
    Bears, 24-17 (GB)
(RS Pts.—Bears 2,890, Packers 2,772)
(PS Pts.—Bears 33, Packers 14)
*Bears known as Staleys prior to 1922
**Division Playoff

CHICAGO vs. HOUSTON
RS: Texans lead series, 1-0
2004—Texans, 24-5 (C)
(RS Pts.—Texans 24, Bears 5)

CHICAGO vs. *INDIANAPOLIS
RS: Colts lead series, 22-17
1953—Colts, 13-9 (B)
    Colts, 16-14 (C)
1954—Bears, 28-9 (C)
    Bears, 28-13 (B)
1955—Colts, 23-17 (B)
    Bears, 38-10 (C)
1956—Colts, 28-21 (B)
    Bears, 58-27 (C)
1957—Colts, 21-10 (B)
    Colts, 29-14 (C)
1958—Colts, 51-38 (B)
    Colts, 17-0 (C)
1959—Bears, 26-21 (B)
    Colts, 21-7 (C)
1960—Colts, 42-7 (B)
    Colts, 24-20 (C)
1961—Bears, 24-10 (C)
    Bears, 21-20 (B)
1962—Bears, 35-15 (C)
    Bears, 57-0 (B)
1963—Bears, 10-3 (C)
    Bears, 17-7 (B)
1964—Colts, 52-0 (B)
    Colts, 40-24 (C)
1965—Colts, 26-21 (C)
    Bears, 13-0 (B)
1966—Bears, 27-17 (C)
    Colts, 21-16 (B)
1967—Colts, 24-3 (C)
1968—Colts, 28-7 (B)
1969—Colts, 24-21 (C)
1970—Colts, 21-20 (B)
1975—Colts, 35-7 (C)
1983—Colts, 22-19 (B) OT
1985—Bears, 17-10 (C)
1988—Bears, 17-13 (I)
1991—Bears, 31-17 (I)
2000—Bears, 27-24 (C)
2004—Colts, 41-10 (C)
(RS Pts.—Colts 835, Bears 779)
*Franchise in Baltimore prior to 1984

CHICAGO vs. JACKSONVILLE
RS: Series tied, 2-2
1995—Bears, 30-27 (J)
1998—Jaguars, 24-23 (C)
2001—Bears, 33-13 (C)
2004—Jaguars, 22-3 (J)
(RS Pts.—Bears 89, Jaguars 86)

CHICAGO vs. KANSAS CITY
RS: Bears lead series, 5-4
1973—Chiefs, 19-7 (KC)
1977—Bears, 28-27 (C)
1981—Bears, 16-13 (KC) OT
1987—Bears, 31-28 (C)
1990—Chiefs, 21-10 (C)
1993—Bears, 19-17 (KC)
1996—Chiefs, 14-10 (KC)
1999—Bears, 20-17 (C)

2003—Chiefs, 31-3 (KC)
(RS Pts.—Chiefs 187, Bears 144)

CHICAGO vs. MIAMI
RS: Dolphins lead series, 6-3
1971—Dolphins, 34-3 (M)
1975—Dolphins, 46-13 (C)
1979—Dolphins, 31-16 (M)
1985—Dolphins, 38-24 (M)
1988—Bears, 34-7 (C)
1991—Dolphins, 16-13 (C) OT
1994—Bears, 17-14 (M)
1997—Bears, 36-33 (M) OT
2002—Dolphins, 27-9 (M)
(RS Pts.—Dolphins 246, Bears 165)

CHICAGO vs. MINNESOTA
RS: Vikings lead series, 48-39-2
PS: Bears lead series, 1-0
1961—Vikings, 37-13 (M)
    Bears, 52-35 (C)
1962—Bears, 13-0 (M)
    Bears, 31-30 (C)
1963—Bears, 28-7 (M)
    Tie, 17-17 (C)
1964—Bears, 34-28 (M)
    Vikings, 41-14 (C)
1965—Bears, 45-37 (M)
    Vikings, 24-17 (C)
1966—Bears, 13-10 (M)
    Bears, 41-28 (C)
1967—Bears, 17-7 (M)
    Tie, 10-10 (C)
1968—Bears, 27-17 (M)
    Bears, 26-24 (C)
1969—Vikings, 31-0 (C)
    Vikings, 31-14 (M)
1970—Vikings, 24-0 (C)
    Vikings, 16-13 (M)
1971—Bears, 20-17 (M)
    Vikings, 27-10 (C)
1972—Bears, 13-10 (C)
    Vikings, 23-10 (M)
1073—Vikings, 22-13 (C)
    Vikings, 31-13 (M)
1974—Vikings, 11-7 (M)
    Vikings, 17-0 (C)
1975—Vikings, 28-3 (M)
    Vikings, 13-9 (C)
1976—Vikings, 20-19 (M)
    Bears, 14-13 (C)
1977—Vikings, 22-16 (M) OT
    Bears, 10-7 (C)
1978—Vikings, 24-20 (M)
    Vikings, 17-14 (M)
1979—Bears, 26-7 (C)
    Vikings, 30-27 (M)
1980—Vikings, 34-14 (C)
    Vikings, 13-7 (M)
1981—Vikings, 24-21 (M)
    Bears, 10-9 (C)
1982—Vikings, 35-7 (M)
1983—Vikings, 23-14 (C)
    Bears, 19-13 (M)
1984—Bears, 16-7 (C)
    Bears, 34-3 (M)
1985—Bears, 33-24 (M)
    Bears, 27-9 (C)
1986—Bears, 23-0 (C)
    Vikings, 23-7 (M)
1987—Bears, 27-7 (C)
    Bears, 30-24 (M)

1988—Vikings, 31-7 (C)
    Vikings, 28-27 (M)
1989—Bears, 38-7 (C)
    Vikings, 27-16 (M)
1990—Bears, 19-16 (C)
    Vikings, 41-13 (M)
1991—Bears, 10-6 (C)
    Bears, 34-17 (M)
1992—Vikings, 21-20 (M)
    Vikings, 38-10 (C)
1993—Vikings, 10-7 (M)
    Vikings, 19-12 (C)
1994—Vikings, 42-14 (C)
    Vikings, 33-27 (M) OT
    *Bears, 35-18 (M)
1995—Bears, 31-14 (C)
    Bears, 14-6 (M)
1996—Vikings, 20-14 (C)
    Bears, 15-13 (M)
1997—Vikings, 27-24 (C)
    Vikings, 29-22 (M)
1998—Vikings, 31-28 (C)
    Vikings, 48-22 (M)
1999—Bears, 24-22 (M)
    Vikings, 27-24 (C) OT
2000—Vikings, 30-27 (M)
    Vikings, 28-16 (C)
2001—Bears, 17-10 (C)
    Bears, 13-6 (M)
2002—Bears, 27-23 (C)
    Vikings, 25-7 (M)
2003—Vikings, 24-13 (M)
    Bears, 13-10 (C)
2004—Vikings, 27-22 (M)
    Bears, 24-14 (C)
2005—Bears, 28-3 (C)
    Vikings, 34-10 (M)
RS Pts.—Vikings 1,848, Bears 1,647)
(PS Pts.—Bears 35, Vikings 18)
*NFC First-Round Playoff

CHICAGO vs. NEW ENGLAND
RS: Patriots lead series, 6-3
PS: Bears lead series, 1-0
1973—Patriots, 13-10 (C)
1979—Patriots, 27-7 (C)
1982—Bears, 26-13 (C)
1985—Bears, 20-7 (C)
    *Bears, 46-10 (New Orleans)
1988—Patriots, 30-7 (NE)
1994—Patriots, 13-3 (C)
1997—Patriots, 31-3 (NE)
2000—Bears, 24-17 (C)
2002—Patriots, 33-30 (C)
(RS Pts.—Patriots 184, Bears 130)
(PS Pts.—Bears 46, Patriots 10)
*Super Bowl XX

CHICAGO vs. NEW ORLEANS
RS: Series tied, 11-11
PS: Bears lead series, 1-0
1968—Bears, 23-17 (NO)
1970—Bears, 24-3 (NO)
1971—Bears, 35-14 (C)
1973—Saints, 21-16 (NO)
1974—Bears, 24-10 (C)
1975—Bears, 42-17 (NO)
1977—Saints, 42-24 (C)
1980—Bears, 22-3 (C)
1982—Saints, 10-0 (C)
1983—Saints, 34-31 (NO) OT
1984—Bears, 20-7 (C)

1987—Saints, 19-17 (C)
1990—*Bears, 16-6 (C)
1991—Bears, 20-17 (NO)
1992—Saints, 28-6 (NO)
1994—Bears, 17-7 (C)
1996—Saints, 27-24 (NO)
1997—Saints, 20-17 (C)
1999—Bears, 14-10 (C)
2000—Saints, 31-10 (C)
2002—Saints, 29-23 (C)
2003—Bears, 20-13 (NO)
2005—Bears, 20-17 (Baton Rouge)
(RS Pts.—Bears 442, Saints 403)
(PS Pts.—Bears 16, Saints 6)
*NFC First-Round Playoff
CHICAGO vs. N.Y. GIANTS
RS: Bears lead series, 26-17-2
PS: Bears lead series, 5-3
1925—Bears, 19-7 (NY)
  Giants, 9-0 (C)
1926—Bears, 7-0 (C)
1927—Giants, 13-7 (NY)
1928—Bears, 13-0 (C)
1929—Bears, 26-14 (C)
  Giants, 34-0 (NY)
  Giants, 14-9 (C)
1930—Giants, 12-0 (C)
  Bears, 12-0 (NY)
1931—Bears, 6-0 (C)
  Bears, 12-6 (NY)
  Giants, 25-6 (C)
1932—Bears, 28-8 (NY)
  Bears, 6-0 (C)
1933—Bears, 14-10 (C)
  Giants, 3-0 (NY)
  *Bears, 23-21 (C)
1934—Bears, 27-7 (C)
  Bears, 10-9 (NY)
  *Giants, 30-13 (NY)
1935—Bears, 20-3 (NY)
  Giants, 3-0 (C)
1936—Bears, 25-7 (NY)
1937—Tie, 3-3 (NY)
1939—Giants, 16-13 (NY)
1940—Bears, 37-21 (NY)
1941—*Bears, 37-9 (C)
1942—Bears, 26-7 (NY)
1943—Bears, 56-7 (NY)
1946—Giants, 14-0 (NY)
  *Bears, 24-14 (NY)
1948—Bears, 35-14 (C)
1949—Giants, 35-28 (NY)
1956—Tie, 17-17 (NY)
  *Giants, 47-7 (NY)
1962—Giants, 26-24 (C)
1963—*Bears, 14-10 (C)
1965—Bears, 35-14 (NY)
1967—Bears, 34-7 (C)
1969—Giants, 28-24 (NY)
1970—Bears, 24-16 (NY)
1974—Bears, 16-13 (C)
1977—Bears, 12-9 (NY) OT
1985—**Bears, 21-0 (C)
1987—Bears, 34-19 (C)
1990—**Giants, 31-3 (NY)
1991—Bears, 20-17 (C)
1992—Giants, 27-14 (C)
1993—Giants, 26-20 (C)
1995—Bears, 27-24 (NY)
2000—Giants, 14-7 (C)

2004—Bears, 28-21 (NY)
(RS Pts.—Bears 769, Giants 591)
(PS Pts.—Giants 162, Bears 142)
*NFL Championship
**NFC Divisional Playoff
CHICAGO vs. N.Y. JETS
RS: Bears lead series, 5-3
1974—Jets, 23-21 (C)
1979—Bears, 23-13 (C)
1985—Bears, 19-6 (NY)
1991—Bears, 19-13 (C) OT
1994—Bears, 19-7 (NY)
1997—Jets, 23-15 (C)
2000—Jets, 17-10 (NY)
2002—Bears, 20-13 (C)
(RS Pts.—Bears 146, Jets 115)
CHICAGO vs. *OAKLAND
RS: Raiders lead series, 6-5
1972—Raiders, 28-21 (O)
1976—Bears, 28-27 (C)
1978—Raiders, 25-19 (C) OT
1981—Bears, 23-6 (O)
1984—Bears, 17-6 (C)
1987—Bears, 6-3 (LA)
1990—Raiders, 24-10 (LA)
1993—Raiders, 16-14 (C)
1996—Bears, 19-17 (C)
1999—Raiders, 24-17 (O)
2003—Bears, 24-21 (O)
(RS Pts.—Raiders 198, Bears 197)
*Franchise in Los Angeles from 1982-1994
CHICAGO vs. PHILADELPHIA
RS: Bears lead series, 24-8-1
PS: Eagles lead series, 2-1
1933—Tie, 3-3 (P)
1935—Bears, 39-0 (P)
1936—Bears, 17-0 (P)
  Bears, 28-7 (P)
1938—Bears, 28-6 (P)
1939—Bears, 27-14 (C)
1941—Bears, 49-14 (P)
1942—Bears, 45-14 (C)
1944—Bears, 28-7 (P)
1946—Bears, 21-14 (C)
1947—Bears, 40-7 (C)
1948—Eagles, 12-7 (P)
1949—Bears, 38-21 (C)
1955—Bears, 17-10 (C)
1961—Eagles, 16-14 (P)
1963—Bears, 16-7 (C)
1968—Bears, 29-16 (P)
1970—Bears, 20-16 (C)
1972—Bears, 21-12 (P)
1975—Bears, 15-13 (C)
1979—*Eagles, 27-17 (P)
1980—Eagles, 17-14 (P)
1983—Bears, 7-6 (P)
  Bears, 17-14 (C)
1986—Bears, 13-10 (C) OT
1987—Bears, 35-3 (P)
1988—**Bears, 20-12 (C)
1989—Bears, 27-13 (C)
1993—Bears, 17-6 (P)
1994—Eagles, 30-22 (P)
1995—Bears, 20-14 (C)
1999—Eagles, 20-16 (C)
2000—Eagles, 13-9 (P)
2001—**Eagles, 33-19 (C)
2002—Eagles, 19-13 (C)
2004—Eagles, 19-9 (C)

(RS Pts.—Bears 721, Eagles 393)
(PS Pts.—Eagles 72, Bears 56)
*NFC First-Round Playoff
**NFC Divisional Playoff
CHICAGO vs. *PITTSBURGH
RS: Bears lead series, 16-7-1
1934—Bears, 28-0 (P)
1935—Bears, 23-7 (P)
1936—Bears, 27-9 (P)
  Bears, 26-6 (C)
1937—Bears, 7-0 (P)
1939—Bears, 32-0 (P)
1941—Bears, 34-7 (C)
1945—Bears, 28-7 (C)
1947—Bears, 49-7 (C)
1949—Bears, 30-21 (C)
1958—Steelers, 24-10 (P)
1959—Bears, 27-21 (C)
1963—Tie, 17-17 (P)
1967—Steelers, 41-13 (P)
1969—Bears, 38-7 (C)
1971—Bears, 17-15 (C)
1975—Steelers, 34-3 (P)
1980—Steelers, 38-3 (P)
1986—Bears, 13-10 (C) OT
1989—Bears, 20-0 (P)
1992—Bears, 30-6 (C)
1995—Steelers, 37-34 (C) OT
1998—Steelers, 17-12 (P)
2005—Steelers, 21-9 (P)
(RS Pts.—Bears 530, Steelers 352)
*Steelers known as Pirates prior to 1941
CHICAGO vs. *ST. LOUIS
RS: Bears lead series, 47-34-3
PS: Series tied, 1-1
1937—Bears, 20-2 (Clev)
  Bears, 15-7 (C)
1938—Rams, 14-7 (C)
  Rams, 23-21 (Clev)
1939—Bears, 30-21 (Clev)
  Bears, 35-21 (C)
1940—Bears, 21-14 (Clev)
  Bears, 47-25 (C)
1941—Bears, 48-21 (Clev)
  Bears, 31-13 (C)
1942—Bears, 21-7 (Clev)
  Bears, 47-0 (C)
1944—Rams, 19-7 (Clev)
  Bears, 28-21 (C)
1945—Rams, 17-0 (Clev)
  Rams, 41-21 (C)
1946—Tie, 28-28 (C)
  Bears, 27-21 (LA)
1947—Bears, 41-21 (C)
  Rams, 17-14 (C)
1948—Bears, 42-21 (C)
  Bears, 21-6 (LA)
1949—Rams, 31-16 (C)
  Rams, 27-24 (LA)
1950—Bears, 24-20 (LA)
  Bears, 24-14 (C)
  **Rams, 24-14 (LA)
1951—Rams, 42-17 (C)
1952—Rams, 31-7 (LA)
  Rams, 40-24 (C)
1953—Rams, 38-24 (LA)
  Bears, 24-21 (C)
1954—Rams, 42-38 (LA)
  Bears, 24-13 (C)
1955—Bears, 31-20 (LA)

Bears, 24-3 (C)
1956—Bears, 35-24 (LA)
Bears, 30-21 (C)
1957—Bears, 34-26 (C)
Bears, 16-10 (LA)
1958—Bears, 31-10 (C)
Rams, 41-35 (LA)
1959—Bears, 28-21 (C)
Bears, 26-21 (LA)
1960—Bears, 34-27 (C)
Tie, 24-24 (LA)
1961—Bears, 21-17 (LA)
Bears, 28-24 (C)
1962—Bears, 27-23 (LA)
Bears, 30-14 (C)
1963—Bears, 52-14 (LA)
Bears, 6-0 (C)
1964—Bears, 38-17 (C)
Bears, 34-24 (LA)
1965—Rams, 30-28 (LA)
Bears, 31-6 (C)
1966—Rams, 31-17 (LA)
Bears, 17-10 (C)
1967—Rams, 28-17 (C)
1968—Bears, 17-16 (LA)
1969—Rams, 9-7 (C)
1971—Rams, 17-3 (LA)
1972—Tie, 13-13 (C)
1973—Rams, 26-0 (C)
1975—Rams, 38-10 (LA)
1976—Rams, 20-12 (LA)
1977—Bears, 24-23 (C)
1979—Bears, 27-23 (C)
1981—Rams, 24-7 (C)
1982—Bears, 34-26 (LA)
1983—Rams, 21-14 (LA)
1984—Rams, 29-13 (LA)
1985—***Bears, 24-0 (C)
1986—Rams, 20-17 (C)
1988—Rams, 23-3 (LA)
1989—Bears, 20-10 (C)
1990—Bears, 38-9 (C)
1993—Rams, 20-6 (LA)
1994—Bears, 27-13 (C)
1995—Rams, 34-28 (StL)
1996—Bears, 35-9 (C)
1997—Bears, 13-10 (StL)
1998—Rams, 20-12 (C)
1999—Rams, 34-12 (StL)
2002—Rams, 21-16 (StL)
2003—Rams, 23-21 (C)
(RS Pts.—Bears 1,934, Rams 1,723)
(PS Pts.—Bears 38, Rams 24)
*Franchise in Los Angeles prior to 1995
and in Cleveland prior to 1946
**Conference Playoff
***NFC Championship
CHICAGO vs. SAN DIEGO
RS: Bears lead series, 5-4
1970—Chargers, 20-7 (C)
1974—Chargers, 28-21 (SD)
1978—Chargers, 40-7 (SD)
1981—Bears, 20-17 (C) OT
1984—Chargers, 20-7 (SD)
1993—Bears, 16-13 (SD)
1996—Bears, 27-14 (C)
1999—Bears, 23-20 (SD) OT
2003—Bears, 20-7 (C)
(RS Pts.—Chargers 179, Bears 148)

CHICAGO vs. SAN FRANCISCO
RS: Bears lead series, 28-27-1
PS: 49ers lead series, 3-0
1950—Bears, 32-20 (SF)
Bears, 17-0 (C)
1951—Bears, 13-7 (C)
1952—49ers, 40-16 (C)
Bears, 20-17 (SF)
1953—49ers, 35-28 (C)
49ers, 24-14 (SF)
1954—49ers, 31-24 (C)
Bears, 31-27 (SF)
1955—49ers, 20-19 (C)
Bears, 34-23 (SF)
1956—Bears, 31-7 (C)
Bears, 38-21 (SF)
1957—49ers, 21-17 (C)
49ers, 21-17 (SF)
1958—Bears, 28-6 (C)
Bears, 27-14 (SF)
1959—49ers, 20-17 (SF)
Bears, 14-3 (C)
1960—Bears, 27-10 (C)
49ers, 25-7 (SF)
1961—Bears, 31-0 (C)
49ers, 41-31 (SF)
1962—Bears, 30-14 (SF)
49ers, 34-27 (C)
1963—49ers, 20-14 (SF)
Bears, 27-7 (C)
1964—49ers, 31-21 (SF)
Bears, 23-21 (C)
1965—49ers, 52-24 (SF)
Bears, 61-20 (C)
1966—Tie, 30-30 (C)
49ers, 41-14 (SF)
1967—Bears, 28-14 (SF)
1968—Bears, 27-19 (C)
1969—49ers, 42-21 (SF)
1970—Bears, 37-16 (C)
1971—49ers, 13-0 (SF)
1972—49ers, 34-21 (C)
1974—49ers, 34-0 (C)
1975—49ers, 31-3 (SF)
1976—Bears, 19-12 (SF)
1978—Bears, 16-13 (SF)
1979—Bears, 28-27 (SF)
1981—49ers, 28-17 (SF)
1983—Bears, 13-3 (C)
1984—*49ers, 23-0 (SF)
1985—Bears, 26-10 (SF)
1987—49ers, 41-0 (SF)
1988—Bears, 10-9 (C)
*49ers, 28-3 (C)
1989—49ers, 26-0 (SF)
1991—49ers, 52-14 (SF)
1994—**49ers, 44-15 (SF)
2000—49ers, 17-0 (C)
2001—Bears, 37-31 (C) OT
2003—49ers, 49-7 (SF)
2004—Bears, 23-13 (C)
2005—Bears, 17-9 (C)
(RS Pts.—49ers 1,267, Bears 1,147)
(PS Pts.—49ers 95, Bears 18)
*NFC Championship
**NFC Divisional Playoff
CHICAGO vs. SEATTLE
RS: Seahawks lead series, 6-2
1976—Bears, 34-7 (S)
1978—Seahawks, 31-29 (C)

1982—Seahawks, 20-14 (S)
1984—Seahawks, 38-9 (S)
1987—Seahawks, 34-21 (C)
1990—Bears, 17-0 (C)
1999—Seahawks, 14-13 (C)
2003—Seahawks, 24-17 (S)
(RS Pts.—Seahawks 168, Bears 154)
CHICAGO vs. TAMPA BAY
RS: Bears lead series, 34-17
1977—Bears, 10-0 (TB)
1978—Buccaneers, 33-19 (TB)
Bears, 14-3 (C)
1979—Buccaneers, 17-13 (C)
Bears, 14-0 (TB)
1980—Bears, 23-0 (C)
Bears, 14-13 (TB)
1981—Bears, 28-17 (C)
Buccaneers, 20-10 (TB)
1982—Buccaneers, 26-23 (TB) OT
1983—Bears, 17-10 (C)
Bears, 27-0 (TB)
1984—Bears, 34-14 (C)
Bears, 44-9 (TB)
1985—Bears, 38-28 (C)
Bears, 27-19 (TB)
1986—Bears, 23-3 (TB)
Bears, 48-14 (C)
1987—Bears, 20-3 (C)
Bears, 27-26 (TB)
1988—Bears, 28-10 (C)
Bears, 27-15 (TB)
1989—Buccaneers, 42-35 (TB)
Buccaneers, 32-31 (C)
1990—Bears, 26-6 (TB)
Bears, 27-14 (C)
1991—Bears, 21-20 (TB)
Bears, 27-0 (C)
1992—Bears, 31-14 (C)
Buccaneers, 20-17 (TB)
1993—Bears, 47-17 (C)
Buccaneers, 13-10 (TB)
1994—Bears, 21-9 (C)
Bears, 20-6 (TB)
1995—Bears, 25-6 (TB)
Bears, 31-10 (C)
1996—Bears, 13-10 (C)
Buccaneers, 34-19 (TB)
1997—Bears, 13-7 (C)
Buccaneers, 31-15 (TB)
1998—Buccaneers, 27-15 (TB)
Buccaneers, 31-17 (C)
1999—Buccaneers, 6-3 (TB)
Buccaneers, 20-6 (C)
2000—Buccaneers, 41-0 (TB)
Bears, 13-10 (C)
2001—Bears, 27-24 (TB)
Bears, 27-3 (C)
2002—Buccaneers, 15-0 (C)
2004—Buccaneers, 19-7 (TB)
2005—Bears, 13-10 (TB)
(RS Pts.—Bears 1,085, Buccaneers 777)
CHICAGO vs. *TENNESSEE
RS: Bears lead series, 5-4
1973—Bears, 35-14 (C)
1977—Oilers, 47-0 (H)
1980—Oilers, 10-6 (C)
1986—Bears, 20-7 (H)
1989—Oilers, 33-28 (C)
1992—Oilers, 24-7 (H)
1995—Bears, 35-32 (C)

1998—Bears, 23-20 (T)
2004—Bears, 19-17 (T) OT
(RS Pts.—Titans 204, Bears 173)
*Franchise in Houston prior to 1997;
known as Oilers prior to 1999*
CHICAGO vs. *WASHINGTON
RS: Bears lead series, 20-17-1
PS: Redskins lead series, 4-3
1932—Tie, 7-7 (B)
1933—Bears, 7-0 (C)
    Redskins, 10-0 (B)
1934—Bears, 21-0 (B)
1935—Bears, 30-14 (B)
1936—Bears, 26-0 (B)
1937—**Redskins, 28-21 (C)
1938—Bears, 31-7 (C)
1940—Redskins, 7-3 (W)
    **Bears, 73-0 (W)
1941—Bears, 35-21 (C)
1942—**Redskins, 14-6 (W)
1943—Redskins, 21-7 (W)
    **Bears, 41-21 (C)
1945—Redskins, 28-21 (W)
1946—Bears, 24-20 (C)
1947—Bears, 56-20 (W)
1948—Bears, 48-13 (C)
1949—Bears, 31-21 (W)
1951—Bears, 27-0 (W)
1953—Bears, 27-24 (W)
1957—Redskins, 14-3 (C)
1964—Redskins, 27-20 (W)
1968—Redskins, 38-28 (C)
1971—Bears, 16-15 (C)
1974—Redskins, 42-0 (W)
1976—Bears, 33-7 (C)
1978—Bears, 14-10 (W)
1980—Bears, 35-21 (C)
1981—Redskins, 24-7 (C)
1984—***Bears, 23-19 (W)
1985—Bears, 45-10 (C)
1986—***Redskins, 27-13 (C)
1987—***Redskins, 21-17 (C)
1988—Bears, 34-14 (W)
1989—Redskins, 38-14 (W)
1990—Redskins, 10-9 (W)
1991—Redskins, 20-7 (C)
1996—Redskins, 10-3 (C)
1997—Redskins, 31-8 (C)
1999—Redskins, 48-22 (W)
2001—Bears, 20-15 (W)
2003—Bears, 27-24 (C)
2004—Redskins, 13-10 (C)
2005—Redskins, 9-7 (W)
(RS Pts.—Bears 763, Redskins 653)
(PS Pts.—Bears 194, Redskins 130)
*Franchise in Boston prior to 1937 and
known as Braves prior to 1933*
**NFL Championship
***NFC Divisional Playoff

CINCINNATI vs. ARIZONA
RS: Bengals lead series, 5-3;
See Arizona vs. Cincinnati
CINCINNATI vs. ATLANTA
RS: Bengals lead series, 7-3;
See Atlanta vs. Cincinnati
CINCINNATI vs. BALTIMORE
RS: Ravens lead series, 12-8;
See Baltimore vs. Cincinnati

CINCINNATI vs. BUFFALO
RS: Bills lead series, 13-9
PS: Bengals lead series, 2-0;
See Buffalo vs. Cincinnati
CINCINNATI vs. CAROLINA
RS: Panthers lead series, 2-0;
See Carolina vs. Cincinnati
CINCINNATI vs. CHICAGO
RS: Bengals lead series, 5-3;
See Chicago vs. Cincinnati
CINCINNATI vs. CLEVELAND
RS: Browns lead series, 33-32
1970—Browns, 30-27 (Cle)
    Bengals, 14-10 (Cin)
1971—Browns, 27-24 (Cin)
    Browns, 31-27 (Cle)
1972—Browns, 27-6 (Cle)
    Browns, 27-24 (Cin)
1973—Browns, 17-10 (Cle)
    Bengals, 34-17 (Cin)
1974—Bengals, 33-7 (Cin)
    Bengals, 34-24 (Cle)
1975—Bengals, 24-17 (Cin)
    Browns, 35-23 (Cle)
1976—Bengals, 45-24 (Cle)
    Bengals, 21-6 (Cin)
1977—Browns, 13-3 (Cin)
    Bengals, 10-7 (Cle)
1978—Browns, 13-10 (Cle) OT
    Bengals, 48-16 (Cin)
1979—Browns, 28-27 (Cle)
    Bengals, 16-12 (Cin)
1980—Browns, 31-7 (Cle)
    Browns, 27-24 (Cin)
1981—Browns, 20-17 (Cin)
    Bengals, 41-21 (Cle)
1982—Bengals, 23-10 (Cin)
1983—Browns, 17-7 (Cle)
    Bengals, 28-21 (Cin)
1984—Bengals, 12-9 (Cin)
    Bengals, 20-17 (Cle) OT
1985—Bengals, 27-10 (Cin)
    Browns, 24-6 (Cle)
1986—Bengals, 30-13 (Cle)
    Browns, 34-3 (Cin)
1987—Browns, 34-0 (Cin)
    Browns, 38-24 (Cle)
1988—Bengals, 24-17 (Cin)
    Browns, 23-16 (Cle)
1989—Bengals, 21-14 (Cin)
    Bengals, 21-0 (Cle)
1990—Bengals, 34-13 (Cle)
    Bengals, 21-14 (Cin)
1991—Browns, 14-13 (Cle)
    Bengals, 23-21 (Cin)
1992—Bengals, 30-10 (Cin)
    Browns, 37-21 (Cle)
1993—Browns, 27-14 (Cle)
    Browns, 28-17 (Cin)
1994—Browns, 28-20 (Cin)
    Browns, 37-13 (Cle)
1995—Browns, 29-26 (Cin) OT
    Browns, 26-10 (Cle)
1999—Bengals, 18-17 (Cle)
    Bengals, 44-28 (Cin)
2000—Browns, 24-7 (Cin)
    Bengals, 12-3 (Cle)
2001—Bengals, 24-14 (Cin)
    Browns, 18-0 (Cle)
2002—Browns, 20-7 (Cle)

    Browns, 27-20 (Cin)
2003—Bengals, 21-14 (Cle)
    Browns, 22-14 (Cin)
2004—Browns, 34-17 (Cle)
    Bengals, 58-48 (Cin)
2005—Bengals, 27-13 (Cle)
    Bengals, 23-20 (Cin)
(RS Pts.—Browns 1,354, Bengals 1,345)
CINCINNATI vs. DALLAS
RS: Cowboys lead series, 5-4
1973—Cowboys, 38-10 (D)
1979—Cowboys, 38-13 (D)
1985—Bengals, 50-24 (C)
1988—Cowboys, 38-24 (D)
1991—Cowboys, 35-23 (D)
1994—Cowboys, 23-20 (C)
1997—Bengals, 31-24 (C)
2000—Cowboys, 23-6 (D)
2004—Bengals, 26-3 (C)
(RS Pts.—Cowboys 232, Bengals 217)
CINCINNATI vs. DENVER
RS: Broncos lead series, 15-8
1968—Bengals, 24-10 (C)
    Broncos, 10-7 (D)
1969—Bengals, 30-23 (C)
    Broncos, 27-16 (D)
1971—Bengals, 24-10 (D)
1972—Bengals, 21-10 (C)
1973—Broncos, 28-10 (D)
1975—Bengals, 17-16 (D)
1976—Bengals, 17-7 (C)
1977—Broncos, 24-13 (C)
1979—Broncos, 10-0 (D)
1981—Bengals, 38-21 (C)
1983—Broncos, 24-17 (D)
1984—Broncos, 20-17 (D)
1986—Broncos, 34-28 (D)
1991—Broncos, 45-14 (D)
1994—Broncos, 15-13 (C)
1996—Broncos, 14-10 (C)
1997—Broncos, 38-20 (D)
1998—Broncos, 33-26 (C)
2000—Bengals, 31-21 (C)
2003—Broncos, 30-10 (D)
2004—Bengals, 23-10 (C)
(RS Pts.—Broncos 487, Bengals 419)
CINCINNATI vs. DETROIT
RS: Bengals lead series, 6-3
1970—Lions, 38-3 (D)
1974—Lions, 23-19 (C)
1983—Bengals, 17-9 (C)
1986—Bengals, 24-17 (D)
1989—Bengals, 42-7 (C)
1992—Lions, 19-13 (C)
1998—Bengals, 34-28 (D) OT
2001—Bengals, 31-27 (D)
2005—Bengals, 41-17 (D)
(RS Pts.—Bengals 224, Lions 185)
CINCINNATI vs. GREEN BAY
RS: Series tied, 5-5
1971—Packers, 20-17 (GB)
1976—Bengals, 28-7 (C)
1977—Bengals, 17-7 (Mil)
1980—Packers, 14-9 (GB)
1983—Bengals, 34-14 (C)
1986—Bengals, 34-28 (Mil)
1992—Packers, 24-23 (GB)
1995—Packers, 24-10 (GB)
1998—Packers, 13-6 (C)
2005—Bengals, 21-14 (C)

(RS Pts.—Bengals 199, Packers 165)

CINCINNATI vs. HOUSTON
RS: Bengals lead series, 3-0
2002—Bengals, 38-3 (H)
2003—Bengals, 34-27 (C)
2005—Bengals, 16-10 (C)
(RS Pts.—Bengals 88, Texans 40)

CINCINNATI vs. *INDIANAPOLIS
RS: Colts lead series, 13-8
PS: Colts lead series, 1-0
1970—**Colts, 17-0 (B)
1972—Colts, 20-19 (C)
1974—Bengals, 24-14 (B)
1976—Colts, 28-27 (B)
1979—Colts, 38-28 (B)
1980—Bengals, 34-33 (C)
1981—Bengals, 41-19 (B)
1982—Bengals, 20-17 (B)
1983—Colts, 34-31 (C)
1987—Bengals, 23-21 (I)
1989—Colts, 23-12 (C)
1990—Colts, 34-20 (C)
1992—Colts, 21-17 (C)
1993—Colts, 9-6 (C)
1994—Colts, 17-13 (C)
1995—Bengals, 24-21 (I) OT
1996—Bengals, 31-24 (C)
1997—Colts, 28-13 (I)
1998—Colts, 39-26 (I)
1999—Colts, 31-10 (I)
2002—Colts, 28-21 (I)
2005—Colts, 45-37 (C)
(RS Pts.—Colts 529, Bengals 492)
(PS Pts.—Colts 17, Bengals 0)
*Franchise in Baltimore prior to 1984
**AFC Divisional Playoff

CINCINNATI vs. JACKSONVILLE
RS: Jaguars lead series, 11-5
1995—Bengals, 24-17 (C)
       Bengals, 17-13 (J)
1996—Bengals, 28-21 (C)
       Jaguars, 30-27 (J)
1997—Jaguars, 21-13 (J)
       Bengals, 31-26 (C)
1998—Jaguars, 24-11 (J)
       Jaguars, 34-17 (C)
1999—Jaguars, 41-10 (C)
       Jaguars, 24-7 (J)
2000—Jaguars, 13-0 (J)
       Bengals, 17-14 (C)
2001—Jaguars, 30-13 (J)
       Jaguars, 14-10 (C)
2002—Jaguars, 29-15 (C)
2005—Jaguars, 23-20 (J)
(RS Pts.—Jaguars 374, Bengals 260)

CINCINNATI vs. KANSAS CITY
RS: Chiefs lead series, 12-10
1968—Chiefs, 13-3 (KC)
       Chiefs, 16-9 (C)
1969—Bengals, 24-19 (C)
       Chiefs, 42-22 (KC)
1970—Chiefs, 27-19 (C)
1972—Bengals, 23-16 (KC)
1973—Bengals, 14-6 (C)
1974—Bengals, 33-6 (C)
1976—Bengals, 27-24 (KC)
1977—Bengals, 27-7 (KC)
1978—Chiefs, 24-23 (C)
1979—Chiefs, 10-7 (C)
1980—Bengals, 20-6 (KC)

1983—Chiefs, 20-15 (KC)
1984—Chiefs, 27-22 (C)
1986—Chiefs, 24-14 (KC)
1987—Bengals, 30-27 (C) OT
1988—Chiefs, 31-28 (KC)
1989—Bengals, 21-17 (KC)
1993—Chiefs, 17-15 (KC)
2003—Bengals, 24-19 (C)
2005—Chiefs, 37-3 (KC)
(RS Pts.—Chiefs 435, Bengals 423)

CINCINNATI vs. MIAMI
RS: Dolphins lead series, 12-4
PS: Dolphins lead series, 1-0
1968—Dolphins, 24-22 (C)
       Bengals, 38-21 (M)
1969—Bengals, 27-21 (C)
1971—Dolphins, 23-13 (C)
1973—*Dolphins, 34-16 (M)
1974—Bengals, 24-3 (M)
1977—Bengals, 23-17 (C)
1978—Dolphins, 21-0 (M)
1980—Dolphins, 17-16 (M)
1983—Dolphins, 38-14 (M)
1987—Dolphins, 20-14 (C)
1989—Dolphins, 20-13 (C)
1991—Dolphins, 37-13 (M)
1994—Dolphins, 23-7 (C)
1995—Dolphins, 26-23 (C)
2000—Dolphins, 31-16 (C)
2004—Bengals, 16-13 (C)
(RS Pts.—Dolphins 376, Bengals 258)
(PS Pts.—Dolphins 34, Bengals 16)
*AFC Divisional Playoff

CINCINNATI vs. MINNESOTA
RS: Series tied, 5-5
1973—Bengals, 27-0 (C)
1977—Vikings, 42-10 (M)
1980—Bengals, 14-0 (C)
1983—Vikings, 20-14 (M)
1986—Bengals, 24-20 (C)
1989—Vikings, 29-21 (M)
1992—Vikings, 42-7 (C)
1995—Bengals, 27-24 (C)
1998—Vikings, 24-3 (M)
2005—Bengals, 37-8 (C)
(RS Pts.—Vikings 209, Bengals 184)

CINCINNATI vs. *NEW ENGLAND
RS: Patriots lead series, 11-8
1968—Patriots, 33-14 (B)
1969—Patriots, 25-14 (C)
1970—Bengals, 45-7 (C)
1972—Bengals, 31-7 (NE)
1975—Bengals, 27-10 (C)
1978—Patriots, 10-3 (C)
1979—Patriots, 20-14 (C)
1984—Patriots, 20-14 (NE)
1985—Patriots, 34-23 (NE)
1986—Bengals, 31-7 (NE)
1988—Patriots, 27-21 (NE)
1990—Bengals, 41-7 (C)
1991—Bengals, 29-7 (C)
1992—Bengals, 20-10 (C)
1993—Patriots, 7-2 (NE)
1994—Patriots, 31-28 (C)
2000—Patriots, 16-13 (NE)
2001—Bengals, 23-17 (C)
2004—Patriots, 35-28 (NE)
(RS Pts.—Bengals 421, Patriots 330)
*Franchise in Boston prior to 1971

CINCINNATI vs. NEW ORLEANS
RS: Series tied, 5-5
1970—Bengals, 26-6 (C)
1975—Bengals, 21-0 (NO)
1978—Saints, 20-18 (C)
1981—Saints, 17-7 (NO)
1984—Bengals, 24-21 (NO)
1987—Saints, 41-24 (C)
1990—Saints, 21-7 (C)
1993—Saints, 20-13 (NO)
1996—Bengals, 30-15 (C)
2002—Bengals, 20-13 (C)
(RS Pts.—Bengals 190, Saints 174)

CINCINNATI vs. N.Y. GIANTS
RS: Bengals lead series, 5-2
1972—Bengals, 13-10 (C)
1977—Bengals, 30-13 (C)
1985—Bengals, 35-30 (C)
1991—Bengals, 27-24 (C)
1994—Giants, 27-20 (NY)
1997—Giants, 29-27 (NY)
2004—Benglas, 23-22 (C)
(RS Pts.—Bengals 175, Giants 155)

CINCINNATI vs. N.Y. JETS
RS: Jets lead series, 12-6
PS: Jets lead series, 1-0
1968—Jets, 27-14 (NY)
1969—Jets, 21-7 (C)
       Jets, 40-7 (NY)
1971—Jets, 35-21 (NY)
1973—Bengals, 20-14 (C)
1976—Bengals, 42-3 (NY)
1981—Bengals, 31-30 (NY)
1982—*Jets, 44-17 (C)
1984—Jets, 43-23 (NY)
1985—Jets, 29-20 (C)
1986—Bengals, 52-21 (C)
1987—Jets, 27-20 (NY)
1988—Bengals, 36-19 (C)
1990—Bengals, 25-20 (C)
1992—Jets, 17-14 (NY)
1993—Jets, 17-12 (NY)
1997—Jets, 31-14 (C)
2001—Jets, 15-14 (NY)
2004—Jets, 31-24 (NY)
(RS Pts.—Jets 440, Bengals 396)
(PS Pts.—Jets 44, Bengals 17)
*AFC First-Round Playoff

CINCINNATI vs. *OAKLAND
RS: Raiders lead series, 17-7
PS: Raiders lead series, 2-0
1968—Raiders, 31-10 (O)
       Raiders, 34-0 (C)
1969—Bengals, 31-17 (C)
       Raiders, 37-17 (O)
1970—Bengals, 31-21 (C)
1971—Raiders, 31-27 (O)
1972—Raiders, 20-14 (C)
1974—Raiders, 30-27 (O)
1975—Bengals, 14-10 (C)
       **Raiders, 31-28 (O)
1976—Raiders, 35-20 (O)
1978—Raiders, 34-21 (C)
1980—Raiders, 28-17 (O)
1982—Bengals, 31-17 (C)
1983—Raiders, 20-10 (C)
1985—Raiders, 13-6 (LA)
1988—Bengals, 45-21 (LA)
1989—Raiders, 28-7 (LA)
1990—Raiders, 24-7 (LA)

**Raiders, 20-10 (LA)
1991—Raiders, 38-14 (C)
1992—Bengals, 24-21 (C) OT
1993—Bengals, 16-10 (C)
1995—Raiders, 20-17 (C)
1998—Raiders, 27-10 (O)
2003—Raiders, 23-20 (O)
(RS Pts.—Raiders 590, Bengals 436)
(PS Pts.—Raiders 51, Bengals 38)
*Franchise in Los Angeles from 1982-1994
**AFC Divisional Playoff

CINCINNATI vs. PHILADELPHIA
RS: Bengals lead series, 7-3
1971—Bengals, 37-14 (C)
1975—Bengals, 31-0 (P)
1979—Bengals, 37-13 (C)
1982—Bengals, 18-14 (P)
1988—Bengals, 28-24 (P)
1991—Eagles, 17-10 (P)
1994—Bengals, 33-30 (C)
1997—Eagles, 44-42 (P)
2000—Eagles, 16-7 (P)
2004—Bengals, 38-10 (P)
(RS Pts.—Bengals 281, Eagles 182)
CINCINNATI vs. PITTSBURGH
RS: Steelers lead series, 42-29
PS: Steelers lead series, 1-0
1970—Steelers, 21-10 (P)
    Bengals, 34-7 (C)
1971—Steelers, 21-10 (P)
    Steelers, 21-13 (C)
1972—Bengals, 15-10 (C)
    Steelers, 40-17 (P)
1973—Bengals, 19-7 (C)
    Steelers, 20-13 (P)
1974—Bengals, 17-10 (C)
    Steelers, 27-3 (P)
1975—Steelers, 30-24 (C)
    Steelers, 35-14 (P)
1976—Steelers, 23-6 (P)
    Steelers, 7-3 (C)
1977—Steelers, 20-14 (P)
    Bengals, 17-10 (C)
1978—Steelers, 28-3 (C)
    Steelers, 7-6 (P)
1979—Bengals, 34-10 (C)
    Steelers, 37-17 (P)
1980—Bengals, 30-28 (C)
    Bengals, 17-16 (P)
1981—Bengals, 34-7 (C)
    Bengals, 17-10 (P)
1982—Steelers, 26-20 (P) OT
1983—Steelers, 24-14 (C)
    Bengals, 23-10 (P)
1984—Steelers, 38-17 (P)
    Bengals, 22-20 (C)
1985—Bengals, 37-24 (P)
    Bengals, 26-21 (C)
1986—Bengals, 24-22 (C)
    Steelers, 30-9 (P)
1987—Steelers, 23-20 (P)
    Steelers, 30-16 (C)
1988—Bengals, 17-12 (P)
    Bengals, 42-7 (C)
1989—Bengals, 41-10 (C)
    Bengals, 26-16 (P)
1990—Bengals, 27-3 (C)
    Bengals, 16-12 (P)
1991—Steelers, 33-27 (C) OT
    Steelers, 17-10 (P)

1992—Steelers, 20-0 (P)
    Steelers, 21-9 (C)
1993—Steelers, 34-7 (P)
    Steelers, 24-16 (C)
1994—Steelers, 14-10 (P)
    Steelers, 38-15 (C)
1995—Bengals, 27-9 (P)
    Steelers, 49-31 (C)
1996—Steelers, 20-10 (P)
    Bengals, 34-24 (C)
1997—Steelers, 26-10 (C)
    Steelers, 20-3 (P)
1998—Bengals, 25-20 (C)
    Bengals, 25-24 (P)
1999—Steelers, 17-3 (C)
    Bengals, 27-20 (P)
2000—Steelers, 15-0 (P)
    Steelers, 48-28 (C)
2001—Steelers, 16-7 (P)
    Bengals, 26-23 (C) OT
2002—Steelers, 34-7 (C)
    Steelers, 29-21 (P)
2003—Steelers, 17-10 (C)
    Bengals, 24-20 (P)
2004—Steelers, 28-17 (P)
    Steelers, 19-14 (C)
2005—Steelers, 27-13 (C)
    Bengals, 38-31 (P)
    *Steelers, 31-17 (C)
(RS Pts.—Steelers 1,517, Bengals 1,278)
(PS Pts.—Steelers 31, Bengals 17)
*AFC First-Round Playoff
CINCINNATI vs. *ST. LOUIS
RS: Series tied, 5-5
1972—Rams, 15-12 (LA)
1976—Bengals, 20-12 (C)
1978—Bengals, 20-19 (LA)
1981—Bengals, 24-10 (C)
1984—Rams, 24-14 (C)
1990—Bengals, 34-31 (LA) OT
1993—Bengals, 15-3 (C)
1996—Rams, 26-16 (StL)
1999—Rams, 38-10 (C)
2003—Rams, 27-10 (StL)
(RS Pts.—Rams 205, Bengals 175)
*Franchise in Los Angeles prior to 1995
CINCINNATI vs. SAN DIEGO
RS: Chargers lead series, 17-10
PS: Bengals lead series, 1-0
1968—Chargers, 29-13 (SD)
    Chargers, 31-10 (C)
1969—Bengals, 34-20 (C)
    Chargers, 21-14 (SD)
1970—Bengals, 17-14 (SD)
1971—Bengals, 31-0 (C)
1973—Bengals, 20-13 (SD)
1974—Chargers, 20-17 (C)
1975—Bengals, 47-17 (C)
1977—Chargers, 24-3 (SD)
1978—Chargers, 22-13 (SD)
1979—Chargers, 26-24 (C)
1980—Chargers, 31-14 (C)
1981—Bengals, 40-17 (SD)
    *Bengals, 27-7 (C)
1982—Chargers, 50-34 (SD)
1985—Chargers, 44-41 (C)
1987—Chargers, 10-9 (C)
1988—Bengals, 27-10 (C)
1990—Bengals, 21-16 (SD)
1992—Chargers, 27-10 (SD)

1994—Chargers, 27-10 (SD)
1996—Chargers, 27-14 (SD)
1997—Bengals, 38-31 (C)
1999—Chargers, 34-7 (C)
2001—Chargers, 28-14 (SD)
2002—Chargers, 34-6 (C)
2003—Bengals, 34-27 (SD)
(RS Pts.—Chargers 650, Bengals 562)
(PS Pts.—Bengals 27, Chargers 7)
*AFC Championship
CINCINNATI vs. SAN FRANCISCO
RS: 49ers lead series, 7-3
PS: 49ers lead series, 2-0
1974—Bengals, 21-3 (SF)
1978—49ers, 28-12 (SF)
1981—49ers, 21-3 (C)
    *49ers, 26-21 (Detroit)
1984—49ers, 23-17 (SF)
1987—49ers, 27-26 (C)
1988—**49ers, 20-16 (Miami)
1990—49ers, 20-17 (C) OT
1993—49ers, 21-8 (SF)
1996—49ers, 28-21 (SF)
1999—Bengals, 44-30 (C)
2003—Bengals, 41-38 (C)
(RS Pts.—49ers 239, Bengals 210)
(PS Pts.—49ers 46, Bengals 37)
*Super Bowl XVI
**Super Bowl XXIII
CINCINNATI vs. SEATTLE
RS: Series tied, 8-8
PS: Bengals lead series, 1-0
1977—Bengals, 42-20 (C)
1981—Bengals, 27-21 (C)
1982—Bengals, 24-10 (C)
1984—Seahawks, 26-6 (C)
1985—Seahawks, 28-24 (C)
1986—Bengals, 34-7 (C)
1987—Bengals, 17-10 (S)
1988—*Bengals, 21-13 (C)
1989—Seahawks, 24-17 (C)
1990—Seahawks, 31-16 (S)
1991—Seahawks, 13-7 (C)
1992—Bengals, 21-3 (S)
1993—Seahawks, 19-10 (C)
1994—Bengals, 20-17 (S) OT
1995—Seahawks, 24-21 (S)
1999—Seahawks, 37-20 (S)
2003—Bengals, 27-24 (C)
(RS Pts.—Bengals 333, Seahawks 314)
(PS Pts.—Bengals 21, Seahawks 13)
*AFC Divisional Playoff
CINCINNATI vs. TAMPA BAY
RS: Buccaneers lead series, 5-3
1976—Bengals, 21-0 (C)
1980—Buccaneers, 17-12 (C)
1983—Bengals, 23-17 (TB)
1989—Bengals, 56-23 (C)
1995—Buccaneers, 19-16 (TB)
1998—Buccaneers, 35-0 (C)
2001—Buccaneers, 16-13 (C) OT
2002—Buccaneers, 35-7 (C)
(RS Pts.— Buccaneers 162, Bengals 148)
CINCINNATI vs. *TENNESSEE
RS: Titans lead series, 38-30-1
PS: Bengals lead series, 1-0
1968—Oilers, 27-17 (C)
1969—Tie, 31-31 (H)
1970—Oilers, 20-13 (C)
    Bengals, 30-20 (H)

1971—Oilers, 10-6 (H)
　　　Bengals, 28-13 (C)
1972—Bengals, 30-7 (C)
　　　Bengals, 61-17 (H)
1973—Bengals, 24-10 (C)
　　　Bengals, 27-24 (H)
1974—Bengals, 34-21 (C)
　　　Oilers, 20-3 (H)
1975—Bengals, 21-19 (H)
　　　Bengals, 23-19 (C)
1976—Bengals, 27-7 (H)
　　　Bengals, 31-27 (C)
1977—Bengals, 13-10 (C) OT
　　　Oilers, 21-16 (H)
1978—Bengals, 28-13 (C)
　　　Oilers, 17-10 (H)
1979—Oilers, 30-27 (C) OT
　　　Oilers, 42-21 (H)
1980—Oilers, 13-10 (C)
　　　Oilers, 23-3 (H)
1981—Oilers, 17-10 (H)
　　　Bengals, 34-21 (C)
1982—Bengals, 27-6 (C)
　　　Bengals, 35-27 (H)
1983—Bengals, 55-14 (H)
　　　Bengals, 38-10 (C)
1984—Bengals, 13-3 (C)
　　　Bengals, 31-13 (H)
1985—Oilers, 44-27 (H)
　　　Bengals, 45-27 (C)
1986—Bengals, 31-28 (C)
　　　Oilers, 32-28 (H)
1987—Bengals, 31-29 (C)
　　　Oilers, 21-17 (H)
1988—Bengals, 44-21 (C)
　　　Oilers, 41-6 (H)
1989—Bengals, 26-24 (H)
　　　Bengals, 61-7 (C)
1990—Oilers, 48-17 (H)
　　　Bengals, 40-20 (C)
　　　**Bengals, 41-14 (C)
1991—Oilers, 30-7 (C)
　　　Oilers, 35-3 (H)
1992—Oilers, 38-24 (C)
　　　Oilers, 26-10 (H)
1993—Oilers, 28-12 (H)
　　　Oilers, 38-3 (C)
1994—Oilers, 20-13 (H)
　　　Bengals, 34-31 (C)
1995—Oilers, 38-28 (C)
　　　Bengals, 32-25 (H)
1996—Oilers, 30-27 (C) OT
　　　Bengals, 21-13 (H)
1997—Oilers, 30-7 (T)
　　　Bengals, 41-14 (C)
1998—Oilers, 23-14 (C)
　　　Oilers, 44-14 (T)
1999—Titans, 36-35 (T)
　　　Titans, 24-14 (C)
2000—Titans, 23-14 (C)
　　　Titans, 35-3 (T)
2001—Titans, 20-7 (C)
　　　Bengals, 23-21 (T)
2002—Titans, 30-24 (C)
2004—Titans, 27-20 (T)
2005—Bengals, 31-23 (T)
(RS Pts.—Titans 1,633, Bengals 1,594)
(PS Pts.—Bengals 41, Titans 14)
*Franchise in Houston prior to 1997;
known as Oilers prior to 1999

**AFC First-Round Playoff
CINCINNATI vs. WASHINGTON
RS: Redskins lead series, 4-3
1970—Redskins, 20-0 (W)
1974—Bengals, 28-17 (C)
1979—Redskins, 28-14 (W)
1985—Redskins, 27-24 (W)
1988—Bengals, 20-17 (C) OT
1991—Redskins, 34-27 (C)
2004—Bengals, 17-10 (W)
(RS Pts.—Redskins 153, Bengals 130)

CLEVELAND vs. ARIZONA
RS: Browns lead series, 33-11-3;
See Arizona vs. Cleveland
CLEVELAND vs. ATLANTA
RS: Browns lead series, 9-2;
See Atlanta vs. Cleveland
CLEVELAND vs. BALTIMORE
RS: Ravens lead series, 9-5;
See Baltimore vs. Cleveland
CLEVELAND vs. BUFFALO
RS: Browns lead series, 7-5
PS: Browns lead series, 1-0;
See Buffalo vs. Cleveland
CLEVELAND vs. CAROLINA
RS: Panthers lead series, 2-0;
See Carolina vs. Cleveland
CLEVELAND vs. CHICAGO
RS: Browns lead series, 9-4;
See Chicago vs. Cleveland
CLEVELAND vs. CINCINNATI
RS: Browns lead series, 33-32;
See Cincinnati vs. Cleveland
CLEVELAND vs. DALLAS
RS: Browns lead series, 15-10
PS: Browns lead series, 2-1
1960—Browns, 48-7 (D)
1961—Browns, 25-7 (C)
　　　Browns, 38-17 (D)
1962—Browns, 19-10 (C)
　　　Cowboys, 45-21 (D)
1963—Browns, 41-24 (D)
　　　Browns, 27-17 (C)
1964—Browns, 27-6 (C)
　　　Browns, 20-16 (D)
1965—Browns, 23-17 (C)
　　　Browns, 24-17 (D)
1966—Browns, 30-21 (C)
　　　Cowboys, 26-14 (D)
1967—Cowboys, 21-14 (C)
　　　*Cowboys, 52-14 (D)
1968—Cowboys, 28-7 (C)
　　　*Browns, 31-20 (C)
1969—Browns, 42-10 (C)
　　　*Browns, 38-14 (D)
1970—Cowboys, 6-2 (C)
1974—Cowboys, 41-17 (D)
1979—Browns, 26-7 (C)
1982—Cowboys, 31-14 (D)
1985—Cowboys, 20-7 (D)
1988—Cowboys, 24-21 (C)
1991—Cowboys, 26-14 (C)
1994—Browns, 19-14 (D)
2004—Cowboys, 19-12 (D)
(RS Pts.—Browns 555, Cowboys 474)
(PS Pts.—Cowboys 86, Browns 83)
*Conference Championship
CLEVELAND vs. DENVER
RS: Broncos lead series, 15-5

PS: Broncos lead series, 3-0
1970—Browns, 27-13 (D)
1971—Broncos, 27-0 (C)
1972—Browns, 27-20 (D)
1974—Browns, 23-21 (C)
1975—Broncos, 16-15 (D)
1976—Broncos, 44-13 (D)
1978—Broncos, 19-7 (C)
1980—Browns, 19-16 (C)
1981—Broncos, 23-20 (D) OT
1983—Broncos, 27-6 (D)
1984—Broncos, 24-14 (C)
1986—*Broncos, 23-20 (C) OT
1987—*Broncos, 38-33 (D)
1988—Broncos, 30-7 (D)
1989—Browns, 16-13 (C)
　　　*Broncos, 37-21 (D)
1990—Browns, 30-29 (D)
1991—Broncos, 17-7 (C)
1992—Broncos, 12-0 (C)
1993—Browns, 29-14 (C)
1994—Broncos, 26-14 (D)
2000—Broncos, 44-10 (D)
2003—Broncos, 23-20 (D) OT
(RS Pts.—Broncos 476, Browns 286)
(PS Pts.—Broncos 98, Browns 74)
*AFC Championship
CLEVELAND vs. DETROIT
RS: Lions lead series, 13-4
PS: Lions lead series, 3-1
1952—Lions, 17-6 (D)
　　　*Lions, 17-7 (C)
1953—*Lions, 17-16 (D)
1954—Lions, 14-10 (C)
　　　*Browns, 56-10 (C)
1957—Lions, 20-7 (D)
　　　*Lions, 59-14 (D)
1958—Lions, 30-10 (C)
1963—Lions, 38-10 (D)
1964—Browns, 37-21 (C)
1967—Lions, 31-14 (D)
1969—Lions, 28-21 (C)
1970—Lions, 41-24 (C)
1975—Lions, 21-10 (D)
1983—Browns, 31-26 (D)
1986—Browns, 24-21 (C)
1989—Lions, 13-10 (D)
1992—Lions, 24-14 (D)
1995—Lions, 38-20 (D)
2001—Browns, 24-14 (C)
2005—Lions, 13-10 (C)
(RS Pts.—Lions 410, Browns 282)
(PS Pts.—Lions 103, Browns 93)
*NFL Championship
CLEVELAND vs. GREEN BAY
RS: Packers lead series, 9-7
PS: Packers lead series, 1-0
1953—Browns, 27-0 (Mil)
1955—Browns, 41-10 (C)
1956—Browns, 24-7 (Mil)
1961—Packers, 49-17 (C)
1964—Packers, 28-21 (Mil)
1965—*Packers, 23-12 (GB)
1966—Packers, 21-20 (C)
1967—Packers, 55-7 (Mil)
1969—Browns, 20-7 (C)
1972—Packers, 26-10 (C)
1980—Browns, 26-21 (C)
1983—Packers, 35-21 (Mil)
1986—Packers, 17-14 (C)

1992—Browns, 17-6 (C)
1995—Packers, 31-20 (C)
2001—Packers, 30-7 (GB)
2005—Browns, 26-24 (GB)
(RS Pts.—Packers 367, Browns 318)
(PS Pts.—Packers 23, Browns 12)
*NFL Championship
CLEVELAND vs. HOUSTON
RS: Browns lead series, 2-1
2002—Browns, 34-17 (C)
2004—Browns, 22-14 (H)
2005—Texans, 19-16 (H)
(RS Pts.—Browns 72, Texans 50)
CLEVELAND vs. *INDIANAPOLIS
RS: Browns lead series, 13-11
PS: Series tied, 2-2
1956—Colts, 21-7 (C)
1959—Browns, 38-31 (B)
1962—Colts, 36-14 (C)
1964—**Browns, 27-0 (C)
1968—Browns, 30-20 (B)
    **Colts, 34-0 (C)
1971—Browns, 14-13 (B)
    ***Colts, 20-3 (C)
1973—Browns, 24-14 (C)
1975—Colts, 21-7 (B)
1978—Browns, 45-24 (B)
1979—Browns, 13-10 (C)
1980—Browns, 28-27 (B)
1981—Browns, 42-28 (C)
1983—Browns, 41-23 (C)
1986—Colts, 24-9 (I)
1987—Colts, 9-7 (C)
    ***Browns, 38-21 (C)
1988—Browns, 23-17 (C)
1989—Colts, 23-17 (I) OT
1991—Browns, 31-0 (I)
1992—Colts, 14-3 (I)
1993—Colts, 23-10 (I)
1994—Browns, 21-14 (I)
1999—Colts, 29-28 (C)
2002—Colts, 28-23 (C)
2003—Colts, 9-6 (C)
2005—Colts, 13-6 (I)
(RS Pts.—Browns 502, Colts 456)
(PS Pts.—Colts 75, Browns 68)
*Franchise in Baltimore prior to 1984
**NFL Championship
***AFC Divisional Playoff
CLEVELAND vs. JACKSONVILLE
RS: Jaguars lead series, 8-2
1995—Jaguars, 23-15 (C)
    Jaguars, 24-21 (J)
1999—Jaguars, 24-7 (J)
    Jaguars, 24-14 (C)
2000—Jaguars, 27-7 (C)
    Jaguars, 48-0 (J)
2001—Browns, 23-14 (J)
    Jaguars, 15-10 (C)
2002—Browns, 21-20 (J)
2005—Jaguars, 20-14 (C)
(RS Pts.—Jaguars 239, Browns 132)
CLEVELAND vs. KANSAS CITY
RS: Chiefs lead series, 9-8-2
1971—Chiefs, 13-7 (KC)
1972—Chiefs, 31-7 (C)
1973—Tie, 20-20 (KC)
1975—Browns, 40-14 (C)
1976—Chiefs, 39-14 (KC)
1977—Browns, 44-7 (C)

1978—Chiefs, 17-3 (KC)
1979—Browns, 27-24 (KC)
1980—Browns, 20-13 (C)
1984—Chiefs, 10-6 (KC)
1986—Browns, 20-7 (C)
1988—Browns, 6-3 (KC)
1989—Tie, 10-10 (C) OT
1990—Chiefs, 34-0 (KC)
1991—Browns, 20-15 (C)
1994—Chiefs, 20-13 (KC)
1995—Browns, 35-17 (C)
2002—Chiefs, 40-39 (C)
2003—Chiefs, 41-20 (KC)
(RS Pts.—Chiefs 375, Browns 351)
CLEVELAND vs. MIAMI
RS: Dolphins lead series, 7-5
PS: Dolphins lead series, 2-0
1970—Browns, 28-0 (M)
1972—*Dolphins, 20-14 (M)
1973—Dolphins, 17-9 (C)
1976—Browns, 17-13 (C)
1979—Browns, 30-24 (C) OT
1985—*Dolphins, 24-21 (M)
1986—Browns, 26-16 (C)
1988—Dolphins, 38-31 (M)
1989—Dolphins, 13-10 (M) OT
1990—Dolphins, 30-13 (C)
1992—Dolphins, 27-23 (C)
1993—Dolphins, 24-14 (C)
2004—Dolphins, 10-7 (M)
2005—Browns, 22-0 (C)
(RS Pts.—Browns 230, Dolphins 212)
(PS Pts.—Dolphins 44, Browns 35)
*AFC Divisional Playoff
CLEVELAND vs. MINNESOTA
RS: Vikings lead series, 9-3
PS: Vikings lead series, 1-0
1965—Vikings, 27-17 (C)
1967—Browns, 14-10 (C)
1969—Vikings, 51-3 (M)
    *Vikings, 27-7 (M)
1973—Vikings, 26-3 (M)
1975—Vikings, 42-10 (C)
1980—Vikings, 28-23 (M)
1983—Vikings, 27-21 (C)
1986—Browns, 23-20 (M)
1989—Browns, 23-17 (C) OT
1992—Vikings, 17-13 (M)
1995—Vikings, 27-11 (M)
2005—Vikings, 24-12 (M)
(RS Pts.—Vikings 316, Browns 173)
(PS Pts.—Vikings 27, Browns 7)
*NFL Championship
CLEVELAND vs. NEW ENGLAND
RS: Browns lead series, 11-8
PS: Browns lead series, 1-0
1971—Browns, 27-7 (C)
1974—Browns, 21-14 (NE)
1977—Browns, 30-27 (C) OT
1980—Patriots, 34-17 (NE)
1982—Browns, 10-7 (C)
1983—Browns, 30-0 (NE)
1984—Patriots, 17-16 (C)
1985—Browns, 24-20 (C)
1987—Browns, 20-10 (NE)
1991—Browns, 20-0 (NE)
1992—Browns, 19-17 (NE)
1993—Patriots, 20-17 (C)
1994—Browns, 13-6 (C)
    *Browns, 20-13 (C)

1995—Patriots, 17-14 (NE)
1999—Patriots, 19-7 (C)
2000—Browns, 19-11 (C)
2001—Patriots, 27-16 (NE)
2003—Patriots, 9-3 (NE)
2004—Patriots, 42-15 (C)
(RS Pts.—Browns 338, Patriots 304)
(PS Pts.—Browns 20, Patriots 13)
*AFC First-Round Playoff
CLEVELAND vs. NEW ORLEANS
RS: Browns lead series, 11-3
1967—Browns, 42-7 (NO)
1968—Browns, 24-10 (NO)
    Browns, 35-17 (C)
1969—Browns, 27-17 (NO)
1971—Browns, 21-17 (NO)
1975—Browns, 17-16 (C)
1978—Browns, 24-16 (NO)
1981—Browns, 20-17 (C)
1984—Saints, 16-14 (C)
1987—Saints, 28-21 (NO)
1990—Saints, 25-20 (NO)
1993—Browns, 17-13 (C)
1999—Browns, 21-16 (NO)
2002—Browns, 24-15 (NO)
(RS Pts.—Browns 327, Saints 230)
CLEVELAND vs. N.Y. GIANTS
RS: Browns lead series, 25-19-2
PS: Series tied, 1-1
1950—Giants, 6-0 (C)
    Giants, 17-13 (NY)
    *Browns, 8-3 (C)
1951—Browns, 14-13 (C)
    Browns, 10-0 (NY)
1952—Giants, 17-9 (C)
    Giants, 37-34 (NY)
1953—Browns, 7-0 (NY)
    Browns, 62-14 (C)
1954—Browns, 24-14 (C)
    Browns, 16-7 (NY)
1955—Browns, 24-14 (C)
    Tie, 35-35 (NY)
1956—Giants, 21-9 (C)
    Browns, 24-7 (NY)
1957—Browns, 6-3 (C)
    Browns, 34-28 (NY)
1958—Giants, 21-17 (C)
    Giants, 13-10 (NY)
    *Giants, 10-0 (NY)
1959—Browns, 10-6 (C)
    Giants, 48-7 (NY)
1960—Giants, 17-13 (C)
    Browns, 48-34 (NY)
1961—Giants, 37-21 (C)
    Tie, 7-7 (NY)
1962—Browns, 17-7 (C)
    Giants, 17-13 (NY)
1963—Browns, 35-24 (NY)
    Giants, 33-6 (C)
1964—Browns, 42-20 (C)
    Browns, 52-20 (NY)
1965—Browns, 38-14 (NY)
    Browns, 34-21 (C)
1966—Browns, 28-7 (NY)
    Browns, 49-40 (C)
1967—Giants, 38-34 (NY)
    Browns, 24-14 (C)
1968—Browns, 45-10 (C)
1969—Browns, 28-17 (C)
    Giants, 27-14 (NY)

1973—Browns, 12-10 (C)
1977—Browns, 21-7 (NY)
1985—Browns, 35-33 (NY)
1991—Giants, 13-10 (NY)
1994—Giants, 16-13 (C)
2000—Giants, 24-3 (C)
2004—Giants, 27-10 (NY)
(RS Pts.—Browns 1,013, Giants 859)
(PS Pts.—Giants 13, Browns 8)
*Conference Playoff
CLEVELAND vs. N.Y. JETS
RS: Browns lead series, 10-7
PS: Browns lead series, 1-0
1970—Browns, 31-21 (C)
1972—Browns, 26-10 (NY)
1976—Browns, 38-17 (C)
1978—Browns, 37-34 (C) OT
1979—Browns, 25-22 (NY) OT
1980—Browns, 17-14 (C)
1981—Jets, 14-13 (C)
1983—Browns, 10-7 (C)
1984—Jets, 24-20 (C)
1985—Jets, 37-10 (NY)
1986—*Browns, 23-20 (C) OT
1988—Jets, 23-3 (C)
1989—Browns, 38-24 (C)
1990—Jets, 24-21 (NY)
1991—Jets, 17-14 (C)
1994—Browns, 27-7 (C)
2002—Browns, 24-21 (NY)
2004—Jets, 10-7 (C)
(RS Pts.—Browns 361, Jets 326)
(PS Pts.—Browns 23, Jets 20)
*AFC Divisional Playoff
CLEVELAND vs. *OAKLAND
RS: Raiders lead series, 9-6
PS: Raiders lead series, 2-0
1970—Raiders, 23-20 (O)
1971—Raiders, 34-20 (C)
1973—Browns, 7-3 (O)
1974—Raiders, 40-24 (C)
1975—Raiders, 38-17 (O)
1977—Raiders, 26-10 (C)
1979—Raiders, 19-14 (O)
1980—**Raiders, 14-12 (C)
1982—***Raiders, 27-10 (LA)
1985—Raiders, 21-20 (C)
1986—Raiders, 27-14 (LA)
1987—Browns, 24-17 (LA)
1992—Browns, 28-16 (LA)
1993—Browns, 19-16 (LA)
2000—Raiders, 36-10 (O)
2003—Browns, 13-7 (C)
2005—Browns, 9-7 (O)
(RS Pts.—Raiders 330, Browns 249)
(PS Pts.—Raiders 41, Browns 22)
*Franchise in Los Angeles from 1982-1994
**AFC Divisional Playoff
***AFC First-Round Playoff
CLEVELAND vs. PHILADELPHIA
RS: Browns lead series, 31-14-1
1950—Browns, 35-10 (P)
Browns, 13-7 (C)
1951—Browns, 20-17 (C)
Browns, 24-9 (P)
1952—Browns, 49-7 (P)
Eagles, 28-20 (C)
1953—Browns, 37-13 (C)
Eagles, 42-27 (P)
1954—Eagles, 28-10 (P)

Browns, 6-0 (C)
1955—Browns, 21-17 (C)
Eagles, 33-17 (P)
1956—Browns, 16-0 (P)
Browns, 17-14 (C)
1957—Browns, 24-7 (C)
Eagles, 17-7 (P)
1958—Browns, 28-14 (C)
Browns, 21-14 (P)
1959—Browns, 28-7 (C)
Browns, 28-21 (P)
1960—Browns, 41-24 (P)
Eagles, 31-29 (C)
1961—Eagles, 27-20 (P)
Browns, 45-24 (C)
1962—Eagles, 35-7 (P)
Tie, 14-14 (C)
1963—Browns, 37-7 (C)
Browns, 23-17 (P)
1964—Browns, 28-20 (P)
Browns, 38-24 (C)
1965—Browns, 35-17 (C)
Browns, 38-34 (C)
1966—Browns, 27-7 (C)
Eagles, 33-21 (P)
1967—Eagles, 28-24 (P)
1968—Browns, 47-13 (C)
1969—Browns, 27-20 (P)
1972—Browns, 27-17 (P)
1976—Browns, 24-3 (C)
1979—Browns, 24-19 (P)
1982—Eagles, 24-21 (C)
1988—Browns, 19-3 (C)
1991—Eagles, 32-30 (C)
1994—Browns, 26-7 (P)
2000—Eagles, 35-24 (C)
2004—Eagles, 34-31 (C) OT
(RS Pts.—Browns 1,175, Eagles 854)
CLEVELAND vs. PITTSBURGH
RS: Browns lead series, 55-51
PS: Steelers lead series, 2-0
1950—Browns, 30-17 (P)
Browns, 45-7 (C)
1951—Browns, 17-0 (C)
Browns, 28-0 (P)
1952—Browns, 21-20 (P)
Browns, 29-28 (C)
1953—Browns, 34-16 (C)
Browns, 20-16 (P)
1954—Steelers, 55-27 (P)
Browns, 42-7 (C)
1955—Browns, 41-14 (C)
Browns, 30-7 (P)
1956—Browns, 14-10 (P)
Steelers, 24-16 (C)
1957—Browns, 23-12 (P)
Browns, 24-0 (C)
1958—Browns, 45-12 (P)
Browns, 27-10 (C)
1959—Steelers, 17-7 (P)
Steelers, 21-20 (C)
1960—Browns, 28-20 (C)
Steelers, 14-10 (P)
1961—Browns, 30-28 (P)
Steelers, 17-13 (C)
1962—Browns, 41-14 (P)
Browns, 35-14 (C)
1963—Browns, 35-23 (C)
Steelers, 9-7 (P)
1964—Steelers, 23-7 (C)

Browns, 30-17 (P)
1965—Browns, 24-19 (C)
Browns, 42-21 (P)
1966—Browns, 41-10 (C)
Steelers, 16-6 (P)
1967—Browns, 21-10 (C)
Browns, 34-14 (P)
1968—Browns, 31-24 (C)
Browns, 45-24 (P)
1969—Browns, 42-31 (C)
Browns, 24-3 (P)
1970—Browns, 15-7 (C)
Steelers, 28-9 (P)
1971—Browns, 27-17 (C)
Steelers, 26-9 (P)
1972—Browns, 26-24 (C)
Steelers, 30-0 (P)
1973—Steelers, 33-6 (P)
Browns, 21-16 (C)
1974—Steelers, 20-16 (P)
Steelers, 26-16 (C)
1975—Browns, 42-6 (C)
Steelers, 31-17 (P)
1976—Steelers, 31-14 (P)
Browns, 18-16 (C)
1977—Steelers, 28-14 (C)
Steelers, 35-31 (P)
1978—Steelers, 15-9 (P) OT
Steelers, 34-14 (C)
1979—Steelers, 51-35 (C)
Steelers, 33-30 (P) OT
1980—Browns, 27-26 (C)
Steelers, 16-13 (P)
1981—Steelers, 13-7 (P)
Steelers, 32-10 (C)
1982—Browns, 10-9 (C)
Steelers, 37-21 (P)
1983—Steelers, 44-17 (P)
Browns, 30-17 (C)
1984—Browns, 20-10 (C)
Steelers, 23-20 (P)
1985—Browns, 17-7 (C)
Steelers, 10-9 (P)
1986—Browns, 27-24 (P)
Browns, 37-31 (C) OT
1987—Browns, 34-10 (C)
Browns, 19-13 (P)
1988—Browns, 23-9 (P)
Browns, 27-7 (C)
1989—Browns, 51-0 (P)
Steelers, 17-7 (C)
1990—Browns, 13-3 (C)
Steelers, 35-0 (P)
1991—Browns, 17-14 (C)
Steelers, 17-10 (P)
1992—Browns, 17-9 (C)
Steelers, 23-13 (P)
1993—Browns, 28-23 (C)
Steelers, 16-9 (P)
1994—Steelers, 17-10 (C)
Steelers, 17-7 (P)
*Steelers, 29-9 (P)
1995—Browns, 20-3 (P)
Steelers, 20-17 (C)
1999—Steelers, 43-0 (C)
Browns, 16-15 (P)
2000—Browns, 23-20 (C)
Steelers, 22-0 (C)
2001—Steelers, 15-12 (C) OT
Steelers, 28-7 (P)

2002—Steelers, 16-13 (P) OT
　　Steelers, 23-20 (C)
　　**Steelers, 36-33 (P)
2003—Browns, 33-13 (P)
　　Steelers, 13-6 (C)
2004—Steelers, 34-23 (P)
　　Steelers, 24-10 (C)
2005—Steelers, 34-21 (P)
　　Steelers, 41-0 (C)
(RS Pts.—Browns 2,173, Steelers 2,097)
(PS Pts.—Steelers 65, Browns 42)
*AFC Divisional Playoff
**AFC First-Round Playoff
CLEVELAND vs. *ST. LOUIS
RS: Rams lead series, 9-8
PS: Browns lead series, 2-1
1950—**Browns, 30-28 (C)
1951—Browns, 38-23 (LA)
　　**Rams, 24-17 (LA)
1952—Browns, 37-7 (C)
1955—**Browns, 38-14 (LA)
1957—Browns, 45-31 (C)
1958—Browns, 30-27 (LA)
1963—Browns, 20-6 (C)
1965—Rams, 42-7 (LA)
1968—Rams, 24-6 (C)
1973—Rams, 30-17 (LA)
1977—Rams, 9-0 (C)
1978—Browns, 30-19 (C)
1981—Rams, 27-16 (LA)
1984—Rams, 20-17 (LA)
1987—Browns, 30-17 (C)
1990—Rams, 38-23 (C)
1993—Browns, 42-14 (LA)
1999—Rams, 34-3 (StL)
2003—Rams, 26-20 (C)
(RS Pts.—Rams 394, Browns 381)
(PS Pts.—Browns 85, Rams 66)
*Franchise in Los Angeles prior to 1995
**NFL Championship
CLEVELAND vs. SAN DIEGO
RS: Chargers lead series, 12-7-1
1970—Chargers, 27-10 (C)
1972—Browns, 21-17 (SD)
1973—Tie, 16-16 (C)
1974—Chargers, 36-35 (SD)
1976—Browns, 21-17 (C)
1977—Chargers, 37-14 (SD)
1981—Chargers, 44-14 (C)
1982—Chargers, 30-13 (C)
1983—Browns, 30-24 (SD) OT
1985—Browns, 21-7 (SD)
1986—Browns, 47-17 (C)
1987—Chargers, 27-24 (SD) OT
1990—Chargers, 24-14 (C)
1991—Browns, 30-24 (SD) OT
1992—Chargers, 14-13 (C)
1995—Chargers, 31-13 (SD)
1999—Chargers, 23-10 (SD)
2001—Browns, 20-16 (C)
2003—Chargers, 26-20 (C)
2004—Chargers, 21-0 (C)
(RS Pts.—Chargers 478, Browns 386)
CLEVELAND vs. SAN FRANCISCO
RS: Browns lead series, 10-6
1950—Browns, 34-14 (C)
1951—49ers, 24-10 (SF)
1953—Browns, 23-21 (C)
1955—Browns, 38-3 (SF)
1959—49ers, 21-20 (C)

1962—Browns, 13-10 (SF)
1968—Browns, 33-21 (SF)
1970—49ers, 34-31 (SF)
1974—Browns, 7-0 (C)
1978—Browns, 24-7 (C)
1981—Browns, 15-12 (SF)
1984—49ers, 41-7 (C)
1987—49ers, 38-24 (SF)
1990—49ers, 20-17 (SF)
1993—Browns, 23-13 (C)
2003—Browns, 13-12 (SF)
(RS Pts.—Browns 332, 49ers 291)
CLEVELAND vs. SEATTLE
RS: Seahawks lead series, 11-4
1977—Seahawks, 20-19 (S)
1978—Seahawks, 47-24 (C)
1979—Seahawks, 29-24 (C)
1980—Browns, 27-3 (S)
1981—Seahawks, 42-21 (S)
1982—Browns, 21-7 (S)
1983—Seahawks, 24-9 (C)
1984—Seahawks, 33-0 (S)
1985—Seahawks, 31-13 (S)
1988—Seahawks, 16-10 (C)
1989—Browns, 17-7 (S)
1993—Seahawks, 22-5 (S)
1994—Browns, 35-9 (C)
2001—Seahawks, 9-6 (C)
2003—Seahawks, 34-7 (S)
(RS Pts.—Seahawks 333, Browns 238)
CLEVELAND vs. TAMPA BAY
RS: Browns lead series, 5-1
1976—Browns, 24-7 (TB)
1980—Browns, 34-27 (TB)
1983—Browns, 20-0 (C)
1989—Browns, 42-31 (TB)
1995—Browns, 22-6 (C)
2002—Buccaneers 17-3 (TB)
(RS Pts.—Browns 145, Buccaneers 88)
CLEVELAND vs. *TENNESSEE
RS: Browns lead series, 33-26
PS: Titans lead series, 1-0
1970—Browns, 28-14 (C)
　　Browns, 21-10 (H)
1971—Browns, 31-0 (C)
　　Browns, 37-24 (H)
1972—Browns, 23-17 (H)
　　Browns, 20-0 (C)
1973—Browns, 42-13 (C)
　　Browns, 23-13 (H)
1974—Browns, 20-7 (C)
　　Oilers, 28-24 (H)
1975—Oilers, 40-10 (C)
　　Oilers, 21-10 (H)
1976—Browns, 21-7 (H)
　　Browns, 13-10 (C)
1977—Browns, 24-23 (H)
　　Oilers, 19-15 (C)
1978—Oilers, 16-13 (C)
　　Oilers, 14-10 (H)
1979—Oilers, 31-10 (H)
　　Browns, 14-7 (C)
1980—Oilers, 16-7 (C)
　　Browns, 17-14 (H)
1981—Oilers, 9-3 (C)
　　Oilers, 17-13 (H)
1982—Browns, 20-14 (H)
1983—Browns, 25-19 (C) OT
　　Oilers, 34-27 (H)
1984—Browns, 27-10 (C)

　　Browns, 27-20 (H)
1985—Browns, 21-6 (H)
　　Browns, 28-21 (C)
1986—Browns, 23-20 (H)
　　Browns, 13-10 (C) OT
1987—Oilers, 15-10 (C)
　　Browns, 40-7 (H)
1988—Oilers, 24-17 (H)
　　Browns, 28-23 (C)
　　**Oilers, 24-23 (C)
1989—Browns, 28-17 (C)
　　Browns, 24-20 (H)
1990—Oilers, 35-23 (C)
　　Oilers, 58-14 (H)
1991—Oilers, 28-24 (H)
　　Oilers, 17-14 (C)
1992—Browns, 24-14 (H)
　　Oilers, 17-14 (C)
1993—Oilers, 27-20 (C)
　　Oilers, 19-17 (H)
1994—Browns, 11-8 (H)
　　Browns, 34-10 (C)
1995—Browns, 14-7 (H)
　　Oilers, 37-10 (C)
1999—Titans, 26-9 (T)
　　Titans, 33-21 (C)
2000—Titans, 24-10 (T)
　　Titans, 24-0 (C)
2001—Titans, 31-15 (C)
　　Browns, 41-38 (T)
2002—Browns, 31-28 (T) OT
2005—Browns, 20-14 (C)
(RS Pts.—Browns 1,173, Titans 1,125)
(PS Pts.—Titans 24, Browns 23)
*Franchise in Houston prior to 1997;
known as Oilers prior to 1999
**AFC First-Round Playoff
CLEVELAND vs. WASHINGTON
RS: Browns lead series, 33-9-1
1950—Browns, 20-14 (C)
　　Browns, 45-21 (W)
1951—Browns, 45-0 (C)
1952—Browns, 19-15 (C)
　　Browns, 48-24 (W)
1953—Browns, 30-14 (W)
　　Browns, 27-3 (C)
1954—Browns, 62-3 (C)
　　Browns, 34-14 (W)
1955—Redskins, 27-17 (C)
　　Browns, 24-14 (W)
1956—Redskins, 20-9 (W)
　　Redskins, 20-17 (C)
1957—Browns, 21-17 (C)
　　Tie, 30-30 (W)
1958—Browns, 20-10 (W)
　　Browns, 21-14 (C)
1959—Browns, 34-7 (C)
　　Browns, 31-17 (W)
1960—Browns, 31-10 (W)
　　Browns, 27-16 (C)
1961—Browns, 31-7 (C)
　　Browns, 17-6 (W)
1962—Redskins, 17-16 (C)
　　Redskins, 17-9 (W)
1963—Browns, 37-14 (C)
　　Browns, 27-20 (W)
1964—Browns, 27-13 (W)
　　Browns, 34-24 (C)
1965—Browns, 17-7 (W)
　　Browns, 24-16 (C)

1966—Browns, 38-14 (W)
Browns, 14-3 (C)
1967—Browns, 42-37 (C)
1968—Browns, 24-21 (W)
1969—Browns, 27-23 (C)
1971—Browns, 20-13 (W)
1975—Redskins, 23-7 (C)
1979—Redskins, 13-9 (C)
1985—Redskins, 14-7 (C)
1988—Browns, 17-13 (W)
1991—Redskins, 42-17 (W)
2004—Browns, 17-13 (C)
(RS Pts.—Browns 1,090, Redskins 680)

DALLAS vs. ARIZONA
RS: Cowboys lead series, 54-27-1
PS: Cardinals lead series, 1-0;
See Arizona vs. Dallas
DALLAS vs. ATLANTA
RS: Cowboys lead series, 12-8
PS: Cowboys lead series, 2-0;
See Atlanta vs. Dallas
DALLAS vs. BALTIMORE
RS: Ravens lead series, 2-0;
See Baltimore vs. Dallas
DALLAS vs. BUFFALO
RS: Cowboys lead series, 4-3
PS: Cowboys lead series, 2-0;
See Buffalo vs. Dallas
DALLAS vs. CAROLINA
RS: Cowboys lead series, 5-1
PS: Panthers lead series, 2-0;
See Carolina vs. Dallas
DALLAS vs. CHICAGO
RS: Cowboys lead series, 10-8
PS: Cowboys lead series, 2-0;
See Chicago vs. Dallas
DALLAS vs. CINCINNATI
RS: Cowboys lead series, 5-4;
See Cincinnati vs. Dallas
DALLAS vs. CLEVELAND
RS: Browns lead series, 15-10
PS: Browns lead series, 2-1;
See Cleveland vs. Dallas
DALLAS vs. DENVER
RS: Broncos lead series, 5-4
PS: Cowboys lead series, 1-0
1973—Cowboys, 22-10 (Den)
1977—Cowboys, 14-6 (Dal)
*Cowboys, 27-10 (New Orleans)
1980—Broncos, 41-20 (Den)
1986—Broncos, 29-14 (Den)
1992—Cowboys, 31-27 (Den)
1995—Cowboys, 31-21 (Dal)
1998—Broncos, 42-23 (Den)
2001—Broncos, 26-24 (Dal)
2005—Broncos, 24-21 (Dal) OT
(RS Pts.—Broncos 226, Cowboys 200)
(PS Pts.—Cowboys 27, Broncos 10)
*Super Bowl XII
DALLAS vs. DETROIT
RS: Cowboys lead series, 10-8
PS: Series tied, 1-1
1960—Lions, 23-14 (Det)
1963—Cowboys, 17-14 (Dal)
1968—Cowboys, 59-13 (Dal)
1970—*Cowboys, 5-0 (Dal)
1972—Cowboys, 28-24 (Dal)
1975—Cowboys, 36-10 (Det)
1977—Cowboys, 37-0 (Dal)

1981—Lions, 27-24 (Det)
1985—Lions, 26-21 (Det)
1986—Cowboys, 31-7 (Det)
1987—Lions, 27-17 (Det)
1991—Lions, 34-10 (Det)
*Lions, 38-6 (Det)
1992—Cowboys, 37-3 (Det)
1994—Cowboys, 20-17 (Dal) OT
2001—Lions, 15-10 (Det)
2002—Lions, 9-7 (Det)
2003—Cowboys, 38-7 (Det)
2004—Cowboys, 31-21 (Dal)
2005—Cowboys, 20-7 (Dal)
(RS Pts.—Cowboys 454, Lions 287)
(PS Pts.—Lions 38, Cowboys 11)
*NFC Divisional Playoff
DALLAS vs. GREEN BAY
RS: Series tied, 10-10
PS: Cowboys lead series, 4-2
1960—Packers, 41-7 (GB)
1964—Packers, 45-21 (D)
1965—Packers, 13-3 (Mil)
1966—*Packers, 34-27 (D)
1967—*Packers, 21-17 (GB)
1968—Packers, 28-17 (D)
1970—Cowboys, 16-3 (D)
1972—Packers, 16-13 (Mil)
1975—Packers, 19-17 (D)
1978—Cowboys, 42-14 (Mil)
1980—Cowboys, 28-7 (Mil)
1982—**Cowboys, 37-26 (D)
1984—Cowboys, 20-6 (D)
1989—Packers, 31-13 (GB)
Packers, 20-10 (D)
1991—Cowboys, 20-17 (Mil)
1993—Cowboys, 36-14 (D)
***Cowboys, 27-17 (D)
1994—Cowboys, 42-31 (D)
***Cowboys, 35-9 (D)
1995—Cowboys, 34-24 (D)
****Cowboys, 38-27 (D)
1996—Cowboys, 21-6 (D)
1997—Packers, 45-17 (GB)
1999—Cowboys, 27-13 (D)
2004—Packers, 41-20 (GB)
(RS Pts.—Cowboys 434, Packers 424)
(PS Pts.—Cowboys 181, Packers 134)
*NFL Championship
**NFC Second-Round Playoff
***NFC Divisional Playoff
****NFC Championship
DALLAS vs. HOUSTON
RS: Texans lead series, 1-0
2002—Texans, 19-10 (H)
(RS Pts.—Texans 19, Cowboys 10)
DALLAS vs. *INDIANAPOLIS
RS: Cowboys lead series, 7-5
PS: Colts lead series, 1-0
1960—Colts, 45-7 (D)
1967—Colts, 23-17 (B)
1969—Cowboys, 27-10 (D)
1970—**Colts, 16-13 (Miami)
1972—Cowboys, 21-0 (B)
1976—Cowboys, 30-27 (D)
1978—Cowboys, 38-0 (D)
1981—Cowboys, 37-13 (B)
1984—Cowboys, 22-3 (D)
1993—Cowboys, 27-3 (I)
1996—Colts, 25-24 (D)
1999—Colts, 34-24 (I)

2002—Colts, 20-3 (I)
(RS Pts.—Cowboys 277, Colts 203)
(PS Pts.—Colts 16, Cowboys 13)
*Franchise in Baltimore prior to 1984
**Super Bowl V
DALLAS VS. JACKSONVILLE
RS: Cowboys lead series, 2-1
1997—Cowboys, 26-22 (D)
2000—Jaguars, 23-17 (D) OT
2002—Cowboys, 21-19 (D)
(RS Pts.—Cowboys 64, Jaguars 64)
DALLAS vs. KANSAS CITY
RS: Cowboys lead series, 5-3
1970—Cowboys, 27-16 (KC)
1975—Chiefs, 34-31 (D)
1983—Cowboys, 41-21 (D)
1989—Chiefs, 36-28 (KC)
1992—Cowboys, 17-10 (D)
1995—Cowboys, 24-12 (D)
1998—Chiefs, 20-17 (KC)
2005—Cowboys, 31-28 (D)
(RS Pts.—Cowboys 216, Chiefs 177)
DALLAS vs. MIAMI
RS: Dolphins lead series, 7-3
PS: Cowboys lead series, 1-0
1971—*Cowboys, 24-3 (New Orleans)
1973—Dolphins, 14-7 (D)
1978—Dolphins, 23-16 (M)
1981—Cowboys, 28-27 (D)
1984—Dolphins, 28-21 (M)
1987—Dolphins, 20-14 (D)
1989—Dolphins, 17-14 (D)
1993—Dolphins, 16-14 (D)
1996—Cowboys, 29-10 (M)
1999—Cowboys, 20-0 (D)
2003—Dolphins, 40-21 (D)
(RS Pts.—Dolphins 195, Cowboys 184)
(PS Pts.—Cowboys 24, Dolphins 3)
*Super Bowl VI
DALLAS vs. MINNESOTA
RS: Vikings lead series, 10-9
PS: Cowboys lead series, 4-2
1961—Cowboys, 21-7 (D)
Cowboys, 28-0 (M)
1966—Cowboys, 28-17 (D)
1968—Cowboys, 20-7 (M)
1970—Vikings, 54-13 (M)
1971—*Cowboys, 20-12 (M)
1973—**Vikings, 27-10 (D)
1974—Vikings, 23-21 (D)
1975—*Cowboys, 17-14 (M)
1977—Cowboys, 16-10 (M) OT
**Cowboys, 23-6 (D)
1978—Vikings, 21-10 (D)
1979—Cowboys, 36-20 (M)
1982—Vikings, 31-27 (M)
1983—Cowboys, 37-24 (M)
1987—Vikings, 44-38 (D) OT
1988—Vikings, 43-3 (D)
1993—Cowboys, 37-20 (M)
1995—Cowboys, 23-17 (M) OT
1996—***Cowboys, 40-15 (D)
1998—Vikings, 46-36 (D)
1999—Vikings, 27-17 (M)
***Vikings, 27-10 (M)
2000—Vikings, 27-15 (D)
2004—Vikings, 35-17 (M)
(RS Pts.—Vikings 473, Cowboys 443)
(PS Pts.—Cowboys 120, Vikings 101)
*NFC Divisional Playoff

****NFC Championship*
*****NFC First-Round Playoff*

DALLAS vs. NEW ENGLAND
RS: Cowboys lead series, 7-2
1971—Cowboys, 44-21 (D)
1975—Cowboys, 34-31 (NE)
1978—Cowboys, 17-10 (D)
1981—Cowboys, 35-21 (NE)
1984—Cowboys, 20-17 (D)
1987—Cowboys, 23-17 (NE) OT
1996—Cowboys, 12-6 (D)
1999—Patriots, 13-6 (NE)
2003—Patriots, 12-0 (NE)
(RS Pts.—Cowboys 191, Patriots 148)

DALLAS vs. NEW ORLEANS
RS: Cowboys lead series, 14-7
1967—Cowboys, 14-10 (D)
⠀⠀⠀⠀Cowboys, 27-10 (NO)
1968—Cowboys, 17-3 (NO)
1969—Cowboys, 21-17 (NO)
⠀⠀⠀⠀Cowboys, 33-17 (D)
1971—Saints, 24-14 (NO)
1973—Cowboys, 40-3 (D)
1976—Cowboys, 24-6 (NO)
1978—Cowboys, 27-7 (D)
1982—Cowboys, 21-7 (D)
1983—Cowboys, 21-20 (D)
1984—Cowboys, 30-27 (D) OT
1988—Saints, 20-17 (NO)
1989—Saints, 28-0 (NO)
1990—Cowboys, 17-13 (D)
1991—Cowboys, 23-14 (D)
1994—Cowboys, 24-16 (NO)
1998—Saints, 22-3 (NO)
1999—Saints, 31-24 (NO)
2003—Saints, 13-7 (NO)
2004—Saints, 27-13 (D)
(RS Pts.—Cowboys 417, Saints 335)

DALLAS vs. N.Y. GIANTS
RS: Cowboys lead series, 51-34-2
1960—Tie, 31-31 (NY)
1961—Giants, 31-10 (D)
⠀⠀⠀⠀Cowboys, 17-16 (NY)
1962—Giants, 41-10 (D)
⠀⠀⠀⠀Giants, 41-31 (NY)
1963—Giants, 37-21 (NY)
⠀⠀⠀⠀Giants, 34-27 (D)
1964—Tie, 13-13 (D)
⠀⠀⠀⠀Cowboys, 31-21 (NY)
1965—Cowboys, 31-2 (D)
⠀⠀⠀⠀Cowboys, 38-20 (NY)
1966—Cowboys, 52-7 (D)
⠀⠀⠀⠀Cowboys, 17-7 (NY)
1967—Cowboys, 38-24 (D)
1968—Giants, 27-21 (D)
⠀⠀⠀⠀Cowboys, 28-10 (NY)
1969—Cowboys, 25-3 (D)
1970—Cowboys, 28-10 (D)
⠀⠀⠀⠀Giants, 23-20 (NY)
1971—Cowboys, 20-13 (D)
⠀⠀⠀⠀Cowboys, 42-14 (NY)
1972—Cowboys, 23-14 (NY)
⠀⠀⠀⠀Giants, 23-3 (D)
1973—Cowboys, 45-28 (NY)
⠀⠀⠀⠀Cowboys, 23-10 (New Haven)
1974—Giants, 14-6 (D)
⠀⠀⠀⠀Cowboys, 21-7 (New Haven)
1975—Cowboys, 13-7 (NY)
⠀⠀⠀⠀Cowboys, 14-3 (D)
1976—Cowboys, 24-14 (NY)

Cowboys, 9-3 (D)
1977—Cowboys, 41-21 (D)
⠀⠀⠀⠀Cowboys, 24-10 (NY)
1978—Cowboys, 34-24 (NY)
⠀⠀⠀⠀Cowboys, 24-3 (D)
1979—Cowboys, 16-14 (NY)
⠀⠀⠀⠀Cowboys, 28-7 (D)
1980—Cowboys, 24-3 (D)
⠀⠀⠀⠀Giants, 38-35 (NY)
1981—Cowboys, 18-10 (D)
⠀⠀⠀⠀Giants, 13-10 (NY) OT
1983—Cowboys, 28-13 (D)
⠀⠀⠀⠀Cowboys, 38-20 (NY)
1984—Giants, 28-7 (NY)
⠀⠀⠀⠀Giants, 19-7 (D)
1985—Cowboys, 30-29 (NY)
⠀⠀⠀⠀Cowboys, 28-21 (D)
1986—Cowboys, 31-28 (D)
⠀⠀⠀⠀Giants, 17-14 (NY)
1987—Cowboys, 16-14 (NY)
⠀⠀⠀⠀Cowboys, 33-24 (D)
1988—Giants, 12-10 (D)
⠀⠀⠀⠀Giants, 29-21 (NY)
1989—Giants, 30-13 (D)
⠀⠀⠀⠀Giants, 15-0 (NY)
1990—Giants, 28-7 (D)
⠀⠀⠀⠀Giants, 31-17 (NY)
1991—Cowboys, 21-16 (D)
⠀⠀⠀⠀Giants, 22-9 (NY)
1992—Cowboys, 34-28 (NY)
⠀⠀⠀⠀Cowboys, 30-3 (D)
1993—Cowboys, 31-9 (D)
⠀⠀⠀⠀Cowboys, 16-13 (NY) OT
1994—Cowboys, 38-10 (D)
⠀⠀⠀⠀Giants, 15-10 (NY)
1995—Cowboys, 35-0 (NY)
⠀⠀⠀⠀Cowboys, 21-20 (D)
1996—Cowboys, 27-0 (D)
⠀⠀⠀⠀Giants, 20-6 (NY)
1997—Giants, 20-17 (NY)
⠀⠀⠀⠀Giants, 20-7 (D)
1998—Cowboys, 31-7 (NY)
⠀⠀⠀⠀Cowboys, 16-6 (D)
1999—Giants, 13-10 (NY)
⠀⠀⠀⠀Cowboys, 26-18 (D)
2000—Giants, 19-14 (NY)
⠀⠀⠀⠀Giants, 17-13 (D)
2001—Giants, 27-24 (NY) OT
⠀⠀⠀⠀Cowboys, 20-13 (D)
2002—Giants, 21-17 (D)
⠀⠀⠀⠀Giants, 37-7 (NY)
2003—Cowboys, 35-32 (NY) OT
⠀⠀⠀⠀Cowboys, 19-3 (D)
2004—Giants, 26-10 (D)
⠀⠀⠀⠀Giants, 28-24 (NY)
2005—Cowboys, 16-13 (D) OT
⠀⠀⠀⠀Giants, 17-10 (NY)
(RS Pts.—Cowboys 1,880, Giants 1,542)

DALLAS vs. N.Y. JETS
RS: Cowboys lead series, 6-2
1971—Cowboys, 52-10 (D)
1975—Cowboys, 31-21 (NY)
1978—Cowboys, 30-7 (NY)
1987—Cowboys, 38-24 (NY)
1990—Jets, 24-9 (NY)
1993—Cowboys, 28-7 (NY)
1999—Jets, 22-21 (D)
2003—Cowboys, 17-6 (NY)
(RS Pts.—Cowboys 226, Jets 121)

DALLAS vs. *OAKLAND
RS: Raiders lead series, 6-3
1974—Raiders, 27-23 (O)
1980—Cowboys, 19-13 (O)
1983—Raiders, 40-38 (D)
1986—Raiders, 17-13 (D)
1992—Cowboys, 28-13 (LA)
1995—Cowboys, 34-21 (O)
1998—Raiders, 13-12 (D)
2001—Raiders, 28-21 (O)
2005—Raiders, 19-13 (O)
(RS Pts.—Cowboys 201, Raiders 191)
Franchise in Los Angeles from 1982-1994

DALLAS vs. PHILADELPHIA
RS: Cowboys lead series, 51-39
PS: Cowboys lead series, 2-1
1960—Eagles, 27-25 (D)
1961—Eagles, 43-7 (D)
⠀⠀⠀⠀Eagles, 35-13 (P)
1962—Cowboys, 41-19 (D)
⠀⠀⠀⠀Eagles, 28-14 (P)
1963—Eagles, 24-21 (P)
⠀⠀⠀⠀Cowboys, 27-20 (D)
1964—Eagles, 17-14 (D)
⠀⠀⠀⠀Eagles, 24-14 (P)
1965—Eagles, 35-24 (D)
⠀⠀⠀⠀Cowboys, 21-19 (P)
1966—Cowboys, 56-7 (D)
⠀⠀⠀⠀Eagles, 24-23 (P)
1967—Eagles, 21-14 (P)
⠀⠀⠀⠀Cowboys, 38-17 (D)
1968—Cowboys, 45-13 (P)
⠀⠀⠀⠀Cowboys, 34-14 (D)
1969—Cowboys, 38-7 (P)
⠀⠀⠀⠀Cowboys, 49-14 (D)
1970—Cowboys, 17-7 (D)
⠀⠀⠀⠀Cowboys, 21-17 (D)
1971—Cowboys, 42-7 (P)
⠀⠀⠀⠀Cowboys, 20-7 (D)
1972—Cowboys, 28-6 (D)
⠀⠀⠀⠀Cowboys, 28-7 (P)
1973—Eagles, 30-16 (P)
⠀⠀⠀⠀Cowboys, 31-10 (D)
1974—Eagles, 13-10 (P)
⠀⠀⠀⠀Cowboys, 31-24 (D)
1975—Cowboys, 20-17 (P)
⠀⠀⠀⠀Cowboys, 27-17 (D)
1976—Cowboys, 27-7 (D)
⠀⠀⠀⠀Cowboys, 26-7 (P)
1977—Cowboys, 16-10 (P)
⠀⠀⠀⠀Cowboys, 24-14 (D)
1978—Cowboys, 14-7 (D)
⠀⠀⠀⠀Cowboys, 31-13 (P)
1979—Eagles, 31-21 (D)
⠀⠀⠀⠀Cowboys, 24-17 (P)
1980—Eagles, 17-10 (P)
⠀⠀⠀⠀Cowboys, 35-27 (D)
⠀⠀⠀⠀*Eagles, 20-7 (P)
1981—Cowboys, 17-14 (P)
⠀⠀⠀⠀Cowboys, 21-10 (D)
1982—Eagles, 24-20 (D)
1983—Cowboys, 37-7 (D)
⠀⠀⠀⠀Cowboys, 27-20 (P)
1984—Cowboys, 23-17 (D)
⠀⠀⠀⠀Cowboys, 26-10 (P)
1985—Eagles, 16-14 (P)
⠀⠀⠀⠀Cowboys, 34-17 (D)
1986—Cowboys, 17-14 (P)
⠀⠀⠀⠀Eagles, 23-21 (P)
1987—Cowboys, 41-22 (D)

Eagles, 37-20 (P)
1988—Eagles, 24-23 (P)
Eagles, 23-7 (D)
1989—Eagles, 27-0 (D)
Eagles, 20-10 (P)
1990—Eagles, 21-20 (D)
Eagles, 17-3 (P)
1991—Eagles, 24-0 (D)
Cowboys, 25-13 (P)
1992—Eagles, 31-7 (P)
Cowboys, 20-10 (D)
**Cowboys, 34-10 (D)
1993—Cowboys, 23-10 (P)
Cowboys, 23-17 (D)
1994—Cowboys, 24-13 (D)
Cowboys, 31-19 (P)
1995—Cowboys, 34-12 (D)
Eagles, 20-17 (P)
**Cowboys, 30-11 (D)
1996—Cowboys, 23-19 (P)
Eagles, 31-21 (D)
1997—Cowboys, 21-20 (D)
Eagles, 13-12 (P)
1998—Cowboys, 34-0 (P)
Cowboys, 13-9 (D)
1999—Eagles, 13-10 (P)
Cowboys, 20-10 (D)
2000—Eagles, 41-14 (D)
Eagles, 16-13 (P) OT
2001—Eagles, 40-18 (P)
Eagles, 36-3 (D)
2002—Eagles, 44-13 (P)
Cowboys, 27-3 (D)
2003—Cowboys, 23-21 (D)
Eagles, 36-10 (P)
2004—Eagles, 49-21 (D)
Eagles, 12-7 (P)
2005—Cowboys, 33-10 (D)
Cowboys, 21-20 (P)
(RS Pts.—Cowboys 1,955, Eagles 1,719)
(PS Pts.—Cowboys 71, Eagles 41)
*NFC Championship
**NFC Divisional Playoff
DALLAS vs. PITTSBURGH
RS: Cowboys lead series, 14-12
PS: Steelers lead series, 2-1
1960—Steelers, 35-28 (D)
1961—Cowboys, 27-24 (D)
Steelers, 37-7 (P)
1962—Steelers, 30-28 (D)
Cowboys, 42-27 (P)
1963—Steelers, 27-21 (P)
Steelers, 24-19 (D)
1964—Steelers, 23-17 (P)
Cowboys, 17-14 (D)
1965—Steelers, 22-13 (P)
Cowboys, 24-17 (D)
1966—Cowboys, 52-21 (D)
Cowboys, 20-7 (P)
1967—Cowboys, 24-21 (P)
1968—Cowboys, 28-7 (D)
1969—Cowboys, 10-7 (P)
1972—Cowboys, 17-13 (D)
1975—*Steelers, 21-17 (Miami)
1977—Steelers, 28-13 (P)
1978—**Steelers, 35-31 (Miami)
1979—Steelers, 14-3 (P)
1982—Steelers, 36-28 (D)
1985—Cowboys, 27-13 (D)
1988—Steelers, 24-21 (P)

1991—Cowboys, 20-10 (D)
1994—Cowboys, 26-9 (P)
1995—***Cowboys, 27-17 (Tempe)
1997—Cowboys, 37-7 (P)
2004—Steelers, 24-20 (D)
(RS Pts.—Cowboys 589, Steelers 521)
(PS Pts.—Cowboys 75, Steelers 73)
*Super Bowl X
**Super Bowl XIII
***Super Bowl XXX
DALLAS vs. *ST. LOUIS
RS: Rams lead series, 10-9
PS: Series tied, 4-4
1960—Rams, 38-13 (D)
1962—Cowboys, 27-17 (LA)
1967—Rams, 35-13 (D)
1969—Rams, 24-23 (LA)
1971—Cowboys, 28-21 (D)
1973—Rams, 37-31 (LA)
**Cowboys, 27-16 (D)
1975—Cowboys, 18-7 (D)
***Cowboys, 37-7 (LA)
1976—**Rams, 14-12 (D)
1978—Rams, 27-14 (LA)
***Cowboys, 28-0 (LA)
1979—Cowboys, 30-6 (D)
**Rams, 21-19 (D)
1980—Rams, 38-14 (LA)
****Cowboys, 34-13 (D)
1981—Cowboys, 29-17 (D)
1983—****Rams, 24-17 (D)
1984—Cowboys, 20-13 (LA)
1985—^^Rams, 20-0 (LA)
1986—Rams, 29-10 (LA)
1987—Cowboys, 29-21 (LA)
1989—Rams, 35-31 (D)
1990—Cowboys, 24-21 (LA)
1992—Rams, 27-23 (D)
2002—Cowboys, 13-10 (StL)
2005—Rams, 20-10 (D)
(RS Pts.—Rams 443, Cowboys 400)
(PS Pts. Cowboys 174, Rams 115)
*Franchise in Los Angeles prior to 1995
**NFC Divisional Playoff
***NFC Championship
****NFC First-Round Playoff
DALLAS vs. SAN DIEGO
RS: Cowboys lead series, 6-2
1972—Cowboys, 34-28 (SD)
1980—Cowboys, 42-31 (D)
1983—Chargers, 24-23 (SD)
1986—Cowboys, 24-21 (SD)
1990—Cowboys, 17-14 (D)
1995—Cowboys, 23-9 (SD)
2001—Chargers, 32-21 (D)
2005—Cowboys, 28-24 (SD)
(RS Pts.—Cowboys 212, Chargers 183)
DALLAS vs. SAN FRANCISCO
RS: 49ers lead series, 14-9-1
PS: Cowboys lead series, 5-2
1960—49ers, 26-14 (D)
1963—49ers, 31-24 (SF)
1965—Cowboys, 39-31 (D)
1967—49ers, 24-16 (SF)
1969—Tie, 24-24 (D)
1970—*Cowboys, 17-10 (SF)
1971—*Cowboys, 14-3 (D)
1972—49ers, 31-10 (D)
**Cowboys, 30-28 (SF)
1974—Cowboys, 20-14 (D)

1977—Cowboys, 42-35 (SF)
1979—Cowboys, 21-13 (SF)
1980—Cowboys, 59-14 (D)
1981—49ers, 45-14 (SF)
*49ers, 28-27 (SF)
1983—49ers, 42-17 (SF)
1985—49ers, 31-16 (SF)
1989—49ers, 31-14 (D)
1990—49ers, 24-6 (D)
1992—*Cowboys, 30-20 (SF)
1993—Cowboys, 26-17 (D)
*Cowboys, 38-21 (D)
1994—49ers, 21-14 (SF)
*49ers, 38-28 (SF)
1995—49ers, 38-20 (D)
1996—Cowboys, 20-17 (SF) OT
1997—49ers, 17-10 (SF)
2000—49ers, 41-24 (D)
2001—Cowboys, 27-21 (D)
2002—49ers, 31-27 (D)
2005—Cowboys, 34-31 (D)
(RS Pts.—49ers 650, Cowboys 538)
(PS Pts.—Cowboys 184, 49ers 148)
*NFC Championship
**NFC Divisional Playoff
DALLAS vs. SEATTLE
RS: Cowboys lead series, 6-4
1976—Cowboys, 28-13 (S)
1980—Cowboys, 51-7 (D)
1983—Cowboys, 35-10 (D)
1986—Seahawks, 31-14 (D)
1992—Cowboys, 27-0 (D)
1998—Cowboys, 30-22 (D)
2001—Seahawks, 29-3 (S)
2002—Seahawks, 17-14 (D)
2004—Cowboys, 43-39 (S)
2005—Seahawks, 13-10 (S)
(RS Pts.—Cowboys 255, Seahawks 181)
DALLAS vs. TAMPA BAY
RS: Cowboys lead series, 6-3
PS: Cowboys lead series, 2-0
1977—Cowboys, 23-7 (D)
1980—Cowboys, 28-17 (D)
1981—*Cowboys, 38-0 (D)
1982—Cowboys, 14-9 (D)
**Cowboys, 30-17 (D)
1983—Cowboys, 27-24 (D) OT
1990—Cowboys, 14-10 (D)
Cowboys, 17-13 (TB)
2000—Buccaneers, 27-7 (TB)
2001—Buccaneers, 10-6 (D)
2003—Buccaneers, 16-0 (TB)
(RS Pts.—Cowboys 136, Buccaneers 133)
(PS Pts.—Cowboys 68, Buccaneers 17)
*NFC Divisional Playoff
**NFC First-Round Playoff
DALLAS vs. *TENNESSEE
RS: Cowboys lead series, 6-5
1970—Cowboys, 52-10 (D)
1974—Cowboys, 10-0 (H)
1979—Oilers, 30-24 (D)
1982—Cowboys, 37-7 (H)
1985—Cowboys, 17-10 (H)
1988—Oilers, 25-17 (D)
1991—Oilers, 26-23 (H) OT
1994—Cowboys, 20-17 (D)
1997—Oilers, 27-14 (D)
2000—Titans, 31-0 (T)
2002—Cowboys, 21-13 (D)
(RS Pts.—Cowboys 235, Titans 196)

Franchise in Houston prior to 1997; known as Oilers prior to 1999

DALLAS vs. WASHINGTON
RS: Cowboys lead series, 54-34-2
PS: Redskins lead series, 2-0
1960—Redskins, 26-14 (W)
1961—Tie, 28-28 (D)
    Redskins, 34-24 (W)
1962—Tie, 35-35 (D)
    Cowboys, 38-10 (W)
1963—Redskins, 21-17 (W)
    Cowboys, 35-20 (D)
1964—Cowboys, 24-18 (D)
    Redskins, 28-16 (W)
1965—Cowboys, 27-7 (D)
    Redskins, 34-31 (W)
1966—Cowboys, 31-30 (W)
    Redskins, 34-31 (D)
1967—Cowboys, 17-14 (W)
    Redskins, 27-20 (D)
1968—Cowboys, 44-24 (W)
    Cowboys, 29-20 (D)
1969—Cowboys, 41-28 (W)
    Cowboys, 20-10 (D)
1970—Cowboys, 45-21 (W)
    Cowboys, 34-0 (D)
1971—Redskins, 20-16 (D)
    Cowboys, 13-0 (W)
1972—Redskins, 24-20 (W)
    Cowboys, 34-24 (D)
    *Redskins, 26-3 (W)
1973—Redskins, 14-7 (W)
    Cowboys, 27-7 (D)
1974—Redskins, 28-21 (W)
    Cowboys, 24-23 (D)
1975—Redskins, 30-24 (W) OT
    Cowboys, 31-10 (D)
1976—Cowboys, 20-7 (W)
    Redskins, 27-14 (D)
1977—Cowboys, 34-16 (D)
    Cowboys, 14-7 (W)
1978—Redskins, 9-5 (W)
    Cowboys, 37-10 (D)
1979—Redskins, 34-20 (W)
    Cowboys, 35-34 (D)
1980—Cowboys, 17-3 (W)
    Cowboys, 14-10 (D)
1981—Cowboys, 26-10 (W)
    Cowboys, 24-10 (D)
1982—Cowboys, 24-10 (W)
    *Redskins, 31-17 (W)
1983—Cowboys, 31-30 (W)
    Redskins, 31-10 (D)
1984—Redskins, 34-14 (W)
    Redskins, 30-28 (D)
1985—Cowboys, 44-14 (D)
    Cowboys, 13-7 (W)
1986—Cowboys, 30-6 (D)
    Redskins, 41-14 (W)
1987—Cowboys, 13-7 (D)
    Redskins, 24-20 (W)
1988—Redskins, 35-17 (D)
    Cowboys, 24-17 (W)
1989—Redskins, 30-7 (D)
    Cowboys, 13-3 (W)
1990—Redskins, 19-15 (W)
    Cowboys, 27-17 (D)
1991—Redskins, 33-31 (W)
    Cowboys, 24-21 (W)
1992—Cowboys, 23-10 (D)

Redskins, 20-17 (W)
1993—Redskins, 35-16 (W)
    Cowboys, 38-3 (D)
1994—Cowboys, 34-7 (W)
    Cowboys, 31-7 (D)
1995—Redskins, 27-23 (W)
    Redskins, 24-17 (D)
1996—Cowboys, 21-10 (D)
    Redskins, 37-10 (W)
1997—Redskins, 21-16 (W)
    Cowboys, 17-14 (D)
1998—Cowboys, 31-10 (W)
    Cowboys, 23-7 (D)
1999—Cowboys, 41-35 (W) OT
    Cowboys, 38-20 (D)
2000—Cowboys, 27-21 (W)
    Cowboys, 32-13 (D)
2001—Cowboys, 9-7 (D)
    Cowboys, 20-14 (W)
2002—Cowboys, 27-20 (D)
    Redskins, 20-14 (W)
2003—Cowboys, 21-14 (D)
    Cowboys, 27-0 (W)
2004—Cowboys, 21-18 (W)
    Cowboys, 13-10 (D)
2005—Redskins, 14-13 (D)
    Redskins, 35-7 (W)
(RS Pts.—Cowboys 2,098, Redskins 1,714)
(PS Pts.—Redskins 57, Cowboys 20)
NFC Championship

DENVER vs. ARIZONA
RS: Broncos lead series, 6-0-1;
See Arizona vs. Denver
DENVER vs. ATLANTA
RS: Broncos lead series, 7-4
PS: Broncos lead series, 1-0;
See Atlanta vs. Denver
DENVER vs. BALTIMORE
RS: Ravens lead series, 3-2
PS: Ravens lead series, 1-0;
See Baltimore vs. Denver
DENVER vs. BUFFALO
RS: Bills lead series, 17-14-1
PS: Bills lead series, 1-0;
See Buffalo vs. Denver
DENVER vs. CAROLINA
RS: Broncos lead series, 2-0;
See Carolina vs. Denver
DENVER vs. CHICAGO
RS: Series tied, 6-6;
See Chicago vs. Denver
DENVER vs. CINCINNATI
RS: Broncos lead series, 15-8;
See Cincinnati vs. Denver
DENVER vs. CLEVELAND
RS: Broncos lead series, 15-5
PS: Broncos lead series, 3-0;
See Cleveland vs. Denver
DENVER vs. DALLAS
RS: Broncos lead series, 5-4
PS: Cowboys lead series, 1-0;
See Dallas vs. Denver
DENVER vs. DETROIT
RS: Broncos lead series, 6-3
1971—Lions, 24-20 (Den)
1974—Broncos, 31-27 (Det)
1978—Lions, 17-14 (Det)
1981—Broncos, 27-21 (Den)
1984—Broncos, 28-7 (Det)

1987—Broncos, 34-0 (Den)
1990—Lions, 40-27 (Det)
1999—Broncos, 17-7 (Det)
2003—Broncos, 20-16 (Den)
(RS Pts.—Broncos 218, Lions 159)
DENVER vs. GREEN BAY
RS: Broncos lead series, 5-4-1
PS: Broncos lead series, 1-0
1971—Packers, 34-13 (Mil)
1975—Broncos, 23-13 (D)
1978—Broncos, 16-3 (D)
1984—Broncos, 17-14 (D)
1987—Tie, 17-17 (Mil) OT
1990—Broncos, 22-13 (D)
1993—Packers, 30-27 (GB)
1996—Packers, 41-6 (GB)
1997—*Broncos, 31-24 (San Diego)
1999—Broncos, 31-10 (D)
2003—Packers, 31-3 (GB)
(RS Pts.—Packers 206, Broncos 175)
(PS Pts.—Broncos 31, Packers 24)
Super Bowl XXXII
DENVER vs. HOUSTON
RS: Broncos lead series, 1-0
2004—Broncos, 31-13 (D)
(RS Pts.—Broncos 31, Texans 13)
DENVER vs. *INDIANAPOLIS
RS: Broncos lead series, 11-4
PS: Colts lead series, 2-0
1974—Broncos, 17-6 (B)
1977—Broncos, 27-13 (D)
1978—Colts, 7-6 (B)
1981—Broncos, 28-10 (D)
1983—Broncos, 17-10 (B)
    Broncos, 21-19 (D)
1985—Broncos, 15-10 (I)
1988—Colts, 55-23 (I)
1989—Broncos, 14-3 (D)
1990—Broncos, 27-17 (I)
1993—Broncos, 35-13 (D)
2001—Colts, 29-10 (I)
2002—Colts, 23-20 (D) OT
2003—Broncos, 31-17 (I)
    **Colts, 41-10 (I)
2004—Broncos, 33-14 (D)
    **Colts, 49-24 (I)
(RS Pts.—Broncos 324, Colts 246)
(PS Pts.—Colts 90, Broncos 34)
Franchise in Baltimore prior to 1984
**AFC First-Round Playoff*
DENVER vs. JACKSONVILLE
RS: Broncos lead series, 3-2
PS: Series tied, 1-1
1995—Broncos, 31-23 (D)
1996—*Jaguars, 30-27 (D)
1997—**Broncos, 42-17 (D)
1998—Broncos, 37-24 (D)
1999—Jaguars, 27-24 (J)
2004—Jaguars, 7-6 (J)
2005—Broncos, 20-7 (J)
(RS Pts.—Broncos 118, Jaguars 88)
(PS Pts.—Broncos 69, Jaguars 47)
AFC Divisional Playoff
**AFC First-Round Playoff*
DENVER vs. *KANSAS CITY
RS: Chiefs lead series, 51-40
PS: Broncos lead series, 1-0
1960—Texans, 17-14 (D)
    Texans, 34-7 (Dal)
1961—Texans, 19-12 (D)

Texans, 49-21 (Dal)
1962—Texans, 24-3 (D)
Texans, 17-10 (Dal)
1963—Chiefs, 59-7 (D)
Chiefs, 52-21 (KC)
1964—Broncos, 33-27 (D)
Chiefs, 49-39 (KC)
1965—Chiefs, 31-23 (D)
Chiefs, 45-35 (KC)
1966—Chiefs, 37-10 (KC)
Chiefs, 56-10 (D)
1967—Chiefs, 52-9 (KC)
Chiefs, 38-24 (D)
1968—Chiefs, 34-2 (KC)
Chiefs, 30-7 (D)
1969—Chiefs, 26-13 (D)
Chiefs, 31-17 (KC)
1970—Broncos, 26-13 (D)
Chiefs, 16-0 (KC)
1971—Chiefs, 16-3 (D)
Chiefs, 28-10 (KC)
1972—Chiefs, 45-24 (D)
Chiefs, 24-21 (KC)
1973—Chiefs, 16-14 (KC)
Broncos, 14-10 (D)
1974—Broncos, 17-14 (KC)
Chiefs, 42-34 (D)
1975—Broncos, 37-33 (D)
Chiefs, 26-13 (KC)
1976—Broncos, 35-26 (KC)
Broncos, 17-16 (D)
1977—Broncos, 23-7 (D)
Broncos, 14-7 (KC)
1978—Broncos, 23-17 (KC) OT
Broncos, 24-3 (D)
1979—Broncos, 24-10 (KC)
Broncos, 20-3 (D)
1980—Chiefs, 23-17 (D)
Chiefs, 31-14 (KC)
1981—Chiefs, 28-14 (KC)
Broncos, 16-13 (D)
1982—Chiefs, 37-16 (D)
1983—Broncos, 27-24 (D)
Chiefs, 48-17 (KC)
1984—Broncos, 21-0 (D)
Chiefs, 16-13 (KC)
1985—Broncos, 30-10 (KC)
Broncos, 14-13 (D)
1986—Broncos, 38-17 (D)
Chiefs, 37-10 (KC)
1987—Broncos, 26-17 (KC)
Broncos, 20-17 (D)
1988—Chiefs, 20-13 (KC)
Broncos, 17-11 (D)
1989—Broncos, 34-20 (D)
Broncos, 16-13 (KC)
1990—Broncos, 24-23 (D)
Chiefs, 31-20 (KC)
1991—Broncos, 19-16 (D)
Broncos, 24-20 (KC)
1992—Broncos, 20-19 (D)
Chiefs, 42-20 (KC)
1993—Chiefs, 15-7 (KC)
Broncos, 27-21 (D)
1994—Chiefs, 31-28 (D)
Broncos, 20-17 (KC) OT
1995—Chiefs, 21-7 (D)
Chiefs, 20-17 (KC)
1996—Chiefs, 17-14 (KC)
Broncos, 34-7 (D)

1997—Broncos, 19-3 (D)
Chiefs, 24-22 (KC)
**Broncos, 14-10 (KC)
1998—Broncos, 30-7 (KC)
Broncos, 35-31 (D)
1999—Chiefs, 26-10 (KC)
Chiefs, 16-10 (D)
2000—Chiefs, 23-22 (D)
Chiefs, 20-7 (KC)
2001—Broncos, 20-6 (D)
Chiefs, 26-23 (KC) OT
2002—Broncos, 37-34 (KC) OT
Broncos, 31-24 (D)
2003—Chiefs, 24-23 (KC)
Broncos, 45-27 (D)
2004—Broncos, 34-24 (D)
Chiefs, 45-17 (KC)
2005—Broncos, 30-10 (D)
Chiefs, 31-27 (KC)
(RS Pts.—Chiefs 2,195, Broncos 1,806)
(PS Pts.—Broncos 14, Chiefs 10)
*Franchise in Dallas prior to 1963 and
known as Texans
**AFC Divisional Playoff
DENVER vs. MIAMI
RS: Dolphins lead series, 10-3-1
PS: Broncos lead series, 1-0
1966—Dolphins, 24-7 (M)
Broncos, 17-7 (D)
1967—Dolphins, 35-21 (M)
1968—Broncos, 21-14 (D)
1969—Dolphins, 27-24 (M)
1971—Tie, 10-10 (D)
1975—Dolphins, 14-13 (M)
1985—Dolphins, 30-26 (D)
1998—Dolphins, 31-21 (M)
*Broncos, 38-3 (D)
1999—Dolphins, 38-21 (D)
2001—Dolphins, 21-10 (M)
2002—Dolphins, 24-22 (D)
2004—Broncos, 20-17 (D)
2005—Dolphins, 34-10 (M)
(RS Pts.—Dolphins 326, Broncos 243)
(PS Pts.—Broncos 38, Dolphins 3)
*AFC Divisional Playoff
DENVER vs. MINNESOTA
RS: Vikings lead series, 7-4
1972—Vikings, 23-20 (D)
1978—Vikings, 12-9 (M) OT
1981—Broncos, 19-17 (D)
1984—Broncos, 42-21 (D)
1987—Vikings, 34-27 (M)
1990—Vikings, 27-22 (M)
1991—Broncos, 13-6 (M)
1993—Vikings, 26-23 (D)
1996—Broncos, 21-17 (M)
1999—Vikings, 23-20 (D)
2003—Vikings, 28-20 (M)
(RS Pts.—Broncos 236, Vikings 234)
DENVER vs. *NEW ENGLAND
RS: Broncos lead series, 23-15
PS: Broncos lead series, 2-0
1960—Broncos, 13-10 (B)
Broncos, 31-24 (D)
1961—Patriots, 45-17 (B)
Patriots, 28-24 (D)
1962—Patriots, 41-16 (B)
Patriots, 33-29 (D)
1963—Broncos, 14-10 (D)
Patriots, 40-21 (B)

1964—Patriots, 39-10 (D)
Patriots, 12-7 (B)
1965—Broncos, 27-10 (B)
Patriots, 28-20 (D)
1966—Patriots, 24-10 (D)
Broncos, 17-10 (B)
1967—Broncos, 26-21 (D)
1968—Patriots, 20-17 (D)
Broncos, 35-14 (B)
1969—Broncos, 35-7 (D)
1972—Broncos, 45-21 (D)
1976—Patriots, 38-14 (NE)
1979—Broncos, 45-10 (D)
1980—Patriots, 23-14 (NE)
1984—Broncos, 26-19 (D)
1986—Broncos, 27-20 (D)
**Broncos, 22-17 (D)
1987—Broncos, 31-20 (D)
1988—Broncos, 21-10 (D)
1991—Broncos, 9-6 (D)
Broncos, 20-3 (D)
1995—Broncos, 37-3 (NE)
1996—Broncos, 34-8 (NE)
1997—Broncos, 34-13 (D)
1998—Broncos, 27-21 (D)
1999—Patriots, 24-23 (NE)
2000—Patriots, 28-19 (D)
2001—Broncos, 31-20 (D)
2002—Broncos, 24-16 (NE)
2003—Patriots, 30-26 (D)
2005—Broncos, 28-20 (D)
**Broncos, 27-13 (D)
(RS Pts.—Broncos 904, Patriots 769)
(PS Pts.—Broncos 49, Patriots 30)
*Franchise in Boston prior to 1971
**AFC Divisional Playoff
DENVER vs. NEW ORLEANS
RS: Broncos lead series, 6-2
1970—Broncos, 31-6 (NO)
1974—Broncos, 33-17 (D)
1979—Broncos, 10-3 (D)
1985—Broncos, 34-23 (D)
1988—Saints, 42-0 (NO)
1994—Saints, 30-28 (D)
2000—Broncos, 38-23 (NO)
2004—Broncos, 34-13 (NO)
(RS Pts.—Broncos 208, Saints 157)
DENVER vs. N.Y. GIANTS
RS: Giants lead series, 5-4
PS: Giants lead series, 1-0
1972—Giants, 29-17 (NY)
1976—Broncos, 14-13 (D)
1980—Broncos, 14-9 (NY)
1986—Giants, 19-16 (NY)
*Giants, 39-20 (Pasadena)
1989—Giants, 14-7 (D)
1992—Broncos, 27-13 (D)
1998—Giants, 20-16 (NY)
2001—Broncos, 31-20 (D)
2005—Giants, 24-23 (NY)
(RS Pts.—Broncos 165, Giants 161)
(PS Pts.—Giants 39, Broncos 20)
*Super Bowl XXI
DENVER vs. *N.Y. JETS
RS: Broncos lead series, 15-14-1
PS: Broncos lead series, 1-0
1960—Titans, 28-24 (NY)
Titans, 30-27 (D)
1961—Titans, 35-28 (NY)
Broncos, 27-10 (D)

1962—Broncos, 32-10 (NY)
Titans, 46-45 (D)
1963—Tie, 35-35 (NY)
Jets, 14-9 (D)
1964—Jets, 30-6 (NY)
Broncos, 20-16 (D)
1965—Broncos, 16-13 (D)
Jets, 45-10 (NY)
1966—Jets, 16-7 (D)
1967—Jets, 38-24 (D)
Broncos, 33-24 (NY)
1968—Broncos, 21-13 (NY)
1969—Broncos, 21-19 (D)
1973—Broncos, 40-28 (NY)
1976—Broncos, 46-3 (D)
1978—Jets, 31-28 (D)
1980—Broncos, 31-24 (D)
1986—Jets, 22-10 (NY)
1992—Broncos, 27-16 (D)
1993—Broncos, 26-20 (NY)
1994—Jets, 25-22 (NY) OT
1996—Broncos, 31-6 (D)
1998—**Broncos, 23-10 (D)
1999—Jets, 21-13 (D)
2000—Broncos, 30-23 (NY)
2002—Jets, 19-13 (NY)
2005—Broncos, 27-0 (D)
(RS Pts.—Broncos 729, Jets 660)
(PS Pts.—Broncos 23, Jets 10)
*Jets known as Titans prior to 1963
**AFC Championship
DENVER vs. *OAKLAND
RS: Raiders lead series, 53-36-2
PS: Series tied, 1-1
1960—Broncos, 31-14 (D)
Raiders, 48-10 (O)
1961—Raiders, 33-19 (O)
Broncos, 27-24 (D)
1962—Broncos, 44-7 (D)
Broncos, 23-6 (O)
1963—Raiders, 26-10 (D)
Raiders, 35-31 (O)
1964—Raiders, 40-7 (O)
Tie, 20-20 (D)
1965—Raiders, 28-20 (D)
Raiders, 24-13 (O)
1966—Raiders, 17-3 (D)
Raiders, 28-10 (O)
1967—Raiders, 51-0 (O)
Raiders, 21-17 (D)
1968—Raiders, 43-7 (D)
Raiders, 33-27 (O)
1969—Raiders, 24-14 (O)
Raiders, 41-10 (D)
1970—Raiders, 35-23 (O)
Raiders, 24-19 (D)
1971—Raiders, 27-16 (D)
Raiders, 21-13 (O)
1972—Broncos, 30-23 (O)
Raiders, 37-20 (D)
1973—Tie, 23-23 (D)
Raiders, 21-17 (O)
1974—Raiders, 28-17 (D)
Broncos, 20-17 (O)
1975—Raiders, 42-17 (D)
Raiders, 17-10 (O)
1976—Raiders, 17-10 (D)
Raiders, 19-6 (O)
1977—Broncos, 30-7 (D)
Raiders, 24-14 (D)

**Broncos, 20-17 (D)
1978—Broncos, 14-6 (D)
Broncos, 21-6 (O)
1979—Raiders, 27-3 (O)
Raiders, 14-10 (D)
1980—Raiders, 9-3 (O)
Raiders, 24-21 (D)
1981—Broncos, 9-7 (D)
Broncos, 17-0 (O)
1982—Raiders, 27-10 (LA)
1983—Raiders, 22-7 (D)
Raiders, 22-20 (LA)
1984—Broncos, 16-13 (D)
Broncos, 22-19 (LA) OT
1985—Raiders, 31-28 (LA) OT
Raiders, 17-14 (D) OT
1986—Broncos, 38-36 (D)
Broncos, 21-10 (LA)
1987—Broncos, 30-14 (D)
Broncos, 23-17 (LA)
1988—Raiders, 30-27 (D) OT
Raiders, 21-20 (LA)
1989—Broncos, 31-21 (D)
Raiders, 16-13 (LA) OT
1990—Raiders, 14-9 (LA)
Raiders, 23-20 (D)
1991—Raiders, 16-13 (LA)
Raiders, 17-16 (D)
1992—Broncos, 17-13 (D)
Raiders, 24-0 (LA)
1993—Raiders, 23-20 (D)
Raiders, 33-30 (LA) OT
***Raiders, 42-24 (LA)
1994—Raiders, 48-16 (D)
Raiders, 23-13 (LA)
1995—Broncos, 27-0 (D)
Broncos, 31-28 (O)
1996—Broncos, 22-21 (O)
Broncos, 24-19 (D)
1997—Raiders, 28-25 (O)
Broncos, 31-3 (D)
1998—Broncos, 34-17 (O)
Broncos, 40-14 (D)
1999—Broncos, 16-13 (O)
Broncos, 27-21 (D) OT
2000—Broncos, 33-24 (O)
Broncos, 27-24 (D)
2001—Raiders, 38-28 (O)
Broncos, 23-17 (D)
2002—Raiders, 34-10 (D)
Raiders, 28-16 (O)
2003—Broncos, 31-10 (D)
Broncos, 22-8 (O)
2004—Broncos, 31-3 (D)
Raiders, 25-24 (O)
2005—Broncos, 31-17 (O)
Broncos, 22-3 (D)
(RS Pts.—Raiders 1,983, Broncos 1,775)
(PS Pts.—Raiders 59, Broncos 44)
*Franchise in Los Angeles from 1982-1994
**AFC Championship
***AFC First-Round Playoff
DENVER vs. PHILADELPHIA
RS: Eagles lead series, 6-4
1971—Eagles, 17-16 (P)
1975—Broncos, 25-10 (D)
1980—Eagles, 27-6 (P)
1983—Eagles, 13-10 (D)
1986—Broncos, 33-7 (P)
1989—Eagles, 28-24 (D)

1992—Eagles, 30-0 (P)
1995—Eagles, 31-13 (P)
1998—Broncos, 41-16 (D)
2005—Broncos, 49-21 (D)
(RS Pts.—Broncos 217, Eagles 200)
DENVER vs. PITTSBURGH
RS: Broncos lead series, 11-6-1
PS: Series tied, 3-3
1970—Broncos, 16-13 (D)
1971—Broncos, 22-10 (P)
1973—Broncos, 23-13 (P)
1974—Tie, 35-35 (D) OT
1975—Steelers, 20-9 (P)
1977—Broncos, 21-7 (D)
*Broncos, 34-21 (D)
1978—Steelers, 21-17 (D)
*Steelers, 33-10 (P)
1979—Steelers, 42-7 (P)
1983—Broncos, 14-10 (P)
1984—*Steelers, 24-17 (D)
1985—Broncos, 31-23 (P)
1986—Broncos, 21-10 (P)
1988—Steelers, 39-21 (P)
1989—Broncos, 34-7 (D)
*Broncos, 24-23 (D)
1990—Steelers, 34-17 (D)
1991—Broncos, 20-13 (D)
1993—Broncos, 37-13 (D)
1997—Steelers, 35-24 (P)
**Broncos, 24-21 (P)
2003—Broncos, 17-14 (D)
2005—**Steelers, 34-17 (D)
(RS Pts.—Broncos 386, Steelers 359)
(PS Pts.—Steelers 156, Broncos 126)
*AFC Divisional Playoff
**AFC Championship
DENVER vs. *ST. LOUIS
RS: Series tied, 5-5
1972—Broncos, 16-10 (LA)
1974—Rams, 17-10 (D)
1979—Rams, 13-9 (D)
1982—Broncos, 27-24 (LA)
1985—Rams, 20-16 (LA)
1988—Broncos, 35-24 (D)
1994—Rams, 27-21 (LA)
1997—Broncos, 35-14 (D)
2000—Rams, 41-36 (StL)
2002—Broncos, 23-16 (D)
(RS Pts.—Broncos 228, Rams 206)
*Franchise in Los Angeles prior to 1995
DENVER vs. *SAN DIEGO
RS: Broncos lead series, 52-39-1
1960—Chargers, 23-19 (D)
Chargers, 41-33 (LA)
1961—Chargers, 37-0 (SD)
Chargers, 19-16 (D)
1962—Broncos, 30-21 (D)
Broncos, 23-20 (SD)
1963—Broncos, 50-34 (D)
Chargers, 58-20 (SD)
1964—Chargers, 42-14 (D)
Chargers, 31-20 (D)
1965—Chargers, 34-31 (SD)
Chargers, 33-21 (D)
1966—Chargers, 24-17 (SD)
Broncos, 20-17 (D)
1967—Chargers, 38-21 (D)
Chargers, 24-20 (SD)
1968—Chargers, 55-24 (SD)
Chargers, 47-23 (D)

1969—Broncos, 13-0 (D)
    Chargers, 45-24 (SD)
1970—Chargers, 24-21 (SD)
    Tie, 17-17 (D)
1971—Broncos, 20-16 (D)
    Chargers, 45-17 (SD)
1972—Chargers, 37-14 (SD)
    Broncos, 38-13 (D)
1973—Broncos, 30-19 (D)
    Broncos, 42-28 (SD)
1974—Broncos, 27-7 (D)
    Chargers, 17-0 (SD)
1975—Broncos, 27-17 (SD)
    Broncos, 13-10 (D) OT
1976—Broncos, 26-0 (D)
    Broncos, 17-0 (SD)
1977—Broncos, 17-14 (SD)
    Broncos, 17-9 (D)
1978—Broncos, 27-14 (D)
    Chargers, 23-0 (SD)
1979—Broncos, 7-0 (D)
    Chargers, 17-7 (SD)
1980—Chargers, 30-13 (D)
    Broncos, 20-13 (SD)
1981—Broncos, 42-24 (D)
    Chargers, 34-17 (SD)
1982—Chargers, 23-3 (D)
    Chargers, 30-20 (SD)
1983—Broncos, 14-6 (D)
    Chargers, 31-7 (SD)
1984—Broncos, 16-13 (SD)
    Broncos, 16-13 (D)
1985—Chargers, 30-10 (SD)
    Broncos, 30-24 (D) OT
1986—Broncos, 31-14 (SD)
    Chargers, 9-3 (D)
1987—Broncos, 31-17 (SD)
    Broncos, 24-0 (D)
1988—Broncos, 34-3 (D)
    Broncos, 12-0 (SD)
1989—Broncos, 16-10 (D)
    Chargers, 19-16 (SD)
1990—Chargers, 19-7 (SD)
    Broncos, 20-10 (D)
1991—Broncos, 27-19 (D)
    Broncos, 17-14 (SD)
1992—Broncos, 21-13 (D)
    Chargers, 24-21 (SD)
1993—Broncos, 34-17 (D)
    Chargers, 13-10 (SD)
1994—Chargers, 37-34 (D)
    Broncos, 20-15 (SD)
1995—Chargers, 17-6 (SD)
    Broncos, 30-27 (D)
1996—Broncos, 28-17 (D)
    Chargers, 16-10 (SD)
1997—Broncos, 38-28 (SD)
    Broncos, 38-3 (D)
1998—Broncos, 27-10 (D)
    Broncos, 31-16 (SD)
1999—Broncos, 33-17 (SD)
    Chargers, 12-6 (D)
2000—Broncos, 21-7 (SD)
    Broncos, 38-37 (D)
2001—Chargers, 27-10 (SD)
    Broncos, 26-16 (D)
2002—Broncos, 26-9 (D)
    Chargers, 30-27 (SD) OT
2003—Broncos, 37-13 (SD)
    Broncos, 37-8 (D)

2004—Broncos, 23-13 (D)
    Chargers, 20-17 (SD)
2005—Broncos, 20-17 (D)
    Broncos, 23-7 (SD)
(RS Pts.—Broncos 1,961, Chargers 1,863)
*Franchise in Los Angeles prior to 1961

DENVER vs. SAN FRANCISCO
RS: Broncos lead series, 6-4
PS: 49ers lead series, 1-0
1970—49ers, 19-14 (SF)
1973—49ers, 36-34 (D)
1979—Broncos, 38-28 (SF)
1982—Broncos, 24-21 (D)
1985—Broncos, 17-16 (D)
1988—Broncos, 16-13 (SF) OT
1989—*49ers, 55-10 (New Orleans)
1994—49ers, 42-19 (SF)
1997—49ers, 34-17 (SF)
2000—Broncos, 38-9 (D)
2002—Broncos, 24-14 (SF)
(RS Pts.—Broncos 241, 49ers 232)
(PS Pts.—49ers 55, Broncos 10)
*Super Bowl XXIV

DENVER vs. SEATTLE
RS: Broncos lead series, 33-17
PS: Seahawks lead series, 1-0
1977—Broncos, 24-13 (S)
1978—Broncos, 28-7 (D)
    Broncos, 20-17 (S) OT
1979—Broncos, 37-34 (D)
    Seahawks, 28-23 (S)
1980—Broncos, 36-20 (D)
    Broncos, 25-17 (S)
1981—Seahawks, 13-10 (S)
    Broncos, 23-13 (D)
1982—Seahawks, 17-10 (D)
    Seahawks, 13-11 (S)
1983—Seahawks, 27-19 (S)
    Broncos, 38-27 (D)
    *Seahawks, 31-7 (S)
1984—Seahawks, 27-24 (D)
    Broncos, 31-14 (S)
1985—Broncos, 13-10 (D) OT
    Broncos, 27-24 (S)
1986—Broncos, 20-13 (D)
    Seahawks, 41-16 (S)
1987—Broncos, 40-17 (D)
    Seahawks, 28-21 (S)
1988—Seahawks, 21-14 (D)
    Seahawks, 42-14 (S)
1989—Broncos, 24-21 (S) OT
    Broncos, 41-14 (D)
1990—Broncos, 34-31 (D) OT
    Seahawks, 17-12 (S)
1991—Broncos, 16-10 (D)
    Seahawks, 13-10 (S)
1992—Seahawks, 16-13 (S) OT
    Broncos, 10-6 (D)
1993—Broncos, 28-17 (D)
    Broncos, 17-9 (S)
1994—Broncos, 16-9 (S)
    Broncos, 17-10 (D)
1995—Seahawks, 27-10 (S)
    Seahawks, 31-27 (D)
1996—Broncos, 30-20 (S)
    Broncos, 34-7 (D)
1997—Broncos, 35-14 (S)
    Broncos, 30-27 (D)
1998—Broncos, 21-16 (S)
    Broncos, 28-21 (D)

1999—Seahawks, 20-17 (S)
    Broncos, 36-30 (D) OT
2000—Broncos, 38-31 (S)
    Broncos, 31-24 (D)
2001—Seahawks, 34-21 (S)
    Broncos, 20-7 (D)
2002—Broncos, 31-9 (S)
(RS Pts.—Broncos 1,171, Seahawks 974)
(PS Pts.—Seahawks 31, Broncos 7)
*AFC First-Round Playoff

DENVER vs. TAMPA BAY
RS: Broncos lead series, 4-2
1976—Broncos, 48-13 (D)
1981—Broncos, 24-7 (TB)
1993—Buccaneers, 17-10 (D)
1996—Broncos, 27-23 (D)
1999—Buccaneers, 13-10 (TB)
2004—Broncos, 16-13 (TB)
(RS Pts.—Broncos 135, Buccaneers 86)

DENVER vs. *TENNESSEE
RS: Titans lead series, 20-12-1
PS: Broncos lead series, 2-1
1960—Oilers, 45-25 (D)
    Oilers, 20-10 (H)
1961—Oilers, 55-14 (D)
    Oilers, 45-14 (H)
1962—Broncos, 20-10 (D)
    Oilers, 34-17 (H)
1963—Broncos, 20-14 (D)
    Oilers, 33-24 (D)
1964—Oilers, 38-17 (D)
    Oilers, 34-15 (H)
1965—Broncos, 28-17 (D)
    Broncos, 31-21 (H)
1966—Oilers, 45-7 (H)
    Broncos, 40-38 (D)
1967—Oilers, 10-6 (H)
    Oilers, 20-18 (D)
1968—Oilers, 38-17 (H)
    Oilers, 24-21 (H)
1969—Oilers, 24-21 (H)
    Tie, 20-20 (D)
1970—Oilers, 31-21 (D)
1972—Broncos, 30-17 (D)
1973—Broncos, 48-20 (H)
1974—Broncos, 37-14 (D)
1976—Oilers, 17-3 (H)
1977—Broncos, 24-14 (H)
1979—**Oilers, 13-7 (H)
1980—Oilers, 20-16 (D)
1983—Broncos, 26-14 (H)
1985—Broncos, 31-20 (D)
1987—Oilers, 40-10 (D)
    ***Broncos, 34-10 (D)
1991—Oilers, 42-14 (H)
    ***Broncos, 26-24 (D)
1992—Broncos, 27-21 (D)
1995—Oilers, 42-33 (H)
2004—Broncos, 37-16 (T)
(RS Pts.—Titans 895, Broncos 715)
(PS Pts.—Broncos 67, Titans 47)
*Franchise in Houston prior to 1997;
known as the Oilers prior to 1999
**AFC First-Round Playoff
***AFC Divisional Playoff

DENVER vs. WASHINGTON
RS: Broncos lead series, 6-4
PS: Redskins lead series, 1-0
1970—Redskins, 19-3 (D)
1974—Redskins, 30-3 (W)
1980—Broncos, 20-17 (D)

1986—Broncos, 31-30 (D)
1987—*Redskins, 42-10 (San Diego)
1989—Broncos, 14-10 (W)
1992—Redskins, 34-3 (W)
1995—Broncos, 38-31 (D)
1998—Broncos, 38-16 (W)
2001—Redskins, 17-10 (D)
2005—Broncos, 21-19 (D)
(RS Pts.—Redskins 223, Broncos 181)
(PS Pts.—Redskins 42, Broncos 10)
*Super Bowl XXII

DETROIT vs. ARIZONA
RS: Lions lead series, 31-21-5;
See Arizona vs. Detroit
DETROIT vs. ATLANTA
RS: Lions lead series, 22-9;
See Atlanta vs. Detroit
DETROIT vs. BALTIMORE
RS: Series tied, 1-1;
See Baltimore vs. Detroit
DETROIT vs. BUFFALO
RS: Series tied, 3-3-1;
See Buffalo vs. Detroit
DETROIT vs. CAROLINA
RS: Panthers lead series, 3-1;
See Carolina vs. Detroit
DETROIT vs. CHICAGO
RS: Bears lead series, 85-62-5;
See Chicago vs. Detroit
DETROIT vs. CINCINNATI
RS: Bengals lead series, 6-3;
See Cincinnati vs. Detroit
DETROIT vs. CLEVELAND
RS: Lions lead series, 13-4
PS: Lions lead series, 3-1;
See Cleveland vs. Detroit
DETROIT vs. DALLAS
RS: Cowboys lead series, 10-8
PS: Series tied, 1-1;
See Dallas vs. Detroit
DETROIT vs. DENVER
RS: Broncos lead series, 6-3;
See Denver vs. Detroit
*DETROIT vs. GREEN BAY
RS: Packers lead series, 80-64-7
PS: Packers lead series, 2-0
1930—Packers, 47-13 (GB)
    Tie, 6-6 (P)
1932—Packers, 15-10 (GB)
    Spartans, 19-0 (P)
1933—Packers, 17-0 (GB)
    Spartans, 7-0 (P)
1934—Lions, 3-0 (GB)
    Packers, 3-0 (D)
1935—Packers, 13-9 (Mil)
    Packers, 31-7 (GB)
    Lions, 20-10 (D)
1936—Packers, 20-18 (GB)
    Packers, 26-17 (D)
1937—Packers, 26-6 (GB)
    Packers, 14-13 (D)
1938—Lions, 17-7 (GB)
    Packers, 28-7 (D)
1939—Packers, 26-7 (GB)
    Packers, 12-7 (D)
1940—Lions, 23-14 (GB)
    Packers, 50-7 (D)
1941—Packers, 23-0 (GB)
    Packers, 24-7 (D)

1942—Packers, 38-7 (Mil)
    Packers, 28-7 (D)
1943—Packers, 35-14 (GB)
    Packers, 27-6 (D)
1944—Packers, 27-6 (Mil)
    Packers, 14-0 (D)
1945—Packers, 57-21 (Mil)
    Lions, 14-3 (D)
1946—Packers, 10-7 (Mil)
    Packers, 9-0 (D)
1947—Packers, 34-17 (GB)
    Packers, 35-14 (D)
1948—Packers, 33-21 (GB)
    Lions, 24-20 (D)
1949—Packers, 16-14 (Mil)
    Lions, 21-7 (D)
1950—Lions, 45-7 (GB)
    Lions, 24-21 (D)
1951—Lions, 24-17 (GB)
    Lions, 52-35 (D)
1952—Lions, 52-17 (GB)
    Lions, 48-24 (D)
1953—Lions, 14-7 (GB)
    Lions, 34-15 (D)
1954—Lions, 21-17 (GB)
    Lions, 28-24 (D)
1955—Packers, 20-17 (GB)
    Lions, 24-10 (D)
1956—Lions, 20-16 (GB)
    Packers, 24-20 (D)
1957—Lions, 24-14 (GB)
    Lions, 18-6 (D)
1958—Tie, 13-13 (GB)
    Lions, 24-14 (D)
1959—Packers, 28-10 (GB)
    Packers, 24-17 (D)
1960—Packers, 28-9 (GB)
    Lions, 23-10 (D)
1961—Lions, 17-13 (Mil)
    Packers, 17-9 (D)
1962—Packers, 9-7 (GB)
    Lions, 26-14 (D)
1963—Packers, 31-10 (Mil)
    Tie, 13-13 (D)
1964—Packers, 14-10 (D)
    Packers, 30-7 (GB)
1965—Packers, 31-21 (D)
    Lions, 12-7 (GB)
1966—Packers, 23-14 (GB)
    Packers, 31-7 (D)
1967—Tie, 17-17 (GB)
    Packers, 27-17 (D)
1968—Lions, 23-17 (GB)
    Tie, 14-14 (D)
1969—Packers, 28-17 (GB)
    Lions, 16-10 (GB)
1970—Lions, 40-0 (GB)
    Lions, 20-0 (D)
1971—Lions, 31-28 (D)
    Tie, 14-14 (Mil)
1972—Packers, 24-23 (D)
    Packers, 33-7 (GB)
1973—Tie, 13-13 (GB)
    Lions, 34-0 (D)
1974—Packers, 21-19 (Mil)
    Lions, 19-17 (D)
1975—Lions, 30-16 (Mil)
    Lions, 13-10 (D)
1976—Packers, 24-14 (GB)
    Lions, 27-6 (D)

1977—Lions, 10-6 (D)
    Packers, 10-9 (GB)
1978—Packers, 13-7 (D)
    Packers, 35-14 (Mil)
1979—Packers, 24-16 (Mil)
    Packers, 18-13 (D)
1980—Lions, 29-7 (Mil)
    Lions, 24-3 (D)
1981—Lions, 31-27 (D)
    Packers, 31-17 (GB)
1982—Lions, 30-10 (GB)
    Lions, 27-24 (D)
1983—Lions, 38-14 (D)
    Lions, 23-20 (Mil) OT
1984—Packers, 41-9 (GB)
    Lions, 31-28 (D)
1985—Packers, 43-10 (GB)
    Packers, 26-23 (D)
1986—Lions, 21-14 (GB)
    Packers, 44-40 (D)
1987—Lions, 19-16 (GB) OT
    Packers, 34-33 (D)
1988—Lions, 19-9 (Mil)
    Lions, 30-14 (D)
1989—Packers, 23-20 (Mil) OT
    Lions, 31-22 (D)
1990—Packers, 24-21 (D)
    Lions, 24-17 (GB)
1991—Lions, 23-14 (D)
    Lions, 21-17 (GB)
1992—Packers, 27-13 (D)
    Packers, 38-10 (Mil)
1993—Packers, 26-17 (Mil)
    Lions, 30-20 (D)
    **Packers, 28-24 (D)
1994—Packers, 38-30 (Mil)
    Lions, 34-31 (D)
    **Packers, 16-12 (GB)
1995—Packers, 30-21 (GB)
    Lions, 24-16 (D)
1996—Packers, 28-18 (GB)
    Packers, 31-3 (D)
1997—Lions, 26-15 (D)
    Packers, 20-10 (GB)
1998—Packers, 38-19 (GB)
    Lions, 27-20 (D)
1999—Lions, 23-15 (D)
    Packers, 26-17 (GB)
2000—Lions, 31-24 (D)
    Packers, 26-13 (GB)
2001—Packers, 28-6 (GB)
    Packers, 29-27 (D)
2002—Packers, 37-31 (D)
    Packers, 40-14 (GB)
2003—Packers, 31-6 (GB)
    Lions, 22-14 (D)
2004—Packers, 38-10 (D)
    Packers, 16-13 (GB)
2005—Lions, 17-3 (D)
    Packers, 16-13 (GB) OT
(RS Pts.—Packers 3,097, Lions 2,726)
(PS Pts.—Packers 44, Lions 36)
*Franchise in Portsmouth prior to 1934
and known as the Spartans
**NFC First-Round Playoff
DETROIT vs. HOUSTON
RS: Lions lead series, 1-0
2004—Lions, 28-16 (D)
(RS Pts.—Lions 28, Texans 16)

DETROIT vs. *INDIANAPOLIS
RS: Colts lead series, 19-18-2
1953—Lions, 27-17 (B)
    Lions, 17-7 (D)
1954—Lions, 35-0 (D)
    Lions, 27-3 (B)
1955—Colts, 28-13 (B)
    Lions, 24-14 (D)
1956—Lions, 31-14 (B)
    Lions, 27-3 (D)
1957—Colts, 34-14 (B)
    Lions, 31-27 (D)
1958—Colts, 28-15 (B)
    Colts, 40-14 (D)
1959—Colts, 21-9 (B)
    Colts, 31-24 (D)
1960—Lions, 30-17 (D)
    Lions, 20-15 (B)
1961—Lions, 16-15 (B)
    Colts, 17-14 (D)
1962—Lions, 29-20 (B)
    Lions, 21-14 (D)
1963—Lions, 25-21 (D)
    Colts, 24-21 (B)
1964—Colts, 34-0 (D)
    Lions, 31-14 (B)
1965—Colts, 31-7 (B)
    Tie, 24-24 (D)
1966—Colts, 45-14 (B)
    Lions, 20-14 (D)
1967—Colts, 41-7 (B)
1968—Colts, 27-10 (D)
1969—Tie, 17-17 (B)
1973—Colts, 29-27 (D)
1977—Lions, 13-10 (B)
1980—Colts, 10-9 (D)
1985—Colts, 14-6 (I)
1991—Lions, 33-24 (I)
1997—Lions, 32-10 (D)
2000—Colts, 30-18 (I)
2004—Colts, 41-9 (D)
(RS Pts.—Colts 829, Lions 757)
Franchise in Baltimore prior to 1984
DETROIT vs. JACKSONVILLE
RS: Jaguars lead series, 2-1
1995—Lions, 44-0 (D)
1998—Jaguars, 37-22 (J)
2004—Jaguars, 23-17 (J) OT
(RS Pts.—Lions 83, Jaguars 60)
DETROIT vs. KANSAS CITY
RS: Chiefs lead series, 7-3
1971—Lions, 32-21 (D)
1975—Chiefs, 24-21 (KC) OT
1980—Chiefs, 20-17 (KC)
1981—Lions, 27-10 (D)
1987—Chiefs, 27-20 (D)
1988—Lions, 7-6 (KC)
1990—Chiefs, 43-24 (KC)
1996—Chiefs, 28-24 (D)
1999—Chiefs, 31-21 (KC)
2003—Chiefs, 45-17 (KC)
(RS Pts.—Chiefs 255, Lions 210)
DETROIT vs. MIAMI
RS: Dolphins lead series, 6-2
1973—Dolphins, 34-7 (M)
1979—Dolphins, 28-10 (D)
1985—Lions, 31-21 (D)
1991—Lions, 17-13 (D)
1994—Dolphins, 27-20 (M)
1997—Dolphins, 33-30 (M)

2000—Dolphins, 23-8 (D)
2002—Dolphins, 49-21 (M)
(RS Pts.—Dolphins 228, Lions 144)
DETROIT vs. MINNESOTA
RS: Vikings lead series, 58-29-2
1961—Lions, 37-10 (M)
    Lions, 13-7 (D)
1962—Lions, 17-6 (M)
    Lions, 37-23 (D)
1963—Lions, 28-10 (D)
    Vikings, 34-31 (M)
1964—Lions, 24-20 (M)
    Tie, 23-23 (D)
1965—Lions, 31-29 (M)
    Vikings, 29-7 (D)
1966—Lions, 32-31 (M)
    Vikings, 28-16 (D)
1967—Tie, 10-10 (M)
    Lions, 14-3 (D)
1968—Vikings, 24-10 (M)
    Vikings, 13-6 (D)
1969—Vikings, 24-10 (M)
    Vikings, 27-0 (D)
1970—Vikings, 30-17 (D)
    Vikings, 24-20 (M)
1971—Vikings, 16-13 (D)
    Vikings, 29-10 (M)
1972—Vikings, 34-10 (D)
    Vikings, 16-14 (M)
1973—Vikings, 23-9 (D)
    Vikings, 28-7 (M)
1974—Vikings, 7-6 (D)
    Lions, 20-16 (M)
1975—Vikings, 25-19 (M)
    Lions, 17-10 (D)
1976—Vikings, 10-9 (D)
    Vikings, 31-23 (M)
1977—Vikings, 14-7 (M)
    Vikings, 30-21 (D)
1978—Vikings, 17-7 (M)
    Lions, 45-14 (D)
1979—Vikings, 13-10 (D)
    Vikings, 14-7 (M)
1980—Lions, 27-7 (D)
    Vikings, 34-0 (M)
1981—Vikings, 26-24 (M)
    Lions, 45-7 (D)
1982—Vikings, 34-31 (D)
1983—Vikings, 20-17 (M)
    Lions, 13-2 (D)
1984—Vikings, 29-28 (D)
    Lions, 16-14 (M)
1985—Vikings, 16-13 (M)
    Lions, 41-21 (D)
1986—Lions, 13-10 (M)
    Vikings, 24-10 (D)
1987—Vikings, 34-19 (M)
    Vikings, 17-14 (D)
1988—Vikings, 44-17 (M)
    Vikings, 23-0 (D)
1989—Vikings, 24-17 (M)
    Vikings, 20-7 (D)
1990—Lions, 34-27 (M)
    Vikings, 17-7 (D)
1991—Lions, 24-20 (D)
    Lions, 34-14 (M)
1992—Lions, 31-17 (D)
    Vikings, 31-14 (M)
1993—Lions, 30-27 (M)
    Vikings, 13-0 (D)

1994—Vikings, 10-3 (M)
    Lions, 41-19 (D)
1995—Vikings, 20-10 (M)
    Lions, 44-38 (D)
1996—Vikings, 17-13 (M)
    Vikings, 24-22 (D)
1997—Lions, 38-15 (D)
    Lions, 14-13 (M)
1998—Vikings, 29-6 (M)
    Vikings, 34-13 (D)
1999—Lions, 25-23 (D)
    Vikings, 24-17 (M)
2000—Vikings, 31-24 (D)
    Vikings, 24-17 (M)
2001—Vikings, 31-26 (M)
    Lions, 27-24 (D)
2002—Vikings, 31-24 (M)
    Vikings, 38-36 (D)
2003—Vikings, 23-13 (D)
    Vikings, 24-14 (M)
2004—Vikings, 22-19 (M)
    Vikings, 28-27 (D)
2005—Vikings, 27-14 (M)
    Vikings, 21-16 (D)
(RS Pts.—Vikings 1,914, Lions 1,666)
DETROIT vs. NEW ENGLAND
RS: Series tied, 4-4
1971—Lions, 34-7 (NE)
1976—Lions, 30-10 (D)
1979—Patriots, 24-17 (NE)
1985—Patriots, 23-6 (NE)
1993—Lions, 19-16 (NE) OT
1994—Patriots, 23-17 (D)
2000—Lions, 34-9 (D)
2002—Patriots, 20-12 (D)
(RS Pts.—Lions 169, Patriots 132)
DETROIT vs. NEW ORLEANS
RS: Lions lead series, 9-8-1
1968—Tie, 20-20 (D)
1970—Saints, 19-17 (NO)
1972—Lions, 27-14 (D)
1973—Saints, 20-13 (NO)
1974—Lions, 19-14 (D)
1976—Saints, 17-16 (NO)
1977—Lions, 23-19 (D)
1979—Saints, 17-7 (NO)
1980—Lions, 24-13 (D)
1988—Saints, 22-14 (D)
1989—Lions, 21-14 (D)
1990—Lions, 27-10 (NO)
1992—Saints, 13-7 (D)
1993—Saints, 14-3 (NO)
1997—Saints, 35-17 (NO)
2000—Lions, 14-10 (NO)
2002—Lions, 26-21 (D)
2005—Lions, 13-12 (San Antonio)
(RS Pts.—Lions 308, Saints 304)
*DETROIT vs. N.Y. GIANTS
RS: Lions lead series, 20-17-1
PS: Lions lead series, 1-0
1930—Giants, 19-6 (P)
1931—Spartans, 14-6 (P)
    Giants, 14-0 (NY)
1932—Spartans, 7-0 (P)
    Spartans, 6-0 (NY)
1933—Spartans, 17-7 (P)
    Giants, 13-10 (NY)
1934—Lions, 9-0 (D)
1935—**Lions, 26-7 (D)
1936—Giants, 14-7 (NY)

Lions, 38-0 (D)
1937—Lions, 17-0 (NY)
1939—Lions, 18-14 (D)
1941—Giants, 20-13 (NY)
1943—Tie, 0-0 (D)
1945—Giants, 35-14 (NY)
1947—Lions, 35-7 (D)
1949—Lions, 45-21 (NY)
1953—Lions, 27-16 (NY)
1955—Giants, 24-19 (D)
1958—Giants, 19-17 (D)
1962—Giants, 17-14 (NY)
1964—Lions, 26-3 (D)
1967—Lions, 30-7 (NY)
1969—Lions, 24-0 (D)
1972—Lions, 30-16 (D)
1974—Lions, 20-19 (D)
1976—Giants, 24-10 (NY)
1982—Giants, 13-6 (D)
1983—Lions, 15-9 (D)
1988—Giants, 30-10 (NY)
Giants, 13-10 (D) OT
1989—Giants, 24-14 (NY)
1990—Giants, 20-0 (NY)
1994—Lions, 28-25 (NY) OT
1996—Giants, 35-7 (D)
1997—Giants, 26-20 (D) OT
2000—Lions, 31-21 (NY)
2004—Lions, 28-13 (NY)
(RS Pts.—Lions 642, Giants 544)
(PS Pts.—Lions 26, Giants 7)
*Franchise in Portsmouth prior to 1934
and known as the Spartans
**NFL Championship
DETROIT vs. N.Y. JETS
RS: Lions lead series, 6-4
1972—Lions, 37-20 (D)
1979—Jets, 31-10 (NY)
1982—Jets, 28-13 (D)
1985—Lions, 31-20 (D)
1988—Jets, 17-10 (D)
1991—Lions, 34-20 (D)
1994—Lions, 18-7 (NY)
1997—Lions, 13-10 (D)
2000—Lions, 10-7 (NY)
2002—Jets, 31-14 (D)
(RS Pts.—Jets 191, Lions 190)
DETROIT vs. *OAKLAND
RS: Raiders lead series, 6-3
1970—Lions, 28-14 (D)
1974—Raiders, 35-13 (O)
1978—Raiders, 29-17 (O)
1981—Lions, 16-0 (D)
1984—Raiders, 24-3 (D)
1987—Raiders, 27-7 (LA)
1990—Raiders, 38-31 (D)
1996—Raiders, 37-21 (O)
2003—Lions, 23-13 (D)
(RS Pts.—Raiders 217, Lions 159)
*Franchise in Los Angeles from 1982-1994
***DETROIT vs. PHILADELPHIA**
RS: Series tied, 12-12-2
PS: Eagles lead series, 1-0
1933—Spartans, 25-0 (P)
1934—Lions, 10-0 (P)
1935—Lions, 35-0 (D)
1936—Lions, 23-0 (P)
1938—Eagles, 21-7 (D)
1940—Lions, 21-0 (P)
1941—Lions, 21-17 (D)

1945—Lions, 28-24 (D)
1948—Eagles, 45-21 (P)
1949—Eagles, 22-14 (D)
1951—Lions, 28-10 (P)
1954—Tie, 13-13 (D)
1957—Lions, 27-16 (P)
1960—Eagles, 28-10 (P)
1961—Eagles, 27-24 (D)
1965—Lions, 35-28 (P)
1968—Eagles, 12-0 (D)
1971—Eagles, 23-20 (D)
1974—Eagles, 28-17 (P)
1977—Lions, 17-13 (D)
1979—Eagles, 44-7 (P)
1984—Tie, 23-23 (D) OT
1986—Lions, 13-11 (P)
1995—**Eagles, 58-37 (P)
1996—Eagles, 24-17 (P)
1998—Eagles, 10-9 (P)
2004—Eagles, 30-13 (D)
(RS Pts.—Lions 478, Eagles 469)
(PS Pts.—Eagles 58, Lions 37)
*Franchise in Portsmouth prior to 1934
and known as the Spartans
**NFC First-Round Playoff
DETROIT vs. *PITTSBURGH
RS: Series tied, 14-14-1
1934—Lions, 40-7 (D)
1936—Lions, 28-3 (D)
1937—Lions, 7-3 (D)
1938—Lions, 16-7 (D)
1940—Pirates, 10-7 (D)
1942—Steelers, 35-7 (D)
1946—Lions, 17-7 (D)
1947—Steelers, 17-10 (P)
1948—Lions, 17-14 (D)
1949—Steelers, 14-7 (P)
1950—Lions, 10-7 (D)
1952—Lions, 31-6 (P)
1953—Lions, 38-21 (D)
1955—Lions, 31-28 (P)
1956—Lions, 45-7 (D)
1959—Tie, 10-10 (P)
1962—Lions, 45-7 (D)
1966—Steelers, 17-3 (P)
1967—Steelers, 24-14 (D)
1969—Steelers, 16-13 (P)
1973—Steelers, 24-10 (P)
1983—Lions, 45-3 (D)
1986—Steelers, 27-17 (P)
1989—Steelers, 23-3 (D)
1992—Steelers, 17-14 (P)
1995—Steelers, 23-20 (P)
1998—Lions, 19-16 (D) OT
2001—Steelers, 47-14 (P)
2005—Steelers, 35-21 (P)
(RS Pts.—Lions 559, Steelers 475)
*Steelers known as Pirates prior to 1941
DETROIT vs. *ST. LOUIS
RS: Rams lead series, 40-37-1
PS: Lions lead series, 1-0
1937—Lions, 28-0 (C)
Lions, 27-7 (D)
1938—Rams, 21-17 (C)
Lions, 6-0 (D)
1939—Lions, 15-7 (D)
Rams, 14-3 (C)
1940—Lions, 6-0 (D)
Rams, 24-0 (C)
1941—Lions, 17-7 (D)

Lions, 14-0 (C)
1942—Rams, 14-0 (D)
Rams, 27-7 (C)
1944—Rams, 20-17 (D)
Lions, 26-14 (C)
1945—Rams, 28-21 (D)
1946—Rams, 35-14 (LA)
Rams, 41-20 (D)
1947—Rams, 27-13 (D)
Rams, 28-17 (LA)
1948—Rams, 44-7 (LA)
Rams, 34-27 (D)
1949—Rams, 27-24 (LA)
Rams, 21-10 (D)
1950—Rams, 30-28 (D)
Rams, 65-24 (LA)
1951—Rams, 27-21 (D)
Lions, 24-22 (LA)
1952—Lions, 17-14 (LA)
Lions, 24-16 (D)
**Lions, 31-21 (D)
1953—Rams, 31-19 (D)
Rams, 37-24 (LA)
1954—Lions, 21-3 (D)
Lions, 27-24 (LA)
1955—Rams, 17-10 (D)
Rams, 24-13 (LA)
1956—Rams, 24-21 (D)
Lions, 16-7 (LA)
1957—Lions, 10-7 (D)
Rams, 35-17 (LA)
1958—Rams, 42-28 (D)
Lions, 41-24 (LA)
1959—Lions, 17-7 (LA)
Lions, 23-17 (D)
1960—Rams, 48-35 (LA)
Lions, 12-10 (D)
1961—Lions, 14-13 (D)
Lions, 28-10 (LA)
1962—Lions, 13-10 (D)
Lions, 12-3 (LA)
1963—Lions, 23-2 (LA)
Rams, 28-21 (D)
1964—Tie, 17-17 (LA)
Lions, 37-17 (D)
1965—Lions, 20-0 (D)
Lions, 31-7 (LA)
1966—Rams, 14-7 (D)
Rams, 23-3 (LA)
1967—Rams, 31-7 (D)
1968—Rams, 10-7 (LA)
1969—Lions, 28-0 (D)
1970—Lions, 28-23 (LA)
1971—Rams, 21-13 (D)
1972—Lions, 34-17 (LA)
1974—Rams, 16-13 (LA)
1975—Rams, 20-0 (D)
1976—Rams, 20-17 (D)
1980—Lions, 41-20 (LA)
1981—Rams, 20-13 (LA)
1982—Lions, 19-14 (LA)
1983—Rams, 21-10 (LA)
1986—Rams, 14-10 (LA)
1987—Rams, 37-16 (D)
1988—Rams, 17-10 (LA)
1991—Rams, 21-10 (D)
1993—Lions, 16-13 (LA)
1999—Lions, 31-27 (D)
2001—Rams, 35-0 (D)
2003—Lions, 30-20 (D)

(RS Pts.—Rams 1,518, Lions 1,401)
(PS Pts.—Lions 31, Rams 21)
*Franchise in Los Angeles prior to 1995
and in Cleveland prior to 1946
**Conference Playoff

DETROIT vs. SAN DIEGO
RS: Chargers lead series, 5-3
1972—Lions, 34-20 (D)
1977—Lions, 20-0 (D)
1978—Lions, 31-14 (D)
1981—Chargers, 28-23 (SD)
1984—Chargers, 27-24 (SD)
1996—Chargers, 27-21 (SD)
1999—Chargers, 20-10 (D)
2003—Chargers, 14-7 (D)
(RS Pts.—Lions 170, Chargers 150)

DETROIT vs. SAN FRANCISCO
RS: 49ers lead series, 31-26-1
PS: Series tied, 1-1
1950—Lions, 24-7 (D)
　　　49ers, 28-27 (SF)
1951—49ers, 20-10 (D)
　　　49ers, 21-17 (SF)
1952—49ers, 17-3 (SF)
　　　49ers, 28-0 (D)
1953—Lions, 24-21 (D)
　　　Lions, 14-10 (SF)
1954—49ers, 37-31 (SF)
　　　Lions, 48-7 (D)
1955—49ers, 27-24 (D)
　　　49ers, 38-21 (SF)
1956—Lions, 20-17 (D)
　　　Lions, 17-13 (SF)
1957—49ers, 35-31 (SF)
　　　Lions, 31-10 (D)
　　　*Lions, 31-27 (SF)
1958—49ers, 24-21 (SF)
　　　Lions, 35-21 (D)
1959—49ers, 34-13 (D)
　　　49ers, 33-7 (SF)
1960—49ers, 14-10 (D)
　　　Lions, 24-0 (SF)
1961—49ers, 49-0 (D)
　　　Tie, 20-20 (SF)
1962—Lions, 45-24 (D)
　　　Lions, 38-24 (SF)
1963—Lions, 26-3 (D)
　　　Lions, 45-7 (SF)
1964—Lions, 26-17 (SF)
　　　Lions, 24-7 (D)
1965—49ers, 27-21 (D)
　　　49ers, 17-14 (SF)
1966—49ers, 27-24 (SF)
　　　49ers, 41-14 (D)
1967—Lions, 45-3 (SF)
1968—49ers, 14-7 (D)
1969—Lions, 26-14 (SF)
1970—Lions, 28-7 (D)
1971—49ers, 31-27 (SF)
1973—Lions, 30-20 (D)
1974—Lions, 17-13 (D)
1975—Lions, 28-17 (SF)
1977—49ers, 28-7 (SF)
1978—Lions, 33-14 (D)
1980—Lions, 17-13 (D)
1981—Lions, 24-17 (D)
1983—**49ers, 24-23 (SF)
1984—49ers, 30-27 (D)
1985—Lions, 23-21 (D)
1988—49ers, 20-13 (SF)

1991—49ers, 35-3 (SF)
1992—49ers, 24-6 (SF)
1993—49ers, 55-17 (D)
1994—49ers, 27-21 (D)
1995—Lions, 27-24 (D)
1996—49ers, 24-14 (SF)
1998—49ers, 35-13 (SF)
2001—49ers, 21-13 (SF)
2003—49ers, 24-17 (SF)
(RS Pts.—49ers 1,256, Lions 1,232)
(PS Pts.—Lions 54, 49ers 51)
*Conference Playoff
**NFC Divisional Playoff

DETROIT vs. SEATTLE
RS: Seahawks lead series, 5-4
1976—Lions, 41-14 (S)
1978—Seahawks, 28-16 (S)
1984—Seahawks, 38-17 (S)
1987—Seahawks, 37-14 (D)
1990—Seahawks, 30-10 (S)
1993—Lions, 30-10 (D)
1996—Lions, 17-16 (D)
1999—Lions, 28-20 (S)
2003—Seahawks, 35-14 (S)
(RS Pts.—Seahawks 228, Lions 187)

DETROIT vs. TAMPA BAY
RS: Lions lead series, 26-24
PS: Buccaneers lead series, 1-0
1977—Lions, 16-7 (D)
1978—Lions, 15-7 (TB)
　　　Lions, 34-23 (D)
1979—Buccaneers, 31-16 (TB)
　　　Buccaneers, 16-14 (D)
1980—Lions, 24-10 (TB)
　　　Lions, 27-14 (D)
1981—Buccaneers, 28-10 (TB)
　　　Buccaneers, 20-17 (D)
1982—Buccaneers, 23-21 (TB)
1983—Lions, 11-0 (TB)
　　　Lions, 23-20 (D)
1984—Buccaneers, 21-17 (TB)
　　　Lions, 13-7 (D) OT
1985—Lions, 30-9 (D)
　　　Buccaneers, 19-16 (TB) OT
1986—Buccaneers, 24-20 (D)
　　　Lions, 38-17 (TB)
1987—Buccaneers, 31-27 (D)
　　　Lions, 20-10 (TB)
1988—Buccaneers, 23-20 (D)
　　　Buccaneers, 21-10 (TB)
1989—Lions, 17-16 (TB)
　　　Lions, 33-7 (D)
1990—Buccaneers, 38-21 (D)
　　　Buccaneers, 23-20 (TB)
1991—Lions, 31-3 (D)
　　　Buccaneers, 30-21 (TB)
1992—Buccaneers, 27-23 (D)
　　　Lions, 38-7 (TB)
1993—Buccaneers, 27-10 (TB)
　　　Lions, 23-0 (D)
1994—Buccaneers, 24-14 (TB)
　　　Lions, 14-9 (D)
1995—Lions, 27-24 (D)
　　　Lions, 37-10 (TB)
1996—Lions, 21-6 (D)
　　　Lions, 27-0 (TB)
1997—Buccaneers, 24-17 (D)
　　　Lions, 27-9 (TB)
　　　*Buccaneers, 20-10 (TB)
1998—Lions, 27-6 (D)

　　　Lions, 28-25 (TB)
1999—Lions, 20-3 (D)
　　　Buccaneers, 23-16 (TB)
2000—Buccaneers, 31-10 (D)
　　　Lions, 28-14 (TB)
2001—Buccaneers, 20-17 (D)
　　　Buccaneers, 15-12 (TB)
2002—Buccaneers, 23-20 (D)
2005—Buccaneers, 17-13 (TB)
(RS Pts—Lions 1,051, Buccaneers 842)
(PS Pts.—Buccaneers 20, Lions 10)
*NFC First-Round Playoff

DETROIT vs. *TENNESSEE
RS: Titans lead series, 6-3
1971—Lions, 31-7 (H)
1975—Oilers, 24-8 (H)
1983—Oilers, 27-17 (H)
1986—Lions, 24-13 (D)
1989—Oilers, 35-31 (H)
1992—Oilers, 24-21 (D)
1995—Lions, 24-17 (H)
2001—Titans, 27-24 (D)
2004—Titans, 24-19 (T)
(RS Pts.—Lions 199, Titans 198)
*Franchise in Houston prior to 1997;
known as Oilers prior to 1999

*DETROIT vs. **WASHINGTON
RS: Redskins lead series, 25-10
PS: Redskins lead series, 3-0
1932—Spartans, 10-0 (P)
1933—Spartans, 13-0 (B)
1934—Lions, 24-0 (D)
1935—Lions, 17-7 (B)
　　　Lions, 14-0 (D)
1938—Redskins, 7-5 (D)
1939—Redskins, 31-7 (W)
1940—Redskins, 20-14 (D)
1942—Redskins, 15-3 (D)
1943—Redskins, 42-20 (W)
1946—Redskins, 17-16 (W)
1947—Lions, 38-21 (D)
1948—Redskins, 46-21 (W)
1951—Lions, 35-17 (D)
1956—Redskins, 18-17 (W)
1965—Lions, 14-10 (D)
1968—Redskins, 14-3 (W)
1970—Redskins, 31-10 (W)
1973—Redskins, 20-0 (D)
1976—Redskins, 20-7 (W)
1978—Redskins, 21-19 (D)
1979—Redskins, 27-24 (D)
1981—Redskins, 33-31 (W)
1982—***Redskins, 31-7 (W)
1983—Redskins, 38-17 (W)
1984—Redskins, 28-14 (W)
1985—Redskins, 24-3 (W)
1987—Redskins, 20-13 (W)
1990—Redskins, 41-38 (D) OT
1991—Redskins, 45-0 (W)
　　　****Redskins, 41-10 (W)
1992—Redskins, 13-10 (W)
1995—Redskins, 36-30 (W) OT
1997—Redskins, 30-7 (W)
1999—Lions, 33-17 (D)
　　　***Redskins, 27-13 (W)
2000—Lions, 15-10 (D)
2004—Redskins, 17-10 (D)
(RS Pts.—Redskins 736, Lions 552)
(PS Pts.—Redskins 99, Lions 30)

Franchise in Portsmouth prior to 1934 and known as the Spartans.
**Franchise in Boston prior to 1937*
***NFC First-Round Playoff*
****NFC Championship*

GREEN BAY vs. ARIZONA
RS: Packers lead series, 41-22-4
PS: Packers lead series, 1-0;
See Arizona vs. Green Bay

GREEN BAY vs. ATLANTA
RS: Packers lead series, 12-10
PS: Series tied, 1-1;
See Atlanta vs. Green Bay

GREEN BAY vs. BALTIMORE
RS: Packers lead series, 2-1;
See Baltimore vs. Green Bay

GREEN BAY vs. BUFFALO
RS: Bills lead series, 6-3;
See Buffalo vs. Green Bay

GREEN BAY vs. CAROLINA
RS: Packers lead series, 5-3
PS: Packers lead series, 1-0;
See Carolina vs. Green Bay

GREEN BAY vs. CHICAGO
RS: Bears lead series, 86-78-6
PS: Bears lead series, 1-0;
See Chicago vs. Green Bay

GREEN BAY vs. CINCINNATI
RS: Series tied, 5-5;
See Cincinnati vs. Green Bay

GREEN BAY vs. CLEVELAND
RS: Packers lead series, 9-7
PS: Packers lead series, 1-0;
See Cleveland vs. Green Bay

GREEN BAY vs. DALLAS
RS: Series tied, 10-10
PS: Cowboys lead series, 4-2;
See Dallas vs. Green Bay

GREEN BAY vs. DENVER
RS: Broncos lead series, 5-4-1
PS: Broncos lead series, 1-0;
See Denver vs. Green Bay

GREEN BAY vs. DETROIT
RS: Packers lead series, 80-64-7
PS: Packers lead series, 2-0;
See Detroit vs. Green Bay

GREEN BAY vs. HOUSTON
RS: Franchise lead series, 1-0
2004—Packers, 16-13 (H)
(RS Pts.—Packers 16, Texans 13)

GREEN BAY vs. *INDIANAPOLIS
RS: Colts lead series, 20-19-1
PS: Packers lead series, 1-0
1953—Packers, 37-14 (GB)
         Packers, 35-24 (B)
1954—Packers, 7-6 (B)
         Packers, 24-13 (Mil)
1955—Colts, 24-20 (Mil)
         Colts, 14-10 (B)
1956—Packers, 38-33 (Mil)
         Colts, 28-21 (B)
1957—Colts, 45-17 (Mil)
         Packers, 24-21 (B)
1958—Colts, 24-17 (Mil)
         Colts, 56-0 (B)
1959—Colts, 38-21 (B)
         Colts, 28-24 (Mil)
1960—Packers, 35-21 (GB)
         Colts, 38-24 (B)

1961—Packers, 45-7 (GB)
         Colts, 45-21 (B)
1962—Packers, 17-6 (B)
         Packers, 17-13 (GB)
1963—Packers, 31-20 (GB)
         Packers, 34-20 (B)
1964—Colts, 21-20 (GB)
         Colts, 24-21 (B)
1965—Packers, 20-17 (Mil)
         Packers, 42-27 (B)
         **Packers, 13-10 (GB) OT
1966—Packers, 24-3 (Mil)
         Packers, 14-10 (B)
1967—Colts, 13-10 (B)
1968—Colts, 16-3 (GB)
1969—Colts, 14-6 (B)
1970—Colts, 13-10 (Mil)
1974—Packers, 20-13 (B)
1982—Tie, 20-20 (B) OT
1985—Colts, 37-10 (I)
1988—Colts, 20-13 (GB)
1991—Packers, 14-10 (Mil)
1997—Colts, 41-38 (I)
2000—Packers, 26-24 (GB)
2004—Colts, 45-31 (I)
(RS Pts.—Colts 906, Packers 861)
(PS Pts.—Packers 13, Colts 10)
Franchise in Baltimore prior to 1984
**Conference Playoff*

GREEN BAY vs. JACKSONVILLE
RS: Packers lead series, 2-1
1995—Packers, 24-14 (J)
2001—Packers, 28-21 (J)
2004—Jaguars, 28-25 (GB)
(RS Pts.—Packers 77, Jaguars 63)

GREEN BAY vs. KANSAS CITY
RS: Chiefs lead series, 6-1-1
PS: Packers lead series, 1-0
1966—*Packers, 35-10 (Los Angeles)
1973—Tie, 10-10 (Mil)
1977—Chiefs, 20-10 (KC)
1987—Packers, 23-3 (KC)
1989—Chiefs, 21-3 (GB)
1990—Chiefs, 17-3 (GB)
1993—Chiefs, 23-16 (KC)
1996—Chiefs, 27-20 (KC)
2003—Chiefs, 40-34 (GB) OT
(RS Pts.—Chiefs 161, Packers 119)
(PS Pts.—Packers 35, Chiefs 10)
Super Bowl I

GREEN BAY vs. MIAMI
RS: Dolphins lead series, 9-2
1971—Dolphins, 27-6 (Mia)
1975—Dolphins, 31-7 (GB)
1979—Dolphins, 27-7 (Mia)
1985—Dolphins, 34-24 (GB)
1988—Dolphins, 24-17 (Mia)
1989—Dolphins, 23-20 (Mia)
1991—Dolphins, 16-13 (Mia)
1994—Dolphins, 24-14 (Mil)
1997—Packers, 23-18 (GB)
2000—Dolphins, 28-20 (Mia)
2002—Packers, 24-10 (GB)
(RS Pts.—Dolphins 262, Packers 175)

GREEN BAY vs. MINNESOTA
RS: Series tied, 44-44-1
PS: Vikings lead series, 1-0
1961—Packers, 33-7 (Minn)
         Packers, 28-10 (Mil)
1962—Packers, 34-7 (GB)

         Packers, 48-21 (Minn)
1963—Packers, 37-28 (Minn)
         Packers, 28-7 (GB)
1964—Vikings, 24-23 (GB)
         Packers, 42-13 (Minn)
1965—Packers, 38-13 (Minn)
         Packers, 24-19 (GB)
1966—Vikings, 20-17 (GB)
         Packers, 28-16 (Minn)
1967—Vikings, 10-7 (Mil)
         Packers, 30-27 (Minn)
1968—Vikings, 26-13 (Mil)
         Vikings, 14-10 (Minn)
1969—Vikings, 19-7 (Mil)
         Vikings, 9-7 (Minn)
1970—Packers, 13-10 (Mil)
         Vikings, 10-3 (Minn)
1971—Vikings, 24-13 (GB)
         Vikings, 3-0 (Minn)
1972—Vikings, 27-13 (GB)
         Packers, 23-7 (Minn)
1973—Vikings, 11-3 (Minn)
         Vikings, 31-7 (GB)
1974—Vikings, 32-17 (GB)
         Packers, 19-7 (Minn)
1975—Vikings, 28-17 (GB)
         Vikings, 24-3 (Minn)
1976—Vikings, 17-10 (Mil)
         Vikings, 20-9 (Minn)
1977—Vikings, 19-7 (Minn)
         Vikings, 13-6 (GB)
1978—Vikings, 21-7 (Minn)
         Tie, 10-10 (GB) OT
1979—Vikings, 27-21 (Minn) OT
         Packers, 19-7 (Mil)
1980—Packers, 16-3 (GB)
         Packers, 25-13 (Minn)
1981—Vikings, 30-13 (Mil)
         Packers, 35-23 (Minn)
1982—Packers, 26-7 (Mil)
1983—Vikings, 20-17 (GB) OT
         Packers, 29-21 (Minn)
1984—Packers, 45-17 (Mil)
         Packers, 38-14 (Minn)
1985—Packers, 20-17 (Mil)
         Packers, 27-17 (Minn)
1986—Vikings, 42-7 (Minn)
         Vikings, 32-6 (GB)
1987—Packers, 23-16 (Minn)
         Packers, 16-10 (Mil)
1988—Packers, 34-14 (Minn)
         Packers, 18-6 (GB)
1989—Vikings, 26-14 (Minn)
         Packers, 20-19 (Mil)
1990—Packers, 24-10 (Mil)
         Vikings, 23-7 (Minn)
1991—Vikings, 35-21 (GB)
         Packers, 27-7 (Minn)
1992—Vikings, 23-20 (GB) OT
         Vikings, 27-7 (Minn)
1993—Vikings, 15-13 (Minn)
         Vikings, 21-17 (Mil)
1994—Vikings, 16-10 (Minn)
         Vikings, 13-10 (Minn) OT
1995—Packers, 38-21 (GB)
         Vikings, 27-24 (Minn)
1996—Vikings, 30-21 (Minn)
         Packers, 38-10 (GB)
1997—Packers, 38-32 (GB)
         Packers, 27-11 (Minn)

1998—Vikings, 37-24 (GB)
    Vikings, 28-14 (Minn)
1999—Packers, 23-20 (GB)
    Vikings, 24-20 (Minn)
2000—Packers, 26-20 (GB) OT
    Packers, 33-28 (Minn)
2001—Vikings, 35-13 (Minn)
    Packers, 24-13 (GB)
2002—Vikings, 31-21 (Minn)
    Packers, 26-22 (GB)
2003—Vikings, 30-25 (M)
    Packers, 30-27 (M)
2004—Packers, 34-31 (GB)
    Packers, 34-31 (M)
    *Vikings, 31-17 (GB)
2005—Packers, 23-20 (M)
    Vikings, 20-17 (GB)
(RS Pts.—Packers 1,835, Vikings 1,720)
(PS Pts.—Vikings 31, Packers 17)
*NFC First-Round Playoff
GREEN BAY vs. NEW ENGLAND
RS: Packers lead series, 4-3
PS: Packers lead series, 1-0
1973—Patriots, 33-24 (NE)
1979—Packers, 27-14 (GB)
1985—Patriots, 26-20 (NE)
1988—Packers, 45-3 (Mil)
1994—Patriots, 17-16 (NE)
1996—*Packers, 35-21 (New Orleans)
1997—Packers, 28-10 (NE)
2002—Packers, 28-10 (NE)
(RS Pts.—Packers 188, Patriots 113)
(PS Pts.—Packers 35, Patriots 21)
*Super Bowl XXXI
GREEN BAY vs. NEW ORLEANS
RS: Packers lead series, 14-5
1968—Packers, 29-7 (Mil)
1971—Saints, 29-21 (Mil)
1972—Packers, 30-20 (NO)
1973—Packers, 30-10 (Mil)
1975—Saints, 20-19 (NO)
1976—Packers, 32-27 (Mil)
1977—Packers, 24-20 (NO)
1978—Packers, 28-17 (Mil)
1979—Packers, 28-19 (Mil)
1981—Packers, 35-7 (NO)
1984—Packers, 23-13 (GB)
1985—Packers, 38-14 (Mil)
1986—Saints, 24-10 (NO)
1987—Saints, 33-24 (NO)
1989—Packers, 35-34 (GB)
1993—Packers, 19-17 (NO)
1995—Packers, 34-23 (NO)
2002—Saints, 35-20 (NO)
2005—Packers, 52-3 (GB)
(RS Pts.—Packers 531, Saints 372)
GREEN BAY vs. N.Y. GIANTS
RS: Packers lead series, 24-21-2
PS: Packers lead series, 4-1
1928—Giants, 6-0 (GB)
    Packers, 7-0 (NY)
1929—Packers, 20-6 (NY)
1930—Packers, 14-7 (GB)
    Giants, 13-6 (NY)
1931—Packers, 27-7 (GB)
    Packers, 14-10 (NY)
1932—Packers, 13-0 (GB)
    Giants, 6-0 (NY)
1933—Giants, 10-7 (Mil)
    Giants, 17-6 (NY)

1934—Packers, 20-6 (Mil)
    Giants, 17-3 (NY)
1935—Packers, 16-7 (GB)
1936—Packers, 26-14 (NY)
1937—Giants, 10-0 (NY)
1938—Giants, 15-3 (NY)
    *Giants, 23-17 (NY)
1939—*Packers, 27-0 (Mil)
1940—Giants, 7-3 (NY)
1942—Tie, 21-21 (NY)
1943—Packers, 35-21 (NY)
1944—Giants, 24-0 (NY)
    *Packers, 14-7 (NY)
1945—Packers, 23-14 (NY)
1947—Tie, 24-24 (NY)
1948—Giants, 49-3 (Mil)
1949—Giants, 30-10 (GB)
1952—Packers, 17-3 (NY)
1957—Giants, 31-17 (GB)
1959—Giants, 20-3 (NY)
1961—Packers, 20-17 (Mil)
    *Packers, 37-0 (GB)
1962—*Packers, 16-7 (NY)
1967—Packers, 48-21 (NY)
1969—Packers, 20-10 (Mil)
1971—Giants, 42-40 (GB)
1973—Packers, 16-14 (New Haven)
1975—Packers, 40-14 (Mil)
1980—Giants, 27-21 (NY)
1981—Packers, 27-14 (NY)
    Packers, 26-24 (Mil)
1982—Packers, 27-19 (NY)
1983—Giants, 27-3 (NY)
1985—Packers, 23-20 (GB)
1986—Giants, 55-24 (NY)
1987—Giants, 20-10 (NY)
1992—Giants, 27-7 (NY)
1995—Packers, 14-6 (GB)
1998—Packers, 37-3 (NY)
2001—Packers, 34-25 (NY)
2004—Giants, 14-7 (GB)
(RS Pts.—Giants 794, Packers 782)
(PS Pts.—Packers 111, Giants 37)
*NFL Championship
GREEN BAY vs. N.Y. JETS
RS: Jets lead series, 7-2
1973—Packers, 23-7 (Mil)
1979—Jets, 27-22 (GB)
1981—Jets, 28-3 (NY)
1982—Jets, 15-13 (NY)
1985—Jets, 24-3 (Mil)
1991—Jets, 19-16 (NY) OT
1994—Packers, 17-10 (GB)
2000—Jets, 20-16 (GB)
2002—Jets, 42-17 (NY)
(RS Pts.—Jets 192, Packers 130)
GREEN BAY vs. *OAKLAND
RS: Raiders lead series, 5-4
PS: Packers lead series, 1-0
1967—**Packers, 33-14 (Miami)
1972—Raiders, 20-14 (GB)
1976—Raiders, 18-14 (O)
1978—Raiders, 28-3 (GB)
1984—Raiders, 28-7 (LA)
1987—Raiders, 20-0 (GB)
1990—Packers, 29-16 (LA)
1993—Packers, 28-0 (GB)
1999—Packers, 28-24 (GB)
2003—Packers, 41-7 (O)
(RS Pts.—Packers 164, Raiders 161)

(PS Pts.—Packers 33, Raiders 14)
*Franchise in Los Angeles from 1982-1994
**Super Bowl II
GREEN BAY vs. PHILADELPHIA
RS: Packers lead series, 22-12
PS: Eagles lead series, 2-0
1933—Packers, 35-9 (GB)
    Packers, 10-0 (P)
1934—Packers, 19-6 (GB)
1935—Packers, 13-6 (P)
1937—Packers, 37-7 (Mil)
1939—Packers, 23-16 (P)
1940—Packers, 27-20 (GB)
1942—Packers, 7-0 (P)
1946—Packers, 19-7 (P)
1947—Eagles, 28-14 (P)
1951—Packers, 37-24 (GB)
1952—Packers, 12-10 (Mil)
1954—Packers, 37-14 (P)
1958—Packers, 38-35 (GB)
1960—*Eagles, 17-13 (P)
1962—Packers, 49-0 (P)
1968—Packers, 30-13 (GB)
1970—Packers, 30-17 (Mil)
1974—Eagles, 36-14 (P)
1976—Packers, 28-13 (GB)
1978—Eagles, 10-3 (P)
1979—Eagles, 21-10 (GB)
1987—Packers, 16-10 (GB) OT
1990—Eagles, 31-0 (P)
1991—Eagles, 20-3 (GB)
1992—Packers, 27-24 (Mil)
1993—Eagles, 20-17 (GB)
1994—Eagles, 13-7 (P)
1996—Packers, 39-13 (GB)
1997—Eagles, 10-9 (P)
1998—Packers, 24-16 (GB)
2000—Packers, 6-3 (GB)
2003—Eagles, 17-14 (GB)
    **Eagles, 20-17 (P) OT
2004—Eagles, 47-17 (P)
2005—Eagles, 19-14 (P)
(RS Pts.—Packers 685, Eagles 535)
(PS Pts.—Eagles 37, Packers 30)
*NFL Championship
**NFC Divisional Playoff
GREEN BAY vs. *PITTSBURGH
RS: Packers lead series, 18-13
1933—Packers, 47-0 (GB)
1935—Packers, 27-0 (GB)
    Packers, 34-14 (P)
1936—Packers, 42-10 (Mil)
1938—Packers, 20-0 (GB)
1940—Packers, 24-3 (Mil)
1941—Packers, 54-7 (P)
1942—Packers, 24-21 (Mil)
1946—Packers, 17-7 (GB)
1947—Steelers, 18-17 (Mil)
1948—Steelers, 38-7 (P)
1949—Steelers, 30-7 (Mil)
1951—Packers, 35-33 (Mil)
    Steelers, 28-7 (P)
1953—Steelers, 31-14 (P)
1954—Steelers, 21-20 (GB)
1957—Packers, 27-10 (P)
1960—Packers, 19-13 (P)
1963—Packers, 33-14 (Mil)
1965—Packers, 41-9 (P)
1967—Steelers, 24-17 (GB)
1969—Packers, 38-34 (P)

1970—Packers, 20-12 (P)
1975—Steelers, 16-13 (Mil)
1980—Steelers, 22-20 (P)
1983—Steelers, 25-21 (GB)
1986—Steelers, 27-3 (P)
1992—Packers, 17-3 (GB)
1995—Packers, 24-19 (GB)
1998—Steelers, 27-20 (P)
2005—Steelers, 20-10 (GB)
(RS Pts.—Packers 719, Steelers 536)
Steelers known as Pirates prior to 1941
GREEN BAY vs. *ST. LOUIS
RS: Rams lead series, 44-40-2
PS: Series tied, 1-1
1937—Packers, 35-10 (C)
       Packers, 35-7 (GB)
1938—Packers, 26-17 (GB)
       Packers, 28-7 (C)
1939—Rams, 27-24 (GB)
       Packers, 7-6 (C)
1940—Packers, 31-14 (GB)
       Tie, 13-13 (C)
1941—Packers, 24-7 (Mil)
       Packers, 17-14 (C)
1942—Packers, 45-28 (GB)
       Packers, 30-12 (C)
1944—Packers, 30-21 (GB)
       Packers, 42-7 (C)
1945—Rams, 27-14 (GB)
       Rams, 20-7 (C)
1946—Rams, 21-17 (Mil)
       Rams, 38-17 (LA)
1947—Packers, 17-14 (Mil)
       Packers, 30-10 (LA)
1948—Packers, 16-0 (GB)
       Rams, 24-10 (LA)
1949—Packers, 48-7 (GB)
       Rams, 35-7 (LA)
1950—Rams, 45-14 (Mil)
       Rams, 51-14 (LA)
1951—Rams, 28-0 (Mil)
       Rams, 42-14 (LA)
1952—Rams, 30-28 (Mil)
       Rams, 45-27 (LA)
1953—Rams, 38-20 (Mil)
       Rams, 33-17 (LA)
1954—Packers, 35-17 (Mil)
       Rams, 35-27 (LA)
1955—Packers, 30-28 (Mil)
       Rams, 31-17 (LA)
1956—Packers, 42-17 (Mil)
       Rams, 49-21 (LA)
1957—Rams, 31-27 (Mil)
       Rams, 42-17 (LA)
1958—Rams, 20-7 (GB)
       Rams, 34-20 (LA)
1959—Rams, 45-6 (Mil)
       Packers, 38-20 (LA)
1960—Rams, 33-31 (Mil)
       Packers, 35-21 (LA)
1961—Packers, 35-17 (GB)
       Packers, 24-17 (LA)
1962—Packers, 41-10 (Mil)
       Packers, 20-17 (LA)
1963—Packers, 42-10 (GB)
       Packers, 31-14 (LA)
1964—Rams, 27-17 (Mil)
       Tie, 24-24 (LA)
1965—Packers, 6-3 (Mil)
       Rams, 21-10 (LA)

1966—Packers, 24-13 (GB)
       Packers, 27-23 (LA)
1967—Rams, 27-24 (LA)
       **Packers, 28-7 (Mil)
1968—Rams, 16-14 (Mil)
1969—Rams, 34-21 (LA)
1970—Rams, 31-21 (GB)
1971—Rams, 30-13 (LA)
1973—Rams, 24-7 (LA)
1974—Packers, 17-6 (Mil)
1975—Rams, 22-5 (LA)
1977—Rams, 24-6 (Mil)
1978—Rams, 31-14 (LA)
1980—Rams, 51-21 (LA)
1981—Rams, 35-23 (LA)
1982—Rams, 35-23 (Mil)
1983—Rams, 27-24 (Mil)
1984—Packers, 31-6 (Mil)
1985—Rams, 34-17 (LA)
1988—Rams, 34-7 (GB)
1989—Rams, 41-38 (LA)
1990—Packers, 36-24 (GB)
1991—Rams, 23-21 (LA)
1992—Packers, 28-13 (GB)
1993—Packers, 36-6 (Mil)
1994—Packers, 24-17 (GB)
1995—Rams, 17-14 (GB)
1996—Packers, 24-9 (StL)
1997—Packers, 17-7 (GB)
2001—***Rams, 45-17 (StL)
2003—Rams, 34-24 (StL)
2004—Packers, 45-17 (GB)
(RS Pts.—Rams 2,018, Packers 1,927)
(PS Pts.—Rams 52, Packers 45)
*Franchise in Los Angeles prior to 1995
and in Cleveland prior to 1946*
**Conference Championship*
***NFC Divisional Playoff*
GREEN BAY vs. SAN DIEGO
RS: Packers lead series, 7-1
1970—Packers, 22-20 (SD)
1974—Packers, 34-0 (GB)
1978—Packers, 24-3 (SD)
1984—Chargers, 34-28 (GB)
1993—Packers, 20-13 (SD)
1996—Packers, 42-10 (GB)
1999—Packers, 31-3 (SD)
2003—Packers, 38-21 (SD)
(RS Pts.—Packers 239, Chargers 104)
GREEN BAY vs. SAN FRANCISCO
RS: Packers lead series, 27-25-1
PS: Packers lead series, 4-1
1950—Packers, 25-21 (GB)
       49ers, 30-14 (SF)
1951—49ers, 31-19 (GB)
1952—49ers, 24-14 (SF)
1953—49ers, 37-7 (Mil)
       49ers, 48-14 (SF)
1954—49ers, 23-17 (Mil)
       49ers, 35-0 (SF)
1955—Packers, 27-21 (Mil)
       Packers, 28-7 (SF)
1956—49ers, 17-16 (Mil)
       49ers, 38-20 (SF)
1957—49ers, 24-14 (Mil)
       49ers, 27-20 (SF)
1958—49ers, 33-12 (Mil)
       49ers, 48-21 (SF)
1959—Packers, 21-20 (GB)
       Packers, 36-14 (SF)

1960—Packers, 41-14 (Mil)
       Packers, 13-0 (SF)
1961—Packers, 30-10 (GB)
       49ers, 22-21 (SF)
1962—Packers, 31-13 (Mil)
       Packers, 31-21 (SF)
1963—Packers, 28-10 (Mil)
       Packers, 21-17 (SF)
1964—Packers, 24-14 (Mil)
       49ers, 24-14 (SF)
1965—Packers, 27-10 (GB)
       Tie, 24-24 (SF)
1966—49ers, 21-20 (SF)
       Packers, 20-7 (Mil)
1967—Packers, 13-0 (GB)
1968—49ers, 27-20 (SF)
1969—Packers, 14-7 (Mil)
1970—49ers, 26-10 (SF)
1972—Packers, 34-24 (Mil)
1973—49ers, 20-6 (SF)
1974—49ers, 7-6 (SF)
1976—49ers, 26-14 (GB)
1977—Packers, 16-14 (Mil)
1980—Packers, 23-16 (Mil)
1981—49ers, 13-3 (Mil)
1986—49ers, 31-17 (Mil)
1987—49ers, 23-12 (GB)
1989—Packers, 21-17 (SF)
1990—49ers, 24-20 (GB)
1995—*Packers, 27-17 (SF)
1996—Packers, 23-20 (GB) OT
       *Packers, 35-14 (GB)
1997—**Packers, 23-10 (SF)
1998—Packers, 36-22 (GB)
       ***49ers, 30-27 (SF)
1999—Packers, 20-3 (SF)
2000—Packers, 31-28 (GB)
2001—***Packers, 25-15 (GB)
2002—Packers, 20-14 (SF)
2003—Packers, 20-10 (GB)
(RS Pts.—49ers 1,077, Packers 1,049)
(PS Pts.—Packers 137, 49ers 86)
NFC Divisional Playoff
**NFC Championship*
***NFC First-Round Playoff*
GREEN BAY vs. SEATTLE
RS: Packers lead series, 6-4
PS: Packers lead series, 1-0
1976—Packers, 27-20 (Mil)
1978—Packers, 45-28 (Mil)
1981—Packers, 34-24 (GB)
1984—Seahawks, 30-24 (Mil)
1987—Seahawks, 24-13 (S)
1990—Seahawks, 20-14 (Mil)
1996—Packers, 31-10 (S)
1999—Seahawks, 27-7 (GB)
2003—Packers, 35-13 (GB)
       *Packers, 33-27 (GB) OT
2005—Packers, 23-17 (GB)
(RS Pts.—Packers 253, Seahawks 213)
(PS Pts.—Packers 33, Seahawks 27)
NFC First-Round Playoff
GREEN BAY vs. TAMPA BAY
RS: Packers lead series, 29-19-1
PS: Packers lead series, 1-0
1977—Packers, 13-0 (TB)
1978—Packers, 9-7 (GB)
       Packers, 17-7 (TB)
1979—Buccaneers, 21-10 (GB)
       Buccaneers, 21-3 (TB)

1980—Tie, 14-14 (TB) OT
    Buccaneers, 20-17 (Mil)
1981—Buccaneers, 21-10 (GB)
    Buccaneers, 37-3 (TB)
1983—Packers, 55-14 (GB)
    Packers, 12-9 (TB) OT
1984—Buccaneers, 30-27 (TB) OT
    Packers, 27-14 (GB)
1985—Packers, 21-0 (GB)
    Packers, 20-17 (TB)
1986—Packers, 31-7 (Mil)
    Packers, 21-7 (TB)
1987—Buccaneers, 23-17 (Mil)
1988—Buccaneers, 13-10 (GB)
    Buccaneers, 27-24 (TB)
1989—Buccaneers, 23-21 (GB)
    Packers, 17-16 (TB)
1990—Buccaneers, 26-14 (TB)
    Packers, 20-10 (Mil)
1991—Packers, 15-13 (GB)
    Packers, 27-0 (TB)
1992—Buccaneers, 31-3 (TB)
    Packers, 19-14 (Mil)
1993—Packers, 37-14 (TB)
    Packers, 13-10 (GB)
1994—Packers, 30-3 (GB)
    Packers, 34-19 (TB)
1995—Packers, 35-13 (GB)
    Buccaneers, 13-10 (TB) OT
1996—Packers, 34-3 (TB)
    Packers, 13-7 (GB)
1997—Packers, 21-16 (GB)
    Packers, 17-6 (TB)
    *Packers, 21-7 (GB)
1998—Packers, 23-15 (GB)
    Buccaneers, 24-22 (TB)
1999—Packers, 26-23 (GB)
    Buccaneers, 29-10 (TB)
2000—Buccaneers, 20-15 (TB)
    Packers, 17-14 (GB) OT
2001—Buccaneers, 14-10 (TB)
    Packers, 21-20 (GB)
2002—Buccaneers, 21-7 (TB)
2003—Packers, 20-13 (TB)
2005—Buccaneers, 17-16 (GB)
(RS Pts.—Packers 928, Buccaneers 756)
(PS Pts.—Packers 21, Buccaneers 7)
*NFC Divisional Playoff
GREEN BAY vs. *TENNESSEE
RS: Titans lead series, 5-4
1972—Packers, 23-10 (H)
1977—Oilers, 16-10 (GB)
1980—Oilers, 22-3 (GB)
1983—Packers, 41-38 (H) OT
1986—Oilers, 31-3 (GB)
1992—Packers, 16-14 (H)
1998—Packers, 30-22 (GB)
2001—Titans, 26-20 (T)
2004—Titans, 48-27 (GB)
(RS Pts.—Titans 227, Packers 173)
*Franchise in Houston prior to 1997;
known as Oilers prior to 1999
GREEN BAY vs. *WASHINGTON
RS: Packers lead series, 16-12-1
PS: Series tied, 1-1
1932—Packers, 21-0 (B)
1933—Tie, 7-7 (GB)
    Redskins, 20-7 (B)
1934—Packers, 10-0 (B)
1936—Packers, 31-2 (GB)

Packers, 7-3 (B)
    **Packers, 21-6 (New York)
1937—Redskins, 14-6 (W)
1939—Packers, 24-14 (Mil)
1941—Packers, 22-17 (W)
1943—Redskins, 33-7 (Mil)
1946—Packers, 20-7 (W)
1947—Packers, 27-10 (Mil)
1948—Redskins, 23-7 (Mil)
1949—Redskins, 30-0 (W)
1950—Packers, 35-21 (Mil)
1952—Packers, 35-20 (Mil)
1958—Redskins, 37-21 (W)
1959—Packers, 21-0 (GB)
1968—Packers, 27-7 (W)
1972—Packers, 21-16 (W)
    ***Redskins, 16-3 (W)
1974—Redskins, 17-6 (GB)
1977—Redskins, 10-9 (W)
1979—Redskins, 38-21 (W)
1983—Packers, 48-47 (GB)
1986—Redskins, 16-7 (GB)
1988—Redskins, 20-17 (Mil)
2001—Packers, 37-0 (GB)
2002—Packers, 30-9 (GB)
2004—Packers, 28-14 (W)
(RS Pts.—Packers 554, Redskins 457)
(PS Pts.—Packers 24, Redskins 22)
*Franchise in Boston prior to 1937 and
known as Braves prior to 1933
**NFL Championship
***NFC Divisional Playoff

HOUSTON vs. ARIZONA
RS: Texans lead series, 1-0;
See Arizona vs. Houston
HOUSTON vs. ATLANTA
RS: Texans lead series, 1-0;
See Atlanta vs. Houston
HOUSTON vs. BALTIMORE
RS: Ravens lead series, 2-0;
See Baltimore vs. Houston
HOUSTON vs. BUFFALO
RS: Bills lead series, 2-1;
See Buffalo vs. Houston
HOUSTON vs. CAROLINA
RS: Texans lead series, 1-0;
See Carolina vs. Houston
HOUSTON vs. CHICAGO
RS: Texans lead series, 1-0;
See Chicago vs. Houston
HOUSTON vs. CINCINNATI
RS: Bengals lead series, 3-0;
See Cincinnati vs. Houston
HOUSTON vs. CLEVELAND
RS: Browns lead series, 2-1;
See Cleveland vs. Houston
HOUSTON vs. DALLAS
RS: Texans lead series, 1-0;
See Dallas vs. Houston
HOUSTON vs. DENVER
RS: Broncos lead series, 1-0;
See Denver vs. Houston
HOUSTON vs. DETROIT
RS: Lions lead series 1-0;
See Detroit vs. Houston
HOUSTON vs. GREEN BAY
RS: Packers lead series, 1-0;
See Green Bay vs. Houston

HOUSTON vs. INDIANAPOLIS
RS: Colts lead series, 8-0
2002—Colts, 23-3 (H)
    Colts, 19-3 (I)
2003—Colts, 30-21 (I)
    Colts, 20-17 (H)
2004—Colts, 49-14 (I)
    Colts, 23-14 (H)
2005—Colts, 38-20 (H)
    Colts, 31-17 (I)
(RS Pts.—Colts 233, Texans 109)
HOUSTON vs. JACKSONVILLE
RS: Series tied, 4-4
2002—Texans, 21-19 (J)
    Jaguars, 24-21 (H)
2003—Texans, 24-20 (H)
    Jaguars, 27-0 (I)
2004—Texans, 20-6 (H)
    Texans, 21-0 (J)
2005—Jaguars, 21-14 (J)
    Jaguars, 38-20 (H)
(RS Pts.—Jaguars 155, Texans 141)
HOUSTON vs. KANSAS CITY
RS: Chiefs lead series, 2-1
2003—Chiefs, 42-14 (H)
2004—Texans, 24-21 (KC)
2005—Chiefs, 45-17 (H)
(RS Pts.—Chiefs 108, Texans 55)
HOUSTON vs. MIAMI
RS: Texans lead series, 1-0
2003—Texans, 21-20 (M)
(RS Pts.—Texans 21, Dolphins 20)
HOUSTON vs. MINNESOTA
RS: Vikings lead series, 1-0
2004—Vikings, 34-28 (H) OT
(RS Pts.—Vikings 34, Texans 28)
HOUSTON vs. NEW ENGLAND
RS: Patriots lead series, 1-0
2003—Patriots, 23-20 (H) OT
(RS Pts.—Patriots 23, Texans 20)
HOUSTON vs. NEW ORLEANS
RS: Saints lead series, 1-0
2003—Saints, 31-10 (NO)
(RS Pts.—Saints 31, Texans 10)
HOUSTON vs. N.Y. GIANTS
RS: Texans lead series, 1-0
2002—Texans, 16-14 (H)
(RS Pts.—Texans 16, Giants 14)
HOUSTON vs. N.Y. JETS
RS: Jets lead series, 2-0
2003—Jets, 19-14 (H)
2004—Jets, 29-7 (NY)
(RS Pts.—Jets 48, Texans 21)
HOUSTON vs. OAKLAND
RS: Texans lead series, 1-0
2004—Texans, 30-17 (H)
(RS Pts.—Texans 30, Raiders 17)
HOUSTON vs. PHILADELPHIA
RS: Eagles lead series, 1-0
2002—Eagles, 35-17 (P)
(RS Pts.—Eagles 35, Texans 17)
HOUSTON vs. PITTSBURGH
RS: Series tied, 1-1
2002—Texans, 24-6 (P)
2005—Steelers, 27-7 (H)
(RS Pts.—Steelers 33, Texans 31)
HOUSTON vs. ST. LOUIS
RS: Rams lead series, 1-0
2005—Rams, 33-27 (H) OT
(RS Pts.—Rams 33, Texans 27)

HOUSTON vs. SAN DIEGO
RS: Chargers lead series, 2-0
2002—Chargers, 24-3 (SD)
2004—Chargers, 27-20 (H)
(RS Pts.—Chargers 51, Texans 23)
HOUSTON vs. SAN FRANCISCO
RS: 49ers lead series, 1-0
2005—49ers, 20-17 (SF) OT
(RS Pts.—49ers 20, Texans 17)
HOUSTON vs. SEATTLE
RS: Seahawks lead series, 1-0
2005—Seahawks, 42-10
(RS Pts.—Seahawks 42, Texans 10)
HOUSTON vs. TAMPA BAY
RS: Buccaneers lead series, 1-0
2003—Buccaneers, 16-3 (TB)
(RS Pts.—Buccaneers 16, Texans 3)
HOUSTON vs. TENNESSEE
RS: Titans lead series, 6-2
2002—Titans, 17-10 (T)
            Titans, 13-3 (H)
2003—Titans, 38-17 (T)
            Titans, 27-24 (H)
2004—Texans, 20-10 (T)
            Texans, 31-21 (H)
2005—Titans, 34-20 (H)
            Titans, 13-10 (T)
(RS Pts.—Titans 173, Texans 135)
HOUSTON vs. WASHINGTON
RS: Redskins lead series, 1-0
2002—Redskins, 26-10 (W)
(RS Pts.—Redskins 26, Texans 10)

INDIANAPOLIS vs. ARIZONA
RS: Colts lead series, 7-6;
See Arizona vs. Indianapolis
INDIANAPOLIS vs. ATLANTA
RS: Colts lead series, 12-1;
See Atlanta vs. Indianapolis
INDIANAPOLIS vs. BALTIMORE
RS: Colts lead series, 4-2;
See Baltimore vs. Indianapolis
INDIANAPOLIS vs. BUFFALO
RS: Bills lead series, 34-29-1;
See Buffalo vs. Indianapolis
INDIANAPOLIS vs. CAROLINA
RS: Panthers lead series, 3-0;
See Carolina vs. Indianapolis
INDIANAPOLIS vs. CHICAGO
RS: Colts lead series, 22-17;
See Chicago vs. Indianapolis
INDIANAPOLIS vs. CINCINNATI
RS: Colts lead series, 13-8
PS: Colts lead series, 1-0;
See Cincinnati vs. Indianapolis
INDIANAPOLIS vs. CLEVELAND
RS: Browns lead series, 13-11
PS: Series tied, 2-2;
See Cleveland vs. Indianapolis
INDIANAPOLIS vs. DALLAS
RS: Cowboys lead series, 7-5
PS: Colts lead series, 1-0;
See Dallas vs. Indianapolis
INDIANAPOLIS vs. DENVER
RS: Broncos lead series, 11-4
PS: Colts lead series, 2-0;
See Denver vs. Indianapolis
INDIANAPOLIS vs. DETROIT
RS: Colts lead series, 19-18-2;
See Detroit vs. Indianapolis

INDIANAPOLIS vs. GREEN BAY
RS: Colts lead series, 20-19-1
PS: Packers lead series, 1-0;
See Green Bay vs. Indianapolis
INDIANAPOLIS vs. HOUSTON
RS: Colts lead series, 8-0;
See Houston vs. Indianapolis
INDIANAPOLIS vs. JACKSONVILLE
RS: Colts lead series, 8-2
1995—Colts, 41-31 (J)
2000—Colts, 43-14 (I)
2002—Colts, 28-25 (J)
            Colts, 20-13 (I)
2003—Colts, 23-13 (I)
            Jaguars, 28-23 (J)
2004—Colts, 24-17 (J)
            Jaguars, 27-24 (I)
2005—Colts, 10-3 (I)
            Colts, 26-18 (J)
(RS Pts.—Colts 262, Jaguars 189)
*INDIANAPOLIS vs. KANSAS CITY
RS: Colts lead series, 8-7
PS: Colts lead series, 2-0
1970—Chiefs, 44-24 (B)
1972—Chiefs, 24-10 (KC)
1975—Colts, 28-14 (B)
1977—Colts, 17-6 (KC)
1979—Chiefs, 14-0 (KC)
            Chiefs, 10-7 (B)
1980—Colts, 31-24 (KC)
            Chiefs, 38-28 (B)
1985—Chiefs, 20-7 (KC)
1990—Colts, 23-19 (I)
1995—**Colts, 10-7 (KC)
1996—Colts, 24-19 (KC)
1999—Colts, 25-17 (I)
2000—Colts, 27-14 (KC)
2001—Colts, 35-28 (KC)
2003—**Colts, 38-31 (KC)
2004—Chiefs, 45-35 (KC)
(RS Pts.—Chiefs 336, Colts 321)
(PS Pts.—Colts 48, Chiefs 38)
*Franchise in Baltimore prior to 1984
**AFC Divisional Playoff
*INDIANAPOLIS vs. MIAMI
RS: Dolphins lead series, 44-22
PS: Dolphins lead series, 2-0
1970—Colts, 35-0 (B)
            Dolphins, 34-17 (M)
1971—Dolphins, 17-14 (M)
            Colts, 14-3 (B)
            **Dolphins, 21-0 (M)
1972—Dolphins, 23-0 (B)
            Dolphins, 16-0 (M)
1973—Dolphins, 44-0 (M)
            Colts, 16-3 (B)
1974—Dolphins, 17-7 (M)
            Dolphins, 17-16 (B)
1975—Colts, 33-17 (M)
            Colts, 10-7 (B) OT
1976—Colts, 28-14 (B)
            Colts, 17-16 (M)
1977—Colts, 45-28 (B)
            Dolphins, 17-6 (M)
1978—Dolphins, 42-0 (B)
            Dolphins, 26-8 (M)
1979—Dolphins, 19-0 (M)
            Dolphins, 28-24 (B)
1980—Colts, 30-17 (M)
            Dolphins, 24-14 (B)

1981—Dolphins, 31-28 (B)
            Dolphins, 27-10 (M)
1982—Dolphins, 24-20 (M)
            Dolphins, 34-7 (B)
1983—Dolphins, 21-7 (B)
            Dolphins, 37-0 (M)
1984—Dolphins, 44-7 (M)
            Dolphins, 35-17 (I)
1985—Dolphins, 30-13 (M)
            Dolphins, 34-20 (I)
1986—Dolphins, 30-10 (M)
            Dolphins, 17-13 (I)
1987—Dolphins, 23-10 (I)
            Colts, 40-21 (M)
1988—Colts, 15-13 (I)
            Colts, 31-28 (M)
1989—Dolphins, 19-13 (M)
            Colts, 42-13 (I)
1990—Dolphins, 27-7 (I)
            Dolphins, 23-17 (M)
1991—Dolphins, 17-6 (M)
            Dolphins, 10-6 (I)
1992—Colts, 31-20 (M)
            Dolphins, 28-0 (I)
1993—Dolphins, 24-20 (I)
            Dolphins, 41-27 (M)
1994—Dolphins, 22-21 (M)
            Colts, 10-6 (I)
1995—Colts, 27-24 (M) OT
            Colts, 36-28 (I)
1996—Colts, 10-6 (I)
            Dolphins, 37-13 (M)
1997—Dolphins, 16-10 (M)
            Colts, 41-0 (I)
1998—Dolphins, 24-15 (I)
            Dolphins, 27-14 (M)
1999—Dolphins, 34-31 (I)
            Colts, 37-34 (M)
2000—Dolphins, 17-14 (I)
            Colts, 20-13 (M)
            ***Dolphins 23-17 (M) OT
2001—Dolphins, 27-24 (I)
            Dolphins, 41-6 (M)
2002—Dolphins, 21-13 (I)
2003—Colts, 23-17 (M)
(RS Pts.—Dolphins 1,494, Colts 1,116)
(PS Pts.—Dolphins 44, Colts 17)
*Franchise in Baltimore prior to 1984
**AFC Championship
***AFC First-Round Playoff
*INDIANAPOLIS vs. MINNESOTA
RS: Colts lead series, 13-7-1
PS: Colts lead series, 1-0
1961—Colts, 34-33 (B)
            Vikings, 28-20 (M)
1962—Colts, 34-7 (M)
            Colts, 42-17 (B)
1963—Colts, 37-34 (M)
            Colts, 41-10 (B)
1964—Vikings, 34-24 (M)
            Colts, 17-14 (B)
1965—Colts, 35-16 (B)
            Colts, 41-21 (M)
1966—Colts, 38-23 (M)
            Colts, 20-17 (B)
1967—Tie, 20-20 (M)
1968—Colts, 21-9 (B)
            **Colts, 24-14 (B)
1969—Vikings, 52-14 (M)
1971—Vikings, 10-3 (M)

1982—Vikings, 13-10 (M)
1988—Vikings, 12-3 (M)
1997—Vikings, 39-28 (M)
2000—Colts, 31-10 (I)
2004—Colts, 31-28 (I)
(RS Pts.—Colts 544, Vikings 447)
(PS Pts.—Colts 24, Vikings 14)
Franchise in Baltimore prior to 1984
**Conference Championship*
INDIANAPOLIS vs. **NEW ENGLAND
RS: Patriots lead series, 41-25
PS: Patriots lead series, 2-0
1970—Colts, 14-6 (Bos)
    Colts, 27-3 (Balt)
1971—Colts, 23-3 (NE)
    Patriots, 21-17 (Balt)
1972—Colts, 24-17 (NE)
    Colts, 31-0 (Balt)
1973—Patriots, 24-16 (NE)
    Colts, 18-13 (Balt)
1974—Patriots, 42-3 (NE)
    Patriots, 27-17 (Balt)
1975—Patriots, 21-10 (NE)
    Colts, 34-21 (Balt)
1976—Colts, 27-13 (NE)
    Patriots, 21-14 (Balt)
1977—Patriots, 17-3 (NE)
    Colts, 30-24 (Balt)
1978—Colts, 34-27 (NE)
    Patriots, 35-14 (Balt)
1979—Colts, 31-26 (Balt)
    Patriots, 50-21 (NE)
1980—Patriots, 37-21 (Balt)
    Patriots, 47-21 (NE)
1981—Colts, 29-28 (NE)
    Colts, 23-21 (Balt)
1982—Patriots, 24-13 (Balt)
1983—Colts, 29-23 (NE) OT
    Colts, 12-7 (Balt)
1984—Patriots, 50-17 (I)
    Patriots, 16-10 (NE)
1985—Patriots, 34-15 (NE)
    Patriots, 38-31 (I)
1986—Patriots, 33-3 (NE)
    Patriots, 30-21 (I)
1987—Colts, 30-16 (I)
    Patriots, 24-0 (NE)
1988—Patriots, 21-17 (NE)
    Colts, 24-21 (I)
1989—Patriots, 23-20 (I) OT
    Patriots, 22-16 (NE)
1990—Patriots, 16-14 (I)
    Colts, 13-10 (NE)
1991—Patriots, 16-7 (I)
    Patriots, 23-17 (NE) OT
1992—Patriots, 37-34 (I) OT
    Colts, 6-0 (NE)
1993—Colts, 9-6 (I)
    Patriots, 38-0 (NE)
1994—Patriots, 12-10 (I)
    Patriots, 28-13 (NE)
1995—Colts, 24-10 (NE)
    Colts, 10-7 (I)
1996—Patriots, 27-9 (I)
    Patriots, 27-13 (NE)
1997—Patriots, 31-6 (I)
    Patriots, 20-17 (NE)
1998—Patriots, 29-6 (NE)
    Patriots, 21-16 (I)
1999—Patriots, 31-28 (NE)

Colts, 20-15 (I)
2000—Patriots, 24-16 (NE)
    Colts, 30-23 (I)
2001—Patriots, 44-13 (NE)
    Patriots, 38-17 (I)
2003—Patriots, 38-34 (I)
    ***Patriots, 24-14 (NE)
2004—Patriots, 27-24 (NE)
    ****Patriots, 20-3 (NE)
2005—Colts, 40-21 (NE)
(RS Pts.—Patriots 1,545, Colts 1,206)
(PS Pts.—Patriots 44, Colts 17)
Franchise in Baltimore prior to 1984
**Franchise in Boston prior to 1971*
***AFC Championship*
****AFC Divisional Playoff*
INDIANAPOLIS vs. NEW ORLEANS
RS: Saints lead series, 5-4
1967—Colts, 30-10 (B)
1969—Colts, 30-10 (NO)
1973—Colts, 14-10 (B)
1986—Saints, 17-14 (I)
1989—Saints, 41-6 (NO)
1995—Saints, 17-14 (NO)
1998—Saints, 19-13 (I) OT
2001—Saints, 34-20 (NO)
2003—Colts, 55-21 (NO)
(RS Pts.—Colts 196, Saints 179)
Franchise in Baltimore prior to 1984
INDIANAPOLIS vs. N.Y. GIANTS
RS: Series tied, 6-6
PS: Colts lead series, 2-0
1954—Colts, 20-14 (B)
1955—Giants, 17-7 (NY)
1958—Giants, 24-21 (NY)
    **Colts, 23-17 (NY) OT
1959—**Colts, 31-16 (B)
1963—Giants, 37-28 (B)
1968—Colts, 26-0 (NY)
1971—Colts, 31-7 (NY)
1975—Colts, 21-0 (NY)
1979—Colts, 31-7 (NY)
1990—Giants, 24-7 (I)
1993—Giants, 20-6 (NY)
1999—Colts, 27-19 (NY)
2002—Giants, 44-27 (I)
(RS Pts.—Colts 252, Giants 213)
(PS Pts.—Colts 54, Giants 33)
Franchise in Baltimore prior to 1984
**NFL Championship*
INDIANAPOLIS vs. N.Y. JETS
RS: Colts lead series, 39-25
PS: Jets lead series, 2-0
1968—**Jets 16-7 (Miami)
1970—Colts, 29-22 (NY)
    Colts, 35-20 (B)
1971—Colts, 22-0 (B)
    Colts, 14-13 (NY)
1972—Jets, 44-34 (B)
    Jets, 24-20 (NY)
1973—Jets, 34-10 (B)
    Jets, 20-17 (NY)
1974—Colts, 35-20 (NY)
    Jets, 45-38 (B)
1975—Colts, 45-28 (NY)
    Colts, 52-19 (B)
1976—Colts, 20-0 (NY)
    Colts, 33-16 (B)
1977—Colts, 20-12 (NY)
    Colts, 33-12 (B)

1978—Jets, 33-10 (B)
    Jets, 24-16 (NY)
1979—Colts, 10-8 (B)
    Jets, 30-17 (NY)
1980—Colts, 17-14 (NY)
    Colts, 35-21 (B)
1981—Jets, 41-14 (B)
    Jets, 25-0 (NY)
1982—Jets, 37-0 (NY)
1983—Colts, 17-14 (NY)
    Jets, 10-6 (B)
1984—Jets, 23-14 (I)
    Colts, 9-5 (NY)
1985—Jets, 25-20 (NY)
    Jets, 35-17 (I)
1986—Jets, 26-7 (I)
    Jets, 31-16 (NY)
1987—Colts, 6-0 (I)
    Colts, 19-14 (NY)
1988—Colts, 38-14 (I)
    Jets, 34-16 (NY)
1989—Colts, 17-10 (NY)
    Colts, 27-10 (I)
1990—Colts, 17-14 (I)
    Colts, 29-21 (NY)
1991—Jets, 17-6 (I)
    Colts, 28-27 (NY)
1992—Colts, 6-3 (I) OT
    Colts, 10-6 (NY)
1993—Jets, 31-17 (I)
    Colts, 9-6 (NY)
1994—Jets, 16-6 (NY)
    Colts, 28-25 (I)
1995—Colts, 27-24 (NY) OT
    Colts, 17-10 (I)
1996—Colts, 21-7 (NY)
    Colts, 34-29 (I)
1997—Jets, 16-12 (I)
    Colts, 22-14 (NY)
1998—Jets, 44-6 (NY)
    Colts, 24-23 (I)
1999—Colts, 16-13 (NY)
    Colts, 13-6 (I)
2000—Colts, 23-15 (I)
    Jets, 27-17 (NY)
2001—Colts, 45-24 (NY)
    Jets, 29-28 (I)
2002—***Jets, 41-0 (NY)
2003—Colts, 38-31 (I)
(RS Pts.—Colts 1,304, Jets 1,291)
(PS Pts.—Jets 57, Colts 7)
Franchise in Baltimore prior to 1984
**Super Bowl III*
***AFC First-Round Playoff*
INDIANAPOLIS vs **OAKLAND
RS: Raiders lead series, 7-3
PS: Series tied, 1-1
1970—***Colts, 27-17 (B)
1971—Colts, 37-14 (O)
1973—Raiders, 34-21 (B)
1975—Raiders, 31-20 (B)
1977—****Raiders, 37-31 (B) OT
1984—Raiders, 21-7 (LA)
1986—Colts, 30-24 (LA)
1991—Raiders, 16-0 (LA)
1995—Raiders, 30-17 (O)
2000—Raiders, 38-31 (I)
2001—Raiders, 23-18 (I)
2004—Colts, 35-14 (I)
(RS Pts.—Raiders 245, Colts 216)

(PS Pts.—Colts 58, Raiders 54)
Franchise in Baltimore prior to 1984
**Franchise in Los Angeles from 1982-1994*
***AFC Championship*
****AFC Divisional Playoff*

*INDIANAPOLIS vs. PHILADELPHIA
RS: Colts lead series, 9-6
1953—Eagles, 45-14 (P)
1965—Colts, 34-24 (B)
1967—Colts, 38-6 (P)
1969—Colts, 24-20 (B)
1970—Colts, 29-10 (B)
1974—Eagles, 30-10 (P)
1978—Eagles, 17-14 (B)
1981—Eagles, 38-13 (P)
1983—Colts, 22-21 (P)
1984—Eagles, 16-7 (P)
1990—Colts, 24-23 (P)
1993—Eagles, 20-10 (I)
1996—Colts, 37-10 (I)
1999—Colts, 44-17 (P)
2002—Colts, 35-13 (P)
(RS Pts.—Colts 355, Eagles 310)
Franchise in Baltimore prior to 1984

*INDIANAPOLIS vs. PITTSBURGH
RS: Steelers lead series, 13-5
PS: Steelers lead series, 5-0
1957—Steelers, 19-13 (B)
1968—Colts, 41-7 (P)
1971—Colts, 34-21 (B)
1974—Steelers, 30-0 (P)
1975—**Steelers, 28-10 (P)
1976—**Steelers, 40-14 (B)
1977—Colts, 31-21 (B)
1978—Steelers, 35-13 (P)
1979—Steelers, 17-13 (P)
1980—Steelers, 20-17 (B)
1983—Steelers, 24-13 (B)
1984—Colts, 17-16 (I)
1985—Steelers, 45-3 (P)
1987—Steelers, 21-7 (P)
1991—Steelers, 21-3 (I)
1992—Steelers, 30-14 (P)
1994—Steelers, 31-21 (P)
1995—***Steelers, 20-16 (P)
1996—****Steelers, 42-14 (P)
1997—Steelers, 24-22 (P)
2002—Steelers, 28-10 (P)
2005—Colts, 26-7 (I)
　　　**Steelers, 21-18 (I)
(RS Pts.—Steelers 417, Colts 298)
(PS Pts.—Steelers 151, Colts 72)
Franchise in Baltimore prior to 1984
**AFC Divisional Playoff*
***AFC Championship*
****AFC First-Round Playoff*

*INDIANAPOLIS vs. **ST. LOUIS
RS: Colts lead series, 22-17-2
1953—Rams, 21-13 (B)
　　　Rams, 45-2 (LA)
1954—Rams, 48-0 (B)
　　　Colts, 22-21 (LA)
1955—Tie, 17-17 (B)
　　　Rams, 20-14 (LA)
1956—Colts, 56-21 (B)
　　　Rams, 31-7 (LA)
1957—Colts, 31-14 (B)
　　　Rams, 37-21 (LA)
1958—Colts, 34-7 (B)

Rams, 30-28 (LA)
1959—Colts, 35-21 (B)
　　　Colts, 45-26 (LA)
1960—Colts, 31-17 (B)
　　　Rams, 10-3 (LA)
1961—Colts, 27-24 (B)
　　　Rams, 34-17 (LA)
1962—Colts, 30-27 (B)
　　　Colts, 14-2 (LA)
1963—Rams, 17-16 (LA)
　　　Colts, 19-16 (B)
1964—Colts, 35-20 (B)
　　　Colts, 24-7 (LA)
1965—Colts, 35-20 (B)
　　　Colts, 20-17 (LA)
1966—Colts, 17-3 (LA)
　　　Rams, 23-7 (B)
1967—Tie, 24-24 (B)
　　　Rams, 34-10 (LA)
1968—Colts, 27-10 (B)
　　　Colts, 28-24 (LA)
1969—Rams, 27-20 (B)
　　　Colts, 13-7 (LA)
1971—Colts, 24-17 (B)
1975—Rams, 24-13 (LA)
1986—Rams, 24-7 (I)
1989—Rams, 31-17 (LA)
1995—Colts, 21-18 (I)
2001—Rams, 42-17 (StL)
2005—Colts, 45-28 (I)
(RS Pts.—Rams 906, Colts 886)
Franchise in Baltimore prior to 1984
**Franchise in Los Angeles prior to 1995*

*INDIANAPOLIS vs. SAN DIEGO
RS: Chargers lead series, 13-8
PS: Colts lead series, 1-0
1970—Colts, 16-14 (SD)
1972—Chargers, 23-20 (B)
1976—Colts, 37-21 (SD)
1981—Chargers, 43-14 (B)
1982—Chargers, 44-26 (SD)
1984—Chargers, 38-10 (I)
1986—Chargers, 17-3 (I)
1987—Chargers, 16-13 (I)
　　　Colts, 20-7 (SD)
1988—Colts, 16-0 (SD)
1989—Colts, 10-6 (I)
1992—Chargers, 34-14 (I)
　　　Chargers, 26-0 (SD)
1993—Chargers, 31-0 (I)
1995—Chargers, 27-24 (I)
　　　**Colts, 35-20 (SD)
1996—Chargers, 26-19 (I)
1997—Chargers, 35-19 (SD)
1998—Colts, 17-12 (I)
1999—Colts, 27-19 (SD)
2004—Colts, 34-31 (I) OT
2005—Chargers, 26-17 (I)
(RS Pts.—Chargers 496, Colts 356)
(PS Pts.—Colts 35, Chargers 20)
Franchise in Baltimore prior to 1984
**AFC First-Round Playoff*

*INDIANAPOLIS vs. SAN FRANCISCO
RS: Colts lead series, 23-18
1953—49ers, 38-21 (B)
　　　49ers, 45-14 (SF)
1954—Colts, 17-13 (B)
　　　49ers, 10-7 (SF)
1955—Colts, 26-14 (B)
　　　49ers, 35-24 (SF)

1956—49ers, 20-17 (B)
　　　49ers, 30-17 (SF)
1957—Colts, 27-21 (B)
　　　49ers, 17-13 (SF)
1958—Colts, 35-27 (B)
　　　49ers, 21-12 (SF)
1959—Colts, 45-14 (B)
　　　Colts, 34-14 (SF)
1960—49ers, 30-22 (B)
　　　49ers, 34-10 (SF)
1961—Colts, 20-17 (B)
　　　Colts, 27-24 (SF)
1962—49ers, 21-13 (B)
　　　Colts, 22-3 (SF)
1963—Colts, 20-14 (SF)
　　　Colts, 20-3 (B)
1964—Colts, 37-7 (B)
　　　Colts, 14-3 (SF)
1965—Colts, 27-24 (B)
　　　Colts, 34-28 (SF)
1966—Colts, 36-14 (B)
　　　Colts, 30-14 (SF)
1967—Colts, 41-7 (B)
　　　Colts, 26-9 (SF)
1968—Colts, 27-10 (B)
　　　Colts, 42-14 (SF)
1969—49ers, 24-21 (B)
　　　49ers, 20-17 (SF)
1972—49ers, 24-21 (SF)
1986—49ers, 35-14 (SF)
1989—49ers, 30-24 (I)
1995—Colts, 18-17 (I)
1998—49ers, 34-31 (SF)
2001—49ers, 40-21 (I)
2005—Colts, 28-3 (SF)
(RS Pts.—Colts 972, 49ers 822)
Franchise in Baltimore prior to 1984

*INDIANAPOLIS vs. SEATTLE
RS: Colts lead series, 5-4
1977—Colts, 29-14 (S)
1978—Colts, 17-14 (S)
1991—Seahawks, 31-3 (S)
1994—Colts, 17-15 (I)
　　　Colts, 31-19 (S)
1997—Seahawks, 31-3 (I)
1998—Seahawks, 27-23 (S)
2000—Colts, 37-24 (S)
2005—Seahawks, 28-13 (S)
(RS Pts.—Seahawks 203, Colts 173)
Franchise in Baltimore prior to 1984

*INDIANAPOLIS vs. TAMPA BAY
RS: Colts lead series, 6-4
1976—Colts, 42-17 (B)
1979—Buccaneers, 29-26 (B) OT
1985—Colts, 31-23 (TB)
1987—Colts, 24-6 (I)
1988—Colts, 35-31 (B)
1991—Buccaneers, 17-3 (TB)
1992—Colts, 24-14 (TB)
1994—Buccaneers, 24-10 (TB)
1997—Buccaneers, 31-28 (I)
2003—Colts, 38-35 (TB) OT
(RS Pts.—Colts 261, Buccaneers 227)
Franchise in Baltimore prior to 1984

*INDIANAPOLIS vs. **TENNESSEE
RS: Colts lead series, 13-9
PS: Titans lead series, 1-0
1970—Colts, 24-20 (H)
1973—Oilers, 31-27 (B)
1976—Colts, 38-14 (B)

1979—Oilers, 28-16 (B)
1980—Oilers, 21-16 (H)
1983—Colts, 20-10 (B)
1984—Colts, 35-21 (H)
1985—Colts, 34-16 (I)
1986—Oilers, 31-17 (H)
1987—Colts, 51-27 (I)
1988—Oilers, 17-14 (I) OT
1990—Oilers, 24-10 (H)
1992—Oilers, 20-10 (I)
1994—Colts, 45-21 (I)
1999—***Titans, 19-16 (I)
2002—Titans, 23-15 (I)
    Titans, 27-17 (T)
2003—Colts, 33-7 (I)
    Colts, 29-27 (T)
2004—Colts, 31-17 (T)
    Colts, 51-24 (I)
2005—Colts, 31-10 (T)
    Colts, 35-3 (I)
(RS Pts.—Colts 599, Titans 439)
(PS Pts.—Titans 19, Colts 16)
*Franchise in Baltimore prior to 1984
**Franchise in Houston prior to 1997;
known as Oilers prior to 1999
***AFC Divisional Playoff
INDIANAPOLIS vs. WASHINGTON
RS: Colts lead series, 17-10
1953—Colts, 27-17 (B)
1954—Redskins, 24-21 (W)
1955—Redskins, 14-13 (B)
1956—Colts, 19-17 (B)
1957—Colts, 21-17 (W)
1958—Colts, 35-10 (B)
1959—Redskins, 27-24 (W)
1960—Colts, 20-0 (B)
1961—Colts, 27-6 (W)
1962—Colts, 34-21 (B)
1963—Colts, 36-20 (W)
1964—Colts, 45-17 (B)
1965—Colts, 38-7 (W)
1966—Colts, 37-10 (B)
1967—Colts, 17-13 (W)
1969—Colts, 41-17 (B)
1973—Redskins, 22-14 (W)
1977—Colts, 10-3 (B)
1978—Colts, 21-17 (B)
1981—Redskins, 38-14 (W)
1984—Redskins, 35-7 (I)
1990—Colts, 35-28 (I)
1993—Redskins, 30-24 (W)
1994—Redskins, 41-27 (I)
1996—Redskins, 31-16 (W)
1999—Colts, 24-21 (I)
2002—Redskins, 26-21 (W)
(RS Pts.—Colts 668, Redskins 529)
*Franchise in Baltimore prior to 1984

JACKSONVILLE vs. ARIZONA
RS: Jaguars lead series, 2-0;
See Arizona vs. Jacksonville
JACKSONVILLE vs. ATLANTA
RS: Jaguars lead series, 2-1;
See Atlanta vs. Jacksonville
JACKSONVILLE vs. BALTIMORE
RS: Jaguars lead series, 9-6;
See Baltimore vs. Jacksonville
JACKSONVILLE vs. BUFFALO
RS: Bills lead series, 3-2
PS: Jaguars lead series, 1-0;

See Buffalo vs. Jacksonville
JACKSONVILLE vs. CAROLINA
RS: Jaguars lead series, 2-1;
See Carolina vs. Jacksonville
JACKSONVILLE vs. CHICAGO
RS: Series tied, 2-2;
See Chicago vs. Jacksonville
JACKSONVILLE vs. CINCINNATI
RS: Jaguars lead series, 11-5;
See Cincinnati vs. Jacksonville
JACKSONVILLE vs. CLEVELAND
RS: Jaguars lead series, 8-2;
See Cleveland vs. Jacksonville
JACKSONVILLE vs. DALLAS
RS: Cowboys lead series, 2-1;
See Dallas vs. Jacksonville
JACKSONVILLE vs. DENVER
RS: Broncos lead series, 3-2
PS: Series tied, 1-1;
See Denver vs. Jacksonville
JACKSONVILLE vs. DETROIT
RS: Jaguars lead series, 2-1;
See Detroit vs. Jacksonville
JACKSONVILLE vs. GREEN BAY
RS: Packers lead series, 2-1;
See Green Bay vs. Jacksonville
JACKSONVILLE vs. HOUSTON
RS: Series tied, 4-4;
See Houston vs. Jacksonville
JACKSONVILLE vs. INDIANAPOLIS
RS: Colts lead series, 8-2;
See Indianapolis vs. Jacksonville
JACKSONVILLE vs. KANSAS CITY
RS: Jaguars lead series, 4-1
1997—Jaguars, 24-10 (J)
1998—Jaguars, 21-16 (J)
2001—Chiefs, 30-26 (J)
2002—Jaguars, 23-16 (KC)
2004—Jaguars, 22-16 (J)
(RS Pts.—Jaguars 116, Chiefs 88)
JACKSONVILLE vs. MIAMI
RS: Series tied, 1-1
PS: Jaguars lead series, 1-0
1998—Jaguars, 28-21 (J)
1999—*Jaguars, 62-7 (J)
2003—Dolphins, 24-10 (J)
(RS Pts.—Dolphins 45, Jaguars 38)
(PS Pts.—Jaguars 62, Dolphins 7)
*AFC Divisional Playoff
JACKSONVILLE vs. MINNESOTA
RS: Vikings lead series, 2-1
1998—Vikings, 50-10 (M)
2001—Jaguars, 33-3 (M)
2004—Vikings, 27-16 (M)
(RS Pts.—Vikings 80, Jaguars 59)
JACKSONVILLE vs. NEW ENGLAND
RS: Patriots lead series, 3-0
PS: Patriots lead series, 2-1
1996—Patriots, 28-25 (NE) OT
    *Patriots, 20-6 (NE)
1997—Patriots, 26-20 (J)
1998—**Jaguars, 25-10 (J)
2003—Patriots, 27-13 (NE)
2005—**Patriots, 28-3 (NE)
(RS Pts.—Patriots 81, Jaguars 58)
(PS Pts.—Patriots 58, Jaguars 34)
*AFC Championship
**AFC First-Round Playoff
JACKSONVILLE vs. NEW ORLEANS
RS: Jaguars lead series, 2-1

1996—Saints, 17-13 (NO)
1999—Jaguars, 41-23 (J)
2003—Jaguars, 20-19 (J)
(RS Pts.—Jaguars 74, Saints 59)
JACKSONVILLE vs. N.Y. GIANTS
RS: Giants lead series, 2-1
1997—Jaguars, 40-13 (J)
2000—Giants, 28-25 (NY)
2002—Giants, 24-17 (NY)
(RS Pts.—Jaguars 82, Giants 65)
JACKSONVILLE vs. N.Y. JETS
RS: Jaguars lead series, 4-2
PS: Jets lead series, 1-0
1995—Jets, 27-10 (NY)
1996—Jaguars, 21-17 (J)
1998—*Jets, 34-24 (NY)
1999—Jaguars, 16-6 (NY)
2002—Jaguars, 28-3 (J)
2003—Jets, 13-10 (NY)
2005—Jaguars, 26-20 (NY) OT
(RS Pts.—Jaguars 111, Jets 86)
(PS Pts.—Jets 34, Jaguars 24)
*AFC Divisional Playoff
JACKSONVILLE vs. OAKLAND
RS: Jaguars lead series, 2-1
1996—Raiders, 17-3 (O)
1997—Jaguars, 20-9 (O)
2004—Jaguars, 13-6 (O)
(RS Pts.—Jaguars 36, Raiders 32)
JACKSONVILLE vs. PHILADELPHIA
RS: Jaguars lead series, 2-0
1997—Jaguars, 38-21 (J)
2002—Jaguars, 28-25 (J)
(RS Pts.—Jaguars 66, Eagles 46)
JACKSONVILLE vs. PITTSBURGH
RS: Jaguars lead series, 9-8
1995—Jaguars, 20-16 (J)
    Steelers, 24-7 (P)
1996—Jaguars, 24-9 (J)
    Steelers, 28-3 (P)
1997—Jaguars, 30-21 (J)
    Steelers, 23-17 (P) OT
1998—Steelers, 30-15 (P)
    Jaguars, 21-3 (J)
1999—Jaguars, 17-3 (P)
    Jaguars, 20-6 (J)
2000—Steelers, 24-13 (J)
    Jaguars, 34-24 (P)
2001—Jaguars, 21-3 (J)
    Steelers, 20-7 (P)
2002—Steelers, 25-23 (J)
2004—Steelers, 17-16 (J)
2005—Jaguars, 23-17 (P) OT
(RS Pts.—Jaguars 311, Steelers 293)
JACKSONVILLE vs. ST. LOUIS
RS: Rams lead series, 2-0
1996—Rams, 17-14 (StL)
2005—Rams, 24-21 (StL)
(RS Pts.—Rams 41, Jaguars 35)
JACKSONVILLE vs. SAN DIEGO
RS: Series tied, 1-1
2003—Jaguars, 27-21 (J)
2004—Chargers, 34-21 (SD)
(RS Pts.—Chargers 55, Jaguars 48)
JACKSONVILLE vs. SAN FRANCISCO
RS: Jaguars lead series, 2-0
1999—Jaguars, 41-3 (J)
2005—Jaguars, 10-9 (J)
(RS Pts.—Jaguars 51, 49ers 12)

ALL-TIME TEAM VS. TEAM RESULTS

JACKSONVILLE vs. SEATTLE
RS: Seahawks lead series, 3-2
1995—Seahawks, 47-30 (J)
1996—Jaguars, 20-13 (J)
2000—Seahawks, 28-21 (J)
2001—Seahawks, 24-15 (S)
2005—Jaguars, 26-14 (J)
(RS Pts.—Seahawks 126, Jaguars 112)
JACKSONVILLE vs. TAMPA BAY
RS: Jaguars lead series, 2-1
1995—Buccaneers, 17-16 (TB)
1998—Jaguars, 29-24 (J)
2003—Jaguars, 17-10 (J)
(RS Pts.—Jaguars 62, Buccaneers 51)
JACKSONVILLE vs. *TENNESSEE
RS: Titans lead series, 12-10
PS: Titans lead, 1-0
1995—Oilers, 10-3 (J)
    Jaguars, 17-16 (H)
1996—Oilers, 34-27 (J)
    Jaguars, 23-17 (H)
1997—Jaguars, 30-24 (T)
    Jaguars, 17-9 (J)
1998—Jaguars, 27-22 (T)
    Oilers, 16-13 (J)
1999—Titans, 20-19 (J)
    Titans, 41-14 (T)
    **Titans, 33-14 (J)
2000—Titans, 27-13 (T)
    Jaguars, 16-13 (J)
2001—Jaguars, 13-6 (J)
    Titans, 28-24 (T)
2002—Titans, 23-14 (T)
    Titans, 28-10 (J)
2003—Titans, 30-17 (J)
    Titans, 10-3 (T)
2004—Jaguars, 15-12 (T)
    Titans, 18-15 (J)
2005—Jaguars, 31-28 (T)
    Jaguars, 40-13 (J)
(RS Pts.—Titans 445, Jaguars 401)
(PS Pts.—Titans 33, Jaguars 14)
*Franchise in Houston prior to 1997;
known as Oilers prior to 1999
**AFC Championship
JACKSONVILLE vs. WASHINGTON
RS: Redskins lead series, 2-1
1997—Redskins, 24-12 (W)
2000—Redskins, 35-16 (J)
2002—Jaguars, 26-7 (J)
(RS Pts.—Redskins 66, Jaguars 54)

KANSAS CITY vs. ARIZONA
RS: Chiefs lead series, 6-2-1;
See Arizona vs. Kansas City
KANSAS CITY vs. ATLANTA
RS: Chiefs lead series, 5-1;
See Atlanta vs. Kansas City
KANSAS CITY vs. BALTIMORE
RS: Chiefs lead series, 3-0;
See Baltimore vs. Kansas City
KANSAS CITY vs. BUFFALO
RS: Bills lead series, 19-16-1
PS: Bills lead series, 2-1;
See Buffalo vs. Kansas City
KANSAS CITY vs. CAROLINA
RS: Chiefs lead series, 2-1;
See Carolina vs. Kansas City
KANSAS CITY vs. CHICAGO
RS: Bears lead series, 5-4;

See Chicago vs. Kansas City
KANSAS CITY vs. CINCINNATI
RS: Chiefs lead series, 12-10;
See Cincinnati vs. Kansas City
KANSAS CITY vs. CLEVELAND
RS: Chiefs lead series, 9-8-2;
See Cleveland vs. Kansas City
KANSAS CITY vs. DALLAS
RS: Cowboys lead series, 5-3;
See Dallas vs. Kansas City
KANSAS CITY vs. DENVER
RS: Chiefs lead series, 51-40
PS: Broncos lead series, 1-0;
See Denver vs. Kansas City
KANSAS CITY vs. DETROIT
RS: Chiefs lead series, 7-3;
See Detroit vs. Kansas City
KANSAS CITY vs. GREEN BAY
RS: Chiefs lead series, 6-1-1
PS: Packers lead series, 1-0;
See Green Bay vs. Kansas City
KANSAS CITY vs. HOUSTON
RS: Chiefs lead series, 2-1;
See Houston vs. Kansas City
KANSAS CITY vs. INDIANAPOLIS
RS: Colts lead series, 8-7
PS: Colts lead series, 2-0;
See Indianapolis vs. Kansas City
KANSAS CITY vs. JACKSONVILLE
RS: Jaguars lead series, 4-1;
See Jacksonville vs. Kansas City
KANSAS CITY vs. MIAMI
RS: Chiefs lead series, 12-10
PS: Dolphins lead series, 3-0
1966—Chiefs, 34-16 (KC)
    Chiefs, 19-18 (M)
1967—Chiefs, 24-0 (M)
    Chiefs, 41-0 (KC)
1968—Chiefs, 48-3 (M)
1969—Chiefs, 17-10 (KC)
1971—*Dolphins, 27-24 (KC) OT
1972—Dolphins, 20-10 (KC)
1974—Dolphins, 9-3 (M)
1976—Chiefs, 20-17 (M) OT
1981—Dolphins, 17-7 (KC)
1983—Dolphins, 14-6 (M)
1985—Dolphins, 31-0 (M)
1987—Dolphins, 42-0 (M)
1989—Chiefs, 26-21 (KC)
    Chiefs, 27-24 (M)
1990—**Dolphins, 17-16 (M)
1991—Chiefs, 42-7 (KC)
1993—Dolphins, 30-10 (M)
1994—Dolphins, 45-28 (M)
    **Dolphins, 27-17 (M)
1995—Dolphins, 13-6 (M)
1997—Dolphins, 17-14 (M)
2002—Chiefs, 48-30 (KC)
2005—Chiefs, 30-20 (M)
(RS Pts.—Chiefs 460, Dolphins 404)
(PS Pts.—Dolphins 71, Chiefs 57)
*AFC Divisional Playoff
**AFC First-Round Playoff
KANSAS CITY vs. MINNESOTA
RS: Series tied, 4-4
PS: Chiefs lead series, 1-0
1969—*Chiefs, 23-7 (New Orleans)
1970—Vikings, 27-10 (M)
1974—Vikings, 35-15 (KC)
1981—Chiefs, 10-6 (M)

1990—Chiefs, 24-21 (KC)
1993—Vikings, 30-10 (M)
1996—Chiefs, 21-6 (M)
1999—Chiefs, 31-28 (KC)
2003—Vikings, 45-20 (M)
(RS Pts.—Vikings 198, Chiefs 141)
(PS Pts.—Chiefs 23, Vikings 7)
*Super Bowl IV
KANSAS CITY vs. **NEW ENGLAND
RS: Chiefs lead series, 16-11-3
1960—Patriots, 42-14 (B)
    Texans, 34-0 (D)
1961—Patriots, 18-17 (D)
    Patriots, 28-21 (B)
1962—Texans, 42-28 (D)
    Texans, 27-7 (B)
1963—Tie, 24-24 (B)
    Chiefs, 35-3 (KC)
1964—Patriots, 24-7 (B)
    Patriots, 31-24 (KC)
1965—Chiefs, 27-17 (KC)
    Tie, 10-10 (B)
1966—Chiefs, 43-24 (B)
    Tie, 27-27 (KC)
1967—Chiefs, 33-10 (B)
1968—Chiefs, 31-17 (KC)
1969—Chiefs, 31-0 (B)
1970—Chiefs, 23-10 (KC)
1973—Chiefs, 10-7 (NE)
1977—Patriots, 21-17 (NE)
1981—Patriots, 33-17 (NE)
1990—Chiefs, 37-7 (NE)
1992—Chiefs, 27-20 (KC)
1995—Chiefs, 31-26 (KC)
1998—Patriots, 40-10 (NE)
1999—Chiefs, 16-14 (KC)
2000—Patriots, 30-24 (NE)
2002—Patriots, 41-38 (NE) OT
2004—Patriots, 27-19 (KC)
2005—Chiefs, 26-16 (KC)
(RS Pts.—Chiefs 742, Patriots 602)
*Franchise located in Dallas prior to 1963
and known as Texans
**Franchise in Boston prior to 1971
KANSAS CITY vs. NEW ORLEANS
RS: Series tied, 4-4
1972—Chiefs, 20-17 (NO)
1976—Saints, 27-17 (KC)
1982—Saints, 27-17 (NO)
1985—Chiefs, 47-27 (NO)
1991—Saints, 17-10 (NO)
1994—Chiefs, 30-17 (NO)
1997—Chiefs, 25-13 (KC)
2004—Saints, 27-20 (NO)
(RS Pts.—Chiefs 186, Saints 172)
KANSAS CITY vs. N.Y. GIANTS
RS: Giants lead series, 9-2
1974—Giants, 33-27 (KC)
1978—Giants, 26-10 (NY)
1979—Giants, 21-17 (KC)
1983—Chiefs, 38-17 (KC)
1984—Giants, 28-27 (NY)
1988—Giants, 28-12 (NY)
1992—Giants, 35-21 (NY)
1995—Chiefs, 20-17 (KC) OT
1998—Giants, 28-7 (NY)
2001—Giants, 13-3 (KC)
2005—Giants, 27-17 (NY)
(RS Pts.—Giants 273, Chiefs 199)

*KANSAS CITY vs. **N.Y. JETS
RS: Chiefs lead series, 16-14-1
PS: Series tied, 1-1
1960—Titans, 37-35 (D)
　　　Titans, 41-35 (NY)
1961—Titans, 28-7 (NY)
　　　Texans, 35-24 (D)
1962—Texans, 20-17 (D)
　　　Texans, 52-31 (NY)
1963—Jets, 17-0 (NY)
　　　Chiefs, 48-0 (KC)
1964—Jets, 27-14 (NY)
　　　Chiefs, 24-7 (KC)
1965—Chiefs, 14-10 (NY)
　　　Jets, 13-10 (KC)
1966—Chiefs, 32-24 (NY)
1967—Chiefs, 42-18 (NY)
　　　Chiefs, 21-7 (NY)
1968—Jets, 20-19 (KC)
1969—Chiefs, 34-16 (NY)
　　　***Chiefs, 13-6 (NY)
1971—Jets, 13-10 (NY)
1974—Chiefs, 24-16 (KC)
1975—Jets, 30-24 (KC)
1982—Chiefs, 37-13 (KC)
1984—Jets, 17-16 (KC)
　　　Jets, 28-7 (NY)
1986—****Jets, 35-15 (NY)
1987—Jets, 16-9 (KC)
1988—Tie, 17-17 (NY)
　　　Chiefs, 38-34 (KC)
1992—Chiefs, 23-7 (NY)
1998—Jets, 20-17 (KC)
2001—Jets, 27-7 (NY)
2002—Chiefs, 29-25 (NY)
2005—Cheifs, 27-7 (KC)
(RS Pts.—Chiefs 727, Jets 607)
(PS Pts.—Jets 41, Chiefs 28)
**Franchise in Dallas prior to 1963 and
known as Texans*
**Jets known as Titans prior to 1963
***Inter-Divisional Playoff
****AFC First-Round Playoff
*KANSAS CITY vs. **OAKLAND
RS: Chiefs lead series, 47-42-2
PS: Chiefs lead series, 2-1
1960—Texans, 34-16 (O)
　　　Raiders, 20-19 (D)
1961—Texans, 42-35 (O)
　　　Texans, 43-11 (D)
1962—Texans, 26-16 (O)
　　　Texans, 35-7 (D)
1963—Raiders, 10-7 (O)
　　　Raiders, 22-7 (KC)
1964—Chiefs, 21-9 (O)
　　　Chiefs, 42-7 (KC)
1965—Raiders, 37-10 (O)
　　　Chiefs, 14-7 (KC)
1966—Chiefs, 32-10 (O)
　　　Raiders, 34-13 (KC)
1967—Raiders, 23-21 (O)
　　　Raiders, 44-22 (KC)
1968—Chiefs, 24-10 (KC)
　　　Raiders, 38-21 (O)
　　　***Raiders, 41-6 (O)
1969—Raiders, 27-24 (KC)
　　　Raiders, 10-6 (O)
　　　****Chiefs, 17-7 (O)
1970—Tie, 17-17 (KC)
　　　Raiders, 20-6 (O)

1971—Tie, 20-20 (O)
　　　Chiefs, 16-14 (KC)
1972—Chiefs, 27-14 (KC)
　　　Raiders, 26-3 (O)
1973—Chiefs, 16-3 (KC)
　　　Raiders, 37-7 (O)
1974—Raiders, 27-7 (O)
　　　Raiders, 7-6 (KC)
1975—Chiefs, 42-10 (KC)
　　　Raiders, 28-20 (O)
1976—Raiders, 24-21 (KC)
　　　Raiders, 21-10 (O)
1977—Raiders, 37-28 (KC)
　　　Raiders, 21-20 (O)
1978—Raiders, 28-6 (O)
　　　Raiders, 20-10 (KC)
1979—Chiefs, 35-7 (KC)
　　　Chiefs, 24-21 (O)
1980—Raiders, 27-14 (KC)
　　　Chiefs, 31-17 (O)
1981—Chiefs, 27-0 (KC)
　　　Chiefs, 28-17 (O)
1982—Raiders, 21-16 (KC)
1983—Raiders, 21-20 (LA)
　　　Raiders, 28-20 (KC)
1984—Raiders, 22-20 (KC)
　　　Raiders, 17-7 (LA)
1985—Chiefs, 36-20 (KC)
　　　Raiders, 19-10 (LA)
1986—Raiders, 24-17 (KC)
　　　Chiefs, 20-17 (LA)
1987—Raiders, 35-17 (LA)
　　　Chiefs, 16-10 (KC)
1988—Raiders, 27-17 (KC)
　　　Raiders, 17-10 (LA)
1989—Chiefs, 24-19 (KC)
　　　Raiders, 20-14 (LA)
1990—Chiefs, 9-7 (KC)
　　　Chiefs, 27-24 (LA)
1991—Chiefs, 24-21 (KC)
　　　Chiefs, 27-21 (LA)
　　　*****Chiefs, 10-6 (KC)
1992—Chiefs, 27-7 (KC)
　　　Raiders, 28-7 (LA)
1993—Chiefs, 24-9 (KC)
　　　Chiefs, 31-20 (LA)
1994—Chiefs, 13-3 (KC)
　　　Chiefs, 19-9 (LA)
1995—Chiefs, 23-17 (KC) OT
　　　Chiefs, 29-23 (O)
1996—Chiefs, 19-3 (KC)
　　　Raiders, 26-7 (O)
1997—Chiefs, 28-27 (O)
　　　Chiefs, 30-0 (KC)
1998—Chiefs, 28-8 (KC)
　　　Chiefs, 31-24 (O)
1999—Chiefs, 37-34 (O)
　　　Raiders, 41-38 (KC) OT
2000—Raiders, 20-17 (KC)
　　　Raiders, 49-31 (O)
2001—Raiders, 27-24 (KC)
　　　Raiders, 28-26 (O)
2002—Chiefs, 20-10 (KC)
　　　Raiders, 24-0 (O)
2003—Chiefs, 17-10 (O)
　　　Chiefs, 27-24 (KC)
2004—Chiefs, 34-27 (O)
　　　Chiefs, 31-30 (KC)
2005—Chiefs, 23-17 (O)
　　　Chiefs, 27-23 (KC)

(RS Pts.—Chiefs 1,923, Raiders 1,814)
(PS Pts.—Raiders 54, Chiefs 33)
**Franchise in Dallas prior to 1963 and
known as Texans*
***Franchise in Los Angeles from
1982-1994*
***Division Playoff
****AFL Championship
*****AFC First-Round Playoff
KANSAS CITY vs. PHILADELPHIA
RS: Eagles lead series, 3-2
1972—Eagles, 21-20 (KC)
1992—Chiefs, 24-17 (KC)
1998—Chiefs, 24-21 (P)
2001—Eagles, 23-10 (KC)
2005—Eagles, 37-31 (KC)
(RS Pts.—Eagles 119, Chiefs 109)
KANSAS CITY vs. PITTSBURGH
RS: Steelers lead series, 16-8
PS: Chiefs lead series, 1-0
1970—Chiefs, 31-14 (P)
1971—Chiefs, 38-16 (KC)
1972—Steelers, 16-7 (P)
1974—Steelers, 34-24 (KC)
1975—Steelers, 28-3 (P)
1976—Steelers, 45-0 (KC)
1978—Steelers, 27-24 (P)
1979—Steelers, 30-3 (KC)
1980—Steelers, 21-16 (P)
1981—Chiefs, 37-33 (P)
1982—Steelers, 35-14 (P)
1984—Chiefs, 37-27 (P)
1985—Steelers, 36-28 (KC)
1986—Chiefs, 24-19 (P)
1987—Steelers, 17-16 (KC)
1988—Steelers, 16-10 (P)
1989—Steelers, 23-17 (P)
1992—Steelers, 27-3 (KC)
1993—*Chiefs, 27-24 (KC) OT
1996—Steelers, 17-7 (KC)
1997—Chiefs, 13-10 (KC)
1998—Steelers, 20-13 (KC)
1999—Chiefs, 35-19 (KC)
2001—Steelers, 20-17 (KC)
2003—Chiefs, 41-20 (KC)
(RS Pts.—Steelers 570, Chiefs 458)
(PS Pts.—Chiefs 27, Steelers 24)
*AFC First-Round Playoff
KANSAS CITY vs. *ST. LOUIS
RS: Series tied, 4-4
1973—Rams, 23-13 (KC)
1982—Rams, 20-14 (LA)
1985—Rams, 16-0 (KC)
1991—Chiefs, 27-20 (LA)
1994—Rams, 16-0 (KC)
1997—Chiefs, 28-20 (StL)
2000—Chiefs, 54-34 (KC)
2002—Chiefs, 49-10 (KC)
(RS Pts.—Chiefs 185, Rams 159)
*Franchise in Los Angeles prior to 1995
*KANSAS CITY vs. **SAN DIEGO
RS: Chiefs lead series, 48-42-1
PS: Chargers lead series, 1-0
1960—Chargers, 21-20 (LA)
　　　Texans, 17-0 (D)
1961—Chargers, 26-10 (D)
　　　Chargers, 24-14 (SD)
1962—Chargers, 32-28 (SD)
　　　Texans, 26-17 (D)
1963—Chargers, 24-10 (SD)

Chargers, 38-17 (KC)
1964—Chargers, 28-14 (KC)
Chiefs, 49-6 (SD)
1965—Tie, 10-10 (SD)
Chiefs, 31-7 (KC)
1966—Chiefs, 24-14 (KC)
Chiefs, 27-17 (SD)
1967—Chargers, 45-31 (SD)
Chargers, 17-16 (KC)
1968—Chiefs, 27-20 (KC)
Chiefs, 40-3 (SD)
1969—Chiefs, 27-9 (SD)
Chiefs, 27-3 (KC)
1970—Chiefs, 26-14 (KC)
Chargers, 31-13 (SD)
1971—Chargers, 21-14 (SD)
Chiefs, 31-10 (KC)
1972—Chiefs, 26-14 (SD)
Chargers, 27-17 (KC)
1973—Chiefs, 19-0 (SD)
Chiefs, 33-6 (KC)
1974—Chiefs, 24-14 (SD)
Chargers, 14-7 (KC)
1975—Chiefs, 12-10 (SD)
Chargers, 28-20 (KC)
1976—Chargers, 30-16 (KC)
Chiefs, 23-20 (KC)
1977—Chargers, 23-7 (KC)
Chiefs, 21-16 (SD)
1978—Chargers, 29-23 (SD) OT
Chiefs, 23-0 (KC)
1979—Chargers, 20-14 (KC)
Chargers, 28-7 (SD)
1980—Chargers, 24-7 (KC)
Chargers, 20-7 (SD)
1981—Chargers, 42-31 (KC)
Chargers, 22-20 (SD)
1982—Chiefs, 19-12 (KC)
1983—Chiefs, 17-14 (KC)
Chargers, 41-38 (SD)
1984—Chiefs, 31-13 (KC)
Chiefs, 42-21 (SD)
1985—Chargers, 31-20 (SD)
Chiefs, 38-34 (KC)
1986—Chiefs, 42-41 (KC)
Chiefs, 24-23 (SD)
1987—Chiefs, 20-13 (KC)
Chargers, 42-21 (SD)
1988—Chargers, 24-23 (KC)
Chargers, 24-13 (SD)
1989—Chargers, 21-6 (SD)
Chargers, 20-13 (KC)
1990—Chiefs, 27-10 (KC)
Chiefs, 24-21 (SD)
1991—Chiefs, 14-13 (SD)
Chiefs, 20-17 (KC) OT
1992—Chiefs, 24-10 (SD)
Chiefs, 16-14 (KC)
***Chargers, 17-0 (SD)
1993—Chiefs, 17-14 (SD)
Chiefs, 28-24 (KC)
1994—Chargers, 20-6 (SD)
Chargers, 14-13 (KC)
1995—Chiefs, 29-23 (KC) OT
Chiefs, 22-7 (SD)
1996—Chargers, 22-19 (SD)
Chargers, 28-14 (KC)
1997—Chiefs, 31-3 (SD)
Chiefs, 29-7 (SD)
1998—Chiefs, 23-7 (KC)

Chargers, 38-37 (SD)
1999—Chargers, 21-14 (SD)
Chiefs, 34-0 (KC)
2000—Chiefs, 42-10 (KC)
Chargers, 17-16 (SD)
2001—Chiefs, 25-20 (SD)
Chiefs, 20-17 (KC)
2002—Chargers, 35-34 (SD)
Chiefs, 24-22 (KC)
2003—Chiefs, 27-14 (KC)
Chiefs, 28-24 (SD)
2004—Chargers, 34-31 (KC)
Chargers, 24-17 (SD)
2005—Chargers, 28-20 (SD)
Chiefs, 20-7 (KC)
(RS Pts.—Chiefs 2,015, Chargers 1,766)
(PS Pts.—Chargers 17, Chiefs 0)
*Franchise in Dallas prior to 1963 and
known as Texans
**Franchise in Los Angeles prior to 1961
***AFC First-Round Playoff
KANSAS CITY vs. SAN FRANCISCO
RS: 49ers lead series, 6-3
1971—Chiefs, 26-17 (SF)
1975—49ers, 20-3 (KC)
1982—49ers, 26-13 (KC)
1985—49ers, 31-3 (SF)
1991—49ers, 28-14 (SF)
1994—Chiefs, 24-17 (KC)
1997—Chiefs, 44-9 (KC)
2000—49ers, 21-7 (SF)
2002—49ers, 17-13 (SF)
(PS Pts.—49ers 186, Chiefs 147)
KANSAS CITY vs. SEATTLE
RS: Chiefs lead series, 30-18
1977—Seahawks, 34-31 (KC)
1978—Seahawks, 13-10 (KC)
Seahawks, 23-19 (S)
1979—Chiefs, 24-6 (S)
Chiefs, 37-21 (KC)
1980—Seahawks, 17-16 (KC)
Chiefs, 31-30 (S)
1981—Chiefs, 20-14 (S)
Chiefs, 40-13 (KC)
1983—Chiefs, 17-13 (KC)
Seahawks, 51-48 (S) OT
1984—Seahawks, 45-0 (S)
Chiefs, 34-7 (KC)
1985—Chiefs, 28-7 (KC)
Seahawks, 24-6 (S)
1986—Seahawks, 23-17 (S)
Chiefs, 27-7 (KC)
1987—Seahawks, 43-14 (S)
Chiefs, 41-20 (KC)
1988—Seahawks, 31-10 (S)
Chiefs, 27-24 (KC)
1989—Chiefs, 20-16 (S)
Chiefs, 20-10 (KC)
1990—Seahawks, 19-7 (S)
Seahawks, 17-16 (KC)
1991—Chiefs, 20-13 (S)
Chiefs, 19-6 (S)
1992—Chiefs, 26-7 (KC)
Chiefs, 24-14 (S)
1993—Chiefs, 31-16 (S)
Chiefs, 34-24 (KC)
1994—Chiefs, 38-23 (KC)
Seahawks, 10-9 (S)
1995—Chiefs, 34-10 (S)
Chiefs, 26-3 (KC)

1996—Chiefs, 35-17 (S)
Chiefs, 34-16 (KC)
1997—Chiefs, 20-17 (KC) OT
Chiefs, 19-14 (S)
1998—Chiefs, 17-6 (KC)
Seahawks, 24-12 (S)
1999—Seahawks, 31-19 (KC)
Seahawks, 23-14 (S)
2000—Chiefs, 24-17 (KC)
Chiefs, 24-19 (S)
2001—Chiefs, 19-7 (KC)
Seahawks, 21-18 (S)
2002—Seahawks, 39-32 (S)
(RS Pts.—Chiefs 1,108, Seahawks 905)
KANSAS CITY vs. TAMPA BAY
RS: Chiefs lead series, 5-4
1976—Chiefs, 28-19 (TB)
1978—Buccaneers, 30-13 (KC)
1979—Buccaneers, 3-0 (TB)
1981—Chiefs, 19-10 (KC)
1984—Chiefs, 24-20 (KC)
1986—Chiefs, 27-20 (KC)
1993—Chiefs, 27-3 (TB)
1999—Buccaneers, 17-10 (TB)
2004—Buccaneers, 34-31 (TB)
(RS Pts.—Chiefs 179, Buccaneers 156)
*KANSAS CITY vs. **TENNESSEE
RS: Chiefs lead series, 25-18
PS: Chiefs lead series, 2-0
1960—Oilers, 20-10 (H)
Texans, 24-0 (D)
1961—Texans, 26-21 (D)
Oilers, 38-7 (H)
1962—Texans, 31-7 (H)
Oilers, 14-6 (D)
***Texans, 20-17 (H) OT
1963—Chiefs, 28-7 (KC)
Oilers, 28-7 (H)
1964—Chiefs, 28-7 (KC)
Chiefs, 28-19 (H)
1965—Chiefs, 52-21 (KC)
Oilers, 38-36 (H)
1966—Chiefs, 48-23 (KC)
1967—Chiefs, 25-20 (H)
Oilers, 24-19 (KC)
1968—Chiefs, 26-21 (H)
Chiefs, 24-10 (KC)
1969—Chiefs, 24-0 (KC)
1970—Chiefs, 24-9 (KC)
1971—Chiefs, 20-16 (H)
1973—Chiefs, 38-14 (KC)
1974—Chiefs, 17-7 (H)
1975—Oilers, 17-13 (KC)
1977—Oilers, 34-20 (H)
1978—Chiefs, 20-17 (KC)
1979—Oilers, 20-6 (H)
1980—Chiefs, 21-20 (KC)
1981—Chiefs, 23-10 (KC)
1983—Chiefs, 13-10 (H) OT
1984—Chiefs, 17-16 (KC)
1985—Oilers, 23-20 (H)
1986—Chiefs, 27-13 (KC)
1988—Oilers, 7-6 (H)
1989—Chiefs, 34-0 (KC)
1990—Oilers, 27-10 (KC)
1991—Oilers, 17-7 (H)
1992—Oilers, 23-20 (H) OT
1993—Oilers, 30-0 (H)
****Chiefs, 28-20 (H)
1994—Chiefs, 31-9 (H)

1995—Chiefs, 20-13 (KC)
1996—Chiefs, 20-19 (H)
2000—Titans, 17-14 (T) OT
2004—Chiefs, 49-38 (T)
(RS Pts.—Chiefs 935, Titans 748)
(PS Pts.—Chiefs 48, Titans 37)
*Franchise in Dallas prior to 1963 and known as Texans
**Franchise in Houston prior to 1997; known as Oilers prior to 1999
***AFL Championship
****AFC Divisional Playoff

KANSAS CITY vs. WASHINGTON
RS: Chiefs lead series, 6-1
1971—Chiefs, 27-20 (KC)
1976—Chiefs, 33-30 (W)
1983—Redskins, 27-12 (W)
1992—Chiefs, 35-16 (KC)
1995—Chiefs, 24-3 (KC)
2001—Chiefs, 45-13 (W)
2005—Chiefs, 28-21, (KC)
(RS Pts.—Chiefs 204, Redskins 130)

MIAMI vs. ARIZONA
RS: Dolphins lead series, 8-1;
See Arizona vs. Miami
MIAMI vs. ATLANTA
RS: Dolphins lead series, 7-3;
See Atlanta vs. Miami
MIAMI vs. BALTIMORE
RS: Dolphins lead series, 4-1
PS: Ravens lead series, 1-0;
See Baltimore vs. Miami
MIAMI vs. BUFFALO
RS: Dolphins lead series, 49-30-1
PS: Bills lead series, 3-1;
See Buffalo vs. Miami
MIAMI vs. CAROLINA
RS: Dolphins lead series, 3-0;
See Carolina vs. Miami
MIAMI vs. CHICAGO
RS: Dolphins lead series, 6-3;
See Chicago vs. Miami
MIAMI vs. CINCINNATI
RS: Dolphins lead series, 12-4
PS: Dolphins lead series, 1-0;
See Cincinnati vs. Miami
MIAMI vs. CLEVELAND
RS: Dolphins lead series, 7-5
PS: Dolphins lead series, 2-0;
See Cleveland vs. Miami
MIAMI vs. DALLAS
RS: Dolphins lead series, 7-3
PS: Cowboys lead series, 1-0;
See Dallas vs. Miami
MIAMI vs. DENVER
RS: Dolphins lead series, 10-3-1
PS: Broncos lead series, 1-0;
See Denver vs. Miami
MIAMI vs. DETROIT
RS: Dolphins lead series, 6-2;
See Detroit vs. Miami
MIAMI vs. GREEN BAY
RS: Dolphins lead series, 9-2;
See Green Bay vs. Miami
MIAMI vs. HOUSTON
RS: Texans lead series, 1-0;
See Houston vs. Miami
MIAMI vs. INDIANAPOLIS
RS: Dolphins lead series, 44-22

PS: Dolphins lead series, 2-0;
See Indianapolis vs. Miami
MIAMI vs. JACKSONVILLE
RS: Series tied, 1-1
PS: Jaguars lead series, 1-0;
See Jacksonville vs. Miami
MIAMI vs. KANSAS CITY
RS: Chiefs lead series, 12-10
PS: Dolphins lead series, 3-0;
See Kansas City vs. Miami
MIAMI vs. MINNESOTA
RS: Series tied, 4-4
PS: Dolphins lead series, 1-0
1972—Dolphins, 16-14 (Minn)
1973—*Dolphins, 24-7 (Houston)
1976—Vikings, 29-7 (Mia)
1979—Dolphins, 27-12 (Minn)
1982—Dolphins, 22-14 (Mia)
1988—Dolphins, 24-7 (Mia)
1994—Vikings, 38-35 (Minn)
2000—Vikings, 13-7 (Minn)
2002—Vikings, 20-17 (Minn)
(RS Pts.—Dolphins 155, Vikings 147)
(PS Pts.—Dolphins 24, Vikings 7)
*Super Bowl VIII
MIAMI vs. *NEW ENGLAND
RS: Dolphins lead series, 46-32
PS: Patriots lead series, 2-1
1966—Patriots, 20-14 (M)
1967—Patriots, 41-10 (B)
        Dolphins, 41-32 (M)
1968—Dolphins, 34-10 (B)
        Dolphins, 38-7 (M)
1969—Dolphins, 17-16 (B)
        Patriots, 38-23 (Tampa)
1970—Patriots, 27-14 (B)
        Dolphins, 37-20 (M)
1971—Dolphins, 41-3 (M)
        Patriots, 34-13 (NE)
1972—Dolphins, 52-0 (M)
        Dolphins, 37-21 (NE)
1973—Dolphins, 44-23 (M)
        Dolphins, 30-14 (M)
1974—Patriots, 34-24 (NE)
        Dolphins, 34-27 (M)
1975—Dolphins, 22-14 (NE)
        Dolphins, 20-7 (M)
1976—Patriots, 30-14 (NE)
        Dolphins, 10-3 (M)
1977—Dolphins, 17-5 (M)
        Patriots, 14-10 (NE)
1978—Patriots, 33-24 (NE)
        Dolphins, 23-3 (M)
1979—Patriots, 28-13 (NE)
        Dolphins, 39-24 (M)
1980—Patriots, 34-0 (NE)
        Dolphins, 16-13 (M) OT
1981—Dolphins, 30-27 (NE) OT
        Dolphins, 24-14 (M)
1982—Patriots, 3-0 (NE)
        **Dolphins, 28-13 (M)
1983—Dolphins, 34-24 (M)
        Patriots, 17-6 (NE)
1984—Dolphins, 28-7 (M)
        Dolphins, 44-24 (NE)
1985—Patriots, 17-13 (NE)
        Dolphins, 30-27 (M)
        ***Patriots, 31-14 (M)
1986—Patriots, 34-7 (NE)
        Patriots, 34-27 (M)

1987—Patriots, 28-21 (NE)
        Patriots, 24-10 (M)
1988—Patriots, 21-10 (NE)
        Patriots, 6-3 (M)
1989—Dolphins, 24-10 (NE)
        Dolphins, 31-10 (M)
1990—Dolphins, 27-24 (NE)
        Dolphins, 17-10 (M)
1991—Dolphins, 20-10 (NE)
        Dolphins, 30-20 (M)
1992—Dolphins, 38-17 (M)
        Dolphins, 16-13 (NE) OT
1993—Dolphins, 17-13 (M)
        Patriots, 33-27 (NE) OT
1994—Dolphins, 39-35 (M)
        Dolphins, 23-3 (NE)
1995—Dolphins, 20-3 (NE)
        Patriots, 34-17 (M)
1996—Dolphins, 24-10 (M)
        Patriots, 42-23 (NE)
1997—Patriots, 27-24 (NE)
        Patriots, 14-12 (M)
        **Patriots, 17-3 (NE)
1998—Dolphins, 12-9 (M) OT
        Patriots, 26-23 (NE)
1999—Dolphins, 31-30 (NE)
        Dolphins, 27-17 (M)
2000—Dolphins, 10-3 (M)
        Dolphins, 27-24 (NE)
2001—Dolphins, 30-10 (M)
        Patriots, 20-13 (NE)
2002—Dolphins, 26-13 (M)
        Patriots, 27-24 (NE) OT
2003—Patriots, 19-13 (M) OT
        Patriots, 12-0 (NE)
2004—Patriots, 24-10 (NE)
        Dolphins, 29-28 (M)
2005—Patriots, 23-16 (M)
        Dolphins, 28-26 (NE)
(RS Pts.—Dolphins 1,746, Patriots 1,521)
(PS Pts.—Patriots 61, Dolphins 45)
*Franchise in Boston prior to 1971
**AFC First-Round Playoff
***AFC Championship
MIAMI vs. NEW ORLEANS
RS: Dolphins lead series, 6-3
1970—Dolphins, 21-10 (M)
1974—Dolphins, 21-0 (NO)
1980—Dolphins, 21-16 (M)
1983—Saints, 17-7 (NO)
1986—Dolphins, 31-27 (NO)
1992—Saints, 24-13 (NO)
1995—Saints, 33-30 (NO)
1998—Dolphins, 30-10 (M)
2005—Dolphins, 21-6 (Baton Rouge)
(RS Pts.—Dolphins 195, Saints 143)
MIAMI vs. N.Y. GIANTS
RS: Giants lead series, 3-2
1972—Dolphins, 23-13 (NY)
1990—Giants, 20-3 (NY)
1993—Giants, 19-14 (M)
1996—Giants, 17-7 (M)
2003—Dolphins, 23-10 (NY)
(RS Pts.—Giants 79, Dolphins 70)
MIAMI vs. N.Y. JETS
RS: Jets lead series, 41-38-1
PS: Dolphins lead series, 1-0
1966—Jets, 19-14 (M)
        Jets, 30-13 (NY)
1967—Jets, 29-7 (NY)

Jets, 33-14 (M)
1968—Jets, 35-17 (NY)
Jets, 31-7 (M)
1969—Jets, 34-31 (NY)
Jets, 27-9 (M)
1970—Dolphins, 20-6 (NY)
Dolphins, 16-10 (M)
1971—Jets, 14-10 (M)
Dolphins, 30-14 (NY)
1972—Dolphins, 27-17 (NY)
Dolphins, 28-24 (M)
1973—Dolphins, 31-3 (M)
Dolphins, 24-14 (NY)
1974—Dolphins, 21-17 (M)
Jets, 17-14 (NY)
1975—Dolphins, 43-0 (NY)
Dolphins, 27-7 (M)
1976—Dolphins, 16-0 (M)
Dolphins, 27-7 (NY)
1977—Dolphins, 21-17 (M)
Dolphins, 14-10 (NY)
1978—Jets, 33-20 (NY)
Jets, 24-13 (M)
1979—Jets, 33-27 (NY)
Jets, 27-24 (M)
1980—Jets, 17-14 (NY)
Jets, 24-17 (M)
1981—Tie, 28-28 (M) OT
Jets, 16-15 (NY)
1982—Dolphins, 45-28 (NY)
Dolphins, 20-19 (M)
*Dolphins, 14-0 (M)
1983—Dolphins, 32-14 (NY)
Dolphins, 34-14 (M)
1984—Dolphins, 31-17 (NY)
Dolphins, 28-17 (M)
1985—Jets, 23-7 (NY)
Dolphins, 21-17 (M)
1986—Jets, 51-45 (NY) OT
Dolphins, 45-3 (M)
1987—Jets, 37-31 (NY) OT
Dolphins, 37-28 (M)
1988—Jets, 44-30 (M)
Jets, 38-34 (NY)
1989—Jets, 40-33 (M)
Dolphins, 31-23 (NY)
1990—Dolphins, 20-16 (M)
Dolphins, 17-3 (NY)
1991—Jets, 41-23 (NY)
Jets, 23-20 (M) OT
1992—Jets, 26-14 (NY)
Dolphins, 19-17 (M)
1993—Jets, 24-14 (M)
Jets, 27-10 (NY)
1994—Dolphins, 28-14 (M)
Dolphins, 28-24 (NY)
1995—Dolphins, 52-14 (M)
Jets, 17-16 (NY)
1996—Dolphins, 36-27 (M)
Dolphins, 31-28 (NY)
1997—Dolphins, 31-20 (NY)
Dolphins, 24-17 (M)
1998—Jets, 20-9 (NY)
Jets, 21-16 (M)
1999—Jets, 28-20 (NY)
Jets, 38-31 (M)
2000—Jets, 40-37 (NY) OT
Jets, 20-3 (M)
2001—Jets, 21-17 (NY)
Jets, 24-0 (M)

2002—Dolphins, 30-3 (M)
Jets, 13-10 (NY)
2003—Dolphins, 21-10 (NY)
Dolphins, 23-21 (M)
2004—Jets, 17-9 (M)
Jets, 41-14 (NY)
2005—Jets, 17-7 (NY)
Dolphins, 24-20 (M)
(RS Pts.—Dolphins 1,797, Jets 1,722)
(PS Pts.—Dolphins 14, Jets 0)
*AFC Championship
MIAMI vs. *OAKLAND
RS: Raiders lead series, 15-11-1
PS: Raiders lead series, 3-1
1966—Raiders, 23-14 (M)
Raiders, 21-10 (O)
1967—Raiders, 31-17 (O)
1968—Raiders, 47-21 (M)
1969—Raiders, 20-17 (O)
Tie, 20-20 (M)
1970—Dolphins, 20-13 (M)
**Raiders, 21-14 (O)
1973—Raiders, 12-7 (O)
***Dolphins, 27-10 (M)
1974—**Raiders, 28-26 (O)
1975—Raiders, 31-21 (M)
1978—Dolphins, 23-6 (M)
1979—Raiders, 13-3 (O)
1980—Raiders, 16-10 (O)
1981—Raiders, 33-17 (M)
1983—Raiders, 27-14 (LA)
1984—Raiders, 45-34 (M)
1986—Raiders, 30-28 (M)
1988—Dolphins, 24-14 (LA)
1990—Raiders, 13-10 (M)
1992—Dolphins, 20-7 (M)
1994—Dolphins, 20-17 (M) OT
1996—Raiders, 17-7 (O)
1997—Dolphins, 34-16 (O)
1998—Dolphins, 27-17 (O)
1999—Dolphins, 16-9 (O)
2000—**Raiders, 27-0 (O)
2001—Dolphins, 18-15 (M)
2002—Dolphins, 23-17 (M)
2005—Dolphins, 33-21 (O)
(RS Pts.—Raiders 551, Dolphins 508)
(PS Pts.—Raiders 86, Dolphins 67)
*Franchise in Los Angeles from 1982-1994
**AFC Divisional Playoff
***AFC Championship
MIAMI vs. PHILADELPHIA
RS: Dolphins lead series, 7-4
1970—Eagles, 24-17 (P)
1975—Dolphins, 24-16 (M)
1978—Eagles, 17-3 (P)
1981—Dolphins, 13-10 (M)
1984—Dolphins, 24-23 (M)
1987—Dolphins, 28-10 (P)
1990—Dolphins, 23-20 (M) OT
1993—Dolphins, 19-14 (P)
1996—Eagles, 35-28 (P)
1999—Dolphins, 16-13 (M)
2003—Eagles, 34-27 (M)
(RS Pts.—Dolphins 222, Eagles 216)
MIAMI vs. PITTSBURGH
RS: Dolphins lead series, 9-8
PS: Dolphins lead series, 2-1
1971—Dolphins, 24-21 (M)
1972—*Dolphins, 21-17 (P)
1973—Dolphins, 30-26 (M)

1976—Steelers, 14-3 (P)
1979—**Steelers, 34-14 (P)
1980—Steelers, 23-10 (P)
1981—Dolphins, 30-10 (M)
1984—Dolphins, 31-7 (P)
*Dolphins, 45-28 (M)
1985—Dolphins, 24-20 (M)
1987—Dolphins, 35-24 (M)
1988—Steelers, 40-24 (P)
1989—Steelers, 34-14 (M)
1990—Dolphins, 28-6 (P)
1993—Steelers, 21-20 (M)
1994—Steelers, 16-13 (P) OT
1995—Dolphins, 23-10 (M)
1996—Steelers, 24-17 (M)
1998—Dolphins, 21-0 (M)
2004—Steelers, 13-3 (M)
(RS Pts.—Dolphins 350, Steelers 309)
(PS Pts.—Dolphins 80, Steelers 79)
*AFC Championship
**AFC Divisional Playoff
MIAMI vs. *ST. LOUIS
RS: Dolphins lead series, 8-2
1971—Dolphins, 20-14 (LA)
1976—Rams, 31-28 (M)
1980—Dolphins, 35-14 (LA)
1983—Dolphins, 30-14 (M)
1986—Dolphins, 37-31 (LA) OT
1992—Dolphins, 26-10 (M)
1995—Dolphins, 41-22 (StL)
1998—Dolphins, 14-0 (M)
2001—Rams, 42-10 (StL)
2004—Dolphins, 31-14 (M)
(RS Pts.—Dolphins 272, Rams 192)
*Franchise in Los Angeles prior to 1995
MIAMI vs. SAN DIEGO
RS: Dolphins lead series, 11-10
PS: Series tied, 2-2
1966—Chargers, 44-10 (SD)
1967—Chargers, 24-0 (SD)
Dolphins, 41-24 (M)
1968—Chargers, 34-28 (SD)
1969—Chargers, 21-14 (M)
1972—Dolphins, 24-10 (M)
1974—Dolphins, 28-21 (SD)
1977—Chargers, 14-13 (M)
1978—Dolphins, 28-21 (SD)
1980—Chargers, 27-24 (M) OT
1981—*Chargers, 41-38 (M) OT
1982—**Dolphins, 34-13 (M)
1984—Chargers, 34-28 (SD) OT
1986—Chargers, 50-28 (SD)
1988—Dolphins, 31-28 (M)
1991—Chargers, 38-30 (SD)
1992—*Dolphins, 31-0 (M)
1993—Chargers, 45-20 (SD)
1994—*Chargers, 22-21 (SD)
1995—Dolphins, 24-14 (SD)
1999—Dolphins, 12-9 (M)
2000—Dolphins, 17-7 (SD)
2002—Dolphins, 30-3 (M)
2003—Dolphins, 26-10 (Ariz)
2005—Dolphins, 23-21 (SD)
(RS Pts.—Chargers 499, Dolphins 479)
(PS Pts.—Dolphins 124, Chargers 76)
*AFC Divisional Playoff
**AFC Second-Round Playoff
MIAMI vs. SAN FRANCISCO
RS: Dolphins lead series, 5-4
PS: 49ers lead series, 1-0

1973—Dolphins, 21-13 (M)
1977—Dolphins, 19-15 (SF)
1980—Dolphins, 17-13 (M)
1983—Dolphins, 20-17 (SF)
1984—*49ers, 38-16 (Stanford)
1986—49ers, 31-16 (M)
1992—49ers, 27-3 (SF)
1995—49ers, 44-20 (M)
2001—49ers, 21-0 (SF)
2004—Dolphins, 24-17 (SF)
(RS Pts.—49ers 198, Dolphins 140)
(PS Pts.—49ers 30, Dolphins 16)
*Super Bowl XIX
MIAMI vs. SEATTLE
RS: Dolphins lead series, 6-3
PS: Dolphins lead series, 2-1
1977—Dolphins, 31-13 (M)
1979—Dolphins, 19-10 (M)
1983—*Seahawks, 27-20 (M)
1984—*Dolphins, 31-10 (M)
1987—Seahawks, 24-20 (S)
1990—Dolphins, 24-17 (M)
1992—Dolphins, 19-17 (S)
1996—Seahawks, 22-15 (M)
1999—**Dolphins, 20-17 (S)
2000—Dolphins, 23-0 (M)
2001—Dolphins, 24-20 (S)
2004—Seahawks, 24-17 (S)
(RS Pts.—Dolphins 192, Seahawks 147)
(PS Pts.—Dolphins 71, Seahawks 54)
*AFC Divisional Playoff
**AFC First-Round Playoff
MIAMI vs. TAMPA BAY
RS: Series tied, 4-4
1976—Dolphins, 23-20 (TB)
1982—Buccaneers, 23-17 (TB)
1985—Dolphins, 41-38 (M)
1988—Dolphins, 17-14 (TB)
1991—Dolphins, 33-14 (M)
1997—Buccaneers, 31-21 (TB)
2000—Buccaneers, 16-13 (M)
2005—Buccaneers, 27-13 (TB)
(RS Pts.—Buccaneers 183, Dolphins 178)
MIAMI vs. *TENNESSEE
RS: Dolphins lead series, 16-13
PS: Titans lead series, 1-0
1966—Dolphins, 20-13 (H)
      Dolphins, 29-28 (M)
1967—Oilers, 17-14 (H)
      Oilers, 41-10 (M)
1968—Oilers, 24-10 (M)
      Dolphins, 24-7 (H)
1969—Oilers, 22-10 (H)
      Oilers, 32-7 (M)
1970—Dolphins, 20-10 (H)
1972—Dolphins, 34-13 (M)
1975—Oilers, 20-19 (H)
1977—Dolphins, 27-7 (M)
1978—Oilers, 35-30 (H)
      **Oilers, 17-9 (M)
1979—Oilers, 9-6 (H)
1981—Dolphins, 16-10 (H)
1983—Dolphins, 24-17 (H)
1984—Dolphins, 28-10 (M)
1985—Oilers, 26-23 (H)
1986—Dolphins, 28-7 (M)
1989—Oilers, 39-7 (H)
1991—Oilers, 17-13 (M)
1992—Dolphins, 19-16 (M)
1996—Dolphins, 23-20 (H)

1997—Dolphins, 16-13 (M) OT
1999—Dolphins, 17-0 (M)
2001—Dolphins, 31-23 (T)
2003—Titans, 31-7 (T)
2004—Titans, 17-7 (M)
2005—Dolphins, 24-10 (M)
(RS Pts.—Dolphins 543, Titans 534)
(PS Pts.—Titans 17, Dolphins 9)
*Franchise in Houston prior to 1997;
known as Oilers prior to 1999
**AFC First-Round Playoff
MIAMI vs. WASHINGTON
RS: Dolphins lead series, 6-3
PS: Series tied, 1-1
1972—*Dolphins, 14-7 (Los Angeles)
1974—Redskins, 20-17 (W)
1978—Dolphins, 16-0 (W)
1981—Dolphins, 13-10 (M)
1982—**Redskins, 27-17 (Pasadena)
1984—Dolphins, 35-17 (W)
1987—Dolphins, 23-21 (M)
1990—Redskins, 42-20 (W)
1993—Dolphins, 17-10 (M)
1999—Redskins, 21-10 (W)
2003—Dolphins, 24-23 (M)
(RS Pts.—Dolphins 175, Redskins 164)
(PS Pts.—Redskins 34, Dolphins 31)
*Super Bowl VII
**Super Bowl XVII

MINNESOTA vs. ARIZONA
RS: Cardinals lead series, 9-8
PS: Vikings lead series, 2-0;
See Arizona vs. Minnesota
MINNESOTA vs. ATLANTA
RS: Vikings lead series, 14-8
PS: Series tied, 1-1;
See Atlanta vs. Minnesota
MINNESOTA vs. BALTIMORE
RS: Ravens lead series, 2-1;
See Baltimore vs. Minnesota
MINNESOTA vs. BUFFALO
RS: Vikings lead series, 7-3;
See Buffalo vs. Minnesota
MINNESOTA vs. CAROLINA
RS: Series tied, 3-3;
See Carolina vs. Minnesota
MINNESOTA vs. CHICAGO
RS: Vikings lead series, 48-39-2
PS: Bears lead series, 1-0;
See Chicago vs. Minnesota
MINNESOTA vs. CINCINNATI
RS: Series tied, 5-5;
See Cincinnati vs. Minnesota
MINNESOTA vs. CLEVELAND
RS: Vikings lead series, 9-3
PS: Vikings lead series, 1-0;
See Cleveland vs. Minnesota
MINNESOTA vs. DALLAS
RS: Vikings lead series, 10-9
PS: Cowboys lead series, 4-2;
See Dallas vs. Minnesota
MINNESOTA vs. DENVER
RS: Vikings lead series, 7-4;
See Denver vs. Minnesota
MINNESOTA vs. DETROIT
RS: Vikings lead series, 58-29-2;
See Detroit vs. Minnesota
MINNESOTA vs. GREEN BAY
RS: Series tied, 44-44-1

PS: Vikings lead series, 1-0;
See Green Bay vs. Minnesota
MINNESOTA vs. HOUSTON
RS: Vikings lead series, 1-0;
See Houston vs. Minnesota
MINNESOTA vs. INDIANAPOLIS
RS: Colts lead series, 13-7-1
PS: Colts lead series, 1-0;
See Indianapolis vs. Minnesota
MINNESOTA vs. JACKSONVILLE
RS: Vikings lead series, 2-1;
See Jacksonville vs. Minnesota
MINNESOTA vs. KANSAS CITY
RS: Series tied, 4-4
PS: Chiefs lead series, 1-0;
See Kansas City vs. Minnesota
MINNESOTA vs. MIAMI
RS: Series tied, 4-4
PS: Dolphins lead series, 1-0;
See Miami vs. Minnesota
MINNESOTA vs. *NEW ENGLAND
RS: Patriots lead series, 5-4
1970—Vikings, 35-14 (B)
1974—Patriots, 17-14 (M)
1979—Patriots, 27-23 (NE)
1988—Vikings, 36-6 (M)
1991—Patriots, 26-23 (NE) OT
1994—Patriots, 26-20 (NE) OT
1997—Vikings, 23-18 (M)
2000—Vikings, 21-13 (NE)
2002—Patriots, 24-17 (NE)
(RS Pts.—Vikings 212, Patriots 171)
*Franchise in Boston prior to 1971
MINNESOTA vs. NEW ORLEANS
RS: Vikings lead series, 17-7
PS: Vikings lead series, 2-0
1968—Saints, 20-17 (NO)
1970—Vikings, 26-0 (M)
1971—Vikings, 23-10 (NO)
1972—Vikings, 37-6 (M)
1974—Vikings, 29-9 (M)
1975—Vikings, 20-7 (NO)
1976—Vikings, 40-9 (NO)
1978—Saints, 31-24 (NO)
1980—Vikings, 23-20 (NO)
1981—Vikings, 20-10 (M)
1983—Saints, 17-16 (NO)
1985—Saints, 30-23 (M)
1986—Vikings, 33-17 (M)
1987—*Vikings, 44-10 (NO)
1988—Vikings, 45-3 (M)
1990—Vikings, 32-3 (M)
1991—Saints, 26-0 (NO)
1993—Saints, 17-14 (M)
1994—Vikings, 21-20 (M)
1995—Vikings, 43-24 (M)
1998—Vikings, 31-24 (M)
2000—**Vikings, 34-16 (M)
2001—Saints, 28-15 (NO)
2002—Vikings, 32-31 (NO)
2004—Vikings, 38-31 (NO)
2005—Vikings, 33-16 (M)
(RS Pts.—Vikings 635, Saints 409)
(PS Pts.—Vikings 78, Saints 26)
*NFC First-Round Playoff
**NFC Divisional Playoff
MINNESOTA vs. N.Y. GIANTS
RS: Vikings lead series, 10-8
PS: Giants lead series, 2-1
1964—Vikings, 30-21 (NY)

1965—Vikings, 40-14 (M)
1967—Vikings, 27-24 (M)
1969—Giants, 24-23 (NY)
1971—Vikings, 17-10 (NY)
1973—Vikings, 31-7 (New Haven)
1976—Vikings, 24-7 (M)
1986—Giants, 22-20 (M)
1989—Giants, 24-14 (NY)
1990—Giants, 23-15 (NY)
1993—*Giants, 17-10 (NY)
1994—Vikings, 27-10 (NY)
1996—Giants, 15-10 (NY)
1997—*Vikings, 23-22 (NY)
1999—Vikings, 34-17 (NY)
2000—**Giants, 41-0 (NY)
2001—Vikings, 28-16 (M)
2002—Giants, 27-20 (M)
2003—Giants, 29-17 (M)
2004—Giants, 34-13 (M)
2005—Vikings, 24-21 (NY)
(RS Pts.—Vikings 414, Giants 345)
(PS Pts.—Giants 80, Vikings 33)
*NFC First-Round Playoff
**NFC Championship
MINNESOTA vs. N.Y. JETS
RS: Jets lead series, 6-1
1970—Jets, 20-10 (NY)
1975—Vikings, 29-21 (M)
1979—Jets, 14-7 (NY)
1982—Jets, 42-14 (M)
1994—Jets, 31-21 (M)
1997—Jets, 23-21 (NY)
2002—Jets, 20-7 (NY)
(RS Pts.—Jets 171, Vikings 109)
MINNESOTA vs. *OAKLAND
RS: Raiders lead series, 8-3
PS: Raiders lead series, 1-0
1973—Vikings, 24-16 (M)
1976—**Raiders, 32-14 (Pasadena)
1977—Raiders, 35-13 (O)
1978—Raiders, 27-20 (O)
1981—Raiders, 36-10 (M)
1984—Raiders, 23-20 (LA)
1987—Vikings, 31-20 (M)
1990—Raiders, 28-24 (M)
1993—Raiders, 24-7 (LA)
1996—Vikings, 16-13 (O) OT
1999—Raiders, 22-17 (M)
2003—Raiders, 28-18 (O)
(RS Pts.—Raiders 272, Vikings 200)
(PS Pts.—Raiders 32, Vikings 14)
*Franchise in Los Angeles from 1982-1994
**Super Bowl XI
MINNESOTA vs. PHILADELPHIA
RS: Vikings lead series, 11-8
PS: Eagles lead series, 2-0
1962—Vikings, 31-21 (M)
1963—Vikings, 34-13 (P)
1968—Vikings, 24-17 (P)
1971—Vikings, 13-0 (P)
1973—Vikings, 28-21 (M)
1976—Vikings, 31-12 (P)
1978—Vikings, 28-27 (M)
1980—Eagles, 42-7 (M)
      *Eagles, 31-16 (P)
1981—Vikings, 35-23 (M)
1984—Eagles, 19-17 (P)
1985—Vikings, 28-23 (P)
      Eagles, 37-35 (M)
1988—Vikings, 23-21 (M)

1989—Eagles, 10-9 (P)
1990—Eagles, 32-24 (P)
1992—Eagles, 28-17 (P)
1997—Vikings, 28-19 (M)
2001—Eagles, 48-17 (P)
2004—Eagles, 27-16 (P)
      *Eagles, 27-14 (P)
(RS Pts.—Vikings 445, Eagles 440)
(PS Pts.—Eagles 58, Vikings 30)
*NFC Divisional Playoff
MINNESOTA vs. PITTSBURGH
RS: Vikings lead series, 8-6
PS: Steelers lead series, 1-0
1962—Steelers, 39-31 (P)
1964—Vikings, 30-10 (M)
1967—Vikings, 41-27 (M)
1969—Vikings, 52-14 (M)
1972—Steelers, 23-10 (P)
1974—*Steelers, 16-6 (New Orleans)
1976—Vikings, 17-6 (M)
1980—Steelers, 23-17 (M)
1983—Vikings, 17-14 (P)
1986—Vikings, 31-7 (M)
1989—Steelers, 27-14 (P)
1992—Vikings, 6-3 (P)
1995—Vikings, 44-24 (P)
2001—Steelers, 21-16 (P)
2005—Steelers, 18-3 (M)
(RS Pts.—Vikings 329, Steelers 256)
(PS Pts.—Steelers 16, Vikings 6)
*Super Bowl IX
MINNESOTA vs. *ST. LOUIS
RS: Vikings lead series, 17-13-2
PS: Vikings lead series, 5-2
1961—Rams, 31-17 (LA)
      Vikings, 42-21 (M)
1962—Vikings, 38-14 (LA)
      Tie, 24-24 (M)
1963—Rams, 27-24 (LA)
      Vikings, 21-13 (M)
1964—Rams, 22-13 (LA)
      Vikings, 34-13 (M)
1965—Vikings, 38-35 (LA)
      Vikings, 24-13 (M)
1966—Vikings, 35-7 (M)
      Rams, 21-6 (LA)
1967—Rams, 39-3 (LA)
1968—Rams, 31-3 (M)
1969—Vikings, 20-13 (LA)
      **Vikings, 23-20 (M)
1970—Vikings, 13-3 (M)
1972—Vikings, 45-41 (LA)
1973—Vikings, 10-9 (M)
1974—Rams, 20-17 (LA)
      ***Vikings, 14-10 (M)
1976—Tie, 10-10 (M) OT
      ***Vikings, 24-13 (M)
1977—Rams, 35-3 (LA)
      ****Vikings, 14-7 (LA)
1978—Rams, 34-17 (M)
      ****Rams, 34-10 (LA)
1979—Rams, 27-21 (LA) OT
1985—Rams, 13-10 (LA)
1987—Vikings, 21-16 (LA)
1988—*****Vikings, 28-17 (M)
1989—Vikings, 23-21 (M) OT
1991—Vikings, 20-14 (M)
1992—Vikings, 31-17 (LA)
1998—Vikings, 38-31 (StL)
1999—****Rams, 49-37 (StL)

2000—Rams, 40-29 (StL)
2003—Rams, 48-17 (StL)
2005—Vikings, 27-13 (M)
(RS Pts.—Rams 716, Vikings 694)
(PS Pts.—Rams 150, Vikings 150)
*Franchise in Los Angeles prior to 1995
**Conference Championship
***NFC Championship
****NFC Divisional Playoff
*****NFC First-Round Playoff
MINNESOTA vs. SAN DIEGO
RS: Chargers lead series, 5-4
1971—Chargers, 30-14 (SD)
1975—Vikings, 28-13 (M)
1978—Chargers, 13-7 (M)
1981—Vikings, 33-31 (SD)
1984—Chargers, 42-13 (M)
1985—Vikings, 21-17 (M)
1993—Chargers, 30-17 (M)
1999—Vikings, 35-27 (M)
2003—Chargers, 42-28 (SD)
(RS Pts.—Chargers 245, Vikings 196)
MINNESOTA vs. SAN FRANCISCO
RS: Vikings lead series, 18-17-1
PS: 49ers lead series, 4-1
1961—49ers, 38-24 (M)
      49ers, 38-28 (SF)
1962—49ers, 21-7 (SF)
      49ers, 35-12 (M)
1963—Vikings, 24-20 (SF)
      Vikings, 45-14 (M)
1964—Vikings, 27-22 (SF)
      Vikings, 24-7 (M)
1965—Vikings, 42-41 (SF)
      49ers, 45-24 (M)
1966—Tie, 20-20 (SF)
      Vikings, 28-3 (SF)
1967—49ers, 27-21 (M)
1968—Vikings, 30-20 (SF)
1969—Vikings, 10-7 (M)
1970—*49ers, 17-14 (M)
1971—49ers, 13-9 (M)
1972—49ers, 20-17 (SF)
1973—Vikings, 17-13 (SF)
1975—Vikings, 27-17 (M)
1976—49ers, 20-16 (M)
1977—Vikings, 28-27 (M)
1979—Vikings, 28-22 (M)
1983—49ers, 48-17 (M)
1984—49ers, 51-7 (SF)
1985—Vikings, 28-21 (M)
1986—Vikings, 27-24 (SF) OT
1987—*Vikings, 36-24 (SF)
1988—49ers, 24-21 (SF)
      *49ers, 34-9 (SF)
1989—*49ers, 41-13 (SF)
1990—49ers, 20-17 (M)
1991—Vikings, 17-14 (M)
1992—49ers, 20-17 (M)
1993—49ers, 38-19 (M)
1994—Vikings, 21-14 (M)
1995—49ers, 37-30 (M)
1997—49ers, 28-17 (SF)
      *49ers, 38-22 (SF)
1999—Vikings, 40-16 (M)
2003—Vikings, 35-7 (M)
(RS Pts.—49ers 852, Vikings 821)
(PS Pts.—49ers 154, Vikings 94)
*NFC Divisional Playoff

MINNESOTA vs. SEATTLE
RS: Seahawks lead series, 6-3
1976—Vikings, 27-21 (M)
1978—Seahawks, 29-28 (S)
1984—Seahawks, 20-12 (M)
1987—Seahawks, 28-17 (S)
1990—Vikings, 24-21 (S)
1996—Seahawks, 42-23 (S)
2002—Seahawks, 48-23 (S)
2003—Vikings, 34-7 (M)
2004—Seahawks, 27-23 (M)
(RS Pts.—Seahawks 243, Vikings 211)
MINNESOTA vs. TAMPA BAY
RS: Vikings lead series, 31-19
1977—Vikings, 9-3 (TB)
1978—Buccaneers, 16-10 (M)
　　　Vikings, 24-7 (TB)
1979—Buccaneers, 12-10 (M)
　　　Vikings, 23-22 (TB)
1980—Vikings, 38-30 (M)
　　　Vikings, 21-10 (TB)
1981—Buccaneers, 21-13 (TB)
　　　Vikings, 25-10 (M)
1982—Vikings, 17-10 (M)
1983—Vikings, 19-16 (TB) OT
　　　Buccaneers, 17-12 (M)
1984—Buccaneers, 35-31 (TB)
　　　Vikings, 27-24 (M)
1985—Vikings, 31-16 (TB)
　　　Vikings, 26-7 (M)
1986—Vikings, 23-10 (TB)
　　　Vikings, 45-13 (M)
1987—Buccaneers, 20-10 (TB)
　　　Vikings, 23-17 (M)
1988—Vikings, 14-13 (M)
　　　Vikings, 49-20 (TB)
1989—Vikings, 17-3 (M)
　　　Vikings, 24-10 (TB)
1990—Buccaneers, 23-20 (M) OT
　　　Buccaneers, 26-13 (TB)
1991—Vikings, 28-13 (M)
　　　Vikings, 26-24 (TB)
1992—Vikings, 26-20 (M)
　　　Vikings, 35-7 (TB)
1993—Vikings, 15-0 (M)
　　　Buccaneers, 23-10 (TB)
1994—Vikings, 36-13 (M)
　　　Buccaneers, 20-17 (M) OT
1995—Buccaneers, 20-17 (TB) OT
　　　Vikings, 31-17 (M)
1996—Buccaneers, 24-13 (TB)
　　　Vikings, 21-10 (M)
1997—Buccaneers, 28-14 (M)
　　　Vikings, 10-6 (TB)
1998—Vikings, 31-7 (M)
　　　Buccaneers, 27-24 (TB)
1999—Vikings, 21-14 (M)
　　　Buccaneers, 24-17 (TB)
2000—Vikings, 30-23 (M)
　　　Buccaneers, 41-13 (TB)
2001—Vikings, 20-16 (M)
　　　Buccaneers, 41-14 (TB)
2002—Buccaneers, 38-24 (TB)
2005—Buccaneers, 24-13 (M)
(RS Pts.—Vikings 1,080, Buccaneers 891)
MINNESOTA vs. *TENNESSEE
RS: Vikings lead series, 7-3
1974—Vikings, 51-10 (M)
1980—Oilers, 20-16 (H)
1983—Vikings, 34-14 (M)

1986—Oilers, 23-10 (H)
1989—Vikings, 38-7 (M)
1992—Oilers, 17-13 (M)
1995—Vikings, 23-17 (M) OT
1998—Vikings, 26-16 (T)
2001—Vikings, 42-24 (M)
2004—Vikings, 20-3 (M)
(RS Pts.—Vikings 273, Titans 151)
*Franchise in Houston prior to 1997;
known as Oilers prior to 1999
MINNESOTA vs. WASHINGTON
RS: Redskins lead series, 7-5
PS: Redskins lead series, 3-2
1968—Vikings, 27-14 (M)
1970—Vikings, 19-10 (W)
1972—Redskins, 24-21 (M)
1973—*Vikings, 27-20 (M)
1975—Redskins, 31-30 (W)
1976—*Vikings, 35-20 (M)
1980—Vikings, 39-14 (M)
1982—**Redskins, 21-7 (W)
1984—Redskins, 31-17 (M)
1986—Redskins, 44-38 (W) OT
1987—Redskins, 27-24 (M) OT
　　　***Redskins, 17-10 (W)
1992—Redskins, 15-13 (M)
　　　****Redskins, 24-7 (M)
1993—Vikings, 14-9 (W)
1998—Vikings, 41-7 (M)
2004—Redskins, 21-18 (W)
(RS Pts.—Vikings 301, Redskins 247)
(PS Pts.—Redskins 102, Vikings 86)
*NFC Divisional Playoff
**NFC Second-Round Playoff
***NFC Championship
****NFC First-Round Playoff

NEW ENGLAND vs. ARIZONA
RS: Cardinals lead series, 6-5;
See Arizona vs. New England
NEW ENGLAND vs. ATLANTA
RS: Falcons lead series, 6-5;
See Atlanta vs. New England
NEW ENGLAND vs. BALTIMORE
RS: Patriots lead series, 3-0;
See Baltimore vs. New England
NEW ENGLAND vs. BUFFALO
RS: Patriots lead series, 50-40-1
PS: Patriots lead series, 1-0;
See Buffalo vs. New England
NEW ENGLAND vs. CAROLINA
RS: Panthers lead series, 2-1
PS: Patriots lead series, 1-0;
See Carolina vs. New England
NEW ENGLAND vs. CHICAGO
RS: Patriots lead series, 6-3
PS: Bears lead series, 1-0;
See Chicago vs. New England
NEW ENGLAND vs. CINCINNATI
RS: Patriots lead series, 11-8;
See Cincinnati vs. New England
NEW ENGLAND vs. CLEVELAND
RS: Browns lead series, 11-8
PS: Browns lead series, 1-0;
See Cleveland vs. New England
NEW ENGLAND vs. DALLAS
RS: Cowboys lead series, 7-2;
See Dallas vs. New England
NEW ENGLAND vs. DENVER
RS: Broncos lead series, 23-15

PS: Broncos lead series, 2-0;
See Denver vs. New England
NEW ENGLAND vs. DETROIT
RS: Series tied, 4-4;
See Detroit vs. New England
NEW ENGLAND vs. GREEN BAY
RS: Packers lead series, 4-3
PS: Packers lead series, 1-0;
See Green Bay vs. New England
NEW ENGLAND vs. HOUSTON
RS: Patriots lead series, 1-0;
See Houston vs. New England
NEW ENGLAND vs. INDIANAPOLIS
RS: Patriots lead series, 41-25
PS: Patriots lead series, 2-0;
See Indianapolis vs. New England
NEW ENGLAND vs. JACKSONVILLE
RS: Patriots lead series, 3-0
PS: Patriots lead series, 2-1;
See Jacksonville vs. New England
NEW ENGLAND vs. KANSAS CITY
RS: Chiefs lead series, 16-11-3;
See Kansas City vs. New England
NEW ENGLAND vs. MIAMI
RS: Dolphins lead series, 46-32
PS: Patriots lead series, 2-1;
See Miami vs. New England
NEW ENGLAND vs. MINNESOTA
RS: Patriots lead series, 5-4;
See Minnesota vs. New England
NEW ENGLAND vs. NEW ORLEANS
RS: Patriots lead series, 8-3
1972—Patriots, 17-10 (NO)
1976—Patriots, 27-6 (NE)
1980—Patriots, 38-27 (NO)
1983—Patriots, 7-0 (NE)
1986—Patriots, 21-20 (NO)
1989—Saints, 28-24 (NE)
1992—Saints, 31-14 (NE)
1995—Saints, 31-17 (NE)
1998—Patriots, 30-27 (NO)
2001—Patriots, 34-17 (NE)
2005—Patriots, 24-17 (NE)
(RS Pts.—Patriots 253, Saints 214)
***NEW ENGLAND vs. N.Y. GIANTS**
RS: Patriots lead series, 4-3
1970—Giants, 16-0 (B)
1974—Patriots, 28-20 (New Haven)
1987—Giants, 17-10 (NY)
1990—Giants, 13-10 (NE)
1996—Patriots, 23-22 (NY)
1999—Patriots, 16-14 (NE)
2003—Patriots, 17-6 (NE)
(RS Pts.—Giants 108, Patriots 104)
*Franchise in Boston prior to 1971
***NEW ENGLAND vs. **N.Y. JETS**
RS: Jets lead series, 47-43-1
PS: Patriots lead series, 1-0
1960—Patriots, 28-24 (NY)
　　　Patriots, 38-21 (B)
1961—Titans, 21-20 (B)
　　　Titans, 37-30 (NY)
1962—Patriots, 43-14 (NY)
　　　Patriots, 24-17 (B)
1963—Patriots, 38-14 (B)
　　　Jets, 31-24 (NY)
1964—Patriots, 26-10 (B)
　　　Jets, 35-14 (NY)
1965—Jets, 30-20 (B)
　　　Patriots, 27-23 (NY)

1966—Tie, 24-24 (B)
    Jets, 38-28 (NY)
1967—Jets, 30-23 (NY)
    Jets, 29-24 (B)
1968—Jets, 47-31 (Birmingham)
    Jets, 48-14 (NY)
1969—Jets, 23-14 (B)
    Jets, 23-17 (NY)
1970—Jets, 31-21 (B)
    Jets, 17-3 (NY)
1971—Patriots, 20-0 (NE)
    Jets, 13-6 (NY)
1972—Patriots, 41-13 (NE)
    Jets, 34-10 (NY)
1973—Jets, 9-7 (NE)
    Jets, 33-13 (NY)
1974—Patriots, 24-0 (NY)
    Jets, 21-16 (NE)
1975—Jets, 36-7 (NY)
    Jets, 30-28 (NE)
1976—Patriots, 41-7 (NE)
    Patriots, 38-24 (NY)
1977—Jets, 30-27 (NY)
    Patriots, 24-13 (NE)
1978—Patriots, 55-21 (NE)
    Patriots, 19-17 (NY)
1979—Patriots, 56-3 (NE)
    Jets, 27-26 (NY)
1980—Patriots, 21-11 (NY)
    Patriots, 34-21 (NE)
1981—Jets, 28-24 (NY)
    Jets, 17-6 (NE)
1982—Jets, 31-7 (NE)
1983—Jets, 23-13 (NE)
    Jets, 26-3 (NY)
1984—Patriots, 28-21 (NY)
    Patriots, 30-20 (NE)
1985—Patriots, 20-13 (NE)
    Jets, 16-13 (NY) OT
    ***Patriots, 26-14 (NY)
1986—Patriots, 20-6 (NY)
    Jets, 31-24 (NE)
1987—Jets, 43-24 (NY)
    Patriots, 42-20 (NE)
1988—Patriots, 28-3 (NE)
    Patriots, 14-13 (NY)
1989—Patriots, 27-24 (NY)
    Jets, 27-26 (NE)
1990—Jets, 37-13 (NE)
    Jets, 42-7 (NY)
1991—Jets, 28-21 (NE)
    Patriots, 6-3 (NY)
1992—Jets, 30-21 (NY)
    Patriots, 24-3 (NE)
1993—Jets, 45-7 (NY)
    Jets, 6-0 (NE)
1994—Jets, 24-17 (NY)
    Patriots, 24-13 (NE)
1995—Patriots, 20-7 (NY)
    Patriots, 31-28 (NE)
1996—Patriots, 31-27 (NY)
    Patriots, 34-10 (NE)
1997—Patriots, 27-24 (NE) OT
    Jets, 24-19 (NY)
1998—Jets, 24-14 (NE)
    Jets, 31-10 (NY)
1999—Patriots, 30-28 (NY)
    Jets, 24-17 (NE)
2000—Jets, 20-19 (NE)
    Jets, 34-17 (NE)

2001—Jets, 10-3 (NE)
    Patriots, 17-16 (NY)
2002—Patriots, 44-7 (NY)
    Jets, 30-17 (NE)
2003—Patriots, 23-16 (NE)
    Patriots, 21-16 (NY)
2004—Patriots, 13-7 (NE)
    Patriots, 23-7 (NY)
2005—Patriots, 16-3 (NE)
    Patriots, 31-21 (NY)
(RS Pts.—Patriots 1,992, Jets 1,975)
(PS Pts.—Patriots 26, Jets 14)
*Franchise in Boston prior to 1971
**Jets known as Titans prior to 1963
***AFC First-Round Playoff
NEW ENGLAND vs. **OAKLAND
RS: Raiders lead series, 14-13-1
PS: Patriots lead series, 2-1
1960—Raiders, 27-14 (O)
    Patriots, 34-28 (B)
1961—Patriots, 20-17 (B)
    Patriots, 35-21 (O)
1962—Patriots, 26-16 (B)
    Raiders, 20-0 (O)
1963—Patriots, 20-14 (O)
    Patriots, 20-14 (B)
1964—Patriots, 17-14 (O)
    Tie, 43-43 (B)
1965—Raiders, 24-10 (B)
    Raiders, 30-21 (O)
1966—Patriots, 24-21 (B)
1967—Raiders, 35-7 (O)
    Raiders, 48-14 (B)
1968—Raiders, 41-10 (O)
1969—Raiders, 38-23 (B)
1971—Patriots, 20-6 (NE)
1974—Raiders, 41-26 (O)
1976—Patriots, 48-17 (NE)
    ***Raiders, 24-21 (O)
1978—Patriots, 21-14 (O)
1981—Raiders, 27-17 (O)
1985—Raiders, 35-20 (NE)
    ***Patriots, 27-20 (LA)
1987—Patriots, 26-23 (NE)
1989—Raiders, 24-21 (LA)
1994—Raiders, 21-17 (NE)
2001—***Patriots, 16-13 (NE) OT
2002—Patriots, 27-20 (O)
2005—Patriots, 30-20 (NE)
(RS Pts.—Raiders 706, Patriots 604)
(PS Pts.—Patriots 64, Raiders 57)
*Franchise in Boston prior to 1971
**Franchise in Los Angeles from
1982-1994
***AFC Divisional Playoff
NEW ENGLAND vs. PHILADELPHIA
RS: Eagles lead series, 6-3
PS: Patriots lead series, 1-0
1973—Eagles, 24-23 (P)
1977—Patriots, 14-6 (NE)
1978—Patriots, 24-14 (NE)
1981—Eagles, 13-3 (P)
1984—Eagles, 27-17 (P)
1987—Patriots, 34-31 (NE) OT
1990—Eagles, 48-20 (P)
1999—Eagles, 24-9 (P)
2003—Patriots, 31-10 (P)
2004—*Patriots, 24-21 (Jacksonvillle)
(RS Pts.—Eagles 200, Patriots 172)
(PS Pts.—Patriots 24, Eagles 21)

*Super Bowl XXXIX
NEW ENGLAND vs. PITTSBURGH
RS: Steelers lead series, 12-6
PS: Patriots lead series, 3-1
1972—Steelers, 33-3 (P)
1974—Steelers, 21-17 (NE)
1976—Patriots, 30-27 (P)
1979—Steelers, 16-13 (NE) OT
1981—Steelers, 27-21 (P) OT
1982—Steelers, 37-14 (P)
1983—Patriots, 28-23 (P)
1986—Patriots, 34-0 (P)
1989—Steelers, 28-10 (P)
1990—Steelers, 24-3 (P)
1991—Patriots, 20-6 (P)
1993—Steelers, 17-14 (P)
1995—Steelers, 41-27 (P)
1996—*Patriots, 28-3 (NE)
1997—Steelers, 24-21 (NE) OT
    *Steelers, 7-6 (P)
1998—Patriots, 23-9 (P)
2001—**Patriots, 24-17 (P)
2002—Patriots, 30-14 (NE)
2004—Steelers, 34-20 (P)
    **Patriots, 41-27 (P)
2005—Patriots, 23-20 (P)
(RS Pts.—Steelers 415, Patriots 337)
(PS Pts.—Patriots 99, Steelers 54)
*AFC Divisional Playoff
**AFC Championship
NEW ENGLAND vs. *ST. LOUIS
RS: Rams lead series, 5-4
PS: Patriots lead series, 1-0
1974—Patriots, 20-14 (NE)
1980—Rams, 17-14 (NE)
1983—Patriots, 21-7 (LA)
1986—Patriots, 30-28 (LA)
1989—Rams, 24-20 (NE)
1992—Rams, 14-0 (LA)
1998—Rams, 32-18 (StL)
2001—Rams, 24-17 (NE)
    **Patriots, 20-17 (New Orleans)
2004—Patriots, 40-22 (StL)
(RS Pts.—Rams 182, Patriots 180)
(PS Pts.—Patriots 20, Rams 17)
*Franchise in Los Angeles prior to 1995
**Super Bowl XXXVI
NEW ENGLAND vs. **SAN DIEGO
RS: Patriots lead series, 17-13-2
PS: Chargers lead series, 1-0
1960—Patriots, 35-0 (LA)
    Chargers, 45-16 (B)
1961—Chargers, 38-27 (B)
    Patriots, 41-0 (SD)
1962—Patriots, 24-20 (B)
    Patriots, 20-14 (SD)
1963—Chargers, 17-13 (SD)
    Chargers, 7-6 (B)
    ***Chargers, 51-10 (SD)
1964—Patriots, 33-28 (SD)
    Chargers, 26-17 (B)
1965—Tie, 10-10 (B)
    Patriots, 22-6 (SD)
1966—Chargers, 24-0 (SD)
    Patriots, 35-17 (B)
1967—Chargers, 28-14 (SD)
    Tie, 31-31 (SD)
1968—Chargers, 27-17 (B)
1969—Chargers, 13-10 (B)
    Chargers, 28-18 (SD)

1970—Chargers, 16-14 (B)
1973—Patriots, 30-14 (NE)
1975—Patriots, 33-19 (SD)
1977—Patriots, 24-20 (SD)
1978—Patriots, 28-23 (NE)
1979—Patriots, 27-21 (NE)
1983—Patriots, 37-21 (NE)
1994—Patriots, 23-17 (NE)
1996—Patriots, 45-7 (SD)
1997—Patriots, 41-7 (NE)
2001—Patriots, 29-26 (NE) OT
2002 Chargers, 21-14 (SD)
2005—Chargers, 41-17 (NE)
(RS Pts.—Patriots 751, Chargers 632)
(PS Pts.—Chargers 51, Patriots 10)
*Franchise in Boston prior to 1971
**Franchise in Los Angeles prior to 1961
***AFL Championship
NEW ENGLAND vs. SAN FRANCISCO
RS: 49ers lead series, 7-3
1971—49ers, 27-10 (SF)
1975—Patriots, 24-16 (NE)
1980—49ers, 21-17 (SF)
1983—49ers, 33-13 (NE)
1986—49ers, 29-24 (NE)
1989—49ers, 37-20 (SF)
1992—Patriots, 24-12 (NE)
1995—49ers, 28-3 (SF)
1998—Patriots, 24-21 (NE)
2004—Patriots, 21-7 (NE)
(RS Pts.—49ers 243, Patriots 168)
NEW ENGLAND vs. SEATTLE
RS: Series tied, 7-7
1977—Patriots, 31-0 (NE)
1980—Patriots, 37-31 (S)
1982—Patriots, 16-0 (S)
1983—Seahawks, 24-6 (S)
1984—Patriots, 38-23 (NE)
1985—Patriots, 20-13 (S)
1986—Seahawks, 38-31 (NE)
1988—Patriots, 13-7 (NE)
1989—Seahawks, 24-3 (NE)
1990—Seahawks, 33-20 (NE)
1992—Seahawks, 10-6 (NE)
1993—Seahawks, 17-14 (NE)
        Seahawks, 10-9 (S)
2004—Patriots, 30-20 (NE)
(RS Pts.—Patriots 274, Seahawks 250)
NEW ENGLAND vs. TAMPA BAY
RS: Patriots lead series, 4-2
1976—Patriots, 31-14 (TB)
1985—Patriots, 32-14 (TB)
1988—Patriots, 10-7 (NE) OT
1997—Buccaneers, 27-7 (TB)
2000—Buccaneers, 21-16 (NE)
2005—Patriots, 28-0 (NE)
(RS Pts.—Patriots 124, Buccaneers 83)
***NEW ENGLAND vs. **TENNESSEE**
RS: Patriots lead series, 19-15-1
PS: Series tied, 1-1
1960—Oilers, 24-10 (B)
        Oilers, 37-21 (H)
1961—Tie, 31-31 (B)
        Oilers, 27-15 (H)
1962—Patriots, 34-21 (B)
        Oilers, 21-17 (H)
1963—Patriots, 45-3 (B)
        Patriots, 46-28 (H)
1964—Patriots, 25-24 (B)
        Patriots, 34-17 (H)

1965—Oilers, 31-10 (H)
        Patriots, 42-14 (B)
1966—Patriots, 27-21 (B)
        Patriots, 38-14 (H)
1967—Patriots, 18-7 (B)
        Oilers, 27-6 (H)
1968—Oilers, 16-0 (B)
        Oilers, 45-17 (H)
1969—Patriots, 24-0 (B)
        Oilers, 27-23 (H)
1971—Patriots, 28-20 (NE)
1973—Patriots, 32-0 (H)
1975—Oilers, 7-0 (NE)
1978—Oilers, 26-23 (NE)
        ***Oilers, 31-14 (NE)
1980—Oilers, 38-34 (H)
1981—Patriots, 38-10 (NE)
1982—Patriots, 29-21 (NE)
1987—Patriots, 21-7 (H)
1988—Oilers, 31-6 (H)
1989—Patriots, 23-13 (NE)
1991—Patriots, 24-20 (NE)
1993—Oilers, 28-14 (NE)
1998—Patriots, 27-16 (NE)
2002—Titans, 24-7 (T)
2003—Patriots, 38-30 (NE)
        ***Patriots, 17-14 (NE)
(RS Pts.—Patriots 827, Titans 726)
(PS Pts.—Titans 45, Patriots 31)
*Franchise in Boston prior to 1971
**Franchise in Houston prior to 1997;
known as Oilers prior to 1999
***AFC Divisional Playoff
NEW ENGLAND vs. WASHINGTON
RS: Redskins lead series, 6-1
1972—Patriots, 24-23 (NE)
1978—Redskins, 16-14 (NE)
1981—Redskins, 24-22 (W)
1984—Redskins, 26-10 (NE)
1990—Redskins, 25-10 (NE)
1996—Redskins, 27-22 (NE)
2003—Redskins, 20-17 (W)
(RS Pts.—Redskins 161, Patriots 119)

NEW ORLEANS vs. ARIZONA
RS: Cardinals lead series, 13-11;
See Arizona vs. New Orleans
NEW ORLEANS vs. ATLANTA
RS: Falcons lead series, 43-30
PS: Falcons lead series, 1-0;
See Atlanta vs. New Orleans
NEW ORLEANS vs. BALTIMORE
RS: Ravens lead series, 2-1;
See Baltimore vs. New Orleans
NEW ORLEANS vs. BUFFALO
RS: Series tied, 4-4;
See Buffalo vs. New Orleans
NEW ORLEANS vs. CAROLINA
RS: Series tied, 11-11;
See Carolina vs. New Orleans
NEW ORLEANS vs. CHICAGO
RS: Series tied, 11-11
PS: Bears lead series, 1-0;
See Chicago vs. New Orleans
NEW ORLEANS vs. CINCINNATI
RS: Series tied, 5-5;
See Cincinnati vs. New Orleans
NEW ORLEANS vs. CLEVELAND
RS: Browns lead series, 11-3;
See Cleveland vs. New Orleans

NEW ORLEANS vs. DALLAS
RS: Cowboys lead series, 14-7;
See Dallas vs. New Orleans
NEW ORLEANS vs. DENVER
RS: Broncos lead series, 6-2;
See Denver vs. New Orleans
NEW ORLEANS vs. DETROIT
RS: Lions lead series, 9-8-1;
See Detroit vs. New Orleans
NEW ORLEANS vs. GREEN BAY
RS: Packers lead series, 14-5;
See Green Bay vs. New Orleans
NEW ORLEANS vs. HOUSTON
RS: Saints lead series, 1-0;
See Houston vs. New Orleans
NEW ORLEANS vs. INDIANAPOLIS
RS: Saints lead series, 5-4;
See Indianapolis vs. New Orleans
NEW ORLEANS vs. JACKSONVILLE
RS: Jaguars lead series, 2-1;
See Jacksonville vs. New Orleans
NEW ORLEANS vs. KANSAS CITY
RS: Series tied, 4-4;
See Kansas City vs. New Orleans
NEW ORLEANS vs. MIAMI
RS: Dolphins lead series, 6-3;
See Miami vs. New Orleans
NEW ORLEANS vs. MINNESOTA
RS: Vikings lead series, 17-7
PS: Vikings lead series, 2-0;
See Minnesota vs. New Orleans
NEW ORLEANS vs. NEW ENGLAND
RS: Patriots lead series, 8-3;
See New England vs. New Orleans
NEW ORLEANS vs. N.Y. GIANTS
RS: Giants lead series, 14-9
1967—Giants, 27-21 (NY)
1968—Giants, 38-21 (NY)
1969—Saints, 25-24 (NY)
1970—Saints, 14-10 (NO)
1972—Giants, 45-21 (NY)
1975—Saints, 28-14 (NY)
1978—Saints, 28-17 (NO)
1979—Saints, 24-14 (NO)
1981—Giants, 20-7 (NY)
1984—Saints, 10-3 (NY)
1985—Giants, 21-13 (NO)
1986—Giants, 20-17 (NY)
1987—Saints, 23-14 (NO)
1988—Giants, 13-12 (NY)
1993—Saints, 24-14 (NO)
1994—Saints, 27-22 (NO)
1995—Giants, 45-29 (NY)
1996—Saints 17-3 (NY)
1997—Giants, 14-9 (NY)
1999—Giants, 31-3 (NY)
2001—Giants, 21-13 (NY)
2003—Saints, 45-7 (NO)
2005—Giants, 27-10 (NY*)
(RS Pts.—Giants 488, Saints 417)
*Saints home game
NEW ORLEANS vs. N.Y. JETS
RS: Series tied, 5-5
1972—Jets, 18-17 (NY)
1977—Jets, 16-13 (NY)
1980—Saints, 21-20 (NY)
1983—Jets, 31-28 (NO)
1986—Jets, 28-23 (NY)
1989—Saints, 29-14 (NO)
1992—Saints, 20-0 (NY)

1995—Saints, 12-0 (NY)
2001—Jets, 16-9 (NO)
2005—Saints, 21-19 (NY)
(RS Pts.—Saints 193, Jets 162)
NEW ORLEANS vs. *OAKLAND
RS: Raiders lead series, 5-4-1
1971—Tie, 21-21 (NO)
1975—Raiders, 48-10 (O)
1979—Raiders, 42-35 (NO)
1985—Raiders, 23-13 (LA)
1988—Saints, 20-6 (NO)
1991—Saints, 27-0 (NO)
1994—Raiders, 24-19 (LA)
1997—Saints, 13-10 (O)
2000—Raiders, 31-22 (NO)
2004—Saints, 31-26 (O)
(RS Pts.—Raiders 231, Saints 211)
Franchise in Los Angeles from 1982-1994
NEW ORLEANS vs. PHILADELPHIA
RS: Eagles lead series, 14-8
PS: Eagles lead series, 1-0
1967—Saints, 31-24 (NO)
       Eagles, 48-21 (P)
1968—Eagles, 29-17 (P)
1969—Eagles, 13-10 (P)
       Saints, 26-17 (NO)
1972—Saints, 21-3 (NO)
1974—Saints, 14-10 (NO)
1977—Eagles, 28-7 (P)
1978—Eagles, 24-17 (NO)
1979—Eagles, 26-14 (NO)
1980—Eagles, 34-21 (NO)
1981—Eagles, 31-14 (NO)
1983—Saints, 20-17 (P) OT
1985—Saints, 23-21 (NO)
1987—Eagles, 27-17 (NO)
1989—Saints, 30-20 (NO)
1991—Saints, 13-6 (P)
1992—Eagles, 15-13 (P)
       *Eagles, 36-20 (NO)
1993—Eagles, 37-26 (P)
1995—Eagles, 15-10 (NO)
2000—Saints, 21-7 (NO)
2003—Eagles, 33-20 (P)
(RS Pts.—Eagles 499, Saints 392)
(PS Pts.—Eagles 36, Saints 20)
NFC First-Round Playoff
NEW ORLEANS vs. PITTSBURGH
RS: Series tied, 6-6
1967—Steelers, 14-10 (NO)
1968—Saints, 16-12 (P)
       Saints, 24-14 (NO)
1969—Saints, 27-24 (NO)
1974—Steelers, 28-7 (NO)
1978—Steelers, 20-14 (P)
1981—Steelers, 20-6 (NO)
1984—Saints, 27-24 (NO)
1987—Saints, 20-16 (P)
1990—Steelers, 9-6 (NO)
1993—Steelers, 37-14 (P)
2002—Saints, 32-29 (NO)
(RS Pts.—Steelers 247, Saints 203)
NEW ORLEANS vs. *ST. LOUIS
RS: Rams lead series, 37-29
PS: Saints lead series, 1-0
1967—Rams, 27-13 (NO)
1969—Rams, 36-17 (LA)
1970—Rams, 30-17 (NO)
       Rams, 34-16 (LA)
1971—Saints, 24-20 (NO)

Rams, 45-28 (LA)
1972—Rams, 34-14 (LA)
       Saints, 19-16 (NO)
1973—Rams, 29-7 (LA)
       Rams, 24-13 (NO)
1974—Rams, 24-0 (LA)
       Saints, 20-7 (NO)
1975—Rams, 38-14 (LA)
       Rams, 14-7 (NO)
1976—Rams, 16-10 (NO)
       Rams, 33-14 (LA)
1977—Rams, 14-7 (LA)
       Saints, 27-26 (NO)
1978—Rams, 26-20 (NO)
       Saints, 10-3 (LA)
1979—Rams, 35-17 (NO)
       Saints, 29-14 (LA)
1980—Rams, 45-31 (LA)
       Rams, 27-7 (NO)
1981—Saints, 23-17 (NO)
       Saints, 21-13 (LA)
1983—Rams, 30-27 (LA)
       Rams, 26-24 (NO)
1984—Rams, 28-10 (NO)
       Rams, 34-21 (NO)
1985—Rams, 28-10 (LA)
       Saints, 29-3 (NO)
1986—Saints, 6-0 (NO)
       Rams, 26-13 (LA)
1987—Saints, 37-10 (NO)
       Saints, 31-14 (LA)
1988—Rams, 12-10 (NO)
       Saints, 14-10 (LA)
1989—Saints, 40-21 (NO)
       Rams, 20-17 (NO) OT
1990—Saints, 24-20 (LA)
       Saints, 20-17 (NO)
1991—Saints, 24-7 (NO)
       Saints, 24-17 (LA)
1992—Saints, 13-10 (NO)
       Saints, 37-14 (LA)
1993—Saints, 37-6 (LA)
       Rams, 23-20 (NO)
1994—Saints, 37-34 (NO)
       Saints, 31-15 (LA)
1995—Rams, 17-13 (StL)
       Saints, 19-10 (NO)
1996—Rams, 26-10 (NO)
       Rams, 14-13 (StL)
1997—Rams, 38-24 (StL)
       Rams, 34-27 (NO)
1998—Saints, 24-17 (StL)
       Saints, 24-3 (NO)
1999—Rams, 43-12 (StL)
       Rams, 30-14 (NO)
2000—Saints, 31-24 (StL)
       Rams, 26-21 (NO)
       **Saints, 31-28 (NO)
2001—Saints, 34-31 (StL)
       Rams, 34-21 (NO)
2004—Saints, 28-25 (StL) OT
2005—Rams, 28-17 (StL)
(RS Pts.—Rams 1,472, Saints 1,313)
(PS Pts.—Saints 31, Rams 28)
Franchise in Los Angeles prior to 1995
**NFC First-Round Playoff*
NEW ORLEANS vs. SAN DIEGO
RS: Chargers lead series, 7-2
1973—Chargers, 17-14 (SD)
1977—Chargers, 14-0 (NO)

1979—Chargers, 35-0 (NO)
1988—Saints, 23-17 (SD)
1991—Chargers, 24-21 (SD)
1994—Chargers, 36-22 (NO)
1997—Chargers, 20-6 (NO)
2000—Saints, 28-27 (SD)
2004—Chargers, 43-17 (SD)
(RS Pts.—Chargers 233, Saints 131)
NEW ORLEANS vs. SAN FRANCISCO
RS: 49ers lead series, 45-20-2
1967—49ers, 27-13 (SF)
1969—Saints, 43-38 (NO)
1970—Tie, 20-20 (SF)
       49ers, 38-27 (SF)
1971—49ers, 38-20 (NO)
       Saints, 26-20 (SF)
1972—49ers, 37-2 (NO)
       Tie, 20-20 (SF)
1973—49ers, 40-0 (SF)
       Saints, 16-10 (NO)
1974—49ers, 17-13 (NO)
       49ers, 35-21 (SF)
1975—49ers, 35-21 (SF)
       49ers, 16-6 (NO)
1976—49ers, 33-3 (SF)
       49ers, 27-7 (NO)
1977—49ers, 10-7 (NO) OT
       49ers, 20-17 (SF)
1978—Saints, 14-7 (SF)
       Saints, 24-13 (NO)
1979—Saints, 30-21 (SF)
       Saints, 31-20 (NO)
1980—49ers, 26-23 (NO)
       49ers, 38-35 (SF) OT
1981—49ers, 21-14 (SF)
       49ers, 21-17 (NO)
1982—Saints, 23-20 (SF)
1983—49ers, 32-13 (NO)
       49ers, 27-0 (SF)
1984—49ers, 30-20 (SF)
       49ers, 35-3 (NO)
1985—Saints, 20-17 (SF)
       49ers, 31-19 (NO)
1986—49ers, 26-17 (SF)
       Saints, 23-10 (NO)
1987—49ers, 24-22 (NO)
       Saints, 26-24 (SF)
1988—49ers, 34-33 (NO)
       49ers, 30-17 (SF)
1989—49ers, 24-20 (NO)
       49ers, 31-13 (SF)
1990—49ers, 13-12 (NO)
       Saints, 13-10 (SF)
1991—Saints, 10-3 (NO)
       49ers, 38-24 (SF)
1992—49ers, 16-10 (NO)
       49ers, 21-20 (SF)
1993—Saints, 16-13 (NO)
       49ers, 42-7 (SF)
1994—49ers, 24-13 (SF)
       49ers, 35-14 (NO)
1995—49ers, 24-22 (NO)
       Saints, 11-7 (SF)
1996—49ers, 27-11 (SF)
       49ers, 24-17 (NO)
1997—49ers, 33-7 (SF)
       49ers, 23-0 (NO)
1998—49ers, 31-0 (NO)
       49ers, 31-20 (SF)
1999—49ers, 28-21 (SF)

Saints, 24-6 (NO)
2000—Saints, 31-15 (NO)
Saints, 31-27 (SF)
2001—49ers, 28-27 (SF)
49ers, 38-0 (NO)
2002—Saints, 35-27 (NO)
2004—Saints, 30-27 (NO)
(RS Pts.—49ers 1,654, Saints 1,165)
NEW ORLEANS vs. SEATTLE
RS: Seahawks lead series, 5-4
1976—Saints, 51-27 (S)
1979—Seahawks, 38-24 (S)
1985—Seahawks, 27-3 (NO)
1988—Saints, 20-19 (S)
1991—Saints, 27-24 (NO)
1997—Saints, 20-17 (NO) OT
2000—Seahawks, 20-10 (S)
2003—Seahawks, 27-10 (S)
2004—Seahawks, 21-7 (NO)
(RS Pts.—Seahawks 220, Saints 172)
NEW ORLEANS vs. TAMPA BAY
RS: Saints lead series, 17-11
1977—Buccaneers, 33-14 (NO)
1978—Saints, 17-10 (TB)
1979—Saints, 42-14 (TB)
1981—Buccaneers, 31-14 (NO)
1982—Buccaneers, 13-10 (NO)
1983—Saints, 24-21 (TB)
1984—Saints, 17-13 (NO)
1985—Saints, 20-13 (NO)
1986—Saints, 38-7 (NO)
1987—Saints, 44-34 (NO)
1988—Saints, 13-9 (NO)
1989—Buccaneers, 20-10 (TB)
1990—Saints, 35-7 (NO)
1991—Saints, 23-7 (NO)
1992—Saints, 23-21 (NO)
1994—Saints, 9-7 (TB)
1996—Buccaneers, 13-7 (TB)
1998—Saints, 9-3 (NO)
1999—Buccaneers, 31-16 (NO)
2001—Buccaneers, 48-21 (TB)
2002—Buccaneers, 26-20 (TB) OT
Saints, 23-20 (NO)
2003—Saints, 17-14 (TB)
Buccaneers, 14-7 (NO)
2004—Buccaneers, 20-17 (NO)
Saints, 21-17 (TB)
2005—Buccaneers, 10-3 (Baton Rouge)
Buccaneers, 27-13 (TB)
(RS Pts.—Saints 533, Buccaneers 497)
NEW ORLEANS vs. *TENNESSEE
RS: Titans lead series, 6-4-1
1971—Tie, 13-13 (H)
1976—Oilers, 31-26 (NO)
1978—Oilers, 17-12 (NO)
1981—Saints, 27-24 (H)
1984—Saints, 27-10 (H)
1987—Saints, 24-10 (NO)
1990—Oilers, 23-10 (H)
1993—Saints, 33-21 (NO)
1996—Oilers, 31-14 (NO)
1999—Titans, 24-21 (NO)
2003—Titans, 27-12 (T)
(RS Pts.—Titans 231, Saints 219)
*Franchise in Houston prior to 1997;
known as Oilers prior to 1999
NEW ORLEANS vs. WASHINGTON
RS: Redskins lead series, 13-7
1967—Redskins, 30-10 (NO)

Saints, 30-14 (W)
1968—Saints, 37-17 (NO)
1969—Redskins, 26-20 (NO)
Redskins, 17-14 (W)
1971—Redskins, 24-14 (W)
1973—Saints, 19-3 (NO)
1975—Redskins, 41-3 (W)
1979—Saints, 14-10 (W)
1980—Redskins, 22-14 (W)
1982—Redskins, 27-10 (NO)
1986—Redskins, 14-6 (NO)
1988—Redskins, 27-24 (W)
1989—Redskins, 16-14 (NO)
1990—Redskins, 31-17 (W)
1992—Saints, 20-3 (NO)
1994—Redskins, 38-24 (NO)
2001—Redskins, 40-10 (NO)
2002—Saints, 43-27 (W)
2003—Saints, 24-20 (W)
(RS Pts.—Redskins 447, Saints 367)

N.Y. GIANTS vs. ARIZONA
RS: Giants lead series, 78-41-2;
See Arizona vs. N.Y. Giants
N.Y. GIANTS vs. ATLANTA
RS: Falcons lead series, 10-7;
See Atlanta vs. N.Y. Giants
N.Y. GIANTS vs. BALTIMORE
RS: Ravens lead series, 2-0
PS: Ravens lead series, 1-0;
See Baltimore vs. N.Y. Giants
N.Y. GIANTS vs. BUFFALO
RS: Bills lead series, 6-3
PS: Giants lead series, 1-0;
See Buffalo vs. N.Y. Giants
N.Y. GIANTS vs. CAROLINA
RS: Panthers lead series, 2-0
PS: Panthers lead series, 1-0;
See Carolina vs. N.Y. Giants
N.Y. GIANTS vs. CHICAGO
RS: Bears lead series, 26-17-2
PS: Bears lead series, 5-3;
See Chicago vs. N.Y. Giants
N.Y. GIANTS vs. CINCINNATI
RS: Bengals lead series, 5-2;
See Cincinnati vs. N.Y. Giants
N.Y. GIANTS vs. CLEVELAND
RS: Browns lead series, 25-19-2
PS: Series tied, 1-1;
See Cleveland vs. N.Y. Giants
N.Y. GIANTS vs. DALLAS
RS: Cowboys lead series, 51-34-2;
See Dallas vs. N.Y. Giants
N.Y. GIANTS vs. DENVER
RS: Giants lead series, 5-4
PS: Giants lead series, 1-0;
See Denver vs. N.Y. Giants
N.Y. GIANTS vs. DETROIT
RS: Lions lead series, 20-17-1
PS: Lions lead series, 1-0;
See Detroit vs. N.Y. Giants
N.Y. GIANTS vs. GREEN BAY
RS: Packers lead series, 24-21-2
PS: Packers lead series, 4-1;
See Green Bay vs. N.Y. Giants
N.Y. GIANTS vs. HOUSTON
RS: Texans lead series, 1-0;
See Houston vs. N.Y. Giants
N.Y. GIANTS vs. INDIANAPOLIS
RS: Series tied, 6-6

PS: Colts lead series, 2-0;
See Indianapolis vs. N.Y. Giants
N.Y. GIANTS vs. JACKSONVILLE
RS: Giants lead series, 2-1;
See Jacksonville vs. N.Y. Giants
N.Y. GIANTS vs. KANSAS CITY
RS: Giants lead series, 9-2;
See Kansas City vs. N.Y. Giants
N.Y. GIANTS vs. MIAMI
RS: Giants lead series, 3-2;
See Miami vs. N.Y. Giants
N.Y. GIANTS vs. MINNESOTA
RS: Vikings lead series, 10-8
PS: Giants lead series, 2-1;
See Minnesota vs. N.Y. Giants
N.Y. GIANTS vs. NEW ENGLAND
RS: Patriots lead series, 4-3;
See New England vs. N.Y. Giants
N.Y. GIANTS vs. NEW ORLEANS
RS: Giants lead series, 14-9;
See New Orleans vs. N.Y. Giants
N.Y. GIANTS vs. N.Y. JETS
RS: Giants lead series, 6-4
1970—Giants, 22-10 (NYJ)
1974—Jets, 26-20 (New Haven) OT
1981—Jets, 26-7 (NYG)
1984—Giants, 20-10 (NYJ)
1987—Giants, 20-7 (NYG)
1988—Jets, 27-21 (NYJ)
1993—Jets, 10-6 (NYG)
1996—Giants, 13-6 (NYJ)
1999—Giants, 41-28 (NYG)
2003—Giants, 31-28 (NYJ) OT
(RS Pts.—Giants 201, Jets 178)
N.Y. GIANTS vs. *OAKLAND
RS: Raiders lead series, 7-3
1973—Raiders, 42-0 (O)
1980—Raiders, 33-17 (NY)
1983—Raiders, 27-12 (LA)
1986—Giants, 14-9 (LA)
1989—Giants, 34-17 (NY)
1992—Raiders, 13-10 (LA)
1995—Raiders, 17-13 (NY)
1998—Raiders, 20-17 (O)
2001—Raiders, 28-10 (NY)
2005—Giants, 30-21 (O)
(RS Pts.—Raiders 227, Giants 157)
*Franchise in Los Angeles from 1982-1994
N.Y. GIANTS vs. PHILADELPHIA
RS: Giants lead series, 75-65-2
PS: Giants lead series, 2-0
1933—Giants, 56-0 (NY)
Giants, 20-14 (P)
1934—Giants, 17-0 (NY)
Eagles, 6-0 (P)
1935—Giants, 10-0 (NY)
Giants, 21-14 (P)
1936—Eagles, 10-7 (P)
Giants, 21-17 (NY)
1937—Giants, 16-7 (P)
Giants, 21-0 (NY)
1938—Eagles, 14-10 (P)
Giants, 17-7 (NY)
1939—Giants, 13-3 (P)
Giants, 27-10 (NY)
1940—Giants, 20-14 (P)
Giants, 17-7 (NY)
1941—Giants, 24-0 (P)
Giants, 16-0 (NY)
1942—Giants, 35-17 (NY)

Giants, 14-0 (P)
1944—Eagles, 24-17 (NY)
Tie, 21-21 (P)
1945—Eagles, 38-17 (P)
Giants, 28-21 (NY)
1946—Eagles, 24-14 (P)
Giants, 45-17 (NY)
1947—Eagles, 23-0 (P)
Eagles, 41-24 (NY)
1948—Eagles, 45-0 (P)
Eagles, 35-14 (NY)
1949—Eagles, 24-3 (NY)
Eagles, 17-3 (P)
1950—Giants, 7-3 (NY)
Giants, 9-7 (P)
1951—Giants, 26-24 (NY)
Giants, 23-7 (P)
1952—Giants, 31-7 (P)
Eagles, 14-10 (NY)
1953—Eagles, 30-7 (P)
Giants, 37-28 (NY)
1954—Giants, 27-14 (NY)
Eagles, 29-14 (P)
1955—Eagles, 27-17 (P)
Giants, 31-7 (NY)
1956—Giants, 20-3 (NY)
Giants, 21-7 (P)
1957—Giants, 24-20 (P)
Giants, 13-0 (NY)
1958—Eagles, 27-24 (P)
Giants, 24-10 (NY)
1959—Eagles, 49-21 (P)
Giants, 24-7 (NY)
1960—Eagles, 17-10 (NY)
Eagles, 31-23 (P)
1961—Giants, 38-21 (NY)
Giants, 28-24 (P)
1962—Giants, 29-13 (P)
Giants, 19-14 (NY)
1963—Giants, 37-14 (P)
Giants, 42-14 (NY)
1964—Eagles, 38-7 (P)
Eagles, 23-17 (NY)
1965—Giants, 16-14 (P)
Giants, 35-27 (NY)
1966—Eagles, 35-17 (P)
Eagles, 31-3 (NY)
1967—Giants, 44-7 (NY)
1968—Giants, 34-25 (P)
Giants, 7-6 (NY)
1969—Eagles, 23-20 (NY)
1970—Giants, 30-23 (NY)
Eagles, 23-20 (P)
1971—Eagles, 23-7 (P)
Eagles, 41-28 (NY)
1972—Eagles, 27-12 (P)
Giants, 62-10 (NY)
1973—Tie, 23-23 (NY)
Eagles, 20-16 (P)
1974—Eagles, 35-7 (P)
Eagles, 20-7 (New Haven)
1975—Giants, 23-14 (P)
Eagles, 13-10 (NY)
1976—Eagles, 20-7 (P)
Eagles, 10-0 (NY)
1977—Eagles, 28-10 (NY)
Eagles, 17-14 (P)
1978—Eagles, 19-17 (NY)
Eagles, 20-3 (P)
1979—Eagles, 23-17 (P)

Eagles, 17-13 (NY)
1980—Eagles, 35-3 (P)
Eagles, 31-16 (NY)
1981—Eagles, 24-10 (NY)
Giants, 20-10 (P)
*Giants, 27-21 (P)
1982—Giants, 23-7 (NY)
Giants, 26-24 (P)
1983—Eagles, 17-13 (NY)
Giants, 23-0 (P)
1984—Giants, 28-27 (NY)
Eagles, 24-10 (P)
1985—Giants, 21-0 (NY)
Giants, 16-10 (P) OT
1986—Giants, 35-3 (NY)
Giants, 17-14 (P)
1987—Giants, 20-17 (P)
Giants, 23-20 (NY) OT
1988—Eagles, 24-13 (P)
Eagles, 23-17 (NY) OT
1989—Eagles, 21-19 (P)
Eagles, 24-17 (NY)
1990—Giants, 27-20 (NY)
Eagles, 31-13 (P)
1991—Eagles, 30-7 (P)
Eagles, 19-14 (NY)
1992—Eagles, 47-34 (NY)
Eagles, 20-10 (P)
1993—Giants, 21-10 (NY)
Giants, 7-3 (P)
1994—Giants, 28-23 (NY)
Giants, 16-13 (P)
1995—Eagles, 17-14 (NY)
Eagles, 28-19 (P)
1996—Eagles, 19-10 (NY)
Eagles, 24-0 (P)
1997—Giants, 31-17 (NY)
Giants, 31-21 (P)
1998—Giants, 20-0 (NY)
Giants, 20-10 (P)
1999—Giants, 16-15 (NY)
Giants, 23-17 (P) OT
2000—Giants, 33-18 (P)
Giants, 24-7 (NY)
**Giants, 20-10 (NY)
2001—Eagles, 10-9 (NY)
Eagles, 24-21 (P)
2002—Eagles, 17-3 (P)
Giants, 10-7 (NY) OT
2003—Eagles, 14-10 (NY)
Eagles, 28-10 (P)
2004—Eagles, 31-17 (P)
Eagles, 27-6 (NY)
2005—Giants, 27-17 (NY)
Giants, 26-23 (P) OT
(RS Pts.—Giants 2,672, Eagles 2,540)
(PS Pts.—Giants 47, Eagles 31)
*NFC First-Round Playoff
**NFC Divisional Playoff
N.Y. GIANTS vs. *PITTSBURGH
RS: Giants lead series, 43-28-3
1933—Giants, 23-2 (P)
Giants, 27-3 (NY)
1934—Giants, 14-12 (P)
Giants, 17-7 (NY)
1935—Giants, 42-7 (P)
Giants, 13-0 (NY)
1936—Pirates, 10-7 (P)
1937—Giants, 10-7 (P)
Giants, 17-0 (NY)

1938—Giants, 27-14 (P)
Pirates, 13-10 (NY)
1939—Giants, 14-7 (P)
Giants, 23-7 (NY)
1940—Tie, 10-10 (P)
Giants, 12-0 (NY)
1941—Giants, 37-10 (P)
Giants, 28-7 (NY)
1942—Steelers, 13-10 (P)
Steelers, 17-9 (NY)
1945—Giants, 34-6 (P)
Steelers, 21-7 (NY)
1946—Giants, 17-14 (P)
Giants, 7-0 (NY)
1947—Steelers, 38-21 (NY)
Steelers, 24-7 (P)
1948—Steelers, 34-27 (NY)
Steelers, 38-28 (P)
1949—Steelers, 28-7 (P)
Steelers, 21-17 (NY)
1950—Giants, 18-7 (P)
Steelers, 17-6 (NY)
1951—Tie, 13-13 (P)
Giants, 14-0 (NY)
1952—Steelers, 63-7 (P)
1953—Steelers, 24-14 (P)
Steelers, 14-10 (NY)
1954—Giants, 30-6 (P)
Giants, 24-3 (NY)
1955—Steelers, 30-23 (P)
Steelers, 19-17 (NY)
1956—Giants, 38-10 (NY)
Giants, 17-14 (P)
1957—Giants, 35-0 (NY)
Steelers, 21-10 (P)
1958—Giants, 17-6 (NY)
Steelers, 31-10 (P)
1959—Giants, 21-16 (P)
Steelers, 14-9 (NY)
1960—Giants, 19-17 (P)
Giants, 27-24 (NY)
1961—Giants, 17-14 (P)
Giants, 42-21 (NY)
1962—Giants, 31-27 (P)
Steelers, 20-17 (NY)
1963—Steelers, 31-0 (P)
Giants, 33-17 (NY)
1964—Steelers, 27-24 (P)
Steelers, 44-17 (NY)
1965—Giants, 23-13 (P)
Giants, 35-10 (NY)
1966—Tie, 34-34 (P)
Steelers, 47-28 (NY)
1967—Giants, 27-24 (P)
Pirates, 28-20 (NY)
1968—Giants, 34-20 (P)
1969—Giants, 10-7 (NY)
Giants, 21-17 (P)
1971—Steelers, 17-13 (P)
1976—Steelers, 27-0 (NY)
1985—Giants, 28-10 (NY)
1991—Giants, 23-20 (P)
1994—Steelers, 10-6 (NY)
2000—Giants, 30-10 (NY)
2004—Steelers, 33-30 (NY)
(RS Pts.—Giants 1,459, Steelers 1,232)
*Steelers known as Pirates prior to 1941
N.Y. GIANTS vs. *ST. LOUIS
RS: Rams lead series, 25-12
PS: Series tied, 1-1

1938—Giants, 28-0 (NY)
1940—Rams, 13-0 (NY)
1941—Giants, 49-14 (NY)
1945—Rams, 21-17 (NY)
1946—Rams, 31-21 (NY)
1947—Rams, 34-10 (LA)
1948—Rams, 52-37 (NY)
1953—Rams, 21-7 (LA)
1954—Rams, 17-16 (NY)
1959—Giants, 23-21 (LA)
1961—Giants, 24-14 (NY)
1966—Rams, 55-14 (LA)
1968—Rams, 24-21 (LA)
1970—Rams, 31-3 (NY)
1973—Rams, 40-6 (LA)
1976—Rams, 24-10 (LA)
1978—Rams, 20-17 (NY)
1979—Giants, 20-14 (LA)
1980—Rams, 28-7 (NY)
1981—Giants, 10-7 (NY)
1983—Rams, 16-6 (NY)
1984—Rams, 33-12 (LA)
　　　**Giants, 16-13 (LA)
1985—Giants, 24-19 (NY)
1988—Rams, 45-31 (NY)
1989—Rams, 31-10 (LA)
　　　***Rams, 19-13 (NY) OT
1990—Giants, 31-7 (LA)
1991—Rams, 19-13 (NY)
1992—Rams, 38-17 (LA)
1993—Giants, 20-10 (NY)
1994—Rams, 17-10 (LA)
1997—Rams, 13-3 (StL)
1999—Rams, 31-10 (StL)
2000—Rams, 38-24 (NY)
2001—Rams, 15-14 (StL)
2002—Giants, 26-21 (StL)
2003—Giants, 23-13 (NY)
2005—Giants, 44-24 (NY)
(RS Pts.—Rams 871, Giants 658)
(PS Pts.—Rams 32, Giants 29)
*Franchise in Los Angeles prior to 1995
and in Cleveland prior to 1946
**NFC First-Round Playoff
***NFC Divisional Playoff
N.Y. GIANTS vs. SAN DIEGO
RS: Giants lead series, 5-4
1971—Giants, 35-17 (NY)
1975—Giants, 35-24 (NY)
1980—Chargers, 44-7 (SD)
1983—Chargers, 41-34 (NY)
1986—Giants, 20-7 (NY)
1989—Giants, 20-13 (SD)
1995—Chargers, 27-17 (NY)
1998—Giants, 34-16 (SD)
2005—Chargers, 45-23 (SD)
(RS Pts.—Chargers 234, Giants 225)
N.Y. GIANTS vs. SAN FRANCISCO
RS: 49ers lead series, 13-12
PS: 49ers lead series, 4-3
1952—Giants, 23-14 (NY)
1956—Giants, 38-21 (SF)
1957—49ers, 27-17 (NY)
1960—Giants, 21-19 (SF)
1963—Giants, 48-14 (NY)
1968—49ers, 26-10 (NY)
1972—Giants, 23-17 (SF)
1975—Giants, 26-23 (SF)
1977—Giants, 20-17 (NY)
1978—Giants, 27-10 (NY)

1979—Giants, 32-16 (NY)
1980—49ers, 12-0 (SF)
1981—49ers, 17-10 (SF)
　　　*49ers, 38-24 (SF)
1984—49ers, 31-10 (NY)
　　　*49ers, 21-10 (SF)
1985—**Giants, 17-3 (NY)
1986—Giants, 21-17 (SF)
　　　*Giants, 49-3 (NY)
1987—49ers, 41-21 (NY)
1988—49ers, 20-17 (NY)
1909—49ers, 34-24 (SF)
1990—49ers, 7-3 (SF)
　　　***Giants, 15-13 (SF)
1991—Giants, 16-14 (NY)
1992—49ers, 31-14 (NY)
1993—*49ers, 44-3 (SF)
1995—49ers, 20-6 (SF)
1998—49ers, 31-7 (SF)
2002—49ers, 16-13 (NY)
　　　**49ers, 39-38 (SF)
2005—Giants, 24-6 (SF)
(RS Pts.—49ers 501, Giants 471)
(PS Pts.—49ers 161, Giants 156)
*NFC Divisional Playoff
**NFC First-Round Playoff
***NFC Championship
N.Y. GIANTS vs. SEATTLE
RS: Giants lead series, 7-4
1976—Giants, 28-16 (NY)
1980—Giants, 27-21 (S)
1981—Giants, 32-0 (S)
1983—Seahawks, 17-12 (NY)
1986—Seahawks, 17-12 (S)
1989—Giants, 15-3 (NY)
1992—Giants, 23-10 (NY)
1995—Seahawks, 30-28 (S)
2001—Giants, 27-24 (NY)
2002—Giants, 9-6 (NY)
2005—Seahawks, 24-21 (S) OT
(RS Pts.—Giants 234, Seahawks 168)
N.Y. GIANTS vs. TAMPA BAY
RS: Giants lead series, 9-6
1977—Giants, 10-0 (TB)
1978—Giants, 19-13 (TB)
　　　Giants, 17-14 (NY)
1979—Giants, 17-14 (NY)
　　　Buccaneers, 31-3 (TB)
1980—Buccaneers, 30-13 (TB)
1984—Giants, 17-14 (NY)
　　　Buccaneers, 20-17 (TB)
1985—Giants, 22-20 (NY)
1991—Giants, 21-14 (TB)
1993—Giants, 23-7 (NY)
1997—Buccaneers, 20-8 (NY)
1998—Buccaneers, 20-3 (TB)
1999—Giants, 17-13 (TB)
2003—Buccaneers, 19-13 (TB)
(RS Pts.—Buccaneers 249, Giants 220)
N.Y. GIANTS vs. *TENNESSEE
RS: Giants lead series, 5-3
1973—Giants, 34-14 (NY)
1982—Giants, 17-14 (NY)
1985—Giants, 35-14 (H)
1991—Giants, 24-20 (NY)
1994—Giants, 13-10 (H)
1997—Oilers, 10-6 (T)
2000—Titans, 28-14 (T)
2002—Titans, 32-29 (NY) OT
(RS Pts.—Giants 172, Titans 142)

*Franchise in Houston prior to 1997;
known as Oilers prior to 1999
N.Y. GIANTS vs. *WASHINGTON
RS: Giants lead series, 82-60-4
PS: Series tied, 1-1
1932—Braves, 14-6 (B)
　　　Tie, 0-0 (NY)
1933—Redskins, 21-20 (B)
　　　Giants, 7-0 (NY)
1934—Giants, 16-13 (B)
　　　Giants, 3-0 (NY)
1935—Giants, 20-12 (B)
　　　Giants, 17-6 (NY)
1936—Giants, 7-0 (B)
　　　Redskins, 14-0 (NY)
1937—Redskins, 13-3 (W)
　　　Redskins, 49-14 (NY)
1938—Giants, 10-7 (W)
　　　Giants, 36-0 (NY)
1939—Tie, 0-0 (W)
　　　Giants, 9-7 (NY)
1940—Redskins, 21-7 (W)
　　　Giants, 21-7 (NY)
1941—Giants, 17-10 (W)
　　　Giants, 20-13 (NY)
1942—Giants, 14-7 (W)
　　　Redskins, 14-7 (NY)
1943—Giants, 14-10 (NY)
　　　Giants, 31-7 (W)
　　　**Redskins, 28-0 (NY)
1944—Giants, 16-13 (NY)
　　　Giants, 31-0 (W)
1945—Redskins, 24-14 (NY)
　　　Redskins, 17-0 (W)
1946—Redskins, 24-14 (W)
　　　Giants, 31-0 (NY)
1947—Redskins, 28-20 (W)
　　　Giants, 35-10 (NY)
1948—Redskins, 41-10 (W)
　　　Redskins, 28-21 (NY)
1949—Giants, 45-35 (W)
　　　Giants, 23-7 (NY)
1950—Giants, 21-17 (W)
　　　Giants, 24-21 (NY)
1951—Giants, 35-14 (W)
　　　Giants, 28-14 (NY)
1952—Giants, 14-10 (W)
　　　Redskins, 27-17 (NY)
1953—Redskins, 13-9 (W)
　　　Redskins, 24-21 (NY)
1954—Giants, 51-21 (W)
　　　Giants, 24-7 (NY)
1955—Giants, 35-7 (NY)
　　　Giants, 27-20 (W)
1956—Redskins, 33-7 (W)
　　　Giants, 28-14 (NY)
1957—Giants, 24-20 (W)
　　　Redskins, 31-14 (NY)
1958—Giants, 21-14 (W)
　　　Giants, 30-0 (NY)
1959—Giants, 45-14 (W)
　　　Giants, 24-10 (NY)
1960—Tie, 24-24 (NY)
　　　Giants, 17-3 (W)
1961—Giants, 24-21 (W)
　　　Giants, 53-0 (NY)
1962—Giants, 49-34 (NY)
　　　Giants, 42-24 (W)
1963—Giants, 24-14 (W)
　　　Giants, 44-14 (NY)

1964—Giants, 13-10 (NY)
    Redskins, 36-21 (W)
1965—Redskins, 23-7 (NY)
    Giants, 27-10 (W)
1966—Giants, 13-10 (NY)
    Redskins, 72-41 (W)
1967—Redskins, 38-34 (W)
1968—Giants, 48-21 (NY)
    Giants, 13-10 (W)
1969—Redskins, 20-14 (W)
1970—Giants, 35-33 (NY)
    Giants, 27-24 (W)
1971—Redskins, 30-3 (NY)
    Redskins, 23-7 (W)
1972—Redskins, 23-16 (NY)
    Redskins, 27-13 (W)
1973—Redskins, 21-3 (New Haven)
    Redskins, 27-24 (W)
1974—Redskins, 13-10 (New Haven)
    Redskins, 24-3 (W)
1975—Redskins, 49-13 (W)
    Redskins, 21-13 (W)
1976—Redskins, 19-17 (W)
    Giants, 12-9 (NY)
1977—Giants, 20-17 (NY)
    Giants, 17-6 (W)
1978—Giants, 17-6 (NY)
    Redskins, 16-13 (W) OT
1979—Redskins, 27-0 (W)
    Giants, 14-6 (NY)
1980—Redskins, 23-21 (NY)
    Redskins, 16-13 (W)
1981—Giants, 17-7 (W)
    Redskins, 30-27 (NY) OT
1982—Redskins, 27-17 (W)
    Redskins, 15-14 (W)
1983—Redskins, 33-17 (NY)
    Redskins, 31-22 (W)
1984—Redskins, 30-14 (W)
    Giants, 37-13 (NY)
1985—Giants, 17-3 (NY)
    Redskins, 23-21 (W)
1986—Giants, 27-20 (NY)
    Giants, 24-14 (W)
    ***Giants, 17-0 (NY)
1987—Redskins, 38-12 (NY)
    Redskins, 23-19 (W)
1988—Giants, 27-20 (NY)
    Giants, 24-23 (W)
1989—Giants, 27-24 (W)
    Giants, 20-17 (NY)
1990—Giants, 24-20 (W)
    Giants, 21-10 (NY)
1991—Redskins, 17-13 (NY)
    Redskins, 34-17 (W)
1992—Giants, 24-7 (W)
    Redskins, 28-10 (NY)
1993—Giants, 41-7 (W)
    Giants, 20-6 (NY)
1994—Giants, 31-23 (W)
    Giants, 21-19 (W)
1995—Giants, 24-15 (W)
    Giants, 20-13 (NY)
1996—Redskins, 31-10 (NY)
    Redskins, 31-21 (W)
1997—Tie, 7-7 (W) OT
    Giants, 30-10 (NY)
1998—Giants, 31-24 (NY)
    Redskins, 21-14 (W)
1999—Redskins, 50-21 (NY)

Redskins, 23-13 (W)
2000—Redskins, 16-6 (NY)
    Giants, 9-7 (W)
2001—Giants, 23-9 (NY)
    Redskins, 35-21 (W)
2002—Giants, 19-17 (NY)
    Giants, 27-21 (W)
2003—Giants, 24-21 (W) OT
    Redskins, 20-7 (NY)
2004—Giants, 20-14 (NY)
    Redskins, 31-7 (W)
2005—Giants, 36-0 (NY)
    Redskins, 35-20 (W)
(RS Pts.—Giants 2,892, Redskins 2,660)
(PS Pts.—Redskins 28, Giants 17)
*Franchise in Boston prior to 1937 and known as Braves prior to 1933
**Division Playoff
***NFC Championship

N.Y. JETS vs. ARIZONA
RS: Jets lead series, 4-2;
See Arizona vs. N.Y. Jets
N.Y. JETS vs. ATLANTA
RS: Falcons lead series, 5-4;
See Atlanta vs. N.Y. Jets
N.Y. JETS vs BALTIMORE
RS: Ravens lead series, 4-1;
See Baltimore vs. N.Y. Jets
N.Y. JETS vs. BUFFALO
RS: Bills lead series, 49-41
PS: Bills lead series, 1-0;
See Buffalo vs. N.Y. Jets
N.Y. JETS vs. CAROLINA
RS: Series tied, 2-2;
See Carolina vs. N.Y. Jets
N.Y. JETS vs. CHICAGO
RS: Bears lead series, 5-3;
See Chicago vs. N.Y. Jets
N.Y. JETS vs. CINCINNATI
RS: Jets lead series, 12-6
PS: Jets lead series, 1-0;
See Cincinnati vs. N.Y. Jets
N.Y. JETS vs. CLEVELAND
RS: Browns lead series, 10-7
PS: Browns lead series, 1-0;
See Cleveland vs. N.Y. Jets
N.Y. JETS vs. DALLAS
RS: Cowboys lead series, 6-2;
See Dallas vs. N.Y. Jets
N.Y. JETS vs. DENVER
RS: Broncos lead series, 15-14-1
PS: Broncos lead series, 1-0;
See Denver vs. N.Y. Jets
N.Y. JETS vs. DETROIT
RS: Lions lead series, 6-4;
See Detroit vs. N.Y. Jets
N.Y. JETS vs. GREEN BAY
RS: Jets lead series, 7-2;
See Green Bay vs. N.Y. Jets
N.Y. JETS vs. HOUSTON
RS: Jets lead series, 2-0;
See Houston vs. N.Y. Jets
N.Y. JETS vs. INDIANAPOLIS
RS: Colts lead series, 39-25
PS: Jets lead series, 2-0;
See Indianapolis vs. N.Y. Jets
N.Y. JETS vs. JACKSONVILLE
RS: Jaguars lead series, 4-2
PS: Jets lead series, 1-0;

See Jacksonville vs. N.Y. Jets
N.Y. JETS vs. KANSAS CITY
RS: Chiefs lead series, 16-14-1
PS: Series tied, 1-1;
See Kansas City vs. N.Y. Jets
N.Y. JETS vs. MIAMI
RS: Jets lead series, 41-38-1
PS: Dolphins lead series, 1-0;
See Miami vs. N.Y. Jets
N.Y. JETS vs. MINNESOTA
RS: Jets lead series, 6-1;
See Minnesota vs. N.Y. Jets
N.Y. JETS vs. NEW ENGLAND
RS: Jets lead series, 47-43-1
PS: Patriots lead series, 1-0;
See New England vs. N.Y. Jets
N.Y. JETS vs. NEW ORLEANS
RS: Series tied, 5-5;
See New Orleans vs. N.Y. Jets
N.Y. JETS vs. N.Y. GIANTS
RS: Giants lead series, 6-4;
See N.Y. Giants vs. N.Y. Jets
*N.Y. JETS vs. **OAKLAND
RS: Raiders lead series, 19-13-2
PS: Series tied, 2-2
1960—Raiders, 28-27 (NY)
    Titans, 31-28 (O)
1961—Titans, 14-6 (O)
    Titans, 23-12 (NY)
1962—Titans, 28-17 (O)
    Titans, 31-21 (NY)
1963—Jets, 10-7 (NY)
    Raiders, 49-26 (O)
1964—Jets, 35-13 (NY)
    Raiders, 35-26 (O)
1965—Tie, 24-24 (NY)
    Raiders, 24-14 (O)
1966—Raiders, 24-21 (NY)
    Tie, 28-28 (O)
1967—Jets, 27-14 (NY)
    Raiders, 38-29 (O)
1968—Raiders, 43-32 (O)
    ***Jets, 27-23 (NY)
1969—Raiders, 27-14 (NY)
1970—Raiders, 14-13 (NY)
1972—Raiders, 24-16 (O)
1977—Raiders, 28-27 (NY)
1979—Jets, 28-19 (NY)
1982—****Jets, 17-14 (LA)
1985—Raiders, 31-0 (LA)
1989—Raiders, 14-7 (NY)
1993—Raiders, 24-20 (LA)
1995—Raiders, 47-10 (NY)
1996—Raiders, 34-13 (NY)
1997—Jets 23-22 (NY)
1999—Raiders, 24-23 (NY)
2000—Raiders, 31-7 (O)
2001—Jets, 24-22 (O)
    *****Raiders, 38-24 (O)
2002—Raiders, 26-20 (O)
    ****Raiders, 30-10 (O)
2003—Jets, 27-24 (O) OT
2005—Jets, 26-10 (NY)
(RS Pts.—Raiders 832, Jets 724)
(PS Pts.—Raiders 105, Jets 78)
*Jets known as Titans prior to 1963
**Franchise in Los Angeles from 1982-1994
***AFL Championship
****AFC Second-Round Playoff

*****AFC First-Round Playoff*
N.Y. JETS vs. PHILADELPHIA
RS: Eagles lead series, 7-0
1973—Eagles, 24-23 (P)
1977—Eagles, 27-0 (P)
1978—Eagles, 17-9 (P)
1987—Eagles, 38-27 (NY)
1993—Eagles, 35-30 (NY)
1996—Eagles, 21-20 (NY)
2003—Eagles, 24-17 (P)
(RS Pts.—Eagles 186, Jets 126)
N.Y. JETS vs. PITTSBURGH
RS: Steelers lead series, 15-2
PS: Steelers lead series, 1-0
1970—Steelers, 21-17 (P)
1973—Steelers, 26-14 (P)
1975—Steelers, 20-7 (NY)
1977—Steelers, 23-20 (NY)
1978—Steelers, 28-17 (NY)
1981—Steelers, 38-10 (P)
1983—Steelers, 34-7 (NY)
1984—Steelers, 23-17 (NY)
1986—Steelers, 45-24 (NY)
1988—Jets, 24-20 (NY)
1989—Steelers, 13-0 (NY)
1990—Steelers, 24-7 (NY)
1992—Steelers, 27-10 (P)
2000—Steelers, 20-3 (NY)
2001—Steelers, 18-7 (P)
2003—Jets, 6-0 (NY)
2004—Steelers, 17-6 (P)
     *Steelers, 20-17 (P) OT
(RS Pts.—Steelers 397, Jets 196)
(PS Pts.—Steelers 20, Jets 17)
AFC Divisional Playoff
N.Y. JETS vs. *ST. LOUIS
RS: Rams lead series, 9-2
1970—Jets, 31-20 (LA)
1974—Rams, 20-13 (NY)
1980—Rams, 38-13 (LA)
1983—Jets, 27-24 (NY) OT
1986—Rams, 17-3 (NY)
1989—Rams, 38-14 (LA)
1992—Rams, 18-10 (LA)
1995—Rams, 23-20 (NY)
1998—Rams, 30-10 (StL)
2001—Rams, 34-14 (NY)
2004—Rams, 32-29 (StL) OT
(RS Pts.—Rams 294, Jets 184)
Franchise in Los Angeles prior to 1995
*N.Y. JETS vs. **SAN DIEGO
RS: Chargers lead series, 18-11-1
PS: Jets lead series, 1-0
1960—Chargers, 21-7 (NY)
     Chargers, 50-43 (LA)
1961—Chargers, 25-10 (NY)
     Chargers, 48-13 (SD)
1962—Chargers, 40-14 (SD)
     Titans, 23-3 (NY)
1963—Chargers, 24-20 (SD)
     Chargers, 53-7 (NY)
1964—Tie, 17-17 (NY)
     Chargers, 38-3 (SD)
1965—Chargers, 34-9 (NY)
     Chargers, 38-7 (SD)
1966—Jets, 17-16 (NY)
     Chargers, 42-27 (SD)
1967—Jets, 42-31 (SD)
1968—Jets, 23-20 (NY)
     Jets, 37-15 (SD)

1969—Chargers, 34-27 (SD)
1971—Chargers, 49-21 (SD)
1974—Jets, 27-14 (NY)
1975—Chargers, 24-16 (SD)
1983—Jets, 41-29 (SD)
1989—Jets, 20-17 (SD)
1990—Chargers, 39-3 (NY)
     Chargers, 38-17 (SD)
1991—Jets, 24-3 (NY)
1994—Chargers, 21-6 (NY)
2002—Jets, 44-13 (SD)
2004—Jets, 34-28 (SD)
     ***Jets, 20-17 (SD) OT
2005—Chargers, 31-26 (NY)
(RS Pts.—Chargers 855, Jets 625)
(PS Pts.—Jets 20, Chargers 17)
Jets known as Titans prior to 1963
**Franchise in Los Angeles prior to 1961*
***AFC First-Round Playoff*
N.Y. JETS vs. SAN FRANCISCO
RS: 49ers lead series, 8-2
1971—49ers, 24-21 (NY)
1976—49ers, 17-6 (SF)
1980—49ers, 37-27 (NY)
1983—Jets, 27-13 (SF)
1986—49ers, 24-10 (SF)
1989—49ers, 23-10 (NY)
1992—49ers, 31-14 (NY)
1998—49ers, 36-30 (SF) OT
2001—49ers, 19-17 (NY)
2004—Jets, 22-14 (NY)
(RS Pts.—49ers 238, Jets 184)
N.Y. JETS vs. SEATTLE
RS: Series tied, 8-8
1977—Seahawks, 17-0 (NY)
1978—Seahawks, 24-17 (NY)
1979—Seahawks, 30-7 (S)
1980—Seahawks, 27-17 (NY)
1981—Seahawks, 19-3 (NY)
     Seahawks, 27-23 (S)
1983—Seahawks, 17-10 (NY)
1985—Jets, 17-14 (NY)
1986—Jets, 38-7 (S)
1987—Jets, 30-14 (NY)
1991—Seahawks, 20-13 (S)
1995—Jets, 16-10 (S)
1997—Jets, 41-3 (S)
1998—Jets, 32-31 (NY)
1999—Jets, 19-9 (NY)
2004—Jets, 37-14 (NY)
(RS Pts.—Jets 320, Seahawks 283)
N.Y. JETS vs. TAMPA BAY
RS: Jets lead series, 8-1
1976—Jets, 34-0 (NY)
1982—Jets, 32-17 (NY)
1984—Buccaneers, 41-21 (TB)
1985—Jets, 62-28 (NY)
1990—Jets, 16-14 (TB)
1991—Jets, 16-13 (NY)
1997—Jets, 31-0 (NY)
2000—Jets, 21-17 (TB)
2005—Jets, 14-12 (NY)
(RS Pts.—Jets 247, Buccaneers 142)
*N.Y. JETS vs. **TENNESSEE
RS: Titans lead series, 20-14-1
PS: Titans lead series, 1-0
1960—Oilers, 27-21 (H)
     Oilers, 42-28 (NY)
1961—Oilers, 49-13 (H)
     Oilers, 48-21 (NY)

1962—Oilers, 56-17 (H)
     Oilers, 44-10 (NY)
1963—Jets, 24-17 (NY)
     Oilers, 31-27 (H)
1964—Jets, 24-21 (NY)
     Oilers, 33-17 (H)
1965—Oilers, 27-21 (H)
     Jets, 41-14 (NY)
1966—Jets, 52-13 (NY)
     Oilers, 24-0 (H)
1967—Tie, 28-28 (NY)
1968—Jets, 20-14 (H)
     Jets, 26-7 (NY)
1969—Jets, 26-17 (NY)
     Jets, 34-26 (H)
1972—Oilers, 26-20 (H)
1974—Oilers, 27-22 (NY)
1977—Oilers, 20-0 (H)
1979—Oilers, 27-24 (H) OT
1980—Jets, 31-28 (NY) OT
1981—Jets, 33-17 (NY)
1984—Oilers, 31-20 (H)
1988—Jets, 45-3 (NY)
1990—Jets, 17-12 (H)
1991—Oilers, 23-20 (NY)
     ***Oilers, 17-10 (H)
1993—Oilers, 24-0 (H)
1994—Oilers, 24-10 (H)
1995—Oilers, 23-6 (H)
1996—Oilers, 35-10 (NY)
1998—Jets, 24-3 (T)
2003—Jets, 24-17 (NY)
(RS Pts.—Titans 878, Jets 756)
(PS Pts.—Titans 17, Jets 10)
Jets known as Titans prior to 1963
**Franchise in Houston prior to 1997;*
known as Oilers prior to 1999
***AFC First-Round Playoff*
N.Y. JETS vs. WASHINGTON
RS: Redskins lead series, 7-1
1972—Redskins, 35-17 (NY)
1976—Redskins, 37-16 (NY)
1978—Redskins, 23-3 (W)
1987—Redskins, 17-16 (W)
1993—Jets, 3-0 (W)
1996—Redskins, 31-16 (W)
1999—Redskins, 27-20 (W)
2003—Redskins, 16-13 (W)
(RS Pts.—Redskins 186, Jets 104)

OAKLAND vs. ARIZONA
RS: Raiders lead series, 4-2;
See Arizona vs. Oakland
OAKLAND vs. ATLANTA
RS: Raiders lead series, 7-4;
See Atlanta vs. Oakland
OAKLAND vs. BALTIMORE
RS: Ravens lead series, 2-1
PS: Ravens lead series, 1-0;
See Baltimore vs. Oakland
OAKLAND vs. BUFFALO
RS: Raiders lead series, 19-15
PS: Bills lead series, 2-0;
See Buffalo vs. Oakland
OAKLAND vs CAROLINA
RS: Raiders lead series, 2-1;
See Carolina vs. Oakland
OAKLAND vs. CHICAGO
RS: Raiders lead series, 6-5;
See Chicago vs. Oakland

OAKLAND vs. CINCINNATI
RS: Raiders lead series, 17-7
PS: Raiders lead series, 2-0;
See Cincinnati vs. Oakland
OAKLAND vs. CLEVELAND
RS: Raiders lead series, 9-6
PS: Raiders lead series, 2-0;
See Cleveland vs. Oakland
OAKLAND vs. DALLAS
RS: Raiders lead series, 6-3;
See Dallas vs. Oakland
OAKLAND vs. DENVER
RS: Raiders lead series, 53-36-2
PS: Series tied, 1-1;
See Denver vs. Oakland
OAKLAND vs. DETROIT
RS: Raiders lead series, 6-3;
See Detroit vs. Oakland
OAKLAND vs. GREEN BAY
RS: Raiders lead series, 5-4
PS: Packers lead series, 1-0;
See Green Bay vs. Oakland
OAKLAND vs. HOUSTON
RS: Texans lead series, 1-0
See Houston vs. Oakland
OAKLAND vs. INDIANAPOLIS
RS: Raiders lead series, 7-3
PS: Series tied, 1-1;
See Indianapolis vs. Oakland
OAKLAND vs. JACKSONVILLE
RS: Jaguars lead series, 2-1;
See Jacksonville vs. Oakland
OAKLAND vs. KANSAS CITY
RS: Chiefs lead series, 47-42-2
PS: Chiefs lead series, 2-1;
See Kansas City vs. Oakland
OAKLAND vs. MIAMI
RS: Raiders lead series, 15-11-1
PS: Raiders lead series, 3-1;
See Miami vs. Oakland
OAKLAND vs. MINNESOTA
RS: Raiders lead series, 8-3
PS: Raiders lead series, 1-0;
See Minnesota vs. Oakland
OAKLAND vs. NEW ENGLAND
RS: Raiders lead series, 14-13-1
PS: Patriots lead series, 2-1;
See New England vs. Oakland
OAKLAND vs. NEW ORLEANS
RS: Raiders lead series, 5-4-1;
See New Orleans vs. Oakland
OAKLAND vs. N.Y. GIANTS
RS: Raiders lead series, 7-3;
See N.Y. Giants vs. Oakland
OAKLAND vs. N.Y. JETS
RS: Raiders lead series, 19-13-2
PS: Series tied, 2-2;
See N.Y. Jets vs. Oakland
*OAKLAND vs. PHILADELPHIA
RS: Eagles lead series, 5-4
PS: Raiders lead series, 1-0
1971—Raiders, 34-10 (O)
1976—Raiders, 26-7 (P)
1980—Eagles, 10-7 (P)
      **Raiders, 27-10 (New Orleans)
1986—Eagles, 33-27 (LA) OT
1989—Eagles, 10-7 (P)
1992—Eagles, 31-10 (P)
1995—Raiders, 48-17 (O)
2001—Raiders, 20-10 (P)

2005—Eagles, 23-20 (P)
(RS Pts.—Raiders 199, Eagles 151)
(PS Pts.—Raiders 27, Eagles 10)
Franchise in Los Angeles from 1982-1994
**Super Bowl XV
*OAKLAND vs. PITTSBURGH
RS: Series tied, 8-8
PS: Series tied, 3-3
1970—Raiders, 31-14 (O)
1972—Steelers, 34-28 (P)
      **Steelers, 13-7 (P)
1973—Steelers, 17-9 (O)
      **Raiders, 33-14 (O)
1974—Raiders, 17-0 (P)
      ***Steelers, 24-13 (O)
1975—***Steelers, 16-10 (P)
1976—Raiders, 31-28 (O)
      ***Raiders, 24-7 (O)
1977—Raiders, 16-7 (P)
1980—Raiders, 45-34 (P)
1981—Raiders, 30-27 (O)
1983—**Raiders, 38-10 (LA)
1984—Steelers, 13-7 (LA)
1990—Raiders, 20-3 (LA)
1994—Steelers, 21-3 (LA)
1995—Steelers, 29-10 (LA)
2000—Steelers, 21-20 (P)
2002—Raiders, 30-17 (P)
2003—Steelers, 27-7 (P)
2004—Steelers, 24-21 (P)
(RS Pts.—Raiders 325, Steelers 316)
(PS Pts.—Raiders 125, Steelers 84)
Franchise in Los Angeles from 1982-1994
**AFC Divisional Playoff
***AFC Championship
*OAKLAND vs. **ST. LOUIS
RS: Raiders lead series, 7-3
1972—Raiders, 45-17 (O)
1977—Rams, 20-14 (LA)
1979—Raiders, 24-17 (LA)
1982—Raiders, 37-31 (LA Raiders)
1985—Raiders, 16-6 (LA Rams)
1988—Rams, 22-17 (LA Raiders)
1991—Raiders, 20-17 (LA Raiders)
1994—Raiders, 20-17 (LA Rams)
1997—Raiders, 35-17 (O)
2002—Rams, 28-13 (StL)
(RS Pts.—Raiders 241, Rams 192)
Franchise in Los Angeles from 1982-1994
**Franchise in Los Angeles prior to 1995
*OAKLAND vs. **SAN DIEGO
RS: Raiders lead series, 54-36-2
PS: Raiders lead series, 1-0
1960—Chargers, 52-28 (LA)
      Chargers, 41-17 (O)
1961—Chargers, 44-0 (SD)
      Chargers, 41-10 (O)
1962—Chargers, 42-33 (O)
      Chargers, 31-21 (SD)
1963—Raiders, 34-33 (O)
      Raiders, 41-27 (O)
1964—Chargers, 31-17 (SD)
      Raiders, 21-20 (O)
1965—Chargers, 17-6 (O)
      Chargers, 24-14 (SD)
1966—Chargers, 29-20 (O)
      Raiders, 41-19 (SD)
1967—Raiders, 51-10 (O)
      Raiders, 41-21 (SD)
1968—Chargers, 23-14 (O)

Raiders, 34-27 (SD)
1969—Raiders, 24-12 (SD)
      Raiders, 21-16 (O)
1970—Tie, 27-27 (SD)
      Raiders, 20-17 (O)
1971—Raiders, 34-0 (O)
      Raiders, 34-33 (O)
1972—Tie, 17-17 (O)
      Raiders, 21-19 (SD)
1973—Raiders, 27-17 (SD)
      Raiders, 31-3 (O)
1974—Raiders, 14-10 (SD)
      Raiders, 17-10 (O)
1975—Raiders, 6-0 (SD)
      Raiders, 25-0 (O)
1976—Raiders, 27-17 (SD)
      Raiders, 24-0 (O)
1977—Raiders, 24-0 (O)
      Chargers, 12-7 (SD)
1978—Raiders, 21-20 (SD)
      Chargers, 27-23 (O)
1979—Chargers, 30-10 (SD)
      Raiders, 45-22 (O)
1980—Chargers, 30-24 (SD) OT
      Raiders, 38-24 (O)
      ***Raiders, 34-27 (SD)
1981—Chargers, 55-21 (O)
      Chargers, 23-10 (SD)
1982—Raiders, 28-24 (LA)
      Raiders, 41-34 (SD)
1983—Raiders, 42-10 (SD)
      Raiders, 30-14 (LA)
1984—Raiders, 33-30 (LA)
      Raiders, 44-37 (SD)
1985—Raiders, 34-21 (LA)
      Chargers, 40-34 (SD) OT
1986—Raiders, 17-13 (LA)
      Raiders, 37-31 (SD) OT
1987—Chargers, 23-17 (LA)
      Chargers, 16-14 (SD)
1988—Raiders, 24-13 (LA)
      Raiders, 13-3 (SD)
1989—Raiders, 40-14 (LA)
      Chargers, 14-12 (SD)
1990—Raiders, 24-9 (SD)
      Raiders, 17-12 (LA)
1991—Chargers, 21-13 (LA)
      Raiders, 9-7 (SD)
1992—Chargers, 27-3 (SD)
      Chargers, 36-14 (LA)
1993—Chargers, 30-23 (LA)
      Raiders, 12-7 (SD)
1994—Chargers, 26-24 (LA)
      Raiders, 24-17 (SD)
1995—Raiders, 17-7 (O)
      Chargers, 12-6 (SD)
1996—Chargers, 40-34 (O)
      Raiders, 23-14 (SD)
1997—Chargers, 25-10 (O)
      Raiders, 38-13 (SD)
1998—Raiders, 7-6 (O)
      Raiders, 17-10 (SD)
1999—Raiders, 28-9 (O)
      Chargers, 23-20 (SD)
2000—Raiders, 9-6 (O)
      Raiders, 15-13 (SD)
2001—Raiders, 34-24 (O)
      Raiders, 13-6 (SD)
2002—Chargers, 27-21 (O) OT
      Raiders, 27-7 (SD)

2003—Raiders, 34-31 (O) OT
    Chargers, 21-14 (SD)
2004—Chargers, 42-14 (SD)
    Chargers, 23-17 (O)
2005—Chargers, 27-14 (O)
    Chargers, 34-10 (SD)
(RS Pts.—Raiders 2,080, Chargers 1,922)
(PS Pts.—Raiders 34, Chargers 27)
*Franchise in Los Angeles from 1982-1994
**Franchise in Los Angeles prior to 1961
***AFC Championship
OAKLAND vs. SAN FRANCISCO
RS: Raiders lead series, 6-4
1970—49ers, 38-7 (O)
1974—Raiders, 35-24 (SF)
1979—Raiders, 23-10 (O)
1982—Raiders, 23-17 (SF)
1985—49ers, 34-10 (LA)
1988—Raiders, 9-3 (SF)
1991—Raiders, 12-6 (LA)
1994—49ers, 44-14 (SF)
2000—Raiders, 34-28 (SF) OT
2002—49ers, 23-20 (O) OT
(RS Pts.—49ers 227, Raiders 187)
*Franchise in Los Angeles from 1982-1994
OAKLAND vs. SEATTLE
RS: Raiders lead series, 27-22
PS: Series tied, 1-1
1977—Raiders, 44-7 (O)
1978—Seahawks, 27-7 (S)
    Seahawks, 17-16 (O)
1979—Seahawks, 27-10 (S)
    Seahawks, 29-24 (O)
1980—Raiders, 33-14 (O)
    Raiders, 19-17 (S)
1981—Raiders, 20-10 (O)
    Raiders, 32-31 (S)
1982—Raiders, 28-23 (LA)
1983—Seahawks, 38-36 (S)
    Seahawks, 34-21 (LA)
    **Raiders, 30-14 (LA)
1984—Raiders, 28-14 (LA)
    Seahawks, 17-14 (S)
    ***Seahawks, 13-7 (S)
1985—Seahawks, 33-3 (S)
    Raiders, 13-3 (LA)
1986—Raiders, 14-10 (LA)
    Seahawks, 37-0 (S)
1987—Seahawks, 35-13 (LA)
    Raiders, 37-14 (S)
1988—Seahawks, 35-27 (S)
    Seahawks, 43-37 (LA)
1989—Seahawks, 24-20 (LA)
    Seahawks, 23-17 (S)
1990—Raiders, 17-13 (S)
    Raiders, 24-17 (LA)
1991—Raiders, 23-20 (S) OT
    Raiders, 31-7 (LA)
1992—Raiders, 19-0 (S)
    Raiders, 20-3 (LA)
1993—Raiders, 17-13 (S)
    Raiders, 27-23 (LA)
1994—Seahawks, 38-9 (LA)
    Raiders, 17-16 (S)
1995—Raiders, 34-14 (O)
    Seahawks, 44-10 (S)
1996—Raiders, 27-21 (S)
    Seahawks, 28-21 (O)
1997—Seahawks, 45-34 (S)
    Seahawks, 22-21 (O)

1998—Raiders, 31-18 (S)
    Raiders, 20-17 (O)
1999—Seahawks, 22-21 (S)
    Raiders, 30-21 (O)
2000—Raiders, 31-3 (O)
    Seahawks, 27-24 (S)
2001—Raiders, 38-14 (O)
    Seahawks, 34-27 (S)
2002—Raiders, 31-17 (O)
(RS Pts.—Raiders 1,117, Seahawks 1,059)
(PS Pts.—Raiders 37, Seahawks 27)
*Franchise in Los Angeles from 1982-1994
**AFC Championship
***AFC First-Round Playoff
OAKLAND vs. TAMPA BAY
RS: Raiders lead series, 5-1
PS: Buccaneers lead series, 1-0
1976—Raiders, 49-16 (O)
1981—Raiders, 18-16 (O)
1993—Raiders, 27-20 (LA)
1996—Buccaneers, 20-17 (TB) OT
1999—Raiders, 45-0 (O)
2002—**Buccaneers, 48-21 (San Diego)
2004—Raiders, 30-20 (O)
(RS Pts.—Raiders 186, Buccaneers 92)
(PS Pts.—Buccaneers 48, Raiders 21)
*Franchise in Los Angeles from 1982-1994
**Super Bowl XXXVII
OAKLAND vs. **TENNESSEE
RS: Raiders lead series, 23-17
PS: Raiders lead series, 4-0
1960—Oilers, 37-22 (O)
    Raiders, 14-13 (H)
1961—Oilers, 55-0 (H)
    Oilers, 47-16 (O)
1962—Oilers, 28-20 (O)
    Oilers, 32-17 (H)
1963—Raiders, 24-13 (H)
    Raiders, 52-49 (O)
1964—Oilers, 42-28 (H)
    Raiders, 20-10 (O)
1965—Raiders, 21-17 (O)
    Raiders, 33-21 (H)
1966—Oilers, 31-0 (H)
    Raiders, 38-23 (O)
1967—Raiders, 19-7 (H)
    ***Raiders, 40-7 (O)
1968—Raiders, 24-15 (H)
1969—Raiders, 21-17 (O)
    ****Raiders, 56-7 (O)
1971—Raiders, 41-21 (O)
1972—Raiders, 34-0 (H)
1973—Raiders, 17-6 (H)
1975—Oilers, 27-26 (O)
1976—Raiders, 14-13 (H)
1977—Raiders, 34-29 (O)
1978—Raiders, 21-17 (O)
1979—Oilers, 31-17 (H)
1980—*****Raiders, 27-7 (O)
1981—Oilers, 17-16 (H)
1983—Raiders, 20-6 (LA)
1984—Raiders, 24-14 (H)
1986—Raiders, 28-17 (H)
1988—Oilers, 38-35 (H)
1989—Oilers, 23-7 (H)
1991—Oilers, 47-17 (H)
1994—Raiders, 17-14 (LA)
1997—Oilers, 24-21 (T) OT
1999—Titans, 21-14 (T)
2001—Titans, 13-10 (O)

2002—Raiders, 52-25 (O)
    ******Raiders, 41-24 (O)
2003—Titans, 25-20 (T)
2004—Raiders, 40-35 (O)
2005—Raiders, 34-25 (T)
(RS Pts.—Titans 945, Raiders 928)
(PS Pts.—Raiders 164, Titans 45)
*Franchise in Los Angeles from 1982-1994
**Franchise in Houston prior to 1997;
known as Oilers prior to 1999
***AFL Championship
****Inter-Divisional Playoff
*****AFC First-Round Playoff
******AFC Championship
OAKLAND vs. WASHINGTON
RS: Raiders lead series, 7-3
PS: Raiders lead series, 1-0
1970—Raiders, 34-20 (O)
1975—Raiders, 26-23 (W) OT
1980—Raiders, 24-21 (O)
1983—Redskins, 37-35 (W)
    **Raiders, 38-9 (Tampa)
1986—Redskins, 10-6 (W)
1989—Raiders, 37-24 (LA)
1992—Raiders, 21-20 (W)
1995—Raiders, 20-8 (W)
1998—Redskins, 29-19 (O)
2005—Raiders, 16-13 (W)
(RS Pts.—Raiders 238, Redskins 205)
(PS Pts.—Raiders 38, Redskins 9)
*Franchise in Los Angeles from
1982-1994
**Super Bowl XVIII

PHILADELPHIA vs. ARIZONA
RS: Cardinals lead series, 53-52-5
PS: Series tied, 1-1;
See Arizona vs. Philadelphia
PHILADELPHIA vs. ATLANTA
RS: Eagles lead series, 11-10-1
PS: Eagles lead series, 2-1;
See Atlanta vs. Philadelphia
PHILADELPHIA vs. BALTIMORE
RS: Eagles lead series, 1-0-1;
See Baltimore vs. Philadelphia
PHILADELPHIA vs. BUFFALO
RS: Series tied, 5-5;
See Buffalo vs. Philadelphia
PHILADELPHIA vs. CAROLINA
RS: Eagles lead series, 3-1
PS: Panthers lead series, 1-0;
See Carolina vs. Philadelphia
PHILADELPHIA vs. CHICAGO
RS: Bears lead series, 24-8-1
PS: Eagles lead series, 2-1;
See Chicago vs. Philadelphia
PHILADELPHIA vs. CINCINNATI
RS: Bengals lead series, 7-3;
See Cincinnati vs. Philadelphia
PHILADELPHIA vs. CLEVELAND
RS: Browns lead series, 31-14-1;
See Cleveland vs. Philadelphia
PHILADELPHIA vs. DALLAS
RS: Cowboys lead series, 51-39
PS: Cowboys lead series, 2-1;
See Dallas vs. Philadelphia
PHILADELPHIA vs. DENVER
RS: Eagles lead series, 6-4;
See Denver vs. Philadelphia

PHILADELPHIA vs. DETROIT
RS: Series tied, 12-12-2
PS: Eagles lead series, 1-0;
See Detroit vs. Philadelphia

PHILADELPHIA vs. GREEN BAY
RS: Packers lead series, 22-12
PS: Eagles lead series, 2-0;
See Green Bay vs. Philadelphia

PHILADELPHIA vs. HOUSTON
RS: Eagles lead series, 1-0;
See Houston vs. Philadelphia

PHILADELPHIA vs. INDIANAPOLIS
RS: Colts lead series, 9-6;
See Indianapolis vs. Philadelphia

PHILADELPHIA vs. JACKSONVILLE
RS: Jaguars lead series, 2-0;
See Jacksonville vs. Philadelphia

PHILADELPHIA vs. KANSAS CITY
RS: Eagles lead series, 3-2;
See Kansas City vs. Philadelphia

PHILADELPHIA vs. MIAMI
RS: Dolphins lead series, 7-4;
See Miami vs. Philadelphia

PHILADELPHIA vs. MINNESOTA
RS: Vikings lead series, 11-8
PS: Eagles lead series, 2-0;
See Minnesota vs. Philadelphia

PHILADELPHIA vs. NEW ENGLAND
RS: Eagles lead series, 6-3
PS: Patriots lead series, 1-0;
See New England vs. Philadelphia

PHILADELPHIA vs. NEW ORLEANS
RS: Eagles lead series, 14-8
PS; Eagles lead series, 1-0;
See New Orleans vs. Philadelphia

PHILADELPHIA vs. N.Y. GIANTS
RS: Giants lead series, 75-65-2
PS: Giants lead series, 2-0;
See N.Y. Giants vs. Philadelphia

PHILADELPHIA vs. N.Y. JETS
RS: Eagles lead series, 7-0;
See N.Y. Jets vs. Philadelphia

PHILADELPHIA vs. OAKLAND
RS: Eagles lead series, 5-4
PS: Raiders lead series, 1-0;
See Oakland vs. Philadelphia

PHILADELPHIA vs. *PITTSBURGH
RS: Eagles lead series, 45-27-3
PS: Eagles lead series, 1-0
1933—Eagles, 25-6 (Phila)
1934—Eagles, 17-0 (Pitt)
　　　Pirates, 9-7 (Phila)
1935—Pirates, 17-7 (Phila)
　　　Eagles, 17-6 (Pitt)
1936—Pirates, 17-0 (Pitt)
　　　Pirates, 6-0 (Johnstown, Pa.)
1937—Pirates, 27-14 (Pitt)
　　　Pirates, 16-7 (Pitt)
1938—Eagles, 27-7 (Buffalo)
　　　Eagles, 14-7 (Charleston, W. Va.)
1939—Eagles, 17-14 (Phila)
　　　Pirates, 24-12 (Pitt)
1940—Pirates, 7-3 (Pitt)
　　　Eagles, 7-0 (Phila)
1941—Eagles, 10-7 (Pitt)
　　　Tie, 7-7 (Phila)
1942—Eagles, 24-14 (Pitt)
　　　Steelers, 14-0 (Phila)
1945—Eagles, 45-3 (Pitt)
　　　Eagles, 30-6 (Phila)

1946—Steelers, 10-7 (Pitt)
　　　Eagles, 10-7 (Phila)
1947—Steelers, 35-24 (Pitt)
　　　Eagles, 21-0 (Phila)
　　　**Eagles, 21-0 (Pitt)
1948—Eagles, 34-7 (Pitt)
　　　Eagles, 17-0 (Phila)
1949—Eagles, 38-7 (Pitt)
　　　Eagles, 34-17 (Phila)
1950—Eagles, 17-10 (Pitt)
　　　Steelers, 9-7 (Phila)
1951—Eagles, 34-13 (Pitt)
　　　Steelers, 17-13 (Phila)
1952—Eagles, 31-25 (Pitt)
　　　Eagles, 26-21 (Phila)
1953—Eagles, 23-17 (Phila)
　　　Eagles, 35-7 (Pitt)
1954—Eagles, 24-22 (Phila)
　　　Steelers, 17-7 (Pitt)
1955—Steelers, 13-7 (Pitt)
　　　Eagles, 24-0 (Phila)
1956—Eagles, 35-21 (Pitt)
　　　Eagles, 14-7 (Phila)
1957—Steelers, 6-0 (Pitt)
　　　Eagles, 7-6 (Phila)
1958—Steelers, 24-3 (Pitt)
　　　Steelers, 31-24 (Phila)
1959—Eagles, 28-24 (Phila)
　　　Steelers, 31-0 (Pitt)
1960—Eagles, 34-7 (Phila)
　　　Steelers, 27-21 (Pitt)
1961—Eagles, 21-16 (Phila)
　　　Eagles, 35-24 (Pitt)
1962—Steelers, 13-7 (Pitt)
　　　Steelers, 26-17 (Phila)
1963—Tie, 21-21 (Phila)
　　　Tie, 20-20 (Pitt)
1964—Eagles, 21-7 (Phila)
　　　Eagles, 34-10 (Pitt)
1965—Steelers, 20-14 (Phila)
　　　Eagles, 47-13 (Pitt)
1966—Eagles, 31-14 (Phila)
　　　Eagles, 27-23 (Phila)
1967—Eagles, 34-24 (Phila)
1968—Steelers, 6-3 (Pitt)
1969—Eagles, 41-27 (Phila)
1970—Eagles, 30-20 (Phila)
1974—Steelers, 27-0 (Pitt)
1979—Eagles, 17-14 (Phila)
1988—Eagles, 27-26 (Pitt)
1991—Eagles, 23-14 (Phila)
1994—Steelers, 14-3 (Pitt)
1997—Eagles, 23-20 (Phila)
2000—Eagles, 26-23 (Pitt) OT
2004—Steelers, 27-3 (Pitt)
(RS Pts.—Eagles 1,414, Steelers 1,091)
(PS Pts.—Eagles 21, Steelers 0)
*Steelers known as Pirates prior to 1941
**Division Playoff

PHILADELPHIA vs. *ST. LOUIS
RS: Rams lead series, 17-16-1
PS: Rams lead series, 2-1
1937—Rams, 21-3 (P)
1939—Rams, 35-13 (Colorado Springs)
1940—Rams, 21-13 (C)
1942—Rams, 24-14 (Akron)
1944—Eagles, 26-13 (P)
1945—Eagles, 28-14 (P)
1946—Eagles, 25-14 (LA)
1947—Eagles, 14-7 (P)

1948—Tie, 28-28 (LA)
1949—Eagles, 38-14 (P)
　　　**Eagles, 14-0 (LA)
1950—Eagles, 56-20 (P)
1955—Rams, 23-21 (P)
1956—Rams, 27-7 (LA)
1957—Rams, 17-13 (LA)
1959—Eagles, 23-20 (P)
1964—Rams, 20-10 (LA)
1967—Rams, 33-17 (LA)
1969—Rams, 23-17 (P)
1972—Rams, 34-3 (P)
1975—Rams, 42-3 (P)
1977—Rams, 20-0 (LA)
1978—Rams, 16-14 (P)
1983—Eagles, 13-9 (P)
1985—Rams, 17-6 (P)
1986—Eagles, 34-20 (P)
1988—Eagles, 30-24 (P)
1989—***Rams, 21-7 (P)
1990—Eagles, 27-21 (LA)
1995—Eagles, 20-9 (P)
1998—Eagles, 17-14 (P)
1999—Eagles, 38-31 (P)
2001—Rams, 20-17 (P) OT
　　　****Rams, 29-24 (StL)
2002—Eagles, 10-3 (P)
2004—Rams, 20-7 (StL)
2005—Eagles, 17-16 (StL)
(RS Pts.—Rams 690, Eagles 622)
(PS Pts.—Rams 50, Eagles 45)
*Franchise in Los Angeles prior to 1995
and in Cleveland prior to 1946
**NFL Championship
***NFC First-Round Playoff
****NFC Championship

PHILADELPHIA vs. SAN DIEGO
RS: Chargers lead series, 5-4
1974—Eagles, 13-7 (SD)
1980—Chargers, 22-21 (SD)
1985—Chargers, 20-14 (SD)
1986—Eagles, 23-7 (P)
1989—Chargers, 20-17 (SD)
1995—Eagles, 27-21 (P)
1998—Chargers, 13-10 (SD)
2001—Eagles, 24-14 (P)
2005—Eagles, 20-17 (P)
(RS Pts.—Eagles 163, Chargers 147)

PHILADELPHIA vs. SAN FRANCISCO
RS: 49ers lead series, 16-8-1
PS: 49ers lead series, 1-0
1951—Eagles, 21-14 (P)
1953—49ers, 31-21 (SF)
1956—Tie, 10-10 (P)
1958—49ers, 30-24 (P)
1959—49ers, 24-14 (SF)
1964—49ers, 28-24 (P)
1966—Eagles, 35-34 (SF)
1967—49ers, 28-27 (P)
1969—49ers, 14-13 (SF)
1971—49ers, 31-3 (P)
1973—49ers, 38-28 (SF)
1975—Eagles, 27-17 (P)
1983—49ers, 22-17 (SF)
1984—49ers, 21-9 (P)
1985—49ers, 24-13 (SF)
1989—49ers, 38-28 (P)
1991—49ers, 23-7 (P)
1992—49ers, 20-14 (SF)
1993—Eagles, 37-34 (SF) OT

1994—Eagles, 40-8 (SF)
1996—*49ers, 14-0 (SF)
1997—49ers, 24-12 (P)
2001—49ers, 13-3 (SF)
2002—Eagles, 38-17 (SF)
2003—49ers, 31-28 (P) OT
2005—Eagles, 42-3 (P)
(RS Pts.—49ers 572, Eagles 540)
(PS Pts.—49ers 14, Eagles 0)
*NFC First-Round Playoff

PHILADELPHIA vs. SEATTLE
RS: Eagles lead series, 6-4
1976—Eagles, 27-10 (P)
1980—Eagles, 27-20 (S)
1986—Seahawks, 24-20 (S)
1989—Eagles, 31-7 (P)
1992—Eagles, 20-17 (S) OT
1995—Seahawks, 26-14 (S)
1998—Seahawks, 38-0 (P)
2001—Eagles, 27-3 (S)
2002—Eagles, 27-20 (S)
2005—Seahawks, 42-0 (S)
(RS Pts.—Seahawks 207, Eagles 193)

PHILADELPHIA vs. TAMPA BAY
RS: Eagles lead series, 5-4
PS: Series tied, 2-2
1977—Eagles, 13-3 (P)
1979—*Buccaneers, 24-17 (TB)
1981—Eagles, 20-10 (P)
1988—Eagles, 41-14 (TB)
1991—Buccaneers, 14-13 (TB)
1995—Buccaneers, 21-6 (P)
1999—Buccaneers, 19-5 (P)
2000—**Eagles, 21-3 (P)
2001—Eagles, 17-13 (TB)
      **Eagles, 31-9 (P)
2002—Eagles, 20-10 (P)
      ***Buccaneers, 27-10 (P)
2003—Buccaneers, 17-0 (P)
(RS Pts.—Eagles 135, Buccaneers 121)
(PS Pts.—Eagles 79, Buccaneers 63)
*NFC Divisional Playoff
**NFC First-Round Playoff
***NFC Championship

PHILADELPHIA vs. *TENNESSEE
RS: Eagles lead series, 6-2
1972—Eagles, 18-17 (H)
1979—Eagles, 26-20 (H)
1982—Eagles, 35-14 (P)
1988—Eagles, 32-23 (P)
1991—Eagles, 13-6 (H)
1994—Eagles, 21-6 (P)
2000—Titans, 15-13 (P)
2002—Titans, 27-24 (T)
(RS Pts.—Eagles 182, Titans 128)
*Franchise in Houston prior to 1997;
known as Oilers prior to 1999

PHILADELPHIA vs. *WASHINGTON
RS: Redskins lead series, 74-62-5
PS: Redskins lead series, 1-0
1934—Redskins, 6-0 (B)
      Redskins, 14-7 (P)
1935—Eagles, 7-6 (B)
1936—Redskins, 26-3 (P)
      Redskins, 17-7 (B)
1937—Eagles, 14-0 (W)
      Redskins, 10-7 (P)
1938—Redskins, 26-23 (P)
      Redskins, 20-14 (W)
1939—Redskins, 7-0 (P)

1940—Redskins, 7-6 (W)
      Redskins, 34-17 (P)
      Redskins, 13-6 (W)
1941—Redskins, 21-17 (P)
      Redskins, 20-14 (W)
1942—Redskins, 14-10 (P)
      Redskins, 30-27 (W)
1944—Tie, 31-31 (P)
      Eagles, 37-7 (W)
1945—Redskins, 24-14 (W)
      Eagles, 16-0 (P)
1946—Eagles, 28-24 (W)
      Redskins, 27-10 (P)
1947—Eagles, 45-42 (P)
      Eagles, 38-14 (W)
1948—Eagles, 45-0 (W)
      Eagles, 42-21 (P)
1949—Eagles, 49-14 (P)
      Eagles, 44-21 (W)
1950—Eagles, 35-3 (P)
      Eagles, 33-0 (W)
1951—Redskins, 27-23 (P)
      Eagles, 35-21 (W)
1952—Eagles, 38-20 (P)
      Redskins, 27-21 (W)
1953—Tie, 21-21 (P)
      Redskins, 10-0 (W)
1954—Eagles, 49-21 (W)
      Eagles, 41-33 (P)
1955—Redskins, 31-30 (P)
      Redskins, 34-21 (W)
1956—Eagles, 13-9 (P)
      Redskins, 19-17 (W)
1957—Eagles, 21-12 (P)
      Redskins, 42-7 (W)
1958—Redskins, 24-14 (P)
      Redskins, 20-0 (W)
1959—Eagles, 30-23 (P)
      Eagles, 34-14 (W)
1960—Eagles, 19-13 (P)
      Eagles, 38-28 (W)
1961—Eagles, 14-7 (P)
      Eagles, 27-24 (W)
1962—Redskins, 27-21 (P)
      Eagles, 37-14 (W)
1963—Eagles, 37-24 (W)
      Redskins, 13-10 (P)
1964—Redskins, 35-20 (W)
      Redskins, 21-10 (P)
1965—Redskins, 23-21 (W)
      Eagles, 21-14 (P)
1966—Redskins, 27-13 (P)
      Eagles, 37-28 (W)
1967—Eagles, 35-24 (P)
      Tie, 35-35 (W)
1968—Redskins, 17-14 (W)
      Redskins, 16-10 (P)
1969—Tie, 28-28 (W)
      Redskins, 34-29 (P)
1970—Redskins, 33-21 (P)
      Redskins, 24-6 (W)
1971—Tie, 7-7 (W)
      Redskins, 20-13 (P)
1972—Redskins, 14-0 (W)
      Redskins, 23-7 (P)
1973—Redskins, 28-7 (P)
      Redskins, 38-20 (W)
1974—Redskins, 27-20 (P)
      Redskins, 26-7 (W)
1975—Eagles, 26-10 (P)

      Eagles, 26-3 (W)
1976—Redskins, 20-17 (P) OT
      Redskins, 24-0 (W)
1977—Redskins, 23-17 (W)
      Redskins, 17-14 (P)
1978—Redskins, 35-30 (W)
      Eagles, 17-10 (P)
1979—Eagles, 28-17 (P)
      Redskins, 17-7 (W)
1980—Eagles, 24-14 (P)
      Eagles, 24-0 (W)
1981—Eagles, 36-13 (P)
      Redskins, 15-13 (W)
1982—Redskins, 37-34 (P) OT
      Redskins, 13-9 (W)
1983—Redskins, 23-13 (P)
      Redskins, 28-24 (W)
1984—Redskins, 20-0 (W)
      Eagles, 16-10 (P)
1985—Eagles, 19-6 (W)
      Redskins, 17-12 (P)
1986—Redskins, 41-14 (W)
      Redskins, 21-14 (P)
1987—Redskins, 34-24 (W)
      Eagles, 31-27 (P)
1988—Redskins, 17-10 (W)
      Redskins, 20-19 (P)
1989—Eagles, 42-37 (W)
      Redskins, 10-3 (P)
1990—Redskins, 13-7 (W)
      Eagles, 28-14 (P)
      **Redskins, 20-6 (P)
1991—Redskins, 23-0 (W)
      Eagles, 24-22 (P)
1992—Redskins, 16-12 (W)
      Eagles, 17-13 (P)
1993—Eagles, 34-31 (P)
      Eagles, 17-14 (W)
1994—Eagles, 21-17 (P)
      Eagles, 31-29 (W)
1995—Eagles, 37-34 (P) (OT)
      Eagles, 14-7 (W)
1996—Eagles, 17-14 (W)
      Redskins, 26-21 (P)
1997—Eagles, 24-10 (P)
      Redskins, 35-32 (W)
1998—Eagles, 17-12 (P)
      Redskins, 28-3 (W)
1999—Eagles, 35-28 (P)
      Redskins, 20-17 (W) OT
2000—Redskins, 17-14 (P)
      Eagles, 23-20 (W)
2001—Redskins, 13-3 (P)
      Eagles, 20-6 (W)
2002—Eagles, 37-7 (W)
      Eagles, 34-21 (P)
2003—Eagles, 27-25 (P)
      Eagles, 31-7 (W)
2004—Eagles, 28-6 (P)
      Eagles, 17-14 (W)
2005—Redskins, 17-10 (W)
      Redskins, 31-20 (P)
(RS Pts.—Eagles 2,880, Redskins 2,768)
(PS Pts.—Redskins 20, Eagles 6)
*Franchise in Boston prior to 1937
**NFC First-Round Playoff

PITTSBURGH vs. ARIZONA
RS: Steelers lead series, 31-22-3;
See Arizona vs. Pittsburgh

PITTSBURGH vs. ATLANTA
RS: Steelers lead series, 11-1-1;
See Atlanta vs. Pittsburgh
PITTSBURGH vs. BALTIMORE
RS: Steelers lead series, 13-7
PS: Steelers lead series, 1-0;
See Baltimore vs. Pittsburgh
PITTSBURGH vs. BUFFALO
RS: Steelers lead series, 10-8
PS: Steelers lead series, 2-1;
See Buffalo vs. Pittsburgh
PITTSBURGH vs. CAROLINA
RS: Steelers lead series, 2-1;
See Carolina vs. Pittsburgh
PITTSBURGH vs. CHICAGO
RS: Bears lead series, 16-7-1;
See Chicago vs. Pittsburgh
PITTSBURGH vs. CINCINNATI
RS: Steelers lead series, 42-29
PS: Steelers lead series, 1-0;
See Cincinnati vs. Pittsburgh
PITTSBURGH vs. CLEVELAND
RS: Browns lead series, 55-51
PS: Steelers lead series, 2-0;
See Cleveland vs. Pittsburgh
PITTSBURGH vs. DALLAS
RS: Cowboys lead series, 14-12
PS: Steelers lead series, 2-1;
See Dallas vs. Pittsburgh
PITTSBURGH vs. DENVER
RS: Broncos lead series, 11-6-1
PS: Series tied, 3-3;
See Denver vs. Pittsburgh
PITTSBURGH vs. DETROIT
RS: Series tied, 14-14-1;
See Detroit vs. Pittsburgh
PITTSBURGH vs. GREEN BAY
RS: Packers lead series, 18-13;
See Green Bay vs. Pittsburgh
PITTSBURGH vs. HOUSTON
RS: Series tied, 1-1;
See Houston vs. Pittsburgh
PITTSBURGH vs. INDIANAPOLIS
RS: Steelers lead series, 13-5
PS: Steelers lead series, 5-0;
See Indianapolis vs. Pittsburgh
PITTSBURGH vs. JACKSONVILLE
RS: Jaguars lead series, 9-8;
See Jacksonville vs. Pittsburgh
PITTSBURGH vs. KANSAS CITY
RS: Steelers lead series, 16-8
PS: Chiefs lead series, 1-0;
See Kansas City vs. Pittsburgh
PITTSBURGH vs. MIAMI
RS: Dolphins lead series, 9-8
PS: Dolphins lead series, 2-1;
See Miami vs. Pittsburgh
PITTSBURGH vs. MINNESOTA
RS: Vikings lead series, 8-6
PS: Steelers lead series, 1-0;
See Minnesota vs. Pittsburgh
PITTSBURGH vs. NEW ENGLAND
RS: Steelers lead series, 12-6
PS: Patriots lead series, 3-1;
See New England vs. Pittsburgh
PITTSBURGH vs. NEW ORLEANS
RS: Series tied, 6-6;
See New Orleans vs. Pittsburgh
PITTSBURGH vs. N.Y. GIANTS
RS: Giants lead series, 43-28-3;

See N.Y. Giants vs. Pittsburgh
PITTSBURGH vs. N.Y. JETS
RS: Steelers lead series, 15-2
PS: Steelers lead series, 1-0;
See N.Y. Jets vs. Pittsburgh
PITTSBURGH vs. OAKLAND
RS: Series tied, 8-8
PS: Series tied, 3-3;
See Oakland vs. Pittsburgh
PITTSBURGH vs. PHILADELPHIA
RS: Eagles lead series, 45-27-3
PS: Eagles lead series, 1-0;
See Philadelphia vs. Pittsburgh
*PITTSBURGH vs. **ST. LOUIS
RS: Rams lead series, 15-5-2
PS: Steelers lead series, 1-0
1938—Rams, 13-7 (New Orleans)
1939—Tie, 14-14 (C)
1941—Rams, 17-14 (Akron)
1947—Rams, 48-7 (P)
1948—Rams, 31-14 (LA)
1949—Tie, 7-7 (P)
1952—Rams, 28-14 (LA)
1955—Rams, 27-26 (LA)
1956—Steelers, 30-13 (P)
1961—Rams, 24-14 (LA)
1964—Rams, 26-14 (P)
1968—Rams, 45-10 (LA)
1971—Rams, 23-14 (P)
1975—Rams, 10-3 (LA)
1978—Rams, 10-7 (LA)
1979—***Steelers, 31-19 (Pasadena)
1981—Steelers, 24-0 (P)
1984—Steelers, 24-14 (P)
1987—Rams, 31-21 (LA)
1990—Steelers, 41-10 (P)
1993—Rams, 27-0 (LA)
1996—Steelers, 42-6 (P)
2003—Rams, 33-21 (P)
(RS Pts.—Rams 457, Steelers 368)
(PS Pts.—Steelers 31, Rams 19)
*Steelers known as Pirates prior to 1941
**Franchise in Los Angeles prior to 1995
and in Cleveland prior to 1946
***Super Bowl XIV
PITTSBURGH vs. SAN DIEGO
RS: Steelers lead series, 19-5
PS: Chargers lead series, 2-0
1971—Steelers, 21-17 (P)
1972—Steelers, 24-2 (SD)
1973—Steelers, 38-21 (P)
1975—Steelers, 37-0 (SD)
1976—Steelers, 23-0 (P)
1977—Steelers, 10-9 (SD)
1979—Chargers, 35-7 (SD)
1980—Chargers, 26-17 (SD)
1982—*Chargers, 31-28 (P)
1983—Steelers, 26-3 (P)
1984—Steelers, 52-24 (P)
1985—Chargers, 54-44 (SD)
1987—Steelers, 20-16 (SD)
1988—Chargers, 20-14 (SD)
1989—Steelers, 20-17 (P)
1990—Steelers, 36-14 (P)
1991—Steelers, 26-20 (P)
1992—Steelers, 23-6 (SD)
1993—Steelers,.16-3 (P)
1994—Chargers, 37-34 (SD)
        **Chargers, 17-13 (P)
1995—Steelers, 31-16 (P)

1996—Steelers, 16-3 (P)
2000—Steelers, 34-21 (SD)
2003—Steelers, 40-24 (P)
2005—Steelers, 24-22 (SD)
(RS Pts.—Steelers 633, Chargers 410)
(PS Pts.—Chargers 48, Steelers 41)
*AFC First-Round Playoff
**AFC Championship
PITTSBURGH vs. SAN FRANCISCO
RS: 49ers lead series, 10-8
1951—49ers, 28-24 (P)
1952—Steelers, 24-7 (SF)
1954—49ers, 31-3 (SF)
1958—49ers, 23-20 (SF)
1961—Steelers, 20-10 (P)
1965—49ers, 27-17 (SF)
1968—49ers, 45-28 (P)
1973—Steelers, 37-14 (SF)
1977—Steelers, 27-0 (P)
1978—Steelers, 24-7 (SF)
1981—49ers, 17-14 (P)
1984—Steelers, 20-17 (SF)
1987—49ers, 30-17 (P)
1990—49ers, 27-7 (SF)
1993—49ers, 24-13 (P)
1996—49ers, 25-15 (P)
1999—Steelers, 27-6 (SF)
2003—49ers, 30-14 (SF)
(RS Pts.—Steelers 364, 49ers 355)
PITTSBURGH vs. SEATTLE
RS: Seahawks lead series, 8-6
PS: Steelers lead series, 1-0
1977—Steelers, 30-20 (P)
1978—Steelers, 21-10 (P)
1981—Seahawks, 24-21 (S)
1982—Seahawks, 16-0 (S)
1983—Steelers, 27-21 (S)
1986—Seahawks, 30-0 (S)
1987—Steelers, 13-9 (P)
1991—Seahawks, 27-7 (P)
1992—Seahawks, 20-14 (P)
1993—Seahawks, 16-6 (S)
1994—Seahawks, 30-13 (S)
1998—Steelers, 13-10 (P)
1999—Steelers, 29-10 (P)
2003—Seahawks, 23-16 (S)
2005—*Steelers, 21-10 (Detroit)
(RS Pts.—Seahawks 279, Steelers 197)
(PS Pts.—Steelers 21, Seahawks 10)
*Super Bowl XL
PITTSBURGH vs. TAMPA BAY
RS: Steelers lead series, 6-1
1976—Steelers, 42-0 (P)
1980—Steelers, 24-21 (TB)
1983—Steelers, 17-12 (P)
1989—Steelers, 31-22 (TB)
1998—Buccaneers, 16-3 (TB)
2001—Steelers, 17-10 (P)
2002—Steelers, 17-7 (TB)
(RS Pts.—Steelers 151, Buccaneers 88)
PITTSBURGH vs. *TENNESSEE
RS: Steelers lead series, 38-28
PS: Steelers lead series, 3-1
1970—Oilers, 19-7 (P)
        Steelers, 7-3 (H)
1971—Steelers, 23-16 (P)
        Oilers, 29-3 (H)
1972—Steelers, 24-7 (P)
        Steelers, 9-3 (H)
1973—Steelers, 36-7 (H)

Steelers, 33-7 (P)
1974—Steelers, 13-7 (H)
Oilers, 13-10 (P)
1975—Steelers, 24-17 (P)
Steelers, 32-9 (H)
1976—Steelers, 32-16 (P)
Steelers, 21-0 (H)
1977—Oilers, 27-10 (H)
Steelers, 27-10 (P)
1978—Oilers, 24-17 (P)
Steelers, 13-3 (H)
**Steelers, 34-5 (P)
1979—Steelers, 38-7 (P)
Oilers, 20-17 (H)
**Steelers, 27-13 (P)
1980—Steelers, 31-17 (P)
Oilers, 6-0 (H)
1981—Steelers, 26-13 (P)
Oilers, 21-20 (H)
1982—Steelers, 24-10 (H)
1983—Steelers, 40-28 (H)
Steelers, 17-10 (P)
1984—Steelers, 35-7 (P)
Oilers, 23-20 (H) OT
1985—Steelers, 20-0 (P)
Steelers, 30-7 (H)
1986—Steelers, 22-16 (H) OT
Steelers, 21-10 (P)
1987—Oilers, 23-3 (P)
Oilers, 24-16 (H)
1988—Oilers, 34-14 (P)
Steelers, 37-34 (H)
1989—Oilers, 27-0 (H)
Oilers, 23-16 (P)
***Steelers, 26-23 (H) OT
1990—Steelers, 20-9 (P)
Oilers, 34-14 (H)
1991—Steelers, 26-14 (P)
Oilers, 31-6 (H)
1992—Steelers, 29-24 (H)
Steelers, 21-20 (P)
1993—Oilers, 23-3 (H)
Oilers, 26-17 (P)
1994—Steelers, 30-14 (P)
Steelers, 12-9 (H) OT
1995—Steelers, 34-17 (H)
Steelers, 21-7 (P)
1996—Steelers, 30-16 (P)
Oilers, 23-13 (H)
1997—Steelers, 37-24 (P)
Oilers, 16-6 (T)
1998—Oilers, 41-31 (P)
Oilers, 23-14 (T)
1999—Titans, 16-10 (T)
Titans, 47-36 (P)
2000—Titans, 23-20 (P)
Titans, 9-7 (T)
2001—Steelers, 34-7 (P)
Steelers, 34-24 (T)
2002—Titans, 31-23 (T)
****Titans, 34-31 (T) OT
2003—Titans, 30-13 (P)
2005—Steelers, 34-7 (P)
(RS Pts.—Steelers 1,363, Titans 1,142)
(PS Pts.—Steelers 118, Titans 75)
*Franchise in Houston prior to 1997;
known as Oilers prior to 1999
**AFC Championship
***AFC First-Round Playoff
****AFC Divisional Playoff

*PITTSBURGH vs. **WASHINGTON
RS: Redskins lead series, 42-30-3
1933—Redskins, 21-6 (P)
Pirates, 16-14 (B)
1934—Redskins, 7-0 (P)
Redskins, 39-0 (B)
1935—Pirates, 6-0 (P)
Redskins, 13-3 (B)
1936—Pirates, 10-0 (P)
Redskins, 30-0 (B)
1937—Redskins, 34-20 (W)
Pirates, 21-13 (P)
1938—Redskins, 7-0 (P)
Redskins, 15-0 (W)
1939—Redskins, 44-14 (W)
Redskins, 21-14 (P)
1940—Redskins, 40-10 (P)
Redskins, 37-10 (W)
1941—Redskins, 24-20 (P)
Redskins, 23-3 (W)
1942—Redskins, 28-14 (W)
Redskins, 14-0 (P)
1945—Redskins, 14-0 (P)
Redskins, 24-0 (W)
1946—Tie, 14-14 (W)
Steelers, 14-7 (P)
1947—Redskins, 27-26 (W)
Steelers, 21-14 (P)
1948—Redskins, 17-14 (W)
Steelers, 10-7 (P)
1949—Redskins, 27-14 (P)
Redskins, 27-14 (W)
1950—Steelers, 26-7 (W)
Redskins, 24-7 (P)
1951—Redskins, 22-7 (P)
Steelers, 20-10 (W)
1952—Redskins, 28-24 (P)
Steelers, 24-23 (W)
1953—Redskins, 17-9 (P)
Steelers, 14-13 (W)
1954—Steelers, 37-7 (P)
Redskins, 17-14 (W)
1955—Redskins, 23-14 (P)
Redskins, 28-17 (W)
1956—Steelers, 30-13 (P)
Steelers, 23-0 (W)
1957—Steelers, 28-7 (P)
Redskins, 10-3 (W)
1958—Steelers, 24-16 (P)
Tie, 14-14 (W)
1959—Redskins, 23-17 (P)
Steelers, 27-6 (W)
1960—Tie, 27-27 (W)
Steelers, 22-10 (P)
1961—Steelers, 20-0 (P)
Steelers, 30-14 (W)
1962—Steelers, 23-21 (P)
Steelers, 27-24 (W)
1963—Steelers, 38-27 (P)
Steelers, 34-28 (W)
1964—Redskins, 30-0 (P)
Steelers, 14-7 (W)
1965—Redskins, 31-3 (P)
Redskins, 35-14 (W)
1966—Redskins, 33-27 (P)
Redskins, 24-10 (W)
1967—Redskins, 15-10 (P)
1968—Redskins, 16-13 (W)
1969—Redskins, 14-7 (P)
1973—Steelers, 21-16 (P)

1979—Steelers, 38-7 (P)
1985—Redskins, 30-23 (P)
1988—Redskins, 30-29 (W)
1991—Redskins, 41-14 (P)
1997—Steelers, 14-13 (P)
2000—Steelers, 24-3 (P)
2004—Steelers, 16-7 (P)
(RS Pts.—Redskins 1,413, Steelers 1,171)
*Steelers known as Pirates prior to 1941
**Franchise in Boston prior to 1937

ST. LOUIS vs. ARIZONA
RS: Rams lead series, 29-23-2
PS: Rams lead series, 1-0;
See Arizona vs. St. Louis
ST. LOUIS vs. ATLANTA
RS: Rams lead series, 46-24-2
PS: Falcons lead series, 1-0;
See Atlanta vs. St. Louis
ST. LOUIS vs. BALTIMORE
RS: Rams lead series, 2-1;
See Baltimore vs. St. Louis
ST. LOUIS vs. BUFFALO
RS: Bills lead series, 5-4;
See Buffalo vs. St. Louis
ST. LOUIS vs. CAROLINA
RS: Panthers lead series, 8-7
PS: Panthers lead series, 1-0;
See Carolina vs. St. Louis
ST. LOUIS vs. CHICAGO
RS: Bears lead series, 47-34-3
PS: Series tied, 1-1;
See Chicago vs. St. Louis
ST. LOUIS vs. CINCINNATI
RS: Series tied, 5-5;
See Cincinnati vs. St. Louis
ST. LOUIS vs. CLEVELAND
RS: Rams lead series, 9-8
PS: Browns lead series, 2-1;
See Cleveland vs. St. Louis
ST. LOUIS vs. DALLAS
RS: Rams lead series, 10-9
PS: Series tied, 4-4;
See Dallas vs. St. Louis
ST. LOUIS vs. DENVER
RS: Series tied, 5-5;
See Denver vs. St. Louis
ST. LOUIS vs. DETROIT
RS: Rams lead series, 40-37-1
PS: Lions lead series, 1-0;
See Detroit vs. St. Louis
ST. LOUIS vs. GREEN BAY
RS: Rams lead series, 44-40-2
PS: Series tied, 1-1;
See Green Bay vs. St. Louis
ST. LOUIS vs. HOUSTON
RS: Rams lead series, 1-0;
See Houston vs. St. Louis
ST. LOUIS vs. INDIANAPOLIS
RS: Colts lead series, 22-17-2;
See Indianapolis vs. St. Louis
ST. LOUIS vs. JACKSONVILLE
RS: Rams lead series, 2-0;
See Jacksonville vs. St. Louis
ST. LOUIS vs. KANSAS CITY
RS: Series tied, 4-4;
See Kansas City vs. St. Louis
ST. LOUIS vs. MIAMI
RS: Dolphins lead series, 8-2;
See Miami vs. St. Louis

ST. LOUIS vs. MINNESOTA
RS: Vikings lead series, 17-13-2
PS: Vikings lead series, 5-2;
See Minnesota vs. St. Louis
ST. LOUIS vs. NEW ENGLAND
RS: Rams lead series, 5-4
PS: Patriots lead series, 1-0;
See New England vs. St. Louis
ST. LOUIS vs. NEW ORLEANS
RS: Rams lead series, 37-29
PS: Saints lead series, 1-0;
See New Orleans vs. St. Louis
ST. LOUIS vs. N.Y. GIANTS
RS: Rams lead series, 25-12
PS: Series tied, 1-1;
See N.Y. Giants vs. St. Louis
ST. LOUIS vs. N.Y. JETS
RS: Rams lead series, 9-2;
See N.Y. Jets vs. St. Louis
ST. LOUIS vs. OAKLAND
RS: Raiders lead series, 7-3;
See Oakland vs. St. Louis
ST. LOUIS vs. PHILADELPHIA
RS: Rams lead series, 17-16-1
PS: Rams lead series, 2-1;
See Philadelphia vs. St. Louis
ST. LOUIS vs. PITTSBURGH
RS: Rams lead series, 15-5-2
PS: Steelers lead series, 1-0;
See Pittsburgh vs. St. Louis
*ST. LOUIS vs. SAN DIEGO
RS: Rams lead series, 5-3
1970—Rams, 37-10 (LA)
1975—Rams, 13-10 (SD) OT
1979—Chargers, 40-16 (LA)
1988—Chargers, 38-24 (LA)
1991—Rams, 30-24 (LA)
1994—Chargers, 31-17 (SD)
2000—Rams, 57-31 (StL)
2002—Rams, 28-24 (StL)
(RS Pts.—Rams 222, Chargers 208)
Franchise in Los Angeles prior to 1995
*ST. LOUIS vs. SAN FRANCISCO
RS: Rams lead series, 58-52-2
PS: 49ers lead series, 1-0
1950—Rams, 35-14 (SF)
    Rams, 28-21 (LA)
1951—49ers, 44-17 (SF)
    Rams, 23-16 (LA)
1952—Rams, 35-9 (LA)
    Rams, 34-21 (SF)
1953—49ers, 31-30 (SF)
    49ers, 31-27 (LA)
1954—Tie, 24-24 (LA)
    Rams, 42-34 (SF)
1955—Rams, 23-14 (SF)
    Rams, 27-14 (LA)
1956—49ers, 33-30 (SF)
    Rams, 30-6 (LA)
1957—49ers, 23-20 (SF)
    Rams, 37-24 (LA)
1958—Rams, 33-3 (SF)
    Rams, 56-7 (LA)
1959—49ers, 34-0 (SF)
    49ers, 24-16 (LA)
1960—49ers, 13-9 (SF)
    49ers, 23-7 (LA)
1961—49ers, 35-0 (SF)
    Rams, 17-7 (LA)
1962—Rams, 28-14 (SF)

49ers, 24-17 (LA)
1963—Rams, 28-21 (LA)
    Rams, 21-17 (SF)
1964—Rams, 42-14 (LA)
    49ers, 28-7 (SF)
1965—49ers, 45-21 (LA)
    49ers, 30-27 (SF)
1966—Rams, 34-3 (LA)
    49ers, 21-13 (SF)
1967—49ers, 27-24 (LA)
    Rams, 17-7 (SF)
1968—Rams, 24-10 (LA)
    Tie, 20-20 (SF)
1969—Rams, 27-21 (SF)
    Rams, 41-30 (LA)
1970—49ers, 20-6 (LA)
    Rams, 30-13 (SF)
1971—Rams, 20-13 (LA)
    Rams, 17-6 (LA)
1972—Rams, 31-7 (LA)
    Rams, 26-16 (SF)
1973—Rams, 40-20 (SF)
    Rams, 31-13 (LA)
1974—Rams, 37-14 (LA)
    Rams, 15-13 (SF)
1975—Rams, 23-14 (SF)
    49ers, 24-23 (LA)
1976—49ers, 16-0 (LA)
    Rams, 23-3 (SF)
1977—Rams, 34-14 (LA)
    Rams, 23-10 (SF)
1978—Rams, 27-10 (LA)
    Rams, 31-28 (SF)
1979—Rams, 27-24 (LA)
    Rams, 26-20 (SF)
1980—Rams, 48-26 (LA)
    Rams, 31-17 (SF)
1981—49ers, 20-17 (SF)
    49ers, 33-31 (LA)
1982—49ers, 30-24 (LA)
    Rams, 21-20 (SF)
1983—Rams, 10-7 (SF)
    49ers, 45-35 (LA)
1984—49ers, 33-0 (LA)
    49ers, 19-16 (SF)
1985—49ers, 28-14 (LA)
    Rams, 27-20 (SF)
1986—Rams, 16-13 (LA)
    49ers, 24-14 (SF)
1987—49ers, 31-10 (LA)
    49ers, 48-0 (SF)
1988—49ers, 24-21 (LA)
    Rams, 38-16 (SF)
1989—Rams, 13-12 (SF)
    49ers, 30-27 (LA)
    **49ers, 30-3 (SF)
1990—Rams, 28-17 (SF)
    49ers, 26-10 (LA)
1991—49ers, 27-10 (SF)
    49ers, 33-10 (LA)
1992—49ers, 27-24 (SF)
    49ers, 27-10 (LA)
1993—49ers, 40-17 (SF)
    49ers, 35-10 (LA)
1994—49ers, 34-19 (LA)
    49ers, 31-27 (SF)
1995—49ers, 44-10 (StL)
    49ers, 41-13 (SF)
1996—49ers, 34-0 (SF)
    49ers, 28-11 (StL)

1997—49ers, 15-12 (StL)
    49ers, 30-10 (SF)
1998—49ers, 28-10 (StL)
    49ers, 38-19 (SF)
1999—Rams, 42-20 (StL)
    Rams, 23-7 (SF)
2000—Rams, 41-24 (StL)
    Rams, 34-24 (SF)
2001—Rams, 30-26 (SF)
    Rams, 27-14 (StL)
2002—49ers, 37-13 (SF)
    Rams, 31-20 (StL)
2003—Rams, 27-24 (StL) OT
    49ers, 30-10 (SF)
2004—Rams, 24-14 (SF)
    Rams, 16-6 (StL)
2005—49ers, 28-25 (SF)
    49ers, 24-20 (StL)
(RS Pts.—Rams 2,507, 49ers 2,484)
(PS Pts.—49ers 30, Rams 3)
Franchise in Los Angeles prior to 1995
*NFC Championship
*ST. LOUIS vs. SEATTLE
RS: Rams lead series, 9-6
PS: Rams lead series, 1-0
1976—Rams, 45-6 (LA)
1979—Rams, 24-0 (S)
1985—Rams, 35-24 (S)
1988—Rams, 31-10 (LA)
1991—Seahawks, 23-9 (S)
1997—Seahawks, 17-9 (StL)
2000—Rams, 37-34 (Sea)
2002—Rams, 37-20 (StL)
    Seahawks, 30-10 (Sea)
2003—Seahawks, 24-23 (Sea)
    Rams, 27-22 (StL)
2004—Rams, 33-27 (Sea) OT
    Rams, 23-12 (StL)
    **Rams, 27-20 (Sea)
2005—Seahawks, 37-31 (StL)
    Seahawks, 31-16 (Sea)
(RS Pts.—Rams 390, Seahawks 317)
(PS Pts.—Rams 27, Seahawks 20)
Franchise in Los Angeles prior to 1995
*NFC First-Round Playoff
*ST. LOUIS vs. TAMPA BAY
RS: Rams lead series, 9-6
PS: Rams lead series, 2-0
1977—Rams, 31-0 (LA)
1978—Rams, 26-23 (LA)
1979—Buccaneers, 21-6 (TB)
    **Rams, 9-0 (TB)
1980—Buccaneers, 10-9 (TB)
1984—Rams, 34-33 (TB)
1985—Rams, 31-27 (TB)
1986—Rams, 26-20 (LA) OT
1987—Rams, 35-3 (LA)
1990—Rams, 35-14 (TB)
1992—Rams, 31-27 (TB)
1994—Buccaneers, 24-14 (TB)
1999—**Rams, 11-6 (StL)
2000—Buccaneers, 38-35 (TB)
2001—Buccaneers, 24-17 (StL)
2002—Buccaneers, 26-14 (TB)
2004—Rams, 28-21 (StL)
(RS Pts.—Rams 372, Buccaneers 311)
(PS Pts.—Rams 20, Buccaneers 6)
Franchise in Los Angeles prior to 1995
*NFC Championship

*ST. LOUIS vs. **TENNESSEE
RS: Rams lead series, 6-3
PS: Rams lead series, 1-0
1973—Rams, 31-26 (H)
1978—Rams, 10-6 (H)
1981—Oilers, 27-20 (LA)
1984—Rams, 27-16 (LA)
1987—Oilers, 20-16 (H)
1990—Rams, 17-13 (LA)
1993—Rams, 28-13 (H)
1999—Titans, 24-21 (T)
　　　***Rams, 23-16 (Atlanta)
2005—Rams, 31-27 (StL)
(RS Pts.—Rams 201, Titans 172)
(PS Pts.—Rams 23, Titans 16)
Franchise in Los Angeles prior to 1995
**Franchise in Houston prior to 1997;
known as Oilers prior to 1999
***Super Bowl XXXIV

*ST. LOUIS vs. WASHINGTON
RS: Redskins lead series, 20-6-1
PS: Series tied, 2-2
1937—Redskins, 16-7 (C)
1938—Redskins, 37-13 (W)
1941—Redskins, 17-13 (W)
1942—Redskins, 33-14 (W)
1944—Redskins, 14-10 (W)
1945—**Rams, 15-14 (C)
1948—Rams, 41-13 (W)
1949—Rams, 53-27 (LA)
1951—Redskins, 31-21 (W)
1962—Redskins, 20-14 (W)
1963—Redskins, 37-14 (LA)
1967—Tie, 28-28 (LA)
1969—Rams, 24-13 (W)
1971—Redskins, 38-24 (LA)
1974—Redskins, 23-17 (LA)
　　　***Rams, 19-10 (LA)
1977—Redskins, 17-14 (W)
1981—Redskins, 30-7 (LA)
1983—Redskins, 42-20 (LA)
　　　***Redskins, 51-7 (W)
1986—****Redskins, 19-7 (W)
1987—Rams, 30-26 (W)
1991—Redskins, 27-6 (LA)
1993—Rams, 10-6 (LA)
1994—Redskins, 24-21 (LA)
1995—Redskins, 35-23 (StL)
1996—Redskins, 17-10 (StL)
1997—Rams, 23-20 (W)
2000—Redskins, 33-20 (StL)
2002—Redskins, 20-17 (W)
2005—Redskins, 24-9 (StL)
(RS Pts.—Redskins 668, Rams 503)
(PS Pts.—Redskins 94, Rams 48)
Franchise in Los Angeles prior to 1995
and in Cleveland prior to 1946
**NFL Championship
***NFC Divisional Playoff
****NFC First-Round Playoff

SAN DIEGO vs. ARIZONA
RS: Chargers lead series, 7-3;
See Arizona vs. San Diego
SAN DIEGO vs. ATLANTA
RS: Falcons lead series, 6-1;
See Atlanta vs. San Diego
SAN DIEGO vs BALTIMORE
RS: Series tied, 2-2;
See Baltimore vs. San Diego

SAN DIEGO vs. BUFFALO
RS: Chargers lead series, 19-9-2
PS: Bills lead series, 2-1;
See Buffalo vs. San Diego
SAN DIEGO vs. CAROLINA
RS: Panthers lead series, 2-1;
See Carolina vs. San Diego
SAN DIEGO vs. CHICAGO
RS: Bears lead series, 5-4;
See Chicago vs. San Diego
SAN DIEGO vs. CINCINNATI
RS: Chargers lead series, 17-10
PS: Bengals lead series, 1-0;
See Cincinnati vs. San Diego
SAN DIEGO vs. CLEVELAND
RS: Chargers lead series, 12-7-1;
See Cleveland vs. San Diego
SAN DIEGO vs. DALLAS
RS: Cowboys lead series, 6-2;
See Dallas vs. San Diego
SAN DIEGO vs. DENVER
RS: Broncos lead series, 52-39-1;
See Denver vs. San Diego
SAN DIEGO vs. DETROIT
RS: Chargers lead series, 5-3;
See Detroit vs. San Diego
SAN DIEGO vs. GREEN BAY
RS: Packers lead series, 7-1;
See Green Bay vs. San Diego
SAN DIEGO vs. HOUSTON
RS: Chargers lead series, 2-0;
See Houston vs. San Diego
SAN DIEGO vs. INDIANAPOLIS
RS: Chargers lead series, 13-8
PS: Colts lead series, 1-0;
See Indianapolis vs. San Diego
SAN DIEGO vs. JACKSONVILLE
RS: Series tied, 1-1;
See Jacksonville vs. San Diego
SAN DIEGO vs. KANSAS CITY
RS: Chiefs lead series, 48-42-1
PS: Chargers lead series, 1-0;
See Kansas City vs. San Diego
SAN DIEGO vs. MIAMI
RS: Dolphins lead series, 11-10
PS: Series tied, 2-2;
See Miami vs. San Diego
SAN DIEGO vs. MINNESOTA
RS: Chargers lead series, 5-4;
See Minnesota vs. San Diego
SAN DIEGO vs. NEW ENGLAND
RS: Patriots lead series, 17-13-2
PS: Chargers lead series, 1-0;
See New England vs. San Diego
SAN DIEGO vs. NEW ORLEANS
RS: Chargers lead series, 7-2;
See New Orleans vs. San Diego
SAN DIEGO vs. N.Y. GIANTS
RS: Giants lead series, 5-4;
See N.Y. Giants vs. San Diego
SAN DIEGO vs. N.Y. JETS
RS: Chargers lead series, 18-11-1
PS: Jets lead series, 1-0;
See N.Y. Jets vs. San Diego
SAN DIEGO vs. OAKLAND
RS: Raiders lead series, 54-36-2
PS: Raiders lead series, 1-0;
See Oakland vs. San Diego
SAN DIEGO vs. PHILADELPHIA
RS: Chargers lead series, 5-4;

See Philadelphia vs. San Diego
SAN DIEGO vs. PITTSBURGH
RS: Steelers lead series, 19-5
PS: Chargers lead series, 2-0;
See Pittsburgh vs. San Diego
SAN DIEGO vs. ST. LOUIS
RS: Rams lead series, 5-3;
See St. Louis vs. San Diego
SAN DIEGO vs. SAN FRANCISCO
RS: 49ers lead series, 6-4
PS: 49ers lead series, 1-0
1972—49ers, 34-3 (SF)
1976—Chargers, 13-7 (SD) OT
1979—Chargers, 31-9 (SD)
1982—49ers, 41-37 (SF)
1988—49ers, 48-10 (SD)
1991—49ers, 34-14 (SF)
1994—49ers, 38-15 (SD)
　　　*49ers, 49-26 (Miami)
1997—49ers, 17-10 (SF)
2000—49ers, 45-17 (SD)
2002—Chargers, 20-17 (SD) OT
(RS Pts.—49ers 286, Chargers 174)
(PS Pts.—49ers 49, Chargers 26)
*Super Bowl XXIX
SAN DIEGO vs. SEATTLE
RS: Seahawks lead series, 25-22
1977—Chargers, 30-28 (S)
1978—Chargers, 24-20 (S)
　　　Chargers, 37-10 (SD)
1979—Chargers, 33-16 (S)
　　　Chargers, 20-10 (SD)
1980—Chargers, 34-13 (S)
　　　Chargers, 21-14 (SD)
1981—Chargers, 24-10 (SD)
　　　Seahawks, 44-23 (S)
1983—Seahawks, 34-31 (S)
　　　Chargers, 28-21 (SD)
1984—Seahawks, 31-17 (S)
　　　Seahawks, 24-0 (SD)
1985—Seahawks, 49-35 (SD)
　　　Seahawks, 26-21 (S)
1986—Seahawks, 33-7 (S)
　　　Seahawks, 34-24 (SD)
1987—Seahawks, 34-3 (S)
1988—Chargers, 17-6 (SD)
　　　Seahawks, 17-14 (S)
1989—Seahawks, 17-16 (S)
　　　Seahawks, 10-7 (S)
1990—Chargers, 31-14 (S)
　　　Seahawks, 13-10 (SD) OT
1991—Seahawks, 20-9 (S)
　　　Chargers, 17-14 (SD)
1992—Chargers, 17-6 (SD)
　　　Chargers, 31-14 (S)
1993—Chargers, 18-12 (SD)
　　　Seahawks, 31-14 (S)
1994—Chargers, 24-10 (S)
　　　Chargers, 35-15 (SD)
1995—Chargers, 14-10 (SD)
　　　Chargers, 35-25 (S)
1996—Chargers, 29-7 (SD)
　　　Seahawks, 32-13 (S)
1997—Seahawks, 26-22 (S)
　　　Seahawks, 37-31 (SD)
1998—Seahawks, 27-20 (SD)
　　　Seahawks, 38-17 (S)
1999—Chargers, 13-10 (SD)
　　　Chargers, 19-16 (S)
2000—Seahawks, 20-12 (SD)

Seahawks, 17-15 (S)
2001—Seahawks, 13-10 (S) OT
Seahawks, 25-22 (SD)
2002—Seahawks, 31-28 (SD) OT
(RS Pts.—Seahawks 984, Chargers 972)
SAN DIEGO vs. TAMPA BAY
RS: Chargers lead series, 7-1
1976—Chargers, 23-0 (TB)
1981—Chargers, 24-23 (TB)
1987—Chargers, 17-13 (TB)
1990—Chargers, 41-10 (SD)
1992—Chargers, 29-14 (SD)
1993—Chargers, 32-17 (TB)
1996—Buccaneers, 25-17 (SD)
2004—Chargers, 31-24 (SD)
(RS Pts.—Chargers 214, Buccaneers 126)
*SAN DIEGO vs. **TENNESSEE
RS: Chargers lead series, 20-13-1
PS: Titans lead series, 3-0
1960—Oilers, 38-28 (H)
Chargers, 24-21 (LA)
***Oilers, 24-16 (H)
1961—Chargers, 34-24 (SD)
Oilers, 33-13 (H)
***Oilers, 10-3 (SD)
1962—Oilers, 42-17 (SD)
Oilers, 33-27 (H)
1963—Chargers, 27-0 (SD)
Chargers 20-14 (H)
1964—Chargers, 27-21 (SD)
Chargers, 20-17 (H)
1965—Chargers, 31-14 (SD)
Chargers, 37-26 (H)
1966—Chargers, 28-22 (H)
1967—Chargers, 13-3 (SD)
Oilers, 24-17 (H)
1968—Chargers, 30-14 (SD)
1969—Chargers, 21-17 (H)
1970—Tie, 31-31 (SD)
1971—Oilers, 49-33 (H)
1972—Chargers, 34-20 (SD)
1974—Oilers, 21-14 (H)
1975—Oilers, 33-17 (H)
1976—Chargers, 30-27 (SD)
1978—Chargers, 45-24 (H)
1979—****Oilers, 17-14 (SD)
1984—Chargers, 31-14 (SD)
1985—Oilers, 37-35 (H)
1986—Chargers, 27-0 (SD)
1987—Oilers, 33-18 (H)
1989—Oilers, 34-27 (SD)
1990—Oilers, 17-7 (SD)
1992—Oilers, 27-0 (H)
1993—Chargers, 18-17 (SD)
1998—Chargers, 13-7 (T)
2004—Chargers, 38-17 (SD)
(RS Pts.—Chargers 832, Titans 771)
(PS Pts.—Titans 51, Chargers 33)
*Franchise in Los Angeles prior to 1961
**Franchise in Houston prior to 1997;
known as Oilers prior to 1999
***AFC Championship
****AFC Divisional Playoff
SAN DIEGO vs. WASHINGTON
RS: Redskins lead series, 6-2
1973—Redskins, 38-0 (W)
1980—Redskins, 40-17 (W)
1983—Redskins, 27-24 (SD)
1986—Redskins, 30-27 (SD)
1989—Redskins, 26-21 (W)

1998—Redskins, 24-20 (W)
2001—Chargers, 30-3 (SD)
2005—Chargers, 23-17 (W) OT
(RS Pts.—Redskins 205, Chargers 162)

SAN FRANCISCO vs. ARIZONA
RS: 49ers lead series, 17-12;
See Arizona vs. San Francisco
SAN FRANCISCO vs. ATLANTA
RS: 49ers lead series, 44-26-1
PS: Falcons lead series, 1-0;
See Atlanta vs. San Francisco
SAN FRANCISCO vs. BALTIMORE
RS: Series tied, 1-1;
See Baltimore vs. San Francisco
SAN FRANCISCO vs. BUFFALO
RS: Bills lead series, 5-4;
See Buffalo vs. San Francisco
SAN FRANCISCO vs. CAROLINA
RS: Panthers lead series, 8-7;
See Carolina vs. San Francisco
SAN FRANCISCO vs. CHICAGO
RS: Bears lead series, 28-27-1
PS: 49ers lead series, 3-0;
See Chicago vs. San Francisco
SAN FRANCISCO vs. CINCINNATI
RS: 49ers lead series, 7-3
PS: 49ers lead series, 2-0;
See Cincinnati vs. San Francisco
SAN FRANCISCO vs. CLEVELAND
RS: Browns lead series, 10-6;
See Cleveland vs. San Francisco
SAN FRANCISCO vs. DALLAS
RS: 49ers lead series, 14-9-1
PS: Cowboys lead series, 5-2;
See Dallas vs. San Francisco
SAN FRANCISCO vs. DENVER
RS: Broncos lead series, 6-4
PS: 49ers lead series, 1-0;
See Denver vs. San Francisco
SAN FRANCISCO vs. DETROIT
RS: 49ers lead series, 31-26-1
PS: Series tied, 1-1;
See Detroit vs. San Francisco
SAN FRANCISCO vs. GREEN BAY
RS: Packers lead series, 27-25-1
PS: Packers lead series, 4-1;
See Green Bay vs. San Francisco
SAN FRANCISCO vs. HOUSTON
RS: 49ers lead series, 1-0;
See Houston vs. San Francisco
SAN FRANCISCO vs. INDIANAPOLIS
RS: Colts lead series, 23-18;
See Indianapolis vs. San Francisco
SAN FRANCISCO vs. JACKSONVILLE
RS: Jaguars lead series, 2-0;
See Jacksonville vs. San Francisco
SAN FRANCISCO vs. KANSAS CITY
RS: 49ers lead series, 6-3;
See Kansas City vs. San Francisco
SAN FRANCISCO vs. MIAMI
RS: Dolphins lead series, 5-4
PS: 49ers lead series, 1-0;
See Miami vs. San Francisco
SAN FRANCISCO vs. MINNESOTA
RS: Vikings lead series, 18-17-1
PS: 49ers lead series, 4-1;
See Minnesota vs. San Francisco
SAN FRANCISCO vs. NEW ENGLAND
RS: 49ers lead series, 7-3;

See New England vs. San Francisco
SAN FRANCISCO vs. NEW ORLEANS
RS: 49ers lead series, 45-20-2;
See New Orleans vs. San Francisco
SAN FRANCISCO vs. N.Y. GIANTS
RS: 49ers lead series, 13-12
PS: 49ers lead series, 4-3;
See N.Y. Giants vs. San Francisco
SAN FRANCISCO vs. N.Y. JETS
RS: 49ers lead series, 8-2;
See N.Y. Jets vs. San Francisco
SAN FRANCISCO vs. OAKLAND
RS: Raiders lead series, 6-4;
See Oakland vs. San Francisco
SAN FRANCISCO vs. PHILADELPHIA
RS: 49ers lead series, 16-8-1
PS: 49ers lead series, 1-0;
See Philadelphia vs. San Francisco
SAN FRANCISCO vs. PITTSBURGH
RS: 49ers lead series, 10-8;
See Pittsburgh vs. San Francisco
SAN FRANCISCO vs. ST. LOUIS
RS: Rams lead series, 58-52-2
PS: 49ers lead series, 1-0;
See St. Louis vs. San Francisco
SAN FRANCISCO vs. SAN DIEGO
RS: 49ers lead series, 6-4
PS: 49ers lead series, 1-0;
See San Diego vs. San Francisco
SAN FRANCISCO vs. SEATTLE
RS: Seahawks lead series, 8-6
1976—49ers, 37-21 (Sea)
1979—Seahawks, 35-24 (SF)
1985—49ers, 19-6 (SF)
1988—49ers, 38-7 (Sea)
1991—49ers, 24-22 (Sea)
1997—Seahawks, 38-9 (Sea)
2002—49ers, 28-21 (Sea)
49ers, 31-24 (SF)
2003—Seahawks, 20-19 (Sea)
Seahawks, 24-17 (SF)
2004—Seahawks, 34-0 (Sea)
Seahawks, 42-27 (SF)
2005—Seahawks, 27-25 (SF)
Seahawks, 41-3 (Sea)
(RS Pts.—Seahawks 362, 49ers 301)
SAN FRANCISCO vs. TAMPA BAY
RS: 49ers lead series, 14-3
PS: Buccaneers lead series, 1-0
1977—49ers, 20-10 (SF)
1978—49ers, 6-3 (SF)
1979—49ers, 23-7 (SF)
1980—Buccaneers, 24-23 (SF)
1983—49ers, 35-21 (SF)
1984—49ers, 24-17 (SF)
1986—49ers, 31-7 (TB)
1987—49ers, 24-10 (TB)
1989—49ers, 20-16 (TB)
1990—49ers, 31-7 (SF)
1992—49ers, 21-14 (SF)
1993—49ers, 45-21 (TB)
1994—49ers, 41-16 (SF)
1997—Buccaneers, 13-6 (TB)
2002—*Buccaneers, 31-6 (TB)
2003—49ers, 24-7 (SF)
2004—Buccaneers, 35-3 (TB)
2005—49ers, 15-10 (TB)
(RS Pts.—49ers 392, Buccaneers 238)
(PS Pts.—Buccaneers 31, 49ers 6)
*NFC Divisional Playoff

SAN FRANCISCO vs. *TENNESSEE
RS: 49ers lead series, 7-4
1970—49ers, 30-20 (H)
1975—Oilers, 27-13 (SF)
1978—Oilers, 20-19 (H)
1981—49ers, 28-6 (SF)
1984—49ers, 34-21 (H)
1987—49ers, 27-20 (H)
1990—49ers, 24-21 (H)
1993—Oilers, 10-7 (SF)
1996—49ers, 10-9 (H)
1999—49ers, 24-22 (SF)
2005—Titans, 33-22 (T)
(RS Pts.—49ers 238, Titans 209)
*Franchise in Houston prior to 1997;
known as Oilers prior to 1999

SAN FRANCISCO vs. WASHINGTON
RS: 49ers lead series, 13-9-1
PS: 49ers lead series, 3-1
1952—49ers, 23-17 (W)
1954—49ers, 41-7 (SF)
1955—Redskins, 7-0 (W)
1961—49ers, 35-3 (W)
1967—Redskins, 31-28 (W)
1969—Tie, 17-17 (SF)
1970—49ers, 26-17 (SF)
1971—*49ers, 24-20 (SF)
1973—Redskins, 33-9 (W)
1976—Redskins, 24-21 (SF)
1978—Redskins, 38-20 (W)
1981—49ers, 30-17 (W)
1983—**Redskins, 24-21 (W)
1984—49ers, 37-31 (SF)
1985—49ers, 35-8 (W)
1986—Redskins, 14-6 (W)
1988—49ers, 37-21 (SF)
1990—49ers, 26-13 (SF)
    *49ers, 28-10 (SF)
1992—*49ers, 20-13 (SF)
1994—49ers, 37-22 (W)
1996—49ers, 19-16 (W) OT
1998—49ers, 45-10 (W)
1999—Redskins, 26-20 (SF) OT
2002—49ers, 20-10 (SF)
2004—Redskins, 26-16 (SF)
2005—Redskins, 52-17 (W)
(RS Pts.—49ers 565, Redskins 460)
(PS Pts.—49ers 93, Redskins 67)
*NFC Divisional Playoff
**NFC Championship

SEATTLE vs. ARIZONA
RS: Series tied, 7-7;
See Arizona vs. Seattle
SEATTLE vs. ATLANTA
RS: Seahawks lead series, 8-2;
See Atlanta vs. Seattle
SEATTLE vs. BALTIMORE
RS: Ravens lead series, 2-0;
See Baltimore vs. Seattle
SEATTLE vs. BUFFALO
RS: Seahawks lead series, 6-4;
See Buffalo vs. Seattle
SEATTLE vs. CAROLINA
RS: Series tied, 1-1
PS: Seahawks lead series, 1-0;
See Carolina vs. Seattle
SEATTLE vs. CHICAGO
RS: Seahawks lead series, 6-2;
See Chicago vs. Seattle

SEATTLE vs. CINCINNATI
RS: Series tied, 8-8
PS: Bengals lead series, 1-0;
See Cincinnati vs. Seattle
SEATTLE vs. CLEVELAND
RS: Seahawks lead series, 11-4;
See Cleveland vs. Seattle
SEATTLE vs. DALLAS
RS: Cowboys lead series, 6-4;
See Dallas vs. Seattle
SEATTLE vs. DENVER
RS: Broncos lead series, 33-17
PS: Seahawks lead series, 1-0;
See Denver vs. Seattle
SEATTLE vs. DETROIT
RS: Seahawks lead series, 5-4;
See Detroit vs. Seattle
SEATTLE vs. GREEN BAY
RS: Packers lead series, 6-4
PS: Packers lead series, 1-0;
See Green Bay vs. Seattle
SEATTLE vs. HOUSTON
RS: Seahawks lead series, 1-0;
See Houston vs. Seattle
SEATTLE vs. INDIANAPOLIS
RS: Colts lead series, 5-4;
See Indianapolis vs. Seattle
SEATTLE vs. JACKSONVILLE
RS: Seahawks lead series, 3-2;
See Jacksonville vs. Seattle
SEATTLE vs. KANSAS CITY
RS: Chiefs lead series, 30-18;
See Kansas City vs. Seattle
SEATTLE vs. MIAMI
RS: Dolphins lead series, 6-3
PS: Dolphins lead series, 2-1;
See Miami vs. Seattle
SEATTLE vs. MINNESOTA
RS: Seahawks lead series, 6-3;
See Minnesota vs. Seattle
SEATTLE vs. NEW ENGLAND
RS: Series tied, 7-7;
See New England vs. Seattle
SEATTLE vs. NEW ORLEANS
RS: Seahawks lead series, 5-4;
See New Orleans vs. Seattle
SEATTLE vs. N.Y. GIANTS
RS: Giants lead series, 7-4;
See N.Y. Giants vs. Seattle
SEATTLE vs. N.Y. JETS
RS: Series tied, 8-8;
See N.Y. Jets vs. Seattle
SEATTLE vs. OAKLAND
RS: Raiders lead series, 27-22
PS: Series tied, 1-1;
See Oakland vs. Seattle
SEATTLE vs. PHILADELPHIA
RS: Eagles lead series, 6-4;
See Philadelphia vs. Seattle
SEATTLE vs. PITTSBURGH
RS: Seahawks lead series, 8-6
PS: Steelers lead series, 1-0;
See Pittsburgh vs. Seattle
SEATTLE vs. ST. LOUIS
RS: Rams lead series, 9-6
PS: Rams lead series, 1-0;
See St. Louis vs. Seattle
SEATTLE vs. SAN DIEGO
RS: Seahawks lead series, 25-22;
See San Diego vs. Seattle

SEATTLE vs. SAN FRANCISCO
RS: Seahawks lead series, 8-6;
See San Francisco vs. Seattle
SEATTLE vs. TAMPA BAY
RS: Seahawks lead series, 5-1
1976—Seahawks, 13-10 (TB)
1977—Seahawks, 30-23 (S)
1994—Seahawks, 22-21 (S)
1996—Seahawks, 17-13 (TB)
1999—Buccaneers, 16-3 (S)
2004—Seahawks, 10-6 (TB)
(RS Pts.—Seahawks 95, Buccaneers 89)
SEATTLE vs. *TENNESSEE
RS: Seahawks lead series, 9-4
PS: Titans lead series, 1-0
1977—Oilers, 22-10 (S)
1979—Seahawks, 34-14 (S)
1980—Seahawks, 26-7 (H)
1981—Oilers, 35-17 (H)
1982—Oilers, 23-21 (H)
1987—**Oilers, 23-20 (H) OT
1988—Seahawks, 27-24 (S)
1990—Seahawks, 13-10 (S) OT
1993—Oilers, 24-14 (H)
1994—Seahawks, 16-14 (H)
1996—Seahawks, 23-16 (S)
1997—Seahawks, 16-13 (S)
1998—Seahawks, 20-18 (S)
2005—Seahawks, 28-24 (T)
(RS Pts.—Seahawks 265, Titans 244)
(PS Pts.—Titans 23, Seahawks 20)
*Franchise in Houston prior to 1997;
known as Oilers prior to 1999
**AFC First-Round Playoff
SEATTLE vs. WASHINGTON
RS: Redskins lead series, 9-4
PS: Seahawks lead series, 1-0
1976—Redskins, 31-7 (W)
1980—Seahawks, 14-0 (W)
1983—Redskins, 27-17 (S)
1986—Redskins, 19-14 (W)
1989—Redskins, 29-0 (S)
1992—Redskins, 16-3 (S)
1994—Seahawks, 28-7 (W)
1995—Seahawks, 27-20 (W)
1998—Seahawks, 24-14 (S)
2001—Redskins, 27-14 (W)
2002—Redskins, 14-3 (S)
2003—Redskins, 27-20 (W)
2005—Redskins, 20-17 (W) OT
    *Seahawks, 20-10 (S)
(RS Pts.—Redskins 251, Seahawks 188)
(PS Pts.—Seahawks 20, Redskins 10)
*NFC Divisional Playoff

TAMPA BAY vs. ARIZONA
RS: Cardinals lead series, 8-7;
See Arizona vs. Tampa Bay
TAMPA BAY vs. ATLANTA
RS: Buccaneers lead series, 15-10;
See Atlanta vs. Tampa Bay
TAMPA BAY vs. BALTIMORE
RS: Buccaneers lead series, 2-0;
See Baltimore vs. Tampa Bay
TAMPA BAY vs. BUFFALO
RS: Buccaneers lead series, 6-2;
See Buffalo vs. Tampa Bay
TAMPA BAY vs. CAROLINA
RS: Panthers lead series, 6-5;
See Carolina vs. Tampa Bay

TAMPA BAY vs. CHICAGO
RS: Bears lead series, 34-17;
See Chicago vs. Tampa Bay
TAMPA BAY vs. CINCINNATI
RS: Buccaneers lead series, 5-3;
See Cincinnati vs. Tampa Bay
TAMPA BAY vs. CLEVELAND
RS: Browns lead series, 5-1;
See Cleveland vs. Tampa Bay
TAMPA BAY vs. DALLAS
RS: Cowboys lead series, 6-3
PS: Cowboys lead series, 2-0;
See Dallas vs. Tampa Bay
TAMPA BAY vs. DENVER
RS: Broncos lead series, 4-2;
See Denver vs. Tampa Bay
TAMPA BAY vs. DETROIT
RS: Lions lead series, 26-24
PS: Buccaneers lead series, 1-0;
See Detroit vs. Tampa Bay
TAMPA BAY vs. GREEN BAY
RS: Packers lead series, 29-19-1
PS: Packers lead series, 1-0;
See Green Bay vs. Tampa Bay
TAMPA BAY vs. HOUSTON
RS: Buccaneers lead series, 1-0;
See Houston vs. Tampa Bay
TAMPA BAY vs. INDIANAPOLIS
RS: Colts lead series, 6-4;
See Indianapolis vs. Tampa Bay
TAMPA BAY vs. JACKSONVILLE
RS: Jaguars lead series, 2-1;
See Jacksonville vs. Tampa Bay
TAMPA BAY vs. KANSAS CITY
RS: Chiefs lead series, 5-4;
See Kansas City vs. Tampa Bay
TAMPA BAY vs. MIAMI
RS: Series tied, 4-4;
See Miami vs. Tampa Bay
TAMPA BAY vs. MINNESOTA
RS: Vikings lead series, 31-19;
See Minnesota vs. Tampa Bay
TAMPA BAY vs. NEW ENGLAND
RS: Patriots lead series, 4-2;
See New England vs. Tampa Bay
TAMPA BAY vs. NEW ORLEANS
RS: Saints lead series, 17-11;
See New Orleans vs. Tampa Bay
TAMPA BAY vs. N.Y. GIANTS
RS: Giants lead series, 9-6;
See N.Y. Giants vs. Tampa Bay
TAMPA BAY vs. N.Y. JETS
RS: Jets lead series, 8-1;
See N.Y. Jets vs. Tampa Bay
TAMPA BAY vs. OAKLAND
RS: Raiders lead series, 5-1
PS: Buccaneers lead series, 1-0;
See Oakland vs. Tampa Bay
TAMPA BAY vs. PHILADELPHIA
RS: Eagles lead series, 5-4
PS: Series tied, 2-2;
See Philadelphia vs. Tampa Bay
TAMPA BAY vs. PITTSBURGH
RS: Steelers lead series, 6-1;
See Pittsburgh vs. Tampa Bay
TAMPA BAY vs. ST. LOUIS
RS: Rams lead series, 9-6
PS: Rams lead series, 2-0;
See St. Louis vs. Tampa Bay

TAMPA BAY vs. SAN DIEGO
RS: Chargers lead series, 7-1;
See San Diego vs. Tampa Bay
TAMPA BAY vs. SAN FRANCISCO
RS: 49ers lead series, 14-3
PS: Buccaneers lead series, 1-0;
See San Francisco vs. Tampa Bay
TAMPA BAY vs. SEATTLE
RS: Seahawks lead series, 5-1;
See Seattle vs. Tampa Bay
TAMPA BAY vs. *TENNESSEE
RS: Titans lead series, 7-1
1976—Oilers, 20-0 (H)
1980—Oilers, 20-14 (H)
1983—Buccaneers, 33-24 (TB)
1989—Oilers, 20-17 (H)
1995—Oilers, 19-7 (H)
1998—Oilers, 31-22 (TB)
2001—Titans, 31-28 (Tenn) OT
2003—Titans, 33-13 (T)
(RS Pts.—Titans 198, Buccaneers 134)
*Franchise in Houston prior to 1997;
known as Oilers prior to 1999
TAMPA BAY vs. WASHINGTON
RS: Redskins lead series, 7-6
PS: Series tied, 1-1
1977—Redskins, 10-0 (TB)
1982—Redskins, 21-13 (TB)
1989—Redskins, 32-28 (W)
1993—Redskins, 23-17 (TB)
1994—Buccaneers, 26-21 (TB)
⠀⠀⠀⠀Buccaneers, 17-14 (W)
1995—Buccaneers, 14-6 (TB)
1996—Buccaneers, 24-10 (TB)
1998—Redskins, 20-16 (W)
1999—*Buccaneers, 14-13 (TB)
2000—Redskins, 20-17 (W) OT
2003—Buccaneers, 35-13 (W)
2004—Redskins, 16-10 (W)
2005—Buccaneers, 36-35 (TB)
⠀⠀⠀⠀**Redskins, 17-10 (TB)
(RS Pts.—Buccaneers 253, Redskins 241)
(PS Pts.—Redskins 30, Buccaneers 24)
*NFC Divisional Playoff
**NFC First-Round Playoff

TENNESSEE VS. ARIZONA
RS: Cardinals lead series, 5-3;
See Arizona vs. Tennessee
TENNESSEE vs. ATLANTA
RS: Titans lead series, 6-5;
See Atlanta vs. Tennessee
TENNESSEE vs. BALTIMORE
RS: Series tied, 7-7
PS: Series tied, 1-1;
See Baltimore vs. Tennessee
TENNESSEE vs. BUFFALO
RS: Titans lead series, 23-14
PS: Bills lead series, 2-1;
See Buffalo vs. Tennessee
TENNESSEE vs. CAROLINA
RS: Series tied, 1-1;
See Carolina vs. Tennessee
TENNESSEE vs. CHICAGO
RS: Bears lead series, 5-4;
See Chicago vs. Tennessee
TENNESSEE vs. CINCINNATI
RS: Titans lead series, 38-30-1
PS: Bengals lead series, 1-0;
See Cincinnati vs. Tennessee

TENNESSEE vs. CLEVELAND
RS: Browns lead series, 33-26
PS: Titans lead series, 1-0;
See Cleveland vs. Tennessee
TENNESSEE vs. DALLAS
RS: Cowboys lead series, 6-5;
See Dallas vs. Tennessee
TENNESSEE vs. DENVER
RS: Titans lead series, 20-12-1
PS: Broncos lead series, 2-1;
See Denver vs. Tennessee
TENNESSEE vs. DETROIT
RS: Titans lead series, 6-3;
See Detroit vs. Tennessee
TENNESSEE vs. GREEN BAY
RS: Titans lead series, 5-4;
See Green Bay vs. Tennessee
TENNESSEE vs. HOUSTON
RS: Titans lead series, 6-2;
See Houston vs. Tennessee
TENNESSEE vs. INDIANAPOLIS
RS: Colts lead series, 13-9
PS: Titans lead series, 1-0;
See Indianapolis vs. Tennessee
TENNESSEE vs. JACKSONVILLE
RS: Titans lead series, 12-10
PS: Titans lead series, 1-0;
See Jacksonville vs. Tennessee
TENNESSEE vs. KANSAS CITY
RS: Chiefs lead series, 25-18
PS: Chiefs lead series, 2-0;
See Kansas City vs. Tennessee
TENNESSEE vs. MIAMI
RS: Dolphins lead series, 16-13
PS: Titans lead series, 1-0;
See Miami vs. Tennessee
TENNESSEE vs. MINNESOTA
RS: Vikings lead series, 7-3;
See Minnesota vs. Tennessee
TENNESSEE vs. NEW ENGLAND
RS: Patriots lead series, 19-15-1
PS: Series tied, 1-1;
See New England vs. Tennessee
TENNESSEE vs. NEW ORLEANS
RS: Titans lead series, 6-4-1;
See New Orleans vs. Tennessee
TENNESSEE vs. N.Y. GIANTS
RS: Giants lead series, 5-3;
See N.Y. Giants vs. Tennessee
TENNESSEE vs. N.Y. JETS
RS: Titans lead series, 20-14-1
PS: Titans lead series, 1-0;
See N.Y. Jets vs. Tennessee
TENNESSEE vs. OAKLAND
RS: Raiders lead series, 23-17
PS: Raiders lead series, 4-0;
See Oakland vs. Tennessee
TENNESSEE vs. PHILADELPHIA
RS: Eagles lead series, 6-2;
See Philadelphia vs. Tennessee
TENNESSEE vs. PITTSBURGH
RS: Steelers lead series, 38-28
PS: Steelers lead series, 3-1;
See Pittsburgh vs. Tennessee
TENNESSEE vs. ST. LOUIS
RS: Rams lead series, 6-3
PS: Rams lead series, 1-0;
See St. Louis vs. Tennessee
TENNESSEE vs. SAN DIEGO
RS: Chargers lead series, 20-13-1

PS: Titans lead series, 3-0;
See San Diego vs. Tennessee
TENNESSEE vs. SAN FRANCISCO
RS: 49ers lead series, 7-4;
See San Francisco vs. Tennessee
TENNESSEE vs. SEATTLE
RS: Seahawks lead series, 9-4
PS: Titans lead series, 1-0;
See Seattle vs. Tennessee
TENNESSEE vs. TAMPA BAY
RS: Titans lead series, 7-1;
See Tampa Bay vs. Tennessee
*TENNESSEE vs. WASHINGTON
RS: Titans lead series, 5-4
1971—Redskins, 22-13 (W)
1975—Oilers, 13-10 (H)
1979—Oilers, 29-27 (W)
1985—Redskins, 16-13 (W)
1988—Oilers, 41-17 (H)
1991—Redskins, 16-13 (W) OT
1997—Oilers, 28-14 (T)
2000—Titans, 27-21 (W)
2002—Redskins, 31-14 (T)
(RS—Titans 191, Redskins 174)
*Franchise in Houston prior to 1997;
known as Oilers prior to 1999*

WASHINGTON vs. ARIZONA
RS: Redskins lead series, 71-44-2;
See Arizona vs. Washington
WASHINGTON vs. ATLANTA
RS: Redskins lead series, 14-4-1
PS: Redskins lead series, 1-0;
See Atlanta vs. Washington
WASHINGTON vs BALTIMORE
RS: Ravens lead series, 2-1;
See Baltimore vs. Washington
WASHINGTON vs. BUFFALO
RS: Bills lead series, 6-4
PS: Redskins lead series, 1-0;
See Buffalo vs. Washington
WASHINGTON vs. CAROLINA
RS: Redskins lead series, 6-1;
See Carolina vs. Washington
WASHINGTON vs. CHICAGO
RS: Bears lead series, 20-17-1
PS: Redskins lead series, 4-3;
See Chicago vs. Washington
WASHINGTON vs. CINCINNATI
RS: Redskins lead series, 4-3;
See Cincinnati vs. Washington
WASHINGTON vs. CLEVELAND
RS: Browns lead series, 33-9-1;
See Cleveland vs. Washington
WASHINGTON vs. DALLAS
RS: Cowboys lead series, 54-34-2
PS: Redskins lead series, 2-0;
See Dallas vs. Washington
WASHINGTON vs. DENVER
RS: Broncos lead series, 6-4
PS: Redskins lead series, 1-0;
See Denver vs. Washington
WASHINGTON vs. DETROIT
RS: Redskins lead series, 25-10
PS: Redskins lead series, 3-0;
See Detroit vs. Washington
WASHINGTON vs. GREEN BAY
RS: Packers lead series, 16-12-1
PS: Series tied, 1-1;
See Green Bay vs. Washington

WASHINGTON vs. HOUSTON
RS: Redskins lead series, 1-0;
See Houston vs. Washington
WASHINGTON vs. INDIANAPOLIS
RS: Colts lead series, 17-10;
See Indianapolis vs. Washington
WASHINGTON vs. JACKSONVILLE
RS: Redskins lead series, 2-1;
See Jacksonville vs. Washington
WASHINGTON vs. KANSAS CITY
RS: Chiefs lead series, 6-1;
See Kansas City vs. Washington
WASHINGTON vs. MIAMI
RS: Dolphins lead series, 6-3
PS: Series tied, 1-1;
See Miami vs. Washington
WASHINGTON vs. MINNESOTA
RS: Redskins lead series, 7-5
PS: Redskins lead series, 3-2;
See Minnesota vs. Washington
WASHINGTON vs. NEW ENGLAND
RS: Redskins lead series, 6-1;
See New England vs. Washington
WASHINGTON vs. NEW ORLEANS
RS: Redskins lead series, 13-7;
See New Orleans vs. Washington
WASHINGTON vs. N.Y. GIANTS
RS: Giants lead series, 82-60-4
PS: Series tied, 1-1;
See N.Y. Giants vs. Washington
WASHINGTON vs. N.Y. JETS
RS: Redskins lead series, 7-1;
See N.Y. Jets vs. Washington
WASHINGTON vs. OAKLAND
RS: Raiders lead series, 7-3
PS: Raiders lead series, 1-0;
See Oakland vs. Washington
WASHINGTON vs. PHILADELPHIA
RS: Redskins lead series, 74-62-5
PS: Redskins lead series, 1-0;
See Philadelphia vs. Washington
WASHINGTON vs PITTSBURGH
RS: Redskins lead series, 42-30-3;
See Pittsburgh vs. Washington
WASHINGTON vs. ST. LOUIS
RS: Redskins lead series, 20-6-1
PS: Series tied, 2-2;
See St. Louis vs. Washington
WASHINGTON vs. SAN DIEGO
RS: Redskins lead series, 6-2;
See San Diego vs. Washington
WASHINGTON vs. SAN FRANCISCO
RS: 49ers lead series, 13-9-1
PS: 49ers lead series, 3-1;
See San Francisco vs. Washington
WASHINGTON vs. SEATTLE
RS: Redskins lead series, 9-4
PS: Seahawks lead series, 1-0;
See Seattle vs. Washington
WASHINGTON vs. TAMPA BAY
RS: Redskins lead series, 7-6
PS: Series tied, 1-1;
See Tampa Bay vs. Washington
WASHINGTON vs. TENNESSEE
RS: Titans lead series, 5-4;
See Tennessee vs. Washington

INTERCONFERENCE GAMES

AFC VS. NFC (REGULAR SEASON), 1970-2005

	Balt	Buff	Cin	Cle	Den	Hou	Ind	Jax	KC	Mia
1970		0-3	1-2	0-3	2-2		3-0		0-2-1	2-1
1971		0-3	1-2	2-1	1-3		2-1		2-1	3-0
1972		2-0-1	2-1	1-2	1-3		0-3		2-1	3-0
1973		2-1	2-1	1-2	0-3-1		2-1		1-1-1	3-0
1974		2-1	2-1	1-2	2-2		1-2		1-2	2-1
1975		1-2	3-0	1-3	2-1		2-1		2-1	3-0
1976		0-2	2-0	2-0	2-0		0-2		1-1	0-2
1977		1-1	2-1	1-1	1-1		1-1		1-1	2-0
1978		1-1	2-2	4-0	2-2		2-2		0-2	3-1
1979		2-2	2-2	3-1	3-1		1-1		0-2	4-0
1980		3-1	2-2	3-1	3-1		1-1		2-0	4-0
1981		1-3	2-2	3-1	3-1		0-4		2-2	3-1
1982		1-2	1-0	0-2	2-1		0-1-1		0-3	1-1
1983		1-3	3-1	2-2	0-2		2-0		2-2	3-1
1984		1-3	2-2	1-3	3-1		0-4		1-1	4-0
1985		0-2	2-2	1-3	3-1		3-1		2-2	3-1
1986		1-1	3-1	2-2	3-1		1-3		1-1	2-2
1987		1-2	1-2	2-2	2-1-1		1-0		1-2	3-0
1988		2-2	4-0	4-0	3-1		2-2		0-2	3-1
1989		1-3	2-2	3-1	2-2		1-3		2-0	2-0
1990		3-1	1-3	1-3	1-3		2-2		4-0	2-2
1991		3-1	1-3	0-4	2-0		0-4		2-2	3-1
1992		4-0	1-3	2-2	1-3		2-0		2-2	2-2
1993		4-0	2-2	3-1	1-3		0-4		2-2	3-1
1994		1-3	1-3	3-1	1-3		0-2		3-1	2-2
1995		3-1	2-2	1-3	2-2		2-2	0-4	3-1	2-2
1996	2-2	4-0	2-2		3-1		3-1	2-2	4-0	1-3
1997	2-1-1	1-3	2-2		3-1		1-3	2-2	4-0	1-3
1998	1-3	3-1	1-3		3-1		0-4	3-1	3-1	3-1
1999	2-1	3-1	1-2	1-2	2-2		4-0	4-0	2-2	2-2
2000	2-1	2-2	1-2	0-3	3-1		2-2	2-2	2-2	2-2
2001	2-2	1-3	1-2	1-2	3-1		1-3	1-2	1-3	2-2
2002	0-4	3-1	1-3	2-2	4-0	2-2	2-2	2-2	2-2	2-2
2003	3-1	2-2	2-2	2-2	1-3	2-2	3-1	2-2	3-1	3-1
2004	3-1	4-0	4-0	1-3	3-1	1-3	4-0	3-1	1-3	2-2
2005	2-2	0-4	4-0	2-2	3-1	1-3	3-1	3-1	1-3	2-2
Total	19-18-1	64-61-1	68-60	56-62	76-56-2	6-10	54-64-1	24-19	62-54-2	87-42

	NE	NYJ	Oak	Pitt	SD	Sea	TB	Tenn	TOTALS
1970	0-3	2-1	1-2	0-3	1-2			0-3	12-27-1
1971	0-3	0-3	1-1-1	1-2	2-1			0-2-1	15-23-2
1972	3-0	1-2	3-0	2-1	0-3			0-3	20-19-1
1973	2-1	0-3	2-1	3-0	1-2			0-3	19-19-2
1974	3-0	2-1	3-0	3-0	1-2			0-3	23-17
1975	1-2	0-3	3-0	2-1	0-3			3-0	23-17
1976	1-1	0-2	3-0	1-1	2-0		0-1	2-0	16-12
1977	2-0	1-1	1-1	2-0	1-1	1-0		2-0	19-9
1978	2-2	1-3	4-0	3-1	2-2	3-1		2-2	31-21
1979	3-1	3-1	4-0	3-1	3-1	3-1		2-2	36-16
1980	1-3	1-3	2-2	4-0	2-2	1-3		4-0	33-19
1981	0-4	2-0	2-2	3-1	2-2	0-2		1-3	24-28
1982	0-1	4-0	3-0	1-0	1-0	1-0		0-3	15-14-1
1983	2-2	3-1	2-2	2-2	2-2	1-3		1-3	26-26
1984	0-4	0-2	3-1	3-1	4-0	4-0		0-4	26-26
1985	3-1	2-2	3-1	1-3	1-1	2-2		1-3	27-25
1986	3-1	2-2	1-3	2-2	0-4	3-1		2-2	26-26
1987	0-3	0-4	2-2	2-2	2-0	4-0		2-2	23-22-1
1988	2-2	2-0	1-3	1-3	2-2	1-3		3-1	30-22
1989	0-4	1-3	2-2	3-1	2-2	0-4		3-1	24-28
1990	0-4	2-0	3-1	3-1	1-1	2-2		1-3	26-26
1991	1-1	2-2	2-2	0-4	1-3	1-3		1-3	19-33
1992	0-4	0-4	2-2	1-3	2-0	0-4		3-1	22-30
1993	1-1	2-2	3-1	2-2	2-2	0-2		2-2	27-25
1994	4-0	1-3	3-1	2-2	2-2	2-0		0-4	25-27
1995	0-4	0-4	3-1	2-2	3-1	3-1		1-3	27-33
1996	2-2	1-3	1-3	2-2	1-3	2-2		2-2	32-28
1997	1-3	3-1	2-2	2-2	1-3	2-2		4-0	31-28-1
1998	2-2	2-2	3-1	2-2	1-3	3-1		1-3	31-29
1999	3-1	2-2	3-1	3-0	1-3	2-2		3-1	38-22
2000	0-4	3-1	4-0	1-2	0-4	2-2		4-0	30-30
2001	3-1	2-2	3-1	3-0	2-2	1-3		3-1	30-30
2002	3-1	3-1	2-2	2-1-1	2-2			2-2	34-29-1
2003	3-1	0-4	1-3	1-3	2-2			4-0	34-30
2004	4-0	3-1	2-2	4-0	3-1			2-2	44-20
2005	3-1	1-3	2-2	4-0	2-2			1-3	34-30
Total	58-68	54-72	85-48-1	76-51-1	57-66	44-44	0-1	62-70-1	952-866-10

NFC VS. AFC (REGULAR SEASON), 1970-2005

	Ariz	Atl	Car	Chi	Dall	Det	GB	Minn	NO
1970	2-0-1	1-2		1-2	3-0	3-0	2-1	2-1	0-3
1971	2-1	3-0		1-2	3-0	4-0	2-1	2-1	0-1-2
1972	1-2	2-2		1-2	3-0	2-0-1	2-1	1-2	0-3
1973	0-2-1	2-1		2-2	2-1	0-3	1-1-1	2-1	1-2
1974	2-1	0-3		0-3	2-1	1-2	2-1	2-1	0-3
1975	2-1	1-2		0-3	2-1	1-2	0-3	4-0	0-3
1976	1-1	0-2		0-2	2-0	2-0	0-2	2-0	1-2
1977	0-2	0-2		1-1	1-1	2-0	0-3	1-1	0-2
1978	0-4	1-3		0-4	3-1	2-2	2-2	1-3	1-3
1979	1-3	1-3		2-2	1-3	0-4	1-3	1-3	0-4
1980	1-1	2-2		0-4	3-1	0-2	1-3	1-3	1-3
1981	3-1	1-3		4-0	4-0	2-2	1-1	1-3	2-2
1982		1-1		1-1	2-1	0-1	1-1-1	1-3	1-0
1983	3-1	3-1		1-1	2-2	1-3	2-2	4-0	1-3
1984	3-1	1-3		2-2	2-2	0-4	0-4	0-4	3-1
1985	2-2	0-4		3-1	3-1	2-2	0-4	2-0	0-4
1986	1-1	1-3		4-0	1-3	1-3	1-3	1-3	1-3
1987	0-1	0-4		2-2	2-1	0-4	1-2-1	2-1	4-0
1988	1-3	1-3		3-1	0-4	1-1	1-3	2-2	4-0
1989	1-3	2-2		2-2	0-2	1-3	0-2	2-2	4-0
1990	2-2	2-2		2-2	1-1	1-3	1-3	2-2	2-2
1991	1-1	3-1		2-2	3-1	4-0	1-3	0-2	3-1
1992	0-2	2-2		1-3	4-0	2-2	3-1	3-1	3-1
1993	1-1	1-3		2-2	2-2	2-0	3-1	2-2	2-2
1994	3-1	1-3		3-1	3-1	2-2	1-3	2-2	1-3
1995	1-3	2-2	3-1	2-2	4-0	3-1	4-0	3-1	4-0
1996	0-4	0-4	3-1	2-2	2-2	1-3	3-1	1-3	1-3
1997	1-3	2-2	2-2	2-2	2-2	2-2	3-1	3-1	2-2
1998	1-3	3-1	1-3	2-2	1-3	1-3	3-1	4-0	1-3
1999	0-4	0-4	2-2	2-2	1-3	1-3	2-2	2-2	0-4
2000	1-3	1-3	2-2	2-2	1-3	2-2	1-3	3-1	1-3
2001	3-1	1-3	0-4	3-1	0-4	0-4	3-1	1-3	2-2
2002	0-4	2-1-1	3-1	1-3	2-2	0-4	3-1	1-3	2-2
2003	1-3	1-3	2-2	3-1	2-2	1-3	3-1	2-2	1-3
2004	1-3	3-1	1-3	1-3	1-3	1-3	1-3	3-1	2-2
2005	1-3	3-1	3-1	1-3	2-2	2-2	0-4	1-3	2-2
Total	43-72-2	50-82-1	22-22	61-70	72-56	50-75-1	55-72-3	67-63	53-77-2

	NYG	Phil	StL	SF	Sea	TB	Wash	TOTALS
1970	3-0	2-1	2-1	4-0			2-1	27-12-1
1971	1-2	1-2	1-2	2-1			1-2	23-15-2
1972	1-2	2-1	1-2	2-1			1-2	19-20-1
1973	1-2	2-1	3-0	1-2			2-1	19-19-2
1974	1-2	2-1	3-1	0-3			2-1	17-23
1975	2-1	0-3	3-0	1-2			1-2	17-23
1976	0-2	0-2	1-1	1-1	1-0		1-1	12-16
1977	0-2	1-1	2-0	0-2		0-1	1-1	9-19
1978	1-1	3-1	2-2	1-3		2-0	2-2	21-31
1979	1-1	2-2	2-2	0-4		2-0	2-2	16-36
1980	1-3	3-1	2-2	2-2		1-3	1-3	19-33
1981	1-1	3-1	1-3	3-1		0-4	2-2	28-24
1982	1-0	2-1	1-2	1-3		2-1		14-15-1
1983	0-4	1-1	1-3	2-2		1-3	4-0	26-26
1984	2-0	3-1	3-1	3-1		1-1	3-1	26-26
1985	2-2	1-1	3-1	3-1		0-4	4-0	25-27
1986	3-1	2-2	2-2	4-0		1-1	3-1	26-26
1987	2-1	3-1	1-2	3-1		0-2	2-1	22-23-1
1988	1-1	2-2	2-2	2-2		1-3	1-3	22-30
1989	4-0	3-1	3-1	4-0		0-4	2-2	28-24
1990	3-1	1-3	2-2	4-0		0-2	3-1	26-26
1991	3-1	4-0	1-3	3-1		1-3	4-0	33-19
1992	2-2	3-1	2-2	3-1		0-2	2-2	30-22
1993	2-2	2-2	2-2	2-2		1-3	1-3	25-27
1994	3-1	1-3	2-2	3-1		1-1	1-1	27-25
1995	0-4	1-3	1-3	3-1		2-2	0-4	33-27
1996	2-2	2-2	2-2	4-0		2-2	3-1	28-32
1997	1-3	2-1-1	0-4	2-2		3-1	1-3	28-31-1
1998	3-1	0-4	3-1	2-2		2-2	2-2	29-31
1999	2-2	1-3	3-1	1-3		3-1	2-2	22-38
2000	3-1	3-1	3-1	2-2		3-1	2-2	30-30
2001	2-2	3-1	4-0	4-0		2-2	2-2	30-30
2002	2-2	1-3	2-2	2-2	2-2	3-1	3-1	29-34-1
2003	1-3	3-1	4-0	1-3	2-2	1-3	2-2	30-34
2004	1-3	2-2	1-3	0-4	1-3	1-3	0-4	20-44
2005	3-1	3-1	3-1	1-3	3-1	2-2	0-4	30-34
Total	61-59	70-58-1	74-59	76-59	9-8	38-58	65-62	866-952-10

INTERCONFERENCE GAMES

2005 INTERCONFERENCE GAMES
(Home Team in CAPITAL letters)

AFC 34, NFC 30

AFC Victories
JACKSONVILLE 26, Seattle 14
CINCINNATI 37, Minnesota 8
Cleveland 26, GREEN BAY 24
Cincinnati 24, CHICAGO 7
MIAMI 27, Carolina 24
SAN DIEGO 45, New York Giants 23
OAKLAND 19, Dallas 13
CLEVELAND 20, Chicago 10
DENVER 21, Washington 19
Indianapolis 28, SAN FRANCISCO 3
New England 31, ATLANTA 28
NEW YORK JETS 14, Tampa Bay 12
INDIANAPOLIS 45, St. Louis 28
KANSAS CITY 28, Washington 21
CINCINNATI 21, Green Bay 14
DENVER 49, Philadelphia 21
Miami 21, NEW ORLEANS 6
Pittsburgh 20, GREEN BAY 10
NEW ENGLAND 24, New Orleans 17
Oakland 16, WASHINGTON 13
Denver 24, DALLAS 21 (OT)
Jacksonville 24, ARIZONA 17
San Diego 23, WASHINGTON 17 (OT)
TENNESSEE 33, San Francisco 22
PITTSBURGH 21, Chicago 9
NEW ENGLAND 28, Tampa Bay 0
Cincinnati 41, DETROIT 17
HOUSTON 30, Arizona 19
JACKSONVILLE 10, San Francisco 9
Pittsburgh 18, MINNESOTA 3
BALTIMORE 48, Green Bay 3
BALTIMORE 30, Minnesota 23
INDIANAPOLIS 17, Arizona 13
PITTSBURGH 35, Detroit 21

NFC Victories
Dallas 28, SAN DIEGO 24
CAROLINA 27, New England 17
TAMPA BAY 19, Buffalo 3
Atlanta 24, BUFFALO 16
PHILADELPHIA 23, Oakland 20
ST. LOUIS 31, Tennessee 27
NEW ORLEANS 19, Buffalo 7
Philadelphia 37, KANSAS CITY 31
DETROIT 35, Baltimore 17
SEATTLE 42, Houston 10
TAMPA BAY 27, Miami 13
ARIZONA 20, Tennessee 10
ATLANTA 27, New York Jets 14
CHICAGO 10, Baltimore 6
Detroit 13, CLEVELAND 10
NEW YORK GIANTS 24, Denver 23
PHILADELPHIA 20, San Diego 17
ST. LOUIS 24, Jacksonville 21
Atlanta 17, MIAMI 10
CAROLINA 30, New York Jets 3
Carolina 13, BUFFALO 9
MINNESOTA 24, Cleveland 12
New Orleans 21, NEW YORK JETS 19
St. Louis 33, HOUSTON 27 (OT)
DALLAS 31, Kansas City 28
NEW YORK GIANTS 27, Kansas City 17
Seattle 28, TENNESSEE 24
SEATTLE 28, Indianapolis 13
New York Giants 30, OAKLAND 21
SAN FRANCISCO 20, Houston 17 (OT)

REGULAR SEASON INTERCONFERENCE RECORDS, 1970-2005

AMERICAN FOOTBALL CONFERENCE

East	W	L	T	Pct.
Miami	87	42	0	.674
Buffalo	64	61	1	.512
New England	58	68	0	.460
New York Jets	54	72	0	.429
North	**W**	**L**	**T**	**Pct.**
Pittsburgh	76	51	1	.598
Cincinnati	68	60	0	.531
Baltimore	19	18	1	.513
Cleveland	56	62	0	.475
South	**W**	**L**	**T**	**Pct.**
Jacksonville	24	19	0	.558
Tennessee	62	70	1	.470
Indianapolis	54	64	1	.458
Houston	6	10	0	.375
West	**W**	**L**	**T**	**Pct.**
Oakland	85	48	1	.639
Denver	76	56	2	.575
Kansas City	62	54	2	.534
San Diego	57	66	0	.463

NATIONAL FOOTBALL CONFERENCE

East	W	L	T	Pct.
Dallas	72	56	0	.563
Philadelphia	70	58	1	.547
Washington	65	62	0	.512
New York Giants	61	59	0	.508
North	**W**	**L**	**T**	**Pct.**
Minnesota	67	63	0	.515
Chicago	61	70	0	.466
Green Bay	55	72	3	.435
Detroit	50	75	1	.401
South	**W**	**L**	**T**	**Pct.**
Carolina	22	22	0	.500
New Orleans	53	77	2	.408
Tampa Bay*	38	59	0	.392
Atlanta	50	82	1	.380
West	**W**	**L**	**T**	**Pct.**
San Francisco	76	59	0	.563
St. Louis	74	59	0	.556
Seattle* #	53	52	0	.505
Arizona	43	72	2	.375

* Records include one game played between Seattle and Tampa Bay, won by the Seahawks 13-10, in their inaugural season (1976) when Seattle competed in the NFC and Tampa Bay in the AFC.

\# Seattle was a member of the AFC from 1977-2001.

INTERCONFERENCE VICTORIES, 1970-2005

	REGULAR SEASON				PRESEASON		
	AFC	**NFC**	**Tie**		**AFC**	**NFC**	**Tie**
1970	12	27	1	1970	21	28	1
1971	15	23	2	1971	28	28	3
1972	20	19	1	1972	27	25	4
1973	19	19	2	1973	23	35	2
1974	23	17	0	1974	35	25	0
1975	23	17	0	1975	30	26	1
1976	16	12	0	1976	30	31	0
1977	19	9	0	1977	38	25	0
1978	31	21	0	1978	20	19	0
1979	36	16	0	1979	25	18	0
1980	33	19	0	1980	22	20	1
1981	24	28	0	1981	18	19	0
1982	15	14	1	1982	25	16	0
1983	26	26	0	1983	15	24	0
1984	26	26	0	1984	16	19	0
1985	27	25	0	1985	10	22	1
1986	26	26	0	1986	22	17	0
1987	23	22	1	1987	22	22	0
1988	30	22	0	1988	23	16	1
1989	24	28	0	1989	16	27	0
1990	26	26	0	1990	15	29	0
1991	19	33	0	1991	19	27	0
1992	22	30	0	1992	30	22	0
1993	27	25	0	1993	17	22	0
1994	25	27	0	1994	22	16	0
1995	27	33	0	1995	19	26	0
1996	32	28	0	1996	27	19	0
1997	31	28	1	1997	26	17	0
1998	31	29	0	1998	34	16	0
1999	38	22	0	1999	22	25	0
2000	30	30	0	2000	34	17	0
2001	30	30	0	2001	28	23	0
2002	34	29	1	2002	25	24	0
2003	34	30	0	2003	25	21	0
2004	44	20	0	2004	21	18	0
2005	34	30	0	2005	21	29	0
Total	952	866	10	Total	851	813	14

SUPER BOWL COMPOSITE STANDINGS

	W	L	Pct.	Pts.	OP
San Francisco 49ers	5	0	1.000	188	89
Baltimore Ravens	1	0	1.000	34	7
Chicago Bears	1	0	1.000	46	10
New York Jets	1	0	1.000	16	7
Tampa Bay Buccaneers	1	0	1.000	48	21
Pittsburgh Steelers	5	1	.833	141	110
Green Bay Packers	3	1	.750	127	76
New York Giants	2	1	.667	66	73
Dallas Cowboys	5	3	.625	221	132
New England Patriots	3	2	.600	107	148
Oakland/L.A. Raiders	3	2	.600	132	114
Washington Redskins	3	2	.600	122	103
Baltimore Colts	1	1	.500	23	29
Kansas City Chiefs	1	1	.500	33	42
Miami Dolphins	2	3	.400	74	103
Denver Broncos	2	4	.333	115	206
St. Louis/L.A. Rams	1	2	.333	59	67
Atlanta Falcons	0	1	.000	19	34
Carolina Panthers	0	1	.000	29	32
San Diego Chargers	0	1	.000	26	49
Seattle Seahawks	0	1	.000	10	21
Tennessee Titans	0	1	.000	16	23
Cincinnati Bengals	0	2	.000	37	46
Philadelphia Eagles	0	2	.000	31	51
Buffalo Bills	0	4	.000	73	139
Minnesota Vikings	0	4	.000	34	95

SUPER BOWL HOST CITIES

New Orleans	9	
Miami	8	
Los Angeles	7	(LA Coliseum 2, Rose Bowl 5)
San Diego	3	
Tampa	3	
Atlanta	2	
Detroit	2	
Houston	2	
Jacksonville	1	
Minneapolis	1	
Stanford	1	
Tempe	1	

FUTURE SUPER BOWL SITES

Super Bowl XLI	Feb. 4, 2007	Dolphin Stadium, South Florida
Super Bowl XLII	Feb. 3, 2008	Cardinals Stadium, Arizona
Super Bowl XLIII	Feb. 1, 2009*	Raymond James Stadium, Tampa, Florida
Super Bowl XLIV	Feb. 7, 2010*	Dolphin Stadium, South Florida

*Tentative Date

PETE ROZELLE TROPHY/SUPER BOWL MVPs*

Super Bowl I	— QB Bart Starr, Green Bay
Super Bowl II	— QB Bart Starr, Green Bay
Super Bowl III	— QB Joe Namath, N.Y. Jets
Super Bowl IV	— QB Len Dawson, Kansas City
Super Bowl V	— LB Chuck Howley, Dallas
Super Bowl VI	— QB Roger Staubach, Dallas
Super Bowl VII	— S Jake Scott, Miami
Super Bowl VIII	— RB Larry Csonka, Miami
Super Bowl IX	— RB Franco Harris, Pittsburgh
Super Bowl X	— WR Lynn Swann, Pittsburgh
Super Bowl XI	— WR Fred Biletnikoff, Oakland
Super Bowl XII	— DT Randy White and DE Harvey Martin, Dallas
Super Bowl XIII	— QB Terry Bradshaw, Pittsburgh
Super Bowl XIV	— QB Terry Bradshaw, Pittsburgh
Super Bowl XV	— QB Jim Plunkett, Oakland
Super Bowl XVI	— QB Joe Montana, San Francisco
Super Bowl XVII	— RB John Riggins, Washington
Super Bowl XVIII	— RB Marcus Allen, L.A. Raiders
Super Bowl XIX	— QB Joe Montana, San Francisco
Super Bowl XX	— DE Richard Dent, Chicago
Super Bowl XXI	— QB Phil Simms, N.Y. Giants
Super Bowl XXII	— QB Doug Williams, Washington
Super Bowl XXIII	— WR Jerry Rice, San Francisco
Super Bowl XXIV	— QB Joe Montana, San Francisco
Super Bowl XXV	— RB Ottis Anderson, N.Y. Giants
Super Bowl XXVI	— QB Mark Rypien, Washington
Super Bowl XXVII	— QB Troy Aikman, Dallas
Super Bowl XXVIII	— RB Emmitt Smith, Dallas
Super Bowl XXIX	— QB Steve Young, San Francisco
Super Bowl XXX	— CB Larry Brown, Dallas
Super Bowl XXXI	— KR-PR Desmond Howard, Green Bay
Super Bowl XXXII	— RB Terrell Davis, Denver
Super Bowl XXXIII	— QB John Elway, Denver
Super Bowl XXXIV	— QB Kurt Warner, St. Louis
Super Bowl XXXV	— LB Ray Lewis, Baltimore
Super Bowl XXXVI	— QB Tom Brady, New England
Super Bowl XXXVII	— S Dexter Jackson, Tampa Bay
Super Bowl XXXVIII	— QB Tom Brady, New England
Super Bowl XXXIX	— WR Deion Branch, New England
Super Bowl XL	— WR Hines Ward, Pittsburgh

* Award named Pete Rozelle Trophy since Super Bowl XXV.

SUPER BOWL MVP BY POSITION

Quarterback	20
Running Back	7
Wide Receiver	5
Defensive End	2
Linebacker	2
Safety	2
Cornerback	1
Defensive Tackle	1
Kick Returner-Punt Returner	1

A defensive end and defensive tackle shared the Super Bowl XII MVP award.

RESULTS

NFC leads AFC, 21-19

Super Bowl	Date	Winner (Share)	Loser (Share)	Score	Site	Attendance
XL	2-5-06	Pittsburgh ($73,000)	Seattle ($38,000)	21-10	Detroit	68,206
XXXIX	2-6-05	New England ($68,000)	Philadelphia ($36,500)	24-21	Jacksonville	78,125
XXXVIII	2-1-04	New England ($68,000)	Carolina ($36,500)	32-29	Houston	71,525
* XXXVII	1-26-03	Tampa Bay ($63,000)	Oakland ($35,000)	48-21	San Diego	67,603
* XXXVI	2-3-02	New England ($63,000)	St. Louis ($34,500)	20-17	New Orleans	72,922
XXXV	1-28-01	Baltimore ($58,000)	N.Y. Giants ($34,500)	34-7	Tampa	71,921
* XXXIV	1-30-00	St. Louis ($58,000)	Tennessee ($33,000)	23-16	Atlanta	72,625
XXXIII	1-31-99	Denver ($53,000)	Atlanta ($32,500)	34-19	Miami	74,803
XXXII	1-25-98	Denver ($48,000)	Green Bay ($29,000)	31-24	San Diego	68,912
XXXI	1-26-97	Green Bay ($48,000)	New England ($29,000)	35-21	New Orleans	72,301
XXX	1-28-96	Dallas ($42,000)	Pittsburgh ($27,000)	27-17	Tempe	76,347
XXIX	1-29-95	San Francisco ($42,000)	San Diego ($26,000)	49-26	Miami	74,107
* XXVIII	1-30-94	Dallas ($38,000)	Buffalo ($23,500)	30-13	Atlanta	72,817
XXVII	1-31-93	Dallas ($36,000)	Buffalo ($18,000)	52-17	Pasadena	98,374
XXVI	1-26-92	Washington ($36,000)	Buffalo ($18,000)	37-24	Minneapolis	63,130
* XXV	1-27-91	N.Y. Giants ($36,000)	Buffalo ($18,000)	20-19	Tampa	73,813
XXIV	1-28-90	San Francisco ($36,000)	Denver ($18,000)	55-10	New Orleans	72,919
XXIII	1-22-89	San Francisco ($36,000)	Cincinnati ($18,000)	20-16	Miami	75,129
XXII	1-31-88	Washington ($36,000)	Denver ($18,000)	42-10	San Diego	73,302
XXI	1-25-87	N.Y. Giants ($36,000)	Denver ($18,000)	39-20	Pasadena	101,063
XX	1-26-86	Chicago ($36,000)	New England ($18,000)	46-10	New Orleans	73,818
XIX	1-20-85	San Francisco ($36,000)	Miami ($18,000)	38-16	Stanford	84,059
XVIII	1-22-84	L.A. Raiders ($36,000)	Washington ($18,000)	38-9	Tampa	72,920
* XVII	1-30-83	Washington ($36,000)	Miami ($18,000)	27-17	Pasadena	103,667
XVI	1-24-82	San Francisco ($18,000)	Cincinnati ($9,000)	26-21	Pontiac	81,270
XV	1-25-81	Oakland ($18,000)	Philadelphia ($9,000)	27-10	New Orleans	76,135
XIV	1-20-80	Pittsburgh ($18,000)	Los Angeles ($9,000)	31-19	Pasadena	103,985
XIII	1-21-79	Pittsburgh ($18,000)	Dallas ($9,000)	35-31	Miami	79,484
XII	1-15-78	Dallas ($18,000)	Denver ($9,000)	27-10	New Orleans	75,583
XI	1-9-77	Oakland ($15,000)	Minnesota ($7,500)	32-14	Pasadena	103,438
X	1-18-76	Pittsburgh ($15,000)	Dallas ($7,500)	21-17	Miami	80,187
IX	1-12-75	Pittsburgh ($15,000)	Minnesota ($7,500)	16-6	New Orleans	80,997
VIII	1-13-74	Miami ($15,000)	Minnesota ($7,500)	24-7	Houston	71,882
VII	1-14-73	Miami ($15,000)	Washington ($7,500)	14-7	Los Angeles	90,182
VI	1-16-72	Dallas ($15,000)	Miami ($7,500)	24-3	New Orleans	81,023
V	1-17-71	Baltimore ($15,000)	Dallas ($7,500)	16-13	Miami	79,204
* IV	1-11-70	Kansas City ($15,000)	Minnesota ($7,500)	23-7	New Orleans	80,562
III	1-12-69	N.Y. Jets ($15,000)	Baltimore ($7,500)	16-7	Miami	75,389
II	1-14-68	Green Bay ($15,000)	Oakland ($7,500)	33-14	Miami	75,546
I	1-15-67	Green Bay ($15,000)	Kansas City ($7,500)	35-10	Los Angeles	61,946

* One week between conference championship games and Super Bowl; all others had two weeks between conference championship games and Super Bowl.

SUPER BOWL XL

Ford Field, Detroit, Michigan
February 5, 2006, Attendance: 68,206
PITTSBURGH 21, SEATTLE 10—at Ford Field, attendance 68,206. The Steelers made three big plays on offense and played a bend-but-don't-break defense to win their record-tying fifth Super Bowl title. The Seahawks lost despite winning the turnover battle (2-1), having more total yards (396-339), and consuming more of the clock (33:02-26:58). The Seahawks crossed midfield on 9 of their 12 possessions, but scored just twice. Late in the first quarter, Darrell Jackson's 16-yard touchdown catch was nullified by pass interference. The Seahawks settled for Josh Brown's 47-yard field goal. With 3:58 left in the second quarter, faced with third-and-28 from the Seahawks' 40, Ben Roethlisberger eluded the rush, rolled left

and threw a deep pass across field. Hines Ward outleaped Michael Boulware at the 3-yard line for a 37-yard pass play. Two plays later, on a broken play, Roethlisberger dove over left tackle and reached the goal line for a touchdown. The Seahawks reached the Steelers' 40 with 54 seconds left, but Matt Hasselbeck's third-and-6 pass fell incomplete and Brown's 54-yard field-goal attempt sailed wide right. On the second play of the second half, Willie Parker set a Super Bowl record with his 75-yard touchdown run over right tackle. Brown's 50-yard field-goal attempt sailed wide left on the next possession, and the Steelers drove to the Seahawks' 7. On third-and-6, Roethlisberger's pass to the right flat was intercepted by Kelly Herndon, who returned the ball a Super Bowl-record 76 yards to the Steelers' 20. Three plays later, Jerramy Stevens caught

Hasselbeck's 16-yard touchdown pass to cut the deficit to 14-10 with 6:45 left in the third quarter. Early in the fourth quarter, the Seahawks drove to the Steelers' 19. On first down, Stevens caught an 18-yard pass, but a holding penalty nullified the catch and Ike Taylor intercepted Hasselbeck's pass a few plays later. Three plays later, Parker took a handoff and gave the ball to Antwaan Randle El on a reverse. Rolling to his right, Randle El fired a perfect 43-yard touchdown pass to Ward for a 21-10 lead with 8:56 to play. The Seahawks punted and then did not get the ball back until there was 1:51 remaining. Seattle reached the Steelers' 26 with 35 seconds left. From the Steelers' 23, Hasselbeck's fourth-and-7 pass to Stevens fell incomplete at the 2-yard line with three seconds remaining. Roethlisberger, who became the youngest quarterback to win the Super Bowl, was 9 of 21 for 123 yards, with 2 interceptions. Ward had 5 catches for 123 yards to earn the Pete Rozelle Trophy as the game's most valuable player. Hasselbeck was 26 of 49 for 273 yards and 1 touchdown, with 1 interception.

Seattle (10)	Offense	Pittsburgh (21)
Bobby Engram	WR	Antwaan Randle El
Walter Jones	LT	Marvel Smith
Steve Hutchinson	LG	Alan Faneca
Robbie Tobeck	C	Jeff Hartings
Chris Gray	RG	Kendall Simmons
Sean Locklear	RT	Max Starks
Jerramy Stevens	TE	Heath Miller
Darrell Jackson	WR	Hines Ward
Matt Hasselbeck	QB	Ben Roethlisberger
Mack Strong	FB	Dan Kreider
Shaun Alexander	RB	Willie Parker
	Defense	
Bryce Fisher	LDE	Aaron Smith
Chuck Darby	LDT-NT	Casey Hampton
Rocky Bernard	RDT-DE	Kimo von Oelhoffen
Grant Wistrom	RDE-LOLB	Clark Haggans
LeRoy Hill	OLB-LILB	James Farrior
Lofa Tatupu	MLB-RILB	Larry Foote
D.D. Lewis	OLB-ROLB	Joey Porter
Andre Dyson	LCB	Ike Taylor
Marcus Trufant	RCB	Deshea Townsend
Michael Boulware	SS	Troy Polamalu
Marquand Manuel	FS	Chris Hope

SUBSTITUTIONS

SEATTLE—Specialists: K—Josh Brown. P—Tom Rouen. LS—Jean-Philippe Darche. Offense: QB—Seneca Wallace. RB—Maurice Morris, Josh Scobey. WR—D.J. Hackett, Joe Jurevicius, Peter Warrick. TE—Ryan Hannam. T/G—Floyd Womack. Defense: DT—Craig Terrill, Marcus Tubbs. DE—Joe Tafoya. LB—Kevin Bentley, Isaiah Kacyvenski, Niko Koutouvides, Cornelius Wortham. CB—Jordan Babineaux, Kelly Herndon, Jimmy Williams. S—Etric Pruitt. DNP: C—Chris Spencer. Inactive: QB—David Greene. FB—Leonard Weaver. TE—Itula Mili. T—Wayne Hunter, Ray Willis. DT—Rodney Bailey. DE—Robert Pollard. CB—Michael Harden.

PITTSBURGH—Specialists: K—Jeff Reed. P—Chris Gardocki. LS—Greg Warren. Offense: RB—Jerome Bettis, Verron Haynes. WR—Sean Morey, Nate Washington, Cedrick Wilson. TE—Jerame Tuman. G—Barrett Brooks. C—Chukky Okobi. Defense: DE—Brett Keisel, Travis Kirschke. DT—Chris Hoke. LB—James Harrison, Clint Kriewaldt. CB—Ricardo Colclough, Chidi Iwuoma, Bryant McFadden. S—Tyrone Carter, Mike Logan. DNP: QB—Charlie Batch. RB—Duce Staley. Inactive: QB—Tommy Maddox. WR—Lee Mays. T—Trai Essex. G—Chris Kemoeatu. DE—Shaun Nua. LB—Arnold Harrison, Rian Wallace. CB—Willie Williams.

OFFICIALS

Referee—Bill Leavy. Umpire—Garth DeFelice. Line Judge—Mark Perlman. Side Judge—Tom Hill. Head Linesman—

Mark Hittner. Back Judge—Bob Waggoner. Field Judge—Steve Zimmer. Replay Official—Bob Boylston. Video Operator—David Coleman.

SCORING

Seattle (NFC)	3	0	7	0	— 10
Pittsburgh (AFC)	0	7	7	7	— 21

Sea— FG J. Brown 47 (0:22)
Pitt— Roethlisberger 1 run (Reed kick) (1:55)
Pitt— Parker 75 run (Reed kick) (14:38)
Sea— Stevens 16 pass from Hasselbeck (J. Brown kick) (6:45)
Pitt— Ward 43 pass from Randle El (Reed kick) (8:56)

TEAM STATISTICS

	SEA	PITT
Total First Downs	20	14
Rushing	5	6
Passing	15	8
Penalty	0	0
Total Net Yardage	396	339
Total Offensive Plays	77	56
Avg. Gain Per Offensive Play	5.1	6.1
Rushes	25	33
Yards Gained Rushing (Net)	137	181
Avg. Yards per Rush	5.5	5.5
Passes Attempted	49	22
Passes Completed	26	10
Had Intercepted	1	2
Tackled Attempting to Pass	3	1
Yards Lost Attempting to Pass	14	8
Yards Gained Passing (Net)	259	158
Punts	6	6
Avg. Distance	50.2	48.7
Punt Returns	4	2
Punt Return Yardage	27	32
Kickoff Returns	4	2
Kickoff Return Yardage	71	43
Interception Return Yardage	76	24
Total Return Yardage	174	99
Fumbles	0	0
Fumbles Lost	0	0
Own Fumbles Recovered	0	0
Opponent Fumbles Recovered	0	0
Penalties	7	3
Yards Penalized	70	20
Field Goals	1	0
Field Goals Attempted	3	0
Third-Down Efficiency	5/17	8/15
Fourth-Down Efficiency	1/2	0/0
Time of Possession	33:02	26:58

INDIVIDUAL STATISTICS

RUSHING: SEA: Alexander 20-95-0, Hasselbeck 3-35-0, Strong 2-7-0. PITT: Parker 10-93-1, Bettis 14-43-0, Roethlisberger 7-25-1, Ward 1-18-0, Haynes 1-2-0.
PASSING: SEA: Hasselbeck 49-26-273-1-1. PITT: Roethlisberger 21-9-123-0-2, Randle El 1-1-43-1-0.
RECEIVING: SEA: Engram 6-70-0, Jurevicius 5-93-0, Jackson 5-50-0, Stevens 3-25-1, Strong 2-15-0, Hannam 2-12-0, Alexander 2-2-0, Morris 1-6-0. PITT: Ward 5-123-1, Randle El 3-22-0, Wilson 1-20-0, Parker 1-1-0.

KICKOFF RETURNS: SEA: Scoby 3-55-0, Morris 1-16-0. PITT: Colclough 2-43-0.
PUNT RETURNS: SEA: Warrick 4-27-0. PITT: Randle El 2-32-0.
PUNTING: SEA: Rouen 6-301-50.2. PITT: Gardocki 6-292-48.7.
INTERCEPTIONS: SEA: Herndon 1-76-0, Boulware 1-0-0. PITT: Taylor 1-24-0.
SACKS: SEA: Wistrom. PITT: Haggans, Hampton, Townsend.

SUPER BOWL XXXIX

Alltel Stadium, Jacksonville, Florida
February 6, 2005, Attendance: 78,125
NEW ENGLAND 24, PHILADELPHIA 21—Deion Branch had 11 receptions for 133 yards and the Patriots' defense forced 4 turnovers en route to becoming the eighth team to post consecutive Super Bowl titles. The Patriots matched the Dallas Cowboys (XXVII, XXVIII, and XXX) as the only team with three Super Bowl victories in the span of four seasons. The Eagles threatened first, driving to the Patriots' 8 late in the first quarter. On first down, Mike Vrabel sacked Donovan McNabb for a 16-yard loss and, after a penalty overturned an interception, Rodney Harrison stepped in front of a pass for an interception at the Eagles' 4. Early in the second quarter the Eagles drove 81 yards, keyed by Todd Pinkston's 40-yard catch, and capped by McNabb's 6-yard touchdown pass to L.J. Smith for a 7-0 lead. The Patriots responded by driving to the Eagles' 4, but Tom Brady fumbled on a fake handoff attempt and Darwin Walker recovered. Later in the quarter, a 29-yard punt by Dirk Johnson allowed the Patriots to drive just 37 yards, keyed by Branch's 7-yard catch on third-and-3, and capped by Brady's pass to David Givens on the right side of the end zone to tie the game with 1:10 left in the half. New England began the second half with a 9-play, 69-yard drive, including 4 receptions, 2 on third down, by Branch, and capped by Vrabel's 2-yard catch. The Eagles put together a 10-play, 74-yard drive later in the third quarter, keyed by Brian Westbrook's 4-yard catch on third-and-3, and followed on the next play by his 10-yard touchdown catch to tie the game. On the ensuing drive, Kevin Faulk caught screen passes of 13 and 14 yards, and had a 12-yard run, and Corey Dillon capped the possession with a 2-yard run with 13:44 remaining for a 21-14 lead. The Patriots' defense forced a three-and-out, and Branch's 19-yard catch set up Adam Vinatieri's 22-yard field goal with 8:40 to play. Tedy Bruschi intercepted McNabb's pass at the Patriots' 24 with 7:20 remaining. The Eagles forced a punt and, beginning at their own 21 with 5:40 to play, needed 13 plays to drive 79 yards, capped by McNabb's 30-yard touchdown pass on a post-pattern to Greg Lewis with 1:48 to play. Christian Fauria recovered the onside kick, but the Eagles' defense

forced a punt. Dexter Reid downed Josh Miller's 32-yard punt at the Eagles' 4 with 46 seconds left, and Harrison intercepted McNabb's pass three plays later to clinch the title. Brady was 23 of 33 for 236 yards and 2 touchdowns. Branch earned MVP honors with his Super Bowl-record-tying 11 catches. McNabb was 30 of 51 for 357 yards and 3 touchdowns, with 3 interceptions. Terrell Owens had 9 receptions for 122 yards.

New England (AFC)	0 7 7 10	— 24
Philadelphia (NFC)	0 7 7 7	— 21

Phil— Smith 6 pass from McNabb (Akers kick) (9:55)
NE— Givens 4 pass from Brady (Vinatieri kick) (1:10)
NE — Vrabel 2 pass from Brady (Vinatieri kick) (11:04)
Phil— Westbrook 10 pass from McNabb (Akers kick) (3:35)
NE — Dillon 2 run (Vinatieri kick) (13:44)
NE— FG Vinatieri 22 (8:40)
Phil— G. Lewis 30 pass from McNabb (Akers kick) (1:48)

SUPER BOWL XXXVIII
Reliant Stadium, Houston, Texas
February 1, 2004, Attendance: 71,525
NEW ENGLAND 32, CAROLINA 29— Adam Vinatieri kicked a 41-yard field goal with four seconds remaining as the Patriots won their second Super Bowl in three seasons. While it took a Super Bowl-record 26 minutes and 55 seconds for the first points to be scored, the teams combined for 868 yards (481 by New England) and the game also featured the highest scoring quarter (combined 37 points in the fourth). Vinatieri missed a 31-yard field goal on the Patriots' first possession, and had a 36-yard attempt blocked by Shane Burton with 6:00 left in the second quarter. But three plays later, Mike Vrabel sacked Jake Delhomme and forced him to fumble. Richard Seymour recovered at the Panthers' 20, and a 12-yard scramble by Tom Brady on third-and-7 set up his 5-yard touchdown pass to Deion Branch with 3:05 left in the first half. The Panthers responded with an 8-play, 95-yard drive capped by Delhomme's 39-yard perfectly placed touchdown pass to Steve Smith with 1:07 left in the half. Delhomme beat the blitz by lofting the pass deep down the left sideline. Brady's 52-yard pass to Branch with 37 seconds left in the half set up David Givens' 5-yard touchdown catch with 18 seconds left. New England squibbed the ensuing kickoff and Kris Mangum returned it 12 yards to the Panthers' 47. A 21-yard run by Stephen Davis set up John Kasay's 50-yard field goal as the half expired for a 14-10 New England lead. Neither team scored in the third quarter, but Antowain Smith's 2-yard touchdown run two plays into the final quarter capped a 71-yard drive and gave the Patriots a 21-10 lead. Undaunted, Car-

olina scored on its next two possessions. First, Delhomme completed passes of 18 and 22 yards to Smith to set up DeShaun Foster's 33-yard touchdown run to cut the deficit to 21-16 with 12:39 to play. Carolina went for the 2-point conversion, but Delhomme's pass was incomplete. New England marched to the Panthers' 9 with the ensuing kickoff, but Reggie Howard intercepted Brady's third-and-goal pass in the end zone. Two plays later, Delhomme rolled left and fired a Super Bowl-record 85-yard touchdown pass to Muhammad for a 22-21 lead with 6:53 left. Once again, the Panthers went for 2 points and Delhomme's pass was incomplete. New England drove 68 yards on its next possession, with Givens catching a 25-yard pass and 18-yard pass on third-and-9, to set up Brady's 1-yard touchdown pass to Vrabel, who was lined up as a tight end. A direct snap to Kevin Faulk resulted in a 2-point conversion for a 29-22 lead with 2:51 left. Delhomme completed passes of 19 yards to Muhammad and 31 yards to Ricky Proehl before finding Proehl with 12 yards for the tying touchdown with 1:08 remaining. Kasay's ensuing kickoff went out of bounds, giving New England the ball at their own 40. Five plays later, faced with third-and-3 from the Panthers' 40 with 14 seconds left, Brady fired a 17-yard pass to Branch to set up Vinatieri's Super Bowl-winning 41-yard field goal. Brady, who was named the Super Bowl most valuable player for the second time in his career, was 32 of 48 for 354 yards and 3 touchdowns, with 1 interception. Branch had 10 receptions for 143 yards. Delhomme was 16 of 33 for 323 yards and 3 touchdowns, and Muhammad had 4 catches for 140 yards.

Carolina (NFC)	0 10 0 19	— 29
New England (AFC)	0 14 0 18	— 32

NE — Branch 5 pass from Brady (Vinatieri kick) (3:05)
Car— Smith 39 pass from Delhomme (Kasay kick) (1:07)
NE — Givens 5 pass from Brady (Vinatieri kick) (0:18)
Car— FG Kasay 50 (0:00)
NE — Smith 2 run (Vinatieri kick) (14:49)
Car— Foster 33 run (pass failed) (12:39)
Car— Muhammad 85 pass from Delhomme (pass failed) (6:53)
NE — Vrabel 1 pass from Brady (Faulk run) (2:51)
Car— Proehl 12 pass from Delhomme (Kasay kick) (1:08)
NE — FG Vinatieri 41 (0:04)

SUPER BOWL XXXVII
Qualcomm Stadium, San Diego, CA
January 26, 2003, Attendance: 67,603
TAMPA BAY 48, OAKLAND 21—The Buccaneers' defense intercepted 5 passes, 3 of which were returned for touchdowns, and recorded 5 sacks as Tampa Bay

scored 34 unanswered points en route to its first Super Bowl victory. Charles Woodson intercepted Brad Johnson three plays into the game to give Oakland the ball at the Buccaneers' 36. But Simeon Rice sacked Rich Gannon on third down to force the Raiders to settle for Sebastian Janikowski's 40-yard field goal. On their next nine possessions, the Raiders registered just 2 first downs and did not run a play inside the Buccaneers' 40 as Tampa Bay scored the next 34 points. The Buccaneers answered Janikowski's field goal with Martin Gramatica's 31-yard boot to tie the game. An interception by Dexter Jackson set up Gramatica's go-ahead field goal early in the second quarter. Midway through the second quarter, a 25-yard punt return by Karl Williams and a 19-yard run by Michael Pittman led to Mike Alstott's 2-yard touchdown run. Late in the half, the Buccaneers drove 77 yards, aided by 3 defensive penalties and pass receptions of 16 and 12 yards by Alstott, to set up Brad Johnson's 5-yard touchdown pass to Keenan McCardell with 30 seconds left in the half, which gave Tampa Bay a 20-3 lead. With their first possession of the second half, the Buccaneers put together a 14-play, 89-yard drive that consumed 7:52 and was culminated by Johnson's 8-yard scoring toss to McCardell. Two plays later, Dwight Smith intercepted Gannon's pass and returned it 44 yards for a touchdown and a 34-3 lead with 4:47 left in the third quarter. Tampa Bay scored 4 touchdowns in a span of 16:37. Jerry Porter's 39-yard touchdown catch in the back of the end zone made it 34-9. Less than three minutes later, Tim Johnson blocked Tom Tupa's punt. Eric Johnson caught the ball and dove into the end zone for a touchdown to cut the deficit to 34-15 with 14:16 remaining. The Buccaneers drove deep downfield again, but Tupa mishandled the snap for a field-goal attempt, allowing the Raiders to regain possession. Gannon hit Jerry Rice with a 48-yard touchdown pass with 6:06 left to trim the lead to 34-21. A 9-yard pass by Johnson to Alstott on third-and-7 allowed Tampa Bay to take another two minutes off the clock before Tupa punted with 2:44 remaining. On third-and-18 from the Raiders' 29, Derrick Brooks intercepted Gannon's pass and raced 44 yards down the left sideline for a touchdown with 1:18 remaining to give Tampa Bay a commanding 41-21 lead. Smith intercepted a tipped pass and returned it 50 yards for a touchdown with two seconds left to finish the scoring. Johnson was 18 of 34 for 215 yards and 2 touchdowns, with 1 interception. Pittman had 29 carries for 124 yards. Gannon was 24 of 44 for 272 yards and 2 touchdowns, with a Super Bowl record 5 interceptions. Jackson, who had the first 2 interceptions, 1 of which led to the go-ahead field goal, was named the game's most valuable player.

| Oakland (AFC) | 3 0 6 12 — 21 |
| Tampa Bay (NFC) | 3 17 14 14 — 48 |

Oak — FG Janikowski 40 (10:40)
TB — FG Gramatica 31 (7:51)
TB — FG Gramatica 43 (11:16)
TB — Alstott 2 run (Gramatica kick) (6:24)
TB — McCardell 5 pass from B. Johnson (Gramatica kick) (0:30)
TB — McCardell 8 pass from B. Johnson (Gramatica kick) (5:30)
TB — D. Smith 44 interception return (Gramatica kick) (4:47)
Oak — Porter 39 pass from Gannon (pass failed) (2:14)
Oak — E. Johnson 13 return of blocked punt (pass failed) (14:16)
Oak — Rice 48 pass from Gannon (pass failed) (6:06)
TB — Brooks 44 interception return (Gramatica kick) (1:18)
TB — D. Smith 50 interception return (Gramatica kick) (0:02)

SUPER BOWL XXXVI

Louisiana Superdome, New Orleans, LA
February 3, 2002, Attendance: 72,922
NEW ENGLAND 20, ST. LOUIS 17—Adam Vinatieri's 48-yard field goal as time expired gave the New England Patriots their first Super Bowl title. The Rams outgained the Patriots 427-267 in total yards, but the Patriots forced 3 turnovers, which resulted in 17 points, while committing no turnovers. Jeff Wilkins' 50-yard field goal capped a 10-play, 48-yard drive midway through the first quarter to give the Rams a 3-0 lead. The first turnover came with 8:49 left in the second quarter, when Ty Law stepped in front of an out-pattern pass intended for Isaac Bruce and raced 47 yards untouched down the left sideline into the end zone. Late in the first half, Kurt Warner completed a 15-yard pass to Ricky Proehl to the Patriots' 40, but Antwan Harris forced Proehl to fumble and Terrell Buckley recovered. Five plays later, Tom Brady's 8-yard touchdown pass to David Patten with 31 seconds left in the quarter gave New England a 14-3 halftime lead. Late in the third quarter, Torry Holt slipped coming off the line of scrimmage, and Otis Smith intercepted Warner's pass and returned it 30 yards to the Rams' 33 to set up Vinatieri's 37-yard field goal and a 17-3 lead. The Rams responded by driving to the Patriots' 3. On fourth-and-goal, Warner scrambled, was tackled by Roman Phifer, and fumbled. Tebucky Jones picked up the ball and raced the length of the field for an apparent touchdown, but the play was negated by Willie McGinest's holding penalty. Warner scored two plays later to trim the deficit to 17-10 with 9:31 left. The Patriots went three and out on their next two possessions, giving the Rams the ball

on their 45-yard-line with 1:51 left. Warner completed an 18-yard pass to Az-Zahir Hakim and an 11-yard pass to Yo Murphy before connecting on a 26-yard touchdown pass to Proehl with 1:30 left to tie the game. Operating without any time outs, Brady completed 3 short passes to J.R. Redmond to reach the Patriots' 41 with 33 seconds left. After an incompletion, Brady completed 23- and 16-yard passes to Troy Brown and Jermaine Wiggins, respectively, to reach the Rams' 30, and then spiked the ball with 7 seconds remaining. Vinatieri drilled the 48-yard field-goal attempt, marking the first time in Super Bowl history the game had been won on the final play. Brady, who earned most valuable player honors, was 16 of 27 for 145 yards and 1 touchdown. Warner was 28 of 44 for 365 yards and 1 touchdown, with 2 interceptions.

| St. Louis (NFC) | 3 0 0 14 — 17 |
| New England (AFC) | 0 14 3 3 — 20 |

StL — FG Wilkins 50 (3:10)
NE — Law 47 interception return (Vinatieri kick) (8:49)
NE — Patten 8 pass from Brady (Vinatieri kick) (0:31)
NE — FG Vinatieri 37 (1:18)
StL — Warner 2 run (Wilkins kick) (9:31)
StL — Proehl 26 pass from Warner (Wilkins kick) (1:30)
NE — FG Vinatieri 48 (0:00)

SUPER BOWL XXXV

Raymond James Stadium, Tampa, Florida
January 28, 2001, Attendance: 71,921
BALTIMORE 34, N.Y. GIANTS 7—The Ravens' defense completed a dominating season by permitting just 152 yards, forcing 5 turnovers, recording 4 sacks, and not allowing an offensive touchdown en route to the franchise's first Super Bowl victory. Jermaine Lewis' punt return into Giants' territory midway through the first quarter was followed two plays later by Trent Dilfer's 38-yard touchdown pass to Brandon Stokley, which gave the Ravens a 7-0 lead. Early in the second quarter, Jessie Armstead intercepted a short pass by Dilfer and returned it 43 yards for a touchdown, but the play was nullified by a penalty. Dilfer's 36-yard pass to Qadry Ismail in the second quarter set up Matt Stover's 47-yard field goal with 1:48 left in the half. Tiki Barber's 27-yard run gave the Giants their deepest penetration of the game, to the Ravens' 29, but Chris McAlister intercepted Kerry Collins' pass on the next play to preserve a 10-0 lead. In the third quarter, Duane Starks stepped in front of Amani Toomer and intercepted Collins' pass. Starks returned it 49 yards untouched for a 17-0 lead. The Giants immediately cut the lead to 10 points when Ron Dixon returned the ensuing kickoff 97 yards for a touchdown. However, Jermaine Lewis then matched Dixon's kickoff return as he cut across the field

and raced 84 yards for a 24-7 lead with 3:13 left in the third quarter. The 3 touchdowns in 36 seconds were a Super Bowl record. The Giants gained just 1 first down on their final four possessions. Jamal Lewis' 3-yard touchdown run midway through the fourth quarter gave Baltimore a 31-7 lead, and Robert Bailey recovered Dixon's fumble on the ensuing kickoff return to set up Stover's 34-yard field goal with 5:27 remaining to finish the scoring. Dilfer completed 12 of 25 passes for 153 yards and 1 touchdown. Jamal Lewis had 27 carries for 102 yards. Collins was 15 of 39 for 112 yards, with 4 interceptions. Ray Lewis was named Super Bowl most valuable player.

| Baltimore (AFC) | 7 3 14 10 — 34 |
| N.Y. Giants (NFC) | 0 0 7 0 — 7 |

Balt — Stokley 38 pass from Dilfer (Stover kick) (6:50)
Balt — FG Stover 47 (1:41)
Balt — Starks 49 interception return (Stover kick) (3:49)
NYG — Dixon 97 kickoff return (Daluiso kick) (3:31)
Balt — Je. Lewis 84 kickoff return (Stover kick) (3:13)
Balt — Ja. Lewis 3 run (Stover kick) (8:45)
Balt — FG Stover 34 (5:27)

SUPER BOWL XXXIV

Georgia Dome, Atlanta, Georgia
January 30, 2000, Attendance: 72,625
ST. LOUIS 23, TENNESSEE 16—Mike Jones tackled Kevin Dyson at the 1-yard line as time expired, preserving the Rams' first-ever Super Bowl title. The Rams drove inside the Titans' 20 with each of their first six possessions, but compiled just 3 field goals and 1 touchdown to take a 16-0 lead. Holder Mike Horan's bobbled snap averted a 35-yard field-goal attempt to conclude the Rams' first drive. The Titans responded with a 42-yard drive, their longest of the half, but Al Del Greco missed a 47-yard attempt. Jeff Wilkins added 3 field goals and missed a 34-yard attempt while the Titans did not threaten the rest of the half, giving the Rams a 9-0 lead at intermission despite outgaining the Titans in total yards (294-89). Tennessee drove 43 yards with the second half's opening kickoff, but Todd Lyght blocked Del Greco's 47-yard attempt to keep the Titans off the board. Kurt Warner's 31-yard pass to Isaac Bruce keyed the ensuing drive that was capped by Warner's 9-yard touchdown pass to Torry Holt with 7:20 left in the third quarter to give the Rams a 16-0 lead. The Titans responded with touchdown drives in excess of seven minutes on each of their next two possessions. Steve McNair's 23-yard scramble set up Eddie George's 1-yard run in the final minute of the third quarter. McNair's 2-point conversion pass to Frank Wycheck was incomplete, but the Titans' defense forced a punt and the offense

drove 79 yards in 13 plays, highlighted by 21-yard passes from McNair to Isaac Byrd and Jackie Harris, and capped by George's 2-yard run to cut the deficit to 16-13 with 7:21 remaining. The Rams once again failed to get a first down, and following a punt, the Titans needed just 28 yards to set up Del Greco's game-tying 43-yard kick with 2:12 left. On the next play from scrimmage, Warner fired a deep pass down the right sideline to Bruce, who caught the ball at the Titans' 38, cut toward the inside, and outran the defense to the end zone to give the Rams a 23-16 lead with 1:54 left. The Titans drove downfield, and McNair avoided a sack and completed a 16-yard pass to Kevin Dyson at the Rams' 10 with six seconds remaining. With no timeouts, McNair attempted a quick pass to a slanting Dyson, who caught the ball in stride at the Rams' 3. However, Jones reacted quickly and stepped up to tackle Dyson at the 1-yard line as time expired. Warner, who was named the game's most valuable player, was 24 of 45 for a Super Bowl-record 414 yards and 2 touchdowns. Bruce had 6 catches for 162 yards, and Holt had 7 for 109 yards. McNair was 22 of 36 for 214 yards. The Titans were the first team in Super Bowl history to come back from a 16-point deficit.

St. Louis (NFC)	3 6 7 7	— 23
Tennessee (AFC)	0 0 6 10	— 16

StL — FG Wilkins 27 (3:00)
StL — FG Wilkins 29 (4:16)
StL — FG Wilkins 28 (0:15)
StL — Holt 9 pass from Warner (Wilkins kick) (3:59)
Tenn — George 1 run (pass failed) (0:14)
Tenn — George 2 run (Del Greco kick) (7:21)
Tenn — FG Del Greco 43 (2:12)
StL — Bruce 73 pass from Warner (Wilkins kick) (1:54)

SUPER BOWL XXXIII
Pro Player Stadium, Miami, Florida
January 31, 1999, Attendance: 74,803
DENVER 34, ATLANTA 19—John Elway, in his last game, passed for 336 yards and ran for a touchdown to earn most valuable player honors as the Broncos became the first AFC team to win consecutive Super Bowls since the Steelers won XIII and XIV. A 25-yard pass interference penalty on Ray Crockett assisted the Falcons' nine-play, 48-yard game-opening drive that was capped by Morten Andersen's 32-yard field goal. Elway's 41-yard pass to Rod Smith kept alive Denver's ensuing drive and led to Howard Griffith's 1-yard touchdown run. Ronnie Bradford's interception and return to the Broncos' 35 late in the first quarter gave Atlanta excellent field position. However, Jamal Anderson was stopped for no gain on third-and-1 and thrown for a 2-yard loss on fourth down. Denver capitalized on its defensive

effort with Jason Elam's 26-yard field goal. The Falcons responded by driving to the Broncos' 8, but Andersen's 26-yard field-goal attempt sailed wide right and on the next play, Elway fired an 80-yard touchdown pass to Smith to turn a possible 10-6 game into a 17-3 Broncos lead. Andersen's 28-yard field goal and 2 misses by Elam on the Broncos' first two second-half possessions gave Atlanta an opportunity to climb back into the game. However, Darrien Gordon dashed the Falcons' hopes with interceptions on consecutive possessions inside the Broncos' 20 to stop drives and set up Broncos touchdowns. Gordon returned the first interception, on a tipped pass, 58 yards to the Falcons' 24 to set up Griffith's second touchdown five plays later, and picked the second pass off at the Broncos' 2 and returned it 50 yards. Terrell Davis turned a short pass into a 39-yard gain, and Elway scored two plays later to give Denver a 31-6 lead. Tim Dwight returned the ensuing kickoff for a touchdown, and, after a field goal by Elam, the Falcons' offense scored with 2:04 remaining on Chandler's 3-yard pass to Terance Mathis. Byron Chamberlain recovered the ensuing onside kick, but Tyrone Braxton recovered Anderson's fumble at the Falcons' 33 with 1:30 remaining to ice the game. The Falcons drove inside the Broncos' 30 seven times, but tallied just 1 touchdown and 2 field goals, throwing 2 interceptions, missing 1 field goal, and turning the ball over 1 time on downs during the other possessions. Elway was 18 of 29 for 336 yards and 1 touchdown, with 1 interception. Davis had 25 carries for 102 yards. Smith had 5 receptions for 152 yards. Chandler was 19 of 35 for 219 yards and 1 touchdown, with 3 interceptions.

Denver (AFC)	7 10 0 17	— 34
Atlanta (NFC)	3 3 0 13	— 19

Atl — FG Andersen 32 (9:35)
Den — Griffith 1 run (Elam kick) (3:55)
Den — FG Elam 26 (9:17)
Den — R. Smith 80 pass from Elway (Elam kick) (4:54)
Atl — FG Andersen 28 (2:25)
Den — Griffith 1 run (Elam kick) (14:56)
Den — Elway 3 run (Elam kick) (11:20)
Atl — Dwight 94 kickoff return (Andersen kick) (11:01)
Den — FG Elam 37 (7:08)
Atl — Mathis 3 pass from Chandler (pass failed) (2:04)

SUPER BOWL XXXII
Qualcomm Stadium, San Diego, California
January 25, 1998, Attendance: 68,912
DENVER 31, GREEN BAY 24—Terrell Davis rushed for 157 yards and a Super Bowl-record 3 touchdowns to lead the Broncos to their first NFL championship and break the NFC's streak of Super Bowl

victories at 13. The defending Super Bowl champion Packers took the opening kick-off and marched 76 yards in just over four minutes, scoring the first points on Brett Favre's 22-yard touchdown pass to Antonio Freeman. The Broncos responded with a 10-play, 58-yard drive capped by Davis' 1-yard run to tie the game. Tyrone Braxton intercepted Favre two plays later, and John Elway scored on a third-and-goal play to begin the second quarter. Steve Atwater forced Favre to fumble three plays later, and Neil Smith recovered at the Packers' 33. Jason Elam converted a 51-yard field goal, the second longest in Super Bowl history, to give the Broncos a 17-7 lead with 12:21 left in the half. After an exchange of punts, the Packers produced a 17-play, 95-yard drive that consumed 7:26 and finished with Favre's 6-yard touchdown pass to Mark Chmura on third-and-5 with 12 seconds left in the half. Tyrone Williams forced and recovered Davis' fumble at the Broncos' 26 on the first play from scrimmage in the second half. However, the Broncos' defense kept the Packers out of the end zone as Ryan Longwell's 27-yard field goal tied the game with 11:59 left in the third quarter. After another exchange of punts, Elway's 36-yard pass to Ed McCaffrey keyed a 13-play, 92-yard drive capped by Davis' 1-yard touchdown run with 34 seconds left in the third quarter. Tim McKyer recovered Freeman's fumble at the Packers' 22 on the ensuing kickoff return, giving the Broncos a golden opportunity, but Eugene Robinson intercepted Elway's pass in the end zone on the next play. Sparked by Robinson's play, the Packers took just four plays, three on passes to Freeman, to score the tying touchdown with 13:32 remaining. Each defense stiffened, forcing two punts, but the Broncos got great field position following Craig Hentrich's 39-yard punt to the Packers' 49 with 3:27 left and the score tied 24-24. Davis rushed for 2 yards on the first play, but Darrius Holland's 15-yard facemask penalty moved the ball to the Packers' 32. Elway threw a 23-yard pass to Howard Griffith two plays later, and after a holding penalty, Davis rushed 17 yards to the Packers' 1 with 1:47 left. After a timeout, Davis waltzed into the end zone to give Denver a 31-24 lead with 1:45 remaining. Freeman returned the kickoff 22 yards to the Broncos' 30, and Favre completed 22- and 13-yard screen passes to Dorsey Levens to reach the Broncos' 35 with 1:04 left. But after a 4-yard pass to Levens and incompletions to Freeman and Brooks, John Mobley knocked away Favre's pass to Chmura with 32 seconds left to give the Broncos the Vince Lombardi Trophy. Elway was 12 of 22 for 123 yards, with 1 interception. Favre was 25 of 42 for 256 yards and 1 touchdown, with 1 interception. Freeman had 9 receptions for 126 yards. Davis was named the game's most valuable player.

Green Bay (NFC)	7	7	3	7 — 24
Denver (AFC)	7	10	7	7 — 31

GB — Freeman 22 pass from Favre (Longwell kick) (10:58)
Den — Davis 1 run (Elam kick) (5:39)
Den — Elway 1 run (Elam kick) (14:55)
Den — FG Elam 51 (12:21)
GB — Chmura 6 pass from Favre (Longwell kick) (0:12)
GB — FG Longwell 27 (11:59)
Den — Davis 1 run (Elam kick) (0:34)
GB — Freeman 13 pass from Favre (Longwell kick) (13:32)
Den — Davis 1 run (Elam kick) (1:45)

SUPER BOWL XXXI

Louisiana Superdome, New Orleans, LA
January 26, 1997, Attendance: 72,301
GREEN BAY 35, NEW ENGLAND 21—
Desmond Howard returned a kickoff 99 yards for a touchdown and Brett Favre passed for 2 touchdowns and ran for a score as the Packers won their first Super Bowl in twenty-nine years. Howard, en route to garnering the MVP trophy, equaled a Super Bowl record with 244 total return yards. It was Favre's arm that struck first, as he hit Andre Rison on a 54-yard touchdown pass on the Packers' second play from scrimmage to take a 7-0 lead. Two plays later Doug Evans made a diving interception of Drew Bledsoe's pass at the 28-yard line, setting up Chris Jacke's field goal and giving the Packers a 10-0 lead just 6:18 into the Super Bowl. The Patriots answered with touchdowns on their next two possessions. Craig Newsome's pass interference penalty set up the first touchdown and a 44-yard completion from Bledsoe to Terry Glenn preceeding Ben Coates' touchdown gave New England its first and only lead. The 24 combined first quarter points were the most in Super Bowl history. Green Bay struck again 56 seconds into the second quarter as Favre hit Antonio Freeman with a Super Bowl-record 81-yard touchdown bomb. Jacke booted his second field goal on Green Bay's next possession. After a Mike Prior interception, Favre orchestrated a 74-yard, nearly 6-minute drive that concluded with a diving Favre touching the ball against the pylon to give Green Bay a 27-14 halftime lead. Curtis Martin brought the Patriots to within a score by running in from 18 yards out with 3:27 left in the third quarter. But Howard broke the Patriots' spirit by returning the ensuing kickoff a Super Bowl-record 99 yards. Favre found Mark Chmura for the 2-point conversion to finish the scoring. Bledsoe was intercepted twice in the fourth quarter as the Patriots never crossed midfield in 4 fourth-quarter possessions. Reggie White set a Super Bowl record with 3 sacks. Favre completed 14 of 27 passes for 246 yards, with no interceptions. Bledsoe completed 11

more passes than Favre, but for just 7 more yards, and threw 4 interceptions.

New England (AFC)	14	0	7	0 — 21
Green Bay (NFC)	10	17	8	0 — 35

GB — Rison 54 pass from Favre (Jacke kick) (11:28)
GB — FG Jacke 37 (8:42)
NE — Byars 1 pass from Bledsoe (Vinatieri kick) (6:35)
NE — Coates 4 pass from Bledsoe (Vinatieri kick) (2:33)
GB — Freeman 81 pass from Favre (Jacke kick) (14:04)
GB — FG Jacke 31 (8:15)
GB — Favre 2 run (Jacke kick) (1:11)
NE — Martin 18 run (Vinatieri kick) (3:27)
GB — Howard 99 kickoff return (Chmura pass from Favre) (3:10)

SUPER BOWL XXX

Sun Devil Stadium, Tempe, Arizona
January 28, 1996, Attendance: 76,347
DALLAS 27, PITTSBURGH 17—Cornerback Larry Brown's 2 interceptions led to 14 second-half points and helped lift the Cowboys to their third Super Bowl victory in the last four seasons and their record-tying fifth title overall. Brown's interceptions foiled the comeback efforts of the Steelers, and earned him the Pete Rozelle Trophy as the game's most valuable player. Dallas scored on each of its first three possessions, taking a 13-0 lead on Troy Aikman's 3-yard touchdown pass to Jay Novacek and a pair of field goals by Chris Boniol. Neil O'Donnell's 6-yard touchdown pass to Yancey Thigpen 13 seconds before halftime pulled Pittsburgh within 6 points, and the Steelers had the ball near midfield midway through the third quarter. But O'Donnell's third-down pass was intercepted by Brown at the Cowboys' 38-yard line, and his 44-yard return carried to Pittsburgh's 18. After Aikman's 17-yard completion to Michael Irvin, Emmitt Smith ran 1 yard for the touchdown that put Dallas ahead again by 13 points. The Steelers rallied, though, behind Norm Johnson's 46-yard field goal, a successful surprise onside kick, and Byron (Bam) Morris' 1-yard touchdown run with 6:36 to play in the game. And when they forced a punt and took possession at their own 32-yard line trailing only 20-17 with 4:15 remaining, it appeared they might have a chance to break the NFC's recent domination in the Super Bowl. But on second down, Brown struck again, intercepting O'Donnell's pass at the 39 and returning it 33 yards to the 6. Two plays later, Smith reeled over from 4 yards out for the clinching touchdown with 3:43 to go. Pittsburgh limited the Cowboys' powerful running game to only 56 yards and enjoyed a whopping 201-61 advantage in total yards in the second half, but could not overcome the 3 interceptions (another came

on the game's final play) thrown by O'Donnell, the NFL's career leader for fewest interceptions per pass attempt. In all, O'Donnell completed 28 of 49 passes for 239 yards. Morris rushed for a game-high 73 yards on 19 carries. For Dallas, Aikman completed 15 of 23 pass attempts for 209 yards. The Cowboys' victory was the twelfth in a row for NFC teams over AFC teams in the Super Bowl.

Dallas (NFC)	10	3	7	7 — 27
Pittsburgh (AFC)	0	7	0	10 — 17

Dall — FG Boniol 42 (12:05)
Dall — Novacek 3 pass from Aikman (Boniol kick) (5:23)
Dall — FG Boniol 35 (6:03)
Pitt — Thigpen 6 pass from O'Donnell (N. Johnson kick) (0:13)
Dall — E. Smith 1 run (Boniol kick) (6:42)
Pitt — FG N. Johnson 46 (11:20)
Pitt — Morris 1 run (N. Johnson kick) (6:36)
Dall — E. Smith 4 run (Boniol kick) (3:43)

SUPER BOWL XXIX

Joe Robbie Stadium, Miami, Florida
January 29, 1995, Attendance: 74,107
SAN FRANCISCO 49, SAN DIEGO 26—
Steve Young passed for a record 6 touchdowns, and the 49ers became the first team to win five Super Bowls when they routed the Chargers. Young, the game's most valuable player, directed an explosive offense that generated 7 touchdowns, 28 first downs, and 455 total yards. He completed 24 of 36 passes for 325 yards, and broke the record of 5 touchdown passes set by fromer 49ers quarterback Joe Montana in Super Bowl XXIV. San Francisco wasted little time scoring, taking the lead for good on Young's 44-yard touchdown pass to Jerry Rice only three plays and 1:24 into the game. The next time they had the ball, the 49ers marched 79 yards in four plays, taking a 14-0 lead when Young teamed with running back Ricky Watters on a 51-yard touchdown pass with 10:05 still to play in the opening period. San Diego then put together its most impressive possession of the game, a 13-play, 78-yard drive that consumed more than 7 minutes and was capped by Natrone Means' 1-yard touchdown run, to cut its deficit to 14-7 late in the quarter. But San Francisco countered with a 70-yard drive of its own, and Young's 5-yard touchdown pass to fullback William Floyd made it 21-7. Young's fourth touchdown pass of the half, 8 yards to Watters 4:44 before halftime, increased the advantage to 28-7, and the Chargers could get no closer than 18 points after that. Watters, who ran 9 yards for a touchdown in the third quarter, equaled the Super Bowl record with 3 touchdowns. Rice also scored 3 touchdowns (the second time in his career he'd

done that in a Super Bowl) while catching 10 passes for 149 yards. He established career records for receptions, yards, and touchdowns in a Super Bowl. Young, who scrambled 21 yards and 15 yards to set up touchdowns in the first half, was the game's leading rusher with 49 yards on 5 carries. San Diego's Means, who rushed for 1,350 yards during the regular season, was limited to 33 yards on 13 attempts. Chargers quarterback Stan Humphries completed 24 of 49 passes for 275 yards. Rookie Andre Coleman became only the third player in Super Bowl history to return a kickoff for a touchdown, going 98 yards in the third quarter. The 75 points scored by the two teams established another record, breaking the previous mark of 69 set in Dallas' 52-17 victory over Buffalo in XXVII. The 49ers' victory was the eleventh straight for NFC teams over AFC teams in the Super Bowl.

San Diego (AFC)	7 3 8 8	—	26
San Francisco (NFC)	14 14 14 7	—	49

SF	—	Rice 44 pass from S. Young (Brien kick) (13:36)
SF	—	Watters 51 pass from S. Young (Brien kick) (10:05)
SD	—	Means 1 run (Carney kick) (2:44)
SF	—	Floyd 5 pass from S. Young (Brien kick) (13:02)
SF	—	Watters 8 pass from S. Young (Brien kick) (4:44)
SD	—	FG Carney 31 (1:44)
SF	—	Watters 9 run (Brien kick) (9:35)
SF	—	Rice 15 pass from S. Young (Brien kick) (3:18)
SD	—	Coleman 98 kickoff return (Seay pass from Humphries) (3:01)
SF	—	Rice 7 pass from S. Young (Brien kick) (13:49)
SD	—	Martin 30 pass from Humphries (Pupunu pass from Humphries) (2:25)

SUPER BOWL XXVIII

Georgia Dome, Atlanta, Georgia
January 30, 1994, Attendance: 72,817
DALLAS 30, BUFFALO 13—Emmitt Smith rushed for 132 yards and 2 second-half touchdowns to power the Cowboys to their second consecutive NFL title. By winning, Dallas joined San Francisco and Pittsburgh as the only franchises with four Super Bowl victories. The Bills, meanwhile, extended a dubious string by losing in the Super Bowl for the fourth consecutive year. To win, the Cowboys had to rally from a 13-6 halftime deficit. Buffalo had forged its lead on Thurman Thomas' 4-yard touchdown run and a pair of field goals by Steve Christie, including a 54-yard kick, the longest in Super Bowl history. But just 55 seconds into the second half, Thomas was stripped of the ball by Dallas defensive tackle Leon Lett. Safety James Washington recovered and weaved

his way 46 yards for a touchdown to tie the game at 13-13. After forcing the Bills to punt, the Cowboys began their next possession on their 36-yard line and Smith, the game's most valuable player, took over. He carried 7 times for 61 yards on the ensuing 8-play, 64-yard drive, capping the march with a 15-yard touchdown run to give Dallas the lead for good with 8:42 remaining in the third quarter. Early in the fourth quarter, Washington intercepted Jim Kelly's pass and returned it 12 yards to Buffalo's 34. A penalty moved the ball back to the 39, but Smith carried twice for 10 yards and caught a screen pass for 9, and quarterback Troy Aikman completed a 16-yard pass to Alvin Harper to give the Cowboys a first-and-goal at the 6. Smith took it from there, cracking the end zone on fourth-and-goal from the 1 to put Dallas ahead 27-13 with 9:50 remaining. Eddie Murray's third field goal, from 20 yards with 2:50 left, ended any doubt about the game's outcome. Smith had 30 carries in all, with 19 of his attempts and 92 yards coming after intermission. Washington, normally a reserve who played most of the game because the Cowboys used five defensive backs to combat the Bills' No-Huddle offense, had 11 tackles and forced another fumble by Thomas in the first quarter. Aikman completed 19 of 27 passes for 207 yards. Buffalo's Kelly completed a Super Bowl-record 31 passes in 50 attempts for 260 yards. Dallas, the first team in NFL history to begin the regular season 0-2 and go on to win the Super Bowl, became the fifth to win back-to-back titles, following Green Bay, Miami, Pittsburgh (the Steelers did it twice), and San Francisco. Buffalo became the third team, along with Minnesota and Denver, to lose four Super Bowls. The Cowboys' victory was the tenth in succession for the NFC over the AFC.

Dallas (NFC)	6 0 14 10	—	30
Buffalo (AFC)	3 10 0 0	—	13

Dall	—	FG Murray 41 (12:41)
Buff	—	FG Christie 54 (10:19)
Dall	—	FG Murray 24 (3:55)
Buff	—	Thomas 4 run (Christie kick) (12:26)
Buff	—	FG Christie 28 (0:00)
Dall	—	Washington 46 fumble return (Murray kick) (14:05)
Dall	—	E. Smith 15 run (Murray kick) (8:42)
Dall	—	E. Smith 1 run (Murray kick) (9:50)
Dall	—	FG Murray 20 (2:50)

SUPER BOWL XXVII

Rose Bowl, Pasadena, California
January 31, 1993, Attendance: 98,374
DALLAS 52, BUFFALO 17—Troy Aikman passed for 4 touchdowns, Emmitt Smith rushed for 108 yards, and the Cowboys converted 9 turnovers into 35 points while coasting to the victory. Dallas' win was its

third in its record sixth Super Bowl appearance; the Bills became the first team to drop three in succession. Buffalo led 7-0 until the first 2 of its record number of turnovers helped the Cowboys take the lead for good late in the opening quarter. First, Dallas safety James Washington intercepted Jim Kelly's pass and returned it 13 yards to the Bills' 47, setting up Aikman's 23-yard touchdown pass to tight end Jay Novacek with 1:36 remaining in the period. On the next play from scrimmage, Kelly was sacked by Charles Haley and fumbled at the Bills' 2-yard line where the Cowboys' Jimmie Jones picked up the loose ball and ran 2 yards for a touchdown. Dallas, which recovered 5 fumbles and intercepted 4 passes, struck just as quickly late in the first half, when Aikman tossed 19- and 18-yard touchdown passes to Michael Irvin 18 seconds apart to give the Cowboys a 28-10 lead at intermission. The second score was set up when Bills running back Thurman Thomas lost a fumble at his 19-yard line. Buffalo scored for the last time when backup quarterback Frank Reich, playing because Kelly was injured while attempting to pass midway through the second quarter, threw a 40-yard touchdown pass to Don Beebe on the final play of the third period to trim the deficit to 31-17. But Dallas put the game out of reach by scoring three times in a span of 2:33 of the fourth quarter. Aikman, the game's most valuable player, completed 22 of 30 passes for 273 yards. The victory was the ninth in succession for the NFC over the AFC.

Buffalo (AFC)	7 3 7 0	—	17
Dallas (NFC)	14 14 3 21	—	52

Buff	—	Thomas 2 run (Christie kick) (10:00)
Dall	—	Novacek 23 pass from Aikman (Elliott kick) (1:36)
Dall	—	J. Jones 2 fumble recovery return (Elliott kick) (1:21)
Buff	—	FG Christie 21 (3:24)
Dall	—	Irvin 19 pass from Aikman (Elliott kick) (1:54)
Dall	—	Irvin 18 pass from Aikman (Elliott kick) (1:36)
Dall	—	FG Elliott 20 (8:21)
Buff	—	Beebe 40 pass from Reich (Christie kick) (0:00)
Dall	—	Harper 45 pass from Aikman (Elliott kick) (10:04)
Dall	—	E. Smith 10 run (Elliott kick) (8:12)
Dall	—	Norton 9 fumble recovery return (Elliott kick) (7:31)

SUPER BOWL XXVI

Metrodome, Minneapolis, Minnesota
January 26, 1992, Attendance: 63,130
WASHINGTON 37, BUFFALO 24—Mark Rypien passed for 292 yards and 2 touchdowns as the Redskins overwhelmed the Bills to win their third Super Bowl in the past 10 years. Rypien, the game's most valuable player, completed 18 of 33 pass-

es, including a 10-yard scoring strike to Earnest Byner and a 30-yard touchdown to Gary Clark. The latter came late in the third quarter after Buffalo had trimmed a 24-0 deficit to 24-10, and effectively put the game out of reach. Washington went on to lead by as much as 37-10 before the Bills made it close wih a pair of touchdowns in the final six minutes. Though the Redskins struggled early, converting their first three drives inside the Bills' 20-yard line into only 3 points, they built a 17-0 halftime lead. And they made it 24-0 just 16 seconds into the second half, after Kurt Gouveia intercepted Buffalo quarterback Jim Kelly's pass on the first play of the third quarter and returned it 23 yards to the Bills' 2. One play later, Gerald Riggs scored his second touchdown of the game to make it 24-0. Kelly, forced to bring Buffalo from behind, completed 28 of a Super Bowl-record 58 passes for 275 yards and 2 touchdowns, but was intercepted 4 tlmes. Bills running back Thurman Thomas, who had an AFC-high 1,407 yards rushing and an NFL-best 2,038 total yards from scrimmage during the regular season, ran for only 13 yards on 10 carries and was limited to 27 yards on 4 receptions. Clark had 7 catches for 114 yards and Art Monk added 7 for 113 for the Redskins, who amassed 417 yards of total offense while limiting the explosive Bills to 283. Washington's Joe Gibbs became only the third head coach to win three Super Bowls.

Washington (NFC)	0 17 14	6 — 37
Buffalo (AFC)	0 0 10	14 — 24

Wash — FG Lohmiller 34 (13:02)
Wash — Byner 10 pass from Rypien (Lohmiller kick) (9:54)
Wash — Riggs 1 run (Lohmiller kick) (7:17)
Wash — Riggs 2 run (Lohmiller kick) (14:44)
Buff — FG Norwood 21 (11:59)
Buff — Thomas 1 run (Norwood kick) (5:58)
Wash — Clark 30 pass from Rypien (Lohmiller kick) (1:24)
Wash — FG Lohmiller 25 (14:54)
Wash — FG Lohmiller 39 (11:36)
Buff — Metzelaars 2 pass from Kelly (Norwood kick) (5:59)
Buff — Beebe 4 pass from Kelly (Norwood kick) (3:55)

SUPER BOWL XXV
Tampa Stadium, Tampa, Florida
January 27, 1991, Attendance: 73,813
NEW YORK GIANTS 20, BUFFALO 19—
The NFC champion New York Giants won their second Super Bowl in five years with a 20-19 victory over AFC titlist Buffalo. New York, employing its ball-control offense, had possession for 40 minutes, 33 seconds, a Super Bowl record. The Bills, who scored 95 points in their previous two playoff games leading to Super Bowl XXV, had the ball for less than eight

minutes in the second half and just 19:27 for the game. Fourteen of New York's 73 plays came on its initial drive of the third quarter, which covered 75 yards and consumed a Super Bowl-record 9:29 before running back Ottis Anderson ran 1 yard for a touchdown. Giants quarterback Jeff Hostetler kept the long drive going by converting three third-down plays—an 11-yard pass to running back David Meggett on third-and-eight, a 14-yard toss to wide receiver Mark Ingram on third-and-13, and a 9-yard pass to Howard Cross on third-and-four—to give New York a 17-12 lead in the third quarter. Buffalo jumped to a 12-3 lead midway through the second quarter before Hostetler completed a 14-yard scoring strike to wide receiver Stephen Baker to close the score to 12-10 at halftime. Buffalo's Thurman Thomas ran 31 yards for a touchdown on the opening play of the fourth quarter to help Buffalo recapture the lead 19-17. Matt Bahr's 21-yard field goal gave the Giants a 20-19 lead, but Buffalo's Scott Norwood had a chance to win the game with seconds remaining before his 47-yard field-goal attempt sailed wide right. Hostetler completed 20 of 32 passes for 222 yards and 1 touchdown. Anderson rushed 21 times for 102 yards and 1 touchdown to capture most-valuable-player honors. Thomas totaled 190 scrimmage yards, rushing 15 times for 135 yards and catching 5 passes for 55 yards.

Buffalo (AFC)	3 9 0	7 — 19
N.Y. Giants (NFC)	3 7 7	3 — 20

NYG — FG Bahr 28 (7:14)
Buff — FG Norwood 23 (5:51)
Buff — D. Smith 1 run (Norwood kick) (12:30)
Buff — Safety, B. Smith tackled Hostetler in end zone (8:27)
NYG — Baker 14 pass from Hostetler (Bahr kick) (0:25)
NYG — Anderson 1 run (Bahr kick) (5:31)
Buff — Thomas 31 run (Norwood kick) (14:52)
NYG — FG Bahr 21 (7:20)

SUPER BOWL XXIV
Louisiana Superdome, New Orleans, LA
January 28, 1990, Attendance: 72,919
SAN FRANCISCO 55, DENVER 10—NFC titlist San Francisco won its fourth Super Bowl championship with a 55-10 victory over AFC champion Denver. The 49ers, who also won Super Bowls XVI, XIX, and XXIII, tied the Pittsburgh Steelers for most Super Bowl victories. The Steelers captured Super Bowls IX, X, XIII, and XIV. San Francisco's 55 points broke the previous Super Bowl scoring mark of 46 points by Chicago in Super Bowl XX. San Francisco scored touchdowns on four of its six first-half possessions to hold a 27-3 lead at halftime. Interceptions by Michael Walter and Chet Brooks ended the Broncos' first two possessions of the second half. San

Francisco quarterback Joe Montana was named the Super Bowl most valuable player for a record third time. Montana completed 22 of 29 passes for 297 yards and a Super Bowl-record 5 touchdowns. Jerry Rice, Super Bowl XXIII most valuable player, caught 7 passes for 148 yards and 3 touchdowns. The 49ers' domination included first downs (28 to 12), net yards (461 to 167), and time of possession (39:31 to 20:29).

San Francisco (NFC)	13 14 14 14 — 55
Denver (AFC)	3 0 7 0 — 10

SF — Rice 20 pass from Montana (Cofer kick) (10:06)
Den — FG Treadwell 42 (6:47)
SF — Jones 7 pass from Montana (kick failed) (0:03)
SF — Rathman 1 run (Cofer kick) (7:15)
SF — Rice 38 pass from Montana (Cofer kick) (0:34)
SF — Rice 28 pass from Montana (Cofer kick) (12:48)
SF — Taylor 35 pass from Montana (Cofer kick) (9:44)
Den — Elway 3 run (Treadwell kick) (6:53)
SF — Rathman 3 run (Cofer kick) (14:57)
SF — Craig 1 run (Cofer kick) (13:47)

SUPER BOWL XXIII
Joe Robbie Stadium, Miami, Florida
January 22, 1989, Attendance: 75,129
SAN FRANCISCO 20, CINCINNATI 16—
NFC champion San Francisco captured its third Super Bowl of the 1980s by defeating AFC champion Cincinnati 20-16. The 49ers, who also won Super Bowls XVI and XIX, became the first NFC team to win three Super Bowls. Pittsburgh, with four Super Bowl titles (IX, X, XIII, and XIV), and the Oakland/Los Angeles Raiders, with three (XI, XV, and XVIII), lead AFC franchises. Even though San Francisco held an advantage in total net yards (453 to 229), the 49ers found themselves trailing the Bengals late in the game. With the score 13-13, Cincinnati took a 16-13 lead on Jim Breech's 40-yard field goal with 3:20 remaining. It was Breech's third field goal of the day, following earlier successes from 34 and 43 yards. The 49ers started their winning drive at their 8-yard line. Over the next 11 plays, San Francisco covered 92 yards with the decisive score coming on a 10-yard pass from quarterback Joe Montana to wide receiver John Taylor with 34 seconds remaining. At halftime, the score was 3-3, the first time in Super Bowl history the game was tied at intermission. After the teams traded third-period field goals, the Bengals jumped ahead 13-6 on Stanford Jennings' 93-yard kickoff return for a touchdown with 34 seconds remaining in the quarter. The 49ers didn't waste any time coming back as they covered 85 yards in four plays,

concluding with Montana's 14-yard scoring pass to Jerry Rice 57 seconds into the final stanza. Rice was named the game's most valuable player after compiling 11 catches for a Super Bowl-record 215 yards. Montana completed 23 of 36 passes for a Super Bowl-record 357 yards and 2 touchdowns.

Cincinnati (AFC)	0	3	10	3	—	16
San Francisco (NFC)	3	0	3	14	—	20

SF	—	FG Cofer 41 (3:14)
Cin	—	FG Breech 34 (1:15)
Cin	—	FG Breech 43 (5:39)
SF	—	FG Cofer 32 (0:50)
Cin	—	Jennings 93 kickoff return (Breech kick) (0:34)
SF	—	Rice 14 pass from Montana (Cofer kick) (14:03)
Cin	—	FG Breech 40 (3:20)
SF	—	Taylor 10 pass from Montana (Cofer kick) (0:34)

SUPER BOWL XXII

San Diego Jack Murphy Stadium, San Diego, CA
January 31, 1988, Attendance: 73,302
WASHINGTON 42, DENVER 10—NFC champion Washington won Super Bowl XXII and its second NFL championship of the 1980s with a 42-10 decision over AFC champion Denver. The Redskins, who also won Super Bowl XVII, enjoyed a record-setting second quarter en route to the victory. The Broncos broke in front 10-0 when quarterback John Elway threw a 56-yard touchdown pass to wide receiver Ricky Nattiel on the Broncos' first play from scrimmage. Following a Washington punt, Denver's Rich Karlis kicked a 24-yard field goal to cap a seven-play, 61-yard scoring drive. The Redskins then erupted for 35 points on five straight possessions in the second period and coasted thereafter. The 35 points established an NFL postseason mark for most points in a period. Redskins quarterback Doug Williams led the second-period explosion by passing for a Super Bowl record-tying 4 touchdowns, including 80- and 50-yard passes to wide receiver Ricky Sanders, a 27-yard toss to wide receiver Gary Clark, and an 8-yard pass to tight end Clint Didier. Washington scored 5 touchdowns in 18 plays with total time of possession of only 5:47. Overall, Williams completed 18 of 29 passes for 340 yards and was named the game's most valuable player. His pass-yardage total eclipsed the Super Bowl record of 331 yards by Joe Montana of San Francisco in Super Bowl XIX. Sanders ended with 193 yards on 8 catches, breaking the previous Super Bowl yardage record of 161 yards by Lynn Swann of Pittsburgh in Game X. Rookie running back Timmy Smith was the game's leading rusher with 22 carries for a Super Bowl-record 204 yards, breaking the previous mark of 191 yards by Marcus Allen of the Raiders in Game XVIII. Smith also scored twice on runs of 58 and 4 yards. Washington's 6 touch-

downs and 602 total yards gained also set Super Bowl records. Redskins cornerback Barry Wilburn had 2 of the team's 3 interceptions, and strong safety Alvin Walton had 2 of Washington's 5 sacks.

Washington (NFC)	0	35	0	7	—	42
Denver (AFC)	10	0	0	0	—	10

Den	—	Nattiel 56 pass from Elway (Karlis kick) (13:03)
Den	—	FG Karlis 24 (9:09)
Wash	—	Sanders 80 pass from Williams (Haji-Sheikh kick) (14:07)
Wash	—	Clark 27 pass from Williams (Haji-Sheikh kick) (10:15)
Wash	—	Smith 58 run (Haji-Sheikh kick) (6:27)
Wash	—	Sanders 50 pass from Williams (Haji-Sheikh kick) (3:42)
Wash	—	Didier 8 pass from Williams (Haji-Sheikh kick) (1:04)
Wash	—	Smith 4 run (Haji-Sheikh kick) (13:09)

SUPER BOWL XXI

Rose Bowl, Pasadena, California
January 25, 1987, Attendance: 101,063
NEW YORK GIANTS 39, DENVER 20—The NFC champion New York Giants captured their first NFL title since 1956 when they downed the AFC champion Denver Broncos 39-20 in Super Bowl XXI. The victory marked the NFC's fifth NFL title in the past six seasons. The Broncos, behind the passing of quarterback John Elway, who was 13 of 20 for 187 yards in the first half, held a 10-9 lead at intermission, the narrowest halftime margin in Super Bowl history. Denver's Rich Karlis opened the scoring with a Super Bowl record-tying 48-yard field goal. New York drove 78 yards in nine plays on the next series to take a 7-3 lead on quarterback Phil Simms' 6-yard touchdown pass to tight end Zeke Mowatt. The Broncos came right back with a 58-yard scoring drive on six plays capped by Elway's 4-yard touchdown run. The only scoring in the second period was the sack of Elway in the end zone by defensive end George Martin for a New York safety. The Giants produced a key defensive stand early in the second quarter when the Broncos had a first down at the New York 1-yard line, but failed to score on three running plays and Karlis' 23-yard missed field-goal attempt. The Giants took command of the game in the third period en route to a 30-point second half, the most ever scored in one half of Super Bowl play. New York took the lead for good on tight end Mark Bavaro's 13-yard touchdown catch 4:52 into the third period. The nine-play, 63-yard scoring drive included the successful conversion of a fourth-and-1 play on the New York 46-yard line. Denver was limited to only 2 net yards on 10 offensive plays in the third period. Simms set Super Bowl records for most consecutive completions

(10) and highest completion percentage (88 percent on 22 completions in 25 attempts). He also passed for 268 yards and 3 touchdowns and was named the game's most valuable player. New York running back Joe Morris was the game's leading rusher with 20 carries for 67 yards. Denver wide receiver Vance Johnson led all receivers with 5 catches for 121 yards.

Denver (AFC)	10	0	0	10	—	20
N.Y. Giants (NFC)	7	2	17	13	—	39

Den	—	FG Karlis 48 (10:51)
NYG	—	Mowatt 6 pass from Simms (Allegre kick) (5:27)
Den	—	Elway 4 run (Karlis kick) (2:06)
NYG	—	Safety, Martin tackled Elway in end zone (2:46)
NYG	—	Bavaro 13 pass from Simms (Allegre kick) (10:08)
NYG	—	FG Allegre 21 (3:54)
NYG	—	Morris 1 run (Allegre kick) (0:24)
NYG	—	McConkey 6 pass from Simms (Allegre kick) (10:56)
Den	—	FG Karlis 28 (6:01)
NYG	—	Anderson 2 run (kick failed) (4:18)
Den	—	V. Johnson 47 pass from Elway (Karlis kick) (2:06)

SUPER BOWL XX

Louisiana Superdome, New Orleans, LA
January 26, 1986, Attendance: 73,818
CHICAGO 46, NEW ENGLAND 10—The NFC champion Chicago Bears, seeking their first NFL title since 1963, scored a Super Bowl-record 46 points in downing AFC champion New England 46-10 in Super Bowl XX. The previous record for most points in a Super Bowl was 38, shared by San Francisco in XIX and the Los Angeles Raiders in XVIII. The Bears' league-leading defense tied the Super Bowl record for sacks (7) and limited the Patriots to a record-low 7 rushing yards. New England took the quickest lead in Super Bowl history when Tony Franklin kicked a 36-yard field goal with 1:19 elapsed in the first period. The score came about because of Larry McGrew's fumble recovery at the Chicago 19-yard line. However, the Bears rebounded for a 23-3 first-half lead, while building a yardage advantage of 236 total yards to New England's minus 19. Running back Matt Suhey rushed 8 times for 37 yards, including an 11-yard touchdown run, and caught 1 pass for 24 yards in the first half. After the Patriot's first drive of the second half ended with a punt to the Bears' 4-yard line, Chicago marched 96 yards in nine plays with quarterback Jim McMahon's 1-yard scoring run capping the drive. McMahon became the first quarterback in Super Bowl history to rush for a pair of touchdowns. The Bears completed their scoring via a 28-yard interception return by reserve cornerback Reggie Phillips, a

1-yard run by defensive tackle/fullback William Perry, and a safety when defensive end Henry Waechter tackled Patriots quarterback Steve Grogan in the end zone. Bears defensive end Richard Dent became the fourth defender to be named the game's most valuable player after contributing 1 1/2 sacks. The Bears' victory margin of 36 points was the largest in Super Bowl history, bettering the previous mark of 29 by the Los Angeles Raiders when they topped Washington 38-9 in Game XVIII. McMahon completed 12 of 20 passes for 256 yards before leaving the game in the fourth period with a wrist injury. The NFL's all-time leading rusher, Bears running back Walter Payton, carried 22 times for 61 yards. Wide receiver Willie Gault caught 4 passes for 129 yards, the fourth-most receiving yards in a Super Bowl. Chicago coach Mike Ditka became the second man (Tom Flores of Raiders was the other) to win a Super Bowl ring as a player and as a coach.

Chicago (NFC)		13 10 21 2 — 46	
New England (AFC)		3 0 0 7 — 10	
NE	—	FG Franklin 36 (13:41)	
Chi	—	FG Butler 28 (9:20)	
Chi	—	FG Butler 24 (1:26)	
Chi	—	Suhey 11 run (Butler kick) (0:23)	
Chi	—	McMahon 2 run (Butler kick) (7:24)	
Chi	—	FG Butler 24 (0:00)	
Chi	—	McMahon 1 run (Butler kick) (7:22)	
Chi	—	Phillips 28 interception return (Butler kick) (6:16)	
Chi	—	Perry 1 run (Butler kick) (3:22)	
NE	—	Fryar 8 pass from Grogan (Franklin kick) (13:14)	
Chi	—	Safety, Waechter tackled Grogan in end zone (5:36)	

SUPER BOWL XIX
Stanford Stadium, Stanford, California
January 20, 1985, Attendance: 84,059
SAN FRANCISCO 38, MIAMI 16—The San Francisco 49ers captured their second Super Bowl title with a dominating offense and a defense that tamed Miami's explosive passing attack. The Dolphins held a 10-7 lead at the end of the first period, which represented the most points scored by two teams in an opening quarter of a Super Bowl. However, the 49ers used excellent field position in the second period to build a 28-16 halftime lead. Running back Roger Craig set a Super Bowl record by scoring 3 touchdowns on pass receptions of 8 and 16 yards and a run of 2 yards. San Francisco's Joe Montana was voted the game's most valuable player. He joined Green Bay's Bart Starr and Pittsburgh's Terry Bradshaw as the only two-time Super Bowl most valuable players. Montana completed 24 of 35 passes for a Super Bowl-record 331 yards and 3 touchdowns, and rushed 5 times for 59

yards, including a 6-yard touchdown. Craig had 58 yards on 15 carries and caught 7 passes for 77 yards. Wendell Tyler rushed 13 times for 65 yards and had 4 catches for 70 yards. Dwight Clark had 6 receptions for 77 yards, while Russ Francis had 5 for 60. San Francisco's 537 total net yards bettered the previous Super Bowl record of 429 yards by Oakland in Super Bowl XI. The 49ers also held a time of possession advantage over the Dolphins of 37:11 to 22:49.

Miami (AFC)		10 6 0 0 — 16	
San Francisco (NFC)		7 21 10 0 — 38	
Mia	—	FG von Schamann 37 (7:24)	
SF	—	Monroe 33 pass from Montana (Wersching kick) (3:12)	
Mia	—	D. Johnson 2 pass from Marino (von Schamann kick) (0:45)	
SF	—	Craig 8 pass from Montana (Wersching kick) (11:34)	
SF	—	Montana 6 run (Wersching kick) (6:58)	
SF	—	Craig 2 run (Wersching kick) (2:05)	
Mia	—	FG von Schamann 31 (0:12)	
Mia	—	FG von Schamann 30 (0:00)	
SF	—	FG Wersching 27 (10:12)	
SF	—	Craig 16 pass from Montana (Wersching kick) (6:18)	

SUPER BOWL XVIII
Tampa Stadium, Tampa, Florida
January 22, 1984, Attendance: 72,920
LOS ANGELES RAIDERS 38, WASHINGTON 9—The Los Angeles Raiders dominated the Washington Redskins from the beginning in Super Bowl XVIII and achieved the most lopsided victory in Super Bowl history, surpassing Green Bay's 35-10 win over Kansas City in Super Bowl I. The Raiders took a 7-0 lead 4:52 into the game when Derrick Jensen blocked Jeff Hayes' punt and recovered it in the end zone for a touchdown. With 9:14 remaining in the first half, Raiders quarterback Jim Plunkett fired a 12-yard touchdown pass to wide receiver Cliff Branch to complete a three-play, 65-yard drive. Washington cut the Raiders' lead to 14-3 on a 24-yard field goal by Mark Moseley. With seven seconds left in the first half, Raiders linebacker Jack Squirek intercepted Joe Theismann's pass at the Redskins' 5-yard line and ran it in for a touchdown to give Los Angeles a 21-3 halftime lead. In the third period, running back Marcus Allen, who rushed for a Super Bowl-record 191 yards on 20 carries, increased the Raiders' lead to 35-9 on touchdown runs of 5 and 74 yards, the latter erasing the Super Bowl record of 58 yards set by Baltimore's Tom Matte in Game III. Allen was named the game's most valuable player. The victory over Washington raised Raiders coach Tom Flores' playoff record to 8-1, including a 27-10 win against Philadelphia in Super

Bowl XV. The 38 points scored by the Raiders were the highest total by a Super Bowl team. The previous high was 35 points by Green Bay in Game I.

Washington (NFC)		0 3 6 0 — 9	
L.A. Raiders (AFC)		7 14 14 3 — 38	
Raiders	—	Jensen recovered blocked punt in end zone (Bahr kick) (10:08)	
Raiders	—	Branch 12 pass from Plunkett (Bahr kick) (9:14)	
Wash	—	FG Moseley 24 (3:05)	
Raiders	—	Squirek 5 interception return (Bahr kick) (0:07)	
Wash	—	Riggins 1 run (kick blocked) (10:52)	
Raiders	—	Allen 5 run (Bahr kick) (7:06)	
Raiders	—	Allen 74 run (Bahr kick) (0:00)	
Raiders	—	FG Bahr 21 (2:24)	

SUPER BOWL XVII
Rose Bowl, Pasadena, California
January 30, 1983, Attendance: 103,667
WASHINGTON 27, MIAMI 17—Fullback John Riggins ran for a Super Bowl-record 166 yards on 38 carries to spark Washington to a 27-17 victory over AFC champion Miami. It was Riggins' fourth straight 100-yard rushing game during the playoffs, also a record. The win marked Washington's first NFL title since 1942, and was only the second time in Super Bowl history NFL/NFC teams scored consecutive victories (Green Bay did it in Super Bowls I and II and San Francisco won Super Bowl XVI). The Redskins, under second-year head coach Joe Gibbs, used a balanced offense that accounted for 400 total yards (a Super Bowl-record 276 yards rushing and 124 passing), second in Super Bowl history to 429 yards by Oakland in Super Bowl XI. The Dolphins built a 17-10 halftime lead on a 76-yard touchdown pass from quarterback David Woodley to wide receiver Jimmy Cefalo 6:49 into the first period, a 20-yard field goal by Uwe von Schamann with 6:00 left in the half, and a Super Bowl-record 98-yard kickoff return by Fulton Walker with 1:38 remaining. Washington had tied the score at 10-10 with 1:51 left on a 4-yard touchdown pass from Joe Theismann to wide receiver Alvin Garrett. Mark Moseley started the Redskins' scoring with a 31-yard field goal late in the first period, and added a 20-yard kick midway through the third period to cut the Dolphins' lead to 17-13. Riggins, who was voted the game's most valuable player, gave Washington its first lead of the game with 10:01 left when he ran 43 yards off left tackle for a touchdown in a fourth-and-1 situation. Wide receiver Charlie Brown caught a 6-yard scoring pass from Theismann with 1:55 left to complete the scoring. The Dolphins managed only 176 yards (142 in first half). Theismann completed 15 of 23 passes for 143 yards, with 2 touchdowns

and 2 interceptions. For Miami, Woodley was 4 of 14 for 97 yards, with 1 touchdown, and 1 interception. Don Strock was 0 for 3 in relief.

Miami (AFC)		7 10 0 0 — 17
Washington (NFC)		0 10 3 14 — 27

Mia — Cefalo 76 pass from Woodley (von Schamann kick) (8:11)
Wash — FG Moseley 31 (0:39)
Mia — FG von Schamann 20 (6:00)
Wash — Garrett 4 pass from Theismann (Moseley kick) (1:51)
Mia — Walker 98 kickoff return (von Schamann kick) (1:38)
Wash — FG Moseley 20 (8:09)
Wash — Riggins 43 run (Moseley kick) (10:01)
Wash — Brown 6 pass from Theismann (Moseley kick) (1:55)

SUPER BOWL XVI

Pontiac Silverdome, Pontiac, Michigan
January 24, 1982, Attendance: 81,270
SAN FRANCISCO 26, CINCINNATI 21—Ray Wersching's Super Bowl record-tying 4 field goals and Joe Montana's controlled passing helped lift the San Francisco 49ers to their first NFL championship with a 26-21 victory over Cincinnati. The 49ers built a game-record 20-0 halftime lead via Montana's 1-yard touchdown run, which capped an 11-play, 68-yard drive; fullback Earl Cooper's 11-yard scoring pass from Montana, which climaxed a Super Bowl record 92-yard drive on 12 plays; and Wersching's 22- and 26-yard field goals. The Bengals rebounded in the second half, closing the gap to 20-14 on quarterback Ken Anderson's 5-yard run and Dan Ross' 4-yard reception from Anderson, who established Super Bowl passing records for completions (25) and completion percentage (73.5 percent on 25 of 34). Wersching added early fourth-period field goals of 40 and 23 yards to increase the 49ers' lead to 26-14. The Bengals managed to score on an Anderson-to-Ross 3-yard pass with only 16 seconds remaining. Ross set a Super Bowl record with 11 receptions for 104 yards. Montana, the game's most valuable player, completed 14 of 22 passes for 157 yards. Cincinnati compiled 356 yards to San Francisco's 275, which marked the first time in Super Bowl history that the team that gained the most yards from scrimmage lost the game.

San Francisco (NFC)		7 13 0 6 — 26
Cincinnati (AFC)		0 0 7 14 — 21

SF — Montana 1 run (Wersching kick) (5:52)
SF — Cooper 11 pass from Montana (Wersching kick) (6:53)
SF — FG Wersching 22 (0:15)
SF — FG Wersching 26 (0:02)
Cin — Anderson 5 run (Breech kick) (11:25)
Cin — Ross 4 pass from Anderson (Breech kick) (10:06)

SF — FG Wersching 40 (5:25)
SF — FG Wersching 23 (1:57)
Cin — Ross 3 pass from Anderson (Breech kick) (0:16)

SUPER BOWL XV

Louisiana Superdome, New Orleans, LA
January 25, 1981, Attendance: 76,135
OAKLAND 27, PHILADELPHIA 10—Jim Plunkett passed for 3 touchdowns, including an 80-yard strike to Kenny King, as the Raiders became the first wild-card team to win the Super Bowl. Plunkett's touchdown bomb to King—the longest play in Super Bowl history—gave Oakland a decisive 14-0 lead with nine seconds left in the first period. Linebacker Rod Martin had set up Oakland's first touchdown, a 2-yard reception by Cliff Branch, with a 17-yard interception return to the Eagles' 30-yard line. The Eagles never recovered from that early deficit, managing only Tony Franklin's field goal (30 yards) and an 8-yard touchdown pass from Ron Jaworski to Keith Krepfle. Plunkett, who became a starter in the sixth game of the season, completed 13 of 21 for 261 yards and was named the game's most valuable player. Oakland won 9 of 11 games with Plunkett starting, but that was good enough only for second place in the AFC West, although they tied division winner San Diego with an 11-5 record. The Raiders, who had previously won Super Bowl XI over Minnesota, had to win three playoff games to get to the championship game. Oakland defeated Houston 27-7 at home followed by road victories over Cleveland (14-12) and San Diego (34-27). Oakland's Mark van Eeghen was the game's leading rusher with 75 yards on 18 carries. Philadelphia's Wilbert Montgomery led all receivers with 6 receptions for 91 yards. Branch had 5 for 67 and Harold Carmichael of Philadelphia 5 for 83. Martin finished the game with 3 interceptions, a Super Bowl record.

Oakland (AFC)		14 0 10 3 — 27
Philadelphia (NFC)		0 3 0 7 — 10

Oak — Branch 2 pass from Plunkett (Bahr kick) (8:56)
Oak — King 80 pass from Plunkett (Bahr kick) (0:09)
Phil — FG Franklin 30 (10:28)
Oak — Branch 29 pass from Plunkett (Bahr kick) (12:24)
Oak — FG Bahr 46 (4:35)
Phil — Krepfle 8 pass from Jaworski (Franklin kick) (13:59)
Oak — FG Bahr 35 (8:29)

SUPER BOWL XIV

Rose Bowl, Pasadena, California
January 20, 1980, Attendance: 103,985
PITTSBURGH 31, LOS ANGELES 19—Terry Bradshaw completed 14 of 21 passes for 309 yards and set two passing records as the Steelers became the first team to win four Super Bowls. Despite 3 interceptions by the Rams, Bradshaw kept

his poise and brought the Steelers from behind twice in the second half. Trailing 13-10 at halftime, Pittsburgh went ahead 17-13 when Bradshaw hit Lynn Swann with a 47-yard touchdown pass after 2:48 of the third quarter. On the Rams' next possession Vince Ferragamo, who was 15 of 25 for 212 yards, responded with a 50-yard pass to Billy Waddy that moved Los Angeles from its 26 to the Steelers' 24. On the following play, Lawrence McCutcheon connected with Ron Smith on a halfback option pass that gave the Rams a 19-17 lead. On Pittsburgh's initial possession of the final period, Bradshaw lofted a 73-yard scoring pass to John Stallworth to put the Steelers in front to stay 24-19. Franco Harris scored on a 1-yard run later in the quarter to seal the verdict. A 45-yard pass from Bradshaw to Stallworth was the key play in the drive to Harris' score. Bradshaw, the game's most valuable player for the second straight year, set career Super Bowl records for most touchdown passes (9) and most passing yards (932). Larry Anderson gave the Steelers excellent field position throughout the game with 5 kickoff returns for a record 162 yards.

Los Angeles (NFC)		7 6 6 0 — 19
Pittsburgh (AFC)		3 7 7 14 — 31

Pitt — FG Bahr 41 (7:31)
LA — Bryant 1 run (Corral kick) (2:44)
Pitt — Harris 1 run (Bahr kick) (12:52)
LA — FG Corral 31 (7:21)
LA — FG Corral 45 (0:14)
Pitt — Swann 47 pass from Bradshaw (Bahr kick) (12:12)
LA — Smith 24 pass from McCutcheon (kick failed) (10:15)
Pitt — Stallworth 73 pass from Bradshaw (Bahr kick) (12:04)
Pitt — Harris 1 run (Bahr kick) (1:49)

SUPER BOWL XIII

Orange Bowl, Miami, Florida
January 21, 1979, Attendance: 79,484
PITTSBURGH 35, DALLAS 31—Terry Bradshaw passed for a record 4 touchdowns to lead the Steelers to victory. The Steelers became the first team to win three Super Bowls, mostly because of Bradshaw's accurate arm. Bradshaw, voted the game's most valuable player, completed 17 of 30 passes for 318 yards, a personal high. Four of those passes went for touchdowns—2 to John Stallworth and the third, with 26 seconds remaining in the second period, to Rocky Bleier for a 21-14 halftime lead. The Cowboys scored twice before intermission on Roger Staubach's 39-yard pass to Tony Hill and a 37-yard fumble return by linebacker Mike Hegman, who stole the ball from Bradshaw. The Steelers broke open the contest with 2 touchdowns in a span of 19 seconds midway through the final

period. Franco Harris rambled 22 yards up the middle to give the Steelers a 28-17 lead with 7:10 left. Pittsburgh got the ball right back when Randy White fumbled the kickoff and Dennis Winston recovered for the Steelers. On first down, Bradshaw fired his fourth touchdown pass, an 18-yard pass to Lynn Swann to boost the Steelers' lead to 35-17 with 6:51 to play. The Cowboys refused to let the Steelers run away with the contest. Staubach connected with Billy Joe DuPree on a 7-yard scoring pass with 2:23 left. Then the Cowboys recovered an onside kick and Staubach took them in for another score, passing 4 yards to Butch Johnson with 22 seconds remaining. Bleier recovered another onside kick with 17 seconds left to seal the victory for the Steelers.

Pittsburgh (AFC)	7 14 0 14 —	35
Dallas (NFC)	7 7 3 14 —	31
Pitt	—	Stallworth 28 pass from Bradshaw (Gerela kick) (9:47)
Dall	—	Hill 39 pass from Staubach (Septien kick) (0:00)
Dall	—	Hegman 37 fumble recovery return (Septien kick) (12:08)
Pitt	—	Stallworth 75 pass from Bradshaw (Gerela kick) (10:25)
Pitt	—	Bleier 7 pass from Bradshaw (Gerela kick) (0:26)
Dall	—	FG Septien 27 (2:36)
Pitt	—	Harris 22 run (Gerela kick) (7:10)
Pitt	—	Swann 18 pass from Bradshaw (Gerela kick) (6:51)
Dall	—	DuPree 7 pass from Staubach (Septien kick) (2:23)
Dall	—	B. Johnson 4 pass from Staubach (Septien kick) (0:22)

SUPER BOWL XII

Louisiana Superdome, New Orleans, LA
January 15, 1978, Attendance: 75,583
DALLAS 27, DENVER 10—The Cowboys evened their Super Bowl record at 2-2 by defeating Denver before a sellout crowd plus 102,010,000 television viewers, the largest audience ever to watch a sporting event. Dallas converted 2 interceptions into 10 points and Efren Herrera added a 35-yard field goal for a 13-0 halftime advantage. In the third period Craig Morton engineered a drive to the Cowboys' 30 and Jim Turner's 47-yard field goal made the score 13-3. After an exchange of punts, Butch Johnson made a spectacular diving catch in the end zone to complete a 45-yard pass from Roger Staubach and put the Cowboys ahead 20-3. Following Rick Upchurch's 67-yard kickoff return, Norris Weese guided the Broncos to a touchdown to cut the deficit to 20-10. Dallas clinched the victory when running back Robert Newhouse tossed a 29-yard touchdown pass to Golden Richards with 7:04 left in the game. It was the first pass thrown by Newhouse since 1975. Harvey Martin and Randy White, who were

named co-most valuable players, led the Cowboys' defense, which recovered 4 fumbles and intercepted 4 passes.

Dallas (NFC)	10 3 7 7 —	27
Denver (AFC)	0 0 10 0 —	10
Dall	—	Dorsett 3 run (Herrera kick) (4:29)
Dall	—	FG Herrera 35 (1:31)
Dall	—	FG Herrera 43 (11:16)
Den	—	FG Turner 47 (12:32)
Dall	—	Johnson 45 pass from Staubach (Herrera kick) (6.59)
Den	—	Lytle 1 run (Turner kick) (5:39)
Dall	—	Richards 29 pass from Newhouse (Herrera kick) (7:04)

SUPER BOWL XI

Rose Bowl, Pasadena, California
January 9, 1977, Attendance: 103,438
OAKLAND 32, MINNESOTA 14—The Raiders won their first NFL championship before a record Super Bowl crowd plus 81 million television viewers, the largest audience ever to watch a sporting event. The Raiders gained a record-breaking 429 yards, including running back Clarence Davis' 137 rushing yards. Wide receiver Fred Biletnikoff made 4 key receptions, which earned him the game's most valuable player trophy. Oakland scored on three successive possessions in the second quarter to build a 16-0 halftime lead. Errol Mann's 24-yard field goal opened the scoring, then the AFC champions put together drives of 64 and 35 yards, scoring on a 1-yard pass from Ken Stabler to Dave Casper and a 1-yard run by Pete Banaszak. The Raiders increased their lead to 19-0 on a 40-yard field goal in the third quarter, but Minnesota responded with a 12-play, 58-yard drive late in the period, with Fran Tarkenton passing 8 yards to wide receiver Sammy White to cut the deficit to 19-7. Two fourth-quarter interceptions clinched the title for the Raiders. One set up Banaszak's second touchdown run, the other resulted in cornerback Willie Brown's Super Bowl-record 75-yard interception return.

Oakland (AFC)	0 16 3 13 —	32
Minnesota (NFC)	0 0 7 7 —	14
Oak	—	FG Mann 24 (14:12)
Oak	—	Casper 1 pass from Stabler (Mann kick) (7:10)
Oak	—	Banaszak 1 run (kick failed) (3:33)
Oak	—	FG Mann 40 (5:16)
Minn	—	S. White 8 pass from Tarkenton (Cox kick) (0:47)
Oak	—	Banaszak 2 run (Mann kick) (7:39)
Oak	—	Brown 75 interception return (kick failed) (5:43)
Minn	—	Voigt 13 pass from Lee (Cox kick) (0:25)

SUPER BOWL X

Orange Bowl, Miami, Florida
January 18, 1976, Attendance: 80,187
PITTSBURGH 21, DALLAS 17—The Steelers won the Super Bowl for the second year in a row on Terry Bradshaw's 64-yard touchdown pass to Lynn Swann and an aggressive defense that snuffed out a late rally by the Cowboys with an end-zone interception on the final play of the game. In the fourth quarter, Pittsburgh ran on fourth down and gave up the ball on the Cowboys' 39 with 1:22 to play. Roger Staubach ran and passed for 2 first downs but his last desperation pass was picked off by Glen Edwards. Dallas' scoring was the result of 2 touchdown passes by Staubach, one to Drew Pearson for 29 yards and the other to Percy Howard for 34 yards. Howard's reception was the only catch of his NFL career. Toni Fritsch had a 36-yard field goal. The Steelers scored on 2 touchdown passes by Bradshaw, 1 to Randy Grossman for 7 yards and the long bomb to Swann. Roy Gerela had 36- and 18-yard field goals. Reggie Harrison blocked a punt through the end zone for a safety. Swann set a Super Bowl record by gaining 161 yards on his 4 receptions.

Dallas (NFC)	7 3 0 7 —	17
Pittsburgh (AFC)	7 0 0 14 —	21
Dall	—	D. Pearson 29 pass from Staubach (Fritsch kick) (10:24)
Pitt	—	Grossman 7 pass from Bradshaw (Gerela kick) (5:57)
Dall	—	FG Fritsch 36 (14:45)
Pitt	—	Safety, Harrison blocked Hoopes' punt through end zone (11:28)
Pitt	—	FG Gerela 36 (8:41)
Pitt	—	FG Gerela 18 (6:37)
Pitt	—	Swann 64 pass from Bradshaw (kick failed) (3:02)
Dall	—	P. Howard 34 pass from Staubach (Fritsch kick) (1:48)

SUPER BOWL IX

Tulane Stadium, New Orleans, Louisiana
January 12, 1975, Attendance: 80,997
PITTSBURGH 16, MINNESOTA 6—AFC champion Pittsburgh, in its initial Super Bowl appearance, and NFC champion Minnesota, making a third bid for its first Super Bowl title, struggled through a first half in which the only score was produced by the Steelers' defense when Dwight White downed Vikings' quarterback Fran Tarkenton in the end zone for a safety 7:49 into the second period. The Steelers forced another break and took advantage on the second-half kickoff when Minnesota's Bill Brown fumbled and Marv Kellum recovered for Pittsburgh on the Vikings' 30. After Rocky Bleier failed to gain on first down, Franco Harris carried 3 consecutive times for 24 yards, a loss of 3, and a 9-yard touchdown and a 9-0 lead. Though its offense was completely

stymied by Pittsburgh's defense, Minnesota managed to move into a threatening position after 4:27 of the final period when Matt Blair blocked Bobby Walden's punt and Terry Brown recovered the ball in the end zone for a touchdown. Fred Cox's kick failed and the Steelers led 9-6. Pittsburgh wasted no time putting the victory away. The Steelers took the ensuing kickoff and marched 66 yards in 11 plays, climaxed by Terry Bradshaw's 4-yard scoring pass to Larry Brown with 3:31 left. Pittsburgh's defense permitted Minnesota only 119 yards total offense, including a Super Bowl low of 17 rushing yards. The Steelers, meanwhile, gained 333 yards, including Harris' record 158 yards on 34 carries.

Pittsburgh (AFC)	0 2 7 7 — 16		
Minnesota (NFC)	0 0 0 6 — 6		

Pitt — Safety, White downed Tarkenton in end zone (7:11)
Pitt — Harris 9 run (Gerela kick) (13:25)
Minn — T. Brown recovered blocked punt in end zone (kick failed) (10:33)
Pitt — L. Brown 4 pass from Bradshaw (Gerela kick) (3:31)

SUPER BOWL VIII
Rice Stadium, Houston, Texas
January 13, 1974, Attendance: 71,882
MIAMI 24, MINNESOTA 7—The defending NFL champion Dolphins, representing the AFC for the third straight year, scored the first two times they had possession on marches of 62 and 56 yards while the Miami defense limited the Vikings to only seven plays in the first period. Larry Csonka climaxed the initial 10-play drive with a 5-yard touchdown bolt through right guard after 5:27 had elapsed. Four plays later, Miami began another 10-play scoring drive, which ended with Jim Kiick bursting 1 yard through the middle for another touchdown after 13:38 of the period. Garo Yepremian added a 28-yard field goal midway in the second period for a 17-0 Miami lead. Minnesota then drove from its 20 to a second-and-2 situation on the Miami 7 yard line with 1:18 left in the half. But on two plays, Miami limited Oscar Reed to 1 yard. On fourth-and-1 from the Miami 2, Reed went over right tackle, but Dolphins middle linebacker Nick Buoniconti jarred the ball loose and Jake Scott recovered for Miami to halt the Minnesota threat. The Vikings were unable to muster enough offense in the second half to threaten the Dolphins. Csonka rushed 33 times for a Super Bowl-record 145 yards. Bob Griese of Miami completed 6 of 7 passes for 73 yards.

Minnesota (NFC)	0 0 0 7 — 7		
Miami (AFC)	14 3 7 0 — 24		

Mia — Csonka 5 run (Yepremian kick) (5:27)
Mia — Kiick 1 run (Yepremian kick) (1:22)
Mia — FG Yepremian 28 (6:02)
Mia — Csonka 2 run (Yepremian kick) (8:44)
Minn — Tarkenton 4 run (Cox kick) (13:25)

SUPER BOWL VII
Memorial Coliseum, Los Angeles, CA
January 14, 1973, Attendance: 90,182
MIAMI 14, WASHINGTON 7—The Dolphins played virtually perfect football in the first half as their defense permitted the Redskins to cross midfield only once and their offense turned good field position into 2 touchdowns. On its third possession, Miami opened its first scoring drive from the Dolphins' 37 yard line. An 18-yard pass from Bob Griese to Paul Warfield preceded by three plays Griese's 28-yard touchdown pass to Howard Twilley. After Washington moved from its 17 to the Miami 48 with two minutes remaining in the first half, Dolphins linebacker Nick Buoniconti intercepted Billy Kilmer's pass at the Miami 41 and returned it to the Washington 27. Jim Kiick ran for 3 yards, Larry Csonka for 3, Griese passed to Jim Mandich for 19, and Kiick gained 1 to the 1-yard line. With 18 seconds left until intermission, Kiick scored from the 1. Washington's only touchdown came with 2:07 left in the game and resulted from a misplayed field-goal attempt and fumble by Garo Yepremian, with the Redskins' Mike Bass picking the ball out of the air and running 49 yards for the score. Dolphins safety Jake Scott, who had 2 interceptions, including 1 in the end zone to kill a Redskins' drive, was voted the game's most valuable player.

Miami (AFC)	7 7 0 0 — 14		
Washington (NFC)	0 0 0 7 — 7		

Mia — Twilley 28 pass from Griese (Yepremian kick) (0:01)
Mia — Kiick 1 run (Yepremian kick) (0:18)
Wash — Bass 49 fumble recovery return (Knight kick) (2:07)

SUPER BOWL VI
Tulane Stadium, New Orleans, Louisiana
January 16, 1972, Attendance: 81,023
DALLAS 24, MIAMI 3—The Cowboys rushed for a record 252 yards and their defense limited the Dolphins to a low of 185 yards while not permitting a touchdown for the first time in Super Bowl history. Dallas converted Chuck Howley's recovery of Larry Csonka's first fumble of the season into a 3-0 advantage and led at halftime 10-3. After Dallas received the second-half kickoff, Duane Thomas led a 71-yard march in eight plays for a 17-3 margin. Howley intercepted Bob Griese's pass at the 50 and returned it to the Miami 9 early in the fourth period, and three plays later Roger Staubach passed 7 yards to Mike Ditka for the final touchdown. Thomas rushed for 95 yards and Walt Garrison gained 74. Staubach, voted the game's most valuable player, completed 12 of 19 passes for 119 yards and 2 touchdowns.

Dallas (NFC)	3 7 7 7 — 24		
Miami (AFC)	0 3 0 0 — 3		

Dall — FG Clark 9 (1:23)
Dall — Alworth 7 pass from Staubach (Clark kick) (1:15)
Mia — FG Yepremian 31 (0:04)
Dall — D. Thomas 3 run (Clark kick) (9:43)
Dall — Ditka 7 pass from Staubach (Clark kick) (11:42)

SUPER BOWL V
Orange Bowl, Miami, Florida
January 17, 1971, Attendance: 79,204
BALTIMORE 16, DALLAS 13—A 32-yard field goal by rookie kicker Jim O'Brien brought the Baltimore Colts a victory over the Dallas Cowboys in the final five seconds of Super Bowl V. The game between the champions of the AFC and NFC was played on artificial turf for the first time. Dallas led 13-6 at the half but interceptions by Rick Volk and Mike Curtis set up a Baltimore touchdown and O'Brien's decisive kick in the fourth period. Earl Morrall relieved an injured Johnny Unitas late in the first half, although Unitas completed the Colts' only scoring pass. It caromed off receiver Eddie Hinton's fingertips, off Dallas defensive back Mel Renfro, and finally settled into the grasp of John Mackey, who went 45 yards to score on a 75-yard play.

Baltimore (AFC)	0 6 0 10 — 16		
Dallas (NFC)	3 10 0 0 — 13		

Dall — FG Clark 14 (5:32)
Dall — FG Clark 30 (14:52)
Balt — Mackey 75 pass from Unitas (kick blocked) (14:55)
Dall — Thomas 7 pass from Morton (Clark kick) (7:53)
Balt — Nowatzke 2 run (O'Brien kick) (7:35)
Balt — FG O'Brien 32 (0:05)

SUPER BOWL IV
Tulane Stadium, New Orleans, Louisiana
January 11, 1970, Attendance: 80,562
KANSAS CITY 23, MINNESOTA 7—The AFL squared the Super Bowl at two games apiece with the NFL, building a 16-0 halftime lead behind Len Dawson's superb quarterbacking and a powerful defense. Dawson, the fourth consecutive quarterback to be chosen the Super Bowl's top player, called an almost flawless game, completing 12 of 17 passes and hitting Otis Taylor on a 46-yard play for the final Chiefs touchdown. The Kansas City defense limited Minnesota's strong rushing game to 67 yards and had 3 interceptions and 2 fumble recoveries. The crowd of 80,562 set a Super Bowl record, as did the gross receipts of $3,817,872.69.

Minnesota (NFL)	0	0	7	0	—	7
Kansas City (AFL)	3	13	7	0	—	23

KC   — FG Stenerud 48 (6:52)
KC   — FG Stenerud 32 (13:20)
KC   — FG Stenerud 25 (7:52)
KC   — Garrett 5 run (Stenerud kick)
         (5:34)
Minn — Osborn 4 run (Cox kick)
         (4:32)
KC   — Taylor 46 pass from Dawson
         (Stenerud kick) (1:22)

SUPER BOWL III

Orange Bowl, Miami, Florida
January 12, 1969, Attendance: 75,389
NEW YORK JETS 16, BALTIMORE 7—
Jets quarterback Joe Namath "guaranteed" victory on the Thursday before the
game, then went out and led the AFL to its
first Super Bowl victory over a Baltimore
team that had lost only once in 16 games
all season. Namath, chosen the outstanding player, completed 17 of 28 passes for
206 yards and directed a steady attack
that dominated the NFL champions after
the Jets' defense had intercepted Colts
quarterback Earl Morrall 3 times in the
first half. The Jets had 337 total yards,
including 121 rushing yards by Matt Snell.
Johnny Unitas, who had missed most of
the season with a sore elbow, came off
the bench and led Baltimore to its only
touchdown late in the fourth quarter after
New York led 16-0.

New York Jets (AFL)	0	7	6	3	—	16
Baltimore (NFL)	0	0	0	7	—	7

NYJ   — Snell 4 run (Turner kick)
         (9:03)
NYJ   — FG Turner 32 (10:08)
NYJ   — FG Turner 30 (3:58)
NYJ   — FG Turner 9 (13:26)
Balt — Hill 1 run (Michaels kick)
         (3:19)

SUPER BOWL II

Orange Bowl, Miami, Florida
January 14, 1968, Attendance: 75,546
GREEN BAY 33, OAKLAND 14—Green
Bay, after winning its third consecutive
NFL championship, won the Super Bowl
title for the second straight year, defeating
the AFL champion Raiders in a game that
drew the first $3-million gate in football
history. Bart Starr again was chosen the
game's most valuable player as he completed 13 of 24 passes for 202 yards and
1 touchdown and directed a Packers'
attack that was in control all the way after
building a 16-7 halftime lead. Don Chandler kicked 4 field goals and all-pro cornerback Herb Adderley capped the Green
Bay scoring with a 60-yard interception
return. The game marked the last for
Vince Lombardi as Packers coach, ending
nine years at Green Bay in which he won
six Western Conference championships,
five NFL championships, and two Super
Bowls.

Green Bay (NFL)	3	13	10	7	—	33
Oakland (AFL)	0	7	0	7	—	14

GB   — FG Chandler 39 (9:53)
GB   — FG Chandler 20 (11:52)
GB   — Dowler 62 pass from Starr
         (Chandler kick) (10:50)
Oak   — Miller 23 pass from Lamonica
         (Blanda kick) (6:15)
GB   — FG Chandler 43 (0:01)
GB   — Anderson 2 run (Chandler
         kick) (5:54)
GB   — FG Chandler 31 (0:02)
GB   — Adderley 60 interception
         return (Chandler kick) (11:03)
Oak   — Miller 23 pass from Lamonica
         (Blanda kick) (9:13)

SUPER BOWL I

Memorial Coliseum, Los Angeles, CA
January 15, 1967, Attendance: 61,946
GREEN BAY 35, KANSAS CITY 10—The
Green Bay Packers opened the Super
Bowl series by defeating the AFL champion Chiefs behind the passing of Bart Starr,
the receiving of Max McGee, and a key
interception by all-pro safety Willie Wood.
Green Bay broke open the game with 3
second-half touchdowns, the first of
which was set up by Wood's 50-yard
return of an interception. McGee, filling in
for ailing Boyd Dowler after having caught
only 4 passes all season, caught 7 from
Starr for 138 yards and 2 touchdowns.
Elijah Pitts ran for 2 other scores. The
Chiefs' 10 points came in the second
quarter, the only touchdown on a 7-yard
pass from Len Dawson to Curtis McClinton. Starr completed 16 of 23 passes for
250 yards and 2 touchdowns and was
chosen the most valuable player. The
Packers collected $15,000 per man and
the Chiefs $7,500—the largest single-
game shares in the history of team
sports.

Kansas City (AFL)	0	10	0	0	—	10
Green Bay (NFL)	7	7	14	7	—	35

GB   — McGee 37 pass from Starr
         (Chandler kick) (6:04)
KC   — McClinton 7 pass from
         Dawson (Mercer kick) (10:40)
GB   — Taylor 14 run (Chandler kick)
         (4:37)
KC   — FG Mercer 31 (0:54)
GB   — Pitts 5 run (Chandler kick)
         (12:33)
GB   — McGee 13 pass from Starr
         (Chandler kick) (0:51)
GB   — Pitts 1 run (Chandler kick)
         (6:35)

AFC CHAMPIONSHIP GAME RESULTS
Includes AFL Championship Games (1960-69)

Season	Date	Winner (Share)	Loser (Share)	Score	Site	Attendance
2005	Jan. 22	Pittsburgh ($37,000)	Denver ($37,000)	34-17	Denver	76,775
2004	Jan. 23	New England ($36,500)	Pittsburgh ($36,500)	41-27	Pittsburgh	65,242
2003	Jan. 18	New England ($36,500)	Indianapolis ($36,500)	24-14	Foxborough	68,436
2002	Jan. 19	Oakland ($35,000)	Tennessee ($35,000)	41-24	Oakland	62,544
2001	Jan. 27	New England ($34,500)	Pittsburgh ($34,500)	24-17	Pittsburgh	64,704
2000	Jan. 14	Baltimore ($34,500)	Oakland ($34,500)	16-3	Oakland	62,784
1999	Jan. 23	Tennessee ($33,000)	Jacksonville ($33,000)	33-14	Jacksonville	75,206
1998	Jan. 17	Denver ($32,500)	N.Y. Jets ($32,500)	23-10	Denver	75,482
1997	Jan. 11	Denver ($30,000)	Pittsburgh ($30,000)	24-21	Pittsburgh	61,382
1996	Jan. 12	New England ($29,000)	Jacksonville ($29,000)	20-6	Foxborough	60,190
1995	Jan. 14	Pittsburgh ($27,000)	Indianapolis ($27,000)	20-16	Pittsburgh	61,062
1994	Jan. 15	San Diego ($26,000)	Pittsburgh ($26,000)	17-13	Pittsburgh	61,545
1993	Jan. 23	Buffalo ($23,500)	Kansas City ($23,500)	30-13	Buffalo	76,642
1992	Jan. 17	Buffalo ($18,000)	Miami ($18,000)	29-10	Miami	72,703
1991	Jan. 12	Buffalo ($18,000)	Denver ($18,000)	10-7	Buffalo	80,272
1990	Jan. 20	Buffalo ($18,000)	L.A. Raiders ($18,000)	51-3	Buffalo	80,325
1989	Jan. 14	Denver ($18,000)	Cleveland ($18,000)	37-21	Denver	76,046
1988	Jan. 8	Cincinnati ($18,000)	Buffalo ($18,000)	21-10	Cincinnati	59,747
1987	Jan. 17	Denver ($18,000)	Cleveland ($18,000)	38-33	Denver	76,197
1986	Jan. 11	Denver ($18,000)	Cleveland ($18,000)	23-20*	Cleveland	79,973
1985	Jan. 12	New England ($18,000)	Miami ($18,000)	31-14	Miami	75,662
1984	Jan. 6	Miami ($18,000)	Pittsburgh ($18,000)	45-28	Miami	76,029
1983	Jan. 8	L.A. Raiders ($18,000)	Seattle ($18,000)	30-14	Los Angeles	91,445
1982	Jan. 23	Miami ($18,000)	N.Y. Jets ($18,000)	14-0	Miami	67,396
1981	Jan. 10	Cincinnati ($9,000)	San Diego ($9,000)	27-7	Cincinnati	46,302
1980	Jan. 11	Oakland ($9,000)	San Diego ($9,000)	34-27	San Diego	52,675
1979	Jan. 6	Pittsburgh ($9,000)	Houston ($9,000)	27-13	Pittsburgh	50,475
1978	Jan. 7	Pittsburgh ($9,000)	Houston ($9,000)	34-5	Pittsburgh	50,725
1977	Jan. 1	Denver ($9,000)	Oakland ($9,000)	20-17	Denver	75,044
1976	Dec. 26	Oakland ($8,500)	Pittsburgh ($5,500)	24-7	Oakland	53,821
1975	Jan. 4	Pittsburgh ($8,500)	Oakland ($5,500)	16-10	Pittsburgh	50,609
1974	Dec. 29	Pittsburgh ($8,500)	Oakland ($5,500)	24-13	Oakland	53,800
1973	Dec. 30	Miami ($8,500)	Oakland ($5,500)	27-10	Miami	79,325
1972	Dec. 31	Miami ($8,500)	Pittsburgh ($5,500)	21-17	Pittsburgh	50,845
1971	Jan. 2	Miami ($8,500)	Baltimore ($5,500)	21-0	Miami	76,622
1970	Jan. 3	Baltimore ($8,500)	Oakland ($5,500)	27-17	Baltimore	54,799
1969	Jan. 4	Kansas City ($7,755)	Oakland ($6,252)	17-7	Oakland	53,564
1968	Dec. 29	N.Y. Jets ($7,007)	Oakland ($5,349)	27-23	New York	62,627
1967	Dec. 31	Oakland ($6,321)	Houston ($4,996)	40-7	Oakland	53,330
1966	Jan. 1	Kansas City ($5,309)	Buffalo ($3,799)	31-7	Buffalo	42,080
1965	Dec. 26	Buffalo ($5,189)	San Diego ($3,447)	23-0	San Diego	30,361
1964	Dec. 26	Buffalo ($2,668)	San Diego ($1,738)	20-7	Buffalo	40,242
1963	Jan. 5	San Diego ($2,498)	Boston ($1,596)	51-10	San Diego	30,127
1962	Dec. 23	Dallas ($2,206)	Houston ($1,471)	20-17*	Houston	37,981
1961	Dec. 24	Houston ($1,792)	San Diego ($1,111)	10-3	San Diego	29,556
1960	Jan. 1	Houston ($1,025)	L.A. Chargers ($718)	24-16	Houston	32,183

*Sudden death overtime

AFC CHAMPIONSHIP GAME COMPOSITE STANDINGS

	W	L	Pct.	Pts.	OP
Cincinnati Bengals	2	0	1.000	48	17
Baltimore Ravens	1	0	1.000	16	3
New England Patriots**	5	1	.833	150	129
Buffalo Bills	6	2	.750	180	92
Denver Broncos	6	2	.750	189	166
Kansas City Chiefs*	3	1	.750	81	61
Miami Dolphins	5	2	.714	152	115
Pittsburgh Steelers	6	7	.462	285	270
Tennessee Titans##	3	5	.375	133	195
Oakland Raiders###	5	9	.357	272	304
New York Jets	1	2	.333	37	60
San Diego Chargers***	2	6	.250	128	161
Indianapolis Colts#	1	3	.250	57	82
Seattle Seahawks	0	1	.000	14	30
Jacksonville Jaguars	0	2	.000	20	53
Cleveland Browns	0	3	.000	74	98

* *One game played when franchise was in Dallas (Texans) (Won 20-17)*

** *One game played when franchise was in Boston (Lost 51-10)*

*** *One game played when franchise was in Los Angeles (Lost 24-16)*

\# *Two games played when franchise was in Baltimore (Won 27-17, lost 21-0)*

\## *Six games played when franchise was in Houston and known as Oilers (Won 2, lost 4)*

\### *Two games played when franchise was in Los Angeles (Won 30-14, lost 51-3)*

2005 AFC CHAMPIONSHIP GAME
INVESCO Field at Mile High, Denver, Colorado
January 22, 2006, Attendance: 76,775
PITTSBURGH 34, DENVER 17—Ben Roethlisberger passed for 2 touchdowns and ran for another as the Steelers earned the sixth AFC title in franchise history. The Steelers were the first team to

beat the first-, second-, and third-seed in the same postseason, and became just the second team to win three playoff road games to reach the Super Bowl (1985 Patriots). The Steelers converted 10 of 16 third-down situations to maintain possession for 36:07, and forced 4 turnovers that led to 21 points. Pittsburgh scored on each of its four first-half possessions to take a 24-3 halftime lead. On their first drive, Roethlisberger's third-and-3 pass intended for Hines Ward was nearly intercepted by Champ Bailey, but the ball was tipped and caught by Ward for a first down. Jeff Reed's 47-yard field goal completed the drive, and three plays later Joey Porter forced Jake Plummer to fumble. Casey Hampton recovered at the Broncos' 39. Five plays later, on third-and-8, Roethlisberger lofted a touchdown pass to Cedrick Wilson in the back left corner of the end zone. The Broncos answered with a field goal, but the Steelers responded with a 14-play, 80-yard drive capped by Jerome Bettis' 3-yard run with 1:55 left in the half for a 17-3 lead. On the next play from scrimmage, Ike Taylor intercepted Plummer's pass, and Ward caught Roethlisberger's 17-yard scoring toss with seven seconds left in the half for a 24-3 lead. Plummer's 32-yard pass to Rod Smith on third-and-1 led to Ashley Lelie's 30-yard touchdown catch to pull within 24-10. Reed's 42-yard field goal capped the ensuing drive, and Larry Foote intercepted Plummer on the next play from scrimmage. Denver forced a punt and Mike Anderson scored with 7:52 left to pull within 10 points. The Broncos' defense forced a three-and-out, but on fourth-and-10 from their own 20 with 4:52 left, Brett Keisel sacked Plummer and forced him to fumble. Travis Kirschke recovered and Roethlisberger scored on a bootleg run five plays later with 2:59 remaining to clinch the victory. Roethlisberger was 21 of 29 for 275 yards and 2 touchdowns. Plummer was 18 of 30 for 223 yards and 1 touchdown, with 2 interceptions.

Pittsburgh (34)	Offense	Denver (17)
Antwaan Randle El	WR	Rod Smith
Marvel Smith	LT	Matt Lepsis
Alan Faneca	LG	Ben Hamilton
Jeff Hartings	C	Tom Nalen
Kendall Simmons	RG	Cooper Carlisle
Max Starks	RT	George Foster
Heath Miller	TE	Stephen Alexander
Hines Ward	WR-TE	Wesley Duke
Ben Roethlisberger	QB	Jake Plummer
Willie Parker	RB	Mike Anderson
Dan Kreider	FB	Kyle Johnson
	Defense	
Aaron Smith	LE	Courtney Brown
Casey Hampton	LT-LT	Michael Myers
Kimo von Oelhoffen	RE-RT	Gerard Warren
Clark Haggans	LOLB-RE	Trevor Pryce
James Farrior	LILB-WLB	Ian Gold
Larry Foote	RILB-MLB	Al Wilson
Joey Porter	ROLB-SLB	D.J. Williams
Ike Taylor	LCB	Champ Bailey
Deshea Townsend	RCB	Domonique Foxworth
Troy Polamalu	SS	Nick Ferguson
Chris Hope	FS	John Lynch

SUBSTITUTIONS
Pittsburgh—Specialists: K—Jeff Reed. P—Chris Gardocki.. LS—Greg Warren. Offense: RB—Jerome Bettis, Verron Haynes. WR—Sean Morey, Nate Washington, Cedrick Wilson. TE—Jerame Tuman. T—Barrett Brooks. C—Chukky Okobi. Defense: DT—Chris Hoke, Travis Kirschke. DE—Brett Keisel. LB—Andre Frazier, Clint Kriewaldt, Rian Wallace. CB—Ricardo Colclough, Chidi Iwuoma, Bryant McFadden. S—Tyrone Carter, Mike Logan. DNP: QB—Charlie Batch.
Denver—Specialists: K—Jason Elam. P—Todd Sauerbrun. LS/TE—Mike Leach. Offense: RB—Tatum Bell, Ron Dayne, Cecil Sapp. WR—Charlie Adams, Todd Devoe, Ashley Lelie. TE—Jeb Putzier. T—Cornell Green. C/G—Chris Myers. Defense: DT—Demetrin Veal. DE—Marco Coleman, Ebenezer Ekuban. LB—

Keith Burns, Patrick Chukwurah, Louis Green. CB—Karl Paymah, Darrent Williams. S—Sam Brandon, Curome Cox. DNP: QB—Bradlee Van Pelt.

OFFICIALS
Referee—Terry McAulay. Umpire—Scott Dawson. Line Judge—Mark Steinkerchner. Side Judge—Doug Toole. Head Linesman—Derick Bowers. Back Judge—Keith Ferguson. Field Judge—Gene Steratore.

SCORING
Pittsburgh	3	21	0	10	—	34
Denver	0	3	7	7	—	17

Pitt — FG Reed 47
Pitt — Wilson 12 pass from Roethlisberger (Reed kick)
Den — FG Elam 23
Pitt — Bettis 3 run (Reed kick)
Pitt — Ward 17 pass from Roethlisberger (Reed kick)
Den — Lelie 30 pass from Plummer (Elam kick)
Pitt — FG Reed 42
Den — Anderson 3 run (Elam kick)
Pitt — Roethlisberger 4 run (Reed kick)

TEAM STATISTICS	PITT	DEN
Total First Downs	20	16
Rushing	5	5
Passing	15	8
Penalty	0	3
Total Net Yardage	358	308
Total Offensive Plays	64	54
Average Gain Per Offensive Play	5.6	5.7
Rushes	33	21
Yards Gained Rushing (Net)	90	97
Average Yards per Rush	2.7	4.6
Passes Attempted	29	30
Passes Completed	21	18
Had Intercepted	0	2
Tackled Attempting to Pass	2	3
Yards Lost Attempting to Pass	7	12
Yards Gained Passing (Net)	268	211
Punts	4	2
Average Distance	37.0	43.5
Punt Returns	1	0
Punt Return Yardage	13	0
Kickoff Returns	2	5
Kickoff Return Yardage	42	121
Interception Return Yardage	15	0
Total Return Yardage	70	121
Fumbles	1	2
Fumbles Lost	0	2
Own Fumbles Recovered	1	0
Opponent Fumbles Recovered	2	0
Penalties	8	4
Yards Penalized	61	20
Field Goals	2	1
Field Goals Attempted	2	1
Third-Down Efficiency	10/16	5/11
Fourth-Down Efficiency	0/0	2/3
Time of Possession	36:07	23:53

INDIVIDUAL STATISTICS
RUSHING: PITT: Bettis 15-39-1, Parker 14-35-0, Roethlisberger 3-12-1, Ward 1-4-0. DEN: Anderson 9-36-1, Bell 5-31-0, Plummer 7-30-0.
PASSING: PITT: Roethlisberger 29-21-275-2-0. DEN: Plummer 30-18-223-1-2.
RECEIVING: PITT: Wilson 5-92-1, Ward 5-59-1, Randle El 4-52-0, Parker 3-20-0, Miller 2-31-0, Washington 1-13-0, Haynes 1-8-0. DEN: Bell 5-28-0, R. Smith 4-61-0, Putzier 4-55-0, Anderson 3-11-0, Lelie 2-68-1.
KICKOFF RETURNS: PITT: Taylor 2-42-0. DEN: Adams 4-110-0, Sapp 1-11-0.

PUNT RETURNS: PITT: Randle El 1-13-0. DEN: Adams 0-0-0.
PUNTING: PITT: Gardocki 4-148-37.0. DEN: Sauerbrun 2-87-43.5.

INTERCEPTIONS: PITT: Foote 1-14-0, Taylor 1-1-0. DEN: None.
SACKS: PITT: Keisel 2, Porter. DEN: Myers, D.J. Williams.

NFC CHAMPIONSHIP GAME RESULTS
Includes NFL Championship Games (1933-1969)

Season	Date	Winner (Share)	Loser (Share)	Score	Site	Attendance
2005	Jan. 22	Seattle ($37,000)	Carolina ($37,000)	34-14	Seattle	67,837
2004	Jan. 23	Philadelphia ($36,500)	Atlanta ($36,500)	27-10	Philadelphia	67,717
2003	Jan. 18	Carolina ($36,500)	Philadelphia ($36,500)	14-3	Philadelphia	67,862
2002	Jan. 19	Tampa Bay ($35,000)	Philadelphia ($35,000)	27-10	Philadelphia	66,713
2001	Jan. 27	St. Louis ($34,500)	Philadelphia ($34,500)	29-24	St. Louis	66,502
2000	Jan. 14	N.Y. Giants ($34,500)	Minnesota ($34,500)	41-0	East Rutherford	79,310
1999	Jan. 23	St. Louis ($33,000)	Tampa Bay ($33,000)	11-6	St. Louis	66,396
1998	Jan. 17	Atlanta ($32,500)	Minnesota ($32,500)	30-27*	Minneapolis	64,060
1997	Jan. 11	Green Bay ($30,000)	San Francisco ($30,000)	23-10	San Francisco	68,987
1996	Jan. 12	Green Bay ($29,000)	Carolina ($29,000)	30-13	Green Bay	60,216
1995	Jan. 14	Dallas ($27,000)	Green Bay ($27,000)	38-27	Dallas	65,135
1994	Jan. 15	San Francisco ($26,000)	Dallas ($26,000)	38-28	San Francisco	69,125
1993	Jan. 23	Dallas ($23,500)	San Francisco ($23,500)	38-21	Dallas	64,902
1992	Jan. 17	Dallas ($18,000)	San Francisco ($18,000)	30-20	San Francisco	64,920
1991	Jan. 12	Washington ($18,000)	Detroit ($18,000)	41-10	Washington	55,585
1990	Jan. 20	N.Y. Giants ($18,000)	San Francisco ($18,000)	15-13	San Francisco	65,750
1989	Jan. 14	San Francisco ($18,000)	L.A. Rams ($18,000)	30-3	San Francisco	65,634
1988	Jan. 8	San Francisco ($18,000)	Chicago ($18,000)	28-3	Chicago	66,946
1987	Jan. 17	Washington ($18,000)	Minnesota ($18,000)	17-10	Washington	55,212
1986	Jan. 11	New York Giants ($18,000)	Washington ($18,000)	17-0	East Rutherford	76,891
1985	Jan. 12	Chicago ($18,000)	L.A. Rams ($18,000)	24-0	Chicago	66,030
1984	Jan. 6	San Francisco ($18,000)	Chicago ($18,000)	23-0	San Francisco	61,336
1983	Jan. 8	Washington ($18,000)	San Francisco ($18,000)	24-21	Washington	55,363
1982	Jan. 22	Washington ($18,000)	Dallas ($18,000)	31-17	Washington	55,045
1981	Jan. 10	San Francisco ($9,000)	Dallas ($9,000)	28-27	San Francisco	60,525
1980	Jan. 11	Philadelphia ($9,000)	Dallas ($9,000)	20-7	Philadelphia	71,522
1979	Jan. 6	Los Angeles ($9,000)	Tampa Bay ($9,000)	9-0	Tampa	72,033
1978	Jan. 7	Dallas ($9,000)	Los Angeles ($9,000)	28-0	Los Angeles	71,086
1977	Jan. 1	Dallas ($9,000)	Minnesota ($9,000)	23-6	Dallas	64,293
1976	Dec. 26	Minnesota ($8,500)	Los Angeles ($5,500)	24-13	Minneapolis	48,379
1975	Jan. 4	Dallas ($8,500)	Los Angeles ($5,500)	37-7	Los Angeles	88,919
1974	Dec. 29	Minnesota ($8,500)	Los Angeles ($5,500)	14-10	Minneapolis	48,444
1973	Dec. 30	Minnesota ($8,500)	Dallas ($5,500)	27-10	Dallas	64,422
1972	Dec. 31	Washington ($8,500)	Dallas ($5,500)	26-3	Washington	53,129
1971	Jan. 2	Dallas ($8,500)	San Francisco ($5,500)	14-3	Dallas	63,409
1970	Jan. 3	Dallas ($8,500)	San Francisco ($5,500)	17-10	San Francisco	59,364
1969	Jan. 4	Minnesota ($7,930)	Cleveland ($5,118)	27-7	Minneapolis	46,503
1968	Dec. 29	Baltimore ($9,306)	Cleveland ($5,963)	34-0	Cleveland	78,410
1967	Dec. 31	Green Bay ($7,950)	Dallas ($5,299)	21-17	Green Bay	50,861
1966	Jan. 1	Green Bay ($9,813)	Dallas ($6,527)	34-27	Dallas	74,152
1965	Jan. 2	Green Bay ($7,819)	Cleveland ($5,288)	23-12	Green Bay	50,777
1964	Dec. 27	Cleveland ($8,052)	Baltimore ($5,571)	27-0	Cleveland	79,544
1963	Dec. 29	Chicago ($5,899)	New York ($4,218)	14-10	Chicago	45,801
1962	Dec. 30	Green Bay ($5,888)	New York ($4,166)	16-7	New York	64,892
1961	Dec. 31	Green Bay ($5,195)	New York ($3,339)	37-0	Green Bay	39,029
1960	Dec. 26	Philadelphia ($5,116)	Green Bay ($3,105)	17-13	Philadelphia	67,325
1959	Dec. 27	Baltimore ($4,674)	New York ($3,083)	31-16	Baltimore	57,545
1958	Dec. 28	Baltimore ($4,718)	New York ($3,111)	23-17*	New York	64,185
1957	Dec. 29	Detroit ($4,295)	Cleveland ($2,750)	59-14	Detroit	55,263
1956	Dec. 30	New York ($3,779)	Chi. Bears ($2,485)	47-7	New York	56,836
1955	Dec. 26	Cleveland ($3,508)	Los Angeles ($2,316)	38-14	Los Angeles	85,693
1954	Dec. 26	Cleveland ($2,478)	Detroit ($1,585)	56-10	Cleveland	43,827
1953	Dec. 27	Detroit ($2,424)	Cleveland ($1,654)	17-16	Detroit	54,577
1952	Dec. 28	Detroit ($2,274)	Cleveland ($1,712)	17-7	Cleveland	50,934
1951	Dec. 23	Los Angeles ($2,108)	Cleveland ($1,483)	24-17	Los Angeles	57,522
1950	Dec. 24	Cleveland ($1,113)	Los Angeles ($686)	30-28	Cleveland	29,751
1949	Dec. 18	Philadelphia ($1,094)	Los Angeles ($739)	14-0	Los Angeles	27,980
1948	Dec. 19	Philadelphia ($1,540)	Chi. Cardinals ($874)	7-0	Philadelphia	36,309
1947	Dec. 28	Chi. Cardinals ($1,132)	Philadelphia ($754)	28-21	Chicago	30,759
1946	Dec. 15	Chi. Bears ($1,975)	New York ($1,295)	24-14	New York	58,346

Season	Date	Winner (Share)	Loser (Share)	Score	Site	Attendance
1945	Dec. 16	Cleveland ($1,469)	Washington ($902)	15-14	Cleveland	32,178
1944	Dec. 17	Green Bay ($1,449)	New York ($814)	14-7	New York	46,016
1943	Dec. 26	Chi. Bears ($1,146)	Washington ($765)	41-21	Chicago	34,320
1942	Dec. 13	Washington ($965)	Chi. Bears ($637)	14-6	Washington	36,006
1941	Dec. 21	Chi. Bears ($430)	New York ($288)	37-9	Chicago	13,341
1940	Dec. 8	Chi. Bears ($873)	Washington ($606)	73-0	Washington	36,034
1939	Dec. 10	Green Bay ($703.97)	New York ($455.57)	27-0	Milwaukee	32,279
1938	Dec. 11	New York ($504.45)	Green Bay ($368.81)	23-17	New York	48,120
1937	Dec. 12	Washington ($225.90)	Chi. Bears ($127.78)	28-21	Chicago	15,870
1936	Dec. 13	Green Bay ($250)	Boston ($180)	21-6	New York	29,545
1935	Dec. 15	Detroit ($313.35)	New York ($200.20)	26-7	Detroit	15,000
1934	Dec. 9	New York ($621)	Chi. Bears ($414.02)	30-13	New York	35,059
1933	Dec. 17	Chi. Bears ($210.34)	New York ($140.22)	23-21	Chicago	26,000

*Sudden death overtime

NFC CHAMPIONSHIP GAME COMPOSITE STANDINGS

	W	L	Pct.	Pts.	OP
Seattle Seahawks	1	0	1.000	34	14
Green Bay Packers	10	3	.769	303	177
Baltimore Colts	3	1	.750	88	60
Detroit Lions	4	2	.667	139	141
Washington Redskins*	7	5	.583	222	255
Philadelphia Eagles	5	4	.556	143	128
Chicago Bears	7	6	.538	286	245
Dallas Cowboys	8	8	.500	361	319
Minnesota Vikings	4	4	.500	135	151
Arizona Cardinals**	1	1	.500	28	28
Atlanta Falcons	1	1	.500	40	54
San Francisco 49ers	5	7	.417	245	222
Cleveland Browns	4	7	.364	224	253
St. Louis Rams***	5	9	.357	163	300
New York Giants	6	11	.353	281	322
Carolina Panthers	1	2	.333	41	67
Tampa Bay Buccaneers	1	2	.333	33	30

*One game played when franchise was in Boston (Lost 21-6)
**Both games played when franchise was in Chicago (Won 28-21, lost 7-0)
***One game played when franchise was in Cleveland (Won 15-14), and 11 games when franchise was in Los Angeles (Won 2, lost 9, scored 108 points, allowed 256 points).

2005 NFC CHAMPIONSHIP GAME

Qwest Field, Seattle, Washington
January 22, 2006, Attendance: 67,837
SEATTLE 34, CAROLINA 14—Matt Hasselbeck passed for 2 touchdowns and Shaun Alexander rushed for 132 yards and 2 scores as the Seahawks earned their first-ever Super Bowl appearance. The Seahawks forced 4 turnovers, outgained the Panthers 393-212 total yards, and held the ball for 41:51. The Seahawks scored 17 points in a span of 5:38 in the first half to pull away. Midway through the first quarter, Hasselbeck completed a 28-yard pass to backup quarterback Seneca Wallace, who had lined up split left. On the next play, Jerramy Stevens caught a 17-yard touchdown pass. Three plays later, Lofa Tatupu intercepted Jake Delhomme's pass to set up Josh Brown's 24-yard field goal. After Marquand Manuel intercepted Delhomme's pass, Alexander scored four plays later for a 17-0 lead with 14:53 left in the half. Steve Smith returned a punt 59 yards for a touchdown with 9:05 remaining in the half, but the Seahawks responded with a 10-play drive to set up Brown's second field goal. Seattle opened the second half with a 65-yard drive capped by Darrell Jackson's 20-yard touchdown catch for a 27-7 lead with 11:09 left in the third quarter. The Panthers never ran a play inside the Seahawks' 32. Hasselbeck was 20 of 28 for 219 yards and 2 touchdowns. Delhomme was 15 of 35 for 196 yards and 1 touchdown, with 3 interceptions.

Carolina (14)	Offense	Seattle (34)
Steve Smith	WR	Bobby Engram
Travelle Wharton	LT	Walter Jones
Mike Wahle	LG	Steve Hutchinson
Jeff Mitchell	C	Robbie Tobeck
Tutan Reyes	RG	Chris Gray
Jordan Gross	RT	Sean Locklear
Michael Gaines	TE-WR	Joe Jurevicius
Keary Colbert	WR	Darrell Jackson
Jake Delhomme	QB	Matt Hasselbeck
Nick Goings	RB	Shaun Alexander
Brad Hoover	FB	Mack Strong
	Defense	
Julius Peppers	LE	Bryce Fisher
Brentson Buckner	LT	Chuck Darby
Jordan Carstens	RT	Rocky Bernard
Micheal Rucker	RE	Grant Wistrom
Brandon Short	SLB-OLB	LeRoy Hill
Dan Morgan	MLB	Lofa Tatupu
Will Witherspoon	WLB-OLB	D.D. Lewis
Chris Gamble	LCB	Andre Dyson
Ken Lucas	RCB	Marcus Trufant
Marlon McCree	SS	Michael Boulware
Mike Minter	FS	Marquand Manuel

SUBSTITUTIONS

Carolina—Specialists: K—John Kasay. P—Jason Baker. Offense: FB—Casey Cramer. RB—Jamal Robertson, Rod Smart. WR—Drew Carter, Karl Hankton, Ricky Proehl. TE—Kris Mangum. T—Todd Fordham. C—Geoff Hangartner. Defense: DT—Kindal Moorehead. DE—Kemp Rasmussen, Al Wallace. LB—Vinny Ciurciu, Chris Draft, Jason Kyle, Sean Tufts. CB—Ricky Manning Jr., Dante Wesley. S—Thomas Davis. DNP: QB—Chris Weinke. TE—Mike Seidman.
Seattle—Specialists: K—Josh Brown. P—Tom Rouen. LS—Jean-Philippe Darche. Offense: QB—Seneca Wallace. RB—Maurice Morris, Josh Scobey. WR—D.J. Hackett, Peter Warrick. TE—Ryan Hannam, Jerramy Stevens. T/G—Floyd Womack. Defense: DT—Craig Terrill, Marcus Tubbs. DE—Joe Tafoya. LB—Kevin Bentley, Isaiah Kacyvenski, Niko Koutouvides, Cornelius Wortham. CB—Jordan Babineaux, Kelly Herndon, Jimmy Williams. S—Etric Pruitt. DNP: C—Chris Spencer.

OFFICIALS

Referee—Ed Hochuli. Umpire—Carl Paganelli. Line Judge—Byron Boston. Side Judge—Carl Cheffers. Head Linesman—Tom Stabile. Back Judge—Steve Freeman. Field Judge—Buddy Horton.

SCORING

Carolina	0	7	0	7	—	14
Seattle	10	10	7	7	—	34

Sea — Stevens 17 pass from Hasselbeck (J. Brown kick)
Sea — FG J. Brown 24
Sea — Alexander 1 run (J. Brown kick)
Car — S. Smith 59 punt return (Kasay kick)
Sea — FG J. Brown 39
Sea — Jackson 20 pass from Hasselbeck (J. Brown kick)
Sea — Alexander 1 run (J. Brown kick)
Car — Carter 47 pass from Delhomme (Kasay kick)

TEAM STATISTICS

	CAR	SEA
Total First Downs	11	27
Rushing	2	13
Passing	7	11
Penalty	2	3
Total Net Yardage	212	393
Total Offensive Plays	49	81
Average Gain Per Offensive Play	4.3	4.9
Rushes	12	51
Yards Gained Rushing (Net)	36	190
Average Yards per Rush	3.0	3.7
Passes Attempted	35	28
Passes Completed	15	20
Had Intercepted	3	0
Tackled Attempting to Pass	2	2
Yards Lost Attempting to Pass	20	16
Yards Gained Passing (Net)	176	203
Punts	7	5
Average Distance	34.7	38.8
Punt Returns	1	2
Punt Return Yardage	59	7
Kickoff Returns	7	2
Kickoff Return Yardage	143	51
Interception Return Yardage	0	67
Total Return Yardage	202	125
Fumbles	1	0
Fumbles Lost	1	0
Own Fumbles Recovered	0	0
Opponent Fumbles Recovered	0	1
Penalties	5	7
Yards Penalized	57	63
Field Goals	0	2
Field Goals Attempted	0	3
Third-Down Efficiency	1/9	8/18
Fourth-Down Efficiency	0/0	0/1
Time of Possession	18:09	41:51

INDIVIDUAL STATISTICS

RUSHING: CAR: Robertson 4-19-0, Delhomme 3-15-0, Goings 5-2-0. SEA: Alexander 34-132-2, Hasselbeck 6-27-0, Morris 7-24-0, Strong 4-7-0.
PASSING: CAR: Delhomme 35-15-196-1-3. SEA: Hasselbeck 28-20-219-2-0.
RECEIVING: CAR: Robertson 5-37-0, S. Smith 5-33-0, Carter 2-88-1, Proehl 1-19-0, Mangum 1-10-0, Hoover 1-9-0. SEA: Jackson 6-75-1, Stevens 6-66-1, Engram 3-34-0, Wallace 1-28-0, Hannam 1-7-0, Jurevicius 1-6-0, Strong 1-3-0, Alexander 1-0-0.
KICKOFF RETURNS: CAR: Smart 4-74-0, Robertson 3-69-0. SEA: Scobey 2-51-0.
PUNT RETURNS: CAR: S. Smith 1-59-1. SEA: Warrick 2-7-0.
PUNTING: CAR: Baker 7-243-34.7. SEA: Rouen 4-169-42.3, J. Brown 1-25-25.0.
INTERCEPTIONS: CAR: None. SEA: Manuel 1-32-0, Tatupu 1-21-0, Boulware 1-14-0.
SACKS: CAR: Morgan, Rucker. SEA: Bernard 2.

AFC DIVISIONAL PLAYOFFS RESULTS

Includes Second-Round Playoff Games (1982), AFC Inter-Divisional Games (1969), and special playoff games to break ties for AFL Division Championships (1963, 1968)

Season	Date	Winner (Share)	Loser (Share)	Score	Site	Attendance
2005	Jan. 15	Pittsburgh ($19,000)	Indianapolis ($19,000)	21-18	Indianapolis	57,449
	Jan. 14	Denver ($19,000)	New England ($19,000)	27-13	Denver	76,238
2004	Jan. 16	New England ($18,000)	Indianapolis ($18,000)	20-3	Foxborough	68,756
	Jan. 15	Pittsburgh ($18,000)	N.Y. Jets ($18,000)	20-17*	Pittsburgh	64,915
2003	Jan. 11	Indianapolis ($18,000)	Kansas City ($18,000)	38-31	Kansas City	79,159
	Jan. 10	New England ($18,000)	Tennessee ($18,000)	17-14	Foxborough	68,436
2002	Jan. 12	Oakland ($17,000)	N.Y. Jets ($17,000)	30-10	Oakland	62,207
	Jan. 11	Tennessee ($17,000)	Pittsburgh ($17,000)	34-31*	Nashville	68,809
2001	Jan. 20	Pittsburgh ($17,000)	Baltimore ($17,000)	27-10	Pittsburgh	63,976
	Jan. 19	New England ($17,000)	Oakland ($17,000)	16-13*	Foxborough	60,292
2000	Jan. 7	Baltimore ($16,000)	Tennessee ($16,000)	24-10	Nashville	68,527
	Jan. 6	Oakland ($16,000)	Miami ($16,000)	27-0	Oakland	61,998
1999	Jan. 16	Tennessee ($16,000)	Indianapolis ($16,000)	19-16	Indianapolis	57,097
	Jan. 15	Jacksonville ($16,000)	Miami ($16,000)	62-7	Jacksonville	75,173
1998	Jan. 10	N.Y. Jets ($15,000)	Jacksonville ($15,000)	34-24	East Rutherford	78,817
	Jan. 9	Denver ($15,000)	Miami ($15,000)	38-3	Denver	75,729
1997	Jan. 4	Denver ($15,000)	Kansas City ($15,000)	14-10	Kansas City	76,965
	Jan. 3	Pittsburgh ($15,000)	New England ($15,000)	7-6	Pittsburgh	61,228
1996	Jan. 5	New England ($14,000)	Pittsburgh ($14,000)	28-3	Foxborough	60,188
	Jan. 4	Jacksonville ($14,000)	Denver ($14,000)	30-27	Denver	75,678
1995	Jan. 7	Indianapolis ($13,000)	Kansas City ($13,000)	10-7	Kansas City	77,594
	Jan. 6	Pittsburgh ($13,000)	Buffalo ($13,000)	40-21	Pittsburgh	59,072
1994	Jan. 8	San Diego ($12,000)	Miami ($12,000)	22-21	San Diego	63,381
	Jan. 7	Pittsburgh ($12,000)	Cleveland ($12,000)	29-9	Pittsburgh	58,185
1993	Jan. 16	Kansas City ($12,000)	Houston ($12,000)	28-20	Houston	64,011
	Jan. 15	Buffalo ($12,000)	L.A. Raiders ($12,000)	29-23	Buffalo	61,923
1992	Jan. 10	Miami ($10,000)	San Diego ($10,000)	31-0	Miami	71,224
	Jan. 9	Buffalo ($10,000)	Pittsburgh ($10,000)	24-3	Pittsburgh	60,407

Season	Date	Winner (Share)	Loser (Share)	Score	Site	Attendance
1991	Jan. 5	Buffalo ($10,000)	Kansas City ($10,000)	37-14	Buffalo	80,182
	Jan. 4	Denver ($10,000)	Houston ($10,000)	26-24	Denver	75,301
1990	Jan. 13	L.A. Raiders ($10,000)	Cincinnati ($10,000)	20-10	Los Angeles	92,045
	Jan. 12	Buffalo ($10,000)	Miami ($10,000)	44-34	Buffalo	77,087
1989	Jan. 7	Denver ($10,000)	Pittsburgh ($10,000)	24-23	Denver	75,477
	Jan. 6	Cleveland ($10,000)	Buffalo ($10,000)	34-30	Cleveland	78,921
1988	Jan. 1	Buffalo ($10,000)	Houston ($10,000)	17-10	Buffalo	79,532
	Dec. 31	Cincinnati ($10,000)	Seattle ($10,000)	21-13	Cincinnati	58,560
1987	Jan. 10	Denver ($10,000)	Houston ($10,000)	34-10	Denver	75,440
	Jan. 9	Cleveland ($10,000)	Indianapolis ($10,000)	38-21	Cleveland	79,372
1986	Jan. 4	Denver ($10,000)	New England ($10,000)	22-17	Denver	75,262
	Jan. 3	Cleveland ($10,000)	N.Y. Jets ($10,000)	23-20*	Cleveland	79,720
1985	Jan. 5	New England ($10,000)	L.A. Raiders ($10,000)	27-20	Los Angeles	87,163
	Jan. 4	Miami ($10,000)	Cleveland ($10,000)	24-21	Miami	74,667
1984	Dec. 30	Pittsburgh ($10,000)	Denver ($10,000)	24-17	Denver	74,981
	Dec. 29	Miami ($10,000)	Seattle ($10,000)	31-10	Miami	73,469
1983	Jan. 1	L.A. Raiders ($10,000)	Pittsburgh ($10,000)	38-10	Los Angeles	90,380
	Dec. 31	Seattle ($10,000)	Miami ($10,000)	27-20	Miami	74,136
1982	Jan. 16	Miami ($10,000)	San Diego ($10,000)	34-13	Miami	71,383
	Jan. 15	N.Y. Jets ($10,000)	L.A. Raiders ($10,000)	17-14	Los Angeles	90,038
1981	Jan. 3	Cincinnati ($5,000)	Buffalo ($5,000)	28-21	Cincinnati	55,420
	Jan. 2	San Diego ($5,000)	Miami ($5,000)	41-38*	Miami	73,735
1980	Jan. 4	Oakland ($5,000)	Cleveland ($5,000)	14-12	Cleveland	78,245
	Jan. 3	San Diego ($5,000)	Buffalo ($5,000)	20-14	San Diego	52,253
1979	Dec. 30	Pittsburgh ($5,000)	Miami ($5,000)	34-14	Pittsburgh	50,214
	Dec. 29	Houston ($5,000)	San Diego ($5,000)	17-14	San Diego	51,192
1978	Dec. 31	Houston ($5,000)	New England ($5,000)	31-14	Foxborough	60,735
	Dec. 30	Pittsburgh ($5,000)	Denver ($5,000)	33-10	Pittsburgh	50,230
1977	Dec. 24	Oakland ($5,000)	Baltimore ($5,000)	37-31*	Baltimore	59,925
	Dec. 24	Denver ($5,000)	Pittsburgh ($5,000)	34-21	Denver	75,059
1976	Dec. 19	Pittsburgh [$]	Baltimore [$]	40-14	Baltimore	59,296
	Dec. 18	Oakland [$]	New England [$]	24-21	Oakland	53,050
1975	Dec. 28	Oakland [$]	Cincinnati [$]	31-28	Oakland	53,030
	Dec. 27	Pittsburgh [$]	Baltimore [$]	28-10	Pittsburgh	49,557
1974	Dec. 22	Pittsburgh [$]	Buffalo [$]	32-14	Pittsburgh	49,841
	Dec. 21	Oakland [$]	Miami [$]	28-26	Oakland	53,023
1973	Dec. 23	Miami [$]	Cincinnati [$]	34-16	Miami	78,928
	Dec. 22	Oakland [$]	Pittsburgh [$]	33-14	Oakland	52,646
1972	Dec. 24	Miami [$]	Cleveland [$]	20-14	Miami	78,916
	Dec. 23	Pittsburgh [$]	Oakland [$]	13-7	Pittsburgh	50,327
1971	Dec. 26	Baltimore [$]	Cleveland [$]	20-3	Cleveland	70,734
	Dec. 25	Miami [$]	Kansas City [$]	27-24*	Kansas City	50,374
1970	Dec. 27	Oakland [$]	Miami [$]	21-14	Oakland	52,594
	Dec. 26	Baltimore [$]	Cincinnati [$]	17-0	Baltimore	49,694
1969	Dec. 21	Oakland [$]	Houston [$]	56-7	Oakland	53,539
	Dec. 20	Kansas City [$]	N.Y. Jets [$]	13-6	New York	62,977
1968	Dec. 22	Oakland [$]	Kansas City [$]	41-6	Oakland	53,605
1963	Dec. 28	Boston [$]	Buffalo [$]	26-8	Buffalo	33,044

*Sudden death overtime
$ Players received 1/14 of annual salary for playoff appearances.

2005 AFC DIVISIONAL PLAYOFF GAMES

RCA Dome, Indianapolis, Indiana
January 15, 2006, Attendance: 57,449

PITTSBURGH 21, INDIANAPOLIS 18—Mike Vanderjagt missed a 46-yard field goal with 17 seconds left to cap a wild finish and send the Steelers to their sixth AFC Championship Game in Bill Cowher's 14 seasons as head coach. The Steelers became the first sixth-seed to reach a conference championship game. The Steelers opened the game with a 10-play, 84-yard touchdown drive, and two possessions later drove 72 yards to take a 14-0 lead less than 12 minutes into the game. The Colts had a 15-play, 96-yard drive that consumed 9:39 from the clock, but were forced to settle for Vanderjagt's 20-yard field goal with 1:20 left in the second quarter to pull within 14-3. Antwaan Randle El's 20-yard punt return set up Jerome Bettis' 1-yard touchdown run with 1:26 left in the third quarter for a 21-3 lead. On the final play of the third quarter, Peyton Manning completed a 13-yard pass to Brandon Stokley on fourth-and-2 to keep alive the drive and set up his 50-yard scoring pass to Dallas Clark. The Steelers responded by barely converting 2 fourth-and-1 situations before punting with 6:03 to play. Troy Polamalu nearly intercepted a pass near midfield with 5:33 left, but the Colts maintained possession and Edgerrin James scored four plays later to pull within 21-16. Reggie Wayne caught the 2-point conversion pass in the back left corner of the end zone to cut the deficit to 21-18 with 4:24 remaining. The Colts' defense forced a three-and-out, but on fourth-and-16 Joey Porter and James Farrior sacked Manning at the Colts' 2 with 1:20 to play. Since the Colts had all 3 timeouts, the Steelers could not kneel on the ball. On the first play, Gary Brackett forced Bettis to fumble. Nick Harper scooped up the ball and returned it 35 yards to the Colts' 42, where Ben Roethlisberger made a touchdown-saving tackle. The Colts drove to the

Steelers' 28, but Manning's passes on second- and third-and-2 fell incomplete. Vanderjagt's 46-yard attempt sailed wide right. Roethlisberger was 14 of 24 for 197 yards and 2 touchdowns, with 1 interception. Manning was 22 of 38 for 290 yards and 1 touchdown.

Pittsburgh	14	0	7	0 —	21
Indianapolis	0	3	0	15 —	18

Pitt — Randle El 6 pass from Roethlisberger (Reed kick)
Pitt — Miller 7 pass from Roethlisberger (Reed kick)
Ind — FG Vanderjagt 20
Pitt — Bettis 1 run (Reed kick)
Ind — Clark 50 pass from Manning (Vanderjagt kick)
Ind — James 3 run (Wayne pass from Manning)

INVESCO Field at Mile High, Denver, Colorado
January 14, 2006, Attendance: 76,238
DENVER 27, NEW ENGLAND 13—Denver's defense forced 5 turnovers that led to 24 points as the Patriots had their NFL record 10-game postseason winning streak snapped. The Patriots outgained the Broncos 420-286 in total yards, but committed 5 turnovers. The Patriots led 3-0 and had the ball with 2:00 left in the second quarter, but Courtney Brown forced Kevin Faulk to fumble. Ian Gold recovered at the Patriots' 40. On the next play, a 39-yard pass interference penalty set up Mike Anderson's 1-yard run. On the ensuing kickoff, kicker Todd Sauerbrun forced Ellis Hobbs to fumble and Cecil Sapp emerged from the pile with the ball. Three plays later, Jason Elam kicked a 50-yard field goal for a 10-3 halftime lead. Adam Vinatieri capped the Patriots' first drive of the second half with a field goal, and New England drove to the Broncos' 5 on their next possession. On third-and-goal, Champ Bailey intercepted Tom Brady's pass and returned it 100 yards to the Patriots' 1, where Ben Watson forced him to fumble the ball out of bounds. It was the longest non-scoring play in postseason history, and Anderson scored on the next snap for a 17-6 lead. New England drove to the Broncos' 25, but Vinatieri missed a 43-yard attempt wide right. The Patriots then forced a punt, but Troy Brown muffed it and Mike Leach recovered at the Patriots' 15. Three plays later, Rod Smith caught a 4-yard touchdown pass from Jake Plummer for a 24-6 lead with 8:38 remaining. Deion Branch's 73-yard catch was followed by David Givens' 4-yard touchdown with 8:05 to play, but Elam kicked a 34-yard field goal with 3:20 remaining, and John Lynch intercepted Brady's long pass with 2:56 to play to clinch the victory. Plummer was 15 of 26 for 197 yards and 1 touchdown, with 1 interception. Brady was 20 of 36 for 341 yards and 1 touchdown, with 2 interceptions. Branch had 8 receptions for 153 yards.

New England	0	3	3	7 —	13
Denver	0	10	7	10 —	27

NE — FG Vinatieri 40
Den — Anderson 1 run (Elam kick)
Den — FG Elam 50
NE — FG Vinatieri 32
Den — Anderson 1 run (Elam kick)
Den — Smith 4 pass from Plummer (Elam kick)
NE — Givens 4 pass from Brady (Vinatieri kick)
Den — FG Elam 34

NFC DIVISIONAL PLAYOFFS RESULTS
Includes Second-Round Playoff Games (1982), NFL Conference Championship Games (1967-69), and special playoff games to break ties for NFL Division or Conference Championships (1941, 1943, 1947, 1950, 1952, 1957, 1958, 1965)

Season	Date	Winner (Share)	Loser (Share)	Score	Site	Attendance
2005	Jan. 15	Carolina ($19,000)	Chicago ($19,000)	29-21	Chicago	62,209
	Jan. 14	Seattle ($19,000)	Washington ($19,000)	20-10	Seattle	67,551
2004	Jan. 16	Philadelphia ($18,000)	Minnesota ($18,000)	27-14	Philadelphia	67,722
	Jan. 15	Atlanta ($18,000)	St. Louis ($18,000)	47-17	Atlanta	70,709
2003	Jan. 11	Philadelphia ($18,000)	Green Bay ($18,000)	20-17*	Philadelphia	67,707
	Jan. 10	Carolina ($18,000)	St. Louis ($18,000)	29-23*	St. Louis	66,165
2002	Jan. 12	Tampa Bay ($17,000)	San Francisco ($17,000)	31-6	Tampa	65,599
	Jan. 11	Philadelphia ($17,000)	Atlanta ($17,000)	20-6	Philadelphia	66,452
2001	Jan. 20	St. Louis ($17,000)	Green Bay ($17,000)	45-17	St. Louis	66,338
	Jan. 19	Philadelphia ($17,000)	Chicago ($17,000)	33-19	Chicago	66,944
2000	Jan. 7	N.Y. Giants ($16,000)	Philadelphia ($16,000)	20-10	East Rutherford	78,765
	Jan. 6	Minnesota ($16,000)	New Orleans ($16,000)	34-16	Minneapolis	63,881
1999	Jan. 16	St. Louis ($16,000)	Minnesota ($16,000)	49-37	St. Louis	66,194
	Jan. 15	Tampa Bay ($16,000)	Washington ($16,000)	14-13	Tampa	65,835
1998	Jan. 10	Minnesota ($15,000)	Arizona ($15,000)	41-21	Minneapolis	63,760
	Jan. 9	Atlanta ($15,000)	San Francisco ($15,000)	20-18	Atlanta	70,262
1997	Jan. 4	Green Bay ($15,000)	Tampa Bay ($15,000)	21-7	Green Bay	60,327
	Jan. 3	San Francisco ($15,000)	Minnesota ($15,000)	38-22	San Francisco	65,018
1996	Jan. 5	Carolina ($14,000)	Dallas ($14,000)	26-17	Charlotte	72,808
	Jan. 4	Green Bay ($14,000)	San Francisco ($14,000)	35-14	Green Bay	60,787
1995	Jan. 7	Dallas ($13,000)	Philadelphia ($13,000)	30-11	Dallas	64,371
	Jan. 6	Green Bay ($13,000)	San Francisco ($13,000)	27-17	San Francisco	69,311
1994	Jan. 8	Dallas ($12,000)	Green Bay ($12,000)	35-9	Dallas	64,745
	Jan. 7	San Francisco ($12,000)	Chicago ($12,000)	44-15	San Francisco	64,644
1993	Jan. 16	Dallas ($12,000)	Green Bay ($12,000)	27-17	Dallas	64,790
	Jan. 15	San Francisco ($12,000)	N.Y. Giants ($12,000)	44-3	San Francisco	67,143
1992	Jan. 10	Dallas ($10,000)	Philadelphia ($10,000)	34-10	Dallas	63,721
	Jan. 9	San Francisco ($10,000)	Washington ($10,000)	20-13	San Francisco	64,991
1991	Jan. 5	Detroit ($10,000)	Dallas ($10,000)	38-6	Detroit	78,290
	Jan. 4	Washington ($10,000)	Atlanta ($10,000)	24-7	Washington	55,181
1990	Jan. 13	N.Y. Giants ($10,000)	Chicago ($10,000)	31-3	East Rutherford	77,025
	Jan. 12	San Francisco ($10,000)	Washington ($10,000)	28-10	San Francisco	65,292
1989	Jan. 7	L.A. Rams ($10,000)	N.Y. Giants ($10,000)	19-13*	East Rutherford	76,526
	Jan. 6	San Francisco ($10,000)	Minnesota ($10,000)	41-13	San Francisco	64,918
1988	Jan. 1	San Francisco ($10,000)	Minnesota ($10,000)	34-9	San Francisco	61,848
	Dec. 31	Chicago ($10,000)	Philadelphia ($10,000)	20-12	Chicago	65,534

Season	Date	Winner (Share)	Loser (Share)	Score	Site	Attendance
1987	Jan. 10	Washington ($10,000)	Chicago ($10,000)	21-17	Chicago	65,268
	Jan. 9	Minnesota ($10,000)	San Francisco ($10,000)	36-24	San Francisco	63,008
1986	Jan. 4	N.Y. Giants ($10,000)	San Francisco ($10,000)	49-3	East Rutherford	75,691
	Jan. 3	Washington ($10,000)	Chicago ($10,000)	27-13	Chicago	65,524
1985	Jan. 5	Chicago ($10,000)	N.Y. Giants ($10,000)	21-0	Chicago	65,670
	Jan. 4	L.A. Rams ($10,000)	Dallas ($10,000)	20-0	Anaheim	66,581
1984	Dec. 30	Chicago ($10,000)	Washington ($10,000)	23-19	Washington	55,431
	Dec. 29	San Francisco ($10,000)	N.Y. Giants ($10,000)	21-10	San Francisco	60,303
1983	Jan. 1	Washington ($10,000)	L.A. Rams ($10,000)	51-7	Washington	54,440
	Dec. 31	San Francisco ($10,000)	Detroit ($10,000)	24-23	San Francisco	59,979
1982	Jan. 16	Dallas ($10,000)	Green Bay ($10,000)	37-26	Dallas	63,972
	Jan. 15	Washington ($10,000)	Minnesota ($10,000)	21-7	Washington	54,593
1981	Jan. 3	San Francisco ($5,000)	N.Y. Giants ($5,000)	38-24	San Francisco	58,360
	Jan. 2	Dallas ($5,000)	Tampa Bay ($5,000)	38-0	Dallas	64,848
1980	Jan. 4	Dallas ($5,000)	Atlanta ($5,000)	30-27	Atlanta	59,793
	Jan. 3	Philadelphia ($5,000)	Minnesota ($5,000)	31-16	Philadelphia	70,178
1979	Dec. 30	Los Angeles ($5,000)	Dallas ($5,000)	21-19	Dallas	64,792
	Dec. 29	Tampa Bay ($5,000)	Philadelphia ($5,000)	24-17	Tampa	71,402
1978	Dec. 31	Los Angeles ($5,000)	Minnesota ($5,000)	34-10	Los Angeles	70,436
	Dec. 30	Dallas ($5,000)	Atlanta ($5,000)	27-20	Dallas	63,406
1977	Dec. 26	Dallas ($5,000)	Chicago ($5,000)	37-7	Dallas	63,260
	Dec. 26	Minnesota ($5,000)	Los Angeles ($5,000)	14-7	Los Angeles	70,203
1976	Dec. 19	Los Angeles [$]	Dallas [$]	14-12	Dallas	63,283
	Dec. 18	Minnesota [$]	Washington [$]	35-20	Minneapolis	47,466
1975	Dec. 28	Dallas [$]	Minnesota [$]	17-14	Minneapolis	48,050
	Dec. 27	Los Angeles [$]	St. Louis [$]	35-23	Los Angeles	73,459
1974	Dec. 22	Los Angeles [$]	Washington [$]	19-10	Los Angeles	77,925
	Dec. 21	Minnesota [$]	St. Louis [$]	30-14	Minneapolis	48,150
1973	Dec. 23	Dallas [$]	Los Angeles [$]	27-16	Dallas	63,272
	Dec. 22	Minnesota [$]	Washington [$]	27-20	Minneapolis	48,040
1972	Dec. 24	Washington [$]	Green Bay [$]	16-3	Washington	52,321
	Dec. 23	Dallas [$]	San Francisco [$]	30-28	San Francisco	59,746
1971	Dec. 26	San Francisco [$]	Washington [$]	24-20	San Francisco	45,327
	Dec. 25	Dallas [$]	Minnesota [$]	20-12	Minneapolis	47,307
1970	Dec. 27	San Francisco [$]	Minnesota [$]	17-14	Minneapolis	45,103
	Dec. 26	Dallas [$]	Detroit [$]	5-0	Dallas	69,613
1969	Dec. 28	Cleveland [$]	Dallas [$]	38-14	Dallas	69,321
	Dec. 27	Minnesota [$]	Los Angeles [$]	23-20	Minneapolis	47,900
1968	Dec. 22	Baltimore [$]	Minnesota [$]	24-14	Baltimore	60,238
	Dec. 21	Cleveland [$]	Dallas [$]	31-20	Cleveland	81,497
1967	Dec. 24	Dallas [$]	Cleveland [$]	52-14	Dallas	70,786
	Dec. 23	Green Bay [$]	Los Angeles [$]	28-7	Milwaukee	49,861
1965	Dec. 26	Green Bay [$]	Baltimore [$]	13-10*	Green Bay	50,484
1958	Dec. 21	N.Y. Giants (#)	Cleveland (#)	10-0	New York	61,274
1957	Dec. 22	Detroit (#)	San Francisco (#)	31-27	San Francisco	60,118
1952	Dec. 21	Detroit (#)	Los Angeles (#)	31-21	Detroit	47,645
1950	Dec. 17	Los Angeles (#)	Chicago Bears (#)	24-14	Los Angeles	83,501
	Dec. 17	Cleveland (#)	N.Y. Giants (#)	8-3	Cleveland	33,054
1947	Dec. 21	Philadelphia (#)	Pittsburgh (#)	21-0	Pittsburgh	35,729
1943	Dec. 19	Washington (¢)	N.Y. Giants (¢)	28-0	New York	42,800
1941	Dec. 14	Chicago Bears (¢)	Green Bay (¢)	33-14	Chicago	43,425

*Sudden death overtime
Players received 1/12 of annual salary for playoff appearances.
$ Players received 1/14 of annual salary for playoff appearances.
¢ Players received 1/10 of annual salary for playoff appearances.

2005 NFC DIVISIONAL PLAYOFF GAMES

Soldier Field, Chicago, Illinois
January 15, 2006, Attendance: 62,209

CAROLINA 29, CHICAGO 21—Steve Smith had 12 receptions for 218 yards and 2 touchdowns as the Panthers knocked off the second-seeded Bears. Despite facing a defense that had set a modern NFL record by allowing just 61 points in eight home games, the Panthers tallied 434 total yards. Smith caught a 58-yard touchdown pass from Jake Delhomme deep down the right sideline on the game's second play to set the tone. Smith outleaped Charles Tillman for a 46-yard catch later in the quarter to set up John Kasay's 20-yard field goal for a 10-0 lead. Kasay added a second field goal for a 13-0 lead before the Bears answered with a 67-yard drive capped by Adrian Peterson's 1-yard scoring run on fourth-and-goal with 1:57 left in the half. The Panthers responded with Kasay's third field goal of the quarter, ending the half with a 37-yard boot to extend the lead to nine points. The Bears drove 68 yards to begin the second half, highlighted by Bernard Berrian holding onto a 17-yard catch at the Bears' 1 despite a strong tackle by Mike Minter. Desmond Clark capped the drive with a 1-yard catch to pull within 16-14. DeShaun Foster broke his ankle on the next play from scrimmage, but the Panthers scored later in the quarter on Smith's 39-yard touchdown catch down the left sideline to take a 23-14 lead. Smith had set up the touchdown with his 21-yard reception on third-and-9 two plays earlier. The Bears answered with a 66-yard drive, kept alive by a facemask penalty that nullified a fumble for a touchback. Jason McKie culminated the drive with a 3-yard run with 12:23 to play. The Panthers needed just seven plays to answer, highlighted by Smith's 22-yard run, and capped by Kris Mangum's 1-yard scoring catch with 8:04 remaining. Kasay slipped and his extra-point attempt hit the right upright, allowing the Bears to trail by just eight points. After an exchange of punts, the Bears drove to the Panthers' 37, but Ken Lucas intercepted

Rex Grossman's third-and-10 pass with 2:26 to play, and after a punt, Grossman's fourth-and-1 pass from the Bears' 45 fell incomplete with 41 seconds left to clinch the victory. Delhomme was 24 of 33 for 319 yards and 3 touchdowns, with 1 interception. Smith had 12 catches for 218 yards, the fourth-best receiving yardage total in postseason history, and had 3 carries for 26 yards. Grossman, who had made just one start during the season, was 17 of 41 for 192 yards and 1 touchdown, with 1 interception.

Carolina	7	9	7	6	—	29
Chicago	0	7	7	7	—	21

Car — S. Smith 58 pass from Delhomme (Kasay kick)
Car — FG Kasay 20
Car — FG Kasay 38
Chi — Peterson 1 run (Gould kick)
Car — FG Kasay 37
Chi — Clark 1 pass from Grossman (Gould kick)
Car — S. Smith 39 pass from Delhomme (Kasay kick)
Chi — McKie 3 run (Gould kick)
Car — Mangum 1 pass from Delhomme (kick failed)

Qwest Field, Seattle, Washington
January 14, 2006, Attendance: 67,551
SEATTLE 20, WASHINGTON 10— Matt Hasselbeck passed for 1 touchdown and ran for another as the Seahawks posted their first playoff victory since 1984. Shaun Alexander suffered a concussion late in the first quarter, and a muffed punt set up a field goal to give the Redskins a 3-0 lead. Seattle responded with a 12-play, 74-yard touchdown drive, capped by Darrell Jackson's 29-yard touchdown catch. Joe Jurevicius' 31-yard reception led to Hasselbeck's scrambling 6-yard touchdown run on third-and-5 for a 14-3 lead with 9:35 left in the third quarter. Seattle extended the lead to 17-3, but Mark Brunell completed a 52-yard pass to Chris Cooley to set up Santana Moss' 20-yard touchdown catch off of a deflection to pull the Redskins within 17-10 with 11:51 remaining. John Hall then recovered a fumble on the ensuing kickoff, but he missed a 36-yard field-goal attempt wide left with 8:01 to play. Mack Strong's 32-yard run on third-and-6 set up Josh Brown's 31-yard field goal with 2:54 remaining. Brunell's fourth-and-2 pass intended for Moss was batted down in the end zone by Michael Boulware with 47 seconds left to quell their final scoring chance. Hasselbeck was 16 of 26 for 215 yards and 1 touchdown. Jackson had 9 receptions for 143 yards. Brunell was 22 of 37 for 242 yards and 1 touchdown. Moss had 7 catches for 103 yards.

Washington	0	3	0	7	—	10
Seattle	0	7	7	6	—	20

Wash — FG Hall 26
Sea — D. Jackson 29 pass from Hasselbeck (J. Brown kick)
Sea — Hasselbeck 6 run (J. Brown kick)
Sea — FG J. Brown 33
Wash — Moss 20 pass from Brunell (Hall kick)
Sea — FG J. Brown 31

AFC WILD CARD PLAYOFF GAMES RESULTS

Season	Date	Winner (Share)	Loser (Share)	Score	Site	Attendance
2005	Jan. 8	Pittsburgh ($17,000)	Cincinnati ($19,000)	31-17	Cincinnati	65,870
	Jan. 7	New England ($19,000)	Jacksonville ($17,000)	28-3	Foxborough	68,756
2004	Jan. 9	Indianapolis ($18,000)	Denver ($15,000)	49-24	Indianapolis	56,609
	Jan. 8	N.Y. Jets ($15,000)	San Diego ($18,000)	20-17*	San Diego	67,536
2003	Jan. 4	Indianapolis ($18,000)	Denver ($15,000)	41-10	Indianapolis	56,586
	Jan. 3	Tennessee ($15,000)	Baltimore ($18,000)	20-17	Baltimore	69,452
2002	Jan. 5	Pittsburgh ($17,000)	Cleveland ($12,500)	36-33	Pittsburgh	62,595
	Jan. 4	N.Y. Jets ($17,000)	Indianapolis ($12,500)	41-0	East Rutherford	78,524
2001	Jan. 13	Baltimore ($12,500)	Miami ($12,500)	20-3	Miami	72,251
	Jan. 12	Oakland ($17,000)	N.Y. Jets ($12,500)	38-24	Oakland	61,503
2000	Dec. 31	Baltimore (12,500)	Denver ($12,500)	21-3	Baltimore	69,638
	Dec. 30	Miami ($16,000)	Indianapolis ($12,500)	23-17*	Miami	73,193
1999	Jan. 9	Miami ($10,000)	Seattle ($16,000)	20-17	Seattle	66,170
	Jan. 8	Tennessee ($10,000)	Buffalo ($10,000)	22-16	Nashville	66,672
1998	Jan. 3	Jacksonville ($15,000)	New England ($10,000)	25-10	Jacksonville	71,139
	Jan. 2	Miami ($10,000)	Buffalo ($10,000)	24-17	Miami	72,698
1997	Dec. 28	New England ($15,000)	Miami ($10,000)	17-3	Foxborough	60,041
	Dec. 27	Denver ($10,000)	Jacksonville ($10,000)	42-17	Denver	74,481
1996	Dec. 29	Pittsburgh ($14,000)	Indianapolis ($10,000)	42-14	Pittsburgh	58,078
	Dec. 28	Jacksonville ($10,000)	Buffalo ($10,000)	30-27	Buffalo	70,213
1995	Dec. 31	Indianapolis ($7,500)	San Diego ($7,500)	35-20	San Diego	61,182
	Dec. 30	Buffalo ($13,000)	Miami ($7,500)	37-22	Buffalo	73,103
1994	Jan. 1	Cleveland ($7,500)	New England ($7,500)	20-13	Cleveland	77,452
	Dec. 31	Miami ($12,000)	Kansas City ($7,500)	27-17	Miami	67,487
1993	Jan. 9	L.A. Raiders ($7,500)	Denver ($7,500)	42-24	Los Angeles	65,314
	Jan. 8	Kansas City ($12,000)	Pittsburgh ($7,500)	27-24*	Kansas City	74,515
1992	Jan. 3	Buffalo ($6,000)	Houston ($6,000)	41-38*	Buffalo	75,141
	Jan. 2	San Diego ($10,000)	Kansas City ($6,000)	17-0	San Diego	58,278
1991	Dec. 29	Houston ($10,000)	N.Y. Jets ($6,000)	17-10	Houston	61,485
	Dec. 28	Kansas City ($6,000)	L.A. Raiders ($6,000)	10-6	Kansas City	75,827
1990	Jan. 6	Cincinnati ($10,000)	Houston ($6,000)	41-14	Cincinnati	60,012
	Jan. 5	Miami ($6,000)	Kansas City ($6,000)	17-16	Miami	67,276
1989	Dec. 31	Pittsburgh ($6,000)	Houston ($6,000)	26-23*	Houston	59,406
1988	Dec. 26	Houston ($6,000)	Cleveland ($6,000)	24-23	Cleveland	75,896
1987	Jan. 3	Houston ($6,000)	Seattle ($6,000)	23-20*	Houston	50,519
1986	Dec. 28	N.Y. Jets ($6,000)	Kansas City ($6,000)	35-15	East Rutherford	75,210
1985	Dec. 28	New England ($6,000)	N.Y. Jets ($6,000)	26-14	East Rutherford	75,945
1984	Dec. 22	Seattle ($6,000)	L.A. Raiders ($6,000)	13-7	Seattle	62,049
1983	Dec. 24	Seattle ($6,000)	Denver ($6,000)	31-7	Seattle	64,275

Season	Date	Winner (Share)	Loser (Share)	Score	Site	Attendance
1982	Jan. 9	N.Y. Jets ($6,000)	Cincinnati ($6,000)	44-17	Cincinnati	57,560
	Jan. 9	San Diego ($6,000)	Pittsburgh ($6,000)	31-28	Pittsburgh	53,546
	Jan. 8	L.A. Raiders ($6,000)	Cleveland ($6,000)	27-10	Los Angeles	56,555
	Jan. 8	Miami ($6,000)	New England ($6,000)	28-13	Miami	68,842
1981	Dec. 27	Buffalo ($3,000)	N.Y. Jets ($3,000)	31-27	New York	57,050
1980	Dec. 28	Oakland ($3,000)	Houston ($3,000)	27-7	Oakland	53,333
1979	Dec. 23	Houston ($3,000)	Denver ($3,000)	13-7	Houston	48,776
1978	Dec. 24	Houston ($3,000)	Miami ($3,000)	17-9	Miami	72,445

*Sudden death overtime

2005 AFC WILD CARD PLAYOFF GAMES
Paul Brown Stadium, Cincinnati, Ohio
January 8, 2006, Attendance: 65,870
PITTSBURGH 31, CINCINNATI 17—Ben Roethlisberger passed for 3 touchdowns and the Steelers' defense shutout the Bengals in the second half to post the first postseason road victory of Bill Cowher's 14-year coaching career. Carson Palmer injured his knee on the Bengals' second play of the game. Kimo von Oelhoffen was blocked into Palmer's knee. The play resulted in a 66-yard pass to Chris Henry, who also was injured on the play. The pass set up Shayne Graham's 23-yard field goal, and Jon Kitna engineered touchdown drives of 76 and 57 yards on the next two possessions to take a 17-7 lead with 6:13 left in the second quarter. Roethlisberger's 54-yard pass to Cedrick Wilson set up Hines Ward's 5-yard touchdown grab on third-and-goal. On the opening possession of the second half, the Bengals led 17-14 and drove to the Steelers' 15, but from field-goal formation Brad St. Louis' snap was high and holder Kyle Larson could not hold onto the ball. The Steelers responded with a 66-yard touchdown drive to take the lead. After forcing a punt, the Steelers were faced with third-and-3 from the Bengals' 43. Antwaan Randle El took the Shotgun snap, rolled right, passed backwards across the field to Roethlisberger, who then fired long downfield to a wide open Wilson, who caught the ball at the 5-yard line and jogged into the end zone for a 28-17 lead. James Farrior's interception on the next drive led to Jeff Reed's field goal with 10:29 to play. The Bengals drove to the Steelers' 45 with 4:12 to play, but Troy Polamalu's diving interception ended the Bengals' final hope. Roethlisberger was 14 of 19 for 208 yards and 3 touchdowns. Wilson had 3 catches for 104 yards. Kitna was 24 of 40 for 197 yards and 1 touchdowns, with 2 interceptions.

Pittsburgh	0	14	14	3	—	31
Cincinnati	10	7	0	0	—	17

Cin — FG Graham 23
Cin — R. Johnson 20 run (Graham kick)
Pitt — Parker 19 pass from Roethlisberger (Reed kick)
Cin — Houshmandzadeh 7 pass from Kitna (Graham kick)
Pitt — Ward 5 pass from Roethlisberger (Reed kick)
Pitt — Bettis 5 run (Reed kick)
Pitt — Wilson 43 pass from Roethlisberger (Reed kick)
Pitt — FG Reed 21

Gillette Stadium, Foxborough, Massachusetts
January 7, 2006, Attendance: 68,756
NEW ENGLAND 28, JACKSONVILLE 3—Tom Brady passed for 3 touchdowns and Willie McGinest registered an NFL-postseason record 4 1/2 sacks as the Patriots won their NFL record 10th consecutive postseason game. Brady improved to 10-0 as a postseason starter, and McGinest set a career postseason record with 16 sacks, surpassing Bruce Smith's mark of 14 1/2. Tim Dwight's 27-yard punt return set up Troy Brown's 11-yard touchdown catch on third-and-5. The Jaguars had a 12-play drive just before halftime that culminated with Josh Scobee's 36-yard field goal to pull within 7-3. New England forced a punt to begin the second half, and the offense drove 81 yards in 12 plays, highlighted by Andre' Davis' fumble recovery of Ben Watson's bouncing fumble at the Jaguars' 3, and capped on the next play by Brady's 3-yard touchdown toss to Givens in the back of the end zone. The touchdown marked Givens' sixth consecutive postseason game with a scoring catch, second in NFL history, and two games shy of John Stallworth's record. The Patriots forced another punt, and on third-and-13 Brady completed a short pass to Watson, who broke three tackles en route to a Patriots' postseason-record long 63-yard touchdown for a 21-3 lead with 3:03 left in the third quarter. The Jaguars' drove to the Patriots' 32, but on fourth-and-5, Asante Samuel stepped in front of Byron Leftwich's pass and returned it untouched 73 yards on the first play of the fourth quarter to complete the scoring. Brady was 15 of 27 for 201 yards and 3 touchdowns. Leftwich, making his first start since missing the final five games with an ankle injury, was 18 of 31 for 179 yards, with 1 interception. David Garrard played the final two drives and was 3 of 8 for 68 yards.

Jacksonville	0	3	0	0	—	3
New England	0	7	14	7	—	28

NE — T. Brown 11 pass from Brady (Vinatieri kick)
Jax — FG Scobee 36
NE — Givens 3 pass from Brady (Vinatieri kick)
NE — Watson 63 pass from Brady (Vinatieri kick)
NE — Samuel 73 interception return (Vinatieri kick)

NFC WILD CARD PLAYOFF GAMES RESULTS

Season	Date	Winner (Share)	Loser (Share)	Score	Site	Attendance
2005	Jan. 8	Carolina ($17,000)	N.Y. Giants ($19,000)	23-0	East Rutherford	79,378
	Jan. 7	Washington ($17,000)	Tampa Bay ($19,000)	17-10	Tampa	65,514
2004	Jan. 9	Minnesota ($15,000)	Green Bay ($18,000)	31-17	Green Bay	71,075
	Jan. 8	St. Louis ($15,000)	Seattle ($18,000)	27-20	Seattle	65,397
2003	Jan. 4	Green Bay ($18,000)	Seattle ($15,000)	33-27*	Green Bay	71,457
	Jan. 3	Carolina ($18,000)	Dallas ($15,000)	29-10	Charlotte	73,014
2002	Jan. 5	San Francisco ($17,000)	N.Y. Giants ($12,500)	39-38	San Francisco	66,318
	Jan. 4	Atlanta ($12,500)	Green Bay ($17,000)	27-7	Green Bay	65,358
2001	Jan. 13	Green Bay ($12,500)	San Francisco ($12,500)	25-15	Green Bay	59,825
	Jan. 12	Philadelphia ($17,000)	Tampa Bay ($12,500)	31-9	Philadelphia	65,847
2000	Dec. 31	Philadelphia ($12,500)	Tampa Bay ($12,500)	21-3	Philadelphia	65,813
	Dec. 30	New Orleans ($16,000)	St. Louis ($12,500)	31-28	New Orleans	64,900
1999	Jan. 9	Minnesota ($10,000)	Dallas ($10,000)	27-10	Minneapolis	64,056
	Jan. 8	Washington ($16,000)	Detroit ($10,000)	27-13	Washington	79,411

PLAYOFF GAME SUMMARIES

Season	Date	Winner (Share)	Loser (Share)	Score	Site	Attendance
1998	Jan. 3	San Francisco ($10,000)	Green Bay ($10,000)	30-27	San Francisco	66,506
	Jan. 2	Arizona ($10,000)	Dallas ($15,000)	20-7	Dallas	62,969
1997	Dec. 28	Tampa Bay ($10,000)	Detroit ($10,000)	20-10	Tampa	73,361
	Dec. 27	Minnesota ($10,000)	N.Y. Giants ($15,000)	23-22	East Rutherford	77,497
1996	Dec. 29	San Francisco ($10,000)	Philadelphia ($10,000)	14-0	San Francisco	56,460
	Dec. 28	Dallas ($14,000)	Minnesota ($10,000)	40-15	Dallas	64,682
1995	Dec. 31	Green Bay ($13,000)	Atlanta ($7,500)	37-20	Green Bay	60,453
	Dec. 30	Philadelphia ($7,500)	Detroit ($7,500)	58-37	Philadelphia	66,099
1994	Jan. 1	Chicago ($7,500)	Minnesota ($12,000)	35-18	Minnesota	60,347
	Dec. 31	Green Bay ($7,500)	Detroit ($7,500)	16-12	Green Bay	58,125
1993	Jan. 9	N.Y. Giants ($7,500)	Minnesota ($7,500)	17-10	East Rutherford	75,089
	Jan. 8	Green Bay ($7,500)	Detroit ($12,000)	28-24	Detroit	68,479
1992	Jan. 3	Philadelphia ($6,000)	New Orleans ($6,000)	36-20	New Orleans	68,893
	Jan. 2	Washington ($6,000)	Minnesota ($10,000)	24-7	Minnesota	57,353
1991	Dec. 29	Dallas ($6,000)	Chicago ($6,000)	17-13	Chicago	62,594
	Dec. 28	Atlanta ($6,000)	New Orleans ($10,000)	27-20	New Orleans	68,794
1990	Jan. 6	Chicago ($10,000)	New Orleans ($6,000)	16-6	Chicago	60,767
	Jan. 5	Washington ($6,000)	Philadelphia ($6,000)	20-6	Philadelphia	65,287
1989	Dec. 31	L.A. Rams ($6,000)	Philadelphia ($6,000)	21-7	Philadelphia	65,479
1988	Dec. 26	Minnesota ($6,000)	L.A. Rams ($6,000)	28-17	Minnesota	61,204
1987	Jan. 3	Minnesota ($6,000)	New Orleans ($6,000)	44-10	New Orleans	68,546
1986	Dec. 28	Washington ($6,000)	L.A. Rams ($6,000)	19-7	Washington	54,567
1985	Dec. 29	N.Y. Giants ($6,000)	San Francisco ($6,000)	17-3	East Rutherford	75,131
1984	Dec. 23	N.Y. Giants ($6,000)	L.A. Rams ($6,000)	16-13	Anaheim	67,037
1983	Dec. 26	L.A. Rams ($6,000)	Dallas ($6,000)	24-17	Dallas	62,118
1982	Jan. 9	Dallas ($6,000)	Tampa Bay ($6,000)	30-17	Dallas	65,042
	Jan. 9	Minnesota ($6,000)	Atlanta ($6,000)	30-24	Minnesota	60,560
	Jan. 8	Green Bay ($6,000)	St. Louis ($6,000)	41-16	Green Bay	54,282
	Jan. 8	Washington ($6,000)	Detroit ($6,000)	31-7	Washington	55,045
1981	Dec. 27	N.Y. Giants ($3,000)	Philadelphia ($3,000)	27-21	Philadelphia	71,611
1980	Dec. 28	Dallas ($3,000)	Los Angeles ($3,000)	34-13	Dallas	63,052
1979	Dec. 23	Philadelphia ($3,000)	Chicago ($3,000)	27-17	Philadelphia	69,397
1978	Dec. 24	Atlanta ($3,000)	Philadelphia ($3,000)	14-13	Atlanta	59,403

*Sudden death overtime

2005 NFC WILD CARD PLAYOFF GAMES

Giants Stadium, East Rutherford, New Jersey
January 8, 2006, Attendance: 79,378

CAROLINA 23, N.Y. GIANTS 0—at Giants Stadium, attendance 79,378. Steve Smith scored 2 touchdowns and the Panthers' defense allowed just 132 yards and forced 5 turnovers to post the NFL's first road postseason shutout in 25 years. The Panthers held the ball for 42:45 of the 60 minutes, and did not commit a turnover. In the second quarter, Jake Delhomme's 22-yard touchdown pass to Smith capped a 12-play, 77-yard drive that included 3 third-down conversions. With 1:28 left in the first half, Dante Wesley recovered Gibril Wilson's muffed punt at the Giants' 15 to set up a field goal. In the third quarter, Ken Lucas intercepted a pass and returned it 14 yards to the Giants' 12. On the next play, Smith scored on an end around for a 17-0 lead. Marlon McCree intercepted passes on the next two possessions that resulted in John Kasay field goals for a 23-0 lead with 2:40 to play. Delhomme was 15 of 22 for 140 yards and 1 touchdown. Smith had 10 catches for 84 yards. DeShaun Foster rushed 27 times for 151 yards. Eli Manning was 10 of 18 for 113 yards, with 3 interceptions.

Carolina	0	10	7	6	—	23
N.Y. Giants	0	0	0	0	—	0

Car — S. Smith 22 pass from Delhomme (Kasay kick)
Car — FG Kasay 31
Car — S. Smith 12 run (Kasay kick)
Car — FG Kasay 45
Car — FG Kasay 18

Raymond James Stadium, Tampa, Florida
January 7, 2006, Attendance: 65,514

WASHINGTON 17, TAMPA BAY 10—The Redskins' defense scored 14 points off turnovers as Washington won its first postseason game since 1999. The Redskins won despite gaining just 120 yards of offense, the lowest output ever by a winning playoff team in NFL history. LaVar Arrington intercepted a pass and returned it 21 yards to the Buccaneers' 6 to set up Clinton Portis' touchdown run on the next play for a 7-0 lead with 8:45 left in the first quarter. On the ensuing drive, Marcus Washington forced Carnell Williams to fumble. Washington picked up the loose ball, ran 7 yards, and he fumbled. Sean Taylor picked up the bouncing ball and raced 51 yards for a touchdown and 14-0 lead with 4:15 remaining in the first quarter. With the score 17-3, the Buccaneers opened the second half by forcing a punt and Chris Simms' 22-yard pass to Michael Pittman on third-and-5 set up Simms' 2-yard dive over the left pylon on third-and-goal to pull Tampa Bay within 17-10. With 7:41 remaining in the game, the Buccaneers drove to the Redskins' 19, but Mike Alstott was stopped on third-and-1, and Simms' fourth-and-1 pass fell incomplete. Brian Kelly intercepted a pass at the Redskins' 35 with 3:43 remaining. On third-and-10 with 2:48 left, Simms' long pass into the end zone was nearly caught by Edell Shepherd. Simms tried for Shepherd again on fourth down, but just overthrew him. The Buccaneers forced a punt with 1:05 left and had the ball on their own 46-yard line, but Washington intercepted Simms' pass to clinch the victory. Mark Brunell was 7 of 15 for 41 yards, with 1 interception. Simms was 25 of 38 for 198 yards, with 2 interceptions.

Washington	14	3	0	0	—	17
Tampa Bay	0	3	7	0	—	10

Wash — Portis 6 run (Hall kick)
Wash — Taylor 51 fumble return (Hall kick)
TB — FG Bryant 43
Wash — FG Hall 47
TB — Simms 2 run (Bryant kick)

AFC-NFC PRO BOWL RESULTS (1971-2006)
Series tied, 18-18

Year	Date	Winner (Share)	Loser (Share)	Score	Site	Attendance
2006	Feb. 12	NFC ($40,000)	AFC ($20,000)	23-17	Honolulu	50,190
2005	Feb. 13	AFC ($35,000)	NFC ($17,500)	38-27	Honolulu	50,225
2004	Feb. 8	NFC ($35,000)	AFC ($17,500)	55-52	Honolulu	50,127
2003	Feb. 2	AFC ($30,000)	NFC ($15,000)	45-20	Honolulu	50,125
2002	Feb. 9	AFC ($30,000)	NFC ($15,000)	38-30	Honolulu	50,301
2001	Feb. 4	AFC ($30,000)	NFC ($15,000)	38-17	Honolulu	50,128
2000	Feb. 6	NFC ($25,000)	AFC ($12,500)	51-31	Honolulu	50,112
1999	Feb. 7	AFC ($25,000)	NFC ($12,500)	23-10	Honolulu	50,075
1998	Feb. 1	AFC ($25,000)	NFC ($12,500)	29-24	Honolulu	49,995
1997	Feb. 2	AFC ($20,000)	NFC ($10,000)	26-23 (OT)	Honolulu	50,031
1996	Feb. 4	NFC ($20,000)	AFC ($10,000)	20-13	Honolulu	50,034
1995	Feb. 5	AFC ($20,000)	NFC ($10,000)	41-13	Honolulu	50,529
1994	Feb. 6	NFC ($20,000)	AFC ($10,000)	17-3	Honolulu	50,026
1993	Feb. 7	AFC ($10,000)	NFC ($5,000)	23-20 (OT)	Honolulu	50,007
1992	Feb. 2	NFC ($10,000)	AFC ($5,000)	21-15	Honolulu	50,209
1991	Feb. 3	AFC ($10,000)	NFC ($5,000)	23-21	Honolulu	50,345
1990	Feb. 4	NFC ($10,000)	AFC ($5,000)	27-21	Honolulu	50,445
1989	Jan. 29	NFC ($10,000)	AFC ($5,000)	34-3	Honolulu	50,113
1988	Feb. 7	AFC ($10,000)	NFC ($5,000)	15-6	Honolulu	50,113
1987	Feb. 1	AFC ($10,000)	NFC ($5,000)	10-6	Honolulu	50,101
1986	Feb. 2	NFC ($10,000)	AFC ($5,000)	28-24	Honolulu	50,101
1985	Jan. 27	AFC ($10,000)	NFC ($5,000)	22-14	Honolulu	50,385
1984	Jan. 29	NFC ($10,000)	AFC ($5,000)	45-3	Honolulu	50,445
1983	Feb. 6	NFC ($10,000)	AFC ($5,000)	20-19	Honolulu	49,883
1982	Jan. 31	AFC ($5,000)	NFC ($2,500)	16-13	Honolulu	50,402
1981	Feb. 1	NFC ($5,000)	AFC ($2,500)	21-7	Honolulu	50,360
1980	Jan. 27	NFC ($5,000)	AFC ($2,500)	37-27	Honolulu	49,800
1979	Jan. 29	NFC ($5,000)	AFC ($2,500)	13-7	Los Angeles	46,281
1978	Jan. 23	NFC ($5,000)	AFC ($2,500)	14-13	Tampa	51,337
1977	Jan. 17	AFC ($2,000)	NFC ($1,500)	24-14	Seattle	64,752
1976	Jan. 26	NFC ($2,000)	AFC ($1,500)	23-20	New Orleans	30,546
1975	Jan. 20	NFC ($2,000)	AFC ($1,500)	17-10	Miami	26,484
1974	Jan. 20	AFC ($2,000)	NFC ($1,500)	15-13	Kansas City	66,918
1973	Jan. 21	AFC ($2,000)	NFC ($1,500)	33-28	Dallas	37,091
1972	Jan. 23	AFC ($2,000)	NFC ($1,500)	26-13	Los Angeles	53,647
1971	Jan. 24	NFC ($2,000)	AFC ($1,500)	27-6	Los Angeles	48,222

2006 AFC-NFC PRO BOWL
Aloha Stadium, Honolulu, Hawaii
February 12, 2006, Attendance: 50,190
NFC 23, AFC 17—at Aloha Stadium, attendance 50,190. Derrick Brooks returned an interception 59 yards for a touchdown, and Neil Rackers added 3 field goals, as the NFC held off the AFC. The series is now tied 18-18. The defenses dominated, as the game featured 7 sacks and 10 turnovers. John Lynch's interception and 40-yard return to the NFC 45-yard line set up Peyton Manning's 16-yard touchdown pass to Chris Chambers. With the ball at midfield and holding a 10-3 lead and 48 seconds left in the half, Manning was intercepted for the third time. Roy Williams picked off the pass at the NFC 12, ran 11 yards, handed off to DeAngelo Hall, who raced 57 yards to the AFC 20-yard line. Three plays later, Michael Vick completed a 14-yard touchdown pass to Alge Crumpler to tie the game with two seconds left in the half. In the middle of the third quarter, Brooks intercepted Trent Green's short pass intended for Antonio Gates and returned it 59 yards for a touchdown. Champ Bailey recovered Santana Moss' fumble to spark a 10-play, 68-yard drive capped by Green's 1-yard run to tie the game 17-17 with 12:47 to play. Matt Hasselbeck engineered a 13-play, 59-yard drive on the ensuing possession to set up Rackers' 22-yard field goal for a 20-17 lead with 6:29 to play. Jeremiah Trotter recovered Steve McNair's fumbled snap at the AFC 18-yard line with 3:42 to play, and Rackers added a 20-yard field goal with 1:10 remaining. The AFC reached the NFC 49-yard line with 29 seconds left, but McNair threw 3 consecutive incompletions and Michael Strahan ended the game with a sack. Brooks was selected the game's outstanding player.

AFC (17)	Offense	NFC (23)
Marvin Harrison (Indianapolis)	WR	Santana Moss (Washington)
Willie Anderson (Cincinnati)	LT	Walter Jones (Seattle)
Alan Faneca (Pittsburgh)	LG	Larry Allen (Dallas)
Jeff Saturday (Indianapolis)	C	LeCharles Bentley (New Orleans)
Will Shields (Kansas City)	RG	Steve Hutchinson (Seattle)
Jonathan Ogden (Baltimore)	RT	Orlando Pace (St. Louis)
Antonio Gates (San Diego)	TE	Alge Crumpler (Atlanta)
Chad Johnson (Cincinnati)	WR	Steve Smith (Carolina)
Peyton Manning (Indianapolis)	QB	Matt Hasselbeck (Seattle)
Lorenzo Neal (San Diego)	FB-WR	Torry Holt (St. Louis)
Edgerrin James (Indianapolis)	RB	Tiki Barber (N.Y. Giants)
	Defense	
Derrick Burgess (Oakland)	DE	Julius Peppers (Carolina)
Marcus Stroud (Jacksonville)	DT	Tommie Harris (Chicago)
Jamal Williams (San Diego)	DT	Shaun Rogers (Detroit)
Dwight Freeney (Indianapolis)	DE	Michael Strahan (N.Y. Giants)
Joey Porter (Pittsburgh)	LOLB	Keith Brooking (Atlanta)
Al Wilson (Denver)	ILB	Jeremiah Trotter (Philadelphia)
Shawne Merriman (San Diego)	ROLB	Derrick Brooks (Tampa Bay)

Champ Bailey	LCB	Ronde Barber
(Denver)		(Tampa Bay)
Deltha O'Neal	RCB	DeAngelo Hall
(Cincinnati)		(Atlanta)
Troy Polamalu	SS	Roy Williams
(Pittsburgh)		(Dallas)
Bob Sanders	FS	Darren Sharper
(Indianapolis)		(Minnesota)

SUBSTITUTIONS

AFC—Specialists: K—Shayne Graham (Cincinnati). P—Brian Moorman (Buffalo). KR—Jerome Mathis (Houston). LS—Mike Schneck (Pittsburgh). ST—Hanik Milligan (San Diego). Offense: QB—Trent Green (Kansas City), Steve McNair (Tennessee). RB—Larry Johnson (Kansas City), LaDainian Tomlinson (San Diego). WR—Chris Chambers (Miami), Rod Smith (Denver). TE—Tony Gonzalez (Kansas City). G—Brian Waters (Kansas City). C—Jeff Hartings (Pittsburgh). Defense: DL—Casey Hampton (Pittsburgh). DE—Kyle Vanden Bosch (Tennessee). LB—Cato June (Indianapolis), Jonathan Vilma (N.Y. Jets). CB—Ty Law (N.Y. Jets). S—John Lynch (Denver). Not Active: QB—Tom Brady (New England), Carson Palmer (Cincinnati). T—Willie Roaf (Kansas City). DL—Richard Seymour (New England). DE—Jason Taylor (Miami). LB—Zach Thomas (Miami). **NFC**—Specialists: K—Neil Rackers (Arizona). P—Josh Bidwell (Tampa Bay). KR—Koren Robinson (Minnesota). LS—Mike Bartrum (Philadelphia). ST—David Tyree (N.Y. Giants). Offense: QB—Jake Delhomme (Carolina), Michael Vick (Atlanta). RB—Warrick Dunn (Atlanta). FB—Mack Strong (Seattle). WR—Larry Fitzgerald (Arizona). TE—Jason Witten (Dallas). G—Mike Wahle (Carolina). T—Chris Samuels (Washington). C—Robbie Tobeck (Seattle). Defense: DL—La'Roi Glover (Dallas), Osi Umenyiora (N.Y. Giants). LB—Lance Briggs (Chicago), Lofa Tatupu (Seattle). CB—Nathan Vasher (Chicago). S—Brian Dawkins (Philadelphia). Did Not Play: RB—Shaun Alexander (Seattle). Not Active: C—Olin Kreutz (Chicago). TE—Jeremy Shockey (N.Y. Giants). DL—Rod Coleman (Atlanta). LB—Brian Urlacher (Chicago). S—Mike Brown (Chicago).

HEAD COACHES
AFC—Mike Shanahan (Denver)
NFC—John Fox (Carolina)

OFFICIALS
Referee—Gerry Austin. Umpire—Steve Wilson. Side Judge—Laird Hayes. Head Linesman—John Schleyer. Back Judge—Phil Luckett. Field Judge—Scott Steenson. Line Judge—Carl Johnson.

AFC	7	3	0	7	—		17
NFC	0	10	7	6	—		23

AFC — Chambers 16 pass from Manning (Graham kick)

NFC — FG Rackers 32
AFC — FG Graham 31
NFC — Crumpler 14 pass from Vick (Rackers kick)
NFC — D. Brooks 59 interception return (Rackers kick)
AFC — T. Green 1 run (Graham kick)
NFC — FG Rackers 22
NFC — FG Rackers 20

TEAM STATISTICS

	AFC	NFC
Total First Downs	19	18
Rushing	6	4
Passing	11	12
Penalty	2	2
Total Net Yardage	260	279
Total Offensive Plays	71	69
Avg. Gain Per Offensive Play	3.7	4.0
Rushes	24	25
Yards Gained Rushing (Net)	71	98
Avg. Yards per Rush	3.0	3.9
Passes Attempted	45	39
Passes Completed	20	21
Had Intercepted	4	2
Tackled Attempting to Pass	2	5
Yards Lost Attempting to Pass	14	26
Yards Gained Passing (Net)	189	181
Punts	4	5
Avg. Distance	48.5	48.4
Punt Returns	1	2
Punt Return Yardage	12	7
Kickoff Returns	5	4
Kickoff Return Yardage	119	94
Interception Return Yardage	73	192
Total Return Yardage	85	199
Fumbles	3	6
Fumbles Lost	2	2
Own Fumbles Recovered	1	4
Opponent Fumbles Recovered	2	2
Penalties	8	8
Yards Penalized	59	55
Field Goals	1	3
Field Goals Attempted	1	3
Third-Down Efficiency	4/13	8/18
Fourth-Down Efficiency	0/1	0/0
Time of Possession	27:59	32:01

INDIVIDUAL STATISTICS

RUSHING: AFC: L. Johnson 8-33-0, James 6-22-0, Tomlinson 5-13-0, Green 3-3-1, McNair 2-0-0. NFC: T. Barber 11-33-0, S. Moss 1-18-0, Vick 2-17-0, Dunn 7-12-0, Fitzgerald 1-12-0, S. Smith 1-6-0, Hasselbeck 1-0-0, Strong 1-0-0.

PASSING: AFC: Manning 26-13-139-1-3, Green 11-5-39-0-1, McNair 8-2-25-0-0. NFC: Hasselbeck 17-10-85-0-1, Vick 12-4-69-1-1, Delhomme 10-7-53-0-0.

RECEIVING: AFC: Gonzalez 5-36-0, Harrison 4-74-0, Chambers 2-34-1, Tomlinson 2-18-0, C. Johnson 2-15-0, R. Smith 2-13-0, Gates 2-7-0, Neal 1-6-0. NFC: S. Smith 8-46-0, S. Moss 3-39-0, Crumpler 3-35-1, Holt 2-18-0, Strong 2-17-0, Fitzgerald 1-32-0, Dunn 1-14-0, T. Barber 1-6-0.

KICKOFF RETURNS: AFC: Mathis 4-109-0, Neal 1-10-0. NFC: K. Robinson 4-94-0.

PUNT RETURNS: AFC: Mathis 1-12-0. NFC: S. Moss 1-12-0, S. Smith 1-(-6)-0,

---

Hall 0-1-0.
PUNTING: AFC: Moorman 4-194-48.5. NFC: Bidwell 5-242-48.4.
INTERCEPTIONS: AFC: Lynch 1-40-0, Bailey 1-33-0. NFC: D. Brooks 1-59-1, Sharper 1-35-0, Vasher 1-30-0, R. Williams 1-11-0, Hall 1-7-0.
SACKS: AFC: Vanden Bosch 2, Stroud 1.5, Hampton 1, Burgess 0.5. NFC: Rogers 1, Strahan 1.

2005 AFC-NFC PRO BOWL
Aloha Stadium, Honolulu, Hawaii
February 13, 2005, Attendance: 50,225
AFC 38, NFC 27—Peyton Manning passed for 130 yards and 3 touchdowns as the AFC won for the fourth time in five years. The NFC outgained the AFC 492-343, but committed 3 turnovers and allowed an onside kick for a touchdown. David Akers missed a 43-yard field goal in the first quarter, and the AFC responded with touchdowns on its next four possessions. Manning completed 3 touchdown passes in the stretch, and Hines Ward registered the first onside kick returned for a touchdown in Pro Bowl history. Manning's final scoring pass, a 12-yard toss to Antonio Gates, was set up by Takeo Spikes' interception near midfield, to take a 28-7 lead with 5:50 left in the half. Michael Vick began the second half for the NFC, and engineered a 73-yard drive, capped by Torry Holt's 27-yard touchdown catch. Lito Sheppard intercepted Tom Brady's pass four plays later, and Vick culminated a 69-yard drive with a 3-yard run to cut the deficit to 28-24 with 3:53 left in the third quarter. An exchange of field goals made the score 31-27 with 9:04 remaining, but Drew Brees connected on a 33-yard pass to Gates on a flea-flicker, and LaDainian Tomlinson scored on third-and-goal from the NFC's 4 with 5:15 to play. Nate Clements' interception of Vick's pass with 2:00 remaining clinched the victory. Manning was 6 of 10 for 130 yards and 3 touchdowns to earn the game's most valuable player award. Brady was 4 of 9 for 48 yards, with 1 interception, and Brees was 2 of 2 for 58 yards. Donovan McNabb was 1 of 8 for 24 yards, with 1 interception. Daunte Culpepper was 9 of 15 for 124 yards, with 1 interception. Vick was 14 of 24 for 205 yards and 1 touchdown, with 1 interception, and became the first player to pass and run for a touchdown in the same Pro Bowl game.

NFC	0	10	14	3	—	27
AFC	14	14	0	10	—	38

AFC — Harrison 62 pass from Manning (Vinatieri kick)
AFC — Ward 41 pass from Manning (Vinatieri kick)
NFC — Westbrook 12 run (Akers kick)
AFC — Ward 39 kickoff return (Vinatieri kick)
AFC — Gates 12 pass from Manning (Vinatieri kick)

NFC — FG Akers 33
NFC — Holt 27 pass from Vick
    (Akers kick)
NFC — Vick 3 run (Akers kick)
AFC — FG Vinatieri 44
NFC — FG Akers 29
AFC — Tomlinson 4 run
    (Vinatieri kick)

2004 AFC-NFC PRO BOWL

Aloha Stadium, Honolulu, Hawaii
February 8, 2004, Attendance: 50,127
NFC 55, AFC 52—Marc Bulger passed for a Pro Bowl-record 4 touchdowns as the NFC rallied from a 25-point deficit to win the highest scoring game in Pro Bowl history. The AFC set a record with 626 yards, but committed 6 turnovers which led to 35 points. Steve McNair fired a 90-yard touchdown pass to Chad Johnson on the AFC's first play, and Ed Reed blocked Todd Sauerbrun's punt and returned it 23 yards for a touchdown for a 14-0 lead 3:58 into the game. The AFC led 17-13 in the second quarter when Peyton Manning fired a 50-yard touchdown pass to Marvin Harrison, and his 9-yard scoring pass to Tony Gonzalez on the next possession gave the AFC a 31-13 lead. Jamal Lewis' 22-yard touchdown run gave the AFC a 38-13 lead with 11:08 left in the third quarter. The comeback started when Trent Green fumbled and Leonard Little recovered. Bulger completed a 12-yard touchdown pass to Torry Holt two plays later with 8:08 left in the third quarter. Two plays later, Derrick Mason fumbled and Jerry Azumah returned it 36 yards to the AFC's 7 to set up Bulger's 2-yard touchdown toss to Keenan McCardell. But following an exchange of punts, Green completed a 23-yard touchdown pass to Clinton Portis to give the AFC a 45-27 lead with 13:14 left. The NFC scored 28 points in the next 9:42, set up by Azumah's 60-yard kickoff return, Champ Bailey's interception of a pass by Harrison, and interception returns by Dre' Bly, 32 yards for a touchdown, and Corey Chavous, 39 yards to set up Shaun Alexander's 2-yard touchdown run with 3:32 left, for a 55-45 NFC lead. Manning's 10-yard touchdown pass to Hines Ward with 1:54 left pulled the AFC within three points, and Bulger was intercepted by Brock Marion on fourth-and-10 from the AFC's 28-yard line with 1:15 left. The AFC drove to the NFC 21, but Kris Jenkins sacked Manning for a 12-yard loss, forcing Vanderjagt, who was 37-for-37 on the season but missed from 52 yards just before halftime, to attempt a 51-yard field goal as time expired. But the kick sailed wide right and the NFC prevailed. Bulger was 12 of 21 for 152 yards and 4 touchdowns, with 1 interception, and was selected as the player of the game. Holt had 7 receptions for 128 yards. Manning was 22 of 41 for 342 yards and 3 touchdowns, with 2 interceptions. Mason had 6 catches for 113 yards, and Johnson had 5 receptions for 156 yards.

AFC	17	14	7	14	— 52
NFC	10	3	14	28	— 55

AFC — C. Johnson 90 pass from
    McNair (Vanderjagt kick)
AFC — Reed 23 return of blocked
    punt (Vanderjagt kick)
NFC — Alexander 12 run
    (Wilkins kick)
NFC — FG Wilkins 28
AFC — FG Vanderjagt 27
NFC — FG Wilkins 38
AFC — Harrison 50 pass from
    Manning (Vanderjagt kick)
AFC — Gonzalez 9 pass from
    Manning (Vanderjagt kick)
AFC — J. Lewis 22 run
    (Vanderjagt kick)
NFC — Holt 12 pass from Bulger
    (Wilkins kick)
NFC — McCardell 2 pass from Bulger
    (Wilkins kick)
AFC — Portis 23 pass from Green
    (Vanderjagt kick)
NFC — Crumpler 33 pass from Bulger
    (Wilkins kick)
NFC — Alexander 5 pass from Bulger
    (pass failed)
NFC — Bly 32 interception return
    (Green run)
NFC — Alexander 2 run (Wilkins kick)
AFC — Ward 10 pass from Manning
    (Vanderjagt kick)

2003 AFC-NFC PRO BOWL

Aloha Stadium, Honolulu, Hawaii
February 2, 2003, Attendance: 50,125
AFC 45, NFC 20—Ricky Williams rushed for a game-high 56 yards, scored 2 touchdowns, and forced a fumble on special teams to earn player of the game honors. The AFC, which led by as many as 39 points, won for the third consecutive time. Jason Taylor's interception three plays into the game set up Williams' first touchdown run, and Rich Gannon's 11-yard touchdown pass to Tony Gonzalez capped a 71-yard drive on the AFC's next possession to take a 14-3 lead. Rod Woodson's interception early in the second quarter led to Gannon's 13-yard touchdown pass to Travis Henry, and Williams capped another 71-yard drive with a 1-yard run with 47 seconds left in the half to give the AFC a 28-6 lead. Brad Johnson began the game in the fourth quarter, and Ty Law intercepted a pass and returned it 43 yards for a touchdown on his first possession, and Sam Madison intercepted Johnson during his second drive to set up Peyton Manning's 32-yard touchdown pass to Hines Ward, which gave the AFC a 45-6 lead with 7:31 left. Johnson guided the NFC to touchdowns on its next two possessions, with the help of Julian Peterson's onside kick recovery, for the game's final points. All three AFC quarterbacks passed for at least 100 yards, led by Drew Bledsoe's 9 of 18 for 122-yard perfor-mance. Gonzalez had 5 receptions for 98 yards to lead all receivers. The AFC's defense had 6 interceptions, 3 of which were thrown by NFC starter Jeff Garcia.

NFC	3	3	0	14	— 20
AFC	14	14	3	14	— 45

AFC — R. Williams 1 run
    (Vinatieri kick)
NFC — FG Akers 45
AFC — Gonzalez 11 pass from
    Gannon (Vinatieri kick)
AFC — Henry 13 pass from Gannon
    (Vinatieri kick)
NFC — FG Akers 53
AFC — R. Williams 1 run
    (Vinatieri kick)
AFC — FG Vinatieri 20
AFC — Law 43 interception return
    (Vinatieri kick)
AFC — Ward 32 pass from Manning
    (Vinatieri kick)
NFC — Horn 12 pass from
    B. Johnson (Akers kick)
NFC — Alstott 4 pass from
    B. Johnson (Akers kick)

2002 AFC-NFC PRO BOWL

Aloha Stadium, Honolulu, Hawaii
February 9, 2002, Attendance: 50,301
AFC 38, NFC 30—Rich Gannon passed for 137 yards and 2 touchdowns to become the first player to earn back-to-back Pro Bowl player of the game honors. The game had an inauspicious beginning for Gannon, who fumbled the game's first snap. Hugh Doulgas recovered the fumble and returned the ball to the AFC's 2-yard line to set up Ahman Green's touchdown 27 seconds into the game. After a three-and-out series, Kurt Warner's 23-yard pass to David Boston set up David Akers' 29-yard field goal to give the NFC a 10-0 lead. Gannon responded two plays later with a 55-yard touchdown pass to Marvin Harrison. Deltha O'Neal's 24-yard interception return to the NFC's 6-yard line moments later set up Curtis Martin's 4-yard touchdown run and gave the AFC a 14-10 lead. After the NFC went three-and-out, the AFC needed just five plays, keyed by Gannon's 30-yard pass to Troy Brown, and capped by Priest Holmes' 39-yard touchdown run to give the AFC its third touchdown in less than six minutes and a 21-10 lead. A 10-play NFC drive led to Akers' second field goal, but Jermaine Lewis' 54-yard kickoff return set up Gannon's 18-yard touchdown pass to Ken Dilger and gave the AFC a 28-10 lead with 12:03 left in the first half. The NFC overcame Shane Lechler's Pro Bowl-record 73-yard punt with Akers' 49-yard field goal just before halftime to cut the deficit to 28-16. Junior Seau's interception at the AFC's 5-yard line early in the fourth quarter thrwarted one NFC rally, but Champ Bailey's interception led to Donovan McNabb's 8-yard touchdown pass to Terrell Owens to cut the deficit to 28-23 with 8:12 left. Runs of 29 and 16 yards by Corey Dillon led to Jason Elam's 38-yard

field goal and, two plays later, Ty Law intercepted McNabb at the NFC 44-yard line, returned the ball to the NFC 13 before lateralling to Ray Lewis, who dragged three players into the end zone for a 38-23 lead with 2:49 remaining. McNabb's 15-yard touchdown pass to Garrison Hearst with 1:32 left cut the deficit to 38-30, but Rod Woodson recovered the ensuing onside kick to clinch the victory. Gannon was 8 of 10 for 137 yards and 2 touchdowns. McNabb was 12 of 25 for 149 yards and 2 touchdowns, with 2 interceptions, to lead the NFC. Owens had 8 receptions for 122 yards and 1 touchdown.

AFC	21	7	0	10	—	38
NFC	13	3	0	14	—	30

NFC — Green 2 run (Akers kick)
NFC — FG Akers 29
AFC — Harrison 55 pass from Gannon (Elam kick)
AFC — Martin 4 run (Elam kick)
AFC — Holmes 39 run (Elam kick)
NFC — FG Akers 41
AFC — Dilger 18 pass from Gannon (Elam kick)
NFC — FG Akers 49
NFC — Owens 8 pass from McNabb (Akers kick)
AFC — FG Elam 38
AFC — R. Lewis 13 lateral from Law (Elam kick)
NFC — Hearst 15 pass from McNabb (Akers kick)

2001 AFC-NFC PRO BOWL
Aloha Stadium, Honolulu, Hawaii
February 4, 2001, Attendance: 50,128
AFC 38, NFC 17—Rich Gannon completed 12 of 14 passes for 160 yards during the game's first two possessions to win player of the game honors and lead the AFC to victory. Gannon's touchdown passes capped 87- and 90-yard drives and staked the AFC to a 14-0 lead. Gannon, who was still recovering from a separated non-throwing shoulder suffered in the AFC Championship Game, was replaced by Peyton Manning. The Colts' quarterback engineered a scoring drive, capped by Matt Stover's field goal, to give the AFC a 17-0 lead early in the second quarter. At that point, the AFC had 14 first downs and 231 yards of offense while limiting the NFC to no first downs and 6 yards. Jimmy Smith caught a 2-yard touchdown pass 54 seconds before halftime to give the AFC a 24-3 lead. Third-quarter touchdown passes by Donovan McNabb and Daunte Culpepper trimmed the AFC's lead to 31-17, but Jason Taylor batted down Culpepper's fourth-and-1 pass early in the fourth quarter, and Edgerrin James' 20-yard touchdown run a few plays later iced the game. The NFC attempted a Pro Bowl record 56 pass attempts, and the two teams combined for a Pro Bowl record 98 pass attempts. Tony Gonzalez had 6 receptions for 108 yards, all in the first half, for the AFC. Torry Holt

had 7 receptions for 103 yards. Smith's touchdown reception gives him 5 for his career, an AFC-NFC Pro Bowl record.

NFC	0	3	14	0	—	17
AFC	14	10	7	7	—	38

AFC — Gonzalez 8 pass from Gannon (Stover kick)
AFC — Harrison 16 pass from Gannon (Stover kick)
AFC — FG Stover 29
NFC — FG Gramatica 48
AFC — J. Smith 2 pass from Manning (Stover kick)
NFC — Owens 17 pass from McNabb (Gramatica kick)
AFC — Harrison 24 pass from Manning (Stover kick)
NFC — Holt 20 pass from Culpepper (Gramatica kick)
AFC — James 20 run (Stover kick)

2000 AFC-NFC PRO BOWL
Aloha Stadium, Honolulu, Hawaii
February 6, 2000, Attendance: 50,112
NFC 51, AFC 31—Randy Moss earned player of the game honors by setting records with 9 receptions for 212 yards as the NFC defeated the AFC in the highest-scoring Pro Bowl ever. Aeneas Williams intercepted Peyton Manning's pass and raced 62 yards down the left sideline to give the NFC an early 7-0 lead. Kurt Warner's 48-yard pass to Moss on the NFC's first possession set up Jason Hanson's first field goal. Mike Alstott and Jimmy Smith each scored twice in the first half, and Michael Bates' 66-yard kickoff return led to Hanson's Pro Bowl-record tying 51-yard field goal as the half expired to give the NFC a 27-21 lead. Alstott's third touchdown increased the NFC's lead to 37-21, and Derrick Brooks' interception of Mark Brunell and 20-yard return staked the NFC to a 44-24 lead with 11:12 left. The AFC responded with Manning's 52-yard touchdown pass to Smith with 6:30 remaining, but Steve Beuerlein found Moss with a 25-yard scoring pass with 1:05 left to finish the scoring. Warner led the three NFC quarterbacks by completing 8 of 11 passes for 123 yards. Alstott led all rushers with 13 carries for 67 yards. The NFC forced 6 turnovers. Manning was 17 of 23 for 270 yards and 2 touchdowns, with 2 interceptions. Smith had 8 receptions for 119 yards. The previous record, 64 points, was set in 1980.

AFC	7	14	0	10	—	31
NFC	10	17	10	14	—	51

NFC — A. Williams 62 interception return (Hanson kick)
NFC — FG Hanson 21
AFC — J. Smith 5 pass from Brunell (Mare kick)
NFC — Alstott 1 run (Hanson kick)
AFC — Gonzalez 10 pass from Gannon (Mare kick)
NFC — Alstott 3 run (Hanson kick)

AFC — J. Smith 21 pass from Manning (Mare kick)
NFC — FG Hanson 51
NFC — Alstott 1 run (Hanson kick)
NFC — FG Hanson 23
AFC — FG Mare 33
NFC — Brooks 20 interception return (Hanson kick)
AFC — J. Smith 52 pass from Manning (Mare kick)
NFC — Moss 25 pass from Beuerlein (Hanson kick)

1999 AFC-NFC PRO BOWL
Aloha Stadium, Honolulu, Hawaii
February 7, 1999, Attendance: 50,075
AFC 23, NFC 10—John Elway, appearing in uniform on a football field for the final time, drove the AFC to its initial touchdown and then watched a strong defensive effort as the AFC won the Pro Bowl for the third consecutive season. Elway capped a game-opening 61-yard drive with a touchdown pass to Sam Gash. The AFC led 10-3 late in the first half when Deion Sanders intercepted a Vinny Testaverde pass at the NFC's 10 and raced downfield, only to be caught by Ed McCaffrey at the AFC 3-yard line as the half expired. The NFC drove into AFC territory early in the second half, but Ty Law thwarted the NFC's spirits with a 67-yard interception return for a touchdown to give the AFC a 17-3 lead with 9:42 left in the third quarter. The NFC reached the end zone three minutes later as Emmitt Smith scored, but the AFC responded with a field goal on its ensuing possession. Jason Elam's third field goal with 1:02 remaining finished the scoring. Elway played just one drive and was 4 of 5 for 55 yards and 1 touchdown. Keyshawn Johnson had 7 catches for 87 yards and shared player of the game honors with Law. Chandler completed 9 of 25 passes for 133 yards en route to leading the NFC to its only touchdown. Randy Moss had 7 catches for 108 yards.

NFC	3	0	7	0	—	10
AFC	7	3	10	3	—	23

AFC — Gash 3 pass from Elway (Elam kick)
NFC — FG Anderson 23
AFC — FG Elam 23
AFC — Law 67 interception return (Elam kick)
NFC — E. Smith 3 run (Anderson kick)
AFC — FG Elam 46
AFC — FG Elam 26

1998 AFC-NFC PRO BOWL
Aloha Stadium, Honolulu, Hawaii
February 1, 1998, Attendance: 49,995
AFC 29, NFC 24—Warren Moon guided the AFC to points on all three of his drives, including the winning touchdown from 1 yard with 1:49 left as the AFC scored the game's final 15 points to beat the NFC. Steve Young threw a 22-yard touchdown

pass to Herman Moore to cap the game's opening drive and give the NFC a 7-0 lead. Late in the first quarter, Mark Brunell threw a 17-yard touchdown pass to Andre Rison to tie the game. Both touchdown passes came on third-and-8 plays. The NFC responded with a 7-play, 71-yard drive capped by Young's 36-yard touchdown pass to Rob Moore. Trent Dilfer guided the NFC to its third touchdown, keyed by a 21-yard pass to Irving Fryar and 23-yard pass to Mike Alstott, and capped by Dorsey Levens' 12-yard touchdown run with 1:36 left in the half to give the NFC a 21-7 lead. The NFC had a chance to pad its lead on its first possession of the second half, but Jason Hanson missed a 44-yard field goal. The AFC bounced back with a 10-play, 65-yard drive that culminated with Drew Bledsoe's 14-yard touchdown pass to Jimmy Smith late in the third quarter. After Hanson's 35-yard field goal gave the NFC a 24-14 lead with 13:42 left, Moon entered the game and drove the AFC into field-goal range, where Mike Hollis drilled a 48-yard attempt with 8:51 left. Attempting to grind out the clock, Warrick Dunn fumbled, and Darryl Williams recovered at the AFC's 49 with 3:03 remaining. After a holding penalty moved the AFC back 10 yards, Moon fired a 57-yard pass to Tim Brown to set up Eddie George's 4-yard run with 2:31 left. The AFC went for the lead instead of a tie, but Moon's pass to Rison fell incomplete. However, the AFC got the ball back when Chris Chandler fumbled the snap on the NFC's first play, and Michael Sinclair recovered at the NFC's 16 with 2:19 left. Three runs by George set up Moon's winning sneak with 1:49 remaining. Moon's 2-point conversion pass to Brown was incomplete, keeping the AFC's lead at 29-24. The NFC was unable to move beyond its own 31-yard line in the final moments, and the AFC prevailed. Tim Brown had 5 receptions for 129 yards. Moon, who was 4 of 8 for 89 yards, earned player of the game honors.

| AFC | 7 | 0 | 7 | 15 | — | 29 |
| NFC | 7 | 14 | 0 | 3 | — | 24 |

NFC — H. Moore 22 pass from Young (Hanson kick)
AFC — Rison 17 pass from Brunell (Hollis kick)
NFC — R. Moore 36 pass from Young (Hanson kick)
NFC — Levens 12 run (Hanson kick)
AFC — J. Smith 14 pass from Bledsoe (Hollis kick)
NFC — FG Hanson 35
AFC — FG Hollis 48
AFC — George 4 run (pass failed)
AFC — Moon 1 run (pass failed)

1997 AFC-NFC PRO BOWL
Aloha Stadium, Honolulu, Hawaii
February 2, 1997, Attendance: 50,031
AFC 26, NFC 23 (OT)—Cary Blanchard's 37-yard field goal 8:16 into overtime gave

the AFC a 26-23 victory. The field goal was an ironic ending to a game that saw Blanchard and NFC kicker John Kasay, who each broke the previous single-season record of 35 field goals, combine to miss 5 of 8 field-goal attempts. The NFC scored on its first two possessions, with Vikings guard Randall McDaniel, who lined up as a fullback, scoring his first professional touchdown to give the NFC a 9-0 lead. However, the follies of the kicking unit began as holder Matt Turk muffed the snap on the extra point attempt. Blanchard booted a 28-yard field goal with 27 seconds left in the half to cut the NFC's lead to 9-3. In the third quarter, Barry Sanders scored from 6 yards out, but Kerry Collins was sacked on the 2-point attempt. A 41-yard pass from Drew Bledsoe to Tony Martin led to Curtis Martin's 3-yard run, and after Ashley Ambrose ran an interception back 54 yards for a touchdown 11 seconds into the fourth quarter, the AFC found itself with a 16-15 lead. The NFC drove for more than six minutes, only to have Kasay miss a 40-yard field goal attempt. After an AFC punt, Cris Carter caught a 47-yard touchdown bomb from Gus Frerotte to put the NFC ahead 23-16. After each team punted, the AFC got the ball on its own 20-yard line with 55 seconds left. Mark Brunell hit Tim Brown with an 80-yard bomb down the right sideline to tie the game with 44 seconds left. Wesley Walls caught a 33-yard pass to give the NFC a chance to win in regulation, but Kasay missed a 39-yard attempt and the game went to overtime. The AFC won the overtime toss, but Blanchard missed a 41-yard field goal attempt. The NFC had to punt after three plays, and Brunell hit Ben Coates with a 43-yard pass on the AFC's first play. After three running plays failed to gain a first down, Blanchard trotted onto the field and made the game-winning kick. The teams combined for a Pro Bowl record 962 total yards. Brunell, who completed 12 of 22 pass attempts for 236 yards, was selected as the player of the game.

| AFC | 0 | 3 | 7 | 13 | 3 | — | 26 |
| NFC | 9 | 0 | 6 | 8 | 0 | — | 23 |

NFC — FG Kasay 20
NFC — R. McDaniel 5 pass from Favre (muffed snap)
AFC — FG Blanchard 28
NFC — Sanders 6 run (pass failed)
AFC — Martin 3 run (Blanchard kick)
AFC — Ambrose 54 interception return (pass failed)
NFC — Carter 53 pass from Frerotte (Walls pass from Frerotte)
AFC — T. Brown 80 pass from Brunell (Blanchard kick)
AFC — FG Blanchard 37

1996 AFC-NFC PRO BOWL
Aloha Stadium, Honolulu, Hawaii
February 4, 1996, Attendance: 50,034
NFC 20, AFC 13—Jerry Rice had 6

receptions for 82 yards and 1 touchdown to earn player of the game honors in the NFC's victory. The 49ers' wide receiver, who was named to the Pro Bowl for the tenth consecutive year, caught a 1-yard touchdown pass from Packers quarterback Brett Favre 1:41 into the second quarter to cap an 80-yard drive and give the NFC the lead for good at 10-7. The AFC had taken a 7-0 lead 2:26 into the game when Bengals quarterback Jeff Blake connected with Steelers wide receiver Yancey Thigpen on a Pro Bowl-record 93-yard touchdown pass. The NFC increased its advantage to 20-7 at halftime on Redskins linebacker Ken Harvey's 36-yard interception return for a touchdown and Falcons kicker Morten Andersen's 24-yard field goal. The AFC trimmed its deficit to 20-13 when Colts quarterback Jim Harbaugh teamed with Patriots running back Curtis Martin on a 17-yard touchdown pass in the final minute of the third quarter, but its bid to win or tie was rebuffed twice in the final minutes of the fourth quarter. First, 49ers safety Tim McDonald intercepted Harbaugh's pass in the end zone with 1:50 remaining. Then, after the AFC forced a punt and got the ball back near midfield, Harbaugh drove his team to the NFC's 9-yard line in the closing seconds. But he spiked the ball once to stop the clock and threw 3 consecutive incompletions as time ran out. The AFC outgained the NFC 390 total yards to 287, but its quarterbacks suffered 4 interceptions, including 3 off Harbaugh, the NFL's leading passer during the regular season. The NFC raised its edge to 15-11 in Pro Bowl games since the AFL-NFL merger in 1970.

| NFC | 3 | 17 | 0 | 0 | — | 20 |
| AFC | 7 | 0 | 6 | 0 | — | 13 |

AFC — Thigpen 93 pass from Blake (Elam kick)
NFC — FG Andersen 36
NFC — Rice 1 pass from Favre (Andersen kick)
NFC — Harvey 36 interception return (Andersen kick)
NFC — FG Andersen 24
AFC — Martin 17 pass from Harbaugh (kick failed)

1995 AFC-NFC PRO BOWL
Aloha Stadium, Honolulu, Hawaii
February 5, 1995, Attendance: 50,529
AFC 41, NFC 13—Colts rookie Marshal Faulk rushed for a Pro Bowl-record 180 yards to key the AFC's rout of the NFC. Faulk, who earned the Dan McGuire Trophy as the player of the game, averaged nearly 14 yards on his 13 carries and shattered the previous rushing mark of 112 yards set by O.J. Simpson in the 1973 game. Faulk's 49-yard touchdown run from punt formation in the fourth quarter was the longest in Pro Bowl history. The Seahawks' Chris Warren added 127 yards on 14 carries as the AFC

amassed records for rushing yards (400) and total yards (552). Steelers tight end Eric Green caught 2 touchdown passes for the victors. The NFC managed only 196 total yards, a large chunk coming when 49ers quarterback Steve Young and Vikings wide receiver Cris Carter teamed on a 51-yard touchdown pass in the first quarter. That gave the NFC a 10-0 advantage, but the AFC rallied in the second quarter and took the lead for good when the Browns' Leroy Hoard scored on a 4-yard touchdown run 2:07 before halftime.

AFC	0	17	3	21	—	41
NFC	10	0	3	0	—	13

NFC — FG Reveiz 28
NFC — Carter 51 pass from Young (Reveiz kick)
AFC — Green 22 pass from Elway (Carney kick)
AFC — FG Carney 22
AFC — Hoard 4 run (Carney kick)
NFC — FG Reveiz 49
AFC — FG Carney 23
AFC — Warren 11 run (Carney kick)
AFC — Green 16 pass from Hostetler (Carney kick)
AFC — Faulk 49 run (Carney kick)

1994 AFC-NFC PRO BOWL

Aloha Stadium, Honolulu, Hawaii
February 6, 1994, Attendance: 50,026
NFC 17, AFC 3—The NFC converted a blocked punt and a fumble recovery into touchdowns just 2:20 apart in the second half of its victory over the AFC. With the score tied 3-3 late in the third quarter, Saints linebacker Renaldo Turnbull deflected a punt by the Oilers' Greg Montgomery, and the NFC took possession at the AFC's 48-yard line. A 32-yard pass from Bobby Hebert to Falcons teammate Andre Rison positioned Rams running back Jerome Bettis for a 4-yard touchdown run with 1:27 left in the third quarter. Moments later, Rams defensive tackle Sean Gilbert recovered a fumble by Oilers quarterback Warren Moon at the AFC's 19. Hebert then teamed with the Vikings' Cris Carter on a 15-yard touchdown pass 53 seconds into the fourth period. The NFC kept the AFC out of the end zone by maintaining possession for more than 38 minutes and forcing 6 turnovers. Rison earned the Dan McGuire Trophy as the player of the game by catching 6 passes for 86 yards. The victory was the fourth in the last six years for the NFC, which leads the series 14-10.

NFC	3	0	7	7	—	17
AFC	0	3	0	0	—	3

NFC — FG Johnson 35
AFC — FG Anderson 25
NFC — Bettis 4 run (Johnson kick)
NFC — Carter 15 pass from Hebert (Johnson kick)

1993 AFC-NFC PRO BOWL

Aloha Stadium, Honolulu, Hawaii
February 7, 1993, Attendance: 50,007
AFC 23, NFC 20—Nick Lowery's 33-yard field goal 4:09 into overtime gave the American Conference all-stars an unlikely 23-20 victory over the National Conference. Despite being overwhelmed by the NFC in first downs (30-9), and total yards (471-114), the AFC won because it forced 6 turnovers, blocked a pair of field goals (1 of which was returned for a touchdown), and returned an interception for a score. Special-teams star Steve Tasker of the Bills earned the Dan McGuire Trophy as the player of the game for making 4 tackles, forcing a fumble, and blocking a field goal. The block came with eight minutes left in regulation and the game tied at 13-13. The Raiders' Terry McDaniel picked up the loose ball and ran 28 yards for a touchdown and a 20-13 AFC lead. The NFC rallied behind 49ers quarterback Steve Young, whose fourth-down, 23-yard touchdown pass to Giants running back Rodney Hampton tied the game at 20-20 with 10 seconds left in regulation. Young completed 18 of 32 passes for 196 yards but was intercepted 3 times and lost a fumble when sacked in overtime. Raiders defensive end Howie Long fell on that fumble at the NFC 28-yard line, and five plays later, Lowery converted the winning field goal.

AFC	0	10	3	7	3	—	23
NFC	3	10	0	7	0	—	20

NFC — FG Andersen 27
AFC — Seau 31 interception return (Lowery kick)
NFC — FG Andersen 37
NFC — Irvin 9 pass from Aikman (Andersen kick)
AFC — FG Lowery 42
AFC — FG Lowery 29
AFC — McDaniel 28 blocked field goal return (Lowery kick)
NFC — Hampton 23 pass from Young (Andersen kick)
AFC — FG Lowery 33

1992 AFC-NFC PRO BOWL

Aloha Stadium, Honolulu, Hawaii
February 2, 1992, Attendance: 50,209
NFC 21, AFC 15—Atlanta's Chris Miller threw an 11-yard touchdown pass to San Francisco's Jerry Rice with 4:04 remaining in the game to lift the NFC over the AFC. It was the NFC's thirteenth win in the 22-game series. The AFC had taken a 15-14 lead when the Raiders' Jeff Jaeger kicked a 27-yard field goal 1:49 into the fourth quarter. But the NFC, aided by a key roughing-the-passer penalty on a third-down incompletion from the AFC 24-yard line, drove 85 yards to the winning score. The Cowboys' Michael Irvin, playing in his first Pro Bowl, caught 8 passes for 125 yards, including a 13-yard touchdown in the first quarter, and was named the player of the game. Rice had 7 catches for 77

yards. Mark Rypien of Washington, the Super Bowl most valuable player one week earlier, completed 11 of 18 passes for 165 yards and 2 touchdowns for the NFC, including a 35-yard pass to Redskins teammate Gary Clark just 26 seconds before halftime. Miller completed 7 of his 10 attempts for 85 yards.

NFC	7	7	0	7	—	21
AFC	7	5	0	3	—	15

AFC — Clayton 4 pass from Kelly (Jaeger kick)
NFC — Irvin 13 pass from Rypien (Lohmiller kick)
AFC — Safety, Townsend tackled Byner in end zone
AFC — FG Jaeger 48
NFC — Clark 35 pass from Rypien (Lohmiller kick)
AFC — FG Jaeger 27
NFC — Rice 11 pass from Miller (Lohmiller kick)

1991 AFC-NFC PRO BOWL

Aloha Stadium, Honolulu, Hawaii
February 3, 1991, Attendance: 50,345
AFC 23, NFC 21—Buffalo's Jim Kelly and Houston's Ernest Givins combined for a 13-yard scoring pass late in the fourth quarter to rally the AFC over the NFC. Phoenix rookie Johnny Johnson scored on runs of 1 and 9 yards to put the NFC ahead 14-3 in the third quarter. Buffalo's Andre Reed, who led all receivers with 4 catches for 80 yards, caught a 20-yard scoring reception from Kelly early in the fourth quarter to move the AFC to within 1 point. Barry Sanders ran 22 yards for a touchdown to increase the NFC's lead to 21-13. Miami's Jeff Cross blocked a 46-yard field-goal attempt by New Orleans' Morten Andersen with seven seconds remaining to preserve the win. Buffalo's Bruce Smith recorded 3 sacks and also had a blocked field goal. Kelly, who completed 13 of 19 passes for 210 yards and 2 touchdowns, was presented the Dan McGuire Award as player of the game. The AFC's victory narrowed the NFC's Pro Bowl series lead to 12-9.

AFC	3	0	3	17	—	23
NFC	0	7	7	7	—	21

AFC — FG Lowery 26
NFC — J. Johnson 1 run (Andersen kick)
AFC — FG Lowery 43
NFC — J. Johnson 9 run (Andersen kick)
AFC — Reed 20 pass from Kelly (Lowery kick)
NFC — Sanders 22 run (Andersen kick)
AFC — FG Lowery 34
AFC — Givins 13 pass from Kelly (Lowery kick)

1990 AFC-NFC PRO BOWL

Aloha Stadium, Honolulu, Hawaii
February 4, 1990, Attendance: 50,445
NFC 27, AFC 21—The NFC captured its

second straight Pro Bowl as the defense accounted for a pair of touchdowns and forced 5 turnovers before the eleventh consecutive sellout crowd at Aloha Stadium. The AFC held a 7-6 halftime edge on a 1-yard scoring run by Christian Okoye of the Chiefs. The NFC then rallied with 21 unanswered points in the third quarter. David Meggett of the Giants began the comeback with an 11-yard touchdown reception from Philadelphia's Randall Cunningham. The Rams' Jerry Gray followed with a 51-yard interception return for a score and the Vikings' Keith Millard added an 8-yard fumble return for a touchdown four minutes later to give the NFC a commanding 27-7 lead. Seattle's Dave Krieg rallied the AFC with a 5-yard touchdown pass to Miami's Ferrell Edmunds. Cleveland's Mike Johnson then returned an interception 22 yards for a score to pull the AFC to within 27-21. Gray, who was credited with 7 tackles, was given the Dan McGuire Award as player of the game. Krieg led all quarterbacks by completing 15 of 23 for 148 yards and 1 touchdown. Buffalo's Thurman Thomas topped all receivers with 5 catches for 47 yards, while Indianapolis' Eric Dickerson led all rushers with 46 yards on 15 carries. The win gave the NFC a 12-8 advantage in Pro Bowl games since 1971.

NFC	3	3	21	0	— 27
AFC	0	7	0	14	— 21

NFC — FG Murray 23
NFC — FG Murray 41
AFC — Okoye 1 run (Treadwell kick)
NFC — Meggett 11 pass from Cunningham (Murray kick)
NFC — Gray 51 interception return (Murray kick)
NFC — Millard 8 fumble recovery return (Murray kick)
AFC — Edmunds 5 pass from Krieg (Treadwell kick)
AFC — M. Johnson 22 interception return (Treadwell kick)

1989 AFC-NFC PRO BOWL
Aloha Stadium, Honolulu, Hawaii
January 29, 1989, Attendance: 50,113
NFC 34, AFC 3—The NFC scored 34 unanswered points to snap a two-game losing streak to the AFC before the tenth straight sellout crowd in Honolulu's Aloha Stadium. Bills kicker Scott Norwood provided the AFC's only points on a 38-yard field goal 6:23 into the game. Touchdown runs by Dallas' Herschel Walker (4 yards) and Atlanta's John Settle (1) brought the NFC a 14-3 halftime lead. Walker added a 7-yard scoring run, the Saints' Morten Andersen kicked field goals of 27 and 51 yards, and Los Angeles Rams' wide receiver Henry Ellard caught an 8-yard scoring pass from Minnesota quarterback Wade Wilson in the second half to complete the scoring. Chicago running back Neal Anderson and Philadelphia quarter-

back Randall Cunningham, who were both appearing in their first Pro Bowl, also played major roles in the NFC's victory. Anderson rushed 13 times for 85 yards and had 2 receptions for 17. Cunningham, who was voted the game's outstanding player, completed 10 of 14 passes for 63 yards and rushed for 49 yards. The NFC, which had 5 takeaways, outgained the AFC 355 yards to 167 and held a time-of-possession advantage of 35:18 to 24:42. Houston quarterback Warren Moon completed 13 of 20 passes for 134 yards for the AFC. The win gave the NFC an 11-8 advantage in Pro Bowl games.

AFC	3	0	0	0	— 3
NFC	7	7	10	10	— 34

AFC — FG Norwood 38
NFC — Walker 4 run (Andersen kick)
NFC — Settle 1 run (Andersen kick)
NFC — FG Andersen 27
NFC — Walker 7 run (Andersen kick)
NFC — FG Andersen 51
NFC — Ellard 8 pass from Wilson (Andersen kick)

1988 AFC-NFC PRO BOWL
Aloha Stadium, Honolulu, Hawaii
February 7, 1988, Attendance: 50,113
AFC 15, NFC 6—Led by a tenacious pass rush, the AFC defeated the NFC for the second consecutive year before the ninth straight sellout crowd in Honolulu's Aloha Stadium. Buffalo quarterback Jim Kelly scored the game's lone touchdown on a 1-yard run for a 7-6 halftime lead. Colts kicker Dean Biasucci added field goals from 37 and 30 yards to complete the AFC's scoring. Saints kicker Morten Andersen had 25- and 36-yard field goals to account for the NFC's points. AFC defenders held the NFC to 213 yards and recorded 8 sacks. Bills defensive end Bruce Smith, who had 2 sacks among his 5 tackles, was voted the game's outstanding player. Oilers running back Mike Rozier led all rushers with 49 yards on 9 carries. Jets wide receiver Al Toon had 5 receptions for 75 yards. The AFC generated 341 yards total offense and held a time-of-possession advantage of 34:14 to 25:46. By winning, the AFC cut the NFC's lead in the Pro Bowl series to 10-8.

NFC	0	6	0	0	— 6
AFC	0	7	6	2	— 15

NFC — FG Andersen 25
AFC — Kelly 1 run (Biasucci kick)
NFC — FG Andersen 36
AFC — FG Biasucci 37
AFC — FG Biasucci 30
AFC — Safety, Montana forced out of end zone

1987 AFC-NFC PRO BOWL
Aloha Stadium, Honolulu, Hawaii
February 1, 1987, Attendance: 50,101
AFC 10, NFC 6—The AFC defeated the NFC in the lowest-scoring game in AFC-NFC Pro Bowl history. The AFC took a 10-0 halftime lead on Broncos quarterback

John Elway's 10-yard touchdown pass to Raiders tight end Todd Christensen and Patriots kicker Tony Franklin's 26-yard field goal. The AFC defense made the lead stand by forcing the NFC to settle for a pair of field goals from 38 and 19 yards by Saints kicker Morten Andersen after the NFC had first downs at the AFC 31-, 7-, 16-, 15-, 5-, and 7-yard lines. Both AFC scores were set up by fumble recoveries by Seahawks linebacker Fredd Young and Dolphins linebacker John Offerdahl, respectively. Eagles defensive end Reggie White, who tied a Pro Bowl record with 4 sacks among his 7 solo tackles, was voted the game's outstanding player. The AFC victory cut the NFC's lead in the Pro Bowl series to 10-7.

AFC	7	3	0	0	— 10
NFC	0	0	3	3	— 6

AFC — Christensen 10 pass from Elway (Franklin kick)
AFC — FG Franklin 26
NFC — FG Andersen 38
NFC — FG Andersen 19

1986 AFC-NFC PRO BOWL
Aloha Stadium, Honolulu, Hawaii
February 2, 1986, Attendance: 50,101
NFC 28, AFC 24—New York Giants quarterback Phil Simms brought the NFC back from a 24-7 halftime deficit to defeat the AFC. Simms, who completed 15 of 27 passes for 212 yards and 3 touchdowns, was named the most valuable player of the game. The AFC had taken its first-half lead behind a 2-yard run by Los Angeles Raiders running back Marcus Allen, who also threw a 51-yard scoring pass to San Diego wide receiver Wes Chandler, an 11-yard touchdown catch by Pittsburgh wide receiver Louis Lipps, and a 34-yard field goal by Steelers kicker Gary Anderson. Minnesota's Joey Browner accounted for the NFC's only score before halftime on a 48-yard interception return. After intermission, the NFC blanked the AFC while scoring 3 touchdowns via a 15-yard catch by Washington wide receiver Art Monk, a 2-yard reception by Dallas tight end Doug Cosbie, and a 15-yard catch by Tampa Bay tight end Jimmie Giles with 2:47 remaining in the game. The victory gave the NFC a 10-6 Pro Bowl record against the AFC.

NFC	0	7	7	14	— 28
AFC	7	17	0	0	— 24

AFC — Allen 2 run (Anderson kick)
NFC — Browner 48 interception return (Andersen kick)
AFC — Chandler 51 pass from Allen (Anderson kick)
AFC — FG Anderson 34
AFC — Lipps 11 pass from O'Brien (Anderson kick)
NFC — Monk 15 pass from Simms (Andersen kick)
NFC — Cosbie 2 pass from Simms (Andersen kick)

NFC — Giles 15 pass from Simms (Andersen kick)

1985 AFC-NFC PRO BOWL

Aloha Stadium, Honolulu, Hawaii
January 27, 1985, Attendance: 50,385
AFC 22, NFC 14—Defensive end Art Still of the Kansas City Chiefs recovered a fumble and returned it 83 yards for a touchdown to clinch the AFC's victory over the NFC. Still's touchdown came in the fourth period with the AFC trailing 14-12 and was one of several outstanding defensive plays in a Pro Bowl dominated by two record-breaking defenses. The teams combined for a Pro Bowl-record 17 sacks, including 4 by New York Jets defensive end Mark Gastineau, who was named the game's outstanding player. The AFC's first score came on a safety when Gastineau tackled running back Eric Dickerson of the Los Angeles Rams in the end zone. The AFC's second score, a 6-yard pass from Miami's Dan Marino to Los Angeles Raiders running back Marcus Allen, was set up by a partial block of a punt by Seahawks linebacker Fredd Young. The NFC leads the series 9-6.

AFC	0	9	0	13	—	22
NFC	0	0	7	7	—	14

AFC — Safety, Gastineau tackled Dickerson in end zone
AFC — Allen 6 pass from Marino (Johnson kick)
NFC — Lofton 13 pass from Montana (Stenerud kick)
NFC — Payton 1 run (Stenerud kick)
AFC — FG Johnson 33
AFC — Still 83 fumble recovery return (Johnson kick)
AFC — FG Johnson 22

1984 AFC-NFC PRO BOWL

Aloha Stadium, Honolulu, Hawaii
January 29, 1984, Attendance: 50,445
NFC 45, AFC 3—The NFC won its sixth Pro Bowl in the last seven seasons by routing the AFC. The NFC was led by the passing of most valuable player Joe Theismann of Washington, who completed 21 of 27 passes for 242 yards and 3 touchdowns. Theismann set Pro Bowl records for completions and touchdown passes. The NFC established Pro Bowl marks for most points scored and fewest points allowed. Running back William Andrews of Atlanta had 6 carries for 43 yards and caught 4 passes for 49 yards, including scoring receptions of 16 and 2 yards. Los Angeles Rams rookie Eric Dickerson gained 46 yards on 11 carries, including a 14-yard touchdown run, and had 45 yards on 5 catches. Rams safety Nolan Cromwell had a 44-yard interception return for a touchdown early in the third period to give the NFC a commanding 24-3 lead. Green Bay wide receiver James Lofton caught an 8-yard touchdown pass, while tight end teammate Paul Coffman had a 6-yard scoring catch.

NFC	3	14	14	14	—	45
AFC	0	3	0	0	—	3

NFC — FG Haji-Sheikh 23
NFC — Andrews 16 pass from Theismann (Haji-Sheikh kick)
NFC — Andrews 2 pass from Montana (Haji-Sheikh kick)
AFC — FG Anderson 43
NFC — Cromwell 44 interception return (Haji-Sheikh kick)
NFC — Lofton 8 pass from Theismann (Haji-Sheikh kick)
NFC — Coffman 6 pass from Theismann (Haji-Sheikh kick)
NFC — Dickerson 14 run (Haji-Sheikh kick)

1983 AFC-NFC PRO BOWL

Aloha Stadium, Honolulu, Hawaii
February 6, 1983, Attendance: 49,883
NFC 20, AFC 19—Dallas' Danny White threw an 11-yard touchdown pass to the Packers' John Jefferson with 35 seconds remaining to rally the NFC over the AFC. White, who completed 14 of 26 passes for 162 yards, kept the winning 65-yard drive alive with a 14-yard completion to Jefferson on a fourth-and-7 play at the AFC 25. The AFC was ahead 12-10 at halftime and increased the lead to 19-10 in the third period, when Marcus Allen scored on a 1-yard run. San Diego's Dan Fouts, who attempted 30 passes, set Pro Bowl records for most completions (17) and yards (274). Pittsburgh's John Stallworth was the AFC's leading receiver with 7 catches for 67 yards. William Andrews topped the NFC with 5 receptions for 48 yards. Fouts and Jefferson were co-winners of the player of the game award.

AFC	9	3	7	0	—	19
NFC	0	10	0	10	—	20

AFC — Walker 34 pass from Fouts (Benirschke kick)
AFC — Safety, Still tackled Theismann in end zone
NFC — Andrews 3 run (Moseley kick)
NFC — FG Moseley 35
AFC — FG Benirschke 29
AFC — Allen 1 run (Benirschke kick)
NFC — FG Moseley 41
NFC — Jefferson 11 pass from D. White (Moseley kick)

1982 AFC-NFC PRO BOWL

Aloha Stadium, Honolulu, Hawaii
January 31, 1982, Attendance: 50,402
AFC 16, NFC 13—Nick Lowery of Kansas City kicked a 23-yard field goal with three seconds remaining to give the AFC a last-second victory over the NFC. Lowery's kick climaxed a 69-yard drive directed by quarterback Dan Fouts. The NFC gained a 13-13 tie with 2:43 to go when Dallas' Tony Dorsett ran 4 yards for a touchdown. In the drive to the winning field goal, Fouts completed 3 passes, including a 23-yard toss to San Diego teammate Kellen Winslow that put the ball on the NFC's 5-yard line. Two plays later, Lowery kicked

the field goal. Winslow, who caught 6 passes for 86 yards, was named co-player of the game along with Tampa Bay defensive end Lee Roy Selmon.

NFC	0	6	0	7	—	13
AFC	0	0	13	3	—	16

NFC — Giles 4 pass from Montana (kick blocked)
AFC — Muncie 2 run (kick failed)
AFC — Campbell 1 run (Lowery kick)
NFC — Dorsett 4 run (Septien kick)
AFC — FG Lowery 23

1981 AFC-NFC PRO BOWL

Aloha Stadium, Honolulu, Hawaii
February 1, 1981, Attendance: 50,360
NFC 21, AFC 7—Eddie Murray kicked 4 field goals and Steve Bartkowski fired a 55-yard scoring pass to Alfred Jenkins to lead the NFC to its fourth straight victory over the AFC and a 7-4 edge in the series. Murray was named the game's most valuable player and missed tying Garo Yepremian's Pro Bowl record of 5 field goals when a 37-yard attempt hit the crossbar with 22 seconds left. The AFC's only score came on a 9-yard pass from Brian Sipe to Stanley Morgan. Bartkowski completed 9 of 21 passes for 173 yards, while Sipe connected on 10 of 15 for 142 yards. Ottis Anderson led all rushers with 70 yards on 10 carries. Earl Campbell, the NFL's leading rusher in 1980, was limited to 24 yards on 8 attempts.

AFC	0	7	0	0	—	7
NFC	3	6	0	12	—	21

NFC — FG Murray 31
AFC — Morgan 9 pass from Sipe (J. Smith kick)
NFC — FG Murray 31
NFC — FG Murray 34
NFC — Jenkins 55 pass from Bartkowski (Murray kick)
NFC — FG Murray 36
NFC — Safety, Shell called for holding in end zone

1980 AFC-NFC PRO BOWL

Aloha Stadium, Honolulu, Hawaii
January 27, 1980, Attendance: 49,800
NFC 37, AFC 27—Chuck Muncie ran for 2 touchdowns and threw a 25-yard option pass for another score to give the NFC its third consecutive victory over the AFC. The Saints' Muncie, who was selected the game's most valuable player, snapped a 3-3 tie on a 1-yard touchdown run at 1:41 of the second quarter, then scored on an 11-yard run in the fourth quarter for the NFC's final touchdown. Two scoring records were set in the game—37 points by the NFC, eclipsing the 33 by the AFC in 1973, and the 64 points by both teams, surpassing the 61 scored in 1973.

NFC	3	20	7	7	—	37
AFC	3	7	10	7	—	27

NFC — FG Moseley 37
AFC — FG Fritsch 19
NFC — Muncie 1 run (Moseley kick)

AFC — Pruitt 1 pass from Bradshaw
(Fritsch kick)
NFC — D. Hill 13 pass from Manning
(kick failed)
NFC — T. Hill 25 pass from Muncie
(Moseley kick)
NFC — Henry 86 punt return (Moseley
kick)
AFC — Campbell 2 run (Fritsch kick)
AFC — FG Fritsch 29
NFC — Muncie 11 run (Moseley kick)
AFC — Campbell 1 run (Fritsch kick)

1979 AFC-NFC PRO BOWL

Memorial Coliseum, Los Angeles, CA
January 29, 1979, Attendance: 46,281
NFC 13, AFC 7—Roger Staubach completed 9 of 15 passes for 125 yards, including the winning touchdown on a 19-yard strike to Dallas Cowboys teammate Tony Hill in the third period. The winning drive began at the AFC's 45-yard line after a shanked punt. Staubach hit Ahmad Rashad with passes of 15 and 17 yards to set up Hill's decisive catch. The victory gave the NFC a 5-4 advantage in Pro Bowl games. Rashad, who accounted for 89 yards on 5 receptions, was named the player of the game. The AFC led 7-6 at halftime on Bob Griese's 8-yard scoring toss to Steve Largent late in the second quarter. Largent had 5 receptions for 84 yards. The NFC scored first as Archie Manning marched his team 70 yards in 11 plays, capped by Wilbert Montgomery's 2-yard touchdown run. The AFC's Earl Campbell was the game's leading rusher with 66 yards on 12 carries.

AFC	0	7	0	0	—	7
NFC	0	6	7	0	—	13

NFC — Montgomery 2 run
(kick failed)
AFC — Largent 8 pass from Griese
(Yepremian kick)
NFC — T. Hill 19 pass from Staubach
(Corral kick)

1978 AFC-NFC PRO BOWL

Tampa Stadium, Tampa, Florida
January 23, 1978, Attendance: 51,337
NFC 14, AFC 13—Walter Payton, the NFL's leading rusher in 1977, sparked a second-half comeback to give the NFC the win and tie the series between the two conferences at four victories each. Payton, who was the game's most valuable player, gained 77 yards on 13 carries and scored the tying touchdown on a 1-yard burst with 7:37 left in the game. Efren Herrera kicked the winning extra point. The AFC dominated the first half of the game, taking a 13-0 lead on field goals of 21 and 39 yards by Toni Linhart and a 10-yard touchdown pass from Ken Stabler to Oakland teammate Cliff Branch. On the NFC's first possession of the second half, Pat Haden put together the first touchdown drive after Eddie Brown returned a punt to the AFC 46-yard line. Haden connected on all 4 of his passes on that drive,

finally hitting Terry Metcalf with a 4-yard scoring toss. The NFC continued to rally and, with Jim Hart at quarterback, moved 63 yards in 12 plays for the go-ahead score. During the winning drive, Hart completed 5 of 6 passes for 38 yards and Payton picked up 20 more on the ground.

AFC	3	10	0	0	—	13
NFC	0	0	7	7	—	14

AFC — FG Linhart 21
AFC — Branch 10 pass from Stabler
(Linhart kick)
AFC — FG Linhart 39
NFC — Metcalf 4 pass from Haden
(Herrera kick)
NFC — Payton 1 run (Herrera kick)

1977 AFC-NFC PRO BOWL

Kingdome, Seattle, Washington
January 17, 1977, Attendance: 64,752
AFC 24, NFC 14—O.J. Simpson's 3-yard touchdown burst at 7:03 of the first quarter gave the AFC a lead it would not surrender, breaking a two-game NFC win streak and giving the AFC stars a 4-3 series lead. The AFC took a 17-7 lead midway through the second period on the first of 2 Ken Anderson touchdown passes, a 12-yard toss to Charlie Joiner. But the NFC mounted a 73-yard drive capped by Lawrence McCutcheon's 1-yard touchdown plunge to pull within 17-14 at the half. Following a scoreless third quarter, player of the game Mel Blount thwarted a possible NFC score when he intercepted Jim Hart's pass in the end zone. Less than three minutes later, Blount again picked off a Hart pass. That set up Anderson's 27-yard touchdown strike to Cliff Branch for the final score.

NFC	0	14	0	0	—	14
AFC	10	7	0	7	—	24

AFC — Simpson 3 run (Linhart kick)
AFC — FG Linhart 31
NFC — Thomas 15 run (Bakken kick)
AFC — Joiner 12 pass from Anderson
(Linhart kick)
NFC — McCutcheon 1 run (Bakken
kick)
AFC — Branch 27 pass from Anderson (Linhart kick)

1976 AFC-NFC PRO BOWL

Superdome, New Orleans, Louisiana
January 26, 1976, Attendance: 30,546
NFC 23, AFC 20—Mike Boryla, a late substitute who did not enter the game until 5:39 remained, lifted the National Football Conference to the victory over the American Football Conference with 2 touchdown passes in the final minutes. It was the second straight NFC win, squaring the series at 3-3. Until Boryla started firing the ball the AFC was in control, leading 13-0 at the half. Boryla entered the game after Billy Johnson had raced 90 yards with a punt to give the AFC a 20-9 lead. He floated a 14-yard touchdown pass to Terry Metcalf and later fired an 8-yard scoring pass to Mel Gray for the winner.

AFC	0	13	0	7	—	20
NFC	0	0	9	14	—	23

AFC — FG Stenerud 20
AFC — FG Stenerud 35
AFC — Burrough 64 pass from Pastorini (Stenerud kick)
NFC — FG Bakken 42
NFC — Foreman 4 pass from Hart
(kick blocked)
AFC — Johnson 90 punt return
(Stenerud kick)
NFC — Metcalf 14 pass from Boryla
(Bakken kick)
NFC — Gray 8 pass from Boryla
(Bakken kick)

1975 AFC-NFC PRO BOWL

Orange Bowl, Miami, Florida
January 20, 1975, Attendance: 26,484
NFC 17, AFC 10—Los Angeles quarterback James Harris, who took over the NFC offense after Jim Hart of St. Louis suffered a laceration above his right eye in the second period, threw 2 touchdown passes early in the fourth period to pace the NFC to its second victory in the five-game Pro Bowl series. The NFC win snapped a three-game AFC victory string. Harris, who was named the player of the game, connected with St. Louis' Mel Gray for an 8-yard touchdown 2:03 into the final period. One minute and 24 seconds later, following a fumble recovery by Washington's Ken Houston, Harris tossed another 8-yard scoring pass to Washington's Charley Taylor for the decisive points.

NFC	0	3	0	14	—	17
AFC	0	0	10	0	—	10

NFC — FG Marcol 33
AFC — Warfield 32 pass from Griese
(Gerela kick)
AFC — FG Gerela 33
NFC — Gray 8 pass from J. Harris
(Marcol kick)
NFC — Taylor 8 pass from J. Harris
(Marcol kick)

1974 AFC-NFC PRO BOWL

Arrowhead Stadium, Kansas City, MO
January 20, 1974, Attendance: 66,918
AFC 15, NFC 13—Miami's Garo Yepremian's fifth field goal—a 42-yard kick with 21 seconds remaining—gave the AFC its third straight victory since the NFC won the inaugural game following the 1970 season. The field goal by Yepremian, who was voted the game's outstanding player, offset a 21-yard field goal by Atlanta's Nick Mike-Mayer that had given the NFC a 13-12 advantage with 1:41 remaining. The only touchdown in the game was scored by the NFC on a 14-yard pass from Philadelphia's Roman Gabriel to the Rams' Lawrence McCutcheon.

NFC	0	10	0	3	—	13
AFC	3	3	3	6	—	15

AFC — FG Yepremian 16
NFC — FG Mike-Mayer 27

NFC	—	McCutcheon 14 pass from Gabriel (Mike-Mayer kick)
AFC	—	FG Yepremian 37
AFC	—	FG Yepremian 27
AFC	—	FG Yepremian 41
NFC	—	FG Mike-Mayer 21
AFC	—	FG Yepremian 42

1973 AFC-NFC PRO BOWL

Texas Stadium, Irving, Texas
January 21, 1973, Attendance: 37,091
AFC 33, NFC 28—Paced by the rushing and receiving of player of the game O.J. Simpson, the AFC erased a 14-0 first period deficit and built a commanding 33-14 lead midway through the fourth period before the NFC managed 2 touchdowns in the final minute of play. Simpson rushed for 112 yards and caught 3 passes for 58 more to gain unanimous recognition in the balloting for player of the game. Green Bay Packers running back John Brockington scored 3 touchdowns for the NFC.

AFC	0	10	10	13	—	33
NFC	14	0	0	14	—	28

NFC	—	Brockington 1 run (Marcol kick)
NFC	—	Brockington 3 pass from Kilmer (Marcol kick)
AFC	—	Simpson 7 run (Gerela kick)
AFC	—	FG Gerela 18
AFC	—	FG Gerela 22
AFC	—	Hubbard 11 run (Gerela kick)
AFC	—	O. Taylor 5 pass from Lamonica (kick failed)
AFC	—	Bell 12 interception return (Gerela kick)
NFC	—	Brockington 1 run (Marcol kick)
NFC	—	Kwalick 12 pass from Snead (Marcol kick)

1972 AFC-NFC PRO BOWL

Memorial Coliseum, Los Angeles, CA
January 23, 1972, Attendance: 53,647
AFC 26, NFC 13—Kansas City's Jan Stenerud kicked 4 field goals to lead the AFC from a 6-0 deficit to victory. The AFC defense picked off 3 passes. Stenerud was selected as the outstanding offensive player and his Kansas City teammate, linebacker Willie Lanier, was the game's outstanding defensive player.

AFC	0	3	13	10	—	26
NFC	0	6	0	7	—	13

NFC	—	Grim 50 pass from Landry (kick failed)
AFC	—	FG Stenerud 25
AFC	—	FG Stenerud 23
AFC	—	FG Stenerud 48
AFC	—	Morin 5 pass from Dawson (Stenerud kick)
AFC	—	FG Stenerud 42
NFC	—	V. Washington 2 run (Knight kick)
AFC	—	F. Little 6 run (Stenerud kick)

1971 AFC-NFC PRO BOWL

Memorial Coliseum, Los Angeles, CA
January 24, 1971, Attendance: 48,222
NFC 27, AFC 6—Mel Renfro of Dallas broke open the first meeting between the American Football Conference and National Football Conference all-star teams as he returned a pair of punts 82 and 56 yards for touchdowns in the final period to clinch the NFC victory over the AFC. Renfro was voted the game's outstanding back and linebacker Fred Carr of Green Bay the outstanding lineman.

AFC	0	3	3	0	—	6
NFC	0	3	10	14	—	27

AFC	—	FG Stenerud 37
NFC	—	FG Cox 13
NFC	—	Osborn 23 pass from Brodie (Cox kick)
NFC	—	FG Cox 35
AFC	—	FG Stenerud 16
NFC	—	Renfro 82 punt return (Cox kick)
NFC	—	Renfro 56 punt return (Cox kick)

Includes AFL All-Star Game played after the 1961-69 seasons.

Date	Result/Honored players	Site (attendance)
Jan. 15, 1939	New York Giants 13, Pro All-Stars 10	Wrigley Field, Los Angeles (20,000)
Jan. 14, 1940	Green Bay 16, NFL All-Stars 7	Gilmore Stadium, Los Angeles (18,000)
Dec. 29, 1940	Chicago Bears 28, NFL All-Stars 14	Gilmore Stadium, Los Angeles (21,624)
Jan. 4, 1942	Chicago Bears 35, NFL All-Stars 24	Polo Grounds, New York (17,725)
Dec. 27, 1942	NFL All-Stars 17, Washington 14	Shibe Park, Philadelphia (18,671)
Jan. 14, 1951	American Conf. 28, National Conf. 27	Los Angeles Memorial Coliseum (53,676)
	Otto Graham, Cleveland, player of the game	
Jan. 12, 1952	National Conf. 30, American Conf. 13	Los Angeles Memorial Coliseum (19,400)
	Dan Towler, Los Angeles, player of the game	
Jan. 10, 1953	National Conf. 27, American Conf. 7	Los Angeles Memorial Coliseum (34,208)
	Don Doll, Detroit, player of the game	
Jan. 17, 1954	East 20, West 9	Los Angeles Memorial Coliseum (44,214)
	Chuck Bednarik, Philadelphia, player of the game	
Jan. 16, 1955	West 26, East 19	Los Angeles Memorial Coliseum (43,972)
	Billy Wilson, San Francisco, player of the game	
Jan. 15, 1956	East 31, West 30	Los Angeles Memorial Coliseum (37,867)
	Ollie Matson, Chi. Cardinals, player of the game	
Jan. 13, 1957	West 19, East 10	Los Angeles Memorial Coliseum (44,177)
	Bert Rechichar, Baltimore, outstanding back	
	Ernie Stautner, Pittsburgh, outstanding lineman	
Jan. 12, 1958	West 26, East 7	Los Angeles Memorial Coliseum (66,634)
	Hugh McElhenny, San Francisco, outstanding back	
	Gene Brito, Washington, outstanding lineman	
Jan. 11, 1959	East 28, West 21	Los Angeles Memorial Coliseum (72,250)
	Frank Gifford, N.Y. Giants, outstanding back	
	Doug Atkins, Chi. Bears, outstanding lineman	
Jan. 17, 1960	West 38, East 21	Los Angeles Memorial Coliseum (56,876)
	Johnny Unitas, Baltimore, outstanding back	
	Gene (Big Daddy) Lipscomb, Baltimore, outstanding lineman	
Jan. 15, 1961	West 35, East 31	Los Angeles Memorial Coliseum (62,971)
	Johnny Unitas, Baltimore, outstanding back	
	Sam Huff, N.Y. Giants, outstanding lineman	
Jan. 7, 1962	AFL West 47, East 27	Balboa Stadium, San Diego (20,973)
	Cotton Davidson, Dallas Texans, player of the game	
Jan. 14, 1962	NFL West 31, East 30	Los Angeles Memorial Coliseum (57,409)
	Jim Brown, Cleveland, outstanding back	
	Henry Jordan, Green Bay, outstanding lineman	
Jan. 13, 1963	AFL West 21, East 14	Balboa Stadium, San Diego (27,641)
	Curtis McClinton, Dallas Texans, outstanding offensive player	
	Earl Faison, San Diego, outstanding defensive player	
Jan. 13, 1963	NFL East 30, West 20	Los Angeles Memorial Coliseum (61,374)
	Jim Brown, Cleveland, outstanding back	
	Gene (Big Daddy) Lipscomb, Pittsburgh, outstanding lineman	
Jan. 12, 1964	NFL West 31, East 17	Los Angeles Memorial Coliseum (67,242)
	Johnny Unitas, Baltimore, player of the game	
	Gino Marchetti, Baltimore, outstanding lineman	
Jan. 19, 1964	AFL West 27, East 24	Balboa Stadium, San Diego (20,016)
	Keith Lincoln, San Diego, outstanding offensive player	
	Archie Matsos, Oakland, outstanding defensive player	
Jan. 10, 1965	NFL West 34, East 14	Los Angeles Memorial Coliseum (60,598)
	Fran Tarkenton, Minnesota, outstanding back	
	Terry Barr, Detroit, outstanding lineman	
Jan. 16, 1965	AFL West 38, East 14	Jeppesen Stadium, Houston (15,446)
	Keith Lincoln, San Diego, outstanding offensive player	
	Willie Brown, Denver, outstanding defensive player	
Jan. 15, 1966	AFL All-Stars 30, Buffalo 19	Rice Stadium, Houston (35,572)
	Joe Namath, N.Y. Jets, most valuable player, offense	
	Frank Buncom, San Diego, most valuable player, defense	
Jan. 15, 1966	NFL East 36, West 7	Los Angeles Memorial Coliseum (60,124)
	Jim Brown, Cleveland, outstanding back	
	Dale Meinert, St. Louis, outstanding lineman	
Jan. 21, 1967	AFL East 30, West 23	Oakland-Alameda County Coliseum (18,876)
	Babe Parilli, Boston, outstanding offensive player	
	Verlon Biggs, N.Y. Jets, outstanding defensive player	
Jan. 22, 1967	NFL East 20, West 10	Los Angeles Memorial Coliseum (15,062)
	Gale Sayers, Chicago, outstanding back	
	Floyd Peters, Philadelphia, outstanding lineman	

Jan. 21, 1968 AFL East 25, West 24 ....Gator Bowl, Jacksonville, Fla. (40,103)
    Joe Namath and Don Maynard, N.Y. Jets, out. off. players
    Leslie (Speedy) Duncan, San Diego, out. def. player
Jan. 21, 1968 NFL West 38, East 20 ....Los Angeles Memorial Coliseum (53,289)
    Gale Sayers, Chicago, outstanding back
    Dave Robinson, Green Bay, outstanding lineman
Jan. 19, 1969 AFL West 38, East 25 ....Gator Bowl, Jacksonville, Fla. (41,058)
    Len Dawson, Kansas City, outstanding offensive player
    George Webster, Houston, outstanding defensive player
Jan. 19, 1969 NFL West 10, East 7 ....Los Angeles Memorial Coliseum (32,050)
    Roman Gabriel, Los Angeles, outstanding back
    Merlin Olsen, Los Angeles, outstanding lineman
Jan. 17, 1970 AFL West 26, East 3 ....Astrodome, Houston (30,170)
    John Hadl, San Diego, player of the game
Jan. 18, 1970 NFL West 16, East 13 ....Los Angeles Memorial Coliseum (57,786)
    Gale Sayers, Chicago, outstanding back
    George Andrie, Dallas, outstanding lineman
Jan. 24, 1971 NFC 27, AFC 6 ....Los Angeles Memorial Coliseum (48,222)
    Mel Renfro, Dallas, outstanding back
    Fred Carr, Green Bay, outstanding lineman
Jan. 23, 1972 AFC 26, NFC 13 ....Los Angeles Memorial Coliseum (53,647)
    Jan Stenerud, Kansas City, outstanding offensive player
    Willie Lanier, Kansas City, outstanding defensive player
Jan. 21, 1973 AFC 33, NFC 28 ....Texas Stadium, Irving (37,091)
    O.J. Simpson, Buffalo, player of the game
Jan. 20, 1974 AFC 15, NFC 13 ....Arrowhead Stadium, Kansas City (66,918)
    Garo Yepremian, Miami, player of the game
Jan. 20, 1975 NFC 17, AFC 10 ....Orange Bowl, Miami (26,484)
    James Harris, Los Angeles, player of the game
Jan. 26, 1976 NFC 23, AFC 20 ....Louisiana Superdome, New Orleans (30,546)
    Billy Johnson, Houston, player of the game
Jan. 17, 1977 AFC 24, NFC 14 ....Kingdome, Seattle (64,752)
    Mel Blount, Pittsburgh, player of the game
Jan. 23, 1978 NFC 14, AFC 13 ....Tampa Stadium (51,337)
    Walter Payton, Chicago, player of the game
Jan. 29, 1979 NFC 13, AFC 7 ....Los Angeles Memorial Coliseum (46,281)
    Ahmad Rashad, Minnesota, player of the game
Jan. 27, 1980 NFC 37, AFC 27 ....Aloha Stadium, Honolulu (49,800)
    Chuck Muncie, New Orleans, player of the game
Feb. 1, 1981 NFC 21, AFC 7 ....Aloha Stadium, Honolulu (50,360)
    Eddie Murray, Detroit, player of the game
Jan. 31, 1982 AFC 16, NFC 13 ....Aloha Stadium, Honolulu (50,402)
    Kellen Winslow, San Diego, and Lee Roy Selmon, Tampa Bay, players of the game
Feb. 6, 1983 NFC 20, AFC 19 ....Aloha Stadium, Honolulu (49,883)
    Dan Fouts, San Diego, and John Jefferson, Green Bay, players of the game
Jan. 29, 1984 NFC 45, AFC 3 ....Aloha Stadium, Honolulu (50,445)
    Joe Theismann, Washington, player of the game
Jan. 27, 1985 AFC 22, NFC 14 ....Aloha Stadium, Honolulu (50,385)
    Mark Gastineau, N.Y. Jets, player of the game
Feb. 2, 1986 NFC 28, AFC 24 ....Aloha Stadium, Honolulu (50,101)
    Phil Simms, N.Y. Giants, player of the game
Feb. 1, 1987 AFC 10, NFC 6 ....Aloha Stadium, Honolulu (50,101)
    Reggie White, Philadelphia, player of the game
Feb. 7, 1988 AFC 15, NFC 6 ....Aloha Stadium, Honolulu (50,113)
    Bruce Smith, Buffalo, player of the game
Jan. 29, 1989 NFC 34, AFC 3 ....Aloha Stadium, Honolulu (50,113)
    Randall Cunningham, Philadelphia, player of the game
Feb. 4, 1990 NFC 27, AFC 21 ....Aloha Stadium, Honolulu (50,445)
    Jerry Gray, L.A. Rams, player of the game
Feb. 3, 1991 AFC 23, NFC 21 ....Aloha Stadium, Honolulu (50,345)
    Jim Kelly, Buffalo, player of the game
Feb. 2, 1992 NFC 21, AFC 15 ....Aloha Stadium, Honolulu (50,209)
    Michael Irvin, Dallas, player of the game
Feb. 7, 1993 AFC 23, NFC 20 (OT) ....Aloha Stadium, Honolulu (50,007)
    Steve Tasker, Buffalo, player of the game
Feb. 6, 1994 NFC 17, AFC 3 ....Aloha Stadium, Honolulu (50,026)
    Andre Rison, Atlanta, player of the game
Feb. 5, 1995 AFC 41, NFC 13 ....Aloha Stadium, Honolulu (50,529)
    Marshall Faulk, Indianapolis, player of the game

Feb. 4, 1996   NFC 20, AFC 13..Aloha Stadium, Honolulu (50,034)
       Jerry Rice, San Francisco, player of the game
Feb. 2, 1997   AFC 26, NFC 23 (OT)...Aloha Stadium, Honolulu (50,031)
       Mark Brunell, Jacksonville, player of the game
Feb. 1, 1998   AFC 29, NFC 24...Aloha Stadium, Honolulu (49,995)
       Warren Moon, Seattle, player of the game
Feb. 7, 1999   AFC 23, NFC 10...Aloha Stadium, Honolulu (50,075)
       Keyshawn Johnson, N.Y. Jets and Ty Law, New England, co-players of the game
Feb. 6, 2000   NFC 51, AFC 31...Aloha Stadium, Honolulu (50,112)
       Randy Moss, Minnesota, player of the game
Feb. 4, 2001   AFC 38, NFC 17...Aloha Stadium, Honolulu (50,128)
       Rich Gannon, Oakland, player of the game
Feb. 9, 2002   AFC 38, NFC 30...Aloha Stadium, Honolulu (50,301)
       Rich Gannon, Oakland, player of the game
Feb. 2, 2003   AFC 45, NFC 20...Aloha Stadium, Honolulu (50,125)
       Ricky Williams, Miami, player of the game
Feb. 8, 2004   NFC 55, AFC 52...Aloha Stadium, Honolulu (50,127)
       Marc Bulger, St. Louis, player of the game
Feb. 13, 2005   AFC 38, NFC 27...Aloha Stadium, Honolulu (50,225)
       Peyton Manning, Indianapolis, player of the game
Feb. 12, 2006   NFC 23, AFC 17...Aloha Stadium, Honolulu (50,190)
       Derrick Brooks, Tampa Bay, player of the game

Compiled by Elias Sports Bureau
*NFL record.

MONDAY NIGHT RECORDS

SCORING
TOUCHDOWNS
Most Touchdowns, Career
- 36   Jerry Rice, San Francisco, 1985-2000; Oakland, 2001-04; Seattle 2004
- 24   Emmitt Smith, Dallas, 1990-2002; Arizona 2003-04
- 19   Marcus Allen, L.A. Raiders, 1982-1992; Kansas City, 1993-97

Most Touchdowns, Game
- 4   Ron Johnson, N.Y. Giants at Philadelphia, Oct. 2, 1972
-     Earl Campbell, Houston vs. Miami, Nov. 20, 1978
-     Marcus Allen, L.A. Raiders vs. San Diego, Sept. 24, 1984
-     Eric Dickerson, Indianapolis vs. Denver, Oct. 31, 1988
-     Emmitt Smith, Dallas at N.Y. Giants, Sept. 4, 1995
-     Marshall Faulk, St. Louis at Tampa Bay, Dec. 18, 2000

FIELD GOALS
Most Field Goals, Career
- 51   Gary Anderson, Pittsburgh, 1982-1994; Philadelphia, 1995-96; San Francisco, 1997; Minnesota, 1998-2002; Tennessee, 2003-04
- 41   Jason Elam, Denver, 1993-2005
- 34   Morten Andersen, New Orleans 1982-1994; Atlanta, 1995-2000; N.Y. Giants, 2001; Kansas City, 2002-03; Minnesota, 2004

Most Field Goals, Game
- 7   Chris Boniol, Dallas vs. Green Bay, Nov. 18, 1996* Billy Cundiff, Dallas at N.Y. Giants, Sept. 15, 2003 (OT)*
- 5   Tim Mazzetti, Atlanta vs. Los Angeles, Oct. 30, 1978
-     Roger Ruzek, Dallas at L.A. Rams, Dec. 21, 1987
-     Rich Karlis, Minnesota vs. Cincinnati, Dec. 25, 1989
-     Nick Lowery, Kansas City vs. Denver, Sept. 20, 1993
-     Chris Jacke, Green Bay vs. San Francisco, Oct. 14, 1996 (OT)
-     Richie Cunningham, Dallas vs. Philadelphia, Sept. 15, 1997

RUSHING
YARDS GAINED
Most Yards Gained, Career
- 2,434   Emmitt Smith, Dallas, 1990-2002; Arizona, 2003-04
- 1,897   Tony Dorsett, Dallas, 1977-1987; Denver, 1988
- 1,769   Thurman Thomas, Buffalo, 1988-1999; Miami, 2000

Most Yards Gained, Game
- 221   Bo Jackson, L.A. Raiders at Seattle, Nov. 30, 1987
- 216   Ricky Williams, Miami vs. Chicago, Dec. 9, 2002
- 214   Thurman Thomas, Buffalo at N.Y. Jets, Sept. 24, 1990

Longest Run From Scrimage, Game
- 99   Tony Dorsett, Dallas at Minnesota, Jan. 3, 1983 (TD)*
- 91   Bo Jackson, L.A. Raiders at Seattle, Nov. 30, 1987 (TD)
- 83   James Lofton, Green Bay at N.Y. Giants, Sept. 20, 1982 (TD)

TOUCHDOWNS
Most Rushing Touchdowns, Career
- 23   Emmitt Smith, Dallas, 1990-2002; Arizona 2003-04
- 17   Marcus Allen, L.A. Raiders, 1982-1992; Kansas City, 1993-97
- 14   Eric Dickerson, L.A. Rams, 1983-87; Indianapolis, 1987-1991; L.A. Raiders, 1992; Atlanta, 1993

Most Rushing Touchdowns, Game
- 4   Earl Campbell, Houston vs. Miami, Nov. 20, 1978
-     Eric Dickerson, Indianapolis vs. Denver, Oct. 31, 1988
-     Emmitt Smith, Dallas at N.Y. Giants, Sept. 4, 1995

PASSING
YARDS GAINED
Most Yards Gained, Career
- 9,654   Dan Marino, Miami, 1983-1999
- 7,076   Brett Favre, Atlanta, 1991; Green Bay, 1992-2005
- 5,148   Joe Montana, San Francisco, 1979-1992; Kansas City, 1993-94

Most Yards Gained, Game
- 458   Joe Montana, San Francisco at L.A. Rams, Dec. 11, 1989
- 448   Marc Bulger, St. Louis at Green Bay, Nov. 29, 2004
- 447   Ken Anderson, Cincinnati vs. Buffalo, Nov. 17, 1975

Longest Pass Play
- 99   Brett Favre to Robert Brooks, Green Bay at Chicago, Sept. 11, 1995 (TD)*
- 97   Bernie Kosar to Webster Slaughter, Cleveland vs. Chicago, Oct. 23, 1989 (TD)
- 95   Joe Montana to John Taylor, San Francisco at L.A. Rams, Dec. 11, 1989 (TD)

TOUCHDOWNS
Most Touchdown Passes, Career
- 74   Dan Marino, Miami, 1983-1999
- 54   Brett Favre, Atlanta, 1991; Green Bay, 1992-2005
- 42   Steve Young, Tampa Bay, 1985-86; San Francisco, 1987-1999

Most Touchdown Passes, Game
- 5   Dave Krieg, Seattle vs. L.A. Raiders, Nov. 28, 1988
-     Jim Kelly, Buffalo vs. Cincinnati, Oct. 21, 1991
-     Vinny Testaverde, N.Y. Jets vs. Miami, Oct. 23, 2000 (OT)

RECEIVING
PASS RECEPTIONS
Most Pass Receptions, Career
- 254   Jerry Rice, San Francisco, 1985-2000; Oakland, 2001-04; Seattle, 2004
- 124   Andre Reed, Buffalo, 1985-1999; Washington, 2000
- 123   Cris Carter, Philadelphia, 1987-89; Minnesota, 1990-2001; Miami, 2002

Most Pass Receptions, Game
- 14   Herman Moore, Detroit vs. Chicago, Dec. 4, 1995
-     Jerry Rice, San Francisco vs. Minnesota, Dec. 18, 1995
- 13   Andre Reed, Buffalo vs. Denver, Sept. 18, 1989
-     Terrell Owens, San Francisco vs. Philadelphia, Nov. 25, 2002

YARDS GAINED
Most Yards Gained, Career
- 4,029   Jerry Rice, San Francisco, 1985-2000; Oakland, 2001-04; Seattle, 2004
- 1,783   Andre Reed, Buffalo, 1985-1999; Washington, 2000
- 1,537   Art Monk, Washington, 1980-1993; N.Y. Jets, 1994; Philadelphia, 1995

Most Yards Gained, Game
- 289   Jerry Rice, San Francisco vs. Minnesota, Dec. 18, 1995
- 286   John Taylor, San Francisco at L.A. Rams, Dec. 11, 1989
- 260   Wes Chandler, San Diego vs. Cincinnati, Dec. 20, 1982

TOUCHDOWNS
Most Receiving Touchdowns, Career
- 34   Jerry Rice, San Francisco, 1985-2000; Oakland, 2001-04; Seattle, 2004
- 15   Mark Clayton, Miami, 1983-1992; Green Bay, 1993 Terrell Owens, San Francisco, 1996-2003; Philadelphia, 2004-05
- 13   Andre Reed, Buffalo, 1985-1999; Washington, 2000

Most Receiving Touchdowns, Game
- 3   Ron Johnson, N.Y. Giants at Philadelphia, Oct. 2, 1972
  - Wesley Walker, N.Y. Jets at Detroit, Dec. 6, 1982
  - Steve Largent, Seattle at San Diego, Oct. 29, 1984
  - Mark Clayton, Miami vs. Dallas, Dec. 17, 1984
  - Jerry Rice, San Francisco vs. Chicago, Dec. 14, 1987
  - Jerry Rice, San Francisco vs. Minnesota, Dec. 18, 1995
  - Lamar Thomas, Miami vs. Denver, Dec. 21, 1998
  - Ed McCaffrey, Denver vs. Miami, Sept. 13, 1999
  - Randy Moss, Minnesota vs. N.Y. Giants, Nov. 19, 2001
  - Isaac Bruce, St. Louis at New Orleans, Dec. 17, 2001
  - Terrell Owens, Philadelphia at Dallas, Nov. 15, 2004
  - Drew Bennett, Tennessee vs. Kansas City, Dec. 13, 2004

YARDS FROM SCRIMMAGE
Most Scrimmage Yards, Career
- 4,116   Jerry Rice, San Francisco, 1985-2000; Oakland, 2001-04; Seattle, 2004
- 2,836   Emmitt Smith, Dallas, 1990-2002; Arizona, 2003-04
- 2,567   Tony Dorsett, Dallas, 1977-1987; Denver, 1988

INTERCEPTIONS BY
Most Interceptions, Career
- 11   Everson Walls, Dallas, 1981-89; N.Y. Giants, 1990-92; Cleveland, 1992-93
- 9   Merton Hanks, San Francisco, 1991-98; Seattle, 1999
- 8   Emmitt Thomas, Kansas City, 1966-1978

Most Interceptions, Game
- 4   Dick Anderson, Miami vs. Pittsburgh, Dec. 3, 1973*
- 3   Johnny Robinson, Kansas City at Baltimore, Sept. 28, 1970
  - Charlie Babb, Miami vs. Oakland, Sept. 22, 1975
  - Charles Phillips, Oakland vs. Denver, Dec. 8, 1975
  - Mark Murphy, Washington at San Diego, Oct. 31, 1983
  - Ken Easley, Seattle at San Diego, Oct. 29, 1984
  - Dwayne Harper, San Diego vs. Oakland, Nov. 27, 1995
  - Marcus Coleman, N.Y. Jets vs. Miami, Oct. 23, 2000 (OT)

Longest Interception Return
- 102   Eddie Anderson, L.A. Raiders at Miami, Dec. 14, 1992 (TD)
- 101   Lito Sheppard, Philadelphia at Dallas, Nov. 15, 2004 (TD)
- 98   Marcus Coleman, N.Y. Jets vs. Miami, Dec. 27, 1999 (TD)
  - Rod Woodson, Oakland at Denver, Nov. 11, 2002 (TD)

SACKS
Most Sacks, Career
- 24.5   Bruce Smith, Buffalo, 1985-1999; Washington, 2000-03
- 20.0   Richard Dent, Chicago, 1983-1993, 1995; San Francisco, 1994; Indianapolis, 1996; Philadelphia, 1997
- 18.0   Kevin Greene, L.A. Rams, 1985-1992; Pittsburgh, 1993-95; Carolina, 1996, 1998-99; San Francisco, 1997

PUNTING
Highest Punt Average, Career (Minimum: 25 Punts)
- 47.3   Shane Lechler, Oakland, 2000-05
- 45.2   Hunter Smith, Indianapolis, 1999-2005
- 44.5   Tom Tupa, Phoenix, 1988-1991; Indianapolis, 1992; Cleveland, 1994-95; New England, 1996-98; N.Y. Jets, 1999-2001; Tampa Bay, 2002-03; Washington, 2004

Longest Punt
- 90   Rodney Williams, N.Y. Giants at Denver, Sept. 10, 2001
- 83   Bryan Barker, Jacksonville vs. N.Y. Jets, Oct. 11, 1999
- 74   Craig Colquitt, Pittsburgh vs. Oakland, Dec. 7, 1981

PUNT RETURNS
Longest Punt Return
- 95   John Taylor, San Francisco vs. Washington, Nov. 21, 1988 (TD)
- 94   Dennis McKinnon, Chicago vs. N.Y. Giants, Sept. 14, 1987 (TD)
- 91   JoJo Townsell, N.Y. Jets vs. Seattle, Nov. 9, 1987 (TD)
  - Nate Burleson, Minnesota at Indianapolis, Nov. 8, 2004 (TD)

KICKOFF RETURNS
Longest Kickoff Return
- 105   Terry Fair, Detroit vs. Tampa Bay, Sept. 28, 1998 (TD)
- 102   Harold Hart, Oakland at Miami, Sept. 22, 1975 (TD)
- 101   Roell Preston, Green Bay vs. Minnesota, Oct. 5, 1998 (TD)

FUMBLES
Longest Fumble Return
- 99   Don Griffin, San Francisco vs. Chicago, Dec. 23, 1991 (TD)
- 96   Joe Lavender, Philadelphia vs. Dallas, Sept. 23, 1974 (TD)
- 93   Adam Archuleta, St. Louis vs. Tampa Bay, Oct. 18, 2004 (TD)

MONDAY NIGHT FOOTBALL, 1970-2005

(Home Team in capitals, games listed in chronological order.)

2005
ATLANTA 14, Philadelphia 10
New York Giants 27, NEW ORLEANS 10
Washington 14, DALLAS 13
DENVER 30, Kansas City 10
CAROLINA 32, Green Bay 29
Pittsburgh 24, SAN DIEGO 22
INDIANAPOLIS 45, St. Louis 28
ATLANTA 27, New York Jets 14
PITTSBURGH 20, Baltimore 19
Indianapolis 40, NEW ENGLAND 21
Dallas 21, PHILADELPHIA 20
Minnesota 20, GREEN BAY 17
INDIANAPOLIS 26, Pittsburgh 7
Seattle 42, PHILADELPHIA 0
ATLANTA 36, New Orleans 17
BALTIMORE 48, Green Bay 3
New England 31, NEW YORK JETS 21

2004
Green Bay 24, CAROLINA 14
PHILADELPHIA 27, Minnesota 16
Dallas 21, WASHINGTON 18
Kansas City 27, BALTIMORE 24
Tennessee 48, GREEN BAY 27
ST. LOUIS 28, Tampa Bay 21
CINCINNATI 23, Denver 10
NEW YORK JETS 41, Miami 14
INDIANAPOLIS 31, Minnesota 28
Philadelphia 49, DALLAS 21
New England 27, KANSAS CITY 19
GREEN BAY 45, St. Louis 17
Dallas 43, SEATTLE 39
Kansas City 49, TENNESSEE 38
MIAMI 29, New England 28
ST. LOUIS 20, Philadelphia 7

2003
Tampa Bay 17, Philadelphia 0
Dallas 35, NEW YORK GIANTS 32 (OT)
DENVER 31, Oakland 10
Green Bay 38, CHICAGO 23
Indianapolis 38, TAMPA BAY 35 (OT)
ST. LOUIS 36, Atlanta 0
Kansas City 17, OAKLAND 10
Miami 26, SAN DIEGO 10
New England 30, DENVER 26
Philadelphia 17, GREEN BAY 14
SAN FRANCISCO 30, Pittsburgh 14
TAMPA BAY 19, New York Giants 13
NEW YORK JETS 24, Tennessee 17
St. Louis 26, CLEVELAND 20
Philadelphia 34, MIAMI 27
Green Bay 41, OAKLAND 7

2002
NEW ENGLAND 30, Pittsburgh 14
Philadelphia 37, WASHINGTON 7
TAMPA BAY 26, St. Louis 14
BALTIMORE 34, Denver 23
Green Bay 34, CHICAGO 21
San Francisco 28, SEATTLE 21
PITTSBURGH 28, Indianapolis 10
PHILADELPHIA 17, New York Giants 3
GREEN BAY 24, Miami 10
Oakland 34, DENVER 10
ST. LOUIS 21, Chicago 16
Philadelphia 38, SAN FRANCISCO 17
OAKLAND 26, New York Jets 20
MIAMI 27, Chicago 9
TENNESSEE 24, New England 7
Pittsburgh 17, TAMPA BAY 7
ST. LOUIS 31, San Francisco 20

2001
DENVER 31, New York Giants 20
GREEN BAY 37, Washington 0
San Francisco 19, NEW YORK JETS 17
St. Louis 35, DETROIT 0
DALLAS 9, Washington 7
Philadelphia 10, NEW YORK GIANTS 9
PITTSBURGH 34, Tennessee 7
OAKLAND 38, Denver 28
Baltimore 16, TENNESSEE 10
MINNESOTA 28, New York Giants 16
Tampa Bay 24, ST. LOUIS 17
Green Bay 28, JACKSONVILLE 21
MIAMI 41, Indianapolis 6
St. Louis 34, NEW ORLEANS 21
BALTIMORE 19, Minnesota 3

2000
ST. LOUIS 41, Denver 36
NEW YORK JETS 20, New England 19
Dallas 27, WASHINGTON 21
INDIANAPOLIS 43, Jacksonville 14
KANSAS CITY 24, Seattle 17
MINNESOTA 30, Tampa Bay 23
TENNESSEE 27, Jacksonville 13
NEW YORK JETS 40, Miami 37 (OT)
Tennessee 27, WASHINGTON 21
GREEN BAY 26, Minnesota 20 (OT)
DENVER 27, Oakland 24
Washington 33, ST. LOUIS 20
CAROLINA 31, Green Bay 14
NEW ENGLAND 30, Kansas City 24
INDIANAPOLIS 44, Buffalo 20
TAMPA BAY 38, St. Louis 35
TENNESSEE 31, Dallas 0

1999
Miami 38, DENVER 21
DALLAS 24, Atlanta 7
San Francisco 24, ARIZONA 10
Buffalo 23, MIAMI 18
Jacksonville 16, NEW YORK JETS 6
NEW YORK GIANTS 13, Dallas 10
PITTSBURGH 13, Atlanta 9
Seattle 27, GREEN BAY 7
MINNESOTA 27, Dallas 17
New York Jets 24, NEW ENGLAND 17
DENVER 27, Oakland 21 (OT)
Green Bay 20, SAN FRANCISCO 3
TAMPA BAY 24, Minnesota 17
JACKSONVILLE 27, Denver 24
MINNESOTA 24, Green Bay 20
New York Jets 38, MIAMI 31
ATLANTA 34, San Francisco 29

1998
DENVER 27, New England 21
San Francisco 45, WASHINGTON 10
Dallas 31, NEW YORK GIANTS 7
DETROIT 27, Tampa Bay 6
Minnesota 37, GREEN BAY 24
JACKSONVILLE 28, Miami 21
New York Jets 24, NEW ENGLAND 14
Pittsburgh 20, KANSAS CITY 13
Dallas 34, PHILADELPHIA 0
PITTSBURGH 27, Green Bay 20
Denver 30, KANSAS CITY 7
NEW ENGLAND 26, Miami 23
SAN FRANCISCO 31, New York Giants 7
TAMPA BAY 24, Green Bay 22
SAN FRANCISCO 35, Detroit 13
MIAMI 31, Denver 21
JACKSONVILLE 21, Pittsburgh 3

1997
GREEN BAY 38, Chicago 24
Kansas City 28, OAKLAND 27
DALLAS 21, Philadelphia 20
JACKSONVILLE 30, Pittsburgh 21
San Francisco 34, CAROLINA 21
DENVER 34, New England 13
WASHINGTON 21, Dallas 16
Buffalo 9, INDIANAPOLIS 6
Green Bay 28, NEW ENGLAND 10
Chicago 36, MIAMI 33 (OT)
KANSAS CITY 13, Pittsburgh 10
San Francisco 24, PHILADELPHIA 12
MIAMI 30, Buffalo 13
DENVER 31, Oakland 3
Green Bay 27, MINNESOTA 11
Carolina 23, DALLAS 13
SAN FRANCISCO 34, Denver 17
New England 14, MIAMI 12

1996
CHICAGO 22, Dallas 6
GREEN BAY 39, Philadelphia 13
PITTSBURGH 24, Buffalo 6
INDIANAPOLIS 10, Miami 6
Dallas 23, PHILADELPHIA 19
Pittsburgh 17, KANSAS CITY 7
GREEN BAY 23, San Francisco 20 (OT)
Oakland 23, SAN DIEGO 14
Chicago 15, MINNESOTA 13
Denver 22, OAKLAND 21
SAN DIEGO 27, Detroit 21
DALLAS 21, Green Bay 6
Pittsburgh 24, MIAMI 17
San Francisco 34, ATLANTA 10
OAKLAND 26, Kansas City 7
MIAMI 16, Buffalo 14
SAN FRANCISCO 24, Detroit 14

1995
Dallas 35, NEW YORK GIANTS 0
Green Bay 27, CHICAGO 24
MIAMI 23, Pittsburgh 10
DETROIT 27, San Francisco 24
Buffalo 22, CLEVELAND 19
KANSAS CITY 29, San Diego 23 (OT)
DENVER 27, Oakland 0
NEW ENGLAND 27, Buffalo 14
Chicago 14, MINNESOTA 6
DALLAS 34, Philadelphia 12
PITTSBURGH 20, Cleveland 3
San Francisco 44, MIAMI 20
SAN DIEGO 12, Oakland 6
DETROIT 27, Chicago 7
MIAMI 13, Kansas City 6
SAN FRANCISCO 37, Minnesota 30
Dallas 37, ARIZONA 13

1994
SAN FRANCISCO 44, L.A. Raiders 14
PHILADELPHIA 30, Chicago 22
Detroit 20, DALLAS 17 (OT)
BUFFALO 27, Denver 20
PITTSBURGH 30, Houston 14
Minnesota 27, NEW YORK GIANTS 10
Kansas City 31, DENVER 28
PHILADELPHIA 21, Houston 6
Green Bay 33, CHICAGO 6
DALLAS 38, New York Giants 10
PITTSBURGH 23, Buffalo 10
New York Giants 13, HOUSTON 10
San Francisco 35, NEW ORLEANS 14
L.A. Raiders 24, SAN DIEGO 17
MIAMI 45, Kansas City 28
Dallas 24, NEW ORLEANS 16
MINNESOTA 21, San Francisco 14

1993
WASHINGTON 35, Dallas 16
CLEVELAND 23, San Francisco 13
KANSAS CITY 15, Denver 7
Pittsburgh 45, ATLANTA 17
MIAMI 17, Washington 10
BUFFALO 35, Houston 7
L.A. Raiders 23, DENVER 20
Minnesota 19, CHICAGO 12
BUFFALO 24, Washington 10
KANSAS CITY 23, Green Bay 16
PITTSBURGH 23, Buffalo 0
SAN FRANCISCO 42, New Orleans 7
San Diego 31, INDIANAPOLIS 0
DALLAS 23, Philadelphia 17
Pittsburgh 21, MIAMI 20
New York Giants 24, NEW ORLEANS 14
SAN DIEGO 45, Miami 20
Philadelphia 37, SAN FRANCISCO 34 (OT)

1992
DALLAS 23, Washington 10
Miami 27, CLEVELAND 23
New York Giants 27, CHICAGO 14
KANSAS CITY 27, L.A. Raiders 7
PHILADELPHIA 31, Dallas 7
WASHINGTON 34, Denver 3
PITTSBURGH 20, Cincinnati 0
Buffalo 24, NEW YORK JETS 20
Minnesota 38, CHICAGO 10
San Francisco 41, ATLANTA 3
Buffalo 26, MIAMI 20
NEW ORLEANS 20, Washington 3
SEATTLE 16, Denver 13 (OT)
HOUSTON 24, Chicago 7
MIAMI 20, L.A. Raiders 7
Dallas 41, ATLANTA 17
SAN FRANCISCO 24, Detroit 6

1991
NEW YORK GIANTS 16, San Francisco 14
Washington 33, DALLAS 31
HOUSTON 17, Kansas City 7
CHICAGO 19, New York Jets 13 (OT)
WASHINGTON 23, Philadelphia 0
KANSAS CITY 33, Buffalo 6
New York Giants 23, PITTSBURGH 20
BUFFALO 35, Cincinnati 16
KANSAS CITY 24, L.A. Raiders 21
PHILADELPHIA 30, New York Giants 7
Chicago 34, MINNESOTA 17
Buffalo 41, MIAMI 27
San Francisco 33, L.A. RAMS 10
Philadelphia 13, HOUSTON 6
MIAMI 37, Cincinnati 13
NEW ORLEANS 27, L.A. Raiders 0
SAN FRANCISCO 52, Chicago 14

1990
San Francisco 13, NEW ORLEANS 12
DENVER 24, Kansas City 23
Buffalo 30, NEW YORK JETS 7
SEATTLE 31, Cincinnati 16
Cleveland 30, DENVER 29
PHILADELPHIA 32, Minnesota 24
Cincinnati 34, CLEVELAND 13
PITTSBURGH 41, L.A. Rams 10
New York Giants 24, INDIANAPOLIS 7
PHILADELPHIA 28, Washington 14
L.A. Raiders 13, MIAMI 10
HOUSTON 27, Buffalo 24
SAN FRANCISCO 7, New York Giants 3
L.A. Raiders 38, DETROIT 31
San Francisco 26, L.A. RAMS 10
NEW ORLEANS 20, L.A. Rams 17

1989
New York Giants 27, WASHINGTON 24
Denver 28, BUFFALO 14
CINCINNATI 21, Cleveland 14
CHICAGO 27, Philadelphia 13
L.A. Raiders 14, NEW YORK JETS 7
BUFFALO 23, L.A. Rams 20
CLEVELAND 27, Chicago 7
NEW YORK GIANTS 24, Minnesota 14
SAN FRANCISCO 31, New Orleans 13
HOUSTON 26, Cincinnati 24
Denver 14, WASHINGTON 10
SAN FRANCISCO 34, New York Giants 24
SEATTLE 17, Buffalo 16
San Francisco 30, L.A. RAMS 27
NEW ORLEANS 30, Philadelphia 20
MINNESOTA 29, Cincinnati 21

1988
NEW YORK GIANTS 27, Washington 20
Dallas 17, PHOENIX 14
CLEVELAND 23, Indianapolis 17
L.A. Raiders 30, DENVER 27 (OT)
NEW ORLEANS 20, Dallas 17
PHILADELPHIA 24, New York Giants 13
Buffalo 37, NEW YORK JETS 14
CHICAGO 10, San Francisco 9
INDIANAPOLIS 55, Denver 23
HOUSTON 24, Cleveland 17
Buffalo 31, MIAMI 6
SAN FRANCISCO 37, Washington 21
SEATTLE 35, L.A. Raiders 27
L.A. RAMS 23, Chicago 3
MIAMI 38, Cleveland 31
MINNESOTA 28, Chicago 27

1987

CHICAGO 34, New York Giants 19
NEW YORK JETS 43, New England 24
San Francisco 41, NEW YORK GIANTS 21
DENVER 30, L.A. Raiders 14
Washington 13, DALLAS 7
CLEVELAND 30, L.A. Rams 17
MINNESOTA 34, Denver 27
DALLAS 33, New York Giants 24
NEW YORK JETS 30, Seattle 14
DENVER 31, Chicago 29
L.A. Rams 30, WASHINGTON 26
L.A. Raiders 37, SEATTLE 14
MIAMI 37, New York Jets 28
SAN FRANCISCO 41, Chicago 0
Dallas 29, L.A. RAMS 21
New England 24, MIAMI 10

1986

DALLAS 31, New York Giants 28
Denver 21, PITTSBURGH 10
Chicago 25, GREEN BAY 12
Dallas 31, ST. LOUIS 7
SEATTLE 33, San Diego 7
CINCINNATI 24, Pittsburgh 22
NEW YORK JETS 22, Denver 10
NEW YORK GIANTS 27, Washington 20
L.A. Rams 20, CHICAGO 17
CLEVELAND 26, Miami 16
WASHINGTON 14, San Francisco 6
MIAMI 45, New York Jets 3
New York Giants 21, SAN FRANCISCO 17
SEATTLE 37, L.A. Raiders 0
Chicago 16, DETROIT 13
New England 34, MIAMI 27

1985

DALLAS 44, Washington 14
CLEVELAND 17, Pittsburgh 7
L.A. Rams 35, SEATTLE 24
Cincinnati 37, PITTSBURGH 24
WASHINGTON 27, St. Louis 10
NEW YORK JETS 23, Miami 7
CHICAGO 23, Green Bay 7
L.A. RAIDERS 34, San Diego 21
ST. LOUIS 21, Dallas 10
DENVER 17, San Francisco 16
WASHINGTON 23, New York Giants 21
SAN FRANCISCO 19, Seattle 6
MIAMI 38, Chicago 24
L.A. Rams 27, SAN FRANCISCO 20
MIAMI 30, New England 27
L.A. Raiders 16, L.A. RAMS 6

1984

Dallas 20, L.A. RAMS 13
SAN FRANCISCO 37, Washington 31
Miami 21, BUFFALO 17
L.A. RAIDERS 33, San Diego 30
PITTSBURGH 38, Cincinnati 17
San Francisco 31, NEW YORK GIANTS 10
DENVER 17, Green Bay 14
L.A. Rams 24, ATLANTA 10
Seattle 24, SAN DIEGO 0
WASHINGTON 27, Atlanta 14
SEATTLE 17, L.A. Raiders 14
NEW ORLEANS 27, Pittsburgh 24
MIAMI 28, New York Jets 17
SAN DIEGO 20, Chicago 7
L.A. Raiders 24, DETROIT 3
MIAMI 28, Dallas 21

1983

Dallas 31, WASHINGTON 30
San Diego 17, KANSAS CITY 14
L.A. RAIDERS 27, Miami 14
NEW YORK GIANTS 27, Green Bay 3
New York Jets 34, BUFFALO 10
Pittsburgh 24, CINCINNATI 14
GREEN BAY 48, Washington 47
ST. LOUIS 20, NEW YORK Giants 20 (OT)
Washington 27, SAN DIEGO 24
DETROIT 15, New York Giants 9
L.A. Rams 36, ATLANTA 13
New York Jets 31, NEW ORLEANS 28
MIAMI 38, Cincinnati 14
DETROIT 13, Minnesota 2
Green Bay 12, TAMPA BAY 9 (OT)
SAN FRANCISCO 42, Dallas 17

1982

Pittsburgh 36, DALLAS 28
Green Bay 27, NEW YORK GIANTS 19
L.A. RAIDERS 28, San Diego 24
TAMPA BAY 23, Miami 17
New York Jets 28, DETROIT 13
Dallas 37, HOUSTON 7
SAN DIEGO 50, Cincinnati 34
MIAMI 27, Buffalo 10
MINNESOTA 31, Dallas 27

1981

San Diego 44, CLEVELAND 14
Oakland 36, MINNESOTA 10
Dallas 35, NEW ENGLAND 21
Los Angeles 24, CHICAGO 7
PHILADELPHIA 16, Atlanta 13
BUFFALO 31, Miami 21
DETROIT 48, Chicago 17
PITTSBURGH 26, Houston 13
DENVER 19, Minnesota 17
DALLAS 27, Buffalo 14
SEATTLE 44, San Diego 23
ATLANTA 31, Minnesota 30
MIAMI 13, Philadelphia 10
OAKLAND 30, Pittsburgh 27
LOS ANGELES 21, Atlanta 16
SAN DIEGO 23, Oakland 10

1980

Dallas 17, WASHINGTON 3
Houston 16, CLEVELAND 7
PHILADELPHIA 35, New York Giants 3
NEW ENGLAND 23, Denver 14
CHICAGO 23, Tampa Bay 0
DENVER 20, Washington 17
Oakland 45, PITTSBURGH 34
NEW YORK JETS 17, Miami 14
CLEVELAND 27, Chicago 21
HOUSTON 38, New England 34
Oakland 19, SEATTLE 17
Los Angeles 27, NEW ORLEANS 7
OAKLAND 9, Denver 3
MIAMI 16, New England 13 (OT)
LOS ANGELES 38, Dallas 14
SAN DIEGO 26, Pittsburgh 17

1979

Pittsburgh 16, NEW ENGLAND 13 (OT)
Atlanta 14, PHILADELPHIA 10
WASHINGTON 27, New York Giants 0
CLEVELAND 26, Dallas 7
GREEN BAY 27, New England 14
OAKLAND 13, Miami 3
NEW YORK JETS 14, Minnesota 7
PITTSBURGH 42, Denver 7
Seattle 31, ATLANTA 28
Houston 9, MIAMI 6
Philadelphia 31, DALLAS 21
LOS ANGELES 20, Atlanta 14
SEATTLE 30, New York Jets 7
Oakland 42, NEW ORLEANS 35
HOUSTON 20, Pittsburgh 17
SAN DIEGO 17, Denver 7

1978

DALLAS 38, Baltimore 0
MINNESOTA 12, Denver 9 (OT)
Baltimore 34, NEW ENGLAND 27
Minnesota 24, CHICAGO 20
WASHINGTON 9, Dallas 5
MIAMI 21, Cincinnati 0
DENVER 16, Chicago 7
Houston 24, PITTSBURGH 17
ATLANTA 15, Los Angeles 7
BALTIMORE 21, Washington 17
Oakland 34, CINCINNATI 21
HOUSTON 35, Miami 30
Pittsburgh 24, SAN FRANCISCO 7
SAN DIEGO 40, Chicago 7
Cincinnati 20, LOS ANGELES 19
MIAMI 23, New England 3

1977

PITTSBURGH 27, San Francisco 0
CLEVELAND 30, New England 27 (OT)
Oakland 37, KANSAS CITY 28
CHICAGO 24, Los Angeles 23
PITTSBURGH 20, Cincinnati 14
LOS ANGELES 35, Minnesota 3
ST. LOUIS 28, New York Giants 0
BALTIMORE 10, Washington 3
St. Louis 24, DALLAS 17
WASHINGTON 10, Green Bay 9
OAKLAND 34, Buffalo 13
MIAMI 17, Baltimore 6
Dallas 42, SAN FRANCISCO 35

1976
Miami 30, BUFFALO 21
Oakland 24, KANSAS CITY 21
Washington 20, PHILADELPHIA 17 (OT)
MINNESOTA 17, Pittsburgh 6
San Francisco 16, LOS ANGELES 0
NEW ENGLAND 41, New York Jets 7
WASHINGTON 20, St. Louis 10
BALTIMORE 38, Houston 14
CINCINNATI 20, Los Angeles 12
DALLAS 17, Buffalo 10
Baltimore 17, MIAMI 16
SAN FRANCISCO 20, Minnesota 16
OAKLAND 35, Cincinnati 20

1975
Oakland 31, MIAMI 21
DENVER 23, Green Bay 13
Dallas 36, DETROIT 10
WASHINGTON 27, St. Louis 17
New York Giants 17, BUFFALO 14
Minnesota 13, CHICAGO 9
Los Angeles 42, PHILADELPHIA 3
Kansas City 34, DALLAS 31
CINCINNATI 33, Buffalo 24
Pittsburgh 32, HOUSTON 9
MIAMI 20, New England 7
OAKLAND 17, Denver 10
SAN DIEGO 24, New York Jets 16

1974
BUFFALO 21, Oakland 20
PHILADELPHIA 13, Dallas 10
WASHINGTON 30, Denver 3
MIAMI 21, New York Jets 17
DETROIT 17, San Francisco 13
CHICAGO 10, Green Bay 9
PITTSBURGH 24, Atlanta 17
Los Angeles 15, SAN FRANCISCO 13
Minnesota 28, ST. LOUIS 24
Kansas City 42, DENVER 34
Pittsburgh 28, NEW ORLEANS 7
MIAMI 24, Cincinnati 3
Washington 23, LOS ANGELES 17

1973
GREEN BAY 23, New York Jets 7
DALLAS 40, New Orleans 3
DETROIT 31, Atlanta 6
WASHINGTON 14, Dallas 7
Miami 17, CLEVELAND 9
DENVER 23, Oakland 23
BUFFALO 23, Kansas City 14
PITTSBURGH 21, Washington 16
KANSAS CITY 19, Chicago 7
ATLANTA 20, Minnesota 14
SAN FRANCISCO 20, Green Bay 6
MIAMI 30, Pittsburgh 26
LOS ANGELES 40, New York Giants 6

1972
Washington 24, MINNESOTA 21
Kansas City 20, NEW ORLEANS 17
New York Giants 27, PHILADELPHIA 12
Oakland 34, HOUSTON 0
Green Bay 24, DETROIT 23
CHICAGO 13, Minnesota 10
DALLAS 28, Detroit 24
Baltimore 24, NEW ENGLAND 17
Cleveland 21, SAN DIEGO 17
WASHINGTON 24, Atlanta 13
MIAMI 31, St. Louis 10
Los Angeles 26, SAN FRANCISCO 16
OAKLAND 24, New York Jets 16

1971
Minnesota 16, DETROIT 13
ST. LOUIS 17, New York Jets 10
Oakland 34, CLEVELAND 20
DALLAS 20, New York Giants 13
KANSAS CITY 38, Pittsburgh 16
MINNESOTA 10, Baltimore 3
GREEN BAY 14, Detroit 14
BALTIMORE 24, Los Angeles 17
SAN DIEGO 20, St. Louis 17
ATLANTA 28, Green Bay 21
MIAMI 34, Chicago 3
Kansas City 26, SAN FRANCISCO 17
Washington 38, LOS ANGELES 24

1970
CLEVELAND 31, New York Jets 21
Kansas City 44, BALTIMORE 24
DETROIT 28, Chicago 14
Green Bay 22, SAN DIEGO 20
OAKLAND 34, Washington 20
MINNESOTA 13, Los Angeles 3
PITTSBURGH 21, Cincinnati 10
Baltimore 13, GREEN BAY 10
St. Louis 38, DALLAS 0
PHILADELPHIA 23, New York Giants 20
Miami 20, ATLANTA 7
Cleveland 21, HOUSTON 10
Detroit 28, LOS ANGELES 23

MONDAY NIGHT WON-LOST RECORDS, 1970-2005
AMERICAN FOOTBALL CONFERENCE

	Balt.	Buff.	Cin.	Cle.	Den.	Hou.	Ind.	Jax.	K.C.	Mia.	N.E.	N.Y.J.	Oak.	Pitt.	S.D.	Tenn.
Total	4-2	17-20	8-16	13-12	23-29-1	0-0	17-10	5-3	20-15	39-32	12-21	16-21	36-21-1	33-21	14-14	16-15
2005	1-1			1-0			3-0		0-1		1-1	0-2		2-1	0-1	
2004	0-1		1-0	0-1	1-0		2-1		1-1	1-1	1-0					1-1
2003			0-1	1-1	1-0		1-0		1-1	1-0			0-3	0-1	0-1	0-1
2002	1-0			0-2	0-1				1-1	1-1	0-1		2-0	2-1		1-0
2001	2-0			1-1			0-1	0-1	1-0			0-1	1-0	1-0		0-2
2000		0-1		1-1	2-0		0-2	1-1	0-1	1-1	2-0		0-1			3-0
1999		1-0		1-2				2-0	1-2	0-1	2-1		0-1	1-0		
1998				2-1			2-0	0-2	1-2	1-2	1-0			2-1		
1997		1-1		2-1			0-1	1-0	2-0	1-2	1-2		0-2	0-2		
1996		0-2		1-0	1-0				0-2	1-2			2-1	3-0	1-1	
1995		1-1	0-2	1-0					1-1	2-1	1-0		0-2	1-1	1-1	
1994		1-1		0-2					1-1	1-0			1-1	2-0	0-1	0-3
1993		2-1	1-0	0-2	0-1				2-0	1-2			1-0	3-0	2-0	0-1
1992		2-0	0-1	0-1	0-2				1-0	2-1		0-1	0-2	1-0		1-0
1991		2-1	0-2						2-1	1-1		0-1	0-2	0-1		1-1
1990		1-1	1-1	1-1	1-1		0-1		0-1	0-1		0-1	2-0	1-0		1-0
1989		1-2	1-2	1-1	2-0							0-1	1-0			1-0
1988		2-0		1-2	0-2		1-1		1-1			0-1	1-1			1-0
1987			1-0	2-1					1-1		1-1	2-1	1-1			
1986		1-0	1-0	1-1					1-2	1-0	1-1		0-1	0-2	0-1	
1985		1-0	1-0	1-0					2-1	0-1	1-0		2-0	0-2	0-1	
1984	0-1	0-1		1-0						3-0	0-1		2-1	1-1	1-2	
1983	0-1	0-2					0-1		1-1				2-0	1-0	1-1	
1982	0-1	0-1							1-1				1-0	1-0	1-1	0-1
1981	1-1		0-1	1-0					1-1	0-1			2-1	1-1	2-1	0-1
1980		1-1	1-2						1-1	1-2	1-0		3-0	0-2	1-0	2-0
1979		1-0	0-2						0-2	0-2	1-1		2-0	2-1	1-0	2-0
1978		1-2		1-1			2-1		2-1	0-2			1-0	1-1	1-0	2-0
1977	0-1	0-1	1-0				1-1		0-1	1-0	0-1		2-0	2-0		
1976		0-2	1-1				2-0		0-1	1-1	1-0	0-1	2-0	0-1		0-1
1975		0-2	1-0		1-1		1-0		1-1		0-1	0-1	2-0	1-0	1-0	0-1
1974	1-0	0-1		0-2					1-0	2-0		0-1	0-1	2-0		
1973	1-0		0-1	0-0-1					1-1	2-0		0-1	0-0-1	1-1		
1972			1-0				1-0		1-0	1-0	0-1	0-1	2-0		0-1	0-1
1971			0-1						1-1	2-0	1-0		0-1	1-0	0-1	1-0
1970			0-1	2-0			1-1		1-0	1-0		0-1	1-0	1-0	0-1	0-1

MONDAY NIGHT FOOTBALL ALL-TIME STANDINGS
AMERICAN FOOTBALL CONFERENCE

East	W	L	T	Pct.	South	W	L	T	Pct.
Miami	39	32	0	.549	Indianapolis	17	10	0	.630
Buffalo	17	20	0	.459	Jacksonville	5	3	0	.625
New York Jets	16	21	0	.432	Tennessee	16	15	0	.516
New England	12	21	0	.364	Houston	0	0	0	.000

North	W	L	T	Pct.	West	W	L	T	Pct.
Baltimore	4	2	0	.667	Oakland	36	21	1	.629
Pittsburgh	33	21	0	.611	Kansas City	20	15	0	.571
Cleveland	13	12	0	.520	San Diego	14	14	0	.500
Cincinnati	8	16	0	.333	Denver	23	29	1	.443

MONDAY NIGHT WON-LOST RECORDS, 1970-2005
NATIONAL FOOTBALL CONFERENCE

	Ariz.	Atl.	Car.	Chi.	Dall.	Det.	G.B.	Minn.	N.O.	N.Y.G.	Phil.	St.L.	S.F.	Sea.	T.B.	Wash.
Total	5-10-1	9-18	3-2	16-32	39-28	11-13-1	24-23-1	22-22	6-15	16-29-1	22-20	26-26	37-22	13-8	8-7	25-28
2005		3-0	1-0	1-1			0-3	1-0	0-2	1-0	0-3	0-1		1-0		1-0
2004			0-1	2-1		2-1		0-2			2-1	2-1		0-1	0-1	0-1
2003		0-1	0-1	1-0			2-1			0-2	2-1	2-0	1-0		2-1	
2002			0-3				2-0			0-1	3-0	2-1	1-2	0-1	1-1	0-1
2001				1-0	0-1		2-0	1-1	0-1	0-3	1-0	2-1	1-0		1-0	0-2
2000			1-0	1-1			1-1	1-1				1-2		0-1	1-1	1-2
1999	0-1	1-2		1-2			1-2	2-1		1-0			1-2	1-0	1-0	
1998				2-0	1-1		0-3	1-0		0-2	0-1		3-0		1-1	0-1
1997			1-1	1-1	1-2		3-0	0-1				0-2	3-0			1-0
1996		0-1	2-0	2-1	0-2	2-1	0-1					0-2	2-1			
1995	0-1		1-2	3-0	2-0		1-0	0-2		0-1	0-1		2-1			
1994			0-2	2-1	1-0		1-0	2-0	0-2	1-2	2-0		2-1			
1993		0-1	0-1	1-1		0-1	1-0	0-2		1-0	1-1		1-2			1-2
1992		0-2	0-3	2-1	0-1		1-0	1-0		1-0	1-0		2-0	1-0		1-2
1991			2-1	0-1				0-1	1-0	2-1	2-1	0-1	2-1			2-0
1990				0-1				0-1	1-1	1-1	2-0	0-3	3-0	1-0		0-1
1989		1-1						1-1	1-1	2-1	0-2	0-2	3-0	1-0		0-2
1988	0-1		1-2	1-1			1-0	1-0	1-1	1-0	1-0	1-1	1-0			0-2
1987			1-2	2-1			1-0			0-3		1-2	2-0	0-2		1-1
1986	0-1		2-1	2-0	0-1	0-1				2-1	1-0	0-2	2-0			1-1
1985	1-1		1-1	1-1		0-1				0-1	2-1	1-2	0-2			2-1
1984		0-2	0-1	1-1	0-1	0-1			1-0	0-1		1-1	2-0	2-0		
1983	0-0-1	0-1		1-1	2-0	2-1	0-1	0-1	1-1-1			1-0	1-0		0-1	1-2
1982		1-2	0-1	1-0			1-0	0-1							1-0	
1981		1-2	0-2	2-0	1-0		0-3					1-1	2-0	1-0		
1980		1-1	1-1						0-1	0-1	1-0	2-0		0-1	0-1	0-2
1979		1-2		0-2		1-0	0-1	0-1	0-1	1-1	1-0		2-0			1-0
1978		1-0	0-3	1-1			2-0					0-2		0-1		1-1
1977	2-0		1-0	1-1		0-1	0-1		0-1			1-1	0-2			1-1
1976	0-1			1-0			1-1				0-1	0-2	2-0			2-0
1975	0-1		0-1	1-1	0-1	0-1	1-0			1-0	0-1	1-0				1-0
1974	0-1	0-1	1-0	0-1	1-0	0-1	1-0	0-1		1-0	1-1	0-2				2-0
1973		1-1	0-1	1-1	1-0	1-1	0-1	0-1	0-1			1-0	1-0			1-1
1972	0-1	0-1	1-0	1-0	0-2	1-0	0-2	0-1	1-0		0-1	1-0	0-1			2-0
1971	1-1	1-0	0-1	1-0	0-1-1	0-1-1	2-0		0-1			0-2	0-1			1-0
1970	1-0	0-1	0-1	0-1	2-0	1-1	1-0		0-1	1-0		0-2				0-1

MONDAY NIGHT FOOTBALL ALL-TIME STANDINGS
NATIONAL FOOTBALL CONFERENCE

East	W	L	T	Pct.	South	W	L	T	Pct.
Dallas	39	28	0	.582	Carolina	3	2	0	.600
Philadelphia	22	20	0	.524	Tampa Bay	8	7	0	.533
Washington	25	28	0	.472	Atlanta	9	18	0	.333
New York Giants	16	29	1	.359	New Orleans	6	15	0	.286

North	W	L	T	Pct.	West	W	L	T	Pct.
Green Bay	24	23	1	.511	San Francisco	37	22	0	.627
Minnesota	22	22	0	.500	Seattle	13	8	0	.619
Detroit	11	13	1	.460	St. Louis	26	26	0	.500
Chicago	16	32	0	.333	Arizona	5	10	1	.344

THURSDAY-SATURDAY-SUNDAY NIGHT FOOTBALL, 1974-2005
(Home Team in capitals, games listed in chronological order.)

2005
NEW ENGLAND 30, Oakland 20 (Thurs.)
Indianapolis 24, BALTIMORE 7 (Sun.)
Kansas City 23, OAKLAND 17 (Sun.)
SAN DIEGO 45, New York Giants 23 (Sun.)
ARIZONA 31, San Francisco 14 (Sun.)
JACKSONVILLE 23, Cincinnati 20 (Sun.)
SEATTLE 42, Houston 10 (Sun.)
Kansas City 30, MIAMI 20 (Fri.)
NEW ENGLAND 21, Buffalo 16 (Sun.)
WASHINGTON 17, Philadelphia 10 (Sun.)
PITTSBURGH 34, Cleveland 21 (Sun.)
Kansas City 45, HOUSTON 17 (Sun.)
New Orleans 21, NEW YORK JETS 19 (Sun.)
SAN DIEGO 34, Oakland 10 (Sun.)
GREEN BAY 16, Detroit 13 (Sun.)
Denver 28, BUFFALO 17 (Sat.)
CHICAGO 16, Atlanta 3 (Sun.)
BALTIMORE 30, Minnesota 23 (Sun.)
New York Giants 30, OAKLAND 21 (Sat.)
St. Louis 20, DALLAS 10 (Sun.)

2004
NEW ENGLAND 27, Indianapolis 24 (Thurs.)
DENVER 34, Kansas City 24 (Sun.)
CINCINNATI 16, Miami 13 (Sun.)
OAKLAND 30, Tampa Bay 20 (Sun.)
Pittsburgh 13, MIAMI 3 (Sun.)
St. Louis 24, SAN FRANCISCO 14 (Sun.)
Baltimore 17, WASHINGTON 10 (Sun.)
Minnesota 38, NEW ORLEANS 31 (Sun.)
CHICAGO 23, San Francisco 13 (Sun.)
BALTIMORE 27, Cleveland 13 (Sun.)
NEW ENGLAND 29, Buffalo 6 (Sun.)
Green Bay 16, HOUSTON 13 (Sun.)
Oakland 25, DENVER 24 (Sun.)
Pittsburgh 17, JACKSONVILLE 16 (Sun.)
Philadelphia 17, WASHINGTON 14 (Sun.)
ATLANTA 34, Carolina 31 (OT) (Sat.)
INDIANAPOLIS 20, Baltimore 10 (Sun.)
Denver 37, TENNESSEE 16 (Sat.)
MIAMI 10, Cleveland 7 (Sun.)
NEW YORK GIANTS 28, Dallas 24 (Sun.)

2003
WASHINGTON 16, New York Jets 13 (Thurs.)
TENNESSEE 25, Oakland 20 (Sun.)
MINNESOTA 24, Chicago 13 (Sun.)
MIAMI 17, Buffalo 7 (Sun.)
Indianapolis 55, NEW ORLEANS 21 (Sun.)
Cleveland 33, PITTSBURGH 13 (Sun.)
SEATTLE 20, San Francisco 19 (Sun.)
KANSAS CITY 38, Buffalo 5 (Sun.)
Green Bay 30, MINNESOTA 27 (Sun.)
ST. LOUIS 33, Baltimore 22 (Sun.)
NEW ENGLAND 12, Dallas 0 (Sun.)
MIAMI 24, Washington 23 (Sun.)
JACKSONVILLE 17, Tampa Bay 10 (Sun.)
ATLANTA 20, Carolina 14 (OT) (Sun.)
NEW ORLEANS 45, New York Giants 7 (Sun.)
New England 21, NEW YORK JETS 16 (Sat.)
Denver 31, INDIANAPOLIS 17 (Sun.)
Philadelphia 31, WASHINGTON 7 (Sat.)
BALTIMORE 13, Pittsburgh 10 (OT) (Sun.)

2002
San Francisco 16, NEW YORK GIANTS 13 (Thurs.)
HOUSTON 19, Dallas 10 (Sun.)
Oakland 30, PITTSBURGH 17 (Sun.)
ATLANTA 30, Cincinnati 3 (Sun.)
SEATTLE 48, Minnesota 23 (Sun.)
Baltimore 26, CLEVELAND 21 (Sun.)
Miami 24, DENVER 22 (Sun.)
WASHINGTON 26, Indianapolis 21 (Sun.)
NEW YORK GIANTS 24, Jacksonville 17 (Sun.)
NEW YORK JETS 13, Miami 10 (Sun.)
OAKLAND 27, New England 20 (Sun.)
Indianapolis 23, DENVER 20 (OT) (Sun.)
NEW ORLEANS 23, Tampa Bay 20 (Sun.)
GREEN BAY 26, Minnesota 22 (Sun.)
ST. LOUIS 30, Arizona 28 (Sun.)
Philadelphia 27, DALLAS 3 (Sat.)
New York Jets 30, NEW ENGLAND 17 (Sun.)
Tampa Bay 15, CHICAGO 0 (Sun.)

2001
Miami 31, TENNESSEE 23 (Sun.)
Denver 38, ARIZONA 17 (Sun.)
PHILADELPHIA 40, Dallas 18 (Sun.)
SAN FRANCISCO 24, Carolina 14 (Sun.)
Oakland 23, INDIANAPOLIS 18 (Sun.)
Buffalo 13, JACKSONVILLE 10 (Thurs.)
Indianapolis 35, KANSAS CITY 28 (Thurs.)
New York Jets 16, NEW ORLEANS 9 (Sun.)
SEATTLE 34, Oakland 27 (Sun.)
St. Louis 24, NEW ENGLAND 17 (Sun.)
Chicago 13, MINNESOTA 6 (Sun.)
SAN FRANCISCO 35, Buffalo 0 (Sun.)
DENVER 20, Seattle 7 (Sun.)
Pittsburgh 26, BALTIMORE 21 (Sun.)
Tennessee 13, OAKLAND 10 (Sat.)
New York Jets 29, INDIANAPOLIS 28 (Sun.)
TAMPA BAY 22, Baltimore 10 (Sat.)
Washington 40, NEW ORLEANS 10 (Sun.)
Philadelphia 17, TAMPA BAY 13 (Sun.)

2000
BUFFALO 16, Tennessee 13 (Sun.)
ARIZONA 32, Dallas 31 (Sun.)
MIAMI 19, Baltimore 6 (Sun.)
Washington 16, NEW YORK GIANTS 6 (Sun.)
PHILADELPHIA 38, Atlanta 10 (Sun.)
Baltimore 15, JACKSONVILLE 10 (Sun.)
Minnesota 28, CHICAGO 16 (Sun.)
Detroit 28, TAMPA BAY 14 (Thurs.)
Oakland 15, SAN DIEGO 13 (Sun.)
Carolina 27, ST. LOUIS 24 (Sun.)
INDIANAPOLIS 23, New York Jets 15 (Sun.)
Jacksonville 34, PITTSBURGH 24 (Sun.)
New York Giants 31, ARIZONA 7 (Sun.)
MINNESOTA 24, Detroit 17 (Thurs.)
Green Bay 28, CHICAGO 6 (Sun.)
OAKLAND 31, New York Jets 7 (Sun.)
New York Giants 17, DALLAS 13 (Sun.)
Buffalo 42, SEATTLE 23 (Sat.)

1999

Pittsburgh 43, CLEVELAND 0 (Sun.)
BUFFALO 17, N.Y. Jets 3 (Sun.)
NEW ENGLAND 16, N.Y. Giants 14 (Sun.)
SEATTLE 22, Oakland 21 (Sun.)
GREEN BAY 26, Tampa Bay 23 (Sun.)
Washington 24, ARIZONA 10 (Sun.)
Kansas City 35, BALTIMORE 8 (Thurs.)
DETROIT 20, Tampa Bay 3 (Sun.)
MIAMI 17, Tennessee 0 (Sun.)
SEATTLE 20, Denver 17 (Sun.)
JACKSONVILLE 41, New Orleans 23 (Sun.)
CAROLINA 34, Atlanta 28 (Sun.)
JACKSONVILLE 20, Pittsburgh 6 (Thurs.)
NEW ENGLAND 13, Dallas 6 (Sun.)
TENNESSEE 21, Oakland 14 (Thurs.)
KANSAS CITY 31, Minnesota 28 (Sun.)
Buffalo 31, ARIZONA 21 (Sun.)
Washington 26, SAN FRANCISCO 20 (OT) (Sun.)

1998

KANSAS CITY 28, Oakland 8 (Sun.)
NEW ENGLAND 29, Indianapolis 6 (Sun.)
ARIZONA 17, Philadelphia 3 (Sun.)
BALTIMORE 31, Cincinnati 24 (Sun.)
KANSAS CITY 17, Seattle 6 (Sun.)
Atlanta 34, NEW YORK GIANTS 20 (Sun.)
DETROIT 27, Green Bay 20 (Thurs.)
Buffalo 30, CAROLINA 14 (Sun.)
Oakland 31, SEATTLE 18 (Sun.)
Tennessee 31, TAMPA BAY 22 (Sun.)
DETROIT 26, Chicago 3 (Sun.)
SAN FRANCISCO 31, New Orleans 20 (Sun.)
Denver 31, SAN DIEGO 16 (Sun.)
PHILADELPHIA 17, St. Louis 14 (Thurs.)
MINNESOTA 48, Chicago 22 (Sun.)
New York Jets 21, MIAMI 16 (Sun.)
MINNESOTA 50, Jacksonville 10 (Sun.)
DALLAS 23, Washington 7 (Sun.)

1997

Washington 24, CAROLINA 10 (Sun.)
ARIZONA 25, Dallas 22 (OT) (Sun.)
NEW ENGLAND 27, New York Jets 24 (OT) (Sun.)
TAMPA BAY 31, Miami 21 (Sun.)
MINNESOTA 28, Philadelphia 19 (Sun.)
New Orleans 20, CHICAGO 17 (Sun.)
PITTSBURGH 24, Indianapolis 22 (Sun.)
KANSAS CITY 31, San Diego 3 (Thurs.)
CAROLINA 21, Atlanta 12 (Sun.)
GREEN BAY 20, Detroit 10 (Sun.)
PITTSBURGH 37, Baltimore 0 (Sun.)
Oakland 38, SAN DIEGO 13 (Sun.)
WASHINGTON 7, New York Giants 7 (OT) (Sun.)
Denver 38, SAN DIEGO 28 (Sun.)
CINCINNATI 41, Tennessee 14 (Thurs.)
MIAMI 33, Detroit 30 (Sun.)
Chicago 13, ST. LOUIS 10 (Sun.)
SEATTLE 38, San Francisco 9 (Sun.)

1996

Buffalo 23, NEW YORK GIANTS 20 (OT) (Sun.)
Miami 38, ARIZONA 10 (Sun.)
DENVER 27, Tampa Bay 23 (Sun.)
Philadelphia 33, ATLANTA 18 (Sun.)
WASHINGTON 31, New York Jets 16 (Sun.)
Houston 30, CINCINNATI 27 (OT) (Sun.)
INDIANAPOLIS 26, Baltimore 21 (Sun.)
KANSAS CITY 34, Seattle 16 (Thurs.)
NEW ENGLAND 28, Buffalo 25 (Sun.)
San Francisco 24, NEW ORLEANS 17 (Sun.)
CAROLINA 27, New York Giants 17 (Sun.)
Minnesota 16, OAKLAND 13 (OT) (Sun.)
Green Bay 24, ST. LOUIS 9 (Sun.)
New England 45, SAN DIEGO 7 (Sun.)
INDIANAPOLIS 37, Philadelphia 10 (Thurs.)
Minnesota 24, DETROIT 22 (Sun.)
JACKSONVILLE 20, Seattle 13 (Sun.)
SAN DIEGO 16, Denver 10 (Sun.)

1995

DENVER 22, Buffalo 7 (Sun.)
Philadelphia 31, ARIZONA 19 (Sun.)
Dallas 23, MINNESOTA 17 (OT) (Sun.)
Green Bay 24, JACKSONVILLE 14 (Sun.)
Oakland 47, NEW YORK JETS 10 (Sun.)
Denver 37, NEW ENGLAND 3 (Sun.)
ST. LOUIS 21, Atlanta 19 (Thurs.)
Cincinnati 27, PITTSBURGH 9 (Thurs.)
New York Giants 24, WASHINGTON 15 (Sun.)
Miami 24, SAN DIEGO 14 (Sun.)
PHILADELPHIA 31, Denver 13 (Sun.)
KANSAS CITY 20, Houston 13 (Sun.)
NEW ORLEANS 34, Carolina 26 (Sun.)
New York Giants 10, ARIZONA 6 (Thurs.)
SAN FRANCISCO 27, Buffalo 17 (Sun.)
TAMPA BAY 13, Green Bay 10 (OT) (Sun.)
SEATTLE 44, Oakland 10 (Sun.)
Indianapolis 10, New England 7 (Sat.)

1994

San Diego 17, DENVER 34 (Sun.)
New York Giants 20, ARIZONA 17 (Sun.)
Kansas City 30, ATLANTA 10 (Sun.)
Chicago 19, NEW YORK JETS 7 (Sun.)
Miami 23, CINCINNATI 7 (Sun.)
PHILADELPHIA 21, Washington 17 (Sun.)
Cleveland 11, HOUSTON 8 (Thurs.)
MINNESOTA 13, Green Bay 10 (OT) (Thurs.)
ARIZONA 20, Pittsburgh 17 (OT) (Sun.)
KANSAS CITY 13, Los Angeles Raiders 3 (Sun.)
DETROIT 14, Tampa Bay 9 (Sun.)
SAN FRANCISCO 31, Los Angeles Rams 27 (Sun.)
New England 12, INDIANAPOLIS 10 (Sun.)
MINNESOTA 33, Chicago 27 (OT) (Thurs.)
Buffalo 42, MIAMI 31 (Sun.)
New Orleans 29, ATLANTA 20 (Sun.)
Los Angeles Raiders 17, SEATTLE 16 (Sun.)
MIAMI 27, Detroit 20 (Sun.)

1993
NEW ORLEANS 33, Houston 21 (Sun.)
Los Angeles Raiders 17, SEATTLE 13 (Sun.)
Dallas 17, PHOENIX 10 (Sun.)
NEW YORK JETS 45, New England 7 (Sun.)
BUFFALO 17, New York Giants 14 (Sun.)
GREEN BAY 30, Denver 27 (Sun.)
ATLANTA 30, Los Angeles Rams 24 (Thurs.)
MIAMI 41, Indianapolis 27 (Sun.)
Detroit 30, MINNESOTA 27 (Sun.)
WASHINGTON 30, Indianapolis 24 (Sun.)
Chicago 16, SAN DIEGO 13 (Sun.)
TAMPA BAY 23, Minnesota 10 (Sun.)
HOUSTON 23, Pittsburgh 3 (Sun.)
SAN FRANCISCO 21, Cincinnati 8 (Sun.)
Green Bay 20, SAN DIEGO 13 (Sun.)
Philadelphia 20, INDIANAPOLIS 10 (Sun.)
MINNESOTA 30, Kansas City 10 (Sun.)
HOUSTON 24, New York Jets 0 (Sun.)

1992
DENVER 17, Los Angeles Raiders 13 (Sun.)
Philadelphia 31, PHOENIX 14 (Sun.)
BUFFALO 38, Indianapolis 0 (Sun.)
San Francisco 16, NEW ORLEANS 10 (Sun.)
NEW YORK JETS 30, New England 21 (Sun.)
NEW ORLEANS 13, Los Angeles Rams 10 (Sun.)
MINNESOTA 31, Detroit 14 (Thurs.)
Pittsburgh 27, KANSAS CITY 3 (Sun.)
New York Giants 24, WASHINGTON 7 (Sun.)
Cincinnati 31, CHICAGO 28 (OT) (Sun.)
DENVER 27, New York Giants 13 (Sun.)
Kansas City 24, SEATTLE 14 (Sun.)
SAN DIEGO 27, Los Angeles Raiders 3 (Sun.)
NEW ORLEANS 22, Atlanta 14 (Thurs.)
Los Angeles Rams 31, TAMPA BAY 27 (Sun.)
Green Bay 16, HOUSTON 14 (Sun.)
MIAMI 19, New York Jets 17 (Sun.)
HOUSTON 27, Buffalo 3 (Sun.)

1991
WASHINGTON 45, Detroit 0 (Sun.)
Houston 30, CINCINNATI 7 (Sun.)
NEW ORLEANS 24, Los Angeles Rams 7 (Sun.)
Dallas 17, PHOENIX 9 (Sun.)
Denver 13, MINNESOTA 6 (Sun.)
Pittsburgh 21, INDIANAPOLIS 3 (Sun.)
Los Angeles Raiders 23, SEATTLE 20 (Sun.)
Chicago 10, GREEN BAY 0 (Thurs.)
Washington 17, NEW YORK GIANTS 13 (Sun.)
DENVER 20, Pittsburgh 13 (Sun.)
MIAMI 30, New England 20 (Sun.)
HOUSTON 28, Cleveland 24 (Sun.)
Atlanta 23, NEW ORLEANS 20 (OT) (Sun.)
Los Angeles Raiders 9, SAN DIEGO 7 (Sun.)
Minnesota 26, TAMPA BAY 24 (Sun.)
Buffalo 35, INDIANAPOLIS 7 (Sun.)
SEATTLE 23, Los Angeles Rams 9 (Sun.)

1990
NEW YORK GIANTS 27, Philadelphia 20 (Sun.)
PITTSBURGH 20, Houston 9 (Sun.)
TAMPA BAY 23, Detroit 20 (Sun.)
Washington 38, PHOENIX 10 (Sun.)
BUFFALO 38, Los Angeles Raiders 24 (Sun.)
CHICAGO 38, Los Angeles Rams 9 (Sun.)
MIAMI 17, New England 10 (Thurs.)
ATLANTA 38, Cincinnati 17 (Sun.)
MINNESOTA 27, Denver 22 (Sun.)
San Francisco 24, DALLAS 6 (Sun.)
CINCINNATI 27, Pittsburgh 3 (Sun.)
Seattle 13, SAN DIEGO 10 (Sun.)
MINNESOTA 23, Green Bay 7 (Sun.)
MIAMI 23, Philadelphia 20 (Sun.)
DETROIT 38, Chicago 21 (Sun.)
INDIANAPOLIS 35, Washington 28 (Sat.)
SEATTLE 17, Denver 12 (Sun.)
HOUSTON 34, Pittsburgh 14 (Sun.)

1989
Dallas 13, WASHINGTON 3 (Sun.)
SAN DIEGO 14, Los Angeles Raiders 12 (Sun.)
INDIANAPOLIS 27, New York Jets 10 (Sun.)
Los Angeles Rams 20, NEW ORLEANS 17 (Sun.)
MINNESOTA 27, Chicago 16 (Sun.)
MIAMI 31, New England 10 (Sun.)
SEATTLE 23, Los Angeles Raiders 17 (Sun.)
Cleveland 24, HOUSTON 20 (Sat.)

1988
HOUSTON 41, Washington 17 (Sun.)
Los Angeles Raiders 13, SAN DIEGO 3 (Sun.)
Minnesota 43, DALLAS 3 (Sun.)
New England 6, MIAMI 3 (Sun.)
New York Giants 13, NEW ORLEANS 12 (Sun.)
Pittsburgh 37, HOUSTON 34 (Sun.)
SEATTLE 42, Denver 14 (Sun.)
Los Angeles Rams 38, SAN FRANCISCO 16 (Sun.)

1987
NEW YORK GIANTS 17, New England 10 (Sun.)
SAN DIEGO 16, Los Angeles Raiders 14 (Sun.)
Miami 20, DALLAS 14 (Sun.)
SAN FRANCISCO 38, Cleveland 24 (Sun.)
Chicago 30, MINNESOTA 24 (Sun.)
SEATTLE 28, Denver 21 (Sun.)
MIAMI 23, Washington 21 (Sun.)
SAN FRANCISCO 48, Los Angeles Rams 0 (Sun.)

1986
New England 20, NEW YORK JETS 6 (Thurs.)
Cincinnati 30, CLEVELAND 13 (Thurs.)
Los Angeles Raiders 37, SAN DIEGO 31 (OT) (Thurs.)
LOS ANGELES RAMS 29, Dallas 10 (Sun.)
SAN FRANCISCO 24, Los Angeles Rams 14 (Fri.)

1985
KANSAS CITY 36, Los Angeles Raiders 20 (Thurs.)
Chicago 33, MINNESOTA 24 (Thurs.)
Dallas 30, NEW YORK GIANTS 29 (Sun.)
SAN DIEGO 54, Pittsburgh 44 (Sun.)
Denver 27, SEATTLE 24 (Fri.)

1984
Pittsburgh 23, NEW YORK JETS 17 (Thurs.)
Denver 24, CLEVELAND 14 (Sun.)
DALLAS 30, New Orleans 27 (Sun.)
Washington 31, MINNESOTA 17 (Thurs.)
SAN FRANCISCO 19, Los Angeles Rams 16 (Fri.)

1983
San Francisco 48, MINNESOTA 17 (Thurs.)
CLEVELAND 17, Cincinnati 7 (Thurs.)
Los Angeles Raiders 40, DALLAS 38 (Sun.)
Los Angeles Raiders 42, SAN DIEGO 10 (Thurs.)
MIAMI 34, New York Jets 14 (Fri.)

1982
BUFFALO 23, Minnesota 22 (Thurs.)
SAN FRANCISCO 30, Los Angeles Rams 24 (Thurs.)
ATLANTA 17, San Francisco 7 (Sun.)

1981
MIAMI 30, Pittsburgh 10 (Thurs.)
Philadelphia 20, BUFFALO 14 (Thurs.)
DALLAS 29, Los Angeles 17 (Sun.)
HOUSTON 17, Cleveland 13 (Thurs.)

1980
TAMPA BAY 10, Los Angeles 9 (Thurs.)
DALLAS 42, San Diego 31 (Sun.)
San Diego 27, MIAMI 24 (OT) (Thurs.)
HOUSTON 6, Pittsburgh 0 (Thurs.)

1979
Los Angeles 13, DENVER 9 (Thurs.)
DALLAS 30, Los Angeles 6 (Sun.)
OAKLAND 45, San Diego 22 (Thurs.)
MIAMI 39, New England 24 (Thurs.)

1978
New England 21, OAKLAND 14 (Sun.)
Minnesota 21, DALLAS 10 (Thurs.)
LOS ANGELES 10, Pittsburgh 7 (Sun.)
Denver 21, OAKLAND 6 (Sun.)

1977
Minnesota 30, DETROIT 21 (Sat.)

1976
Los Angeles 20, DETROIT 17 (Sat.)

1975
LOS ANGELES 10, Pittsburgh 3 (Sat.)

1974
OAKLAND 27, Dallas 23 (Sat.)

THANKSGIVING DAY FOOTBALL, 1920-2005
(Home Team in capitals, games listed in chronological order.)
(AFL)-American Football League, 1960-69.

Nov. 25, 1920
AKRON PROS 7, Canton Bulldogs 0
Decatur Staleys 6, CHICAGO TIGERS 0
ELYRIA (OH) ATHLETICS* 0, Columbus Panhandles 0
DAYTON TRIANGLES 28, Detroit Heralds 0
CHICAGO BOOSTERS* 27, Hammond Pros 0
All-Tonawanda (NY) 14, ROCHESTER JEFFERSONS 3
* Non league team. Games between league teams and non league teams counted in standings in 1920.

Nov. 24, 1921
Canton Bulldogs 14, AKRON PROS 0
Buffalo All-Americans 7, CHICAGO STALEYS 6

Nov. 30, 1922
Buffalo All-Americans 21, ROCHESTER JEFFERSONS 0
CHICAGO CARDINALS 6, Chicago Bears 0
RACINE LEGION 3, Milwaukee Badgers 0
Oorang Indians 18, COLUMBUS PANHANDLES 6
CANTON BULLDOGS 14, Akron Pros 0

Nov. 29, 1923
CANTON BULLDOGS 28, Toledo Maroons 0
CHICAGO BEARS 3, Chicago Cardinals 0
GREEN BAY PACKERS 19, Hammond Pros 0
Milwaukee Badgers 16, RACINE LEGION 0
AKRON PROS 2, Buffalo All-Americans 0

Nov. 27, 1924
AKRON PROS 22, Buffalo Bisons 0
Chicago Bears 21, CHICAGO CARDINALS 0
FRANKFORD YELLOWJACKETS 32, Dayton Triangles 7
CLEVELAND BULLDOGS 53, Milwaukee Badgers 10 (at Canton, Ohio)
Green Bay Packers 17, KANSAS CITY BLUES 6

Nov. 26, 1925
CHICAGO BEARS 0, Chicago Cardinals 0
Kansas City Cowboys 17, CLEVELAND BULLDOGS 0 (at Hartford, Connecticut)
Rock Island Independents 6, DETROIT PANTHERS 3
POTTSVILLE MAROONS 31, Green Bay Packers 0

Nov. 25, 1926
New York Giants 17, BROOKLYN LIONS 0
Los Angeles Buccaneers 9, DETROIT PANTHERS 6
CHICAGO BEARS 0, Chicago Cardinals 0
FRANKFORD YELLOWJACKETS 20, Green Bay Packers 14
POTTSVILLE MAROONS 8, Providence Steam Roller 0
CANTON BULLDOGS 0, Akron Pros 0

Nov. 24, 1927
Chicago Cardinals 3, CHICAGO BEARS 0
POTTSVILLE MAROONS 6, Providence Steam Roller 0
Green Bay Packers 17, FRANKFORD YELLOWJACKETS 9
Cleveland Bulldogs 30, NEW YORK YANKEES 19

Nov. 29, 1928
Providence Steam Roller 7, POTTSVILLE MAROONS 0
DETROIT WOLVERINES 33, Dayton Triangles 0
FRANKFORD YELLOWJACKETS 2, Green Bay Packers 0
CHICAGO BEARS 34, Chicago Cardinals 0

Nov. 28, 1929
New York Giants 21, STATEN ISLAND STAPLETONS 7
FRANKFORD YELLOWJACKETS 0, Green Bay Packers 0
Chicago Cardinals 40, CHICAGO BEARS 6

Nov. 27, 1930
STATEN ISLAND STAPLETONS 7, New York Giants 6
BROOKLYN DODGERS 33, Providence Steam Roller 12
Green Bay Packers 25, FRANKFORD YELLOWJACKETS 7
CHICAGO BEARS 6, Chicago Cardinals 0

Nov. 26, 1931
Green Bay Packers 38, PROVIDENCE STEAM ROLLER 7
STATEN ISLAND STAPLETONS 9, New York Giants 6
CHICAGO BEARS 18, Chicago Cardinals 7

Nov. 24, 1932
CHICAGO BEARS 34, Chicago Cardinals 0
Green Bay Packers 7, BROOKLYN DODGERS 0
STATEN ISLAND STAPLETONS 13, New York Giants 13

Nov. 30, 1933
Chicago Bears 22, CHICAGO CARDINALS 6
New York Giants 10, BROOKLYN DODGERS 0

Nov. 29, 1934	CHICAGO CARDINALS 6, Green Bay Packers 0 Chicago Bears 19, DETROIT LIONS 16 New York Giants 27, BROOKLYN DODGERS 0
Nov. 28, 1935	New York Giants 21, BROOKLYN DODGERS 0 CHICAGO CARDINALS 9, Green Bay Packers 7 DETROIT LIONS 14, Chicago Bears 2
Nov. 26, 1936	DETROIT LIONS 13, Chicago Bears 7 New York Giants 14, BROOKLYN DODGERS 0
Nov. 25, 1937	Chicago Bears 13, DETROIT LIONS 0 BROOKLYN DODGERS 13, New York Giants 13
Nov. 24, 1938	DETROIT LIONS 14, Chicago Bears 7 BROOKLYN DODGERS 7, New York Giants 7
Nov. 23, 1939#	PHILADELPHIA EAGLES 17, Pittsburgh Steelers 14
Nov. 28, 1940#	Pittsburgh Steelers 7, PHILADELPHIA EAGLES 0

In 1939 and 1940, President Roosevelt moved Thanksgiving one week earlier. Various states celebrated on the date declared by the President, while other states recognized the traditional fourth Thursday of the month. In 1941, Thanksgiving was sanctioned by Congress to be celebrated on the fourth Thursday of November, which it has been ever since.

Nov. 22, 1945	Cleveland Rams 28, DETROIT LIONS 21
Nov. 28, 1946	Boston Yanks 34, DETROIT LIONS 10
Nov. 27, 1947	Chicago Bears 34, DETROIT LIONS 14
Nov. 25, 1948	Chicago Cardinals 28, DETROIT LIONS 14
Nov. 24, 1949	Chicago Bears 28, DETROIT LIONS 7
Nov. 23, 1950	DETROIT LIONS 49, New York Yanks 14 Pittsburgh Steelers 28, CHICAGO CARDINALS 17
Nov. 22, 1951	DETROIT LIONS 52, Green Bay Packers 35
Nov. 27, 1952	DETROIT LIONS 48, Green Bay Packers 24 DALLAS TEXANS 27, Chicago Bears 23 (at Akron, Ohio)
Nov. 26, 1953	DETROIT LIONS 34, Green Bay Packers 15
Nov. 25, 1954	DETROIT LIONS 28, Green Bay Packers 24
Nov. 24, 1955	DETROIT LIONS 24, Green Bay Packers 10
Nov. 22, 1956	Green Bay Packers 24, DETROIT LIONS 20
Nov. 28, 1957	DETROIT LIONS 18, Green Bay Packers 6
Nov. 27, 1958	DETROIT LIONS 24, Green Bay Packers 14
Nov. 26, 1959	Green Bay Packers 24, DETROIT LIONS 17
Nov. 24, 1960	DETROIT LIONS 23, Green Bay Packers 10 (AFL) - NEW YORK TITANS 41, Dallas Texans 35
Nov. 23, 1961	Green Bay Packers 17, DETROIT LIONS 9 (AFL) - NEW YORK TITANS 21, Buffalo Bills 14
Nov. 22, 1962	DETROIT LIONS 26, Green Bay Packers 14 (AFL) - New York Titans 46, DENVER BRONCOS 45
Nov. 28, 1963	DETROIT LIONS 13, Green Bay Packers 13 (AFL) - Oakland Raiders 26, DENVER BRONCOS 10
Nov. 26, 1964	Chicago Bears 27, DETROIT LIONS 24 (AFL) - Buffalo Bills 27, SAN DIEGO CHARGERS 24
Nov. 25, 1965	DETROIT LIONS 24, Baltimore Colts 24 (AFL) - SAN DIEGO CHARGERS 20, Buffalo Bills 20
Nov. 24, 1966	San Francisco 49ers 41, DETROIT LIONS 14 DALLAS COWBOYS 26, Cleveland Browns 14 (AFL) - Buffalo Bills 31, OAKLAND RAIDERS 10

Nov. 23, 1967	Los Angeles Rams 31, DETROIT LIONS 7 DALLAS COWBOYS 46, St. Louis Cardinals 21 (AFL) - Oakland Raiders 44, KANSAS CITY CHIEFS 22 (AFL) - SAN DIEGO CHARGERS 24, Denver Broncos 20
Nov. 28, 1968	Philadelphia Eagles 12, DETROIT LIONS 0 DALLAS COWBOYS 29, Washington Redskins 20 (AFL) - OAKLAND RAIDERS 13, Buffalo Bills 10 (AFL) - KANSAS CITY CHIEFS 24, Houston Oilers 10
Nov. 27, 1969	Minnesota Vikings 27, DETROIT LIONS 0 DALLAS COWBOYS 24, San Francisco 49ers 24 (AFL) - KANSAS CITY CHIEFS 31, Denver Broncos 17 (AFL) - San Diego Chargers 21, HOUSTON OILERS 17
Nov. 26, 1970	DETROIT LIONS 28, Oakland Raiders 14 DALLAS COWBOYS 16, Green Bay Packers 3
Nov. 25, 1971	DETROIT LIONS 32, Kansas City Chiefs 21 DALLAS COWBOYS 28, Los Angeles Rams 21
Nov. 23, 1972	DETROIT LIONS 37, New York Jets 20 San Francisco 49ers 31, DALLAS COWBOYS 10
Nov. 22, 1973	Washington Redskins 20, DETROIT LIONS 0 Miami Dolphins 14, DALLAS COWBOYS 7
Nov. 28, 1974	Denver Broncos 31, DETROIT LIONS 27 DALLAS COWBOYS 24, Washington Redskins 23
Nov. 27, 1975	Los Angeles Rams 20, DETROIT LIONS 0 Buffalo Bills 32, ST. LOUIS CARDINALS 14
Nov. 25, 1976	DETROIT LIONS 27, Buffalo Bills 14 DALLAS COWBOYS 19, St. Louis Cardinals 14
Nov. 24, 1977	Chicago Bears 31, DETROIT LIONS 14 Miami Dolphins 55, ST. LOUIS CARDINALS 14
Nov. 23, 1978	DETROIT LIONS 17, Denver Broncos 14 DALLAS COWBOYS 37, Washington Redskins 10
Nov. 22, 1979	DETROIT LIONS 20, Chicago Bears 0 Houston Oilers 30, DALLAS COWBOYS 24
Nov. 27, 1980	Chicago Bears 23, DETROIT LIONS 17 (OT) DALLAS COWBOYS 51, Seattle Seahawks 7
Nov. 26, 1981	DETROIT LIONS 27, Kansas City Chiefs 10 DALLAS COWBOYS 10, Chicago Bears 9
Nov. 25, 1982	New York Giants 13, DETROIT LIONS 6 DALLAS COWBOYS 31, Cleveland Browns 14
Nov. 24, 1983	DETROIT LIONS 45, Pittsburgh Steelers 3 DALLAS COWBOYS 35, St. Louis Cardinals 17
Nov. 22, 1984	DETROIT LIONS 31, Green Bay Packers 28 DALLAS COWBOYS 20, New England Patriots 17
Nov. 28, 1985	DETROIT LIONS 31, New York Jets 20 DALLAS COWBOYS 35, St. Louis Cardinals 17
Nov. 27, 1986	Green Bay Packers 44, DETROIT LIONS 40 Seattle Seahawks 31, DALLAS COWBOYS 14
Nov. 26, 1987	Kansas City Chiefs 27, DETROIT LIONS 20 Minnesota Vikings 44, DALLAS COWBOYS 38 (OT)
Nov. 24, 1988	Minnesota Vikings 23, DETROIT LIONS 0 Houston Oilers 25, DALLAS COWBOYS 17
Nov. 23, 1989	DETROIT LIONS 13, Cleveland Browns 10 Philadelphia Eagles 27, DALLAS COWBOYS 0
Nov. 22, 1990	DETROIT LIONS 40, Denver Broncos 27 DALLAS COWBOYS 27, Washington Redskins 17

Nov. 28, 1991	DETROIT LIONS 16, Chicago Bears 6
	DALLAS COWBOYS 20, Pittsburgh Steelers 10
Nov. 26, 1992	Houston Oilers 24, DETROIT LIONS 21
	DALLAS COWBOYS 30, New York Giants 3
Nov. 25, 1993	Chicago Bears 10, DETROIT LIONS 6
	Miami Dolphins 16, DALLAS COWBOYS 14
Nov. 24, 1994	DETROIT LIONS 35, Buffalo Bills 21
	DALLAS COWBOYS 42, Green Bay Packers 31
Nov. 23, 1995	DETROIT LIONS 44, Minnesota Vikings 38
	DALLAS COWBOYS 24, Kansas City Chiefs 12
Nov. 28, 1996	Kansas City Chiefs 28, DETROIT LIONS 24
	DALLAS COWBOYS 21, Washington Redskins 10
Nov. 27, 1997	DETROIT LIONS 55, Chicago Bears 20
	Tennessee Titans 27, DALLAS COWBOYS 14
Nov. 26, 1998	DETROIT LIONS 19, Pittsburgh Steelers 16 (OT)
	Minnesota Vikings 46, DALLAS COWBOYS 36
Nov. 25, 1999	DETROIT LIONS 21, Chicago Bears 17
	DALLAS COWBOYS 20, Miami Dolphins 0
Nov. 23, 2000	DETROIT LIONS 34, New England Patriots 9
	Minnesota Vikings 27, DALLAS COWBOYS 15
Nov. 22, 2001	Green Bay Packers 29, DETROIT LIONS 27
	Denver Broncos 26, DALLAS COWBOYS 24
Nov. 28, 2002	New England Patriots 20, DETROIT LIONS 12
	DALLAS COWBOYS 27, Washington Redskins 20
Nov. 27, 2003	DETROIT LIONS 22, Green Bay Packers 14
	Miami Dolphins 40, DALLAS COWBOYS 21
Nov. 25, 2004	Indianapolis Colts 41, DETROIT LIONS 9
	DALLAS COWBOYS 21, Chicago Bears 7
Nov. 24, 2005	Atlanta Falcons 27, DETROIT LIONS 7
	Denver Broncos 24, DALLAS COWBOYS 21

THANKSGIVING DAY RECORDS
*NFL record; stats compiled by Elias Sports Bureau.

SCORING / Most Touchdowns, Game
    6   Ernie Nevers, Chi. Cardinals vs. Chi. Bears, Nov. 28, 1929*
    4   Sterling Sharpe, Green Bay at Dallas, Nov. 24, 1994
    3   By many players

RUSHING / Most Yards Rushing, Game
    273   O.J. Simpson, Buffalo at Detroit, Nov. 25, 1976
    198   Bob Hoernschemeyer, Detroit vs. N.Y. Yankees, Nov. 23, 1950
    195   Earl Campbell, Houston at Dallas, Nov. 22, 1979

PASSING / Most Yards Passing, Game
    455   Troy Aikman, Dallas vs. Minnesota, Nov. 26, 1998
    410   Scott Mitchell, Detroit vs. Minnesota, Nov. 23, 1995
    384   Warren Moon, Minnesota at Detroit, Nov. 23, 1995

PASS RECEIVING
RECEPTIONS / Most Pass Receptions, Game
    12   Brett Perriman, Detroit vs. Minnesota, Nov. 23, 1995
         Marvin Harrison, Indianapolis at Detroit, Nov. 25, 2004
    11   Daryl Johnston, Dallas vs. Miami, Nov. 25, 1993
         Michael Irvin, Dallas vs. Kansas City, Nov. 23, 1995
YARDS GAINED / Most Yards on Pass Receptions, Game
    303   Jim Benton, Cleveland at Detroit, Nov. 22, 1945
    185   Lance Alworth, San Diego vs. Buffalo, Nov. 26, 1964
    184   Anthony Carter, Minnesota at Dallas, Nov. 26, 1987 (OT)

HISTORY OF OVERTIME GAMES
PRESEASON

Aug. 28, 1955	Los Angeles 23, New York Giants 17, at Portland, Oregon
Aug. 24, 1962	Denver 27, Dallas Texans 24, at Fort Worth, Texas
Aug. 10, 1974	San Diego 20, New York Jets 14, at San Diego
Aug. 17, 1974	Pittsburgh 33, Philadelphia 30, at Philadelphia
Aug. 17, 1974	Dallas 19, Houston 13, at Dallas
Aug. 17, 1974	Cincinnati 13, Atlanta 7, at Atlanta
Sept. 6, 1974	Buffalo 23, New York Giants 17, at Buffalo
Aug. 9, 1975	Baltimore 23, Denver 20, at Denver
Aug. 30, 1975	New England 20, Green Bay 17, at Milwaukee
Sept. 13, 1975	Minnesota 14, San Diego 14, at San Diego
Aug. 1, 1976	New England 13, New York Giants 7, at New England
Aug. 2, 1976	Kansas City 9, Houston 3, at Kansas City
Aug. 20, 1976	New Orleans 26, Baltimore 20, at Baltimore
Sept. 4, 1976	Dallas 26, Houston 20, at Dallas
Aug. 13, 1977	Seattle 23, Dallas 17, at Seattle
Aug. 28, 1977	New England 13, Pittsburgh 10, at New England
Aug. 28, 1977	New York Giants 24, Buffalo 21, at East Rutherford, N.J.
Aug. 2, 1979	Seattle 12, Minnesota 9, at Minnesota
Aug. 4, 1979	Los Angeles 20, Oakland 14, at Los Angeles
Aug. 24, 1979	Denver 20, New England 17, at Denver
Aug. 23, 1980	Tampa Bay 20, Cincinnati 14, at Tampa Bay
Aug. 5, 1981	San Francisco 27, Seattle 24, at Seattle
Aug. 29, 1981	New Orleans 20, Detroit 17, at New Orleans
Aug. 28, 1982	Miami 17, Kansas City 17, at Kansas City
Sept. 3, 1982	Miami 16, New York Giants 13, at Miami
Aug. 6, 1983	L.A. Raiders 26, San Francisco 23, at Los Angeles
Aug. 6, 1983	Atlanta 13, Washington 10, at Atlanta
Aug. 13, 1983	St. Louis 27, Chicago 24, at St. Louis
Aug. 18, 1983	New York Jets 20, Cincinnati 17, at Cincinnati
Aug. 27, 1983	Chicago 20, Kansas City 17, at Chicago
Aug. 11, 1984	Pittsburgh 20, Philadelphia 17, at Pittsburgh
Aug. 9, 1985	Buffalo 10, Detroit 10, at Pontiac, Mich.
Aug. 10, 1985	Minnesota 16, Miami 13, at Miami
Aug. 17, 1985	Dallas 27, San Diego 24, at San Diego
Aug. 24, 1985	N.Y. Giants 34, N.Y. Jets 31, at East Rutherford, N.J.
Aug. 15, 1986	Washington 27, Pittsburgh 24, at Washington
Aug. 15, 1986	Detroit 30, Seattle 27, at Detroit
Aug. 23, 1986	Los Angeles Rams 20, San Diego 17, at Anaheim
Aug. 30, 1986	Minnesota 23, Indianapolis 20, at Indianapolis
Aug. 23, 1987	Philadelphia 19, New England 13, at New England
Sept. 5, 1987	Cleveland 30, Green Bay 24, at Milwaukee
Sept. 6, 1987	Kansas City 13, St. Louis 10, at Memphis, Tenn.
Aug. 11, 1988	Seattle 16, Detroit 13, at Detroit
Aug. 19, 1988	Miami 16, Denver 13, at Miami
Aug. 19, 1988	Green Bay 21, Kansas City 21, at Milwaukee
Aug. 20, 1988	Houston 20, Los Angeles Rams 17, at Anaheim
Aug. 21, 1988	Minnesota 19, Phoenix 16, at Phoenix
Aug. 5, 1989	Los Angeles Rams 16, San Francisco 13, at Tokyo, Japan
Aug. 26, 1989	Denver 24, Dallas 21, at Denver
Sept. 1, 1989	N.Y. Jets 15, Kansas City 13, at Kansas City
Aug. 24, 1990	Cincinnati 13, New England 10, at New England
Aug. 16, 1991	Cleveland 24, Washington 21, at Washington
Aug. 17, 1991	Cincinnati 27, Minnesota 24, at Cincinnati
Aug. 23, 1991	Dallas 20, Atlanta 17, at Dallas
Aug. 24, 1991	Cincinnati 19, Green Bay 16, at Green Bay
Aug. 22, 1992	Los Angeles Rams 16, Green Bay 13, at Anaheim
Aug. 8, 1993	Dallas 13, Detroit 13, at London, England
Aug. 12, 1995	Washington 16, Houston 13, at Knoxville, Tenn.
Aug. 19, 1995	Indianapolis 20, Green Bay 17, at Green Bay
Aug. 3, 1996	Minnesota 23, San Diego 20, at Minnesota
Aug. 10, 1996	San Francisco 16, San Diego 13, at San Francisco
Aug. 1, 1998	Green Bay 27, Kansas City 24, at Tokyo, Japan
Aug. 7, 1998	Detroit 13, Arizona 10, at Pontiac, Mich.
Aug. 22, 1998	Minnesota 25, Carolina 22, at Charlotte, N.C.
Aug. 9, 1999	Cleveland 20, Dallas 17, at Canton, Ohio
Aug. 4, 2001	Chicago 16, Cincinnati 13, at Chicago
Aug. 18, 2001	San Diego 23, Miami 20, at Miami
Aug. 18, 2001	Arizona 16, Seattle 13, at Seattle
Aug. 25, 2001	San Diego 13, St. Louis 10, at San Diego
Aug. 10, 2002	Kansas City 17, San Francisco 14, at San Francisco

* indicates Monday-night game
 # indicates Thursday/Saturday/Sunday-night game
+ indicates Thanksgiving Day game

REGULAR SEASON

Sept. 22, 1974—Pittsburgh 35, Denver 35, at Denver; Steelers win toss. Gilliam's pass intercepted and returned by Rowser to Denver's 42. Turner misses 41-yard field goal. Walden punts and Greer returns to Broncos' 39. Van Heusen punts and Edwards returns to Steelers' 16. Game ends with Steelers on own 26.

Nov. 10, 1974—New York Jets 26, New York Giants 20, at New Haven, Conn.; Giants win toss. Gogolak misses 42-yard field goal. Namath passes to Boozer for five yards and touchdown at 6:53.

Sept. 28, 1975—Dallas 37, St. Louis 31, at Dallas; Cardinals win toss. Hart's pass intercepted and returned by Jordan to Cardinals' 37. Staubach passes to DuPree for three yards and touchdown at 7:53.

Oct. 12, 1975—Los Angeles 13, San Diego 10, at San Diego; Chargers win toss. Partee punts to Rams' 14. Dempsey kicks 22-yard field goal at 9:27.

Nov. 2, 1975—Washington 30, Dallas 24, at Washington; Cowboys win toss. Staubach's pass intercepted and returned by Houston to Cowboys' 35. Kilmer runs one yard for touchdown at 6:34.

Nov. 16, 1975—St. Louis 20, Washington 17, at St. Louis; Cardinals win toss. Bakken kicks 37-yard field goal at 7:00.

Nov. 23, 1975—Kansas City 24, Detroit 21, at Kansas City; Lions win toss. Chiefs take over on downs at own 38. Stenerud kicks 26-yard field goal at 6:44.

Nov. 23, 1975—Oakland 26, Washington 23, at Washington; Redskins win toss. Bragg punts to Raiders' 42. Blanda kicks 27-yard field goal at 7:13.

Nov. 30, 1975—Denver 13, San Diego 10, at Denver; Broncos win toss. Turner kicks 25-yard field goal at 4:13.

Nov. 30, 1975—Oakland 37, Atlanta 34, at Oakland; Falcons win toss. James punts to Raiders' 16. Guy punts and Herron returns to Falcons' 41. Nick Mike-Mayer misses 45-yard field goal. Guy punts into Falcons' end zone. James punts to Raiders' 39. Blanda kicks 36-yard field goal at 15:00.

Dec. 14, 1975—Baltimore 10, Miami 7, at Baltimore; Dolphins win toss. Seiple punts to Colts' 4. Linhart kicks 31-yard field goal at 12:44.

Sept. 19, 1976—Minnesota 10, Los Angeles 10, at Minnesota; Vikings win toss. Tarkenton's pass intercepted by Monte Jackson and returned to Minnesota 16. Allen blocks Dempsey's 30-yard field goal attempt, ball rolls into end zone for touchback. Clabo punts and Scribner returns to Rams' 20. Rusty Jackson punts to Vikings' 35. Tarkenton's pass intercepted by Kay at Rams' 1, no return. Game ends with Rams on own 3.

* **Sept. 27, 1976—Washington 20, Philadelphia 17**, at Philadelphia; Eagles win toss. Jones punts and E. Brown loses one yard on return to Redskins' 40. Bragg punts 51 yards into end zone for touchback. Jones punts and E. Brown returns to Redskins' 42. Bragg punts and Marshall returns to Eagles' 41. Boryla's pass intercepted by Dusek at Redskins' 37, no return. Bragg punts and Bradley returns. Philadelphia holding penalty moves ball back to Eagles' 8. Boryla pass intercepted by E. Brown and returned to Eagles' 22. Moseley kicks 29-yard field goal at 12:49.

Oct. 17, 1976—Kansas City 20, Miami 17, at Miami; Chiefs win toss. Wilson punts into end zone for touchback. Bulaich fumbles into Kansas City end zone, Collier recovers for touchback. Stenerud kicks 34-yard field goal at 14:48.

Oct. 31, 1976—St. Louis 23, San Francisco 20, at St. Louis; Cardinals win toss. Joyce punts and Leonard fumbles on return, Jones recovers at 49ers' 43. Bakken kicks 21-yard field goal at 6:42.

Dec. 5, 1976—San Diego 13, San Francisco 7, at San Diego; Chargers win toss. Morris runs 13 yards for touchdown at 5:12.

Sept. 18, 1977—Dallas 16, Minnesota 10, at Minnesota; Vikings win toss. Dallas starts on Vikings' 47 after a punt early in the overtime period. Staubach scores seven plays later on a four-yard run at 6:14.

* **Sept. 26, 1977—Cleveland 30, New England 27**, at Cleveland; Browns win toss. Sipe throws a 22-yard pass to Logan at Patriots' 19. Cockroft kicks 35-yard field goal at 4:45.

Oct. 16, 1977—Minnesota 22, Chicago 16, at Minnesota; Bears win toss. Parsons punts 53 yards to Vikings' 18. Minnesota drives to Bears' 11. On a first-and-10, Vikings fake a field goal and holder Krause hits Voigt with a touchdown pass at 6:45.

Oct. 30, 1977—Cincinnati 13, Houston 10, at Cincinnati; Bengals win toss. Bahr kicks a 22-yard field goal at 5:51.

Nov. 13, 1977—San Francisco 10, New Orleans 7, at New Orleans; Saints win toss. Saints fail to move ball and Blanchard punts to 49ers' 41. Wersching kicks a 33-yard field goal at 6:33.

Dec. 18, 1977—Chicago 12, New York Giants 9, at East Rutherford, N.J.; Giants win toss. The ball changes hands eight times before Thomas kicks a 28-yard field goal at 14:51.

Sept. 10, 1978—Cleveland 13, Cincinnati 10, at Cleveland; Browns win toss. Collins returns kickoff 41 yards to Browns' 47. Cockroft kicks 27-yard field goal at 4:30.

* **Sept. 11, 1978—Minnesota 12, Denver 9**, at Minnesota; Vikings win toss. Danmeier kicks 44-yard field goal at 2:56.

Sept. 24, 1978—Pittsburgh 15, Cleveland 9, at Pittsburgh; Steelers win toss. Cunningham scores on a 37-yard "gadget" pass from Bradshaw at 3:43. Steelers start winning drive on their 21.

Sept. 24, 1978—Denver 23, Kansas City 17, at Kansas City; Broncos win toss. Dilts punts to Kansas City. Chiefs advance to Broncos' 40 where Reed fails to make first down on fourth-and-one situation. Broncos march downfield. Preston scores two-yard touchdown at 10:28.

Oct. 1, 1978—Oakland 25, Chicago 19, at Chicago; Bears win toss. Both teams punt on first possession. On Chicago's second offensive series, Colzie intercepts Avellini's pass and returns it to Bears' 3. Three plays later, Whittington runs two yards for a touchdown at 5:19.

Oct. 15, 1978—Dallas 24, St. Louis 21, at St. Louis; Cowboys win toss. Dallas drives from its 23 into field goal range. Septien kicks 27-yard field goal at 3:28.

Oct. 29, 1978—Denver 20, Seattle 17, at Seattle; Broncos win toss. Ball changes hands four times before Turner kicks 18-yard field goal at 12:59.

Nov. 12, 1978—San Diego 29, Kansas City 23, at San Diego; Chiefs win toss. Fouts hits Jefferson for decisive 14-yard touchdown pass on the last play (15:00) of overtime period.

Nov. 12, 1978—Washington 16, New York Giants 13, at Washington; Redskins win toss. Moseley kicks winning 45-yard field goal at 8:32 after missing first down field goal attempt of 35 yards at 4:50.

Nov. 26, 1978—Green Bay 10, Minnesota 10, at Green Bay; Packers win toss. Both teams have possession of the ball four times.

Dec. 9, 1978—Cleveland 37, New York Jets 34, at Cleveland; Browns win toss. Cockroft kicks 22-yard field goal at 3:07.

Sept. 2, 1979—Atlanta 40, New Orleans 34, at New Orleans; Falcons win toss. Bartkowski's pass intercepted by Myers and returned to Falcons' 46. Erxleben punts to Falcons' 4. James punts to Chandler on Saints' 43. Erxleben punts and Ryckman returns to Falcons' 28. James punts and Chandler returns to Saints' 36. Erxleben retrieves punt snap on Saints' 1 and attempts pass. Mayberry intercepts and returns six yards for touchdown at 8:22.

Sept. 2, 1979—Cleveland 25, New York Jets 22, at New York;

Jets win toss. Leahy's 43-yard field goal attempt goes wide right at 4:41. Evans's punt blocked by Dykes is recovered by Newton. Ramsey punts into end zone for touchback. Evans punts and Harper returns to Jets' 24. Robinson's pass intercepted by Davis and returned 33 yards to Jets' 31. Cockroft kicks 27-yard field goal at 14:45.

* **Sept. 3, 1979—Pittsburgh 16, New England 13**, at Foxboro; Patriots win toss. Hare punts to Swann at Steelers' 31. Bahr kicks 41-yard field goal at 5:10.

Sept. 9, 1979—Tampa Bay 29, Baltimore 26, at Baltimore; Colts win toss. Landry fumbles, recovered by Kollar at Colts' 14. O'Donoghue kicks 31-yard, first-down field goal at 1:41.

Sept. 16, 1979—Denver 20, Atlanta 17, at Atlanta; Broncos win toss. Broncos march 65 yards to Falcons' 7. Turner kicks 24-yard field goal at 6:15.

Sept. 23, 1979—Houston 30, Cincinnati 27, at Cincinnati; Oilers win toss. Parsley punts and Lusby returns to Bengals' 33. Bahr's 32-yard field goal attempt is wide right at 8:05. Parsley's punt downed on Bengals' 5. McInally punts and Ellender returns to Bengals' 42. Fritsch's third down, 29-yard field goal attempt hits left upright and bounces through at 14:28.

Sept. 23, 1979—Minnesota 27, Green Bay 21, at Minnesota; Vikings win toss. Kramer throws 50-yard touchdown pass to Rashad at 3:18.

Oct. 28, 1979—Houston 27, New York Jets 24, at Houston; Oilers win toss. Oilers march 58 yards to Jets' 18. Fritsch kicks 35-yard field goal at 5:10.

Nov. 18, 1979—Cleveland 30, Miami 24, at Cleveland; Browns win toss. Sipe passes 39 yards to Rucker for touchdown at 1:59.

Nov. 25, 1979—Pittsburgh 33, Cleveland 30, at Pittsburgh; Browns win toss. Sipe's pass intercepted by Blount on Steelers' 4. Bradshaw pass intercepted by Bolton on Browns' 12. Evans punts and Bell returns to Steelers' 17. Bahr kicks 37-yard field goal at 14:51.

Nov. 25, 1979—Buffalo 16, New England 13, at Foxboro; Patriots win toss. Hare's punt downed on Bills' 38. Jackson punts and Morgan returns to Patriots' 20. Grogan's pass intercepted by Haslett and returned to Bills' 42. Ferguson's 51-yard pass to Butler sets up N. Mike-Mayer's 29-yard field goal at 9:15.

Dec. 2, 1979—Los Angeles 27, Minnesota 21, at Los Angeles; Rams win toss. Clark punts and Miller returns to Vikings' 25. Kramer's pass intercepted by Brown and returned to Rams' 40. Cromwell, holding for 22-yard field goal attempt, runs around left end untouched for winning score at 6:53.

Sept. 7, 1980—Green Bay 12, Chicago 6, at Green Bay; Bears win toss. Parsons punts and Nixon returns 16 yards. Five plays later, Marcol returns own blocked field goal attempt 24 yards for touchdown at 6:00.

Sept. 14, 1980—San Diego 30, Oakland 24, at San Diego; Raiders win toss. Pastorini's first-down pass intercepted by Edwards. Millen intercepts Fouts' first-down pass and returns to San Diego 46. Bahr's 50-yard field goal attempt partially blocked by Williams and recovered on Chargers' 32. Eight plays later, Fouts throws 24-yard touchdown pass to Jefferson at 8:09.

Sept. 14, 1980—San Francisco 24, St. Louis 21, at San Francisco; Cardinals win toss. Swider punts and Robinson returns to 49ers' 32. San Francisco drives 52 yards to St. Louis 16, where Wersching kicks 33-yard field goal at 4:12.

Oct. 12, 1980—Green Bay 14, Tampa Bay 14, at Tampa Bay; Packers win toss. Teams trade punts twice. Lee returns second Tampa Bay punt to Green Bay 42. Dickey completes three passes to Buccaneers' 18, where Birney's 36-yard field goal attempt is wide right as time expires.

Nov. 9, 1980—Atlanta 33, St. Louis 27, at St. Louis; Falcons win toss. Strong runs 21 yards for touchdown at 4:20.

Nov. 20, 1980—San Diego 27, Miami 24, at Miami; Chargers win toss. Partridge punts into end zone, Dolphins take over on their own 20. Woodley's pass for Nathan intercepted by Lowe

and returned 28 yards to Dolphins' 12. Benirschke kicks 28-yard field goal at 7:14.

Nov. 23, 1980—New York Jets 31, Houston 28, at New York; Jets win toss. Leahy kicks 38-yard field goal at 3:58.

+ **Nov. 27, 1980—Chicago 23, Detroit 17**, at Detroit; Bears win toss. Williams returns kickoff 95 yards for touchdown at 0:21.

Dec. 7, 1980—Buffalo 10, Los Angeles 7, at Buffalo; Rams win toss. Corral punts and Hooks returns to Bills' 34. Ferguson's 30-yard pass to Lewis sets up N. Mike-Mayer's 30-yard field goal at 5:14.

Dec. 7, 1980—San Francisco 38, New Orleans 35, at San Francisco; Saints win toss. Erxleben's punt downed by Hardy on 49ers' 27. Wersching kicks 36-yard field goal at 7:40.

* **Dec. 8, 1980—Miami 16, New England 13**, at Miami; Dolphins win toss. Von Schamann kicks 23-yard field goal at 3:20.

Dec. 14, 1980—Cincinnati 17, Chicago 14, at Chicago; Bengals win toss. Breech kicks 28-yard field goal at 4:23.

Dec. 21, 1980—Los Angeles 20, Atlanta 17, at Los Angeles; Rams win toss. Corral's punt downed at Rams' 37. James punts into end zone for touchback. Corral's punt downed on Falcons' 17. Bartkowski fumbles when hit by Harris, recovered by Delaney. Corral kicks 23-yard field goal on first play of possession at 7:00.

Sept. 27, 1981—Cincinnati 27, Buffalo 24, at Cincinnati; Bills win toss. Cater punts into end zone for touchback. Bengals drive to the Bills' 10 where Breech kicks 28-yard field goal at 9:33.

Sept. 27, 1981—Pittsburgh 27, New England 21, at Pittsburgh; Patriots win toss. Hubach punts and Smith returns five yards to midfield. Four plays later Bradshaw throws 24-yard touchdown pass to Swann at 3:19.

Oct. 4, 1981—Miami 28, New York Jets 28, at Miami; Jets win toss. Teams trade punts twice. Leahy's 48-yard field goal attempt is wide right as time expires.

Oct. 25, 1981—New York Giants 27, Atlanta 24, at Atlanta; Giants win toss. Jennings' punt goes out of bounds at New York 47. Bright returns Atlanta punt to Giants' 14. Woerner fair catches punt at own 28. Andrews fumbles on first play, recovered by Van Pelt. Danelo kicks 40-yard field goal four plays later at 9:20.

Oct. 25, 1981—Chicago 20, San Diego 17, at Chicago; Bears win toss. Teams trade punts. Bears' second punt returned by Brooks to Chargers' 33. Fouts pass intercepted by Fencik and returned 32 yards to San Diego 27. Roveto kicks 27-yard field goal seven plays later at 9:30.

Nov. 8, 1981—Chicago 16, Kansas City 13, at Kansas City; Bears win toss. Teams trade punts. Kansas City takes over on downs on its own 38. Fuller's fumble recovered by Harris on Chicago 36. Roveto's 37-yard field goal wide, but Chiefs penalized for leverage. Roveto's 22-yard field goal attempt three plays later is good at 13:07.

Nov. 8, 1981—Denver 23, Cleveland 20, at Denver; Browns win toss. D. Smith recovers Hill's fumble at Denver 48. Morton's 33-yard pass to Upchurch and 6-yard run by Preston set up Steinfort's 30-yard field goal at 4:10.

Nov. 8, 1981—Miami 30, New England 27, at New England; Dolphins win toss. Orosz punts and Morgan returns six yards to New England 26. Grogan's pass intercepted by Brudzinski who returns 19 yards to Patriots' 26. Von Schamann kicks 30-yard field goal on first down at 7:09.

Nov. 15, 1981—Washington 30, New York Giants 27, at New York; Giants win toss. Nelms returns Giants' punt 26 yards to New York 47. Five plays later Moseley kicks 48-yard field goal at 3:44.

Dec. 20, 1981—New York Giants 13, Dallas 10, at New York; Cowboys win toss and kick off. Jennings punts to Dallas 40. Taylor recovers Dorsett's fumble on second down. Danelo's 33-yard field goal attempt hits right upright and bounces back. White's pass for Pearson intercepted by Hunt and returned seven yards to Dallas 24. Four plays later Danelo kicks 35-yard field goal at 6:19.

Sept. 12, 1982—Washington 37, Philadelphia 34, at Philadelphia; Redskins win toss. Theismann completes five passes for 63 yards to set up Moseley's 26-yard field goal at 4:47.

Sept. 19, 1982—Pittsburgh 26, Cincinnati 20, at Pittsburgh; Bengals win toss. Anderson's pass intended for Kreider intercepted by Woodruff and returned 30 yards to Cincinnati 2. Bradshaw completes two-yard touchdown pass to Stallworth on first down at 1:08.

Dec. 19, 1982—Baltimore 20, Green Bay 20, at Baltimore; Packers win toss. K. Anderson intercepts Dickey's first-down pass and returns to Packers' 42. Miller's 44-yard field goal attempt blocked by G. Lewis. Teams trade punts before Stenerud's 47-yard field goal attempt is wide right. Teams trade punts again before time expires in Colts possession.

Jan. 2, 1983—Tampa Bay 26, Chicago 23, at Tampa; Bears win toss. Parsons punts to T. Bell at Buccaneers' 40. Capece kicks 33-yard field goal at 3:14.

Sept. 4, 1983—Baltimore 29, New England 23, at New England; Patriots win toss. Cooks runs 52 yards with fumble recovery three plays into overtime at 0:30.

Sept. 4, 1983—Green Bay 41, Houston 38, at Houston; Packers win toss. Stenerud kicks 42-yard field goal at 5:55.

Sept. 11, 1983—New York Giants 16, Atlanta 13, at Atlanta; Giants win toss. Dennis returns kickoff 54 yards to Atlanta 41. Haji-Sheikh kicks 30-yard field goal at 3:38.

Sept. 18, 1983—New Orleans 34, Chicago 31, at New Orleans; Bears win toss. Parsons punts and Groth returns five yards to New Orleans 34. Stabler pass intercepted by Schmidt at Chicago 47. Parsons punt downed by Gentry at New Orleans 2. Stabler gains 36 yards in four passes; Wilson 38 on six carries. Andersen kicks 41-yard field goal at 10:57.

Sept. 18, 1983—Minnesota 19, Tampa Bay 16, at Tampa; Vikings win toss. Coleman punts and Bell returns eight yards to Tampa Bay 47. Capece's 33-yard field goal attempt sails wide at 7:26. Dils and Young combine for 48-yard gain to Tampa Bay 27. Ricardo kicks 42-yard field goal at 9:27.

Sept. 25, 1983—Baltimore 22, Chicago 19, at Baltimore; Colts win toss. Allegre kicks 33-yard field goal nine plays later at 4:51.

Sept. 25, 1983—Cleveland 30, San Diego 24, at San Diego; Browns win toss. Walker returns kickoff 33 yards to Cleveland 37. Sipe completes 48-yard touchdown pass to Holt four plays later at 1:53.

Sept. 25, 1983—New York Jets 27, Los Angeles Rams 24, at New York; Jets win toss. Ramsey punts to Irvin who returns to 25 but penalty puts Rams on own 13. Holmes 30-yard interception return sets up Leahy's 26-yard field goal at 3:22.

Oct. 9, 1983—Buffalo 38, Miami 35, at Miami; Dolphins win toss. Von Schamann's 52-yard field goal attempt goes wide at 12:36. Cater punts to Clayton who loses 11 to own 13. Von Schamann's 43-yard field goal attempt sails wide at 5:15. Danelo kicks 36-yard field goal nine plays later at 13:58.

Oct. 9, 1983—Dallas 27, Tampa Bay 24, at Dallas; Cowboys win toss. Septien's 51-yard field-goal attempt goes wide but Buccaneers penalized for roughing kicker. Septien kicks 42-yard field goal at 4:38.

Oct. 23, 1983—Kansas City 13, Houston 10, at Houston; Chiefs win toss. Lowery kicks 41-yard field goal 13 plays later at 7:41.

Oct. 23, 1983—Minnesota 20, Green Bay 17, at Green Bay; Packers win toss. Scribner's punt downed on Vikings' 42. Ricardo kicks 32-yard field goal eight plays later at 5:05.

* **Oct. 24, 1983—New York Giants 20, St. Louis 20,** at St. Louis; Cardinals win toss. Teams trade punts before O'Donoghue's 44-yard field goal attempt is wide left. Jennings' punt returned by Bird to St. Louis 21. Lomax pass intercepted by Haynes who loses six yards to New York 33. Jennings' punt downed on St. Louis 17. O'Donoghue's 19-yard field goal

attempt is wide right. Rutledge's pass intercepted by L. Washington who returns 25 yards to New York 25. O'Donoghue's 42-yard field goal attempt is wide right. Rutledge's pass intercepted by W. Smith at St. Louis 33 to end game.

Oct. 30, 1983—Cleveland 25, Houston 19, at Cleveland; Oilers win toss. Teams trade punts. Nielsen's pass intercepted by Whitwell who returns to Houston 20. Green runs 20 yards for touchdown on first down at 6:34.

Nov. 20, 1983—Detroit 23, Green Bay 20, at Milwaukee; Packers win toss. Scribner punts and Jenkins returns 14 yards to Green Bay 45. Murray's 33-yard field goal attempt is wide left at 9:32. Whitehurst's pass intercepted by Watkins and returned to Green Bay 27. Murray kicks 37-yard field goal four plays later at 8:30.

Nov. 27, 1983—Atlanta 47, Green Bay 41, at Atlanta; Packers win toss. K. Johnson returns interception 31 yards for touchdown at 2:13.

Nov. 27, 1983—Seattle 51, Kansas City 48, at Seattle; Seahawks win toss. Dixon's 47-yard kickoff return sets up N. Johnson's 42-yard field goal at 1:36.

Dec. 11, 1983—New Orleans 20, Philadelphia 17, at Philadelphia; Eagles win toss. Runager punts to Groth who fair catches on New Orleans 32. Stabler completes two passes for 36 yards to Goodlow to set up Andersen's 50-yard field goal at 5:30.

* **Dec. 12, 1983—Green Bay 12, Tampa Bay 9,** at Tampa; Packers win toss. Stenerud kicks 23-yard field goal 11 plays later at 4:07.

Sept. 9, 1984—Detroit 27, Atlanta 24, at Atlanta; Lions win toss. Murray kicks 48-yard field goal nine plays later at 5:06.

Sept. 30, 1984—Tampa Bay 30, Green Bay 27, at Tampa; Packers win toss. Scribner punts 44 yards to Tampa Bay 2. Epps returns Garcia's punt three yards to Green Bay 27. Scribner's punt downed on Buccaneers' 33. Ariri kicks 46-yard field goal 11 plays later at 10:32.

Oct. 14, 1984—Detroit 13, Tampa Bay 7, at Detroit; Buccaneers win toss. Tampa Bay drives to Lions' 39 before Wilder fumbles. Five plays later Danielson hits Thompson with 37-yard touchdown pass at 4:34.

Oct. 21, 1984—Dallas 30, New Orleans 27, at Dallas; Cowboys win toss. Septien kicks 41-yard field goal eight plays later at 3:42.

Oct. 28, 1984—Denver 22, Los Angeles Raiders 19, at Los Angeles; Raiders win toss. Hawkins fumble recovered by Foley at Denver 7. Teams trade punts. Karlis' 42-yard field goal attempt is wide left. Teams trade punts. Wilson pass intercepted by R. Jackson at Los Angeles 45, returned 23 yards to Los Angeles 22. Karlis kicks 35-yard field goal two plays later at 15:00.

Nov. 4, 1984—Philadelphia 23, Detroit 23, at Detroit; Lions win toss. Lions drive to Eagles' 3 in eight plays. Murray's 21-yard field goal attempt hits right upright and bounces back. Jaworski's pass intercepted by Watkins at Detroit 5. Teams trade punts. Cooper returns Black's punt five yards to Eagles' 14. Time expires four plays later with Eagles on own 21.

Nov. 18, 1984—San Diego 34, Miami 28, at San Diego; Chargers win toss. McGee scores eight plays later on a 25-yard run at 3:17.

Dec. 2, 1984—Cincinnati 20, Cleveland 17, at Cleveland; Browns win toss. Simmons returns Cox's punt 30 yards to Cleveland 35. Breech kicks 35-yard field goal seven plays later at 4:34.

Dec. 2, 1984—Houston 23, Pittsburgh 20, at Houston; Oilers win toss. Cooper kicks 30-yard field goal 16 plays later at 5:53.

Sept. 8, 1985—St. Louis 27, Cleveland 24, at Cleveland; Cardinals win toss. O'Donoghue kicks 35-yard field goal nine plays later at 5:27.

Sept. 29, 1985—New York Giants 16, Philadelphia 10, at Philadelphia; Eagles win toss. Jaworski's pass tipped by Quick and intercepted by Patterson who returns 29 yards for touchdown at 0:55.

Oct. 20, 1985—Denver 13, Seattle 10, at Denver; Seahawks win toss. Teams trade punts twice. Krieg's pass intercepted by Hunter and returned to Seahawks' 15. Karlis kicks 24-yard field goal four plays later at 9:19.

Nov. 10, 1985—Philadelphia 23, Atlanta 17, at Philadelphia; Falcons win toss. Donnelly's 62-yard punt goes out of bounds at Eagles' 1. Jaworski completes 99-yard touchdown pass to Quick two plays later at 1:49.

Nov. 10, 1985—San Diego 40, Los Angeles Raiders 34, at San Diego; Chargers win toss. James scores on 17-yard run seven plays later at 3:44.

Nov. 17, 1985—Denver 30, San Diego 24, at Denver; Chargers win toss. Thomas' 40-yard field goal attempt blocked by Smith and returned 60 yards by Wright for touchdown at 4:45.

Nov. 24, 1985—New York Jets 16, New England 13, at New York; Jets win toss. Teams trade punts twice. Patriots' second punt returned 46 yards by Sohn to Patriots' 15. Leahy kicks 32-yard field goal one play later at 10:05.

Nov. 24, 1985—Tampa Bay 19, Detroit 16, at Tampa; Lions win toss. Teams trade punts. Lions' punt downed on Buccaneers' 38. Igwebuike kicks 24-yard field goal 11 plays later at 12:31.

Nov. 24, 1985—Los Angeles Raiders 31, Denver 28, at Los Angeles; Raiders win toss. Bahr kicks 32-yard field goal six plays later at 2:42.

Dec. 8, 1985—Los Angeles Raiders 17, Denver 14, at Denver; Broncos win toss. Teams trade punts twice. Elway's fumble recovered by Townsend at Broncos' 8. Bahr kicks 26-yard field goal one play later at 4:55.

Sept. 14, 1986—Chicago 13, Philadelphia 10, at Chicago; Eagles win toss. Crawford's fumble of kickoff recovered by Jackson at Eagles' 35. Butler kicks 23-yard field goal 10 plays later at 5:56.

Sept. 14, 1986—Cincinnati 36, Buffalo 33, at Cincinnati; Bills win toss. Zander intercepts Kelly's first-down pass and returns it to Bills' 17. Breech kicks 20-yard field goal two plays later at 0:56.

Sept. 21, 1986—New York Jets 51, Miami 45, at New York; Jets win toss. O'Brien completes 43-yard touchdown pass to Walker five plays later at 2:35.

Sept. 28, 1986—Pittsburgh 22, Houston 16, at Houston; Oilers win toss. Johnson's punt returned 41 yards by Woods to Oilers' 15. Abercrombie scores on three-yard run three plays later at 2:35.

Sept. 28, 1986—Atlanta 23, Tampa Bay 20, at Tampa; Falcons win toss. Teams trade punts. Luckhurst kicks 34-yard field goal 10 plays later at 12:35.

Oct. 5, 1986—Los Angeles Rams 26, Tampa Bay 20, at Anaheim; Rams win toss. Dickerson scores four plays later on 42-yard run at 2:16.

Oct. 12, 1986—Minnesota 27, San Francisco 24, at San Francisco; Vikings win toss. C. Nelson kicks 28-yard field goal nine plays later at 4:27.

Oct. 19, 1986—San Francisco 10, Atlanta 10, at Atlanta; Falcons win toss. Teams trade punts twice. Donnelly punts to 49ers' 27. The following play Wilson recovers Rice's fumble at 49ers' 46 as time expires.

Nov. 2, 1986—Washington 44, Minnesota 38, at Washington; Redskins win toss. Schroeder completes 38-yard touchdown pass to Clark four plays later at 1:46.

#Nov. 20, 1986—Los Angeles Raiders 37, San Diego 31, at San Diego; Raiders win toss. Teams trade punts. Allen scores five plays later on 28-yard run at 8:33.

Nov. 23, 1986—Cleveland 37, Pittsburgh 31, at Cleveland; Browns win toss. Teams trade punts. Six plays later Kosar hits Slaughter with 36-yard touchdown pass at 6:37.

Nov. 30, 1986—Chicago 13, Pittsburgh 10, at Chicago; Bears win toss and kick off. Newsome's punt returned by Barnes to Chicago 49. Butler kicks 42-yard field goal five plays later at

3:55.

Nov. 30, 1986—Philadelphia 33, Los Angeles Raiders 27, at Los Angeles; Eagles win toss. Teams trade punts. Long recovers Cunningham's fumble at Philadelphia 42. Waters returns Allen's fumble 81 yards to Los Angeles 4. Cunningham scores on one-yard run two plays later at 6:53.

Nov. 30, 1986—Cleveland 13, Houston 10, at Cleveland; Oilers win toss and kick off. Gossett punts to Houston 39. Luck's pass intercepted by Minnifield at Cleveland 21. Gossett punts to Houston 34. Luck's pass intercepted by Minnifield at Cleveland 43 who returns 20 yards to Houston 37. Moseley kicks 29-yard field goal nine plays later at 14:44.

Dec. 7, 1986—St. Louis 10, Philadelphia 10, at Philadelphia; Cardinals win toss. White blocks Schubert's 40-yard field goal attempt. Teams trade punts. McFadden's 43-yard field goal attempt is wide left. Schubert's 37-yard field goal attempt is wide right. Cavanaugh's pass intercepted by Carter and returned to Eagles' 48 to end game.

Dec. 14, 1986—Miami 37, Los Angeles Rams 31, at Anaheim; Dolphins win toss. Marino completes 20-yard touchdown pass to Duper six plays later at 3:04.

Sept. 20, 1987—Denver 17, Green Bay 17, at Milwaukee; Packers win toss. Del Greco's 47-yard field goal attempt is short. Teams trade punts. Elway intercepted by Noble who returns 10 yards to Green Bay 34. Davis fumbles on next play and Smith recovers. Two plays later, Karlis's 40-yard field goal attempt is wide left. Time expires two plays later with Packers on own 23.

Oct. 11, 1987—Detroit 19, Green Bay 16, at Green Bay; Lions win toss. Prindle's 42-yard field goal attempt is wide left. Packers punt downed on Detroit 17. Prindle kicks 31-yard field goal 16 plays later at 12:26.

Oct. 18, 1987—New York Jets 37, Miami 31, at New York; Jets win toss. Teams trade punts. Ryan intercepted by Hooper at Jets' 47 who returns 11 yards. Mackey intercepted by Haslett at Jets' 37 who returns 9 yards. Jets punt. Mackey intercepted by Radachowsky who returns 45 yards to Miami 24. Ryan completes eight-yard touchdown pass to Hunter five plays later at 14:26.

Oct. 18, 1987—Green Bay 16, Philadelphia 10, at Green Bay; Packers win toss. Hargrove scores on seven-yard run 10 plays later at 5:04.

Oct. 18, 1987—Buffalo 6, New York Giants 3, at Buffalo; Bills win toss. Schlopy's 28-yard field goal attempt is wide left. Teams trade punts. Rutledge intercepted by Clark who returns 23 yards to Buffalo 40. Schlopy kicks 27-yard field goal nine plays later at 14:41.

Oct. 25, 1987—Buffalo 34, Miami 31, at Miami; Bills win toss. Norwood kicks 27-yard field goal seven plays later at 4:12.

Nov. 1, 1987—San Diego 27, Cleveland 24, at San Diego; Browns win toss. Kosar intercepted by Glenn who returns 20 yards to Browns' 25. Abbott kicks 33-yard field goal three plays later at 2:16.

Nov. 15, 1987—Dallas 23, New England 17, at New England; Cowboys win toss. Walker scores on 60-yard run four plays later at 1:50.

+Nov. 26, 1987—Minnesota 44, Dallas 38, at Dallas; Vikings win toss. Coleman's punt downed by Hilton at Cowboys' 37. White intercepted by Studwell who returns 12 yards to Vikings' 37. D. Nelson scores on 24-yard run seven plays later at 7:51.

Nov. 29, 1987—Philadelphia 34, New England 31, at New England; Patriots win toss. Ramsey intercepted by Joyner who returns 29 yards to Eagles' 32. Fryar fair catches Teltschik's punt at Patriots' 13. Franklin's 46-yard field-goal attempt is short. McFadden's 39-yard field goal attempt is wide left. Tatupu fumbles on next play and Cobb recovers. McFadden kicks 38-yard field goal four plays later at 12:16.

Dec. 6, 1987—New York Giants 23, Philadelphia 20, at New York; Giants win toss and kick off. Teams trade punts twice.

Teltschik's punt is returned 16 yards by McConkey to Eagles' 33. Three plays later, Allegre's 50-yard field goal attempt is blocked by Joyner and returned 25 yards by Hoage to Eagles' 30. McConkey returns Teltschik's punt four yards to Giants' 44. Allegre kicks 28-yard field goal four plays later at 10:42.

Dec. 6, 1987—Cincinnati 30, Kansas City 27, at Cincinnati; Bengals win toss. Teams trade punts. Breech kicks 32-yard field goal 16 plays later at 9:44.

Dec. 26, 1987—Washington 27, Minnesota 24, at Minnesota; Redskins win toss. Haji-Sheikh kicks 26-yard field goal six plays later at 2:09.

Sept. 4, 1988—Houston 17, Indianapolis 14, at Indianapolis; Colts win toss. Dickerson fumble recovered by Lyles who returns six yards to Colts' 42. Zendejas kicks 35-yard field goal six plays later at 3:51.

* **Sept. 26, 1988—Los Angeles Raiders 30, Denver 27,** at Denver; Broncos win toss. Teams trade punts twice. Elway intercepted by Lee who returns 20 yards to Broncos' 31. Bahr kicks 35-yard field goal four plays later at 12:35.

Oct. 2, 1988—New York Jets 17, Kansas City 17, at New York; Chiefs win toss. Chiefs punt goes into end zone for touchback. Leahy's 44-yard field goal attempt is wide right. Chiefs punt is returned by Townsell to Jets' 26. Burruss recovers McNeil's fumble at Chiefs' 11. DeBerg intercepted by Humphery at Jets' 49. Three plays later, time expires.

Oct. 9, 1988—Denver 16, San Francisco 13, at San Francisco; Broncos win toss and kick off. Young intercepted by Haynes at Broncos' 32. Denver punt downed at 49ers' 5. Young intercepted by Wilson who returns seven yards to 49ers' 5. Karlis kicks 22-yard field goal two plays later at 8:11.

Oct. 30, 1988—New York Giants 13, Detroit 10, at Detroit; Lions win toss. James's fumble recovered by Taylor at Lions' 22. Three plays later, McFadden kicks 33-yard field goal at 1:13.

Nov. 20, 1988—Buffalo 9, New York Jets 6, at Buffalo; Jets win toss. Vick's fumble recovered by Bennett at Bills' 32. Norwood kicks 30-yard field goal five plays later at 3:47.

Nov. 20, 1988—Philadelphia 23, New York Giants 17, at New York; Eagles win toss. Philadelphia's punt goes into end zone for touchback. Hostetler intercepted by Hoage who returns 11 yards to Giants' 41. Six plays later, Zendejas's 30-yard field-goal attempt is blocked and ball is recovered behind line of scrimmage by Eagles' Simmons, who runs 15 yards for touchdown at 3:09.

Dec. 11, 1988—New England 10, Tampa Bay 7, at New England; Buccaneers win toss and kick off. Staurovsky kicks 27-yard field goal six plays later at 3:08.

Dec. 17, 1988—Cincinnati 20, Washington 17, at Cincinnati; Bengals win toss. Cincinnati's punt returned by Oliphant to Redskins' 16. Grant recovers Williams's fumble at Redskins' 17. Breech kicks 20-yard field goal three plays later at 7:01.

Sept. 24, 1989—Buffalo 47, Houston 41, at Houston; Oilers win toss. Johnson returns Brady's kickoff 17 yards to Oilers' 19. Oilers drive to Buffalo 25, Zendejas's 37-yard field goal blocked, but Bills offsides and Zendejas's second attempt is wide left. Bills' ball and Kelly completes series of passes, including 28-yard game-winner to Andre Reed, at 8:42.

Oct. 8, 1989—Miami 13, Cleveland 10, at Miami; Browns win toss. Metcalf returns Stoyanovich's kickoff 20 yards to Browns' 28. Browns drive bad 46 yards in eight plays; Bahr wide left on 44-yard field goal attempt. Dolphins ball. Browns called for pass interference on Marino pass to Banks at Cleveland 47. Two plays later, Banks's 20-yard reception at Browns' 23 sets up winning 35-yard field goal by Stoyanovich at 6:23.

Oct. 22, 1989—Denver 24, Seattle 21, at Seattle; Seahawks win toss. Treadwell's 56-yard kickoff returned 18 yards by Jefferson to Seahawks' 27. Seahawks drive to Broncos' 22 in 10 plays, but Johnson's 40-yard field goal attempt wide left. Smith intercepts a Krieg pass and returns it 28 yards to Seahawks' 10. Treadwell kicks winning 27-yard field goal at 7:46.

Oct. 29, 1989—New England 23, Indianapolis 20, at Indi-

anapolis; Patriots win toss. Biasucci kickoff returned 13 yards to Patriots' 23 by Martin. Holding penalty brings ball back to Patriots' 13. After six plays, Feagles punt returned 11 yards by Verdin to Colts' 28. Six plays later, Colts punt to Martin at Patriots' 12. Grogan completes three straight passes to Patriots' 44. Five consecutive runs put New England on Colts' 33. Davis kicks a 51-yard winning field goal for Patriots at 9:46.

Oct. 29, 1989—Green Bay 23, Detroit 20, at Milwaukee; Lions win toss. Sanders touchback on Jacke kickoff. On first play, Murphy intercepts Lions' Peete and returns it three yards to Lions' 26. Fullwood gains five yards on three plays to set up Jacke's 38-yard field goal at 2:14.

Nov. 5, 1989—Minnesota 23, Los Angeles Rams 21, at Minneapolis; Rams win toss. Karlis's kick returned 18 yards by Delpino to Rams' 19. Drive stops at Rams' 28. Merriweather blocks Hatcher's punt at 12. Ball rolls out of end zone for safety.

Nov. 19, 1989—Cleveland 10, Kansas City 10, at Cleveland; Browns win toss. Browns punt three times; Chiefs twice; before Kansas City's Lowery misses 47-yard field goal with 17 seconds remaining in overtime. Kosar's pass intercepted as time expired.

Nov. 26, 1989—Los Angeles Rams 20, New Orleans 17, at New Orleans; Saints win toss. Lansford's kickoff returned 27 yards to Saints' 30. After four plays, Barnhardt punts to Rams' 15. Saints penalized 35 yards for interference to Rams' 43. Three plays later, Everett hits Anderson with 14-yard pass to Saints' 40, then 26-yarder to put Rams in field goal position. Lansford kicks 31-yard field goal at 6:38.

Dec. 3, 1989—Los Angeles Raiders 16, Denver 13, at Los Angeles; Broncos win toss. Bell returns Jaeger kickoff 14 yards to Broncos' 18. Broncos' penalized for illegal block to Broncos' 9. Elway completes three passes for two first downs. On third and eight Elway sacked for 10-yard loss. Horan punts, Adams calls for fair catch at Raiders' 29. Dyal's 26-yard reception moves Raiders to Denver 43. Raiders move ball 34 yards in three plays to set up Jaeger's 26-yard field goal at 7:02.

Dec. 10, 1989—Indianapolis 23, Cleveland 17, at Indianapolis; Browns win toss. Teams trade punts. McNeil returns Colts' punt 42 yards to 42. Seven plays later, Bahr misses 35-yard field goal attempt. Three plays later, Stark punts and McNeil returns ball to 50-yard line. Two plays later, Prior intercepts Kosar's pass at Colts' 42 and returns it 58 yards for touchdown at 10:54.

Dec. 17, 1989—Cleveland 23, Minnesota 17, at Cleveland; Browns win toss. Browns punt to Vikings' 18. Six plays later, Vikings punt to Browns' 22. Nine plays later, Bahr lines up to attempt 31-yard field goal. Holder Pagel takes snap and passes 14 yards to Waiters for touchdown at 9:30.

Sept. 23, 1990—Denver 34, Seattle 31, at Denver; Seahawks win toss. Loville returns kickoff 19 yards to Seahawks' 27. Seahawks drive to Broncos' 26, where Johnson misses 44-yard field goal wide right. Broncos take over and Elway completes series of passes to set up Treadwell's 25-yard field goal at 9:14.

Sept. 30, 1990—Tampa Bay 23, Minnesota 20, at Minnesota; Vikings win toss. Vikings drive to Buccaneers' 31; Igwebuike's 48-yard field goal attempt wide left. Buccaneers drive to Vikings' 43 and punt. Gannon's pass is intercepted at Vikings' 26 by Wayne Haddix. Buccaneers drive to Vikings' 19 to set up Christie's 36-yard field goal at 9:11.

Oct. 7, 1990—Cincinnati 34, Los Angeles Rams 31, at Anaheim; Rams win toss. Berry returns kickoff to Rams' 21. After 3 plays, English punts and Green downs ball at Bengals' 25. After 3 plays, Johnson punts and Sutton downs ball at Rams' 29-yard line. After 3 plays, English punts and Price signals fair catch at Bengals' 47. Esiason completes series of passes to 26-yard line to set up Breech's 44-yard field goal at 11:56.

Nov. 4, 1990—Washington 41, Detroit 38, at Detroit; Redskins win toss. Howard downs kickoff on Redskins' 15. After 3 plays, Mojsiejenko punts to Redskins' 45. After 3 plays, Arnold punts to Redskins' 10. Rutledge completes series of passes to set up

Lohmiller's 34-yard field goal at 9:10.

Nov. 18, 1990—Chicago 16, Denver 13, at Denver; Broncos win toss. Ezor returns kickoff to Broncos' 12. Both teams have ball twice and have to punt after each possession. Broncos punt after third possession of overtime and Bailey returns 20 yards to Broncos' 34. Harbaugh completes 10-yard pass to Thornton to set up Butler's 44-yard field goal at 13:14.

Nov. 25, 1990—Seattle 13, San Diego 10, at San Diego; Chargers win toss. Lewis returns kickoff to Chargers' 22. After 2 plays, Cox fumbles and ball is recovered by Porter at Chargers' 23. After two plays, Johnson kicks 40-yard field goal at 3:01.

Dec. 2, 1990—Chicago 23, Detroit 17, at Chicago; Lions win toss. Gray returns kickoff to Lions' 35. After 10 plays, Murray misses 35-yard field goal. Bears take possession at Chicago 20. Harbaugh completes 50-yard game-winning pass to Anderson at 10:57.

Dec. 2, 1990—Seattle 13, Houston 10, at Seattle; Seahawks win toss. Warren returns kickoff to Seahawks' 13. After 5 plays, Donnelly punts to Oilers' 23-yard line. Ford's fumble recovered by Wyman. Seahawks take possession at Oilers' 27. After 2 plays, Johnson kicks 42-yard field goal at 4:25.

Dec. 9, 1990—Miami 23, Philadelphia 20, at Miami; Eagles win toss. After 11 plays, Feagles punts to Dolphins' 26. After 6 plays, Roby punts to Eagles' 14 and Harris returns to 25. After 3 plays, Feagles punts to Dolphins' 43. Marino completes series of passes to Eagles' 22. Stoyanovich kicks 39-yard field goal at 12:32.

Dec. 9, 1990—San Francisco 20, Cincinnati 17, at Cincinnati; 49ers win toss. Carter returns kickoff to 49ers' 19. After 10 plays, Cofer kicks 23-yard field goal at 6:12.

* **Sept. 23, 1991—Chicago 19, New York Jets 13,** at Chicago; Jets win toss. Mathis returns kickoff seven yards to New York's 12. Jets drive to New York 26; Bailey returns punt to Chicago 39. Bears drive to Jets' 44-yard line and punt into the end zone. Jets drive to Bears' 11 where Leahy's 28-yard field goal attempt is wide left. Bears drive from 20 to Jets' 1 where Harbaugh runs for touchdown at 14:42.

Oct. 13, 1991—Los Angeles Raiders 23, Seattle 20, at Seattle; Seahawks win toss. Seahawks begin on 20. After 5 plays, Tuten punts and Brown signals fair catch at Raiders' 24. After 3 plays, Gossett punts and Land downs ball at Seattle 9. After 1 play, Lott intercepts at Seahawks' 19 to set up Jaeger's game-winning 37-yard field goal at 6:37.

Oct. 20, 1991—Cleveland 30, San Diego 24, at San Diego; Chargers win toss. After kickoff, Chargers drive to Browns' 45 and punt to Browns' 6 where Hendrickson downs ball. Browns drive to 38 and punt; Taylor fair catches on Chargers' 14. After 3 plays, Brandon intercepts at Chargers' 30 and scores at 5:58.

Oct. 20, 1991—New England 26, Minnesota 23, at New England; Patriots win toss. Martin returns kickoff 18 yards to New England 22. Patriots drive to Minnesota 19. Staurovsky's 36-yard field goal attempt is wide left. Minnesota drives to the 50 where Newsome punts into end zone. On first play, McMillian intercepts at the 40 for Minnesota. After 2 plays, Marion causes Jordan fumble and Pool recovers at New England 20. New England drives to Minnesota 24 where Staurovsky kicks 42-yard field goal as time expires.

Nov. 3, 1991—New York Jets 19, Green Bay 16, at New York; Packers win toss. Thompson returns kickoff 30 yards to Packers' 39. Green Bay drives to New York 24 where Jacke's 42-yard field-goal attempt is wide right. Jets drive to 50. Aguiar's punt is fumbled by Sikahema and recovered by New York at Packers' 23. After 2 plays, Leahy kicks 37-yard field goal at 9:40.

Nov. 3, 1991—Washington 16, Houston 13, at Washington; Redskins win toss. Mitchell returns kickoff 9 yards to Washington 14. After 4 plays, Goodburn punts and Givins returns to Houston 31. After 1 play, Moon's pass is intercepted by Green at Oilers' 35. After 3 plays, Lohmiller kicks 41-yard field goal at 4:01.

Nov. 10, 1991—Houston 26, Dallas 23, at Houston; Oilers win

toss. Pinkett returns kickoff 20 yards to Houston 24. After 6 plays, Montgomery punts and Martin returns to Dallas 24. Cowboys drive to Oilers' 24 where Smith fumbles and McDowell recovers at Oilers' 15. Houston drives to Dallas 5 where Del Greco kicks 23-yard field goal at 14:31.

Nov. 10, 1991—Pittsburgh 33, Cincinnati 27, at Cincinnati; Steelers wins toss. Woodson downs kickoff for touchback. After 3 plays, Stryzinski punts and Barber returns 7 yards to Cincinnati 38. Bengals drive to Pittsburgh 37 where Woods fumbles and Lloyd returns recovery to Cincinnati 44. After 2 plays, O'Donnell passes to Green for 26-yard touchdown at 6:32.

#**Nov. 24, 1991—Atlanta 23, New Orleans 20,** at New Orleans; Falcons win toss. Falcons begin at 20. After 3 plays, Fulhage punts and Fenerty signals fair catch at New Orleans 43. After 3 plays, Barnhardt punts and Thompson downs ball at Atlanta 23. After 3 plays, Fulhage punts and Fenerty fair catches at New Orleans 25. Saints drive to Atlanta 38 where Andersen misses 55-yard field-goal attempt. After 1 play, Rozier fumbles and Martin recovers on 50. Saints drive to Atlanta 38 where Barnhardt punts to Falcons' 2. Atlanta drives to New Orleans 33 where Johnson kicks 50-yard field goal at 13:03.

Nov. 24, 1991—Miami 16, Chicago 13, at Chicago; Dolphins wins toss. Butler kicks to Miami 20 where Paige returns kickoff 15 yards to 35. Miami drives to Chicago 9 where Stoyanovich kicks 27-yard field goal at 4:11.

Dec. 8, 1991—Buffalo 30, Los Angeles Raiders 27, at Los Angeles; Raiders win toss. Daluiso kicks into end zone for touchback. On third play, Kelso intercepts for Buffalo and returns ball to Bills' 36. Bills drive to Los Angeles 24 where Norwood kicks 42-yard field goal at 2:34.

Dec. 8, 1991—Kansas City 20, San Diego 17, at Kansas City; Chiefs win toss. Carney kicks to Kansas City 10 where Stradford returns 23 yards to 33. After 3 plays, Barker punts to San Diego 4. Chargers drive to 40 where Kidd punts 60 yards into end zone for touchback. Kansas City drives to San Diego 39 where Barker punts 38 yards to 1. After 3 plays, Kidd punts 41 yards to San Diego 42 where Stradford returns 12 yards to 30. Chiefs drive to San Diego 1 where Lowery kicks 18-yard field goal at 11:26.

Dec. 8, 1991—New England 23, Indianapolis 17, at New England; Colts wins toss. Baumann kicks off to Indianapolis 2 where Martin returns 23 yards to 25. After 3 downs, Stark punts to New England 17 where Henderson returns 8 yards to 25. New England drives to 50 where McCarthy punts and Prior signals fair catch at Indianapolis 15. After 3 plays, Stark punts to New England 40 where Henderson returns 7 yards to 47. After 2 plays, Millen passes to Timpson for 45-yard touchdown at 8:55.

Dec. 22, 1991—Detroit 17, Buffalo 14, at Buffalo; Lions wins toss. Daluiso kicks off to Detroit 20 where Dozier returns 15 yards to Lions 35. Lions drive to Bills' 3 where Murray kicks 21-yard field goal at 4:23.

Dec. 22, 1991—New York Jets 23, Miami 20, at Miami; Jets win toss. Aguiar kicks to Miami's 30 where Logan returns 3 yards to the 33. After 4 downs, Stoyanovich punts to Jets' 15 where Baty returns 8 yards to 23. Jets drive to Miami 12 where Allegre kicks 30-yard field goal at 6:33.

Sept. 6, 1992—Minnesota 23, Green Bay 20, at Green Bay; Vikings win toss. Nelson returns kickoff 14 yards to the Minnesota 23. After 5 plays, Newsome punts 49 yards to Green Bay 21 where Brooks returns 12 yards to the 33. After 2 plays, Glenn intercepts pass at the Vikings' 30. On first play, Allen fumbles and Billups recovers at Green Bay 35. After 3 plays, McJulien punts 33 yards to Vikings' 35. Vikings drive to Minnesota 48; Newsome punts 52 yards for touchback. After 3 plays, McJulien punts and Parker returns 10 yards to Green Bay 48. Vikings drive to Packers' 9 where Reveiz kicks 26-yard field goal at 10:20.

Sept. 13, 1992—Cincinnati 24, Los Angeles Raiders 21, at Cincinnati; Raiders win toss. Land returns kickoff 13 yards but fumbles at Los Angeles' 20; ball recovered by Bengals' Bennett at Raiders' 21. After 1 play, Breech kicks 34-yard field goal at

1:01.

Sept. 20, 1992—Houston 23, Kansas City 20, at Houston; Chiefs win toss. Carter returns kickoff 25 yards to Kansas City 28. On third play of drive, Birden fumbles at Kansas City 34; ball recovered by Houston's D. Smith at Chiefs' 23. After one play, Del Greco kicks 39-yard field goal at 1:55.

Oct. 11, 1992—Indianapolis 6, New York Jets 3, at Indianapolis; Colts win toss. Verdin returns kickoff 33 yards to Colts' 36. Colts drive to Jets' 30 where Biasucci kicks 47-yard field goal at 3:01.

#Nov. 8, 1992—Cincinnati 31, Chicago 28, at Chicago; Bears win toss. Lewis returns kickoff 22 yards to Chicago's 29. Bears drive to Chicago's 46 where Gardocki punts; fair catch by Wright at the Cincinnati 17. Bengals drive to Bears' 18 where Breech kicks 36-yard field goal at 8:39.

Nov. 15, 1992—New England 37, Indianapolis 34, at Indianapolis; Colts win toss. Verdin returns kickoff 10 yards to Colts' 20; holding penalty brings ball back to Colts' 10. After two plays, Henderson intercepts pass at Colts' 38 and returns it 9 yards to the 29. In three plays, Patriots drive to 1 where Baumann kicks 18-yard field goal at 3:25.

Nov. 29, 1992—Indianapolis 16, Buffalo 13, at Indianapolis; Colts win toss. Verdin returns kickoff 24 yards to Colts' 22. Colts drive to Buffalo 22 where Biasucci kicks 40-yard field goal at 3:51.

* Nov. 30, 1992—Seattle 16, Denver 13, at Seattle; Seahawks win toss. Daluiso kicks through end zone for touchback. After three plays, Tuten punts 53 yards to Denver 18 where Marshall returns for no gain. After three plays, Rodriguez punts 29 yards to Seattle 45 where Warren signals fair catch. Seahawks drive to Denver 15 where Kasay's 33-yard field goal attempt misses. Broncos take over at Denver 20. After three plays, Rodriguez punts 43 yards to Seattle 38 where Warren signals for fair catch. After four plays, Tuten punts 39 yards to Denver 4 where Daniels downs punt. After three plays, Rodriguez punts 46 yards to Denver 48 where Warren returns 10 yards to the 38. Seahawks drive to Denver 14 where Kasay kicks 32-yard field goal at 11:10.

Dec. 13, 1992—Philadelphia 20, Seattle 17, at Seattle; Eagles win toss. Sydner returns kick 12 yards to Eagles' 16; illegal block penalty brings ball back to 8. Eagles drive to Philadelphia 45 where Feagles punts for a touchback. After 6 plays, Tuten punts 45 yards to Philadelphia 22 where Sydner returns 7 yards to 29. After 6 plays, Feagles punts 44 yards to Seattle 26 where Warren returns 5 yards to 31. After 5 plays, Tuten punts 32 yards to Philadelphia 20 where Sydner signals for fair catch. Eagles drive to Seattle 8 where Ruzek kicks 44-yard field goal with no time remaining.

Dec. 27, 1992—Miami 16, New England 13, at New England; Patriots win toss. Lockwood returns kickoff 15 yards to Patriots' 21. After three plays, McCarthy punts 39 yards to Miami 33 where Miller returns 2 yards to the 35. Miami drives to New England 18 where Stoyanovich kicks 35-yard field goal at 8:17.

Sept. 12, 1993—Detroit 19, New England 16, at New England; Patriots win toss. Patriots begin at 20. After 3 plays, Saxon punts 42 yards to Detroit 29 where Gray returns 12 yards to the 41. After 3 plays, Arnold punts 41 yards to New England 12 where Brown returns 16 yards to the 28. Patriots drive to Detroit 44 where Saxon punts into the end zone for a touchback. Detroit drives to New England 20 where Hanson kicks 38-yard field goal at 11:04.

Nov. 7, 1993—Buffalo 13, New England 10, at New England; Patriots win toss. T. Brown returns kickoff 27 yards to Patriots 30. Patriots drive to Buffalo 48 where Bills take over on downs. Bills drive to New England 25 where Metzelaars fumbles, and C. Brown recovers. After 3 plays, Saxon punts 46 yards to Buffalo 24 where Copeland returns 11 yards to the 35. Bills drive to New England 14 where Christie kicks 32-yard field goal at 9:22.

Dec. 19, 1993—Phoenix 30, Seattle 27, at Seattle; Cardinals win toss. Bailey returns kickoff 14 yards to Cardinals 20. Cardinals drive to Seattle 23 where Davis kicks 41-yard field goal at

6:45.

Jan. 2, 1994—Dallas 16, New York Giants 13, at New York; Giants win toss. Meggett returns kickoff 19 yards to Giants 19. After 6 plays, Horan punts 45 yards to Cowboys 25 where Widmer downs punt. Cowboys drive to Giants' 23 where Murray kicks 41-yard field goal at 10:44.

Jan. 2, 1994—New England 33, Miami 27, at New England; Dolphins win toss. McDuffie returns kickoff 21 yards to Miami 27. After 3 plays, Hatcher punts 43 yards to New England 29 where Harris returns 6 yards to the 35. After 2 plays, Brown intercepts pass from Bledsoe and returns 3 yards to Miami 44. After 3 plays, Hatcher punts 37 yards to New England 14 where Harris returns 18 yards to the 32. After 2 plays, Bledsoe passes 36 yards to Timpson for touchdown at 4:44.

Jan. 2, 1994—Los Angeles Raiders 33, Denver 30, at Los Angeles; Broncos win toss. Delpino returns kickoff 12 yards to Denver 25. Broncos drive to Los Angeles 22 where Elam's 40-yard field goal attempt is wide left. Raiders drive to Denver 29 where Jaeger kicks 47-yard field goal at 7:10.

* Jan. 3, 1994—Philadelphia 37, San Francisco 34, at San Francisco; 49ers win toss. Walker returns kickoff, 19 yards to San Francisco 27. 49ers drive to Philadelphia 14 where Cofer misses 32-yard field goal. Eagles start at their 20-yard line, and, after 3 plays, Feagles punts 48 yards to San Francisco 36 where Carter fumbles and 49ers recover. After 7 plays, Wilmsmeyer punts 57 yards to Philadelphia 6 where Sikahema returns 16 yards to the 22. Eagles drive to San Francisco 10 where Ruzek kicks 28-yard field goal with no time remaining.

Sept. 4, 1994—Detroit 31, Atlanta 28, at Detroit; Falcons win toss. Falcons start at their own 16 after holding penalty on kickoff. After 3 plays, Alexander punts 41 yards to Detroit 39 where Clay returns 12 yards to Atlanta 49. Detroit drives to Atlanta 20 where Hanson kicks 37-yard field goal at 5:14.

Sept. 11, 1994—New York Jets 25, Denver 22, at New York; Jets win toss. Murrell returns kickoff 24 yards to New York 33. Jets drive to Denver 22 where Lowery kicks 39-yard field goal at 3:57.

* Sept. 19, 1994—Detroit 20, Dallas 17, at Dallas; Lions win toss. Gray returns kickoff 24 yards to Detroit 32. Lions drive to Dallas 34 where Hanson's 51-yard field-goal attempt is blocked by Lett. Cowboys take possession at Dallas 42. Cowboys drive to Detroit 37 where Kennard fumbles and Swilling recovers. Lions take possession at Detroit 45. After 6 plays, Montgomery punts 31 yards to Dallas 16. Cowboys drive to Dallas 49 where Aikman fumbles and Thomas recovers at Dallas 43. Lions drive to Dallas 26 where Hanson kicks 44-yard field goal at 14:33.

Oct. 16, 1994—Arizona 19, Washington 16, at Washington; Redskins win toss. Mitchell returns kickoff 27 yards to Washington 41. Redskins drive to Arizona 34 where Lohmiller's 51-yard field-goal attempt is blocked by Joyner and recovered by Williams who returns it to the Washington 37. After 5 plays, Peterson's 45-yard field-goal attempt is wide right. Redskins take possession at the Washington 36. After 3 plays, Roby punts 36 yards to the Arizona 37 where Robinson returns 3 yards to the 40. After 3 plays, Feagles punts 51 yards for a touchback. After 1 play, Shuler's pass is intercepted by Hoage who returns it to the Washington 12. Peterson kicks 29-yard field goal at 10:00.

Oct. 16, 1994—Miami 20, Los Angeles Raiders 17, at Miami; Dolphins win toss. McDuffie returns kickoff 19 yards to Miami 23. Dolphins drive to Los Angeles 12 where Stoyanovich kicks 29-yard field goal at 5:46.

#Oct. 20, 1994—Minnesota 13, Green Bay 10, at Minnesota; Vikings win toss. Ismail returns kickoff 22 yards to Minnesota 29. Vikings drive to Green Bay 9 where Fuad Reveiz kicks 27-yard field goal at 4:26.

Oct. 30, 1994—Detroit 28, New York Giants 25, at New York; Giants win toss. Lewis returns kickoff 16 yards to New York 27. After 3 plays, Horan punts 42 yards to Detroit 24 where Gray calls for fair catch. Detroit drives to New York 6 where Hanson kicks 24-yard field goal at 6:43.

#**Oct. 30, 1994—Arizona 20, Pittsburgh 17,** at Arizona; Steelers win toss. Johnson returns kickoff 24 yards to Pittsburgh 30 where he fumbles and Arizona's Merritt recovers at Pittsburgh 32. After 3 plays, Davis kicks 51-yard field goal at 1:40.

Nov. 6, 1994—Cincinnati 20, Seattle 17, at Seattle; Seahawks win toss. Warren returns kickoff 32 yards to Seattle 33. After 3 plays, Tuten punts 37 yards to Cincinnati 28 where Sawyer calls for fair catch. After 3 plays, Johnson punts 64 yards to Seattle 2 where Truitt downs ball. Seahawks drive to Seattle 38 where Tuten punts 50 yards to Cincinnati 12 and Sawyer returns 5 yards to 17. Blake passes to Scott for 76 yards to Seattle 7. Pelfrey kicks 26-yard field goal at 8:14.

Nov. 6, 1994—Pittsburgh 12, Houston 9, at Houston; Steelers win toss. Stone returns kickoff 15 yards to Pittsburgh 28. After 3 plays, Royals punts 53 yards to Houston 13 where Givins downs ball. After 3 plays, Camarillo punts 57 yards to Pittsburgh 31 where Woodson returns 20 yards to Houston 49. After 3 plays, Royals punts 43 yards to Houston 15 where Coleman returns 3 yards to 18. After 5 plays, Camarillo punts 57 yards to Pittsburgh 12 where Hastings returns 12 yards to 24. Steelers drive to Houston 41 where Royals punts 29 yards to Houston 12, and Coleman calls for fair catch. Brown fumbles on first play and Jones recovers at Houston 22. After 1 play, Anderson kicks 40-yard field goal at 11:24.

Nov. 13, 1994—New England 26, Minnesota 20, at New England; Patriots win toss. Thompson returns kickoff 27 yards to New England 33. Patriots drive to Minnesota 14 where Bledsoe passes 14 yards to Turner for touchdown at 4:10.

Nov. 20, 1994—Pittsburgh 16, Miami 13, at Pittsburgh; Steelers win toss. Stone returns kickoff 15 yards to Pittsburgh 16. Steelers drive to Miami 39 where they lose possession on downs. Dolphins drive to Pittsburgh 47 where Arnold punts 35 yards to Pittsburgh 12 and Oliver downs ball. Steelers drive to Miami 21 where Anderson kicks 39-yard field goal at 10:19.

Nov. 27, 1994—Chicago 19, Arizona 16, at Arizona; Cardinals win toss. Levy returns kickoff 31 yards to Arizona 45. After 5 plays, Feagles punts 38 yards to the end zone for a touchback. Bears drive to Arizona 10 where Butler kicks 27-yard field goal at 8:11.

Nov. 27, 1994—Tampa Bay 20, Minnesota 17, at Minnesota; Buccaneers win toss. Harris returns kickoff 12 yards to Tampa Bay 38. After 6 plays, Stryzinski punts 40 yards to Minnesota 4 where Guliford muffs punt and Buccaneers' Brady recovers. Husted kicks 22-yard field goal at 2:08.

Dec. 1, 1994—Minnesota 33, Chicago 27, at Minnesota; Bears win toss. Lewis returns kickoff 23 yards to Chicago 33. Bears drive to Minnesota 22 where Butler's 40-yard field goal attempt is wide left. After 1 play, Moon passes 65 yards to Carter for touchdown at 5:46.

Dec. 4, 1994—Denver 20, Kansas City 17, at Kansas City; Broncos win toss. Milburn returns kickoff 24 yards to Denver 29. After 3 plays, Millen fumbles and Phillips recovers at Denver 35. After 4 plays, Allen fumbles and Smith recovers at Denver 27. After 3 plays, Rouen punts 45 yards to Kansas City 25 where Hughes calls for fair catch. After 3 plays, Aguiar punts 33 yards to Denver 42 where Chiefs down ball. Broncos drive to Kansas City 17 where Elam kicks 34-yard field goal at 12:12.

Sept. 3, 1995—Cincinnati 24, Indianapolis 21, at Indianapolis; Bengals win toss. Dunn returns kickoff 15 yards to Bengals' 17. Cincinnati drives to Indianapolis 29 where Pelfrey kicks 47-yard field goal at 2:36.

Sept. 3, 1995—Atlanta 23, Carolina 20, at Atlanta; Panthers win toss. Baldwin downs kickoff for touchback. Panthers drive to Carolina 42 where Reich fumbles and ball is recovered by Archambeau at Carolina 31. Falcons drive to Panthers' 16 where Andersen kicks 35-yard field goal at 6:17.

Sept. 10, 1995—Indianapolis 27, New York Jets 24, at New York; Jets win toss. Carter downs kickoff for touchback. Jets punt downed at Colts' 37. Colts drive to Jets' 35 where Cofer kicks 52-yard field goal at 4:27.

Sept. 10, 1995—Kansas City 20, New York Giants 17, at Kansas City; Chiefs win toss. Vanover returns kickoff 30 yards to Chiefs' 28. Aguiar punts to Giants' 3. Horan punts to Chiefs' 49. Chiefs drive to Giants' 6 where Elliott kicks 23-yard field goal at 7:49.

Sept. 17, 1995—Kansas City 23, Oakland 17, at Kansas City; Chiefs win toss. Vanover returns kickoff 28 yards to Chiefs' 41. M. Allen fumbles, ball recovered by Robbins at Raiders' 38. Hasty intercepts pass at Chiefs' 36 and returns it 64 yards for touchdown at 4:27.

Sept. 17, 1995—Atlanta 27, New Orleans 24, at Atlanta; Saints win toss. Hughes returns kickoff 21 yards to Saints' 17. Metcalf returns Wilmsmeyer's punt 18 yards to Saints' 39. Stryzinski punts, fair catch by Hughes at Saints' 14. Wilmsmeyer punt downed at Falcons' 6. Falcons drive to Saints' 3 where Andersen kicks 21-yard field goal at 7:58.

#**Sept. 17, 1995—Dallas 23, Minnesota 17,** at Minnesota; Cowboys win toss. K. Williams returns kickoff 23 yards to Cowboys' 27. E. Smith scores on 31-yard run at 2:26.

Oct. 8, 1995—Indianapolis 27, Miami 24, at Miami; Colts win toss. Warren returns kickoff 25 yards to Colts' 33. Colts drive to Dolphins' 10 where Blanchard kicks 27-yard field goal at 4:58.

Oct. 8, 1995—New York Giants 27, Arizona 21, at New York; Cardinals win toss. Terry returns kickoff 20 yards to Cardinals' 23. Hamilton recovers Krieg's fumble at Cardinals' 36. Lynch recovers Brown's fumble at Cardinals' 38. Armstead intercepts pass at Giants' 42 and returns it 58 yards for touchdown at 4:05.

Oct. 8, 1995—Minnesota 23, Houston 17, at Minnesota; Vikings win toss. Palmer returns kickoff 10 yards to Vikings' 15. Saxon's punt downed at Oilers' 8. Washington intercepts pass at Vikings' 47 and returns it 25 yards to Oilers' 28. R. Smith scores on 20-yard run at 7:10.

Oct. 8, 1995—Philadelphia 37, Washington 34, at Philadelphia; Redskins win toss. Redskins take possession at their 20 after touchback. Turk punt out of bounds at Eagles' 9. Eagles drive to Redskins' 18 where Anderson kicks 35-yard field goal at 10:06.

* **Oct. 9, 1995—Kansas City 29, San Diego 23,** at Kansas City; Chargers win toss. Coleman returns kickoff 24 yards to Chargers' 28. Vanover makes fair catch of Bennett's punt at Chiefs' 15. Coleman makes fair catch of Aguiar's punt at Chargers' 43. Vanover returns Bennett's punt 86 yards for a touchdown at 7:27.

Oct. 15, 1995—Tampa Bay 20, Minnesota 17, at Tampa Bay; Buccaneers win toss. Edmonds returns kickoff 19 yards to Buccaneers' 22. A. Lee returns Roby's punt to Vikings' 48. Vikings drive to Tampa Bays' 35 where Reveiz's 53-yard field-goal attempt is wide right. Buccaneers take over at own 43 and drive to Vikings' 33 where Husted kicks 51-yard field goal at 6:23.

Oct. 22, 1995—Washington 36, Detroit 30, at Washington; Redskins win toss. B. Mitchell returns kickoff 16 yards to Redskins' 27. Turk's punt downed at Lions' 4. D. Green intercepts S. Mitchell's pass and returns it 7 yards for touchdown at 3:41.

Oct. 29, 1995—Carolina 20, New England 17, at New England; Panthers win toss. Baldwin returns kickoff 22 yards to Panthers' 25. Meggett makes fair catch of Barnhardt's punt at Patriots' 9. Guliford returns O'Neill's punt 9 yards to Patriots' 32. Panthers drive to Patriots' 12 where Kasay kicks 29-yard field goal at 7:08.

Oct. 29, 1995—Cleveland 29, Cincinnati 26, at Cincinnati; Browns win toss. Hunter returns kickoff 31 yards to Browns' 31. Bieniemy returns Tupa's punt 9 yards to Bengals' 37. McCardell makes fair catch of Johnson's punt at Browns' 12. Bieniemy returns Tupa's punt 0 yards to Bengals' 38. Hall intercepts Blake's pass and returns it 5 yards to Bengals' 45. Browns drive to Bengals' 11 where Stover kicks 28-yard field goal at 6:30.

Oct. 29, 1995—Arizona 20, Seattle 14, at Arizona; Cardinals win toss. Dowdell returns kickoff 16 yards to Cardinals' 25. Cardinals drive to Seahawks' 10 where G. Davis' 27-yard field goal attempt is blocked. L. Lynch intercepts Friesz's pass at Cardinals' 28 and returns it 72 yards for a touchdown at 11:16.

Nov. 5, 1995—Pittsburgh 37, Chicago 34, at Chicago; Bears win toss. Timpson returns kickoff 23 yards to Bears' 33. Hastings returns Sauerbrun's punt 2 yards to Steelers' 31. Steelers drive to Bears' 6 where N. Johnson kicks 24-yard field goal at 8:19.

Nov. 12, 1995—Minnesota 30, Arizona 24, at Arizona; Vikings win toss. A. Lee returns kickoff 20 yards to Vikings' 25. Moon throws 50-yard touchdown pass to Ismail at 2:16.

Nov. 26, 1995—Arizona 40, Atlanta 37, at Arizona; Falcons win loss. J. Anderson returns kickoff 20 yards to Falcons' 20. Stryzinski fumbles punt snap. Recovered by England at Falcons' 10 where G. Davis kicks 28-yard field goal at 1:43.

#Dec. 10, 1995—Tampa Bay 13, Green Bay 10, at Tampa Bay; Buccaneers win toss. Edmonds returns kickoff 24 yards to Buccaneers' 23. Tampa Bay drives to Packers' 29 where Husted kicks 47-yard field goal at 3:46.

#Sept. 1, 1996—Buffalo 23, New York Giants 20, at New York; Bills win toss. Daluiso kick is a touchback. Bills drive to Buffalo 46. Toomer returns Mohr's punt to Giants' 16. Dave Brown's fumble recovered by Spielman at Giants' 33. Bills drive to Giants' 16 where Christie kicks 34-yard field goal at 9:08.

Sept. 22, 1996—New England 28, Jacksonville 25, at New England; Patriots win toss. T. Brown returns kickoff 18 yards to Patriots' 29. Patriots drive to Jaguars' 22 where Vinatieri kicks 40-yard field goal at 2:36.

Sept. 29, 1996—Arizona 31, St. Louis 28, at Arizona; Cardinals win toss. Lohmiller kick is a touchback. Cardinals drive to Rams' 7 where G. Davis kicks 24-yard field goal at 1:54.

Oct. 6, 1996—Buffalo 16, Indianapolis 13, at Buffalo; Colts win toss. Christie kick is a touchback. Colts drive to Indianapolis 32. Burris returns Gardocki's punt to Bills' 35. Bills drive to Colts' 48. Mohr punts out of bounds at Colts' 14. Colts drive to Indianapolis 9. Burris returns Gardocki's punt to Colts' 48. Bills drive to Colts' 22 where Christie kicks 39-yard field goal at 9:22.

#Oct. 6, 1996—Houston 30, Cincinnati 27, at Cincinnati; Bengals win toss. Dunn returns kickoff 23 yards to Bengals' 34. Bengals drive to Cincinnati 36. Floyd returns L. Johnson's punt to Oilers' 18. Oilers drive to Bengals' 31 where Del Greco kicks 49-yard field goal at 7:07.

* Oct. 14, 1996—Green Bay 23, San Francisco 20, at Green Bay; 49ers win toss. D. Carter returns kickoff 23 yards to 49ers' 22. 49ers' drive to San Francisco 25. Howard makes fair catch of Thompson's punt at Packers' 44. Packers drive to 49ers' 35 where Jacke kicks 53-yard field goal at 3:41.

Oct. 27, 1996—Baltimore 37, St. Louis 31, at Baltimore; Rams win toss. J. Thomas returns kickoff 17 yard to Rams' 17. Rams drive to Ravens' 15. F. Miller fumble in field goal formation recovered by S. Moore at Ravens' 17. Ravens drive to Baltimore 49 and turn ball over on downs. Rams drive to Ravens' 40 and turn ball over on downs. Testaverde throws 22-yard scoring pass to M. Jackson at 14:50.

Nov. 10, 1996—Dallas 20, San Francisco 17, at San Francisco; Cowboys win toss. H. Walker returns kickoff 10 yards to Cowboys' 23. Cowboys drive to 49ers' 11 where Boniol kicks 29-yard field goal at 6:17.

Nov. 10, 1996—Arizona 37, Washington 34, at Washington; Cardinals win toss. Blanton's kickoff is a touchback. Cardinals drive to Redskins' 15 where Butler misses 32-yard field goal. Redskins drive to Cardinals' 43 where Turk punts for touchback. L. Johnson fumble returned by Morrison to Cardinals' 27. Redskins drive to Cardinals' 31 where Blanton misses 48-yard field goal. Cardinals drive to Redskins' 15 where Butler kicks 32-yard field goal at 14:27.

Nov. 10, 1996—Tampa Bay 20, Oakland 17, at Tampa Bay; Buccaneers win toss. M. Marshall returns kickoff 15 yards to Bucs' 17. Bucs drive to Tampa Bay 36. T. Brown returns Barnhardt's punt four yards to Raiders' 22. Raiders drive to Oakland

25. M. Marshall returns Gossett's punt nine yards to Bucs' 39. Bucs drive to Raiders' 4 where Husted kicks 23-yard field goal at 11:56.

#Nov. 17, 1996—Minnesota 16, Oakland 13, at Oakland; Raiders win toss. Kaufman returns kickoff 32 yards to Raiders' 27. Raiders drive to Oakland 46 where Gossett punts to Vikings' 17. Vikings drive to Raiders' 12 where Sisson kicks 31-yard field goal at 11:53.

Nov. 24, 1996—Jacksonville 28, Baltimore 25, at Baltimore; Jaguars win toss. Jordon returns kickoff 16 yards to Jaguars' 30. Jaguars drive to Jacksonville 37. Barker's punt is downed at Ravens' 6. Ravens drive to Jaguars' 37 where Pritchett recovers Byner's fumble. Jaguars drive to Ravens' 15 where Hollis kicks 34-yard field goal at 9:06.

Nov. 24, 1996—San Francisco 19, Washington 16, at Washington; 49ers win toss. D. Carter returns kickoff 20 yards to 49ers' 32. 49ers drive to Redskins' 20 where Wilkins kicks 38-yard field goal at 3:24.

Dec. 1, 1996—Indianapolis 13, Buffalo 10, at Indianapolis; Bills win toss. Moulds returns kickoff 26 yards to Bills' 25. Bills drive to Buffalo 49. Stock returns Mohr's punt one yard to Colts' 16. Colts drive to Bills' 32 where Blanchard kicks 49-yard field goal at 10:46.

Aug. 31, 1997—Tennessee 24, Oakland 21, at Tennessee; Oilers win toss. Gray returns kickoff 32 yards to Tennessee 33. Oilers drive to Tennessee 38. Roby's punt is downed at the Oakland 33. Raiders drive to Oakland 32. Gray returns Araguz punt to Tennessee 35. Oilers drive to Oakland 15 where Del Greco kicks 33-yard field goal at 6:57.

Sept. 7, 1997—Miami 16, Tennessee 13, at Miami; Dolphins win toss. Spikes returns kickoff 48 yards to Tennessee 45. Dolphins drive to Tennessee 11 where Mare kicks 29-yard field goal at 2:15.

#Sept. 7, 1997— Arizona 25, Dallas 22, at Arizona; Cowboys win toss. Walker returns kickoff 21 yards to Dallas 25. Cowboys drive to Arizona 43. Gowin punts 43 yards for a touchback. Cardinals drive to Dallas 44. Graham fumbles. Cowboys drive to Arizona 42. Williams fumbles. Cardinals drive to Dallas 3 where Butler kicks 20-yard field goal at 8:30.

Sept. 14, 1997—Washington 19, Arizona 13, at Washington; Cardinals win toss. K. Williams returns kickoff 27 yards to Arizona 34. Cardinals drive to Arizona 40. McElroy fumbles. Redskins drive to Arizona 40. Westbrook catches 40-yard touchdown pass from Frerotte at 1:36.

#Sept. 14, 1997—New England 27, New York Jets 24, at New England; Patriots win toss. Hall's kickoff is a touchback. Patriots drive to New England 15. Bledsoe pass intercepted by O. Smith. Jets drive to New York 46. Hansen punts 47 yards. Meggett returns to New England 21. Patriots drive to New York 17 where Vinatieri kicks 34-yard field goal at 8:03.

Sept. 28, 1997—Kansas City 20, Seattle 17, at Kansas City; Seahawks win toss. Broussard returns kickoff 12 yards to Seattle 14. Seahawks drive to Seattle 17. Vanover returns Tuten punt 8 yards to Kansas City 26. Chiefs drive to Seattle 44. Aguiar punt downed at Seattle 11. Seahawks drive to Seattle 26. Moon pass intercepted by Woods and returned 13 yards to 50. Chiefs drive to Seattle 23 where Stoyanovich kicks 41-yard field goal at 13:04.

Oct. 19, 1997—Philadelphia 13, Arizona 10, at Philadelphia; Cardinals win toss. K. Williams returns kickoff 28 yards to Arizona 42. Cardinals drive to Philadelphia 48. Feagles punts 48 yards for touchback. Eagles drive to Arizona 7 where Boniol kicks 24-yard field goal at 4:02.

Oct. 19, 1997—New York Giants 26, Detroit 20, at Detroit; Giants win toss. Pegram returns kickoff 16 yards to New York 18. Giants drive to New York 32. Calloway catches 68-yard touchdown pass from Kanell at 1:40.

Oct. 26, 1997—Denver 23, Buffalo 20, at Buffalo; Broncos win toss and elects to kickoff. Holmes returns kickoff 20 yards to Buffalo 25. Bills drive to Buffalo 23. Mohr punt downed at

Denver 40. Broncos drive to Buffalo 48. Rouen punt downed at Buffalo 1. Bills drive to Buffalo 20. Gordon returns Mohr punt to Denver 42. Broncos drive to Buffalo 15 where Elam kicks 33-yard field goal at 13:04.

Oct. 26, 1997—Pittsburgh 23, Jacksonville 17, at Pittsburgh; Steelers win toss. Coleman returns kickoff 23 yards to Pittsburgh 23. Steelers drive to Jacksonville 17. Bettis catches 17-yard touchdown pass from Stewart at 3:47.

* **Oct. 27, 1997—Chicago 36, Miami 33,** at Miami; Dolphins win toss. McPhail returns kickoff 23 yards to Miami 27. Dolphins drive to Miami 36. Kidd punts out of bounds at Chicago 10. Bears drive to the Chicago 39. Sauerbrun punt out of bounds at Miami 27. Reeves recovers Marino fumble at Miami 17. Bears drive to Miami 17 where Jaeger kicks 35-yard field goal at 9:25.

Nov. 2, 1997—New York Jets 19, Baltimore 16, at New York; Jets win toss. Stover's kickoff is a touchback. Jets drive to Baltimore 20 where Hall kicks 37-yard field goal at 4:58.

Nov. 16, 1997—Philadelphia 10, Baltimore 10, at Baltimore; Eagles win toss. Stover's kickoff is a touchback. Eagles drive to Philadelphia 19. Hutton punts 36 yards to Baltimore 45. Ravens drive to Baltimore 36 where Eagles take over on downs. Eagles drive to Baltimore 33 where Ravens take over on downs. Ravens drive to Baltimore 37. Montgomery punts 55 yards, and Solomon returns to Philadelphia 22. Eagles drive to Philadelphia 16. Hutton punts 41 yards, and Roe returns to Baltimore 46. Ravens drive to Philadelphia 35 where Stover's 53-yard field-goal attempt is no good. Eagles drive to Baltimore 22 where Boniol's 40-yard field-goal is no good as time expires.

Nov. 16, 1997—New Orleans 20, Seattle 17, at New Orleans; Seahawks win toss. Brien's kickoff is a touchback. Seahawks start at Seattle 20 where Moon's pass intercepted by Tubbs who returns 15 yards to Seattle 20. Saints Brien kicks 38-yard field goal at 17 seconds.

#**Nov. 23, 1997—New York Giants 7, Washington 7,** at Washington; Redskins win toss. Davis returns kickoff 28 yards to Washington 39. Redskins drive to Washington 36 where Hostetler's pass intercepted by Sehorn who returns minus–2 yards before lateralling to Wooten who returns 5 yards to New York 41. Giants drive to New York 26 where Maynard punts 37 yards to Washington 37. Redskins drive to New York 39 where Hostetler fumble is recovered by Harris at New York 40. Giants drive to New York 43 where Maynard punts 57 yards for a touchback. Washington drives to New York 41. Giants take over on downs at New York 40. Giants drive to Washington 36 where Daluiso's 54-yard field-goal attempt is no good. Redskins drive to Washington 45 where Hostetler's pass intercepted by Sparks at New York 49. Giants drive to Washington 36 where Maynard punts 36 yards for a touchback. Redskins drive to New York 36 where Blanton's 54-yard field-goal attempt is no good. Giants drive to New York 45 where Kanell's pass intercepted by Patton who laterals to Pounds who returns 11 yards to Washington 24 as time expires.

Nov. 30, 1997—Pittsburgh 26, Arizona 20, at Arizona; Cardinals win toss. K. Williams returns kickoff 11 yards to Arizona 23. Cardinals drive to Arizona 18 where Feagles punts 43 yards. Hawkins returns punt 9 yards to Pittsburgh 48. Steelers drive to Arizona 10 where Bettis scores on a 10-yard touchdown run at 5:34.

Dec. 13, 1997—Pittsburgh 24, New England 21, at New England; Steelers win toss. Coleman returns kickoff 19 yards to Pittsburgh 26. Steelers drive to New England 13 where Johnson kicks a 31-yard field goal at 4:43.

Sept. 6, 1998—San Francisco 36, New York Jets 30, at San Francisco; Jets win toss. Richey's kickoff is a touchback. Jets drive to New York 11. Gallery punts 48 yards. McQuarters returns to New York 43. 49ers drive to New York 44. Howard punts 23 yards to New York 21. Johnson calls fair catch. Jets drive to New York 47. Gallery's 49-yard punt downed at San Francisco 4. Hearst runs for a 96-yard touchdown at 4:08.

Sept. 13, 1998—Cincinnati 34, Detroit 28, at Detroit; Lions win toss. Johnson's kickoff is a touchback. Lions drive to Detroit 47 where Mitchell's pass is intercepted by Sawyer and returned for a 58-yard touchdown at 2:06.

Sept. 27, 1998—New Orleans 19, Indianapolis 13, at Indianapolis; Saints win toss. Gardocki's kickoff is returned by Ismail to New Orleans 28. Saints drive to New Orleans 30. Royals punts 64 yards. Poole returns to Indianapolis 12. Colts drive to Indianapolis 20. Gardocki punts 58 yards. Hastings returns to New Orleans 29. Saints drive to New Orleans 32. Royals punts 59 yards. Punt downed at Indianapolis 9. Colts drive to Indianapolis 44 where Manning's pass is intercepted by Drakeford and returned to Indianapolis 36. Saints drive to Indianapolis 33. Wuerffel throws 33-yard touchdown pass to Cleeland at 6:10.

Oct. 25, 1998—Miami 12, New England 9, at Miami; Dolphins win toss. Vinatieri's kickoff is returned by Avery to Miami 15. Dolphins drive to New England 26 where Mare kicks 43-yard field goal at 4:36.

+**Nov. 26, 1998—Detroit 19, Pittsburgh 16,** at Detroit; Lions win toss. Johnson's kickoff is returned by Fair to Detroit 35. Lions drive to Pittsburgh 24 where Hanson kicks 42-yard field goal at 2:52.

Dec. 6, 1998—San Francisco 31, Carolina 28, at Carolina; Panthers win toss. Richey's kickoff is returned by Floyd to Carolina 36. Panthers drive to Carolina 38 where Beuerlein's fumble is recovered by Doleman at Carolina 30. 49ers drive to Carolina 5 where Richey kicks 23-yard field goal at 4:16.

Dec. 13, 1998—Arizona 20, Philadelphia 17, at Philadelphia; Cardinals win toss. Boniol's kickoff is returned by Metcalf to Arizona 28. Cardinals drive to Philadelphia 15 where Jacke kicks 32-yard field goal at 4:30.

Sept. 12, 1999—Dallas 41, Washington 35, at Washington; Redskins win toss. Gowin's kickoff is returned by B. Mitchell to Washington 24. Redskins drive to Washington 47. M. Turk punts 48 yards. Punt downed at Dallas 5. Cowboys drive to Dallas 24. Aikman passes 76-yard touchdown to R. Ismail at 4:09.

Oct. 3, 1999—Baltimore 19, Atlanta 13, at Atlanta; Falcons win toss. Stover's kickoff is returned by Oliver to Atlanta 18. Falcons drive to Atlanta 23. Stryzinski punts 41 yards, out of bounds at Baltimore 36. Baltimore drives to Baltimore 46. Case passes 54-yard touchdown to Armour at 2:29.

Oct. 31, 1999—New York Giants 23, Philadelphia 17, at Philadelphia; Giants win toss. Akers' kickoff is returned by Levingston to New York 27. New York drives to Giants 31. Maynard punts 43 yards to Philadelphia 26. Rossum returns to Eagles 28. Pederson drives to New York 45. Pederson's pass is intercepted by Strahan at Philadelphia 44. Giants' Peter batted ball up in the air as Pederson backpedaled. Strahan for 44 yards and touchdown at 4:24.

Nov. 14, 1999—Minnesota 27, Chicago 24, at Chicago; Vikings win toss. Boniol kicks to Minnesota 2, Williams touchback. Minnesota starts on own 20. George's pass is intercepted by Harris at Minnesota 29 for -1 yard. Chicago starts at Minnesota 29 and moves to Minnesota 23. Boniol's 41-yard field goal is no good. Minnesota starts from own 31 and drives to Chicago 20. Anderson kicks 38-yard field goal at 9:02.

Nov. 21, 1999—Chicago 23, San Diego 20, at San Diego; Bears win toss. Chicago starts from own 22. Miller completes four consecutive passes and Bears drive to San Diego 22. Enis rushes twice to San Diego 19. Boniol kicks 36-yard field goal at 4:58.

* **Nov. 22, 1999—Denver 27, Oakland 21,** at Denver; Broncos win toss. Denver starts from own 33 and drives to Broncos' 35. Rouen punts 46 yards to Oakland 19. Oakland starts at own 19 and drives to Raiders' 25. Gannon fumbles and Broncos' Pryce recovers at Oakland 25. Denver running back Gary scores on 24-yard run at 2:40.

Nov. 28, 1999—Washington 20, Philadelphia 17, at Washington; Redskins win toss. Akers' kickoff is returned by Thrash for 48 yards to Philadelphia 46. Johnson completes 20-yard pass to Connell to Philadelphia 26. Johnson completes 9-yard pass to Mitchell to Philadelphia 9. Mitchell runs for seven yards to Philadelphia 2. On third down, Washington attempts field goal from Philadelphia 2. Johnson fumbles and recovers at Philadelphia 9. Conway kicks 27-yard field goal at 4:34.

Dec. 19, 1999—Denver 36, Seattle 30, at Denver; Broncos win toss. Peterson kicks to Denver 8. Watson returns kick to Denver 27 for 19 yards. Broncos do not convert a first down. Rouen punts 46 yards, out of bounds at Seattle 25. Kitna passes to Dawkins for 17 yards at Seattle 47. Watters runs for 6 yards to Denver 47. Kitna sacked for 11-yard loss by Crockett. Kitna fumbles, forced by Crockett, recovered by Cadrez at Seattle 37. Cadrez for 37 yards and touchdown at 2:34.

Dec. 26, 1999—Buffalo 13, New England 10, at New England; Patriots win toss. New England's Vinatieri misses 44-yard field goal from Buffalo 26. Buffalo takes over at Bills 34. Flutie passes to Moulds to New England 21 for 17 yards. Moulds fumbles, recovered by Bruschi at Patriots 21. New England drives to own 34. Johnson punts from New England 34 to Buffalo 42. Flutie passes to Price for 7 yards to New England 44. Flutie passes to Moulds for 11 yards to New England 27. Thomas runs for 9 yards to New England 6. Christie kicks 23-yard field goal at 13:12.

#Dec. 26, 1999—Washington 26, San Francisco 20, at San Francisco; Redskins win toss. Richey kicks to Washington 9, Thrash returns 13 yards to Washington 22. Johnson passes to Hicks for 25 yards to Washington 47. Centers runs for 12 yards to San Francisco 33. Johnson passes to Centers for 33 yards and touchdown at 2:00.

Jan. 2, 2000—Oakland 41, Kansas City 38, at Kansas City; Raiders win toss. Baker kicks 69 yards from Kansas City 30 to Oakland 1 and out of bounds. Oakland starts at Raiders 40. Gannon passes to Dudley for 21 yards to Kansas City 40. Gannon passes to Brown at Kansas City 16 for 24 yards. Crockett runs to Kansas City 15 for 1 yard. Nedney kicks 33-yard field goal at 3:13.

Sept. 10, 2000—Tennessee 17, Kansas City 14, at Tennessee; Titans win toss. Mason returns kickoff 28 yards to Tennessee 29. Face-mask penalty on Kansas City, 5 yards, enforced at 29. Titans drive to Kansas City 18 where Del Greco kicks 36-yard field goal at 2:58.

Oct. 1, 2000—Dallas 16, Carolina 13, at Carolina; Cowboys win toss. Tucker returns kickoff 20 yards to Dallas 26. Dallas drives to Carolina 6 where Seder kicks 24-yard field goal at 3:52.

Oct. 1, 2000—Washington 20, Tampa Bay 17, at Washington; Redskins win toss. Thrash returns kickoff 32 yards to Washington 30. Washington gains five yards where Barnhardt punts 52 yards to Tampa Bay 13. Green returns for one yard to Tampa Bay 14. Buccaneers gain one yard to Tampa Bay 15 where Royals punts 50 yards to Washington 35. Sanders returns punt 57 yards to Tampa Bay 8. Davis rushes three times and gets to Tampa Bay 2 where Husted kicks 20-yard field goal at 4:09.

Oct. 8, 2000—Oakland 34, San Francisco 28, at San Francisco; Raiders win toss. Dunn returns kickoff 20 yards to Oakland 19. Raiders drive to San Francisco 17 where Janikowski misses 35-yard field-goal attempt wide right. San Francisco drives to Oakland 11 where Richey's 29-yard field-goal attempt is blocked by Dorsett. Raiders recover at Oakland 16. Oakland drives to San Francisco 31 where Gannon passes to Brown for 31-yard touchdown at 10:15.

Oct. 15, 2000—Buffalo 27, San Diego 24, at Buffalo; Bills win toss. Bills drive to Buffalo 47. Mohr punts 42 yards to San Diego 11. Chargers drive to San Diego 38 where Harbaugh is intercepted at Buffalo 41. Flutie in for injured Johnson. Bills drive to San Diego 28. Christie kicks 46-yard field goal at 8:26.

* **Oct. 23, 2000—New York Jets 40, Miami 37,** at New York; Dolphins win toss. Marion returns kickoff 31 yards to Miami 37. Fielder is intercepted at Miami 46 by Coleman, who returns ball to 39 where he fumbles. Gadsden recovers ball for Dolphins and runs out of bounds at Miami 34. Dolphins drive to New York 43 where Fiedler is intercepted again by Coleman at the Jets 34. Jets drive to Miami 23 where Hall kicks 40-yard field goal at 6:47.

Oct. 29, 2000—Jacksonville 23, Dallas 17, at Dallas; Jaguars win toss. Stith returns kickoff 24 yards to Jacksonville 34. Jaguars drive to Dallas 37 where Brunell passes to Whitted for a 37 yard touchdown at 3.02.

Nov. 5, 2000—Buffalo 16, New England 13, at New England; Patriots win toss. Faulk returns kickoff 38 yards to New England 43. Penalty on New England for offensive holding, 10 yards, enforced at New England 33. Patriots lose one yard on three plays. Johnson punts 43 yards to Buffalo 35. Bills drive to New England 13 where Christie kicks 32-yard field goal at 4:21.

Nov. 5, 2000—Philadelphia 16, Dallas 13, at Philadelphia; Eagles win toss. Mitchell returns kickoff 30 yards to Philadelphia 34. Eagles drive to Dallas 36 where McNabb is intercepted by Wortham at Dallas 30. Wortham returns interception to Dallas 31. Cowboys drive to Dallas 48 where Thomas fumbles. Recovered by Hauck at Dallas 48. Eagles drive to Dallas 13 where Akers kicks 32-yard field goal at 7:52.

* **Nov. 6, 2000—Green Bay 26, Minnesota 20,** at Green Bay; Packers win toss. Rossum returns kickoff 13 yards to Green Bay 18. Packers drive to Minnesota 43 where Favre passes to Freeman for a 43-yard touchdown at 3:27.

Nov. 12, 2000—Philadelphia 26, Pittsburgh 23, at Pittsburgh; Eagles win toss. Mitchell returns kickoff 24 yards to Philadelphia 37. Eagles drive to Pittsburgh 24 where Akers kicks 42-yard field goal at 4:09.

Dec. 17, 2000—New England 13, Buffalo 10, at Buffalo; Bills win toss and elect to defend the South goal. Patriots elect to receive. Jackson returns kickoff 38 yards to New England 48. Patriots drive to Buffalo 31 where they turn the ball over on downs. Bills drive to New England 12 where Christie's 30-yard field goal attempt is blocked by Eaton. Patriots recover at New England 11. Patriots drive to Buffalo 6 where Vinatieri kicks 24-yard field goal at 14:37.

Dec. 24, 2000—Green Bay 17, Tampa Bay 14, at Green Bay; Packers win toss. Rossum returns kickoff 29 yards to Green Bay 38. Packers drive to Tampa Bay 4 where Longwell kicks 22-yard field goal at 6:28.

Sept. 9, 2001—St. Louis 20, Philadelphia 17, at Philadelphia; Eagles win toss. Wilkins' kickoff is a touchback. Eagles drive to Philadelphia 30. Landeta punts 34 yards to St. Louis 36. Rams drive to Philadelphia 8. Wilkins kicks 26-yard field goal at 7:56.

Sept. 9, 2001—San Francisco 16, Atlanta 13, at San Francisco; 49ers win toss. Feely's kickoff is a touchback. 49ers drive to Atlanta 6. Cortez kicks 24-yard field goal at 4:04.

Oct. 14, 2001—New England 29, San Diego 26, at New England; Chargers win toss. Jenkins returns kickoff 39 yards to San Diego 40. Chargers drive to San Diego 45. Bennett punts 32 yards to New England 23. Patriots drive to San Diego 26. Vinatieri kicks 44-yard field goal at 4:00.

Oct. 14, 2001—San Francisco 37, Atlanta 31, at Atlanta; 49ers win toss. Sutherland returns kickoff 24 yards to San Francisco 24. 49ers drive to Atlanta 14. Garcia fumbles, Hall recovers at Atlanta 16. Falcons drive to Atlanta 23. Mohr punts 44 yards to San Francisco 33. Garcia throws 52-yard touchdown to Owens at 8:34.

Oct. 14, 2001—Tennessee 31, Tampa Bay 28, at Tennessee; Buccaneers win toss. D. Smith returns kickoff 17 yards to Tampa Bay 18. Buccaneers forced back to Tampa Bay 9. Royals punts 45 yards to Tennessee 46. Titans drive to Tampa Bay 32. Nedney kicks 49-yard field goal at 1:52.

Oct. 21, 2001—Washington 17, Carolina 14, at Washington; Redskins win toss. Bates returns kickoff 17 yards to Washington 14. Redskins drive to Carolina 5. Conway kicks 23-yard field goal at 1:47.

Oct. 28, 2001—Chicago 37, San Francisco 31, at Chicago; 49ers win toss. Edinger's kickoff is a touchback. M. Brown intercepts Garcia pass and returns it 33 yards for touchdown at 16 seconds.

Nov. 4, 2001—Chicago 27, Cleveland 21, at Chicago; Bears win toss. L. Johnson returns kickoff 31 yards to Chicago 32. Bears drive to Chicago 40. Maynard punts 52 yards to Cleveland 8. M. Brown intercepts Couch pass and returns it 16 yards for touchdown at 2:50.

Nov. 4, 2001—New York Giants 27, Dallas 24, at New York; Cowboys win toss. Swinton returns kickoff 21 yards to Dallas 29. Cowboys drive to New York 48. Knorr punts 33 yards to New York 15. Giants drive to Dallas 24. Andersen kicks 42-yard field goal at 7:12.

Nov. 11, 2001—Pittsburgh 15, Cleveland 12, at Cleveland; Steelers win toss. T. Edwards returns kickoff 21 yards to Pittsburgh 28. Steelers drive to Cleveland 14. Brown kicks 32-yard field goal at 5:22.

Nov. 18, 2001—San Francisco 25, Carolina 22, at Carolina; 49ers win toss. Sutherland returns kickoff 24 yards to San Francisco 26. 49ers drive to Carolina 8. Cortez kicks 26-yard field goal at 4:41.

Dec. 2, 2001—Arizona 34, Oakland 31, at Oakland; Raiders win toss. Gramatica's kickoff is a touchback. Raiders drive to Oakland 40. Lechler punts 37 yards to Arizona 23. Cardinals drive to Arizona 48. Stanley punts 29 yards to Oakland 23. Woods recovers Dunn fumble on Oakland 25. Arizona drives to Oakland 18. Gramatica kicks 36-yard field goal at 7:29.

Dec. 2, 2001—Seattle 13, San Diego 10, at Seattle; Seahawks win toss. Rogers returns kickoff 33 yards to Seattle 32. Seahawks drive to San Diego 6. Lindell kicks 24-yard field goal at 6:23.

Dec. 2, 2001—Tampa Bay 16, Cincinnati 13, at Cincinnati; Buccaneers win toss. F. Murphy returns kickoff 20 yards to Tampa Bay 38. Buccaneers drive to Cincinnati 35. Royals punts 31 yards to Cincinnati 4. Lynch recovers Dillon fumble on Cincinnati 3. Gramatica kicks 21-yard field goal at 5:06.

Dec. 16, 2001—Kansas City 26, Denver 23, at Kansas City; Broncos win toss. Carter returns kickoff 24 yards to Denver 41. Broncos drive to Denver 35. Rouen punts 35 yards to Kansas City 30. Chiefs drive to Denver 23. T. Peterson misses 41-yard field-goal attempt. Broncos drive to Denver 32. Rouen punts 38 yards to Kansas City 30. Chiefs drive to Denver 14. T. Peterson kicks 32-yard field goal at 9:04.

Dec. 16, 2001—New England 12, Buffalo 9, at Buffalo; Bills win toss. Bryson returns kickoff 23 yards to Buffalo 28. Bills drive to Buffalo 48. Moorman punts 52 yards to end zone. Patriots drive to Buffalo 5. Vinatieri kicks 23-yard field goal at 5:45.

Dec. 30, 2001—Cincinnati 26, Pittsburgh 23, at Cincinnati; Steelers win toss. Geason returns kickoff and laterals to Logan who carries ball 9 yards to Pittsburgh 38. Steelers drive to Cincinnati 39. Miller punts 38 yards to Cincinnati 1. Bengals drive to Pittsburgh 13. Rackers kicks 31-yard field goal at 10:52.

Sept. 8, 2002—New York Jets 37, Buffalo 31, at Buffalo; Jets win toss. Morton returns kickoff 96 yards for touchdown at 14 seconds.

Sept. 8, 2002—Green Bay 37, Atlanta 34, at Green Bay; Packers win toss. J. Walker returns kickoff 26 yards to Green Bay 34. Packers drive to Atlanta 39. Bidwell punts 27 yards to Atlanta 12. Falcons drive to Atlanta 14. Mohr punts 46 yards to Green Bay 40. Packers drive to Atlanta 19. Longwell kicks 34-yard field goal at 9:40.

Sept. 8, 2002—New Orleans 26, Tampa Bay 20, at Tampa Bay; Tampa Bay wins toss. Stecker returns kickoff 31 yards to Tampa Bay 42. Buccaneers drive to New Orleans 39. Tupa punts 39 yards into end zone. Saints drive to New Orleans 20. Williams returns Johnson's punt 4 yards to Tampa Bay 46. Buccaneers drive to Tampa Bay 48. Tupa punts 52 yards into end zone. Saints drive to New Orleans 41. Williams returns Johnson's punt -4 yards to Tampa Bay 6. Buccaneers drive to Tampa Bay 5. Tupa pass intercepted by Allen in Tampa Bay end zone at 12:01.

Sept. 15, 2002—Buffalo 45, Minnesota 39, at Minnesota; Buffalo wins toss. Rodgers returns kickoff 22 yards to Buffalo 22. Bills drive to Buffalo 48. Moorman punts 27 yards, downed at Minnesota 25. Vikings drive to Minnesota 32. Richardson punts 45 yards. Downed at Buffalo 23. Bills drive to Minnesota 26. Hollis' 44-yard field-goal attempt is no good. Vikings take over on Minnesota 35. Drive to Minnesota 41. Richardson punts 52 yards. Returned by Rogers 16 yards to Buffalo 24. Bills drive to Minnesota 48. Bledsoe throws 48-yard pass to Price for touchdown at 10:12.

Sept. 22, 2002—Cleveland 31, Tennessee 28, at Tennessee; Cleveland wins toss. White returns kickoff 6 yards to Tennessee 26. Browns drive to Tennessee 15. Dawson kicks 33-yard field goal at 4:09.

Sept. 22, 2002—New England 41, Kansas City 38, at New England; New England wins toss. Branch returns kickoff 30 yards to New England 30. Patriots drive to Kansas City 17. Vinatieri kicks 35-yard field goal at 4:36.

Sept. 29, 2002—Buffalo 33, Chicago 27, at Buffalo; Chicago wins toss. Johnson returns kickoff 19 yards to Chicago 20. Bears drive to Chicago 25. Maynard punts 31 yards to Buffalo 44. Fair catch by Mannelly. Buffalo drives to Chicago 26. Bledsoe throws 26-yard pass to Henry for touchdown at 2:48.

Sept. 29, 2002—Pittsburgh 16, Cleveland 13, at Pittsburgh; Pittsburgh wins toss. Mays returns kickoff 32 yards to Pittsburgh 32. Maddox's pass intercepted by Davis at Pittsburgh 34, returned for no gain. Cleveland drives to Pittsburgh 27. Dawson's 45-yard field-goal attempt no good, tipped at line of scrimmage by Flowers. Steelers take over at Pittsburgh 35. Steelers drive to Cleveland 6, and 24-yard field-goal attempt by Peterson blocked by McKinley, recovered by Peterson, fumbles, recovered by Fiala. Peterson's 31-yard field goal is good at 6:58.

Oct. 20, 2002—Denver 37, Kansas City 34, at Denver; Denver wins toss. Kasper returns kickoff 15 yards to Denver 24. Broncos drive to Denver 33. Rouen punts 43 yards to Kansas City 24. Hall returns punt 13 yards to Kansas City 37. Chiefs drive to Kansas City 43. Stryzinski's punt is blocked and recovered by Burns at Kansas City 32. Denver drives to Kansas City 7. Elam's 25-yard field goal is good at 2:52.

Oct. 20, 2002—Detroit 23, Chicago 20, at Detroit; Detroit wins toss. Edinger's kickoff goes out of bounds at Detroit 2. Lions take over at Detroit 40. Lions drive to Chicago 30. Hanson's 48-yard field goal is good at 4:42.

Oct. 20, 2002—San Diego 27, Oakland 21, at Oakland; San Diego wins toss. Chargers start at San Diego 20 after touchback. Chargers drive to Oakland 19. Tomlinson runs 19 yards for touchdown at 3:33.

Oct. 20, 2002—Arizona 9, Dallas 6, at Arizona; Dallas wins toss. Swinton returns kickoff 26 yards to Dallas 24. Cowboys drive to Dallas 29. Knorr punts 45 yards to Arizona 26. Jackson returns 5 yards to Arizona 31. Cardinals drive to Dallas 38. Player punts 38 yards into end zone. Cowboys take over at Dallas 20. Cowboys drive to Arizona 49. Knorr punts 31 yards to Arizona 18. Fair catch by Jackson. Cardinals drive to Dallas 22. Gramatica's 40-yard field goal is good at 11:45.

Nov. 3, 2002—San Francisco 23, Oakland 20, at Oakland; San Francisco wins toss. Janikowski's kickoff returned to SF 22 by J. Williams. 49ers drive to Oakland 5. Cortez's 23-yard field goal at 8:41.

Nov. 10, 2002—Atlanta 34, Pittsburgh 34, at Pittsburgh; Pittsburgh wins toss. Touchback on Feely kickoff. Pittsburgh starts at own 20, drives to Atlanta 30. Peterson's 48-yard field-goal attempt blocked by Finneran. Atlanta takes over at own 47, drives to Atlanta 33. Mohr punts 47 yards to Randle El, who returns to Pittsburgh 18. Steelers drive to Atlanta 33. Miller punts 22 yards to Atlanta 12, no return. Falcons drive to Atlanta 23. Mohr punts 52 yards. Randle El returns 1 yard to Pittsburgh 26. Steelers drive to Pittsburgh 44. Maddox intercepted by Mathis at Atlanta 43. Mathis returns to Pittsburgh 44. Atlanta drives to Pittsburgh 37. Feely's 56-yard field-goal attempt blocked by Farrior. Pittsburgh takes over on own 49. Maddox pass to Burress downed at Atlanta 1 as time expires.

Nov. 17, 2002—San Diego 20, San Francisco 17, at San Diego; San Diego wins toss. Jenkins returns Cortez kickoff 39 yards to San Diego 38. Chargers drive to San Diego 38. Bennett punts 47 yards to San Francisco 15. Williams returns 9 yards to San Francisco 24. 49ers drive to San Diego 23. Cortez's 41-yard field-goal attempt is no good. San Diego takes over on San Diego 31. Chargers drive to San Francisco 22. Christie's 40-yard field goal is good at 10:49.

Nov. 24, 2002—Chicago 20, Detroit 17, at Chicago; Detroit wins toss. Elects to defend the north goal. Hanson kicks 72 yards. Kick returned 37 yards to Chicago 35. Chicago drives to Detroit 22. Edinger's 40-yard field-goal attempt is good at 6:02.

#Nov. 24, 2002—Indianapolis 23, Denver 20, at Denver; Indianapolis wins toss. Knorr kicks 66 yards. Returned by Walters 28 yards to Indianapolis 32. Colts drive to Denver 33. Vanderjagt's 51-yard field-goal attempt is good at 5:38.

Dec. 1, 2002—Atlanta 30, Minnesota 24, at Minnesota; Minnesota wins toss. Feely kicks 60 yards. Returned by Carter 10 yards to Minnesota 20. Vikings drive to Minnesota 11. Richardson punts 47 yards to Atlanta 42. Returned by Rossum 10 yards to Minnesota 48. Falcons drive to Minnesota 46. Vick runs 46 yards for touchdown at 2:25.

Dec. 1, 2002—Tennessee 32, New York Giants 29, at New York; New York wins toss. Nedney kicks 68 yards. Returned by Joyce 38 yards to New York 40. Giants drive to New York 46. Allen punts 34 yards to Tennessee 20. Fair catch by O'Leary. Titans drive to New York 20. Nedney's 38-yard field goal good at 5:00.

Dec. 1, 2002—San Diego 30, Denver 27, at San Diego; Denver wins toss. Christie kicks 65 yards. Droughns returns 27 yards to Denver 32. Broncos drive to Denver 23. Knorr punts 36 yards to San Diego 41. Fair catch by Dwight. Chargers drive to Denver 19. Christie's 38-yard field-goal attempt blocked. Denver takes over on own 27. Broncos drive to San Diego 34. Elam's 53-yard field-goal attempt is no good. San Diego takes over on own 43. Chargers drive to Denver 9. Christie's field goal is good from 27 yards at 11:59.

Dec. 8, 2002—Arizona 23, Detroit 20, at Arizona; Arizona wins toss. Hanson kicks 64 yards. Kasper returns 19 yards to Arizona 30. Cardinals drive to Detroit 24. Gramatica's 42-yard field-goal attempt is good at 4:12.

Dec. 15, 2002—Seattle 30, Atlanta 24, at Atlanta; Atlanta wins toss. Lindell kicks 69 yards. Returned 17 yards to Atlanta 18 by Rossum. Atlanta drives to Seattle 18. Feely's 36-yard field-goal attempt wide right. Seattle takes over at own 26. Seahawks drive to Atlanta 27. Alexander runs 27 yards for a touchdown at 10:36.

Dec. 29, 2002—New York Giants 10, Philadelphia 7, at N.Y. Giants; Philadelphia wins toss. Bryant kicks 57 yards. Returned by Mitchell 32 yards to Philadelphia 45. Eagles drive to mid-field. Feeley's pass intercepted by Williams at New York 37, returned for no gain. Giants drive to Philadelphia 22. Bryant's 39-yard field-goal attempt is good at 5:10.

Dec. 29, 2002—New England 27, Miami 24, at New England; New England wins toss. Mare kicks 68 yards out of bounds. Patriots begin at own 40. New England drives to Miami 17. Vinatieri's 35-yard field goal is good at 2:03.

Dec. 29, 2002—Seattle 31, San Diego 28, at San Diego;

Seattle wins toss. Christie kicks 64 yards. Returned by Williams 26 yards to Seattle 32. Seahawks drive to San Diego 28. Hasselbeck's pass is intercepted by Molden at San Diego 20 and returned 1 yard to the 21. Chargers drive to San Diego 12. Bennett punts 48 yards to Seattle 40. Returned by Engram 8 yards to Seattle 48. Seahawks drive to San Diego 6. Lindell's 24-yard field goal is good at 9:58.

Sept. 14, 2003—St. Louis 27, San Francisco 24, at St. Louis; Rams win the toss. Harris returns kick 42 yards to St. Louis 48. Rams drive to San Francisco 10. Wilkins kicks 28-yard field goal at 1:56.

Sept. 14, 2003—Carolina 12, Tampa Bay 9, at Tampa Bay; Panthers win toss. Touchback. Carolina starts at own 20, drives to own 37. Sauerbrun punts 45 yards to Tampa Bay 18. Buccaneers drive to Carolina 42. Tupa punts 34 yards to Carolina 8. Smith returns punt 52 yards to Tampa Bay 40. Panthers drive to Tampa Bay 29. Kasay kicks 47-yard field goal at 11:26.

* **Sept. 15, 2003—Dallas 35, New York Giants 32**, at New York; Cowboys win toss. Smith returns kickoff 21 yards to Dallas 29. Cowboys drive to Dallas 48. Gowin punts 32 yards to Giants 20. Giants drive to New York 15. Feagles punts 42 yards to Dallas 43. Cowboys drive to New York 6. Cundiff kicks 25-yard field goal at 9:04.

Sept. 21, 2003—New York Giants 24, Washington 21, at Washington; Giants win toss. Begin drive on New York 6 due to penalty on kickoff return. Giants drive to Washington 11. Bryant kicks 29-yard field goal at 4:15.

Sept. 28, 2003—Oakland 34, San Diego 31, at Oakland; Chargers win toss. Johnson returns kickoff to San Diego 24. Chargers drive to San Diego 36. Bennett punts 46 yards to Oakland 18. Raiders drive to Oakland 8. Lechler punts 49 yards to San Diego 43. Chargers drive to San Diego 39. Bennett punts to Oakland 8. Raiders drive to San Diego 28. Janikowski kicks 46-yard field goal at 9:59.

Oct. 5, 2003—Buffalo 22, Cincinnati 16, at Buffalo; Bengals win toss. Begin drive on Cincinnati 20 after touchback. Bengals drive to Cincinnati 28. Harris punts 29 yards to Buffalo 43. Bills drive to Cincinnati 2. Henry scores on 2-yard touchdown run at 3:53.

* **Oct. 6, 2003—Indianapolis 38, Tampa Bay 35**, at Tampa Bay; Buccaneers win toss. Barlow returns kickoff 30 yards to Tampa Bay 30. Buccaneers drive to Indianapolis 41. Tupa punts to Indianapolis 13. Colts drive to Tampa Bay 11. Vanderjagt kicks 29-yard field goal at 11:13.

Oct. 12, 2003—Carolina 23, Indianapolis 20, at Indianapolis; Panthers win toss. Smart returns kickoff to Carolina 27. Panthers drive to Indianapolis 30. Kasay kicks 47-yard field goal at 5:39.

Oct. 12, 2003—Kansas City 40, Green Bay 34, at Green Bay; Chiefs win toss. Hall returns kick to Kansas City 29. Chiefs drive to Green Bay 30. Andersen misses 48-yard field goal (ball tipped at line). Packers take over possession at Green Bay 39. A. Green fumbles after eight-yard run. Chiefs recover at Kansas City 49. T. Green throws 51-yard touchdown pass to Kennison at 6:18.

Oct. 19, 2003—New England 19, Miami 13, at Miami; Dolphins win toss. Rogers returns kickoff 24 yards to Miami 26. Dolphins drive to New England 17. Mare's 35-yard field-goal attempt no good. Patriots take over on New England 26. Patriots drive to New England 40. Walter punts to Miami 21. Returned by Rogers to Miami 30. Dolphins drive to Miami 45. Fiedler pass intercepted by Poole at New England 18. Brady passes 82 yards to Brown for touchdown at 9:15.

Oct. 26, 2003—Carolina 23, New Orleans 20, at New Orleans; Saints win toss. Lewis returns kickoff 53 yards to Carolina 46. Saints drive to Carolina 37. McAllister fumbles on fourth-and-one. Panthers take over at Carolina 38 and drive to New Orleans 12. Kasay kicks 31-yard field goal at 4:36.

Oct. 26, 2003—Arizona 16, San Francisco 13, at Arizona; Cardinals win toss. 49ers' Pochman kicks out of bounds. Cardinals take possession at Arizona 40 and drive to San Francisco 22. Duncan kicks 39-yard field goal at 4:59.

Nov. 2, 2003—New York Giants 31, New York Jets 28, at New York Jets; Giants win toss. Mitchell returns kick 26 yards to Giants 34. Giants drive to Jets 21. Conway misses 39-yard field-goal attempt. Jets take over on own 30. Drive to Giants 49. Stryzinski's punt returned by Mitchell two yards to Giants 18. Giants drive to own 35. Feagles' punt returned six yards by Moss to Jets 29. Jets drive to Giants 32. Brien's 51-yard field goal attempt is blocked by Allen. Giants take over on own 36, drive to Jets 11. Conway kicks 29-yard field goal at 14:56.

Nov. 9, 2003—New York Jets 27, Oakland 24, at Oakland; Jets win toss. Jordan returns kick 12 yards to New York 25. Jets drive to Oakland 21. Brien kicks 38-yard field goal at 5:56.

Nov. 16, 2003—Miami 9, Baltimore 6, at Miami; Dolphins win toss. Dolphins start at Miami 20 after touchdown, drive to Baltimore 45. Turk punts 36 yards to Baltimore 9. Ravens drive to Baltimore 36. Lewis fumbles, recovered by Dolphins' Thomas. Dolphins drive to Baltimore 25. Mare kicks 43-yard field goal at 6:12.

Nov. 16, 2003—New Orleans 23, Atlanta 20, at New Orleans; Saints win toss. Lewis returns kick 39 yards to New Orleans 38. Saints drive to New Orleans 40. McAllister fumbles on Atlanta 2 after 58-yard run. Ball recovered by Falcons' Stewart for touchdown. Falcons drive to New Orleans 37. Feely's 54-yard field-goal attempt no good. Saints take over on New Orleans 45. Drive to Atlanta 18. Carney kicks 36-yard field goal at 3:59.

Nov. 23, 2003—New England 23, Houston 20, at Houston; Texans win toss, take over possession at own 13 after penalty on Hollings' return. Patriots intercept Texans at Houston 23. Patriots drive to Houston 19. Vinatieri's 37-yard field-goal attempt blocked. Texans take over at own 27, drive to New England 40. Stanley punts 31 yards to New England 9. Patriots drive to New England 4. Walter punts 31 yards to New England 35. Texans drive to New England 40. Stanley punts 26 yards to New England 14. Patriots drive to Houston 10. Vinatieri kicks 28-yard field goal at 14:19.

Nov. 23, 2003—Baltimore 44, Seattle 41, at Baltimore; Seahawks win toss. Morris returns kick to Seattle 27. Seahawks drive to Seattle 30. Rouen punts 50 yards to Baltimore 20, returned 1 yard by Brightful to Baltimore 21. Ravens drive to Seattle 24. Stover kicks 42-yard field goal at 8:28.

Nov. 23, 2003—St. Louis 30, Arizona 27, at Arizona; Rams win toss. Harris returns kick to St. Louis 14. Rams drive to Arizona 31. Wilkins kicks 49-yard field goal at 3:38.

 # Dec. 7, 2003—Atlanta 20, Carolina 14, at Atlanta; Panthers win toss. Smart returns kickoff 19 yards to Carolina 22. Panthers drive to Carolina 29. Delhomme's pass intercepted by Mathis at Carolina 32 and returned for touchdown at 1:19.

Dec. 14, 2003—Denver 23, Cleveland 20, at Cleveland; Browns win toss, start on Cleveland 20 after touchback. Browns drive to Cleveland 17. Gardocki punts 42 yards, returned by O'Neal 6 yards to Denver 47. Broncos drive to Cleveland 7. Elam kicks 25-yard field goal at 5:10.

Dec. 21, 2003—San Francisco 31, Philadelphia 28, at Philadelphia; Eagles win toss, start on Philadelphia 21 after penalty on Thrash's return. McNabb's pass intercepted by 49ers' Parrish and returned 29 yards to Philadelphia 4. On second down, Peterson kicks 22-yard field goal at 1:05.

 # Dec. 28, 2003—Baltimore 13, Pittsburgh 10, at Baltimore; Steelers win toss. Mays returns kick to Pittsburgh 20. Steelers drive to Pittsburgh 27. Miller punts 43 yards, returned 6 yards by Brightful to Baltimore 36. Ravens drive to Pittsburgh 29. Stover kicks 47-yard field goal at 3:28.

Sept. 26, 2004—New Orleans 28, St. Louis 25, at St. Louis; Rams win the toss. Furrey returns kick 23 yards to St. Louis 32. Rams drive to own 41. Landeta punts 41 yards to New Orleans 18. Lewis returns punt 15 yards to New Orleans 33. Saints drive to St. Louis 13. Carney kicks 31-yard field goal at 7:04.

Oct. 10, 2004—Minnesota 34, Houston 28, at Houston; Vikings win the toss. Burleson returns kick 29 yards to Minnesota 30. Vikings drive to own 35. Bennett punts 47 yards to Houston 18. Houston drives to own 38. Stanley punts 43 yards to Minnesota 19. Minnesota drives to the 50. Culpepper passes to Robinson for 50-yard touchdown at 7:55.

Oct. 10, 2004—St. Louis 33, Seattle 27, at Seattle; Rams win the toss. Harris returns kick 17 yards to St. Louis 29. Rams drive to own 48. Bulger passes to McDonald for 52-yard touchdown at 3:02.

Oct. 10, 2004—San Francisco 31, Arizona 28, at San Francisco; 49ers win the toss. Jackson returns kick 14 yards to San Francisco 39. 49ers drive to Arizona 14. Peterson kicks 32-yard field goal at 3:23.

Oct. 24, 2004—Philadelphia 34, Cleveland 31, at Cleveland; Eagles win the toss. Reed returns kick 27 yards to Philadelphia 30. Eagles drive to Cleveland 37. Johnson punts 47 yards for touchback. Cleveland drives to own 47. Frost punts 30 yards to Eagles 22. Philadelphia drives to Cleveland 32. Akers kicks 50-yard field goal at 9:58.

Nov. 14, 2004—Jacksonville 23, Detroit 17, at Jacksonville; Jaguars win the toss. Lewis returns kick 17 yards to the Jacksonville 24. Jaguars drive to the Detroit 38. Garrard passes to Smith for 38-yard touchdown at 5:28.

Nov. 14, 2004—Chicago 19, Tennessee 17, at Tennessee; Bears win the toss. Azumarh returns kick 22 yards to Chicago 26. Bears drive to own 48. Maynard punts 43 yards to Tennessee. Fair catch by Mason. Volek sacked at Tennessee 0 and fumble is recovered by Miller who is tackled in the end zone for safety at 3:17.

Nov. 14, 2004—Baltimore 20, New York Jets 17, at New York; Jets win the toss. Touchback. Jets drive to own 24. Gowin punts to Baltimore 35. Sams returns punt 9 yards to Baltimore 44. Ravens drive to own 49. Stewart punts 42 yards and ball is downed at the New York 9. Jets drive to own 16. Gowin punts 43 yards to Baltimore 41. Sams returns punt to Baltimore 44. Baltimore drives to New York 24. Stover kicks 42-yard field goal at 7:25.

Dec. 12, 2004—San Francisco 31, Arizona 28, at Arizona; 49ers win the toss. Touchback. 49ers drive to Arizona 37. Lee punts to 34 yards and is downed at Arizona 3. Cardinals drive to own 7. Player punts 51 yards and is returned to Arizona 49. 49ers drive to own 13. Peterson kicks 31-yard field goal at 6:22.

 # Dec. 18, 2004—Atlanta 34, Carolina 31, at Atlanta; Panthers win the toss. Broussard returns kick 16 yards to Carolina 19. Delhomme intercepted by Beasley returns pass 30 yards to Carolina 23. Atlanta drives to Carolina 20. Feely kicks 38-yard field goal at 2:25.

Dec. 26, 2004—Indianapolis 34, San Diego 31, at Indianapolis; Colts win the toss. Rhodes returns kick 17 yards to Indianpolis 27. Colts drive to San Diego 17. Vanderjagt kicks 30-yard field goal at 2:47.

Jan. 2, 2005—St. Louis 32, New York Jets 29, at St. Louis; Rams win the toss. Cason returns kick to St. Louis 24. Rams drive to New York 44. Stemke punts into endzone for touchback. Jets drive to own 44. Gowin punts 33 yards. Fair catch at St. Louis 23. Rams drive to own 31. Stemke punts to New York 27 and returned by McCareins two yards. Jets drive to St. Louis 35. Brien misses 53-yard field goal wide right. Rams begin drive from own 43. Rams drive to Jets 13. Wilkins kicks 31-yard field goal at 11:58.

Sept. 25, 2005—Jacksonville 26, New York Jets 20, at New York; Jets win the toss. Miller returns kick for 29 yards to Jets 21. Mathis intercepts Pennington pass and returns to Jets 46. Rhodes intercepts Leftwich pass at Jets 12 for no return. Jets drive ends at own 1. Graham punts 44 yards. Pearman returns punt 11 yards to Jets 34. Leftwich passes to Smith for 36-yard touchdown at 6:05.

Oct. 2, 2005—Washington 20, Seattle 17, at Washington; Redskins win the toss. Betts returns kick for 24 yards to Washington 23. Redskins drive to Seattle 22. Novak kicks a 39-yard field goal at 5:31.

Oct. 16, 2005—Jacksonville 23, Pittsburgh 17, at Pittsburgh; Steelers win the toss. Morgan returns kick for 74 yards to Jacksonville 26. Maddox fumbles and ball is recovered by Jaguars on own 36. Jaguars drive ends on own 16. Hanson punts 48 yards. Randel El returns punt 2 yards to Pittsburgh 35. Mathis intercepts Maddox pass and returned 41 yards for a touchdown at 3:36.

Oct. 16, 2005—Dallas 16, New York Giants 13, at Dallas; Cowboys win the toss. Thompson returns kick 23 yards to Dallas 23. Cowboys drive to Giants 26. Cortez kicks a 45-yard field goal at 3:47.

Oct. 30, 2005—Chicago 19, Detroit 13, at Detroit; Lions win the toss. Drummond returns kick 15 yards to Detroit 22. Lions drive to own 28. Harris punts 45 yards. Wade returns to Chicago 23 for no gain. Bears drive to own 48. Maynard punts 39 yards. Fair catch by Drummond at Detroit 13. Garcia pass intercepted by Tillman and returned 22 yards for a touchdown at 6:17.

Nov. 20, 2005—Baltimore 16, Pittsburgh 13, at Baltimore; Steelers win the toss. Colclough returns kick 16 yards to Pittsburgh 18. Steelers drive ends at own 36. Gardocki punts 27 yards. Ball downed at Baltimore 37. Ravens drive to own 39. Zastudil punts 26 yards. Ball downed at Pittsburgh 35. Steelers drive ends at own 33. Gardocki punts 37 yards. Sams returns punt 14 yards to Baltimore 44. Ravens drive to Pittsburgh 26. Stover kicks 44-yard field goal at 10:51.

Nov. 24, 2005—Denver 24, Dallas 21, at Dallas; Broncos win the toss. Da. Williams returns kick 27 yards to own 32. Broncos drive to Dallas 7. Elam kicks 24-yard field goal at 1:11.

Nov. 27, 2005—St. Louis 33, Houston 27, at Houston; Texans win the toss. Touchback. Drive begins at Houston 20. Texans drive to St. Louis 47. Stanley punts 47 yards. Touchback. Drive begins at St. Louis 20. Fitzpatrick passes to Curtis for 56-yard touchdown at 6:14.

Nov. 27, 2005—San Diego 23, Washington 17, at Washington; Chargers win the toss. Sproles returns kick 22 yards to San Diego 35. Tomlinson runs 41 yards for a touchdown at 34 seconds.

Nov. 27, 2005—Seattle 24, New York Giants 21, at Seattle; Seahawks win the toss. Scobey returns kick 24 yards to Seattle 22. Seahawks drive ends at own 13. Rouen punts 40 yards. Morton returns punt 2 yards to Giants 49. Giants drive to Seattle 36. Feely misses 54-yard field goal. Seahawks drive begins at own 44. Drive ends at Giants 46. Rouen punts 46 yards. Touchback. Drive begins at Giants 20. Seahawks drive to own 27. Feely misses 45-yard field goal. Drive begins at Seattle 35. Seahawks drive to Giants 18. Brown kicks 36-yard field goal at 12:15.

Dec. 11, 2005—Green Bay 16, Detroit 13, at Green Bay; Packers win the toss. Chatman returns kick 33 yards to Green Bay 35. Packers drive to Lions 11. Longwell kicks 28-yard field goal at 5:17.

Dec. 11, 2005—New York Giants 26, Philadelphia 23, at Philadelphia; Eagles win the toss. Hood returns kick 27 yards to Philadelphia 33. Eagles drive ends on own 33. Landeta punts 41 yards. Morton returns punt 7 yards to Giants 33. Manning pass intercepted by Dawkins at Philadelphia 37 and returned for no gain. McMahon fumbles and ball recovered by K. Allen. Fumble returned 2 yards. Giants drive begins on Philadelphia 37. Giants drive to Philadelphia 18. Feely kicks 36-yard field goal at 11:05.

Dec. 24, 2005—Tampa Bay 27, Falcons 24, at Tampa Bay; Buccaneers win the toss. Shepherd returns kick 18 yards and fumbles. Ball is recovered by Falcons' Heard at Tampa Bay 18. Falcons drive to Tampa Bay 10. Peterson field goal blocked by White. Ball recovered by Kelley and returned 9 yards to Tampa Bay 31. Buccaneers drive to Atlanta 9. Bryant misses 27-yard field goal. Falcons begin drive at own 20. Falcons drive to own

46. Koenen punts 49 yards. Jones returns punt 4 yards to Tampa Bay 9. Buccaneers drive to own 47. Bidwell punts 37 yards out of bounds at Atlanta 16. Falcons drive to Atlanta 24. Koenen punts 53 yards. Jones returns punt 28 yards to Atlanta 49. Buccaneers drive to Atlanta 23. Bryant kicks 41-yard field goal at 14:45.

Jan. 1, 2006—San Francisco 20, Houston 17, at San Francisco; 49ers win the toss. Amey returns kick 15 yards to San Francisco 21. 49ers drive to own 30. Lee punts 39 yards. Ball downed at Houston 31. Texans drive to San Francisco 44. Stanley punts 39 yards. Ball downed at San Francisco 5. 49ers drive to own 49. Lee punts 47 yards. Ball downed at Houston 4. Banks pass intercepted by Adams and laterals to Emanuel. Ball returned 35 yards to Houston 21. 49ers drive to Houston 15. Nedney kicks 31-yard field goal at 11:08.

POSTSEASON

Dec. 28, 1958—Baltimore 23, New York Giants 17, at New York in NFL Championship Game; Giants win toss. Maynard returns kickoff to Giants' 20. Chandler punts and Taseff returns one yard to Colts' 20. Ameche scores on 1-yard run at 8:15.

Dec. 23, 1962—Dallas Texans 20, Houston Oilers 17, at Houston in AFL Championship Game; Texans win toss and kick off. Jancik returns kickoff to Oilers' 33. Norton punts and Jackson makes fair catch on Texans' 22. Wilson punts and Jancik makes fair catch on Oilers' 45. Robinson intercepts Blanda's pass and returns 13 yards to Oilers' 47. Wilson's punt rolls dead at Oilers' 12. Hull intercepts Blanda's pass and returns 23 yards to midfield. Brooker kicks 25-yard field goal at 17:54.

Dec. 26, 1965—Green Bay 13, Baltimore 10, at Green Bay in NFL Divisional Playoff Game; Packers win toss. Moore returns kickoff to Packers' 22. Chandler punts and Haymond returns nine yards to Colts' 41. Gilburg punts and Wood makes fair catch at Packers' 21. Chandler punts and Haymond returns one yard to Colts' 41. Michaels misses 47-yard field goal. Chandler kicks 25-yard field goal at 13:39.

Dec. 25, 1971—Miami 27, Kansas City 24, at Kansas City in AFC Divisional Playoff Game; Chiefs win toss. Podolak, after a lateral from Buchanan, returns kickoff to Chiefs' 46. Stenerud's 42-yard field goal is blocked. Seiple punts and Podolak makes fair catch at Chiefs' 17. Wilson punts and Scott returns 18 yards to Dolphins' 39. Yepremian misses 62-yard field goal. Scott intercepts Dawson's pass and returns 13 yards to Dolphins' 46. Seiple punts and Podolak loses one yard to Chiefs' 15. Wilson punts and Scott makes fair catch on Dolphins' 30. Yepremian kicks 37-yard field goal at 22:40.

Dec. 24, 1977—Oakland 37, Baltimore 31, at Baltimore in AFC Divisional Playoff Game; Colts win toss. Raiders start on own 42 following a punt late in the first overtime. Oakland works way into field-goal range on Stabler's 19-yard pass to Branch at Colts' 26. Four plays later, on the second play of the second overtime, Stabler hits Casper with a 10-yard touchdown pass at 15:43.

Jan. 2, 1982—San Diego 41, Miami 38, at Miami in AFC Divisional Playoff Game; Chargers win toss. San Diego drives from its 13 to Miami 8. On second-and-goal, Benirschke misses 27-yard field goal attempt wide left at 9:15. Miami has the ball twice and San Diego twice more before the Dolphins get their third possession. Miami drives from the San Diego 46 to Chargers' 17 and on fourth-and-two, von Schamann's 34-yard field goal attempt is blocked by San Diego's Winslow after 11:27. Fouts then completes four of five passes, including a 39-yarder to Joiner that puts the ball on Dolphins' 10. On first down, Benirschke kicks a 29-yard field goal at 13:52.

Jan. 3, 1987—Cleveland 23, New York Jets 20, at Cleveland in AFC Divisional Playoff Game; Jets win toss. Jets' punt downed at Browns' 26. Moseley's 23-yard field goal attempt is wide right. Teams trade punts. Jets' second punt downed at Browns' 31. First overtime period expires eight plays later with Browns in possession at Jets' 42. Moseley kicks 27-yard field

OVERTIME GAMES

goal four plays into second overtime at 17:02.

Jan. 11, 1987—Denver 23, Cleveland 20, at Cleveland in AFC Championship Game; Browns win toss. Broncos hold Browns on four downs. Browns' punt returned four yards to Denver's 25. Elway completes 22- and 28-yard passes to set up Karlis's 33-yard field goal nine plays into drive at 5:38.

Jan. 3, 1988—Houston 23, Seattle 20, at Houston in AFC Wild Card Game; Seahawks win toss. Rodriguez punts to K. Johnson who returns one yard to Houston 15. Zendejas kicks 32-yard field goal 12 plays later at 8:05.

Dec. 31, 1989—Pittsburgh 26, Houston 23, at Houston in AFC Wild Card Playoff Game; Steelers win toss. Steelers punt to Oilers. Oilers' fumble recovered by Woodson and returned three yards. Four plays and 13 yards later, Anderson kicks a 50-yard field goal at 3:26.

Jan. 7, 1990—Los Angeles Rams 19, New York Giants 13, at New York in NFC Divisional Game; Rams win toss. Everett completes two passes to move ball to Giants' 48. White called for pass interference; ball spotted on Giants' 25. Everett hits Anderson with a 30-yard touchdown pass at 1:06.

Jan. 3, 1993—Buffalo 41, Houston 38, at Buffalo in AFC Wild Card Game; Oilers win toss. Oilers begin at 20. After 2 plays, Moon's pass is intercepted by Odomes who returns ball 2 yards to Houston 35. After 2 plays, Christie kicks 32-yard field goal at 3:06.

Jan. 8, 1994—Kansas City 27, Pittsburgh 24, at Kansas City in AFC Wild Card Game; Chiefs win toss. Hughes returns kickoff 20 yards to Kansas City 25. After 3 plays, Barker punts 48 yards to Pittsburgh 18 where Woodson returns 8 yards to the 26. After 6 plays, Royals punts 30 yards to Kansas City 20. Kansas City drives to Pittsburgh 14 where Lowery kicks 32-yard field goal at 11:03.

Jan. 17, 1999—Atlanta 30, Minnesota 27, at Minnesota in NFC Championship Game; Vikings win toss. Palmer returns kickoff 30 yards to Minnesota 29. After four plays, Berger punts 51 yards to Atlanta 7 where Dwight returns 8 yards to Atlanta 15. Falcons drive to Atlanta 36. Stryzinski punts 37 yards to Vikings' 27. Palmer calls fair catch. Vikings drive to Minnesota 39. Berger punts 52 yards to Atlanta 9. Downed by Vikings. Atlanta drives to Minnesota 21 where Andersen kicks 38-yard field goal at 11:52.

Dec. 30, 2000—Miami 23, Indianapolis 17, at Miami in AFC Wild Card Game; Dolphins win toss. Williams returns kickoff 18 yards to Miami 20. Offensive holding penalty on Freeman, 10 yards, ball spotted on Miami 10. Dolphins drive to Miami 29 where Turk punts 53 yards to Indianapolis 18. Colts drive to Miami 31 where Vanderjagt misses 49-yard field-goal attempt wide right. Dolphins drive to Indianapolis 17 where Smith rushes for a 17-yard touchdown at 11:16.

Jan. 19, 2002—New England 16, Oakland 13, at New England in AFC Divisional Playoff Game; Patriots win toss. Pass returns kickoff 24 yards to New England 34. Patriots drive to Oakland 5. Vinatieri kicks 23-yard field goal at 8:29.

Jan. 11, 2003—Tennessee 34, Pittsburgh 31, at Tennessee in AFC Divisional Playoff Game; Tennessee wins toss. Reed kicks 60 yards. Returned by Simon 21 yards to Tennessee 31. Titans drive to Pittsburgh 8. Nedney's 26-yard field goal is good at 2:15.

Jan. 4, 2004—Green Bay 33, Seattle 27, at Green Bay in NFC Wild Card Game; Seahawks win toss. Morris returns kick to Seattle 33. Seahawks drive to Seattle 42. Rouen's 44-yard punt returned by Chatman to Green Bay 26. Packers drive to Green Bay 31. Bidwell punts 35 yards to Seattle 34. Seahawks drive to Seattle 45. Hasselbeck's pass to Bannister intercepted by Packers' Harris and returned 52 yards for touchdown at 4:25.

Jan. 10, 2004—Carolina 29, St. Louis 23, at St. Louis in NFC Divisional Game; Panthers win toss. Smart returns kick to Carolina 32. Panthers drive to St. Louis 27. Kasay's 45-yard field-goal attempt no good. Rams take over at own 35 and drive to Carolina 35. Wilkins' 53-yard field-goal attempt no good. Pan-

thers take over at Carolina 43, drive to Carolina 47. Sauerbrun punts 40 yards to St. Louis 13. Rams drive to Carolina 38. Bulger's pass intercepted by Manning at Carolina 35. Panthers drive to Carolina 31. First overtime ends. On first play of second overtime, Delhomme passes to Smith for 69-yard touchdown at 15:10.

Jan. 11, 2004—Philadelphia 20, Green Bay 17, at Philadelphia in NFC Divisional Game; Eagles win toss. Thrash returns kick to Philadelphia 28. Eagles drive to Philadelphia 24. Johnson punts 49 yards and Packers start at own 32 after holding penalty. Favre's pass intercepted by Dawkins at Philadelphia 31 and returned to Green Bay 34. Eagles drive to Green Bay 13. Akers kicks 31-yard field goal at 4:48.

Jan. 8, 2005—New York Jets 20, San Diego 17, at San Diego in AFC Wild Card Game; Chargers win toss. Dwight returns kick to San Diego 26. Chargers drive to San Diego 35. Scifres punts 39 yards and ball is downed at the New York 26. Jets gain no yards. Gowin punts 41 yards. Parker loses 3 yards on return. San Diego starts on own 30. Chargers drive to New York 22. Kaeding's 40-yard field-goal attempt no good. Jets drive to San Diego 10. Brien kicks 28-yard field goal at 14:55.

Jan. 15, 2005—Pittsburgh 20, New York Jets 17, at Pittsburgh in AFC Divisional Game; Jets win toss. Cotchery returns kick to New York 31. Jets drive to New York 41. Gowin punts 54 yards. Randle El returns 8 yards to Pittsburgh 13. Steelers drive to New York 15. Reed kicks 33-yard field goal at 11:04.

NFL POSTSEASON OVERTIME GAMES
(BY LENGTH OF GAME)

Dec. 25, 1971	Miami 27, KANSAS CITY 24	82:40
Dec. 23, 1962	Dallas Texans 20, HOUSTON 17	77:54
Jan. 3 1987	CLEVELAND 23, N.Y. Jets 20	77:02
Dec. 24, 1977	Oakland 37, BALTIMORE 31	75:43
Jan. 10, 2004	Carolina 29, ST. LOUIS 23	75:10
Jan. 8, 2005	New York Jets 20, SAN DIEGO 17	74:55
Jan 2, 1982	San Diego 41, MIAMI 38	73:52
Dec. 26, 1965	GREEN BAY 13, Baltimore 10	73:39
Jan 17, 1999	Atlanta 30, MINNESOTA 27	71:52
Dec. 30, 2000	MIAMI 23, Indianapolis 17	71:16
Jan. 15, 2005	PITTSBURGH 20, New York Jets 17	71:04
Jan 8, 1994	KANSAS CITY 27, Pittsburgh 24	71:03
Jan. 19, 2002	NEW ENGLAND 16, Oakland 13	68:29
Dec. 28, 1958	Baltimore 23, N.Y. GIANTS 17	68:15
Jan. 3, 1988	HOUSTON 23, Seattle 20	68:05
Jan. 11, 1987	Denver 23, CLEVELAND 20	65:38
Jan. 11, 2004	PHILADELPHIA 20, Green Bay 17	64:48
Jan. 4, 2004	GREEN BAY 33, Seattle 27	64:25
Dec. 31, 1989	Pittsburgh 26, HOUSTON 23	63:26
Jan. 3, 1993	BUFFALO 41, Houston 38	63:06
Jan. 11, 2003	TENNESSEE 34, Pittsburgh 31	62:15
Jan. 7, 1990	L.A. Rams 19, N.Y. GIANTS 13	61:06

Home team in CAPS

There have been 22 overtime postseason games dating back to 1958. In 19 cases, both teams have had at least one possession. Last time: 1/15/05, PITTSBURGH 20, New York Jets 17.

OVERTIME WON-LOST RECORDS, 1974-2005
(REGULAR SEASON)

Team	Win	Loss	Tie	Pct.
AFC				
Baltimore	6	3	1	.650
Buffalo	17	9	0	.654
Cincinnati	14	9	0	.609
Cleveland	13	13	1	.500
Denver	18	12	2	.594
Houston	0	4	0	.000
Indianapolis	12	9	1	.568
Jacksonville	4	2	0	.666
Kansas City	10	11	2	.478
Miami	11	17	1	.397
New England	16	18	0	.470
N.Y. Jets	13	13	2	.500
Oakland	13	16	0	.448
Pittsburgh	15	10	2	.592
San Diego	11	17	0	.393
Tennessee	11	15	0	.423
NFC				
Arizona	16	13	2	.548
Atlanta	10	16	2	.392
Carolina	4	7	0	.363
Chicago	17	14	0	.548
Dallas	13	11	0	.542
Detroit	11	15	1	.426
Green Bay	10	11	4	.480
Minnesota	15	15	2	.500
New Orleans	7	8	0	.466
N.Y. Giants	14	14	2	.500
Philadelphia	11	15	3	.431
St. Louis	12	8	1	.595
San Francisco	15	13	1	.534
Seattle	8	15	0	.348
Tampa Bay	11	13	1	.460
Washington	16	10	1	.611

OVERTIME GAMES BY YEAR
(REGULAR SEASON)

2005-14	1997-17	1989-11	1981-10
2004-12	1996-14	1988- 9	1980-13
2003-23	1995-21	1987-13	1979-12
2002-25*	1994-16	1986-16	1978-11
2001-17	1993-7	1985-10	1977-6
2000-13	1992-10	1984- 9	1976-5
1999-11	1991-15	1983-19	1975-9
1998-7	1990-10	1982- 4	1974-2

*Record

OVERTIME GAME SUMMARY—1974-2005

There have been 391 overtime games in regular season play since the rule was adopted in 1974 (14 in 2005 season). Breakdown follows:

RESULTS
- **206 (8)** times the team which won the toss won the game (52.7%)
- **169 (6)** times the team which lost the toss won the game (43.2%)
- **16 (0)** games ended tied (4.1%). Last time: Nov. 10, 2002, Atlanta 34 at Pittsburgh 34.

POSSESSIONS
- **279 (9)** times both teams had at least one possession (71.4%)
- **112 (5)** times the team which won the toss drove for winning score (81 FG, 31 TD) (28.6%)

Of the 391 overtime games, there were 12 miscellaneous situations in which non-standard possessions took place:
- **8 (0)** times the defense or special teams won without registering an official possession (5 interceptions, 1 fumble recovery, 1 blocked punt, 1 blocked field goal)(2.0%)
- **1 (0)** times the special teams forced a fumble on the opening kickoff and drove for the winning score (0.26%)
- **1 (0)** times the punting team recovered a muffed punt and drove for winning score with team muffing punt having no official possessions (0.26%)
- **2 (0)** times the team that won the toss elected to kick and the team receiving the ball drove for winning score (0.51%)

SCORING
- **272 (9)** games were decided by a field goal (69.6%)
- **101 (5)** games were decided by a touchdown (25.8%)
- **2 (0)** games were decided by a safety (0.51%)
- **16 (0)** games ended tied (4.1%). Last time: Nov. 10, 2002, Atlanta 34 at Pittsburgh 34.

COIN TOSS
- **382(14)** times the team which won the toss elected to receive (97.7%)
- **9 (0)** times the team which won the toss elected to kick off (4 wins) (2.3%)

Note: The number in parentheses represents 2005 Season Total in each category.

MOST OVERTIME GAMES, SEASON

5	Green Bay Packers, 1983
4	Denver Broncos, 1985
	Cleveland Browns, 1989
	Minnesota Vikings, 1994
	Arizona Cardinals, 1995
	Minnesota Vikings, 1995
	Arizona Cardinals, 1997
	San Francisco 49ers, 2001
	Atlanta Falcons, 2002
	San Diego Chargers, 2002
	Carolina Panthers, 2003

LONGEST CONSECUTIVE GAME STREAKS
WITHOUT OVERTIME (Current)

43   Buffalo Bills (Last OT Game, 10/5/03
        vs. Cincinnati Bengals)
        Cincinnati Bengals (Last OT Game, 10/5/03
        at Buffalo Bills)
(Record: 110, St. Louis/Phoenix Cardinals, 12/7/86-12/19/93)

SHORTEST OVERTIME GAMES

0:14	New York Jets 37, BUFFALO 31; 9/8/02
0:16	CHICAGO 37, San Francisco 31; 10/28/01
0:17	NEW ORLEANS 20, Seattle 17; 11/16/97
0:21	Chicago 23, DETROIT 17; 11/27/80
0:30	Baltimore 29, NEW ENGLAND 23; 9/4/83
0:34	San Diego 23, WASHINGTON 17; 11/27/05
0:55	New York Giants 16, PHILADELPHIA 10; 9/29/85

LONGEST OVERTIME GAMES
(ALL POSTSEASON GAMES)

22:40	Miami 27, KANSAS CITY 24; 12/25/71
17:54	Dallas Texans 20, HOUSTON 17; 12/23/62
17:02	CLEVELAND 23, New York Jets 20; 1/3/87
15:43	Oakland 37, BALTIMORE 31; 12/24/77
15:10	Carolina 29, ST. LOUIS 23; 1/10/04

Home team in CAPS
There have been 22 overtime postseason games dating back to 1958. In 19 cases, both teams have had at least one possession. Last time: 1/15/05, PITTSBURGH 20, New York Jets 17.

OVERTIME SCORING SUMMARY

272   were decided by a field goal
46   were decided by a touchdown pass
27   were decided by a touchdown run
17   were decided by an interception (Atlanta 40, New Orleans 34, 9/2/79; Atlanta 47, Green Bay 41, 11/27/83; New York Giants 16, Philadelphia 10, 9/29/85; Indianapolis 23, Cleveland 17, 12/10/89; Cleveland 30, San Diego 24, 10/20/91; Kansas City 23, Oakland 17, 9/17/95; New York Giants 27, Arizona 21, 10/8/95; Washington 36, Detroit 30, 10/22/95; Arizona 20, Seattle 14, 10/29/95; Cincinnati 34, Detroit 28, 9/13/98; New York Giants 23, Philadelphia 17, 10/31/99; Chicago 37, San Francisco 31, 10/28/01; Chicago 27, Cleveland 21, 11/4/01; New Orleans 26, Tampa Bay 20, 9/8/02; Atlanta 20, Carolina 14, 12/7/03; Jacksonville 23, Pittsburgh 17, 10/16/05; Chicago 19, Detroit 13, 10/30/05)
2   were decided on a fake field goal/touchdown pass (Minnesota 22, Chicago 16, 10/16/77; Cleveland 23, Minnesota 17, 12/17/89)
2   were decided by a fumble recovery (Baltimore 29, New England 23, 9/4/83; Denver 36, Seattle 30, 12/19/99)
2   were decided by a kickoff return (Chicago 23, Detroit 17, 11/27/80; New York Jets 37, Buffalo 31, 9/8/02)
2   was decided by a safety (Minnesota 23, Los Angeles Rams 21, 11/5/89; Chicago 19, Tennessee 17, 11/14/04)
1   was decided by a punt return (Kansas City 29, San Diego 23, 10/9/95)
1   was decided on a fake field goal/touchdown run (Los Angeles Rams 27, Minnesota 21, 12/2/79)
1   was decided on a blocked field goal (Denver 30, San Diego 24, 11/17/85)
1   was decided on a blocked field goal/recovery by kicker (Green Bay 12, Chicago 6, 9/7/80)
1   was decided on a blocked field goal/recovery by kicking team (Philadelphia 23, New York Giants 17, 11/20/88)
16   ended tied

OVERTIME RECORDS
Longest Touchdown Pass

99 Yards — Ron Jaworski to Mike Quick, Philadelphia 23, Atlanta 17 (11/10/85)
82 Yards — Tom Brady to Troy Brown, New England 19, Miami 13 (10/19/03)
76 Yards — Troy Aikman to Raghib Ismail, Dallas 41, Washington 35 (9/12/99)

Longest Touchdown Run

96 Yards — Garrison Hearst, San Francisco 36, New York Jets 30 (9/6/98)
60 Yards — Herschel Walker, Dallas 23, New England 17 (11/15/87)
46 Yards — Michael Vick, Atlanta 30, Minnesota 24 (12/1/02)

Longest Field Goal

53 Yards — Chris Jacke, Green Bay 23, San Francisco 20 (10/4/96)
52 Yards — Mike Cofer, Indianapolis 27, New York Jets 24 (9/10/95)
51 Yards — Greg Davis, New England 23, Indianapolis 20 (10/29/89); Greg Davis, Arizona 20, Pittsburgh 17 (10/30/94); Michael Husted, Tampa Bay 20, Minnesota 17 (10/15/95); Mike Vanderjagt, Indianapolis 23, Denver 20 (11/24/02)

Longest Touchdown Plays

99 Yards — (Pass) Ron Jaworski to Mike Quick, Philadelphia 23, Atlanta 17 (11/10/85)
96 Yards — (Run) Garrison Hearst, San Francisco 36, New York Jets 30 (9/6/98)
96 Yards — (Kickoff return) Chad Morton, New York Jets 37, Buffalo 31 (9/8/02)
95 Yards — (Kickoff return) Dave Williams, Chicago 23, Detroit 17 (11/27/80)
86 Yards — (Punt return) Tamarick Vanover, Kansas City 29, San Diego 23 (10/9/95)

FIRST-ROUND SELECTIONS

If club had no first-round selection, first player drafted is listed with round in parentheses.

ARIZONA CARDINALS
Year   Player, College, Position
1936   Jim Lawrence, Texas Christian, B
1937   Ray Buivid, Marquette, B
1938   Jack Robbins, Arkansas, B
1939   Charles (Ki) Aldrich, TCU, C
1940   George Cafego, Tennessee, B
1941   John Kimbrough, Texas A&M, B
1942   Steve Lach, Duke, B
1943   Glenn Dobbs, Tulsa, B
1944   Pat Harder, Wisconsin, B
1945   Charley Trippi, Georgia, B
1946   Dub Jones, Louisiana State, B
1947   DeWitt (Tex) Coulter, Army, T
1948   Jim Spavital, Oklahoma A&M, B
1949   Bill Fischer, Notre Dame, G
1950   Jack Jennings, Ohio State, T (2)
1951   Jerry Groom, Notre Dame, C
1952   Ollie Matson, San Francisco, B
1953   Johnny Olszewski, California, B
1954   Lamar McHan, Arkansas, B
1955   Max Boydston, Oklahoma, E
1956   Joe Childress, Auburn, B
1957   Jerry Tubbs, Oklahoma, C
1958   King Hill, Rice, B
         John David Crow, Texas A&M, B
1959   Bill Stacy, Mississippi State, B
1960   George Izo, Notre Dame, QB
1961   Ken Rice, Auburn, T
1962   Fate Echols, Northwestern, DT
         Irv Goode, Kentucky, C
1963   Jerry Stovall, Louisiana State, S
         Don Brumm, Purdue, DE
1964   Ken Kortas, Louisville, DT
1965   Joe Namath, Alabama, QB
1966   Carl McAdams, Oklahoma, LB
1967   Dave Williams, Washington, WR
1968   MacArthur Lane, Utah State, RB
1969   Roger Wehrli, Missouri, DB
1970   Larry Stegent, Texas A&M, RB
1971   Norm Thompson, Utah, CB
1972   Bobby Moore, Oregon, RB-WR
1973   Dave Butz, Purdue, DT
1974   J.V. Cain, Colorado, TE
1975   Tim Gray, Texas A&M, DB
1976   Mike Dawson, Arizona, DT
1977   Steve Pisarkiewicz, Missouri, QB
1978   Steve Little, Arkansas, K
         Ken Greene, Washington State, DB
1979   Ottis Anderson, Miami, RB
1980   Curtis Greer, Michigan, DE
1981   E.J. Junior, Alabama, LB
1982   Luis Sharpe, UCLA, T
1983   Leonard Smith, McNeese St., DB
1984   Clyde Duncan, Tennessee, WR
1985   Freddie Joe Nunn, Mississippi, LB
1986   Anthony Bell, Michigan State, LB
1987   Kelly Stouffer, Colorado State, QB
1988   Ken Harvey, California, LB
1989   Eric Hill, Louisiana State, LB
         Joe Wolf, Boston College, G
1990   Anthony Thompson, Indiana, RB (2)
1991   Eric Swann, No College, DE
1992   Tony Sacca, Penn State, QB (2)

1993   Garrison Hearst, Georgia, RB
         Ernest Dye, South Carolina, T
1994   Jamir Miller, UCLA, LB
1995   Frank Sanders, Auburn, WR (2)
1996   Simeon Rice, Illinois, DE
1997   Tom Knight, Iowa, DB
1998   Andre Wadsworth, Florida St., DE
1999   David Boston, Ohio State, WR
         L.J. Shelton, Eastern Michigan, T
2000   Thomas Jones, Virginia, RB
2001   Leonard Davis, Texas, T
2002   Wendell Bryant, Wisconsin, DT
2003   Bryant Johnson, Penn State, WR
         Calvin Pace, Wake Forest, DE
2004   Larry Fitzgerald, Pittsburgh, WR
2005   Antrel Rolle, Miami, DB
2006   Matt Leinart, So. California, QB

ATLANTA FALCONS
Year   Player, College, Position
1966   Tommy Nobis, Texas, LB
         Randy Johnson, Texas A&I, QB
1967   Leo Carroll, San Diego St., DE (2)
1968   Claude Humphrey, Tennessee St., DE
1969   George Kunz, Notre Dame, T
1970   John Small, Citadel, LB
1971   Joe Profit, Northeast Louisiana, RB
1972   Clarence Ellis, Notre Dame, DB
1973   Greg Marx, Notre Dame, DT (2)
1974   Gerald Tinker, Kent State, WR (2)
1975   Steve Bartkowski, California, QB
1976   Bubba Bean, Texas A&M, RB
1977   Warren Bryant, Kentucky, T
         Wilson Faumuina, San Jose St., DT
1978   Mike Kenn, Michigan, T
1979   Don Smith, Miami, DE
1980   Junior Miller, Nebraska, TE
1981   Bobby Butler, Florida State, DB
1982   Gerald Riggs, Arizona State, RB
1983   Mike Pitts, Alabama, DE
1984   Rick Bryan, Oklahoma, DT
1985   Bill Fralic, Pittsburgh, T
1986   Tony Casillas, Oklahoma, NT
         Tim Green, Syracuse, LB
1987   Chris Miller, Oregon, QB
1988   Aundray Bruce, Auburn, LB
1989   Deion Sanders, Florida State, DB
         Shawn Collins, No. Arizona, WR
1990   Steve Broussard, Washington St., RB
1991   Bruce Pickens, Nebraska, DB
         Mike Pritchard, Colorado, WR
1992   Bob Whitfield, Stanford, T
         Tony Smith, So. Mississippi, RB
1993   Lincoln Kennedy, Washington, T
1994   Bert Emanuel, Rice, WR (2)
1995   Devin Bush, Florida State, DB
1996   Shannon Brown, Alabama, DT (3)
1997   Michael Booker, Nebraska, DB
1998   Keith Brooking, Georgia Tech, LB
1999   Patrick Kerney, Virginia, DE
2000   Travis Claridge, So. California, T (2)
2001   Michael Vick, Virginia Tech, QB
2002   T.J. Duckett, Michigan State, RB
2003   Bryan Scott, Penn State, DB (2)
2004   DeAngelo Hall, Virginia Tech, DB
         Michael Jenkins, Ohio State, WR
2005   Roddy White, Ala.-Birmingham, WR
2006   Jimmy Williams, Virginia Tech, DB (2)

BALTIMORE RAVENS
Year   Player, College, Position
1996   Jonathan Ogden, UCLA, T
         Ray Lewis, Miami, LB
1997   Peter Boulware, Florida State, DE
1998   Duane Starks, Miami, DB
1999   Chris McAlister, Arizona, DB
2000   Jamal Lewis, Tennessee, RB
         Travis Taylor, Florida, WR
2001   Todd Heap, Arizona State, TE
2002   Ed Reed, Miami, DB
2003   Terrell Suggs, Arizona State, DE
         Kyle Boller, California, QB
2004   Dwan Edwards, Oregon St., DT (2)
2005   Mark Clayton, Oklahoma, WR
2006   Haloti Ngata, Oregon, DT

BUFFALO BILLS
Year   Player, College, Position
1960   Richie Lucas, Penn State, QB
1961   Ken Rice, Auburn, T
1962   Ernie Davis, Syracuse, RB
1963   Dave Behrman, Michigan State, C
1964   Carl Eller, Minnesota, DE
1965   Jim Davidson, Ohio State, T
1966   Mike Dennis, Mississippi, RB
1967   John Pitts, Arizona State, S
1968   Haven Moses, San Diego St., WR
1969   O.J. Simpson, So. California, RB
1970   Al Cowlings, So. California, DE
1971   J.D. Hill, Arizona State, WR
1972   Walt Patulski, Notre Dame, DE
1973   Paul Seymour, Michigan, TE
         Joe DeLamielleure, Michigan St., G
1974   Reuben Gant, Oklahoma State, TE
1975   Tom Ruud, Nebraska, LB
1976   Mario Clark, Oregon, DB
1977   Phil Dokes, Oklahoma State, DT
1978   Terry Miller, Oklahoma State, RB
1979   Tom Cousineau, Ohio State, LB
         Jerry Butler, Clemson, WR
1980   Jim Ritcher, North Carolina St., C
1981   Booker Moore, Penn State, RB
1982   Perry Tuttle, Clemson, WR
1983   Tony Hunter, Notre Dame, TE
         Jim Kelly, Miami, QB
1984   Greg Bell, Notre Dame, RB
1985   Bruce Smith, Virginia Tech, DE
         Derrick Burroughs, Memphis St., DB
1986   Ronnie Harmon, Iowa, RB
         Will Wolford, Vanderbilt, T
1987   Shane Conlan, Penn State, LB
1988   Thurman Thomas, Oklahoma St., RB (2)
1989   Don Beebe, Chadron, Neb., WR (3)
1990   James Williams, Fresno State, DB
1991   Henry Jones, Illinois, DB
1992   John Fina, Arizona, T
1993   Thomas Smith, North Carolina, DB
1994   Jeff Burris, Notre Dame, DB
1995   Ruben Brown, Pittsburgh, G
1996   Eric Moulds, Mississippi St., WR
1997   Antowain Smith, Houston, RB
1998   Sam Cowart, Florida State, LB (2)
1999   Antoine Winfield, Ohio State, DB
2000   Erik Flowers, Arizona State, DE
2001   Nate Clements, Ohio State, DB
2002   Mike Williams, Texas, T
2003   Willis McGahee, Miami, RB
2004   Lee Evans, Wisconsin, WR
         J.P. Losman, Tulane, QB

2005 Roscoe Parrish, Miami, WR (2)
2006 Donte' Whitner, Ohio State, DB
      John McCargo, North Carolina St., DT

CAROLINA PANTHERS
Year Player, College, Position
1995 Kerry Collins, Penn State, QB
      Tyrone Poole, Ft. Valley State, DB
      Blake Brockermeyer, Texas, T
1996 Tim Biakabutuka, Michigan, RB
1997 Rae Carruth, Colorado, WR
1998 Jason Peter, Nebraska, DT
1999 Chris Terry, Georgia, T (2)
2000 Rashard Anderson, Jackson St., DB
2001 Dan Morgan, Miami, LB
2002 Julius Peppers, North Carolina, DE
2003 Jordan Gross, Utah, T
2004 Chris Gamble, Ohio State, DB
2005 Thomas Davis, Georgia, DB
2006 DeAngelo Williams, Memphis, RB

CHICAGO BEARS
Year Player, College, Position
1936 Joe Stydahar, West Virginia, T
1937 Les McDonald, Nebraska, E
1938 Joe Gray, Oregon State, B
1939 Sid Luckman, Columbia, QB
      Bill Osmanski, Holy Cross, B
1940 Clyde (Bulldog) Turner, Hardin-Simmons, C
1941 Tom Harmon, Michigan, B
      Norm Standlee, Stanford, B
      Don Scott, Ohio State, B
1942 Frankie Albert, Stanford, B
1943 Bob Steber, Missouri, B
1944 Ray Evans, Kansas, B
1945 Don Lund, Michigan, B
1946 Johnny Lujack, Notre Dame, QB
1947 Bob Fenimore, Oklahoma State, B
      Don Kindt, Wisconsin, B
1948 Bobby Layne, Texas, QB
      Max Bumgardner, Texas, E
1949 Dick Harris, Texas, C
1950 Chuck Hunsinger, Florida, B
      Fred Morrison, Ohio State, B
1951 Bob Williams, Notre Dame, B
      Billy Stone, Bradley, B
      Gene Schroeder, Virginia, E
1952 Jim Dooley, Miami, B
1953 Billy Anderson, Compton (Calif.) J.C., B
1954 Stan Wallace, Illinois, B
1955 Ron Drzewiecki, Marquette, B
1956 Menan (Tex) Schriewer, Texas, E
1957 Earl Leggett, Louisiana State, T
1958 Chuck Howley, West Virginia, G
1959 Don Clark, Ohio State, B
1960 Roger Davis, Syracuse, G
1961 Mike Ditka, Pittsburgh, E
1962 Ronnie Bull, Baylor, RB
1963 Dave Behrman, Michigan State, C
1964 Dick Evey, Tennessee, DT
1965 Dick Butkus, Illinois, LB
      Gale Sayers, Kansas, RB
      Steve DeLong, Tennessee, T
1966 George Rice, Louisiana State, DT
1967 Loyd Phillips, Arkansas, DE
1968 Mike Hull, Southern California, RB
1969 Rufus Mayes, Ohio State, T
1970 George Farmer, UCLA, WR (3)
1971 Joe Moore, Missouri, RB

1972 Lionel Antoine, Southern Illinois, T
      Craig Clemons, Iowa, DB
1973 Wally Chambers, Eastern Kentucky, DE
1974 Waymond Bryant, Tennessee St., LB
      Dave Gallagher, Michigan, DT
1975 Walter Payton, Jackson State, RB
1976 Dennis Lick, Wisconsin, T
1977 Ted Albrecht, California, T
1978 Brad Shearer, Texas, DT (3)
1979 Dan Hampton, Arkansas, DT
      Al Harris, Arizona State, DE
1980 Otis Wilson, Louisville, LB
1981 Keith Van Horne, So. California, T
1982 Jim McMahon, Brigham Young, QB
1983 Jim Covert, Pittsburgh, T
      Willie Gault, Tennessee, WR
1984 Wilber Marshall, Florida, LB
1985 William Perry, Clemson, DT
1986 Neal Anderson, Florida, RB
1987 Jim Harbaugh, Michigan, QB
1988 Brad Muster, Stanford, RB
      Wendell Davis, Louisiana St., WR
1989 Donnell Woolford, Clemson, DB
      Trace Armstrong, Florida, DE
1990 Mark Carrier, So. California, DB
1991 Stan Thomas, Texas, T
1992 Alonzo Spellman, Ohio State, DE
1993 Curtis Conway, So. California, WR
1994 John Thierry, Alcorn State, DE
1995 Rashaan Salaam, Colorado, RB
1996 Walt Harris, Mississippi State, DB
1997 John Allred, So. California, TE (2)
1998 Curtis Enis, Penn State, RB
1999 Cade McNown, UCLA, QB
2000 Brian Urlacher, New Mexico, LB
2001 David Terrell, Michigan, WR
2002 Marc Colombo, Boston College, T
2003 Michael Haynes, Penn State, DE
      Rex Grossman, Florida, QB
2004 Tommie Harris, Oklahoma, DT
2005 Cedric Benson, Texas, RB
2006 Danieal Manning, Abilene Christian, DB (2)

CINCINNATI BENGALS
Year Player, College, Position
1968 Bob Johnson, Tennessee, C
1969 Greg Cook, Cincinnati, QB
1970 Mike Reid, Penn State, DT
1971 Vernon Holland, Tennessee St., T
1972 Sherman White, California, DE
1973 Isaac Curtis, San Diego State, WR
1974 Bill Kollar, Montana State, DT
1975 Glenn Cameron, Florida, LB
1976 Billy Brooks, Oklahoma, WR
      Archie Griffin, Ohio State, RB
1977 Eddie Edwards, Miami, DT
      Wilson Whitley, Houston, DT
      Mike Cobb, Michigan State, TE
1978 Ross Browner, Notre Dame, DT
      Blair Bush, Washington, C
1979 Jack Thompson, Washington St., QB
      Charles Alexander, Louisiana St., RB
1980 Anthony Muñoz, So. California, T
1981 David Verser, Kansas, WR
1982 Glen Collins, Mississippi State, DE
1983 Dave Rimington, Nebraska, C
1984 Ricky Hunley, Arizona, LB
      Pete Koch, Maryland, DE
      Brian Blados, North Carolina, T

1985 Eddie Brown, Miami, WR
      Emanuel King, Alabama, LB
1986 Joe Kelly, Washington, LB
      Tim McGee, Tennessee, WR
1987 Jason Buck, Brigham Young, DE
1988 Rickey Dixon, Oklahoma, DB
1989 Eric Ball, UCLA, RB (2)
1990 James Francis, Baylor, LB
1991 Alfred Williams, Colorado, LB
1992 David Klingler, Houston, QB
      Darryl Williams, Miami, DB
1993 John Copeland, Alabama, DE
1994 Dan Wilkinson, Ohio State, DT
1995 Ki-Jana Carter, Penn State, RB
1996 Willie Anderson, Auburn, T
1997 Reinard Wilson, Florida State, LB
1998 Takeo Spikes, Auburn, LB
      Brian Simmons, North Carolina, LB
1999 Akili Smith, Oregon, QB
2000 Peter Warrick, Florida State, WR
2001 Justin Smith, Missouri, DE
2002 Levi Jones, Arizona State, T
2003 Carson Palmer, Southern California, QB
2004 Chris Perry, Michigan, RB
2005 David Pollack, Georgia, LB
2006 Johnathan Joseph, South Carolina, DB

CLEVELAND BROWNS
Year Player, College, Position
1950 Ken Carpenter, Oregon State, B
1951 Ken Konz, Louisiana State, B
1952 Bert Rechichar, Tennessee, DB
      Harry Agganis, Boston U., QB
1953 Doug Atkins, Tennessee, DE
1954 Bobby Garrett, Stanford, QB
      John Bauer, Illinois, G
1955 Kurt Burris, Oklahoma, C
1956 Preston Carpenter, Arkansas, B
1957 Jim Brown, Syracuse, RB
1958 Jim Shofner, Texas Christian, DB
1959 Rich Kreitling, Illinois, DE
1960 Jim Houston, Ohio State, DE
1961 Bobby Crespino, Mississippi, TE
1962 Gary Collins, Maryland, WR
      Leroy Jackson, Western Illinois, RB
1963 Tom Hutchinson, Kentucky, WR
1964 Paul Warfield, Ohio State, WR
1965 James Garcia, Purdue, T (2)
1966 Milt Morin, Massachusetts, TE
1967 Bob Matheson, Duke, LB
1968 Marvin Upshaw, Trinity, Tex., DT-DE
1969 Ron Johnson, Michigan, RB
1970 Mike Phipps, Purdue, QB
      Bob McKay, Texas, T
1971 Clarence Scott, Kansas State, CB
1972 Thom Darden, Michigan, DB
1973 Steve Holden, Arizona State, WR
      Pete Adams, Southern California, T
1974 Billy Corbett, Johnson C. Smith, T (2)
1975 Mack Mitchell, Houston, DE
1976 Mike Pruitt, Purdue, RB
1977 Robert Jackson, Texas A&M, LB
1978 Clay Matthews, So. California, LB
      Ozzie Newsome, Alabama, TE
1979 Willis Adams, Houston, WR
1980 Charles White, So. California, RB
1981 Hanford Dixon, So. Mississippi, DB
1982 Chip Banks, So. California, LB
1983 Ron Brown, Arizona State, WR (2)
1984 Don Rogers, UCLA, DB

1985 Greg Allen, Florida State, RB (2)
1986 Webster Slaughter, San Diego St., WR (2)
1987 Mike Junkin, Duke, LB
1988 Clifford Charlton, Florida, LB
1989 Eric Metcalf, Texas, RB
1990 Leroy Hoard, Michigan, RB (2)
1991 Eric Turner, UCLA, DB
1992 Tommy Vardell, Stanford, RB
1993 Steve Everitt, Michigan, C
1994 Antonio Langham, Alabama, DB
     Derrick Alexander, Michigan, WR
1995 Craig Powell, Ohio State, LB
1999 Tim Couch, Kentucky, QB
2000 Courtney Brown, Penn State, DE
2001 Gerard Warren, Florida, DT
2002 William Green, Boston College, RB
2003 Jeff Faine, Norte Dame, C
2004 Kellen Winslow, Miami, TE
2005 Braylon Edwards, Michigan, WR
2006 Kamerion Wimbley, Florida St., DE

DALLAS COWBOYS
Year Player, College, Position
1960 None
1961 Bob Lilly, Texas Christian, DT
1962 Sonny Gibbs, TCU, QB (2)
1963 Lee Roy Jordan, Alabama, LB
1964 Scott Appleton, Texas, DT
1965 Craig Morton, California, QB
1966 John Niland, Iowa, G
1967 Phil Clark, Northwestern, DB (3)
1968 Dennis Homan, Alabama, WR
1969 Calvin Hill, Yale, RB
1970 Duane Thomas, West Texas St., RB
1971 Tody Smith, So. California, DE
1972 Bill Thomas, Boston College, RB
1973 Billy Joe DuPree, Michigan St., TE
1974 Ed (Too Tall) Jones, Tennessee St., DE
     Charley Young, North Carolina St., RB
1975 Randy White, Maryland, LB
     Thomas Henderson, Langston, LB
1976 Aaron Kyle, Wyoming, DB
1977 Tony Dorsett, Pittsburgh, RB
1978 Larry Bethea, Michigan State, DE
1979 Robert Shaw, Tennessee, C
1980 Bill Roe, Colorado, LB (3)
1981 Howard Richards, Missouri, T
1982 Rod Hill, Kentucky State, DB
1983 Jim Jeffcoat, Arizona State, DE
1984 Billy Cannon, Jr., Texas A&M, LB
1985 Kevin Brooks, Michigan, DE
1986 Mike Sherrard, UCLA, WR
1987 Danny Noonan, Nebraska, DT
1988 Michael Irvin, Miami, WR
1989 Troy Aikman, UCLA, QB
1990 Emmitt Smith, Florida, RB
1991 Russell Maryland, Miami, DT
     Alvin Harper, Tennessee, WR
     Kelvin Pritchett, Mississippi, DT
1992 Kevin Smith, Texas A&M, DB
     Robert Jones, East Carolina, LB
1993 Kevin Williams, Miami, WR (2)
1994 Shante Carver, Arizona State, DE
1995 Sherman Williams, Alabama, RB (2)
1996 Kavika Pittman, McNeese St., DE (2)
1997 David LaFleur, Louisiana State, TE
1998 Greg Ellis, North Carolina, DE
1999 Ebenezer Ekuban, North Carolina, DE
2000 Dwayne Goodrich, Tennessee, DB (2)
2001 Quincy Carter, Georgia, QB (2)

2002 Roy Williams, Oklahoma, DB
2003 Terence Newman, Kansas State, DB
2004 Julius Jones, Notre Dame, RB (2)
2005 Demarcus Ware, Troy, DE
     Marcus Spears, Louisiana St., DE
2006 Bobby Carpenter, Ohio State, LB

DENVER BRONCOS
Year Player, College, Position
1960 Roger LeClerc, Trinity, Conn., C
1961 Bob Gaiters, New Mexico St., RB
1962 Merlin Olsen, Utah State, DT
1963 Kermit Alexander, UCLA, CB
1964 Bob Brown, Nebraska, T
1965 Dick Butkus, Illinois, LB (2)
1966 Jerry Shay, Purdue, DT
1967 Floyd Little, Syracuse, RB
1968 Curley Culp, Arizona State, DE (2)
1969 Grady Cavness, Texas-El Paso, DB (2)
1970 Bob Anderson, Colorado, RB
1971 Marv Montgomery, So. California, T
1972 Riley Odoms, Houston, TE
1973 Otis Armstrong, Purdue, RB
1974 Randy Gradishar, Ohio State, LB
1975 Louis Wright, San Jose State, DB
1976 Tom Glassic, Virginia, G
1977 Steve Schindler, Boston College, G
1978 Don Latimer, Miami, DT
1979 Kelvin Clark, Nebraska, T
1980 Rulon Jones, Utah State, DE (2)
1981 Dennis Smith, So. California, DB
1982 Gerald Willhite, San Jose St., RB
1983 Chris Hinton, Northwestern, G
1984 Andre Townsend, Mississippi, DE (2)
1985 Steve Sewell, Oklahoma, RB
1986 Jim Juriga, Illinois, T (4)
1987 Ricky Nattiel, Florida, WR
1988 Ted Gregory, Syracuse, NT
1989 Steve Atwater, Arkansas, DB
1990 Alton Montgomery, Houston, DB (2)
1991 Mike Croel, Nebraska, LB
1992 Tommy Maddox, UCLA, QR
1993 Dan Williams, Toledo, DE
1994 Allen Aldridge, Houston, LB (2)
1995 Jamie Brown, Florida A&M, T (4)
1996 John Mobley, Kutztown, LB
1997 Trevor Pryce, Clemson, DT
1998 Marcus Nash, Tennessee, WR
1999 Al Wilson, Tennessee, LB
2000 Deltha O'Neal, California, DB
2001 Willie Middlebrooks, Minnesota, DB
2002 Ashley Lelie, Hawaii, WR
2003 George Foster, Georgia, T
2004 D.J. Williams, Miami, LB
2005 Darrent Wiliams, Oklahoma St., DB (2)
2006 Jay Cutler, Vanderbilt, QB

DETROIT LIONS
Year Player, College, Position
1936 Sid Wagner, Michigan State, G
1937 Lloyd Cardwell, Nebraska, B
1938 Alex Wojciechowicz, Fordham, C
1939 John Pingel, Michigan State, B
1940 Doyle Nave, Southern California, B
1941 Jim Thomason, Texas A&M, B
1942 Bob Westfall, Michigan, B
1943 Frank Sinkwich, Georgia, B
1944 Otto Graham, Northwestern, B
1945 Frank Szymanski, Notre Dame, C
1946 Bill Dellastatious, Missouri, B

1947 Glenn Davis, Army, B
1948 Y.A. Tittle, Louisiana State, B
1949 John Rauch, Georgia, B
1950 Leon Hart, Notre Dame, E
     Joe Watson, Rice, C
1951 Dick Stanfel, San Francisco, G (2)
1952 Yale Lary, Texas A&M, B (3)
1953 Harley Sewell, Texas, G
1954 Dick Chapman, Rice, T
1955 Dave Middleton, Auburn, B
1956 Hopalong Cassady, Ohio State, B
1957 Bill Glass, Baylor, G
1958 Alex Karras, Iowa, T
1959 Nick Pietrosante, Notre Dame, B
1960 John Robinson, Louisiana State, S
1961 Danny LaRose, Missouri, T (2)
1962 John Hadl, Kansas, QB
1963 Daryl Sanders, Ohio State, T
1964 Pete Beathard, So. California, QB
1965 Tom Nowatzke, Indiana, RB
1966 Nick Eddy, Notre Dame, RB (2)
1967 Mel Farr, UCLA, RB
1968 Greg Landry, Massachusetts, QB
     Earl McCullouch, So. California, WR
1969 Altie Taylor, Utah State, RB (2)
1970 Steve Owens, Oklahoma, RB
1971 Bob Bell, Cincinnati, DT
1972 Herb Orvis, Colorado, DE
1973 Ernie Price, Texas A&I, DE
1974 Ed O'Neil, Penn State, LB
1975 Lynn Boden, South Dakota St., G
1976 James Hunter, Grambling, DB
     Lawrence Galnes, Wyoming, RB
1977 Walt Williams, New Mexico St., DB (2)
1978 Luther Bradley, Notre Dame, DB
1979 Keith Dorney, Penn State, T
1980 Billy Sims, Oklahoma, RB
1981 Mark Nichols, San Jose State, WR
1982 Jimmy Williams, Nebraska, LB
1983 James Jones, Florida, RB
1984 David Lewis, California, TE
1985 Lomas Brown, Florida, T
1986 Chuck Long, Iowa, QB
1987 Reggie Rogers, Washington, DE
1988 Bennie Blades, Miami, DB
1989 Barry Sanders, Oklahoma St., RB
1990 Andre Ware, Houston, QB
1991 Herman Moore, Virginia, WR
1992 Robert Porcher, South Carolina St., DE
1993 Ryan McNeil, Miami, DB (2)
1994 Johnnie Morton, So. California, WR
1995 Luther Elliss, Utah, DT
1996 Reggie Brown, Texas A&M, LB
     Jeff Hartings, Penn State, G
1997 Bryant Westbrook, Texas, DB
1998 Terry Fair, Tennessee, DB
1999 Chris Claiborne, So. California, LB
     Aaron Gibson, Wisconsin, T
2000 Stockar McDougle, Oklahoma, T
2001 Jeff Backus, Michigan, T
2002 Joey Harrington, Oregon, QB
2003 Charles Rogers, Michigan State, WR
2004 Roy Williams, Texas, WR
     Kevin Jones, Virginia Tech, RB
2005 Mike Wiliams, So. California, WR
2006 Ernie Sims, Florida State, LB

GREEN BAY PACKERS
Year Player, College, Position
1936 Russ Letlow, San Francisco, G

1937 Eddie Jankowski, Wisconsin, B
1938 Cecil Isbell, Purdue, B
1939 Larry Buhler, Minnesota, B
1940 Harold Van Every, Minnesota, B
1941 George Paskvan, Wisconsin, B
1942 Urban Odson, Minnesota, T
1943 Dick Wildung, Minnesota, T
1944 Merv Pregulman, Michigan, G
1945 Walt Schlinkman, Texas Tech, B
1946 Johnny Strzykalski, Marquette, B
1947 Ernie Case, UCLA, B
1948 Earl (Jug) Girard, Wisconsin, B
1949 Stan Heath, Nevada, B
1950 Clayton Tonnemaker, Minnesota, C
1951 Bob Gain, Kentucky, T
1952 Babe Parilli, Kentucky, QB
1953 Al Carmichael, So. California, B
1954 Art Hunter, Notre Dame, T
　　　Veryl Switzer, Kansas State, B
1955 Tom Bettis, Purdue, G
1956 Jack Losch, Miami, B
1957 Paul Hornung, Notre Dame, B
　　　Ron Kramer, Michigan, E
1958 Dan Currie, Michigan State, C
1959 Randy Duncan, Iowa, B
1960 Tom Moore, Vanderbilt, RB
1961 Herb Adderley, Michigan State, CB
1962 Earl Gros, Louisiana State, RB
1963 Dave Robinson, Penn State, LB
1964 Lloyd Voss, Nebraska, DT
1965 Donny Anderson, Texas Tech, RB
　　　Lawrence Elkins, Baylor, E
1966 Jim Grabowski, Illinois, RB
　　　Gale Gillingham, Minnesota, T
1967 Bob Hyland, Boston College, C
　　　Don Horn, San Diego State, QB
1968 Fred Carr, Texas-El Paso, LB
　　　Bill Lueck, Arizona, G
1969 Rich Moore, Villanova, DT
1970 Mike McCoy, Notre Dame, DT
　　　Rich McGeorge, Elon, TE
1971 John Brockington, Ohio State, RB
1972 Willie Buchanon, San Diego St., DB
　　　Jerry Tagge, Nebraska, QB
1973 Barry Smith, Florida State, WR
1974 Barty Smith, Richmond, RB
1975 Bill Bain, So. California, G (2)
1976 Mark Koncar, Colorado, T
1977 Mike Butler, Kansas, DE
　　　Ezra Johnson, Morris Brown, DE
1978 James Lofton, Stanford, WR
　　　John Anderson, Michigan, LB
1979 Eddie Lee Ivery, Georgia Tech, RB
1980 Bruce Clark, Penn State, DE
　　　George Cumby, Oklahoma, LB
1981 Rich Campbell, California, QB
1982 Ron Hallstrom, Iowa, G
1983 Tim Lewis, Pittsburgh, DB
1984 Alphonso Carreker, Florida St., DE
1985 Ken Ruettgers, So. California, T
1986 Kenneth Davis, TCU, RB (2)
1987 Brent Fullwood, Auburn, RB
1988 Sterling Sharpe, South Carolina, WR
1989 Tony Mandarich, Michigan State, T
1990 Tony Bennett, Mississippi, LB
　　　Darrell Thompson, Minnesota, RB
1991 Vinnie Clark, Ohio State, DB
1992 Terrell Buckley, Florida State, DB
1993 Wayne Simmons, Clemson, LB
　　　George Teague, Alabama, DB

1994 Aaron Taylor, Notre Dame, T
1995 Craig Newsome, Arizona State, DB
1996 John Michels, Southern California, T
1997 Ross Verba, Iowa, T
1998 Vonnie Holliday, North Carolina, DT
1999 Antuan Edwards, Clemson, DB
2000 Bubba Franks, Miami, TE
2001 Jamal Reynolds, Florida State, DE
2002 Javon Walker, Florida State, WR
2003 Nick Barnett, Oregon State, LB
2004 Ahmad Carroll, Arkansas, DB
2005 Aaron Rodgers, California, QB
2006 A.J. Hawk, Ohio State, LB

HOUSTON TEXANS
Year Player, College, Position
2002 David Carr, Fresno State, QB
2003 Andre Johnson, Miami, WR
2004 Dunta Robinson, South Carolina, DB
　　　Jason Babin, Western Michigan, LB
2005 Travis Johnson, Florida State, DE
2006 Mario Williams, North Carolina St., DE

INDIANAPOLIS COLTS
Year Player, College, Position
1953 Billy Vessels, Oklahoma, B
1954 Cotton Davidson, Baylor, B
1955 George Shaw, Oregon, B
　　　Alan Ameche, Wisconsin, FB
1956 Lenny Moore, Penn State, B
1957 Jim Parker, Ohio State, G
1958 Lenny Lyles, Louisville, B
1959 Jackie Burkett, Auburn, C
1960 Ron Mix, Southern California, T
1961 Tom Matte, Ohio State, RB
1962 Wendell Harris, Louisiana State, S
1963 Bob Vogel, Ohio State, T
1964 Marv Woodson, Indiana, CB
1965 Mike Curtis, Duke, LB
1966 Sam Ball, Kentucky, T
1967 Bubba Smith, Michigan State, DT
　　　Jim Detwiler, Michigan, RB
1968 John Williams, Minnesota, G
1969 Eddie Hinton, Oklahoma, WR
1970 Norman Bulaich, Texas Christian, RB
1971 Don McCauley, North Carolina, RB
　　　Leonard Dunlap, North Texas St., DB
1972 Tom Drougas, Oregon, T
1973 Bert Jones, Louisiana State, QB
　　　Joe Ehrmann, Syracuse, DT
1974 John Dutton, Nebraska, DE
　　　Roger Carr, Louisiana Tech, WR
1975 Ken Huff, North Carolina, G
1976 Ken Novak, Purdue, DT
1977 Randy Burke, Kentucky, WR
1978 Reese McCall, Auburn, TE
1979 Barry Krauss, Alabama, LB
1980 Curtis Dickey, Texas A&M, RB
　　　Derrick Hatchett, Texas, DB
1981 Randy McMillan, Pittsburgh, RB
　　　Donnell Thompson, North Carolina, DT
1982 Johnie Cooks, Mississippi St., LB
　　　Art Schlichter, Ohio State, QB
1983 John Elway, Stanford, QB
1984 Leonard Coleman, Vanderbilt, DB
　　　Ron Solt, Maryland, G
1985 Duane Bickett, So. California, LB
1986 Jon Hand, Alabama, DE
1987 Cornelius Bennett, Alabama, LB
1988 Chris Chandler, Washington, QB (3)

1989 Andre Rison, Michigan State, WR
1990 Jeff George, Illinois, QB
1991 Shane Curry, Miami, DE (2)
1992 Steve Emtman, Washington, DT
　　　Quentin Coryatt, Texas A&M, LB
1993 Sean Dawkins, California, WR
1994 Marshall Faulk, San Diego St., RB
　　　Trev Alberts, Nebraska, LB
1995 Ellis Johnson, Florida, DT
1996 Marvin Harrison, Syracuse, WR
1997 Tarik Glenn, California, T
1998 Peyton Manning, Tennessee, QB
1999 Edgerrin James, Miami, RB
2000 Rob Morris, Brigham Young, LB
2001 Reggie Wayne, Miami, WR
2002 Dwight Freeney, Syracuse, DE
2003 Dallas Clark, Iowa, TE
2004 Bob Sanders, Iowa, DB (2)
2005 Marlin Jackson, Michigan, DB
2006 Joseph Addai, Louisiana State, RB

JACKSONVILLE JAGUARS
Year Player, College, Position
1995 Tony Boselli, Southern California, T
　　　James Stewart, Tennessee, RB
1996 Kevin Hardy, Illinois, LB
1997 Renaldo Wynn, Notre Dame, DT
1998 Fred Taylor, Florida, RB
　　　Donovin Darius, Syracuse, DB
1999 Fernando Bryant, Alabama, DB
2000 R. Jay Soward, So. California, WR
2001 Marcus Stroud, Georgia, DT
2002 John Henderson, Tennessee, DT
2003 Byron Leftwich, Marshall, QB
2004 Reggie Williams, Washington, WR
2005 Matt Jones, Arkansas, WR
2006 Marcedes Lewis, UCLA, TE

KANSAS CITY CHIEFS
Year Player, College, Position
1960 Don Meredith, So. Methodist, QB
1961 E.J. Holub, Texas Tech, C
1962 Ronnie Bull, Baylor, RB
1963 Buck Buchanan, Grambling, DT
　　　Ed Budde, Michigan State, G
1964 Pete Beathard, So. California, QB
1965 Gale Sayers, Kansas, RB
1966 Aaron Brown, Minnesota, DE
1967 Gene Trosch, Miami, DE-DT
1968 Mo Moorman, Texas A&M, G
　　　George Daney, Texas-El Paso, G
1969 Jim Marsalis, Tennessee State, CB
1970 Sid Smith, Southern California, T
1971 Elmo Wright, Houston, WR
1972 Jeff Kinney, Nebraska, RB
1973 Gary Butler, Rice, TE (2)
1974 Woody Green, Arizona State, RB
1975 Elmore Stephens, Kentucky, TE (2)
1976 Rod Walters, Iowa, G
1977 Gary Green, Baylor, DB
1978 Art Still, Kentucky, DE
1979 Mike Bell, Colorado State, DE
　　　Steve Fuller, Clemson, QB
1980 Brad Budde, Southern California, G
1981 Willie Scott, South Carolina, TE
1982 Anthony Hancock, Tennessee, WR
1983 Todd Blackledge, Penn State, QB
1984 Bill Maas, Pittsburgh, DT
　　　John Alt, Iowa, T
1985 Ethan Horton, North Carolina, RB

1986 Brian Jozwiak, West Virginia, T
1987 Paul Palmer, Temple, RB
1988 Neil Smith, Nebraska, DE
1989 Derrick Thomas, Alabama, LB
1990 Percy Snow, Michigan State, LB
1991 Harvey Williams, Louisiana St., RB
1992 Dale Carter, Tennessee, DB
1993 Will Shields, Nebraska, G (3)
1994 Greg Hill, Texas A&M, RB
1995 Trezelle Jenkins, Michigan, T
1996 Jerome Woods, Memphis, DB
1997 Tony Gonzalez, California, TE
1998 Victor Riley, Auburn, T
1999 John Tait, Brigham Young, T
2000 Sylvester Morris, Jackson St., WR
2001 Eric Downing, Syracuse, DT (3)
2002 Ryan Sims, North Carolina, DT
2003 Larry Johnson, Penn State, RB
2004 Junior Siavii, Oregon, DT (2)
2005 Derrick Johnson, Texas, LB
2006 Tamba Hali, Penn State, DE

MIAMI DOLPHINS
Year Player, College, Position
1966 Jim Grabowski, Illinois, RB
      Rick Norton, Kentucky, QB
1967 Bob Griese, Purdue, QB
1968 Larry Csonka, Syracuse, RB
      Doug Crusan, Indiana, T
1969 Bill Stanfill, Georgia, DE
1970 Jim Mandich, Michigan, TE (2)
1971 Otto Stowe, Iowa State, WR (2)
1972 Mike Kadish, Notre Dame, DT
1973 Chuck Bradley, Oregon, C (2)
1974 Donald Reese, Jackson State, DE
1975 Darryl Carlton, Tampa, T
1976 Larry Gordon, Arizona State, LB
      Kim Bokamper, San Jose State, LB
1977 A.J. Duhe, Louisiana State, DT
1978 Guy Benjamin, Stanford, QB (2)
1979 Jon Giesler, Michigan, T
1980 Don McNeal, Alabama, DB
1981 David Overstreet, Oklahoma, RB
1982 Roy Foster, Southern California, G
1983 Dan Marino, Pittsburgh, QB
1984 Jackie Shipp, Oklahoma, LB
1985 Lorenzo Hampton, Florida, RB
1986 John Offerdahl, Western Michigan, LB (2)
1987 John Bosa, Boston College, DE
1988 Eric Kumerow, Ohio State, DE
1989 Sammie Smith, Florida State, RB
      Louis Oliver, Florida, DB
1990 Richmond Webb, Texas A&M, T
1991 Randal Hill, Miami, WR
1992 Troy Vincent, Wisconsin, DB
      Marco Coleman, Georgia Tech, LB
1993 O.J. McDuffie, Penn State, WR
1994 Tim Bowens, Mississippi, DT
1995 Billy Milner, Houston, T
1996 Daryl Gardener, Baylor, DT
1997 Yatil Green, Miami, WR
1998 John Avery, Mississippi, RB
1999 J.J. Johnson, Mississippi St., RB (2)
2000 Todd Wade, Mississippi, T (2)
2001 Jamar Fletcher, Wisconsin, DB
2002 Seth McKinney, Texas A&M, C (3)
2003 Eddie Moore, Tennessee, LB (2)
2004 Vernon Carey, Miami, T
2005 Ronnie Brown, Auburn, RB
2006 Jason Allen, Tennessee, DB

MINNESOTA VIKINGS
Year Player, College, Position
1961 Tommy Mason, Tulane, RB
1962 Bill Miller, Miami, WR (3)
1963 Jim Dunaway, Mississippi, T
1964 Carl Eller, Minnesota, DE
1965 Jack Snow, Notre Dame, WR
1966 Jerry Shay, Purdue, DT
1967 Clint Jones, Michigan State, RB
      Gene Washington, Michigan St., WR
      Alan Page, Notre Dame, DT
1968 Ron Yary, Southern California, T
1969 Ed White, California, G (2)
1970 John Ward, Oklahoma State, DT
1971 Leo Hayden, Ohio State, RB
1972 Jeff Siemon, Stanford, LB
1973 Chuck Foreman, Miami, RB
1974 Fred McNeill, UCLA, LB
      Steve Riley, Southern California, T
1975 Mark Mullaney, Colorado State, DE
1976 James White, Oklahoma State, DT
1977 Tommy Kramer, Rice, QB
1978 Randy Holloway, Pittsburgh, DE
1979 Ted Brown, North Carolina St., RB
1980 Doug Martin, Washington, DT
1981 Mardye McDole, Mississippi St., WR (2)
1982 Darrin Nelson, Stanford, RB
1983 Joey Browner, So. California, DB
1984 Keith Millard, Washington St., DE
1985 Chris Doleman, Pittsburgh, LB
1986 Gerald Robinson, Auburn, DE
1987 D.J. Dozier, Penn State, RB
1988 Randall McDaniel, Arizona State, G
1989 David Braxton, Wake Forest, LB (2)
1990 Mike Jones, Texas A&M, TE (3)
1991 Carlos Jenkins, Michigan St., LB (3)
1992 Robert Harris, Southern Univ., DE (2)
1993 Robert Smith, Ohio State, RB
1994 DeWayne Washington, N. Carolina St., DB
      Todd Steussie, California, T
1995 Derrick Alexander, Florida St., DE
      Korey Stringer, Ohio State, T
1996 Duane Clemons, California, DE
1997 Dwayne Rudd, Alabama, LB
1998 Randy Moss, Marshall, WR
1999 Daunte Culpepper, Central Florida, QB
      Dimitrius Underwood, Michigan St., DE
2000 Chris Hovan, Boston College, DT
2001 Michael Bennett, Wisconsin, RB
2002 Bryant McKinnie, Miami, T
2003 Kevin Williams, Oklahoma State, DT
2004 Kenechi Udeze, Southern California, DE
2005 Troy Williamson, South Carolina, WR
      Erasmus James, Wisconsin, DE
2006 Chad Greenway, Iowa, LB

NEW ENGLAND PATRIOTS
Year Player, College, Position
1960 Ron Burton, Northwestern, RB
1961 Tommy Mason, Tulane, RB
1962 Gary Collins, Maryland, WR
1963 Art Graham, Boston College, WR
1964 Jack Concannon, Boston College, QB
1965 Jerry Rush, Michigan State, DE
1966 Karl Singer, Purdue, T
1967 John Charles, Purdue, S
1968 Dennis Byrd, North Carolina St., DE
1969 Ron Sellers, Florida State, WR
1970 Phil Olsen, Utah State, DE
1971 Jim Plunkett, Stanford, QB

1972 Tom Reynolds, San Diego St., WR (2)
1973 John Hannah, Alabama, G
      Sam Cunningham, So. California, RB
      Darryl Stingley, Purdue, WR
1974 Steve Corbett, Boston College, G (2)
1975 Russ Francis, Oregon, TE
1976 Mike Haynes, Arizona State, DB
      Pete Brock, Colorado, C
      Tim Fox, Ohio State, DB
1977 Raymond Clayborn, Texas, DB
      Stanley Morgan, Tennessee, WR
1978 Bob Cryder, Alabama, G
1979 Rick Sanford, South Carolina, DB
1980 Roland James, Tennessee, DB
      Vagas Ferguson, Notre Dame, RB
1981 Brian Holloway, Stanford, T
1982 Kenneth Sims, Texas, DT
      Lester Williams, Miami, DT
1983 Tony Eason, Illinois, QB
1984 Irving Fryar, Nebraska, WR
1985 Trevor Matich, Brigham Young, C
1986 Reggie Dupard, So. Methodist, RB
1987 Bruce Armstrong, Louisville, T
1988 John Stephens, Northwestern St., La., RB
1989 Hart Lee Dykes, Oklahoma St., WR
1990 Chris Singleton, Arizona, LB
      Ray Agnew, North Carolina St., DE
1991 Pat Harlow, Southern California, T
      Leonard Russell, Arizona St., RB
1992 Eugene Chung, Virginia Tech, T
1993 Drew Bledsoe, Washington St., QB
1994 Willie McGinest, So. California, DE
1995 Ty Law, Michigan, DB
1996 Terry Glenn, Ohio State, WR
1997 Chris Canty, Kansas State, DB
1998 Robert Edwards, Georgia, RB
      Tebucky Jones, Syracuse, DB
1999 Damien Woody, Boston College, C
      Andy Katzenmoyer, Ohio State, LB
2000 Adrian Klemm, Hawaii, T (2)
2001 Richard Seymour, Georgia, DT
2002 Daniel Graham, Colorado, TE
2003 Ty Warren, Texas A&M, DT
2004 Vince Wilfork, Miami, DT
      Ben Watson, Georgia, TE
2005 Logan Mankins, Fresno State, G
2006 Laurence Maroney, Minnesota, RB

NEW ORLEANS SAINTS
Year Player, College, Position
1967 Les Kelley, Alabama, RB
1968 Kevin Hardy, Notre Dame, DE
1969 John Shinners, Xavier, G
1970 Ken Burrough, Texas Southern, WR
1971 Archie Manning, Mississippi, QB
1972 Royce Smith, Georgia, G
1973 Derland Moore, Oklahoma, DE (2)
1974 Rick Middleton, Ohio State, LB
1975 Larry Burton, Purdue, WR
      Kurt Schumacher, Ohio State, T
1976 Chuck Muncie, California, RB
1977 Joe Campbell, Maryland, DE
1978 Wes Chandler, Florida, WR
1979 Russell Erxleben, Texas, P-K
1980 Stan Brock, Colorado, T
1981 George Rogers, South Carolina, RB
1982 Lindsay Scott, Georgia, WR
1983 Steve Korte, Arkansas, G (2)
1984 James Geathers, Wichita State, DE
1985 Alvin Toles, Tennessee, LB

1986 Jim Dombrowski, Virginia, T
1987 Shawn Knight, Brigham Young, DT
1988 Craig Heyward, Pittsburgh, RB
1989 Wayne Martin, Arkansas, DE
1990 Renaldo Turnbull, West Virginia, DE
1991 Wesley Carroll, Miami, WR (2)
1992 Vaughn Dunbar, Indiana, RB
1993 Willie Roaf, Louisiana Tech, T
        Irv Smith, Notre Dame, TE
1994 Joe Johnson, Louisville, DE
1995 Mark Fields, Washington State, LB
1996 Alex Molden, Oregon, DB
1997 Chris Naeole, Colorado, G
1998 Kyle Turley, San Diego State, T
1999 Ricky Williams, Texas, RB
2000 Darren Howard, Kansas St., DE (2)
2001 Deuce McAllister, Mississippi, RB
2002 Donte' Stallworth, Tennessee, WR
        Charles Grant, Georgia, DE
2003 Johnathan Sullivan, Georgia, DT
2004 Will Smith, Ohio State, DE
2005 Jammal Brown, Oklahoma, T
2006 Reggie Bush, So. California, RB

NEW YORK GIANTS
Year Player, College, Position
1936 Art Lewis, Ohio U., T
1937 Ed Widseth, Minnesota, T
1938 George Karamatic, Gonzaga, B
1939 Walt Neilson, Arizona, B
1940 Grenville Lansdell, So. California, B
1941 George Franck, Minnesota, B
1942 Merle Hapes, Mississippi, B
1943 Steve Filipowicz, Fordham, B
1944 Billy Hillenbrand, Indiana, B
1945 Elmer Barbour, Wake Forest, B
1946 George Connor, Notre Dame, T
1947 Vic Schwall, Northwestern, B
1948 Tony Minisi, Pennsylvania, B
1949 Paul Page, Southern Methodist, B
1950 Travis Tidwell, Auburn, B
1951 Kyle Rote, Southern Methodist, B
        Jim Spavital, Oklahoma A&M, B
1952 Frank Gifford, Southern California, B
1953 Bobby Marlow, Alabama, B
1954 Ken Buck, Pacific, C (2)
1955 Joe Heap, Notre Dame, B
1956 Henry Moore, Arkansas, B (2)
1957 Sam DeLuca, South Carolina, T (2)
1958 Phil King, Vanderbilt, B
1959 Lee Grosscup, Utah, B
1960 Lou Cordileone, Clemson, G
1961 Bruce Tarbox, Syracuse, G (2)
1962 Jerry Hillebrand, Colorado, LB
1963 Frank Lasky, Florida, T (2)
1964 Joe Don Looney, Oklahoma, RB
1965 Tucker Frederickson, Auburn, RB
1966 Francis Peay, Missouri, T
1967 Louis Thompson, Alabama, DT (4)
1968 Dick Buzin, Penn State, T (2)
1969 Fred Dryer, San Diego State, DE
1970 Jim Files, Oklahoma, LB
1971 Rocky Thompson, West Texas St., WR
1972 Eldridge Small, Texas A&I, DB
        Larry Jacobson, Nebraska, DE
1973 Brad Van Pelt, Michigan St., LB (2)
1974 John Hicks, Ohio State, G
1975 Al Simpson, Colorado State, T (2)
1976 Troy Archer, Colorado, DE
1977 Gary Jeter, Southern California, DT

1978 Gordon King, Stanford, T
1979 Phil Simms, Morehead State, QB
1980 Mark Haynes, Colorado, DB
1981 Lawrence Taylor, North Carolina, LB
1982 Butch Woolfolk, Michigan, RB
1983 Terry Kinard, Clemson, DB
1984 Carl Banks, Michigan State, LB
        William Roberts, Ohio State, T
1985 George Adams, Kentucky, RB
1986 Eric Dorsey, Notre Dame, DE
1987 Mark Ingram, Michigan State, WR
1988 Eric Moore, Indiana, T
1989 Brian Williams, Minnesota, C-G
1990 Rodney Hampton, Georgia, RB
1991 Jarrod Bunch, Michigan, RB
1992 Derek Brown, Notre Dame, TE
1993 Michael Strahan, Texas Southern, DE (2)
1994 Thomas Lewis, Indiana, WR
1995 Tyrone Wheatley, Michigan, RB
1996 Cedric Jones, Oklahoma, DE
1997 Ike Hilliard, Florida, WR
1998 Shaun Williams, UCLA, DB
1999 Luke Petitgout, Notre Dame, T
2000 Ron Dayne, Wisconsin, RB
2001 Will Allen, Syracuse, DB
2002 Jeremy Shockey, Miami, TE
2003 William Joseph, Miami, DT
2004 Philip Rivers, North Carolina St., QB
2005 Corey Webster, Louisiana St., DB (2)
2006 Mathias Kiwanuka, Boston College, DE

NEW YORK JETS
Year Player, College, Position
1960 George Izo, Notre Dame, QB
1961 Tom Brown, Minnesota, G
1962 Sandy Stephens, Minnesota, QB
1963 Jerry Stovall, Louisiana State, S
1964 Matt Snell, Ohio State, RB
1965 Joe Namath, Alabama, QB
        Tom Nowatzke, Indiana, RB
1966 Bill Yearby, Michigan, DT
1967 Paul Seiler, Notre Dame, T
1968 Lee White, Weber State, RB
1969 Dave Foley, Ohio State, T
1970 Steve Tannen, Florida, CB
1971 John Riggins, Kansas, RB
1972 Jerome Barkum, Jackson St., WR
        Mike Taylor, Michigan, LB
1973 Burgess Owens, Miami, DB
1974 Carl Barzilauskas, Indiana, DT
1975 Anthony Davis, So. California, RB (2)
1976 Richard Todd, Alabama, QB
1977 Marvin Powell, So. California, T
1978 Chris Ward, Ohio State, T
1979 Marty Lyons, Alabama, DE
1980 Johnny (Lam) Jones, Texas, WR
1981 Freeman McNeil, UCLA, RB
1982 Bob Crable, Notre Dame, LB
1983 Ken O'Brien, Cal-Davis, QB
1984 Russell Carter, So. Methodist, DB
        Ron Faurot, Arkansas, DE
1985 Al Toon, Wisconsin, WR
1986 Mike Haight, Iowa, T
1987 Roger Vick, Texas A&M, RB
1988 Dave Cadigan, So. California, T
1989 Jeff Lageman, Virginia, LB
1990 Blair Thomas, Penn State, RB
1991 Browning Nagle, Louisville, QB (2)
1992 Johnny Mitchell, Nebraska, TE
1993 Marvin Jones, Florida State, LB

1994 Aaron Glenn, Texas A&M, DB
1995 Kyle Brady, Penn State, TE
        Hugh Douglas, Central St., Ohio, DE
1996 Keyshawn Johnson, So. California, WR
1997 James Farrior, Virginia, LB
1998 Dorian Boose, Washington St., DE (2)
1999 Randy Thomas, Mississippi St., G (2)
2000 Shaun Ellis, Tennessee, DE
        John Abraham, South Carolina, LB
        Chad Pennington, Marshall, QB
        Anthony Becht, West Virginia, TE
2001 Santana Moss, Miami, WR
2002 Bryan Thomas, Ala.-Birmingham, DE
2003 Dewayne Robertson, Kentucky, DT
2004 Jonathan Vilma, Miami, LB
2005 Mike Nugent, Ohio State, K (2)
2006 D'Brickashaw Ferguson, Virginia, T
        Nick Mangold, Ohio State, C

OAKLAND RAIDERS
Year Player, College, Position
1960 Dale Hackbart, Wisconsin, CB
1961 Joe Rutgens, Illinois, DT
1962 Roman Gabriel, North Carolina St., QB
1963 George Wilson, Alabama, RB (6)
1964 Tony Lorick, Arizona State, RB
1965 Harry Schuh, Memphis State, T
1966 Rodger Bird, Kentucky, S
1967 Gene Upshaw, Texas A&I, G
1968 Eldridge Dickey, Tennessee St., QB
1969 Art Thoms, Syracuse, DT
1970 Raymond Chester, Morgan St., TE
1971 Jack Tatum, Ohio State, S
1972 Mike Siani, Villanova, WR
1973 Ray Guy, Southern Mississippi, P
1974 Henry Lawrence, Florida A&M, T
1975 Neal Colzie, Ohio State, DB
1976 Charles Philyaw, Texas Southern, DT (2)
1977 Mike Davis, Colorado, DB (2)
1978 Dave Browning, Washington, DE (2)
1979 Willie Jones, Florida State, DE (2)
1980 Marc Wilson, Brigham Young, QB
1981 Ted Watts, Texas Tech, DB
        Curt Marsh, Washington, T
1982 Marcus Allen, So. California, RB
1983 Don Mosebar, So. California, T
1984 Sean Jones, Northeastern, DE (2)
1985 Jessie Hester, Florida State, WR
1986 Bob Buczkowski, Pittsburgh, DE
1987 John Clay, Missouri, T
1988 Tim Brown, Notre Dame, WR
        Terry McDaniel, Tennessee, DB
        Scott Davis, Illinois, DE
1989 Jeff Francis, Tennessee, QB (6)
1990 Anthony Smith, Arizona, DE
1991 Todd Marinovich, So. California, QB
1992 Chester McGlockton, Clemson, DE
1993 Patrick Bates, Texas A&M, DB
1994 Rob Fredrickson, Michigan St., LB
1995 Napoleon Kaufman, Washington, RB
1996 Rickey Dudley, Ohio State, TE
1997 Darrell Russell, Southern
        California, DT
1998 Charles Woodson, Michigan, DB
        Mo Collins, Florida, T
1999 Matt Stinchcomb, Georgia, T
2000 Sebastian Janikowski, Florida St., K
2001 Derrick Gibson, Florida State, DB
2002 Phillip Buchanon, Miami, DB
        Napoleon Harris, Northwestern, LB

2003	Nnamdi Asomugha, California, DB
	Tyler Brayton, Colorado, DE
2004	Robert Gallery, Iowa, T
2005	Fabian Washington, Nebraska, DB
2006	Michael Huff, Texas, DB

PHILADELPHIA EAGLES
Year Player, College, Position

1936	Jay Berwanger, Chicago, B
1937	Sam Francis, Nebraska, B
1938	Jim McDonald, Ohio State, B
1939	Davey O'Brien, Texas Christian, B
1940	George McAfee, Duke, B
1941	Art Jones, Richmond, B (2)
1942	Pete Kmetovic, Stanford, B
1943	Joe Muha, Virginia Military, B
1944	Steve Van Buren, Louisiana St., B
1945	John Yonaker, Notre Dame, E
1946	Leo Riggs, Southern California, B
1947	Neill Armstrong, Oklahoma A&M, E
1948	Clyde (Smackover) Scott, Arkansas, B
1949	Chuck Bednarik, Pennsylvania, C
	Frank Tripucka, Notre Dame, B
1950	Harry (Bud) Grant, Minnesota, E
1951	Ebert Van Buren, Louisiana St., B
	Chet Mutryn, Xavier, B
1952	Johnny Bright, Drake, B
1953	Al Conway, Army, B (2)
1954	Neil Worden, Notre Dame, B
1955	Dick Bielski, Maryland, B
1956	Bob Pellegrini, Maryland, C
1957	Clarence Peaks, Michigan State, B
1958	Walt Kowalczyk, Michigan State, B
1959	J.D. Smith, Rice, T (2)
1960	Ron Burton, Northwestern, RB
1961	Art Baker, Syracuse, RB
1962	Pete Case, Georgia, G (2)
1963	Ed Budde, Michigan State, G
1964	Bob Brown, Nebraska, T
1965	Ray Rissmiller, Georgia, T (2)
1966	Randy Beisler, Indiana, DE
1967	Harry Jones, Arkansas, RB
1968	Tim Rossovich, So. California, DE
1969	Leroy Keyes, Purdue, RB
1970	Steve Zabel, Oklahoma, TE
1971	Richard Harris, Grambling, DE
1972	John Reaves, Florida, QB
1973	Jerry Sisemore, Texas, T
	Charle Young, So. California, TE
1974	Mitch Sutton, Kansas, DT (3)
1975	Bill Capraun, Miami, T (7)
1976	Mike Smith, Florida, DE (4)
1977	Skip Sharp, Kansas, DB (5)
1978	Reggie Wilkes, Georgia Tech, LB (3)
1979	Jerry Robinson, UCLA, LB
1980	Roynell Young, Alcorn State, DB
1981	Leonard Mitchell, Houston, DE
1982	Mike Quick, North Carolina St., WR
1983	Michael Haddix, Mississippi St., RB
1984	Kenny Jackson, Penn State, WR
1985	Kevin Allen, Indiana, T
1986	Keith Byars, Ohio State, RB
1987	Jerome Brown, Miami, DT
1988	Keith Jackson, Oklahoma, TE
1989	Jessie Small, Eastern Kentucky, LB (2)
1990	Ben Smith, Georgia, DB
1991	Antone Davis, Tennessee, T
1992	Siran Stacy, Alabama, RB (2)
1993	Lester Holmes, Jackson State, T
	Leonard Renfro, Colorado, DT

1994	Bernard Williams, Georgia, T
1995	Mike Mamula, Boston College, DE
1996	Jermane Mayberry, Texas A&M-Kingsville, T
1997	Jon Harris, Virginia, DE
1998	Tra Thomas, Florida State, T
1999	Donovan McNabb, Syracuse, QB
2000	Corey Simon, Florida State, DT
2001	Freddie Mitchell, UCLA, WR
2002	Lito Sheppard, Florida, DB
2003	Jerome McDougle, Miami, DE
2004	Shawn Andrews, Arkansas, T
2005	Mike Patterson, So. California, DT
2006	Brodrick Bunkley, Florida State, DT

PITTSBURGH STEELERS
Year Player, College, Position

1936	Bill Shakespeare, Notre Dame, B
1937	Mike Basrak, Duquesne, C
1938	Byron (Whizzer) White, Colorado, B
1939	Bill Patterson, Baylor, B (3)
1940	Kay Eakin, Arkansas, B
1941	Chet Gladchuk, Boston College, C (2)
1942	Bill Dudley, Virginia, B
1943	Bill Daley, Minnesota, B
1944	Johnny Podesto, St. Mary's, Calif., B
1945	Paul Duhart, Florida, B
1946	Felix (Doc) Blanchard, Army, B
1947	Hub Bechtol, Texas, E
1948	Dan Edwards, Georgia, E
1949	Bobby Gage, Clemson, B
1950	Lynn Chandnois, Michigan St., B
1951	Butch Avinger, Alabama, B
1952	Ed Modzelewski, Maryland, B
1953	Ted Marchibroda, St. Bonaventure, B
1954	Johnny Lattner, Notre Dame, B
1955	Frank Varrichione, Notre Dame, T
1956	Gary Glick, Colorado A&M, B
	Art Davis, Mississippi State, B
1957	Len Dawson, Purdue, B
1958	Larry Krutko, West Virginia, B (2)
1959	Tom Barnett, Purdue, B (8)
1960	Jack Spikes, Texas Christian, RB
1961	Myron Pottios, Notre Dame, LB (2)
1962	Bob Ferguson, Ohio State, RB
1963	Frank Atkinson, Stanford, T (8)
1964	Paul Martha, Pittsburgh, S
1965	Roy Jefferson, Utah, WR (2)
1966	Dick Leftridge, West Virginia, RB
1967	Don Shy, San Diego State, RB (2)
1968	Mike Taylor, Southern California, T
1969	Joe Greene, North Texas State, DT
1970	Terry Bradshaw, Louisiana Tech, QB
1971	Frank Lewis, Grambling, WR
1972	Franco Harris, Penn State, RB
1973	J.T. Thomas, Florida State, DB
1974	Lynn Swann, So. California, WR
1975	Dave Brown, Michigan, DB
1976	Bennie Cunningham, Clemson, TE
1977	Robin Cole, New Mexico, LB
1978	Ron Johnson, Eastern Michigan, DB
1979	Greg Hawthorne, Baylor, RB
1980	Mark Malone, Arizona State, QB
1981	Keith Gary, Oklahoma, DE
1982	Walter Abercrombie, Baylor, RB
1983	Gabriel Rivera, Texas Tech, DT
1984	Louis Lipps, So. Mississippi, WR
1985	Darryl Sims, Wisconsin, DE
1986	John Rienstra, Temple, G
1987	Rod Woodson, Purdue, DB
1988	Aaron Jones, Eastern Kentucky, DE

1989	Tim Worley, Georgia, RB
	Tom Ricketts, Pittsburgh, T
1990	Eric Green, Liberty, TE
1991	Huey Richardson, Florida, DE
1992	Leon Searcy, Miami, T
1993	Deon Figures, Colorado, DB
1994	Charles Johnson, Colorado, WR
1995	Mark Bruener, Washington, TE
1996	Jamain Stephens, North Carolina A&T, T
1997	Chad Scott, Maryland, DB
1998	Alan Faneca, Louisiana State, G
1999	Troy Edwards, Louisiana Tech, WR
2000	Plaxico Burress, Michigan St., WR
2001	Casey Hampton, Texas, DT
2002	Kendall Simmons, Auburn, G
2003	Troy Polamalu, Southern California, DB
2004	Ben Roethlisberger, Miami (OH), QB
2005	Heath Miller, Virginia, TE
2006	Santonio Holmes, Ohio State, WR

ST. LOUIS RAMS
Year Player, College, Position

1937	Johnny Drake, Purdue, B
1938	Corbett Davis, Indiana, B
1939	Parker Hall, Mississippi, B
1940	Ollie Cordill, Rice, B
1941	Rudy Mucha, Washington, C
1942	Jack Wilson, Baylor, B
1943	Mike Holovak, Boston College, B
1944	Tony Butkovich, Illinois, B
1945	Elroy (Crazylegs) Hirsch, Wisconsin, B
1946	Emil Sitko, Notre Dame, B
1947	Herman Wedemeyer, St. Mary's, Calif., B
1948	Tom Keane, West Virginia, B (2)
1949	Bobby Thomason, Virginia Military, B
1950	Ralph Pasquariello, Villanova, B
	Stan West, Oklahoma, G
1951	Bud McFadin, Texas, G
1952	Bill Wade, Vanderbilt, QB
	Bob Carey, Michigan State, E
1953	Donn Moomaw, UCLA, C
	Ed Barker, Washington State, E
1954	Ed Beatty, Cincinnati, C
1955	Larry Morris, Georgia Tech, C
1956	Joe Marconi, West Virginia, B
	Charles Horton, Vanderbilt, B
1957	Jon Arnett, Southern California, B
	Del Shofner, Baylor, E
1958	Lou Michaels, Kentucky, T
	Jim Phillips, Auburn, E
1959	Dick Bass, Pacific, B
	Paul Dickson, Baylor, T
1960	Billy Cannon, Louisiana State, RB
1961	Marlin McKeever, So. California, E-LB
1962	Roman Gabriel, North Carolina St., QB
	Merlin Olsen, Utah State, DT
1963	Terry Baker, Oregon State, QB
	Rufus Guthrie, Georgia Tech, G
1964	Bill Munson, Utah State, QB
1965	Clancy Williams, Washington St., CB
1966	Tom Mack, Michigan, G
1967	Willie Ellison, Texas Southern, RB (2)
1968	Gary Beban, UCLA, QB (2)
1969	Larry Smith, Florida, RB
	Jim Seymour, Notre Dame, WR
	Bob Klein, Southern California, TE
1970	Jack Reynolds, Tennessee, LB
1971	Isiah Robertson, Southern, LB
	Jack Youngblood, Florida, DE
1972	Jim Bertelsen, Texas, RB (2)

1973 Cullen Bryant, Colorado, DB (2)
1974 John Cappelletti, Penn State, RB
1975 Mike Fanning, Notre Dame, DT
     Dennis Harrah, Miami, T
     Doug France, Ohio State, T
1976 Kevin McLain, Colorado State, LB
1977 Bob Brudzinski, Ohio State, LB
1978 Elvis Peacock, Oklahoma, RB
1979 George Andrews, Nebraska, LB
     Kent Hill, Georgia Tech, T
1980 Johnnie Johnson, Texas, DB
1981 Mel Owens, Michigan, LB
1982 Barry Redden, Richmond, RB
1983 Eric Dickerson, So. Methodist, RB
1984 Hal Stephens, East Carolina, DE (5)
1985 Jerry Gray, Texas, DB
1986 Mike Schad, Queen's Univ., Canada, T
1987 Donald Evans, Winston-Salem, DE (2)
1988 Gaston Green, UCLA, RB
     Aaron Cox, Arizona State, WR
1989 Bill Hawkins, Miami, DE
     Cleveland Gary, Miami, RB
1990 Bern Brostek, Washington, C
1991 Todd Lyght, Notre Dame, DB
1992 Sean Gilbert, Pittsburgh, DE
1993 Jerome Bettis, Notre Dame, RB
1994 Wayne Gandy, Auburn, T
1995 Kevin Carter, Florida, DE
1996 Lawrence Phillips, Nebraska, RB
     Eddie Kennison, Louisiana St., WR
1997 Orlando Pace, Ohio State, T
1998 Grant Wistrom, Nebraska, DE
1999 Torry Holt, North Carolina St., WR
2000 Trung Canidate, Arizona, RB
2001 Damione Lewis, Miami, DT
     Adam Archuleta, Arizona State, DB
     Ryan Pickett, Ohio State, DT
2002 Robert Thomas, UCLA, LB
2003 Jimmy Kennedy, Penn State, DT
2004 Steven Jackson, Oregon State, RB
2005 Alex Barron, Florida State, T
2006 Tye Hill, Clemson, DB

SAN DIEGO CHARGERS
Year Player, College, Position
1960 Monty Stickles, Notre Dame, E
1961 Earl Faison, Indiana, DE
1962 Bob Ferguson, Ohio State, RB
1963 Walt Sweeney, Syracuse, G
1964 Ted Davis, Georgia Tech, LB
1965 Steve DeLong, Tennessee, DE
1966 Don Davis, Cal St.-Los Angeles, DT
1967 Ron Billingsley, Wyoming, DE
1968 Russ Washington, Missouri, DT
     Jimmy Hill, Texas A&I, DB
1969 Marty Domres, Columbia, QB
     Bob Babich, Miami, Ohio, LB
1970 Walker Gillette, Richmond, WR
1971 Leon Burns, Long Beach State, RB
1972 Pete Lazetich, Stanford, DE (2)
1973 Johnny Rodgers, Nebraska, WR
1974 Bo Matthews, Colorado, RB
     Don Goode, Kansas, LB
1975 Gary Johnson, Grambling, DT
     Mike Williams, Louisiana State, DB
1976 Joe Washington, Oklahoma, RB
1977 Bob Rush, Memphis State, C
1978 John Jefferson, Arizona State, WR
1979 Kellen Winslow, Missouri, TE
1980 Ed Luther, San Jose State, QB (4)

1981 James Brooks, Auburn, RB
1982 Hollis Hall, Clemson, DB (7)
1983 Billy Ray Smith, Arkansas, LB
     Gary Anderson, Arkansas, WR
     Gill Byrd, San Jose State, DB
1984 Mossy Cade, Texas, DB
1985 Jim Lachey, Ohio State, G
1986 Leslie O'Neal, Oklahoma State, DE
     James FitzPatrick, So. California, T
1987 Rod Bernstine, Texas A&M, TE
1988 Anthony Miller, Tennessee, WR
1989 Burt Grossman, Pittsburgh, DE
1990 Junior Seau, So. California, LB
1991 Stanley Richard, Texas, DB
1992 Chris Mims, Tennessee, DE
1993 Darrien Gordon, Stanford, DB
1994 Isaac Davis, Arkansas, G (2)
1995 Terrance Shaw, Stephen F. Austin, DB (2)
1996 Bryan Still, Virginia Tech, WR (2)
1997 Freddie Jones, North Carolina, TE (2)
1998 Ryan Leaf, Washington State, QB
1999 Jermaine Fazande, Oklahoma, RB (2)
2000 Rogers Beckett, Marshall, DB (2)
2001 LaDainian Tomlinson, TCU, RB
2002 Quentin Jammer, Texas, DB
2003 Sammy Davis, Texas A&M, DB
2004 Eli Manning, Mississippi, QB
2005 Shawne Merriman, Maryland, LB
     Luis Castillo, Northwestern, DT
2006 Antonio Cromartie, Florida State, DB

SAN FRANCISCO 49ERS
Year Player, College, Position
1950 Leo Nomellini, Minnesota, T
1951 Y.A. Tittle, Louisiana State, B
1952 Hugh McElhenny, Washington, B
1953 Harry Babcock, Georgia, E
     Tom Stolhandske, Texas, E
1954 Bernie Faloney, Maryland, B
1955 Dickie Moegle, Rice, B
1956 Earl Morrall, Michigan State, B
1957 John Brodie, Stanford, B
1958 Jim Pace, Michigan, B
     Charlie Krueger, Texas A&M, T
1959 Dave Baker, Oklahoma, B
     Dan James, Ohio State, C
1960 Monty Stickles, Notre Dame, E
1961 Jimmy Johnson, UCLA, CB
     Bernie Casey, Bowling Green, WR
     Bill Kilmer, UCLA, QB
1962 Lance Alworth, Arkansas, WR
1963 Kermit Alexander, UCLA, CB
1964 Dave Parks, Texas Tech, WR
1965 Ken Willard, North Carolina, RB
     George Donnelly, Illinois, DB
1966 Stan Hindman, Mississippi, DE
1967 Steve Spurrier, Florida, QB
     Cas Banaszek, Northwestern, T
1968 Forrest Blue, Auburn, C
1969 Ted Kwalick, Penn State, TE
     Gene Washington, Stanford, WR
1970 Cedrick Hardman, North Texas St., DE
     Bruce Taylor, Boston U., DB
1971 Tim Anderson, Ohio State, DB
1972 Terry Beasley, Auburn, WR
1973 Mike Holmes, Texas Southern, DB
1974 Wilbur Jackson, Alabama, RB
     Bill Sandifer, UCLA, DT
1975 Jimmy Webb, Mississippi St., DT
1976 Randy Cross, UCLA, C (2)

1977 Elmo Boyd, Eastern Kentucky, WR (3)
1978 Ken MacAfee, Notre Dame, TE
     Dan Bunz, Cal St.-Long Beach, LB
1979 James Owens, UCLA, WR (2)
1980 Earl Cooper, Rice, RB
     Jim Stuckey, Clemson, DT
1981 Ronnie Lott, So. California, DB
1982 Bubba Paris, Michigan, T (2)
1983 Roger Craig, Nebraska, RB (2)
1984 Todd Shell, Brigham Young, LB
1985 Jerry Rice, Mississippi Valley St., WR
1986 Larry Roberts, Alabama, DE (2)
1987 Harris Barton, North Carolina, T
     Terrence Flagler, Clemson, RB
1988 Danny Stubbs, Miami, DE (2)
1989 Keith DeLong, Tennessee, LB
1990 Dexter Carter, Florida State, RB
1991 Ted Washington, Louisville, DT
1992 Dana Hall, Washington, DB
1993 Dana Stubblefield, Kansas, DT
     Todd Kelly, Tennessee, DE
1994 Bryant Young, Notre Dame, DT
     William Floyd, Florida State, RB
1995 J.J. Stokes, UCLA, WR
1996 Israel Ifeanyi, So.California, DE (2)
1997 Jim Druckenmiller, Virginia Tech, QB
1998 R.W. McQuarters, Oklahoma St., DB
1999 Reggie McGrew, Florida, DT
2000 Julian Peterson, Michigan St., LB
     Ahmed Plummer, Ohio State, DB
2001 Andre Carter, California, DE
2002 Mike Rumph, Miami, DB
2003 Kwame Harris, Stanford, T
2004 Rashaun Woods, Oklahoma St., WR
2005 Alex Smith, Utah, QB
2006 Vernon Davis, Maryland, TE
     Manny Lawson, North Carolina St., DE

SEATTLE SEAHAWKS
Year Player, College, Position
1976 Steve Niehaus, Notre Dame, DT
1977 Steve August, Tulsa, G
1978 Keith Simpson, Memphis St., DB
1979 Manu Tuiasosopo, UCLA, DT
1980 Jacob Green, Texas A&M, DE
1981 Ken Easley, UCLA, DB
1982 Jeff Bryant, Clemson, DE
1983 Curt Warner, Penn State, RB
1984 Terry Taylor, Southern Illinois, DB
1985 Owen Gill, Iowa, RB (2)
1986 John L. Williams, Florida, RB
1987 Tony Woods, Pittsburgh, LB
1988 Brian Blades, Miami, WR (2)
1989 Andy Heck, Notre Dame, T
1990 Cortez Kennedy, Miami, DT
1991 Dan McGwire, San Diego St., QB
1992 Ray Roberts, Virginia, T
1993 Rick Mirer, Notre Dame, QB
1994 Sam Adams, Texas A&M, DT
1995 Joey Galloway, Ohio State, WR
1996 Pete Kendall, Boston College, T
1997 Shawn Springs, Ohio State, DB
     Walter Jones, Florida State, T
1998 Anthony Simmons, Clemson, LB
1999 Lamar King, Saginaw Valley St., DE
2000 Shaun Alexander, Alabama, RB
     Chris McIntosh, Wisconsin, T
2001 Koren Robinson, North Carolina St., WR
     Steve Hutchinson, Michigan, G
2002 Jerramy Stevens, Washington, TE

2003 Marcus Trufant, Washington State, DB
2004 Marcus Tubbs, Texas, DT
2005 Chris Spencer, Mississippi, C
2006 Kelly Jennings, Miami, DB

TAMPA BAY BUCCANEERS

Year Player, College, Position
1976 Lee Roy Selmon, Oklahoma, DT
1977 Ricky Bell, Southern California, RB
1978 Doug Williams, Grambling, QB
1979 Greg Roberts, Oklahoma, G (2)
1980 Ray Snell, Wisconsin, G
1981 Hugh Green, Pittsburgh, LB
1982 Sean Farrell, Penn State, G
1983 Randy Grimes, Baylor, C (2)
1984 Keith Browner, So. California, LB (2)
1985 Ron Holmes, Washington, DE
1986 Bo Jackson, Auburn, RB
     Roderick Jones, So. Methodist, DB
1987 Vinny Testaverde, Miami, QB
1988 Paul Gruber, Wisconsin, T
1989 Broderick Thomas, Nebraska, LB
1990 Keith McCants, Alabama, LB
1991 Charles McRae, Tennessee, T
1992 Courtney Hawkins, Michigan St., WR (2)
1993 Eric Curry, Alabama, DE
1994 Trent Dilfer, Fresno State, QB
1995 Warren Sapp, Miami, DT
     Derrick Brooks, Florida State, LB
1996 Regan Upshaw, California, DE
     Marcus Jones, North Carolina, DT
1997 Warrick Dunn, Florida State, RB
     Reidel Anthony, Florida, WR
1998 Jacquez Green, Florida, WR (2)
1999 Anthony McFarland, Louisiana St., DT
2000 Cosey Coleman, Tennessee, G (2)
2001 Kenyatta Walker, Florida, T
2002 Marquise Walker, Michigan, WR (3)
2003 Dewayne White, Louisville, DE (2)
2004 Michael Clayton, Louisiana St., WR
2005 Carnell Williams, Auburn, RB
2006 Davin Joseph, Oklahoma, G

TENNESSEE TITANS

Year Player, College, Position
1960 Billy Cannon, Louisiana State, RB
1961 Mike Ditka, Pittsburgh, E
1962 Ray Jacobs, Howard Payne, DT
1963 Danny Brabham, Arkansas, LB
1964 Scott Appleton, Texas, DT
1965 Lawrence Elkins, Baylor, WR
1966 Tommy Nobis, Texas, LB
1967 George Webster, Michigan St., LB
     Tom Regner, Notre Dame, G
1968 Mac Haik, Mississippi, WR (2)
1969 Ron Pritchard, Arizona State, LB
1970 Doug Wilkerson, N. Carolina Central, G
1971 Dan Pastorini, Santa Clara, QB
1972 Greg Sampson, Stanford, DE
1973 John Matuszak, Tampa, DE
     George Amundson, Iowa State, RB
1974 Steve Manstedt, Nebraska, LB (4)
1975 Robert Brazile, Jackson State, LB
     Don Hardeman, Texas A&I, RB
1976 Mike Barber, Louisiana Tech, TE (2)
1977 Morris Towns, Missouri, T
1978 Earl Campbell, Texas, RB
1979 Mike Stensrud, Iowa State, DE (2)
1980 Angelo Fields, Michigan St., T (2)
1981 Michael Holston, Morgan St., WR (3)

1982 Mike Munchak, Penn State, G
1983 Bruce Matthews, So. California, T
1984 Dean Steinkuhler, Nebraska, T
1985 Ray Childress, Texas A&M, DE
     Richard Johnson, Wisconsin, DB
1986 Jim Everett, Purdue, QB
1987 Alonzo Highsmith, Miami, RB
     Haywood Jeffires, North Carolina St., WR
1988 Lorenzo White, Michigan State, RB
1989 David Williams, Florida, T
1990 Lamar Lathon, Houston, LB
1991 Mike Dumas, Indiana, DB (2)
1992 Eddie Robinson, Alabama St., LB (2)
1993 Brad Hopkins, Illinois, T
1994 Henry Ford, Arkansas, DE
1995 Steve McNair, Alcorn State, QB
1996 Eddie George, Ohio State, RB
1997 Kenny Holmes, Miami, DE
1998 Kevin Dyson, Utah, WR
1999 Jevon Kearse, Florida, DE
2000 Keith Bulluck, Syracuse, LB
2001 Andre Dyson, Utah, DB (2)
2002 Albert Haynesworth, Tennessee, DT
2003 Andre Woolfolk, Oklahoma, DB
2004 Ben Troupe, Florida, TE (2)
2005 Adam Jones, West Virginia, DB
2006 Vince Young, Texas, QB

WASHINGTON REDSKINS

Year Player, College, Position
1936 Riley Smith, Alabama, B
1937 Sammy Baugh, Texas Christian, B
1938 Andy Farkas, Detroit, B
1939 I.B. Hale, Texas Christian, T
1940 Ed Boell, New York U., B
1941 Forest Evashevski, Michigan, B
1942 Orban (Spec) Sanders, Texas, B
1943 Jack Jenkins, Missouri, B
1944 Mike Micka, Colgate, B
1945 Jim Hardy, Southern California, B
1946 Cal Rossi, UCLA, B*
1947 Cal Rossi, UCLA, B
1948 Harry Gilmer, Alabama, B
     Lowell Tew, Alabama, B
1949 Rob Goode, Texas A&M, B
1950 George Thomas, Oklahoma, B
1951 Leon Heath, Oklahoma, B
1952 Larry Isbell, Baylor, B
1953 Jack Scarbath, Maryland, B
1954 Steve Meilinger, Kentucky, E
1955 Ralph Guglielmi, Notre Dame, B
1956 Ed Vereb, Maryland, B
1957 Don Bosseler, Miami, B
1958 Mike Sommer, George
     Washington, B (2)
1959 Don Allard, Boston College, B
1960 Richie Lucas, Penn State, QB
1961 Norman Snead, Wake Forest, QB
     Joe Rutgens, Illinois, DT
1962 Ernie Davis, Syracuse, RB
1963 Pat Richter, Wisconsin, TE
1964 Charley Taylor, Arizona St., RB-WR
1965 Bob Breitenstein, Tulsa, T (2)
1966 Charlie Gogolak, Princeton, K
1967 Ray McDonald, Idaho, RB
1968 Jim Smith, Oregon, DB
1969 Eugene Epps, Texas-El Paso, DB (2)
1970 Bill Bundige, Colorado, DT (2)
1971 Cotton Speyrer, Texas, WR (2)
1972 Moses Denson, Maryland St., RB (8)

1973 Charles Cantrell, Lamar, G (5)
1974 Jon Keyworth, Colorado, TE (6)
1975 Mike Thomas, Nevada-Las Vegas, RB (6)
1976 Mike Hughes, Baylor, G (5)
1977 Duncan McColl, Stanford, DE (4)
1978 Tony Green, Florida, RB (6)
1979 Don Warren, San Diego St., TE (4)
1980 Art Monk, Syracuse, WR
1981 Mark May, Pittsburgh, T
1982 Vernon Dean, San Diego St., DB (2)
1983 Darrell Green, Texas A&I, DB
1984 Bob Slater, Oklahoma, DT (2)
1985 Tory Nixon, San Diego St., DB (2)
1986 Markus Koch, Boise State, DE (2)
1987 Brian Davis, Nebraska, DB (2)
1988 Chip Lohmiller, Minnesota, K (2)
1989 Tracy Rocker, Auburn, DT (3)
1990 Andre Collins, Penn State, LB (2)
1991 Bobby Wilson, Michigan State, DT
1992 Desmond Howard, Michigan, WR
1993 Tom Carter, Notre Dame, DB
1994 Heath Shuler, Tennessee, QB
1995 Michael Westbrook, Colorado, WR
1996 Andre Johnson, Penn State, T
1997 Kenard Lang, Miami, DE
1998 Stephen Alexander, Oklahoma, TE (2)
1999 Champ Bailey, Georgia, DB
2000 LaVar Arrington, Penn State, LB
     Chris Samuels, Alabama, T
2001 Rod Gardner, Clemson, WR
2002 Patrick Ramsey, Tulane, QB
2003 Taylor Jacobs, Florida, WR (2)
2004 Sean Taylor, Miami, DB
2005 Carlos Rogers, Auburn, DB
     Jason Campbell, Auburn, QB
2006 Rocky McIntosh, Miami, LB (2)
Choice lost because of ineligibility

NUMBER-ONE DRAFT CHOICES

Season	Date	Team	Player	Position	College
2006	April 29-30	Houston	Mario Williams	DE	North Carolina State
2005	April 23-24	San Francisco	Alex Smith	QB	Utah
2004	April 24-25	San Diego	Eli Manning	QB	Mississippi
2003	April 26-27	Cincinnati	Carson Palmer	QB	Southern California
2002	April 20-21	Houston	David Carr	QB	Fresno State
2001	April 21-22	Atlanta	Michael Vick	QB	Virginia Tech
2000	April 15-16	Cleveland	Courtney Brown	DE	Penn State
1999	April 17-18	Cleveland	Tim Couch	QB	Kentucky
1998	April 18-19	Indianapolis	Peyton Manning	QB	Tennessee
1997	April 19-20	St. Louis	Orlando Pace	T	Ohio State
1996	April 20-21	New York Jets	Keyshawn Johnson	WR	Southern California
1995	April 22-23	Cincinnati	Ki-Jana Carter	RB	Penn State
1994	April 24-25	Cincinnati	Dan Wilkinson	DT	Ohio State
1993	April 25-26	New England	Drew Bledsoe	QB	Washington State
1992	April 26-27	Indianapolis	Steve Emtman	DT	Washington
1991	April 21-22	Dallas	Russell Maryland	DT	Miami
1990	April 22-23	Indianapolis	Jeff George	QB	Illinois
1989	April 23-24	Dallas	Troy Aikman	QB	UCLA
1988	April 24-25	Atlanta	Aundray Bruce	LB	Auburn
1987	April 28-29	Tampa Bay	Vinny Testaverde	QB	Miami
1986	April 29-30	Tampa Bay	Bo Jackson	RB	Auburn
1985	April 30-May 1	Buffalo	Bruce Smith	DE	Virginia Tech
1984	May 1-2	New England	Irving Fryar	WR	Nebraska
1983	April 26-27	Baltimore	John Elway	QB	Stanford
1982	April 27-28	New England	Kenneth Sims	DT	Texas
1981	April 28-29	New Orleans	George Rogers	RB	South Carolina
1980	April 29-30	Detroit	Billy Sims	RB	Oklahoma
1979	May 3-4	Buffalo	Tom Cousineau	LB	Ohio State
1978	May 2-3	Houston	Earl Campbell	RB	Texas
1977	May 3-4	Tampa Bay	Ricky Bell	RB	Southern California
1976	April 8-9	Tampa Bay	Lee Roy Selmon	DE	Oklahoma
1975	January 28-29	Atlanta	Steve Bartkowski	QB	California
1974	January 29-30	Dallas	Ed Jones	DE	Tennessee State
1973	January 30-31	Houston	John Matuszak	DE	Tampa
1972	February 1-2	Buffalo	Walt Patulski	DE	Notre Dame
1971	January 28-29	New England	Jim Plunkett	QB	Stanford
1970	January 27-28	Pittsburgh	Terry Bradshaw	QB	Louisiana Tech
1969	January 28-29	Buffalo (AFL)	O.J. Simpson	RB	Southern California
1968	January 30-31	Minnesota	Ron Yary	T	Southern California
1967	March 14	Baltimore	Bubba Smith	DT	Michigan State
1966	November 27, 1965	Atlanta	Tommy Nobis	LB	Texas
	November 28, 1965	Miami (AFL)	Jim Grabowski	RB	Illinois
1965	November 28, 1964	New York Giants	Tucker Frederickson	RB	Auburn
	November 28, 1964	Houston (AFL)	Lawrence Elkins	E	Baylor
1964	December 2, 1963	San Francisco	Dave Parks	E	Texas Tech
	November 30, 1963	Boston (AFL)	Jack Concannon	QB	Boston College
1963	December 3, 1962	Los Angeles	Terry Baker	QB	Oregon State
	December 1, 1962	Kansas City (AFL)	Buck Buchanan	DT	Grambling
1962	December 4, 1961	Washington	Ernie Davis	RB	Syracuse
	December 2, 1961	Oakland (AFL)	Roman Gabriel	QB	North Carolina State
1961	December 27-28, 1960	Minnesota	Tommy Mason	RB	Tulane
	November 23, 1960	Buffalo (AFL)	Ken Rice	G	Auburn
1960	Secret Draft	Los Angeles	Billy Cannon	RB	Louisiana State
	November 22, December 2, 1959	(AFL had no formal first pick)			
1959	December 2, 1958	Green Bay	Randy Duncan	QB	Iowa
1958	December 2, 1957	Chicago Cardinals	King Hill	QB	Rice
1957	November 27, 1956	Green Bay	Paul Hornung	HB	Notre Dame
1956	November 29, 1955	Pittsburgh	Gary Glick	DB	Colorado A&M
1955	January 27-28	Baltimore	George Shaw	QB	Oregon
1954	January 28	Cleveland	Bobby Garrett	QB	Stanford
1953	January 22	San Francisco	Harry Babcock	E	Georgia

Season	Date	Team	Player	Position	College
1952	January 17	Los Angeles	Bill Wade	QB	Vanderbilt
1951	January 18-19	New York Giants	Kyle Rote	HB	Southern Methodist
1950	January 21-22	Detroit	Leon Hart	E	Notre Dame
1949	December 21, 1948	Philadelphia	Chuck Bednarik	C	Pennsylvania
1948	December 19, 1947	Washington	Harry Gilmer	QB	Alabama
1947	December 16, 1946	Chicago Bears	Bob Fenimore	HB	Oklahoma A&M
1946	January 14	Boston	Frank Dancewicz	QB	Notre Dame
1945	April 6	Chicago Cardinals	Charley Trippi	HB	Georgia
1944	April 19	Boston	Angelo Bertelli	QB	Notre Dame
1943	April 8	Detroit	Frank Sinkwich	HB	Georgia
1942	December 22, 1941	Pittsburgh	Bill Dudley	HB	Virginia
1941	December 10, 1940	Chicago Bears	Tom Harmon	HB	Michigan
1940	December 9, 1939	Chicago Cardinals	George Cafego	HB	Tennessee
1939	December 8, 1938	Chicago Cardinals	Ki Aldrich	C	Texas Christian
1938	December 12, 1937	Cleveland	Corbett Davis	FB	Indiana
1937	December 12, 1936	Philadelphia	Sam Francis	FB	Nebraska
1936	February 8	Philadelphia	Jay Berwanger	HB	Chicago

Note: From 1947 through 1958, the first selection in the draft was a Bonus pick, awarded to the winner of a random draw. That club, in turn, forfeited its last-round draft choice. The winner of the Bonus choice was eliminated from future draws. The system was abolished after 1958, by which time all clubs had received a Bonus choice.

NUMBER-ONE DRAFT CHOICES BY POSITION

Quarterbacks:	26
Running Backs:	23
Defenisve Linemen:	13
Wide Receivers:	6
Offensive Linemen:	5
Linebackers:	3
Defensive Backs:	1

THE FOLLOWING AWARDS WERE NAMED BY *ASSOCIATED PRESS* IN BALLOTING BY A NATIONWIDE PANEL OF MEDIA.

NFL MOST VALUABLE PLAYER AWARD

YEAR	PLAYER	POS.	TEAM	ACCOMPLISHMENTS
1957	Jim Brown	RB	Cleveland Browns	Rushed for league-leading 942 yards and added 9 touchdowns as a rookie.
1958	Gino Marchetti	DE	Baltimore Colts	Leader of defense that permitted league-low 1,291 rushing yards and division-low 203 points.
1959	Charley Conerly	QB	New York Giants	Passed for 14 touchdowns and only 4 interceptions. Led offense to division-leading 284 points.
1960*	Norm Van Brocklin	QB	Philadelphia Eagles	Guided Eagles to first division title since 1949. Passed for 2,471 yards and 24 touchdowns.
	Joe Schmidt	LB	Detroit Lions	After 0-3 start, team went 7-2 when he returned from injury. Scored 2 defensive touchdowns.
1961	Paul Hornung	RB	Green Bay Packers	Led league in scoring for second straight season with 146 points (10 TD, 15 FG, 41 PAT).
1962	Jim Taylor	RB	Green Bay Packers	League rushing champion with 1,474 yards. Scored all-time record 19 touchdowns.
1963	Y.A. Tittle	QB	New York Giants	Set all-time season record with 36 touchdown passes. Guided league's top offense (5,024 yards).
1964	Johnny Unitas	QB	Baltimore Colts	Guided Colts to NFL's best record (12-2) and league's top offensive attack (4,779 yards).
1965	Jim Brown	RB	Cleveland Browns	Leader of NFL's top rushing attack. Led league with 1,544 yards, added 21 total touchdowns.
1966	Bart Starr	QB	Green Bay Packers	Passed for 14 touchdowns and only 3 interceptions. Led Packers to league-best 12-2 record.
1967	Johnny Unitas	QB	Baltimore Colts	Passed for 3,428 yards and 20 touchdowns. Led Colts to 11-1-2 record.
1968	Earl Morrall	QB	Baltimore Colts	Guided Colts to NFL-best 13-1 record. Led league with 26 touchdown passes.
1969	Roman Gabriel	QB	Los Angeles Rams	Led NFL with 24 touchdown passes. Guided Rams to 11-3 record.
1970	John Brodie	QB	San Francisco 49ers	Took 49ers to first division title. Threw NFL-best 24 touchdown passes.
1971	Alan Page	DT	Minnesota Vikings	Led defense that allowed NFL-low 139 points. Vikings won fourth straight NFC Central title.
1972	Larry Brown	RB	Washington Redskins	Led conference with 1,216 rushing yards. Redskins had NFC-best 11-3 record.
1973	O.J. Simpson	RB	Buffalo Bills	Rushed for all-time record 2,003 yards, including three 200-yard performances.
1974	Ken Stabler	QB	Oakland Raiders	Led league with 26 touchdown passes and only 12 interceptions. Raiders had NFL-best 12-2 record.
1975	Fran Tarkenton	QB	Minnesota Vikings	Tied for league-best 12-2 record. Led NFC with 91.7 passer rating.
1976	Bert Jones	QB	Baltimore Colts	Threw 24 touchdowns and only 9 interceptions for 102.5 passer rating.
1977	Walter Payton	RB	Chicago Bears	Rushed for league-leading 1,852 yards and 16 total touchdowns.
1978	Terry Bradshaw	QB	Pittsburgh Steelers	Led Steelers to league-leading 14-2 mark. Set club record with 28 touchdown passes.
1979	Earl Campbell	RB	Houston Oilers	Led league with 1,697 rushing yards and 19 touchdowns.
1980	Brian Sipe	QB	Cleveland Browns	NFL-best 91.4 passer rating. Set Browns' records with 30 touchdown passes and 4,132 yards.
1981	Ken Anderson	QB	Cincinnati Bengals	Led Bengals to first division title since 1973. NFL-high 98.5 passer rating.
1982	Mark Moseley	K	Washington Redskins	Converted 20 of 21 FGs. Set consecutive field-goal record at 23 (including last three in '81).
1983	Joe Theismann	QB	Washington Redskins	Leader of offense that scored NFL record 541 points. Redskins had NFL-best 14-2 record.
1984	Dan Marino	QB	Miami Dolphins	Set NFL records with 5,084 yards and 48 touchdown passes. Led Dolphins to AFC-best 14-2 mark.
1985	Marcus Allen	RB	Los Angeles Raiders	Rushed for league-leading 1,759 yards. Tied for AFC lead with 11 rushing touchdowns.
1986	Lawrence Taylor	LB	New York Giants	Recorded league-high 20.5 sacks, and led Giants' second-ranked defense (297.3).
1987	John Elway	QB	Denver Broncos	In 12 games, passed for 19 touchdowns and 3,198 yards, including four 300-yard games.
1988	Boomer Esiason	QB	Cincinnati Bengals	Led NFL with 97.4 passer rating. Tied for AFC lead with 28 TD passes.
1989	Joe Montana	QB	San Francisco 49ers	Set NFL record with 112.4 passer rating, including 70.2 completion percentage.
1990	Joe Montana	QB	San Francisco 49ers	Led 49ers to league-best 14-2 record. Completed NFC-high 61.7 percent of passes.
1991	Thurman Thomas	RB	Buffalo Bills	Recorded league-high 2,038 yards from scrimmage (1,407 rushing, 631 receiving).

1992	Steve Young	QB	San Francisco 49ers	NFL's top passer with 107.0 rating. Led 49ers to league-best 14-2 record.
1993	Emmitt Smith	RB	Dallas Cowboys	Led league in rushing (1,486 yards) for third straight year despite missing first two games.
1994	Steve Young	QB	San Francisco 49ers	Compiled NFL all-time best 112.8 passer rating. Completed more than 70 percent of his passes.
1995	Brett Favre	QB	Green Bay Packers	Led league with 38 touchdown passes and NFC with 99.5 passer rating.
1996	Brett Favre	QB	Green Bay Packers	Led Packers to top conference record (13-3). Threw NFL-best 39 touchdown passes.
1997*	Brett Favre	QB	Green Bay Packers	Led league with 35 touchdown passes. Led NFC with 3,867 passing yards.
	Barry Sanders	RB	Detroit Lions	Rushed for all-time second-best 2,053 yards, including record 14 straight 100-yard games.
1998	Terrell Davis	RB	Denver Broncos	Rushed for 2,008 yards and scored league-best 23 total touchdowns.
1999	Kurt Warner	QB	St. Louis Rams	Became the second QB in history to have 40 touchdown passes in a season (41).
2000	Marshall Faulk	RB	St. Louis Rams	Set NFL record with 26 touchdowns and led NFC with 2,189 yards from scrimmage.
2001	Kurt Warner	QB	St. Louis Rams	Led NFL with 4,830 passing yards, 36 touchdowns, 68.7 completion percentage, and 101.4 passer rating.
2002	Rich Gannon	QB	Oakland Raiders	Set single-season records with 10 300-yard passing games and 418 completions, and led NFL with 4,689 passing yards.
2003*	Peyton Manning	QB	Indianapolis Colts	Led NFL with 4,267 passing yards, had AFC-best 29 touchdown passes, and posted 99.0 passer rating.
	Steve McNair	QB	Tennessee Titans	Posted NFL-best 100.4 passer rating, passing for 3,215 yards with 24 touchdowns against 7 interceptions.
2004	Peyton Manning	QB	Indianapolis Colts	Set NFL records with 49 touchdown passes and 121.1 passer rating while passing for 4,557 yards.
2005	Shaun Alexander	RB	Seattle Seahawks	Set NFL record with 28 touchdowns and led league with 1,880 rushing yards.

Total *Associated Press* NFL MVPs: 52
Two-time Winners: Jim Brown, Brett Favre (3), Peyton Manning, Joe Montana, Johnny Unitas, Kurt Warner, Steve Young
* The award was shared in 1960, 1997, and 2003.

ASSOCIATED PRESS MVPs WHO WON SUPER BOWL/ NFL CHAMPIONSHIP IN SAME SEASON: 15

1958	Gino Marchetti	Baltimore Colts
1960	Norm Van Brocklin	Philadelphia Eagles
1961	Paul Hornung	Green Bay Packers
1962	Jim Taylor	Green Bay Packers
1966	Bart Starr	Green Bay Packers
1968	Earl Morrall	Baltimore Colts
1978	Terry Bradshaw	Pittsburgh Steelers
1982	Mark Moseley	Washington Redskins
1986	Lawrence Taylor	New York Giants
1989	Joe Montana	San Francisco 49ers
1993	Emmitt Smith	Dallas Cowboys
1994	Steve Young	San Francisco 49ers
1996	Brett Favre	Green Bay Packers
1998	Terrell Davis	Denver Broncos
1999	Kurt Warner	St. Louis Rams

ASSOCIATED PRESS NFL MVP BY POSITION

Quarterback:	32	Defensive End:	1
Running Back:	15	Defensive Tackle:	1
Linebacker:	2	Kicker:	1

ASSOCIATED PRESS MVPs BY TEAM

7	Indianapolis/Baltimore Colts	1	Chicago Bears
			Dallas Cowboys
6	Green Bay Packers		Houston Oilers
			Miami Dolphins
5	San Francisco 49ers		Philadelphia Eagles
			Pittsburgh Steelers
4	St. Louis/Los Angeles Rams		Seattle Seahawks
			Tennessee Titans
3	Cleveland Browns		
	New York Giants		
	Oakland/Los Angeles Raiders		
	Washington Redskins		
2	Buffalo Bills		
	Cincinnati Bengals		
	Denver Broncos		
	Detroit Lions		
	Minnesota Vikings		

AP OFFENSIVE PLAYER OF THE YEAR

1973	O.J. Simpson	RB	Buffalo Bills
1974	Ken Stabler	QB	Oakland Raiders
1975	Fran Tarkenton	QB	Minnesota Vikings
1976	Bert Jones	QB	Baltimore Colts
1977	Walter Payton	RB	Chicago Bears
1978	Earl Campbell	RB	Houston Oilers
1979	Earl Campbell	RB	Houston Oilers
1980	Earl Campbell	RB	Houston Oilers
1981	Ken Anderson	QB	Cincinnati Bengals
1982	Dan Fouts	QB	San Diego Chargers
1983	Joe Theismann	QB	Washington Redskins
1984	Dan Marino	QB	Miami Dolphins
1985	Marcus Allen	RB	Los Angeles Raiders
1986	Eric Dickerson	RB	Los Angeles Rams
1987	Jerry Rice	WR	San Francisco 49ers
1988	Roger Craig	RB	San Francisco 49ers
1989	Joe Montana	QB	San Francisco 49ers
1990	Warren Moon	QB	Houston Oilers
1991	Thurman Thomas	RB	Buffalo Bills
1992	Steve Young	QB	San Francisco 49ers
1993	Jerry Rice	WR	San Francisco 49ers
1994	Barry Sanders	RB	Detroit Lions
1995	Brett Favre	QB	Green Bay Packers
1996	Terrell Davis	RB	Denver Broncos
1997	Barry Sanders	RB	Detroit Lions
1998	Terrell Davis	RB	Denver Broncos
1999	Marshall Faulk	RB	St. Louis Rams
2000	Marshall Faulk	RB	St. Louis Rams
2001	Marshall Faulk	RB	St. Louis Rams
2002	Priest Holmes	RB	Kansas City Chiefs
2003	Jamal Lewis	RB	Baltimore Ravens
2004	Peyton Manning	QB	Indianapolis Colts
2005	Shaun Alexander	RB	Seattle Seahawks

AP OFFENSIVE ROOKIE OF THE YEAR

1957	Jim Brown	RB	Cleveland Browns
1958	Jimmy Orr	WR	Pittsburgh Steelers
1959	Nick Pietrosante	RB	Detroit Lions
1960	Gail Cogdill	WR	Detroit Lions
1961	Mike Ditka	TE	Chicago Bears
1962	Ron Bull	RB	Chicago Bears
1963	Paul Flatley	WR	Minnesota Vikings
1964	Charley Taylor	WR	Washington Redskins
1965	Gale Sayers	RB	Chicago Bears
1966	Johnny Roland	RB	St. Louis Cardinals
1967	Mel Farr	RB	Detroit Lions
1968	Earl McCullouch	WR	Detroit Lions
1969	Calvin Hill	RB	Dallas Cowboys
1970	Duane Thomas	RB	Dallas Cowboys
1971	John Brockington	RB	Green Bay Packers
1972	Franco Harris	RB	Pittsburgh Steelers
1973	Chuck Foreman	RB	Minnesota Vikings
1974	Don Woods	RB	San Diego Chargers
1975	Mike Thomas	RB	Washington Redskins
1976	Sammy White	WR	Minnesota Vikings
1977	Tony Dorsett	RB	Dallas Cowboys
1978	Earl Campbell	RB	Houston Oilers
1979	Ottis Anderson	RB	St. Louis Cardinals
1980	Billy Sims	RB	Detroit Lions
1981	George Rogers	RB	New Orleans Saints
1982	Marcus Allen	RB	Los Angeles Raiders
1983	Eric Dickerson	RB	Los Angeles Rams
1984	Louis Lipps	WR	Pittsburgh Steelers
1985	Eddie Brown	WR	Cincinnati Bengals
1986	Rueben Mayes	RB	New Orleans Saints
1987	Troy Stradford	RB	Miami Dolphins
1988	John Stephens	RB	New England Patriots

1989	Barry Sanders	RB	Detroit Lions
1990	Emmitt Smith	RB	Dallas Cowboys
1991	Leonard Russell	RB	New England Patriots
1992	Carl Pickens	WR	Cincinnati Bengals
1993	Jerome Bettis	RB	Los Angeles Rams
1994	Marshall Faulk	RB	Indianapolis Colts
1995	Curtis Martin	RB	New England Patriots
1996	Eddie George	RB	Houston Oilers
1997	Warrick Dunn	RB	Tampa Bay Buccaneers
1998	Randy Moss	WR	Minnesota Vikings
1999	Edgerrin James	RB	Indianapolis Colts
2000	Mike Anderson	RB	Denver Broncos
2001	Anthony Thomas	RB	Chicago Bears
2002	Clinton Portis	RB	Denver Broncos
2003	Anquan Boldin	WR	Arizona Cardinals
2004	Ben Roethlisberger	QB	Pittsburgh Steelers
2005	Carnell Williams	RB	Tampa Bay Buccaneers

AP DEFENSIVE PLAYER OF THE YEAR

1971	Alan Page	DT	Minnesota Vikings
1972	Joe Greene	DT	Pittsburgh Steelers
1973	Dick Anderson	S	Miami Dolphins
1974	Joe Greene	DT	Pittsburgh Steelers
1975	Mel Blount	CB	Pittsburgh Steelers
1976	Jack Lambert	LB	Pittsburgh Steelers
1977	Harvey Martin	DE	Dallas Cowboys
1978	Randy Gradishar	LB	Denver Broncos
1979	Lee Roy Selmon	DE	Tampa Bay Buccaneers
1980	Lester Hayes	CB	Oakland Raiders
1981	Lawrence Taylor	LB	New York Giants
1982	Lawrence Taylor	LB	New York Giants
1983	Doug Betters	DE	Miami Dolphins
1984	Kenny Easley	S	Seattle Seahawks
1985	Mike Singletary	LB	Chicago Bears
1986	Lawrence Taylor	LB	New York Giants
1987	Reggie White	DT	Philadelphia Eagles
1988	Mike Singletary	LB	Chicago Bears
1989	Keith Millard	DT	Minnesota Vikings
1990	Bruce Smith	DE	Buffalo Bills
1991	Pat Swilling	LB	New Orleans Saints
1992	Cortez Kennedy	DT	Seattle Seahawks
1993	Rod Woodson	CB	Pittsburgh Steelers
1994	Deion Sanders	CB	San Francisco 49ers
1995	Bryce Paup	LB	Buffalo Bills
1996	Bruce Smith	DE	Buffalo Bills
1997	Dana Stubblefield	DT	San Francisco 49ers
1998	Reggie White	DE	Green Bay Packers
1999	Warren Sapp	DT	Tampa Bay Buccaneers
2000	Ray Lewis	LB	Baltimore Ravens
2001	Michael Strahan	DE	New York Giants
2002	Derrick Brooks	LB	Tampa Bay Buccaneers
2003	Ray Lewis	LB	Baltimore Ravens
2004	Ed Reed	S	Baltimore Ravens
2005	Brian Urlacher	LB	Chicago Bears

AP DEFENSIVE ROOKIE OF THE YEAR

1967	Lem Barney	CB	Detroit Lions
1968	Claude Humphrey	DE	Atlanta Falcons
1969	Joe Greene	DT	Pittsburgh Steelers
1970	Bruce Taylor	CB	San Franicsco 49ers
1971	Isiah Robertson	LB	Los Angeles Rams
1972	Willie Buchanon	CB	Green Bay Packers
1973	Wally Chambers	DT	Chicago Bears
1974	Jack Lambert	LB	Pittsburgh Steelers
1975	Robert Brazile	LB	Houston Oilers
1976	Mike Haynes	S	New England Patriots
1977	A.J. Duhe	DT	Miami Dolphins
1978	Al Baker	DE	Detroit Lions

1979	Jim Haslett	LB	Buffalo Bills
1980*	Buddy Curry	LB	Atlanta Falcons
	Al Richardson	LB	Atlanta Falcons
1981	Lawrence Taylor	LB	New York Giants
1982	Chip Banks	LB	Cleveland Browns
1983	Vernon Maxwell	LB	Baltimore Colts
1984	Bill Maas	NT	Kansas City Chiefs
1985	Duane Bickett	LB	Indianapolis Colts
1986	John Offerdahl	LB	Miami Dolphins
1987	Shane Conlan	LB	Buffalo Bills
1988	Erik McMillan	S	New York Jets
1989	Derrick Thomas	LB	Kansas City Chiefs
1990	Mark Carrier	S	Chicago Bears
1991	Mike Croel	LB	Denver Broncos
1992	Dale Carter	CB	Kansas City Chiefs
1993	Dana Stubblefield	DT	San Francisco 49ers
1994	Tim Bowens	DT	Miami Dolphins
1995	Hugh Douglas	DE	New York Jets
1996	Simeon Rice	DE	Arizona Cardinals
1997	Peter Boulware	LB	Baltimore Ravens
1998	Charles Woodson	CB	Oakland Raiders
1999	Jevon Kearse	DE	Tennessee Titans
2000	Brian Urlacher	LB	Chicago Bears
2001	Kendrell Bell	LB	Pittsburgh Steelers
2002	Julius Peppers	DE	Carolina Panthers
2003	Terrell Suggs	LB	Baltimore Ravens
2004	Jonathan Vilma	LB	New York Jets
2005	Shawne Merriman	LB	San Diego Chargers

*The award was shared in 1980.

1981	Bill Walsh	San Francisco 49ers
1982	Joe Gibbs	Washington Redskins
1983	Joe Gibbs	Washington Redskins
1984	Chuck Knox	Seattle Seahawks
1985	Mike Ditka	Chicago Bears
1986	Bill Parcells	New York Giants
1987	Jim Mora	New Orleans Saints
1988	Mike Ditka	Chicago Bears
1989	Lindy Infante	Green Bay Packers
1990	Jimmy Johnson	Dallas Cowboys
1991	Wayne Fontes	Detroit Lions
1992	Bill Cowher	Pittsburgh Steelers
1993	Dan Reeves	New York Giants
1994	Bill Parcells	New England Patriots
1995	Ray Rhodes	Philadelphia Eagles
1996	Dom Capers	Carolina Panthers
1997	Jim Fassel	New York Giants
1998	Dan Reeves	Atlanta Falcons
1999	Dick Vermeil	St. Louis Rams
2000	Jim Haslett	New Orleans Saints
2001	Dick Jauron	Chicago Bears
2002	Andy Reid	Philadelphia Eagles
2003	Bill Belichick	New England Patriots
2004	Marty Schottenheimer	San Diego Chargers
2005	Lovie Smith	Chicago Bears

*The award was shared in 1967.

AP COMEBACK PLAYER OF THE YEAR

1998	Doug Flutie	QB	Buffalo Bills
1999	Bryant Young	DT	San Francisco 49ers
2000	Joe Johnson	DE	New Orleans Saints
2001	Garrison Hearst	RB	San Francisco 49ers
2002	Tommy Maddox	QB	Pittsburgh Steelers
2003	Jon Kitna	QB	Cincinnati Bengals
2004	Drew Brees	QB	San Diego Chargers
2005*	Steve Smith	WR	Carolina Panthers
	Tedy Bruschi	LB	New England Patriots

*The award was shared in 2005.

AP COACH OF THE YEAR

1957	George Wilson	Detroit Lions
1958	Weeb Ewbank	Baltimore Colts
1959	Vince Lombardi	Green Bay Packers
1960	Buck Shaw	Philadelphia Eagles
1961	Allie Sherman	New York Giants
1962	Allie Sherman	New York Giants
1963	George Halas	Chicago Bears
1964	Don Shula	Baltimore Colts
1965	George Halas	Chicago Bears
1966	Tom Landry	Dallas Cowboys
1967*	George Allen	Los Angeles Rams
	Don Shula	Baltimore Colts
1968	Don Shula	Baltimore Colts
1969	Bud Grant	Minnesota Vikings
1970	Paul Brown	Cincinnati Bengals
1971	George Allen	Washington Redskins
1972	Don Shula	Miami Dolphins
1973	Chuck Knox	Los Angeles Rams
1974	Don Coryell	St. Louis Cardinals
1975	Ted Marchibroda	Baltimore Colts
1976	Forrest Gregg	Cleveland Browns
1977	Red Miller	Denver Broncos
1978	Jack Patera	Seattle Seahawks
1979	Jack Pardee	Washington Redskins
1980	Chuck Knox	Buffalo Bills

WALTER PAYTON NFL MAN OF THE YEAR

The Walter Payton NFL Man of the Year Award is the only NFL award that recognizes a player for his community service activities as well as his excellence on the field. Renamed in 1999 for the legendary Chicago Bears Pro Football Hall of Fame running back, the Walter Payton NFL Man of the Year Award has been given annually since 1970.

YEAR	PLAYER	POS.	TEAM
1970	Johnny Unitas	QB	Baltimore Colts
1971	John Hadl	QB	San Diego Chargers
1972	Willie Lanier	LB	Kansas City Chiefs
1973	Len Dawson	QB	Kansas City Chiefs
1974	George Blanda	QB	Oakland Raiders
1975	Ken Anderson	QB	Cincinnati Bengals
1976	Franco Harris	RB	Pittsburgh Steelers
1977	Walter Payton	RB	Chicago Bears
1978	Roger Staubach	QB	Dallas Cowboys
1979	Joe Greene	DT	Pittsburgh Steelers
1980	Harold Carmichael	WR	Philadelphia Eagles
1981	Lynn Swann	WR	Pittsburgh Steelers
1982	Joe Theismann	QB	Washington Redskins
1983	Rolf Benirschke	K	San Diego Chargers
1984	Marty Lyons	T	New York Jets
1985	Dwight Stephenson	C	Miami Dolphins
1986	Reggie Williams	LB	Cincinnati Bengals
1987	Dave Duerson	S	Chicago Bears
1988	Steve Largent	WR	Seattle Seahawks
1989	Warren Moon	QB	Houston Oilers
1990	Mike Singletary	LB	Chicago Bears
1991	Anthony Muñoz	T	Cincinnati Bengals
1992	John Elway	QB	Denver Broncos
1993	Derrick Thomas	LB	Kansas City Chiefs
1994	Junior Seau	LB	San Diego Chargers
1995	Boomer Esiason	QB	New York Jets
1996	Darrell Green	CB	Washington Redskins
1997	Troy Aikman	QB	Dallas Cowboys
1998	Dan Marino	QB	Miami Dolphins
1999	Cris Carter	WR	Minnesota Vikings
2000*	Derrick Brooks	LB	Tampa Bay Buccaneers
	Jim Flanigan	DT	Chicago Bears
2001	Jerome Bettis	RB	Pittsburgh Steelers
2002	Troy Vincent	CB	Philadelphia Eagles
2003	Will Shields	G	Kansas City Chiefs
2004	Warrick Dunn	RB	Atlanta Falcons
2005	Peyton Manning	QB	Indianapolis Colts

* The award was shared in 2000.

NFL'S 10 HIGHEST SCORING WEEKENDS

Point Total	Date	Weekend
788	December 5-6, 2004	13th
788	September 5, 8-9, 2002	1st
762	November 10-11, 1996	11th
761	October 16-17, 1983	7th
753	December 8-9, 2002	14th
748	December 18-20, 2004	15th
740	November 29-30, 1998	13th
739	November 23, 26-27, 1995	13th
736	October 25-26, 1987	7th
734	November 19-20, 1995	12th

TOP 10 TELEVISED SPORTS EVENTS OF ALL-TIME
(Based on A.C. Nielsen Figures)

Program	Date	Network	Share	Rating
Super Bowl XVI	1/24/82	CBS	73%	49.1
Super Bowl XVII	1/30/83	NBC	69%	48.6
Winter Olympics	2/23/94	CBS	64%	48.5
Super Bowl XX	1/26/86	NBC	70%	48.3
Super Bowl XII	1/15/78	CBS	67%	47.2
Super Bowl XIII	1/21/79	NBC	74%	47.1
Super Bowl XVIII	1/22/84	CBS	71%	46.4
Super Bowl XIX	1/20/85	ABC	63%	46.4
Super Bowl XIV	1/20/80	CBS	67%	46.3
Super Bowl XXX	1/28/96	NBC	68%	46.0

TEN MOST WATCHED TV PROGRAMS & ESTIMATED TOTAL NUMBER OF VIEWERS
(Based on A.C. Nielsen Figures)

Program	Date	Network	*Total Viewers
Super Bowl XXXVIII	Feb. 1, 2004	CBS	144,400,000
Super Bowl XL	Feb. 5, 2006	ABC	141,400,000
Super Bowl XXXVII	Jan. 26, 2003	ABC	138,900,000
Super Bowl XXX	Jan. 28, 1996	NBC	138,488,000
Super Bowl XXVIII	Jan. 30, 1994	NBC	134,800,000
Super Bowl XXXIX	Feb. 6, 2005	FOX	133,700,000
Super Bowl XXXII	Jan. 25, 1998	NBC	133,400,000
Super Bowl XXVII	Jan. 31, 1993	NBC	133,400,000
Super Bowl XXXVI	Feb. 3, 2002	FOX	131,700,000
Super Bowl XXXV	Jan. 28, 2001	CBS	131,200,000

*Watched some portion of the broadcast

NFL'S TOP FIVE PAID ATTENDANCE TOTALS FOR ALL GAMES

Year	Preseason	Regular Season	Postseason	All Games
2005	3,977,388	17,012,453	802,255	21,792,096
2004	3,918,848	17,000,811	788,965	21,708,624
2003	3,919,910	16,913,584	805,546	21,639,040
2002	3,889,884	16,833,310	781,944	21,505,138
2000	3,757,231	16,387,289	809,132	20,953,652

TEN HIGHEST-RATED ABC *NFL MONDAY NIGHT FOOTBALL* GAMES OF ALL-TIME
(Based on A.C. Nielsen Figures)

Game	Date	Share	Rating
Chicago at Miami	12/2/85	46%	29.6
N.Y. Giants at San Francisco	12/3/90	42%	26.9
Dallas at Washington	10/2/78	43%	26.8
Pittsburgh at San Diego	12/22/80	40%	25.3
Philadelphia at Miami	11/30/81	40%	25.3
Pittsburgh at Houston	12/10/79	40%	25.1
Dallas at Miami	12/17/84	40%	25.1
Pittsburgh at Dallas	9/13/82	42%	24.9
Cincinnati at Oakland	12/6/76	40%	24.7
Dallas at Washington	10/8/73	40%	24.6
Minnesota at Atlanta	11/19/73	40%	24.6

NFL'S 10 BIGGEST SINGLE-GAME ATTENDANCE TOTALS

Date	Site	Game	Teams	Attendance
August 15, 1994	Azteca Stadium	American Bowl (Mexico City)	Cowboys vs. Oilers	112,376
August 17, 1998	Azteca Stadium	American Bowl (Mexico City)	Cowboys vs. Patriots	106,424
August 22, 1947	Soldier Field	College All-Star	Bears vs. All-Stars	105,840
August 4, 1997	Estadio Guillermo Canedo	American Bowl (Mexico City)	Broncos vs. Dolphins	104,629
January 20, 1980	Rose Bowl	Super Bowl XIV	Steelers vs. Rams	103,985
January 30, 1983	Rose Bowl	Super Bowl XVII	Redskins vs. Dolphins	103,667
October 2, 2005	Azteca Stadium	Regular Season	49ers at Cardinals	103,467
January 9, 1977	Rose Bowl	Super Bowl XI	Raiders vs. Vikings	103,438
November 10, 1957	L.A. Coliseum	Regular Season	49ers at Rams	102,368
January 25, 1987	Rose Bowl	Super Bowl XXI	Giants vs. Broncos	101,643

For detailed 2005 attendance, see page 344.

NFL'S TOP 10 PAID ATTENDANCE WEEKENDS

Weekend	Games	Attendance
September 8, 11-12, 2005	16	1,115,018
November 20-21, 2005	16	1,112,555
December 27-28, 2003	16	1,106,818
December 24-26, 2005	16	1,102,701
September 9, 12-13, 2004	16	1,101,332
September 4, 7-8, 2003	16	1,095,720
November 23-24, 2003	16	1,087,869
September 15-16, 2002	16	1,081,206
December 7-8, 2003	16	1,078,229
November 24-25, 2002	16	1,078,011

NFL'S TOP 10 TEAM SINGLE-SEASON HOME PAID ATTENDANCE TOTALS

Year	Club	Games	Attendance
2004	Washington Redskins	8	707,920
2005	Washington Redskins	8	707,614
2003	Washington Redskins	8	667,033
2002	Washington Redskins	8	663,536
2001	Washington Redskins	8	661,970
2000	Washington Redskins	8	656,599
1980	Detroit Lions	8	634,204
1988	Buffalo Bills	8	631,818
1991	Buffalo Bills	8	631,786
1992	Buffalo Bills	8	630,978

NFL PAID ATTENDANCE

Year	Regular Season			Average	Postseason	Total
2005	#17,012,453	(256 games)		#66,455	802,255 (12)	#17,814,708
2004	17,000,811	(256 games)		66,409	788,965 (12)	17,789,776
2003	16,913,584	(255 games***)		66,328	805,546 (12)	17,719,130
2002	16,833,310	(256 games)		65,755	781,944 (12)	17,615,254
2001	16,166,258	(248 games)		65,187	766,905 (12)	16,933,163
2000	16,387,289	(248 games)		66,078	809,132 (12)	17,196,421
1999	16,206,640	(248 games)		65,349	793,759 (12)	17,000,399
1998	15,364,873	(240 games)		64,020	822,885 (12)	16,187,758
1997	14,967,314	(240 games)		62,364	801,879 (12)	15,769,193
1996	14,612,417	(240 games)		60,885	769,310 (12)	15,381,727
1995	15,043,562	(240 games)		62,682	790,906 (12)	15,834,468
1994	14,030,435	(224 games)		62,636	779,738 (12)	14,810,173
1993	13,966,843	(224 games)		62,352	814,607 (12)	14,781,450
1992	13,828,887	(224 games)		61,736	815,910 (12)	14,644,797
1991	13,841,459	(224 games)		61,792	813,247 (12)	14,654,706
1990	13,959,896	(224 games)		62,321	847,543 (12)	14,807,439
1989	13,625,662	(224 games)		60,829	685,771 (10)	14,311,433
1988	13,539,848	(224 games)		60,446	658,317 (10)	14,198,165
1987	11,406,166	(210 games**)		54,315	656,977 (10)	12,063,143
1986	13,588,551	(224 games)		60,663	734,002 (10)	14,322,553
1985	13,345,047	(224 games)		59,567	710,768 (10)	14,055,815
1984	13,398,112	(224 games)		59,813	665,194 (10)	14,063,306
1983	13,277,222	(224 games)		59,273	675,513 (10)	13,952,735
1982	7,367,438	(126 games*)		58,472	1,033,153 (16)	8,400,591
1981	13,606,990	(224 games)		60,745	637,763 (10)	14,244,753
1980	13,392,230	(224 games)		59,787	624,430 (10)	14,016,660
1979	13,182,039	(224 games)		58,848	630,326 (10)	13,812,365
1978	12,771,800	(224 games)		57,017	624,388 (10)	13,396,188
1977	11,018,632	(196 games)		56,218	534,925 (8)	11,553,557
1976	11,070,543	(196 games)		56,482	492,884 (8)	11,563,427
1975	10,213,193	(182 games)		56,116	475,919 (8)	10,689,112
1974	10,236,322	(182 games)		56,244	438,664 (8)	10,674,986
1973	10,730,933	(182 games)		58,961	525,433 (8)	11,256,366
1972	10,445,827	(182 games)		57,395	483,345 (8)	10,929,172
1971	10,076,035	(182 games)		55,363	483,891 (8)	10,559,926
1970	9,533,333	(182 games)		52,381	458,493 (8)	9,991,826
1969	6,096,127	(112 games)	NFL	54,430	162,279 (3)	6,258,406
	2,843,373	(70 games)	AFL	40,620	167,088 (3)	3,010,461
1968	5,882,313	(112 games)	NFL	52,521	215,902 (3)	6,098,215
	2,635,004	(70 games)	AFL	37,643	114,438 (2)	2,749,442
1967	5,938,924	(112 games)	NFL	53,026	166,208 (3)	6,105,132
	2,295,697	(63 games)	AFL	36,439	53,330 (1)	2,349,027
1966	5,337,044	(105 games)	NFL	50,829	74,152 (1)	5,411,196
	2,160,369	(63 games)	AFL	34,291	42,080 (1)	2,202,449
1965	4,634,021	(98 games)	NFL	47,286	100,304 (2)	4,734,325
	1,782,384	(56 games)	AFL	31,828	30,361 (1)	1,812,745
1964	4,563,049	(98 games)	NFL	46,562	79,544 (1)	4,642,593
	1,447,875	(56 games)	AFL	25,855	40,242 (1)	1,488,117
1963	4,163,643	(98 games)	NFL	42,486	45,801 (1)	4,209,444
	1,208,697	(56 games)	AFL	21,584	63,171 (2)	1,271,868
1962	4,003,421	(98 games)	NFL	40,851	64,892 (1)	4,068,313
	1,147,302	(56 games)	AFL	20,487	37,981 (1)	1,185,283

Year	Regular Season			Average	Postseason	Total
1961	3,986,159	(98 games)	NFL	40,675	39,029 (1)	4,025,188
	1,002,657	(56 games)	AFL	17,904	29,556 (1)	1,032,213
1960	3,128,296	(78 games)	NFL	40,106	67,325 (1)	3,195,621
	926,156	(56 games)	AFL	16,538	32,183 (1)	958,339
1959	3,140,000	(72 games)		43,617	57,545 (1)	3,197,545
1958	3,006,124	(72 games)		41,752	123,659 (2)	3,129,783
1957	2,836,318	(72 games)		39,393	119,579 (2)	2,955,897
1956	2,551,263	(72 games)		35,434	56,836 (1)	2,608,099
1955	2,521,836	(72 games)		35,026	85,693 (1)	2,607,529
1954	2,190,571	(72 games)		30,425	43,827 (1)	2,234,398
1953	2,164,585	(72 games)		30,064	54,577 (1)	2,219,162
1952	2,052,126	(72 games)		28,502	97,507 (2)	2,149,633
1951	1,913,019	(72 games)		26,570	57,522 (1)	1,970,541
1950	1,977,753	(78 games)		25,356	136,647 (3)	2,114,400
1949	1,391,735	(60 games)		23,196	27,980 (1)	1,419,715
1948	1,525,243	(60 games)		25,421	36,309 (1)	1,561,552
1947	1,837,437	(60 games)		30,624	66,268 (2)	1,903,705
1946	1,732,135	(55 games)		31,493	58,346 (1)	1,790,481
1945	1,270,401	(50 games)		25,408	32,178 (1)	1,302,579
1944	1,019,649	(50 games)		20,393	46,016 (1)	1,065,665
1943	969,128	(40 games)		24,228	71,315 (2)	1,040,443
1942	887,920	(55 games)		16,144	36,006 (1)	923,926
1941	1,108,615	(55 games)		20,157	55,870 (2)	1,164,485
1940	1,063,025	(55 games)		19,328	36,034 (1)	1,099,059
1939	1,071,200	(55 games)		19,476	32,279 (1)	1,103,479
1938	937,197	(55 games)		17,040	48,120 (1)	985,317
1937	963,039	(55 games)		17,510	15,878 (1)	978,917
1936	816,007	(54 games)		15,111	29,545 (1)	845,552
1935	638,178	(53 games)		12,041	15,000 (1)	653,178
1934	492,684	(60 games)		8,211	35,059 (1)	527,743

Record

*Players' 57-day strike reduced 224-game schedule to 126 games.
**Players' 24-day strike reduced 224-game schedule to 210 games.
***The Week 8 Miami at San Diego game is not included. The game was moved to Arizona due to the San Diego wildfires and tickets were distributed at no charge.

INTERNATIONAL GAMES

NFL INTERNATIONAL GAMES (57)

Date	Site	Teams
August 12, 1950	Ottawa, Canada	N.Y. Giants 27, Ottawa Rough Riders 6
August 11, 1951	Ottawa, Canada	N.Y. Giants 41, Ottawa Rough Riders 18
August 5, 1959	Toronto, Canada	Chi. Cardinals 55, Tor. Argonauts 26
August 3, 1960	Toronto, Canada	Pittsburgh 43, Toronto Argonauts 16
August 15, 1960	Toronto, Canada	Chicago 16, N.Y. Giants 7
August 2, 1961	Toronto, Canada	St. Louis 36, Toronto Argonauts 7
August 5, 1961	Montreal, Canada	Chicago 34, Montreal Allouettes 16
August 8, 1961	Hamilton, Canada	Hamilton Tiger-Cats 38, Buffalo 21
August 25, 1969	Montreal, Canada	Detroit 22, Boston 9
September 11, 1969	Montreal, Canada	Pittsburgh 17, N.Y. Giants 13
August 16, 1976	Tokyo, Japan	St. Louis 20, San Diego 10
August 5, 1978	Mexico City, Mexico	New Orleans 14, Philadelphia 7
August 6, 1983	London, England	Minnesota 28, St. Louis 10
* August 3, 1986	London, England	Chicago 17, Dallas 6
* August 9, 1987	London, England	L.A. Rams 28, Denver 27
* July 31, 1988	London, England	Miami 27, San Francisco 21
August 14, 1988	Goteborg, Sweden	Minnesota 28, Chicago 21
August 18, 1988	Montreal, Canada	N.Y. Jets 11, Cleveland 7
* August 5, 1989	Tokyo, Japan	L.A. Rams 16, San Francisco 13 (OT)
* August 6, 1989	London, England	Philadelphia 17, Cleveland 13
* August 4, 1990	Tokyo, Japan	Denver 10, Seattle 7
* August 5, 1990	London, England	New Orleans 17, L.A. Raiders 10
* August 9, 1990	Montreal, Canada	Pittsburgh 30, New England 14
* August 11, 1990	Berlin, Germany	L.A. Rams 19, Kansas City 3
* July 28, 1991	London, England	Buffalo 17, Philadelphia 13
* August 3, 1991	Berlin, Germany	San Francisco 21, Chicago 7
* August 3, 1991	Tokyo, Japan	Miami 19, L.A. Raiders 17
* August 1, 1992	Tokyo, Japan	Houston 34, Dallas 23
* August 15, 1992	Berlin, Germany	Miami 31, Denver 27
* August 16, 1992	London, England	San Francisco 17, Washington 15
* July 31, 1993	Tokyo, Japan	New Orleans 28, Philadelphia 16
* August 1, 1993	Barcelona, Spain	San Francisco 21, Pittsburgh 14
* August 7, 1993	Berlin, Germany	Minnesota 20, Buffalo 6
* August 8, 1993	London, England	Dallas 13, Detroit 13 (OT)
August 14, 1993	Toronto, Canada	Cleveland 12, New England 9
* July 31, 1994	Barcelona, Spain	L.A. Raiders 25, Denver 22
* August 6, 1994	Tokyo, Japan	Minnesota 17, Kansas City 9
* August 13, 1994	Berlin, Germany	N.Y. Giants 28, San Diego 20
* August 15, 1994	Mexico City, Mexico	Houston 6, Dallas 0
* August 5, 1995	Tokyo, Japan	Denver 24, San Francisco 10
* August 12, 1995	Toronto, Canada	Buffalo 9, Dallas 7
* July 27, 1996	Tokyo, Japan	San Diego 20, Pittsburgh 10
* August 5, 1996	Monterrey, Mexico	Kansas City 32, Dallas 6
* July 27, 1997	Dublin, Ireland	Pittsburgh 30, Chicago 17
* August 4, 1997	Mexico City, Mexico	Miami 38, Denver 19
* August 16, 1997	Toronto, Canada	Green Bay 35, Buffalo 3
* August 1, 1998	Tokyo, Japan	Green Bay 27, Kansas City 24 (OT)
* August 15, 1998	Vancouver, Canada	San Francisco 24, Seattle 21
* August 17, 1998	Mexico City, Mexico	New England 21, Dallas 3
* August 7, 1999	Sydney, Australia	Denver 20, San Diego 17
* August 5, 2000	Tokyo, Japan	Atlanta 20, Dallas 9
* August 19, 2000	Mexico City, Mexico	Indianapolis 24, Pittsburgh 23
* August 27, 2001	Mexico City, Mexico	Dallas 21, Oakland 6
* August 3, 2002	Osaka, Japan	Washington 38, San Francisco 7
* August 2, 2003	Tokyo, Japan	Tampa Bay 30, N.Y. Jets 14
* August 6, 2005	Tokyo, Japan	Atlanta 27, Indianapolis 21
** October 2, 2005	Mexico City, Mexico	Arizona 31, San Francisco 14

* *American Bowl Game*
** *Regular-season Game*

CHICAGO ALL-STAR GAME

Pro teams won 31, lost 9, and tied 2. The game was discontinued after 1976.

Date	Winner	Loser	Attendance
August 31, 1934	Chicago Bears 0	All-Stars 0 (tie)	79,432
August 29, 1935	Chicago Bears 5	All-Stars 0	77,450
September 3, 1936	Detroit Lions 7	All-Stars 7 (tie)	76,000
September 1, 1937	All-Stars 6	Green Bay Packers 0	84,560
August 31, 1938	All-Stars 28	Washington Redskins 16	74,250
August 30, 1939	N.Y. Giants 9	All-Stars 0	81,456
August 29, 1940	Green Bay Packers 45	All-Stars 28	84,567
August 28, 1941	Chicago Bears 37	All-Stars 13	98,203
August 28, 1942	Chicago Bears 21	All-Stars 0	101,100
August 25, 1943	All-Stars 27	Washington Redskins 7	48,471
August 30, 1944	Chicago Bears 24	All-Stars 21	48,769
August 30, 1945	Green Bay Packers 19	All-Stars 7	92,753
August 23, 1946	All-Stars 16	Los Angeles Rams 0	97,380
August 22, 1947	All-Stars 16	Chicago Bears 0	105,840
August 20, 1948	Chicago Cardinals 28	All-Stars 0	101,220
August 12, 1949	Philadelphia Eagles 38	All-Stars 0	93,780
August 11, 1950	All-Stars 17	Philadelphia Eagles 7	88,885
August 17, 1951	Cleveland Browns 33	All-Stars 0	92,180
August 15, 1952	Los Angeles Rams 10	All-Stars 7	88,316
August 14, 1953	Detroit Lions 24	All-Stars 10	93,818
August 13, 1954	Detroit Lions 31	All-Stars 6	93,470
August 12, 1955	All-Stars 30	Cleveland Browns 27	75,000
August 10, 1956	Cleveland Browns 26	All-Stars 0	75,000
August 9, 1957	N.Y. Giants 22	All-Stars 12	75,000
August 15, 1958	All-Stars 35	Detroit Lions 19	70,000
August 14, 1959	Baltimore Colts 29	All-Stars 0	70,000
August 12, 1960	Baltimore Colts 32	All-Stars 7	70,000
August 4, 1961	Philadelphia Eagles 28	All-Stars 14	66,000
August 3, 1962	Green Bay Packers 42	All-Stars 20	65,000
August 2, 1963	All-Stars 20	Green Bay Packers 17	65,000
August 7, 1964	Chicago Bears 28	All-Stars 17	65,000
August 6, 1965	Cleveland Browns 24	All-Stars 16	68,000
August 5, 1966	Green Bay Packers 38	All-Stars 0	72,000
August 4, 1967	Green Bay Packers 27	All-Stars 0	70,934
August 2, 1968	Green Bay Packers 34	All-Stars 17	69,917
August 1, 1969	N.Y. Jets 26	All-Stars 24	74,208
July 31, 1970	Kansas City Chiefs 24	All-Stars 3	69,940
July 30, 1971	Baltimore Colts 24	All-Stars 17	52,289
July 28, 1972	Dallas Cowboys 20	All-Stars 7	54,162
July 27, 1973	Miami Dolphins 14	All-Stars 3	54,103
1974	No game was played		
August 1, 1975	Pittsburgh Steelers 21	All-Stars 14	54,103
July 23, 1976*	Pittsburgh Steelers 24	All-Stars 0	52,895

Game shortened because of thunderstorms.

NFL PLAYOFF BOWL

Consolation game that matched conference runners-up.
Western Conference won 8, Eastern Conference won 2.
All games played at Miami's Orange Bowl.

January 7, 1961	Detroit Lions 17, Cleveland Browns 16
January 6, 1962	Detroit Lions 38, Philadelphia Eagles 10
January 6, 1963	Detroit Lions 17, Pittsburgh Steelers 10
January 5, 1964	Green Bay Packers 40, Cleveland Browns 23
January 3, 1965	St. Louis Cardinals 24, Green Bay Packers 17
January 9, 1966	Baltimore Colts 35, Dallas Cowboys 3
January 8, 1967	Baltimore Colts 20, Philadelphia Eagles 14
January 7, 1968	Los Angeles Rams 30, Cleveland Browns 6
January 5, 1969	Dallas Cowboys 17, Minnesota Vikings 13
January 3, 1970	Los Angeles Rams 31, Dallas Cowboys 0

75TH ANNIVERSARY ALL-TIME TEAM
Chosen by a selection committee of media and league personnel in 1994.

Position	Name	Team(s)	Ht.	Wt.	College
OFFENSE					
QB	Sammy Baugh	Washington Redskins (1937-52)	6-2	180	Texas Christian
QB	Otto Graham	Cleveland Browns (1946-55)	6-1	195	Northwestern
QB	Joe Montana	San Francisco 49ers (1979-92), Kansas City Chiefs (1993-94)	6-2	195	Notre Dame
QB	Johnny Unitas	Baltimore Colts (1956-72), San Diego Chargers (1973)	6-1	195	Louisville
RB	Jim Brown	Cleveland Browns (1957-65)	6-2	232	Syracuse
RB	Marion Motley	Cleveland Browns (1946-53), Pittsburgh Steelers (1955)	6-1	238	Nevada-Reno
RB	Bronko Nagurski	Chicago Bears (1930-37, 1943)	6-2	225	Minnesota
RB	Walter Payton	Chicago Bears (1975-87)	5-10	202	Jackson State
RB	Gale Sayers	Chicago Bears (1965-71)	6-0	200	Kansas
RB	O.J. Simpson	Buffalo Bills (1969-77), San Francisco 49ers (1978-79)	6-1	212	Southern California
RB	Steve Van Buren	Philadelphia Eagles (1944-51)	6-1	200	Louisiana State
WR	Lance Alworth	San Diego Chargers (1962-70), Dallas Cowboys (1971-72)	6-0	184	Arkansas
WR	Raymond Berry	Baltimore Colts (1955-67)	6-2	187	Southern Methodist
WR	Don Hutson	Green Bay Packers (1935-45)	6-1	180	Alabama
WR	Jerry Rice	San Francisco 49ers (1985-2000), Oakland Raiders (2001-04), Seattle Seahawks (2004)	6-2	200	Miss. Valley State
TE	Mike Ditka	Chicago Bears (1961-66), Philadelphia Eagles (1967-68), Dallas Cowboys (1969-72)	6-3	225	Pittsburgh
TE	Kellen Winslow	San Diego Chargers (1979-87)	6-5	250	Missouri
T	Roosevelt Brown	New York Giants (1953-65)	6-3	255	Morgan State
T	Forrest Gregg	Green Bay Packers (1956, 1958-70)	6-4	250	Southern Methodist
T	Anthony Muñoz	Cincinnati Bengals (1980-92)	6-6	285	Southern California
G	John Hannah	New England Patriots (1973-85)	6-3	265	Alabama
G	Jim Parker	Baltimore Colts (1957-67)	6-3	273	Ohio State
G	Gene Upshaw	Oakland Raiders (1967-81)	6-5	255	Texas A&I
C	Mel Hein	New York Giants (1931-45)	6-2	225	Washington State
C	Mike Webster	Pittsburgh Steelers (1974-88), Kansas City Chiefs (1989-90)	6-2	250	Wisconsin
DEFENSE					
DE	David (Deacon) Jones	Los Angeles Rams (1961-71), San Diego Chargers (1972-73), Washington Redskins (1974)	6-5	250	Miss. Vocational-South Carolina St.
DE	Gino Marchetti	Dallas Texans (1952), Baltimore Colts (1953-64, 1966)	6-4	245	San Francisco
DE	Reggie White	Philadelphia Eagles (1985-92), Green Bay Packers (1993-1998), Carolina Panthers (2000)	6-5	290	Tennessee
DT	Joe Greene	Pittsburgh Steelers (1969-81)	6-4	260	North Texas State
DT	Bob Lilly	Dallas Cowboys (1961-74)	6-5	260	Texas Christian
DT	Merlin Olsen	Los Angeles Rams (1962-76)	6-5	270	Utah State
LB	Dick Butkus	Chicago Bears (1965-73)	6-3	245	Illinois
LB	Jack Ham	Pittsburgh Steelers (1971-82)	6-1	225	Penn State
LB	Ted Hendricks	Baltimore Colts (1969-73), Green Bay Packers (1974), Oakland/L.A. Raiders (1975-83)	6-7	235	Miami
LB	Jack Lambert	Pittsburgh Steelers (1974-84)	6-4	220	Kent State
LB	Willie Lanier	Kansas City Chiefs (1967-77)	6-1	245	Morgan State
LB	Ray Nitschke	Green Bay Packers (1958-72)	6-3	235	Illinois
LB	Lawrence Taylor	New York Giants (1981-93)	6-3	243	North Carolina
CB	Mel Blount	Pittsburgh Steelers (1970-83)	6-3	205	Southern
CB	Mike Haynes	New England Patriots (1976-82), Los Angeles Raiders (1983-89)	6-2	190	Arizona State
CB	Dick (Night Train) Lane	Los Angeles Rams (1952-53), Chicago Cardinals (1954-59), Detroit Lions (1960-65)	6-2	210	Scottsbluff JC
CB	Rod Woodson	Pittsburgh Steelers (1987-96), San Francisco 49ers (1997), Baltimore Ravens (1998-2001), Oakland Raiders (2002-2003)	6-0	200	Purdue
S	Ken Houston	Houston Oilers (1967-72), Washington Redskins (1973-80)	6-3	198	Prairie View A&M
S	Ronnie Lott	San Francisco 49ers (1981-90), Los Angeles Raiders (1991-92), New York Jets (1993-94)	6-0	200	Southern California
S	Larry Wilson	St. Louis Cardinals (1960-72)	6-0	190	Utah
SPECIAL TEAMS					
P	Ray Guy	Oakland/L.A. Raiders (1973-86)	6-3	190	Southern Mississippi
K	Jan Stenerud	Kansas City Chiefs (1967-79), Green Bay Packers (1980-83), Minnesota Vikings (1984-85)	6-2	190	Montana State
PR	Billy (White Shoes) Johnson	Houston Oilers (1974-80), Atlanta Falcons (1982-87), Washington Redskins (1988)	5-9	170	Widener
KR	Gale Sayers	Chicago Bears (1965-71)	6-0	200	Kansas

75TH ANNIVERSARY ALL-TWO-WAY TEAM
Positions

Quarterback, Defensive Halfback, Punter	Sammy Baugh
Center, Linebacker	Chuck Bednarik
Quarterback, Defensive Halfback, Punter	Earl (Dutch) Clark
Tackle, Defensive Tackle	George Connor
Guard, Defensive Tackle	Danny Fortmann
Center, Defensive Tackle	Mel Hein
Tackle, Defensive Tackle, Punter	Wilbur (Pete) Henry
Back, Defensive Halfback	Bill Hewitt
Fullback, Linebacker, Kicker	Clarke Hinkle
Tackle, Defensive Tackle	Cal Hubbard
End, Defensive Halfback	Don Hutson
Back, Defensive Back	George McAfee
Fullback, Linebacker	Marion Motley
Guard-Tackle, Defensive Tackle	George Musso
Fullback, Linebacker	Bronko Nagurski
Halfback, Defensive Halfback	Ernie Nevers
End, Defensive Back	Pete Pihos
Tackle, Defensive Tackle	Joe Stydahar
Running Back, Defensive Back	Steve Van Buren

50TH ANNIVERSARY TEAM
Chosen by the Hall of Fame Selection Committee in 1969.
Offense

Split End	Don Hutson
Tight End	John Mackey
Tackle	Cal Hubbard
Guard	Jerry Kramer
Center	Chuck Bednarik
Flanker	Elroy Hirsch
Quarterback	Johnny Unitas
Halfback	Jim Thorpe
Halfback	Gale Sayers
Fullback	Jim Brown
Kicker	Lou Groza

Defense

End	Gino Marchetti
Tackle	Leo Nomellini
Linebacker	Ray Nitschke
Cornerback	Dick (Night Train) Lane
Safety	Emlen Tunnell

SUPER BOWL SILVER ANNIVERSARY TEAM
Chosen by the fans in 1990 prior to Super Bowl XXV.

Head Coach	Vince Lombardi
Offense	
Quarterback	Joe Montana
Running Back	Franco Harris
Running Back	Larry Csonka
Wide Receiver	Lynn Swann
Wide Receiver	Jerry Rice
Tight End	Dave Casper
Tackle	Art Shell
Tackle	Forrest Gregg
Guard	Gene Upshaw
Guard	Jerry Kramer
Center	Mike Webster
Defense	
Defensive End	L.C. Greenwood
Defensive End	Ed (Too Tall) Jones
Defensive Tackle	Joe Greene
Defensive Tackle	Randy White
Inside Linebacker	Jack Lambert
Inside Linebacker	Mike Singletary
Outside Linebacker	Jack Ham
Outside Linebacker	Ted Hendricks
Cornerback	Ronnie Lott
Cornerback	Mel Blount
Safety	Donnie Shell
Safety	Willie Wood
Special Teams	
Punter	Ray Guy
Kicker	Jan Stenerud
Kick Returner	John Taylor

All-Decade teams chosen by the Hall of Fame Selection Committee members.

1920s ALL-DECADE TEAM

End	Guy Chamberlin
End	Lavern Dilweg
End	George Halas
Tackle	Ed Healey
Tackle	Wilbur (Pete) Henry
Tackle	Cal Hubbard
Tackle	Steve Owen
Guard	Hunk Anderson
Guard	Walt Kiesling
Guard	Mike Michalske
Center	George Trafton
Quarterback	Jimmy Conzelman
Quarterback	John (Paddy) Driscoll
Halfback	Harold (Red) Grange
Halfback	Joe Guyon
Halfback	Earl (Curly) Lambeau
Halfback	Jim Thorpe
Fullback	Ernie Nevers

1930s ALL-DECADE TEAM

End	Bill Hewitt
End	Don Hutson
End	Wayne Millner
End	Gaynell Tinsley
Tackle	George Christensen
Tackle	Frank Cope
Tackle	Glen (Turk) Edwards
Tackle	Bill Lee
Tackle	Joe Stydahar
Guard	Grover (Ox) Emerson
Guard	Dan Fortmann
Guard	Charles (Buckets) Goldenberg
Guard	Russ Letlow
Center	Mel Hein
Center	George Svendsen
Quarterback	Earl (Dutch) Clark
Quarterback	Arnie Herber
Quarterback	Cecil Isbell
Halfback	Cliff Battles
Halfback	Johnny (Blood) McNally
Halfback	Beattie Feathers
Halfback	Alphonse (Tuffy) Leemans
Halfback	Ken Strong
Fullback	Clarke Hinkle
Fullback	Bronko Nagurski

1940s ALL-DECADE TEAM

End	Jim Benton
End	Jack Ferrante
End	Ken Kavanaugh
End	Dante Lavelli
End	Pete Pihos
End	Mac Speedie
End	Ed Sprinkle
Tackle	Al Blozis
Tackle	George Connor
Tackle	Frank (Bucko) Kilroy
Tackle	Buford (Baby) Ray
Tackle	Vic Sears
Tackle	Al Wistert
Guard	Bruno Banducci
Guard	Bill Edwards
Guard	Garrard (Buster) Ramsey
Guard	Bill Willis
Guard	Len Younce
Center	Charley Brock
Center	Clyde (Bulldog) Turner
Center	Alex Wojciechowicz
Quarterback	Sammy Baugh
Quarterback	Sid Luckman
Quarterback	Bob Waterfield
Halfback	Tony Canadeo
Halfback	Bill Dudley
Halfback	George McAfee
Halfback	Charley Trippi
Halfback	Steve Van Buren
Halfback	Byron (Whizzer) White
Fullback	Pat Harder
Fullback	Marion Motley
Fullback	Bill Osmanski

1950s ALL-DECADE TEAM

Offense

End	Raymond Berry
End	Tom Fears
End	Bobby Walston
Halfback-End	Elroy (Crazylegs) Hirsch
Tackle	Roosevelt Brown
Tackle	Bob St. Clair
Guard	Dick Barwegan
Guard	Jim Parker
Guard	Dick Stanfel
Center	Chuck Bednarik
Quarterback	Otto Graham
Quarterback	Bobby Layne
Quarterback	Norm Van Brocklin
Halfback	Frank Gifford
Halfback	Ollie Matson
Halfback	Hugh McElhenny
Halfback	Lenny Moore
Fullback	Alan Ameche
Fullback	Joe Perry
Kicker	Lou Groza

Defense

End	Len Ford
End	Gino Marchetti
Tackle	Art Donovan
Tackle	Leo Nomellini
Tackle	Ernie Stautner
Linebacker	Joe Fortunato
Linebacker	Bill George
Linebacker	Sam Huff
Linebacker	Joe Schmidt
Halfback	Jack Butler

Halfback	Dick (Night Train) Lane
Safety	Jack Christiansen
Safety	Yale Lary
Safety	Emlen Tunnell

1960s ALL-DECADE TEAM

Offense

Split End	Del Shofner
Split End	Charley Taylor
Flanker	Gary Collins
Flanker	Boyd Dowler
Tight End	John Mackey
Tackle	Bob Brown
Tackle	Forrest Gregg
Tackle	Ralph Neely
Guard	Gene Hickerson
Guard	Jerry Kramer
Guard	Howard Mudd
Center	Jim Ringo
Quarterback	Sonny Jurgensen
Quarterback	Bart Starr
Quarterback	Johnny Unitas
Halfback	John David Crow
Halfback	Paul Hornung
Halfback	Leroy Kelly
Halfback	Gale Sayers
Fullback	Jim Brown
Fullback	Jim Taylor
Kicker	Jim Bakken

Defense

End	Doug Atkins
End	Willie Davis
End	David (Deacon) Jones
Tackle	Alex Karras
Tackle	Bob Lilly
Tackle	Merlin Olsen
Linebacker	Dick Butkus
Linebacker	Larry Morris
Linebacker	Ray Nitschke
Linebacker	Tommy Nobis
Linebacker	Dave Robinson
Cornerback	Herb Adderley
Cornerback	Lem Barney
Cornerback	Bobby Boyd
Safety	Eddie Meador
Safety	Larry Wilson
Safety	Willie Wood
Punter	Don Chandler

1970s ALL-DECADE TEAM

Offense

Wide Receiver	Harold Carmichael
Wide Receiver	Drew Pearson
Wide Receiver	Lynn Swann
Wide Receiver	Paul Warfield
Tight End	Dave Casper
Tight End	Charlie Sanders
Tackle	Dan Dierdorf
Tackle	Art Shell
Tackle	Rayfield Wright
Tackle	Ron Yary
Guard	Joe DeLamielleure
Guard	John Hannah
Guard	Larry Little
Guard	Gene Upshaw
Center	Jim Langer
Center	Mike Webster
Quarterback	Terry Bradshaw
Quarterback	Ken Stabler
Quarterback	Roger Staubach
Running Back	Earl Campbell
Running Back	Franco Harris
Running Back	Walter Payton
Running Back	O.J. Simpson
Kicker	Garo Yepremian

Defense

End	Carl Eller
End	L.C. Greenwood
End	Harvey Martin
End	Jack Youngblood
Tackle	Joe Greene
Tackle	Bob Lilly
Tackle	Merlin Olsen
Tackle	Alan Page
Linebacker	Bobby Bell
Linebacker	Robert Brazile
Linebacker	Dick Butkus
Linebacker	Jack Ham
Linebacker	Ted Hendricks
Linebacker	Jack Lambert
Cornerback	Willie Brown
Cornerback	Jimmy Johnson
Cornerback	Roger Wehrli
Cornerback	Louis Wright
Safety	Dick Anderson
Safety	Cliff Harris
Safety	Ken Houston
Safety	Larry Wilson
Punter	Ray Guy

1980s ALL-DECADE TEAM

Offense

Wide Receiver	Jerry Rice
Wide Receiver	Steve Largent
Wide Receiver	James Lofton
Wide Receiver	Art Monk
Tight End	Kellen Winslow
Tight End	Ozzie Newsome
Tackle	Anthony Munoz
Tackle	Jim Covert
Tackle	Gary Zimmerman
Tackle	Joe Jacoby
Guard	John Hannah
Guard	Russ Grimm
Guard	Bill Fralic
Guard	Mike Munchak
Center	Dwight Stephenson
Center	Mike Webster
Quarterback	Joe Montana
Quarterback	Dan Fouts
Running Back	Walter Payton
Running Back	Eric Dickerson
Running Back	Roger Craig
Running Back	John Riggins

Defense

End	Reggie White
End	Howie Long
End	Lee Roy Selmon
End	Bruce Smith
Tackle	Randy White
Tackle	Dan Hampton
Tackle	Keith Millard
Tackle	Dave Butz
Linebacker	Mike Singletary
Linebacker	Lawrence Taylor
Linebacker	Ted Hendricks
Linebacker	Jack Lambert
Linebacker	Andre Tippett
Linebacker	John Anderson
Linebacker	Carl Banks
Cornerback	Mike Haynes
Cornerback	Mel Blount
Cornerback	Frank Minnifield
Cornerback	Lester Hayes
Safety	Ronnie Lott
Safety	Kenny Easley
Safety	Deron Cherry
Safety	Joey Browner
Safety	Nolan Cromwell

Specialists

Punter	Sean Landeta
Punter	Reggie Roby
Kicker	Morten Andersen
Kicker	Gary Anderson
Kicker	Eddie Murray
Punt Returner	Billy (White Shoes) Johnson
Punt Returner	John Taylor
Kick Returner	Mike Nelms
Kick Returner	Rick Upchurch
Coach	Bill Walsh
Coach	Chuck Noll

1990s ALL-DECADE TEAM

Offense

Wide Receiver	Cris Carter
Wide Receiver	Jerry Rice
Wide Receiver	Tim Brown
Wide Receiver	Michael Irvin
Tight End	Shannon Sharpe
Tight End	Ben Coates
Tackle	William Roaf
Tackle	Gary Zimmerman
Tackle	Tony Boselli
Tackle	Richmond Webb
Guard	Bruce Matthews
Guard	Randall McDaniel
Guard	Larry Allen
Guard	Steve Wisniewski
Center	Dermontti Dawson
Center	Mark Stepnoski
Quarterback	John Elway
Quarterback	Brett Favre
Running Back	Barry Sanders
Running Back	Emmitt Smith
Running Back	Terrell Davis
Running Back	Thurman Thomas

Defense

End	Bruce Smith
End	Reggie White
End	Chris Doleman
End	Neil Smith
Tackle	Cortez Kennedy
Tackle	John Randle
Tackle	Warren Sapp
Tackle	Bryant Young
Linebacker	Kevin Greene
Linebacker	Junior Seau
Linebacker	Derrick Thomas
Linebacker	Cornelius Bennett
Linebacker	Hardy Nickerson
Linebacker	Levon Kirkland
Cornerback	Deion Sanders
Cornerback	Rod Woodson
Cornerback	Darrell Green
Cornerback	Aeneas Williams
Safety	Steve Atwater
Safety	LeRoy Butler
Safety	Carnell Lake
Safety	Ronnie Lott

Specialists

Punter	Darren Bennett
Punter	Sean Landeta
Kicker	Morten Andersen
Kicker	Gary Anderson
Punt Returner	Deion Sanders
Punt Returner	Mel Gray
Kick Returner	Michael Bates
Kick Returner	Mel Gray
Coach	Bill Parcells
Coach	Marv Levy

ALL-TIME AFL TEAM
Chosen by 1969 AFL Hall of Fame Selection Committee members.
Offense
Flanker	Lance Alworth
End	Don Maynard
Tight End	Fred Arbanas
Tackle	Ron Mix
Tackle	Jim Tyrer
Guard	Ed Budde
Guard	Billy Shaw
Center	Jim Otto
Quarterback	Joe Namath
Running Back	Clem Daniels
Running Back	Paul Lowe

Defense
End	Jerry Mays
End	Gerry Philbin
Tackle	Houston Antwine
Tackle	Tom Sestak
Linebacker	Bobby Bell
Linebacker	George Webster
Linebacker	Nick Buoniconti
Cornerback	Willie Brown
Cornerback	Dave Grayson
Safety	Johnny Robinson
Safety	George Saimes

Special Teams
Kicker	George Blanda
Punter	Jerrel Wilson

ALL-TIME NFL TEAM
Chosen by members of the Hall of Fame Selection Committee in 2000 for the book NFL's Greatest.
Offense
Wide Receiver	Don Hutson
Wide Receiver	Jerry Rice
Tight End	John Mackey
Tackle	Roosevelt Brown
Tackle	Anthony Muñoz
Guard	John Hannah
Guard	Jim Parker
Center	Mike Webster
Quarterback	Johnny Unitas
Running Back	Jim Brown
Running Back	Walter Payton

Defense
End	Deacon Jones
End	Reggie White
Tackle	Joe Greene
Tackle	Bob Lilly
Middle Linebacker	Dick Butkus
Outside Linebacker	Jack Ham
Outside Linebacker	Lawrence Taylor
Cornerback	Mel Blount
Cornerback	Dick (Night Train) Lane
Safety	Ronnie Lott
Safety	Larry Wilson

Special Teams
Kicker	Jan Stenerud
Punter	Ray Guy
Kick Returner	Gale Sayers
Punt Returner	Deion Sanders
Special Teams	Steve Tasker

AFL-NFL 1960-1984 ALL-STAR TEAM
Chosen by the Hall of Fame Selection Committee in 1985.
Offense
Quarterback	Johnny Unitas
Running Back	Jim Brown
Running Back	O.J. Simpson
Wide Receiver	Lance Alworth
Wide Receiver	Raymond Berry
Tight End	Kellen Winslow
Tight End	Forrest Gregg
Tight End	Ron Mix
Guard	Jim Parker
Guard	John Hannah
Center	Jim Otto

Defense
End	Gino Marchetti
End	Willie Davis
Tackle	Bob Lilly
Tackle	Merlin Olsen
Linebacker	Dick Butkus
Linebacker	Jack Lambert
Linebacker	Ray Nitschke
Cornerback	Willie Brown
Cornerback	Dick (Night Train) Lane
Safety	Larry Wilson
Safety	Yale Lary

Special Teams
Punter	Ray Guy
Kicker	Jan Stenerud
Kick Returner	Gale Sayers
Kick Returner	Rick Upchurch
Coach	Don Shula
Coach	Vince Lombardi

Records

Compiled by Elias Sports Bureau

The following records reflect all available official information on the National Football League from its formation in 1920 to date. Also included are all applicable records from the American Football League, 1960-69.

Individuals eligible for Rookie records are players who were in their first season of professional football and had not been on the roster of another professional football team, including teams in other leagues, for any regular-season or postseason games in a previous season. Eligible players, therefore, include those who were under contract to a National Football League club for a previous season but were terminated prior to their club's first regular-season game and not re-signed, or who were placed on Reserve/Injured (or another category of the Reserve List) prior to their club's first regular-season game and were not activated during the rest of the regular season or postseason.

INDIVIDUAL RECORDS

SERVICE
Most Seasons
- 26 George Blanda, Chi. Bears, 1949, 1950-58; Baltimore, 1950; Houston, 1960-66; Oakland, 1967-1975
- 23 Morten Andersen, New Orleans, 1982-1994; Atlanta, 1995-2000; N.Y. Giants, 2001; Kansas City, 2002-03; Minnesota, 2004
  Gary Anderson, Pittsburgh, 1982-1994; Philadelphia, 1995-96; San Francisco, 1997; Minnesota, 1998-2002; Tennessee, 2003-04
- 21 Earl Morrall, San Francisco, 1956; Pittsburgh, 1957-58; Detroit, 1958-1964; N.Y. Giants, 1965-67; Baltimore, 1968-1971; Miami, 1972-76
  Sean Landeta, N.Y. Giants, 1985-1993; L.A. Rams, 1993-94; St. Louis, 1995-96; Tampa Bay, 1997; Green Bay, 1998; Philadelphia, 1999-2002; St. Louis, 2003-04; Philadelphia, 2005

Most Seasons, One Club
- 20 Jackie Slater, L.A. Rams, 1976-1994; St. Louis, 1995
  Darrell Green, Washington, 1983-2002
- 19 Jim Marshall, Minnesota, 1961-1979
  Bruce Matthews, Houston, 1983-1996; Tennessee, 1997-2001
- 18 Jim Hart, St. Louis, 1966-1983
  Jeff Van Note, Atlanta, 1969-1986
  Pat Leahy, N.Y. Jets, 1974-1991

Most Games Played, Career
- 354 Morten Andersen, New Orleans, 1982-1994; Atlanta, 1995-2000; N.Y. Giants, 2001; Kansas City, 2002-03; Minnesota, 2004
- 353 Gary Anderson, Pittsburgh, 1982-1994; Philadelphia, 1995-96; San Francisco, 1997; Minnesota, 1998-2002; Tennessee, 2003-04
- 340 George Blanda, Chi. Bears, 1949, 1950-58; Baltimore, 1950; Houston, 1960-66; Oakland, 1967-1975

Most Consecutive Games Played, Career
- 288 Jeff Feagles, New England, 1988-89; Philadelphia, 1990-93; Arizona, 1994-97; Seattle, 1998-2002; N.Y. Giants, 2003-05 (current)
- 282 Jim Marshall, Cleveland, 1960; Minnesota, 1961-1979
- 248 Morten Andersen, New Orleans, 1987-1994; Atlanta, 1995-2000; N.Y. Giants, 2001; Kansas City, 2002

SCORING
Most Seasons Leading League
- 5 Don Hutson, Green Bay, 1940-44
  Gino Cappelletti, Boston, 1961, 1963-66
- 3 Earl (Dutch) Clark, Portsmouth, 1932; Detroit, 1935-36
  Pat Harder, Chi. Cardinals, 1947-49
  Paul Hornung, Green Bay, 1959-1961

- 2 Jack Manders, Chi. Bears, 1934, 1937
  Gordy Soltau, San Francisco, 1952-53
  Doak Walker, Detroit, 1950, 1955
  Gene Mingo, Denver, 1960, 1962
  Jim Turner, N.Y. Jets, 1968-69
  Fred Cox, Minnesota, 1969-1970
  Chester Marcol, Green Bay, 1972, 1974
  John Smith, New England, 1979-1980
  Marshall Faulk, St. Louis, 2000-01

Most Consecutive Seasons Leading League
- 5 Don Hutson, Green Bay, 1940-44
- 4 Gino Cappelletti, Boston, 1963-66
- 3 Pat Harder, Chi. Cardinals, 1947-49
  Paul Hornung, Green Bay, 1959-1961

POINTS
Most Points, Career
- 2,434 Gary Anderson, Pittsburgh, 1982-1994; Philadelphia 1995-96; San Francisco, 1997; Minnesota, 1998-2002; Tennessee, 2003-04 (820-pat, 538-fg)
- 2,358 Morten Andersen, New Orleans, 1982-1994; Atlanta, 1995-2000; N.Y. Giants, 2001; Kansas City, 2002-03; Minnesota, 2004 (798-pat, 520-fg)
- 2,002 George Blanda, Chi. Bears, 1949, 1950-58; Baltimore, 1950; Houston, 1960-66; Oakland, 1967-1975 (9-td, 943-pat, 335-fg)

Most Points, Season
- 176 Paul Hornung, Green Bay, 1960 (15-td, 41-pat, 15-fg)
- 168 Shaun Alexander, Seattle, 2005 (28-td)
- 164 Gary Anderson, Minnesota, 1998 (59-pat, 35-fg)

Most Points, No Touchdowns, Season
- 164 Gary Anderson, Minnesota, 1998 (59-pat, 35-fg)
- 163 Jeff Wilkins, St. Louis, 2003 (46-pat, 39-fg)
- 161 Mark Moseley, Washington, 1983 (62-pat, 33-fg)

Most Seasons, 100 or More Points
- 14 Gary Anderson, Pittsburgh, 1982-1994; Philadelphia 1995-96; San Francisco, 1997; Minnesota, 1998-2002; Tennessee, 2003
  Morten Andersen, New Orleans, 1982-1994; Atlanta, 1995-2000; N.Y. Giants, 2001; Kansas City, 2002-03
- 13 Jason Elam, Denver, 1993-2005
- 11 Nick Lowery, Kansas City, 1981, 1983-86, 1988-1993

Most Points, Rookie, Season
- 144 Kevin Butler, Chicago, 1985 (51-pat, 31-fg)
- 132 Gale Sayers, Chicago, 1965 (22-td)
- 128 Doak Walker, Detroit, 1950 (11-td, 38-pat, 8-fg)
  Chester Marcol, Green Bay, 1972 (29-pat, 33-fg)

Most Points, Game
- 40 Ernie Nevers, Chi. Cardinals vs. Chi. Bears, Nov. 28, 1929 (6-td, 4-pat)
- 36 Dub Jones, Cleveland vs. Chi. Bears, Nov. 25, 1951 (6-td)
  Gale Sayers, Chicago vs. San Francisco, Dec. 12, 1965 (6-td)
- 33 Paul Hornung, Green Bay vs. Baltimore, Oct. 8, 1961 (4-td, 6-pat, 1-fg)

Most Consecutive Games Scoring
- 332 Morten Andersen, New Orleans, 1983-1994; Atlanta, 1995-2000; N.Y. Giants, 2001; Kansas City, 2002-03; Minnesota, 2004 (current)
- 204 Jason Elam, Denver, 1993-2005 (current)
- 186 Jim Breech, Oakland, 1979; Cincinnati, 1980-1992

TOUCHDOWNS
Most Seasons Leading League
- 8 Don Hutson, Green Bay, 1935-38, 1941-44
- 3 Jim Brown, Cleveland, 1958-59, 1963
  Lance Alworth, San Diego, 1964-66

Emmitt Smith, Dallas, 1992, 1994-95

2 By many players

Most Consecutive Seasons Leading League

4 Don Hutson, Green Bay, 1935-38, 1941-44

3 Lance Alworth, San Diego, 1964-66

2 By many players

Most Touchdowns, Career

208 Jerry Rice, San Francisco, 1985-2000;
Oakland, 2001-04; Seattle, 2004
(10-r, 197-p, 1-ret)

175 Emmitt Smith, Dallas, 1990-2002; Arizona, 2003-04
(164-r, 11-p)

145 Marcus Allen, L.A. Raiders, 1982-1992; Kansas City,
1993-97 (123-r, 21-p, 1-ret)

Most Touchdowns, Season

28 Shaun Alexander, Seattle, 2005 (27-r, 1-p)

27 Priest Holmes, Kansas City, 2003 (27-r)

26 Marshall Faulk, St. Louis, 2000 (18-r, 8-p)

Most Touchdowns, Rookie, Season

22 Gale Sayers, Chicago, 1965 (14-r, 6-p, 2-ret)

20 Eric Dickerson, L.A. Rams, 1983 (18-r, 2-p)

17 Randy Moss, Minnesota, 1998 (17-p)
Fred Taylor, Jacksonville, 1998 (14-r, 3-p)
Edgerrin James, Indianapolis, 1999 (13-r, 4-p)
Clinton Portis, Denver, 2002 (15-r, 2-p)

Most Touchdowns, Game

6 Ernie Nevers, Chi. Cardinals vs. Chi. Bears,
Nov. 28, 1929 (6-r)
Dub Jones, Cleveland vs. Chi. Bears, Nov. 25, 1951
(4-r, 2-p)
Gale Sayers, Chicago vs. San Francisco, Dec. 12, 1965
(4-r, 1-p, 1-ret)

5 Jimmy Conzelman, Rhode Island vs. Evansville,
Oct. 15, 1922 (5-r)
Bob Shaw, Chi. Cardinals vs. Baltimore, Oct. 2, 1950
(5-p)
Jim Brown, Cleveland vs. Baltimore, Nov. 1, 1959 (5-r)
Abner Haynes, Dall. Texans vs. Oakland,
Nov. 26, 1961 (4-r, 1-p)
Billy Cannon, Houston vs. N.Y. Titans, Dec. 10, 1961
(3-r, 2-p)
Cookie Gilchrist, Buffalo vs. N.Y. Jets, Dec. 8, 1963 (5-r)
Paul Hornung, Green Bay vs. Baltimore,
Dec. 12, 1965 (3-r, 2-p)
Kellen Winslow, San Diego vs. Oakland,
Nov. 22, 1981 (5-p)
Jerry Rice, San Francisco vs. Atlanta, Oct. 14, 1990
(5-p)
James Stewart, Jacksonville vs. Philadelphia,
Oct. 12, 1997 (5-r)
Shaun Alexander, Seattle vs. Minnesota,
Sept. 29, 2002 (4-r, 1-p)
Clinton Portis, Denver vs. Kansas City, Dec. 7, 2003
(5-r)

4 By many players. Last time: LaDainian Tomlinson,
San Diego vs. N.Y. Jets, Nov. 6, 2005

Most Consecutive Games Scoring Touchdowns

18 Lenny Moore, Baltimore, 1963-65
LaDainian Tomlinson, San Diego, 2004-05

14 O.J. Simpson, Buffalo, 1975

13 John Riggins, Washington, 1982-83
George Rogers, Washington, 1985-86
Jerry Rice, San Francisco, 1986-87

POINTS AFTER TOUCHDOWN

Most Seasons Leading League

8 George Blanda, Chi. Bears, 1956; Houston,
1961-62; Oakland, 1967-69, 1972, 1974

4 Bob Waterfield, Cleveland, 1945; Los Angeles, 1946,
1950, 1952

3 Earl (Dutch) Clark, Portsmouth, 1932; Detroit,
1935-36 Jack Manders, Chi. Bears, 1933-35
Don Hutson, Green Bay, 1941-42, 1945

Most (Kicking) Points After Touchdown Attempted, Career

959 George Blanda, Chi. Bears, 1949, 1950-58; Baltimore,
1950; Houston, 1960-66; Oakland, 1967-1975

827 Gary Anderson, Pittsburgh, 1982-1994; Philadelphia
1995-96; San Francisco, 1997; Minnesota,
1998-2002; Tennessee, 2003-04

808 Morten Andersen, New Orleans, 1982-1994;
Atlanta, 1995-2000; N.Y. Giants, 2001;
Kansas City, 2002-03; Minnesota, 2004

Most (Kicking) Points After Touchdown Attempted, Season

70 Uwe von Schamann, Miami, 1984

65 George Blanda, Houston, 1961

64 Jeff Wilkins, St. Louis, 1999

Most (Kicking) Points After Touchdown Attempted, Game

10 Charlie Gogolak, Washington vs. N.Y. Giants,
Nov. 27, 1966

9 Pat Harder, Chi. Cardinals vs. N.Y. Giants,
Oct. 17, 1948; vs. N.Y. Bulldogs, Nov. 13, 1949
Bob Waterfield, Los Angeles vs. Baltimore,
Oct. 22, 1950
Bob Thomas, Chicago vs. Green Bay, Dec. 7, 1980

8 By many players

Most (One-Point) Points After Touchdown, Career

943 George Blanda, Chi. Bears, 1949, 1950-58; Baltimore,
1950; Houston, 1960-66; Oakland, 1967-1975

820 Gary Anderson, Pittsburgh, 1982-1994; Philadelphia
1995-96; San Francisco, 1997; Minnesota,
1998-2002; Tennessee, 2003-04

798 Morten Andersen, New Orleans, 1982-1994; Atlanta,
1995-2000; N.Y. Giants, 2001; Kansas City,
2002-03; Minnesota, 2004

Most (One-Point) Points After Touchdown, Season

66 Uwe von Schamann, Miami, 1984

64 George Blanda, Houston, 1961
Jeff Wilkins, St. Louis, 1999

62 Mark Moseley, Washington, 1983

Most (One-Point) Points After Touchdown, Game

9 Pat Harder, Chi. Cardinals vs. N.Y. Giants,
Oct. 17, 1948
Bob Waterfield, Los Angeles vs. Baltimore,
Oct. 22, 1950
Charlie Gogolak, Washington vs. N.Y. Giants,
Nov. 27, 1966

8 By many players

Most Consecutive (Kicking) Points After Touchdown

371 Jason Elam, Denver, 1993-2002

311 Jeff Wilkins, St. Louis, 1999-2005 (current)

301 Norm Johnson, Atlanta, 1991-94; Pittsburgh,
1995-98; Philadelphia, 1999

**Highest (Kicking) Points After Touchdown Percentage, Career
(200 points after touchdown)**

99.44 Jason Elam, Denver, 1993-2005 (534-537)

99.43 Tommy Davis, San Francisco, 1959-1969 (350-348)

99.42 Mike Vanderjagt, Indianapolis, 1998-2005 (344-346)

Most (Kicking) Points After Touchdown, No Misses, Season

64 Jeff Wilkins, St. Louis, 1999

59 Gary Anderson, Minnesota, 1998

58 Jason Elam, Denver, 1998
Jeff Wilkins, St. Louis, 2001

Most (Kicking) Points After Touchdown, No Misses, Game

9 Pat Harder, Chi. Cardinals vs. N.Y. Giants,
Oct. 17, 1948
Bob Waterfield, Los Angeles vs. Baltimore,
Oct. 22, 1950

8 By many players

Most Two-Point Conversions, Career

Two-point conversions include AFL (1960-69) and NFL (since 1994).

- 7 Marshall Faulk, Indianapolis, 1994-98; St. Louis, 1999-2005
- 6 Terance Mathis, Atlanta, 1994-2001; Pittsburgh, 2002
- 5 Cris Carter, Minnesota, 1994-2001; Miami, 2002
  - Rob Moore, N.Y. Jets, 1994; Arizona, 1995-99
  - Willie Jackson, Jacksonville, 1995-97; Cincinnati, 1998-99; New Orleans, 2000-01; Washington, 2002
  - Keenan McCardell, Cleveland, 1994-95; Jacksonville, 1996-2001; Tampa Bay, 2002-03; San Diego, 2004-05
  - Marvin Harrison, Indianapolis, 1996-2005
  - Marcus Pollard, Indianapolis, 1995-2004; Detroit, 2005
  - Todd Heap, Baltimore, 2001-05

Most Two-Point Conversions, Season

- 4 Todd Heap, Baltimore, 2003
- 3 Gino Cappelletti, Boston, 1960
  - Richie Lucas, Buffalo, 1961
  - Ronnie Harmon, San Diego, 1994
  - Haywood Jeffires, Houston, 1994
  - Tom Tupa, Cleveland, 1994
  - Terance Mathis, Atlanta, 1995
  - Lamar Smith, Seattle, 1996
  - Cris Carter, Minnesota, 1997
  - Terrell Davis, Denver, 1997
  - James Stewart, Detroit, 2000
  - Hines Ward, Pittsburgh, 2002
  - Brian Finneran, Atlanta, 2005
- 2 By many players

Most Two-Point Conversions, Game

- 2 Brett Perriman, Detroit vs. Green Bay, Nov. 6, 1994
  - Michael Jackson, Baltimore vs. New England, Oct. 6, 1996
  - Terrell Davis, Denver vs. Atlanta, Sept. 28, 1997
  - Charles Johnson, Pittsburgh vs. Tennessee, Nov. 1, 1998
  - Marshall Faulk, St. Louis vs. Atlanta, Oct. 15, 2000
  - Todd Heap, Baltimore vs. Cincinnati, Oct. 19, 2003

FIELD GOALS

Most Seasons Leading League

- 5 Lou Groza, Cleveland, 1950, 1952-54, 1957
- 4 Jack Manders, Chi. Bears, 1933-34, 1936-37
  - Ward Cuff, N.Y. Giants, 1938-39, 1943; Green Bay, 1947
  - Mark Moseley, Washington, 1976-77, 1979, 1982
- 3 Bob Waterfield, Los Angeles, 1947, 1949, 1951
  - Gino Cappelletti, Boston, 1961, 1963-64
  - Fred Cox, Minnesota, 1965, 1969-1970
  - Jan Stenerud, Kansas City, 1967, 1970, 1975

Most Consecutive Seasons Leading League

- 3 Lou Groza, Cleveland, 1952-54
- 2 Jack Manders, Chi. Bears, 1933-34
  - Armand Niccolai, Pittsburgh, 1935-36
  - Jack Manders, Chi. Bears, 1936-37
  - Ward Cuff, N.Y. Giants, 1938-39
  - Clark Hinkle, Green Bay, 1940-41
  - Cliff Patton, Philadelphia, 1948-49
  - Gino Cappelletti, Boston, 1963-64
  - Jim Turner, N.Y. Jets, 1968-69
  - Fred Cox, Minnesota, 1969-1970
  - Mark Moseley, Washington, 1976-77
  - Chip Lohmiller, Washington, 1991-92
  - Pete Stoyanovich, Miami, 1991-92

Most Field Goals Attempted, Career

- 672 Gary Anderson, Pittsburgh, 1982-1994; Philadelphia 1995-96; San Francisco, 1997; Minnesota,
  - 1998-2002; Tennessee, 2003-04
- 658 Morten Andersen, New Orleans, 1982-1994; Atlanta, 1995-2000; N.Y. Giants, 2001; Kansas City, 2002-03; Minnesota, 2004
- 637 George Blanda, Chi. Bears, 1949, 1950-58; Baltimore, 1950; Houston, 1960-66; Oakland, 1967-1975

Most Field Goals Attempted, Season

- 49 Bruce Gossett, Los Angeles, 1966
  - Curt Knight, Washington, 1971
- 48 Chester Marcol, Green Bay, 1972
- 47 Jim Turner, N.Y. Jets, 1969
  - David Ray, Los Angeles, 1973
  - Mark Moseley, Washington, 1983

Most Field Goals Attempted, Game

- 9 Jim Bakken, St. Louis vs. Pittsburgh, Sept. 24, 1967
- 8 Lou Michaels, Pittsburgh vs. St. Louis, Dec. 2, 1962
  - Garo Yepremian, Detroit vs. Minnesota, Nov. 13, 1966
  - Jim Turner, N.Y. Jets vs. Buffalo, Nov. 3, 1968
  - Billy Cundiff, Dallas vs. N.Y. Giants, Sept. 15, 2003 (OT)
- 7 By many players

Most Field Goals, Career

- 538 Gary Anderson, Pittsburgh, 1982-1994; Philadelphia, 1995-96; San Francisco, 1997; Minnesota, 1998-2002; Tennessee, 2003-04
- 520 Morten Andersen, New Orleans, 1982-1994; Atlanta, 1995-2000; N.Y. Giants, 2001; Kansas City, 2002-03; Minnesota, 2004
- 390 John Carney, Tampa Bay, 1988-89; L.A. Rams, 1990; San Diego, 1990-2000; New Orleans, 2001-05

Most Field Goals, Season

- 40 Neil Rackers, Arizona, 2005
- 39 Olindo Mare, Miami, 1999
  - Jeff Wilkins, St. Louis, 2003
- 37 John Kasay, Carolina, 1996
  - Mike Vanderjagt, Indianapolis, 2003

Most Field Goals, Rookie, Season

- 35 Ali Haji-Sheikh, N.Y. Giants, 1983
- 34 Richie Cunningham, Dallas, 1997
- 33 Chester Marcol, Green Bay, 1972

Most Field Goals, Game

- 7 Jim Bakken, St. Louis vs. Pittsburgh, Sept. 24, 1967
  - Rich Karlis, Minnesota vs. L.A. Rams, Nov. 5, 1989 (OT)
  - Chris Boniol, Dallas vs. Green Bay, Nov. 18, 1996
  - Billy Cundiff, Dallas vs. N.Y. Giants, Sept. 15, 2003 (OT)
- 6 Gino Cappelletti, Boston vs. Denver, Oct. 4, 1964
  - Garo Yepremian, Detroit vs. Minnesota, Nov. 13, 1966
  - Jim Turner, N.Y. Jets vs. Buffalo, Nov. 3, 1968
  - Tom Dempsey, Philadelphia vs. Houston, Nov. 12, 1972
  - Bobby Howfield, N.Y. Jets vs. New Orleans, Dec. 3, 1972
  - Jim Bakken, St. Louis vs. Atlanta, Dec. 9, 1973
  - Joe Danelo, N.Y. Giants vs. Seattle, Oct. 18, 1981
  - Ray Wersching, San Francisco vs. New Orleans, Oct. 16, 1983
  - Gary Anderson, Pittsburgh vs. Denver, Oct. 23, 1988
  - John Carney, San Diego vs. Seattle, Sept. 5, 1993
  - John Carney, San Diego vs. Houston, Sept. 19, 1993
  - Doug Pelfrey, Cincinnati vs. Seattle, Nov. 6, 1994 (OT)
  - Norm Johnson, Atlanta vs. New Orleans, Nov. 13, 1994
  - Jeff Wilkins, San Francisco vs. Atlanta, Sept. 29, 1996
  - Steve Christie, Buffalo vs. N.Y. Jets, Oct. 20, 1996
  - Greg Davis, San Diego vs. Oakland, Oct. 5, 1997
  - Gary Anderson, Minnesota vs. Baltimore, Dec. 13, 1998
  - Olindo Mare, Miami vs. New England, Oct. 17, 1999
  - Jason Hanson, Detroit vs. Minnesota, Oct. 17, 1999
  - Jeff Reed, Pittsburgh vs. Jacksonville, Dec. 1, 2002

John Kasay, Carolina vs. New Orleans, Dec. 5, 2004
Neil Rackers, Arizona vs. San Francisco,
Oct. 2, 2005
5 By many players

Most Field Goals, One Quarter
4 Garo Yepremian, Detroit vs. Minnesota, Nov. 13, 1966
(second quarter)
Curt Knight, Washington vs. N.Y. Giants, Nov. 15, 1970
(second quarter)
Roger Ruzek, Dallas vs. N.Y. Giants, Nov. 2, 1987
(fourth quarter)
Cary Blanchard, Indianapolis vs. Buffalo,
Sept. 21 1997 (second quarter)
Sebastian Janikowski, Oakland vs. Chicago,
Oct. 5, 2003 (second quarter)
Jeff Wilkins, St. Louis vs. Baltimore, Nov. 9, 2003
(fourth quarter)
Lawrence Tynes, Kansas City vs. New England,
Nov. 27, 2005 (second quarter)
3 By many players

Most Consecutive Games Scoring Field Goals
38 Matt Stover, Baltimore, 1999-2001
31 Fred Cox, Minnesota, 1968-1970
28 Jim Turner, N.Y. Jets, 1970; Denver, 1971-72
Chip Lohmiller, Washington, 1988-1990

Most Consecutive Field Goals
42 Mike Vanderjagt, Indianapolis, 2002-04
40 Gary Anderson, San Francisco, 1997; Minnesota,
1998
31 Fuad Reveiz, Minnesota, 1994-95
Neil Rackers, Arizona, 2005

Longest Field Goal
63 Tom Dempsey, New Orleans vs. Detroit, Nov. 8, 1970
Jason Elam, Denver vs. Jacksonville, Oct. 25, 1998
60 Steve Cox, Cleveland vs. Cincinnati, Oct. 21, 1984
Morten Andersen, New Orleans vs. Chicago,
Oct. 27, 1991
59 Tony Franklin, Philadelphia vs. Dallas, Nov. 12, 1979
Pete Stoyanovich, Miami vs. N.Y. Jets, Nov. 12, 1989
Steve Christie, Buffalo vs. Miami, Sept. 26, 1993
Morten Andersen, Atlanta vs. San Francisco,
Dec. 24, 1995

Highest Field Goal Percentage, Career (100 field goals)
87.50 Mike Vanderjagt, Indianapolis, 1998-2005 (217-248)
83.85 Phil Dawson, Cleveland, 1999-2005 (135-161)
83.15 Matt Stover, Cleveland, 1991-95; Baltimore,
1996-2005 (380-457)

Highest Field Goal Percentage, Season (Qualifiers)
100.00 Tony Zendejas, L.A. Rams, 1991 (17-17)
Gary Anderson, Minnesota, 1998 (35-35)
Jeff Wilkins, St. Louis, 2000 (17-17)
Mike Vanderjagt, Indianapolis, 2003 (37-37)
96.43 Chris Boniol, Dallas, 1995 (28-27)
96.30 Norm Johnson, Atlanta, 1993 (27-26)
Pete Stoyanovich, Kansas City, 1997 (27-26)

Most Field Goals, No Misses, Game
7 Rich Karlis, Minnesota vs. L.A. Rams, Nov. 5, 1989
(OT)
Chris Boniol, Dallas vs. Green Bay, Nov. 18, 1996
6 Gino Cappelletti, Boston vs. Denver, Oct. 4, 1964
Joe Danelo, N.Y. Giants vs. Seattle, Oct. 18, 1981
Ray Wersching, San Francisco vs. New Orleans,
Oct. 16, 1983
Gary Anderson, Pittsburgh vs. Denver, Oct. 23, 1988
John Carney, San Diego vs. Seattle, Sept. 5, 1993
John Carney, San Diego vs. Houston, Sept. 19, 1993
Doug Pelfrey, Cincinnati vs. Seattle, Nov. G, 1994 (OT)
Norm Johnson, Atlanta vs. New Orleans,
Nov. 13, 1994

Jeff Wilkins, San Francisco vs. Atlanta,
Sept. 29, 1996
Greg Davis, San Diego vs. Oakland, Oct. 5, 1997
Gary Anderson, Minnesota vs. Baltimore,
Dec. 13, 1998
Olindo Mare, Miami vs. New England, Oct. 17, 1999
Jeff Reed, Pittsburgh vs. Jacksonville, Dec. 1, 2002
John Kasay, Carolina vs. New Orleans, Dec. 5, 2004
Neil Rackers, Arizona vs. San Francisco,
Oct. 2, 2005
5 By many players

Most Field Goals, 50 or More Yards, Career
40 Morten Andersen, New Orleans, 1982-1994;
Atlanta, 1995-2000; N.Y. Giants, 2001;
Kansas City, 2002-03; Minnesota, 2004
35 Jason Elam, Denver, 1993-2005
29 John Kasay, Seattle, 1991-94; Carolina, 1995-2005

Most Field Goals, 50 or More Yards, Season
8 Morten Andersen, Atlanta, 1995
6 Dean Biasucci, Indianapolis, 1988
Chris Jacke, Green Bay, 1993
Tony Zendejas, L.A. Rams, 1993
Mike Vanderjagt, Indianapolis, 1998
Neil Rackers, Arizona, 2005
5 Fred Steinfort, Denver, 1980
Norm Johnson, Seattle, 1986
Kevin Butler, Chicago, 1993
Jason Elam, Denver, 1995
Cary Blanchard, Indianapolis, 1996
Jason Elam, Denver, 1999
Martín Gramatica, Tampa Bay, 2000, 2002
Paul Edinger, Chicago, 2002
Neil Rackers, Arizona, 2004
Josh Brown, Seattle, 2005

Most Field Goals, 50 or More Yards, Game
3 Morten Andersen, Atlanta vs. New Orleans,
Dec. 10, 1995
Neil Rackers, Arizona vs. Seattle, Oct. 24, 2004
2 By many players. Last time: Jeff Wilkins,
St. Louis, vs. San Francisco, Dec. 24, 2005

SAFETIES
Most Safeties, Career
4 Ted Hendricks, Baltimore, 1969-1973; Green Bay,
1974; Oakland, 1975-1981; L.A. Raiders, 1982-83
Doug English, Detroit, 1975-79, 1981-85
3 Bill McPeak, Pittsburgh, 1949-1957
Charlie Krueger, San Francisco, 1959-1973
Ernie Stautner, Pittsburgh, 1950-1963
Jim Katcavage, N.Y. Giants, 1956-1968
Roger Brown, Detroit, 1960-66; Los Angeles,
1967-69
Bruce Maher, Detroit, 1960-67; N.Y. Giants, 1968-69
Ron McDole, St. Louis, 1961; Houston, 1962;
Buffalo, 1963-1970; Washington, 1971-78
Alan Page, Minnesota, 1967-1978; Chicago,
1979-1981
Lyle Alzado, Denver, 1971-78; Cleveland,
1979-1981; L.A. Raiders, 1982-85
Rulon Jones, Denver, 1980-88
Steve McMichael, New England, 1980; Chicago,
1981-1993; Green Bay, 1994
Kevin Greene, L.A. Rams, 1985-1992; Pittsburgh,
1993-95; Carolina, 1996, 1998-99;
San Francisco, 1997
Burt Grossman, San Diego, 1989-1993;
Philadelphia, 1994
Eric Swann, Phoenix, 1991-93; Arizona, 1994-99;
Carolina, 2000

Dan Saleaumua, Detroit, 1987-88; Kansas City,
  1989-1996; Seattle, 1997-98
Derrick Thomas, Kansas City, 1989-1999
Bryant Young, San Francisco, 1994-2005
2 By many players

Most Safeties, Season
2 Tom Nash, Green Bay, 1932
    Roger Brown, Detroit, 1962
    Ron McDole, Buffalo, 1964
    Alan Page, Minnesota, 1971
    Fred Dryer, Los Angeles, 1973
    Benny Barnes, Dallas, 1973
    James Young, Houston, 1977
    Doug English, Detroit, 1983
    Don Blackmon, New England, 1985
    Tim Harris, Green Bay, 1988
    Brian Jordan, Atlanta, 1991
    Burt Grossman, San Diego, 1992
    Rod Stephens, Seattle, 1993
    Bryant Young, San Francisco, 1996

Most Safeties, Game
2 Fred Dryer, Los Angeles vs. Green Bay,
    Oct. 21, 1973

RUSHING

Most Seasons Leading League
8 Jim Brown, Cleveland, 1957-1961, 1963-65
4 Steve Van Buren, Philadelphia, 1945, 1947-49
    O.J. Simpson, Buffalo, 1972-73; 1975-76
    Eric Dickerson, L.A. Rams, 1983-84; 1986;
      Indianapolis, 1988
    Emmitt Smith, Dallas, 1991-93, 1995
    Barry Sanders, Detroit, 1990, 1994, 1996-97
3 Earl Campbell, Houston, 1978-1980

Most Consecutive Seasons Leading League
5 Jim Brown, Cleveland, 1957-1961
3 Steve Van Buren, Philadelphia, 1947-49
    Jim Brown, Cleveland, 1963-65
    Earl Campbell, Houston, 1978-1980
    Emmitt Smith, Dallas, 1991-93
2 Bill Paschal, N.Y. Giants, 1943-44
    Joe Perry, San Francisco, 1953-54
    Jim Nance, Boston, 1966-67
    Leroy Kelly, Cleveland, 1967-68
    O.J. Simpson, Buffalo, 1972-73; 1975-76
    Eric Dickerson, L.A. Rams, 1983-84
    Barry Sanders, Detroit, 1996-97
    Edgerrin James, Indianapolis, 1999-2000

ATTEMPTS

Most Seasons Leading League
6 Jim Brown, Cleveland, 1958-59, 1961, 1963-65
4 Steve Van Buren, Philadelphia, 1947-1950
    Walter Payton, Chicago, 1976-79
3 Cookie Gilchrist, Buffalo, 1963-64; Denver, 1965
    Jim Nance, Boston, 1966-67, 1969
    O.J. Simpson, Buffalo, 1973-75
    Eric Dickerson, L.A. Rams, 1983, 1986;
      Indianapolis, 1988
    Emmitt Smith, Dallas, 1991, 1994-95

Most Consecutive Seasons Leading League
4 Steve Van Buren, Philadelphia, 1947-1950
    Walter Payton, Chicago, 1976-79
3 Jim Brown, Cleveland, 1963-65
    Cookie Gilchrist, Buffalo, 1963-64; Denver, 1965
    O.J. Simpson, Buffalo, 1973-75
2 By many players

Most Attempts, Career
4,409 Emmitt Smith, Dallas, 1990-2002; Arizona, 2003-04
3,838 Walter Payton, Chicago, 1975-1987

3,518 Curtis Martin, New England, 1995-97; N.Y. Jets,
      1998-2005

Most Attempts, Season
410 Jamal Anderson, Atlanta, 1998
407 James Wilder, Tampa Bay, 1984
404 Eric Dickerson, L.A. Rams, 1986

Most Attempts, Rookie, Season
390 Eric Dickerson, L.A. Rams, 1983
378 George Rogers, New Orleans, 1981
369 Edgerrin James, Indianapolis, 1999

Most Attempts, Game
45 Jamie Morris, Washington vs. Cincinnati,
    Dec. 17, 1988 (OT)
43 Butch Woolfolk, N.Y. Giants vs. Philadelphia,
    Nov. 20, 1983
    James Wilder, Tampa Bay vs. Green Bay,
    Sept. 30, 1984 (OT)
    Rudi Johnson, Cincinnati vs. Houston, Nov. 9, 2003
42 James Wilder, Tampa Bay vs. Pittsburgh,
    Oct. 30, 1983
    Terrell Davis, Denver vs. Buffalo, Oct. 26, 1997 (OT)
    Ricky Williams, Miami vs. Buffalo, Sept. 21, 2003

YARDS GAINED

Most Yards Gained, Career
18,355 Emmitt Smith, Dallas, 1990-2002; Arizona, 2003-04
16,726 Walter Payton, Chicago, 1975-1987
15,269 Barry Sanders, Detroit, 1989-1998

Most Seasons, 1,000 or More Yards Rushing
11 Emmitt Smith, Dallas, 1991-2001
10 Walter Payton, Chicago, 1976-1981, 1983-86
    Barry Sanders, Detroit, 1989-1998
    Curtis Martin, New England, 1995-97; N.Y. Jets,
      1998-2004
8 Franco Harris, Pittsburgh, 1972, 1974-79, 1983
    Tony Dorsett, Dallas, 1977-1981, 1983-85
    Thurman Thomas, Buffalo, 1989-1996
    Jerome Bettis, L.A. Rams, 1993-94; Pittsburgh,
      1996-2001

Most Consecutive Seasons, 1,000 or More Yards Rushing
11 Emmitt Smith, Dallas, 1991-2001
10 Barry Sanders, Detroit, 1989-1998
    Curtis Martin, New England, 1995-97; N.Y. Jets,
      1998-2004
8 Thurman Thomas, Buffalo, 1989-1996

Most Yards Gained, Season
2,105 Eric Dickerson, L.A. Rams, 1984
2,066 Jamal Lewis, Baltimore, 2003
2,053 Barry Sanders, Detroit, 1997

Most Yards Gained, Rookie, Season
1,808 Eric Dickerson, L.A. Rams, 1983
1,674 George Rogers, New Orleans, 1981
1,605 Ottis Anderson, St. Louis, 1979

Most Yards Gained, Game
295 Jamal Lewis, Baltimore vs. Cleveland, Sept. 14, 2003
278 Corey Dillon, Cincinnati vs. Denver, Oct. 22, 2000
275 Walter Payton, Chicago vs. Minnesota,
    Nov. 20, 1977

Most Games, 200 or More Yards Rushing, Career
6 O.J. Simpson, Buffalo, 1969-1977; San Francisco,
    1978-79
4 Jim Brown, Cleveland, 1957-1965
    Earl Campbell, Houston, 1978-1984; New Orleans,
      1984-85
    Barry Sanders, Detroit, 1989-1998
    LaDainian Tomlinson, San Diego, 2001-05
    Tiki Barber, N.Y. Giants, 1997-2005
3 Eric Dickerson, L.A. Rams, 1983-87; Indianapolis,
    1987-1991; L.A. Raiders, 1992; Atlanta, 1993

Greg Bell, Buffalo, 1984-87; L.A. Rams, 1987-89;
L.A. Raiders, 1990
Terrell Davis, Denver, 1995-2001
Corey Dillon, Cincinnati, 1997-2003; New England,
2004-05
Marshall Faulk, Indianapolis, 1994-98; St. Louis,
1999-2005

Most Games, 200 or More Yards Rushing, Season
4   Earl Campbell, Houston, 1980
3   O.J. Simpson, Buffalo, 1973
    Tiki Barber, N.Y. Giants, 2005
2   Jim Brown, Cleveland, 1963
    O.J. Simpson, Buffalo, 1976
    Walter Payton, Chicago, 1977
    Eric Dickerson, L.A. Rams, 1984
    Greg Bell, L.A. Rams, 1989
    Terrell Davis, Denver, 1997
    Barry Sanders, Detroit, 1997
    Corey Dillon, Cincinnati, 2000
    Marshall Faulk, St. Louis, 2000
    LaDainian Tomlinson, San Diego, 2002
    Ricky Williams, Miami, 2002
    Jamal Lewis, Baltimore, 2003
    LaDainian Tomlinson, San Diego, 2003
    Larry Johnson, Kansas City, 2005

Most Consecutive Games, 200 or More Yards Rushing
2   O.J. Simpson, Buffalo, 1973, 1976
    Earl Campbell, Houston, 1980
    Ricky Williams, Miami, 2002

Most Games, 100 or More Yards Rushing, Career
78   Emmitt Smith, Dallas, 1990-2002; Arizona, 2003-04
77   Walter Payton, Chicago, 1975-1987
76   Barry Sanders, Detroit, 1989-1998

Most Games, 100 or More Yards Rushing, Season
14   Barry Sanders, Detroit, 1997
12   Eric Dickerson, L.A. Rams, 1984
     Barry Foster, Pittsburgh, 1992
     Jamal Anderson, Atlanta, 1998
     Jamal Lewis, Baltimore, 2003
11   O.J. Simpson, Buffalo, 1973
     Earl Campbell, Houston, 1979
     Marcus Allen, L.A. Raiders, 1985
     Eric Dickerson, L.A. Rams, 1986
     Emmitt Smith, Dallas, 1995
     Terrell Davis, Denver, 1998
     Shaun Alexander, Seattle, 2005

Most Consecutive Games, 100 or More Yards Rushing
14   Barry Sanders, Detroit, 1997
11   Marcus Allen, L.A. Raiders, 1985-86
9   Walter Payton, Chicago, 1985
     Fred Taylor, Jacksonville, 2000
     Deuce McAllister, New Orleans, 2003
     Larry Johnson, Kansas City, 2005

Longest Run From Scrimmage
99   Tony Dorsett, Dallas vs. Minnesota, Jan. 3, 1983
     (TD)
98   Ahman Green, Green Bay vs. Denver, Dec. 28, 2003
     (TD)
97   Andy Uram, Green Bay vs. Chi. Cardinals,
     Oct. 8, 1939 (TD)
     Bob Gage, Pittsburgh vs. Chi. Bears, Dec. 4, 1949
     (TD)

AVERAGE GAIN
Highest Average Gain, Career (750 attempts)
6.36   Randall Cunningham, Philadelphia, 1985-1995;
       Minnesota, 1997-99; Dallas, 2000; Baltimore,
       2001 (775-4,928)
5.22   Jim Brown, Cleveland, 1957-1965 (2,359-12,312)

5.14   Eugene (Mercury) Morris, Miami, 1969-1975;
       San Diego, 1976 (804-4,133)
Highest Average Gain, Season (Qualifiers)
8.44   Beattie Feathers, Chi. Bears, 1934 (119-1,004)
7.98   Randall Cunningham, Philadelphia, 1990 (118-942)
7.52   Michael Vick, Atlanta, 2004 (120-902)
Highest Average Gain, Game (10 attempts)
17.30   Michael Vick, Atlanta vs. Minnesota, Dec. 1, 2002
        (OT) (10-173)
17.09   Marion Motley, Cleveland vs. Pittsburgh,
        Oct. 29, 1950 (11-188)
16.70   Bill Grimes, Green Bay vs. N.Y. Yanks, Oct. 8, 1950
        (10-167)

TOUCHDOWNS
Most Seasons Leading League
5   Jim Brown, Cleveland, 1957-59, 1963, 1965
4   Steve Van Buren, Philadelphia, 1945, 1947-49
3   Abner Haynes, Dall. Texans, 1960-62
    Cookie Gilchrist, Buffalo, 1962-64
    Paul Lowe, L.A. Chargers, 1960; San Diego, 1961,
    1965
    Leroy Kelly, Cleveland, 1966-68
    Emmitt Smith, Dallas, 1992, 1994-95

Most Consecutive Seasons Leading League
3   Steve Van Buren, Philadelphia, 1947-49
    Jim Brown, Cleveland, 1957-59
    Abner Haynes, Dall. Texans, 1960-62
    Cookie Gilchrist, Buffalo, 1962-64
    Leroy Kelly, Cleveland, 1966-68

Most Touchdowns, Career
164   Emmitt Smith, Dallas, 1990-2002; Arizona, 2003-04
123   Marcus Allen, L.A. Raiders, 1982-1992; Kansas City,
      1993-97
110   Walter Payton, Chicago, 1975-1987

Most Touchdowns, Season
27   Priest Holmes, Kansas City, 2003
     Shaun Alexander, Seattle, 2005
25   Emmitt Smith, Dallas, 1995
24   John Riggins, Washington, 1983

Most Touchdowns, Rookie, Season
18   Eric Dickerson, L.A. Rams, 1983
15   Ickey Woods, Cincinnati, 1988
     Mike Anderson, Denver, 2000
     Clinton Portis, Denver, 2002
14   Gale Sayers, Chicago, 1965
     Barry Sanders, Detroit, 1989
     Curtis Martin, New England, 1995
     Fred Taylor, Jacksonville, 1998

Most Touchdowns, Game
6   Ernie Nevers, Chi. Cardinals vs. Chi. Bears,
    Nov. 28, 1929
5   Jimmy Conzelman, Rhode Island vs. Evansville,
    Oct. 15, 1922
    Jim Brown, Cleveland vs. Baltimore, Nov. 1, 1959
    Cookie Gilchrist, Buffalo vs. N.Y. Jets, Dec. 8, 1963
    James Stewart, Jacksonville vs. Philadelphia,
    Oct. 12, 1997
    Clinton Portis, Denver vs. Kansas City, Dec. 7, 2003
4   By many players

Most Consecutive Games Rushing for Touchdowns
18   LaDainian Tomlinson, San Diego, 2004-05
13   John Riggins, Washington, 1982-83
     George Rogers, Washington, 1985-86
11   Lenny Moore, Baltimore, 1963-64
     Emmitt Smith, Dallas, 1994-95
     Emmitt Smith, Dallas, 1995
     Priest Holmes, Kansas City, 2002

PASSING

Most Seasons Leading League
- 6   Sammy Baugh, Washington, 1937, 1940, 1943,
   1945, 1947, 1949
   Steve Young San Francisco, 1991-94, 1996-97
- 4   Len Dawson, Dall. Texans; 1962; Kansas City, 1964,
   1966, 1968
   Roger Staubach, Dallas, 1971, 1973, 1978-79
   Ken Anderson, Cincinnati, 1974-75, 1981-82
- 3   Arnie Herber, Green Bay, 1932, 1934, 1936
   Norm Van Brocklin, Los Angeles, 1950, 1952, 1954
   Bart Starr, Green Bay, 1962, 1964, 1966

Most Consecutive Seasons Leading League
- 4   Steve Young, San Francisco, 1991-94
- 2   Cecil Isbell, Green Bay, 1941-42
   Milt Plum, Cleveland, 1960-61
   Ken Anderson, Cincinnati, 1974-75, 1981-82
   Roger Staubach, Dallas, 1978-79
   Steve Young, San Francisco, 1996-97
   Peyton Manning, Indianapolis, 2004-05

PASSER RATING

Highest Passer Rating, Career (1,500 attempts)
- 96.8   Steve Young, Tampa Bay, 1985-86; San Francisco,
   1987-1999
- 94.1   Kurt Warner, St. Louis, 1998-2003; N.Y. Giants,
   2004, Arizona, 2005
- 93.5   Peyton Manning, Indianapolis, 1998-2005

Highest Passer Rating, Season (Qualifiers)
- 121.1   Peyton Manning, Indianapolis, 2004
- 112.8   Steve Young, San Francisco, 1994
- 112.4   Joe Montana, San Francisco, 1989

Highest Passer Rating, Rookie, Season (Qualifiers)
- 98.1   Ben Roethlisberger, Pittsburgh, 2004
- 96.0   Dan Marino, Miami, 1983
- 88.2   Greg Cook, Cincinnati, 1969

ATTEMPTS

Most Seasons Leading League
- 5   Dan Marino, Miami, 1984, 1986, 1988, 1992, 1997
- 4   Sammy Baugh, Washington, 1937, 1943, 1947-48
   Johnny Unitas, Baltimore, 1957, 1959-1961
   George Blanda, Chi. Bears, 1953; Houston, 1963-65
- 3   Arnie Herber, Green Bay, 1932, 1934, 1936
   Sonny Jurgensen, Washington, 1966-67, 1969
   Drew Bledsoe, New England, 1994-96

Most Consecutive Seasons Leading League
- 3   Johnny Unitas, Baltimore, 1959-1961
   George Blanda, Houston, 1963-65
   Drew Bledsoe, New England, 1994-96
- 2   By many players

Most Passes Attempted, Career
- 8,358   Dan Marino, Miami, 1983-1999
- 7,610   Brett Favre, Atlanta, 1991; Green Bay, 1992-2005
- 7,250   John Elway, Denver, 1983-1998

Most Passes Attempted, Season
- 691   Drew Bledsoe, New England, 1994
- 655   Warren Moon, Houston, 1991
- 636   Drew Bledsoe, New England, 1995

Most Passes Attempted, Rookie, Season
- 575   Peyton Manning, Indianapolis, 1998
- 540   Chris Weinke, Carolina, 2001
- 486   Rick Mirer, Seattle, 1993

Most Passes Attempted, Game
- 70   Drew Bledsoe, New England vs. Minnesota, Nov. 13,
   1994 (OT)
- 69   Vinny Testaverde, N.Y. Jets vs. Baltimore, Dec. 24,
   2000
- 68   George Blanda, Houston vs. Buffalo, Nov. 1, 1964

Jon Kitna, Cincinnati vs. Pittsburgh, Dec. 30, 2001
(OT)

COMPLETIONS

Most Seasons Leading League
- 6   Dan Marino, Miami, 1984-86, 1988, 1992, 1997
- 5   Sammy Baugh, Washington, 1937, 1943, 1945,
   1947-48
- 4   George Blanda, Chi. Bears, 1953; Houston, 1963-65
   Sonny Jurgensen, Philadelphia, 1961; Washington,
   1966-67, 1969

Most Consecutive Seasons Leading League
- 3   George Blanda, Houston, 1963-65
   Dan Marino, Miami, 1984-86
- 2   By many players

Most Passes Completed, Career
- 4,967   Dan Marino, Miami, 1983-1999
- 4,678   Brett Favre, Atlanta, 1991; Green Bay, 1992-2005
- 4,123   John Elway, Denver, 1983-1998

Most Passes Completed, Season
- 418   Rich Gannon, Oakland, 2002
- 404   Warren Moon, Houston, 1991
- 400   Drew Bledsoe, New England, 1994

Most Passes Completed, Rookie, Season
- 326   Peyton Manning, Indianapolis, 1998
- 293   Chris Weinke, Carolina, 2001
- 274   Rick Mirer, Seattle, 1993

Most Passes Completed, Game
- 45   Drew Bledsoe, New England vs. Minnesota,
   Nov. 13, 1994 (OT)
- 43   Rich Gannon, Oakland vs. Pittsburgh, Sept. 15, 2002
- 42   Richard Todd, N.Y. Jets vs. San Francisco,
   Sept. 21, 1980
   Vinny Testaverde, N.Y. Jets vs. Seattle, Dec. 6, 1998

Most Consecutive Passes Completed
- 24   Donovan McNabb, Philadelphia vs. N.Y. Giants (10),
   Nov. 28, 2004; vs. Green Bay (14),
   Dec. 5, 2004
- 22   Joe Montana, San Francisco vs. Cleveland (5),
   Nov. 29, 1987; vs. Green Bay (17), Dec. 6, 1987
- 21   Rich Gannon, Oakland vs. Denver, Nov. 11, 2002

COMPLETION PERCENTAGE

Most Seasons Leading League
- 8   Len Dawson, Dall. Texans, 1962; Kansas City,
   1964-69, 1975
- 7   Sammy Baugh, Washington, 1940, 1942-43, 1945,
   1947-49
- 5   Joe Montana, San Francisco, 1980-81, 1985, 1987,
   1989
   Steve Young, San Francisco, 1992, 1994-97

Most Consecutive Seasons Leading League
- 6   Len Dawson, Kansas City, 1964-69
- 4   Steve Young, San Francisco, 1994-97
- 3   Sammy Baugh, Washington, 1947-49
   Otto Graham, Cleveland, 1953-55
   Milt Plum, Cleveland, 1960-61
   Kurt Warner, St. Louis, 1999-2001

Highest Completion Percentage, Career (1,500 attempts)
- 65.68   Kurt Warner, St. Louis, 1998-2003; N.Y. Giants,
   2004, Arizona, 2005 (2,340-1,537)
- 65.02   Marc Bulger, St. Louis, 2002-05 (1,518-987)
- 64.37   Daunte Culpepper, Minnesota, 1999-2005
   (2,607-1,678)

Highest Completion Percentage, Season (Qualifiers)
- 70.55   Ken Anderson, Cincinnati, 1982 (309-218)
- 70.33   Sammy Baugh, Washington, 1945 (182-128)
- 70.28   Steve Young, San Francisco, 1994 (461-324)

Highest Completion Percentage, Rookie, Season (Qualifiers)
- 66.44   Ben Roethlisberger, Pittsburgh, 2004 (295-196)

58.45   Dan Marino, Miami, 1983 (296-173)
57.18   Byron Leftwich, Jacksonville, 2003 (418-239)

Highest Completion Percentage, Game (20 attempts)
91.30   Vinny Testaverde, Cleveland vs. L.A. Rams,
           Dec. 26, 1993 (23-21)
90.91   Ken Anderson, Cincinnati vs. Pittsburgh,
           Nov. 10, 1974 (22-20)
90.48   Lynn Dickey, Green Bay vs. New Orleans,
           Dec. 13, 1981 (21-19)

YARDS GAINED

Most Seasons Leading League
5   Sonny Jurgensen, Philadelphia, 1961-62;
      Washington, 1966-67, 1969
      Dan Marino, Miami, 1984-86, 1988, 1992
4   Sammy Baugh, Washington, 1937, 1940, 1947-48
      Johnny Unitas, Baltimore, 1957, 1959-1960, 1963
      Dan Fouts, San Diego, 1979-1982
3   Arnie Herber, Green Bay, 1932, 1934, 1936
      Sid Luckman, Chi. Bears, 1943, 1945-46
      John Brodie, San Francisco, 1965, 1968, 1970
      John Hadl, San Diego, 1965, 1968, 1971
      Joe Namath, N.Y. Jets, 1966-67, 1972

Most Consecutive Seasons Leading League
4   Dan Fouts, San Diego, 1979-1982
3   Dan Marino, Miami, 1984-86
2   By many players

Most Yards Gained, Career
61,361   Dan Marino, Miami, 1983-1999
53,615   Brett Favre, Atlanta, 1991; Green Bay, 1992-2005
51,475   John Elway, Denver, 1983-1998

Most Seasons, 3,000 or More Yards Passing
14   Brett Favre, Green Bay, 1992-2005
13   Dan Marino, Miami, 1984-1992, 1994-95, 1997-98
12   John Elway, Denver, 1985-1991, 1993-97

Most Yards Gained, Season
5,084   Dan Marino, Miami, 1984
4,830   Kurt Warner, St. Louis, 2001
4,802   Dan Fouts, San Diego, 1981

Most Yards Gained, Rookie, Season
3,739   Peyton Manning, Indianapolis, 1998
2,931   Chris Weinke, Carolina, 2001
2,833   Rick Mirer, Seattle, 1993

Most Yards Gained, Game
554   Norm Van Brocklin, Los Angeles vs. N.Y. Yanks,
       Sept. 28, 1951
527   Warren Moon, Houston vs. Kansas City,
       Dec. 16, 1990
522   Boomer Esiason, Arizona vs. Washington,
       Nov. 10, 1996

Most Games, 400 or More Yards Passing, Career
13   Dan Marino, Miami, 1983-1999
7   Joe Montana, San Francisco, 1979-1990, 1992;
     Kansas City, 1993-94
     Warren Moon, Houston, 1984-1993; Minnesota,
     1994-96; Seattle, 1997-98; Kansas City,
     1999-2000
6   Dan Fouts, San Diego, 1973-1987
     Drew Bledsoe, New England, 1993-2001; Buffalo,
     2002-03
     Peyton Manning, Indianapolis, 1998-2005

Most Games, 400 or More Yards Passing, Season
4   Dan Marino, Miami, 1984
3   Dan Marino, Miami, 1986
2   By many players

Most Consecutive Games, 400 or More Yards Passing
2   Dan Fouts, San Diego, 1982
     Dan Marino, Miami, 1984
     Phil Simms, N.Y. Giants, 1985
     Billy Volek, Tennessee, 2004

Most Games, 300 or More Yards Passing, Career
63   Dan Marino, Miami, 1983-1999
51   Dan Fouts, San Diego, 1973-1987
49   Warren Moon, Houston, 1984-1993; Minnesota,
     1994-96; Seattle, 1997-98; Kansas City,
     1999-2000

Most Games, 300 or More Yards Passing, Season
10   Rich Gannon, Oakland, 2002
9   Dan Marino, Miami, 1984
    Warren Moon, Houston, 1990
    Kurt Warner, St. Louis, 1999
    Kurt Warner, St. Louis, 2001
8   Dan Fouts, San Diego, 1980
    Kurt Warner, St. Louis, 2000
    Trent Green, Kansas City, 2004

Most Consecutive Games, 300 or More Yards Passing
6   Steve Young, San Francisco, 1998
    Kurt Warner, St. Louis, 2000
    Rich Gannon, Oakland, 2002
5   Joe Montana, San Francisco, 1982
    Kerry Collins, N.Y. Giants, 2001-02
4   Dan Fouts, San Diego, 1979
    Dan Fouts, San Diego, 1980-81
    Bill Kenney, Kansas City, 1983
    Joe Montana, San Francisco, 1985-86
    Joe Montana, San Francisco, 1990
    Warren Moon, Houston, 1990
    Drew Bledsoe, New England, 1993-94
    Kurt Warner, St. Louis, 1999
    Brian Griese, Denver, 2000
    Daunte Culpepper, Minnesota, 2004
    Trent Green, Kansas City, 2004

Longest Pass Completion (All TDs except as noted)
99   Frank Filchock (to Farkas), Washington vs.
     Pittsburgh, Oct. 15, 1939
     George Izo (to Mitchell), Washington vs. Cleveland,
     Sept. 15, 1963
     Karl Sweetan (to Studstill), Detroit vs. Baltimore,
     Oct. 16, 1966
     Sonny Jurgensen (to Allen), Washington vs.
     Chicago, Sept. 15, 1968
     Jim Plunkett (to Branch), L.A. Raiders vs.
     Washington, Oct. 2, 1983
     Ron Jaworski (to Quick), Philadelphia vs. Atlanta,
     Nov. 10, 1985
     Stan Humphries (to Martin), San Diego vs. Seattle,
     Sept. 18, 1994
     Brett Favre (to Brooks), Green Bay vs. Chicago,
     Sept. 11, 1995
     Trent Green (to Boerigter), Kansas City vs.
     San Diego, Dec. 22, 2002
     Jeff Garcia, (to Davis), Cleveland vs. Cincinnati,
     Oct. 17, 2004
98   Doug Russell (to Tinsley), Chi. Cardinals vs.
     Cleveland, Nov. 27, 1938
     Ogden Compton (to Lane), Chi. Cardinals vs.
     Green Bay, Nov. 13, 1955
     Bill Wade (to Farrington), Chicago Bears vs. Detroit,
     Oct. 8, 1961
     Jacky Lee (to Dewveall), Houston vs. San Diego,
     Nov. 25, 1962
     Earl Morrall (to Jones), N.Y. Giants vs. Pittsburgh,
     Sept. 11, 1966
     Jim Hart (to Moore), St. Louis vs. Los Angeles,
     Dec. 10, 1972 (no TD)
     Bobby Hebert (to Haynes), Atlanta vs. New Orleans,
     Sept. 12, 1993
     Charlie Batch (to Morton), Detroit vs. Chicago,
     Oct. 4, 1998

97   Pat Coffee (to Tinsley), Chi. Cardinals vs. Chi. Bears,
      Dec. 5, 1937
      Bobby Layne (to Box), Detroit vs. Green Bay,
      Nov. 26, 1953
      George Shaw (to Tarr), Denver vs. Boston,
      Sept. 21, 1962
      Bernie Kosar (to Slaughter), Cleveland vs. Chicago,
      Oct. 23, 1989
      Steve Young (to Taylor), San Francisco vs. Atlanta,
      Nov. 3, 1991

AVERAGE GAIN
Most Seasons Leading League
7   Sid Luckman, Chi. Bears, 1939-1943, 1946-47
5   Steve Young, San Francisco, 1991-94, 1997
3   Arnie Herber, Green Bay, 1932, 1934, 1936
    Norm Van Brocklin, Los Angeles, 1950, 1952, 1954
    Len Dawson, Dall. Texans, 1962; Kansas City, 1966, 1968
    Bart Starr, Green Bay, 1966-68
    Kurt Warner, St. Louis, 1999-2001

Most Consecutive Seasons Leading League
5   Sid Luckman, Chi. Bears, 1939-1943
4   Steve Young, San Francisco, 1991-94
3   Bart Starr, Green Bay, 1966-68
    Kurt Warner, St. Louis, 1999-2001

Highest Average Gain, Career (1,500 attempts)
8.63   Otto Graham, Cleveland, 1950-55 (1,565-13,499)
8.42   Sid Luckman, Chi. Bears, 1939-1950
      (1,744-14,686)
8.21   Kurt Warner, St. Louis, 1998-2003; N.Y. Giants,
      2004; Arizona, 2005 (2,340-19,214)

Highest Average Gain, Season (Qualifiers)
11.17   Tommy O'Connell, Cleveland, 1957 (110-1,229)
10.86   Sid Luckman, Chi. Bears, 1943 (202-2,194)
10.55   Otto Graham, Cleveland, 1953 (258-2,722)

Highest Average Gain, Rookie, Season (Qualifiers)
9.411   Greg Cook, Cincinnati, 1969 (197-1,854)
9.409   Bob Waterfield, Cleveland, 1945 (171-1,609)
8.88   Ben Roethlisberger, Pittsburgh, 2004 (295-2,621)

Highest Average Gain, Game (20 attempts)
18.58   Sammy Baugh, Washington vs. Boston,
      Oct. 31, 1948 (24-446)
18.50   Johnny Unitas, Baltimore vs. Atlanta, Nov. 12, 1967
      (20-370)
17.71   Joe Namath, N.Y. Jets vs. Baltimore, Sept. 24, 1972
      (28-496)

TOUCHDOWNS
Most Seasons Leading League
4   Johnny Unitas, Baltimore, 1957-1960
    Len Dawson, Dall. Texans, 1962; Kansas City, 1963,
    1965-66
    Steve Young, San Francisco, 1992-94, 1998
    Brett Favre, Green Bay, 1995-97, 2003
3   Arnie Herber, Green Bay, 1932, 1934, 1936
    Sid Luckman, Chi. Bears, 1943, 1945-46
    Y.A. Tittle, San Francisco, 1955; N.Y. Giants, 1962-63
    Dan Marino, Miami, 1984-86
2   By many players

Most Consecutive Seasons Leading League
4   Johnny Unitas, Baltimore, 1957-1960
3   Dan Marino, Miami, 1984-86
    Steve Young, San Francisco, 1992-94
    Brett Favre, Green Bay, 1995-97
2   By many players

Most Touchdown Passes, Career
420   Dan Marino, Miami, 1983-1999
396   Brett Favre, Atlanta, 1991; Green Bay, 1992-2005

342   Fran Tarkenton, Minnesota, 1961-66, 1972-78;
      N.Y. Giants, 1967-1971

Most Touchdown Passes, Season
49   Peyton Manning, Indianapolis, 2004
48   Dan Marino, Miami, 1984
44   Dan Marino, Miami, 1986

Most Touchdown Passes, Rookie, Season
26   Peyton Manning, Indianapolis, 1998
22   Charlie Conerly, N.Y. Giants, 1948
20   Dan Marino, Miami, 1983

Most Touchdown Passes, Game
7   Sid Luckman, Chi. Bears vs. N.Y. Giants,
    Nov. 14, 1943
    Adrian Burk, Philadelphia vs. Washington,
    Oct. 17, 1954
    George Blanda, Houston vs. N.Y. Titans,
    Nov. 19, 1961
    Y.A. Tittle, N.Y. Giants vs. Washington, Oct. 28, 1962
    Joe Kapp, Minnesota vs. Baltimore, Sept. 28, 1969
6   By many players. Last time:
    Peyton Manning, Indianapolis vs. Detroit,
    Nov. 25, 2004

Most Games, Four or More Touchdown Passes, Career
21   Dan Marino, Miami, 1983-1999
19   Brett Favre, Atlanta, 1991; Green Bay, 1992-2005
17   Johnny Unitas, Baltimore, 1956-1972; San Diego, 1973

Most Games, Four or More Touchdown Passes, Season
6   Dan Marino, Miami, 1984
    Peyton Manning, Indianapolis, 2004
5   Dan Marino, Miami, 1986
    Brett Favre, Green Bay, 1996
    Donovan McNabb, Philadelphia, 2004
4   George Blanda, Houston, 1961
    Vince Ferragamo, Los Angeles, 1980
    Steve Young, San Francisco, 1994
    Randall Cunningham, Minnesota, 1998
    Daunte Culpepper, Minnesota, 2004

Most Consecutive Games, Four or More Touchdown Passes
5   Peyton Manning, Indianapolis, 2004
4   Dan Marino, Miami, 1984
2   By many players

Most Consecutive Games, Touchdown Passes
47   Johnny Unitas, Baltimore, 1956-1960
36   Brett Favre, Green Bay, 2002-2004
30   Dan Marino, Miami, 1985-87

HAD INTERCEPTED
Most Consecutive Passes Attempted, None Intercepted
308   Bernie Kosar, Cleveland, 1990-91
294   Bart Starr, Green Bay, 1964-65
279   Jeff George, Indianapolis, 1993; Atlanta, 1994

Most Passes Had Intercepted, Career
277   George Blanda, Chi. Bears, 1949, 1950-58; Baltimore,
      1950; Houston, 1960-66; Oakland, 1967-1975
268   John Hadl, San Diego, 1962-1972; Los Angeles,
      1973-74; Green Bay, 1974-75; Houston, 1976-77
266   Fran Tarkenton, Minnesota, 1961-66, 1972-78;
      N.Y. Giants, 1967-1971

Most Passes Had Intercepted, Season
42   George Blanda, Houston, 1962
35   Vinny Testaverde, Tampa Bay, 1988
34   Frank Tripucka, Denver, 1960

Most Passes Had Intercepted, Game
8   Jim Hardy, Chi. Cardinals vs. Philadelphia,
    Sept. 24, 1950
7   Parker Hall, Cleveland vs. Green Bay, Nov. 8, 1942
    Frank Sinkwich, Detroit vs. Green Bay, Oct. 24, 1943
    Bob Waterfield, Los Angeles vs. Green Bay,
    Oct. 17, 1948

Zeke Bratkowski, Chicago vs. Baltimore,
Oct. 2, 1960
Tommy Wade, Pittsburgh vs. Philadelphia,
Dec. 12, 1965
Ken Stabler, Oakland vs. Denver, Oct. 16, 1977
Steve DeBerg, Tampa Bay vs. San Francisco,
Sept. 7, 1986
Ty Detmer, Detroit vs. Cleveland, Sept. 23, 2001
6 By many players

Most Attempts, No Interceptions, Game
70 Drew Bledsoe, New England vs. Minnesota,
Nov. 13, 1994 (OT)
63 Rich Gannon, Minnesota vs. New England,
Oct. 20, 1991 (OT)
60 Davey O'Brien, Philadelphia vs. Washington,
Dec. 1, 1940

LOWEST PERCENTAGE, PASSES HAD INTERCEPTED
Most Seasons Leading League, Lowest Percentage, Passes Had Intercepted
5 Sammy Baugh, Washington, 1940, 1942, 1944-45,
1947
3 Charlie Conerly, N.Y. Giants, 1950, 1956, 1959
Bart Starr, Green Bay, 1962, 1964, 1966
Roger Staubach, Dallas, 1971, 1977, 1979
Ken Anderson, Cincinnati, 1972, 1981-82
Ken O'Brien, N.Y. Jets, 1985, 1987-88
2 By many players

Lowest Percentage, Passes Had Intercepted, Career (1,500 attempts)
2.11 Neil O'Donnell, Pittsburgh, 1991-95; N.Y. Jets,
1996-97; Cincinnati, 1998; Tennessee,
1999-2003 (3,229-68)
2.24 Donovan McNabb, Philadelphia, 1999-2005
(2,943-66)
2.35 Mark Brunell, Green Bay, 1994; Jacksonville,
1995-2003; Washington, 2004-05 (4,334-102)

Lowest Percentage, Passes Had Intercepted, Season (Qualifiers)
0.66 Joe Ferguson, Buffalo, 1976 (151-1)
0.90 Steve DeBerg, Kansas City, 1990 (444-4)
1.16 Steve Bartkowski, Atlanta, 1983 (432-5)

Lowest Percentage, Passes Had Intercepted, Rookie, Season (Qualifiers)
1.98 Charlie Batch, Detroit, 1998 (303-6)
2.03 Dan Marino, Miami, 1983 (296-6)
2.10 Gary Wood, N.Y. Giants, 1964 (143-3)

TIMES SACKED
Times Sacked has been compiled since 1963.
Most Times Sacked, Career
516 John Elway, Denver, 1983-1998
494 Dave Krieg, Seattle, 1980-1991; Kansas City,
1992-93; Detroit, 1994; Arizona, 1995;
Chicago, 1996; Tennessee, 1997-98
484 Randall Cunningham, Philadelphia, 1985-1995;
Minnesota, 1997-99; Dallas, 2000; Baltimore,
2001

Most Times Sacked, Season
76 David Carr, Houston, 2002
72 Randall Cunningham, Philadelphia, 1986
68 David Carr, Houston, 2005

Most Times Sacked, Game
12 Bert Jones, Baltimore vs. St. Louis, Oct. 26, 1980
Warren Moon, Houston vs. Dallas, Sept. 29, 1985
11 Charley Johnson, St. Louis vs. N.Y. Giants,
Nov. 1, 1964
Bart Starr, Green Bay vs. Detroit, Nov. 7, 1965
Jack Kemp, Buffalo vs. Oakland, Oct. 15, 1967
Bob Berry, Atlanta vs. St. Louis, Nov. 24, 1968

Greg Landry, Detroit vs. Dallas, Oct. 6, 1975
Ron Jaworski, Philadelphia vs. St. Louis,
Dec. 18, 1983
Paul McDonald, Cleveland vs. Kansas City,
Sept. 30, 1984
Archie Manning, Minnesota vs. Chicago,
Oct. 28, 1984
Steve Pelluer, Dallas vs. San Diego, Nov. 16, 1986
Randall Cunningham, Philadelphia vs. L.A. Raiders,
Nov. 30, 1986 (OT)
David Norrie, N.Y. Jets vs. Dallas, Oct. 4, 1987
Troy Aikman, Dallas vs. Philadelphia, Sept. 15, 1991
Bernie Kosar, Cleveland vs. Indianapolis,
Sept. 6, 1992
10 By many players

RECEIVING
Most Seasons Leading League
8 Don Hutson, Green Bay, 1936-37, 1939, 1941-45
5 Lionel Taylor, Denver, 1960-63, 1965
3 Tom Fears, Los Angeles, 1948-1950
Pete Pihos, Philadelphia, 1953-55
Billy Wilson, San Francisco, 1954, 1956-57
Raymond Berry, Baltimore, 1958-1960
Lance Alworth, San Diego, 1966, 1968-69
Sterling Sharpe, Green Bay, 1989, 1992-93

Most Consecutive Seasons Leading League
5 Don Hutson, Green Bay, 1941-45
4 Lionel Taylor, Denver, 1960-63
3 Tom Fears, Los Angeles, 1948-1950
Pete Pihos, Philadelphia, 1953-55
Raymond Berry, Baltimore, 1958-1960

Most Pass Receptions, Career
1,549 Jerry Rice, San Francisco, 1985-2000; Oakland,
2001-04; Seattle, 2004
1,101 Cris Carter, Philadelphia, 1987-89; Minnesota,
1990-2001; Miami, 2002
1,094 Tim Brown, L.A. Raiders, 1988-1994; Oakland,
1995-2003; Tampa Bay, 2004

Most Seasons, 50 or More Pass Receptions
17 Jerry Rice, San Francisco, 1986-1996, 1998-2000;
Oakland, 2001-03
13 Andre Reed, Buffalo, 1986-1994, 1996-99
11 Cris Carter, Minnesota, 1991-2001
Tim Brown, L.A. Raiders, 1993-1994; Oakland,
1995-2003
Shannon Sharpe, Denver 1992-98; Baltimore,
2000-01; Denver, 2002-03

Most Pass Receptions, Season
143 Marvin Harrison, Indianapolis, 2002
123 Herman Moore, Detroit, 1995
122 Cris Carter, Minnesota, 1994
Cris Carter, Minnesota, 1995
Jerry Rice, San Francisco, 1995

Most Pass Receptions, Rookie, Season
101 Anquan Boldin, Arizona, 2003
90 Terry Glenn, New England, 1996
83 Earl Cooper, San Francisco, 1980

Most Pass Receptions, Game
20 Terrell Owens, San Francisco vs. Chicago,
Dec. 17, 2000
18 Tom Fears, Los Angeles vs. Green Bay, Dec. 3, 1950
17 Clark Gaines, N.Y. Jets vs. San Francisco,
Sept. 21, 1980

Most Consecutive Games, Pass Receptions
274 Jerry Rice, San Francisco, 1985-2000; Oakland,
2001-04
183 Art Monk, Washington, 1983-1993; N.Y. Jets, 1994;
Philadelphia, 1995

179   Tim Brown, L.A. Raiders, 1993-94; Oakland, 1995-2003; Tampa Bay, 2004

YARDS GAINED

Most Seasons Leading League

7   Don Hutson, Green Bay, 1936, 1938-39, 1941-44
6   Jerry Rice, San Francisco, 1986, 1989-1990, 1993-95
3   Raymond Berry, Baltimore, 1957, 1959-1960
   Lance Alworth, San Diego, 1965-66, 1968

Most Consecutive Seasons Leading League

4   Don Hutson, Green Bay, 1941-44
3   Jerry Rice, San Francisco, 1993-95
2   By many players

Most Yards Gained, Career

22,895   Jerry Rice, San Francisco, 1985-2000; Oakland, 2001-04; Seattle, 2004
14,934   Tim Brown, L.A. Raiders, 1988-1994; Oakland, 1995-2003; Tampa Bay, 2004
14,004   James Lofton, Green Bay, 1978-1986; L.A. Raiders, 1987-88; Buffalo, 1989-1992; L.A. Rams, 1993; Philadelphia, 1993

Most Seasons, 1,000 or More Yards, Pass Receiving

14   Jerry Rice, San Francisco, 1986-1996, 1998; Oakland, 2001-02
9   Tim Brown, L.A. Raiders, 1993-94; Oakland, 1995-2001
   Jimmy Smith, Jacksonville, 1996-2002, 2004-05
8   Steve Largent, Seattle, 1978-1981, 1983-86
   Cris Carter, Minnesota, 1993-2000
   Rod Smith, Denver, 1997-2002, 2004-05

Most Yards Gained, Season

1,848   Jerry Rice, San Francisco, 1995
1,781   Isaac Bruce, St. Louis, 1995
1,746   Charley Hennigan, Houston, 1961

Most Yards Gained, Rookie, Season

1,473   Bill Groman, Houston, 1960
1,377   Anquan Boldin, Arizona, 2003
1,313   Randy Moss, Minnesota, 1998

Most Yards Gained, Game

336   Willie Anderson, L.A. Rams vs. New Orleans, Nov. 26, 1989 (OT)
309   Stephone Paige, Kansas City vs. San Diego, Dec. 22, 1985
303   Jim Benton, Cleveland vs. Detroit, Nov. 22, 1945

Most Games, 200 or More Yards Pass Receiving, Career

5   Lance Alworth, San Diego, 1962-1970; Dallas, 1971-72
4   Don Hutson, Green Bay, 1935-45
   Charley Hennigan, Houston, 1960-66
   Jerry Rice, San Francisco, 1985-2000; Oakland, 2001-04; Seattle, 2004
3   Don Maynard, N.Y. Giants, 1958; N.Y. Jets, 1960-1972; St. Louis, 1973
   Wes Chandler, New Orleans, 1978-1981; San Diego, 1981-87; San Francisco, 1988
   Isaac Bruce, L.A. Rams, 1994; St. Louis, 1995-2005

Most Games, 200 or More Yards Pass Receiving, Season

3   Charley Hennigan, Houston, 1961
2   Don Hutson, Green Bay, 1942
   Gene Roberts, N.Y. Giants, 1949
   Lance Alworth, San Diego, 1963
   Don Maynard, N.Y. Jets, 1968

Most Games, 100 or More Yards Pass Receiving, Career

76   Jerry Rice, San Francisco, 1985-2000; Oakland, 2001-04; Seattle, 2004
53   Marvin Harrison, Indianapolis, 1996-2005
50   Don Maynard, N.Y. Giants, 1958; N.Y. Jets, 1960-1972; St. Louis, 1973

Most Games, 100 or More Yards Pass Receiving, Season

11   Michael Irvin, Dallas, 1995
10   Charley Hennigan, Houston, 1961
   Herman Moore, Detroit, 1995
   Marvin Harrison, Indianapolis, 2002
   Torry Holt, St. Louis, 2003
9   Elroy (Crazylegs) Hirsch, Los Angeles, 1951
   Bill Groman, Houston, 1960
   Lance Alworth, San Diego, 1965
   Don Maynard, N.Y. Jets, 1967
   Stanley Morgan, New England, 1986
   Mark Carrier, Tampa Bay, 1989
   Robert Brooks, Green Bay, 1995
   Isaac Bruce, St. Louis, 1995
   Jerry Rice, San Francisco, 1995
   Marvin Harrison, Indianapolis, 1999
   Jimmy Smith, Jacksonville, 1999
   David Boston, Arizona, 2001
   Steve Smith, Carolina, 2005

Most Consecutive Games, 100 or More Yards Pass Receiving

7   Charley Hennigan, Houston, 1961
   Michael Irvin, Dallas, 1995
6   Raymond Berry, Baltimore, 1960
   Bill Groman, Houston, 1961
   Pat Studstill, Detroit, 1966
   Isaac Bruce, St. Louis, 1995
5   Elroy (Crazylegs) Hirsch, Los Angeles, 1951
   Bob Boyd, Los Angeles, 1954
   Terry Barr, Detroit, 1963
   Lance Alworth, San Diego, 1966
   Don Maynard, N.Y. Jets, 1968-69
   Harold Jackson, Philadelphia, 1971-72
   Patrick Jeffers, Carolina, 1999
   Terrell Owens, Philadelphia, 2004
   Anquan Boldin, Arizona, 2005

Longest Pass Reception (All TDs except as noted)

99   Andy Farkas (from Filchock), Washington vs. Pittsburgh, Oct. 15, 1939
   Bobby Mitchell (from Izo), Washington vs. Cleveland, Sept. 15, 1963
   Pat Studstill (from Sweetan), Detroit vs. Baltimore, Oct. 16, 1966
   Gerry Allen (from Jurgensen), Washington vs. Chicago, Sept. 15, 1968
   Cliff Branch (from Plunkett), L.A. Raiders vs. Washington, Oct. 2, 1983
   Mike Quick (from Jaworski), Philadelphia vs. Atlanta, Nov. 10, 1985
   Tony Martin (from Humphries), San Diego vs. Seattle, Sept. 18, 1994
   Robert Brooks (from Favre), Green Bay vs. Chicago, Sept. 11, 1995
   Marc Boerigter (from Green), Kansas City vs. San Diego, Dec. 22, 2002
   Andre Davis (from Garcia), Cleveland vs. Cincinnati, Oct. 17, 2004
98   Gaynell Tinsley (from Russell), Chi. Cardinals vs. Cleveland, Nov. 17, 1938
   Dick (Night Train) Lane (from Compton), Chi. Cardinals vs. Green Bay, Nov. 13, 1955
   John Farrington (from Wade), Chicago vs. Detroit, Oct. 8, 1961
   Willard Dewveall (from Lee), Houston vs. San Diego, Nov. 25, 1962
   Homer Jones (from Morrall), N.Y. Giants vs. Pittsburgh, Sept. 11, 1966
   Bobby Moore (from Hart), St. Louis vs. Los Angeles, Dec. 10, 1972 (no TD)
   Michael Haynes (from Hebert), Atlanta vs. New Orleans, Sept. 12, 1993

Johnnie Morton (from Batch), Detroit vs. Chicago,
Oct. 4, 1998
  97 Gaynell Tinsley (from Coffee), Chi. Cardinals vs.
Chi. Bears, Dec. 5, 1937
Cloyce Box (from Layne), Detroit vs. Green Bay,
Nov. 26, 1953
Jerry Tarr (from Shaw), Denver vs. Boston,
Sept. 21, 1962
Webster Slaughter (from Kosar), Cleveland vs.
Chicago, Oct. 23, 1989
John Taylor (from Young), San Francisco vs. Atlanta,
Nov. 3, 1991

AVERAGE GAIN
Highest Average Gain, Career (200 receptions)
  22.26 Homer Jones, N.Y. Giants, 1964-69; Cleveland, 1970
(224-4,986)
  20.83 Buddy Dial, Pittsburgh, 1959-1963; Dallas, 1964-66
(261-5,436)
  20.24 Harlon Hill, Chi. Bears, 1954-1961; Pittsburgh,
1962; Detroit, 1962 (233-4,717)
Highest Average Gain, Season (24 receptions)
  32.58 Don Currivan, Boston, 1947 (24-782)
  31.44 Bucky Pope, Los Angeles, 1964 (25-786)
  28.60 Bobby Duckworth, San Diego, 1984 (25-715)
Highest Average Gain, Game (3 receptions)
  63.00 Torry Holt, St. Louis vs. Atlanta, Sept. 24, 2000
(3-189)
  60.67 Bill Groman, Houston vs. Denver, Nov. 20, 1960
(3-182)
Homer Jones, N.Y. Giants vs. Washington,
Dec. 12, 1965 (3-182)
  60.33 Don Currivan, Boston vs. Washington,
Nov. 30, 1947 (3-181)

TOUCHDOWNS
Most Seasons Leading League
  9 Don Hutson, Green Bay, 1935-38, 1940-44
  6 Jerry Rice, San Francisco, 1986-87, 1989-1991,
1993
  3 Lance Alworth, San Diego, 1964-66
Cris Carter, Minnesota, 1995, 1997, 1999
Randy Moss, Minnesota, 1998, 2000, 2003
Most Consecutive Seasons Leading League
  5 Don Hutson, Green Bay, 1940-44
  4 Don Hutson, Green Bay, 1935-38
  3 Lance Alworth, San Diego, 1964-66
Jerry Rice, San Francisco, 1989-1991
Most Touchdowns, Career
  197 Jerry Rice, San Francisco, 1985-2000; Oakland,
2001-04; Seattle, 2004
  130 Cris Carter, Philadelphia, 1987-89; Minnesota,
1990-2001; Miami, 2002
  110 Marvin Harrison, Indianapolis, 1996-2005
Most Touchdowns, Season
  22 Jerry Rice, San Francisco, 1987
  18 Mark Clayton, Miami, 1984
Sterling Sharpe, Green Bay, 1994
  17 Don Hutson, Green Bay, 1942
Elroy (Crazylegs) Hirsch, Los Angeles, 1951
Bill Groman, Houston, 1961
Jerry Rice, San Francisco, 1989
Cris Carter, Minnesota, 1995
Carl Pickens, Cincinnati, 1995
Randy Moss, Minnesota, 1998
Randy Moss, Minnesota, 2003
Most Touchdowns, Rookie, Season
  17 Randy Moss, Minnesota, 1998
  13 Bill Howton, Green Bay, 1952
John Jefferson, San Diego, 1978

  12 Harlon Hill, Chi. Bears, 1954
Bill Groman, Houston, 1960
Mike Ditka, Chicago, 1961
Bob Hayes, Dallas, 1965
Most Touchdowns, Game
  5 Bob Shaw, Chi. Cardinals vs. Baltimore, Oct. 2, 1950
Kellen Winslow, San Diego vs. Oakland, Nov. 22, 1981
Jerry Rice, San Francisco vs. Atlanta, Oct. 14, 1990
  4 By many players. Last time: Joe Horn,
New Orleans vs. N.Y. Giants, Dec. 14, 2003
Most Consecutive Games, Touchdowns
  13 Jerry Rice, San Francisco, 1986-87
  11 Elroy (Crazylegs) Hirsch, Los Angeles, 1950-51
Buddy Dial, Pittsburgh, 1959-1960
  10 Carl Pickens, Cincinnati, 1994-95
Randy Moss, Minnesota, 2003-04

YARDS FROM SCRIMMAGE
Most Scrimmage Yards, Career
  23,540 Jerry Rice, San Francisco 1985-2000; Oakland,
2001-04; Seattle, 2004
  21,579 Emmitt Smith, Dallas, 1990-2002; Arizona, 2003-04
  21,264 Walter Payton, Chicago, 1975-1987
Most Scrimmage Yards, Season
  2,429 Marshall Faulk, St. Louis, 1999 (1,381 rush.,
1,048 rec.)
  2,390 Tiki Barber, N.Y. Giants, 2005 (1,860 rush., 530 rec.)
  2,370 LaDainian Tomlinson, San Diego, 2003 (1,645 rush.,
725 rec.)
Most Scrimmage Yards, Rookie, Season
  2,212 Eric Dickerson, L.A. Rams, 1983 (1,808 rush.,
404 rec.)
  2,139 Edgerrin James, Indianapolis, 1999 (1,553 rush.,
586 rec.)
  1,924 Billy Sims, Detroit, 1980 (1,303 rush., 621 rec.)
Most Scrimmage Yards, Game
  336 Flipper Anderson, L.A. Rams vs. New Orleans,
Nov. 26, 1989 (OT) (336 rec.)
  330 Billy Cannon, Houston vs. N.Y. Titans, Dec. 10, 1961
(216 rush., 114 rec.)
  309 Stephone Paige, Kansas City vs. San Diego,
Dec. 22, 1985 (309 rec.)

INTERCEPTIONS BY
Most Seasons Leading League
  3 Everson Walls, Dallas, 1981-82, 1985
  2 Dick (Night Train) Lane, Los Angeles, 1952;
Chi. Cardinals, 1954
Jack Christiansen, Detroit, 1953, 1957
Milt Davis, Baltimore, 1957, 1959
Dick Lynch, N.Y. Giants, 1961, 1963
Johnny Robinson, Kansas City, 1966, 1970
Bill Bradley, Philadelphia, 1971-72
Emmitt Thomas, Kansas City, 1969, 1974
Ronnie Lott, San Francisco, 1986; L.A. Raiders, 1991
Rod Woodson, Baltimore, 1999; Oakland, 2002
Ty Law, New England, 1998; N.Y. Jets, 2005
Most Interceptions By, Career
  81 Paul Krause, Washington, 1964-67; Minnesota,
1968-1979
  79 Emlen Tunnell, N.Y. Giants, 1948-1958; Green Bay,
1959-1961
  71 Rod Woodson, Pittsburgh, 1987-1996; San Francisco,
1997; Baltimore, 1998-2001; Oakland, 2002-03
Most Interceptions By, Season
  14 Dick (Night Train) Lane, Los Angeles, 1952
  13 Dan Sandifer, Washington, 1948
Orban (Spec) Sanders, N.Y. Yanks, 1950
Lester Hayes, Oakland, 1980
  12 By nine players

Most Interceptions By, Rookie, Season
- 14   Dick (Night Train) Lane, Los Angeles, 1952
- 13   Dan Sandifer, Washington, 1948
- 12   Woodley Lewis, Los Angeles, 1950
  - Paul Krause, Washington, 1964

Most Interceptions By, Game
- 4   Sammy Baugh, Washington vs. Detroit, Nov. 14, 1943
  - Dan Sandifer, Washington vs. Boston, Oct. 31, 1948
  - Don Doll, Detroit vs. Chi. Cardinals, Oct. 23, 1949
  - Bob Nussbaumer, Chi. Cardinals vs. N.Y. Bulldogs, Nov. 13, 1949
  - Russ Craft, Philadelphia vs. Chi. Cardinals, Sept. 24, 1950
  - Bobby Dillon, Green Bay vs. Detroit, Nov. 26, 1953
  - Jack Butler, Pittsburgh vs. Washington, Dec. 13, 1953
  - Austin (Goose) Gonsoulin, Denver vs. Buffalo, Sept. 18, 1960
  - Jerry Norton, St. Louis vs. Washington, Nov. 20, 1960; vs. Pittsburgh, Nov. 26, 1961
  - Dave Baker, San Francisco vs. L.A. Rams, Dec. 4, 1960
  - Bobby Ply, Dall. Texans vs. San Diego, Dec. 16, 1962
  - Bobby Hunt, Kansas City vs. Houston, Oct. 4, 1964
  - Willie Brown, Denver vs. N.Y. Jets, Nov. 15, 1964
  - Dick Anderson, Miami vs. Pittsburgh, Dec. 3, 1973
  - Willie Buchanon, Green Bay vs. San Diego, Sept. 24, 1978
  - Deron Cherry, Kansas City vs. Seattle, Sept. 29, 1985
  - Kwamie Lassiter, Arizona vs. San Diego, Dec. 27, 1998
  - Deltha O'Neal, Denver vs. Kansas City, Oct. 7, 2001

Most Consecutive Games, Passes Intercepted By
- 8   Tom Morrow, Oakland, 1962-63
- 7   Tom Landry, N.Y. Giants, 1950-51
  - Paul Krause, Washington, 1964
  - Larry Wilson, St. Louis, 1966
  - Ben Davis, Cleveland, 1968
- 6   By many players.
  - Last time: Brian Russell, Minnesota, 2003

YARDS GAINED

Most Seasons Leading League
- 2   Dick (Night Train) Lane, Los Angeles, 1952; Chi. Cardinals, 1954
  - Herb Adderley, Green Bay, 1965, 1969
  - Dick Anderson, Miami, 1968, 1970
  - Darren Sharper, Green Bay, 2002; Minnesota, 2005

Most Yards Gained, Career
- 1,483   Rod Woodson, Pittsburgh, 1987-1996; San Francisco, 1997; Baltimore, 1998-2001; Oakland, 2002-03
- 1,331   Deion Sanders, Atlanta, 1989-1993; San Francisco, 1994; Dallas, 1995-99; Washington, 2000; Baltimore, 2004-05
- 1,282   Emlen Tunnell, N.Y. Giants, 1948-1958; Green Bay, 1959-1961

Most Yards Gained, Season
- 358   Ed Reed, Baltimore, 2004
- 349   Charlie McNeil, San Diego, 1961
- 303   Deion Sanders, San Francisco, 1994

Most Yards Gained, Rookie, Season
- 301   Don Doll, Detroit, 1949
- 298   Dick (Night Train) Lane, Los Angeles, 1952
- 275   Woodley Lewis, Los Angeles, 1950

Most Yards Gained, Game
- 177   Charlie McNeil, San Diego vs. Houston, Sept. 24, 1961
- 170   Louis Oliver, Miami vs. Buffalo, Oct. 4, 1992
- 167   Dick Jauron, Detroit vs. Chicago, Nov. 18, 1973

Longest Return (All TDs)
- 106   Ed Reed, Baltimore vs. Cleveland, Nov. 7, 2004

- 103   Vencie Glenn, San Diego vs. Denver, Nov. 29, 1987
  - Louis Oliver, Miami vs. Buffalo, Oct. 4, 1992
- 102   Bob Smith, Detroit vs. Chi. Bears, Nov. 24, 1949
  - Erich Barnes, N.Y. Giants vs. Dall. Cowboys, Oct. 15, 1961
  - Gary Barbaro, Kansas City vs. Seattle, Dec. 11, 1977
  - Louis Breeden, Cincinnati vs. San Diego, Nov. 8, 1981
  - Eddie Anderson, L.A. Raiders vs. Miami, Dec. 14, 1992
  - Donald Frank, San Diego vs. L.A. Raiders, Oct. 31, 1993
  - Artrell Hawkins, Cincinnati vs. Houston, Nov. 3, 2002
  - Marcus Coleman, Houston vs. Kansas City, Sept. 26, 2004

TOUCHDOWNS

Most Touchdowns, Career
- 12   Rod Woodson, Pittsburgh, 1987-1996; San Francisco, 1997; Baltimore, 1998-2001; Oakland, 2002-03
- 9   Ken Houston, Houston, 1967-1972; Washington, 1973-1980
  - Aeneas Williams, Phoenix, 1991-93; Arizona, 1994-2000; St. Louis, 2001-04
  - Deion Sanders, Atlanta, 1989-1993; San Francisco, 1994; Dallas, 1995-99; Washington, 2000; Baltimore, 2004-05
- 8   Eric Allen, Philadelphia, 1988-1994; New Orleans, 1995-97; Oakland, 1998-2001

Most Touchdowns, Season
- 4   Ken Houston, Houston, 1971
  - Jim Kearney, Kansas City, 1972
  - Eric Allen, Philadelphia, 1993
- 3   Dick Harris, San Diego, 1961
  - Dick Lynch, N.Y. Giants, 1963
  - Herb Adderley, Green Bay, 1965
  - Lem Barney, Detroit, 1967
  - Miller Farr, Houston, 1967
  - Monte Jackson, Los Angeles, 1976
  - Rod Perry, Los Angeles, 1978
  - Ronnie Lott, San Francisco, 1981
  - Lloyd Burruss, Kansas City, 1986
  - Wayne Haddix, Tampa Bay, 1990
  - Robert Massey, Phoenix, 1992
  - Ray Buchanan, Indianapolis, 1994
  - Deion Sanders, San Francisco, 1994
  - Mark McMillian, Kansas City, 1997
  - Otis Smith, N.Y. Jets, 1997
  - Jimmy Hitchcock, Minnesota, 1998
  - Eric Allen, Oakland, 2000
  - Derrick Brooks, Tampa Bay, 2002
- 2   By many players

Most Touchdowns, Rookie, Season
- 3   Lem Barney, Detroit, 1967
  - Ronnie Lott, San Francisco, 1981
- 2   By many players

Most Touchdowns, Game
- 2   Bill Blackburn, Chi. Cardinals vs. Boston, Oct. 24, 1948
  - Dan Sandifer, Washington vs. Boston, Oct. 31, 1948
  - Bob Franklin, Cleveland vs. Chicago, Dec. 11, 1960
  - Bill Stacy, St. Louis vs. Dall. Cowboys, Nov. 5, 1961
  - Jerry Norton, St. Louis vs. Pittsburgh, Nov. 26, 1961
  - Miller Farr, Houston vs. Buffalo, Dec. 7, 1968
  - Ken Houston, Houston vs. San Diego, Dec. 19, 1971
  - Jim Kearney, Kansas City vs. Denver, Oct. 1, 1972
  - Lemar Parrish, Cincinnati vs. Houston, Dec. 17, 1972
  - Dick Anderson, Miami vs. Pittsburgh, Dec. 3, 1973
  - Prentice McCray, New England vs. N.Y. Jets, Nov. 21, 1976
  - Kenny Johnson, Atlanta vs. Green Bay, Nov. 27, 1983 (OT)

Mike Kozlowski, Miami vs. N.Y. Jets, Dec. 16, 1983
Dave Brown, Seattle vs. Kansas City, Nov. 4, 1984
Lloyd Burruss, Kansas City vs. San Diego,
   Oct. 19, 1986
Henry Jones, Buffalo vs. Indianapolis, Sept. 20, 1992
Robert Massey, Phoenix vs. Washington, Oct. 4, 1992
Eric Allen, Philadelphia vs. New Orleans,
   Dec. 26, 1993
Ken Norton, San Francisco vs. St. Louis,
   Oct. 22, 1995
Otis Smith, N.Y. Jets vs. Tampa Bay, Dec. 14, 1997
Dewayne Washington, Pittsburgh vs. Jacksonville,
   Nov. 22, 1998
Aaron Glenn, Houston vs. Pittsburgh, Dec. 8, 2002

PUNTING
Most Seasons Leading League
  4 Sammy Baugh, Washington, 1940-43
     Jerrel Wilson, Kansas City, 1965, 1968, 1972-73
  3 Yale Lary, Detroit, 1959, 1961, 1963
     Jim Fraser, Denver, 1962-64
     Ray Guy, Oakland, 1974-75, 1977
     Rohn Stark, Baltimore, 1983; Indianapolis, 1985-86
  2 By many players
Most Consecutive Seasons Leading League
  4 Sammy Baugh, Washington, 1940-43
  3 Jim Fraser, Denver, 1962-64
  2 By many players

PUNTS
Most Punts, Career
1,437 Jeff Feagles, New England, 1988-89; Philadelphia,
      1990-93; Arizona, 1994-97; Seattle, 1998-2002;
      N.Y. Giants, 2003-05
1,401 Sean Landeta, N.Y. Giants, 1985-1993; L.A. Rams,
      1993-94; St. Louis, 1995-96; Tampa Bay, 1997;
      Green Bay, 1998; Philadelphia, 1999-2002;
      St. Louis, 2003-04; Philadelphia, 2005
1,226 Lee Johnson, Houston, 1985-87; Cleveland, 1987-
      88; Cincinnati, 1988-1998; New England, 1999-
      2001; Minnesota, 2001; Philadelphia, 2002
Most Punts, Season
  114 Bob Parsons, Chicago, 1981
      Chad Stanley, Houston, 2002
  111 Brad Maynard, N.Y. Giants, 1997
  109 John James, Atlanta, 1978
Most Punts, Rookie, Season
  111 Brad Maynard, N.Y. Giants, 1997
  108 John Teltschik, Philadelphia, 1986
  101 Daniel Pope, Kansas City, 1999
Most Punts, Game
  16 Leo Araguz, Oakland vs. San Diego, Oct. 11, 1998
  15 John Teltschik, Philadelphia vs. N.Y. Giants,
     Dec. 6, 1987 (OT)
  14 Dick Nesbitt, Chi. Cardinals vs. Chi. Bears,
     Nov. 30, 1933
     Keith Molesworth, Chi. Bears vs. Green Bay,
     Dec. 10, 1933
     Sammy Baugh, Washington vs. Philadelphia,
     Nov. 5, 1939
     Carl Kinscherf, N.Y. Giants vs. Detroit, Nov. 7, 1943
     George Taliaferro, N.Y. Yanks vs. Los Angeles,
     Sept. 28, 1951
Longest Punt
  98 Steve O'Neal, N.Y. Jets vs. Denver, Sept. 21, 1969
  94 Joe Lintzenich, Chi. Bears vs. N.Y. Giants, Nov. 16, 1931
  93 Shawn McCarthy, New England vs. Buffalo,
     Nov. 3, 1991

AVERAGE YARDAGE
Highest Average, Punting, Career (250 punts)
  45.85 Shane Lechler, Oakland, 2000-05 (442-20,266)
  45.10 Sammy Baugh, Washington, 1937-1952
       (338-15,245)
  44.68 Tommy Davis, San Francisco, 1959-1969
       (511-22,833)
Highest Average, Punting, Season (Qualifiers)
  51.40 Sammy Baugh, Washington, 1940 (35-1,799)
  48.94 Yale Lary, Detroit, 1963 (35-1,713)
  48.73 Sammy Baugh, Washington, 1941 (30-1,462)
Highest Average, Punting, Rookie, Season (Qualifiers)
  45.92 Frank Sinkwich, Detroit, 1943 (12-551)
  45.91 Shane Lechler, Oakland, 2000 (65-2,984)
  45.66 Tommy Davis, San Francisco, 1959 (59-2,694)
Highest Average, Punting, Game (4 punts)
  61.75 Bob Cifers, Detroit vs. Chi. Bears, Nov. 24, 1946
       (4-247)
  61.60 Roy McKay, Green Bay vs. Chi. Cardinals,
       Oct. 28, 1945 (5-308)
  59.50 Darren Bennett, San Diego vs. Pittsburgh,
       Oct. 1, 1995 (4-238)

PUNTS HAD BLOCKED
Most Consecutive Punts, None Blocked
1,112 Chris Gardocki, Chicago, 1992-94; Indianapolis,
      1995-98; Cleveland, 1999-2003; Pittsburgh,
      2004-05 (current)
  878 Bryan Barker, Kansas City, 1993; Philadelphia, 1994;
      Jacksonville, 1995-2000; Washington, 2001-03
      Green Bay, 2004; St. Louis, 2005 (current)
  638 Tom Tupa, New England, 1997-98; N.Y. Jets,
      1999-2001; Tampa Bay, 2002-03;
      Washington, 2004
Most Punts Had Blocked, Career
  14 Herman Weaver, Detroit, 1970-76; Seattle, 1977-1980
     Harry Newsome, Pittsburgh, 1985-89; Minnesota,
     1990-93
  12 Jerrel Wilson, Kansas City, 1963-1977;
     New England, 1978
     Tom Blanchard, N.Y. Giants, 1971-73; New Orleans,
     1974-78; Tampa Bay, 1979-1981
  11 David Lee, Baltimore, 1966-1978
     Jeff Feagles, New England, 1988-89; Philadelphia,
     1990-93; Arizona, 1994-97; Seattle, 1998-2002;
     N.Y. Giants, 2003-05
Most Punts Had Blocked, Season
  6 Harry Newsome, Pittsburgh, 1988
  4 Bryan Wagner, Cleveland, 1990
  3 By many players

PUNTS INSIDE THE 20
Punts Inside the 20 have been compiled since 1976.
Most Punts Inside the 20, Career
  456 Jeff Feagles, New England, 1988-89; Philadelphia,
      1990-93; Arizona, 1994-97; Seattle, 1998-2002;
      N.Y. Giants, 2003-05
  381 Sean Landeta, N.Y. Giants, 1985-1993; L.A. Rams,
      1993-94; St. Louis, 1995-96; Tampa Bay, 1997;
      Green Bay, 1998; Philadelphia, 1999-2002;
      St. Louis, 2003-04; Philadelphia, 2005
  326 Bryan Barker, Kansas City, 1990-93; Philadelphia,
      1994; Jacksonville, 1995-2000; Washington,
      2001-03; Green Bay, 2004; St. Louis, 2005
Most Punts Inside the 20, Season
  39 Kyle Richardson, Baltimore, 1999
  36 Brad Maynard, Chicago, 2001
     Chad Stanley, Houston, 2002
     Chad Stanley, Houston, 2003

35 Rich Camarillo, Houston, 1994
Mark Royals, Pittsburgh, 1994
Craig Hentrich, Tennessee, 1999
Kyle Richardson, Baltimore, 2000
Todd Sauerbrun, Carolina, 2001

Most Punts Inside the 20, Game
8 Mark Royals, Pittsburgh vs. Houston, Nov. 6, 1994 (OT)
Bryan Barker, Jacksonville vs. Baltimore, Nov. 14, 1999
7 Josh Miller, Pittsburgh vs. Cincinnati, Dec. 20, 1998
6 By many players

PUNT RETURNS
Most Seasons Leading League
3 Les (Speedy) Duncan, San Diego, 1965-66; Washington, 1971
Rick Upchurch, Denver, 1976, 1978, 1982
2 Dick Christy, N.Y. Titans, 1961-62
Claude Gibson, Oakland, 1963-64
Billy (White Shoes) Johnson, Houston, 1975, 1977
Mel Gray, New Orleans, 1987; Detroit, 1991
Jermaine Lewis, Baltimore, 1997, 2000

PUNT RETURNS
Most Punt Returns, Career
463 Brian Mitchell, Washington, 1990-99; Philadelphia, 2000-02; N.Y. Giants, 2003
351 Eric Metcalf, Cleveland, 1989-1994; Atlanta, 1995-96; San Diego, 1997; Arizona, 1998; Carolina, 1999; Washington, 2001; Green Bay, 2002
349 David Meggett, N.Y. Giants, 1989-1994; New England, 1995-97; N.Y. Jets, 1998

Most Punt Returns, Season
70 Danny Reece, Tampa Bay, 1979
62 Fulton Walker, Miami-L.A. Raiders, 1985
58 J.T. Smith, Kansas City, 1979
Greg Pruitt, L.A. Raiders, 1983
Leo Lewis, Minnesota, 1988
Desmond Howard, Green Bay, 1996

Most Punt Returns, Rookie, Season
57 Lew Barnes, Chicago, 1986
55 B.J. Sams, Baltimore, 2004
54 James Jones, Dallas, 1980

Most Punt Returns, Game
11 Eddie Brown, Washington vs. Tampa Bay, Oct. 9, 1977
10 Theo Bell, Pittsburgh vs. Buffalo, Dec. 16, 1979
Mike Nelms, Washington vs. New Orleans, Dec. 26, 1982
Ronnie Harris, New England vs. Pittsburgh, Dec. 5, 1993
9 Rodger Bird, Oakland vs. Denver, Sept. 10, 1967
Ralph McGill, San Francisco vs. Atlanta, Oct. 29, 1972
Ed Podolak, Kansas City vs. San Diego, Nov. 10, 1974
Anthony Leonard, San Francisco vs. New Orleans, Oct. 17, 1976
Butch Johnson, Dallas vs. Buffalo, Nov. 15, 1976
Larry Marshall, Philadelphia vs. Tampa Bay, Sept. 18, 1977
Nesby Glasgow, Baltimore vs. Kansas City, Sept. 2, 1979
Mike Nelms, Washington vs. St. Louis, Dec. 21, 1980
Leon Bright, N.Y. Giants vs. Philadelphia, Dec. 11, 1982
Pete Shaw, N.Y. Giants vs. Philadelphia, Nov. 20, 1983

Cleotha Montgomery, L.A. Raiders vs. Detroit, Dec. 10, 1984
Phil McConkey, N.Y. Giants vs. Philadelphia, Dec. 6, 1987 (OT)
Andre Hastings, Pittsburgh vs. Cleveland, Nov. 13, 1995
Steve Smith, Carolina vs. Detroit, Sept. 15, 2002
Reggie Swinton, Arizona vs. Philadelphia, Dec. 24, 2005

FAIR CATCHES
Most Fair Catches, Career
231 Brian Mitchell, Washington, 1990-99; Philadelphia, 2000-02; N.Y. Giants, 2003
162 Tim Brown, L.A. Raiders, 1988-1994; Oakland, 1995-2003; Tampa Bay, 2004
144 Glyn Milburn, Denver, 1993-95; Detroit, 1996-97; Chicago, 1998-2001; San Diego, 2001

Most Fair Catches, Season
33 Brian Mitchell, Philadelphia, 2000
27 Leo Lewis, Minnesota, 1989
Antonio Chatman, Green Bay, 2004
26 Eric Guliford, New Orleans, 1997
Glyn Milburn, Detroit, 1997
Glyn Milburn, Chicago, 2000

Most Fair Catches, Game
7 Bake Turner, N.Y. Jets vs. Miami, Nov. 20, 1966
Lem Barney, Detroit vs. Chicago, Nov. 21, 1976
Bobby Morse, Philadelphia vs. Buffalo, Dec. 27, 1987
6 Jake Scott, Miami vs. Buffalo, Dec. 20, 1970
Greg Pruitt, L.A. Raiders vs. Seattle, Oct. 7, 1984
Phil McConkey, San Diego vs. Kansas City, Dec. 17, 1989
Gerald McNeil, Houston vs. Pittsburgh, Sept. 16, 1990
Bobby Engram, Chicago vs. Minnesota, Sept. 15, 1996
Eddie Kennison, New Orleans vs. Baltimore, Dec. 19, 1999
5 By many players

YARDS GAINED
Most Seasons Leading League
3 Alvin Haymond, Baltimore, 1965-66; Los Angeles, 1969
2 Bill Dudley, Pittsburgh, 1942, 1946
Emlen Tunnell, N.Y. Giants, 1951-52
Dick Christy, N.Y. Titans, 1961-62
Claude Gibson, Oakland, 1963-64
Rodger Bird, Oakland, 1966-67
J.T. Smith, Kansas City, 1979-1980
Vai Sikahema, St. Louis, 1986-87
David Meggett, N.Y. Giants, 1989-1990
Tamarick Vanover, Kansas City, 1995, 1999

Most Yards Gained, Career
4,999 Brian Mitchell, Washington, 1990-99; Philadelphia, 2000-02; N.Y. Giants, 2003
3,708 David Meggett, N.Y. Giants, 1989-1994; New England, 1995-97; N.Y. Jets, 1998
3,601 Darrien Gordon, San Diego, 1993-94, 1996; Denver, 1997-98; Oakland, 1999-2000; Atlanta, 2001; Green Bay, 2002

Most Yards Gained, Season
875 Desmond Howard, Green Bay, 1996
692 Fulton Walker, Miami-L.A. Raiders, 1985
666 Greg Pruitt, L.A. Raiders, 1983

Most Yards Gained, Rookie, Season
656 Louis Lipps, Pittsburgh, 1984
655 Neal Colzie, Oakland, 1975
619 Leon Johnson, N.Y. Jets, 1997

Most Yards Gained, Game
- 207 LeRoy Irvin, Los Angeles vs. Atlanta, Oct. 11, 1981
- 205 George Atkinson, Oakland vs. Buffalo, Sept. 15, 1968
- 199 Eddie Drummond, Detroit vs. Jacksonville, Nov. 14, 2004 (OT)

Longest Punt Return (All TDs)
- 103 Robert Bailey, L.A. Rams vs. New Orleans, Oct. 23, 1994
- 98 Gil LeFebvre, Cincinnati vs. Brooklyn, Dec. 3, 1933
  Charlie West, Minnesota vs. Washington, Nov. 3, 1968
  Dennis Morgan, Dallas vs. St. Louis, Oct. 13, 1974
  Terance Mathis, N.Y. Jets vs. Dallas, Nov. 4, 1990
- 97 Greg Pruitt, L.A. Raiders vs. Washington, Oct. 2, 1983

AVERAGE YARDAGE
Highest Average, Career (75 returns)
- 12.78 George McAfee, Chi. Bears, 1940-41, 1945-1950 (112-1,431)
- 12.75 Jack Christiansen, Detroit, 1951-58 (85-1,084)
- 12.55 Claude Gibson, San Diego, 1961-62; Oakland, 1963-65 (110-1,381)

Highest Average, Season (Qualifiers)
- 23.00 Herb Rich, Baltimore, 1950 (12-276)
- 21.47 Jack Christiansen, Detroit, 1952 (15-322)
- 21.28 Dick Christy, N.Y. Titans, 1961 (18-383)

Highest Average, Rookie, Season (Qualifiers)
- 23.00 Herb Rich, Baltimore, 1950 (12-276)
- 20.88 Jerry Davis, Chi. Cardinals, 1948 (16-334)
- 20.73 Frank Sinkwich, Detroit, 1943 (11-228)

Highest Average, Game (3 returns)
- 51.00 Steve Smith, Carolina vs. Cincinnati, Dec. 8, 2002 (3-153)
- 47.67 Chuck Latourette, St. Louis vs. New Orleans, Sept. 29, 1968 (3-143)
- 47.33 Johnny Roland, St. Louis vs. Philadelphia, Oct. 2, 1966 (3-142)

TOUCHDOWNS
Most Touchdowns, Career
- 10 Eric Metcalf, Cleveland, 1989-1994; Atlanta, 1995-96; San Diego, 1997; Arizona, 1998; Carolina, 1999; Washington, 2001; Green Bay, 2002
- 9 Brian Mitchell, Washington, 1990-99; Philadelphia 2000-02; N.Y. Giants, 2003
- 8 Jack Christiansen, Detroit, 1951-58
  Rick Upchurch, Denver, 1975-1983
  Desmond Howard, Washington, 1992-94; Jacksonville, 1995; Green Bay, 1996, 1999; Oakland, 1997-98; Detroit, 1999-2002

Most Touchdowns, Season
- 4 Jack Christiansen, Detroit, 1951
  Rick Upchurch, Denver, 1976
- 3 Emlen Tunnell, N.Y. Giants, 1951
  Billy (White Shoes) Johnson, Houston, 1975
  LeRoy Irvin, Los Angeles, 1981
  Desmond Howard, Green Bay, 1996
  Darrien Gordon, Denver, 1997
  Eric Metcalf, San Diego, 1997
- 2 By many players

Most Touchdowns, Rookie, Season
- 4 Jack Christiansen, Detroit, 1951
- 2 By many players

Most Touchdowns, Game
- 2 Jack Christiansen, Detroit vs. Los Angeles, Oct. 14, 1951; vs. Green Bay, Nov. 22, 1951
  Dick Christy, N.Y. Titans vs. Denver, Sept. 24, 1961
  Rick Upchurch, Denver vs. Cleveland, Sept. 26, 1976
  LeRoy Irvin, Los Angeles vs. Atlanta, Oct. 11, 1981

Vai Sikahema, St. Louis vs. Tampa Bay, Dec. 21, 1986
Todd Kinchen, L.A. Rams vs. Atlanta, Dec. 27, 1992
Eric Metcalf, Cleveland vs. Pittsburgh, Oct. 24, 1993; San Diego vs. Cincinnati, Nov. 2, 1997
Darrien Gordon, Denver vs. Carolina, Nov. 9, 1997
Jermaine Lewis, Baltimore vs. Seattle, Dec. 7, 1997; Baltimore vs. N.Y. Jets, Dec. 24, 2000
Steve Smith, Carolina vs. Cincinnati, Dec. 8, 2002
Eddie Drummond, Detroit vs. Jacksonville, Nov. 14, 2004 (OT)

KICKOFF RETURNS
Most Seasons Leading League
- 3 Abe Woodson, San Francisco, 1959, 1962-63
- 2 Lynn Chandnois, Pittsburgh, 1951-52
  Bobby Jancik, Houston, 1962-63
  Travis Williams, Green Bay, 1967; Los Angeles, 1971
  Mel Gray, Detroit, 1991, 1994
  Michael Bates, Carolina, 1996-97

KICKOFF RETURNS
Most Kickoff Returns, Career
- 607 Brian Mitchell, Washington, 1990-99; Philadelphia 2000-02; N.Y. Giants, 2003
- 421 Mel Gray, New Orleans, 1986-88; Detroit, 1989-1994; Houston, 1995-96; Tennessee, 1997; Philadelphia, 1997
- 407 Glyn Milburn, Denver, 1993-95; Detroit, 1996-97; Chicago, 1998-2001; San Diego, 2001

Most Kickoff Returns, Season
- 82 MarTay Jenkins, Arizona, 2000
- 73 Josh Scobey, Arizona, 2003
  Chris Carr, Oakland, 2005
- 70 Tyrone Hughes, New Orleans, 1996
  Michael Lewis, New Orleans, 2002

Most Kickoff Returns, Rookie, Season
- 73 Josh Scobey, Arizona, 2003
  Chris Carr, Oakland, 2005
- 67 Ronney Jenkins, San Diego, 2000
- 64 Tab Perry, Cincinnati, 2005

Most Kickoff Returns, Game
- 10 Desmond Howard, Oakland vs. Seattle, Oct. 26, 1997
  Richard Alston, Cleveland vs. Cincinnati, Nov. 28, 2004
- 9 Noland Smith, Kansas City vs. Oakland, Nov. 23, 1967
  Dino Hall, Cleveland vs. Pittsburgh, Oct. 7, 1979
  Paul Palmer, Kansas City vs. Seattle, Sept. 20, 1987
  Eric Metcalf, Atlanta vs. San Francisco, Sept. 29, 1996; vs. St. Louis, Nov. 10, 1996
  Michael Bates, Carolina vs. Atlanta, Oct. 4, 1998
  Nate Jacquet, Minnesota vs. Philadelphia, Nov. 11, 2001
  Ahmad Merritt, Chicago vs. San Francisco, Sept. 7, 2003
  Josh Scobey, Arizona vs. Cleveland, Nov. 16, 2003
- 8 By many players

YARDS GAINED
Most Seasons Leading League
- 3 Bruce Harper, N.Y. Jets, 1977-79
  Tyrone Hughes, New Orleans, 1994-96
- 2 Marshall Goldberg, Chi. Cardinals, 1941-42
  Woodley Lewis, Los Angeles, 1953-54
  Al Carmichael, Green Bay, 1956-57
  Timmy Brown, Philadelphia, 1961, 1963
  Bobby Jancik, Houston, 1963, 1966
  Ron Smith, Atlanta, 1966-67

Most Yards Gained, Career

14,014   Brian Mitchell, Washington, 1990-99; Philadelphia, 2000-02; N.Y. Giants, 2003

10,250   Mel Gray, New Orleans, 1986-88; Detroit, 1989-1994; Houston, 1995-96; Tennessee, 1997; Philadelphia, 1997

9,788   Glyn Milburn, Denver, 1993-95; Detroit, 1996-97; Chicago, 1998-2001; San Diego, 2001

Most Yards Gained, Season

2,186   MarTay Jenkins, Arizona, 2000

1,807   Michael Lewis, New Orleans, 2002

1,791   Tyrone Hughes, New Orleans, 1996

Most Yards Gained, Rookie, Season

1,752   Chris Carr, Oakland, 2005

1,684   Josh Scobey, Arizona, 2003

1,577   Justin Miller, N.Y. Jets, 2005

Most Yards Gained, Game

304   Tyrone Hughes, New Orleans vs. L.A. Rams, Oct. 23, 1994

294   Wally Triplett, Detroit vs. Los Angeles, Oct. 29, 1950

278   Chad Morton, N.Y. Jets vs. Buffalo, Sept. 8, 2002 (OT)

Longest Kickoff Return (All TDs)

106   Al Carmichael, Green Bay vs. Chi. Bears, Oct. 7, 1956

Noland Smith, Kansas City vs. Denver, Dec. 17, 1967

Roy Green, St. Louis vs. Dallas, Oct. 21, 1979

105   Frank Seno, Chi. Cardinals vs. N.Y. Giants, Oct. 20, 1946

Ollie Matson, Chi. Cardinals vs. Washington, Oct. 14, 1956

Abe Woodson, San Francisco vs. Los Angeles, Nov. 8, 1959

Timmy Brown, Philadelphia vs. Cleveland, Sept. 17, 1961

Jon Arnett, Los Angeles vs. Detroit, Oct. 29, 1961

Eugene (Mercury) Morris, Miami vs. Cincinnati, Sept. 14, 1969

Travis Williams, Los Angeles vs. New Orleans, Dec. 5, 1971

Terry Fair, Detroit vs. Tampa Bay, Sept. 28, 1998

104   By many players

AVERAGE YARDAGE

Highest Average, Career (75 returns)

30.56   Gale Sayers, Chicago, 1965-1971 (91-2,781)

29.57   Lynn Chandnois, Pittsburgh, 1950-56 (92-2,720)

28.69   Abe Woodson, San Francisco, 1958-1964; St. Louis, 1965-66 (193-5,538)

Highest Average, Season (Qualifiers)

41.06   Travis Williams, Green Bay, 1967 (18-739)

37.69   Gale Sayers, Chicago, 1967 (16-603)

35.50   Ollie Matson, Chi. Cardinals, 1958 (14-497)

Highest Average, Rookie, Season (Qualifiers)

41.06   Travis Williams, Green Bay, 1967 (18-739)

33.08   Tom Moore, Green Bay, 1960 (12-397)

32.88   Duriel Harris, Miami, 1976 (17-559)

Highest Average, Game (3 returns)

73.50   Wally Triplett, Detroit vs. Los Angeles, Oct. 29, 1950 (4-294)

67.33   Lenny Lyles, San Francisco vs. Baltimore, Dec. 18, 1960 (3-202)

65.33   Ken Hall, Houston vs. N.Y. Titans, Oct. 23, 1960 (3-196)

TOUCHDOWNS

Most Touchdowns, Career

6   Ollie Matson, Chi. Cardinals, 1952, 1954-58; L.A. Rams, 1959-1962; Detroit, 1963; Philadelphia, 1964

Gale Sayers, Chicago, 1965-1971

Travis Williams, Green Bay, 1967-1970; Los Angeles, 1971

Mel Gray, New Orleans, 1986-88; Detroit, 1989-1994; Houston, 1995-96; Tennessee, 1997; Philadelphia, 1997

Dante Hall, Kansas City, 2000-05

5   Bobby Mitchell, Cleveland, 1958-1961; Washington, 1962-68

Abe Woodson, San Francisco, 1958-1964; St. Louis, 1965-66

Timmy Brown, Green Bay, 1959; Philadelphia, 1960-67; Baltimore, 1968

Michael Bates, Seattle, 1993-94; Cleveland, 1995; Carolina, 1996-2000, 2002; Washington, 2001; N.Y. Jets, 2003; Dallas, 2003

4   Cecil Turner, Chicago, 1968-1973

Ron Brown, L.A. Rams, 1984-89, 1991; L.A. Raiders, 1990

Jon Vaughn, New England, 1991-92; Seattle, 1993-94; Kansas City, 1994

Andre Coleman, San Diego, 1994-96; Seattle, 1997; Pittsburgh, 1997-98

Tamarick Vanover, Kansas City, 1995-99, San Diego, 2002

Tony Horne, St. Louis, 1998-2000

Brian Mitchell, Washington, 1990-99; Philadelphia, 2000-02; N.Y. Giants, 2003

Darrick Vaughn, Atlanta, 2000-01; Houston, 2003

Terrence McGee, Buffalo, 2003-05

Most Touchdowns, Season

4   Travis Williams, Green Bay, 1967

Cecil Turner, Chicago, 1970

3   Verda (Vitamin T) Smith, Los Angeles, 1950

Abe Woodson, San Francisco, 1963

Gale Sayers, Chicago, 1967

Raymond Clayborn, New England, 1977

Ron Brown, L.A. Rams, 1985

Mel Gray, Detroit, 1994

Darrick Vaughn, Atlanta, 2000

Terrence McGee, Buffalo, 2004

2   By many players

Most Touchdowns, Rookie, Season

4   Travis Williams, Green Bay, 1967

3   Raymond Clayborn, New England, 1977

Darrick Vaughn, Atlanta, 2000

2   By many players

Most Touchdowns, Game

2   Timmy Brown, Philadelphia vs. Dallas, Nov. 6, 1966

Travis Williams, Green Bay vs. Cleveland, Nov. 12, 1967

Ron Brown, L.A. Rams vs. Green Bay, Nov. 24, 1985

Tyrone Hughes, New Orleans vs. L.A. Rams, Oct. 23, 1994

Chad Morton, N.Y. Jets vs. Buffalo, Sept. 8, 2002 (OT)

COMBINED KICK RETURNS

Most Combined Kick Returns, Career

1,070   Brian Mitchell, Washington, 1990-99; Philadelphia, 2000-02; N.Y. Giants, 2003 (p-463, k-607)

711   Glyn Milburn, Denver, 1993-95; Detroit, 1996-97; Chicago, 1998-2001; San Diego, 2001 (p-304, k-407)

673   Mel Gray, New Orleans, 1986-88; Detroit, 1989-1994; Houston, 1995-96; Tennessee, 1997; Philadelphia, 1997 (p-252, k-421)

Most Combined Kick Returns, Season

114   Michael Lewis, New Orleans, 2002 (p-44, k-70)

B.J. Sams, Baltimore, 2004 (p-55, k-59)

107   Chris Carr, Oakland, 2005 (p-34, k-73)

Dante Hall, Kansas City, 2005 (p-42, k-65)

105 Reggie Swinton, Arizona, 2005 (p-42, k-63)

Most Combined Kick Returns, Game
13 Stump Mitchell, St. Louis vs. Atlanta, Oct. 18, 1981
    (p-6, k-7)
    Ronnie Harris, New England vs. Pittsburgh,
    Dec. 5, 1993 (p-10, k-3)
12 Mel Renfro, Dallas vs. Green Bay, Nov. 29, 1964
    (p-4, k-8)
    Larry Jones, Washington vs. Dallas, Dec. 13, 1975
    (p-6, k-6)
    Eddie Brown, Washington vs. Tampa Bay,
    Oct. 9, 1977 (p-11, k-1)
    Nesby Glasgow, Baltimore vs. Denver, Sept. 2, 1979
    (p-9, k-3)
    Tim Dwight, Atlanta vs. Detroit, Nov. 12, 2000
    (p-8, k-4)
    Wes Welker, Miami vs. Buffalo, Dec. 5, 2004
    (p-6, k-6)
11 By many players

YARDS GAINED
Most Yards Returned, Career
19,013 Brian Mitchell, Washington, 1990-99; Philadelphia,
        2000-02; N.Y. Giants, 2003 (p-4,999; k-14,014)
13,003 Mel Gray, New Orleans, 1986-88; Detroit,
        1989-1994; Houston, 1995-96; Tennessee,
        1997; Philadelphia, 1997 (p-2,753; k-10,250)
12,772 Glyn Milburn, Denver, 1993-95; Detroit, 1996-97;
        Chicago, 1998-2001; San Diego, 2001
        (p-2,984; k-9,788)

Most Yards Returned, Season
2,432 Michael Lewis, New Orleans, 2002 (p-625, k-1,807)
2,187 MarTay Jenkins, Arizona, 2000 (p-1, k-2,186)
1,992 Charlie Rogers, Seattle, 2000 (p-363, k-1,629)

Most Yards Returned, Game
347 Tyrone Hughes, New Orleans vs. L.A. Rams,
     Oct. 23, 1994 (p-43, k-304)
294 Wally Triplett, Detroit vs. Los Angeles, Oct. 29, 1950
     (k-294)
     Woodley Lewis, Los Angeles vs. Detroit,
     Oct. 18, 1953 (p-120, k-174)
289 Eddie Payton, Detroit vs. Minnesota, Dec. 17, 1977
     (p-105, k-184)

TOUCHDOWNS
Most Touchdowns, Career
13 Brian Mitchell, Washington, 1990-99; Philadelphia,
    2000-02; N.Y. Giants, 2003 (p-9, k-4)
12 Eric Metcalf, Cleveland, 1989-1994; Atlanta,
    1995-96; San Diego, 1997; Arizona, 1998;
    Carolina, 1999; Washington, 2001; Green Bay,
    2002 (p-10, k-2)
10 Dante Hall, Kansas City, 2000-05 (p-4, k-6)

Most Touchdowns, Season
4 Jack Christiansen, Detroit, 1951 (p-4)
   Emlen Tunnell, N.Y. Giants, 1951 (p-3, k-1)
   Gale Sayers, Chicago, 1967 (p-1, k-3)
   Travis Williams, Green Bay, 1967 (k-4)
   Cecil Turner, Chicago, 1970 (k-4)
   Billy Johnson, Houston, 1975 (p-3, k-1)
   Rick Upchurch, Denver, 1976 (p-4)
   Dante Hall, Kansas City, 2003 (p-2, r-2)
   Eddie Drummond, Detroit, 2004 (p-2, k-2)
3 Verda (Vitamin T) Smith, Los Angeles, 1950 (k-3)
   Abe Woodson, San Francisco, 1963 (k-3)
   Raymond Clayborn, New England, 1977 (k-3)
   Billy Johnson, Houston, 1977 (p-2, k-1)
   LeRoy Irvin, Los Angeles, 1981 (p-3)
   Ron Brown, L.A. Rams, 1985 (k-3)
   Tyrone Hughes, New Orleans, 1993 (p-2, k-1)

Mel Gray, Detroit, 1994 (k-3)
Andre Coleman, San Diego, 1995 (p-2; k-1)
Tamarick Vanover, Kansas City, 1995 (p-1, k-2)
Desmond Howard, Green Bay, 1996 (p-3)
Darrien Gordon, Denver, 1997 (p-3)
Eric Metcalf, San Diego, 1997 (p-3)
Glyn Milburn, Chicago, 1998 (p-2, k-1)
Roell Preston, Green Bay, 1998 (p-2, k-1)
Darrick Vaughn, Atlanta, 2000 (k-3)
Steve Smith, Carolina, 2001 (p-1, k-2)
Michael Lewis, New Orleans, 2002 (p-1, k-2)
Dante Hall, Kansas City, 2002 (p-2, k-1)
Terrence McGee, Buffalo, 2004 (k-3)
2 By many players

Most Touchdowns, Game
2 Jack Christiansen, Detroit vs. Los Angeles,
   Oct. 14, 1951 (p-2); vs. Green Bay,
   Nov. 22, 1951 (p-2)
   Jim Patton, N.Y. Giants vs. Washington,
   Oct. 30, 1955 (p-1, k-1)
   Bobby Mitchell, Cleveland vs. Philadelphia,
   Nov. 23, 1958 (p-1, k-1)
   Dick Christy, N.Y. Titans vs. Denver, Sept. 24, 1961
   (p-2)
   Al Frazier, Denver vs. Boston, Dec. 3, 1961 (p-1, k-1)
   Timmy Brown, Philadelphia vs. Dallas, Nov. 6, 1966
   (k-2)
   Travis Williams, Green Bay vs. Cleveland,
   Nov. 12, 1967 (k-2); vs. Pittsburgh,
   Nov. 2, 1969 (p-1, k-1)
   Gale Sayers, Chicago vs. San Francisco,
   Dec. 3, 1967 (p-1, k-1)
   Rick Upchurch, Denver vs. Cleveland,
   Sept. 26, 1976 (p-2)
   Eddie Payton, Detroit vs. Minnesota, Dec. 17, 1977
   (p-1, k-1)
   LeRoy Irvin, Los Angeles vs. Atlanta, Oct. 11, 1981
   (p-2)
   Ron Brown, L.A. Rams vs. Green Bay,
   Nov. 24, 1985 (k-2)
   Vai Sikahema, St. Louis vs. Tampa Bay,
   Dec. 21, 1986 (p-2)
   Todd Kinchen, L.A. Rams vs. Atlanta, Dec. 27, 1992
   (p-2)
   Eric Metcalf, Cleveland vs. Pittsburgh, Oct. 24, 1993
   (p-2); San Diego vs. Cincinnati, Nov. 2, 1997
   (p-2)
   Tyrone Hughes, New Orleans vs. L.A. Rams,
   Oct. 23, 1994 (k-2)
   Darrien Gordon, Denver vs. Carolina, Nov. 9, 1997
   (p-2)
   Jermaine Lewis, Baltimore vs. Seattle, Dec. 7, 1997
   (p-2); Baltimore vs. N.Y. Jets, Dec. 24, 2000
   (p-2)
   Chad Morton, N.Y. Jets vs. Buffalo, Sept. 8, 2002
   (OT) (k-2)
   Michael Lewis, New Orleans vs. Washington,
   Oct. 13, 2002 (p-1, k-1)
   Dante Hall, Kansas City vs. St. Louis, Dec. 8, 2002
   (p-1, k-1)
   Steve Smith, Carolina vs. Cincinnati, Dec. 8, 2002
   (p-2)
   Eddie Drummond, Detroit vs. Jacksonville,
   Nov. 14, 2004 (OT) (p-2)

FUMBLES
Most Fumbles, Career
161 Warren Moon, Houston, 1984-1993; Minnesota,
     1994-96; Seattle, 1997-98; Kansas City,
     1999-2000

153 Dave Krieg, Seattle, 1980-1991; Kansas City,
     1992-93; Detroit, 1994; Arizona, 1995;
     Chicago, 1996; Tennessee, 1997-98
137 John Elway, Denver, 1983-1998

Most Fumbles, Season
  23 Kerry Collins, N.Y. Giants, 2001
      Daunte Culpepper, Minnesota, 2002
  21 Tony Banks, St. Louis, 1996
      David Carr, Houston, 2002
  18 Dave Krieg, Seattle, 1989
      Warren Moon, Houston, 1990

Most Fumbles, Game
   7 Len Dawson, Kansas City vs. San Diego,
     Nov. 15, 1964
   6 Sam Etcheverry, St. Louis vs. N.Y. Giants,
     Sept. 17, 1961
     Dave Krieg, Seattle vs. Kansas City, Nov. 5, 1989
     Brett Favre, Green Bay vs. Tampa Bay, Dec. 7, 1998
     Kurt Warner, St. Louis vs. N.Y. Giants, Sept. 7, 2003
     Chad Pennington, N.Y. Jets vs. Kansas City,
     Sept. 11, 2005
   5 Paul Christman, Chi. Cardinals vs. Green Bay,
     Nov. 10, 1946
     Charlie Conerly, N.Y. Giants vs. San Francisco,
     Dec. 1, 1957
     Jack Kemp, Buffalo vs. Houston, Oct. 29, 1967
     Roman Gabriel, Philadelphia vs. Oakland,
     Nov. 21, 1976
     Randall Cunningham, Philadelphia vs. L.A. Raiders,
     Nov. 30, 1986 (OT)
     Willie Totten, Buffalo vs. Indianapolis, Oct. 4, 1987
     Dave Walter, Cincinnati vs. Seattle, Oct. 11, 1987
     Dave Krieg, Seattle vs. San Diego, Nov. 25, 1990 (OT)
     Andre Ware, Detroit vs. Green Bay, Dec. 6, 1992
     Steve Beuerlein, Carolina vs. San Francisco,
     Nov. 8, 1998
     Patrick Ramsey, Washington vs. Green Bay,
     Oct. 20, 2002

FUMBLES RECOVERED

Most Fumbles Recovered, Career, Own and Opponents'
  56 Warren Moon, Houston, 1984-1993; Minnesota,
     1994-96; Seattle, 1997-98; Kansas City,
     1999-2000 (56 own)
  47 Dave Krieg, Seattle, 1980-1991; Kansas City,
     1992-93; Detroit, 1994; Arizona, 1995; Chica-
     go, 1996; Tennessee, 1997-98 (47 own)
  45 Boomer Esiason, Cincinnati, 1984-1992, 1997;
     N.Y. Jets, 1993-95; Arizona, 1996 (45 own)

Most Fumbles Recovered, Season, Own and Opponents'
  12 David Carr, Houston, 2002 (12 own)
   9 Don Hultz, Minnesota, 1963 (9 opp)
     Dave Krieg, Seattle, 1989 (9 own)
     Brian Griese, Denver, 1999 (9 own)
     Jon Kitna, Seattle, 2000 (9 own)
   8 Paul Christman, Chi. Cardinals, 1945 (8 own)
     Joe Schmidt, Detroit, 1955 (8 opp)
     Bill Butler, Minnesota, 1963 (8 own)
     Kermit Alexander, San Francisco, 1965
     (4 own, 4 opp)
     Jack Lambert, Pittsburgh, 1976 (1 own, 7 opp)
     Danny White, Dallas, 1981 (8 own)
     Dan Marino, Miami, 1988 (7 own, 1 opp)
     Tony Banks, St. Louis, 1998 (8 own)

Most Fumbles Recovered, Game, Own and Opponents'
   4 Otto Graham, Cleveland vs. N.Y. Giants,
     Oct. 25, 1953 (4 own)
     Sam Etcheverry, St. Louis vs. N.Y. Giants,
     Sept. 17, 1961 (4 own)

Roman Gabriel, Los Angeles vs. San Francisco,
     Oct. 12, 1969 (4 own)
Joe Ferguson, Buffalo vs. Miami, Sept. 18, 1977
     (4 own)
Randall Cunningham, Philadelphia vs. L.A. Raiders,
     Nov. 30, 1986 (OT) (4 own)
   3 By many players

OWN FUMBLES RECOVERED

Most Own Fumbles Recovered, Career
  56 Warren Moon, Houston, 1984-1993; Minnesota,
     1994-96; Seattle, 1997-98; Kansas City,
     1999-2000
  47 Dave Krieg, Seattle, 1980-1991; Kansas City,
     1992-93; Detroit, 1994; Arizona, 1995;
     Chicago, 1996; Tennessee, 1997-98
  45 Boomer Esiason, Cincinnati, 1984-1992, 1997;
     N.Y. Jets, 1993-95; Arizona, 1996

Most Own Fumbles Recovered, Season
  12 David Carr, Houston, 2002
   9 Dave Krieg, Seattle, 1989
     Brian Griese, Denver, 1999
     Jon Kitna, Seattle, 2000
   8 Paul Christman, Chi. Cardinals, 1945
     Bill Butler, Minnesota, 1963
     Danny White, Dallas, 1981
     Tony Banks, St. Louis, 1998

Most Own Fumbles Recovered, Game
   4 Otto Graham, Cleveland vs. N.Y. Giants, Oct. 25, 1953
     Sam Etcheverry, St. Louis vs. N.Y. Giants,
     Sept. 17, 1961
     Roman Gabriel, Los Angeles vs. San Francisco,
     Oct. 12, 1969
     Joe Ferguson, Buffalo vs. Miami, Sept. 18, 1977
     Randall Cunningham, Philadelphia vs. L.A. Raiders,
     Nov. 30, 1986 (OT)
   3 By many players

OPPONENTS' FUMBLES RECOVERED

Most Opponents' Fumbles Recovered, Career
  29 Jim Marshall, Cleveland, 1960; Minnesota, 1961-1979
  28 Rickey Jackson, New Orleans, 1981-1993;
     San Francisco, 1994-95
  26 Kevin Greene, L.A. Rams, 1985-1992; Pittsburgh,
     1993-95; Carolina, 1996, 1998-99;
     San Francisco, 1997
     Cornelius Bennett, Buffalo, 1987-1995; Atlanta,
     1996-98; Indianapolis, 1999-2000

Most Opponents' Fumbles Recovered, Season
   9 Don Hultz, Minnesota, 1963
   8 Joe Schmidt, Detroit, 1955
   7 Alan Page, Minnesota, 1970
     Jack Lambert, Pittsburgh, 1976
     Ray Childress, Houston, 1988
     Rickey Jackson, New Orleans, 1990

Most Opponents' Fumbles Recovered, Game
   3 Corwin Clatt, Chi. Cardinals vs. Detroit, Nov. 6, 1949
     Vic Sears, Philadelphia vs. Green Bay, Nov. 2, 1952
     Ed Beatty, San Francisco vs. Los Angeles,
     Oct. 7, 1956
     Ron Carroll, Houston vs. Cincinnati, Oct. 27, 1974
     Maurice Spencer, New Orleans vs. Atlanta,
     Oct. 10, 1976
     Steve Nelson, New England vs. Philadelphia,
     Oct. 8, 1978
     Charles Jackson, Kansas City vs. Pittsburgh,
     Sept. 6, 1981
     Willie Buchanon, San Diego vs. Denver,
     Sept. 27, 1981

Joey Browner, Minnesota vs. San Francisco,
Sept. 8, 1985
Ray Childress, Houston vs. Washington, Oct. 30, 1988
John Thierry, Chicago vs. Houston, Oct. 22, 1995
Stephen Boyd, Detroit vs. Chicago, Oct. 4, 1998
Darryl Williams, Seattle vs. Kansas City, Oct. 4, 1998
Rod Woodson, Oakland vs. Pittsburgh, Sept. 15, 2002
Brian Young, St. Louis vs. Baltimore, Nov. 9, 2003
2 By many players

YARDS RETURNING FUMBLES
Longest Fumble Run (All TDs)
104 Jack Tatum, Oakland vs. Green Bay, Sept. 24, 1972
Aeneas Williams, Arizona vs. Washington,
Nov. 5, 2000
102 Travis Davis, Pittsburgh vs. Carolina, Dec. 26, 1999
100 Chris Martin, Kansas City vs. Miami, Oct. 13, 1991

TOUCHDOWNS
Most Touchdowns, Career (Total)
5 Jessie Tuggle, Atlanta, 1987-2000
Jason Taylor, Miami, 1997-2005
4 Bill Thompson, Denver, 1969-1981
Derrick Thomas, Kansas City, 1989-1999
3 By many players
Most Touchdowns, Season (Total)
2 Harold McPhail, Boston, 1934
Harry Ebding, Detroit, 1937
John Morelli, Boston, 1944
Frank Maznicki, Boston, 1947
Fred (Dippy) Evans, Chi. Bears, 1948
Ralph Heywood, Boston, 1948
Art Tait, N.Y. Yanks, 1951
John Dwyer, Los Angeles, 1952
Leo Sugar, Chi. Cardinals, 1957
Doug Cline, Houston, 1961
Jim Bradshaw, Pittsburgh, 1964
Royce Berry, Cincinnati, 1970
Ahmad Rashad, Buffalo, 1974
Tim Gray, Kansas City, 1977
Charles Phillips, Oakland, 1978
Kenny Johnson, Atlanta, 1981
George Martin, N.Y. Giants, 1981
Del Rodgers, Green Bay, 1982
Mike Douglass, Green Bay, 1983
Shelton Robinson, Seattle, 1983
Erik McMillan, N.Y. Jets, 1989
Les Miller, San Diego, 1990
Seth Joyner, Philadelphia, 1991
Robert Goff, New Orleans, 1992
Willie Clay, Detroit, 1993
Tyrone Hughes, New Orleans, 1994
Chad Brown, Seattle, 1997
Marcus Robertson, Tennessee, 1997
Dwayne Rudd, Minnesota, 1998
Keith McKenzie, Green Bay, 1999
Ronde Barber, Tampa Bay, 2004
Leonard Little, St. Louis, 2004
Antwan Odom, Tennessee, 2005
Adalius Thomas, Baltimore, 2005
Most Touchdowns, Career (Own recovered)
2 Ken Kavanaugh, Chi. Bears, 1940-41, 1945-1950
Mike Ditka, Chicago, 1961-66; Philadelphia,
1967-68; Dallas, 1969-1972
Gail Cogdill, Detroit, 1960-68; Baltimore, 1968;
Atlanta, 1969-1970
Ahmad Rashad, St. Louis, 1972-73; Buffalo, 1974;
Minnesota, 1976-1982
Jim Mitchell, Atlanta, 1969-1979
Drew Pearson, Dallas, 1973-1983

Del Rodgers, Green Bay, 1982, 1984; San Francisco,
1987-88
Alan Ricard, Baltimore, 2001-05
Most Touchdowns, Season (Own recovered)
2 Ahmad Rashad, Buffalo, 1974
Del Rodgers, Green Bay, 1982
1 By many players
Most Touchdowns, Career (Opponents' recovered)
5 Jessie Tuggle, Atlanta, 1987-2000
Jason Taylor, Miami, 1997-2005
4 Derrick Thomas, Kansas City, 1989-1999
3 By many players
Most Touchdowns, Season (Opponents' recovered)
2 Harold McPhail, Boston, 1934
Harry Ebding, Detroit, 1937
John Morelli, Boston, 1944
Frank Maznicki, Boston, 1947
Fred (Dippy) Evans, Chi. Bears, 1948
Ralph Heywood, Boston, 1948
Art Tait, N.Y. Yanks, 1951
John Dwyer, Los Angeles, 1952
Leo Sugar, Chi. Cardinals, 1957
Doug Cline, Houston, 1961
Jim Bradshaw, Pittsburgh, 1964
Royce Berry, Cincinnati, 1970
Tim Gray, Kansas City, 1977
Charles Phillips, Oakland, 1978
Kenny Johnson, Atlanta, 1981
George Martin, N.Y. Giants, 1981
Mike Douglass, Green Bay, 1983
Shelton Robinson, Seattle, 1983
Erik McMillan, N.Y. Jets, 1989
Les Miller, San Diego, 1990
Seth Joyner, Philadelphia, 1991
Robert Goff, New Orleans, 1992
Willie Clay, Detroit, 1993
Tyrone Hughes, New Orleans, 1994
Chad Brown, Seattle, 1997
Marcus Robertson, Tennessee, 1997
Dwayne Rudd, Minnesota, 1998
Keith McKenzie, Green Bay, 1999
Ronde Barber, Tampa Bay, 2004
Leonard Little, St. Louis, 2004
Antwan Odom, Tennessee, 2005
Adalius Thomas, Baltimore, 2005
Most Touchdowns, Game (Opponents' recovered)
2 Fred (Dippy) Evans, Chi. Bears vs. Washington,
Nov. 28, 1948

COMBINED NET YARDS GAINED
Rushing, receiving, interception returns, punt returns, kickoff
returns, and fumble returns
Most Seasons Leading League
5 Jim Brown, Cleveland, 1958-1961, 1964
4 Brian Mitchell, Washington, 1994-96, 1998
3 Cliff Battles, Boston, 1932-33; Washington, 1937
Gale Sayers, Chicago, 1965-67
Eric Dickerson, L.A. Rams, 1983-84, 1986
Thurman Thomas, Buffalo, 1989, 1991-92
Most Consecutive Seasons Leading League
4 Jim Brown, Cleveland, 1958-1961
3 Gale Sayers, Chicago, 1965-67
Brian Mitchell, Washington, 1994-96
2 Cliff Battles, Boston, 1932-33
Charley Trippi, Chi. Cardinals, 1948-49
Timmy Brown, Philadelphia, 1962-63
Floyd Little, Denver, 1967-68
James Brooks, San Diego, 1981-82
Eric Dickerson, L.A. Rams, 1983-84

Thurman Thomas, Buffalo, 1991-92
Dante Hall, Kansas City, 2003-04

ATTEMPTS
Most Attempts, Career
4,939 Emmitt Smith, Dallas, 1990-2002; Arizona, 2003-04
4,368 Walter Payton, Chicago, 1975-1987
4,016 Curtis Martin, New England, 1995-97; N.Y. Jets, 1998-2005
Most Attempts, Season
496 James Wilder, Tampa Bay, 1984
455 Eddie George, Tennessee, 2000
451 LaDainian Tomlinson, San Diego, 2002
Most Attempts, Rookie, Season
442 Eric Dickerson, L.A. Rams, 1983
433 Edgerrin James, Indianapolis, 1999
401 Curtis Martin, New England, 1995
Most Attempts, Game
48 James Wilder, Tampa Bay vs. Pittsburgh, Oct. 30, 1983
LaDainian Tomlinson, San Diego vs. Denver, Dec. 1, 2002 (OT)
47 James Wilder, Tampa Bay vs. Green Bay, Sept. 30, 1984 (OT)
Terrell Davis, Denver vs. Buffalo, Oct. 26, 1997 (OT)
46 Gerald Riggs, Atlanta vs. L.A. Rams, Nov. 17, 1985

YARDS GAINED
Most Yards Gained, Career
23,546 Jerry Rice, San Francisco, 1985-2000; Oakland, 2001-04; Seattle, 2004
23,330 Brian Mitchell, Washington, 1990-99; Philadelphia, 2000-02; N.Y. Giants, 2003
21,803 Walter Payton, Chicago, 1975-1987
Most Yards Gained, Season
2,690 Derrick Mason, Tennessee, 2000
2,647 Michael Lewis, New Orleans, 2002
2,535 Lionel James, San Diego, 1985
Most Yards Gained, Rookie, Season
2,317 Tim Brown, L.A. Raiders, 1988
2,272 Gale Sayers, Chicago, 1965
2,212 Eric Dickerson, L.A. Rams, 1983
Most Yards Gained, Game
404 Glyn Milburn, Denver vs. Seattle, Dec. 10, 1995
373 Billy Cannon, Houston vs. N.Y. Titans, Dec. 10, 1961
356 Michael Lewis, New Orleans vs. Washington, Oct. 13, 2002

SACKS
Sacks have been compiled since 1982.
Most Seasons Leading League
2 Mark Gastineau, N.Y. Jets, 1983-84
Reggie White, Philadelphia, 1987-88
Kevin Greene, Pittsburgh, 1994; Carolina, 1996
Michael Strahan, N.Y. Giants, 2001, 2003
Most Sacks, Career
200.0 Bruce Smith, Buffalo, 1985-1999; Washington, 2000-03
198.0 Reggie White, Philadelphia, 1985-1992; Green Bay, 1993-98; Carolina, 2000
160.0 Kevin Greene, L.A. Rams, 1985-1992; Pittsburgh, 1993-95; Carolina, 1996, 1998-99; San Francisco, 1997
Most Sacks, Season
22.5 Michael Strahan, N.Y. Giants, 2001
22.0 Mark Gastineau, N.Y. Jets, 1984
21.0 Reggie White, Philadelphia, 1987
Chris Doleman, Minnesota, 1989
Most Sacks, Rookie, Season
14.5 Jevon Kearse, Tennessee, 1999
13.0 Dwight Freeney, Indianapolis, 2002

12.5 Leslie O'Neal, San Diego, 1986
Simeon Rice, Arizona, 1996
Most Sacks, Game
7.0 Derrick Thomas, Kansas City vs. Seattle, Nov. 11, 1990
6.0 Fred Dean, San Francisco vs. New Orleans, Nov. 13, 1983
Derrick Thomas, Kansas City vs. Oakland, Sept. 6, 1998
5.5 William Gay, Detroit vs. Tampa Bay, Sept. 4, 1983
Most Seasons, 10 or More Sacks
13 Bruce Smith, Buffalo, 1986-1990, 1992-98; Washington, 2000
12 Reggie White, Philadelphia, 1985-1992; Green Bay, 1993, 1995, 1997-98
10 Kevin Greene, L.A. Rams, 1988-1990, 1992; Pittsburgh, 1993-94; Carolina, 1996, 1998-99; San Francisco, 1997
Most Consecutive Seasons, 10 or More Sacks
9 Reggie White, Philadelphia, 1985-1992; Green Bay, 1993
8 John Randle, Minnesota, 1992-99
7 Lawrence Taylor, N.Y. Giants, 1984-1990
Bruce Smith, Buffalo, 1992-98
Most Consecutive Games, Sack
10 Simon Fletcher, Denver, Nov. 15, 1992-Sept. 20, 1993
9 Bruce Smith, Buffalo, Nov. 16, 1986-Oct. 25, 1987
Kevin Greene, San Francisco-Carolina, Dec. 7, 1997-Oct. 18, 1998
8 By many players

MISCELLANEOUS
Longest Return of Missed Field Goal (All TDs)
108 Nathan Vasher, Chicago vs. San Francisco, Nov. 13, 2005
107 Chris McAlister, Baltimore vs. Denver, Sept. 30, 2002
104 Aaron Glenn, N.Y. Jets vs. Indianapolis, Nov. 15, 1998

TEAM RECORDS

CHAMPIONSHIPS
Most Seasons League Champion
12 Green Bay, 1929-1931, 1936, 1939, 1944, 1961-62, 1965-67, 1996
9 Chi. Bears, 1921, 1932-33, 1940-41, 1943, 1946, 1963, 1985
6 N.Y. Giants, 1927, 1934, 1938, 1956, 1986, 1990
Most Consecutive Seasons League Champion
3 Green Bay, 1929-1931
Green Bay, 1965-67
2 Canton, 1922-23
Chi. Bears, 1932-33
Chi. Bears, 1940-41
Philadelphia, 1948-49
Detroit, 1952-53
Cleveland, 1954-55
Baltimore, 1958-59
Houston, 1960-61
Green Bay, 1961-62
Buffalo, 1964-65
Miami, 1972-73
Pittsburgh, 1974-75
Pittsburgh, 1978-79
San Francisco, 1988-89
Dallas, 1992-93
Denver, 1997-98
New England, 2003-04

Most Times Finishing First, Regular Season
- 21   N.Y. Giants, 1927, 1933-35, 1938-39, 1941, 1944, 1946, 1956, 1958-59, 1961-63, 1986, 1989-1990, 1997, 2000, 2005
- 20   Green Bay, 1929-1931, 1936, 1938-39, 1944, 1960-62, 1965-67, 1972, 1995-97, 2002-04
-     Chi. Bears, 1921, 1932-34, 1937, 1940-43, 1946, 1956, 1963, 1984-88, 1990, 2001, 2005
- 19   Dallas, 1966-1971, 1973, 1976-79, 1981, 1985, 1992-96, 1998

Most Consecutive Times Finishing First, Regular Season
- 7   Los Angeles, 1973-79
- 6   Cleveland, 1950-55
-    Dallas, 1966-1971
-    Minnesota, 1973-78
-    Pittsburgh, 1974-79
- 5   Oakland, 1972-76
-    Chicago, 1984-88
-    San Francisco, 1986-1990
-    Dallas, 1992-96

GAMES WON

Most Consecutive Games Won
- 18   New England, 2003-04
- 17   Chi. Bears, 1933-34
- 16   Chi. Bears, 1941-42
-     Miami, 1971-73
-     Miami, 1983-84
-     Pittsburgh, 2004-05

Most Consecutive Games Without Defeat
- 25   Canton, 1921-23 (won 22, tied 3)
- 24   Chi. Bears, 1941-43 (won 23, tied 1)
- 23   Green Bay, 1928-1930 (won 21, tied 2)

Most Games Won, Season
- 15   San Francisco, 1984
-     Chicago, 1985
-     Minnesota, 1998
-     Pittsburgh, 2004
- 14   Frankford, 1926
-     Miami, 1972
-     Pittsburgh, 1978
-     Washington, 1983
-     Miami, 1984
-     Chicago, 1986
-     N.Y. Giants, 1986
-     San Francisco, 1989
-     San Francisco, 1990
-     Washington, 1991
-     San Francisco, 1992
-     Atlanta, 1998
-     Denver, 1998
-     Jacksonville, 1999
-     St. Louis, 2001
-     New England, 2003
-     New England, 2004
-     Indianapolis, 2005
- 13   By many teams

Most Consecutive Games Won, Season
- 14   Miami, 1972
-     Pittsburgh, 2004
- 13   Chi. Bears, 1934
-     Denver, 1998
-     Indianapolis, 2005
- 12   Minnesota, 1969
-     Chicago, 1985
-     New England, 2003

Most Consecutive Games Won, Start of Season
- 14   Miami, 1972, entire season
- 13   Chi. Bears, 1934, entire season
-     Denver, 1998

-     Indianapolis, 2005
- 12   Chicago, 1985

Most Consecutive Games Won, End of Season
- 14   Miami, 1972, entire season
-     Pittsburgh, 2004
- 13   Chi. Bears, 1934, entire season
- 12   New England, 2003

Most Consecutive Games Without Defeat, Season
- 14   Miami, 1972 (won 14)
-     Pittsburgh, 2004 (won 14)
- 13   Chi. Bears, 1926 (won 11, tied 2)
-     Green Bay, 1929 (won 12, tied 1)
-     Chi. Bears, 1934 (won 13)
-     Baltimore, 1967 (won 11, tied 2)
-     Denver, 1998 (won 13)
-     Indianapolis, 2005 (won 13)
- 12   Canton, 1922 (won 10, tied 2)
-     Canton, 1923 (won 11, tied 1)
-     Minnesota, 1969 (won 12)
-     Chicago, 1985 (won 12)
-     New England, 2003 (won 12)

Most Consecutive Games Without Defeat, Start of Season
- 14   Miami, 1972 (won 14), entire season
- 13   Chi. Bears, 1926 (won 11, tied 2)
-     Green Bay, 1929 (won 12, tied 1), entire season
-     Chi. Bears, 1934 (won 13), entire season
-     Baltimore, 1967 (won 11, tied 2)
-     Denver, 1998 (won 13)
-     Indianapolis, 2005 (won 13)
- 12   Canton, 1922 (won 10, tied 2), entire season
-     Canton, 1923 (won 11, tied 1), entire season
-     Chicago, 1985 (won 12)

Most Consecutive Games Without Defeat, End of Season
- 14   Miami, 1972 (won 14), entire season
-     Pittsburgh, 2004 (won 14)
- 13   Green Bay, 1929 (won 12, tied 1), entire season
-     Chi. Bears, 1934 (won 13), entire season
- 12   Canton, 1922 (won 10, tied 2), entire season
-     Canton, 1923 (won 11, tied 1), entire season
-     New England, 2003 (won 12)

Most Consecutive Home Games Won
- 27   Miami, 1971-74
- 25   Green Bay, 1995-98
- 24   Denver, 1996-98

Most Consecutive Home Games Without Defeat
- 30   Green Bay, 1928-1933 (won 27, tied 3)
- 27   Miami, 1971-74 (won 27)
- 25   Chi. Bears, 1923-25 (won 19, tied 6)
-     Green Bay, 1995-98 (won 25)

Most Consecutive Road Games Won
- 18   San Francisco, 1988-1990
- 11   L.A. Chargers/San Diego, 1960-61
-     San Francisco, 1987-88
-     Pittsburgh, 2004-05
- 10   Chi. Bears, 1941-42
-     Dallas, 1968-69
-     New Orleans, 1987-88

Most Consecutive Road Games Without Defeat
- 18   San Francisco, 1988-1990 (won 18)
- 13   Chi. Bears, 1941-43 (won 12, tied 1)
- 12   Green Bay, 1928-1930 (won 10, tied 2)

Most Shutout Games Won or Tied, Season
- 10   Pottsville, 1926 (won 9, tied 1)
-     N.Y. Giants, 1927 (won 9, tied 1)
- 9   Akron, 1921 (won 8, tied 1)
-    Canton, 1922 (won 7, tied 2)
-    Frankford, 1926 (won 9)
-    Frankford, 1929 (won 6, tied 3)
- 8   By many teams

Most Consecutive Shutout Games Won or Tied
- 13 Akron, 1920-21 (won 10, tied 3)
- 7 Pottsville, 1926 (won 6, tied 1)
  Detroit, 1934 (won 7)
- 6 Buffalo, 1920-21 (won 5, tied 1)
  Frankford, 1926 (won 6)
  Detroit, 1926 (won 4, tied 2)
  N.Y. Giants, 1926-27 (won 5, tied 1)

GAMES LOST

Most Consecutive Games Lost
- 26 Tampa Bay, 1976-1977
- 19 Chi. Cardinals, 1942-43, 1945
  Oakland, 1961-62
- 18 Houston, 1972-73

Most Consecutive Games Without Victory
- 26 Tampa Bay, 1976-77 (lost 26)
- 23 Rochester, 1922-25 (lost 21, tied 2)
  Washington, 1960-61 (lost 20, tied 3)
- 19 Dayton, 1927-29 (lost 18, tied 1)
  Chi. Cardinals, 1942-43, 1945 (lost 19)
  Oakland, 1961-62 (lost 19)

Most Games Lost, Season
- 15 New Orleans, 1980
  Dallas, 1989
  New England, 1990
  Indianapolis, 1991
  N.Y. Jets, 1996
  San Diego, 2000
  Carolina, 2001
- 14 By many teams

Most Consecutive Games Lost, Season
- 15 Carolina, 2001
- 14 Tampa Bay, 1976
  New Orleans, 1980
  Baltimore, 1981
  New England, 1990
- 13 Oakland, 1962
  Pittsburgh, 1969
  Indianapolis, 1986

Most Consecutive Games Lost, Start of Season
- 14 Tampa Bay, 1976, entire season
  New Orleans, 1980
- 13 Oakland, 1962
  Indianapolis, 1986
- 12 Tampa Bay, 1977
  Detroit, 2001

Most Consecutive Games Lost, End of Season
- 15 Carolina, 2001
- 14 Tampa Bay, 1976, entire season
  New England, 1990
- 13 Pittsburgh, 1969

Most Consecutive Games Without Victory, Season
- 15 Carolina, 2001 (lost 15)
- 14 Tampa Bay, 1976 (lost 14), entire season
  New Orleans, 1980 (lost 14)
  Baltimore, 1981 (lost 14)
  New England, 1990 (lost 14)
- 13 Washington, 1961 (lost 12, tied 1)
  Oakland, 1962 (lost 13)
  Pittsburgh, 1969 (lost 13)
  Indianapolis, 1986 (lost 13)

Most Consecutive Games Without Victory, Start of Season
- 14 Tampa Bay, 1976 (lost 14), entire season
  New Orleans, 1980 (lost 14)
- 13 Washington, 1961 (lost 12, tied 1)
  Oakland, 1962 (lost 13)
  Indianapolis, 1986 (lost 13)
- 12 Dall. Cowboys, 1960 (lost 11, tied 1), entire season
  Tampa Bay, 1977 (lost 12)

Detroit, 2001 (lost 12)

Most Consecutive Games Without Victory, End of Season
- 15 Carolina, 2001
- 14 Tampa Bay, 1976, (lost 14), entire season
  New England, 1990 (lost 14)
- 13 Pittsburgh, 1969 (lost 13)

Most Consecutive Home Games Lost
- 14 Dallas, 1988-89
- 13 Houston, 1972-73
  Tampa Bay, 1976-77
  N.Y. Jets, 1995-97
- 11 Oakland, 1961-62
  Los Angeles, 1961-63
  Cincinnati, 1998-99

Most Consecutive Home Games Without Victory
- 14 Dallas, 1988-89 (lost 14)
- 13 Houston, 1972-73 (lost 13)
  Tampa Bay, 1976-77 (lost 13)
  N.Y. Jets, 1995-97 (lost 13)
- 12 Philadelphia, 1936-38 (lost 11, tied 1)

Most Consecutive Road Games Lost
- 24 Detroit, 2001-03
- 23 Houston, 1981-84
- 22 Buffalo, 1983-86

Most Consecutive Road Games Without Victory
- 24 Detroit, 2001-03 (lost 24)
- 23 Houston, 1981-84 (lost 23)
- 22 Buffalo, 1983-86 (lost 22)

Most Shutout Games Lost or Tied, Season
- 8 Frankford, 1927 (lost 6, tied 2)
  Brooklyn, 1931 (lost 8)
- 7 Dayton, 1925 (lost 6, tied 1)
  Orange, 1929 (lost 4, tied 3)
  Frankford, 1931 (lost 6, tied 1)
- 6 By many teams

Most Consecutive Shutout Games Lost or Tied
- 8 Rochester, 1922-24 (lost 8)
- 7 Hammond, 1922-23 (lost 6, tied 1)
- 6 Providence, 1926-27 (lost 5, tied 1)
  Brooklyn, 1942-43 (lost 6)

TIE GAMES

Most Tie Games, Season
- 6 Chi. Bears, 1932
- 5 Frankford, 1929
- 4 Chi. Bears, 1924
  Orange, 1929
  Portsmouth, 1932

Most Consecutive Tie Games
- 3 Chi. Bears, 1932
- 2 By many teams

SCORING

Most Seasons Leading League
- 10 Chi. Bears, 1932, 1934-35, 1939, 1941-43,
  1946-47, 1956
- 9 San Francisco, 1953, 1965, 1970, 1987, 1989,
  1992-95
  L.A./St. Louis Rams, 1950-52, 1957, 1967, 1973,
  1999-2001
- 7 Green Bay, 1931, 1936-38, 1961-62, 1996

Most Consecutive Seasons Leading League
- 4 San Francisco, 1992-1995
- 3 Green Bay, 1936-38
  Chi. Bears, 1941-43
  Los Angeles, 1950-52
  Oakland, 1967-69
  St. Louis, 1999-2001
- 2 By many teams

POINTS

Most Points, Season
556   Minnesota, 1998
541   Washington, 1983
540   St. Louis, 2000

Fewest Points, Season (Since 1932)
37   Cincinnati/St. Louis, 1934
38   Cincinnati, 1933
     Detroit, 1942
51   Pittsburgh, 1934
     Philadelphia, 1936

Most Points, Game
72   Washington vs. N.Y. Giants, Nov. 27, 1966
70   Los Angeles vs. Baltimore, Oct. 22, 1950
66   Rochester vs. *Fort Porter, Oct. 10, 1920
     *Not a member of the American Professional
     Football Association

Most Points, Both Teams, Game
113   Washington (72) vs. N.Y. Giants (41), Nov. 27, 1966
106   Cincinnati (58) vs. Cleveland (48), Nov. 28, 2004
101   Oakland (52) vs. Houston (49), Dec. 22, 1963

Fewest Points, Both Teams, Game
0   In many games. Last time: N.Y. Giants vs. Detroit,
     Nov. 7, 1943

Most Points, Shutout Victory, Game
66   Rochester vs. *Fort Porter, Oct. 10, 1920
     *Not a member of the American Professional
     Football Association
64   Philadelphia vs. Cincinnati, Nov. 6, 1934
62   Akron vs. Oorang, Oct. 29, 1922

Fewest Points, Shutout Victory, Game
2   Akron vs. Buffalo, Nov. 29, 1923
     Kansas City vs. Buffalo, Nov. 21, 1926
     Frankford vs. Green Bay, Nov. 29, 1928
     Green Bay vs. Chi. Bears, Oct. 16, 1932
     Chi. Bears vs. Green Bay, Sept. 18, 1938

Most Points Overcome to Win Game
28   San Francisco vs. New Orleans, Dec. 7, 1980 (OT)
     (trailed 7-35, won 38-35)
26   Buffalo vs. Indianapolis, Sept., 21, 1997
     (trailed 0-26, won 37-35)
25   St. Louis vs. Tampa Bay, Nov. 8, 1987
     (trailed 3-28, won 31-28)

Most Points Overcome to Tie Game
31   Denver vs. Buffalo, Nov. 27, 1960
     (trailed 7-38, tied 38-38)
28   Los Angeles vs. Philadelphia, Oct. 3, 1948
     (trailed 0-28, tied 28-28)

Most Points, Each Half
1st: 49   Green Bay vs. Tampa Bay, Oct. 2, 1983
     48   Buffalo vs. Miami, Sept. 18, 1966
     45   Green Bay vs. Cleveland, Nov. 12, 1967
         Indianapolis vs. Denver, Oct. 31, 1988
         Houston vs. Cleveland, Dec. 9, 1990
         Seattle vs. Minnesota, Sept. 29, 2002
2nd: 49   Chi. Bears vs. Philadelphia, Nov. 30, 1941
     48   Chi. Cardinals vs. Baltimore, Oct. 2, 1950
         N.Y. Giants vs. Baltimore, Nov. 19, 1950
     45   Cincinnati vs. Houston, Dec. 17, 1972

Most Points, Both Teams, Each Half
1st: 70   Houston (35) vs. Oakland (35), Dec. 22, 1963
     62   N.Y. Jets (41) vs. Tampa Bay (21), Nov. 17, 1985
         Indianapolis (35) vs. Cincinnati (27), Nov. 20, 2005
     59   St. Louis (31) vs. Philadelphia (28), Dec. 16, 1962
2nd: 66   Cleveland (35) vs. Cincinnati (31), Nov. 28, 2004
     65   Washington (38) vs. N.Y. Giants (27), Nov. 27, 1966
     62   L.A. Raiders (31) vs. San Diego (31), Jan. 2, 1983
         Baltimore (38) vs. Seattle (24), Nov. 23, 2003

Most Points, One Quarter
41   Green Bay vs. Detroit, Oct. 7, 1945 (second quarter)
     Los Angeles vs. Detroit, Oct. 29, 1950
     (third quarter)
37   Los Angeles vs. Green Bay, Sept. 21, 1980
     (second quarter)
35   Chi. Cardinals vs. Boston, Oct. 24, 1948
     (third quarter)
     Green Bay vs. Cleveland, Nov. 12, 1967 (first quarter)
     Green Bay vs. Tampa Bay, Oct. 2, 1983
     (second quarter)

Most Points, Both Teams, One Quarter
49   Oakland (28) vs. Houston (21), Dec. 22, 1963
     (second quarter)
48   Green Bay (41) vs. Detroit (7), Oct. 7, 1945
     (second quarter)
     Los Angeles (41) vs. Detroit (7), Oct. 29, 1950
     (third quarter)
47   St. Louis (27) vs. Philadelphia (20), Dec. 13, 1964
     (second quarter)

Most Points, Each Quarter
1st: 35   Green Bay vs. Cleveland, Nov. 12, 1967
     31   Buffalo vs. Kansas City, Sept. 13, 1964
     28   By eight teams
2nd: 41   Green Bay vs. Detroit, Oct. 7, 1945
     37   Los Angeles vs. Green Bay, Sept. 21, 1980
     35   Green Bay vs. Tampa Bay, Oct. 2, 1983
3rd: 41   Los Angeles vs. Detroit, Oct. 29, 1950
     35   Chi. Cardinals vs. Boston, Oct. 24, 1948
     28   By 10 teams
4th: 31   Oakland vs. Denver, Dec. 17, 1960
         Oakland vs. San Diego, Dec. 8, 1963
         Atlanta vs. Green Bay, Sept. 13, 1981
     30   N.Y. Jets vs. Miami, Oct. 23, 2000
     28   By many teams

Most Points, Both Teams, Each Quarter
1st: 42   Green Bay (35) vs. Cleveland (7), Nov. 12, 1967
     41   Tennessee (24) vs. Indianapolis (17), Dec. 5, 2004
     35   Dall. Texans (21) vs. N.Y. Titans (14), Nov. 11, 1962
         Dallas (28) vs. Philadelphia (7), Oct. 19, 1969
         Kansas City (21) vs. Seattle (14), Dec. 11, 1977
         Detroit (21) vs. L.A. Raiders (14), Dec. 10, 1990
         Dallas (21) vs. Atlanta (14), Dec. 22, 1991
         Indianapolis (21) vs. Green Bay (14), Sept 26, 2004
         Miami (21) vs. Buffalo (14), Dec. 5, 2004
2nd: 49   Oakland (28) vs. Houston (21), Dec. 22, 1963
     48   Green Bay (41) vs. Detroit (7), Oct. 7, 1945
     47   St. Louis (27) vs. Philadelphia (20), Dec. 13, 1964
3rd: 48   Los Angeles (41) vs. Detroit (7), Oct. 29, 1950
     42   Washington (28) vs. Philadelphia (14), Oct. 1, 1955
     41   Green Bay (21) vs. N.Y. Yanks (20), Oct. 8, 1950
4th: 42   Chi. Cardinals (28) vs. Philadelphia (14), Dec. 7, 1947
         Green Bay (28) vs. Chi. Bears (14), Nov. 6, 1955
         N.Y. Jets (28) vs. Boston (14), Oct. 27, 1968
         Pittsburgh (21) vs. Cleveland (21), Oct. 18, 1969
         New England (21) vs. Kansas City (21),
         Sept. 22, 2002
     41   Baltimore (27) vs. New England (14), Sept. 18, 1978
         New England (27) vs. Baltimore (14), Nov. 23, 1980
     40   Chicago (21) vs. Tampa Bay (19), Nov. 19, 1989

Most Consecutive Games Scoring
420   San Francisco, 1977-2004
274   Cleveland, 1950-1971
236   Minnesota, 1991-2005 (current)

TOUCHDOWNS

Most Seasons Leading League, Touchdowns
13   Chi. Bears, 1932, 1934-35, 1939, 1941-44,
     1946-48, 1956, 1965

7   Dallas, 1966, 1968, 1971, 1973, 1977-78, 1980
    San Francisco, 1953, 1970, 1987, 1992-95
    L.A./St. Louis Rams, 1949-1952, 1999-2001

6   Oakland, 1967-69, 1972, 1974, 1977
    San Diego, 1963, 1965, 1979, 1981-82, 1985
    Green Bay, 1932, 1937-38, 1961-62, 1996
    Baltimore/Indianapolis Colts, 1957-59, 1964, 1976, 2004

Most Consecutive Seasons Leading League, Touchdowns

4   Chi. Bears, 1941-44
    Los Angeles, 1949-1952
    San Francisco, 1992-95

3   Chi. Bears, 1946-48
    Baltimore, 1957-59
    Oakland, 1967-69
    St. Louis, 1999-2001

2   By many teams

Most Touchdowns, Season

70   Miami, 1984

67   St. Louis, 2000

66   Houston, 1961
    San Francisco, 1994
    St. Louis, 1999
    Indianapolis, 2004

Fewest Touchdowns, Season (Since 1932)

3   Cincinnati, 1933

4   Cincinnati/St. Louis, 1934

5   Detroit, 1942

Most Touchdowns, Game

10   Rochester vs. *Fort Porter, Oct. 10, 1920
    *Not a member of the American Professional
    Football Association
    Philadelphia vs. Cincinnati, Nov. 6, 1934
    Los Angeles vs. Baltimore, Oct. 22, 1950
    Washington vs. N.Y. Giants, Nov. 27, 1966

9   Rock Island vs. Evansville, Oct. 15, 1922
    Akron vs. Oorang, Oct. 29, 1922
    Racine vs. Louisville, Nov. 5, 1922
    Chi. Cardinals vs. Rochester, Oct. 7, 1923
    Chi. Cardinals vs. Milwaukee, Dec. 10, 1925
    Chi. Cardinals vs. N.Y. Giants, Oct. 17, 1948
    Chi. Cardinals vs. N.Y. Bulldogs, Nov. 13, 1949
    Los Angeles vs. Detroit, Oct. 29, 1950
    Pittsburgh vs. N.Y. Giants, Nov. 30, 1952
    Chicago vs. San Francisco, Dec. 12, 1965
    Chicago vs. Green Bay, Dec. 7, 1980

8   By many teams

Most Touchdowns, Both Teams, Game

16   Washington (10) vs. N.Y. Giants (6), Nov. 27, 1966

14   Chi. Cardinals (9) vs. N.Y. Giants (5), Oct. 17, 1948
    Los Angeles (10) vs. Baltimore (4), Oct. 22, 1950
    Houston (7) vs. Oakland (7), Dec. 22, 1963

13   New Orleans (7) vs. St. Louis (6), Nov. 2, 1969
    Kansas City (7) vs. Seattle (6), Nov. 27, 1983 (OT)
    San Diego (8) vs. Pittsburgh (5), Dec. 8, 1985
    N.Y. Jets (7) vs. Miami (6), Sept. 21, 1986 (OT)
    Cincinnati (7) vs. Cleveland (6), Nov. 28, 2004

Most Consecutive Games Scoring Touchdowns

166   Cleveland, 1957-1969

97   Oakland, 1966-1973
    Minnesota, 1995-2001

96   Kansas City, 1963-1970

POINTS AFTER TOUCHDOWN

Most (One-Point) Points After Touchdown, Season

66   Miami, 1984

65   Houston, 1961

64   St. Louis, 1999
    Indianapolis, 2004

Fewest (One-Point) Points After Touchdown, Season

2   Chi. Cardinals, 1933

3   Cincinnati, 1933
    Pittsburgh, 1934

4   Cincinnati/St. Louis, 1934

Most (One-Point) Points After Touchdown, Game

10   Los Angeles vs. Baltimore, Oct. 22, 1950

9   Chi. Cardinals vs. N.Y. Giants, Oct. 17, 1948
    Pittsburgh vs. N.Y. Giants, Nov. 30, 1952
    Washington vs. N.Y. Giants, Nov. 27, 1966

8   By many teams

Most (One-Point) Points After Touchdown, Both Teams, Game

14   Chi. Cardinals (9) vs. N.Y. Giants (5), Oct. 17, 1948
    Houston (7) vs. Oakland (7), Dec. 22, 1963
    Washington (9) vs. N.Y. Giants (5), Nov. 27, 1966

13   Los Angeles (10) vs. Baltimore (3), Oct. 22, 1950
    Cincinnati (7) vs. Cleveland (6), Nov. 28, 2004

12   In many games

Most Two-Point Conversions, Season

6   Miami, 1994
    Minnesota, 1997

5   Arizona, 1995
    Baltimore, 1996
    Jacksonville, 1996
    Chicago, 1997
    San Francisco, 1998
    Pittsburgh, 2002

4   By many teams

Most Two-Point Conversions, Game

4   St. Louis vs. Atlanta, Oct. 15, 2000

3   Baltimore vs. New England, Oct. 6, 1996
    Pittsburgh vs. Tennessee, Nov. 1, 1998

2   By many teams

Most Two-Point Conversions, Both Teams, Game

5   Baltimore (3) vs. New England (2), Oct. 6, 1996
    St. Louis (4) vs. Atlanta (1), Oct. 15, 2000

3   Seattle (2) vs. Kansas City (1), Oct. 23, 1994
    Minnesota (2) vs. Seattle (1), Nov. 10, 1996
    Pittsburgh (3) vs. Tennessee (0), Nov. 1, 1998

2   In many games

FIELD GOALS

Most Seasons Leading League, Field Goals

11   Green Bay, 1935-36, 1940-43, 1946-47, 1955, 1972, 1974

8   Washington, 1945, 1956, 1971, 1976-77, 1979, 1982, 1992

7   N.Y. Giants, 1933, 1937, 1939, 1941, 1944, 1959, 1983
    L.A./St. Louis Rams, 1949, 1951, 1958, 1966, 1973, 1978, 2003

Most Consecutive Seasons Leading League, Field Goals

4   Green Bay, 1940-43

3   Cleveland, 1952-54

2   By many teams

Most Field Goals Attempted, Season

49   Los Angeles, 1966
    Washington, 1971

48   Green Bay, 1972

47   N.Y. Jets, 1969
    Los Angeles, 1973
    Washington, 1983

Fewest Field Goals Attempted, Season (Since 1938)

0   Chi. Bears, 1944

2   Cleveland, 1939
    Card-Pitt, 1944
    Boston, 1946
    Chi. Bears, 1947

3   Chi. Bears, 1945
    Cleveland, 1945

Most Field Goals Attempted, Game
- 9   St. Louis vs. Pittsburgh, Sept. 24, 1967
- 8   Pittsburgh vs. St. Louis, Dec. 2, 1962
  - Detroit vs. Minnesota, Nov. 13, 1966
  - N.Y. Jets vs. Buffalo, Nov. 3, 1968
  - Dallas vs. N.Y. Giants, Sept. 15, 2003 (OT)
- 7   By many teams

Most Field Goals Attempted, Both Teams, Game
- 11   St. Louis (6) vs. Pittsburgh (5), Nov. 13, 1966
  - Washington (6) vs. Chicago (5), Nov. 14, 1971
  - Green Bay (6) vs. Detroit (5), Sept. 29, 1974
  - Washington (6) vs. N.Y. Giants (5), Nov. 14, 1976
- 10   In many games

Most Field Goals, Season
- 43   Arizona, 2005
- 39   Miami, 1999
  - St. Louis, 2003
- 37   Carolina, 1996
  - Indianapolis, 2003

Fewest Field Goals, Season (Since 1932)
- 0   Boston, 1932, 1935
  - Chi. Cardinals, 1932, 1945
  - Green Bay, 1932, 1944
  - N.Y. Giants, 1932
  - Brooklyn, 1944
  - Card-Pitt, 1944
  - Chi. Bears, 1944, 1947
  - Boston, 1946
  - Baltimore, 1950
  - Dallas, 1952

Most Field Goals, Game
- 7   St. Louis vs. Pittsburgh, Sept. 24, 1967
  - Minnesota vs. L.A. Rams, Nov. 5, 1989 (OT)
  - Dallas vs. Green Bay, Nov. 18, 1996
  - Dallas vs. N.Y. Giants, Sept. 15, 2003 (OT)
- 6   Boston vs. Denver, Oct. 4, 1964
  - Detroit vs. Minnesota, Nov. 13, 1966
  - N.Y. Jets vs. Buffalo, Nov. 3, 1968
  - Philadelphia vs. Houston, Nov. 12, 1972
  - N.Y. Jets vs. New Orleans, Dec. 3, 1972
  - St. Louis vs. Atlanta, Dec. 9, 1973
  - N.Y. Giants vs. Seattle, Oct. 18, 1981
  - San Francisco vs. New Orleans, Oct. 16, 1983
  - Pittsburgh vs. Denver, Oct. 23, 1988
  - San Diego vs. Seattle, Sept. 5, 1993
  - San Diego vs. Houston, Sept. 19, 1993
  - Cincinnati vs. Seattle, Nov. 6, 1994
  - Atlanta vs. New Orleans, Nov. 13, 1994
  - San Francisco vs. Atlanta, Sept. 29, 1996
  - Buffalo vs. N.Y. Jets, Oct. 20, 1996
  - San Diego vs. Oakland, Oct. 5, 1997
  - Minnesota vs. Baltimore, Dec. 13, 1998
  - Detroit vs. Minnesota, Oct. 17, 1999
  - Miami vs. New England, Oct. 17, 1999
  - Pittsburgh vs. Jacksonville, Dec. 1, 2002
  - Carolina vs. New Orleans, Dec. 5, 2004
  - Arizona vs. San Francisco, Oct. 2, 2005
- 5   By many teams

Most Field Goals, Both Teams, Game
- 9   San Diego (5) vs. Kansas City (4), Sept. 29, 1996
  - Miami (6) vs. New England (3), Oct. 17, 1999
- 8   Cleveland (4) vs. St. Louis (4), Sept. 20, 1964
  - Chicago (5) vs. Philadelphia (3), Oct. 20, 1968
  - Washington (5) vs. Chicago (3), Nov. 14, 1971
  - Kansas City (5) vs. Buffalo (3), Dec. 19, 1971
  - Detroit (4) vs. Green Bay (4), Sept. 29, 1974
  - Cleveland (5) vs. Denver (3), Oct. 19, 1975
  - New England (4) vs. San Diego (4), Nov. 9, 1975
  - San Francisco (6) vs. New Orleans (2), Oct. 16, 1983
  - Seattle (5) vs. L.A. Raiders (3), Dec. 18, 1988

Atlanta (6) vs. New Orleans (2), Nov. 13, 1994
Indianapolis (4) vs. San Diego (4), Nov. 3, 1996
Dallas (7) vs. N.Y. Giants (1), Sept. 15, 2003 (OT)
Oakland (5) vs. Chicago (3), Oct. 5, 2003
- 7   In many games

Most Consecutive Games Scoring Field Goals
- 38   Baltimore, 1999-2001
- 31   Minnesota, 1968-1970
- 28   Washington, 1988-1990

SAFETIES

Most Safeties, Season
- 4   Cleveland, 1927
  - Detroit, 1962
  - Seattle, 1993
  - San Francisco, 1996
  - Tennessee, 1999
- 3   By many teams

Most Safeties, Game
- 3   L.A. Rams vs. N.Y. Giants, Sept. 30, 1984
- 2   N.Y. Giants vs. Pottsville, Oct. 30, 1927
  - Chi. Bears vs. Pottsville, Nov. 13, 1927
  - Detroit vs. Brooklyn, Dec. 1, 1935
  - N.Y. Giants vs. Pittsburgh, Sept. 17, 1950
  - N.Y. Giants vs. Washington, Nov. 5, 1961
  - Chicago vs. Pittsburgh, Nov. 9, 1969
  - Dallas vs. Philadelphia, Nov. 19, 1972
  - Los Angeles vs. Green Bay, Oct. 21, 1973
  - Oakland vs. San Diego, Oct. 26, 1975
  - Denver vs. Seattle, Jan. 2, 1983
  - New Orleans vs. Cleveland, Sept. 13, 1987
  - Buffalo vs. Denver, Nov. 8, 1987
  - San Francisco vs. St. Louis, Sept. 8, 1996
  - Jacksonville vs. Pittsburgh, Oct. 3, 1999
  - Minnesota vs. Atlanta, Oct. 5, 2003
  - Dallas vs. Arizona, Oct. 5, 2003
  - Buffalo vs. Houston, Nov. 16, 2003

Most Safeties, Both Teams, Game
- 3   L.A. Rams (3) vs. N.Y. Giants (0), Sept. 30, 1984
- 2   Chi. Cardinals (1) vs. Frankford (1), Nov. 19, 1927
  - Chi. Cardinals (1) vs. Cincinnati (1), Nov. 12, 1933
  - Chi. Bears (1) vs. San Francisco (1), Oct. 19, 1952
  - Cincinnati (1) vs. Los Angeles (1), Oct. 22, 1972
  - Chi. Bears (1) vs. San Francisco (1), Sept. 19, 1976
  - Baltimore (1) vs. Miami (1), Oct. 29, 1978
  - Atlanta (1) vs. Detroit (1), Oct. 5, 1980
  - Houston (1) vs. Philadelphia (1), Oct. 2, 1988
  - Cleveland (1) vs. Seattle (1), Nov. 14, 1993
  - Arizona (1) vs. Houston (1), Dec. 4, 1994
  - (Also see previous record)

FIRST DOWNS

Most Seasons Leading League
- 9   Chi. Bears, 1935, 1939, 1941, 1943, 1945, 1947-49, 1955
- 7   San Diego, 1965, 1969, 1980-83, 1985
  - L.A./St. Louis Rams, 1946, 1950-51, 1954, 1957, 1973, 2001
- 6   San Francisco, 1965, 1987, 1989, 1993-94, 1998

Most Consecutive Seasons Leading League
- 4   San Diego, 1980-83
- 3   Chi. Bears, 1947-49
- 2   By many teams

Most First Downs, Season
- 398   Kansas City, 2004
- 387   Miami, 1984
- 383   Denver, 2000

Fewest First Downs, Season
- 51   Cincinnati, 1933
- 64   Pittsburgh, 1935

67 Philadelphia, 1937
Most First Downs, Game
39 N.Y. Jets vs. Miami, Nov. 27, 1988
   Washington vs. Detroit, Nov. 4, 1990 (OT)
38 Los Angeles vs. N.Y. Giants, Nov. 13, 1966
37 Green Bay vs. Philadelphia, Nov. 11, 1962
Fewest First Downs, Game
0 N.Y. Giants vs. Green Bay, Oct. 1, 1933
   Pittsburgh vs. Boston, Oct. 29, 1933
   Philadelphia vs. Detroit, Sept. 20, 1935
   N.Y. Giants vs. Washington, Sept. 27, 1942
   Denver vs. Houston, Sept. 3, 1966
Most First Downs, Both Teams, Game
64 Seattle (32) vs. Kansas City (32), Nov. 24, 2002
62 San Diego (32) vs. Seattle (30), Sept. 15, 1985
   Oakland (31) vs. Kansas City (31), Nov. 5, 2000
59 Miami (31) vs. Buffalo (28), Oct. 9, 1983 (OT)
   Seattle (33) vs. Kansas City (26), Nov. 27, 1983 (OT)
   N.Y. Jets (32) vs. Miami (27), Sept. 21, 1986 (OT)
   N.Y. Jets (39) vs. Miami (20), Nov. 27, 1988
   Oakland (31) vs. San Francisco (28), Oct. 8, 2000 (OT)
Fewest First Downs, Both Teams, Game
7 Chi. Cardinals (2) vs. Detroit (5), Sept. 15, 1940
9 Pittsburgh (1) vs. Boston (8), Oct. 27, 1935
   Boston (4) vs. Brooklyn (5), Nov. 24, 1935
   N.Y. Giants (3) vs. Detroit (6), Nov. 7, 1943
   Pittsburgh (4) vs. Chi. Cardinals (5), Nov. 11, 1945
   N.Y. Bulldogs (1) vs. Philadelphia (8), Sept. 22, 1949
10 N.Y. Giants (4) vs. Washington (6), Dec. 11, 1960
Most First Downs, Rushing, Season
181 New England, 1978
177 Los Angeles, 1973
176 Chicago, 1985
Fewest First Downs, Rushing, Season
36 Cleveland, 1942
   Boston, 1944
39 Brooklyn, 1943
40 Philadelphia, 1940
   Detroit, 1945
Most First Downs, Rushing, Game
25 Philadelphia vs. Washington, Dec. 2, 1951
23 St. Louis vs. New Orleans, Oct. 5, 1980
21 Cleveland vs. Philadelphia, Dec. 13, 1959
   Green Bay vs. Philadelphia, Nov. 11, 1962
   Los Angeles vs. New Orleans, Nov. 25, 1973
   Pittsburgh vs. Kansas City, Nov. 7, 1976
   New England vs. Denver, Nov. 28, 1976
   Oakland vs. Green Bay, Sept. 17, 1978
   Buffalo vs. Washington, Nov. 3, 1996
   San Francisco vs. Detroit, Dec. 14, 1998
   Kansas City vs. Atlanta, Oct. 24, 2004
Fewest First Downs, Rushing, Game
0 By many teams. Last time: Indianapolis vs. Arizona,
   Jan. 1, 2006
Most First Downs, Rushing, Both Teams, Game
36 Philadelphia (25) vs. Washington (11), Dec. 2, 1951
31 Detroit (18) vs. Washington (13), Sept. 30, 1951
30 Los Angeles (17) vs. Minnesota (13), Nov. 5, 1961
   New Orleans (17) vs. Green Bay (13), Sept. 9, 1979
   New Orleans (16) vs. San Francisco (14), Nov. 11, 1979
   New England (16) vs. Kansas City (14), Oct. 4, 1981
Fewest First Downs, Rushing, Both Teams, Game
1 Oakland (0) vs. Tennessee (1), Sept. 7, 2003
   Carolina (0) vs. Detroit (1), Oct. 16, 2005
2 Houston (0) vs. Denver (2), Dec. 2, 1962
   N.Y. Jets, (1) vs. St. Louis (1), Dec. 3, 1995
   Miami (1) vs. San Diego (1), Dec. 19, 1999
   New Orleans (0) vs. Baltimore (2), Dec. 19, 1999
   Baltimore (0) vs. Tennessee (2), Sept. 18, 2005
3 In many games

Most First Downs, Passing, Season
259 San Diego, 1985
251 Houston, 1990
250 Miami, 1986
Fewest First Downs, Passing, Season
18 Pittsburgh, 1941
23 Brooklyn, 1942
   N.Y. Giants, 1944
24 N.Y. Giants, 1943
Most First Downs, Passing, Game
29 N.Y. Giants vs. Cincinnati, Oct. 13, 1985
28 Tennessee vs. Oakland, Dec. 19, 2004
27 San Diego vs. Seattle, Sept. 15, 1985
Fewest First Downs, Passing, Game
0 By many teams. Last time: Cleveland vs.
   Jacksonville, Dec. 3, 2000
Most First Downs, Passing, Both Teams, Game
43 San Diego (23) vs. Cincinnati (20), Dec. 20, 1982
   Miami (24) vs. N.Y. Jets (19), Sept. 21, 1986 (OT)
   Tennessee (28) vs. Oakland (15), Dec. 19, 2004
42 San Francisco (22) vs. San Diego (20), Dec. 11, 1982
41 San Diego (27) vs. Seattle (14), Sept. 15, 1985
   Miami (26) vs. Cleveland (15), Dec. 12, 1988
   Kansas City (23) vs. Oakland (18), Nov. 5, 2000
Fewest First Downs, Passing, Both Teams, Game
0 Brooklyn vs. Pittsburgh, Nov. 29, 1942
1 Green Bay (0) vs. Cleveland (1), Sept. 21, 1941
   Pittsburgh (0) vs. Brooklyn (1), Oct. 11, 1942
   N.Y. Giants (0) vs. Detroit (1), Nov. 7, 1943
   Pittsburgh (0) vs. Chi. Cardinals (1), Nov. 11, 1945
   N.Y. Bulldogs (0) vs. Philadelphia (1), Sept. 22, 1949
   Chicago (0) vs. Buffalo (1), Oct. 7, 1979
2 In many games
Most First Downs, Penalty, Season
47 Buffalo, 2002
   Indianapolis, 2004
44 Dallas, 2005
43 Denver, 1994
Fewest First Downs, Penalty, Season
2 Brooklyn, 1940
4 Chi. Cardinals, 1940
   N.Y. Giants, 1942, 1944
   Washington, 1944
   Cleveland, 1952
   Kansas City, 1969
5 Brooklyn, 1939
   Chi. Bears, 1939
   Detroit, 1953
   Los Angeles, 1953
   Houston, 1982
Most First Downs, Penalty, Game
11 Denver vs. Houston, Oct. 6, 1985
9 Chi. Bears vs. Cleveland, Nov. 25, 1951
   Baltimore vs. Pittsburgh, Oct. 30, 1977
   N.Y. Jets vs. Houston, Sept. 18, 1988
   Dallas vs. Detroit, Nov. 20, 2005
8 Philadelphia vs. Detroit, Dec. 2, 1979
   Cincinnati vs. N.Y. Jets, Oct. 6, 1985
   Buffalo vs. Houston, Sept. 20, 1987
   Houston vs. Atlanta, Sept. 9, 1990
   Kansas City vs. L.A. Raiders, Oct. 3, 1993
   San Francisco vs. New Orleans, Oct. 11, 1998
   Oakland vs. San Francisco, Oct. 8, 2000 (OT)
   Philadelphia vs. Chicago, Nov. 3, 2002
   Detroit vs. Baltimore, Oct. 9, 2005
Most First Downs, Penalty, Both Teams, Game
12 Buffalo (7) vs. San Francisco (5), Oct. 4, 1998
   Detroit (8) vs. Baltimore (4), Oct. 9, 2005
11 Chi. Bears (9) vs. Cleveland (2), Nov. 25, 1951
   Cincinnati (8) vs. N.Y. Jets (3), Oct. 6, 1985

Denver (11) vs. Houston (0), Oct. 6, 1985
Detroit (6) vs. Dallas (5), Nov. 8, 1987
N.Y. Jets (9) vs. Houston (2), Sept. 18, 1988
Kansas City (8) vs. L.A. Raiders (3), Oct. 3, 1993
Detroit (6) vs. San Diego (5), Nov. 11, 1996
Philadelphia (8) vs. Chicago (3), Nov. 3, 2002
10   In many games

NET YARDS GAINED RUSHING AND PASSING
Most Seasons Leading League
12   Chi. Bears, 1932, 1934-35, 1939, 1941-44, 1947,
      1949, 1955-56
9   L.A./St. Louis Rams, 1946, 1950-51, 1954, 1957,
      1973, 1999-2001
7   San Diego, 1963, 1965, 1980-83, 1985
Most Consecutive Seasons Leading League
4   Chi. Bears, 1941-44
      San Diego, 1980-83
3   Baltimore, 1958-1960
      Houston, 1960-62
      Oakland, 1968-1970
      St. Louis, 1999-2001
2   By many teams
Most Yards Gained, Season
7,075   St. Louis, 2000
6,936   Miami, 1984
6,800   San Francisco, 1998
Fewest Yards Gained, Season
1,150   Cincinnati, 1933
1,443   Chi. Cardinals, 1934
1,486   Chi. Cardinals, 1933
Most Yards Gained, Game
735   Los Angeles vs. N.Y. Yanks, Sept. 28, 1951
683   Pittsburgh vs. Chi. Cardinals, Dec. 13, 1958
682   Chi. Bears vs. N.Y. Giants, Nov. 14, 1943
Fewest Yards Gained, Game
−7   Seattle vs. Los Angeles, Nov. 4, 1979
−5   Denver vs. Oakland, Sept. 10, 1967
14   Chi. Cardinals vs. Detroit, Sept. 15, 1940
Most Yards Gained, Both Teams, Game
1,133   Los Angeles (636) vs. N.Y. Yanks (497), Nov. 19, 1950
1,102   San Diego (661) vs. Cincinnati (441), Dec. 20, 1982
1,095   Kansas City (590) vs. Indianapolis (505),
         Oct. 31, 2004
Fewest Yards Gained, Both Teams, Game
30   Chi. Cardinals (14) vs. Detroit (16), Sept. 15, 1940
136   Chi. Cardinals (50) vs. Green Bay (86), Nov. 18, 1934
154   N.Y. Giants (51) vs. Washington (103), Dec. 11, 1960
Most Consecutive Games, 400 or More Yards Gained
11   San Diego, 1982-83
8   St. Louis, 1999-2000
6   Houston, 1961-62
      San Diego, 1981
      San Francisco, 1987
Most Consecutive Games, 300 or More Yards Gained
36   Minnesota, 2002-04
30   Minnesota, 1999-2000
      St. Louis, 2000-02
29   Los Angeles, 1949-1951

RUSHING
Most Seasons Leading League
16   Chi. Bears, 1932, 1934-35, 1939-1942, 1951,
      1955-56, 1968, 1977, 1983-86
7   Buffalo, 1962, 1964, 1973, 1975, 1982, 1991-92
6   Cleveland, 1958-59, 1963, 1965-67
      San Francisco, 1952-54, 1987, 1998-99
Most Consecutive Seasons Leading League
4   Chi. Bears, 1939-1942
      Chi. Bears, 1983-86

3   Detroit, 1936-38
      San Francisco, 1952-54
      Cleveland, 1965-67
2   By many teams

ATTEMPTS
Most Rushing Attempts, Season
681   Oakland, 1977
674   Chicago, 1984
671   New England, 1978
Fewest Rushing Attempts, Season
211   Philadelphia, 1982
219   San Francisco, 1982
225   Houston, 1982
Most Rushing Attempts, Game
72   Chi. Bears vs. Brooklyn, Oct. 20, 1935
70   Chi. Cardinals vs. Green Bay, Dec. 5, 1948
69   Chi. Cardinals vs. Green Bay, Dec. 6, 1936
      Kansas City vs. Cincinnati, Sept. 3, 1978
Fewest Rushing Attempts, Game
6   Chi. Cardinals vs. Boston, Oct. 29, 1933
      New England vs. Pittsburgh, Oct. 31, 2004
7   Oakland vs. Buffalo, Oct. 15, 1963
      Houston vs. N.Y. Giants, Dec. 8, 1985
      Seattle vs. L.A. Raiders, Nov. 17, 1991
      Green Bay vs. Miami, Sept. 11, 1994
8   Denver vs. Oakland, Dec. 17, 1960
      Buffalo vs. St. Louis, Sept. 9, 1984
      Detroit vs. San Francisco, Oct. 20, 1991
      Atlanta vs. Detroit, Sept. 5, 1993
      St. Louis vs. San Francisco, Nov. 2, 2003
      N.Y. Jets vs. Denver, Nov. 20, 2005
Most Rushing Attempts, Both Teams, Game
108   Chi. Cardinals (70) vs. Green Bay (38), Dec. 5, 1948
105   Oakland (62) vs. Atlanta (43), Nov. 30, 1975 (OT)
104   Chi. Bears (64) vs. Pittsburgh (40), Oct. 18, 1936
Fewest Rushing Attempts, Both Teams, Game
34   Atlanta (12) vs. Houston (22), Dec. 5, 1993
      Atlanta (15) vs. San Francisco (19), Dec. 24, 1995
      Philadelphia (14) vs. San Diego (20), Oct. 23, 2005
35   Seattle (15) vs. New Orleans (20), Sept. 1, 1991
      Oakland (17) vs. Pittsburgh (18), Sept. 15, 2002
36   Houston (15) vs. N.Y. Jets (21), Oct. 13, 1991
      St. Louis (16) vs. Detroit (20), Nov. 7, 1999
      Detroit (15) vs. Washington (21), Dec. 5, 1999
      Tennessee (14) vs. Baltimore (22), Dec. 5, 1999
      Tampa Bay (16) vs. St. Louis (20), Sept. 23, 2002
      Oakland (14) vs. Denver (22), Nov. 11, 2002
      Philadelphia (17) vs. Minnesota (19), Sept. 20, 2004

YARDS GAINED
Most Yards Gained Rushing, Season
3,165   New England, 1978
3,088   Buffalo, 1973
2,986   Kansas City, 1978
Fewest Yards Gained Rushing, Season
298   Philadelphia, 1940
467   Detroit, 1946
471   Boston, 1944
Most Yards Gained Rushing, Game
426   Detroit vs. Pittsburgh, Nov. 4, 1934
423   N.Y. Giants vs. Baltimore, Nov. 19, 1950
420   Boston vs. N.Y. Giants, Oct. 8, 1933
Fewest Yards Gained Rushing, Game
−53   Detroit vs. Chi. Cardinals, Oct. 17, 1943
−36   Philadelphia vs. Chi. Bears, Nov. 19, 1939
−33   Phil-Pitt vs. Brooklyn, Oct. 2, 1943
Most Yards Gained Rushing, Both Teams, Game
595   Los Angeles (371) vs. N.Y. Yanks (224),
         Nov. 18, 1951

574 Chi. Bears (396) vs. Pittsburgh (178), Oct. 10, 1934
558 Boston (420) vs. N.Y. Giants (138), Oct. 8, 1933

Fewest Yards Gained Rushing, Both Teams, Game
–15 Detroit (–53) vs. Chi. Cardinals (38), Oct. 17, 1943
4 Detroit (–10) vs. Chi. Cardinals (14), Sept. 15, 1940
45 San Diego (21) vs. Philadelphia (24), Oct. 23, 2005

AVERAGE GAIN
Highest Average Gain, Rushing, Season
5.74 Cleveland, 1963
5.65 San Francisco, 1954
5.56 San Diego, 1963

Lowest Average Gain, Rushing, Season
0.94 Philadelphia, 1940
1.45 Boston, 1944
1.55 Pittsburgh, 1935

TOUCHDOWNS
Most Touchdowns, Rushing, Season
36 Green Bay, 1962
33 Pittsburgh, 1976
32 Kansas City, 2003

Fewest Touchdowns, Rushing, Season
1 Brooklyn, 1934
2 Chi. Cardinals, 1933
Cincinnati, 1933
Pittsburgh, 1934
Philadelphia, 1935
Philadelphia, 1936
Philadelphia, 1937
Philadelphia, 1938
Pittsburgh, 1940
Philadelphia, 1972
N.Y. Jets, 1995
Arizona, 2005
3 By many teams

Most Touchdowns, Rushing, Game
9 Rock Island vs. Evansville, Oct. 15, 1922
Racine vs. Louisville, Nov. 5, 1922
8 Chi. Cardinals vs. Rochester, Oct. 7, 1923
Kansas City vs. Atlanta, Oct. 24, 2004
7 By many teams

Most Touchdowns, Rushing, Both Teams, Game
9 Rock Island (9) vs. Evansville (0), Oct. 15, 1922
Racine (9) vs. Louisville (0), Nov. 5, 1922
8 Chi. Cardinals (8) vs. Rochester (0), Oct. 7, 1923
Canton (7) vs. Cleveland (1), Nov. 25, 1923
Los Angeles (6) vs. N.Y. Yanks (2), Nov. 18, 1951
Chi. Bears (5) vs. Green Bay (3), Nov. 6, 1955
Denver (5) vs. Kansas City (3), Dec. 7, 2003
Kansas City (8) vs. Atlanta (0), Oct. 24, 2004
7 In many games

PASSING
ATTEMPTS
Most Passes Attempted, Season
709 Minnesota, 1981
699 New England, 1994
686 New England, 1995

Fewest Passes Attempted, Season
102 Cincinnati, 1933
106 Boston, 1933
120 Detroit, 1937

Most Passes Attempted, Game
70 New England vs. Minnesota, Nov. 13, 1994 (OT)
69 N.Y. Jets vs. Baltimore, Dec. 24, 2000
68 Houston vs. Buffalo, Nov 1, 1964
Cincinnati vs. Pittsburgh, Dec. 30, 2001 (OT)

Fewest Passes Attempted, Game
0 Green Bay vs. Portsmouth, Oct. 8, 1933

Detroit vs. Cleveland, Sept. 10, 1937
Pittsburgh vs. Brooklyn, Nov. 16, 1941
Pittsburgh vs. Los Angeles, Nov. 13, 1949
Cleveland vs. Philadelphia, Dec. 3, 1950

Most Passes Attempted, Both Teams, Game
112 New England (70) vs. Minnesota (42), Nov. 13, 1994
104 Miami (55) vs. N.Y. Jets (49), Oct. 18, 1987 (OT)
N.Y. Jets (58) vs. San Francisco (46), Sept. 6, 1998 (OT)
103 Cincinnati (68) vs. Pittsburgh (35), Dec. 30, 2001 (OT)
Seattle (53) vs. San Diego (50), Dec. 29, 2002 (OT)

Fewest Passes Attempted, Both Teams, Game
4 Chi. Cardinals (1) vs. Detroit (3), Nov. 3, 1935
Detroit (0) vs. Cleveland (4), Sept. 10, 1937
6 Chi. Cardinals (2) vs. Detroit (4), Sept. 15, 1940
8 Brooklyn (2) vs. Philadelphia (6), Oct. 1, 1939

COMPLETIONS
Most Passes Completed, Season
432 San Francisco, 1995
419 Arizona, 2005
418 Oakland, 2002

Fewest Passes Completed, Season
25 Cincinnati, 1933
33 Boston, 1933
34 Chi. Cardinals, 1934
Detroit, 1934

Most Passes Completed, Game
45 New England vs. Minnesota, Nov. 13, 1994 (OT)
43 Washington vs. Detroit, Nov. 4, 1990 (OT)
Oakland vs. Pittsburgh, Sept. 15, 2002
42 N.Y. Jets vs. San Francisco, Sept. 21, 1980
N.Y. Jets vs. Seattle, Dec. 6, 1998

Fewest Passes Completed, Game
0 By many teams. Last time: Buffalo vs. N.Y. Jets, Sept. 29, 1974

Most Passes Completed, Both Teams, Game
71 New England (45) vs. Minnesota (26), Nov. 13, 1994
68 San Francisco (37) vs. Atlanta (31), Oct. 6, 1985
Denver (34) vs. Oakland (34), Nov. 11, 2002
66 Cincinnati (40) vs. San Diego (26), Dec. 20, 1982

Fewest Passes Completed, Both Teams, Game
1 Chi. Cardinals (0) vs. Philadelphia (1), Nov. 8, 1936
Detroit (0) vs. Cleveland (1), Sept. 10, 1937
Chi. Cardinals (0) vs. Detroit (1), Sept. 15, 1940
Brooklyn (0) vs. Pittsburgh (1), Nov. 29, 1942
2 Chi. Cardinals (0) vs. Detroit (2), Nov. 3, 1935
Buffalo (0) vs. N.Y. Jets (2), Sept. 29, 1974
Chi. Cardinals (0) vs. Green Bay (2), Nov. 18, 1934
3 In seven games

YARDS GAINED
Most Seasons Leading League, Passing Yardage
10 San Diego, 1965, 1968, 1971, 1978-1983, 1985
8 Chi. Bears, 1932, 1939, 1941, 1943, 1945, 1949, 1954, 1964
Washington, 1938, 1940, 1944, 1947-48, 1967, 1974, 1989
7 Houston, 1960-61, 1963-64, 1990-92
L.A./St. Louis Rams, 1946, 1950-51, 1956, 1999-2001
Balt./Indianapolis, 1957, 1959, 1960, 1963, 1976, 2003-04

Most Consecutive Seasons Leading League, Passing Yardage
6 San Diego, 1978-1983
4 Green Bay, 1934-37
3 Miami, 1986-88
Houston, 1990-92
St. Louis, 1999-2001

Most Yards Gained, Passing, Season
5,232 St. Louis, 2000

5,018   Miami, 1984
4,870   San Diego, 1985

Fewest Yards Gained, Passing, Season
302   Chi. Cardinals, 1934
357   Cincinnati, 1933
459   Boston, 1934

Most Yards Gained, Passing, Game
554   Los Angeles vs. N.Y. Yanks, Sept. 28, 1951
530   Minnesota vs. Baltimore, Sept. 28, 1969
521   Miami vs. N.Y. Jets, Oct. 23, 1988

Fewest Yards Gained, Passing, Game
−53   Denver vs. Oakland, Sept. 10, 1967
−52   Cincinnati vs. Houston, Oct. 31, 1971
−39   Atlanta vs. San Francisco, Oct. 23, 1976

Most Yards Gained, Passing, Both Teams, Game
884   N.Y. Jets (449) vs. Miami (435), Sept. 21, 1986 (OT)
883   San Diego (486) vs. Cincinnati (397), Dec. 20, 1982
874   Miami (456) vs. New England (418), Sept. 4, 1994

Fewest Yards Gained, Passing, Both Teams, Game
−11   Green Bay (−10) vs. Dallas (−1), Oct. 24, 1965
  1   Chi. Cardinals (0) vs. Philadelphia (1), Nov. 8, 1936
  7   Brooklyn (0) vs. Pittsburgh (7), Nov. 29, 1942

TIMES SACKED

Most Seasons Leading League, Fewest Times Sacked
10   Miami, 1973, 1982-1990
 5   N.Y. Jets, 1965-66, 1968, 1993, 2000
 4   San Diego, 1963-64, 1967-68
     San Francisco, 1964-65, 1970-71
     Indianapolis, 1999-2000, 2004-05

Most Consecutive Seasons Leading League, Fewest Times Sacked
 9   Miami, 1982-1990
 3   St. Louis, 1974-76
 2   By many teams

Most Times Sacked, Season
104   Philadelphia, 1986
 78   Arizona, 1997
 76   Houston, 2002

Fewest Times Sacked, Season
 7   Miami, 1988
 8   San Francisco, 1970
     St. Louis, 1975
 9   N.Y. Jets, 1966
     Washington, 1991

Most Times Sacked, Game
12   Pittsburgh vs. Dallas, Nov. 20, 1966
     Baltimore vs. St. Louis, Oct. 26, 1980
     Detroit vs. Chicago, Dec. 16, 1984
     Houston vs. Dallas, Sept. 29, 1985
11   St. Louis vs. N.Y. Giants, Nov. 1, 1964
     Los Angeles vs. Baltimore, Nov. 22, 1964
     Denver vs. Buffalo, Dec. 13, 1964
     Green Bay vs. Detroit, Nov. 7, 1965
     Buffalo vs. Oakland, Oct. 15, 1967
     Denver vs. Oakland, Nov. 5, 1967
     Atlanta vs. St. Louis, Nov. 24, 1968
     Detroit vs. Dallas, Oct. 6, 1975
     Philadelphia vs. St. Louis, Dec. 18, 1983
     Cleveland vs. Kansas City, Sept. 30, 1984
     Minnesota vs. Chicago, Oct. 28, 1984
     Atlanta vs. Cleveland, Nov. 18, 1984
     Dallas vs. San Diego, Nov. 16, 1986
     Philadelphia vs. Detroit, Nov. 16, 1986
     Philadelphia vs. L.A. Raiders, Nov. 30, 1986 (OT)
     L.A. Raiders vs. Seattle, Dec. 8, 1986
     N.Y. Jets vs. Dallas, Oct. 4, 1987
     Philadelphia vs. Chicago, Oct. 4, 1987
     Dallas vs. Philadelphia, Sept. 15, 1991
     Cleveland vs. Indianapolis, Sept. 6, 1992
10   By many teams

Most Times Sacked, Both Teams, Game
18   Green Bay (10) vs. San Diego (8), Sept. 24, 1978
17   Buffalo (10) vs. N.Y. Titans (7), Nov. 23, 1961
     Pittsburgh (12) vs. Dallas (5), Nov. 20, 1966
     Atlanta (9) vs. Philadelphia (8), Dec. 16, 1984
     Philadelphia (11) vs. L.A. Raiders (6), Nov. 30, 1986 (OT)
16   Los Angeles (11) vs. Baltimore (5), Nov. 22, 1964
     Buffalo (11) vs. Oakland (5), Oct. 15, 1967

COMPLETION PERCENTAGE

Most Seasons Leading League, Completion Percentage
14   San Francisco, 1952, 1957-58, 1965, 1981, 1983,
     1987, 1989, 1992-97
11   Washington, 1937, 1939-1940, 1942-45, 1947-48,
     1969-1970
 8   Green Bay, 1936, 1941, 1961-62, 1964, 1966,
     1968, 1998

Most Consecutive Seasons Leading League, Completion Percentage
 6   San Francisco, 1992-97
 4   Washington, 1942-45
     Kansas City, 1966-69
 3   Cleveland, 1953-55
     St. Louis, 1999-2001

Highest Completion Percentage, Season
70.65   Cincinnati, 1982 (310-219)
70.25   San Francisco, 1994 (511-359)
70.19   San Francisco, 1989 (483-339)

Lowest Completion Percentage, Season
22.9   Philadelphia, 1936 (170-39)
24.5   Cincinnati, 1933 (102-25)
25.0   Pittsburgh, 1941 (168-42)

TOUCHDOWNS

Most Touchdowns, Passing, Season
51   Indianapolis, 2004
49   Miami, 1984
48   Houston, 1961

Fewest Touchdowns, Passing, Season
0   Cincinnati, 1933
    Pittsburgh, 1945
1   Boston, 1932
    Boston, 1933
    Chi. Cardinals, 1934
    Cincinnati/St. Louis, 1934
    Detroit, 1942
2   Chi. Cardinals, 1932
    Stapleton, 1932
    Chi. Cardinals, 1935
    Brooklyn, 1936
    Pittsburgh, 1942

Most Touchdowns, Passing, Game
7   Chi. Bears vs. N.Y. Giants, Nov. 14, 1943
    Philadelphia vs. Washington, Oct. 17, 1954
    Houston vs. N.Y. Titans, Nov. 19, 1961
    Houston vs. N.Y. Titans, Oct. 14, 1962
    N.Y. Giants vs. Washington, Oct. 28, 1962
    Minnesota vs. Baltimore, Sept. 28, 1969
    San Diego vs. Oakland, Nov. 22, 1981
6   By many teams

Most Touchdowns, Passing, Both Teams, Game
12   New Orleans (6) vs. St. Louis (6), Nov. 2, 1969
11   N.Y. Giants (7) vs. Washington (4), Oct. 28, 1962
     Oakland (6) vs. Houston (5), Dec. 22, 1963
10   San Diego (5) vs. Seattle (5), Sept. 15, 1985
     Miami (6) vs. N.Y. Jets (4), Sept. 21, 1986 (OT)
     San Francisco (6) vs. Atlanta (4), Oct. 14, 1990

PASSES HAD INTERCEPTED

Most Passes Had Intercepted, Season
- 48 Houston, 1962
- 45 Denver, 1961
- 41 Card-Pitt, 1944

Fewest Passes Had Intercepted, Season
- 5 Cleveland, 1960
  - Green Bay, 1966
  - Kansas City, 1990
  - N.Y. Giants, 1990
- 6 Green Bay, 1964
  - St. Louis, 1982
  - Dallas, 1993
  - Jacksonville, 2005
- 7 Los Angeles, 1969
  - Denver, 2005

Most Passes Had Intercepted, Game
- 9 Detroit vs. Green Bay, Oct. 24, 1943
  - Pittsburgh vs. Philadelphia, Dec. 12, 1965
- 8 Green Bay vs. N.Y. Giants, Nov. 21, 1948
  - Chi. Cardinals vs. Philadelphia, Sept. 24, 1950
  - N.Y. Yanks vs. N.Y. Giants, Dec. 16, 1951
  - Denver vs. Houston, Dec. 2, 1962
  - Chi. Bears vs. Detroit, Sept. 22, 1968
  - Baltimore vs. N.Y. Jets, Sept. 23, 1973
- 7 By many teams. Last time: Detroit vs. Cleveland, Sept. 23, 2001

Most Passes Had Intercepted, Both Teams, Game
- 13 Denver (8) vs. Houston (5), Dec. 2, 1962
- 11 Philadelphia (7) vs. Boston (4), Nov. 3, 1935
  - Boston (6) vs. Pittsburgh (5), Dec. 1, 1935
  - Cleveland (7) vs. Green Bay (4), Oct. 30, 1938
  - Green Bay (7) vs. Detroit (4), Oct. 20, 1940
  - Detroit (7) vs. Chi. Bears (4), Nov. 22, 1942
  - Detroit (7) vs. Cleveland (4), Nov. 26, 1944
  - Chi. Cardinals (8) vs. Philadelphia (3), Sept. 24, 1950
  - Washington (7) vs. N.Y. Giants (4), Dec. 8, 1963
  - Pittsburgh (9) vs. Philadelphia (2), Dec 12, 1965
- 10 In many games

PUNTING

Most Seasons Leading League (Average Distance)
- 7 Denver 1962-64, 1966-67, 1982, 1999
- 6 Washington, 1940-43, 1945, 1958
  - Kansas City, 1968, 1971-73, 1979, 1984
  - Oakland, 1974-75, 1977-78, 2003-04
- 5 L.A. Rams, 1946, 1949, 1955-56, 1994

Most Consecutive Seasons Leading League (Average Distance)
- 4 Washington, 1940-43
- 3 Cleveland, 1950-52
  - Denver, 1962-64
  - Kansas City, 1971-73

Most Punts, Season
- 116 Houston, 2002
- 114 Chicago, 1981
- 113 Boston, 1934
  - Brooklyn, 1934
  - Dallas, 2002

Fewest Punts, Season
- 23 San Diego, 1982
- 31 Cincinnati, 1982
- 32 Chi. Bears, 1941

Most Punts, Game
- 17 Chi. Bears vs. Green Bay, Oct. 22, 1933
  - Cincinnati vs. Pittsburgh, Oct. 22, 1933
- 16 Cincinnati vs. Portsmouth, Sept. 17, 1933
  - Chi. Cardinals vs. Chi. Bears, Nov. 30, 1933
  - Chi. Cardinals vs. Detroit, Sept. 15, 1940
  - Oakland vs. San Diego, Oct. 11, 1998

- 15 N.Y. Giants vs. Chi. Bears, Nov. 17, 1935
  - Philadelphia vs. N.Y. Giants, Dec. 6, 1987 (OT)

Fewest Punts, Game
- 0 By many teams. Last time:
  - Indianapolis vs. Houston, Oct. 23, 2005

Most Punts, Both Teams, Game
- 31 Chi. Bears (17) vs. Green Bay (14), Oct. 22, 1933
  - Cincinnati (17), vs. Pittsburgh (14), Oct. 22, 1933
- 29 Chi. Cardinals (15) vs. Cincinnati (14), Nov. 12, 1933
  - Chi. Cardinals (16) vs. Chi. Bears (13), Nov. 30, 1933
  - Chi. Cardinals (16) vs. Detroit (13), Sept. 15, 1940
- 28 Philadelphia (14) vs. Washington (14), Nov. 5, 1939

Fewest Punts, Both Teams, Game
- 0 Buffalo vs. San Francisco, Sept. 13, 1992
- 1 Baltimore (0) vs. Cleveland (1), Nov. 1, 1959
  - Dall. Cowboys (0) vs. Cleveland (1), Dec. 3, 1961
  - Chicago (0) vs. Detroit (1), Oct. 1, 1972
  - San Francisco (0) vs. N.Y. Giants (1), Oct. 15, 1972
  - Green Bay (0) vs. Buffalo (1), Dec. 5, 1982
  - Miami (0) vs. Buffalo (1), Oct. 12, 1986
  - Green Bay (0) vs. Chicago (1), Dec. 17, 1989
  - Oakland (0) vs. Seattle (1), Dec. 5, 1999
  - Tampa Bay (0) vs. Minnesota (1), Oct. 29, 2000
  - New Orleans (0) vs. San Francisco (1), Oct. 20, 2002
- 2 In many games

AVERAGE YARDAGE

Highest Average Distance, Punting, Season
- 47.6 Detroit, 1961 (56-2,664)
- 47.2 Tennessee, 1998 (69-3,258)
- 47.0 Carolina, 2001 (94-4,419)

Lowest Average Distance, Punting, Season
- 32.7 Card-Pitt, 1944 (60-1,964)
- 33.8 Cincinnati, 1986 (59-1,996)
- 33.9 Detroit, 1969 (74-2,510)

PUNT RETURNS

Most Seasons Leading League (Average Return)
- 9 Detroit, 1943-45, 1951-52, 1962, 1966, 1969, 1991
- 7 Chi. Cardinals/St. Louis, 1948-49, 1955-56, 1959, 1986-87
- 6 Green Bay, 1950, 1953-54, 1961, 1972, 1996
  - Dallas/Kansas City, 1960, 1968, 1970, 1979-1980, 2003

Most Consecutive Seasons Leading League (Average Return)
- 3 Detroit, 1943-45
- 2 By many teams

Most Punt Returns, Season
- 71 Pittsburgh, 1976
  - Tampa Bay, 1979
  - L.A. Raiders, 1985
- 67 Pittsburgh, 1974
  - Los Angeles, 1978
  - L.A. Raiders, 1984
- 65 San Francisco, 1976

Fewest Punt Returns, Season
- 12 Baltimore, 1981
  - San Diego, 1982
- 14 Los Angeles, 1961
  - Philadelphia, 1962
  - Baltimore, 1982
- 15 Houston, 1960
  - Washington, 1960
  - Oakland, 1961
  - N.Y. Giants, 1969
  - Philadelphia, 1973
  - Kansas City, 1982

Most Punt Returns, Game
- 12 Philadelphia vs. Cleveland, Dec. 3, 1950
- 11 Chi. Bears vs. Chi. Cardinals, Oct. 8, 1950

Washington vs. Tampa Bay, Oct. 9, 1977
10 Philadelphia vs. N.Y. Giants, Nov. 26, 1950
Philadelphia vs. Tampa Bay, Sept. 18, 1977
Pittsburgh vs. Buffalo, Dec. 16, 1979
Washington vs. New Orleans, Dec. 26, 1982
Philadelphia vs. Seattle, Dec. 13, 1992 (OT)
New England vs. Pittsburgh, Dec. 5, 1993

Most Punt Returns, Both Teams, Game
17 Philadelphia (12) vs. Cleveland (5), Dec. 3, 1950
16 N.Y. Giants (9) vs. Philadelphia (7), Dec. 12, 1954
Washington (11) vs. Tampa Bay (5), Oct. 9, 1977
Oakland (8) vs. San Diego (8), Oct. 11, 1998
15 Detroit (8) vs. Cleveland (7), Sept. 27, 1942
Los Angeles (8) vs. Baltimore (7), Nov. 27, 1966
Pittsburgh (8) vs. Houston (7), Dec. 1, 1974
Philadelphia (10) vs. Tampa Bay (5), Sept. 18, 1977
Baltimore (9) vs. Kansas City (6), Sept. 2, 1979
Washington (10) vs. New Orleans (5), Dec. 26, 1982
L.A. Raiders (8) vs. Cleveland (7), Nov. 16, 1986

FAIR CATCHES
Most Fair Catches, Season
34 Baltimore, 1971
33 Philadelphia, 2000
32 San Diego, 1969
Oakland, 2001
Fewest Fair Catches, Season
0 San Diego, 1975
New England, 1976
Tampa Bay, 1976
Pittsburgh, 1977
Dallas, 1982
1 Cleveland, 1974
San Francisco, 1975
Kansas City, 1976
St. Louis, 1976
San Diego, 1976
L.A. Rams, 1982
St. Louis, 1982
Tampa Bay, 1982
Arizona, 2001
2 By many teams
Most Fair Catches, Game
7 Minnesota vs. Dallas, Sept. 25, 1966
N.Y. Jets vs. Miami, Nov. 20, 1966
Detroit vs. Chicago, Nov. 21, 1976
Philadelphia vs. Buffalo, Dec. 27, 1987
6 By many teams

YARDS GAINED
Most Yards, Punt Returns, Season
875 Green Bay, 1996
785 L.A. Raiders, 1985
781 Chi. Bears, 1948
Fewest Yards, Punt Returns, Season
27 St. Louis, 1965
35 N.Y. Giants, 1965
37 New England, 1972
Most Yards, Punt Returns, Game
231 Detroit vs. San Francisco, Oct. 6, 1963
225 Oakland vs. Buffalo, Sept. 15, 1968
219 Los Angeles vs. Atlanta, Oct. 11, 1981
Fewest Yards, Punt Returns, Game
-28 Washington vs. Dallas, Dec. 11, 1966
-23 N.Y. Giants vs. Buffalo, Oct. 20, 1975
Pittsburgh vs. Houston, Sept. 20, 1970
-20 New Orleans vs. Pittsburgh, Oct. 20, 1968
Most Yards, Punt Returns, Both Teams, Game
282 Los Angeles (219) vs. Atlanta (63), Oct. 11, 1981
245 Detroit (231) vs. San Francisco (14), Oct. 6, 1963

244 Oakland (225) vs. Buffalo (19), Sept. 15, 1968
Fewest Yards, Punt Returns, Both Teams, Game
-18 Buffalo (-18) vs. Pittsburgh (0), Oct. 29, 1972
-14 Miami (-14) vs. Boston (0), Nov. 30, 1969
Tennessee (-14) vs. New Orleans (0),
Sept. 21, 2003
-13 N.Y. Giants (-13) vs. Cleveland (0), Nov. 14, 1965

AVERAGE YARDS RETURNING PUNTS
Highest Average, Punt Returns, Season
20.2 Chi. Bears, 1941 (27-546)
19.1 Chi. Cardinals, 1948 (35-669)
18.2 Chi. Cardinals, 1949 (30-546)
Lowest Average, Punt Returns, Season
1.2 St. Louis, 1965 (23-27)
1.5 N.Y. Giants, 1965 (24-35)
1.7 Washington, 1970 (27-45)

TOUCHDOWNS RETURNING PUNTS
Most Touchdowns, Punt Returns, Season
5 Chi. Cardinals, 1959
4 Chi. Cardinals, 1948
Detroit, 1951
N.Y. Giants, 1951
Denver, 1976
3 Washington, 1941
Detroit, 1952
Pittsburgh, 1952
Houston, 1975
Los Angeles, 1981
Cleveland, 1993
Green Bay, 1996
Denver, 1997
San Diego, 1997
Most Touchdowns, Punt Returns, Game
2 Detroit vs. Los Angeles, Oct. 14, 1951
Detroit vs. Green Bay, Nov. 22, 1951
Chi. Cardinals vs. Pittsburgh, Nov. 1, 1959
Chi. Cardinals vs. N.Y. Giants, Nov. 22, 1959
N.Y. Titans vs. Denver, Sept. 24, 1961
Denver vs. Cleveland, Sept. 26, 1976
Los Angeles vs. Atlanta, Oct. 11, 1981
St. Louis vs. Tampa Bay, Dec. 21, 1986
L.A. Rams vs. Atlanta, Dec. 27, 1992
Cleveland vs. Pittsburgh, Oct. 24, 1993
San Diego vs. Cincinnati, Nov. 2, 1997
Denver vs. Carolina, Nov. 9, 1997
Baltimore vs. Seattle, Dec. 7, 1997
Baltimore vs. N.Y. Jets, Dec. 24, 2000
Oakland vs. Tennessee, Sept. 29, 2002
Carolina vs. Cincinnati, Dec. 8, 2002
Detroit at Jacksonville, Nov. 14, 2004 (OT)
Most Touchdowns, Punt Returns, Both Teams, Game
2 Philadelphia (1) vs. Washington (1), Nov. 9, 1952
Kansas City (1) vs. Buffalo (1), Sept. 11, 1966
Baltimore (1) vs. New England (1), Nov. 18, 1979
L.A. Raiders (1) vs. Philadelphia (1),
Nov. 30, 1986 (OT)
Cincinnati (1) vs. Green Bay (1), Sept. 20, 1992
Oakland (1) vs. Seattle (1), Nov. 15, 1998
Atlanta (1) vs. Tennessee (1), Nov. 23, 2003
(Also see previous record)

KICKOFF RETURNS
Most Seasons Leading League (Average Return)
8 Washington, 1942, 1947, 1962-63, 1973-74, 1981,
1995
6 Chicago Bears, 1943, 1948, 1958, 1966, 1972, 1985
N.Y. Giants, 1944, 1946, 1949, 1951, 1953, 2004
5 Green Bay, 1954, 1964, 1967, 1993, 1998

Most Consecutive Seasons Leading League (Average Return)
- 3   Denver, 1965-67
- 2   By many teams

Most Kickoff Returns, Season
- 89   Cleveland, 1999
- 88   New Orleans, 1980
- 87   Atlanta, 1996
-      New Orleans, 2001

Fewest Kickoff Returns, Season
- 17   N.Y. Giants, 1944
- 20   N.Y. Giants, 1941, 1943
-      Chi. Bears, 1942
- 23   Washington, 1942

Most Kickoff Returns, Game
- 12   N.Y. Giants vs. Washington, Nov. 27, 1966
- 10   By many teams

Most Kickoff Returns, Both Teams, Game
- 19   N.Y. Giants (12) vs. Washington (7), Nov. 27, 1966
-      Cleveland (10) vs. Cincinnati (9), Nov. 28, 2004
- 18   Houston (10) vs. Oakland (8), Dec. 22, 1963
- 17   Washington (9) vs. Green Bay (8), Oct. 17, 1983
-      San Diego (9) vs. Pittsburgh (8), Dec. 8, 1985
-      Detroit (9) vs. Green Bay (8), Nov. 27, 1986
-      L.A. Raiders (9) vs. Seattle (8), Dec. 18, 1988
-      Oakland (10) vs. Seattle (7), Oct. 26, 1997
-      Buffalo (9) vs. Minnesota (8), Sept. 15, 2002 (OT)

YARDS GAINED

Most Yards, Kickoff Returns, Season
- 2,296   Arizona, 2000
- 2,173   Houston, 2005
- 2,039   Detroit, 2002

Fewest Yards, Kickoff Returns, Season
- 282   N.Y. Giants, 1940
- 381   Green Bay, 1940
- 424   Chicago, 1963

Most Yards, Kickoff Returns, Game
- 367   Baltimore vs. Minnesota, Dec. 13, 1998
- 362   Detroit vs. Los Angeles, Oct. 29, 1950
- 304   Chi. Bears vs. Green Bay, Nov. 9, 1952
-      New Orleans vs. L.A. Rams, Oct. 23, 1994

Most Yards, Kickoff Returns, Both Teams, Game
- 560   Detroit (362) vs. Los Angeles (198), Oct. 29, 1950
- 511   Baltimore (367) vs. Minnesota (144), Dec. 13, 1998
- 501   New Orleans (304) vs. L.A. Rams (197), Oct. 23, 1994

AVERAGE YARDAGE

Highest Average, Kickoff Returns, Season
- 29.4   Chicago, 1972 (52-1,528)
- 28.9   Pittsburgh, 1952 (39-1,128)
- 28.2   Washington, 1962 (61-1,720)

Lowest Average, Kickoff Returns, Season
- 14.7   N.Y. Jets, 1993 (46-675)
- 15.8   N.Y. Giants, 1993 (32-507)
- 15.9   Tampa Bay, 1993 (58-922)

TOUCHDOWNS

Most Touchdowns, Kickoff Returns, Season
- 4   Green Bay, 1967
-    Chicago, 1970
-    Detroit, 1994
- 3   Los Angeles, 1950
-    Chi. Cardinals, 1954
-    San Francisco, 1963
-    Denver, 1966
-    Chicago, 1967
-    New England, 1977
-    L.A. Rams, 1985
-    Atlanta, 2000

-    Buffalo, 2004
- 2   By many teams

Most Touchdowns, Kickoff Returns, Game
- 2   Chi. Bears vs. Green Bay, Sept. 22, 1940
-    Chi. Bears vs. Green Bay, Nov. 9, 1952
-    Philadelphia vs. Dallas, Nov. 6, 1966
-    Green Bay vs. Cleveland, Nov. 12, 1967
-    L.A. Rams vs. Green Bay, Nov. 24, 1985
-    New Orleans vs. L.A. Rams, Oct. 23, 1994
-    Baltimore vs. Minnesota, Dec. 13, 1998
-    N.Y. Jets vs. Buffalo, Sept. 8, 2002 (OT)

Most Touchdowns, Kickoff Returns, Both Teams, Game
- 3   Baltimore (2) vs. Minnesota (1), Dec. 13, 1998
- 2   In many games

FUMBLES

Most Fumbles, Season
- 56   Chi. Bears, 1938
-      San Francisco, 1978
- 54   Philadelphia, 1946
- 51   New England, 1973

Fewest Fumbles, Season
- 7   Kansas City, 2002
- 8   Cleveland, 1959
- 10   Indianapolis, 1998
-      Minnesota, 1998

Most Fumbles, Game
- 10   Phil-Pitt vs. N.Y. Giants, Oct. 9, 1943
-      Detroit vs. Minnesota, Nov. 12, 1967
-      Kansas City vs. Houston, Oct. 12, 1969
-      San Francisco vs. Detroit, Dec. 17, 1978
- 9   Philadelphia vs. Green Bay, Oct. 13, 1946
-    Boston at Oakland, Dec. 16, 1962
-    Kansas City vs. San Diego, Nov. 15, 1964
-    N.Y. Giants vs. Buffalo, Oct. 20, 1975
-    St. Louis vs. Washington, Oct. 25, 1976
-    San Diego vs. Green Bay, Sept. 24, 1978
-    Pittsburgh vs. Cincinnati, Oct. 14, 1979
-    Cleveland vs. Seattle, Dec. 20, 1981
-    Cleveland vs. Pittsburgh, Dec. 23, 1990
-    Oakland vs. Seattle, Dec. 22, 1996
- 8   By many teams

Most Fumbles, Both Teams, Game
- 14   Washington (8) vs. Pittsburgh (6), Nov. 14, 1937
-      Chi. Bears (7) vs. Cleveland (7), Nov. 24, 1940
-      St. Louis (8) vs. N.Y. Giants (6), Sept. 17, 1961
-      Kansas City (10) vs. Houston (4), Oct. 12, 1969
- 13   Washington (8) vs. Pittsburgh (5), Nov. 14, 1937
-      Philadelphia (7) vs. Boston (6), Dec. 8, 1946
-      N.Y. Giants (7) vs. Washington (6), Nov. 5, 1950
-      Kansas City (9) vs. San Diego (4), Nov. 15, 1964
-      Buffalo (7) vs. Denver (6), Dec. 13, 1964
-      N.Y. Jets (7) vs. Houston (6), Sept. 12, 1965
-      Cleveland (7) vs. New Orleans (6), Dec. 12, 1971
-      Houston (8) vs. Pittsburgh (5), Dec. 9, 1973
-      St. Louis (9) vs. Washington (4), Oct. 25, 1976
-      Cleveland (9) vs. Seattle (4), Dec. 20, 1981
-      Green Bay (7) vs. Detroit (6), Oct. 6, 1985
- 12   In many games

FUMBLES LOST

Most Fumbles Lost, Season
- 36   Chi. Cardinals, 1959
- 31   Green Bay, 1952
- 29   Chi. Cardinals, 1946
-      Pittsburgh, 1950
-      Cleveland, 1978

Fewest Fumbles Lost, Season
- 2   Kansas City, 2002

3   Philadelphia, 1938
     Minnesota, 1980
4   San Francisco, 1960
     Kansas City, 1982
     Minnesota, 1998
     Detroit, 2003

Most Fumbles Lost, Game
8   St. Louis vs. Washington, Oct. 25, 1976
     Cleveland vs. Pittsburgh, Dec. 23, 1990
7   Cincinnati vs. Buffalo, Nov. 30, 1969
     Pittsburgh vs. Cincinnati, Oct. 14, 1979
     Cleveland vs. Seattle, Dec. 20, 1981
6   By many teams

FUMBLES RECOVERED

Most Fumbles Recovered, Season, Own and Opponents'
58   Minnesota, 1963 (27 own, 31 opp)
51   Chi. Bears, 1938 (37 own, 14 opp)
     San Francisco, 1978 (24 own, 27 opp)
50   Philadelphia, 1987 (23 own, 27 opp)

Fewest Fumbles Recovered, Season, Own and Opponents'
9   San Francisco, 1982 (5 own, 4 opp)
11   Cincinnati, 1982 (5 own, 6 opp)
12   Washington, 1994 (6 own, 6 opp)
     Arizona, 1997 (7 own, 5 opp)
     New Orleans, 2005 (3 own, 9 opp)

Most Fumbles Recovered, Game, Own and Opponents'
10   Denver vs. Buffalo, Dec. 13, 1964 (5 own, 5 opp)
     Pittsburgh vs. Houston, Dec. 9, 1973 (5 own, 5 opp)
     Washington vs. St. Louis, Oct. 25, 1976
        (2 own, 8 opp)
9   St. Louis vs. N.Y. Giants, Sept. 17, 1961
        (6 own, 3 opp)
     Houston vs. Cincinnati, Oct. 27, 1974 (4 own, 5 opp)
     Kansas City vs. Dallas, Nov. 10, 1975 (4 own, 5 opp)
     Green Bay vs. Detroit, Oct. 6, 1985 (5 own, 4 opp)
     Pittsburgh vs. Cleveland, Dec. 23, 1990
        (1 own, 8 opp)
8   By many teams

Most Own Fumbles Recovered, Season
37   Chi. Bears, 1938
28   Pittsburgh, 1987
27   Philadelphia, 1946
     Minnesota, 1963

Fewest Own Fumbles Recovered, Season
2   Washington, 1958
     Miami, 2000
3   Detroit, 1956
     Cleveland, 1959
     Houston, 1982
     New Orleans, 2005
4   By many teams

Most Opponents' Fumbles Recovered, Season
31   Minnesota, 1963
29   Cleveland, 1951
28   Green Bay, 1946
     Houston, 1977
     Seattle, 1983

Fewest Opponents' Fumbles Recovered, Season
3   Los Angeles, 1974
     Green Bay, 1995
4   Philadelphia, 1944
     San Francisco, 1982
5   Baltimore, 1982
     Arizona, 1997
     Baltimore, 1998
     Chicago, 2003

Most Opponents' Fumbles Recovered, Game
8   Washington vs. St. Louis, Oct. 25, 1976
     Pittsburgh vs. Cleveland, Dec. 23, 1990

7   Buffalo vs. Cincinnati, Nov. 30, 1969
     Cincinnati vs. Pittsburgh, Oct. 14, 1979
     Seattle vs. Cleveland, Dec. 20, 1981
6   By many teams

TOUCHDOWNS

Most Touchdowns, Fumbles Recovered, Season, Own and Opponents'
5   Chi. Bears, 1942 (1 own, 4 opp)
     Los Angeles, 1952 (1 own, 4 opp)
     San Francisco, 1965 (1 own, 4 opp)
     Oakland, 1978 (2 own, 3 opp)
4   Chi. Bears, 1948 (1 own, 3 opp)
     Boston, 1948 (4 opp)
     Denver, 1979 (1 own, 3 opp)
     Atlanta, 1981 (1 own, 3 opp)
     Denver, 1984 (4 opp)
     St. Louis, 1987 (4 opp)
     Minnesota, 1989 (4 opp)
     Atlanta, 1991 (4 opp)
     Philadelphia, 1995 (4 opp)
     Atlanta, 1998 (4 opp)
     New Orleans, 1998 (4 opp)
     Kansas City, 1999 (4 opp)
3   By many teams

Most Touchdowns, Own Fumbles Recovered, Season
2   Chi. Bears, 1953
     New England, 1973
     Buffalo, 1974
     Denver, 1975
     Oakland, 1978
     Green Bay, 1982
     New Orleans, 1983
     Cleveland, 1986
     Green Bay, 1989
     Miami, 1996
     Buffalo, 2000

Most Touchdowns, Opponents' Fumbles Recovered, Season
4   Detroit, 1937
     Chi. Bears, 1942
     Boston, 1948
     Los Angeles, 1952
     San Francisco, 1965
     Denver, 1984
     St. Louis, 1987
     Minnesota, 1989
     Atlanta, 1991
     Philadelphia, 1995
     Atlanta, 1998
     New Orleans, 1998
     Kansas City, 1999
3   By many teams

Most Touchdowns, Fumbles Recovered, Game, Own and Opponents'
2   By many teams

Most Touchdowns, Fumbles Recovered, Game, Both Teams, Own and Opponents'
3   Detroit (2) vs. Minnesota (1), Dec. 9, 1962
        (2 own, 1 opp)
     Green Bay (2) vs. Dallas (1), Nov. 29, 1964 (3 opp)
     Oakland (2) vs. Buffalo (1), Dec. 24, 1967 (3 opp)
     Oakland (2) vs. Philadelphia (1), Sept. 24, 1995
        (3 opp)
     Tennessee (2) vs. Pittsburgh (1), Jan. 2, 2000
        (3 opp)

Most Touchdowns, Own Fumbles Recovered, Game
2   Miami vs. New England, Sept.1, 1996

Most Touchdowns, Opponents' Fumbles Recovered, Game
2   Many times. Last time:
     Green Bay vs. St. Louis, Nov. 29, 2004

Most Touchdowns, Opponents' Fumbles Recovered, Game, Both Teams

3 Green Bay (2) vs. Dallas (1), Nov. 29, 1964
    Oakland (2) vs. Buffalo (1), Dec. 24, 1967
    Oakland (2) vs. Philadelphia (1), Sept. 24, 1995
    Tennessee (2) vs. Pittsburgh (1), Jan. 2, 2000

TURNOVERS
(Number of times losing the ball on interceptions and fumbles.)

Most Turnovers, Season
65 Denver, 1961
63 San Francisco, 1978
58 Chi. Bears, 1947
    Pittsburgh, 1950
    N.Y. Giants, 1983

Fewest Turnovers, Season
12 Kansas City, 1982
14 N.Y. Giants, 1943
    Cleveland, 1959
    N.Y. Giants, 1990
15 Dallas, 1998
    Jacksonville, 2002
    Kansas City, 2002

Most Turnovers, Game
12 Detroit vs. Chi. Bears, Nov. 22, 1942
    Chi. Cardinals vs. Philadelphia, Sept. 24, 1950
    Pittsburgh vs. Philadelphia, Dec. 12, 1965
11 San Diego vs. Green Bay, Sept. 24, 1978
10 Washington vs. N.Y. Giants, Dec. 4, 1938
    Pittsburgh vs. Green Bay, Nov. 23, 1941
    Detroit vs. Green Bay, Oct. 24, 1943
    Chi. Cardinals vs. Green Bay, Nov. 10, 1946
    Chi. Cardinals vs. N.Y. Giants, Nov. 2, 1952
    Minnesota vs. Detroit, Dec. 9, 1962
    Houston vs. Oakland, Sept. 7, 1963
    Washington vs. N.Y. Giants, Dec. 8, 1963
    Chicago vs. Detroit, Sept. 22, 1968
    St. Louis vs. Washington, Oct. 25, 1976
    N.Y. Jets vs. New England, Nov. 21, 1976
    San Francisco vs. Dallas, Oct. 12, 1980
    Cleveland vs. Seattle, Dec. 20, 1981
    Detroit vs. Denver, Oct. 7, 1984

Most Turnovers, Both Teams, Game
17 Detroit (12) vs. Chi. Bears (5), Nov. 22, 1942
    Boston (9) vs. Philadelphia (8), Dec. 8, 1946
16 Chi. Cardinals (12) vs. Philadelphia (4), Sept. 24, 1950
    Chi. Cardinals (8) vs. Chi. Bears (8), Dec. 7, 1958
    Minnesota (10) vs. Detroit (6), Dec. 9, 1962
    Houston (9) vs. Kansas City (7), Oct. 12, 1969
15 Philadelphia (8) vs. Chi. Cardinals (7), Oct. 3, 1954
    Denver (9) vs. Houston (6), Dec. 2, 1962
    Washington (10) vs. N.Y. Giants (5), Dec. 8, 1963
    St. Louis (9) vs. Kansas City (6), Oct. 2, 1983

PENALTIES

Most Seasons Leading League, Fewest Penalties
13 Miami, 1968, 1976-1984, 1986, 1990-91
9 Pittsburgh, 1946-47, 1950-52, 1954, 1963, 1965, 1968
7 Boston/New England, 1962, 1964-65, 1973, 1987, 1989, 1993

Most Consecutive Seasons Leading League, Fewest Penalties
9 Miami, 1976-1984
3 Pittsburgh, 1950-52
2 By many teams

Most Seasons Leading League, Most Penalties
16 Chi. Bears, 1941-44, 1946-49, 1951, 1959-1961, 1963, 1965, 1968, 1976

15 Oakland/L.A. Raiders, 1963, 1966, 1968-69, 1975, 1982, 1984, 1991, 1993-96, 2003-05
7 L.A./St. Louis Rams, 1950, 1952, 1962, 1969, 1978, 1980, 1997

Most Consecutive Seasons Leading League, Most Penalties
4 Chi. Bears, 1941-44, 1946-49
    Oakland/L.A. Raiders, 1993-96
3 Chi. Cardinals, 1954-56
    Chi. Bears, 1959-1961
    Oakland, 2003-05 (current)

Fewest Penalties, Season
19 Detroit, 1937
21 Boston, 1935
24 Philadelphia, 1936

Most Penalties, Season
158 Kansas City, 1998
156 L.A. Raiders, 1994
     Oakland, 1996
149 Houston, 1989

Fewest Penalties, Game
0 By many teams. Last time:
    Oakland vs. San Diego, Dec. 4, 2005

Most Penalties, Game
22 Brooklyn vs. Green Bay, Sept. 17, 1944
    Chi. Bears vs. Philadelphia, Nov. 26, 1944
    San Francisco vs. Buffalo, Oct. 4, 1998
21 Cleveland vs. Chi. Bears, Nov. 25, 1951
    Baltimore vs. Detroit, Oct. 9, 2005
20 Tampa Bay vs. Seattle, Oct. 17, 1976
    Oakland vs. Denver, Dec. 15, 1996

Fewest Penalties, Both Teams, Game
0 Brooklyn vs. Pittsburgh, Oct. 28, 1934
    Brooklyn vs. Boston, Sept. 28, 1936
    Cleveland vs. Chi. Bears, Oct. 9, 1938
    Pittsburgh vs. Philadelphia, Nov. 10, 1940

Most Penalties, Both Teams, Game
37 Cleveland (21) vs. Chi. Bears (16), Nov. 25, 1951
35 Tampa Bay (20) vs. Seattle (15), Oct. 17, 1976
34 San Francisco (22) vs. Buffalo (12), Oct. 4, 1998

YARDS PENALIZED

Most Seasons Leading League, Fewest Yards Penalized
13 Miami, 1967-68, 1973, 1977-1984, 1990-91
10 Boston/Washington, 1935, 1953-54, 1956-58, 1970, 1985, 1995, 1997
7 Pittsburgh, 1946-47, 1950, 1952, 1962, 1965, 1968
    Boston/New England, 1962, 1964-66, 1987, 1989, 1993

Most Consecutive Seasons Leading League, Fewest Yards Penalized
8 Miami, 1977-1984
3 Washington, 1956-58
    Boston, 1964-66
2 By many teams

Most Seasons Leading League, Most Yards Penalized
15 Chi. Bears, 1935, 1937, 1939-1944, 1946-47, 1949, 1951, 1961-62, 1968
12 Oakland/L.A. Raiders, 1963-64, 1968-69, 1975, 1982, 1984, 1991, 1993-94, 1996, 2003
6 Buffalo, 1962, 1967, 1970, 1972, 1981, 1983
    Houston, 1961, 1985-86, 1988-1990

Most Consecutive Seasons Leading League, Most Yards Penalized
6 Chi. Bears, 1939-1944
3 Houston, 1988-1990
2 By many teams

Fewest Yards Penalized, Season
139 Detroit, 1937
146 Philadelphia, 1937
159 Philadelphia, 1936

Most Yards Penalized, Season
- 1,304 Kansas City, 1998
- 1,274 Oakland, 1969
- 1,266 Oakland, 1996

Fewest Yards Penalized, Game
- 0 By many teams. Last time:
      Oakland vs. San Diego, Dec. 4, 2005

Most Yards Penalized, Game
- 212 Tennessee vs. Baltimore, Oct. 10, 1999
- 209 Cleveland vs. Chi. Bears, Nov. 25, 1951
- 191 Philadelphia vs. Seattle, Dec. 13, 1992 (OT)

Fewest Yards Penalized, Both Teams, Game
- 0 Brooklyn vs. Pittsburgh, Oct. 28, 1934
      Brooklyn vs. Boston, Sept. 28, 1936
      Cleveland vs. Chi. Bears, Oct. 9, 1938
      Pittsburgh vs. Philadelphia, Nov. 10, 1940

Most Yards Penalized, Both Teams, Game
- 374 Cleveland (209) vs. Chi. Bears (165), Nov. 25, 1951
- 310 Tampa Bay (190) vs. Seattle (120), Oct. 17, 1976
- 309 Green Bay (184) vs. Boston (125), Oct. 21, 1945

DEFENSE

SCORING
Most Seasons Leading League, Fewest Points Allowed
- 11 N.Y. Giants, 1927, 1935, 1938-39, 1941, 1944, 1958-59, 1961, 1990, 1993
      Chi. Bears, 1932, 1936-37, 1942, 1948, 1963, 1985-86, 1988, 2001, 2005
- 7 Cleveland, 1951, 1953-57, 1994
      Green Bay, 1929, 1935, 1947, 1962, 1965-66, 1996
- 6 Dallas/Kansas City, 1960, 1962, 1968-69, 1995, 1997

Most Consecutive Seasons Leading League, Fewest Points Allowed
- 5 Cleveland, 1953-57
- 3 Buffalo, 1964-66
      Minnesota, 1969-1971
- 2 By many teams

Fewest Points Allowed, Season (Since 1932)
- 44 Chi. Bears, 1932
- 54 Brooklyn, 1933
- 59 Detroit, 1934

Most Points Allowed, Season
- 533 Baltimore, 1981
- 501 N.Y. Giants, 1966
- 487 New Orleans, 1980

Fewest Touchdowns Allowed, Season (Since 1932)
- 6 Chi. Bears, 1932
      Brooklyn, 1933
- 7 Detroit, 1934
- 8 Green Bay, 1932

Most Touchdowns Allowed, Season
- 68 Baltimore, 1981
- 66 N.Y. Giants, 1966
- 63 Baltimore, 1950

FIRST DOWNS
Fewest First Downs Allowed Season
- 77 Detroit, 1935
- 79 Boston, 1935
- 82 Washington, 1937

Most First Downs Allowed, Season
- 406 Baltimore, 1981
- 371 Seattle, 1981
- 368 Cleveland, 1999

Fewest First Downs Allowed, Rushing, Season
- 35 Chi. Bears, 1942
- 40 Green Bay, 1939
- 41 Brooklyn, 1944

Most First Downs Allowed, Rushing, Season
- 179 Detroit, 1985
- 178 New Orleans, 1980
- 175 Seattle, 1981

Fewest First Downs Allowed, Passing, Season
- 33 Chi. Bears, 1943
- 34 Pittsburgh, 1941
      Washington, 1943
- 35 Detroit, 1940
      Philadelphia, 1940, 1944

Most First Downs Allowed, Passing, Season
- 230 Atlanta, 1995
- 227 Kansas City, 2002
- 221 Detroit, 2002

Fewest First Downs Allowed, Penalty, Season
- 1 Boston, 1944
- 3 Philadelphia, 1940
      Pittsburgh, 1945
      Washington, 1957
- 4 Cleveland, 1940
      Green Bay, 1943
      N.Y. Giants, 1943

Most First Downs Allowed, Penalty, Season
- 56 Kansas City, 1998
- 48 Houston, 1985
- 46 Houston, 1986

NET YARDS ALLOWED RUSHING AND PASSING
Most Seasons Leading League, Fewest Yards Allowed
- 8 Chi. Bears, 1942-43, 1948, 1958, 1963, 1984-86
- 6 N.Y. Giants, 1938, 1940-41, 1951, 1956, 1959
      Philadelphia, 1944-45, 1949, 1953, 1981, 1991
      Minnesota, 1969-1970, 1975, 1988-89, 1993
      Pittsburgh, 1957, 1974, 1976, 1990, 2001, 2004
- 5 Boston/Washington, 1935-37, 1939, 1946

Most Consecutive Seasons Leading League, Fewest Yards Allowed
- 3 Boston/Washington, 1935-37
      Chicago, 1984-86
- 2 By many teams

Fewest Yards Allowed, Season
- 1,539 Chi. Cardinals, 1934
- 1,703 Chi. Bears, 1942
- 1,789 Brooklyn, 1933

Most Yards Allowed, Season
- 6,793 Baltimore, 1981
- 6,403 Green Bay, 1983
- 6,391 Seattle, 2000

RUSHING
Most Seasons Leading League, Fewest Yards Allowed
- 10 Chi. Bears, 1937, 1939, 1942, 1946, 1949, 1963, 1984-85, 1987-88
- 7 Detroit, 1938, 1950, 1952, 1962, 1970, 1980-81
      Philadelphia, 1944-45, 1947-48, 1953, 1990-91
      Dallas, 1966-69, 1972, 1978, 1992
      Pittsburgh, 1961, 1976, 1982, 1997, 2001-02, 2004
- 5 N.Y. Giants, 1940, 1951, 1956, 1959, 1986
      L.A./St. Louis Rams, 1964-65, 1973-74, 1999

Most Consecutive Seasons Leading League, Fewest Yards Allowed
- 4 Dallas, 1966-69
- 2 By many teams

Fewest Yards Allowed, Rushing, Season
- 519 Chi. Bears, 1942
- 558 Philadelphia, 1944
- 762 Pittsburgh, 1982

Most Yards Allowed, Rushing, Season
- 3,228 Buffalo, 1978
- 3,106 New Orleans, 1980
- 3,010 Baltimore, 1978

Fewest Touchdowns Allowed, Rushing, Season
- 2   Detroit, 1934
-     N.Y. Giants, 1944
-     Dallas, 1968
-     Minnesota, 1971
- 3   By many teams

Most Touchdowns Allowed, Rushing, Season
- 36   Oakland, 1961
- 31   N.Y. Giants, 1980
-     Tampa Bay, 1986
- 30   Baltimore, 1981

PASSING

Most Seasons Leading League, Fewest Yards Allowed
- 10   Green Bay, 1947-48, 1962, 1964-68, 1996, 2005
- 7   Washington, 1939, 1942, 1945, 1952-53, 1980, 1985
-    Philadelphia 1934, 1936, 1940, 1949, 1981, 1991, 1998
- 6   Chi. Bears, 1938, 1943-44, 1958, 1960, 1963
-    Minnesota, 1969-1970, 1972, 1975-76, 1989
-    Pittsburgh, 1941, 1946, 1951, 1955, 1974, 1990

Most Consecutive Seasons Leading League, Fewest Yards Allowed
- 5   Green Bay, 1964-68
- 2   By many teams

Fewest Yards Allowed, Passing, Season
- 545   Philadelphia, 1934
- 558   Portsmouth, 1933
- 585   Chi. Cardinals, 1934

Most Yards Allowed, Passing, Season
- 4,541   Atlanta, 1995
- 4,427   San Francisco, 2005
- 4,389   N.Y. Jets, 1986

Fewest Touchdowns Allowed, Passing, Season
- 1   Portsmouth, 1932
-    Philadelphia, 1934
- 2   Brooklyn, 1933
-    Chi. Bears, 1934
- 3   Chi. Bears, 1932
-    Green Bay, 1932
-    Green Bay, 1934
-    Chi. Bears, 1936
-    New York, 1939
-    New York, 1944

Most Touchdowns Allowed, Passing, Season
- 40   Denver, 1963
- 38   St. Louis, 1969
- 37   Washington, 1961
-    Baltimore, 1981

SACKS

Most Seasons Leading League
- 5   Oakland/L.A. Raiders, 1966-68, 1982, 1986
- 4   New England/Boston, 1961, 1963, 1977, 1979
-    Dallas, 1966, 1968-69, 1978
-    Dallas/Kansas City, 1960, 1965, 1969, 1990
-    L.A./St. Louis Rams, 1968, 1970, 1988, 1999
- 3   San Francisco, 1967, 1972, 1976
-    N.Y. Giants, 1963, 1985, 1998
-    New Orleans, 1992, 1997, 2000
-    Pittsburgh, 1974, 1994, 2001

Most Consecutive Seasons Leading League
- 3   Oakland, 1966-68
- 2   Dallas, 1968-69

Most Sacks, Season
- 72   Chicago, 1984
- 71   Minnesota, 1989
- 70   Chicago, 1987

Fewest Sacks, Season
- 11   Baltimore, 1982
- 12   Buffalo, 1982
- 13   Baltimore, 1981

Most Sacks, Game
- 12   Dallas vs. Pittsburgh, Nov. 20, 1966
-    St. Louis vs. Baltimore, Oct. 26, 1980
-    Chicago vs. Detroit, Dec. 16, 1984
-    Dallas vs. Houston, Sept. 29, 1985
- 11   N.Y. Giants vs. St. Louis, Nov. 1, 1964
-    Baltimore vs. Los Angeles, Nov. 22, 1964
-    Buffalo vs. Denver, Dec. 13, 1964
-    Detroit vs. Green Bay, Nov. 7, 1965
-    Oakland vs. Buffalo, Oct. 15, 1967
-    Oakland vs. Denver, Nov. 5, 1967
-    St. Louis vs. Atlanta, Nov. 24, 1968
-    Dallas vs. Detroit, Oct. 6, 1975
-    St. Louis vs. Philadelphia, Dec. 18, 1983
-    Kansas City vs. Cleveland, Sept. 30, 1984
-    Chicago vs. Minnesota, Oct. 28, 1984
-    Cleveland vs. Atlanta, Nov. 18, 1984
-    Detroit vs. Philadelphia, Nov. 16, 1986
-    San Diego vs. Dallas, Nov. 16, 1986
-    L.A. Raiders vs. Philadelphia, Nov. 30, 1986 (OT)
-    Seattle vs. L.A. Raiders, Dec. 8, 1986
-    Chicago vs. Philadelphia, Oct. 4, 1987
-    Dallas vs. N.Y. Jets, Oct. 4, 1987
-    Philadelphia vs. Dallas, Sept. 15, 1991
-    Indianapolis vs. Cleveland, Sept. 6, 1992
- 10   By many teams

Most Opponents Yards Lost Attempting to Pass, Season
- 666   Oakland, 1967
- 583   Chicago, 1984
- 573   San Francisco, 1976

Fewest Opponents Yards Lost Attempting to Pass, Season
- 72   Jacksonville, 1995
- 75   Green Bay, 1956
- 77   N.Y. Bulldogs, 1949

INTERCEPTIONS BY

Most Seasons Leading League
- 10   N.Y. Giants, 1933, 1937-39, 1944, 1948, 1951, 1954, 1961, 1997
- 8   Green Bay, 1940, 1942-43, 1947, 1955, 1957, 1962, 1965
-    Chi. Bears, 1935-36, 1941-42, 1946, 1963, 1985, 1990
- 6   Kansas City, 1966-1970, 1974

Most Consecutive Seasons Leading League
- 5   Kansas City, 1966-1970
- 3   N.Y. Giants, 1937-39
- 2   By many teams

Most Passes Intercepted By, Season
- 49   San Diego, 1961
- 42   Green Bay, 1943
- 41   N.Y. Giants, 1951

Fewest Passes Intercepted By, Season
- 3   Houston, 1982
- 5   Baltimore, 1982
-    Oakland, 2005
- 6   Houston, 1972
-    St. Louis, 1982
-    Atlanta, 1996
-    St. Louis, 2004

Most Passes Intercepted By, Game
- 9   Green Bay vs. Detroit, Oct. 24, 1943
-    Philadelphia vs. Pittsburgh, Dec. 12, 1965
- 8   N.Y. Giants vs. Green Bay, Nov. 21, 1948
-    Philadelphia vs. Chi. Cardinals, Sept. 24, 1950
-    N.Y. Giants vs. N.Y. Yanks, Dec. 16, 1951

Houston vs. Denver, Dec. 2, 1962
Detroit vs. Chicago, Sept. 22, 1968
N.Y. Jets vs. Baltimore, Sept. 23, 1973
7   By many teams. Last time:
      Cleveland vs. Detroit, Sept. 23, 2001

Most Consecutive Games, One or More Interceptions By
46 L.A. Chargers/San Diego, 1960-63
37 Detroit, 1960-63
36 Boston, 1944-47

Most Yards Returning Interceptions, Season
929 San Diego, 1961
712 Los Angeles, 1952
700 Baltimore, 2004

Fewest Yards Returning Interceptions, Season
5   Los Angeles, 1959
37 Dallas, 1989
38 Oakland, 2005

Most Yards Returning Interceptions, Game
325 Seattle vs. Kansas City, Nov. 4, 1984
314 Los Angeles vs. San Francisco, Oct. 18, 1964
245 Houston vs. N.Y. Jets, Oct. 15, 1967

Most Yards Returning Interceptions, Both Teams, Game
356 Seattle (325) vs. Kansas City (31), Nov. 4, 1984
338 Los Angeles (314) vs. San Francisco (24),
      Oct. 18, 1964
308 Dallas (182) vs. Los Angeles (126), Nov. 2, 1952

Most Touchdowns, Returning Interceptions, Season
9   San Diego, 1961
8   Seattle, 1998
7   Seattle, 1984
   St. Louis, 1999

Most Touchdowns Returning Interceptions, Game
4   Seattle vs. Kansas City, Nov. 4, 1984
3   Baltimore vs. Green Bay, Nov. 5, 1950
   Cleveland vs. Chicago, Dec. 11, 1960
   Philadelphia vs. Pittsburgh, Dec. 12, 1965
   Baltimore vs. Pittsburgh, Sept. 29, 1968
   Buffalo vs. N.Y. Jets, Sept. 29, 1968
   Houston vs. San Diego, Dec. 19, 1971
   Cincinnati vs. Houston, Dec. 17, 1972
   Tampa Bay vs. New Orleans, Dec. 11, 1977
2   By many teams

Most Touchdown Returning Interceptions, Both Teams, Game
4   Philadelphia (3) vs. Pittsburgh (1), Dec. 12, 1965
   Seattle (4) vs. Kansas City (0), Nov. 4, 1984
3   Los Angeles (2) vs. Detroit (1), Nov. 1, 1953
   Cleveland (2) vs. N.Y. Giants (1), Dec. 18, 1960
   Pittsburgh (2) vs. Cincinnati (1), Oct. 10, 1983
   Kansas City (2) vs. San Diego (1), Oct. 19, 1986
   (Also see previous record)

PUNT RETURNS
Fewest Opponents Punt Returns, Season
7   Washington, 1962
   San Diego, 1982
10 Buffalo, 1982
11 Boston, 1962

Most Opponents Punt Returns, Season
71 Tampa Bay, 1976, 1977
69 N.Y. Giants, 1953
   Cleveland, 2000
68 Cleveland, 1974
   Cleveland, 1999

Fewest Yards Allowed, Punt Returns, Season
22 Green Bay, 1967
30 Buffalo, 1982
34 Washington, 1962

Most Yards Allowed, Punt Returns, Season
932 Green Bay, 1949
913 Boston, 1947

906 New Orleans, 1974

Lowest Average Allowed, Punt Returns, Season
1.20 Chi. Cardinals, 1954 (46-55)
1.22 Cleveland, 1959 (32-39)
1.55 Chi. Cardinals, 1953 (44-68)

Highest Average Allowed, Punt Returns, Season
18.6 Green Bay, 1949 (50-932)
18.0 Cleveland, 1977 (31-558)
17.9 Boston, 1960 (20-357)

Most Touchdowns Allowed, Punt Returns, Season
4   New York, 1959
   Atlanta, 1992
3   Green Bay, 1949
   Chi. Cardinals, 1951
   L.A. Rams, 1951, 1994
   Washington, 1952
   Dallas, 1952
   Pittsburgh, 1959, 1993
   N.Y. Jets, 1968
   Cleveland, 1977
   Atlanta, 1986
   Tampa Bay, 1986
   Arizona, 2002
   Cincinnati, 2002
   Tennessee, 2002
2   By many teams

KICKOFF RETURNS
Fewest Opponents Kickoff Returns, Season
10 Brooklyn, 1943
13 Denver, 1992
15 Detroit, 1942
   Brooklyn, 1944

Most Opponents Kickoff Returns, Season
93 Indianapolis, 2003
92 Indianapolis, 2004
91 Washington, 1983

Fewest Yards Allowed, Kickoff Returns, Season
225 Brooklyn, 1943
254 Denver, 1992
293 Brooklyn, 1944

Most Yards Allowed, Kickoff Returns, Season
2,194 St. Louis, 2001
2,115 St. Louis, 1999
2,053 Kansas City, 2005

Lowest Average Allowed, Kickoff Returns, Season
14.3 Cleveland, 1980 (71-1,018)
14.9 Indianapolis, 1993 (37-551)
15.0 Seattle, 1982 (24-361)

Highest Average Allowed, Kickoff Returns, Season
29.5 N.Y. Jets, 1972 (47-1,386)
29.4 Los Angeles, 1950 (48-1,411)
29.1 New England, 1971 (49-1,427)

Most Touchdowns Allowed, Kickoff Returns, Season
4   Minnesota, 1998
3   Minnesota, 1963, 1970
   Dallas, 1966
   Detroit, 1980
   Pittsburgh, 1986
   Buffalo, 1997
   Atlanta, 2000
   Arizona, 2005
2   By many teams

FUMBLES
Fewest Opponents Fumbles, Season
11 Cleveland, 1956
   Baltimore, 1982
   Tennessee, 1998

  12 Green Bay, 1995
      Cincinnati, 1998
  13 Los Angeles, 1956
      Chicago, 1960
      Cleveland, 1963
      Cleveland, 1965
      Detroit, 1967
      San Diego, 1969
      New England, 2005

Most Opponents Fumbles, Season
  50 Minnesota, 1963
      San Francisco, 1978
  48 N.Y. Giants, 1980
      N.Y. Jets, 1986
  47 N.Y. Giants, 1977
      Seattle, 1984

TURNOVERS
(Number of times losing the ball on interceptions and fumbles.)

Fewest Opponents Turnovers, Season
  11 Baltimore, 1982
  13 San Francisco, 1982
  15 St. Louis, 1982
      Green Bay, 2004
      St. Louis, 2004

Most Opponents Turnovers, Season
  66 San Diego, 1961
  63 Seattle, 1984
  61 Washington, 1983

Most Opponents Turnovers, Game
  12 Chi. Bears vs. Detroit, Nov. 22, 1942
      Philadelphia vs. Chi. Cardinals, Sept. 24, 1950
      Philadelphia vs. Pittsburgh, Dec. 12, 1965
  11 Green Bay vs. San Diego, Sept. 24, 1978
  10 By 14 teams

ANNUAL SCORING LEADERS

Year	Player, Team	TD	FG	PAT	TP
2005	Shaun Alexander, Seattle, NFC	28	0	0	168
	Shayne Graham, Cincinnati, AFC	0	28	47	131
2004	Adam Vinatieri, New England, AFC	0	31	48	141
	David Akers, Philadelphia, NFC	0	27	41	122
2003	Jeff Wilkins, St. Louis, NFC	0	39	46	163
	Priest Holmes, Kansas City, AFC	27	0	0	162
2002	Priest Holmes, Kansas City, AFC	24	0	0	144
	Jay Feely, Atlanta, NFC	0	32	42	138
2001	Marshall Faulk, St. Louis, NFC	21	0	0	#128
	Mike Vanderjagt, Indianapolis, AFC	0	28	41	125
2000	Marshall Faulk, St. Louis, NFC	26	0	0	##160
	Matt Stover, Baltimore, AFC	0	35	30	135
1999	Mike Vanderjagt, Indianapolis, AFC	0	34	43	145
	Jeff Wilkins, St. Louis, NFC	0	20	64	124
1998	Gary Anderson, Minnesota, NFC	0	35	59	164
	Steve Christie, Buffalo, AFC	0	33	41	140
1997	Mike Hollis, Jacksonville, AFC	0	31	41	134
	Richie Cunningham, Dallas, NFC	0	34	24	126
1996	John Kasay, Carolina, NFC	0	37	34	145
	Cary Blanchard, Indianapolis, AFC	0	36	27	135
1995	Emmitt Smith, Dallas, NFC	25	0	0	150
	Norm Johnson, Pittsburgh, AFC	0	34	39	141
1994	John Carney, San Diego, AFC	0	34	33	135
	Fuad Reveiz, Minnesota, NFC	0	34	30	132
1993	Jeff Jaeger, L.A. Raiders, AFC	0	35	27	132
	Jason Hanson, Detroit, NFC	0	34	28	130
1992	Pete Stoyanovich, Miami, AFC	0	30	34	124
	Morten Andersen, New Orleans, NFC	0	29	33	120
	Chip Lohmiller, Washington, NFC	0	30	30	120
1991	Chip Lohmiller, Washington, NFC	0	31	56	149
	Pete Stoyanovich, Miami, AFC	0	31	28	121
1990	Nick Lowery, Kansas City, AFC	0	34	37	139
	Chip Lohmiller, Washington, NFC	0	30	41	131
1989	Mike Cofer, San Francisco, NFC	0	29	49	136
	*David Treadwell, Denver, AFC	0	27	39	120
1988	Scott Norwood, Buffalo, AFC	0	32	33	129
	Mike Cofer, San Francisco, NFC	0	27	40	121
1987	Jerry Rice, San Francisco, NFC	23	0	0	138
	Jim Breech, Cincinnati, AFC	0	24	25	97
1986	Tony Franklin, New England, AFC	0	32	44	140
	Kevin Butler, Chicago, NFC	0	28	36	120
1985	*Kevin Butler, Chicago, NFC	0	31	51	144
	Gary Anderson, Pittsburgh, AFC	0	33	40	139
1984	Ray Wersching, San Francisco, NFC	0	25	56	131
	Gary Anderson, Pittsburgh, AFC	0	24	45	117
1983	Mark Moseley, Washington, NFC	0	33	62	161
	Gary Anderson, Pittsburgh, AFC	0	27	38	119
1982	*Marcus Allen, L.A. Raiders, AFC	14	0	0	84
	Wendell Tyler, L.A. Rams, NFC	13	0	0	78
1981	Ed Murray, Detroit, NFC	0	25	46	121
	Rafael Septien, Dallas, NFC	0	27	40	121
	Jim Breech, Cincinnati, AFC	0	22	49	115
	Nick Lowery, Kansas City, AFC	0	26	37	115
1980	John Smith, New England, AFC	0	26	51	129
	*Ed Murray, Detroit, NFC	0	27	35	116
1979	John Smith, New England, AFC	0	23	46	115
	Mark Moseley, Washington, NFC	0	25	39	114
1978	*Frank Corral, Los Angeles, NFC	0	29	31	118
	Pat Leahy, N.Y. Jets, AFC	0	22	41	107
1977	Errol Mann, Oakland, AFC	0	20	39	99
	Walter Payton, Chicago, NFC	16	0	0	96
1976	Toni Linhart, Baltimore, AFC	0	20	49	109
	Mark Moseley, Washington, NFC	0	22	31	97
1975	O.J. Simpson, Buffalo, AFC	23	0	0	138
	Chuck Foreman, Minnesota, NFC	22	0	0	132
1974	Chester Marcol, Green Bay, NFC	0	25	19	94
	Roy Gerela, Pittsburgh, AFC	0	20	33	93

Year	Player, Team	TD	FG	PAT	TP
1973	David Ray, Los Angeles, NFC	0	30	40	130
	Roy Gerela, Pittsburgh, AFC	0	29	36	123
1972	*Chester Marcol, Green Bay, NFC	0	33	29	128
	Bobby Howfield, N.Y. Jets, AFC	0	27	40	121
1971	Garo Yepremian, Miami, AFC	0	28	33	117
	Curt Knight, Washington, NFC	0	29	27	114
1970	Fred Cox, Minnesota, NFC	0	30	35	125
	Jan Stenerud, Kansas City, AFC	0	30	26	116
1969	Jim Turner, N.Y. Jets, AFL	0	32	33	129
	Fred Cox, Minnesota, NFL	0	26	43	121
1968	Jim Turner, N.Y. Jets, AFL	0	34	43	145
	Leroy Kelly, Cleveland, NFL	20	0	0	120
1967	Jim Bakken, St. Louis, NFL	0	27	36	117
	George Blanda, Oakland, AFL	0	20	56	116
1966	Gino Cappelletti, Boston, AFL	6	16	35	119
	Bruce Gossett, Los Angeles, NFL	0	28	29	113
1965	*Gale Sayers, Chicago, NFL	22	0	0	132
	Gino Cappelletti, Boston, AFL	9	17	27	132
1964	Gino Cappelletti, Boston, AFL	7	25	36	#155
	Lenny Moore, Baltimore, NFL	20	0	0	120
1963	Gino Cappelletti, Boston, AFL	2	22	35	113
	Don Chandler, N.Y. Giants, NFL	0	18	52	106
1962	Gene Mingo, Denver, AFL	4	27	32	137
	Jim Taylor, Green Bay, NFL	19	0	0	114
1961	Gino Cappelletti, Boston, AFL	8	17	48	147
	Paul Hornung, Green Bay, NFL	10	15	41	146
1960	Paul Hornung, Green Bay, NFL	15	15	41	176
	*Gene Mingo, Denver, AFL	6	18	33	123
1959	Paul Hornung, Green Bay	7	7	31	94
1958	Jim Brown, Cleveland	18	0	0	108
1957	Sam Baker, Washington	1	14	29	77
	Lou Groza, Cleveland	0	15	32	77
1956	Bobby Layne, Detroit	5	12	33	99
1955	Doak Walker, Detroit	7	9	27	96
1954	Bobby Walston, Philadelphia	11	4	36	114
1953	Gordy Soltau, San Francisco	6	10	48	114
1952	Gordy Soltau, San Francisco	7	6	34	94
1951	Elroy (Crazylegs) Hirsch, Los Angeles	17	0	0	102
1950	*Doak Walker, Detroit	11	8	38	128
1949	Pat Harder, Chi. Cardinals	8	3	45	102
	Gene Roberts, N.Y. Giants	17	0	0	102
1948	Pat Harder, Chi. Cardinals	6	7	53	110
1947	Pat Harder, Chi. Cardinals	7	7	39	102
1946	Ted Fritsch, Green Bay	10	9	13	100
1945	Steve Van Buren, Philadelphia	18	0	2	110
1944	Don Hutson, Green Bay	9	0	31	85
1943	Don Hutson, Green Bay	12	3	36	117
1942	Don Hutson, Green Bay	17	1	33	138
1941	Don Hutson, Green Bay	12	1	20	95
1940	Don Hutson, Green Bay	7	0	15	57
1939	Andy Farkas, Washington	11	0	2	68
1938	Clarke Hinkle, Green Bay	7	3	7	58
1937	Jack Manders, Chi. Bears	5	8	15	69
1936	Earl (Dutch) Clark, Detroit	7	4	19	73
1935	Earl (Dutch) Clark, Detroit	6	1	16	55
1934	Jack Manders, Chi. Bears	3	10	31	79
1933	Ken Strong, N.Y. Giants	6	5	13	64
	Glenn Presnell, Portsmouth	6	6	10	64
1932	Earl (Dutch) Clark, Portsmouth	6	3	10	55

*First season of professional football.
#Cappelletti's total and Faulk's total in 2001 include a two-point conversion.
##Faulk's total in 2000 includes 2 two-point conversions.

ANNUAL TOUCHDOWN LEADERS

Year	Player, Team	TD	Rush	Pass	Ret.
2005	Shaun Alexander, Seattle, NFC	28	27	1	0
	Larry Johnson, Kansas City, AFC	21	20	1	0
2004	Shaun Alexander, Seattle, NFC	20	16	4	0
	LaDainian Tomlinson, San Diego, AFC	18	17	1	0

Year	Player, Team	TD	Rush	Pass	Ret.
2003	Priest Holmes, Kansas City, AFC	27	27	0	0
	Ahman Green, Green Bay, NFC	20	15	5	0
2002	Priest Holmes, Kansas City, AFC	24	21	3	0
	Shaun Alexander, Seattle, NFC	18	16	2	0
2001	Marshall Faulk, St. Louis, NFC	21	12	9	0
	Shaun Alexander, Seattle, AFC	16	14	2	0
2000	Marshall Faulk, St. Louis, NFC	26	18	8	0
	Edgerrin James, Indianapolis, AFC	18	13	5	0
1999	Stephen Davis, Washington, NFC	17	17	0	0
	*Edgerrin James, Indianapolis, AFC	17	13	4	0
1998	Terrell Davis, Denver, AFC	23	21	2	0
	*Randy Moss, Minnesota, NFC	17	0	17	0
1997	Karim Abdul-Jabbar, Miami, AFC	16	15	1	0
	Barry Sanders, Detroit, NFC	14	11	3	0
1996	Terry Allen, Washington, NFC	21	21	0	0
	Curtis Martin, New England, AFC	17	14	3	0
1995	Emmitt Smith, Dallas, NFC	25	25	0	0
	Carl Pickens, Cincinnati, AFC	17	0	17	0
1994	Emmitt Smith, Dallas, NFC	22	21	1	0
	*Marshall Faulk, Indianapolis, AFC	12	11	1	0
	Natrone Means, San Diego, AFC	12	12	0	0
1993	Jerry Rice, San Francisco, NFC	16	1	15	0
	Marcus Allen, Kansas City, AFC	15	12	3	0
1992	Emmitt Smith, Dallas, NFC	19	18	1	0
	Thurman Thomas, Buffalo, AFC	12	9	3	0
1991	Barry Sanders, Detroit, NFC	17	16	1	0
	Mark Clayton, Miami, AFC	12	0	12	0
	Thurman Thomas, Buffalo, AFC	12	7	5	0
1990	Barry Sanders, Detroit, NFC	16	13	3	0
	Derrick Fenner, Seattle, AFC	15	14	1	0
1989	Dalton Hilliard, New Orleans, NFC	18	13	5	0
	Christian Okoye, Kansas City, AFC	12	12	0	0
	Thurman Thomas, Buffalo, AFC	12	6	6	0
1988	Greg Bell, L.A. Rams, NFC	18	16	2	0
	Eric Dickerson, Indianapolis, AFC	15	14	1	0
	*Ickey Woods, Cincinnati, AFC	15	15	0	0
1987	Jerry Rice, San Francisco, NFC	23	1	22	0
	Johnny Hector, N.Y. Jets, AFC	11	11	0	0
1986	George Rogers, Washington, NFC	18	18	0	0
	Sammy Winder, Denver, AFC	14	9	5	0
1985	Joe Morris, N.Y. Giants, NFC	21	21	0	0
	Louis Lipps, Pittsburgh, AFC	15	1	12	2
1984	Marcus Allen, L.A. Raiders, AFC	18	13	5	0
	Mark Clayton, Miami, AFC	18	0	18	0
	Eric Dickerson, L.A. Rams, NFC	14	14	0	0
	John Riggins, Washington, NFC	14	14	0	0
1983	John Riggins, Washington, NFC	24	24	0	0
	Pete Johnson, Cincinnati, AFC	14	14	0	0
	*Curt Warner, Seattle, AFC	14	13	1	0
1982	*Marcus Allen, L.A. Raiders, AFC	14	11	3	0
	Wendell Tyler, L.A. Rams, NFC	13	9	4	0
1981	Chuck Muncie, San Diego, AFC	19	19	0	0
	Wendell Tyler, Los Angeles, NFC	17	12	5	0
1980	*Billy Sims, Detroit, NFC	16	13	3	0
	Earl Campbell, Houston, AFC	13	13	0	0
	*Curtis Dickey, Baltimore, AFC	13	11	2	0
	John Jefferson, San Diego, AFC	13	0	13	0
1979	Earl Campbell, Houston, AFC	19	19	0	0
	Walter Payton, Chicago, NFC	16	14	2	0
1978	David Sims, Seattle, AFC	15	14	1	0
	Terdell Middleton, Green Bay, NFC	12	11	1	0
1977	Walter Payton, Chicago, NFC	16	14	2	0
	Nat Moore, Miami, AFC	13	1	12	0
1976	Chuck Foreman, Minnesota, NFC	14	13	1	0
	Franco Harris, Pittsburgh, AFC	14	14	0	0
1975	O.J. Simpson, Buffalo, AFC	23	16	7	0
	Chuck Foreman, Minnesota, NFC	22	13	9	0
1974	Chuck Foreman, Minnesota, NFC	15	9	6	0
	Cliff Branch, Oakland, AFC	13	0	13	0

Year	Player, Team	TD	Rush	Pass	Ret.
1973	Larry Brown, Washington, NFC	14	8	6	0
	Floyd Little, Denver, AFC	13	12	1	0
1972	Emerson Boozer, N.Y. Jets, AFC	14	11	3	0
	Ron Johnson, N.Y. Giants, NFC	14	9	5	0
1971	Duane Thomas, Dallas, NFC	13	11	2	0
	Leroy Kelly, Cleveland, AFC	12	10	2	0
1970	Dick Gordon, Chicago, NFC	13	0	13	0
	MacArthur Lane, St. Louis, NFC	13	11	2	0
	Gary Garrison, San Diego, AFC	12	0	12	0
1969	Warren Wells, Oakland, AFL	14	0	14	0
	Tom Matte, Baltimore, NFL	13	11	2	0
	Lance Rentzel, Dallas, NFL	13	0	12	1
1968	Leroy Kelly, Cleveland, NFL	20	16	4	0
	Warren Wells, Oakland, AFL	12	1	11	0
1967	Homer Jones, N.Y. Giants, NFL	14	1	13	0
	Emerson Boozer, N.Y. Jets, AFL	13	10	3	0
1966	Leroy Kelly, Cleveland, NFL	16	15	1	0
	Dan Reeves, Dallas, NFL	16	8	8	0
	Lance Alworth, San Diego, AFL	13	0	13	0
1965	*Gale Sayers, Chicago, NFL	22	14	6	2
	Lance Alworth, San Diego, AFL	14	0	14	0
	Don Maynard, N.Y. Jets, AFL	14	0	14	0
1964	Lenny Moore, Baltimore, NFL	20	16	3	1
	Lance Alworth, San Diego, AFL	15	2	13	0
1963	Art Powell, Oakland, AFL	16	0	16	0
	Jim Brown, Cleveland, NFL	15	12	3	0
1962	Abner Haynes, Dallas, AFL	19	13	6	0
	Jim Taylor, Green Bay, NFL	19	19	0	0
1961	Bill Groman, Houston, AFL	18	1	17	0
	Jim Taylor, Green Bay, NFL	16	15	1	0
1960	Paul Hornung, Green Bay, NFL	15	13	2	0
	Sonny Randle, St. Louis, NFL	15	0	15	0
	Art Powell, N.Y. Titans, AFL	14	0	14	0
1959	Raymond Berry, Baltimore	14	0	14	0
	Jim Brown, Cleveland	14	14	0	0
1958	Jim Brown, Cleveland	18	17	1	0
1957	Lenny Moore, Baltimore	11	3	7	1
1956	Rick Casares, Chi. Bears	14	12	2	0
1955	*Alan Ameche, Baltimore	9	9	0	0
	Harlon Hill, Chi. Bears	9	0	9	0
1954	*Harlon Hill, Chi. Bears	12	0	12	0
1953	Joseph Perry, San Francisco	13	10	3	0
1952	Cloyce Box, Detroit	15	0	15	0
1951	Elroy (Crazylegs) Hirsch, Los Angeles	17	0	17	0
1950	Bob Shaw, Chi. Cardinals	12	0	12	0
1949	Gene Roberts, N.Y. Giants	17	9	8	0
1948	Mal Kutner, Chi. Cardinals	15	1	14	0
1947	Steve Van Buren, Philadelphia	14	13	0	1
1946	Ted Fritsch, Green Bay	10	9	1	0
1945	Steve Van Buren, Philadelphia	18	15	2	1
1944	Don Hutson, Green Bay	9	0	9	0
	Bill Paschal, N.Y. Giants	9	9	0	0
1943	Don Hutson, Green Bay	12	0	11	1
	*Bill Paschal, N.Y. Giants	12	10	2	0
1942	Don Hutson, Green Bay	17	0	17	0
1941	Don Hutson, Green Bay	12	2	10	0
	George McAfee, Chi. Bears	12	6	3	3
1940	John Drake, Cleveland	9	9	0	0
	Richard Todd, Washington	9	4	4	1
1939	Andrew Farkas, Washington	11	5	5	1
1938	Don Hutson, Green Bay	9	0	9	0
1937	Cliff Battles, Washington	7	5	1	1
	Clarke Hinkle, Green Bay	7	5	2	0
	Don Hutson, Green Bay	7	0	7	0
1936	Don Hutson, Green Bay	9	0	8	1
1935	*Don Hutson, Green Bay	7	0	6	1
1934	*Beattie Feathers, Chi. Bears	9	8	1	0

Year	Player, Team	TD	Rush	Pass	Ret.
1933	*Charlie (Buckets) Goldenberg, Green Bay	7	4	1	2
	John (Shipwreck) Kelly, Brooklyn	7	2	3	2
	*Elvin (Kink) Richards, N.Y. Giants	7	4	3	0
1932	Earl (Dutch) Clark, Portsmouth	6	3	3	0
	Red Grange, Chi. Bears	6	3	3	0

*First season of professional football.

ANNUAL LEADERS—MOST FIELD GOALS MADE

Year	Player, Team	Att.	Made	Pct.
2005	Neil Rackers, Arizona, NFC	42	40	95.2
	Matt Stover, Baltimore, AFC	34	30	88.2
2004	Adam Vinatieri, New England, AFC	33	31	93.9
	David Akers, Philadelphia, NFC	32	27	84.4
2003	Jeff Wilkins, St. Louis, NFC	42	39	92.9
	Mike Vanderjagt, Indianapolis, AFC	37	37	100.0
2002	Jay Feely, Atlanta, NFC	40	32	80.0
	Martín Gramatica, Tampa Bay, NFC	39	32	82.1
	Adam Vinatieri, New England, AFC	30	27	90.0
2001	Jason Elam, Denver, AFC	36	31	86.1
	*Jay Feely, Atlanta, NFC	37	29	78.4
2000	Matt Stover, Baltimore, AFC	39	35	89.7
	Ryan Longwell, Green Bay, NFC	38	33	86.8
1999	Olindo Mare, Miami, AFC	46	39	84.8
	*Martin Gramatica, Tampa Bay, NFC	32	27	84.4
1998	Al Del Greco, Tennessee, AFC	39	36	92.3
	Gary Anderson, Minnesota, NFC	35	35	100.0
1997	Richie Cunningham, Dallas, NFC	37	34	91.9
	Cary Blanchard, Indiapolis, AFC	41	32	78.1
1996	John Kasay, Carolina, NFC	45	37	82.2
	Cary Blanchard, Indiapolis, AFC	40	36	90.0
1995	Norm Johnson, Pittsburgh, AFC	41	34	82.9
	Morten Andersen, Atlanta, NFC	37	31	83.8
1994	John Carney, San Diego, AFC	38	34	89.5
	Fuad Reveiz, Minnesota, NFC	39	34	87.2
1993	Jeff Jaeger, L.A. Raiders, AFC	44	35	79.5
	Jason Hanson, Detroit, NFC	43	34	79.1
1992	Pete Stoyanovich, Miami, AFC	37	30	81.1
	Chip Lohmiller, Washington, NFC	40	30	75.0
1991	Pete Stoyanovich, Miami, AFC	37	31	83.8
	Chip Lohmiller, Washington, NFC	43	31	72.1
1990	Nick Lowery, Kansas City, AFC	37	34	91.9
	Chip Lohmiller, Washington, NFC	40	30	75.0
1989	Rich Karlis, Minnesota, NFC	39	31	79.5
	*David Treadwell, Denver, AFC	33	27	81.8
1988	Scott Norwood, Buffalo, AFC	37	32	86.5
	Mike Cofer, San Francisco, NFC	38	27	71.1
1987	Morten Andersen, New Orleans, NFC	36	28	77.8
	Dean Biasucci, Indianpolis, AFC	27	24	88.9
	Jim Breech, Cincinnati, AFC	30	24	80.0
1986	Tony Franklin, New England, AFC	41	32	78.0
	Kevin Butler, Chicago, NFC	41	28	68.3
1985	Gary Anderson, Pittsburgh, AFC	42	33	78.6
	Morten Andersen, New Orleans, NFC	35	31	88.6
	*Kevin Butler, Chicago, NFC	37	31	83.8
1984	*Paul McFadden, Philadelphia, NFC	37	30	81.1
	Gary Anderson, Pittsburgh, AFC	32	24	75.0
	Matt Bahr, Cleveland, AFC	32	24	75.0
1983	*Ali-Haji-Sheikh, N.Y. Giants, NFC	42	35	83.3
	*Raul Allegre, Baltimore, AFC	35	30	85.7
1982	Mark Moseley, Washington, NFC	21	20	95.2
	Nick Lowery, Kansas City, AFC	24	19	79.2
1981	Rafael Septien, Dallas, NFC	35	27	77.1
	Nick Lowery, Kansas City, AFC	36	26	72.2
1980	*Ed Murray, Detroit, NFC	42	27	64.3
	John Smith, New England, AFC	34	26	76.5
	Fred Steinfort, Denver, AFC	34	26	76.5
1979	Mark Moseley, Washington, NFC	33	25	75.8
	John Smith, New England, AFC	33	23	69.7

Year	Player, Team	Att.	Made	Pct.
1978	*Frank Corral, Los Angeles, NFC	43	29	67.4
	Pat Leahy, N.Y. Jets, AFC	30	22	73.3
1977	Mark Moseley, Washington, NFC	37	21	56.8
	Errol Mann, Oakland, AFC	28	20	71.4
1976	Mark Moseley, Washington, NFC	34	22	64.7
	Jan Stenerud, Kansas City, AFC	38	21	55.3
1975	Jan Stenerud, Kansas City, AFC	32	22	68.8
	Toni Fritsch, Dallas, NFC	35	22	62.9
1974	Chester Marcol, Green Bay, NFC	39	25	64.1
	Roy Gerela, Pittsburgh, AFC	29	20	69.0
1973	David Ray, Los Angeles, NFC	47	30	63.8
	Roy Gerela, Pittsburgh, AFC	43	29	67.4
1972	*Chester Marcol, Green Bay, NFC	48	33	68.8
	Roy Gerela, Pittsburgh, AFC	41	28	68.3
1971	Curt Knight, Washington, NFC	49	29	59.2
	Garo Yepremian, Miami, AFC	40	28	70.0
1970	Jan Stenerud, Kansas City, AFC	42	30	71.4
	Fred Cox, Minnesota, NFC	46	30	65.2
1969	Jim Turner, N.Y. Jets, AFL	47	32	68.1
	Fred Cox, Minnesota, NFL	37	26	70.3
1968	Jim Turner, N.Y. Jets, AFL	46	34	73.9
	Mac Percival, Chicago, NFL	36	25	69.4
1967	Jim Bakken, St. Louis, NFL	39	27	69.2
	Jan Stenerud, Kansas City, AFL	36	21	58.3
1966	Bruce Gossett, Los Angeles, NFL	49	28	57.1
	Mike Mercer, Oakland-Kansas City, AFL	30	21	70.0
1965	Pete Gogolak, Buffalo, AFL	46	28	60.9
	Fred Cox, Minnesota, NFL	35	23	65.7
1964	Jim Bakken, St. Louis, NFL	38	25	65.8
	Gino Cappelletti, Boston, AFL	39	25	64.1
1963	Jim Martin, Baltimore, NFL	39	24	61.5
	Gino Cappelletti, Boston, AFL	38	22	57.9
1962	Gene Mingo, Denver, AFL	39	27	69.2
	Lou Michaels, Pittsburgh, NFL	42	26	61.9
1961	Steve Myhra, Baltimore, NFL	39	21	53.8
	Gino Cappelletti, Boston, AFL	32	17	53.1
1960	Tommy Davis, San Francisco, NFL	32	19	59.4
	*Gene Mingo, Denver, AFL	28	18	64.3
1959	Pat Summerall, N.Y. Giants	29	20	69.0
1958	Paige Cothren, Los Angeles	25	14	56.0
	*Tom Miner, Pittsburgh	28	14	50.0
1957	Lou Groza, Cleveland	22	15	68.2
1956	Sam Baker, Washington	25	17	68.0
1955	Fred Cone, Green Bay	24	16	66.7
1954	Lou Groza, Cleveland	24	16	66.7
1953	Lou Groza, Cleveland	26	23	88.5
1952	Lou Groza, Cleveland	33	19	57.6
1951	Bob Waterfield, Los Angeles	23	13	56.5
1950	Lou Groza, Cleveland	19	13	68.4
1949	Cliff Patton, Philadelphia	18	9	50.0
	Bob Waterfield, Los Angeles	16	9	56.3
1948	Cliff Patton, Philadelphia	12	8	66.7
1947	Ward Cuff, Green Bay	16	7	43.8
	Pat Harder, Chi. Cardinals	10	7	70.0
	Bob Waterfield, Los Angeles	16	7	43.8
1946	Ted Fritsch, Green Bay	17	9	52.9
1945	Joe Aguirre, Washington	13	7	53.8
1944	Ken Strong, N.Y. Giants	12	6	50.0
1943	Ward Cuff, N.Y. Giants	9	3	33.3
	Don Hutson, Green Bay	5	3	60.0
1942	Bill Daddio, Chi. Cardinals	10	5	50.0
1941	Clarke Hinkle, Green Bay	14	6	42.9
1940	Clarke Hinkle, Green Bay	14	9	64.3
1939	Ward Cuff, N.Y. Giants	16	7	43.8
1938	Ward Cuff, N.Y. Giants	9	5	55.6
	Ralph Kercheval, Brooklyn	13	5	38.5
1937	Jack Manders, Chi. Bears		8	
1936	Jack Manders, Chi. Bears		7	
	Armand Niccolai, Pittsburgh		7	

Year	Player, Team	Att.	Made	Pct.
1935	Armand Niccolai, Pittsburgh		6	
	Bill Smith, Chi. Cardinals		6	
1934	Jack Manders, Chi. Bears		10	
1933	*Jack Manders, Chi. Bears		6	
	Glenn Presnell, Portsmouth		6	
1932	Earl (Dutch) Clark, Portsmouth		3	

*First season of professional football.

ANNUAL RUSHING LEADERS

Year	Player, Team	Att.	Yards	Avg.	TD
2005	Shaun Alexander, Seattle, NFC	370	1,880	5.1	27
	Larry Johnson, Kansas City, AFC	336	1,750	5.2	20
2004	Curtis Martin, N.Y. Jets, AFC	371	1,697	4.6	12
	Shaun Alexander, Seattle, NFC	353	1,696	4.8	16
2003	Jamal Lewis, Baltimore, AFC	387	2,066	5.3	14
	Ahman Green, Green Bay, NFC	355	1,883	5.3	15
2002	Ricky Williams, Miami, AFC	383	1,853	4.8	16
	Deuce McAllister, New Orleans, NFC	325	1,388	4.3	13
2001	Priest Holmes, Kansas City, AFC	327	1,555	4.8	8
	Stephen Davis, Washington, NFC	356	1,432	4.0	5
2000	Edgerrin James, Indianapolis, AFC	387	1,709	4.4	13
	Robert Smith, Minnesota, NFC	295	1,521	5.2	7
1999	*Edgerrin James, Indianapolis, AFC	369	1,553	4.2	13
	Stephen Davis, Washington, NFC	290	1,405	4.8	17
1998	Terrell Davis, Denver, AFC	392	2,008	5.1	21
	Jamal Anderson, Atlanta, NFC	410	1,846	4.5	14
1997	Barry Sanders, Detroit, NFC	335	2,053	6.1	11
	Terrell Davis, Denver, AFC	369	1,750	4.7	15
1996	Barry Sanders, Detroit, NFC	307	1,553	5.1	11
	Terrell Davis, Denver, AFC	345	1,538	4.5	13
1995	Emmitt Smith, Dallas, NFC	377	1,773	4.7	25
	*Curtis Martin, New England, AFC	368	1,487	4.0	14
1994	Barry Sanders, Detroit, NFC	331	1,883	5.7	7
	Chris Warren, Seattle, AFC	333	1,545	4.6	9
1993	Emmitt Smith, Dallas, NFC	283	1,486	5.3	9
	Thurman Thomas, Buffalo, AFC	355	1,315	3.7	6
1992	Emmitt Smith, Dallas, NFC	373	1,713	4.6	18
	Barry Foster, Pittsburgh, AFC	390	1,690	4.3	11
1991	Emmitt Smith, Dallas, NFC	365	1,563	4.3	12
	Thurman Thomas, Buffalo, AFC	288	1,407	4.9	7
1990	Barry Sanders, Detroit, NFC	255	1,304	5.1	13
	Thurman Thomas, Buffalo, AFC	271	1,297	4.8	11
1989	Christian Okoye, Kansas City, AFC	370	1,480	4.0	12
	*Barry Sanders, Detroit, NFC	280	1,470	5.3	14
1988	Eric Dickerson, Indianapolis, AFC	388	1,659	4.3	14
	Herschel Walker, Dallas, NFC	361	1,514	4.2	5
1987	Charles White, L.A. Rams, NFC	324	1,374	4.2	11
	Eric Dickerson, Indianapolis, AFC	223	1,011	4.5	5
1986	Eric Dickerson, L.A. Rams, NFC	404	1,821	4.5	11
	Curt Warner, Seattle, AFC	319	1,481	4.6	13
1985	Marcus Allen, L.A. Raiders, AFC	380	1,759	4.6	11
	Gerald Riggs, Atlanta, NFC	397	1,719	4.3	10
1984	Eric Dickerson, L.A. Rams, NFC	379	2,105	5.6	14
	Earnest Jackson, San Diego, AFC	296	1,179	4.0	8
1983	*Eric Dickerson, L.A. Rams, NFC	390	1,808	4.6	18
	*Curt Warner, Seattle, AFC	335	1,449	4.3	13
1982	Freeman McNeil, N.Y. Jets, AFC	151	786	5.2	6
	Tony Dorsett, Dallas, NFC	177	745	4.2	5
1981	*George Rogers, New Orleans, NFC	378	1,674	4.4	13
	Earl Campbell, Houston, AFC	361	1,376	3.8	10
1980	Earl Campbell, Houston, AFC	373	1,934	5.2	13
	Walter Payton, Chicago, NFC	317	1,460	4.6	6
1979	Earl Campbell, Houston, AFC	368	1,697	4.6	19
	Walter Payton, Chicago, NFC	369	1,610	4.4	14
1978	*Earl Campbell, Houston, AFC	302	1,450	4.8	13
	Walter Payton, Chicago, NFC	333	1,395	4.2	11
1977	Walter Payton, Chicago, NFC	339	1,852	5.5	14
	Mark van Eeghen, Oakland, AFC	324	1,273	3.9	7

Year	Player, Team	Att.	Yards	Avg.	TD
1976	O.J. Simpson, Buffalo, AFC	290	1,503	5.2	8
	Walter Payton, Chicago, NFC	311	1,390	4.5	13
1975	O.J. Simpson, Buffalo, AFC	329	1,817	5.5	16
	Jim Otis, St. Louis, NFC	269	1,076	4.0	5
1974	Otis Armstrong, Denver, AFC	263	1,407	5.3	9
	Lawrence McCutcheon, Los Angeles, NFC	236	1,109	4.7	3
1973	O.J. Simpson, Buffalo, AFC	332	2,003	6.0	12
	John Brockington, Green Bay, NFC	265	1,144	4.3	3
1972	O.J. Simpson, Buffalo, AFC	292	1,251	4.3	6
	Larry Brown, Washington, NFC	285	1,216	4.3	8
1971	Floyd Little, Denver, AFC	284	1,133	4.0	6
	*John Brockington, Green Bay, NFC	216	1,105	5.1	4
1970	Larry Brown, Washington, NFC	237	1,125	4.7	5
	Floyd Little, Denver, AFC	209	901	4.3	3
1969	Gale Sayers, Chicago, NFL	236	1,032	4.4	8
	Dickie Post, San Diego, AFL	182	873	4.8	6
1968	Leroy Kelly, Cleveland, NFL	248	1,239	5.0	16
	*Paul Robinson, Cincinnati, AFL	238	1,023	4.3	8
1967	Jim Nance, Boston, AFL	269	1,216	4.5	7
	Leroy Kelly, Cleveland, NFL	235	1,205	5.1	11
1966	Jim Nance, Boston, AFL	299	1,458	4.9	11
	Gale Sayers, Chicago, NFL	229	1,231	5.4	8
1965	Jim Brown, Cleveland, NFL	289	1,544	5.3	17
	Paul Lowe, San Diego, AFL	222	1,121	5.0	7
1964	Jim Brown, Cleveland, NFL	280	1,446	5.2	7
	Cookie Gilchrist, Buffalo, AFL	230	981	4.3	6
1963	Jim Brown, Cleveland, NFL	291	1,863	6.4	12
	Clem Daniels, Oakland, AFL	215	1,099	5.1	3
1962	Jim Taylor, Green Bay, NFL	272	1,474	5.4	19
	Cookie Gilchrist, Buffalo, AFL	214	1,096	5.1	13
1961	Jim Brown, Cleveland, NFL	305	1,408	4.6	8
	Billy Cannon, Houston, AFL	200	948	4.7	6
1960	Jim Brown, Cleveland, NFL	215	1,257	5.8	9
	*Abner Haynes, Dall. Texans, AFL	156	875	5.6	9
1959	Jim Brown, Cleveland	290	1,329	4.6	14
1958	Jim Brown, Cleveland	257	1,527	5.9	17
1957	*Jim Brown, Cleveland	202	942	4.7	9
1956	Rick Casares, Chi. Bears	234	1,126	4.8	12
1955	*Alan Ameche, Baltimore	213	961	4.5	9
1954	Joe Perry, San Francisco	173	1,049	6.1	8
1953	Joe Perry, San Francisco	192	1,018	5.3	10
1952	Dan Towler, Los Angeles	156	894	5.7	10
1951	Eddie Price, N.Y. Giants	271	971	3.6	7
1950	Marion Motley, Cleveland	140	810	5.8	3
1949	Steve Van Buren, Philadelphia	263	1,146	4.4	11
1948	Steve Van Buren, Philadelphia	201	945	4.7	10
1947	Steve Van Buren, Philadelphia	217	1,008	4.6	13
1946	Bill Dudley, Pittsburgh	146	604	4.1	3
1945	Steve Van Buren, Philadelphia	143	832	5.8	15
1944	Bill Paschal, N.Y. Giants	196	737	3.8	9
1943	*Bill Paschal, N.Y. Giants	147	572	3.9	10
1942	*Bill Dudley, Pittsburgh	162	696	4.3	5
1941	Clarence (Pug) Manders, Brooklyn	111	486	4.4	5
1940	Byron (Whizzer) White, Detroit	146	514	3.5	5
1939	*Bill Osmanski, Chicago	121	699	5.8	7
1938	*Byron (Whizzer) White, Pittsburgh	152	567	3.7	4
1937	Cliff Battles, Washington	216	874	4.0	5
1936	*Alphonse (Tuffy) Leemans, N.Y. Giants	206	830	4.0	2
1935	Doug Russell, Chi. Cardinals	140	499	3.6	0
1934	*Beattie Feathers, Chi. Bears	119	1,004	8.4	8
1933	Jim Musick, Boston	173	809	4.7	5
1932	*Cliff Battles, Boston	148	576	3.9	3

*First season of professional football.

ANNUAL PASSING LEADERS

(Current rating system implemented in 1973)

Year	Player, Team	Att.	Comp.	Yards	TD	Int.	Rating
2005	Peyton Manning, Indianapolis, AFC	453	305	3,747	28	10	104.1
	Matt Hasselbeck, Seattle, NFC	449	294	3,459	24	9	98.2

Year	Player, Team	Att.	Comp.	Yards	TD	Int.	Rating
2004	Peyton Manning, Indianapolis, AFC	497	336	4,557	49	10	121.1
	Daunte Culpepper, Minnesota, NFC	548	379	4,717	39	11	110.9
2003	Steve McNair, Tennessee, AFC	400	250	3,215	24	7	100.4
	Daunte Culpepper, Minnesota, NFC	454	295	3,479	25	11	96.4
2002	Chad Pennington, N.Y. Jets, AFC	399	275	3,120	22	6	104.2
	Brad Johnson, Tampa Bay, NFC	451	281	3,049	22	6	92.9
2001	Kurt Warner, St. Louis, NFC	546	375	4,830	36	22	101.4
	Rich Gannon, Oakland, AFC	549	361	3,828	27	9	95.5
2000	Brian Griese, Denver, AFC	336	216	2,688	19	4	102.9
	Trent Green, St. Louis, NFC	240	145	2,063	16	5	101.8
1999	Kurt Warner, St. Louis, NFC	499	325	4,353	41	13	109.2
	Peyton Manning, Indianapolis, AFC	533	331	4,135	26	15	90.7
1998	Randall Cunningham, Minnesota, NFC	425	259	3,704	34	10	106.0
	Vinny Testaverde, N.Y. Jets, AFC	421	259	3,256	29	7	101.6
1997	Steve Young, San Francisco, NFC	356	241	3,029	19	6	104.7
	Mark Brunell, Jacksonville, AFC	435	264	3,281	18	7	91.2
1996	Steve Young, San Francisco NFC	316	214	2,410	14	6	97.2
	John Elway, Denver, AFC	466	287	3,328	26	14	89.2
1995	Jim Harbaugh, Indianapolis, AFC	314	200	2,575	17	5	100.7
	Brett Favre, Green Bay, NFC	570	359	4,413	38	13	99.5
1994	Steve Young, San Francisco, NFC	461	324	3,969	35	10	112.8
	Dan Marino, Miami, AFC	615	385	4,453	30	17	89.2
1993	Steve Young, San Francisco, NFC	462	314	4,023	29	16	101.5
	John Elway, Denver, AFC	551	348	4,030	25	10	92.8
1992	Steve Young, San Francisco, NFC	402	268	3,465	25	7	107.0
	Warren Moon, Houston, AFC	346	224	2,521	18	12	89.3
1991	Steve Young, San Francisco, NFC	279	180	2,517	17	8	101.8
	Jim Kelly, Buffalo, AFC	474	304	3,844	33	17	97.6
1990	Jim Kelly, Buffalo, AFC	346	219	2,829	24	9	101.2
	Phil Simms, N.Y. Giants, NFC	311	184	2,284	15	4	92.7
1989	Joe Montana, San Francisco, NFC	386	271	3,521	26	8	112.4
	Boomer Esiason, Cincinnati, AFC	455	258	3,525	28	11	92.1
1988	Boomer Esiason, Cincinnati, AFC	388	223	3,572	28	14	97.4
	Wade Wilson, Minnesota, NFC	332	204	2,746	15	9	91.5
1987	Joe Montana, San Francisco, NFC	398	266	3,054	31	13	102.1
	Bernie Kosar, Cleveland, AFC	389	241	3,033	22	9	95.4
1986	Tommy Kramer, Minnesota, NFC	372	208	3,000	24	10	92.6
	Dan Marino, Miami, AFC	623	378	4,746	44	23	92.5
1985	Ken O'Brien, N.Y. Jets, AFC	488	297	3,888	25	8	96.2
	Joe Montana, San Francisco, NFC	494	303	3,653	27	13	91.3
1984	Dan Marino, Miami, AFC	564	362	5,084	48	17	108.9
	Joe Montana, San Francisco, NFC	432	279	3,630	28	10	102.9
1983	Steve Bartkowski, Atlanta, NFC	432	274	3,167	22	5	97.6
	*Dan Marino, Miami, AFC	296	173	2,210	20	6	96.0
1982	Ken Anderson, Cincinnati, AFC	309	218	2,495	12	9	95.3
	Joe Theismann, Washington, NFC	252	161	2,033	13	9	91.3
1981	Ken Anderson, Cincinnati, AFC	479	300	3,754	29	10	98.4
	Joe Montana, San Francisco, NFC	488	311	3,565	19	12	88.4
1980	Brian Sipe, Cleveland, AFC	554	337	4,132	30	14	91.4
	Ron Jaworski, Philadelphia, NFC	451	257	3,529	27	12	91.0
1979	Roger Staubach, Dallas, NFC	461	267	3,586	27	11	92.3
	Dan Fouts, San Diego, AFC	530	332	4,082	24	24	82.6
1978	Roger Staubach, Dallas, NFC	413	231	3,190	25	16	84.9
	Terry Bradshaw, Pittsburgh, AFC	368	207	2,915	28	20	84.7
1977	Bob Griese, Miami, AFC	307	180	2,252	22	13	87.8
	Roger Staubach, Dallas, NFC	361	210	2,620	18	9	87.0
1976	Ken Stabler, Oakland, AFC	291	194	2,737	27	17	103.4
	James Harris, Los Angeles, NFC	158	91	1,460	8	6	89.6
1975	Ken Anderson, Cincinnati, AFC	377	228	3,169	21	11	93.9
	Fran Tarkenton, Minnesota, NFC	425	273	2,994	25	13	91.8
1974	Ken Anderson, Cincinnati, AFC	328	213	2,667	18	10	95.7
	Sonny Jurgensen, Washington, NFC	167	107	1,185	11	5	94.5
1973	Roger Staubach, Dallas, NFC	286	179	2,428	23	15	94.6
	Ken Stabler, Oakland, AFC	260	163	1,997	14	10	88.3
1972	Norm Snead, N.Y. Giants, NFC	325	196	2,307	17	12	
	Earl Morrall, Miami, AFC	150	83	1,360	11	7	
1971	Roger Staubach, Dallas, NFC	211	126	1,882	15	4	
	Bob Griese, Miami, AFC	263	145	2,089	19	9	

Year	Player, Team	Att.	Comp.	Yards	TD	Int.	Rating
1970	John Brodie, San Francisco, NFC	378	223	2,941	24	10	
	Daryle Lamonica, Oakland, AFC	356	179	2,516	22	15	
1969	Sonny Jurgensen, Washington, NFL	442	274	3,102	22	15	
	*Greg Cook, Cincinnati, AFL	197	106	1,854	15	11	
1968	Len Dawson, Kansas City, AFL	224	131	2,109	17	9	
	Earl Morrall, Baltimore, NFL	317	182	2,909	26	17	
1967	Sonny Jurgensen, Washington, NFL	508	288	3,747	31	16	
	Daryle Lamonica, Oakland, AFL	425	220	3,228	30	20	
1966	Bart Starr, Green Bay, NFL	251	156	2,257	14	3	
	Len Dawson, Kansas City, AFL	284	159	2,527	26	10	
1965	Rudy Bukich, Chicago, NFL	312	176	2,641	20	9	
	John Hadl, San Diego, AFL	348	174	2,798	20	21	
1964	Len Dawson, Kansas City, AFL	354	199	2,879	30	18	
	Bart Starr, Green Bay, NFL	272	163	2,144	15	4	
1963	Y.A. Tittle, N.Y. Giants, NFL	367	221	3,145	36	14	
	Tobin Rote, San Diego, AFL	286	170	2,510	20	17	
1962	Len Dawson, Dallas Texans, AFL	310	189	2,759	29	17	
	Bart Starr, Green Bay, NFL	285	178	2,438	12	9	
1961	George Blanda, Houston, AFL	362	187	3,330	36	22	
	Milt Plum, Cleveland, NFL	302	177	2,416	18	10	
1960	Milt Plum, Cleveland, NFL	250	151	2,297	21	5	
	Jack Kemp, L.A. Chargers, AFL	406	211	3,018	20	25	
1959	Charlie Conerly, N.Y. Giants	194	113	1,706	14	4	
1958	Eddie LeBaron, Washington	145	79	1,365	11	10	
1957	Tommy O'Connell, Cleveland	110	63	1,229	9	8	
1956	Ed Brown, Chicago Bears	168	96	1,667	11	12	
1955	Otto Graham, Cleveland	185	98	1,721	15	8	
1954	Norm Van Brocklin, Los Angeles	260	139	2,637	13	21	
1953	Otto Graham, Cleveland	258	167	2,722	11	9	
1952	Norm Van Brocklin, Los Angeles	205	113	1,736	14	17	
1951	Bob Waterfield, Los Angeles	176	88	1,566	13	10	
1950	Norm Van Brocklin, Los Angeles	233	127	2,061	18	14	
1949	Sammy Baugh, Washington	255	145	1,903	18	14	
1948	Tommy Thompson, Philadelphia	246	141	1,965	25	11	
1947	Sammy Baugh, Washington	354	210	2,938	25	15	
1946	Bob Waterfield, Los Angeles	251	127	1,747	18	17	
1945	Sammy Baugh, Washington	182	128	1,669	11	4	
	Sid Luckman, Chicago Bears	217	117	1,725	14	10	
1944	Frank Filchock, Washington	147	84	1,139	13	9	
1943	Sammy Baugh, Washington	239	133	1,754	23	19	
1942	Cecil Isbell, Green Bay	268	146	2,021	24	14	
1941	Cecil Isbell, Green Bay	206	117	1,479	15	11	
1940	Sammy Baugh, Washington	177	111	1,367	12	10	
1939	*Parker Hall, Cleveland	208	106	1,227	9	13	
1938	Ed Danowski, N.Y. Giants	129	70	848	7	8	
1937	*Sammy Baugh, Washington	171	81	1,127	8	14	
1936	Arnie Herber, Green Bay	173	77	1,239	11	13	
1935	Ed Danowski, N.Y. Giants	113	57	794	10	9	
1934	Arnie Herber, Green Bay	115	42	799	8	12	
1933	*Harry Newman, N.Y. Giants	136	53	973	11	17	
1932	Arnie Herber, Green Bay	101	37	639	9	9	

First season of professional football.

ANNUAL PASSING TOUCHDOWN LEADERS

Year	Player, Team	TD
2005	Carson Palmer, Cincinnati, AFC	32
	Jake Delhomme, Carolina, NFC	24
	Matt Hasselbeck, Seattle, NFC	24
	Eli Manning, N.Y. Giants, NFC	24
2004	Peyton Manning, Indianapolis, AFC	49
	Daunte Culpepper, Minnesota, NFC	39
2003	Brett Favre, Green Bay, NFC	32
	Peyton Manning, Indianapolis, AFC	29
2002	Tom Brady, New England, AFC	28
	Aaron Brooks, New Orleans, NFC	27
	Brett Favre, Green Bay, NFC	27
2001	Kurt Warner, St. Louis, NFC	36
	Rich Gannon, Oakland, AFC	27

Year	Player, Team	TD
2000	Daunte Culpepper, Minnesota, NFC	33
	Peyton Manning, Indianapolis, AFC	33
1999	Kurt Warner, St. Louis, NFC	41
	Peyton Manning, Indianapolis, AFC	26
1998	Steve Young, San Francisco, NFC	36
	Vinny Testaverde, N.Y. Jets, AFC	29
1997	Brett Favre, Green Bay, NFC	35
	Jeff George, Oakland, AFC	29
1996	Brett Favre, Green Bay, NFC	39
	Vinny Testaverde, Baltimore, AFC	33
1995	Brett Favre, Green Bay, NFC	38
	Jeff Blake, Cincinnati, AFC	28
1994	Steve Young, San Francisco, NFC	35
	Dan Marino, Miami, AFC	30

Year	Player, Team	TD
1993	Steve Young, San Francisco, NFC	29
	John Elway, Denver, AFC	25
1992	Steve Young, San Francisco, NFC	25
	Dan Marino, Miami, AFC	24
1991	Jim Kelly, Buffalo, AFC	33
	Mark Rypien, Washington, NFC	28
1990	Warren Moon, Houston, AFC	33
	Randall Cunningham, Philadelphia, NFC	30
1989	Jim Everett, L.A. Rams, NFC	29
	Boomer Esiason, Cincinnati, AFC	28
1988	Jim Everett, L.A. Rams, NFC	31
	Boomer Esiason, Cincinnati, AFC	28
	Dan Marino, Miami, AFC	28
1987	Joe Montana, San Francisco, NFC	31
	Dan Marino, Miami, AFC	26
1986	Dan Marino, Miami, AFC	44
	Tommy Kramer, Minnesota, NFC	24
1985	Dan Marino, Miami, AFC	30
	Joe Montana, San Francisco, NFC	27
1984	Dan Marino, Miami, AFC	48
	Neil Lomax, St. Louis, NFC	28
	Joe Montana, San Francisco, NFC	28
1983	Lynn Dickey, Green Bay, NFC	32
	Joe Ferguson, Buffalo, AFC	26
	Brian Sipe, Cleveland, AFC	26
1982	Terry Bradshaw, Pittsburgh, AFC	17
	Dan Fouts, San Diego, AFC	17
	Joe Montana, San Francisco, NFC	17
1981	Dan Fouts, San Diego, AFC	33
	Steve Bartkowski, Atlanta, NFC	30
1980	Steve Bartkowski, Atlanta, NFC	31
	Dan Fouts, San Diego, AFC	30
	Brian Sipe, Cleveland, AFC	30
1979	Steve Grogan, New England, AFC	28
	Brian Sipe, Cleveland, AFC	28
	Roger Staubach, Dallas, NFC	27
1978	Terry Bradshaw, Pittsburgh, AFC	28
	Roger Staubach, Dallas, NFC	25
	Fran Tarkenton, Minnesota, NFC	25
1977	Bob Griese, Miami, AFC	22
	Ron Jaworski, Philadelphia, NFC	18
	Roger Staubach, Dallas, NFC	18
1976	Ken Stabler, Oakland, AFC	27
	Jim Hart, St. Louis, NFC	18
1975	Joe Ferguson, Buffalo, AFC	25
	Fran Tarkenton, Minnesota, NFC	25
1974	Ken Stabler, Oakland, AFC	26
	Jim Hart, St. Louis, NFC	20
1973	Roman Gabriel, Philadelphia, NFC	23
	Roger Staubach, Dallas, NFC	23
	Charley Johnson, Denver, AFC	20
1972	Billy Kilmer, Washington, NFC	19
	Joe Namath, N.Y. Jets, AFC	19
1971	John Hadl, San Diego, AFC	21
	John Brodie, San Francisco, NFC	18

Year	Player, Team	TD
1970	John Brodie, San Francisco, NFC	24
	John Hadl, San Diego, AFC	22
	Daryle Lamonica, Oakland, AFC	22
1969	Daryle Lamonica, Oakland, AFL	34
	Roman Gabriel, Los Angeles, NFL	24
1968	John Hadl, San Diego, AFL	27
	Earl Morrall, Baltimore, NFL	26
1967	Sonny Jurgensen, Washington, NFL	31
	Daryle Lamonica, Oakland, AFL	30
1966	Frank Ryan, Cleveland, NFL	29
	Len Dawson, Kansas City, AFL	26
1965	John Brodie, San Francisco, NFL	30
	Len Dawson, Kansas City, AFL	21
1964	Babe Parilli, Boston, AFL	31
	Frank Ryan, Cleveland, NFL	25
1963	Y.A. Tittle, N.Y. Giants, NFL	36
	Len Dawson, Kansas City, AFL	26
1962	Y.A. Tittle, N.Y. Giants, NFL	33
	Len Dawson, Dallas, AFL	29
1961	George Blanda, Houston, AFL	36
	Sonny Jurgensen, Philadelphia, NFL	32
1960	Al Dorow, N.Y. Titans, AFL	26
	Johnny Unitas, Baltimore, NFL	25
1959	Johnny Unitas, Baltimore	32
1958	Johnny Unitas, Baltimore	19
1957	Johnny Unitas, Baltimore	24
1956	Tobin Rote, Green Bay	18
1955	Tobin Rote, Green Bay	17
	Y.A. Tittle, San Francisco	17
1954	Adrian Burk, Philadelphia	23
1953	Robert Thomason, Philadelphia	21
1952	Jim Finks, Pittsburgh	20
	Otto Graham, Cleveland	20
1951	Bobby Layne, Detroit	26
1950	George Ratterman, N.Y. Yanks	22
1949	Johnny Lujack, Chi. Bears	23
1948	Tommy Thompson, Philadelphia	25
1947	Sammy Baugh, Washington	25
1946	Sid Luckman, Chi. Bears	17
	Bob Waterfield, Los Angeles	17
1945	Sid Luckman, Chi. Bears	14
	*Bob Waterfield, Cleveland	14
1944	Frank Filchock, Washington	13
1943	Sid Luckman, Chi. Bears	28
1942	Cecil Isbell, Green Bay	24
1941	Cecil Isbell, Green Bay	15
1940	Sammy Baugh, Washington	12
1939	Frank Filchock, Washington	11
1938	Bob Monnett, Green Bay	9
1937	Bernie Masterson, Chi. Bears	9
1936	Arnie Herber, Green Bay	11
1935	Ed Danowski, N.Y. Giants	10
1934	Arnie Herber, Green Bay	8
1933	*Harry Newman, N.Y. Giants	11
1932	Arnie Herber, Green Bay	9

First season of professional football.

ANNUAL PASS RECEIVING LEADERS

Year	Player, Team	No.	Yards	Avg.	TD
2005	Steve Smith, Carolina, NFC	103	1,563	15.2	12
	Larry Fitzgerald, Arizona, NFC	103	1,409	13.7	10
	Chad Johnson, Cincinnati, AFC	97	1,432	14.8	9
2004	Tony Gonzalez, Kansas City, AFC	102	1,258	12.3	7
	Joe Horn, New Orleans, NFC	94	1,399	14.9	11
	Torry Holt, St. Louis, NFC	94	1,372	14.6	10
2003	Torry Holt, St. Louis, NFC	117	1,696	14.5	12
	LaDainian Tomlinson, San Diego, AFC	100	725	7.3	4

Year	Player, Team	No.	Yards	Avg.	TD
2002	Marvin Harrison, Indianapolis, AFC	143	1,722	12.0	11
	Randy Moss, Minnesota, NFC	106	1,347	12.7	7
2001	Rod Smith, Denver, AFC	113	1,343	11.9	11
	Keyshawn Johnson, Tampa Bay, NFC	106	1,266	11.9	1
2000	Marvin Harrison, Indianapolis, AFC	102	1,413	13.9	14
	Muhsin Muhammad, Carolina, NFC	102	1,183	11.6	6
1999	Jimmy Smith, Jacksonville, AFC	116	1,636	14.1	6
	Muhsin Muhammad, Carolina, NFC	96	1,253	13.1	8
1998	O.J. McDuffie, Miami, AFC	90	1,050	11.7	7
	Frank Sanders, Arizona, NFC	89	1,145	12.9	3
1997	Tim Brown, Oakland, AFC	104	1,408	13.5	5
	Herman Moore, Detroit, NFC	104	1,293	12.4	8
1996	Jerry Rice, San Francisco, NFC	108	1,254	11.6	8
	Carl Pickens, Cincinnati, AFC	100	1,180	11.8	12
1995	Herman Moore, Detroit, NFC	123	1,686	13.7	14
	Carl Pickens, Cincinnati, AFC	99	1,234	12.5	17
1994	Cris Carter, Minnesota, NFC	122	1,256	10.3	7
	Ben Coates, New England, AFC	96	1,174	12.2	7
1993	Sterling Sharpe, Green Bay, NFC	112	1,274	11.4	11
	Reggie Langhorne, Indianapolis, AFC	85	1,038	12.2	3
1992	Sterling Sharpe, Green Bay, NFC	108	1,461	13.5	13
	Haywood Jeffires, Houston, AFC	90	913	10.1	9
1991	Haywood Jeffires, Houston, AFC	100	1,181	11.8	7
	Michael Irvin, Dallas, NFC	93	1,523	16.4	8
1990	Jerry Rice, San Francisco, NFC	100	1,502	15.0	13
	Haywood Jeffires, Houston, AFC	74	1,048	14.2	8
	Drew Hill, Houston, AFC	74	1,019	13.8	5
1989	Sterling Sharpe, Green Bay, NFC	90	1,423	15.8	12
	Andre Reed, Buffalo, AFC	88	1,312	14.9	9
1988	Al Toon, N.Y. Jets, AFC	93	1,067	11.5	5
	Henry Ellard, L.A. Rams, NFC	86	1,414	16.4	10
1987	J.T. Smith, St. Louis, NFC	91	1,117	12.3	8
	Al Toon, N.Y. Jets, AFC	68	976	14.4	5
1986	Todd Christensen, L.A. Raiders, AFC	95	1,153	12.1	8
	Jerry Rice, San Francisco, NFC	86	1,570	18.3	15
1985	Roger Craig, San Francisco, NFC	92	1,016	11.0	6
	Lionel James, San Diego, AFC	86	1,027	11.9	6
1984	Art Monk, Washington, NFC	106	1,372	12.9	7
	Ozzie Newsome, Cleveland, AFC	89	1,001	11.2	5
1983	Todd Christensen, L.A. Raiders, AFC	92	1,247	13.6	12
	Roy Green, St. Louis, NFC	78	1,227	15.7	14
	Charlie Brown, Washington, NFC	78	1,225	15.7	8
	Earnest Gray, N.Y. Giants, NFC	78	1,139	14.6	5
1982	Dwight Clark, San Francisco, NFC	60	913	15.2	5
	Kellen Winslow, San Diego, AFC	54	721	13.4	6
1981	Kellen Winslow, San Diego, AFC	88	1,075	12.2	10
	Dwight Clark, San Francisco, NFC	85	1,105	13.0	4
1980	Kellen Winslow, San Diego, AFC	89	1,290	14.5	9
	*Earl Cooper, San Francisco, NFC	83	567	6.8	4
1979	Joe Washington, Baltimore, AFC	82	750	9.1	3
	Ahmad Rashad, Minnesota, NFC	80	1,156	14.5	9
1978	Rickey Young, Minnesota, NFC	88	704	8.0	5
	Steve Largent, Seattle, AFC	71	1,168	16.5	8
1977	Lydell Mitchell, Baltimore, AFC	71	620	8.7	4
	Ahmad Rashad, Minnesota, NFC	51	681	13.4	2
1976	MacArthur Lane, Kansas City, AFC	66	686	10.4	1
	Drew Pearson, Dallas, NFC	58	806	13.9	6
1975	Chuck Foreman, Minnesota, NFC	73	691	9.5	9
	Reggie Rucker, Cleveland, AFC	60	770	12.8	3
	Lydell Mitchell, Baltimore, AFC	60	544	9.1	4
1974	Lydell Mitchell, Baltimore, AFC	72	544	7.6	2
	Charles Young, Philadelphia, NFC	63	696	11.0	3
1973	Harold Carmichael, Philadelphia, NFC	67	1,116	16.7	9
	Fred Willis, Houston, AFC	57	371	6.5	1
1972	Harold Jackson, Philadelphia, NFC	62	1,048	16.9	4
	Fred Biletnikoff, Oakland, AFC	58	802	13.8	7
1971	Fred Biletnikoff, Oakland, AFC	61	929	15.2	9
	Bob Tucker, N.Y. Giants, NFC	59	791	13.4	4

Year	Player, Team	No.	Yards	Avg.	TD
1970	Dick Gordon, Chicago, NFC	71	1,026	14.5	13
	Marlin Briscoe, Buffalo, AFC	57	1,036	18.2	8
1969	Dan Abramowicz, New Orleans, NFL	73	1,015	13.9	7
	Lance Alworth, San Diego, AFL	64	1,003	15.7	4
1968	Clifton McNeil, San Francisco, NFL	71	994	14.0	7
	Lance Alworth, San Diego, AFL	68	1,312	19.3	10
1967	George Sauer, N.Y. Jets, AFL	75	1,189	15.9	6
	Charley Taylor, Washington, NFL	70	990	14.1	9
1966	Lance Alworth, San Diego, AFL	73	1,383	18.9	13
	Charley Taylor, Washington, NFL	72	1,119	15.5	12
1965	Lionel Taylor, Denver, AFL	85	1,131	13.3	6
	Dave Parks, San Francisco, NFL	80	1,344	16.8	12
1964	Charley Hennigan, Houston, AFL	101	1,546	15.3	8
	Johnny Morris, Chicago, NFL	93	1,200	12.9	10
1963	Lionel Taylor, Denver, AFL	78	1,101	14.1	10
	Bobby Joe Conrad, St. Louis, NFL	73	967	13.2	10
1962	Lionel Taylor, Denver, AFL	77	908	11.8	4
	Bobby Mitchell, Washington, NFL	72	1,384	19.2	11
1961	Lionel Taylor, Denver, AFL	100	1,176	11.8	4
	Jim (Red) Phillips, Los Angeles, NFL	78	1,092	14.0	5
1960	Lionel Taylor, Denver, AFL	92	1,235	13.4	12
	Raymond Berry, Baltimore, NFL	74	1,298	17.5	10
1959	Raymond Berry, Baltimore	66	959	14.5	14
1958	Raymond Berry, Baltimore	56	794	14.2	9
	Pete Retzlaff, Philadelphia	56	766	13.7	2
1957	Billy Wilson, San Francisco	52	757	14.6	6
1956	Billy Wilson, San Francisco	60	889	14.8	5
1955	Pete Pihos, Philadelphia	62	864	13.9	7
1954	Pete Pihos, Philadelphia	60	872	14.5	10
	Billy Wilson, San Francisco	60	830	13.8	5
1953	Pete Pihos, Philadelphia	63	1,049	16.7	10
1952	Mac Speedie, Cleveland	62	911	14.7	5
1951	Elroy (Crazylegs) Hirsch, Los Angeles	66	1,495	22.7	17
1950	Tom Fears, Los Angeles	84	1,116	13.3	7
1949	Tom Fears, Los Angeles	77	1,013	13.2	9
1948	*Tom Fears, Los Angeles	51	698	13.7	4
1947	Jim Keane, Chi. Bears	64	910	14.2	10
1946	Jim Benton, Los Angeles	63	981	15.6	6
1945	Don Hutson, Green Bay	47	834	17.7	9
1944	Don Hutson, Green Bay	58	866	14.9	9
1943	Don Hutson, Green Bay	47	776	16.5	11
1942	Don Hutson, Green Bay	74	1,211	16.4	17
1941	Don Hutson, Green Bay	58	738	12.7	10
1940	*Don Looney, Philadelphia	58	707	12.2	4
1939	Don Hutson, Green Bay	34	846	24.9	6
1938	Gaynell Tinsley, Chi. Cardinals	41	516	12.6	1
1937	Don Hutson, Green Bay	41	552	13.5	7
1936	Don Hutson, Green Bay	34	536	15.8	8
1935	*Tod Goodwin, N.Y. Giants	26	432	16.6	4
1934	Joe Carter, Philadelphia	16	238	14.9	4
	Morris (Red) Badgro, N.Y. Giants	16	206	12.9	1
1933	John (Shipwreck) Kelly, Brooklyn	22	246	11.2	3
1932	Ray Flaherty, N.Y. Giants	21	350	16.7	3

First season of professional football.

ANNUAL PASS RECEIVING LEADERS (YARDS)

Year	Player, Team	No.	Yards	Avg.	TD
2005	Steve Smith, Carolina, NFC	103	1,563	15.2	12
	Chad Johnson, Cincinnati, AFC	97	1,432	14.8	9
2004	Muhsin Muhammad, Carolina, NFC	93	1,405	15.1	16
	Chad Johnson, Cincinnati, AFC	95	1,274	13.4	9
2003	Torry Holt, St. Louis, NFC	117	1,696	14.5	12
	Chad Johnson, Cincinnati, AFC	90	1,355	15.1	10
2002	Marvin Harrison, Indianapolis, AFC	143	1,722	12.0	11
	Randy Moss, Minnesota, NFC	106	1,347	12.7	7
2001	David Boston, Arizona, NFC	98	1,598	16.3	8
	Marvin Harrison, Indianapolis, AFC	109	1,524	14.0	15
2000	Torry Holt, St. Louis, NFC	82	1,635	19.9	6
	Rod Smith, Denver, AFC	100	1,602	16.0	8

Year	Player, Team	No.	Yards	Avg.	TD
1999	Marvin Harrison, Indianapolis, AFC	115	1,663	14.5	12
	Randy Moss, Minnesota, NFC	80	1,413	17.7	11
1998	Antonio Freeman, Green Bay, NFC	84	1,424	17.0	14
	Eric Moulds, Buffalo, AFC	67	1,368	20.4	9
1997	Rob Moore, Arizona, NFC	97	1,584	16.3	8
	Tim Brown, Oakland, AFC	104	1,408	13.5	5
1996	Isaac Bruce, St. Louis, NFC	84	1,338	15.9	7
	Jimmy Smith, Jacksonville, AFC	83	1,244	15.0	7
1995	Jerry Rice, San Francisco, NFC	122	1,848	15.1	15
	Tim Brown, Oakland, AFC	89	1,342	15.1	10
1994	Jerry Rice, San Francisco, NFC	112	1,499	13.4	13
	Tim Brown, L.A. Raiders, AFC	89	1,309	14.7	9
1993	Jerry Rice, San Francisco, NFC	98	1,503	15.3	15
	Tim Brown, L.A. Raiders, AFC	80	1,180	14.8	7
1992	Sterling Sharpe, Green Bay, NFC	108	1,461	13.5	13
	Anthony Miller, San Diego, AFC	72	1,060	14.7	7
1991	Michael Irvin, Dallas, NFC	93	1,523	16.4	8
	Haywood Jeffires, Houston, AFC	100	1,181	11.8	7
1990	Jerry Rice, San Francisco, NFC	100	1,502	15.0	13
	Haywood Jeffires, Houston, AFC	74	1,048	14.2	8
1989	Jerry Rice, San Francisco, NFC	82	1,483	18.1	17
	Andre Reed, Buffalo, AFC	88	1,312	14.9	9
1988	Henry Ellard, L.A. Rams, NFC	86	1,414	16.4	10
	Eddie Brown, Cincinnati, AFC	53	1,273	24.0	9
1987	J.T. Smith, St. Louis, NFC	91	1,117	12.3	8
	Carlos Carson, Kansas City, AFC	55	1,044	19.0	7
1986	Jerry Rice, San Francisco, NFC	86	1,570	18.3	15
	Stanley Morgan, New England, AFC	84	1,491	17.8	10
1985	Steve Largent, Seattle, AFC	79	1,287	16.3	6
	Mike Quick, Philadelphia, NFC	73	1,247	17.1	11
1984	Roy Green, St. Louis, NFC	78	1,555	19.9	12
	John Stallworth, Pittsburgh, AFC	80	1,395	17.4	11
1983	Mike Quick, Philadelphia, NFC	69	1,409	20.4	13
	Carlos Carson, Kansas City, AFC	80	1,351	16.9	7
1982	Wes Chandler, San Diego, AFC	49	1,032	21.1	9
	Dwight Clark, San Francisco, NFC	60	913	15.2	5
1981	Alfred Jenkins, Atlanta, NFC	70	1,358	19.4	13
	Frank Lewis, Buffalo, AFC	70	1,244	17.8	4
	Steve Watson, Denver, AFC	60	1,244	20.7	13
1980	John Jefferson, San Diego, AFC	82	1,340	16.3	13
	James Lofton, Green Bay, NFC	71	1,226	17.3	4
1979	Steve Largent, Seattle, AFC	66	1,237	18.7	9
	Ahmad Rashad, Minnesota, NFC	80	1,156	14.5	9
1978	Wesley Walker, N.Y. Jets, AFC	48	1,169	24.4	8
	Harold Carmichael, Philadelphia, NFC	55	1,072	19.5	8
1977	Drew Pearson, Dallas, NFC	48	870	18.1	2
	Ken Burrough, Houston, AFC	43	816	19.0	8
1976	Roger Carr, Baltimore, AFC	43	1,112	25.9	11
	*Sammy White, Minnesota, NFC	51	906	17.8	10
1975	Ken Burrough, Houston, AFC	53	1,063	20.1	8
	Mel Gray, St. Louis, NFC	48	926	19.3	11
1974	Cliff Branch, Oakland, AFC	60	1,092	18.2	13
	Drew Pearson, Dallas, NFC	62	1,087	17.5	2
1973	Harold Carmichael, Philadelphia, NFC	67	1,116	16.7	9
	*Isaac Curtis, Cincinnati, AFC	45	843	18.7	9
1972	Harold Jackson, Philadelphia, NFC	62	1,048	16.9	4
	Rich Caster, N.Y. Jets, AFC	39	833	21.4	10
1971	Otis Taylor, Kansas City, AFC	57	1,110	19.5	7
	Gene Washington, San Francisco, NFC	46	884	19.2	4
1970	Gene Washington, San Francisco, NFC	53	1,100	20.8	12
	Marlin Briscoe, Buffalo, AFC	57	1,036	18.2	8
1969	Warren Wells, Oakland, AFL	47	1,260	26.8	14
	Harold Jackson, Philadelphia, NFL	65	1,116	17.2	9
1968	Lance Alworth, San Diego, AFL	68	1,312	19.3	10
	Roy Jefferson, Pittsburgh, NFL	58	1,074	18.5	11
1967	Don Maynard, N.Y. Jets, AFL	71	1,434	20.3	10
	Ben Hawkins, Philadelphia, NFL	59	1,265	21.4	10
1966	Lance Alworth, San Diego, AFL	73	1,383	18.9	13
	Pat Studstill, Detroit, NFL	67	1,266	18.9	5

Year	Player, Team	No.	Yards	Avg.	TD
1965	Lance Alworth, San Diego, AFL	69	1,602	23.2	14
	Dave Parks, San Francisco, NFL	80	1,344	16.8	12
1964	Charley Hennigan, Houston, AFL	101	1,546	15.3	8
	Johnny Morris, Chicago, NFL	93	1,200	12.9	10
1963	Bobby Mitchell, Washington, NFL	69	1,436	20.8	7
	Art Powell, Oakland, AFL	73	1,304	17.8	16
1962	Bobby Mitchell, Washington, NFL	72	1,384	19.2	11
	Art Powell, N.Y. Titans, AFL	64	1,130	17.6	8
1961	Charley Hennigan, Houston, AFL	82	1,746	21.3	12
	Tommy McDonald, Philadelphia, NFL	64	1,144	17.9	13
1960	*Bill Groman, Houston, AFL	72	1,473	20.5	12
	Raymond Berry, Baltimore, NFL	74	1,298	17.5	10
1959	Raymond Berry, Baltimore	66	959	14.5	14
1958	Del Shofner, Los Angeles	51	1,097	21.5	8
1957	Raymond Berry, Baltimore	47	800	17.0	6
1956	Billy Howton, Green Bay	55	1,188	21.6	12
1955	Pete Pihos, Philadelphia	62	864	13.9	7
1954	Bob Boyd, Los Angeles	53	1,212	22.9	6
1953	Pete Pihos, Philadelphia	63	1,049	16.7	10
1952	*Bill Howton, Green Bay	53	1,231	23.2	13
1951	Elroy (Crazylegs) Hirsch, Los Angeles	66	1,495	22.7	17
1950	Tom Fears, Los Angeles	84	1,116	13.3	7
1949	Bob Mann, Detroit	66	1,014	15.4	4
1948	Mal Kutner, Chi. Cardinals	41	943	23.0	14
1947	Mal Kutner, Chi. Cardinals	43	944	21.9	7
1946	Jim Benton, Los Angeles	63	981	15.5	6
1945	Jim Benton, Cleveland	45	1,067	23.7	8
1944	Don Hutson, Green Bay	58	866	14.6	9
1943	Don Hutson, Green Bay	47	776	16.5	11
1942	Don Hutson, Green Bay	74	1,211	16.4	17
1941	Don Hutson, Green Bay	58	738	12.7	10
1940	*Don Looney, Philadelphia	58	707	12.2	4
1939	Don Hutson, Green Bay	34	846	24.9	6
1938	Don Hutson, Green Bay	32	548	17.1	9
1937	*Gaynell Tinsley, Chi. Cardinals	36	675	18.8	5
1936	Don Hutson, Green Bay	34	526	15.5	8
1935	Charley Malone, Boston	22	433	19.7	2
1934	Harry Ebding, Detroit	9	257	28.6	2
1933	*Paul Moss, Pittsburgh	18	383	21.3	2
1932	Johnny (Blood) McNally, Green Bay	19	326	17.2	3

First season of professional football.

ANNUAL PUNT RETURN LEADERS

Year	Player, Team	No.	Yards	Avg.	Long	TD
2005	Reno Mahe, Philadelphia, NFC	21	269	12.8	44	0
	B.J. Sams, Baltimore, AFC	33	401	12.2	51	0
2004	Eddie Drummond, Detroit, NFC	24	316	13.2	83	2
	Dennis Northcutt, Cleveland, AFC	36	432	12.0	44	0
2003	Dante Hall, Kansas City, AFC	29	472	16.3	93	2
	Brian Westbrook, Philadelphia, NFC	20	306	15.3	84	2
2002	Jimmy Williams, San Francisco, NFC	20	336	16.8	89	1
	Santana Moss, N.Y. Jets, AFC	25	413	16.5	63	2
2001	Troy Brown, New England, AFC	29	413	14.2	85	2
	Darrien Gordon, Atlanta, NFC	31	437	14.1	74	0
2000	Jermaine Lewis, Baltimore, AFC	36	578	16.1	89	2
	Az-Zahir Hakim, St. Louis, NFC	32	489	15.3	86	1
1999	*Charlie Rogers, Seattle, AFC	22	318	14.5	94	1
	*Mac Cody, Arizona, NFC	32	373	11.7	31	0
1998	Deion Sanders, Dallas, NFC	24	375	15.6	69	2
	Reggie Barlow, Jacksonville, AFC	43	555	12.9	85	1
1997	Jermaine Lewis, Baltimore, AFC	28	437	15.6	89	2
	David Palmer, Minnesota, NFC	34	444	13.1	57	0
1996	Desmond Howard, Green Bay, NFC	58	875	15.1	92	3
	Darrien Gordon, San Diego, AFC	36	537	14.9	81	1
1995	David Palmer, Minnesota, NFC	26	342	13.2	74	1
	Andre Coleman, San Diego, AFC	28	326	11.6	88	1
1994	Brian Mitchell, Washington, NFC	32	452	14.1	78	2
	Darrien Gordon, San Diego, AFC	36	475	13.2	90	2

Year	Player, Team	No.	Yards	Avg.	Long	TD
1993	*Tyrone Hughes, New Orleans, NFC	37	503	13.6	83	2
	Eric Metcalf, Cleveland, AFC	36	464	12.9	91	2
1992	Johnny Bailey, Phoenix, NFC	20	263	13.2	65	0
	Rod Woodson, Pittsburgh, AFC	32	364	11.4	80	1
1991	Mel Gray, Detroit, NFC	25	385	15.4	78	1
	Rod Woodson, Pittsburgh, AFC	28	320	11.4	40	0
1990	Clarence Verdin, Indianapolis, AFC	31	396	12.8	36	0
	*Johnny Bailey, Chicago, NFC	36	399	11.1	95	1
1989	Walter Stanley, Detroit, NFC	36	496	13.8	74	0
	Clarence Verdin, Indianapolis, AFC	23	296	12.9	49	1
1988	John Taylor, San Francisco, NFC	44	556	12.6	95	2
	JoJo Townsell, N.Y. Jets, AFC	35	409	11.7	59	1
1987	Mel Gray, New Orleans, NFC	24	352	14.7	80	0
	Bobby Joe Edmonds, Seattle, AFC	20	251	12.6	40	0
1986	*Bobby Joe Edmonds, Seattle, AFC	34	419	12.3	75	1
	*Vai Sikahema, St. Louis, NFC	43	522	12.1	71	2
1985	Irving Fryar, New England, AFC	37	520	14.1	85	2
	Henry Ellard, L.A. Rams, NFC	37	501	13.5	80	1
1984	Mike Martin, Cincinnati, AFC	24	376	15.7	55	0
	Henry Ellard, L.A. Rams, NFC	30	403	13.4	83	2
1983	*Henry Ellard, L.A. Rams, NFC	16	217	13.6	72	1
	Kirk Springs, N.Y. Jets, AFC	23	287	12.5	76	1
1982	Rick Upchurch, Denver, AFC	15	242	16.1	78	2
	Billy Johnson, Atlanta, NFC	24	273	11.4	71	0
1981	LeRoy Irvin, Los Angeles, NFC	46	615	13.4	84	3
	*James Brooks, San Diego, AFC	22	290	13.2	42	0
1980	J.T. Smith, Kansas City, AFC	40	581	14.5	75	2
	*Kenny Johnson, Atlanta, NFC	23	281	12.2	56	0
1979	John Sciarra, Philadelphia, NFC	16	182	11.4	38	0
	*Tony Nathan, Miami, AFC	28	306	10.9	86	1
1978	Rick Upchurch, Denver, AFC	36	493	13.7	75	1
	Jackie Wallace, Los Angeles, NFC	52	618	11.9	58	0
1977	Billy Johnson, Houston, AFC	35	539	15.4	87	2
	Larry Marshall, Philadelphia, NFC	46	489	10.6	48	0
1976	Rick Upchurch, Denver, AFC	39	536	13.7	92	4
	Eddie Brown, Washington, NFC	48	646	13.5	71	1
1975	Billy Johnson, Houston, AFC	40	612	15.3	83	3
	Terry Metcalf, St. Louis, NFC	23	285	12.4	69	1
1974	Lemar Parrish, Cincinnati, AFC	18	338	18.8	90	2
	Dick Jauron, Detroit, NFC	17	286	16.8	58	0
1973	Bruce Taylor, San Francisco, NFC	15	207	13.8	61	0
	Ron Smith, San Diego, AFC	27	352	13.0	84	2
1972	Ken Ellis, Green Bay, NFC	14	215	15.4	80	1
	Chris Farasopoulos, N.Y. Jets, AFC	17	179	10.5	65	1
1971	Les (Speedy) Duncan, Washington, NFC	22	233	10.6	33	0
	Leroy Kelly, Cleveland, AFC	30	292	9.7	74	0
1970	Ed Podolak, Kansas City, AFC	23	311	13.5	60	0
	*Bruce Taylor, San Francisco, NFC	43	516	12.0	76	0
1969	Alvin Haymond, Los Angeles, NFL	33	435	13.2	52	0
	*Bill Thompson, Denver, AFL	25	288	11.5	40	0
1968	Bob Hayes, Dallas, NFL	15	312	20.8	90	2
	Noland Smith, Kansas City, AFL	18	270	15.0	80	1
1967	Floyd Little, Denver, AFL	16	270	16.9	72	1
	Ben Davis, Cleveland, NFL	18	229	12.7	52	1
1966	Les (Speedy) Duncan, San Diego, AFL	18	238	13.2	81	1
	Johnny Roland, St. Louis, NFL	20	221	11.1	86	1
1965	Leroy Kelly, Cleveland, NFL	17	265	15.6	67	2
	Les (Speedy) Duncan, San Diego, AFL	30	464	15.5	66	2
1964	Bobby Jancik, Houston, AFL	12	220	18.3	82	1
	Tommy Watkins, Detroit, NFL	16	238	14.9	68	2
1963	Dick James, Washington, NFL	16	214	13.4	39	0
	Claude (Hoot) Gibson, Oakland, AFL	26	307	11.8	85	2
1962	Dick Christy, N.Y. Titans, AFL	15	250	16.7	73	2
	Pat Studstill, Detroit, NFL	29	457	15.8	44	0
1961	Dick Christy, N.Y. Titans, AFL	18	383	21.3	70	2
	Willie Wood, Green Bay, NFL	14	225	16.1	72	2
1960	*Abner Haynes, Dall. Texans, AFL	14	215	15.4	46	0
	Abe Woodson, San Francisco, NFL	13	174	13.4	48	0
1959	Johnny Morris, Chi. Bears	14	171	12.2	78	1

Year	Player, Team	No.	Yards	Avg.	Long	TD
1958	Jon Arnett, Los Angeles	18	223	12.4	58	0
1957	Bert Zagers, Washington	14	217	15.5	76	2
1956	Ken Konz, Cleveland	13	187	14.4	65	1
1955	Ollie Matson, Chi. Cardinals	13	245	18.8	78	2
1954	*Veryl Switzer, Green Bay	24	306	12.8	93	1
1953	Charley Trippi, Chi. Cardinals	21	239	11.4	38	0
1952	Jack Christiansen, Detroit	15	322	21.5	79	2
1951	Claude (Buddy) Young, N.Y. Yanks	12	231	19.3	79	1
1950	*Herb Rich, Baltimore	12	276	23.0	86	1
1949	Verda (Vitamin T) Smith, Los Angeles	27	427	15.8	85	1
1948	George McAfee, Chi. Bears	30	417	13.9	60	1
1947	*Walt Slater, Pittsburgh	28	435	15.5	33	0
1946	Bill Dudley, Pittsburgh	27	385	14.3	52	0
1945	*Dave Ryan, Detroit	15	220	14.7	56	0
1944	*Steve Van Buren, Philadelphia	15	230	15.3	55	1
1943	Andy Farkas, Washington	15	168	11.2	33	0
1942	Merlyn Condit, Brooklyn	21	210	10.0	23	0
1941	Byron (Whizzer) White, Detroit	19	262	13.8	64	0

*First season of professional football.

ANNUAL KICKOFF RETURN LEADERS

Year	Player, Team	No.	Yards	Avg.	Long	TD
2005	Terrence McGee, Buffalo, AFC	46	1,391	30.2	99	1
	Koren Robinson, Minnesota, NFC	47	1,221	26.0	86	1
2004	Willie Ponder, N.Y. Giants, NFC	36	967	26.9	91	1
	Terrence McGee, Buffalo, AFC	52	1,370	26.3	104	3
2003	Jerry Azumah, Chicago, NFC	41	1,191	29.0	89	2
	*Bethel Johnson, New England, AFC	30	847	28.2	92	1
2002	MarTay Jenkins, Arizona, NFC	20	559	28.0	95	1
	Kevin Faulk, New England, AFC	26	725	27.9	87	2
2001	Ronney Jenkins, San Diego, AFC	58	1,541	26.6	93	2
	*Steve Smith, Carolina, NFC	56	1,431	25.6	99	2
2000	*Darrick Vaughn, Atlanta, NFC	39	1,082	27.7	100	3
	Derrick Mason, Tennessee, AFC	42	1,132	27.0	66	0
1999	Tony Horne, St. Louis, NFC	30	892	29.7	101	2
	Tremain Mack, Cincinnati, AFC	51	1,382	27.1	99	1
1998	*Terry Fair, Detroit, NFC	51	1,428	28.0	105	2
	Corey Harris, Baltimore, AFC	35	965	27.6	95	1
1997	Michael Bates, Carolina, NFC	47	1,281	27.3	56	0
	Aaron Glenn, N.Y. Jets, AFC	28	741	26.5	96	1
1996	Michael Bates, Carolina, NFC	33	998	30.2	93	1
	Tamarick Vanover, Kansas City, AFC	33	854	25.9	97	1
1995	Ron Carpenter, N.Y. Jets, AFC	20	553	27.7	58	0
	Brian Mitchell, Washington, NFC	55	1,408	25.6	59	0
1994	Mel Gray, Detroit, NFC	45	1,276	28.4	102	3
	Randy Baldwin, Cleveland, AFC	28	753	26.9	85	1
1993	Robert Brooks, Green Bay, NFC	23	611	26.6	95	1
	*Raghib Ismail, L.A. Raiders, AFC	25	605	24.2	66	0
1992	Jon Vaughn, New England, AFC	20	564	28.2	100	1
	Deion Sanders, Atlanta, NFC	40	1,067	26.7	99	2
1991	Mel Gray, Detroit, NFC	36	929	25.8	71	0
	Nate Lewis, San Diego, AFC	23	578	25.1	95	1
1990	Kevin Clark, Denver, AFC	20	505	25.3	75	0
	David Meggett, N.Y. Giants, NFC	21	492	23.4	58	0
1989	Rod Woodson, Pittsburgh, AFC	36	982	27.3	84	1
	Mel Gray, Detroit, NFC	24	640	26.7	57	0
1988	*Tim Brown, L.A. Raiders, AFC	41	1,098	26.8	97	1
	Donnie Elder, Tampa Bay, NFC	34	772	22.7	51	0
1987	Sylvester Stamps, Atlanta, NFC	24	660	27.5	97	1
	Paul Palmer, Kansas City, AFC	38	923	24.3	95	2
1986	Dennis Gentry, Chicago, NFC	20	576	28.8	91	1
	Lupe Sanchez, Pittsburgh, AFC	25	591	23.6	64	0
1985	Ron Brown, L.A. Rams, NFC	28	918	32.8	98	3
	Glen Young, Cleveland, AFC	35	898	25.7	63	0
1984	*Bobby Humphery, N.Y. Jets, AFC	22	675	30.7	97	1
	Barry Redden, L.A. Rams, NFC	23	530	23.0	40	0
1983	Fulton Walker, Miami, AFC	36	962	26.7	78	0
	Darrin Nelson, Minnesota, NFC	18	445	24.7	50	0

Year	Player, Team	No.	Yards	Avg.	Long	TD
1982	*Mike Mosley, Buffalo, AFC	18	487	27.1	66	0
	Alvin Hall, Detroit, NFC	16	426	26.6	96	1
1981	Mike Nelms, Washington, NFC	37	1,099	29.7	84	0
	Carl Roaches, Houston, AFC	28	769	27.5	96	1
1980	Horace Ivory, New England, AFC	36	992	27.6	98	1
	Rich Mauti, New Orleans, NFC	31	798	25.7	52	0
1979	Larry Brunson, Oakland, AFC	17	441	25.9	89	0
	Jimmy Edwards, Minnesota, NFC	44	1,103	25.1	83	0
1978	Steve Odom, Green Bay, NFC	25	677	27.1	95	1
	*Keith Wright, Cleveland, AFC	30	789	26.3	86	0
1977	*Raymond Clayborn, New England, AFC	28	869	31.0	101	3
	*Wilbert Montgomery, Philadelphia, NFC	23	619	26.9	99	1
1976	*Duriel Harris, Miami, AFC	17	559	32.9	69	0
	Cullen Bryant, Los Angeles, NFC	16	459	28.7	90	1
1975	*Walter Payton, Chicago, NFC	14	444	31.7	70	0
	Harold Hart, Oakland, AFC	17	518	30.5	102	1
1974	Terry Metcalf, St. Louis, NFC	20	623	31.2	94	1
	Greg Pruitt, Cleveland, AFC	22	606	27.5	88	1
1973	Carl Garrett, Chicago, NFC	16	486	30.4	67	0
	*Wallace Francis, Buffalo, AFC	23	687	29.9	101	2
1972	Ron Smith, Chicago, NFC	30	924	30.8	94	1
	*Bruce Laird, Baltimore, AFC	29	843	29.1	73	0
1971	Travis Williams, Los Angeles, NFC	25	743	29.7	105	1
	Eugene (Mercury) Morris, Miami, AFC	15	423	28.2	94	1
1970	Jim Duncan, Baltimore, AFC	20	707	35.4	99	1
	Cecil Turner, Chicago, NFC	23	752	32.7	96	4
1969	Bobby Williams, Detroit, NFL	17	563	33.1	96	1
	*Bill Thompson, Denver, AFL	18	513	28.5	63	0
1968	Preston Pearson, Baltimore, NFL	15	527	35.1	102	2
	*George Atkinson, Oakland, AFL	32	802	25.1	60	0
1967	*Travis Williams, Green Bay, NFL	18	739	41.1	104	4
	*Zeke Moore, Houston, AFL	14	405	28.9	92	1
1966	Gale Sayers, Chicago, NFL	23	718	31.2	93	2
	*Goldie Sellers, Denver, AFL	19	541	28.5	100	2
1965	Tommy Watkins, Detroit, NFL	17	584	34.4	94	0
	Abner Haynes, Denver, AFL	34	901	26.5	60	0
1964	*Clarence Childs, N.Y. Giants, NFL	34	987	29.0	100	1
	Bo Roberson, Oakland, AFL	36	975	27.1	59	0
1963	Abe Woodson, San Francisco, NFL	29	935	32.2	103	3
	Bobby Jancik, Houston, AFL	45	1,317	29.3	53	0
1962	Abe Woodson, San Francisco, NFL	37	1,157	31.3	79	0
	*Bobby Jancik, Houston, AFL	24	826	30.3	61	0
1961	Dick Bass, Los Angeles, NFL	23	698	30.3	64	0
	*Dave Grayson, Dall. Texans, AFL	16	453	28.3	73	0
1960	*Tom Moore, Green Bay, NFL	12	397	33.1	84	0
	Ken Hall, Houston, AFL	19	594	31.3	104	1
1959	Abe Woodson, San Francisco	13	382	29.4	105	1
1958	Ollie Matson, Chi. Cardinals	14	497	35.5	101	2
1957	*Jon Arnett, Los Angeles	18	504	28.0	98	1
1956	*Tom Wilson, Los Angeles	15	477	31.8	103	1
1955	Al Carmichael, Green Bay	14	418	29.9	100	1
1954	Billy Reynolds, Cleveland	14	413	29.5	51	0
1953	Joe Arenas, San Francisco	16	551	34.4	82	0
1952	Lynn Chandnois, Pittsburgh	17	599	35.2	93	2
1951	Lynn Chandnois, Pittsburgh	12	390	32.5	55	0
1950	Verda (Vitamin T) Smith, Los Angeles	22	742	33.7	97	3
1949	*Don Doll, Detroit	21	536	25.5	56	0
1948	*Joe Scott, N.Y. Giants	20	569	28.5	99	1
1947	Eddie Saenz, Washington	29	797	27.5	94	2
1946	Abe Karnofsky, Boston	21	599	28.5	97	1
1945	Steve Van Buren, Philadelphia	13	373	28.7	98	1
1944	Bob Thurbon, Card.-Pitt.	12	291	24.3	55	0
1943	Ken Heineman, Brooklyn	16	444	27.8	69	0
1942	Marshall Goldberg, Chi. Cardinals	15	393	26.2	95	1
1941	Marshall Goldberg, Chi. Cardinals	12	290	24.2	41	0

*First season of professional football.

ANNUAL INTERCEPTION LEADERS

Year	Player, Team	No.	Yards	TD
2005	Ty Law, N.Y. Jets, AFC	10	195	1
	Deltha O'Neal, Cincinnati, AFC	10	103	0
	Darren Sharper, Minnesota, NFC	9	276	2
2004	Ed Reed, Baltimore, AFC	9	358	1
	Ken Lucas, Seattle, NFC	6	46	1
	*Chris Gamble, Carolina, NFC	6	15	0
2003	Tony Parrish, San Francisco, NFC	9	202	1
	Brian Russell, Minnesota, NFC	9	185	0
	Ed Reed, Baltimore, AFC	7	132	1
	Marcus Coleman, Houston, AFC	7	95	0
	Patrick Surtain, Miami, AFC	7	59	0
2002	Rod Woodson, Oakland, AFC	8	225	2
	Brian Kelly, Tampa Bay, NFC	8	68	0
2001	*Anthony Henry, Cleveland, AFC	10	177	1
	Ronde Barber, Tampa Bay, NFC	10	86	1
2000	Darren Sharper, Green Bay, NFC	9	109	1
	Samari Rolle, Tennessee, AFC	7	140	1
	Brian Walker, Miami, AFC	7	80	0
1999	Rod Woodson, Baltimore, AFC	7	195	2
	Sam Madison, Miami, AFC	7	164	1
	James Hasty, Kansas City, AFC	7	98	2
	Donnie Abraham, Tampa Bay, NFC	7	115	2
	Troy Vincent, Philadelphia, NFC	7	91	0
1998	Ty Law, New England, AFC	9	133	1
	Kwamie Lassiter, Arizona, NFC	8	80	0
1997	Ryan McNeil, St. Louis, NFC	9	127	1
	Mark McMillian, Kansas City, AFC	8	274	3
	Darryl Williams, Seattle, AFC	8	172	1
1996	Tyrone Braxton, Denver, AFC	9	128	1
	Keith Lyle, St. Louis, NFC	9	152	0
1995	*Orlando Thomas, Minnesota, NFC	9	108	1
	Willie Williams, Pittsburgh, AFC	7	122	1
1994	Eric Turner, Cleveland, AFC	9	199	1
	Aeneas Williams, Arizona, NFC	9	89	0
1993	Eugene Robinson, Seattle, AFC	9	80	1
	Nate Odomes, Buffalo, AFC	9	65	0
	Deion Sanders, Atlanta, NFC	7	91	0
1992	Henry Jones, Buffalo, AFC	8	263	2
	Audray McMillian, Minnesota, NFC	8	157	2
1991	Ronnie Lott, L.A. Raiders, AFC	8	52	0
	Ray Crockett, Detroit, NFC	6	141	1
	Deion Sanders, Atlanta, NFC	6	119	1
	*Aeneas Williams, Phoenix, NFC	6	60	0
	Tim McKyer, Atlanta, NFC	6	24	0
1990	*Mark Carrier, Chicago, NFC	10	39	0
	Richard Johnson, Houston, AFC	8	100	1
1989	Felix Wright, Cleveland, AFC	9	91	1
	Eric Allen, Philadelphia, NFC	8	38	0
1988	Scott Case, Atlanta, NFC	10	47	0
	Erik McMillan, N.Y. Jets, AFC	8	168	2
1987	Barry Wilburn, Washington, NFC	9	135	1
	Mike Prior, Indianapolis, AFC	6	57	0
	Mark Kelso, Buffalo, AFC	6	25	0
	Keith Bostic, Houston, AFC	6	-14	0
1986	Ronnie Lott, San Francisco, NFC	10	134	1
	Deron Cherry, Kansas City, AFC	9	150	0
1985	Everson Walls, Dallas, NFC	9	31	0
	Albert Lewis, Kansas City, AFC	8	59	0
	Eugene Daniel, Indianapolis, AFC	8	53	0
1984	Ken Easley, Seattle, AFC	10	126	2
	*Tom Flynn, Green Bay, NFC	9	106	0
1983	Mark Murphy, Washington, NFC	9	127	0
	Ken Riley, Cincinnati, AFC	8	89	2
	Vann McElroy, L.A. Raiders, AFC	8	68	0

Year	Player, Team	No.	Yards	TD
1982	Everson Walls, Dallas, NFC	7	61	0
	Ken Riley, Cincinnati, AFC	5	88	1
	Bobby Jackson, N.Y Jets, AFC	5	84	1
	Dwayne Woodruff, Pittsburgh, AFC	5	53	0
	Donnie Shell, Pittsburgh, AFC	5	27	0
1981	*Everson Walls, Dallas, NFC	11	133	0
	John Harris, Seattle, AFC	10	155	2
1980	Lester Hayes, Oakland, AFC	13	273	1
	Nolan Cromwell, Los Angeles, NFC	8	140	1
1979	Mike Reinfeldt, Houston, AFC	12	205	0
	Lemar Parrish, Washiongton, NFC	9	65	0
1978	Thom Darden, Cleveland, AFC	10	200	0
	Ken Stone, St. Louis, NFC	9	139	0
	Willie Buchanon, Green Bay, NFC	9	93	1
1977	Lyle Blackwood, Baltimore, AFC	10	163	0
	Rolland Lawrence, Atlanta, NFC	7	138	0
1976	Monte Jackson, Los Angeles, NFC	10	173	3
	Ken Riley, Cincinnati, AFC	9	141	1
1975	Mel Blount, Pittsburgh, AFC	11	121	0
	Paul Krause, Minnesota, NFC	10	201	0
1974	Emmitt Thomas, Kansas City, AFC	12	214	2
	Ray Brown, Atlanta, NFC	8	164	1
1973	Dick Anderson, Miami, AFC	8	163	2
	Mike Wagner, Pittsburgh, AFC	8	134	0
	Bobby Bryant, Minnesota, NFC	7	105	1
1972	Bill Bradley, Philadelphia, NFC	9	73	0
	Mike Sensibaugh, Kansas City, AFC	8	65	0
1971	Bill Bradley, Philadelphia, NFC	11	248	0
	Ken Houston, Houston, AFC	9	220	4
1970	Johnny Robinson, Kansas City, AFC	10	155	0
	Dick LeBeau, Detroit, NFC	9	96	0
1969	Mel Renfro, Dallas, NFL	10	118	0
	Emmitt Thomas, Kansas City, AFL	9	146	1
1968	Dave Grayson, Oakland, AFL	10	195	1
	Willie Williams, N.Y. Giants, NFL	10	103	0
1967	Miller Farr, Houston, AFL	10	264	3
	*Lem Barney, Detroit, NFL	10	232	3
	Tom Janik, Buffalo, AFL	10	222	2
	Dave Whitsell, New Orleans, NFL	10	178	2
	Dick Westmoreland, Miami, AFL	10	127	1
1966	Larry Wilson, St. Louis, NFL	10	180	2
	Johnny Robinson, Kansas City, AFL	10	136	1
	Bobby Hunt, Kansas City, AFL	10	113	0
1965	W.K. Hicks, Houston, AFL	9	156	0
	Bobby Boyd, Baltimore, NFL	9	78	1
1964	Dainard Paulson, N.Y. Jets, AFL	12	157	1
	*Paul Krause, Washington, NFL	12	140	1
1963	Fred Glick, Houston, AFL	12	180	1
	Dick Lynch, N.Y. Giants, NFL	9	251	3
	Roosevelt Taylor, Chicago, NFL	9	172	1
1962	Lee Riley, N.Y. Titans, AFL	11	122	0
	Willie Wood, Green Bay, NFL	9	132	0
1961	Billy Atkins, Buffalo, AFL	10	158	0
	Dick Lynch, N.Y. Giants, NFL	9	60	0
1960	*Austin (Goose) Gonsoulin, Denver, AFL	11	98	0
	Dave Baker, San Francisco, NFL	10	96	0
	Jerry Norton, St. Louis, NFL	10	96	0
1959	Dean Derby, Pittsburgh	7	127	0
	Milt Davis, Baltimore	7	119	1
	Don Shinnick, Baltimore	7	70	0
1958	Jim Patton, N.Y. Giants	11	183	0
1957	Milt Davis, Baltimore	10	219	2
	Jack Christiansen, Detroit	10	137	1
	Jack Butler, Pittsburgh	10	85	0
1956	Linden Crow, Chi. Cardinals	11	170	0
1955	Will Sherman, Los Angeles	11	101	0
1954	Dick (Night Train) Lane, Chi. Cardinals	10	181	0
1953	Jack Christiansen, Detroit	12	238	1

Year	Player, Team	No.	Yards	TD
1952	*Dick (Night Train) Lane, Los Angeles	14	298	2
1951	Otto Schnellbacher, N.Y. Giants	11	194	2
1950	Orban (Spec) Sanders, N.Y. Yanks	13	199	0
1949	Bob Nussbaumer, Chi. Cardinals	12	157	0
1948	*Dan Sandifer, Washington	13	258	2
1947	Frank Reagan, N.Y. Giants	10	203	0
	Frank Seno, Boston	10	100	0
1946	Bill Dudley, Pittsburgh	10	242	1
1945	Roy Zimmerman, Philadelphia	7	90	0
1944	*Howard Livingston, N.Y. Giants	9	172	1
1943	Sammy Baugh, Washington	11	112	0
1942	Clyde (Bulldog) Turner, Chi. Bears	8	96	1
1941	Marshall Goldberg, Chi. Cardinals	7	54	0
	*Art Jones, Pittsburgh	7	35	0
1940	Clarence (Ace) Parker, Brooklyn	6	146	1
	Kent Ryan, Detroit	6	65	0
	Don Hutson, Green Bay	6	24	0

First season of professional football.

ANNUAL PUNTING LEADERS

Year	Player, Team	No.	Avg.	Long
2005	Brian Moorman, Buffalo, AFC	71	45.7	68
	Josh Bidwell, Tampa Bay, NFC	90	45.6	61
2004	Shane Lechler, Oakland, AFC	73	46.7	67
	Tom Tupa, Washington, NFC	103	44.1	61
2003	Shane Lechler, Oakland, AFC	96	46.9	73
	Todd Sauerbrun, Carolina, NFC	77	44.6	64
2002	Todd Sauerbrun, Carolina, NFC	104	44.2	64
	Chris Hanson, Jacksonville, AFC	81	44.2	64
2001	Todd Sauerbrun, Carolina, NFC	93	47.5	73
	Shane Lechler, Oakland, AFC	73	46.2	65
2000	Darren Bennett, San Diego, AFC	92	46.2	66
	Mitch Berger, Minnesota, NFC	62	44.7	60
1999	Tom Rouen, Denver, AFC	84	46.5	65
	Mitch Berger, Minnesota, NFC	61	45.4	75
1998	Craig Hentrich, Tennessee, AFC	69	47.2	71
	Mark Royals, New Orleans, NFC	88	45.6	64
1997	Mark Royals, New Orleans, NFC	88	45.9	66
	Tom Tupa, New England, AFC	78	45.8	73
1996	John Kidd, Miami, AFC	78	46.3	63
	Matt Turk, Washington, NFC	75	45.1	63
1995	Rick Tuten, Seattle, AFC	83	45.0	73
	Sean Landeta, St. Louis, NFC	83	44.3	63
1994	Sean Landeta, L.A. Rams, NFC	78	44.8	62
	Jeff Gossett, L.A. Raiders, AFC	77	43.9	65
1993	Greg Montgomery, Houston, AFC	54	45.6	77
	Jim Arnold, Detroit, NFC	72	44.5	68
1992	Greg Montgomery, Houston, AFC	53	46.9	66
	Harry Newsome, Minnesota, NFC	72	45.0	84
1991	Reggie Roby, Miami, AFC	54	45.7	64
	Harry Newsome, Minnesota, AFC	68	45.5	65
1990	Mike Horan, Denver, AFC	58	44.4	67
	Sean Landeta, N.Y. Giants, NFC	75	44.1	67
1989	Rich Camarillo, Phoenix, NFC	76	43.4	58
	Greg Montgomery, Houston, AFC	56	43.3	63
1988	Harry Newsome, Pittsburgh, AFC	65	45.4	62
	Jim Arnold, Detroit, NFC	97	42.4	69
1987	Rick Donnelly, Atlanta, NFC	61	44.0	62
	Ralf Mojsiejenko, San Diego, AFC	67	42.9	57
1986	Rohn Stark, Indianapolis, AFC	76	45.2	63
	Sean Landeta, N.Y. Giants, NFC	79	44.8	61
1985	Rohn Stark, Indianapolis, AFC	78	45.9	68
	*Rick Donnelly, Atlanta, NFC	59	43.6	68
1984	Jim Arnold, Kansas City, AFC	98	44.9	63
	*Brian Hansen, New Orleans, NFC	69	43.8	66
1983	Rohn Stark, Baltimore, AFC	91	45.3	68
	Frank Garcia, Tampa Bay, NFC	95	42.2	64
1982	Luke Prestridge, Denver, AFC	45	45.0	65
	Carl Birdsong, St. Louis, NFC	54	43.8	65

Year	Player, Team	No.	Avg.	Long
1981	Pat McInally, Cincinnati, AFC	72	45.4	62
	Tom Skladany, Detroit, NFC	64	43.5	74
1980	Dave Jennings, N.Y. Giants, NFC	94	44.8	63
	Luke Prestridge, Denver, AFC	70	43.9	57
1979	*Bob Grupp, Kansas City, AFC	89	43.6	74
	Dave Jennings, N.Y. Giants, NFC	104	42.7	72
1978	Pat McInally, Cincinnati, AFC	91	43.1	65
	*Tom Skladany, Detroit, NFC	86	42.5	63
1977	Ray Guy, Oakland, AFC	59	43.3	74
	Tom Blanchard, New Orleans, NFC	82	42.4	66
1976	Marv Bateman, Buffalo, AFC	86	42.8	78
	John James, Atlanta, NFC	101	42.1	67
1975	Ray Guy, Oakland, AFC	68	43.8	64
	Herman Weaver, Detroit, NFC	80	42.0	61
1974	Ray Guy, Oakland, AFC	74	42.2	66
	Tom Blanchard, New Orleans, NFC	88	42.1	71
1973	Jerrel Wilson, Kansas City, AFC	80	45.5	68
	*Tom Wittum, San Francisco, NFC	79	43.7	62
1972	Jerrel Wilson, Kansas City, AFC	66	44.8	69
	Dave Chapple, Los Angeles, NFC	53	44.2	70
1971	Dave Lewis, Cincinnati, AFC	72	44.8	56
	Tom McNeill, Philadelphia, NFC	73	42.0	64
1970	Dave Lewis, Cincinnati, AFC	79	46.2	63
	*Julian Fagan, New Orleans, NFC	77	42.5	64
1969	David Lee, Baltimore, NFL	57	45.3	66
	Dennis Partee, San Diego, AFL	71	44.6	62
1968	Jerrel Wilson, Kansas City, AFL	63	45.1	70
	Billy Lothridge, Atlanta, NFL	75	44.3	70
1967	Bob Scarpitto, Denver, AFL	105	44.9	73
	Billy Lothridge, Atlanta, NFL	87	43.7	62
1966	Bob Scarpitto, Denver, AFL	76	45.8	70
	*David Lee, Baltimore, NFL	49	45.6	64
1965	Gary Collins, Cleveland, NFL	65	46.7	71
	Jerrel Wilson, Kansas City, AFL	69	45.4	64
1964	Bobby Walden, Minnesota, NFL	72	46.4	73
	Jim Fraser, Denver, AFL	73	44.2	67
1963	Yale Lary, Detroit, NFL	35	48.9	73
	Jim Fraser, Denver, AFL	81	44.4	66
1962	Tommy Davis, San Francisco, NFL	48	45.6	82
	Jim Fraser, Denver, AFL	55	43.6	75
1961	Yale Lary, Detroit, NFL	52	48.4	71
	Billy Atkins, Buffalo, AFL	85	44.5	70
1960	Jerry Norton, St. Louis, NFL	39	45.6	62
	*Paul Maguire, L.A. Chargers, AFL	43	40.5	61
1959	Yale Lary, Detroit	45	47.1	67
1958	Sam Baker, Washington	48	45.4	64
1957	Don Chandler, N.Y. Giants	60	44.6	61
1956	Norm Van Brocklin, Los Angeles	48	43.1	72
1955	Norm Van Brocklin, Los Angeles	60	44.6	61
1954	Pat Brady, Pittsburgh	66	43.2	72
1953	Pat Brady, Pittsburgh	80	46.9	64
1952	Horace Gillom, Cleveland	61	45.7	73
1951	Horace Gillom, Cleveland	73	45.5	66
1950	*Fred (Curly) Morrison, Chi. Bears	57	43.3	65
1949	*Mike Boyda, N.Y. Bulldogs	56	44.2	61
1948	Joe Muha, Philadelphia	57	47.3	82
1947	Jack Jacobs, Green Bay	57	43.5	74
1946	Roy McKay, Green Bay	64	42.7	64
1945	Roy McKay, Green Bay	44	41.2	73
1944	Frank Sinkwich, Detroit	45	41.0	73
1943	Sammy Baugh, Washington	50	45.9	81
1942	Sammy Baugh, Washington	37	48.2	74
1941	Sammy Baugh, Washington	30	48.7	75
1940	Sammy Baugh, Washington	35	51.4	85
1939	*Parker Hall, Cleveland	58	40.8	80

First season of professional football.

ANNUAL LEADERS IN SACKS (SINCE 1982)

Year	Player, Team	Sacks
2005	Derrick Burgess, Oakland, AFC	16.0
	Osi Umenyiora, N.Y. Giants, NFC	14.5
2004	Dwight Freeney, Indianapolis, AFC	16.0
	Bertrand Berry, Arizona, NFC	14.5
2003	Michael Strahan, N.Y. Giants, NFC	18.5
	Adewale Ogunleye, Miami, AFC	15.0
2002	Jason Taylor, Miami, AFC	18.5
	Simeon Rice, Tampa Bay, NFC	15.5
2001	Michael Strahan, N.Y. Giants, NFC	22.5
	Peter Boulware, Baltimore, AFC	15.0
2000	La'Roi Glover, New Orleans, NFC	17.0
	Trace Armstrong, Miami, AFC	16.5
1999	Kevin Carter, St. Louis, NFC	17.0
	*Jevon Kearse, Tennessee, AFC	14.5
1998	Michael Sinclair, Seattle, AFC	16.5
	Reggie White, Green Bay, NFC	16.0
1997	John Randle, Minnesota, NFC	15.5
	Bruce Smith, Buffalo, AFC	14.0
1996	Kevin Greene, Carolina, NFC	14.5
	Michael McCrary, Seattle, AFC	13.5
	Bruce Smith, Buffalo, AFC	13.5
1995	Bryce Paup, Buffalo, AFC	17.5
	William Fuller, Philadelphia, NFC	13.0
	Wayne Martin, New Orleans, NFC	13.0
1994	Kevin Greene, Pittsburgh, AFC	14.0
	Ken Harvey, Washington, NFC	13.5
	John Randle, Minnesota, NFC	13.5
1993	Neil Smith, Kansas City, AFC	15.0
	Renaldo Turnbull, New Orleans, NFC	13.0
	Reggie White, Green Bay, NFC	13.0
1992	Clyde Simmons, Philadelphia, NFC	19.0
	Leslie O'Neal, San Diego, AFC	17.0
1991	Pat Swilling, New Orleans, NFC	17.0
	William Fuller, Houston, AFC	15.0
1990	Derrick Thomas, Kansas City, AFC	20.0
	Charles Haley, San Francisco, NFC	16.0
1989	Chris Doleman, Minnesota, NFC	21.0
	Lee Williams, San Diego, AFC	14.0
1988	Reggie White, Philadelphia, NFC	18.0
	Greg Townsend, L.A. Raiders, AFC	11.5
1987	Reggie White, Philadelphia, NFC	21.0
	Andre Tippett, New England, AFC	12.5
1986	Lawrence Taylor, N.Y. Giants, NFC	20.5
	Sean Jones, L.A. Raiders, AFC	15.5
1985	Richard Dent, Chicago, NFC	17.0
	Andre Tippett, New England, AFC	16.5
1984	Mark Gastineau, N.Y. Jets, AFC	22.0
	Richard Dent, Chicago, NFC	17.5
1983	Mark Gastineau, N.Y. Jets, AFC	19.0
	Fred Dean, San Francisco, NFC	17.5
1982	Doug Martin, Minnesota, NFC	11.5
	Jesse Baker, Houston, AFC	7.5

*First season of professional football.

POINTS SCORED

Year	Team	Points
2005	Seattle, NFC	452
	Indianapolis, AFC	439
2004	Indianapolis, AFC	522
	Green Bay, NFC	424
2003	Kansas City, AFC	484
	St. Louis, NFC	447
2002	Kansas City, AFC	467
	New Orleans, NFC	432
2001	St. Louis, NFC	503
	Indianapolis, AFC	413
2000	St. Louis, NFC	540
	Denver, AFC	485
1999	St. Louis, NFC	526
	Indianapolis, AFC	423
1998	Minnesota, NFC	556
	Denver, AFC	501
1997	Denver, AFC	472
	Green Bay, NFC	422
1996	Green Bay, NFC	456
	New England, AFC	418
1995	San Francisco, NFC	457
	Pittsburgh, AFC	407
1994	San Francisco, NFC	505
	Miami, AFC	389
1993	San Francisco, NFC	473
	Denver, AFC	373
1992	San Francisco, NFC	431
	Buffalo, AFC	381
1991	Washington, NFC	485
	Buffalo, AFC	458
1990	Buffalo, AFC	428
	Philadelphia, NFC	396
1989	San Francisco, NFC	442
	Buffalo, AFC	409
1988	Cincinnati, AFC	448
	L.A. Rams, NFC	407
1987	San Francisco, NFC	459
	Cleveland, AFC	390
1986	Miami, AFC	430
	Minnesota, NFC	398
1985	San Diego, AFC	467
	Chicago, NFC	456
1984	Miami, AFC	513
	San Francisco, NFC	475
1983	Washington, NFC	541
	L.A. Raiders, AFC	442
1982	San Diego, AFC	288
	Dallas, NFC	226
	Green Bay, NFC	226
1981	San Diego, AFC	478
	Atlanta, NFC	426
1980	Dallas, NFC	454
	New England, AFC	441
1979	Pittsburgh, AFC	416
	Dallas, NFC	371
1978	Dallas, NFC	384
	Miami, AFC	372
1977	Oakland, AFC	351
	Dallas, NFC	345
1976	Baltimore, AFC	417
	Los Angeles, NFC	351
1975	Buffalo, AFC	420
	Minnesota, NFC	377
1974	Oakland, AFC	355
	Washington, NFC	320
1973	Los Angeles, NFC	388
	Denver, AFC	354
1972	Miami, AFC	385
	San Francisco, NFC	353
1971	Dallas, NFC	406
	Oakland, AFC	344
1970	San Francisco, NFC	352
	Baltimore, AFC	321
1969	Minnesota, NFL	379
	Oakland, AFL	377
1968	Oakland, AFL	453
	Dallas, NFL	431
1967	Oakland, AFL	468
	Los Angeles, NFL	398
1966	Kansas City, AFL	448
	Dallas, NFL	445

Year	Team	Points
1965	San Francisco, NFL	421
	San Diego, AFL	340
1964	Baltimore, NFL	428
	Buffalo, AFL	400
1963	N.Y. Giants, NFL	448
	San Diego, AFL	399
1962	Green Bay, NFL	415
	Dall. Texans, AFL	389
1961	Houston, AFL	513
	Green Bay, NFL	391
1960	N.Y. Titans, AFL	382
	Cleveland, NFL	362
1959	Baltimore	374
1958	Baltimore	381
1957	Los Angeles	307
1956	Chi. Bears	363
1955	Cleveland	349
1954	Detroit	337
1953	San Francisco	372
1952	Los Angeles	349
1951	Los Angeles	392
1950	Los Angeles	466
1949	Philadelphia	364
1948	Chi. Cardinals	395
1947	Chi. Bears	363
1946	Chi. Bears	289
1945	Philadelphia	272
1944	Philadelphia	267
1943	Chi. Bears	303
1942	Chi. Bears	376
1941	Chi. Bears	396
1940	Washington	245
1939	Chi. Bears	298
1938	Green Bay	223
1937	Green Bay	220
1936	Green Bay	248
1935	Chi. Bears	192
1934	Chi. Bears	286
1933	N.Y. Giants	244
1932	Chi. Bears	160

TOTAL YARDS GAINED

Year	Team	Yards
2005	Kansas City, AFC	6,192
	Seattle, NFC	5,915
2004	Kansas City, AFC	6,695
	Green Bay, NFC	6,357
2003	Minnesota, NFC	6,294
	Kansas City, AFC	5,910
2002	Oakland, AFC	6,237
	Minnesota, NFC	6,192
2001	St. Louis, NFC	6,690
	Indianapolis, AFC	5,955
2000	St. Louis, NFC	7,075
	Denver, AFC	6,554
1999	St. Louis, NFC	6,412
	Indianapolis, AFC	5,726
1998	San Francisco, NFC	6,800
	Denver, AFC	6,092
1997	Denver, AFC	5,872
	Detroit, NFC	5,798
1996	Denver, AFC	5,791
	Philadelphia, NFC	5,627
1995	Detroit, NFC	6,113
	Denver, AFC	6,040
1994	Miami, AFC	6,078
	San Francisco, NFC	6,060
1993	San Francisco, NFC	6,435
	Miami, AFC	5,812

Year	Team	Yards
1992	San Francisco, NFC	6,195
	Buffalo, AFC	5,893
1991	Buffalo, AFC	6,252
	San Francisco, NFC	5,858
1990	Houston, AFC	6,222
	San Francisco, NFC	5,895
1989	San Francisco, NFC	6,268
	Cincinnati, AFC	6,101
1988	Cincinnati, AFC	6,057
	San Francisco, NFC	5,900
1987	San Francisco, NFC	5,987
	Denver, AFC	5,624
1986	Cincinnati, AFC	6,490
	San Francisco, NFC	6,082
1985	San Diego, AFC	6,535
	San Francisco, NFC	5,920
1984	Miami, AFC	6,936
	San Francisco, NFC	6,366
1983	San Diego, AFC	6,197
	Green Bay, NFC	6,172
1982	San Diego, AFC	4,048
	San Francisco, NFC	3,242
1981	San Diego, AFC	6,744
	Detroit, NFC	5,933
1980	San Diego, AFC	6,410
	Los Angeles, NFC	6,006
1979	Pittsburgh, AFC	6,258
	Dallas, NFC	5,968
1978	New England, AFC	5,965
	Dallas, NFC	5,959
1977	Dallas, NFC	4,812
	Oakland, AFC	4,736
1976	Baltimore, AFC	5,236
	St. Louis, NFC	5,136
1975	Buffalo, AFC	5,467
	Dallas, NFC	5,025
1974	Dallas, NFC	4,983
	Oakland, AFC	4,718
1973	Los Angeles, NFC	4,906
	Oakland, AFC	4,773
1972	Miami, AFC	5,036
	N.Y. Giants, NFC	4,483
1971	Dallas, NFC	5,035
	San Diego, AFC	4,738
1970	Oakland, AFC	4,829
	San Francisco, NFC	4,503
1969	Dallas, NFL	5,122
	Oakland, AFL	5,036
1968	Oakland, AFL	5,696
	Dallas, NFL	5,117
1967	N.Y. Jets, AFL	5,152
	Baltimore, NFL	5,008
1966	Dallas, NFL	5,145
	Kansas City, AFL	5,114
1965	San Francisco, NFL	5,270
	San Diego, AFL	5,188
1964	Buffalo, AFL	5,206
	Baltimore, NFL	4,779
1963	San Diego, AFL	5,153
	N.Y. Giants, NFL	5,024
1962	N.Y. Giants, NFL	5,005
	Houston, AFL	4,971
1961	Houston, AFL	6,288
	Philadelphia, NFL	5,112
1960	Houston, AFL	4,936
	Baltimore, NFL	4,245
1959	Baltimore	4,458
1958	Baltimore	4,539
1957	Los Angeles	4,143

Year	Team	Yards	Year	Team	Yards
1956	Chi. Bears	4,537	1985	Chicago, NFC	2,761
1955	Chi. Bears	4,316		Indianapolis, AFC	2,439
1954	Los Angeles	5,187	1984	Chicago, NFC	2,974
1953	Philadelphia	4,811		N.Y. Jets, AFC	2,189
1952	Cleveland	4,352	1983	Chicago, NFC	2,727
1951	Los Angeles	5,506		Baltimore, AFC	2,695
1950	Los Angeles	5,420	1982	Buffalo, AFC	1,371
1949	Chi. Bears	4,873		Dallas, NFC	1,313
1948	Chi. Cardinals	4,705	1981	Detroit, NFC	2,795
1947	Chi. Bears	5,053		Kansas City, AFC	2,633
1946	Los Angeles	3,703	1980	Los Angeles, NFC	2,799
1945	Washington	3,549		Houston, AFC	2,635
1944	Chi. Bears	3,239	1979	N.Y. Jets, AFC	2,646
1943	Chi. Bears	4,045		St. Louis, NFC	2,582
1942	Chi. Bears	3,900	1978	New England, AFC	3,165
1941	Chi. Bears	4,265		Dallas, NFC	2,783
1940	Green Bay	3,400	1977	Chicago, NFC	2,811
1939	Chi. Bears	3,988		Oakland, AFC	2,627
1938	Green Bay	3,037	1976	Pittsburgh, AFC	2,971
1937	Green Bay	3,201		Los Angeles, NFC	2,528
1936	Detroit	3,703	1975	Buffalo, AFC	2,974
1935	Chi. Bears	3,454		Dallas, NFC	2,432
1934	Chi. Bears	3,900	1974	Dallas, NFC	2,454
1933	N.Y. Giants	2,973		Pittsburgh, AFC	2,417
1932	Chi. Bears	2,755	1973	Buffalo, AFC	3,088
				Los Angeles, NFC	2,925

YARDS RUSHING

Year	Team	Yards	Year	Team	Yards
2005	Atlanta, NFC	2,546	1972	Miami, AFC	2,960
	Denver, AFC	2,539		Chicago, NFC	2,360
2004	Atlanta, NFC	2,672	1971	Miami, AFC	2,429
	Pittsburgh, AFC	2,464		Detroit, NFC	2,376
2003	Baltimore, AFC	2,674	1970	Dallas, NFC	2,300
	Green Bay, NFC	2,558		Miami, AFC	2,082
2002	Minnesota, NFC	2,507	1969	Dallas, NFL	2,276
	Miami, AFC	2,502		Kansas City, AFL	2,220
2001	Pittsburgh, AFC	2,774	1968	Chicago, NFL	2,377
	San Francisco, NFC	2,244		Kansas City, AFL	2,227
2000	Oakland, AFC	2,470	1967	Cleveland, NFL	2,139
	Minnesota, NFC	2,129		Houston, AFL	2,122
1999	San Francisco, NFC	2,095	1966	Kansas City, AFL	2,274
	Jacksonville, AFC	2,091		Cleveland, NFL	2,166
1998	San Francisco, NFC	2,544	1965	Cleveland, NFL	2,331
	Denver, AFC	2,468		San Diego, AFL	2,085
1997	Pittsburgh, AFC	2,479	1964	Green Bay, NFL	2,276
	Detroit, NFC	2,464		Buffalo, AFL	2,040
1996	Denver, AFC	2,362	1963	Cleveland, NFL	2,639
	Washington, NFC	1,910		San Diego, AFL	2,203
1995	Kansas City, AFC	2,222	1962	Buffalo, AFL	2,480
	Dallas, NFC	2,201		Green Bay, NFL	2,460
1994	Pittsburgh, AFC	2,180	1961	Green Bay, NFL	2,350
	Detroit, NFC	2,080		Dall. Texans, AFL	2,189
1993	N.Y. Giants, NFC	2,210	1960	St. Louis, NFL	2,356
	Seattle, AFC	2,015		Oakland, AFL	2,056
1992	Buffalo, AFC	2,436	1959	Cleveland	2,149
	Philadelphia, NFC	2,388	1958	Cleveland	2,526
1991	Buffalo, AFC	2,381	1957	Los Angeles	2,142
	Minnesota, NFC	2,201	1956	Chi. Bears	2,468
1990	Philadelphia, NFC	2,556	1955	Chi. Bears	2,388
	San Diego, AFC	2,257	1954	San Francisco	2,498
1989	Cincinnati, AFC	2,483	1953	San Francisco	2,230
	Chicago, NFC	2,287	1952	San Francisco	1,905
1988	Cincinnati, AFC	2,710	1951	Chi. Bears	2,408
	San Francisco, NFC	2,523	1950	N.Y. Giants	2,336
1987	San Francisco, NFC	2,237	1949	Philadelphia	2,607
	L.A. Raiders, AFC	2,197	1948	Chi. Cardinals	2,560
1986	Chicago, NFC	2,700	1947	Los Angeles	2,171
	Cincinnati, AFC	2,533	1946	Green Bay	1,765
			1945	Cleveland	1,714
			1944	Philadelphia	1,661
			1943	Phil-Pitt	1,730

Year	Team	Yards
1942	Chi. Bears	1,881
1941	Chi. Bears	2,263
1940	Chi. Bears	1,818
1939	Chi. Bears	2,043
1938	Detroit	1,893
1937	Detroit	2,074
1936	Detroit	2,885
1935	Chi. Bears	2,096
1934	Chi. Bears	2,847
1933	Boston	2,260
1932	Chi. Bears	1,770

YARDS PASSING

Leadership in this category has been based on net yards since 1952.

Year	Team	Yards
2005	Arizona, NFC	4,437
	New England, AFC	4,120
2004	Indianapolis, AFC	4,623
	Minnesota, NFC	4,516
2003	Indianapolis, AFC	4,179
	St. Louis, NFC	3,961
2002	Oakland, AFC	4,475
	St. Louis, NFC	4,154
2001	St. Louis, NFC	4,663
	Indianapolis, AFC	3,989
2000	St. Louis, NFC	5,232
	Indianapolis, AFC	4,282
1999	St. Louis, NFC	4,353
	Indianapolis, AFC	4,066
1998	Minnesota, NFC	4,328
	N.Y. Jets, AFC	3,836
1997	Seattle, AFC	3,959
	Green Bay, NFC	3,705
1996	Jacksonville, AFC	4,110
	Philadelphia, AFC	3,745
1995	San Francisco, NFC	4,608
	Miami, AFC	4,210
1994	New England, AFC	4,444
	Minnesota, NFC	4,324
1993	Miami, AFC	4,353
	San Francisco, NFC	4,302
1992	Houston, AFC	4,029
	San Francisco, NFC	3,880
1991	Houston, AFC	4,621
	San Francisco, NFC	3,997
1990	Houston, AFC	4,805
	San Francisco, NFC	4,177
1989	Washington, NFC	4,349
	Miami, AFC	4,216
1988	Miami, AFC	4,516
	Washington, NFC	4,136
1987	Miami, AFC	3,876
	San Francisco, NFC	3,750
1986	Miami, AFC	4,779
	San Francisco, NFC	4,096
1985	San Diego, AFC	4,870
	Dallas, NFC	3,861
1984	Miami, AFC	5,018
	St. Louis, NFC	4,257
1983	San Diego, AFC	4,661
	Green Bay, NFC	4,365
1982	San Diego, AFC	2,927
	San Francisco, NFC	2,502
1981	San Diego, AFC	4,739
	Minnesota, NFC	4,333
1980	San Diego, AFC	4,531
	Minnesota, NFC	3,688

Year	Team	Yards
1979	San Diego, AFC	3,915
	San Francisco, NFC	3,641
1978	San Diego, AFC	3,375
	Minnesota, NFC	3,243
1977	Buffalo, AFC	2,530
	St. Louis, NFC	2,499
1976	Baltimore, AFC	2,933
	Minnesota, NFC	2,855
1975	Cincinnati, AFC	3,241
	Washington, NFC	2,917
1974	Washington, NFC	2,978
	Cincinnati, AFC	2,804
1973	Philadelphia, NFC	2,998
	Denver, AFC	2,519
1972	N.Y. Jets, AFC	2,777
	San Francisco, NFC	2,735
1971	San Diego, AFC	3,134
	Dallas, NFC	2,786
1970	San Francisco, NFC	2,923
	Oakland, AFC	2,865
1969	Oakland, AFL	3,271
	San Francisco, NFL	3,158
1968	San Diego, AFL	3,623
	Dallas, NFL	3,026
1967	N.Y. Jets, AFL	3,845
	Washington, NFL	3,730
1966	N.Y. Jets, AFL	3,464
	Dallas, NFL	3,023
1965	San Francisco, NFL	3,487
	San Diego, AFL	3,103
1964	Houston, AFL	3,527
	Chicago, NFL	2,841
1963	Baltimore, NFL	3,296
	Houston, AFL	3,222
1962	Denver, AFL	3,404
	Philadelphia, NFL	3,385
1961	Houston, AFL	4,392
	Philadelphia, NFL	3,605
1960	Houston, AFL	3,203
	Baltimore, NFL	2,956
1959	Baltimore	2,753
1958	Pittsburgh	2,752
1957	Baltimore	2,388
1956	Los Angeles	2,419
1955	Philadelphia	2,472
1954	Chi. Bears	3,104
1953	Philadelphia	3,089
1952	Cleveland	2,566
1951	Los Angeles	3,296
1950	Los Angeles	3,709
1949	Chi. Bears	3,055
1948	Washington	2,861
1947	Washington	3,336
1946	Los Angeles	2,080
1945	Chi. Bears	1,857
1944	Washington	2,021
1943	Chi. Bears	2,310
1942	Green Bay	2,407
1941	Chi. Bears	2,002
1940	Washington	1,887
1939	Chi. Bears	1,965
1938	Washington	1,536
1937	Green Bay	1,398
1936	Green Bay	1,629
1935	Green Bay	1,449
1934	Green Bay	1,165
1933	N.Y. Giants	1,348
1932	Chi. Bears	1,013

FEWEST POINTS ALLOWED

Year	Team	Points
2005	Chicago, NFC	202
	Indianapolis, AFC	247
2004	Pittsburgh, AFC	251
	Philadelphia, NFC	260
2003	New England, AFC	238
	Dallas, NFC	260
2002	Tampa Bay, NFC	196
	Miami, AFC	301
2001	Chicago, NFC	203
	Pittsburgh, AFC	212
2000	Baltimore, AFC	165
	Philadelphia, NFC	245
1999	Jacksonville, AFC	217
	Tampa Bay, NFC	235
1998	Miami, AFC	265
	Dallas, NFC	275
1997	Kansas City, AFC	232
	Tampa Bay, NFC	263
1996	Green Bay, NFC	210
	Pittsburgh, AFC	257
1995	Kansas City, AFC	241
	San Francisco, NFC	258
1994	Cleveland, AFC	204
	Dallas, NFC	248
1993	N.Y. Giants, NFC	205
	Houston, AFC	238
1992	New Orleans, NFC	202
	Pittsburgh, AFC	225
1991	New Orleans, NFC	211
	Denver, AFC	235
1990	N.Y. Giants, NFC	211
	Pittsburgh, AFC	240
1989	Denver, AFC	226
	N.Y. Giants, NFC	252
1988	Chicago, NFC	215
	Buffalo, AFC	237
1987	Indianapolis, AFC	238
	San Francisco, NFC	253
1986	Chicago, NFC	187
	Seattle, AFC	293
1985	Chicago, NFC	198
	N.Y. Jets, AFC	264
1984	San Francisco, NFC	227
	Denver, AFC	241
1983	Miami, AFC	250
	Detroit, NFC	286
1982	Washington, NFC	128
	Miami, AFC	131
1981	Philadelphia, NFC	221
	Miami, AFC	275
1980	Philadelphia, NFC	222
	Houston, AFC	251
1979	Tampa Bay, NFC	237
	San Diego, AFC	246
1978	Pittsburgh, AFC	195
	Dallas, NFC	208
1977	Atlanta, NFC	129
	Denver, AFC	148
1976	Pittsburgh, AFC	138
	Minnesota, NFC	176
1975	Los Angeles, NFC	135
	Pittsburgh, AFC	162
1974	Los Angeles, NFC	181
	Pittsburgh, AFC	189
1973	Miami, AFC	150
	Minnesota, NFC	168
1972	Miami, AFC	171
	Washington, NFC	218

Year	Team	Points
1971	Minnesota, NFC	139
	Baltimore, AFC	140
1970	Minnesota, NFC	143
	Miami, AFC	228
1969	Minnesota, NFL	133
	Kansas City, AFL	177
1968	Baltimore, NFL	144
	Kansas City, AFL	170
1967	Los Angeles, NFL	196
	Houston, AFL	199
1966	Green Bay, NFL	163
	Buffalo, AFL	255
1965	Green Bay, NFL	224
	Buffalo, AFL	226
1964	Baltimore, NFL	225
	Buffalo, AFL	242
1963	Chicago, NFL	144
	San Diego, AFL	255
1962	Green Bay, NFL	148
	Dall. Texans, AFL	233
1961	San Diego, AFL	219
	N.Y. Giants, NFL	220
1960	San Francisco, NFL	205
	Dall. Texans, AFL	253
1959	N.Y. Giants	170
1958	N.Y. Giants	183
1957	Cleveland	172
1956	Cleveland	177
1955	Cleveland	218
1954	Cleveland	162
1953	Cleveland	162
1952	Detroit	192
1951	Cleveland	152
1950	Philadelphia	141
1949	Philadelphia	134
1948	Chi. Bears	151
1947	Green Bay	210
1946	Pittsburgh	117
1945	Washington	121
1944	N.Y. Giants	75
1943	Washington	137
1942	Chi. Bears	84
1941	N.Y. Giants	114
1940	Brooklyn	120
1939	N.Y. Giants	85
1938	N.Y. Giants	79
1937	Chi. Bears	100
1936	Chi. Bears	94
1935	Green Bay	96
	N.Y. Giants	96
1934	Detroit	59
1933	Brooklyn	54
1932	Chi. Bears	44

FEWEST TOTAL YARDS ALLOWED

Year	Team	Yards
2005	Tampa Bay, NFC	4,444
	Pittsburgh, AFC	4,544
2004	Pittsburgh, AFC	4,134
	Washington, NFC	4,281
2003	Dallas, NFC	4,056
	Buffalo, AFC	4,313
2002	Tampa Bay, NFC	4,044
	Miami, AFC	4,656
2001	Pittsburgh, AFC	4,137
	St. Louis, NFC	4,471
2000	Tennessee, AFC	3,813
	Washington, NFC	4,474

Year	Team	Yards
1999	Buffalo, AFC	4,045
	Tampa Bay, NFC	4,280
1998	San Diego, AFC	4,208
	Tampa Bay, NFC	4,345
1997	San Francisco, NFC	4,013
	Denver, AFC	4,671
1996	Green Bay, NFC	4,156
	Pittsburgh, AFC	4,362
1995	San Francisco, NFC	4,398
	Kansas City, AFC	4,549
1994	Dallas, NFC	4,313
	Pittsburgh, AFC	4,326
1993	Minnesota, NFC	4,406
	Pittsburgh, AFC	4,531
1992	Dallas, NFC	3,931
	Houston, AFC	4,211
1991	Philadelphia, NFC	3,549
	Denver, AFC	4,549
1990	Pittsburgh, AFC	4,115
	N.Y. Giants, NFC	4,206
1989	Minnesota, NFC	4,184
	Kansas City, AFC	4,293
1988	Minnesota, NFC	4,091
	Buffalo, AFC	4,578
1987	San Francisco, NFC	4,095
	Cleveland, AFC	4,264
1986	Chicago, NFC	4,130
	L.A. Raiders, AFC	4,804
1985	Chicago, NFC	4,135
	L.A. Raiders, AFC	4,603
1984	Chicago, NFC	3,863
	Cleveland, AFC	4,641
1983	Cincinnati, AFC	4,327
	New Orleans, NFC	4,691
1982	Miami, AFC	2,312
	Tampa Bay, NFC	2,442
1981	Philadelphia, NFC	4,447
	N.Y. Jets, AFC	4,871
1980	Buffalo, AFC	4,101
	Philadelphia, NFC	4,443
1979	Tampa Bay, NFC	3,949
	Pittsburgh, AFC	4,270
1978	Los Angeles, NFC	3,893
	Pittsburgh, AFC	4,168
1977	Dallas, NFC	3,213
	New England, AFC	3,638
1976	Pittsburgh, AFC	3,323
	San Francisco, NFC	3,562
1975	Minnesota, NFC	3,153
	Oakland, AFC	3,629
1974	Pittsburgh, AFC	3,074
	Washington, NFC	3,285
1973	Los Angeles, NFC	2,951
	Oakland, AFC	3,160
1972	Miami, AFC	3,297
	Green Bay, NFC	3,474
1971	Baltimore, AFC	2,852
	Minnesota, NFC	3,406
1970	Minnesota, NFC	2,803
	N.Y. Jets, AFC	3,655
1969	Minnesota, NFL	2,720
	Kansas City, AFL	3,163
1968	Los Angeles, NFL	3,118
	N.Y. Jets, AFL	3,363
1967	Oakland, AFL	3,294
	Green Bay, NFL	3,300
1966	St. Louis, NFL	3,492
	Oakland, AFL	3,910
1965	San Diego, AFL	3,262
	Detroit, NFL	3,557
1964	Green Bay, NFL	3,179
	Buffalo, AFL	3,878
1963	Chicago, NFL	3,176
	Boston, AFL	3,834
1962	Detroit, NFL	3,217
	Dall. Texans, AFL	3,951
1961	San Diego, AFL	3,726
	Baltimore, NFL	3,782
1960	St. Louis, NFL	3,029
	Buffalo, AFL	3,866
1959	N.Y. Giants	2,843
1958	Chi. Bears	3,066
1957	Pittsburgh	2,791
1956	N.Y. Giants	3,081
1955	Cleveland	2,841
1954	Cleveland	2,658
1953	Philadelphia	2,998
1952	Cleveland	3,075
1951	N.Y. Giants	3,250
1950	Cleveland	3,154
1949	Philadelphia	2,831
1948	Chi. Bears	2,931
1947	Green Bay	3,396
1946	Washington	2,451
1945	Philadelphia	2,073
1944	Philadelphia	1,943
1943	Chi. Bears	2,262
1942	Chi. Bears	1,703
1941	N.Y. Giants	2,368
1940	N.Y. Giants	2,219
1939	Washington	2,116
1938	N.Y. Giants	2,029
1937	Washington	2,123
1936	Boston	2,181
1935	Boston	1,996
1934	Chi. Cardinals	1,539
1933	Brooklyn	1,789

FEWEST RUSHING YARDS ALLOWED

Year	Team	Yards
2005	San Diego, AFC	1,349
	Carolina, NFC	1,465
2004	Pittsburgh, AFC	1,299
	Washington, NFC	1,304
2003	Tennessee, AFC	1,295
	Dallas, NFC	1,425
2002	Pittsburgh, AFC	1,375
	Tampa Bay, NFC	1,554
2001	Pittsburgh, AFC	1,195
	Chicago, NFC	1,313
2000	Baltimore, AFC	970
	N.Y. Giants, NFC	1,156
1999	St. Louis, NFC	1,189
	Baltimore, AFC	1,231
1998	San Diego, AFC	1,140
	Atlanta, NFC	1,203
1997	Pittsburgh, AFC	1,318
	San Francisco, NFC	1,366
1996	Denver, AFC	1,331
	Green Bay, NFC	1,416
1995	San Francisco, NFC	1,061
	Pittsburgh, AFC	1,321
1994	Minnesota, NFC	1,090
	San Diego, AFC	1,404
1993	Houston, AFC	1,273
	Minnesota, NFC	1,536

Year	Team	Yards
1992	Dallas, NFC	1,244
	Buffalo, AFC	1,395
	San Diego, AFC	1,395
1991	Philadelphia, NFC	1,136
	N.Y. Jets, AFC	1,442
1990	Philadelphia, NFC	1,169
	San Diego, AFC	1,515
1989	New Orleans, NFC	1,326
	Denver, AFC	1,580
1988	Chicago, NFC	1,326
	Houston, AFC	1,592
1987	Chicago, NFC	1,413
	Cleveland, AFC	1,433
1986	N.Y. Giants, NFC	1,284
	Denver, AFC	1,651
1985	Chicago, NFC	1,319
	N.Y. Jets, AFC	1,516
1984	Chicago, NFC	1,377
	Pittsburgh, AFC	1,617
1983	Washington, NFC	1,289
	Cincinnati, AFC	1,499
1982	Pittsburgh, AFC	762
	Detroit, NFC	854
1981	Detroit, NFC	1,623
	Kansas City, AFC	1,747
1980	Detroit, NFC	1,599
	Cincinnati, AFC	1,680
1979	Denver, AFC	1,693
	Tampa Bay, NFC	1,873
1978	Dallas, NFC	1,721
	Pittsburgh, AFC	1,774
1977	Denver, AFC	1,531
	Dallas, NFC	1,651
1976	Pittsburgh, AFC	1,457
	Los Angeles, NFC	1,564
1975	Minnesota, NFC	1,532
	Houston, AFC	1,680
1974	Los Angeles, NFC	1,302
	New England, AFC	1,587
1973	Los Angeles, NFC	1,270
	Oakland, AFC	1,470
1972	Dallas, NFC	1,515
	Miami, AFC	1,548
1971	Baltimore, AFC	1,113
	Dallas, NFC	1,144
1970	Detroit, NFC	1,152
	N.Y. Jets, AFC	1,283
1969	Dallas, NFL	1,050
	Kansas City, AFL	1,091
1968	Dallas, NFL	1,195
	N.Y. Jets, AFL	1,195
1967	Dallas, NFL	1,081
	Oakland, AFL	1,129
1966	Buffalo, AFL	1,051
	Dallas, NFL	1,176
1965	San Diego, AFL	1,094
	Los Angeles, NFL	1,409
1964	Buffalo, AFL	913
	Los Angeles, NFL	1,501
1963	Boston, AFL	1,107
	Chicago, NFL	1,442
1962	Detroit, NFL	1,231
	Dall. Texans, AFL	1,250
1961	Boston, AFL	1,041
	Pittsburgh, NFL	1,463
1960	St. Louis, NFL	1,212
	Dall. Texans, AFL	1,338
1959	N.Y. Giants	1,261
1958	Baltimore	1,291

Year	Team	Yards
1957	Baltimore	1,174
1956	N.Y. Giants	1,443
1955	Cleveland	1,189
1954	Cleveland	1,050
1953	Philadelphia	1,117
1952	Detroit	1,145
1951	N.Y. Giants	913
1950	Detroit	1,367
1949	Chi. Bears	1,196
1948	Philadelphia	1,209
1947	Philadelphia	1,329
1946	Chi. Bears	1,060
1945	Philadelphia	817
1944	Philadelphia	558
1943	Phil-Pitt	793
1942	Chi. Bears	519
1941	Washington	1,042
1940	N.Y. Giants	977
1939	Chi. Bears	812
1938	Detroit	1,081
1937	Chi. Bears	933
1936	Boston	1,148
1935	Boston	998
1934	Chi. Cardinals	954
1933	Brooklyn	964

FEWEST PASSING YARDS ALLOWED

Leadership in this category has been based on net yards since 1952.

Year	Team	Yards
2005	Green Bay, NFC	2,680
	N.Y. Jets, AFC	2,755
2004	Tampa Bay, NFC	2,579
	Miami, AFC	2,592
2003	Dallas, NFC	2,631
	Buffalo, AFC	2,707
2002	Tampa Bay, NFC	2,490
	Indianapolis, AFC	2,917
2001	Miami, AFC	2,829
	Philadelphia, NFC	2,864
2000	Tennessee, AFC	2,423
	Washington, NFC	2,621
1999	Buffalo, AFC	2,675
	Tampa Bay, NFC	2,873
1998	Philadelphia, NFC	2,720
	Oakland, AFC	2,876
1997	Dallas, NFC	2,522
	Indianapolis, AFC	2,820
1996	Green Bay, NFC	2,740
	Pittsburgh, AFC	2,947
1995	N.Y. Jets, AFC	2,740
	Philadelphia, NFC	2,816
1994	Dallas, NFC	2,752
	Houston, AFC	2,795
1993	New Orleans, NFC	2,606
	Cincinnati, AFC	2,798
1992	New Orleans, NFC	2,470
	Kansas City, AFC	2,537
1991	Philadelphia, AFC	2,413
	Denver, AFC	2,755
1990	Pittsburgh, AFC	2,500
	Dallas, NFC	2,639
1989	Minnesota, NFC	2,501
	Kansas City, AFC	2,527
1988	Kansas City, AFC	2,434
	Minnesota, NFC	2,489
1987	San Francisco, NFC	2,484
	L.A. Raiders, AFC	2,727

YEARLY STATISTICAL LEADERS

Year	Team	Yards
1986	St. Louis, NFC	2,637
	New England, AFC	2,978
1985	Washington, NFC	2,746
	Pittsburgh, AFC	2,783
1984	New Orleans, NFC	2,453
	Cleveland, AFC	2,696
1983	New Orleans, NFC	2,691
	Cincinnati, AFC	2,828
1982	Miami, AFC	1,027
	Tampa Bay, NFC	1,384
1981	Philadelphia, NFC	2,696
	Buffalo, AFC	2,870
1980	Washington, NFC	2,171
	Buffalo, AFC	2,282
1979	Tampa Bay, NFC	2,076
	Buffalo, AFC	2,530
1978	Buffalo, AFC	1,960
	Los Angeles, NFC	2,048
1977	Atlanta, NFC	1,384
	San Diego, AFC	1,725
1976	Minnesota, NFC	1,575
	Cincinnati, AFC	1,758
1975	Minnesota, NFC	1,621
	Cincinnati, AFC	1,729
1974	Pittsburgh, AFC	1,466
	Atlanta, NFC	1,572
1973	Miami, AFC	1,290
	Atlanta, NFC	1,430
1972	Minnesota, NFC	1,699
	Cleveland, AFC	1,736
1971	Atlanta, NFC	1,638
	Baltimore, AFC	1,739
1970	Minnesota, NFC	1,438
	Kansas City, AFC	2,010
1969	Minnesota, NFL	1,631
	Kansas City, AFL	2,072
1968	Houston, AFL	1,671
	Green Bay, NFL	1,796
1967	Green Bay, NFL	1,377
	Buffalo, AFL	1,825
1966	Green Bay, NFL	1,959
	Oakland, AFL	2,118
1965	Green Bay, NFL	1,981
	San Diego, AFL	2,168
1964	Green Bay, NFL	1,647
	San Diego, AFL	2,518
1963	Chicago, NFL	1,734
	Oakland, AFL	2,589
1962	Green Bay, NFL	1,746
	Oakland, AFL	2,306
1961	Baltimore, NFL	1,913
	San Diego, AFL	2,363
1960	Chicago, NFL	1,388
	Buffalo, AFL	2,124
1959	N.Y. Giants	1,582
1958	Chi. Bears	1,769
1957	Cleveland	1,300
1956	Cleveland	1,103
1955	Pittsburgh	1,295
1954	Cleveland	1,608
1953	Washington	1,751
1952	Washington	1,580
1951	Pittsburgh	1,687
1950	Cleveland	1,581
1949	Philadelphia	1,607
1948	Green Bay	1,626
1947	Green Bay	1,790
1946	Pittsburgh	939
1945	Washington	1,121

Year	Team	Yards
1944	Chi. Bears	1,052
1943	Chi. Bears	980
1942	Washington	1,093
1941	Pittsburgh	1,168
1940	Philadelphia	1,012
1939	Washington	1,116
1938	Chi. Bears	897
1937	Detroit	804
1936	Philadelphia	853
1935	Chi. Cardinals	793
1934	Philadelphia	545
1933	Portsmouth	558

1,000 YARDS RUSHING IN A SEASON

Year	Player, Team	Att.	Yards	Avg.	Long	TD
2005	Shaun Alexander, Seattle[5]	370	1,880	5.1	88	27
	Tiki Barber, N.Y. Giants[5]	357	1,860	5.2	95	9
	Larry Johnson, Kansas City	336	1,750	5.2	49	20
	Clinton Portis, Washington[4]	352	1,516	4.3	47	11
	Edgerrin James, Indianapolis[5]	360	1,506	4.2	33	13
	LaDainian Tomlinson, San Diego[5]	339	1,462	4.3	62	18
	Rudi Johnson, Cincinnati[2]	337	1,458	4.3	33	12
	Warrick Dunn, Atlanta[4]	280	1,416	5.1	65	3
	Thomas Jones, Chicago	314	1,335	4.3	42	9
	Willis McGahee, Buffalo[2]	325	1,247	3.8	27	5
	Reuben Droughns, Cleveland[2]	309	1,232	4.0	75	2
	Willie Parker, Pittsburgh	255	1,202	4.7	80	4
	*Carnell Williams, Tampa Bay	290	1,178	4.1	71	6
	Steven Jackson, St. Louis	254	1,046	4.1	51	8
	LaMont Jordan, Oakland	272	1,025	3.8	26	9
	Mike Anderson, Denver[2]	239	1,014	4.2	44	12
2004	Curtis Martin, N.Y. Jets[10]	371	1,697	4.6	25	12
	Shaun Alexander, Seattle[4]	353	1,696	4.8	44	16
	Corey Dillon, New England[7]	345	1,635	4.7	44	12
	Edgerrin James, Indianapolis[4]	334	1,548	4.6	40	9
	Tiki Barber, N.Y. Giants[4]	322	1,518	4.7	72	13
	Rudi Johnson, Cincinnati	361	1,454	4.0	52	12
	LaDainian Tomlinson, San Diego[4]	339	1,335	3.9	42	17
	Clinton Portis, Washington[3]	343	1,315	3.8	64	5
	Reuben Droughns, Denver	275	1,240	4.5	51	6
	Fred Taylor, Jacksonville[5]	260	1,224	4.7	46	2
	Domanick Davis, Houston[2]	302	1,188	3.9	44	13
	Ahman Green, Green Bay[6]	259	1,163	4.5	90	7
	*Kevin Jones, Detroit	241	1,133	4.7	74	5
	Willis McGahee, Buffalo	284	1,128	4.0	41	13
	Warrick Dunn, Atlanta[3]	265	1,106	4.2	60	9
	Deuce McAllister, New Orleans[3]	269	1,074	4.0	71	9
	Chris Brown, Tennessee	220	1,067	4.9	52	6
	Jamal Lewis, Baltimore[4]	235	1,006	4.3	75	7
2003	Jamal Lewis, Baltimore[3]	387	2,066	5.3	82	14
	Ahman Green, Green Bay[4]	355	1,883	5.3	98	15
	LaDainian Tomlinson, San Diego[3]	313	1,645	5.3	73	13
	Deuce McAllister, New Orleans[2]	351	1,641	4.7	76	8
	Clinton Portis, Denver[2]	290	1,591	5.5	65	14
	Fred Taylor, Jacksonville[4]	345	1,572	4.6	62	6
	Stephen Davis, Carolina[4]	318	1,444	4.5	40	8
	Shaun Alexander, Seattle[3]	326	1,435	4.4	55	14
	Priest Holmes, Kansas City[4]	320	1,420	4.4	31	27
	Ricky Williams, Miami[4]	392	1,372	3.5	45	9
	Travis Henry, Buffalo[2]	331	1,356	4.1	64	10
	Curtis Martin, N.Y. Jets[9]	323	1,308	4.1	56	2
	Edgerrin James, Indianapolis[3]	310	1,259	4.1	43	11
	Tiki Barber, N.Y. Giants[3]	278	1,216	4.4	27	2
	*Domanick Davis, Houston	238	1,031	4.3	51	8
	Eddie George, Tennessee[7]	312	1,031	3.3	27	5
	Kevan Barlow, San Francisco	201	1,024	5.1	78	6
	Anthony Thomas, Chicago[2]	244	1,024	4.2	67	6
2002	Ricky Williams, Miami[3]	383	1,853	4.8	63	16
	LaDainian Tomlinson, San Diego[2]	372	1,683	4.5	76	14
	Priest Holmes, Kansas City[3]	313	1,615	5.2	56	21
	*Clinton Portis, Denver	273	1,508	5.5	59	15
	Travis Henry, Buffalo	325	1,438	4.4	34	13
	Deuce McAllister, New Orleans	325	1,388	4.3	62	13
	Tiki Barber, N.Y. Giants[2]	304	1,387	4.6	70	11
	Jamal Lewis, Baltimore[2]	308	1,327	4.3	75	6
	Fred Taylor, Jacksonville[3]	287	1,314	4.6	63	8
	Corey Dillon, Cincinnati[6]	314	1,311	4.2	67	7
	Michael Bennett, Minnesota	255	1,296	5.1	85	5
	Ahman Green, Green Bay[3]	286	1,240	4.3	43	7
	Shaun Alexander, Seattle[2]	295	1,175	4.0	88	16
	Eddie George, Tennessee[6]	343	1,165	3.4	35	12
	Curtis Martin, N.Y. Jets[8]	261	1,094	4.2	35	7
	Duce Staley, Philadelphia[3]	269	1,029	3.8	57	5

Year	Player, Team	Att.	Yards	Avg.	Long	TD
	James Stewart, Detroit[2]	231	1,021	4.4	56	4
2001	Priest Holmes, Kansas City[2]	327	1,555	4.8	41	8
	Curtis Martin, N.Y. Jets[7]	333	1,513	4.5	47	10
	Stephen Davis, Washington[3]	356	1,432	4.0	32	5
	Ahman Green, Green Bay[2]	304	1,387	4.6	83	9
	Marshall Faulk, St. Louis[7]	260	1,382	5.3	71	12
	Shaun Alexander, Seattle	309	1,318	4.3	88	14
	Corey Dillon, Cincinnati[5]	340	1,315	3.9	96	10
	Ricky Williams, New Orleans[2]	313	1,245	4.0	46	6
	*LaDainian Tomlinson, San Diego	339	1,236	3.6	54	10
	Garrison Hearst, San Francisco[4]	252	1,206	4.8	43	4
	*Anthony Thomas, Chicago	278	1,183	4.3	46	7
	Antowain Smith, New England[2]	287	1,157	4.0	44	12
	*Dominic Rhodes, Indianapolis	233	1,104	4.7	77	9
	Jerome Bettis, Pittsburgh[8]	225	1,072	4.8	48	4
	Emmitt Smith, Dallas[11]	261	1,021	3.9	44	3
2000	Edgerrin James, Indianapolis[2]	387	1,709	4.4	30	13
	Robert Smith, Minnesota[4]	295	1,521	5.2	72	7
	Eddie George, Tennessee[5]	403	1,509	3.7	35	14
	*Mike Anderson, Denver	297	1,487	5.0	80	15
	Corey Dillon, Cincinnati[4]	315	1,435	4.6	80	7
	Fred Taylor, Jacksonville[2]	292	1,399	4.8	71	12
	*Jamal Lewis, Baltimore	309	1,364	4.4	45	6
	Marshall Faulk, St. Louis[6]	253	1,359	5.4	36	18
	Jerome Bettis, Pittsburgh[7]	355	1,341	3.8	30	8
	Stephen Davis, Washington[2]	332	1,318	4.0	50	11
	Ricky Watters, Seattle[7]	278	1,242	4.5	55	7
	Curtis Martin, N.Y. Jets[6]	316	1,204	3.8	55	9
	Emmitt Smith, Dallas[10]	294	1,203	4.1	52	9
	James Stewart, Detroit	339	1,184	3.5	34	10
	Ahman Green, Green Bay	263	1,175	4.5	39	10
	Charlie Garner, San Francisco[2]	258	1,142	4.4	42	7
	Lamar Smith, Miami	309	1,139	3.7	68	14
	Warrick Dunn, Tampa Bay[2]	248	1,133	4.6	70	8
	James Allen, Chicago	290	1,120	3.9	29	2
	Tyrone Wheatley, Oakland	232	1,046	4.5	80	9
	Jamal Anderson, Atlanta[4]	282	1,024	3.6	42	6
	Tiki Barber, N.Y. Giants	213	1,006	4.7	78	8
	Ricky Williams, New Orleans	248	1,000	4.0	26	8
1999	*Edgerrin James, Indianapolis	369	1,553	4.2	72	13
	Curtis Martin, N.Y. Jets[5]	367	1,464	4.0	50	5
	Stephen Davis, Washington	290	1,405	4.8	76	17
	Emmitt Smith, Dallas[9]	329	1,397	4.3	63	11
	Marshall Faulk, St. Louis[5]	253	1,381	5.5	58	7
	Eddie George, Tennessee[4]	320	1,304	4.1	40	9
	Duce Staley, Philadelphia[2]	325	1,273	3.9	29	4
	Charlie Garner, San Francisco	241	1,229	5.1	53	4
	Ricky Watters, Seattle[6]	325	1,210	3.7	45	5
	Corey Dillon, Cincinnati[3]	263	1,200	4.6	50	5
	*Olandis Gary, Denver	276	1,159	4.2	71	7
	Jerome Bettis, Pittsburgh[6]	299	1,091	3.7	35	7
	Dorsey Levens, Green Bay[2]	279	1,034	3.7	36	9
	Robert Smith, Minnesota[3]	221	1,015	4.6	70	2
1998	Terrell Davis, Denver[4]	392	2,008	5.1	70	21
	Jamal Anderson, Atlanta[3]	410	1,846	4.5	48	14
	Garrison Hearst, San Francisco[3]	310	1,570	5.1	96	7
	Barry Sanders, Detroit[10]	343	1,491	4.3	73	4
	Emmitt Smith, Dallas[8]	319	1,332	4.2	32	13
	Marshall Faulk, Indianapolis[4]	324	1,319	4.1	68	6
	Eddie George, Tennessee[3]	348	1,294	3.7	37	5
	Curtis Martin, N.Y. Jets[4]	369	1,287	3.5	60	8
	Ricky Watters, Seattle[5]	319	1,239	3.9	39	9
	*Fred Taylor, Jacksonville	264	1,223	4.6	77	14
	Robert Smith, Minnesota[2]	249	1,187	4.8	74	6
	Jerome Bettis, Pittsburgh[5]	316	1,185	3.8	42	3
	Corey Dillon, Cincinnati[2]	262	1,130	4.3	66	4
	Antowain Smith, Buffalo	300	1,124	3.7	30	8
	*Robert Edwards, New England	291	1,115	3.8	53	9
	Duce Staley, Philadelphia	258	1,065	4.1	64	5

Year	Player, Team	Att.	Yards	Avg.	Long	TD
	Gary Brown, N.Y. Giants[2]	247	1,063	4.3	45	5
	Adrian Murrell, Arizona[3]	274	1,042	3.8	32	8
	Warrick Dunn, Tampa Bay	245	1,026	4.2	50	2
	Priest Holmes, Baltimore	233	1,008	4.3	56	7
1997	Barry Sanders, Detroit[8]	335	2,053	6.1	82	11
	Terrell Davis, Denver[3]	369	1,750	4.7	50	15
	Jerome Bettis, Pittsburgh[4]	375	1,665	4.4	34	7
	Dorsey Levens, Green Bay	329	1,435	4.4	52	7
	Eddie George, Tennessee[2]	357	1,399	3.9	30	6
	Napoleon Kaufman, Oakland	272	1,294	4.8	83	6
	Robert Smith, Minnesota	232	1,266	5.5	78	6
	Curtis Martin, New England[3]	274	1,160	4.2	70	4
	*Corey Dillon, Cincinnati	233	1,129	4.8	71	10
	Ricky Watters, Philadelphia[4]	285	1,110	3.9	28	7
	Adrian Murrell, N.Y. Jets[2]	300	1,086	3.6	43	7
	Emmitt Smith, Dallas[7]	261	1,074	4.1	44	4
	Marshall Faulk, Indianapolis[3]	264	1,054	4.0	45	7
	Raymont Harris, Chicago	275	1,033	3.8	68	10
	Garrison Hearst, San Francisco[2]	234	1,019	4.4	51	4
	Jamal Anderson, Atlanta[2]	290	1,002	3.5	39	7
1996	Barry Sanders, Detroit[8]	307	1,553	5.1	54	11
	Terrell Davis, Denver[2]	345	1,538	4.5	71	13
	Jerome Bettis, Pittsburgh[3]	320	1,431	4.5	50	11
	Ricky Watters, Philadelphia[3]	353	1,411	4.0	56	13
	*Eddie George, Houston	335	1,368	4.1	76	8
	Terry Allen, Washington[4]	347	1,353	3.9	49	21
	Adrian Murrell, N.Y. Jets	301	1,249	4.1	78	6
	Emmitt Smith, Dallas[6]	327	1,204	3.7	42	12
	Curtis Martin, New England[2]	316	1,152	3.6	57	14
	Anthony Johnson, Carolina	300	1,120	3.7	29	6
	*Karim Abdul-Jabbar, Miami	307	1,116	3.6	29	11
	Jamal Anderson, Atlanta	232	1,055	4.5	32	5
	Thurman Thomas, Buffalo[8]	281	1,033	3.7	36	8
1995	Emmitt Smith, Dallas[5]	377	1,773	4.7	60	25
	Barry Sanders, Detroit[7]	314	1,500	4.8	75	11
	*Curtis Martin, New England	368	1,487	4.0	49	14
	Chris Warren, Seattle[4]	310	1,346	4.3	52	15
	Terry Allen, Washington[3]	338	1,309	3.9	28	10
	Ricky Watters, Philadelphia[2]	337	1,273	3.8	57	11
	Errict Rhett, Tampa Bay[2]	332	1,207	3.6	21	11
	Rodney Hampton, N.Y. Giants[5]	306	1,182	3.9	32	10
	*Terrell Davis, Denver	237	1,117	4.7	60	7
	Harvey Williams, Oakland	255	1,114	4.4	60	9
	Craig Heyward, Atlanta	236	1,083	4.6	31	6
	Marshall Faulk, Indianapolis[2]	289	1,078	3.7	40	11
	*Rashaan Salaam, Chicago	296	1,074	3.6	42	10
	Garrison Hearst, Arizona	284	1,070	3.8	38	1
	Edgar Bennett, Green Bay	316	1,067	3.4	23	3
	Thurman Thomas, Buffalo[7]	267	1,005	3.8	49	6
1994	Barry Sanders, Detroit[6]	331	1,883	5.7	85	7
	Chris Warren, Seattle[3]	333	1,545	4.6	41	9
	Emmitt Smith, Dallas[4]	368	1,484	4.0	46	21
	Natrone Means, San Diego	343	1,350	3.9	25	12
	*Marshall Faulk, Indianapolis	314	1,282	4.1	52	11
	Thurman Thomas, Buffalo[8]	287	1,093	3.8	29	7
	Rodney Hampton, N.Y. Giants[4]	327	1,075	3.3	27	6
	Terry Allen, Minnesota[2]	255	1,031	4.0	45	8
	Jerome Bettis, L.A. Rams[2]	319	1,025	3.2	19	3
	*Errict Rhett, Tampa Bay	284	1,011	3.6	27	7
1993	Emmitt Smith, Dallas[3]	283	1,486	5.3	62	9
	*Jerome Bettis, L.A. Rams	294	1,429	4.9	71	7
	Thurman Thomas, Buffalo[5]	355	1,315	3.7	27	6
	Erric Pegram, Atlanta	292	1,185	4.1	29	3
	Barry Sanders, Detroit[5]	243	1,115	4.6	42	3
	Leonard Russell, New England	300	1,088	3.6	21	7
	Rodney Hampton, N.Y. Giants[3]	292	1,077	3.7	20	5
	Chris Warren, Seattle[2]	273	1,072	3.9	45	7
	*Reggie Brooks, Washington	223	1,063	4.8	85	3
	*Ron Moore, Phoenix	263	1,018	3.9	20	9

Year	Player, Team	Att.	Yards	Avg.	Long	TD
	Gary Brown, Houston	195	1,002	5.1	26	6
1992	Emmitt Smith, Dallas[2]	373	1,713	4.6	68	18
	Barry Foster, Pittsburgh	390	1,690	4.3	69	11
	Thurman Thomas, Buffalo[4]	312	1,487	4.8	44	9
	Barry Sanders, Detroit[4]	312	1,352	4.3	55	9
	Lorenzo White, Houston	265	1,226	4.6	44	7
	Terry Allen, Minnesota	266	1,201	4.5	51	13
	Reggie Cobb, Tampa Bay	310	1,171	3.8	25	9
	Harold Green, Cincinnati	265	1,170	4.4	53	2
	Rodney Hampton, N.Y. Giants[2]	257	1,141	4.4	63	14
	Cleveland Gary, L.A. Rams	279	1,125	4.0	63	7
	Herschel Walker, Philadelphia[2]	267	1,070	4.0	38	8
	Chris Warren, Seattle	223	1,017	4.6	52	3
	Ricky Watters, San Francisco	206	1,013	4.9	43	9
1991	Emmitt Smith, Dallas	365	1,563	4.3	75	12
	Barry Sanders, Detroit[3]	342	1,548	4.5	69	16
	Thurman Thomas, Buffalo[3]	288	1,407	4.9	33	7
	Rodney Hampton, N.Y. Giants	256	1,059	4.1	44	10
	Earnest Byner, Washington[3]	274	1,048	3.8	32	5
	Gaston Green, Denver	261	1,037	4.0	63	4
	Christian Okoye, Kansas City[2]	225	1,031	4.6	48	9
1990	Barry Sanders, Detroit[2]	255	1,304	5.1	45	13
	Thurman Thomas, Buffalo[2]	271	1,297	4.8	80	11
	Marion Butts, San Diego	265	1,225	4.6	52	8
	Earnest Byner, Washington[2]	297	1,219	4.1	22	6
	Bobby Humphrey, Denver[2]	288	1,202	4.2	37	7
	Neal Anderson, Chicago[3]	260	1,078	4.1	52	10
	Barry Word, Kansas City	204	1,015	5.0	53	4
	James Brooks, Cincinnati[3]	195	1,004	5.1	56	5
1989	Christian Okoye, Kansas City	370	1,480	4.0	59	12
	*Barry Sanders, Detroit	280	1,470	5.3	34	14
	Eric Dickerson, Indianapolis[7]	314	1,311	4.2	21	7
	Neal Anderson, Chicago[2]	274	1,275	4.7	73	11
	Dalton Hilliard, New Orleans	344	1,262	3.7	40	13
	Thurman Thomas, Buffalo	298	1,244	4.2	38	6
	James Brooks, Cincinnati[2]	221	1,239	5.6	65	7
	*Bobby Humphrey, Denver	294	1,151	3.9	40	7
	Greg Bell, L.A. Rams[3]	272	1,137	4.2	47	15
	Roger Craig, San Francisco[3]	271	1,054	3.9	27	6
	Ottis Anderson, N.Y. Giants[6]	325	1,023	3.1	36	14
1988	Eric Dickerson, Indianapolis[6]	388	1,659	4.3	41	14
	Herschel Walker, Dallas	361	1,514	4.2	38	5
	Roger Craig, San Francisco[2]	310	1,502	4.8	46	9
	Greg Bell, L.A. Rams[2]	288	1,212	4.2	44	16
	*John Stephens, New England	297	1,168	3.9	52	4
	Gary Anderson, San Diego	225	1,119	5.0	36	3
	Neal Anderson, Chicago	249	1,106	4.4	80	12
	Joe Morris, N.Y. Giants[3]	307	1,083	3.5	27	5
	*Ickey Woods, Cincinnati	203	1,066	5.3	56	15
	Curt Warner, Seattle[4]	266	1,025	3.9	29	10
	John Settle, Atlanta	232	1,024	4.4	62	7
	Mike Rozier, Houston	251	1,002	4.0	28	10
1987	Charles White, L.A. Rams	324	1,374	4.2	58	11
	Eric Dickerson, L.A. Rams-Indianapolis[5]	283	1,288	4.6	57	6
1986	Eric Dickerson, L.A. Rams[4]	404	1,821	4.5	42	11
	Joe Morris, N.Y. Giants[2]	341	1,516	4.4	54	14
	Curt Warner, Seattle[3]	319	1,481	4.6	60	13
	*Rueben Mayes, New Orleans	286	1,353	4.7	50	8
	Walter Payton, Chicago[10]	321	1,333	4.2	41	8
	Gerald Riggs, Atlanta[3]	343	1,327	3.9	31	9
	George Rogers, Washington[4]	303	1,203	4.0	42	18
	James Brooks, Cincinnati	205	1,087	5.3	56	5
1985	Marcus Allen, L.A. Raiders[3]	390	1,759	4.6	61	11
	Gerald Riggs, Atlanta[2]	397	1,719	4.3	50	10
	Walter Payton, Chicago[9]	324	1,551	4.8	40	9
	Joe Morris, N.Y. Giants	294	1,336	4.5	65	21
	Freeman McNeil, N.Y. Jets[2]	294	1,331	4.5	69	3
	Tony Dorsett, Dallas[8]	305	1,307	4.3	60	7
	James Wilder, Tampa Bay[2]	365	1,300	3.6	28	10

Year	Player, Team	Att.	Yards	Avg.	Long	TD
	Eric Dickerson, L.A. Rams[3]	292	1,234	4.2	43	12
	Craig James, New England	263	1,227	4.7	65	5
	Kevin Mack, Cleveland	222	1,104	5.0	61	7
	Curt Warner, Seattle[2]	291	1,094	3.8	38	8
	George Rogers, Washington[3]	231	1,093	4.7	35	7
	Roger Craig, San Francisco	214	1,050	4.9	62	9
	Earnest Jackson, Philadelphia[2]	282	1,028	3.6	59	5
	Stump Mitchell, St. Louis	183	1,006	5.5	64	7
	Earnest Byner, Cleveland	244	1,002	4.1	36	8
1984	Eric Dickerson, L.A. Rams[2]	379	2,105	5.6	66	14
	Walter Payton, Chicago[8]	381	1,684	4.4	72	11
	James Wilder, Tampa Bay	407	1,544	3.8	37	13
	Gerald Riggs, Atlanta	353	1,486	4.2	57	13
	Wendell Tyler, San Francisco[3]	246	1,262	5.1	40	7
	John Riggins, Washington[5]	327	1,239	3.8	24	14
	Tony Dorsett, Dallas[7]	302	1,189	3.9	31	6
	Earnest Jackson, San Diego	296	1,179	4.0	32	8
	Ottis Anderson, St. Louis[5]	289	1,174	4.1	24	6
	Marcus Allen, L.A. Raiders[2]	275	1,168	4.2	52	13
	Sammy Winder, Denver	296	1,153	3.9	24	4
	*Greg Bell, Buffalo	262	1,100	4.2	85	7
	Freeman McNeil, N.Y. Jets	229	1,070	4.7	53	5
1983	*Eric Dickerson, L.A. Rams	390	1,808	4.6	85	18
	William Andrews, Atlanta[4]	331	1,567	4.7	27	7
	*Curt Warner, Seattle	335	1,449	4.3	60	13
	Walter Payton, Chicago[7]	314	1,421	4.5	49	6
	John Riggins, Washington[4]	375	1,347	3.6	44	24
	Tony Dorsett, Dallas[6]	289	1,321	4.6	77	8
	Earl Campbell, Houston[5]	322	1,301	4.0	42	12
	Ottis Anderson, St. Louis[4]	296	1,270	4.3	43	5
	Mike Pruitt, Cleveland[4]	293	1,184	4.0	27	10
	George Rogers, New Orleans[2]	256	1,144	4.5	76	5
	Joe Cribbs, Buffalo[3]	263	1,131	4.3	45	3
	Curtis Dickey, Baltimore	254	1,122	4.4	56	4
	Tony Collins, New England	219	1,049	4.8	50	10
	Billy Sims, Detroit[3]	220	1,040	4.7	41	7
	Marcus Allen, L.A. Raiders	266	1,014	3.8	19	9
	Franco Harris, Pittsburgh[8]	279	1,007	3.6	19	5
1981	*George Rogers, New Orleans	378	1,674	4.4	79	13
	Tony Dorsett, Dallas[5]	342	1,646	4.8	75	4
	Billy Sims, Detroit[2]	296	1,437	4.9	51	13
	Wilbert Montgomery, Philadelphia[3]	286	1,402	4.9	41	8
	Ottis Anderson, St. Louis[3]	328	1,376	4.2	28	9
	Earl Campbell, Houston[4]	361	1,376	3.8	43	10
	William Andrews, Atlanta[3]	289	1,301	4.5	29	10
	Walter Payton, Chicago[6]	339	1,222	3.6	39	6
	Chuck Muncie, San Diego[2]	251	1,144	4.6	73	19
	*Joe Delaney, Kansas City	234	1,121	4.8	82	3
	Mike Pruitt, Cleveland[3]	247	1,103	4.5	21	7
	Joe Cribbs, Buffalo[2]	257	1,097	4.3	35	3
	Pete Johnson, Cincinnati	274	1,077	3.9	39	12
	Wendell Tyler, Los Angeles[2]	260	1,074	4.1	69	12
	Ted Brown, Minnesota	274	1,063	3.9	34	6
1980	Earl Campbell, Houston[3]	373	1,934	5.2	55	13
	Walter Payton, Chicago[5]	317	1,460	4.6	69	6
	Ottis Anderson, St. Louis[2]	301	1,352	4.5	52	9
	William Andrews, Atlanta[2]	265	1,308	4.9	33	4
	*Billy Sims, Detroit	313	1,303	4.2	52	13
	Tony Dorsett, Dallas[4]	278	1,185	4.3	56	11
	*Joe Cribbs, Buffalo	306	1,185	3.9	48	11
	Mike Pruitt, Cleveland[2]	249	1,034	4.2	56	6
1979	Earl Campbell, Houston[2]	368	1,697	4.6	61	19
	Walter Payton, Chicago[4]	369	1,610	4.4	43	14
	*Ottis Anderson, St. Louis	331	1,605	4.8	76	8
	Wilbert Montgomery, Philadelphia[2]	338	1,512	4.5	62	9
	Mike Pruitt, Cleveland	264	1,294	4.9	77	9
	Ricky Bell, Tampa Bay	283	1,263	4.5	49	7
	Chuck Muncie, New Orleans	238	1,198	5.0	69	11
	Franco Harris, Pittsburgh[7]	267	1,186	4.4	71	11

Year	Player, Team	Att.	Yards	Avg.	Long	TD
	John Riggins, Washington[3]	260	1,153	4.4	66	9
	Wendell Tyler, Los Angeles	218	1,109	5.1	63	9
	Tony Dorsett, Dallas[3]	250	1,107	4.4	41	6
	*William Andrews, Atlanta	239	1,023	4.3	23	3
1978	*Earl Campbell, Houston	302	1,450	4.8	81	13
	Walter Payton, Chicago[3]	333	1,395	4.2	76	11
	Tony Dorsett, Dallas[2]	290	1,325	4.6	63	7
	Delvin Williams, Miami[2]	272	1,258	4.6	58	8
	Wilbert Montgomery, Philadelphia	259	1,220	4.7	47	9
	Terdell Middleton, Green Bay	284	1,116	3.9	76	11
	Franco Harris, Pittsburgh[6]	310	1,082	3.5	37	8
	Mark van Eeghen, Oakland[3]	270	1,080	4.0	34	9
	*Terry Miller, Buffalo	238	1,060	4.5	60	7
	Tony Reed, Kansas City	206	1,053	5.1	62	5
	John Riggins, Washington[2]	248	1,014	4.1	31	5
1977	Walter Payton, Chicago[2]	339	1,852	5.5	73	14
	Mark van Eeghen, Oakland[2]	324	1,273	3.9	27	7
	Lawrence McCutcheon, Los Angeles[4]	294	1,238	4.2	48	7
	Franco Harris, Pittsburgh[5]	300	1,162	3.9	61	11
	Lydell Mitchell, Baltimore[3]	301	1,159	3.9	64	3
	Chuck Foreman, Minnesota[3]	270	1,112	4.1	51	6
	Greg Pruitt, Cleveland[3]	236	1,086	4.6	78	3
	Sam Cunningham, New England	270	1,015	3.8	31	4
	*Tony Dorsett, Dallas	208	1,007	4.8	84	12
1976	O.J. Simpson, Buffalo[5]	290	1,503	5.2	75	8
	Walter Payton, Chicago	311	1,390	4.5	60	13
	Delvin Williams, San Francisco	248	1,203	4.9	80	7
	Lydell Mitchell, Baltimore[2]	289	1,200	4.2	43	5
	Lawrence McCutcheon, Los Angeles[3]	291	1,168	4.0	40	9
	Chuck Foreman, Minnesota[2]	278	1,155	4.2	46	13
	Franco Harris, Pittsburgh[4]	289	1,128	3.9	30	14
	Mike Thomas, Washington	254	1,101	4.3	28	5
	Rocky Bleier, Pittsburgh	220	1,036	4.7	28	5
	Mark van Eeghen, Oakland	233	1,012	4.3	21	3
	Otis Armstrong, Denver[2]	247	1,008	4.1	31	5
	Greg Pruitt, Cleveland[2]	209	1,000	4.8	64	4
1975	O.J. Simpson, Buffalo[4]	329	1,817	5.5	88	16
	Franco Harris, Pittsburgh[3]	262	1,246	4.8	36	10
	Lydell Mitchell, Baltimore	289	1,193	4.1	70	11
	Jim Otis, St. Louis	269	1,076	4.0	30	5
	Chuck Foreman, Minnesota	280	1,070	3.8	31	13
	Greg Pruitt, Cleveland	217	1,067	4.9	50	8
	John Riggins, N.Y. Jets	238	1,005	4.2	42	8
	Dave Hampton, Atlanta	250	1,002	4.0	22	5
1974	Otis Armstrong, Denver	263	1,407	5.3	43	9
	*Don Woods, San Diego	227	1,162	5.1	56	7
	O.J. Simpson, Buffalo[3]	270	1,125	4.2	41	3
	Lawrence McCutcheon, Los Angeles[2]	236	1,109	4.7	23	3
	Franco Harris, Pittsburgh[2]	208	1,006	4.8	54	5
1973	O.J. Simpson, Buffalo[2]	332	2,003	6.0	80	12
	John Brockington, Green Bay[3]	265	1,144	4.3	53	3
	Calvin Hill, Dallas[2]	273	1,142	4.2	21	6
	Lawrence McCutcheon, Los Angeles	210	1,097	5.2	37	2
	Larry Csonka, Miami[3]	219	1,003	4.6	25	5
1972	O.J. Simpson, Buffalo	292	1,251	4.3	94	6
	Larry Brown, Washington[2]	285	1,216	4.3	38	8
	Ron Johnson, N.Y. Giants[2]	298	1,182	4.0	35	9
	Larry Csonka, Miami[2]	213	1,117	5.2	45	6
	Marv Hubbard, Oakland	219	1,100	5.0	39	4
	*Franco Harris, Pittsburgh	188	1,055	5.6	75	10
	Calvin Hill, Dallas	245	1,036	4.2	26	6
	Mike Garrett, San Diego[2]	272	1,031	3.8	41	6
	John Brockington, Green Bay[2]	274	1,027	3.7	30	8
	Eugene (Mercury) Morris, Miami	190	1,000	5.3	33	12
1971	Floyd Little, Denver	284	1,133	4.0	40	6
	*John Brockington, Green Bay	216	1,105	5.1	52	4
	Larry Csonka, Miami	195	1,051	5.4	28	7
	Steve Owens, Detroit	246	1,035	4.2	23	8
	Willie Ellison, Los Angeles	211	1,000	4.7	80	4

Year	Player, Team	Att.	Yards	Avg.	Long	TD
1970	Larry Brown, Washington	237	1,125	4.7	75	5
	Ron Johnson, N.Y. Giants	263	1,027	3.9	68	8
1969	Gale Sayers, Chicago[2]	236	1,032	4.4	28	8
1968	Leroy Kelly, Cleveland[3]	248	1,239	5.0	65	16
	*Paul Robinson, Cincinnati	238	1,023	4.3	87	8
1967	Jim Nance, Boston[2]	269	1,216	4.5	53	7
	Leroy Kelly, Cleveland[2]	235	1,205	5.1	42	11
	Hoyle Granger, Houston	236	1,194	5.1	67	6
	Mike Garrett, Kansas City	236	1,087	4.6	58	9
1966	Jim Nance, Boston	299	1,458	4.9	65	11
	Gale Sayers, Chicago	220	1,231	5.4	58	8
	Leroy Kelly, Cleveland	209	1,141	5.5	70	15
	Dick Bass, Los Angeles[2]	248	1,090	4.4	50	8
1965	Jim Brown, Cleveland[7]	289	1,544	5.3	67	17
	Paul Lowe, San Diego[2]	222	1,121	5.0	59	7
1964	Jim Brown, Cleveland[6]	280	1,446	5.2	71	7
	Jim Taylor, Green Bay[5]	235	1,169	5.0	84	12
	John Henry Johnson, Pittsburgh[2]	235	1,048	4.5	45	7
1963	Jim Brown, Cleveland[5]	291	1,863	6.4	80	12
	Clem Daniels, Oakland	215	1,099	5.1	74	3
	Jim Taylor, Green Bay[4]	248	1,018	4.1	40	9
	Paul Lowe, San Diego	177	1,010	5.7	66	8
1962	Jim Taylor, Green Bay[3]	272	1,474	5.4	51	19
	John Henry Johnson, Pittsburgh	251	1,141	4.5	40	7
	Cookie Gilchrist, Buffalo	214	1,096	5.1	44	13
	Abner Haynes, Dall. Texans	221	1,049	4.7	71	13
	Dick Bass, Los Angeles	196	1,033	5.3	57	6
	Charlie Tolar, Houston	244	1,012	4.1	25	7
1961	Jim Brown, Cleveland[4]	305	1,408	4.6	38	8
	Jim Taylor, Green Bay[2]	243	1,307	5.4	53	15
1960	Jim Brown, Cleveland[3]	215	1,257	5.8	71	9
	Jim Taylor, Green Bay	230	1,101	4.8	32	11
	John David Crow, St. Louis	183	1,071	5.9	57	6
1959	Jim Brown, Cleveland[2]	290	1,329	4.6	70	14
	J.D. Smith, San Francisco	207	1,036	5.0	73	10
1958	Jim Brown, Cleveland	257	1,527	5.9	65	17
1956	Rick Casares, Chi. Bears	234	1,126	4.8	68	12
1954	Joe Perry, San Francisco[2]	173	1,049	6.1	58	8
1953	Joe Perry, San Francisco	192	1,018	5.3	51	10
1949	Steve Van Buren, Philadelphia[2]	263	1,146	4.4	41	11
	Tony Canadeo, Green Bay	208	1,052	5.1	54	4
1947	Steve Van Buren, Philadelphia	217	1,008	4.6	45	13
1934	*Beattie Feathers, Chi. Bears	119	1,004	8.4	82	8

*First season of professional football.

200 YARDS RUSHING IN A GAME

Date	Player, Team, Opponent	Att.	Yards	TD
Jan. 1, 2006	Larry Johnson, Kansas City vs. Cincinnati	26	201	3
Dec. 31, 2005	Tiki Barber, N.Y. Giants vs. Oakland	28	203	1
Dec. 17, 2005	Tiki Barber, N.Y. Giants vs. Kansas City	29	220	2
Nov. 20, 2005	Larry Johnson, Kansas City vs. Houston	36	211	2
Oct. 30, 2005	Tiki Barber, N.Y. Giants vs. Washington	24	206	1
Nov. 28, 2004	Rudi Johnson, Cincinnati vs. Cleveland	26	202	2
Nov. 21, 2004	Edgerrin James, Indianapolis vs. Chicago	23	204	1
Dec. 28, 2003	Ahman Green, Green Bay vs. Denver	20	218	2
Dec. 28, 2003	LaDainian Tomlinson, San Diego vs. Oakland	31	243	2
Dec. 21, 2003	Jamal Lewis, Baltimore vs. Cleveland	22	205	2
Dec. 7, 2003	Clinton Portis, Denver vs. Kansas City	22	218	5
Oct. 19, 2003	LaDainian Tomlinson, San Diego vs. Cleveland	26	200	1
Sept. 14, 2003	Jamal Lewis, Baltimore vs. Cleveland	30	295	2
Dec. 29, 2002	*Clinton Portis, Denver vs. Arizona	24	228	2
Dec. 28, 2002	Tiki Barber, N.Y. Giants vs. Philadelphia	32	203	0
Dec. 9, 2002	Ricky Williams, Miami vs. Chicago	31	216	2
Dec. 1, 2002	LaDainian Tomlinson, San Diego vs. Denver	37	220	3
Dec. 1, 2002	Ricky Williams, Miami vs. Buffalo	27	228	2
Sept. 29, 2002	LaDainian Tomlinson, San Diego vs. New England	27	217	2
Dec. 23, 2001	Marshall Faulk, St. Louis vs. Carolina	30	202	2
Nov. 11, 2001	Shaun Alexander, Seattle vs. Oakland	35	266	3
Dec. 24, 2000	Marshall Faulk, St. Louis vs. New Orleans	32	220	2

Date	Player, Team, Opponent	Att.	Yards	TD
Dec. 3, 2000	Corey Dillon, Cincinnati vs. Arizona	35	216	1
Dec. 3, 2000	Warrick Dunn, Tampa Bay vs. Dallas	22	210	2
Dec. 3, 2000	*Mike Anderson, Denver vs. New Orleans	37	251	4
Dec. 3, 2000	Curtis Martin, N.Y. Jets vs. Indianapolis	30	203	1
Nov. 19, 2000	Fred Taylor, Jacksonville vs. Pittsburgh	30	234	3
Oct. 22, 2000	Corey Dillon, Cincinnati vs. Denver	22	278	2
Oct. 15, 2000	Marshall Faulk, St. Louis vs. Atlanta	25	208	1
Oct. 15, 2000	Edgerrin James, Indianapolis vs. Seattle	38	219	3
Sept. 24, 2000	Charlie Garner, San Francisco vs. Dallas	36	201	1
Sept. 3, 2000	Duce Staley, Philadelphia vs. Dallas	26	201	1
Nov. 22, 1998	Priest Holmes, Baltimore vs. Cincinnati	36	227	1
Oct. 11, 1998	Terrell Davis, Denver vs Seattle	30	208	1
Dec. 4, 1997	*Corey Dillon, Cincinnati vs. Tennessee	39	246	4
Nov. 23, 1997	Barry Sanders, Detroit vs. Indianapolis	24	216	2
Oct. 26, 1997	Terrell Davis, Denver vs. Buffalo (OT)	42	207	1
Oct. 19, 1997	Napoleon Kaufman, Oakland vs. Denver	28	227	1
Oct. 12, 1997	Barry Sanders, Detroit vs. Tampa Bay	24	215	2
Sept. 21, 1997	Terrell Davis, Denver vs. Cincinnati	27	215	1
Aug. 31, 1997	Eddie George, Tennessee vs. Oakland (OT)	35	216	1
Sept. 22, 1996	LeShon Johnson, Arizona vs. New Orleans	21	214	2
Nov. 13, 1994	Barry Sanders, Detroit vs. Tampa Bay	26	237	0
Dec. 12, 1993	*Jerome Bettis, L.A. Rams vs. New Orleans	28	212	1
Oct. 31, 1993	Emmitt Smith, Dallas vs. Philadelphia	30	237	1
Nov. 24, 1991	Barry Sanders, Detroit vs. Minnesota	23	220	4
Dec. 23, 1990	James Brooks, Cincinnati vs. Houston	20	201	1
Oct. 14, 1990	Barry Word, Kansas City vs. Detroit	18	200	2
Sept. 24, 1990	Thurman Thomas, Buffalo vs. N.Y. Jets	18	214	0
Dec. 24, 1989	Greg Bell, L.A. Rams vs. New England	26	210	1
Sept. 24, 1989	Greg Bell, L.A. Rams vs. Green Bay	28	221	2
Sept. 17, 1989	Gerald Riggs, Washington vs. Philadelphia	29	221	1
Dec. 18, 1988	Gary Anderson, San Diego vs. Kansas City	34	217	1
Nov. 30, 1987	*Bo Jackson, L.A. Raiders vs. Seattle	18	221	2
Nov. 15, 1987	Charles White, L.A. Rams vs. St. Louis	34	213	1
Dec. 7, 1986	Rueben Mayes, New Orleans vs. Miami	28	203	2
Oct. 5, 1986	Eric Dickerson, L.A. Rams vs. Tampa Bay (OT)	30	207	2
Dec. 21, 1985	George Rogers, Washington vs. St. Louis	34	206	1
Dec. 21, 1985	Joe Morris, N.Y. Giants vs. Pittsburgh	36	202	3
Dec. 9, 1984	Eric Dickerson, L.A. Rams vs. Houston	27	215	2
Nov. 18, 1984	*Greg Bell, Buffalo vs. Dallas	27	206	1
Nov. 4, 1984	Eric Dickerson, L.A. Rams vs. St. Louis	21	208	0
Sept. 2, 1984	Gerald Riggs, Atlanta vs. New Orleans	35	202	2
Nov. 27, 1983	*Curt Warner, Seattle vs. Kansas City (OT)	32	207	3
Nov. 6, 1983	James Wilder, Tampa Bay vs. Minnesota	31	219	1
Sept. 18, 1983	Tony Collins, New England vs. N.Y. Jets	23	212	3
Sept. 4, 1983	George Rogers, New Orleans vs. St. Louis	24	206	2
Dec. 21, 1980	Earl Campbell, Houston vs. Minnesota	29	203	1
Nov. 16, 1980	Earl Campbell, Houston vs. Chicago	31	206	0
Oct. 26, 1980	Earl Campbell, Houston vs. Cincinnati	27	202	2
Oct. 19, 1980	Earl Campbell, Houston vs. Tampa Bay	33	203	0
Nov. 26, 1978	*Terry Miller, Buffalo vs. N.Y. Giants	21	208	2
Dec. 4, 1977	*Tony Dorsett, Dallas vs. Philadelphia	23	206	2
Nov. 20, 1977	Walter Payton, Chicago vs. Minnesota	40	275	1
Oct. 30, 1977	Walter Payton, Chicago vs. Green Bay	23	205	2
Dec. 5, 1976	O.J. Simpson, Buffalo vs. Miami	24	203	1
Nov. 25, 1976	O.J. Simpson, Buffalo vs. Detroit	29	273	2
Oct. 24, 1976	Chuck Foreman, Minnesota vs. Philadelphia	28	200	2
Dec. 14, 1975	Greg Pruitt, Cleveland vs. Kansas City	26	214	3
Sept. 28, 1975	O.J. Simpson, Buffalo vs. Pittsburgh	28	227	1
Dec. 16, 1973	O.J. Simpson, Buffalo vs. N.Y. Jets	34	200	1
Dec. 9, 1973	O.J. Simpson, Buffalo vs. New England	22	219	1
Sept. 16, 1973	O.J. Simpson, Buffalo vs. New England	29	250	2
Dec. 5, 1971	Willie Ellison, Los Angeles vs. New Orleans	26	247	1
Dec. 20, 1970	John (Frenchy) Fuqua, Pittsburgh vs. Philadelphia	20	218	2
Nov. 3, 1968	Gale Sayers, Chicago vs. Green Bay	24	205	0
Oct. 30, 1966	Jim Nance, Boston vs. Oakland	38	208	2
Oct. 10, 1964	John Henry Johnson, Pittsburgh vs. Cleveland	30	200	3
Dec. 8, 1963	Cookie Gilchrist, Buffalo vs. N.Y. Jets	36	243	5
Nov. 3, 1963	Jim Brown, Cleveland vs. Philadelphia	28	223	1
Oct. 20, 1963	Clem Daniels, Oakland vs. N.Y. Jets	27	200	2
Sept. 22, 1963	Jim Brown, Cleveland vs. Dallas	20	232	2
Dec. 10, 1961	Billy Cannon, Houston vs. N.Y. Titans	25	216	3

Date	Player, Team, Opponent	Att.	Yards	TD
Nov. 19, 1961	Jim Brown, Cleveland vs. Philadelphia	34	237	4
Dec. 18, 1960	John David Crow, St. Louis vs. Pittsburgh	24	203	0
Nov. 15, 1959	Bobby Mitchell, Cleveland vs. Washington	14	232	3
Nov. 24, 1957	*Jim Brown, Cleveland vs. Los Angeles	31	237	4
Dec. 16, 1956	*Tom Wilson, Los Angeles vs. Green Bay	23	223	0
Nov. 22, 1953	Dan Towler, Los Angeles vs. Baltimore	14	205	1
Nov. 12, 1950	Gene Roberts, N.Y. Giants vs. Chi. Cardinals	26	218	2
Nov. 27, 1949	Steve Van Buren, Philadelphia vs. Pittsburgh	27	205	0
Oct. 8, 1933	Cliff Battles, Boston vs. N.Y. Giants	16	215	1

*First season of professional football.

TIMES 200 OR MORE

102 times by 64 players…Simpson 6; Barber, Brown, Campbell, Sanders, Tomlinson 4; Bell, Davis, Dickerson, Dillon, Faulk 3; James, Johnson, Lewis, Payton, Portis, Riggs, Rogers, Williams 2.

4,000 YARDS PASSING IN A SEASON

Year	Player, Team	Att.	Comp.	Pct.	Yards	TD	Int.
2005	Tom Brady, New England	530	334	63.0	4,110	26	14
	Trent Green, Kansas City[3]	507	317	62.5	4,014	17	10
2004	Daunte Culpepper, Minnesota	548	379	69.2	4,717	39	11
	Trent Green, Kansas City[2]	556	369	66.4	4,591	27	17
	Peyton Manning, Indianapolis[6]	497	336	67.6	4,557	49	10
	Jake Plummer, Denver	521	303	58.2	4,089	27	20
	Brett Favre, Green Bay[4]	540	346	64.1	4,088	30	17
2003	Peyton Manning, Indianapolis[5]	566	379	67.0	4,267	29	10
	Trent Green, Kansas City	523	330	63.1	4,039	24	12
2002	Rich Gannon, Oakland	618	418	67.6	4,689	26	10
	Drew Bledsoe, Buffalo[3]	610	375	61.5	4,359	24	15
	Peyton Manning, Indianapolis[4]	591	392	66.3	4,200	27	19
	Kerry Collins, N.Y. Giants	545	335	61.5	4,073	19	14
2001	Kurt Warner, St. Louis[2]	546	375	68.7	4,830	36	22
	Peyton Manning, Indianapolis[3]	547	343	62.7	4,131	26	23
2000	Peyton Manning, Indianapolis[2]	571	357	62.5	4,413	33	15
	Jeff Garcia, San Francisco	561	355	63.3	4,278	31	10
	Elvis Grbac, Kansas City	547	326	59.6	4,169	28	14
1999	Steve Beuerlein, Carolina	571	343	60.1	4,436	36	15
	Kurt Warner, St. Louis	499	325	65.1	4,353	41	13
	Peyton Manning, Indianapolis	533	331	62.1	4,135	26	15
	Brett Favre, Green Bay[3]	595	341	57.3	4,091	22	23
	Brad Johnson, Washington	519	316	60.9	4,005	24	13
1998	Brett Favre, Green Bay[2]	551	347	63.0	4,212	31	23
	Steve Young, San Francisco[2]	517	322	62.3	4,170	36	12
1996	Mark Brunell, Jacksonville	557	353	63.4	4,367	19	20
	Vinny Testaverde, Baltimore	549	325	59.2	4,177	33	19
	Drew Bledsoe, New England[2]	623	373	59.9	4,086	27	15
1995	Brett Favre, Green Bay	570	359	63.0	4,413	38	13
	Scott Mitchell, Detroit	583	346	59.3	4,338	32	12
	Warren Moon, Minnesota[4]	606	377	62.2	4,228	33	14
	Jeff George, Atlanta	557	336	60.3	4,143	24	11
1994	Drew Bledsoe, New England	691	400	57.9	4,555	25	27
	Dan Marino, Miami[6]	615	385	62.6	4,453	30	17
	Warren Moon, Minnesota[3]	601	371	61.7	4,264	18	19
1993	John Elway, Denver	551	348	63.2	4,030	25	10
	Steve Young, San Francisco	462	314	68.0	4,023	29	16
1992	Dan Marino, Miami[5]	554	330	59.6	4,116	24	16
1991	Warren Moon, Houston[2]	655	404	61.7	4,690	23	21
1990	Warren Moon, Houston	584	362	62.0	4,689	33	13
1989	Don Majkowski, Green Bay	599	353	58.9	4,318	27	20
	Jim Everett, L.A. Rams	518	304	58.7	4,310	29	17
1988	Dan Marino, Miami[4]	606	354	58.4	4,434	28	23
1986	Dan Marino, Miami[3]	623	378	60.7	4,746	44	23
	Jay Schroeder, Washington	541	276	51.0	4,109	22	22
1985	Dan Marino, Miami[2]	567	336	59.3	4,137	30	21
1984	Dan Marino, Miami	564	362	64.2	5,084	48	17
	Neil Lomax, St. Louis	560	345	61.6	4,614	28	16
	Phil Simms, N.Y. Giants	533	286	53.7	4,044	22	18
1983	Lynn Dickey, Green Bay	484	289	59.7	4,458	32	29
	Bill Kenney, Kansas City	603	346	57.4	4,348	24	18

Year	Player, Team	Att.	Comp.	Pct.	Yards	TD	Int.
1981	Dan Fouts, San Diego[3]	609	360	59.1	4,802	33	17
1980	Dan Fouts, San Diego[2]	589	348	59.1	4,715	30	24
	Brian Sipe, Cleveland	554	337	60.8	4,132	30	14
1979	Dan Fouts, San Diego	530	332	62.6	4,082	24	24
1967	Joe Namath, N.Y. Jets	491	258	52.5	4,007	26	28

400 YARDS PASSING IN A GAME

Date	Player, Team, Opponent	Att.	Comp.	Yards	TD
Oct. 2, 2005	Marc Bulger, St. Louis vs. N.Y. Giants	62	40	442	2
Jan. 2, 2005	Marc Bulger, St. Louis vs. N.Y. Jets (OT)	39	29	450	3
Dec. 19, 2004	Daunte Culpepper, Minnesota vs. Detroit	35	25	404	3
Dec. 19, 2004	Billy Volek, Tennessee vs. Oakland	60	40	492	4
Dec. 13, 2004	Billy Volek, Tennessee vs. Kansas City	43	29	426	4
Dec. 6, 2004	Matt Hasselbeck, Seattle vs. Dallas	40	28	414	3
Dec. 5, 2004	Peyton Manning, Indianapolis vs. Tennessee	33	25	425	3
Dec. 5, 2004	Donovan McNabb, Philadelphia vs. Green Bay	43	32	464	5
Nov. 29, 2004	Marc Bulger, St. Louis vs. Green Bay	53	35	448	2
Nov. 28, 2004	Kelly Holcomb, Cleveland vs. Cincinnati	39	30	413	5
Oct. 31, 2004	Peyton Manning, Indianapolis vs. Kansas City	44	25	472	5
Oct. 31, 2004	Jake Plummer, Denver vs. Atlanta	55	31	499	4
Oct. 17, 2004	Daunte Culpepper, Minnesota vs. New Orleans	37	26	425	5
Oct. 10. 2004	Tim Rattay, San Francisco vs. Arizona (OT)	57	38	417	2
Nov. 16, 2003	Peyton Manning, Indianapolis vs. N.Y. Jets	36	27	401	1
Oct. 12, 2003	Trent Green, Kansas City vs. Green Bay (OT)	45	27	400	3
Oct. 12, 2003	Steve McNair, Tennessee vs. Houston	27	18	421	3
Dec. 29, 2002	Matt Hasselbeck, Seattle vs. San Diego (OT)	53	36	449	2
Dec. 1, 2002	Matt Hasselbeck, Seattle vs. San Francisco	55	30	427	3
Nov. 10, 2002	Marc Bulger, St. Louis vs. San Diego	48	36	453	4
Nov. 10, 2002	Tommy Maddox, Pittsburgh vs. Atlanta (OT)	41	28	473	4
Oct. 6, 2002	Drew Bledsoe, Buffalo vs. Oakland	53	32	417	2
Sept. 22, 2002	Tom Brady, New England vs. Kansas City (OT)	54	39	410	4
Sept. 15, 2002	Drew Bledsoe, Buffalo vs. Minnesota (OT)	49	35	463	3
Sept. 15, 2002	Rich Gannon, Oakland vs. Pittsburgh	64	43	403	1
Dec. 30, 2001	Jon Kitna, Cincinnati vs. Pittsburgh	68	35	411	2
Dec. 23, 2001	Chris Chandler, Atlanta vs. Buffalo	40	28	431	2
Nov. 18, 2001	Charlie Batch, Detroit vs. Arizona	62	36	436	3
Nov. 18, 2001	Kurt Warner, St. Louis vs. New England	42	30	401	3
Sept. 23, 2001	Peyton Manning, Indianapolis vs. Buffalo	29	23	421	4
Dec. 24, 2000	Vinny Testaverde, N.Y. Jets vs. Baltimore	69	36	481	2
Dec. 17, 2000	Jeff Garcia, San Francisco vs. Chicago	44	36	402	2
Dec. 3, 2000	Aaron Brooks, New Orleans vs. Denver	48	30	441	2
Nov. 19, 2000	Gus Frerotte, Denver vs. San Diego	58	36	462	5
Nov. 5, 2000	Elvis Grbac, Kansas City vs. Oakland	53	39	504	2
Nov. 5, 2000	Trent Green, St. Louis vs. Carolina	42	29	431	2
Sept. 25, 2000	Peyton Manning, Indianapolis vs. Jacksonville	36	23	440	4
Sept. 4, 2000	Kurt Warner, St. Louis vs. Denver	35	25	441	3
Dec. 26, 1999	Brad Johnson, Washington vs. San Francisco (OT)	47	32	471	2
Dec. 5, 1999	Jeff Garcia, San Francisco vs. Cincinnati	49	33	437	3
Nov. 28, 1999	Jim Harbaugh, San Diego vs. Minnesota	39	25	404	1
Nov. 14, 1999	Jim Miller, Chicago vs. Minnesota (OT)	48	34	422	3
Sept. 26, 1999	Peyton Manning, Indianapolis vs. San Diego	54	29	404	2
Dec. 6, 1998	Vinny Testaverde, N.Y. Jets vs. Seattle	63	42	418	2
Dec. 6, 1998	John Elway, Denver vs. Kansas City	32	22	400	2
Nov. 26, 1998	Troy Aikman, Dallas vs. Minnesota	57	34	455	1
Nov. 23, 1998	Drew Bledsoe, New England vs. Miami	54	28	423	2
Nov. 15, 1998	Jake Plummer, Arizona vs. Dallas	56	31	465	3
Oct. 5, 1998	Randall Cunningham, Minnesota vs. Green Bay	32	20	442	4
Sept. 6, 1998	Glenn Foley, N.Y. Jets vs. San Francisco (OT)	58	30	415	3
Nov. 2, 1997	Tony Banks, St. Louis vs. Atlanta	34	23	401	2
Oct. 26, 1997	Warren Moon, Seattle vs. Oakland	44	28	409	5
Nov. 10, 1996	Boomer Esiason, Arizona vs. Washington (OT)	59	35	522	3
Nov. 3, 1996	Drew Bledsoe, New England vs. Miami	41	30	419	3
Oct. 27, 1996	Vinny Testaverde, Baltimore vs. St. Louis (OT)	51	31	429	3
Oct. 20, 1996	Mark Brunell, Jacksonville vs. St. Louis	52	37	421	0
Sept. 22, 1996	Mark Brunell, Jacksonville vs. New England (OT)	39	23	432	3
Dec. 18, 1995	Steve Young, San Francisco vs. Minnesota	49	30	425	3
Nov. 26, 1995	Dave Krieg, Arizona vs. Atlanta (OT)	43	27	413	4
Nov. 23, 1995	Scott Mitchell, Detroit vs. Minnesota	45	30	410	4
Oct. 1, 1995	Dan Marino, Miami vs. Cincinnati	48	33	450	2

Date	Player, Team, Opponent	Att.	Comp.	Yards	TD
Nov. 20, 1994	Warren Moon, Minnesota vs. N.Y. Jets	50	33	400	2
Nov. 13, 1994	Drew Bledsoe, New England vs. Minnesota (OT)	70	45	426	3
Nov. 6, 1994	Warren Moon, Minnesota vs. New Orleans	57	33	420	3
Sept. 25, 1994	Dan Marino, Miami vs. Minnesota	54	29	431	3
Sept. 4, 1994	Dan Marino, Miami vs. New England (OT)	42	23	473	5
Sept. 4, 1994	Drew Bledsoe, New England vs. Miami (OT)	51	32	421	4
Dec. 19, 1993	Steve Beuerlein, Phoenix vs. Seattle	53	34	431	3
Dec. 5, 1993	Brett Favre, Green Bay vs. Chicago	54	36	402	2
Nov. 28, 1993	Steve Young, San Francisco vs. L.A. Rams	32	26	462	4
Oct. 31, 1993	Jeff Hostetler, L.A. Raiders vs. San Diego	32	20	424	2
Sept. 13, 1992	Steve Young, San Francisco vs. Buffalo	37	26	449	3
Sept. 13, 1992	Jim Kelly, Buffalo vs. San Francisco	33	22	403	3
Nov. 10, 1991	Warren Moon, Houston vs. Dallas (OT)	56	41	432	0
Nov. 10, 1991	Mark Rypien, Washington vs. Atlanta	31	16	442	6
Oct. 13, 1991	Warren Moon, Houston vs. N.Y. Jets	50	35	423	2
Dec. 16, 1990	Warren Moon, Houston vs. Kansas City	45	27	527	3
Nov. 4, 1990	Joe Montana, San Francisco vs. Green Bay	40	25	411	3
Oct. 14, 1990	Joe Montana, San Francisco vs. Atlanta	49	32	476	6
Oct. 7, 1990	Boomer Esiason, Cincinnati vs. L.A. Rams (OT)	45	31	490	3
Dec. 23, 1989	Warren Moon, Houston vs. Cleveland	51	32	414	2
Dec. 11, 1989	Joe Montana, San Francisco vs. L.A. Rams	42	30	458	3
Nov. 26, 1989	Jim Everett, L.A. Rams vs. New Orleans (OT)	51	29	454	1
Nov. 26, 1989	Mark Rypien, Washington vs. Chicago	47	30	401	4
Oct. 2, 1989	Randall Cunningham, Philadelphia vs. Chicago	62	32	401	1
Sept. 24, 1989	Joe Montana, San Francisco vs. Philadelphia	34	25	428	5
Sept. 24, 1989	Dan Marino, Miami vs. N.Y. Jets	55	33	427	3
Sept. 17, 1989	Randall Cunningham, Philadelphia vs. Washington	46	34	447	5
Dec. 18, 1988	Dave Krieg, Seattle vs. L.A. Raiders	32	19	410	4
Dec. 12, 1988	Dan Marino, Miami vs. Cleveland	50	30	404	4
Oct. 23, 1988	Dan Marino, Miami vs. N.Y. Jets	60	35	521	3
Oct. 16, 1988	Vinny Testaverde, Tampa Bay vs. Indianapolis	42	25	469	2
Sept. 11, 1988	Doug Williams, Washington vs. Pittsburgh	52	30	430	2
Nov. 29, 1987	Tom Ramsey, New England vs. Philadelphia	53	34	402	3
Nov. 22, 1987	Boomer Esiason, Cincinnati vs. Pittsburgh	53	30	409	0
Sept. 20, 1987	Neil Lomax, St. Louis vs. San Diego	61	32	457	3
Dec. 21, 1986	Boomer Esiason, Cincinnati vs. N.Y. Jets	30	23	425	5
Dec. 14, 1986	Dan Marino, Miami vs. L.A. Rams (OT)	46	29	403	5
Nov. 23, 1986	Bernie Kosar, Cleveland vs. Pittsburgh (OT)	46	28	414	2
Nov. 17, 1986	Joe Montana, San Francisco vs. Washington	60	33	441	0
Nov. 16, 1986	Dan Marino, Miami vs. Buffalo	54	39	404	4
Nov. 10, 1986	Bernie Kosar, Cleveland vs. Miami	50	32	401	0
Nov. 2, 1986	Tommy Kramer, Minnesota vs. Washington (OT)	35	20	490	4
Nov. 2, 1986	Ken O'Brien, N.Y. Jets vs. Seattle	32	26	431	4
Oct. 27, 1986	Jay Schroeder, Washington vs. N.Y. Giants	40	22	420	1
Oct. 12, 1986	Steve Grogan, New England vs. N.Y. Jets	42	23	401	3
Sept. 21, 1986	Ken O'Brien, N.Y. Jets vs. Miami (OT)	43	29	479	4
Sept. 21, 1986	Dan Marino, Miami vs. N.Y. Jets (OT)	50	30	448	6
Sept. 21, 1986	Tony Eason, New England vs. Seattle	45	26	414	3
Dec. 20, 1985	John Elway, Denver vs. Seattle	42	24	432	1
Nov. 10, 1985	Dan Fouts, San Diego vs. L.A. Raiders (OT)	41	26	436	4
Oct. 13, 1985	Phil Simms, N.Y. Giants vs. Cincinnati	62	40	513	1
Oct. 13, 1985	Dave Krieg, Seattle vs. Atlanta	51	33	405	4
Oct. 6, 1985	Phil Simms, N.Y. Giants vs. Dallas	36	18	432	3
Oct. 6, 1985	Joe Montana, San Francisco vs. Atlanta	57	37	429	5
Sept. 19, 1985	Tommy Kramer, Minnesota vs. Chicago	55	28	436	3
Sept. 15, 1985	Dan Fouts, San Diego vs. Seattle	43	29	440	4
Dec. 16, 1984	Neil Lomax, St. Louis vs. Washington	46	37	468	2
Dec. 9, 1984	Dan Marino, Miami vs. Indianapolis	41	29	404	4
Dec. 2, 1984	Dan Marino, Miami vs. L.A. Raiders	57	35	470	4
Nov. 25, 1984	Dave Krieg, Seattle vs. Denver	44	30	406	3
Nov. 4, 1984	Dan Marino, Miami vs. N.Y. Jets	42	23	422	2
Oct. 21, 1984	Dan Fouts, San Diego vs. L.A. Raiders	45	24	410	2
Sept. 30, 1984	Dan Marino, Miami vs. St. Louis	36	24	429	3
Sept. 2, 1984	Phil Simms, N.Y. Giants vs. Philadelphia	30	23	409	4
Dec. 11, 1983	Bill Kenney, Kansas City vs. San Diego	41	31	411	4
Nov. 20, 1983	Dave Krieg, Seattle vs. Denver	42	31	418	3
Oct. 9, 1983	Joe Ferguson, Buffalo vs. Miami (OT)	55	38	419	5
Oct. 2, 1983	Joe Theismann, Washington vs. L.A. Raiders	39	23	417	3
Sept. 25, 1983	Richard Todd, N.Y. Jets vs. L.A. Rams (OT)	50	37	446	2

Date	Player, Team, Opponent	Att.	Comp.	Yards	TD
Dec. 26, 1982	Vince Ferragamo, L.A. Rams vs. Chicago	46	30	509	3
Dec. 20, 1982	Dan Fouts, San Diego vs. Cincinnati	40	25	435	1
Dec. 20, 1982	Ken Anderson, Cincinnati vs. San Diego	56	40	416	2
Dec. 11, 1982	Dan Fouts, San Diego vs. San Francisco	48	33	444	5
Nov. 21, 1982	Joe Montana, San Francisco vs. St. Louis	39	26	408	3
Nov. 15, 1981	Steve Bartkowski, Atlanta vs. Pittsburgh	50	33	416	2
Oct. 25, 1981	Brian Sipe, Cleveland vs. Baltimore	41	30	444	4
Oct. 25, 1981	David Woodley, Miami vs. Dallas	37	21	408	3
Oct. 11, 1981	Tommy Kramer, Minnesota vs. San Diego	43	27	444	4
Dec. 14, 1980	Tommy Kramer, Minnesota vs. Cleveland	49	38	456	4
Nov. 16, 1980	Doug Williams, Tampa Bay vs. Minnesota	55	30	486	4
Oct. 19, 1980	Dan Fouts, San Diego vs. N.Y. Giants	41	26	444	3
Oct. 12, 1980	Lynn Dickey, Green Bay vs. Tampa Bay (OT)	51	35	418	1
Sept. 21, 1980	Richard Todd, N.Y. Jets vs. San Francisco	60	42	447	3
Oct. 3, 1976	James Harris, Los Angeles vs. Miami	29	17	436	2
Nov. 17, 1975	Ken Anderson, Cincinnati vs. Buffalo	46	30	447	2
Nov. 18, 1974	Charley Johnson, Denver vs. Kansas City	42	28	445	2
Dec. 11, 1972	Joe Namath, N.Y. Jets vs. Oakland	46	25	403	1
Sept. 24, 1972	Joe Namath, N.Y. Jets vs. Baltimore	28	15	496	6
Dec. 21, 1969	Don Horn, Green Bay vs. St. Louis	31	22	410	5
Sept. 28, 1969	Joe Kapp, Minnesota vs. Baltimore	43	28	449	7
Sept. 9, 1968	Pete Beathard, Houston vs. Kansas City	48	23	413	2
Nov. 26, 1967	Sonny Jurgensen, Washington vs. Cleveland	50	32	418	3
Oct. 1, 1967	Joe Namath, N.Y. Jets vs. Miami	39	23	415	3
Sept. 17, 1967	Johnny Unitas, Baltimore vs. Atlanta	32	22	401	2
Nov. 13, 1966	Don Meredith, Dallas vs. Washington	29	21	406	2
Nov. 28, 1965	Sonny Jurgensen, Washington vs. Dallas	43	26	411	3
Oct. 24, 1965	Fran Tarkenton, Minnesota vs. San Francisco	35	21	407	3
Nov. 1, 1964	Len Dawson, Kansas City vs. Denver	38	23	435	6
Oct. 25, 1964	Cotton Davidson, Oakland vs. Denver	36	23	427	5
Oct. 16, 1964	Babe Parilli, Boston vs. Oakland	47	25	422	4
Dec. 22, 1963	Tom Flores, Oakland vs. Houston	29	17	407	6
Nov. 17, 1963	Norm Snead, Washington vs. Pittsburgh	40	23	424	2
Nov. 10, 1963	Don Meredith, Dallas vs. San Francisco	48	30	460	3
Oct. 13, 1963	Charley Johnson, St. Louis vs. Pittsburgh	41	20	428	2
Dec. 16, 1962	Sonny Jurgensen, Philadelphia vs. St. Louis	34	15	419	5
Nov. 18, 1962	Bill Wade, Chicago vs. Dall. Cowboys	46	28	466	2
Oct. 28, 1962	Y.A. Tittle, N.Y. Giants vs. Washington	39	27	505	7
Sept. 15, 1962	Frank Tripucka, Denver vs. Buffalo	56	29	447	2
Dec. 17, 1961	Sonny Jurgensen, Philadelphia vs. Detroit	42	27	403	3
Nov. 19, 1961	George Blanda, Houston vs. N.Y. Titans	32	20	418	7
Oct. 29, 1961	George Blanda, Houston vs. Buffalo	32	18	464	4
Oct. 29, 1961	Sonny Jurgensen, Philadelphia vs. Washington	41	27	436	3
Oct. 13, 1961	Jacky Lee, Houston vs. Boston	41	27	457	2
Dec. 13, 1958	Bobby Layne, Pittsburgh vs. Chi. Cardinals	49	23	409	2
Nov. 8, 1953	Bobby Thomason, Philadelphia vs. N.Y. Giants	44	22	437	4
Oct. 4, 1952	Otto Graham, Cleveland vs. Pittsburgh	49	21	401	3
Sept. 28, 1951	Norm Van Brocklin, Los Angeles vs. N.Y. Yanks	41	27	554	5
Dec. 11, 1949	Johnny Lujack, Chi. Bears vs. Chi. Cardinals	39	24	468	6
Oct. 31, 1948	Sammy Baugh, Washington vs. Boston	24	17	446	4
Oct. 31, 1948	Jim Hardy, Los Angeles vs. Chi. Cardinals	53	28	406	3
Nov. 14, 1943	Sid Luckman, Chi. Bears vs. N.Y. Giants	32	21	433	7

TIMES 400 OR MORE

182 times by 95 players...Marino 13; Montana, Moon 7; Bledsoe, Fouts, Manning 6; Jurgensen, Krieg 5; Bulger, Esiason, Kramer, Testaverde 4; Cunningham, Hasselbeck, Namath, Simms, Young 3; Anderson, Blanda, Brunell, Culpepper, Elway, Garcia, Green, Johnson, Kosar, Lomax, Meredith, O'Brien, Plummer, Rypien, Todd, Volek, Warner, Williams 2.

100 PASS RECEPTIONS IN A SEASON

Year	Player, Team	No.	Yards	Avg.	Long	TD
2005	Larry Fitzgerald, Arizona	103	1,409	13.7	47	10
	Steve Smith, Carolina	103	1,563	15.2	80	12
	Anquan Boldin, Arizona[2]	102	1,402	13.7	54	7
	Torry Holt, St. Louis[2]	102	1,331	13.0	44	9
2004	Tony Gonzalez, Kansas City	102	1,258	12.3	32	7
2003	Torry Holt, St. Louis	117	1,696	14.5	48	12
	Randy Moss, Minnesota[2]	111	1,632	14.7	72	17
	*Anquan Boldin, Arizona	101	1,377	13.6	71	8
	LaDainian Tomlinson, San Diego	100	725	7.3	73	4
2002	Marvin Harrison, Indianapolis[4]	143	1,722	12.0	69	11
	Hines Ward, Pittsburgh	112	1,329	11.9	72	12
	Randy Moss, Minnesota	106	1,347	12.7	60	7
	Eric Moulds, Buffalo	100	1,292	12.9	70	10
	Terrell Owens, San Francisco	100	1,300	13.0	76	13
2001	Rod Smith, Denver[2]	113	1,343	11.9	65	11
	Jimmy Smith, Jacksonville[2]	112	1,373	12.3	35	8
	Marvin Harrison, Indianapolis[3]	109	1,524	14.0	68	15
	Keyshawn Johnson, Tampa Bay	106	1,266	11.9	47	1
	Troy Brown, New England	101	1,199	11.9	60	5
	Marty Booker, Chicago	100	1,071	10.7	66	8
2000	Marvin Harrison, Indianapolis[2]	102	1,413	13.9	78	14
	Muhsin Muhammad, Carolina	102	1,183	11.6	36	6
	Ed McCaffrey, Denver	101	1,317	13.0	61	9
	Rod Smith, Denver	100	1,602	16.0	49	8
1999	Jimmy Smith, Jacksonville	116	1,636	14.1	62	6
	Marvin Harrison, Indianapolis	115	1,663	14.5	57	12
1997	Tim Brown, Oakland	104	1,408	13.5	59	5
	Herman Moore, Detroit[3]	104	1,293	12.4	79	8
1996	Jerry Rice, San Francisco[4]	108	1,254	11.6	39	8
	Herman Moore, Detroit[2]	106	1,296	12.2	50	9
	Carl Pickens, Cincinnati	100	1,180	11.8	61	12
1995	Herman Moore, Detroit	123	1,686	13.7	69	14
	Jerry Rice, San Francisco[3]	122	1,848	15.1	81	15
	Cris Carter, Minnesota[2]	122	1,371	11.2	60	17
	Isaac Bruce, St. Louis	119	1,781	15.0	72	13
	Michael Irvin, Dallas	111	1,603	14.4	50	10
	Brett Perriman, Detroit	108	1,488	13.8	91	9
	Eric Metcalf, Atlanta	104	1,189	11.4	62	8
	Robert Brooks, Green Bay	102	1,497	14.7	99	13
	Larry Centers, Arizona	101	962	9.5	32	2
1994	Cris Carter, Minnesota	122	1,256	10.3	65	7
	Jerry Rice, San Francisco[2]	112	1,499	13.4	69	13
	Terance Mathis, Atlanta	111	1,342	12.1	81	11
1993	Sterling Sharpe, Green Bay[2]	112	1,274	11.4	54	11
1992	Sterling Sharpe, Green Bay	108	1,461	13.5	76	13
1991	Haywood Jeffires, Houston	100	1,181	11.8	44	7
1990	Jerry Rice, San Francisco	100	1,502	15.0	64	13
1984	Art Monk, Washington	106	1,372	12.9	72	7
1964	Charley Hennigan, Houston	101	1,546	15.3	53	8
1961	Lionel Taylor, Denver	100	1,176	11.8	52	4

1,000 YARDS PASS RECEIVING IN A SEASON

Year	Player, Team	No.	Yards	Avg.	Long	TD
2005	Steve Smith, Carolina[2]	103	1,563	15.2	80	12
	Santana Moss, Washington[2]	84	1,483	17.7	78	9
	Chad Johnson, Cincinnati[4]	97	1,432	14.8	70	9
	Larry Fitzgerald, Arizona	103	1,409	13.7	47	10
	Anquan Boldin, Arizona[2]	102	1,402	13.7	54	7
	Torry Holt, St. Louis[6]	102	1,331	13.0	44	9
	Joey Galloway, Tampa Bay[4]	83	1,287	15.5	80	10
	Donald Driver, Green Bay[3]	86	1,221	14.2	59	5
	Plaxico Burress, N.Y. Giants[3]	76	1,214	16.0	78	7
	Marvin Harrison, Indianapolis[7]	82	1,146	14.0	80	12
	Terry Glenn, Dallas[3]	62	1,136	18.3	71	7
	Chris Chambers, Miami	82	1,118	13.6	77	11
	Rod Smith, Denver[8]	85	1,105	13.0	72	6
	Eddie Kennison, Kansas City[2]	68	1,102	16.2	55	5
	Antonio Gates, San Diego	89	1,101	12.4	38	10

Year	Player, Team	No.	Yards	Avg.	Long	TD
	Derrick Mason, Baltimore[5]	86	1,073	12.5	39	3
	Reggie Wayne, Indianapolis[2]	83	1,055	12.7	66	5
	Jimmy Smith, Jacksonville[9]	70	1,023	14.6	45	6
	Antonio Bryant, Cleveland	69	1,009	14.6	54	4
	Randy Moss, Oakland[7]	60	1,005	16.8	79	8
2004	Muhsin Muhammad, Carolina[3]	93	1,405	15.1	51	16
	Joe Horn, New Orleans[4]	94	1,399	14.9	57	11
	Javon Walker, Green Bay	89	1,382	15.5	79	12
	Torry Holt, St. Louis[5]	94	1,372	14.6	75	10
	Isaac Bruce, St. Louis[7]	89	1,292	14.5	56	6
	Chad Johnson, Cincinnati[3]	95	1,274	13.4	53	9
	Tony Gonzalez, Kansas City[2]	102	1,258	12.3	32	7
	Drew Bennett, Tennessee	80	1,247	15.6	48	11
	Reggie Wayne, Indianapolis	77	1,210	15.7	71	12
	Donald Driver, Green Bay[2]	84	1,208	14.4	50	9
	Terrell Owens, Philadelphia[6]	77	1,200	15.6	59	14
	Darrell Jackson, Seattle[3]	87	1,199	13.8	56	7
	*Michael Clayton, Tampa Bay	80	1,193	14.9	75	7
	Jimmy Smith, Jacksonville[8]	74	1,172	15.8	65	6
	Derrick Mason, Tennessee[4]	96	1,168	12.2	37	7
	Rod Smith, Denver[7]	79	1,144	14.5	85	7
	Andre Johnson, Houston	79	1,142	14.5	54	6
	Marvin Harrison, Indianapolis[6]	86	1,113	12.9	59	15
	Eddie Kennison, Kansas City	62	1,086	17.5	70	8
	Ashley Lelie, Denver	54	1,084	20.1	58	7
	Brandon Stokley, Indianapolis	68	1,077	15.8	69	10
	Eric Moulds, Buffalo[4]	88	1,043	11.9	49	5
	Nate Burleson, Minnesota	68	1,006	14.8	68	9
	Hines Ward, Pittsburgh[4]	80	1,004	12.6	58	4
2003	Torry Holt, St. Louis[4]	117	1,696	14.5	48	12
	Randy Moss, Minnesota[6]	111	1,632	14.7	72	17
	*Anquan Boldin, Arizona	101	1,377	13.6	71	8
	Chad Johnson, Cincinnati[2]	90	1,355	15.1	82	10
	Derrick Mason, Tennessee[3]	95	1,303	13.7	50	8
	Marvin Harrison, Indianapolis[5]	94	1,272	13.5	79	10
	Laveranues Coles, Washington[2]	82	1,204	14.7	64	6
	Keenan McCardell, Tampa Bay[5]	84	1,174	14.0	76	8
	Hines Ward, Pittsburgh[3]	95	1,163	12.2	50	10
	Darrell Jackson, Seattle[2]	68	1,137	16.7	80	9
	Steve Smith, Carolina	88	1,110	12.6	67	7
	Santana Moss, N.Y. Jets	74	1,105	14.9	65	10
	Terrell Owens, San Francisco[5]	80	1,102	13.8	75	9
	Amani Toomer, N.Y. Giants[5]	63	1,057	16.8	77	5
2002	Marvin Harrison, Indianapolis[4]	143	1,722	12.0	69	11
	Randy Moss, Minnesota[5]	106	1,347	12.7	60	7
	Amani Toomer, N.Y. Giants[4]	82	1,343	16.4	82	8
	Hines Ward, Pittsburgh[2]	112	1,329	11.9	72	12
	Plaxico Burress, Pittsburgh[2]	78	1,325	17.0	62	7
	Joe Horn, New Orleans[3]	88	1,312	14.9	63	7
	Torry Holt, St. Louis[3]	91	1,302	14.3	58	4
	Terrell Owens, San Francisco[4]	100	1,300	13.0	76	13
	Eric Moulds, Buffalo[3]	100	1,292	12.9	70	10
	Laveranues Coles, N.Y. Jets	89	1,264	14.2	43	5
	Peerless Price, Buffalo	94	1,252	13.3	73	9
	Koren Robinson, Seattle	78	1,240	15.9	83	5
	Jerry Rice, Oakland[14]	92	1,211	13.2	75	7
	Marty Booker, Chicago[2]	97	1,189	12.3	54	6
	Chad Johnson, Cincinnati	69	1,166	16.9	72	5
	Keyshawn Johnson, Tampa Bay[4]	76	1,088	14.3	76	5
	Isaac Bruce, St. Louis[6]	79	1,075	13.6	34	7
	Donald Driver, Green Bay	70	1,064	15.2	85	9
	Jimmy Smith, Jacksonville[7]	80	1,027	12.8	47	7
	Rod Smith, Denver[6]	89	1,027	11.5	46	5
	Derrick Mason, Tennessee[2]	79	1,012	12.8	40	5
	Rod Gardner, Washington	71	1,006	14.2	43	8
2001	David Boston, Arizona[2]	98	1,598	16.3	61	8
	Marvin Harrison, Indianapolis[3]	109	1,524	14.0	68	15
	Terrell Owens, San Francisco[3]	93	1,412	15.2	60	16
	Jimmy Smith, Jacksonville[6]	112	1,373	12.3	35	8

Year	Player, Team	No.	Yards	Avg.	Long	TD
	Torry Holt, St. Louis[2]	81	1,363	16.8	51	7
	Rod Smith, Denver[6]	113	1,343	11.9	65	11
	Keyshawn Johnson, Tampa Bay[3]	106	1,266	11.9	47	1
	Joe Horn, New Orleans[2]	83	1,265	15.2	56	9
	Randy Moss, Minnesota[4]	82	1,233	15.0	73	10
	Troy Brown, New England	101	1,199	11.9	60	5
	Tim Brown, Oakland[9]	91	1,165	12.8	46	9
	Johnnie Morton, Detroit[4]	77	1,154	15.0	76	4
	Jerry Rice, Oakland[13]	83	1,139	13.7	40	9
	Derrick Mason, Tennessee	73	1,128	15.5	71	9
	Curtis Conway, San Diego[3]	71	1,125	15.8	72	6
	Keenan McCardell, Jacksonville[4]	93	1,110	11.9	45	6
	Isaac Bruce, St. Louis[5]	64	1,106	17.3	51	6
	Kevin Johnson, Cleveland	84	1,097	13.1	55	9
	Darrell Jackson, Seattle	70	1,081	15.4	64	8
	Marty Booker, Chicago	100	1,071	10.7	66	8
	Qadry Ismail, Baltimore[2]	74	1,059	14.3	77	7
	Amani Toomer, N.Y. Giants[3]	72	1,054	14.6	60	5
	Willie Jackson, New Orleans	81	1,046	12.9	63	5
	Plaxico Burress, Pittsburgh	66	1,008	15.3	43	6
	Hines Ward, Pittsburgh	94	1,003	10.7	34	4
2000	Torry Holt, St. Louis	82	1,635	19.9	85	6
	Rod Smith, Denver[4]	100	1,602	16.0	49	8
	Isaac Bruce, St. Louis[4]	87	1,471	16.9	78	9
	Terrell Owens, San Francisco[2]	97	1,451	15.0	69	13
	Randy Moss, Minnesota[3]	77	1,437	18.7	78	15
	Marvin Harrison, Indianapolis[2]	102	1,413	13.9	78	14
	Derrick Alexander, Kansas City[3]	78	1,391	17.8	81	10
	Joe Horn, New Orleans	94	1,340	14.3	52	8
	Eric Moulds, Buffalo[2]	94	1,326	14.1	52	5
	Ed McCaffrey, Denver[3]	101	1,317	13.0	61	9
	Cris Carter, Minnesota[8]	96	1,274	13.3	53	9
	Jimmy Smith, Jacksonville[5]	91	1,213	13.3	65	8
	Keenan McCardell, Jacksonville[3]	94	1,207	12.8	67	5
	Tony Gonzalez, Kansas City	93	1,203	12.9	39	9
	Muhsin Muhammad, Carolina[2]	102	1,183	11.6	36	6
	David Boston, Arizona	71	1,156	16.3	70	7
	Tim Brown, Oakland[8]	76	1,128	14.8	45	11
	Amani Toomer, N.Y. Giants[2]	78	1,094	14.0	54	7
1999	Marvin Harrison, Indianapolis	115	1,663	14.5	57	12
	Jimmy Smith, Jacksonville[4]	116	1,636	14.1	62	6
	Randy Moss, Minnesota[2]	80	1,413	17.7	67	11
	Marcus Robinson, Chicago	84	1,400	16.7	80	9
	Tim Brown, Oakland[7]	90	1,344	14.9	47	6
	Germane Crowell, Detroit	81	1,338	16.5	77	7
	Muhsin Muhammad, Carolina	96	1,253	13.1	60	8
	Cris Carter, Minnesota[7]	90	1,241	13.8	68	13
	Michael Westbrook, Washington	65	1,191	18.3	65	9
	Amani Toomer, N.Y. Giants	79	1,183	15.0	80	6
	Keyshawn Johnson, N.Y. Jets[2]	89	1,170	13.2	65	8
	Isaac Bruce, St. Louis[3]	77	1,165	15.1	60	12
	Terry Glenn, New England[2]	69	1,147	16.6	67	4
	Albert Connell, Washington	62	1,132	18.3	62	7
	Johnnie Morton, Detroit[3]	80	1,129	14.1	48	5
	Qadry Ismail, Baltimore	68	1,105	16.3	76	6
	Raghib Ismail, Dallas[2]	80	1,097	13.7	76	6
	Patrick Jeffers, Carolina	63	1,082	17.2	88	12
	Antonio Freeman, Green Bay[3]	74	1,074	14.5	51	6
	Bill Schroeder, Green Bay	74	1,051	14.2	51	5
	Marshall Faulk, St. Louis	87	1,048	12.1	57	5
	Tony Martin, Miami[4]	67	1,037	15.5	69	5
	Darnay Scott, Cincinnati	68	1,022	15.0	76	7
	Rod Smith, Denver[3]	79	1,020	12.9	71	4
	Ed McCaffrey, Denver[2]	71	1,018	14.3	78	7
	Terance Mathis, Atlanta[4]	81	1,016	12.5	52	6
1998	Antonio Freeman, Green Bay[2]	84	1,424	17.0	84	14
	Eric Moulds, Buffalo	67	1,368	20.4	84	9
	*Randy Moss, Minnesota	69	1,313	19.0	61	17
	Rod Smith, Denver[2]	86	1,222	14.2	58	6

Year	Player, Team	No.	Yards	Avg.	Long	TD
	Jimmy Smith, Jacksonville[3]	78	1,182	15.2	72	8
	Tony Martin, Atlanta[3]	66	1,181	17.9	62	6
	Jerry Rice, San Francisco[12]	82	1,157	14.1	75	9
	Frank Sanders, Arizona[2]	89	1,145	12.9	42	3
	Terance Mathis, Atlanta[3]	64	1,136	17.8	78	11
	Keyshawn Johnson, N.Y. Jets	83	1,131	13.6	41	10
	Terrell Owens, San Francisco	67	1,097	16.4	79	14
	Wayne Chrebet, N.Y. Jets	75	1,083	14.4	63	8
	Michael Irvin, Dallas[7]	74	1,057	14.3	51	1
	Ed McCaffrey, Denver	64	1,053	16.5	48	10
	O.J. McDuffie, Miami	90	1,050	11.7	61	7
	Joey Galloway, Seattle[3]	65	1,047	16.1	81	10
	Johnnie Morton, Detroit[2]	69	1,028	14.9	98	2
	Raghib Ismail, Carolina	69	1,024	14.8	62	8
	Carl Pickens, Cincinnati[4]	82	1,023	12.5	67	5
	Tim Brown, Oakland[6]	81	1,012	12.5	49	9
	Cris Carter, Minnesota[6]	78	1,011	13.0	54	12
1997	Rob Moore, Arizona[3]	97	1,584	16.3	47	8
	Tim Brown, Oakland[5]	104	1,408	13.5	59	5
	Yancey Thigpen, Pittsburgh[2]	79	1,398	17.7	69	7
	Jimmy Smith, Jacksonville[2]	82	1,324	16.1	75	4
	Irving Fryar, Philadelphia[5]	86	1,316	15.3	72	6
	Herman Moore, Detroit[4]	104	1,293	12.4	79	8
	Antonio Freeman, Green Bay	81	1,243	15.3	58	12
	Michael Irvin, Dallas[6]	75	1,180	15.7	55	9
	Rod Smith, Denver	70	1,180	16.9	78	12
	Keenan McCardell, Jacksonville[2]	85	1,164	13.7	60	5
	Jake Reed, Minnesota[4]	68	1,138	16.7	56	6
	Shannon Sharpe, Denver[3]	72	1,107	15.4	68	3
	Andre Rison, Kansas City[5]	72	1,092	15.2	45	7
	Cris Carter, Minnesota[5]	89	1,069	12.0	43	13
	Johnnie Morton, Detroit	80	1,057	13.2	73	6
	Joey Galloway, Seattle[2]	72	1,049	14.6	53	12
	Frank Sanders, Arizona	75	1,017	13.6	70	4
	Robert Brooks, Green Bay[2]	60	1,010	16.8	48	7
	Derrick Alexander, Baltimore[2]	65	1,009	15.5	92	9
1996	Isaac Bruce, St. Louis[2]	84	1,338	15.9	70	7
	Jake Reed, Minnesota[3]	72	1,320	18.3	82	7
	Herman Moore, Detroit[3]	106	1,296	12.2	50	9
	Jerry Rice, San Francisco[11]	108	1,254	11.6	39	8
	Jimmy Smith, Jacksonville	83	1,244	15.0	62	7
	Michael Jackson, Baltimore	76	1,201	15.8	86	14
	Irving Fryar, Philadelphia[4]	88	1,195	13.6	42	11
	Carl Pickens, Cincinnati[3]	100	1,180	11.8	61	12
	Tony Martin, San Diego[2]	85	1,171	13.8	55	14
	Cris Carter, Minnesota[4]	96	1,163	12.1	43	10
	*Terry Glenn, New England	90	1,132	12.6	37	6
	Keenan McCardell, Jacksonville	85	1,129	13.3	52	3
	Tim Brown, Oakland[4]	90	1,104	12.3	42	9
	Derrick Alexander, Baltimore	62	1,099	17.7	64	9
	Shannon Sharpe, Denver[2]	80	1,062	13.3	51	10
	Curtis Conway, Chicago[2]	81	1,049	13.0	58	7
	Andre Reed, Buffalo[4]	66	1,036	15.7	67	6
	Brett Perriman, Detroit[2]	94	1,021	10.9	44	5
	Rob Moore, Arizona[2]	58	1,016	17.5	69	4
	Henry Ellard, Washington[7]	52	1,014	19.5	51	2
	Charles Johnson, Pittsburgh	60	1,008	16.8	70	3
1995	Jerry Rice, San Francisco[10]	122	1,848	15.1	81	15
	Isaac Bruce, St. Louis	119	1,781	15.0	72	13
	Herman Moore, Detroit[2]	123	1,686	13.7	69	14
	Michael Irvin, Dallas[5]	111	1,603	14.4	50	10
	Robert Brooks, Green Bay	102	1,497	14.7	99	13
	Brett Perriman, Detroit	108	1,488	13.8	91	9
	Cris Carter, Minnesota[3]	122	1,371	11.2	60	17
	Tim Brown, Oakland[3]	89	1,342	15.1	80	10
	Yancey Thigpen, Pittsburgh	85	1,307	15.4	43	5
	Jeff Graham, Chicago	82	1,301	15.9	51	4
	Carl Pickens, Cincinnati[2]	99	1,234	12.5	68	17
	Tony Martin, San Diego	90	1,224	13.6	51	6

Year	Player, Team	No.	Yards	Avg.	Long	TD
	Eric Metcalf, Atlanta	104	1,189	11.4	62	8
	Jake Reed, Minnesota[2]	72	1,167	16.2	55	9
	Quinn Early, New Orleans	81	1,087	13.4	70	8
	Anthony Miller, Denver[5]	59	1,079	18.3	62	14
	Bert Emanuel, Atlanta	74	1,039	14.0	52	5
	*Joey Galloway, Seattle	67	1,039	15.5	59	7
	Terance Mathis, Atlanta[2]	78	1,039	13.3	54	9
	Curtis Conway, Chicago	62	1,037	16.7	76	12
	Henry Ellard, Washington[6]	56	1,005	17.9	59	5
	Mark Carrier, Carolina[2]	66	1,002	15.2	66	3
	Brian Blades, Seattle[4]	77	1,001	13.0	49	4
1994	Jerry Rice, San Francisco[9]	112	1,499	13.4	69	13
	Henry Ellard, Washington[5]	74	1,397	18.9	73	6
	Terance Mathis, Atlanta	111	1,342	12.1	81	11
	Tim Brown, L.A. Raiders[2]	89	1,309	14.7	77	9
	Andre Reed, Buffalo[2]	90	1,303	14.5	83	8
	Irving Fryar, Miami[3]	73	1,270	17.4	54	7
	Cris Carter, Minnesota[2]	122	1,256	10.3	65	7
	Michael Irvin, Dallas[4]	79	1,241	15.7	65	6
	Jake Reed, Minnesota	85	1,175	13.8	59	4
	Ben Coates, New England	96	1,174	12.2	62	7
	Herman Moore, Detroit	72	1,173	16.3	51	11
	Fred Barnett, Philadelphia[2]	78	1,127	14.4	54	5
	Carl Pickens, Cincinnati	71	1,127	15.9	70	11
	Sterling Sharpe, Green Bay[4]	94	1,119	11.9	49	18
	Anthony Miller, Denver[4]	60	1,107	18.5	76	5
	Andre Rison, Atlanta[3]	81	1,088	13.4	69	8
	Brian Blades, Seattle[3]	81	1,088	13.4	45	4
	Rob Moore, N.Y. Jets	78	1,010	12.9	41	6
	Shannon Sharpe, Denver	87	1,010	11.6	44	4
1993	Jerry Rice, San Francisco[8]	98	1,503	15.3	80	15
	Michael Irvin, Dallas[3]	88	1,330	15.1	61	7
	Sterling Sharpe, Green Bay[4]	112	1,274	11.4	54	11
	Andre Rison, Atlanta[3]	86	1,242	14.4	53	15
	Tim Brown, L.A. Raiders	80	1,180	14.8	71	7
	Anthony Miller, San Diego[3]	84	1,162	13.8	66	7
	Cris Carter, Minnesota	86	1,071	12.5	58	9
	Reggie Langhorne, Indianapolis	85	1,038	12.2	72	3
	Irving Fryar, Miami[2]	64	1,010	15.8	65	5
1992	Sterling Sharpe, Green Bay[3]	108	1,461	13.5	76	13
	Michael Irvin, Dallas[2]	78	1,396	17.9	87	7
	Jerry Rice, San Francisco[7]	84	1,201	14.3	80	10
	Andre Rison, Atlanta[2]	93	1,119	12.0	71	11
	Fred Barnett, Philadelphia	67	1,083	16.2	71	6
	Anthony Miller, San Diego[2]	72	1,060	14.7	67	7
	Eric Martin, New Orleans[3]	68	1,041	15.3	52	5
1991	Michael Irvin, Dallas	93	1,523	16.4	66	8
	Gary Clark, Washington[5]	70	1,340	19.1	82	10
	Jerry Rice, San Francisco[6]	80	1,206	15.1	73	14
	Haywood Jeffires, Houston[2]	100	1,181	11.8	44	7
	Michael Haynes, Atlanta	50	1,122	22.4	80	11
	Andre Reed, Buffalo[2]	81	1,113	13.7	55	10
	Drew Hill, Houston[5]	90	1,109	12.3	61	4
	Mark Duper, Miami[4]	70	1,085	15.5	43	5
	James Lofton, Buffalo[6]	57	1,072	18.8	77	8
	Mark Clayton, Miami[5]	70	1,053	15.0	43	12
	Henry Ellard, L.A. Rams[4]	64	1,052	16.4	38	3
	Art Monk, Washington[5]	71	1,049	14.8	64	8
	Irving Fryar, New England	68	1,014	14.9	56	3
	John Taylor, San Francisco[2]	64	1,011	15.8	97	9
	Brian Blades, Seattle[2]	70	1,003	14.3	52	2
1990	Jerry Rice, San Francisco[5]	100	1,502	15.0	64	13
	Henry Ellard, L.A. Rams[3]	76	1,294	17.0	50	4
	Andre Rison, Atlanta	82	1,208	14.7	75	10
	Gary Clark, Washington[4]	75	1,112	14.8	53	8
	Sterling Sharpe, Green Bay[2]	67	1,105	16.5	76	6
	Willie Anderson, L.A. Rams[2]	51	1,097	21.5	55	4
	Haywood Jeffires, Houston	74	1,048	14.2	87	8
	Stephone Paige, Kansas City	65	1,021	15.7	86	5

Year	Player, Team	No.	Yards	Avg.	Long	TD
	Drew Hill, Houston[4]	74	1,019	13.8	57	5
	Anthony Carter, Minnesota[3]	70	1,008	14.4	56	8
1989	Jerry Rice, San Francisco[4]	82	1,483	18.1	68	17
	Sterling Sharpe, Green Bay	90	1,423	15.8	79	12
	Mark Carrier, Tampa Bay	86	1,422	16.5	78	9
	Henry Ellard, L.A. Rams[2]	70	1,382	19.7	53	8
	Andre Reed, Buffalo	88	1,312	14.9	78	9
	Anthony Miller, San Diego	75	1,252	16.7	69	10
	Webster Slaughter, Cleveland	65	1,236	19.0	97	6
	Gary Clark, Washington[3]	79	1,229	15.6	80	9
	Tim McGee, Cincinnati	65	1,211	18.6	74	8
	Art Monk, Washington[4]	86	1,186	13.8	60	8
	Willie Anderson, L.A. Rams	44	1,146	26.0	78	5
	Ricky Sanders, Washington[2]	80	1,138	14.2	68	4
	Vance Johnson, Denver	76	1,095	14.4	69	7
	Richard Johnson, Detroit	70	1,091	15.6	75	8
	Eric Martin, New Orleans[2]	68	1,090	16.0	53	8
	John Taylor, San Francisco	60	1,077	18.0	95	10
	Mervyn Fernandez, L.A. Raiders	57	1,069	18.8	75	9
	Anthony Carter, Minnesota[2]	65	1,066	16.4	50	4
	Brian Blades, Seattle	77	1,063	13.8	60	5
	Mark Clayton, Miami[4]	64	1,011	15.8	78	9
1988	Henry Ellard, L.A. Rams	86	1,414	16.4	68	10
	Jerry Rice, San Francisco[3]	64	1,306	20.4	96	9
	Eddie Brown, Cincinnati	53	1,273	24.0	86	9
	Anthony Carter, Minnesota	72	1,225	17.0	67	6
	Ricky Sanders, Washington	73	1,148	15.7	55	12
	Drew Hill, Houston[3]	72	1,141	15.8	57	10
	Mark Clayton, Miami[3]	86	1,129	13.1	45	14
	Roy Green, Phoenix[3]	68	1,097	16.1	52	7
	Eric Martin, New Orleans	85	1,083	12.7	40	7
	Al Toon, N.Y. Jets[2]	93	1,067	11.5	42	5
	Bruce Hill, Tampa Bay	58	1,040	17.9	42	9
	Lionel Manuel, N.Y. Giants	65	1,029	15.8	46	4
1987	J.T. Smith, St. Louis[2]	91	1,117	12.3	38	8
	Jerry Rice, San Francisco[2]	65	1,078	16.6	57	22
	Gary Clark, Washington[2]	56	1,066	19.0	84	7
	Carlos Carson, Kansas City[3]	55	1,044	19.0	81	7
1986	Jerry Rice, San Francisco	86	1,570	18.3	66	15
	Stanley Morgan, New England[3]	84	1,491	17.8	44	10
	Mark Duper, Miami[3]	67	1,313	19.6	85	11
	Gary Clark, Washington	74	1,265	17.1	55	7
	Al Toon, N.Y. Jets	85	1,176	13.8	62	8
	Todd Christensen, L.A. Raiders[3]	95	1,153	12.1	35	8
	Mark Clayton, Miami[2]	60	1,150	19.2	68	10
	*Bill Brooks, Indianapolis	65	1,131	17.4	84	8
	Drew Hill, Houston[2]	65	1,112	17.1	81	5
	Steve Largent, Seattle[8]	70	1,070	15.3	38	9
	Art Monk, Washington[3]	73	1,068	14.6	69	4
	*Ernest Givins, Houston	61	1,062	17.4	60	3
	Cris Collinsworth, Cincinnati[4]	62	1,024	16.5	46	10
	Wesley Walker, N.Y. Jets[2]	49	1,016	20.7	83	12
	J.T. Smith, St. Louis	80	1,014	12.7	45	6
	Mark Bavaro, N.Y. Giants	66	1,001	15.2	41	4
1985	Steve Largent, Seattle[7]	79	1,287	16.3	43	6
	Mike Quick, Philadelphia[3]	73	1,247	17.1	99	11
	Art Monk, Washington[2]	91	1,226	13.5	53	2
	Wes Chandler, San Diego[4]	67	1,199	17.9	75	10
	Drew Hill, Houston	64	1,169	18.3	57	9
	James Lofton, Green Bay[5]	69	1,153	16.7	56	4
	Louis Lipps, Pittsburgh	59	1,134	19.2	51	12
	Cris Collinsworth, Cincinnati[3]	65	1,125	17.3	71	5
	Tony Hill, Dallas[3]	74	1,113	15.0	53	7
	Lionel James, San Diego	86	1,027	11.9	67	6
	Roger Craig, San Francisco	92	1,016	11.0	73	6
1984	Roy Green, St. Louis[2]	78	1,555	19.9	83	12
	John Stallworth, Pittsburgh[3]	80	1,395	17.4	51	11
	Mark Clayton, Miami	73	1,389	19.0	65	18
	Art Monk, Washington	106	1,372	12.9	72	7

Year	Player, Team	No.	Yards	Avg.	Long	TD
	James Lofton, Green Bay[4]	62	1,361	22.0	79	7
	Mark Duper, Miami[2]	71	1,306	18.4	80	8
	Steve Watson, Denver[3]	69	1,170	17.0	73	7
	Steve Largent, Seattle[6]	74	1,164	15.7	65	12
	Tim Smith, Houston[2]	69	1,141	16.5	75	4
	Stacey Bailey, Atlanta	67	1,138	17.0	61	6
	Carlos Carson, Kansas City[2]	57	1,078	18.9	57	4
	Mike Quick, Philadelphia[2]	61	1,052	17.2	90	9
	Todd Christensen, L.A. Raiders[2]	80	1,007	12.6	38	7
	Kevin House, Tampa Bay[2]	76	1,005	13.2	55	5
	Ozzie Newsome, Cleveland[2]	89	1,001	11.2	52	5
1983	Mike Quick, Philadelphia	69	1,409	20.4	83	13
	Carlos Carson, Kansas City	80	1,351	16.9	50	7
	James Lofton, Green Bay[3]	58	1,300	22.4	74	8
	Todd Christensen, L.A. Raiders	92	1,247	13.6	45	12
	Roy Green, St. Louis	78	1,227	15.7	71	14
	Charlie Brown, Washington	78	1,225	15.7	75	8
	Tim Smith, Houston	83	1,176	14.2	47	6
	Kellen Winslow, San Diego[3]	88	1,172	13.3	46	8
	Earnest Gray, N.Y. Giants	78	1,139	14.6	62	5
	Steve Watson, Denver[2]	59	1,133	19.2	78	5
	Cris Collinsworth, Cincinnati[2]	66	1,130	17.1	63	5
	Steve Largent, Seattle[5]	72	1,074	14.9	46	11
	Mark Duper, Miami	51	1,003	19.7	85	10
1982	Wes Chandler, San Diego[3]	49	1,032	21.1	66	9
1981	Alfred Jenkins, Atlanta[2]	70	1,358	19.4	67	13
	James Lofton, Green Bay[2]	71	1,294	18.2	75	8
	Steve Watson, Denver	60	1,244	20.7	95	13
	Frank Lewis, Buffalo[2]	70	1,244	17.8	33	4
	Steve Largent, Seattle[4]	75	1,224	16.3	57	9
	Charlie Joiner, San Diego[4]	70	1,188	17.0	57	7
	Kevin House, Tampa Bay	56	1,176	21.0	84	9
	Wes Chandler, N.O.-San Diego[2]	69	1,142	16.6	51	6
	Dwight Clark, San Francisco	85	1,105	13.0	78	4
	John Stallworth, Pittsburgh[2]	63	1,098	17.4	55	5
	Kellen Winslow, San Diego[2]	88	1,075	12.2	67	10
	Pat Tilley, St. Louis	66	1,040	15.8	75	3
	Stanley Morgan, New England[2]	44	1,029	23.4	76	6
	Harold Carmichael, Philadelphia[3]	61	1,028	16.9	85	6
	Freddie Scott, Detroit	53	1,022	19.3	48	5
	*Cris Collinsworth, Cincinnati	67	1,009	15.1	74	8
	Joe Senser, Minnesota	79	1,004	12.7	53	8
	Ozzie Newsome, Cleveland	69	1,002	14.5	62	6
	Sammy White, Minnesota	66	1,001	15.2	53	3
1980	John Jefferson, San Diego[3]	82	1,340	16.3	58	13
	Kellen Winslow, San Diego	89	1,290	14.5	65	9
	James Lofton, Green Bay	71	1,226	17.3	47	4
	Charlie Joiner, San Diego[3]	71	1,132	15.9	51	4
	Ahmad Rashad, Minnesota[2]	69	1,095	15.9	76	5
	Steve Largent, Seattle[3]	66	1,064	16.1	67	6
	Tony Hill, Dallas[2]	60	1,055	17.6	58	8
	Alfred Jenkins, Atlanta	57	1,026	18.0	57	6
1979	Steve Largent, Seattle[2]	66	1,237	18.7	55	9
	John Stallworth, Pittsburgh	70	1,183	16.9	65	8
	Ahmad Rashad, Minnesota	80	1,156	14.5	52	9
	John Jefferson, San Diego[2]	61	1,090	17.9	65	10
	Frank Lewis, Buffalo	54	1,082	20.0	55	2
	Wes Chandler, New Orleans	65	1,069	16.4	85	6
	Tony Hill, Dallas	60	1,062	17.7	75	10
	Drew Pearson, Dallas[2]	55	1,026	18.7	56	8
	Wallace Francis, Atlanta	74	1,013	13.7	42	8
	Harold Jackson, New England[3]	45	1,013	22.5	59	7
	Charlie Joiner, San Diego[2]	72	1,008	14.0	39	4
	Stanley Morgan, New England	44	1,002	22.8	63	12
1978	Wesley Walker, N.Y. Jets	48	1,169	24.4	77	8
	Steve Largent, Seattle	71	1,168	16.5	57	8
	Harold Carmichael, Philadelphia[2]	55	1,072	19.5	56	8
	*John Jefferson, San Diego	56	1,001	17.9	46	13
1976	Roger Carr, Baltimore	43	1,112	25.9	79	11

Year	Player, Team	No.	Yards	Avg.	Long	TD
	Cliff Branch, Oakland[2]	46	1,111	24.2	88	12
	Charlie Joiner, San Diego	50	1,056	21.1	81	7
1975	Ken Burrough, Houston	53	1,063	20.1	77	8
1974	Cliff Branch, Oakland	60	1,092	18.2	67	13
	Drew Pearson, Dallas	62	1,087	17.5	50	2
1973	Harold Carmichael, Philadelphia	67	1,116	16.7	73	9
1972	Harold Jackson, Philadelphia[2]	62	1,048	16.9	77	4
	John Gilliam, Minnesota	47	1,035	22.0	66	7
1971	Otis Taylor, Kansas City[2]	57	1,110	19.5	82	7
1970	Gene Washington, San Francisco	53	1,100	20.8	79	12
	Marlin Briscoe, Buffalo	57	1,036	18.2	48	8
	Dick Gordon, Chicago	71	1,026	14.5	69	13
	Gary Garrison, San Diego[2]	44	1,006	22.9	67	12
1969	Warren Wells, Oakland[2]	47	1,260	26.8	80	14
	Harold Jackson, Philadelphia	65	1,116	17.2	65	9
	Roy Jefferson, Pittsburgh[2]	67	1,079	16.1	63	9
	Dan Abramowicz, New Orleans	73	1,015	13.9	49	7
	Lance Alworth, San Diego[7]	64	1,003	15.7	76	4
1968	Lance Alworth, San Diego[6]	68	1,312	19.3	80	10
	Don Maynard, N.Y. Jets[5]	57	1,297	22.8	87	10
	George Sauer, N.Y. Jets[3]	66	1,141	17.3	43	3
	Warren Wells, Oakland	53	1,137	21.5	94	11
	Gary Garrison, San Diego	52	1,103	21.2	84	10
	Roy Jefferson, Pittsburgh	58	1,074	18.5	62	11
	Paul Warfield, Cleveland	50	1,067	21.3	65	12
	Homer Jones, N.Y. Giants[3]	45	1,057	23.5	84	7
	Fred Biletnikoff, Oakland	61	1,037	17.0	82	6
	Lance Rentzel, Dallas	54	1,009	18.7	65	6
1967	Don Maynard, N.Y. Jets[4]	71	1,434	20.2	75	10
	Ben Hawkins, Philadelphia	59	1,265	21.4	87	10
	Homer Jones, N.Y. Giants[2]	49	1,209	24.7	70	13
	Jackie Smith, St. Louis	56	1,205	21.5	76	9
	George Sauer, N.Y. Jets[2]	75	1,189	15.9	61	6
	Lance Alworth, San Diego[5]	52	1,010	19.4	71	9
1966	Lance Alworth, San Diego[4]	73	1,383	18.9	78	13
	Otis Taylor, Kansas City	58	1,297	22.4	89	8
	Pat Studstill, Detroit	67	1,266	18.9	99	5
	Bob Hayes, Dallas[2]	64	1,232	19.3	95	13
	Charlie Frazier, Houston	57	1,129	19.8	79	12
	Charley Taylor, Washington	72	1,119	15.5	86	12
	George Sauer, N.Y. Jets	63	1,081	17.2	77	5
	Homer Jones, N.Y. Giants	48	1,044	21.8	98	8
	Art Powell, Oakland[5]	53	1,026	19.4	46	11
1965	Lance Alworth, San Diego[3]	69	1,602	23.2	85	14
	Dave Parks, San Francisco	80	1,344	16.8	53	12
	Don Maynard, N.Y. Jets[3]	68	1,218	17.9	56	14
	Pete Retzlaff, Philadelphia	66	1,190	18.0	78	10
	Lionel Taylor, Denver[4]	85	1,131	13.3	63	6
	Tommy McDonald, Los Angeles[3]	67	1,036	15.5	51	9
	*Bob Hayes, Dallas	46	1,003	21.8	82	12
1964	Charley Hennigan, Houston[3]	101	1,546	15.3	53	8
	Art Powell, Oakland[4]	76	1,361	17.9	77	11
	Lance Alworth, San Diego[2]	61	1,235	20.2	82	13
	Johnny Morris, Chicago	93	1,200	12.9	63	10
	Elbert Dubenion, Buffalo	42	1,139	27.1	72	10
	Terry Barr, Detroit[2]	57	1,030	18.1	58	9
1963	Bobby Mitchell, Washington[2]	69	1,436	20.8	99	7
	Art Powell, Oakland[3]	73	1,304	17.9	85	16
	Buddy Dial, Pittsburgh[2]	60	1,295	21.6	83	9
	Lance Alworth, San Diego	61	1,205	19.8	85	11
	Del Shofner, N.Y. Giants[4]	64	1,181	18.5	70	9
	Lionel Taylor, Denver[3]	78	1,101	14.1	72	10
	Terry Barr, Detroit	66	1,086	16.5	75	13
	Charley Hennigan, Houston[2]	61	1,051	17.2	83	10
	Sonny Randle, St. Louis[2]	51	1,014	19.9	68	12
	Bake Turner, N.Y. Jets	71	1,009	14.2	53	6
1962	Bobby Mitchell, Washington	72	1,384	19.2	81	11
	Sonny Randle, St. Louis	63	1,158	18.4	86	7
	Tommy McDonald, Philadelphia[2]	58	1,146	19.8	60	10

Year	Player, Team	No.	Yards	Avg.	Long	TD
	Del Shofner, N.Y. Giants[3]	53	1,133	21.4	69	12
	Art Powell, N.Y. Titans[2]	64	1,130	17.7	80	8
	Frank Clarke, Dall. Cowboys	47	1,043	22.2	66	14
	Don Maynard, N.Y. Titans[2]	56	1,041	18.6	86	8
1961	Charley Hennigan, Houston	82	1,746	21.3	80	12
	Lionel Taylor, Denver[2]	100	1,176	11.8	52	4
	Bill Groman, Houston[2]	50	1,175	23.5	80	17
	Tommy McDonald, Philadelphia	64	1,144	17.9	66	13
	Del Shofner, N.Y. Giants[2]	68	1,125	16.5	46	11
	Jim Phillips, Los Angeles	78	1,092	14.0	69	5
	*Mike Ditka, Chicago	56	1,076	19.2	76	12
	Dave Kocourek, San Diego	55	1,055	19.2	76	4
	Buddy Dial, Pittsburgh	53	1,047	19.8	88	12
	R.C. Owens, San Francisco	55	1,032	18.8	54	5
1960	*Bill Groman, Houston	72	1,473	20.5	92	12
	Raymond Berry, Baltimore	74	1,298	17.5	70	10
	Don Maynard, N.Y. Titans	72	1,265	17.6	65	6
	Lionel Taylor, Denver	92	1,235	13.4	80	12
	Art Powell, N.Y. Titans	69	1,167	16.9	76	14
1958	Del Shofner, Los Angeles	51	1,097	21.5	92	8
1956	Bill Howton, Green Bay[2]	55	1,188	21.6	66	12
	Harlon Hill, Chi. Bears[2]	47	1,128	24.0	79	11
1954	Bob Boyd, Los Angeles	53	1,212	22.9	80	6
	*Harlon Hill, Chi. Bears	45	1,124	25.0	76	12
1953	Pete Pihos, Philadelphia	63	1,049	16.7	59	10
1952	*Bill Howton, Green Bay	53	1,231	23.2	90	13
1951	Elroy (Crazylegs) Hirsch, Los Angeles	66	1,495	22.7	91	17
1950	Tom Fears, Los Angeles[2]	84	1,116	13.3	53	7
	Cloyce Box, Detroit	50	1,009	20.2	82	11
1949	Bob Mann, Detroit	66	1,014	15.4	64	4
	Tom Fears, Los Angeles	77	1,013	13.2	51	9
1945	Jim Benton, Cleveland	45	1,067	23.7	84	8
1942	Don Hutson, Green Bay	74	1,211	16.4	73	17

*First season of professional football.

250 YARDS PASS RECEIVING IN A GAME

Date	Player, Team, Opponent	No.	Yards	TD
Nov. 10, 2002	Plaxico Burress, Pittsburgh vs. Atlanta (OT)	9	253	2
Dec. 17, 2000	Terrell Owens, San Francisco vs. Chicago	20	283	1
Sept. 10, 2000	Jimmy Smith, Jacksonville vs. Baltimore	15	291	3
Dec. 12, 1999	Qadry Ismail, Baltimore vs. Pittsburgh	6	258	3
Dec. 18, 1995	Jerry Rice, San Francisco vs. Minnesota	14	289	3
Dec. 11, 1989	John Taylor, San Francisco vs. L.A. Rams	11	286	2
Nov. 26, 1989	Willie Anderson, L.A. Rams vs. New Orleans (OT)	15	336	1
Oct. 18, 1987	Steve Largent, Seattle vs. Detroit	15	261	3
Oct. 4, 1987	Anthony Allen, Washington vs. St. Louis	7	255	3
Dec. 22, 1985	Stephone Paige, Kansas City vs. San Diego	8	309	2
Dec. 20, 1982	Wes Chandler, San Diego vs. Cincinnati	10	260	2
Sept. 23, 1979	*Jerry Butler, Buffalo vs. N.Y. Jets	10	255	4
Nov. 4, 1962	Sonny Randle, St. Louis vs. N.Y. Giants	16	256	1
Oct. 28, 1962	Del Shofner, N.Y. Giants vs. Washington	11	269	1
Oct. 13, 1961	Charley Hennigan, Houston vs. Boston	13	272	1
Oct. 21, 1956	Billy Howton, Green Bay vs. Los Angeles	7	257	2
Dec. 3, 1950	Cloyce Box, Detroit vs. Baltimore	12	302	4
Nov. 22, 1945	Jim Benton, Cleveland vs. Detroit	10	303	1

*First season of professional football.

2,000 COMBINED NET YARDS GAINED IN A SEASON

Year	Player, Team	Rushing Att.-Yds.	Pass Rec.	Punt Ret.	Kickoff Ret.	Fum. Ret.	Total Yds.
2005	Tiki Barber, N.Y. Giants[3]	357-1,860	54-530	0-0	0-0	1-0	412-2,390
	Dante Hall, Kansas City[4]	7-11	34-436	42-276	65-1,560	2-0	150-2,283
	Wes Welker, Miami	1-5	29-434	43-390	61-1,379	4-0	138-2,208
	Larry Johnson, Kansas City	336-1,750	33-343	0-0	0-0	3-0	372-2,093
2004	Dante Hall, Kansas City[3]	8-56	25-230	23-232	68-1,718	0-0	124-2,236
	Tiki Barber, N.Y. Giants[2]	322-1,518	52-578	0-0	0-0	2-0	376-2,096
	Edgerrin James, Indianapolis[3]	334-1,548	51-483	0-0	0-0	1-0	386-2,031
2003	Dante Hall, Kansas City[2]	16-73	40-423	29-472	57-1,478	0-0	142-2,446

Year	Player, Team	Rushing Att.-Yds.	Pass Rec.	Punt Ret.	Kickoff Ret.	Fum. Ret.	Total Yds.
	LaDainian Tomlinson, San Diego[2]	313-1,645	100-725	0-0	0-0	2-0	415-2,370
	Jamal Lewis, Baltimore	387-2,066	26-205	0-0	0-0	1-0	414-2,271
	Ahman Green, Green Bay	355-1,883	50-367	0-0	0-0	2-0	407-2,250
	Deuce McAllister, New Orleans	351-1,641	69-516	0-0	0-0	3-(-3)	423-2,154
	Priest Holmes, Kansas City[3]	320-1,420	74-690	0-0	0-0	0-0	394-2,110
2002	Michael Lewis, New Orleans	1-15	8-200	44-625	70-1,807	2-0	125-2,647
	Priest Holmes, Kansas City[2]	313-1,615	70-672	0-0	0-0	0-0	383-2,287
	Ricky Williams, Miami	383-1,853	47-363	0-0	0-0	1-0	431-2,216
	LaDainian Tomlinson, San Diego	372-1,683	79-489	0-0	0-0	0-0	451-2,172
	Dante Hall, Kansas City	11-54	20-322	29-390	57-1,354	1-0	118-2,120
2001	Priest Holmes, Kansas City	327-1,555	62-614	0-0	0-0	0-0	389-2,169
	Marshall Faulk, St. Louis[4]	260-1,382	83-765	0-0	0-0	2-0	345-2,147
	Derrick Mason, Tennessee[2]	0-0	73-1,128	20-128	34-748	1-0	128-2,004
2000	Derrick Mason, Tennessee	1-1	63-895	51-662	42-1,132	1-0	158-2,690
	MarTay Jenkins, Arizona	1-(-4)	17-219	1-1	82-2,186	0-0	101-2,402
	Edgerrin James, Indianapolis[2]	387-1,709	63-594	0-0	0-0	0-0	450-2,303
	Marshall Faulk, St. Louis[3]	253-1,359	81-830	0-0	1-18	2-0	337-2,207
	Tiki Barber, N.Y. Giants	213-1,006	70-719	39-332	1-28	5-0	328-2,085
1999	Marshall Faulk, St. Louis[2]	253-1,381	87-1,048	0-0	0-0	0-0	340-2,429
	*Edgerrin James, Indianapolis	369-1,553	62-586	0-0	0-0	2-0	433-2,139
	*Terrence Wilkins, Indianapolis	1-2	42-565	41-388	51-1,134	1-0	136-2,089
	Glyn Milburn, Chicago[2]	16-102	20-151	30-346	61-1,426	2-0	129-2,025
1998	Brian Mitchell, Washington[4]	39-208	44-306	44-506	59-1,337	0-0	186-2,357
	Marshall Faulk, Indianapolis	324-1,319	86-908	0-0	0-0	2-13	412-2,240
	Terrell Davis, Denver[2]	392-2,008	25-217	0-0	0-0	1-0	418-2,225
	Jamal Anderson, Atlanta	410-1,846	27-319	0-0	0-0	1-0	438-2,165
	Garrison Hearst, San Francisco	310-1,570	39-535	0-0	0-0	1-0	350-2,105
1997	Barry Sanders, Detroit[2]	335-2,053	33-305	0-0	0-0	1-0	369-2,358
	Kevin Williams, Arizona	1-(-2)	20-273	40-462	59-1,458	1-0	121-2,191
	Brian Mitchell, Washington[3]	23-107	36-438	38-442	47-1,094	0-0	144-2,081
	Terrell Davis, Denver	369-1,750	42-287	0-0	0-0	2-(-7)	413-2,030
	Jermaine Lewis, Baltimore	3-35	42-648	28-437	41-905	2-0	116-2,025
1995	Brian Mitchell, Washington[2]	46-301	38-324	25-315	55-1,408	0-0	164-2,348
	Emmitt Smith, Dallas[2]	377-1,773	62-375	0-0	0-0	0-0	439-2,148
	Glyn Milburn, Denver	49-266	22-191	31-354	47-1,269	0-0	149-2,080
	Ernie Mills, Pittsburgh	5-39	39-679	0-0	54-1,306	0-0	98-2,024
1994	Brian Mitchell, Washington	78-311	26-236	32-452	58-1,478	0-0	194-2,477
	Barry Sanders, Detroit	331-1,883	44-283	0-0	0-0	0-0	375-2,166
1992	Thurman Thomas, Buffalo[2]	312-1,487	58-626	0-0	0-0	1-0	371-2,113
	Emmitt Smith, Dallas	373-1,713	59-335	0-0	0-0	1-0	433-2,048
	Barry Foster, Pittsburgh	390-1,690	36-344	0-0	0-0	2-(−20)	428-2,014
1991	Thurman Thomas, Buffalo	288-1,407	62-631	0-0	0-0	0-0	350-2,038
1990	Herschel Walker, Minnesota[2]	184-770	35-315	0-0	44-966	4-0	267-2,051
1988	*Tim Brown, L.A. Raiders	14-50	43-725	49-444	41-1,098	7-0	154-2,317
	Roger Craig, San Francisco[2]	310-1,502	76-534	0-0	2-32	2-0	390-2,068
	Eric Dickerson, Indianapolis[4]	388-1,659	36-377	0-0	0-0	1-0	425-2,036
	Herschel Walker, Dallas	361-1,514	53-505	0-0	0-0	3-0	417-2,019
1986	Eric Dickerson, L.A. Rams[3]	404-1,821	26-205	0-0	0-0	2-0	432-2,026
	Gary Anderson, San Diego	127-442	80-871	25-227	24-482	2-0	258-2,022
1985	Lionel James, San Diego	105-516	86-1,027	25-213	36-779	1-0	253-2,535
	Marcus Allen, L.A. Raiders	380-1,759	67-555	0-0	0-0	2-(−6)	449-2,308
	Roger Craig, San Francisco	214-1,050	92-1,016	0-0	0-0	0-0	306-2,066
	Walter Payton, Chicago[4]	324-1,551	49-483	0-0	0-0	1-0	374-2,034
1984	Eric Dickerson, L.A. Rams[2]	379-2,105	21-139	0-0	0-0	4-15	404-2,259
	James Wilder, Tampa Bay	407-1,544	85-685	0-0	0-0	4-0	496-2,229
	Walter Payton, Chicago[3]	381-1,684	45-368	0-0	0-0	1-0	427-2,052
1983	*Eric Dickerson, L.A. Rams	390-1,808	51-404	0-0	0-0	1-0	442-2,212
	William Andrews, Atlanta[2]	331-1,567	59-609	0-0	0-0	2-0	392-2,176
	Walter Payton, Chicago[2]	314-1,421	53-607	0-0	0-0	2-0	369-2,028
1981	*James Brooks, San Diego	109-525	46-329	22-290	40-949	2-0	219-2,093
	William Andrews, Atlanta	289-1,301	81-735	0-0	0-0	0-0	370-2,036
1980	Bruce Harper, N.Y. Jets[2]	45-126	50-634	28-242	49-1,070	3-0	175-2,072
1979	Wilbert Montgomery, Philadelphia	338-1,512	41-494	0-0	1-6	2-0	382-2,012
1978	Bruce Harper, N.Y. Jets	58-303	13-196	30-378	55-1,280	1-0	157-2,157
1977	Walter Payton, Chicago[2]	339-1,852	27-269	0-0	2-95	5-0	373-2,216
	Terry Metcalf, St. Louis[3]	149-739	34-403	14-108	32-772	1-0	230-2,022
1975	Terry Metcalf, St. Louis[2]	165-816	43-378	23-285	35-960	2-23	268-2,462
	O.J. Simpson, Buffalo[2]	329-1,817	28-426	0-0	0-0	1-0	358-2,243

Year	Player, Team	Rushing Att.-Yds.	Pass Rec.	Punt Ret.	Kickoff Ret.	Fum. Ret.	Total Yds.
1974	Mack Herron, New England	231-824	38-474	35-517	28-629	3-0	335-2,444
	Otis Armstrong, Denver	263-1,407	38-405	0-0	16-386	1-0	318-2,198
	Terry Metcalf, St. Louis	152-718	50-377	26-340	20-623	7-0	255-2,058
1973	O.J. Simpson, Buffalo	332-2,003	6-70	0-0	0-0	0-0	338-2,073
1966	Gale Sayers, Chicago[2]	229-1,231	34-447	6-44	23-718	3-0	295-2,440
	Leroy Kelly, Cleveland	209-1,141	32-366	13-104	19-403	0-0	273-2,014
1965	*Gale Sayers, Chicago	166-867	29-507	16-238	21-660	4-0	236-2,272
1963	Timmy Brown, Philadelphia[2]	192-841	36-487	16-152	33-945	2-3	279-2,428
	Jim Brown, Cleveland	291-1,863	24-268	0-0	0-0	0-0	315-2,131
1962	Timmy Brown, Philadelphia	137-545	52-849	6-81	30-831	4-0	229-2,306
	Dick Christy, N.Y. Titans	114-535	62-538	15-250	38-824	2-0	231-2,147
1961	Billy Cannon, Houston	200-948	43-586	9-70	18-439	2-0	272-2,043
1960	*Abner Haynes, Dallas Texans	156-875	55-576	14-215	19-434	4-0	248-2,100

*First season of professional football.

300 COMBINED NET YARDS GAINED IN A GAME

Date	Player, Team, Opponent	No.	Yards	TD
Dec. 14, 2003	Derrick Mason, Tennessee vs. Buffalo	21	302	0
Nov. 16, 2003	Jonathan Carter, N.Y. Jets vs. Indianapolis	7	304	2
Dec. 8, 2002	Steve Smith, Carolina vs. Cincinnati	9	313	3
Nov. 24, 2002	Priest Holmes, Kansas City vs. Seattle	30	307	3
Oct. 13, 2002	Michael Lewis, New Orleans vs. Washington	8	356	2
Dec. 24, 1999	Jason Tucker, Dallas vs. New Orleans	13	331	1
Dec. 7, 1997	Jermaine Lewis, Baltimore vs. Seattle	10	308	3
Dec. 25, 1995	Kevin Williams, Dallas vs. Arizona	16	307	2
Dec. 10, 1995	Glyn Milburn, Denver vs. Seattle	33	404	0
Oct. 23, 1994	Tyrone Hughes, New Orleans vs. L.A. Rams	11	347	2
Dec. 11, 1989	John Taylor, San Francisco vs. L.A. Rams	14	321	2
Nov. 26, 1989	Willie Anderson, L.A. Rams vs. New Orleans (OT)	15	336	1
Nov. 28, 1988	*Tim Brown, L.A. Raiders vs. Seattle	12	308	1
Dec. 22, 1985	Stephone Paige, Kansas City vs. San Diego	8	309	2
Nov. 10, 1985	Lionel James, San Diego vs. L.A. Raiders (OT)	23	345	0
Sept. 22, 1985	Lionel James, San Diego vs. Cincinnati	20	316	2
Dec. 21, 1975	*Walter Payton, Chicago vs. New Orleans	32	300	1
Nov. 23, 1975	Greg Pruitt, Cleveland vs. Cincinnati	28	304	2
Nov. 1, 1970	Eugene (Mercury) Morris, Miami vs. Baltimore	17	302	0
Oct. 4, 1970	O.J. Simpson, Buffalo vs. N.Y. Jets	26	303	2
Dec. 6, 1969	Jerry LeVias, Houston vs. N.Y. Jets	18	329	1
Nov. 2, 1969	Travis Williams, Green Bay vs. Pittsburgh	11	314	3
Dec. 18, 1966	Gale Sayers, Chicago vs. Minnesota	20	339	2
Dec. 12, 1965	*Gale Sayers, Chicago vs. San Francisco	17	336	6
Nov. 17, 1963	Gary Ballman, Pittsburgh vs. Washington	12	320	2
Dec. 16, 1962	Timmy Brown, Philadelphia vs. St. Louis	19	341	2
Dec. 10, 1961	Billy Cannon, Houston vs. N.Y. Titans	32	373	5
Nov. 19, 1961	Jim Brown, Cleveland vs. Philadelphia	38	313	4
Dec. 3, 1950	Cloyce Box, Detroit vs. Baltimore	13	302	4
Oct. 29, 1950	Wally Triplett, Detroit vs. Los Angeles	11	331	1
Nov. 22, 1945	Jim Benton, Cleveland vs. Detroit	10	303	1

*First season of professional football.

2,000 SCRIMMAGE YARDS GAINED IN A SEASON

Year	Player, Team	Att.	Rushing Yards	Receptions	Receiving Yards	Scrimm. Yards
2005	Tiki Barber, N.Y. Giants[2]	357	1,860	54	530	2,390
	Larry Johnson, Kansas City	336	1,750	33	343	2,093
2004	Tiki Barber, N.Y. Giants	322	1,518	52	578	2,096
	Edgerrin James, Indianapolis[3]	334	1,548	51	483	2,031
2003	LaDainian Tomlinson, San Diego[2]	313	1,645	100	725	2,370
	Jamal Lewis, Baltimore	387	2,066	26	205	2,271
	Ahman Green, Green Bay	355	1,883	50	367	2,250
	Deuce McAllister, New Orleans	351	1,641	69	516	2,157
	Priest Holmes, Kansas City[3]	320	1,420	74	690	2,110
2002	Priest Holmes, Kansas City[2]	313	1,615	70	672	2,287
	Ricky Williams, Miami	383	1,853	47	363	2,216
	LaDainian Tomlinson, San Diego	372	1,683	79	489	2,172
2001	Priest Holmes, Kansas City	327	1,555	62	614	2,169
	Marshall Faulk, St. Louis[4]	260	1,382	83	765	2,147
2000	Edgerrin James, Indianapolis[2]	387	1,709	63	594	2,303
	Marshall Faulk, St. Louis[3]	253	1,359	81	830	2,189

Year	Player, Team	Att.	Rushing Yards	Receptions	Receiving Yards	Scrimm. Yards
1999	Marshall Faulk, St. Louis[2]	253	1,381	87	1,048	2,429
	*Edgerrin James, Indianapolis	369	1,553	62	586	2,139
1998	Marshall Faulk, Indianapolis	324	1,319	86	908	2,227
	Terrell Davis, Denver[2]	392	2,008	25	217	2,225
	Jamal Anderson, Atlanta	410	1,846	27	319	2,165
	Garrison Hearst, San Francisco	310	1,570	39	535	2,105
1997	Barry Sanders, Detroit[2]	335	2,053	33	305	2,358
	Terrell Davis, Denver	369	1,750	42	287	2,037
1995	Emmitt Smith, Dallas[2]	377	1,773	62	375	2,148
1994	Barry Sanders, Detroit	331	1,883	44	283	2,166
1992	Thurman Thomas, Buffalo[2]	312	1,487	58	626	2,113
	Emmitt Smith, Dallas	373	1,713	59	335	2,048
	Barry Foster, Pittsburgh	390	1,690	36	344	2,034
1991	Thurman Thomas, Buffalo	288	1,407	62	631	2,038
1988	Roger Craig, San Francisco[2]	310	1,502	76	534	2,036
	Eric Dickerson, Indianapolis[4]	388	1,659	36	377	2,036
	Herschel Walker, Dallas	361	1,514	53	505	2,019
1986	Eric Dickerson, L.A. Rams[3]	404	1,821	26	205	2,026
1985	Marcus Allen, L.A. Raiders	380	1,759	67	555	2,314
	Roger Craig, San Francisco	214	1,050	92	1,016	2,066
	Walter Payton, Chicago[4]	324	1,551	49	483	2,034
1984	Eric Dickerson, L. A. Rams[2]	379	2,105	21	139	2,244
	James Wilder, Tampa Bay	407	1,544	85	685	2,229
	Walter Payton, Chicago[3]	381	1,684	45	368	2,052
1983	*Eric Dickerson, L.A. Rams	390	1,808	51	404	2,212
	William Andrews, Atlanta[2]	331	1,567	59	609	2,176
	Walter Payton, Chicago[2]	314	1,421	53	607	2,028
1981	William Andrews, Atlanta	289	1,301	81	735	2,036
1979	Wilbert Montgomery, Philadelphia	338	1,512	41	494	2,006
1977	Walter Payton, Chicago	339	1,852	27	269	2,121
1975	O.J. Simpson, Buffalo[2]	329	1,817	28	426	2,243
1973	O.J. Simpson, Buffalo	332	2,003	6	70	2,073
1963	Jim Brown, Cleveland	91	1,863	24	268	2,131

*First season of professional football.

300 SCRIMMAGE YARDS GAINED IN A GAME

Date	Player, Team, Opponent	Att.	Yards	TD
Nov. 24, 2002	Priest Holmes, Kansas City vs. Seattle	30	307	3
Nov. 26, 1989	Flipper Anderson, L.A. Rams vs. New Orleans (OT)	15	336	1
Dec. 22, 1985	Stephone Paige, Kansas City vs. San Diego	8	309	2
Dec. 10, 1961	Billy Cannon, Houston vs. N.Y. Titans	30	330	5
Dec. 3, 1950	Cloyce Box, Detroit vs. Baltimore	12	302	4
Nov. 22, 1945	Jim Benton, Cleveland vs. Detroit	10	303	1

TOP 20 SCORERS

Player	Years	TD	FG	PAT	TP
Gary Anderson	23	0	538	820	2,434
Morten Andersen	23	0	520	798	2,358
George Blanda	26	9	335	942	2,002
Norm Johnson	18	0	366	638	1,736
Nick Lowery	18	0	383	562	1,711
Jan Stenerud	19	0	373	580	1,699
John Carney	18	0	390	464	1,634
Eddie Murray	19	0	352	538	1,594
Matt Stover	15	0	380	454	1,594
Al Del Greco	17	0	347	543	1,584
Jason Elam	13	0	341	534	1,557
Steve Christie	15	0	336	468	1,476
Pat Leahy	18	0	304	558	1,470
Jim Turner	16	1	304	521	1,439
Matt Bahr	17	0	300	522	1,422
Jason Hanson	14	0	327	439	1,420
Mark Moseley	16	0	300	482	1,382
Jim Bakken	17	0	282	534	1,380
Fred Cox	15	0	282	519	1,365
Lou Groza	17	1	234	641	1,349

TOP 20 TOUCHDOWN SCORERS

Player	Years	Rush	Rec.	Total Returns	TD
Jerry Rice	20	10	197	1	208
Emmitt Smith	15	164	11	0	175
Marcus Allen	16	123	21	1	145
Marshall Faulk	12	100	36	0	136
Cris Carter	16	0	130	1	131
Jim Brown	9	106	20	0	126
Walter Payton	13	110	15	0	125
John Riggins	14	104	12	0	116
Lenny Moore	12	63	48	2	113
Marvin Harrison	10	0	110	0	110
Barry Sanders	10	99	10	0	109
Tim Brown	17	1	100	4	105
Don Hutson	11	3	99	3	105
Terrell Owens	10	2	101	0	103
Steve Largent	14	1	100	0	101
Shaun Alexander	6	89	11	0	100
Franco Harris	13	91	9	0	100
Curtis Martin	11	90	10	0	100
Randy Moss	8	0	98	1	99
Eric Dickerson	11	90	6	0	96

TOP 20 RUSHERS

Player	Years	Att.	Yards	Avg.	Long	TD
Emmitt Smith	15	4,409	18,355	4.2	75	164
Walter Payton	13	3,838	16,726	4.4	76	110
Barry Sanders	10	3,062	15,269	5.0	85	99
Curtis Martin	11	3,518	14,101	4.0	70	90
Jerome Bettis	13	3,479	13,662	3.9	71	91
Eric Dickerson	11	2,996	13,259	4.4	85	90
Tony Dorsett	12	2,936	12,739	4.3	99	77
Jim Brown	9	2,359	12,312	5.2	80	106
Marshall Faulk	12	2,836	12,279	4.3	71	100
Marcus Allen	16	3,022	12,243	4.1	61	123
Franco Harris	13	2,949	12,120	4.1	75	91
Thurman Thomas	13	2,877	12,074	4.2	80	65
John Riggins	14	2,916	11,352	3.9	66	104
O.J. Simpson	11	2,404	11,236	4.7	94	61
Ricky Watters	10	2,622	10,643	4.1	57	78
Eddie George	9	2,865	10,441	3.6	76	68
Corey Dillon	9	2,419	10,429	4.3	96	69
Ottis Anderson	14	2,562	10,273	4.0	76	81
Earl Campbell	9	2,187	9,407	4.3	81	74
Edgerrin James	7	2,188	9,226	4.2	72	64

OUTSTANDING PERFORMERS

TOP 20 COMBINED YARDS GAINED

Player	Years	Tot.	Rush.	Rec.	Int. Ret.	Punt Ret.	Kickoff Ret.	Fumble Ret.
Jerry Rice	20	23,546	645	22,895	0	0	6	0
Brian Mitchell	14	23,330	1,967	2,336	0	4,999	14,014	14
Walter Payton	13	21,803	16,726	4,538	0	0	539	0
Emmitt Smith	15	21,564	18,355	3,224	0	0	0	-15
Tim Brown	17	19,682	190	14,934	0	3,320	1,235	3
Marshall Faulk	12	19,190	12,279	6,875	0	0	18	18
Barry Sanders	10	18,308	15,269	2,921	0	0	118	0
Herschel Walker	12	18,168	8,225	4,859	0	0	5,084	0
Marcus Allen	16	17,648	12,243	5,411	0	0	0	-6
Curtis Martin	11	17,421	14,101	3,329	0	0	0	-9
Eric Metcalf	13	17,230	2,392	5,572	0	3,453	5,813	0
Thurman Thomas	13	16,532	12,074	4,458	0	0	0	0
Tony Dorsett	12	16,326	12,739	3,554	0	0	0	54
Henry Ellard	16	15,718	50	13,777	0	1,527	364	0
Irving Fryar	17	15,594	242	12,785	0	2,055	505	7
Jim Brown	9	15,459	12,312	2,499	0	0	648	0
Eric Dickerson	11	15,411	13,259	2,137	0	0	0	15
Tiki Barber	9	15,232	8,787	4,718	0	1,181	544	2
Jerome Bettis	13	15,113	13,662	1,449	0	0	0	2
Glyn Milburn	9	14,911	817	1,322	0	2,984	9,788	0

TOP 20 YARDS FROM SCRIMMAGE

Player	Years	Scrimmage Yards	Rushing Yards	Receiving Yards
Jerry Rice	20	23,540	645	22,895
Emmitt Smith	15	21,579	18,355	3,224
Walter Payton	13	21,264	16,726	4,538
Marshall Faulk	12	19,154	12,279	6,875
Barry Sanders	10	18,190	15,269	2,921
Marcus Allen	16	17,654	12,243	5,411
Curtis Martin	11	17,430	14,101	3,329
Thurman Thomas	13	16,532	12,074	4,458
Tony Dorsett	12	16,293	12,739	3,554
Eric Dickerson	11	15,396	13,259	2,137
Tim Brown	17	15,124	190	14,934
Jerome Bettis	13	15,111	13,662	1,449
Ricky Watters	10	14,891	10,643	4,248
Jim Brown	9	14,811	12,312	2,499
Franco Harris	13	14,407	12,120	2,287
James Lofton	16	14,250	246	14,004
Cris Carter	16	13,940	41	13,899
Henry Ellard	16	13,827	50	13,777
Andre Reed	16	13,698	500	13,198
Tiki Barber	9	13,505	8,787	4,718

TOP 20 PASSERS

Player	Years	Att.	Comp.	Pct. Comp.	Yards	Avg. Gain	TD	Pct. TD	Int.	Pct. Int.	Rating
Steve Young	15	4,149	2,667	64.3	33,124	7.98	232	5.6	107	2.6	96.8
Kurt Warner	8	2,340	1,537	65.7	19,214	8.21	119	5.1	78	3.3	94.1
Peyton Manning	8	4,333	2,769	63.9	33,189	7.66	244	5.6	130	3.0	93.5
Joe Montana	15	5,391	3,409	63.2	40,551	7.52	273	5.1	139	2.6	92.3
Daunte Culpepper	7	2,607	1,678	64.4	20,162	7.73	135	5.2	86	3.3	91.5
Marc Bulger	4	1,518	987	65.0	11,932	7.86	71	4.7	51	3.4	90.6
Tom Brady	6	2,548	1,577	61.9	18,035	7.08	123	4.8	66	2.6	88.5
Trent Green	8	3,329	2,022	60.7	25,621	7.70	150	4.5	92	2.8	88.3
Matt Hasselbeck	7	2,205	1,342	60.9	15,925	7.22	96	4.4	57	2.6	86.6
Dan Marino	17	8,358	4,967	59.4	61,361	7.34	420	5.0	252	3.0	86.4
Brett Favre	15	7,610	4,678	61.5	53,615	7.05	396	5.2	255	3.4	86.0
Jeff Garcia	7	2,785	1,695	60.9	19,076	6.85	126	4.5	71	2.5	85.8
Drew Brees	5	1,809	1,125	62.2	12,348	6.83	80	4.4	53	2.9	84.9
Brian Griese	8	2,318	1,463	63.1	16,344	7.05	103	4.4	78	3.4	84.8
Rich Gannon	16	4,206	2,533	60.2	28,743	6.83	180	4.3	104	2.5	84.7
Jake Delhomme	5	1,503	888	59.1	11,160	7.43	75	5.0	52	3.5	84.5
Jim Kelly	11	4,779	2,874	60.1	35,467	7.42	237	5.0	175	3.7	84.4
Brad Johnson	12	3,798	2,350	61.9	25,798	6.79	155	4.1	102	2.7	84.4
Donovan McNabb	7	2,943	1,718	58.4	19,433	6.60	134	4.6	66	2.2	84.1
Mark Brunell	12	4,334	2,576	59.4	30,037	6.93	174	4.0	102	2.4	84.1

1,500 or more attempts. The passing ratings are based on performance standards established for completion percentage, interception percentage, touchdown percentage, and average gain. Please consult page 364 for more information.

2006 NFL Record & Fact Book

TOP 20 LEADERS IN PASSES COMPLETED

Dan Marino	4,967
Brett Favre	4,678
John Elway	4,123
Warren Moon	3,988
Drew Bledsoe	3,749
Vinny Testaverde	3,691
Fran Tarkenton	3,686
Joe Montana	3,409
Dan Fouts	3,297
Dave Krieg	3,105
Boomer Esiason	2,969
Troy Aikman	2,898
Steve DeBerg	2,874
Jim Kelly	2,874
Jim Everett	2,841
Johnny Unitas	2,830
Kerry Collins	2,826
Peyton Manning	2,769
Steve Young	2,667
Ken Anderson	2,654

TOP 20 LEADERS IN TOUCHDOWN PASSES

Dan Marino	420
Brett Favre	396
Fran Tarkenton	342
John Elway	300
Warren Moon	291
Johnny Unitas	290
Joe Montana	273
Vinny Testaverde	269
Dave Krieg	261
Sonny Jurgensen	255
Dan Fouts	254
Boomer Esiason	247
Drew Bledsoe	244
John Hadl	244
Peyton Manning	244
Len Dawson	239
Jim Kelly	237
George Blanda	236
Steve Young	232
John Brodie	214

TOP 20 LEADERS IN PASSING YARDS

Dan Marino	61,361
Brett Favre	53,615
John Elway	51,475
Warren Moon	49,325
Fran Tarkenton	47,003
Vinny Testaverde	45,252
Drew Bledsoe	43,447
Dan Fouts	43,040
Joe Montana	40,551
Johnny Unitas	40,239
Dave Krieg	38,147
Boomer Esiason	37,920
Jim Kelly	35,467
Jim Everett	34,837
Jim Hart	34,665
Steve DeBerg	34,241
Kerry Collins	33,637
John Hadl	33,503
Phil Simms	33,462
Peyton Manning	33,189

TOP 20 LEADERS IN RECEPTION YARDS

Jerry Rice	22,895
Tim Brown	14,934
James Lofton	14,004
Cris Carter	13,899
Henry Ellard	13,777
Andre Reed	13,198
Steve Largent	13,089
Irving Fryar	12,785
Art Monk	12,721
Marvin Harrison	12,331
Jimmy Smith	12,287
Isaac Bruce	12,278
Charlie Joiner	12,146
Michael Irvin	11,904
Don Maynard	11,834
Rod Smith	10,877
Gary Clark	10,856
Stanley Morgan	10,716
Keenan McCardell	10,680
Terrell Owens	10,535

TOP 20 PASS RECEIVERS

Player	Years	No.	Yards	Avg.	Long	TD
Jerry Rice	20	1,549	22,895	14.8	96	197
Cris Carter	16	1,101	13,899	12.6	80	130
Tim Brown	17	1,094	14,934	13.7	80	100
Andre Reed	16	951	13,198	13.9	83	87
Art Monk	16	940	12,721	13.5	79	68
Marvin Harrison	10	927	12,331	13.3	80	110
Jimmy Smith	12	862	12,287	14.3	75	67
Irving Fryar	17	851	12,785	15.0	80	84
Larry Centers	14	827	6,797	8.2	54	28
Keenan McCardell	14	825	10,680	12.9	76	62
Steve Largent	14	819	13,089	16.0	74	100
Shannon Sharpe	14	815	10,060	12.3	82	62
Henry Ellard	16	814	13,777	16.9	81	65
Isaac Bruce	12	813	12,278	15.1	80	77
Rod Smith	11	797	10,877	13.6	85	65
Marshall Faulk	12	767	6,875	9.0	85	36
James Lofton	16	764	14,004	18.3	80	75
Michael Irvin	12	750	11,904	15.9	87	65
Charlie Joiner	18	750	12,146	16.2	87	65
Keyshawn Johnson	10	744	9,756	13.1	76	60

TOP 20 INTERCEPTORS

Player	Years	No.	Yards	Avg.	Long	TD
Paul Krause	16	81	1,185	14.6	81	3
Emlen Tunnell	14	79	1,282	16.2	55	4
Rod Woodson	17	71	1,483	20.9	98	12
Dick (Night Train) Lane	14	68	1,207	17.8	80	5
Ken Riley	15	65	596	9.2	66	5
Ronnie Lott	14	63	730	11.6	83	5
Dave Brown	15	62	698	11.3	90	5
Dick LeBeau	14	62	762	12.3	70	3
Emmitt Thomas	13	58	937	16.2	73	5
Mel Blount	14	57	736	12.9	52	2
Bobby Boyd	9	57	994	17.4	74	4
Eugene Robinson	16	57	762	13.4	49	1
Johnny Robinson	12	57	741	13.0	57	1
Everson Walls	13	57	504	8.8	40	1
Lem Barney	11	56	1,077	19.2	71	7
Pat Fischer	17	56	941	16.8	69	4
Aeneas Williams	14	55	807	14.7	65	9
Eric Allen	14	54	826	15.3	94	8
Willie Brown	16	54	472	8.7	45	2
Darrell Green	20	54	621	11.5	83	6

TOP 20 PUNTERS (MINIMUM 250 PUNTS)

Player	Years	No.	Yards	Avg.	Long	Blk.
Shane Lechler	6	442	20,266	45.9	73	2
Sammy Baugh	16	338	15,245	45.1	85	9
Tommy Davis	11	511	22,833	44.7	82	2
Yale Lary	11	503	22,279	44.3	74	4
Todd Sauerbrun	11	832	36,600	44.0	73	7
Bob Scarpitto	8	283	12,408	43.8	87	4
Horace Gillom	7	385	16,872	43.8	80	5
Jerry Norton	11	358	15,671	43.8	78	2
Dave Lewis	4	285	12,447	43.7	63	0
Greg Montgomery	9	524	22,831	43.6	77	8
Don Chandler	12	660	28,678	43.5	90	4
Tom Rouen	12	810	35,189	43.4	76	9
Rick Tuten	11	741	32,190	43.4	73	2
Darren Bennett	11	836	36,316	43.4	66	3
Brian Moorman	5	379	16,461	43.4	84	1
Tom Tupa	17	873	37,862	43.4	73	2
Hunter Smith	7	425	18,429	43.4	69	4
Rohn Stark	16	1,141	49,471	43.4	72	7
Chris Hanson	6	356	15,427	43.3	74	2
Sean Landeta	21	1,401	60,707	43.3	74	6

TOP 20 KICKOFF RETURNERS (MINIMUM 75 RETURNS)

Player	Years	No.	Yards	Avg.	Long	TD
Gale Sayers	7	91	2,781	30.6	103	6
Lynn Chandnois	7	92	2,720	29.6	93	3
Abe Woodson	9	193	5,538	28.7	105	5
Buddy Young	6	90	2,514	27.9	104	2
Terrence McGee	3	106	2,921	27.6	104	4
Travis Williams	5	102	2,801	27.5	105	6
Joe Arenas	7	139	3,798	27.3	96	1
Clarence Davis	8	79	2,140	27.1	76	0
Steve Van Buren	8	76	2,030	26.7	98	3
Lonny Lyles	12	81	2,161	26.7	103	3
Mercury Morris	8	111	2,947	26.5	105	3
Bobby Jancik	6	158	4,185	26.5	61	0
Mel Renfro	14	85	2,246	26.4	100	2
Bobby Mitchell	14	102	2,690	26.4	98	5
Ollie Matson	14	143	3,746	26.2	105	6
Alvin Haymond	10	170	4,438	26.1	98	2
Noland Smith	3	82	2,137	26.1	106	1
Al Nelson	9	101	2,625	26.0	78	0
Timmy Brown	11	184	4,781	26.0	105	5
Vic Washington	6	129	3,341	25.9	98	1

TOP 20 PUNT RETURNERS (MINIMUM 75 RETURNS)

Player	Years	No.	Yards	Avg.	Long	TD
George McAfee	8	112	1,431	12.8	74	2
Jack Christiansen	8	85	1,084	12.8	89	8
Claude Gibson	5	110	1,381	12.6	85	3
Bill Dudley	9	124	1,515	12.2	96	3
Rick Upchurch	9	248	3,008	12.1	92	8
Desmond Howard	11	244	2,895	11.9	95	8
Billy Johnson	14	282	3,317	11.8	87	6
Mack Herron	3	84	982	11.7	66	0
Billy Thompson	13	157	1,814	11.6	60	0
Santana Moss	5	95	1,092	11.5	63	2
Darrien Gordon	9	314	3,601	11.5	94	6
Henry Ellard	16	135	1,527	11.3	83	4
Rodger Bird	3	94	1,063	11.3	78	0
Bosh Pritchard	6	95	1,072	11.3	81	2
Terry Metcalf	6	84	936	11.1	69	1
Bob Hayes	11	104	1,158	11.1	90	3
Jermaine Lewis	9	295	3,282	11.1	89	6
B.J. Sams	2	88	976	11.1	78	2
Floyd Little	9	81	893	11.0	72	2
Louis Lipps	9	112	1,234	11.0	76	3

TOP 20 LEADERS IN SACKS

Player	*Years	No.
Bruce Smith	19	200.0
Reggie White	15	198.0
Kevin Greene	15	160.0
Chris Doleman	15	150.5
Richard Dent	15	137.5
John Randle	14	137.5
Leslie O'Neal	13	132.5
Lawrence Taylor	12	132.5
Michael Strahan	13	129.5
Rickey Jackson	14	128.0
Derrick Thomas	11	126.5
Clyde Simmons	15	121.5
Simeon Rice	10	119.0
Sean Jones	13	113.0
Greg Townsend	13	109.5
Pat Swilling	12	107.5
Trace Armstrong	15	106.0
Neil Smith	13	104.5
Jim Jeffcoat	15	102.5
William Fuller	13	100.5
Charles Haley	12	100.5

*Years played since 1982 when sacks became an official statistic.

POSTSEASON LEADERS
TOP 10 POSTSEASON RUSHERS

Player	Att.	Yards	Avg.	Long	TD
Emmitt Smith	349	1,586	4.5	65	19
Franco Harris	400	1,556	3.9	50	16
Thurman Thomas	339	1,442	4.3	40	16
Tony Dorsett	302	1,383	4.6	53	9
Marcus Allen	267	1,347	5.0	74	11
Terrell Davis	204	1,140	5.6	62	12
John Riggins	251	996	4.0	43	12
Larry Csonka	225	891	4.0	49	9
Chuck Foreman	229	860	3.8	62	7
Roger Craig	208	841	4.0	80	7

TOP 10 POSTSEASON PASSERS

Player	Att.	Comp.	Pct. Comp.	Yards	Avg. Gain	TD	Pct. TD	Int.	Pct. Int.	Rating
Bart Starr	213	130	61.0	1,753	8.23	15	7.0	3	1.4	104.8
Joe Montana	734	460	62.7	5,772	7.86	45	6.1	21	2.9	95.6
Jake Delhomme	192	113	58.9	1,642	8.55	11	5.7	5	2.6	95.0
Ken Anderson	166	110	66.3	1,321	7.96	9	5.4	6	3.6	93.5
Kurt Warner	268	169	63.1	2,221	8.29	15	5.6	10	3.7	92.3
Joe Theismann	211	128	60.7	1,782	8.45	11	5.2	7	3.3	91.4
Tom Brady	367	225	61.3	2,493	6.79	15	4.1	5	1.4	89.4
Peyton Manning	321	193	60.1	2,462	7.67	15	4.7	8	2.5	89.3
Troy Aikman	502	320	63.7	3,849	7.67	23	4.6	17	3.4	88.3
Steve Young	471	292	62.0	3,326	7.06	20	4.2	13	2.8	85.8

TOP 10 POSTSEASON PASS RECEIVERS

Player	No.	Yards	Avg.	Long	TD
Jerry Rice	151	2,245	14.9	72	22
Micahel Irvin	87	1,315	15.1	53	8
Andre Reed	85	1,229	14.5	72	9
Thurman Thomas	76	672	8.8	27	5
Cliff Branch	73	1,289	17.7	72	5
Fred Biletnikoff	70	1,167	16.7	57	10
Art Monk	69	1,062	15.4	48	7
Drew Pearson	67	1,105	16.5	83	8
Tony Nathan	65	649	10.0	39	2
Cris Carter	63	870	13.8	66	8
Roger Craig	63	606	9.6	40	2

TOP 10 POSTSEASON INTERCEPTION LEADERS

Player	Interceptions
Ronnie Lott	9
Bill Simpson	9
Charlie Waters	9
Lester Hayes	8
Willie Brown	7
Dennis Thurman	7
Bobby Bryant	6
Eric Davis	6
Glen Edwards	6
Darrell Green	6
Cliff Harris	6
Rodney Harrison	6
Vernon Perry	6
Aeneas Williams	6

TOP 10 POSTSEASON SACK LEADERS

Player	Sacks
Willie McGinest	16.0
Bruce Smith	14.5
Reggie White	12.0
Charles Haley	11.0
Richard Dent	10.5
Trace Armstrong	10.0
Charles Mann	10.0
Tony Tolbert	10.0
Neil Smith	9.5
Jeff Wright	9.0

*Sacks became an official statistic in 1982.

Compiled by Elias Sports Bureau

Super Bowl I, 1/15/67	Super Bowl XXI, 1/25/87
Super Bowl II, 1/14/68	Super Bowl XXII, 1/31/88
Super Bowl III, 1/12/69	Super Bowl XXIII, 1/22/89
Super Bowl IV, 1/11/70	Super Bowl XXIV, 1/28/90
Super Bowl V, 1/17/71	Super Bowl XXV, 1/27/91
Super Bowl VI, 1/16/72	Super Bowl XXVI, 1/26/92
Super Bowl VII, 1/14/73	Super Bowl XXVII, 1/31/93
Super Bowl VIII, 1/13/74	Super Bowl XXVIII, 1/30/94
Super Bowl IX, 1/12/75	Super Bowl XXIX, 1/29/95
Super Bowl X, 1/18/76	Super Bowl XXX, 1/28/96
Super Bowl XI, 1/9/77	Super Bowl XXXI, 1/26/97
Super Bowl XII, 1/15/78	Super Bowl XXXII, 1/25/98
Super Bowl XIII, 1/21/79	Super Bowl XXXIII, 1/31/99
Super Bowl XIV, 1/20/80	Super Bowl XXXIV, 1/30/00
Super Bowl XV, 1/25/81	Super Bowl XXXV, 1/28/01
Super Bowl XVI, 1/24/82	Super Bowl XXXVI, 2/3/02
Super Bowl XVII, 1/30/83	Super Bowl XXXVII, 1/26/03
Super Bowl XVIII, 1/22/84	Super Bowl XXXVIII, 2/1/04
Super Bowl XIX, 1/20/85	Super Bowl XXXIX, 2/6/05
Super Bowl XX, 1/26/86	Super Bowl XL, 2/5/06

INDIVIDUAL RECORDS

SERVICE
Most Games
- 6 Mike Lodish, Buffalo, XXV-XXVIII; Denver, XXXII-XXXIII
- 5 Marv Fleming, Green Bay, I-II; Miami, VI-VIII
  - Larry Cole, Dallas, V-VI, X, XII-XIII
  - Cliff Harris, Dallas, V-VI, X, XII-XIII
  - Charles Haley, San Francisco, XXIII-XXIV; Dallas, XXVII-XXVIII, XXX
  - D.D. Lewis, Dallas, V-VI, X, XII-XIII
  - Preston Pearson, Baltimore, III; Pittsburgh, IX; Dallas, X, XII-XIII
  - Charlie Waters, Dallas, V-VI, X, XII-XIII
  - Rayfield Wright, Dallas, V-VI, X, XII-XIII
  - Cornelius Bennett, Buffalo, XXV-XXVIII; Atlanta, XXXIII
  - John Elway, Denver, XXI-XXII, XXIV, XXXII-XXXIII
  - Glenn Parker, Buffalo, XXV-XXVIII; N.Y. Giants, XXXV
  - Bill Romanowski, San Francisco, XXIII-XXIV; Denver, XXXII-XXXIII; Oakland, XXXVII
- 4 By many players

Most Games, Winning Team
- 5 Charles Haley, San Francisco, XXIII-XXIV; Dallas, XXVII-XXVIII, XXX
- 4 By many players

Most Games, Coach
- 6 Don Shula, Baltimore, III; Miami, VI-VIII, XVII, XIX
- 5 Tom Landry, Dallas, V-VI, X, XII-XIII
- 4 Bud Grant, Minnesota, IV, VIII-IX, XI
  - Chuck Noll, Pittsburgh, IX-X, XIII-XIV
  - Joe Gibbs, Washington, XVII-XVIII, XXII, XXVI
  - Marv Levy, Buffalo, XXV-XXVIII
  - Dan Reeves, Denver, XXI-XXII, XXIV; Atlanta, XXXIII

Most Games, Winning Team, Coach
- 4 Chuck Noll, Pittsburgh, IX-X, XIII-XIV
- 3 Bill Walsh, San Francisco, XVI, XIX, XXIII
  - Joe Gibbs, Washington, XVII, XXII, XXVI
  - Bill Belichick, New England, XXXVI, XXXVIII-XXXIX
- 2 Vince Lombardi, Green Bay, I-II
  - Tom Landry, Dallas, VI, XII
  - Don Shula, Miami, VII-VIII
  - Tom Flores, Oakland, XV; L.A. Raiders, XVIII
  - Bill Parcells, N.Y. Giants, XXI, XXV
  - Jimmy Johnson, Dallas, XXVII-XXVIII
  - George Seifert, San Francisco, XXIV, XXIX
  - Mike Shanahan, Denver, XXXII-XXXIII

Most Games, Losing Team, Coach
- 4 Bud Grant, Minnesota, IV, VIII-IX, XI

Don Shula, Baltimore, III; Miami, VI, XVII, XIX
Marv Levy, Buffalo, XXV-XXVIII
Dan Reeves, Denver, XXI-XXII, XXIV; Atlanta, XXXIII
- 3 Tom Landry, Dallas, V, X, XIII

SCORING
POINTS
Most Points, Career
- 48 Jerry Rice, San Francisco-Oakland, 4 games (8-td)
- 30 Emmitt Smith, Dallas, 3 games (5-td)
- 24 Franco Harris, Pittsburgh, 4 games (4-td)
  - Roger Craig, San Francisco, 3 games (4-td)
  - Thurman Thomas, Buffalo, 4 games (4-td)
  - John Elway, Denver, 5 games (4-td)

Most Points, Game
- 18 Roger Craig, San Francisco vs. Miami, XIX (3-td)
  - Jerry Rice, San Francisco vs. Denver, XXIV (3-td); vs. San Diego, XXIX (3-td)
  - Ricky Watters, San Francisco vs. San Diego, XXIX (3-td)
  - Terrell Davis, Denver vs. Green Bay, XXXII (3-td)
- 15 Don Chandler, Green Bay vs. Oakland, II (3-pat, 4-fg)
- 14 Ray Wersching, San Francisco vs. Cincinnati, XVI (2-pat, 4-fg)
  - Kevin Butler, Chicago vs. New England, XX (5-pat, 3-fg)

TOUCHDOWNS
Most Touchdowns, Career
- 8 Jerry Rice, San Francisco-Oakland, 4 games (8-p)
- 5 Emmitt Smith, Dallas, 3 games (5-r)
- 4 Franco Harris, Pittsburgh, 4 games (4-r)
  - Roger Craig, San Francisco, 3 games (2-r, 2-p)
  - Thurman Thomas, Buffalo, 4 games (4-r)
  - John Elway, Denver, 5 games (4-r)

Most Touchdowns, Game
- 3 Roger Craig, San Francisco vs. Miami, XIX (1-r, 2-p)
  - Jerry Rice, San Francisco. vs. Denver, XXIV (3-p); vs. San Diego, XXIX (3-p)
  - Ricky Watters, San Francisco vs. San Diego, XXIX (1-r, 2-p)
  - Terrell Davis, Denver vs. Green Bay, XXXII (3-r)
- 2 Max McGee, Green Bay vs. Kansas City, I (2-p)
  - Elijah Pitts, Green Bay vs. Kansas City, I (2-r)
  - Bill Miller, Oakland vs. Green Bay, II (2-p)
  - Larry Csonka, Miami vs. Minnesota, VIII (2-r)
  - Pete Banaszak, Oakland vs. Minnesota, XI (2-r)
  - John Stallworth, Pittsburgh vs. Dallas, XIII (2-p)
  - Franco Harris, Pittsburgh vs. Los Angeles, XIV (2-r)
  - Cliff Branch, Oakland vs. Philadelphia, XV (2-p)
  - Dan Ross, Cincinnati vs. San Francisco, XVI (2-p)
  - Marcus Allen, L.A. Raiders vs. Washington, XVIII (2-r)
  - Jim McMahon, Chicago vs. New England, XX (2-r)
  - Ricky Sanders, Washington vs. Denver, XXII (2-p)
  - Timmy Smith, Washington vs. Denver, XXII (2-r)
  - Tom Rathman, San Francisco vs. Denver, XXIV (2-r)
  - Gerald Riggs, Washington vs. Buffalo, XXVI (2-r)
  - Michael Irvin, Dallas vs. Buffalo, XXVII (2-p)
  - Emmitt Smith, Dallas vs. Buffalo, XXVIII (2-r)
  - Emmitt Smith, Dallas vs. Pittsburgh, XXX (2-r)
  - Antonio Freeman, Green Bay vs. Denver, XXXII (2-p)
  - Howard Griffith, Denver vs. Atlanta, XXXIII (2-r)
  - Eddie George, Tennessee vs. St. Louis, XXXIV (2-r)
  - Keenan McCardell, Tampa Bay vs. Oakland, XXXVII (2-r)
  - Dwight Smith, Tampa Bay vs. Oakland, XXXVII (2-ret)

POINTS AFTER TOUCHDOWN
Most (One-Point) Points After Touchdown, Career
- 11 Adam Vinatieri, New England, 4 games (11 att)

9 Mike Cofer, San Francisco, 2 games (10 att)
8 Don Chandler, Green Bay, 2 games (8 att)
Roy Gerela, Pittsburgh, 3 games (9 att)
Chris Bahr, Oakland-L.A. Raiders, 2 games (8 att)
Jason Elam, Denver, 2 games (8 att)

Most (One-Point) Points After Touchdown, Game

7 Mike Cofer, San Francisco vs. Denver, XXIV (8 att)
Lin Elliott, Dallas vs. Buffalo, XXVII (7 att)
Doug Brien, San Francisco vs. San Diego, XXIX (7 att)
6 Ali Hají-Sheikh, Washington vs. Denver, XXII (6 att)
Martín Gramatica, Tampa Bay vs. Oakland, XXXVII (6 att)
5 Don Chandler, Green Bay vs. Kansas City, I (5 att)
Roy Gerela, Pittsburgh vs. Dallas, XIII (5 att)
Chris Bahr, L.A. Raiders vs. Washington, XVIII (5 att)
Ray Wersching, San Francisco vs. Miami, XIX (5 att)
Kevin Butler, Chicago vs. New England, XX (5 att)

Most Two-Point Conversions, Game

1 Mark Seay, San Diego vs. San Francisco, XXIX
Alfred Pupunu, San Diego vs. San Francisco, XXIX
Mark Chmura, Green Bay vs. New England, XXXI
Kevin Faulk, New England vs. Carolina, XXXVIII

FIELD GOALS
Field Goals Attempted, Career

6 Jim Turner, N.Y. Jets-Denver, 2 games
Roy Gerela, Pittsburgh, 3 games
Rich Karlis, Denver, 2 games
Jeff Wilkins, St. Louis, 2 games
Adam Vinatieri, New England, 4 games
5 Efren Herrera, Dallas, 1 game
Ray Wersching, San Francisco, 2 games
Jason Elam, Denver, 2 games

Most Field Goals Attempted, Game

5 Jim Turner, N.Y. Jets vs. Baltimore, III
Efren Herrera, Dallas vs. Denver, XII
4 Don Chandler, Green Bay vs. Oakland, II
Roy Gerela, Pittsburgh vs. Dallas, X
Ray Wersching, San Francisco vs. Cincinnati, XVI
Rich Karlis, Denver vs. N.Y. Giants, XXI
Mike Cofer, San Francisco vs. Cincinnati, XXIII
Jason Elam, Denver vs. Atlanta, XXXIII
Jeff Wilkins, St. Louis vs. Tennessee, XXXIV

Most Field Goals, Career

5 Ray Wersching, San Francisco, 2 games (5 att)
4 Don Chandler, Green Bay, 2 games (4 att)
Jim Turner, N.Y. Jets-Denver, 2 games (6 att)
Uwe von Schamann, Miami, 2 games (4 att)
Jeff Wilkins, St. Louis, 2 games (6 att)
Adam Vinatieri, New England, 4 games (6 att)
3 Mike Clark, Dallas, 2 games (3 att)
Jan Stenerud, Kansas City, 1 game (3 att)
Chris Bahr, Oakland-L.A. Raiders, 2 games (4 att)
Mark Moseley, Washington, 2 games (4 att)
Kevin Butler, Chicago, 1 game (3 att)
Rich Karlis, Denver, 2 games (6 att)
Jim Breech, Cincinnati, 2 games (3 att)
Matt Bahr, Pittsburgh-N.Y. Giants, 2 games (3 att)
Chip Lohmiller, Washington, 1 game (3 att)
Steve Christie, Buffalo, 2 games (3 att)
Eddie Murray, Dallas, 1 game (3 att)
Jason Elam, Denver, 2 games (5 att)

Most Field Goals, Game

4 Don Chandler, Green Bay vs. Oakland, II
Ray Wersching, San Francisco vs. Cincinnati, XVI
3 Jim Turner, N.Y. Jets vs. Baltimore, III
Jan Stenerud, Kansas City vs. Minnesota, IV
Uwe von Schamann, Miami vs. San Francisco, XIX
Kevin Butler, Chicago vs. New England, XX
Jim Breech, Cincinnati vs. San Francisco, XXIII

Chip Lohmiller, Washington vs. Buffalo, XXVI
Eddie Murray, Dallas vs. Buffalo, XXVIII
Jeff Wilkins, St. Louis vs. Tennessee, XXXIV

Longest Field Goal

54 Steve Christie, Buffalo vs. Dallas, XXVIII
51 Jason Elam, Denver vs. Green Bay, XXXII
50 Jeff Wilkins, St. Louis vs. New England, XXXVI
John Kasay, Carolina vs. New England, XXXVIII

SAFETIES
Most Safeties, Game

1 Dwight White, Pittsburgh vs. Minnesota, IX
Reggie Harrison, Pittsburgh vs. Dallas, X
Henry Waechter, Chicago vs. New England, XX
George Martin, N.Y. Giants vs. Denver, XXI
Bruce Smith, Buffalo vs. N.Y. Giants, XXV

RUSHING
ATTEMPTS
Most Attempts, Career

101 Franco Harris, Pittsburgh, 4 games
70 Emmitt Smith, Dallas, 3 games
64 John Riggins, Washington, 2 games

Most Attempts, Game

38 John Riggins, Washington vs. Miami, XVII
34 Franco Harris, Pittsburgh vs. Minnesota, IX
33 Larry Csonka, Miami vs. Minnesota, VIII

YARDS GAINED
Most Yards Gained, Career

354 Franco Harris, Pittsburgh, 4 games
297 Larry Csonka, Miami, 3 games
289 Emmitt Smith, Dallas, 3 games

Most Yards Gained, Game

204 Timmy Smith, Washington vs. Denver, XXII
191 Marcus Allen, L.A. Raiders vs. Washington, XVIII
166 John Riggins, Washington vs. Miami, XVII

Longest Run From Scrimmage

75 Willie Parker, Pittsburgh vs. Seattle, XL (TD)
74 Marcus Allen, L.A. Raiders vs. Washington, XVIII (TD)
58 Tom Matte, Baltimore vs. N.Y. Jets, III
Timmy Smith, Washington vs. Denver, XXII (TD)

AVERAGE GAIN
Highest Average Gain, Career (20 attempts)

9.6 Marcus Allen, L.A. Raiders, 1 game (20-191)
9.3 Timmy Smith, Washington, 1 game (22-204)
5.3 Walt Garrison, Dallas, 2 games (26-139)

Highest Average Gain, Game (10 attempts)

10.5 Tom Matte, Baltimore vs. N.Y. Jets, III (11-116)
9.6 Marcus Allen, L.A. Raiders vs. Washington, XVIII (20-191)
9.3 Willie Parker, Pittsburgh vs. Seattle, XL (10-93)

TOUCHDOWNS
Most Touchdowns, Career

5 Emmitt Smith, Dallas, 3 games
4 Franco Harris, Pittsburgh, 4 games
Thurman Thomas, Buffalo, 4 games
John Elway, Denver, 5 games
3 Terrell Davis, Denver, 2 games

Most Touchdowns, Game

3 Terrell Davis, Denver vs. Green Bay, XXXII
2 Elijah Pitts, Green Bay vs. Kansas City, I
Larry Csonka, Miami vs. Minnesota, VIII
Pete Banaszak, Oakland vs. Minnesota, XI
Franco Harris, Pittsburgh vs. Los Angeles, XIV
Marcus Allen, L.A. Raiders vs. Washington, XVIII
Jim McMahon, Chicago vs. New England, XX
Timmy Smith, Washington vs. Denver, XXII

Tom Rathman, San Francisco vs. Denver, XXIV
Gerald Riggs, Washington vs. Buffalo, XXVI
Emmitt Smith, Dallas vs. Buffalo, XXVIII
Emmitt Smith, Dallas vs. Pittsburgh, XXX
Howard Griffith, Denver vs. Atlanta, XXXIII
Eddie George, Tennessee vs. St. Louis, XXXIV

PASSING
PASSER RATING
Highest Passer Rating, Career (40 attempts)
- 127.8 Joe Montana, San Francisco, 4 games
- 122.8 Jim Plunkett, Oakland-L.A. Raiders, 2 games
- 112.8 Terry Bradshaw, Pittsburgh, 4 games

ATTEMPTS
Most Passes Attempted, Career
- 152 John Elway, Denver, 5 games
- 145 Jim Kelly, Buffalo, 4 games
- 122 Joe Montana, San Francisco, 4 games

Most Passes Attempted, Game
- 58 Jim Kelly, Buffalo vs. Washington, XXVI
- 51 Donovan McNabb, Philadelphia vs. New England, XXXIX
- 50 Dan Marino, Miami vs. San Francisco, XIX
  Jim Kelly, Buffalo vs. Dallas, XXVIII

COMPLETIONS
Most Passes Completed, Career
- 83 Joe Montana, San Francisco, 4 games
- 81 Jim Kelly, Buffalo, 4 games
- 76 John Elway, Denver, 5 games

Most Passes Completed, Game
- 32 Tom Brady, New England vs. Carolina, XXXVIII
- 31 Jim Kelly, Buffalo vs. Dallas, XXVIII
- 30 Donovan McNabb, Philadelphia vs. New England, XXXIX

Most Consecutive Completions, Game
- 13 Joe Montana, San Francisco vs. Denver, XXIV
- 10 Phil Simms, N.Y. Giants vs. Denver, XXI
  Troy Aikman, Dallas vs. Pittsburgh, XXX
- 9 Jim Kelly, Buffalo vs. Dallas, XXVIII
  Neil O'Donnell, Pittsburgh vs. Dallas, XXX
  Steve McNair, Tennessee vs. St. Louis, XXXIV

COMPLETION PERCENTAGE
Highest Completion Percentage, Career (40 attempts)
- 70.0 Troy Aikman, Dallas, 3 games, (80-56)
- 68.0 Joe Montana, San Francisco, 4 games (122-83)
- 65.7 Tom Brady, New England, 3 games (108-71)

Highest Completion Percentage, Game (20 attempts)
- 88.0 Phil Simms, N.Y. Giants vs. Denver, XXI (25-22)
- 75.9 Joe Montana, San Francisco vs. Denver, XXIV (29-22)
- 73.5 Ken Anderson, Cincinnati vs. San Francisco, XVI (34-25)

YARDS GAINED
Most Yards Gained, Career
- 1,142 Joe Montana, San Francisco, 4 games
- 1,128 John Elway, Denver, 5 games
- 932 Terry Bradshaw, Pittsburgh, 4 games

Most Yards Gained, Game
- 414 Kurt Warner, St. Louis vs. Tennessee, XXXIV
- 365 Kurt Warner, St. Louis vs. New England, XXXVI
- 357 Joe Montana, San Francisco vs. Cincinnati, XXIII
  Donovan McNabb, Philadelphia vs. New England, XXXIX

Longest Pass Completion
- 85 Jake Delhomme (to Muhammad), Carolina vs. New England, XXXVIII (TD)

- 81 Brett Favre (to Freeman), Green Bay vs. New England, XXXI (TD)
- 80 Jim Plunkett (to King), Oakland vs. Philadelphia, XV (TD)
  Doug Williams (to Sanders), Washington vs. Denver, XXII (TD)
  John Elway (to R. Smith), Denver vs. Atlanta, XXXIII (TD)

AVERAGE GAIN
Highest Average Gain, Career (40 attempts)
- 11.10 Terry Bradshaw, Pittsburgh, 4 games (84-932)
- 9.62 Bart Starr, Green Bay, 2 games (47-452)
- 9.41 Jim Plunkett, Oakland-L.A. Raiders, 2 games (46-433)

Highest Average Gain, Game (20 attempts)
- 14.71 Terry Bradshaw, Pittsburgh vs. Los Angeles, XIV (21-309)
- 12.80 Jim McMahon, Chicago vs. New England, XX (20-256)
- 12.43 Jim Plunkett, Oakland vs. Philadelphia, XV (21-261)

TOUCHDOWNS
Most Touchdown Passes, Career
- 11 Joe Montana, San Francisco, 4 games
- 9 Terry Bradshaw, Pittsburgh, 4 games
- 8 Roger Staubach, Dallas, 4 games

Most Touchdown Passes, Game
- 6 Steve Young, San Francisco vs. San Diego, XXIX
- 5 Joe Montana, San Francisco vs. Denver, XXIV
- 4 Terry Bradshaw, Pittsburgh vs. Dallas, XIII
  Doug Williams, Washington vs. Denver, XXII
  Troy Aikman, Dallas vs. Buffalo, XXVII

HAD INTERCEPTED
Lowest Percentage, Passes Had Intercepted, Career (40 attempts)
- 0.00 Jim Plunkett, Oakland-L.A. Raiders, 2 games (46-0)
  Joe Montana, San Francisco, 4 games (122-0)
- 0.93 Tom Brady, New England, 3 games (108-1)
- 1.25 Troy Aikman, Dallas, 3 games (80-1)

Most Attempts, Without Interception, Game
- 45 Kurt Warner, St. Louis vs. Tennessee, XXXIV
- 36 Joe Montana, San Francisco vs. Cincinnati, XXIII
  Steve Young, San Francisco vs. San Diego, XXIX
  Steve McNair, Tennessee vs. St. Louis, XXXIV
- 35 Joe Montana, San Francisco vs. Miami, XIX

Most Passes Had Intercepted, Career
- 8 John Elway, Denver, 5 games
- 7 Craig Morton, Dallas-Denver, 2 games
  Jim Kelly, Buffalo, 4 games
- 6 Fran Tarkenton, Minnesota, 3 games

Most Passes Had Intercepted, Game
- 5 Rich Gannon, Oakland vs. Tampa Bay, XXXVII
- 4 Craig Morton, Denver vs. Dallas, XII
  Jim Kelly, Buffalo vs. Washington, XXVI
  Drew Bledsoe, New England vs. Green Bay, XXXI
  Kerry Collins, N.Y. Giants vs. Baltimore, XXXV
- 3 By 11 players

PASS RECEIVING
RECEPTIONS
Most Receptions, Career
- 33 Jerry Rice, San Francisco-Oakland, 4 games
- 27 Andre Reed, Buffalo, 4 games
- 21 Deion Branch, New England, 2 games

Most Receptions, Game
- 11 Dan Ross, Cincinnati vs. San Francisco, XVI
  Jerry Rice, San Francisco vs. Cincinnati, XXIII
  Deion Branch, New England vs. Philadelphia, XXXIX
- 10 Tony Nathan, Miami vs. San Francisco, XIX
  Jerry Rice, San Francisco vs. San Diego, XXIX
  Andre Hastings, Pittsburgh vs. Dallas, XXX

Deion Branch, New England vs. Carolina, XXXVIII
9 Ricky Sanders, Washington vs. Denver, XXII
Antonio Freeman, Green Bay vs. Denver, XXXII
Terrell Owens, Philadelphia vs. New England, XXXIX

YARDS GAINED
Most Yards Gained, Career
589 Jerry Rice, San Francisco-Oakland, 4 games
364 Lynn Swann, Pittsburgh, 4 games
323 Andre Reed, Buffalo, 4 games
Most Yards Gained, Game
215 Jerry Rice, San Francisco vs. Cincinnati, XXIII
193 Ricky Sanders, Washington vs. Denver, XXII
162 Isaac Bruce, St. Louis vs. Tennessee, XXXIV
Longest Reception
85 Muhsin Muhammad (from Delhomme), Carolina vs. New England, XXXVIII
81 Antonio Freeman (from Favre), Green Bay vs. New England, XXXI (TD)
80 Kenny King (from Plunkett), Oakland vs. Philadelphia, XV (TD)
Ricky Sanders (from Williams), Washington vs. Denver, XXII (TD)
Rod Smith (from Elway), Denver vs. Atlanta, XXXIII

AVERAGE GAIN
Highest Average Gain, Career (8 receptions)
24.4 John Stallworth, Pittsburgh, 4 games (11-268)
23.4 Ricky Sanders, Washington, 2 games (10-234)
22.8 Lynn Swann, Pittsburgh, 4 games (16-364)
Highest Average Gain, Game (3 receptions)
40.33 John Stallworth, Pittsburgh vs. Los Angeles, XIV (3-121)
40.25 Lynn Swann, Pittsburgh vs. Dallas, X (4-161)
38.33 John Stallworth, Pittsburgh vs. Dallas, XIII (3-115)

TOUCHDOWNS
Most Touchdowns, Career
8 Jerry Rice, San Francisco-Oakland, 4 games
3 John Stallworth, Pittsburgh, 4 games
Lynn Swann, Pittsburgh, 4 games
Cliff Branch, Oakland-L.A. Raiders, 3 games
Antonio Freeman, Green Bay, 2 games
2 Max McGee, Green Bay, 2 games
Bill Miller, Oakland, 1 game
Butch Johnson, Dallas, 2 games
Dan Ross, Cincinnati, 1 game
Roger Craig, San Francisco, 3 games
Ricky Sanders, Washington, 2 games
John Taylor, San Francisco, 3 games
Gary Clark, Washington, 2 games
Don Beebe, Buffalo-Green Bay, 4 games
Michael Irvin, Dallas, 3 games
Ricky Watters, San Francisco, 1 game
Jay Novacek, Dallas, 3 games
Keenan McCardell, Tampa Bay, 1 game
Ricky Proehl, St. Louis-Carolina, 3 games
David Givens, New England, 2 games
Mike Vrabel, New England, 3 games
Most Touchdowns, Game
3 Jerry Rice, San Francisco vs. Denver, XXIV; vs. San Diego, XXIX
2 Max McGee, Green Bay vs. Kansas City, I
Bill Miller, Oakland vs. Green Bay, II
John Stallworth, Pittsburgh vs. Dallas, XIII
Cliff Branch, Oakland vs. Philadelphia, XV
Dan Ross, Cincinnati vs. San Francisco, XVI
Roger Craig, San Francisco vs. Miami, XIX
Ricky Sanders, Washington vs. Denver, XXII
Michael Irvin, Dallas vs. Buffalo, XXVII

Ricky Watters, San Francisco vs. San Diego, XXIX
Antonio Freeman, Green Bay vs. Denver, XXXII
Keenan McCardell, Tampa Bay vs. Oakland, XXXVII

INTERCEPTIONS BY
Most Interceptions By, Career
3 Chuck Howley, Dallas, 2 games
Rod Martin, Oakland-L.A. Raiders, 2 games
Larry Brown, Dallas, 3 games
2 Randy Beverly, N.Y. Jets, 1 game
Jake Scott, Miami, 3 games
Mike Wagner, Pittsburgh, 3 games
Mel Blount, Pittsburgh, 4 games
Eric Wright, San Francisco, 4 games
Barry Wilburn, Washington, 1 game
Brad Edwards, Washington, 1 game
Thomas Everett, Dallas, 2 games
James Washington, Dallas, 2 games
Darrien Gordon, San Diego-Denver-Oakland, 4 games
Dexter Jackson, Tampa Bay, 1 game
Dwight Smith, Tampa Bay, 1 game
Rodney Harrison, San Diego-New England, 3 games
Most Interceptions By, Game
3 Rod Martin, Oakland vs. Philadelphia, XV
2 Randy Beverly, N.Y. Jets vs. Baltimore, III
Chuck Howley, Dallas vs. Baltimore, V
Jake Scott, Miami vs. Washington, VII
Barry Wilburn, Washington vs. Denver, XXII
Brad Edwards, Washington vs. Buffalo, XXVI
Thomas Everett, Dallas vs. Buffalo, XXVII
Larry Brown, Dallas vs. Pittsburgh, XXX
Darrien Gordon, Denver vs. Atlanta, XXXIII
Dexter Jackson, Tampa Bay vs. Oakland, XXXVII
Dwight Smith, Tampa Bay vs. Oakland, XXXVII
Rodney Harrison, New England vs. Philadelphia, XXXIX

YARDS GAINED
Most Yards Gained, Career
108 Darrien Gordon, San Diego-Denver-Oakland, 4 games
94 Dwight Smith, Tampa Bay, 1 game
77 Larry Brown, Dallas, 3 games
Most Yards Gained, Game
108 Darrien Gordon, Denver vs. Atlanta, XXXIII
94 Dwight Smith, Tampa Bay vs. Oakland, XXXVII
77 Larry Brown, Dallas vs. Pittsburgh, XXX
Longest Return
76 Kelly Herndon, Seattle vs. Pittsburgh, XL
75 Willie Brown, Oakland vs. Minnesota, XI (TD)
60 Herb Adderley, Green Bay vs. Oakland, II (TD)

TOUCHDOWNS
Most Touchdowns, Game
2 Dwight Smith, Tampa Bay vs. Oakland, XXXVII
1 Herb Adderley, Green Bay vs. Oakland, II
Willie Brown, Oakland vs. Minnesota, XI
Jack Squirek, L.A. Raiders vs. Washington, XVIII
Reggie Phillips, Chicago vs. New England, XX
Duane Starks, Baltimore vs. N.Y. Giants, XXXV
Ty Law, New England vs. St. Louis, XXXVI
Derrick Brooks, Tampa Bay vs. Oakland, XXXVII

PUNTING
Most Punts, Career
17 Mike Eischeid, Oakland-Minnesota, 3 games
Mike Horan, Denver-St. Louis, 4 games
15 Larry Seiple, Miami, 3 games
14 Ron Widby, Dallas, 2 games

Ray Guy, Oakland-L.A. Raiders, 3 games
Chris Mohr, Buffalo, 3 games
Craig Hentrich, Green Bay-Tennessee, 3 games

Most Punts, Game
11 Brad Maynard, N.Y. Giants vs. Baltimore, XXXV
10 Kyle Richardson, Baltimore vs. N.Y. Giants, XXXV
9 Ron Widby, Dallas vs. Baltimore, V

Longest Punt
63 Lee Johnson, Cincinnati vs. San Francisco, XXIII
62 Rich Camarillo, New England vs. Chicago, XX
61 Jerrel Wilson, Kansas City vs. Green Bay, I

AVERAGE YARDAGE
Highest Average, Punting, Career (10 punts)
46.5 Jerrel Wilson, Kansas City, 2 games (11-511)
43.8 Tom Rouen, Denver-Seattle, 3 games (11-482)
43.0 Kyle Richardson, Baltimore, 1 game (10-430)
Tom Tupa, New England-Tampa Bay, 2 games
(12-516)
Highest Average, Punting, Game (4 punts)
50.2 Tom Rouen, Seattle vs. Pittsburgh, XL (6-301)
48.8 Bryan Wagner, San Diego vs. San Francisco, XXIX
(4-195)
48.7 Chris Gardocki, Pittsburgh vs. Seattle, XL (6-292)

PUNT RETURNS
Most Punt Returns, Career
8 Troy Brown, New England, 3 games
6 Willie Wood, Green Bay, 2 games
Jake Scott, Miami, 3 games
Theo Bell, Pittsburgh, 2 games
Mike Nelms, Washington, 1 game
John Taylor, San Francisco, 3 games
Desmond Howard, Green Bay, 1 game
David Meggett, N.Y. Giants-New England, 2 games
Darrien Gordon, San Diego-Denver-Oakland,
4 games
5 Dana McLemore, San Francisco, 1 game
Most Punt Returns, Game
6 Mike Nelms, Washington vs. Miami, XVII
Desmond Howard, Green Bay vs. New England, XXXI
5 Willie Wood, Green Bay vs. Oakland, II
Dana McLemore, San Francisco vs. Miami, XIX
4 By nine players
Most Fair Catches, Game
4 Jermaine Lewis, Baltimore vs. N.Y. Giants, XXXV
Karl Williams, Tampa Bay vs. Oakland, XXXVII
3 Ron Gardin, Baltimore vs. Dallas, V
Golden Richards, Dallas vs. Pittsburgh, X
Greg Pruitt, L.A. Raiders vs. Washington, XVIII
Al Edwards, Buffalo vs. N.Y. Giants, XXV
David Meggett, N.Y. Giants vs. Buffalo, XXV

YARDS GAINED
Most Yards Gained, Career
94 John Taylor, San Francisco, 3 games
90 Desmond Howard, Green Bay, 1 game
67 David Meggett, N.Y. Giants-New England, 2 games
Most Yards Gained, Game
90 Desmond Howard, Green Bay vs. New England, XXXI
56 John Taylor, San Francisco vs. Cincinnati, XXIII
52 Mike Nelms, Washington vs. Miami, XXII
Longest Return
45 John Taylor, San Francisco vs. Cincinnati, XXIII
34 Darrell Green, Washington vs. L.A. Raiders, XVIII
Desmond Howard, Green Bay vs. New England, XXXI
Jermaine Lewis, Baltimore vs. N.Y. Giants, XXXV
32 Desmond Howard, Green Bay vs. New England, XXXI

AVERAGE YARDAGE
Highest Average, Career (4 returns)
15.7 John Taylor, San Francisco, 3 games (6-94)
15.0 Desmond Howard, Green Bay, 1 game (6-90)
11.2 David Meggett, N.Y. Giants-New England, 2 games
(6-67)
Highest Average, Game (3 returns)
18.7 John Taylor, San Francisco vs. Cincinnati, XXIII (3-56)
15.0 Desmond Howard, Green Bay vs. New England, XXXI
(6-90)
12.7 John Taylor, San Francisco vs. Denver, XXIV (3-38)

TOUCHDOWNS
Most Touchdowns, Game
None

KICKOFF RETURNS
Most Kickoff Returns, Career
10 Ken Bell, Denver, 3 games
8 Larry Anderson, Pittsburgh, 2 games
Fulton Walker, Miami, 2 games
Andre Coleman, San Diego, 1 game
Marcus Knight, Oakland, 1 game
7 Preston Pearson, Baltimore-Pittsburgh-Dallas, 5 games
Stephen Starring, New England, 1 game
David Meggett, N.Y. Giants-New England, 2 games
Most Kickoff Returns, Game
8 Andre Coleman, San Diego vs. San Francisco, XXIX
Marcus Knight, Oakland vs. Tampa Bay, XXXVII
7 Stephen Starring, New England vs. Chicago, XX
6 Darren Carrington, Denver vs. San Francisco, XXIV
Antonio Freeman, Green Bay vs. Denver, XXXII
Ron Dixon, N.Y. Giants vs. Baltimore, XXXV

YARDS GAINED
Most Yards Gained, Career
283 Fulton Walker, Miami, 2 games
244 Andre Coleman, San Diego, 1 game
210 Tim Dwight, Atlanta, 1 game
Most Yards Gained, Game
244 Andre Coleman, San Diego vs. San Francisco, XXIX
210 Tim Dwight, Atlanta vs. Denver, XXXIII
190 Fulton Walker, Miami vs. Washington, XVII
Longest Return
99 Desmond Howard, Green Bay vs. New England, XXXI
(TD)
98 Fulton Walker, Miami vs. Washington, XVII (TD)
Andre Coleman, San Diego vs. San Francisco, XXIX
(TD)
97 Ron Dixon, N.Y. Giants vs. Baltimore, XXXV (TD)

AVERAGE YARDAGE
Highest Average, Career (4 returns)
42.0 Tim Dwight, Atlanta, 1 game (5-210)
38.5 Desmond Howard, Green Bay, 1 game (4-154)
35.4 Fulton Walker, Miami, 2 games (8-283)
Highest Average, Game (3 returns)
47.5 Fulton Walker, Miami vs. Washington, XVII (4-190)
42.0 Tim Dwight, Atlanta vs. Denver, XXXIII (5-210)
38.5 Desmond Howard, Green Bay vs. New England, XXXI
(4-154)

TOUCHDOWNS
Most Touchdowns, Game
1 Fulton Walker, Miami vs. Washington, XVII
Stanford Jennings, Cincinnati vs. San Francisco, XXIII
Andre Coleman, San Diego vs. San Francisco, XXIX
Desmond Howard, Green Bay vs. New England, XXXI
Tim Dwight, Atlanta vs. Denver, XXXIII
Ron Dixon, N.Y. Giants vs. Baltimore, XXXV

Jermaine Lewis, Baltimore vs. N.Y. Giants, XXXV

FUMBLES
Most Fumbles, Career
5 Roger Staubach, Dallas, 4 games
4 Jim Kelly, Buffalo, 4 games
3 Franco Harris, Pittsburgh, 4 games
Terry Bradshaw, Pittsburgh, 4 games
John Elway, Denver, 5 games
Frank Reich, Buffalo, 4 games
Thurman Thomas, Buffalo, 4 games

Most Fumbles, Game
3 Roger Staubach, Dallas vs. Pittsburgh, X
Jim Kelly, Buffalo vs. Washington, XXVI
Frank Reich, Buffalo vs. Dallas, XXVII
2 Franco Harris, Pittsburgh vs. Minnesota, IX
Butch Johnson, Dallas vs. Denver, XII
Terry Bradshaw, Pittsburgh vs. Dallas, XIII
Joe Montana, San Francisco vs. Cincinnati, XXIII
John Elway, Denver vs. San Francisco, XXIV
Thurman Thomas, Buffalo vs. Dallas, XXVIII

RECOVERIES
Most Fumbles Recovered, Career
2 Jake Scott, Miami, 3 games (1 own, 1 opp)
Fran Tarkenton, Minnesota, 3 games (2 own)
Franco Harris, Pittsburgh, 4 games (2 own)
Roger Staubach, Dallas, 4 games (2 own)
Bobby Walden, Pittsburgh, 2 games (2 own)
John Fitzgerald, Dallas, 4 games (2 own)
Randy Hughes, Dallas, 3 games (2 opp)
Butch Johnson, Dallas, 2 games (2 own)
Mike Singletary, Chicago, 1 game (2 opp)
John Elway, Denver, 5 games (2 own)
Jimmie Jones, Dallas, 2 games (2 opp)
Kenneth Davis, Buffalo, 4 games (2 own)
Kurt Warner, St. Louis, 2 games (2 own)

Most Fumbles Recovered, Game
2 Jake Scott, Miami vs. Minnesota, VIII (1 own, 1 opp)
Roger Staubach, Dallas vs. Pittsburgh, X (2 own)
Randy Hughes, Dallas vs. Denver, XII (2 opp)
Butch Johnson, Dallas vs. Denver, XII (2 own)
Mike Singletary, Chicago vs. New England, XX (2 opp)
Jimmie Jones, Dallas vs. Buffalo, XXVII (2 opp)

YARDS GAINED
Most Yards Gained, Game
64 Leon Lett, Dallas vs. Buffalo, XXVII (opp)
49 Mike Bass, Washington vs. Miami, VII (opp)
46 James Washington, Dallas vs. Buffalo, XXVIII (opp)
Longest Return
64 Leon Lett, Dallas vs. Buffalo, XXVII
49 Mike Bass, Washington vs. Miami, VII (TD)
46 James Washington, Dallas vs. Buffalo, XXVIII (TD)

TOUCHDOWNS
Most Touchdowns, Game
1 Mike Bass, Washington vs. Miami, VII (opp 49 yds)
Mike Hegman, Dallas vs. Pittsburgh, XIII (opp 37 yds)
Jimmie Jones, Dallas vs. Buffalo, XXVII (opp 2 yds)
Ken Norton, Dallas vs. Buffalo, XXVII (opp 9 yds)
James Washington, Dallas vs. Buffalo, XXVIII
(opp 46 yds)

COMBINED NET YARDS GAINED
(Rushing, receiving, interception returns, punt returns, kickoff returns, and fumble returns)
ATTEMPTS
Most Attempts, Career
108 Franco Harris, Pittsburgh, 4 games

81 Emmitt Smith, Dallas, 3 games
72 Roger Craig, San Francisco, 3 games
Thurman Thomas, Buffalo, 4 games
Most Attempts, Game
39 John Riggins, Washington vs. Miami, XVII
35 Franco Harris, Pittsburgh vs. Minnesota, IX
34 Matt Snell, N.Y. Jets vs. Baltimore, III
Emmitt Smith, Dallas vs. Buffalo, XXVIII

YARDS GAINED
Most Yards Gained, Career
604 Jerry Rice, San Francisco-Oakland, 4 games
468 Franco Harris, Pittsburgh, 4 games
410 Roger Craig, San Francisco, 3 games
Most Yards Gained, Game
244 Andre Coleman, San Diego vs. San Francisco, XXIX
Desmond Howard, Green Bay vs. New England, XXXI
235 Ricky Sanders, Washington vs. Denver, XXII
230 Antonio Freeman, Green Bay vs. Denver, XXXII

SACKS
Sacks have been compiled since XVII.
Most Sacks, Career
4.5 Charles Haley, San Francisco-Dallas, 5 games
3.0 Danny Stubbs, San Francisco, 2 games
Leonard Marshall, N.Y. Giants, 2 games
Jeff Wright, Buffalo, 4 games
Reggie White, Green Bay, 2 games
Willie McGinest, New England, 4 games
Tedy Bruschi, New England, 4 games
Mike Vrabel, New England, 3 games
2.5 Dexter Manley, Washington, 3 games
Most Sacks, Game
3.0 Reggie White, Green Bay vs. New England, XXXI
2.0 Dwaine Board, San Francisco vs. Miami, XIX
Dennis Owens, New England vs. Chicago, XX
Otis Wilson, Chicago vs. New England, XX
Leonard Marshall, N.Y. Giants vs. Denver, XXI
Alvin Walton, Washington vs. Denver, XXII
Charles Haley, San Francisco vs. Cincinnati, XXIII
Danny Stubbs, San Francisco vs. Denver, XXIV
Jeff Wright, Buffalo vs. Dallas, XXVIII
Raylee Johnson, San Diego vs. San Francisco, XXIX
Chad Hennings, Dallas vs. Pittsburgh, XXX
Tedy Bruschi, New England vs. Green Bay, XXXI
Michael McCrary, Baltimore vs. N.Y. Giants, XXXV
Simeon Rice, Tampa Bay vs. Oakland, XXXVII
Mike Vrabel, New England vs. Carolina, XXXVIII

TEAM RECORDS

GAMES, VICTORIES, DEFEATS
Most Games
8 Dallas, V-VI, X, XII-XIII, XXVII-XXVIII, XXX
6 Denver, XII, XXI-XXII, XXIV, XXXII-XXXIII
Pittsburgh, IX-X, XIII-XIV, XXX, XL
5 Miami, VI-VIII, XVII, XIX
Washington, VII, XVII-XVIII, XXII, XXVI
San Francisco, XVI, XIX, XXIII-XXIV, XXIX
Oakland/L.A. Raiders, II, XI, XV, XVIII, XXXVII
New England, XX, XXXI, XXXVI, XXXVIII-XXXIX
Most Consecutive Games
4 Buffalo, XXV-XXVIII
3 Miami, VI-VIII
2 Green Bay, I-II; XXXI-XXXII
Dallas, V-VI; XII-XIII; XXVII-XXVIII
Minnesota, VIII-IX
Pittsburgh, IX-X; XIII-XIV
Washington, XVII-XVIII
Denver, XXI-XXII; XXXII-XXXIII

San Francisco, XXIII-XXIV
New England, XXXVIII-XXXIX

Most Games Won

5   San Francisco, XVI, XIX, XXIII-XXIV, XXIX
    Dallas, VI, XII, XXVII-XXVIII, XXX
    Pittsburgh, IX-X, XIII-XIV, XL

3   Oakland/L.A. Raiders, XI, XV, XVIII
    Washington, XVII, XXII, XXVI
    Green Bay, I-II, XXXI
    New England, XXXVI, XXXVIII-XXXIX

2   Miami, VII-VIII
    N.Y. Giants, XXI, XXV
    Denver, XXXII, XXXIII

Most Consecutive Games Won

2   Green Bay, I-II
    Miami, VII-VIII
    Pittsburgh, IX-X, XIII-XIV
    San Francisco, XXIII-XXIV
    Dallas, XXVII-XXVIII
    Denver, XXXII-XXXIII
    New England, XXXVIII-XXXIX

Most Games Lost

4   Minnesota, IV, VIII-IX, XI
    Denver, XII, XXI-XXII, XXIV
    Buffalo, XXV-XXVIII

3   Dallas, V, X, XIII
    Miami, VI, XVII, XIX

2   Washington, VII, XVIII
    Cincinnati, XVI, XXIII
    New England, XX, XXXI
    L.A./St. Louis Rams, XIV, XXXVI
    Oakland/L.A. Raiders, II, XXXVII
    Philadelphia, XV, XXXIX

Most Consecutive Games Lost

4   Buffalo, XXV-XXVIII
2   Minnesota, VIII-IX
    Denver, XXI-XXII

SCORING

Most Points, Game

55   San Francisco vs. Denver, XXIV
52   Dallas vs. Buffalo, XXVII
49   San Francisco vs. San Diego, XXIX

Fewest Points, Game

3   Miami vs. Dallas, VI
6   Minnesota vs. Pittsburgh, IX
7   By five teams

Most Points, Both Teams, Game

75   San Francisco (49) vs. San Diego (26), XXIX
69   Dallas (52) vs. Buffalo (17), XXVII
     Tampa Bay (48) vs. Oakland (21), XXXVII
66   Pittsburgh (35) vs. Dallas (31), XIII

Fewest Points, Both Teams, Game

21   Washington (7) vs. Miami (14), VII
22   Minnesota (6) vs. Pittsburgh (16), IX
23   Baltimore (7) vs. N.Y. Jets (16), III

Largest Margin of Victory, Game

45   San Francisco vs. Denver, XXIV (55-10)
36   Chicago vs. New England, XX (46-10)
35   Dallas vs. Buffalo, XXVII (52-17)

Most Points, Each Half

1st: 35   Washington vs. Denver, XXII
2nd: 30   N.Y. Giants vs. Denver, XXI

Most Points, Each Quarter

1st: 14   Miami vs. Minnesota, VIII
          Oakland vs. Philadelphia, XV
          Dallas vs. Buffalo, XXVII
          San Francisco vs. San Diego, XXIX
          New England vs. Green Bay, XXXI
2nd: 35   Washington vs. Denver, XXII

3rd: 21   Chicago vs. New England, XX
4th: 21   Dallas vs. Buffalo, XXVII

Most Points, Both Teams, Each Half

1st: 45   Washington (35) vs. Denver (10), XXII
2nd: 46   Tampa Bay (28) vs. Oakland (18), XXXVII

Fewest Points, Both Teams, Each Half

1st: 2   Minnesota (0) vs. Pittsburgh (2), IX
2nd: 7   Miami (0) vs. Washington (7), VII
         Denver (0) vs. Washington (7), XXII

Most Points, Both Teams, Each Quarter

1st: 24   New England (14) vs. Green Bay (10), XXXI
2nd: 35   Washington (35) vs. Denver (0), XXII
3rd: 24   Washington (14) vs. Buffalo (10), XXVI
4th: 37   Carolina (19) vs. New England (18), XXXVIII

TOUCHDOWNS

Most Touchdowns, Game

8   San Francisco vs. Denver, XXIV
7   Dallas vs. Buffalo, XXVII
    San Francisco vs. San Diego, XXIX
6   Washington vs. Denver, XXII
    Tampa Bay vs. Oakland, XXXVII

Fewest Touchdowns, Game

0   Miami vs. Dallas, VI
1   By 19 teams

Most Touchdowns, Both Teams, Game

10   San Francisco (7) vs. San Diego (3), XXIX
9   Pittsburgh (5) vs. Dallas (4), XIII
     San Francisco (8) vs. Denver (1), XXIV
     Dallas (7) vs. Buffalo (2), XXVII
     Tampa Bay (6) vs. Oakland (3), XXXVII
8   Carolina (4) vs. New England (4), XXXVIII

Fewest Touchdowns, Both Teams, Game

2   Baltimore (1) vs. N.Y. Jets (1), III
3   In six games

POINTS AFTER TOUCHDOWN

Most (One-Point) Points After Touchdown, Game

7   San Francisco vs. Denver, XXIV
    Dallas vs. Buffalo, XXVII
    San Francisco vs. San Diego, XXIX
6   Washington vs. Denver, XXII
    Tampa Bay vs. Oakland, XXXVII
5   Green Bay vs. Kansas City, I
    Pittsburgh vs. Dallas, XIII
    L.A. Raiders vs. Washington, XVIII
    San Francisco vs. Miami, XIX
    Chicago vs. New England, XX

Most (One-Point) Points After Touchdown, Both Teams, Game

9   Pittsburgh (5) vs. Dallas (4), XIII
    Dallas (7) vs. Buffalo (2), XXVII
8   San Francisco (7) vs. Denver (1), XXIV
    San Francisco (7) vs. San Diego (1), XXIX
7   Washington (6) vs. Denver (1), XXII
    Washington (4) vs. Buffalo (3), XXVI
    Denver (4) vs. Green Bay (3), XXXII

Fewest (One-Point) Points After Touchdown, Both Teams, Game

2   Baltimore (1) vs. N.Y. Jets (1), III
    Baltimore (1) vs. Dallas (1), V
    Minnesota (0) vs. Pittsburgh (2), IX

Most Two-Point Conversions, Game

2   San Diego vs. San Francisco, XXIX

Most Two-Point Conversions, Both Teams, Game

2   San Diego (2) vs. San Francisco (0), XXIX

FIELD GOALS

Most Field Goals Attempted, Game

5   N.Y. Jets vs. Baltimore, III
    Dallas vs. Denver, XII
4   Green Bay vs. Oakland, II

Pittsburgh vs. Dallas, XX
San Francisco vs. Cincinnati, XVI; XXIII
Denver vs. N.Y. Giants, XXI
Denver vs. Atlanta, XXXIII
St. Louis vs. Tennessee, XXXIV

Most Field Goals Attempted, Both Teams, Game
- 7 N.Y. Jets (5) vs. Baltimore (2), III
  San Francisco (4) vs. Cincinnati (3), XXIII
  St. Louis (4) vs. Tennessee (3), XXXIV
  Denver (4) vs. Atlanta (3), XXXIII
- 6 Dallas (5) vs. Denver (1), XII
- 5 Green Bay (4) vs. Oakland (1), II
  Pittsburgh (4) vs. Dallas (1), X
  Oakland (3) vs. Philadelphia (2), XV
  Denver (4) vs. N.Y. Giants (1), XXI
  Dallas (3) vs. Buffalo (2), XXVIII

Fewest Field Goals Attempted, Both Teams, Game
- 1 Minnesota (0) vs. Miami (1), VIII
  San Francisco (0) vs. Denver (1), XXIV
  Philadelphia (0) vs. New England (1), XXXIX
- 2 Green Bay (0) vs. Kansas City (2), I
  Miami (1) vs. Washington (1), VII
  Minnesota (1) vs. Pittsburgh (1), IX
  Dallas (1) vs. Pittsburgh (1), XIII
  Dallas (1) vs. Buffalo (1), XXVII
  San Diego (1) vs. San Francisco (1), XXIX
  Denver (1) vs. Green Bay (1), XXXII

Most Field Goals, Game
- 4 Green Bay vs. Oakland, II
  San Francisco vs. Cincinnati, XVI
- 3 N.Y. Jets vs. Baltimore, III
  Kansas City vs. Minnesota, IV
  Miami vs. San Francisco, XIX
  Chicago vs. New England, XX
  Cincinnati vs. San Francisco, XXIII
  Washington vs. Buffalo, XXVI
  Dallas vs. Buffalo, XXVIII
  St. Louis vs. Tennessee, XXXIV

Most Field Goals, Both Teams, Game
- 5 Cincinnati (3) vs. San Francisco (2), XXIII
  Dallas (3) vs. Buffalo (2), XXVIII
- 4 Green Bay (4) vs. Oakland (0), II
  San Francisco (4) vs. Cincinnati (0), XVI
  Miami (3) vs. San Francisco (1), XIX
  Chicago (3) vs. New England (1), XX
  Washington (3) vs. Buffalo (1), XXVI
  Atlanta (2) vs. Denver (2), XXXIII
  St. Louis (3) vs. Tennessee (1), XXXIV
- 3 In 13 games

Fewest Field Goals, Both Teams, Game
- 0 Miami vs. Washington, VII
  Pittsburgh vs. Minnesota, IX
- 1 Green Bay (0) vs. Kansas City (1), I
  Minnesota (0) vs. Miami (1), VIII
  Pittsburgh (0) vs. Dallas (1), XIII
  Washington (0) vs. Denver (1), XXII
  San Francisco (0) vs. Denver (1), XXIV
  San Francisco (0) vs. San Diego (1), XXIX
  Philadelphia (0) vs. New England (1), XXXIX
  Pittsburgh (0) vs. Seattle (1), XL

SAFETIES
Most Safeties, Game
- 1 Pittsburgh vs. Minnesota, IX; vs. Dallas, X
  Chicago vs. New England, XX
  N.Y. Giants vs. Denver, XXI
  Buffalo vs. N.Y. Giants, XXV

FIRST DOWNS
Most First Downs, Game
- 31 San Francisco vs. Miami, XIX
- 29 New England vs. Carolina, XXXVIII
- 28 San Francisco vs. Denver, XXIV
  San Francisco vs. San Diego, XXIX

Fewest First Downs, Game
- 9 Minnesota vs. Pittsburgh, IX
  Miami vs. Washington, XVII
- 10 Dallas vs. Baltimore, V
  Miami vs. Dallas, VI
- 11 Denver vs. Dallas, XII
  N.Y. Giants vs. Baltimore, XXXV
  Oakland vs. Tampa Bay, XXXVII

Most First Downs, Both Teams, Game
- 50 San Francisco (31) vs. Miami (19), XIX
  Tennessee (27) vs. St. Louis (23), XXXIV
- 49 Buffalo (25) vs. Washington (24), XXVI
- 48 San Francisco (28) vs. San Diego (20), XXIX

Fewest First Downs, Both Teams, Game
- 24 Dallas (10) vs. Baltimore (14), V
  N.Y. Giants (11) vs. Baltimore (13), XXXV
- 26 Minnesota (9) vs. Pittsburgh (17), IX
- 27 Pittsburgh (13) vs. Dallas (14), X

RUSHING
Most First Downs, Rushing, Game
- 16 San Francisco vs. Miami, XIX
- 15 Dallas vs. Miami, VI
- 14 Washington vs. Miami, XVII
  San Francisco vs. Denver, XXIV
  Denver vs. Green Bay, XXXII

Fewest First Downs, Rushing, Game
- 1 New England vs. Chicago, XX
  St. Louis vs. Tennessee, XXXIV
  Oakland vs. Tampa Bay, XXXVII
- 2 Minnesota vs. Kansas City, IV; vs. Pittsburgh, IX;
  vs. Oakland, XI
  Pittsburgh vs. Dallas, XIII
  Miami vs. San Francisco, XIX
  N.Y. Giants vs. Baltimore, XXXV
- 3 Miami vs. Dallas, VI
  Philadelphia vs. Oakland, XV
  New England vs. Green Bay, XXXI
  Carolina vs. New England, XXXVIII

Most First Downs, Rushing, Both Teams, Game
- 21 Washington (14) vs. Miami (7), XVII
- 19 Washington (13) vs. Denver (6), XXII
  San Francisco (14) vs. Denver (5), XXIV
- 18 Dallas (15) vs. Miami (3), VI
  Miami (13) vs. Minnesota (5), VIII
  San Francisco (16) vs. Miami (2), XIX
  N.Y. Giants (10) vs. Buffalo (8), XXV
  Denver (14) vs. Green Bay (4), XXXII

Fewest First Downs, Rushing, Both Teams, Game
- 7 Oakland (1) vs. Tampa Bay (6), XXXVII
- 8 Baltimore (4) vs. Dallas (4), V
  Pittsburgh (2) vs. Dallas (6), XIII
  N.Y. Giants (2) vs. Baltimore (6), XXXV
- 9 Philadelphia (3) vs. Oakland (6), XV

PASSING
Most First Downs, Passing, Game
- 19 New England vs. Carolina, XXXVIII
- 18 Buffalo vs. Washington, XXVI
  St. Louis vs. Tennessee, XXXIV
  Philadelphia vs. New England, XXXIX
- 17 Miami vs. San Francisco, XIX
  San Francisco vs. San Diego, XXIX

Fewest First Downs, Passing, Game
- 1 Denver vs. Dallas, XII
- 2 Miami vs. Washington, XVII
- 4 Miami vs. Minnesota, VIII

Most First Downs, Passing, Both Teams, Game
- 32 Miami (17) vs. San Francisco (15), XIX
  - Philadelphia (18) vs. New England (14), XXXIX
- 31 San Francisco (17) vs. San Diego (14), XXIX
  - St. Louis (18) vs. Tennessee (13), XXXIV
  - New England (19) vs. Carolina (12), XXXVIII
- 30 Buffalo (18) vs. Washington (12), XXVI

Fewest First Downs, Passing, Both Teams, Game
- 9 Denver (1) vs. Dallas (8), XII
- 10 Minnesota (5) vs. Pittsburgh (5), IX
- 11 Dallas (5) vs. Baltimore (6), V
  - Miami (2) vs. Washington (9), XVII

PENALTY
Most First Downs, Penalty, Game
- 4 Baltimore vs. Dallas, V
  - Miami vs. Minnesota, VIII
  - Cincinnati vs. San Francisco, XVI
  - Buffalo vs. Dallas, XXVII
  - St. Louis vs. Tennessee, XXXIV
- 3 Kansas City vs. Minnesota, IV
  - Minnesota vs. Oakland, XI
  - Buffalo vs. Washington, XXVI
  - Green Bay vs. Denver, XXXII
  - N.Y. Giants vs. Baltimore, XXXV
  - St. Louis vs. New England, XXXVI
  - Tampa Bay vs. Oakland, XXXVII
  - New England vs. Carolina, XXXVIII

Most First Downs, Penalty, Both Teams, Game
- 6 Cincinnati (4) vs. San Francisco (2), XVI
  - St. Louis (4) vs. Tennessee (2), XXXIV
- 5 Baltimore (4) vs. Dallas (1), V
  - Miami (4) vs. Minnesota (1), VIII
  - Buffalo (3) vs. Washington (2), XXVI
  - Green Bay (3) vs. Denver (2), XXXII
  - New England (3) vs. Carolina (2), XXXVIII
- 4 Kansas City (3) vs. Minnesota (1), IV
  - Buffalo (4) vs. Dallas (0), XXVII
  - N.Y. Giants (3) vs. Baltimore (1), XXXV
  - St. Louis (3) vs. New England (1), XXXVI
  - Tampa Bay (3) vs Oakland (1), XXXVII

Fewest First Downs, Penalty, Both Teams, Game
- 0 Dallas vs. Miami, VI
  - Miami vs. Washington, VII
  - Dallas vs. Pittsburgh, X
  - Miami vs. San Francisco, XIX
  - Pittsburgh vs. Seattle, XL
- 1 Green Bay (0) vs. Kansas City (1), I
  - Miami (0) vs. Washington (1), XVII
  - Cincinnati (0) vs. San Francisco (1), XXIII
  - San Francisco (0) vs. Denver (1), XXIV
  - Dallas (0) vs. Buffalo (1), XXVIII
  - Dallas (0) vs. Pittsburgh (1), XXX
  - Denver (0) vs. Atlanta (1), XXXIII

NET YARDS GAINED RUSHING AND PASSING
Most Yards Gained, Game
- 602 Washington vs. Denver, XXII
- 537 San Francisco vs. Miami, XIX
- 481 New England vs. Carolina, XXXVIII

Fewest Yards Gained, Game
- 119 Minnesota vs. Pittsburgh, IX
- 123 New England vs. Chicago, XX
- 152 N.Y. Giants vs. Baltimore, XXXV

Most Yards Gained, Both Teams, Game
- 929 Washington (602) vs. Denver (327), XXII

- 868 New England (481) vs. Carolina (387), XXXVIII
- 851 San Francisco (537) vs. Miami (314), XIX

Fewest Yards Gained, Both Teams, Game
- 396 N.Y. Giants (152) vs. Baltimore (244), XXXV
- 452 Minnesota (119) vs. Pittsburgh (333), IX
- 481 Washington (228) vs. Miami (253), VII
  - Denver (156) vs. Dallas (325), XII

RUSHING
ATTEMPTS
Most Attempts, Game
- 57 Pittsburgh vs. Minnesota, IX
- 53 Miami vs. Minnesota, VIII
- 52 Oakland vs. Minnesota, XI
  - Washington vs. Miami, XVII

Fewest Attempts, Game
- 9 Miami vs. San Francisco, XIX
- 11 New England vs. Chicago, XX
  - Oakland vs. Tampa Bay, XXXVII
- 13 New England vs. Green Bay, XXXI
  - St. Louis vs. Tennessee, XXXIV

Most Attempts, Both Teams, Game
- 81 Washington (52) vs. Miami (29), XVII
- 78 Pittsburgh (57) vs. Minnesota (21), IX
  - Oakland (52) vs. Minnesota (26), XI
- 77 Miami (53) vs. Minnesota (24), VIII
  - Pittsburgh (46) vs. Dallas (31), X

Fewest Attempts, Both Teams, Game
- 45 Philadelphia (17) vs. New England (28), XXXIX
- 47 St. Louis (22) vs. New England (25), XXXVI
- 49 Miami (9) vs. San Francisco (40), XIX
  - New England (13) vs. Green Bay (36), XXXI
  - St. Louis (13) vs. Tennessee (36), XXXIV
  - N.Y. Giants (16) vs. Baltimore (33), XXXV

YARDS GAINED
Most Yards Gained, Game
- 280 Washington vs. Denver, XXII
- 276 Washington vs. Miami, XVII
- 266 Oakland vs. Minnesota, XI

Fewest Yards Gained, Game
- 7 New England vs. Chicago, XX
- 17 Minnesota vs. Pittsburgh, IX
- 19 Oakland vs. Tampa Bay, XXXVII

Most Yards Gained, Both Teams, Game
- 377 Washington (280) vs. Denver (97), XXII
- 372 Washington (276) vs. Miami (96), XVII
- 338 N.Y. Giants (172) vs. Buffalo (166), XXV

Fewest Yards Gained, Both Teams, Game
- 157 Philadelphia (45) vs. New England (112), XXXIX
- 158 New England (43) vs. Green Bay (115), XXXI
- 159 Dallas (56) vs. Pittsburgh (103), XXX

AVERAGE GAIN
Highest Average Gain, Game
- 7.00 L.A. Raiders vs. Washington, XVIII (33-231)
  - Washington vs. Denver, XXII (40-280)
- 6.64 Buffalo vs. N.Y. Giants, XXV (25-166)
- 6.22 Baltimore vs. N.Y. Jets, III (23-143)

Lowest Average Gain, Game
- 0.64 New England vs. Chicago, XX (11-7)
- 0.81 Minnesota vs. Pittsburgh, IX (21-17)
- 1.73 Oakland vs. Tampa Bay, XXXVII (11-19)

TOUCHDOWNS
Most Touchdowns, Game
- 4 Chicago vs. New England, XX
  - Denver vs. Green Bay, XXXII
- 3 Green Bay vs. Kansas City, I
  - Miami vs. Minnesota, VIII

San Francisco vs. Denver, XXIV
Denver vs. Atlanta, XXXIII
2 Oakland vs. Minnesota, XI
Pittsburgh vs. Los Angeles, XIV
L.A. Raiders vs. Washington, XVIII
San Francisco vs. Miami, XIX
N.Y. Giants vs. Denver, XXI
Washington vs. Denver, XXII; vs. Buffalo, XXVI
Buffalo vs. N.Y. Giants, XXV
Dallas vs. Buffalo, XXVIII; vs. Pittsburgh, XXX
Tennessee vs. St. Louis, XXXIV
Pittsburgh vs. Seattle, XL

Fewest Touchdowns, Game
0 By 26 teams

Most Touchdowns, Both Teams, Game
4 Miami (3) vs. Minnesota (1), VIII
Chicago (4) vs. New England (0), XX
San Francisco (3) vs. Denver (1), XXIV
Denver (4) vs. Green Bay (0), XXXII
3 In nine games

Fewest Touchdowns, Both Teams, Game
0 Pittsburgh vs. Dallas, X
Oakland vs. Philadelphia, XV
Cincinnati vs. San Francisco, XXIII
1 In 11 games

PASSING
ATTEMPTS
Most Passes Attempted, Game
59 Buffalo vs. Washington, XXVI
55 San Diego vs. San Francisco, XXIX
51 Philadelphia vs. New England, XXXIX

Fewest Passes Attempted, Game
7 Miami vs. Minnesota, VIII
11 Miami vs. Washington, VII
14 Pittsburgh vs. Minnesota, IX

Most Passes Attempted, Both Teams, Game
93 San Diego (55) vs. San Francisco (38), XXIX
92 Buffalo (59) vs. Washington (33), XXVI
85 Miami (50) vs. San Francisco (35), XIX

Fewest Passes Attempted, Both Teams, Game
35 Miami (7) vs. Minnesota (28), VIII
39 Miami (11) vs. Washington (28), VII
40 Pittsburgh (14) vs. Minnesota (26), IX
Miami (17) vs. Washington (23), XVII

COMPLETIONS
Most Passes Completed, Game
32 New England vs. Carolina, XXXVIII
31 Buffalo vs. Dallas, XXVIII
30 Philadelphia vs. New England, XXXIX

Fewest Passes Completed, Game
4 Miami vs. Washington, XVII
6 Miami vs. Minnesota, VIII
8 Miami vs. Washington, VII
Denver vs. Dallas, XII

Most Passes Completed, Both Teams, Game
53 Miami (29) vs. San Francisco (24), XIX
Philadelphia (30) vs. New England (23), XXXIX
52 San Diego (27) vs. San Francisco (25), XXIX
50 Buffalo (31) vs. Dallas (19), XXVIII

Fewest Passes Completed, Both Teams, Game
19 Miami (4) vs. Washington (15), XVII
20 Pittsburgh (9) vs. Minnesota (11), IX
22 Miami (8) vs. Washington (14), VII

COMPLETION PERCENTAGE
Highest Completion Percentage, Game (20 attempts)
88.0 N.Y. Giants vs. Denver, XXI (25-22)
75.0 San Francisco vs. Denver, XXIV (32-24)

73.5 Cincinnati vs. San Francisco, XVI (34-25)

Lowest Completion Percentage, Game (20 attempts)
32.0 Denver vs. Dallas, XII (25-8)
37.9 Denver vs. San Francisco, XXIV (29-11)
38.5 Denver vs. Washington, XXII (39-15)
N.Y. Giants vs. Baltimore, XXXV (39-15)

YARDS GAINED
Most Yards Gained, Game
407 St. Louis vs. Tennessee, XXXIV
354 New England vs. Carolina, XXXVIII
341 San Francisco vs. Cincinnati, XXIII

Fewest Yards Gained, Game
35 Denver vs. Dallas, XII
63 Miami vs. Minnesota, VIII
69 Miami vs. Washington, VII

Most Yards Gained, Both Teams, Game
649 New England (354) vs. Carolina (295), XXXVIII
615 San Francisco (326) vs. Miami (289), XIX
St. Louis (407) vs. Tennessee (208), XXXIV
603 San Francisco (316) vs. San Diego (287), XXIX

Fewest Yards Gained, Both Teams, Game
156 Miami (69) vs. Washington (87), VII
186 Pittsburgh (84) vs. Minnesota (102), IX
204 Miami (80) vs. Washington (124), XVII

TIMES SACKED
Most Times Sacked, Game
7 Dallas vs. Pittsburgh, X
New England vs. Chicago, XX
6 Kansas City vs. Green Bay, I
Washington vs. L.A. Raiders, XVIII
Denver vs. San Francisco, XXIV
5 Dallas vs. Denver, XII; vs. Pittsburgh, XIII
Cincinnati vs. San Francisco, XVI; XXIII
Denver vs. Washington, XXII
Buffalo vs. Washington, XXVI
Green Bay vs. New England, XXXI
New England vs. Green Bay, XXXI
Oakland vs. Tampa Bay, XXXVII

Fewest Times Sacked, Game
0 Baltimore vs. N.Y. Jets, III; vs. Dallas, V
Minnesota vs. Pittsburgh, IX
Pittsburgh vs. Los Angeles, XIV
Philadelphia vs. Oakland, XV
Washington vs. Buffalo, XXVI
Denver vs. Green Bay, XXXII; vs. Atlanta, XXXIII
Tampa Bay vs. Oakland, XXXVII
New England vs. Carolina, XXXVIII
1 By 14 teams

Most Times Sacked, Both Teams, Game
10 New England (7) vs. Chicago (3), XX
Green Bay (5) vs. New England (5), XXXI
9 Kansas City (6) vs. Green Bay (3), I
Dallas (7) vs. Pittsburgh (2), X
Dallas (5) vs. Denver (4), XII
Dallas (5) vs. Pittsburgh (4), XIII
Cincinnati (5) vs. San Francisco (4), XXIII
8 Washington (6) vs. L.A. Raiders (2), XVIII

Fewest Times Sacked, Both Teams, Game
1 Philadelphia (0) vs. Oakland (1), XV
Denver (0) vs. Green Bay (1), XXXII
2 Baltimore (0) vs. N.Y. Jets (2), III
Baltimore (0) vs. Dallas (2), V
Minnesota (0) vs. Pittsburgh (2), IX
Denver (0) vs. Atlanta (2), XXXIII
3 In five games

TOUCHDOWNS
Most Touchdowns, Game
- 6 San Francisco vs. San Diego, XXIX
- 5 San Francisco vs. Denver, XXIV
- 4 Pittsburgh vs. Dallas, XIII
    Washington vs. Denver, XXII
    Dallas vs. Buffalo, XXVII

Fewest Touchdowns, Game
- 0 By 19 teams

Most Touchdowns, Both Teams, Game
- 7 Pittsburgh (4) vs. Dallas (3), XIII
    San Francisco (6) vs. San Diego (1), XXIX
- 6 Carolina (3) vs. New England (3), XXXVIII
- 5 Washington (4) vs. Denver (1), XXII
    San Francisco (5) vs. Denver (0), XXIV
    Dallas (4) vs. Buffalo (1), XXVII
    Philadelphia (3) vs. New England (2), XXXIX

Fewest Touchdowns, Both Teams, Game
- 0 N.Y. Jets vs. Baltimore, III
    Miami vs. Minnesota, VIII
    Buffalo vs. Dallas, XXVIII
- 1 In seven games

INTERCEPTIONS BY
Most Interceptions By, Game
- 5 Tampa Bay vs. Oakland, XXXVII
- 4 N.Y. Jets vs. Baltimore, III
    Dallas vs. Denver, XII
    Washington vs. Buffalo, XXVI
    Dallas vs. Buffalo, XXVII
    Green Bay vs. New England, XXXI
    Baltimore vs. N.Y. Giants, XXXV
- 3 By 13 teams

Most Interceptions By, Both Teams, Game
- 6 Baltimore (3) vs. Dallas (3), V
    Tampa Bay (5) vs. Oakland (1), XXXVII
- 5 Washington (4) vs. Buffalo (1), XXVI
- 4 In 10 games

Fewest Interceptions By, Both Teams, Game
- 0 Buffalo vs. N.Y. Giants, XXV
    St. Louis vs. Tennessee, XXXIV
- 1 Oakland (0) vs. Green Bay (1), II
    Miami (0) vs. Dallas (1), VI
    Minnesota (0) vs. Miami (1), VIII
    N.Y. Giants (0) vs. Denver (1), XXI
    Cincinnati (0) vs. San Francisco (1), XXIII
    New England (0) vs. Carolina (1), XXXVIII

YARDS GAINED
Most Yards Gained, Game
- 172 Tampa Bay vs. Oakland, XXXVII
- 136 Denver vs. Atlanta, XXXIII
- 95 Miami vs. Washington, VII

Most Yards Gained, Both Teams, Game
- 184 Tampa Bay (172) vs. Oakland (12), XXXVII
- 137 Denver (136) vs. Atlanta (1), XXXIII
- 100 Seattle (76) vs. Pittsburgh (24), XL

TOUCHDOWNS
Most Touchdowns, Game
- 3 Tampa Bay vs. Oakland, XXXVII
- 1 Green Bay vs. Oakland, II
    Oakland vs. Minnesota, XI
    L.A. Raiders vs. Washington, XVIII
    Chicago vs. New England, XX
    Baltimore vs. N.Y. Giants, XXXV
    New England vs. St. Louis, XXXVI

PUNTING
Most Punts, Game
- 11 N.Y. Giants vs. Baltimore, XXXV
- 10 Baltimore vs. N.Y. Giants, XXXV
- 9 Dallas vs. Baltimore, V

Fewest Punts, Game
- 1 Atlanta vs. Denver, XXXIII
    Denver vs. Atlanta, XXXIII
- 2 Pittsburgh vs. Los Angeles, XIV
    Denver vs. N.Y. Giants, XXI
    St. Louis vs. Tennessee, XXXIV
- 3 By 11 teams

Most Punts, Both Teams, Game
- 21 N.Y. Giants (11) vs. Baltimore (10), XXXV
- 15 Washington (8) vs. L.A. Raiders (7), XVIII
    New England (8) vs. Green Bay (7), XXXI
- 13 Dallas (9) vs. Baltimore (4), V
    Pittsburgh (7) vs. Minnesota (6), IX

Fewest Punts, Both Teams, Game
- 2 Atlanta (1) vs. Denver (1), XXXIII
- 5 Denver (2) vs. N.Y. Giants (3), XXI
    St. Louis (2) vs. Tennessee (3), XXXIV
- 6 Oakland (3) vs. Philadelphia (3), XV

AVERAGE YARDAGE
Highest Average, Game (4 punts)
- 50.17 Seattle vs. Pittsburgh, XL (6-301)
- 48.75 San Diego vs. San Francisco, XXIX (4-195)
- 48.67 Pittsburgh vs. Seattle, XL (6-292)

Lowest Average, Game (4 punts)
- 31.00 Tampa Bay vs. Oakland, XXXVII (5-155)
- 31.20 Washington vs. Miami, VII (5-156)
- 32.38 Washington vs. L.A. Raiders, XVIII (8-259)

PUNT RETURNS
Most Punt Returns, Game
- 6 Washington vs. Miami, XVII
    Green Bay vs. New England, XXXI
- 5 By seven teams

Fewest Punt Returns, Game
- 0 Minnesota vs. Miami, VIII
    Buffalo vs. N.Y. Giants, XXV
    Washington vs. Buffalo, XXVI
    Denver vs. Green Bay, XXXII
    Green Bay vs. Denver, XXXII
    Atlanta vs. Denver, XXXIII
    Denver vs. Atlanta, XXXIII
- 1 By 19 teams

Most Punt Returns, Both Teams, Game
- 10 Green Bay (6) vs. New England (4), XXXI
- 9 Pittsburgh (5) vs. Minnesota (4), IX
- 8 Green Bay (5) vs. Oakland (3), II
    Baltimore (5) vs. Dallas (3), V
    Washington (6) vs. Miami (2), XVII
    N.Y. Giants (5) vs. Baltimore (3), XXXV

Fewest Punt Returns, Both Teams, Game
- 0 Denver vs. Green Bay, XXXII
    Atlanta vs. Denver, XXXIII
- 2 Dallas (1) vs. Miami (1), VI
    Denver (1) vs. N.Y. Giants (1), XXI
    Buffalo (0) vs. N.Y. Giants (2), XXV
    Buffalo (1) vs. Dallas (1), XXVIII
- 3 Kansas City (1) vs. Minnesota (2), IV
    Minnesota (0) vs. Miami (3), VIII
    Washington (1) vs. Denver (2), XXII
    Washington (0) vs. Buffalo (3), XXVI
    Dallas (1) vs. Pittsburgh (2), XXX
    Tennessee (1) vs. St. Louis (2), XXXIV

YARDS GAINED
Most Yards Gained, Game
- 90 Green Bay vs. New England, XXXI
- 56 San Francisco vs. Cincinnati, XXIII
- 52 Washington vs. Miami, XVII

Fewest Yards Gained, Game
- –1 Dallas vs. Miami, VI
  Tennessee vs. St. Louis, XXXIV
- 0 By 12 teams

Most Yards Gained, Both Teams, Game
- 120 Green Bay (90) vs. New England (30), XXXI
- 80 N.Y. Giants (46) vs. Baltimore (34), XXXV
- 74 Washington (52) vs. Miami (22), XVII

Fewest Yards Gained, Both Teams, Game
- 0 Denver vs. Green Bay, XXXII
  Atlanta vs. Denver, XXXIII
- 7 Tennessee (-1) vs. St. Louis (8), XXXIV
- 9 Washington (0) vs. Bufffalo (9), XXVI

AVERAGE RETURN
Highest Average, Game (3 returns)
- 18.7 San Francisco vs. Cincinnati, XXIII (3-56)
- 15.0 Green Bay vs. New England, XXXI (6-90)
- 12.7 San Francisco vs. Denver, XXIV (3-38)

TOUCHDOWNS
Most Touchdowns, Game
- None

KICKOFF RETURNS
Most Kickoff Returns, Game
- 9 Denver vs. San Francisco, XXIV
  Oakland vs. Tampa Bay, XXXVII
- 8 San Diego vs. San Francisco, XXIX
- 7 By eight teams

Fewest Kickoff Returns, Game
- 1 N.Y. Jets vs. Baltimore, III
  L.A. Raiders vs. Washington, XVIII
  Washington vs. Buffalo, XXVI
- 2 By nine teams

Most Kickoff Returns, Both Teams, Game
- 13 Oakland (9) vs. Tampa Bay (4), XXXVII
- 12 Denver (9) vs. San Francisco (3), XXIV
  San Diego (8) vs. San Francisco (4), XXIX
- 11 Los Angeles (6) vs. Pittsburgh (5), XIV
  Miami (7) vs. San Francisco (4), XIX
  New England (7) vs. Chicago (4), XX
  Green Bay (6) vs. Denver (5), XXXII

Fewest Kickoff Returns, Both Teams, Game
- 5 N.Y. Jets (1) vs. Baltimore (4), III
  Miami (2) vs. Washington (3), VII
  Washington (1) vs. Buffalo (4), XXVI
- 6 In four games

YARDS GAINED
Most Yards Gained, Game
- 244 San Diego vs. San Francisco, XXIX
- 227 Atlanta vs. Denver, XXXIII
- 222 Miami vs. Washington, XVII

Fewest Yards Gained, Game
- 16 Washington vs. Buffalo, XXVI
- 17 L.A. Raiders vs. Washington, XVIII
- 25 N.Y. Jets vs. Baltimore, III

Most Yards Gained, Both Teams, Game
- 292 San Diego (244) vs. San Francisco (48), XXIX
- 289 Green Bay (154) vs. New England (135), XXXI
- 281 N.Y. Giants (170) vs. Baltimore (111), XXXV

Fewest Yards Gained, Both Teams, Game
- 78 Miami (33) vs. Washington (45), VII
- 82 Pittsburgh (32) vs. Minnesota (50), IX

- 92 San Francisco (40) vs. Cincinnati (52), XVI

AVERAGE GAIN
Highest Average, Game (3 returns)
- 44.0 Cincinnati vs. San Francisco, XXIII (3-132)
- 38.5 Green Bay vs. New England, XXXI (4-154)
- 37.0 Miami vs. Washington, XVII (6-222)

TOUCHDOWNS
Most Touchdowns, Game
- 1 Miami vs. Washington, XVII
  Cincinnati vs. San Francisco, XXIII
  San Diego vs. San Francisco, XXIX
  Green Bay vs. New England, XXXI
  Atlanta vs. Denver, XXXIII
  Baltimore vs. N.Y. Giants, XXXV
  N.Y. Giants vs. Baltimore, XXXV

Most Touchdowns, Both Teams, Game
- 2 Baltimore (1) vs. N.Y. Giants (1), XXXV

PENALTIES
Most Penalties, Game
- 12 Dallas vs. Denver, XII
  Carolina vs. New England, XXXVIII
- 10 Dallas vs. Baltimore, V
- 9 Dallas vs. Pittsburgh, XIII
  Green Bay vs. Denver, XXXII
  Baltimore vs. N.Y. Giants, XXXV

Fewest Penalties, Game
- 0 Miami vs. Dallas, VI
  Pittsburgh vs. Dallas, X
  Denver vs. San Francisco, XXIV
  Atlanta vs. Denver, XXXIII
- 1 Green Bay vs. Oakland, II
  Miami vs. Minnesota, VIII; vs. San Francisco, XIX
  Buffalo vs. Dallas, XXVIII
- 2 By six teams

Most Penalties, Both Teams, Game
- 20 Dallas (12) vs. Denver (8), XII
  Carolina (12) vs. New England (8), XXXVIII
- 16 Cincinnati (8) vs. San Francisco (8), XVI
  Green Bay (9) vs. Denver (7), XXXII
- 15 St. Louis (8) vs. Tennessee (7), XXXIV
  Baltimore (9) vs. N.Y. Giants (6), XXXV

Fewest Penalties, Both Teams, Game
- 2 Pittsburgh (0) vs. Dallas (2), X
- 3 Miami (0) vs. Dallas (3), VI
  Miami (1) vs. San Francisco (2), XIX
- 4 Denver (0) vs. San Francisco (4), XXIV
  Atlanta (0) vs. Denver (4), XXXIII

YARDS PENALIZED
Most Yards Penalized, Game
- 133 Dallas vs. Baltimore, X
- 122 Pittsburgh vs. Minnesota, IX
- 94 Dallas vs. Denver, XII

Fewest Yards Penalized, Game
- 0 Miami vs. Dallas, VI
  Pittsburgh vs. Dallas, X
  Denver vs. San Francisco, XXIV
  Atlanta vs. Denver, XXXIII
- 4 Miami vs. Minnesota, VIII
- 10 Miami vs. San Francisco, XIX
  San Francisco vs. Miami, XIX
  Buffalo vs. Dallas, XXVIII

Most Yards Penalized, Both Teams, Game
- 164 Dallas (133) vs. Baltimore (31), V
- 154 Dallas (94) vs. Denver (60), XII
- 140 Pittsburgh (122) vs. Minnesota (18), IX

Fewest Yards Penalized, Both Teams, Game
- 15　Miami (0) vs. Dallas (15), VI
- 20　Pittsburgh (0) vs. Dallas (20), X
- 　　Miami (10) vs. San Francisco (10), XIX
- 38　Denver (0) vs. San Francisco (38), XXIV

FUMBLES

Most Fumbles, Game
- 8　Buffalo vs. Dallas, XXVII
- 6　Dallas vs. Denver, XII
- 　　Buffalo vs. Washington, XXVI
- 5　Baltimore vs. Dallas, V

Fewest Fumbles, Game
- 0　By 19 teams

Most Fumbles, Both Teams, Game
- 12　Buffalo (8) vs. Dallas (4), XXVII
- 10　Dallas (6) vs. Denver (4), XII
- 8　Dallas (4) vs. Pittsburgh (4), X

Fewest Fumbles, Both Teams, Game
- 0　Los Angeles vs. Pittsburgh, XIV
- 　　Green Bay vs. New England, XXXI
- 　　Pittsburgh vs. Seattle, XL
- 1　Oakland (0) vs. Minnesota (1), XI
- 　　Oakland (0) vs. Philadelphia (1), XV
- 　　Denver (0) vs. Washington (1), XXII
- 　　N.Y. Giants (0) vs. Buffalo (1), XXV
- 　　Denver (0) vs. Atlanta (1), XXXIII
- 2　In eight games

Most Fumbles Lost, Game
- 5　Buffalo vs. Dallas, XXVII
- 4　Baltimore vs. Dallas, V
- 　　Denver vs. Dallas, XII
- 　　New England vs. Chicago, XX
- 2　In many games

Most Fumbles Lost, Both Teams, Game
- 7　Buffalo (5) vs. Dallas (2), XXVII
- 6　Denver (4) vs. Dallas (2), XII
- 　　New England (4) vs. Chicago (2), XX
- 5　Baltimore (4) vs. Dallas (1), V

Fewest Fumbles Lost, Both Teams, Game
- 0　Green Bay vs. Kansas City, I
- 　　Dallas vs. Pittsburgh, X
- 　　Los Angeles vs. Pittsburgh, XIV
- 　　Denver vs. N.Y. Giants, XXI; vs. Washington, XXII
- 　　Buffalo vs. N.Y. Giants, XXV
- 　　San Diego vs. San Francisco, XXIX
- 　　Dallas vs. Pittsburgh, XXX
- 　　Green Bay vs. New England, XXXI
- 　　St. Louis vs. Tennessee, XXXIV
- 　　Oakland vs. Tampa Bay, XXXVII
- 　　Pittsburgh vs. Seattle, XL

Most Fumbles Recovered, Game
- 8　Dallas vs. Denver, XII (4 own, 4 opp.)
- 6　Dallas vs. Buffalo, XXVII (1 own, 5 opp.)
- 5　Chicago vs. New England, XX (1 own, 4 opp.)

TURNOVERS

(Number of times losing the ball on interceptions and fumbles.)

Most Turnovers, Game
- 9　Buffalo vs. Dallas, XXVII
- 8　Denver vs. Dallas, XII
- 7　Baltimore vs. Dallas, V

Fewest Turnovers, Game
- 0　Green Bay vs. Oakland, II
- 　　Miami vs. Minnesota, VIII
- 　　Pittsburgh vs. Dallas, X
- 　　Oakland vs. Minnesota, XI; vs. Philadelphia, XV
- 　　N.Y. Giants vs. Denver, XXI; vs. Buffalo, XXV
- 　　San Francisco vs. Denver, XXIV; vs. San Diego, XXIX
- 　　Buffalo vs. N.Y. Giants, XXV

　　Dallas vs. Pittsburgh, XXX
　　Green Bay vs. New England, XXXI
　　St. Louis vs. Tennessee, XXXIV
　　Tennessee vs. St. Louis, XXXIV
　　Baltimore vs. N.Y. Giants, XXXV
　　New England vs. St. Louis, XXXVI
- 1　By many teams

Most Turnovers, Both Teams, Game
- 11　Baltimore (7) vs. Dallas (4), V
- 　　Buffalo (9) vs. Dallas (2), XXVII
- 10　Denver (8) vs. Dallas (2), XII
- 8　New England (6) vs. Chicago (2), XX

Fewest Turnovers, Both Teams, Game
- 0　Buffalo vs. N.Y. Giants, XXV
- 　　St. Louis vs. Tennessee, XXXIV
- 1　N.Y. Giants (0) vs. Denver (1), XXI
- 2　Green Bay (1) vs. Kansas City (1), I
- 　　Miami (0) vs. Minnesota (2), VIII
- 　　Cincinnati (1) vs. San Francisco (1), XXIII
- 　　Carolina (1) vs. New England (1), XXXVIII

Compiled by Elias Sports Bureau

Throughout this all-time postseason record section, the following abbreviations are used to indicate various levels of postseason games:

SB — Super Bowl (1966 to date)

AFC — AFC Championship Game (1970 to date) or AFL Championship Game (1960-69)

NFC — NFC Championship Game (1970 to date) or NFL Championship Game (1933-69)

AFC-D — AFC Divisional Playoff Game (1970 to date), AFC Second-Round Playoff Game (1982), AFL Inter-Divisional Playoff Game (1969), or special playoff game to break tie for AFL Division Championship (1963, 1968)

NFC-D — NFC Divisional Playoff Game (1970 to date), NFC Second-Round Playoff Game (1982), NFL Conference Championship Game (1967-69), or special playoff game to break tie for NFL Division or Conference Championship (1941, 1943, 1947, 1950, 1952, 1957, 1958, 1965)

AFC-FR — AFC First-Round Playoff Game (1978 to date)

NFC-FR — NFC First-Round Playoff Game (1978 to date)

Year indicates season in which game took place and does not necessarily reflect calendar year.

POSTSEASON GAME COMPOSITE STANDINGS

	W	L	PCT.	PTS.	OP
Baltimore Ravens	5	2	.714	142	73
Carolina Panthers	6	3	.667	206	170
Green Bay Packers	24	14	.632	888	723
Pittsburgh Steelers	28	18	.609	1,066	928
New England Patriots#	17	11	.607	569	542
San Francisco 49ers	25	17	.595	1,044	853
Dallas Cowboys	32	22	.593	1,281	1,008
Washington Redskins*	23	16	.590	805	672
Oakland Raiders**	25	18	.581	1,028	797
Denver Broncos	17	15	.531	694	794
Miami Dolphins	20	19	.513	780	848
Philadelphia Eagles	16	16	.500	606	561
Buffalo Bills	14	15	.483	681	658
Chicago Bears	14	16	.467	619	614
Tennessee Titans†	14	17	.452	563	732
Indianapolis Colts***	13	16	.448	556	602
Jacksonville Jaguars	4	5	.444	211	228
New York Jets	8	10	.444	372	352
St. Louis Rams††	19	24	.442	770	944
Atlanta Falcons	6	8	.429	298	331
Minnesota Vikings	18	24	.429	824	957
Tampa Bay Buccaneers	6	8	.429	216	255
New York Giants	16	22	.421	647	722
Detroit Lions	7	10	.412	365	404
Kansas City Chiefs****	8	12	.400	332	422
Cincinnati Bengals	5	8	.385	263	288
Seattle Seahawks	5	8	.385	256	264
San Diego Chargers†††	7	12	.368	349	448
Cleveland Browns	11	20	.355	629	728
Arizona Cardinals††††	2	5	.286	122	182
New Orleans Saints	1	5	.167	103	185

   * *One game played when franchise was in Boston (lost 21-6).*

   ** *12 games played when franchise was in Los Angeles (won 6, lost 6, 268 points scored, 224 points allowed).*

   *** *15 games played when franchise was in Baltimore (won 8, lost 7, 264 points scored, 262 points allowed).*

   **** *One game played when franchise was Dallas Texans (won 20-17).*

   # *Two games played when franchise was in Boston (won 26-8, lost 51-10).*

   † *22 games played when franchise was in Houston and known as the Oilers (won 9, lost 13, 371 points scored, 533 points allowed).*

   †† *One game played when franchise was in Cleveland (won 15-14), 32 games played when franchise was in Los Ange-*

les (won 12, lost 20, 486 points scored, 683 points allowed).

   ††† *One game played when franchise was in Los Angeles (lost 24-16).*

   †††† *Two games played when franchise was in Chicago (won 28-21, lost 7-0), three games played when franchise was in St. Louis (lost 30-14, lost 35-23, lost 41-16).*

INDIVIDUAL RECORDS

SERVICE

Most Games, Career

29   Jerry Rice, San Francisco-Oakland-Seattle (SB 4, NFC 6, AFC 1, NFC-D 11, AFC-D 2, NFC-FR 4, AFC-FR 1)

27   D.D. Lewis, Dallas (SB 5, NFC 9, NFC-D 12, NFC-FR 1)

26   Larry Cole, Dallas (SB 5, NFC 8, NFC-D 12, NFC-FR 1)
Bill Romanowski, San Francisco-Philadelphia-Denver-Oakland (SB 5, NFC 5, AFC 3, NFC-D 6, AFC-D 4, NFC-FR 1, AFC-FR 2)

Most Games, Head Coach

36   Tom Landry, Dallas
Don Shula, Baltimore-Miami

24   Chuck Noll, Pittsburgh

23   Joe Gibbs, Washington

Most Games Won, Head Coach

20   Tom Landry, Dallas

19   Don Shula, Baltimore-Miami

17   Joe Gibbs, Washington

Most Games Lost, Head Coach

17   Don Shula, Baltimore-Miami

16   Tom Landry, Dallas

12   Bud Grant, Minnesota
Marty Schottenheimer, Cleveland-Kansas City-San Diego

SCORING

POINTS

Most Points, Career

153   Gary Anderson, Pittsburgh-Philadelphia-San Francisco-Minnesota-Tennessee, (57-pat, 32-fg)

132   Jerry Rice, San Francisco-Oakland-Seattle, 29 games (22-td)

126   Thurman Thomas, Buffalo, 21 games (21-td)
Emmitt Smith, Dallas, 17 games (21-td)

Most Points, Game

30   Ricky Watters, NFC-D: San Francisco vs. N.Y. Giants, 1993 (5-td)

19   Pat Harder, NFC-D: Detroit vs. Los Angeles, 1952 (2-td, 4-pat, 1-fg)
Paul Hornung, NFC: Green Bay vs. N.Y. Giants, 1961 (1-td, 4-pat, 3-fg)

18   By many players

Most Consecutive Games Scoring

19   George Blanda, Chi. Bears-Houston-Oakland, 1956-1975

17   Adam Vinatieri, New England, 1996-2005 (current)

16   Norm Johnson, Seattle-Atlanta-Pittsburgh, 1983-1997

TOUCHDOWNS

Most Touchdowns, Career

22   Jerry Rice, San Francisco-Oakland-Seattle, 29 games (22-p)

21   Thurman Thomas, Buffalo, 21 games (16-r, 5-p)
Emmitt Smith, Dallas, 17 games (19-r, 2-p)

17   Franco Harris, Pittsburgh, 19 games (16-r, 1-p)

Most Touchdowns, Game

5   Ricky Watters, NFC-D: San Francisco vs. N.Y. Giants, 1993 (5-r)

3   Andy Farkas, NFC-D: Washington vs. N.Y. Giants, 1943 (3-r)
Tom Fears, NFC-D: Los Angeles vs. Chi. Bears, 1950 (3-p)
Otto Graham, NFC: Cleveland vs. Detroit, 1954 (3-r)

Gary Collins, NFC: Cleveland vs. Baltimore, 1964 (3-p)
Craig Baynham, NFC-D: Dallas vs. Cleveland, 1967
  (2-r, 1-p)
Fred Biletnikoff, AFC-D: Oakland vs. Kansas City, 1968 (3-p)
Tom Matte, NFC: Baltimore vs. Cleveland, 1968 (3-r)
Larry Schreiber, NFC-D: San Francisco vs. Dallas, 1972 (3-r)
Larry Csonka, AFC: Miami vs. Oakland, 1973 (3-r)
Franco Harris, AFC-D: Pittsburgh vs. Buffalo, 1974 (3-r)
Preston Pearson, NFC: Dallas vs. Los Angeles, 1975 (3-p)
Dave Casper, AFC-D: Oakland vs. Baltimore, 1977 (OT) (3-p)
Alvin Garrett, NFC-FR: Washington vs. Detroit, 1982 (3-p)
John Riggins, NFC-D: Washington vs. L.A. Rams, 1983 (3-r)
Roger Craig, SB: San Francisco vs. Miami, 1984 (1-r, 2-p)
Jerry Rice, NFC-D: San Francisco vs. Minnesota, 1988 (3-p)
Jerry Rice, SB: San Francisco vs. Denver, 1989 (3-p)
Kenneth Davis, AFC: Buffalo vs. L.A. Raiders, 1990 (3-r)
Andre Reed, AFC-FR: Buffalo vs. Houston, 1992 (OT)
  (3-p)
Sterling Sharpe, NFC-FR: Green Bay vs. Detroit, 1993 (3-p)
Napoleon McCallum, AFC-FR: L.A. Raiders vs. Denver,
  1993 (3-r)
Thurman Thomas, AFC: Buffalo vs. Kansas City, 1993 (3-r)
William Floyd, NFC-D: San Francisco vs. Chicago, 1994 (3-r)
Ricky Watters, SB: San Francisco vs. San Diego, 1994
  (1-r, 2-p)
Jerry Rice, SB: San Francisco vs. San Diego, 1994 (3-p)
Emmitt Smith, NFC: Dallas vs. Green Bay, 1995 (3-r)
Curtis Martin, AFC-D: New England vs. Pittsburgh, 1996 (3-r)
Terrell Davis, SB: Denver vs. Green Bay, 1997 (3-r)
Mario Bates, NFC-D: Arizona vs. Minnesota, 1998 (3-r)
Leroy Hoard, NFC-D: Minnesota vs. Arizona, 1998 (2-r, 1-p)
Willie Jackson, NFC-FR: New Orleans vs. St. Louis, 2000
  (3-p)
Amani Toomer, NFC-FR: N.Y. Giants vs. San Francisco,
  2002 (3-p)
Shaun Alexander, NFC-FR: Seattle vs. Green Bay, 2003
  (OT) (3-r)

Most Consecutive Games Scoring Touchdowns
9   Thurman Thomas, Buffalo, 1992-98
8   John Stallworth, Pittsburgh, 1978-1983
    Emmitt Smith, Dallas, 1993-96
7   John Riggins, Washington, 1982-84
    Marcus Allen, L.A. Raiders, 1982-85
    Terrell Davis, Denver, 1996-98
    David Givens, New England, 2003-05 (current)

POINTS AFTER TOUCHDOWN
Most (One-Point) Points After Touchdown, Career
57   Gary Anderson, Pittsburgh-Philadelphia-San Francisco-
     Minnesota-Tennessee, 22 games (57 att)
49   George Blanda, Chi. Bears-Houston-Oakland, 19 games
     (49 att)
42   Mike Cofer, San Francisco, 12 games (46 att)
Most (One-Point) Points After Touchdown, Game
8   Lou Groza, NFC: Cleveland vs. Detroit, 1954 (8 att)
     Jim Martin, NFC: Detroit vs. Cleveland, 1957 (8 att)
     George Blanda, AFC-D: Oakland vs. Houston, 1969 (8 att)
     Mike Hollis, AFC-D: Jacksonville vs. Miami, 1999 (8 att)
7   Danny Villanueva, NFC-D: Dallas vs. Cleveland, 1967 (7 att)
     Raul Allegre, NFC-D: N.Y. Giants vs. San Francisco, 1986
     (7 att)
     Mike Cofer, SB: San Francisco vs. Denver, 1989 (8 att)
     Lin Elliott, SB: Dallas vs. Buffalo, 1992 (7 att)
     Doug Brien, SB: San Francisco vs. San Diego, 1994 (7 att)
     Gary Anderson, NFC-FR: Philadelphia vs. Detroit, 1995 (7 att)
     Jeff Wilkins, NFC-D: St. Louis vs. Minnesota, 1999 (7 att)
     Mike Vanderjagt, AFC-FR: Indianapolis vs. Denver, 2004
     (7 att)
6   George Blair, AFC: San Diego vs. Boston, 1963 (6 att)
     Mark Moseley, NFC-D: Washington vs. L.A. Rams, 1983 (6 att)

Uwe von Schamann, AFC: Miami vs. Pittsburgh, 1984 (6 att)
Ali Haji-Sheikh, SB: Washington vs. Denver, 1987 (6 att)
Scott Norwood, AFC: Buffalo vs. L.A. Raiders, 1990 (7 att)
Jeff Jaeger, AFC-FR: L.A. Raiders vs. Denver, 1993 (6 att)
Jason Elam, AFC-FR: Denver vs. Jacksonville, 1997 (6 att)
Jeff Wilkins, NFC-D: St. Louis vs. Green Bay, 2001 (6 att)
Martín Gramatica, SB: Tampa Bay vs. Oakland, 2002 (6 att)
Jay Feely, NFC-D: Atlanta vs. St. Louis, 2004 (6 att)

Most (Kicking) Points After Touchdown, No Misses, Career
57   Gary Anderson, Pittsburgh-Philadelphia-San Francisco-
     Minnesota-Tennessee, 22 games
49   George Blanda, Chi. Bears-Houston-Oakland, 19 games
41   Rafael Septien, L.A. Rams-Dallas, 15 games
Most Two-Point Conversions, Career
2   Terrell Owens, San Francisco-Philadelphia, 10 games
Most Two-Point Conversions, Game
2   Terrell Owens, NFC-FR: San Francisco vs. N.Y. Giants,
     2002

FIELD GOALS
Most Field Goals Attempted, Career
40   Gary Anderson, Pittsburgh-Philadelphia-San Francisco-
     Minnesota-Tennessee, 22 games
39   George Blanda, Chi. Bears-Houston-Oakland, 19 games
34   Adam Vinatieri, New England, 17 games
Most Field Goals Attempted, Game
6   George Blanda, AFC: Oakland vs. Houston, 1967
     David Ray, NFC-D: Los Angeles vs. Dallas, 1973
     Mark Moseley, AFC-D: Cleveland vs. N.Y. Jets, 1986 (OT)
     Matt Bahr, NFC: N.Y. Giants vs. San Francisco, 1990
     Steve Christie, AFC: Buffalo vs. Miami, 1992
     Jeff Wilkins, NFC-D: St. Louis vs. Carolina, 2003 (2 OT)
5   By many players
Most Field Goals, Career
32   Gary Anderson, Pittsburgh-Philadelphia-San Francisco-
     Minnesota-Tennessee, 22 games
26   Adam Vinatieri, New England, 17 games
22   George Blanda, Chi. Bears-Houston-Oakland, 19 games
     Steve Christie, Buffalo, 12 games
Most Field Goals, Game
5   Chuck Nelson, NFC-D: Minnesota vs. San Francisco, 1987
     Matt Bahr, NFC: N.Y. Giants vs. San Francisco, 1990
     Steve Christie, AFC: Buffalo vs. Miami, 1992
     Brad Daluiso, NFC-FR: N.Y. Giants vs. Minnesota, 1997
     John Kasay, NFC-FR: Carolina vs. Dallas, 2003
     Jeff Wilkins, NFC-D: St. Louis vs. Carolina, 2003 (2 OT)
     Adam Vinatieri, AFC: New England vs. Indianapolis, 2003
4   Gino Cappelletti, AFC-D: Boston vs. Buffalo, 1963
     George Blanda, AFC: Oakland vs. Houston, 1967
     Don Chandler, SB: Green Bay vs. Oakland, 1967
     Curt Knight, NFC: Washington vs. Dallas, 1972
     George Blanda, AFC-D: Oakland vs. Pittsburgh, 1973
     Ray Wersching, SB: San Francisco vs. Cincinnati, 1981
     Tony Franklin, AFC-FR: New England vs. N.Y. Jets, 1985
     Jess Atkinson, NFC-FR: Washington vs. L.A. Rams, 1986
     Luis Zendejas, NFC-D: Philadelphia vs. Chicago, 1988
     Gary Anderson, AFC-FR: Pittsburgh vs. Houston, 1989 (OT)
     Norm Johnson, AFC-D: Pittsburgh vs. Buffalo, 1995
     Chris Boniol, NFC: Dallas vs. Minnesota, 1996
     John Kasay, NFC-D: Carolina vs. Dallas, 1996
     Mike Hollis, AFC-D: Jacksonville vs. New England, 1998
     Al Del Greco, AFC-D: Tennessee vs. Indianapolis, 1999
     David Akers, NFC-D: Philadelphia vs. Chicago, 2001
3   By many players
Most Consecutive Games Scoring Field Goals
13   Toni Fritsch, Dallas-Houston, 1972-79
12   Adam Vinatieri, New England, 1997-2004 (current)
10   David Akers, Philadelphia, 2000-04
     Morten Andersen, New Orleans-Atlanta-Kansas City-
     Minnesota, 1987-2004

Jason Elam, Denver, 1997-2000, 2003-05 (current)

Most Consecutive Field Goals

16 Gary Anderson, Pittsburgh-Philadelphia, 1989-1995
15 Rafael Septien, Dallas, 1978-1982
14 Mike Hollis, Jacksonville, 1996-99
John Kasay, Carolina, 1996-2003

Longest Field Goal

58 Pete Stoyanovich, AFC-FR: Miami vs. Kansas City, 1990
55 Jeff Wilkins, NFC-D: St. Louis vs. Atlanta, 2004
54 Ed Murray, NFC-D: Detroit vs. San Francisco, 1983
Steve Christie, SB: Buffalo vs. Dallas, 1993
John Carney, AFC-FR: San Diego vs. Indianapolis, 1995

Highest Field Goal Percentage, Career (10 field goals)

91.7 Martín Gramatica, Tampa Bay-Indianapolis, 8 games (12-11)
91.3 John Kasay, Carolina, 9 games (23-21)
90.9 Chuck Nelson, L.A. Rams-Minnesota, 6 games (11-10)

SAFETIES
Most Safeties, Game

1 Bill Willis, NFC-D: Cleveland vs. N.Y. Giants, 1950
Carl Eller, NFC-D: Minnesota vs. Los Angeles, 1969
George Andrie, NFC-D: Dallas vs. Detroit, 1970
Alan Page, NFC-D: Minnesota vs. Dallas, 1971
Dwight White, SB: Pittsburgh vs. Minnesota, 1974
Reggie Harrison, SB: Pittsburgh vs. Dallas, 1975
Jim Jensen, NFC-D: Dallas vs. Los Angeles, 1976
Ted Washington, AFC: Houston vs. Pittsburgh, 1978
Randy White, NFC-D: Dallas vs. Los Angeles, 1979
Henry Waechter, SB: Chicago vs. New England, 1985
Rulon Jones, AFC-FR: Denver vs. New England, 1986
George Martin, SB: N.Y. Giants vs. Denver, 1986
D.D. Hoggard, AFC: Cleveland vs. Denver, 1987
Bruce Smith, SB: Buffalo vs. N.Y. Giants, 1990
Reggie White, NFC-FR: Philadelphia vs. New Orleans, 1992
Willie Clay, NFC-FR: Detroit vs. Green Bay, 1994
Carnell Lake, AFC-D: Pittsburgh vs. Cleveland, 1994
Reuben Davis, AFC-D: San Diego vs. Miami, 1994
Jevon Kearse, AFC-FR: Tennessee vs. Buffalo, 1999
Brady Smith, NFC-D: Atlanta vs. St. Louis, 2004

RUSHING
ATTEMPTS
Most Attempts, Career

400 Franco Harris, Pittsburgh, 19 games
349 Emmitt Smith, Dallas, 17 games
339 Thurman Thomas, Buffalo, 21 games

Most Attempts, Game

40 Lamar Smith, AFC-FR: Miami vs. Indianapolis, 2000 (OT)
38 Ricky Bell, NFC-D: Tampa Bay vs. Philadelphia, 1979
John Riggins, SB: Washington vs. Miami, 1982
37 Lawrence McCutcheon, NFC-D: Los Angeles vs. St. Louis, 1975
John Riggins, NFC-D: Washington vs. Minnesota, 1982

YARDS GAINED
Most Yards Gained, Career

1,586 Emmitt Smith, Dallas, 17 games
1,556 Franco Harris, Pittsburgh, 19 games
1,442 Thurman Thomas, Buffalo, 21 games

Most Yards Gained, Game

248 Eric Dickerson, NFC-D: L.A. Rams vs. Dallas, 1985
209 Lamar Smith, AFC-FR: Miami vs. Indianapolis, 2000 (OT)
206 Keith Lincoln, AFC: San Diego vs. Boston, 1963

Most Games, 100 or More Yards Rushing, Career

7 Emmitt Smith, Dallas, 17 games
Terrell Davis, Denver, 8 games
6 John Riggins, Washington, 9 games
Thurman Thomas, Buffalo, 21 games
5 Franco Harris, Pittsburgh, 19 games

Marcus Allen, L.A. Raiders-Kansas City, 16 games

Most Consecutive Games, 100 or More Yards Rushing

7 Terrell Davis, Denver, 1997-98
6 John Riggins, Washington, 1982-83
4 Thurman Thomas, Buffalo, 1990-91

Longest Run From Scrimmage

90 Fred Taylor, AFC-D: Jacksonville vs. Miami, 1999 (TD)
80 Roger Craig, NFC-D: San Francisco vs. Minnesota, 1988 (TD)
Charlie Garner, AFC-FR: Oakland vs. N.Y. Jets, 2001 (TD)
78 Curtis Martin, AFC-D: New England vs. Pittsburgh, 1996 (TD)

AVERAGE GAIN
Highest Average Gain, Career (100 attempts)

5.59 Terrell Davis, Denver, 8 games (204-1,140)
5.04 Marcus Allen, L.A. Raiders-Kansas City, 16 games (267-1,347)
4.89 Eric Dickerson, L.A. Rams-Indianapolis, 7 games (148-724)

Highest Average Gain, Game (10 attempts)

15.90 Elmer Angsman, NFC: Chi. Cardinals vs. Philadelphia, 1947 (10-159)
15.85 Keith Lincoln, AFC: San Diego vs. Boston, 1963 (13-206)
11.31 Zack Crockett, AFC-FR: Indianapolis vs. San Diego, 1995 (13-147)

TOUCHDOWNS
Most Touchdowns, Career

19 Emmitt Smith, Dallas, 17 games
16 Franco Harris, Pittsburgh, 19 games
Thurman Thomas, Buffalo, 21 games
12 John Riggins, Washington, 9 games
Terrell Davis, Denver, 8 games

Most Touchdowns, Game

5 Ricky Watters, NFC-D: San Francisco vs. N.Y. Giants, 1993
3 Andy Farkas, NFC-D: Washington vs. N.Y. Giants, 1943
Otto Graham, NFC: Cleveland vs. Detroit, 1954
Tom Matte, NFC: Baltimore vs. Cleveland, 1968
Larry Schreiber, NFC-D: San Francisco vs. Dallas, 1972
Larry Csonka, AFC: Miami vs. Oakland, 1973
Franco Harris, AFC-D: Pittsburgh vs. Buffalo, 1974
John Riggins, NFC-D: Washington vs. L.A. Rams, 1983
Kenneth Davis, AFC: Buffalo vs. L.A. Raiders, 1990
Napoleon McCallum, AFC-FR: L.A. Raiders vs. Denver, 1993
Thurman Thomas, AFC: Buffalo vs. Kansas City, 1993
William Floyd, NFC-D: San Francisco vs. Chicago, 1994
Emmitt Smith, NFC: Dallas vs. Green Bay, 1995
Curtis Martin, AFC-D: New England vs. Pittsburgh, 1996
Terrell Davis, SB: Denver vs. Green Bay, 1997
Mario Bates, NFC-D: Arizona vs. Minnesota, 1998
Shaun Alexander, NFC-FR: Seattle vs. Green Bay, 2003 (OT)

Most Consecutive Games Rushing for Touchdowns

8 Emmitt Smith, Dallas, 1993-96
Thurman Thomas, Buffalo, 1992-98
7 John Riggins, Washington, 1982-84
Terrell Davis, Denver, 1996-98
5 Franco Harris, Pittsburgh, 1974-75
Franco Harris, Pittsburgh, 1977-79
Curtis Martin, New England-N.Y. Jets, 1996-98
Jerome Bettis, Pittsburgh, 2004-05

PASSING
PASSER RATING
Highest Passer Rating, Career (150 attempts)

104.8 Bart Starr, Green Bay, 10 games
95.6 Joe Montana, San Francisco-Kansas City, 23 games
95.0 Jake Delhomme, Carolina, 7 games

ATTEMPTS
Most Passes Attempted, Career

734 Joe Montana, San Francisco-Kansas City, 23 games
687 Dan Marino, Miami, 18 games

663 Brett Favre, Green Bay, 20 games

Most Passes Attempted, Game

65 Steve Young, NFC-D: San Francisco vs. Green Bay, 1995
64 Bernie Kosar, AFC-D: Cleveland vs. N.Y. Jets, 1986 (OT)
   Dan Marino, AFC-FR: Miami vs. Buffalo, 1995
58 Jim Kelly, SB: Buffalo vs. Washington, 1991

COMPLETIONS

Most Passes Completed, Career

460 Joe Montana, San Francisco-Kansas City, 23 games
401 Brett Favre, Green Bay, 20 games
385 Dan Marino, Miami, 18 games

Most Passes Completed, Game

36 Warren Moon, AFC-FR: Houston vs. Buffalo, 1992 (OT)
33 Dan Fouts, AFC-D: San Diego vs. Miami, 1981 (OT)
   Bernie Kosar, AFC-D: Cleveland vs. N.Y. Jets, 1986 (OT)
   Dan Marino, AFC-FR: Miami vs. Buffalo, 1995
32 Neil Lomax, NFC-FR: St. Louis vs. Green Bay, 1982
   Danny White, NFC-FR: Dallas vs. L.A. Rams, 1983
   Warren Moon, AFC-D: Houston vs. Kansas City, 1993
   Neil O'Donnell, AFC: Pittsburgh vs. San Diego, 1994
   Steve Young, NFC-D: San Francisco vs. Green Bay, 1995
   Tom Brady, AFC-D: New England vs. Oakland, 2001 (OT)
   Tom Brady, SB: New England vs. Carolina, 2003

COMPLETION PERCENTAGE

Highest Completion Percentage, Career (150 attempts)

66.3 Ken Anderson, Cincinnati, 6 games (166-110)
64.3 Warren Moon, Houston-Minnesota, 10 games (403-259)
64.2 Rich Gannon, Minnesota-Kanas City-Oakland, 10 games
    (240-154)

Highest Completion Percentage, Game (15 completions)

88.0 Phil Simms, SB: N.Y. Giants vs. Denver, 1986 (25-22)
86.7 Joe Montana, NFC: San Francisco vs. L.A. Rams, 1989
    (30-26)
84.6 Peyton Manning, AFC-FR: Indianapolis vs. Denver, 2003
    (26-22)

YARDS GAINED

Most Yards Gained, Career

5,772 Joe Montana, San Francisco-Kansas City, 23 games
4,964 John Elway, Denver, 22 games
4,902 Brett Favre, Green Bay, 20 games

Most Yards Gained, Game

489 Bernie Kosar, AFC-D: Cleveland vs. N.Y. Jets, 1986 (OT)
458 Peyton Manning, AFC-FR: Indianapolis vs. Denver, 2004
433 Dan Fouts, AFC-D: San Diego vs. Miami, 1981 (OT)

Most Games, 300 or More Yards Passing, Career

6 Joe Montana, San Francisco-Kansas City, 23 games
5 Dan Fouts, San Diego, 7 games
4 Warren Moon, Houston-Minnesota, 10 games
  Troy Aikman, Dallas, 16 games
  Dan Marino, Miami, 18 games
  John Elway, Denver, 22 games
  Kurt Warner, St. Louis, 7 games

Most Consecutive Games, 300 or More Yards Passing

4 Dan Fouts, San Diego, 1979-1981
3 Jim Kelly, Buffalo, 1989-1990
  Warren Moon, Houston, 1991-93
2 Daryle Lamonica, Oakland, 1968
  Ken Anderson, Cincinnati, 1981-82
  Terry Bradshaw, Pittsburgh, 1979-1982
  Joe Montana, San Francisco, 1983-84
  Dan Marino, Miami, 1984
  Troy Aikman, Dallas, 1994
  Steve Young, San Francisco, 1994-95
  Kurt Warner, St. Louis, 1999-2000
  Peyton Manning, Indianapolis, 2003
  Marc Bulger, St. Louis, 2003-04
  Matt Hasselbeck, Seattle, 2003-04

Longest Pass Completion

96 Trent Dilfer (to Sharpe), AFC: Baltimore vs. Oakland, 2000 (TD)
94 Troy Aikman (to Harper), NFC-D: Dallas vs. Green Bay, 1994 (TD)
93 Daryle Lamonica (to Dubenion), AFC-D: Buffalo vs. Boston, 1963 (TD)

AVERAGE GAIN

Highest Average Gain, Career (150 attempts)

8.55 Jake Delhomme, Carolina, 7 games (192-1,642)
8.45 Joe Theismann, Washington, 10 games (211-1,782)
8.43 Jim Plunkett, Oakland/L.A.Raiders, 10 games (272-2,293)

Highest Average Gain, Game (20 attempts)

14.71 Terry Bradshaw, SB: Pittsburgh vs. Los Angeles, 1979 (21-309)
14.50 Peyton Manning, AFC-FR: Indianapolis vs. Denver, 2003 (26-377)
13.88 Peyton Manning, AFC-FR: Indianapolis vs. Denver, 2004 (33-458)

TOUCHDOWNS

Most Touchdown Passes, Career

45 Joe Montana, San Francisco-Kansas City, 23 games
34 Brett Favre, Green Bay, 20 games
32 Dan Marino, Miami, 18 games

Most Touchdown Passes, Game

6 Daryle Lamonica, AFC-D: Oakland vs. Houston, 1969
  Steve Young, SB: San Francisco vs. San Diego, 1994
5 Sid Luckman, NFC: Chi. Bears vs. Washington, 1943
  Daryle Lamonica, AFC-D: Oakland vs. Kansas City, 1968
  Joe Montana, SB: San Francisco vs. Denver, 1989
  Kurt Warner, NFC-D: St. Louis vs. Minnesota, 1999
  Kerry Collins, NFC: N.Y. Giants vs. Minnesota, 2000
  Peyton Manning, AFC-FR: Indianapolis vs. Denver, 2003
4 Otto Graham, NFC: Cleveland vs. Los Angeles, 1950
  Tobin Rote, NFC: Detroit vs. Cleveland, 1957
  Bart Starr, NFC: Green Bay vs. Dallas, 1966
  Ken Stabler, AFC-D: Oakland vs. Miami, 1974
  Roger Staubach, NFC: Dallas vs. Los Angeles, 1975
  Terry Bradshaw, SB: Pittsburgh vs. Dallas, 1978
  Don Strock, AFC-D: Miami vs. San Diego, 1981 (OT)
  Lynn Dickey, NFC-FR: Green Bay vs. St. Louis, 1982
  Dan Marino, AFC: Miami vs. Pittsburgh, 1984
  Phil Simms, NFC-D: N.Y. Giants vs. San Francisco, 1986
  Doug Williams, SB: Washington vs. Denver, 1987
  Jim Kelly, AFC-D: Buffalo vs. Cleveland, 1989
  Joe Montana, NFC-D: San Francisco vs. Minnesota, 1989
  Warren Moon, AFC-FR: Houston vs. Buffalo, 1992 (OT)
  Frank Reich, AFC-FR: Buffalo vs. Houston, 1992 (OT)
  Troy Aikman, SB: Dallas vs. Buffalo, 1992
  Jeff George, NFC-D: Minnesota vs. St. Louis, 1999
  Aaron Brooks, NFC-FR: New Orleans vs. St. Louis, 2000
  Kerry Collins, NFC-FR: N.Y. Giants vs. San Francisco, 2002
  Peyton Manning, AFC-FR: Indianapolis vs. Denver, 2004
  Daunte Culpepper, NFC-FR: Minnesota vs. Green Bay, 2004

Most Consecutive Games, Touchdown Passes

16 Brett Favre, Green Bay, 1995-2004 (current)
13 Dan Marino, Miami, 1983-1995
10 Ken Stabler, Oakland, 1973-77
  Joe Montana, San Francisco-Kansas City, 1988-1993

HAD INTERCEPTED

Lowest Percentage, Passes Had Intercepted, Career (150 attempts)

1.36 Tom Brady, New England, 11 games (367-5)
1.41 Bart Starr, Green Bay, 10 games (213-3)
1.57 Matt Hasselbeck, Seattle, 3 games (191-3)

Most Attempts Without Interception, Game

54 Neil O'Donnell, AFC: Pittsburgh vs. San Diego, 1994
48 Warren Moon, AFC-FR: Houston vs. Pittsburgh, 1989 (OT)
  Randall Cunningham, NFC: Minnesota vs. Atlanta, 1998 (OT)
47 Daryle Lamonica, AFC: Oakland vs. N.Y. Jets, 1968

Most Passes Had Intercepted, Career

28   Jim Kelly, Buffalo, 17 games
26   Terry Bradshaw, Pittsburgh, 19 games
     Brett Favre, Green Bay, 20 games
24   Dan Marino, Miami, 18 games

Most Passes Had Intercepted, Game

6   Frank Filchock, NFC: N.Y. Giants vs. Chi. Bears, 1946
    Bobby Layne, NFC: Detroit vs. Cleveland, 1954
    Norm Van Brocklin, NFC: Los Angeles vs. Cleveland, 1955
    Brett Favre, NFC-D: Green Bay vs. St. Louis, 2001
5   Frank Filchock, NFC: Washington vs. Chi. Bears, 1940
    George Blanda, AFC: Houston vs. San Diego, 1961
    George Blanda, AFC: Houston vs. Dall. Texans, 1962 (OT)
    Y.A. Tittle, NFC: N.Y. Giants vs. Chicago, 1963
    Mike Phipps, AFC-D: Cleveland vs. Miami, 1972
    Dan Pastorini, AFC: Houston vs. Pittsburgh, 1978
    Dan Fouts, AFC-D: San Diego vs. Houston, 1979
    Tommy Kramer, NFC-D: Minnesota vs. Philadelphia, 1980
    Dan Fouts, AFC-D: San Diego vs. Miami, 1982
    Richard Todd, AFC: N.Y. Jets vs Miami, 1982
    Gary Danielson, NFC-D: Detroit vs. San Francisco, 1983
    Jay Schroeder, AFC: L.A. Raiders vs. Buffalo, 1990
    Rich Gannon, SB: Oakland vs. Tampa Bay, 2002
4   By many players

PASS RECEIVING

RECEPTIONS

Most Receptions, Career

151   Jerry Rice, San Francisco-Oakland-Seattle, 29 games
87   Michael Irvin, Dallas, 16 games
85   Andre Reed, Buffalo, 21 games

Most Receptions, Game

13   Kellen Winslow, AFC-D: San Diego vs. Miami, 1981 (OT)
    Thurman Thomas, AFC-D: Buffalo vs. Cleveland, 1989
    Shannon Sharpe, AFC-FR: Denver vs. L.A. Raiders, 1993
    Chad Morton, NFC-D: New Orleans vs. Minnesota, 2000
12   Raymond Berry, NFC: Baltimore vs. N.Y. Giants, 1958
    Michael Irvin, NFC: Dallas vs. San Francisco, 1994
    Darrell Jackson, NFC-FR: Seattle vs. St. Louis, 2004
    Steve Smith, NFC-D: Carolina vs. Chicago, 2005
11   Dante Lavelli, NFC: Cleveland vs. Los Angeles, 1950
    Dan Ross, SB: Cincinnati vs. San Francisco, 1981
    Franco Harris, AFC-FR: Pittsburgh vs. San Diego, 1982
    Steve Watson, AFC-D: Denver vs. Pittsburgh, 1984
    John L. Williams, AFC-D: Seattle vs. Cincinnati, 1988
    Jerry Rice, SB: San Francisco vs. Cincinnati, 1988
    Ernest Givins, AFC-FR: Houston vs. Pittsburgh, 1989 (OT)
    Amp Lee, NFC-D: Minnesota vs. Chicago, 1994
    Jay Novacek, NFC-D: Dallas vs. Green Bay, 1994
    O.J. McDuffie, AFC-FR: Miami vs. Buffalo, 1995
    Jerry Rice, NFC-C: San Francisco vs. Green Bay, 1995
    Hines Ward, AFC-FR: Pittsburgh vs. Cleveland, 2002
    Deion Branch, SB: New England vs. Philadelphia, 2004

Most Consecutive Games, Pass Receptions

28   Jerry Rice, San Francisco-Oakland, 1985-2002
22   Drew Pearson, Dallas, 1973-1983
18   Paul Warfield, Cleveland-Miami, 1964-1974
    Cliff Branch, Oakland/L.A. Raiders, 1974-1983
    Thurman Thomas, Buffalo, 1989-1998
    Shannon Sharpe, Denver-Baltimore-Denver, 1991-2003

YARDS GAINED

Most Yards Gained, Career

2,245   Jerry Rice, San Francisco-Oakland-Seattle, 29 games
1,315   Michael Irvin, Dallas, 16 games
1,289   Cliff Branch, Oakland/L.A. Raiders, 22 games

Most Yards Gained, Game

240   Eric Moulds, AFC-FR: Buffalo vs. Miami, 1998
227   Anthony Carter, NFC-D: Minnesota vs. San Francisco, 1987
221   Reggie Wayne, AFC-FR: Indianapolis vs. Denver, 2004

Most Games, 100 or More Yards Receiving, Career

8   Jerry Rice, San Francisco-Oakland-Seattle, 29 games
6   Michael Irvin, Dallas, 16 games
5   John Stallworth, Pittsburgh, 18 games
    Andre Reed, Buffalo, 21 games

Most Consecutive Games, 100 or More Yards Receiving, Career

3   Tom Fears, Los Angeles, 1950-51
    Jerry Rice, San Francisco, 1988-89
    Randy Moss, Minnesota, 1999-2000
2   By many players

Longest Reception

96   Shannon Sharpe (from Dilfer), AFC: Baltimore vs. Oakland, 2000 (TD)
94   Alvin Harper (from Aikman), NFC-D: Dallas vs. Green Bay, 1994 (TD)
93   Elbert Dubenion (from Lamonica), AFC-D: Buffalo vs. Boston, 1963 (TD)

AVERAGE GAIN

Highest Average Gain, Career (20 receptions)

27.3   Alvin Harper, Dallas, 10 games (24-655)
23.7   Willie Gault, Chicago-L.A. Raiders, 12 games (21-497)
22.8   Harold Jackson, L.A. Rams-New England-Minnesota-Seattle, 14 games (24-548)

Highest Average Gain, Game (3 receptions)

46.3   Harold Jackson, NFC: Los Angeles vs. Minnesota, 1974 (3-139)
42.7   Billy Cannon, AFC: Houston vs. L.A. Chargers, 1960 (3-128)
42.0   Lenny Moore, NFC: Baltimore vs. N.Y. Giants, 1959 (3-126)

TOUCHDOWNS

Most Touchdowns, Career

22   Jerry Rice, San Francisco-Oakland-Seattle, 29 games
12   John Stallworth, Pittsburgh, 18 games
10   Fred Biletnikoff, Oakland, 19 games
    Antonio Freeman, Green Bay-Philadelphia-Green Bay, 16 games

Most Touchdowns, Game

3   Tom Fears, NFC-D: Los Angeles vs. Chi. Bears, 1950
    Gary Collins, NFC: Cleveland vs. Baltimore, 1964
    Fred Biletnikoff, AFC-D: Oakland vs. Kansas City, 1968
    Preston Pearson, NFC: Dallas vs. Los Angeles, 1975
    Dave Casper, AFC-D: Oakland vs. Baltimore, 1977 (OT)
    Alvin Garrett, NFC-FR: Washington vs. Detroit, 1982
    Jerry Rice, NFC-D: San Francisco vs. Minnesota, 1988
    Jerry Rice, SB: San Francisco vs. Denver, 1989
    Andre Reed, AFC-FR: Buffalo vs. Houston, 1992 (OT)
    Sterling Sharpe, NFC-FR: Green Bay vs. Detroit, 1993
    Jerry Rice, SB: San Francisco vs. San Diego, 1994
    Willie Jackson, NFC-FR: New Orleans vs. St. Louis, 2000
    Amani Toomer, NFC-FR: N.Y. Giants vs. San Francisco, 2002

Most Consecutive Games, Touchdown Passes Caught

8   John Stallworth, Pittsburgh, 1978-1983
7   David Givens, New England, 2003-05 (current)
5   James Lofton, Green Bay-Buffalo, 1982-1990
    Randy Moss, Minnesota, 1998-2000
    Antonio Freeman, Green Bay, 1997-2001
    Hines Ward, Pittsburgh, 2002-05

INTERCEPTIONS BY

Most Interceptions, Career

9   Charlie Waters, Dallas, 25 games
    Bill Simpson, Los Angeles-Buffalo, 11 games
    Ronnie Lott, San Francisco-L.A. Raiders, 20 games
8   Lester Hayes, Oakland/L.A. Raiders, 13 games
7   Willie Brown, Oakland, 17 games
    Dennis Thurman, Dallas, 14 games

Most Interceptions, Game

4   Vernon Perry, AFC-D: Houston vs. San Diego, 1979
3   Joe Laws, NFC: Green Bay vs. N.Y. Giants, 1944
    Charlie Waters, NFC-D: Dallas vs. Chicago, 1977

Rod Martin, SB: Oakland vs. Philadelphia, 1980
Dennis Thurman, NFC-D: Dallas vs. Green Bay, 1982
A.J. Duhe, AFC: Miami vs. N.Y. Jets, 1982
Ty Law, AFC: New England vs. Indianapolis, 2003
Ricky Manning Jr., NFC: Carolina vs. Philadelphia, 2003
2 By many players

Most Consecutive Games, Interceptions
4 Aeneas Williams, Arizona-St. Louis, 1998-2001
3 By many players. Last time:
     Rodney Harrison, New England, 2004 (current)

YARDS GAINED
Most Yards Gained, Career
196 Willie Brown, Oakland, 17 games
187 Ronnie Lott, San Francisco-L.A.-Raiders, 20 games
160 George Teague, Green Bay-Dallas-Miami-Dallas, 12 games

Most Yards Gained, Game
108 Darrien Gordon, SB: Denver vs. Atlanta, 1998
101 George Teague, NFC-FR: Green Bay vs. Detroit, 1993
100 Champ Bailey, AFC-D: Denver vs. New England, 2005

Longest Return
101 George Teague, NFC-FR: Green Bay vs. Detroit, 1993 (TD)
100 Champ Bailey, AFC-D: Denver vs. New England, 2005
98 Darrol Ray, AFC-FR: N.Y. Jets vs. Cincinnati, 1982 (TD)

TOUCHDOWNS
Most Touchdowns, Career
3 Willie Brown, Oakland, 17 games
2 Lester Hayes, Oakland/L.A. Raiders, 13 games
   Ronnie Lott, San Francisco-L.A. Raiders, 20 games
   Darrell Green, Washington, 18 games
   Melvin Jenkins, Seattle-Detroit, 5 games
   George Teague, Green Bay-Dallas-Miami-Dallas, 12 games
   Aeneas Williams, Arizona-St. Louis, 6 games
   Dwight Smith, Tampa Bay, 4 games

Most Touchdowns, Game
2 Aeneas Williams, NFC-D: St. Louis vs. Green Bay, 2001
   Dwight Smith, SB: Tampa Bay vs. Oakland, 2002
1 By many players

PUNTING
Most Punts, Career
111 Ray Guy, Oakland/L.A. Raiders, 22 games
92 Craig Hentrich, Green Bay-Tennessee, 20 games
84 Danny White, Dallas, 18 games
   Sean Landeta, N.Y. Giants-Tampa Bay-Green Bay-
     Philadelphia-St. Louis, 18 games

Most Punts, Game
14 Dave Jennings, AFC-D: N.Y. Jets vs. Cleveland, 1986 (OT)
12 David Lee, AFC-D: Baltimore vs. Oakland, 1977 (OT)
11 Ken Strong, NFC: N.Y. Giants vs. Chi. Bears, 1933
   Jim Norton, AFC: Houston vs. Oakland, 1967
   Ode Burrell, AFC-D: Houston vs. Oakland, 1969
   Dale Hatcher, NFC: L.A. Rams vs. Chicago, 1985
   Brad Maynard, SB: N.Y. Giants vs. Baltimore, 2000

Longest Punt
76 Ed Danowski, NFC: N.Y. Giants vs. Detroit, 1935
   Mike Horan, AFC: Denver vs. Buffalo, 1991
72 Charlie Conerly, NFC-D: N.Y. Giants vs. Cleveland, 1950
   Yale Lary, NFC: Detroit vs. Cleveland, 1953
71 Ray Guy, AFC: Oakland vs. San Diego, 1980

AVERAGE YARDAGE
Highest Average, Career (25 punts)
44.5 Rich Camarillo, New England, 6 games (35-1,559)
43.8 Todd Sauerbrun, Carolina-Denver, 8 games (29-1,271)
43.5 Jeff Feagles, Philadelphia-Seattle-N.Y. Giants, 5 games
     (30-1,306)

Highest Average, Game (4 punts)
56.0 Ray Guy, AFC: Oakland vs. San Diego, 1980 (4-224)

52.5 Sammy Baugh, NFC: Washington vs. Chi. Bears, 1942
     (6-315)
52.0 Craig Hentrich, AFC-D: Tennessee vs. Indianapolis, 1999
     (5-260)

PUNT RETURNS
Most Punt Returns, Career
34 David Meggett, N.Y. Giants-New England-N.Y. Jets,
     13 games
   Brian Mitchell, Washington-Philadelphia, 16 games
30 Troy Brown, New England, 17 games
25 Theo Bell, Pittsburgh-Tampa Bay, 10 games

Most Punt Returns, Game
7 Ron Gardin, AFC-D: Baltimore vs. Cincinnati, 1970
   Carl Roaches, AFC-FR: Houston vs. Oakland, 1980
   Gerald McNeil, AFC-D: Cleveland vs. N.Y. Jets, 1986 (OT)
   Phil McConkey, NFC-D: N.Y. Giants vs. San Francisco,
     1986
   David Meggett, AFC-D: New England vs. Pittsburgh, 1996
   Reggie Barlow, AFC-FR: Jacksonville vs. New England,
     1998
6 George McAfee, NFC-D: Chi. Bears vs. Los Angeles, 1950
   Eddie Brown, NFC-D: Washington vs. Minnesota, 1976
   Theo Bell, AFC: Pittsburgh vs. Houston, 1978
   Eddie Brown, NFC: Los Angeles vs. Tampa Bay, 1979
   John Sciarra, NFC: Philadelphia vs. Dallas, 1980
   Kurt Sohn, AFC: N.Y. Jets vs. Miami, 1982
   Mike Nelms, SB: Washington vs. Miami, 1982
   Anthony Carter, NFC-FR: Minnesota vs. New Orleans,
     1987
   Desmond Howard, SB: Green Bay vs. New England, 1996
   Nate Jacquet, AFC-FR: Miami vs. Seattle, 1999
   Derrick Mason, AFC-FR: Tennessee vs. Baltimore, 2003
   Antonio Chatman, AFC-D: Green Bay vs. Philadelphia,
     2003
5 By many players

YARDS GAINED
Most Yards Gained, Career
339 Brian Mitchell, Washington-Philadelphia, 16 games
312 David Meggett, N.Y. Giants-New England-N.Y. Jets,
     13 games
276 Troy Brown, New England, 17 games

Most Yards Gained, Game
152 Allen Rossum, NFC-D: Atlanta vs. St. Louis, 2004
143 Anthony Carter, NFC-FR: Minnesota vs. New Orleans,
     1987
141 Bob Hayes, NFC-D: Dallas vs. Cleveland, 1967

Longest Return
88 Jermaine Lewis, AFC-D: Baltimore vs. Pittsburgh, 2001
     (TD)
84 Anthony Carter, NFC-FR: Minnesota vs. New Orleans, 1987
     (TD)
81 Hugh Gallarneau, NFC-D: Chi. Bears vs. Green Bay, 1941
     (TD)

AVERAGE YARDAGE
Highest Average, Career (10 returns)
23.9 Allen Rossum, Green Bay-Atlanta, 6 games (10-239)
15.3 Robert Brooks, Green Bay, 11 games (14-214)
15.2 Anthony Carter, Minnesota-Detroit, 9 games (17-259)

Highest Average Gain, Game (3 returns)
50.7 Allen Rossum, NFC-D: Atlanta vs. St. Louis, 2004 (3-152)
47.0 Bob Hayes, NFC-D: Dallas vs. Cleveland, 1967 (3-141)
33.0 Jermaine Lewis, AFC-D: Baltimore vs. Pittsburgh, 2001
     (3-99)

TOUCHDOWNS
Most Touchdowns
1 Hugh Gallarneau, NFC-D: Chicago Bears vs. Green Bay, 1941

Bosh Pritchard, NFC-D: Philadelphia vs. Pittsburgh, 1947

Charley Trippi, NFC: Chicago Cardinals vs. Philadelphia, 1947

Verda (Vitamin T) Smith, NFC-D: Los Angeles vs. Detroit, 1952

George (Butch) Byrd, AFC: Buffalo vs. San Diego, 1965

Golden Richards, NFC: Dallas vs. Minnesota, 1973

Wes Chandler, AFC-D: San Diego vs. Miami, 1981 (OT)

Shaun Gayle, NFC-D: Chicago vs. N.Y. Giants, 1985

Anthony Carter, NFC-FR: Minnesota vs. New Orleans, 1987

Darrell Green, NFC-D: Washington vs. Chicago, 1987

Antonio Freeman, NFC-FR: Green Bay vs. Atlanta, 1995

Desmond Howard, NFC-D: Green Bay vs. San Francisco, 1996

Jermaine Lewis, AFC-D: Baltimore vs. Pittsburgh, 2001

Troy Brown, AFC: New England vs. Pittsburgh, 2001

Antwaan Randle El, AFC-FR: Pittsburgh vs. Cleveland, 2002

Santana Moss, AFC-D: N.Y. Jets vs. Pittsburgh, 2004 (OT)

Allen Rossum, NFC-D: Atlanta vs. St. Louis, 2004

Steve Smith, NFC: Carolina vs. Seattle, 2005

KICKOFF RETURNS
Most Kickoff Returns, Career
36 Brian Mitchell, Washington-Philadelphia, 16 games
31 Kevin Williams, Dallas-Buffalo, 12 games
29 Fulton Walker, Miami-L.A. Raiders, 10 games
Most Kickoff Returns, Game
8 Marc Logan, AFC-D: Miami vs. Buffalo, 1990
Andre Coleman, SB: San Diego vs. San Francisco, 1994
Marcus Knight, SB: Oakland vs. Tampa Bay, 2002
7 Don Bingham, NFC: Chi. Bears vs. N.Y. Giants, 1956
Reggie Brown, NFC-FR: Atlanta vs. Minnesota, 1982
David Verser, AFC-FR: Cincinnati vs. N.Y. Jets, 1982
Del Rodgers, NFC-D: Green Bay vs. Dallas, 1982
Henry Ellard, NFC-D: L.A. Rams vs. Washington, 1983
Stephen Starring, SB: New England vs. Chicago, 1985
Darick Holmes, AFC-D: Buffalo vs. Pittsburgh, 1995
Antonio Freeman, NFC: Green Bay vs. Dallas, 1995
Roell Preston, NFC-FR: Green Bay vs. San Francisco, 1998
Robert Tate, NFC-D: Minnesota vs. St. Louis, 1999
Fred McAfee, NFC-D: New Orleans vs. Minnesota, 2000
Michael Bates, NFC-FR: Dallas vs. Carolina, 2003
Dante Hall, AFC-D: Kansas City vs. Indianapolis, 2003
6 By many players

YARDS GAINED
Most Yards Gained, Career
875 Brian Mitchell, Washington-Philadelphia, 16 games
677 Fulton Walker, Miami-L.A. Raiders, 10 games
632 Kevin Williams, Dallas-Buffalo, 12 games
Most Yards Gained, Game
244 Andre Coleman, SB: San Diego vs. San Francisco, 1994
210 Tim Dwight, SB: Atlanta vs. Denver, 1998
208 Dante Hall, AFC-D: Kansas City vs. Indianapolis, 2003
Longest Return
100 Brian Mitchell, NFC-D: Washington vs. Tampa Bay, 1999 (TD)
99 Desmond Howard, SB: Green Bay vs. New England, 1996 (TD)
98 Fulton Walker, SB: Miami vs. Washington, 1982 (TD)
Andre Coleman, SB: San Diego vs. San Francisco, 1994 (TD)

AVERAGE YARDAGE
Highest Average, Career (10 returns)
30.1 Carl Garrett, Oakland, 5 games (16-481)
30.0 Reggie Barlow, Jacksonville, 8 games (12-360)
29.2 Chad Morton, New Orleans-N.Y. Jets-N.Y. Giants, 6 games (14-409)
Highest Average, Game (3 returns)
56.7 Les (Speedy) Duncan, NFC-D: Washington vs. San Francisco, 1971 (3-170)
51.3 Ed Podolak, AFC-D: Kansas City vs. Miami, 1971 (OT) (3-154)
49.0 Les (Speedy) Duncan, AFC: San Diego vs. Buffalo, 1964 (3-147)

TOUCHDOWNS
Most Touchdowns, Career
2 Ron Dixon, N.Y. Giants, 4 games
1 By many players
Most Touchdowns, Game
1 Vic Washington, NFC-D: San Francisco vs. Dallas, 1972
Nat Moore, AFC-D: Miami vs. Oakland, 1974
Marshall Johnson, AFC-D: Baltimore vs. Oakland, 1977 (OT)
Fulton Walker, SB: Miami vs. Washington, 1982
Stanford Jennings, SB: Cincinnati vs. San Francisco, 1988
Eric Metcalf, AFC-D: Cleveland vs. Buffalo, 1989
Andre Coleman, SB: San Diego vs. San Francisco, 1994
Desmond Howard, SB: Green Bay vs. New England, 1996
Chuck Levy, NFC: San Franisco vs. Green Bay, 1997
Tim Dwight, SB: Atlanta vs. Denver, 1998
Kevin Dyson, AFC-FR: Tennessee vs. Buffalo, 1999
Charlie Rogers, AFC-FR: Seattle vs. Miami, 1999
Brian Mitchell, NFC-D: Washington vs. Tampa Bay, 1999
Tony Horne, NFC-D: St. Louis vs. Minnesota, 1999
Derrick Mason, AFC: Tennessee vs. Jacksonville, 1999
Ron Dixon, NFC-D: N.Y. Giants vs. Philadelphia, 2000;
  SB: N.Y. Giants vs. Baltimore, 2000
Jermaine Lewis, SB: Baltimore vs. N.Y. Giants, 2000
Dante Hall, AFC-D: Kansas City vs. Indianapolis, 2003

FUMBLES
Most Fumbles, Career
16 Warren Moon, Houston-Minnesota, 10 games
14 John Elway, Denver, 22 games
13 Tony Dorsett, Dallas, 17 games
Most Fumbles, Game
5 Warren Moon, AFC-D: Houston vs. Kansas City, 1993
4 Brian Sipe, AFC-D: Cleveland vs. Oakland, 1980
Randall Cunningham, NFC-FR: Minnesota vs. N.Y. Giants, 1997
3 By many players

RECOVERIES
Most Own Fumbles Recovered, Career
8 Warren Moon, Houston-Minnesota, 10 games
7 John Elway, Denver, 22 games
6 Jim Kelly, Buffalo, 17 games
Most Opponents' Fumbles Recovered, Career
4 Cliff Harris, Dallas, 21 games
Harvey Martin, Dallas, 22 games
Ted Hendricks, Baltimore-Oakland/L.A. Raiders, 21 games
Alvin Walton, Washington, 9 games
Monte Coleman, Washington, 21 games
Dave Thomas, Dallas-Jacksonville-N.Y. Giants, 13 games
3 Paul Krause, Minnesota, 19 games
Jack Lambert, Pittsburgh, 18 games
Fred Dryer, Los Angeles, 14 games
Charlie Waters, Dallas, 25 games
Jack Ham, Pittsburgh, 16 games
Mike Hegman, Dallas, 16 games

Tom Jackson, Denver, 10 games
Rich Milot, Washington, 13 games
Mike Singletary, Chicago, 12 games
Darryl Grant, Washington, 16 games
Wes Hopkins, Philadelphia, 3 games
Wilber Marshall, Chicago-Washington, 15 games
Tyrone Braxton, Denver-Miami-Denver, 19 games
Neil Smith, Kansas City-Denver, 16 games
Tony Brackens, Jacksonville, 7 games
Phil Hansen, Buffalo, 14 games
Carnell Lake, Pittsburgh-Jacksonville-Baltimore, 17 games
Jason Gildon, Pittsburgh, 13 games
Tedy Bruschi, New England, 16 games

2   By many players

Most Fumbles Recovered, Game, Own and Opponents'

3   Jack Lambert, AFC: Pittsburgh vs. Oakland, 1975 (3 opp)
    Ron Jaworski, NFC-FR: Philadelphia vs. N.Y. Giants, 1981 (3 own)

2   By many players

YARDS GAINED
Longest Return

93   Andy Russell, AFC-D: Pittsburgh vs. Baltimore, 1975 (opp, TD)
79   Neil Smith, AFC-D: Denver vs. Miami, 1998 (opp, TD)
64   Leon Lett, SB: Dallas vs. Buffalo, 1992 (opp)

TOUCHDOWNS
Most Touchdowns

1   By many players

COMBINED NET YARDS GAINED
Rushing, receiving, interception returns, punt returns, kickoff returns, and fumble returns.

ATTEMPTS
Most Attempts, Career

454   Franco Harris, Pittsburgh, 19 games
417   Thurman Thomas, Buffalo, 21 games
397   Emmitt Smith, Dallas, 17 games

Most Attempts, Game

43   Lamar Smith, AFC-FR: Miami vs. Indianapolis, 2000 (OT)
42   Curtis Martin, AFC-D: N.Y. Jets vs. Jacksonville, 1998
40   Lawrence McCutcheon, NFC-D: Los Angeles vs. St. Louis, 1975

YARDS GAINED
Most Yards Gained, Career

2,289   Jerry Rice, San Francisco-Oakland-Seattle, 29 games
2,124   Thurman Thomas, Buffalo, 21 games
2,060   Franco Harris, Pittsburgh, 19 games

Most Yards Gained, Game

350   Ed Podolak, AFC-D: Kansas City vs. Miami, 1971 (OT)
329   Keith Lincoln, AFC: San Diego vs. Boston, 1963
285   Bob Hayes, NFC-D: Dallas vs. Cleveland, 1967

SACKS
Sacks have been compiled since 1982.

Most Sacks, Career

16.0   Willie McGinest, New England, 18 games
14.5   Bruce Smith, Buffalo, 20 games
12.0   Reggie White, Philadelphia-Green Bay, 19 games

Most Sacks, Game

4.5   Willie McGinest, AFC-FR: New England vs. Jacksonville, 2005
3.5   Rich Milot, NFC-D: Washington vs. Chicago, 1984
    Richard Dent, NFC-D: Chicago vs. N.Y. Giants, 1985
3.0   Richard Dent, NFC-D: Chicago vs. Washington, 1984
    Garin Veris, AFC-FR: New England vs. N.Y. Jets, 1985
    Gary Jeter, NFC-D: L.A. Rams vs. Dallas, 1985
    Carl Hairston, AFC-D: Cleveland vs. N.Y. Jets, 1986 (OT)

Charles Mann, NFC-D: Washington vs. Chicago, 1987
Kevin Greene, NFC-FR: L.A. Rams vs. Minnesota, 1988
Greg Townsend, AFC-D: L.A. Raiders vs. Cincinnati, 1990
Wilber Marshall, NFC: Washington vs. Detroit, 1991
Fred Stokes, NFC-FR: Washington vs. Minnesota, 1992
Pierce Holt, NFC-D: San Francisco vs. Washington, 1992
Tony Casillas, NFC: Dallas vs. San Francisco, 1992
Gerald Williams, AFC-FR: Pittsburgh vs. Kansas City, 1993
Chad Brown, AFC-FR: Pittsburgh vs. Indianapolis, 1996
Reggie White, SB: Green Bay vs. New England, 1996
Warren Sapp, NFC-D: Tampa Bay vs. Green Bay, 1997
Trace Armstrong, AFC-FR: Miami vs. Seattle, 1999
Michael McCrary, AFC-FR: Baltimore vs. Denver, 2000
Willie McGinest, AFC-D: New England vs. Tennessee, 2003

TEAM RECORDS

GAMES, VICTORIES, DEFEATS
Most Seasons Participating in Postseason Games

27   Dallas, 1966-1973, 1975-1983, 1985, 1991-96, 1998-99, 2003
    Cleveland/L.A./St. Louis Rams, 1945, 1949-1952, 1955, 1967, 1969, 1973-1980, 1983-86, 1988-89, 1999-2001, 2003-04
    N.Y. Giants, 1933-35, 1938-39, 1941, 1943-44, 1946, 1950, 1956, 1958-59, 1961-63, 1981, 1984-86, 1989-1990, 1993, 1997, 2000, 2002, 2005
24   Cleveland, 1950-55, 1957-58, 1964-65, 1967-69, 1971-72, 1980, 1982, 1985-89, 1994, 2002
    Minnesota, 1968-1971, 1973-78, 1980, 1982, 1987-89, 1992-94, 1996-2000, 2004
23   Green Bay, 1936, 1938-39, 1941, 1944, 1960-62, 1965-67, 1972, 1982, 1993-98, 2001-04
    Chi. Bears, 1933-34, 1937, 1940-43, 1946, 1950, 1956, 1963, 1977, 1979, 1984-88, 1990-91, 1994, 2001, 2005
    Pittsburgh, 1947, 1972-79, 1982-84, 1989, 1992-97, 2001-02, 2004-05

Most Consecutive Seasons Participating in Postseason Games

9   Dallas, 1975-1983
8   Dallas, 1966-1973
    Pittsburgh, 1972-79
    Los Angeles, 1973-1980
    San Francisco, 1983-1990
7   Houston, 1987-1993
    San Francisco, 1992-98

Most Games

54   Dallas, 1966-1973, 1975-1983, 1985, 1991-96, 1998-99, 2003
46   Pittsburgh, 1947, 1972-79, 1982-84, 1989, 1992-97, 2001-02, 2004-05
43   Oakland/L.A. Raiders, 1967-1970, 1972-77, 1980, 1982-85, 1990-91, 1993, 2000-02
    Cleveland/L.A./St. Louis Rams, 1945, 1949-1952, 1955, 1967, 1969, 1973-1980, 1983-86, 1988-89, 1999-2001, 2003-04

Most Games Won

32   Dallas, 1967, 1970-73, 1975, 1977-78, 1980-82, 1991-96
28   Pittsburgh, 1972, 1974-76, 1978-79, 1984, 1989, 1994-97, 2001-02, 2004-05
25   Oakland/L.A. Raiders, 1967-1970, 1973-77, 1980, 1982-83, 1990, 1993, 2000-02
    San Francisco, 1970-71, 1981, 1983-84, 1988-1990, 1992-94, 1996-98, 2002

Most Consecutive Games Won

10   New England, 2001, 2003-05
9   Green Bay, 1961-62, 1965-67
7   Pittsburgh, 1974-76

San Francisco, 1988-1990
Dallas, 1992-94
Denver, 1997-98

Most Games Lost
24 Minnesota, 1968-1971, 1973-78, 1980, 1982, 1987-89,
1992-94, 1996-2000, 2004
L.A./St. Louis Rams, 1949-1950, 1952, 1955, 1967,
1969, 1973-1980, 1983-86, 1988-89, 2000-01,
2003-04
22 Dallas, 1966-1970, 1972-73, 1975-76, 1978-1983, 1985,
1991, 1994, 1996, 1998-99, 2003
N.Y. Giants, 1993, 1935, 1939, 1941, 1943-44, 1946,
1950, 1958-59, 1961-63, 1981, 1984-85, 1989,
1993, 1997, 2000, 2002, 2005
20 Cleveland, 1951-53, 1957-58, 1965, 1967-69, 1971-72,
1980, 1982, 1985-89, 1994, 2002

Most Consecutive Games Lost
6 N.Y. Giants, 1939, 1941, 1943-44, 1946, 1950
Cleveland, 1969, 1971-72, 1980, 1982, 1985
Minnesota, 1988-89, 1992-94, 1996
Detroit, 1991, 1993-95, 1997, 1999 (current)
Seattle, 1984, 1987-88, 1999, 2003-04
5 N.Y. Giants, 1958-59, 1961-63
Los Angeles, 1952, 1955, 1967, 1969, 1973
Denver, 1977-79, 1983-84
Baltimore/Indianapolis, 1971, 1975-77, 1987
Philadelphia, 1980-81, 1988-1990
Indianapolis, 1995-96, 1999-2000, 2002
Kansas City, 1993-95, 1997, 2003 (current)
4 Washington, 1972-74, 1976
Miami, 1974, 1978-79, 1981
Chi. Cardinals/St. Louis, 1948, 1974-75, 1982
Boston/New England, 1963, 1976, 1978, 1982
New Orleans, 1987, 1990-92
Buffalo, 1995-96, 1998-99 (current)
Dallas, 1996, 1998-99, 2003 (current)

SCORING
Most Points, Game
73 NFC: Chi. Bears vs. Washington, 1940
62 AFC-D: Jacksonville vs. Miami, 1999
59 NFC: Detroit vs. Cleveland, 1957

Most Points, Both Teams, Game
95 NFC-FR: Philadelphia (58) vs. Detroit (37), 1995
86 NFC-D: St. Louis (49) vs. Minnesota (37), 1999
79 AFC-D: San Diego (41) vs. Miami (38), 1981 (OT)
AFC-FR: Buffalo (41) vs. Houston (38), 1992 (OT)

Fewest Points, Both Teams, Game
5 NFC-D: Detroit (0) vs. Dallas (5), 1970
7 NFC: Chi. Cardinals (0) vs. Philadelphia (7), 1948
9 NFC: Tampa Bay (0) vs. Los Angeles (9), 1979

Largest Margin of Victory, Game
73 NFC: Chi. Bears vs. Washington, 1940 (73-0)
55 AFC-D: Jacksonville vs. Miami, 1999 (62-7)
49 AFC-D: Oakland vs. Houston, 1969 (56-7)

Most Points, Shutout Victory, Game
73 NFC: Chi. Bears vs. Washington, 1940
41 NFC: N.Y. Giants vs. Minnesota, 2000
AFC-FR: N.Y. Jets vs. Indianapolis, 2002
38 NFC-D: Dallas vs. Tampa Bay, 1981

Most Points Overcome to Win Game
32 AFC-FR: Buffalo vs. Houston, 1992 (trailed 3-35,
won 41-38) (OT)
24 NFC-FR: San Francisco vs. N.Y. Giants, 2002 (trailed
14-38, won 39-38)
20 NFC-D: Detroit vs. San Francisco, 1957 (trailed 7-27,
won 31-27)

Most Points, Each Half
1st: 41 AFC: Buffalo vs. L.A. Raiders, 1990

AFC-D: Jacksonville vs. Miami, 1999
38 NFC-D: Washington vs. L.A. Rams, 1983
NFC-FR: Philadelphia vs. Detroit, 1995
35 NFC: Cleveland vs. Detroit, 1954
AFC-D: Oakland vs. Houston, 1969
SB: Washington vs. Denver, 1987
AFC-FR: Indianapolis vs. Denver, 2004
2nd: 45 NFC: Chi. Bears vs. Washington, 1940
35 AFC-FR: Buffalo vs. Houston, 1992
NFC-D: St. Louis vs. Minnesota, 1999
30 SB: N.Y. Giants vs. Denver, 1986
AFC: Cleveland vs. Denver, 1987
NFC-FR: Detroit vs. Philadelphia, 1995

Most Points, Each Quarter
1st: 28 AFC-D: Oakland vs. Houston, 1969
24 AFC-D: San Diego vs. Miami, 1981
AFC-D: Jacksonville vs. Miami, 1999
21 NFC: Chi. Bears vs. Washington, 1940
AFC: San Diego vs. Boston, 1963
AFC-D: Oakland vs. Kansas City, 1968
AFC: Oakland vs. San Diego, 1980
AFC: Buffalo vs. L.A. Raiders, 1990
NFC: San Francisco vs. Dallas, 1994
2nd: 35 SB: Washington vs. Denver, 1987
31 NFC-FR: Philadelphia vs. Detroit, 1995
26 AFC-D: Pittsburgh vs. Buffalo, 1974
3rd: 28 AFC-FR: Buffalo vs. Houston, 1992
26 NFC: Chi. Bears vs. Washington, 1940
21 NFC-D: Dallas vs. Cleveland, 1967
NFC-D: Dallas vs. Tampa Bay, 1981
AFC-D: L.A. Raiders vs. Pittsburgh, 1983
SB: Chicago vs. New England, 1985
NFC-FR: N.Y. Giants vs. San Francisco, 1986
AFC: Cleveland vs. Denver, 1987
AFC: Cleveland vs. Denver, 1989
NFC-D: St. Louis vs. Minnesota, 1999
4th: 27 NFC: N.Y. Giants vs. Chi. Bears, 1934
26 NFC-FR: Philadelphia vs. New Orleans, 1992
24 NFC: Baltimore vs. N.Y. Giants, 1959
OT: 6 NFC: Baltimore vs. N.Y. Giants, 1958
AFC-D: Oakland vs. Baltimore, 1977
NFC-D: L.A. Rams vs. N.Y. Giants, 1989
AFC-FR: Miami vs. Indianapolis, 2000
NFC-FR: Green Bay vs. Seattle, 2003
NFC-D: Carolina vs. St. Louis, 2003

TOUCHDOWNS
Most Touchdowns, Game
11 NFC: Chi. Bears vs. Washington, 1940
8 NFC: Cleveland vs. Detroit, 1954
NFC: Detroit vs. Cleveland, 1957
AFC-D: Oakland vs. Houston, 1969
SB: San Francisco vs. Denver, 1989
AFC-D: Jacksonville vs. Miami, 1999
7 AFC: San Diego vs. Boston, 1963
NFC-D: Dallas vs. Cleveland, 1967
NFC-FR: N.Y. Giants vs. San Francisco, 1986
AFC: Buffalo vs. L.A. Raiders, 1990
SB: Dallas vs. Buffalo, 1992
SB: San Francisco vs. San Diego, 1994
NFC-FR: Philadelphia vs. Detroit, 1995
NFC-D: St. Louis vs. Minnesota, 1999
AFC-FR: Indianapolis vs. Denver, 2004

Most Touchdowns, Both Teams, Game
12 NFC-FR: Philadelphia (7) vs. Detroit (5), 1995
NFC-D: St. Louis (7) vs. Minnesota (5), 1999
11 NFC: Chi. Bears (11) vs. Washington (0), 1940
10 NFC: Detroit (8) vs. Cleveland (2), 1957
AFC-D: Miami (5) vs. San Diego (5), 1981 (OT)
AFC: Miami (6) vs. Pittsburgh (4), 1984

AFC-FR: Buffalo (5) vs. Houston (5), 1992 (OT)
SB: San Francisco (7) vs. San Diego (3), 1994
NFC-FR: San Francisco (5) vs. N.Y. Giants (5), 2002
AFC-FR: Indianapolis (7) vs. Denver (3), 2004

Fewest Touchdowns, Both Teams, Game
0 NFC-D: N.Y. Giants vs. Cleveland, 1950
   NFC-D: Dallas vs. Detroit, 1970
   NFC: Los Angeles vs. Tampa Bay, 1979
1 NFC: Chi. Cardinals (0) vs. Philadelphia (1), 1948
   NFC-D: Cleveland (0) vs. N.Y. Giants (1), 1958
   AFC: San Diego (0) vs. Houston (1), 1961
   AFC-D: N.Y .Jets (0) vs. Kansas City (1), 1969
   NFC-D: Green Bay (0) vs. Washington (1), 1972
   NFC-FR: New Orleans (0) vs. Chicago (1), 1990
   NFC: N.Y. Giants (0) vs. San Francisco (1), 1990
   AFC-FR: L.A. Raiders (0) vs. Kansas City (1), 1991
   AFC-D: New England (0) vs. Pittsburgh (1), 1997
   NFC: Tampa Bay (0) vs. St. Louis (1), 1999
   AFC: Oakland (0) vs. Baltimore (1), 2000
2 In many games

POINTS AFTER TOUCHDOWN
Most (One-Point) Points After Touchdown, Game
8 NFC: Cleveland vs. Detroit, 1954
   NFC: Detroit vs. Cleveland, 1957
   AFC-D: Oakland vs. Houston, 1969
   AFC-D: Jacksonville vs. Miami, 1999
7 NFC: Chi. Bears vs. Washington, 1940
   NFC-D: Dallas vs. Cleveland, 1967
   NFC-D: N.Y. Giants vs. San Francisco, 1986
   SB: San Francisco vs. Denver, 1989
   SB: Dallas vs. Buffalo, 1992
   SB: San Francisco vs. San Diego, 1994
   NFC-FR: Philadelphia vs. Detroit, 1995
   NFC-D: St. Louis vs. Minnesota, 1999
   AFC-FR: Indianapolis vs. Denver, 2004
6 AFC: San Diego vs. Boston, 1963
   NFC-D: Washington vs. L.A. Rams, 1983
   AFC: Miami vs. Pittsburgh, 1984
   SB: Washington vs. Denver, 1987
   AFC: Buffalo vs. L.A. Raiders, 1990
   AFC-FR: L.A. Raiders vs. Denver, 1993
   AFC-FR: Denver vs. Jacksonville, 1997
   NFC-D: St. Louis vs. Green Bay, 2001
   SB: Tampa Bay vs. Oakland, 2002
   NFC-D: Atlanta vs. St. Louis, 2004

Most (One-Point) Points After Touchdown, Both Teams, Game
10 NFC: Detroit (8) vs. Cleveland (2), 1957
    AFC-D: Miami (5) vs. San Diego (5), 1981 (OT)
    AFC: Miami (6) vs. Pittsburgh (4), 1984
    AFC-FR: Buffalo (5) vs. Houston (5), 1992 (OT)
    NFC-FR: Philadelphia (7) vs. Detroit (3), 1995
    AFC-FR: Indianapolis (7) vs. Denver (3), 2004
9 In many games

Fewest (One-Point) Points After Touchdown, Both Teams, Game
0 NFC-D: N.Y. Giants vs. Cleveland, 1950
   NFC-D: Dallas vs. Detroit, 1970
   NFC: Los Angeles vs. Tampa Bay, 1979
   NFC: St. Louis vs. Tampa Bay, 1999

Most Two-Point Conversions, Game
2 SB: San Diego vs. San Francisco, 1994
   NFC-FR: Detroit vs. Philadelphia, 1995
   NFC-FR: San Francisco vs.. N.Y. Giants, 2002
1 By many teams

FIELD GOALS
Most Field Goals, Game
5 NFC-D: Minnesota vs. San Francisco, 1987
   NFC: N.Y. Giants vs. San Francisco, 1990
   AFC: Buffalo vs. Miami, 1992

NFC-FR: N.Y. Giants vs. Minnesota, 1997
NFC-FR: Carolina vs. Dallas, 2003
NFC-D: St. Louis vs. Carolina, 2003 (2 OT)
AFC: New England vs. Indianapolis, 2003
4 AFC-D: Boston vs. Buffalo, 1963
   AFC: Oakland vs. Houston, 1967
   SB: Green Bay vs. Oakland, 1967
   NFC: Washington vs. Dallas, 1972
   AFC-D: Oakland vs. Pittsburgh, 1973
   SB: San Francisco vs. Cincinnati, 1981
   AFC-FR: New England vs. N.Y. Jets, 1985
   NFC-FR: Washington vs. L.A. Rams, 1986
   NFC-D: Philadelphia vs. Chicago, 1988
   AFC-FR: Pittsburgh vs. Houston, 1989 (OT)
   AFC-D: Pittsburgh vs. Buffalo, 1995
   NFC-FR: Dallas vs. Minnesota, 1996
   NFC-D: Carolina vs. Dallas, 1996
   AFC-FR: Jacksonville vs. New England, 1998
   AFC-D: Tennessee vs. Indianapolis, 1999
   NFC-D: Philadelphia vs. Chicago, 2001
3 By many teams

Most Field Goals, Both Teams, Game
8 NFC-FR: N.Y. Giants (5) vs. Minnesota (3), 1997
   NFC-D: St. Louis (5) vs. Carolina (3), 2003 (2 OT)
7 AFC-FR: Pittsburgh (4) vs. Houston (3), 1989 (OT)
   NFC: N.Y. Giants (5) vs. San Francisco (2), 1990
   NFC-D: Carolina (4) vs. Dallas (3), 1996
   AFC-D: Tennessee (4) vs. Indianapolis (3), 1999
6 NFC-D: Minnesota (5) vs. San Francisco (1), 1987
   NFC-D: Philadelphia (4) vs. Chicago (2), 1988
   AFC: Buffalo (5) vs. Miami (1), 1992
   NFC-FR: Carolina (5) vs. Dallas (1), 2003

Most Field Goals Attempted, Game
6 AFC: Oakland vs. Houston, 1967
   NFC-D: Los Angeles vs. Dallas, 1973
   AFC-D: Cleveland vs. N.Y. Jets, 1986 (OT)
   NFC: N.Y. Giants vs. San Francisco, 1990
   AFC: Buffalo vs. Miami, 1992
   NFC-D: St. Louis vs. Carolina, 2003 (2 OT)
5 By many teams

Most Field Goals Attempted, Both Teams, Game
11 NFC-D: St. Louis (6) vs. Carolina (5), 2003 (2 OT)
9   NFC-D: Philadelphia (5) vs. Chicago (4), 1988
    NFC-FR: N.Y. Giants (5) vs. Minnesota (4), 1997
8   NFC-D: Los Angeles (6) vs. Dallas (2), 1973
    NFC-D: Detroit (5) vs. San Francisco (3), 1983
    AFC-D: Cleveland (6) vs. N.Y. Jets (2), 1986 (OT)
    NFC-D: Minnesota (5) vs. San Francisco (3), 1987
    AFC-FR: Houston (4) vs. Pittsburgh (4), 1989 (OT)
    NFC-FR: Chicago (4) vs. New Orleans (4), 1990
    NFC: N.Y. Giants (6) vs. San Francisco (2), 1990

SAFETIES
Most Safeties, Game
1 By many teams
Most Safeties, Both Teams, Game
1 In many games

FIRST DOWNS
Most First Downs, Game
34 AFC-D: San Diego vs. Miami, 1981 (OT)
33 AFC-D: Cleveland vs. N.Y. Jets, 1986 (OT)
31 SB: San Francisco vs. Miami, 1984
    NFC-D: San Francisco vs. Minnesota, 1997
    NFC: N.Y. Giants vs. Minnesota, 2000
Fewest First Downs, Game
6   NFC: N.Y. Giants vs. Green Bay, 1961
    AFC-D: Baltimore vs. Tennessee, 2000
7   NFC: Green Bay vs. Boston, 1936
    NFC-D: Pittsburgh vs. Philadelphia, 1947

NFC: Chi. Cardinals vs. Philadelphia, 1948
NFC: Los Angeles vs. Philadelphia, 1949
NFC-D: Cleveland vs. N.Y. Giants, 1958
AFC-D: Cincinnati vs. Baltimore, 1970
NFC-D: Detroit vs. Dallas, 1970
NFC: Tampa Bay vs. Los Angeles, 1979
AFC-D: Baltimore vs. Pittsburgh, 2001
8 By many teams

Most First Downs, Both Teams, Game
59 AFC-D: San Diego (34) vs. Miami (25), 1981 (OT)
55 AFC-FR: San Diego (29) vs. Pittsburgh (26), 1982
54 AFC-D: Buffalo (28) vs. Miami (26), 1995

Fewest First Downs, Both Teams, Game
15 NFC: Green Bay (7) vs. Boston (8), 1936
19 NFC: N.Y. Giants (9) vs. Green Bay (10), 1939
     NFC: Washington (9) vs. Chi. Bears (10), 1942
20 NFC-D: Cleveland (9) vs. N.Y. Giants (11), 1950

RUSHING
Most First Downs, Rushing, Game
19 NFC-FR: Dallas vs. Los Angeles, 1980
18 AFC-D: Miami vs. Cincinnati, 1973
     AFC: Miami vs. Oakland, 1973
     AFC-D: Pittsburgh vs. Buffalo, 1974
     AFC-FR: Buffalo vs. Miami, 1995
     AFC-FR: Denver vs. Jacksonville, 1997
17 AFC-D: Cincinnati vs. Seattle, 1988
     AFC: Buffalo vs. Kansas City, 1993

Fewest First Downs, Rushing, Game
0 NFC: Los Angeles vs. Philadelphia, 1949
   AFC-D: Buffalo vs. Boston, 1963
   AFC: Oakland vs. Pittsburgh, 1974
   NFC-FR: New Orleans vs. Minnesota, 1987
   NFC: L.A. Rams vs. San Francisco, 1989
   NFC-D: Chicago vs. N.Y. Giants, 1990
   AFC-FR: Indianapolis vs. Pittsburgh, 1996
   AFC-FR: Seattle vs. Miami, 1999
   AFC-D: Miami vs. Jacksonville, 1999
   AFC-D: Miami vs. Oakland, 2000
   AFC-D: Baltimore vs. Pittsburgh, 2001
   AFC-D: Indianapolis vs. New England, 2004
1 By many teams

Most First Downs, Rushing, Both Teams, Game
26 AFC: Buffalo (14) vs. L.A. Raiders (12), 1990
25 NFC-FR: Dallas (19) vs. Los Angeles (6), 1980
23 NFC: Cleveland (15) vs. Detroit (8), 1952
     AFC-D: Miami (18) vs. Cincinnati (5), 1973
     AFC-D: Pittsburgh (18) vs. Buffalo (5), 1974
     AFC-FR: Buffalo (18) vs. Miami (5), 1995

Fewest First Downs, Rushing, Both Teams, Game
2 NFC-FR: New Orleans (1) vs. St. Louis (1), 2000
5 AFC-D: Buffalo (0) vs. Boston (5), 1963
   NFC-D: Washington (1) vs. Tampa Bay (4), 1999
   AFC-FR: Cleveland (2) vs. Pittsburgh (3), 2002
6 NFC: Green Bay (2) vs. Boston (4), 1936
   NFC-D: Baltimore (2) vs. Minnesota (4), 1968
   AFC-D: Houston (1) vs. Oakland (5), 1969
   AFC-FR: N.Y. Jets (1) vs. Houston (5), 1991
   AFC-FR: Denver (1) vs. Baltimore (5), 2000

PASSING
Most First Downs, Passing, Game
24 AFC-FR: Pittsburgh vs. Cleveland, 2002
21 AFC-D: Miami vs. San Diego, 1981 (OT)
     AFC-D: San Diego vs. Miami, 1981 (OT)
     AFC-D: Cleveland vs. N.Y. Jets, 1986 (OT)
     NFC-D: Philadelphia vs. Chicago, 1988
20 NFC-FR: Dallas vs. L.A. Rams, 1983
     AFC-D: Buffalo vs. Cleveland, 1989
     AFC-FR: Miami vs. Buffalo, 1995

NFC-FR: Detroit vs. Philadelphia, 1995
AFC-FR: San Diego vs. Indianapolis, 1995
NFC-D: Minnesota vs. St. Louis, 1999

Fewest First Downs, Passing, Game
0 NFC: Philadelphia vs. Chi. Cardinals, 1948
1 NFC-D: N.Y. Giants vs. Washington, 1943
   NFC: Cleveland vs. Detroit, 1953
   SB: Denver vs. Dallas, 1977
2 By many teams

Most First Downs, Passing, Both Teams, Game
42 AFC-D: Miami (21) vs. San Diego (21), 1981 (OT)
     AFC-FR: Pittsburgh (24) vs. Cleveland (18), 2002
38 AFC-FR: Pittsburgh (19) vs. San Diego (19), 1982
     NFC-D: Minnesota (20) vs. St. Louis (18), 1999
36 NFC: Minnesota (19) vs. Atlanta (17), 1998 (OT)

Fewest First Downs, Passing, Both Teams, Game
2 NFC: Philadelphia (0) vs. Chi. Cardinals (2), 1948
4 NFC-D: Cleveland (2) vs. N.Y. Giants (2), 1950
5 NFC: Detroit (2) vs. N.Y. Giants (3), 1935
   NFC: Green Bay (2) vs. N.Y. Giants (3), 1939

PENALTY
Most First Downs, Penalty, Game
7 AFC-D: New England vs. Oakland, 1976
   AFC: Tennessee vs. Oakland, 2002
6 AFC-D: Cleveland vs. N.Y. Jets, 1986 (OT)
   NFC-D: Chicago vs. Carolina, 2005
5 AFC-FR: Cleveland vs. L. A. Raiders, 1982
   NFC-D: San Francisco vs. Minnesota, 1997
   AFC-FR: Miami vs. Buffalo, 1998
   NFC-D: Arizona vs. Minnesota, 1998
   AFC: Pittsburgh vs. New England, 2001
   AFC-D: Pittsburgh vs. Tennessee, 2002 (OT)

Most First Downs, Penalty, Both Teams, Game
10 AFC: Tennessee (7) vs. Oakland (3), 2002
9 AFC-D: New England (7) vs. Oakland (2), 1976
8 NFC-FR: Atlanta (4) vs. Minnesota (4), 1982
   AFC-FR: Miami (5) vs. Buffalo (3), 1998

NET YARDS GAINED RUSHING AND PASSING
Most Yards Gained, Game
610 AFC: San Diego vs. Boston, 1963
602 SB: Washington vs. Denver, 1987
569 AFC: Miami vs. Pittsburgh, 1984

Fewest Yards Gained, Game
86 NFC-D: Cleveland vs. N.Y. Giants, 1958
99 NFC: Chi. Cardinals vs. Philadelphia, 1948
114 NFC-D: N.Y. Giants vs. Washington, 1943
     NFC: Minnesota vs. N.Y. Giants, 2000

Most Yards Gained, Both Teams, Game
1,038 AFC-FR: Buffalo (536) vs. Miami (502), 1995
1,036 AFC-D: San Diego (564) vs. Miami (472), 1981 (OT)
1,024 AFC: Miami (569) vs. Pittsburgh (455), 1984

Fewest Yards Gained, Both Teams, Game
331 NFC: Chi. Cardinals (99) vs. Philadelphia (232), 1948
332 NFC-D: N.Y. Giants (150) vs. Cleveland (182), 1950
336 NFC: Boston (116) vs. Green Bay (220), 1936

RUSHING
ATTEMPTS
Most Attempts, Game
65 NFC: Detroit vs. N.Y. Giants, 1935
61 NFC: Philadelphia vs. Los Angeles, 1949
59 AFC: New England vs. Miami, 1985

Fewest Attempts, Game
8 AFC-D: Miami vs. San Diego, 1994
9 SB: Miami vs. San Francisco, 1984
   NFC: Minnesota vs. N.Y. Giants, 2000
10 NFC: L.A. Rams vs. San Francisco, 1989
    NFC-FR: Atlanta vs. Green Bay, 1995

NFC-FR: Detroit vs. Washington, 1999

Most Attempts, Both Teams, Game
- 109 NFC: Detroit (65) vs. N.Y. Giants (44), 1935
- 97 AFC-D: Baltimore (50) vs. Oakland (47), 1977 (OT)
- 91 NFC: Philadelphia (57) vs. Chi. Cardinals (34), 1948

Fewest Attempts, Both Teams, Game
- 32 AFC-D: Houston (14) vs. Kansas City (18), 1993
- 38 NFC-D: Detroit (16) vs. Dallas (22), 1991
- 39 NFC-FR: Atlanta (10) vs. Green Bay (29), 1995

YARDS GAINED
Most Yards Gained, Game
- 382 NFC: Chi. Bears vs. Washington, 1940
- 341 AFC-D: Buffalo vs. Miami, 1995
- 338 NFC-FR: Dallas vs. Los Angeles, 1980

Fewest Yards Gained, Game
- – 4 NFC-FR: Detroit vs. Green Bay, 1994
- 7 AFC-D: Buffalo vs. Boston, 1963
  SB: New England vs. Chicago, 1985
- 14 AFC-D: Miami vs. Denver, 1998
  AFC: N.Y. Jets vs. Denver, 1998

Most Yards Gained, Both Teams, Game
- 430 NFC-FR: Dallas (338) vs. Los Angeles (92), 1980
- 426 NFC: Cleveland (227) vs. Detroit (199), 1952
- 411 AFC-FR: Buffalo (341) vs. Miami (70), 1995

Fewest Yards Gained, Both Teams, Game
- 77 NFC-FR: Detroit (–4) vs. Green Bay (81), 1994
- 84 NFC-FR: St. Louis (34) vs. New Orleans (50), 2000
- 90 AFC-D: Buffalo (7) vs. Boston (83), 1963
  NFC-D: Tampa Bay (44) vs. Washington (46), 1999

AVERAGE GAIN
Highest Average Gain, Game
- 9.94 AFC: San Diego vs. Boston, 1963 (32-318)
- 9.29 NFC: Green Bay vs. Dallas, 1982 (17-158)
- 8.18 NFC-D: Atlanta vs. St. Louis, 2004 (40-327)

Lowest Average Gain, Game
- – 0.27 NFC-FR: Detroit vs. Green Bay, 1994 (15-(– 4))
- 0.58 AFC-D: Buffalo vs. Boston, 1963 (12-7)
- 0.64 SB: New England vs. Chicago, 1985 (11-7)

TOUCHDOWNS
Most Touchdowns, Game
- 7 NFC: Chi. Bears vs. Washington, 1940
- 6 NFC-D: San Francisco vs. N.Y. Giants, 1993
- 5 NFC: Cleveland vs. Detroit, 1954
  NFC-D: San Francisco vs. Chicago, 1994
  AFC-FR: Pittsburgh vs. Indianapolis, 1996
  AFC-FR: Denver vs. Jacksonville, 1997

Most Touchdowns, Both Teams, Game
- 7 NFC: Chi. Bears (7) vs. Washington (0), 1940
- 6 NFC: Cleveland (5) vs. Detroit (1), 1954
  NFC-D: San Francisco (6) vs. N.Y. Giants (0), 1993
  NFC-D: San Francisco (5) vs. Chicago (1), 1994
  AFC-FR: Denver (5) vs. Jacksonville (1), 1997
- 5 NFC: Chi. Cardinals (3) vs. Philadelphia (2), 1947
  AFC: San Diego (4) vs. Boston (1), 1963
  AFC-D: Cincinnati (3) vs. Buffalo (2), 1981
  AFC-FR: Pittsburgh (5) vs. Indianapolis (0), 1996
  NFC-D: Arizona (3) vs. Minnesota (2), 1998
  NFC-FR: Seattle (3) vs. Green Bay (2), 2003 (OT)

PASSING
ATTEMPTS
Most Attempts, Game
- 66 AFC-FR: Miami vs. Buffalo, 1995
- 65 AFC-D: Cleveland vs. N.Y. Jets, 1986 (OT)
  NFC-D: San Francisco vs. Green Bay, 1995
- 61 NFC-FR: Minnesota vs. Chicago, 1994

Fewest Attempts, Game
- 5 NFC: Detroit vs. N.Y. Giants, 1935
- 6 AFC: Miami vs. Oakland, 1973
- 7 SB: Miami vs. Minnesota, 1973

Most Attempts, Both Teams, Game
- 102 AFC-D: San Diego (54) vs. Miami (48), 1981 (OT)
- 96 NFC: N.Y. Jets (49) vs. Oakland (47), 1968
- 95 AFC-D: Cleveland (65) vs. N.Y. Jets (30), 1986 (OT)

Fewest Attempts, Both Teams, Game
- 18 NFC: Detroit (5) vs. N.Y. Giants (13), 1935
- 23 NFC: Chi. Cardinals (11) vs. Philadelphia (12), 1948
- 24 NFC-D: Cleveland (9) vs. N.Y. Giants (15), 1950

COMPLETIONS
Most Completions, Game
- 36 AFC-FR: Houston vs. Buffalo, 1992 (OT)
- 34 AFC-D: Cleveland vs. N.Y. Jets, 1986 (OT)
  AFC-FR: Miami vs. Buffalo, 1995
- 33 AFC-D: San Diego vs. Miami, 1981 (OT)
  NFC-FR: Minnesota vs. Chicago, 1994

Fewest Completions, Game
- 2 NFC: Detroit vs. N.Y. Giants, 1935
  NFC: Philadelphia vs. Chi. Cardinals, 1948
- 3 NFC: N.Y. Giants vs. Chi. Bears, 1941
  NFC: Green Bay vs. N.Y. Giants, 1944
  NFC: Chi. Cardinals vs. Philadelphia, 1947
  NFC: Chi. Cardinals vs. Philadelphia, 1948
  NFC-D: Cleveland vs. N.Y. Giants, 1950
  NFC: N.Y. Giants vs. Cleveland, 1950
  NFC: Cleveland vs. Detroit, 1953
  AFC: Miami vs. Oakland, 1973
- 4 NFC: N.Y. Giants vs. Detroit, 1935
  NFC-D: N.Y. Giants vs. Washington, 1943
  NFC-D: Pittsburgh vs. Philadelphia, 1947
  NFC-D: Dallas vs. Detroit, 1970
  AFC: Miami vs. Baltimore, 1971
  SB: Miami vs. Washington, 1982
  AFC-FR: Seattle vs. L.A. Raiders, 1984

Most Completions, Both Teams, Game
- 64 AFC-D: San Diego (33) vs. Miami (31), 1981 (OT)
- 57 AFC-FR: Houston (36) vs. Buffalo (21), 1992 (OT)
  NFC-FR: N.Y. Giants (29) vs. San Francisco (28), 2002
- 56 NFC-D: Dallas (28) vs. Green Bay (28), 1993
  NFC: Minnesota (29) vs. Atlanta (27), 1998 (OT)
  NFC-D: Minnesota (29) vs. St. Louis (27), 1999
  AFC-FR: Pittsburgh (30) vs. Cleveland (26), 2002

Fewest Completions, Both Teams, Game
- 5 NFC: Philadelphia (2) vs. Chi. Cardinals (3), 1948
- 6 NFC: Detroit (2) vs. N.Y. Giants (4), 1935
  NFC-D: Cleveland (3) vs. N.Y. Giants (3), 1950
- 11 NFC: Green Bay (3) vs. N.Y. Giants (8), 1944
  NFC-D: Dallas (4) vs. Detroit (7), 1970

COMPLETION PERCENTAGE
Highest Completion Percentage, Game (20 attempts)
- 88.0 SB: N.Y. Giants vs. Denver, 1986 (25-22)
- 87.1 NFC: San Francisco vs. L.A. Rams, 1989 (31-27)
- 83.9 AFC-FR: Indianapolis vs. Denver, 2003

Lowest Completion Percentage, Game (20 attempts)
- 18.5 NFC: Tampa Bay vs. Los Angeles, 1979 (27-5)
- 20.0 NFC-D: N.Y. Giants vs. Washington, 1943 (20-4)
- 25.8 NFC: Chi. Bears vs. Washington, 1937 (31-8)

YARDS GAINED
Most Yards Gained, Game
- 483 AFC-D: Cleveland vs. N.Y. Jets, 1986 (OT)
- 454 AFC-FR: Indianapolis vs. Denver, 2004
- 435 AFC: Miami vs. Pittsburgh, 1984

Fewest Yards Gained, Game
- 3 NFC: Chi. Cardinals vs. Philadelphia, 1948

7 NFC: Philadelphia vs. Chi. Cardinals, 1948
9 NFC-D: N.Y. Giants vs. Cleveland, 1950
NFC: Cleveland vs. Detroit, 1953

Most Yards Gained, Both Teams, Game
809 AFC-D: San Diego (415) vs. Miami (394), 1981 (OT)
762 NFC-D: Minnesota (388) vs. St. Louis (374), 1999
752 AFC-FR: Cleveland (409) vs. Pittsburgh (343), 2002

Fewest Yards Gained, Both Teams, Game
10 NFC: Chi. Cardinals (3) vs. Philadelphia (7), 1948
38 NFC-D: N.Y. Giants (9) vs. Cleveland (29), 1950
102 NFC-D: Dallas (22) vs. Detroit (80), 1970

TIMES SACKED
Most Times Sacked, Game
9 AFC: Kansas City vs. Buffalo, 1966
NFC: Chicago vs. San Francisco, 1984
AFC-D: N.Y. Jets vs. Cleveland, 1986 (OT)
AFC-D: Houston vs. Kansas City, 1993
8 NFC: Green Bay vs. Dallas, 1967
NFC: Minnesota vs. Washington, 1987
NFC-D: Philadelphia vs. Green Bay, 2003 (OT)
7 NFC-D: Dallas vs. Los Angeles, 1973
SB: Dallas vs. Pittsburgh, 1975
AFC-FR: Houston vs. Oakland, 1980
NFC-D: Washington vs. Chicago, 1984
SB: New England vs. Chicago, 1985
AFC-FR: Kansas City vs. San Diego, 1992
AFC-D: Pittsburgh vs. Buffalo, 1992

Most Times Sacked, Both Teams, Game
13 AFC: Kansas City (9) vs. Buffalo (4), 1966
AFC-D: N.Y. Jets (9) vs. Cleveland (4), 1986 (OT)
12 NFC-D: Dallas (7) vs. Los Angeles (5), 1973
NFC-D: Washington (7) vs. Chicago (5), 1984
NFC: Chicago (9) vs. San Francisco (3), 1984
AFC-FR: Kansas City (7) vs. San Diego (5), 1992
11 AFC-D: Houston (9) vs. Kansas City (2), 1993

Fewest Times Sacked, Both Teams, Game
0 AFC-D: Buffalo vs. Pittsburgh, 1974
AFC-FR: Pittsburgh vs. San Diego, 1982
AFC: Miami vs. Pittsburgh, 1984
AFC-D: Buffalo vs. Miami, 1990
AFC-D: Denver vs. Houston, 1991
AFC-FR: Buffalo vs. Miami, 1995
AFC-D: Indianapolis vs. Tennessee, 1999
1 In many games

TOUCHDOWNS
Most Touchdowns, Game
6 AFC-D: Oakland vs. Houston, 1969
SB: San Francisco vs. San Diego, 1994
5 NFC: Chi. Bears vs. Washington, 1943
NFC: Detroit vs. Cleveland, 1957
AFC-D: Oakland vs. Kansas City, 1968
SB: San Francisco vs. Denver, 1989
NFC-D: St. Louis vs. Minnesota, 1999
NFC: N.Y. Giants vs. Minnesota, 2000
AFC-FR: Indianapolis vs. Denver, 2003
4 By many teams

Most Touchdowns, Both Teams, Game
9 NFC-D: St. Louis (5) vs. Minnesota (4), 1999
8 AFC-FR: Buffalo (4) vs. Houston (4), 1992 (OT)
7 NFC: Chi. Bears (5) vs. Washington (2), 1943
AFC-D: Oakland (6) vs. Houston (1), 1969
SB: Pittsburgh (4) vs. Dallas (3), 1978
AFC-D: Miami (4) vs. San Diego (3), 1981 (OT)
AFC: Miami (4) vs. Pittsburgh (3), 1984
AFC-D: Buffalo (4) vs. Cleveland (3), 1989
SB: San Francisco (6) vs. San Diego (1), 1994
NFC-FR: Detroit (4) vs. Philadelphia (3), 1995
NFC-FR: New Orleans (4) vs. St. Louis (3), 2000

NFC-FR: N.Y. Giants (4) vs. San Francisco (3), 2002

INTERCEPTIONS BY
Most Interceptions By, Game
8 NFC: Chi. Bears vs. Washington, 1940
7 NFC: Cleveland vs. Los Angeles, 1955
6 NFC: Green Bay vs. N.Y. Giants, 1939
NFC: Chi. Bears vs. N.Y. Giants, 1946
NFC: Cleveland vs. Detroit, 1954
AFC: San Diego vs. Houston, 1961
AFC: Buffalo vs. L.A. Raiders, 1990
NFC-FR: Philadelphia vs. Detroit, 1995
NFC-D: St. Louis vs. Green Bay, 2001

Most Interceptions By, Both Teams, Game
10 NFC: Cleveland (7) vs. Los Angeles (3), 1955
AFC: San Diego (6) vs. Houston (4), 1961
9 NFC: Green Bay (6) vs. N.Y. Giants (3), 1939
8 NFC: Chi. Bears (8) vs. Washington (0), 1940
NFC: Chi. Bears (6) vs. N.Y. Giants (2), 1946
NFC: Cleveland (6) vs. Detroit (2), 1954
AFC-FR: Buffalo (4) vs. N.Y. Jets (4), 1981
AFC: Miami (5) vs. N.Y. Jets (3), 1982

YARDS GAINED
Most Yards Gained, Game
172 SB: Tampa Bay vs. Oakland, 2002
161 NFC-D: St. Louis vs. Green Bay, 2001
138 AFC-FR: N.Y. Jets vs. Cincinnati, 1982

Most Yards Gained, Both Teams, Game
184 SB: Tampa Bay (172) vs. Oakland (12), 2002
161 NFC-D: St. Louis (161) vs. Green Bay (0), 2001
156 NFC: Green Bay (123) vs. N.Y. Giants (33), 1939

TOUCHDOWNS
Most Touchdowns, Game
3 NFC: Chi. Bears vs. Washington, 1940
NFC-D: St. Louis vs. Green Bay, 2001
SB: Tampa Bay vs Oakland, 2002
2 NFC-D: Los Angeles vs. St. Louis, 1975
NFC-FR: Philadelphia vs. Detroit, 1995
1 In many games

Most Touchdowns, Both Teams, Game
3 NFC: Chi. Bears (3) vs. Washington (0), 1940
NFC-D: St. Louis (3) vs. Green Bay (0), 2001
SB: Tampa Bay (3) vs. Oakland (0), 2002
2 NFC-D: Los Angeles (2) vs. St. Louis(0), 1975
NFC-D: Dallas (1) vs. Green Bay (1), 1982
NFC-D: Minnesota (1) vs. San Francisco (1), 1987
NFC-FR: Detroit (1) vs. Green Bay (1), 1993
NFC-FR: Philadelphia (2) vs. Detroit (0), 1995
AFC-FR: Buffalo (1) vs. Jacksonville (1), 1996
1 In many games

PUNTING
Most Punts, Game
14 AFC-D: N.Y. Jets vs. Cleveland, 1986 (OT)
13 NFC: N.Y. Giants vs. Chi. Bears, 1933
AFC-D: Baltimore vs. Oakland, 1977 (OT)
11 AFC: Houston vs. Oakland, 1967
AFC-D: Houston vs. Oakland, 1969
NFC: L.A. Rams vs. Chicago, 1985
SB: N.Y. Giants vs. Baltimore, 2000

Fewest Punts, Game
0 NFC-FR: St. Louis vs. Green Bay, 1982
AFC-FR: N.Y. Jets vs. Cincinnati, 1982
AFC-FR: Indianapolis vs. Denver, 2003
AFC-D: Kansas City vs. Indianapolis, 2003
AFC-D: Indianapolis vs. Kansas City, 2003
1 By many teams

Most Punts, Both Teams, Game
- 23 NFC: N.Y. Giants (13) vs. Chi. Bears (10), 1933
- 22 AFC-D: N.Y. Jets (14) vs. Cleveland (8), 1986 (OT)
- 21 AFC-D: Baltimore (13) vs. Oakland (8), 1977 (OT)
-     NFC: L.A. Rams (11) vs. Chicago (10), 1985
-     SB: N.Y. Giants (11) vs. Baltimore (10), 2000

Fewest Punts, Both Teams, Game
- 0 AFC-FR: Kansas City vs. Indianapolis, 2003
- 1 NFC-FR: St. Louis (0) vs. Green Bay (1), 1982
- 2 AFC-FR: N.Y. Jets (0) vs. Cincinnati (2), 1982
-    SB: Atlanta (1) vs. Denver (1), 1998
-    AFC-FR: Indianapolis (0) vs. Denver (2), 2003

AVERAGE YARDAGE

Highest Average, Punting, Game (4 punts)
- 56.0 AFC: Oakland vs. San Diego, 1980
- 52.5 NFC: Washington vs. Chi. Bears, 1942
- 52.0 AFC-D: Tennessee vs. Indianapolis, 1999

Lowest Average, Punting, Game (4 punts)
- 24.9 NFC: Washington vs. Chi. Bears, 1937
- 25.3 AFC-FR: Pittsburgh vs. Houston, 1989
- 25.5 NFC: Green Bay vs. N.Y. Giants, 1962

PUNT RETURNS

Most Punt Returns, Game
- 8 NFC: Green Bay vs. N.Y. Giants, 1944
- 7 By many teams

Most Punt Returns, Both Teams, Game
- 13 AFC-FR: Houston (7) vs. Oakland (6), 1980
- 12 AFC-D: New England (7) vs. Pittsburgh (5), 1996
- 11 NFC: Green Bay (8) vs. N.Y. Giants (3), 1944
-     NFC-D: Green Bay (6) vs. Baltimore (5), 1965
-     AFC-FR: Jacksonville (7) vs. New England (4), 1998

Fewest Punt Returns, Both Teams, Game
- 0 NFC: Chi. Bears vs. N.Y. Giants, 1941
-    AFC: Boston vs. San Diego, 1963
-    NFC-FR: Green Bay vs. St. Louis, 1982
-    AFC-FR: Houston vs. N.Y. Jets, 1991
-    AFC-D: Denver vs. Houston, 1991
-    NFC-D: San Francisco vs. Washington, 1992
-    SB: Denver vs. Green Bay, 1997
-    SB: Atlanta vs. Denver, 1998
-    AFC-FR: Oakland vs. N.Y. Jets, 2001
-    AFC-D: N.Y. Jets vs. Oakland, 2002
-    AFC-FR: Denver vs. Indianapolis, 2003
-    NFC-D: Carolina vs. St. Louis, 2003
-    AFC D: Indianapolis vs. Kansas City, 2003
- 1 In many games

YARDS GAINED

Most Yards Gained, Game
- 155 NFC-D: Dallas vs. Cleveland, 1967
- 152 NFC-D: Atlanta vs. St. Louis, 2004
- 150 NFC: Chi. Cardinals vs. Philadelphia, 1947

Fewest Yards Gained, Game
- −10 NFC: Green Bay vs. Cleveland, 1965
- −9 NFC: Dallas vs. Green Bay, 1966
-     AFC-D: Kansas City vs. Oakland, 1968
- −7 NFC-D: San Francisco vs. Atlanta, 1998

Most Yards Gained, Both Teams, Game
- 166 NFC-D: Dallas (155) vs. Cleveland (11), 1967
-     AFC-D: Baltimore (99) vs. Pittsburgh (67), 2001
- 160 NFC: Chi. Cardinals (150) vs. Philadelphia (10), 1947
- 152 NFC-D: Atlanta (152) vs. St. Louis (0), 2004

Fewest Yards Gained, Both Teams, Game
- −9 NFC: Dallas (−9) vs. Green Bay (0), 1966
- −6 AFC: Miami (−5) vs. Oakland (−1), 1970
- −3 NFC-D: San Francisco (−5) vs. Dallas (2), 1972

TOUCHDOWNS

Most Touchdowns, Game
- 1 By 18 teams

KICKOFF RETURNS

Most Kickoff Returns, Game
- 10 NFC-D: L.A. Rams vs. Washington, 1983
-     NFC-FR: Detroit vs. Philadelphia, 1995
- 9 NFC: Chi. Bears vs. N.Y. Giants, 1956
-    AFC: Boston vs. San Diego, 1963
-    AFC: Houston vs. Oakland, 1967
-    SB: Denver vs. San Francisco, 1989
-    AFC-D: Miami vs. Buffalo, 1990
-    AFC: L.A. Raiders vs. Buffalo, 1990
-    AFC-D: Miami vs. Jacksonville, 1999
-    SB: Oakland vs. Tampa Bay, 2002
- 8 By many teams

Most Kickoff Returns, Both Teams, Game
- 15 AFC-D: Miami (9) vs. Buffalo (6), 1990
- 14 NFC-FR: Detroit (10) vs. Philadelphia (4), 1995
- 13 NFC-D: Green Bay (7) vs. Dallas (6), 1982
-     NFC-FR: Green Bay (7) vs. San Francisco (6), 1998
-     AFC-FR: N.Y. Jets (8) vs. Oakland (5), 2001
-     NFC-FR: San Francisco (7) vs. N.Y. Giants (6), 2002
-     AFC-D: Tennessee (7) vs. Pittsburgh (6), 2002
-     SB: Oakland (9) vs. Tampa Bay (4), 2002
-     NFC-FR: Seattle (7) vs. Green Bay (6), 2003 (OT)
-     AFC-D: Kansas City (7) vs. Indianapolis (6), 2003
-     AFC: Pittsburgh (8) vs. New England (5), 2004

Fewest Kickoff Returns, Both Teams, Game
- 1 NFC: Green Bay (0) vs. Boston (1), 1936
-    AFC-FR: San Diego (0) vs. Kansas City (1), 1992
- 2 NFC-D: Los Angeles (0) vs. Chi. Bears (2), 1950
-    AFC: Houston (0) vs. San Diego (2), 1961
-    AFC-D: Oakland (1) vs. Pittsburgh (1), 1972
-    AFC-D: N.Y. Jets (0) vs. L.A. Raiders (2), 1982
-    AFC: Miami (1) vs. N.Y. Jets (1), 1982
-    NFC: N.Y. Giants (0) vs. Washington (2), 1986
- 3 In many games

YARDS GAINED

Most Yards Gained, Game
- 244 SB: San Diego vs. San Francisco, 1994
- 227 SB: Atlanta vs. Denver, 1998
- 225 NFC: Washington vs. Chi. Bears, 1940

Most Yards Gained, Both Teams, Game
- 379 AFC D: Baltimore (193) vs. Oakland (186), 1977 (OT)
- 348 NFC-D: Minnesota (174) vs. St. Louis (174), 1999
- 322 NFC-D: Green Bay (194) vs. San Francisco (128), 1998

Fewest Yards Gained, Both Teams, Game
- 5 AFC-FR: San Diego (0) vs. Kansas City (5), 1992
- 15 NFC: N.Y. Giants (0) vs. Washington (15), 1986
- 31 NFC-D: Los Angeles (0) vs. Chi. Bears (31), 1950

TOUCHDOWNS

Most Touchdowns, Game
- 1 NFC-D: San Francisco vs. Dallas, 1972
-    AFC-D: Miami vs. Oakland, 1974
-    AFC-D: Baltimore vs. Oakland, 1977 (OT)
-    SB: Miami vs. Washington, 1982
-    SB: Cincinnati vs. San Francisco, 1988
-    AFC-D: Cleveland vs. Buffalo, 1989
-    SB: San Diego vs. San Francisco, 1994
-    SB: Green Bay vs. New England, 1996
-    NFC: San Francisco vs. Green Bay, 1997
-    SB: Atlanta vs. Denver, 1998
-    AFC-FR: Tennessee vs. Buffalo, 1999
-    AFC-FR: Seattle vs. Miami, 1999
-    NFC-D: Washington vs. Tampa Bay, 1999
-    NFC: St. Louis vs. Minnesota, 1999

AFC: Tennessee vs. Jacksonville, 1999
NFC-D: N.Y. Giants vs. Philadelphia, 2000
SB: Baltimore vs. N.Y. Giants, 2000
SB: N.Y. Giants vs. Baltimore, 2000
AFC-D: Kansas City vs. Indianapolis, 2003
Most Touchdowns, Both Teams, Game
   2 SB: Baltimore (1) vs. N.Y. Giants (1), 2000

PENALTIES
Most Penalties, Game
  17 AFC-FR: L.A. Raiders vs. Denver, 1993
  14 AFC-FR: Oakland vs. Houston, 1980
       NFC-D: San Francisco vs. N.Y. Giants, 1981
       AFC: Oakland vs. Tennessee, 2002
  13 AFC-FR: Houston vs. Cleveland, 1988
       AFC: Houston vs. Denver, 1991
       NFC-D: Arizona vs. Minnesota, 1998
       NFC-D: Carolina vs. St. Louis, 2003 (2 OT)
Fewest Penalties, Game
   0 NFC: Philadelphia vs. Green Bay, 1960
       NFC-D: Detroit vs. Dallas, 1970
       AFC-D: Miami vs. Oakland, 1970
       SB: Miami vs. Dallas, 1971
       NFC-D: Washington vs. Minnesota, 1973
       SB: Pittsburgh vs. Dallas, 1975
       NFC: San Francisco vs. Chicago, 1988
       SB: Denver vs. San Francisco, 1989
       AFC-D: L.A. Raiders vs. Cincinnati, 1990
       AFC-D: Miami vs. San Diego, 1992
       SB: Atlanta vs. Denver, 1998
       AFC-FR: N.Y. Jets vs. Oakland, 2001
       NFC-FR: Carolina vs. Dallas, 2003
   1 By many teams
Most Penalties, Both Teams, Game
  27 AFC-FR: L.A. Raiders (17) vs. Denver (10), 1993
  22 AFC-FR: Oakland (14) vs. Houston (8), 1980
       NFC-D: San Francisco (14) vs. N.Y. Giants (8), 1981
       AFC-FR: Houston (13) vs. Cleveland (9), 1988
       NFC-D: Arizona (13) vs. Minnesota (9), 1998
  21 AFC-D: Oakland (11) vs. New England (10), 1976
       AFC: Oakland (14) vs. Tennessee (7), 2002
Fewest Penalties, Both Teams, Game
   1 AFC-D: L.A. Raiders (0) vs. Cincinnati (1), 1990
   2 NFC: Washington (1) vs. Chi. Bears (1), 1937
       NFC-D: Washington (0) vs. Minnesota (2), 1973
       SB: Pittsburgh (0) vs. Dallas (2), 1975
       NFC-FR: Carolina (0) vs. Dallas (2), 2003
   3 AFC: Miami (1) vs. Baltimore (2), 1971
       NFC: San Francisco (1) vs. Dallas (2), 1971
       SB: Miami (0) vs. Dallas (3), 1971
       AFC-D: Pittsburgh (1) vs. Oakland (2), 1972
       AFC-D: Miami (1) vs. Cincinnati (2), 1973
       SB: Miami (1) vs. San Francisco (2), 1984
       NFC: San Francisco (0) vs. Chicago (3), 1988
       AFC: New England (1) vs. Pittsburgh (2), 2004

YARDS PENALIZED
Most Yards Penalized, Game
 145 NFC-D: San Francisco vs. N.Y. Giants, 1981
 133 SB: Dallas vs. Baltimore, 1970
 130 AFC-FR: L.A. Raiders vs. Denver, 1993
Fewest Yards Penalized, Game
   0 By many teams
Most Yards Penalized, Both Teams, Game
 227 AFC-FR: L.A. Raiders (130) vs. Denver (97), 1993
 206 NFC-D: San Francisco (145) vs. N.Y. Giants (61), 1981
 201 NFC-FR: Detroit (126) vs. Washington (75), 1999
Fewest Yards Penalized, Both Teams, Game
   5 AFC-D: L.A. Raiders (0) vs. Cincinnati (5), 1990
   9 NFC-D: Washington (0) vs. Minnesota (9), 1973

  11 NFC-FR: Carolina (0) vs. Dallas (11), 2003

FUMBLES
Most Fumbles, Game
   8 SB: Buffalo vs. Dallas, 1992
   7 AFC-D: Houston vs. Kansas City, 1993
   6 By 12 teams
Most Fumbles, Both Teams, Game
  12 AFC: Houston (6) vs. Pittsburgh (6), 1978
       SB: Buffalo (8) vs. Dallas (4), 1992
  10 NFC: Chi. Bears (5) vs. N.Y. Giants (5), 1934
       SB: Dallas (6) vs. Denver (4), 1977
       AFC: Jacksonville (5) vs. Tennessee (5), 1999
   9 NFC-D: San Francisco (6) vs. Detroit (3), 1957
       NFC-D: San Francisco (5) vs. Dallas (4), 1972
       NFC: Dallas (5) vs. Philadelphia (4), 1980
Most Fumbles Lost, Game
   5 SB: Buffalo vs. Dallas, 1992
       AFC-D: Miami vs. Jacksonville, 1999
   4 NFC: N.Y. Giants vs. Baltimore, 1958 (OT)
       AFC: Kansas City vs. Oakland, 1969
       SB: Baltimore vs. Dallas, 1970
       AFC: Pittsburgh vs. Oakland, 1975
       SB: Denver vs. Dallas, 1977
       AFC: Houston vs. Pittsburgh, 1978
       AFC: Miami vs. New England, 1985
       SB: New England vs. Chicago, 1985
       NFC-FR: L.A. Rams vs. Washington, 1986
       NFC-FR: Minnesota vs. Dallas, 1996
       AFC-FR: Buffalo vs. Miami, 1998
       AFC: N.Y. Jets vs. Denver, 1998
       AFC: Jacksonville vs. Tennessee, 1999
   3 By many teams
Fewest Fumbles, Both Teams, Game
   0 NFC: Green Bay vs. Cleveland, 1965
       AFC-D: Houston vs. San Diego, 1979
       NFC-D: Dallas vs. Los Angeles, 1979
       SB: Los Angeles vs. Pittsburgh, 1979
       AFC-D: Buffalo vs. Cincinnati, 1981
       NFC: Minnesota vs. Washington, 1987
       NFC-D: San Francisco vs. Washington, 1990
       NFC: Dallas vs. Green Bay, 1995
       AFC-D: New England vs. Pittsburgh, 1996
       SB: Green Bay vs. New England, 1996
       AFC-FR: Miami vs. Seattle, 1999
       AFC-FR: Miami vs. Indianapolis, 2000 (OT)
       AFC-D: Baltimore vs. Tennessee, 2000
       SB: Pittsburgh vs. Seattle, 2005
   1 In many games

RECOVERIES
Most Total Fumbles Recovered, Game
   8 SB: Dallas vs. Denver, 1977 (4 own, 4 opp)
   7 NFC: Chi. Bears vs. N.Y. Giants, 1934 (5 own, 2 opp)
       NFC-D: San Francisco vs. Detroit, 1957 (4 own, 3 opp)
       NFC-D: San Francisco vs. Dallas, 1972 (4 own, 3 opp)
       AFC: Pittsburgh vs. Houston, 1978 (3 own, 4 opp)
   6 AFC: Houston vs. San Diego, 1961 (4 own, 2 opp)
       AFC-D: Cleveland vs. Baltimore, 1971 (4 own, 2 opp)
       AFC-D: Cleveland vs. Oakland, 1980 (5 own, 1 opp)
       NFC: Philadelphia vs. Dallas, 1980 (3 own, 3 opp)
       SB: Dallas vs. Buffalo, 1992 (1 own, 5 opp)
       NFC-D: Green Bay vs. San Francisco, 1996
         (4 own, 2 opp)
       AFC: Denver vs. N.Y. Jets, 1998 (2 own, 4 opp)
       AFC: Tennessee vs. Jacksonville, 1999 (2 own, 4 opp)
Most Own Fumbles Recovered, Game
   5 NFC: Chi. Bears vs. N.Y. Giants, 1934
       AFC-D: Cleveland vs. Oakland, 1980

4   By many teams

TOUCHDOWNS
Most Touchdowns, Game
2   SB: Dallas vs. Buffalo, 1992

TURNOVERS
Numbers of times losing the ball on interceptions and fumbles.
Most Turnovers, Game
9   NFC: Washington vs. Chi. Bears, 1940
    NFC: Detroit vs. Cleveland, 1954
    AFC: Houston vs. Pittsburgh, 1978
    SB: Buffalo vs. Dallas, 1992
8   NFC: N.Y. Giants vs. Chi. Bears, 1946
    NFC: Los Angeles vs. Cleveland, 1955
    NFC: Cleveland vs. Detroit, 1957
    SB: Denver vs. Dallas, 1977
    NFC-D: Minnesota vs. Philadelphia, 1980
    NFC-D: Green Bay vs. St. Louis, 2001
7   In many games
Fewest Turnovers, Game
0   By many teams
Most Turnovers, Both Teams, Game
14 AFC: Houston (9) vs. Pittsburgh (5), 1978
13 NFC: Detroit (9) vs. Cleveland (4), 1954
    AFC: Houston (7) vs. San Diego (6), 1961
12 AFC: Pittsburgh (7) vs. Oakland (5), 1975
Fewest Turnovers, Both Teams, Game
0   SB: Buffalo vs. N.Y. Giants, 1990
    AFC-FR: Kansas City vs Pittsburgh, 1993 (OT)
    NFC-FR: Detroit vs. Green Bay, 1994
    AFC-FR: Denver vs. Jacksonville, 1996
    SB: St. Louis vs. Tennessee, 1999
1   AFC-D: Baltimore (0) vs. Cincinnati (1), 1970
    AFC-D: Pittsburgh (0) vs. Buffalo (1), 1974
    AFC: Oakland (0) vs. Pittsburgh (1), 1976
    NFC-D: Minnesota (0) vs. Washington (1), 1982
    NFC-D: Chicago (0) vs. N.Y. Giants (1), 1985
    SB: N.Y. Giants (0) vs. Denver (1), 1986
    NFC: Washington (0) vs. Minnesota (1), 1987
    AFC-D: Cincinnati (0) vs. L.A. Raiders (1), 1990
    NFC: N.Y. Giants (0) vs. San Francisco (1), 1990
    NFC-FR: N.Y. Giants (0) vs. Minnesota (1), 1993
    AFC-FR: L.A. Raiders (0) vs. Denver (1), 1993
    NFC: Dallas (0) vs. San Francisco (1), 1993
    AFC: Indianapolis (0) vs. Pittsburgh (1), 1995
    NFC-D: San Francisco (0) vs. Minnesota (1), 1997
    AFC-D: Indianapolis (0) vs. Tennessee (1), 1999
    AFC-FR: Baltimore (0) vs. Denver (1), 2000
    AFC-D: Baltimore (0) vs. Tennessee (1), 2000
    AFC-D: Oakland (0) vs. New England (1), 2001
    NFC-FR: Green Bay (0) vs. Seattle (1), 2003 (OT)
    AFC-D: Indianapolis (0) vs. Kansas City (1), 2003
    AFC-FR: N.Y. Jets (0) vs. San Diego (1), 2004 (OT)
    NFC: Philadelphia (0) vs. Atlanta (1), 2004
2   In many games

Includes records of AFC-NFC Pro Bowls, 1971-2006
Compiled by Elias Sports Bureau

INDIVIDUAL RECORDS

SERVICE
Most Games
- 12 Randall McDaniel, Minnesota 1990-2000; Tampa Bay 2001
- 11 *Reggie White, Philadelphia, 1987-1993; Green Bay, 1994, 1996-97, 1999
   Junior Seau, San Diego, 1992-2002
   Rod Woodson, Pittsburgh, 1990-95, 1997; Baltimore, 2000-02; Oakland, 2003
   Will Shields, Kansas City, 1996-2006
- 10 Lawrence Taylor, N.Y. Giants, 1982-1991
   Ronnie Lott, San Francisco, 1982-85, 1987-1991; L.A. Raiders 1992
   Mike Singletary, Chicago, 1984-1993
   **Bruce Matthews, Houston, 1989-1995, 1997; Tennessee, 2000, 2002
   ***Jerry Rice, San Francisco, 1987-88, 1990-94, 1996, 1999; Oakland, 2003

*Also selected, but did not play, in two additional games
**Also selected, but did not play, in four additional games
***Also selected but did not play, in three additional games

SCORING
POINTS
Most Points, Career
- 45 Morten Andersen, New Orleans, 1986-89, 1991, 1993; Atlanta, 1996 (15-pat, 10-fg)
- 30 Jan Stenerud, Kansas City, 1971-72, 1976; Minnesota, 1985 (6-pat, 8-fg)
   Jimmy Smith, Jacksonville, 1998-2001 (5-td)
   Marvin Harrison, Indianapolis, 2000-06 (5-td)
- 29 David Akers, Philadelphia, 2002-03, 2005 (8-pat, 7-fg)

Most Points, Game
- 18 John Brockington, Green Bay, 1973 (3-td)
   Mike Alstott, Tampa Bay, 2000 (3-td)
   Jimmy Smith, Jacksonville, 2000 (3-td)
   Shaun Alexander, Seattle, 2004 (3-td)
- 15 Garo Yepremian, Miami, 1974 (5-fg)
   Jason Hanson, Detroit, 2000 (6-pat, 3-fg)
- 14 Jan Stenerud, Kansas City, 1972 (2-pat, 4-fg)

TOUCHDOWNS
Most Touchdowns, Career
- 5 Jimmy Smith, Jacksonville, 1998-2001 (5-p)
   Marvin Harrison, Indianapolis, 2000-06 (5-p)
- 4 Mike Alstott, Tampa Bay, 1998-2003 (3-r, 1-p)
   Tony Gonzalez, Kansas City, 2000-01, 2003-06 (4-p)
   Hines Ward, Pittsburgh, 2002-05 (3-p, 1-ret)
- 3 John Brockington, Green Bay, 1972-74 (2-r, 1-p)
   Earl Campbell, Houston, 1979-1982, 1984 (3-r)
   Chuck Muncie, New Orleans, 1980; San Diego, 1982-83 (3-r)
   William Andrews, Atlanta, 1981-84 (1-r, 2-p)
   Marcus Allen, L.A. Raiders, 1983, 1985-86, 1988; Kansas City, 1994 (2-r, 1-p)
   Cris Carter, Minnesota, 1994-2001 (3-p)
   Curtis Martin, New England, 1996-97; N.Y. Jets, 1999, 2002 (2-r, 1-p)
   Shaun Alexander, Seattle, 2004 (2-r, 1-p)
   Torry Holt, St. Louis, 2001-02, 2004-06 (3-p)

Most Touchdowns, Game
- 3 John Brockington, Green Bay, 1973 (2-r, 1-p)
   Mike Alstott, Tampa Bay, 2000 (3-r)

Jimmy Smith, Jacksonville, 2000 (3-p)
Shaun Alexander, Seattle, 2004 (2-r, 1-p)
- 2 Mel Renfro, Dallas, 1971 (2-ret)
   Earl Campbell, Houston, 1980 (2-r)
   Chuck Muncie, New Orleans, 1980 (2-r)
   William Andrews, Atlanta, 1984 (2-p)
   Herschel Walker, Dallas, 1989 (2-r)
   Johnny Johnson, Phoenix, 1991 (2-r)
   Eric Green, Pittsburgh, 1995 (2-p)
   Marvin Harrison, Indianapolis, 2001 (2-p)
   Ricky Wiilliams, Miami, 2003 (2-r)
   Hines Ward, Pittsburgh, 2005 (1-p, 1-ret)

POINTS AFTER TOUCHDOWN
Most Points After Touchdown, Career
- 15 Morten Andersen, New Orleans, 1986-89, 1991, 1993; Atlanta, 1996 (15 att)
- 11 Adam Vinatieri, New England, 2003, 2005 (11 att)
- 9 Jason Hanson, Detroit, 1998, 2000 (9 att)

Most Points After Touchdown, Game
- 7 Mike Vanderjagt, Indianapolis, 2004 (7 att)
- 6 Ali Haji-Sheikh, N.Y. Giants, 1984 (6 att)
   Jason Hanson, Detroit, 2000 (6 att)
   Adam Vinatieri, New England, 2003 (6 att)
- 5 John Carney, San Diego, 1995 (5 att)
   Matt Stover, Baltimore, 2001 (5 att)
   Jason Elam, Denver, 2002 (5 att)
   Jeff Wilkins, St. Louis, 2004 (5 att)
   Adam Vinatieri, New England, 2005 (5 att)

FIELD GOALS
Most Field Goals Attempted, Career
- 18 Morten Andersen, New Orleans, 1986-89, 1991, 1993; Atlanta, 1996
- 15 Jan Stenerud, Kansas City, 1971-72, 1976; Minnesota, 1985
- 10 Nick Lowery, Kansas City, 1982, 1991, 1993

Most Field Goals Attempted, Game
- 6 Jan Stenerud, Kansas City, 1972
   Eddie Murray, Detroit, 1981
   Mark Moseley, Washington, 1983
- 5 Garo Yepremian, Miami, 1974
- 4 Jan Stenerud, Kansas City, 1976
   Nick Lowery, Kansas City, 1991, 1993
   Morten Andersen, New Orleans, 1993
   Cary Blanchard, Indianapolis, 1997
   John Kasay, Carolina, 1997
   David Akers, Philadelphia, 2002
   Jeff Wilkins, St. Louis, 2004

Most Field Goals, Career
- 10 Morten Andersen, New Orleans, 1986-89, 1991, 1993; Atlanta, 1996
- 8 Jan Stenerud, Kansas City, 1971-72, 1976; Minnesota, 1985
- 7 Nick Lowery, Kansas City, 1982, 1991, 1993
   David Akers, Philadelphia, 2002-03, 2005

Most Field Goals, Game
- 5 Garo Yepremian, Miami, 1974 (5 att)
- 4 Jan Stenerud, Kansas City, 1972 (6 att)
   Eddie Murray, Detroit, 1981 (6 att)
- 3 Nick Lowery, Kansas City, 1991 (4 att)
   Nick Lowery, Kansas City, 1993 (4 att)
   Jason Elam, Denver, 1999 (3 att)
   Jason Hanson, Detroit, 2000 (3 att)
   David Akers, Philadelphia, 2002 (4 att)
   Neil Rackers, Arizona, 2006 (3 att)

Longest Field Goal
- 53 David Akers, Philadelphia, 2003
- 51 Morten Andersen, New Orleans, 1989
   Jason Hanson, Detroit, 2000

49   Fuad Reveiz, Minnesota, 1995
     David Akers, Philadelphia, 2002

SAFETIES
Most Safeties, Game
1   Art Still, Kansas City, 1983
    Mark Gastineau, N.Y. Jets, 1985
    Greg Townsend, L.A. Raiders, 1992

RUSHING
ATTEMPTS
Most Attempts, Career
81   Walter Payton, Chicago, 1977-1981, 1984-87
68   O.J. Simpson, Buffalo, 1973-77
66   Barry Sanders, Detroit, 1990-93, 1995-98
Most Attempts, Game
19   O.J. Simpson, Buffalo, 1974
17   Marv Hubbard, Oakland, 1974
16   O.J. Simpson, Buffalo, 1973
     Marcus Allen, L.A. Raiders, 1986

YARDS GAINED
Most Yards Gained, Career
368   Walter Payton, Chicago, 1977-1981, 1984-87
356   O.J. Simpson, Buffalo, 1973-77
271   Marshall Faulk, Indianapolis, 1995-96, 1999;
      St. Louis, 2000, 2002-03
Most Yards Gained, Game
180   Marshall Faulk, Indianapolis, 1995
127   Chris Warren, Seattle, 1995
112   O. J. Simpson, Buffalo, 1973
Longest Run From Scrimmage
49   Marshall Faulk, Indianapolis, 1995 (TD)
41   Lawrence McCutcheon, Los Angeles, 1976
     Natrone Means, San Diego, 1995
     Marshall Faulk, Indianapolis, 1995
39   Chris Warren, Seattle, 1994
     Priest Holmes, Kansas City, 2002

AVERAGE GAIN
Highest Average Gain, Career (20 attempts)
9.36   Chris Warren, Seattle, 1994-96, (25-234)
6.45   Marshall Faulk, Indianapolis, 1995-96, 1999;
       St. Louis, 2000, 2002-03 (42-271)
5.81   Marv Hubbard, Oakland, 1972-74 (36-209)
Highest Average Gain, Game (10 attempts)
13.85   Marshall Faulk, Indianapolis, 1995 (13-180)
9.07   Chris Warren, Seattle, 1995 (14-127)
7.00   O.J. Simpson, Buffalo, 1973 (16-112)
       Ottis Anderson, St. Louis, 1981 (10-70)

TOUCHDOWNS
Most Touchdowns, Career
3   Earl Campbell, Houston, 1979-1982, 1984
    Chuck Muncie, New Orleans, 1980; San Diego,
      1982-83
    Mike Alstott, Tampa Bay, 1998-2003
2   John Brockington, Green Bay, 1972-74
    O.J. Simpson, Buffalo, 1973-77
    Walter Payton, Chicago, 1977-1981, 1984-87
    Marcus Allen, L.A. Raiders, 1983, 1985-86, 1988;
      Kansas City, 1994
    Herschel Walker, Dallas, 1988-89
    Johnny Johnson, Phoenix, 1991
    Barry Sanders, Detroit, 1990-93, 1995-98
    Curtis Martin, New England, 1996-97; N.Y. Jets,
      1999, 2002
    Ricky Williams, Miami, 2003
    Shaun Alexander, Seattle, 2004

Most Touchdowns, Game
3   Mike Alstott, Tampa Bay, 2000
2   John Brockington, Green Bay, 1973
    Earl Campbell, Houston, 1980
    Chuck Muncie, New Orleans, 1980
    Herschel Walker, Dallas, 1989
    Johnny Johnson, Phoenix, 1991
    Ricky Williams, Miami, 2003
    Shaun Alexander, Seattle, 2004

PASSING
ATTEMPTS
Most Attempts, Career
134   Peyton Manning, Indianapolis, 2000-01, 2003-06
120   Dan Fouts, San Diego, 1980-84, 1986
101   Steve Young, San Francisco, 1993-96, 1998-99
Most Attempts, Game
41   Peyton Manning, Indianapolis, 2004
32   Bill Kenney, Kansas City, 1984
     Steve Young, San Francisco, 1993
30   Dan Fouts, San Diego, 1983

COMPLETIONS
Most Completions, Career
79   Peyton Manning, Indianapolis, 2000-01, 2003-06
63   Dan Fouts, San Diego, 1980-84, 1986
48   Steve Young, San Francisco, 1993-96, 1998-99
Most Completions, Game
22   Peyton Manning, Indianapolis, 2004
21   Joe Theismann, Washington, 1984
18   Steve Young, San Francisco, 1993

COMPLETION PERCENTAGE
Highest Completion Percentage, Career (40 attempts)
68.9   Joe Theismann, Washington, 1983-84 (45-31)
67.9   Rich Gannon, Oakland, 2000-03 (53-36)
64.4   Jim Kelly, Buffalo, 1988, 1991-92 (45-29)
Highest Completion Percentage, Game (10 attempts)
90.0   Archie Manning, New Orleans, 1980 (10-9)
85.7   Rich Gannon, Oakland, 2001 (14-12)
80.0   Rich Gannon, Oakland, 2002 (10-8)

YARDS GAINED
Most Yards Gained, Career
1,131   Peyton Manning, Indianapolis, 2000-01, 2003-06
890   Dan Fouts, San Diego, 1980-84, 1986
614   Steve Young, San Francisco, 1993-96, 1998-99
Most Yards Gained, Game
342   Peyton Manning, Indianapolis, 2004
274   Dan Fouts, San Diego, 1983
270   Peyton Manning, Indianapolis, 2000
Longest Completion
93   Jeff Blake, Cincinnati (to Thigpen, Pittsburgh),
       1996 (TD)
90   Steve McNair, Tennessee (to Johnson, Cincinnati),
       2004 (TD)
80   Mark Brunell, Jacksonville (to Brown, Oakland),
       1997 (TD)

AVERAGE GAIN
Highest Average Gain, Career (40 attempts)
8.44   Peyton Manning, Indianapolis, 2000-01,
       2003-06 (134-1,131)
8.19   Rich Gannon, Oakland, 2000-03 (53-434)
8.12   Brett Favre, Green Bay, 1993-94, 1996-97 (57-463)
Highest Average Gain, Game (10 attempts)
15.27   Randall Cunningham, Philadelphia, 1991 (11-168)
13.70   Rich Gannon, Oakland, 2002 (10-137)

13.00 Brett Favre, Green Bay, 1997 (11-143)
      Peyton Manning, Indianapolis, 2005 (10-130)

TOUCHDOWNS
Most Touchdowns, Career
12 Peyton Manning, Indianapolis, 2000-01, 2003-06
7 Rich Gannon, Oakland, 2000-03
4 Steve Young, San Francisco, 1993-96, 1998-99
  Marc Bulger, St. Louis, 2004
Most Touchdowns, Game
4 Marc Bulger, St. Louis, 2004
3 Joe Theismann, Washington, 1984
  Phil Simms, N.Y. Giants, 1986
  Peyton Manning, Indianapolis, 2004
  Peyton Manning, Indianapolis, 2005
2 James Harris, Los Angeles, 1975
  Mike Boryla, Philadelphia, 1976
  Ken Anderson, Cincinnati, 1977
  Jim Kelly, Buffalo, 1991
  Mark Rypien, Washington, 1992
  Steve Young, San Francisco, 1998
  Peyton Manning, Indianapolis, 2000
  Rich Gannon, Oakland, 2001
  Peyton Manning, Indianapolis, 2001
  Rich Gannon, Oakland, 2002
  Donovan McNabb, Philadelphia, 2002
  Rich Gannon, Oakland, 2003
  Brad Johnson, Tampa Bay, 2003

HAD INTERCEPTED
Most Passes Had Intercepted, Career
8 Dan Fouts, San Diego, 1980-84, 1986
  Peyton Manning, Indianapolis, 2000-01, 2003-06
6 Jim Hart, St. Louis, 1975-78
5 Ken Stabler, Oakland, 1974-75, 1978
  Donovan McNabb, Philadelphia, 2001-03, 2005
Most Passes Had Intercepted, Game
5 Jim Hart, St. Louis, 1977
4 Ken Stabler, Oakland, 1974
3 Dan Fouts, San Diego, 1986
  Mark Rypien, Washington, 1990
  Steve Young, San Francisco, 1993
  Jim Harbaugh, Indianapolis, 1996
  Vinny Testaverde, N.Y. Jets, 1999
  Jeff Garcia, San Francisco, 2003
  Peyton Manning, Indianapolis, 2006
Most Attempts, Without Interception, Game
27 Joe Theismann, Washington, 1984
   Phil Simms, N.Y. Giants, 1986
26 John Brodie, San Francisco, 1971
   Danny White, Dallas, 1983
23 Dave Krieg, Seattle, 1990

PERCENTAGE, PASSES HAD INTERCEPTED
Lowest Percentage, Passes Had Intercepted, Career
(40 attempts)
0.00 Joe Theismann, Washington, 1983-84 (45-0)
1.89 Rich Gannon, Oakland, 2000-03 (53-1)
2.13 Dave Krieg, Seattle, 1985, 1989-1990 (47-1)

PASS RECEIVING
RECEPTIONS
Most Receptions, Career
37 Jerry Rice, San Francisco, 1987-88, 1990-94, 1996,
   1999; Oakland, 2003
30 Marvin Harrison, Indianapolis, 2000-06
27 Cris Carter, Minnesota, 1994-2001
Most Receptions, Game
9 Randy Moss, Minnesota, 2000

8 Steve Largent, Seattle, 1986
  Michael Irvin, Dallas, 1992
  Andre Rison, Atlanta, 1993
  Jimmy Smith, Jacksonville, 2000
  Marvin Harrison, Indianapolis, 2001
  Terrell Owens, San Francisco, 2002
  Steve Smith, Carolina, 2006
7 John Stallworth, Pittsburgh, 1983
  Jerry Rice, San Francisco, 1992
  Isaac Bruce, St. Louis, 1997
  Keyshawn Johnson, N.Y. Jets, 1999
  Randy Moss, Minnesota, 1999
  Warrick Dunn, Tampa Bay, 2001
  Torry Holt, St. Louis, 2001
  Torry Holt, St. Louis, 2004

YARDS GAINED
Most Yards Gained, Career
495 Jerry Rice, San Francisco, 1987-88, 1990-94, 1996,
    1999; Oakland, 2003
462 Marvin Harrison, Indianapolis, 2000-06
408 Tim Brown, L.A. Raiders, 1989, 1992, 1994-95;
    Oakland, 1996-98, 2002
Most Yards Gained, Game
212 Randy Moss, Minnesota, 2000
156 Chad Johnson, Cincinnati, 2004
137 Tim Brown, Oakland, 1997
Longest Reception
93 Yancey Thigpen, Pittsburgh (from Blake, Cincinnati),
   1996 (TD)
90 Chad Johnson, Cincinnati (from McNair, Tennessee),
   2004 (TD)
80 Tim Brown, Oakland (from Brunell, Jacksonville),
   1997 (TD)

TOUCHDOWNS
Most Touchdowns, Career
5 Jimmy Smith, Jacksonville, 1998-2001
  Marvin Harrison, Indianapolis, 2000-06
4 Tony Gonzalez, Kansas City, 2000-01, 2003-06
3 Cris Carter, Minnesota, 1994-2001
  Torry Holt, St. Louis, 2001-02, 2004-06
  Hines Ward, Pittsburgh, 2002-05
Most Touchdowns, Game
3 Jimmy Smith, Jacksonville, 2000
2 William Andrews, Atlanta, 1984
  Eric Green, Pittsburgh, 1995
  Marvin Harrison, Indianapolis, 2001

INTERCEPTIONS BY
Most Interceptions By, Career
4 Everson Walls, Dallas, 1982-84, 1986
  Deion Sanders, Atlanta, 1992-94; San Francisco,
  1995; Dallas, 1999
  Champ Bailey, Washington, 2001-04; Denver,
  2005-06
3 Ken Houston, Houston, 1971-73; Washington,
  1974-79
  Jack Lambert, Pittsburgh, 1976-1984
  Ted Hendricks, Baltimore, 1972-74; Green Bay, 1975;
  Oakland, 1981-82; L.A. Raiders, 1983-84
  Mike Haynes, New England, 1978-1981, 1983;
  L.A. Raiders, 1985-87
  Ty Law, New England, 1999, 2002-04;
  N.Y. Jets, 2006
2 By 18 players
Most Interceptions By, Game
2 Mel Blount, Pittsburgh, 1977
  Everson Walls, Dallas, 1982, 1983
  LeRoy Irvin, L.A. Rams, 1986

David Fulcher, Cincinnati, 1990
Brian Dawkins, Philadelphia, 2000
Rod Woodson, Oakland, 2003

YARDS GAINED
Most Yards Gained, Career
147   Ty Law, New England, 1999, 2002-04;
      N.Y. Jets, 2006
103   Deion Sanders, Atlanta, 1992-94; San Francisco,
      1995; Dallas, 1999
 88   Rod Woodson, Pittsburgh, 1990-95, 1997;
      Baltimore, 2000-02; Oakland, 2003
Most Yards Gained, Game
 87   Deion Sanders, Dallas, 1999
 73   Rod Woodson, Pittsburgh, 1994
 67   Ty Law, New England, 1999
Longest Gain
 87   Deion Sanders, Dallas, 1999
 73   Rod Woodson, Pittsburgh, 1994 (lateral)
 67   Ty Law, New England, 1999 (TD)

TOUCHDOWNS
Most Touchdowns, Career
 2   Ty Law, New England, 1999, 2002-04;
      N.Y. Jets, 2006
      Derrick Brooks, Tampa Bay, 1998-2001, 2003, 2006
 1   By many
Most Touchdowns, Game
 1   Bobby Bell, Kansas City, 1973
      Nolan Cromwell, L.A. Rams, 1984
      Joey Browner, Minnesota, 1986
      Jerry Gray, L.A. Rams, 1990
      Mike Johnson, Cleveland, 1990
      Junior Seau, San Diego, 1993
      Ken Harvey, Washington, 1996
      Ashley Ambrose, Cincinnati, 1997
      Ty Law, New England, 1999
      Derrick Brooks, Tampa Bay, 2000
      Aeneas Williams, Arizona, 2000
      Ray Lewis, Baltimore, 2002
      Ty Law, New England, 2003
      Dre' Bly, Detroit, 2004
      Derrick Brooks, Tampa Bay, 2006

PUNTING
Most Punts, Career
33   Ray Guy, Oakland, 1974-79, 1981
23   Rohn Stark, Indianapolis, 1986-87, 1991, 1993
22   Reggie Roby, Miami, 1985, 1990; Washington, 1995
Most Punts, Game
10   Reggie Roby, Miami, 1985
 9   Tom Wittum, San Francisco, 1974
      Rohn Stark, Indianapolis, 1987
 8   Jerrel Wilson, Kansas City, 1971
      Tom Skladany, Detroit, 1982
      Reggie Roby, Washington, 1995
Longest Punt
73   Shane Lechler, Oakland, 2002
70   Shane Lechler, Oakland, 2002
64   Tom Wittum, San Francisco, 1974
      Darren Bennett, San Diego, 1996

AVERAGE YARDAGE
Highest Average, Career (10 punts)
46.73   Reggie Roby, Miami, 1985, 1990; Washington, 1995
      (22-1,028)
45.27   Matt Turk, Washington, 1997-99 (15-679)
45.25   Jerrel Wilson, Kansas City, 1971-73 (16-724)
Highest Average, Game (4 punts)
60.75   Shane Lechler, Oakland, 2002 (4-243)

55.50   Darren Bennett, San Diego, 1996 (4-222)
52.00   Matt Turk, Washington, 1999 (4-208)

PUNT RETURNS
Most Punt Returns, Career
13   Rick Upchurch, Denver, 1977, 1979-1980, 1983
11   Vai Sikahema, St. Louis, 1987-88
      Eric Metcalf, Cleveland 1994-95; San Diego 1998
10   Mike Nelms, Washington, 1981-83
Most Punt Returns, Game
 7   Vai Sikahema, St. Louis, 1987
 6   Henry Ellard, L.A. Rams, 1985
      Gerald McNeil, Cleveland, 1988
      Eric Metcalf, Cleveland, 1995
 5   Rick Upchurch, Denver, 1980
      Mike Nelms, Washington, 1981
      Carl Roaches, Houston, 1982
      Johnny Bailey, Phoenix, 1993
Most Fair Catches, Game
 2   Jerry Logan, Baltimore, 1971
      Dick Anderson, Miami, 1974
      Henry Ellard, L.A. Rams, 1985
      Isaac Bruce, St. Louis, 1997
      Desmond Howard, Detroit, 2001

YARDS GAINED
Most Yards Gained, Career
183   Billy Johnson, Houston, 1976, 1978; Atlanta, 1984
138   Mel Renfro, Dallas, 1971-72, 1974
      Rick Upchurch, Denver, 1977, 1979-1980, 1983
135   Eric Metcalf, Cleveland, 1994-95; San Diego 1998
Most Yards Gained, Game
159   Billy Johnson, Houston, 1976
138   Mel Renfro, Dallas, 1971
117   Wally Henry, Philadelphia, 1980
Longest Punt Return
90   Billy Johnson, Houston, 1976 (TD)
86   Wally Henry, Philadelphia, 1980 (TD)
82   Mel Renfro, Dallas, 1971 (TD)

AVERAGE YARDAGE
Highest Average, Career (4 returns)
22.88   Billy Johnson, Houston, 1976, 1978; Atlanta, 1984
      (8-183)
21.50   Tony Green, Washington, 1979 (4-86)
15.67   David Meggett, N.Y. Giants, 1990; New England, 1997
Highest Average, Game (3 returns)
39.75   Billy Johnson, Houston, 1976 (4-159)
39.00   Wally Henry, Philadelphia, 1980 (3-117)
21.50   Tony Green, Washington, 1979 (4-86)

TOUCHDOWNS
Most Touchdowns, Game
 2   Mel Renfro, Dallas, 1971
 1   Billy Johnson, Houston, 1976
      Wally Henry, Philadelphia, 1980

KICKOFF RETURNS
Most Kickoff Returns, Career
17   Michael Bates, Carolina, 1997-2001
14   Mel Gray, Detroit, 1991-92, 1995
11   Eric Metcalf, Cleveland, 1994-95; San Diego, 1998
      Derrick Mason, Tennessee, 2001, 2004
Most Kickoff Returns, Game
 8   Derrick Mason, Tennessee, 2004
 7   Mel Gray, Detroit, 1995
      Jerry Azumah, Chicago, 2004
 6   Greg Pruitt, L.A. Raiders, 1984
      David Meggett, New England, 1997
      Michael Bates, Carolina, 1998

Steve Smith, Carolina, 2002

YARDS GAINED
Most Yards Gained, Career
- 488 Michael Bates, Carolina, 1997-2001
- 309 Greg Pruitt, Cleveland, 1974-75, 1977-78;
       L.A. Raiders, 1984
- 294 Mel Gray, Detroit, 1991-92, 1995

Most Yards Gained, Game
- 228 Jerry Azumah, Chicago, 2004
- 217 Michael Lewis, New Orleans, 2003
- 192 Greg Pruitt, L.A. Raiders, 1984

Longest Kickoff Return
- 66 Michael Bates, Carolina, 2000
- 62 Greg Pruitt, L.A. Raiders, 1984
- 61 Eugene (Mercury) Morris, Miami, 1972

AVERAGE YARDAGE
Highest Average, Career (4 returns)
- 43.40 Michael Lewis, New Orleans, 2003 (5-217)
- 35.00 Les (Speedy) Duncan, Washington, 1972 (5-175)
- 32.57 Jerry Azumah, Chicago, 2004 (7-228)

Highest Average, Game (3 returns)
- 43.40 Michael Lewis, New Orleans, 2003 (5-217)
- 42.00 Michael Bates, Carolina, 2000 (4-168)
- 35.00 Les (Speedy) Duncan, Washington, 1972 (5-175)

TOUCHDOWNS
Most Touchdowns, Game
- 1 Hines Ward, Pittsburgh, 2005

FUMBLES
Most Fumbles, Career
- 6 Dan Fouts, San Diego, 1980-84, 1986
- 4 Lawrence McCutcheon, Los Angeles, 1974-78
     Franco Harris, Pittsburgh, 1973-76, 1978-1981
     Jay Schroeder, Washington, 1987
     Vai Sikahema, St. Louis, 1987-88
     Trent Green, Kansas City, 2004, 2006
- 3 O.J. Simpson, Buffalo, 1973-77
     William Andrews, Atlanta, 1981-84
     Joe Montana, San Francisco, 1982, 1984-85, 1988
     Walter Payton, Chicago, 1977-1981, 1984-87
     Neil Lomax, St. Louis, 1985, 1988
     Jim Kelly, Buffalo, 1988, 1991-92
     Chris Chandler, Atlanta, 1998-99
     Peyton Manning, Indianapolis, 2000-01, 2003-06

Most Fumbles, Game
- 4 Jay Schroeder, Washington, 1987
     Trent Green, Kansas City, 2004
- 3 Dan Fouts, San Diego, 1982
     Vai Sikahema, St. Louis, 1987
- 2 By 15 players

RECOVERIES
Most Fumbles Recovered, Career
- 3 Harold Jackson, Philadelphia, 1973; Los Angeles,
     1974, 1976, 1978 (3-own)
     Dan Fouts, San Diego, 1980-84, 1986 (3-own)
     Randy White, Dallas, 1978, 1980-86 (3-opp)
     Trent Green, Kansas City, 2004, 2006 (3-own)
- 2 By many players

Most Fumbles Recovered, Game
- 3 Trent Green, Kansas City, 2004 (3-own)
- 2 Dick Anderson, Miami, 1974 (1-own, 1-opp)
     Harold Jackson, Los Angeles, 1974 (2-own)
     Dan Fouts, San Diego, 1982 (2-own)
     Joey Browner, Minnesota, 1990 (2-opp)
     Jessie Armstead, N.Y. Giants, 1999 (1-own, 1-opp)8

Steve Beuerlein, Carolina, 2000 (2-own)

YARDAGE
Longest Fumble Return
- 83 Art Still, Kansas City, 1985 (TD, opp)
- 51 Phil Villapiano, Oakland, 1974 (opp)
- 37 Sam Mills, New Orleans, 1988 (opp)

TOUCHDOWNS
Most Touchdowns, Game
- 1 Art Still, Kansas City, 1985
     Keith Millard, Minnesota, 1990

SACKS
Sacks have been compiled since 1983.
Most Sacks, Career
- 9.5 Reggie White, Philadelphia, 1987-1993; Green Bay,
       1994, 1996-97, 1999
- 9.0 Howie Long, L.A. Raiders, 1984-88, 1990, 1993-1994
- 7.5 Bruce Smith, Buffalo, 1988-1991, 1995-96, 1998-99

Most Sacks, Game
- 4 Mark Gastineau, N.Y. Jets, 1985
     Reggie White, Philadelphia, 1987
- 3 Richard Dent, Chicago, 1985
     Bruce Smith, Buffalo, 1991
- 2.5 Bruce Smith, Buffalo, 1998

TEAM RECORDS

SCORING
Most Points, Game
- 55 NFC, 2004

Fewest Points, Game
- 3 AFC, 1984, 1989, 1994

Most Points, Both Teams, Game
- 107 NFC (55) vs. AFC (52), 2004

Fewest Points, Both Teams, Game
- 16 NFC (6) vs. AFC (10), 1987

TOUCHDOWNS
Most Touchdowns, Game
- 7 AFC, 2004
    NFC, 2004

Fewest Touchdowns, Game
- 0 AFC, 1971, 1974, 1984, 1989, 1994
    NFC, 1987, 1988

Most Touchdowns, Both Teams, Game
- 14 AFC (7) vs. NFC (7), 2004

Fewest Touchdowns, Both Teams, Game
- 1 AFC (0) vs. NFC (1), 1974
    NFC (0) vs. AFC (1), 1987
    NFC (0) vs. AFC (1), 1988

POINTS AFTER TOUCHDOWN
Most Points After Touchdown, Game
- 7 AFC, 2004

Most Points After Touchdown, Both Teams, Game
- 12 AFC (7) vs. NFC (5), 2004

FIELD GOALS
Most Field Goals Attempted, Game
- 6 AFC, 1972
    NFC, 1981, 1983

Most Field Goals Attempted, Both Teams, Game
- 9 NFC (6) vs. AFC (3), 1983

Most Field Goals, Game
- 5 AFC, 1974

Most Field Goals, Both Teams, Game
- 7 AFC (5) vs. NFC (2), 1974

NET YARDS GAINED RUSHING AND PASSING
Most Yards Gained, Game
626   AFC, 2004
Fewest Yards Gained, Game
114   AFC, 1993
Most Yards Gained, Both Teams, Game
1,022   AFC (626) vs. NFC (396), 2004
Fewest Yards Gained, Both Teams, Game
424   AFC (202) vs. NFC (222), 1987

RUSHING
ATTEMPTS
Most Attempts, Game
50   AFC, 1974
Fewest Attempts, Game
9   NFC, 2001
Most Attempts, Both Teams, Game
80   AFC (50) vs. NFC (30), 1974
Fewest Attempts, Both Teams, Game
32   NFC (9) vs. AFC (23), 2001

YARDS GAINED
Most Yards Gained, Game
400   AFC, 1995
Fewest Yards Gained, Game
28   NFC, 1992
Most Yards Gained, Both Teams, Game
441   AFC (400) vs. NFC (41), 1995
Fewest Yards Gained, Both Teams, Game
119   NFC (36) vs. AFC (83), 2001

TOUCHDOWNS
Most Touchdowns, Game
3   NFC, 1989, 1991, 2000
AFC, 1995
Most Touchdowns, Both Teams, Game
4   AFC (2) vs. NFC (2), 1973
AFC (2) vs. NFC (2), 1980

PASSING
ATTEMPTS
Most Attempts, Game
58   NFC, 2002
Fewest Attempts, Game
17   NFC, 1972
Most Attempts, Both Teams, Game
101   NFC (54) vs. AFC (47), 2003
Fewest Attempts, Both Teams, Game
42   NFC (17) vs. AFC (25), 1972

COMPLETIONS
Most Completions, Game
32   NFC, 1993
AFC, 2001
Fewest Completions, Game
7   NFC, 1972, 1982
Most Completions, Both Teams, Game
60   AFC (32) vs. NFC (28), 2001
Fewest Completions, Both Teams, Game
18   NFC (7) vs. AFC (11), 1972

YARDS GAINED
Most Yards Gained, Game
515   AFC, 2004
Fewest Yards Gained, Game
42   NFC, 1982
Most Yards Gained, Both Teams, Game
775   AFC (515) vs. NFC (260), 2004

Fewest Yards Gained, Both Teams, Game
215   NFC (89) vs. AFC (126), 1972

TIMES SACKED
Most Times Sacked, Game
9   NFC, 1985
Fewest Times Sacked, Game
0   AFC, 1998, 1999, 2000, 2003
NFC, 1971, 1997, 2001
Most Times Sacked, Both Teams, Game
17   NFC (9) vs. AFC (8), 1985
Fewest Times Sacked, Both Teams, Game
1   NFC (0) vs. AFC (1), 1997

TOUCHDOWNS
Most Touchdowns, Game
5   AFC, 2004
Most Touchdowns, Both Teams, Game
9   AFC (5) vs. NFC (4), 2004

INTERCEPTIONS BY
Most Interceptions By, Game
6   AFC, 1977, 2003
Most Interceptions By, Both Teams, Game
8   AFC (6) vs. NFC (2), 2003

YARDS GAINED
Most Yards Gained, Game
192   NFC, 2006
Most Yards Gained, Both Teams, Game
265   NFC (192) vs. AFC (73), 2006

TOUCHDOWNS
Most Touchdowns, Game
2   NFC, 2000

PUNTING
Most Punts, Game
10   AFC, 1985
Fewest Punts, Game
0   NFC, 1989
Most Punts, Both Teams, Game
16   AFC (10) vs. NFC (6), 1985
Fewest Punts, Both Teams, Game
3   NFC (1) vs. AFC (2), 2005

PUNT RETURNS
Most Punt Returns, Game
7   NFC, 1985, 1987
AFC, 1995
Fewest Punt Returns, Game
0   AFC, 1984, 1989
NFC, 2005
Most Punt Returns, Both Teams, Game
11   NFC (7) vs. AFC (4), 1985
Fewest Punt Returns, Both Teams, Game
1   NFC (0) vs. AFC (1), 2005

YARDS GAINED
Most Yards Gained, Game
177   AFC, 1976
Fewest Yards Gained, Game
−1   NFC, 1991
Most Yards Gained, Both Teams, Game
263   AFC (177) vs. NFC (86), 1976
Fewest Yards Gained, Both Teams, Game
7   NFC (0) vs. AFC (7), 2005

TOUCHDOWNS
Most Touchdowns, Game
   2 NFC, 1971

KICKOFF RETURNS
Most Kickoff Returns, Game
   10 AFC, 2004
Fewest Kickoff Returns, Game
   1 NFC, 1971, 1984, 1994
      AFC, 1988, 1991
Most Kickoff Returns, Both Teams, Game
   18 AFC (10) vs. NFC (8), 2004
Fewest Kickoff Returns, Both Teams, Game
   5 NFC (2) vs. AFC (3), 1979
     AFC (1) vs. NFC (4), 1988
     NFC (2) vs. AFC (3), 1992
     NFC (1) vs. AFC (4), 1994

YARDS GAINED
Most Yards Gained, Game
   247 NFC, 2004
Fewest Yards Gained, Game
   6 NFC, 1971
Most Yards Gained, Both Teams, Game
   461 NFC (247) vs. AFC (214), 2004
Fewest Yards Gained, Both Teams, Game
   99 NFC (48) vs. AFC (51), 1987

TOUCHDOWNS
Most Touchdowns, Game
   1 AFC, 2005

FUMBLES
Most Fumbles, Game
   10 NFC, 1974
Most Fumbles, Both Teams, Game
   15 NFC (10) vs. AFC (5), 1974

RECOVERIES
Most Fumbles Recovered, Game
   10 NFC, 1974 (6 own, 4 opp)
Most Fumbles Lost, Game
   4 AFC, 1974, 1988
     NFC, 1974

YARDS GAINED
Most Yards Gained, Game
   87 AFC, 1985

TOUCHDOWNS
Most Touchdowns, Game
   1 AFC, 1985
     NFC, 1990

TURNOVERS
(Number of times losing the ball on interceptions and fumbles.)
Most Turnovers, Game
   8 AFC, 1974
Fewest Turnovers, Game
   0 AFC, 1991, 1997
     NFC, 1991, 1995, 1996, 2001
Most Turnovers, Both Teams, Game
   12 AFC (8) vs. NFC (4), 1974
Fewest Turnovers, Both Teams, Game
   0 AFC vs. NFC, 1991

Rules

2006 NFL ROSTER OF OFFICIALS

Mike Pereira, Vice President of Officiating
Larry Upson, Director of Officiating Operations
Jim Daopoulos, Supervisor of Officials

Ron Baynes, Supervisor of Officials
Neely Dunn, Supervisor of Officials
Johnny Grier, Supervisor of Officials

No.	Name	Position	College
66	Anderson, Walt	Referee	Texas
108	Arthur, Gary	Line Judge	Wright State
34	Austin, Gerald	Referee	Western Carolina
26	Baltz, Mark	Head Linesman	Ohio University
72	Banks, Michael	Side Judge	Illinois State
55	Barnes, Tom	Line Judge	Minnesota
32	Bergman, Jeff	Line Judge	Robert Morris
91	Bergman, Jerry	Head Linesman	Robert Morris
7	Blum, Ron	Line Judge	Marin College
109	Boger, Jerome	Referee	Morehouse College
18	Boston, Byron	Line Judge	Austin
74	Bowers, Derick	Line Judge	Oklahoma
31	Brown, Chad	Umpire	East Texas State
134	Camp, Ed	Head Linesman	William Paterson
126	Carey, Don	Back Judge	UC Riverside
94	Carey, Mike	Referee	Santa Clara
39	Carlsen, Don	Side Judge	Cal State-Chico
63	Carollo, Bill	Referee	Wisconsin-Milwaukee
11	Carroll, Duke	Field Judge	Ithaca
60	Cavaletto, Gary	Field Judge	Hancock
41	Cheek, Boris	Field Judge	Morgan State
51	Cheffers, Carl	Side Judge	UC Irvine
95	Coleman, James	Side Judge	Arkansas
65	Coleman, Walt	Referee	Arkansas
99	Corrente, Tony	Referee	Cal State-Fullerton
71	Coukart, Ed	Umpire	Northwestern
70	Dawson, Scott	Umpire	Virginia Tech
53	DeFelice, Garth	Umpire	San Diego State
113	Dorkowski, Don	Back Judge	Cal State-Los Angeles
6	Dornan, Kirk	Back Judge	Central Washington
27	Dyer, Lee	Field Judge	Tennessee-Chattanooga
3	Edwards, Scott	Field Judge	Alabama
81	Ellison, Roy	Umpire	Savannah State
61	Ferguson, Keith	Back Judge	San Jose State
64	Ferrell, Dan	Umpire	Cal State-Fullerton
47	Fincken, Tom	Side Judge	Kansas State
133	Freeman, Steve	Back Judge	Mississippi State
80	Gautreaux, Greg	Field Judge	Southwestern Louisiana
19	Green, Scott	Referee	Delaware
49	Hall, Rich	Umpire	Arizona
40	Hannah, Butch	Umpire	Middle Tennessee State
125	Hayes, Laird	Side Judge	Princeton
54	Hayward, George	Head Linesman	Missouri Western
93	Helverson, Scott	Back Judge	Iowa
97	Hill, Tom	Side Judge	Carson-Newman
28	Hittner, Mark	Head Linesman	Pittsburg State
85	Hochuli, Ed	Referee	Texas-El Paso
82	Horton, Buddy	Field Judge	Oregon State
37	Howey, Jim	Back Judge	Erskine College
35	Hussey, John	Line Judge	Idaho State
76	Jenkins, Darrell	Umpire	San Jose State
101	Johnson, Carl	Line Judge	Nicholls State
103	Lamberth, Jeff	Side Judge	Texas A&M
73	Larrew, Joe	Side Judge	St. Louis University
17	Lawing, Bob	Back Judge	North Carolina State
127	Leavy, Bill	Referee	San Jose State
130	Lewis, Darryll	Line Judge	Dartmouth
98	Lovett, Bill	Field Judge	Maryland

No.	Name	Position	College
92	Madsen, Carl	Umpire	Washington
107	Marinucci, Ron	Head Linesman	Glassboro State
77	McAulay, Terry	Referee	Louisiana State
120	McGrath, John	Head Linesman	Kentucky
110	McKinnely, Phil	Head Linesman	UCLA
48	Mello, Jim	Head Linesman	Northeastern
78	Meyer, Greg	Side Judge	TCU
115	Michalek, Tony	Umpire	Indiana
135	Morelli, Pete	Referee	St. Mary's College
20	Nemmers, Larry	Referee	Upper Iowa
124	Paganelli, Carl	Umpire	Michigan State
46	Paganelli, Perry	Back Judge	Hope College
132	Parry, John	Side Judge	Purdue
15	Patterson, Rick	Side Judge	Wofford
79	Payne, Kent	Head Linesman	Nebraska-Wesleyan
9	Perlman, Mark	Line Judge	Salem
10	Phares, Ron	Head Linesman	Virginia Tech
38	Powers, Eddy	Field Judge	Tennessee
5	Quirk, Jim	Umpire	Delaware
83	Reels, Richard	Back Judge	Chicago State
44	Rice, Jeff	Umpire	Northwestern
57	Riveron, Alberto	Side Judge	Miami
128	Rose, Larry	Side Judge	Florida
67	Rosenbaum, Doug	Field Judge	Illinois Wesleyan
58	Saracino, Jim	Field Judge	Northern Colorado
21	Schleyer, John	Head Linesman	Millersville
122	Schmitz, Bill	Back Judge	Colorado State
129	Schuster, Blll	Umpire	Alfred
45	Seeman, Jeff	Line Judge	Minnesota
118	Sifferman, Tom	Field Judge	Seattle
30	Slaughter, Gary	Head Linesman	East Texas State
2	Smith, Billy	Back Judge	East Carolina
90	Spanier, Michael	Line Judge	St. Cloud State
8	Spyksma, Bill	Line Judge	South Dakota
24	Stabile, Tom	Head Linesman	Slippery Rock
12	Steed, Greg	Back Judge	Howard
88	Steenson, Scott	Field Judge	North Texas
84	Steinkerchner, Mark	Line Judge	Akron
22	Stelljes, Steve	Head Linesman	Friends University
68	Stephan, Tom	Line Judge	Pittsburg State
114	Steratore, Gene	Referee	Kent State
112	Steratore, Tony	Back Judge	California (Penn.)
62	Stewart, Charles	Line Judge	Long Beach State
4	Toole, Doug	Side Judge	Utah State
42	Triplette, Jeff	Referee	Wake Forest
75	Vernatchi, Rob	Side Judge	UC Riverside
36	Veteri, Tony	Head Linesman	Manhattan College
52	Vinovich, Bill	Referee	San Diego
25	Waggoner, Bob	Back Judge	Juniata College
96	Wash, Undrey	Umpire	Texas-Arlington
116	Weatherford, Mike	Side Judge	Oklahoma State
87	Weidner, Paul	Head Linesman	Cincinnati
50	Weir, Mike	Field Judge	Missouri
29	Wilson, Steve	Umpire	Whitworth College
14	Winter, Ron	Referee	Michigan State
89	Wrolstad, Craig	Field Judge	Washington
16	Wyant, David	Side Judge	Virginia
33	Zimmer, Steve	Field Judge	Hofstra

Roster as of May 2006

NUMERICAL ROSTER

No.	Name	Position
2	Billy Smith	BJ
3	Scott Edwards	FJ
4	Doug Toole	SJ
5	Jim Quirk	U
6	Kirk Dornan	BJ
7	Ron Blum	LJ
8	Bill Spyksma	LJ
9	Mark Perlman	LJ
10	Ron Phares	HL
11	Duke Carroll	FJ
12	Greg Steed	BJ
14	Ron Winter	R
15	Rick Patterson	SJ
16	David Wyant	SJ
17	Bob Lawing	BJ
18	Byron Boston	LJ
19	Scott Green	R
20	Larry Nemmers	R
21	John Schleyer	HL
22	Steve Stelljes	HL
24	Tom Stabile	HL
25	Bob Waggoner	BJ
26	Mark Baltz	HL
27	Lee Dyer	FJ
28	Mark Hittner	HL
29	Steve Wilson	U
30	Gary Slaughter	HL
31	Chad Brown	U
32	Jeff Bergman	LJ
33	Steve Zimmer	FJ
34	Gerry Austin	R
35	John Hussey	LJ
36	Tony Veteri	HL
37	Jim Howey	BJ
38	Eddy Powers	FJ
39	Don Carlsen	SJ
40	Butch Hannah	U
41	Boris Cheek	FJ
42	Jeff Triplette	R
44	Jeff Rice	U
45	Jeff Seeman	LJ
46	Perry Paganelli	BJ
47	Tom Fincken	SJ
48	Jim Mello	HL
49	Rich Hall	U
50	Mike Weir	FJ
51	Carl Cheffers	SJ
52	Bill Vinovich	R
53	Garth DeFelice	U
54	George Hayward	HL
55	Tom Barnes	LJ
57	Alberto Riveron	SJ
58	Jim Saracino	FJ
60	Gary Cavaletto	FJ
61	Keith Ferguson	BJ
62	Charles Stewart	LJ
63	Bill Carollo	R
64	Dan Ferrell	U
65	Walt Coleman	R
66	Walt Anderson	R
67	Doug Rosenbaum	FJ
68	Tom Stephan	LJ
70	Scott Dawson	U
71	Ed Coukart	U
72	Michael Banks	SJ
73	Joe Larrew	SJ
74	Derick Bowers	LJ
75	Rob Vernatchi	SJ
76	Darrell Jenkins	U
77	Terry McAulay	R
78	Greg Meyer	SJ
79	Kent Payne	HL
80	Greg Gautreaux	FJ
81	Roy Ellison	U
82	Buddy Horton	FJ
83	Richard Reels	BJ
84	Mark Steinkerchner	LJ
85	Ed Hochuli	R
87	Paul Weidner	HL
88	Scott Steenson	FJ
89	Craig Wrolstad	FJ
90	Michael Spanier	LJ
91	Jerry Bergman	HL
92	Carl Madsen	U
93	Scott Helverson	BJ
94	Mike Carey	R
95	James Coleman	SJ
96	Undrey Wash	U
97	Tom Hill	SJ
98	Bill Lovett	FJ
99	Tony Corrente	R
101	Carl Johnson	LJ
103	Jeff Lamberth	SJ
107	Ron Marinucci	HL
108	Gary Arthur	LJ
109	Jerome Boger	R
110	Phil McKinnely	HL
112	Tony Steratore	BJ
113	Don Dorkowski	BJ
114	Gene Steratore	R
115	Tony Michalek	BJ
116	Mike Weatherford	SJ
118	Tom Sifferman	FJ
120	John McGrath	HL
122	Bill Schmitz	BJ
124	Carl Paganelli	U
125	Laird Hayes	SJ
126	Don Carey	BJ
127	Bill Leavy	R
128	Larry Rose	SJ
129	Bill Schuster	U
130	Darryll Lewis	LJ
132	John Parry	SJ
133	Steve Freeman	BJ
134	Ed Camp	HL
135	Pete Morelli	R

Roster as of May 2006

OFFICIALS

2006 OFFICIALS AT A GLANCE
REFEREES
Walt Anderson, No. **66,** Texas, college officiating coordinator, 11th year.

Gerry Austin, No. **34,** Western Carolina, president, leadership development group, 25th year.

Jerome Boger, No. **109,** Morehouse College, commercial insurance underwriter, 3rd year.

Mike Carey, No. **94,** Santa Clara, owner, skiing accessories, 17th year.

Bill Carollo, No. **63,** Wisconsin-Milwaukee, marketing executive, 18th year.

Walt Coleman, No. **65,** Arkansas, manager, dairy processor, 18th year.

Tony Corrente, No. **99,** Cal State-Fullerton, educator, 12th year.

Scott Green, No. **19,** Delaware, vice-president, government relations, 16th year.

Ed Hochuli, No. **85,** Texas-El Paso, attorney, 17th year.

Bill Leavy, No. **127,** San Jose State, retired firefighter, 12th year.

Terry McAulay, No. **77,** Louisiana State, senior computer scientist, 9th year.

Pete Morelli, No. **135,** St. Mary's, high school principal, 10th year.

Larry Nemmers, No. **20,** Upper Iowa, motivational speaker, 22nd year.

Gene Steratore, No. **114,** Kent State, co-owner, supply company, 4th year.

Jeff Triplette, No. **42,** Wake Forest, vice president, world-wide energy company, 11th year.

Bill Vinovich, No. **52,** San Diego, certified public accountant, 6th year.

Ron Winter, No. **14,** Michigan State, university professor, 12th year.

UMPIRES
Chad Brown, No. **31,** East Texas State, manager, intramural/sports clubs, 15th year.

Ed Coukart, No. **71,** Northwestern, vice-president, commercial bank, 18th year.

Scott Dawson, No. **70,** Virginia Tech, president/owner, commercial construction company, 12th year.

Garth DeFelice, No. **53,** San Diego State, director of distributing, beverage company, 9th year.

Roy Ellison, No. **81,** Savannah State, technical staff member, 4th year.

Dan Ferrell, No. **64,** Cal State-Fullerton, regional manager, parts distribution and logistics, 4th year.

Rich Hall, No. **49,** Arizona, custom cabinetry, 3rd year.

Butch Hannah, No. **40,** Middle Tennessee State, federal probation officer, 8th year.

Darrell Jenkins, No. **76,** San Jose State, retired, 5th year.

Carl Madsen, No. **92,** Washington, partner/owner, office furniture dealership, 10th year.

Tony Michalek, No. **115,** Indiana, eurodollar future trader, 5th year.

Carl Paganelli, No. **124,** Michigan State, federal probation officer, 8th year.

Jim Quirk, No. **5,** Delaware, consultant, 19th year.

Jeff Rice, No. **44,** Northwestern, attorney, 12th year.

Bill Schuster, No. **129,** Alfred, insurance broker, 7th year.

Undrey Wash, No. **96,** Texas-Arlington, claims manager, 7th year.

Steve Wilson, No. **29,** Whitworth College, pastor, 8th year.

HEAD LINESMEN
Mark Baltz, No. **26,** Ohio University, sales consultant, 18th year.

Jerry Bergman, No. **91,** Robert Morris, sales executive, 5th year.

Ed Camp, No. **134,** William Paterson, teacher, 7th year.

George Hayward, No. **54,** Missouri Western, vice-president and manager, warehouse company, 16th year.

Mark Hittner, No. **28,** Pittsburg State, investment banker, 10th year.

Ron Marinucci, No. **107,** Glassboro State, novelty cone company, 9th year.

John McGrath, No. **120,** Kentucky, senior account executive, 5th year.

Phil McKinnely, No. **110,** UCLA, inventory control, former NFL player, 4th year.

Jim Mello, No. **48,** Northeastern, facilities management, 3rd year.

Kent Payne, No. **79,** Nebraksa-Wesleyan, 3rd year.

Ron Phares, No. **10,** Virginia Tech, president, construction company, 22nd year.

John Schleyer, No. **21,** Millersville, medical sales, 17th year.

Gary Slaughter, No. **30,** East Texas State, general manager, 11th year.

Tom Stabile, No. **24,** Slippery Rock, secondary educational administrator, 12th year.

Steve Stelljes, No. **22,** Friends University, business planning manager, 5th year.

Tony Veteri, No. **36,** Manhattan, director of athletics, 15th year.

Paul Weidner, No. **87,** Cincinnati, marketing manager, 21st year.

LINE JUDGES
Gary Arthur, No. **108,** Wright State, president, commercial printing company, 10th year.

Tom Barnes, No. **55,** Minnesota, manufacturing representative, 21st year.

Jeff Bergman, No. **32,** Robert Morris, president and chief executive officer, medical services, 15th year.

Ron Blum, No. **7,** Marin College, professional golfer, 22nd year.

Byron Boston, No. **18,** Austin, tax consultant, 4th year.

Derick Bowers, No. **74,** East Central University, purchasing supervisor, 4th year.

John Hussey, No. **35,** Idaho State, sales representative, retail logistics group, 5th year.

Carl Johnson, No. **101,** Nicholls State, district sales manager, 6th year.

Darryll Lewis, No. **130,** Dartmouth, associate professor, 8th year.

Mark Perlman, No. **9,** Salem, teacher, 6th year.

Jeff Seeman, No. **45,** Minnesota, brokerage sales, 5th year.

Mike Spanier, No. **90,** St. Cloud State, middle school principal, 8th year.

Bill Spyksma, No. **8,** South Dakota, managing partner, marina, 12th year.

Mark Steinkerchner, No. **84,** Akron, vice-president, 13th year.

Tom Stephan, No. **68,** Pittsburg State, business broker, 8th year.

Charles Stewart, No. **62,** Long Beach State, retired human services administrator, 15th year.

Roster as of May 2006

FIELD JUDGES

Duke Carroll, No. **11,** Ithaca, insurance sales, 12th year.
Gary Cavaletto, No. **60,** Hancock, general manager, agricultural operations, 4th year.
Boris Cheek, No. **41,** Morgan State, director of operations and management, 11th year.
Lee Dyer, No. **27,** Tennessee-Chattanooga, sales manager, 4th year.
Scott Edwards, No. **3,** Alabama, environmental engineer, 8th year.
Greg Gautreaux, No. **80,** Southwestern Louisiana, athletic programs manager, 5th year.
Buddy Horton, No. **82,** Oregon State, water service worker, 8th year.
Bill Lovett, No. **98,** Maryland, managing partner, financial sales, 17th year.
Eddy Powers, No. **38,** Tennessee, sales/design office supply, 5th year.
Doug Rosenbaum, No. **67,** Illinois Wesleyan, financial advisor, 6th year.
Jim Saracino, No. **58,** Northern Colorado, secondary educator, 12th year.
Tom Sifferman, No. **118,** Seattle, manufacturer's representative, 21st year.
Scott Steenson, No. **88,** North Texas, commercial real estate broker, 16th year.
Mike Weir, No. **50,** Missouri, owner, sporting goods store, 5th year.
Craig Wrolstad, No. **89,** Washington, education, 4th year.
Steve Zimmer, No. **33,** Hofstra, attorney, 10th year.

SIDE JUDGES

Michael Banks, No. **72,** Illinois State, carpenter foreman, 5th year.
Don Carlsen, No. **39,** Cal State-Chico, retired county school superintendent, 18th year.
Carl Cheffers, No. **51,** UC Irvine, sales manager, 7th year.
James Coleman, No. **95,** Arkansas, 2nd year.
Tom Fincken, No. **47,** Emporia State, retired educational administrator, 23rd year.
Laird Hayes, No. **125,** Princeton, professor, physical education & athletics, 12th year.
Tom Hill, No. **97,** Carson Newman, teacher, 8th year.
Jeff Lamberth, No. **103,** Texas A&M, attorney, 5th year.
Joe Larrew, No. **73,** St. Louis University, attorney, 5th year.
Greg Meyer, No. **78,** TCU, banker, 5th year.
John Parry, No. **132,** Purdue, corporate pilot, 7th year.
Rick Patterson, No. **15,** Wofford, banker, 11th year.
Alberto Riveron, No. **57,** Miami, commercial restaurant equipment, 3rd year.
Larry Rose, No. **128,** Florida, financial planner, 10th year.
Doug Toole, No. **4,** Utah State, physical therapist, 19th year.
Rob Vernatchi, No. **75,** UC Riverside, enforcement investigator, 3rd year.
Mike Weatherford, No. **116,** Oklahoma State, energy trader, 5th year.
David Wyant, No. **16,** Virginia, consulting engineer, 16th year.

BACK JUDGES

Don Carey, No. **126,** UC Riverside, contract manager, 12th year.
Don Dorkowski, No. **113,** Cal State-Los Angeles, pump manufacturer, 21st year.
Kirk Dornan, No. **6,** Central Washington, purchasing manager, 13th year.
Keith Ferguson, No. **61,** San Jose State, sales, 7th year.
Steve Freeman, No. **133,** Mississippi State, custom home builder, 6th year.
Scott Helverson, No. **93,** Iowa, sales, printing and promotions, 4th year.
Jim Howey, No. **37,** Erskine College, director of adult education, 8th year.
Bob Lawing, No. **17,** North Carolina State, real estate management, 10th year.
Perry Paganelli, No. **46,** Hope College, high school administrator, 9th year.
Richard Reels, No. **83,** Chicago State, director of security, court services, 14th year.
Bill Schmitz, No. **122,** Colorado State, general sales manager, 18th year.
Billy Smith, No. **2,** East Carolina, federal government, 12th year.
Greg Steed, No. **12,** Howard, computer systems analyst, 4th year.
Tony Steratore, No. **112,** California (Penn.), co-owner, supply company, 7th year.
Bob Waggoner, No. **25,** Juniata College, probation officer, 10th year.

Roster as of May 2006

1

TOUCHDOWN, FIELD GOAL, or SUCCESSFUL TRY
Both arms extended above head.

2

SAFETY
Palms together above head.

3

FIRST DOWN
Arm pointed toward defensive team's goal.

4

CROWD NOISE, DEAD BALL, or NEUTRAL ZONE ESTABLISHED
One arm above head with an open hand.
With fist closed: **Fourth Down.**

5

BALL ILLEGALLY TOUCHED, KICKED, or BATTED
Fingertips tap both shoulders.

6

TIME OUT
Hands crisscrossed above head.
Same signal followed by placing one hand on top of cap: **Referee's Time Out.**
Same signal followed by arm swung at side: **Touchback.**

7

**NO TIME OUT or
TIME IN WITH WHISTLE**
Full arm circled to
simulate moving clock.

8

**DELAY OF GAME
or EXCESS TIME OUT**
Folded arms.

9

**FALSE START,
ILLEGAL FORMATION, or
KICKOFF or SAFETY KICK
OUT OF BOUNDS or
KICKING TEAM PLAYER
VOLUNTARILY OUT OF BOUNDS
DURING A PUNT**
Forearms rotated over and over
in front of body.

10

PERSONAL FOUL
One wrist striking the other above head.
Same signal followed by swinging leg:
Roughing the Kicker.
Same signal followed by raised arm
swinging forward:
Roughing the Passer.
Same signal followed by grasping
facemask: **Major Facemask.**

11

HOLDING
Grasping one wrist,
the fist clenched,
in front of chest.

12

**ILLEGAL USE OF HANDS,
ARMS, or BODY**
Grasping one wrist,
the hand open and facing
forward, in front of chest.

13

PENALTY REFUSED, INCOMPLETE PASS, PLAY OVER, or MISSED FIELD GOAL or EXTRA POINT
Hands shifted in horizontal plane.

14

PASS JUGGLED INBOUNDS AND CAUGHT OUT OF BOUNDS
Hands up and down in front of chest (following incomplete pass signal).

15

ILLEGAL FORWARD PASS
One hand waved behind back followed by loss of down signal (23), when appropriate.

16

INTENTIONAL GROUNDING OF PASS
Parallel arms waved in a diagonal plane across body. Followed by loss of down signal (23).

17

INTERFERENCE WITH FORWARD PASS or FAIR CATCH
Hands open and extended forward from shoulders with hands vertical.

18

INVALID FAIR-CATCH SIGNAL
One hand waved above head.

19

**INELIGIBLE RECEIVER
or INELIGIBLE
MEMBER OF KICKING TEAM
DOWNFIELD**
Right hand touching top of cap.

20

ILLEGAL CONTACT
One open hand extended forward.

21

**OFFSIDE, ENCROACHMENT, or
NEUTRAL ZONE INFRACTION**
Hands on hips.

22

ILLEGAL MOTION AT SNAP
Horizontal arc with one hand.

23

LOSS OF DOWN
Both hands held behind head.

24

**INTERLOCKING
INTERFERENCE, PUSHING, or
HELPING RUNNER**
Pushing movement of hands
to front with arms downward.

25

**TOUCHING A FORWARD
PASS or SCRIMMAGE KICK**
Diagonal motion of
one hand across another.

26

**UNSPORTSMANLIKE
CONDUCT**
Arms outstretched,
palms down.

27

ILLEGAL CUT
Hand striking front of thigh.
ILLEGAL BLOCK BELOW THE WAIST
One hand striking front of thigh
preceded by personal-foul signal (10).
CHOP BLOCK
Both hands striking side of thighs
preceded by personal-foul signal (10).
CLIPPING
One hand striking back of calf
preceded by personal-foul signal (10).

28

ILLEGAL CRACKBACK
Strike of an
open right hand
against the right mid-thigh
preceded by personal foul
signal (10).

29

PLAYER DISQUALIFIED
Ejection signal.

30

TRIPPING
Repeated action of right foot
in back of left heel.

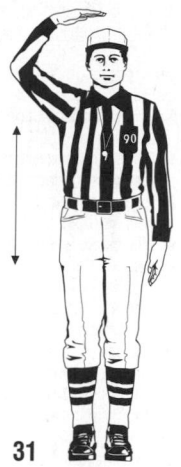

31

UNCATCHABLE FORWARD PASS
Palm of right hand held parallel to ground above head and moved back and forth.

32

TWELVE MEN IN OFFENSIVE HUDDLE or TOO MANY MEN ON THE FIELD
Both hands on top of head.

33

FACEMASK
Grasping facemask with one hand.

34

ILLEGAL SHIFT
Horizontal arcs with two hands.

35

RESET PLAY CLOCK– 25 SECONDS
Pump one arm vertically.

36

RESET PLAY CLOCK– 40 SECONDS
Pump two arms vertically.

NFL DIGEST OF RULES

This Digest of Rules of the National Football League has been prepared to aid players, fans, and members of the press, radio, and television media in their understanding of the game.

It is not meant to be a substitute for the official rule book. In any case of conflict between these explanations and the official rules, the rules always have precedence.

In order to make it easier to coordinate the information in this digest, the topics discussed generally follow the order of the rule book.

OFFICIALS' JURISDICTIONS, POSITIONS, AND DUTIES

Referee—General oversight and control of game. Gives signals for all fouls and is final authority for rule interpretations. Takes a position in backfield 10 to 12 yards behind line of scrimmage, favors right side (if quarterback is right-handed passer). Determines legality of snap, observes deep back(s) for legal motion. On running plays, observes quarterback during and after handoff, remains with him until action has cleared away, then proceeds downfield, checking on runner and contact behind him. When runner is downed, Referee determines forward progress from wing official and, if necessary, adjusts final position of ball.

On pass plays, drops back as quarterback begins to fade back, picks up legality of tackle on Head Linesman's side. Changes to complete concentration on quarterback as defenders approach. Primarily responsible to rule on possible roughing action on passer and if ball becomes loose, rules whether ball is free on a fumble or dead on an incomplete pass. Shares responsibility with Umpire, Linesman, and Line Judge on intentional grounding.

During kicking situations, Referee has primary responsibility to rule on kicker's actions and whether or not any subsequent contact by a defender is legal. During punt plays, Referee's position is parallel to kicker and wide. The Referee will announce on the microphone when each period is ended, penalties, a charged team time out, and when the two-minute warning for each half is reached.

Umpire—Primary responsibility are to rule on players' conduct and actions on scrimmage line, as well as check on their equipment. Lines up approximately four to five yards downfield, varying position from the outside shoulder of one guard to outside shoulder of opposite guard. Looks for possible false start by offensive linemen. Observes legality of contact by both offensive linemen while blocking and by defensive players while they attempt to ward off blockers. Is prepared to call rule infractions if they occur on offense or defense. Moves forward to line of scrimmage when pass play develops in order to insure that interior linemen do not move illegally downfield. If offensive linemen indicate screen pass is to be attempted, Umpire shifts his attention toward screen side, picks up potential receiver in order to insure that he will legally be permitted to run his pattern and continues to rule on action of blockers. Umpire is to assist in ruling on incomplete or trapped passes when ball is thrown overhead or short. On field goal and try-kick attempts, he will become a second umpire with the Side Judge.

Head Linesman—Primarily responsible for ruling on offside, encroachment, and actions pertaining to scrimmage line prior to or at snap. Takes a position straddling the line of scrimmage. Keys on closest setback on his side of the field. On pass plays, Linesman is responsible to clear his receiver approximately seven yards downfield as he moves to a point five yards beyond the line. Linesman's secondary responsibility is to rule on any illegal action taken by defenders on any delay receiver moving downfield. Has full responsibility for ruling on sideline plays on his side, e.g., pass receiver or runner in or out of bounds. Together with Referee, Linesman is responsible for keeping track of number of downs and is in charge of mechanics of his chain crew in connection with its duties.

Linesman must be prepared to assist in determining forward progress by a runner on play directed toward middle or into his side zone. He, in turn, is to signal Referee or Umpire what forward

point ball has reached. Linesman is also responsible to rule on legality of action involving any receiver who approaches his side zone. He is to call pass interference when the infraction occurs and is to rule on legality of blockers and defenders on plays involving ball carriers, whether it is entirely a running play, a combination pass and run, or a play involving a kick. Also assists referee with intentional grounding.

Line Judge—Straddles line of scrimmage on side of field opposite Linesman. Keeps time of game as a backup for official clock operator. However, should official clock malfunction or be operated improperly, the time kept by the Line Judge is official. Along with Linesman is responsible for offside, encroachment, and actions pertaining to scrimmage line prior to or at snap. Line Judge keys on closest setback on his side of field. Line Judge is to observe his receiver until he moves at least seven yards downfield. He then moves toward backfield side, being especially alert to rule on any back in motion and on flight of ball when pass is made (he must rule whether forward or backward). Line Judge has primary responsibility to rule whether or not passer is behind or beyond line of scrimmage when pass is made. He also assists in observing actions by blockers and defenders who are on his side of field. After pass is thrown, Line Judge directs attention toward activities that occur in back of Umpire. During punting situations, Line Judge remains at line of scrimmage to be sure that only the end men move downfield until kick has been made. He also rules whether or not the kick crossed line and then observes action by members of the kicking team who are moving downfield to cover the kick. The Line Judge will advise the Referee when time has expired at the end of each period.

Field Judge—Operates on same side of field as Line Judge, 20 yards deep. Keys on widest receiver on his side. Concentrates on path of end or back, observing legality of his potential block(s) or of actions taken against him. Is prepared to rule from deep position on holding or illegal use of hands by end or back or on defensive infractions committed by player guarding him. Has primary responsibility to make decisions involving sideline on his side of field, e.g., pass receiver or runner in or out of bounds.

Field Judge makes decisions involving catching, recovery, or illegal touching of a loose ball beyond line of scrimmage. Rules on plays involving pass receiver, including legality of catch or pass interference. Assists in covering actions of runner, including blocks by teammates and that of defenders. Rules on blocking during punt returns and, together with Back Judge, rules whether or not field goal and try-kick attempts are successful.

Side Judge—Operates on same side of field as Linesman, 20 yards deep. Keys on widest receiver on his side. Concentrates on path of this receiver, observing legality of his potential block(s) or of actions taken against him. Is prepared to rule from deep position on holding or illegal use of hands by the receiver or on defensive infractions committed by player defending him. Has primary responsibility to make decisions involving sideline on his side of field, e.g., pass receiver or runner in or out of bounds.

Side Judge makes decisions involving catching, recovery, or illegal touching of a loose ball beyond line of scrimmage. Rules on plays involving pass receiver, including legality of catch or pass interference. Assists in covering actions of runner, including blocks by teammates and that of defenders and rules on blocking during punt returns. On field goals and try-kick attempts, he becomes a second umpire.

Back Judge—Takes a position 25 yards downfield. In general, favors the tight end's side of field. Usually keys on tight end, concentrates on his path and observes legality of tight end's potential block(s) or of actions taken against him. Is prepared to rule from deep position on holding or illegal use of hands by end or back or on defensive infractions committed by player defending him.

Back Judge times interval between plays on 40/25-second clock plus intermission between two periods of each half. Makes decisions involving catching, recovery, or illegal touching of a loose ball beyond line of scrimmage. Is responsible to rule on plays involving end line. Calls pass interference, fair-catch infractions, and blocking during kick returns and, together with Field Judge, rules whether or not field goal and try-kick attempts are successful.

DEFINITIONS

1. **Chucking:** Warding off an opponent who is in front of a defender by contacting him with a quick extension of arm or arms, followed by the return of arm(s) to a flexed position, thereby breaking the original contact.
2. **Clipping:** Throwing the body across the back of an opponent's leg or hitting him from the back below the waist while moving up from behind unless the opponent is a runner or the contact is above the knee in close line play.
3. **Close Line Play:** The area between the positions normally occupied by the offensive tackles, extending three yards on each side of the line of scrimmage. It is legal to clip above the knee.
4. **Crackback:** Eligible receivers who take or move to a position more than two yards outside the tackle or a player in a backfielf position may not block an opponent below the waist toward the ball at the snap and within five yards of the line of scrimmage.
5. **Dead Ball:** Ball not in play.
6. **Double Foul:** A foul by each team during the same down.
7. **Down:** The period of action that starts when the ball is put in play and ends when it is dead.
8. **Encroachment:** When a defensive player enters the neutral zone and makes contact with an opponent before the ball is snapped.
9. **Fair Catch:** An unhindered catch of a kick by a member of the receiving team who must raise one arm a full length above his head and wave his arm from side to side while the kick is in flight.
10. **Foul:** Any violation of a playing rule.
11. **Free Kick:** A kickoff or safety kick. It may be a placekick, dropkick, or punt, except a punt may not be used on a kickoff following a touchdown, successful field goal, or to begin each half or overtime period. A tee cannot be used on a fair-catch or safety kick.
12. **Fumble:** The unintentional loss of player possession of the ball.
13. **Game Clock:** Scoreboard game clock.
14. **Impetus:** The action of a player that gives momentum to the ball and sends it into the end zone.
15. **Live Ball:** A ball legally free-kicked or snapped. It continues in play until the down ends.
16. **Loose Ball:** A live ball not in possession of any player.
17. **Muff:** The touching of a loose ball by a player in an unsuccessful attempt to obtain possession.
18. **Neutral Zone:** The space the length of a ball between the two scrimmage lines. The offensive team and defensive team must remain behind their end of the ball.
    Exception: The offensive player who snaps the ball.
19. **Offside:** A player is offside when any part of his body is beyond his scrimmage or free kick line when the ball is snapped or kicked. Exception: Snapper, holder of placekick or kicker.
20. **Own Goal:** The goal a team is defending.
21. **Play Clock:** 40/25 second clock.
22. **Pocket Area:** Applies from a point two yards outside of either offensive tackle and includes the tight end if he drops off the line of scrimmage to pass protect. Pocket extends longitudinally behind the line back to offensive team's own end line. For purposes of intentional grounding, the pocket is considered tackle to tackle.
23. **Possession of a Pass:** When a player controls the ball throughout the act of clearly touching both feet, or any other part of his body other than his hand(s), to the ground inbounds.
24. **Post-Possession Foul:** A foul by the receiving team that occurs after a ball is legally kicked from scrimmage prior to possession changing. The ball must cross the line of scrimmage and the receiving team must retain the kicked ball unless it is part of a double foul.
25. **Punt:** A kick made when a player drops the ball and kicks it while it is in flight.
26. **Safety:** The situation in which the ball is dead on or behind a team's own goal if the impetus comes from a player on that team. Two points are scored for the opposing team.
27. **Shift:** The movement of two or more offensive players at the same time before the snap.
28. **Striking:** The act of swinging, clubbing, or propelling the arm or forearm in contacting an opponent.
29. **Sudden Death:** The continuation of a tied game into sudden death overtime in which the team scoring first (by safety, field goal, or touchdown) wins.
30. **Touchback:** When a ball is dead on or behind a team's own goal line, provided the impetus came from an opponent and provided it is not a touchdown or a missed field goal attempt when the ball was kicked outside the 20-yard line.
31. **Touchdown:** When any part of the ball, legally in possession of a player inbounds, breaks the plane of the opponent's goal line, provided it is not a touchback.
32. **Unsportsmanlike Conduct:** Any act contrary to the generally understood principles of sportsmanship.

SUMMARY OF PENALTIES
Automatic First Down

1. Awarded to offensive team on all <u>defensive fouls</u> with these exceptions:
   (a) Offside.
   (b) Encroachment.
   (c) Delay of game.
   (d) Illegal substitution.
   (e) Excessive time out(s).
   (f) Incidental grasp of facemask.
   (g) Neutral zone infraction.
   (h) Running into the kicker.
   (i) More than 11 players on the field at the snap for either team.

Five Yards

1. Defensive holding or illegal use of hands (automatic first down).
2. Delay of game on offense or defense.
3. Delay of kickoff.
4. Encroachment.
5. Excessive time out(s).
6. False start.
7. Illegal formation.
8. Illegal shift.
9. Illegal motion.
10. Illegal substitution.
11. First onside kickoff out of bounds between goal lines and untouched or last touched by kickers.
12. Invalid fair catch signal.
13. More than 11 players on the field at snap for either team.
14. Less than seven men on offensive line at snap.
15. Offside.
16. Failure to pause one second after shift or huddle.
17. Running into kicker.
18. More than one man in motion at snap.
19. Grasping facemask of the ball carrier or quarterback.
20. Player out of bounds at snap.
21. Ineligible member(s) of kicking team going beyond line of scrimmage before ball is kicked.
22. Illegal return.
23. Failure to report change of eligibility.
24. Neutral zone infraction.

25. Loss of team time out(s) or five-yard penalty on the defense for excessive crowd noise. Offensive team's quarterback can be penalized if he does not make every effort to put the ball in play.
26. Ineligible player downfield during passing down.
27. Second forward pass behind the line.
28. Forward pass is first touched by eligible receiver who has gone out of bounds and returned.
29. Forward pass touches or is caught by an ineligible receiver on or behind line.
30. Forward pass thrown from behind line of scrimmage after ball once crossed the line.
31. Kicking team player voluntarily out of bounds during a punt.
32. Twelve (12) men in the huddle.

Ten Yards
1. Offensive pass interference.
2. Holding, illegal use of hands, arms, or body by offense.
3. Tripping by a member of either team.
4. Helping the runner.
5. Deliberately batting or punching a loose ball.
6. Deliberately kicking a loose ball.
7. Illegal block above the waist.

Fifteen Yards
1. Chop block.
2. Clipping below the waist.
3. Fair catch interference.
4. Illegal crackback block by offense.
5. Piling on.
6. Roughing the kicker.
7. Roughing the passer.
8. Twisting, turning, or pulling an opponent by the facemask.
9. Unnecessary roughness.
10. Unsportsmanlike conduct.
11. Delay of game at start of either half.
12. Illegal low block.
13. A tackler using his helmet to butt, spear, or ram an opponent.
14. Any player who uses the top of his helmet unnecessarily.
15. A punter, placekicker, or holder who simulates being roughed by a defensive player.
16. Leaping.
17. Leverage.
18. Any player who removes his helmet after a play while on the field.
19. Taunting.

Five Yards and Loss of Down (Combination Penalty)
1. Forward pass thrown from beyond line of scrimmage.

Ten Yards and Loss of Down (Combination Penalty)
1. Intentional grounding of forward pass (safety if passer is in own end zone). If foul occurs more than 10 yards behind line, play results in loss of down at spot of foul.

Fifteen Yards and Loss of Coin Toss Option
1. Team's late arrival on the field prior to scheduled kickoff.
2. Captains not appearing for coin toss.

Fifteen Yards (and disqualification if flagrant)
1. Striking opponent with fist.
2. Kicking or kneeing opponent.
3. Striking opponent on head or neck with forearm, elbow, or hands whether or not the initial contact is made below the neck area.
4. Roughing kicker.
5. Roughing passer.
6. Malicious unnecessary roughness.
7. Unsportsmanlike conduct.
8. Palpably unfair act. (Distance penalty determined by the Referee after consultation with other officials.)

Fifteen Yards and Automatic Disqualification
1. Using a helmet (not worn) as a weapon.
2. Striking or purposely shoving a game official.

Suspension From Game For One Down
1. Illegal equipment. (Player may return after one down when legally equipped.)

Touchdown Awarded (Palpably Unfair Act)
1. When Referee determines a palpably unfair act deprived a team of a touchdown. (Example: Player comes off bench and tackles runner apparently en route to touchdown.)

FIELD
1. Sidelines and end lines are out of bounds. The goal line is actually in the end zone. A player with the ball in his possession scores a touchdown when the ball is on, above, or over the goal line.
2. The field is rimmed by a white border, six feet wide, along the sidelines. All of this is out of bounds.
3. The hashmarks (inbound lines) are 70 feet, 9 inches from each sideline.
4. Goal posts must be single-standard type, offset from the end line and painted bright gold. The goal posts must be 18 feet, 6 inches wide and the top face of the crossbar must be 10 feet above the ground. Vertical posts extend at least 30 feet above the crossbar. A ribbon 4 inches by 42 inches long is to be attached to the top of each post. The actual goal is the plane extending indefinitely above the crossbar and between the outer edges of the posts.
5. The field is 360 feet long and 160 feet wide. The end zones are 30 feet deep. The line used in try-for-point plays is two yards out from the goal line.
6. Chain crew members and ball boys must be uniformly identifiable.
7. All clubs must use standardized sideline markers. Pylons must be used for goal line and end line markings.
8. End zone markings and club identification at 50 yard line must be approved by the Commissioner to avoid any confusion as to delineation of goal lines, sidelines, and end lines.

BALL
1. The home club shall have 36 balls for outdoor games and 24 for indoor games available for testing with a pressure gauge by the referee two hours prior to the starting time of the game to meet with League requirements. Twelve (12) new footballs, sealed in a special box and shipped by the manufacturer, will be opened in the officials' locker room two hours prior to the starting time of the game. These balls are to be specially marked with the letter "k" and used exclusively for the kicking game.

COIN TOSS
1. The toss of coin will take place within three minutes of kickoff in center of field. The toss will be called by the visiting captain before the coin is flipped. The winner may choose one of two privileges and the loser gets the other:
   (a) Receive or kick
   (b) Goal his team will defend
2. Immediately prior to the start of the second half, the captains of both teams must inform the officials of their respective choices. The loser of the original coin toss gets first choice.

TIMING
1. The stadium game clock is official. In case it stops or is operating incorrectly, the Line Judge takes over the official timing on the field.
2. Each period is 15 minutes. The intermission between the periods is two minutes. Halftime is 12 minutes, unless otherwise specified.
3. On charged team time outs, the Back Judge starts watch and blows whistle after 1 minute 50 seconds, unless television does not utilize the time for commercial. In this case the length of the time out is reduced to 30 seconds.

4. The Referee will allow necessary time to attend to an injured player, or repair a legal player's equipment.
5. Each team is allowed three time outs each half.
6. Time between plays will be 40 seconds from the end of a given play until the snap of the ball for the next play, or a 25-second interval after certain administrative stoppages and game delays.
7. Clock will start running when ball is snapped following all changes of team possession.
8. With the exception of the last two minutes of the first half and the last five minutes of the second half, the game clock will be restarted following a player going out of bounds on a play from scrimmage, or after declined penalties when appropriate on the referee's signal.
9. Consecutive team time outs can be taken by opposing teams but the length of the second time out will be reduced to 30 seconds.
10. When, in the judgment of the Referee, the level of crowd noise prevents the offense from hearing its signals, he can institute a series of procedures which can result in a loss of team time outs or a five-yard penalty against the defensive team.
11. On kickoff, clock does not start until the ball has been legally touched by player of either team in the field of play.

SUDDEN DEATH

1. The sudden death system of determining the winner shall prevail when score is tied at the end of the regulation playing time of all NFL games. The team scoring first during overtime play shall be the winner and the game automatically ends upon any score (by safety, field goal, or touchdown) or when a score is awarded by Referee for a palpably unfair act.
2. At the end of regulation time the Referee will immediately toss coin at center of field in accordance with rules pertaining to the usual pregame toss. The captain of the visiting team will call the toss prior to the coin being flipped.
3. Following a three-minute intermission after the end of the regulation game, play will be continued in 15-minute periods or until there is a score. There is a two-minute intermission between subsequent periods. The teams change goals at the start of each period. Each team has three time outs per half and all general timing provisions apply as during a regular game. Disqualified players are not allowed to return.
   Exception: In preseason and regular season games there shall be a maximum of 15 minutes of sudden death with two time outs instead of three. General provisions that apply for the fourth quarter will prevail. Try not attempted if touchdown scored.

TIMING IN FINAL TWO MINUTES OF EACH HALF

1. A team cannot buy an excess time out for a penalty. However, a fourth time out is allowed without penalty for an injured player, who must be removed immediately. A fifth time out or more is allowed for an injury and a five-yard penalty is assessed. Additionally, if the clock was running and the score is tied or the team in possession is losing, the ball cannot be put in play for at least 10 seconds on the fourth or more time out. The half or game can end while those 10 seconds are run off on the clock.
2. If the defensive team is behind in the score and commits a foul when it has no time outs left in the final 40 seconds of either half, the offensive team can decline the penalty for the foul and have the time on the clock expire.
3. Fouls that occur in the last five minutes of the fourth quarter as well as the last two minutes of the first half will result in the clock starting on the snap.

TRY

1. After a touchdown, the scoring team is allowed a try during one scrimmage down. The ball may be spotted anywhere between the inbounds lines, two or more yards from the goal line. The successful conversion counts one point by kick; two points for a successful conversion by touchdown; or one point for a safety.
2. The defensive team never can score on a try. As soon as defense gets possession or the kick is blocked or a touchdown is not scored, the try is over.
3. Any distance penalty for fouls committed by the defense that prevent the try from being attempted can be enforced on the succeeding try or succeeding kickoff. Any foul committed on a successful try will result in a distance penalty being assessed on the ensuing kickoff.
4. Only the fumbling player can recover and advance a fumble during a try.

PLAYERS-SUBSTITUTIONS

1. Each team is permitted 11 men on the field at the snap.
2. Unlimited substitution is permitted. However, players may enter the field only when the ball is dead. Players who have been substituted for are not permitted to linger on the field. Such lingering will be interpreted as unsportsmanlike conduct.
3. Players leaving the game must be out of bounds on their own side, clearing the field between the end lines, before a snap or free kick. If player crosses end line leaving field, it is delay of game (five-yard penalty).
4. Offensive substitutes who remain in the game must move onto the field as far as the inside of the field numerals before moving to a wide position.
5. With the exception of the last two minutes of either half, the offensive team, while in the process of substitution or simulated substitution, is prohibited from rushing quickly to the line and snapping the ball with the obvious attempt to cause a defensive foul; i.e., too many men on the field.
6. There never can be 12 or more players in the offensive huddle.

KICKOFF

1. The kickoff shall be from the kicking team's 30-yard line at the start of each half and after a field goal and try. A kickoff is one type of free kick.
2. A one-inch tee may be used (no tee permitted for field goal, safety kick, or try attempt) on a kickoff. The ball is put in play by a placekick.
3. A kickoff may not score a field goal.
4. A kickoff is illegal unless it travels 10 yards OR is touched by the receiving team. Once the ball is touched by the receiving team or has gone 10 yards, it is a free ball. Receivers may recover and advance. Kicking team may recover but NOT advance UNLESS receiver had possession and lost the ball.
5. When a kickoff goes out of bounds between the goal lines without being touched by the receiving team, the ball belongs to the receivers 30 yards from the spot of the kick or at the out-of-bounds spot unless the ball went out-of-bounds the first time an onside kick was attempted. In this case, the kicking team is penalized five yards and the ball must be kicked again.
6. When a kickoff goes out of bounds between the goal lines and is touched last by receiving team, it is receiver's ball at out-of-bounds spot.
7. If the kicking team either illegally kicks off out of bounds or is guilty of a short free kick on two or more consecutive onside kicks, receivers may take possession of the ball at the dead ball spot, out-of-bounds spot, or spot of illegal touch.

SAFETY

1. In addition to a kickoff, the other free kick is a kick after a safety (safety kick). A punt may be used (a punt may not be used on a kickoff).
2. On a safety kick, the team scored upon puts ball in play by a punt, dropkick, or placekick without tee. No score can be

made on a free kick following a safety, even if a series of penalties places team in position. (A field goal can be scored only on a play from scrimmage or a free kick after a fair catch.)

FAIR CATCH KICK

1. After a fair catch, the receiving team has the option to put the ball in play by a snap or a fair catch kick (field goal attempt), with fair catch kick lines established ten yards apart. All general rules apply as for a field goal attempt from scrimmage. The clock starts when the ball is kicked. (No tee permitted.)

FIELD GOAL

1. All field goals attempted (kicker) and missed from beyond the 20-yard line will result in the defensive team taking possession of the ball at the spot of the kick. On any field goal attempted and missed where the spot of the kick is on or inside the 20-yard line, ball will revert to defensive team at the 20-yard line.

SAFETY

1. The important factor in a safety is impetus. Two points are scored for the opposing team when the ball is dead on or behind a team's own goal line if the impetus came from a player on that team.

Examples of Safety:

(a) Blocked punt goes out of kicking team's end zone. Impetus was provided by punting team. The block only changes direction of ball, not impetus.

(b) Ball carrier retreats from field of play into his own end zone and is downed. Ball carrier provides impetus.

(c) Offensive team commits a foul and spot of enforcement is behind its own goal line.

(d) Player on receiving team muffs punt and, trying to get ball, forces or illegally kicks (creating new impetus) it into end zone where it goes out of the end zone or is recovered by a member of the receiving team in the end zone.

Examples of Non-Safety:

(a) Player intercepts a pass with both feet inbounds in the field of play and his momentum carries him into his own end zone. Ball is put in play at spot of interception.

(b) Player intercepts a pass in his own end zone and is downed in the end zone, even after recovering in the end zone. Impetus came from passing team, not from defense. (Touchback)

(c) Player passes from behind his own goal line. Opponent bats down ball in end zone. (Incomplete pass)

MEASURING

1. The forward point of the ball is used when measuring.

POSITION OF PLAYERS AT SNAP

1. Offensive team must have at least seven players on line.

2. Offensive players, not on line, must be at least one yard back at snap.

   (Exception: player who takes snap.)

3. No interior lineman may move abruptly after taking or simulating a three-point stance.

4. No player of either team may enter neutral zone before snap.

5. No player of offensive team may charge or move abruptly, after assuming set position, in such manner as to lead defense to believe snap has started. No player of the defensive team within one yard of the line of scrimmage may make an abrupt movement in an attempt to cause the offense to false start.

6. If a player changes his eligibility, the Referee must alert the defensive captain after player has reported to him.

7. All players of offensive team must be stationary at snap, except one back who may be in motion parallel to scrimmage line or backward (not forward).

8. After a shift or huddle all players on offensive team must come to an absolute stop for at least one second with no movement of hands, feet, head, or swaying of body.

9. Quarterbacks can be called for a false start penalty (five yards) if their actions are judged to be an obvious attempt to draw an opponent offside.

10. Offensive linemen are permitted to interlock legs.

USE OF HANDS, ARMS, AND BODY

1. No player on offense may assist a runner except by blocking for him. There shall be no interlocking interference.

2. A runner may ward off opponents with his hands and arms but no other player on offense may use hands or arms to obstruct an opponent by grasping with hands, pushing, or encircling any part of his body during a block. Hands (open or closed) can be thrust forward to initially contact an opponent on or outside the opponent's frame, but the blocker immediately must work to bring his hands on or inside the frame.

   Note: Pass blocking: Hand(s) thrust forward that slip outside the body of the defender will be legal if blocker immediately worked to bring them back inside. Hand(s) or arm(s) that encircle a defender—i.e., hook an opponent—are to be considered illegal and officials are to call a foul for holding. Blocker cannot use his hands or arms to push from behind, hang onto, or encircle an opponent in a manner that restricts his movement as the play develops.

3. Hands cannot be thrust forward above the frame to contact an opponent on the neck, face or head.

   Note: The frame is defined as the part of the opponent's body below the neck that is presented to the blocker.

4. A defensive player may not tackle or hold an opponent other than a runner. Otherwise, he may use his hands, arms, or body only:

   (a) To defend or protect himself against an obstructing opponent.

      Exception: An eligible receiver is considered to be an obstructing opponent ONLY to a point five yards beyond the line of scrimmage unless the player who receives the snap clearly demonstrates no further intention to pass the ball. Within this five-yard zone, a defensive player may chuck an eligible player in front of him. A defensive player is allowed to maintain continuous and unbroken contact within the five-yard zone until a point when the receiver is even with the defender. The defensive player cannot use his hands or arms to push from behind, hang onto, or encircle an eligible receiver in a manner that restricts movement as the play develops. Beyond this five-yard limitation, a defender may use his hands or arms ONLY to defend or protect himself against impending contact caused by a receiver. In such reaction, the defender may not contact a receiver who attempts to take a path to evade him.

   (b) To push or pull opponent out of the way on line of scrimmage.

   (c) In actual attempt to get at or tackle runner.

   (d) To push or pull opponent out of the way in a legal attempt to recover a loose ball.

   (e) During a legal block on an opponent who is not an eligible pass receiver.

   (f) When legally blocking an eligible pass receiver above the waist.

      Exception: Eligible receivers lined up within two yards of the tackle, whether on or immediately behind the line, may be blocked below the waist at or behind the line of scrimmage. NO eligible receiver may be blocked below the waist after he goes beyond the line. (Illegal cut)

Note: Once the quarterback hands off or pitches the ball to a back, or if the quarterback leaves the pocket area, the restrictions (illegal chuck, illegal cut) on the defensive team relative to the offensive receivers will end, provided the ball is not in the air.

5. A defensive player may not contact an opponent above the shoulders with the palm of his hand except to ward him off on the line. This exception is permitted only if it is not a repeated act against the same opponent during any one contact. In all other cases the palms may be used on head, neck, or face only to ward off or push an opponent in legal attempt to get at the ball.

6. Any offensive player who pretends to possess the ball or to whom a teammate pretends to give the ball may be tackled provided he is crossing his scrimmage line between the ends of a normal tight offensive line.

7. An offensive player who lines up more than two yards outside his own tackle or a player who, at the snap, is in a backfield position and subsequently takes a position more than two yards outside a tackle may not clip an opponent anywhere nor may he contact an opponent below the waist if the blocker is moving toward the ball and if contact is made within an area five yards on either side of the ball. (crackback)

8. A player of either team may block at any time provided it is not pass interference, fair catch interference, or unnecessary roughness.

9. A player may not bat or punch:
   (a) A loose ball (in field of play) toward his opponent's goal line or in any direction in either end zone.
   (b) A ball in player possession.
   Note: If there is any question as to whether a defender is stripping or batting a ball in player possession, the official(s) will rule the action as a legal act (stripping the ball).
   Exception: A forward or backward pass may be batted, tipped, or deflected in any direction at any time by either the offense or the defense.
   Note: A pass in flight that is controlled or caught may only be thrown backward, if it is thrown forward it is considered an illegal bat.

10. No player may deliberately kick any ball except as a punt, dropkick, or placekick.

FORWARD PASS

1. A forward pass may be touched or caught by any eligible receiver. All members of the defensive team are eligible. Eligible receivers on the offensive team are players on either end of line (other than center, guard, or tackle) or players at least one yard behind the line at the snap. A T-formation quarterback is not eligible to receive a forward pass during a play from scrimmage.
   Exception: T-formation quarterback becomes eligible if pass is previously touched by an eligible receiver.

2. An offensive team may make only one forward pass during each play from scrimmage (Loss of 5 yards).

3. The passer must be behind his line of scrimmage (Loss of down and five yards, enforced from the spot of pass).

4. Any eligible offensive player may catch a forward pass. If a pass is touched by one eligible offensive player and touched or caught by a second offensive player, pass completion is legal. Further, all offensive players become eligible once a pass is touched by an eligible receiver or any defensive player.

5. The rules concerning a forward pass and ineligible receivers:
   (a) If ball is touched accidentally by an ineligible receiver on or behind his line: loss of five yards.
   (b) If ineligible receiver is illegally downfield: loss of five yards.
   (c) If touched or caught (intentionally or accidentally) by ineligible receiver beyond the line: loss of 5 yards.

6. The player who first controls and continues to maintain control of a pass will be awarded the ball even though his opponent later establishes joint control of the ball.

7. Any forward pass becomes incomplete and ball is dead if:
   (a) Pass hits the ground or goes out of bounds.
   (b) Pass hits the goal post or the crossbar of either team.

8. A forward pass is complete when a receiver clearly possesses the pass and touches the ground with both feet inbounds while in possession of the ball. If a receiver would have landed inbounds with both feet but is carried or pushed out of bounds while maintaining possession of the ball, pass is complete at the out-of-bounds spot.

9. If a personal foul is committed by the defense prior to the completion of a pass, the penalty is 15 yards from the spot where ball becomes dead.

10. If a personal foul is committed by the offense prior to the completion of a pass, the penalty is 15 yards from the previous line of scrimmage.

INTENTIONAL GROUNDING OF FORWARD PASS

1. Intentional grounding of a forward pass is a foul: loss of down and 10 yards from previous spot if passer is in the field of play or loss of down at the spot of the foul if it occurs more than 10 yards behind the line or safety if passer is in his own end zone when ball is released.

2. Intentional grounding will be called when a passer, facing an imminent loss of yardage due to pressure from the defense, throws a forward pass without a realistic chance of completion.

3. Intentional grounding will not be called when a passer, while out of the pocket and facing an imminent loss of yardage, throws a pass that lands at or beyond the line of scrimmage, even if no offensive player(s) have a realistic chance to catch the ball (including if the ball lands out of bounds over the sideline or end line).

PROTECTION OF PASSER

1. By interpretation, a pass begins when the passer—with possession of ball—starts to bring his hand forward. If ball strikes ground after this action has begun, play is ruled an incomplete pass. If passer loses control of ball prior to his bringing his hand forward, play is ruled a fumble.

2. When a passer is holding the ball to pass it forward, any intentional movement forward of his hand starts a forward pass. If a defensive player contacts the passer or the ball after forward movement begins, and the ball leaves the passer's hand, a forward pass is ruled, regardless of where the ball strikes the ground or a player.

3. No defensive player may run into a passer of a legal forward pass after the ball has left his hand (15 yards). The Referee must determine whether opponent had a reasonable chance to stop his momentum during an attempt to block the pass or tackle the passer while he still had the ball.

4. No defensive player who has an unrestricted path to the quarterback may hit him flagrantly in the area of the knee(s) or below when approaching in any direction.

5. Officials are to blow the play dead as soon as the quarterback is clearly in the grasp and control of any tackler, and his safety is in jeopardy.

6. No defensive player may hit the quarterback in the head, face, or neck.

PASS INTERFERENCE

1. There shall be no interference with a forward pass thrown from behind the line. The restriction for the passing team starts with the snap. The restriction on the defensive team starts when the ball leaves the passer's hand. Both restrictions end when the ball is touched by anyone.

2. The penalty for defensive pass interference is an automatic first down at the spot of the foul. If interference is in the end

zone, it is first down for the offense on the defense's 1-yard line. If previous spot was inside the defense's 1-yard line, penalty is half the distance to the goal line.

3. The penalty for offensive pass interference is 10 yards from the previous spot.

4. It is pass interference by either team when any player movement beyond the line of scrimmage significantly hinders the progress of an eligible player of such player's opportunity to catch the ball. Offensive pass interference rules apply from the time the ball is snapped until the ball is touched. Defensive pass interference rules apply from the time the ball is thrown until the ball is touched.

Actions that constitute defensive pass interference include but are not limited to:

(a) Contact by a defender who is not playing the ball and such contact restricts the receiver's opportunity to make the catch.

(b) Playing through the back of a receiver in an attempt to make a play on the ball.

(c) Grabbing a receiver's arm(s) in such a manner that restricts his opportunity to catch a pass.

(d) Extending an arm across the body of a receiver thus restricting his ability to catch a pass, regardless of whether the defender is playing the ball.

(e) Cutting off the path of a receiver by making contact with him without playing the ball.

(f) Hooking a receiver in an attempt to get to the ball in such a manner that it causes the receiver's body to turn prior to the ball arriving.

Actions that do not constitute pass interference include but are not limited to:

(a) Incidental contact by a defender's hands, arms, or body when both players are competing for the ball, or neither player is looking for the ball. If there is any question whether contact is incidental, the ruling shall be no interference.

(b) Inadvertent tangling of feet when both players are playing the ball or neither player is playing the ball.

(c) Contact that would normally be considered pass interference, but the ball is clearly uncatchable by the involved players.

(d) Laying a hand on a receiver that does not restrict the receiver in an attempt to make a play on the ball.

(e) Contact by a defender who has gained position on a receiver in an attempt to catch the ball.

Actions that constitute offensive pass interference include but are not limited to:

(a) Blocking downfield by an offensive player prior to the ball being touched.

(b) Initiating contact with a defender by shoving or pushing off thus creating a separation in an attempt to catch a pass.

(c) Driving through a defender who has established a position on the field.

Actions that do not constitute offensive pass interference include but are not limited to:

(a) Incidental contact by a receiver's hands, arms, or body when both players are competing for the ball or neither player is looking for the ball.

(b) Inadvertent touching of feet when both players are playing the ball or neither player is playing the ball.

(c) Contact that would normally be considered pass interference, but the ball is clearly uncatchable by involved players.

Note 1: If there is any question whether player contact is incidental, the ruling should be no interference.

Note 2: Defensive players have as much right to the path of the ball as eligible offensive players.

Note 3: Pass interference for both teams ends when the pass is touched.

Note 4: There can be no pass interference at or behind the line of scrimmage, but defensive actions such as tackling a receiver can still result in a 5-yard penalty for defensive holding, if accepted.

Note 5: Whenever a team presents an apparent punting formation, defensive pass interference is not to be called for action on the end man on the line of scrimmage, or an eligible receiver behind the line of scrimmage who is aligned or in motion more than one yard outside the end man on the line. Defensive holding, such as tackling a receiver, still can be called and result in a 5-yard penalty and automatic first down from the previous spot, if accepted. Offensive pass interference rules still apply.

BACKWARD PASS

1. Any pass not forward is regarded as a backward pass. A pass parallel to the line is a backward pass. A runner may pass backward at any time.

2. A backward pass that strikes the ground can be recovered and advanced by either team.

3. A backward pass caught in the air can be advanced by either team.

4. A backward pass in flight may not be batted forward by an offensive player.

FUMBLE

1. The distinction between a fumble and a muff should be kept in mind in considering rules about fumbles. A fumble is the loss of player possession of the ball. A muff is the touching of a loose ball by a player in an unsuccessful attempt to obtain possession.

2. A fumble may be advanced by any player on either team regardless of whether recovered before or after ball hits the ground.

3. A fumble that goes forward and out of bounds will return to the fumbling team at the spot of the fumble unless the ball goes out of bounds in the opponent's end zone. In this case, it is a touchback.

4. On a play from scrimmage, if an offensive player fumbles anywhere on the field during fourth down, only the fumbling player is permitted to recover and/or advance the ball. If any player fumbles after the two-minute warning in a half, only the fumbling player is permitted to recover and/or advance the ball. If recovered by any other offensive player, the ball is dead at the spot of the fumble unless it is recovered behind the spot of the fumble. In that case, the ball is dead at the spot of recovery. Any defensive player may recover and/or advance any fumble at any time.

5. A muffed hand-to-hand snap from center is treated as a fumble.

KICKS FROM SCRIMMAGE

1. Any kick from scrimmage must be made from behind the line to be legal.

2. Any punt or missed field goal that touches a goal post is dead.

3. During a kick from scrimmage, only the end men, as eligible receivers on the line of scrimmage at the time of the snap, are permitted to go beyond the line before the ball is kicked.

Exception: An eligible receiver who, at the snap, is aligned or in motion behind the line and more than one yard outside the end man on his side of the line, clearly making him the outside receiver, replaces that end man as the player eligible to go downfield after the snap. All other members of the kicking team must remain at the line of scrimmage until the ball has been kicked.

4. Any punt that is blocked and does not cross the line of scrimmage can be recovered and advanced by either team. However, if offensive team recovers it must make the yardage necessary for its first down to retain possession if punt was

on fourth down.

5. The kicking team may never advance its own kick even though legal recovery is made beyond the line of scrimmage. Possession only.

6. A member of the receiving team may not run into or rough a kicker who kicks from behind his line unless contact is:
   (a) Incidental to and after he had touched ball in flight.
   (b) Caused by kicker's own motions.
   (c) Occurs during a quick kick, or a kick made after a run behind the line, or after kicker recovers a loose ball on the ground. Ball is loose when kicker muffs snap or snap hits ground.
   (d) Defender Is blocked into kicker.
   The penalty for running into the kicker is 5 yards. For roughing the kicker: 15 yards, an automatic first down and disqualification if flagrant.

7. If a member of the kicking team attempting to down the ball on or inside opponent's 5-yard line carries the ball into the end zone, it is a touchback.

8. Fouls during a punt are enforced from the previous spot (line of scrimmage).
   Exception: Illegal touching, fair-catch interference, invalid fair-catch signal, or personal foul (blocking after a fair-catch signal).

9. While the ball is in the air or rolling on the ground following a punt or field-goal attempt and receiving team commits a foul only before or after gaining possession, receiving team will retain possession and will be penalized for its foul.

10. It will be illegal for a defensive player to jump or stand on any player, or be picked up by a teammate or to use a hand or hands on a teammate to gain additional height in an attempt to block a kick (Penalty: 15 yards, unsportsmanlike conduct).

11. A punted ball remains a kicked ball until it is declared dead or in possession of either team.

12. Any member of the punting team may down the ball anywhere in the field of play. However, it is illegal touching (Official's time out and receiver's ball at spot of illegal touching). This foul does not offset any foul by receivers during the down.

13. Defensive team may advance all kicks from scrimmage (including unsuccessful field goal) whether or not ball crosses defensive team's goal line. Rules pertaining to kicks from scrimmage apply until defensive team gains possession.

14. When a team presents a punt formation, defensive pass interference is not to be called for actions on the widest player eligible to go beyond line. Defensive holding may be called.

FAIR CATCH

1. The member of the receiving team must raise one arm a full length above his head and wave it from side to side while kick is in flight. (Failure to give proper sign: receivers' ball five yards behind spot of signal.) **Note:** It is legal for the receiver to shield his eyes from the sun by raising one hand no higher than the helmet.

2. No opponent may interfere with the fair catcher, the ball, or his path to the ball. Penalty: 15 yards from spot of foul and fair catch is awarded.

3. A player who signals for a fair catch is not required to catch the ball. However, if a player signals for a fair catch, he may not block or initiate contact with any player on the kicking team until the ball touches a player. Penalty: snap 15 yards.

4. If ball is touched by member of kicking team in flight, fair catch signal is off and all rules for a kicked ball apply.

5. Any undue advance by a fair catch receiver is delay of game. No specific distance is specified for undue advance as ball is dead at spot of catch. If player comes to a reasonable stop, no penalty. For penalty, five yards.

6. If time expires while ball is in play and a fair catch is awarded,

receiving team may choose to extend the period with one fair catch kick down. However, placekicker may not use tee.

FOUL ON LAST PLAY OF HALF OR GAME

1. On a foul by defense on last play of half or game, the down is replayed if penalty is accepted.

2. On a foul by the offense on last play of half or game, the down is not replayed and the play in which the foul is committed is nullified.
   Exception: Fair catch interference, foul following change of possession, illegal touching. No score by offense counts.

SPOT OF ENFORCEMENT OF FOUL

1. There are four basic spots at which a penalty for a foul is enforced:
   (a) Spot of foul: The spot where the foul is committed.
   (b) Previous spot: The spot where the ball was put in play.
   (c) Spot of snap, backward pass or fumble: The spot where the foul occurred or the spot where the penalty is to be enforced.
   (d) Succeeding spot: The spot where the ball next would be put in play if no distance penalty were to be enforced.
   Exception: If foul occurs after a touchdown and before the whistle for a try, succeeding spot is spot of next kickoff.

2. All fouls committed by offensive team behind the line of scrimmage (except in the end zone) shall be penalized from the previous spot. If the foul is in the end zone, it is a safety.

3. When spot of enforcement for fouls involving defensive holding or illegal use of hands by the defense is behind the line of scrimmage, any penalty yardage to be assessed on that play shall be measured from the line if the foul occurred beyond the line.

DOUBLE FOUL

1. If there is a double foul during a down in which there is a change of possession, the team last gaining possession may keep the ball unless its foul was committed prior to the change of possession.

2. If double foul occurs after a change of possession, the defensive team retains the ball at the spot of its foul or dead ball spot.

3. If one of the fouls of a double foul involves disqualification, that player must be removed, but no penalty yardage is to be assessed.

4. If the kickers foul during a kickoff, punt, safety kick, or field-goal attempt before possession changes, the receivers will have the option of replaying the down at the previous spot (offsetting fouls), or keeping the ball after enforcement for its fouls.

PENALTY ENFORCED ON FOLLOWING KICKOFF

1. When a team scores by touchdown, field goal, extra point, or safety and either team commits a personal foul, unsportsmanlike conduct, or obvious unfair act during the down, the penalty will be assessed on the following kickoff.

EMERGENCIES AND UNFAIR ACTS
Emergencies—Policy

The National Football League requires all League personnel, including game officials, League office employees, players, coaches, and other club employees to use best effort to see that each game—preseason, regular season, and postseason—is played to its conclusion. The League recognizes, however, that emergencies may arise that make a game's completion impossible or inadvisable. Such circumstances may include, but are not limited to, severely inclement weather, natural or manmade disaster, power failure, and spectator interference. Games should be suspended, cancelled, postponed, or terminated when circumstances exist such that comencement or continuation of play would pose a threat to the safety of participants or spectators.

Authority of Commissioner's Office

1. Authority to cancel, postpone, or terminate games is vested only in the Commissioner and the League President (other League office representatives and referees may suspend play temporarily; see point No. 3 under this section and point No. 1 under "Authority of Referee" below). The following definitions apply:

   - **Cancel.** To cancel a game is to nullify it either before or after it begins and to make no provision for rescheduling it or for including its score or other performance statistics in League records.

   - **Postpone.** To postpone a game is (a) to defer its starting time to a later date, or (b) to suspend it after play has begun and to make provision to resume at a later date with all scores and other performance statistics up to the point of postponement added to those achieved in the resumed portion of the game.

   - **Terminate.** To terminate a game is to end it short of a full 60 minutes of play, to record it officially as a completed game, and to make no provision to resume it at a later date. The Commissioner or League President may terminate a game in an emergency if, in his opinion, it is reasonable to project that its resumption (a) would not change its ultimate result or (b) would not adversely affect any other interteam competitive issue.

   - **Forfeit.** The Commissioner, (except in cases of disciplinary action; see last section on "Removing Team from Field"), League President, and their representatives, including referees, are not authorized unilaterally to declare forfeits. A forfeit occurs only when a game is not played because of the failure or refusal of *one* team to participate. In that event, the other team, if ready and willing to play, is the winner by a score of 2-0.

2. If an emergency arises that may require cancellation, postponement, or termination (see above), the highest ranking representative from the Commissioner's office working the game in a "control" capacity will consult with the Commissioner, League President, or game-day duty officer designated by the League (by telephone, if that person is not in attendance) concerning such decision. If circumstances warrant, the League representative should also attempt to consult with the weather bureau and with appropriate security personnel of the League, club, stadium, and local authorities. If no representative from the Commissioner's office is working the game in a "control" capacity, the referee will be in charge (see "Authority of Referee" below).

3. In circumstances where safety is of immediate concern, the Commissioner's office representative may, after consulting with the referee, authorize a temporary suspension in play and, if warranted, removal of the participants from the playing field. The representative should be mindful of the safety of spectators, players, game officials, nonplayer personnel in the bench areas, and other field-level personnel such as photographers and cheerleaders.

4. If possible, the League-office representative should consult with authorized representatives of the two participating clubs before any decision involving cancellation, postponement, or termination is made by the Commissioner or League President.

5. If the Commissioner or League President decides to cancel, postpone, or terminate a game, his representative at the game or the game-day duty officer will then determine the method(s) for announcing such decision, e.g., by public-address announcement over referee's wireless microphone, by public-address announcement by home club, or by communication to radio, television, and other news media.

Authority of Referee

1. If a referee determines that an emergency warrants immediate removal of participants from the playing field for safety reasons, he may do so on his own authority. If, however, circumstances allow him the time, he must reach the highest ranking full-time League office representative working at the game in a "control" capacity or the game-day duty officer designated by the League (by telephone, if that person is not in attendance) and discuss the actual or potential emergency with such representative or duty officer. That representative or duty officer then will make the final decision on removal of participants from the field or obtain a decision from the Commissioner or League President.

2. If a referee removes participants from the playing field under No. 1 above, he may order them to their respective bench areas or to their locker rooms, whichever is appropriate in the circumstances.

3. After appropriate consultation under No. 1 above, the referee must advise the two participating head coaches of the nature of the emergency and the action contemplated (if the decision has not yet been reached) or of the final decision.

4. The referee must *not*, before a decision is reached, make an announcement on his microphone concerning the possibility of a cancellation, postponement, or termination unless instructed to do so by an appropriate representative of the Commissioner's office.

5. The referee must *not* discuss a forfeit with head coaches or club personnel and must *not* use that term over the referee's microphone (see definition of *forfeit* under No. 1 of "Authority of Commissioner's Office" above).

6. The referee must *not* assess an unsportsmanlike-conduct penalty on the home team for actions of fans that cause or contribute to an emergency.

7. The referee should be mindful of the safety of not only players and officials, but also of the spectators and other nonparticipants.

8. If an emergency involves spectator interference (for example, nonparticipants on the field or thrown objects), the referee immediately should contact the appropriate club or League representative for additional security assistance, including, if applicable, involvement of the League's security representative(s) assigned to the game.

9. The referee may order the resumption of play when he deems conditions safe for all concerned and, if circumstances warrant, after consultation with appropriate representatives of the Commissioner's office.

10. Under no circumstances is the referee authorized to cancel, postpone, terminate, or declare forfeiture of a game unilaterally.

Procedures for Starting and Resuming Games

Subject to the points of authority listed above, League personnel and referees will be guided by the following procedures for starting and resuming games that are affected by emergencies.

1. If, because of an emergency, a regular-season or postseason game is not started at its scheduled time and cannot be played at any later time that same day, the game nevertheless must be played on a subsequent date to be determined by the Commissioner.

2. If an emergency threatens to occur during the playing of a game (for example, an incoming tropical storm), the starting time of the game will not be moved to an earlier time unless there is clearly sufficient time to make an orderly change.

3. All games that are suspended temporarily and resumed on the same day, and all suspended games that are postponed to a later date, will be resumed at the point of suspension. On suspension, the referee will call timeout and make a record of the following: team possessing the ball, direction in which its offense was headed, position of the ball on the field, down, distance, period, time remaining in the period, and any other pertinent information required for an orderly and equitable resumption of play.

4. For regular-season postponements, the Commissioner will make every effort to set the game for no later than two days

after its originally scheduled date and at the same site. If
unable to schedule at the same site, he will select an
appropriate alternative site. If it is impossible to schedule the
game within two days after its original date, the
Commissioner will attempt to schedule it on the Tuesday of
the next calendar week. The Commissioner will keep in mind
the potential for competitive inequities if one or both of the
involved clubs has already been scheduled for a game close
to the Tuesday of that week (for example, a Thursday game).

5. For postseason postponements, the Commissioner will make
every effort to set the game as soon as possible after its
originally scheduled date and at the same site. If unable to
schedule at the same site, he will select an appropriate
alternative site.

6. Whenever postponement is attributable to negligence by a
club, the negligent club is responsible for all home club costs
and expenses, including, subject to approval by the
Commissioner, gate receipts and television-contract income.
[See Section 19.11 (C) of the NFL Constitution and Bylaws.]

7. Each home club is strictly responsible for having the playing
surface of its stadium well maintained and suitable for NFL
play.

UNFAIR ACTS
Commissioner's Authority
The Commissioner has sole authority to investigate and to take
appropriate disciplinary or corrective measures if any club action,
nonparticipant interference, or emergency occurs in an NFL game
which he deems so unfair or outside the accepted tactics
encountered in professional football that such action has a major
effect on the result of a game.
No Club Protests
The authority and measures provided for in this section (UNFAIR
ACTS) do not constitute a protest machinery for NFL clubs to
dispute the result of a game. The Commissioner will conduct an
investigation under this section only to review an act or occurrence
that he deems so unfair that the result of the game in question may
be inequitable to one of the participating teams. The Commissioner
will not apply his authority under this section when a club registers
a complaint concerning judgmental errors or routine errors of
omission by game officials. Games involving such complaints will
continue to stand as completed.
Penalties for Unfair Acts
The Commissioner's powers under this section (UNFAIR ACTS)
include the imposition of monetary fines and draft choice
forfeitures, suspension of persons involved, and, if appropriate, the
reversal of a game's result or the rescheduling of a game, either
from the beginning or from the point at which the extraordinary act
occurred. In the event of rescheduling a game, the Commissioner
will be guided by the procedures specified above ("Procedures for
Starting and Resuming Games" under EMERGENCIES). In all
cases, the Commissioner will conduct a full investigation, including
the opportunity for hearings, use of game videotape, and any other
procedures he deems appropriate.

REMOVING TEAM FROM FIELD
No player, coach, or other person affiliated with a club may remove
that club's team from the field during the playing of any game,
including preseason, except at the direction of the referee. Any club
violating this rule will be subject to disciplinary action by the
Commissioner, including possible game forfeiture and sole liability
for financial losses suffered by the opposing club and any other
affected member clubs of the League. [See Section 9.1 (E) of the
NFL Constitution and Bylaws.]

General Information

AMERICAN FOOTBALL CONFERENCE

BALTIMORE RAVENS
1 Winning Drive
Owings Mills, MD 21117
410/701-4000

BUFFALO BILLS
One Bills Drive
Orchard Park, NY 14127
716/648-1800

CINCINNATI BENGALS
One Paul Brown Stadium
Cincinnati, OH 45202
513/621-3550

CLEVELAND BROWNS
76 Lou Groza Boulevard
Berea, OH 44017
440/891-5000

DENVER BRONCOS
13655 Broncos Parkway
Englewood, CO 80112
303/649-9000

HOUSTON TEXANS
Two Reliant Park
Houston, TX 77054
832/667-2000

INDIANAPOLIS COLTS
P.O. Box 535000
Indianapolis, IN 46253
317/297-2658

JACKSONVILLE JAGUARS
Alltel Stadium
One Alltel Stadium Place
Jacksonville, FL 32202
904/633-6000

KANSAS CITY CHIEFS
One Arrowhead Drive
Kansas City, MO 64129
816/920-9300

MIAMI DOLPHINS
7500 S.W. 30th Street
Davie, FL 33314
954/452-7000

NEW ENGLAND PATRIOTS
Gillette Stadium
One Patriot Place
Foxborough, MA 02035
508/543-8200

NEW YORK JETS
1000 Fulton Avenue
Hempstead, NY 11550
516/560-8100

OAKLAND RAIDERS
1220 Harbor Bay Parkway
Alameda, CA 94502
510/864-5000

PITTSBURGH STEELERS
3400 South Water Street
Pittsburgh, PA 15203
412/432-7800

SAN DIEGO CHARGERS
P.O. Box 609609
San Diego, CA 92160
858/874-4500

TENNESSEE TITANS
460 Great Circle Road
Nashville, TN 37228
615/565-4000

NATIONAL FOOTBALL CONFERENCE

ARIZONA CARDINALS
P.O. Box 888
Phoenix, AZ 85001
602/379-0101

ATLANTA FALCONS
4400 Falcon Parkway
Flowery Branch, GA 30542
770/965-3115

CAROLINA PANTHERS
800 South Mint Street
Charlotte, NC 28202
704/358-7000

CHICAGO BEARS
Halas Hall at Conway Park
1000 Football Drive
Lake Forest, IL 60045
847/295-6600

DALLAS COWBOYS
Cowboys Center
One Cowboys Parkway
Irving, TX 75063
972/556-9900

DETROIT LIONS
Detroit Lions Practice & Training Facility
222 Republic Drive
Allen Park, MI 48101
313/216-4000

GREEN BAY PACKERS
Lambeau Field Atrium
1265 Lombardi Avenue
Green Bay, WI 54304
920/569-7500

MINNESOTA VIKINGS
9520 Viking Drive
Eden Prairie, MN 55344
952/828-6500

NEW ORLEANS SAINTS
5800 Airline Drive
Metairie, LA 70003
504/733-0255

NEW YORK GIANTS
Giants Stadium
East Rutherford, NJ 07073
201/935-8111

PHILADELPHIA EAGLES
NovaCare Complex
One NovaCare Way
Philadelphia, PA 19145
215/463-2500

ST. LOUIS RAMS
One Rams Way
St. Louis, MO 63045
314/982-7267

SAN FRANCISCO 49ERS
4949 Centennial Boulevard
Santa Clara, CA 95054
408/562-4949

SEATTLE SEAHAWKS
11220 N.E. 53rd Street
Kirkland, WA 98033
425/827-9777

TAMPA BAY BUCCANEERS
One Buccaneer Place
Tampa, FL 33607
813/870-2700

WASHINGTON REDSKINS
Redskins Park
21300 Redskin Park Drive
Ashburn, VA 20147
703/726-7000

AMERICAN FOOTBALL CONFERENCE

BALTIMORE RAVENS
Stadium: M&T Bank Stadium
(opened in 1998)
• **Capacity:** 70,107
1101 Russell Street
Baltimore, MD 21230
Playing Surface: Sportexe Momentum

BUFFALO BILLS
Stadium: Ralph Wilson Stadium
(opened in 1973)
• **Capacity:** 73,967
One Bills Drive
Orchard Park, NY 14127
Playing Surface: AstroPlay

CINCINNATI BENGALS
Stadium: Paul Brown Stadium
(opened in 2000)
• **Capacity:** 65,378
One Paul Brown Stadium
Cincinnati, OH 45202
Playing Surface: Synthetic

CLEVELAND BROWNS
Stadium: Cleveland Browns Stadium
(opened in 1999)
• **Capacity:** 73,300
100 Alfred Lerner Way
Cleveland, OH 44114
Playing Surface: Grass

DENVER BRONCOS
Stadium: INVESCO Field at Mile High
(opened in 2001)
• **Capacity:** 76,125
1701 Bryant Street
Denver, CO 80204
Playing Surface: Grass (PAT)

HOUSTON TEXANS
Stadium: Reliant Stadium
(opened in 2002)
• **Capacity:** 71,054
Houston, TX 77054
Playing Surface: Grass

INDIANAPOLIS COLTS
Stadium: RCA Dome
(opened in 1983)
• **Capacity:** 55,531
100 South Capitol Avenue
Indianapolis, IN 46225
Playing Surface: FieldTurf

JACKSONVILLE JAGUARS
Stadium: Alltel Stadium
(opened in 1995)
• **Capacity:** 67,164
One Alltel Stadium Place
Jacksonville, FL 32202
Playing Surface: Grass

KANSAS CITY CHIEFS
Stadium: Arrowhead Stadium
(opened in 1972)
• **Capacity:** 79,451
One Arrowhead Drive
Kansas City, MO 64129
Playing Surface: Grass

MIAMI DOLPHINS
Stadium: Dolphin Stadium
(opened in 1987)
• **Capacity:** 75,192
2269 Dan Marino Blvd.
Miami Gardens, FL 33056
Playing Surface: Grass (PAT)

NEW ENGLAND PATRIOTS
Stadium: Gillette Stadium
(opened in 2002)
• **Capacity:** 68,756
One Patriot Place
Foxborough, MA 02035
Playing Surface: Grass

NEW YORK JETS
Stadium: Meadowlands
(opened in 1976)
• **Capacity:** 79,466
East Rutherford, NJ 07073
Playing Surface: FieldTurf

OAKLAND RAIDERS
Stadium: McAfee Coliseum
(opened in 1966)
• **Capacity:** 63,132
7000 Coliseum Way
Oakland, CA 94621
Playing Surface: Grass

PITTSBURGH STEELERS
Stadium: Heinz Field
(opened in 2001)
• **Capacity:** 64,350
100 Art Rooney Avenue
Pittsburgh, PA 15212
Playing Surface: DD GrassMaster

SAN DIEGO CHARGERS
Stadium: Qualcomm Stadium
(opened in 1967)
• **Capacity:** 70,000
9449 Friars Road
San Diego, CA 92108
Playing Surface: Grass

TENNESSEE TITANS
Stadium: LP Field
(opened in 1999)
• **Capacity:** 68,809
One Titans Way
Nashville, TN 37213
Playing Surface: Natural Grass

NATIONAL FOOTBALL CONFERENCE

ARIZONA CARDINALS
Stadium: Cardinals Stadium
(opened in 2006)
• **Capacity:** 63,400
Maryland Avenue
Glendale, AZ 85305
Playing Surface: Grass

ATLANTA FALCONS
Stadium: Georgia Dome
(opened in 1992)
• **Capacity:** 71,228
One Georgia Dome Drive
Atlanta, GA 30313
Playing Surface: FieldTurf

CAROLINA PANTHERS
Stadium: Bank of America Stadium
(opened in 1996)
• **Capacity:** 73,298
Charlotte, NC 28202
Playing Surface: Grass

CHICAGO BEARS
Stadium: Soldier Field
(opened in 1924)
• **Capacity:** 61,500
1410 S. Museum Campus Dr.
Chicago, IL 60605
Playing Surface: Natural Grass

DALLAS COWBOYS
Stadium: Texas Stadium
(opened in 1971)
• **Capacity:** 65,529
2401 E. Airport Freeway
Irving, TX 75062
Playing Surface: Sportfield Realgrass

DETROIT LIONS
Stadium: Ford Field
(opened in 2002)
• **Capacity:** 64,500
2000 Brush Street
Detroit, MI 48226
Playing Surface: FieldTurf

GREEN BAY PACKERS
Stadium: Lambeau Field
(opened in 1957)
• **Capacity:** 72,922
1265 Lombardi Avenue
Green Bay, WI 54304
Playing Surface: Grass

MINNESOTA VIKINGS
Stadium: Hubert H. Humphrey Metrodome
(opened in 1982)
• **Capacity:** 64,121
500 11th Avenue South
Minneapolis, MN 55415
Playing Surface: FieldTurf

NEW ORLEANS SAINTS
Stadium: Louisiana Superdome
(opened in 1975)
• **Capacity:** 65,000
1500 Poydras Street
New Orleans, LA 70112
Playing Surface: Sportexe Momentum

NEW YORK GIANTS
Stadium: Giants Stadium
(opened In 1976)
• **Capacity:** 80,242
East Rutherford, NJ 07073
Playing Surface: FieldTurf

PHILADELPHIA EAGLES
Stadium: Lincoln Financial Field
(opened in 2003)
• **Capacity:** 68,400
One Lincoln Financial Field Way
Philadelphia, PA 19148
Playing Surface: Natural Grass

ST. LOUIS RAMS
Stadium: Edward Jones Dome
(opened in 1995)
• **Capacity:** 66,000
701 Convention Plaza
St. Louis, MO 63101
Playing Surface: FieldTurf

SAN FRANCISCO 49ERS
Stadium: Monster Park
(opened in 1958)
• **Capacity:** 69,732
San Francisco, CA 94124
Playing Surface: Natural Grass

SEATTLE SEAHAWKS
Stadium: Qwest Field
(opened in 2002)
• **Capacity:** 67,000
800 Occidental Ave South, #200
Seattle, WA 98134
Playing Surface: FieldTurf

TAMPA BAY BUCCANEERS
Stadium: Raymond James Stadium
(opened in 1998)
• **Capacity:** 65,657
Tampa, FL 33607
Playing Surface: Grass

WASHINGTON REDSKINS
Stadium: FedExField
(opened in 1997)
• **Capacity:** 91,704
1600 FedEx Way
Landover, MD 20785
Playing Surface: Natural Grass

280 Park Avenue, New York, New York 10017 (212) 450-2000

NFL Internet Network: www.NFL.com

Commissioner: Paul Tagliabue

Executive Vice President/Chief Operating Officer: Roger Goodell

Executive Vice President/Chief Administrative Officer-Counsel: Jeff Pash

Executive Vice President of Labor Relations/Chairman NFLMC: Harold Henderson

Executive Vice President of Communications and Public Affairs: Joe Browne

Executive Vice President of Media/President and Chief Executive Officer of NFL Network: Steve Bornstein

Executive Vice President of Finance and Strategic Transactions: Eric Grubman